DRIVE HISTORY HOME

TO YOUR STUDENTS

American Odyssey
The United States in the 20th Century

★ ★ ★ ★ ★

GLENCOE

McGraw-Hill

Hit a Home Run with *American Odyssey.*

Chapters that grab student's interest and focus their attention.

Learning history is much more than memorizing facts. It's also discovering relationships, interpreting evidence, and connecting past to present. That's what *American Odyssey: The United States in the Twentieth Century* is all about.

★ ★ ★ ★ ★ ★ ★ ★ ★ ★

Compelling Chapter Openers and Section Openers put students on the battlefield, in the unemployment line, and at the shuttle launch. Thrust into the action, students realize that they too are participants in history—not just spectators.

The **Narrative** of each section introduces students not only to important leaders, but also to the lives of ordinary people. Students hear the stories of all Americans.

Journal Writing is included in every chapter opener and chapter review. This active learning exercise challenges students to develop their writing and critical thinking skills.

CHAPTER
10

Expansionism and World War I

MARCH 1901: GEORGE WASHINGTON OF THE PHILIPPINES CAPTURED

Senator George F. Hoar once called Emilio Aguinaldo the "George Washington of the Philippines" when Aguinaldo sought to liberate his country from foreign rule. When that rule was Spanish, Hoar and others had encouraged the Philippine liberation struggle.

Aguinaldo had responded in kind, shouting "Viva los Americanos!" This enthusiasm, however, did not last long. The United States had promised its support of Philippine independence if Aguinaldo joined the United States in its fight against Spain. After the war, that promise was not kept. President McKinley wanted to "civilize" the Filipinos before granting independence.

When the United States refused to accept Aguinaldo as the legitimate head of government, a struggle ensued. American officials no longer

praised him as a founder of his country. Instead, they plotted his capture. Aguinaldo marked the United States as an enemy and led a guerrilla war to rid his country of American forces.

Aguinaldo's capture in 1901 did not end the Filipino struggle. The war lasted for another year.

How the United States became the enemy of Aguinaldo is only part of the larger story of American foreign policy under the progressives— a policy guided by an uneasy mixture of idealism and self-interest. ■

HISTORY JOURNAL

Study the illustration of this famous piece of sheet music, and write your reaction to the mood it creates.
Do you think American soldiers were always welcome in foreign countries? Why or why not?

292

Your Song—My Song—Our Boys' Song
OVER THERE

WORDS AND MUSIC BY GEORGE M. COHAN

LEO. FEIST NEW YORK

THIS SPIRITED PATRIOTIC SONG GLORIFIED THE ROLE OF THE UNITED STATES IN WORLD WAR I.

293

Toward a New Century

JULY 6, 1995: RUSSIANS AND AMERICANS LINK UP IN SPACE

NEARLY 240 MILES (386 KM) ABOVE THE EARTH, THE SPACE SHUTTLE *ATLANTIS* MOVED INTO ORBIT WITH *MIR* (MEANING *PEACE*), THE RUSSIAN SPACE STATION LAUNCHED IN 1986, SLOWLY CLOSING THE 4,000-MILE (6,436-KM) GAP BETWEEN THEM. By the next day, only 250 feet (76 m) separated the 2 crafts, which were circling at 17,500 miles (28,158 km) per hour. Tension increased as American astronauts Hoot Gibson and Charles Precourt continued the delicate maneuvers necessary to link the 2 ships. Inch by inch, they guided *Atlantis* until they had jockeyed the 100-ton spacecraft to within 3 inches of the Russian station. Soon the 2 were linked, soaring through space together. Russian cosmonauts and American astronauts swung open the hatches, and the 2 crews grasped each others' hands in joyous greeting. The moment was symbolic of the huge changes that had reshaped the map of the planet below.

Atlantis and Mir Hook Up
American astronaut Robert L. Gibson shakes hands with *Mir* cosmonaut Vladimir N. Dezhurov in 1995.

Both the Russians and the Americans, faced with cutbacks in funding for their space programs, envisioned a future of cooperation. Plans are under way for a new space station, with modules supplied and assembled by both nations. Once it is in place, the plan is to invite the European Space Agency, Canada, and Japan to participate in and expand the facility. While questions remained about the commitment of the American and Russian governments to such an ambitious project, the fact that cosmonauts and astronauts were cruising above the earth in the summer of 1995 seemed to most observers a reason for optimism.

At its inception, the space program was an arm of the cold war. For both the USSR and the United States, the goal had been to beat the other in the space race. Winning meant setting records: first to orbit the earth, first to walk in space, first to set foot on the moon. Today in a new

AS YOU READ

Vocabulary
▸ militia group
▸ community policing

Think About . . .
▸ arguments for and against gerrymandering.
▸ the changing nature of work in an increasingly technological society.
▸ the financial and educational challenges facing schools and educators as the United States moves toward the twenty-first century.

Words and images that speak directly from the past.

American Odyssey makes history unforgettable by integrating gripping narrative with exciting visuals and the practical skills lessons that students need.

Words alone can't always capture the flavor of an era. Period photographs and art communicate struggle, triumph, and everyday life in a way that words cannot.

Dynamic graphics, maps, and the creative use of photos enhance each chapter and entice students to spend more time with the material.

Geography: Impact on History

MOVEMENT
Route 66

The construction of U.S. Route 66 provided Americans with a main artery for travel that linked the Midwest with the Far West. The ensuing movement of people and goods had dramatic effects on the nation's culture and economy.

Building a Spirit of Travel

Pulitzer Prize–winning author James Agee described the American story as having five main characters: the continent, the people, the automobile, the road, and the roadside. According to Agee, these five characters met because of the restless nature of Americans:

The twenties made him [the American] rich and more restive still and he found the automobile not merely good but better and better. It was good because continually it satisfied and at the same time greatly sharpened his hunger for movement.

—James Agee, *Fortune*, September 1934

Cars alone could not satisfy the American hunger for movement. Only the construction of a vast network of highways would finally enable Americans to travel freely. This increased movement of people and goods contributed to the reduction of regional differences.

One famous highway, U.S. Route 66, allowed Americans to fulfill their desire to take to the road. How did the United States highway system, including roads such as Route 66, develop?

Building the Roadway

Americans enjoyed driving their cars and soon wanted better roads. People were interested in what Americans in other parts of the country were doing and how they lived.

Car owners and manufacturers were not the only ones demanding new roads. Since the early 1900s, farmers in the Midwest and the Southwest had cried out for roads on which to transport their products to market. Farmers had been dependent on trains to freight their produce at whatever rate the railroad monopoly set.

Local political-action groups pressed Congress to legislate highway building and to break the railroad's stranglehold over transportation. In 1916 the Federal Aid Road Act responded to the pleas of these groups. The Road Act provided federal aid for half of the construction costs of any rural highway intended to carry mail. The new state highway departments were to plan the routes of the new roads. A second federal provision in 1921 granted money to states that would connect their roads to the roads of other states, forming a main thoroughfare. These acts set the basis for a national highway system.

When U.S. Route 66 officially opened on November 11, 1926, it became one of the main arteries of the national highway system. This "great diagonal highway" between Chicago and Los Angeles cut through the Middle West, straddled the Great Plains, crossed the deserts of the Southwest, and reached to the very edge of the Pacific Ocean. Route 66 spanned 8 states and ran through 200 towns, covering 2,400 miles (38,616 km). In the late 1920s, Route 66 was an autotourist's vacationland.

During the Depression of the 1930s, Route 66 became famous as the road that migrants in search of jobs in California followed. John Steinbeck once wrote, "66 is the mother road, the road of flight."

A Roadside Autocamp Americans enjoyed the fresh air and fellowship found at roadside autocamps. *What goods and services did these autotourists require?*

Building the Roadside

The car and the highways provided Americans with a new form of recreation and business in the 1920s: autocamping. Millions of Americans packed tents and headed for the countryside. Car dealers even advertised autotourism as a way to strengthen the family. They pictured the prosperous middle-class family traveling down Route 66 exploring the United States.

Much of the land Route 66 crossed had not experienced the same prosperity as the rest of the nation in the 1920s. The same technology that brought cars and highways also revolutionized farming with new machinery. When the overproduction of grains glutted the market, however, prices fell. Many farmers went bust, losing their farms as well as their jobs.

The unemployed farmers and other people who lived in rural areas throughout the western states were not quite sure what the new highways were, nor what businesses the highways could bring to their communities. When Route 66 opened, though, they soon found out.

Many unemployed farmers enthusiastically joined the retail petroleum business selling gasoline, oil, and other services to passing tourists. After these new entrepreneurs opened gas stations, they went on to build tourist courts and cafes where tourists could rest and try local foods. Billboards began advertising such roadside attractions as man-eating pythons. In those days any promise became fair in the battle to get the tourist to stop and spend money.

THE PATH OF U.S. ROUTE 66, 1926

The path of U.S. Route 66 was the subject of intense negotiating as many small towns petitioned to have the road run through their community. *What other points of interest besides towns were located on Route 66?*

MAKING THE GEOGRAPHIC CONNECTION

1. What did Americans want to learn as they drove to other parts of the United States?

2. What events led to the establishment of a national highway system?

3. **Movement** As Americans traveled along roads such as Route 66, what impact did they have on the economy of local cities and towns?

Geography emphasis puts history on the map. Every unit contains a *Geography: Impact on History* section featuring articles and large, colorful maps. Integration with geography reinforces students' development of skills and concepts essential to understanding history.

Exciting features give your students a front- row seat to the 20th century.

In *American Odyssey*, features don't interrupt the narrative—they complement it, adding life and depth of understanding.

★ ★ ★ ★ ★ ★ ★ ★ ★

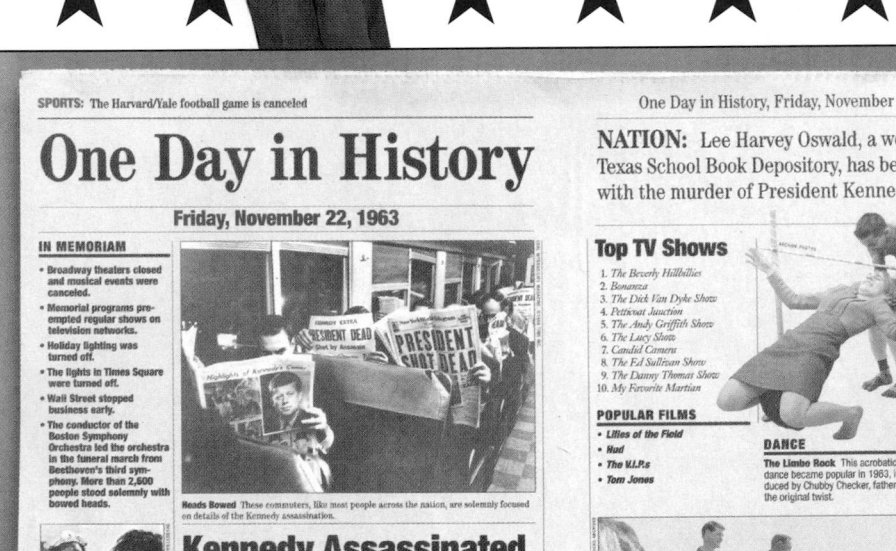

◀ One Day in History
Reminiscent of a daily newspaper, these "front pages" recall the dramatic—and the ordinary— events of ten special days in history. A look at top TV shows, movies, fashions, fads, music, and what things cost give students an understanding of what life was like on that day in history.

▶ Then and Now
With photos and fun facts, students can examine in detail an artifact or phenomenon from each unit's time period and see how it has evolved into what it is today.

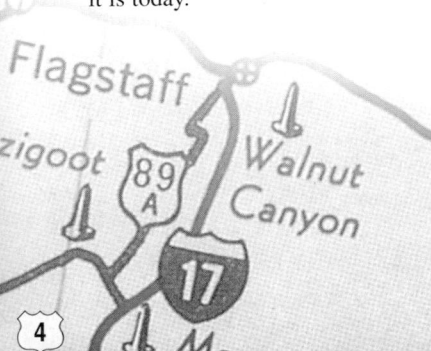

Flagstaff

zigoot 89 Walnut Canyon

17

Holbrook

Petrified

Grar

Case Study Turning Point

Give your students an inside look at pivotal issues and events in history. Show students the decision-making process and how these decisions affected the course of our history. By studying both sides of an issue, students form their own opinions and develop critical thinking skills.

Science, Technology, and Society

Using an exciting combination of text, visuals, and a timeline, this feature focuses on a technological advance and its impact on society. Students gain real insight into how these advances affect their lives.

Additional Features

Culture of Our Time

Visual and verbal displays appearing once per unit capture the popular culture of the time.

Literature

A variety of literature selections at the beginning of each unit communicate the thoughts, feelings, and life experiences of people, past and present.

Be a Hero to All Your Students.

Guide your students' learning with our comprehensive Teacher's Wraparound Edition.

The multimedia Teacher's Wraparound Edition gives you direct access to an impressive collection of videodisc and CD-ROM programs referenced throughout the text. In seconds, you can bring the latest technology into your classroom presentations.

★ ★ ★ ★ ★ ★ ★ ★ ★ ★ ★ ★ ★ ★ ★

A wide range of *teaching strategies* lets you select the approaches that fit your teaching style and classroom needs. Strategies include:

- *Linking Past and Present*
- *Cooperative Learning Activities*
- *Performance Assessment*
- *Multi Cultural Perspectives*
- *And More!*

Chapter 17 SECTION 1

Facts on File
Landmark Documents in American History Have students review "Yalta Agreement, 1945" and "United Nations Charter, 1945" and write a paragraph about the intent of one of the documents.

GLENCOE TECHNOLOGY

Videodisc
Focus on Government

Side 3, Chapter 55
Title: Electronic Field Trip to the United Nations
Subject: Tour the United Nations
Ask: Why was the United Nations founded? (to help preserve world peace)

Focus on Government is also available on videotape.

VISUAL INSTRUCTION

The Big Three Meet Ask whether it was fair that the Yalta Conference involved leaders of only three nations. Have students discuss whether this type of conference would be acceptable today.

Answer: to divide Germany and settle the war payments question later

---

Turning Point at Yalta
Soviets Take Power in Eastern Europe

In February 1945, near the end of the war, the Big Three—Roosevelt, Churchill, and Stalin—met in the Soviet city of Yalta to work out control of the postwar world. The three men and their advisers arrived at a moment when victorious Soviet armies were sweeping across Eastern Europe.

Each leader brought his own concerns to the table. Churchill hoped to save the British Empire; Stalin intended to protect his borders and rebuild his country. Unlike Churchill and Stalin, who believed in great powers controlling spheres of influence, Roosevelt sought the worldwide spread of democracy and free trade. The American President, however, also needed Soviet aid in the war against Japan. All agreed, ultimately, that working out these interests together was the only path to peace.

Every day for a week, the Big Three met in the ballroom of the former czar's palace along the Black Sea. They talked, debated, and compromised.

The meeting at Yalta marked a high point of cooperation among the Big Three. It also became a turning point in the relationship between the major powers, and in many ways it determined the form the postwar world would take.

Big Three Agreements

Many key agreements came out of the Yalta talks. Much to Roosevelt's relief, Stalin agreed to join the fight against Japan "two or three" months after Germany

The Big Three Meet At Yalta, Churchill, Roosevelt, and Stalin reached a number of historic agreements. *Which of these agreements affected the future of Germany?*

surrendered. In return, Stalin would receive territories in Asia. Stalin also pledged Soviet support for the United Nations (UN), an international body that would be formed to help keep world peace.

Agreement broke down over Germany and Eastern Europe. Even though all three leaders feared a rearmed Germany, they disagreed on how to keep Germany under control. Stalin wanted to punish Germany by demanding $20 billion in war payments. Half of the money would go to the Soviet Union to help rebuild its shattered economy. Roosevelt and Churchill knew that Germany could not afford the payments without their help; they feared having to support Germany so it could pay Stalin.

Rather than debate the issue, the three agreed that each nation would control the part of Germany its troops held at the end of the war. Later a commission would solve the problem of war payments.

Control in Eastern Europe

Eastern Europe and Poland were even touchier issues. Stalin demanded recognition of Soviet power in Poland, Romania, Bulgaria, Austria, Hungary, and Czechoslovakia to protect his western border. Soviet forces already occupied much of Eastern Europe, and Stalin had installed a government in Poland. Roosevelt and Churchill protested strongly. Britain went to war "so that Poland should be free," Churchill exclaimed.

In the end, however, Roosevelt and Churchill had little choice but to give in. With the Pacific war still raging, they had no means of forcing Stalin to back down. Reluctantly they agreed to Soviet influence in Eastern Europe but insisted that Stalin hold "free and unfettered elections" at an "early date."

In the weeks after the conference at Yalta, Roosevelt worried as the Soviets installed Communist governments in country after country. Still, he had faith in his ability to win Stalin's trust of the West. Newly elected to a fourth term, Roosevelt believed he could persuade Stalin that the Soviets had nothing to fear and could relax their iron grip on Eastern Europe. Any such hopes were dashed, however, when Roosevelt died suddenly on April 12, 1945.

Truman Comes to Power
Truman Gets Tough With Stalin

"I don't know whether you fellows ever had a load of hay or a bull fall on you, but last night the moon, stars, and all the planets fell on me." Harry S Truman could well feel overwhelmed on his first day as President—April 13, 1945. Nations were still battling, and the world had reached a turning point in its history: The old system of

564   CHAPTER 17 THE UNEASY PEACE

power was crumbling and a new, unknown system remained to be built.

Truman stepped into the presidency unprepared. Raised in a small Missouri town with little chance for an education, the gritty, intelligent Truman worked his way up from the farm to business and finally to the United States Senate. Nominated as Roosevelt's running mate in 1944, he spent only 12 weeks as Vice President before Roosevelt's death.

During those 83 days, Truman got little information from Roosevelt. The President shared no details of key military or foreign policies with him, and Truman received only two short foreign relations briefings. According to Roosevelt's key adviser, Harry Hopkins, Truman himself knew "absolutely nothing of world affairs." Yet only 10 days after Truman assumed the presidency, international events took center stage.

Formation of the United Nations

At Yalta, the Big Three had agreed in principle to an international peacekeeping organization. On April 25, 1945, 50 countries met in San Francisco to draft the charter for the United Nations. United States support

was voiced in Truman's address to the conference: "We must build a new world, a far better world—one in which the eternal dignity of man is respected."

The first article of the charter stated that the purpose of the United Nations was to maintain international peace and security. By October 1945, a majority of the participating nations had ratified the charter, and the United Nations officially came into existence.

The United States hoped that the United Nations would help to bring about a world in which every country would be free to run its own government. The Soviet Union—and to a lesser extent Great Britain—believed, however, that self-determination applied only to those countries that did not have strategic value to Soviet, or British, interests. In particular, the Soviets were determined to control Eastern Europe as a protection against future aggression from the West.

Truman's advisers urged him to get tough with the Soviets, and Truman exhibited his hard-line approach during the visit of Soviet ambassador V.M. Molotov. Truman sharply criticized Molotov for failing to support the Yalta agreements. Specifically, Truman demanded to know why the Soviets had not held free elections in Poland.

SECTION ONE   565

EUROPE AT THE END OF WORLD WAR II

At the close of World War II, the political map of Europe underwent massive changes. Which European nations fell under the control of the Soviet Union at the end of the war?

Chapter 17 SECTION 1

MAP STUDY

Stalin wanted control of Eastern Europe to protect the western border of the Soviet Union from invasion.

Answer: Eastern Europe: Estonia, Latvia, Lithuania, East Prussia, East Germany, Czechoslovakia, Hungary, Romania, Yugoslavia, Bulgaria, Poland, Albania

ABC NEWS INTERACTIVE

Videodisc
Communism and the Cold War

Side 2, Chapter 3
Title: United Nations
Subject: The development of the United Nations and the organization's assistance to developing countries
Ask: Why was the UN formed? (to promote world peace and cooperation)

See Communism and the Cold War Guidebook page 48 for complete lesson plan.

Facts on File
Landmark Documents in American History Have students review "United Nations Charter, 1945" and write a paragraph about the intent of the document.

Meeting Special Needs

Visual Learners Have students who learn best visually make a time line of the years from January 1945 to December 1947. As students read, they should enter dates and key events on the time line. Encourage students to refer to their time lines as they discuss events.

Reading Disability Have students with reading comprehension problems skim the section to find the vocabulary words that are introduced. Be certain that students understand each term before they read the section. After reading, have students listen to the Chapter 17, Section 1 portion of the audiocassette.

Portfolio Project

Constructing a Graph To calculate the relative influence of the United States, Great Britain, and the Soviet Union, students should consult an atlas to find the number of square miles in the countries under the control of the United States, Great Britain, and the Soviet Union in 1945. Students can then make a graph of the results to put in their portfolios.

Mapping Have students find out what the geographic conditions were in areas of Europe in which World War II was fought. They should consider the season of the year and the probable effects of weather and terrain on battle action. Then have students draw a map that shows the influence of geography on one battle. Have students put their maps in their portfolios.

564

565

✔ Performance Assessment

Cooperative Project

Organize students into groups of four or five. Have the groups investigate the economic aspects of the arms buildup. Students might create a line graph showing the growth of the defense budget and pie graphs showing the defense budgets as a percentage of the federal budget. Have the groups present their results to the class. **LEP** 🔲

Suggested Rubrics: An Oral Presentation, Group Work and the Individual. See Performance Assessment Strategies and Activites, pp. 33 and 49.

Individual Project

Before students read about the end of the cold war, point out that reduced tensions between the superpowers led to reduced military spending. Have students identify which problems in United States society most deserve the government funds spent on the military. Have them write up their ideas in a report or present them to the class orally. 🔲

Suggested Rubric: An Oral Presentation. See Performance Assessment Strategies and Activites, pp. 33 and 49.

Performance Assessment strategies are prepared for you; two alternate strategies measure student understanding in each chapter.

Key to Ability Levels

Teaching strategies have been coded for varying learning styles and abilities.

L1 **BASIC** activities for all students

L2 **AVERAGE** activities for average to above-average students

L3 **CHALLENGING** activities for above-average students

LEP **LIMITED ENGLISH PROFICIENCY** activities

Block Scheduling

Block scheduling differs from traditional class scheduling in the amount of time allotted to each period. The extended timeframe provided by block scheduling affords you the opportunity to implement a greater number of research-oriented and activity-intense projects to motivate and involve your students. Activities that are particularly suited to use within the block scheduling framework are identified throughout this chapter by the following designation. 🔲

Block Scheduling suggestions are available at the point of use in the Teacher's Wraparound Edition. These strategies provide instructional variety for your students throughout the course.

TEACHER'S CORNER

NATIONAL GEOGRAPHIC SOCIETY

INDEX TO NATIONAL GEOGRAPHIC MAGAZINE

The following articles may be used for research relating to this chapter:

- "Information Revolution," by Joel L. Swerdlow, October 1995.
- "Russia: Playing by New Rules," by Mike Edwards, March 1993.
- "The Bolshevik Revolution," By Dusko Doder, October 1992
- "East Europe's Dark Dawn," by Jon Thompson, June 1991.
- "Computer Rebuilds the Ancient Sphinx," by Mark Lehner, April 1991.
- "Dispatches From Eastern Europe," by Tad Szulc, March 1991.

- "Mother Russia on a New Course," by Mike Edwards, February 1991.
- "Berlin's Ode to Joy," by Priit J. Vesilind, April 1990.
- "Advanced Materials—Reshaping Our Lives " by Thomas Y. Canby, December 1989.
- "High Tech: The Future is Now," by Michael E. Long, July 1989.

NATIONAL GEOGRAPHIC SOCIETY PRODUCTS AVAILABLE FROM GLENCOE

To order the following products for use with this chapter, contact your local Glencoe sales representative or call Glencoe at 1-800-334-7344:

- *The Presidents: A Picture History of Our Nation* (CD-ROM)
- *GTV: The American People: Fabric of a Nation* (Videodisc)

- *GTV: A Geographic Perspective on American History* (Videodisc)

ADDITIONAL NATIONAL GEOGRAPHIC SOCIETY PRODUCTS

To order the following products for use with this chapter, call National Geographic Society at 1-800-368-2728:

- *The Changing Faces of Communism Series*: Poland. (Video)
- *The Rise and Fall of the Soviet Union* (Video)
- *Russia: After the U.S.S.R.* (Video)

- *The Soviet World in Transition* (Filmstrip)
- *The American Presidency* (Filmstrip)
- *Miniature Miracle: The Computer Chip* (Video)

854B

The *National Geographic Teacher's Corner* correlates *National Geographic* magazines articles, key technology, and other media to *American Odyssey*.

NATIONAL GEOGRAPHIC SOCIETY

Videodisc Bar Code and other multimedia references at point-of-use make it easy to use these resources in every lesson.

Keep in Step with All Your Students' Needs.

Teacher's Classroom Resources help you design the course the way you want.

Teacher Planning and Support

Enable you to focus more time and attention on teaching.
• *Reproducible Lesson Plans*
• *Block Scheduling Implementation Guide*
• *Videodisc Bar Code Correlation*

Transparencies

A wide array of transparencies enhance each lesson.
• *Section Focus Transparencies*
• *Teaching Transparencies*
    • *Beginnings to 1900 Review Transparencies:*
    • *Chapter Teaching Transparencies*
    • *Map Transparencies*
    • *Unit Time Line Transparancies*
Each transparency is accompanied by a Teaching
Strategy and Activity.

Review and Reinforcement

Helps students comprehend concepts they may not have
learned the first time, without additional preparation on
your part.
• *Vocabulary and Guided Reading Activities*
• *Reteaching Activities*
• *Skill Reinforcement Activities*

Enrichment and Applications

Issues that reinforce students' learning and allow them to develop critical thinking skills. Provides variety to daily lessons with high-interest activities.

- *Enrichment Activities*
- *Supreme Court Case Studies*
- *Great Debates in History*
- *Political Cartoons Activities*
- *Case Studies*
- *Cooperative Learning*
- *American Portraits*

Geography in History Activities

Give students graphic opportunities to understand the impact of geography on the historical development of the United States

- *Geography in History Activities*
- *Outline Map Resource Book*
- *Building Skills in Geography*

Art and Humanities

A look at our rich national heritage in the arts and humanities.

- *American Literature: Readings and Activities*
- *The Spirit of America: Art and Music*
- *American Music: Cultural Traditions*
- *Focus on American Art Prints*

Assessment and Evaluation

Contains alternative assessment activities for each chapter.

- *Performance Assessment Strategies and Activities*
- *Section Quizzes*
- *Chapter and Unit Test: Forms A & B*

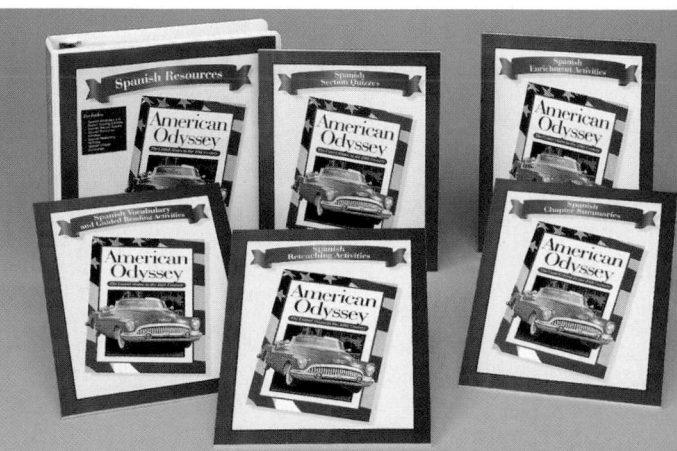

Spanish Resources

Extra support to help Spanish-speaking students succeed.

- *Vocabulary and Guided Reading Activities*
- *Section Quizzes*
- *Enrichment Activities*
- *Reteaching Activities*
- *Chapter Summaries*

The Sights, the Sounds, and All That Jazz.

Award-winning technology and multimedia capture the drama of history.

★ ★ ★ ★ ★ ★ ★ ★ ★ ★

Videodisc Programs

NATIONAL GEOGRAPHIC SOCIETY

Award-Winning Programs

- *GTV: A Geographic Perspective on American History* is an exciting exploration of American history, from pre-Colombian days to the present.
- *GTV: The American People: Fabric of a Nation* allows you to present an inclusive story of American history, highlighting the contributions of all Americans.

ABCNEWS INTERACTIVE™

Award-Winning Programs

- *Lessons of War* examines the causes of war, how wars are actually fought, and how they can be resolved.
- *Communism and the Cold War* helps your students understand the historical context of the U.S.-Soviet rivalry and portrays the events that led to the collapse of communism and the end of the Cold War.
- *Martin Luther King, Jr.* is a tribute to the life and work of one of America's greatest civil rights leaders. The program provides a chronology of his participation in the Civil Rights Movement and explores the impact of the movement on today's society.
- *Powers of the U.S. Government* (3 videodiscs) details the powers of the Supreme Court, the Congress, and the President. Chief Justice William Rehnquist, former Speaker of the House Tom Foley, and former President Jimmy Carter lead the discussions of their respective branches of government.
- **NEW!** *Historic America: Electronic Field Trips* lets your students experience the sights and sounds of America's historic landmarks without ever leaving the classroom. Journey from coast to coast with ABC News correspondents as your tour guides to The Vietnam Veterans Memorial, the Alamo, and many more historic sites.

Glencoe Videodisc

- *Set on Freedom: The American Civil Rights Movement* lets your students meet the movement's greatest leaders, hear the major speeches, and witness pivotal events of the Civil Rights Era.

CD-ROM/Software Programs

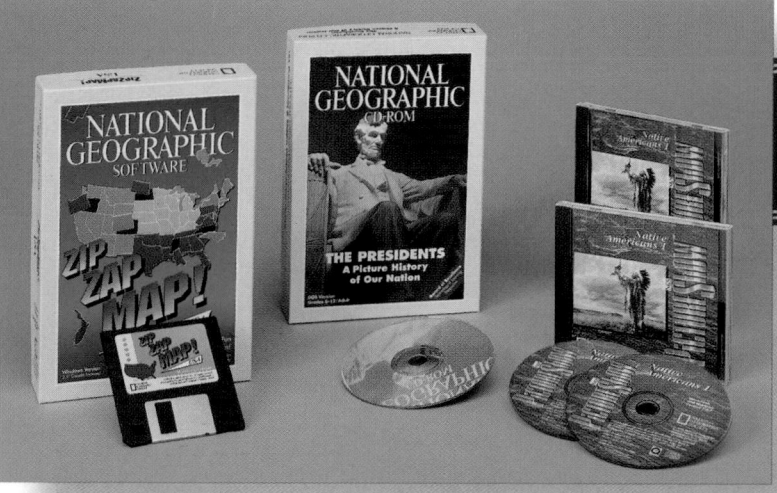

National Geographic Society

- *The Presidents: A Picture History of Our Nation* CD-ROM offers a spellbinding look at the presidency in an easy-to-use multimedia format.
- *NGS PictureShow: Native Americans* CD-ROM Part One introduces the major Native American tribes that inhabited the Eastern Woodlands and the Great Plains. Part Two introduces the Native Americans of the Southwest, Northwest Coast, and Arctic.
- *ZipZapMap! USA* is a fast-paced software game that quickly increases your students' grasp of U.S. geography.

More Technology

- *Facts on File* CD-ROM programs
  - Landmark Documents in American History
  - The American Indian
- *Student Self-Test & Review* software lets students review the key concepts of every chapter at their own pace. Incorrect responses activate a built-in tutorial function.
- *Vocabulary Puzzlemaker* software lets you to create various types of word puzzles that help students learn vocabulary terms from each chapter.
- *Testmaker* software (DOS, Macintosh) has over 3,000 questions and offers the flexibility of adding your own questions or editing existing questions.

Transparencies, Audiocassettes, Compact Discs, and Posters

- *Teaching Transparencies with Strategies and Activities* allow you to introduce, reteach, and reinforce chapter and unit concepts with:
  - Chapter Teaching Transparencies
  - Map Transparencies
  - Beginnings to 1900 Transparencies
  - Unit Time Line Activities Transparencies
- *Section Focus Transparencies with Strategies and Activities* give you easy-to-use motivational activities to begin every lesson in the textbook.
- *Chapter Digest Audiocassettes* (English and Spanish) reinforce major concepts. Perfect for auditory learners and students who need to review or catch up because of missed classes. Includes reproducible student activities and tests.
- *American Music: Cultural Traditions* (*audiocassettes* and *Compact Disc* version) provide a music review of the major time periods of American history.
- *U.S. History and Art*
  - *U.S. History and Art Transparencies* offer a multifaceted look at our nation's history through its art and include teaching strategies, learning objectives, teacher-guided activities, and student worksheets.
  - *Focus on American Art Prints* are display-quality, laminated posters that portray the cultural heritage of America. Complete with a Teacher's Guide and Student Worksheets.

NEW! USA Desk Map

Glencoe offers you a dynamic tool for hands-on geography. This double-sided desk map is both a political and physical map of the U. S. for truly interactive learning. (World Desk Maps are also available.)

AMERICAN ODYSSEY ©1997 COMPONENT LIST

Student Edition 0-02-822259-8
TWE 0-02-822261-X
Building Skills in Geography 0-02-823724-2
Teacher's Classroom Resources 0-02-822262-8
   Reproducible Lesson Plans
   Block Scheduling Implementation Guide
   Videodisc Bar Code Correlation
   Vocabulary and Guided Reading Activities
   Reteaching Activities
   Skill Reinforcement Activities
   Geography in History Activities
* Building Skills in Geography TAE 0-02-823725-0
   Outline Map Resource Book
   Enrichment Activities
   Supreme Court Case Studies
   Great Debates in History
   Political Cartoon Activities
   Case Studies
   Cooperative Learning Activities
   American Portraits
   American Literature: Readings and Activities
   The Spirit of American Art and Music
   Writer's Guidebook
   American Literary Heritage
   Performance Assessment Strategies and Activities
   Section Quizzes
   Chapter and Unit Tests: Forms A & B
* Teaching Transparencies 0-02-822294-6
   Beginnings to 1900 Review Transparencies
   Unit Time Line Transparencies
   Map Transparencies
   Chapter Teaching Transparencies
* Section Focus Transparencies 0-02-822293-8
U.S. History and Art Transparencies.........0-02-662292-0
Focus on American History
   Fine Art Prints......................................0-02-822354-3

American Music: Cultural Traditions
   CD 0-02-823803-6
   Audiocassettes....................................0-02-823805-2
English Chapter Digest Audiocassettes.....0-02-822295-4
Spanish Chapter Digest Audiocassettes 0-02-822296-2
Spanish Resources...................................0-02-822282-2
   Spanish Vocabulary and Guided Reading Activities
   Spanish Reteaching Activities
   Spanish Enrichment Activities
   Spanish Chapter Summaries
   Spanish Section Quizzes
Vocabulary PuzzleMaker
   DOS/Macintosh....................................0-02-822299-7
Testmaker 0-02-822297-0
   (includes DOS 3.5" & 5.25", and Macintosh 3.5")
Student Self-Test & Review Software
   DOS/Macintosh....................................0-02-822302-0
U.S. Desk Maps (Package of 30) 0-02-822469-8
World Desk Maps (Package of 30) 0-02-823770-6
Great Speeches (Abridged Edition) 0-02-822568-6
Set on Freedom: The American Civil Rights
Movement™ Videodisc Program
   Level I Videodisc Program 0-02-823432-4
   Level III MS-DOS Videodisc Program.0-02-823433-2
National Geographic Society
   GTV The American People:
     Fabric of a Nation Level I ** 0-02-823639-4
   GTV A Geographic Perspective
     on American History Level I**........0-02-823631-9
   The Presidents: A Picture History of Our Nation
     CD-ROM Program (DOS Version) ..0-02-823657-2
   NGS PictureShow Native Americans
     CD-ROM Program
      Part I...0-02-823679-3
      Part II 0-02-823692-0

ZipZapMap! USA Software
   Windows Version 0-02-823646-7
   DOS Version 0-02-823647-5
   Macintosh Version 0-02-823648-3
STV North America Level I** 0-02-823615-7
NGS Picture Atlas of the World
   DOS Version .,.....................................0-02-823652-1
NGS Picture Atlas of the World
   Macintosh/Windows Version 0-02-823654-8
Facts on File
   The American Indian CD-ROM 0-02-823462-6
   Landmark Documents in
     American History CD-ROM 0-02-822773-5
ABCNews InterActive™
   Powers of the U.S. Government 0-02-823690-4
   Communism and the Cold War**.........0-02-822925-8
   Lessons of War**.................................0-02-822926-6
   Martin Luther King, Jr. Level I**.........0-02-822932-0
   NEW! Historic America:
     Electronic Field Trips Level I...........0-02-821671-7

  * INCLUDED IN TEACHER'S CLASSROOM RESOURCES
  ** ALSO AVAILABLE AS LEVEL III

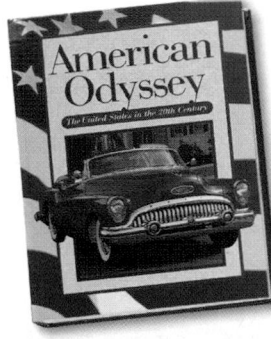

GLENCOE
McGraw-Hill

For more information contact your nearest regional office or call 1-800-334-7344.

1. Northeast Region
Glencoe/McGraw-Hill
15 Trafalgar Square #201
Nashua, NH 03063-1968
Phone: 603-880-4701
Phone: 800-424-3451
Fax: 603-595-0204

2. Mid-Atlantic Region
Glencoe/McGraw-Hill
P.O. Box 458
Hightstown, NJ 08520-0458
Phone: 609-426-5560
Phone: 800-553-7515
Fax: 609-426-7063

3. Atlantic-Southeast Region
Glencoe/McGraw-Hill
Brookside Park
One Harbison Way, Suite 101
Columbia, SC 29212
Phone: 803-732-2365
Phone: 800-731-2365
Fax: 803-732-4582

4. Southeast Region
Glencoe/McGraw-Hill
6510 Jimmy Carter Boulevard
Norcross, GA 30071
Phone: 770-446-7493
Phone: 800-982-3992
Fax: 770-446-2356

5. Mid-America Region
Glencoe/McGraw-Hill
936 Eastwind Drive
Westerville, OH 43081
Phone: 614-890-1111
Phone: 800-848-1567
Fax: 614-899-4905

6. Great Lakes Region
Glencoe/McGraw-Hill
846 East Algonquin Road
Schaumburg, IL 60173
Phone: 708-397-8448
Phone: 800-762-4876
Fax: 708-397-9472

7. Mid-Continent Region
Glencoe/McGraw-Hill
846 East Algonquin Road
Schaumburg, IL 60173
Phone: 708-397-8448
Phone: 800-762-4876
Fax: 708-397-9472

8. Southwest Region
Glencoe/McGraw-Hill
320 Westway Place, Suite 550
Arlington, TX 76018
Phone: 817-784-2113
Phone: 800-828-5096
Fax: 817-784-2116

9. Texas Region
Glencoe/McGraw-Hill
320 Westway Place, Suite 550
Arlington, TX 76018
Phone: 817-784-2100
Phone: 800-828-5096
Fax: 817-784-2116

10. Western Region
Glencoe/McGraw-Hill
709 E. Riverpark Lane,
Suite 150
Boise, ID 83706
Phone: 208-368-0300
Phone: 800-452-6126
Fax: 208-368-0303

11. California Region
Glencoe/McGraw-Hill
15319 Chatsworth Street
P. O. Box 9609
Mission Hills, CA 91346
Phone: 818-898-1391
Phone: 800-423-9534
Fax: 818-898-3864

**Glencoe Catholic
School Region**
Glencoe/McGraw-Hill
25 Crescent Street, 1st Floor
Stamford, CT 06906
Phone: 203-964-9109
Phone: 800-551-8766
Fax: 203-967-3108

Canada
McGraw-Hill Ryerson Ltd.
300 Water Street
Whitby, Ontario
L1N 9B6, Canada
Phone: 905-430-5088
Fax: 905-430-5194

International
The McGraw-Hill Companies
International Marketing
1221 Avenue of the Americas
28th Floor
New York, NY 10020
Phone: 212-512-3641
Fax: 212-512-2186

DoDDS and Pacific Territories
McGraw-Hill School
Publishing Company
600 Delran Parkway, Suite 640
Delran, NJ 08075
Phone: 609-764-4586
Fax: 609-764-4587

 Printed on recycled paper.

*A Division of The **McGraw·Hill** Companies*

Multimedia Edition
Teacher's Wraparound Edition

American Odyssey

★ ★ ★

The United States in the Twentieth Century

Gary B. Nash

PROFESSOR OF HISTORY
UNIVERSITY OF CALIFORNIA AT LOS ANGELES

GLENCOE

McGraw-Hill

New York, New York   Columbus, Ohio   Mission Hills, California   Peoria, Illinois

AUTHOR

Gary B. Nash is Professor of History at the University of California at Los Angeles and Associate Director of the National Center for History in the Schools. He is author of *Red, White, and Black: The People of Early America* (Prentice-Hall, 1982) and *Forging Freedom: The Formation of Philadelphia's Black Community, 1720–1840* (Harvard University Press, 1988), among other publications.

CONSULTANTS

Program Consultants

Geography Consultant
Christopher L. Salter
Professor and Chair
Department of Geography
University of Missouri
Columbia, Missouri

Educational Consultant
Allan H. Scholl
Former Secondary Social Science Specialist
Office of Instruction
Los Angeles Unified School District
Los Angeles, California

Contributing Consultants

Multicultural Education
Gloria Contreras
Professor of Secondary Education
University of North Texas
Denton, Texas

American West Frontiers
Albert L. Hurtado
Associate Professor of History
Arizona State University
Tempe, Arizona

Reading and Bilingual Education
Eileen Mortensen
Assistant Professor of Education
National Louis University
Evanston, Illinois

Women's Studies and African American History
Cheryl Johnson Odim
Assistant Professor of History
Loyola University
Chicago, Illinois

Asian Studies
Gary Okihiro
Associate Professor of History
Cornell University
Ithaca, New York

African American History
Julius S. Scott
Assistant Professor of History
Duke University
Durham, North Carolina

Mexican American Women's History
Vicki L. Ruiz
Associate Professor of History
University of California
Davis, California

Native American History
John Waukechan, M.A.
Member, American Indian Resource and Education Coalition
Austin, Texas

Glencoe/McGraw-Hill
A Division of The **McGraw-Hill** *Companies*

Printed in the United States of America.

Send all inquiries to:
Glencoe/McGraw-Hill
936 Eastwind Drive
Westerville, Ohio 43081

ISBN 0-02-822259-8 (student text)
ISBN 0-02-822261-X (teacher's wraparound edition)

1 2 3 4 5 6 7 8 9 VH/LP 00 99 98 97 96

Cover: 1953 Buick Skylark convertible

Development by Ligature, Inc.

REVIEWERS

Content Reviewers

David Anderson
Department of History and
  Political Science
University of Indianapolis
Indianapolis, Indiana

D'Ann Campbell
Department of History
U.S. Military Academy
West Point, New York

Lynn Dumenil
History Department
Claremont-McKenna College
Claremont, California

Paula Fass
Department of History
University of California
Berkeley, California

Otis Graham
Department of History
University of California
Santa Barbara, California

James R. Grossman
Director, Family and
  Community History Center
Newberry Library
Chicago, Illinois

Warren F. Kimball
Department of History
Rutgers University
Newark, New Jersey

John Martz
Department of Political
  Science
Pennsylvania State University
University Park, Pennsylvania

Allen J. Matusow
School of Humanities
Rice University
Houston, Texas

David Oshinsky
Department of History
Rutgers University
New Brunswick, New Jersey

Herbert Parmet
Department of History
Queensborough Community
  College
Bayside, New York

Richard Polenberg
Department of History
Cornell University
Ithaca, New York

Bernard Reich
Professor of Political Science
  and International Affairs
George Washington
  University
Washington, D.C.

Athan Theoharis
Department of History
Marquette University
Milwaukee, Wisconsin

Educational Reviewers

David Bardow
Carmel High School
Carmel, Indiana

Edward Brickner
Woodbury High School
Woodbury, Minnesota

Carolyn Conner
Westbury High School
Houston Independent
  School District
Houston, Texas

Bruce Eddy
Evanston Township High
  School
Evanston, Illinois

Brook A. Goddard
Miami Norland Senior High
  School
Dade County Public Schools
Miami, Florida

Ronnie Granade
Arkadelphia High School
Arkadelphia, Arkansas

Robert Griesing
Toms River Regional School
  District
Toms River, New Jersey

Sonya Heckman
Greencastle-Antrim Middle
  School
Greencastle, Pennsylvania

Merle Knight
Lewis S. Mills High School
Burlington, Connecticut

Tom Laiches
Crossroads School
Santa Monica, California

Doris B. Meyers
Huntington High School
Huntington, West Virginia

Sheldon Obelsky
Arlington High School
Arlington, Massachusetts

Dennis Schillings
Homewood-Flossmoor High
  School
Flossmoor, Illinois

Jacob R. Seitz
Morgantown High School
Morgantown, West Virginia

Gloria Sesso
Half Hollow Hills School
  District
Dix Hills, New York

Louise Stricklin
Redondo Union High
  School
Redondo Beach, California

Larry Sutton
Madison High School
San Diego Unified School
  District
San Diego, California

Darla Weissenberg
Lincoln Park High School
Chicago, Illinois

Teacher's Wraparound Edition Contents

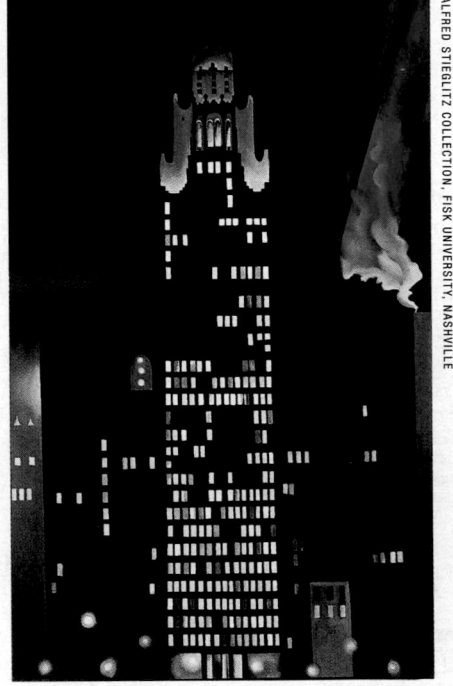

ALFRED STIEGLITZ COLLECTION, FISK UNIVERSITY, NASHVILLE

Student Edition Table of Contents

BROWN BROTHERS

WHITE HOUSE HISTORICAL ASSOCIATION

Student Edition Features

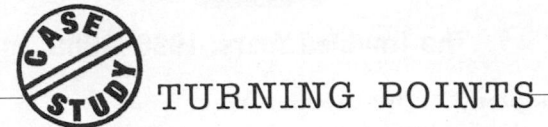

TURNING POINTS

By examining pivotal decisions made by leaders and ordinary people, the cases provide insight into the decision-making process and highlight the significance of these historic events.

LITERATURE

A variety of literature selections at the beginning of each unit communicate the thoughts, feelings, and life experiences of people, past and present.

© FAITH RINGGOLD INC.

One Day in History

Reminiscent of a daily newspaper, these "front pages" recall the dramatic—and the ordinary—events of ten special days in history.

CULTURE OF THE TIME

Visual and verbal displays appearing once per unit capture the popular culture of the time.

Then and Now...

With photos and fun facts each feature examines in detail an artifact or phenomenon from each unit's time period and the influence of that item on what exists now.

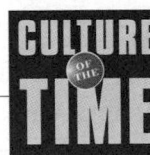

PHOTOPLAY ARCHIVES/LGI

Science, TECHNOLOGY, and Society

Through text, visuals, and a time line, this feature focuses on a technological advance and its short and long term impact on society.

Geography: Impact on History

The five geographic themes are explored through pivotal developments in United States history.

Social Studies Skill

Social Studies Skills provide learning and practice in the context of historical and geographical topics.

DIAGRAPHICS

Through diagrams, maps, statistical information, and annotated visuals, complex concepts are clearly and accurately depicted.

Defining Performance Assessment

In response to the growing demand for accountability in the classroom, many educators are advocating new approaches to assessment. One such approach is performance assessment, which measures student achievement in a more constructive and interactive manner than traditional tests do. In general, performance assessment includes performance-based activities and tests, and portfolios.

Performance tests ask students to effectively and creatively apply the knowledge they have gained. These tests require the application of problem-solving skills rather than mere recall. Instead of using a multiple-choice test to assess knowledge of a specific history concept, for example, a performance-based test asks students to actually utilize the concept. In designing performance-based tests, educators devise tasks that have more than one correct answer and that require more than one answer to complete. A key element in scoring such tests is to analyze the process the students use to clarify and solve the problem. Scoring involves rating students' performance on multiple factors, resulting in a descriptive profile of performance.

The portfolio approach is often used with performance-based assessment. Portfolios contain samples of students' work collected over a period of time—an entire grading period or even a semester. Students often help choose which items will be included in their portfolios. Portfolios allow for assessing a broad range of skills. Students can see how much progress they are making by comparing the work that they have completed throughout the course.

Performance Assessment Activities

Performance assessment is a way of teaching and learning that involves both process and product. It is not just a testing strategy.

Performance assessment activities provide hands-on approaches to learning concepts. Through the activities students are able to actually experience these concepts rather than just reading, writing, and listening about them. Each performance assessment is designed to allow the teacher to give a guided practice of the concepts being taught. At the end of each activity, the student is assigned a performance task that checks understanding of the lesson's concepts.

Performance assessment tasks get students involved in constructing various types of products for diverse audiences. Students also are involved in developing the process that leads to the finished product.

Performance assessment measures what you can do with what you know, not how much you know. Performance assessment tasks are based on what is most essential in the curriculum and what is interesting to a student.

More Like Playing Baseball Than Just Playing Catch

Many concepts, skills, and attitudes are important if an athlete is to develop into an accomplished baseball player. A coach teaches and drills players and promotes appropriate attitudes. However, if the training stopped there, the players would never learn the game. They must play baseball. Similarly, teachers can present the information and skills of a discipline and quiz the students on the details, but students also must "play the game." Students need the opportunity to put the concepts, skills, and attitudes together. Performance assessment allows students to demonstrate how effectively they can put the pieces together in ways similar to how information is used in the larger world.

Performance Assessment in the *American Odyssey: The United States in the 20th Century* Program

The *American Odyssey: The United States in the 20th Century* program provides a variety of performance assessment suggestions and options. The Teacher's Wraparound Edition provides Portfolio Project suggestions throughout the textbook.

Performance Assessment Activities are included on each Chapter Planning Guide. Additional performance assessment activities and rubrics are provided in the Performance Assessment Strategies and Activities booklet found in the Teacher's Classroom Resources.

Professional Notes

Block scheduling differs from traditional scheduling in that fewer class sessions are scheduled for larger blocks of time over fewer days. For example, in block scheduling, a course might meet for 90 minutes a day for 90 days, or half a school year. Does this type of scheduling have any advantage over more traditional scheduling methods? Those schools that have tried it believe that it does.

Advantages for School Systems

For the schools themselves, the greatest advantage of block scheduling is that there is a better use of resources. No additional teachers or classrooms may be needed, and more efficient use is made of those resources presently in schools. These advantages are accompanied by an increase in the quality of teacher instruction and students' time on task.

Advantages for Teachers

The advantages for teachers who are in schools that use block scheduling are many. Teacher-student relationships are improved. In traditional scheduling, teachers may teach five or six (or more) classes a day with as many different preparations. They are expected to know and teach 150 or more students in a day's time. With block scheduling, teachers have responsibility for a smaller number of students at a time, so students and teachers get to know each other better. With more time, teachers are able to provide additional time and resources for meeting the individual needs of students.

Teachers can also be more focused on what they are teaching. In fact, block scheduling seems to result in changes in teaching approaches, classrooms that are more student-centered, improved teacher morale, and increased teacher effectiveness. Teachers feel free to venture away from discussion and lecture to use more productive models of teaching.

If school days are of the same length as those that are more traditionally scheduled, teachers find the block approach more time-efficient. Block scheduling cuts in half the time needed for introducing and closing classes. Block scheduling also eliminates half of the time needed for class changes. If two six-minute class changes are eliminated each day, an hour of teaching time is gained in just one week. Fewer class changes also result in fewer discipline problems.

Advantages for Students

The benefits of block scheduling are not limited to teachers. Student success rate is found to be greater than is found with traditional scheduling because students seem to learn more and retain it better. Problem-solving skills are better developed, grades are improved, and the failure rate is lower.

Some of the advantages for teachers also are advantages for students. Improved student-teacher relationships and a more manageable work load help students. Students feel better about what they are learning, outside interference is reduced, and students are better able to concentrate. Generally, students feel better organized and are more aware of their progress in the class.

Parents report that there are many home-related benefits to block scheduling. There are fewer hassles about school, and students have a more positive attitude in general and take more responsibility for their homework. All of this results in a more relaxed family environment.

Modified Block Scheduling

Some schools use a modified form of block scheduling that combines two core classes. Under this system students might study social studies for 90 minutes each day during the first semester, science during the second semester. Another modification has students taking English and social studies blocks in one semester and science and mathematics blocks the second. Such scheduling encourages the teachers to institute team teaching or similar interdisciplinary approaches.

Professional Notes

Block Scheduling

90-MINUTE BLOCK SCHEDULE PLANNING GUIDE

The following is a suggested planning guide for using *American Odyssey: The United States in the 20th Century* in 90-minute periods for a total of 90 days. It can easily be adjusted for alternative lengths or for varied course emphasis.

Professional Notes

90-MINUTE BLOCK SCHEDULE PLANNING GUIDE

Professional Notes

CULTURAL PERSPECTIVES

The study of history furnishes a wealth of material that can help students learn to appreciate the cultural diversity of the United States. By reading *American Odyssey: The United States in the 20th Century,* students receive a broad view of the people and events that have contributed to the foundation of this country and the smooth operation of our system of democracy.

As immigration continues to make the United States a multicultural society, it is increasingly important for students to see peoples different from themselves as interesting neighbors who have different ideas, customs, and languages, but who also share many of the same values. By studying all aspects of our multicultural society, students gain a keen understanding of the roles that all Americans have played and continue to play in our government. The following five points have been identified as some of the major goals of multicultural education:

- Promoting the strength and value of cultural diversity.
- Promoting human rights and respect for those who are different from oneself.
- Promoting alternative life choices for people.
- Promoting social justice and equal opportunity for all people.
- Promoting equity in the distribution of power among groups.

—from *Making Choices for Multicultural Education: Five Approaches to Race, Class, and Gender* by Sleeter, Grant. Columbus: Merrill Publishing, 1988.

CRITICAL THINKING

To learn about history in a way that prepares students to become thoughtful participants in our society, students must learn to think critically. They need to be able to evaluate and to question the meaning of what they see, read, and hear. The teacher plays a crucial role in this development by creating a classroom climate that actively encourages critical thinking. To help teach critical thinking, teachers may wish to refer to Benjamin Bloom's *Taxonomy of Cognitive Behavior.* Bloom's *Taxonomy* organizes cognitive learning into six hierarchical classes:

- Knowledge involves recalling, identifying, and defining.
- Comprehension includes describing, explaining, summarizing and interpreting.
- Application entails applying, solving, and predicting.
- Analysis involves organizing, comparing, differentiating, relating, and inferring.
- Synthesis includes combining, producing, proposing, and hypothesizing.
- Evaluation entails appraising, judging, and deciding.

The Classroom Climate

The teacher can promote critical thinking in the classroom by asking questions that encourage students to analyze, synthesize, apply, and evaluate the information they hear and read daily. Sources for critical thinking activities or discussions range from the textbooks to newspaper and magazine stories and television news reports. Questions dealing with what happened, when it happened, or who was involved check the student's comprehension of facts. Questions that ask them to compare or explain events require that they dig deeper.

Critical Thinking in the *American Odyssey: The United States in the 20th Century* Program

Critical thinking is taught, reviewed, and reinforced throughout the *American Odyssey: The United States in the 20th Century* program. The Student Edition teaches the skills used in critical thinking, such as distinguishing between fact and opinion, determining cause and effect, and recognizing bias. Each of the skill pages provides opportunities for students to both learn and practice the skill being taught. Additional practice is provided in each Section Review and Chapter Review to continually reinforce the critical thinking process.

The Teacher's Wraparound Edition includes additional critical thinking activities. These are found at the bottom of pages throughout the lessons.

Professional Notes

DIFFERENT LEARNING STYLES

Your classroom undoubtedly contains students from a variety of backgrounds and with a variety of learning styles. In order to reach all of your students and make their learning experiences the most rewarding for their individual needs, *American Odyssey: The United States in the 20th Century* provides a wealth of instructional approaches and strategies.

Visual Learners

Visual learners benefit the most when they can carefully look at the material to be studied. In general, visual learners retain more information if they are able to visualize what they are learning. These types of learners benefit from laser disc presentations as well as from CD-ROMs. Visual learners also benefit from reading the text and studying the accompanying visuals.

Auditory Learners

Auditory learners retain the most information when they hear what they are to learn. Oral instructions from the teacher are ideal ways to introduce these learners to new concepts. Technology also plays an essential role in helping these learners master the course content. For example, audiocassette transcripts of chapters or lessons provide these students with invaluable learning aids. These students also benefit from laser disc presentations because the soundtracks help them comprehend the information with a higher retention rate. These learners also benefit from CD-ROMs, which provide them with instant auditory directions and feedback.

Kinesthetic Learners

Kinesthetic learners retain information more easily when they can actually perform basic tasks using the information. For these students, individual or group projects in which they construct models, charts, or graphs are ideal.

AT-RISK STUDENTS

Most educators today agree that the nation's schools are facing an epidemic of students who are at risk of failure. If their special needs are not met, these students usually drop out of school. Without a high school education, these young people face a life of low wages and menial jobs. Occupying the lowest ranks of our society, these young people seldom have the opportunity to enjoy the advantages that most Americans take for granted. These young people also make up a disproportionate number of prison inmates, with little hope for escape from the cycle of poverty.

Identifying At-Risk Students

It is difficult to define exactly what constitutes an at-risk student because being at risk is not linked to a single cause. Rather it is often linked to several environmental causes such as limited English proficiency, poverty, low self-esteem, homelessness, substance abuse, or pregnancy. Whatever the causes, at-risk students share a common characteristic. They have extreme difficulty with learning and are almost always low achievers.

Teaching Methods

Current educational research has shown that certain teaching methods can make a difference with at-risk students and help keep them from dropping out. One method is to maximize time-on-task. By doing so, teachers can help students overcome the outside stimuli that distract them from academic work.

Another method is to establish high expectations and a school climate that supports learning. Expecting students to succeed will help them believe that they are capable of succeeding. Many schools actively involve parents in this process so that the expectations for success are not left inside the classroom after school is out. By including the parents in decision making, many teachers have found that the entire school community benefits.

Because at-risk students have often failed in school, it is important to give them as much positive feedback as possible. Many teachers try to give this feedback at the end of each successfully completed assignment and regularly include awards ceremonies for those students who are meeting expectations.

COOPERATIVE LEARNING

Although cooperative learning is a useful teaching strategy in many subjects, it occupies a special place in the social studies curriculum because of its success in imparting the abilities needed to work effectively in a group. Such social studies skills are beneficial for all citizens living in a democracy.

Research suggests that mixed ability grouping in learning activities leads to higher student achievement, especially for lower ability level students. More able students benefit as well, however, from the reinforcement of learning that occurs as they assist their peers or justify their opinions.

Defining Cooperative Learning

Cooperative learning requires students to work together to pursue a common goal. Each member of the group has a specific task to accomplish in achieving the group's goal. Because part of each student's evaluation is determined by the overall quality of the group's work, there are incentives for students to help one another accomplish tasks assigned to the group as a whole. In such approaches, cooperation replaces the competitiveness of more traditional classroom activities, and students learn effective interpersonal communication skills.

Cooperative learning requires careful structuring and monitoring by the teacher if it is to be something more than a group activity. Characteristics of cooperative learning include the following:

- Students work face-to-face in heterogeneous groups.
- The activity promotes a sense of positive interdependence.
- Each member of a group has individual accountability.
- The group has a common product or goal.

Role of the Teacher

Although successful Cooperative Learning groups may appear to work independently, this is no doubt due to the astute coaching of a good teacher. Groups may need the teacher's assistance at key moments during a project, such as in agreeing on goals, establishing a structure of accountability, or evaluating their success. In particular, the teacher

needs to assure that no one student in a group does most of the work.

In their efforts to achieve group goals or objectives, students practice such social skills as listening critically, consensus building, conflict resolution, and offering and accepting constructive feedback.

Cooperative Learning in the *American Odyssey: The United States in the 20th Century* Program

Throughout the *American Odyssey: The United States in the 20th Century* program, students are asked to work together to address significant questions and resolve pertinent issues raised in their study. Activities require students to work together to analyze, synthesize, and apply lesson content. These cooperative learning activities challenge groups to solve problems, to make decisions, and to explain or justify conclusions. Many activities involve students in hands-on research and in presenting learning to others.

Depending on the nature of the activity, the strategies suggest that students approach tasks in pairs, small groups, or larger groups. Generally, the ideal group size will be four to six students. The teacher should structure each group to obtain a mix of high, average, and low achievers. In addition, gender and ethnic balance should be sought.

The Student Edition includes cooperative learning activities in each of the Chapter Reviews. They provide a variety of opportunities for students to work together on activities related to the chapter content.

The Teacher's Wraparound Edition contains both individual and cooperative learning activities. The cooperative learning suggestions, found in each Chapter Planning Guide as well as at the bottom of the pages throughout the lessons, offer a variety of interesting, activity-based teaching ideas.

The Teacher's Classroom Resources includes a Cooperative Learning Acivities booklet containing blackline master cooperative learnng activities for each chapter. These activities reinforce learning and build management and interpersonal skills by requiring students to work together to acquire, organize, and present information.

Professional Notes

TECHNOLOGY IN THE CLASSROOM

Advances in technology are continually being made, and these advances dramatically affect all aspects of the social studies. Social studies instruction should include an awareness of advances in technology. Wherever possible, discuss technology with your students as an ongoing part of the social studies courses.

Using Software With Limited Hardware

As with many other types of instructional tools, the more equipment available, the more flexibility your program can have. The ideal situation is to have one computer for each member of the class. You also might have access several times a week to a school computer lab. If either of these situations exists, you have unlimited opportunities for providing a wide range of computer activities. It is possible, however, to provide some computer activities with limited computer hardware.

• **One Computer for 25 Students.** With 1 computer, 3 to 5 students can be accommodated in an average class period by rotating students at the computer. Rather than have each student complete a specific exercise, form teams of 2 or possibly 3 students and assign each a portion of the software for the chapter. All students can then gain some computer experience without taking an excessive amount of classroom time. The 1-computer classroom is also ideal for demonstration using an electronic display device hooked up to a computer and an overhead projector. Remember that computerized student demonstrations of social studies concepts are excellent learning situations that develop not only content knowledge, but also software and communication skills as well.

• **3 to 5 Computers for 25 Students.** Three to 5 students can be accommodated at each computer in an average class period. All students should be able to complete review and reinforcement activities and become familiar with computers.

• **7 to 10 Computers for 25 Students.** Review and reinforcement programs can all be completed on an individual basis. With proper scheduling, students should have sufficient time to complete several computer activities without intruding on instructional time.

Multimedia

As a social studies teacher, you know that your students have varying learning styles. Some students are print-dominant learners; others are non-print-dominant learners. To help you accommodate these varying learning styles and to integrate listening, hands-on application, and more frequent stimulation and interactivity into the classroom, Glencoe offers a variety of multimedia programs, including software, laser discs, CD-ROMs, and audiocassettes.

Laser discs

If your school has a basic system consisting of a video-disc player and a television receiver, Glencoe laser discs provide an effective tool for classroom presentations. Students can see the connection between concepts and the real world. Students are also given opportunities to apply what they have learned.

CD-ROMs

CD-ROM programs provide large databases of information, as well as sound and motion. A display panel allows for large-screen display.

Computer Training for Teachers

You must have a general knowledge of computer operation, but you do not have to have a knowledge of internal hardware elements or programming languages. Resources exist in every school or district for help in using any troubleshooting equipment. These resources include other computer teachers, lab assistants, and technology supervisors. Concentrate on becoming familiar with the operation of your software programs. Remember that software hotlines are one of your best resources when using any type of software. Glencoe's software HOTLINE is 1-800-437-3715.

Professional Notes

RESOURCES

Using the following resources will help enrich student understanding of key concepts and provide useful background information for teachers. Most resources are available in your community library. They can also be ordered directly from the publisher.

Chapter 1 A Geographic Perspective on History

Readings for the Student
Farndon, John. *How the Earth Works.* The Reader's Digest Association, 1992.
The Usborner Geography Encyclopedia. Usborner, 1992.

Readings for the Teacher
Davis, Kenneth C. *Don't Know Much About Geography.* William Morrow, 1992.
Grillet, Donnat V. *Where on Earth?* Prentice Hall, 1991.

Multimedia Resources
Understanding Globes. United Learning. (videocassette, 15 minutes).World Atlas. The Software Toolworks. (CD-ROM for Macintosh or IBM).

Chapter 2 Encounters and Colonies

Literature From the Period
Brandon, William, ed., *The Magic World: American Indian Songs and Poems.* William Morrow, 1971.
Callaway, Sydney M., et al. *Grandfather Stories of the Navajos.* Navajo Curriculum Press, 1979.
Hammon, Jupiter. *America's First Negro Poet: The Complete Works of Jupiter Hammon of Long Island.* Stanley Austin Ransom, Jr., Kennikat Press, 1970.

Readings for the Student
Brandon, William. *Indians.* American Heritage, 1985.
Nash, Gary B. *Red, White, and Black: The Peoples of Early America,* 2nd ed. Prentice-Hall, 1982.
Swanson, Earl H., et al. *The Ancient Americas.* Peter Bedrick Books, 1990.

Readings for the Teacher
Brandon, William. *The Last Americans: The Indian in American Culture.* McGraw-Hill, 1974.
Hawke, David Freeman. *Everyday Life in Early America.* Perennial Library, 1988.

Multimedia Resources
Asia, 1600-1800. Landmark Films. (VHS, 26 minutes)
Colonial America. Mastervision. (VHS, 60 minutes)
Mexico Before Cortez. Social Studies School Service. (VHS, 14 minutes)
Peru: Inca Heritage. Social Studies School Service. (VHS, 18 minutes)

Chapter 3 The American Revolution

Literature From the Period
Franklin, Benjamin. *The Autobiography.* 1771.
Paine, Thomas. *Common Sense.* 1776
Wheatley, Phillis. "To His Excellency, General Washington." 1775

Readings for the Student
Applebaum, Diane Karter. *The Glorious Fourth.* Facts On File, 1989.
Bober, Natalie S. *Thomas Jefferson: Man on a Mountain.* Atheneum, 1988.
DePauw, Linda Grant. *Founding Mothers: Women in the Revolutionary Era.* Houghton Mifflin, 1975.
Langguth, A. J. *Patriots: The Men Who Started the American Revolution.* Simon and Schuster, 1988.

Readings for the Teacher
Greene, Jack P. *The Reinterpretation of the American Revolution, 1763–1789.* Greenwood Press, 1979.
Wood, W. J. *Battles of the Revolutionary War, 1775–1781.* Algonquin, 1990.

Multimedia Resources
Independence: Birth of a Free Nation. Finley-Holiday Film Corporation. (VHS, 28 minutes)
Paul Revere: The Messenger of Liberty. (VHS, 24 minutes)
Revolution '76. Britannica Software. (Apple IIGS or IBM diskette)
To Keep Our Liberty. National Park Service. (VHS, 23 minutes)

Chapter 4 A New Nation

Literature From the Period
Henry, Patrick. "Speech in the Virginia Ratifying Convention."
Jefferson, Thomas. *Notes on the State of Virginia.* 1787.

Readings for the Student
Kennedy, Caroline, and Ellen Alderman. *In Our Defense: The Bill Of Rights in Action.* Morrow, 1991
Rossiter, Clinton. 1787: *The Grand Convention.* Norton, 1987.

Readings for the Teacher
Gaustad, Edwin S. *Faith of Our Fathers: Religion and the New Nation.* Harper, 1987.
Norton, Mary Beth. *Liberty's Daughters: The Revolutionary Experiences of American Women, 1750-1800.* Scott, Foresman, 1980.

Multimedia Resources
The Constitution as a Living Document. Close-Up Foundation. (VHS, 57 minutes)
To Form a More Perfect Union. National Geographic. (film, teacher's guide)
Meet George Washington. NBC Project 20 Series. (VHS, 54 minutes)

Chapter 5 The Expanding Nation

Literature From the Period
De Tocqueville, Alexis. *Democracy in America.* 1835.
Jackson, Andrew. "Farewell Address." March 4, 1837.
Irving, Washington. "The Legend of Sleepy Hollow." 1819–1820.

Readings for the Student
"Robert Fulton Through Nineteenth Century Eyes." American History Illustrated. Vol. 21, No. 8, December 1986.

Readings for the Teacher
Brown, Richard D. *Modernization: The Transformation of American Life: 1600–1865.* Hill and Wang, 1976.
Dangerfield, George. *The Awakening of American Nationalism: 1815–1828.* Harper, 1980.

Multimedia Resources
Mill Girls, Intellectuals and the Southern Myth. Random House. (color, sound filmstrip)
The Monroe Doctrine Applied: US Policy Toward Latin America. VMA.(VHS, 16 minutes)
The New American Worker. Random House. (color, sound filmstrip)

Chapter 6 Civil War and Reconstruction

Literature From the Period
Alcott, Louisa May. *Hospital Sketches.* 1863.
Douglass, Frederick. "What the Black Man Wants." 1865.
Lee, Robert E. "Letter to His Son." 1863.
Stevens, Thaddeus. "Speech in the U.S. House of Representatives." January 3, 1867.

Readings for the Student
Catton, Bruce. *The Civil War.* American Heritage, 1971.
Cook, Fred. *The Ku Klux Klan: America's Recurring Nightmare.* Messner, 1989.
Woodward, C. Vann. *The Strange Career of Jim Crow.* Oxford. 1974.

Readings for the Teacher
Catton, Bruce. *A Stillness at Appomattox.* Washington Square, 1970.

Professional Notes

RESOURCES

Foner, Eric. *Reconstruction: America's Unfinished Revolution.* Harper, 1988.
Foote, Shelby. *The Civil War.* Random House, 1958.
Sernett, Milton C., ed. *Afro-American Religious History: A Documentary Witness.* Duke University Press, 1985.
Ward, Geoffrey C., with Ric and Ken Burns. *The Civil War: An Illustrated History.* Knopf, 1990.

Multimedia Resources
Frederick Douglass: An American Life. Your World Video. (VHS, 30 minutes)
Reconstruction. Dallas Community College. (VHS, 30 minutes)
Abraham Lincoln. Atlas Video. (VHS, 35 minutes)
The Civil War. Time-Life Video. (VHS, 9 episodes)
Slavery: America's Peculiar Institution. Zenger Productions. (VHS, 30 minutes)

Chapter 7 New Frontiers

Literature From the Period
Chief Joseph. *Chief Joseph's Own Story.* Montana Council for Indian Education, 1983.
_____. "I Will Fight No More Forever." 1877.
Harte, Bret. "The Outcasts of Poker Flat." 1869.

Readings for the Student
Brown, Dee. *Hear That Lonesome Whistle Blow.* Holt, 1977.
Freedman, Russell. *Buffalo Hunt.* Holiday House, 1988.
"Joseph, A Chief of the Nez Perce." Cobblestone, Vol. 2, No. 9, September 1990.
Walker, Robert H. *Everyday Life in the Age of Enterprise: 1865–1900.* Putnam, 1967.

Readings for the Teacher
Dale, Edward E. *Frontier Ways: Sketches of Life in the Old West.* University of Texas, 1989.
Moyniham, Ruth B., et. al., eds. *So Much to Be Done: Women Settlers on the Mining and Ranching Frontier.* University of Nebraska Press, 1990.
Takaki, Ronald. *Strangers From a Different Shore.* Little, Brown, 1989.
Vine, Robert V. *Community on the American Frontier: Separate But Not Alone.* University of Oklahoma Press, 1980.

Multimedia Resources
The Entrepreneurs: An American Adventure. Martin Sandler. (6 VHS, 5 hours)
Famous Women of the West. Multi-Media Productions. (filmstrip, cassette, guide)
Nez Perce: Portrait of a People. National Park Service. (VHS, 23 minutes)
Vaquero: The Forgotten Cowboy. PBS (VHS, 60 minutes)

Chapter 8 Progressive Reforms

Literature From the Period
Sinclair, Upton. *The Jungle.* 1906.
Tarbell, Ida. *History of the Standard Oil Company.* 1904.

Readings for the Student
Marshall, Megan. "Three Sisters Who Showed the Way." American Heritage, Vol. 38, No. 6, September/October 1987.
Mitelman, Bonnie. "Rose Schneiderman and the Triangle Fire." American History Illustrated. Vol. 16, No. 4, July 1981.

Readings for the Teacher
Filler, Louis. *The Muckrakers.* Rev. ed. Pennsylvania State University, 1980.
Hopkins, C. Howard. *The Rise of the Social Gospel in American Protestantism, 1865–1895.* Yale University Press, 1967.

Multimedia Resources
Progressives, Populists, and Reform in America. Guidance Associates (VHS, 32 minutes)

Chapter 9 Progressivism Takes Hold

Literature From the Period
Dreiser, Theodore. *The Financier.* 1912.
Du Bois, W.E.B. "Of the Meaning of Progress." 1903.

Readings for the Student
"Environmentalism." Cobblestone, Vol. 10, No. 8, August 1988.
Morris, Edmund. *The Rise of Theodore Roosevelt.* Ballantine Books, 1980.

Readings for the Teacher
Harbaugh, William H. *The Life and Times of Teddy Roosevelt.* Oxford University Press, 1975.
Link, Arthur S. *Woodrow Wilson: Revolution, War and Peace.* Harlan Davidson, 1979.

Multimedia Resources
The Federal Reserve System. Federal Reserve Board. (VHS, 30 minutes)
Theodore Roosevelt—Cowboy in the White House. Centron (29 minutes)
The U.S. Economic System. United Learning. (VHS, 75 minutes)

Chapter 10 Expansionism and World War I

Literature From the Period
Norris, George. "Opposition to War." April 4, 1917.
Wilson, Woodrow. "Appeal for Neutrality." August 19, 1914.
_____. "Fourteen Points." January 8, 1918.

Readings for the Student
McGinty, Brian. "Alvin York." American History Illustrated, Vol. 21, No. 7, November 1986.

Readings for the Teacher
Coffman, Edward M. *The War to End All Wars.* University of Wisconsin Press, 1968.
Greenwald, Maurine W. *Women, War and Work.* Greenwood Press, 1980.
Lemann, Nicholas. *The Promised Land: The Great Black Migration and How It Changed America.* Knopf, 1991.

Multimedia Resources
Mirror of America. National Archives. (VHS, 36 minutes)
The Ordeal of Woodrow Wilson. NBC. (VHS, 26 minutes)
The United States in World War I: Witness to History. Guidance Associates. (VHS, 15 minutes)
World War I: 1914–1918. Films for the Humanities. (VHS, 52 minutes)

Chapter 11 Getting on With Business

Literature From the Period
Fitzgerald, F. Scott. *The Great Gatsby.* 1925.
Lewis, Sinclair. *Babbit.* 1922.

Readings for the Student
Mowry, George E. *The Twenties—Fords, Flappers, and Fanatics.* Prentice-Hall, Inc., 1963.

Readings for the Teacher
Nash, Roderick. *The Nervous Generation: American Thought, 1917–1930.* Yale University Press, 1970.

Multimedia Resources
The Spirit of St. Louis. Warners (VHS, 137 minutes)

Chapter 12 A Prospering Society

Literature From the Period
Hughes, Langston. *The Weary Blues.* 1926.
Lewis, Sinclair. *Main Street.* Buccaneer Books, 1984.

Readings for the Student
Lyons, Mary E. *Sorrow's Kitchen: The Life and Folklore of Zora Neale Hurston.* Charles Scribner's Sons, 1990.

RESOURCES

Readings for the Teacher
The American Heritage History of the 20s and 30s. American Heritage Company, 1970.
McCay, Claude. *Home in Harlem.* Northeastern University Press, 1987.

Multimedia Resources
Cultural Contributions of Black Americans: A Literary Renaissance. SVE (color filmstrips)
Inherit the Wind. MGM/United Artists Entertainment. (film, 127 min.).

Chapter 13 The Great Depression
Literature From the Period
Hemingway, Ernest. *A Farewell to Arms.* 1929.
Hoover, Herbert. "Speech at New York City." October 22, 1928.

Readings for the Student
Meltzer, Milton. *Brother, Can You Spare a Dime? The Great Depression 1929–1933.* Mentor, 1977.
Scraff, Anne E. *The Great Depression and the New Deal: America's Economic Collapse and Recovery.* Watts, 1980.

Readings for the Teacher
Terkel, Studs. *Hard Times: An Oral History of the Depression.* Random House, 1980.

Multimedia Resources
Brother, Can You Spare a Dime? History in Action. Films for the Humanities. (VHS, 20 minutes)

Chapter 14 The New Deal
Literature From the Period
Roosevelt, Franklin D. "First Inaugural Address." March 4, 1933.
Steinbeck, John. *The Grapes of Wrath.* 1939.

Readings for the Student
Dillon, Richard. "Spanning the Golden Gate." American History Illustrated, Vol. 22, No. 3, May 1987.

Readings for the Teacher
McElvaine, Thomas Gordon. *The Great Depression.* Time Books, 1985.
Sternsher, Bernard, and Judith Sealander, eds. *Women of Valor: The Struggle Against the Great Depression as Told in Their Own Life Stories.* Ivan R. Dee, 1990.

Multimedia Resources
The Grapes of Wrath. 20th Century Fox. (VHS, 129 minutes)

Chapter 15 World War II
Literature From the Period
Parker, Dorothy. "Soldiers of the Republic." 1938.
Roosevelt, Franklin D. "Radio Address." September 3, 1939.

Readings for the Student
Berenbaum, Michael. *The World Must Know: The History of the Holocaust as Told in the United States Holocaust Memorial Museum.* Little Brown, 1993.
Gregory, Ross. *America 1941: A Nation at the Crossroads.* The Free Press, 1989.

Readings for the Teacher
Hosokawa, Bill. *Nisei: The Quiet Americans.* William Morrow, Inc., 1969.
Terkel, Studs. "The Good War." New York, 1984.

Multimedia Resources
December 7th. National Archives. (VHS, 34 minutes)

Chapter 16 The Home Front
Literature From the Period
Pyle, Ernie, *Dispatches From the Front.* 1944

Readings for the Student
Anderson, Karen T. *Wartime Women: Sex Roles, Family Relations, and the Status of Women During World War II.* Greenwood Press, 1981.
McGuire, Philip. *Taps for a Jim Crow Army: Letters From Black Soldiers in World War II.* ABC-Clio, Inc., 1983.

Readings for the Teacher
Davis, Daniel S. *Behind Barbed Wire: The Imprisonment of Japanese Americans During World War II.* Dutton, 1982.

Multimedia Resources
Home Front, World War II. Multi-Media Productions. (2 filmstrips, cassette)

Chapter 17 The Uneasy Peace
Literature From the Period
Churchill, Winston. "Speech at Fulton, Missouri." March 5, 1946.
Williams, Tennessee. *The Glass Menagerie.* 1945.

Readings for the Student
Caute, David. *The Great Fear.* Simon and Schuster, 1978.

Readings for the Teacher
Weisberger, Bernard *A. Cold War, Cold Peace: The United States and Russia since 1945.* American Heritage, 1985.

Multimedia Resources
America and the World Since World War II, 1945–1952: Volume 1. ABC (VHS, 52 minutes)

Chapter 18 The Postwar Era
Literature From the Period
Ellison, Ralph. *Invisible Man.* 1952.
Galbraith, John Kenneth. *The Affluent Society.* 1958.
Hansberry, Lorraine. *A Raisin in the Sun.* 1959.

Readings for the Student
Cheney, Glenn Alan. *Television in American Society.* Franklin Watts, 1983.
Divine, Robert. *Eisenhower and the Cold War.* Oxford University Press, 1981.

Readings for the Teacher
Girling, John L. S. *America and the Third World.* Routledge and Kegan, 1980.

Multimedia Resources
The Cold War. Educational Environment. (VHS, 31 minutes)

Chapter 19 Cold War Politics
Literature From the Period
Schute, Neville, *On the Beach,* 1958

Readings for the Student
Divine, Robert. *Eisenhower and the Cold War.* Oxford University Press, 1981.

Readings for the Teacher
Fried, Richard M. *Nightmare in Red: The McCarthy Era in Perspective.* Oxford, 1990.
Ingalls, Robert. *Point of Order—A Profile of Senator Joe McCarthy.* Putnam, 1981.

Multimedia Resources
The Cold War. Educational Environment. (VHS, 31 minutes)

Chapter 20 The Civil Rights Struggle
Literature From the Period
Brown, et. al. v. *Board of Education of Topeka, KA. et al.* May 17, 1954.
Ellison, Ralph. *Shadow and Act.* Random House, 1964.
King, Jr., Martin Luther. "I Have a Dream." 1963.

Professional Notes

RESOURCES

Readings for the Student
Durham, Michael S. *Powerful Days: The Civil Rights Photography of Charles Moore.* Stewart, Tabori, and Chang, 1991.

Patterson, Lillie. *Martin Luther King, Jr. and the Freedom Movement.* Facts on File, 1989.

Readings for the Teacher
King, Jr., Martin Luther. *Stride Toward Freedom.* Harper, 1958.

Powledge, Fred. *Free at Last? The Civil Rights Movement and the People Who Made It.* Little, Brown, 1991.

Multimedia Resources
All the Unsung Heroes. American Heritage Group. (VHS, 30 minutes)

King. Filmways. (VHS, 254 minutes)

Chapter 21 The Kennedy and Johnson Years

Literature From the Period
Kennedy, John F. "Inaugural Address." January 20, 1961.

Readings for the Student
Cummins, Duane. *Conflict and Compromise: The 1960s and 1970s.* Glencoe, 1980.

Oxford, Edward. "Destiny in Dallas." American History Illustrated, Vol. 23, No. 7, November 1988.

Readings for the Teacher
Barnet, Richard J. *The Giants: Russia and America.* Touchstone, 1977.

Goodwin, Richard. *Remembering America: A Voice from the Sixties.* Little, Brown, 1988.

Multimedia Resources
America and the World Since World War II, 1961–1975, Volume III. ABC News. (VHS, 52 minutes)

America and the World Since World War II, 1961–1975, Volume IX. ABC News. (VHS, 52 minutes)

That Memorable Year: 1963. Media Access Corp. (VHS, 50 minutes)

Chapter 22 Voices of Protest

Literature From the Period
Brown, Dee. *Bury My Heart at Wounded Knee.* Holt, Rinehart, and Winston, 1970

Friedan, Betty. *The Feminine Mystique.* Dell, 1984.

Resources for the Student
Lewis, Oscar. *La Vida: A Puerto Rican Family in the Culture of Poverty— San Juan and New York.* Irvington, 1966.

Pirsig, Robert M. *Zen and the Art of Motorcycle Maintenance.* Morrow, 1974.

Resources for the Teacher
Evans, Sara M. *Born for Liberty: A History of Women in America.* The Free Press, 1989.

Chapter 23 The Vietnam War

Literature From the Period
Kovic, Ron. *Born on the Fourth of July,* Dell, 1984.

Readings for the Student
Lawson, Don. *The United States in the Vietnam War.* Crowell, 1981.

Readings for the Teacher
Karnow, Stanley. *Vietnam: A History.* Viking, 1983.

Lacouture, Jean. *Ho Chi Minh: A Political Biography.* Random House, 1968.

Multimedia Resources
America and the World Since World War II, 1961–1975, Volume III. ABC News. (VHS, 52 minutes)

America and the World Since World War II, 1961–1975, Volume IX. ABC News. (VHS, 52 minutes)

Chapter 24 From Nixon to Carter

Literature From the Period
Nixon, Richard M. "Farewell Address." August 1974.

Readings for the Student
Cummins, Duane. *Conflict and Compromise: The 1960s and 1970s.* Glencoe, 1980.

"Energy: Powering Our Nation." Cobblestone, Vol. 2, No 10, October 1990.

Readings for the Teacher
Ambrose, Stephen E. *Nixon: The Triumph of a Politician.* Simon and Schuster, 1989.

Goodwin, Richard. *Remembering America: A Voice from the Sixties.* Little, Brown, 1988.

Multimedia Resources
All the President's Men. Warner. (VHS, 135 minutes)

Watergate Hearings: Summer of Judgment. WETA (VHS, 120 minutes)

Chapter 25 The Reagan and Bush Years

Literature From the Period
White, Theodore H. *America in Search of Itself: The Making of the President.* Warner Books, 1983.

Readings for the Student
Hewett, Ed. A., and Victor H. Winston, eds. *Milestones in Glasnost and Perestroyka: Politics and People.* Brookings, 1991.

Readings for the Teacher
Hyde, Margaret O. *The Homeless: Profiling the Problem.* Enslow Publishers, 1989.

Multimedia Resources
Contemporary America—1960–1980: A History of the United States. Encyclopaedia Britannica. (film, 84 minutes).

Chapter 26 A Changing Nation in a Changing World

Literature From the Period
Takaki, Ronald. *A Different Mirror: A History of Multicultural America.* Little, Brown, 1993.

Readings for the Student
Parillo, Vincent N., ed. *Rethinking Today's Minorities.* Greenwood Press, 1991.

Readings for the Teacher
Dinnerstein, Leonard, et al. *Natives and Strangers: Blacks, Indians, and Immigrants in America.* Oxford University Press, 1990.

Multimedia Resources
Energy: The Key to Our Future. United Learning. (VHS, 60 minutes)

Spaceship Earth: Our Global Environment. WORLDLINK. (VHS, 25 minutes)

Reading Comprehension

Name _____ Class _____ Date _____

CHAPTER 23

VOCABULARY AND GUIDED READING ACTIVITY

Section 1: War in Southeast Asia

The Vietnam War

Understanding Vocabulary

Fill in the blanks with vocabulary words from the section.

- national liberation
- containment
- domino theory
- guerrilla warfare
- pacification program

1. Opposing communism to keep it from spreading:

   _____

2. Using sabotage, hit-and-run, and ambushes to fight:

   _____

3. Fear that if South Vietnam became Communist, the rest of Southeast Asia would too:

   _____

4. Freeing a country from foreign control:

   _____

5. Relocating peasants so they couldn't assist the enemy:

   _____

UNDERSTANDING CONCEPTS

❶ *As you read Section 1, fill in the blanks in the following section outline.*

I. The French War in Indochina

  A. France and Vietnam fought a war because _____ wanted freedom from _____ control.

  B. The United States financially supported the French because of a commitment to stop the spread of _____ .

II. The United States Enters the War

  A. The United States supported the Vietnamese leader _____ because he was against communism.

  B. In 1960 the Vietminh and other groups joined forces in South Vietnam and became the _____ , also called the _____ .

  C. President Diem was overthrown because he did not help improve the conditions of the peasants and he severely repressed the _____ .

III. Johnson's War

  A. After the assassinations of _____ and _____ , President Johnson continued to support intervention in Vietnam.

  B. Through the Gulf of Tonkin Resolution, Johnson was able to get _____ approval to escalate involvement in Vietnam.

  C. Operation Rolling Thunder tried to stop the flow of supplies from _____ Vietnam into rebel camps in _____ Vietnam.

  D. By the end of 1967, _____ American troops were in Vietnam.

IV. Fighting the War

  A. The Vietcong had two advantages: they could move easily through the terrain, and they had the support of many _____ .

  B. Many American soldiers began to lose _____ because the war seemed unwinnable and its goals were unclear.

❷ *Write the number to show the correct order of the events below.*

a. ____ Kennedy assassinated

b. ____ NLF campaign of terror

c. ____ Ho Chi Minh declared independence.

d. ____ Ho Chi Minh Trail bombed

Also Available in Spanish!

Reteaching

Reteaching Activities provide students with comprehensive reinforcement of chapter information and history study skills.

Name _____ Class _____ Date _____

CHAPTER 23

RETEACHING ACTIVITY

The Vietnam War

Chapter Link

Between 1950 and 1968 the war that had begun as the struggle of the Vietnamese to throw off French colonial rule became a United States war to halt the spread of communism in Southeast Asia.

DIRECTIONS

The outline below lists five generalizations that show the progress of the war in Vietnam as it developed between 1950 and 1968. List pieces of evidence that support each generalization from the choices at the bottom of the page. You may want to review pages 768–775 before you begin.

THE EARLY VIETNAM WAR

❶ The Vietnamese people rebelled against French colonial rulers.

A Ho Chi Minh, a Communist, led a nationalist force that won control in the north.

B _____

❷ The United States entered the war on the side of the French.

A United States feared the spread of communism from China after 1949.

B _____

❸ The United States supported the unpopular anti-Communist regime of Diem in South Vietnam.

A _____

B United States staged overthrow of Diem when his policies were denounced worldwide.

❹ President Johnson increased American involvement in Vietnam.

A _____

B _____

❺ United States troops were not successful against the Vietcong.

A _____

B _____

Evidence

- Vietcong channeled supplies through underground tunnels.
- United States feared Soviet atomic power and needed France as an ally against the Soviets.
- Vietminh goals included land reform and a united, independent Vietnam.
- United States bombed North Vietnam nonstop.
- Diem refused to hold free elections, fearing Ho Chi Minh's popular support.
- Vietcong used guerrilla warfare against American troops.
- Almost 500,000 American troops were in Vietnam by December 1967.

AMERICAN ODYSSEY: Chapter 23   **23**

Also Available in Spanish!

Skills

Name _____ Class _____ Date _____

CHAPTER 23

SKILL REINFORCEMENT ACTIVITY

Understanding Public Opinion Polls

The Vietnam War

Skill Review

Public opinion polls can help you to understand what your fellow citizens think about current issues.

- To analyze a poll, first note the date and subject of the poll.
- Then note the sample size and margin of error.
- Next, decide if the questions asked were unbiased. Note the differences in responses from the sample's subgroups.
- Finally, translate the responses that are given in percentages into a statement summarizing the results of the poll.

Study the poll below and then answer the questions.

The United States and Vietnam

Interviewing dates: October 6–11, 1967   **Sample size:** 1,500   **Margin of error:** +/-3.5%

A. *In view of the developments since we entered the fighting in Vietnam, do you think the United States made a mistake sending troops to fight there?*

Yes	46%
No	44%
No opinion	10%

B. *Some people say that the war in Vietnam may prevent World War III. Others say it may start World War III. With which group are you more inclined to agree?*

May prevent	40%
May start	40%
No opinion	20%

C. *Do you think the Johnson administration is or is not telling the public all they should know about the Vietnam War?*

Is	21%
Is not	70%
No opinion	9%

D. *If a situation like Vietnam were to develop in another part of the world, do you think the United States should or should not send troops?*

Should	28%
Should not	57%
No opinion	15%

❶ Was this poll taken toward the beginning, middle, or end of the war?

_____

❷ According to the sample size, how many people thought the Vietnam War could prevent World War III?

_____

_____

❸ Were any of the statements phrased in a biased way? Which one(s)? Explain what made the question(s) biased.

_____

_____

❹ If 44% of those surveyed thought the United States belonged in the Vietnam War, how would you explain the fact that only 28% thought we should do the same again elsewhere?

_____

_____

_____

_____

❺ Based on this poll, how would you describe the public's outlook on the Vietnam War in 1967?

_____

Extension and Enrichment

Name _____ Class _____ Date _____

CHAPTER 23

ENRICHMENT ACTIVITY

The Vietnam War

Chapter Link

Section 2 (pages 664–671) describes the tumultuous domestic unrest of 1968. Discontent over the war festered in mass demonstrations. Race riots erupted following Martin Luther King Jr.'s assassination. The presidential election that year was also filled with turmoil and conflict over civil rights issues and American participation in Vietnam.

COMPLETE ONE OF THE FOLLOWING ACTIVITIES

❶ Imagine you are a reporter for a large urban daily newspaper. You have been invited to serve on a panel during a televised debate of presidential candidates Nixon, Humphrey, and Wallace. Write two questions to ask each candidate during the debate.

Nixon

- Republican   • Promises "peace with honor"
....
....
....
....
....
....

Humphrey

- Democrat   • Supports Johnson's war policies
....
....
....
....
....
....

Wallace

- Independent   • "Victory in Vietnam"
....
....
....
....
....
....

❷ Imagine you are a college student who has decided to leave school for a semester to campaign for Eugene McCarthy for President in 1968. Your parents support the United States's actions in Vietnam. Write a letter to your parents seeking their approval and explain what you plan to do and why.

AMERICAN ODYSSEY: Chapter 23   **23**

Also Available in Spanish!

Extension and Enrichment

Name _____   Class _____   Date _____

CHAPTER 23

COOPERATIVE LEARNING ACTIVITY

The Vietnam War

Chapter Link

Chapter 23 (pages 766–805) describes how the Vietnam War divided the people of the United States as no other issue had since the Civil War. More than 20 years after the war ended, Americans continue to debate social and political issues related to the war.

GROUP RESEARCH DIRECTIONS

The list below suggests some subtopics for a research report on the Vietnam War. Use Chapter 23 and library resources to find answers to these or other questions raised by the Vietnam War.

> **Vietnam**
>
> - Why did the U.S. become involved in Vietnam?
> - How did the student protest movement influence the war effort?
> - Why did United States policy fail in Vietnam?
> - Who fought in the war and how was the war fought?
> - What are the legacies of the Vietnam War?
> - How does the music of the 1960s and 1970s reflect feelings about the war?

COOPERATIVE GROUP PROCESS

❶ **Decision Making** Decide which subtopic your group would like to research. Brainstorm possible answers to the selected subtopic question and record these answers on a sheet of paper. Then identify possible resources, such as books, magazines, song books, or interviews. Assign each group member a different resource.

❷ **Individual Work** Research the subtopic using the assigned resource and take notes.

❸ **Group Sharing** Researchers share their notes and create an outline for an essay answering the subtopic question. Group members review the outline and decide what additional information is needed. Select a writer, editor, and proofreader to put the notes into an essay.

❹ **Individual Work** Group members gather additional information if necessary. The writer uses the notes to write the paper based on the outline. The editor reads and revises the rough draft. The proofreader examines the paper for spelling and grammatical errors.

❺ **Decision Making** All group members read the final draft and decide if additional changes are needed before the final copy is written.

Group Process Questions

Write your comments about the following questions on a separate piece of paper.

❑ Were the goals of this assignment clear?

❑ Did members work well together?

❑ Did each member contribute ideas at group meetings?

❑ Did members respect one another's point of view?

AMERICAN ODYSSEY: Chapter 23   **23**

Cooperative Learning Activities for each chapter reinforce chapter content and build management and interpersonal skills by requiring students to work together to acquire, organize, and present information.

Extension and Enrichment

Name _____ Class _____ Date _____

SUPREME COURT CASE 37

May be used with
Chapter 23, Section 3

Background

John Tinker and Christopher Eckhardt were high school students in Des Moines, Iowa. Along with John's sister, Mary Beth, a junior high school student, they were involved in planning a protest against United States's involvement in Vietnam. In December 1965, with their parents and others, the trio met to consider ways to publicize their protest. They decided that on December 16 and on New Year's Eve they would wear a black armband in order to indicate their support for a truce.

School authorities learned of these plans and on December 14 announced that any student wearing an armband would be asked to remove it or be suspended. Mary Beth and Christopher wore their armbands to school on December 16. John wore his the following day. All were suspended. The fathers of the students then filed a complaint in the United States District Court for the Southern District of Iowa seeking an injunction against the disciplinary action of the school authorities; they also sought nominal damages.

In the legal actions that followed, the district court sided with school authorities. The decision was upheld by an appeals court. The case then went on appeal to the United States Supreme Court.

Tinker v. Des Moines School District (1969)

CONSTITUTIONAL ISSUE

Was the wearing of armbands as a political protest in the public schools protected by the First Amendment's guarantee of freedom of speech?

THE COURT'S DECISION

The Court held 7 to 2 that this form of expression was protected by the First Amendment. Justice Abe Fortas wrote for the Court.

On the one hand, Justice Fortas observed, "It can hardly be argued that either students or teachers shed their constitutional rights to freedom of speech or expression at the schoolhouse gate. . . . the Court has repeatedly emphasized the need for affirming the comprehensive authority of the States and of school officials, consistent with fundamental constitutional safeguards, to prescribe and control conduct in the schools. . . ."

The Court found that there had been no evidence of any interference with the rights of other students or any disruption of classes. Yet the district court had supported school authorities because their fear of a potential disturbance was reasonable. The Court took note of this possibility but stated that "our Constitution says we must take this risk."

The Court also found it relevant that no general prohibition existed against wearing any controversial or political symbol, only black armbands. Such selective prohibition was held to be unconstitutional. Fortas went on to write, "If a regulation were adopted by school officials forbidding discussion of the Vietnam conflict, or the expression by any student of opposition to it anywhere on school property except as part of a prescribed classroom exercise, it would be obvious that the regulation would violate the constitutional rights of students, at least if it could not be justified by a showing that the students' activities would materially and substantially disrupt the work and the discipline of the school."

Students, whether in or out of school, were held to be "persons" under the Constitution, according to Justice Fortas. They have fundamental rights that must be respected. He emphasized, "In our system, students may not be regarded as closed-circuit recipients of only that which the State chooses to communicate. They may not be confined to the expression of those sentiments that are officially approved."

The Court's ruling concluded that "the wearing of armbands in the circumstances of this case was entirely divorced from actually or potentially disruptive conduct by those participating in it. It was closely akin to 'pure speech' which, we have repeatedly held, is entitled to comprehensive protection under the First Amendment."

Class _____ Date _____

dissenting opinion. He felt that the state's
the courts should have the right to decide
ns are "reasonable." He felt that there was evi-
rmbands and all the controversy that sur-
, disrupt school routine and classwork. Overall,
gave too much power to the students and
from the states and the school authorities.

_____ hools not absolute?

_____ rson" under the Constitution?

Extension and Enrichment

Name _____ Class _____ Date _____

CHAPTER 23

GEOGRAPHY IN HISTORY ACTIVITY

MOVEMENT: Trekking Through South Vietnam

The Vietnam War

Topographic Maps

Sharp jungle grasses, swarms of mosquitoes, steep and slippery inclines—each variety of terrain caused its own complications for the American troops as they moved through South Vietnam searching for guerrillas.

Maps like this one informed troops about the types of obstacles they should prepare for with each mission.

MAP KEY

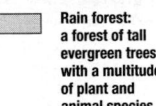

Rain forest: a forest of tall evergreen trees with a multitude of plant and animal species

Monsoon forest: open woodland typified by tall teak trees and thickets of bamboo

Cleared area

Savanna: a grassland with widely scattered trees and shrubs

Mangroves: trees that grow in shallow waters supported by a visible network of stilt-like roots

Use the map to answer the following questions. A dictionary or encyclopedia may help.

TERRAIN IN SOUTH VIETNAM, 1967

Gulf of Tonkin
NORTH VIETNAM
★Vientiane
N
LAOS
THAILAND
CAMBODIA
SOUTH VIETNAM
Phnom Penh ★
Saigon
SOUTH CHINA SEA
Gulf of Siam

0   100   200 mi.
0 100 200 km
Conic projection

❶ What kinds of terrain did American soldiers find in South Vietnam?

_____
_____
_____
_____

❷ What kind of terrain might be best for searching for guerrillas? Why?

_____
_____
_____
_____
_____

❸ Do you think troops would want to remain in one type of environment? Why?

_____
_____
_____
_____

❹ Compare the different types of terrain.

_____
_____
_____
_____

MAPPING ACTIVITY

❺ Create a map like the one above showing an area you are familiar with that has various types of terrain, or fill in an outline map from the back of the book.

Extension and Enrichment

Name _____ Class _____ Date _____

UNIT 9

The Troubled Years

AMERICAN LITERATURE

"How to Tell a True War Story"
by Tim O'Brien

Shortly after graduating from college, Tim O'Brien was drafted and sent to Vietnam. In this excerpt from his realistic short story, O'Brien shares his feelings about being in Vietnam. When he tries to tell "a true war story," he finds that some stories can't be told. No words can convey their meaning.

It's all exactly true.

It happened, to me, nearly twenty years ago, and I still remember that trail junction and those giant trees and a soft dripping sound somewhere beyond the trees. I remember the smell of moss. Up in the canopy there were tiny white blossoms, but no sunlight at all, and I remember the shadows spreading out under the

Even during the Vietnam War, the beauty of the land existed along with war's ugliness.

trees where Curt Lemon and Rat Kiley were playing catch with smoke grenades. Mitchell Sanders sat flipping his yo-yo. Norman Bowker and Kiowa and Dave Jensen were dozing, or half dozing, and all around us were those ragged green mountains.

Except for the laughter things were quiet.

At one point, I remember, Mitchell Sanders turned and looked at me, not quite nodding, as if to warn me about something, as if he already knew, then after a while he rolled up his yo-yo and moved away.

It's hard to tell you what happened next. They were just goofing. There was a noise, I suppose, which must've been the detonator, so I glanced behind me and watched Lemon step from the shade into bright sunlight. His face was suddenly

brown and shining. A handsome kid, really sharp gray eyes, lean and narrow-waisted, and when he died it was almost beautiful, the way the sunlight came around him and lifted him up and sucked him high into a tree full of moss and vines and white blossoms. . . .

How do you generalize?

War is hell, but that's not the half of it, because war is also mystery and terror and adventure and courage and discovery and holiness and pity and despair and longing and love. War is nasty; war is fun. War is thrilling; war is drudgery. War makes you a man; war makes you dead.

The truths are contradictory. It can be argued, for instance, that war is grotesque. But in truth war is also beauty. For all its horror, you can't help but gape at the awful majesty of combat. You stare out at tracer rounds unwinding through the dark like brilliant red ribbons. You crouch in ambush as a cool, impassive moon rises over the nighttime paddies. You admire the fluid symmetries of troops on the move, the harmonies of sound and shape and proportion, the great sheets of metal-fire streaming

the mountains and do terrible things , even so, you find yourself studying n the river, you feel wonder and awe f the sun, and you are filled with a hard, aching love for how the world could be and always should be, but now is not. Mitchell Sanders [a fellow soldier] was right. For the common soldier, at least, war has the feel—the spiritual texture—of a great ghostly fog, thick and permanent. rity. Everything swirls. The old rules nding, the old truths no longer true. er into wrong. Order blends into o hate, ugliness into beauty, law into y into savagery. The vapors suck you l where you are, or why you're there, ertainty is overwhelming ambiguity. ose your sense of the definite, hence ruth itself, and therefore it's safe to e war story nothing is ever absolutely

DING TO LITERATURE

ien says, "For all its horror, you but gape at the awful majesty of n your opinion, can war be both and grotesque? Why might people rent perspectives on the beauty or war? Explain your answer.

Tim O'Brien's feelings can you identify with? When have you experienced similar feelings?

world, all that might be lost. At the hour of dusk you sit at your foxhole and look out on a wide river turning pinkish red, and at the mountains beyond, and although in the morning you must cross the riv-

Extension and Enrichment

Name _____ Class _____ Date _____

UNIT 9 — CASE STUDY

The Troubled Years

CASE STUDY — Turning Point

LBJ, Vietnam, and the Troop Request

MARCH, 1968

MEMORANDUM

To: The Secretary of Defense

Subject: The Infeasibility of Military Victory in Vietnam

As a contribution to current deliberations and your own ongoing review of the situation, this memorandum argues the case that the idea of military victory in Vietnam is a dangerous illusion at any price that would be compatible with the U.S. interests, the interests of the people of South Vietnam, or the cause of world peace. . . .

Townsend Hoopes
Under Secretary of the Air Force
March 14, 1968

The Case

On February 28, 1968, General Earle G. Wheeler arrived at Andrews Air Force Base, Maryland, from Vietnam and went directly to the White House. Wheeler, the chairman of the Joint Chiefs of Staff, carried a report that he and General Westmoreland had prepared in Vietnam. Wheeler met with President Johnson and his senior advisers to present a summary of the report.

Wheeler and Westmoreland asked for 206,000 more troops to counteract the recent Tet offensive.

The magnitude of the request shocked some, including the President. In a grim outline of the situation, Wheeler focused on the political and military weakness of the South Vietnamese and stressed that the Tet offensive had not yet run its course.

The choices open to the President were not attractive ones, especially in an election year. Meeting the troop request would require calling up reserves, an unpopular act that would put the country in a state of wartime readiness. Funding such an escalation would require new taxes as well as cuts in domestic programs vital to the Great Society. On the other hand, denying the request, or supplying only a fraction of the troops requested, would signal to the enemy that the American war effort had limits.

The Background

The Tet offensive was a watershed for American policy in Vietnam. Both those who supported the war and those who opposed it saw in Tet an opportunity—and a need—to change the American war effort radically. Neither group believed any longer in the strategy of a limited war won by wearing down the North Vietnamese. For hawks, Tet was the act of a desperate enemy, a last-ditch effort to strike a crippling blow. The hawks hoped for a change in United States strategy that would support new offensives against a

Copyright ©The McGraw-Hill Companies, Inc.

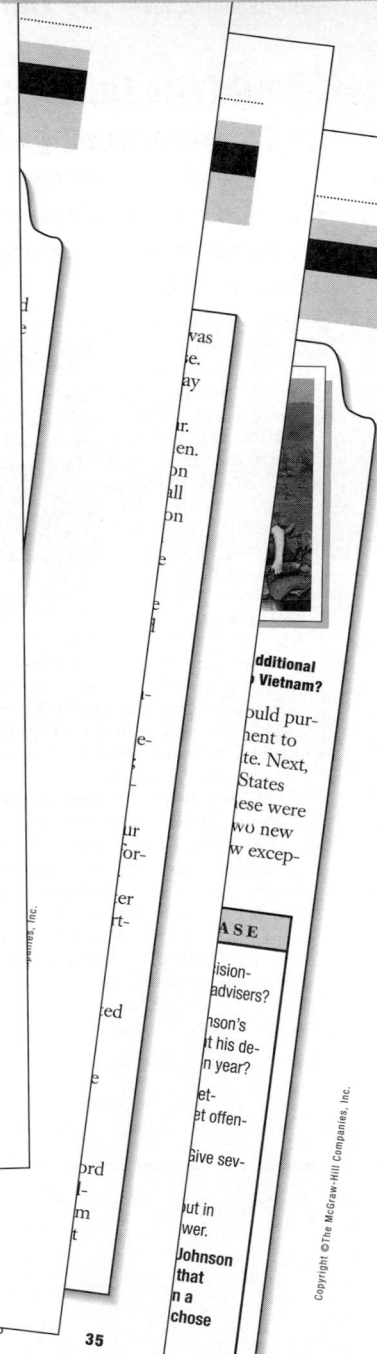

Copyright ©The McGraw-Hill Companies, Inc.

Extension and Enrichment

Name _____ Class _____ Date _____

GREAT DEBATES IN AMERICAN HISTORY
United States Involvement in Vietnam

The Troubled Years

Should the United States Discontinue Its Involvement in Vietnam?

The role of the United States in Vietnam, almost from the beginning, was a cause of great controversy. People of all walks of life–ordinary citizens, as well as politicians and other prominent people–disagreed on whether or not American troops should be fighting there.

The United States became more and more involved in Vietnam in the early sixties. By July 1965, the Pentagon had begun urging President Johnson to intervene more strongly in order to avoid the collapse of the government of South Vietnam. In June, Secretary of Defense Robert McNamara asked the President to send 200,000 American troops to aid the South Vietnamese. On July 21 and 22 the White House held meetings to discuss the issue. Among those present were George Ball, Undersecretary of State, and Henry Cabot Lodge, the American Ambassador to Vietnam.

Pro

George Ball thought that the United States should withdraw from Vietnam. He was against sending more troops and had sent memos and spoken many times about the issue. Here is one of his statements from the July 1965 meeting.

We cannot win, Mr. President. This war will be long and protracted. The most we can hope for is a messy conclusion. There remains a great danger of intrusion by the Chinese. But the biggest problem is the problem of the long war. . . . As casualties increase, the pressure to strike at the very jugular of North Vietnam will become very great. I am concerned about world opinon. If we could win in a year's time, and win decisively, world opinion would be all right. However, if the war is long and protracted, as I believe it will be, then we will suffer because the world's greatest power cannot

defeat guerrillas. Then there is the problem of national politics. Every great captain in history was not afraid to make a tactical withdrawal if conditions were unfavorable to him. The enemy cannot even be seen in Vietnam. He is indigenous to the country. I truly have serious doubts that an army of Westerners can successfully fight Orientals in an Asian jungle.

I think we all have understimated the seriousness of this situation. It is like giving cobalt treatment to a terminal cancer case. I think a long, protracted war will disclose our weakness, not our strength.

AMERICAN ODYSSEY: Unit 9   **37**

(overlapping pages, partial text)

gles. If we can secure
namese can secure, in
rement to, one, appre-
and two, give intel-
overnment. . . . The
n dealt more casual-
we suffered in the
ese soldier is an un-
le has ideas he will

ps to Vietnam,
s began to

l by the war,
r in Vietnam"
ing told his
t before, and
rays of
States involve-
g other civil
vil rights
es presence
as his duty

y were
r King.
etween
of Ne-
s circle
impris-
des the

itical play-
war, and I
invest the
ehabilita-
n contin-
oney like
n tube.
see the
attack

ietnam
reover,
aft age
ns and
ectors.
ust de-
is con-

young men of his time.

40   AMERICAN ODYSSEY: UNIT 9

AMERICAN ODYSSEY: Unit 9   **39**

Extension and Enrichment

Interpreting Political Cartoons enrich and motivate by providing visual activities that challenge students with provocative perspectives on key issues.

Name _____ Date _____ Class _____

ACTIVITY 23
Interpreting Political Cartoons ★★★★★★★★★★★★★★★★★★★★★★★★★★★★★★★★★

New Deal Policies

The New Deal had three main goals: to provide immediate help to millions of Americans, to improve the economy, and to reform laws that favored the rich and powerful over the poor and powerless. People called these the "Three Rs" of relief, recovery, and reform. Several relief measures became law during the first 100 days.

Study the cartoon below, then answer the questions that follow.

Library of Congress

Political Cartoons in American History   **45**

Extension and Enrichment

SPIRIT OF AMERICAN ART AND MUSIC

Name_____ Date_____ Class _____

Spirit of American Art and Music

★ ★ ★ ★ ★ ★ ★ ★ ★ ★ ★ **Maya Angelou** ★ ★ ★ ★ ★ ★ ★ ★ ★ ★ ★

As a writer, a poet, a composer of music, a performer, and a professor of American Studies, Maya Angelou has often been described as a modern rendition of the Renaissance woman. She has indeed achieved much in her life and is today recognized as one of the great voices in contemporary African American literature.

Maya Angelou was born on April 4, 1928, in St. Louis, Missouri. Her childhood was tumultuous at best. After her parents separated, she went to live with her grandmother in Arkansas. At the age of eight, she was raped, and for the next five years of her life remained mute.

As a young woman, she traveled to New York and joined the Harlem Writer's Guild.

Meanwhile, she earned a living singing in nightclubs, waitressing, and doing whatever she could to stay afloat amidst hard times. In her twenties, Angelou joined a performing arts group and toured through Europe and Africa in the musical "Porgy and Bess."

The decade of the 1960s saw the emergence of the civil rights movement in America and gave Angelou a new focus to her life. At the request of Dr. Martin Luther King, Jr., she became the National Coordinator for the Southern Christian Leadership Conference. From there, Angelou went on to write her most famous work—an autobiography titled *I Know Why the Caged Bird Sings*, published in 1970. This story is an account, often humorous, of her childhood

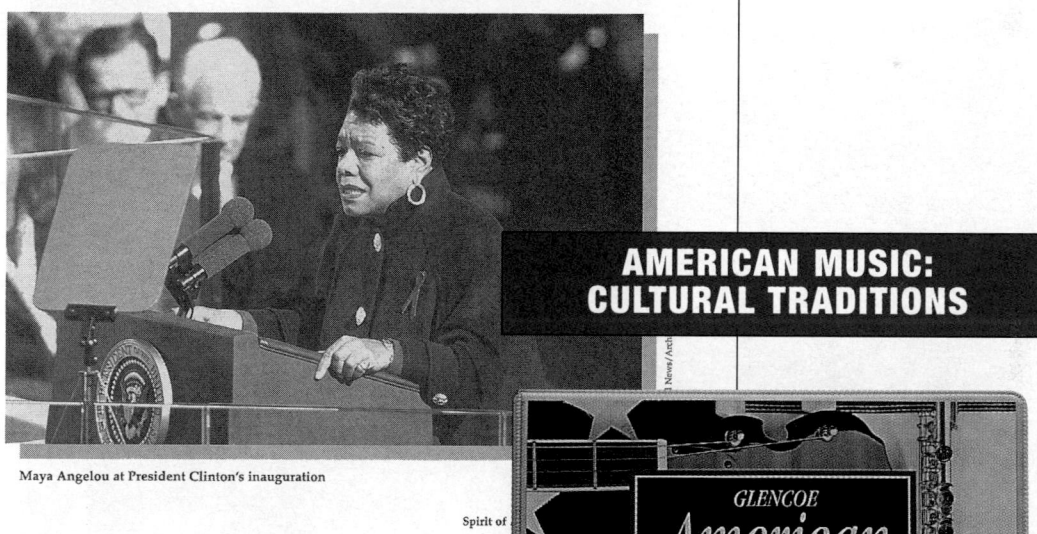

Maya Angelou at President Clinton's inauguration

Spirit of

Spirit of American Art and Music blackline masters provide biographical material on American artists, musicians, and architects who made significant contributions throughout American history.

AMERICAN MUSIC: CULTURAL TRADITIONS

GLENCOE
American Music
★ ★ ★ ★ ★ ★ ★ ★
Cultural Traditions

GLENCOE
American Music
★ ★ ★ ★ ★ ★ ★
Cultural Traditions
Volume 1

Includes:
Teacher's Guide • Student Activities
Compact Discs, Volume I and II

American Music: Cultural Traditions brings students into contact with American music from the pre-colonial period through today's contemporary music.

Extension and Enrichment

Focus on American Fine Art Prints includes 20 colorful, laminated fine-art posters that decorate your classroom and show students how the cultural heritage of the United States is reflected through the arts. Includes a Teacher's Guide.

Ellen Day Hale (American 1855–1940)
June

ca. 1905, oil on canvas, 24 x 18⅝".
The National Museum of Women in the Arts, Gift of Wallace and Wilhelmina Holladay.

Spanish Resources

Spanish Resources include *Spanish Chapter Summaries* as well as Spanish translations of *Vocabulary and Guided Reading Activities, Section Quizzes, Enrichment Activities,* and *Reteaching Activities. Spanish Chapter Digests Audiocassettes* with Activities and Tests are also available.

Spanish Resources

Includes
- Spanish Vocabulary and Guided Reading Activities
- Spanish Section Quizzes
- Spanish Enrichment Activities
- Spanish Reteaching Activities
- Spanish Chapter Summaries

American Odyssey
The United States in the 20th Century

G22822.01

Evaluation

Name   Class   Date   Score

CHAPTER 23

SECTION QUIZ

Section 1: War in Southeast Asia

The Vietnam War

MULTIPLE CHOICE (10 points each)

In the space at the left, write the letter of the choice that best completes the statement or answers the question.

_____ **1** One of the goals of the Vietminh leaders in the 1940s was
   a. to split Vietnam into two countries.
   b. to rid the country of communism.
   c. to find a nation to control Vietnam.
   d. extensive land reform.

_____ **2** The capture of Dien Bien Phu by the Vietminh in 1954
   a. signaled the end of United States control of Vietnam.
   b. resulted in the end of Communist rule in Vietnam.
   c. resulted in a victory for the French.
   d. signaled the end of French control of Vietnam.

_____ **3** Which of the following statements does NOT describe a term of the Geneva peace agreement of 1954?
   a. Vietnam would be temporarily divided along the 17th parallel.
   b. The Vietminh would withdraw to the north of the 17th parallel.
   c. Vietnam would be under the control of the United States.
   d. Vietnam would be reunified in 1956 after national elections.

_____ **4** Most of the money pumped into South Vietnam by the United States between 1954 and 1961 was
   a. used to provide free elections.
   b. used to improve agriculture in the country.
   c. used for economic development.
   d. spent on the military.

_____ **5** In the mid-1960s, the United States relied on air power in Vietnam because
   a. bombing cost fewer American lives than ground combat.
   b. bombing would guarantee an American victory in Vietnam.
   c. the Vietcong had a very efficient air force.
   d. it did not want to involve civilians.

MATCHING (10 points each)

In the blank at the left of each term, name, or date, write the letter of the statement that best defines or describes the item.

_____ **6** Ho Chi Minh   **a.** a fierce nationalist and anti-Communist leader
_____ **7** Pleiku, South Vietnam   **b.** United States military base
_____ **8** Ngo Dinh Diem   **c.** Vietminh leader
_____ **9** Vietminh   **d.** Communist, anti-Diem group in South Vietnam
_____ **10** National Liberation Front   **e.** Vietnamese nationalist group

72   AMERICAN ODYSSEY: Chapter 23

Also Available in Spanish!

Evaluation

Name _____ Class _____ Date _____ Score _____

| CHAPTER 23 | TEST: FORM A |

The Vietnam War

COMPLETION (5 points each)

In the space provided, write the word or words that best complete the sentence.

_____ **1** The French surrendered to the Vietminh at_____, signaling the end of French rule in Vietnam.

_____ **2** _____ was the first United States President to provide aid in the struggle in Vietnam.

_____ **3** Groups opposed to Diem formed the National Liberation Front, also known as the _____.

_____ **4** _____ gave President Johnson the authority to increase United States involvement in Vietnam.

_____ **5** First a general and then President, _____ led South Vietnam throughout most of the war.

_____ **6** The Tet offensive made Americans _____ Johnson's policies in Vietnam.

_____ **7** Running as an antiwar Democrat, _____ won the New Hampshire primary election in 1968.

_____ **8** The system for selecting individuals for military service is called the _____.

_____ **9** Student protests and the _____ helped to mold public opinion about the war.

_____ **10** The protests at Columbia University linked two issues, the Vietnam War and _____.

MULTIPLE CHOICE (5 points each)

In the space at the left, write the letter of the choice that best completes the statement or answers the question.

_____ **11** American generals in Vietnam insisted that the war could be won, while many civilians called for negotiations to end the conflict. Opinions differed because

a. the generals were only looking for a military solution and did not consider the eroding lack of political support for war.
b. the generals wanted a war.
c. civilians did not understand all the facts about the war.
d. they just didn't want to agree with one another.

_____ **12** The Vietminh were fighting the French so that

a. they could take over all the land and wealth.
b. they could take control of North Vietnam.
c. they could get aid from the United States.
d. they could undertake land reform.

Date _____ Score _____

he letter of the statement that best defines

ent

s, Cambodia and North Vietnam
rd assault on students
litary service
nam
in Vietnam
sm to prevent its spread
s of the Vietnam War
munist group

est completes the statement or answers

Testmaker

American Odyssey

135

137

Evaluation

Name _____ Class _____ Date _____

CHAPTER 23

✓ PERFORMANCE ASSESSMENT

Student Activism During the Vietnam War

The Vietnam War

Background	TASK
In the early 1960s, when the United States began sending large numbers of troops to fight in Vietnam, students at various American colleges and universities formed groups to protest this involvement.	You are a newspaper reporter during the time of the Vietnam War. Your assignment is to write an article about the student movement of the 1960s. You will describe the beginnings of the movement, and then you will report on one particular group and its leader or leaders. Your article will state what the group hoped to accomplish, and what, if anything, it did accomplish.

AUDIENCE

Your audience is readers of a student newspaper.

PURPOSE

Your article should inform your audience about the student movement during the Vietnam War, including the origins of the movement and the accomplishments of one student group.

PROCEDURE

1. Consult the Assessment Lists for a Newspaper Article and a Research Report.

2. Research the various student groups. Then make a list of these groups and choose the one you want to focus on. Continue your research, using your text and your school or public library to find sources of information. Take notes.

3. Use your notes to write a first draft of your article, and create a title that will grab the attention of your readers.

4. Share your draft with a classmate. Ask for feedback, and then revise your draft, eliminating parts that do not work and adding vivid, supporting details, if necessary. Check for accuracy.

5. Write the final draft of your article.

Assessment

☐ Use the Assessment Lists for a Newspaper Article and a Research Report to evaluate your newspaper article.

☐ Check to be sure that you have included all elements.

☐ Complete a final self-assessment of your work before you share it with your class.

Performance Assessment Strategies and Activities provide alternative assessment strategies for greater flexibility in evaluation. The booklet also contains classroom assessment lists and scoring rubrics.

Evaluation

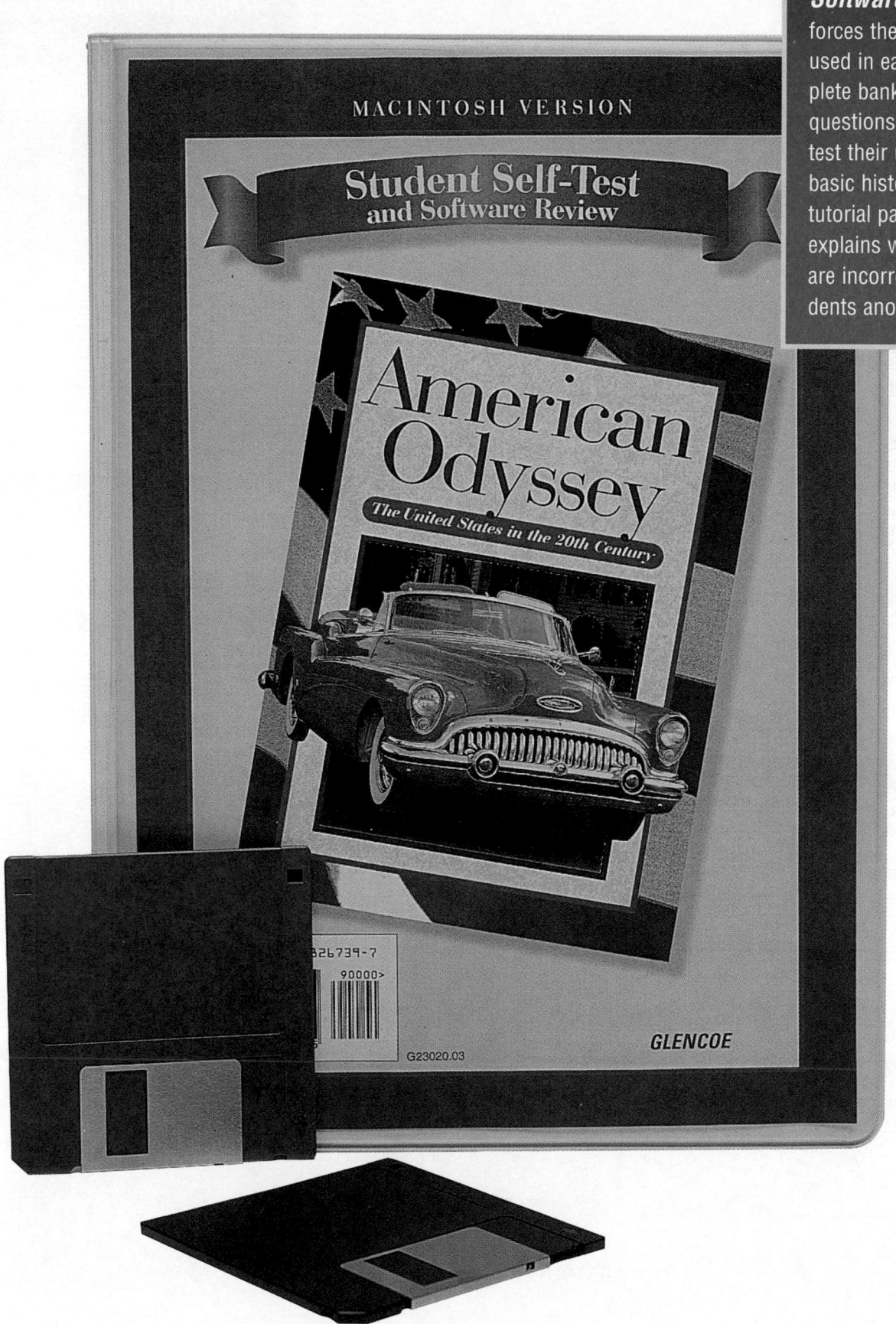

MACINTOSH VERSION

Student Self-Test
and Software Review

American Odyssey

The United States in the 20th Century

826739-7

90000>

G23020.03

GLENCOE

Student Self-Test and Software Review rein-forces the history concepts used in each chapter. A com-plete bank of multiple-choice questions allows students to test their understanding of basic history concepts. The tutorial part of the program explains why certain responses are incorrect and gives stu-dents another chance.

Multimedia

Copyright©The McGraw-Hill Companies, Inc.

CHAPTER 23

SECTION FOCUS TRANSPARENCY 72

Section 1

ANSWERS
1. 12
2. 15
3. no
4. yes

The Spread of Communism Before the Vietnam War

PACIFIC OCEAN

ATLANTIC OCEAN

INDIAN OCEAN

NUMBER OF COMMUNIST COUNTRIES AND TERRITORIES

Turned Communist before 1940

Turned Communist during the 1940s

0   5   10   15

0   1,000   2,000 mi.

0   1,000   2,000 km
Robinson projection

RESPONDING TO THE TRANSPARENCY

❶ How many countries and territories were Communist by 1940?

❷ How many turned Communist during the 1940s?

❸ Did Communism stop spreading by 1940?

❹ Since 27 countries and territories had turned Communist by 1950, were fears about the continued spread of communism reasonable?

Section Focus Transparencies offer a variety of formats that may be used as Bellringer Motivational Activities for each of the 85 lessons in the text. Each activity is also available as a blackline master.

Multimedia

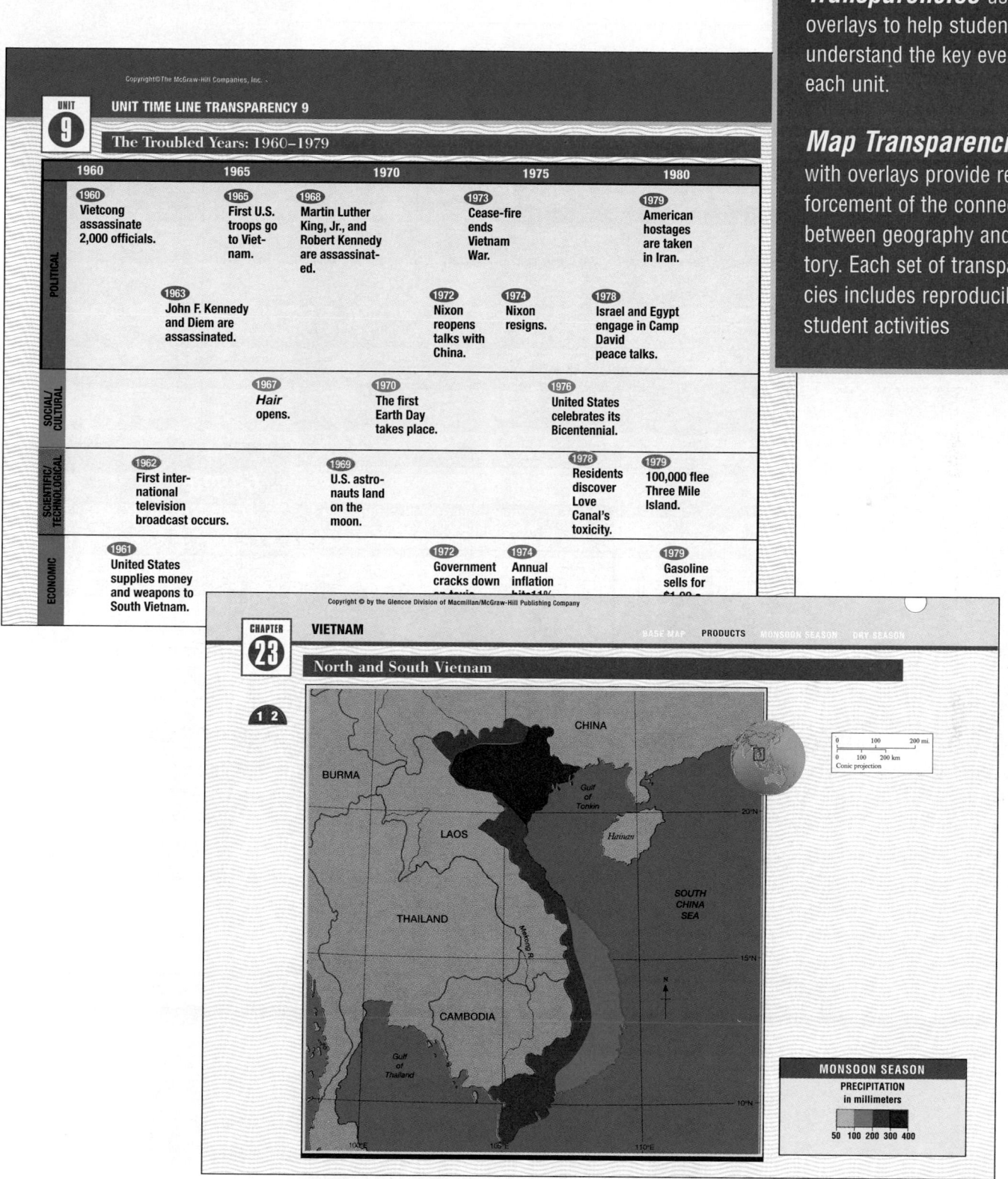

Copyright©The McGraw-Hill Companies, Inc.

UNIT 9

UNIT TIME LINE TRANSPARENCY 9

The Troubled Years: 1960–1979

	1960	1965	1970	1975	1980

POLITICAL

1960
Vietcong assassinate 2,000 officials.

1965
First U.S. troops go to Vietnam.

1968
Martin Luther King, Jr., and Robert Kennedy are assassinated.

1973
Cease-fire ends Vietnam War.

1979
American hostages are taken in Iran.

1963
John F. Kennedy and Diem are assassinated.

1972
Nixon reopens talks with China.

1974
Nixon resigns.

1978
Israel and Egypt engage in Camp David peace talks.

SOCIAL/ CULTURAL

1967
Hair opens.

1970
The first Earth Day takes place.

1976
United States celebrates its Bicentennial.

SCIENTIFIC/ TECHNOLOGICAL

1962
First international television broadcast occurs.

1969
U.S. astronauts land on the moon.

1978
Residents discover Love Canal's toxicity.

1979
100,000 flee Three Mile Island.

ECONOMIC

1961
United States supplies money and weapons to South Vietnam.

1972
Government cracks down on tuxic

1974
Annual inflation hits 11%.

1979
Gasoline sells for $1.00 a

Copyright © by the Glencoe Division of Macmillan/McGraw-Hill Publishing Company

CHAPTER 23

VIETNAM

BASE MAP   PRODUCTS   MONSOON SEASON   DRY SEASON

North and South Vietnam

1 2

CHINA

BURMA

Gulf of Tonkin

Hainan

LAOS

THAILAND

Mekong R.

SOUTH CHINA SEA

CAMBODIA

Gulf of Thailand

N

0   100   200 mi.
0   100   200 km
Conic projection

20°N
15°N
10°N
105°E
110°E

MONSOON SEASON

PRECIPITATION in millimeters

50 100 200 300 400

T41

Multimedia

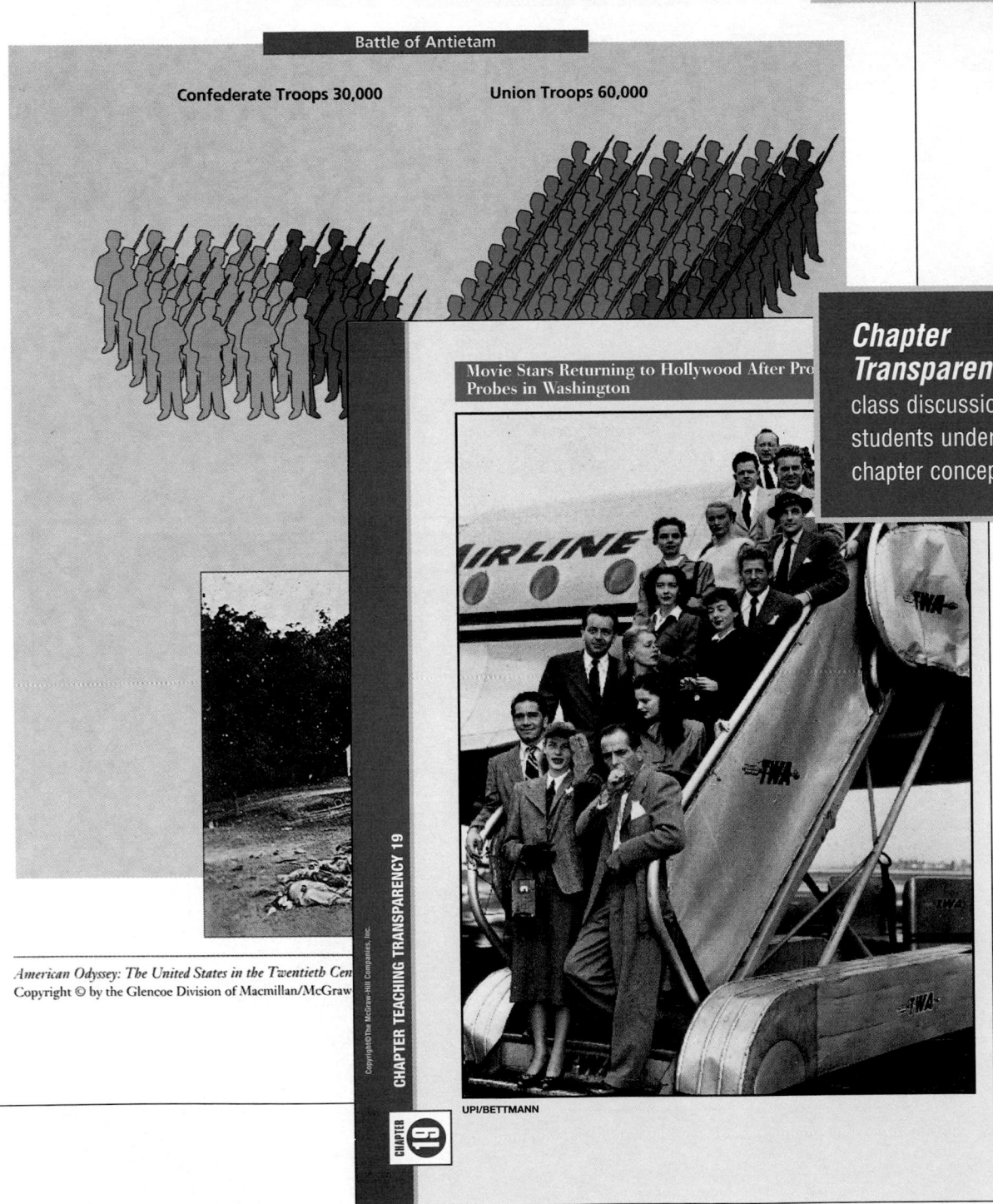

TRANSPARENCY 14

Civil War Casualties

Battle of Antietam

Confederate Troops 30,000   Union Troops 60,000

American Odyssey: The United States in the Twentieth Cen...
Copyright © by the Glencoe Division of Macmillan/McGraw...

Copyright © The McGraw-Hill Companies, Inc.

CHAPTER TEACHING TRANSPARENCY 19

CHAPTER 19

Movie Stars Returning to Hollywood After Pro...
Probes in Washington

UPI/BETTMANN

Multimedia

UNITED STATES HISTORY & ART

Allies Day, May 1917 (1917)
Childe Hassam

National Gallery of Art, Washington

Chapter Digest Audiocassettes summarize each chapter and include student activities and tests, providing yet another means to review, reteach, reinforce, or condense chapter content.

Also Available in Spanish!

Multimedia

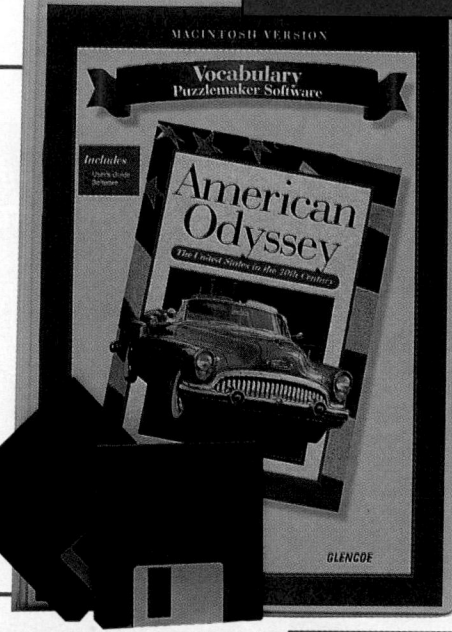

Vocabulary PuzzleMaker (DOS and Macintosh) reinforces chapter vocabulary terms by allowing you to generate your own crossword puzzles and word searches, so students can have fun while they learn the language of history.

Student Self-Test and Software Review (DOS and Macintosh) allows students to test their understanding of basic concepts at the unit, chapter, and section levels. A tutorial explains why incorrect answers to the questions are wrong.

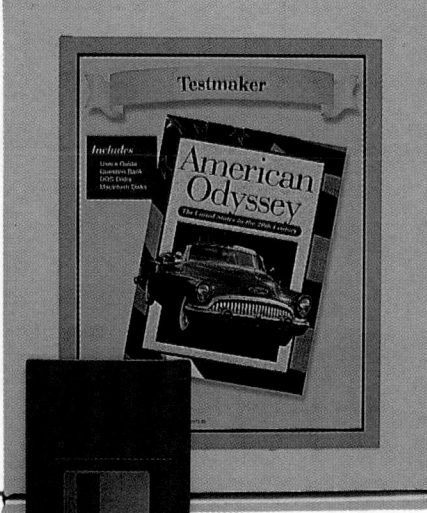

Testmaker Software (DOS and Macintosh) offers a bank of more than 3,000 questions, and provides the flexibility to edit existing questions and add new ones.

Multimedia

GLENCOE VIDEODISCS

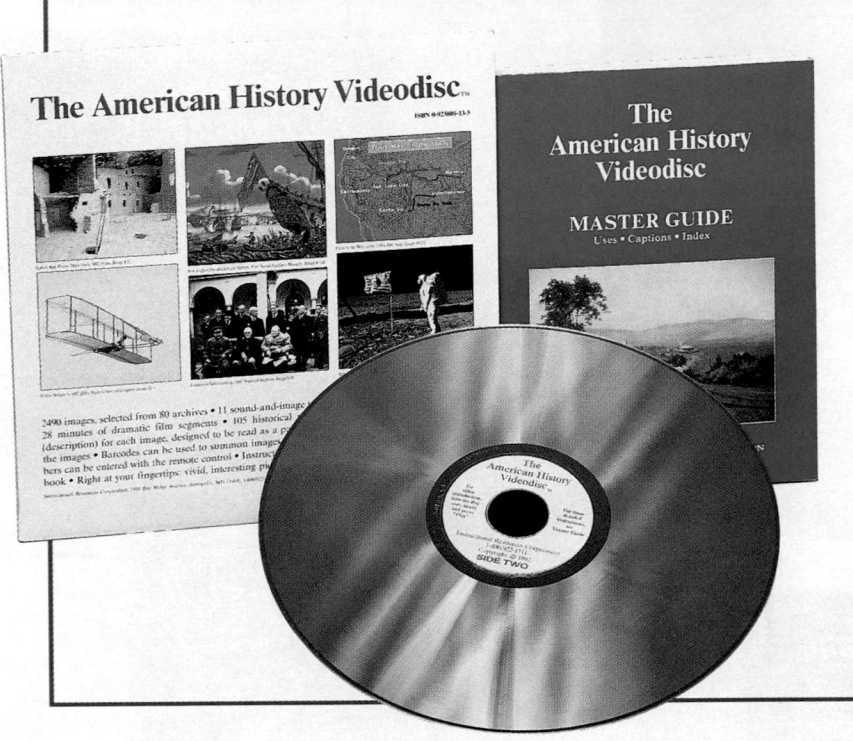

American History Videodisc includes narrated overviews of key periods and more than 2,000 images that show your students American history with a touch of your finger.

Set on Freedom provides award-winning footage detailing the civil rights movement in the United States. Available as a Level I and III videodisc program. Interactive computer software for both Windows™ and Macintosh® users.

Multimedia

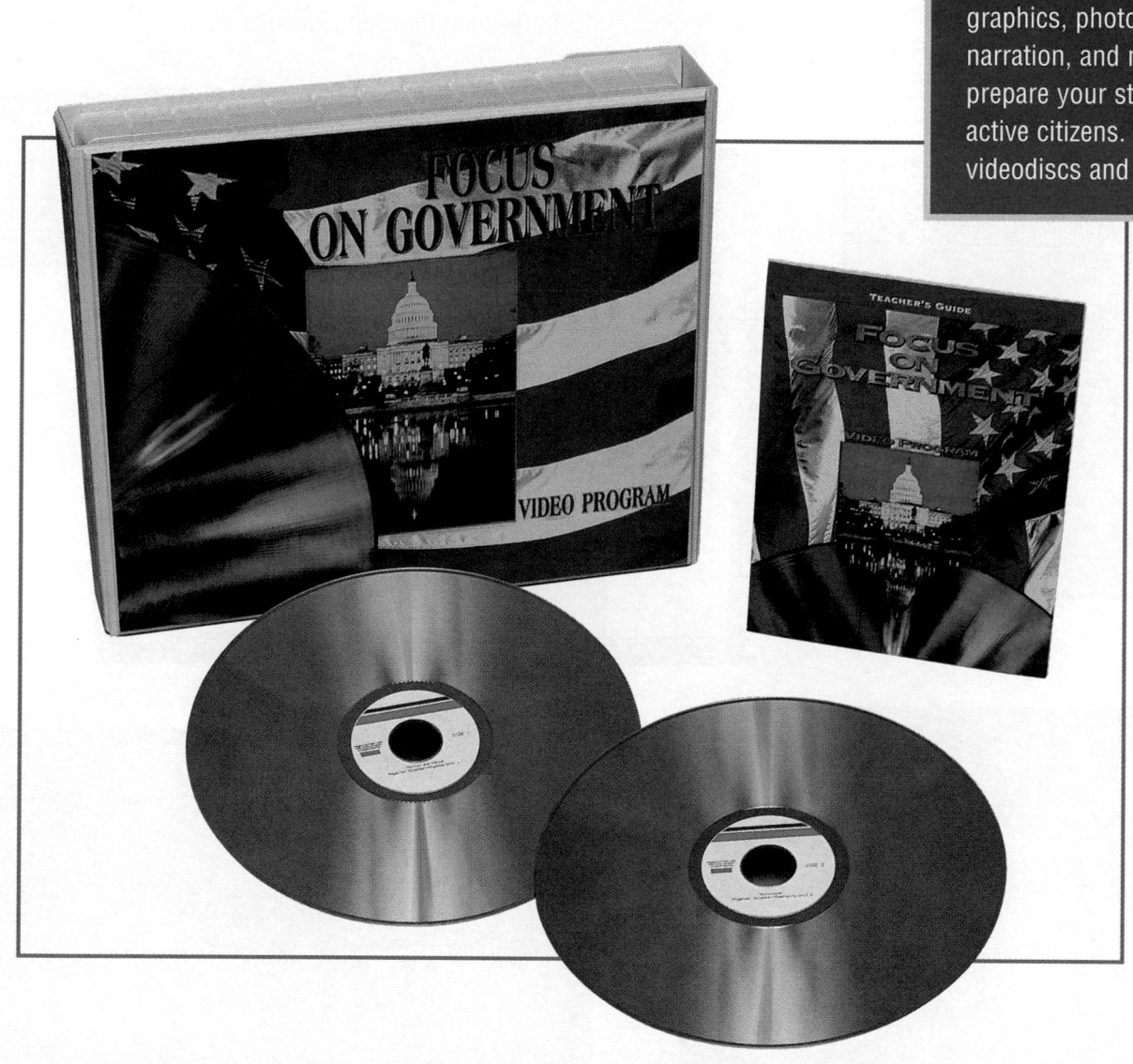

Focus on Government combines archival footage, graphics, photographs, narration, and music to help prepare your students to be active citizens. Available on videodiscs and videotapes.

Multimedia

ABCNEWS INTERACTIVE™

Historic America: Electronic Field Trips

takes students visit important sites where many of the momentous events in our nation's history took place.

Each of these titles includes a double-sided videodisc, as well as a guidebook with barcoded lesson plans. Ted Koppel of ABCNews Nightline provides the editorial framework for each videodisc.

Lessons of War looks at conflicts from World War I to the Persian Gulf.

Martin Luther King, Jr.,
is a tribute to the life and work of one of America's civil rights advocates and details his commitment to nonviolence, equal rights, and the end of segregation.

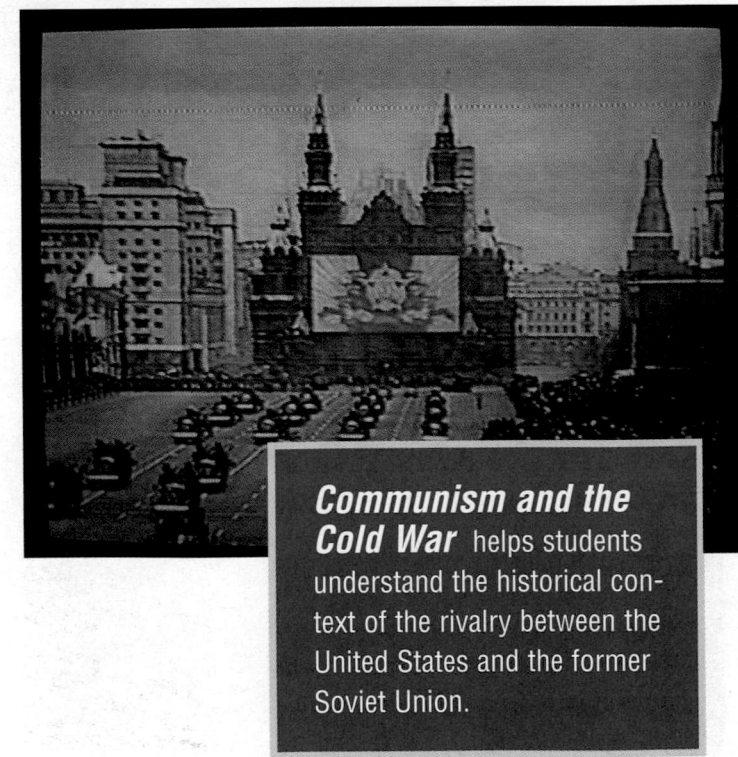

Communism and the Cold War helps students understand the historical context of the rivalry between the United States and the former Soviet Union.

Multimedia

ABC NEWS INTERACTIVE™

Powers of the President examines the constitutional role of the President as narrated by former President Jimmy Carter.

Powers of the Supreme Court reviews the Court's landmark decisions as narrated by Chief Justice of the United States William Rehnquist.

Powers of the Congress discusses the role Congress plays in governing as explained by former Speaker of the House Thomas Foley.

Multimedia

NATIONAL GEOGRAPHIC SOCIETY

The prestigious National Geographic Society has teamed with Glencoe to provide your students with a variety of interactive videodiscs to extend and enrich the study of American history.

GTV: A Geographic Perspective on American History provides a series of topics, from the American landscape to European settlement to Native Americans to modern immigration patterns—and more.

Multimedia

NATIONAL GEOGRAPHIC SOCIETY

GTV: The American People: Fabric of a Nation traces the changing makeup of the American population to help students understand the rich cultural heritage of our nation's.

CD-ROMs

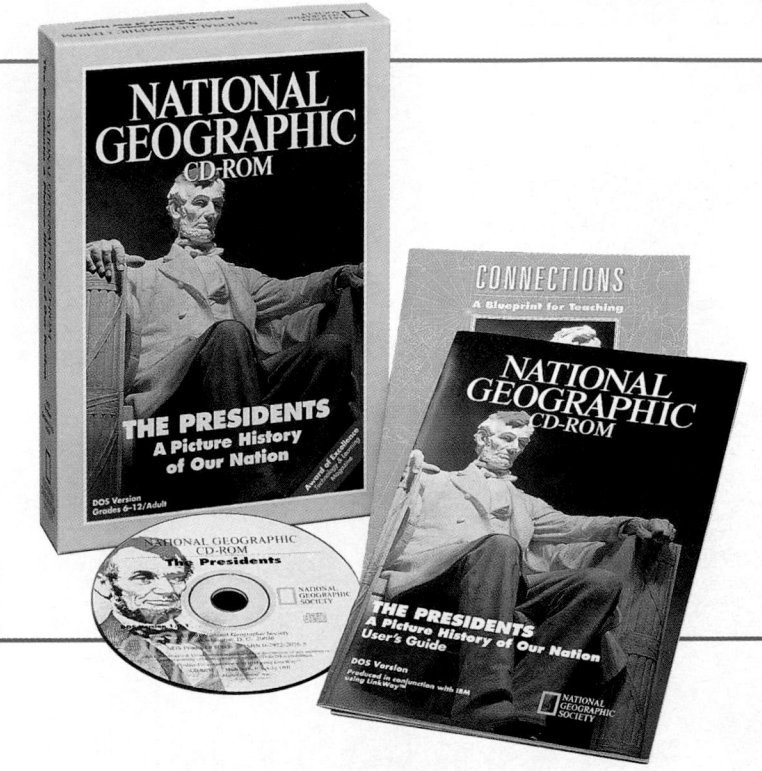

National Geographic Society

The Presidents: A Picture History of Our Nation includes more than 1,400 full-screen, captioned photographs and 33 videoclips of significant presidential events.

Native Americans provides extensive information on the saga of Native Americans.

The American Indian

provides the largest collection of rare documents ever available from one source. Historical treasures include maps, photos, illustrations, treaties, land grants—and much more. From Facts on File

Landmark Documents in American History

Reports includes more than 1,000 full text sources, 200 biographies, and 200 photographs and illustrations to enhance the documents. From Facts on File

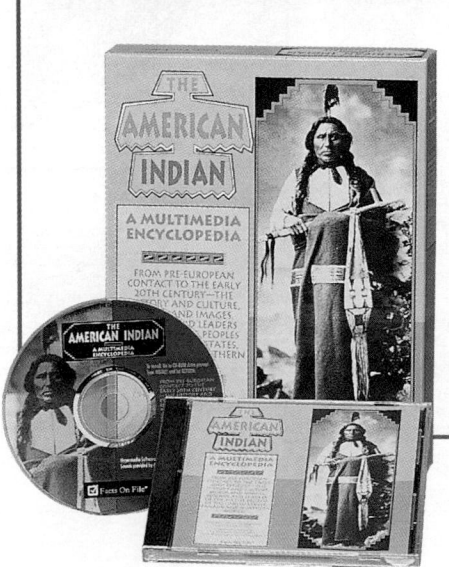

Classroom Management

Teacher's Name _____ Date _____

Grade _____ Class(es) _____ Date(s) _____ M Tu W Th F

CHAPTER 23

LESSON PLAN

Section 1 War in Southeast Asia

The Vietnam War

KEY
TWE = Teacher's Wraparound Edition
TCR = Teacher's Classroom Resources
Transparency   Videodisc
CDROM   Audio Cassettes

OBJECTIVES
- Understand why most of the Vietnamese wanted a Communist government
- Understand why the United States feared the spread of Communism in Asia
- Analyze the reasons why the United States brought military forces into Vietnam
- Understand why the United States was unable to defeat the Vietcong guerrillas

LOCAL OBJECTIVES	FOCUS
	_____ Bellringer Activity, **TWE,** p. 768
	_____ Section Focus Transparencies, Transparency 72 **TCR** <icon>
	_____ Unit Time Line Transparencies, Transparency 9 **TCR** <icon>
	TEACH
	Guided Practice
	_____ Activity, **TWE,** p.769
	_____ Cooperative Learning, **TWE,** p. 769
	_____ Meeting Special Needs, **TWE,** p. 770
	_____ Extending the Content, **TWE,** p. 772
	_____ Cultural Perspectives, **TWE,** p. 773
	_____ Critical Thinking, **TWE,** p. 774
	_____ Map Transparency 23 **TCR** <icon>
	_____ Chapter Teaching Transparency 23 **TCR** <icon>
	_____ ABC News Interactive Videodiscs <icon>
	_____ Facts on File <icon>
	Independent Practice
	_____ Activity, **TWE,** p. 773
	_____ Portfolio Project, **TWE,** p. 771
	_____ Vocabulary and Guided Reading Activities (English and Spanish), **TCR**
	_____ Great Debate, **TCR**
	ASSESS
	Evaluate
	_____ Meeting Lesson Objectives, **TWE,** p.774
	_____ Evaluate, **TWE,** p. 775
	_____ Section Quizzes, Chapter 23, Section 1 (English and Spanish), **TCR**
	_____ Testmaker <icon>
	_____ Student Self-Test: A Software Review <icon>
	Reteach
	_____ Reteach, **TWE,** p.427
	_____ Chapter Digest Audiocassettes (English and Spanish) <icon>
	Enrich
	_____ Enrich, **TWE,** p.775
	_____ American Literature: Readings and Activities
	_____ Geography in History Activity, **TCR**
	CLOSE
	_____ Close, **TWE,** p.775

UNIT

A Nation of Nations

The Unit at a Glance

Chapter 1

An understanding of geographic concepts illuminates the study of history. The five themes of geography—location, place, movement, human/environment interaction, and region—help explain the way history unfolds.

Chapter 2

In the millenia before 1492, Native Americans populated the Americas. The advent of Europeans set the stage for complex interactions between the Native Americans, the Europeans, and the arriving enslaved Africans. After 1763 Great Britain was the dominant power in North America, but the colonists began to question British authority.

Chapter 3

Britain's hold on the colonies weakened when colonists protested land restrictions and taxation they considered unfair. From 1775 to 1781, the colonists waged and won the Revolutionary War against Great Britain. State governments were formed and the idea of liberty was strengthened.

Chapter 4

After public debate, the Constitution of the new United States, including a Bill of Rights, was ratified. As rival political parties emerged, the nation stabilized its new government and successfully fought Great Britain in the War of 1812.

Portfolio Project

A Research Report Have students research and create a brief report about the Inca or any other Native American culture that existed in the Americas before the Europeans came. Encourage students to collect or draw images of Native American artifacts. Have students include their reports in their portfolios.

1

00:00 **Out of Time?**

If time does not permit teaching every chapter in this unit, use the Chapter Digest Audiocassettes and the accompanying student activities and tests. The Chapter Digest Audiocassettes are available in Spanish.

Introducing the Unit

Show students the Unit 1 Time Line Transparency and/or assign the accompanying activity sheet. This Unit covers from 40,000 B.C. through the early 1800s.

NATIONAL GEOGRAPHIC SOCIETY

 Videodisc

STV: North America

Side 3, Chapter 5
Title: The Pacific Edge
Subject: The landscapes, climate, and region of the Pacific Edge
Ask: In recent years, many residents of the Pacific Edge have opposed further development. Why? *(Answers will vary, but students might suggest that the residents want to preserve their beautiful surroundings.)*

Side 4, Chapter 6
Title: The Western Dry Lands
Subject: Physical characteristics of subregions of the Western Dry Lands
Ask: Why is irrigation so important in this region? *(Rainfall is insufficient for crops without irrigation.)*

Examining the Visual

Gold Artifacts Point out that the Inca made this beautiful gold knife handle. The Inca established an extensive empire in what is now South America long before they were conquered by the Spanish in 1532. Help students appreciate the intricacy of this artifact. Discuss how valuable golden objects like this one would have interested the Spaniards.

LITERATURE

TEACH

Making the Historical Connection

In the first few decades of the 1500s, Spaniards explored the northern Caribbean and began to understand the shape of the Florida peninsula (which they believed to be an island at first). In 1513 Ponce de León sailed down the eastern coast and around the tip of Florida. By 1526 Spaniards had roughly charted the Gulf of Mexico. The great wealth found in Central America among the Inca and the Aztec led the Spaniards to believe that there were more riches for the taking in North America, and so expeditions were launched. Cabeza de Vaca's adventure (1528–36) was unprofitable, but the rumors of wealth he heard from the Native Americans only encouraged his compatriots such as Hernando de Soto, who launched an expedition into Florida in 1539.

VISUAL INSTRUCTION

Exploration This work is by Flemish-born engraver Theodor de Bry (1528–1598), whose greatest achievement may have been the illustrations he engraved for a book of narratives about voyages and travels known as *Collected Travels in the East Indies and West Indies.* **Several other people, including de Bry's sons, worked on the book, which was not completed until 1634.**

Castaways

BY ALVAR NÚÑEZ CABEZA DE VACA

Alvar Núñez Cabeza de Vaca landed in present-day Florida in 1528, part of an expedition that was to explore and claim territory for Spain. After losing contact with their ships, the Spaniards found themselves stranded in a harsh land with no supplies, among often hostile local peoples. Cabeza de Vaca and 3 others reached Spanish territory (in present-day Mexico) after an 8-year odyssey; the 4 were the only survivors from a group of 300. This excerpt from Cabeza de Vaca's account of the expedition concerns an attack on the Spaniards as they were crossing one of many lakes in Florida.

SUPERSTOCK/NEW YORK PUBLIC LIBRARY

F. Delfinum.

Exploration European explorers approach the coast of Florida. Native Americans are gathered along the shore.

In view of this [the Indians' aggression] the governor ordered the horsemen to dismount and attack them on foot. The auditor dismounted with them, and they attacked the Indians and they all fought together in the lake, and so we forced our way through. In this affray some of our men were wounded, and the good weapons they carried were of no use; and there were men that day who swore they had seen two oak trees, each as thick as the lower part of a man's leg, shot clear through by the Indians' arrows. And this is not so much to be wondered at considering the strength and skill with which they shoot them, for I myself saw an arrow at the foot of a poplar tree that had penetrated into it two handbreadths. All the Indians that we saw, from Florida to here, use arrows; and they are so tall . . . they look like giants when seen from a distance. They are wonderfully handsome folk, very lean and extremely strong and agile. The bows they use are as thick as a man's arm and eleven or twelve handbreadths long, which they shoot at a distance of two hundred paces, so surely that they never miss anything. After we had made this crossing, a league farther on we came to another that was very like it, except for the fact that, as it was half a league wide, it was much worse; this one we crossed without hin-

Background Information

Survival Skills In order to exist, Cabeza de Vaca and his companions learned native ways and languages. After losing all their belongings while attempting to sail to New Spain in home-made boats, the Spaniards went without shoes or clothing and lived on nothing but prickly pear cactus. At times the Spaniards were enslaved by Native Americans. Later they gained status as shamans and were often called upon to perform healing rituals. Cabeza de Vaca writes that when contact was finally made with other Spanish near the Texas/Mexico border, the Native Americans refused to believe that he and his companions were related to the conquistadors because "we cured the sick and they killed the healthy" and "we came naked and barefoot and they were well dressed and on horses and with lances."

drance and without attacks by Indians, for as they had used up all their supplies of arrows in the first encounter, they had nothing left with which they dared to confront us. On the following day, as we made another similar crossing, I found traces of people who had gone ahead of us and warned the governor of it, for he was in the rear guard; and so, although the Indians attacked us, they were unable to harm us because we were forewarned, and when we emerged on level ground they continued to follow us. We attacked them on two sides and killed two Indians, and they wounded me and two or three other Spaniards, and because they took shelter in the woods we were unable to do them any more harm or damage. We marched like this for eight days, and after the crossing I have described no more Indians attacked us until a league farther on, which is the place that, as I have said, we were going.

> WE ATTACKED THEM ON TWO SIDES AND KILLED TWO INDIANS, AND THEY WOUNDED ME AND TWO OR THREE OTHER SPANIARDS . . .

As we were going our way, Indians came out of the woods without our hearing them and attacked the rear guard, and among them was a hidalgo [a man of the lower nobility in Spain] named Avellaneda who turned around on hearing the cries of a lad who was a servant of his and went to his aid, and the Indians hit him with an arrow at the edge of his cuirass [breastplate], and the wound was so severe that almost all the arrow went into his neck and he died on the spot, and we carried him to Aute [community near present-day Tallahassee, Florida]. We arrived after nine days of journeying from Apalachee [village near present-day Tallahassee], and when we reached there we found all the people fled, and the houses burned, and a great quantity of maize and pumpkins and beans, all ready to be harvested. We rested there for two days, and after that the governor asked me to go

and find the sea, for the Indians said it was very close by: during this journey we thought we had discovered it because of a very large river that we found, which we named the Magdalena. In view of this, on the next day I set off to find it, along with the commissary and Captain Castillo and Andrés Dorantes and seven other mounted men and fifty on foot, and we marched until the hour of vespers, when we reached an inlet or arm of the sea where we found many oysters, which the men enjoyed greatly, and we gave great thanks to God for having brought us there.

Next morning I sent twenty men to explore the coast and find out what it was like; they returned on the following night saying that those inlets and bays were very large and entered so deeply into the land that they made it extremely difficult to find out what we wished to know, and that the coast was very far away. Once we had learned this, and considering the fact that we were ill prepared and ill equipped to explore the coast, I returned to the governor. When we arrived we found him and many others sick, and the previous night the Indians had come upon them and placed them in great peril owing to the illness they had suffered; also, one of the horses had died. I reported to him what I had done, and the unfavorable lie of the land. That day we stayed there.

> ### RESPONDING TO LITERATURE
>
> 1. What difficulties did Cabeza de Vaca encounter while trying to explore Florida?
>
> 2. Do you find Cabeza de Vaca to be a careful observer? Support your answer with examples from the selection.

Team Teaching This excerpt from *Castaways* can be presented in a team teaching context, in conjunction with English or Language Arts.

CLOSE

Ask a volunteer to summarize what the reader now knows about the circumstances of Cabeza de Vaca's expedition. How might these have affected interactions with Native Americans? *(Sample: The Spaniards will need to depend on the Native Americans for help. The Spanish will not be in a position to oppress the Native Americans.)* Why do students think so many members of the expedition died? *(Sample: The land they traveled was very inhospitable and the native peoples often hostile. The Spaniards were weakened by exposure and lack of food and shelter.)*

Responding to Literature Answers

1. He encountered hostile Native Americans, difficult terrain, lack of equipment, and illness.
2. Students may answer that Cabeza de Vaca is a careful observer because he notes details such as the size of the Native Americans' bows, the size of the lake, and the particular crops the Spaniards find in Aute.

A Geographic Perspective on History

DAILY LESSON OBJECTIVES	REPRODUCIBLE RESOURCES	MULTIMEDIA RESOURCES
SECTION 1 The Five Themes of Geography 1. Define geography and give examples of what it reveals about people, places, and environments. 2. Explain how the five themes of geography help organize geographic information.	➧ Reproducible Lesson Plans ➧ Vocabulary and Guided Reading Activities (English or Spanish) ➧ Cooperative Learning Activities ➧ Skill Reinforcement Activities ➧ Section Quizzes (English or Spanish)	⬛ Chapter Teaching Transparencies ⬛ Section Focus Transparencies ⬛ Map Transparencies ⬛ Student Self-Test: A Software Review ⬛ Testmaker
SECTION 2 The Themes as Guides to History 1. Explain how understanding geography helps people understand history. 2. Describe ways the five themes of geography relate to United States history.	➧ Reproducible Lesson Plans ➧ Vocabulary and Guided Reading Activities (English or Spanish) ➧ Reteaching Activities (English or Spanish) ➧ Enrichment Activities (English or Spanish) ➧ Geography in History Activities ➧ Section Quizzes (English or Spanish)	⬛ Section Focus Transparencies ⬛ Beginnings to 1900 Transparencies ⬛ North America ⬛ Student Self-Test: A Software Review ⬛ Testmaker
CHAPTER REVIEW AND EVALUATION	➧ Chapter 1 Test, Forms A and B ➧ Performance Assessment Strategies and Activities	⬛ Student Self-Test: A Software Review ⬛ Vocabulary PuzzleMaker ⬛ Testmaker ⌢ Chapter Digests Audiocassettes

00:00 If time does not permit teaching the entire chapter, summarize using the Chapter 1 Digests Audiocassettes and the accompanying activities and tests. (Available in English and Spanish.)

Cooperative Project

Organize the class into small groups and ask each of them to research one result of human/environment interaction via migratory movement. Possibilities include how types of foods and natural resources spread from continent to continent. Have them share their group's results with the class. **LEP**

Suggested Rubric: An Oral Presentation. See Performance Assessment Strategies and Activities, p. 33.

Individual Project

Have students research the types of satellite technology that allow access to information about short-term geographic factors such as daily weather and to long-term geographic factors such as changes in vegetation and pollution.

Suggested Rubric: A Research Report. See Performance Assessment Strategies and Activities, p. 39.

Key to Ability Levels

Teaching strategies have been coded for varying learning styles and abilities.

L1 **BASIC** activities for all students

L2 **AVERAGE** activities for average to above-average students

L3 **CHALLENGING** activities for above-average students

LEP **LIMITED ENGLISH PROFICIENCY** activities

 Block Scheduling

Block scheduling differs from traditional class scheduling in the amount of time allotted to each period. The extended timeframe provided by block scheduling affords you the opportunity to implement a greater number of research-oriented and activity-intense projects to motivate and involve your students. Activities that are particularly suited to use within the block scheduling framework are identified throughout this chapter by the following designation.

T E A C H E R ' S   C O R N E R

 NATIONAL GEOGRAPHIC SOCIETY

INDEX TO NATIONAL GEOGRAPHIC MAGAZINE

The following articles may be used for research relating to this chapter:

- "Living with California's Faults," by Rick Gore, April 1995.
- "The Sonoran Desert," By Priit J. Vesilind, September 1994.
- *Water: The Power, Promise, and Turmoil of North America's Fresh Water,* (A Special Edition), November 1993.
- "The American Prairie: Roots of the Sky," by Douglas H. Chadwick, October 1993.
- "Chesapeake Bay—Hanging in the Balance," by Tom Horton, June 1993.
- "Our Disappearing Wetlands," by John G. Mitchell, October 1992.
- "The Colorado: A River Drained Dry," by Jim Richardson, June 1991.
- "Sagebrush Country: America's Outback," by Douglas H. Chadwick, January 1989.
- "The John Muir Trail: Along the High Wild Sierra," by Galen Rowell, April 1989.

NATIONAL GEOGRAPHIC SOCIETY PRODUCTS AVAILABLE FROM GLENCOE

To order the following products for use with this chapter, contact your local Glencoe sales representative or call Glencoe at 1-800-334-7344:

- *ZipZapMap! USA* (Software)
- *STV: North America* (Videodisc)
- *GTV: A Geographic Perspective on American History* (Videodisc)
- *GTV: The American People: Fabric of a Nation* (Videodisc)
- *Geography of North America* (Transparencies)

ADDITIONAL NATIONAL GEOGRAPHIC SOCIETY PRODUCTS

To order the following products for use with this chapter, call National Geographic Society at 1-800-368-2728:

- *The Water's Edge: Life Along the Great Rivers,* "The Mississippi." (Filmstrip)
- *Great Lakes, Fragile Seas* (Video)
- *Chesapeake Borne* (Video)

Chapter Overview

Chapter 1 defines geography and presents the five themes of location, place, movement, human/environment interaction, and region. It then demonstrates how an understanding of geographical concepts can illuminate one's study of history.

Introducing the Chapter

Point out to students that the Chapter Teaching Transparency shows one example of artwork based on Marco Polo's journal. Have students read about the impact of Polo's journal in the narrative on this page.

Display Chapter Teaching Transparency 1 on the board and distribute copies of the activity sheet.

Extension Activity

Have students complete Beyond the Transparency on the activity sheet for Chapter 1 and present their projects after the class has completed the chapter.

History Journal

Ask students to select and share a journal entry that would tell a visitor to their locale something important about the area's geography and history.

CHAPTER
1

A Geographic Perspective on History

LATE 1400s: EAGER EXPLORERS PORE OVER TRAVEL JOURNALS AND MAPS

"Just as we roof our houses or churches with lead, so this palace is roofed with fine gold. And the value of it is almost beyond computation."

Thus did Marco Polo describe Japan, a country he had never visited. Polo, a trader from Venice, lived in China for about 20 years in the late 1200s. He saw many amazing events, and heard stories about a mysterious country now called Japan. After returning home, Polo was commanding a Venetian ship in a war against Genoa when he was captured and held prisoner. During his imprisonment, he recorded the story of his travels.

During the 1200s, people copied books by hand, so books were scarce. About 1440, however, Johannes Gutenberg invented the printing press. By the century's end, printing presses were common, and Europeans were exchanging ideas at an unprecedented rate. Polo's journal was now available to explorers, including the Genoese Christopher Columbus. In 1492 when Columbus set sail to find the riches of Japan and China, he took along Polo's book as a guide. ■

HISTORY JOURNAL

As you read this chapter, write a description of the ways that the geography of your locale has affected the events that have occurred there in the past and in the present.

4

✚ EXTRA CREDIT PROJECT

Focus on One Theme Invite students to select 1 of the 5 themes of geography and to use that theme as a focus for presenting additional information about the time period of Unit 1. Explain that students may not simply duplicate information that is given elsewhere in the unit, so they may need to look ahead to Chapters 2, 3, and 4 as well as at Chapter 1. Urge them to use visuals, especially maps, to enrich their written or oral presentations. Samples of possible topics include events in the history of mapmaking, ways that early sailors navigated, the instruments that sailors used to determine location, and famous people of the time.

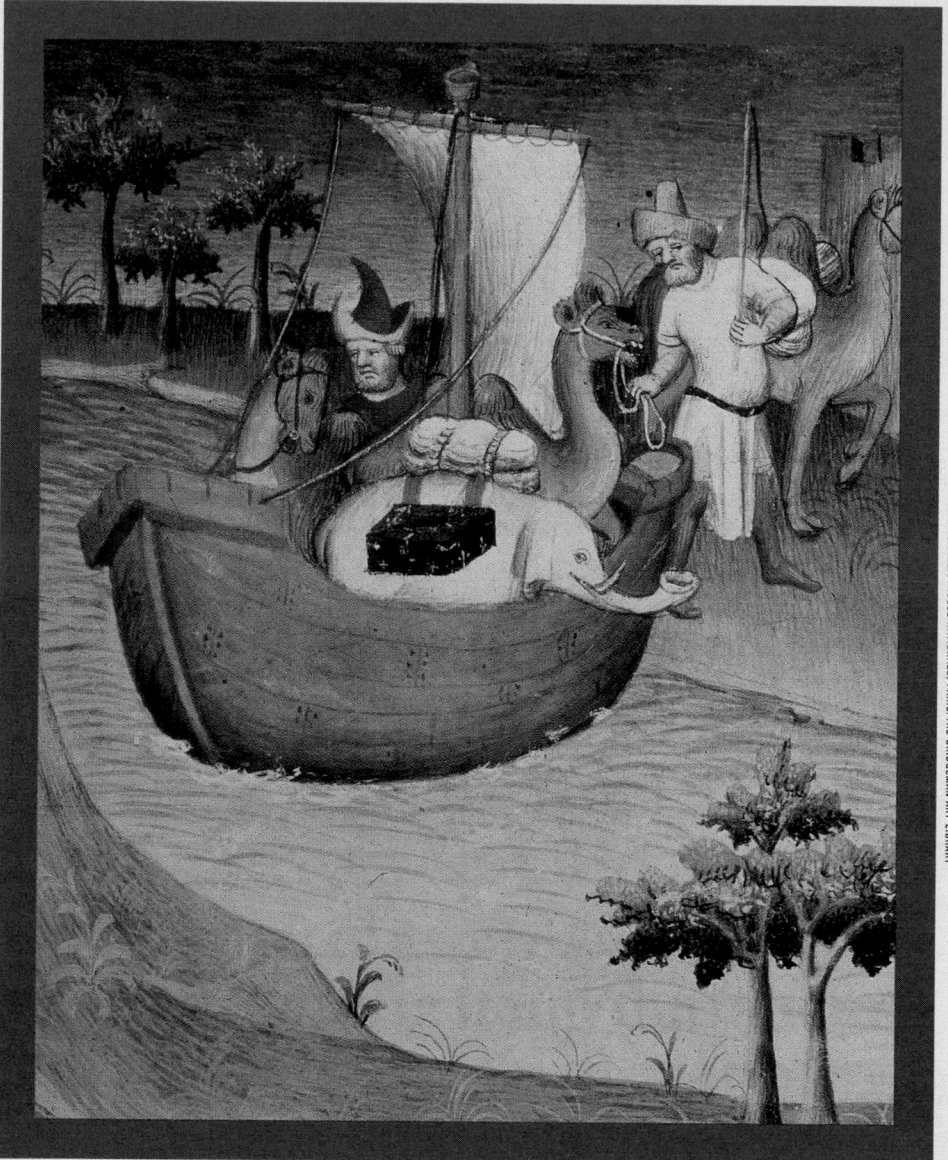

FROM "LIVRE DES MERVEILLES" (DETAIL) MARCO POLO WITH ELEPHANTS AND CAMELS ARRIVING AT HORMUZ/BIBLIOTHEQUE NATIONALE, PARIS/THE BRIDGEMAN ART LIBRARY

BY SHARING HIS DISCOVERIES ABOUT THE
GEOGRAPHY OF ASIA, MARCO POLO
INFLUENCED THE HISTORY OF THE WORLD.

5

NATIONAL GEOGRAPHIC SOCIETY

Videodisc

GTV: A Geographic Perspective on American History

Side 1, Chapter 1
Title: The Lay of the Land
Subject: Overview of the American landscape and physical features
Ask: What are the two major mountain ranges of the continental United States? *(Appalachians and Rockies)*

✔ Performance Assessment

Refer to page 4B for performance assessment activities for this chapter.

 Also see Activity 1 in the Performance Assessment Strategies and Activities for an additional activity as well as for suggested rubrics.

Examining the Visual

A Book of Marvels This scene from *Livre des Merveilles du Monde,* which is at the Bibliothèque Nationale in Paris, France, shows Marco Polo arriving at Hormuz in the Gulf of Persia. The camel and elephant shown here, as well as other animals Polo described, would have been unknown to many of the traveler's fellow Europeans. Marco Polo's story of unfamiliar sights and experiences captivated the imaginations of Europeans at a time when very few people traveled from their birthplace. Some of Polo's contemporaries considered his tales so outlandish that when Polo was dying they urged him to retract his story. Polo refused, telling them that, on the contrary, his journal did not fully describe all the wondrous things he had observed.

SECTION

1

FOCUS

Section Objectives

1. Define geography and give examples of what it reveals about people, places, and environments.
2. Explain how the five themes of geography help organize geographic information.

Bellringer Activity

While taking attendance at the beginning of the class period, display **Section Focus Transparency 1,** and have students answer the questions. (Or use the blackline master.)

VISUAL INSTRUCTION

A Land of Great Variety Often Native Americans taught newcomers about unfamiliar foods.

Ask: What does the image on page 6 show about the foods eaten by the Native Americans? *(It shows that they ate a wide variety of animals, including fish, reptiles, and mammals.)*

The Five Themes of Geography

1542: EXPLORER PUBLISHES SENSATIONAL TRAVEL JOURNAL

© SUPERSTOCK

A Land of Great Variety
Newcomers to the Americas saw animals and plants that they had never seen before.

IT WAS A GRIPPING STORY OF SURVIVAL THAT ALVAR NÚÑEZ CABEZA DE VACA HAD TO TELL. This Spanish noble had been a member of an expedition sent to claim new lands in America for the Spanish king. The explorers experienced terrible misfortunes, including shipwreck and disease. In presenting his journal to King Charles V, Cabeza de Vaca admitted that the expedition had failed to achieve its goals. He was convinced, however, that his journal was a worthwhile offering to the king.

The value of his report, Cabeza de Vaca wrote, was its information about the new lands, including descrip-

tions of native peoples, the environment, the kinds of food people ate, and the location of places and the distances between them.

In describing these discoveries to the king, Cabeza de Vaca was writing about **geography,** the study of people, places, and environments. Geography looks at space on the earth and how specific spaces are alike or different. It is a rich subject filled with intriguing, even astonishing information. To help organize such a huge body of information, today's geographers cluster their subject matter around five themes: location, place, movement, human/environment interaction, and region.

AS YOU READ

Vocabulary
► geography
► location
► place
► movement
► human/environment interaction
► region

Think About . . .
► what geography is and what it reveals about people, places, and environments.

► how the five themes of geography help organize geographical information.

---

6   CHAPTER 1   A GEOGRAPHIC PERSPECTIVE ON HISTORY

Section 1 Resources

REPRODUCIBLE RESOURCES

📂 Lesson Plan 1-1
📂 Vocabulary and Guided Reading Activity 1-1
📂 Cooperative Learning Activity 1-1
📂 Section 1 Quiz
📂 Skill Reinforcement Activity 1

MULTIMEDIA RESOURCES

📃 Chapter Teaching Transparency 1
📃 Section Focus Transparency 1
📃 Map Transparency 1
💿 Testmaker
🎧 Chapter 1 Digest Audiocassette
💿 Student Self-Test: A Software Review

TYPVS ORBIS TERRARVM

A World Map From 1570 This map shows many misunderstandings about the size and shape of North America, South America, Australia, and Antarctica. *Which parts of this map look like maps of today?*

Location

Finding Places Anywhere on Earth

The theme of **location** focuses on a specific place and considers the question of its position on the earth's surface. People may talk about the location of a place just out of curiosity, or they may actually want to travel to a place.

Absolute Location

In 25 B.C. a young man named Strabo had the chance to visit Alexandria, then the Roman capital of Egypt and a cosmopolitan meeting place for travelers. In a library built by Egyptian royalty, Strabo found an enormous collection of scholarly writings. He pored over those works, especially those related to geography and mapmaking, and evaluated what he read. He eventually published his conclusions in an 18-volume book on world geography. Two of Strabo's central conclusions were that the earth had the shape of a sphere, and that the best map of the earth would employ a grid of intersecting lines, a plan that is still in use today.

One set of grid lines consists of the lines of latitude, which circle the earth parallel to each other and to the Equator, an imaginary line around the center of the

earth. The Equator is measured at 0°, and the poles are measured at 90° N (north) or S (south). The other set of lines comprises longitude lines, which run from pole to pole and measure distance east or west of a starting line called the Prime Meridian. During most of the history of mapmaking, individual mapmakers chose where to locate the Prime Meridian—usually placing it where they lived. Finally, in 1884, the United States held the First International Meridian Conference. The delegates decided to locate the Prime Meridian at an observatory in Greenwich, England. The other meridians are measured east or west of the Prime Meridian up to 180°. This grid system enables people to give the exact, or absolute, location for any place on the earth.

Relative Location

In everyday life people usually think of a place's location in relation to other known places, a concept called relative location. Even before there was a written language, people showed each other relative location by using simple maps such as those drawn in sand or made with sticks and stones. They also spoke of relative location, saying, for example, that Europe is north of Africa. Today following oral or written directions that are based on relative location continues to be a common way for people to get to their destinations.

SECTION ONE 7

BRITISH LIBRARY, LONDON/BRIDGEMAN ART LIBRARY, LONDON

TEACH

Guided Practice

L1 Map Reading Discuss the value of map reading skills for the average person. Encourage students to identify instances when people might benefit from knowing how to use a map. Be sure students consider the various types of maps that are used in everyday life. (You may wish to pair this discussion with the teaching of the skill on page 10.)

Show students Map Transparency 1 and have them complete the activity sheet. **LEP**

Independent Practice

L2 How Maps Were Made Individually or in small groups, students can research the history of how maps were made. Encourage them to bring in books showing examples of old historical maps and to explain what the maps show about people's understanding of the world at that time.

Have students complete the Chapter 1, Section 1 Vocabulary and Guided Reading Activity. (Also in Spanish.) **LEP**

Have students complete the Chapter 1 Cooperative Learning Activity. **LEP**

Cooperative Learning

Giving Directions Students can reinforce their understanding of the concept of relative location by writing directions. Organize the class into small groups, and have each group select a place that is a five-minute walk or a five-minute ride away from school. Direct each group to write one set of directions that could be given orally and also to draw a map that shows all the directions visually. Encourage

students to consider when it would be best to use compass directions and when it would be clearer to use other kinds of descriptions, such as references to distinctive landmarks. Each group can then exchange their directions with another group, and together the groups can discuss whether their sets of directions are accurate and easy to follow.

VISUAL INSTRUCTION

A World Map From 1570 The Latin title of the map can be translated as "map of the world."

Answer: *Europe, Africa, the western parts of Asia, and the surrounding waters.*

ASSESS

Meeting Lesson Objectives

Each section objective is tested by the section review question(s) that follows it in parentheses.

1. Define geography and give examples of what it reveals about people, places, and environments. (1, 3)

2. Explain how the five themes of geography help organize geographic information. (2, 4, 5)

Place
Describing a Location

Every **place**, or specific location, on the earth has a set of characteristics that distinguish it from other places. When geographers focus on place, they look at the physical features of a location as well as its human features. A place's physical features include the nature of the land and water as well as the weather, soil, plants, and animals. The human features include the number and kinds of people who live in a place, the activities that occur there, and the cultures, languages, and religions represented. The combination of all these different characteristics gives each place its own distinctive flavor.

In 1596 explorer William Barents and his crew experienced the extremes of a place in the Arctic when their ship was frozen in the ice at 76° N latitude. Gerrit de Veer, one of the crew, recorded their experiences in a detailed account accompanied by illustrations.

Movement
Monitoring a Continuing Flow

From the beginning of human history, people have moved from one location to another, sometimes migrating great distances. They may have moved out of necessity, because of catastrophic natural events such as droughts or because of conflicts with other people. They may also have moved out of curiosity or from a desire to seek a better life. Such movements may be temporary, such as the travels of explorers or traders, or permanent, when people move to a new location and settle there. Geographers are also interested in the transfer of goods from place to place and the spread of information and ideas. All these activities are examples of the theme of **movement.**

Moving Into the Unknown Determining location at sea or in a new land presented explorers with a challenge. They used an astrolabe like the one shown (upper left) to determine latitude. *Which geography themes does this painting illustrate?*

Meeting Special Needs

Visual Learners and LEP To help students who learn best visually, create an ongoing Geography Themes bulletin board of photographs and newspaper articles about the students' local community. For each bulletin board item, label one or more of the five themes exemplified by the item. For LEP students, add theme labels in their first language. It may also be helpful to add key words or phrases to summarize how the event relates to one or more themes. Some examples of bulletin board items might be stories about a community discussion concerning the location of a new mall or factory (location, human/environment interaction) and stories about how to create or improve public transportation (movement).

Human/ Environment Interaction
A Story of a Close Relationship

The theme of **human/ environment interaction** explores the interdependence of people and their surroundings. People are totally dependent on the environment for fresh water, food, and shelter, their three most basic needs. Throughout most of human history, people have chosen to live near rivers, lakes, or other sources of fresh water.

The simplest and earliest way that people obtained food was as hunter-gatherers. They hunted for meat and collected vegetables and fruits that they found growing in their surroundings. Of all the ways that people have lived, the hunter-gatherer way of life produces the fewest environmental changes.

About 10,000 B.C., some hunter-gatherer societies began to experiment with the domestication of plants and animals, events that led to the development of agriculture. Agriculture revolutionized the way people interacted with their surroundings, for they could now exert a new level of control. It also changed the environment far more extensively than had their former way of life. Even today agriculture continues to bring about environmental changes.

Region
A Versatile Organizing Concept

The theme of region is the most flexible of the five themes. A **region** is an area that is defined according to one or more characteristics. Those characteristics may be physical features or they may be based on other types of human concepts such as political divisions, kinds of languages, or types of industry.

Geographers often need to consider the physical features of an area, even when they are focusing on another type of region concept. The physical features of a region, such as the type of land, the bodies of water, the climate, and the vegetation, often influence whether or not the region will be heavily populated and what types of industries will flourish there.

Picturing New Discoveries Explorers returned to their European homelands with tales of new regions such as the Arctic (above). Books illustrated new kinds of plants (right). *What does the image above tell you about the explorer's life in the Arctic?*

SECTION REVIEW

Vocabulary
1. Define: geography, location, place, movement, human/environment interaction, region.

Checking Facts
2. What is the difference between absolute and relative location?

3. What is the simplest method people have used to obtain food?

Critical Thinking
Evaluating Information
4. Do you agree that region is the most flexible of the five geographic themes? Why or why not?

Linking Across Time
5. How can using the five themes of geography promote an understanding of current events?

SECTION ONE   9

Evaluate
Have students complete the Section Review.

⬤ Assign the Section 1 Quiz or use the Testmaker to develop a customized quiz. (Also in Spanish.) **LEP**

Reteach
🎧 Have students listen to the Chapter 1, Section 1 Audiocassette. (Also in Spanish.) **LEP**

Enrich
Have volunteers find and share illustrations of exploration made during the time period covered in Unit 1.

VISUAL INSTRUCTION

Picturing New Discoveries Barents's crew suffered from scurvy because foods containing vitamin C were scarce. Some members of the crew were killed by polar bears.

Answer: *Explorers in the Arctic had to endure extremely cold temperatures, snow and ice, and a scarcity of food.*

CLOSE

Ask: What can a historian learn by focusing on the geographic theme of movement? What are some examples of historical events that illustrate this theme? (*The theme of movement emphasizes the migration of people as well as the transfer of goods and the spread of information and ideas. Related historical events include exploration, migration, trade, the spread of information such as the location of trade routes, and the spread of ideas such as the concept of freedom.*)

Section 1 Review Answers

1. geography (6), **location** (7), **place** (8), **movement** (8), **human/environment interaction** (9), **region** (9)
2. Absolute location is the position of a place given in terms of the grid of latitude and longitude lines. Relative location is the position of a place given in relation to other places.
3. The simplest way of getting food is the method used by hunter-gatherers.
4. Region is the most flexible of the five themes because it can be based on any characteristic(s) a person chooses.
5. Location, place, movement, human/environment interaction, and region influence current events just as much as they have influenced historical events.

Social Studies Skill
READING A MAP

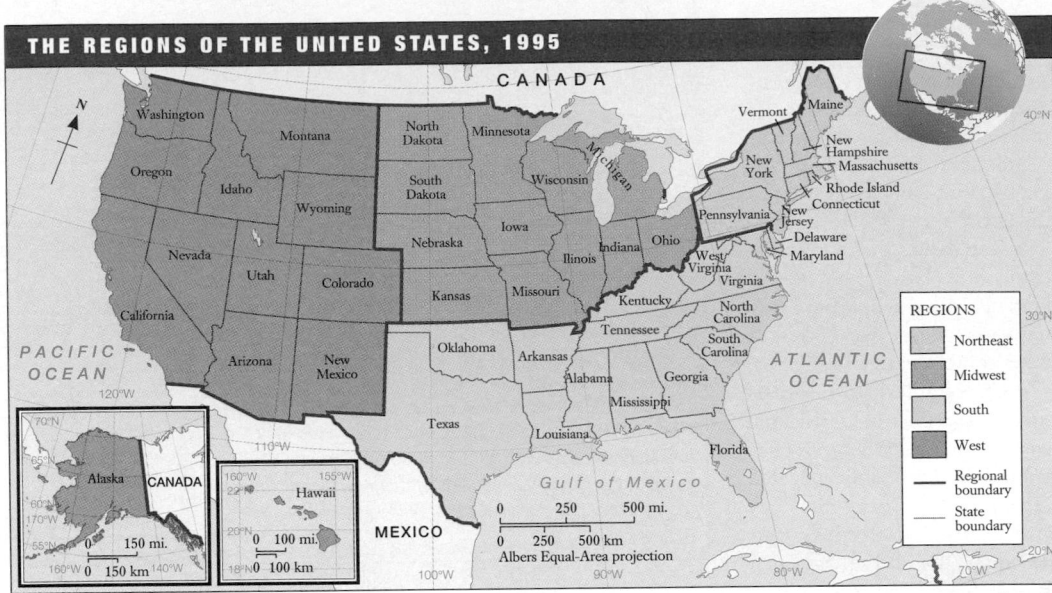

THE REGIONS OF THE UNITED STATES, 1995

REGIONS
- Northeast
- Midwest
- South
- West
- Regional boundary
- State boundary

The four regions shown here are based partly on geographical location and partly on history and other factors such as climate. *In which region do you live? Which regions border your region?*

TEACH

This feature teaches the social studies skill of map reading. It presents students with some of the features common to most maps: title, scale, latitude, longitude, color, boundaries, and symbols. In addition to looking for these features on this map, students can examine the variety of other maps that are presented in the Atlas, beginning on page 940.

Additional Practice

☞ Have students complete the Chapter 1 Skill Reinforcement Activity.

Notes

Learning the Skill

Maps are visual tools that show to scale the relative size, location, or even environmental aspects of specific geographic areas. Maps contain symbols and other elements that enable you to interpret them accurately.

Reading a Map

To read a map, follow these steps:

a. Examine the title to determine the map's content.

b. Examine the map's scale, which indicates the ratio between the map's size and the actual area being represented. A scale also shows the ratio between distance on the map and real distance on the earth.

c. Look for a compass rose or directional arrow to find the map's directions.

d. Examine the lines of latitude and longitude to find the absolute location of specific places. Express the latitude and longitude in degrees and direction. For example, the tip of Florida is about 80° W and 25° N.

e. Read the legend, or key, to interpret any boundary lines, shapes, or other symbols.

Practicing the Skill

Study the map below and answer the following questions.

1. Which region has no coastline?

2. Which region has the greatest number of states? Which has the fewest?

3. Which state is closest to the Equator?

4. Which state has a place with a location of 120° W and 45° N?

5. Approximately how long is the western border of the state of Idaho?

Applying the Skill

Look at the map on pages 932–933. Write three statements about different kinds of information from the map, for example, statements about absolute location, relative location, and distance.

Additional Practice

For additional practice, see Reinforcing Skills on page 19.

10   SOCIAL STUDIES SKILL

Practicing the Skill Answers

1. the Midwest
2. The South has the greatest number (16). The Northeast has the fewest (9).
3. Hawaii, at about 20°N of the Equator, is the state closest to it.

4. Oregon
5. about 500 miles or 800 km

SECTION 2

The Themes as Guides to History

EARLY 1500s: TRANSFER OF MAP A CRIMINAL ACT

Sailors Gossip
In the busy ports of Europe, sailors often spread news of new discoveries that rulers tried to keep secret.

"IT IS IMPOSSIBLE TO GET A CHART OF THE VOYAGE BECAUSE THE KING HAS DECREED THE DEATH PENALTY FOR ANYONE SENDING ONE ABROAD." The king was Manuel I of Portugal, and the chart was a map of Vasco da Gama's travel route from Lisbon around Africa to India. The person making the complaint was a visitor to Portugal frantically trying to discover exactly how da Gama had accomplished his historic voyage.

Today, when many kinds of maps are freely available, people may find it hard to imagine that maps were once kept strictly secret. In the past, possession of a map could mean great power, in this case, control of the lucrative spice trade.

Spices were valuable because Europeans lacked the fodder to keep domesticated flocks alive through the winter. Each fall people butchered many of their animals and then salted the meat to keep it from spoiling. If the meat spoiled, people masked the taste of decay with spices.

Before da Gama's voyage, the merchants of Venice had monopolized trade in the spices that came westward by the traditional route from Asia. Now the Venetians saw their wealth disappearing, and they were desperate to counter Portugal's threat. This series of events was only one of countless occasions when knowledge about geography has had a major impact on historical events.

AS YOU READ

Vocabulary
► history
► climate
► vegetation

Think About . . .
► how understanding geography helps people understand history.
► the ways in which the five themes of geography relate to United States history.

SECTION TWO **11**

MAP STUDY

Guide students in examining the altitude legend. Point out that the blue in the bottom layer represents the ocean, and that the land in the bottom layer is land that is below sea level.

Answer: *Landforms influence lifestyles, types of industries, and so on.*

NATIONAL GEOGRAPHIC SOCIETY

 Videodisc

STV: North America

Side 1, Chapter 1
Title: The East
Subject: Physical characteristics of the eastern region of North America
Ask: What is the major mountain range of the East? *(the Appalachians)*

Side 1, Chapter 1
Title: The East
Subject: The Appalachian Mountains
Ask: How did the Appalachian Mountains impact early European settlement? *(The mountains kept most early settlers from penetrating the continent.)*

The altitude key shows that the United States has land at most of the different altitude levels on the earth. *What are some of the ways that the presence of these different landforms might influence people and events?*

12 CHAPTER 1 A GEOGRAPHIC PERSPECTIVE ON HISTORY

Cooperative Learning

Map-Reading Challenge Have students form small groups to write 5 questions and answers based on the map on page 12. When the questions are ready, ask each group to exchange questions with another group. Stress that the questions should be fair and answerable. Encourage students to base the different questions on a variety of map elements, such as latitude and longitude lines, the color code for altitude, distance, and state outlines. (Students may want to refer to the map with state names on page 10.) After the groups have answered all the questions, ask each group to talk about 1 question and its answer, describing the strategies that students used to find that answer.

A Country Characterized by Diversity These four locations—Oregon, Hawaii, New York, and Alaska (moving from left to right)—look very different from each other. *What are some of those differences?*

History is the study of people and events over time. Geography looks at people and events not over time but in space. Focusing on geographic concepts such as the five themes can illuminate the study of the past as well as make it easier to understand the present and the future.

The Location of the United States
Forty-eight Plus Two

The United States is located in the Northern Hemisphere west of the Prime Meridian. The United States currently includes 48 states that are contiguous, that is, that share borders, and 2 other states. The state of Alaska shares a border with Canada. The state of Hawaii is a group of islands located in the central Pacific Ocean.

A consideration of such a location can raise many questions about the history of the United States. How and when did the 48 states come together as a single political body? How and when did Alaska and Hawaii join the contiguous states? How has the location of the United States affected its relations with other nations in different parts of the world? The location of the United States has influenced many events in its history, including events that are occurring today.

Places in the United States
Richness and Variety

When a person pictures the physical characteristics of all the places in the United States, an extraordinary variety of environments becomes apparent. When the influences of all the different cultural heritages are added, the picture becomes even more amazingly diverse.

The concept of "place" can illuminate the study of history by showing how different people at different times came to this land and chose where to live. The earliest Americans settled in many diverse environments and developed ways of life that harmonized with those diverse places. Later settlers from Europe looked for harbors or farmland or opportunities for fur trapping. At each new stage of United States history, people have come seeking a place where they could live and prosper.

Regions of the United States
Natural Versus Human Divisions

The map on page 10 shows various political regions—areas defined by governments acting individually or jointly. The regions that nature has created are equally interesting and important.

Landforms

When someone looks at a physical map of the United States, like the one on page 12, the region that seems most prominent may be that of the mountain ranges that

SECTION TWO   **13**

Meeting Special Needs

Attention Deficit Disorder To help students who have difficulty concentrating, assign to a pair of students a limited task related to reading the map on page 12. Help them find their own location on the map. Then give them a series of questions to answer, such as the following: What is the altitude at your location? Are you

closer to the Atlantic Ocean or the Pacific Ocean? Are you closer to Canada or to Mexico? What altitude would you be at if you moved 1,000 miles (1,609 km) north? South? East? West? Urge each pair of students to talk about each question and the steps they use as they try to answer it.

VISUAL INSTRUCTION

A Country Characterized by Diversity Population density is just one factor that influences the atmosphere of a specific place.

Answer: *Answers will vary but should discuss both physical and human differences.*

TEACH

Guided Practice

L1 **Discussion** Use the map and the images on pages 12–13 to stimulate a discussion about different places in the United States and elsewhere. Urge students to compare places in terms of both physical features and human features.

Show students Beginnings to 1900 Transparency 1 and have them complete the activity sheet.

Independent Practice

L2 **Investigating Vegetation** Individually or in small groups, students can investigate the natural vegetation of places other than those shown on page 15. Remind students to explain how the vegetation relates to the climate and other conditions at each location.

Have students complete the Chapter 1, Section 2 Vocabulary and Guided Reading Activity. (Also in Spanish.) **LEP**

13

Videodisc

STV: North America

Side 1, Chapter 2
Title: The Northlands
Subject: Subregions and climate of the Northlands
Ask: Why do fewer people live in the Northlands than in other regions? *(climate)*

Side 2, Chapter 3
Title: The Central Lowlands
Subject: The Central Lowlands region
Ask: Why is agriculture so important there? *(ideal climate and good soil)*

Side 3, Chapter 4
Title: The Rocky Mountains
Subject: the Rocky Mountains region
Ask: Through what two nations do these mountains run? *(U.S., Canada)*

VISUAL INSTRUCTION

Moving Through the Locks Variations in water level may occur because the land itself varies in altitude or because the tides change water level at a coastline.

Answer: *Locks lift or lower vessels to the water level needed along the next stage of a route involving uneven water levels.*

14

---

run down the west side of the continent. These westernmost mountains make up the Coast Ranges, with the Rocky Mountains slightly to the east. These impressive mountains arose millions of years ago when tectonic plates (the huge pieces of the earth's outer crust) collided.

To the east of the western mountains lies a series of Plains areas. The Plains are generally flat and lack significant changes in landforms, though the elevation drops gradually from west to east.

Between the Plains and the Atlantic Ocean lie the Appalachian Mountains, less impressive in height than their counterparts to the west. East and south of these mountains are the coastal lowlands.

For someone studying history, these landforms can suggest many questions. Where could people settle most easily? Which landforms are the easiest for people to traverse? When the early European settlers tried to migrate, for example, the Appalachian Mountains prevented easy access to western territories. For those hardy people who faced the challenge, moving uphill and through forests often meant carrying possessions on their backs and sometimes canoes as well. Most migrants chose to move along the coastal plain and up low-lying rivers instead, where the geography made movement easier.

Water Systems

Throughout history, people have settled near a supply of fresh water. In North America fresh water in lakes and river systems is abundant. Several lakes are so large that they are easily visible on the map on page 12.

Many lakes were formed as a result of the Ice Age that took place from about 2 million years ago to about 10,000 B.C., when sheets of ice moved down from the north as far as the valleys of the Missouri and Ohio Rivers. The ice blocked the water of some rivers and formed lakes, such as Great Bear Lake in northern Canada. The ice also dug out hollows as it moved over rocks, and water later filled these hollows creating, among other bodies of water, the Great Lakes, which lie between Canada and the United States.

The United States also contains several major river systems, which consist of brooks and streams that flow into small rivers that, in turn, flow into larger ones. The Mississippi River system is the largest in the United States both in the size of its drainage area and in its volume of water.

Throughout history, rivers have been important in the exploration, trade, and control of an area because rivers offer a natural route of transportation. For example, when settlers from the British colonies tried to migrate westward, they found their progress impeded by the French, who had built a network of settlements and forts that helped them control large parts of the Mississippi River system.

Climate Regions

The term **climate** refers to the set of meteorological conditions, including sunlight, temperature, precipitation, and wind, that characterize an area. An area having the same meteorological conditions is called a climate region. The United States has a wide variety of climate regions from the subarctic areas of Alaska to the tropical regions of Hawaii.

The climate of a region is like a meteorological boundary that sets limits for all aspects of life, including the extent to which humans can survive. In particular, climate determines the kinds of plants that can grow in an area and the kinds of animals that can thrive there.

Vegetation Regions

The term **vegetation** refers to the collection of plants that grow in an area. When people travel from one area to another that is very different, it is usually the vegetation that first draws their notice.

Given the variety of climate areas and landforms that characterize the United States, it is not surprising that the vegetation regions of the country are equally diverse. There are several kinds of forests, each with its own distinct family of trees. There are desert areas and flat grassland regions. Each type of vegetation supports a specific type of human lifestyle and activities.

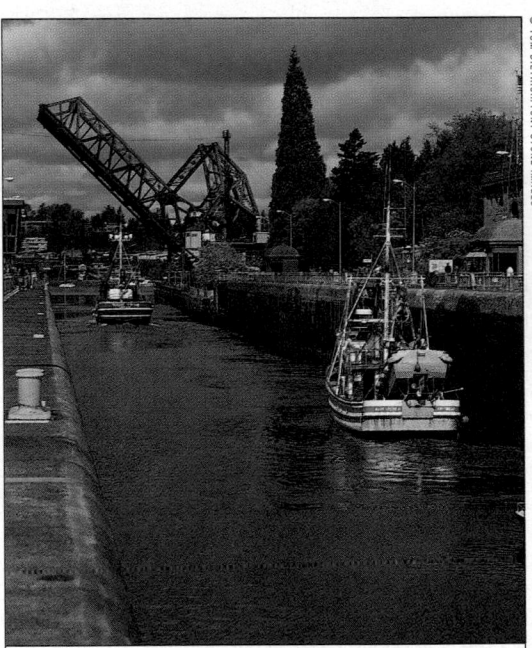

Moving Through the Locks Locks are sections of a waterway that can be closed off with gates so that the water level can be raised or lowered. *How can locks make it easier to travel on waterways that have variations in water level?*

14 CHAPTER 1 A GEOGRAPHIC PERSPECTIVE ON HISTORY

Portfolio Project

Local Weather and Climate Have students look up the difference between weather (conditions such as temperature, moisture, and wind velocity at a given time) and climate (overall year-round weather conditions). Invite them to write about the climate in their locale. They can obtain the annual average temperature from the map on page 15. They can also look up and describe conditions during the four seasons. Encourage students to consider representing some findings visually, for example, in a graph of temperatures. Students may wish to share their plans with a partner before doing their final work, which they will place in a portfolio.

FACTORS INFLUENCING VEGETATION

Climatic factors—such as the amount and intensity of sunlight, annual temperature patterns, and the annual rate of precipitation—limit the kinds of plants that grow naturally in a region. The type of soil and the local landforms also affect a region's vegetation.

GRASSLAND

© DAVID MUENCH

Temperature	Jan.	10°F to 20°F	−12°C to −7°C
	July	80°F to 90°F	27°C to 32°C
Annual Precipitation		Less than 20 in.	Less than 51 cm

Grasses feed animals and people throughout the year. In the winter, cattle and other grazing animals eat dried or fermented grass products. People eat foods made from wheat, oats, corn, and rice.

Agate Fossil Beds, Nebraska

Alaska

0 — 200 mi.
0 — 200 km

0 — 200 mi.
0 — 200 km

Hawaii

MEAN ANNUAL AIR TEMPERATURE	
°F	°C
Over 75	Over 24
70 to 75	21 to 24
65 to 70	18 to 21
60 to 65	16 to 18
55 to 60	13 to 16
50 to 55	10 to 13
45 to 50	7 to 10
40 to 45	4 to 7
35 to 40	2 to 4
30 to 35	−1 to 2
25 to 30	−4 to −1
20 to 25	−7 to −4
15 to 20	−9 to −7
10 to 15	−12 to −9
5 to 10	−15 to −12

0 — 250 — 500 mi.
0 — 250 — 500 km
Albers Equal-Area projection

DESERT

© ROB BOUDREAU/TONY STONE IMAGES

Temperature	Jan.	20°F to 30°F	−7°C to −1°C
	July	74°F to 82°F	23°C to 28°C
Annual Precipitation		8 in. to 12 in.	20 cm to 30 cm

Adaptations enable desert plants to survive in a dry climate. Mesquite tree roots can grow to depths of about 260 feet (79 m). Many cacti expand to store rainwater and then shrink as they use water during dry periods.

Monument Valley, Arizona

The temperature and rainfall statistics given here are averages for these three specific locations. Other grassland, desert, and forest locations may have different climate patterns.

FOREST

© MICHAEL GADOMSKI/PHOTO RESEARCHERS

Temperature	Jan.	24°F to 28°F	−4°C to −2°C
	July	72°F to 74°F	22°C to 23°C
Annual Precipitation		44 in. to 48 in.	112 cm to 122 cm

Every autumn the flat green leaves of this forest change color. The cooler, shorter days cause the breakdown of the green pigment chlorophyll. Other pigments in the leaf now become visible as the yellow, orange, and red colors of fall foliage.

Delaware Water Gap, Pennsylvania

Climate and vegetation are interrelated. *How important is a region's vegetation to the people who live there?*

SECTION TWO   **15**

GRAPH STUDY

Plants determine which herbivores live in an area.

Answer: *Vegetation partly determines people's lifestyles and local industries.*

NATIONAL
GEOGRAPHIC
SOCIETY

 Videodisc

STV: North America

Side 3, Chapter 5
Title: The Pacific Edge
Subject: The Pacific Edge region
Ask: In recent years, many residents of the Pacific Edge have opposed new development. Why do you think this is so? *(The residents may want to preserve their beautiful surroundings.)*

Side 4, Chapter 6
Title: The Western Dry Lands
Subject: The Western Dry Lands region
Ask: Why is irrigation important there? *(Rainfall is too slight for most crops.)*

Extending the Content

Is the World's Climate Changing? Students have probably heard the terms "global warming" and "greenhouse effect." Review the meaning of those terms and explain what could happen (especially to the food supply) if the world became just a little bit hotter or colder. Describe some of the evidence that researchers use to study past climates: evidence of glaciers, presence or absence of pollen, data from tree rings, ice core samples, and so on. To enrich the discussion, volunteers could research and report on the different kinds of evidence and what each reveals. Help students understand how this evidence lays the basis for answering the question of whether today's climate is changing, a question that still has not been reliably answered.

 Curriculum Connection

Science Invite volunteers to investigate why the earth has four seasons and to share their findings with the class.

Facilitating Movement Before 1794, roads in the United States were usually crude surfaces to and from waterways. In 1794 the first sizable hard-surface road was laid in Pennsylvania.

Answer: *Highways make it easier to travel to jobs and other destinations.*

Global Connection

From about 1400 to about 1600, several advanced civilizations were present around the world. It was primarily explorers from the countries of western Europe who made the historic voyages of exploration that changed world history.

ASSESS

Meeting Lesson Objectives

Each section objective is tested by the section review question(s) that follows it in parentheses.

1. Explain how understanding geography helps people understand history. (1, 2, 5)
2. Describe ways the five themes of geography relate to United States history. (3, 4, 5)

Ask: When was writing developed? *(3,000 B.C.)*

© TONY STONE WORLDWIDE

Facilitating Movement Modern highways include many features to improve safety, such as controlled traffic patterns at intersections. *How might a well-planned network of highways influence people's lives?*

Movement
People Come to the Two Continents

Fifty thousand years ago, North and South America were filled with a fascinating array of animals, but there were no people there at all. Anthropologists infer that the first human ancestors appeared in Africa a few million years ago. Their descendants migrated into Europe and Asia slightly less than 1 million years ago.

That migration took place during the most recent Ice Age, which ended about 10,000 years ago. Much of the earth's water was locked up in glaciers, and the ocean level was lower than it is today. Sometime toward

the end of that Ice Age, while the ocean floor between Alaska and Asia was exposed and could serve as a "land bridge," the first humans migrated into North America from Asia.

From that moment until the present, a series of migrations have populated the United States and the other countries of the Americas. A rich understanding of United States history can be developed, in part, by tracing the reasons for and the effects of those migrations. A consideration of the goods, information, and ideas that have flowed into and out of the United States over the centuries can further enhance one's knowledge of history.

Human/Environment Interaction
An Inevitable Interdependence

Groups of people have always interacted with their surroundings in ways that affected the people as well as the environment. These interactions have produced human culture—the combination of institutions, ideas, and products that people have created and passed on from generation to generation. The time line below describes some of the milestones in the development of human culture.

The Early Centuries

The earliest Americans adapted to the variety of environments they discovered on the new continents. Some of their ways of life, for example, hunting and gathering, had a minimal impact on the surroundings. The single human activity that most changed early environments was the clearing of forests for farming and for fuel. Cutting down forests begins a series of changes that includes the loss of topsoil, the silting of rivers, and an overall increase in an area's temperature.

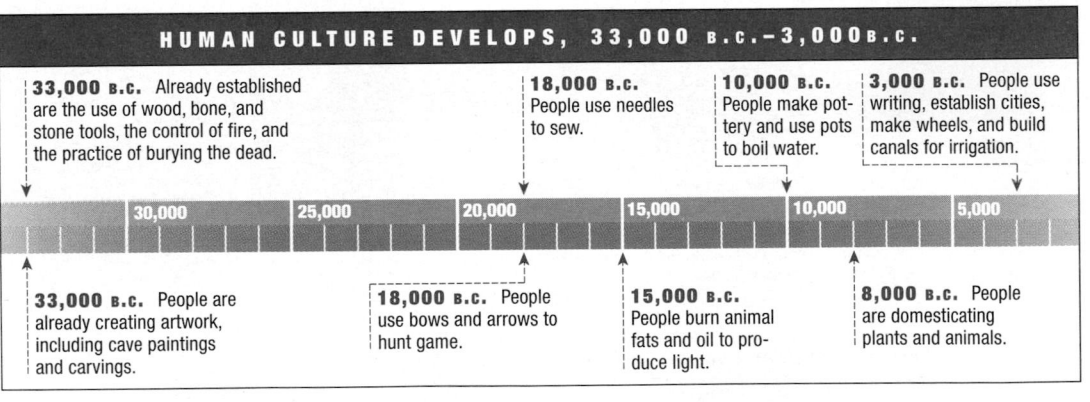

HUMAN CULTURE DEVELOPS, 33,000 B.C.–3,000 B.C.

33,000 B.C. Already established are the use of wood, bone, and stone tools, the control of fire, and the practice of burying the dead.

18,000 B.C. People use needles to sew.

10,000 B.C. People make pottery and use pots to boil water.

3,000 B.C. People use writing, establish cities, make wheels, and build canals for irrigation.

30,000   25,000   20,000   15,000   10,000   5,000

33,000 B.C. People are already creating artwork, including cave paintings and carvings.

18,000 B.C. People use bows and arrows to hunt game.

15,000 B.C. People burn animal fats and oil to produce light.

8,000 B.C. People are domesticating plants and animals.

Cultural Perspectives

Climates Around the World Find a copy of a world climate map based on the work of Wladimir Köppen. *(Harm de Blij's Geography Book* by Harm de Blij, Wiley & Sons, Inc., 1995, contains such a map on pages 96–97.) Help students examine the classification system, looking first at the major categories (represented by the first uppercase letter) and then at the subcategories (represented by a second and sometimes a third letter). Help students find specific climates, for example, all the hot or all the cold, dry climates. If you provide a political map of the world as a reference, students can also consider other questions, such as, if people from a specific climate in India wanted to move to a place with a similar climate in Africa, where could they go?

People's Night Lights This computerized composite image shows the light sensed by a satellite during the night. *In which two areas is the light the most concentrated?*

As the centuries have passed, the magnitude of the environmental changes caused by human activity has increased in a drastic way.

Monitoring Today's Conditions

In the late decades of this century, people have developed an amazing range of tools for looking at the environment. These tools can show the impact of natural events, such as volcanic eruptions, as well as human activities, such as burning fuel. The knowledge obtained from these tools will enable citizens and governments to make intelligent choices about the way people relate to their surroundings.

People can now use a modern understanding of the theme of human/environment interaction along with the other geography themes to illuminate the study of past events. The value of integrating the study of history and geography has been recognized for centuries. As one early historian noted:

A s Geography without History seems as carcass without motion, so History without Geography wanders as vagrant without a certain habitation.
—John Smith, *The General History of Virginia, New-England, and the Summer Isles,* 1624

SECTION REVIEW

Vocabulary

1. Define: history, climate, vegetation.

Checking Facts

2. Give an example of a history question related to the location of the United States.

3. Why did the Mississippi River deter the westward migration of British colonists?

Critical Thinking

Making Inferences

4. *Irrigation* refers to the supplying of water to an area by means of ditches or pipes. What historical changes might irrigation bring about in regions of dry land?

Linking Across Time

5. Describe a current historical event and explain how using one or more of the geography themes helps you to better understand that event.

SECTION TWO **17**

Section 2 Review Answers

1. history (13), **climate** (14), **vegetation** (14)
2. Answers will vary. Example: How has the location of the United States affected the country's relations with other nations in different parts of the world?
3. The French controlled the Mississippi River and prevented the migration of other settlers into that region.

4. Irrigation can lead to farming and the buildup of towns and cities in dry areas.
5. Answers will vary, but students should make a reasonable link between the event and the themes.

VISUAL INSTRUCTION

People's Night Lights Satellite images can show information that cannot be observed without instrumentation.

Answer: *around the southern coast of Lake Michigan and along the Northeast Coast*

Evaluate

Have students complete the Section Review.

☞ 🔲 Assign the Section 2 Quiz or use the Testmaker. **LEP**

☞ 🔲 Assign the Chapter 1 Test or use the Testmaker.

☞ Have students complete the Chapter 1 Performance Assessment Activity.

Reteach

🎧 Have students listen to the Chapter 1, Section 2 Audiocassette. (Also in Spanish.) **LEP**

☞ Have students complete the Chapter 1 Reteaching Activity. **LEP**

Enrich

☞ Have students complete the Chapter 1 Enrichment Activity. (Also in Spanish.) **LEP**

☞ Have students complete the Chapter 1 Geography in History Activity.

CLOSE

Have students name the five themes of geography. *(location, place, movement, human/environment interaction, region)*

Chapter ① Review

Reviewing Key Terms

1. place
2. region
3. human/environment interaction
4. geography
5. movement

Recalling Facts

1. To organize the information covered by geography
2. Position on earth's surface
3. By using a grid of latitude and longitude lines
4. Location of a place in relation to other known places
5. Physical and human features
6. From necessity because of catastrophes or conflicts; to seek a better life
7. Fresh water, food, shelter
8. Domestication of plants and animals, leading to the development of agriculture
9. Political divisions, languages, or industries
10. Landforms, water systems, climate, or vegetation
11. To conceal Vasco da Gama's discovery of a new travel route to India
12. The study of people and events over time
13. West of it
14. 48 states are contiguous; Alaska shares a border with Canada. The Hawaiian Islands are located in the central Pacific Ocean.
15. Regions defined by governments acting individually or jointly
16. Mountains, plains, and coastal lowlands
17. The set of meteorological conditions that characterize an area over time
18. The collection of plants that grow in an area
19. Over a "land bridge" that formed when the Ice Age lowered the ocean level, exposing the ocean floor
20. Clearing of forests for farming and fuel

Reviewing Key Terms

Choose the vocabulary term that best matches each description below. Write your answers on a separate sheet of paper.

human/environment interaction
geography   **location**
movement   **place**
region

1. Theme that focuses on the distinctive characteristics of a specific location

2. An area that is defined according to one or more characteristics

3. Theme that explores the interdependence of people and their surroundings

4. The study of people, places, and environments

5. Theme that focuses on the relocation of people as well as the transfer of goods and information

Recalling Facts

1. Why do geographers often refer to the five themes of geography?

2. What does the theme of location emphasize?

3. How is absolute location described?

4. What is relative location?

5. What types of features describe a specific place?

6. What are some reasons why people migrate?

7. What three basic human needs does the environment satisfy?

8. What revolutionary event took place about 10,000 B.C.?

9. What three examples of region are based on human concepts?

10. What four examples of region are based on physical features?

11. Why did King Manuel I of Portugal want to keep a particular map a secret?

12. What is history?

13. Where is the United States located relative to the Prime Meridian?

14. How are the 50 states of the United States distributed?

15. What are political regions?

16. What are examples of landforms that are present in the United States?

17. What is climate?

18. What does the term *vegetation* mean?

19. How were the first people able to migrate from Asia to North America?

20. What single human activity most changed the environment during the early centuries of life in North America?

Critical Thinking

1. Determining Relevance How does an understanding of geography make it easier to understand history? Give examples to support your reasoning.

2. Making Inferences Write a description of the place shown in the top photograph, below. What event(s) might have produced the conditions shown in that photograph?

PHOTOGRAPH BY CAMILO VERGARA

PHOTOGRAPH BY CAMILO VERGARA

Critical Thinking

1. Answers will vary, but students' explanations should stress that historical events are partly determined by the place(s) where they occur.
2. Inner city scene with abandoned buildings or rubble; people and/or fire destroyed buildings and left trash.

3. Place, because the photos show the characteristics of a specific place at two different times, and human/environment interaction, because they show what improvements people have made to a specific environment.

4. Answers will vary, but students should choose reasonable and significant characteristics to define their region.

CHAPTER
1
REVIEW

3. Making Comparisons The pair of photographs on page 18 show a location in the Bronx, New York, in 1981 (top) and 1994 (bottom). What geographic themes does this pair of photographs illustrate? Explain your answer.

4. Synthesizing Information If you described the region where your school and community are located, what characteristics would you include? Explain your answer.

Portfolio Project

The geographer Harm de Blij has written, "If a picture is worth a thousand words, then a map is worth a million." Respond in writing to this statement, either agreeing or disagreeing with Harm de Blij. Explain the reasons for your opinion. Revise your work before placing it in your portfolio.

Cooperative Learning

In small groups, examine maps and use brainstorming to list the ways that all types of spatial boundaries can be established—from national borders to the property lines of private land. Then each member of the group should investigate one boundary that has changed at least once during its history. Find out what the boundary used to look like, what it looks like now, and why it changed. Report your findings to your group, and then choose one of the group's stories to share with the whole class.

Reinforcing Skills

Reading a Map Examine the map above. Write a set of directions that would help someone read the map accurately and completely.

EXPLORATION BY EARLY SETTLERS

NEW ENGLAND

Kennebec River

Salmon Falls River

Merrimack River

Connecticut River

Hudson River

Boston (1630)

Fort Orange (1623)

Fort Nassau (1614)

Hartford (1637)

Providence (1636)

Plymouth (1620)

Newport (1639)

NEW NETHERLANDS

New Amsterdam (1623)

Breukelen (1646)

ATLANTIC OCEAN

N

0   50   100 mi.
0   50   100 km
Albers Equal-Area projection

- English territory, 1630
- Dutch territory, 1630
- ■ Settlement (date)
- → John Oldham, 1633
- → Darby Field, 1642
- → Simon Willard, 1640s

76°W   74°W   72°W   70°W
44°
42°
40°
38°

Geography and History

Study the map on this page to answer the following questions:

1. Where were the Dutch settlements located?

2. How does the size of New Netherlands compare to the size of the New England region at the time period shown on this map?

3. Describe John Oldham's explorations of 1633.

4. How does this map reinforce the idea that rivers play an important role in history?

HISTORY JOURNAL

Read over the journal entries you made after reading page 4. How has a consideration of the five themes of geography helped you understand and appreciate the history of your locale?

CHAPTER 1   REVIEW   **19**

Geography and History

1. Most were along a river running north from New Amsterdam; Breukelen was on an island near New Amsterdam.
2. The New England region is two to three times as large as New Netherlands.
3. John Oldham explored a route from Boston to Hartford.
4. Many of the settlements are built on rivers, and Simon Willard followed a river route as he explored northward.

History Journal

Student journals should relate local historical events to one or more appropriate themes.

BONUS QUESTION

This question may be used for extra credit on the chapter test.

Where was the Prime Meridian located through most of its history, and where is it located today?

Answer: *Until 1884 the Prime Meridian was located wherever the mapmaker wanted to place it; since 1884 it has been located at an observatory in Greenwich, England.*

Portfolio Project

Answers will vary, but students should provide persuasive reasons for their position and include detailed examples to support their logic.

Cooperative Learning

Students' examples of changing boundaries will vary. They may include boundaries that were established, changed, or eliminated by mutual agreement as well as boundaries that were created, changed, or destroyed by force.

Reinforcing Skills

Answers will vary but should include most or all of the following: reading the title; using the scale and direction arrow; reading the color codes; reading the settlement symbol and related labels; reading the arrows that show routes of exploration.

Encounters and Colonies

DAILY LESSON OBJECTIVES	REPRODUCIBLE RESOURCES	MULTIMEDIA RESOURCES
SECTION 1 The Earliest Americans 1. Examine how people arrived in North America. 2. Understand the origins and life-ways of some Native American groups. 3. Describe the formation of the League of the Iroquois.	▸ Reproducible Lesson Plans ▸ Vocabulary and Guided Reading Activities (English or Spanish) ▸ Cooperative Learning Activities ▸ Section Quizzes (English or Spanish)	▸ Chapter Teaching Transparencies ▸ Section Focus Transparencies ▸ Map Transparencies ▸ U.S. History and Art Transparencies ▸ American Indian ▸ A Geographic Perspective on American History ▸ Native Americans
SECTION 2 Three Worlds Meet 1. Explain European explorers' motives for coming to the Americas. 2. Understand the Europeans' first interactions with Native Americans. 3. Describe why Africans were brought to North America and what their new life was like.	▸ Reproducible Lesson Plans ▸ Vocabulary and Guided Reading Activities (English or Spanish) ▸ Geography in History Activities ▸ Section Quizzes (English or Spanish)	▸ Section Focus Transparencies ▸ U.S. History and Art Transparencies ▸ Beginnings to 1900 Transparenceis ▸ The American People: Fabric of a Nation ▸ A Geographic Perspective on American History ▸ American Music: Cultural Traditions
SECTION 3 Building Colonial America 1. Describe where Spanish, French, and English settlers established claims in the Americas. 2. Explain how the various European settlers adapted to the land and made their livings. 3. Explain the differences in the colonies.	▸ Reproducible Lesson Plans ▸ Vocabulary and Guided Reading Activities (English or Spanish) ▸ Section Quizzes (English or Spanish)	▸ Section Focus Transparencies ▸ U.S. History and Art Transparencies ▸ A Geographic Perspective on American History ▸ Student Self-Test: A Software Review ▸ Testmaker ▸ Focus on American Fine Art Prints
SECTION 4 Conflict and Growth in the Colonies 1. Explain why Native Americans rebelled against the colonists. 2. Relate how England became the dominant power in the colonies. 3. Describe colonial conditions after the Seven Years' War.	▸ Reproducible Lesson Plans ▸ Vocabulary and Guided Reading Activities (English or Spanish) ▸ Reteaching Activities (English or Spanish) ▸ Enrichment Activities (English or Spanish) ▸ Skill Reinforcement Activities ▸ Section Quizzes (English or Spanish)	▸ Section Focus Transparencies ▸ Beginnings to 1900 Transparencies ▸ Student Self-Test: A Software Review ▸ Testmaker
CHAPTER REVIEW AND EVALUATION	▸ Chapter 2 Test, Forms A and B ▸ Performance Assessment Strategies and Activities	▸ Student Self-Test: A Software Review ▸ Vocabulary PuzzleMaker ▸ Testmaker ▸ Chapter Digests Audiocassettes

🕐 **00:00** If time does not permit teaching the entire chapter, summarize using the Chapter 2 Digests Audiocassettes and the accompanying activities and tests. (Available in English and Spanish.)

Cooperative Project

Organize the class into three groups. Have one group research more about the individual Spanish explorers, another the English explorers, and the last more about the French explorers Have them compile their findings and present them to the class. **L1**

Suggested Rubric: An Oral Presentation. See Performance Assessment Strategies and Activities, p. 33.

Individual Project

Have students research more about the cultures that existed in Africa at the time Africans were enslaved and brought to the Americas. Encourage them to collect visuals and information about the art and music of these cultures as well as the other facets of their societies.

Suggested Rubric: A Research Report. See Performance Assessment Strategies and Activities, p. 39.

Key to Ability Levels

Teaching strategies have been coded for varying learning styles and abilities.

L1 **BASIC** activities for all students

L2 **AVERAGE** activities for average to above-average students

L3 **CHALLENGING** activities for above-average students

LEP **LIMITED ENGLISH PROFICIENCY** activities

Block Scheduling

Block scheduling differs from traditional class scheduling in the amount of time allotted to each period. The extended timeframe provided by block scheduling affords you the opportunity to implement a greater number of research-oriented and activity-intense projects to motivate and involve your students. Activities that are particularly suited to use within the block scheduling framework are identified throughout this chapter by the following designation.

TEACHER'S CORNER

NATIONAL GEOGRAPHIC SOCIETY

INDEX TO NATIONAL GEOGRAPHIC MAGAZINE

The following articles may be used for research relating to this chapter:

- "Powwow," by Michael Parfit, June 1994.
- "Geronimo," by David Roberts, October 1992.
- "Search for Columbus," by Eugene Lyon, January 1992.
- *1491: America Before Columbus* (A Special Edition), October 1991.
- "The Battle To Save our Past," by George E. Stuart, March 1989.
- "Exploring Our Forgotten Century: Between Columbus and Jamestown," by Joseph Judge, March 1988.
- "The Fire That Never Dies," by Harvey Arden, September 1987.

NATIONAL GEOGRAPHIC SOCIETY PRODUCTS AVAILABLE FROM GLENCOE

To order the following products for use with this chapter, contact your local Glencoe sales representative or call Glencoe at 1-800-334-7344:

- *GTV: A Geographic Perspective on American History* (Videodisc)
- *GTV: The American People: Fabric of a Nation* (Videodisc)
- *Native Americans, Part I* (CD-ROM)
- *Native Americans, Part II* (CD-ROM)
- *Native Americans: Eastern Woodlands and Plains* (Transparencies)
- *Native Americans: Southwest, Northwest Coast, Arctic* (Transparencies)

ADDITIONAL NATIONAL GEOGRAPHIC SOCIETY PRODUCTS

To order the following products for use with this chapter, call National Geographic Society at 1-800-368-2728:

- *Digging Up America's Past,* "North America Before Columbus," "The First Europeans in the Americas," "Colonization and After," (Filmstrip)

Chapter Overview

Chapter 2 relates the arrivals and interactions of the Native Americans who had come across the Beringia land bridge and established themselves throughout the Americas, the Europeans who set up colonies in the Americas, and the Africans forcibly brought to the Americas as slaves.

Introducing the Chapter

Point out to students that the interactions of the three cultures that settled in the Americas varied widely. Sometimes the cultures engaged beneficially with each other; sometimes they did not.

Display the Chapter Teaching Transparency on the board and distribute copies of the activity sheet.

Extension Activity

Have students complete Beyond the Transparency on the activity sheet for Chapter 2 and present their projects after the class has completed the chapter.

History Journal

Have students choose an interesting image from the chapter and write their responses to that image in their journals.

CHAPTER
2

Encounters and Colonies

APRIL 5, 1614: A WEDDING IS CELEBRATED IN JAMESTOWN

The bride was a Native American princess, the favorite daughter of King Powhatan. The groom, an English settler named John Rolfe, had been obliged to plead for the right to marry Pocahontas.

Rolfe received permission from Virginia's Governor Thomas Dale to wed for "the good of this plantation." The wedding brought a temporary if uneasy truce between the Powhatans and the English settlers of Jamestown, who would have starved if not for the Powhatans' gifts of corn.

Six years earlier, at the age of 12, Pocahontas had saved the life of Jamestown's leader, John Smith, by interposing herself between Smith and his Powhatan combatants. This intervention, which ended in Smith's being adopted into King Powhatan's family, allowed for the Powhatans to demonstrate their strength by establishing trade relations with the English settlers. When Smith re-turned to England, the settlers captured Pocahontas, holding her hostage in exchange for the release of English prisoners and food. In captivity, she became an English-speaking Christian and met Rolfe.

When the Rolfes traveled to England with their infant son, the beautiful Pocahontas became an instant celebrity. She posed for a portrait, charmed the English king, and established a mythical presence that continues even today. Ironically, Pocahontas's celebrity also aroused the interest of potential English settlers who would soon flood the new colony and wage bloody warfare with her Powhatan relatives. ■

HISTORY JOURNAL

Write your reactions to the treatment of
Pocahontas and the Powhatans by the English.

EXTRA CREDIT PROJECT

Primary Sources Have students find primary sources that help to tell a story of early America. Students should look for quotes or artwork that show the perspectives of Native Americans, European settlers, and African Americans. Each student can present a dramatic reading using the voices of several of these early Americans.

(DETAIL) NATIONAL PORTRAIT GALLERY, SMITHSONIAN INSTITUTION/ART RESOURCE, NY

Ætatis suæ 21. Aº. 1616.

ALTHOUGH POCAHONTAS DIED BEFORE SHE WAS 22 YEARS OLD, SHE LEFT A LASTING MARK ON COLONIAL HISTORY.

21

GLENCOE
TECHNOLOGY

 Videodisc

American History

Side 1, Section A
Title: Prehistory to 1680
Subject: Overview of American history from before European contact to the English settlement of New England
Ask: Where was the first permanent English settlement in North America? *(Jamestown)*

Side 1, Section B
Title: Mature Colonial Life, 1680–1765
Subject: Overview of American history from England's Glorious Revolution and the beginning of the wars for empire to the second phase of the Anglo-French War for empire
Ask: What was the most significant event for the colonies in 1763? *(end of war with France)*

✔ **Performance Assessment**

Refer to page 20B for performance assessment activities for this chapter.

 Also see Activity 2 in the Performance Assessment Strategies and Activities for an additional activity as well as for suggested rubrics.

Examining the Visual

Lady Rebecca During her visit to London, Pocahontas, known as Lady Rebecca in society circles, posed for this portrait, probably painted by Simon Van de Pass, a young Dutch painter. Pocahontas wore lace cuffs, a starched shoulder collar, and a beaver hat, which were considered fashionable for the time.

22

FOCUS

Section Objectives

1. Examine how people first arrived in North America.
2. Understand the origins and lifeways of some Native American groups.
3. Describe the formation of the League of the Iroquois.

Bellringer Activity

 While taking attendance at the beginning of the class period, display **Section Focus Transparency 3,** and have students answer the questions. (Or use the blackline master.)

VISUAL INSTRUCTION

Land of Plenty These bison live in Alberta, in northwestern Canada. Migrants hunted large grazing animals in game drives, stampeding herds over cliffs. In this way several species of animals, including the mammoth, the ground sloth, and the mastodon, were hunted to extinction.

Ask: What other plentiful foods did migrants find in North America? *(antelope, saber-toothed tigers, berries, nuts, and grasses)*

History and the Humanities

U.S. History and Art Transparency 1—Quilled Buckskin Robe

∩ American Music: Cultural Traditions—"Rain Dance, Parts 1 & 2" by George Buck and George Green, leaders

---

SECTION 1

The Earliest Americans

38,000 B.C.–10,000 B.C.: PEOPLE CROSS LAND BRIDGE TO NORTH AMERICA

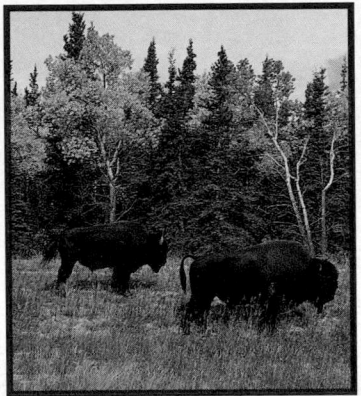

Land of Plenty
As people moved south into the Americas, they found abundant herds of bison and other grazing animals such as mammoths.

ARCHAEOLOGICAL EVIDENCE INDICATES THAT ACROSS THE WIDE, GRASSY LAND BRIDGE THAT ONCE CONNECTED ASIA AND NORTH AMERICA TREKKED THE FIRST PEOPLE TO SETTLE IN NORTH AMERICA. With spears poised they may have pursued a mammoth, the huge game animal that once strode the earth. Today Beringia, the land bridge that allowed passage from Asia to Alaska, lies underwater. At several periods during the Ice Age, the glaciers that covered most of North America lowered sea levels by as much as 300 feet (91.44 m)—sufficient to expose a 1,000-mile (1609-km) wide passageway between continents.

The first settlers stalked big game such as mammoths and bison. Later settlers came by boat, hunting seals and whales. Gradually, over thousands of years, the press of a growing population prompted the southward and eastward migration of smaller groups. Seeking new hunting grounds, the migrants followed their animal prey through the narrow pass between towering glaciers. When they reached the plains of North America, the earliest people beheld a paradise of plenty: animals from the antelope to the saber-toothed tiger; and berries, nuts, and grasses for the picking.

Over the centuries, groups continued breaking off and migrating farther southward and eastward. About 8,000 B.C. melting glaciers again boosted the sea level, burying Beringia underwater and drowning the land bridge back to Asia.

Scientists disagree on when people first came to the Americas and on how many waves of settlement they rode. Beringia, the land bridge, surfaced during 3 separate periods: between 70,000 and 30,000 years ago; between 25,000 and 15,000 years ago; and between 14,000 and 10,000 years ago. Some archaeologists speculate that people arrived from Asia as early as 40,000 years ago. Others suggest a much later date or a series of arrivals. Nevertheless, on several facts scientists do

---

AS YOU READ

Vocabulary
► nomadic
► sedentary
► egalitarian

Think About . . .
► how people first arrived in North America.
► the origins and ways of life of some Native American groups.

► the formation of the League of the Iroquois.

---

22 CHAPTER 2 ENCOUNTERS AND COLONIES

Section 1 Resources

REPRODUCIBLE RESOURCES
📁 Lesson Plan 2-1
📁 Vocabulary and Guided Reading Activity 2-1
📁 Cooperative Learning Activity 2
📁 Section 1 Quiz

MULTIMEDIA RESOURCES
📷 Chapter Teaching Transparency 2
📷 Section Focus Transparency 3
📷 U.S. History and Art Transparency 1
∩ American Music: Cultural Traditions
📷 Map Transparency 2
🌐 The American Indian

🌐 A Geographic Perspective on American History
🌐 Native Americans
💻 Testmaker
∩ Chapter 2 Digest Audiocassette
💻 Student Self-Test: A Software Review

agree: by 10,000 B.C. people had spread 15,000 miles (24,135 km) south to Tierra del Fuego, the southern tip of South America, and 6,000 miles (9,654 km) east to the East Coast of North America.

After generations of adapting to diverse climates and terrains, Native Americans practiced a staggering variety of lifeways and spoke several thousand languages. They became most populous in Mexico and Central America (Mesoamerica), but Native Americans also developed distinctive cultures throughout North America. There—in the deserts of the Southwest, along the fertile banks of the Mississippi, and in the woodlands of the East Coast—three contrasting cultures arose.

Cliff Dwellers of the Southwest

From Nomads to Farmers

During the Ice Age, descendants of the nomadic people who had followed their prey to North America hunted huge game animals such as mastodons in the southwestern part of what is now the United States. In time the weather warmed and the glaciers melted. As the climate grew drier, the larger game disappeared. The challenge of human survival in a newly arid environment launched a desert culture that depended on fishing, hunting small birds and animals, and on collecting edible foods that grew in the wild. This Southwestern desert culture survived for thousands of years.

Development of Agriculture

Between about 8,000 B.C. and 5,000 B.C., agriculture began to develop independently in Europe, Asia, Africa, and the Americas. As in other parts of the world, the cultivation of crops in the Southwest ushered in dramatic social changes. These changes included giving up a **nomadic,** or wandering, lifestyle for a more **sedentary,** or settled, one. A more dependable food supply stimulated population growth and reduced the amount of time people had to work to obtain food. Less time spent foraging afforded people more time for developing socially, politically, and religiously. In most places the growth of agriculture also decreed the division of labor. Now men hunted game and cleared the land that women then planted and cultivated.

Like their modern Pueblo descendants, but unlike most other highly developed early peoples, the Anasazi fostered an **egalitarian** culture in which people functioned as equals. Without kings, chiefs, or other official authority figures to compel cooperation, members of Anasazi farming villages built dams, reservoirs, and irri-

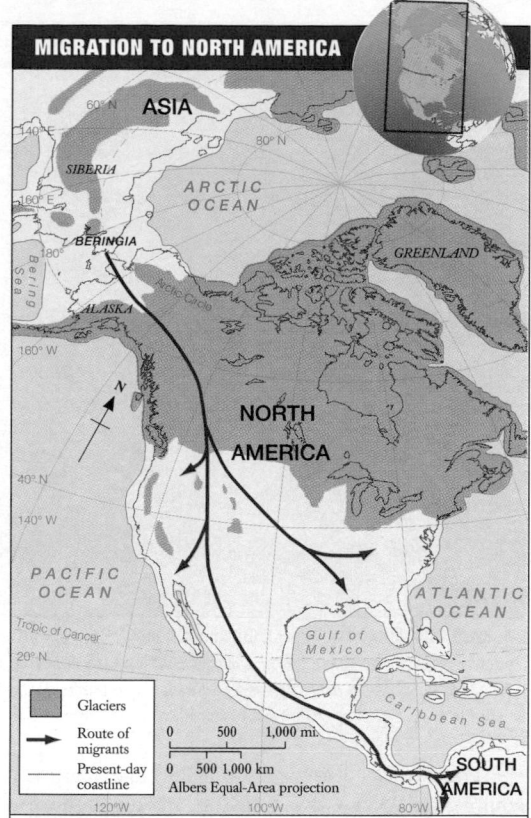

MIGRATION TO NORTH AMERICA

Glaciers

Route of migrants

Present-day coastline

0   500   1,000 mi.

0   500 1,000 km

Albers Equal-Area projection

By 10,000 B.C. people occupied North America from present-day Alaska to the tip of what is now Chile. *In which areas did Native Americans become most populous?*

gation systems that harnessed the region's precious moisture to water corn and other crops. Beginning around A.D. 900, the Anasazi also constructed 400 miles (643.6 km) of roads and broad avenues leading to Chaco Canyon in northwest New Mexico, which became the heart of a thriving turquoise trade.

Anasazi Architecture

The leisure that accompanied the farming culture's prosperity allowed the Anasazi to turn out beautiful baskets and pottery, but their greatest creativity flowered in architecture. Generation after generation of Anasazi had lived in underground houses whose stonework walls and strong roofs provided shelter from the harshness of the seasons. Now, adapting their aboveground food storage houses for living quarters, the Anasazi transformed their underground pit houses into spiritual centers, or kivas. Some kivas in the populous valley held as many as 500 people. Constructing these kivas without horses (which were not brought to the Americas until the 1500s) required people to transport tons of timber to reinforce kiva roofs.

SECTION ONE   23

Cooperative Learning

Debate Organize students into 2 groups to prepare for a debate about when people first came to the Americas. One group will take the position that humans arrived as early as 40,000 years ago and the other group will take the position that the arrival occurred much later.

Students should research the evidence found by archaeologists to support their position. Students may wish to take a different position on the issue if their research turns up new evidence pointing to another arrival date.

TEACH

Guided Practice

L1 Discussion Initiate a discussion with students about how it would feel to be the first human to set foot in a place.

Show students Map Transparency 2 and have them complete the activity sheet.

Independent Practice

L2 Class Presentation Have students choose an aspect of Anasazi culture such as agriculture, social organization, or religion to research in more detail. Encourage them to share their findings with the class.

Have students complete the Chapter 2, Section 1 Vocabulary and Guided Reading Activity. (Also in Spanish.) **LEP**

Have students complete the Chapter 2 Cooperative Learning Activity.

MAP STUDY

During the ice ages, glaciers and ice caps covered northern Europe, Asia, and North America. A glacier forms on land from compacted snow and moves downhill under its own weight. Glaciers can move up to 13–16 feet (4–5 m) per day. The pressure caused by glaciers in the Ice Age carved many valleys and mountains.

Answer: *Mexico and Central America*

Global Connection

In 3500 B.C., while ancestors of today's Inuit were moving across the Arctic, the civilization of Sumer was born in what is now southeastern Iraq. About 500 years later, Sumerians created the first writing system in the world: cuneiform, a collection of wedge-shaped symbols. Cuneiform was written on wet clay tablets, which then hardened into permanence. Thousands of these tablets telling of Sumerian life still exist.

Facts on File

The American Indian Have students review the information about the early Native Americans and write a brief report on one of the groups.

J. BLANK/H. ARMSTRONG ROBERTS

Ancient City In the Southwest, the Anasazi built cities of cliff-side dwellings, such as this one at Mesa Verde, Colorado, which was constructed around 1100. *What are the possible explanations for why the Anasazi abandoned Mesa Verde?*

The Anasazi also began to build huge apartment complexes. At one dwelling site, Pueblo Bonito in Chaco Canyon, more than 1,000 residents lived in a free-standing 600-room structure. From the plaza amphitheater, some apartment sections towered 5 stories above the canyon floor. Until a larger apartment building went up in New York City in 1882, the size of this Anasazi building of the tenth century remained unsurpassed in the world.

When drought or a devaluation of turquoise prompted the Anasazis to abandon Chaco Canyon, about 3,000 Anasazi built stunning multifamily apartments within the protected cliff walls of Mesa Verde in Southwest Colorado. From their rooms in the cliff walls, the farmers used toeholds to clamber to the mesa top, where they cultivated corn, beans, and squash. The largest structure in Mesa Verde, later named the Cliff Palace, boasted 220 rooms that may have housed as many as 350 people.

By 1300, perhaps driven by drought or enemies, the Anasazi abandoned their homes in Mesa Verde. Among their descendants are today's Zuni, Hopi, and Taos Pueblo. The Taos Pueblo people of New Mexico repeat this myth about their beginnings, a story that may well have been told in this part of the world for more than 1,000 years: "The boy cried and cried. The blood came out, and finally he died. With his tears our lakes became. With his blood the red clay became. With his body our mountains became, and that was how Earth became."

Moundbuilders' Rich Culture
Metropolis on the Mississippi

About 1,000 years before the Anasazis began to farm mesa tops and construct apartment buildings in the dry Southwest, a friendlier eastern landscape had given rise to a very different culture. In the lushly watered country near the Ohio River, Native Americans farmed, hunted, and foraged for food. They also built gigantic earth mounds by the tens of thousands.

The First Moundbuilders

Used primarily as burial and ceremonial sites, the earth mounds rose as high as 70 feet (21.3 m). Their grandeur baffled the colonial settlers, who came upon the mounds after crossing the Appalachian Mountains in the late 1700s. Because the settlers had stereotyped eastern Native Americans as primitive forest dwellers, they invented myths to explain the imposing structures. Perhaps, they thought, survivors of the legendary sunken island of Atlantis or descendants of the ancient Egyptians had constructed the huge mounds.

Instead the mounds had been built by Native American people during the first century A.D. The building of such gigantic structures suggests a high degree of cooperation, that required powerful leaders. These leaders were adorned at death and buried in special locations. Many excavations have shown individuals of high rank in the center of a group of people of secondary importance who had died earlier. One archaeologist described a Moundbuilder grave of a high-ranking female:

At the head, neck, hips and knees of the female and completely encircling the skeleton were thousands of pearl beads and buttons of wood and stone covered with copper; extending the full length of the grave along one side was a row of copper ear ornaments; at the wrists of the female were copper bracelets . . . [she wore a necklace] of grizzly bear canines and [a] copper breastplate on the chest.
—quoted in Joy Hakim's *The First Americans,* 1993

The contents of the burial mounds revealed the Moundbuilders as brilliant metalworkers and sculptors. The materials they worked with depended on a far-flung trading network, most likely based on a relay system.

24 CHAPTER 2 ENCOUNTERS AND COLONIES

Meeting Special Needs

Visual Learners To help visual learners, have students use the map of the United States on page 10 and the map on page 23 to trace which present-day states the earliest migrants passed through as they moved into North America.

The tentacles of the Moundbuilders' trading network reached west to Yellowstone (present-day northwest Wyoming) for obsidian, a natural glass used to make ceremonial blades; north to the Great Lakes for copper nuggets to beat out breastplates; east to the Appalachians for mica to fashion into decorated combs; and south to the Gulf of Mexico for turtle shells and alligator teeth to beautify ornaments.

The population of the Moundbuilders, ancestors of today's Creek, Choctaw, and Natchez, began to decline by about A.D. 500, perhaps due to the enmity of rivals or to a lingering cold spell that made farming and foraging less productive. West along the Mississippi River, however, another Moundbuilding culture arose. Centered at what is now East St. Louis, Illinois, on the Missouri border, this Mississippian culture encompassed thousands of villages from Wisconsin to Louisiana and from Oklahoma to Tennessee.

Cahokia

Like the Moundbuilders of the Ohio River valley, the Mississippians had strong leaders who directed the raising of huge mounds for burial and ceremonial purposes. The largest mound, built between A.D. 900 and 1100 rises 100 feet (30.5 m) from a rectangular base covering nearly 15 acres (6.1 ha) and containing 22 million cubic feet (616,000 cubic m) of earth. Its size surpasses that of the base of the Great Pyramid of Egypt.

This gigantic earthwork faces the site of a palisaded city that contains 100 smaller burial mounds and the remains of a busy urban settlement that archaeologists call Cahokia. Deemed "America's first metropolis" by one archaeologist, Cahokia once housed as many as 35,000 people. The city's residents worked at a variety of tasks, from jewelry making and weaving to hide dressing and salt making.

Mysteriously, the metropolis on the Mississippi lay abandoned centuries before the Europeans arrived on the Atlantic Coast. Before they disappeared, however, both the Mississippians and the Ohio River Moundbuilders passed on key agricultural skills to their trading partners in the Eastern Woodlands.

Eastern Woodland Native Americans
From Varied Lifeways, an Alliance

Like the Mississippians, the Native Americans who lived along the Eastern seaboard ate the fish they caught and the animals they hunted. Occasionally the men would don a deer head with antlers as a hunting ruse. Fertilizing the young plants with fish heads, the women cultivated corn, beans, and squash—which were called "the three sisters"—in the same plots. The sister plants supported each other as they grew, bean vines curling themselves around a supporting cornstalk. In addition, the nitrogen that beans brought to the soil benefited the other plants.

Like the Mississippians, the Eastern Woodland Native Americans also cleared their chosen planting grounds by girdling the trees. First they slashed the bark all the way around the trunk, leaving the tree to die.

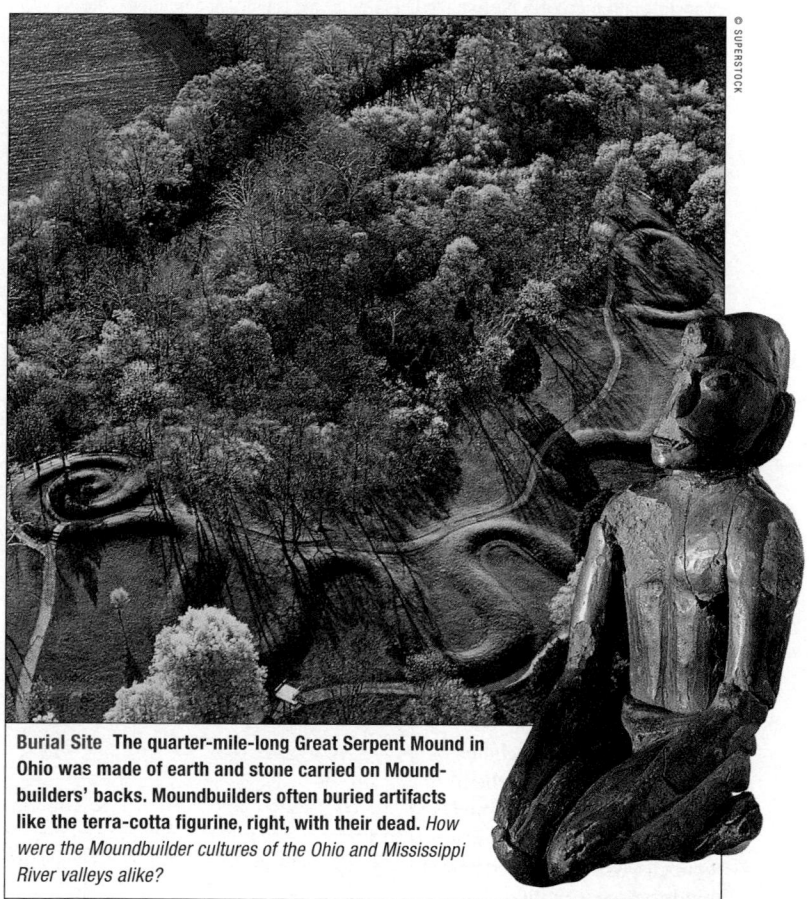

© SUPERSTOCK

Burial Site The quarter-mile-long Great Serpent Mound in Ohio was made of earth and stone carried on Moundbuilders' backs. Moundbuilders often buried artifacts like the terra-cotta figurine, right, with their dead. *How were the Moundbuilder cultures of the Ohio and Mississippi River valleys alike?*

PEABODY MUSEUM OF ARCHAEOLOGY AND ETHNOLOGY, HARVARD UNIVERSITY

SECTION ONE   **25**

NATIONAL GEOGRAPHIC SOCIETY

 Videodisc

GTV: A Geographic Perspective on American History

Side 1, Chapter 2
Title: Linking Life and Land
Subject: The first Americans and the effects of geography on their lives
Ask: How did geography affect the lives of the earliest Americans? *(They had to adapt to their environment with the types of dwellings they built and the clothes they wore.)*

NATIONAL GEOGRAPHIC SOCIETY

 Native Americans

Have students review the information about early Native Americans and create a bulletin board display about their different lifestyles.

VISUAL INSTRUCTION

Burial Site In addition to making serpent-shaped mounds, Moundbuilders constructed earthworks that depicted birds, lizards, turtles, and bears.

Answer: *Both had strong rulers who compelled the creation of ceremonial and burial mounds.*

Portfolio Project

Creation Myths Direct students to reread the Pueblo creation myth on page 24. Then ask students to research the creation myth(s) of another Native American group mentioned in the section and write a brief explanation of the origin, significance, and symbolism of the myth. Students may also wish to create an illustration to accompany their report. Have them place the finished product in their portfolios.

ASSESS

Meeting Lesson Objectives

Each section objective is tested by the section review question(s) that follows it in parentheses.

1. Examine how people first arrived in North America. (2)
2. Understand the origins and lifeways of some Native American groups. (1, 3, 4, 5)
3. Describe the formation of the League of the Iroquois. (3)

Evaluate

Have students complete the Section Review.

👉 💻 Assign the Section 1 Quiz or use the Testmaker to develop a customized quiz. (Also in Spanish.) **LEP**

Reteach

🎧 Have students listen to the Chapter 2, Section 1 Audiocassette. (Also in Spanish.) **LEP**

MAP STUDY

This map is based on descriptions written in the 1500s. Boundaries between groups were rarely fixed.

Answer: *along the coastline*

After burning the branches and leaves, they hoed the rich ash into the ground as a fertilizer.

The Mississippians passed on another influence, too. With their clusters of domed wigwams, occasionally surrounded by a palisade, the villages of many Eastern Woodland groups resembled the villages most Mississippians had called home. No Eastern Woodland village ever competed in size or sophistication with Cahokia. Still, excavation of one Huron town in the Great Lakes region revealed that it had housed about 5,000 people in more than 100 large structures. Its size exceeded that of the average European village of the 1500s.

The Iroquois Alliance

Eventually, the Iroquois became the most populous and powerful of all the groups that lived along the eastern seaboard. The group controlled territory from the Adirondack Mountains to the Great Lakes and from Pennsylvania to northern New York.

The power of the Iroquois derived from a longstanding alliance of 5 Native American groups—the Mohawk, Oneida, Onondaga, Cayuga, and Seneca. Europeans later called the Iroquois alliance the League of the Iroquois. The Iroquois themselves called their alliance *Ganonsyoni,* or The Lodge Extended Lengthwise, after the lodges, or longhouses, that as many as 20 families shared.

In an Iroquois longhouse, a woman and her female relatives ruled. The women owned the house and all its belongings. Women also controlled the fields where they planted their crops. When a son married, he left his mother's longhouse to move in with his wife's family. Iroquois women held power in the outside world as well. They chose the chiefs, or sachems, and could also depose them. Though only men could speak in the community councils, women exerted behind-the-scenes influence—

determining, for example, the fate of captive warriors from enemies.

At one time, the 5 groups that formed the Iroquois League had themselves been enemies. By the late 1400s the constant feuding that had rendered the Iroquois people powerless in the face of their mutual enemy, the powerful Algonquian people, spurred them to form the league for mutual protection.

In Iroquois legend the league began when a Mohawk sachem named Hiawatha had a vision. In Hiawatha's vision a spirit named Dekanawidah dictated how the five groups should affiliate with one another. According to the legend, Dekanawidah spoke these words:

> We bind ourselves together by taking hold of each other's hands so firmly and forming a circle so strong that if a tree should fall upon it, it could not shake nor break it, so that our people and

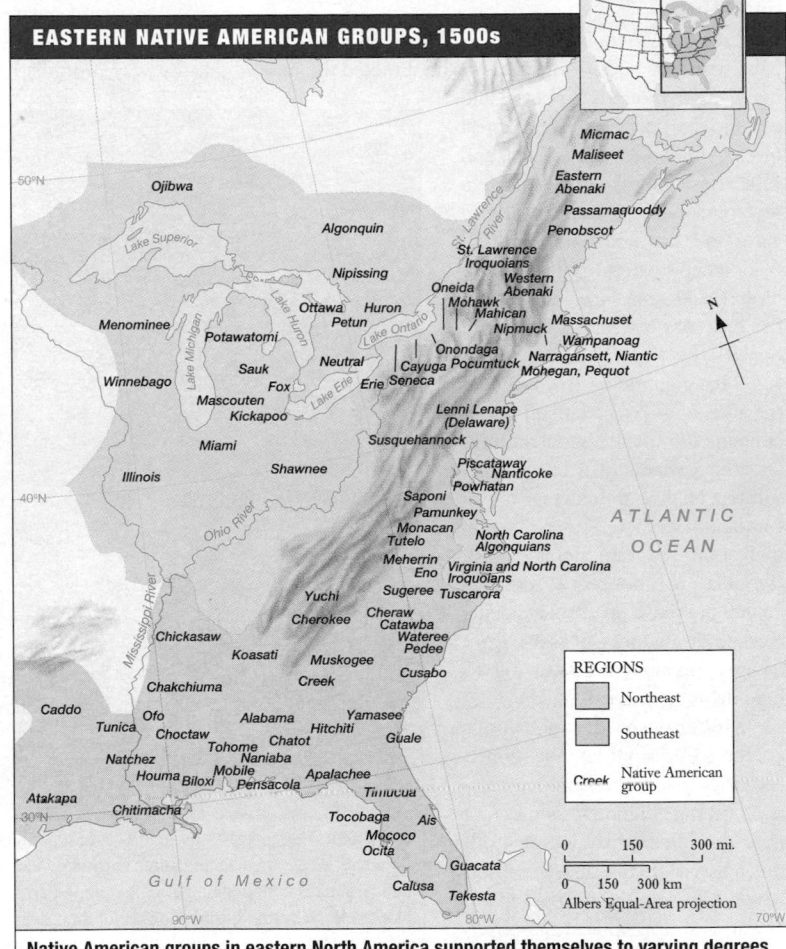

EASTERN NATIVE AMERICAN GROUPS, 1500s

REGIONS
Northeast
Southeast
Creek Native American group

0 150 300 mi.
0 150 300 km
Albers Equal-Area projection

Native American groups in eastern North America supported themselves to varying degrees with agriculture. *In what areas are most groups of Native Americans concentrated?*

Extending the Content

Iroquois Government Today In the 1830s, Iroquois traditionalists and followers of Handsome Lake, a Seneca prophet, revived the ancient Iroquois chief system hoping to replace the elected chief system used on most reservations. Three reservations in New York State have now returned to the traditional system of chief selection. On the Onondaga, Tuscarora, and Tonawanda Seneca reservations, the women of the clans select the chiefs just as their ancestors did. The clans induct the chiefs with a traditional ceremony.

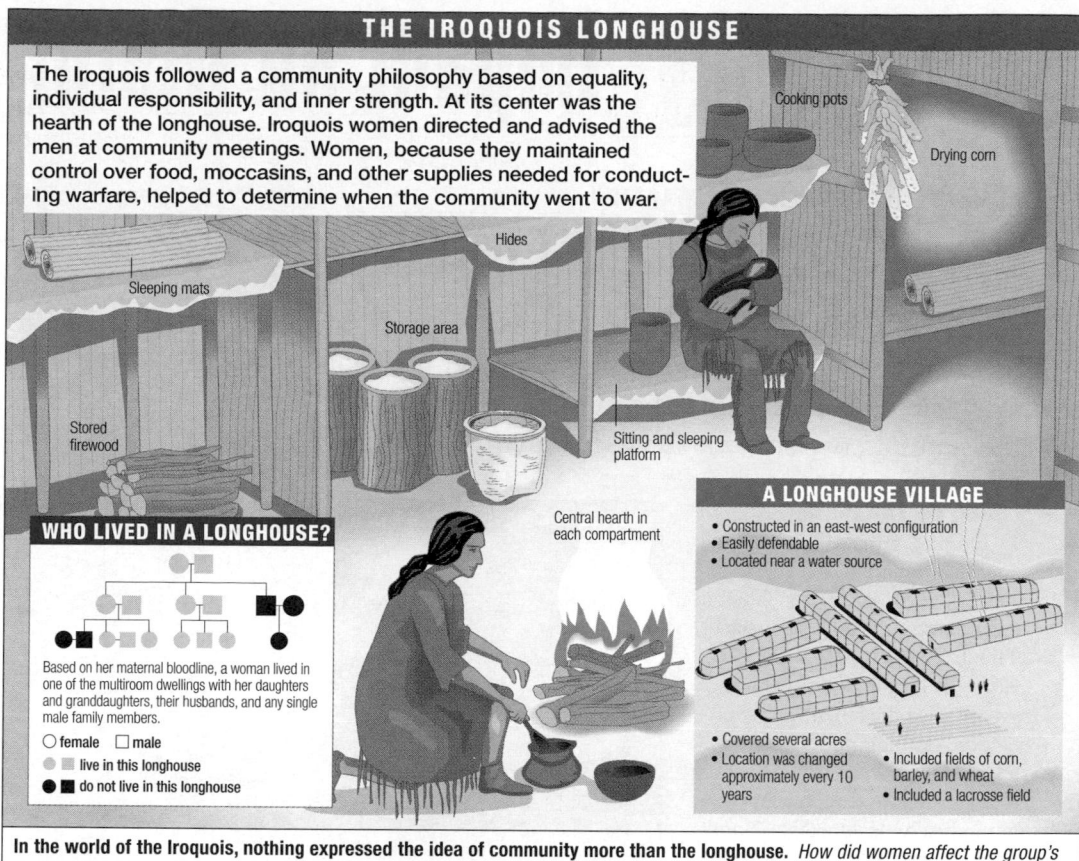

THE IROQUOIS LONGHOUSE

The Iroquois followed a community philosophy based on equality, individual responsibility, and inner strength. At its center was the hearth of the longhouse. Iroquois women directed and advised the men at community meetings. Women, because they maintained control over food, moccasins, and other supplies needed for conducting warfare, helped to determine when the community went to war.

Cooking pots

Drying corn

Hides

Sleeping mats

Storage area

Stored firewood

Sitting and sleeping platform

WHO LIVED IN A LONGHOUSE?

Based on her maternal bloodline, a woman lived in one of the multiroom dwellings with her daughters and granddaughters, their husbands, and any single male family members.

○ female   □ male
● ● live in this longhouse
● ■ do not live in this longhouse

Central hearth in each compartment

A LONGHOUSE VILLAGE
- Constructed in an east-west configuration
- Easily defendable
- Located near a water source

- Covered several acres
- Location was changed approximately every 10 years
- Included fields of corn, barley, and wheat
- Included a lacrosse field

In the world of the Iroquois, nothing expressed the idea of community more than the longhouse. How did women affect the group's decision to go to war?

grandchildren shall remain in the circle in security, peace, and happiness.

—quoted in Gary Nash's *Red, White, and Black: The Peoples of Early America,* 1982

European Attitudes

The Europeans who colonized the eastern seaboard wrongly considered the Native Americans to be ignorant savages. Nevertheless, they praised the organization of the Iroquois League. Benjamin Franklin wrote, "It would be a very strange Thing, if six Nations of ignorant Savages should be capable of forming a Scheme for such a Union . . . and yet that a like Union should be impracticable for ten or a Dozen English Colonies, to whom it is more necessary." For the European colonists, the Iroquois League offered a model for achieving unity among disparate states. For the Native Americans, the Iroquois League proved a powerful tool that enabled them to deal shrewdly with the European newcomers.

SECTION REVIEW

Vocabulary

1. Define: nomadic, sedentary, egalitarian.

Checking Facts

2. Why did people first cross the land bridge into North America?

3. What spurred the Iroquois to form an alliance?

Critical Thinking

Evaluating Information

4. Explain why you agree or disagree with this statement about the Anasazi: "Their greatest creativity flowered in architecture."

Linking Across Time

5. Compare the influence of women in Iroquois society to that of women in modern American society. Do women today have as much power?

Enrich

Have students research how archaeologists investigate people of the past such as the Native Americans who first peopled the Americas. What kind of evidence have they found? How do they interpret that evidence?

CHART STUDY

The traditional Iroquois culture was later severely disrupted by the creation of the United States and by treaties that forced the Iroquois to live on reservations. The traditional male roles of hunter, warrior, and diplomat became less important. Women's political influence was undercut. In the early 1800s, the Seneca prophet Handsome Lake called for the Iroquois to return to traditional values while tolerating the encroaching American culture.

Answer: *by controlling distribution of supplies needed for war*

CLOSE

Ask students to name cultural advances made by each Native American group discussed in the section. Which development do students think was the most important or far-reaching and why? *(Students may answer that the formation of the League of the Iroquois was the most important because it influenced the formation of the United States.)*

Section 1 Review Answers

1. nomadic (23), **sedentary** (23), **egalitarian** (23)

2. They may have been seeking new hunting grounds.

3. The Iroquois banded together to protect themselves from a mutual enemy, the Algonquians.

4. Students may answer that they agree with the statement because the Anasazi built apartment complexes whose size was not surpassed for centuries.

5. Students may answer that women had more power in Iroquois society because they owned most of the property and appointed the chiefs.

Geography: Impact on History

TEACH

Making the Geography Connection

Since humans existed, they have been challenged and supported by the environments in which they live. Extremes of weather in some areas have forced them to create appropriate clothing, housing, and tools. Everywhere people have lived, the natural world has provided them with the food and resources they have needed to survive.

Mapping Activity

Invite students to research the average climate conditions for one area of the map, and the ways in which today's residents of that region interact with the environment.

MAP STUDY

Ask volunteers to research and report on types of housing that are not discussed in the feature.

Answer: *People used available resources to build houses that were suitable to the climate.*

HUMAN/ENVIRONMENT INTERACTION

Native American Housing

Long before European settlers arrived, Native Americans had adapted to a broad range of environments, finding food and building homes using locally available resources. From the upper reaches of the Arctic to the Great Plains, the natural environment shaped Native American cultures.

Living on the Plains

On the Great Plains, Native American hunters and their families followed herds of millions of buffalo across the rolling grasslands. The Dakota, the Blackfeet, the Crow, and other Native American groups used the buffalo as a source of food, clothing, and shelter. They adapted their lifestyles to enable them to follow the buffalo, living nomadically in portable homes called tepees.

The Native Americans of the Plains built conical tepees by stretching buffalo hides across a frame of pine or cedar timbers. The tepees could be assembled and taken apart quickly. Because timber was scarce in the grasslands, the tepee poles were bundled together with the hides and transported from camp to camp. The hides formed a platform for carrying goods and even people across the Plains.

Northwest Coast Villages

In the rainy, mountainous forests of the Northwest Coast of North America, people lived in an environment of abundance. Rivers, streams, and the ocean teemed with fish, and the forest provided wild plants, berries, and a variety of game. Because a reliable supply of food was locally available, the

NATIVE AMERICAN CULTURAL AREAS, 1500s–1800s

Native American Culture Areas
- Arctic
- California
- Great Basin
- Great Plains
- Northeast
- Northwest Coast
- Plateau
- Southeast
- Southwest
- Subarctic

0   300   600 mi.
0 300 600 km
Albers Equal-Area projection

Many Native American groups used more than one type of dwelling, according to the season. *Why did Native American housing types vary by region?*

Geographic Themes

Human/Environment Interaction The ability of the Native Americans of the Plains to hunt buffalo was greatly enhanced by the reintroduction of the horse to North America by Spanish explorers. In what other ways has the domestication of animals helped humans to more easily survive in their environments?

people of the Northwest developed a sedentary culture and lived in permanent homes and villages.

Using timbers hewn from the immense trees that blanketed the coastal mountains, the Native Americans of the Northwest built sturdy multi-family dwellings. Huge beams composed the frameworks of the houses. Planks made from split logs covered the frames. Pitched roofs shed the frequent rains. Craftspeople also made seaworthy canoes from hollowed-out logs. Water travel was a common form of transportation.

Native American villages nestled along narrow beaches or river shores. In only a few months' work each spring, villagers gathered enough food to last for the remainder of the year. Fishers caught large quantities of salmon, halibut, cod, and trout. The fish were dried on racks in the rafters of the houses and used as needed until the following spring.

Abodes of the Arctic

In the icy reaches of the Arctic, the Inuit used a variety of strategies to survive in an often harsh environment. Arctic peoples hunted and fished, moving in a rhythm that followed the seasons and the habits of their prey. Although they sometimes traveled great distances when hunting, the Inuit often built permanent homes and villages to which they returned between expeditions.

The Aleuts lived in small communities beside the sea. They built semisubterranean houses framed

Scraping Hides **Cheyenne women scrape and stretch hides for use in tepee covers.** *Why was the buffalo critical to the livelihood of the Native Americans of the Plains?*

with whale bones and driftwood and covered with dirt, stone, and layers of sod. After a time, grass and other plants created a living roof that insulated against the cold. Most of their sustenance came from the sea, where they caught fish, hunted whales, seals, and other marine mammals, and gathered mussels and seaweed.

During the cold season, Inuit whalers moved north onto the Arctic ice to hunt seals. They traveled by dogsled and on foot, carrying few possessions. Lacking timber and other building materials, the whalers built ingenious dwellings called igloos from blocks of snow. The igloo's walls insulated occupants from the cold and wind. A small oil lamp or fire heated the igloo. Occupants carefully controlled the heat to prevent the igloo from melting.

MAKING THE GEOGRAPHIC CONNECTION

1. For each of the different types of Native American dwellings described, what was the main resource used?

2. What were some advantages of the materials selected for each type of dwelling?

3. **Human/Environment Interaction** How did the Native American groups discussed adapt their dwellings to their specific environments? List at least three examples for each environment.

Making the Geographic Connection Answers

1. tepees: buffalo hide, cedar timbers; homes of Northwest Native Americans: cedar logs and planks; Aleut dwellings: whale bones, driftwood, dirt, stone, and sod; igloo: snow
2. Buffalo hide and cedar timbers were portable and durable; cedar beams and planks were durable and could be fashioned into walls and roofs; whalebone, driftwood, dirt, stone, sod formed a strong and well-insulated dwelling; snow was easily fashioned into insulating blocks.
3. Plains Native Americans: used local materials, built portable shelters, used hides to carry materials; Northwest Native Americans: used local materials, pitched roofs to shed rain, built permanent dwellings; Inuit: built from local materials, used snow and sod for insulation, built both permanent and temporary dwellings.

FYI

Totem Poles Totem poles were characteristically carved by Northwest Native American artisans, and served a number of symbolic and practical functions. Each animal or spirit carved on the pole of cedar had a particular meaning. The poles served as memorials, grave markers, roof supports, portals through which one could enter the house, mortuaries in which the remains of the dead could be placed, and devices to ridicule an important individual who had failed in some way. The poles could also tell a symbolic family or clan history.

VISUAL INSTRUCTION

Scraping Hides By 1870 canvas was widely used for making tepees, so the work of scraping hides could be eliminated.

Answer: *The buffalo was a source of food, clothing, and shelter.*

CLOSE

Encourage students to discuss how cultures continue to be influenced by geography. How do geography and climate conditions affect food production? *(Climate and soil conditions can limit agriculture and affect the ability of people to store food.)* How is population distribution affected by climate? *(Population tends to be less dense in areas of extreme climates.)*

FOCUS

Section Objectives

1. Explain European explorers' motives in coming to the Americas.
2. Understand the Europeans' first interactions with Native Americans.
3. Describe why Africans were brought to North America and what their new lives were like.

Bellringer Activity

 While taking attendance at the beginning of the class period, display **Section Focus Transparency 4,** and have students answer the questions. (Or use the blackline master.)

VISUAL INSTRUCTION

Ask: Why did Columbus's patrons agree to fund more voyages? *(They thought he had found a passage to Asia that would make them rich.)*

NATIONAL GEOGRAPHIC SOCIETY

 Videodisc

GTV: The American People: Fabric of a Nation

Side 1, Chapter 3
Title: Change of Scene
Subject: Why Europeans sought a new home
Ask: Why did many Europeans go to the Americas? *(new opportunities and religious freedoms)*

SECTION 2

Three Worlds Meet

OCTOBER 28, 1492: COLUMBUS EXPLORES CARIBBEAN

AFTER 70 DAYS AT SEA—WEEKS AFTER HE CALCULATED HE WOULD REACH JAPAN AND DAYS AFTER HIS FEARFUL CREW HAD THREATENED MUTINY—A SAILOR AND HIS CREW OF 90 MEN FINALLY MADE LANDFALL ON A TINY ISLAND IN THE BAHAMAS. At first the sailor delighted in everything he saw. The friendly people, whom the sailor called *los indios*, offered gifts of parrots and cotton thread in exchange for little glass beads.

Sixteen days after arriving in the Caribbean on October 12, Christopher Columbus wrote these words:

In Search of Asia
Columbus named the island where he first landed San Salvador—the present-day Bahamas.

T he houses of these Indians are the most beautiful I have ever seen, and I swear that the closer I get to the mainland, the better they become. They're like grand pavilions, like royal tents in an encampment without streets. One here, another there. They are well swept and quite clean inside, and the furnishings are arranged in good order. All are built of very

beautiful palm branches. . . . The island is so beautiful, I could go on praising it forever.
—Journal of Christopher Columbus

The skillful Genoese sailor had reckoned to reach the rich lands of India, China, and Japan by sailing west. Columbus, however, had stumbled upon the populous islands of Hispaniola (now Haiti and the Dominican Republic) and Cuba, which he assumed was the Asian mainland. Convinced that his quest had been successful, Columbus proudly returned to his Spanish royal sponsors. He brought cinnamon, coconuts, and a small amount of gold.

Columbus also carried human cargo: several kidnapped Arawaks. "There cannot be better or more gentle people than these anywhere in the world," Columbus wrote. Indifferent to the fate of the Arawaks and greedy for riches, Columbus's grateful patrons gave him more money and bigger ships to make three more expeditions.

AS YOU READ

Vocabulary
▶ western passage
▶ conquistador
▶ indigenous

Think About . . .
▶ the motives of European explorers in coming to the Americas.
▶ the interactions between Europeans and Native Americans.
▶ why Africans were brought to North America and what their lives were like.

30 CHAPTER 2 ENCOUNTERS AND COLONIES

Section 2 Resources

REPRODUCIBLE RESOURCES
- Lesson Plan 2-2
- Section 2 Quiz
- Vocabulary and Guided Reading Activity 2-2
- Geography in History Activity 2

MULTIMEDIA RESOURCES
- Section Focus Transparency 4
- The American People: Fabric of a Nation
- A Geographic Perspective on American History
- Beginnings to 1900 Transparencies 1, 2, 3

- U.S. History and Art Transparency 3
- American Music: Cultural Traditions
- Testmaker
- Student Self-Test: A Software Review
- Chapter 2 Digest Audiocassette

Columbus died convinced that he had found the **western passage,** or direct western route, to Asia. Instead the sailor had unwittingly accomplished something even more revolutionary. Columbus's voyages across the Atlantic forever connected the old world of Europe to the old world of the Americas and eventually to the old world of Africa. These links would blend the people and cultures of the old worlds. For good and ill a new world was born.

Europeans Cross the Atlantic

Cultures Collide

The first European to reach the shores of America preceded Columbus by almost 500 years. About A.D. 1000 a Viking sailor named Leif Eriksson landed in present-day Newfoundland. Eriksson named the spot Vinland because of its wild vines. The Vikings had sought new fishing grounds; for unknown reasons, their American settlements proved to be short-lived. In contrast the European hunger for gold and spices that fueled the voyages of Columbus forever married three worlds.

As the 1400s ended, Spain vied with its rival, Portugal, to discover western ocean routes offering direct access to the riches of Asia and Africa. Both powers sought to bypass the Middle Eastern merchants who controlled trade along eastern land routes to Asia. Bypassing these merchants would mean sharply higher profits for the Europeans.

Early Portuguese Dominance

Portugal forged an early lead in the race. Under the guidance of Prince Henry the Navigator, Portuguese sailors rounded West Africa, capturing a direct trade in gold and enslaved persons. Eventually, the Portuguese sailed all the way around Africa and onward to India and Asia.

The Portuguese had studied the works of Ptolemy, an astronomer of ancient Egypt. From their studies they knew that the earth was round, that distances on its surface could be measured in degrees, and that they could measure the position of the stars to determine their location on a map.

Two new inventions propelled Portuguese navigation in the second half of the 1400s. The quadrant, invented in 1450, notably improved the precision with which sailors could measure a star's altitude. By using a quadrant, sailors could determine their latitude much more accurately than was possible with a chart and compass.

A Moorish ship design inspired the second invention: the lateen-rigged caravel. A great improvement over European square-rigged vessels, the caravel with its triangular sails permitted Portuguese sailors to sail against the wind down the west coast of Africa.

"PORTUGUESE CARAVELS" FROM AMERICA BY THEODORE DE BRY, 1594. (DETAIL) RARE BOOK AND MANUSCRIPT DIVISION. THE NEW YORK PUBLIC LIBRARY, ASTOR, LENOX AND TILDEN FOUNDATIONS

MAJOR EUROPEAN EXPLORATION, 1492–1550

The European powers vied for ocean routes to Asia and land claims in the Americas. Portugal's invention of the caravel (at left) enabled it to forge a lead in the exploration race. *Who were the French explorers who sailed to North America in 1524 and 1535?*

SECTION TWO   **31**

TEACH

Guided Practice

L1 Discussion Have students discuss the initial meeting between the Spanish and the Arawak. What questions might each group have had about the other? What positive feelings or apprehensions might each group have had?

Show students Beginnings to 1900 Transparencies 1, 2, 3 and have them complete the activity sheets.

Independent Practice

L2 Discussion Invite students to discuss possible reasons early Viking settlements in Newfoundland failed to thrive while Spanish settlements in the Caribbean proved to be long-lived. They might include climate, economics, and technology in their discussion.

Have students complete the Chapter 2, Section 2 Vocabulary and Guided Reading Activity. (Also in Spanish.) **LEP**

MAP STUDY

Although some explorers traveled to the interiors, most early European settlements were located on the coasts.

Answer: *Verrazano in 1524, Cartier in 1535.*

Cooperative Learning

European Exploration Organize the class into four groups and assign each group one of the following countries: England, France, Spain, the Netherlands, and Portugal. Have each group research economic conditions in its country at the time of its exploration of the Americas. Discuss how these conditions influenced the nations' interest in exploration.

NATIONAL GEOGRAPHIC SOCIETY

 Videodisc

GTV: The American People: Fabric of a Nation

Side 1, Chapter 4
Title: Wealth Enough
Subject: Europeans in the Americas
Ask: What was the main source of wealth for European settlers? *(land)*

Side 1, Chapter 5
Title: When Worlds Collide
Subject: European and Native American Encounters
Ask: Why were the contacts between the Europeans and the Native Americans so often violent? *(The Europeans took land that the Native Americans regarded as their own.)*

Conquest The Aztec's defense was thwarted by the superior weapons of the Spanish. *What other advantages did the Spaniards have over the Aztec?*

[The Spaniards] deal with them in any way they wish . . . without regard to sex, age, status, or dignity.

—Bartolomé de Las Casas

Though Las Casas spent his life trying to stop Spanish exploitation of the Native Americans, his carefully documented efforts gained few supporters.

An Uneven Exchange
Livestock, Crops, and Disease

When Columbus first opened the Americas to European settlement, previously separate worlds became forever wed. The exchange favored the Europeans, but both sides contributed to the mix.

The Spaniards had come to the Americas, as one Spanish soldier explained, "to serve God and the king, and also to get rich." To serve God, priests attempted and sometimes succeeded in converting Native Americans to Catholicism. Because the Spanish men who served the king often traveled without women, they frequently took Indian wives, beginning a mixed-race culture that still permeates the Americas. In addition, as Bartolomé de Las Casas's passionate writings revealed, Spaniards forced Native Americans to mine gold and silver under unspeakable conditions.

Under two Spanish policies, known as the *encomienda* and *repartimiento*, Native Americans toiled to enrich Spanish colonists. The *encomienda* policy assigned to the Spanish a group of Native Americans who provided labor in return for protection and religious instruction. In practice this system meant virtual slavery for the Native Americans. As the Native American population fell, *repartimiento* replaced the *encomienda*. Like the *encomienda, repartimiento*—in which adult male Native Americans rotated their labor in Spanish factories, mines, farms, and ranches—also functioned as a slave labor system.

Native Americans did not succumb without a struggle. The European encroachment onto Native American lands engendered lethal warfare that continued for centuries. Disease, however, proved an even bigger killer.

The Scourge of Smallpox

Before 1492 Native Americans on the 2 continents numbered perhaps 50 million. Lacking immunities to smallpox and other European diseases, Native Americans saw their populations diminished by as much as 90 percent within a few generations. Many Native Americans who had never even seen a European perished from the diseases Europeans carried.

While the Portuguese made their way east around the cape of Africa, claiming the lucrative Asian spice trade, Columbus's voyages west staked Spain's title to the Americas. Within decades after Columbus's death in 1506, Spanish **conquistadors,** or conquerors, had cruelly subdued the **indigenous** peoples who inhabited the Americas.

The Conquest of Mexico and Peru

Two wealthy and ancient civilizations—the Aztec and the Inca—fell before the bloody onslaught of the Spanish conquerors. Mexico's Aztec civilization, weakened by internal strife, yielded in 1521 to the horses and firearms of Hernando Cortés's army. Like Mexico's Aztec, the Inca of Peru lived in populous cities under a well-organized social system. Before the Spanish conquest, domestic conflict had also undermined the Inca. Just 12 years after Cortés's bloody victory over the Aztec, the Spanish conquistador Francisco Pizarro led an army of 168 men to subdue the Incan capital of Cuzco. Pizarro's troops then used Cuzco as a base of operations from which to steal gold and silver from the other wealthy cities of the defeated Inca.

By the 1540s Catholic Spain laid exclusive claim to Central America, the southern parts of North America, and all of South America except Brazil, a Portuguese conquest. Spain now controlled an empire larger than the Western world had seen since the fall of Rome. The world would soon feel the effects of the Spanish conquest.

Profiting from the labor of enslaved Native Americans, the Spaniards plundered South American silver mines of millions of pounds of silver. As Spain grew wealthy, millions of Native Americans perished, mostly from disease. Bartolomé de Las Casas, a Dominican friar whose father and uncle had accompanied Columbus on his second voyage, condemned his fellow Spaniards' treatment of indigenous peoples:

Meeting Special Needs

Reading Disability Students with reading disabilities may need additional assistance with reading and pronouncing Spanish words and names. You might pair these students with stronger readers who can help them with reading and pronunciation. Another strategy might be to write Spanish words or names on the chalkboard along with their pronunciations and definitions. Students with reading disabilities can use the chalkboard as a reference in reading and speaking.

Smallpox, for example, a common scourge in the densely populated cities of Europe, had been unknown in the Americas before 1518. The smallpox epidemic that raged through Hispaniola decimated the indigenous people, who had barely survived warfare and enslavement. Las Casas wrote that the population of Hispaniola fell to no more than 1,000 "of that immensity of people that was on this island and which we have seen with our own eyes."

The horror of illness suggested to some Native Americans that their own gods had deserted them, and left many survivors susceptible to the belief that the Christian god had superior power. When the English pirate Sir Francis Drake raided Spanish Florida in the 1580s, he wrote that the Florida natives "died verie fast and said amongst themselves, it was the Inglisshe God that made them die so faste."

The scourge of disease and the promise of a powerful god were not the Europeans' only allies. Numerous European chroniclers of the invasion of the Americas expressed the sentiment that "after God, we owe the victory to the horses." Horses had died out on the American continent 10,000 years earlier. The return of the horse to the Americas on Spanish ships in the 1500s provided mounted Spanish conquistadors an easy victory over Native American foot soldiers. Eventually the

A Conquistador on Horseback Without horses, the Spanish conquistadors might have failed in their conquests. *Why did Native Americans have to fight on foot?*

horse would achieve near-sacred status among the buffalo-hunting Native Americans, whose life the horse revolutionized.

Cultural Exchange

The Europeans also brought cows, chickens, and pigs to the Americas, and exchanged fruits and vegetables with the Native Americans. The exchange went both ways. From Europe Columbus brought oranges and sugarcane to the West Indies. To Europe went corn, beans, and potatoes—staple crops that would prove to be an even greater treasure than gold or silver.

Under optimal growing conditions, potatoes yielded far more calories per acre than the grain crops on which Europeans had traditionally relied. Potatoes carried another advantage. Grains such as rice, rye, or barley needed to be harvested and stored, making them an easy target for rent collectors or pillaging soldiers. Potatoes, however, could be left in the ground to be dug up one at a time, providing insurance against starvation. The potato's superior nutrient value prompted a population surge in Europe that laid the groundwork for the spread of industrialization in the 1700s.

The sugarcane that traveled from Europe to the Americas on Columbus's second voyage in 1493 opened the door to Africa's unwilling entrance into the Americas. The process of refining sugar from cane required backbreaking labor that Spaniards refused to do. The Native American populations that had provided forced labor lay decimated or had fled to the interiors of the North and South American continents. As a result the Spaniards looked to Africa. Enslaved Africans were first

Epidemic This woodcut from the 1500s shows the devastating effects of smallpox on Native Americans. *Why did smallpox cause some Native Americans to turn to Christianity?*

History and the Humanities

🕮 U.S. History and Art Transparency 3—Mission San Xavier del Bac

🎧 American Music: Cultural Traditions—"Yarum Praise Songs" by Fra-Fra Tribesmen; "Ay cómo flecha" by Hesperus; "Ainsworth Psalm 100" and "Standish" by the Gregg Smith Singers

VISUAL INSTRUCTION

A Conquistador on Horseback Early humans hunted horses for food. Horses were domesticated much later than cattle or dogs.

Answer: *Horses had died out on the American continent 10,000 years earlier.*

Epidemic A World Health Organization campaign has eradicated smallpox. No deaths from the disease have been reported since 1978.

Answer: *The numerous deaths convinced them that their own gods had deserted them and that the Christian god was superior.*

Portfolio Project

Native American Life Organize students into small groups. Have each group choose one Native American group encountered by early Spanish explorers of the Caribbean, Central America, or South America. Students can do research about daily life in Native American societies at or shortly after the arrival of the first Europeans. Each student can choose one aspect of Native American life, such as agriculture, technology, travel, or religion, and write a short paper about that aspect. 📄

33

Videodisc

*GTV: A Geographic
Perspective on
American History*

Side 1, Chapter 4
Title: Land of
Opportunity
Subject: Europeans gain
a foothold in the Americas
Ask: What European
nation first sent explorers
to the Americas? *(Spain)*

ASSESS

Meeting Lesson Objectives

Each section objective is
tested by the section
review question(s) that
follows it in parentheses.

1. Explain European
explorers' motives in
coming to the Americas.
(1, 2, 5)
2. Understand the Europeans' first interactions
with Native Americans.
(1, 3)
3. Describe why Africans
were brought to North
America and what their
new lives were like. (4)

VISUAL INSTRUCTION

Answer: *They needed a
rationalization for the profitable business of trading in
human flesh.*

---

brought to the Caribbean as field-workers in 1505. Eventually 1 out of 4 of the 10 to 12 million Africans who were
transported across the Atlantic as slaves would toil on
Caribbean sugar plantations.

Africans in the Americas
A Forced Migration

The earliest Africans came to the Americas not
only as slaves, but also as explorers. An African named
Pedro Alonso Niño served on Columbus's crew. When
the conquistador Hernando Cortés sailed to Mexico, Africans accompanied him; one
African planted and harvested the
first crop of wheat in North
America. An African explorer
named Estevanico opened up
New Mexico and Arizona for the
Spaniards, who followed cautiously when they discovered that
hostile Native Americans had
murdered the unlucky Estevanico.

The enslavement of millions of
Africans followed rapidly upon the
Europeans' arrival on American
shores. The labor-intensive sugar,
coffee, and tobacco plantations
Spain established in the West Indies and in South America fueled
African slavery. In time slavery expanded to North America as well.

A New Type of Slavery

Slavery itself was nothing
new. During centuries of religious
wars, Christians and Muslims
had enslaved one another as in-
fidels or unbelievers. Africans,
too, had been involved for centuries in trading small numbers of
slaves from West Africa across
the Sahara to work as soldiers,
servants, and artisans in Roman Europe and the Middle
East. Before the American slave trade, however, slavery
had never been permanent and irrevocable—nor had enslaved persons ever before been treated as subhuman, denied the rights of education, marriage, and parenthood,
or forced to pass on their slave status to their descendants.

The European myth of African inferiority arose
only after Europeans needed a rationalization for the
profitable business of trading in human flesh. Far different from the European stereotype, West Africa had been

**Elaborate Art This bronze mask from Benin in
Africa shows highly developed skills in metalwork-
ing and aesthetic expression.** *Why did many Europeans believe that Africans were culturally inferior to
them?*

the home of several advanced empires. For example,
between the sixth and tenth centuries, the kingdom of
Ghana ruled the territory between the Sahara and the
Gulf of Guinea and from the Niger River to the Atlantic
Ocean. In time the kingdom of Ghana fell, succeeded by
the empire of Mali. At the center of the empire of Mali,
the city of Timbuktu boasted great wealth and a distinguished Islamic university. Even the lesser kingdoms
of Kongo and Benin boasted towns whose size rivaled
that of European cities.

Life Enslaved

Before his capture from Benin in 1756, 11-year-old
Olaudah Equiano "had never heard of white men
or Europeans, nor of the sea." Equiano
was enslaved in Barbados in the
West Indies, and onboard a ship,
he became the servant of a British
naval officer. After buying his
freedom and settling in Britain,
Equiano published a 2-volume
autobiography that powerfully indicted the slave trade.

Equiano's experience was
atypical. Perhaps one of every
six enslaved Africans died on
the transatlantic journey. Survivors rarely had the opportunity to learn to read or
write. Even fewer won their
freedom. Still, Equiano's story
reveals the harrowing experiences that transplanted Africans
faced.

Captured and thrust onto
a slave ship, Equiano described
the wretched journey:

I was soon put down under
the decks, and there I received such a salutation in my
nostrils as I had never experienced in my life: so that with
the loathsomeness of the
stench and crying together, I became so sick and
low that I was not able to eat . . . but soon, to my
grief, two of the white men offered me eatables, and
on my refusing to eat, one of them held me fast . . .
and laid me across I think the windlass, and tied my
feet while the other flogged me severely . . . One
day, when we had a smooth sea and a moderate
wind, two of my wearied countrymen who were
chained together . . . preferring death to such a life
of misery, somehow made through the nettings and

Extending the Content

Slavery's Impact At the time of contact with
Europeans, many African kingdoms had developed sophisticated cultures and trading systems. Encourage students to discuss the ways
in which the slave trade negatively affected the
kingdoms. How did slavery change the systems

of trade among Africans? How might the slave
trade have altered relations among kingdoms?
How might depopulation have weakened the
kingdoms' abilities to grow food, build cities,
and defend their territory?

Fig.5

Fig.4

Store Room

Store Room

The Middle Passage Illustrations such as this one, which appeared in the early 1700s, showed slave traders how to pack their holds as efficiently as possible. *How many Africans died on slave ships during their journey to the Americas?*

jumped into the sea, immediately another quite de-jected fellow . . . also followed; and I believe many more would very soon have done the same if they had not been prevented by the ship's crew.
—Autobiography of Olaudah Equiano

At least 10 million enslaved Africans made the same journey, unwillingly transported to the Americas in the largest forced migration the world has ever seen. By the mid-1700s, enslaved Africans represented about 40 percent of the population in America's Southern Colonies. In South Carolina after 1710, enslaved Africans outnumbered white colonists.

This massive migration not only enriched the European nations who traded in human flesh, it profoundly changed the character of the Americas. During the 300 years between Columbus's journey and the American Revolution, 6 out of 7 persons who crossed the Atlantic came to the Americas against their will. These Africans soon learned European ways. With their complex religious and musical heritage as well as their agricultural knowledge, they also began to Africanize America's European culture.

SECTION REVIEW

Vocabulary
1. Define: western passage, conquistador, indigenous.

Checking Facts
2. What did Columbus mistakenly believe he had found on his voyages?

3. What was the most common cause of death among Native Americans after contact with Europeans?

Critical Thinking
Predicting Consequences
4. How would the early history of the Americas have been different if there had been no slave trade?

Linking Across Time
5. The quadrant and the caravel helped Portugal gain an early lead in the race to find new ocean routes. Name a recent invention that helps people explore.

SECTION TWO   35

THE LIBRARY COMPANY OF PHILADELPHIA

Chapter 2
SECTION 2

Evaluate
Have students complete the Section Review.

📂 🔘 Assign the Section 2 Quiz or use the Testmaker to develop a customized quiz. (Also in Spanish.) **LEP**

Reteach
🎧 Have students listen to the Chapter 2, Section 2 Audiocassette. (Also in Spanish.) **LEP**

Enrich
📂 Have students complete the Chapter 2 Geography in History Activity.

CLOSE

Have students discuss the impact of the meeting of three worlds in the Americas. Ask: What did the Europeans gain? *(spices, precious metals, new crops, territory, slaves)* How did Europeans disrupt Native American life? *(Europeans killed or enslaved many Native Americans and conquered their kingdoms and cities. Many Native Americans died of disease brought by Europeans)* How did the Europeans' exploitation of American resources fuel the African slave trade? *(Europeans enslaved Africans to provide human labor for mining, industry, and agriculture.)*

VISUAL INSTRUCTION

The Middle Passage The "middle passage" was the brutal period that Africans spent between their initial enslavement and their arrival months later in America.

Answer: *one in six*

Section 2 Review Answers

1. western passage (31), **conquistador** (32), **indigenous** (32)
2. Columbus believed he had found the western passage to Asia.
3. disease
4. Students may answer that sugar, coffee, and tobacco production would have been much more difficult and less lucrative for the Europeans and that agriculture, religion, and music in America would have developed differently.
5. Students may answer that the creation of the space shuttle has made possible more accurate exploration of outer space.

FOCUS

Section Objectives

1. Describe where Spanish, French, and English settlers established claims in the Americas.
2. Explain how the various European settlers adapted to the land and made their livings.
3. Explain the differences in the resources and economies of the New England, Middle, and Southern Colonies.

Bellringer Activity

While taking attendance at the beginning of the class period, display **Section Focus Transparency 5,** and have students answer the questions. (Or use the blackline master.)

VISUAL INSTRUCTION

Arrival of the Puritans
John Winthrop attended Cambridge University in England and practiced law. John Winthrop, Jr., his son, served as the colonial governor of Connecticut.

Ask: What did John Winthrop urge the Puritans to do in his sermon aboard the *Arbella*? *(to form a community that adhered strictly to Christian ideals)*

Building Colonial America

SPRING 1630: PURITANS ESTABLISH MASSACHUSETTS BAY COLONY

© NORTH WIND PICTURE ARCHIVES

Arrival of the Puritans
This etching depicts Winthrop's fleet of ships arriving in New England.

IN THE SPRING OF 1630 THE SHIP *ARBELLA* HEADED A FLEET OF 11 SHIPS SAILING FOR MASSACHU-SETTS. Along with cows, horses, goats, pigs, and chickens, the ships carried 1,000 Puritans. In England these Puritans had failed to purify the Protestant Church of England of rituals they deplored as traces of Catholicism. The Puritans hoped Massachusetts would provide a more hospitable home for their strict religious practices.

Aboard the *Arbella,* John Winthrop, newly elected governor of the Massachusetts Bay Colony, summoned his fellow Puritans for a sermon. Although in England the Puritans had spurned church and state authority, Winthrop urged them to submerge their individuality in favor of a community that would adhere strictly to Christian ideals. Only if the Puritans could "rejoyce together, mourne together, labour and suffer together," Winthrop preached, could their settlement serve as an example to others:

> . . . for wee must Consider that wee shall be as a Citty upon a Hill, the eies [eyes] of all people are uppon us; so that if wee shall deale falsely with our god in this worke . . . wee shall be made a story and a by-word through the world, wee shall open the mouthes of enemies to speake evill of the wayes of god. . . .
> —John Winthrop, "A Model of Christian Charity," 1630

AS YOU READ

Vocabulary
► mission
► presidio
► selectman
► pacifism
► indentured servant

Think About . . .
► where Spanish, French, and English settlers established claims in the Americas.
► how the European settlers adapted to the land and made their livings.
► the differences in the resources and economies of the New England, Middle, and Southern Colonies.

Section 3 Resources

REPRODUCIBLE RESOURCES
Lesson Plans 2-3
Vocabulary and Guided Reading Activity 2-3
Section 3 Quiz

MULTIMEDIA RESOURCES
Section Focus Transparency 5
U.S. History and Art Transparency 2
Focus on American Fine Art Prints, Print 1
A Geographic Perspective on American History
Testmaker

Student Self-Test: A Software Review
Chapter 2 Digest Audiocassette

The Puritans were not the first English people to settle in North America. In 1607 English colonists established a settlement at Jamestown, Virginia. English Pilgrims, even stricter than the Puritans, had landed at Plymouth in 1620. English settlers in New England created communities, experimented with self-government, and struggled to create a "city upon a hill."

The English, however, were latecomers to the colonizing of North America. Well before the English settlements in Jamestown and Plymouth, the Spanish had carved out a much larger empire. Because the French also had made earlier claims, they would control far more territory than did England in the 1600s.

Spain and France in North America

Claiming the Land and Its Resources

Spain assumed a commanding lead in the settlement of the Americas. Within decades after Christopher Columbus died in 1506, Spanish conquistadors explored, conquered, and claimed most of South and Central America, as well as the southern portion of North America from Florida to California. In 1565 Spain built a fort at St. Augustine in what is now Florida, establishing the oldest continuously inhabited town in the continental United States. In the Southwest, as in Florida, the Spanish established **missions** to try to convert Native Americans to Christianity. They also constructed **presidios,** or garrisons, that served a dual purpose: to defend Spanish holdings and to serve as trading centers.

Because of the valuable silver Native American slave labor wrested from mines, Mexico and Peru dominated the Spanish Empire. Next in importance were Spain's Caribbean territories with their lucrative sugar plantations. Because they yielded no obvious riches, the Spanish territories that later became Florida, the Gulf states, Texas, New Mexico, Arizona, and California rep-

resented Spain's least important settlements in the Americas. Though Spain claimed huge territorial holdings in what would become the continental United States, Spanish colonists never settled there in large numbers. As late as 1700, fewer than 4,000 Spaniards dwelled in the northern border lands of Spain's territories.

Like the Spanish, the French staked an early claim to North America. In 1524 Giovanni da Verrazano sailed up the Atlantic coast for France, searching for the fabled passage to India. Though that search proved fruitless, Verrazano charted the Atlantic coastline between Florida and Newfoundland and established important trade contacts with Native American trappers. When he sailed up the St. Lawrence River in 1534, Jacques Cartier made further friendly contacts with Native Americans.

After the Portuguese and Spanish defeated French attempts to colonize Brazil and Florida, France chose to concentrate its settlements on the area around the St. Lawrence River. French fishing boats plied the cold waters of the North Atlantic for cod and salmon, but trading in furs soon proved even more profitable.

The fur trade required few settlers. The French simply brought manufactured goods such as iron and woolens across the Atlantic, anchored their ships in St. Lawrence's sheltered bay, and waited for Native Americans to bring their beaver pelts to barter at French trading posts. As late as 1643 fewer than 400 French people lived in Nova Gallia, or New France.

METROPOLITAN MUSEUM OF ART, NEW YORK/THE BRIDGEMAN ART LIBRARY, LONDON

Fur Traders This painting by George Caleb Bingham depicts fur traders on the Missouri River. *Which European nation established fur trading around the St. Lawrence River?*

Cooperative Learning

Routes of the Explorers Organize students into three groups. Have one group research the the exploration route of Columbus; another, Verrazano; and the third, Cartier. Have each group mark the routes of the explorer they have researched on the same world map, color coding each explorer's travels. Display the map in class. 🖙

TEACH

Guided Practice

L1 Discussion The first explorers of North America hoped to find the riches of India. Discuss with students the "riches"—or resources—they did find.

Independent Practice

L2 Research Have students research more about the trade from the Spanish Caribbean territories. Ask them to explore food products that came from that area.

📁 Have students complete the Chapter 2, Section 3 Vocabulary and Guided Reading Activity. (Also in Spanish.) **LEP**

VISUAL INSTRUCTION

Fur Traders Fur trading was lucrative, so many French farmers turned to it in the 1700s. The resulting decrease in farming slowed the population growth in New France.

Answer: *France*

 History and the Humanities

🕮 U.S. History and Art Transparency 2—*Penn's Treaty with the Indians* by Benjamin West

🎨 Focus on American Fine Art Prints, Print 1—*Mrs. Elizabeth Freake & Baby Mary,* artist unknown

NATIONAL GEOGRAPHIC SOCIETY

 Videodisc

GTV: A Geographic Perspective on American History

Side 1, Chapter 6
Title: Hoping for the Best in America
Subject: Trials and triumphs of English settlers
Ask: What challenges did the settlers face in the Americas? *(They had to build a life in the wilderness, often with opposition from indigenous peoples.)*

Side 1, Chapter 7
Title: A Mixed Bag
Subject: Diversity in the colonies
Ask: What nationalities settled the Middle Colonies? *(English, Swedish, Dutch)*

CHART STUDY

Ask: When did the English establish their first colony?
Answer: *1607*

Most of these settlers were traders or Jesuit priests. According to the royal government of France, the French in America had two concerns: the conversion of beaver and the conversion of souls. Thus, missions were often conveniently located at river junctions where the fur trade took place.

By the early 1600s the French government realized that they needed more settlers to protect understaffed French trading posts from their English and Dutch rivals. In the mid-1600s French explorers canoed down America's inland waterways. By 1660 New France's population was 2,000, and by 1690 France controlled the interior of North America. On the burgeoning coast, however, late-starting England reigned supreme.

Re-creating England in the Colonies
Thousands Settle the Atlantic Seaboard

From the beginning, England's settlements differed from those of Spain and France. Unlike the Spanish and French, whose settlements involved few colonists, the English came in large numbers, founding 13 colonies by 1732. In addition, while the royal governments of Spain and France sponsored and coordinated their settlers' activities, partnerships of merchants, who stood to win or lose large sums of money on the success of the colonies, privately financed the English ventures. As the 1600s drew to a close, moneyed investors became increasingly willing to speculate on the growing agricultural colonies on America's Atlantic seaboard.

Aside from needing money, English agricultural settlements on the Atlantic required a large body of willing migrants. During the 1600s thousands of English migrants streamed westward across the Atlantic, lured by an array of economic, religious, and political factors.

The glut of Spanish silver from the Americas had caused prices to rise on the European continent. When the rise in prices combined with population growth and the dispossession of small landowners, crime and poverty surged. John Winthrop, who would later lead the Puritans in Massachusetts, complained of England, "This land grows weary of her inhabitants, so as a man, which is the most precious of all creatures, is near more vile among us than a horse or a sheep."

In Europe religious wars between Catholics and Protestants made it harder to sell English woolen cloth and devastated once-thriving textile regions. Finally, the bloody political struggles between Catholics and Protestants within England itself made thousands of English settlers willing to brave everything to face an uncertain destiny. Between 1600 and 1640, 80,000 colonists fled England. By 1660 another 80,000 had followed.

Many of these English settlers stayed in the West Indies, but between 1630 and 1640, 20,000 Puritans headed for New England, moving from Hingham in Norfolk County, England, to Hingham, Massachusetts, or from Sudbury in Suffolk County, England, to Sudbury, Massachusetts. More than those who immigrated to the Middle or Southern colonies, English immigrants in New England sought to re-create English life and ways.

New England Colonies
A Puritan Stronghold

Because Puritan intolerance discouraged European immigrants of other countries from settling in the New England Colonies, most of the settlers in the northernmost colonies came from England. The Puritans sought to mold communities of pure Christians who would swear a covenant with God to achieve his ends on earth. As John Winthrop put it, if "the Lord shall please to . . . bring us in peace to the place wee desire, then hath hee

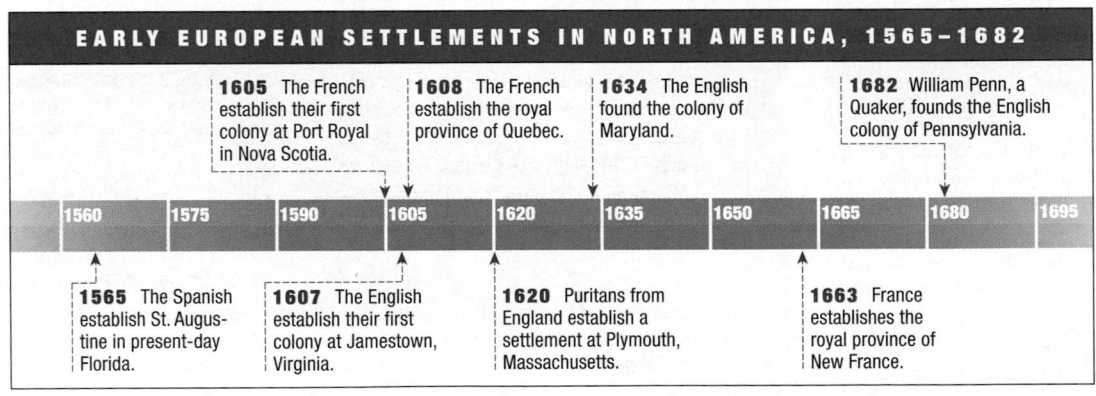

EARLY EUROPEAN SETTLEMENTS IN NORTH AMERICA, 1565–1682

1605 The French establish their first colony at Port Royal in Nova Scotia.

1608 The French establish the royal province of Quebec.

1634 The English found the colony of Maryland.

1682 William Penn, a Quaker, founds the English colony of Pennsylvania.

1560 | 1575 | 1590 | 1605 | 1620 | 1635 | 1650 | 1665 | 1680 | 1695

1565 The Spanish establish St. Augustine in present-day Florida.

1607 The English establish their first colony at Jamestown, Virginia.

1620 Puritans from England establish a settlement at Plymouth, Massachusetts.

1663 France establishes the royal province of New France.

Meeting Special Needs

Reading Disability Have students with reading disabilities work to create a chart with these heads: *New England Colonies, Middle Colonies, Southern Colonies.* As they read the section, ask students to record facts about each region's colonies under the appropriate heads. Have students save their chart to use as a review tool.

ratified this Covenant and . . . will expect a strickt performance of the Articles contained in it." Concerning this "strickt performance," Puritan leaders such as Winthrop brooked no differences of opinion, even among their own members. When the pious Puritans Roger Williams and Anne Hutchinson threatened church authority, first Williams, then Hutchinson, were forced to flee to Rhode Island, where other dissidents soon began to settle.

Establishing Communities

The single-mindedness that drove their religious ideals gave Puritans an economic edge. These New Englanders soon constructed a thriving economy based on agriculture, fishing, lumbering, shipbuilding, wool production, and trading for beaver furs with neighboring Native Americans.

Most Puritans emigrated with their families, or sent for them to come afterward. From New England John Winthrop wrote his wife, "Remember to come well furnished with linen, woollen, some more bedding, peuter, leather bottles, drinking horns . . . and many other necessaries which I can't now think of, as candles, soap, and store of beef suet. . . ."

Striving to do God's work and avoid temptation, Puritan leaders dictated that single men and women not live on their own. Instead Puritan families clustered together in small towns that centered on the village meetinghouse, or "Lord's barn." There, even in New England's frigid winters, townspeople gathered to pray midweek as well as twice on Sundays.

Government and Education

Though the minister headed the community hierarchy, Puritans shared authority and developed a form of self-government. Voters, who were required to be male church members, elected **selectmen.** The selectmen dispensed land, determined taxes, and settled arguments. In addition all townsmen gathered yearly for a town meeting at which they chose town officers for the coming year and determined matters of community importance, such as teachers' salaries.

The Puritans' stress on literacy grew out of their belief that everyone should be able to read the Bible and psalmbooks. To train ministers, Puritans founded Harvard College in 1636, a mere 6 years after they had arrived. To ensure that their fledgling college would attract a healthy supply of students, the Massachusetts Bay Colony passed a law in 1642 dictating

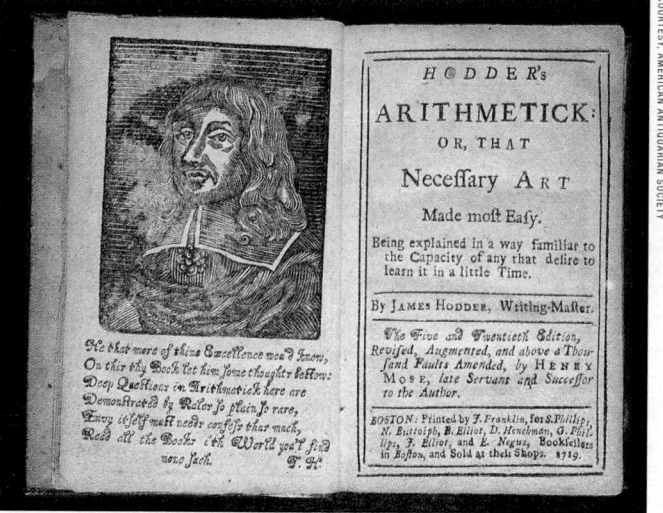

Teaching With the Primer Primers often combined teaching arithmetic or reading with teaching morals. *Why did the Puritans believe it was important that everyone be able to read?*

that parents must teach their children to read. A law that followed in 1647 mandated publicly funded education in towns of more than 50 residents.

In the healthy atmosphere of New England, the colonists' population doubled every generation. Between 1620 and 1700, the original immigrant population of 25,000 had burgeoned to 100,000 second- and third-generation Americans.

Middle Colonies
Northern Europeans Inhabit Farmlands

Unlike rocky New England, which drew most of its settlers from England's Puritan sect, the lush farmland of the Middle Colonies attracted immigrants from most of northern Europe. As one settler wrote in 1681, "For the Soyl [soil] it is Good, and capable to produce any thing that England doth: (and) the Yearly Increase is far greater. The Air Temperate and Healthy." The Dutch established New Amsterdam (which later became New York City) in 1626, after purchasing Manhattan Island from Native Americans with goods worth about $24. Swedish settlers established a settlement called New Sweden along the banks of the Delaware River. New Jersey welcomed immigrants from the Netherlands, Sweden, England, France, and Finland. In addition to these groups, Pennsylvania also boasted immigrants from Denmark, Germany, Ireland, Scotland, and Wales.

NATIONAL GEOGRAPHIC SOCIETY

 Videodisc

GTV: A Geographic Perspective on American History

Side 1, Chapter 9
Title: Settling Down, Moving On
Subject: Regional differences in the colonies
Ask: How did New England differ from the Southern Colonies? *(New England's soil was less productive, and small farms predominated. In the South the long growing season and fertile land made plantation agriculture possible.)*

Side 1, Chapter 12
Title: The Rise of Cities
Subject: Urban life in the colonies
Ask: What were the major cities of the early colonies? *(Boston, Philadelphia, Charleston, Savannah)*

VISUAL INSTRUCTION

Teaching With the Primer This photo shows the frontispiece of the twenty-fifth edition of James Hodder's *Arithmetick,* with a portrait of Hodder on the left.
Answer: *because they wanted everyone to be able to read the Bible*

PORTFOLIO PROJECT

Portfolio Project

A Puritan's Journal Ask students to imagine they are a Puritan man or woman moving from Europe to colonial New England. Ask them to use what they have read to write a journal entry expressing their observations, hopes, and fears as they finally arrive in New England.

ASSESS

Meeting Lesson Objectives

Each section objective is tested by the section review question(s) that follows it in parentheses.

1. Describe where Spanish, French, and English settlers established claims in the Americas. (1, 2)
2. Explain how the various European settlers adapted to the land and made their livings. (3)
3. Explain the differences in the resources and economies of the New England, Middle, and Southern Colonies. (4, 5)

VISUAL INSTRUCTION

A Treaty With Native Americans When William Penn made this treaty of friendship with the Lenni Lenape, he paid them for most of the land in spite of the fact that King Charles II of England had given the land to Penn as a gift.

Answer: *one of openness, brotherhood, and love*

In the late 1600s England moved to expand its North American claims. In 1660 King of Great Britain Charles II granted New Amsterdam and the surrounding land to his brother, the Duke of York. The Duke kept the area he called New York for himself and granted New Jersey to a group of friends.

In 1681 Charles II made an even more generous grant. To repay a debt he had owed William Penn's father, the king offered young Penn a huge expanse of land. The land, including part of what is now the state of Delaware, became Pennsylvania, a holy experiment for its owner.

A Quaker, Penn had faced persecution in England for practicing his religious beliefs in human equality and **pacifism,** opposition to the use of force. Penn offered religious freedom to all Pennsylvanians and optimistically provided a governmental framework: "Let men be good and the government cannot be bad; if it be ill they will cure it." In contrast to New England Puritans, who seized Native American farming and hunting lands, Penn advocated maintaining good relations with the Native Americans. In a treaty in 1682, Penn wrote, "No advantage is to be taken on either side, but all is to be openness, brotherhood, and love."

Penn's enthusiastic advertisements attracted settlers from all over northern Europe. Pennsylvania soon became home to a mosaic of religious groups, including Quakers, Mennonites, Lutherans, the Dutch Reformed Church, Baptists, Anglicans, Presbyterians, Catholics, and Jews.

Lured to emigrate by the lush farmland, farmers in the Middle Colonies raised enough wheat, rye, beef, and pork to export to the other colonies and the West Indies. Prosperity from this agricultural trade turned cities such as Philadelphia, Lancaster, and New York into bustling commercial centers.

Farmers and business owners who needed additional workers often sent to Europe for **indentured servants,** people who would work for a number of years to repay the cost of their passage. An eyewitness account suggests both the harshness of the voyage and the devastating discovery many immigrants made at their destination:

> How sad and miserable is the fate of so many thousand German families who lost all the money they ever owned in the course of the long and difficult voyage, many of whom perished wretchedly and had to be buried at sea and who, once they have arrived in the new country, saw their old and young separated and sold away into places far removed one from the other.
>
> —Gottfried Mittelberger,
> *Journey to Pennsylvania*, 1756

Few indentured servants ever achieved their dream of owning land in America, but their labor boosted the prosperity of the Middle Colonies. In the Southern Colonies, the harshness of indentured servitude quickly gave way to the crueler institution of slavery.

Southern Colonies
Tobacco and Plantation Slavery

While the Middle and New England Colonies attracted people seeking religious freedom and farmland, the Southern Colonies drew fortune hunters. At Jamestown, the first English settlement in Virginia, however, most of the men who came seeking gold found death instead. Of the more than 900 settlers who arrived between 1607 and 1609, only 60 survived dysentery, malaria, and malnutrition.

The settlers who survived, and the land-hungry people who followed, soon discovered that the South's climate and soil were particularly well suited to growing tobacco. In London where tobacco brought high prices, people joked that Virginia had been built on smoke.

The Plantation Economy

By the mid-1600s, a plantation economy had taken root in Maryland, Virginia, and parts of the Carolinas. The

GIRAUDON/ART RESOURCE, NY

A Treaty With Native Americans This painting depicts the signing of a treaty in 1682 between the Native American group the Lenni Lenape and William Penn's agents. *What relationship did Penn strive to have with Native Americans?*

Extending the Content

William Penn Even as a student, William Penn ardently supported freedom of worship. At Oxford University he was expelled for opposing the university rule that all students attend the Church of England. His family then sent him to France and Italy to study, in the hopes that Penn would put aside his religious arguments. When he went to Ireland in 1667, however, he became a Quaker at a time when Quakers were scorned. Penn was imprisoned several times for his Quaker beliefs, once being kept for eight months in the Tower of London. His father finally managed to have him released. Charles II then granted the charter to Penn for the territory that would become Pennsylvania, meaning "Penn's woods."

labor-intensive cultivation of tobacco demanded attention at many stages, from planting up through curing and packing. Other Southern cash crops, such as the rice and indigo that brought wealth to the Carolinas and Georgia, were similarly labor-intensive.

At first Southern planters relied on unskilled indentured servants to supply backbreaking labor in exchange for the hope of freedom and land. Most indentured servants came from the lowest rungs of society in England and Ireland. Probably no more than 1 in 20 indentured servants ever became free landholders. Instead the servants who survived the ocean journey and the unhealthy climate faced years of brutal treatment and an uncertain future.

Beginning in the early 1600s, Spanish and Dutch trading ships began to bring a few Africans to the Southern Colonies. The first Africans worked alongside whites as indentured servants, trading their work for the hope of freedom. By the late 1600s, however, the flow of enslaved Africans increased while the supply of white servants began to diminish. By the early 1700s, there were more enslaved Africans in the tobacco and rice fields than there were white indentured servants.

The institution of slavery quickly became a racial caste system in which even free Africans found their political and human rights obliterated. Laws controlling their rights and activities forbade enslaved persons to testify in court, engage in commerce or politics, travel independently, hold property, congregate in public, or marry. The holders of the enslaved Africans who toiled on Southern plantations viewed and treated African people as their private property.

Slavery Pervades the Colonies

Though the North never adopted plantation slavery, many enslaved Africans worked in Northern cities as artisans or domestic servants or on Northern farms as agricultural laborers. Still, every American colony dirtied its hands in the slave trade, from the wealthy Rhode Island shipbuilders whose fleets carried human cargo, to Pennsylvania wheat farmers whose crops fed the enslaved Africans of the West Indies.

In contrast to white settlers in New England and the Middle Colonies, white settlers in the South remained dispersed and isolated on small farms or plantations, where the gap between rich and poor loomed large. Power remained in the hands of a few wealthy plantation owners who could afford to educate their children privately or send them to Europe to study.

By 1682 English colonies lined the Atlantic seaboard from Massachusetts to South Carolina. In the late 1600s, both New England and Virginia fought major wars against Native Americans who resisted English settlement.

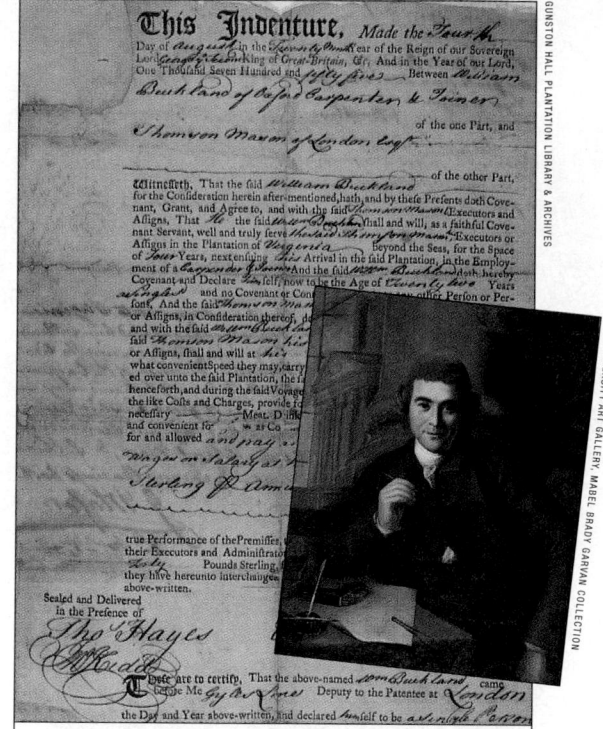

A Contract of Indenture In 1755 William Buckland, a white indentured servant, signed this contract. He was a carpenter who was paid for his years of work, unlike many other indentured servants who labored on tobacco and sugarcane plantations but received no pay. *Why did people sign such contracts?*

SECTION REVIEW

Vocabulary

1. Define: mission, presidio, selectman, pacifism, indentured servant.

Checking Facts

2. Where in North America did France concentrate its settlements?

3. What was the main occupation of the English living in colonies along the Atlantic seaboard?

Critical Thinking

Recognizing Ideologies
4. How did William Penn's ideology compare with that of the Puritans?

Linking Across Time

5. Are the differences between the New England and Southern states as extreme today as they were in colonial times?

Evaluate

Have students complete the Section Review.

Assign the Section 3 Quiz or use the Testmaker to develop a customized quiz. (Also in Spanish.) **LEP**

Reteach

Have students listen to the Chapter 2, Section 3 Audiocassette. (Also in Spanish.) **LEP**

Enrich

Have students research one or more contemporary situations or traditions that are based on life in the early colonies.

CLOSE

Review by asking students the following questions: Who were the major European nations that colonized America? *(Spain, France, England)* Which power dominated? *(England)* How did it dominate? *(through war with France.)*

VISUAL INSTRUCTION

A Contract of Indenture The first African indentured servants were brought to the colony of Virginia in 1619. This practice was short-lived. Most Africans were brought to North America as enslaved persons who had no opportunity to earn freedom.

Answer: *They usually had their trip to America paid for by the person to whom they promised years of work.*

Section 3 Review Answers

1. **mission** (37), **presidio** (37), **selectman** (39), **pacifism** (40), **indentured servant** (40)
2. After being ousted from Florida, the French settled around the St. Lawrence River.
3. agriculture
4. Penn believed in allowing people of various cultures and religions to live in freedom according to their own choices. The Puritans were intolerant of religious beliefs other than their own.
5. Students may answer that the differences are not as extreme as they were in colonial times, but that differences in climate and resources continue to affect occupations in each area.

TEACH

Making the Historical Connection

The founders of the Massachusetts Bay Colony based their government on the framework and ideas of Puritanism, which included the belief that only through conversion to Puritanism could one be redeemed from sin. In the Bay Colony, membership in the church was a requirement for voting or holding public office.

Turning Point

The Hutchinson trials ultimately helped diminish the governmental powers of the Bay Colony's religious leaders. Beginning in 1641, laws in the colony were no longer based on religious leaders' interpretation of the Bible, but on the laws of England. In 1644 the establishment of a two-house legislature further eroded the power of religious leaders. In 1646 laws that discriminated against unpopular religious views were annulled.

Turning Point

The Trial of Anne Hutchinson

NOVEMBER, 1637

> ### TRANSCRIPT
>
> From the Church Trial Against Anne Hutchinson
>
> I look at her as a dangerous instrument of the Devil, raised up by Satan among us. . . . Whereas there was much love and union and sweet agreement amongst us before she came, yet since, all union and love have been broken and there have been censurings and judgings and condemnings one of another. . . . The misgovernment of this woman's tongue has been a great cause of this disorder. . . . Therefore, we should sin against God if we should not put away from us so evil a woman, guilty of such evils.
>
> Reverend John Wilson,
> Pastor, Church of Boston
> March 1638

The Case

The General Court of the Massachusetts Bay Colony tried Anne Hutchinson in November 1637 for sedition, or working against the government. The Church of Boston tried Hutchinson for heresy in March 1638. By modern standards, Hutchinson committed no crimes. She had held meetings at her home to discuss the Sunday sermons given by Boston area ministers. At these meetings, she sometimes subtly criticized the teachings of some of the ministers. Challenging the authority of ministers and disputing their teachings was dangerous—especially for women, who were expected to bow to the authority of men at all times. Opposing the authority of church law was equal to speaking against the state.

The Background

Anne Hutchinson, a Puritan, left England and came to Boston with her family in 1634. They followed the minister John Cotton, who had been silenced in England and fled to the colonies. Anne's husband, William, held a considerable inheritance. He soon became a leading merchant in Boston. Anne worked as a midwife and healer and had contact with many Boston families.

Not long after the Hutchinsons landed in Boston, Anne invited a small group of women to her home to discuss religious doctrine. Anne was smart, eloquent, and well-versed in the Bible; she was also sensitive, supportive, and optimistic about life in the colonies. The gatherings quickly grew; as many as 80 people squeezed into her living room at once. Soon Anne was holding meetings twice a week to accommodate the crowds.

42 CASE STUDY

The Case at a Glance

| Hutchinson and her family arrive, following minister John Cotton from England. | → | Hutchinson begins to hold religious discussions in her home. | → | Hutchinson is tried and convicted of sedition; she is sentenced to be banished. | → | Hutchinson is convicted in a church trial. | → |

Through these meetings many Bostonians became familiar with Hutchinson's unorthodox views. She believed that a person's inner connection to God was more important than the person's appearance of following church laws. She thought that people could receive revelations—direct signs from God—without the help of a minister.

At that time in the Bay Colony many people considered it inappropriate for women to participate in public discourse. Hutchinson challenged this convention, as well as the authority of Boston's leaders, most of whom were men.

The Players

Within about a year of Anne Hutchinson's arrival, Massachusetts Bay Colony was divided into those who supported her and those who did not. Because of her neighborliness, her compelling egalitarian ideas, and her strength as a speaker and a leader, Hutchinson held wide popular support. Many businesspeople supported Hutchinson because religious leaders had placed severe restrictions on business. Some of the colony's most important political and religious figures opposed Hutchinson. John Winthrop, the colony's founder, lived across the street from Hutchinson. Winthrop knew about the popularity of Hutchinson's meetings. He also knew that his most powerful political rivals regularly attended. John Wilson, pastor of the Church of Boston, disliked Hutchinson because she had spoken against his teachings and walked out on his sermons. She had also tried to replace Wilson with Reverend John Wheelwright, her brother-in-law and one of her ardent supporters. John Cotton, Hutchinson's mentor, tried to remain neutral.

The Trial

By the fall of 1637, the balance of power had shifted in favor of the Bay Colony's founders. John Winthrop had recaptured the governorship; former governor Henry Vane, a Hutchinson supporter, had returned to England. Governor Winthrop and Reverend Wilson quickly acted against Hutchinson. First, they called a meeting of the ministers to evaluate her theologies. Not surprisingly, the ministers condemned Hutchinson's views, especially those on revelations. Ministers who preached these views

"... you have maintained a meeting and an assembly in your house that hath been condemned by the general assembly as a thing not tolerable nor comely in the sight of God nor fitting for your sex...."

Governor John Winthrop

CULVER PICTURES

"You have rather been a Husband than a Wife and a preacher than a Hearer; a Magistrate than a Subject."

Reverend Hugh Peter of Salem

"I'll bring you to a woman that preaches better than any of your black-coats ... and for my part, sayeth he, I had rather hear such a one that speaks from the mere motion of the spirit without any study at all, than any of your learned scholars...."

Chronicler Edward Johnson, quoting a male follower of Hutchinson's

"Here is no law of God that she hath broken nor any law of the country that she hath broke, and therefore she deserves no censure."

William Coddington, merchant and civic leader of Boston

CASE STUDY 43

FYI

Early Feminist Anne Hutchinson remained a controversial figure long after her death. In 1920, when the women's suffrage movement was at its peak, a statue of Hutchinson was given to the Commonwealth of Massachusetts by its Women's Clubs. Legislators did not, however, formally accept the statue until 1923. When asked to justify the situation, one legislator explained that the statue represented Hutchinson "as an idealist while many think she was aggressive."

Hutchinson is banished. She and her family move to Rhode Island. → Hutchinson is killed in a Native American attack.

Analyzing the Case

Invite students to read The Background. What qualities made Anne Hutchinson suitable as a leader of religious discussions? (*She was smart, eloquent, and well-versed in the Bible.*) What other traits might have drawn listeners to her discussions? (*She was sensitive, supportive, and optimistic about life in the colonies.*) Which of Hutchinson's views were unorthodox? (*She believed that a person's inner connection to God was more important than outer appearances in following church laws, and that people could receive revelations without the help of a minister.*)

Notes

_____

_____

_____

_____

_____

_____

_____

_____

_____

_____

_____

_____

_____

_____

_____

_____

_____

_____

_____

_____

Turning Point

were called to recant. Reverend Wheelwright refused and was banished from the colony, along with some of his supporters. Many other supporters were stripped of their citizenship.

The court called Anne Hutchinson to trial. Governor Winthrop sat as both judge and chief prosecutor. Anne Hutchinson addressed the court alone, without the benefit of a jury, lawyer, or witnesses.

The Opinions

The quotations on the previous page show divided opinions about Anne Hutchinson. Many in Boston were inspired by her, but they realized it was dangerous to speak against those in power. William Coddington, one of Boston's most successful business leaders, rallied to Hutchinson's defense.

Hutchinson spoke calmly, clearly, and eloquently in her own defense during the two-day trial. Although the governor and the ministers had little evidence against Hutchinson, they spoke strongly. Their strident judgments rang throughout the trial.

The Outcome

The verdict—banishment—surprised neither Hutchinson's supporters nor her detractors. Because winter was near, the court voted to allow Hutchinson to remain in the area under house arrest until spring.

The Bay Colony leaders still felt threatened by Hutchinson, who refused to alter her views. In March, they held a church trial. At the end of the trial, Hutchinson recanted her views in one breath and insulted the ministers in the next. They responded by excommunicating her.

The banishment was carried out a few days later. Hutchinson left with her family for the settlement of Aquidneck in present-day Portsmouth, Rhode Island. This region had become a haven for religious dissenters, including Roger Williams, who had been banished from the Bay Colony in 1635. Harassment by the Bay Colony continued. Ministers came to try to convince Hutchinson to reform; the colony also threatened to take over the Hutchinsons' land.

With the death of her husband in the summer of 1642, Anne Hutchinson decided to try to escape ever-present threats of the Bay Colony. The family eventually moved to the shores of Long Island, near Pelham Bay. Anne Hutchinson was killed there during a Native American attack in 1643.

© FORREST FRAZIEN/COURTESY OF THE DEDHAM HISTORICAL SOCIETY, DEDHAM, MA

Most Puritan households contained only one chair, which was usually reserved for the man of the house. Anne Hutchinson sat in a chair when she held her meetings, thus violating this convention. One Hutchinson critic, Reverend Thomas Weld, sarcastically remarked that "the custom was for her scholars to propound questions and she (gravely sitting in the chair) did make answers thereunto."

Cooperative Learning

Researching Puritan Life Have students work in groups to find out more about life in the Bay Colony of Anne Hutchinson's time. Each group can choose one aspect of colonial life, such as religion, agriculture, or architecture. Once groups have gathered and organized their information, they can give short presentations to the class.

Sir Henry Vane (left), a supporter of Hutchinson's, was governor of the colony from 1636–1637. When John Winthrop (right) succeeded Vane, he used the power of the governor's office against her.

COURTESY, AMERICAN ANTIQUARIAN SOCIETY

COURTESY, AMERICAN ANTIQUARIAN SOCIETY

The Significance

The religious controversy Anne Hutchinson sparked ravaged the Bay Colony. More than two dozen families left. Some followed Reverend Wheelwright to the settlement he founded at Exeter, now in New Hampshire. Most settled with the Hutchinsons in Aquidneck. As John Winthrop later noted, the colony's finest citizens were among the ranks of those who followed Hutchinson.

Winthrop himself eventually became disheartened about Hutchinson's banishment. In 1649 he refused to sign an order banishing another religious dissenter, saying, "No, of that work I have done too much already."

In the years between Hutchinson's banishment and Winthrop's expression of remorse, the Massachusetts Bay Colony slowly and subtly began a transformation. The power of traditional government authority, which had been intimately tied to the church, was curtailed. For instance, the personal power of the colony's main leaders was limited in 1641 when a written code of law was drawn up. The colony's laws were no longer based on the leaders' interpretations of the Bible but on the body of English common law.

The establishment of a two-house legislature in 1644 further cut into the power of the Bay Colony's traditional leadership. In 1646 business leaders who gained power in the lower house of the legislature, pushed to suspend laws that discriminated against people who held unpopular religious views. With these acts, the intertwining of the church and the state gradually began to be disentangled. This separation of church and state became an important principle in the Massachusetts colonial government and a cornerstone of the United States Constitution.

RESPONDING TO THE CASE

1. In what ways was Anne Hutchinson a threat to the Massachusetts Bay Colony?

2. What do you think would have happened in Boston if Hutchinson's supporter Henry Vane had been reelected governor in 1637 and for several subsequent years?

3. Before Hutchinson was called to trial, the leaders of the colony had warned her to tone down her teachings. Do you think Hutchinson could have championed her views better if she had heeded their warnings, thereby avoiding banishment? Do you think she would have gained more influence if she had remained a citizen of Boston? Explain.

4. Many Puritans left England for New England so that they would be able to worship according to their own consciences. As you read in the chapter, however, they tolerated no dissent from their own religious views once they had their own colony. Based on what you know of this contradictory attitude, are you surprised, or do you think it was inevitable that religious toleration would become an issue for Puritans in America? Explain your views either way.

PORTFOLIO PROJECT

Using what you have learned about Anne Hutchinson, write a speech she might have given to the people who came with her to Aquidneck, thanking them for their support. In the speech, look to the future and describe the dreams you have for the settlement.

CASE STUDY

Turning Point

Block Scheduling

The Portfolio Project on this page provides an excellent opportunity to enrich and extend the key elements of this case study.

CLOSE

Invite students to consider how Anne Hutchinson helped direct the colonies toward an increased tolerance of divergent religious views. Why did Hutchinson stand by her beliefs, even though she was threatened with banishment? *(because she believed her ideas important enough to sacrifice for)* How do Hutchinson's ideals of religious tolerance and the controversy surrounding religious freedom live on? *(The United States is now based on the idea of a separation between church and state. People sometimes still try, however, to make laws that reflect their own religious beliefs.)*

Responding to the Case Answers

1. As a woman who spoke out on religious issues, Hutchinson threatened Puritan and male dominance of religion and government in the Bay Colony.

2. Hutchinson might have been allowed to continue with her activities.

3. Some students might argue that it would be better to compromise her position in order to remain in the community and speak; others might argue that compromising her views might have diminished her influence.

4. Answers will vary but students should include logical or factual support for either position.

SECTION

4

FOCUS

Section Objectives

1. Explain why Native Americans rebelled against the colonists.
2. Relate how Britain became the dominant power in the colonies.
3. Describe the conditions in the colonies after the Seven Years' War that fostered new ideas.

Bellringer Activity

While taking attendance at the beginning of the class period, display **Section Focus Transparency 6,** and have students answer the questions. (Or use the blackline master.)

VISUAL INSTRUCTION

A Mohawk Leader The Mohawk were members of the Six Nations, along with the Cayuga, Oneida, Onondaga, Seneca, and Tuscarora. Brant and other leaders of the Six Nations chose to fight for the English during the Revolutionary War.

Ask: What did the chiefs of the Six Nations think of the education provided by the Virginian colonists? *(They thought that it did not make their young men into effective hunters, warriors, or counsellors, so the men were unfit for living amid their Native American groups.)*

Conflict and Growth in the Colonies

1744: VIRGINIANS OFFER EDUCATION TO NATIVE AMERICANS

NATIONAL GALLERY OF CANADA/THE BRIDGEMAN ART LIBRARY

A Mohawk Leader
Joseph Brant, who once served as a missionary among his people, translated part of the New Testament into Mohawk.

BENJAMIN FRANKLIN WAS BORN IN BOSTON IN 1706, THE FIFTEENTH CHILD AND YOUNGEST SON OF A POOR CANDLE MAKER. Fleeing a hateful apprenticeship to his older brother, Franklin crafted a successful life as a printer in the bustling port of Philadelphia. In his pamphlet "Information to Those Who Would Remove to America," Franklin contrasted the world views held by white colonists and Native Americans, saying, "The learning on which we value ourselves, they regard as frivolous and useless." Franklin illustrated his point with the following story.

In 1744 the commissioners of Virginia had invited the chiefs of 6 Native American nations to send 6 of their sons to college in Williamsburg, Virginia. The chiefs declined with thanks and this explanation:

Several of our young people were formerly brought up at the colleges of the Northern Provinces; they were instructed in all your sciences; but when they came back to us, they were bad runners, ignorant of every means of living in the woods, unable to bear either cold or hunger; knew neither how to build a cabin, take a deer, or kill an enemy; spoke our language imperfectly; were therefore neither fit for hunters, warriors, or counsellors; they

As You Read

Vocabulary
► kachina
► legislature
► revivalism

Think About . . .
► why Native Americans rebelled against the colonists.
► how England became the dominant power in the colonies.

► how conditions in the colonies after the Seven Years' War fostered new ideas that foreshadowed independence.

46 CHAPTER 2 ENCOUNTERS AND COLONIES

Section 4 Resources

REPRODUCIBLE RESOURCES

- Lesson Plan 2-4
- Vocabulary and Guided Reading Activity 2-4
- Section 4 Quiz
- Chapter 2 Test
- Performance Assessment Activity 2
- Reteaching Activity 2
- Skill Reinforcement Activity 2
- Enrichment Activity 2

MULTIMEDIA RESOURCES

- Section Focus Transparency 6
- Beginnings to 1900 Transparency 4
- Focus on American Fine Art Prints, Prints 2, 3, 4
- Testmaker
- Student Self-Test: A Software Review
- Chapter 2 Digest Audiocassette

were totally good for nothing. . . . if the Gentlemen of Virginia will send us a dozen of their sons, we will take great care of their education, instruct them in all we know, and make *men* of them.

—Zall, P.M., *Ben Franklin Laughing: Anecdotes from Original Sources by and about Benjamin Franklin*, 1980

In the 1600s and 1700s, conflicts erupted between colonists and Native Americans over such differences in values, but more importantly, over the colonists' persistent encroachment onto Native American territories.

Native American Wars
Colonists Conflict With Native Americans

In the Spanish Southwest, Native Americans succeeded for a time in ridding themselves of a hateful colonial presence. On the Eastern seaboard, however, coastal peoples soon succumbed to the English colonists' superior strength. The more powerful interior peoples would hold onto their own power only as long as France and England vied for supremacy on the continent.

Popé's Rebellion

In the 1600s Spain built missions in New Mexico. Nearby, Spanish soldiers occupied forts called presidios. With the aid of guns and horses, a few Spaniards subdued numerous Native Americans, converted them to Christianity, and forced them to toil for the Spaniards.

To destroy the Native American religion that competed with Christianity, the Spanish priests banned Native American dances, imprisoned and beat Taos Pueblo holy men, and burned sacred **kachina** dolls. In 1676 Spanish priests in New Mexico proudly reported the destruction of 1,600 Native American priestly masks.

Four years later, a Native American religious leader named Popé united Taos Pueblo people who spoke seven different languages into a formidable fighting force. Popé and his fighters leveled all but two Spanish villages in New Mexico and drove the hated priests back to Mexico, where they remained for more than a decade.

Victories such as Popé's did not occur in the East, where Native Americans came into conflict with American colonists who coveted their land. On the East Coast, two major defeats finally overpowered the Native American societies of the Atlantic seaboard.

King Philip's War

Massasoit, the Wampanoag chief, had befriended the earliest English colonists in Massachusetts, even bestowing the English names of Alexander and Philip on

King Philip Almost 100 years after King Philip's War, Paul Revere created this engraved portrait of him. *How many Native Americans died in the war?*

his sons, Wamsutta and Metacom. Eventually, Metacom (Philip) became chief. He detested the colonists, who had greedily overrun Wampanoag hunting and fishing lands. Unwilling to lose any more land or to be pushed westward, Metacom enlisted the aid of other seaboard peoples to fight the English. From 1675 to 1676, about 600 colonists and 3,000 Native Americans lost their lives in the bloody war.

Bacon's Rebellion

While New England colonists were fighting King Philip's War, settlers in Virginia were complaining that Virginia's royal governor, Sir William Berkeley, had reserved too much frontier land for Native Americans. Though his conciliatory policies pleased Native Americans and wealthy plantation owners, Berkeley's rulings infuriated new settlers and former indentured servants who coveted Native American lands.

In 1676 a planter named Nathaniel Bacon rallied troops of angry Virginians. First they declared war on all Native Americans, including those who were friendly, and then they battled the governor and his troops.

TEACH

Guided Practice

L1 Discussion Begin a discussion by asking students the following: What would you have done if you were a Native American and were being pushed off your land by the Europeans?

Show students *Beginnings to 1900* Transparency 4 and have them complete the activity sheet.

Independent Practice

L2 Research Ask students to select either Popé's Rebellion, King Philip's War, or Bacon's Rebellion to research in detail. Have them compile their research to use in oral reports.

Have students complete the Chapter 2, Section 4 Vocabulary and Guided Reading Activity. (Also in Spanish.) **LEP**

VISUAL INSTRUCTION

King Philip This engraving is actually a composite, rather than a true portrait. Paul Revere created it using eighteenth-century prints of four Native American chiefs.
Answer: *3,000*

Cooperative Learning

Native American Cultures Organize students into small groups to research and create reports on one aspect of either the Pueblo or Wampanoag Native American culture.

Students may choose to focus on any aspect of the organization of the Native American society, including its spiritual beliefs or its means of acquiring food.

History and the Humanities

📖 Focus on American Fine Art Prints, Prints 2, 3, and 4—*Dean George Berkeley & His Family (The Bermuda Group)* by John Smibert; *Isaac Royall & Family*, by Robert Feke; *Watson & the Shark* by John Singleton Copley.

MAP STUDY

After making peace with the French, the British government drew a racial boundary from Maine to Georgia in an attempt to separate Native Americans and colonists by keeping Native Americans in territories west of the Appalachian Mountains.

Answer: *Canada and all territory east of the Mississippi River except New Orleans*

EUROPEAN LAND CLAIMS, 1763

UNEXPLORED

Hudson Bay

HUDSON'S BAY COMPANY

Newfoundland

St. Pierre and Miquelon (FR.)

NOVA SCOTIA

QUEBEC

L. Superior
L. Michigan
L. Huron
L. Ontario
L. Erie

THIRTEEN COLONIES

ATLANTIC OCEAN

LOUISIANA

INDIAN RESERVE

NEW SPAIN

PACIFIC OCEAN

FLORIDA

Gulf of Mexico

TERRITORIAL GROWTH
- British
- Spanish
- French

| 0 | 250 | 500 mi. |
| 0 | 250 | 500 km |

Albers Equal-Area projection

The Seven Years' War clearly established Britain as the dominant power in eastern North America. *What territories did France lose to Britain as a result of the war?*

Hundreds of settlers and Native Americans died in what became known as Bacon's Rebellion. Bacon was killed, but his followers later gained seats in the Virginia **legislature,** or lawmaking body, where they immediately voted to legalize Native American slavery. When English investigators arrived in 1677, they condemned the "inconsiderate sort of men who so rashly and causelessly cry up a war and seem to wish and aim at an utter extirpation [elimination] of the Indians."

France and Britain Struggle for Control
Britain Emerges Victorious

The Iroquois, Cherokee, Creek, and Choctaw of North America's interior wielded far greater power than did the smaller coastal peoples who submitted to the colonists in the 1600s. At first the interior Native Americans shrewdly protected their interests and maintained

power by refusing to side with either France or England. As the growing white population of the English colonies pushed up against French-held territory, long-standing religious and commercial hostilities between the European rivals expanded into a deadly territorial struggle.

In 4 wars between 1689 and 1763, Protestant England sought to expel its Catholic French rival from the Americas. Foiled by weather, disease, and the hardship of transporting supplies, France and England each soon discovered that their best chance for success lay in recruiting colonial soldiers and in paying Native American allies to fight for them.

The fourth war, called the Seven Years' War in Europe and the French and Indian War in the colonies, proved climactic. By 1759, after the tide of victory turned indisputably toward Britain, the powerful Iroquois calculated that their interests would be best served by supporting the eventual victors. By the end of the Seven Years' War in 1763, France had lost Canada and all territory east of the Mississippi River except New Orleans; Britain held sway in the eastern part of North America; and thirteen separate colonies congratulated themselves

Meeting Special Needs

Visual Learners Before students who learn visually continue with the remainder of the section, lead them in a discussion about the map on this page. Ask them to trace the coastal locations of the thirteen British colonies and to point out the territories controlled by European powers in 1763 at the end of the Seven Years' War.

on uniting against a common enemy. The Native Americans of North America's interior, however, had forever lost the power they had previously enjoyed from playing off one colonial power against another.

A People Emerges
New Ideas Foreshadow Independence

The Seven Years' War extracted a high price from the colonies. During the course of the long war, most working-class Boston men fought, and many died. In 1764 census takers in Boston counted 3,612 women but only 2,941 men. In addition the peace that put an end to the bloodshed precipitated an economic depression as 40,000 British troops suddenly departed.

Despite its heavy costs, the Seven Years' War left the colonists heady with victory and seeking westward expansion. Territory that had been newly wrested from French control grew even more attractive to colonists who wished to escape the crowded Eastern seaboard.

The Population Explosion

The population of the colonies had increased at an extraordinary rate between 1680 and 1770, rising more than tenfold from 150,000 to 1,700,000. A mere one-fourth of this increase stemmed from the willing immigration of indentured servants from Germany and Ireland, and the forced immigration of Africans. Fully three-quarters of the population explosion stemmed from a high birthrate accompanied by a low death rate. For European colonists and their descendants, North America's pure drinking water, healthful climate, and spacious territory made life both longer and healthier. Enslaved Africans who formed families also began to have children by the 1720s, producing as many children as whites and soon outnumbering enslaved persons who had been born in Africa.

Africans had brought to North America not only the agricultural know-how that enriched Southern farmers, but also the medical expertise that saved many white colonists from smallpox, a dreaded killer. The Boston minister Cotton Mather learned from a "Guramantee" servant—probably a West African man shipped from the

Gold Coast fort at Kormantin—about a method of inoculation common in West Africa. In this method, "juice of small-pox" inserted into a cut produced a weakened form of illness, thereby conferring lifelong immunity. In July 1721 Mather wrote in his diary, "I have instructed our Physicians in the new Method used by the Africans . . . to prevent and abate the Dangers of the Small-Pox, and infallibly to save the Lives of those that have it wisely managed upon them." After inoculation took hold in colonial cities, smallpox virtually disappeared as a major killer.

A Great Awakening

At the same time that the population in the colonies was skyrocketing, many Americans came under the sway of **revivalism**—a movement that emphasized individual religious experience instead of church doctrine. A series of Christian revivals called the Great Awakening swept different regions between 1720 and 1760, arousing a widespread hunger for spiritual renewal. The timing and character of the Great Awakening differed from region to region. Still, regardless of region, revivalism posed a serious challenge to accepted sources of authority and introduced patterns of activity that helped fuel the revolutionary movement of the next generation. George Whitefield, a tiny 24-year-old Anglican priest with a magnificent voice, began by exciting audiences in his native Britain. In 1739 and 1740 Whitefield ignited the American Great Awakening on the first of 7 open-air preaching tours along the Atlantic Coast.

Awakeners like Whitefield preached that established congregations were dead because "dead men preach to them." The Awakeners shocked established clergy by encouraging individuals to participate by "lay exhorting." A lay exhorter could be any converted person—man or woman, young or old, African or white—who wished to preach "the Lord's truth."

Enslaved Africans were especially drawn to the revivalists of the 1740s and 1750s. Unlike professional Protestant clergy, whose sermons were typically dry and uninvolving, the revivalists preached personal rebirth in a freewheeling participatory style that gave Christianity mass appeal. Not surprisingly Africans' conversion experiences prompted many new African Christians to

THE BETTMANN ARCHIVE

George Whitefield Drawn by his riveting style as a performer, more than 20,000 people attended Whitefield's farewell sermon in Boston. *What did revivalism emphasize?*

ASSESS

Meeting Lesson Objectives

Each section objective is tested by the section review question(s) that follows it in parentheses.

1. Explain why Native Americans rebelled against the colonists. (1, 2)
2. Relate how Britain became the dominant power in the colonies. (3, 5)
3. Describe the conditions in the colonies after the Seven Years' War that fostered new ideas. (4)

VISUAL INSTRUCTION

George Whitefield Whitefield's custom of open-air preaching began in England when some Anglican ministers refused to let him give sermons in their churches. Whitefield then started to preach outdoors where great crowds assembled to hear him. In America he continued his successful custom of outdoor sermons.

Answer: *Revivalism emphasized individual religious experience over church doctrine.*

Portfolio Project

A Diary Entry Ask each student to imagine that he or she is an enslaved African American who has heard and been influenced by one of George Whitefield's revival sermons. Have students write fictitious diary entries recording their impressions of the sermon and their feelings about their status as African Americans in colonial society.

Evaluate

Have students complete the Section Review.

📋 🖥 Assign the Section 4 Quiz or use the Testmaker to develop a customized quiz. (Also in Spanish.) **LEP**

📋 🖥 Assign the Chapter 2 Test or use the Testmaker to develop a customized test.

📋 Have students complete the Chapter 2 Performance Assessment Activity. 📀

Reteach

🎧 Have students listen to the Chapter 2, Section 4 Audiocassette. (Also in Spanish.) **LEP**

📋 Have students complete the Chapter 2 Reteaching Activity. (Also in Spanish.) **LEP**

Enrich

Have volunteers research and share additional information about Benjamin Franklin.

📋 Have students complete the Chapter 2 Enrichment Activity. (Also in Spanish.) **LEP**

CLOSE

Ask: Who was Popé? *(a religious leader who led the Pueblo in a successful rebellion against the Spanish)* How did Africans aid the colonists? *(by sharing knowledge about agriculture and healing illness)*

VISUAL INSTRUCTION

Ben Franklin Franklin's inventions included bifocal glasses and the Franklin stove.

Answer: *hard work, education, community responsibility*

question the basis for their enslavement. On May 25, 1774, a group of Africans in Massachusetts addressed the following appeal to Thomas Gage, the royal governor: "There is a great number of us sincear . . . members of the Church of Christ(;) how can the master and the slave be said to fulfil that command Live in love. . . ."

All Americans, not just enslaved Africans, began to question received authority as a result of the Great Awakening. The ideas spread during this period encouraged people to create new churches and to take responsibility in other matters of importance, such as communal betterment and self-government.

Benjamin Franklin, Yankee Paragon

Though he shunned formal religion, the genial Benjamin Franklin offered George Whitefield accommodations on the preacher's 1745 visit to Philadelphia. Even if Franklin did not worship at any particular church, he nevertheless lived the maxim that "a good example is the best sermon." The sermon the self-educated Franklin preached promoted the Puritan virtues of thrift, hard work, education, and community responsibility. In his *Poor Richard's Almanack,* a collection of weather predictions and other useful information, Franklin coined many popular sayings giving practical advice about such subjects as working hard and saving time. Two of these familiar sayings are "A stitch in time saves nine" and "Lost time is never found again." After the Bible, Franklin's annual almanac was the most popular book in the colonies.

Over a career that spanned decades, Franklin became the most famous colonial American. In the second half of the 1700s, thanks to his experiments with electricity and his lightning rod, Franklin's name had traversed the Atlantic and was a household word in France. There the wealthy and famous man who had begun life as a poor boy seemed the embodiment of a freshly minted American spirit.

Colonial Self-Government

The American spirit Franklin celebrated expressed itself in the way the colonies governed themselves. Though each colony's government differed slightly, all the governments shared an important inheritance from

Ben Franklin Franklin's many accomplishments included founding the first city hospital and the University of Pennsylvania. *What virtues did Franklin promote?*

the British system of government: an elected legislature. In most colonies, these legislatures consisted of two chambers that approximated the English House of Lords and House of Commons. As in the House of Lords, members of the council were wealthy appointees of the royal governor. As in the House of Commons, members of the assembly were elected by white male property holders.

The legislatures provided a check on the power of the appointed royal or proprietary governors, many of whom proved to be corrupt at worst or mediocre at best. In the 1700s, the colonies' legislatures won the right to initiate bills, to settle contested elections, and to determine taxes.

Following the Seven Years' War, a French diplomat looked at the colonies' smoothly functioning governments and made an uncanny prediction. The diplomat warned an unbelieving Britain that the colonies no longer needed its protection: "You will call on them to contribute towards supporting the burden which they have helped to bring on you; they will answer you by shaking off all dependence."

SECTION REVIEW

Vocabulary
1. Define: kachina, legislature, revivalism.

Checking Facts
2. What prompted King Philip's War?

3. How did England emerge victorious over France in the struggle for territory in North America?

Critical Thinking
Recognizing Ideologies
4. How did the practice of enslavement conflict with the practice of revivalism?

Linking Across Time
5. How do the struggles between colonial powers for North American territory compare with wars fought over world territory today?

Section 4 Review Answers

1. kachina (47), **legislature** (48), **revivalism** (49)

2. Metacom (Philip) wanted to prevent the English from taking more Native American lands.

3. The British enlisted the help of the powerful Iroquois, resulting in the victory over France.

4. Revivalism encouraged the inclusion and participation of all people, raising questions about conflicts between enslavement and Christianity.

5. Students may answer that such territorial struggles are still going on in the world today, many still spurred by ethnic and religious differences. One example is the war in the former Yugoslavia.

Critical Thinking Skill

MAKING GENERALIZATIONS

Learning the Skill

Any item of information is like an isolated piece of a jigsaw puzzle. You need to look for patterns in information and put those facts together into a larger picture.

Making a generalization is making a general statement about a pattern you find in information you study. This skill helps you clarify your understanding of a situation so you can make decisions and act on your understanding.

Making Generalizations

To make a generalization, follow these steps:

a. Pull together the facts that are relevant to the topic.

b. Figure out categories or ways of grouping the information.

c. Look for patterns and relationships within the categories or groups.

d. Make a general statement based on the information.

Recall that in the last paragraph of the text on page 50, the French diplomat said:

> **Y**ou will call on them to contribute towards supporting the burden which they have helped to bring on you; they will answer you by shaking off all dependence.

This statement may have been based on facts such as the following:

a. Each of the thirteen colonies had an elected legislature to make laws.

b. The colonial governments were maturing and becoming more confident.

c. The legislatures had provided a check on the power of the appointed royal governors.

d. The legislatures won the right to initiate bills and to determine taxes.

You can see that each of these facts relates to the category of government. A pattern you can observe is that the colonists were working together and governing themselves successfully. The French diplomat could make the generalization that the colonial governments were able to function independently. Based on this generalization, the diplomat made his statement to England.

Debating Ideas The colonists discussed news and public events in town meetings and in informal gatherings. *State a generalization that a colonist of the time might have made about government.*

Practicing the Skill

Use the facts below to answer the questions.

Around A.D. 900, the Anasazi built 400 miles (643.6 km) of road to Chaco Canyon and lived in huge apartment complexes housing more than 1,000 people.

Between A.D. 900 and 1100 the Moundbuilders built a gigantic mound. It faces the site of a city that once housed as many as 35,000 people.

1. What facts fit in the category of time?

2. What facts fit in the category of people?

3. What patterns do you see in each category?

4. What common patterns do you see in the histories of the Anasazi and the Moundbuilders?

5. What generalization can you make about the earliest Americans?

Applying the Skill

Read a newspaper or magazine article that contains many facts. Make a list of categories and write down any patterns that you notice. Make a generalization based on those facts.

Additional Practice

For additional practice, see Reinforcing Skills on page 53.

CRITICAL THINKING SKILL   **51**

Students may be aware that they make generalizations on a regular basis in everyday life. Encourage them to test the generalizations that they make by looking for evidence that either supports or contradicts their generalizations. Also, encourage them to evaluate their generalizations to be sure that they are not too narrow or too broad.

VISUAL INSTRUCTION

Debating Ideas Because the colonies were located so far from Britain, the colonists were allowed much more self-government than citizens living in the British Isles had. This strong colonial tradition of self-government made many colonists resist later British attempts to exert more control and eventually led to the Revolution.

Answer: *Answers will vary, but students might suggest that the colonist would say that colonial governments were democratic.*

Additional Practice

☞ Have students complete the Chapter 2 Skill Reinforcement Activity.

Practicing the Skill Answers

Answers will vary

1. About A.D. 900 the Anasazi built roads and huge apartment complexes. Between A.D. 900 and 1100 the Moundbuilders built a huge mound near their city.

2. The Anasazi lived in apartment complexes of more than a thousand people. The Moundbuilders lived in a city of about 35,000 people.

3. In each category, complex human activities are taking place among large numbers of people.

4. Both groups of people completed projects of great complexity.

5. The Anasazi and the Moundbuilders must have had well-organized societies and effective leaders who coordinated large projects requiring cooperation among workers.

Chapter ② Review

Reviewing Key Terms

1. indentured servant
2. egalitarian
3. conquistador
4. pacifism
5. revivalism

Recalling Facts

1. that people in their society had varying ranks and that the Moundbuilders were brilliant metal workers and sculptors
2. Corn, beans, and squash; they supported each other physically and with the nutrients each left in the soil.
3. Mohawks, Oneidas, Onondagas, Cayugas, and Senecas
4. a direct western route to Asia
5. the quadrant and the lateen-rigged caravel
6. Slaves were needed to work the sugar and tobacco plantations.
7. They wanted to establish their own community where they could live according to their strict religious beliefs.
8. The middle colonies had lush farmland; Pennsylvania offered religious freedom and tolerance.
9. The Iroquois fought on the side of the victorious English in the Seven Years' War, defeating the French.
10. Revivalism and the Great Awakening and the success of colonial self-government contributed to the questioning of authority and the spirit of independence.

Critical Thinking

1. that the Iroquois were far more advanced than the Europeans assumed.
2. They assumed that the Native Americans were uncivilized, ignorant savages when, in fact, they had advanced societies and knew more about agriculture and interacting with the environment than the newly arrived Europeans.
3. Some of them used violent means to try to convert Native Americans to Christianity.
4. Students' charts will vary, but should include all of the points covered on pages 38–41.
5. Students' answers will vary. They may answer that this distinction was unfair and just one way that the Europeans tried to justify taking Native American lands for their own use.

Reviewing Key Terms

Choose the vocabulary term that best completes each sentence below. Write your answers on a separate sheet of paper.

conquistador   egalitarian
indigenous   pacifism
indentured   revivalism
servant

1. A wealthy colonist might hire an _____ to work on his plantation for several years in exchange for passage to America.

2. The Anasazi functioned as equals and had no leaders because theirs was an _____ society.

3. Hernando Cortés was a Spanish _____ who conquered the Aztec.

4. As a Quaker, William Penn believed in tolerance of differences among people and in _____, or opposition to the use of force.

5. The Great Awakening, which swept colonial America between the 1720s and 1760s, was based on the movement called _____.

Recalling Facts

1. What did the contents of the burial mounds reveal about the Native American Moundbuilders?

2. What were "the three sisters," and how did they support each other?

3. What five Native American nations combined to form the Iroquois League?

4. What was Columbus trying to find when he first sailed west from Europe?

5. What were the 2 major inventions that helped advance Portuguese navigation in the second half of the 1400s?

6. Why did the enslavement of Africans occur soon after the Europeans explored and began colonizing in the Americas?

7. Why did the Puritans leave their homes in England and come to Massachusetts?

8. What physical and social factors drew people to settle in the Middle Colonies, especially in the colony of Pennsylvania?

9. How were Native Americans instrumental in helping to establish Great Britain, rather than France, as the dominant power in North America?

10. What conditions in the thirteen colonies after the Seven Years' War fostered a growing spirit of independence?

Critical Thinking

1. **Drawing Conclusions** The Iroquois alliance was organized with the major purpose of ending the battles between Native American nations. A council of 49 chiefs, delegated by the 5 participating nations, governed the alliance and had the power to make decisions for all the Iroquois villages. Under this political structure, the people in the Iroquois alliance were more united and stronger than before. What does the success of this ruling body, organized before Columbus arrived in North America, indicate about those who organized it?

2. **Identifying Assumptions** What erroneous assumptions did the Europeans who colonized the Eastern seaboard of North America make about the Native Americans who were living there when the Europeans arrived?

3. **Recognizing Ideologies** Using missions such as the one in the photograph below as their bases, Spanish priests tried to convert the indigenous peoples of the Southwest to Roman Catholicism. How did their treatment of the Native Americans conflict with the ideology of Christianity that they espoused?

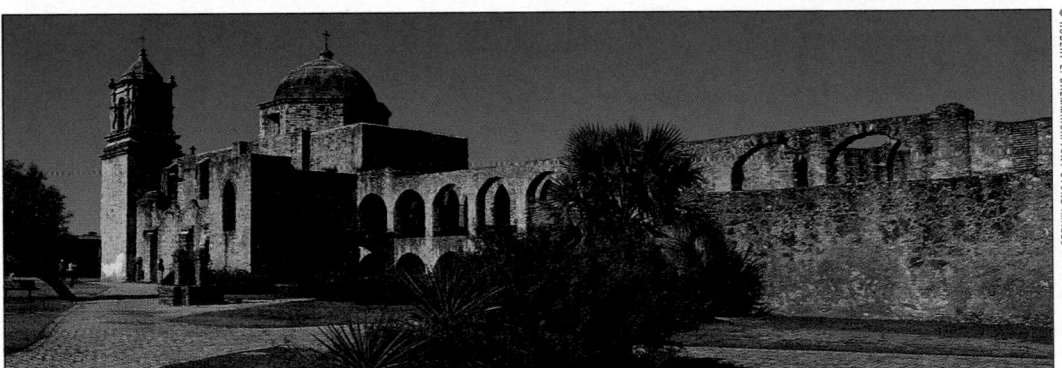

© ROBERT E. DAEMMRICH/TONY STONE IMAGES

4. Making Comparisons Life in the colonies was different depending upon whether a colonist lived in the New England Colonies, the Middle Colonies, or the Southern Colonies. Make a chart that compares the advantages and disadvantages of life in each of these colonial regions. Include social life as well as issues of work and religion.

5. Demonstrating Reasoned Judgment The Puritans followed the European theory that land that was not settled was available to be claimed by them as "civilized" people. In this way, they justified claiming lands where Native Americans "roamed" but had not settled. Do you think this distinction was just? Why or why not?

Portfolio Project

Imagine that you could ask Benjamin Franklin five questions about what life was like in colonial America after the Seven Years' War. Write these questions, and use them to do more research about this historic period. Put the results of your research into your portfolio.

Cooperative Learning

Working in small groups, research factors (other than epidemics) that contributed to the decline in the population of Native Americans and factors that contributed to the increase in the population of Africans in North America by 1750. Present your findings to the rest of the class.

Reinforcing Skills

Making Generalizations Write a letter to a friend from the point of view of a Puritan colonist, expressing generalizations you believe a member of that religious group would make about other religions in North America.

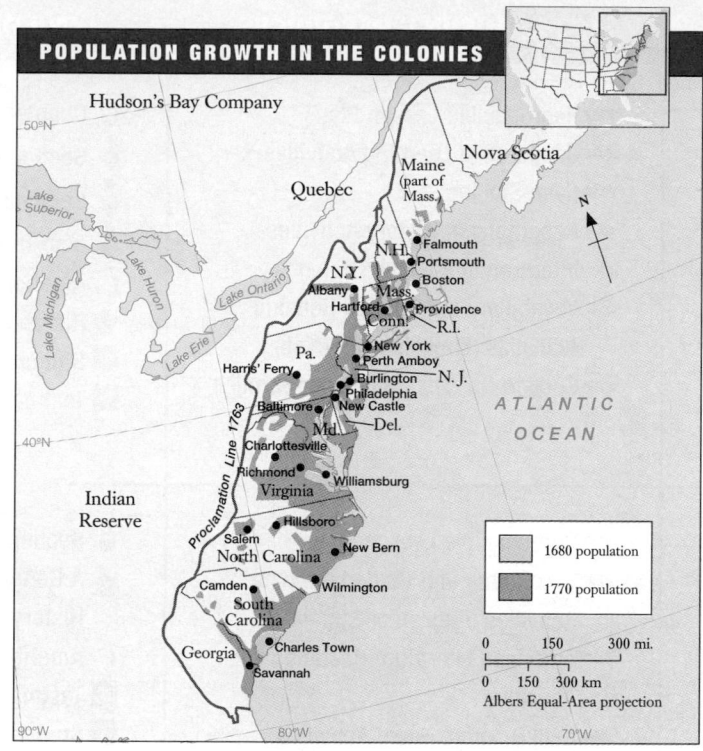

POPULATION GROWTH IN THE COLONIES

Hudson's Bay Company

Quebec

Maine (part of Mass.)

Nova Scotia

N.H.
Falmouth
Portsmouth
N.Y. Mass. Boston
Albany Hartford Providence
Conn. R.I.

Pa.
New York
Perth Amboy
Harris' Ferry Burlington N.J.
Philadelphia
Baltimore New Castle
Md. Del.
Charlottesville
Richmond Williamsburg
Virginia

Indian Reserve

Hillsboro
Salem New Bern
North Carolina
Camden
South Carolina Wilmington

Georgia Charles Town
Savannah

ATLANTIC OCEAN

Proclamation Line 1763

Lake Superior
Lake Michigan
Lake Huron
Lake Erie
Lake Ontario

50°N
40°N
90°W
80°W
70°W

1680 population
1770 population

0   150   300 mi.
0 150 300 km
Albers Equal-Area projection

Geography and History

Study the map on this page to answer the following questions:

1. Which colonies had no significant population in 1680?

2. Which colonies experienced the most growth from 1680 to 1770?

3. Locate the Proclamation Line established in 1763 after the Seven Years' War. Colonial governors were ordered to reserve all lands west of this line for Native Americans. Which colonies had people living closest to that line in 1770?

4. Which colonies—Northern, Middle, or Southern—were more likely to expand westward over the Proclamation Line first? Why?

HISTORY JOURNAL

Write specific facts that you have learned about how the Spanish, French, and English treated indigenous peoples in North America.

Geography and History

1. Georgia and North Carolina
2. Virginia, North Carolina, and Pennsylvania showed the greatest increase in populated areas. Some students may also point out that most of Massachusetts, Connecticut, and New Jersey became populated during this period.
3. New York, Pennsylvania, Maryland, Virginia, and North Carolina
4. The Southern Colonies, especially Virginia and North Carolina, were most likely to expand over the Proclamation Line because they had people living close to the Line and their populations were growing most rapidly.

History Journal

Student journals should include references to the violence against indigenous peoples and the taking of their lands.

? BONUS QUESTION

This question may be used for extra credit on the chapter test.
What led the Spaniards to enslave Africans?
Answer: *The Native Americans they had enslaved had died or fled, and labor was needed to refine sugar from cane—a process requiring physical labor the Spaniards refused to do themselves.*

Portfolio Project

Check to see that students have used research sources to answer adequately the questions they wrote about colonial life. Ask them to summarize what they learned and to share their results with the class.

Cooperative Learning

Criteria for the completion of each project will vary. Projects can be individual or group tasks. Discuss your expectations of students when assigning the project.

Reinforcing Skills

Generalizations expressed in the students' letters should reflect the intolerant Puritan point of view that their religion was the only correct one.

The American Revolution

DAILY LESSON OBJECTIVES	REPRODUCIBLE RESOURCES	MULTIMEDIA RESOURCES
SECTION 1 Toward Revolution 1. Describe life in the thirteen English colonies in the 1760s. 2. Examine the changing relationship between Britain and the American colonies at the dawn of the Revolutionary era. 3. Analyze the origins of the Revolution.	Reproducible Lesson Plans Cooperative Learning Activities Case Studies Geography In History Activities Interpreting Political Cartoons Vocabulary and Guided Reading Activities (English or Spanish) Section Quizzes (English or Spanish)	Chapter Teaching Transparencies Section Focus Transparencies Beginnings to 1900 Transparencies Map Transparencies American Music: Cultural Traditions Historic America: Electronic Field Trips Student Self-Test: A Software Review Testmaker
SECTION 2 War for Independence 1. Describe the steps the Second Continental Congress took to prepare for war with Britain. 2. Explain the strategies used by George Washington to help win the war. 3. Describe ways that the Revolutionary War changed the lives of the colonists on the battlefield and at home.	Reproducible Lesson Plans Vocabulary and Guided Reading Activities (English or Spanish) American Literature Readings and Activities Skill Reinforcement Activities Section Quizzes (English or Spanish)	Section Focus Transparencies A Geographic Perspective on American History American Music: Cultural Traditions Testmaker Student Self-Test: A Software Review
SECTION 3 Creating a New America 1. Explain how the state constitutions differed from the British colonial charters. 2. Describe the major differences between the state constitutions of Virginia, Massachusetts, and Pennsylvania. 3. Explain how the lives of women and African Americans changed in the Revolutionary era.	Reproducible Lesson Plans Vocabulary and Guided Reading Activities (English or Spanish) Reteaching Activites (English or Spanish) Enrichment Activites (English or Spanish) Section Quizzes (English or Spanish)	Section Focus Transparencies American Fine Art Prints American Music: Cultural Traditions Testmaker Student Self-Test: A Software Review
CHAPTER REVIEW AND EVALUATION	Chapter 3 Test, Forms A and B Performance Assessment Strategies and Activities	Vocabulary PuzzleMaker Testmaker Student Self-Test: A Software Review Chapter Digests Audiocassettes

00:00 If time does not permit teaching the entire chapter, summarize using the Chapter 3 Digests Audiocassettes and the accompanying activities and tests. (Available in English or Spanish.)

✔ Performance Assessment

Cooperative Project

Organize the class into groups. Assign each group one of the major battles of the Revolutionary War. Ask each group to prepare a newspaper article about the battle. Invite groups to present their articles on the bulletin board. **LEP**

Suggested Rubrics: A Newspaper Article, A Bulletin Board. See Performance Assessment Strategies and Activities, pp. 31 and 46.

Individual Project

Have students read "On Being Brought From Africa to America" by Phillis Wheatley and contrast it with works by modern African American authors on the forced removal of Africans from their homelands. Ask students to write a journal on the same topic.

Suggested Rubric: A Journal. See Performance Assessment Strategies and Activities, p. 29.

Key to Ability Levels

Teaching strategies have been coded for varying learning styles and abilities.

L1 **BASIC** activities for all students

L2 **AVERAGE** activities for average to above-average students

L3 **CHALLENGING** activities for above-average students

LEP **LIMITED ENGLISH PROFICIENCY** activities

Block Scheduling

Block scheduling differs from traditional class scheduling in the amount of time allotted to each period. The extended timeframe provided by block scheduling affords you the opportunity to implement a greater number of research-oriented and activity-intense projects to motivate and involve your students. Activities that are particularly suited to use within the block scheduling framework are identified throughout this chapter by the following designation.

TEACHER'S CORNER

NATIONAL GEOGRAPHIC SOCIETY

INDEX TO NATIONAL GEOGRAPHIC MAGAZINE

The following articles may be used for research relating to this chapter:

• "Two Revolutions," by Charles McCarry, July 1989.

• "Yorktown Shipwreck," by John D. Broadwater, June 1988

NATIONAL GEOGRAPHIC SOCIETY PRODUCTS AVAILABLE FROM GLENCOE

To order the following products for use with this chapter, contact your local Glencoe sales representative or call Glencoe at 1-800-334-7344:

• *GTV: A Geographic Perspective on American History* (Videodisc)

• *GTV: The American People: Fabric of a Nation* (Videodisc)

ADDITIONAL NATIONAL GEOGRAPHIC SOCIETY PRODUCTS

To order the following products for use with this chapter, call National Geographic Society at 1-800-368-2728:

• *America: Colonization to Constitution* (Filmstrip)

Chapter Overview

Chapter 3 covers British policies, the Revolution, and the creation of state governments following the war.

Introducing the Chapter

Have students read the vignette. Invite students to consider that the American Revolution meant freedom for some residents of the colonies but not for others.

 Display the Chapter Teaching Transparency and distribute copies of the activity sheet.

Extension Activity

Have students complete Beyond the Transparency on the activity sheet for Chapter 3 and present their projects after the class has completed the chapter.

History Journal

Have students write in their journals a letter supporting James Armistead's request for freedom.

CHAPTER
3

The American Revolution

OCTOBER 19, 1781: BRITISH SURRENDER AT YORKTOWN

An enslaved African named James gained permission from his owner, William Armistead, to join the Continental Army stationed nearby. It was March 1781.

The general commanding these American troops was Marie Joseph Lafayette, a young French aristocrat, who had volunteered to serve with the American army. That spring Lafayette sent many spies to the nearby British camp, but no one was as important as James. The secret information James gathered helped Lafayette and the Americans corner the British at Yorktown, Virginia. In October 1781 the British surrendered there, ending the fight for independence. At the end of the war, however, Lafayette went home a hero, and James went home an enslaved person.

Yet, with Lafayette's help, James was to be given his freedom. The Frenchman wrote a letter describing James's "essential services" during the war and urged that James be released by his owner in recognition of the value of those services. In 1786 the Virginia legislature finally freed James in thanks for his military efforts during the American Revolution.

James Armistead's story was exceptional, but the lives of many Americans—African and white, male and female, famous and unknown—changed during the Revolutionary era. Americans tasted new freedoms as they faced new challenges after the Revolutionary War. People of all backgrounds struggled together to forge their new nation. ∎

HISTORY JOURNAL

Before reading the chapter, write about your understanding of the Revolutionary War and how you think the war may have changed people's lives.

54

EXTRA CREDIT PROJECT

African Americans Invite students to explore the experience of African Americans who fought on both sides during the Revolutionary War. How did African Americans respond to the conflict? What were their reasons for supporting the side they chose? What did they gain or lose as a result of the war? Have students present their findings to the class.

VIRGINIA HISTORICAL SOCIETY

JAMES ARMISTEAD BEGAN CALLING HIMSELF
"JAMES LAFAYETTE," IN HONOR OF THE MAN
WHO HELPED FREE HIM.

55

 GLENCOE
TECHNOLOGY

 Videodisc

American History

Side 1, Section C
Title: The American
Revolution and the Early
Republic, 1765–1820
Subject: Overview of
American history from
1765–1820
Ask: Where were the
first shots of the American
Revolution fired? *(Lexington and Concord)*

Focus on Government

Side 1, Chapter 1
Title: Electronic Field
Trip to Independence Hall
Subject: The role of
Independence Hall in
American history
Ask: What two major
documents were debated
in Independence Hall? *(the
Declaration of Independence
and the Constitution)*

 **Focus on Government is also
available on videotape.**

Examining the Visual

The Art of Engraving This image of James Armistead Lafayette is a print made from an engraving. An artist makes an engraving by cutting an image into a flat plate, usually one made of metal. The depth and width of the cuts help to determine the appearance of the engraved image. The artist then inks the engraved plate and rubs it to force ink into the plate's cuts. Finally, the artist prints the image by pressing the inked plate against a surface—often handmade paper of high quality. Encourage students to examine this print and describe the different lines and textures the artist has produced. Ask them what overall effect the artist has achieved. How would students describe Armistead's character based on this engraving? *(Students may say that he appears intelligent, dignified, and self-possessed.)*

✔ **Performance
Assessment**

Refer to page 54B for
performance assessment
activities for this chapter.

☞ Also see Activity 3
in the Performance
Assessment Strategies
and Activities for an
additional activity as well
as for suggested rubrics.

FOCUS

Section Objectives

1. Describe life in the thirteen English colonies in the 1760s.
2. Examine the changing relationship between Britain and the American colonies at the dawn of the Revolutionary era.
3. Analyze the origins of the Revolution.

Bellringer Activity

 While taking attendance at the beginning of the class period, display **Section Focus Transparency 7,** and have students answer the questions. (Or use the blackline master.)

VISUAL INSTRUCTION

Tax Protest This wood engraving by J.W. Barber dates from around 1829. It is an illustration from the book *Interesting Events in the History of the U.S.*

Ask: Why did the colonists resort to violent protest to deal with the British? *(When the British ignored colonists' petitions, the colonists decided that only such action would be effective.)*

History and the Humanities

American Music: Cultural Traditions— "Junto Song" by Seth McCoy, vocal; James Richman, harpsichord.

SECTION 1

Toward Revolution

AUGUST 14, 1765: BOSTON CROWD PROTESTS NEW TAX

Tax Protest
Mobs of colonists vented their anger on stamp officers, who were appointed by the British to see that taxes were collected.

THE SOUND OF SCUFFLING FEET AND SHOUTING VOICES SHATTERED THE QUIET SUMMER EVENING. Hundreds of people, led by a poor, 28-year-old shoemaker named Ebenezer MacIntosh, stormed up the street. Men walking at the head of the crowd carried an effigy—a rag-stuffed dummy.

The effigy represented Andrew Oliver, a wealthy Boston merchant. Oliver had recently been made stamp officer for Massachusetts to help collect from the colonies a British tax authorized by the Stamp Act. Many Bostonians hated the tax; MacIntosh was leading a group to protest it.

The crowd carried the effigy through the streets of Boston. Then, after burning Oliver's effigy on a nearby hill, they attacked Oliver's luxurious house.

Oliver heard the crash of glass, the splintering of wood, and hoarse shouts. When the noise died down,

Oliver found his "garden torn in pieces, his house broken open, his furniture destroyed." Standing before MacIntosh and his mob, Oliver "came to a sudden resolution to resign his office" as stamp agent. The common people had scored a victory.

On that hot August night, Ebenezer MacIntosh, the poor Boston shoemaker, found himself at the forefront of a movement that strained the bonds between Great Britain and its thirteen colonies. Yet MacIntosh did not always oppose the British. Only a few years before, he had proudly fought for Britain's colonies in the French and Indian War (also known as the Seven Years' War). As recently as 1763, he had joined with other colonists in celebrating Britain's victory over France in that war. In the intervening years, Britain's treatment of her subjects ignited the ire of MacIntosh and many other colonists.

AS YOU READ

Vocabulary
► external tax
► internal tax
► treason

Think About . . .
► what life was like in the thirteen English colonies in the 1760s.
► the changing relationship between Great Britain and the colonies in

America at the dawn of the Revolutionary era.
► the origins of the Revolution.

Section 1 Resources

REPRODUCIBLE RESOURCES

📂 Lesson Plan 3-1
📂 Vocabulary and Guided Reading Activity 3-1
📂 Section 1 Quiz
📂 Cooperative Learning Activity 3
📂 Unit 1 Case Study

📂 Geography in History Activity 3
📂 Political Cartoons 1, 2

MULTIMEDIA RESOURCES

🔊 Section Focus Transparency 7
🎧 American Music: Cultural Traditions
📽 Chapter Teaching Transparency 3

📽 Beginnings to 1900 Transparency 5
💿 Historic America: Electronic Field Trips
🎧 Chapter 3 Digest Audiocassette
💿 Student Self-Test: A Software Review
💿 Testmaker
📽 Map Transparency 3

Paying for Security
Parliament Taxes the Colonies

Britain's leaders celebrated the end of the war in Europe and North America as heartily as did the colonists. The British victory ended more than 70 years of fighting with France in North America. As a result of a treaty signed in February 1763, King George III took possession of all French territory east of the Mississippi River, including lands in Canada. Yet the decades of fighting had left the British government struggling with a large national debt. British politicians also faced the expense of paying for an army in North America to secure the new borders and defend the enlarged territory.

The Proclamation of 1763

After the British victory, settlers began moving into the newly acquired lands west of the Appalachians. New settlers claimed the Native American hunting grounds that the French had protected. In May 1763, Native American resentment erupted in a bloody uprising led by Pontiac, an Ottawa chief. Within a few months, Native Americans captured or destroyed British forts on the frontier and killed many settlers.

To prevent another war, which Britain could not afford, King George III issued the Proclamation of 1763. The document proclaimed that all lands west of the Appalachians were reserved for Native Americans and closed to colonial settlement. For the British, the proclamation preserved peace with the Native Americans and prevented colonists from moving westward, farther from Britain's control.

Some colonists, however, felt that Britain had slammed shut a door of opportunity. They deeply resented being forbidden to settle on lands they had helped win from France. The colonists' resentment grew when Parliament demanded that they help pay for the army that Britain maintained to defend the frontier.

The Sugar Act

Beginning in 1764 Parliament tried to collect a series of taxes from the colonies to ease the war debt and strengthen the British Empire. The colonists' reaction was strong; it was most violent in Boston. The Sugar Act hurt Boston especially, because that city depended heavily on shipping and trade. Payment of all duties, or taxes, on

EASTERN NORTH AMERICA, 1763

This 1763 map of North America reflects many national interests. *Who would settlers come in conflict with as they moved westward and claimed lands between the Appalachian Mountains and the Mississippi River?*

molasses and sugar imported to North America from places outside the British Empire would now be strictly enforced. The act also placed new or higher duties on other foreign imports such as textiles, coffee, and wine.

These new duties caused the price of goods in the colonies to skyrocket, hurting businesses and customers alike. Just as important, the act also restricted smugglers by toughening the enforcement of customs laws. Smuggling formed a sizable part of colonial trade, in part because customs duties were high. The act had the overall effect of widening the division between Britain and the colonies. Americans resented having no representatives in Parliament to determine how the British rulers would spend their tax money.

Boston merchants protested the Sugar Act with orderly petitions. "If these taxes are laid upon us, in any shape," one petition read, "without our having a legal representation where they are laid, are we not reduced . . . to the miserable status of tributary slaves?" Yet these petitions had little impact on Parliament, and the Sugar Act remained law.

SECTION ONE   **57**

Cooperative Learning

Debate: Defending the Frontier Organize students into three groups: members of Parliament, wealthy colonists, and other people in the colonies. Have each group select one person to participate in a debate on the topic,

"Should Colonists Help Pay the Cost of an Army to Defend the Frontier?" The members of each group should prepare answers for their panelist and questions for the other panelists. 👝

TEACH

Guided Practice

L1 Discussion Explain that representation in government gives citizens a voice in determining their taxes. Discuss how the issue of representation became linked to the issue of taxation in the colonies.

🔖 Show students Beginnings to 1900 Transparency 5 and have them complete the activity sheet.

🔖 Show students Map Transparency 3 and have them complete the activity sheet.

MAP STUDY

Point out that in the days before paved roads and bridges the Appalachians formed a formidable natural barrier.

Answer: *Native Americans*

Independent Practice

L1 Writing Under the terms of the Treaty of Paris signed in 1763, Britain gained all of Canada and all former French lands east of the Mississippi River. Ask students to write a paragraph explaining how the newly acquired territory presented both advantages and disadvantages to Britain and to the colonists.

👝 Have students complete the Chapter 3, Section 1 Vocabulary and Guided Reading Activity. (Also in Spanish.) **LEP**

👝 Have students complete the Chapter 3 Cooperative Learning Activity.

Block Scheduling

☞ Have students complete the Unit 1 Case Study to enrich their understanding of the debate over the Declaration of Independence.

ABCNEWS INTERACTIVE™

 Videodisc

Historic America: Electronic Field Trips

Side 1, Chapter 6
Title: Lexington/ Concord
Subject: Tour of the site today
Ask: Why are Lexington and Concord so important in American history? *(The American Revolution began there.)*

See Historic America: Electronic Field Trips Guidebook for complete lesson plan.

VISUAL INSTRUCTION

Tea Protests Boycotts of British goods encouraged colonists to purchase plain, practical housewares from local artisans and to drink home-brewed beverages instead of British tea.

Answer: *Colonists resented the Stamp Act for individual reasons, but all agreed that a governing body in which the colonists had no representation should not be allowed to levy internal taxes.*

The Stamp Act

In 1765 Parliament passed a tax on all official documents and publications in the colonies. To be official, marriage licenses, mortgages, diplomas, bills of sale, and newspapers had to bear an official stamp, or seal, showing that a duty had been paid. The tax money was to pay for keeping British troops in North America.

The Stamp Act affected almost everyone, and most colonists hated it. Landowners and business owners despised it because the tax money raised went directly to the colonial governor. Colonists themselves had no say in how it was spent. Poorer people hated the tax because they had to pay extra for everyday items such as newspapers and playing cards.

Opposition to the stamp tax focused not just on the cost of the stamps but also on the method of taxation. Colonists agreed that Parliament had the right to levy an **external tax,** one to regulate trade in goods that came into the colonies. The Stamp Act, however, was an **internal tax,** one levied on goods made within the colonies, and designed only to raise revenue. Colonists argued that only their elected representatives should have the right to levy internal taxes. Because colonists could not elect representatives to Parliament, they believed that the right to levy an internal tax should belong to their elected colonial assemblies.

Protests over the Stamp Act united the colonists. Daniel Dulany, an attorney from Maryland, wrote a

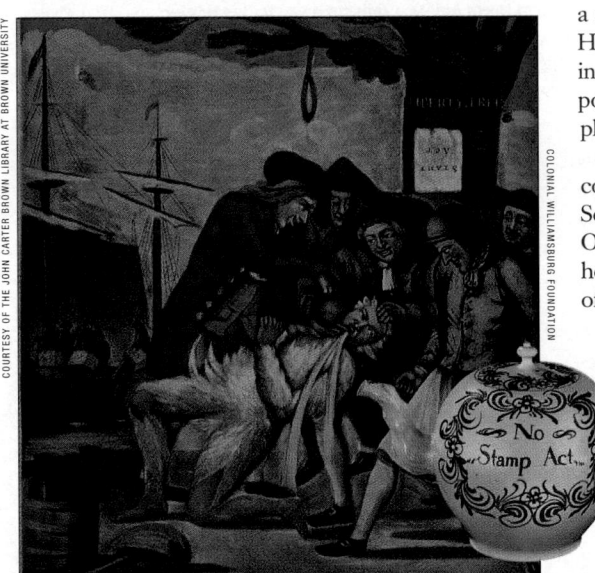

Tea Protests Here colonists have tarred and feathered a tax collector and are forcing him to drink scalding hot tea. *How did the Stamp Act unite both wealthy colonists and common people in protest against Britain?*

---

pamphlet rejecting Britain's right to impose internal taxes on Americans. John Dickinson of Pennsylvania published a pamphlet that denied the authority of Parliament to tax the colonists in any form. It was James Otis, a Massachusetts lawyer, who gave the colonists their rallying cry with his statement, "Taxation without representation is tyranny!"

The Coming of the Revolution
Tensions Explode in the Colonies

The taxation crisis of the 1760s heated the debate between Britain and its colonies. Colonists argued that Parliament violated their cherished right as British subjects to consent to all taxes levied on them. Feelings of resentment grew. People had been asking, Who has the power to tax us? Now the question became, Who has the power to govern? A movement toward self-government began to take shape. Protests against British authority intensified and, in some cases, became violent.

Sons of Liberty

Men like Samuel Adams of Boston felt that speeches and petitions against unjust British laws were not enough. A genial yet cagey politician, Samuel Adams came from a respected family and had attended Harvard College. He ran his own business, but after 20 years he was deep in debt. By the 1760s Adams was very involved in local politics and sought support for his ideas from the people of Boston.

Throughout 1765 Adams and leaders in other colonies formed a network of local groups called the Sons of Liberty to organize opposition to the Stamp Act. Often led by men of high position, these groups did not hesitate to resort to violence. They destroyed the homes of British officials and forced stamp agents to resign. To enforce a boycott of British goods, the Sons of Liberty threatened merchants. Anyone who imported or sold British goods risked being smeared with hot tar and covered with feathers.

In October 1765 delegates from nine colonies met in New York City and drafted a petition demanding repeal of the Stamp Act. This protest was effective, but the economic impact of the boycott was much stronger. The combination forced Parliament to repeal the Stamp Act in 1766. In its place Parliament passed the Declaratory Act. This law flatly declared Parliament's right to make laws concerning the colonists without their consent.

Meeting Special Needs

Visual Learners Have students who are visual learners examine the engraving of the Boston Massacre on page 59 and discuss their reactions. According to the engraving, what is happening? *(British soldiers are firing on the unarmed colonists.)* Who is to blame? *(the British)* Which side do students think the artist was on? *(the colonists' side)*

The Boston Massacre

Conflict over taxation prompted Britain to send troops to Boston to enforce laws and maintain order. The presence of British soldiers only raised tensions. Clashes between citizens and soldiers became common in Boston. On the evening of March 5, 1770, the tensions exploded into violence in an event that came to be called the Boston Massacre.

Accounts of the incident vary, but most agree that it began when a mob of townspeople taunted a British sentry on duty. Other British soldiers, led by Captain Thomas Preston, came to the sentry's aid. Tempers flared. The crowd threw snowballs and rocks at the soldiers. In the confusion, shots rang out. Some reports say that one soldier's musket went off by mistake, and then other soldiers began to fire. Others say an unidentified person commanded the soldiers to fire. Three colonists, including Crispus Attucks, a sailor of African and Native American ancestry, lay dead. Two more colonists later died from their wounds. Captain Preston was put on trial and acquitted. Two of his men were convicted of manslaughter and were branded on the hand.

A period of uneasy calm followed the Boston Massacre. Samuel Adams continued to use the incident to stir up anti-British feelings, but no violent protests resulted.

New trouble began in 1773. Parliament passed the Tea Act to save the East India Company, a British trading company, from bankruptcy. According to this law, only the East India Company could sell tea to the colonies. Though the tea would sell for a lower price than Americans were used to paying, they would still have to pay the import tax on it. Most of all, colonists resented the East India Company's monopoly on selling tea. To protest the tea tax, Boston's Sons of Liberty disguised themselves as Mohawks and went to the pier one night. There they tossed 342 chests of tea into the harbor.

As punishment for the so-called Boston Tea Party, Parliament closed Boston Harbor to all shipping until

COURTESY, AMERICAN ANTIQUARIAN SOCIETY

Violence Erupts This engraving is called *The Bloody Massacre Perpetrated in King Street*. Why would the colonists want to refer to the Boston shootings as a massacre?

the tea was paid for. General Thomas George Gage, commander of British troops in North America, took over as governor of the colony to restore order to the rebellious city.

Committees of Correspondence

While Bostonians fought for their rights, people in other colonies also struggled against British control. Their struggle took different forms as tensions mounted. As early as the Stamp Act crisis in 1765, Virginia's assembly opposed Parliament with decrees worded so strongly that some colonists called them **treason,** or a betrayal of Britain. In 1768 merchants up and down the coast boycotted British goods to protest the Townshend Acts of 1767. Five years later, patriots from New

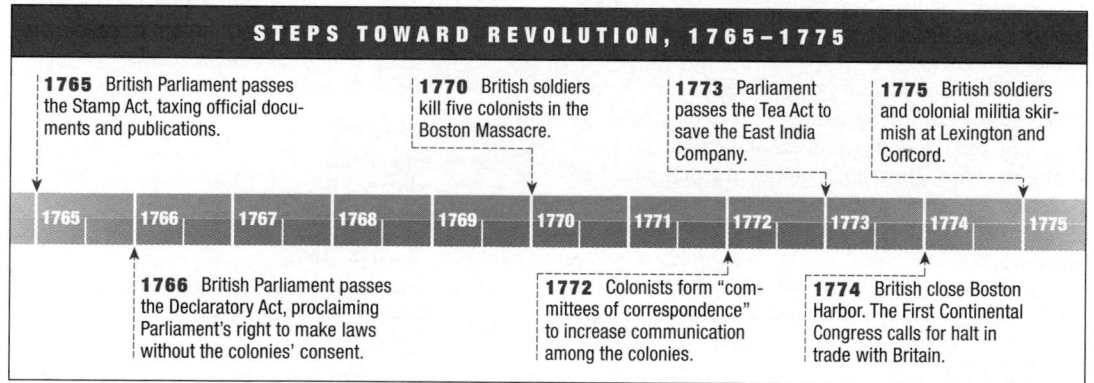

STEPS TOWARD REVOLUTION, 1765–1775

1765 British Parliament passes the Stamp Act, taxing official documents and publications.

1770 British soldiers kill five colonists in the Boston Massacre.

1773 Parliament passes the Tea Act to save the East India Company.

1775 British soldiers and colonial militia skirmish at Lexington and Concord.

1765 | 1766 | 1767 | 1768 | 1769 | 1770 | 1771 | 1772 | 1773 | 1774 | 1775

1766 British Parliament passes the Declaratory Act, proclaiming Parliament's right to make laws without the colonies' consent.

1772 Colonists form "committees of correspondence" to increase communication among the colonies.

1774 British close Boston Harbor. The First Continental Congress calls for halt in trade with Britain.

Portfolio Project

Trial Transcript Have students research the trial of Captain Preston and the soldiers involved in the Boston Massacre. Students should find out who defended the British soldiers and what defense their lawyer used. Then have the students write a one-page excerpt of the trial "transcript," using the information they

found in their research. Have students conclude the project by writing a paragraph or two stating whether they think the trial and the soldiers' punishment was fair, and why. Have them include their transcripts in their portfolios.

VISUAL INSTRUCTION

Violence Erupts This picture was made by Paul Revere. Better known as an accomplished silversmith, Revere also engraved political cartoons that were widely read.

Answer: *The colonists wished to portray the soldiers as brutal murderers to stir up feeling against the British government.*

ASSESS

Meeting Lesson Objectives

Each section objective is tested by the section review question(s) that follows it in parentheses.

1. Describe life in the thirteen English colonies in the 1760s. (3, 4)
2. Examine the changing relationship between Britain and the American colonies at the dawn of the Revolutionary era. (1, 2, 3)
3. Analyze the origins of the Revolution. (1, 4, 5)

CHART STUDY

Point out that several events led to the American Revolution.

Ask: What do you think were the most significant events leading to the Revolution? Why? *(Answers will vary, but most students will probably cite Lexington and Concord because those were the first battles.)*

Old North Bridge At the Old North Bridge, an attack by colonial minutemen forced the British to retreat.

Answer: *This first battle started the revolution that would help bring the idea of democracy to the modern world.*

Evaluate

Have students complete the Section Review.

📎 🔲 Assign the Section 1 Quiz or use the Testmaker to develop a customized quiz. (Also in Spanish.) **LEP**

Reteach

🎧 Have students listen to the Chapter 3, Section 1 Audiocassette. (Also in Spanish.) **LEP**

Enrich

📎 Have students complete the Chapter 3 Geography in History Activity.

📎 Have students complete Interpreting Political Cartoons 1, 2.

CLOSE

Ask students to list the events leading up to the American Revolution. *(Stamp Act, Declaratory Act, Boston Massacre, committees of correspondence, Tea Act, closing of Boston Harbor, battles of Lexington and Concord)*

Hampshire to Virginia dumped or boycotted tea to protest the Tea Act. The Boston Tea Party was only the best known of these protests.

Most colonists, however, viewed the crisis with Britain as a local matter. A Philadelphia lawyer, a New England fisher, and a Carolina planter might all oppose a tax on tea, but they felt little in common with each other beyond that. Many colonists thought that Bostonians had brought trouble on themselves and felt no obligation to solve or share their problems.

A group in Boston tried to change that attitude in 1772 by forming what it called a "committee of correspondence." The committee would "state the rights of the colonists . . . and communicate and publish the same to the several towns and to the world." Within a year dozens of towns in Massachusetts and assemblies from nearly every colony had created similar letter-writing committees.

The letters carried along the muddy roads leading from colony to colony did much to bring North and South, town and country, closer together in the struggle for self-government. Farmers had been slow to join the protests against Britain, but now they too argued against unfair taxes. Many farmers organized against the British as city people had done earlier.

News in 1774 that the British had closed Boston Harbor circulated through the committees of correspondence and outraged Americans everywhere. This news especially distressed merchants and planters, for if Britain closed the main ports of their colonies, they would be ruined. So when Bostonians called for a meeting to discuss the crisis, twelve of the thirteen colonies sent representatives.

Continental Congress

Fifty-six men from twelve colonies traveled to Philadelphia late in the summer of 1774 for the First Continental Congress. Most of them had served in colonial assemblies, but few knew any of the other representatives. John Adams of Massachusetts wrote, "We have numberless prejudices to remove here." Nobody knew what to expect of this unprecedented—and perhaps treasonous—meeting.

The First Continental Congress called for a halt in trade with Great Britain and resolved to meet again in the spring of 1775. In the process of discussing the crisis that had brought them together, the delegates had succeeded in removing some of their prejudices against one another and helped make Boston's crisis an American crisis.

By 1775 the machinery of the British Empire—governors, councils, courts—had broken down. In its place grew a ramshackle system of local committees and congresses of men who ignored British authority.

Old North Bridge At this site in Concord, Massachusetts, militia skirmished with British soldiers sent to destroy rebel supply stores. *Why was the exchange of gunfire at Lexington later referred to as "the shot heard round the world"?*

General Gage, the governor of Massachusetts, received orders from London to arrest just such a group of men. On an April night in 1775, 700 British soldiers marched toward Concord, about 15 miles from Boston. At the town of Lexington, 70 American militia stood waiting. After a brief skirmish at dawn, the British left 8 Americans dead on the village green and marched on to Concord.

At Concord, fighting again broke out. As the British began the return march to Boston, colonists hid behind rocks, trees, and fences all along the road and picked off scores of British troops. By the time the British forces reached Boston, they had suffered 273 casualties, and 88 Americans had fallen. The struggle to defend the colonists' rights had become a war.

SECTION REVIEW

Vocabulary

1. Define: external tax, internal tax, treason.

Checking Facts

2. What were the purposes of the Proclamation of 1763 from the British point of view?

3. What were the consequences of the Sugar Act?

Critical Thinking

Making Inferences

4. What might the British government have done to prevent revolution?

Linking Across Time

5. Under what conditions might the people of a country feel justified in revolting against their government today?

Section 1 Review Answers

1. external tax (58), **internal tax** (58), **treason** (59)

2. The Proclamation of 1763 was intended to preserve peace with Native Americans and to prevent colonists from moving farther from Britain's control.

3. The Sugar Act raised prices of goods for colonial businesses and customers by blocking cheaper goods from smugglers. It widened the division between Britain and the colonies.

4. Students may answer that Britain could have repealed some of the taxes.

5. Students may answer that people might revolt if they believe that their government is oppressive.

The Declaration *of* Independence

In Congress, July 4, 1776. The unanimous Declaration of the thirteen united States of America,

Preamble

When in the Course of human events, it becomes necessary for one people to dissolve the political bands which have connected them with another, and to assume among the powers of the earth, the separate and equal station to which the Laws of Nature and Nature's God entitle them, a decent respect to the opinions of mankind requires that they should declare the causes which impel them to the separation.—

Declaration of Natural Rights

We hold these truths to be self-evident, that all men are created equal, that they are endowed by their Creator with certain unalienable Rights, that among these are Life, Liberty, and the pursuit of Happiness.—

That to secure these rights, Governments are instituted among Men, deriving their just powers from the consent of the governed,—

That whenever any Form of Government becomes destructive of these ends, it is the Right of the People to alter or to abolish it, and to institute new Government, laying its foundation on such principles and organizing its powers in such form, as to them shall seem most likely to effect their Safety and Happiness. Prudence, indeed, will dictate that Governments long established should not be changed for light and transient causes; and accordingly all experience hath shewn, that mankind are more disposed to suffer, while evils are sufferable, than to right themselves by abolishing the forms to which they are accustomed. But when a long train of abuses and usurpations, pursuing invariably the same Object evinces a design to reduce them under absolute Despotism, it is their right, it is their duty, to throw off such Government, and to provide new Guards for their future security.—

List of Grievances

Such has been the patient sufferance of these Colonies; and such is now the necessity which constrains them to alter their former Systems of Government. The history of the present King of Great Britain is a history of repeated injuries and usurpations, all having in direct object the establishment of an absolute Tyranny over these States. To prove this, let Facts be submitted to a candid world.—

He has refused his Assent to Laws, the most wholesome and necessary for the public good.—

He has forbidden his Governors to pass Laws of immediate and pressing importance, unless suspended in their operation till his Assent should be obtained; and when so suspended, he has utterly neglected to attend to them.—

The printed text of the document shows the spelling and punctuation of the parchment original. To aid in comprehension, selected words and their definitions appear in the side margin, along with other explanatory notes.

impel *force*

endowed *provided*

People create governments to ensure that their natural rights are protected.

If a government does not serve its purpose, the people have a right to abolish it. Then the people have the right and duty to create a new government that will safeguard their security.

Despotism *unlimited power*

usurpations *unjust uses of power*

Each paragraph lists alleged injustices of George III.

relinquish *give up*
inestimable *priceless*

Annihilation *destruction*

convulsions
violent disturbances

Naturalization of Foreigners
*process by which foreign-born
persons become citizens*

tenure *term*

Refers to the British troops sent to
the colonies after the French and
Indian War.

Refers to the 1766 Declaratory Act.

quartering *lodging*

Refers to the 1774 Quebec Act.

render *make*

abdicated *given up*

perfidy *violation of trust*

He has refused to pass other Laws for the accommodation of large districts of people, unless those people would relinquish the right of Representation in the Legislature, a right inestimable to them and formidable to tyrants only.—

He has called together legislative bodies at places unusual, uncomfortable, and distant from the depository of their public Records, for the sole purpose of fatiguing them into compliance with his measures.—

He has dissolved Representative Houses repeatedly, for opposing with manly firmness his invasions on the rights of the people.—

He has refused for a long time, after such dissolutions, to cause others to be elected; whereby the Legislative powers, incapable of Annihilation, have returned to the People at large for their exercise; the State remaining in the meantime exposed to all the dangers of invasion from without, and convulsions within.—

He has endeavoured to prevent the population of these States; for that purpose obstructing the Laws for Naturalization of Foreigners; refusing to pass others to encourage their migrations hither, and raising the conditions of new Appropriations of Lands.—

He has obstructed the Administration of Justice, by refusing his Assent to Laws for establishing Judiciary powers.—

He has made Judges dependent on his Will alone, for the tenure of their offices, and the amount and payment of their salaries.—

He has erected a multitude of New Offices, and sent hither swarms of Officers to harass our people, and eat out their substance.—

He has kept among us, in times of peace, Standing Armies without the Consent of our legislatures.—

He has affected to render the Military independent of and superior to the Civil power.—

He has combined with others to subject us to a jurisdiction foreign to our constitution, and unacknowledged by our laws; giving his Assent to their Acts of pretended Legislation:—

For quartering large bodies of troops among us:—

For protecting them, by a mock Trial, from punishment for any Murders which they should commit on the Inhabitants of these States:—

For cutting off our Trade with all parts of the world:—

For imposing Taxes on us without our Consent:—

For depriving us in many cases, of the benefits of Trial by Jury:—

For transporting us beyond Seas to be tried for pretended offences:—

For abolishing the free System of English Laws in a neighbouring Province, establishing therein an Arbitrary government, and enlarging its Boundaries so as to render it at once an example and fit instrument for introducing the same absolute rule into these Colonies:—

For taking away our Charters, abolishing our most valuable Laws, and altering fundamentally the Forms of our Governments:—

For suspending our own Legislatures, and declaring themselves invested with power to legislate for us in all cases whatsoever.—

He has abdicated Government here, by declaring us out of his Protection and waging War against us.—

He has plundered our seas, ravaged our Coasts, burnt our towns, and destroyed the Lives of our people.—

He is at this time transporting large Armies of foreign Mercenaries to compleat the works of death, desolation and tyranny, already begun with circumstances of Cruelty & perfidy scarcely paralleled in the most barbarous ages, and totally unworthy the Head of a civilized nation.—

He has constrained our fellow Citizens taken Captive on the high Seas to bear Arms against their Country, to become the executioners of their friends and Brethren, or to fall themselves by their Hands.—

He has excited domestic insurrections amongst us, and has endeavoured to bring on the inhabitants of our frontiers, the merciless Indian Savages, whose known rule of warfare, is an undistinguished destruction of all ages, sexes and conditions.

In every stage of these Oppressions We have Petitioned for Redress in the most humble terms: Our repeated Petitions have been answered only by repeated injury. A Prince, whose character is thus marked by every act which may define a Tyrant, is unfit to be the ruler of a free people.

Nor have We been wanting in attentions to our British brethren. We have warned them from time to time of attempts by their legislature to extend an unwarrantable jurisdiction over us. We have reminded them of the circumstances of our emigration and settlement here. We have appealed to their native justice and magnanimity, and we have conjured them by the ties of our common kindred to disavow these usurpations, which would inevitably interrupt our connections and correspondence. They too have been deaf to the voice of justice and of consanguinity. We must, therefore, acquiesce in the necessity, which denounces our Separation, and hold them, as we hold the rest of mankind, Enemies in War, in Peace Friends.—

Resolution of Independence by the United States

We, therefore, the Representatives of the united States of America, in General Congress, Assembled, appealing to the Supreme Judge of the world for the rectitude of our intentions, do, in the Name, and by Authority of the good People of these Colonies, solemnly publish and declare, That these United Colonies are, and of Right ought to be Free and Independent States; that they are Absolved from all Allegiance to the British Crown, and that all political connection between them and the State of Great Britain, is and ought to be totally dissolved; and that as Free and Independent States, they have full Power to levy War, conclude Peace, contract Alliances, establish Commerce, and to do all other Acts and Things which Independent States may of right do.—

And for the support of this Declaration, with a firm reliance on the protection of divine Providence, we mutually pledge to each other our Lives, our Fortunes and our sacred Honour.

insurrections *rebellions*

Petitioned for Redress *asked formally for a correction of wrongs*

unwarrantable jurisdiction *unjustified authority*

consanguinity *originating from the same ancestor*

rectitude *rightness*

The signers, as representatives of the American people, declared the colonies independent from Great Britain. Most members signed the document on August 2, 1776.

John Hancock
    President from
    Massachusetts

GEORGIA
Button Gwinnett
Lyman Hall
George Walton

NORTH CAROLINA
William Hooper
Joseph Hewes
John Penn

SOUTH CAROLINA
Edward Rutledge
Thomas Heyward, Jr.
Thomas Lynch, Jr.
Arthur Middleton

MARYLAND
Samuel Chase
William Paca
Thomas Stone
Charles Carroll of
    Carrollton

VIRGINIA
George Wythe
Richard Henry Lee
Thomas Jefferson
Benjamin Harrison
Thomas Nelson, Jr.
Francis Lightfoot Lee
Carter Braxton

PENNSYLVANIA
Robert Morris
Benjamin Rush
Benjamin Franklin
John Morton
George Clymer
James Smith
George Taylor
James Wilson
George Ross

DELAWARE
Caesar Rodney
George Read
Thomas McKean

NEW YORK
William Floyd
Philip Livingston
Francis Lewis
Lewis Morris

NEW JERSEY
Richard Stockton
John Witherspoon
Francis Hopkinson
John Hart
Abraham Clark

NEW HAMPSHIRE
Josiah Bartlett
William Whipple
Matthew Thornton

MASSACHUSETTS
Samuel Adams
John Adams
Robert Treat Paine
Elbridge Gerry

RHODE ISLAND
Stephen Hopkins
William Ellery

CONNECTICUT
Samuel Huntington
William Williams
Oliver Wolcott
Roger Sherman

TEACH

Making the Historical Connection

Tell students that conditions in the colonies just before the outbreak of the Revolutionary War in 1775 all pointed toward conflict. Since the end of the Seven Years' War in 1763, Great Britain had been trying to exact more revenues from the colonies, in part to pay for that war. Taxation on the colonies increased and caused growing resentment against the tyranny of Great Britain. Many uprisings against British colonial government had already occurred, and publications such as Paine's *Common Sense* further fanned the flames of revolution.

ABCNEWS INTERACTIVE™

 Videodisc

Historic America: Electronic Field Trips

Side 1, Chapter 6
Title: Lexington and Concord
Subject: The battle sites
Ask: Why are Lexington and Concord important in American history? *(The Revolution began there.)*

See Historic America: Electronic Field Trips Guidebook for complete lesson plan.

64

One Day in History

Wednesday, April 19, 1775

MARKET BASKET

Here is where money will go:

Ferry prices for taking cargo across the Susquehanna River at Wright's Ferry in Continental currency

A six-horse wagon	$90
A horse and rider	$12

Prices at the Ellery Tavern in Gloucester, Massachusetts: s.=shilling; d.=pence

Lodging for two	6d.
Bread and cheese	7d.
One dinner	9d.
One mug cider	1.5d.
Breakfast	9.5d.
15 lbs. (6.81 kg) tobacco	7s. 6d.

British Assault on Minutemen British troops led by Lieutenant Francis Smith vastly outnumbered the armed minutemen they fired upon in Lexington.

The Shot Heard Around the World

Patriot minutemen and British redcoats clash at Lexington and Concord

LEXINGTON, MA—Fighting broke out today in Lexington and Concord between British troops and volunteer minutemen. An unconfirmed number of deaths and casualties occurred.

Boston patriots learned last night of a plan for a British attack on the colonial arms depot at Concord. Paul Revere and William Dawes rode to warn the people of Lexington and Concord that the British were on the march.

In Lexington about 70 armed minutemen confronted some 700 British troops. Although no one knows who fired the first shot, 8 patriots lay dead when the smoke cleared. One group of redcoats then clashed with minutemen at the North Bridge in Concord, causing more casualties. The British then retreated to Boston, beset by residents who fired at them from behind stone walls and trees. It appears that a war for our freedom has begun.

Background Information

Common Sense Thomas Paine's *Common Sense* contributed greatly to the move away from Great Britain and toward independence. Written in language that the public could understand, Paine made a logical but passionate argument that included economic facts supporting his case. He made the point that there were no advantages to remaining connected to Great Britain. Regarding trade, for example, he states: "Our corn will fetch its price in any market in Europe. . . ." The colonists bought hundreds of thousands of copies of Paine's pamphlet, fueling the spirit of rebellion.

One Day in History, Wednesday, April 19, 1775

NATION: The Continental Congress creates its own postal system and names Benjamin Franklin postmaster general.

Daniel Boone Cuts New Road

FORT BOONE, KY—With about 30 woodchoppers, Daniel Boone completed the Wilderness Road, which is 250 miles (402.25 km) long and runs through the Allegheny Mountains from North Carolina to Otter Creek near the Kentucky River. Settlers from Virginia and North Carolina plan to follow this road to found a fourteenth colony.

Daniel Boone

Treaty With Cherokee

KENTUCKY—By the terms of a treaty with the Cherokee, the Transylvania Land Company acquired all land south of the Ohio River, north of the Cumberland River, and west of the Appalachians in exchange for goods worth $10.

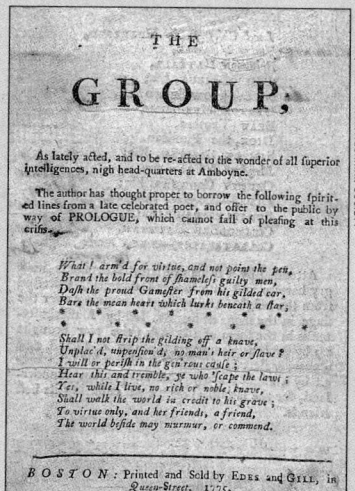

The Group, a play about Puritan leaders written by Mercy Warren, draws enthusiastic audiences.

IN PRINT

Women's Rights Written by Thomas Paine, the first article to expound women's rights in North America appears in *Pennsylvania Magazine*.

Nathaniel Law's *Astronomical Diary,* or *Almanack,* is published for 1775.

MUSIC

• **Popular song:** "Yankee Doodle"
• **First pianoforte:** John Behrent of Philadelphia makes North America's first pianoforte.

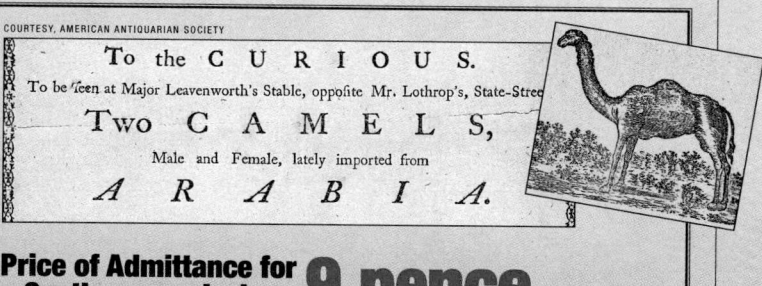

COURTESY, AMERICAN ANTIQUARIAN SOCIETY

To the CURIOUS.
To be seen at Major Leavenworth's Stable, opposite Mr. Lothrop's, State-Street
Two CAMELS,
Male and Female, lately imported from
ARABIA.

Price of Admittance for a Gentleman or Lady **9 pence**

CLOSE

Discuss the events of April 19, 1775 with students. Ask: Why were the colonists prepared for the British at Lexington? What was the intended outcome of the British march to Concord?

Oral History

Student Survey Have students conduct brief interviews with families and friends to find out what people know about the Revolutionary War. As a class or in small groups, students can prepare a set of questions to ask; for example:

When did the war take place? Who were some people who played a major role in the war? What happened on April 19, 1775? Challenge students to report their results in a way that shows any patterns that they find.

PORTFOLIO PROJECT

FOCUS

Section Objectives

1. Describe the steps the Second Continental Congress took to prepare for war with Britain.

2. Explain the strategies used by George Washington to help win the war.

3. Describe ways that the Revolutionary War changed the lives of the colonists on the battlefield and at home.

Bellringer Activity

While taking attendance at the beginning of the class period, display **Section Focus Transparency 8,** and have students answer the questions. (Or use the blackline master.)

VISUAL INSTRUCTION

A Rallying Cry for Independence In 1776 Paine served as a soldier in the war.

Ask: How did *Common Sense* help to unify the colonists? *(Its logical arguments delivered in plain language convinced many to rise up against British rule.)*

War for Independence

MAY 1775: SECOND CONTINENTAL CONGRESS MEETS

BETTMANN ARCHIVES

A Rallying Cry for Independence
Paine's *Common Sense* was the most widely circulated pamphlet in America in 1776.

ON MAY 10, 1775, THREE WEEKS AFTER THE BRITISH SPILLED COLONISTS' BLOOD AT THE BATTLES OF LEXINGTON AND CONCORD, THE DELEGATES OF THE SECOND CONTINENTAL CONGRESS ASSEMBLED IN PHILADELPHIA. They faced the challenge of leading thirteen colonies against the greatest empire and strongest army on earth. The Congress attempted to deal with that awesome task in two ways. First, the delegates called for the formation of a Continental Army of 20,000 men. Second, the delegates attempted to resolve the crisis with Britain. They sent King George III a petition blaming Parliament for the current problems and asking for the King's help in solving them. In December 1775, King George rejected the petition, declared the colonies in rebellion, and sent about 20,000 more British soldiers to America.

One month later, in January 1776, colonists began reading a pamphlet that helped motivate and prepare them for independence. *Common Sense* appeared first in Philadelphia where its author, Thomas Paine, lived. Paine grew up in England and for a time worked as a tax collector. After meeting Benjamin Franklin, then the most famous American alive, Paine decided to move to Philadelphia in 1774 and soon became involved in the colonists' fight for independence.

Unlike other revolutionary writers, Paine wrote in the direct, colorful language of America's farmers and city workers. Paine called King George "the Royal Brute of Britain," and asserted that "a government of our own is our own national right." In 3 months, people purchased about 120,000 copies of *Common Sense*. Paine's arguments persuaded many Americans to join the cause.

AS YOU READ

Vocabulary
▶ revolution
▶ suffrage

Think About . . .
▶ how the Second Continental Congress prepared for war with Britain.
▶ how the strategies used by George Washington helped win the war.

▶ the ways that the Revolutionary War affected the lives of the colonists on the battlefield and at home.

Section 2 Resources

REPRODUCIBLE RESOURCES

📂 Lesson Plan 3-2
📂 Vocabulary and Guided Reading Activity 3-2
📂 Section 2 Quiz
📂 Unit 1 American Literature Reading
📂 Skill Reinforcement Activity 3

MULTIMEDIA RESOURCES

🖼 Section Focus Transparency 8
🌐 A Geographic Perspective on American History
🎧 American Music: Cultural Traditions
💻 Testmaker
🎧 Chapter 3 Digest Audiocassette
💻 Student Self-Test: A Software Review

Declaring Independence

Planning the Revolution

Congress felt this popular push for independence. When it met in Philadelphia in June 1776, the Congress formed a committee to draft a declaration of the colonies' independence. The committee called on 33-year-old Thomas Jefferson, a lawyer from Virginia, to write it. He reluctantly agreed.

The tall, redheaded Jefferson owned a large plantation, and in the leisure hours of a planter's life, he pursued a variety of interests: law, architecture, music, science, and politics. The document this cultured lawyer created consisted of 3 parts. The first part contained a statement of what the Congress believed a government should do. "All men are created equal," Jefferson wrote, ". . . they are endowed by their Creator with certain unalienable Rights; . . . among these are Life, Liberty, and the pursuit of Happiness." Jefferson stated that governments existed to "secure these rights." The second part contained 27 "reasons for separation" from Britain, and the third part consisted of a declaration of independence from Britain.

Congress discussed the declaration for several days before voting unanimously for independence on July 2, 1776. On July 4 the delegates adopted the Declaration of Independence. Congress now turned to the business of steering the new nation, the United States of America, through a **revolution,** a violent struggle to overthrow a government.

Winning the War

Congress had made its most important decision about the war a year earlier when it called for a commander for the Continental Army. John Adams worried that the war would remain New England's war unless a Southerner took command. A Southern commander, reasoned Adams, would bring the whole nation—North, Middle, and South—into the war together.

Adams had in mind for the job a Virginian named George Washington. Washington had fought in the French and Indian War, where he had been an able soldier and leader. Delegates to the Congress approved of the aloof 43-year-old Virginian as the commander of their army. Washington had the qualities they admired in themselves and others: rank, wealth, and integrity.

Washington also had the discipline needed to turn a mass of poorly equipped, poorly trained men into an army that could survive the predicted long years of fighting. During the six years of the war, Washington's army received little support from the Congress or the states, which bickered throughout. Still, Washington managed to maintain order through defeat, freezing winters, and starvation.

REVOLUTIONARY WAR BATTLES, 1775–1781

Compare the number of British and American victories between 1775 and 1781. *Prior to 1777 in what region of the country did most battles occur?*

MAP STUDY

Britain's campaign against the South began in December 1778 with the capture of Savannah, Georgia—a major port. Within a few months, the British were using Georgia as an entry point to the rest of the South.

Answer: *in the North*

NATIONAL GEOGRAPHIC SOCIETY

Videodisc

GTV: A Geographic Perspective on American History

Side 1, Chapter 17
Title: The American Revolution
Subject: The impact of geography and aid from France on the American Revolution
Ask: How did France aid the colonies? *(with money and troops)*

TEACH

Guided Practice

L2 Discussion Loyalists were those who continued to support British control in the colonies. Discuss the possible reasons for such support. *(economic ties to Britain, fear of joining the battle against such a formidable power)*

Cooperative Learning

Revolutionary War Figures Ask small groups of students to research and report on any American prominent in the Revolutionary War. Have them gather facts on the individual's background, characteristics, and specific contributions during the war. Subjects may include American military leaders such as Ethan Allen, Benedict Arnold, Nathanael Greene, George R. Clark, Nathan Hale, John Paul Jones, Henry Knox, or Francis Marion. Other students may choose to focus on civilian leaders such as Samuel Adams, Patrick Henry, or Robert Morris. Encourage the use of visuals and have the groups of students give oral presentations of their reports to the class.

Independent Practice

L3 **Research** Ask students to select one major battle of the Revolutionary War to research in more depth. Have them present their findings to the class in an oral report.

 Have students complete the Chapter 3, Section 2 Vocabulary and Guided Reading Activity. (Also in Spanish.) **LEP**

VISUAL INSTRUCTION

Portrait of a General The artist shows Washington in an easy, informal pose. Following a change in the military uniform code, Peale painted out the blue ribbon that had been worn across the breast.

Answer: *The British did not want to continue fighting and could not afford to.*

Global Connection

France decided to aid the colonists partly because they had lost the French and Indian War to the British. They also wanted to weaken the might of Britain's empire.

CHART STUDY

Ask: Where did the British finally surrender?
Answer: *Yorktown*

Portrait of a General This oil painting, *George Washington at the Battle of Princeton,* was done by Charles Willson Peale.
Why did the British finally surrender in 1781?

victory boosted the Americans' spirits and persuaded the French to enter the war to fight against their British rivals. After Saratoga, the British focused their energies in the South, where they hoped the region's many Loyalists, those who supported the British, might help them.

Washington learned valuable lessons during the first years of the war. The Americans, he knew, must avoid major battles with the better-trained British troops. They had to learn to use surprise tactics and familiar terrain to their advantage. If the Americans could not defeat the British in open combat, at least they could drag the war on until the British no longer cared to fight. This strategy paid off when Washington, supported by French troops and the French navy, trapped a large British force at Chesapeake Bay in Yorktown, Virginia, in 1781. The British surrendered at Yorktown; it became clear that after six years and no conclusive victories, the British no longer cared to fight, nor could they afford to.

The war finally ended in 1783, when Congress sent John Adams, Benjamin Franklin, and John Jay to negotiate a peace treaty with Britain. In the treaty, the British promised to remove their troops from America "with all convenient speed," to recognize officially the independence of the United States of America, and to agree that the Mississippi River was the nation's western border.

Surviving the War
Victory Through Sacrifice

More than 250,000 American soldiers fought for 6 years to break the back of British rule. During that time 1 out of every 10 Americans who fought died; the British captured and occupied most major cities, including Boston, New York, and Philadelphia; and many American lives were reshaped by the American Revolution.

When America mobilized for war in 1775 and 1776, all levels of society became involved. Elite politicians

In the first years of the war, the British aimed to divide the rebellious colonies, cutting New England off from the rest of the nation. Only a surprise American victory at Saratoga, New York, in 1777 foiled their plan. The

REVOLUTIONARY WAR ERA, 1775–1783

APRIL 1775 The British and Americans fight at Lexington and Concord.

JULY 1776 The Continental Congress adopts the Declaration of Independence.

OCTOBER 1777 The Americans defeat the British at Saratoga.

OCTOBER 1781 The British surrender at Yorktown.

1775 | 1776 | 1777 | 1778 | 1779 | 1780 | 1781 | 1782 | 1783

MARCH 1776 The British evacuate Boston.

SEPTEMBER 1777 The British occupy Philadelphia.

FEBRUARY 1778 France enters the war on the American side.

JUNE 1778 The British evacuate Philadelphia.

SEPTEMBER 1783 The United States and Great Britain sign the final peace treaty in Paris.

Meeting Special Needs

Visual Learners To help students who learn visually, have them trace the progress of the Revolutionary War in detail using the dates on the map on page 67.

You might prepare a short list of questions about the war that students can answer using the map. Ask the questions and have the students consult the map for answers.

designed state and national governments. Men with military experience volunteered for army positions. Some merchants loaned money to the army and to the Congress; others made fortunes from wartime government contracts. Farmers tried to provide food for armies.

On the Battlefield

These many groups contributed to the war effort, but the poorest Americans did most of the actual fighting. Young city laborers, farm boys, indentured servants, and sometimes enslaved persons all fought bravely. A lack of money, food, and supplies made the usual wartime experiences—boredom, disease, bloodshed—worse for the soldiers in the Continental Army. In 1778 one young American gave this nightmarish description of a soldier's life: "Poor food, hard lodging, cold weather, fatigue, nasty clothes, nasty cookery."

Only the horror of battle relieved boredom. Ranks of soldiers standing in open fields fired their muskets once, reloaded, and fired again. Orderly troop movements soon broke down into hand-to-hand combat; soldiers inflicted many wounds with bayonets and knives. Mud, smoke, blood, curses, and cannon shot flew about the battlefield. Medical treatment barely existed on or off the battlefield, and most wounds were fatal.

African Americans also stood and fell on the battlefields of the Revolutionary War. One enslaved laborer named Jehu Grant escaped from his master and joined the colonists when he "saw liberty poles and people all engaged for the purpose of freedom." Yet only about 5,000 of the 500,000 African Americans living in the colonies served in the Continental Army during the war. Many more sided with the British, who promised them freedom if they fought. As many as 20,000 enslaved persons in the Carolinas and Georgia joined the British.

Many Native Americans also sided with the British. The British represented a last hope for keeping land-hungry Americans out of Native American territories. During the war, colonists fought Native Americans in bloody battles, creating long-lasting bitter feelings.

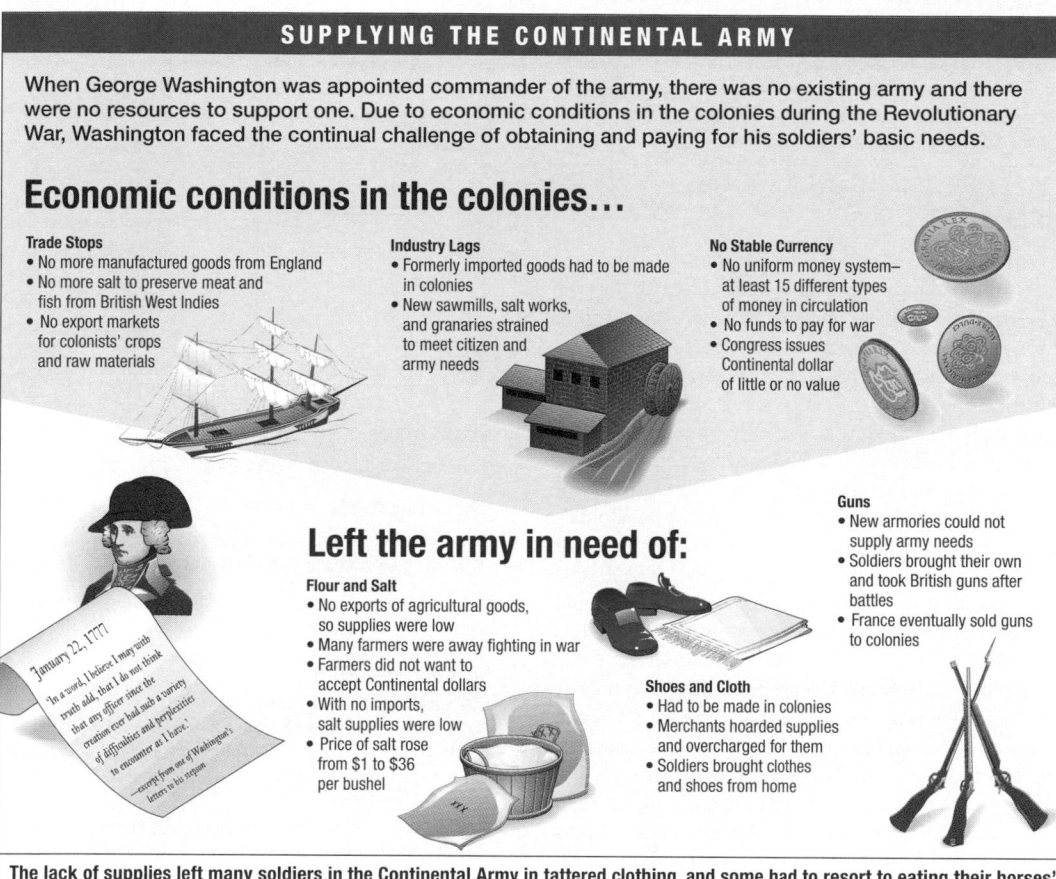

SUPPLYING THE CONTINENTAL ARMY

When George Washington was appointed commander of the army, there was no existing army and there were no resources to support one. Due to economic conditions in the colonies during the Revolutionary War, Washington faced the continual challenge of obtaining and paying for his soldiers' basic needs.

Economic conditions in the colonies...

Trade Stops
• No more manufactured goods from England
• No more salt to preserve meat and fish from British West Indies
• No export markets for colonists' crops and raw materials

Industry Lags
• Formerly imported goods had to be made in colonies
• New sawmills, salt works, and granaries strained to meet citizen and army needs

No Stable Currency
• No uniform money system—at least 15 different types of money in circulation
• No funds to pay for war
• Congress issues Continental dollar of little or no value

Left the army in need of:

Flour and Salt
• No exports of agricultural goods, so supplies were low
• Many farmers were away fighting in war
• Farmers did not want to accept Continental dollars
• With no imports, salt supplies were low
• Price of salt rose from $1 to $36 per bushel

Shoes and Cloth
• Had to be made in colonies
• Merchants hoarded supplies and overcharged for them
• Soldiers brought clothes and shoes from home

Guns
• New armories could not supply army needs
• Soldiers brought their own and took British guns after battles
• France eventually sold guns to colonies

The lack of supplies left many soldiers in the Continental Army in tattered clothing, and some had to resort to eating their horses' food. *What were the three major economic problems in the colonies that caused these conditions?*

Portfolio Project

A Revolutionary War Diary Ask students to use the facts presented in the section as well as additional information found in other school resources to create a Revolutionary War diary entry for one day during the war. They may write their entries from the perspective of a merchant, a farmer, a woman left behind on the home front, or a soldier. Have them place their diary entries in their portfolios.

History and the Humanities

∩ American Music: Cultural Traditions— "British Grenadiers" by the American Fife Ensemble

CHART STUDY

The high cost of waging the Revolutionary War left Congress and the thirteen colonies deeply in debt. In 1788 a new United States Constitution gave Congress the power to tax, but it was not until the early 1800s that most of the war debt was paid.

Answer: *lack of trade, lag in industry, and lack of stable currency*

ASSESS

Meeting Lesson Objectives

Each section objective is tested by the section review question(s) that follows it in parentheses.

1. Describe the steps the Second Continental Congress took to prepare for war with Britain. (1, 2, 4)

2. Explain the strategies used by George Washington to help win the war. (3)

3. Describe ways that the Revolutionary War changed the lives of the colonists on the battlefield and at home. (5)

Evaluate

Have students complete the Section Review.

☞ ▣ Assign the Section 2 Quiz or use the Testmaker to develop a customized quiz. (Also in Spanish.) **LEP**

Reteach

⌒ Have students listen to the Chapter 3, Section 2 Audiocassette. (Also in Spanish.) **LEP**

Enrich

☞ Have students complete the Unit 1 American Literature Reading.

VISUAL INSTRUCTION

Home Front Tactics In wartime throughout history, people have destroyed their possessions rather than allow an enemy to benefit from them.

Answer: *Women managed farms and businesses, worked outside the home as cooks and nurses, and began to express their thoughts on politics.*

CLOSE

Ask: How did the colonists defeat Britain? *(The colonists had Washington as general and the help of the French; they used surprise tactics; they had the advantage of fighting on familiar terrain; and the long duration of the war wore down the British.)* What were the effects of the war? *(There was a new national government; economic conditions worsened; and women took on new roles.)*

Home Front Tactics Artist Emanuel Leutze portrayed the plight of many American colonists during the Revolutionary War in this 1852 painting, *Mrs. Schuyler Burning Her Wheat Fields on the Approach of the British.* *In what other ways did the Revolutionary War change the lives of women?*

At Home

After the war, many soldiers returned to homes that the deaths of fathers, brothers, and sons had forever changed. Families were changed in other ways as well. Wives had managed farms and businesses while husbands served in the army. Other women had traveled with the army, working as cooks and nurses. These experiences gave satisfaction to many women who had never owned property nor had **suffrage,** the right to vote. Women began to express their thoughts more freely on such subjects as politics. As Philadelphia's Anne Emlen wrote to her husband in 1777, "How shall I impose a silence upon myself when the subject is so very interesting, so much engrossing conversation—and what every member of the community is more or less concerned in?"

Women actively and openly participating in politics was a new phenomenon. In less than 20 years American society had changed in unpredictable and lasting ways. A group of colonies had challenged their governing country, fought the best army in the world, and won the right to be self-governing states. As the war ended, many Americans openly wondered how their experiment in self-government would eventually turn out. "The answer to the question," said Thomas Paine, "can America be happy under a government of her own, is short and simple—as happy as she pleases; she hath a blank sheet to write upon."

S E C T I O N   R E V I E W

Vocabulary

1. Define: revolution, suffrage.

Checking Facts

2. What did the Second Continental Congress do to prepare for war with Britain?

3. What battle tactics did George Washington employ with success against the British?

Critical Thinking

Identifying Alternatives

4. What alternatives did the colonists have to fighting the British in the Revolutionary War?

Linking Across Time

5. Explain similarities and differences between the effects of war on the colonists and the effects of war on people today.

Section 2 Review Answers

1. revolution (67), **suffrage** (70)
2. The Congress formed the Continental Army and named George Washington as its leader, tried unsuccessfully to get King George to resolve problems, and adopted the Declaration of Independence.
3. He used surprise tactics and took advantage of terrain familiar to the colonists.

4. They would have had to continue paying taxes to Britain and living under British rule.
5. Students may answer that many of the effects of war such as death and loss of property are the same today, but they are on a larger scale due to more destructive weapons.

Study and Writing Skill

INTERPRETING A PRIMARY SOURCE

Learning the Skill

A primary source is direct evidence of an event, idea, or development. It is obtained firsthand, such as oral or written accounts from actual participants. Examples of such primary sources are official documents, speeches, diaries, autobiographies, and letters. A primary source may also consist of physical objects, such as tools or weapons, or visual evidence such as paintings, photographs, maps, or videotapes.

In contrast with a primary source, a secondary source is a written, oral, or visual account created after an event, usually produced using information from primary sources. Textbooks and biographies are examples of secondary sources.

Interpreting primary sources is a skill you can practice. One primary source to examine is the Declaration of Independence on pages 61–63. As you continue to read *American Odyssey,* you will encounter other primary source documents and speeches. Primary sources help to present a reliable and accurate picture of history. The ability to interpret a primary source allows you to make your own judgment about a historical event, one not based on secondhand interpretations.

Interpreting a Primary Source

To interpret a primary source, use the following steps:

a. Examine the origins of the document or material to determine if it is a primary source.

b. Read the document and summarize the main ideas in your own words.

c. Read through it again, this time looking for details that support the main ideas.

d. Give an interpretation of the material in your own words.

To round out your interpretation, try putting the document or material within the context of what you know about history. It may be necessary to look at the person or people who created the source, to examine why it was created, or to explore the motive behind it. Sometimes, just looking at the title can give you insights.

> *I* long to hear that you have declared independence. And by the way, in the new code of laws that I suppose you will make, I wish you would remember the ladies and be more generous and favorable to them than your ancestors. Do not put such unlimited power in the hands of husbands. Remember, all men would be tyrants if they could. If particular care and attention is not paid to the ladies, we are determined to stir up a rebellion and will not regard ourselves as bound by any laws in which we have had no voice or representation.

A Wife's Request This excerpt is from a letter Abigail Adams wrote to her husband when the Second Continental Congress was considering the Declaration of Independence. *What do her words suggest about her character?*

Practicing the Skill

Read the passage from the Declaration of Independence and answer the questions that follow.

We hold these truths to be self-evident: that all men are created equal, that they are endowed by their Creator with certain unalienable rights; that among these are life, liberty, and the pursuit of happiness.

1. How do you know that the Declaration of Independence is a primary source?

2. What is the main idea of the passage?

3. What are the details?

4. What do you know about the writers of the Declaration of Independence?

5. Explain what you think this passage means.

Applying the Skill

Read the passage from the letter above, and give your interpretation of it as a primary source.

Additional Practice

For additional practice, see Reinforcing Skills on page 77.

STUDY AND WRITING SKILL **71**

TEACH

Students have the opportunity to contrast primary and secondary sources and to practice interpreting primary sources. Primary sources provide a valuable source of insights into past events. Suggest that students deepen their understanding of history by examining and contrasting several primary sources dealing with a given event. Remind them that secondary sources are also valuable, in part because the authors often have a knowledge of subsequent events that was unavailable to those who created the primary sources.

Additional Practice

☞ Have students complete the Chapter 3 Skill Reinforcement Activity.

Practicing the Skill Answers

1. because it is an official document of the United States

2. All people are equal, and every person has rights that cannot be taken away.

3. people's inalienable rights include the rights to life, freedom, and the search for happiness

4. The writers were representatives of the thirteen colonies and met in Philadelphia in June 1776. They asked Thomas Jefferson to draft a declaration of independence, and they voted to adopt it on July 4, 1776.

5. Answers will vary, but students should stress that all individuals have basic rights that no individuals or governments can take away.

SECTION

3

FOCUS

Section Objectives

1. Explain how the state constitutions differed from the British colonial charters.
2. Describe the major differences between the state constitutions of Virginia, Massachusetts, and Pennsylvania.
3. Explain how the lives of women and enslaved African Americans changed in the Revolutionary War era.

Bellringer Activity

While taking attendance at the beginning of the class period, display **Section Focus Transparency 9,** and have students answer the questions. (Or use the blackline master.)

TEACH

Guided Practice

L2 **Discussion** Ask students which of the three featured states they would have preferred to live in and why, based on each state's constitution.

VISUAL INSTRUCTION

A Leader of the Revolutionary Era John Adams was the first President to live in the White House and the only Chief Executive whose son also became President.

Ask: What did Adams urge the Congress to do in 1776? *(He urged Congress to recommend that each colony create its own new state government.)*

Creating a New America

MAY 10, 1776: CONGRESS RECOMMENDS FORMING STATE GOVERNMENTS

ON APRIL 22, 1776, JOHN ADAMS WROTE TO HIS FRIEND, JAMES WARREN, ABOUT THE REVOLUTION THAT HAD JUST BEGUN. Adams wrote that South Carolina had already adopted a constitution:

> The news from South Carolina has aroused and animated all the continent. It has spread a visible joy, and if North Carolina and Virginia should follow the example, it will spread through the rest of the colonies like electric fire.
> —John Adams, from a letter to James Warren

**A Leader of the Revolutionary Era
John Adams served as the second President of the United States from 1797 to 1801.**

At Adams's urging, the Congress officially recommended that each colony "adopt such a government as shall, in the opinion of the representatives of the people, best conduce to the happiness and safety of their constituents in particular, and America in general."

For the colonies, forming new governments was anything but a luxury. In colony after colony, royal colonial governments had collapsed at the onset of the war. After dissolving the colonial assemblies that had so boldly challenged royal authority, the British governors had escaped as best they could. Wartime responsibilities dictated the need for governmental authority to muster troops, collect money, and protect the public safety. Now the colonies hastily embarked on the daunting task of creating their own governments.

The idea that ordinary citizens could plan their own governments, draft written constitutions, and vote their approval of self-government represented something new in history, and Americans knew it. Crafting individual state constitutions also provided a rehearsal for the process of creating the national constitution during the decade that followed.

AS YOU READ

Vocabulary
► constitution
► abolition
► status quo
► coverture

Think About . . .
► how the state constitutions differed from colonial charters under British rule.
► the differences between the state constitutions of Virginia, Massachusetts, and Pennsylvania.

► how the lives of women and enslaved African Americans changed in the Revolutionary War era.

---

72 CHAPTER 3 THE AMERICAN REVOLUTION

Section 3 Resources

REPRODUCIBLE RESOURCES
📋 Lesson Plan 3-3
📋 Section 3 Quiz
📋 Vocabulary and Guided Reading Activity 3-3
📋 Chapter 3 Test

📋 Performance Assessment Activity 3
📋 Reteaching Activity 3
📋 Enrichment Activity 3

MULTIMEDIA RESOURCES
🔊 Section Focus Transparency 9
🖼 Focus on American Fine Art Prints, Print 6
🎧 American Music: Cultural Traditions
💻 Testmaker
🎧 Chapter 3 Digest Audiocassette
💻 Vocabulary PuzzleMaker
💻 Student Self-Test: A Software Review

State Constitutions
A Variety of Democratic Documents

The British system on which colonists based their ideas of government did not reside in a **constitution,** one written document of a plan of government, but rather in a miscellaneous collection of laws and court cases that had developed over centuries. In contrast, American colonial leaders planned that state constitutions, and eventually the national constitution, would be documents written clearly, concisely, and specifically so that anyone who read a copy could understand the law.

Thomas Jefferson realized that the colonies could win the war for independence but lose the Revolution if they failed at these experiments in self-government: "In truth," he said, "self-government is the whole object of the present controversy." During the tumultuous war for independence, each state drafted a constitution that established self-government.

Virtually every state limited voting and government service to white male property holders. Still, most of the new constitutions established state governments that were more democratic than the colonial regimes they replaced. In place of governors appointed by a king, state executives now had to face elections. Furthermore, elected governors would wield less power than had their appointed predecessors, giving greater power to popularly elected assemblies. These assemblies in turn grew larger as farmers and artisans clamored to be represented.

Connecticut and Rhode Island merely adopted their colonial charters, carefully deleting all references to the British Crown. The other 11 states, awed by the opportunity before them, began afresh. In 1776 alone, 8 states crafted new constitutions. By 1780, all 13 states had adopted written constitutions.

Virginia's Conservative Constitution

In several states, conservatives drew up plans for governments that closely resembled the colonial regimes they replaced. For example, the Virginia constitution of 1776, drafted by Thomas Jefferson, preserved intact almost all of the institutions of the colonial era, including slavery. Though Jefferson had inserted a section in the constitution's first draft proposing **abolition,** an end to the practice of slavery, his attempt failed to win approval. Virginia's governor, now elected annually by the legislature and denied the power of the veto, held a somewhat weaker position than before the Revolution. On the other hand, Virginia's new House of Delegates looked nearly identical to its old House of Burgesses. The continuation of prewar property qualifications for voters as well as for officeholders ensured that wealthy landowners would still represent Virginians. Members of many of the same families who had served before the war continued to hold elected office after the war.

If its constitution maintained the **status quo,** or existing conditions, Virginia's Bill of Rights established a bold new tradition. This document, written by George Mason, enumerated rights, such as a jury trial and freedom of the press, that free citizens could expect from their representative governments. The Virginia Bill of Rights prompted other states to include similar documents in their constitutions. It also provided a model for the Bill of Rights that eventually crowned the national Constitution of 1787.

A Radical Document for Pennsylvania

Compared to the conservative Virginians, the liberals who wrote constitutions in other states sought to redistribute power more equitably. Vermont, Georgia, and Pennsylvania—a state that bordered Virginia—crafted the most liberal documents of all.

Pennsylvania, for example, cast off the British model of a balanced government consisting of two legislative houses and an executive, the governor. In the vacuum created by the departure of colonial leaders, the radical politicians who wrote Pennsylvania's constitution established a single legislative house. Its members would be elected each year and its debates would be open to the public. Going even further, the document also abolished the requirement that persons holding public

CULVER PICTURES

The Artisan Spirit Many hardworking blacksmiths and other artisans looked forward to better representation in state government after the Revolution. *How could they participate?*

Independent Practice

L2 **Bill of Rights** Some of the students may wish to research and write a report on state bills of rights and their authors and on how the Virginia bill of rights (and other such bills) later influenced the national Bill of Rights.

 Have students complete the Chapter 3, Section 3 Vocabulary and Guided Reading Activity. (Also in Spanish.) **LEP**

History and the Humanities

American Music: Cultural Traditions— "Kittery" by the Old Sturbridge Singers; "Tunes from Colonial America and The President's March" by E. Power Biggs.

Focus on American Fine Art Prints, Print 6— *The Staircase Group* by Charles Willson Peale.

VISUAL INSTRUCTION

The Artisan Spirit Silversmiths, blacksmiths, shoemakers, cabinetmakers, carpenters, coopers (barrel makers), and tailors were all artisans or mechanics, as they were called in the 1700s.

Answer: *Artisans helped elect representatives to the state assemblies.*

Cooperative Learning

A Constitutional Convention Have students form three groups and designate each group as politicians from the state of Virginia, Pennsylvania, or Massachusetts during the time the politicians wrote their states' constitutions. Ask students to do research to supplement the information in the text, and encourage them to assume the roles of specific historic personalities. Have each group act out the process of drafting the state constitution for its assigned state.

ASSESS

Meeting Lesson Objectives

Each section objective is tested by the section review question(s) that follows it in parentheses.

1. Explain how the state constitutions differed from the British colonial charters. (1, 2, 3)
2. Describe the major differences between the state constitutions of Virginia, Massachusetts, and Pennsylvania. (1, 4)
3. Explain how the lives of women and enslaved African Americans changed in the Revolutionary War era. (5)

VISUAL INSTRUCTION

Abigail Adams Mother of five children, she managed the family farm in Massachusetts while John Adams served in the Continental Congress.

Answer: *that she was a strong proponent of women's rights*

Evaluate

Have students complete the Section Review.

☞ 🖉 Assign the Section 3 Quiz or use the Testmaker to develop a customized quiz. (Also in Spanish.) **LEP**

☞ 🖉 Assign the Chapter 3 Test or use the Testmaker to develop a customized test.

☞ Have students complete the Chapter 3 Performance Assessment Activity.

74

office be property owners and opened the vote to any white male adult who paid taxes. The preamble that began the constitution clearly predicted the end of African slavery with its suggestion that government should "provide for future improvements, without partiality for or prejudice against any particular class, sect, or denomination of men whatever."

Even in liberal Pennsylvania, however, the long list of residents denied the vote included servants, dependent sons, the poor, Native Americans, and women. In only one state, for a brief period, did women get the vote. New Jersey's 1776 constitution granted suffrage to "all free inhabitants" who met property and residency requirements. Property-owning New Jersey women took advantage of their voting rights until their state reversed that ruling in 1807.

Constitutional Convention in Massachusetts

Like Virginia's conservative constitution and unlike Pennsylvania's liberal one, the Massachusetts document divided political power between a governor and two legislative houses. One house, the assembly, would represent the common people. Because the other house, the senate, would look after propertied interests, its members were required to own three times as much property as assemblymen. Constitutional architect John Adams defended this balance of power, saying, "power must be opposed to power, force to force . . . interest to interest . . . and passion to passion."

However conservative its constitution, Massachusetts took a radical new path to writing the document. Opposed to letting the existing legislature write the constitution, as most states had done, a Concord town meeting in October 1776 resolved that "a Constitution alterable by the Supreme Legislation is no security at all." To prevent the abuses that might follow if the legislature drafted the constitution by which it would rule, Concord suggested the novel idea of electing a special convention to do the job and requiring voters to approve the constitution. In 1780 the eligible voters of Massachusetts voted their approval of the document.

The preamble to Massachusetts's constitution read, "All men are born free and equal." Enslaved African men and women as well as white women began to wonder for how long these lofty words would exclude them.

Abigail Adams During the war her letters provided her husband with information about the British in Boston. *What else did her letters to her husband reveal?*

Focus on Reforms
Expanding the Ideas of Liberty

The Revolutionary era fostered a climate of unprecedented political interest; the number of voters casting ballots doubled. A profusion of pamphlets and broadsides offered ordinary citizens instant access to Revolutionary affairs as well as exhortations about domestic matters. In his pamphlet *Common Sense,* Thomas Paine said, "We have it in our power to begin the world over again. The birthday of a new world is at hand." With a sense of unprecedented hopefulness, Americans began to write on the "blank sheet" Thomas Paine had set forth.

Republican Women

White women in Revolutionary America claimed few personal or political rights. For example, under an article of British law called **coverture,** any property a woman inherited passed into her husband's control when she married. Not until the 1900s would most American women regain the vote they so fleetingly enjoyed in New Jersey between 1776 and 1807.

Despite their inferior status compared to that of white men, white women aided the Revolution as nurses, innkeepers, suppliers of food and clothing, fund-raisers, farmers, and even as spies. Nevertheless, only the mediation of their fathers, husbands, brothers, or sons allowed those women who longed to do so to participate in the political ferment of the time.

Abigail Adams's letters to her husband John reveal a keen interest in women's rights. She marveled at the persistence of women's patriotism despite their forced exclusion from the political process: "Deprived of a voice in Legislation, obliged to submit to those Laws which are imposed upon us, is it not sufficient to make us indifferent to the publick Welfare? Yet all History and every age exhibit Instances of patriotic virtue in the female Sex; which considering our situation equals the most Heroick." After assisting at the polls in 1780, she consoled herself that her participation counted for something: "If I cannot be a voter upon this occasion, I will be a writer of votes. I can do some thing in that way."

Meeting Special Needs

Reading Disability To help students with reading disabilities, have them preview the section and create an outline of it using the heads and subheads. After they have finished reading, ask them to use their outlines and fill in important facts under each main head as they read.

Like Abigail Adams, Esther De Berdt Reed felt keenly that women should contribute to the Revolution. In a broadside published in 1780, she wrote, "If opinion and manners did not forbid us to march to glory on the same paths as the Men, we should at least equal, and sometimes surpass them in our love for the public good." Reed helped organize the women of Philadelphia to collect funds for Washington's troops. The women refused George Washington's suggestion that their $300,000 contribution be deposited into the Bank of the United States to be united "with the gentlemen." Instead, they used their money to buy linen shirts so the soldier recipients would recognize that women had sent the gifts.

During the Revolution, the idea took hold that mothers could play a crucial role in educating their sons toward a lifetime of civic participation. This notion of the "Republican mother" expanded the limited domain in which women had lived and gave a rationale for increasing their participation in political life. Many Republican mothers also began to insist on a better education for themselves and their daughters.

COURTESY, THE HENRY FRANCIS DU PONT WINTERTHUR MUSEUM

Dr. Benjamin Rush This influential physician was a member of the Continental Congress and signed the Declaration of Independence. *What did he do to fight slavery?*

Trying to End Slavery

While white Americans waged a revolution to gain liberty from the tyranny of Britain, some enslaved Africans viewed fighting on the British side as their own best chance to grasp liberty from the tyranny of slavery. In Virginia, Lord Dunmore's 1775 proclamation offering freedom to Virginia's enslaved persons and servants "able and willing to bear arms" attracted more than 500 eager African Americans. The first volunteers formed a regiment of African American soldiers wearing chest sashes that proclaimed, "Liberty to Slaves!" As many as 20 percent of African Americans may have crossed behind British lines to struggle for their own freedom. Only a few thousand African Americans fought on the American side during the Revolution because the Americans did not promise them release from slavery.

If the Revolution did not end slavery, it did deal the institution a powerful blow. For one thing, the importation of enslaved persons almost stopped during the war. Though importation resumed briefly afterwards, 11 of the 13 states had outlawed it by 1790.

In addition, the Revolution brought the very institution of slavery under increased attack. In the South, the legislatures of Virginia and Maryland made it easier for slaveholders to free enslaved persons. A rapid increase in the population of freed African Americans fed expanding free African American communities in cities such as Richmond and Baltimore.

In the North, where enslaved persons made up a much smaller percentage of the population, the Revolution prompted states either to abolish slavery outright or to weaken it. In 1773, Dr. Benjamin Rush, the physician and Pennsylvania leader who helped found America's first antislavery society, said, "The plant of liberty is of so tender a Nature, that it cannot thrive long in the neighborhood of slavery." In 1779 Pennsylvania legislated that all children born to enslaved women should be freed at age 21 if female and age 28 if male. Even such cautious steps demonstrated the North's understanding that human slavery could never be reconciled with the ideals of the Revolution.

SECTION REVIEW

Vocabulary

1. Define: constitution, abolition, status quo, coverture.

Checking Facts

2. How did the American colonial leaders plan that state constitutions would differ from British colonial charters?

3. In what ways were state governments more democratic than British colonial regimes?

Critical Thinking

Making Comparisons

4. What were the major differences between the state constitutions of Virginia, Massachusetts, and Pennsylvania?

Linking Across Time

5. Describe at least two negative conditions relating to women and African Americans during the Revolutionary era that do not exist today.

Reteach

🎧 Have students listen to the Chapter 3, Section 3 Audiocassette. (Also in Spanish.) **LEP**

📁 Have students complete the Chapter 3 Reteaching Activity. (Also in Spanish.) **LEP**

Enrich

📁 Have students complete the Chapter 3 Enrichment Activity. (Also in Spanish.) **LEP**

VISUAL INSTRUCTION

Dr. Benjamin Rush In addition to his work with abolition, Rush promoted societal reforms in education. He recommended the establishment of free public schools and encouraged greater education for women.

Answer: *He founded America's first antislavery society in Pennsylvania.*

CLOSE

Ask: Do you think the status of women and free and enslaved African Americans changed much during the Revolutionary era? *(Students may answer that although the lives of women and African Americans did not change dramatically, at least they began to question their restrictions more seriously as a result of the spirit of the Revolution.)*

Section 3 Review Answers

1. constitution (73), **abolition** (73), **status quo** (73), **coverture** (74)

2. They were to be written as single, clearly written documents that could be understood by all.

3. State executives had to be elected rather than appointed and the governors' power would be limited by popularly elected assemblies.

4. Virginia's was conservative, but its Bill of Rights was innovative; Massachusetts's was moderate and written by a special constitutional convention; Pennsylvania's was liberal, with a single, elected legislative house.

5. Negative conditions included slavery and the exclusion of African Americans and women from voting.

Reviewing Key Terms

1. external tax
2. constitution
3. revolution
4. treason
5. internal tax

Recalling Facts

1. Sugar Act, Stamp Act; the acts helped convince colonists that they were not fairly represented.
2. people who helped to spread news and revolutionary ideas throughout the colonies; they helped to unite the North and the South, farmers and merchants in opposition to the British.
3. called for a halt in trade with Britain, resolved to meet again in the spring of 1775
4. Paine's widely circulated *Common Sense* helped convince colonists that "a government of our own is our own national right."
5. to set out the governmental principles supported by the colonists, list reasons for separating from Britain, and declare independence; Thomas Jefferson
6. to cut New England off from the rest of the nation; they focused their energies in the South, where they hoped Loyalists would support them
7. in New England; many revolutionaries lived there
8. so they could organize a new system of government with specific new laws that could be easily read and understood; white males who paid taxes or were property owners, except in New Jersey, where women could also vote
9. Massachusetts; it ensured that all people would have a voice in the formation of the government
10. New Jersey; they had to own property and live in New Jersey

Reviewing Key Terms

Choose the vocabulary word that best completes the sentences below. Write your answers on a separate sheet of paper.

internal tax	revolution
preamble	external tax
treason	constitution

1. Any goods that came into the colonies could be subject to an _____ .

2. Many colonists believed strongly in the idea of a _____ or written plan of government.

3. The Continental Congress heeded the push for independence and began the _____.

4. Colonists meeting to defy the British government could be considered to be committing _____.

5. To raise revenue, Parliament levied an _____ on goods made within the colonies.

Recalling Facts

1. Identify 2 major taxation acts imposed upon the colonies in the 1760s. How did these acts move some colonists to look more favorably upon the idea of self-government?

2. What were committees of correspondence? How did colonists use them to gain sympathy for the revolutionary cause?

3. What action was taken by the First Continental Congress?

4. Who was Thomas Paine and what did he write? How did his publications influence colonial attitudes toward seeking independence?

5. What was the purpose of the Declaration of Independence? Who wrote it?

6. What was the British strategy at the beginning of the war? How did that plan change in 1777?

7. In which region of the colonies were most of the early battles of the Revolution fought? Why might war have broken out there first?

8. Why did each colony create its own constitution? Which people were allowed to vote and participate in government service?

9. Which colony initiated the idea that the Constitution should be ratified by voters? Why was this voter ratification an important development?

10. In what colony were women allowed to vote between 1776 and

LIBRARY OF CONGRESS

Critical Thinking

1. External taxes regulated trade in goods that came into the colonies; internal taxes were levied on goods made in the colonies and were intended only to raise revenue. Supporters of this position might argue that internal taxes required representation; those opposed might argue that Britain ruled the colonies and could do as it pleased.
2. Students might answer that poor people hoped to gain some social or monetary benefit from the war, or that the rich could use their influence to avoid serving.
3. Answers might include the idea that women, too, helped to develop the nation and were influenced by ideas of independence and freedom.
4. People began to debate the idea of freedom and equality and to question their justifications for slavery.

1807? What requirements did these women have to meet to be eligible to vote?

Critical Thinking

1. Making Comparisons Compare external taxes and internal taxes. Were the colonists justified in protesting that Parliament had no right to levy internal taxes on them? Explain.

2. Making Generalizations Why do you think that the poorest Americans did most of the actual fighting in the Revolutionary War?

3. Drawing Conclusions The illustration on page 76 shows Nancy Hart defending her home against the Tories. How did the war encourage women to speak out and to assume new roles?

4. Making Inferences How did the ideals of freedom and independence that many colonists held during the Revolution help to change people's attitudes about slavery?

Portfolio Project

What do you think a good citizen is? Is it someone who follows the law? Or might it be someone who breaks the law in order to stand up for an ideal? Do you think that people like the Sons of Liberty acted as good citizens? Are there groups like the Sons of Liberty today? Do you think they are good citizens? Write a persuasive paper explaining your views.

Cooperative Learning

Work with a group of classmates to determine the positive and negative effects of the Revolutionary War. Who benefited from the war? Whose lives remained the same? Who experienced negative consequences? Consider European American men and women, African Americans, and Native Americans.

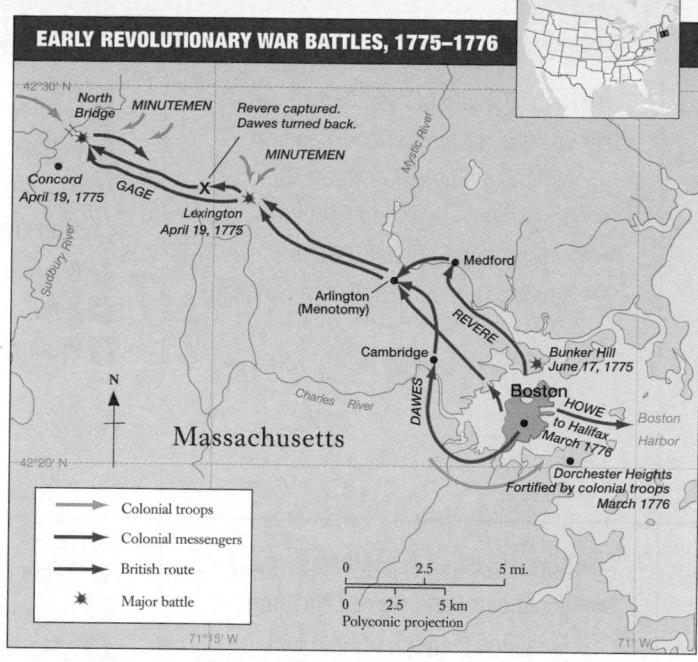

EARLY REVOLUTIONARY WAR BATTLES, 1775–1776

42°30' N

North Bridge

MINUTEMEN

Revere captured. Dawes turned back.

MINUTEMEN

Concord April 19, 1775

GAGE

X

Lexington April 19, 1775

Medford

Arlington (Menotomy)

REVERE

Cambridge

Bunker Hill June 17, 1775

Sudbury River

Mystic River

DAWES

Charles River

Boston

HOWE to Halifax March 1776

Boston Harbor

42°20' N

Massachusetts

Dorchester Heights Fortified by colonial troops March 1776

N

→ Colonial troops
→ Colonial messengers
→ British route
✶ Major battle

0   2.5   5 mi.
0   2.5   5 km
Polyconic projection

71°15' W

71° W

Discuss these issues and make a list of positive and negative consequences for each group. Share your group lists with your classmates.

Reinforcing Skills

Interpreting a Primary Source Read the quotation by Anne Emlen on page 70. How do you know that this is a primary source? In your own words, explain what Anne Emlen means in her statement.

Geography and History

Study the map on this page to answer the following questions:

1. How many major battles did the colonists and the British fight between April 1775 and the time when the British evacuated Boston?

2. Approximately how many miles did the British soldiers march from

Lexington to Concord on April 19, 1775?

3. Describe the route taken by William Dawes when he rode to warn the colonists that the British were on the march.

4. What town marks the western limit of British troop movements on April 19, 1775?

5. For how many months after the start of the war were the British able to keep possession of the city of Boston?

HISTORY JOURNAL

Look back at your journal response to page 54. Write what you learned about how the Revolutionary War changed people's lives. Do you think the changes were positive or negative?

Geography and History

1. three
2. 5 miles (8 km)
3. Dawes rode from Boston to Arlington, then on to Lexington. He turned back partway between Lexington and Concord.
4. Concord
5. about 11 months

History Journal

Student journals should include references to the ways in which the Revolutionary War changed people's lives.

? BONUS QUESTION

This question may be used for extra credit on the chapter test.
In what year did the Virginia legislature free James Armistead?
Answer: *1786*

Portfolio Project

Students' papers should be well organized and include factual and logical support for their position.

Cooperative Learning

Group lists should include factual support of positive and negative effects for each group of people included in their survey.

Reinforcing Skills

It is stated that Anne Emlen wrote the quotation in 1777, and the statement is surrounded by quotation marks.

A New Nation

DAILY LESSON OBJECTIVES	REPRODUCIBLE RESOURCES	MULTIMEDIA RESOURCES
SECTION 1 From Federation to Constitution 1. Describe the successes and failures of government under the Articles of Confederation. 2. Understand the difficulties in creating the Constitution. 3. Show how the Constitution increased the power of the federal government and lessened the power of the state legislatures.	▰ Reproducible Lesson Plans ▰ Vocabulary and Guided Reading Activities (English or Spanish) ▰ Cooperative Learning Activities ▰ Interpreting Political Cartoons ▰ Section Quizzes (English or Spanish)	▰ Section Focus Transparencies ▰ Historic America: Electronic Field Trips ▰ Beginnings to 1900 Transparencies ▰ Map Transparencies ▰ Chapter Teaching Transparencies ▰ Testmaker ▰ Student Self-Test: A Software Review
SECTION 2 Debate and Ratification 1. Explain why opinions were divided about the proposed new Constitution. 2. Describe how the views of the Federalists differed from those of the Anti-Federalists. 3. Explain how the addition of the Bill of Rights enhanced the Constitution.	▰ Reproducible Lesson Plans ▰ Vocabulary and Guided Reading Activities (English or Spanish) ▰ Great Debates in American History ▰ Section Quizzes (English or Spanish)	▰ Section Focus Transparencies ▰ Testmaker ▰ Student Self-Test: A Software Review
SECTION 3 Launching the New Government 1. Explain how federal power was used in the 1790s. 2. Explain the conflicts between the Federalist and Democratic-Republican political parties. 3. Describe the role of the Marshall Court in shaping the government. 4. Explain the emergence of the United States's foreign policy.	▰ Reproducible Lesson Plans ▰ Vocabulary and Guided Reading Activities (English or Spanish) ▰ Supreme Court Case Studies ▰ Reteaching Activities (English or Spanish) ▰ Skill Reinforcement Activities ▰ Enrichment Activities (English or Spanish) ▰ Geography in History Activities ▰ Section Quizzes (English or Spanish)	▰ Section Focus Transparencies ▰ Testmaker ▰ Student Self-Test: A Software Review ▰ American Music: Cultural Traditions ▰ Focus on American Fine Art Prints
CHAPTER REVIEW AND EVALUATION	▰ Chapter 4 Test: Forms A and B ▰ Unit 4 Test: Forms A and B ▰ Performance Assessment Strategies and Activities	▰ Testmaker ▰ Vocabulary PuzzleMaker ▰ Student Self-Test: A Software Review ▰ Chapter Digests Audiocassettes

00:00 If time does not permit teaching the entire chapter, summarize using the Chapter 4 Digests Audiocassettes and the accompanying activities and tests. (Available in English or Spanish.)

Cooperative Project

Ask students to work in pairs or small groups to make charts of the structure of the government established under the Articles of Confederation, the structure defined in the Constitution, and the United States government today. Ask each group to prepare a brief report analyzing the three structures. **LEP**

Suggested Rubric: A Research Report. See Performance Assessment Strategies and Activities, p. 39.

Individual Project

Have students select a nation of the world and prepare a bulletin board display detailing the status of human rights in that country.

Suggested Rubric: A Bulletin Board. See Performance Assessment Strategies and Activities, p. 45.

Key to Ability Levels

Teaching strategies have been coded for varying learning styles and abilities.

L1 **BASIC** activities for all students

L2 **AVERAGE** activities for average to above-average students

L3 **CHALLENGING** activities for above-average students

LEP **LIMITED ENGLISH PROFICIENCY** activities

 Block Scheduling

Block scheduling differs from traditional class scheduling in the amount of time allotted to each period. The extended timeframe provided by block scheduling affords you the opportunity to implement a greater number of research-oriented and activity-intense projects to motivate and involve your students. Activities that are particularly suited to use within the block scheduling framework are identified throughout this chapter by the following designation.

TEACHER'S CORNER

NATIONAL GEOGRAPHIC SOCIETY

INDEX TO NATIONAL GEOGRAPHIC MAGAZINE

The following articles may be used for research relating to this chapter:

- "L'Enfant's Washington," by Alice J. Hall, August 1991.
- "James Madison, Architect of the Constitution," by Alice J. Hall, September 1991.

NATIONAL GEOGRAPHIC SOCIETY PRODUCTS AVAILABLE FROM GLENCOE

To order the following products for use with this chapter, contact your local Glencoe sales representative or call Glencoe at 1-800-334-7344:

- *The Presidents: A Picture History of Our Nation* (CD-ROM)
- *GTV: A Geographic Perspective on American History* (Videodisc)
- *GTV: The American People: Fabric of a Nation* (Videodisc)

ADDITIONAL NATIONAL GEOGRAPHIC SOCIETY PRODUCTS

To order the following products for use with this chapter, call National Geographic Society at 1-800-368-2728:

- *Our Living Constitution* (Filmstrip)
- *America: Colonization to Constitution* (Filmstrip)
- *The American Presidency* (Filmstrip)
- *The United States Congress* (Filmstrip)
- *Democractic Government Series,* "The United States." (Video)
- *Branches of Government Series,* "The Legislative Branch," "The Judicial Branch," "The Executive Branch." (Video)
- *Washington, D.C.* (Video)

Chapter Overview

Chapter 4 describes the United States as a new nation experiencing the successes and failures of government. It discusses the Constitution, which was written in 1787 and created the three-branch system of government that the nation still uses today.

Introducing the Chapter

Ask students to read the Chapter 4 opener. How do students think Jefferson and Adams may have felt about their accomplishments at the end of their lives? Why? *(Sample: They may have felt that with the anniversary of the Declaration of Independence, their life's work, to nurture the United States, had been accomplished.)*

Display Chapter Teaching Transparency 4 on the board and distribute copies of the activity sheet.

Extension Activity

Have students complete Beyond the Transparency on the activity sheet for Chapter 4 and present their projects after the class has completed the chapter.

History Journal

Have students investigate the history of portraying Liberty as a woman and write a brief essay on this topic in their journals.

CHAPTER 4

A New Nation

It was the fiftieth anniversary of the signing of the Declaration of Independence. Thomas Jefferson, the nation's third President and principal author of the Declaration, lay gravely ill at Monticello, his home in Virginia.

Jefferson said to his grandson, "I am like an old watch, with a pinion worn out here, and a wheel there, until it can go no longer." He passed away shortly after noon.

John Adams died later that same day in Massachusetts, on his lips the words, "Thomas Jefferson survives!" He did not know that his old friend and rival was already gone.

Adams's words reflected his hope that at least one Founder would remain to watch over the young nation. While their relationship was strained at times by tensions in the country that pitted Democratic-Republicans against Federalists, Jefferson and Adams were bound together by the experiences they shared in the heady days of the Revolution.

Jefferson spent his vice presidency and two terms as President working to return the country to the Republican ideals of the Declaration of Independence and the Revolutionary era. He believed his predecessors, especially John Adams, had gone too far in strengthening the powers of the federal government. "I am not for transferring all the powers of the States to the general government, and all those of that government to the Executive branch," Jefferson wrote in a letter shortly before his election to the presidency. "I am for a government rigorously frugal and simple. . . ."

Confident in the strength of the American character, Jefferson never lost sight of his belief that the people's experiment in self-government was destined to set an example for the world. ∎

HISTORY JOURNAL

What do you think is the meaning of Liberty feeding the American eagle in the painting at the right? Write your ideas in your journal.

78

✚ **EXTRA CREDIT PROJECT**

Man of Letters Have students research an aspect of Thomas Jefferson's life aside from politics. They may be interested in investigating his work in founding the University of Virginia or his views on slavery. Students' finished products may take the form of written or oral reports or a dramatic presentation.

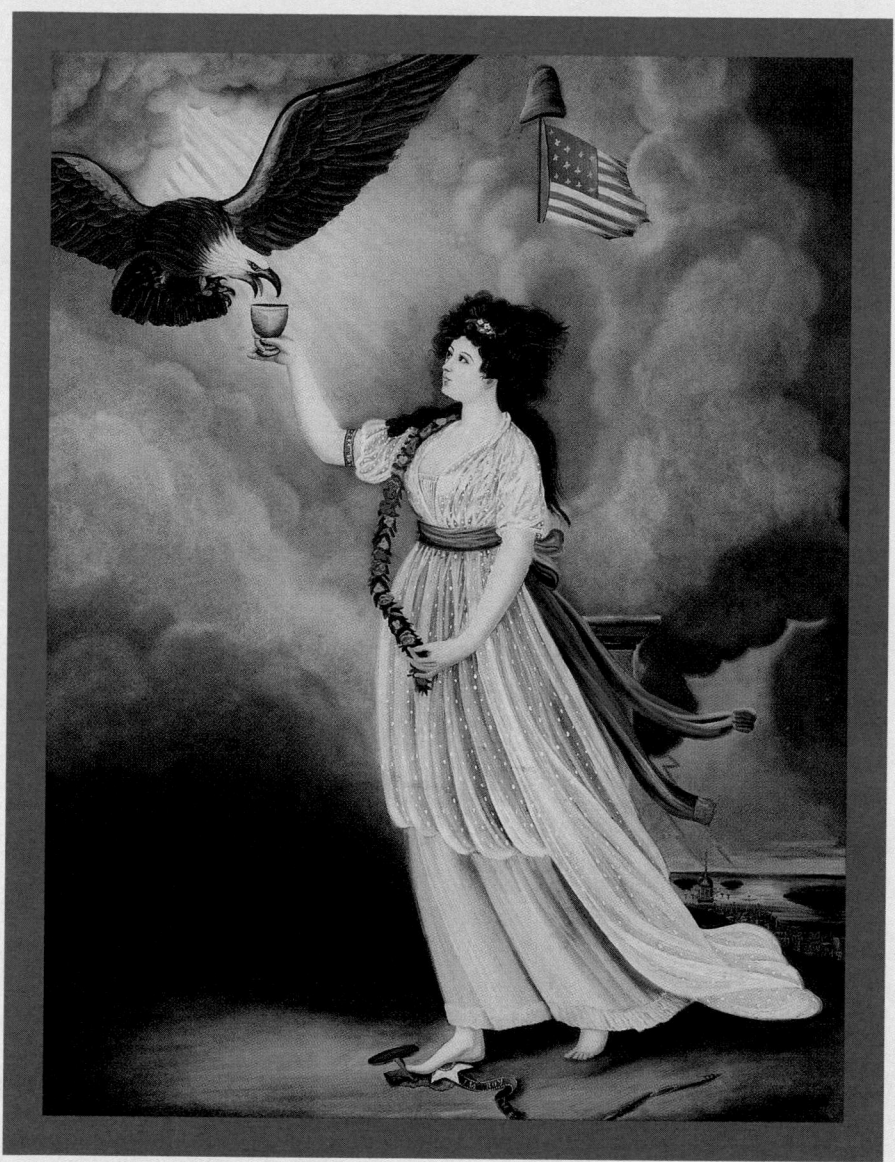

HENRY FORD MUSEUM & GREENFIELD VILLAGE

"LIBERTY" FEEDING THE AMERICAN EAGLE,
CIRCA 1800–1810

79

ABC NEWS
INTERACTIVE™

 Videodisc

Powers of the Congress

Side 1, Chapter 3
Title: Constitutional Government
Subject: Overview of constitutional government
Ask: How does constitutional government help guarantee the rights of citizens? *(The specific rights are usually written out in a constitution.)*

See Powers of the Congress Guidebook page 4 for complete lesson plan.

 Performance Assessment

Refer to page 78B for performance assessment activities for this chapter.

 Also see Activity 4 in the Performance Assessment Strategies and Activities for an additional activity as well as for suggested rubrics.

Examining the Visual

Lady Liberty This work is a reverse painting on glass done in gouache, or opaque watercolors. The artist was Abijah Canfield of Connecticut. Some elements of the painting that may be indistinct or invisible in the detail shown in the pupil's edition include a medal and a key on which Liberty is standing. A seaport during a storm is shown at right in the background. On a border around the central scene is inscribed in gold "LIBERTY/ In the form of the Goddess of Youth: giving Support to the Bald Eagle."

FOCUS

Section Objectives

1. Describe the successes and failures of government under the Articles of Confederation.
2. Understand the difficulties in creating the Constitution.
3. Show how the Constitution increased the power of the federal government and lessened the power of the state legislatures.

Bellringer Activity

 While taking attendance at the beginning of the class period, display **Section Focus Transparency 10,** and have students answer the questions. (Or use the blackline master.)

FYI

Confederation The confederate form of government has seldom been successful. Perhaps the only long-term success has been Switzerland.

VISUAL INSTRUCTION

Anti-Federalist Patrick Henry had been chosen to represent Virginia at the Constitutional Convention but refused to attend.

Ask: Why did Patrick Henry object to the new Constitution? *(Henry did not want powers to be taken away from the states and given to the federal government and he also believed that the authors of the Constitution did not have the authority to do so.)*

SECTION 1

From Federation to Constitution

JUNE 17, 1788: VIRGINIANS DEBATE PROPOSED CONSTITUTION

Anti-Federalist
Patrick Henry led the opposition to the Constitution at Virginia's ratifying convention in 1788.

THE WINDOWS OF THE STATE-HOUSE IN RICHMOND, VIRGINIA, STOOD OPEN ON THE HOT SUMMER AFTERNOON. Impassioned voices boomed from the building's main hall. There, 168 Virginia representatives heard arguments for and against a plan for a new government of the United States.

Patrick Henry stood before his fellow Virginians; they knew him as a former governor of their state and as a great public speaker. Henry explained his opposition to the proposed Constitution. It stripped powers away from the states, he said. It increased the powers of federal government, and it had been written by men with no authority to do so. He twisted the first words of the document into an attack on those men. "What right had they to say *We, the People?*" he asked. "Who authorized them to speak the language of *We, the People,* instead of *We, the States?*"

One of the men who helped design the new plan was at the convention. Edmund Randolph was as well known as Patrick Henry; he, too, had served as governor of the state and came from an old Virginia family. Randolph asked Virginia to accept the Constitution and unite the nation. Raising his right arm, Randolph exclaimed, "I will assent to the lopping of this limb before I assent to the dissolution of the Union."

The men debated the merits and faults of the Constitution through the rest of that warm June of 1788.

AS YOU READ

Vocabulary
► ratify
► hard money
► checks and balances
► representation

Think About . . .
► the successes and failures of government under the Articles of Confederation.
► the difficulties in creating the Constitution.

► how the Constitution increased the power of the federal government and lessened the power of the state legislatures.

Section 1 Resources

REPRODUCIBLE RESOURCES
📁 Lesson Plan 4-1
📁 Vocabulary and Guided Reading Activity 4-1
📁 Cooperative Learning Activity 4
📁 Section 1 Quiz
📁 Political Cartoon 3

MULTIMEDIA RESOURCES
🔦 Section Focus Transparency 10
💿 Historic America: Electronic Field Trips
🔦 Beginnings to 1900 Transparency 6
🔦 Map Transparency 4
🔦 Chapter Teaching Transparency 4

🖥 Testmaker
🎧 Chapter 4 Digest Audiocassette
🖥 Student Self-Test: A Software Review

Patrick Henry and his supporters argued for the rights of the states. Randolph and others urged unity under a strong federal government that the new Constitution offered. The differences between the 2 men summed up tensions that pulled at the fabric of life in the United States in the 1780s.

A Firm League of Friendship
The Articles of Confederation

Hopes for unity under a strong central government stemmed from experiences with the Articles of Confederation, an earlier attempt at a federal constitution. A federal constitution had become necessary because state governments, established in the late 1770s, issued their own money, taxed their own citizens, and competed with other states in trade and for land beyond the Appalachians. By the 1780s states acted more like 13 small independent nations—each with its own government, economy, and interests—than like parts of a larger nation.

The Plan of the Articles

Around the same time that the former colonies were creating their state governments, the Second Continental Congress appointed a committee to draw up a plan for a national government. Congress, preparing for war, wanted its powers to be officially defined and recognized. Other Americans, too, realized that the states could not do everything on their own.

The Articles of Confederation created a national government in the form of a one-house legislature, similar to the Continental Congress. Each state, regardless of its size, had one vote in the Confederation Congress. This body was given only those powers that individual states could not fulfill alone: declaring war, conducting foreign policy, and establishing a postal system were examples. The Articles denied Congress the power to collect taxes, even for the support of an army or to enforce its own laws and treaties. One rule firmly established the power of the states over Congress: only a unanimous vote of the states could change the Articles of Confederation. Many Americans believed that this new system avoided the evils of a strong government—such as Britain's government—but allowed the states to work together for their common good and protection.

Ratification Difficulties

While all the newly formed states wanted a national government, it took almost four years to **ratify,** or officially accept, the Articles of Confederation (which could only be adopted if every state consented). The primary stumbling block to ratification was the question of control of the land between the Appalachian Mountains and the Mississippi River. Larger states such as Virginia claimed these Western lands in their colonial charters and were reluctant to give up control. Small states feared that control of this territory would make large states too powerful. Moreover, if the national government took control of the Western lands, their resources could benefit all the states in the union instead of just a few. States with no claims to Western lands pointed out that it was only fair that these lands be common property because they were being "wrested from the common enemy [the British] by the blood and treasure of the thirteen states." Small states hoped to see the Western lands opened for settlement and farming, so their poorer residents might make a new start.

Eventually most smaller states agreed to ratify the Articles despite their misgivings about control of Western lands. Maryland, however, refused to ratify until New York transferred its Western land claims to Congress in 1780, and Virginia followed suit in 1781. With all states' Western land claims ceded, or formally surrendered, Maryland announced its ratification of the Articles on March 1, 1781.

NATIONAL MUSEUM OF AMERICAN ART, WASHINGTON, DC/ART RESOURCE, NY

Unspoiled Lands The land that became the state of Tennessee (seen here in a later painting) was ceded by North Carolina in 1790. *Why did small states want the federal government to control Western lands?*

TEACH

Guided Practice

L1 **Discussion** Discuss what colonial experiences might have most influenced Americans when they planned a new government. What hopes and fears might they have had? How might their feelings have differed when planning state versus national governments?

Show students Map Transparency 4 and have them complete the activity sheet.

Show students Beginnings to 1900 Transparency 6 and have them complete the activity sheet.

VISUAL INSTRUCTION

Unspoiled Lands Land speculators (companies that invested in undeveloped land hoping its value would increase) encouraged states to cede their Western lands to the government, hoping that the government would honor the speculators' land purchases from Native Americans.

Answer: *So Western lands could benefit all states*

Cooperative Learning

League of Friendship Ask students to prepare for a panel discussion on the topic: The Articles of Confederation: Is Friendship Among States Enough? Organize the class into groups, each with students of varying skills and strengths. Each group should choose a focus for their discussion: for example, international relations, economics, national defense, etc.

Independent Practice

L1 **Making a Time Line**
Have students make individual time lines of the events in this section. The time lines should start with the date 1776 and go through 1787. Some students may wish to do additional research and add events that are not covered in the text, such as scientific discoveries, international events, etc.

☛ Have students complete the Chapter 4, Section 1 Vocabulary and Guided Reading Activity. (Also in Spanish.) **LEP**

☛ Have students complete the Chapter 4 Cooperative Learning Activity.

VISUAL INSTRUCTION

Shays's Rebellion This 1787 woodcut by an unknown artist is the only representation of Shays and Shattuck from the period.
Answer: *The shortage of hard money caused a lack of confidence in paper money. When people who had loaned money asked for repayment in hard money, few farmers could pay their debts. In 1786 the Massachusetts legislature refused Shays and other farmers more time to pay their debts. Shays and the farmers then decided to use force to protect themselves from their creditors.*

The 13 states would now be joined in a "firm league of friendship."

When the states worked together, the Confederation Congress succeeded in passing laws of lasting value. The Northwest Ordinance of 1787, for example, established rules for organizing the lush region west of the Appalachian Mountains. It reached a compromise on slavery, allowing it in territory south of the Ohio River and prohibiting the importation of slaves north of the river. The ordinance also provided rules for electing assemblies in the Western territories and for admitting territories "on an equal footing with the original states."

Although effective in passing the Northwest Ordinance, Congress faced a variety of difficult problems after the war that states refused to help solve. The worst of these problems involved paying off war debts and stabilizing the American economy.

In Debt

Congress had borrowed nearly $60 million from American investors and European governments during the war. After the war Congress lacked cash to pay its old debts. Because Congress was not allowed to tax the states, the only way it could pay its debts was to print massive amounts of paper money.

Continental paper currency was nothing more than a promise that Congress would pay the holder of the bill in **hard money**—gold or silver—at some time in the future. By the end of the war, the United States had a severe shortage of hard money. The more paper money Congress printed, therefore, the less it was worth. By the mid-1780s, Continental currency was worth only one-fortieth of its face value. Since Congress had no hard

In the Backcountry The Massachusetts Supreme Court sentenced Shays to death for his part in the uprising, then pardoned him in 1788. He is shown here with Jacob Shattuck, another leader in the farmers' rebellion. *What conditions in the country led to Shays's Rebellion?*

NATIONAL PORTRAIT GALLERY, SMITHSONIAN INSTITUTION/ART RESOURCE, NY

money to back up the millions of dollars printed during the war, people's confidence in paper money fell. Many merchants refused to accept Continental currency, and few Americans had any hard money to spend.

Desperately in need of a new way to raise taxes, leaders in Congress tried unsuccessfully to convince the states that it should have the power to tax imports. Meanwhile, the money problems began to have dire effects on the lives of common Americans.

Shays's Rebellion

One of those Americans was Daniel Shays. Shays served as a captain in the Continental Army during the Revolution. When the war was over, he returned to his small farm in western Massachusetts. In the best of times, Shays had little extra money. After the war, he had none. In a time before banks, Shays and other farmers sometimes borrowed money from wealthy neighbors to buy food and supplies, or bought goods on credit from a store in town. When the wealthy neighbor or store owner asked the farmers to pay their debts—in hard money, of course—many could not pay.

For people who could not pay their debts, there were two alternatives. If they had property, a local court seized it and sold it to pay off the debt. If they had no property, they were sent to debtors' prison. In 1786 Shays and other farmers begged the Massachusetts legislature for extra time to pay their debts. The legislature ignored the requests, and the county courts continued to seize farms.

Daniel Shays recalled the early days of the crisis with Britain when legal attempts to solve disputes with government failed. He knew what to do in the face of an arrogant legislature. In August and September 1786, disgruntled farmers marched on courthouses in Northampton and Worcester. Muskets in hand, they closed the courthouses and prevented the courts from seizing any more farms or imprisoning any more farmers.

After those successes, Shays's group gathered near Springfield, where the state's supreme court was in session and where the state arsenal also happened to be located. When wealthy New Englanders learned that angry farmers were massing near the arsenal, they feared open rebellion and attacks on their property. They called the farmers traitors and provided the money that induced 4,400 militia from eastern Massachusetts to march against the gathering farmers.

In January 1787, Shays and 1,200 farmers marched on the arsenal. When Shays's men advanced, the militia opened fire. Four farmers died and the rest scattered. The revolt broke up soon afterward.

While Shays and the other farmers believed they were patriotic, other Americans were horrified. Men of wealth and power saw the rebellion as proof of social dis-

---

Meeting Special Needs

Reading Disability To assist students with learning disabilities, discuss the section heads, "A Firm League of Friendship" and "A More Perfect Union." Ask students to define and discuss the terms *friendship* and *union* in the context of government and the needs of Americans in the 1780s.

DEPOSITED BY THE CITY OF BOSTON, COURTESY, MUSEUM OF FINE ARTS, BOSTON

© NORTH WIND PICTURE ARCHIVES

THE THOMAS GILCREASE INSTITUTE OF AMERICAN HISTORY AND ART, TULSA, OKLAHOMA

Constitutional Convention at the Pennsylvania Statehouse James Madison (right) was among the most influential figures at the convention, where delegates shaped the new government and wrote the Constitution. Samuel Adams (above) refused to attend as a protest against the formation of a stronger federal government. *Why was the Confederation congress so anxious to replace the Articles of Confederation?*

order. Congress sent a veteran of Washington's army, General Henry Knox, to investigate. Knox reported that the farmers' uprising had "alarmed men of principle and property." He declared, "What is to afford our security against the violence of lawless men? Our government must be braced, changed, or altered to secure our lives and property."

A More Perfect Union
Reinventing Government

By 1787 the flaws in the Articles of Confederation were obvious to many Americans, including most members of the Confederation congress. A group of these men worried that the nation was headed for disaster unless the Articles were altered. They called on the states to send delegates to a convention where they might correct "such defects as may be discovered to exist" in the present government.

Meeting in Philadelphia

The group that gathered in Philadelphia in May 1787 contained some of the most distinguished men in America. Adoring crowds mobbed stern, proper George Washington, a delegate from Virginia. Americans still hailed him as the hero of the American Revolution. Another Virginia delegate, the short and frail James Madison, had spent much of the previous year reading about governments in past history to prepare for the convention. Benjamin Franklin was the elder statesman of the convention. At age 81, Franklin tired easily and had other Pennsylvania delegates read his speeches for him, but he enjoyed hosting the state delegates in his home city.

The other 52 delegates had experience drafting state constitutions and serving in state governments or the Confederation congress. The delegates' average age was 45, just past the prime of life in the 1700s. Many of them had attended college. All were white, male, and wealthy.

By May 25, delegates from 7 states had arrived and the meeting began. Delegates from 3 more states arrived late; delegates from Rhode Island never showed up.

SECTION ONE **83**

Portfolio Project

Constitutional Models James Madison spent an entire year before the Constitutional Convention studying democratic governments and republics of the past. Students may research and report on the governments Madison studied and how the United States Constitution resembled and differed from those earlier models.

ASSESS

Meeting Lesson Objectives

Each section objective is tested by the section review questions that follow it in parentheses.

1. Describe the successes and failures of government under the Articles of Confederation. (1, 2)
2. Understand the difficulties in creating the Constitution. (1, 3, 4)
3. Show how the Constitution increased the power of the federal government and lessened the power of the state legislatures. (1, 5)

VISUAL INSTRUCTION

Federalist Leader Roger Sherman was one of only two people to sign all three of the founding documents of the United States: the Declaration of Independence, the Articles of Confederation, and the Constitution.

Answer: *Slaves were counted at the ratio of 3:5; slave trade had to be maintained until 1808.*

Sworn to secrecy, and meeting behind closed doors, the delegates began their work at green felt-covered tables in the Pennsylvania statehouse. The delegates quickly agreed that the Articles were beyond repair. The Virginia delegation, headed by Edmund Randolph, proposed an entirely new system of government, based on James Madison's studies. This new government would be larger and more powerful than the Confederation congress.

That plan was the basis for discussion among the delegates throughout the long, hot summer of 1787. Working in a closed hall, the delegates suffered through sweltering heat. Six days a week, from May to September, they proposed and debated idea after idea. Angry delegates threatened to walk out of the convention and some did. Slowly, a plan for a new government emerged.

Reshaping the Government

Unlike the Confederation congress, the new government was to consist of three equal but separate branches: an executive branch, a legislative branch, and a judicial branch, or system of federal courts. The job of the executive branch, headed by a President, was to enforce federal laws. The responsibility of the legislative branch, or Congress, as it was to be called, was to make laws. The judicial branch would rule on cases of federal laws. The responsibilities of these branches would overlap and interlock, creating **checks and balances** that would prevent one branch from being too powerful.

Two major differences between the Confederation government and the new one are notable. First, under the new Constitution, the President held far-reaching powers. The President was commander in chief of the army, he could veto acts of Congress, appoint judges, and put down rebellions. One delegate said that these powers might not have been so great "had not many of the members cast their eyes towards General Washington as president." A second major difference was that the new Constitution curbed the power of state legislatures. States were now prohibited from issuing paper money and from allowing debts and taxes to be paid in produce, such as tobacco and wheat, instead of with hard money.

States were also forbidden from "impairing the obligation of contracts"—meaning interfering with the settlement of contracts, which included debts owed by farmers.

The greatest difficulty the convention faced centered on Congress. The delegates agreed early that Congress should consist of two houses, but the question of **representation,** or how many votes each state should have, nearly broke up the convention. Delegates from small states insisted that each state have an equal vote in Congress. Those from larger states felt that was unfair: representation in Congress should be decided by population.

Learning to Compromise

After seven weeks of deadlock on this issue, the two sides agreed to what historians call the Great Compromise. Both small and large states got part of what they wanted, but neither group got all they had hoped for. In the upper house, or Senate, each state would have two votes, regardless of its size. Representation in the lower house, called the House of Representatives, would be based on each state's population.

Another conflict erupted over the way to figure the number of representatives a state could have. Southern delegates insisted that enslaved African Americans be counted in a state's population. Northern delegates objected to this proposal: some believed slavery was wrong; others realized that counting enslaved

Federalist Leader Roger Sherman of Connecticut was a major architect of the Great Compromise. *How did the delegates decide to compromise on slavery?*

YALE UNIVERSITY ART GALLERY, GIFT OF ROGER SHERMAN WHITE, B.A. 1899, LL.B. 1902

Extending the Content

The Supreme Court The highest court in the government's judicial branch is the Supreme Court. It is the only court specifically created by the Constitution. Ever since the Court was created, there have been disagreements about the extent of its power. Some people believe that the Court should interpret and apply the Constitution only according to the meaning and intent of the men who wrote it. Others believe that the Court should take a more creative role in interpreting and applying the Constitution in order to address the changing problems of the nation. Encourage students to discuss which point of view they agree with and why.

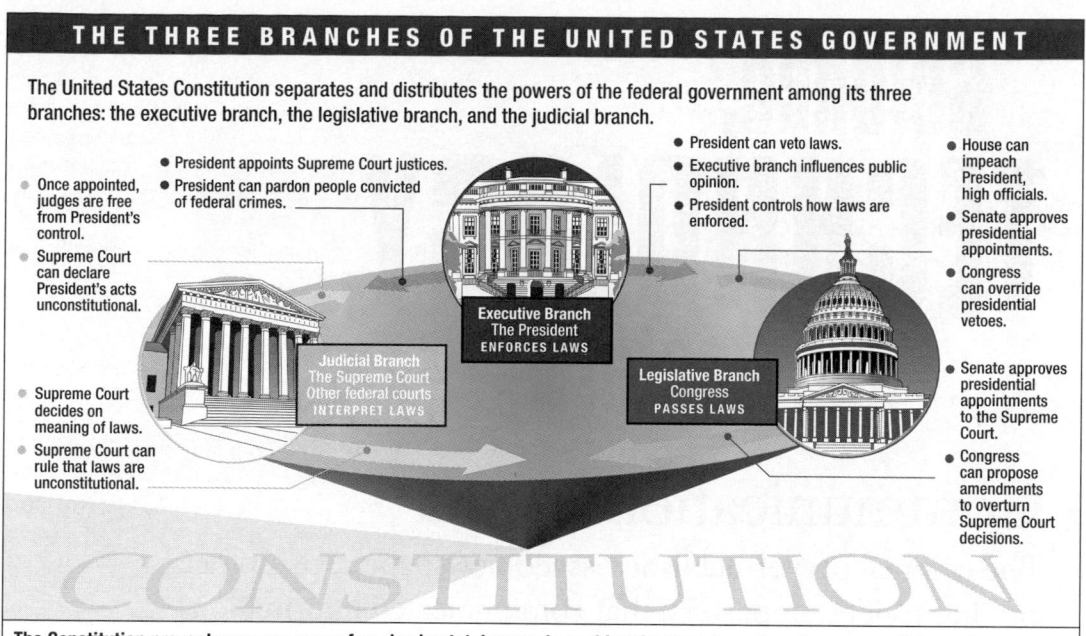

THE THREE BRANCHES OF THE UNITED STATES GOVERNMENT

The United States Constitution separates and distributes the powers of the federal government among its three branches: the executive branch, the legislative branch, and the judicial branch.

- President appoints Supreme Court justices.
- President can pardon people convicted of federal crimes.

- Once appointed, judges are free from President's control.
- Supreme Court can declare President's acts unconstitutional.

- Supreme Court decides on meaning of laws.
- Supreme Court can rule that laws are unconstitutional.

Judicial Branch
The Supreme Court
Other federal courts
INTERPRET LAWS

Executive Branch
The President
ENFORCES LAWS

Legislative Branch
Congress
PASSES LAWS

- President can veto laws.
- Executive branch influences public opinion.
- President controls how laws are enforced.

- House can impeach President, high officials.
- Senate approves presidential appointments.
- Congress can override presidential vetoes.

- Senate approves presidential appointments to the Supreme Court.
- Congress can propose amendments to overturn Supreme Court decisions.

CONSTITUTION

The Constitution prevents any one group from having total power by making the three branches of government depend on one another for their authority. *Using the graphic above, name two examples of the overlapping responsibilities of the branches.*

---

persons would increase the power of Southern states in Congress. To complicate matters, some Northern delegates threatened to outlaw the slave trade.

The 2 sides finally agreed to a compromise over slavery. Representation in the House of Representatives would be based on all of the free inhabitants of a state, plus three-fifths of all enslaved persons, even though they could not vote. The same formula would be used to figure the taxes each state owed to the federal government. The group also agreed that Congress could pass no laws abolishing the slave trade before 1808.

The delegates also decided late in their meetings that the Constitution should be ratified in specially elected conventions of the people, rather than by the state legislatures. Delegates feared that state governments would never approve their new plan, which strengthened the national government. In addition, they agreed that only 9 of the 13 states had to ratify the Constitution before the new government went into effect.

When the delegates saw the final document, many felt disappointed. Many had compromised on issues of great importance to their states. "I confess there are several parts of this constitution which I do not at present approve," said Benjamin Franklin. He also said, however, that the new plan was better than their current government and encouraged the remaining delegates to sign it. All but 3 of them did so on September 17, 1787. (See pages 91–109 to read the Constitution.)

The next day, Major William Jackson, secretary of the convention, left Philadelphia by stagecoach, carrying a copy of the Constitution to the Confederation congress in New York. He also carried a letter from the convention explaining "the necessity of a different organization."

SECTION REVIEW

Vocabulary

1. Define: ratify, hard money, checks and balances, representation.

Checking Facts

2. Why did smaller states want larger states to give up Western land claims?

3. What was the Great Compromise, and how did it satisfy all 13 states?

Critical Thinking

Analyzing Information

4. Why did the delegates at the Constitutional Convention decide to compromise with each other?

Linking Across Time

5. Give an example of a part of the Constitution that might be different if the Constitution were being written today. Explain your answer.

Section 1 Review Answers

1. ratify (81), **hard money** (82), **checks and balances** (84), **representation** (84)
2. They felt they should benefit equally with larger states from the lands.
3. It gave two senators to each state and based House membership on population, which was counted as all free inhabitants of a state

plus three-fifths of all enslaved African Americans.
4. Delegates realized that their diverse interests could be addressed only by compromise.
5. Students may answer that the Constitution, if written today, might specify equal rights for women.

GRAPH STUDY

A veto, or rejection, of a bill by the President can be overridden by a two-thirds vote in both the House and the Senate.

Answer: *Students may answer that the executive branch can veto laws, but the legislative branch can override a veto and that the executive branch appoints judges to the Supreme Court, but the legislative branch must approve the appointments.*

Evaluate

Have students complete the Section Review.

☞ ● Assign the Section 1 Quiz or use the Testmaker to develop a customized quiz. (Also in Spanish.) **LEP**

Reteach

🎧 Have students listen to the Chapter 4, Section 1 Audiocassette. (Also in Spanish.) **LEP**

Enrich

☞ Have students complete Interpreting Political Cartoon 3.

CLOSE

Ask students to explain the major compromises of the Constitutional Convention. *(In the Senate, each state got two votes. In the House, votes were based on population, which was the number of free inhabitants plus three-fifths of slaves. Slave trade could not be abolished before 1808.)*

TEACH

Making the Historical Connection

The world's first printed books appeared in China starting around A.D. 868. Printing was later reinvented in Europe; the first book printed in the West was Johannes Gutenberg's Latin Bible, printed at Mainz, Germany, in 1455. By 1500 more than 200 European cities had printing presses. It took some time for printing to be established in colonies in North America; at first the small, widely separated communities were too busy struggling for survival. A surprising number of colonists, however, packed books among the belongings they brought to their new homes. These were most often practical reference volumes on topics such as medicine or the law.

FYI

Snail Mail Communication in the early colonial period was also made difficult by the lack of a reliable postal system. In the 1600s colonists had to make their own arrangements for delivery of mail through ship captains; communities that had the most overseas trade had the best mail service. Colonists corresponded with relatives in England, but because the Atlantic crossing could take eight weeks or more, they had to wait months for a reply.

Science, TECHNOLOGY, and Society

Communication Media

The colonial printer-publisher issued newspapers, pamphlets, and broadsides, or posters, that communicated information and opinions concerning the debate over British rule.

(DETAIL) PHOTO COURTESY PEABODY ESSEX MUSEUM, SALEM, MASS.. ORIGINAL IN THE COLLECTION OF THE MARBLEHEAD HISTORICAL SOCIETY, MARBLEHEAD, MA

FILE PHOTO BY DOUG MINDELL

KEEPING IN TOUCH
Before the availability of printing presses in the Americas, colonists used letters and journals, such as the one at left, to keep records and disseminate information. These handwritten accounts had the obvious disadvantage of not being reproducible without great effort.

300 YEARS OF COMMUNICATION MEDIA

Pre-1650	1650	1700	1750
FIRST COLONIAL PRINTING PRESS is set up by Stephen Daye of Massachusetts in 1639.		The **BOSTON NEWS-LETTER,** the first successful newspaper in the colonies, is first published in 1704.	**BALTIMORE PRINTER** Mary Katherine Goddard prints and distributes the Declaration of Independence in 1777.

Background Information

Electronic Mail One of the most popular applications of the Internet, and one that has revolutionized communication for those with access to computers, is electronic mail. Internet users anywhere in the world can send each other typewritten messages, and can enclose other documents or software with their messages. In some cases, the transmission is almost instantaneous. The first e-mail messages were sent in 1972–73. Initially, scientists used this capability to exchange information about their research. Soon, though, government workers were using e-mail to keep in touch on a social level and to discuss common interests through massive e-mailings—the first e-mail list was "SF-Lovers," for fans of science fiction.

FREEDOM PRESS

Boston printer Isaiah Thomas learned his trade on this printing press in 1755, when he was 6 years old. At the start of the Revolution, Thomas removed his press to a town outside Boston to keep it out of British hands. There he printed the first accounts of the skirmishes at Lexington and Concord with the headline, "Americans!—Liberty or Death!—Join or Die!"

COURTESY, AMERICAN ANTIQUARIAN SOCIETY

COLONIAL WILLIAMSBURG

COURTESY, AMERICAN ANTIQUARIAN SOCIETY

Or, Thoma...

REASONS
WHY
The *BRITISH* Colonies,
IN
AMERICA,
SHOULD NOT BE CHARGED WITH
INTERNAL TAXES,
By AUTHORITY OF
PARLIAMENT;
HUMBLY OFFERED,
For CONSIDERATION,
In Behalf of the Colony of
CONNECTICUT.

NEW-HAVEN:
Printed by B. MECOM. M,DCC,LXIV.

COURTESY, AMERICAN ANTIQUARIAN SOCIETY

PAPERS AND PAMPHLETS

The growth of small presses and improvements in the postal service made it much easier to find out what was going on. Connecticut Governor Thomas Fitch published a pamphlet (above, right) in 1740 that stated clearly and concisely his colony's objections to taxes. Between 1763 and 1775, the number of newspapers in the colonies doubled. The *Massachusetts Spy* (above, left) was founded in 1770.

COLONIAL WILLIAMSBURG

INTERNET NEWS

PORTFOLIO PROJECT

Comparisons have been made between colonial newspapers and today's electronic bulletin boards on the Internet. Do some research and write a brief report on how these media are alike and different.

1800	1850	1900	1950–1990s

THE TELEPHONE is invented by Alexander Graham Bell in 1876.

FIRST COMMERCIAL RADIO STATION, KDKA in Pittsburgh, goes on the air in 1920.

THE COMPUTER AGE begins when the first automatic digital computer is created in 1942.

THE INTERNET is born in 1969 out of a computer network built to study how the government could maintain communications in the event of nuclear war.

SCIENCE, TECHNOLOGY, AND SOCIETY **87**

The Portfolio Project on this page provides an excellent opportunity to enrich and extend the key elements of this feature.

CLOSE

Engage students in a discussion about how printed matter (pamphlets, newspapers, and broadsides) affected the movement toward independence from Britain. Ask: How might the political discussion have been different if it had occurred before the invention of the printing press? *(Answers will vary. The drive for independence might not have gained popular support if the ideas of the revolutionary leaders and the injustices perpetrated by the British had not been widely disseminated in print.)*

Portfolio Project

Tradeswomen Have students research women printers and publishers or women in other trades during the colonial period. Students might want to find out more about Mary Katherine Goddard of Baltimore (see time line, p. 86) or examine women's participation in printing and trades more generally. Have students write a report on the topic and place it in their portfolio.

FOCUS

Section Objectives

1. Explain why opinions were divided about the proposed new Constitution.
2. Describe how the views of the Federalists differed from those of the Anti-Federalists.
3. Explain how the addition of the Bill of Rights enhanced the Constitution.

Bellringer Activity

 While taking attendance at the beginning of the class period, display **Section Focus Transparency 11,** and have students answer the questions. (Or use the blackline master.)

VISUAL INSTRUCTION

A Staunch Federalist The essays in *The Federalist* were aimed mainly at influencing the New York ratifying convention.

Ask: What did *The Federalist* essays urge? (*That the Constitution be ratified and a strong national government be established*)

Block Scheduling

☞ Have students complete the Unit 1 Great Debate to enrich their understanding of the debate over ratification of the Constitution.

Debate and Ratification

SEPTEMBER 17, 1787: CONSTITUTIONAL CONVENTION ADJOURNS

NATIONAL PORTRAIT GALLERY, SMITHSONIAN INSTITUTION/ART RESOURCE, NY

A Staunch Federalist
Alexander Hamilton was a major author of *The Federalist,* a series of 85 essays defending the Constitution.

As soon as the convention in Philadelphia ended, delegates rushed home to begin the campaign for ratification. That was a novel idea in itself. Never before had the nation's people at large been asked to ratify the laws under which they would live. The process of deciding for or against ratification produced perhaps the biggest, most informed political debate in American history.

News of the new Constitution spread rapidly through the states. Newspapers published the document and strongly worded arguments began to fill their pages. Those who favored the proposed Constitution called themselves Federalists. The Anti-Federalists opposed the new plan of government.

The idea of a strong national government frightened some Americans. Many Anti-Federalists were small farmers who had learned to be self-sufficient and had found most of their contact with government unpleasant. The Anti-Federalist leaders, however, came from all classes and all regions. State politicians who dreaded losing power to the federal government were among the most active supporters of the Anti-Federalists.

The debate over the Constitution in newspapers, letters, and public discussions revealed divisions that remained in American society. One poor Anti-Federalist farmer mistrusted the people of "wealth and talent" who had framed the Constitution:

These lawyers, and men of learning, and moneyed men, that talk so finely, and gloss over matters so smoothly, to make us, poor illiterate people swallow down the pill, expect to get into Congress themselves; they expect to be managers of this Constitution, and get all the power and all the money into their own hands, and then they will swallow up all us little folks, like the great Leviathan, Mr. President; yes, just like the whale swallowed up Jonah.

—Amos Singletary, *Massachusetts Gazette,* January 25, 1788

AS YOU READ

Vocabulary
► majority
► amendment

Think About . . .
► why opinions were divided about the proposed new Constitution.
► how the views of the Federalists differed from those of the Anti-Federalists.
► how the addition of the Bill of Rights enhanced the Constitution.

Section 2 Resources

REPRODUCIBLE RESOURCES
☞ Lesson Plan 4-2
☞ Vocabulary and Guided Reading Activity 4-2
☞ Unit 1 Great Debate
☞ Section 2 Quiz

MULTIMEDIA RESOURCES
🖳 Section Focus Transparency 11
🖥 Testmaker
🎧 Chapter 4 Digest Audiocassette
💿 Student Self-Test: A Software Review

Toward Ratification
The Debate Over Basic Rights

Many of the Anti-Federalists feared that a strong central government would not preserve the essential rights of the people. Even Britain guaranteed certain rights to its citizens, they argued. Why was there no bill of basic American rights?

The leading Federalists, including George Washington, Benjamin Franklin, and James Madison, did not believe a bill of rights was necessary. All basic rights, they argued, were protected by the Constitution or by state constitutions.

The Federalists found support in the area where America's elite had always dominated, the Atlantic Coast. Wealthy landowners in these areas wanted the protection a strong central government could provide. Merchants with overseas connections and artisans in large coastal cities also supported the proposed Constitution. These men had been hard hit by the inability of the Confederation congress to control the nation's economy; they saw a strong government that would pass import taxes on foreign goods as their best chance to succeed in business.

As the ratifying conventions began to convene, the Federalists knew they had clear **majorities,** or more than 50 percent of the votes, in some states. The vote was much closer in others, including large states such as Massachusetts, Virginia, and New York. If any one of those states did not ratify, the Federalists risked total failure.

NORTH WIND PICTURE ARCHIVES

The People Celebrate In this print New Yorkers are shown celebrating the ratification of the Constitution in 1788. *Why was New York a key state in the campaign for ratification?*

The Ratification Debate

Anti-Federalist Objections to the Constitution

The Articles of Confederation were basically a good plan for government that could be amended.

The Constitution made national government too strong.

Strong national government threatened the rights of the common people.

The Constitution favored wealthy men and preserved their power.

The Constitution lacked a bill of rights.

Federalist Defense of the Constitution

The Articles of Confederation were weak and ineffective.

National government needed to be strong in order to function.

Strong national government was needed to quell rebellions by Native Americans and small farmers.

National government would protect the rights of the people.

Men of experience and talent should govern the nation.

Constitutional and state governments protected individual freedoms without a bill of rights.

Both the Anti-Federalists and the Federalists held strong views regarding ratification of the new Constitution. *According to the Federalists, what safeguards would a strong national government provide for citizens?*

SECTION TWO **89**

Cooperative Learning

A Constitutional Debate Have two groups of students form debate teams—one of Federalists and one of Anti-Federalists. Ask them to hold a debate on their opposing political views. Suggest that the rest of the class vote on the outcome of the debate and tell why the team they voted for deserved to win. 🖼

TEACH

Guided Practice

L2 **Discussion** Discuss with students some current political issues that create heated public debate similar to the debate over the ratification of the Constitution.

Independent Practice

L2 **Writing** Have students write a letter to a friend arguing their cause as either a Federalist or an Anti-Federalist in 1787.

📁 Have students complete the Chapter 4, Section 2 Vocabulary and Guided Reading Activity. (Also in Spanish.) **LEP**

VISUAL INSTRUCTION

The People Celebrate

This painting is fairly romanticized. Many Americans doubted whether the new government would work.

Answer: *If New York did not ratify, the nation would be split into two parts.*

CHART STUDY

Lawmakers and judiciary officials continue to weigh the strength of the federal government against the rights of individuals.

Answer: *It could function efficiently, protect against rebellions, defend individual rights, and ensure that the most experienced and talented men would lead the country.*

ASSESS

Meeting Lesson Objectives

Each section objective is tested by the section review question(s) that follows it in parentheses.

1. Explain why opinions were divided about the new Constitution. (2, 3, 4)

2. Describe how the views of the Federalists differed from those of the Anti-Federalists. (2, 3)

3. Explain how the addition of the Bill of Rights enhanced the Constitution. (1, 5)

Evaluate

Have students complete the Section Review.

☞ 🖥 Assign the Section 2 Quiz or use the Testmaker to develop a customized quiz. (Also in Spanish.) **LEP**

Reteach

🎧 Have students listen to the Chapter 4, Section 2 Audiocassette. (Also in Spanish.) **LEP**

Enrich

Have interested students research the architecture of the Federalist era and present their findings to the class.

CLOSE

Ask: What was the Bill of Rights? *(the first 10 amendments to the Constitution, which guaranteed individual rights)*

FROM INDEPENDENCE TO THE CONSTITUTION, 1776–1791

JULY 1776 Colonists sign Declaration of Independence.

FEBRUARY 1787 Massachusetts militia quell Shays's Rebellion, which had started in 1786.

JUNE 1788 Ratification of Constitution by the ninth state (N.H.) makes it official.

DECEMBER 1791 The Bill of Rights is ratified.

1776 1778 1780 1782 1784 1786 1788 1790 1792

MARCH 1781 The Articles of Confederation are ratified.

SEPTEMBER 1783 The Treaty of Paris ends the Revolutionary War.

MAY 1787 Writing of the Constitution begins.

APRIL 1789 George Washington is elected first President.

The People Vote

The first state conventions were held in December 1787 and January 1788. Delaware, New Jersey, Georgia, and Connecticut all ratified the Constitution.

The first real test occurred in Massachusetts. Opponents of the Constitution, including Samuel Adams, held a clear majority when the convention met in January 1788. The state's urban craftspeople—still the source of Samuel Adams's political power—sided with the Federalists, however, and persuaded Adams to vote for ratification. The Massachusetts convention agreed to the Constitution, but only if a bill of rights was added.

In June 1788, New Hampshire became the ninth state to ratify the Constitution. The Federalists had reached the minimum number required to make the new government legal. Virginia and New York, however, still had not yet ratified. Without these 2 large states the new government could hardly succeed.

George Washington and James Madison worked hard for ratification in Virginia, but Patrick Henry and other Anti-Federalists worked just as hard against it. Finally, at the urging of Thomas Jefferson, Madison compromised and agreed to add a bill of rights.

The contest was even closer in New York. Only a last-minute promise to add a bill of rights won ratification in New York. Once New York joined the other states, the Federalists' victory was made more secure.

Adding the Bill of Rights

Five states had ratified the Constitution with the understanding that Congress would add a bill of rights. Many Federalist leaders who had made this promise served in the new Congress. James Madison represented Virginia in the Congress, and in September 1789, he recommended that 12 **amendments,** or written changes, be added to the Constitution.

Over the next 2 years, state legislatures ratified 10 of these 12 amendments. The Constitution now officially protected rights such as freedom of speech, religion,

press, and assembly. In December 1791, these 10 amendments, known as the Bill of Rights, were added to the Constitution.

The Preamble of the United States Constitution states that the Constitution is designed to "promote the general welfare, and secure the blessings of liberty" of "the people of the United States." It did not, however, address the rights of many Americans. The Constitution protected slavery, ignored women, and did not acknowledge Native Americans' rights. It left to future generations problems that it could neither foresee nor solve.

Yet through the process of ratification and with the addition of the Bill of Rights, the Constitution was shaped by more people than the flawed Articles of Confederation. As they headed into the 1790s, the American people watched—with hopes and fears—to see how this latest experiment would turn out.

SECTION REVIEW

Vocabulary

1. Define: majority, amendment.

Checking Facts

2. Why did Anti-Federalists oppose the new Constitution?

3. Why did the Federalists favor the Constitution?

Critical Thinking

Identifying Assumptions

4. What assumptions were many poorer Anti-Federalists making about the Federalists as a group?

Linking Across Time

5. Give an example of an addition to the Bill of Rights that might be made if it were being written today for the first time. Explain your answer.

Section 2 Review Answers

1. majority (89), **amendment** (90)

2. They feared a strong national government as a threat to their rights.

3. They wanted a strong central government to manage the economy and allow them to remain in positions of power.

4. They assumed that the Federalists would hold all the power and enhance their own wealth while ignoring the rights of others.

5. Students' answers may suggest a variety of amendments to add to the Bill of Rights relating to different areas of society. Have students justify their ideas for change.

The Constitution
of the United States

For easier study of the Constitution, those passages that have been set aside or changed by the adoption of the amendments are printed in blue.

Preamble

We, the people of the United States, in Order to form a more perfect Union, establish Justice, insure domestic Tranquility, provide for the common defence, promote the general Welfare, and secure the Blessings of Liberty to ourselves and our Posterity, do ordain and establish this Constitution for the United States of America.

Article I

SECTION 1

All legislative Powers herein granted shall be vested in a Congress of the United States, which shall consist of a Senate and House of Representatives.

SECTION 2

1. The House of Representatives shall be composed of Members chosen every second Year by the People of the several States, and the Electors in each State shall have the Qualifications requisite for Electors of the most numerous Branch of the State Legislature.

2. No Person shall be a Representative who shall not have attained to the Age of twenty-five Years, and been seven Years a Citizen of the United States, and who shall not, when elected, be an Inhabitant of that State in which he shall be chosen.

3. Representatives and direct Taxes shall be apportioned among the several states which may be included within this Union, according to their respective Numbers, which shall be determined by adding to the whole Number of free Persons, including those bound to Service for a Term of Years, and excluding Indians not taxed, three-fifths of all other Persons. The actual Enumeration shall be made within three Years after the first Meeting of the Congress of the United States, and within every subsequent Term of ten Years, in such Manner as they shall by Law direct. The Number of Representatives shall not exceed one for every thirty Thousand, but each state shall have at Least one Representative; and until such enumeration shall be made, the State of New Hampshire shall be entitled to chuse three; Massachusetts eight, Rhode Island and Providence Plantations one, Connecticut five, New York six, New Jersey four, Pennsylvania eight, Delaware one, Maryland six, Virginia ten; North Carolina five, South Carolina five, and Georgia three.

Preamble

The Preamble introduces the Constitution and sets forth the general purposes for which the government was established. The preamble also declares that the power of the government comes from the people.

The printed text of the document shows the spelling and punctuation of the parchment original.

Article I. The Legislative Branch

Section 1. Congress

The power to make laws is given to a Congress made up of two chambers to represent different interests: the Senate to represent the states; the House to be more responsive to the people's will.

Section 2. House of Representatives

1. Elections and Term of Office

"Electors" means voters. Every two years the voters choose new Congress members to serve in the House of Representatives. The Constitution states that each state may specify who can vote. But the 15th, 19th, 24th, and 26th Amendments have established guidelines that all states must follow regarding the right to vote.

2. Qualifications

Representatives must be 25 years old, citizens of the United States for 7 years, and residents of the state they represent.

3. Division of Representatives Among the States

The number of representatives from each state is based on the size of the state's population. Each state is divided into congressional districts, with each district required to be equal in population. Each state is entitled to at least one representative. The number of representatives in the House was set at 435 in 1929. Since then, there has been a reapportionment of seats based on population shifts rather than on addition of seats.

Only three-fifths of a state's slave population was to be counted in determining the number of representatives elected by the state. Native Americans were not counted at all.

The "enumeration" referred to is the census, the population count taken every 10 years since 1790.

4. Vacancies

Vacancies in the House are filled through special elections called by the state's governor.

5. Officers

The speaker is the leader of the majority party in the House and is responsible for choosing the heads of various House committees. "Impeachment" means indictment, or bringing charges against an official.

Section 3. The Senate

1. Number of Members, Terms of Office, and Voting Procedure

Originally, senators were chosen by the state legislators of their own states. The 17th Amendment changed this, so that senators are now elected directly by the people. There are 100 senators, 2 from each state.

2. Staggered Elections; Vacancies

One-third of the Senate is elected every two years. The terms of the first Senate's membership was staggered: one group served two years, one four, and one six. All senators now serve a six-year term.

The 17th Amendment changed the method of filling vacancies in the Senate.

3. Qualifications

Qualifications for the Senate are more restrictive than those for the House. Senators must be at least 30 years old and they must have been citizens of the United States for at least 9 years. The Framers of the Constitution made the Senate a more elite body in order to produce a further check on the powers of the House of Representatives.

4. President of the Senate

The Vice President's only duty listed in the Constitution is to preside over the Senate. The only real power the Vice President has is to cast the deciding vote when there is a tie. However, modern Presidents have given their Vice Presidents new responsibilities.

5. Other Officers

The Senate selects its other officers, including a presiding officer (president pro tempore) who serves when the Vice President is absent or has become President of the United States.

6. Trial of Impeachments

When trying a case of impeachment brought by the House, the Senate convenes as a court. The Chief Justice of the Supreme Court acts as the presiding judge, and the Senate acts as the jury. A two-thirds vote of the members present is necessary to convict officials under impeachment charges.

7. Penalty for Conviction

If the Senate convicts an official, it may only remove the official from office and prevent that person from holding another federal position. However, the convicted official may still be tried for the same offense in a regular court of law.

---

4. When vacancies happen in the Representation from any State, the Executive Authority thereof shall issue Writs of Election to fill such Vacancies.

5. The House of Representatives shall chuse their Speaker and other Officers; and shall have the sole Power of Impeachment.

SECTION 3

1. The Senate of the United States shall be composed of two Senators from each State, chosen by the Legislature thereof, for six Years; and each Senator shall have one Vote.

2. Immediately after they shall be assembled in Consequence of the first Election, they shall be divided as equally as may be into three Classes. The Seats of the Senators of the first Class shall be vacated at the Expiration of the second Year, of the second Class at the Expiration of the fourth Year, and of the third Class at the Expiration of the sixth Year, so that one-third may be chosen every second Year; and if Vacancies happen by Resignations, or otherwise, during the Recess of the Legislature of any State, the Executive thereof may make temporary Appointments until the next Meeting of the Legislature, which shall then fill such Vacancies.

3. No person shall be a Senator who shall not have attained the Age of thirty Years, and been nine Years a Citizen of the United States, and who shall not, when elected, be an Inhabitant of that State in which he shall be chosen.

4. The Vice President of the United States shall be President of the Senate, but shall have no vote, unless they be equally divided.

5. The Senate shall chuse their Officers, and also a President pro tempore, in the absence of the Vice-President or when he shall exercise the Office of the President of the United States.

6. The Senate shall have the sole Power to try all impeachments. When sitting for that purpose they shall be on Oath or Affirmation. When the President of the United States is tried, the Chief Justice shall preside: And no person shall be convicted without the Concurrence of two-thirds of the Members present.

7. Judgment in Cases of Impeachment shall not extend further than to removal from Office, and disqualification to hold and enjoy any Office of Honor, Trust or Profit under the United States: but the Party convicted shall nevertheless be liable and subject to Indictment, Trial, Judgment and Punishment, according to Law.

SECTION 4

1. The Times, Places, and Manner of holding Elections for Senators and Representatives, shall be prescribed in each state by the Legislature thereof; but the Congress may at any time by Law make or alter such Regulations, except as to the Places of Chusing Senators.

2. The Congress shall assemble at least once in every Year, and such Meeting shall be on the first Monday in December, unless they shall by Law appoint a different Day.

SECTION 5

1. Each House shall be the Judge of the Elections, Returns and Qualifications of its own Members, and a Majority of each shall constitute a Quorum to do Business; but a smaller Number may adjourn from day to day, and may be authorized to compel the Attendance of absent Members, in such Manner, and under such Penalties as each House may provide.

2. Each House may determine the Rules of its Proceedings, punish its Members for disorderly Behaviour, and, with the Concurrence of two-thirds, expel a Member.

3. Each House shall keep a Journal of its Proceedings, and from time to time publish the same, excepting such Parts as may in their Judgment require Secrecy; and the Yeas and Nays of the Members of either House on any question shall, at the desire of one-fifth of those Present, be entered on the Journal.

4. Neither House during the Session of Congress, shall, without the Consent of the other, adjourn for more than three days, nor to any other Place than that in which the two Houses shall be sitting.

SECTION 6

1. The Senators and Representatives shall receive a Compensation for their Services, to be ascertained by Law, and paid out of the Treasury of the United States. They shall in all Cases, except Treason, Felony and Breach of the Peace be privileged from Arrest during their attendance at the Session of their respective Houses, and in going to and returning from the same; and for any Speech or Debate in either House, they shall not be questioned in any other place.

2. No Senator or Representative shall, during the Time for which he was elected, be appointed to any civil Office under the Authority of the United States, which shall have been created, or the Emoluments whereof shall have been encreased, during such time; and no Person holding any Office under the United States, shall be a Member of either House during his continuance in Office.

Section 7. Passing Laws
1. Revenue Bills
"Revenue" is income raised by the government. The chief source of government revenue is taxes. All tax laws must originate in the House of Representatives. This insures that the branch of Congress which is elected by the people every two years has the major role in determining taxes. This clause does not prevent the Senate from amending tax bills.

2. How Bills Become Laws
A bill may become a law only by passing both houses of Congress and by being signed by the President. If the President disapproves, or vetoes, the bill, it is returned to the house where it originated, along with a written statement of the President's objections. If two-thirds of each house approves the bill after the President has vetoed it, it becomes law. In voting to override a President's veto, the votes of all members of Congress must be recorded in the journals or official records. If the President does not sign or veto a bill within 10 days (excluding Sundays), it becomes law. However, if Congress has adjourned during this 10-day period, the bill does not become law. This is known as a "pocket veto."

3. Presidential Approval or Veto
The Framers included this paragraph to prevent Congress from passing joint resolutions instead of bills to avoid the possibility of a presidential veto. A bill is a draft of a proposed law, whereas a resolution is the legislature's formal expression of opinion or intent on a matter.

Section 8. Powers Granted to Congress
1. Revenue
This clause gives Congress the power to raise and spend revenue. Taxes must be levied at the same rate throughout the nation.

2. Borrowing
The federal government borrows money by issuing bonds.

3. Commerce
The exact meaning of "commerce" has caused controversy. The trend has been to expand its meaning and, consequently, the extent of Congress's powers.

4. Naturalization and Bankruptcy
"Naturalization" refers to the procedure by which a citizen of a foreign nation becomes a citizen of the United States.

5. Currency
Control over money is an exclusive federal power; the states are forbidden to issue currency.

6. Counterfeiting
"Counterfeiting" means illegally imitating or forging.

7. Post Office
In 1970 the United States Postal Service replaced the Post Office Department.

SECTION 7

1. All Bills for raising Revenue shall originate in the House of Representatives; but the Senate may propose or concur with Amendments as on other bills.

2. Every Bill which shall have passed the House of Representatives and the Senate, shall, before it become a Law, be presented to the President of the United States; If he approve he shall sign it, but if not he shall return it, with his Objections, to that House in which it shall have originated, who shall enter the Objections at large on their Journal, and proceed to reconsider it. If after such Reconsideration two-thirds of that House shall agree to pass the bill, it shall be sent, together with the objections, to the other House, by which it shall likewise be reconsidered, and if approved by two-thirds of that House, it shall become a Law. But in all such Cases the Votes of both Houses shall be determined by Yeas and Nays, and the Names of the Persons voting for and against the Bill shall be entered on the Journal of each House respectively. If any Bill shall not be returned by the President within ten Days (Sundays excepted) after it shall have been presented to him, the Same shall be a Law, in like Manner as if he had signed it, unless the Congress by their Adjournment prevent its Return, in which Case it shall not be a Law.

3. Every Order, Resolution, or Vote to which the Concurrence of the Senate and House of Representatives may be necessary (except on a question of Adjournment) shall be presented to the President of the United States; and before the Same shall take Effect, shall be approved by him, or, being disapproved by him, shall be repassed by two-thirds of the Senate and House of Representatives, according to the Rules and Limitations prescribed in the case of a Bill.

SECTION 8
The Congress shall have the Power

1. To lay and collect Taxes, Duties, Imposts and Excises, to pay the Debts and provide for the common Defence and general Welfare of the United States; but all Duties, Imposts and Excises shall be uniform throughout the United States;

2. To borrow money on the credit of the United States;

3. To regulate Commerce with foreign Nations, and among the several States, and with the Indian Tribes;

4. To establish an uniform Rule of Naturalization, and uniform Laws on the subject of Bankruptcies throughout the United States;

5. To coin Money, regulate the Value thereof, and of foreign Coin, and fix the Standard of Weights and Measures;

6. To provide for the Punishment of counterfeiting the Securities and current Coin of the United States;

7. To establish Post Offices and post Roads;

8. To promote the Progress of Science and useful Arts, by securing for limited Times to Authors and Inventors the exclusive Right to their respective Writings and Discoveries;

9. To constitute Tribunals inferior to the Supreme Court;

10. To define and punish Piracies and Felonies committed on the high Seas, and Offenses against the Law of Nations;

11. To declare War, grant Letters of Marque and Reprisal, and make Rules concerning Captures on Land and Water;

12. To raise and support Armies, but no Appropriation of Money to that Use shall be for a longer Term than two Years;

13. To provide and maintain a Navy;

14. To make Rules for the Government and Regulation of the land and naval forces;

15. To provide for calling forth the Militia to execute the Laws of the Union, suppress Insurrections, and repel Invasions;

16. To provide for organizing, arming, and disciplining, the Militia, and for governing such Part of them as may be employed in the Service of the United States, reserving to the States respectively, the Appointment of the Officers, and the Authority of training the Militia according to the discipline prescribed by Congress;

17. To exercise exclusive Legislation in all Cases whatsoever, over such District (not exceeding ten Miles square) as may, by Cession of particular States, and the acceptance of Congress, become the Seat of Government of the United States, and to exercise like Authority over all Places purchased by the Consent of the Legislature of the State in which the Same shall be, for the Erection of Forts, Magazines, Arsenals, dock-Yards, and other needful Buildings; And

18. To make all Laws which shall be necessary and proper for carrying into Execution the foregoing Powers, and all other Powers vested by this Constitution in the Government of the United States, or in any Department or Officer thereof.

SECTION 9

1. The Migration or Importation of such Persons as any of the States now existing shall think proper to admit, shall not be prohibited by the Congress prior to the Year one thousand eight hundred and eight, but a tax or duty may be imposed on such importation, not exceeding ten dollars for each Person.

2. The privilege of the Writ of Habeas Corpus shall not be suspended, unless when in Cases of Rebellion or Invasion the public Safety may require it.

3. No Bill of Attainder or ex post facto Law shall be passed.

4. No capitation, or other direct, Tax shall be laid unless in Proportion to the Census or Enumeration herein before directed to be taken.

---

8. Copyrights and Patents
Under this provision, Congress has passed copyright and patent laws.

9. Courts
This provision allows Congress to establish a federal court system.

10. Piracy
Congress has the power to protect American ships on the high seas.

11. Declare War
While the Constitution gives Congress the right to declare war, the United States has sent troops into combat without a congressional declaration.

12. Army
This provision reveals the Framers' fears of a standing army.

13. Navy
This clause allows Congress to establish a navy.

14. Rules for Armed Forces
Congress may pass regulations that deal with military discipline.

15. Militia
The "militia" is now called the National Guard. It is organized by the states.

16. National Guard
Even though the National Guard is organized by the states, Congress has the authority to pass rules for governing its behavior.

17. Nation's Capital
This clause grants Congress the right to make laws for Washington, D.C.

18. Elastic Clause
This is the so-called "elastic clause" of the Constitution and one of its most important provisions. The "necessary and proper" laws must be related to one of the 17 enumerated powers.

Section 9. Powers Denied to the Federal Government.

1. Slave Trade
This paragraph contains the compromise the Framers reached regarding regulation of the slave trade in exchange for Congress's exclusive control over interstate commerce.

2. Habeas Corpus
Habeas corpus is a Latin term meaning "you may have the body." A writ of habeas corpus issued by a judge requires a law official to bring a prisoner to court and show cause for holding the prisoner. The writ may be suspended only during wartime.

3. Bills of Attainder
A "bill of attainder" is a bill that punishes a person without a jury trial. An "ex post facto" law is one that makes an act a crime after the act has been committed.

4. Direct Taxes
The 16th Amendment allowed Congress to pass an income tax.

5. Tax on Exports

Congress may not tax goods that move from one state to another.

6. Uniformity of Treatment

This prohibition prevents Congress from favoring one state or region over another in the regulation of trade.

7. Appropriation Law

This clause protects against the misuse of funds. All of the President's expenditures must be made with the permission of Congress.

8. Titles of Nobility

This clause prevents the development of a nobility in the United States.

Section 10. Powers Denied to the States
1. Limitations on Power

The states are prohibited from conducting foreign affairs, carrying on a war, or controlling interstate and foreign commerce. States are also not allowed to pass laws that the federal government is prohibited from passing, such as enacting ex post facto laws or bills of attainder. These restrictions on the states were designed, in part, to prevent an overlapping in functions and authority with the federal government that could create conflict and chaos.

2. Export and Import Taxes

This clause prevents states from levying duties on exports and imports. If states were permitted to tax imports and exports they could use their taxing power in a way that weakens or destroys Congress's power to control interstate and foreign commerce.

3. Duties, Armed Forces, War

This clause prohibits states from maintaining an army or navy and from going to war, except in cases where a state is directly attacked. It also forbids states from collecting fees from foreign vessels or from making treaties with other nations. All of these powers are reserved for the federal government.

Article II. The Executive Branch

Section 1. President and Vice President
1. Term of Office

The President is given power to enforce the laws passed by Congress. Both the President and the Vice President serve four-year terms. The 22nd Amendment limits the number of terms the President may serve to two.

---

5. No Tax or Duty shall be laid on Articles exported from any State.

6. No Preference shall be given by any Regulation of Commerce or Revenue to the Ports of one State over those of another: nor shall Vessels bound to, or from, one State, be obliged to enter, clear, or pay Duties in another.

7. No Money shall be drawn from the Treasury, but in Consequence of Appropriations made by Law; and a regular Statement and Account of the Receipts and Expenditures of all public Money shall be published from time to time.

8. No Title of Nobility shall be granted by the United States: And no Person holding any Office of Profit or Trust under them, shall, without the Consent of the Congress, accept of any present, Emolument, Office, or Title, of any kind whatever, from any King, Prince, or foreign State.

SECTION 10

1. No State shall enter into any Treaty, Alliance, or Confederation; grant Letters of Marque and Reprisal; coin Money; emit Bills of Credit; make any Thing but gold and silver Coin a Tender in Payment of Debts; pass any Bill of Attainder; ex post facto Law, or Law impairing the Obligation of Contracts, or grant any Title of Nobility.

2. No State shall, without the Consent of the Congress, lay any Imposts or Duties on Imports or Exports, except what may be absolutely necessary for executing its inspection Laws: and the net Produce of all Duties and Imposts, laid by any State on Imports and Exports, shall be for the Use of the Treasury of the United States; and all such Laws shall be subject to the Revision and Controul of the Congress.

3. No State shall, without the Consent of Congress, lay any duty on Tonnage, keep Troops, or Ships of War in time of Peace, enter into any Agreement or Compact with another State, or with a foreign Power, or engage in War, unless actually invaded, or in such imminent Danger as will not admit of delay.

Article II
SECTION 1

1. The executive Power shall be vested in a President of the United States of America. He shall hold his Office during the Term of four years, and together with the Vice-President chosen for the same Term, be elected, as follows:

2. Each State shall appoint, in such Manner as the Legislature thereof may direct, a Number of Electors, equal to the whole Number of Senators and Representatives to which the State may be entitled in the Congress: but no Senator or Representative, or Person holding an Office of Trust or Profit under the United States, shall be appointed an Elector.

3. The Electors shall meet in their respective States, and vote by Ballot for two Persons, of whom one at least shall not be an Inhabitant of the same State with themselves. And they shall make a List of all the Persons voted for and of the Number of Votes for each; which List they shall sign and certify, and transmit sealed to the Seat of the Government of the United States, directed to the President of the Senate. The President of the Senate shall, in the Presence of the Senate and House of Representatives, open all the Certificates, and the Votes shall then be counted. The Person having the greatest Number of Votes shall be the President, if such Number be a Majority of the whole Number of Electors appointed; and if there be more than one who have such Majority, and have an equal Number of Votes, then the House of Representatives shall immediately chuse by Ballot one of them for President; and if no Person have a Majority, then from the five highest on the List the said House shall in like Manner chuse the President. But in chusing the President, the Votes shall be taken by States, the Representation from each State having one Vote; a quorum for this Purpose shall consist of a Member or Members from two-thirds of the States, and a Majority of all the States shall be necessary to a Choice. In every Case, after the Choice of the President, the Person having the greatest Number of Votes of the Electors shall be the Vice-President. But if there should remain two or more who have equal votes, the Senate shall chuse from them by Ballot the Vice President.

4. The Congress may determine the Time of chusing the Electors, and the Day on which they shall give their Votes; which Day shall be the same throughout the United States.

5. No person except a natural born Citizen, or a Citizen of the United States, at the time of the Adoption of this Constitution, shall be eligible to the Office of President; neither shall any Person be eligible to that Office who shall not have attained to the Age of thirty-five years, and been fourteen Years a Resident within the United States.

6. In Case of the Removal of the President from Office, or of his Death, Resignation, or Inability to discharge the Powers and Duties of the said Office, the same shall devolve on the Vice-President, and the Congress may by Law provide for the Case of Removal, Death, Resignation or Inability, both of the President and Vice-President, declaring what Officer shall then act as President, and such Officer shall act accordingly, until the disability be removed, or a President shall be elected.

2. Election

The Philadelphia Convention had trouble deciding how the President was to be chosen. The system finally agreed upon was indirect election by "electors" chosen for that purpose. The President and Vice President are not directly elected. Instead, the President and Vice President are elected by presidential electors from each state who form the electoral college. Each state has the number of presidential electors equal to the total number of its senators and representatives. State legislatures determine how the electors are chosen. Originally, the state legislatures chose the electors, but today they are nominated by political parties and elected by the voters. No senator, representative, or any other federal officeholder can serve as an elector.

3. Former Method of Election

This clause describes the original method of electing the President and Vice President. According to this method, each elector voted for two candidates. The candidate with the most votes (as long as it was a majority) became President. The candidate with the second highest number of votes became Vice President. In the election of 1800, the two top candidates received the same number of votes, making it necessary for the House of Representatives to decide the election. To prevent such a situation from recurring, the 12th Amendment was added in 1804.

4. Date of Elections

Congress selects the date when the presidential electors are chosen and when they vote for President and Vice President. All electors must vote on the same day. The first Tuesday after the first Monday in November has been set as the date for presidential elections. Electors cast their votes on the Monday after the second Wednesday in December.

5. Qualifications

The President must be a citizen of the United States by birth, at least 35 years old, and a resident of the United States for 14 years. See Amendment 22.

6. Vacancies

If the President dies, resigns, is removed from office by impeachment, or is unable to carry out the duties of the office, the Vice President becomes President. (Amendment 25 deals with presidential disability.) If both the President and Vice President are unable to serve, Congress has the power to declare by law who acts as President. Congress set the line of succession in the Presidential Succession Act of 1947.

7. Salary

Originally, the President's salary was $25,000 per year. The President's current salary of $200,000 plus a $50,000 taxable expense account per year was enacted in 1969. The President also receives numerous fringe benefits including a $120,000 nontaxable allowance for travel and entertainment, and living accommodations in two residences —the White House and Camp David. However, the President cannot receive any other income from the United States government or state governments while in office.

8. Oath of Office

The oath of office is generally administered by the chief justice, but can be administered by any official authorized to administer oaths. All Presidents-elect except Washington have been sworn into office by the chief justice. Only Vice Presidents John Tyler, Calvin Coolidge, and Lyndon Johnson in succeeding to the office have been sworn in by someone else.

Section 2. Powers of the President
1. Military, Cabinet, Pardons

Mention of "the principal officer in each of the executive departments" is the only suggestion of the President's Cabinet to be found in the Constitution. The Cabinet is a purely advisory body, and its power depends on the President. Each Cabinet member is appointed by the President and must be confirmed by the Senate. This clause also makes the President, a civilian, the head of the armed services. This established the principle of civilian control of the military.

2. Treaties and Appointments

The President is the chief architect of American foreign policy. He or she is responsible for the conduct of foreign relations, or dealings with other countries. All treaties, however, require approval of two-thirds of the senators present. Most federal positions today are filled under the rules and regulations of the civil service system. Most presidential appointees serve at the pleasure of the President. Removal of an official by the President is not subject to congressional approval. But the power can be restricted by conditions set in creating the office.

3. Vacancies in Offices

The President can temporarily appoint officials to fill vacancies when the Senate is not in session.

7. The President shall, at stated Times, receive for his Services a Compensation, which shall neither be encreased nor diminished during the Period for which he shall have been elected, and he shall not receive within that Period any other Emolument from the United States, or any of them.

8. Before he enter on the execution of his office, he shall take the following Oath or Affirmation "I do solemnly swear (or affirm) that I will faithfully execute the Office of President of the United States, and will to the best of my Ability, preserve, protect and defend the Constitution of the United States."

SECTION 2

1. The President shall be Commander in Chief of the Army and Navy of the United States, and of the Militia of the several States, when called into the actual Service of the United States; he may require the Opinion, in writing, of the principal Officer in each of the executive Departments, upon any subject relating to the Duties of their respective Offices, and he shall have Power to Grant Reprieves and Pardons for Offences against the United States, except in Cases of Impeachment.

2. He shall have Power, by and with the Advice and Consent of the Senate, to make Treaties, provided two-thirds of the Senators present concur; and he shall nominate, and by and with the Advice and Consent of the Senate, shall appoint Ambassadors, other public Ministers and Consuls, Judges of the supreme Court, and all other Officers of the United States, whose Appointments are not herein otherwise provided for, and which shall be established by Law. But the Congress may by Law vest the Appointment of such inferior Officers, as they think proper, in the President alone, in the Courts of Law, or in the Heads of Departments.

3. The President shall have Power to fill up all Vacancies that may happen during the Recess of the Senate, by granting Commissions which shall expire at the End of their next Session.

SECTION 3

He shall from time to time give to Congress Information of the State of the Union, and recommend to their Consideration such Measures as he shall judge necessary and expedient; he may, on extraordinary occasions, convene both Houses, or either of them, and in Case of Disagreement between them, with respect to the Time of Adjournment, he may adjourn them to such Time as he shall think proper; he shall receive Ambassadors and other public Ministers; he shall take Care that the Laws be faithfully executed, and shall Commission all the Officers of the United States.

SECTION 4

The President, Vice-President and all civil Officers of the United States, shall be removed from Office on Impeachment for, and Conviction of, Treason, Bribery, or other high Crimes and Misdemeanors.

Article III
SECTION 1

The Judicial Power of the United States, shall be vested in one supreme Court, and in such inferior Courts as the Congress may from time to time ordain and establish. The judges, both of the supreme and inferior Courts, shall hold their Offices during good Behaviour, and shall, at stated Times, receive for their Services, a Compensation, which shall not be diminished during their Continuance in Office.

SECTION 2

1. The judicial Power shall extend to all Cases, in Law and Equity, arising under this Constitution, the Laws of the United States, and treaties made, or which shall be made, under their Authority; to all Cases affecting ambassadors, other public ministers and consuls; to all cases of admiralty and maritime Jurisdiction; to Controversies to which the United States shall be a party; to Controversies between two or more states; between a State and Citizens of another State; between Citizens of different States; between Citizens of the same State claiming Lands under Grants of different States, and between a State, or the Citizens thereof, and foreign States, Citizens or Subjects.

2. In all Cases affecting Ambassadors, other public Ministers and Consuls, and those in which a State shall be Party, the supreme Court shall have original Jurisdiction. In all the other Cases before mentioned, the supreme Court shall have appellate Jurisdiction, both as to Law and Fact, with such Exceptions, and under such Regulations as the Congress shall make.

3. The trial of all Crimes, except in Cases of Impeachment, shall be by Jury; and such Trial shall be held in the State where the said Crimes shall have been committed; but when not committed within any State, the Trial shall be at such Place or Places as the Congress may by Law have directed.

Section 3. Duties of the President

Under this provision the President delivers annual State-of-the-Union messages. On occasion, Presidents have called Congress into special session to consider particular problems.

The President's duty to receive foreign diplomats also includes the power to ask a foreign country to withdraw its diplomatic officials from this country. This is called "breaking diplomatic relations" and often carries with it the implied threat of more drastic action, even war. The President likewise has the power of deciding whether or not to recognize foreign governments.

Section 4. Impeachment

This section states the reasons for which the President and Vice President may be impeached and removed from office. (See annotations of Article I, Section 3, Clauses 6 and 7.)

Article III. The Judicial Branch

Section 1. Federal Courts

The term *judicial* refers to courts. The Constitution set up only the Supreme Court but provided for the establishment of other federal courts. There are presently nine justices on the Supreme Court. Congress has created a system of federal district courts and courts of appeals, which review certain district court cases. Judges of these courts serve during "good behavior," which means that they usually serve for life or until they choose to retire.

Section 2. Jurisdiction
1. General Jurisdiction

Use of the words *in law and equity* reflects the fact that American courts took over two kinds of traditional law from Great Britain. The basic law was the "common law," which was based on over five centuries of judicial decisions. "Equity" was a special branch of British law developed to handle cases where common law did not apply.

Federal courts deal mostly with "statute law," or laws passed by Congress, treaties, and cases involving the Constitution itself. "Admiralty and maritime jurisdiction" covers all sorts of cases involving ships and shipping on the high seas and on rivers, canals, and lakes.

2. The Supreme Court

When a court has "original jurisdiction" over certain kinds of cases, it means that the court has the authority to be the first court to hear a case. A court with "appellate jurisdiction" hears cases that have been appealed from lower courts. Most Supreme Court cases are heard on appeal from lower courts.

3. Jury Trials

Except in cases of impeachment, anyone accused of a crime has the right to a trial by jury. The trial must be held in the state where the crime was committed. Jury trial guarantees were strengthened in the 6th, 7th, 8th, and 9th Amendments.

Section 3. Treason

1. Definition

Knowing that the charge of treason often had been used by monarchs to get rid of people who opposed them, the Framers of the Constitution defined treason carefully, requiring that at least two witnesses be present to testify in court that a treasonable act was committed.

2. Punishment

Congress is given the power to determine the punishment for treason. The children of a person convicted of treason may not be punished nor may the convicted person's property be taken away from the children. Convictions for treason have been relatively rare in the nation's history.

Article IV. Relations Among the States

Section 1. Official Acts

This provision insures that each state recognizes the laws, court decisions, and records of all other states. For example, a marriage license or corporation charter issued by one state must be accepted in other states.

Section 2. Mutual Duties of States

1. Privileges

The "privileges and immunities," or rights of citizens, guarantee each state's citizens equal treatment in all states.

2. Extradition

"Extradition" means that a person convicted of a crime or a person accused of a crime must be returned to the state where the crime was committed. Thus, a person cannot flee to another state hoping to escape the law.

3. Fugitive-Slave Clause

Formerly this clause meant that slaves could not become free persons by escaping to free states.

Section 3. New States and Territories

1. New States

Congress has the power to admit new states. It also determines the basic guidelines for applying for statehood. One state, Maine, was created within the original boundaries of another state (Massachusetts) with the consent of Congress and the state.

2. Territories

Congress has power over federal land. But neither in this clause nor anywhere else in the Constitution is the federal government explicitly empowered to acquire new territory.

Section 4. Federal Protection for States

This section allows the federal government to send troops into a state to guarantee law and order. The President may send in troops even without the consent of the state government involved.

SECTION 3

1. Treason against the United States, shall consist only in levying War against them, or in adhering to their Enemies, giving them Aid and Comfort. No Person shall be convicted of Treason unless on the Testimony of two Witnesses to the same overt Act, or on Confession in open Court.

2. The Congress shall have power to declare the Punishment of Treason, but no Attainder of Treason shall work Corruption of Blood, or Forfeiture except during the Life of the Person attainted.

Article IV

SECTION 1

Full Faith and Credit shall be given in each State to the public Acts, Records, and judicial Proceedings of every other State. And the Congress may by general Laws prescribe the Manner in which such Acts, Records, and Proceedings shall be proved, and the Effect thereof.

SECTION 2

1. The Citizens of each State shall be entitled to all Privileges and Immunities of Citizens in the several States.

2. A Person charged in any State with Treason, Felony, or other Crime, who shall flee from Justice, and be found in another State, shall on demand of the executive Authority of the State from which he fled, be delivered up, to be removed to the State having Jurisdiction of the crime.

3. No Person held to Service of Labour in one State, under the Laws thereof, escaping into another, shall, in Consequence of any Law or Regulation therein, be discharged from such Service or Labour, but shall be delivered up on Claim of the Party to whom such Service or Labour may be due.

SECTION 3

1. New States may be admitted by the Congress into this Union; but no new State shall be formed or erected within the Jurisdiction of any other State; nor any State be formed by the Junction of two or more States, or parts of States, without the Consent of the Legislatures of the States concerned as well as of the Congress.

2. The Congress shall have Power to dispose of and make all needful Rules and Regulations respecting the Territory of other Property belonging to the United States; and nothing in this Constitution shall be so construed as to Prejudice any Claims of the United States, or of any particular State.

SECTION 4

The United States shall guarantee to every State in this Union a Republican Form of Government, and shall protect each of them against Invasion; and on Application of the Legislature, or of the Executive (when the Legislature cannot be convened) against domestic Violence.

Article V

The Congress, whenever two-thirds of both Houses shall deem it necessary, shall propose Amendments to this Constitution, or, on the Application of the Legislatures of two-thirds of the several States, shall call a Convention for proposing Amendments, which, in either Case, shall be valid to all Intents and Purposes, as part of this Constitution, when ratified by the Legislatures of three-fourths of the several States, or by Conventions in three-fourths thereof, as the one or the other Mode of Ratification may be proposed by the Congress; Provided that no Amendment which may be made prior to the Year One thousand eight hundred and eight shall in any Manner affect the first and fourth clauses in the Ninth Section of the first Article; and that no State, without its Consent, shall be deprived of its equal Suffrage in the Senate.

Article V. The Amending Process

There are now 27 Amendments to the Constitution. The Framers of the Constitution deliberately made it difficult to amend or change the Constitution. Two methods of proposing and ratifying amendments are provided for. A two-thirds majority is needed in Congress to propose an amendment, and at least three-fourths of the states (38 states) must accept the amendment before it can become law. No amendment has yet been proposed by a national convention called by the states, though in the 1980s a convention to propose an amendment requiring a balanced budget had been approved by 32 states.

Article VI

1. All Debts contracted and Engagements entered into, before the Adoption of this Constitution, shall be as valid against the United States under this Constitution as under the Confederation.

2. This Constitution, and the Laws of the United States which shall be made in Pursuance thereof; and all Treaties made, or which shall be made, under the Authority of the United States, shall be the supreme Law of the Land; and the Judges in every State shall be bound thereby, any Thing in the Constitution or Laws of any State to the Contrary notwithstanding.

3. The Senators and Representatives before mentioned, and the Members of the several State Legislatures, and all executive and judicial Officers, both of the United States and of the several States, shall be bound by Oath or Affirmation, to support this Constitution; but no religious Test shall ever be required as a Qualification to any Office or public Trust under the United States.

Article VI. National Supremacy

1. Public Debts and Treaties
This section promised that all debts the colonies had incurred during the Revolution and under the Articles of Confederation would be honored by the new United States government.

2. The Supreme Law
The "supremacy clause" recognized the Constitution and federal laws as supreme when in conflict with those of the states. It was largely based on this clause that Chief Justice John Marshall wrote his historic decision in *McCulloch* v. *Maryland*. The 14th Amendment reinforced the supremacy of federal law over state laws.

3. Oaths of Office
This clause also declares that no religious test shall be required as a qualification for holding public office. This principle is also asserted in the First Amendment, which forbids Congress to set up an established church or to interfere with the religious freedom of Americans.

Article VII

The Ratification of the Conventions of nine States shall be sufficient for the Establishment of this Constitution between the States so ratifying the same.

Done in Convention, by the Unanimous Consent of the States present, the Seventeenth Day of September, in the Year of our Lord one thousand seven hundred and Eighty-seven, and of the Independence of the United States of America the Twelfth. In Witness whereof We have hereunto subscribed our Names.

Article VII. Ratification of the Constitution

Unlike the Articles of Confederation, which required approval of all thirteen states for adoption, the Constitution required approval of only nine of thirteen states. Thirty-nine of the 55 delegates at the Constitutional Convention signed the Constitution. The Constitution went into effect in June 1788.

Amendment 1. Freedom of Religion, Speech, Press, and Assembly (1791)

The 1st Amendment protects the civil liberties of individuals in the United States. The 1st Amendment freedoms are not absolute, however. They are limited by the rights of other individuals.

Amendment 2. Right to Bear Arms (1791)

The purpose of this amendment is to guarantee states the right to keep a militia.

Amendment 3. Quartering Troops (1791)

This amendment is based on the principle that people have a right to privacy in their own homes. It also reflects the colonists' grievances against the British government before the Revolution. Britain had angered Americans by quartering (housing) troops in private homes.

Amendment 4. Searches and Seizures (1791)

Like the 3rd Amendment, the 4th amendment reflects the colonists' desire to protect their privacy. Britain had used writs of assistance (general search warrants) to seek out smuggled goods. Americans wanted to make sure that such searches and seizures would be conducted only when a judge felt that there was "reasonable cause" to conduct them. The Supreme Court has ruled that evidence seized illegally without a search warrant may not be used in court.

Amendment I

Congress shall make no law respecting an establishment of religion, or prohibiting the free exercise thereof; or abridging the freedom of speech, or of the press; or the right of the people peaceably to assemble, and to petition the Government for a redress of grievances.

Amendment II

A well-regulated Militia, being necessary to the security of a free State, the right of the people to keep and bear Arms, shall not be infringed.

Amendment III

No soldier shall, in time of peace be quartered in any house, without the consent of the Owner, nor in time of war, but in a manner to be prescribed by law.

Amendment IV

The right of the people to be secure in their persons, houses, papers, and effects, against unreasonable searches and seizures, shall not be violated, and no Warrants shall issue, but upon probable cause, supported by Oath or affirmation, and particularly describing the place to be searched, and the persons or things to be seized.

Amendment V

No person shall be held to answer for a capital, or otherwise infamous crime, unless on a presentment or indictment of a Grand Jury, except in cases arising in the land or naval forces, or in the Militia, when in actual service in time of War or public danger; nor shall any person be subject for the same offence to be twice put in jeopardy of life or limb; nor shall be compelled in any criminal case to be a witness against himself, nor be deprived of life, liberty, or property, without due process of law; nor shall private property be taken for public use, without just compensation.

Amendment VI

In all criminal prosecutions, the accused shall enjoy the right to a speedy and public trial, by an impartial jury of the State and district wherein the crime shall have been committed, which district shall have been previously ascertained by law, and to be informed of the nature and cause of the accusation; to be confronted with the witnesses against him; to have compulsory process for obtaining witnesses in his favor, and to have the Assistance of Counsel for his defence.

Amendment VII

In suits at common law, where the value in controversy shall exceed twenty dollars, the right of trial by jury shall be preserved, and no fact tried by a jury, shall be otherwise reexamined in any Courts of the United States, than according to the rules of common law.

Amendment VIII

Excessive bail shall not be required, nor excessive fines imposed, nor cruel and unusual punishments inflicted.

Amendment IX

The enumeration in the Constitution, of certain rights, shall not be construed to deny or disparage others retained by the people.

Amendment X

The powers not delegated to the United States by the Constitution, nor prohibited by it to the States, are reserved to the States respectively, or to the people.

Amendment 5. Rights of Accused Persons (1791)

To bring a "presentment" or "indictment" means to formally charge a person with committing a crime. It is the function of a grand jury to see whether there is enough evidence to bring the accused person to trial. A person may not be tried more than once for the same crime (double jeopardy).

Members of the armed services are subject to military law. They may be tried in a court martial. In times of war or a natural disaster, civilians may also be put under martial law.

The 5th Amendment also guarantees that persons may not be forced in any criminal case to be a witness against themselves. That is, accused persons may refuse to answer questions on the ground that the answers might tend to incriminate them.

Amendment 6. Right to Speedy, Fair Trial (1791)

The requirement of a "speedy" trial insures that an accused person will not be held in jail for a lengthy period as a means of punishing the accused without a trial. A "fair" trial means that the trial must be open to the public and that a jury must hear witnesses and evidence on both sides before deciding the guilt or innocence of a person charged with a crime. This amendment also provides that legal counsel must be provided to a defendant. In 1963, the Supreme Court ruled, in *Gideon* v. *Wainwright,* that if a defendant cannot afford a lawyer, the government must provide one to defend the accused person.

Amendment 7. Civil Suits (1791)

"Common law" means the law established by previous court decisions. In civil cases where one person sues another for more than $20, a jury trial is provided for. But customarily, federal courts do not hear civil cases unless they involve a good deal more money.

Amendment 8. Bail and Punishment (1791)

"Bail" is money that an accused person provides to the court as a guarantee that he or she will be present for a trial. This amendment insures that neither bail nor punishment for a crime shall be unreasonably severe.

Amendment 9. Powers Reserved to the People (1791)

This amendment provides that the people's rights are not limited to those mentioned in the Constitution.

Amendment 10. Powers Reserved to the States (1791)

This amendment protects the states and the people from an all-powerful federal government. It provides that the states or the people retain all powers except those denied them or those specifically granted to the federal government. This "reserved powers" provision is a check on the "necessary and proper" power of the federal government provided in the "elastic clause" in Article I, Section 8, Clause 18.

Amendment 11. Suits Against States (1795)

This amendment provides that a lawsuit brought by a citizen of the United States or a foreign nation against a state must be tried in a state court, not in a federal court. This amendment was passed after the Supreme Court ruled that a federal court could try a lawsuit brought by citizens of South Carolina against a citizen of Georgia. This case, *Chisholm* v. *Georgia,* decided in 1793, was protested by many Americans, who insisted states would lose authority if they could be sued in federal courts.

Amendment 12. Election of President and Vice President (1804)

This amendment changes the procedure for electing the President and Vice President as outlined in Article II, Section 1, Clause 3.

To prevent the recurrence of the election of 1800 whereby a candidate running for Vice President (Aaron Burr) could tie a candidate running for President (Thomas Jefferson) and thus force the election into the House of Representatives, the Twelfth Amendment specifies that the electors are to cast separate ballots for each office. The votes for each office are counted and listed separately. The results are signed, sealed, and sent to the president of the senate. At a joint session of Congress, the votes are counted. The candidate who receives the most votes, providing it is a majority, is elected President. Other changes include: (1) a reduction from five to the three highest candidates receiving votes among whom the House is to choose if no candidate receives a majority of the electoral votes, and (2) provision for the Senate to choose the Vice President from the two highest candidates if neither has received a majority of the electoral votes.

The Twelfth Amendment does place one restriction on electors. It prohibits electors from voting for two candidates (President and Vice President) from their home state.

Amendment 13. Abolition of Slavery (1865)

This amendment was the final act in ending slavery in the United States. It also prohibits the binding of a person to perform a personal service due to debt. In addition to imprisonment for crime, the Supreme Court has held that the draft is not a violation of the amendment.

This amendment is the first adopted to be divided into sections. It is also the first to contain specifically a provision granting Congress power to enforce it by appropriate legislation.

Amendment XI

The Judicial power of the United States shall not be construed to extend to any suit in law or equity, commenced or prosecuted against one of the United States by Citizens of another State, or by Citizens or Subjects of any Foreign State.

Amendment XII

The Electors shall meet in their respective States and vote by ballot for President and Vice-President, one of whom, at least, shall not be an inhabitant of the same State with themselves; they shall name in their ballots the person voted for as President, and in distinct ballots the person voted for as Vice-President, and they shall make distinct lists of all persons voted for as President, and of all persons voted for as Vice-President, and of the number of votes for each, which lists they shall sign and certify, and transmit sealed to the seat of the government of the United States, directed to the President of the Senate; The President of the Senate shall, in the presence of the Senate and House of Representatives, open all the certificates and the votes shall then be counted; The person having the greatest number of votes for President, shall be the President, if such number be a majority of the whole number of Electors appointed; and if no person have such majority, then from the persons having the highest numbers not exceeding three on the list of those voted for as President, the House of Representatives shall choose immediately, by ballot, the President. But in choosing the President, the votes shall be taken by states, the representation from each state having one vote; a quorum for this purpose shall consist of a member or members from two-thirds of the states, and a majority of all the states shall be necessary to a choice. And if the House of Representatives shall not choose a President whenever the right of choice shall devolve upon them, before the fourth day of March next following, then the Vice-President shall act as President, as in the case of the death or other constitutional disability of the President. The person having the greatest number of votes as Vice-President, shall be the Vice-President, if such number be a majority of the whole number of Electors appointed, and if no person have a majority, then from the two highest numbers on the list, the Senate shall choose the Vice-President; a quorum for the purpose shall consist of two-thirds of the whole number of Senators, and a majority of the whole number shall be necessary to a choice. But no person constitutionally ineligible to the office of President shall be eligible to that of Vice-President of the United States.

Amendment XIII

SECTION 1

Neither slavery nor involuntary servitude, except as a punishment for crime whereof the party shall have been duly convicted, shall exist within the United States, or any place subject to their jurisdiction.

SECTION 2

Congress shall have power to enforce this article by appropriate legislation.

Amendment XIV

SECTION 1

All persons born or naturalized in the United States, and subject to the jurisdiction thereof, are citizens of the United States and of the State wherein they reside. No State shall make or enforce any law which shall abridge the privileges or immunities of citizens of the United States; nor shall any State deprive any person of life, liberty, or property, without due process of law, nor deny to any person within its jurisdiction the equal protection of the laws.

SECTION 2

Representatives shall be apportioned among the several States according to their respective numbers, counting the whole number of persons in each State, excluding Indians not taxed. But when the right to vote at any election for the choice of electors for President and Vice-President of the United States, Representatives in Congress, the Executive and Judicial officers of a State, or the members of the Legislature thereof, is denied to any of the male inhabitants of such State, being twenty-one years of age, and citizens of the United States, or in any way abridged, except for participation in rebellion, or other crime, the basis of representation therein shall be reduced in the proportion which the number of such male citizens shall bear to the whole number of male citizens twenty-one years of age in such State.

SECTION 3

No person shall be a Senator or Representative in Congress, or elector of President and Vice-President, or hold any office, civil or military, under the United States, or under any State, who, having previously taken an oath, as a member of Congress, or as an officer of the United States, or as a member of any State legislature, or as an executive or judicial officer of any State, to support the Constitution of the United States, shall have engaged in insurrection or rebellion against the same, or given aid or comfort to the enemies thereof. But Congress may by a vote of two-thirds of each House, remove such disability.

SECTION 4

The validity of the public debt of the United States incurred for payment of pensions and bounties for service, authorized by law, including debts in suppressing insurrections or rebellion, shall not be questioned. But neither the United States nor any State shall assume or pay any debt or obligation incurred in aid of insurrection or rebellion against the United States, or any claim for the loss or emancipation of any slave; but all such debts, obligations and claims shall be held illegal and void.

SECTION 5

The Congress shall have power to enforce, by appropriate legislation, the provisions of this article.

Amendment 14. Rights of Citizens (1868)

The clauses of this amendment were intended 1) to penalize southern states that refused to grant African Americans the vote, 2) to keep former Confederate leaders from serving in government, 3) to forbid payment of the Confederacy's debt by the federal government, and 4) to insure payment of the war debts owed the federal government.

Section 1. Citizenship Defined

By granting citizenship to all persons born in the United States, this amendment granted citizenship to former slaves. The amendment also guaranteed "due process of law." By the 1950s, Supreme Court rulings used the due process clause to protect civil liberties. The last part of Section 1 establishes the doctrine that all citizens are entitled to equal protection of the laws. In 1954 the Supreme Court ruled, in *Brown* v. *Board of Education of Topeka,* that segregation in public schools was unconstitutional because it denied equal protection.

Section 2. Representation in Congress

This section reduced the number of members a state had in the House of Representatives if it denied its citizens the right to vote. This section was not implemented, however. Later civil rights laws and the 24th Amendment guaranteed the vote to African Americans.

Section 3. Penalty for Engaging in Insurrection

The leaders of the Confederacy were barred from state or federal offices unless Congress agreed to revoke this ban. By the end of Reconstruction all but a few Confederate leaders were allowed to return to public life.

Section 4. Public Debt

The public debt incurred by the federal government during the Civil War was valid and could not be questioned by the South. However, the debts of the Confederacy were declared to be illegal. And former slave owners could not collect compensation for the loss of their slaves.

Section 5. Enforcement

Congress was empowered to pass civil rights bills to guarantee the provisions of the amendment.

Amendment 15. The Right to Vote (1870)
Section 1. Suffrage for African Americans
The 15th Amendment replaced Section 2 of the 14th Amendment in guaranteeing African Americans the right to vote, that is, the right of African Americans to vote was not to be left to the states. Yet, despite this prohibition, African Americans were denied the right to vote by many states by such means as poll taxes, literacy tests, and white primaries.

Section 2. Enforcement
Congress was given the power to enforce this amendment. During the 1950s and 1960s, it passed successively stronger laws to end racial discrimination in voting rights.

Amendment 16. Income Tax (1913)
The origins of this amendment went back to 1895, when the Supreme Court declared a federal income tax unconstitutional. To overcome this Supreme Court decision, this amendment authorized an income tax that was levied on a direct basis.

Amendment 17. Direct Election of Senators (1913)
Section 1. Method of Election
The right to elect senators was given directly to the people of each state. It replaced Article I, Section 3, Clause 1, which empowered state legislatures to elect senators. This amendment was designed not only to make the choice of senators more democratic but also to cut down on corruption and to improve state government.

Section 2. Vacancies
A state must order an election to fill a senate vacancy. A state may empower its governor to appoint a person to fill a Senate seat if a vacancy occurs until an election can be held.

Section 3. Time in Effect
This amendment was not to affect any Senate election or temporary appointment until it was in effect.

Amendment 18. Prohibition of Alcoholic Beverages (1919)
This amendment prohibited the production, sale, or transportation of alcoholic beverages in the United States. Prohibition proved to be difficult to enforce, especially in states with large urban populations. This amendment was later repealed by the 21st Amendment.

Amendment 19. Women's Suffrage (1920)
This amendment, extending the vote to all qualified women in federal and state elections, was a landmark victory for the woman suffrage movement, which had worked to achieve this goal for many years. The women's movement had earlier gained full voting rights for women in four western states in the late nineteenth century.

Amendment XV

SECTION 1
The right of citizens of the United States to vote shall not be denied or abridged by the United States or by any State on account of race, color, or previous condition of servitude.

SECTION 2
The Congress shall have power to enforce this article by appropriate legislation.

Amendment XVI

The Congress shall have power to lay and collect taxes on incomes, from whatever source derived, without apportionment among several States, and without regard to any census or enumeration.

Amendment XVII

SECTION 1
The Senate of the United States shall be composed of two Senators from each State, elected by the people thereof, for six years; and each Senator shall have one vote. The electors in each state shall have the qualifications requisite for electors of the most numerous branch of the state legislatures.

SECTION 2
When vacancies happen in the representation of any State in the Senate, the executive authority of such State shall issue writs of election to fill such vacancies: *Provided,* that the legislature of any State may empower the executive thereof to make temporary appointments until the people fill the vacancies by election as the legislature may direct.

SECTION 3
This amendment shall not be so construed as to affect the election or term of any Senator chosen before it becomes valid as part of the Constitution.

Amendment XVIII

SECTION 1
After one year from ratification of this article the manufacture, sale, or transportation of intoxicating liquors within, the importation thereof into, or the exportation thereof from the United States and all territory subject to the jurisdiction thereof for beverage purposes is hereby prohibited.

SECTION 2
The Congress and the several states shall have concurrent power to enforce this article by appropriate legislation.

SECTION 3
This article shall be inoperative unless it shall have been ratified as an amendment to the Constitution by the legislatures of the several States, as provided in the Constitution, within seven years from the date of the submission hereof to the states of the Congress.

Amendment XIX

SECTION 1
The right of citizens of the United States to vote shall not be denied or abridged by the United States or by any state on account of sex.

SECTION 2
Congress shall have power to enforce this article by appropriate legislation.

Amendment XX

SECTION 1

The terms of the President and Vice President shall end at noon on the 20th day of January, and the terms of the Senators and Representatives at noon on the 3rd day of January, of the years in which such terms would have ended if this article had not been ratified; and the terms of their successors shall then begin.

SECTION 2

The Congress shall assemble at least once in every year, and such meeting shall begin at noon on the 3rd day of January, unless they shall by law appoint a different day.

SECTION 3

If, at the time fixed for the beginning of the term of the President, the President elect shall have died, the Vice President elect shall become President. If a President shall not have been chosen before the time fixed for the beginning of his term, or if the President elect shall have failed to qualify, then the Vice President elect shall act as President until a President shall have qualified; and the Congress may by law provide for the case wherein neither a President elect nor a Vice President elect shall have qualified, declaring who shall then act as President, or the manner in which one who is to act shall be selected, and such person shall act accordingly until a President or Vice President shall have qualified.

SECTION 4

The Congress may by law provide for the case of the death of any of the persons from whom the House of Representatives may choose a President whenever the right of choice shall have devolved upon them, and for the case of the death of any of the persons from whom the Senate may choose a Vice President whenever the right of choice shall have devolved upon them.

SECTION 5

Sections 1 and 2 shall take effect on the 15th day of October following the ratification of this article.

SECTION 6

This article shall be inoperative unless it shall have been ratified as an amendment to the Constitution by the legislatures of three-fourths of the several States within seven years from the date of its submission.

Amendment XXI

SECTION 1

The eighteenth article of amendment to the Constitution of the United States is hereby repealed.

SECTION 2

The transportation or importation into any State, Territory, or possession of the United States for delivery or use therein of intoxicating liquors, in violation of the laws thereof, is hereby prohibited.

SECTION 3

This article shall be inoperative unless it shall have been ratified as an amendment to the Constitution by conventions in the several States, as provided in the Constitution, within seven years from the date of the submission hereof to the States by the Congress.

Amendment 20. "Lame-Duck" Amendment (1933)

Section 1. New Dates of Terms

This amendment had two major purposes: 1) to shorten the time between the President's and Vice President's election and inauguration, and 2) to end "lame-duck" sessions of Congress.

When the Constitution first went into effect, transportation and communication were slow and uncertain. It often took many months after the election in November for the President and Vice President to travel to Washington, D.C., and prepare for their inauguration on March 4. This amendment ended this long wait for a new administration by fixing January 20 as Inauguration Day.

Section 2. Meeting Time of Congress

"Lame-duck" sessions occurred every two years, after the November congressional election. That is, the Congress that held its session in December of an election year was not the newly elected Congress but the old Congress that had been elected two years earlier. This Congress continued to serve for several more months, usually until March of the next year. Often many of its members had failed to be re-elected and were called "lame-ducks." The 20th Amendment abolished this "lame-duck" session, and provided that the new Congress hold its first session soon after the November election, on January 3.

Section 3. Succession of President and Vice President

This amendment provides that if the President-elect dies before taking office, the Vice President-elect becomes President. In the cases described, Congress will decide on a temporary President.

Section 4. Filling Presidential Vacancy

If a presidential candidate dies while an election is being decided in the House, Congress may pass legislation to deal with the situation. Congress has similar power if this occurs when the Senate is deciding a vice-presidential election.

Section 5. Beginning the New Dates

Sections 1 and 2 affected the Congress elected in 1934 and President Roosevelt, elected in 1936.

Section 6. Time Limit on Ratification

The period for ratification by the states was limited to seven years.

Amendment 21. Repeal of Prohibition Amendment (1933)

This amendment nullified the 18th Amendment. It is the only amendment ever passed to overturn an earlier amendment. It remained unlawful to transport alcoholic beverages into states that forbade their use. It is the only amendment ratified by special state conventions instead of state legislatures.

Amendment XXII

SECTION 1

No person shall be elected to the office of the President more than twice, and no person who had held the office of President, or acted as President, for more than two years of a term to which some other person was elected President shall be elected to the office of the President more than once.

But this Article shall not apply to any person holding the office of President when this Article was proposed by the Congress, and shall not prevent any person who may be holding the office of President, or acting as President, during the term within which this Article becomes operative from holding the office of President or acting as President during the remainder of such term.

SECTION 2

This article shall be inoperative unless it shall have been ratified as an amendment to the Constitution by the legislatures of three-fourths of the several States within seven years from the date of its submission to the States by the Congress.

Amendment XXIII

SECTION 1

The District constituting the seat of Government of the United States shall appoint in such manner as the Congress may direct:

A number of electors of President and Vice President equal to the whole number of Senators and Representatives in Congress to which the District would be entitled if it were a State, but in no event more than the least populous State; they shall be in addition to those appointed by the States, but they shall be considered, for the purposes of the election of President and Vice President, to be electors appointed by a State; and they shall meet in the District and perform such duties as provided by the twelfth article of amendment.

SECTION 2

The Congress shall have power to enforce this article by appropriate legislation.

Amendment XXIV

SECTION 1

The right of citizens of the United States to vote in any primary or other election for President or Vice President, for electors for President or Vice President, or for Senator or Representative in Congress, shall not be denied or abridged by the United States or any State by reason of failure to pay any poll tax or other tax.

SECTION 2

The Congress shall have power to enforce this article by appropriate legislation.

Amendment XXV

SECTION 1

In case of the removal of the President from office or his death or resignation, the Vice President shall become President.

SECTION 2

Whenever there is a vacancy in the office of the Vice President, the President shall nominate a Vice President who shall take the office upon confirmation by a majority vote of both houses of Congress.

SECTION 3

Whenever the President transmits to the President pro tempore of the Senate and the Speaker of the House of Representatives his written declaration that he is unable to discharge the powers and duties of his office, and until he transmits to them a written declaration to the contrary, such powers and duties shall be discharged by the Vice President as Acting President.

SECTION 4

Whenever the Vice President and a majority of either the principal officers of the executive departments or of such other body as Congress may by law provide, transmit to the President pro tempore of the Senate and the Speaker of the House of Representatives their written declaration that the President is unable to discharge the powers and duties of his office, the Vice President shall immediately assume the power and duties of the office of Acting President.

Thereafter, when the President transmits to the President pro tempore of the Senate and the Speaker of the House of Representatives his written declaration that no inability exists, he shall resume the powers and duties of his office unless the Vice President and a majority of either the principal officers of the executive departments or of such other body as Congress may by law provide, transmit within four days to the President pro tempore of the Senate and the Speaker of the House of Representatives their written declaration that the President is unable to discharge the powers and duties of his office. Thereupon Congress shall decide the issue, assembling within forty-eight hours for that purpose if not in session. If the Congress within twenty-one days after receipt of the latter written declaration, or, if Congress is not in session, within twenty-one days after Congress is required to assemble, determines by two-thirds vote of both houses that the President is unable to discharge the powers and duties of his office, the Vice President shall continue to discharge the same as Acting President; otherwise, the President shall resume the power and duties of his office.

Amendment XXVI

SECTION 1

The right of citizens of the United States, who are eighteen years of age or older, to vote shall not be denied or abridged by the United States or by any State on account of age.

SECTION 2

The Congress shall have power to enforce this article by appropriate legislation.

Amendment XXVII

No law, varying the compensation for the services of Senators and Representatives, shall take effect, until an election of Representatives shall have intervened.

Section 3. Replacing the President With Consent

If the President informs Congress, in writing, that he or she cannot carry out the duties of the office of President, the Vice President becomes Acting President.

Section 4. Replacing the President Without Consent

If the President is unable to carry out the duties of the office but is unable or unwilling to so notify Congress, the Cabinet and the Vice President are to inform Congress of this fact. The Vice President then becomes Acting President. The procedure by which the President may regain the office if he or she recovers is also spelled out in this amendment.

Amendment 26. Eighteen-Year-Old Vote (1971)

This amendment made 18-year-olds eligible to vote in all federal, state, and local elections. Until then, the minimum age had been 21 in most states.

Amendment 27. Restraint on Congressional Salaries (1992)

Any increase in the salaries of members of Congress will take effect in the subsequent session of Congress.

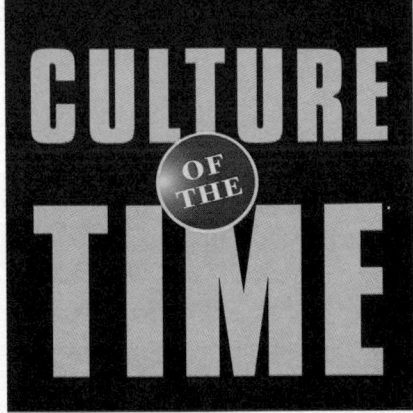

CULTURE
OF THE
TIME

TEACH

Making the Historical Connection

Because of the relatively small capacities of the sailing vessels, early colonists from Europe were able to bring very few possessions with them from their homelands. They could easily bring ideas, however. European customs and traditions found homes in the colonies. From the earliest days of the colonies, craftspeople and traders worked to ensure that familiar material goods would be available to colonists.

FYI

Religion The importance of religion in the new colonies is evidenced by the history of colonial printing. The first book published in the colonies was *The Bay Psalm Book,* printed by Stephen Daye of Cambridge, Massachusetts in 1640.

The Colonial Period

Immigrants brought European customs with them to the colonies. Familiar clothing styles, religious beliefs, amusements, and cookery helped settlers feel at home.

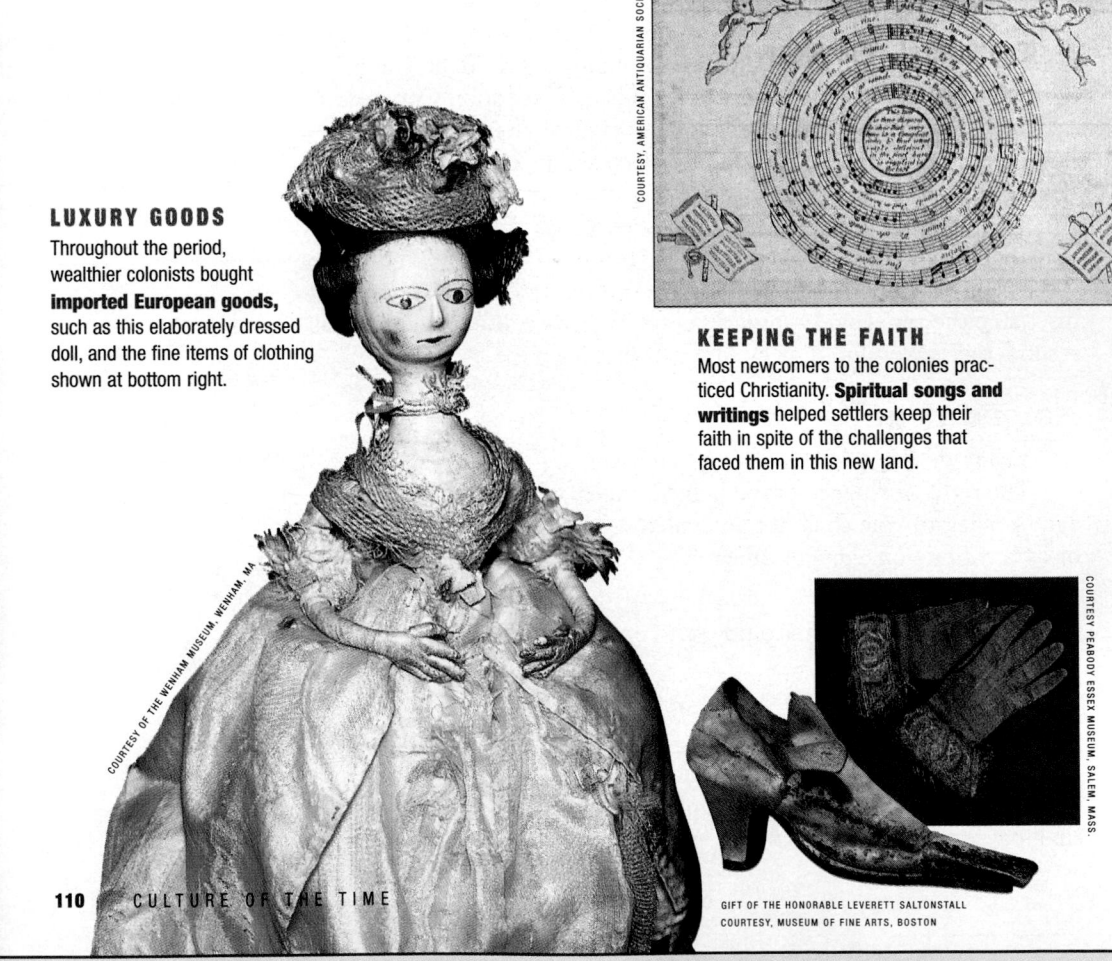

LUXURY GOODS
Throughout the period, wealthier colonists bought **imported European goods,** such as this elaborately dressed doll, and the fine items of clothing shown at bottom right.

COURTESY, AMERICAN ANTIQUARIAN SOCIETY

KEEPING THE FAITH
Most newcomers to the colonies practiced Christianity. **Spiritual songs and writings** helped settlers keep their faith in spite of the challenges that faced them in this new land.

COURTESY OF THE WENHAM MUSEUM, WENHAM, MA.

COURTESY PEABODY ESSEX MUSEUM, SALEM, MASS.

110   CULTURE OF THE TIME

GIFT OF THE HONORABLE LEVERETT SALTONSTALL
COURTESY, MUSEUM OF FINE ARTS, BOSTON

Background Information

Handmade Clothing Many colonists made their clothing by hand. They spun wool or flax into thread on wooden spinning wheels. They used hand looms to make cloth, then cut and sewed the cloth into garments. They also made clothing of leather from deer or cow hides.

COLONIAL CLOTHING

This colonial couple is dressed in clothing typical of the English middle class in the 1620s. Men's full baggy breeches were called **"slops."** Styles, of course, varied from region to region.

COURTESY OF PLIMOTH PLANTATION

GUILFORD COURTHOUSE NATIONAL MILITARY PARK

MAKING MUSIC

Craftspeople made instruments by hand, such as this painted **war drum.** Colonists played traditional European music and composed and played new music of their own.

To make a Cow-heel Pudding.

TAKE a large Cow-heel, and cut off all the Meat but the black Toes; put them away, but mince the reft very fmall, and fhred it over again, with three Quarters of a Pound of Beef-fuet; put to it a Penny Loaf grated, Cloves, Mace, Nutmeg, Sugar, and a little Salt, fome Sack, and Rofe-water; mix thefe well together with fix raw Eggs well beaten; butter a Cloth and put it in, and boil it two Hours. For Sauce, melt Butter, Sack, and Sugar. To

COURTESY, AMERICAN ANTIQUARIAN SOCIETY

HOME ECONOMICS

Colonial cooks adapted to scarcity when necessary. This recipe for **cow-heel pudding** shows one way colonists economized.

CULTURE OF THE TIME **111**

Portfolio Project

Other Immigrants Invite students to work in groups to research immigrants who came to America in a time other than the colonial period. Students might want to focus on cultural elements these immigrants brought from their homelands to America. Have each student write a letter in the voice of an immigrant from the time period they chose, explaining how cultural elements from their homeland help them to feel more at ease in their new home.

CULTURE OF THE TIME

CLOSE

Invite students to discuss the ways in which a continuation of European culture helped colonists to feel more secure in colonial America. *(Students may say that moving to a new place can be difficult and stressful, in part because people have to deal with new, sometimes unexpected experiences. The presence of familiar things and the continuation of traditional customs probably eased the strain of colonial life in a new land.)*

Notes

111

FOCUS

Section Objectives

1. Explain how federal power was used in the 1790s.
2. Explain the conflicts between the Federalist and Democratic-Republican political parties.
3. Describe the role of the Marshall Court in shaping the government.
4. Explain the emergence of the United States's foreign policy.

Bellringer Activity

While taking attendance at the beginning of the period, display **Section Focus Transparency 12,** and have students answer the questions. (Or use the blackline master.)

VISUAL INSTRUCTION

A President for the Common Man Thomas Jefferson was also a leading architect of his day. He designed the Virginia capitol, the University of Virginia, and his home, Monticello.

Ask: How did Jefferson's inaugural address soothe people's fears? *(He said he wanted to put political differences with the Federalists aside for the common good. This would avoid possible violence.)*

SECTION 3

Launching the New Government

MARCH 4, 1801: A NEW PRESIDENT IN A NEW CAPITAL

A President for the Common Man
Thomas Jefferson believed strongly in the people's right to self-government and civil liberties.

JUST BEFORE NOON ON MARCH 4, 1801, THOMAS JEFFERSON LEFT HIS BOARDINGHOUSE AND WALKED THROUGH THE DUSTY STREETS OF WASHINGTON, D.C. As he stepped up the hill toward the unfinished Capitol building, one observer noted that his clothing was "usual, that of a plain citizen, without any distinctive badge of office." Yet that day Jefferson assumed the highest office in the nation: he became the third President of the United States.

Jefferson faced a number of firsts that day. He became the first President to be sworn into office in the nation's new capital city. He also became the first Chief Executive to succeed a political opponent in office. Jefferson had served as Vice President under President John

Adams, but by the time of the election the two men headed conflicting political parties: Adams led the Federalists, and Jefferson led the Democratic-Republicans.

When Jefferson won the presidential election, Americans feared that the transition from one political party to another might result in violence. Many Federalists worried that Jefferson would punish them as political enemies.

In his Inaugural Address, however, Jefferson asked all American people to "unite for the common good." "Every difference of opinion," he explained, "is not a difference of principle. We have called by different names brethren of the same principles. We are all Republicans—we are all Federalists."

AS YOU READ

Vocabulary
► cabinet
► national debt
► speculator
► neutral
► impressed
► embargo

Think About . . .
► how federal power was used in the 1790s.
► the conflicts between the Federalist and Democratic-Republican political parties.

► the role the Marshall Court played in shaping the government.
► how the foreign policy of the United States emerged.

---

112 CHAPTER 4 A NEW NATION

Section 3 Resources

REPRODUCIBLE RESOURCES

- Lesson Plan 4-3
- Vocabulary and Guided Reading Activity 4-3
- Supreme Court Case 1
- Reteaching Activity 4
- Section 3 Quiz
- Chapter 4 Test
- Unit 4 Test
- Skill Reinforcement Activity 4
- Enrichment Activity 4
- Geography in History Activity 4

MULTIMEDIA RESOURCES

- Section Focus Transparency 12
- Testmaker
- Chapter 4 Digest Audiocassette
- Vocabulary PuzzleMaker
- Student Self-Test: A Software Review
- American Music: Cultural Traditions
- Focus on American Fine Art Prints, Print 5

After Jefferson's speech, many Americans breathed a sigh of relief. Yet their fears had been real. The struggles between the two parties threatened the stability of the nation. Even more disturbing, this political conflict had arisen in such a short time.

Washington and the Government
Stabilizing Economic Conditions

Just 12 years earlier, in 1789, George Washington took the same oath after being unanimously elected President. While bonfires and parties marked the people's excitement, Washington himself had grave concerns. "I walk on untrodden ground," he said. As the first President, Washington had no examples to follow. Every move he made set a precedent. He also knew the nation faced dire problems.

Congress created several departments to help the President run the country. The heads of those departments made up the President's **cabinet,** or official advisers. Among others in his cabinet, Washington appointed fellow Virginian Thomas Jefferson as secretary of state, in charge of relations with foreign countries. He named 34-year-old Alexander Hamilton of New York as secretary of the treasury.

The brilliant and handsome Hamilton had served as Washington's assistant during the Revolution, and the two men remained close friends after the war. Both served at the Constitutional Convention, and both fought for ratification. Hamilton felt, however, that the Constitution fell short of providing the type of government the United States needed.

As head of the Treasury Department, Hamilton hoped to increase the powers of the United States government. Under his guidance, he said, the government would work closely with "the rich, the well-born, and the good" to create wealth and stability in the young nation. Starting in 1790 he proposed a series of plans that helped to make this vision a reality.

Hamilton's Plans

The **national debt,** money owed from the American Revolution, remained the country's most serious economic problem. The United States government owed about $12 million to European countries and investors and about $40 million to American citizens. In addition the state governments had war debts of nearly $21 million. Most of these debts took the form of bonds that the government had sold to investors to pay for the costs of the war. Like Continental currency, bonds were worth a fraction of their face value in 1790 because people doubted that bondholders would ever be paid. Hamilton worried that if the United States could not make good on its own bonds, it would never establish credit—or credibility—with other nations or with its own citizens.

In 1790 Hamilton proposed to Congress that the government should pay off its bonds at full value and assume the debts of all the states as well. Congress agreed that foreign debts should be paid, but a storm of controversy arose over the rest of Hamilton's plan.

Some members of Congress argued that paying off domestic bonds at full value was unfair. The people who originally bought the bonds had given up hope of ever collecting on them. Many of them—mostly farmers and others who lacked cash—had sold their bonds at a discount to **speculators,** people who bought the bonds in the hopes that their value would go up again. Under the plan, wealthy speculators, not the common people who originally bought the bonds, would benefit. Hamilton believed that wealthy people were the key to the nation's economic development.

Other members of Congress complained about paying off the states' debts. Some Southern states had already paid their debts, while most New England states had not. Hamilton's plan favored the North, where most speculators lived. Southerners did not want to pay other states' debts after they had paid off their own.

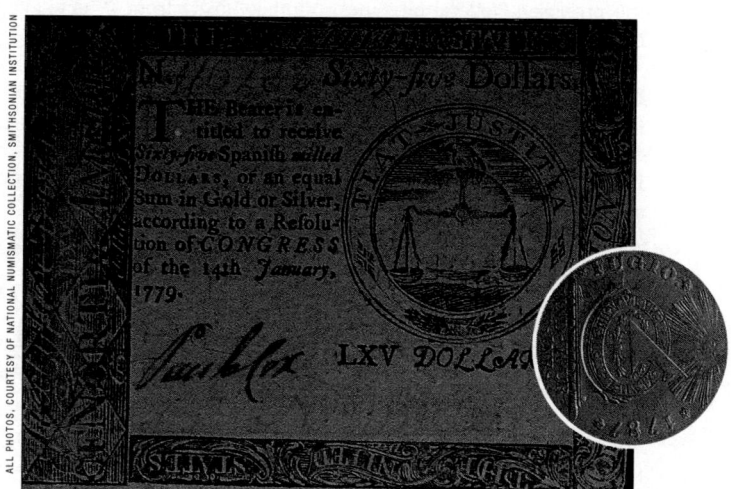

ALL PHOTOS, COURTESY OF NATIONAL NUMISMATIC COLLECTION, SMITHSONIAN INSTITUTION

Money Problems "Not worth a Continental" became a popular saying after the war. *Why were Continental currency and bonds of little value to investors in 1790?*

SECTION THREE **113**

TEACH

Guided Practice

L3 **Discussion** Differences had always existed between people living in different sections of the United States. In the 1790s conflicts emerged between Northerners and Southerners. Discuss some of the differences—in lifeways, economics, and politics—between Northern and Southern states in the 1790s.

CHART STUDY

Explain to students that merely printing currency does not give the currency value. Attempts at creating new currency to solve economic problems have often failed. During the Civil War, for example, the Confederate States of America printed its own currency in an attempt to gain financial stability. The value of the currency declined dramatically.

Answer: *Investors believed that the United States did not have enough money in its treasury to support the currency and pay the bonds.*

Cooperative Learning

A Report on Government Finances

Alexander Hamilton believed that the United States government would survive only if it allied itself with businessmen and investors. Organize students into research teams to learn about the role of big business and finance in government today. Each team might research a particular topic, such as political campaigns, congressional lobbies, political action committees, laws regulating business, tax on businesses, etc. Ask each team to present an oral report of their findings to the class. 📖

TEACH

Independent Practice

L2 Chronology Have each student make a time line of the events discussed in this section. The time line should begin with the year 1790 and go through 1815. Some students may wish to research and add events that occurred during this period but are not covered in the text.

☛ Have students complete the Chapter 4, Section 3 Vocabulary and Guided Reading Activity. (Also in Spanish.) **LEP**

VISUAL INSTRUCTION

Quelling the Whiskey Rebellion For the first time, federal military troops intervened to establish authority within state boundaries.

Answer: *They felt the taxation unfair and feared loss of income from whiskey sales.*

GENERAL GEORGE WASHINGTON.
Reviewing the Western army at Fort Cumberland the 18th of October 1794

Quelling the Whiskey Rebellion In 1794 President Washington reviews federal troops at Fort Cumberland in Maryland. The Maryland militia was called in to help end the Whiskey Rebellion. *Why were the farmers so opposed to the tax on their whiskey?*

Though not entirely convinced by Hamilton's argument, Washington sided with Hamilton and signed the bill in early 1791.

Whiskey and Taxes

Later that year Hamilton proposed a tax on distilled liquor. This tax would increase revenue and test the government's ability to tax—one of its most important powers, Hamilton thought.

The liquor tax aroused strong opposition from farmers in the hills of western Pennsylvania. Most back-country farmers made whiskey to sell in the eastern part of the state. This had always been the best way to transport processed corn, and whiskey proved to be a reliable source of extra cash. Hamilton's tax threatened to make this practice unprofitable.

For these farmers the liquor tax brought back memories of the days before the American Revolution. At first the farmers simply refused to pay. Then they began to tar and feather tax collectors. Finally, in July 1794, 500 armed men surrounded the home of a local tax collector and demanded that he resign. When the farmers discovered soldiers in the house, they opened fire. In the violence that followed, several men were wounded, and the tax collector's house was destroyed.

When the farmers ignored several orders to obey the law and pay their taxes, Washington and Hamilton reacted vigorously. In the fall of 1794, Henry Lee, accompanied by Hamilton, led a federal army to put down the rebels and demonstrate the power of the federal government. Threatened with this force, the "whiskey boys" dispersed and the Whiskey Rebellion ended. Two of the farmers were later convicted of treason, but Washington pardoned them both.

Hamilton brushed these criticisms aside. His intentions were to favor the commercial North over the agricultural South, and he hoped to ally the government with the wealthy men who had speculated in bonds. To get Congress to pass the plan, he struck a deal with Southern leaders. According to that deal, Southerners agreed to support Hamilton's debt plan, while Hamilton and other Northerners agreed to locate the proposed "federal city" near Virginia, away from Northern influence.

Hamilton then proposed the creation of a national bank. As a major stockholder, the government would have much influence on the operations of the Bank of the United States, as it would be called, but private citizens would own most of its stock. The bank would issue money, regulate the nation's financial affairs, and loan money to American citizens.

Before signing the bank bill into law, Washington asked the members of his cabinet to give him a written opinion of the plan. Jefferson argued that the plan was illegal; the Constitution said nothing about the government having the power to create a bank. Hamilton argued that, in addition to powers spelled out, the Constitution gave the government "implied" powers to do anything "necessary and proper" to carry out its responsibilities. The Bank, he said, was necessary for the government to regulate the economy. Washington carefully considered both Jefferson's strict reading of the Constitution and Hamilton's loose interpretation.

Conflicts at Home and Abroad
Party Politics and Foreign Policy

The Whiskey Rebellion confirmed Hamilton's worst fears about the common people—"that great beast," as he called them collectively. "How can you trust people who own no property?" he asked. The army had been needed, Hamilton argued, to enforce the laws of the land and put down a dangerous rebellion.

114 CHAPTER 4 A NEW NATION

Meeting Special Needs

Learning Disability Have students with learning disabilities preview the section by discussing illustrations, charts, captions, and headings. Help students identify and verbalize the main ideas of the section.

Thomas Jefferson, however, believed that "such an armament against people at their ploughs" had shown unnecessary force. The differences between Hamilton and Jefferson went beyond the Whiskey Rebellion, however. The two men had very different ideas of what the United States should be.

Hamilton envisioned a nation with bustling cities, churning factories, big banks, and a powerful government. He found backers for his plans and ideas in large Northern cities and New England—places where trade and manufacturing thrived.

The freedom of the common people thrived in Thomas Jefferson's America. "I know of no safe depository," Jefferson wrote, "of the ultimate powers of the society but the people themselves." Democracy worked best, he believed, in a society of small farmers, living in quiet, rural areas. Jefferson found support on plantations in the South, farms in the Middle Atlantic states, and farms on the Western frontier.

The people that these men attracted formed America's first political parties, groups that promoted ideas and supported candidates. As Hamilton and his Federalists continued to appeal to people with commercial interests, support for Jefferson and the Democratic-Republicans grew among common people. The parties not only differed on domestic issues; their conflicts over foreign policy nearly split the nation in the 1790s.

France and Britain

In 1789 revolution erupted in France. What began as an effort to reform a corrupt monarchy turned into a violent, bloody battle that completely upset French society. Fearing the spread of revolt against monarchy and aristocracy, other nations, including Britain, declared war on France.

Jefferson, formerly the United States minister to France, supported the French. He and other Republicans believed the French Revolution continued the struggle for liberty that America had begun. They also remembered France's support during the American Revolution and argued that the alliance between the two countries remain intact. To Federalists like Hamilton and Vice President Adams, the French Revolution showed the destructiveness of the common people. They sided with the British, admired the stability of the British government, and believed that America's economic livelihood depended on close ties with Britain.

Despite mounting pressure to enter the war on one side or the other, Washington chose to keep the United States **neutral**, or not allied with any side. Washington's decision did nothing to calm tensions in the United States or on the Atlantic Ocean. Both French and British ships seized American merchant vessels bound for Europe, and American trade suffered. The British navy **impressed**, or forced into service, American sailors (and British deserters) and forced them to serve on British ships. In addition the British had not removed all of their troops from forts in the western United States after the American Revolution. In 1794 war between the United States and either France or Britain seemed likely.

Fearing Britain's military power, Washington sent John Jay, a Federalist, to London to negotiate a treaty. When Jay returned home in 1795, however, it became clear that the new treaty was not very successful. The British agreed to remove their troops from the western United States, but not until 1796. To get this, Jay gave up American rights to ship cotton and sugar to British colonies. In addition he resolved nothing about the impressment of American sailors. The treaty seemed to please no one but those Federalists who wanted to maintain good relations with Britain at all costs. Democratic-Republicans called the Jay Treaty "the death warrant of American liberty."

The Beginnings of Party Rivalries

The political harmony of Washington's early years in office had long since disappeared, and Washington decided to leave office in 1797. In his Farewell Address, he

EDWARD S. ELLIS, YOUTH'S HISTORY OF THE U.S., NY, 1887

Citizen Reaction Angry Americans burn an effigy of John Jay upon his return from treaty negotiations in Britain. *Why were Americans so upset by the terms of the Jay Treaty?*

SECTION THREE **115**

🌐 Global Connection

The French adopted many of the ideals of the United States during their Revolution of 1789. The monarchy was dissolved, and the rights of the people were guaranteed. The French, however, launched a reign of terror against the aristocracy, and thousands were executed. Within a few years, the French had a new monarch—Napoleon.

VISUAL INSTRUCTION

Citizen Reaction Although Jay's Treaty was unpopular, it did serve as a model of international arbitration.

Answer: *They felt that too many concessions had been made to Britain, including loss of states' rights to ship cotton and sugar to Britain.*

Portfolio Project

Opinion on the Supreme Court Since the time of John Marshall people of the United States have questioned whether the Supreme Court is a nonpolitical forum or the ultimate political body. Is the Supreme Court too powerful? Should its judges be allowed to serve for life as they do now? Ask students to write their opinions about these and other issues they want to address related to the Supreme Court. Have them share their opinions in a class discussion and add their written opinions to their portfolios.

History and the Humanities

American Music: Cultural Traditions— "Hull's Victory" by L. O. Weeks; "Hunters of Kentucky" by The Yankee Doodle Society

Focus on American Fine Art Prints, Print 5— *George Washington* by Gilbert Stuart

urged the new nation to avoid conflicts with foreign nations and warned about the dangers of political parties.

In 1797 President John Adams ignored Washington's plea and sent 3 Americans to secure a treaty with France. In Paris the French foreign minister demanded a bribe of $240,000 from the Americans and hinted that if they refused to pay it France would declare war on the United States. This threat allowed Adams to sway American public opinion away from the French and the Democratic-Republicans.

The Alien and Sedition Acts

Adams called for the formation of an army to defend against the expected French invasion in 1798; he also signed the Alien Act, giving him the power to expel any aliens, or foreign-born residents of the United States, who were "dangerous to the peace and safety of the United States."

Another law signed by Adams during the crisis—the Sedition Act—was aimed directly at the Democratic-Republicans themselves. This law made it a crime for anyone to "write, print, utter, or publish . . . any false, scandalous, and malicious writing" about the President or the government. As a result, about 10 Democratic-Republican editors, printers, and politicians were jailed.

The Alien and Sedition acts proved very unpopular, and public opinion turned against the President and the Federalists. When peaceful relations with France were restored in 1800, it appeared that the Federalists had manufactured the entire crisis. As a result, Adams and his party were in chaos as the presidential election of 1800 approached. Jefferson and his party were ready to challenge them.

The Election of 1800

In 1800 the American people witnessed a hard-fought and noisy presidential campaign. Democratic-Republicans spread rumors that President Adams would soon name himself "King of America." New England Federalists whispered that Jefferson planned to burn every Bible in the nation. The final count of votes was close, but Jefferson won.

Jefferson chose to let the nation heal rather than churn up old political conflicts. He quietly stopped en-

Tie Vote The Twelfth Amendment, establishing separate balloting for President and Vice President, was ratified in 1804 in response to a tie between Jefferson and Aaron Burr (above) in the election of 1800. *Why were the Federalists in turmoil before the election?*

forcing the Alien and Sedition acts and allowed them to expire. He reduced military spending. He even allowed the Bank of the United States to continue to exist.

John Marshall and Judicial Power
Strengthening the Supreme Court

After losing the election, John Adams sought ways to make Federalist ideas continue in a government dominated by Democratic-Republicans. He found his solution in the judiciary.

Packing the Courts

In the winter before their terms ran out, Adams and the Federalist Congress worked together to pass the Judiciary Act of 1801. This law added 21 positions to the roster of federal judges. Adams named Federalists to these positions. Adams also named John Marshall, a strong Federalist, chief justice of the United States.

Adams signed the appointments of the new Federalist judges the night before Jefferson's inauguration, leaving several of the appointments to be delivered by the new administration. Yet Jefferson's secretary of state, James Madison, refused to do this. When a Federalist named William Marbury did not receive his expected appointment, he appealed to the Supreme Court.

John Marshall found himself in a difficult position. As a Federalist, he would have liked to order Jefferson to make Marbury a federal judge. If he did, however, Jefferson and Madison would probably ignore the order, reducing the authority of the Supreme Court. Yet Marshall could not give in.

Marshall's Solution

Marshall's solution bypassed short-term gains for the Federalists, but it had long-term national effects. In 1803 he ruled that Marbury was entitled to his appointment and that Madison had violated the law in not delivering it. Marshall ruled, however, that the Court could not re-

---

Extending the Content

John Jay Along with Alexander Hamilton and James Madison, John Jay was a collaborating author of some of the essays in *The Federalist*. He served as president of the Continental Congress, and, in 1789, President George Washington appointed him the first Chief Justice of the United States. Before the unpopular Jay Treaty, Jay had been thought of as a possible successor to George Washington. The treaty ended his presidential ambitions, however. New York Federalists elected Jay governor, and he served in that position from 1795 to 1801, after which he retired to his farm.

quire delivery of the appointment because a part of the law giving the Court that right—the Judiciary Act of 1789—was unconstitutional, or violated the Constitution. Marshall had established the right of the Supreme Court to judge an act of Congress illegal. It is "the duty of the judicial department to say what the law is," he wrote. "A law repugnant to the Constitution is void."

What began as a petty political fight ended by strengthening the Supreme Court. John Marshall served as chief justice for 34 years, and during that time he consistently supported the Federalist program of a strong federal government. In this way, Marshall remained the chief adversary of Democratic-Republican Presidents for the next 16 years and helped Federalist policy endure long after the party ceased to exist.

Foreign Policy
The War of 1812: Another War With Britain

Along with the Federalist judiciary, conflicts with European nations troubled Thomas Jefferson's presidency. France and Britain continued to victimize the United States. Navies of the 2 nations seized nearly 1,500 American merchant ships. By 1807 the British had captured as many as 10,000 American sailors. The British fired on the American frigate *Chesapeake,* killing 3 Americans and wounding 18. Across the nation, Americans called for action against the British.

The Embargo Act

Jefferson did not believe that the United States could fight a war against Britain. He also remembered the trouble that foreign conflicts had caused during the 1790s, and he hoped to avoid such conflicts now.

Still, Jefferson knew that something had to be done. He believed that the European powers needed American food and materials. So in 1807 Jefferson signed the Embargo Act. The **embargo** stopped the export of all American goods and forbade American ships from sailing for foreign ports.

Jefferson thought that by depriving European countries of American products they would stop harassing the young nation. He was wrong. The Embargo Act had almost no effect on Britain and France. Instead, it proved

to be a disaster for the United States, especially in the trading centers of New England. Depression and unemployment swept the country. Americans from South Carolina to New Hampshire openly defied the law.

Jefferson left office after 2 terms in 1809, but not before he convinced Congress to repeal the Embargo Act. James Madison won the presidency easily, but opposition to timid Democratic-Republican policies against the British grew. By 1811 a new breed of politician had swept into Congress.

The War Hawks

These politicians came from the West and were the first generation of politicians to come of age after the Revolution. They earned the name "war hawks" for their calls for action against the British.

The British had heaped one insult after another on the American people, the war hawks charged. They impressed American sailors, attacked American ships, and stirred up trouble between settlers and Native Americans. To Westerners accustomed to action, the economic warfare of Jefferson and Madison seemed pathetic. "Is the rod of British power to be forever suspended over our heads?" asked war hawk Henry Clay of Kentucky.

Madison recognized the growing power of these new politicians, and in 1812 he made a deal with them. If they supported him for reelection as President, he would ask for a declaration of war. The war hawks agreed, and by the summer of 1812 the United States and Britain were locked in combat.

COURTESY U.S. NAVAL ACADEMY MUSEUM

A British Defeat at Sea This painting shows the frigate *USS Constitution,* nicknamed "Old Ironsides," defeating the British warship *Guerrière* in the War of 1812. *What actions by the British led to war?*

FYI

Related Opponents John Marshall was one of the American envoys whom the French tried to bribe and threaten in 1797. Hailed as a hero when he returned, Marshall became a strong supporter of John Adams. That made Marshall a rival of his cousin Virginian Thomas Jefferson.

VISUAL INSTRUCTION

A British Defeat at Sea Among navies around the world, the *USS Constitution* is the oldest warship still afloat.

Answer: *They captured American sailors and fired on the American frigate* Chesapeake, *killing and wounding Americans.*

ASSESS

Meeting Lesson Objectives

Each section objective is tested by the section review question(s) that follows it in parentheses.

1. Explain how federal power was used in the 1790s. (1, 2)
2. Explain the conflicts between the Federalist and Democratic-Republican political parties. (3)
3. Describe the role of the Marshall Court in shaping the government. (4)
4. Explain the emergence of the United States's foreign policy. (1, 5)

Cultural Perspectives

Political Philosophies Alexander Hamilton considered the common people "the great beast," and believed that government should be composed of and aligned with "the rich, the well-born, and the good." Thomas Jefferson thought it was proper for the common people to hold the power of government. Invite students

to research how the ideas of each of these statesmen influence today's federal government. Which group has more influence over government—the rich people or the common people? Why? Have students write papers defending their position.

Evaluate

Have students complete the Section Review.

📁 💿 Assign the Section 3 Quiz or use the Testmaker to develop a customized quiz.

📁 💿 Assign the Chapter 4 Test or use the Testmaker to develop a customized test.

📁 Have students complete the Chapter 4 Performance Assessment Activity.

Reteach

🎧 Have students listen to the Chapter 4, Section 3 Audiocassette. Also in Spanish.) **LEP**

📁 Have students complete the Chapter 4 Reteaching Activity. (Also in Spanish.) **LEP**

Enrich

📁 Have students complete the Chapter 4 Enrichment Activity. (Also in Spanish.) **LEP**

📁 Have students complete the Chapter 4 Geography in History Activity.

📁 Have students complete Supreme Court Case Study 1.

CLOSE

Ask students to write their own section quizzes, consisting of five questions, each covering a different major part of the section. Have them exchange quizzes, write the answers to the questions, then check the accuracy of their own answers against the text.

Flames in Washington This British cartoon shows President Madison fleeing the burning capital during the British attack on Washington in 1814. *Why was the War of 1812 so significant for the United States?*

American goals in the war were unclear. The war hawks had boasted of conquering Canada and Florida, but these plans were squelched when the British invaded the United States. Each side scored victories in battles around the Great Lakes, near Washington, D.C., and on the Atlantic Ocean. By the end of 1814, British leaders, more concerned with European matters, wearied of the American war and offered to make peace. The treaty, ratified in 1815, resolved few of the problems that had caused the conflict. It simply ended the fighting and restored everything to what it had been before the war.

The United States had not won the war—no one had—but the War of 1812 became an important event for the young nation. The war hawks hailed it as the "Second War for Independence." United States victories stimulated national pride and confidence. The war, which had been urged by Western politicians, also created a new Western hero: General Andrew Jackson of Tennessee, who scored a sensational victory over the British near New Orleans. The War of 1812 also marked the end of United States involvement with European conflicts for more than a century.

After the war Americans looked eastward to Europe less and looked westward across their own continent more. At last the United States put its colonial past behind it and headed toward its future as a nation of lush prairies, growing cities, and a restless, changing people.

SECTION REVIEW

Vocabulary

1. Define: cabinet, national debt, speculator, neutral, impressed, embargo.

Checking Facts

2. How did Alexander Hamilton increase the powers of the federal government?

3. What were the main conflicts between the Federalists and the Democratic-Republicans?

Critical Thinking

Demonstrating Reasoned Judgment

4. How did John Marshall's actions shape the role of the Supreme Court?

Linking Across Time

5. Impressment was an act of aggression against the United States that led to war. If it occurred today, do you think war would result? Why?

118 CHAPTER 4 A NEW NATION

Section 3 Review Answers

1. **cabinet** (113), **national debt** (113), **speculator** (113), **neutral** (115), **impressed** (115), **embargo** (117)
2. He proposed the creation of a national bank.
3. The Federalists wanted a strong national government run by the elite; the Democratic-Republicans were more concerned about the rights of the common people.

4. By establishing the right of the Supreme Court to judge an act of Congress illegal, Marshall greatly expanded the power and influence of the Supreme Court.
5. Students may answer that such acts of aggression aimed directly at the United States probably would cause war.

Critical Thinking Skill

ANALYZING INFORMATION

Learning the Skill

The newly independent Americans had to vote to ratify the laws under which they would live. They had to analyze information in order to decide how to vote. Analyzing information involves breaking it into meaningful parts so that it can be understood. Subsequently the reader or listener is able to form an opinion about it.

The ability to analyze information is important in deciding your position on a subject that could affect your life. You need to analyze a political document to determine if you should support it. You would analyze a candidate's position statements to determine if you should vote for him or her. You would analyze an article or editorial to arrive at your own opinion of it.

Analyzing Information

To analyze information, use the following steps:

a. Identify the topic that is being discussed.

b. Examine how the information is organized. What are the main points?

c. Summarize the information in your own words, and then make a statement of your own based on your understanding and what you already know.

Read the following passage from Article II, Section 1, of the Constitution of the United States.

No person except a natural-born citizen, or a citizen of the United States, at the time of the adoption of this Constitution, shall be eligible to the office of President; neither shall any person be eligible to that office who shall not have attained to the age of thirty-five years, and been fourteen years a resident within the United States.

The first step is to determine the general topic. This passage is about the qualifications for the President of the United States. Next, identify the three main points: the President must be a citizen of the United States by birth, must be at least thirty-five years old, and must have lived here for at least fourteen years. Then give a brief summary, such as: "People who want to become President must fulfill these three requirements." Finally, make a statement of your own, such as: "These requirements restrict the presidency to people who have a reasonable amount of life experience and keep from power people who were not born in the United States or who have not lived here very long."

ARTICLE II.—Sec. 1.—The power of this government shall be divided into three distinct departments; the Legislative, the Executive, and Judicial. . . .

ARTICLE III.—Sec. 1.—The Legislative power shall be vested in two distinct branches; a Committee and a Council, each to have a negative on the other, and both to be styled the General Council of the Cherokee Nation. . . .

ARTICLE IV.—Sec. 1.—The Supreme Executive Power of this Nation shall be vested in a Principal Chief, who shall be chosen by the General Council and shall hold his office four years. . . .

ARTICLE V.—Sec. 1.—The Judicial Powers shall be vested in a Supreme Court, and such Circuit and Inferior Courts as the General Council may from time to time ordain and establish. . . .

Constitution of the Cherokee Nation **In 1827 elected delegates of the Cherokee Nation met to establish their own constitution.** *How do these excerpts compare with related passages in the Constitution of the United States?*

Practicing the Skill

Read the excerpts above and practice analyzing information by answering these questions.

1. What is the subject of the document?

2. What are the most important points?

3. What do you notice about the organization of the document?

4. What does it mean that the Committee and the Council "each to have a negative on the other"? How is this similar to the "checks and balances" of the United States Constitution?

5. Summarize the passage in your own words, and make a statement of your own regarding it.

Applying the Skill

Find a short, informative piece, such as a political candidate's position paper, an editorial in a newspaper, or an explanation of a new law that will soon be implemented. Analyze the information and make a statement of your own.

Additional Practice

For additional practice, see Reinforcing Skills on page 121.

CRITICAL THINKING SKILL   **119**

TEACH

In this feature students analyze written passages. Analysis involves a methodical examination of the parts of a passage in order to understand the whole passage more deeply. Explain to students that when they analyze a passage, they may sometimes discover that the writer has omitted key information or used illogical thinking. You may want students to find and share examples of such passages.

Additional Practice

☞ Have students complete the Chapter 4 Skill Reinforcement Activity.

Notes

Practicing the Skill Answers

1. the government of the Cherokee Nation
2. There are three branches of government, each with its own powers.
3. The document is organized into sections called "articles," which are devoted to specific topics.

4. The Committee and the Council can each restrain the other, a situation that resembles the system of "checks and balances" that characterizes the Constitution of the United States.
5. Students' statements will vary, but their summaries should describe how the basic powers of the Cherokee Nation government were divided among the three branches of government.

Chapter ④ Review

Reviewing Key Terms

1. representation
2. amendments
3. impressed
4. cabinet
5. ratify

Recalling Facts

1. plan of government that created the Confederation congress; small states did not want to ratify unless Western land claims were ceded
2. Slaves could not be imported north of the Ohio River.
3. Paper money was a promise to pay the holder in gold or silver (hard money); paper money, because Congress had no cash
4. No branch of government could gain too much power.
5. Federalists supported the new Constitution; they favored a strong central government.
6. Articles of Confederation could be fixed; national government would be too strong, would favor the wealthy and preserve their power
7. The Constitution did not protect the rights of the people.
8. freedom of speech, religion, press, assembly, arms-bearing
9. enslaved persons, women, and Native Americans
10. to regulate the economy
11. a tax on liquor; Shays's Rebellion
12. political disharmony
13. Chief Justice; he strengthened the federal government
14. It violates the Constitution; judicial branch
15. like the Revolution, it was fought against Britain

Reviewing Key Terms

Choose the vocabulary term that best completes the sentences below. Write your answers on a separate sheet of paper.

amendments	embargo
cabinet	representation
ratify	impressed

1. The smaller states demanded equal _____.

2. Ten _____, known as the Bill of Rights, were added to the Constitution.

3. American sailors were forcibly _____ into the British navy.

4. The President's _____ consists of department heads who serve as official advisers.

5. The state representatives urged the voters to _____ the Constitution.

Recalling Facts

1. What were the Articles of Confederation? Why were some states reluctant to accept them?

2. What restrictions on slavery were included in the Northwest Ordinance of 1787?

3. What was the difference between hard money and paper money? Which type of money did the Confederation Congress use? Why?

4. Why did the Constitution include a system of checks and balances for the new government?

5. Who were the Federalists? What type of government did they support?

6. What reasons did the Anti-Federalists give for opposing the Constitution?

7. Why did some states demand that a bill of rights be added to the Constitution?

8. Identify at least five rights guaranteed by the Bill of Rights.

9. Which Americans' rights were not guaranteed in the Bill of Rights?

10. Why did Alexander Hamilton feel a national bank was necessary?

11. What events caused the Whiskey Rebellion? What other rebellions did it resemble?

12. Why did George Washington decide to step down as President?

13. Who was John Marshall and what effect did he have on the federal government?

14. What is an unconstitutional law? Which branch of government can declare a law to be unconstitutional?

15. Why was the War of 1812 known as the "Second War of Independence"?

Critical Thinking

1. **Identifying Assumptions** Were Daniel Shays and the farmers who followed him justified in going outside the law to address their grievances? Explain.

2. **Making Comparisons** Compare how class and geographic location affected people's support of the Constitution. Did the groups of supporters and nonsupporters divide along class lines? Explain.

3. **Drawing Conclusions** Under the Alien and Sedition acts, was jailing people for publicly criticizing Federalist policies a violation of the First Amendment, or was it justified by the ongoing crises? Explain.

4. **Making Comparisons** Compare the views of the 2 political parties on economic and foreign policies. Who would be most likely to support the Federalists? Who would support the Democratic-Republicans?

5. **Making Inferences** The illustration below shows the guillotine with which French revolutionaries executed King Louis XVI. What arguments might favor the overthrow of an oppressive government by force? What arguments might favor a political system where tyrants could be removed only by the force of law?

Portfolio Project

Prepare a chart that compares the American and French Revolutions. What were the causes of each? How long did each last? What were the results of each? In what ways were they similar? Different? When you are finished, put the chart in your portfolio.

Cooperative Learning

Working with a small group, read the Bill of Rights that was added to the Constitution (pages 91–109). Rewrite the amendments in your own words. Use modern English. Then compare the rewritings done by various groups of your classmates. How do they differ from the original amendments in the Bill of Rights?

Critical Thinking

1. In the harsh economic climate after the war it was unfair to jail farmers or take away their livelihoods.
2. Federalists: wealthy and middle class, the Atlantic coast; Anti-Federalists: inland farmers and wealthy state politicians
3. a violation of the First Amendment, a way for Adams to keep political power, not for national security
4. Federalists wanted to maintain good relations with England while Democratic-Republicans supported the French Revolution; wealthy people: Federalists, common people: Democratic-Republicans.
5. fast way to get rid of oppressive government versus not allowing civil unrest any time someone was unhappy with government

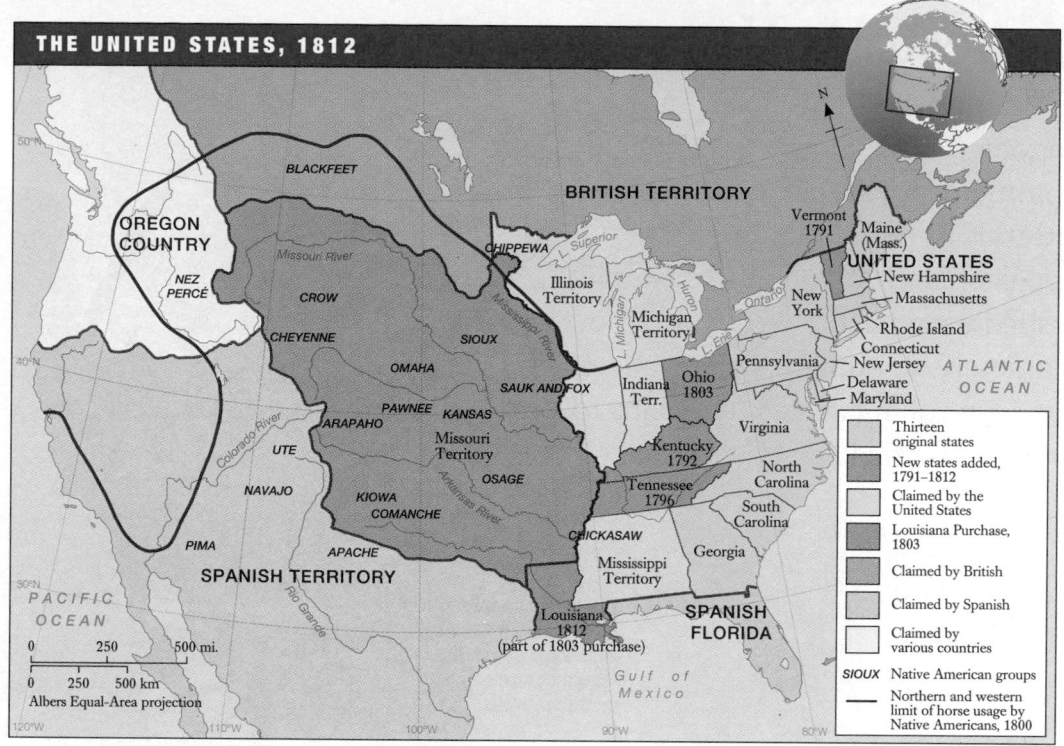

THE UNITED STATES, 1812

OREGON
COUNTRY
NEZ
PERCÉ

BLACKFEET

BRITISH TERRITORY

CHIPPEWA

Vermont
1791

Maine
(Mass.)

UNITED STATES
New Hampshire

Missouri River

CROW

Illinois
Territory

Michigan
Territory

Massachusetts

New York

Rhode Island
Connecticut

CHEYENNE

SIOUX

SAUK AND FOX

Indiana
Terr.

Ohio
1803

Pennsylvania
New Jersey
Delaware
Maryland

ATLANTIC
OCEAN

OMAHA

Colorado River

PAWNEE KANSAS

ARAPAHO

UTE

NAVAJO

KIOWA
COMANCHE

Missouri
Territory

OSAGE

Arkansas River

Virginia

Kentucky
1792

North
Carolina

Tennessee
1796

South
Carolina

PIMA

APACHE

SPANISH TERRITORY

PACIFIC
OCEAN

Rio Grande

0   250   500 mi.

0   250   500 km
Albers Equal-Area projection

CHICKASAW

Louisiana
1812
(part of 1803 purchase)

Mississippi
Territory

SPANISH
FLORIDA

Georgia

Gulf of
Mexico

120°W   110°W   100°W   90°W   80°W

Thirteen
original states

New states added,
1791–1812

Claimed by the
United States

Louisiana Purchase,
1803

Claimed by British

Claimed by Spanish

Claimed by
various countries

SIOUX Native American groups

Northern and western
limit of horse usage by
Native Americans, 1800

Reinforcing Skills

Analyzing Information Find a copy of the Northwest Ordinance in an encyclopedia or history book. Read the slavery clause and analyze the importance of this clause to African Americans.

Geography and History

Study the map on this page to answer the following questions:

1. Notice the five new states that were added to the original colonies. In which direction does the United States seem to be expanding the most? Why do you think this is so?

2. United States territory expanded as a result of the Louisiana Purchase. Why do you think it was advantageous to have a state (Louisiana) in that region?

3. France and the United States negotiated the Louisiana Purchase without consulting the Native Americans who lived west of the Mississippi. How might this have contributed to future conflicts between white settlers and Native Americans?

4. Why might the United States of 1812 have been a more formidable opponent for the British than the thirteen colonies of 1775?

5. Consider the order in which the first 18 states were admitted to the union. Which areas are likely to have been next to gain statehood?

HISTORY JOURNAL

Reread your response to the History Journal activity at the beginning of Chapter 4. Now that you have read the chapter, do you still agree with your interpretation of the painting *Liberty?* Revise your previous journal entry to reflect what you learned in the chapter.

Geography and History

1. west; people wanted new land that they could farm, mine, etc.

2. Louisiana was valuable for shipping because it is on the coast, and it helped the U.S. surround the territories claimed by Spain.

3. Both the white settlers and the Native Americans thought they owned the land in question. As the Native Americans were not included in negotiations there was no reason for them to recognize the settlers' ownership.

4. The United States in 1812 was larger and owned or had claimed more land on waterways that would be useful for fighting a war.

5. Mississippi Territory, Indiana Territory, Michigan Territory

History Journal

Students' revisions should reflect a deeper understanding of American politics around 1800.

? BONUS QUESTION

This question may be used for extra credit on the chapter test.

Why did James Madison refuse to honor William Marbury's appointment to a federal judgeship in 1801?

Answer: *Marbury's appointment was part of the Judiciary Act of 1801, John Adams's attempt to pack the the courts with Federalists.*

Portfolio Project

Students' charts should cite the causes, durations, and results of the American and French Revolutions, and compare and contrast the two.

Cooperative Learning

Criteria for completion of each project will vary. Projects can be individual or group tasks. Discuss your expectations when assigning the project to students.

Reinforcing Skills

Students' papers should reflect an understanding of the importance to African Americans of the slavery clause in the Northwest Ordinance.

TEACH

Making the Historical Connection

The life of the Conestoga wagon spanned the years of the French and Indian War, the Revolutionary War, and the frontier years of Westward expansion. These wagons hauled both war supplies and domestic goods, easing the burdens of transporting heavy loads until the mid-nineteenth century when they were finally replaced by railroads and canalboats.

FYI

Colloquial Expression
"Come home with your bells on" is one that was associated with the Conestoga wagon. It signified a successful trip because drivers often had to trade some of their brass bells when they needed assistance on their journey.

Then...

Conestoga Wagon

By the mid-1700s, sturdy Conestoga wagons, called "Ships of the Inland Commerce," transported settlers and tons of their freight over the Appalachian Mountains. As people pushed even farther westward, the characteristic outline of the Conestoga was seen rolling across the plains toward Oregon and finally to California.

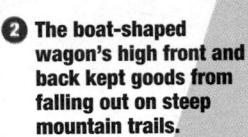
2 The boat-shaped wagon's high front and back kept goods from falling out on steep mountain trails.

NORTH WIND PICTURE ARCHIVES

1 Six to eight draft horses or a dozen oxen pulled the wagon. The driver rode or walked beside the animals.

Fun Facts

CRACKING THE WHIP

Wielding whips equipped with noisemaking "crackers" at the tips, drivers frequently had to snap them within inches of the ears of mules to keep the animals moving on the long treks over difficult terrain.

Background Information

The First Turnpikes The need for better roads for Conestoga wagons and other vehicles led to the construction of such roads as the Philadelphia-Lancaster Turnpike (1792–1794) and the National Road from Baltimore to Wheeling, West Virginia. The word *turnpike* derived from toll houses on those early roads, where a collector would take money from travelers before turning aside a long, pointed pole—or pike—allowing the travelers to continue on their journey.

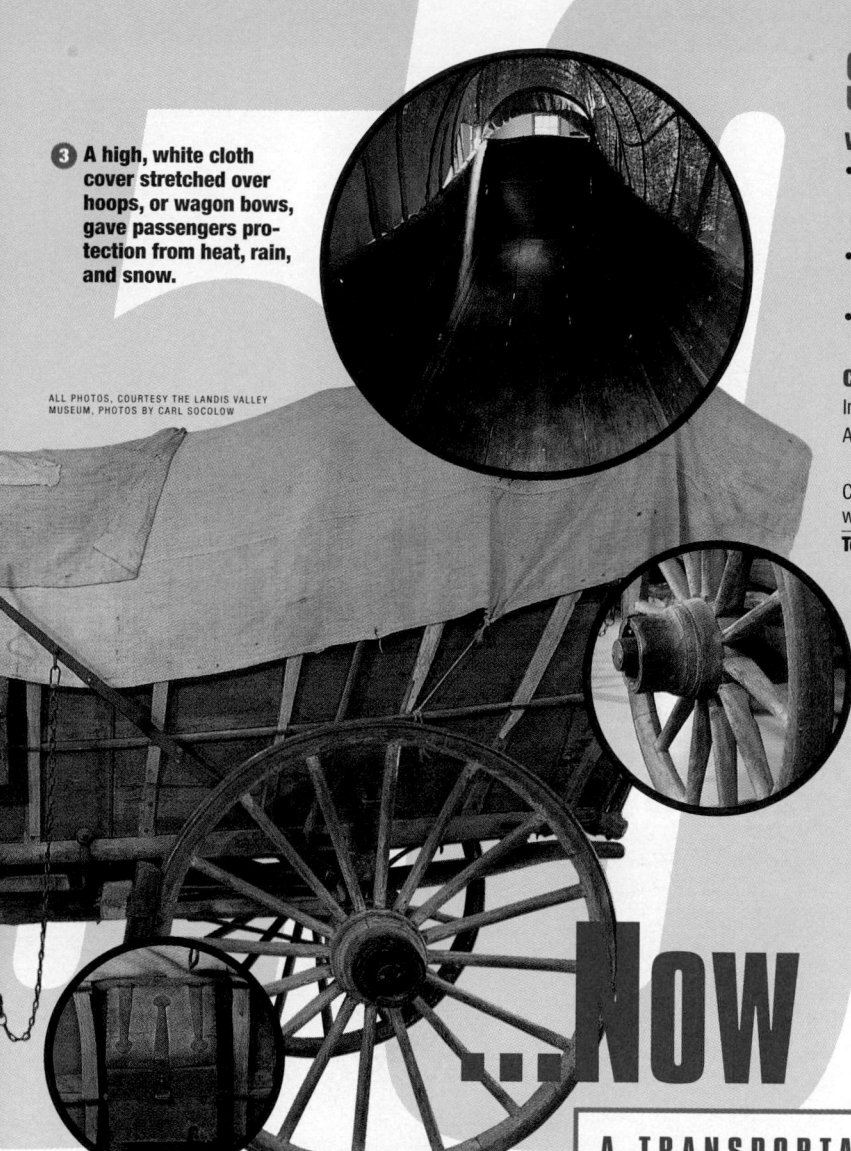

3 A high, white cloth cover stretched over hoops, or wagon bows, gave passengers protection from heat, rain, and snow.

ALL PHOTOS, COURTESY THE LANDIS VALLEY MUSEUM, PHOTOS BY CARL SOCOLOW

4 A toolbox attached to the side of the wagon held spare parts for needed repairs.

...Now

Stats

WAGON NUMBERS

- Average wagon box: 21 feet long, 11 feet high, 4 feet in width and depth
- Average wagon weight: 1.5 to 2 tons (3,000 to 4,000 pounds)
- Wagon capacity: up to 6 tons (12,000 pounds) of cargo

COSTLY TRANSPORT

In the 1800s:

A team of horses:	
Approximately $1,000	
Construction of a	
wagon:	$250
Total:	**$1,250**

5 Broad wheels helped keep the heavy wagon from being mired in the mud.

A TRANSPORTATION REPORT

PORTFOLIO PROJECT

Create a report about the length of Conestoga wagon journeys and how far they could typically travel in a day. Include a list of items that the settlers may have loaded for their trip. Then compare the modes of transportation available today, gathering statistics about how long a specific Conestoga trail would take by automobile or airplane.

THE "CONESTOGA STOGIE"

The wagons were named after the place where they were first built in the 1700s—the Conestoga Creek region of Lancaster, Pennsylvania. The word *stogie* derived from the cigars smoked by Conestoga wagon drivers.

THEN AND NOW **123**

Then & Now

CLOSE

Discuss some of the difficulties that travelers using Conestoga wagons probably faced crossing the Allegheny Mountains. Ask: What kinds of food provisions would settlers probably take? Why would it be important to travel a route near fresh water? What do you think travelers would do if one or more of their horses or mules were disabled? *(Answers will vary. Travelers may have taken preserved foods such as dried or salted meat. They would have had to refill their water containers at rivers or lakes. Wagoners may have sought help from fellow travelers or purchased new animals using some of their bells as currency.)*

PORTFOLIO PROJECT

Portfolio Project

A Diary Entry Have students imagine that they are traveling over the Allegheny Mountains with their family in a Conestoga wagon. Ask students to imagine and record a typical day's events on the trail. Encourage them to include descriptions of chores they might have had to do as well as their thoughts about journeying to an unknown place. Have them save their diary entries in their portfolios.

123

The Unit at a Glance

Chapter 5

As settlers moved westward into newly acquired lands, Native Americans were forced out. Meanwhile, growing industry, urbanization, a transportation revolution, and a more democratic and reform-minded population were changing the direction of the nation.

Chapter 6

Conflict over extending slavery to the new territories and the right of Southern states to secede from the Union brought on the tragedy of the Civil War. Four years of bloodshed ended in Confederate defeat and the assassination of Lincoln. Reconstruction helped newly freed African Americans until the nation reverted to business as usual.

Chapter 7

Homesteading, cattle ranching, and mining drew more Americans to the West, and the transcontinental railroad made it easy to get there. Industrialization brought the growth of national markets and big businesses run by the wealthy; the widening gap between rich and poor brought populism and protest. The United States sought territory and influence abroad.

00:00 Out of Time?

If time does not permit teaching every chapter in this unit, use the Chapter Digest Audiocassettes and the accompanying student activities and tests. The Chapter Digest Audiocassettes are available in Spanish.

UNIT

2

Rift and Reunion

1800

CHAPTER 5
The Expanding Nation

CHAPTER 6
Civil War and Reconstruction

CHAPTER 7
New Frontiers

124

Portfolio Project

Civil War Art Winslow Homer first came to public notice with his Civil War sketches and paintings. Another artist recording the events of those tragic years was Mathew Brady, who practiced the new art of photography. Have students research the life of one of these artists and write a biographical essay. Volunteers may wish to share their essays with the class before putting them in their portfolios.

125

Introducing the Unit

Show students the Unit 2 Time Line Transparency and/or assign the accompanying activity sheet. This unit covers the entire nineteenth century, from the early explorations of the West, through the Civil War, to the nation's international ventures of the late 1800s. Several features illuminate important aspects of the century, and skills lessons help students take charge of their own learning.

Notes

Examining the Visual

A Young Soldier Winslow Homer's painting was part of a series that *Harper's Weekly* magazine commissioned the young artist to do. Homer accompanied the Army of the Potomac during their training. Altogether he produced 180 wartime sketches, wood engravings, watercolors, and oils.

TEACH

Making the Historical Connection

Remind students that there are many ways in which people learn about their history. Invite students to brainstorm some of the ways (for example, documents, museums, history books, ruins). Explain that in order to write the story of a slave ship crossing, Haley undertook an ocean voyage from Africa to the United States, traveling each of 10 nights in the ". . . deep dark cold cargo hold . . . on my back on a wide rough bare dunnage plank." Ask students how imagination might be used to give life to history in a historical novel such as *Roots*.

Block Scheduling

Team Teaching This excerpt from *Roots* can be presented in a team teaching context, in conjunction with English or Language Arts.

Roots

BY ALEX HALEY

Oral history, folklore, and tradition connect us to the past. In this excerpt from the autobiographical novel Roots, *author Alex Haley learns his family history from a Mandinka griot, an elder who commits events of the past to memory and retells them to new generations.*

Recreating Roots LeVar Burton (left) prepares to play author Alex Haley (right) in the 1977 televised version of Haley's family saga. Nightly audiences of 80 million tuned in to the 8-part show, more than half of all American viewers.

There is an expression called "the peak experience"— that which emotionally, nothing in your life ever transcends. I've had mine, that first day in the back country of black West Africa.

When we got within sight of Juffure, the children who were playing outside gave the alert, and the people came flocking from their huts. It's a village of only about seventy people. Like most back-country villages, it was still very much as it was two hundred years ago, with its circular mud houses and their conical thatched roofs. Among the people as they gathered was a small man wearing an off-white robe, a pillbox hat over an aquiline-featured black face, and about him was an aura of "somebodiness" until I knew he was the man we had come to see and hear.

As the three interpreters left our party to converge upon him, the seventy-odd other villagers gathered closely around me, in a kind of horseshoe pattern, three or four deep all around; had I stuck out my arms, my fingers would have touched the nearest ones on either side. They were all staring at me. The eyes just raked me. . . .

One of my interpreters came up quickly and whispered in my ear, "They stare at you so much because they have never here seen a black American." When I grasped the significance, I believe that hit me harder than what had already happened. They hadn't been looking at me as an individual, but I represented in their eyes a symbol of the twenty-five millions of us black people whom they had never seen, who lived beyond an ocean.

The people were clustered thickly about the old man, all of them intermittently flicking glances toward me as they talked animatedly in their Mandinka tongue. After a while, the old man turned, walked briskly through the people, past my three interpreters, and right

Background Information

up to me. His eyes piercing into mine, seeming to feel I should understand his Mandinka, he expressed what they had all decided they *felt* concerning those unseen millions of us who lived in those places that had been slave ships' destinations—and the translation came: "We have been told by the forefathers that there are many of us from this place who are in exile in that place called America—and in other places."

The old man sat down, facing me, as the people hurriedly gathered behind him. Then he began to recite for me the ancestral history of the Kinte clan, as it had been passed along orally down across centuries from the forefathers' time. It was not merely conversational, but more as if a scroll were being read; for the still, silent villagers, it was clearly a formal occasion. The *griot* would speak, bending forward from the waist, his body rigid, his neck cords standing out, his words seeming almost physical objects. After a sentence or two, seeming to go limp, he would lean back, listening to an interpreter's translation. Spilling from the *griot's* head came an incredibly complex Kinte clan lineage that reached back across many generations. . . . To date things the *griot* linked them to events, such as "—in the year of the big water"—a flood—"he slew a water buffalo." To determine the calendar date, you'd have to find out when that particular flood occurred.

Simplifying to its essence the encyclopedic saga that I was told, the griot said that the Kinte clan had begun in the country called Old Mali. Then the Kinte men traditionally were blacksmiths, "who had conquered fire," and the women mostly were potters and weavers. In time, one branch of the clan moved into the country called Mauretania; and it was from Mauretania that one son of this clan, whose name was Kairaba Kunta Kinte—a *marabout*, or holy man of the Moslem faith—journeyed down into the country called The Gambia. He went first to a village called Pakali N'Ding, stayed there for a while, then went to

> ## HE HAD JUST ECHOED WHAT I HAD HEARD ALL THROUGH MY BOYHOOD YEARS.

a village called Jiffarong, and then to the village of Juffure. . . .

[His] youngest son, Omoro, stayed on in Juffure village until he had thirty rains—years—of age, then he took as his wife a Mandinka maiden named Binta Kebba. And by Binta Kebba, roughly between the years 1750 and 1760, Omoro Kinte begat four sons, whose names were, in the order of their birth, Kunta, Lamin, Suwadu, and Madi. . . .

Now after he had just named those four sons, again he appended a detail, and the interpreter translated— "About the time the King's soldiers came"—another of the *griot's* time-fixing references—"the oldest of these four sons, Kunta, went away from his village to chop wood . . . and he was never seen again. . . ." . . .

I sat as if I were carved of stone. My blood seemed to have congealed. This man whose lifetime had been in this back-country African village had no way in the world to know that he had just echoed what I had heard all through my boyhood years on my grandma's front porch in Henning, Tennessee . . . of an African who always had insisted that his name was "Kin-tay"; who had called a guitar a "*ko*," and a river within the state of Virginia, "Kamby Bolongo"; and who had been kidnaped into slavery while not far from his village, chopping wood, to make himself a drum.

 At the Movies

The 1977 television dramatization of *Roots,* based on the book, attracted record numbers of viewers and inspired many Americans to undertake a search for their own roots. Students may wish to view a video recording of this American family saga.

CLOSE

Ask: What was the role of the griot in the story? (*The griot passed along the family history.*)

Notes

_____
_____
_____
_____
_____
_____
_____
_____
_____
_____
_____
_____
_____
_____
_____
_____
_____
_____
_____
_____
_____
_____
_____
_____

Responding to Literature Answers

1. Answers will vary. Students might refer to Haley's experience as the culmination of his work and a chance to transcend time by reclaiming a lost past. A peak experience is a time when the mind opens to new understanding. It might be meeting a physical challenge or a learning challenge. It might be something emotionally new like falling in love.

2. Answers will vary. The griot uses events as reference points, for example, "the time the King's soldiers came." While recorded history can relate measured information using time lines and statistics, the calendar itself relates back to a historic event, the birth of Christ. Written histories often refer to upheavals such as wars to mark time periods.

The Expanding Nation

DAILY LESSON OBJECTIVES	REPRODUCIBLE RESOURCES	MULTIMEDIA RESOURCES
SECTION 1 Territorial Expansion 1. Explain western movement as a central experience of American life in the early nineteenth century. 2. Discuss the relationship between the federal government and the territories. 3. Describe federal policy toward Native Americans before 1860.	☞ Reproducible Lesson Plans ☞ Vocabulary and Guided Reading Activities (English or Spanish) ☞ Cooperative Learning Activities ☞ Supreme Court Case Studies ☞ Geography in History Activities ☞ Section Quizzes (English or Spanish)	🔦 Section Focus Transparencies 🔦 Beginnings to 1900 Transparencies 🔦 Map Transparencies 🔦 Chapter Teaching Transparencies 🔦 U.S. History and Art Transparencies 💿 A Geographic Perspective on American History 💿 Landmark Documents in American History
SECTION 2 The Economy Grows 1. Describe the development of factory manufacturing in the United States. 2. Explain the importance of immigration to the labor force and the growth of American manufacturing. 3. Show how roads, canals, and railroads knitted the country together. 4. Describe the connections between economics, politics, and sectionalism.	☞ Reproducible Lesson Plans ☞ Vocabulary and Guided Reading Activities (English or Spanish) ☞ Supreme Court Case Studies ☞ Section Quizzes (English or Spanish)	🔦 Section Focus Transparencies 📙 Focus on American Fine Art Prints 💿 Landmark Documents in American History 💿 Historic America: Electronic Field Trips 💻 Testmaker 💻 Student Self-Test: A Software Review
SECTION 3 A Changing People 1. Explain the changes in early 1800s political culture that brought Andrew Jackson to power. 2. Demonstrate the connection between evangelical Christianity and social reform in the 1800s. 3. Describe how abolitionism and other social reform movements gave women and African Americans a political voice.	☞ Reproducible Lesson Plans ☞ Vocabulary and Guided Reading Activities (English or Spanish) ☞ Skill Reinforcement Activities ☞ Enrichment Activities (English or Spanish.) ☞ Reteaching Activities (English or Spanish.) ☞ Section Quizzes (English or Spanish)	🔦 Section Focus Transparencies 🔦 Beginnings to 1900 Transparencies 💿 Landmark Documents in American History 🎧 American Music: Cultural Traditions 💻 Testmaker 💻 Student Self-Test: A Software Review
CHAPTER REVIEW AND EVALUATION	☞ Chapter 5 Test, Forms A and B ☞ Performance Assessment Strategies and Activities	💻 Testmaker 💻 Vocabulary PuzzleMaker 💻 Student Self-Test: A Software Review 🎧 Chapter Digests Audiocassettes

⏱ **00:00** If time does not permit teaching the entire chapter, summarize using the Chapter 5 Digests Audiocassettes and the accompanying activities and tests. (Available in English or Spanish.)

Cooperative Project

Have students work in groups of four or five to make time line posters of events discussed in the chapter. Each group's time lines should have a different foucs: political events, westward expansion, economic development, social changes. Later have the groups compare time lines and discuss events that show up for more than one group's focus topic. **LEP**

Suggested Rubric: A Poster. See Performance Assessment Strategies and Activities, p. 37.

Individual Project

Have students imagine that they have settled on the Kentucky frontier. Ask them to write a series of journal letters, one for each section of the chapter. Students should describe the changes that have occurred around them—conflicts in the frontier region, new modes of transportation, religious movements, and others.

Suggested Rubric: A Journal. See Performance Assessment Strategies and Activities, p. 29.

Key to Ability Levels

Teaching strategies have been coded for varying learning styles and abilities.

L1 **BASIC** activities for all students

L2 **AVERAGE** activities for average to above-average students

L3 **CHALLENGING** activities for above-average students

LEP **LIMITED ENGLISH PROFICIENCY** activities

Block Scheduling

Block scheduling differs from traditional class scheduling in the amount of time allotted to each period. The extended timeframe provided by block scheduling affords you the opportunity to implement a greater number of research-oriented and activity-intense projects to motivate and involve your students. Activities that are particularly suited to use within the block scheduling framework are identified throughout this chapter by the following designation.

T E A C H E R ' S   C O R N E R

 NATIONAL GEOGRAPHIC SOCIETY

INDEX TO NATIONAL GEOGRAPHIC MAGAZINE

The following articles may be used for research relating to this chapter:

- "America's Poet: Walt Whitman," by Joel L. Swerdlow, December 1994.
- "The Peales: America's First Family of Art," by Otto Friedrich, December 1990.
- "Erie Canal: Living Link to Our Past," by Joel L. Swerdlow, November 1990.
- "New Life for Ellis Island," by Alice J. Hall, September 1990.
- "George Washington's Patowmack Canal," by Wilbur E. Garrett, June 1987.

NATIONAL GEOGRAPHIC SOCIETY PRODUCTS AVAILABLE FROM GLENCOE

To order the following products for use with this chapter, contact your local Glencoe sales representative or call Glencoe at 1-800-334-7344:

- *The Presidents: A Picture History of Our Nation* (CD-ROM)
- *GTV: A Geographic Perspective on American History* (Videodisc)
- *GTV: The American People: Fabric of a Nation* (Videodisc)

ADDITIONAL NATIONAL GEOGRAPHIC SOCIETY PRODUCTS

To order the following products for use with this chapter, call National Geographic Society at 1-800-368-2728:

- *Building a Nation: The Story of Immigration* (Filmstrip)
- *Immigration: The Triumph of Hope* (Video)

Chapter Overview

After it had won its independence and struggled to create a government, the United States entered the early 1800s, a period of territorial expansion and political change. During this time Americans addressed the question of what they wanted the nation to become.

Introducing the Chapter

Few events captured the spirit of the expanding nation as well as the construction of the Erie Canal. The project opened a major new route to the West using the latest technology. Construction required massive economic resources, and symbolized for many Americans what the young nation could accomplish.

 Display the Chapter Teaching Transparency and distribute the corresponding activity sheet for students to complete.

Extension Activity

Have students complete Beyond the Transparency on the activity sheet for Chapter 5 and present their projects after the class has completed the chapter.

History Journal

Have students describe a recent event that occurred in the United States which represented the same kind of growth and change as the opening of the Erie Canal. Ask them to write what significance the new event had in United States history.

The Expanding Nation

OCTOBER 26, 1825: ERIE CANAL OPENS

A large flatboat, the *Seneca Chief,* strung with flowers, led "a grand aquatic procession" through New York Harbor on November 4, 1825. The fleet sailed to a spot near Sandy Hook, New Jersey, where the other boats circled the *Seneca Chief.*

On deck stood DeWitt Clinton, governor of New York. He raised a small wooden keg, pulled the cork, and said: "May the God of the heavens and the earth smile on this work and render it subservient to the best interests of the human race." Then he emptied the keg, which contained water from Lake Erie, into the Atlantic Ocean.

The "Marriage of the Waters" concluded the official ceremonies marking the opening nine days earlier of the Erie Canal, the most important national waterway built in the United States. It stretched from the Hudson River to Lake Erie and connected New York City with the fertile regions to the West.

The building and subsequent success of the Erie Canal changed the way Americans traveled, conducted business, and practiced politics. This vital link between the East Coast and the Western frontier also changed the way many Americans thought about their country. The canal served as a symbol of pride and economic determination. ■

HISTORY JOURNAL

Write about some of the ways in which the United States might experience growth in the 1800s.

128

EXTRA CREDIT PROJECT

Transportation Debate To deepen students' understanding of the controversy surrounding internal improvements in the early 1800s, have teams re-create a Congressional debate. Each student should prepare a three-paragraph argument for either the benefits or the drawbacks of government funding for roads and canals in the 1820s. Point out that some of the arguments might involve constitutionality. Also, their arguments could take a regional point of view, with Westerners more dependent on improvements than Easterners. The project could culminate in an oral debate with a chance for impromptu rebuttals from both sides.

NORTH WIND PICTURE ARCHIVES

NEW YORK GOVERNOR DEWITT
CLINTON LEADS THE CEREMONIES
OPENING THE ERIE CANAL.

129

 Performance Assessment

Refer to page 125A for a performance assessment activity for this chapter.

📁 Also see Activity 5 in the Performance Assessment Strategies and Activities for an additional activity as well as for suggested rubrics.

Examining the Visual

American Drama Between 1800 and 1850, in the climate of expansion and pioneering, American writers came out from the shadow of European literature. The subjects for this dis-tinctly American brand of writing often came from the nation's recent past. Washington Irving's *History of New York* (1809) combined humor and tall tales to create a mock history of the author's home state. Students might look at some of the literature from this period by American authors such as James Fenimore Cooper or Nathaniel Hawthorne. They can note examples of how these writers helped define the United States by looking at events in the nation's short history.

FOCUS

Section Objectives

1. Explain western movement as a central experience of American life in the early nineteenth century.
2. Discuss the relationship between the federal government and the territories.
3. Describe federal policy toward Native Americans before 1860.

Bellringer Activity

 While taking attendance at the beginning of the class period, display **Section Focus Transparency 33,** and have students answer the questions. (Or use the blackline master.)

VISUAL INSTRUCTION

The Expedition A thousand new words, many borrowed from Native American languages, first appeared in the expedition's journals. Among them were *bayou, bluegrass, maize, moccasin, persimmon, raccoon, squash, tote,* and *Yankee.*

Ask: How did the United States acquire the land that Lewis and Clark explored? *(It was acquired from France in the Louisiana Purchase.)*

History and the Humanities

U.S. History and Art Transparency 6—*The Great Blue Heron* by John James Audubon

---

Territorial Expansion

NOVEMBER 7, 1805: EXPLORERS REACH THE PACIFIC OCEAN

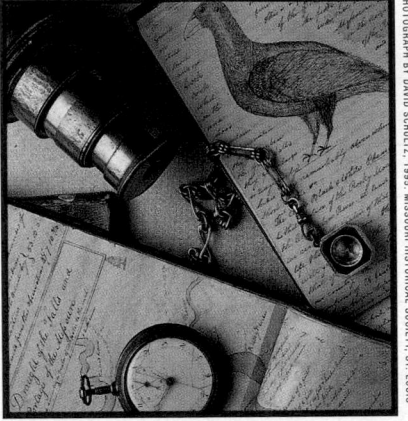

The Expedition
In 1805 Lewis and Clark's tools included some that are still used in exploration today.

A COLD RAIN FELL FROM THE GRAY SKY, DRENCHING THE EXPLORERS AS THEY PULLED THEIR CANOES ASHORE. Giant pines rose above them, green and full. Dense forest lined the sides of the river that emptied into the Pacific Ocean.

One man climbed a muddy hill to get a better look at the vast sea. For a year and a half he had traveled by boat and horseback, on foot and by canoe, to reach this spot. To mark the journey's end, he chose a tall yellow pine tree, pulled a knife from his belt, and began carving. "William Clark," he cut into the bark, dating his entry. "By land from the U. States in 1804 and 1805."

Clark and his friend Meriwether Lewis had set out from St. Louis in May 1804 on orders from President Thomas Jefferson. The United States had just purchased much of the territory west of the Mississippi River, and Jefferson wanted it explored.

Lewis and Clark traveled through the lands of many Native American nations—land unknown to all but a few fur-trading white Americans. When they reached the Pacific, they had pushed the American frontier all the way to the continent's western edge.

The Moving Frontier
Westward Advance

Only 40 years earlier, the **frontier**—the shifting zone where colonist-controlled lands met Native American-controlled lands—began at the Appalachian Mountains. Over the next decades, white settlers steadily displaced Native Americans as they pushed this frontier westward. One of these white men, Daniel Boone, played a major part in this movement.

AS YOU READ

Vocabulary
► frontier
► flatboat

Think About . . .
► westward movement as a central experience of American life in the early nineteenth century.
► the relationship between the federal government and the territories.
► federal policy toward Native Americans before 1860.

130   CHAPTER 5   THE EXPANDING NATION

Section 1 Resources

REPRODUCIBLE RESOURCES
- Lesson Plan 5-1
- Vocabulary and Guided Reading Activity 5-1
- Cooperative Learning Activity 5
- Section 1 Quiz
- Supreme Court Case 2

- Geography in History Activity 5

MULTIMEDIA RESOURCES
- Section Focus Transparency 33
- U.S. History and Art Transparency 6
- Map Transparency 5
- Chapter Teaching Transparency 5

- Beginnings to 1900 Transparencies 7, 8, 9
- A Geographic Perspective on American History
- Landmark Documents in American History
- Testmaker
- Chapter 5 Digest Audiocassette

The Wilderness Road

Daniel Boone first learned about the land west of the Appalachians during the French and Indian War. He had heard a soldier describe a hunter's paradise, a land with buffalo so large that the earth sagged beneath them. The soldier told of a mountain pass, the Cumberland Gap, that led to this paradise.

After the war Boone searched for a route to the West. In 1769 he found a Native American trail across the mountains. Warriors' Path, as it was called, led Boone through the Cumberland Gap to the gentle hills of a land that came to be called Kentucky. For two years, he explored the region's dense forests and lush meadows.

In 1775 Boone rounded up 30 skilled foresters to build a path so that pioneer families could take it west. Boone's crew widened the Warriors' Path, cleared rocks from the Cumberland Gap, cut down trees in Kentucky, and marked the trail. The new Wilderness Road, as it became known, became the main Southern highway from the Eastern states to the West. More than 100,000 people traveled it between 1775 and 1790.

Meanwhile Boone continued his wandering. In 1799 he crossed the Mississippi River into present-day Missouri, then controlled by Spain. The Spanish governor awarded Boone a large piece of land. Boone, however, lost this land when this territory suddenly became the property of the United States in 1803.

The Louisiana Purchase

Boone's land was part of the Louisiana Territory, which included about half the land between the Mississippi River and the Pacific Ocean. Louisiana had once belonged to France, but it came under Spain's control after the French and Indian War. Then, in 1800, French Emperor Napoleon Bonaparte forced Spain to return ownership of Louisiana to France. Napoleon wanted Louisiana in order to expand France's American empire.

President Jefferson grew worried when he learned of this deal. He was anxious to ensure that New Orleans, a vital port, remain open to American trade. His fears turned out to be well founded, for the ruling official at New Orleans closed the port to American trade in 1802. Jefferson quickly planned his response.

Early in 1803 the President sent Virginian James Monroe to Paris with instructions to buy New Orleans. Congress had voted $2 million for the purchase, though Jefferson privately told Monroe to spend up to $10 million.

THE SETTLEMENT OF THE UNITED STATES, 1783–1900

Settled in 1790	
Settled in 1820	
Settled in 1860	
Settled in 1890	
Largely unsettled	
Boundary of Louisiana Purchase	

The settlement of the United States is a story of relentless westward movement. *When was Tennessee settled? When was Iowa settled?*

Cooperative Learning

Planning an Expedition The members of the Lewis and Clark team each contributed specialized skills to the expedition. Ask students to imagine that you are leading them on an expedition (to a nearby campground, to Antarctica, to Mars). Discuss with your class what skills are important to the expedition's success. Organize the class into groups. Have each group decide on a particular expedition and determine which skills individual students can contribute. Groups can share their expedition plans with the class.

TEACH

Guided Practice

L2 Discussion Read aloud the passage from the Northwest Ordinance concerning Native Americans (page 134). Discuss the meaning of "good faith." Ask how students would interpret this statement if they were Native Americans in 1787.

Show students Map Transparency 5 and have them complete the activity sheet.

Show students Beginnings to 1900 Transparencies 7, 8, and 9 and have them complete the activity sheets.

MAP STUDY

Ask students to note that the green line on the map marking the route of the Lewis and Clark expedition extends west of the Louisiana Purchase. The boundaries of the Purchase were disputed for decades. Jefferson seems to have thought that they probably extended to the Pacific.

Answer: *1790–1860; 1860–1890*

Global Connection

The French colony of Saint Domingue became Haiti in 1804 when the enslaved people there revolted, declared independence, and renamed the island.

Independent Practice

L3 **Writing** Jefferson directed Lewis and Clark to keep journals describing the lands they saw. Have students write a description of the geography and natural life of the region they live in.

 Have students complete the Chapter 5, Section 1 Vocabulary and Guided Reading Activity. (Also in Spanish.) **LEP**

 Have students complete the Chapter 5 Cooperative Learning Activity.

VISUAL INSTRUCTION

A Salmon Observed The expedition's records included excellent journals kept by many members of the party, yet none had a formal education—not even Meriwether Lewis, who had been Jefferson's secretary.

Answer: *President Jefferson*

NATIONAL GEOGRAPHIC SOCIETY

 Videodisc

GTV: A Geographic Perspective on American History

Side 2, Chapter 4
Title: Lewis and Clark
Subject: The expedition
Ask: Why were Lewis and Clark sent to Louisiana? *(to explore the new territory)*

When Monroe reached Paris, Napoleon's situation had changed. A successful slave revolt in the French colony of Haiti had ended his hopes for an American empire. In addition war between France and Britain again seemed likely, and Napoleon needed money. The French offered Monroe all of the Louisiana Territory for $15 million. Monroe agreed.

When news of the purchase reached the United States, some people grumbled that the President had no right to buy land without Congress's approval. Ultimately, however, Congress approved the purchase. The United States thus gained nearly 830,000 square miles (2,149,700 sq. km) of land—doubling the size of the country.

Exploring the New Territory

President Jefferson knew that this region had to be explored. He selected Meriwether Lewis, his personal secretary, and army officer William Clark to lead the expedition. Jefferson instructed the explorers to establish friendly relations with Native Americans and to study their habits and languages. Jefferson wanted descriptions of wildlife they saw along the way. He also wanted detailed maps of the region.

Lewis and Clark chose about 45 men for the expedition, including 20 soldiers accustomed to living in the woods. Others were specialists in Native American sign language, gun repair, and carpentry. The group left St. Louis in the spring of 1804, navigating the Missouri River on **flatboats**, the square-ended, flat-bottomed craft used for transporting freight on inland waterways.

The explorers spent the winter of 1804–1805 near a friendly Mandan village in present-day North Dakota. There they met a French-Canadian trader named Toussaint Charbonneau, his Shoshone wife named Sacajawea, and their infant son. Sacajawea and Charbonneau joined up as guides and translators when the expedition set out again in the spring of 1805.

That summer Lewis and Clark crossed the Rocky Mountains. Using horses and supplies the Shoshone provided, they threaded their way through high mountain passes. After a month of climbing, the party reached the Pacific side of the range. From there they traveled quickly, arriving at the Pacific Ocean before the cold weather. The explorers built a fort and spent the winter at the ocean before returning to St. Louis in 1806.

Westward Migration

The reports and maps Lewis and Clark brought back sparked the interest of a nation that was already looking to its western frontier. Thousands of families crossed the Appalachians in the early 1800s. These new Western settlers were anxious to acquire the same political rights they had enjoyed in the East. According to the Northwest Ordinance, which Congress passed in

1787, each Western territory was permitted limited self-government. When its population reached 60,000, a territory could draft a constitution. If Congress approved the document, the territory became a state.

Western territories quickly lined up to join the union. Kentucky became a state in 1792, Tennessee in 1796, Ohio in 1803, and Illinois in 1818. Meanwhile, more settlers flocked to territories farther west. By 1820 more than 2 million Americans—about one-fourth of the population—lived west of the Appalachian Mountains.

Settling the West
Farming the New Frontier

In 1817 an English visitor to Ohio observed, "Old America seems to be breaking up and moving westward." The people who made this move were farmers, hunters,

A Salmon Observed Lewis and Clark kept excellent geographical and naturalistic records, often enhanced by Clark's drawings. *Who instructed them to keep such records?*

Meeting Special Needs

Visual Learners To help students who learn best through visual instruction, direct them to the map on page 131. Discuss what effect certain geographic features—mountains, rivers, lakes, oceans—of North America would have had on western settlement.

European immigrants, army veterans, artisans—a cross section of poor and middling people. The settlers brought their values and culture to their new homes in the West.

Paths to the New Land

Pioneers by the thousands gathered their belongings and loaded them into wooden wagons called Conestogas. These vehicles—20 feet (6.1 m) long and 4 feet (1.2 m) deep—were short on comfort but long on durability. They were also versatile. A Conestoga could serve as a wagon on roads, a sled in the mud, and a cozy camp at night.

Conestogas were a common sight along the rough roads of America. One traveler in New York counted 500 wagons a day rolling west in 1797.

Rivers provided another important route to the West. Some settlers traveled overland to Pittsburgh, Pennsylvania, where they climbed aboard flatboats and floated down the Ohio River. After reaching the desired spot in Ohio or Kentucky or the Indiana Territory, the pioneers unloaded their belongings and headed inland.

When settlers reached a spot they liked, they built a home, often a small log cabin, and began clearing land for farming. One observer in western New York noted in 1805 that "the woods are full of new settlers. Axes are resounding, and the trees literally falling about us as we passed."

Farms in the West

The new frontier farms generally resembled farms in the East. A few Southern settlers used enslaved Africans to plant and harvest cash crops like cotton. Most farmers on the Southern frontier, however, had no slaves, though many hoped to strike it rich and thus join the ranks of wealthy slaveholding planters. North of the Ohio River, where slavery was prohibited, farms were small and most produced only enough food to feed the families that worked them.

Northern and Southern farmers raised crops of corn and wheat and hunted to provide their families with food. "My old daddy," recalled one pioneer woman, "caught rabbits, 'coons, and possums. He would work all day and hunt at night." Women did almost everything else. One farm journal reported that women "spun their own yarn ... made and mended their own chairs, braided their own baskets, wove their own carpets ... picked their own geese, milked their own cows. . . ." They also cooked meals, raised children, and cared for the sick.

Cabin in the West This 1847 oil painting, *Home in the Woods,* is by Thomas Cole, a leader in the painting movement known as the Hudson River School. *In what ways did settlers on the frontier depend on one another?*

Frontier farmers felt close bonds with their neighbors. Community activities—churchgoing and barn raisings, weddings and funerals, barbecues and quilting bees—were necessary diversions from the rough life. Unlike the solitary explorers who first explored the frontiers, most settlers relied on the support of neighbors during good times and bad.

Bad times were an ever-present threat. In the lawless wilderness of the early 1800s, conflicts were often settled with fists and guns. Frigid winters and steamy summers brought disease and death. The land was lush, but a bad harvest could spell disaster for a farm family. The threat pioneers feared most, however, was an attack from Native Americans.

Native Americans and the Settlers

Promises Made and Broken

The greatest threat to Native Americans, in turn, was white settlers. For more than 150 years Native Americans had watched a tide of settlers stream west, threatening their ways of life. Usually, however, the conflicts between settlers and Native Americans arose over land.

In theory the United States government insisted on respect for Native American land claims. In 1787 the Northwest Ordinance declared:

SECTION ONE **133**

 Facts on File

Landmark Documents in American History Have students review "Louisiana Purchase Treaty, 1803" and write a paragraph about the intent of the document.

VISUAL INSTRUCTION

Cabin in the West In the early 1800s, the lone traveler to the West was the exception. To make the perilous trip across the continent safely, settlers had to travel in groups. The Conestoga wagon required group resources for managing steep slopes or deep streams. Some wagon trains were three miles long.

Answer: *They depended on each other for help in hard times and for social life.*

 NATIONAL GEOGRAPHIC SOCIETY

 Videodisc

GTV: A Geographic Perspective on American History

Side 2, Chapter 3
Title: Map Rap
Subject: The growth of the United States, 1776–1867
Ask: What was the first major territorial purchase of the United States government? *(Louisiana Purchase)*

Portfolio Project

Making a Time Line Have students make individual time lines of the events discussed in this section. The time lines should start with 1775 and end with 1840. Some students may wish to add related events not covered in the text. Students can keep these time lines in their portfolios.

> The utmost good faith shall always be observed towards the Indians; their land and property shall never be taken from them without their consent; and, in their property, rights, and liberty, they shall never be invaded or disturbed.
>
> —*The Northwest Ordinance*, 1787

This well-intentioned promise proved flimsy, however, in the face of land-hungry settlers.

Trouble in Ohio

During the 1700s several Native American nations—the Shawnee, the Miami, the Wyandot—shared the land that is today Ohio. They settled in villages and ate what they could hunt and grow. White settlers in this region pushed the Native Americans from their homes and hunting grounds. "Hear the lamentations of our women and children," cried one Shawnee leader. "Stop your people from killing our game."

When the United States government did nothing to stop this conflict, Native Americans in Ohio formed a confederation to halt white settlement. In 1790 and 1791 warriors repeatedly attacked settlers, killing more than 800 soldiers and handing the army several defeats.

In 1792 President Washington gave General Anthony Wayne command of an army in the Ohio country. After drilling some 3,000 soldiers for several months, Wayne led his army against the Ohio confederation. His troops fought about 2,000 warriors in the Battle of Fallen Timbers near Lake Erie in 1794. The Native Americans were soundly defeated. After the battle Wayne torched their homes and fields. Under the Treaty of Greenville that ended the war, Native Americans gave up much of their land.

Tecumseh This oil portrait (artist unknown), painted not later than 1813, is from the collection of the Field Museum in Chicago. It is believed to portray the Shawnee military leader **Tecumseh.** *What was the name of the community Tecumseh and his brother established?*

The Shawnee Solution

After the defeat many Native Americans of the Ohio Valley traveled west across the Mississippi, away from the settlers. Others tried to find new homes in Ohio.

One of those who remained in Ohio was a Shawnee named Tenskwatawa. Around 1805 Tenskwatawa began preaching a message of hope to the Shawnee. If the Shawnee returned to traditional ways, he said, he would lead them to "a rich, fertile country, abounding in game, fish, pleasant hunting grounds, and fine corn fields." Tenskwatawa told them to stop drinking the white man's whiskey, stop using his weapons, and stop eating "the food of the whites." Over time, Tenskwatawa's spiritual message turned into a political program, and his brother Tecumseh joined him as a leader of the Shawnee people.

The two brothers—the mystical prophet Tenskwatawa and the politically shrewd, militarily skillful Tecumseh—spoke of Native American pride, power, and unity. The brothers said they would reclaim lost land and draw a "boundary between Indians and white people." The magnetic presence and convincing speeches of the brothers attracted many im-

After the Battle The Treaty of Greenville marked another loss of Native American lands. *Where did the Native Americans of the Ohio Valley go after the war ended?*

VISUAL INSTRUCTION

Tecumseh He argued that the Northwest Territory and the Ohio Valley belonged to the Native American peoples in common and that no one had the right to sell the land.

Answer: *Prophet's Town*

After the Battle The Treaty of Greenville divided all of the Northwest Territory between Native American lands and lands open to settlers, a division that endured only until contradictory and overlapping treaties and purchases confused the boundaries during the next half-century.

Answer: *Many moved west across the Mississippi while others stayed and tried to live among the white settlers.*

ASSESS

Meeting Lesson Objectives

Each section objective is tested by the section review question(s) that follows it in parentheses.

1. Explain western movement as a central experience of American life in the early nineteenth century. (1, 4, 5)

2. Discuss the relationship between the federal government and the territories. (2)

3. Describe federal policy toward Native Americans before 1860. (3)

Extending the Content

A Military Man William Henry Harrison's victory in the Tippecanoe battle elected him President 30 years later. Campaigning in the 1840 election as the Hero of Tippecanoe—with John Tyler, an old-fashioned Virginian, as his running mate—Harrison rode into office on the Whig ticket using the slogan, Tippecanoe and Tyler Too! He lived only a month after his inauguration. Do students think that Harrison's defeat of the Shawnee was heroic? Can they recall other instances in which a candidate's military exploits influenced an election? *(Students may mention George Washington, Andrew Jackson, Dwight Eisenhower, and others.)*

poverished Native Americans in Ohio and Indiana. In 1808 the two leaders established a community called Prophet's Town along Indiana's Tippecanoe River. William Henry Harrison, governor of the Indiana Territory, grew alarmed at the power of the Shawnee leaders. In 1811 he gathered a force of 1,000 soldiers and attacked and destroyed Prophet's Town. Though Tecumseh and Tenskwatawa survived to continue their resistance, Tecumseh was eventually killed in 1813 while fighting for the British in the War of 1812. With his death came the decline of effective Native American resistance in the North. Soon more Native Americans were moving across the Mississippi River, away from white settlers.

The Cherokee Solution

Not all Native Americans spurned new ways and resisted white trespassers. The Cherokee of the southeastern United States, for example, tried to live in peace with whites.

In many ways Cherokee villages resembled white settlements in the South. The Cherokee built roads and collected taxes. Some adopted the Christian religion most white settlers followed. One man named Sequoyah spent 12 years devising an alphabet for the Cherokee language. Using this alphabet the Cherokee printed a newspaper, the *Cherokee Phoenix*.

The Cherokee learned that many conflicts between white settlers and Native Americans were resolved using the written laws of the state governments. To protect their interests, the Cherokee adopted their own legal code in 1808, combining Cherokee and American laws. In 1827 the Cherokee nation adopted a written constitution based on that of the United States.

These efforts, however, did not protect the Cherokee from Southern whites who hungered to obtain Cherokee land to grow cotton. As the Case Study on pages 136–139 shows, the Cherokee were unable to stop the relentless westward advance of white people.

The Cherokee joined other Native Americans who had been expelled from the East and resettled in the "Great American Desert." Some Native Americans, however, remained in the East, the ancestors of today's Eastern Native Americans. Yet far more common was the experience of those who, in the words of one Native American, were "compelled to seek asylum [protection] from the craving desires of the white man, beyond the great river."

NATIVE AMERICAN REMOVAL

Ceded before 1785
Ceded 1785-1810
Ceded 1810-1850
★ Battle site
← Route of removal

Frontier settlers often came into conflict with Native Americans; sooner or later the Native Americans lost their territories. *Identify the region where the Trail of Tears begins. How many states did the trail cross?*

SECTION REVIEW

Vocabulary
1. Define: frontier, flatboat.

Checking Facts
2. What conditions did a territory have to meet in order to become a state?

3. What policy toward Native Americans did the federal government set forth in the Northwest Ordinance? What policy did it follow in its treatment of the Shawnee and Cherokee?

Critical Thinking
Recognizing Ideologies
4. Did pioneer families who traveled west have any purposes other than to "strike it rich"? Explain your answer.

Linking Across Time
5. Does the frontier as defined in this section still exist? Does any kind of frontier exist today? Explain your answers.

MAP STUDY

Native Americans found it hard to resume their old ways of life in the arid and barren lands to which they were sent.

Answer: *Georgia; seven*

💿 Facts on File

Landmark Documents in American History Have students review "Constitution of the Cherokee Nation, 1827" and write a paragraph about the intent of the document.

Evaluate

Have students complete the Section Review.

📁 💿 Assign the Section 1 Quiz or use the Testmaker to develop a customized quiz. (Also in Spanish.) **LEP**

Reteach

🎧 Have students listen to the Chapter 5, Section 1 Audiocassette. (Also in Spanish.) **LEP**

Enrich

📁 Have students complete the Chapter 5 Geography in History Activity.

📁 Have students complete Supreme Court Case Study 2.

CLOSE

To summarize the section, have students share the most important events on their individual time lines. From these events create one large time line on the board.

Section 1 Review Answers

1. frontier (130), **flatboat** (132)
2. population of 60,000; congressional approval of its constitution
3. to act in "good faith" and to respect their property rights and liberty; destroyed the Shawnee community and drove the Cherokee out of their land

4. Answers will vary. Most pioneers sought land where they could be self-sufficient.
5. Answers will vary. The frontier no longer exists today. There are areas that are considered a frontier—outer space, for example.

135

TEACH

Making the Historical Connection

As white settlers moved west, conflicts with Native Americans arose. Sometimes those conflicts led to violence and bloodshed. In the case of the Cherokee, who had attempted to coexist with white Americans, the situation was more complex. Ask students to recall some of the efforts the Cherokee made to live peacefully with settlers. Discuss the conflicts that occurred between settlers and the Cherokee.

Notes

CASE STUDY Turning Point

Cherokee Expulsion

WINTER 1838

DECISION

Chief Justice: John Marshall

Case: Worcester v. Georgia

Date: 1832

The Cherokee nation, then, is a distinct community, occupying its own territory, with boundaries accurately described, in which the laws of Georgia can have no force, and which the citizens of Georgia have no right to enter, but with the assent of the Cherokees themselves. . . .

It is the opinion of this court that the judgment of the superior court . . . of Georgia, condemning Samuel A. Worcester to hard labour, . . . was pronounced by that court under . . . a law which is void . . . and ought, therefore, to be reversed and nullified.

The Case

The Cherokee and their supporters were jubilant. The case of *Worcester* v. *Georgia* was decided, and the Supreme Court of the United States had ruled in favor of Samuel Worcester, reversing the state's earlier judgment against him.

Worcester, a missionary who had lived among the Cherokee for years, had broken a Georgia state law. This law stated that non-Cherokee people living on Cherokee lands could either sign an oath of allegiance to Georgia or leave the Cherokee land. Worcester refused to do either. Instead, he chose a prison sentence of four years and appealed his case to the United States Supreme Court.

The Supreme Court ruling promised far more than just freedom for Worcester. Chief Justice John Marshall's words implied that the Cherokee would be free to control their own fate, without interference from the state of Georgia. No one could enter the Cherokee Nation without the permission of the Cherokee, and the Cherokee could invite whomever they wanted to live on their land. The United States government would protect their lands.

The victory proved to be an empty one. President Andrew Jackson is said to have remarked, "John Marshall has made his decision; let him enforce it now if he can." It was true—the decision could not be enforced. Jackson did nothing to see that the ruling was obeyed, and Worcester stayed in prison.

The Background

The Cherokee had held their land long before European settlers arrived. Through treaties with the United States government, the Cherokee became a sovereign nation within Georgia.

By the early 1800s the Cherokee were principally an agricultural people, having adopted many of the customs and ways of life of neighboring white

136 CASE STUDY

The Case at a Glance

| The Cherokee become a sovereign nation within Georgia. | → | Settlers desire valuable Cherokee land. | → | Georgia claims Cherokee land and restricts white presence there. | → | Samuel Worcester defies Georgia law, remains on Cherokee land, and is arrested. | → |

farmers. They had their own schools, their own newspaper, their own judicial system, and their own written constitution. Chief Sequoya's invention of a Cherokee alphabet enabled many of the Cherokee to read and write in their own language as well as in English. The Cherokee farmed some of Georgia's richest land, and in 1829 gold was discovered there. Settlers, miners, and land speculators were steadily encroaching on Cherokee territory in pursuit of its riches.

By the time of *Worcester* v. *Georgia* in 1832, federal and state laws had opened the door for Cherokee removal. In 1830 Congress had passed the Indian Removal Act, allowing Jackson to pursue his goal of relocating Eastern Native Americans to lands west of the Mississippi River.

That same year Georgia lawmakers had decreed that all Cherokee lands were under state jurisdiction, erasing Cherokee claims to sovereignty. Furthermore, the Cherokee could not testify against a white person or dig for the gold discovered in their own nation. Their laws were nullified. Finally, in December of 1830, Georgia restricted the presence of white settlers on Cherokee lands, a law that led to the *Worcester* case.

In 1832, when Jackson ignored the Supreme Court's ruling, the Cherokee realized their hopes for federal protection were in vain. Jackson recognized that the Cherokee had not been treated fairly. Nevertheless, he believed that the Eastern Native Americans would have to be relocated, because a separate nation could not continue to exist within an American state. Long before *Worcester* v. *Georgia,* Jackson had warned Congress against "encroachments upon the legitimate sphere of State sovereignty." It was no surprise that Jackson chose not to enforce the Supreme Court's ruling.

The Opinions

Read the opinions of some of the people involved in the Cherokee drama. President Jackson and Governor Lumpkin of Georgia favored removal, while Massachusetts Senator Everett sided with Cherokee Principal Chief Ross in upholding the sovereignty promised in earlier treaties and outlined in the Cherokee Constitution of 1827.

Among both United States and Cherokee officials, people's views on the issue of removal differed

"My opinion remains the same, and I can see no alternative for them but that of their removal to the West or a quiet submission to the State laws."

President Andrew Jackson, 1831

"Any attempt to infringe the evident right of a state to govern the entire population within its territorial limits . . . would be the usurpation of a power never granted by the states."

Wilson Lumpkin, governor of Georgia, 1832

"Whoever read of such a project? Ten or fifteen thousand families, to be rooted up. . . . There is not . . . such a thing in the annals of mankind. . . ."

Edward Everett, senator from Massachusetts, 1830

"The lands solemnly guaranteed and reserved forever to the Cherokee Nation by the Treaties concluded with the United States, . . . shall forever hereafter remain unalterably the same."

Constitution of the Cherokee Nation, formed by a convention of delegates led by Principal Chief John Ross, 1827

LIBRARY OF CONGRESS

LIBRARY OF CONGRESS

MASSACHUSETTS HISTORICAL SOCIETY

ARCHIVES AND MANUSCRIPTS DIVISION OF THE OKLAHOMA HISTORICAL SOCIETY

Turning Point

CASE STUDY

Facts on File
Landmark Documents in American History Have students review "Indian Removal Act, 1830," "*Cherokee Nation* v. *Georgia,* 1831," "*Worcester* v. *Georgia,* 1832," and "Message on Removal of Southern Indians (Seventh Annual Message to Congress), Andrew Jackson, 1835," and write a paragraph about the intent of one of the documents.

FYI

John Ross Although only one-eighth Cherokee by blood, John Ross was raised to consider himself Cherokee. At age 22, he fought under General Andrew Jackson in the War of 1812, and again assisted Jackson's troops in the Creek War of 1813. He then led the Cherokee in forming a government based largely on the United States model. Ross helped to draft the first Cherokee Constitution in 1827, following which he became principal chief of the Cherokee Nation, serving until 1839. Ross led the majority of the Cherokee in resisting the Georgia legislature's claim to the Cherokee lands.

The Supreme Court rules that Cherokee lands are sovereign.	→	President Jackson refuses to enforce the Court decision and favors expulsion of the Cherokee.

137

CASE STUDY Turning Point

Turning Point

The Trail of Tears was not the first organized expulsion of Native Americans, but it represented a dramatic betrayal of past promises and treaties. The Cherokee had worked to exist within the confines of the United States government. Instead of coexisting peacefully, however, white settlers turned resentment over the Native Americans' wealth and land into a crusade to remove the Cherokee. In supporting the demands to push the Cherokee west, Jackson devalued solemn treaties made between the United States and Native Americans.

Analyzing the Case

After students have read the last three sections of this case, have them discuss the following:

1. Which opinion quoted seems to be least motivated by self-interest? *(Answers will vary. Senator Everett takes the side of the Cherokee although he has nothing personal to gain.)*

2. What accounts for the differences in the opinions of Andrew Jackson and Edward Everett? *(Answers will vary. Jackson's assumption that the Cherokee were not as civilized as whites led him to favor removal. Everett held that the Cherokee were equal to whites; this led to his opinion that they had a greater claim to the land.)*

3. If the Cherokee had defended their land, what would they have risked? *(Answers will vary. If the Cherokee had stuck together to defend their land, they would have risked a war with the United States.)*

Robert Lindeux's painting *The Trail of Tears* depicts the Cherokee on the forced march across the Appalachian Mountains from their homes in the Southeast. One soldier noted that he had seen 22 people die in a single night during the journey.

sharply. The government's removal policy would serve the interests of expansionists and miners, who wanted both rich soil and gold. On the other hand, most of the Cherokee wanted to remain on the land of their ancestors. Not only did they have a settled life on that land, they had also heard about the hardship and suffering of those who had already moved west.

The Assumptions

Quotations from the players involved reveal another basis for their opinions—underlying assumptions. For example, President Jackson professed to have "the kindest feelings" toward the Cherokee. Even so, his words and actions reveal a bias against them. On another occasion President Jackson had addressed the Cherokee, saying, "I tell you that you cannot remain where you now are. Circumstances that cannot be controlled, and which are beyond the reach of human laws, render it impossible that you can flourish in the midst of a civilized community." Notice the assumption that underlies Jackson's words in that last sentence.

Jackson based much of his argument for removal on his belief in state sovereignty. Governor Lumpkin had less sympathy for the Cherokee than Jackson and far less knowledge of them. Like Jackson, however, he based much of his argument against the Supreme Court's ruling on his belief that the powers of the state government took precedence over those of the federal government.

Everett's underlying assumptions caused him to speak passionately on behalf of the Cherokee. Unlike Jackson, Everett thought of them as "essentially a civilized people." This assumption led to his vehement expressions of indignation.

What about the Cherokee themselves? What were their assumptions? They at first assumed that the federal government would uphold the promises of previous administrations, such as those made during Thomas Jefferson's presidency. The Cherokee had worked hard, in the words of Cherokee orator John Ridge, ". . . to form a republican government, . . . cultivate the earth, and learn the mechanic arts." They made the basic assumption that the white senators would come to regard Native Americans as equals, with shared values and basic human rights.

138 CASE STUDY

Cooperative Learning

Peaceful Alternatives Have students work together to find peaceful alternatives to the Cherokee expulsion. Organize the class into groups of four. Suggest that they start by splitting their groups into twos. Each pair can represent either the white Georgia government or the Cherokee leaders. Have them identify and record the issues and conflicts between them, then generate and record as many ideas for solving these conflicts as they can. Afterward they can eliminate ideas that might lead to violence or injustice toward one side. Have the groups share their final lists with the class and discuss the implications of their resolutions.

The Outcome

For years John Ross, the principal chief of the Cherokee, was able to maintain unity among his people. He and other Cherokee leaders—such as Major Ridge and his son John Ridge—all opposed the Cherokee removal at first.

John Ridge When news of the *Worcester* v. *Georgia* decision reached John Ridge, he was exuberant. He believed that the Supreme Court, and therefore the Cherokee, would prevail over Georgia. Ridge then spoke to Jackson himself, however, and learned that the President had no intention of enforcing the decision. Jackson told him that the only hope for the Cherokee was in "abandoning their country and removing to the West."

By the mid-1830s John Ridge, his father, Major Ridge, and his cousin Elias Boudinot, the editor of the *Cherokee Phoenix,* had begun to believe that removal was inevitable. These Cherokee leaders and their supporters realized that the United States government would never protect the Cherokee lands in Georgia. They also believed the government was making the Cherokee a better offer in terms of land and assistance than ever before.

Two Factions The two factions that developed among the Cherokee were the Treaty party, which favored removal, and the National party, which continued to oppose it. John Ross and the National party viewed their opponents as traitors. They never came to accept removal. Major Ridge, knowing that many of the people he loved considered him an enemy, pleaded with them:

> I am one of the native sons of these wild woods. I have hunted the deer and turkey here more than fifty years. . . . The Georgians have shown a grasping spirit lately; they have extended their laws, to which we are unaccustomed, which harass our braves and make the children suffer and cry. . . . I know the Indians have an older title than theirs. We obtained the land from the living God above. . . . Yet they are strong and we are weak. We are few, they are many. We cannot remain here in safety and comfort. I know we love the graves of our fathers. . . . We can never forget these homes, I know, but an unbending, iron necessity tells us we must leave them.

Pressure to complete the Cherokee relocation intensified. The National party, representing about 16,000 Cherokee, adamantly resisted the move, yet the administration dealt only with the minority Treaty party. Its leaders signed a relocation treaty, ratified by Congress and the President in 1836.

Still, in 1838 after the deadline set for removal had passed, few Cherokee had moved voluntarily. Soldiers with rifles and bayonets forced more than 18,000 Cherokee from their homes and marched them approximately 1,000 miles to what is now Oklahoma. During the march nearly 4,000 Cherokee died from malnutrition, exposure to the cold, cholera, and physical hardship. Their grueling trek earned the name the Trail of Tears.

RESPONDING TO THE CASE

1. Jackson spoke of the Cherokee as hunters who had no right to "tracts of country on which they have neither dwelt nor made improvements, merely because they have seen them from the mountain or passed them in the chase." Why do you think Jackson made this statement? What was he purposely ignoring?

2. Senator Theodore Frelinghuysen, in a speech on the Indian Removal Act, asked: "Do the obligations of justice change with the color of the skin?" Which views presented on page 137 would Frelinghuysen probably agree with?

3. Before the Trail of Tears, the Ridges had decided that their people had no choice but to go west. Although at first they were opposed to relocation, what events changed their minds? Why?

4. In what respects was Major Ridge in sympathy with the Cherokee who continued to oppose removal? What were some of the values and assumptions he shared with them?

PORTFOLIO PROJECT Imagine that you are a Cherokee leader faced with the threat of removal. Write a speech addressed to the Cherokee people urging the case of either the Treaty party or the National party. Keep the speech in your portfolio.

CASE STUDY **139**

CASE STUDY Turning Point

 Block Scheduling

The Portfolio Project on this page provides an excellent opportunity to enrich and extend the key elements of this case study.

CLOSE

Discuss the values that lay behind the actions and statements of the people involved in the Cherokee expulsion. What values and goals motivated Jackson? What values influenced the actions and responses of the two factions of the Cherokee? (See The Assumptions on page 138.)

Notes

Responding to the Case Answers

1. Answers will vary. Jackson used strong words to support his belief that the Cherokee were less civilized than whites. Jackson purposely ignored the fact that the Cherokee had improved the land, and had homes, businesses, mines, and farms. He also ignored the authority of the Supreme Court ruling.

2. Answers will vary. Frelinghuysen would agree with John Ross and Edward Everett.

3. Answers will vary. Ridge's conversation with Jackson convinced him that there was little hope of the Cherokee keeping their land.

4. Answers will vary. Both parties valued modern education and government. They both shared a longstanding heritage of stewarding the land. They both valued Cherokee unity, although Ridge favored relocation because he feared aggression from the United States government.

FOCUS

Section Objectives

1. Describe the development of factory manufacturing in the United States.
2. Explain the importance of immigration to the labor force and the growth of American manufacturing.
3. Show how roads, canals, and railroads knitted the country together.
4. Describe the connections between economics, politics, and sectionalism.

Bellringer Activity

While taking attendance at the beginning of the class period, display **Section Focus Transparency 35,** and have students answer the questions. (Or use the blackline master.)

VISUAL INSTRUCTION

New Line of Work This photograph, taken about 1860, shows four weavers from the Winthrop, Maine, area.

Ask: How do you think the 70-hour work week in a mill compared with the hours a woman worked on a farm? *(Answers will vary; a woman probably worked as many hours on the farm, but with more flexibility.)*

SECTION 2

The Economy Grows

APRIL 4, 1839: MILLWORKER DESCRIBES FACTORY LIFE

MUSEUM OF AMERICAN TEXTILE HISTORY, NORTH ANDOVER, MA

New Line of Work
The change from farm to factory meant a complete change in lifestyle for these young women.

AFTER 14 HOURS ON THE JOB, MALENDA EDWARDS WALKED TO HER BOARDINGHOUSE, WEARILY CLIMBED THE STAIRS, AND SAT AT THE DESK IN HER ROOM. Her ears still ringing from the din of the mill machinery, Malenda found a piece of paper and began a letter to her cousin Sabrina. "You have been informed, I suppose," she wrote, "that I am a factory girl." She continued:

There are many young ladies at work in the factories that have given up millinery dressmaking and school keeping for to work in the mill. But I would not advise anyone to do it, for I was so sick of it at first I wished a factory had never been thought of. But the longer I stay the better I like it.

—Malenda Edwards, from a letter to Sabrina Bennet, April 4, 1839

In 1839 Malenda Edwards had left her parents' quiet farm and moved to Nashua, New Hampshire, to work in a textile mill. She traded her days of milking cows, spinning thread, and raking hay for work in a 5-story, red-brick factory. Every day but Sunday, she started work at 5:00 A.M. and operated a power loom until 7:00 P.M., with only short breaks for meals. Most of the 250 workers in the factory were women.

Despite the long hours, Malenda was happy to work in the mill. For a 70-hour work week she earned $3.25—more than most women could make as teachers, seamstresses, or servants. In the years between 1839 and 1845, Malenda would work in the factory for part of the year, then return home to enjoy her earnings and take care of her aging parents.

AS YOU READ

Vocabulary
► textile
► wage
► turnpike
► tariff

Think About . . .
► the development of factories in the United States and their features.
► how immigration contributed to the growth of American manufacturing.
► how roads, canals, and railroads united the country.
► the connections between economics and sectional politics.

140 CHAPTER 5 THE EXPANDING NATION

Section 2 Resources

REPRODUCIBLE RESOURCES
📂 Lesson Plan 5-2
📂 Vocabulary and Guided Reading Activity 5-2
📂 Section 2 Quiz
📂 Supreme Court Case 3

MULTIMEDIA RESOURCES
Section Focus Transparency 35
Focus on American Fine Art Prints, Print 7
Landmark Documents in American History
Historic America: Electronic Field Trips
Testmaker
Chapter 5 Digest Audiocassette
Student Self-Test: A Software Review

In 1845 Malenda Edwards got married, stopped working in the mills, and moved to a small town. She was just one of thousands of Americans who made the journey from farm to factory in the 1800s.

From Farms to Factories
Manufacturing Picks Up Speed

In 1800 most Americans worked on farms. Whether raising cotton in the South, planting in the meadow of a Western forest, or farming near an Eastern town, American farmers led a quiet, rural life. They prided themselves on being self-sufficient. Their farm supplied the family with food, and farm women made day-to-day necessities like soap, candles, and maple sugar.

Most other necessities could be found within a few miles of the farm. Items that could not be made at home were manufactured—by hand, one at a time—by local blacksmiths, shoemakers, and tailors in exchange for corn or wheat. In the more populous areas of the nation, small country stores provided farmers with hard-to-find

75 Young Women

From 15 to 35 Years of Age,

WANTED TO WORK IN THE

COTTON MILLS!

IN LOWELL AND CHICOPEE, MASS.

I am authorized by the Agents of said Mills to make the following proposition to persons suitable for their work, viz:—They will be paid $1.00 per week, and board, for the first month. It is presumed they will then be able to go to work at job prices. They will be considered as engaged for one year, cases of sickness excepted. I will pay the expenses of those who have not the means to pay for themselves, and the girls will pay it to the Company by their first labor. All that remain in the employ of the Company eighteen months will have the amount of their expenses to the Mills refunded to them. They will be properly cared for in sickness. It is hoped that none will go except those whose circumstances will admit of their staying at least one year. None but active and healthy girls will be engaged for this work as it would not be advisable for either the girls or the Company.

I shall be at the Howard Hotel, Burlington, on Monday, July 25th; at Farnham's, St Albans, Tuesday forenoon, 26th, at Keyse's, Swanton, in the afternoon; at the Massachusetts' House, Rouses Point, on Wednesday, the 27th, to engage girls,—such as would like a place in the Mills would do well to improve the present opportunity, as new hands will not be wanted late in the season. I shall start with my Company, for the Mills, on Friday morning, the 29th inst., from Rouses Point, at 6 o'clock. Such as do not have an opportunity to see me at the above places, can take the cars and go with me the same as though I had engaged them.

I will be responsible for the safety of all baggage that is marked in care of I. M. BOYNTON, and delivered to my charge.

I. M. BOYNTON,

Agent for Procuring Help for the Mills.

BAKER LIBRARY, HARVARD UNIVERSITY

COURTESY AMERICAN ANTIQUARIAN SOCIETY

Millworkers The Merrimack label shows the weaving and printing of cloth under one roof. Mills recruited young women (poster, above) rather than young men because women were more easily spared from farmwork. *How did the Embargo Act spur the development of factories?*

goods, like gunpowder, coffee, and tea. **Textiles,** or cloth and fabric, from Europe were especially popular in American stores.

By 1800 all but those farmers living on the most remote fringes of the frontier survived on a mix of homemade goods, handcrafted products of local artisans, and store-bought items imported from Europe. This way of living began to change in 1807.

A Changing Economy

Trade between the United States and Europe had increased steadily. In 1803, however, war broke out between Great Britain and France, resulting in harassment and capture of United States merchant ships. To avoid a war with Britain or France, President Jefferson signed the Embargo Act in 1807, stopping all trade between Europe and the United States. Trade remained choked until after the War of 1812. The resulting economic slowdown had several effects. First, the British wool, Irish linen, and Indian cotton that had flooded the American market no longer arrived. As a result, the home manufacture of textiles boomed. A second effect of this situation was that merchants who had traded with Europe now looked for other ways to make money.

One of those merchants, a Bostonian named Francis Cabot Lowell, recognized the demand for textiles in the United States. He had seen dozens of tiny spinning mills crop up across New England. Lowell took advantage of the postwar slowdown in trade with Britain and began a bold experiment. He started to organize an entirely new system of textile production that was bigger, more efficient, and more profitable than any in the United States.

Lowell's Experiment

In 1813 Lowell set about designing a new spinning and weaving machine. With help from employee Paul Moody, the machine was finally perfected. Lowell and his business partners built a three-story factory on the banks of the Charles River in Waltham, Massachusetts. The current of the river turned waterwheels, which were connected to gears and belts that ran the machinery in the factory.

SECTION TWO **141**

TEACH

Guided Practice

L2 Making a Time Line
As students discuss the section, have them make a large time line on the board covering important events between 1800 and 1850. Some students may wish to add events that occurred during the period but are not covered by the text.

VISUAL INSTRUCTION

Millworkers The young farm women who first came to the Lowell mills were expected to work for just a few years. They were to be recruited "from the healthy and virtuous population of the country."

Answer: *Needed textiles could no longer be imported from abroad; also, merchants whose overseas trade was interrupted looked for other ways to make money.*

Curriculum Connection

Economics Before and during the War of 1812, the United States decided to limit its connections with Europe. Discuss the impact of that decision on the nation's economy. What changes would American businesspeople and consumers have had to make?

Cooperative Learning

Role Playing Organize the class into groups of five or six. Have students play the roles of a New England farm family who have just learned about Lowell's textile mill. Each student should express different hopes, fears, and concerns about the mill. The father and the son, for example, might oppose industrialization because of their love of farm life. A daughter might want the money and freedom that mill work would bring. The mother might point out that life on the farm would be easier with more cash income. Some groups may wish to present their sketches to the class.

Independent Practice

L2 Writing The Erie Canal fascinated Americans. Writers, painters, and composers marked its building and completion. Some students may wish to write a report about a song, story, or painting of the canal. Others may wish to write a brief analysis of why it was so important to Americans.

☛ Have students complete the Chapter 5, Section 2 Vocabulary and Guided Reading Activity. (Also in Spanish.) **LEP**

CHART STUDY

Paul Moody, who assisted Lowell in designing a new spinning and weaving machine, was a self-taught inventor, who later established one of the first factories for making textile machinery.

Answer: *57*

Unlike the tiny spinning mills of New England, Lowell's plant contained all the stages of textile production under one roof: spinning, weaving, bleaching, dyeing, and printing. The fabric Lowell's factory turned out was rougher than the fine textiles of Europe, but it suited the needs of Americans who bought his cloth. Lowell's factory—larger and more ambitious than any other in the United States—launched the nation's Industrial Revolution, the change from manufacturing at home to manufacturing in factories.

New Workers

Where would Lowell find workers to operate his spinning and weaving machines? In the rural areas around Waltham, no farmer wanted to give up his property and independence to earn **wages,** or daily pay, in a textile factory. Lowell discovered, however, that the farmers' daughters were happy for an opportunity to earn money. Many parents were also happy to receive some of these earnings.

Lowell began recruiting young (mostly ages 15–29) farm women to live and work at his factory. He promised parents that their daughters would live under strict moral supervision in company dormitories, be required to attend church services, and be held to a nightly curfew. After persuading many parents to allow their daughters to move to Waltham, Lowell opened his factory in 1814.

Lowell's Waltham mill was an enormous success. It was so successful that following Lowell's death in 1817, his partners built a new, larger plant located on the Merrimack River in 1823. The town that grew up at that spot

THE FIRST MODERN FACTORIES

The "Lowell" factory system was designed to bring work and workers together. A typical Lowell textile mill in 1830 housed 4,500 spindles, 120 power looms, and more than 200 employees under one roof. Activities within the mill were organized to speed the flow of materials through a multistep process. The system saved time, increased efficiency, and dramatically boosted production and profits.

Unskilled Labor Factory production taught workers the skills they needed. More experienced employees trained newcomers, and workers often changed jobs to increase their wages or to cope with the dull routine.

Reliance on Power-driven Machines Lowell's improvements in the power loom were essential to the factory system's success.

Yards of Cloth per Day
1 handloom with 1 operator — 18
3 power looms with 1 operator — 75
0 — 100

Cleaning The first steps in production turned loose cotton into crude yarn.

Spinning Spinning transformed the yarn into thread.

Weaving Weaving created coarse cloth.

Finishing Cloth was measured and batched for bleaching, dyeing, or printing.

Increased Production Mill owners continued to improve machines and methods to increase production.

Yards per Year
200,000
100,000
0
50,000 — 1836
167,000 — 1860

Technological innovation and economic opportunity combined to make the first textile mills possible. *How many more yards of cloth could an operator produce each day tending three power looms instead of one handloom?*

Meeting Special Needs

Oral Learners Help oral learners by opening a discussion that links historical and current issues. Discuss with the class the importance and necessity of jobs. Ask which students have jobs, how many hours they work each week, and how old they were when they started working. What do they think makes a job good or bad?

became known as Lowell, Massachusetts. Other textile mills that were located in Lowell also adopted the factory system. By 1840 textile mills employed 8,000 workers, almost 40 percent of Lowell's population.

Business leaders built textile mills all over New England and the mid-Atlantic states in the 1830s and 1840s. Most of the workers in these factories were women like Malenda Edwards. The rest of the labor force was made up of children from local farms and a growing number of men who sought factory work after failing at farming.

After 1840 another source of labor began arriving in the factories of the Northeast. Political turmoil and failed crops drove thousands of Germans and Irish from their European homes. Most of these immigrants arrived on American shores desperate for jobs. Many came to the textile mills of the Northeast and offered to work for lower wages than the farm women.

For factory owners this new, cheap source of labor came just in time. The success of the factory system had created intense competition between textile companies. Mill owners struggled to find ways to increase production and lower costs. Many cut wages and increased the workload of employees. Some women went out on strike to protest wage cuts. In response factory owners began to hire more and more immigrants. By 1860 European immigrants had replaced farm women as the largest group of workers in American factories. This influx of labor willing to work for low wages continued to make the factory system profitable in the United States.

A New Economy

The census of 1850 reported that in the past most "manufacturing was carried on in the shop and the household by the labor of the family." By 1850 it was done by "a system of factory labor, compensated by wages, and assisted by power." Factories producing textiles, shoes, furniture, carriages, and other goods appeared all across the Northeast. Many of these factories were built in growing cities that attracted immigrant workers.

The growth of factories meant that more Americans bought more goods in stores. After 1850 farmers did not get their shoes handmade from a cobbler two miles from home. Instead they bought factory-made shoes from a store that had ordered them from a merchant hundreds of miles away. The transportation revolution that also occurred after 1800 made more goods available to more people in more places than ever before.

The Transportation Revolution
Road, River, and Rail

By 1850 American manufactured goods and farm produce were being transported to most places where people wanted them, whether in Boston or Chicago. Moving goods and people from one place to another had not always been so simple, however.

Roads and Turnpikes

Before 1800 roads and rivers were the most important links between farms, villages, and cities. Yet travel over these roadways and waterways was impossible during some seasons and difficult during the best times. Dry seasons turned many rivers into trickling streams. Hot weather turned roads to dust and rain turned them into muddy troughs. Shipping goods from east to west was expensive: it cost more to haul a ton of goods 9 miles (14.5 km) inland from the ocean than it did to bring that same ton of goods from Europe.

An early solution to American transportation problems was the development of **turnpikes,** roads that required travelers to pay tolls. Private companies built the first turnpikes hoping to earn back the cost of the roads by charging tolls. Turnpike companies often built their roads of stone and gravel, making better traveling conditions. By 1832 the

WELLS FARGO BANK

Riding the Mail Coach Improving the transportation network helped industry and linked the people of different regions. *How might failure to improve transportation have affected the social development of the nation?*

SECTION TWO **143**

VISUAL INSTRUCTION

Riding the Mail Coach The National Road, also called the Cumberland Road, was the main route to the Northwest Territory. It forms part of present-day U.S. 40.

Answer: *The interaction of different peoples would not have occurred as rapidly.*

History and the Humanities

 Focus on American Fine Art Prints, Print 7— *Pat Lyon at the Forge* by John Neagle

ABCNEWS
iNTERACTiVE™

 Videodisc

Historic America: Electronic Field Trips

Side 2, Chapter 3
Title: Lowell Factories
Subject: Tour of early factories in Lowell, Massachusetts
Ask: Why was Lowell chosen as a site for these early factories? *(It was close to a water supply, which could power the machines.)*

See Historic America: Electronic Field Trips Guidebook for complete lesson plan.

Portfolio Project

Conducting an Interview Immigrants supplied factory owners with inexpensive labor in the 1840s, and they continue to be a major component of the nation's labor force. Have students interview an immigrant friend or family member (or someone whose parents were immigrants), asking him or her a number of questions related to employment. Students should prepare questions in advance. They should take notes during the interview, or they may wish to tape-record it. After discussing their results in class, students can file their reports in their portfolios.

VISUAL INSTRUCTION

Big Dig Irish immigrants, who numbered 343,000 in New York State by 1850, supplied much of the labor for the digging of the Erie Canal; many of them settled permanently along the line of the canal.

Answer: *They did not answer the need for cheap, fast transportation over varied terrain.*

Curriculum Connection

Literature Writer Mark Twain was born and raised in the Mississippi River town of Hannibal, Missouri. In *Life on the Mississippi* (1883), Twain described the sights and legends of the river and his days as a riverboat pilot. In his novel *The Adventures of Huckleberry Finn* (1885), the river is such a prominent feature of the story that it almost becomes a character in its own right. Some students may wish to read these books and report on what they say about life on the river.

United States had nearly 2,400 miles (3,861.6 km) of toll roads linking together most important cities.

Roads to the West were the most common projects during the turnpike era. The federal government funded construction of the most important route west, the National Road. This stone road that was 80 feet (24.3 m) wide was started in 1811 and ran westward from Cumberland, Maryland. By 1818 it stretched about 130 miles (209.2 km) to Wheeling, in present-day West Virginia. By 1852 it spanned approximately 600 miles (965.4 km), ending in Vandalia, Illinois.

Rivers and Canals

Transportation by water was much less expensive than by road. During the early 1800s, flatboats floated down the Ohio and Mississippi Rivers, carrying crops raised by Western farmers to export markets and to pioneers in other areas. Upstream travel remained slow and expensive, but rivers were a popular and cheap way to move people and goods from place to place.

The rise of steam power made the nation's rivers even more crowded. After 1810 steamboats began churning up and down the rivers, bringing trade in their wake. Between 1830 and 1860, riverboats were especially important on the Mississippi, where they helped make Western farms profitable.

Of course, rivers had limited usefulness. For one thing, most run from north to south, so travel from east to west was often difficult. "Rivers are ungovernable things," Benjamin Franklin wrote. "Canals are quiet and always manageable." Franklin neglected to note that canals were also expensive and hard to build. Nevertheless, the early 1800s witnessed the growth of a network of canals linking the nation's natural waterways.

After the War of 1812, a group of New Yorkers pushed for a canal connecting the Hudson River to Lake Erie. The Erie Canal was to be 363 miles (584.1 km) long at a time when the longest existing canal in the nation was less than 28 miles (45.1 km) long. Construction began in 1817, and over the next 8 years laborers dug by hand a canal 40 feet (12.2 m) wide and 4 feet (1.2 m) deep through the wilderness of northern New York.

Completed in 1825, the Erie Canal was a phenomenal success. Thanks to the business the canal generated, by 1830 New York City replaced Baltimore as the

THE BETTMANN ARCHIVE

Big Dig The completion of the Erie Canal and other canals, together with the rise of steam power, solved many transportation problems. *What transportation problems could not be solved by the use of waterways?*

Extending the Content

Daily Life American household amenities of the mid-1800s were crude. Most cities lacked water and sewer systems. Residents drew water from a well in the backyard (adjacent to the privy) or from a rainwater cistern in which mosquitoes bred. Insects were the worst pest of the era; window screens were rare. The bathtub was a wooden box lined with copper or zinc; water to fill it was heated on the stove. Houses were heated with wood or coal in fireplaces or parlor stoves. Gaslight had been introduced but whale-oil lamps and candles were still used. Discuss the effect such limitations would have had on the time, energy, and health of people.

major Eastern port leading to the interior of the nation. Freight rates to western New York fell by 90 percent after the canal opened. The benefit of this modification to the nation's geography and transportation system was clear.

The Erie Canal's success spurred the construction of canals throughout the nation between 1830 and 1850. In the East, canals connected the backcountry to the ocean. Further inland canals linked Eastern cities with the growing settlements of the Ohio River valley. In the Midwest, canals connected the Great Lakes with the Mississippi River. By 1840 Americans had constructed more than 3,300 miles (5,309.7 km) of canals. In a land of mountains, forests, and plains, however, canals did not solve every transportation problem. Soon Americans were looking for another way to travel.

Tracks and Steam Engines

The success of the Erie Canal took business away from Baltimore merchants who had profited from their location near the National Road. Some of them hatched a plan to restore Baltimore's importance as a seaport by building a railroad from Maryland to Ohio. In 1828 these merchants launched the Baltimore and Ohio, or B & O, Railroad.

Railroads had been invented in Britain. The idea, however, seemed tailor-made for the United States and its huge, varied landscape. Fast transportation that could cover virtually any terrain offered obvious advantages over canals. As a result, people eagerly invested large sums of money in infant railroad companies. During the 1830s more than 3,300 miles (5,309.7 km) of iron rails were built across the nation. A trip from New York to Cincinnati that had taken 2 months over roads took only 1 week by train in 1850.

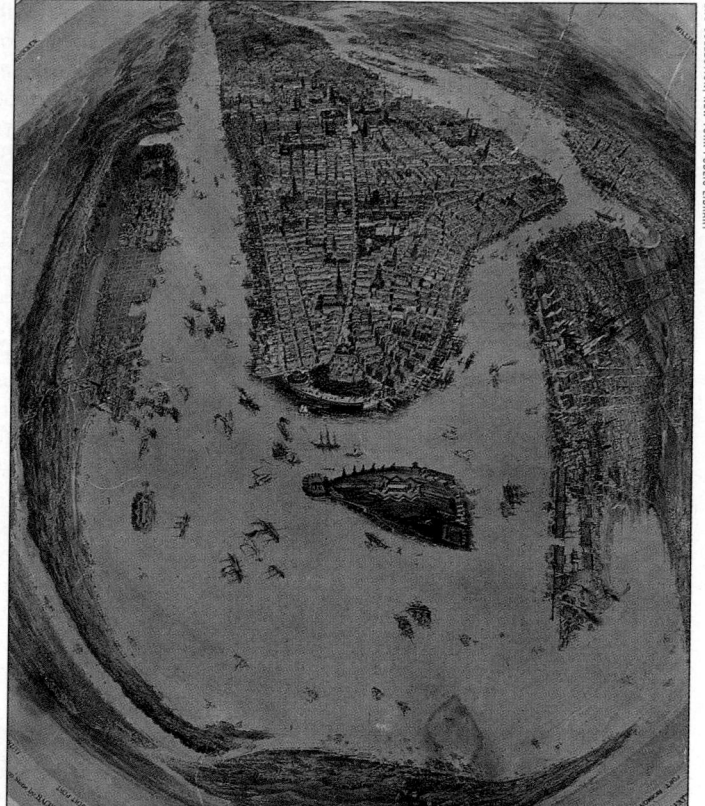

Bird's-Eye View While transportation systems spawned new inland cities, they also built up older port cities such as New York, shown in this 1859 engraving. *What effect did the opening of the Erie Canal have on the commerce of New York City?*

WATER TRANSPORT DEVELOPMENTS, 1811–1850

1811 Robert Fulton's steamboat cruises down the Mississippi River. Previously, flatboats carried cargo along Western rivers.

1825 Erie Canal is completed, connecting New York City to Great Lakes.

1840s Sharp decline in freight rates on canals and increase in allowed tonnage on lakes and rivers leads to heyday for water transport.

1848 Illinois and Michigan Canal connects the Great Lakes to the Mississippi.

1810   1820   1830   1840   1850

1816 Capt. Shreve's steamboat, *The Washington*, travels upstream as well as down on the Ohio River.

1817 Construction on Erie Canal begins. First steamboat travels on the Great Lakes.

1833 Laborers, many of whom had worked on the Erie Canal, complete canal system in Ohio.

1850s Private railroad companies break the transportation monopolies of state waterways. Toll rates decrease. Water and rail transport increase.

Cultural Perspectives

Native Americans in Fact and Fiction In 1826—just after the Erie Canal had been driven through the Mohawk Valley, where the Five Nations of the Iroquois once held sway—James Fenimore Cooper published *The Last of the Mohicans*. The book did nothing to arrest the decline of Native American societies, but it developed the "noble red man" theme that is a staple of American literature. Several films were based on the book, the latest in 1992. Have students discuss this film or others that treat Native American subjects. How does the film compare with what they know about the historical reality? Some students may wish to read Cooper's novel.

VISUAL INSTRUCTION

Bird's-Eye View In the engraving, New Jersey lies to the left, and Staten Island floats in the foreground. Students can compare this view with a modern map of New York.

Answer: *As of 1830 New York replaced Baltimore as the number one supplier to inland areas.*

 Curriculum Connection

Geography The solid rock of the Niagara Escarpment, 17 miles east of Niagara Falls, was the greatest natural barrier in the path of the Erie Canal. It would require eastbound boats to be lowered 70 feet and westbound boats to be raised 70 feet before they could sail on. Builders rose to the challenge by creating the famous locks—two separate flights of five locks each—that made the city of Lockport, New York, out of a wilderness.

CHART STUDY

Ask: When was the Erie Canal completed?
Answer: *1825*
Ask: How long did it take to build?
Answer: *about 8 years*

Meeting Lesson Objectives

Each section objective is tested by the section review question(s) that follows it in parentheses.

1. Describe the development of factory manufacturing in the United States. (2)
2. Explain the importance of immigration to the labor force and the growth of American manufacturing. (4)
3. Show how roads, canals, and railroads knitted the country together. (1, 3)
4. Describe the connections between economics, politics, and sectionalism. (5)

VISUAL INSTRUCTION

Henry Clay for President
The election of 1824 was a four-way tie among Henry Clay, Andrew Jackson, John Calhoun, and John Quincy Adams. Adams won by a vote in the House of Representatives. This situation has not recurred in more than 170 years.

Answer: *He thought it would aid stability and investment.*

 Facts on File

Landmark Documents in American History Have students review "Tariff Act of 1816" and write a paragraph about the intent of the document.

By 1860 railroads carried goods and passengers at lower cost and in less time than roads, canals, or rivers. They made money for investors, merchants who shipped by rail, and people who settled in the towns and cities that sprouted along the track of the locomotive during the 1840s and 1850s. The need for railroads, like roads and canals before, came from industry and trade. The growth of railroads, in turn, created thousands of jobs and stimulated new industries, such as those for iron, steel, and railroad car manufacturing.

Politics and the Economy
National and Regional Interests Clash

"It is an extraordinary era in which we live," said Daniel Webster, a senator from Massachusetts, in 1847. "It is altogether new. The world has seen nothing like it." Revolutions in industry and transportation in the United States made this new world possible. While private investors had funded many of these developments, government also helped nurture America's economic growth in the 1800s.

Henry Clay for President Clay began campaigning for President in 1824 and ran in three elections. Like other candidates of the period, his likeness appeared on practical and playful items, such as this bandanna. *What effect did Clay expect a new Bank of the United States to have on the national economy in 1816?*

One of the strongest supporters of government's role in the economy was Henry Clay. A member of Congress from Kentucky, Clay had gained prominence during the War of 1812 as a Western war hawk. At that time he opposed a strong national government and programs such as the Bank of the United States, which gave the federal government significant centralized economic power.

As America's economic power grew, however, Clay's views changed. He organized his new ideas into an economic plan called the American System.

The American System

Clay's American System was based on the idea that a stronger national government would benefit each of the different sections of the country. As part of this system Clay supported an 1816 bill to increase **tariffs**, or fees on imported goods. The tariffs were designed to protect American manufacturers—nearly all of whom were located in the East—from European competition. Clay believed that healthy Eastern industries would help the whole nation. This bill passed despite the objections of Southerners in Congress. The South, a region with little manufacturing, would gain nothing directly from the tariff. Consequently, the tariff would have the effect of higher prices for the South, because Southerners imported a great deal of foreign goods.

In 1816 Congress faced the decision of whether to charter a new Bank of the United States (the charter of the first Bank expired in 1811). Clay supported the Bank, arguing that it would stabilize the economy and encourage investments. The Bank bill passed.

Another part of Clay's American System met with less success than the first two. Clay wanted the government to supply money for improvements such as road and canal building. Other Westerners in Congress voted for these plans, which would greatly benefit the frontier regions they represented. Southerners in Congress generally favored Clay's plans because the South also stood to benefit from such improvements. Northerners, however, clashed with Clay over these improvements. For one thing, their roads and canals were already built and dug, so they would not

PHOTO BY STEVE LASCHEVER/COURTESY OF MUSEUM OF AMERICAN POLITICAL LIFE, HARTFORD, CT

Critical Thinking

Demonstrating Reasoned Judgment
Henry Clay's American System did not succeed as he hoped, largely because several Presidents were reluctant to spend federal funds on internal improvements. Discuss how the federal government spends money today. Would a proposal like Clay's—to rebuild roads and bridges at federal expense, for example—gain many supporters today?

CARTMEN

Transportation Ticket This silk campaign ribbon shows the loyalty of a strong Clay contingent: the wagoneers, or cartmen. *What specific proposals did Clay put forward that could have won him the wagoneers' support?*

PHOTO BY STEVE LASCHEVER/COURTESY OF MUSEUM OF AMERICAN POLITICAL LIFE, HARTFORD, CT

built many of their canals with state funds. Canal and railroad companies usually obtained land from federal and state governments at bargain prices. The combination of private investments and public policy reshaped American life after 1815.

A New Nation

Shortly after steamboats began to paddle down the nation's rivers, a newspaper editor exclaimed that steam power would "diminish the size of the globe." It would make Americans "one single people, one nation, one mind." In some ways, the nation did seem more unified after the transportation and industrial revolutions. After 1850 the farmer's solitary self-sufficiency no longer seemed practical. Cooperation between people with different interests and from different regions replaced it. New Englanders gave up most of their farming and devoted resources to manufacturing. Farmers from the western side of the Appalachians now produced most of the American grain. Southern planters devoted more land and slave labor to cash crops like cotton.

Regional specialization, however, could lead to conflicts. A law that helped Northern manufacturers, such as the tariff, might hurt Southern planters. Tensions between different sections of the nation and between different groups of people began to grow. The forces that changed America's economy in the 1800s also changed the politics and beliefs of its people.

benefit directly from federal assistance. Also, many Northerners feared the growing power of the Westerners and did not want to help them grow stronger.

The greatest opposition to Clay's plans, however, came from the Executive Office of the President. Between 1817 and 1830, three of Clay's internal improvement bills were passed by Congress and then vetoed by three different Presidents. President James Madison, who argued that the Constitution did not give Congress the power to build roads, vetoed the first. On the same basic grounds, in 1822, President James Monroe vetoed a proposal to improve the National Road. Finally, in 1830 President Andrew Jackson vetoed the use of federal funds to improve Kentucky's Maysville Road.

Clay was disappointed that these Presidents paid so little attention to internal improvements, but the government did encourage the nation's growth in other ways. After 1816 Congress passed a series of tariffs that protected the nation's young industries. Between 1830 and 1860 New York, Pennsylvania, Ohio, and Virginia

SECTION REVIEW

Vocabulary
1. Define: textile, wage, turnpike, tariff.

Checking Facts
2. Describe Lowell's experiment and explain its significance.

3. Explain the success of the Erie Canal and the railroads.

Critical Thinking
Predicting Consequences
4. Why might factory owners have feared labor shortages in the 1830s when they increased production and cut wages? Who helped solve the owners' labor problems?

Linking Across Time
5. In 1816 sectional interests partly determined how people reacted to a proposal such as Clay's tariff bill. How might sectional interests today influence a person's position on, for example, environmental legislation?

Evaluate

Have students complete the Section Review.

📁 🔾 Assign the Section 2 Quiz or use the Testmaker to develop a customized quiz. (Also in Spanish.) **LEP**

Reteach

🎧 Have students listen to the Chapter 5, Section 2 Audiocassette. (Also in Spanish.) **LEP**

Enrich

📁 Have students complete Supreme Court Case Study 3.

VISUAL INSTRUCTION

Transportation Ticket Clay lost three presidential races but held positions as speaker of the House and as secretary of state. He once said that he would "rather be right than be president."

Answer: *His proposed road-building would increase the demand for cartmen.*

CLOSE

Review with students the major topics treated in the section. Ask: How did the events of the early 1800s encourage Americans to think of themselves as "one single people, one nation, one mind"? *(See the last two paragraphs of the section.)*

Section 2 Review Answers

1. **textile** (141), **wage** (142), **turnpike** (143), **tariff** (146)
2. Lowell put all parts of textile manufacturing into one factory. This was an important step in industrialized production.
3. They created interregional markets and opened up trade and travel routes to the western United States.

4. Answers will vary. Factory owners feared that workers would strike. Immigrants willingly worked for lower wages.
5. Answers will vary. Farmers might oppose restrictions on use of fertilizers in watershed areas; fishers might support them.

TEACH

Making the Geography Connection

The building of roads, canals, and railroads aided the economic development of the United States during the 1800s, and also changed how and where Americans lived. St. Louis, Buffalo, and Chicago are examples of communities that boomed as a result of the transportation advances. Discuss the differences between city life and rural life at that time.

MAP STUDY

Ask: What pattern do railroads form around a major city? *(spokes)*

Answer: *Chicago's central location on level land near Lake Michigan made it the nation's rail hub.*

Mapping Activity

Have students use the map to show (1) how a Baltimore spice merchant might transport goods to Nashville, and (2) how a Wisconsin dairy farmer might ship cheese to Richmond.

Geography: Impact on History

The Rise of American Cities

Changes in trade and transportation set off a burst of urban growth from 1800 to 1860. All along trade and transportation routes, older cities grew larger and new ones were born. Topography, too, played a key role in this rise of American cities because terrain usually dictated locations of trade routes.

Early American Cities

Most American cities in the thirteen colonies grew up along the Atlantic coast. The ocean linked them with Britain and other countries. Ports and coastal cities such as New York, Charleston, and Boston are still important centers of transportation and industry today.

Inland cities tended to grow up along rivers that provided easy access to the coast and water power to run industries. As American technology overcame obstacles of distance and rugged terrain, the people moved steadily westward.

Steamboats bucked the currents in inland rivers to carry cargo; mules plodded along towpaths, pulling canal boats laden with everything from beeswax to lumber. Trains, spitting sparks and belching steam, hauled freight at the amazing speed of 15 miles per hour. With these 3 modes of transportation now in full swing west of the Appalachians, the pace of trade in the interior picked up. Soon river outposts, canal communities, and railroad whistle-stops developed into cities, while settlements off the beaten track stagnated, sometimes completely disappearing from the map.

Three cities exemplify how trade, transportation, and topography directed the course of urban growth in the United States.

Riverside City

A bonanza of waterways transformed the fur-trading center of St. Louis into a sizable city. Encircled by farmland, St. Louis is situated on the Mississippi just south of where that mighty river meets the

Illinois and Missouri Rivers. By midcentury steamboats chugged into St. Louis from north and south, so many that sometimes they lined up for a mile along the docks. From St. Louis, both boats and barges traveled along the Illinois to the

TRANSPORTATION ROUTES, 1800–1860

Three kinds of transportation routes linked American cities in the early 1800s.
How did geography help make Chicago a major transportation center?

Geographic Themes

Movement Explain that transportation and trade centers draw population primarily by creating new opportunities for business. As businesses grow and people move into an area, the need for services also grows. Have students consider what services people in a new city might require right away. (medical services, education, entertainment, shelter, food, clothing) When cities are beginning to grow these services are far less available than in older, established cities. Ask students to imagine how inland cities differed from coastal cities in the early to mid-1800s. What did they have in common? (Inland cities were more sparsely populated, with grid-like patterns and more modern architecture. Both the older and the newer cities were ports, and thriving trade centers filled with travelers.)

A Busy Port Between 1800 and 1860, major new cities like Chicago, St. Louis, and Buffalo developed along transportation routes. This print from the 1870s shows heavy traffic at the docks in St. Louis. *What factors made St. Louis an ideal spot for urban growth?*

the same load by wagon cost $100 and took twice as long.

Although railroads soon outran canals, the Erie Canal remained in operation. Today it is part of the 524-mile (843-km) New York State Barge Canal System, and Buffalo remains a major transportation center.

The Hub of the Rails

As the railroad roared westward, Chicago changed its shape from swampy settlement to megacity. In 1840 the community numbered only about 4,500 people. Eight years later, as the first trains rumbled into town, grain, lumber, and livestock began opening up the city's growing market. Population rose to 109,260 by 1860.

Located on level land in the heart of the nation, with Lake Michigan at its front door, Chicago was perfectly placed for a rail center. Rail tycoons bypassed landlocked communities and charted their tracks to Chicago. By 1860 Chicago was the nation's top rail city, with 11 lines radiating from its hub.

Other industrial centers sprang up across Ohio and the Midwest; canal and rail networks gave them access to both raw materials and markets. Gradually these cities developed the political systems, educational facilities, and cultural institutions that were already flourishing in the older port cities.

prairies, along the Missouri to the West, and down the Mississippi to New Orleans, gateway to the Gulf of Mexico. This intense activity helped boost the one-time fur-trade outpost to a city of 160,773 by 1860.

Along the Canal

In 1810, Buffalo, New York, was nothing but a settlement of 1,500 people at the east end of Lake Erie. When the Erie Canal opened in 1825, Buffalo's population grew to more than 2,400, and hundreds of new buildings were added. By 1860 the population had risen to 81,000.

The 363-mile (584-km) canal ran across New York State from Albany to Buffalo. At Albany, the Hudson River linked the canal with the coast, tying the Atlantic seaboard to the Great Lakes. Canal boats poked along at speeds of between 1 and 5 miles an hour, but rates were cheap. Shipping freight from New York City to Buffalo cost as little as $5 a ton. Transporting

MAKING THE GEOGRAPHIC CONNECTION

1. Identify the different kinds of transportation that linked American cities.

2. Trade and transportation often spur urban growth. What factors expand trade and transportation?

3. **Movement** In 1950 railroads carried 56 percent of American intercity freight. By 1988 they only carried 37 percent. What kinds of transportation are greatly affecting urban growth today?

GEOGRAPHY: IMPACT ON HISTORY **149**

VISUAL INSTRUCTION

A Busy Port The expeditions of Lewis and Clark, and Zebulon Pike both started from St. Louis, establishing the city as the gateway to the frontier. The city's population boom continued to a lesser degree until the 1970s when St. Louis lost 27 percent of its population, more than any other American city during that decade.

Answer: *Situated on the Mississippi River near the junction of the Missouri and Illinois Rivers, St. Louis was an ideal port for steamships traveling from east to west as well as from north to south.*

CLOSE

Begin a discussion of early urban growth by asking students what industries might emerge as a result of new transportation routes. *(construction and engineering companies, legal services, grocers and retailers, hotels and restaurants, advertising, and so on)*

Making the Geographic Connection Answers

1. Canals, roads, and railroads
2. Answers will vary. Improved transportation can expand trade as well as negotiation with and exploration of neighboring or foreign countries. Improvements in manufacturing and agricultural production also increase trade.

3. Answers will vary. Commercial shipping today, like passenger travel, relies on trucks and planes more than trains and boats.

SECTION
3

FOCUS

Section Objectives

1. Explain the changes in early nineteenth-century political culture that brought Andrew Jackson to power.
2. Demonstrate the connection between evangelical Christianity and social reform in the nineteenth century.
3. Describe how abolitionism and other social reform movements gave women and African Americans a political voice.

Bellringer Activity

While taking attendance at the beginning of the class period, display **Section Focus Transparency 37,** and have students answer the questions. (Or use the black-line master.)

VISUAL INSTRUCTION

Open-Air Sermon Peter Cartwright, a Methodist, was a popular preacher of revivalist campgrounds for 50 years. When he preached about salvation, hundreds fell to the ground.

Ask: What forces in society contributed to the religious revival of the early 1800s? *(People needed to resolve economic, regional, and racial conflicts.)*

A Changing People

AUGUST 1801: 20,000 WORSHIP AT KENTUCKY CAMP MEETING

COURTESY OF THE NEW YORK HISTORICAL SOCIETY, NEW YORK CITY

Open-Air Sermon
Camp-meeting preachers often
held enormous audiences spellbound.

THE NOISE RISING FROM THE CLEARING IN THE FOREST "WAS LIKE THE ROAR OF NIAGARA." The sound of singing, weeping, shouting, and moaning of thousands of people came from the meadow. "The vast sea of human beings," observed young James Finley, "seemed to be agitated as if by a storm." The power that stirred the people at Cane Ridge, Kentucky, on that warm August afternoon was religion.

The Cane Ridge meeting began early one Friday and continued for 6 full days. More than 20,000 people flocked from the surrounding countryside to attend. For these people camp meetings were a rare chance for contact with others and for a religious service. At night they slept in a city of canvas tents; by day they heard sermons by traveling preachers.

"I counted seven ministers all preaching at once," reported Finley. Some stood on tree stumps, others in wagons. Using vivid images of Satan and fiery hell, the preachers evoked powerful feelings among the listeners. Their sermons offered straightforward choices: sin or salvation, evil or good, wrong or right. The decision was in each person's hands.

Like many others, James Finley was powerfully affected by what he heard at Cane Ridge. "A peculiar strange sensation came over me," he said. "My heart beat tumultuously, my knees trembled, my lips quivered, and I felt as though I must fall to the ground." Finley never forgot this experience; several years later he became a preacher himself.

To many people, religion was the solution to the problems facing the United States in the early 1800s. As the nation expanded, Americans became participants in disturbing conflicts—conflicts between rich and poor, Easterner and Westerner, Northerner and Southerner, African American and white. Some people tried to escape these tensions by joining religious communities.

AS YOU READ

Vocabulary
▶ spoils system
▶ nullification
▶ secede
▶ temperance
▶ abolitionism

Think About . . .
▶ the changes in early nineteenth-century politics that brought Andrew Jackson to power.
▶ the connection between the Second Great Awakening and social reform.

▶ how participation in the abolition movement and other social movements gave women and African Americans a political voice.

Section 3 Resources

REPRODUCIBLE RESOURCES
- Lesson Plan 5-3
- Vocabulary and Guided Reading Activity 5-3
- Section 3 Quiz
- Chapter 5 Test
- Performance Assessment Activity 5
- Reteaching Activity 5
- Enrichment Activity 5
- Skill Reinforcement Activity 5

MULTIMEDIA RESOURCES
- Section Focus Transparency 37
- Landmark Documents in American History
- American Music: Cultural Traditions
- Testmaker
- Chapter 5 Digest Audiocassette
- Vocabulary PuzzleMaker
- Student Self-Test: A Software Review

Others tried to reform American society, while still others turned to politics as a way of bringing change to the nation.

A New Era in Politics
Courting the Common Man

New ideas about politics were sweeping the United States in the early 1800s. The most important of these ideas involved the question of who should be allowed to vote. Many Western states allowed all adult men to vote, regardless of how much land they owned. In the 1820s many Eastern states also eliminated property requirements for voters. During that decade, more white men than ever before gained the vote. Many of these new voters were Westerners, men who had left the East to seek wealth and opportunity on the frontier. These new voters wanted a new type of politician. They found one in Andrew Jackson.

Jackson and the Common Man

Thanks to his exploits in the War of 1812, Andrew Jackson became one of the nation's best-known heroes. Though he professed little interest in politics, friends persuaded him to run for President in 1824.

Jackson entered one of the wildest elections Americans had yet seen. After 23 years of solid control over the presidency, the Democratic-Republican party was split by factions battling along sectional lines. John Q. Adams, a Northerner and son of the second President, had the support of President James Monroe. Another veteran Democratic-Republican, Henry Clay, hoped to be elected by the Westerners he represented. A Southern candidate, William Crawford of Georgia, had won the support of many members of Congress.

Jackson was the fourth candidate. By far the least experienced politically, he nonetheless impressed people. His image as a no-nonsense frontiersman who had worked his way up the ladder of society, appealed to

Andrew Jackson This figurehead representing Jackson was used on a ship in 1834. *Why do you think Jackson made enemies among traditional politicians?*

LABAN S. BEECHER/MUSEUM OF THE CITY OF NEW YORK

many voters. His political ideas were as direct as a frontier preacher's sermon: He favored a "Democracy of Numbers" over the "moneyed aristocracy."

Jackson's supporters in the West and South gave him the most electoral and popular votes in the contest, but no candidate had a clear majority. The contest—according to the Constitution's rule—was turned over to the House of Representatives. Henry Clay, who served as speaker of the House that year, threw his support to Adams. When the House vote was taken in February 1825, Adams won with the votes of 13 states to Jackson's 7 states. Jackson's supporters claimed that Clay and Adams had made a "corrupt bargain," a charge that seemed justified when Adams named Clay secretary of state.

The election of 1824 split the Democratic-Republican party once and for all. Supporters of Adams and Clay began to call themselves National Republicans. Jackson's supporters, calling themselves Democrats, began to make plans for the 1828 presidential election.

The Election of 1828

Both Adams and Jackson had observed the changing political climate, and both designed their campaigns with the "common man" in mind. The result was a mean-spirited but lively campaign that avoided most serious issues.

National Republicans called Jackson "a gambler, a cockfighter, a brawler, a drunkard, and a murderer." The Democrats attacked Adams as a "stingy, undemocratic" aristocrat. They asked Americans to choose between "John Quincy Adams, who can write, and Andrew Jackson, who can fight."

The political tide of democracy favored Jackson in 1828. Almost three times as many people voted as had in 1824, and these new voters helped deliver a resounding victory for Jackson.

After his Inaugural Address in March 1829, Jackson rode down Pennsylvania Avenue to the White House followed by thousands of his celebrating supporters. The crowd swarmed into the White House behind Jackson, grabbing the

TEACH

Guided Practice

L2 **Discussion** Andrew Jackson won strong popular support during the campaigns of 1824 and 1828 despite being the least experienced of all the candidates. Some historians claim that Jackson's image as a frontiersman was more important to voters than political experience. Discuss the roles of image and experience in presidential politics. What image do voters respond to in politicians today?

VISUAL INSTRUCTION

Andrew Jackson Although Jackson's military career was long past by the time of the 1828 election, his victory at the Battle of New Orleans in the War of 1812 still influenced voters. Ironically, the peace treaty ending that war had been signed the week before the battle, unknown to Jackson and his British opponents.

Answer: *Jackson's ideas and frontier personality might not have been accepted during the post-Revolutionary period when the nation still looked to well-born leaders.*

Cooperative Learning

Campaigning for the Presidency Organize students into two groups. Have each group select one student to play the role of a candidate for the 1828 election. One group's candidate will be John Quincy Adams; the other's will be Andrew Jackson. The candidates and remaining students in each group will prepare for a one-hour campaign. Some students may make posters and buttons, while others may help the candidates prepare a short speech. The activity may also include an election. Afterward, discuss which campaign presented issues better and which used the concept of image more successfully.

Independent Practice

 L3 **Research** One aspect of the Second Great Awakening was the urge to create utopian communities. The utopian movement boomed in the United States in the 1830s and 1840s. Have students research and report on one of the utopian communities of the 1800s.

📂 Have students complete the Chapter 5, Section 3 Vocabulary and Guided Reading Activity. (Also in Spanish). **LEP**

💿 Facts on File

Landmark Documents in American History Have students review "Inaugural Address, Andrew Jackson, 1829" and write a paragraph about the intent of the document.

VISUAL INSTRUCTION

People's Reception The rowdy inaugural reception in this drawing exemplified the political style of the era. It was to become known as the Jacksonian Era because Jackson dominated United States politics from 1828 until the Civil War, even after he was out of office.

Answer: *Jackson's headstrong personality and his strong opinions about states' rights alienated him from most Eastern businessmen and Southern politicians.*

---

cakes, ice cream, and punch that had been set out for the inaugural reception. The people broke china, tore curtains, and knocked over furniture. Jackson had to escape the mob through a window. It was apparent to everyone in Washington that a new era in politics had begun.

"The people expect reform," Jackson said. "They shall not be disappointed." One of his first changes was to fire a number of allegedly "lazy" government workers, many of whom had supported Adams. Jackson replaced them with his own supporters.

This practice of rewarding government supporters with government jobs was known as the **spoils system.** Jackson claimed that replacing workers every so often made the government more democratic. The duties in most government jobs, he argued, were so "plain and simple" that anyone could do them. Dismantling the old bureaucracy, however, was a small matter compared with Jackson's war on the powerful Bank of the United States.

The Bank Crisis

The Bank of the United States was an important financial institution that exerted significant influence over Congress and the nation's economy. The United States owned 20 percent of the Bank's stock, and the government's money was deposited there. This money, along with private investments, was used to promote commerce and manufacturing. This had the effect of promoting the interests of Northeastern industries.

To Jackson, the Bank was undemocratic and unconstitutional. It represented the "moneyed aristocracy" that he so hated. He called the Bank a "monster" that threatened to "control the Government and change its character." Henry Clay and Daniel Webster knew how Jackson felt and planned to strengthen the Bank and embarrass the President at the same time. Clay and Webster drafted a bill rechartering the Bank, even though the Bank's original charter still had four years remaining. They reasoned that Jackson would not dare veto a bill—a rare occurrence in that era—in his reelection year. The bill passed Congress and reached the President's desk in July 1832.

Jackson saw this early bank bill as an attack. "The bank . . . is trying to kill me," he told an adviser, "but I will kill the bank." Jackson not only vetoed the Bank bill, he also made it the central issue in his campaign that fall. "When the laws," he said, "make the rich richer and the potent more powerful, the humble members of society—the farmers, mechanics, and laborers—. . . have a right to complain." Many people agreed, and in the 1832 election Jackson defeated his opponent Henry Clay.

LIBRARY OF CONGRESS

People's Reception Andrew Jackson brought to Washington the spirit of the rugged frontier or a shocking lack of refinement, according to how one viewed him. *Do you think Jackson would have been as politically successful earlier in the history of the United States? Why or why not?*

152 CHAPTER 5 THE EXPANDING NATION

Meeting Special Needs

Reading Disability To address the needs of students with reading comprehension difficulties, preview the section with them by discussing illustrations, captions, and headings. Help them to identify the main ideas of the section, pointing out to them the major headings that include the main ideas.

During his second term, Jackson was determined to destroy the Bank. He closed the government's accounts at the Bank and moved federal funds to state banks. In 1836 the Bank's charter expired for good.

The Tariff Controversy

As Jackson battled the Bank, another crisis split his administration and threatened to divide the nation. Tariffs had been part of the country's economic policy since 1816. Tariffs were unpopular in the South, however. When Congress passed a high tariff on some European imports in 1828, many Southerners complained loudly. One of these angry Southerners was Jackson's Vice President, John Calhoun. Calhoun wrote an essay invoking states' rights and the theory of **nullification.** A state, wrote Calhoun, had the right to nullify, or reject, any law that the state felt violated the Constitution.

Jackson supported states' rights, but as President he could not accept nullification because it threatened the federal government's power and the states' unity. Still, some Southerners tried to win Jackson's support by inviting him to a large ceremonial dinner with Calhoun in 1830. When Jackson stood to make the toast before dinner, he let the nullifiers know exactly where he stood on the matter: "Our Federal Union: It must be preserved." Jackson's toast—which plainly put the power of the federal government above the power of the states—silenced the room. A stunned Calhoun rose with his own toast to defend states' rights: "The Union," he said, "next to our liberty, most dear."

In 1832 the controversy became a crisis when Congress passed yet another high tariff. This act enraged politicians in South Carolina. During the fall of 1832 the state legislature nullified the tariff. They also threatened to **secede,** or leave the Union, if the government tried to collect tariff duties in the state. John Calhoun resigned as Vice President and took over one of South Carolina's seats in the Senate.

In December, Jackson directed warships and troops to move toward South Carolina. Then Congress passed a Force Bill permitting the President to use military force to collect the state's tariff duties.

As tensions mounted, Henry Clay designed a compromise plan to reduce all tariffs for 10 years. South Carolina accepted this peace offering and withdrew its nullification of the tariff. Clay's compromise bill resolved the crisis, but states' rights would remain a burning issue for the next 30 years as Southern and Northern politicians battled over slavery.

The Whig Party

While Jackson remained a popular figure, he made many political enemies. By 1834 opposition to Jackson had unified as the Whig party. The new party included Republicans such as Henry Clay and Federalists such as

Daniel Webster, plus supporters of the Bank of the United States, manufacturers who favored tariffs, and wealthy business leaders in large cities. The Democrats maintained their support among working people, immigrants, and the small farmers of the South and West.

The Democrats retained the White House in 1836 as Jackson's chosen successor, Martin Van Buren, won the election. In 1840, however, the Whigs retaliated. They portrayed Van Buren as an aristocrat who ate from gold plates. The Whig candidate was a military hero in the Jackson mold, William Henry Harrison. By ignoring the issues and portraying him as a common, cider-drinking man, the Whigs were able to capture the White House.

In the election of 1840, the Whigs made use of the Jacksonian idea that power and success were available to everyone, not just the elite. That idea was echoed in the sermons of preachers on the Western frontier.

An Awakening Interest in Religion
Revivalism Sweeps the Land

While voters were expressing displeasure toward the "moneyed aristocracy," many Americans were finding they had little in common with the traditional colonial Christian churches: the Anglican (Episcopal), the Congregationalist, and the Presbyterian. These churches often had an air of wealth and privilege. Services tended to be formal affairs that inspired little enthusiasm. As the nation expanded, Americans began seeking new forms of religion more in keeping with the spirit of a restless, growing young nation.

Western Revival

Beginning in the 1790s, a revival in religious interest known as the Second Great Awakening swept the Western frontier. The style of these growing churces—especially Methodist and Baptist—was less formal than the better established churches of the East. Circuit riders, or traveling ministers, rode about the frontier preaching to farmers. Rallies such as the camp meeting at Cane Ridge, Kentucky, attracted people from miles around.

The sermons delivered at these meetings and churches could be frightening—damnation awaited all sinners. The message behind them remained personal, emotional, practical, and even democratic. The idea that anything—even victory over sin—was possible with hard work and prayer appealed to many Americans.

SECTION THREE **153**

 Facts on File

Landmark Documents in American History Have students review "Tariff Act of 1828 (Tariff of Abominations)," "South Carolina Exposition (Protest Against the Tariff of 1828)," "John C. Calhoun, 1828," "Address to the People of South Carolina, John C. Calhoun, 1831," "Fort Hill Letter, John C. Calhoun, 1832," "South Carolina Ordinance of Nullification, 1832," "Nullification Proclamation (Andrew Jackson's proclamation to the people of South Carolina), 1832," "South Carolina's Reply to Jackson's Proclamation, 1832," and "Force Act of 1833" and write a paragraph about the intent of one of these documents.

Notes

Portfolio Project

Speechwriting Discuss with students the controversy over the tariff of 1828 and the related states' rights issues of nullification and secession. Ask them to imagine that they were members of Congress at the time, and have them write a speech either defending or opposing the tariff and/or states' rights. They might wish to deliver their speeches in class. Students can keep their speeches in their portfolios.

History and the Humanities

🎧 American Music: Cultural Traditions—"The Rose Tree" from *The Poor Soldier* (William Shield) by David and Ginger Hildebrand; "Come Life, Shaker Life" and "Tis the Gift to be Simple" by the Sisters of the Sabbathday Lake Shaker Community; "The Handcart Song" by L.M. Hilton

FYI

Some Slavery Ends Between 1800 and 1850 Great Britain and France ended slavery in their American possessions.

Perfecting Society

As the powerful ideas of the Second Great Awakening spread through the country, the nature of its message changed. One preacher who took this message and developed it was Charles Grandison Finney. A tall man with thinning blond hair and blazing eyes, Finney began with the idea that sin was a failure of will. Those who could avoid the temptation of sin could make themselves perfect.

Finney went on to say that not only could Christians make themselves perfect, they could—indeed, must—make the world around them perfect. No Christian could fail to see a thousand evils that needed to be corrected, reformed, and eliminated. The ideas of Finney and other preachers unleashed enormous energy in Americans. The urge to perfect the nation grew stronger during the 1830s and thereafter.

Reforming American Society
Fighting Evils From Alcohol to Slavery

The Second Great Awakening inspired different responses from different groups. Some withdrew to create their own "perfect" communities. For example, the Shakers and the Mormons, two religious groups, attempted to build their own utopia, or ideal world, away from mainstream American life.

Others set about changing the mainstream itself. They saw a host of evils in the rapidly changing society of the 1800s. Churchgoers in the populous areas of the North were among the first to organize reform groups. These groups usually saw social problems in religious terms of "evil" and "sin."

In the Promised Land These survivors of the 1847 Mormon trek across the plains and mountains to the Great Salt Lake were photographed 50 years later. *What other religious society of the time set out to build its own utopia?*

Extending the Content

Mormon Wars The Mormons were industrious and filled with a sense of their special mission. They aroused the jealous suspicion of surrounding communities. Most outrageous to their neighbors was the doctrine of polygamy. Led at first by Joseph Smith, the Mormons fought small-scale wars in Missouri and Illinois. Splinter groups developed among them. Joseph Smith was murdered, and the Mormons moved on to Utah. There they fought a last, losing battle with federal troops. The church forbade polygamy in 1862, but Utah did not achieve statehood until 1896. Ask students what other religious groups have had trouble with the government.

In an era when women had limited opportunities for education or jobs, reform groups offered an outlet for their energy and skills. Women filled the ranks of many reform efforts during the mid-1800s, but others considered it "un-feminine" for women to play an active role in these movements. As a result of these tensions, women's rights became one of the dominant issues during the reform era.

While women's rights concerned some, other evils were more visible and easier to attack. Alcohol, for example, was blamed for crime, insanity, and the breakdown of the family. As a result, the **temperance,** or antidrinking, movement became one of the first organized reform movements in the United States.

Demon Rum

Starting in the 1830s reformers targeted the evils of "demon rum." They flooded the nation with tracts and articles. One of the best-selling novels of the 1850s, *Ten Nights in a Bar Room and What I Saw There,* warned against the excesses of alcohol. Reformed alcoholics traveled to meetings in city after city, telling their stories. These efforts got results. Hard liquor sales fell by half during the 1830s alone.

Gradually the fight against drunkenness became a war on alcohol itself. More and more Americans chose to avoid all liquor and became "teetotalers." Reformers took their case to state legislatures. In 1838 Tennessee passed the first statewide regulation of liquor. Temperance reformers won another victory when Maine passed a tougher liquor law in 1851. While some citizens protested and bootleg liquor poured into the state from Canada, reformers counted the Maine law as a victory.

The success of the temperance movement inspired dozens of other reform efforts: the push for better prisons, mental health care, free public education, and aid for the blind and the deaf. Some reformers, however, perceived an evil much greater than all of these—an evil endorsed by politicians, protected by laws, and defended by an entire section of the nation. That evil was slavery.

Fighting Slavery

Slavery had troubled some Americans since before the Revolution. In 1787 the Northwest Ordinance forbade slavery in territories north of the Ohio River, and by 1804 every Northern state had provided for the end of slavery. Few white Americans, however, took an active stand on slavery between the passage of the Constitution and the 1820s.

At this time dozens of publications appeared spreading the ideas of **abolitionism,** the movement to end slavery. Most of these papers called for a gradual end to slavery, believing that the slow pace would bring liberation while it protected the businesses of Southern planters.

Other abolitionists had less patience. David Walker, a former slave living in Boston, called for an immediate end to slavery in 1829. He argued that enslaved individuals were entitled to use violence to obtain their freedom.

Two years later William Lloyd Garrison began publishing a newspaper called *The Liberator.* In his black suits and steel-rimmed glasses, Garrison looked more like a schoolmaster than a radical reformer. His pen, however, spouted fire as he called for the immediate emancipation of all enslaved persons. "I am in earnest," he wrote. "I will not retreat a single inch—AND I WILL BE HEARD!"

FRUITLANDS MUSEUM

THE DRUNKARD'S PROGRESS.

Nine Steps to Destruction This illustration reflects the temperance movement's belief that alcohol drove people to ruin. *What other reform movements developed in the wake of the temperance movement?*

Curriculum Connection

Literature Students may wish to research John Greenleaf Whittier, a poet who contributed to *The Liberator,* and read some of his abolitionist poems aloud.

ASSESS

Meeting Lesson Objectives

Each section objective is tested by the section review question(s) that follows it in parentheses.

1. Explain the changes in early nineteenth-century political culture that brought Andrew Jackson to power. (1, 2, 5)
2. Demonstrate the connection between evangelical Christianity and social reform in the nineteenth century. (3)
3. Describe how abolitionism and other social reform movements gave women and African Americans a political voice. (3, 4)

Cultural Perspectives

Independent African American Churches
African Americans in the South had organized their own churches before the Civil War, but the history of these churches went unrecorded because they were illegal. Ask students to consider why such churches were illegal. Histories of African American churches usually begin with those founded by two free African American ministers in Philadelphia in the late 1700s. Absalom Jones founded the African Protestant Episcopal Church, and Richard Allen founded the African Methodist Episcopal Church, which later worked with the Underground Railroad. Allen became that church's first bishop in 1816.

Evaluate

Have students complete the Section Review.

📁 💿 Assign the Section 3 Quiz or use the Testmaker to develop a customized quiz. (Also in Spanish.) **LEP**

📁 💿 Assign the Chapter 5 Test or use the Testmaker to develop a customized test.

📁 Have students complete the Chapter 5 Performance Assessment Activity.

Reteach

🎧 Have students listen to the Chapter 5, Section 3 Audiocassette. (Also in Spanish.) **LEP**

📁 Have students complete the Chapter 5 Reteaching Activity. (Also in Spanish.) **LEP**

Enrich

📁 Have students complete the Chapter 5 Enrichment Activity. (Also in Spanish.) **LEP**

VISUAL INSTRUCTION

Freedom Fighters Students may wish to read Frederick Douglass's autobiography.

Answer: *Racial segregation and women's roles in the movement; use of violence*

CLOSE

Discuss the changes in the United States between 1800 and 1850. Ask: What changes in political ideas helped to elect Jackson? *(eliminating property requirements for voting; popular opposition to aristocracy)*

Freedom Fighters The abolition movement brought forth many notable historical figures. From left to right: top, Frederick Douglass and Sojourner Truth, both fugitives from slavery; bottom, William Lloyd Garrison, a member of the clergy, and Lucretia C. Mott, who was also a temperance leader. *What issues divided the abolition movement?*

binding speaker. "I appear before this immense assembly," he addressed one crowd, "as a thief and robber. I stole this head, these limbs, this body from my master, and ran off with them."

Sojourner Truth, a tall, deep-voiced woman, had also become free after serving several masters for 30 years. In the 1840s she attracted large crowds throughout the North and West with her abolitionist speeches.

For all their talent, African American abolitionists found that white opponents of slavery were generally unwilling to accept them into their organizations. In addition, abolitionists often disagreed over how to attack slavery. Some abolitionists advocated the use of violence and urged enslaved persons to revolt. They felt that the speeches and tracts of the American Anti-Slavery Society were useless against a problem like slavery. Others, like Frederick Douglass, believed that change could only come from within the political system.

Women also chafed at their role as second-class citizens within the movement. Recognizing the important contributions of women, Garrison supported women's rights and encouraged their role in the movement. Other male leaders, however, refused to accept women as equals.

In 1840 all these tensions within the American Anti-Slavery Society splintered it. The split in the society, however, was not the end of abolitionism. In the 1840s and 1850s abolitionism was one of the issues—along with western expansion and the nation's changing economic identity—that widened the split between Northern and Southern states.

Garrison was heard. In 1833 a group of his supporters met in Philadelphia and formed the American Anti-Slavery Society. The goals of the society were to end slavery in the United States by stirring up public sentiment and flooding the nation with abolitionist literature. The society grew throughout the 1830s. With success, however, came controversy. Southerners worried about the effect of Garrison's message on their enslaved laborers and mounted vicious verbal attacks on him. Northerners blasted his views on the Constitution, which he called a "compromise with tyranny" and "an agreement with hell" because it allowed slavery.

Tensions Within the Movement

White leaders of the abolitionist movement discovered that African Americans, especially those who had escaped from bondage, made the most convincing arguments against slavery. Soon, fugitives became the star attractions at meetings of the American Anti-Slavery Society. One of the best speakers was Frederick Douglass, a brilliant man who had made a dramatic escape from slavery in 1838 at age 21. Douglass was a spell-

SECTION REVIEW

Vocabulary

1. Define: spoils system, nullification, secede, temperance, abolitionism.

Checking Facts

2. How was William Henry Harrison's appeal to voters similar to Jackson's?

3. How did the Second Great Awakening relate to reform movements of the time?

Critical Thinking

Making Comparisons

4. Abolitionists differed among themselves in their strategies for ending slavery. Compare their opinions.

Linking Across Time

5. How is name-calling used in modern election campaigns? Is it ever effective? Explain your answer.

Section 3 Review Answers

1. **spoils system** (152), **nullification** (153), **secede** (153), **temperance** (155), **abolitionism** (155)
2. Both were portrayed as war heroes and common men.
3. It espoused a simple, direct religion similar to the democratizing of politics and the movement toward states' rights that Jackson advocated.

4. Some abolitionists wanted an immediate end to slavery and advocated slave revolts. Others called for gradual abolition.
5. Answers will vary. Name calling is still used. It is effective when used as a diversionary tactic to avoid discussion of controversial issues.

Social Studies Skill
MAKING TELESCOPING TIME LINES

Learning the Skill

A telescoping time line highlights a relatively short period of time, showing selected events within a larger time span. The activities of abolitionist William Lloyd Garrison can be represented with a part of the time line that telescopes—or extends—from one point along the historically broader part of the time line. The two sections of the time line work together to show a historical movement and a critical point in that movement.

Placing Events on a Telescoping Time Line

To decide where an event belongs, do the following:

a. First examine the subject and dates of the broad part of the time line. The upper time line section on this page shows the growth of slavery and abolitionism in the United States, 1619–1840.

b. Next examine the highlighted part of the time line. Here the lower time line section shows one abolitionist leader's activities beginning in 1828 and continuing to 1840.

c. Choose an occurrence from the general time span and determine where it belongs. For example, the Missouri Compromise occurred before 1826 and relates to abolitionism but not to Garrison. Therefore it belongs on the upper section of the time line.

Practicing the Skill

Study the telescoping time line below and answer the following questions.

1. When did Garrison edit Boston's *National Philanthropist* and Vermont's *Journal of the Times*?

2. Where would you place the start of the abolitionist newspaper the *Liberator* in 1831? Why?

3. Where would you place an entry for abolition of slavery in New York State in 1827? Why?

4. How might the 1688 entry on the upper part of the time line relate to Garrison's activities?

5. Name another time span that could extend or telescope from the broader time line section.

Applying the Skill

Try making a telescoping time line for United States expansion from 1776 through 1850. Choose a focus and a smaller time span to highlight.

Additional Practice

For additional practice, see Reinforcing Skills on page 161.

TEACH

This skill lesson teaches students how to read telescoping time lines as well as how to make their own. Students study the relationship between a short focused time line and a broad contextual time line. Point out that *telescope,* when used in this context, means "to extend." Discuss with students how the relationship between the two sections of a telescoping time line is similar to views through a telescope at different strengths. Explain that on a telescoping time line a specific group of events extends from a broad group because it is a more detailed but narrower view of the time span.

Additional Practice

☞ Have students complete the Chapter 5 Skill Reinforcement Activity.

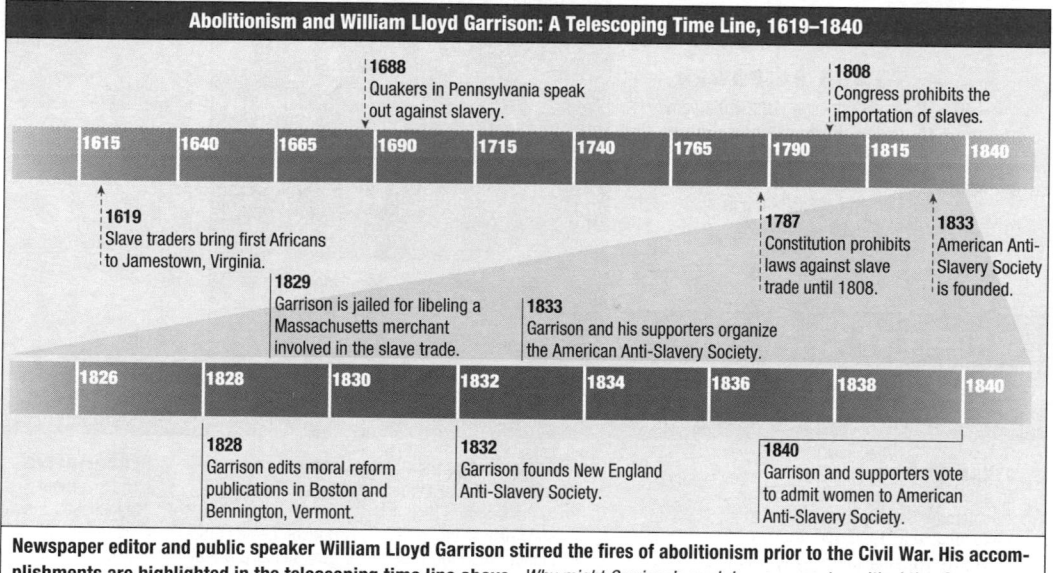

Abolitionism and William Lloyd Garrison: A Telescoping Time Line, 1619–1840

1688 Quakers in Pennsylvania speak out against slavery.

1808 Congress prohibits the importation of slaves.

1615 | 1640 | 1665 | 1690 | 1715 | 1740 | 1765 | 1790 | 1815 | 1840

1619 Slave traders bring first Africans to Jamestown, Virginia.

1787 Constitution prohibits laws against slave trade until 1808.

1833 American Anti-Slavery Society is founded.

1829 Garrison is jailed for libeling a Massachusetts merchant involved in the slave trade.

1833 Garrison and his supporters organize the American Anti-Slavery Society.

1826 | 1828 | 1830 | 1832 | 1834 | 1836 | 1838 | 1840

1828 Garrison edits moral reform publications in Boston and Bennington, Vermont.

1832 Garrison founds New England Anti-Slavery Society.

1840 Garrison and supporters vote to admit women to American Anti-Slavery Society.

Newspaper editor and public speaker William Lloyd Garrison stirred the fires of abolitionism prior to the Civil War. His accomplishments are highlighted in the telescoping time line above. *Why might Garrison's work have come at a critical time?*

SOCIAL STUDIES SKILL   **157**

Practicing the Skill Answers

1. 1828

2. The event would appear on the lower time line, the extension, because it occurs within that time span (1826–1840) and relates specifically to William Lloyd Garrison's achievements.

3. Abolition in the state of New York should appear on the upper, or broad, time line. This event is a landmark in the abolitionist movement but does not relate specifically to Garrison.

4. Answers will vary. Early reformists, such as the Quakers, laid the foundation for the abolitionists of the 1800s. The Quakers set a precedent for making radical views heard.

5. Answers will vary. The extending time line could be The Work of Frederick Douglass: From Freedom to the Civil War, 1838–1860.

Science, Technology, and Society

TEACH

Making the Historical Connection

A preoccupation with the steam engine was a natural outgrowth of the American passion for speed. The high-pressure steam engine developed by Oliver Evans, though more expensive to operate and more dangerous than the low-pressure engine, got steamboat travelers where they were going in a hurry. Then railroads began to attract the steamboat passenger traffic because they could cover in two or three days the distance the steamboat covered in a week. Both steamboats and trains had an appalling record of explosions and wrecks in the mid-1800s, in part because of the general demand for speed.

FYI

American Engine The first steam-powered locomotive to run on American rails was the *Stourbridge Lion,* imported from England, but its heavy, rigid construction proved unsuitable for American railway conditions. American designers then produced lighter, more flexible locomotives that could handle steep grades, sharp curves, and light wooden trestles.

Science, TECHNOLOGY, and Society

The Steam Engine

By the mid-1800s the steam engine had wrought enormous changes in American society, especially in transportation. Steam engines were not only turning the wheels of steamboats and locomotives, but were powering manufacturing, mining, and agricultural machinery as well.

© MICHAEL FREEMAN

TOWER OF POWER

A 40-foot-high (12.2-m) steam engine, built by George Corliss, supplied power to all 8,000 machines on display at the 1876 Centennial Exhibition in Philadelphia.

NATIONAL MUSEUM OF AMERICAN HISTORY, DIVISION OF ENGINEERING AND INDUSTRY, SMITHSONIAN INSTITUTE

HISTORY OF STEAM POWER

1760s	1780s	1800	1820s
STEAM ENGINE Building on earlier work, James Watt, a Scotsman, develops a true steam engine in 1769. He also devises a measure of output—*horsepower*.	**HIGH-PRESSURE STEAM** Oliver Evans in the U.S. and Richard Trevithick in England pioneer the high-pressure engine in 1801.	**STEAMBOAT** Robert Fulton's steamboat on the Hudson begins practical steam-powered travel in 1807.	**LOCOMOTIVE** The Liverpool & Manchester Line is the first public railroad to use steam power, 1830s.

Background Information

Tough Job Before the railroads adopted the air brake, invented by George Westinghouse in the 1860s, the brakeman on a freight train had to stop the cars by hand. Standing on the roof of a car, he slowed or stopped the train by turning a cast-iron wheel connected to a shaft that ran down to the brakes. Many a brakeman lost his life falling from the top of a fast freight on an icy winter's night as he wrestled with the wheel while the train sped around dangerous curves.

GETTING UP STEAM

Steamboats, the floating palaces of their day, plied the Mississippi River from New Orleans to St. Paul. Steamboat captains and the public loved racing, despite its danger. In 1870 in a contest celebrated in story and song, the *Robert E. Lee* beat the *Natchez* in a race from New Orleans to St. Louis.

THE "IRON HORSE"

After the heyday of the steamboat, the steam locomotive took center stage. It sparked the railroad building boom that reached its climax with the completion of the transcontinental railroad in 1869.

RUNNING ON STEAM

PORTFOLIO PROJECT

Research and report on a machine mentioned on these pages— perhaps the steam locomotive or the steamboat—or another steam-driven machine such as the Stanley steamer car. Illustrate your report if you wish. Keep the report in your portfolio.

CULVER PICTURES

FULL SPEED AHEAD

The locomotive engineer was king, but no one worked harder than his understudy, the fireman, to keep the train "highballing"—going at top speed. In the early years the boiler was fueled by wood, but later by coal.

1840s	1860s	1880s	1900s
ON THE WATER The paddle wheeler dominates river transportation, but the young business is reaching its peak by the 1840s.	**ON THE LAND** By the 1860s the locomotive has transformed land transportation. Steam drives the Industrial Revolution in factories and mines, and on farms.	**STEAM TURBINE** In 1879 Irishman Charles Parsons invents a steam turbine to generate electricity to power ocean liners. Steam turbines are still used.	**STEAM TAKES A BACKSEAT** The steam engine gives way to electricity and to the internal combustion engine, though many uses for steam remain. Researchers are now developing steam-driven microchips; possible applications include microsurgery.

SCIENCE, TECHNOLOGY, AND SOCIETY **159**

PORTFOLIO PROJECT

Portfolio Project

Researching Inventors Have students research and report on one of the inventors mentioned in the time line, or on another person associated with the history of steam power. Ask them to include an account of the inventor's scientific or technical contributions. Students can keep their reports in their portfolios.

Chapter ⑤ Review

Reviewing Key Terms

1. turnpike
2. tariffs
3. spoils system
4. frontier
5. temperance

Recalling Facts

1. bought from France in the Louisiana Purchase of 1803; mapping the Louisiana Territory, recording plant and animal life, establishing relations with Native Americans
2. The Northwest Ordinance promised to respect the land rights of Native Americans; after the battle their homes and fields were burned and their lands confiscated.
3. They led the Shawnee resistance; Tenskwatawa was the religious leader and Tecumseh the military leader.
4. He devised a Cherokee alphabet; it was used in publishing a newspaper, the *Cherokee Phoenix*.
5. The current of the rivers powered the machinery. The original labor force was young women from farms.
6. Great Lakes were linked with the Mississippi River, Hudson River with Lake Erie; railroads were fast and could cover any terrain.
7. It promoted a strong central government; it succeeded in increasing tariffs and chartering a new Bank of the United States but failed to get the government to supply money for roads and canals.
8. Property requirements were abandoned; many new voters were westerners. Jackson was regarded as a rugged frontiersman.
9. Women joined abolitionist and temperance movements; many started speaking out for women's rights.
10. Both drew large crowds for their abolitionist speeches in the North and West.

Reviewing Key Terms

Choose the vocabulary term that best completes each sentence below. Write your answers on a separate sheet of paper.

frontier	turnpike
tariffs	spoils system
nullification	temperance

1. Before they could travel on a _____, travelers were required to pay a toll.

2. One provision of Henry Clay's American System aimed to protect American manufacturers by increasing the _____ on imported goods.

3. When Andrew Jackson was elected President, he rewarded his supporters with government jobs, a practice that became known as the _____.

4. Large numbers of new settlers began to take over Native American lands as they continued to push the _____ westward.

5. During the 1830s reformers in the _____ movement attacked the evils of alcohol, which they were able to get prohibited in several states.

Recalling Facts

1. How did the United States acquire the territory that the Lewis and Clark team explored? Identify three purposes of the Lewis and Clark expedition.

2. General Anthony Wayne defeated the Ohio confederation at the Battle of Fallen Timbers and then concluded the Treaty of Greenville. In what way did these events contradict the Northwest Ordinance?

3. Who were the brothers Tecumseh and Tenskwatawa? What was their message to the Shawnee about relations between Native Americans and white settlers?

4. Who was Sequoyah, and what was his contribution to Native American literacy? What was the *Cherokee Phoenix?*

5. Why were the early textile mills of New England built along rivers? What group made up the principal labor force of these mills?

6. What were some bodies of water linked by the canals that were built in the early 1800s? What advantages did the railroads have that allowed them to take business away from the canals?

7. Describe the features of Henry Clay's American System. What parts of it were most successful? What part was less successful?

8. What changes in voting requirements made possible the era of the "common man"? In what ways did President Andrew Jackson represent this new era?

9. How was the question of women's rights related to the reform movement?

10. Describe the abolitionist work of Sojourner Truth and Frederick Douglass.

Critical Thinking

1. **Analyzing Information** How did the Cherokee attempt to adapt to the ways of the white settlers? What was the consequence of their adaptations?

2. **Making Comparisons** Compare the life of a young woman employed in a Lowell mill with the life of a young woman employed on the family farm.

3. **Determining Cause and Effect** After 1850 the system of canals, which had only recently been completed, ceased to be heavily used. What caused the rapid decline of the canals?

4. **Identifying Central Issues** What were the differences of opinion among abolitionists that caused the antislavery movement to break into factions?

5. **Making Inferences** The picture below shows a campaign ribbon used in William Henry Harrison's 1840 presidential campaign. How are campaign paraphernalia such as this used to gain voter support?

COURTESY OF MUSEUM OF AMERICAN POLITICAL LIFE, HARTFORD, CT/PHOTO BY STEVE LASCHEVER

Critical Thinking

1. They built roads, collected taxes, and developed a written language; some became Christians. Nevertheless, they were expelled from their lands and driven west on the Trail of Tears.
2. Young women who worked in the mills lived with others their own age, earned money, and worked long hours. Young farm women worked without pay on their families' farms.
3. The growth of railroads caused the canals to decline.
4. They differed on questions of segregation, the use of violence, and the position of women within the movement.
5. At a time when many voters lived in simple circumstances, this ribbon with its log cabin, American eagle, and boot would have created an attractive "common man" image for Harrison.

Portfolio Project

Choose one of the Native American peoples mentioned in the chapter—Mandan, Shoshone, Shawnee, Miami, Wyandot, or Cherokee—and research their history. Find out about their original way of life, their customs, and the regions they inhabited. Find out where and how they live today. Write a report and keep it in your portfolio.

Cooperative Learning

With a small group, construct a time line for the 1800s showing significant events in the history of industrial development. Beneath it, construct another time line showing the important developments in the history of women's rights. Is there a relationship between the developments in both? Add other time lines for the antislavery movement, the addition of new states to the Union, and the growth of the railroads. Draw your own conclusions about the period from studying these parallel developments. Do they appear to show that progress always occurs steadily?

Reinforcing Skills

Making Telescoping Time Lines

Use the years 1790 to 1840 for a standard time line showing major events discussed in the chapter. Your telescoping time line can focus on events during the presidencies of John Quincy Adams and Andrew Jackson, especially those related to political change and to the development of national political parties.

Geography and History

Study the map on this page to answer the following questions:

1. What does the yellow area on the map indicate?

U.S. TERRITORY, 1776–1803

CANADA

50°N

OREGON COUNTRY (DISPUTED)

Louisiana Purchase

Missouri R.

Colorado R.

40°N

Red R.

30°N

SPANISH TERRITORY

Mississippi R.

Superior

L. Michigan

L. Huron

Ontario

Erie

Maine (part of Mass.)

N.H.

Vt.

Mass.

N.Y.

R.I.

Conn.

Mich. Terr.

Pa.

N.J.

Indiana Territory

Ohio

Md.

Del.

Ohio R.

Va.

Kentucky

N.C.

Tennessee

S.C.

Mississippi Territory

Ga.

ATLANTIC OCEAN

N

SPANISH FLORIDA

Gulf of Mexico

Original Thirteen Colonies, 1776
Gained in Treaty of Paris, 1783
Louisiana Purchase, 1803
Spanish Territory
British Territory
--- Indefinite boundary

0   250   500 mi.
0   250   500 km
Albers Equal-Area projection

110°W   100°W   90°W   80°W

2. How did the United States acquire the territory that became the state of New York?

3. When did the Indiana Territory become a part of the United States?

4. The Spanish government was distressed to learn that France had sold the Louisiana Territory to the United States. What inference can you make from the map about why the Spanish government might have been worried?

5. What was the northern boundary of the Louisiana Purchase? What geographical feature marked the eastern boundary? To what body of water did the southern boundary extend?

HISTORY JOURNAL

Write briefly in your journal about what you learned in this chapter. Include an account of what you understand to be the connection between the westward expansion of the frontier and developments in transportation.

Geography and History

1. the original 13 colonies
2. Western New York was acquired in the Treaty of Paris, 1783; eastern New York was one of the original colonies.
3. in 1783 through the Treaty of Paris
4. Spanish Territory shared a long border with the Louisiana Territory; Spain might have feared encroachment by the United States.
5. The Louisiana Purchase was bounded by Canada on the north and by the Mississippi River on the east; it extended south as far as the Gulf of Mexico.

History Journal

Ask volunteers to share their journal entries with the class. Students should observe that the development of the transcontinental railroad made possible a great increase in settlement of the West.

? BONUS QUESTION

This question may be used for extra credit on the chapter test.

Ask: What were the consequences of the Embargo Act of 1807?

Answer: *It stopped all trade with Europe, thus stimulating textile production in the United States.*

Portfolio Project

Have students try to include in their reports the original and present-day populations of the peoples they are researching. Ask at least one volunteer for each Native American group studied to share their research with the class.

Cooperative Learning

Put some of the best time lines on the board, or distribute photocopies. Have the groups come together as a class to discuss the conclusions they have drawn about the relationships revealed by the time lines.

Reinforcing Skills

The telescoping time line should cover the years 1825–1837. Suggest that students review the material discussed on pages 151–153, paying special attention to the party realignments associated with the major events.

161

Civil War and Reconstruction

DAILY LESSON OBJECTIVES	REPRODUCIBLE RESOURCES	MULTIMEDIA RESOURCES
SECTION 1 Slavery and Politics 1. Identify various forms of resistance to slavery. 2. Contrast the political agendas of the North and the South. 3. Analyze the attempts at compromise over slavery.	Reproducible Lesson Plans Vocabulary and Guided Reading Activities (English or Spanish) Cooperative Learning Activities Supreme Court Case Studies Geography in History Activities Great Debates in American History American Literature Readings and Activities Section Quizzes (English or Spanish)	Section Focus Transparencies Beginnings to 1900 Transparencies Map Transparencies Chapter Teaching Transparencies Landmark Documents in American History Historic America: Electronic Field Trips American Music: Cultural Traditions Testmaker Student Self-Test: A Software Review
SECTION 2 The Civil War 1. Analyze the results of the South's decision to form a separate government based on ideals that conflicted with those of the federal government. 2. Understand the effects on African Americans of the Emancipation Proclamation.	Reproducible Lesson Plans Vocabulary and Guided Reading Activities (English or Spanish) Case Studies Skill Reinforcement Activities Section Quizzes (English or Spanish)	Section Focus Transparencies Beginnings to 1900 Transparencies U.S. History and Art Transparencies American Music: Cultural Traditions Focus on American Fine Art Prints Powers of the Supreme Court Landmark Documents in American History Testmaker
SECTION 3 Reconstruction 1. Explore the possible approaches the North might have taken toward the reconstruction of the South. 2. Explain how Reconstruction altered the relationship between the President and Congress in favor of legislative supremacy. 3. Analyze Reconstruction in terms of gains and losses for African Americans.	Reproducible Lesson Plans Vocabulary and Guided Reading Activities (English or Spanish) Reteaching Activities (English or Spanish) Enrichment Activities (English or Spanish) Geography in History Activities Section Quizzes (English or Spanish)	Section Focus Transparencies Beginnings to 1900 Transparencies Landmark Documents in American History American Music: Cultural Tradition The American People: Fabric of a Nation Testmaker Student Self-Test: A Software Review
CHAPTER REVIEW AND EVALUATION	Chapter 6 Test, Forms A and B Performance Assessment Strategies and Activities	Testmaker Vocabulary PuzzleMaker Student Self-Test: A Software Review Chapter Digests Audiocassettes

 If time does not permit teaching the entire chapter, summarize using the Chapter 6 Digests Audiocassettes and the accompanying activities and tests. (Available in English or Spanish.)

Cooperative Project

Have students work in groups of four or five to write a narrative of the Civil War and perform a choral reading. The narrative should be written in four or five different voices which take turns telling the story. As a group, have students choose different perspectives for each voice, such as plantation owner, abolitionist newspaper editor, Union and Confederate military personnel, freed African American, or other diverse personalities. **LEP**

Suggested Rubric: An Original Song with Lyrics. See Performance Assessment Strategies and Activities, p. 35.

Individual Project

Give students an opportunity to do an in-depth research report on one of the key figures of the Civil War era. Although important leaders may be discussed on several pages in the text, this only scratches the surface of their lives. Through writing a biographical report, students can better understand the complexity of this era.

Suggested Rubric: A Research Report. See Performance Assessment Strategies and Activities, p. 39.

Key to Ability Levels

Teaching strategies have been coded for varying learning styles and abilities.

L1 **BASIC** activities for all students

L2 **AVERAGE** activities for average to above-average students

L3 **CHALLENGING** activities for above-average students

LEP **LIMITED ENGLISH PROFICIENCY** activities

Block Scheduling

Block scheduling differs from traditional class scheduling in the amount of time allotted to each period. The extended timeframe provided by block scheduling affords you the opportunity to implement a greater number of research-oriented and activity-intense projects to motivate and involve your students. Activities that are particularly suited to use within the block scheduling framework are identified throughout this chapter by the following designation.

TEACHER'S CORNER

NATIONAL GEOGRAPHIC SOCIETY

INDEX TO NATIONAL GEOGRAPHIC MAGAZINE

The following articles may be used for research relating to this chapter:

- "C.S.S. Alabama," by Max Guerout, December 1994.
- "The Cruelest Commerce: African Slave Trade," by Colin Palmer, September 1992.
- "The Underground Railroad," by Charles L. Blockson, July 1984

NATIONAL GEOGRAPHIC SOCIETY PRODUCTS AVAILABLE FROM GLENCOE

To order the following products for use with this chapter, contact your local Glencoe sales representative or call Glencoe at 1-800-334-7344:

- *The Presidents: A Picture History of Our Nation* (CD-ROM)
- *GTV: A Geographic Perspective on American History* (Videodisc)
- *GTV: The American People: Fabric of a Nation* (Videodisc)

ADDITIONAL NATIONAL GEOGRAPHIC SOCIETY PRODUCTS

To order the following products for use with this chapter, call National Geographic Society at 1-800-368-2728:

- *The Civil War* (Filmstrip)

Chapter Overview

The Civil War represents the most devastating period in United States history. The conflict resulted in the deaths of about 620,000 people. Almost as many were wounded. At the war's end, 4 million enslaved African Americans won their freedom.

Introducing the Chapter

Politicians tried compromises to avoid the Civil War. When war finally erupted, the devastation lasted through years of fighting and into the following decades.

Display the Chapter Teaching Transparency and distribute the corresponding activity sheet for students to complete.

Extension Activity

Have students complete Beyond the Transparency on the activity sheet for Chapter 6 and present their projects after the class has completed the chapter.

History Journal

Have students write about John Brown's use of violence to end violence. Do they approve of this? Why or why not?

Facts on File

Landmark Documents in American History Have students review "John Brown, Final Speech, 1859" and write a paragraph about the intent of the document.

CHAPTER 6

Civil War and Reconstruction

MAY 1856: POTTAWATOMIE, KANSAS

Proslavery and antislavery forces were fighting for control of Kansas by 1855. Proslavery residents of Missouri had poured into Kansas by the hundreds to elect proslavery leaders to office.

The legislature that they elected then passed harsh laws to prohibit even the free expression of opinions against slavery. By the fall of 1855, however, more Kansas residents opposed slavery than supported it. These antislavery forces, determined to defy the proslavery laws, armed themselves, called for new elections, and then drafted a new state constitution.

In response, in the spring of 1856, a group of proslavery Missourians lugged five cannons to the outskirts of Lawrence, Kansas, the antislavery stronghold. The invaders ransacked and burned homes and businesses and killed several men. Outraged by this action, militant antislavery leader John Brown, with his four sons and two other men, kidnapped and brutally executed five proslavery settlers in Pottawatomie, Kansas.

In subsequent raids by the proslavery and antislavery forces, about 200 people were killed before federal troops could stop the violence. The conflict in "Bleeding Kansas" foreshadowed the turmoil that later would engulf the nation. ∎

H I S T O R Y   J O U R N A L

Write in your journal about your reaction to the story of Pottawatomie and the picture on the opposite page. What kind of man do you think John Brown was?

162

✚ EXTRA CREDIT PROJECT

Primary Source Research Ask students to collect examples of songs, poems, speeches, letters, diaries, or newspaper articles from the Civil War years. To deepen students' understanding of the controversy surrounding the war, ask them to write about the context for the material they have chosen. What political issues influenced the text? What cultural trends are reflected? Ask students to read all or part of their chosen pieces aloud and explain their significance to the class.

IN JOHN STEUART CURRY'S MURAL,
JOHN BROWN CALLS DOWN THE STORM
OF CIVIL WAR.

163

THE STATE HOUSE, TOPEKA, KANSAS/PHOTO COURTESY OF PHOTO ONE

NATIONAL GEOGRAPHIC SOCIETY

Videodisc

GTV: A Geographic Perspective on American History

Side 2, Chapter 16
Title: The Civil War and Reconstruction
Subject: Geography and the Civil War
Ask: How did railroads help the North? *(better troop and supply transport)*

GLENCOE TECHNOLOGY

Videodisc

American History

Side 1, Section E
Title: The Civil War and Reconstruction
Subject: Political crisis; Civil War; Grant's presidency
Ask: Where did the Civil War begin? *(Fort Sumter)*

Performance Assessment

Refer to page 162B for performance assessment activities for this chapter.

 Also see Activity 6 in the Performance Assessment Strategies and Activities for an additional activity as well as for suggested rubrics.

Examining the Visual

Tragic Prelude More than 75 years after John Brown's death, John Steuart Curry painted *Tragic Prelude,* a tribute to Brown's revolutionary politics and actions. In death, Brown became a powerful icon for the antislavery movement. Soldiers marched to war singing his praises in the folk song "John Brown's Body." Northern ministers began calling armed rebellions "divine weapons." Frederick Douglass, who had consulted with Brown before the raid, said that Brown had shown the way to end slavery. According to Douglass, "A system of brute force . . . must be met with its own weapons." Students might discuss how the sacrifice of a martyr can fuel popular support for a cause.

FOCUS

Section Objectives

1. Identify various forms of resistance to slavery.
2. Contrast the political agendas of the North and the South.
3. Analyze the attempts at compromise over slavery.

Bellringer Activity

While taking attendance at the beginning of the class period, display **Section Focus Transparency 39,** and have students answer the questions. (Or use the blackline master.)

VISUAL INSTRUCTION

Landmark Case When the Supreme Court ruled on the *Dred Scott* case, slavery was a hotly debated issue. Ask students to identify issues under debate today and tell why they would or would not be candidates for a Supreme Court case.

Ask: What did the Supreme Court rule unconstitutional in the Dred Scott decision? *(The Missouri Compromise)*

Slavery and Politics

MARCH 6, 1857: SUPREME COURT RULES ON *DRED SCOTT* CASE

Landmark Case
The Supreme Court handed Dred and Harriet Scott a grim decision. The Scotts' daughters, Eliza and Lizzie, are shown above them.

DRED SCOTT AND HIS WIFE, HARRIET SCOTT, ANXIOUSLY AWAITED THE SUPREME COURT DECISION. The Scotts were legally enslaved, but they were hoping the Supreme Court would set them free because they had resided with a former master in Illinois and in the Wisconsin Territory, where the Missouri Compromise prohibited slavery. The year was 1857, however, and people who were enslaved did not have any legal rights in the United States. Furthermore, the Scotts were again living in Missouri, a slave state.

At last Chief Justice Roger Taney read the majority opinion of the Court and crushed the Scotts' hopes for freedom. Enslaved African Americans were considered legal property, and

no state could deprive citizens of their property without due process of law, Taney said. In addition the Court ruled the Missouri Compromise unconstitutional, declaring that Congress could not prohibit slavery in American territories.

Several weeks later the Scotts were again sold. Their new owner freed them, and they slipped quietly into obscurity. The decision from their lawsuit, however, did not travel quietly. The Court's ruling angered Northerners because it meant that new American territories could now become slave states. The ruling threatened to upset the balance of power between free and slave states, fueling a heated debate that in 1861 would erupt into a bloody war.

AS YOU READ

Vocabulary
► sectionalism
► gospel tradition
► fugitive

Think About . . .
► methods of coping with bondage and various forms of resistance to slavery.
► the contrast between the Northern and the Southern political agendas.
► the North's and the South's efforts at compromise and their effects.

---

164 CHAPTER 6 CIVIL WAR AND RECONSTRUCTION

Section 1 Resources

REPRODUCIBLE RESOURCES

📂 Lesson Plan 6-1
📂 Vocabulary and Guided Reading Activity 6-1
📂 Cooperative Learning Activity 6
📂 Unit 2 Great Debate
📂 Supreme Court Case 4
📂 Section 1 Quiz

📂 Geography in History Activity 6
📂 Unit 2 American Literature Reading

MULTIMEDIA RESOURCES

🖥 Section Focus Transparency 39
🖥 Chapter Teaching Transparency 6
🖥 Map Transparency 6

🖥 Beginnings to 1900 Transparencies 10, 11, 12
💿 Landmark Documents in American History
🎧 American Music: Cultural Traditions
💿 Historic America: Electronic Field Trips
🖥 Testmaker
🎧 Chapter 6 Digest Audiocassette

The Roots of Conflict
Diverging Interests of North and South

In the late 1700s, many farmers in the upper South—Maryland, Virginia, and North Carolina—shifted from tobacco to grain crops because these crops required less labor. The result was that a once-booming slave trade declined in this region. In 1793, however, a single event abruptly stopped any possible downward trend in the enslaved labor trade. In that year Eli Whitney introduced the cotton gin, a machine that greatly reduced the amount of time and work required to remove the seeds from cotton.

Suddenly, large quantities of cotton could be profitably grown with the aid of the enslaved labor force. Almost overnight, vast numbers of landowners throughout the South converted their fields to cotton production and thousands of would-be cotton farmers poured into the South from other regions. These new cotton planters figured they could increase their profit margins if they used enslaved laborers to pick and clean their cotton.

With the profitability of cotton production ensured by Whitney's invention, slavery quickly gained a new economic foothold. It was a foothold white Southerners were determined to protect.

By the mid-1800s, the Northern economy relied mostly on manufacturing and an ever-increasing immigrant workforce. Therefore, the Northern economy did not rely on enslaved laborers. Northern workers feared that if slavery were to extend northward, their own jobs

King Cotton A steamship in New Orleans carries a load of cotton bales. Most cotton bales weigh about 500 pounds or 227 kilograms. *How did increased cotton production affect the economies of the North and the South differently?*

THE BETTMANN ARCHIVE

THE COTTON GIN

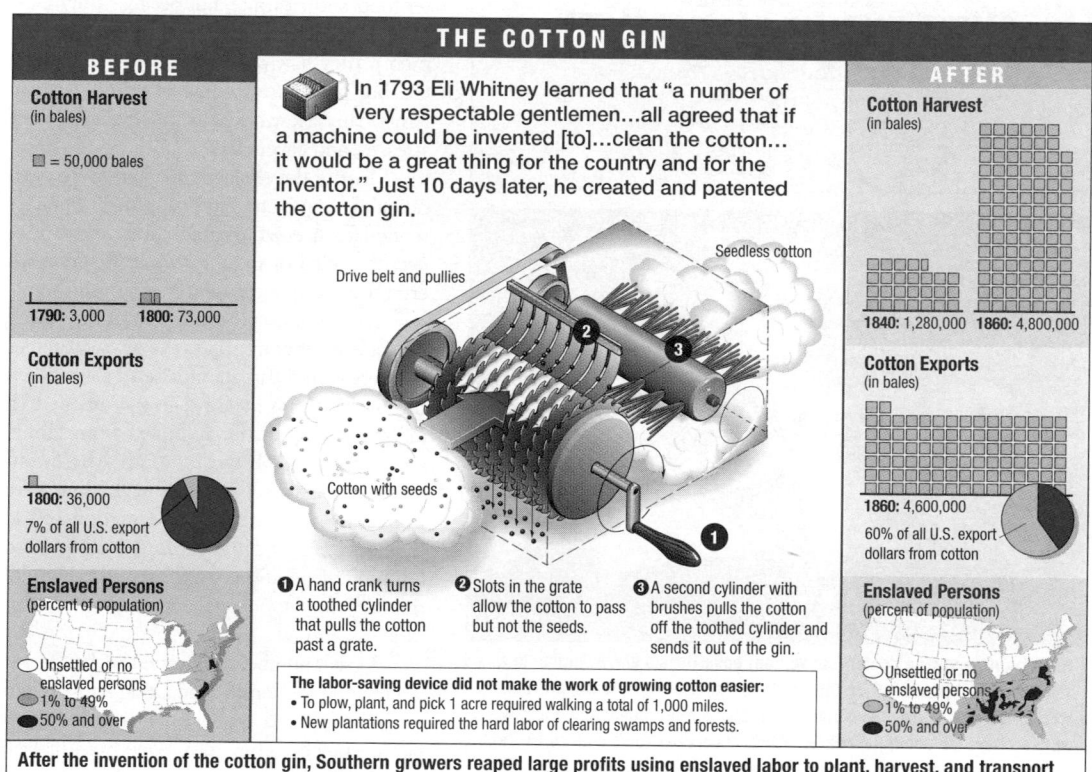

BEFORE

Cotton Harvest (in bales)

☐ = 50,000 bales

1790: 3,000   1800: 73,000

Cotton Exports (in bales)

1800: 36,000

7% of all U.S. export dollars from cotton

Enslaved Persons (percent of population)

○ Unsettled or no enslaved persons
○ 1% to 49%
● 50% and over

In 1793 Eli Whitney learned that "a number of very respectable gentlemen...all agreed that if a machine could be invented [to]...clean the cotton... it would be a great thing for the country and for the inventor." Just 10 days later, he created and patented the cotton gin.

Drive belt and pullies

Seedless cotton

Cotton with seeds

❶ A hand crank turns a toothed cylinder that pulls the cotton past a grate.

❷ Slots in the grate allow the cotton to pass but not the seeds.

❸ A second cylinder with brushes pulls the cotton off the toothed cylinder and sends it out of the gin.

The labor-saving device did not make the work of growing cotton easier:
• To plow, plant, and pick 1 acre required walking a total of 1,000 miles.
• New plantations required the hard labor of clearing swamps and forests.

AFTER

Cotton Harvest (in bales)

1840: 1,280,000   1860: 4,800,000

Cotton Exports (in bales)

1860: 4,600,000

60% of all U.S. export dollars from cotton

Enslaved Persons (percent of population)

○ Unsettled or no enslaved persons
○ 1% to 49%
● 50% and over

After the invention of the cotton gin, Southern growers reaped large profits using enslaved labor to plant, harvest, and transport cotton. *Approximately how closely did the increase in cotton production match the increase in enslaved labor?*

Cooperative Learning

Holding a Team Debate Have the class prepare arguments and debate whether issues such as slavery should be settled at the federal level or at the state level. Students can form teams, with each team member responsible for researching a strand of the argument on either side. Tell students to include quotations from writers and speakers who debated the issue in the 1800s.

TEACH

Guided Practice

L2 **Recognizing Regional Differences** In 1832 South Carolina threatened to secede from the Union. Ask students why Northerners might have felt threatened by such a secession. Ask how Southerners might have felt about Northern pressure to abolish slavery. Then ask if the North and South have different views today.

📽 Show students Map Transparency 6 and have them complete the activity sheet.

📽 Show students Beginnings to 1900 Transparencies 10, 11, and 12 and have them complete the activity sheets.

VISUAL INSTRUCTION

King Cotton Discuss the link between the cotton revolution and the water transport revolution with regard to upstream transportability and tonnage allowances. See time line on page 145.

Answer: *South: more plantations; North: more textile production and transportation*

CHART STUDY

Have students find out from the chart what the cotton harvest was in 1790, before the cotton gin. *(3,000 bales)* Have them note what the harvest was in 1860. *(4,800,000 bales)*

Answer: *There is approximately a 1-to-1 correspondence*

Independent Practice

L2 **Writing a Letter**
Ask students to imagine they are living in Kentucky in the 1850s. Have them write a letter to a Northern friend in which they justify being either an abolitionist or a slaveholder.

📁 Have students complete the Chapter 6, Section 1 Vocabulary and Guided Reading Activity. (Also in Spanish.) **LEP**

📁 Have students complete the Chapter 6 Cooperative Learning Activity.

VISUAL INSTRUCTION

Selling Humans Have students speculate about why painter Eyre Crowe depicted the slave market in such a romanticized way. Direct them to contrast the feeling in the painting with the language in the poster. *(One reveals the humanity of its subjects while the other denies human qualities.)*

Answer: *Examples include threats of separation from kin or of sale to an abusive master.*

---

would be threatened. In addition Northern abolitionists opposed slavery on moral grounds. Abolitionists such as Frederick Douglass, Sojourner Truth, and William Lloyd Garrison had become adamant that slavery be abolished throughout the nation. As Garrison wrote in his antislavery newspaper, *The Liberator,* "I will be as harsh as truth and as uncompromising as justice. On this subject [slavery] I do not wish to think, or speak, or write, with moderation. No! No!"

By midcentury, North and South had developed two different political agendas based on their very different economies. The Northern agenda called for the extension of free labor into new states. The Southern agenda demanded the maintenance of slavery. The two regions drifted toward **sectionalism,** or an extreme allegiance to their own local interests.

Selling Humans The poster (above, top) advertises a slave auction in a matter-of-fact manner. Eyre Crowe's painting (above, bottom), *Slave Market in Richmond, Virginia,* clothes its subjects more finely than most who appeared on the auction block. A British observer, Crowe was one of few painters to dignify the subjects of slavery. *What were some psychological abuses of slavery?*

This sectionalism developed because of Northern politicians' attempts to pass laws settling the slavery debate for the entire nation. White Southerners, angered over increasing federal intervention in their affairs, believed that they should be able to make more decisions—especially about slavery—at the state level of government. Meanwhile millions of African Americans wondered when their oppression would end.

Community Under Slavery
Inhuman Conditions and Human Response

From about 1800 to the Civil War, about half of all Southern African Americans lived on large plantations. On the plantation most enslaved laborers worked in the fields from sunup to sundown, six days a week. Although they were typically given Sundays off, many used that day to cultivate their own garden plots. Some worked as cooks, maids, and nursemaids in the Big House, where the plantation owner lived. There the enslaved servants might receive better food and clothing, but because they lived in Big House slave quarters (often in the basement), they saw their loved ones less often. On big plantations some enslaved African Americans also worked as shoemakers, seamstresses, and carpenters.

Most of the enslaved workers were periodically subject to physical abuse. Planters tended to use whips freely and sometimes even branded or maimed what they considered their human property to punish them.

The emotional torment slavery imposed was at least as common as the physical abuse. Planters would threaten to "sell a slave down the river," which meant selling someone to a distant plantation far removed from family and friends, usually farther south, where conditions were worse. Parents and children were frequently separated on the auction block. One way many families coped with these traumatic separations was by substituting "fictive kin" for blood ties, adopting new comrades as family.

A great number also turned to the Christian religion for comfort, adapting African religious beliefs and practices to suit their new circumstances. They took hope from biblical stories of slavery and liberation and transformed Protestant customs into their own African-

---

Meeting Special Needs

Visual Learners To help visual learners preview and predict the section's content, direct students to look closely at the images on pages 164–167. Have them speculate about the economic differences between the North and South and how these differences might have led to conflicts. Students may also wish to use a map to identify geographic features of the North and South as they were defined in the early 1800s. Guide them to connect geographic differences with the development of a primarily agricultural economy in the South and the development of manufacturing in the North.

Christian blend. African dancing, drumming, music and chanting were incorporated into worship services. During the years of enslavement African Americans created a **gospel tradition,** a unique musical form that combines many African musical styles with the text of Protestant hymns. Characterized by passionate choral harmonizing and preaching through song, the spirituals were born from this tradition.

In the Sea Islands of Georgia and South Carolina, African Americans known as the Gullah people were especially noted for infusing the Christian religion with African cultural practices. One observer described a worship service in 1867, noting, "Song and dance alike are extremely energetic, and often, when the shout lasts into the middle of the night, the monotonous thud, thud, thud of the feet prevents sleep within half a mile of the praisehouse. . . ."

SOPHIA SMITH ARCHIVES, GARRISON COLLECTION

Underground Hero Harriet Tubman (far left) stands with a family she helped to freedom. Despite rewards of $40,000 for her capture, Tubman helped more than 300 people, including her parents, escape from slavery. *What did a conductor on the Underground Railroad do?*

Resistance to Slavery
Escape, Sabotage, and Revolt

Religious beliefs and practices could both offer comfort and inspire action. By the mid-1800s, hundreds were fleeing plantations each year to freedom in the North and in Mexico. Between 1830 and 1860, a network of abolitionists known as the Underground Railroad helped many enslaved African Americans escape by conducting them to safe houses where they could hide on their way to free territories.

One of the most famous "conductors" along the Underground Railroad was Harriet Tubman, a woman who had herself escaped from slavery. Armed with a pistol she was not afraid to use, Tubman guided 19 expeditions of escape out of the South.

Jerry Loguen, another conductor, is said to have helped as many as 1,500 people escape from slavery. When Loguen's former owner, Sarah Logue, discovered his whereabouts, she wrote demanding that he return or pay her $1,000 to purchase his freedom and the horse he had stolen to escape. This was Loguen's reply:

Mrs. Sarah Logue . . . You say you have offers to buy me, and that you shall sell me if I do not send you $1000, and in the same breath and almost in the same sentence, you say, "You know we raised you as we did our own children." Woman, did you raise your own children for the market? Did you raise them for the whipping post? Did you raise them to be driven off, bound to a coffle in chains? . . . Shame on you!

But you say I am a thief, because I took the old mare along with me. Have you got to learn that I had a better right to the old mare, as you call her, than Manasseth Logue had to me? Is it a greater sin for me to steal his horse, than it was for him to rob my mother's cradle, and steal me? . . . Have you got to learn that human rights are mutual and reciprocal, and if you take my liberty and life, you forfeit your own liberty and life? Before God and high heaven, is there a law for one man which is not a law for every other man?

—J.W. Loguen, from a letter reprinted in *The Liberator* in the 1850s

Despite the threat of punishment, some enslaved laborers made annual forays off the plantations to visit family and friends. Others resisted their masters within the confines of the plantation grounds. They held secret meetings, staged work slowdowns, broke tools, feigned illnesses, and set fires.

SECTION ONE **167**

 History and the Humanities

 American Music: Cultural Traditions— "Kneebone Bend" by McIntosh County Shouters; "The Monongahela Waltz" (Francis Johnson) by the Chestnut Brass Company and Friends; "De Boatmen's Dance" by Robert Winans and Ensemble; "Hard Times Come Again No More" by The Hutchinson Family Singers, Wayne Dalton, solo; "Get Off the Track!" by the Hutchinson Family Singers

Curriculum Connection

Literature In 1852 Harriet Beecher Stowe published *Uncle Tom's Cabin,* an antislavery novel, which rapidly became a best-seller. Students may wish to read *Uncle Tom's Cabin.*

 PORTFOLIO PROJECT

Portfolio Project

Making a Time Line As students read the section, encourage them to keep notes for a time line of events preceding the Civil War. They can create time lines showing events that may have led to war, giving some detail about each event and creating illustrations for some. In addition, some students may wish to make telescoping time lines that focus on a particular strand of conflict, such as political compromises, slave revolts, abolitionist protests, technological progress, or territorial expansion. Students should add their time lines to their portfolios.

167

Plantation owners feared open defiance from individuals but were even more afraid of a collective rebellion. A number of early slave revolts—such as Gabriel's Revolt in Richmond in 1800 and the Denmark Vesey Conspiracy in Charleston in 1822—aroused concern. This concern turned into panic in 1831 when, on August 22, an enslaved preacher named Nat Turner led 75 armed followers in a rebellion. During the 2 days before they were subdued, these rebels killed between 55 and 60 whites.

The hysteria that spread throughout the South after the Turner revolt prompted slaveholders to take elaborate precautions to protect themselves. They created a complicated system of permits for slave travel and patrols to enforce the system. Believing that literacy would lead to empowerment and revolt, masters tried to prevent enslaved workers from learning to read and write. Additionally, Southern legislatures passed laws that made it difficult for masters to free captive African Americans. They wanted to prevent the freed population from increasing because free African Americans could organize revolts much more easily than an enslaved group. While these tactics seemed to halt slave rebellion in the South, Northern opposition to the spread of slavery grew.

Conflict and Compromise
The Slavery Debate Gathers Fire

The majority of Northern politicians did not oppose slavery as a labor force or as a way of life. For purely political reasons, they opposed the extension of slavery into the new territories gained by the Louisiana Purchase. If these territories became slave states, the South would have greater representation in the Senate than the North. Greater representation would give Southern politicians a better chance of fulfilling their political agenda.

To protect slavery and their way of life, white Southerners insisted that the federal government keep out of all matters that the Constitution had not clearly defined. In addition, Southerners wanted tariff laws that encouraged Southern development.

As mentioned in Chapter 2, white Southerners opposed high tariff laws, which raised prices on many articles from overseas. Because the South bought large quantities of manufactured goods from Great Britain, which in turn bought the South's cotton for British cotton mills, the high tariffs threatened the South's prosperity. The Southerners argued that Congress did not have the right to make laws that caused one section of the country to suffer unfairly. They were determined to maintain the political balance.

The Missouri Compromise

Until 1818 there had been an equal number of slave and free states, and likewise an equal number of senators representing the interests of North and South. Then, in 1818 when Missouri petitioned to enter the Union as a slave state, this delicate balance of power was threatened. Northern legislators amended Missouri's petition by stipulating that Missouri could become a state only if it outlawed slavery. Southern politicians were outraged.

Lawmakers eventually resolved this conflict with a series of legislative compromises. The northern part of Massachusetts, which had petitioned for statehood soon after Missouri, would be admitted as the separate free state of Maine. Missouri would be admitted to the Union as a slave state. In addition, the region south of the 36°30´ latitude line in the Louisiana territory would be open to slavery, whereas all the land north of it, except Missouri, would be free. These agreements were collectively known as the Missouri Compromise.

White Southerners were unhappy with the compromise because it made more land available for settlement as free territory than as slave territory. Southerners were also concerned because the majority of immigrants pouring into the country were seeking jobs in Northern urban

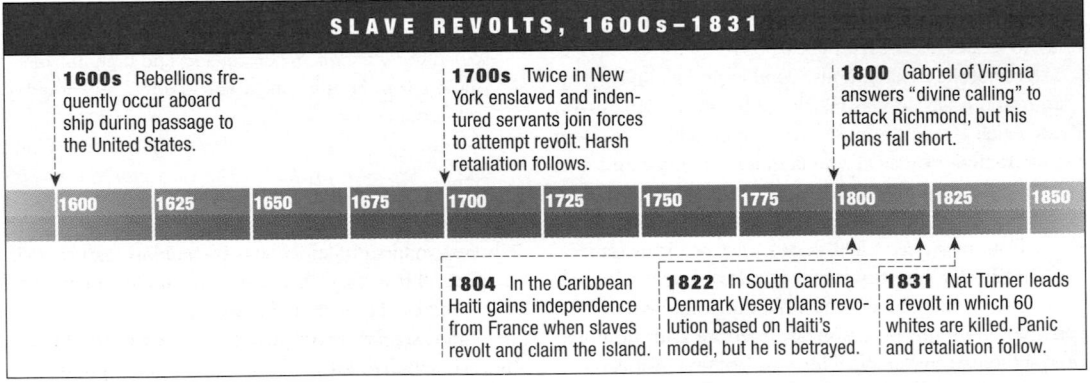

SLAVE REVOLTS, 1600s–1831

1600s Rebellions frequently occur aboard ship during passage to the United States.

1700s Twice in New York enslaved and indentured servants join forces to attempt revolt. Harsh retaliation follows.

1800 Gabriel of Virginia answers "divine calling" to attack Richmond, but his plans fall short.

| 1600 | 1625 | 1650 | 1675 | 1700 | 1725 | 1750 | 1775 | 1800 | 1825 | 1850 |

1804 In the Caribbean Haiti gains independence from France when slaves revolt and claim the island.

1822 In South Carolina Denmark Vesey plans revolution based on Haiti's model, but he is betrayed.

1831 Nat Turner leads a revolt in which 60 whites are killed. Panic and retaliation follow.

168 CHAPTER 6 CIVIL WAR AND RECONSTRUCTION

Extending the Content

Nat Turner's Rebellion Turner's uprising in Virginia was the bloodiest slave revolt in the nation's history. It struck fear into the hearts of whites and effectively ended the organized abolition movement in the South. Turner rebelled not against a particular master—his owner had treated him comparatively well—but against slavery itself. A Baptist preacher who believed he was divinely inspired, Turner saw visions and heard voices. He looked for signs in the heavens; an eclipse of the sun led him to plan the uprising. Ask students if they know of other military leaders who held such beliefs. *(They may mention Joan of Arc or John Brown.)*

centers. This trend meant that the North's population would soon far exceed the South's. The North would then be entitled to far more seats in the House of Representatives and would be able to advance the goals of its free labor agenda. The North already had more seats, and this had helped them push the Missouri Compromise through.

War With Mexico

In 1836 when Texas declared its independence from Mexico, white Southerners hoped to acquire Texas as a new slave state. Northerners feared that the admission of Texas to the Union would not only increase the South's power in Congress but would also embroil the United States in a war with Mexico. Nevertheless by 1845 enough politicians were caught up in the fervor of westward expansion—believing that it was the destiny of the nation to reach from shore to shore—that white Southern politicians were able to prevail in getting Texas admitted to the Union as the twenty-eighth state. Mexico was outraged at this action. After a border skirmish between American troops and Mexican troops, the United States declared war on Mexico in May 1846.

On February 2, 1848, after almost two years of fighting, the nations ended the war by signing the Treaty of Guadalupe Hidalgo. This treaty gave the United States vast new regions that today include California, Arizona, New Mexico, Utah, Nevada, and parts of Colorado and Wyoming. The fear that these territories would organize into states intensified the sectional conflict between the North and the South. Many Northerners opposed the extension of slavery even into the newly acquired lands that lay south of the line established by the Missouri Compromise.

The Compromise of 1850

In 1850, 15 free states and 15 slave states made up the Union. California threatened this delicate balance of power by applying for admission to the Union as a free state. Congress once again faced the need to hammer out a legislative compromise. Senator Henry Clay of Kentucky introduced 4 compromise resolutions that became the basic proposals making up the Compromise of 1850: first, that California be admitted to the Union

A Treaty for Half of Mexico This nineteenth-century engraving shows General Zachary Taylor at Buena Vista, where he defeated General Santa Anna in 1847. Following Buena Vista it took five major battles to win the war. *What modern states are in the lands Mexico surrendered to the United States at the end of the war?*

as a free state; second, that territorial governments in Utah and New Mexico let the people of the territories decide the slavery issue for themselves; third, that the slave trade—but not slavery—be prohibited in the District of Columbia; and fourth, that a new fugitive slave law require federal marshals to assist in recapturing **fugitives**—people who had escaped from slavery and were running from the law.

Clay's proposals touched off months of heated debate in Congress. Some of the greatest orators of the time lined up on opposite sides of the issue. John C. Calhoun of South Carolina bitterly opposed Clay's plan. Weak and near death, Calhoun sat silent while his final speech was read to the Senate. In it he warned that the Union could be saved only by giving the South equal rights in the acquired territory and by halting the agitation over slavery. Daniel Webster, who supported Clay's ideas, captivated the Senate with a sentence that has since become famous:

I wish to speak today, not as a Massachusetts man, nor as a northern man, but as an American. . . . I speak today for the preservation of the Union. "Hear me for my cause."

—Daniel Webster, March 7, 1850

Webster argued that there was no need to exclude slavery from the territories because it would not prosper there due to the soil and climate.

President Taylor opposed a compromise, but his untimely death in July 1850 brought Millard Fillmore to

SECTION ONE **169**

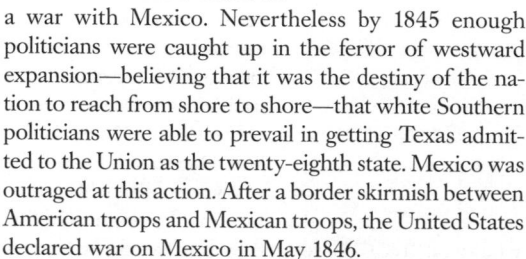

VISUAL INSTRUCTION

A Treaty for Half of Mexico General Taylor's son-in-law, Colonel Jefferson Davis, later to be president of the Confederacy, also distinguished himself at Buena Vista by breaking up a Mexican cavalry charge.

Answer: *Arizona, Utah, Nevada, New Mexico, California, and parts of Colorado and Wyoming*

FYI

Language Derivation On February 25, 1820, when Congress was finally ready to vote on the Missouri Compromise, Felix Walker insisted on making one more speech for Buncombe County, North Carolina. Thereafter, politicians spoke of making an empty political speech as "talking for Buncombe." The term *bunk,* referring to useless verbiage, comes from this expression.

 Facts on File

Landmark Documents in American History Have students review "Compromise of 1850" and "Kansas-Nebraska Act, 1854" and write a paragraph about the intent of one of the documents.

Cultural Perspectives

New Mexico Of all the lands acquired by the United States as a result of the Mexican-American War, none reveals its Hispanic heritage more clearly than the state of New Mexico. Two-fifths of the population is of Hispanic origin. One-half of these are Mexican Americans; the others are descendants of Spanish settlers. Spanish is spoken widely.

Another one-tenth of the population is Native American. The historical fusion of Hispanic, Anglo, and Native American cultures has resulted in a unique art and architecture, to be seen especially in Taos, Santa Fe, and Albuquerque. Students who are familiar with this region may enjoy leading the class discussion.

ASSESS

Meeting Lesson Objectives

Each section objective is tested by the section review question(s) that follows it in parentheses.

1. Identify various forms of resistance to slavery. (1, 3, 5)
2. Contrast the political agendas of the North and the South.
3. Analyze the attempts at compromise over slavery. (4)

Map Study

With its victory in the Mexican-American War, the United States annexed new territories that eventually would become states. Deciding whether these states would be free or slave was one cause of the Civil War.
Answer: In 1820 Congress banned slavery in territories north of 36° 30′ but allowed it south of that line. In 1850 Congress decided to let people in the Utah and New Mexico territories decide the slavery issue for themselves. All of California, including that part south of 36°30′, was admitted as a free state. In 1854 Congress ruled that when Nebraska and Kansas became states, each could decide whether to be slave or free.

---

the presidency. With Fillmore's backing, Clay and his supporters succeeded in pushing the proposals through Congress. The package of four laws that became known as the Compromise of 1850 temporarily settled the question of slavery in the territories. The problems did not go away, however, because they were rooted in the issue of slavery itself.

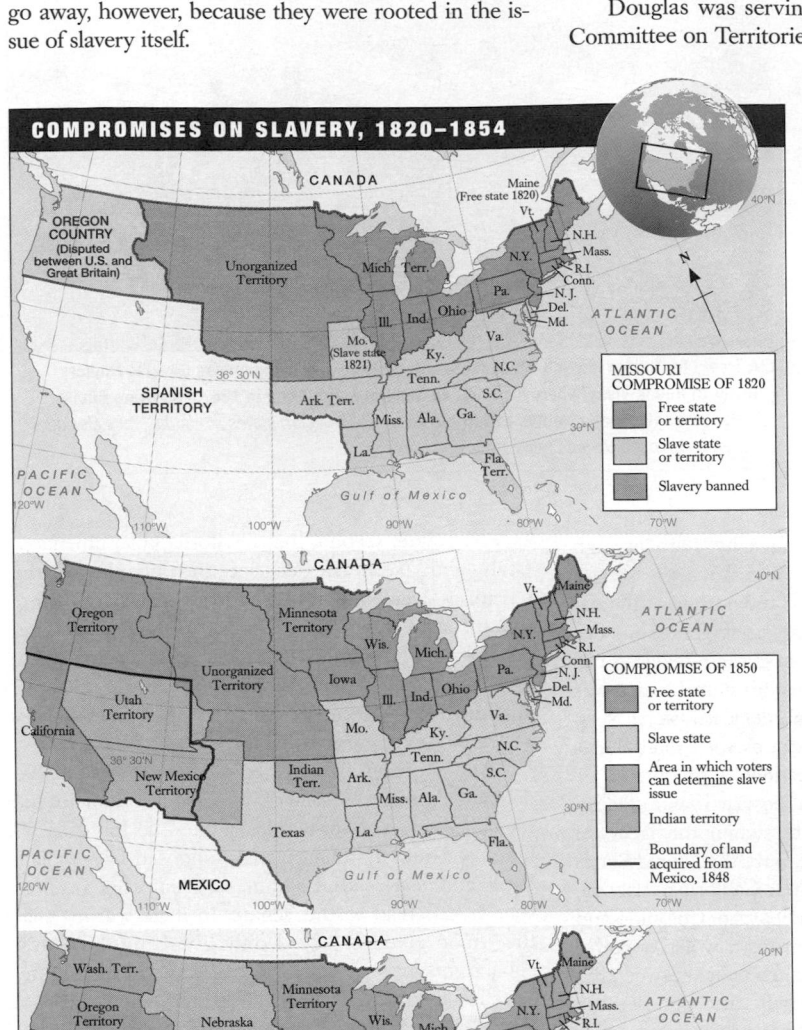

The Kansas-Nebraska Act

Just four years later, in 1854, Illinois senator Stephen A. Douglas guided a highly controversial bill through Congress. This bill was the Kansas-Nebraska Act.

Douglas was serving as chairman of the Senate Committee on Territories. He wanted to see the unorganized territory west of Missouri and Iowa opened for settlement. This land lay north of the line established by the Missouri Compromise. Yet rather than letting the land become a free territory according to this legislation, Douglas proposed that the people in the territory decide for themselves whether or not they wanted slavery.

In 1854, after much negotiation, the Kansas-Nebraska Act was passed. It divided the Nebraska territory into two separate territories, Kansas and Nebraska; and it repealed the prohibition of slavery north of the Missouri Compromise line. The citizens of each territory would be able to determine by vote whether their state would be slave or free. In effect the act voided the Missouri Compromise, enabling slavery to expand northward.

Many of the antislavery politicians detested Douglas's bill as a violation of the "sacred pledge" of the Missouri Compromise: no slavery north of the 36°30′ line. These politicians broke from traditional party politics to form the Republican party in February 1854. The Republicans defended Northern sectional interests under the slogan Free soil, free labor, free speech, free men.

Kansas meanwhile became the battleground for sectional and party conflicts.

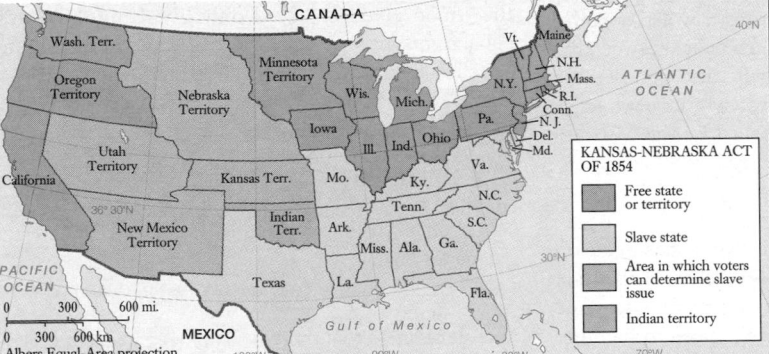

Three important stages in the slavery dispute are shown in these maps: The Missouri Compromise, the Compromise of 1850, and the Kansas-Nebraska Act. Note the status of the territories in each map. *How does the territories' slavery status change from one map to the next?*

170 CHAPTER 6 CIVIL WAR AND RECONSTRUCTION

Critical Thinking

Making Inferences The Kansas-Nebraska Act repealed the 30-year-old Missouri Compromise and brought pro- and antislavery passions to the boiling point. Abraham Lincoln said that the North wanted to give new settlers "a clean bed, with no snakes in it." Ask students to infer what Lincoln meant by this. What were the "snakes" in the territory after the Kansas-Nebraska Act was passed? A Southerner in Boston wrote that because of the act, "the Fugitive Slave Law is a dead letter throughout New England." This proved to be true; Northerners refused to return any more fugitives. Ask students to infer why this was so.

By 1856 Kansas had turned into a cauldron of violence between antislavery and proslavery groups.

Violence Reaches Washington, D.C.

"Bleeding Kansas" became the catchword for the escalating violence over slavery—and the blood spilled all the way to Capitol Hill. In May 1856 Congressman Preston Brooks of South Carolina entered the nearly empty Senate chamber and beat Massachusetts Senator Charles Sumner with a cane. Brooks felt that Sumner's "Crime Against Kansas" speech, which verbally attacked Brooks's kinsman, had warranted this retaliation.

It was in the wake of these events that the Supreme Court handed down its decision in the *Dred Scott* case in March 1857. Naturally enough, this decision gave rise to fear among Northern politicians. The Free-Soil Republicans, worried that the extension of slavery into all the territories was forthcoming, gained more popular support, causing Southern forces to defend slavery even more stubbornly.

An unsettled nation approached the 1858 elections. In this tense atmosphere, Abraham Lincoln, a little-known one-term congressman from Springfield, Illinois, opposed Senator Stephen A. Douglas in the race for the Senate and challenged him to a series of debates. The debates gave Lincoln the opportunity to make his political views, including his defense of Northern interests, nationally known. Lincoln lost the election, but the debates catapulted him into the national spotlight.

Hostilities Intensify

Then, in October 1859 a violent clash captured the nation's attention. Abolitionist John Brown, leading an interracial band of 21 men, attacked the federal arsenal at Harpers Ferry, Virginia. Brown said he hoped to spark a slave rebellion that would end slavery and "purge this land with blood."

Although Brown and his men were captured within 36 hours, the revolt prompted intense public reaction. White Southerners initially responded hysterically, fearing an outbreak of slave insurrections. The fear calmed as they realized that Brown had not, after all, managed to incite even one slave to join him in the Harpers Ferry revolt. Northern response was initially cool. Brown's eloquence during his trial, however, swayed public opinion. Some Northerners, including many African Americans, proclaimed Brown a hero.

By the time Brown was sentenced to hang, writer Ralph Waldo Emerson predicted that Brown would "make the gallows as glorious as the cross." The editor

of a Kansas newspaper supported Emerson's prediction; he wrote, "The death of no man in America has ever produced so profound a sensation. A feeling of deep and sorrowful indignation seems to possess the masses." With Northerners gripped by indignation and most white Southerners gripped by fear or anger, the nation prepared for the upcoming presidential election of 1860.

BOSTON ATHENAEUM

SOUTHERN CHIVALRY.— ARGUMENT versus CLUB'S.

Brawl on the Senate Floor Violence over slavery spread to Congress when a Southern congressman attacked a Northern senator. *Who are the two men pictured in this famous cartoon and what prompted the attack?*

SECTION REVIEW

Vocabulary

1. Define: sectionalism, gospel tradition, fugitive.

Checking Facts

2. What were the economic differences between the North and the South that led to the Civil War?

3. What were some ways that enslaved individuals coped with and fought the conditions of slavery?

Critical Thinking

Identifying Assumptions

4. Northerners strongly opposed the Fugitive Slave Law enacted as part of the Compromise of 1850. Why do you think this was so? What assumptions did the law make about the North?

Linking Across Time

5. Compare efforts of African Americans to resist slavery in the mid-1800s with civil rights protests in the 1960s.

SECTION ONE **171**

VISUAL INSTRUCTION

Brawl on the Senate Floor In an 1849 lawsuit against the city of Boston, Charles Sumner—assisted by Robert Morris, an African American attorney—argued that school segregation was unconstitutional.

Answer: *Preston Brooks, Charles Sumner*

Evaluate

Have students complete the Section Review.

☛ 🖸 Assign the Section 1 Quiz or use the Testmaker to develop a customized quiz. (Also in Spanish.) **LEP**

Reteach

∩ Have students listen to the Chapter 6, Section 1 Audiocassette. (Also in Spanish.) **LEP**

Enrich

☛ Have students complete the Chapter 6 Geography in History Activity.

☛ Have students complete the Unit 2 American Literature Reading.

☛ Have students complete Supreme Court Case Study 4.

CLOSE

Have students suggest ways the conflict between North and South could have been resolved without war. (*Slavery could have been outlawed and slaveholders compensated.*)

Section 1 Review Answers

1. **sectionalism** (166), **gospel tradition** (167), **fugitive** (169)
2. The North had free labor and an industrial economy; the South, plantations and slave labor.
3. Relying on their families, participating in religious activities, slowing down work, breaking equipment, running away and rebelling

4. The law requiring federal marshals to help recapture fugitives in the North assumed that local Northern police would not normally do this.
5. Answers will vary. In the 1960s African Americans had more political power and successfully used nonviolent demonstrations in contrast to the armed rebellions of the 1800s.

FOCUS

Section Objectives

1. Analyze the results of the South's decision to form a separate government based on ideals that conflicted with those of the federal government.
2. Understand the effects on African Americans of the Emancipation Proclamation.

Bellringer Activity

While taking attendance at the beginning of the class period, display **Section Focus Transparency 17,** and have students answer the questions. (Or use the blackline master.)

VISUAL INSTRUCTION

Richmond in Ruins When the Confederate army decided to evacuate the city, escaped convicts and others began looting. The army's decision to burn the city met with protests from the city's own government and community leaders.

Ask: Who set fire to the city of Richmond and why? *(Confederates set fire to it, so that Union soldiers could not take shelter there.)*

SECTION 2

The Civil War

APRIL 2, 1865: THE FALL OF RICHMOND

Richmond in Ruins
Citizens flee the burning Confederate capital, shown in this Currier and Ives print.

ON SUNDAY, APRIL 2, 1865, CONFEDERATE PRESIDENT JEFFERSON DAVIS WAS PRAYING IN A RICHMOND, VIRGINIA, CHURCH WHEN A MESSENGER RUSHED IN. The Union army had broken through Confederate lines and was advancing on the city. In response General Lee had ordered his troops to pull out of Richmond. The city would have to be evacuated.

By midafternoon, troops, cavalry, and townspeople were clogging the roads in a frenzied attempt to escape the city. Then as the sun set, bands of devoted Confederates set fire to their own city of Richmond to destroy any remaining goods and shelter that might be of benefit to the Union soldiers.

On April 4, just 40 hours after Davis had left Richmond, President Lincoln entered the smoldering city. As Lincoln walked the streets of the fallen Confederate capital, freed slaves waved, shouted thanks and praise, and even reached out to touch him. One woman shouted, "I know I am free, for I have seen Father Abraham and felt him."

The Start of the War
"A Hornet's Nest"

In 1860 after a hard-fought campaign, Abraham Lincoln was elected President. Of the 4 candidates who had battled for the presidency, Lincoln had obtained an overwhelming majority of electoral votes—but only 40 percent of the popular vote.

Southerners, aware of Lincoln's pro-Northern political views, reacted by calling for **secession,** or formal withdrawal, from the nation. In December 1860, South Carolina became the first state to secede from the Union. The following year Mississippi, Florida, Alabama, Georgia, Louisiana, and Texas followed, declaring themselves a new nation, the Confederate States of America.

AS YOU READ

Vocabulary
► secession
► emancipation
► lynching
► scorched earth policy

Think About . . .
► what military and political consequences resulted from the decision of the Southern states to form their own government.

► the effects of the Emancipation Proclamation on African Americans in the Southern states.

Section 2 Resources

REPRODUCIBLE RESOURCES
- Lesson Plan 6-2
- Vocabulary and Guided Reading Activity 6-2
- Unit 2 Case Study
- Section 2 Quiz
- Skill Reinforcement Activity 6

MULTIMEDIA RESOURCES
- Section Focus Transparency 17
- Beginnings to 1900 Transparencies, 13–18
- U.S. History and Art Transparency 11
- American Music: Cultural Traditions
- Focus on American Fine Art Prints, Print 10

- Powers of the Supreme Court
- Landmark Documents in American History
- Testmaker
- Chapter 6 Digest Audiocassette
- Student Self-Test: A Software Review

THE UNION AND THE CONFEDERACY

	Free state in the Union
	Slave state in the Union
	Confederate state
	Territory
★	Capital city

The map above shows the opposing sides in the Civil War. *Which states left the Union and decided to join the Confederacy? Which slave states remained in the Union?*

The Fall of Fort Sumter

The Confederacy's first military objective was to obtain control of Fort Sumter, a Union military installation in the harbor of Charleston, South Carolina. A prominent Southerner warned against firing on this army stronghold, "You will wantonly strike a hornet's nest. Legions now quiet will swarm out and sting us to death." Nevertheless, on April 12, 1861, the Confederate army began shelling Fort Sumter until its commander surrendered.

Proclaiming an insurrection in the South, Lincoln called for 75,000 volunteers to suppress the rebellion. In response, Virginia, Arkansas, North Carolina, and Tennessee left the Union to join the Confederacy. Headed by their newly elected president, Jefferson Davis, the Confederates prepared for a war of independence, likening their status to that of the American revolutionaries in 1776.

The Union and the Confederacy Compared

The Union could draw its fighting force from a population of 22 million that included foreign-born immigrants, free African Americans, and escaped slaves. With this size population, the North was able to raise a much larger army than the South. The 11 Confederate states had a population of only 9 million, nearly 3 million of whom the Confederacy refused to let fight because they were enslaved laborers.

What the South lacked in numbers, it made up for in military skill and experience. The Confederacy could draw from a talented pool of military minds that included many officers from West Point and veterans of the

Mexican American War. It was a seasoned West Point general, Robert E. Lee of Virginia, who assumed command of the Confederate army. Also, many white Southerners were members of local militia units and were skilled marksmen.

This superior military training might have given the South a clear advantage over the North were it not for the fact that almost all resources for waging war—steel mills and iron mines, important industries, and transportation facilities—were located in the North. More than 70 percent of the nation's railroads ran through the North. Most naval facilities and ships were in the North as well. By comparison the Confederacy possessed inferior natural resources, industry, and transportation. Furthermore the South lacked the financial resources to manufacture or acquire these necessities of war.

The South tried to make up for its disadvantages by fighting a defensive war. Southerners fortified their cities and waited for the Union to invade. If the Union forces invaded, Confederate strategists reasoned that Southerners would at least be fighting on familiar terrain, amid supporters, and close to supplies.

African American Soldiers

Early in the war, Northern African Americans eagerly tried to enlist in the Union army in order to join the fight to end slavery, but they were not accepted.

African American Troops This print, showing troops training near Philadelphia, appeared on Union recruiting posters. *How did free and fugitive African Americans give the Union an advantage?*

SECTION TWO **173**

TEACH

Guided Practice

L2 Linking Past and Present Point out that the presidential election of 1860 aroused such strong feelings that in its aftermath 11 Southern states seceded. Ask students what, if any, issue might create similar regional strife in an election today.

MAP STUDY

Have students use the map on this page to locate the Union and Confederate capitals. How far apart are the 2 cities? *(about 100 miles, or 160.9 k.)*

Answer: *Virginia, North Carolina, South Carolina, Georgia, Florida, Alabama, Mississippi, Tennessee, Arkansas, Louisiana, and Texas joined the Confederacy. Delaware, Maryland, Kentucky, Missouri, and, in 1863, West Virginia remained a part of the Union.*

VISUAL INSTRUCTION

African American Troops Commanding officers of African American troops were usually white. Some African American surgeons held officer's rank, but Dr. Martin Delany was the only African American major. In February of 1865, Lincoln implemented Delany's plan to create an entirely African American fighting unit.

Answer: *The Union had more than double the South's fighting force, partly due to African Americans in its ranks.*

Cooperative Learning

Making a Time Line in Sections Hang poster board or large paper in the classroom with a time line marked 1861 through 1865. Organize the class into 5 groups and ask each to be responsible for filling in dates in 1 year of the time line. Above the line students should mark Civil War battles, summarizing their significance and listing the number of casualties on both sides of the battle. Below the line other group members should mark significant socioeconomic and political developments, such as the founding of the American Red Cross or the date of the Emancipation Proclamation.

173

174

Show students Beginnings to 1900 Transparencies 13, 14, 15, 16, 17, and 18 and have them complete the activity sheets.

Independent Practice

L1 Responding to Images Explain that photographers and artists were valued at Civil War camps and battlegrounds. Have students examine civil war photography, sketches, and paintings. Ask them to find a particularly moving image. Students can write descriptive paragraphs about the mood or atmosphere of the image and then write a paragraph about its historical significance. The two paragraphs may be worked into poems.

Have students complete the Chapter 6, Section 2 Vocabulary and Guided Reading Activity. (Also in Spanish.) **LEP**

Outraged by the army's refusal, Frederick Douglass wrote: "Why does the Government reject the negro? Is he not a man? Can he not wield a sword, fire a gun, march and . . . obey orders like any other?"

In 1863, desperately needing more soldiers, Lincoln announced his decision to use African American troops. By the end of the war, about 180,000 African Americans served in the Union army. These units took part in more than 500 engagements. During the Mississippi Valley campaign, one observer wrote: "The self-forgetfulness, the undaunted heroism, and the great endurance of the negro . . . created a new chapter in American history." In spite of the Confederate threat to shoot them on capture, 23 African American soldiers won the Medal of Honor.

Major Military Battles
The Bloodiest War

Neither the Union nor the Confederacy imagined that the war would last as long as it did, or that it would exact such a terrible cost in lives and property throughout the nation. During four years of war, hundreds of thousands of Americans were killed in battle and property damage was enormous.

The First Battle of Bull Run

On July 21, 1861, the first battle of the Civil War was fought in Virginia, about 20 miles (32.2 km) southwest of Washington, D.C. Northern civilians, believing that they would be able to witness the easy defeat of the Confederates, came out to picnic and watch the battle. The battle, however, did not end as the North had expected.

Even though Confederate soldiers were outnumbered more than two to one, they managed to hold their ground until reinforcements arrived. The Confederates then counterattacked, letting out bloodcurdling cries— "rebel yells"—that terrified and confused Union troops. Hastily retreating Union soldiers rushed right into the crowds of spectators. According to one witness:

Cruel, crazy, mad, hopeless panic possessed them, and communicated to everybody about in front and rear. The heat was awful, although now about six; the men were exhausted—their mouths gaped, their lips cracked and blackened with the powder of the cartridges they had bitten off in the battle, their eyes starting in frenzy; no mortal ever saw such a mass of ghastly wretches.

—Congressman Albert Riddle

The defeat meant more than losing one battle. It was a psychological setback from which the Union did not quickly recover.

BOSTON ATHENAEUM

Images of War Photography was a relatively new technology during the Civil War. Photographers as well as artists were pressed into service to document the horrors of war. The photo above, taken by Timothy O'Sullivan in 1863, is titled "Harvest of Death." Inexpensive forms of photography made portraits of soldiers and loved ones available to send home or to carry into battle.

How might documentary photos have affected Americans' view of the war in a way that paintings or engravings did not?

Meeting Special Needs

Attention Deficit Disorder To help students with attention deficit disorder understand the issues and conflicts of the Civil War, play recordings of several period marches, including "Dixie" and "The Battle Hymn of the Republic." Discuss with students how the moods of Northern and Southern songs differ.

Have them identify any lyrics that express regional differences. If necessary, explain to students that the words *North, Union, blue,* and *yankees* all refer to one side in the Civil War, while *South, Confederacy, gray,* and *rebels* refer to the other.

Shiloh and Antietam

On April 6 and 7, 1862, the Union and Confederate armies clashed in the first of several massive battles at Shiloh, Tennessee. After the Battle of Shiloh, Americans realized that this conflict was not going to be a gentlemen's war; rather, it would be the wholesale slaughter of ill-fated men and boys. In just those 2 days of fighting at Shiloh, more than 20,000 Union and Confederate soldiers were killed or wounded—8,000 more than in several previous battles combined.

Another violent clash occurred at Antietam Creek on September 17, 1862, when General Lee marched his Confederate troops northward into Maryland. In the ensuing battle, which eventually stopped Lee's advance north, 30,000 soldiers died. The air, one army surgeon commented, was "vocal with the whistle of bullets and scream of shells." A Confederate officer said a nearby cornfield "looked as if it had been struck down by a storm of bloody hail." The Union's victory was of strategic importance because it made Britain reluctant to respond to the South's request for aid.

Gettysburg

In 1863 Confederate general Lee tried once again to invade the North. Union troops met his advance, and during the first 3 days of July the 2 armies battled outside the town of Gettysburg, Pennsylvania. The Union suffered heavy losses on the first day of battle at Seminary Ridge. A gunner recalled "bullets hissing, humming and whistling everywhere; cannon roaring; all crash on crash and peal on peal."

On the third day, Lee ordered General George Pickett to lead 13,000 men in an assault on Union lines.

MAJOR BATTLES OF THE CIVIL WAR

Using the map above, follow the war strategies of the Union and the Confederacy on land and on sea. *How does the location of most of the battles reflect the Confederates' plan to fight a defensive war? Where did the Union army attack along water routes? Why would the Union force want to gain control of the Mississippi River?*

CIVIL WAR TURNING POINTS, 1861–1864

July 21, 1861 First battle of the Civil War brings startling loss to the Union at Bull Run, Virginia.

October 1861 Union initiates a naval blockade of Southern Atlantic coast.

May–July, 1863 Grant sustains siege of last Mississippi River stronghold at Vicksburg. Confederates surrender at Vicksburg and Gettysburg on July 4; celebration throughout the Union follows.

April 1862 Shiloh, Tennessee, runs with the blood of 20,000 soldiers killed or injured in 2 days of fighting.

September 17, 1862 The Union stops Lee's advance northward, but 30,000 die in one day at Antietam Creek, Maryland.

May–September, 1864 General Sherman leads Atlanta campaign, followed by scorched earth campaign throughout the South.

SECTION TWO   **175**

Portfolio Project

Creating Diagrams Have students develop strategies for either side in the Civil War. Ask them what the North's strategy for victory was. Suggest that they create their own maps of the United States and territories at the time of the war and diagram a step-by-step plan for one side or the other that might lead to a speedy victory. Ask students if they can think of some reasons why fighting a defensive war might become a disadvantage for the South. Discuss which side had the more difficult task. After discussing their completed diagrams, students can add them to their portfolios.

CHART STUDY

Ask: What gave the North something to celebrate in 1863? (*Confederate defeats at Gettysburg and Vicksburg.*)

MAP STUDY

Ask students why Lee changed his plan to fight defensively and invaded the North at Antietam and Gettysburg. (*Defensive battles occurred on Southern soil, destroying Southern resources and morale.*)

Answer: *Most battles were in the South. The Union army attacked at Shiloh, Vicksburg, Chattanooga, and Nashville. Union forces wanted to prevent supplies and reinforcements from reaching the South.*

History and the Humanities

 U.S. History and Art Transparency 11— *A Rainy Day in Camp* by Winslow Homer

🎧 American Music: Cultural Traditions— "Bonnie Blue Flag" by 1st Brigade Band; "Glory! Glory! Hallelujah!" ("John Brown's Body") by the Princely Players; "The Vacant Chair, or We Shall Meet But We Shall Miss Him" by the Hutchinson Family Singers

📖 Focus on American Fine Art Prints, Print 10— *Forever Free* by Edmonia Lewis

ABCNEWS INTERACTIVE™

Videodisc

Powers of the Supreme Court

Side 1, Chapter 20
Title: Amendment 13 (1865): Abolition of Slavery
Subject: Historical paintings and illustrations about the Emancipation Proclamation
Ask: What was the Emancipation Proclamation? *(document that freed enslaved persons in the Confederacy)*

See Powers of the Supreme Court Guidebook page 32 for complete lesson plan.

Facts on File

Landmark Documents in American History Have students review "Emancipation Proclamation, Abraham Lincoln, 1863" and write a paragraph about the intent of the document.

Global Connection

A Swiss philanthropist, Jean Henri Dunant, organized volunteers to help the wounded at Solferino, Italy, in 1859. Three years later he published an appeal to found an international organization. In response 12 European countries formed the Red Cross as part of the First Geneva Convention, in 1864.

Nearly half the advancing Confederates were gunned down. By the time the Confederates retreated from Gettysburg, they had sustained 28,000 casualties; the Union had sustained 23,000. As wagons carried the Confederate wounded southward, a Quaker nurse wrote, "There are no words in the English language to express the suffering I witnessed today."

The Gettysburg Address

The Battle of Gettysburg cost both sides heavy casualties, but it was a crushing defeat for the South. The Confederacy would never recover from the losses it had suffered. On November 19, 1863, President Lincoln visited the battle site to dedicate a cemetery to honor the soldiers who had fallen there. In a short and eloquent address, the President stated:

> The world will little note nor long remember what we say here, but it can never forget what they [the fallen soldiers] did here. It is for us, the living, rather, to be dedicated here to the unfinished work which they who fought here have thus far so nobly advanced.
>
> It is rather for us to be here dedicated to the great task remaining before us—that from these honored dead we take increased devotion to that cause for which they gave the last full measure of devotion; that we here highly resolve that these dead shall not have died in vain; that this nation, under God, shall have a new birth of freedom; and that government of the people, by the people, and for the people, shall not perish from the earth.
>
> —Abraham Lincoln, November 19, 1863

Many people who were there that momentous day thought that Lincoln's remarks were too short and simple for such a serious occasion. The Address, however, is one of the significant developments in the history of individual rights in the United States. Here the President was telling a war-weary nation that *all Americans*—regardless of heritage—had a stake in the future of the nation. Along with that stake would eventually come equality.

Vicksburg

Yet the war was far from over in 1863. Union and Confederate forces battled to control the Mississippi River at the same time that troops fought at Gettysburg. Union troops occupied New Orleans, Baton Rouge, Natchez, and Memphis. Finally all that remained in Confederate hands was Vicksburg, located on bluffs high above the river. In mid-May 1863, Union general Ulysses S. Grant ordered a siege of the city. On July 4, the same day Lee began his retreat from Gettysburg, Confederate forces in Vicksburg surrendered. As news of the 2

strategic victories spread throughout the Union, there were, according to Carl Sandburg, "celebrations with torchlight processions, songs, jubilation, refreshments."

The War at Sea

While armies battled their way across the land, another aspect of the war took place in coastal waters and on inland rivers. At the outset of the war, Lincoln had ordered a blockade of all Southern ports. The Union navy's assorted ships patrolled the 3,500 miles (5,631.5 km) of Confederate coastline and eventually cut off Southern trade. The daring blockade runners that managed to escape capture could not carry enough goods to supply the South. The greatest blow to Confederate trade came in April 1862 when Commodore David Farragut sailed a fleet into the mouth of the Mississippi River. He steamed past the forts below New Orleans and went on to capture the South's largest city.

The Confederates almost succeeded in breaking the blockade at Chesapeake Bay. Southerners raised the frigate *Merrimack,* scuttled by Union forces when they abandoned the Norfolk navy yard, and converted it into an ironclad warship. In March 1862, the ship, renamed the *Virginia,* battled the Union's ironclad *Monitor.* Neither ship could sink the other, but the battle marked the beginning of a new era in naval warfare.

Social and Economic Battles
Controversy Over the War

The battles of 1863 turned the tide militarily for the Union, but Northerners still experienced difficulties on the home front. Social and economic difficulties plagued both sides.

Emancipation

Throughout the war, abolitionists pressured President Lincoln to free all enslaved African Americans. Abolitionists argued that Union soldiers were fighting not only to preserve the Union but also to end slavery. They also pointed out that freeing the slaves would create a new pool of recruits that could be drafted to fight for the North. Further, backers of **emancipation,** or liberation from slavery, reasoned that the Fugitive Slave Law no longer applied to Southerners, who after their secession from the Union could no longer claim to be protected by the Union's laws. By this reasoning, the North was finally rid of its obligation to return runaways, and Union troops could confiscate Southern property and slaves as spoils of war.

At first Lincoln evaded the issue of emancipation, fearing it would drive Maryland, Missouri, and

---

Extending the Content

Women and Medicine The year 1864 was a banner year for women in medicine. Elizabeth Blackwell founded the American Women's College. The Women's Medical College opened its doors the same year. The advance of women in medicine was due largely to the efforts of women nurses and doctors during the war.

Students can examine diaries and historical texts about nurses Clara Barton, Phoebe Pember, and Harriet Tubman; Dr. Mary Edwards Walker; hospital supervisor Captain Sally Tompkins; or other women in medicine. They can create visual displays featuring details about one woman's medical achievement during the Civil War.

Kentucky out of the Union. On September 22, 1862, however, under extreme pressure from Republican senators to declare his position on slavery, Lincoln signed a preliminary version of the Emancipation Proclamation, which declared freedom for enslaved persons only in parts of the Confederacy not under the control of the Union army. The proclamation had no effect on enslaved African Americans in the border states that had not joined the Confederacy.

Although this proclamation freed some enslaved African Americans, it did not necessarily express Lincoln's personal views on the subject of slavery. Just a few months earlier, Lincoln had made his position known in a letter to the abolitionist Horace Greeley.

Contributions to the War Effort Mary Rice Livermore worked throughout the Civil War in support of the Union cause. She organized women's aid societies such as the group pictured. The societies raised money and sent food and clothing to Union soldiers on the battlefield. *In what other ways did women's efforts make a difference during the Civil War?*

M y paramount object in this struggle is to save the Union, and is not either to save or destroy Slavery. If I could save the Union without freeing any slave, I would do it; and if I could save it by freeing all the slaves, I would do it; and if I could do it by freeing some and leaving others alone, I would also do that. What I do about Slavery and the colored race, I do because it helps to save this Union; and what I forbear, I forbear because I do not believe it would help to save the Union.

—Abraham Lincoln, from a letter to Horace Greeley, 1862

New Roles

As the war dragged on, Northern and Southern women had to assume many of the roles previously assigned to the men who had gone away to fight. The two armies needed food, clothing, and weapons. Women took responsibility for supplying many of these goods. In addition many women needed jobs to help support their families. So across the country, women managed their family farms, worked in factories, ran printing presses, shod horses, and also filled government positions. A handful of women even disguised themselves as men and fought in the war.

One of the many significant contributions women made to the war effort was caring for the wounded. Three thousand women served as nurses during the war. Nurses were in great demand to tend the wounded because twice as many soldiers died of infectious diseases as died of injuries sustained in combat. Doctors did not yet understand the importance of sanitation, sterile medical equipment, and a balanced diet. As a result deaths from dysentery, malaria, and typhoid were a by-product of war.

Confederacy/Union Resource Comparisons, 1861

	Confederacy	Union
Population	29%	71%
Livestock	40%	60%
Farm acreage	25%	75%
Railroad mileage	29%	71%
Firearm production	3%	97%
Textile production	7%	93%
Coal production	3%	97%
Iron production	6%	94%

Compare the resources of the North and the South at the start of the Civil War. *In what two areas did the Union have the greatest advantage over the Confederacy? What, if any, advantages are shown for the South?*

Cultural Perspectives

Cherokee Heroes The alliance of Cherokee leader Stand Watie with the Confederacy almost caused civil war among the Cherokee. Most Native American groups allied themselves with the Confederacy as a way to "repay" the government for taking their lands. Many of the Cherokee, however, favored Principal Chief John Ross's view that the Southern states were at fault for the Cherokee expulsion. (See Chapter 5 Case Study, page 136.) Ross eventually gave up pleading the Union cause, choosing unity of his own people over all other issues. Watie gained the rank of brigadier general in 1864 for successful campaigns in the West. The last Confederate general to surrender, he continued fighting until June 1865.

VISUAL INSTRUCTION

Contributions to the War Effort Mary Rice Livermore supported the army by speaking, writing, and organizing. She visited hospitals and publicized what she saw. She and her aides sent 18,000 bushels (158,580 l) of vegetables, 3,000 cans of fruit, and 61,000 pounds (27,694 kg) of dried fruit to the army in 1863.

Answer: *Women ran businesses and farms, worked in factories and government, served as medics, spies, and even soldiers.*

 Curriculum Connection

English Have students read and discuss Lincoln's Gettysburg Address, which he delivered four months after the battle.

CHART STUDY

Have students speculate about the advantages and disadvantages the North and South would have in a war.

Answer: *firearm production and iron production; the South had no resource advantage*

 Block Scheduling

☛ Have students complete the Unit 2 Case Study to enrich their understanding of secession.

177

Curriculum Connection

Civics The United States currently has a standby draft. Since 1981 all men have been required to register for the draft when they reach the age of 18. This registration provides the federal government with a list of names to use if a draft is ever necessary. Have students prepare a speech to deliver before a Union draft board, explaining why they should or should not fight in the Civil War.

VISUAL INSTRUCTION

Victory by Siege In appointing Grant commander of the Union forces, Lincoln recognized that Grant was single-minded and tenacious. He did not hesitate (as other generals might) to pursue the total destruction of Lee's army.

Answer: *Grant had more troops than Lee and better access to supplies. He fought head-to-head in the Wilderness, then waited out a siege of Richmond.*

Quotations General Sherman is credited with being the first to say, "War is hell." When there was talk about his running for President in 1884, he said, "I will not accept if nominated, and will not serve if elected."

Riots

As the bloody battles dragged on, both the North and the South experienced difficulties recruiting soldiers as well as raising money needed to keep up the fight. The Union draft law of March 1863 excused men from military service if they paid the government a $300 fee. Many Northerners who thought the law discriminated against the poor angrily took to the streets in protest.

The most violent draft riots erupted in New York City on July 13 in the wake of Union victories at Gettysburg and Vicksburg. There the draft riots had racial overtones as low-paid workers blamed African Americans for the war. Rioters set fire to an African American orphanage and began **lynching** African Americans, murdering them in ruthless mob attacks.

Resentment over the draft was also prevalent in the South. There, however, homelessness and hunger overshadowed the draft issue. Women, being the majority of those left at home to confront these issues, eventually took matters into their own hands. In 1863 riots broke out in which women looted stores, hijacked trains, and attacked Confederate supply depots to get bread and other food stored there.

The Road to Surrender
Smoldering Soil, Smoldering Resentment

Until 1864 Lincoln had been disappointed with the quality of his military commanders. Only General Ulysses S. Grant had performed close to Lincoln's expectations. In March the President appointed Grant commander of all Union forces.

One of Grant's first official actions was to order Generals William Tecumseh Sherman and Philip Henry Sheridan to pursue a **scorched earth policy** in the South. Following Grant's instructions, Sherman's and Sheridan's troops burned farmland, plantation homes, and cities in order to destroy the enemy's food, shelter, and supplies. In so doing they broke the South's will to fight. Sheridan raided the Shenandoah Valley, one of the Confederacy's main sources of food, to starve Lee's hungry troops. Sherman led 60,000 men on a "March to the Sea" from Atlanta to Savannah. On the way they burned homesteads and fields, sacked storehouses, and ripped up and twisted railroad tracks to render them useless. Consequently Savannah fell to Sherman in December 1864.

Meanwhile Grant battled Lee in Virginia, hoping eventually to take the Confederate capital of Richmond. Union and Confederate forces clashed in three major battles: in the Virginia wilderness and at Spotsylvania in

May, and at Cold Harbor in early June. In three battles Grant lost almost as many Union soldiers as there were Confederates serving in Lee's army. Yet because of the Union's population advantage, Grant could replace his soldiers, while Lee could not. Grant then settled down to a long siege of Richmond.

By the fall of 1864, Lincoln called home as many Union troops as he could, hoping to generate support for his reelection. The Union victories in the South helped Lincoln win by an electoral college vote of 212 to 21 and a popular majority of more than 400,000 votes.

The War's End

Increasing desertions among Confederate troops prompted Jefferson Davis in November 1864 to allow enslaved African Americans to enlist. The Confederate Congress did not authorize the act, however, until it was too late to take effect. Still, Davis refused to surrender

BROWN BROTHERS

Victory by Siege General Ulysses S. Grant, commander of all Union forces, exuded the confidence of a capable, aggressive soldier. Grant and General Lee had fought together during the Mexican American War. *What were some of the advantages Grant held over his former compatriot? How did Grant destroy Lee's remaining resources?*

Critical Thinking

Identifying Alternatives Ask students whether they think Lincoln was correct to make the Emancipation Proclamation apply only to most slaves in the Confederacy and not to slaves in the Union. Lincoln's main goal was to preserve the Union, but he realized that the North and South could never unite while slavery was sanctioned. His decision was a wise political and military move, but morally it was a compromise designed to reward Union loyalty. Students may wish to debate whether this compromise was necessary by presenting their ideas about decisions Lincoln could have made about slavery in 1862 and the possible outcomes.

ABOLITION OF SLAVERY, 1777–1865

CANADA

Slavery abolished before statehood

PACIFIC OCEAN

Wash. Territory

Oregon

Montana Territory

Idaho Territory

Nevada

Utah Territory

Calif.

Arizona Territory

New Mexico Territory

Dakota Territory

Nebraska Territory

Colorado Territory

Unorganized Territory

Minn.

Wis.

Iowa

Kansas

Ark.

Texas

Mich.

Ill.

Ind.

Mo.

Miss.

La.

Ohio

Ky.

Tenn.

Ala.

Ga.

Maine

Vt.

N.H.

Mass.

N.Y.

Pa.

N.J.

Del.

Md.

W. Va.

Va.

N.C.

S.C.

Fla.

R.I.

Conn.

Gulf of Mexico

ATLANTIC OCEAN

MEXICO

0   250   500 mi.
0   250   500 km
Albers Equal-Area projection

By state before Constitution, 1777–1783

By provisional government of Oregon in 1843

By Northwest Ordinance, Missouri Compromise, or Compromise of 1850

By state action before Civil War, 1784–1858

Entered the Union as free state during the Civil War

By Emancipation Proclamation, 1863

By state action after Emancipation Proclamation, 1863–1865

By Thirteenth Amendment, 1865

Entered as states after 1865

With the North victorious, the abolition of slavery was assured. The process of emancipation had been a gradual one, the result of long-fought political battles and bloodshed. *What legal action liberated enslaved people in the greatest number of states?*

ASSESS

Meeting Lesson Objectives

Each section objective is tested by the section review questions that follow it in parentheses.

1. Analyze the results of the South's decision to form a separate government based on ideals that conflicted with those of the federal government. (1, 2, 3)

2. Understand the effects on African Americans of the Emancipation Proclamation. (1, 3, 4, 5)

MAP STUDY

Kansas and Nevada entered the Union as free states during the Civil War, and California and several northwestern states became free just before the war. Discuss the advantage in terms of power balance that these states gave to the Union.

Answer: *The Emancipation Proclamation in 1863*

 ### Facts on File

Landmark Documents in American History Have students review "Surrender Terms at Appomattox Court House, 1865" and "Farewell to His Troops, Robert E. Lee, 1865" and write about the intent of one of the documents.

---

unless Lincoln acknowledged the South as an independent nation.

Grant and Sheridan finally took Richmond on April 3, 1865, as the city smoldered from the fires set by retreating Confederates. Union troops pursued Lee and his exhausted army. The Confederates made feeble attempts to hold them off, but Lee's army had been reduced to about 30,000 hungry and demoralized men. On the morning of April 9, Lee led his troops into battle for the last time. Union forces had them almost surrounded and badly outnumbered. Facing an almost certain slaughter, Lee decided to surrender. That afternoon he met Grant at Appomattox Court House in Virginia. Grant's terms of surrender ensured that Confederate soldiers would not be prosecuted for treason and that artillery and cavalry soldiers would be permitted to keep their horses. Grant also arranged for 3 days' rations to be sent to the Confederate soldiers. Lee accepted.

When Union troops heard of the surrender, they began firing their guns to celebrate their victory. Grant put an end to the firing. "The war is over," he said, "the rebels are our countrymen again, and the best sign of rejoicing after the victory will be to abstain from all demonstrations."

Lee echoed these sentiments when he knew the Confederate army was defeated.

> The war being at an end, the southern states having laid down their arms, and the question at issue between them and the northern states having been decided, I believe it to be the duty of everyone to unite in the restoration of the country and the reestablishment of peace and harmony.
>
> —Robert E. Lee, April 1865

The human costs of the war were staggering. About 360,000 Union soldiers and 260,000 Confederates lay dead. Another 375,000 soldiers were wounded. Approximately 1 in 3 Confederate soldiers died in the war. These figures do not include deaths from imprisonment such as at Andersonville, a prison camp operated by Confederates in Georgia, where 13,000 out of 32,000 Union prisoners died.

Lincoln as Commander in Chief

Lincoln's main goal had been to preserve the Union. In his second Inaugural Address, he indicated that he would deal compassionately with the South after the war ended:

SECTION TWO   **179**

Cooperative Learning

Making Civil War Chess Sets Explain that Civil War chess sets are popular with collectors and that soldiers and prisoners of war played chess and cards while stationed in camps during the Civil War. Some even made their own sets. A regular chess set can be labeled with names of presidents, generals, spies, doctors, drummers, and foot soldiers from both of the Civil War armies. Have students work in small groups to create their own set and play team chess. Students who know the game can explain the rules. Teams can decide to set up a tournament ladder or play one game, taking turns with each move.

"Peace Among Ourselves" Lincoln asked citizens to work for peace after the war. Matthew Brady's portrait of Lincoln (above) captures the peaceful spirit of the President. *How did Lincoln's agenda at the start of the war account for his postwar policy of leniency toward the South?*

Mourning Throngs of citizens flocked to view the President's open casket and mourn his untimely death. Parades, banners, and memorials trumpeted Lincoln's victories to those who had been disloyal and might see his death as his defeat. *What public memorials followed Lincoln's death?*

VISUAL INSTRUCTION

"Peace Among Ourselves" This Matthew Brady portrait of President Lincoln appears on the five-dollar bill today.

Answer: *Lincoln wanted to repair the Union. His postwar policy continued this aim.*

Mourning Lincoln's funeral became a symbol of Northern victory.

Answer: *cannon fire, bonfires, and bells greeted the funeral train.*

Evaluate

Have students complete the Section Review.

📩 💻 Assign the Section 2 Quiz or use the Testmaker to develop a customized quiz. (Also in Spanish.) **LEP**

Reteach

🎧 Have students listen to the Chapter 6, Section 2 Audiocassette. (Also in Spanish.) **LEP**

Enrich

📩 Have interested students study one of the many films about the Civil War, such as *Glory*. They could recreate one of the scenes from the film to perform for the class.

CLOSE

Point out that the Civil War was the bloodiest in United States history, resulting in the most American casualties. Ask students why this is so. (*Americans fought against Americans; medical care and facilities were primitive.*)

180

Springfield, Illinois. Millions of people lined the route. At night, bonfires and torches lit the way. By day, bells tolled and cannons fired.

Lincoln's second Inaugural Address, read at the cemetery, reminded Americans of his plan "to do all which may achieve and cherish a just, and a lasting peace, among ourselves, and with all nations." The future, however, was in the hands of those who favored harsher measures against the former Confederates.

W ith malice toward none; with charity for all; with firmness in the right, as God gives us to see the right, let us strive on to finish the work we are in; to bind up the nation's wounds; to care for him who shall have borne the battle, and for his widow, and his orphan. . . .

—Abraham Lincoln,
Second Inaugural Address, March 1865

Unfortunately Lincoln never got to carry out his plan. On April 14, 1865, five days after the South surrendered, Confederate sympathizer John Wilkes Booth shot President Lincoln at a theater in Washington, D.C. Lincoln died the next morning. The nation, and indeed the world, mourned his death.

Even those who had sharply criticized Lincoln's policies acknowledged his leadership and accomplishments. The *New Orleans Tribune* stated: "Brethren, we are mourning for a benefactor of our race." An outpouring of sympathy came from Britain and others who had supported the Confederate cause. Admirers as well as critics agreed that replacing Lincoln would be difficult.

A funeral train carried Lincoln's body on a 1,700-mile (2,735.3-km) journey from Washington, D.C., to

SECTION REVIEW

Vocabulary

1. Define: secession, emancipation, lynching, scorched earth policy.

Checking Facts

2. What advantages did the North have upon entering the war? The South?

3. What were the social and economic battles fought during the Civil War?

Critical Thinking

Analyzing Information

4. From what you have learned about Lincoln, why do you think he initiated a postwar policy of leniency toward the South?

Linking Across Time

5. Lincoln's actions helped bring an end to slavery, but African Americans continued to fight for genuine freedom long after the Civil War. What specific effects of slavery do you see in United States policies and culture today?

Section 2 Review Answers

1. secession (172), **emancipation** (176), **lynching** (178), **scorched earth policy** (178)
2. North: population, resources, factories, money; South: trained officers and militia, fighting on own land
3. freeing of slaves; draft riots; new roles for women in business, nursing, and government

4. He wanted to heal the sectional hostility and reunite the nation.
5. Answers will vary. Students might suggest that although freeing the slaves was crucial, the struggle for true freedom and equality has continued up to the present.

Social Studies Skill

COMBINING INFORMATION FROM MAPS

Learning the Skill

Thematic maps aid in the communication of information by presenting place-related data in a concise way. Sometimes two or more maps can convey information that cannot be presented easily on a single map.

Finding Connections

To find and combine geographic patterns:

a. First examine the map on this page to find information about industry and agriculture in 1860.

b. Note any significant patterns. For example, a quick look reveals that New England farmers mainly raised dairy cattle and hay, which are small farm enterprises.

c. Then examine the map on the abolition of slavery on page 179, which shows, for example, that the New England states prohibited slavery before the framing of the Constitution.

d. Try to visualize relationships between the two maps. In each, there are patterns differentiating the North and the South. Combining these maps suggests a state's decisions about slavery or abolition may have related to how the people in that state made a living.

Practicing the Skill

Study the map below and the map on page 179 and answer the following questions:

1. What relationship do you see between plantation crops and the abolition of slavery?

2. Compare industry in cotton-growing states and in other states. What pattern do you notice?

3. What connection can you make between a state's economy and its stand on slavery?

4. What was produced in the West and Midwest?

5. How might the economies of the West and Midwest have affected the slavery debate nationwide?

Applying the Skill

Using two other maps, draw five conclusions about the combined information they present.

Additional Practice

For additional practice, see Reinforcing Skills on page 193.

AGRICULTURE AND INDUSTRY, 1860

By 1860 textile and shoe factories fueled the economies of New York and New England, while plantation crops such as cotton and tobacco were the mainstay of the Southern economy. *What states depended on flour milling?*

TEACH

This skill teaches students how to use the information from two or more maps in conjunction with each other. Students discover that each map conveys information on its own, but in juxtaposition, two related maps can suggest more than either can alone. Point out that this is a case in which the whole is more than the "sum of its parts."

MAP STUDY

Point out that the map clearly shows industrialization in the North and the agricultural development in the South.

Answer: *Wisconsin, Iowa, Illinois, Indiana, Missouri, Michigan, Ohio, New York, Pennsylvania*

Additional Practice

Have students complete the Chapter 6 Skill Reinforcement Activity.

Practicing the Skill Answers

1. Answers will vary. The plantation economy of the South required large labor forces to be profitable. The South felt that it was dependent upon an enslaved labor force.

2. Answers will vary. Industry was relatively undeveloped in slave states but was a significant part of the economy of the Northeast.

3. Answers will vary. Most states with industrialized economies were among the first to abolish slavery. States with agricultural economies were likely to be slave states.

4. Answers will vary. Most of the Western states depended upon mining raw materials. Midwestern states produced lumber and flour, as well as mining ore.

5. Answers will vary. These economies were not primarily agricultural. Therefore, they may have weakened the case for slavery.

TEACH

Making the Historical Connection

After four years of civil war, the economic condition of the South was disastrous. The states of the Confederacy had no currency and no capital. Banks had failed, shops were empty, and schools were few. Where the troops of Sheridan and Sherman had marched, "scorched earth" was a reality—the material basis of daily life had been destroyed.

FYI

Ely S. Parker When General Lee shook hands with Colonel Parker, the Seneca staff officer who recorded the surrender, he said, "I am glad to see one real American here." Parker answered, "We are all Americans." When Grant became president in 1869, he appointed his former aide Parker as commissioner of Indian affairs.

One Day in History

Sunday, April 9, 1865

MARKET BASKET

Here is where a dollar will go:

Stereoscopic
pictures $1.50/dozen
Barnum's American Museum
ticket . . . . 15¢ child
. . . . 25¢ adult
Theater ticket . . . . 25¢ child
. . . . 50¢ adult
Printing press $3,500

LINEN LINED

Collar $1.25/dozen
Coffee . . . . 7 to 25¢/lb.
Pocket watch $10
Artificial leg $75

HIGH IMPACT PHOTOGRAPHY, TIME-LIFE BOOKS

Daguerreotypes . . . . 25¢ to $1
Medical consultation fee . . $5
Harper's Weekly
magazine . . . . 10¢
New York Times
newspaper . . . . 3¢
Yarn . . . . 2¢/spool
Stove polish . . . . 10¢/cake
Sarsaparilla
compound $1/bottle

LOVELL THOMAS © NATIONAL GEOGRAPHIC SOCIETY

Dignity in Defeat Rising to this sorrowful occasion, General Lee, in full dress uniform, agrees to peace terms with General Grant and signs the articles of surrender.

Confederates Surrender

Union Victory! Peace! General Lee Surrenders

APPOMATTOX COURT HOUSE, VIRGINIA—This afternoon General Robert E. Lee surrendered the Army of Northern Virginia to General Ulysses S. Grant, ending four years of bloody civil war and ensuring the survival of the American Union. Officers and men of the Confederate army will be allowed to return to their homes, and officers will retain their side arms and private property. All former Confederate fighters will be required to swear and sign an oath of loyalty to the Union.

The details of the treaty were negotiated at the home of a man named McLean, the same man who saw the first bombshell of the war fall on his front lawn. Colonel Ely S. Parker, a Seneca man and an aide to General Grant, recorded the proceedings.

Background Information

Flag of Surrender Joshua Chamberlain, who commanded two Union brigades at Appomattox, recorded his first sight of the flag of surrender on the morning of April 9: "Suddenly rose to sight another form . . . a soldierly young figure, a Confederate staff officer undoubtedly. Now I see the white flag earnestly borne . . . like a wraith of morning mist. . . . But it bore a mighty message . . . above the dark and crimsoned streams that never can wash themselves away."

NATION: Maria Mitchell, discoverer of comet, is appointed to chair at Vassar; she becomes the first woman astronomy professor in the nation.

Editorial

APRIL 1, 1865, from the *New Orleans Tribune*, an African American daily newspaper

> *Before 1863, the planters said that it was for the sake of the negroes that they kept them in slavery; it was from a feeling of humanity that they retained in bondage a race of men whom they proclaimed unfit to lie under any other status. . . . going so far as to have them whipped and put into the stocks—as a means of promoting their advancement. . . .*
>
> *The planters defended slavery on the ground of sympathy for the negro. But it was all shame. They clung to slavery for the sake of making money. There is no disputing about it.*

Free Mail Delivery

WASHINGTON, D.C.—Mail will now be delivered free in all cities with populations of 50,000 or more. Recent improvements in rail and steamship transport make this free delivery possible.

Actor Edwin Booth, brother of John Wilkes Booth, appears in *Hamlet*.

MUSIC

"Battle Hymn of the Republic"

"When Johnny Comes Marching Home"

"Follow the Drinking Gourd"

"Many Thousand Gone"

"Oh, Susanna"

"Swanee River"

"My Old Kentucky Home"

Owner P.T. Barnum has improved his museum by hiring trapper Grizzly Adams to stock the menagerie.

AMUSEMENTS

At Barnum's American Museum:

The Great Dancing Giraffe

Punch and Judy

Bohemian Glass Blowers

Two Glass Steam Engines in Motion

Prof. Hutchins, lightning calculator

Poultry, pigeon, and rabbit show

TIME CAPSULE

1865

AMERICAN LIFE

March 3: Freedmen's Bureau is established.

March 4: Lincoln gives his second Inaugural Address.

April 14: Lincoln is shot by John Wilkes Booth.

May 10: Jefferson Davis is captured in Georgia.

June 23: Colonels Stand Watie and Peter B. Pitchlynn, the Confederacy's Native American allies, finally surrender their troops.

December 2: Thirteenth Amendment, prohibiting slavery, is ratified.

Mark Twain leaps to fame with his story "The Celebrated Jumping Frog of Calaveras County."

Walt Whitman's poems in *Drum-Taps* recount his experiences as a nurse.

Atlantic cable is laid.

First oil pipeline is built in Pennsylvania.

Baseball convention is held in New York; beginning of professionalism.

CLOSE

The Civil War dominated American daily life for four years. Ask: How did the popular songs listed on page 183 reflect the war years? (*They included marching songs, spirituals about escape from slavery, and nostalgic songs about the South in peacetime.*)

Oral History

Role Playing Have students pair up. The first student can take the role of a person who was present on April 9, 1865, at Appomattox—perhaps General Lee, General Grant, the recording officer, or a Union or Confederate soldier. The second student can be the interviewer, using questions prepared in advance. Then the second student can choose a role, with the first student acting as interviewer. Students should write up their interview results and keep them in their portfolios.

FOCUS

Section Objectives

1. Explore the possible approaches the North might have taken toward the reconstruction of the South.
2. Explain how Reconstruction altered the relationship between the President and Congress in favor of legislative supremacy.
3. Analyze Reconstruction in terms of gains and losses for African Americans.

Bellringer Activity

While taking attendance at the beginning of the class period, display **Section Focus Transparency 18**, and have students answer the questions. (Or use the blackline master.)

VISUAL INSTRUCTION

Exodusters Frederick Douglass opposed the exodus, arguing that the government should protect citizens wherever they lived and that emigration was not a cure for oppression.

Ask: What were the exodusters fleeing from when they left Louisiana and Mississippi? *(poverty and terrorism)*

SECTION 3

Reconstruction

FEBRUARY 24, 1879: BANKS OF THE MISSISSIPPI RIVER

FROM HARPER'S WEEKLY, MAY 1, 1880

Exodusters
This drawing from an 1880 *Harper's Weekly* contrasts the new exodus with the old (inset), as African Americans fled the South.

HUNDREDS OF AFRICAN AMERI-CANS, WITH THEIR BELONG-INGS BUNDLED ON THEIR BACKS, WAITED ON THE SHORES OF THE MISSISSIPPI RIVER FOR THE STEAMER THAT WOULD CARRY THEM ACROSS TO ST. LOUIS. From there they would head by train to Kansas, where they hoped to begin new lives. These people were called the Exodusters, so named because they left their homes to make better lives in the dusty new land, just as the Israelites had done centuries earlier in their exodus from Egypt to Canaan.

During the exodus of 1879, more than 20,000 African Americans migrated to Kansas, their Canaan, or "promised land." A Louisiana preacher explained that they "were not emigrating because of inducements held out to them by parties in Kansas, but because they were terrorized, robbed, and murdered by the bulldozing desperadoes of Louisiana and Mississippi." The African Americans hoped that their journey to Kansas would take them far from the poverty and terrorism that they experienced in the South despite the many promises of the postwar government.

Presidential Reunion Plans
Attempts at Reconciliation

In 1863 before the war had ended, Lincoln made plans to reestablish state governments in the South that would be loyal to the Union after the war. According to Lincoln's plan, for a state to be recognized as legitimate, 10 percent of the men eligible to vote in 1860 had to have sworn allegiance to the Union.

Andrew Johnson, who assumed the presidency after Lincoln's assassination, had expressed harsh sentiments toward Confederate "traitors" during the war. He therefore surprised many Northerners when he began to promote policies that seemed to continue Lincoln's intentions of "malice toward none." Congress was not in session when Johnson took office, so he proceeded with

AS YOU READ

Vocabulary
▶ amnesty
▶ black codes
▶ sharecropping
▶ carpetbagger
▶ gerrymandering

Think About . . .
▶ the possible approaches the North might have taken toward restoring the economic and social fabric of the defeated South.

▶ how Reconstruction altered the roles of Congress and the President.
▶ how Reconstruction brought both gains and hardships to African Americans.

184 CHAPTER 6 CIVIL WAR AND RECONSTRUCTION

Section 3 Resources

REPRODUCIBLE RESOURCES

📁 Lesson Plan 6-3
📁 Vocabulary and Guided Reading Activity 6-3
📁 Section 3 Quiz
📁 Chapter 6 Test
📁 Performance Assessment Activity 6
📁 Reteaching Activity 6

📁 Enrichment Activity 6
📁 Geography in History Activity 6

MULTIMEDIA RESOURCES

📷 Section Focus Transparency 18
📷 Beginnings to 1900 Transparencies 19, 20, 21

💿 Landmark Documents in American History
💿 The American People: Fabric of a Nation
🎧 American Music: Cultural Traditions
💻 Testmaker and Vocabulary PuzzleMaker
🎧 Chapter 6 Digest Audiocassette

his plans for Reconstruction—the process of restoring relations with the Confederate states.

In a Reconstruction proclamation issued in May of 1865, Johnson granted **amnesty,** or pardon, to Confederates who would sign an oath of loyalty to the Union. Political and military leaders and landowners whose property was worth more than $20,000 had to apply for special pardons. Johnson granted such pardons regularly. In addition Johnson appointed provisional governors and set forth minimal requirements for reorganizing Southern state governments. By December 1865 all former Confederate states except Texas had fulfilled the requirements and had elected representatives to Congress. Johnson announced that the Union had been restored.

When Congress reconvened in December, it refused to seat the newly elected Southern representatives. Some members of Congress criticized Johnson's leniency toward the South. They pointed out that Johnson had done nothing to prevent new Southern state governments from passing **black codes,** laws that severely restricted the rights of newly freed African Americans. In Mississippi, for example, black codes prohibited free African Americans from receiving farmland and stipulated that freed African American orphans could be assigned to forced labor. Throughout 1866 and 1867, tensions increased as the President and Congress battled over Reconstruction.

Military Occupation

In 1867 Congress passed a series of Reconstruction Acts over Johnson's veto. These acts abolished the state governments formed under Johnson's plan. They also divided the South into five military districts, each under the command of a general. Federal troops were stationed in each district to carry out the process of readmitting states to the Union. The functions of the military forces, according to the acts, were "to protect all persons in their rights of person and property, to suppress insurrection, disorder, and violence, and to punish, or cause to be punished, all disturbers of the public peace and criminals."

The provision for military occupation of the Southern states changed the tone of Reconstruction. Leadership was in the hands of Congress, and the army administered Congress's plan. Many Northerners felt that the presence of federal troops was necessary to bring about political and social changes in the South. General Sherman, however, was more astute and ex-

Federal Troops Union soldiers roamed the streets of major Southern cities, protecting the rights of the recently freed. This cartoon shows how two Southern women might have looked upon such troops. *According to Sherman, what changes were impossible to accomplish with military presence?*

HISTORICAL PICTURES/STOCK MONTAGE, INC.

pressed a different view: "No matter what change we may desire in the feelings and thoughts of people South, we cannot accomplish it by force. Nor can we afford to maintain there an army large enough to hold them in subjugation [control]."

The Supreme Court's Role

In the battle between the executive and legislative branches over Reconstruction, the Supreme Court at first seemed to support President Johnson's position. In *ex parte Milligan,* the Court ruled that civilians could not be tried in military courts when civil courts were functioning. Northerners defied this decision, however, and made military tribunals part of legislation. The Court further stated that the administration of military justice in the South was "mere lawless violence." In *ex parte Garland,* a case that involved a law requiring loyalty oaths from former Confederate teachers and others who wanted to resume their jobs, the Court handed down a split decision. The majority opinion ruled that such oaths were invalid. The dissenting opinion held that such requirements were valid qualifications for officeholders and voters.

The Court soon upheld Congress's authority to reconstruct the states. In 1867 Georgia and Mississippi sought an injunction preventing President Johnson from enforcing Congress's Reconstruction Acts. The Supreme Court refused on the grounds that executive functions were not subject to judicial restraint. Johnson, who had relied on the Court's record of sympathy toward the South, began to feel increasingly isolated.

SECTION THREE **185**

Cooperative Learning

Expressing Points of View Organize the class into three groups representing people of the South, people of the North, and freed African Americans. Have each group prepare a presentation in which they explain what they would want President Johnson to do on their behalf. Be sure groups understand that each student should have a role to play. 🖳

TEACH

Guided Practice

L2 **Discussion** Point out to students that no President has faced a greater challenge than Andrew Johnson did at the end of the Civil War. The fact that he had been Vice President for only six weeks when Lincoln was assassinated made it even more difficult. Have students predict whether people of the North or of the South would cause more difficulty for Johnson in the first four years after the war.

Show students Beginnings to 1900 Transparencies 19, 20, and 21 and have them complete the activity sheets.

VISUAL INSTRUCTION

Federal Troops Federal military supervision of Reconstruction was relatively small-scale and short-lived. It did not amount to a full-fledged military occupation of the South. As new state governments became stable, federal troops were withdrawn, and state militias took their place.

Answer: *changes in the feelings and thoughts of the people of the South*

Facts on File

Landmark Documents in American History Have students review "Black Codes (Mississippi), 1865" and write a paragraph about the intent of the document.

VISUAL INSTRUCTION

Influence at the Polls In 1867 referendums in the South on the question of holding constitutional conventions to reconstruct the states drew 703,459 African American voters and 660,181 white voters.

Answer: *the Radical Republican faction*

CHART STUDY

Ask: What was the Enforcement Act?

Answer: *It allowed the government to enforce the provisions of the Fourteenth and Fifteenth Amendments.*

Notes

_____
_____
_____
_____
_____
_____
_____
_____
_____
_____
_____
_____
_____
_____
_____
_____
_____
_____

Congressional Plans
The Push to Reform the South

The Radical Republican faction of Congress had been formulating plans for Reconstruction since the early 1860s. These Republicans earned the label "radical" because they were strongly antislavery and were not willing to forgive the Confederates. Lincoln's leniency had outraged them. They wanted sweeping political change in the South, which they believed would occur only with the strong presence of Union troops. As Thaddeus Stevens, a leading Radical Republican, said, any valid unifying plan "must revolutionize the southern institutions, habits, and manner . . . or all our blood and treasure have been spent in vain."

The Radical Republicans had responded to Lincoln's terms by passing the Wade-Davis Bill in 1864. This bill would have required a majority of a state's white male citizenry to swear both past and future loyalty to the Union; only then would the federal government recognize the state's government. Considering the bill too harsh, Lincoln had vetoed it.

Johnson further outraged the Radical Republicans by promoting Lincoln's lenient policies. In 1866 Northerners fought Johnson's policies by electing a Radical Republican majority to Congress. The Radical Republicans quickly enacted legislation designed to punish the former Confederate states, to increase Republican power in the South, and to create conditions that would promote economic development and racial equality in the South.

Much of the legislation passed during Reconstruction increased the rights and freedoms of African Americans. This benefited the Republicans in two ways: it made the Republicans popular with a large new pool of voters, and it diminished white Southerners' ability to dominate the South politically and economically. In 1866 Congress passed the Civil Rights Act, which granted

THE BETTMANN ARCHIVE

Influence at the Polls *Harper's Weekly* celebrated full citizenship for African Americans with an illustration showing a soldier, a businessman, and an artisan casting their first ballots. *What political faction promoted enfranchisement of African American citizens?*

citizenship to African Americans and prohibited states from diminishing the rights accompanying this citizenship. In addition ratification of the Fourteenth Amendment in 1868 prevented states from denying rights and privileges to any American citizen. The Fifteenth Amendment of 1870 guaranteed that no citizen could be denied the right to vote based on race, color, or former servitude. The Enforcement Act of 1870 empowered federal authorities to prosecute anyone who violated the Fourteenth or Fifteenth Amendments.

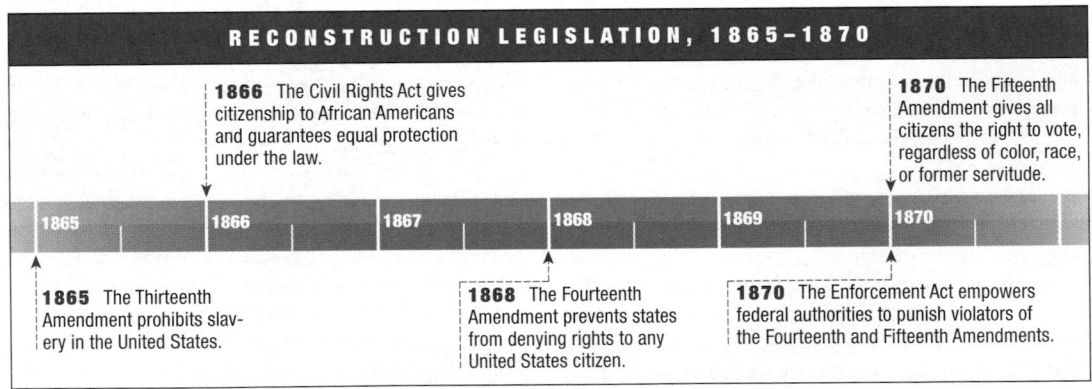

RECONSTRUCTION LEGISLATION, 1865–1870

1866 The Civil Rights Act gives citizenship to African Americans and guarantees equal protection under the law.

1870 The Fifteenth Amendment gives all citizens the right to vote, regardless of color, race, or former servitude.

1865	1866	1867	1868	1869	1870

1865 The Thirteenth Amendment prohibits slavery in the United States.

1868 The Fourteenth Amendment prevents states from denying rights to any United States citizen.

1870 The Enforcement Act empowers federal authorities to punish violators of the Fourteenth and Fifteenth Amendments.

Meeting Special Needs

Oral Learners Help students who learn best orally to set a purpose for reading the section. Have them speculate about the problems that 4 million enslaved people would confront when they were suddenly set free but had no money, houses, farmland, or jobs.

Radical Republican **Thaddeus Stevens,** a Radical Republican leader in Congress, wanted African Americans to receive full rights as citizens. *Who was the chief opponent to Stevens's proposals?*

Radical Reconstruction

New state governments were established under the Reconstruction Acts. White Southerners who protested the acts refused to vote in the elections that set up these governments. Their protest had two results: Republicans, who had little support in the South before the Civil War, won control of every new state government; and African Americans began to exert influence at the polls. One white Southerner wrote in his diary:

> B ills have passed both houses of Congress which repudiate and destroy the present civil government of the lately seceded states and substitute in their place a military government. Most of the whites are disenfranchised [deprived of the right to vote] and ineligible for office, whilst the negroes are invested with the right of voting.
>
> —Henry William Ravenel, South Carolina, February 24, 1867

When African Americans were guaranteed their right to vote, they began to exert influence at the polls in states in which they were a majority of the population: Alabama, Florida, Louisiana, Mississippi, and South Carolina. African American representatives outnumbered white representatives in the South Carolina legislature.

Radical Republicans pushed their legislation through Congress in spite of President Johnson's vetoes. In 1866

Johnson vetoed the Civil Rights Act and a bill that would have enabled the Freedmen's Bureau, an organization that assisted formerly enslaved people, to continue. Congress overrode both vetoes.

The Invisible Empire

At about the same time that Johnson was undermining African Americans' efforts to obtain equality, white supremacist organizations such as the Ku Klux Klan began terrorizing them. These organizations used intimidation and violence to prevent African Americans from voting or holding positions of power. In this environment of violence and hatred, mobs of Southern whites periodically lashed out against the newly freed citizens among them. For example, in May 1866 in Memphis, Tennessee, a crowd of white supremacists killed 46 African Americans and 2 white sympathizers.

The Impeachment Effort

Johnson's attempts to undermine congressional legislation coupled with his inability or lack of desire to control terrorist organizations further angered Radical Republicans. Their anger peaked when the President defied the Tenure of Office Act, which required Senate approval for the removal of cabinet members. Johnson failed to obtain that approval before he fired Secretary of War Edwin Stanton in 1868.

The House responded by voting to impeach the President on 11 charges of misconduct. These included charges that Johnson had violated the Tenure of Office Act. The House appointed 7 representatives to present the charges to the Senate. Johnson was defended by a

The Invisible Empire of the South Two African American attorneys are brutalized by the Ku Klux Klan in Pulaski, Tennessee, on Christmas Eve, 1865. The Klan began as an elite club for Confederate veterans but within months was terrorizing citizens with racist attacks. *What did the Ku Klux Klan seek to prevent?*

NATIONAL GEOGRAPHIC SOCIETY

 Videodisc

GTV: The American People: Fabric of a Nation

Side 2, Chapter 8
Title: *The Dream, Deferred*
Subject: Equal rights during Reconstruction—and now
Ask: How were African Americans able to secure their rights during Reconstruction? *(The federal government protected them.)*

VISUAL INSTRUCTION

Radical Republican In 1867 Stevens said this about African American suffrage: "If it be just, it should not be denied; . . . if it be punishment to traitors, they deserve it."

Answer: *President Johnson*

The Invisible Empire of the South Congress passed laws aimed at the Klan in 1870 and 1871. Hundreds of members were arrested, and many were found guilty of conspiracy.

Answer: *They tried to prevent African Americans from voting and holding positions of power.*

Portfolio Project

African American Higher Education
Suggest that students find out about African American colleges and universities that were established during Reconstruction. These include Fisk University and Howard University among many others. Have each student choose one such school and find out when, where, and how it was founded. Then the student can write a brief report and include it in his or her portfolio.

187

Independent Practice

 Research One issue in President Johnson's impeachment trial was his refusal to ask Congress's approval before dismissing his secretary of war. Ask students if a President today still needs congressional approval to dismiss a cabinet officer. Have them research the impeachment process and write reports to be included in their portfolios.

Have students complete the Chapter 6, Section 3 Vocabulary and Guided Reading Activity. (Also in Spanish.) **LEP**

Facts on File

Landmark Documents in American History Have students review "Tenure of Office Act, 1867" and write a paragraph about the intent of the document.

VISUAL INSTRUCTION

Elected to Office Hiram B. Revels was chosen to fill the unexpired Senate term of Jefferson Davis. Although he was a well-educated pastor and had helped to organize two African American regiments, the Senate debated his credentials for three days.

Answer: *emancipation, equal protection, the right to vote*

---

team of lawyers. Chief Justice Salmon P. Chase presided over the trial. Johnson did not attend.

The trial dragged on for 8 weeks. Johnson's attackers accused him of everything from alcoholism to plotting Lincoln's murder. The President's lawyers presented a purely legal defense, arguing that the Tenure of Office Act was unconstitutional and did not apply to Stanton. Conviction required a two-thirds majority of the Senate. The final tally of 35 for conviction and 19 against acquitted Johnson by 1 vote.

Limits on Freedom
Freed but Not Free

At the end of the Civil War, most African Americans expected their lives to improve radically. A formerly enslaved woman recalled the excitement she and other freed men and women had felt when they learned of the Union victory and their new freedom:

> When the soldiers marched in to tell us that we were free . . . I remember one woman. She jumped on a barrel and she shouted. She jumped off and she shouted. She jumped back on again and shouted some more. She kept that up for a long time, just jumping on a barrel and back off again.
> —Anna Woods, a Federal Writers' Project interview, 1930s

After the initial happiness passed, however, African Americans realized that they would have to struggle to secure their rights as a freed people. At an 1865 convention in Alabama, African Americans demanded "exactly the same rights, privileges, and immunities as are enjoyed by white men—we ask nothing more and will be content with nothing less. . . ."

The Freedmen's Bureau, an office of the War Department, was established to provide freed African Americans with food, teachers, legal aid, and other assistance. The bureau also distributed horses, mules, and land that had been confiscated during the war. With the

THE BETTMANN ARCHIVE

Elected to Office This lithograph shows the first African Americans who served in Congress. Top row, left to right: Representatives Robert C. De Large of South Carolina, Jefferson H. Long of Georgia. Bottom row, left to right: Senator H.R. Revels of Mississippi, Representatives Benjamin Turner of Alabama, Josiah T. Walls of Florida, and Joseph H. Rainy and R. Brown Elliot, both of South Carolina. *What important civil rights did African Americans win during the 1860s?*

Extending the Content

Freedmen's Bureau The bureau's relief efforts compare favorably with the great efforts made in other wars and depressions. Nor was its work confined to African Americans: 21 million rations distributed between 1865 and 1869 included 5.5 million issued to white people. Substantial redistribution of land, however, was not attempted. The "40 acres and a mule" that many freedmen had been led to expect was not to be. Although the Freedmen's Bureau did distribute some confiscated lands to freedmen, it mainly helped them to find employers and work for wages. Ask students why they think land redistribution was so hard to accomplish.

The Freedmen's Bureau Education was the bureau's primary goal. A former Union commander, O.O. Howard (left), led the organization. The children here are students at one of many Freedmen's Bureau schools in the South. *What role did the Freedmen's Bureau play in the fight for equality?*

bureau's help, about 40,000 African Americans were able to establish their own farms in Georgia and South Carolina. In the face of much opposition, African Americans obtained an education. At first, the Freedmen's Bureau and charitable organizations paid the cost of African American education. After 1871 the states began to take over the support of their own segregated schools. Many white Southerners resented African American schools, and teachers often faced intimidation or physical abuse. Progress was slow. Nevertheless, illiteracy among African Americans fell from more than 90 percent in 1860 to about 80 percent in 1870.

Voting Power

During Reconstruction African American voters exercised their political power for the first time. W.E.B. Du Bois, an important African American leader of the early 1900s, wrote: "With northern white leadership, the Negro voters . . . proved apt pupils in politics. They developed their own leadership. They gained clearer and clearer conceptions of how their political powers could be used for their own good."

African Americans were elected to office at the local, state, and national levels. Between 1869 and 1876, 2 African Americans served in the Senate and 14 served in the House of Representatives. Most of these men had been enslaved or were born of enslaved parents. Some critics claimed "they left no mark on the legislation of their time; none of them, in comparison with their white associates, attained the least distinction." Others observed: "The colored men who took seats in both Senate and House did not appear ignorant or helpless. They were as a rule studious, earnest, ambitious men, whose public conduct . . . would be honorable to any race."

Sharecropping

For many formerly enslaved African Americans, life changed little in the years after the Civil War. President Johnson returned confiscated estates to the previous Confederate owners. Freed people who had established farms on that land found themselves back on the plantations. Some worked under contract for meager wages. Others were forced into **sharecropping**, a system in which a wealthy patron would give seeds, supplies, and a small parcel of land to a farmer in exchange for a portion of the crop. If the patron required a large portion of the crop, the sharecropper might not be able to survive on what remained. If the crop failed, the sharecropper usually wound up hopelessly in debt to the patron.

"Freedom wasn't no difference I know of," complained one man. "I works for Marse John just the same." Many newly freed people did stay on the same plantations, where they worked under the same overseer. The wages or share of the crop they received hardly made up for the fact that freedom in no way meant equality.

Grant's Presidency
Corruption and Crisis

In 1868 the Republican Ulysses S. Grant won the presidency by a margin of 300,000 votes. The more than 500,000 African Americans who voted in the election certainly contributed to Grant's victory. Nevertheless, during Grant's two terms in office, from 1869 to 1877, the government began paying less and less attention to the problems of prejudice, discrimination, and racial harassment.

The Freedmen's Bureau The bureau faced chaotic conditions. According to General Howard, "The freed people were in a state of great excitement and uncertainty. . . . Many were afraid to remain on the same soil that they had tilled as slaves lest by some trick they might find themselves again in bondage."

Answer: *It provided food, schools, teachers, legal aid, and other help.*

 History and the Humanities

 American Music: Cultural Traditions— "Roll, Jordan, Roll" by the Fisk University Jubilee Singers

Facts on File

Landmark Documents in American History Have students review "First Inaugural Address, Ulysses S. Grant, 1869" and write a paragraph about the intent of the document.

Cultural Perspectives

Sharecropping More than 75 percent of African Americans were still living in former Confederate states after the Civil War. Most of them had to make some adjustment to the economics of farming, which usually meant sharecropping. Few African Americans had capital with which to buy farmland; those who did often found whites reluctant to sell to them. As late as 1890, African Americans owned only 120,738 farms in the South, always with relatively small acreage. The hard life of the sharecropper was one of the reasons for the northward migration of African Americans that began toward the end of the century.

ASSESS

Meeting Lesson Objectives

Each section objective is tested by the section review question(s) that follows it in parentheses.

1. Explore the possible approaches the North might have taken toward the reconstruction of the South. (1, 5)
2. Explain how Reconstruction altered the relationship between the President and Congress in favor of legislative supremacy. (2, 3)
3. Analyze Reconstruction in terms of gains and losses few African Americans. (4)

Government Scandal

Scandal and corruption plagued Grant's administration. A congressional investigation in the mid-1870s found that whiskey distillers and tax officials were stealing excise taxes from the government, and it linked a member of Grant's staff to the scandal. In addition, Grant's secretary of war, William W. Belknap, was accused of accepting bribes. Even Grant wrongly accepted personal gifts.

At the time successful politicians commonly rewarded their supporters by appointing them to government positions. These appointed individuals often lacked the skills and experience necessary to do their jobs. Quite often they were also greedy and dishonest. This was true of a number of the personal friends, relatives, and fellow army officers Grant appointed.

Such was also the case in the newly created Republican state governments in the South. Although these governments did implement legislation that helped to ease the South's social and economic difficulties, many of the Northerners involved in local Southern administrations were inexperienced and even corrupt. White Southerners called these Northern transplants **carpetbaggers,** mocking them for having arrived in the South with only the possessions they had been able to stuff inside their luggage. Most white Southerners believed the carpetbaggers wanted only to turn a profit or rise to power at the expense of the South. In addition, African Americans newly elected to political positions were often blamed for government wastefulness and dishonesty.

Democratic Success

As one after another of the carpetbag governments came under attack, Democrats began to regain control of Southern legislatures. They also used some underhanded tactics to neutralize the issues of equality that had begun to affect the election process.

One such technique, called **gerrymandering,** involved redividing voting districts to decrease African American representation in a particular area. Another tactic was to institute a poll tax, which the Democrats managed to do in several states. In these states voting became a privilege that required payment of a fee. Poll taxes excluded poor citizens of both races from the voting process. By 1875, aided by these strategies, Democrats had gained control of the House of Representatives for the first time since before the Civil War. By 1877 they had completely reestablished control over Southern state governments.

The Panic of 1873

Grant's administration faced economic as well as political problems. A financial crisis during his second term in office left the country in economic difficulty. The crisis was touched off in 1873 when financier Jay Cooke suddenly closed his Philadelphia bank. The bank closing prompted a panic during which 5,000 businesses closed, and thousands of people lost their jobs.

As the panic spread, concern for economic reform quickly replaced concern for social reform. In the North the demands of unemployed workers for economic relief supplanted demands for racial equality. By 1874 one-quarter of the population of New York City was out of work. In Chicago 20,000 unemployed people protested in the streets, demanding that government officials solve the problems of the economy.

In the South the sharecropping system cheated many African American farmers out of owning land or reaping profits from their labors. Meanwhile white farmers suffered devastating losses during these hard times and often accused African Americans of causing their economic troubles.

African Americans living in Northern states also faced economic and social problems. Although they had gained access to public education and transportation, they were usually trapped in low-paying, unskilled jobs; lived in poor housing; and had little voice in shaping government policies. Unlike the large freed population in the South, Northern African Americans comprised only 2 percent of the population. In both the North and the South, these newly enfranchised citizens had to struggle to claim the political and social rights that Reconstruction promised.

In the midst of the economic and social upheaval of Reconstruction, however, the United States celebrated its centennial in 1876. Ten million people paid 50 cents each to visit the Grand Exposition in Philadelphia. Displays of the nation's art, fashion, produce, appliances, and industrial development greeted the visitors. Many Americans were ready to push the problems of the Civil War into the past and forge on optimistically into the nation's second century.

The End of Reconstruction
Prejudice and Exodus

In the wake of social and economic crises, government scandals, and outbreaks of violence, the Radical Republicans lost their political power. So, too, the Radical Republican program of Reconstruction came to an end. No longer supported by the majority of voters, Republicans attempted to regain their foothold in the South by backing a moderate candidate for President—Rutherford B. Hayes, who appealed to both the North and South.

Hayes ran against Democratic candidate Samuel Tilden in what was possibly the closest presidential election battle in American history. A dispute arose over the

Critical Thinking

Analyzing Information Ulysses S. Grant's second term of office was marked by several financial scandals involving members of his administration. Disappointed, he told Congress that the failures had been "errors of judgment, not of intent." Ask students what qualifications they think Grant had for the presidency. List on the board the qualifications mentioned, and have students rank them in order of importance.

election returns from four states. Three of these states were Southern states still under Reconstruction rule. The Democrats insisted that the majority of the people in these states favored Tilden but had been prevented from registering their votes. To settle the dispute, Congress appointed a special electoral commission.

To get Hayes elected, Republicans made many concessions to the Democrats, among which was the agreement to withdraw the Union troops that had been stationed in the South since the end of the war. These votes assured, Hayes won the election by one electoral vote. Shortly thereafter, the last Union troops withdrew from the South.

Prejudice Persists

Without the presence of the Union army to combat terrorism, the rights of Southern African Americans were gravely jeopardized. Even before Hayes's election, the Supreme Court's 1876 ruling in *United States* v. *Cruikshank* overturned the Enforcement Act of 1870. The Court ruled that a state could not legally discriminate against African Americans, but nonstate institutions and individuals could. Specifically, the Court had overturned the convictions of three whites for their participation in a bloody massacre of African Americans on the grounds that the three individuals did not specify that their actions were racially motivated.

In subsequent administrations, the Supreme Court's support of African American rights diminished still further. For example, in 1883, during Chester A. Arthur's presidency, the Supreme Court nullified the Civil Rights Act of 1875.

Reconstruction Appraised

Although the period of Reconstruction had ended and Republicans and Democrats had temporarily united, African Americans felt as if their needs had been forgotten. Most of the legal decisions that had advanced African American rights during Reconstruction had been overturned. Furthermore the Radical Republican governments had failed to correct the problem of unequal land distribution in the South, a measure that might have provided the economic leverage that African Americans needed to protect their rights.

Discontented and afraid for their lives, African Americans left the South by the thousands. Many moved to Northern urban centers, such as Chicago and New York

NATIONAL MUSEUM OF AMERICAN ART, WASHINGTON DC/ART RESOURCE, NY

Losing Ground By the turn of the century, conditions for African Americans in the South were in many ways indistinguishable from slavery, much like the scene in R.N. Brooke's painting, *Dog Swap.* *How were the civil rights gains during Reconstruction dismantled after 1870?*

City. Some moved to Kansas, a state in which there was an abundance of fertile land open to homesteaders and a strong Republican government that promised unbiased treatment under the law. There, many began to enjoy a decent existence.

SECTION REVIEW

Vocabulary

1. Define: amnesty, black codes, sharecropping, carpetbagger, gerrymandering.

Checking Facts

2. What legislation passed during Reconstruction aided African Americans?

3. How did Congress react to Johnson's vetoes of Radical Republican bills in 1866?

Critical Thinking

Determining Cause and Effect

4. Why did many Northern politicians stop concentrating on securing rights for African Americans after Grant's election?

Linking Across Time

5. Did Reconstruction mend the rift between North and South? Why or why not? What examples of sectionalism exist today within the two regions?

SECTION THREE **191**

VISUAL INSTRUCTION

Losing Ground The rifle is one sign that the people in the painting are free.

Answer: *Withdrawal of Union troops; Enforcement Act and the Civil Rights Act overturned*

Evaluate

Have students complete the Section Review.

☞ 🔘 Assign the Section 3 Quiz or use the Testmaker to develop a customized quiz.

☞ 🔘 Assign the Chapter 6 Test or use the Testmaker to develop a customized test.

☞ 🔘 Have students complete the Chapter 6 Performance Assessment Activity.

Reteach

🎧 Have students listen to the Chapter 6, Section 3 Audiocassette. (Also in Spanish.) **LEP**

☞ Have students complete the Chapter 6 Reteaching Activity. (Also in Spanish.) **LEP**

Enrich

☞ Have students complete the Chapter 6 Enrichment Activity. (Also in Spanish.) **LEP**

☞ Have students complete the Chapter 6 Geography in History Activity.

CLOSE

Ask students how conditions changed for African Americans in the South from before the war to after Reconstruction. *(Though they were free, they had lost rights gained at the start of Reconstruction.)*

Section 3 Review Answers

1. amnesty (185), **black code** (185), **sharecropping** (189), **carpetbagger** (190), **gerrymandering** (190)
2. Civil Rights Act of 1866, Enforcement Act of 1870, and the Fourteenth and Fifteenth Amendments
3. Congress overrode his vetoes, putting the Radical Republicans in control.

4. They were more concerned with government scandal and corruption and the Panic of 1873.
5. partially; differences between the regions today are less pronounced than they were during Reconstruction

Chapter ⑥ Review

Reviewing Key Terms

1. gospel tradition
2. black codes
3. sectionalism
4. gerrymandering
5. scorched earth policy

Recalling Facts

1. The decision reinforced the Southern position that enslaved persons were property that could not be taken away.

2. The cotton gin made cotton plantations more profitable; new plantations required a growing slave labor force, further dividing the South from the North, especially on questions of states' rights and extending slavery into the new states.

3. *(a)* kept Senate vote equal; *(b)* balanced power between North and South; *(c)* allowed slavery in the North

4. They left the Union upon the election of Lincoln, whose views were pro-North.

5. The North was confident because of its resources; the South, because of its military officers and its ability to defend its own territory.

6. Losses at Gettysburg severely weakened the South; loss of Vicksburg cut off the South from the West.

7. It freed enslaved people in the Confederacy, but not in Union states that permitted slavery or in Union-occupied areas of the South.

8. Republicans believed in rights for freed people, and they also wanted to increase political support for their party by giving the vote to African Americans.

9. Gerrymandering and poll taxes limited representation; Union troops withdrew and left no protection.

10. Sectionalism remains; the South was devastated by the war and received no recovery aid for decades.

Reviewing Key Terms

Match each sentence below to the vocabulary term it defines or describes. Write your answers on a separate sheet of paper.

sectionalism	black codes
gospel tradition	scorched earth policy
emancipation	gerrymandering

1. Enslaved African Americans developed a unique musical form by combining African religious practices and beliefs with Christian practices and beliefs.

2. After the war President Johnson permitted Southern state governments to pass laws restricting the rights of newly freed African Americans.

3. In the years leading up to the war, the North and the South had developed entirely different political agendas based on their own regional economic interests.

4. Southern whites sometimes regained control of their state legislatures by the technique of redividing voting districts to dilute African American representation.

5. When General Grant became commander of the Union forces, he ordered his generals to burn and destroy the South's crops, homes, and supplies.

Recalling Facts

1. Why was the *Dred Scott* decision significant?

2. Explain how Eli Whitney's cotton gin contributed to increasing sectionalism. Discuss economic and political factors.

3. How did *(a)* the Missouri Compromise, *(b)* the Compromise of 1850, and *(c)* the Kansas-Nebraska Act reflect sectional interests?

4. What led to the secession of 11 Southern states?

SMITHSONIAN INSTITUTION

5. Why were both Northerners and Southerners at first confident of victory in the Civil War?

6. Explain the significance of the battles in 1863 at Gettysburg and Vicksburg.

7. What was the Emancipation Proclamation? Did it achieve all of the goals of the abolitionists? Explain.

8. What motivated the Radical Republicans to pass civil rights legislation on behalf of African Americans?

9. Despite laws passed during Reconstruction, African Americans in the South lost many of their civil rights until the 1950s and 1960s. Explain.

10. Did the Civil War and Reconstruction end sectionalism? Why or why not?

Critical Thinking

1. Recognizing Bias White Southerners tended to support policies that enlarged the powers of the states, while Northerners supported limiting the powers of the states in certain important ways. What caused this difference in outlook?

2. Making Inferences Explain what Jerry Loguen meant when he said, "Human rights are mutual and reciprocal." How has this idea been applied to other areas, for example, women's rights?

3. Making Comparisons Make a chart showing the strengths and weaknesses of the Union and the Confederacy at the outbreak of the Civil War. What proved to be the determining factors in the war?

4. Drawing Conclusions Playing marches like "The Battle Hymn of the Republic" and "Dixie," drummers as young as 10 and 12 years old—like those in the photo at left—

Critical Thinking

1. Southerners, on plantations, were more independant; Northerners, centralized in cities, found government more acceptable. Conflicts still occur over education and social services.

2. The rights of one group should be enjoyed by all.

3. Strengths: Union—population, resources, factories, transportation; Confederacy—officers, trained men, home territory. Weaknesses: Union—unfamiliar ground, far from supplies; Confederacy—lack of finances, factories, resources. The North's greater population and resources were decisive.

4. It would have encouraged comradeship and patriotism.

5. Reconstruction policies were compassionate toward the freed people, less so toward white Southerners, and were not sustainable.

marched alongside Union and Confederate troops. Why was this music important to soldiers?

5. Determining Cause and Effect
President Lincoln believed that the South should be treated with compassion after the Civil War. Did Reconstruction fulfill this objective? Explain.

Portfolio Project

Civil war has torn apart many countries in the 1900s. Choose one country, such as China, Spain, Yugoslavia, or Mexico, and investigate its civil war period. Identify the causes and effects of its civil war. In what ways was the war similar to the American Civil War? In what ways was it different? Write a report and include it in your portfolio.

Cooperative Learning

The Civil War has inspired numerous books, plays, movies, and TV dramas. For example, Margaret Mitchell's novel *Gone With the Wind,* Stephen Crane's novel *The Red Badge of Courage,* and the 1989 movie *Glory* look at the war from different perspectives. With a group of your classmates, prepare a review of different works on the Civil War. Include answers to the following questions: How historically accurate is the work in question? What evidence is there of character stereotyping? Has stereotyping changed over the years?

Reinforcing Skills

Combining Information From Maps Compare the map of transportation routes on page 148 with the map of Civil War battles on page 175. What inference can you make about why Union victories in Tennessee and battles in New Orleans caused major hardships for the South?

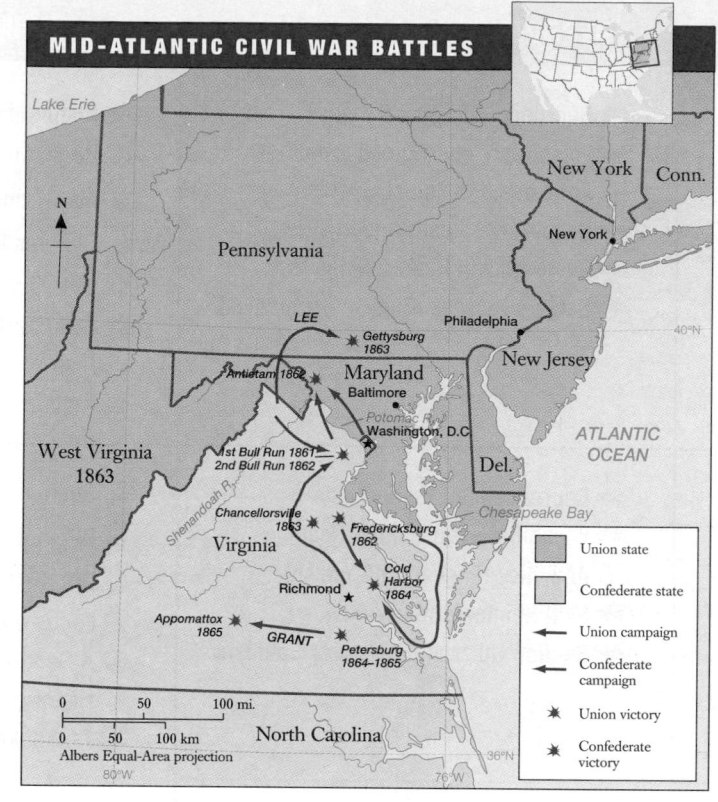

MID-ATLANTIC CIVIL WAR BATTLES

Lake Erie

New York   Conn.

N

Pennsylvania

New York

LEE

Gettysburg 1863   Philadelphia

Antietam 1862

Maryland
Baltimore

New Jersey

Potomac R.
Washington, D.C.

West Virginia 1863

1st Bull Run 1861
2nd Bull Run 1862

Del.

ATLANTIC
OCEAN

Shenandoah R.

Chancellorsville 1863

Fredericksburg 1862

Chesapeake Bay

Virginia

Richmond

Cold Harbor 1864

Appomattox 1865

GRANT

Petersburg 1864–1865

	Union state
	Confederate state
←	Union campaign
←	Confederate campaign
★	Union victory
✷	Confederate victory

0   50   100 mi.
0   50   100 km
Albers Equal-Area projection

North Carolina

80°W   76°W
40°N   36°N

Geography and History

Study the map on this page to answer the following questions:

1. In which mid-Atlantic state did the most battles take place? Which side won most of these battles?

2. Which of the battles shown on the map were victories for the Confederacy?

3. Which battles took place in Union states?

4. In which battles did the Confederate campaign appear to threaten Washington, D.C.?

5. What Confederate general was in command at Gettysburg?

HISTORY JOURNAL

Write a brief account of what you have learned in this chapter. Include a consideration of the ways in which the institution of slavery was related to the Civil War.

Geography and History

1. Virginia; the Confederacy
2. Bull Run, Chancellorsville, Fredericksburg, Cold Harbor
3. Antietam; Gettysburg
4. first and second battles at Bull Run
5. General Lee

History Journal

Ask volunteers to share their journal entries with the class. Students should be aware that slavery was at the root of the economic and political differences that led the South to secede.

BONUS QUESTION

This question may be used for extra credit on the chapter test.

How did sharecropping block African American hopes?

Answer: *Sharecroppers were usually in debt to the landlord and unable to buy land of their own.*

Portfolio Project

Be sure that students have identified causes and effects and that they have compared the subject of their study with the American Civil War. Invite volunteers to share their research with the class.

Cooperative Learning

Bring the groups together to discuss the different works they have reviewed and their answers to the questions. Students may wish to read passages aloud or show film clips to support their answers.

Reinforcing Skills

A Union victory in Tennessee would interrupt the South's east-west supply lines; a Union victory in New Orleans would interrupt the north-south supply lines, including transportation on the Mississippi River.

New Frontiers

DAILY LESSON OBJECTIVES	REPRODUCIBLE RESOURCES	MULTIMEDIA RESOURCES
SECTION 1 Moving West 1. Trace the development of American cowhand culture. 2. Name the factors that led to settlement of the Plains and the West. 3. Describe the construction of the transcontinental railroad. 4. Explain the federal policies that affected Native Americans.	Reproducible Lesson Plans Vocabulary and Guided Reading Activities (English or Spanish) Cooperative Learning Activities Geography in History Activities Section Quizzes (English or Spanish)	Section Focus Transparencies Beginnings to 1900 Transparencies Map Transparencies Chapter Teaching Transparencies U.S. History and Art Transparencies Landmark Documents in American History American Music: Cultural Traditions
SECTION 2 Rise of Industrialism 1. Explain the relationship between inventions and industrialism. 2. Describe how industrialism and national markets changed business. 3. Describe the two types of mergers. 4. Explain Social Darwinism and big business.	Reproducible Lesson Plans Vocabulary and Guided Reading Activities (English or Spanish) Skill Reinforcement Activities Section Quizzes (English or Spanish)	Section Focus Transparencies Beginnings to 1900 Transparencies U.S. History and Art Transparencies Focus on American Fine Art Prints A Geographic Perspective on American History Testmaker
SECTION 3 Populism and Protest 1. Trace the early development of the Populist party. 2. Describe the problems facing farmers and their efforts to solve them. 3. Explain the development of early labor unions in the late 1800s.	Reproducible Lesson Plans Vocabulary and Guided Reading Activities (English or Spanish) Section Quizzes (English or Spanish)	Section Focus Transparencies Beginnings to 1900 Transparencies U.S. History and Art Transparencies Focus on American Fine Art Prints American Music: Cultural Traditions Testmaker Student Self-Test: Software Review
SECTION 4 Reaching for Empire 1. Explain how the United States opened new avenues for trade. 2. Explain how the United States acquired Alaska, Hawaii, and the Phillipines. 3. Understand how the idea of Manifest Destiny related to the expansion of the country's boundaries.	Reproducible Lesson Plans Vocabulary and Guided Reading Activities (English or Spanish) Reteaching Activities (English or Spanish) Enrichment Activities (English or Spanish) Section Quizzes (English or Spanish)	Section Focus Transparencies Beginnings to 1900 Transparencies Landmark Documents in American History American Music: Cultural Traditions Testmaker Student Self-Test: Software Review
CHAPTER REVIEW AND EVALUATION	Chapter 7 Test, Forms A and B Performance Assessment Strategies and Activities Unit 2 Test, Forms A and B	Testmaker Vocabulary PuzzleMaker Student Self-Test: Software Review Chapter Digests Audiocassettes

 If time does not permit teaching the entire chapter, summarize using the Chapter 7 Digests Audiocassettes and the accompanying activities and tests. (Available in English or Spanish.)

Performance Assessment

Cooperative Project

Have students work in groups of four or five to research the history of one region belonging to the United States which is not a state or has become a state within the twentieth century. Groups might choose the Virgin Islands, Alaska, Hawaii, or another region. Have them prepare a journalistic treatment about United States acquistion of the area. They can work together to prepare a newcast or newspaper report. **LEP**

Suggested Rubric: A Newspaper Article. See Performance Assessment Strategies and Activities, p. 31.

Individual Project

One focus of today's environmental movement is preservation and restoration of the tall-grass prairies plowed under during the settlement of the West. Ask students to use persuasive writing to defend preservation of the prairie habitat. They should research descriptions of the prairie in it's original state and detail events of the 1800s that led to the development of the prairie. They should include a comparison of the region then and today.

Suggested Rubric: A Research Report. See Performance Assessment Strategies and Activities, p. 39.

Key to Ability Levels

Teaching strategies have been coded for varying learning styles and abilities.

L1 **BASIC** activities for all students

L2 **AVERAGE** activities for average to above-average students

L3 **CHALLENGING** activities for above-average students

LEP **LIMITED ENGLISH PROFICIENCY** activities

 Block Scheduling

Block scheduling differs from traditional class scheduling in the amount of time allotted to each period. The extended timeframe provided by block scheduling affords you the opportunity to implement a greater number of research-oriented and activity-intense projects to motivate and involve your students. Activities that are particularly suited to use within the block scheduling framework are identified throughout this chapter by the following designation.

TEACHER'S CORNER

NATIONAL GEOGRAPHIC SOCIETY

INDEX TO NATIONAL GEOGRAPHIC MAGAZINE

The following articles may be used for research relating to this chapter:

- "The Cherokee," by Geoffrey Norman, May 1995.
- "John Wesley Powell," by Peter Miller, April 1994.
- "Geronimo," by David Roberts, October 1992.
- "Along the Santa Fe Trail," by Rowe Findley, March 1991.
- "Sagebrush Country: America's Outback," by Douglas Chadwick, January 1989.
- "Seizing the Light: Photography's First Fifty Years," by Erla Zwingle, October 1989.

- "The Life and Times of William Henry Jackson," by Rowe Findley, February 1989.
- "The Itch to Move West: Life and Death on the Oregon Trail," by Boyd Gibbons, August 1986.
- "Sam Houston: A Man Too Big For Texas," by Bart McDowell, March 1986.
- "Daniel Boone, First Hero of the Frontier," by Elizabeth A. Moize, December 1985.

NATIONAL GEOGRAPHIC SOCIETY PRODUCTS AVAILABLE FROM GLENCOE

To order the following products for use with this chapter, contact your local Glencoe sales representative or call Glencoe at 1-800-334-7344:

- *The Presidents: A Picture History of Our Nation* (CD-ROM)
- *Native Americans, Part I* (CD-ROM)
- *Native Americans, Part II* (CD-ROM)
- *Native Americans: Eastern Woodlands and Plains* (Transparencies)

- *Native Americans: Southwest, Northwest Coast, Arctic* (Transparencies)
- *GTV: A Geographic Perspective on American History* (Videodisc)
- *GTV: The American People: Fabric of a Nation* (Videodisc)

ADDITIONAL NATIONAL GEOGRAPHIC SOCIETY PRODUCTS

To order the following products for use with this chapter, call National Geographic Society at 1-800-368-2728:

- *People of America's Western Frontier* (Filmstrip)
- *The Westward Movement* (Filmstrip)

- *The United States as a World Power: From the 1890s to the 1970s* (Filmstrip)

Chapter Overview

This chapter describes the country's transition in the late 1800s as settlers and businesses pushed west of the Mississippi River and on to the Pacific coast. A new industrial society also grew during the era, and the United States became heavily involved in international affairs.

Introducing the Chapter

The Brooklyn Bridge is an appropriate symbol of its age in several ways. It reflected the tremendous technical and industrial advancement of the era. Just as the bridge cost the lives of some who worked on it, so the progress that marked the late 1800s took a toll on human life. Social and economic problems for workers, for Native Americans, for African Americans, for women, and for immigrants would carry over into the next century.

Display the Chapter 7 Teaching Transparency and distribute the corresponding activity sheet for students to complete.

Extension Activity
Have students complete Beyond the Transparency on the activity sheet for Chapter 7 and present their projects after the class has completed the chapter.

History Journal

Have students define *frontier* in their own words, and write how it applies to the United States in the late 1800s.

CHAPTER

7

New Frontiers

MAY 24, 1883: FANFARE MARKS BROOKLYN BRIDGE OPENING

Church bells rang out all over the city. Guns boomed from forts in New York harbor. After 14 years of construction, marred by worker injuries and deaths, New York City celebrated the opening of the Brooklyn Bridge.

President Chester A. Arthur and New York Governor Grover Cleveland joined thousands of New Yorkers in the opening ceremony. The steel bridge stretched over the East River, ready to open the way from the island of Manhattan to the borough of Brooklyn.

At the time it was opened, the bridge was the longest suspension bridge in the world. Costing nearly $15 million, the bridge was suspended by 4 cables. Each cable contained more than 5,000 small wires and could hold nearly 3,000 tons. More than 100,000 people would travel over it each day.

The Brooklyn Bridge reflected the tide of industrial progress sweeping the nation in the years following the Civil War. Factories and cities grew, while advancements in technology and communications transformed the way Americans lived. As the nation continued to push its boundaries outward, the United States emerged as one of the great powers of the 1900s. ■

HISTORY JOURNAL

Write in your journal about your reaction to the story and photograph of the Brooklyn Bridge. What makes a great bridge an appropriate symbol of industrial progress?

194

 EXTRA CREDIT PROJECT

Farming and Industry To deepen students' understanding of the economics of the late 1800s, have students choose one type of farming or manufacturing and research developments that brought a boom in productivity for that industry toward the end of the century.

What new techniques and mechanical devices helped increase production? How was land acquired? How readily available was labor and why? As students share their reports, they can draw comparisons and parallels among the various industries.

ARCHIVE PHOTOS

STROLLERS ENJOY THE BROAD
PROMENADE ABOVE THE ROADWAY
OF THE SOARING BROOKLYN BRIDGE.

195

✔ **Performance Assessment**

Refer to page 194B for performance assessment activities for this chapter.

 Also see Activity 7 in the Performance Assessment Strategies and Activities for an additional activity as well as for suggested rubrics.

Examining the Visual

The Great Suspension Bridge John A. Roebling, originator of the wire suspension bridge was already famous for building such structures across the Niagara and Ohio Rivers, when he undertook plans for the Brooklyn Bridge, the largest and longest one yet. While laying the bridge's foundation in 1869, however, Roebling sustained an injury that led to lockjaw, leaving his son and partner, Washington A.

Roebling to complete the project. Just two years later, Washington too fell ill. He continued to supervise construction, but due to paralysis, he was unable to do the work of drafting. He consulted with his wife, Emily, who for the next five years drew all the plans for the bridge's construction. Ask students to discuss both the dangers and benefits of these huge iron and steel structures that marked the late 1800s.

FOCUS

Section Objectives

1. Trace the development of American cowhand culture.
2. Name the factors that led to settlement of the Plains and the West.
3. Describe the construction of the transcontinental railroad.
4. Explain the federal policies that adversely affected Native Americans.

Bellringer Activity

 While taking attendance at the beginning of the class period, display **Section Focus Transparency 19,** and have students answer the questions. (Or use the blackline master.)

VISUAL INSTRUCTION

Staking Claims The Creek, Cherokee, Choctaw, Chickasaw, and Seminole peoples had been forced to move to Oklahoma after the Louisiana Purchase. Now they were being forced out again.

Ask: What did settlers have to do before they could own the land? *(They had to farm it for at least five years.)*

History and the Humanities

American Music: Cultural Traditions— "Little Old Sod Shanty" by Jimmy Denoon

---

Moving West

APRIL 22, 1889: THOUSANDS GRAB LAND IN OKLAHOMA

ARCHIVES AND MANUSCRIPTS DIVISION OF THE OKLAHOMA HISTORICAL SOCIETY

Staking Claims
The rush into Oklahoma's Cherokee Outlet goes by in a blur of speed. Thousands of Americans claimed free land in the new territories. Claims often sparked violent disputes that took years to settle.

THE CLOCK STRUCK NOON AND GUNSHOTS RANG OUT, BEGINNING ONE OF THE MOST REMARKABLE LAND GRABS IN AMERICAN HISTORY. Yancey Cravat, the hero in Edna Ferber's novel, *Cimarron,* describes the scene on April 22, 1889, when the federal government effectively gave away the almost 2 million acres (0.8 million ha) of land it had purchased from evicted Creek and Seminole.

There we were, the girl on my left, the old plainsman on my right. Eleven forty-five. Along the border were the soldiers, their guns in one hand, their watches in the other. . . . Twelve o'clock. There went up a roar that drowned the crack of the soldiers' musketry as they fired in the air as the signal of noon and the start of the Run. You could see the puffs of smoke from their guns but you couldn't hear a sound. The thousands surged over the Line. It was like running water going over a broken dam. The rush had started, and it was devil take the hindmost. We swept across the prairie in a cloud of black and red dust that covered our faces and hands in a minute. . . .

—Edna Ferber, *Cimarron,* 1930

More than 50,000 men, women, and children participated in the rush. Although the land was free, the settlers would have to **homestead,** or settle on the land, for a number of years before they could own it. Some found their stakes too dry to farm, and disease-causing conditions drove others out; but a year later, the Oklahoma Territory boasted a population of about 259,000 people.

The success of the Oklahoma rush led the government to open more land in the West. The following year

---

AS YOU READ

Vocabulary
► homestead
► transcontinental railroad
► government boarding school

Think About . . .
► what influenced the development of American cowhand culture.
► what geographical, political, and technological factors led to settlement of the Plains and the West.

► how the transcontinental railroad was built.
► how federal policies adversely affected Native Americans.

Section 1 Resources

REPRODUCIBLE RESOURCES
📠 Lesson Plan 7-1
📠 Vocabulary and Guided Reading 7-1
📠 Section 1 Quiz
📠 Cooperative Learning Activity 7
📠 Geography in History Activity 7

MULTIMEDIA RESOURCES
🎞 Section Focus Transparency 19
🎧 American Music: Cultural Traditions
🎞 Map Transparency 7
🎞 U.S. History and Art Transparencies 7, 9, 13, 18
🎞 Beginnings to 1900 Transparencies 22, 23, 24

📖 Focus on American Fine Art Prints, Prints 8, 9
💿 Landmark Documents in American History
💻 Testmaker
🎧 Chapter 7 Digest Audiocassette
💻 Student Self-Test: A Software Review

federal authorities authorized settlement on millions of acres of Sioux land in South Dakota. The government could not hold back the tide of eager settlers, and after 1900 thousands descended on the former Native American reservation.

Expanding Frontiers
Farmers, Ranchers, and Miners Go West

After the Civil War, as the nation's population boomed and Midwestern agricultural land filled up, farmers looked westward to the Great Plains. Completed in 1869, the **transcontinental railroad** spanned the continent from east to west. The railroad companies then encouraged eager farmers to buy some of their enormous land holdings. More encouragement came from the Homestead Act of 1862 that awarded 160 acres (64.8 ha) of public land free to any settler who would farm the land for at least 5 years. So enticed, many settlers, including thousands of newly arrived immigrants from European countries, poured into the lands west of the Mississippi River.

The Cattle Frontier

On the eastern high-grass prairie of the Great Plains, enough rain fell to cultivate grain crops. Settlers used the drier western lands for cattle grazing. Herds of longhorn and other cattle were fattened on the open range lands of Texas, Kansas, Nebraska, the Dakotas, Wyoming, and Montana. They were driven to market and sold to packers and finally were sent east to feed the growing numbers of beef-hungry city dwellers.

The profits from cattle ranching could be enormous. A Texas steer, purchased as a calf for $5–$6, could be set out to graze on public land and later sold for $60–$70. For two decades after the Civil War, the cowhand and the cattle reigned supreme on the Great Plains. By the late 1880s, however, drought and an oversupply of cattle forced beef prices down.

Cowhands

American cowhands have been idealized in popular books and movies. Their unique way of life evolved from that of the vaqueros, their Mexican counterparts. The cattle industry in the United States developed from the livestock and horses that the Spanish introduced into the Americas. Similarly, cowhand culture—the

COLLECTION OF WILLIAM GLADSTONE/PICTURE RESEARCH CONSULTANTS, INC.

BUFFALO BILL HISTORICAL CENTER, CODY, WY

Cowhand Culture Cowhands, one-third of whom were African American or Hispanic American, shared the hardships of the long trail drives as well as the hours of relaxation in town. These two cowhands posed for their photograph in the 1860s. *How did the cattle industry in the United States begin?*

clothing, equipment, work, and entertainment of American cowhands—had a partly Spanish heritage.

Cowhands' chaps—a word based on the vaqueros' word *chaparajos*—protected their legs from thorny brush on the Plains. The words *lariat* and *rodeo* also have Spanish origins. Cowhands' outfits were functional. High-heeled boots kept their feet from slipping out of the stirrups, and broad-brimmed hats kept sun, rain, and dust from their eyes.

A cowhand's work was seasonal. Ranchers hired extra help for the roundup, when cattle were branded. During a trail drive, hired hands kept the herds together and moved them as far as 1,000 miles (1,609 km) in 3 months. The work was exhausting, and the wages were low—$40 or $50 per month. Few cowhands owned their own horses, but every cowhand owned a saddle—a prized possession. The cowhands' worth was measured by their skill at roping and riding. Cattle rancher Joseph G. McCoy said of a cowhand in 1874: "He lives hard, works hard, has but few comforts and fewer necessities. He loves danger but abhors labor of the common kind, and never tires riding."

SECTION ONE   **197**

TEACH

Guided Practice

L2 Discussion Tell students that vaqueros used their rope both as a tool and a weapon; they regarded the cowhands' use of a gun as "unmanly." Most cowhands left their guns in the chuck wagon during trail drives and roundups. Discuss whether movies and TV exaggerate cowhands' reliance on guns.

Show students Map Transparency 7 and have them complete the activity sheet.

Show students Beginnings to 1900 Transparencies 22, 23, and 24 and have them complete the activity sheets.

VISUAL INSTRUCTION

Cowhand Culture On a typical trail drive, 2,500 longhorns might be driven 1,200 miles to the western terminus of a railroad and sold to buyers from Chicago or Kansas City.

Answer: *It began when the Spanish brought livestock and horses to the Americas.*

History and the Humanities

U.S. History and Art Transparencies 7, 9, 13, and 18—The *Buffalo Chase, Mouth of the Yellowstone* by George Catlin; *Shooting for the Beef* by George Caleb Bingham; *Merced River, Yosemite Valley* by Albert Bierstadt; *The Stampede* by Frederic Remington

---

Cooperative Learning

Writing Descriptions Have students work in small groups to make lists of words associated with the cowhand culture and with a particular Plains nation such as the Sioux, noting that both depended on the same grasslands for their livelihood. Students may want to consult an encyclopedia while gathering words. Regroup, with each student taking his or her word list to a new group. Have each group write a collaborative description of both cultures.

Independent Practice

L3 Research Have students investigate and report on California's economy today. Ask them to find out how resources and location have continued to influence the state's development.

 Have students complete the Chapter 7, Section 1 Vocabulary and Guided Reading Activity. (Also in Spanish.) **LEP**

 Have students complete the Chapter 7 Cooperative Learning Activity.

FYI

New Breeds By the 1920s cowhands no longer tended the long-horns because the breed failed to produce much beef in proportion to its size. Ranchers switched to more profitable breeds.

VISUAL INSTRUCTION

Promise of the West The Santa Fe line mentioned in the advertisement started from Atchison, Kansas, went up the Arkansas River, across the Rockies to Santa Fe, through Apache and Navaho country, and finally across the Mojave Desert to reach the coast.

Answer: *Until the railroads were built, much of the West was remote from transportation and markets.*

The profession was more integrated than most walks of American life. African American, Native American, Hispanic, and Anglo cowhands, as well as those of mixed ancestry, all met and worked together. Yet discrimination existed on the frontier as elsewhere. Vaqueros earned less than Anglos and seldom became foremen or trail bosses. Some saloons discriminated against Hispanics, segregated African Americans, and excluded Chinese altogether.

Few women worked as salaried cowhands. Ranchers' wives and daughters did help with many chores, such as tending animals and sewing leather britches. A widow sometimes took over her deceased husband's ranch.

During free time in the bunkhouse, cowhands entertained themselves with card games, tall tales, practical jokes, and songs. In town, after several months on the trail, many of them let off steam by drinking, gambling, and fighting in local saloons. Cow towns, where cattle were loaded on trains for shipment to market, had a reputation for lawlessness. Yet the "Wild West" gained its name not so much for gunfights as for the cowhands' rugged life.

Mountains and Valleys

West of the Great Plains, people sought their fortune from the vast mineral and forest resources of the Rocky Mountain and Sierra Nevada regions. The timberlands of California and the Northwest yielded much of the wood necessary for thousands of miles of railroad ties, fence posts, and the building of hundreds of towns.

Gold and silver provided much of the capital for an industrializing country. The Comstock Lode, a rich vein of silver in Nevada, yielded more than $292 million between 1859 and 1882. Though Western tales celebrate the lone miner toiling with pick and shovel, huge companies did most of the mining of valuable metals. These companies, in pursuit of gold, silver, lead, copper, tin, and zinc, commanded great money and power. They could build railroad lines, bring in heavy machinery, and employ armies of miners.

In California the gold discovered under the ground proved less valuable than the ground itself. As one father told his son: "Plant your lands, these be your best gold fields." Farmland turned out to be California's most valuable asset. Eager miners, believing the California soil unsuitable for crops, willingly paid high prices for farm produce: "watermelon at from one to five dollars each, apples from Oregon at one and two dollars each, potatoes and onions at fifty cents to one dollar a pound . . . eggs at two dollars a dozen," according to one older resident. More often than not, provisioners in the West made money while miners did not. By 1862 California produced a surplus of some crops.

Promise of the West In this government advertisement, the new railroad service is used to attract homesteaders to stake claims. *Why was much of the West sparsely settled before 1870?*

Like the cattle culture of the Great Plains, the agriculture of California had a partly Spanish heritage. Franciscan missionaries introduced grapes and citrus fruits to California's fertile soils in the late 1700s. With the end of the mission system in the mid-1800s, however, the vineyards and orchards fell into neglect. Enterprising settlers, once in search of gold, displaced Mexican ranchers and turned the rich California valleys into cornucopias of the Far West.

Building the Railroad
Across the Continent by Rail

California's population increased dramatically because of its gold rush and its agricultural successes. Other parts of the West remained sparsely settled, usually because they were far from transportation and markets. In the early 1860s, the federal government proposed that railroad lines should cross the entire United States.

Meeting Special Needs

Reading Disability Help students who have difficulty reading to understand the section by reading the main headings aloud. Ask them to find illustrations that go with the headings. Ask a student to volunteer to make an outline of the section on the chalkboard as other students tell the volunteer which headings to include.

The incredible engineering feat that provided transcontinental transportation began with the Pacific Railroad Act. Passed by Congress in 1862, the act authorized the Union Pacific Railroad to lay track westward from a point near Omaha, Nebraska, while the Central Pacific Railroad laid track eastward from Sacramento. The lines were to meet in Utah. In addition to government loans, the railroads received large land grants, 20 square miles (51.8 square km) of land for 1 mile (1.6 km) of track laid. The railroad barons made fortunes by selling this land to settlers.

Both railroads faced enormous challenges that required armies of laborers. The Central Pacific had to cross the Sierra Nevada in eastern California, while the Union Pacific had to cross the Rockies. Blasting and tunneling into rock and working through the winters, the crew suffered many injuries and deaths. In January 1865, the Central Pacific advertised for 5,000 more workers.

The quiet efficiency of Chinese laborers impressed the construction boss, and he began recruiting in China. Before the end of the year, about 7,000 Chinese laborers were at work on the line. The Union Pacific relied heavily on Irish immigrant labor, although one worker described the team as "a crowd of ex-Confederates and Federal soldiers, muleskinners, Mexicans, New York Irish, bushwackers, and ex-convicts," with a few African Americans as well.

By 1868 the work of laying track had become a race between the two railroads. The pace quickened as the lines approached each other. When the two sets of tracks met on May 10, 1869, at Promontory, Utah, special trains carrying railroad officials and their guests arrived for the completion ceremony. Leland Stanford, governor of California, drove in a gold spike, symbolically uniting the rail lines. A telegraph message informed the nation, "It is done!" By the end of the 1800s four more transcontinental rail lines crossed the United States. Passengers and freight began to crisscross the nation.

History and the Humanities

Focus on American Fine Art Prints, Prints 8 and 9—*The Long Story* by William Sydney Mount; *Fur Traders Descending the Missouri by* George Caleb Bingham.

FYI

Leland Stanford As a Californian and as president of the Central Pacific, Stanford benefited from the success of the transcontinental railroad. After first opposing Chinese immigration, he later supported it, saying that California would benefit if half a million Chinese were brought in.

 Facts on File

Landmark Documents in American History Have students review "'I Will Fight No More Forever,' Chief Joseph, 1877" and write a paragraph about the intent of the document.

THE HARRY T. PETERS COLLECTION, MUSEUM OF THE CITY OF NEW YORK

A Dangerous Pass This photo from 1877 shows the Secrettown Trestle, 62 miles (99.8 km) from Sacramento, California. The Chinese laborers shown used picks, chisels, hammers, wheelbarrows, and one-horse carts to build the timber structures and earthen embankments that bridged these chasms in the Sierra Nevada. *When was the Pacific Railroad Act passed by Congress?*

SECTION ONE **199**

VISUAL INSTRUCTION

A Dangerous Pass The wooden trestle, in place of an embankment of earth or stone, was typical of American railroad construction techniques of the time—a technology of haste, with little attention to safety. The accident rate was high in comparison with European railroads.

Answer: *The Pacific Railroad Act was passed by Congress in 1862.*

Portfolio Project

Taking a Stand Discuss the differences in points of view of people who believe in preserving the land and those who believe in using it for human needs. Chief Seattle gave the perspective of Native Americans in a letter to President Pierce: "If we sell you our land, love it as we have loved it. . . . preserve it for your children."

Relate Chief Seattle's views to those of environmentalists today. Ask students to select a local environmental issue and have them write a letter to a public official taking a stand. They can keep their letters in their portfolios.

ASSESS

Meeting Lesson Objectives

Each section objective is tested by the section review question(s) that follows it in parentheses.

1. Trace the development of American cowhand culture. (1, 2)
2. Name the factors that led to settlement of the Plains and the West. (3)
3. Describe the construction of the transcontinental railroad. (1, 3)
4. Explain the federal policies that adversely affected Native Americans. (4, 5)

VISUAL INSTRUCTION

Forced Removal In 1874 some 4,000 Apache were forced to move to a wasteland in Arizona. For years thereafter Geronimo led the Apache in wars against the whites before finally surrendering in 1886.

Answer: *It is bound for the reservation to which the Native Americans of the southern Plains were sent.*

Forced Removal This photograph shows federal agents preparing to relocate a group of Apache from Arizona to Oklahoma by train in the late 1800s. Geronimo, of the Chiricahua Apache, sat third from right in front. *Why is this train bound for Oklahoma?*

The Second Great Removal

Native American Lands Taken

Not everyone benefited from the expansion of the railroads. In the summer of 1860, Lieutenant Henry Maynadier quoted one Sioux elder who warned about the expansion of the West, "We are glad to have the traders, but we don't want you soldiers and roadmakers; the country is ours and we intend to keep it."

The rapid settlement of the lands west of the Mississippi River after the Civil War led to a generation of violent conflict. Settlers fought the dozens of Native American nations that had inhabited these lands for generations.

In 1871 the federal government decreed that all Western Native American nations must agree to relocate to one of two reservation areas. The northern Plains na-

tions were assigned to the western half of present-day South Dakota; the southern Plains nations were assigned to what is now Oklahoma. Once placed on the reservations, they would have to accept the federal government as their guardian.

Government policy, as well as military conflict with those who resisted, undermined Native American cultures. In 1871 the government ended the practice of treating each Native American nation separately. Under the new policy, Native Americans lost two rights. They could no longer negotiate treaties to protect their lands, and they could no longer vote on laws governing their fate. The Dawes Severalty Act of 1887 continued the attempt to break down Native American loyalty to their own nations. This act decreed that parcels of land be given not to nations but to individuals. Each family head was allowed 160 acres (64.8 ha). Reservation land left over was sold to white settlers.

200 CHAPTER 7 NEW FRONTIERS

Extending the Content

Land Allotment System Native American societies were rooted in the idea of communally possessed land. Tecumseh had once declared, "Sell land! As well sell air and water. The Great Spirit gave them in common to all." To allot land to individuals was to destroy the basis of Native American cultures. The Cherokee took their

case to the Supreme Court, invoking their treaty guarantee that their lands would be "secured to the whole Cherokee people for their common use." The Court declined to consider the case. Of the 16 million acres allotted to members of the Five Tribes, all but 1.5 million had passed to whites within 20 years.

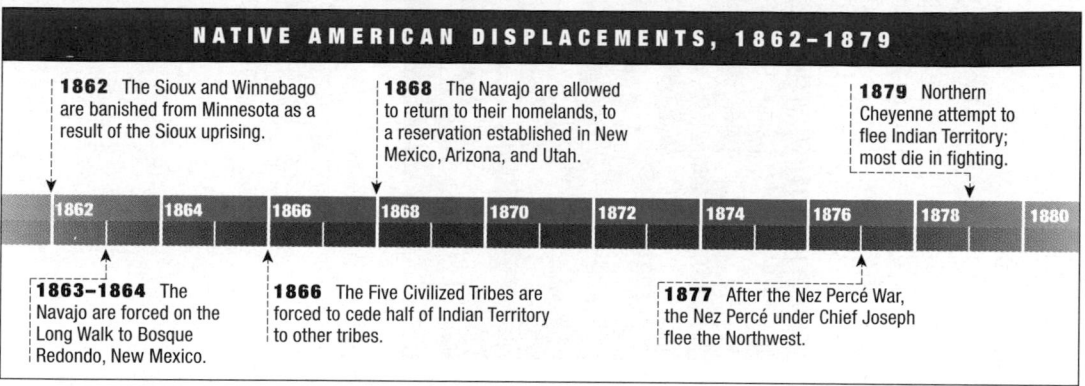

NATIVE AMERICAN DISPLACEMENTS, 1862–1879

1862 The Sioux and Winnebago are banished from Minnesota as a result of the Sioux uprising.

1868 The Navajo are allowed to return to their homelands, to a reservation established in New Mexico, Arizona, and Utah.

1879 Northern Cheyenne attempt to flee Indian Territory; most die in fighting.

| 1862 | 1864 | 1866 | 1868 | 1870 | 1872 | 1874 | 1876 | 1878 | 1880 |

1863–1864 The Navajo are forced on the Long Walk to Bosque Redondo, New Mexico.

1866 The Five Civilized Tribes are forced to cede half of Indian Territory to other tribes.

1877 After the Nez Percé War, the Nez Percé under Chief Joseph flee the Northwest.

CHART STUDY

Ask: In what year were the Navajo able to return to their homelands?
Answer: *1868*

Some reformers compared this act to the Emancipation Proclamation: just as enslaved people were set free, so Native Americans would gradually gain citizenship. Few reformers seemed to notice that sending Native American children to **government boarding schools,** where they were schooled in the white cultural tradition, was breaking down Native American culture.

Within 20 years after the Dawes Act, Native Americans retained control of only 20 percent of their original reservation lands. The southern Plains Native Americans in Oklahoma were severely hurt. By the time of Oklahoma statehood in 1907, most of their original acreage was in the hands of 500,000 white settlers. A newspaper editor in that year summed up the prevailing feeling among the settlers: "Sympathy and sentiment never stand in the way of the onward march of empire." The Oglala Sioux leader Red Cloud, who later represented Arapaho, Crow, and Cheyenne as well, expressed the corresponding Native American lament in 1870: "When we first had all this land we were strong; now we are all melting like snow on the hillside, while you are growing like spring grass."

S.J. MORROW COLLECTION/W.H. OVER MUSEUM

Red Cloud A chief of the Oglala Sioux, Red Cloud led the opposition to the Bozeman Trail through Native American lands in Colorado and Montana. Under his leadership, representatives were able to negotiate removal of federal troops and forts from their lands. *What was the impact of westward expansion on Red Cloud and his people?*

SECTION REVIEW

Vocabulary

1. Define: homestead, transcontinental railroad, government boarding school.

Checking Facts

2. What aspects of American cowhand culture reflect its Spanish heritage?

3. Name some of the natural resources that settlers found on the Great Plains and in the Far West. How did the federal government's transportation policy contribute to the westward movement?

Critical Thinking

Recognizing Points of View
4. How did the Native Americans' view of westward expansion differ from that of the settlers?

Linking Across Time

5. Some reformers compared the Dawes Severalty Act to the Emancipation Proclamation. Just as enslaved people were set free, reformers argued, so Native Americans would gain citizenship. How would you compare the consequences of the Emancipation Proclamation and the Dawes Act? Explain.

SECTION ONE   **201**

Evaluate

Have students complete the Section Review.

☞ ◎ Assign the Section 1 Quiz or use the Testmaker to develop a customized quiz. (Also in Spanish.) **LEP**

Reteach

∩ Have students listen to the Chapter 7, Section 1 Audiocassette. (Also in Spanish.) **LEP**

Enrich

☞ Have students complete the Chapter 7 Geography in History Activity.

VISUAL INSTRUCTION

Red Cloud This short-lived victory was not achieved without bloodshed. The bitter fighting in Red Cloud's War included the 1866 raid known as Fetterman's Massacre, in which Red Cloud's warriors ambushed and killed 80 federal troops.

Answer: *White settlers coming to the West with the advent of railroads drove Red Cloud's people out.*

Section 1 Review Answers

1. homestead (196), **transcontinental railroad** (197), **government boarding school** (201)
2. Cowhands' dress, equipment, and work were borrowed in part from Mexican vaqueros.
3. fertile soil on the Plains, forests and ores in the mountains, all three in California; transcontinental railroad made settlement easier

4. Native Americans viewed it as a threat; settlers viewed it as an opportunity.
5. Answers will vary. Both moved toward giving a minority group citizenship, yet neither benefited the group economically. The Dawes Act was culturally destructive.

CLOSE

Ask: When was the transcontinental railroad completed? *(1869)* What happened in Oklahoma in 1889? *(land rush)*

CULTURE
OF THE
TIME

TEACH

Making the Historical Connection

Discuss the important relationship between post–Civil War economic growth and the burst of ideas, novelties, and patented inventions. Point out that in addition to new inventions, technological improvements such as safer, faster trains began to have an important impact on daily life. Trains allowed traveling shows such as Barnum's circus to reach more people.

Notes

An Age of Ingenuity

After the Civil War, Americans yearned to shed painful memories. They channeled their creative energy into hopes for a brighter future. Inventors filed record numbers of patent applications for everything from the dentist's drill to the corn flake. They contrived new modes of travel and entertainment, and displayed their creations at exhibitions and fairs.

RON LABBE/STUDIO 3-D

SCHMITT COLLECTION RJB

STEREO PHOTOGRAPHY

Stereoscopes filled the imaginations and parlors of Victorian viewers. In 1849 photographers began using a double-lensed camera to capture the perspectives of the left and right eyes. The resulting **stereographs** quickly became the most popular form of photography. Printed side by side, and seen through the little windows of the stereoscope, the two views on the stereograph merged into one and popped to life in 3-D.

Background Information

Cultural Impact With each exhibition of the latest technology, there was excitement about new heights of style and imagination as well as about the inventions themselves. The Ferris wheel was one such case. For years "pleasure wheels" had carried riders at fairs and carnivals, but the 264-foot-high (80.5-m) Ferris wheel towered above even the world's tallest building. At each fair, conventional styles reached their peak or fell away. At the Philadelphia Centennial Exhibition in 1876, Victorian Gothic, French mansard, and Swiss châlet architecture prevailed, while foreign art and crafts left their mark on public taste. The World's Columbian Exposition in Chicago began a trend in Roman Classical architecture that continued through the first decade of the 1900s.

CURIOSITY SEEKERS

Already famous for drawing a crowd, **Phineas T. Barnum** watched 10,000 spectators flock to his first circus in 1871. Three acres of tents housed the likes of Zazel the human cannonball and Alexis the horseback-riding, hoop-jumping goat.

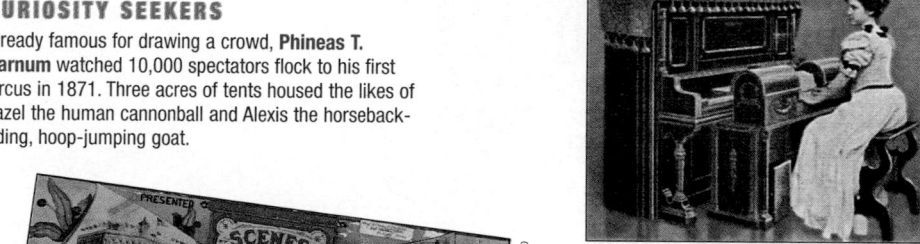

CULVER PICTURES

MECHANICAL MUSIC

Wild saloons and proper parlors alike displayed the newest musical novelty, the **player piano**. Meanwhile, employees of the **United States Patent Office** saw designs for a music-playing sewing machine and a convertible piano bed.

COURTESY OF THE BARNUM MUSEUM, BRIDGEPORT, CT

PATENTED

REINVENTING THE WHEEL

The 1893 World's Columbian Exposition unveiled the first **Ferris wheel**. Inventor Charles Ferris designed the ride to be the United States's answer to France's Eiffel Tower. During the Exposition the wheel carried more than 1.5 million people in its 36 trolley-sized cars.

CHICAGO HISTORICAL SOCIETY

CULTURE OF THE TIME **203**

CULTURE OF THE TIME

FYI

Politics and P.T. Barnum During the Civil War, Barnum supported abolition. He used his influence to have "traitors" punished, and his wealth to pay volunteer soldiers. A group of Confederates unsuccessfully tried to burn the American Museum. Before the war's end, Barnum ran for the state legislature in Connecticut so that he might vote on the Thirteenth Amendment. He served two terms, unsuccessfully supporting a state measure to enfranchise African Americans. Resentment over Southern secession caused Barnum to avoid the South with his touring circus.

CLOSE

Ask students to imagine what it was like to live in a world without movies, television, radio, or cars. Then ask them to describe what it would be like to attend an exhibition of new technology. *(New inventions would revolutionize peoples' lifestyles so much that a trip to the exhibit would be like a glimpse of the future.)*

Portfolio Project

Patent Ideas Have students brainstorm ideas for games, household devices, vehicles, or other inventions. Have them choose their best idea, sketch a design for it, and diagram all pieces and parts. They should give the invention a name and write a brief description of its purpose and unique qualities. Students can keep their patent ideas in their portfolios or take them a step further, building a model of the invention out of recycled materials and photographing it. Some students may want to write to the U.S. Patent and Trademark Office to see what criteria are required for patenting an idea.

203

FOCUS

FOCUS

Section Objectives

1. Explain the relationship between inventions and industrialism.
2. Describe how industrialism and national markets fostered changes in business.
3. Describe the two types of mergers.
4. Explain how industrialists applied Social Darwinism to big business.

Bellringer Activity

While taking attendance at the beginning of the class period, display **Section Focus Transparency 20,** and have students answer the questions. (Or use the blackline master.)

VISUAL INSTRUCTION

Innovator Andrew Carnegie founded the Carnegie Institute of Technology of Carnegie-Mellon University. He also contributed generously to Tuskegee Institute.

Ask: How did Carnegie improve steel production? *(He introduced the Bessemer converter and the open-hearth furnace; he combined smelting, refining, and rolling into one operation.)*

Rise of Industrialism

LATE 1800s: CARNEGIE FORGES A STEEL EMPIRE

BROWN BROTHERS

Innovator
Andrew Carnegie entered business when the use of steel was already widespread. He pioneered techniques to make steel processing more efficient and gradually took over the plants of his suppliers and distributors.

ANDREW CARNEGIE LEARNED ABOUT THE MEANING OF HARD WORK AS A YOUNG BOY. When his family fell on hard times in Scotland, he helped his mother sew shoes by threading her needles. In 1848 after the Carnegies left Scotland for the United States, 12-year-old Andrew worked with his father in a Pennsylvania cotton factory, earning $1.20 for a 72-hour week.

Little by little, Carnegie made himself a business success. At age 14 he started work in a telegraph office as a messenger and then quickly rose to the position of telegraph operator. The Pennsylvania Railroad hired Carnegie when he was 17, and his skills and hard work catapulted him in a few years to the job of assistant to the president. Through smart investments in a railroad car company and in oil wells, Carnegie made a small fortune by his early twenties and left the railroad to start his own business manufacturing iron bridges.

Carnegie was not only a shrewd investor but also a daring industrial innovator. In 1873 he began building a massive steel plant to produce railroad tracks in Pittsburgh, Pennsylvania. Carnegie introduced the revolutionary Bessemer converter and open-hearth steelmaking method, which converted iron ore into steel with much less labor than was previously required. Carnegie's mill also combined all stages of steel production—smelting, refining, and rolling—into one unified operation. As a result, the price of steel rails dropped from $107 per ton in 1870 to $32 per ton in 1890.

Innovation, ambition, and organizational skill made Carnegie hugely wealthy by the time he was 40 years old. Saying that hard work brought success, he also believed that those who acquired great

---

AS YOU READ

Vocabulary
► industrialism
► national market
► merger
► horizontal integration
► vertical integration

Think About . . .
► the relationship between inventions and industrialism.
► how industrialism and the development of national markets affected business.

► the two different types of mergers.
► how industrialists applied Social Darwinism to big business.

204   CHAPTER 7   NEW FRONTIERS

Section 2 Resources

REPRODUCIBLE RESOURCES
- Lesson Plan 7-2
- Vocabulary and Guided Reading 7-2
- Section 2 Quiz
- Skill Reinforcement Activity 7

MULTIMEDIA RESOURCES
- Section Focus Transparency 20
- Beginnings to 1900 Transparencies 25, 26, 28
- U.S. History and Art Transparencies 14, 16, 17
- A Geographic Perspective on American History

- Focus on American Fine Art Prints, Prints, 11, 12
- Testmaker
- Chapter 7 Digest Audiocassette
- Student Self-Test: A Software Review

wealth had a responsibility to return a portion of their profits to society. "The man who dies rich, dies disgraced," the self-made Scottish immigrant avowed.

By the time of his death in 1919, Carnegie had donated more than $350 million to worthy causes, including thousands of libraries, and another $30 million was disbursed through his last will and testament. His generosity was legendary throughout the world.

Industrialism Triumphant
A New World of Manufacturing

The era during which Andrew Carnegie built his steel empire witnessed a dramatic economic transformation. Between the end of the Civil War in 1865 and the end of the 1800s, the United States became an industrial giant. Manufacturing replaced agriculture as the main source of economic growth; growing **industrialism** turned the United States into a land rich with machines, factories, mines, and railroads.

The Rise of Heavy Industry

Before the Civil War, manufacturing in the United States had been tied to the farming economy. Factories processed the products of the farm and forest into consumer goods—turning cotton and wool into cloth; hides into shoes and boots; and trees into ships, barrels, and furniture. After the Civil War, manufacturing branched out and concentrated increased funding and labor in heavy-industry consumer goods such as railroad tracks, steam engines, and farm tractors. Factories could now produce in huge quantities what craftspersons had painstakingly been making by hand.

Steelmaking was central to the new heavy industry. Hand in hand with steel production went the intensive development of the nation's mineral resources. Iron ore deposits in Michigan and Minnesota provided the raw

BROWN BROTHERS

Growing Employment Cotton mills, such as this one in Greensboro, North Carolina, photographed in 1895, provided jobs for many Southerners who were forced out of farming by hard times. Whole families worked in the mills. *How were factories linked to farming?*

substance for the steelmaking centers that sprang up in Illinois, Ohio, and Pennsylvania. Coal was equally important because it became the fuel that powered a nation of steam-run machines.

The Technology Boom

In 1876 the most ingenious American inventor since Benjamin Franklin built a long wooden shed in a little town in New Jersey where he promised to produce "a minor invention every ten days and a big thing every six months or so." Thomas Alva Edison, a brash 29-year-old at the time, was nearly as good as his word.

Edison patented more than 1,000 inventions in his Menlo Park laboratory before his death in 1931. He lit up the nation through his stunning development of an incandescent lightbulb that provided a cheap and

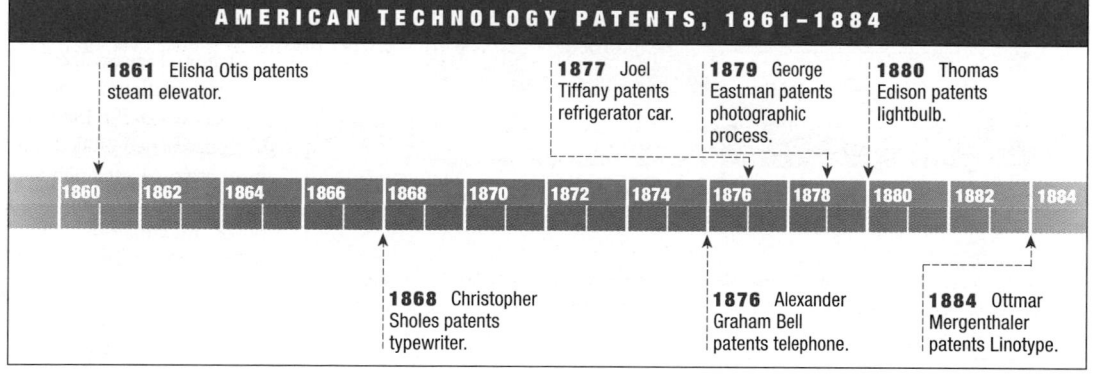

AMERICAN TECHNOLOGY PATENTS, 1861–1884

1861 Elisha Otis patents steam elevator.

1877 Joel Tiffany patents refrigerator car.

1879 George Eastman patents photographic process.

1880 Thomas Edison patents lightbulb.

| 1860 | 1862 | 1864 | 1866 | 1868 | 1870 | 1872 | 1874 | 1876 | 1878 | 1880 | 1882 | 1884 |

1868 Christopher Sholes patents typewriter.

1876 Alexander Graham Bell patents telephone.

1884 Ottmar Mergenthaler patents Linotype.

TEACH

Guided Practice

L2 **Discussion** Point out to students that the oil well and pipeline were two technological breakthroughs that revolutionized industry. By the 1860s prospectors knew how to drill successfully for petroleum, the fossil fuel that today supplies nearly half the world's energy. By the 1870s technicians had built pipelines for carrying crude oil to railroad centers or refineries. By 1900, 14 states had extensive drilling operations. Ask students what they know about the disadvantages of producing and burning oil.

Show students Beginnings to 1900 Transparencies 25, 26, and 28 and have them complete the activity sheets.

VISUAL INSTRUCTION

Growing Employment Cotton mills were multiplying in the South. By 1910 Southern mills had 11 million spindles, 39 percent of the national total.

Answer: *Factories processed the products of the farm.*

CHART STUDY

Ask: In what year did Alexander Graham Bell receive a patent for the telephone?
Answer: *1876*

Cooperative Learning

Researching Inventions Have students work in small groups to research inventions by Thomas Edison, Ottmar Mergenthaler (Linotype), George Westinghouse (air brakes), George Pullman (sleeping car), Andrew S. Hallidie (underground cable railway), Joseph F. Glidden (barbed wire), or John Hyatt (celluloid) and to determine how these inventions affected the nation. Group members should share the results of their research within their own group, then form new groups. Each group should plan and present an inventor roundup in one of these ways: chart, collage, biographical booklet, newspaper page, radio roundtable, or time line.

NATIONAL GEOGRAPHIC SOCIETY

 Videodisc

GTV: A Geographic Perspective on American History

Side 3, Chapter 8
Title: *The March of Industry*
Subject: Growth of American industry
Ask: In what region of the United States did industry first develop? *(the Northeast)*

Independent Practice

L1 Interviewing Have students interview older relatives to find out if they have ever shopped in a Ma and Pa grocery store instead of a supermarket, asking them about the advantages and disadvantages of each. Students should prepare a report.

Have students complete the Chapter 7, Section 2 Vocabulary and Guided Reading Activity. (Also in Spanish.) **LEP**

CHART STUDY

The Pullman sleeping car and the dining car also were introduced in the late 1800s, increasing public demand for passenger trains.

Answer: *1870s; stimulated a nationwide demand for fresh meat shipped by rail*

---

efficient replacement for candles and oil lamps. Of equal importance was his invention of the technology for producing and distributing electrical power.

Between 1860 and 1900, thousands of other inventors pushed forward the new age of machines and electrical energy. The United States Patent Office, which had issued a total of 36,000 patents in the 70 years before 1860, granted 676,000 between 1860 and 1900. Among the most important was Alexander Graham Bell's telephone. Patented in 1876, the telephone revolutionized communications.

By 1884 telephone service from Boston to New York City began the boom in rapid long-distance communication. By 1900 more than 1.3 million telephones were in operation nationwide.

Inventions and entrepreneurial skills combined to reshape the face of American manufacturing. New cotton machinery speeded up textile production. By 1886 a worker laboring for 10 hours could turn out 3 times as much as a worker in 1840 who toiled for 14 hours. Such developments made processed goods and consumer items cheaper and more readily available.

Everywhere in the United States the new technology could be seen in the form of mechanical reapers, blast furnaces, and telegraph offices; in the camera, typewriter, electric motor, and electric light; in the high-speed rotary printing press, iron and steel ships, pressed glass, wire rope, and petroleum. All of these products combined to create a new world of manufacturing, business, and consumerism.

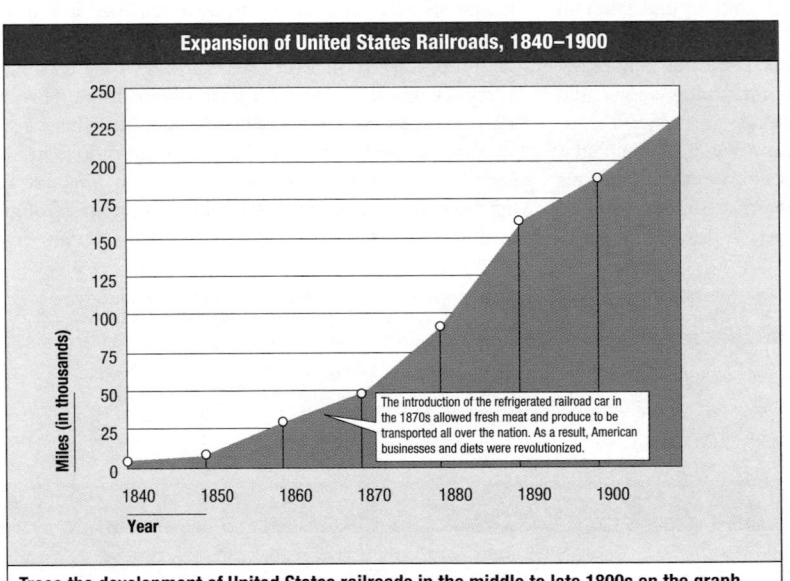

Expansion of United States Railroads, 1840–1900

Miles (in thousands) / Year

The introduction of the refrigerated railroad car in the 1870s allowed fresh meat and produce to be transported all over the nation. As a result, American businesses and diets were revolutionized.

Trace the development of United States railroads in the middle to late 1800s on the graph. *When was the refrigerated railroad car introduced? What inference can you make about how it may have affected the growth of railroads?*

206 CHAPTER 7 NEW FRONTIERS

National Markets
Products Move Across the Nation by Rail

Closely linked to the maturing of the nation's industrial economy was the creation of a transportation network that turned the country into a huge, unified **national market.** Before the Civil War, canal and river boats had carried the bulky farm and forest products from one region to another. After the Civil War, the fledgling railroad system that began in the 1830s surged forward. Soon it became the most popular way of transporting people and goods.

Across these thousands of miles of railroad track, goods could move with such year-round, on-time efficiency that entire industries were revolutionized. One example was the meatpacking industry. Before the Civil War, Americans bought meat from their local butchers, who had purchased livestock from nearby farmers. The railroads, however, allowed for far more efficient cattle raising on the wide-open ranges of the Great Plains. This in turn lowered meat prices for the consumer. From the Great Plains, cattle were shipped in cattle cars to livestock markets— Chicago was the largest—and then were distributed by the railroads to be slaughtered in Eastern and Southern cities.

Refrigerated Railroad Cars

The invention of the refrigerated railroad car further revolutionized the business. Gustavus Swift, a clever Chicago cattle dealer, recognized that if slaughtering and preparing meat for market could be done in one place, money could be saved and meat sold more cheaply. What was needed was the ability to keep meat fresh during its journey to the local butcher shops. The refrigerated railroad car was the answer.

Using the newly invented refrigerated car, Swift created a gigantic national meatpacking network in the 1880s. His wagons carried chilled meat from regional packinghouses to local butcher shops. Four other meatpackers copied Swift's innovations, and by the 1890s these five companies completely dominated the nation's meat business.

Meeting Special Needs

Oral Learners To help oral learners get acquainted with the section, invite them to predict what the rise of industrialism would have been like under somewhat different circumstances. Ask: If Thomas Edison had not invented the light bulb at this time, how would this have affected the growth of United States industry? *(Because other inventors were working on the same task, someone would probably have soon invented a light bulb or similar device. Manufacturing of bulbs and the vast amount of related equipment, however, would have been slowed.)*

New Consumer Markets With the growth of a national market, merchandising took a leap from local department stores to national chain stores. Customers across the country could expect to find F.W. Woolworth stores that looked very similar to this one, which was in New Haven, Connecticut. *What merchandising gimmick is advertised at this store?*

VISUAL INSTRUCTION

New Consumer Markets
The five-and-ten-cent store was a special kind of department store, and F.W. Woolworth was its presiding genius. He established fixed prices in a world where haggling was still customary, and he used attractive window displays and plentiful goods on the counters to entice customers. By 1900 his volume was more than $5 million a year.

Answer: *"Nothing in this store over 10 cents"*

First Train Robbery
The first train holdup took place at North Bend, Ohio in 1865. An Ohio and Mississippi train was derailed. Passengers were robbed and the express car looted.

The refrigerated railroad car also created a national market for fruits and vegetables from the West Coast. By 1888 fresh apricots and cherries were able to survive the train ride from California to New York, and the nation's diet was transformed. Large parts of the country that only ate locally grown fruits and vegetables during the summer months could now have a Florida orange for breakfast, an Oregon apple for lunch, and a California lettuce salad for dinner at any time of the year.

Nationwide Businesses

Other businesses quickly followed the move to identify or create a national market. By the 1880s the McCormick Harvesting Machine Company had a national network of dealers who not only sold mechanized farm equipment that arrived by train but also provided credit and repair services. The Singer Sewing Machine Company dotted the land with retail stores and blanketed the country with door-to-door salespeople.

City dwellers also became connected to huge nationwide chain store systems. F.W. Woolworth's five-and-ten-cent stores sprouted in thousands of towns and cities. The Great Atlantic and Pacific Tea Company replaced "Ma and Pa" grocery stores all over the country because this large grocery chain could undersell the single retailer through mass purchasing. All of the products sold in chain stores moved across the nation by rail.

The Birth of Consumerism

The creation of a national marketplace changed the way people spent their money. In the cities people no longer purchased solely from pushcarts or small shops, but rushed to the new department stores. John Wanamaker of Philadelphia introduced fixed prices and window displays to entice customers in 1861. Macy's in New York, Marshall Field in Chicago, and Jordan Marsh in Boston soon joined him.

These lavish consumer palaces included leaded-glass skylights, polished marble staircases, expensive carpets, and chandeliers. Such stores introduced charge accounts and trained clerks to cater to the customer. They tried to convince buyers that shopping was a great pleasure to be enjoyed. Advertising played a significant role in this buying craze. Between 1870 and 1900 the amount of money spent on advertising increased dramatically, from $50 million to $542 million.

Portfolio Project

National Marketers Have students research and report on one of the entrepreneurs who helped develop national markets. They might select Gustavus Swift of the meatpacking industry, F.W. Woolworth or John Wanamaker of retailing, mail-order innovator Aaron Montgomery Ward, sewing-machine magnate Isaac Merritt Singer, or another person who interests them. You may wish to have students share their reports with the class. Have them keep their reports in their portfolios.

Shopping at Home Montgomery Ward issued mail-order catalogs to rural families across the country. People could buy thousands of items, from barn nails to sunbonnets. *How did the mail-order business depend on railroads?*

The Growth of Big Business
Mergers Create Industrial Giants

The growth of heavy industry and the creation of vast nationwide markets brought about a fundamental change in business organization. Only large businesses gathering capital from many investors could afford to set up huge factories, install modern machinery, and employ hundreds of workers.

At the same time, the vast railroad system allowed national corporations to ship goods almost anywhere. While the typical railroad line in 1865 was only 100 miles long, by 1885 it had expanded to 1,000 miles (1,609 km) of track. Such a large enterprise, with enormous costs of construction, maintenance, and operation, demanded unprecedented amounts of capital and new methods of management.

The Managerial Revolution

In the early days of railroading, a superintendent could give his personal attention to every detail in running a 50- or 100-mile (80.45- or 160.9-km) operation.

How, then, could one person oversee the operations of a business such as the Pennsylvania Railroad? By 1890 this railroad had 50,000 employees, properties spread over great distances, large amounts of capital invested, and hundreds of trains that had to be scheduled and coordinated with precision.

The answer was to separate the various functions of a business into departments and put each one under the direction of a separate manager. In a railroad, for example, one person would be in charge of people who maintained the tracks; another supervised cargo handling; another oversaw traffic. Managers reported to the central office through well-defined lines of communication.

The Merger Movement

Led by the railroads, the American industrial economy grew rapidly in the decades after the Civil War. The cutthroat competition of an uncontrolled marketplace, however, plagued businesses. Business owners feverishly overbuilt their operations in good times and cut back sharply when demand for their products slackened. In such a boom-or-bust marketplace, bankruptcy was common. In the depression of the 1870s, for example, 47,000 firms closed their doors, laying off hundreds of thousands of employees.

Some people felt that the solution to such business instability was a **merger,** or a combining of several competing firms under a single head. By merging companies in a particular industry, a junglelike market could become an orderly, predictable market. "I like a little competition now and then," exclaimed J.P. Morgan, a titan of mergers in the late 1800s, "but I like combination a lot better."

The pioneering figure in the late nineteenth-century merger movement was John D. Rockefeller. Rockefeller started out as a clerk in his boyhood town of Cleveland, Ohio. In the 1860s he founded a business that refined kerosene from petroleum and later became Standard Oil Company. Hundreds of oil refineries, mostly small and badly organized, competed fiercely in the Ohio and Pennsylvania regions.

Both wise and ruthless, Rockefeller purchased as many competing companies as possible, and by the late 1870s Standard Oil controlled almost all the oil refineries in Ohio. By 1882 Standard Oil had gobbled up most of the competition throughout the country. Rockefeller's 40 oil companies owned 90 percent of the nation's

Extending the Content

Creating a Trust Use the oil industry as an example of how a trust was created. A board of directors was formed. Then stockholders in small oil companies, enticed by the promise of better profits, turned their stock over to this board, which held them in trust. "Trustees" gained huge advantages from this innocent-looking maneuver. The trust cut prices, forcing out competing companies. Then the trust limited production and hiked prices, boosting profits. Today, the Federal Trade Commission (FTC) and the Antitrust Division of the Department of Justice enforce antitrust laws. Ask students why a democratic society should control trusts.

pipelines and refined 84 percent of the nation's oil. "The day of individual competition [in the oil business] is past and gone," Rockefeller pronounced.

Because he dominated the market, Rockefeller was able to demand rail shipping rates of ten cents a barrel as compared with his competitors' thirty-five cents. When Rockefeller turned the business over to his son in 1911, his fortune exceeded $1 billion.

The merger of competing companies in one area of business such as occurred to form Rockefeller's oil corporation was known as **horizontal integration.** It was often accompanied by **vertical integration** of industries, in which a firm would strive to control all aspects of production from acquisition of raw materials to final delivery of finished products. In this way a single business might gain total control over a national market, as the chart below shows. Note that when a business integrates horizontally, it merges all competing companies in one area of business. In vertical integration, one business controls all aspects of production.

In the merger movement, Swift and Armour dominated meatpacking, and the Duke family controlled tobacco. Andrew Carnegie, however, had the most success with vertical integration. Carnegie bought up coal mines and iron ore deposits for his steel mills, then bought railroads and ships to transport raw materials and send his products to market. By owning every aspect of steel production he could limit risk and guarantee profit.

When J.P. Morgan bought Carnegie's steel company in 1901, he consolidated it with several other firms to form the U.S. Steel Corporation, which controlled 60 percent of American steel production. It was the nation's first billion-dollar company. By 1913 J.P. Morgan controlled 314 directorships in 112 corporations, with an estimated collective worth of $22 billion.

The Spirit of the Gilded Age
Lavish Spending and Ruthless Competition

The wealth generated by industrial capitalism and big business led to the growth of a "nouveau riche" class with its own philosophy. Many of these self-made people proclaimed their importance with showy displays of wealth, leading humorist Mark Twain to call the late 1800s the Gilded Age.

HORIZONTAL AND VERTICAL INTEGRATION

Business mergers of the late 1800s followed two strategies: **vertical**—joining all areas of one business, and **horizontal**—joining competing businesses in one area. Although the huge companies boosted the nation's production, they exercised unfair control over industry and faced legal battles that limited their size.

VERTICAL

Raw Materials:
mines, oil fields, farms, companies that extract or harvest a natural resource

Production:
refineries, mills, factories, companies that manufacture a product

Distribution:
railroads, ships, trucks, companies that transport a product to market

HORIZONTAL

Vertical Merger
"There is but one rule among Americans—the tools to those who can use them."
—Andrew Carnegie
To streamline business at his steel plants, Carnegie bought iron deposits, coke fields, ships, and railroads. In 1889 he joined these holdings into one company, which J.P. Morgan later reorganized as U.S. Steel.

Horizontal Merger
"I believe it is my duty to make money and still more money, and to use [it] . . . for the good of my fellow man."
—John D. Rockefeller
Rockefeller began by buying refineries around Cleveland. He then expanded to include refineries and pipelines throughout the country. By 1882 his Standard Oil Company owned most of the nation's oil industry.

The chart above illustrates horizontal and vertical business integration. When a business integrates horizontally, it merges all competing companies in one area of business. In vertical integration, one business controls all aspects of production. *What kind of business integration does U.S. Steel represent in the chart? What did it own?*

Cultural Perspectives

Settlement House Immigration supplied a great many of the workers needed for the rise of industrialism at the end of the 1800s. Adult night schools and social settlements helped to teach these newcomers and their children the English language and American customs, and to protect them from exploitation. The first such settlement was Hull House, established by reformer Jane Addams in Chicago in 1889. Addams and her Hull House associates also worked for the enactment of child labor laws and for the development of trade unions.

ASSESS

Meeting Lesson Objectives

Each section objective is tested by the section review question(s) that follows it in parentheses.

1. Explain the relationship between inventions and industrialism. (2, 5)
2. Describe how industrialism and national markets fostered changes in business. (3)
3. Describe the two types of mergers. (1)
4. Explain how industrialists applied Social Darwinism to big business. (4)

CHART STUDY

In 1882 Standard Oil formed a trust, which was declared illegal in 1892. It was then reconstituted as a "holding company." U.S. Steel, too, was formed as a holding company in 1901. Antitrust laws were enacted quickly, but big business grew faster.

Answer: *Vertical integration; raw materials, manufacturing, and distribution*

History and the Humanities

U.S. History and Art Transparencies 14, 16, and 17—*Smoking Room, John D. Rockefeller House; In the Garden* by Mary Cassatt; *Gold Presentation Vase,* Paulding Farnham for Tiffany and Co.

209

History and the Humanities

📖 Focus on American Fine Art Prints, Prints 11 and 12—*The Gulf Stream* by Winslow Homer; *The Boating Party* by Mary Cassatt

Evaluate

Have students complete the Section Review.

📁 💿 Assign the Section 2 Quiz or use the Testmaker to develop a customized quiz. (Also in Spanish.) **LEP**

Reteach

🎧 Have students listen to the Chapter 7, Section 2 Audiocassette. (Also in Spanish.) **LEP**

Enrich

Have interested students research the work of Herbert Spencer and prepare an oral report detailing his beliefs.

VISUAL INSTRUCTION

Newport, Rhode Island The most palatial of Newport's "cottages" was The Breakers, built in 1895 in the Renaissance style for Cornelius Vanderbilt. Many of these mansions are now tourist attractions.

Answer: *People flaunted their new wealth in showy ways.*

CLOSE

Help students develop an outline on the board to recapture the main points of this section. They can use the headings in the text as a framework.

210

Some of these people, known as robber barons, built lavish mansions in New York City complete with solid gold bathroom fixtures. For the summer months many built castlelike estates in Newport, Rhode Island, which they dubbed their "cottages." Railroad tycoon William Vanderbilt's summer home cost $11 million. Outrageous displays of wealth were popular. At one debutante ball in Philadelphia, a young woman's parents ordered thousands of live butterflies (many of which drowned in champagne glasses) as decorations at the $75,000 party.

Social Darwinism

In the heady, expensive atmosphere of the Gilded Age, the struggle for wealth became a way of life for the most ambitious Americans. How did business leaders, bent on killing off competition in order to increase their control of the marketplace and make as much money as possible, justify their activities to a public raised on the ideology of a fair and open society? A new theory of human behavior provided an answer. It rested on the scientific theories of Charles Darwin about the origin of species and the evolution of humankind. Darwin argued that the plant and animal world had reached its present state through a long process of "natural selection" in which only the fittest had survived. Herbert Spencer, an English philosopher, loosely adapted these ideas, in a theory known as Social Darwinism, to explain the evolution of human society.

Progress, Spencer argued, occurred through competition in which the weak fell and the strong forged ahead. His strongest American supporter, William G. Sumner, put it this way: "If we do not like the survival of the fittest, we have only one possible alternative, and that is the survival of the unfittest."

American business leaders flocked to honor Spencer when he visited the United States in 1882. Here was a man whose theories justified their aggressive business practices and their attempts to eliminate weaker competitors. They heaped praise on his notion that government should never interfere with the separation of the weak from the strong because this would only hold back progress.

Concern for the Less Fortunate

Despite their seeming lack of regard for common people, many of the robber barons who had embraced Social Darwinism also supported the spirit of charity. They believed that the more fortunate should give back to society to benefit the public at large. Carnegie was but one of a host of powerful, rich patrons who supported the arts, education, and culture; funded public works; and established foundations.

These individual efforts had their limitations, however. As Jane Addams, a reformer of this time, com-

---

CULVER PICTURES

Newport, Rhode Island While the wealthy lounged on the steps of summer "cottages," others worked in factories and mines. *Why were the late 1800s known as an age of excess?*

mented concerning her native city of Chicago, "Private beneficence [charity] is totally inadequate to deal with vast numbers of the city's disinherited." Americans would have to learn new ways to cope with and solve the enormous problems created by population growth and industrialization in the United States between the Civil War and the end of the nineteenth century.

SECTION REVIEW

Vocabulary

1. Define: industrialism, national market, merger, horizontal integration, vertical integration.

Checking Facts

2. Name two technological advances that spurred industrial growth in the late 1800s.

3. How did the growth of railroads help to create national markets ?

Critical Thinking

Predicting Consequences

4. How might workers have reacted to the theory preached by Social Darwinists?

Linking Across Time

5. How do you think technological advances in computer science have changed the job qualifications that workers need today?

Section 2 Review Answers

1. industrialism (205), **national market** (206), **merger** (208), **horizontal integration** (209), **vertical integration** (209)
2. Possible answers include the steam engine and the Bessemer converter.
3. Railroads carried goods across the nation and reduced the cost and time of transporting them.

4. Survival of the fittest implies aggression. Workers might resent business magnates' self-serving aggression, which for workers meant poor working conditions and long hours.
5. Today's workers require more advanced skills to operate computers and other modern equipment.

Social Studies Skill

READING STATISTICAL TABLES

Learning the Skill

Tables present statistical information by organizing it into categories. A statistical table can help you to identify patterns in employment in the United States.

Finding Information in a Table

To find the answers to statistical questions:

a. Read the title; then make sure that you understand the headings. There are three major headings: Total Labor Force, Labor Force, and Employment. Two of these heads are divided into smaller categories or heads; and of these, Manufacturing, Transport, and Service are subdivided again.

b. The lefthand column, the stub, lists another category of information, in this case, years. Find out which years the stub lists.

c. The columns of figures are the body of the table. They give data, by category, for each year.

d. Read down from one column heading and across from the corresponding year to find a measure of the labor force employed in a trade for that year.

Practicing the Skill

Study the table below, then answer the following questions:

1. In 1960 the Total Labor Force was 74,060,000. Why are there no figures in the next 2 columns?

2. What percentage worked in Trade in 1900?

3. Which category has lost the most workers?

4. By what percentage did employment in this field change?

5. Which categories gained the most workers?

Applying the Skill

Using another table, write 10 questions that can be answered from the table, and their answers.

Additional Practice

For additional practice, see Reinforcing Skills on page 225.

Labor Force and Employment, 1800–1960

Year	TOTAL LABOR FORCE (IN THOUSANDS)	LABOR FORCE (PERCENT) Free	Slave	Agriculture	Fishing	Mining	Construction	Total	Cotton Textiles	Primary Iron and Steel	Trade	Ocean Vessels	Railways	Teachers	Domestics
1800	1,900	72	28	74	0.3	1.0	–	–	0.1	0.1	–	2.0	–	0.3	2
1810	2,330	68	32	84	0.3	0.5	–	3	0.4	0.2	–	3.0	–	1.0	3
1820	3,135	70	30	79	0.4	0.4	–	–	0.4	0.2	–	2.0	–	1.0	4
1830	4,200	72	28	71	0.4	1.0	–	–	1.0	0.5	–	2.0	–	1.0	4
1840	5,660	74	26	63	0.4	1.0	5	9	1.0	0.4	6	2.0	0.1	1.0	4
1850	8,250	76	24	55	0.4	1.0	5	15	1.0	0.4	6	2.0	0.2	1.0	4
1860	11,110	79	21	53	0.3	2.0	5	14	1.0	0.4	8	1.0	1.0	1.0	5
1870	12,930	–	–	53	0.2	1.0	6	19	1.0	1.0	10	1.0	1.0	1.0	8
1880	17,390	–	–	51	0.2	2.0	5	19	1.0	1.0	11	1.0	2.0	1.0	6
1890	23,320	–	–	43	0.3	2.0	6	19	1.0	1.0	13	1.0	3.0	2.0	7
1900	29,070	–	–	40	0.2	2.0	6	20	1.0	1.0	14	0.4	4.0	1.0	6
1910	37,480	–	–	31	0.2	3.0	5	22	1.0	1.0	14	0.4	5.0	2.0	6
1920	41,610	–	–	26	0.1	3.0	3	27	1.0	1.0	14	0.5	5.0	2.0	4
1930	48,830	–	–	22	0.1	2.0	4	20	1.0	1.0	17	0.3	3.0	2.0	5
1940	56,290	–	–	17	0.1	2.0	3	20	1.0	1.0	17	0.3	2.0	2.0	4
1950	65,470	–	–	12	0.1	1.0	5	24	1.0	1.0	19	0.2	2.0	2.0	3
1960	74,060	–	–	8	0.1	1.0	5	23	0.4	1.0	19	0.2	1.0	2.0	3

(EMPLOYMENT (PERCENT); Manufacturing spans Total / Cotton Textiles / Primary Iron and Steel; Transport spans Ocean Vessels / Railways; Service spans Teachers / Domestics)

The United States Bureau of the Census compiled the statistical data for this table on labor and employment. *How many different fields of employment are represented? What are they?*

TEACH

This skill teaches students to glean valuable information from a table of figures. Tell students that many people think statistics are dull or just a dry series of numbers. Point out that when organized into a table, the figures reveal shifts, trends, growth and decline in various categories. Discuss with students what such patterns might tell a reader about people's lives, for instance, how they work, play, and spend money; how healthy they are; and what their beliefs are. This table provides an example. One number alone is meaningless, but when viewed as a whole, the figures in the table tell how the lives of workers changed over a given time period.

MAP STUDY

Point out to students that the table shows data from 1800 to 1960.

Answer: *8; Agriculture, Fishing, Mining, Construction, Manufacturing, Trade, Transport, Service*

Additional Practice

☞ Have students complete the Chapter 7 Skill Reinforcement Activity.

Practicing the Skill Answers

1. The next 2 columns show the division between enslaved and free labor. This differentiation did not exist in 1960, when slavery had long been abolished.

2. 14 percent

3. Agriculture lost the greatest percentage of workers between 1800 and 1960.

4. 66 percent

5. Manufacturing, followed by the trade industry, gained the greatest share of workers.

SECTION

3

FOCUS

Section Objectives

1. Trace the early development of the Populist party.
2. Describe the problems facing farmers and their efforts to solve them.
3. Explain the development of early labor unions in the late 1800s.

Bellringer Activity

While taking attendance at the beginning of the class period, display **Section Focus Transparency 21,** and have students answer the questions. (Or use the blackline master.)

VISUAL INSTRUCTION

Stirring Words Attempts to start a third political party, such as the Populists, have usually occurred during hard economic times, which often impact farmers first and hardest.

Ask: What were some of the Populist ideals? *(Populists believed in a shorter workday, restrictions on immigration, and free coinage of silver.)*

Populism and Protest

JULY 2, 1892: PEOPLE'S PARTY HOLDS FIRST CONVENTION

IN JULY 1892, THE DELEGATES OF A NEW POLITICAL PARTY MET IN OMAHA TO CEMENT THEIR ALLIANCE:

We have witnessed for more than a quarter of a century the struggles of the two great political parties for power and plunder, while grievous wrongs have been inflicted upon the suffering people. . . . Assembled on the anniversary of the birthday of the nation ... we seek to restore the government of the Republic to the hands of "the plain people."
—Omaha Platform, July 1892

Stirring Words
Farmers and laborers listened to Ignatius Donnelly at the first Populist convention in 1892.

The delegates adopted the platform of the People's party, also called the Populist party, with great enthusiasm. The platform not only denounced the existing ills of society but also proposed a third-party remedy. The Populists represented a grand coalition of farmers, laborers, and reformers, which aimed to put government back into the hands of the people.

Populist leaders were as colorful and diverse as the causes they represented. Ignatius Donnelly of Minnesota, who had written the preamble to the party platform, was considered the greatest orator of Populism. Mary E. Lease, who forcefully represented farmers' interests, once advised Kansas farmers to "raise less corn and more hell." "Sockless Jerry" Simpson earned his nickname when he told a Kansas audience that he wore no silk socks like his "princely" Republican opponent. Georgia's Thomas E. Watson left the Democratic party to campaign for Populist ideals.

AS YOU READ

Vocabulary
► union
► strike
► injunction

Think About . . .
► the development of the Populist party.
► the problems facing farmers and their efforts to improve their situation.
► the development of labor unions in the late 1800s.

212 CHAPTER 7 NEW FRONTIERS

Section 3 Resources

REPRODUCIBLE RESOURCES
📁 Lesson Plan 7-3
📁 Vocabulary and Guided Reading 7-3
📁 Section 3 Quiz

MULTIMEDIA RESOURCES
📷 Section Focus Transparency 21
📷 Beginnings to 1900 Transparency 27
🎧 American Music: Cultural Traditions
📖 Focus on American Fine Art Prints, Print 13

💿 Testmaker
🎧 Chapter 7 Digest Audiocassette
💿 Student Self-Test: A Software Review

The Populists chose their candidates amid calls for restricted immigration and a shorter workday for industrial laborers. The party also aimed to convince the government to allow the free coinage of silver, a measure that would make silver, not just gold, legal tender. Many farmers thought this would cause inflation, thereby raising prices for farm goods, and would breathe new life into the faltering economy. The nomination for President in 1892 went to James B. Weaver, a seasoned campaigner from Iowa, who had been the candidate of the Greenback party in 1880. Second place on the ticket went to James G. Field, a former Confederate general from Virginia. As one historian observed, "Whether they knew it or not, the delegates were beginning the last phase of a long and perhaps losing struggle—the struggle to save agricultural America from the devouring jaws of industrial America."

Farmers Beleaguered
Falling Prices, Rising Debts

The rapid development of the agricultural West and the reorganization of Southern agriculture after the Civil War provided new opportunities for millions of American families. The changes also exposed these families to the financial hardships of rural life. The result was the first mass organization of farmers in American history.

Ironically the farmers' problem was rooted in their ability to produce so much. Immigrants as well as American-born farmers were tilling huge tracts of the Great Plains for the first time. Larger acreage, coupled with improved farming methods, meant bumper crops in most years. By the 1870s farmers produced more than the country—or the world—demanded. Prices dropped, as the graph shows. In addition two factors contributed to the farmers' financial problems: many farmers borrowed money to put more land under cultivation, and most of them had to pay high transportation costs to get crops to market.

Falling farm prices brought widespread rural suffering. On the Great Plains, many farmers had to borrow more money to keep afloat financially. In the South many lost their farms and became debt-ridden sharecroppers. When Eastern bankers began to foreclose on farm loans, thousands abandoned their homesteads.

Homesteaders in the late 1800s also faced nature's wrath. In 1874 a plague of grasshoppers devoured crops, clothes, and even plow handles. Droughts parched the earth in 1886. In January 1888, in the northern Plains the School Children's Storm killed more than 200 youngsters who were stranded at school or starting home.

Loneliness could be just as tormenting. One farm mother, who had not seen another woman for a year, walked across the prairie with her small children to see a woman who had come to live several miles away. The two strangers threw their arms around each other and wept.

Some families gave up and headed back East. They left behind bitter slogans: "In God we trusted, in Kansas we busted." The farmers who stayed began to seek political relief. The governor of Kansas received the following letter from a farm woman in 1894:

> I take my pen in hand to let you know we are starving. . . . My husband went away to find work and came home last night and told me that he would have to starve. He had been in 10 counties and did not get no work. . . . I haven't had nothing to eat today and it is 3 o'clock.

Farmers United

Farmers, like other beleaguered groups in society, realized that there is strength in numbers. As early as 1867 farmers banded together to form the Patrons of Husbandry, also known as the Grange. By 1875 there were about 1 million Grange members spread from New England to Texas, concentrated mainly in the South and the Great Plains. The Grangers wanted the government to

Production and Price of Wheat, 1860–1900

The graph on the left shows an increase in wheat production during the late 1800s. The graph on the right shows the price of wheat declining during this same period. *What conclusion can you draw from these two graphs?*

Cooperative Learning

Creating Comparison Charts Have students work together with partners or small groups to research minority political parties in the United States today, such as the Green party, the Libertarian party, or the Socialist party. Have each group create a visual display comparing the platforms of these radical parties to the ideals of the Populist party. Group members should work cooperatively to design a graphic display of their comparisons. 🖥️

TEACH

Guided Practice

L2 Linking Past and Present Although no Populist candidate ever won the presidency, the third party shaped mainstream politics. Ask students to identify the positions of Democrats and Republicans in a recent election. Then discuss how a third party with more radical views than either major party might have affected the election.

🕹️ Show students Beginnings to 1900 Transparency 27 and have them complete the activity sheet.

FYI

Community Organizing A clerk in the Agriculture Department, Oliver Hudson Kelley, organized the Grangers. He recognized that large industries operating without regulations endangered farmers. Members gathered at halls called granges. *Grange* is a British term used to describe a gentleman farmer's residence and outbuildings.

GRAPH STUDY

Farmers produced more than the market demanded, causing prices to drop. As a result, they had to borrow funds to keep going. If a drought or other disaster hit, they had no way to halt foreclosures on their farms.

Answer: *Prices fell as production increased.*

Independent Practice

L2 **Researching Labor Unions** Have students investigate labor unions today. Have them compare the problems and programs of labor today with those of the late 1800s. If they wish, they can narrow their topic to a particular problem. They can begin their research with a recent guide to periodical literature, finding and reading one article. They can also talk with older relatives about their experiences with unions and their opinions of them. Have students report their findings orally or in writing.

📁 Have students complete the Chapter 7, Section 3 Vocabulary and Guided Reading Activity. (Also in Spanish.) **LEP**

MAP STUDY

By 1892, a full generation after the Civil War, some Northerners' allegiance to the Republican party had waned as they confronted new problems and challenges. The Populists illuminated the issues but provided answers too radical for most Northerners. This caused many Northerners to switch their votes to the Democrat, Grover Cleveland, giving him the victory.

Answer: *Populists gained the most support in the Plains states and some Western states—areas where mining and farming were prevalent.*

---

regulate railroad freight rates and to fund agricultural colleges. They also formed sales cooperatives, pooling their products and dividing profits.

In the 1880s farmers stepped up their political activism by forming groups known as Farmers' Alliances— one in the South, another on the Plains. The Alliances pooled the credit resources of their members to free themselves from the high interest rates banks charged. They formed marketing cooperatives to sell directly to large merchants and thus avoided paying extra costs to brokers. Such cooperatives could also buy bulk quantities of the supplies and machinery farmers needed.

The Populist Crusade

Despite action by the Farmers' Alliances and the Grangers, the plight of thousands of farmers worsened. By the 1890s they had become politically active as never before. The platform of the Populist party called for extensive reforms. Reformers believed that farmers and workers should be freed from the exploitative practices of banks, railroads, and merchants. Although James Weaver, the Populist candidate for President, soundly lost to Democrat Grover Cleveland in the election of 1892, his party made headway. The Populists gained 14 seats in Congress, won 2 governorships, and received the largest number of popular votes cast for any third party in the 1800s.

Shortly after the election of 1892, the nation plunged into the deepest depression the country had yet known. In 1893 more than 2.5 million Americans, about 20 percent of the labor force, were unemployed. By the following year, the ranks of the unemployed had swollen to 4 million.

President Cleveland's seeming indifference to the economic problems caused by the depression created a popular revolt. Jacob S. Coxey, a quiet Ohio business owner, led a march of about 500 people from Ohio to Washington, D.C., to dramatize the plight of the jobless. Leaders read their grievances on the steps of the Capitol and were arrested for unlawfully trying to enter the building.

By the time of the 1896 election, the Populist party itself had declined, but some of its ideas entered the mainstream. The continuing depression forced the Democratic party into a more radical position on one key issue—unlimited coinage of silver. This stance led many Populists to support the Democratic candidate, William Jennings Bryan of Nebraska. Bryan waged a campaign in favor of "free silver," and secured endorsement by the Populist party. He traveled extensively, logging 18,000 miles (28,962 km) on the campaign trail.

The Republican nominee, William McKinley, took a more relaxed approach. McKinley had the support of big business. Standard Oil's $250,000 donation to the Republicans nearly exceeded the total amount in the Democrats' treasury. McKinley merely warned voters of the dangers of radicalism.

McKinley won by a comfortable 600,000 votes, suggesting that Americans in towns and cities heeded his warning. The discovery of gold in Alaska in 1898 increased the nation's gold reserves and eased more money into circulation, stemming the money crisis for many farmers. Populism began to decline as a political force.

THE ELECTION OF 1892

VOTING FOR THE PEOPLE'S PARTY, 1892
Popular vote by state for the People's (Populist) party ticket of Weaver and Field

- 50% or more
- 33% to 50%
- 10% to 33%
- 0% to 10%
- Not yet a state in 1892

Nationally, the People's party received 8.54% of the popular vote

0   250   500 mi.
0   250 500 km
Albers Equal-Area projection

The Populist candidates for President and Vice President in 1892 received varying support from one state to the next. In which states or regions did the Populists gain the most votes?

The South Withholds Support

One factor limited Populism's strength in the South. By 1890 more than 1 million farmers belonged to the Southern Alliance—the Southern branch of the two Farmers' Alliances. In December the Southern Alliance met with other farmers' groups at Ocala, Florida, and drew up a list of concerns. These included cheap currency, the abolition of national banks, and the restriction of land ownership to American citizens.

Meeting Special Needs

Limited English Proficiency Help students who are less proficient in English to preview the content of the section. Guide students in scanning the illustrations and discussing their captions and themes. Another useful tactic would be to go over vocabulary terms and objectives in As You Read on page 212. Then be certain that students understand these items. **LEP**

Although this list resembled the Populist platform of 1892, the People's party failed to gain wide support in the South. The Southern Alliance advised its members to support major party candidates who favored agricultural interests.

The underlying reason for the failure of Populism in the South was the issue of white supremacy. The Southern Alliance feared that Populism might lead to gains for African Americans. Populist leader Thomas Watson tried to form an alliance of poor white and African American farmers. He argued that social class was more important than race. He urged citizens of both races to unite against the financial oppression that enslaved them.

Watson's career, however, mirrored the fate of Populism in the South. He was elected to Congress in 1890 but was defeated two years later as Democratic candidates who promised to exclude African Americans from political power gained support. Watson ran for President on the Populist ticket in 1904 and 1908. Embittered by his defeats, he turned against many who had supported him. He became racist, anti-Catholic, and anti-Semitic.

Labor Organizes
Unions for Skilled Workers

As early as the 1810s, skilled workers such as carpenters, printers, and tailors had formed citywide organizations to try to get better pay. Construction workers in many Eastern cities succeeded in getting a 10-hour day in 1834. As the workplace changed, however, so did the labor movement. After the Civil War, factory production replaced skilled labor. Employers often cut the cost of wages by hiring women and children. Workers, like farmers, decided to organize to maintain control over their wages and working conditions.

The first nationwide labor organizations developed during the mid-1800s. In 1867 bootmakers and shoemakers, whose wares were being undersold by machine-made products, formed the Knights of St. Crispin to try to block competition from unskilled workers. By 1870 this **union,** an organization for mutual benefit, had nearly 50,000 members. Like most early unions, however, the Knights of St. Crispin could not survive the high unemployment of the 1870s.

In 1877 a national railroad **strike,** or work stoppage, was the first of many violent confrontations between labor and the large corporations in the post–Civil War era. Clashes between railroad workers and state militias or federal troops sent in to break the strikes recurred in the 1880s. Then in 1885 successful negotiations with railroad magnate Jay Gould helped workers in all fields by convincing millions that they needed stronger unions.

Mother Jones Mary Harris Jones became known by company bosses as "the most dangerous woman in America." *What obstacles did Mother Jones overcome in her early life before becoming a champion for poor workers?*

The Knights of Labor

The first national labor union to remain active for more than a few years was the Knights of Labor. Tailors in Philadelphia formed it as a secret society in 1869, and it grew to national proportions in the 1880s. The Knights of Labor differed from other labor unions by accepting all gainfully employed persons, including farmers, merchants, and unskilled workers. The union proposed new laws, including one to cut the workday to eight hours and one to authorize equal pay for men and women doing the same work. Both of these were radical propositions at the time.

Women workers played a role in this growing labor movement. When Irish immigrant Mary Harris Jones lost her husband and children to yellow fever in 1867, she moved to Chicago to work as a seamstress. After losing everything else in a fire, she turned to the Knights of Labor for help. Soon she was one of its strongest campaigners. She traveled on behalf of labor for nearly 50 years—later organizing for the United Mine Workers. Beloved by her followers, she became known as "Mother Jones." The bosses, however, feared her. A West Virginia lawyer working for the mining companies called her "the most dangerous woman in America."

VISUAL INSTRUCTION

Mother Jones Mother Jones wanted to overthrow the whole concept of private ownership. In 1912 she told a newspaper reporter: "I believe in collective ownership of the means of wealth. . . . My life work has been to educate the worker to a sense of the wrongs he has had to suffer—and to stir up the oppressed to a point of getting off their knees and demanding that which I believe to be rightfully theirs."

Answer: *Mary Jones lost her husband and children and her home and business.*

History and the Humanities

American Music: Cultural Traditions— "The Farmer Is the Man That Feeds Them All" by Fiddlin' John Carson

Focus on American Fine Art Prints, Print 13— *Love's Young Dream* by Jennie Augusta Brownescombe

---

Portfolio Project

Persuasive Writing Use a bulletin board or large posterboard to create a mock-up of an editorial newspaper page. Several student pieces can be mounted together. Ask each student to select a labor clash covered in this section, such as the Haymarket riot or the American Railway Union strike. After researching the events students can create: an editorial supporting labor's role in the clash; an editorial supporting management's role; or a cartoon parodying the government's response. Have students keep copies of their editorials or cartoons in their portfolios.

Meeting Lesson Objectives

Each section objective is tested by the section review question(s) that follows it in parentheses.

1. Trace the early development of the Populist party. (1, 3)
2. Describe the problems facing farmers and their efforts to solve them. (2, 3, 5)
3. Explain the development of early labor unions in the late 1800s. (1, 4)

VISUAL INSTRUCTION

Violent Clash The Homestead workers were defeated partly because Carnegie's other plants kept working, and pig iron from those plants was then used at Homestead. The strike delayed the unionization of steelworkers for more than 40 years.

Answer: *The strike involved the Carnegie Steel Company and the steelworkers' union.*

The American Federation of Labor

In 1886 the Knights of Labor reached its peak with more than 700,000 members. A less reform-minded group, the American Federation of Labor (AFL), soon replaced it as the leading union. Led by Samuel Gompers, a cigar maker born in England, the AFL concentrated on organizing skilled workers. It advocated using strikes to improve wages and hours.

Gompers was willing to accept the new industrial system as it was, but only if labor got greater rewards. He also advocated boycotts—organized agreements to refuse to buy specific products—as one means of peaceful protest. This tactic had only limited success.

Protests and Violence
The Labor Movement Meets Resistance

Workers in the late 1800s customarily worked 10 hours a day, 6 days a week. A strike for an 8-hour workday at the huge McCormick Harvester factory in Chicago led to violent confrontation on May 3, 1886. After police killed 4 strikers in a scuffle outside the plant, about 1,000 workers turned out for a rally at Haymarket Square.

The Haymarket Riot

Someone in the crowd threw a bomb during the Haymarket protest, killing 7 police officers and injuring 67 bystanders. The police then fired into the crowd, killing 10 and wounding 50. Uproar over the Haymar-

CULVER PICTURES

Violent Clash Angry strikers taunt security forces sent to break up the Pennsylvania Homestead strike in this 1892 print. *Which company and which union were involved in the Homestead strike?*

ket riot continued when 8 radical strike leaders were put on trial for murder. Although no direct evidence that any of them had thrown the bomb could be found, 7 of the 8 were sentenced to death, and 4 eventually were hanged. The public outcry against labor organizers helped employers defeat the 8-hour workday reform.

The Homestead Strike

In 1892 another violent dispute took place in Homestead, Pennsylvania. The steelworkers' union called a strike when the Carnegie Steel Company reduced wages. The company hired 300 guards from the Pinkerton Detective Agency to protect its factories. Several people were killed when violence broke out between the strikers and the guards. The Homestead strike failed when most workers quit the union and returned to work.

Coeur d'Alene

Labor unrest spread to the West as well. Disputes arose between miners and mine owners over pay and conditions. Disputes also flared between nonunion miners and members of the Western Federation of Miners. Strikes plagued the Coeur d'Alene mining region of Idaho during the 1890s. Twice the strikes were broken when the governor called in federal troops.

The Pullman Strike

The depression that lasted from 1893 to 1897 brought further setbacks for labor. In 1894 Eugene V. Debs, the founder of the new American Railway Union, led a labor action against the Pullman sleeping car works near Chicago.

George Pullman saw his company town as a model industrial village where workers were paid decently and were also disciplined. "We are born in a Pullman house," said one worker, "fed from the Pullman shop, taught in the Pullman school, catechized in the Pullman church, and when we die we shall be buried in the Pullman cemetery and go to the Pullman hell."

As the depression of 1893 worsened, Pullman cut wages by one-third and fired many workers. Prices in the company stores and rents for the company houses, however, stayed the same. Angry Pullman workers joined Debs's railroad union in droves and went on strike in the spring of 1894.

Debs then led a strike of all American Railway Union members across

---

Extending the Content

Gold and Silver In the 1896 presidential race, William Jennings Bryan promoted "free silver." Farmers became convinced that minting silver coins would be to their benefit. An increased money supply meant inflation, which would bring about higher crop prices, allowing debts to be paid with devalued dollars. In 1900 the United States officially adopted the gold standard. This meant the United States would redeem any of its currency (coin or paper) in gold upon demand. It did keep inflation in check, but did not allow for needed adjustments in the money supply. After going on and off the gold standard, the United States eventually gave it up under FDR.

EARLY LABOR STRUGGLES, 1869–1895

1869 Tailors in Philadelphia organize the first long-standing American union, the Knights of Labor.

1886 A strike at McCormick Harvester culminates in the Haymarket riot after 4 strikers are killed.

1894 Eugene V. Debs leads the Pullman strike, which grows into the American Railway Union strike.

| 1855 | 1860 | 1865 | 1870 | 1875 | 1880 | 1885 | 1890 | 1895 |

1877 A national railroad strike triggers a series of clashes between government troops and rail workers.

1892 Steelworkers in Pennsylvania fight armed guards in the Homestead strike.

1895 The Supreme Court rules that the President has the power to break strikes.

the country in sympathy with the Pullman workers. Debs promised to "use no violence" and to "stop no trains." Instead workers refused to handle trains with Pullman sleeping cars.

Determined to break the growing union movement, 24 railroad owners persuaded President Cleveland to order United States Army troops to disperse the strikers. Violence once again centered in Chicago where strikers fought troops and railroad company guards. Strikers set boxcars on fire and brought rail traffic in the Midwest to a dead halt.

Labor did not stand united, however. Samuel Gompers refused to swing his powerful AFL behind the strike, causing it to collapse. The government arrested Debs and other union leaders and sentenced Debs to 6 months in prison. In 1895 the Supreme Court upheld the President's right to issue an **injunction,** an order to end a strike. Corporations thereby gained a powerful legal weapon that they used against unions for years.

Obstacles to Unity

Government intervention during major strikes repeatedly thwarted the nation's industrial unions. The unions, however, also tended to cripple themselves by largely excluding three important groups: women, members of minority groups, and unskilled workers. By 1900 only about 1 in every 33 American workers belonged to a union, and fewer than 100,000 of the 5.3 million working women belonged to unions.

In the South the great majority of African American workers could join only separate, segregated local unions. In the North and West white unionists feared the competition of African American workers, knowing that many bosses would pay them less.

The hostility of American-born workers toward immigrants also kept the unions weak. Suspicion often centered on German, British, or Russian immigrants, some of whom had more radical ideas about society and labor than Americans usually heard.

American-born workers strongly expressed their resentment of immigrants during the anti-Chinese movement in the West during the 1870s and 1880s. Angry mobs rampaged through Chinese areas in San Francisco, Tacoma, Seattle, and Denver in the 1870s. The Chinese Exclusion Act of 1882 reflected the widespread hostility against immigrant workers. The law halted immigration of Chinese workers and gained wide support from American labor unions.

By the turn of the century, big business had cast its shadow across most of the American economy, and in the turbulent labor struggles of the era, government took its place on the side of the employers against the workers.

SECTION REVIEW

Vocabulary

1. Define: union, strike, injunction.

Checking Facts

2. How did successful growth of bumper crops ultimately hurt farmers?

3. What reforms did the Populist party advocate?

Critical Thinking

Determining Cause and Effect

4. How did attitudes toward women and minorities hurt labor unions in the late 1800s?

Linking Across Time

5. William Jennings Bryan said, "The great cities rest upon our broad and fertile prairies. Burn down your cities and leave our farms, and your cities will spring up again as if by magic. But destroy our farms, and the grass will grow in the streets of every city in the country." What did Bryan mean by this? Is this argument valid today? Why or why not?

SECTION THREE   **217**

CHART STUDY

Ask: How did the Supreme Court help businesses at the expense of unions?

Answer: *It ruled that the President could break strikes.*

Evaluate

Have students complete the Section Review.

📁 💿 Assign the Section 3 Quiz or use the Testmaker to develop a customized quiz. (Also in Spanish.) **LEP**

Reteach

🎧 Have students listen to the Chapter 7, Section 3 Audiocassette. (Also in Spanish.) **LEP**

Enrich

Have interested students prepare a panel discussion to present to the class. Students should organize into two groups. One group should take the role of business owners in 1900. The other group should represent union leaders. Each side should explain why their opinions about the labor movement are best for the future of the nation.

CLOSE

Ask students what the concerns of labor protesters were in the late 1800s. *(shorter work week, job security, good wages)* Were the actions of the protesters effective or ineffective? *(Answers will vary. Refer students to pages 215 and 216.)*

Section 3 Review Answers

1. union (215), **strike** (215), **injunction** (217)
2. When farmers grew surplus wheat and cotton, prices dropped, and many farmers lost their land.
3. Reforms included free silver, restricted immigration, and a shorter workday.

4. By excluding women and immigrants, labor unions lost power and unity.
5. Answers will vary. Fertile land is more difficult to replace than buildings. The statement is still true. The nation is more industrialized, but people still need to eat and still need farmers.

SECTION

4

FOCUS

Section Objectives

1. Explain how the United States opened new avenues for trade in foreign lands.
2. Explain how the United States acquired Alaska, Hawaii, and the Philippines.
3. Understand how the idea of Manifest Destiny related to the expansion of the country's boundaries.

Bellringer Activity

While taking attendance at the beginning of the class period, display **Section Focus Transparency 22**, and have students answer the questions. (Or use the blackline master.)

VISUAL INSTRUCTION

The Rough Riders
Although Roosevelt was only second in command of the Rough Riders, he was not modest about his role. The humorist Finley Peter Dunne, through his Irish saloonkeeper character Mr. Dooley, said that Roosevelt's account of the war should be called "Alone in Cuba."

Ask: What unusual elements made up this cavalry regiment? *(cowhands, college students, ranchers, and rich aristocrats)*

Reaching for Empire

JULY 1, 1898: ROUGH RIDERS STORM SAN JUAN HILL

THEODORE ROOSEVELT COLLECTION,HARVARD COLLEGE LIBRARY

The Rough Riders
Proud of his elite cavalry regiment, Roosevelt spent his own money to buy their rations.

SHOUTS OF "HURRAH!" WELCOMED TEDDY ROOSEVELT AND HIS BAND OF AMERICAN SOLDIERS AS THEY BATTLED THEIR WAY UP SAN JUAN HILL NEAR SANTIAGO, CUBA. Nonetheless Roosevelt barked at his troops: "Don't cheer, but fight. Now's the time to fight."

As the weary force struggled one last time to overpower the Spanish forces at the top of the hill, American wagons appeared, heaped with weapons. Grabbing rapid-fire rifles, American troops and the Cuban freedom fighters they supported finally captured the hill. The American and Cuban fighters won the battle, but the war continued. Finally, 16 days later, the Spanish garrison at Santiago surrendered.

Roosevelt was but one of more than 250,000 Americans who served in the Spanish-American War. When the United States declared war on Spain, Teddy Roosevelt was assistant secretary of the navy. Eager to fight, he resigned his government post, ordered a well-tailored uniform, and rushed to volunteer for military service. The secretary of the navy had mixed feelings about Roosevelt, saying, "He means to be thoroughly loyal, but the very devil seemed to possess him. . . . He has gone at things like a bull in a china shop."

Roosevelt proved to be a popular war figure. He organized the First Voluntary Cavalry Regiment, known as the Rough Riders. This odd collection of cowhands, college students, ranchers, and rich aristocrats fascinated the press. Roosevelt attracted a large following of wartime newspaper reporters with his colorful style and "bully" spirit. Reporters peppered their articles with Roosevelt's colorful quotes about the war.

The brief war with Spain was the climax of an era marked by the United States's growing involvement with foreign nations. In the late 1800s, the American people were in a mood for expansion as they pushed their boundaries westward, gained new lands, and created new businesses and markets in faraway places for American products.

AS YOU READ

Vocabulary
► expansionism
► missionary
► armistice

Think About . . .
► how the United States opened new avenues for trade.
► the reasons for acquiring Alaska, Hawaii, and the Philippines for the United States.
► how Manifest Destiny related to the expansion of the country's boundaries.

Section 4 Resources

REPRODUCIBLE RESOURCES
📂 Lesson Plan 7-4
📂 Vocabulary and Guided Reading Activity 7-4
📂 Section 4 Quiz
📂 Chapter 7 Test
📂 Unit 2 Test
📂 Reteaching Activity 7

📂 Enrichment Activity 7
📂 Performance Assessment Activity 7

MULTIMEDIA RESOURCES
🔖 Section Focus Transparency 22
🔖 Beginnings to 1900 Transparency 29

💿 Landmark Documents in American History
💿 Testmaker
🎧 Chapter 7 Digest Audiocassette
🎧 American Music: Cultural Traditions
💿 Student Self-Test: A Software Review
💿 Vocabulary PuzzleMaker

The Monroe Doctrine
A Legacy of Hemispheric Control

The United States had a long and complex relationship with its neighbors in the Western Hemisphere. President James Monroe's address to Congress in 1823 had a significant impact on this relationship. Monroe's message to the European powers was loud and clear: no more European colonies in the Western Hemisphere.

Any foreign military expeditions sent to the Western Hemisphere for whatever reason would be seen as a threat to the United States, Monroe warned. No European country should interfere in United States affairs, at home or abroad, he continued.

Spain's interest in regaining control over former colonies spurred the President into action. Yet Monroe did have some assurance as he made these bold statements. He knew that Britain was also determined to prevent Spain from gaining any new colonies in the Western Hemisphere.

The President, relying on this information, decided to seize the moment and chart American foreign policy with his strong words. This was a bold move, to volunteer to be the "police force" protecting emerging nations in the entire hemisphere.

At the time there was little discussion of Monroe's ground-breaking pronouncement. It was neither widely liked nor sharply contested. More than 20 years passed before President James K. Polk implemented this so-called Monroe Doctrine and laid a cornerstone for American foreign policy.

From Sea to Shining Sea

American settlers were flooding into territories throughout the country. Settlers in foreign-owned territories such as Oregon, Texas, and California wanted a government of their own, and they wanted to be part of the United States. Taking over these lands, however, would create conflicts with Britain, which owned part of Oregon, and with Mexico, which held Texas and California and much of today's southwestern United States.

James K. Polk was the settlers' champion. When Polk ran for President in 1844, he warmly supported **expansionism,** the process of increasing the territory of the United States. After his election, Polk set out to gain Oregon as well as the Southwest. Polk and many other Americans supported the concept of Manifest Destiny—the notion that the United States was a superior country and had a right to invade, conquer, and occupy the North American continent and beyond.

NATIONAL PORTRAIT GALLERY, SMITHSONIAN INSTITUTION/ART RESOURCE, NY

Manifest Destiny In 1845 Polk's campaigns to control more of the North American continent made him the settlers' champion. *What was Manifest Destiny?*

In 1845 Polk declared that no European colony could occupy the North American continent. When the British insisted that they would continue to share in the rich Northwest Territory, Polk decided to drive the British out.

In a compromise move in 1846, Britain claimed land above the forty-ninth parallel, and the United States retained what has today become the states of Oregon and Washington. War was avoided on the northern border as the United States prepared for battle with Mexico.

Mexico had broken diplomatic relations with the United States when Congress annexed Texas in 1845. In that same year Polk sent negotiators to Mexico in an attempt to buy other Mexican lands, such as California and the area known as New Mexico. Mexico refused the United States's $30 million offer. Shortly after, following a border dispute, war erupted. After 2 years of fighting, the 2 governments negotiated a peace, and the United States laid claim to nearly half of Mexico for the bargain price of $15 million, with an additional $3.25 million to compensate American citizens with claims against Mexico.

Policing the Hemisphere

The Civil War years, 1861 through 1865, considerably limited American dreams of expansion. The war so consumed American arms and energy that during the long conflict, European nations tried to gain control of weak nations south of the Mexican border.

In 1861, despite warnings by Secretary of State William Seward, Spain seized an opportunity to reclaim its former colony, the Dominican Republic, an island in the Caribbean.

SECTION FOUR   **219**

TEACH

Guided Practice

L1 Creating an Outline
Review the major changes that took place on the domestic scene in the late 1880s. Then have students scan the heads and pictures in this section and speculate about changes on the foreign scene. Discuss how a belief in Manifest Destiny prompted expansion. As they read, ask students to list the United States's expansionist activities on this continent and beyond.

Show students Beginnings to 1900 Transparency 29 and have them complete the activity sheet.

VISUAL INSTRUCTION

Manifest Destiny Explain that the term *Manifest Destiny* was used for the first time in an 1845 article in the *United States Magazine and Democratic Review,* which said it was "our Manifest Destiny to overspread the continent allotted by Providence for the free development of our yearly multiplying millions." Other publications soon picked up the phrase. Have students look up the words *manifest* and *destiny* in a dictionary and speculate about why the idea was so appealing in the mid-1800s.

Answer: *the notion that the United States was a superior country destined to occupy and govern North America*

Cooperative Learning

Creating a Newspaper Have students create a newspaper of stories relating to Manifest Destiny and the Monroe Doctrine. Stories should include a page-one editorial, an eyewitness feature, and various news reports relating battles, land acquisitions, treaties, or policy making. Each student should have one responsibility: writing a story, editing, headline writing, page layout, an editorial, or a political cartoon.

Independent Practice

L2 **Writing an Argument**
Explain that in the 1850s expansionism was supported by the "Young America" movement, which wanted the United States to expand into the Southwest, support young republics in the Western Hemisphere, and pursue a liberal trade policy. Many others, however, opposed expansionism, and a strong moral crusade arose against the Mexican-American War, especially among abolitionists in New England. Students can research the issue further and write a persuasive argument supporting or protesting expansionism in the 1800s.

✏ Have students complete the Chapter 7, Section 4 Vocabulary and Guided Reading Activity. (Also in Spanish.) **LEP**

VISUAL INSTRUCTION

Amerikazin The artist of this print described the subject as "Americans enjoying themselves." He used the Roman alphabet to write the Japanese word for "Americans."

Answer: *blouses; skirts; loose hair; dangling earring; a cigar; Victorian-style beard*

At the same time that Spain sailed into the Caribbean, Britain and France sent troops to Mexico, pretending to collect war debts. The British soon retreated, but in 1864 the French leader Napoleon III installed Austrian Archduke Ferdinand Maximilian on the Mexican throne.

After the Union victory in the Civil War, however, American troops massed on the Mexican border, and Secretary of State Seward, citing the Monroe Doctrine, threatened war with France if its troops did not withdraw. By 1867 France complied, bringing new life to the Monroe Doctrine.

Worldwide Ambitions
Markets, Trade Routes, and Territories

Many factors contributed to the spread of expansionist fever in the United States after the Civil War. A patriotic fervor motivated many Americans. They felt that the acquisition of new lands would increase American glory and prestige throughout the world. Others saw the United States as a model country and felt a moral obligation to expand. They wanted to spread the American ideals of democracy and Protestant Christian values to people in other lands. **Missionaries,** or religious teachers, went to foreign lands to convert natives to Christianity. A new brand of American foreign policy maker supported these expansionist sentiments. These newly established foreign policy professionals wanted to make the United States a world power through trade, diplomacy, and conquest.

Perhaps the greatest motivation for expansion was the need for new economic markets. As settlers filled the Western frontier, farms and businesses produced more goods than Americans could buy. Henry Demarest Lloyd, a popular political writer at the time, wrote, "American production has outrun American consumption and we must seek markets for the surplus abroad."

Amerikazin When trade with Japan began, Westerners exchanged culture as well as commodities. This 1861 woodblock print shows a family of American tourists. *What details of the figures and dress portray American style of the era?*

Opening Closed Doors

The United States looked especially to Asia. American involvement in Asia actually began long before the Civil War. In 1844 the United States negotiated trade agreements with China and began to export cloth, iron, and fur to the Chinese in exchange for tea, silk, porcelain, and jade. Far Eastern trade became a boon to New England merchants and expanded naval production, especially after Commodore Matthew Perry "opened" Japan in 1854.

The Japanese had steadfastly refused contact with Western merchants and had closed their ports to European and American traders and missionaries for 250 years. Yet reports of Japan's great coal deposits had filtered out. Coal was an increasingly important resource for American steam-powered transportation and machinery. When Perry was sent to negotiate trade, it was important to the United States to be the first of the Western nations to access this resource. As he sailed into Tokyo's harbor under steam power, he so impressed the authorities that Japan began doing business with the United States.

By the 1880s the United States had made further inroads in the Far East by negotiating commercial treaties with Korea. The growth of these Asian markets stimulated the American economy and became a key factor in the United States's bid for world power.

Acquiring New Lands

Under the leadership of Secretary of State William Seward, foreign policy after the Civil War became more aggressive. Seward dreamed of an American empire that would include Canada, the Caribbean, Mexico, and Central America as well as Hawaii and other Pacific islands.

Meeting Special Needs

Visual Learners Help visual learners and students with Attention Deficit Disorder focus on the physical aspects of American expansion. Help them to locate on a classroom map the areas that play a key part in this section.

Encourage students to refer to an atlas or a globe as they read and review the section. Later, they may wish to create their own maps of a selected area.

Hawaii for Hawaiians Queen Liliuokalani was determined to keep the United States from seizing Hawaii. *Why were the Hawaiian Islands so valuable to American interests in the Pacific?*

In 1867 Seward attempted to purchase Danish islands in the Caribbean for $7.5 million—a move that the Senate rejected. Congress also refused to approve Seward's plans for a United States naval base in the Dominican Republic.

He succeeded elsewhere, however. In 1867 the United States seized the Midway Islands in the Pacific Ocean, strategically located along the trade route to China and Japan. In the same year, Seward bought Alaska from Russia for $7.2 million.

Newspapers mocked Seward, and Alaska became known as "Seward's folly" and a worthless "polar bear garden." Seward, however, was wiser than his critics realized. Alaska paid for itself many times over with the gold that was discovered in the Yukon Valley, and its rich copper and oil resources, as well as seal and whale trade.

Moving into the Pacific

Expansionist ambitions continued in the Pacific in the last three decades of the 1800s. In 1878 the United States acquired rights to a naval station in Samoa, which was astride the trade route to Australia and New Zealand. Because Germany and England also had claims in Samoa, the three powers divided the islands in 1889.

The Hawaiian Islands were another Pacific prize. American planters and missionaries had thrived there after 1875 when the Senate allowed Hawaiian sugar to enter the United States duty-free. By 1881 the secretary of state declared the islands "essentially a part of the American system." In 1887, under strong pressure, King Kalakaua granted the United States rights to build a naval base at Pearl Harbor to protect American interests in the Pacific. Finally in 1893 American sugar planters in Hawaii staged a rebellion, determined to wrest control from Kalakaua's sister, Queen Liliuokalani. The queen had resisted American control with the slogan "Hawaii for the Hawaiians."

The United States Marines surrounded the palace, and the American minister cabled Washington: "The Hawaiian pear is now fully ripe, and this is the golden hour for the United States to pluck it." The palace coup succeeded, leaving American sugar planters and missionaries in political control of the islands. Congress moved toward official annexation, but this process would take another five years to complete.

War With Spain
Reports Become Real

The expansionist moves from the end of the Civil War through the early 1890s reached a peak in 1898 with the Spanish-American War. The war's outcome added significant new territory to the growing American overseas empire, and it demonstrated that the United States could turn its industrial muscle into formidable naval power in both of the oceans surrounding North America.

The origins of the Spanish-American War lay in the troubled island of Cuba, only 90 miles off the southern tip of Florida. The Cuban people had struggled since 1868 for independence from Spain.

Many Americans identified that struggle with their own revolution against Britain. Other Americans, beginning in the 1850s, had regarded Cuba as a natural part of the United States geographically and as an island of great economic potential because of its sugar-growing capability.

In 1895 Cuban rebels led by José Martí renewed their fight for independence, launching their first attacks from American soil. A ferocious war ensued. Spanish troops, commanded by Valeriano Weyler, forced some 300,000 Cubans into concentration camps, where tens of thousands died.

The war continued, and Americans elected William McKinley President in 1896. McKinley's campaign platform included claims to Hawaii and the Virgin Islands

SECTION FOUR   **221**

Portfolio Project

Creating "Yellow" Headlines William Randolph Hearst of the *New York Journal* was the key exponent of "yellow" journalism. Seeing the situation with Spain as a chance to boost circulation, Hearst sent Frederick Remington to Cuba to do sketches. Remington sent a cable, reporting that nothing was happening in Cuba.

Hearst reputedly cabled back, "You furnish the pictures, I'll furnish the war!" Have students bring in current newspapers and create their own "yellow" alternatives for chosen headlines. Students can later add these pages to their portfolios.

ASSESS

Meeting Lesson Objectives

Each section objective is tested by the section review question(s) that follows it in parentheses.

1. Explain how the United States expanded its borders and sought new trade in foreign lands. (1, 3, 4)

2. Explain how the United States acquired Alaska, Hawaii, and the Philippines. (1, 2, 4)

3. Understand how the idea of Manifest Destiny related to the expansion of the country's boundaries. (2, 5)

History and the Humanities

🎧 American Music: Cultural Traditions—"Battleship of Maine" by the New Lost City Ramblers

VISUAL INSTRUCTION

Media Hype President McKinley claimed, "But for the inflamed state of public opinion, and the fact that Congress could no longer be held in check, a peaceful solution might have been had."

Answer: *An accident—possibly a faulty boiler—caused the explosion.*

---

as well as support for Cuban independence. He had no desire for war with Spain, however, and in 1897 the President took encouragement from a new Spanish government that promised reforms in Cuba as well as some independence for Cubans.

Headline Wars

Dramatic events early in 1898 ruined McKinley's desire to avoid war. In February an explosion blew up the battleship *Maine,* killing 260 officers and men. Headlines screamed for revenge: "Remember the *Maine*! To Hell With Spain!" Two days later, a New York newspaper proclaimed: "Whole Country Thrills With the War Fever/Yet President Says 'It Was An Accident'." Most Americans believed the Spanish had blown up the *Maine,* and a naval board of investigation soon concluded that a Spanish mine had caused the explosions.

Against his conscience, President McKinley took action. On April 11, 1898, he sent a message to Congress that called for the use of troops to bring about "a national compromise between the contestants." Congress responded with a more warlike declaration that gave the President authority to use troops to end Spanish control of Cuba and declared the island independent. These acts amounted to a declaration of war against Spain. Spain responded with its own declaration of war on April 24, 1898.

Critics believed that journalists, with their sensational headlines and stories, pressed politicians into declaring war following the explosion of the *Maine.* Their views were justified 78 years later when Admiral Hyman Rickover conducted a study of the sinking of the *Maine.* Rickover concluded that an accident, probably a faulty boiler, caused the explosion—not a mine.

Media Hype Sensational stories and illustrations in newspapers misled the public and stirred Americans to war. *What may have been the real cause of the explosion of the* Maine?

222   CHAPTER 7   NEW FRONTIERS

From Havana to Manila

Although most American citizens focused on Cuba as the primary target for United States military might, others concentrated on the Philippines, a group of Pacific islands also under Spanish control. One reformer asked: "Why should Cuba with its 1.6 million people have a right to freedom and self-government and the 8 million people who dwell in the Philippine Islands be denied the same right?" Also, gaining a foothold in the Philippines would help the United States protect Asian business connections.

Shortly after the *Maine* explosion, Assistant Secretary of the Navy Teddy Roosevelt, anticipating war, instructed Commodore George Dewey to prepare to remove his squadron of six ships from the neutral port of Hong Kong and to attack the Spanish fleet in the Philippines.

Dewey confirmed this plan with President McKinley by cable and steamed across the China Sea to enemy waters more than 600 miles (965 km) away. The commodore sailed into Manila Bay on May 1, 1898, and demolished the old Spanish fleet protecting the city. Before noon every Spanish ship was sunk.

After Dewey's triumph, soldiers training in Florida felt eager to launch their attack in Cuba. The battle began on June 22 with great fanfare.

Within days most of the troops were under fire, wading through waist-deep swamps and dodging shrapnel day and night. American troops finally took San Juan Hill, near the city of Santiago, on July 1, but a strong Spanish naval force remained in the harbor.

On July 3, however, the United States Navy chased Spanish cruisers and defeated their fleet in a dramatic battle that left only 1 American sailor killed and another wounded. By contrast almost 500 Spanish were killed or wounded and 1,700 taken prisoner.

By July 17 the United States had secured Cuba, and only Puerto Rico remained under Spanish control. It fell to the United States in a few days. The United States stepped up the pace of the war in order to bring home the thousands of soldiers who were suffering from yellow fever and malaria. Occupation had proved more deadly than battle. By the end of 1898, the death toll exceeded 5,400 soldiers, fewer than 400 of whom had died in combat.

United States Victorious

On August 12, with two fleets and their colonial armies devastated, Spain signed an **armistice,** or cease-fire. Diplomats met in Paris in October to negotiate a permanent settlement. It took two months to iron out their differences. Spain granted independence to Cuba and ceded Guam, Puerto Rico, and the Philippines to the United States for $20 million.

Although the United States had claimed it was fighting to liberate the Philippines, the American gov-

---

Extending the Content

Seward's Folly In 1867 William Seward's purchase of Alaska seemed like folly. Explain that at 2 cents an acre, Seward swept Russia from the North American continent and gained both gold and oil for the United States. The wealth of the Klondike came to light with the 1896 gold strike. In the 1970s "black gold" flowed freely with the completion of an 800-mile (1287.2-km)

pipeline at a cost of 8 billion dollars. Today, the TransAlaska Pipeline System (TAPS) carries about 2 million barrels of oil daily from Prudhoe Bay on the Arctic Ocean to Valdez, an Alaskan port. Students can locate these areas on a map and discuss the relative value of gold and oil in the 1800s and today.

THE PHILIPPINES, 1898

THE CARIBBEAN, 1898

Fighting during the Spanish-American War took place in the Philippines and in the Caribbean. Note Dewey's successful strike in the Philippines and the United States's blockade of Cuba. *According to the two maps, in which area did more of the fighting take place?*

ernment refused to accept the pleas of Filipino nationalists for independence. The leader of the Filipino rebels against Spain, Emilio Aguinaldo, was deported from the islands when he refused to recognize American rule.

President McKinley felt it would be "cowardly and dishonorable" to return the islands to the Spanish and argued that the Filipinos were "unfit for self-government." To keep Europeans from taking over the Philippines, many Americans said that possession of the islands would uplift and Christianize the Philippines, overlooking the fact that the majority of Filipinos were already Catholic. Actually business interests outweighed all other considerations, as an editor at the *Chicago Times-Herald* wrote: "The commercial and industrial interests of Americans, learning that the islands lie in the gateway of the vast and undeveloped markets of the Orient, say 'Keep the Philippines. . . .'"

The war also gave the nation glory and many new heroes. Although Dewey's command to his subordinate, "You may fire when ready," was hardly stirring, the admiral became a cult figure. Eager for a hero, businesses capitalized on the naval commander's exploits: a song celebrated his bravery and a chewing gum was marketed as "Dewey's Chewies."

Teddy Roosevelt reveled in his image as a Rough Rider charging up San Juan Hill. He effectively used his military adventures during his political career, first as governor of New York and then as President. Roosevelt, like many Americans, believed the Spanish-American War had given the United States a new status. In 1898 he wrote, "the nation now stands as the peer of any of the Great Powers of the world."

By 1899 the United States had expanded its dominion to include Puerto Rico, Hawaii, and many Pacific islands, including the newly acquired Philippines. The consequences of this economic and political expansion would shape the course of the United States's future well into the next century.

SECTION REVIEW

Vocabulary
1. Define: expansionism, missionary, armistice.

Checking Facts
2. Why did Europeans try to create new colonies in the Western Hemisphere during the Civil War years? How did the United States respond?

3. Why did the Japanese finally agree to trade with the United States in 1854?

Critical Thinking
Drawing Conclusions
4. Why did the smaller nations in the Pacific play a large role in the United States's plans for expansion?

Linking Across Time
5. In recent years the United States has become involved in conflicts in such Central American countries as Nicaragua and El Salvador. How does this involvement reflect policies set forth by the Monroe Doctrine?

SECTION FOUR **223**

Section 4 Review Answers

1. **expansionism** (219), **missionary** (220), **armistice** (222)
2. Europeans believed the United States was too busy fighting the Civil War to fight them. The United States invoked the Monroe Doctrine and threatened war.
3. They were impressed with the military power and diplomacy that Matthew Perry displayed.

4. Pacific allies and acquisitions helped protect American military and business interests in the Far East.
5. Answers will vary. American intervention protects countries from foreign intervention, but the United States too is an intervening power.

Reviewing Key Terms

1. injunction
2. homestead
3. expansionism
4. industrialism
5. merger

Recalling Facts

1. Ranchers, cowhands, and people in related occupations came to settle in or near "cow towns" in the West.
2. People who went westward by rail often settled near the railroads, especially because the railroad's land grants were for sale to settlers.
3. The settlers benefited from fertile plains, vast mineral deposits, and open land. Native Americans and Mexican Americans suffered because their land was taken and Native Americans were placed on reservations.
4. Inventions include the incandescent light bulb, electric motor, typewriter, high-speed printing press, and oil-drilling equipment. They helped speed up the manufacturing process and increase worker productivity.
5. Rockefeller merged oil companies into one industry giant, pushing competition out of the market.
6. Industry leaders built business empires by ruthlessly eliminating their competitors.
7. Their goals were to help the indebted farmers and exploited workers whose interests they represented.
8. They could have allowed women, minorities, and unskilled workers to join, but they feared the competition.
9. It warned against outside intervention in hemispheric affairs. It caused France to withdraw from Mexico.
10. McKinley thought Filipinos could not rule themselves. U.S. businesses wanted a foothold in the Philippines.

Reviewing Key Terms

Choose the vocabulary term that best answers the questions below. Write your answers on a separate sheet of paper.

homestead	union
industrialism	injunction
merger	expansionism

1. If a corporation hoped to prohibit a strike or to end a strike, what kind of order might it ask a court to issue?

2. A settler who wanted to claim free land and who was willing to farm it for a number of years might do what?

3. What kind of foreign policy was the United States following when it set out to become a world power by acquiring new lands such as Puerto Rico, Hawaii, and Alaska?

4. What kind of economic and social system is marked by the development of large-scale industries concentrated in urban factories?

5. If a company's managers thought that market competition was too fierce in their industry, what solution might they choose?

Recalling Facts

1. How did cattle ranching and the work of cowhands promote the movement of settlers to the Great Plains?

2. What influence did the early railroad lines have on where people settled on the Plains and in the Far West?

3. Which groups of people benefited from the settlement of the West? Which groups did not benefit? Why not?

4. Identify three important inventions from the era of 1865 to 1900. What effect did these and other inventions have on the productivity of workers?

5. John D. Rockefeller once said, "The day of individual competition is past and gone." How did Rockefeller's own business practices illustrate his statement?

6. Explain the term *robber barons*. Why was it applied to people such as Andrew Carnegie and J.P. Morgan?

7. What were the main goals of the Populist party? Whose interests did the party represent?

8. How could labor unions have dramatically increased their size and power? What prevented them from doing so?

9. What was the Monroe Doctrine? Why was it important to the United States after the Civil War?

10. Why did the United States decide to keep control of the Philippines?

Critical Thinking

1. Predicting Consequences The 1868 Currier and Ives lithograph below captures the American march westward. Do you think the government could have kept settlers from taking Native American lands? What government measures might have been effective?

2. Making Inferences Wanamaker's, Macy's, and other department stores had marble staircases, expensive carpets, and chandeliers. Why do you think the owners spent so much money to decorate their stores? What values were they trying to appeal to in customers?

3. Making Comparisons Explain the difference between horizontal and vertical integration of industry. Why did Carnegie and other business leaders try to achieve both?

4. Making Generalizations Reread the material on the Populist party and on the labor movements. Based on this material, what generalizations can you make about farm and labor movements during the era? What evidence supports your generalizations?

5. Recognizing Bias President McKinley argued that the Filipinos were "unfit for self-government." What bias does this statement reveal? What might account for McKinley's bias?

THE HARRY T. PETERS COLLECTION, MUSEUM OF THE CITY OF NEW YORK

Critical Thinking

1. Answers will vary. As in other regions, settlers probably could not have been stopped except by force.
2. The owners believed that people with money would spend more of it in lavish surroundings. In fact, sales did increase.

3. Horizontal integration merges all competing companies in an industry; vertical integration controls all related aspects of a production process. They wanted total control of a national market.
4. Both movements were fighting for ordinary workers

and urging the government to regulate rising business costs; both made some small gains.
5. McKinley's remark reflects his idea that Filipinos were uncivilized and therefore unable to form a government. He apparently lacked knowledge of foreign cultures.

Portfolio Project

The history of United States expansionism in the 1800s includes efforts to acquire or at least to influence Cuba, Hawaii, Alaska, Puerto Rico, and the Philippines. Choose one of these places and investigate the history of United States involvement there, carrying your research up to the present. Use your research notes to build a time line showing the major events in that involvement. Keep your time line in your portfolio.

Cooperative Learning

Form several groups to discuss the life stories of Carnegie, Rockefeller, and other robber barons. Groups should consider the following questions: Do you admire that kind of success? What is its impact on ordinary citizens? How do the robber barons compare with today's wealthy industrialists? Choose a representative to present your group's conclusions as part of a whole-class discussion.

Reinforcing Skills

Reading Statistical Tables The *Statistical Abstract of the United States* publishes annual statistics from the Bureau of the Census and other governmental agencies. Look at the latest edition in the library for information on a topic discussed in this chapter—for example, labor union membership by state, mergers of corporations, or income levels of households. Pick one table and photocopy it. What information is given in the table's title and subtitle? According to the headings, in what categories and subcategories is the information grouped? Look at the column on the left side of the table to find out how items in the table are organized. Describe any changes or patterns shown by the statistics in the table.

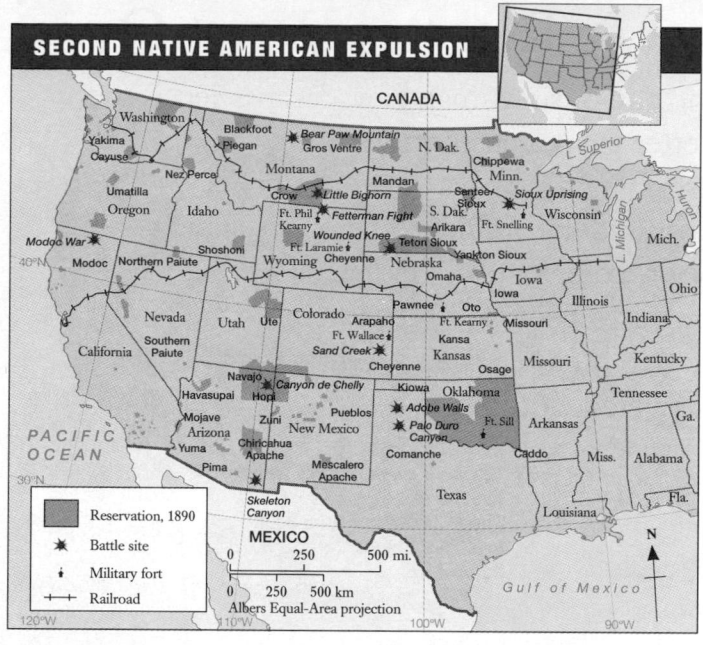

SECOND NATIVE AMERICAN EXPULSION

Reservation, 1890
* Battle site
⚔ Military fort
╀╀╀ Railroad

0   250   500 mi.
0   250   500 km
Albers Equal-Area projection

Geography and History

Study the map on this page to answer the following questions:

1. What Native American lands lay along the routes of the two transcontinental railroads shown on the map?

2. What battle took place in South Dakota? What Native American nation was involved? In what year was the battle fought?

3. What Native American peoples inhabited the lands that are now Arizona and New Mexico?

4. Where did the Battle of the Little Bighorn—sometimes known as Custer's Last Stand—take place? What Native American nations fought there?

5. What army fort was located near Cheyenne and Arapaho lands? What fort was near the Little Bighorn?

HISTORY JOURNAL

Write in your journal about what you have learned in this chapter. You can pull together the diverse subjects covered in the chapter by broadly interpreting "new frontiers" to include national, industrial, political, and international frontiers.

Geography and History

1. northern line: Yakima, Cayuse, Nez Perce, Blackfoot, Piegan, Crow, Mandan, Chippewa, Santee Sioux; southern line: Modoc, Northern Paiute, Shoshoni, Ute, Cheyenne, Teton Sioux, Arapaho, Pawnee, Omaha, Oto, Yankton Sioux
2. Wounded Knee; Teton Sioux
3. Havasupai, Mojave, Yuma, Pima, Navajo, Hopi, Zuni, Chiricahua Apache, Pueblo, Mescalero Apache
4. Montana; Crow
5. Cheyenne: Fort Laramie; Arapaho: Fort Wallace; Fort Phil Kearney

History Journal

Invite volunteers to share their journal entries with the class. Help students to see that industrial development and populism at home, and expansionism abroad, paralleled the westward expansion of the frontier.

? BONUS QUESTION

This question may be used for extra credit on the chapter test.

Ask: What factors made Northern and Northeastern states the center of industry after the Civil War?

Answer: *mines for iron and coal; lakes and rivers for shipping; plentiful labor supply*

Portfolio Project

Invite volunteers to share their time lines with the class, at least one for each place researched. They may wish to read their time line entries aloud or write them on the board. The class can discuss the similarities and differences in the various cases.

Cooperative Learning

For their comparisons, help students to choose appropriate modern industrialists such as Bill Gates of Microsoft.

Reinforcing Skills

You may wish to have students practice this skill together. Make photocopies of one table for all members of the class and have them address the questions as a group.

TEACH

Making the Historical Connection

Levi Strauss arrived in California a year after the forty-niners had begun their mad rush for gold. When an Indiana reporter, John L.B. Soule, advised entrepreneurs to "Go West, young man, go West!" Strauss was already doing business there. He knew the limited equipment that travelling miners could carry. He was also aware of the conditions they had faced crossing deserts, mountains, and lands where Native Americans fought off intruders. With his dry-goods business he could supply the replacement equipment, tents, camping supplies, and warm, sturdy clothing that the growing Western population needed.

Then...

Levi's Riveted Waist Overalls

One day businessman Levi Strauss received a letter from a customer, Jacob Davis, describing a new way to make pants. Davis, a tailor, could not afford to patent the process. Instead, he persuaded Strauss to become his partner. In 1873 the two men received a joint patent for riveted clothing.

❶ The word *denim* comes from the French "de Nimes," or "of Nimes," but the denim used by Strauss came from New Hampshire.

❷ The pants all had button closings. The zipper was invented in 1891, but the Levi Strauss company did not use zippers in jeans until 1954.

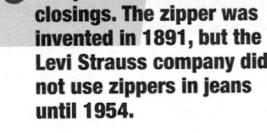

FILE PHOTO BY DOUG MINDELL

Fun Facts

COURTESY LEVI STRAUSS & CO. SAN FRANCISCO

SELLING STRENGTH

A leather patch was added to the design in 1886 depicting two workhorses attempting unsuccessfully to pull apart a pair of Levi pants. The company never tried the stunt, but rather used the patch as a symbol of strength.

Background Information

Far Cry From Fashion Levi Strauss's riveted clothing rarely made it east of the Rocky Mountains in the 1800s. The clothing's value lay in durability, not fashion. The pants, jackets, and overalls became a staple item for ranch hands and miners across the West, and soon came to symbolize the spirit of rugged individualism associated with frontier settlement. It wasn't until the 1930s when the movie business boomed, that all things Californian took on an air of sophistication and Americans clamored to wear "jeans."

3 Copper rivets reinforced pocket corners and the base of the fly. The fly rivet, however, fell by the wayside during World War II when the government ordered conservation of precious metals.

PATENT RIVETED CLOTHING

The Best in USE FOR

FARMERS, Mechanics AND MINERS.

LEVI STRAUSS & CO. SAN FRANCISCO, CAL.

4 During most of the 1800s blue dyes came from a plant called *indigo,* grown on South Carolina plantations. In the 1880s a chemical version, *indigotin,* became available.

Stats

PROFILE

In Buttenheim, Bavaria, Hirsch Strauss taught his peddler's business to his youngest son, Levi. Upon Hirsch's death in 1847, 18-year-old Levi immigrated to New York City.

Hoping prospectors' gold would end up in his cash register, Levi took his dry goods business to San Francisco, where he brought his four nephews on board as partners.

With the success of riveted clothing, Strauss became active in San Francisco's business and cultural community, serving on boards of both utility companies and orphanages. He belonged to San Francisco's first synagogue and helped to fund a gold medal for students of its Sabbath School.

PRICE

Levi Strauss & Co. sold riveted clothing to stores. In 1879, the catalog advertised:

Riveted XXExtra Heavy blue denim pants........$17.50 /doz

...Now

LEVI'S COMPARISON CHART

Consult the *Readers' Guide to Periodical Literature* to obtain information about Levi's clothing of today. Then draw or paste a picture of a pair of jeans in the center of a sheet of paper. Beside the left leg list the similarities between the Levi's jeans of 1873 and today's jeans. List differences beside the right leg. Include information on manufacturing, profitability, business, fashion, or culture.

WHAT'S IN A NAME?

The patented pants were called waist overalls in the Old West. The term *jeans* was not used until the 1900s, and the name "Levi's" meaning riveted denim pants did not emerge in advertising until the 1960s.

Then & Now

FYI

Woolen Lining In 1874 Levi and two associates acquired the Mission and Pacific Woolen Mills from the estate of William Ralston, a silver millionaire. The purchase enabled Strauss to use the mill's woolen fabric in "blanket lined" pants and coats.

FYI

Family History In many ways the Levi Strauss company of today resembles its early beginnings. Levi's great-great-grand-nephew, Robert Haas, the current CEO, has reorganized the Levi Strauss factories to pioneer a "team" system of assembly. In the 1880s Strauss had organized one of the earliest piece-work factories.

CLOSE

Ask students to discuss examples of working people's clothing that have become fashion trends. *(overalls, coveralls, military outfits, bandanas, flannel work shirts, and work boots)*

Portfolio Project

Fashion Patents Have students research types of clothing that have been designed to solve a problem. For example, clothing made from recycled plastics solves a societal problem, while easy-to-clean garments solve an individual's problem. Students can use trade magazines and books about the garment industry to write a brief report on one such innovation. Reports should include details such as: Was there a patent involved? Who benefited? Was there a lasting impact on fashion? Students can keep their reports in their portfolios. Afterward they may wish to present their research with photographs, artifacts, or even a fashion show.

The Unit at a Glance

Chapter 8

Between 1880 and 1920 the United States experienced rapid industrial and economic growth and political change. Immigration accelerated and population exploded; industry flourished and the ranks of labor swelled. Political party "machines" dominated politics. Meanwhile, dramatic problems convulsed the nation: social unrest, labor strife, political corruption, corporate monopolies, and urban decay. In response to the disorder, reformers, called progressives, proposed solutions that would confer on government a more substantive role in the lives of its citizens and in the regulation of society.

Chapter 9

As the power of the presidency expanded and strengthened under Theodore Roosevelt and Woodrow Wilson, the visibility and the role of the President increased. The Progressive movement continued, resulting in political clashes with socialists and other radicals who challenged capitalism.

Chapter 10

Just as government's role expanded during this period of unrest, so too did American activities abroad—from developing new trade markets, to annexing and occupying foreign territories, to fighting in an international conflict—World War I.

UNIT

3

The Roots of a Modern Nation

CHAPTER 8
Progressive Reforms

CHAPTER 9
Progressivism Takes Hold

CHAPTER 10
Expansionism and World War I

228

Portfolio Project

Creating a World Presence Have students create a booklet of information explaining how the United States became a world power. Suggest to students that they categorize information from 1880 to 1920 in the areas of economics, politics, and international relations. Prompt them by listing the following: immigration; urbanization; various progressive social, economic, and political reforms; educational changes; growth in the power of the President; expansionism; World War I. Ask students to include visuals that support their written data. Then invite volunteers to share their booklets before filing them in their portfolios.

Introducing the Unit

Show Students the Unit 3 Time Line Transparency and/or assign the accompanying activity sheet. Tell students that they will learn about the growth of cities and the problems that accompanied urbanization and large-scale immigration. The rise of the Progressive movement and its ideology, which included an expanded role for government in fighting social problems, will be examined. Students will also study the increase in presidential power and the development of the United States as a world leader.

NATIONAL GEOGRAPHIC SOCIETY

Videodisc

GTV: A Geographic Perspective on American History

Side 3, Chapter 10
Title: A New Life
Subject: Migrations from rural to urban areas, 1890–1920
Ask: Why did so many Americans migrate to cities? *(They hoped to find better paying jobs and excitement.)*

LIBRARY OF CONGRESS

229

Examining the Visual

Expanding Modes of Transportation By the end of the 1800s the United States had 5 transcontinental rail lines. Railroads reached their maturity in the early 1900s, as trains carried the bulk of land freight and passenger traffic. In this 1882 chromolithograph entitled *The World's Railroad Scene*, created by Swaim and Lewis, the travelers depicted prepare to depart via one transportation mode or another. Lithography is a printing process in which an image is printed on a flat surface such as stone, sheet zinc, or aluminum. The surface is then treated so that the image areas will retain ink, or in this case colored inks. Color lithographs were developed in the second half of the 1800s. To make a lithograph in more than one color, the artist must prepare a separate surface for each color.

[00:00] Out of Time?

If time does not permit teaching every chapter in this unit, use the Chapter Digest Audiocassettes and the accompanying student activities and tests. The Chapter Digest Audiocassettes are available in Spanish.

TEACH

Making the Historical Connection

At the beginning of the twentieth century, industrialization prompted large numbers of immigrants and many people from rural America to seek their fortune in the nation's burgeoning new cities. In this passage from *Sister Carrie,* Theodore Dreiser depicts Chicago as a dazzling land of promise where people believe that hard work will make that promise a reality. For another perspective, students may want to read Amy Lowell's "New York at Night," which gives a description of people slaving for a city that gives nothing in return.

VISUAL INSTRUCTION

The Frenetic Movement of the City For many artists in the early 1900s, the frantic pace and depersonalization of the cities inspired an abstract, experimental approach. Max Weber's *Rush Hour, New York*, with its sharp edges and discordant imagery, is an example of this abstract approach.

Ask: What kind of job would Carrie most likely obtain? *(a shop girl)*

Team Teaching This excerpt from *Sister Carrie* can be presented in a team teaching context, in conjunction with English or Language Arts.

230

Sister Carrie

BY THEODORE DREISER

In his novel Sister Carrie, *Theodore Dreiser captured the allure of rapidly expanding cities such as Chicago and New York for ambitious men and women in the late 1800s. Because he paid such careful attention to detail, Dreiser's portrait of city life at the time is as accurate as it is vivid.*

When she awoke at eight the next morning, Hanson had gone. Her sister was busy in the dining-room, which was also the sitting-room, sewing. She worked, after dressing, to arrange a little breakfast for herself, and then advised with Minnie as to which way to look. The latter had changed considerably since Carrie had seen her. She was now a thin, though rugged, woman of twenty-seven, with ideas of life coloured by her husband's, and fast hardening into narrower conceptions of pleasure and duty than had ever been hers in a thoroughly circumscribed youth. She had invited Carrie, not because she longed for her presence, but because the latter was dissatisfied at home, and could probably get work and pay her board here. She was pleased to see her in a way but reflected her husband's point of view in the matter of work. Anything was good enough so long as it paid—say, five dollars a week to begin with. A shop girl was the destiny prefigured for the newcomer. She would get in one of the great shops and do well enough

The Frenetic Movement of the City The abstract geometric shapes of Max Weber's *Rush Hour, New York* (1915) convey the hustle and bustle of the burgeoning cities of the early part of the century.

until—well, until something happened. Neither of them knew exactly what. They did not figure on promotion. They did not exactly count on marriage. Things would go on, though, in a dim kind of way until the better thing would eventuate, and Carrie would be rewarded for coming and toiling in the city. It was under such auspicious circumstances that she started out this morning to look for work.

Before following her in her round of seeking, let us look at the sphere in which her future was to lie. In 1889 Chicago had the peculiar qualifications of growth which made such adventuresome pilgrimages even on the part of young girls plausible. Its many and growing commercial opportunities gave it widespread fame, which made of it a giant magnet, drawing to itself, from all quarters, the hopeful and the hopeless—those who had their fortune yet to make and those whose fortunes and affairs had reached a disastrous climax elsewhere. It was a city of over 500,000, with the ambition, the dar-

Background Information

Publishing *Sister Carrie* Theodore Dreiser (1871–1945) was born in Terre Haute, Indiana. His family was very poor, and he soon saw a profound difference between the promise and the reality of American life. This realization was a major source of Dreiser's discontent and an important influence on his works. Dreiser began writing his first novel, *Sister Carrie*, in 1899 at the suggestion of a newspaper colleague. It was partly based on the experiences of one of his sisters. Doubleday, Page, and Co. published the book in 1900. Due to qualms about the story line, which involves a young "kept woman" whose disreputable behavior goes unpunished, Doubleday limited the book's advertising. Consequently, it sold fewer than 500 copies.

ing, the activity of a metropolis of a million. Its streets and houses were already scattered over an area of seventy-five square miles. Its population was not so much thriving upon established commerce as upon the industries which prepared for the arrival of others. The sound of the hammer engaged upon the erection of new structures was everywhere heard. Great industries were moving in. The huge railroad corporations which had long before recognised the prospects of the place had seized upon vast tracts of land for transfer and shipping purposes. Street-car lines had been extended far out into the open country in anticipation of rapid growth. The city had laid miles and miles of streets and sewers through regions where, perhaps, one solitary house stood out alone —a pioneer of the populous ways to be. There were regions open to the sweeping winds and rain, which were yet lighted throughout the night with long, blinking lines of gas-lamps, fluttering in the wind. Narrow board walks extended out, passing here a house, and there a store, at far intervals, eventually ending on the open prairie.

> ANYTHING WAS GOOD ENOUGH SO LONG AS IT PAID—SAY, FIVE DOLLARS A WEEK TO BEGIN WITH.

In the central portion was the vast wholesale and shopping district, to which the uninformed seeker for work usually drifted. It was a characteristic of Chicago then, and one not generally shared by other cities, that individual firms of any pretension occupied individual buildings. The presence of ample ground made this possible. It gave an imposing appearance to most of the wholesale houses, whose offices were upon the ground floor and in plain view of the street. The large plates of window glass, now so common, were then rapidly coming into use, and gave to the ground floor offices a distinguished and prosperous look. The casual wanderer could see as he passed a polished array of office fixtures, much frosted glass, clerks hard at work, and genteel business men in "nobby" suits and clean linen lounging about or sitting in groups. Polished brass or nickel signs at the square stone entrances announced the firm and the nature of the business in rather neat and reserved terms. The entire metropolitan center possessed a high and mighty air calculated to overawe and abash the common applicant, and to make the gulf between poverty and success seem both wide and deep.

Into this important commercial region the timid Carrie went. She walked east along Van Buren Street through a region of lessening importance, until it deteriorated into a mass of shanties and coal-yards, and finally verged upon the river. She walked bravely forward, led by an honest desire to find employment and delayed at every step by the interest of the unfolding scene, and a sense of helplessness amid so much evidence of power and force which she did not understand. These vast buildings, what were they? These strange energies and huge interests, for what purposes were they there? She could have understood the meaning of a little stone-cutter's yard at Columbia City, carving little pieces of marble for individual use, but when the yards of some huge stone corporation came into view, filled with spur tracks and flat cars, transpierced by docks from the river and traversed overhead by immense trundling cranes of wood and steel, it lost all significance in her little world.

RESPONDING TO LITERATURE

1. Would you have wanted to live in a city at the turn of the century? Why or why not?

2. In *Sister Carrie* the main character believes the city will provide her with new opportunities and a new life. Explain why cities would or would not represent to you such a gateway to opportunity today?

FYI

Naturalists Versus Imagists Theodore Dreiser was one of the most prominent naturalist writers in the United States. The naturalist writes in a realistic style, placing people in situations they do not understand and over which they have no control and then reporting the results. Dreiser's vision is of a city that is merely cold and indifferent.

Other writers, such as Amy Lowell, were proponents of the imagist movement. In contrast with the impersonal style of the naturalists, imagists used a vividly pictorial style to create clear, sharp images. Students who choose to read Lowell's description of the city will note that she takes a darker view. Lowell's city is a savage beast that actively devours its inhabitants.

CLOSE

Ask students if they would rather live in a different-sized community than they do now. Why or why not? *(Answers will vary but should refer to and weigh the community's amenities or drawbacks, and compare them to those in a different-sized place.)*

Responding to Literature Answers

1. Answers will vary. Some students will say that they would have been attracted by the city's developing business opportunities, its entertainment resources, or its hustle and bustle. Others will argue that the early cities were only havens for the very rich and that most people worked very hard, often under dehumanizing conditions.

2. Answers will vary. While some students will claim that cities remain the gateway to opportunity for those willing to work, others will disagree. The opposing students may extol the virtues of rural or small-town life, citing the benefits of a healthy environment, relaxed pace, and friendly neighbors.

Progressive Reforms

DAILY LESSON OBJECTIVES	REPRODUCIBLE RESOURCES	MULTIMEDIA RESOURCES
SECTION 1 Facing a New Order 1. Examine the growth of cities in the United States. 2. Analyze the impact of rapid urbanization on American life in the late 1800s. 3. Discuss the experiences of immigrants in the United States. 4. Describe the reaction of middle-class people to industrialization, urbanization, and immigration.	Reproducible Lesson Plans Vocabulary and Guided Reading Activities (English or Spanish) Cooperative Learning Activities Great Debates in American History American Literature Readings and Activities Section Quizzes (English or Spanish)	Section Focus Transparencies Map Transparencies Chapter Teaching Transparencies Beginnings to 1900 Transparencies U.S. History and Art Transparencies The American People: Fabric of a Nation American Music: Cultural Traditions Testmaker Student Self-Test: A Software Review
SECTION 2 A Generation of Reformers 1. Identify the different types of people who became progressives. 2. Analyze the aspects of American society that were criticized by the progressives. 3. List the different ways progressives tried to address problems linked to urbanization and industrialization.	Reproducible Lesson Plans Vocabulary and Guided Reading Activities (English or Spanish) Geography in History Activities Skill Reinforcement Activities Section Quizzes (English or Spanish)	Section Focus Transparencies Landmark Documents in American History Testmaker Student Self-Test: A Software Review
SECTION 3 Progressive Agendas 1. Identify the main elements of progressive reform at the state and local levels. 2. Identify the conflicting motives underlying progressive reforms. 3. Explain how progressives viewed the role of government and how they worked to eliminate political corruption. 4. List reforms designed to help all workers, particularly women and children.	Reproducible Lesson Plans Vocabulary and Guided Reading Activities (English or Spanish) Reteaching Activities (English or Spanish) Enrichment Activities (English or Spanish) Interpreting Political Cartoons Section Quizzes (English or Spanish)	Section Focus Transparencies Landmark Documents in American History Testmaker Student Self-Test: A Software Review
CHAPTER REVIEW AND EVALUATION	Chapter 8 Test, Forms A and B Performance Assessment Strategies and Activities	Student Self-Test: A Software Review Vocabulary PuzzleMaker Testmaker Chapter Digests Audiocassettes

 If time does not permit teaching the entire chapter, summarize using the Chapter 8 Digests Audiocassettes and the accompanying activities and tests. (Available in English or Spanish.)

Cooperative Project

Organize the class into small groups to research and report on progressive reforms from 1880 to 1920 in one particular state. As information is shared, have students develop a chart showing what economic groups supported reforms in each state, what problems they identified, and what they accomplished. Then have the class develop generalizations about the backgrounds, goals, and accomplishments of the progressives.

Suggested Rubric: A Research Report. See Performance Assessment Strategies and Activities, p. 39.

Individual Project

Have students choose a topic of personal interest, such as professional baseball, college football, fashion, or popular music. Direct them to research the history of the topic from 1880 to 1920. Identify any trends or developments that show the influence of urbanization, industrialization, immigration, or the progressive impulse. **LEP**

Suggested Rubric: A Research Report. See Performance Assessment Strategies and Activities, p. 39.

Key to Ability Levels

Teaching strategies have been coded for varying learning styles and abilities.

L1 **BASIC** activities for all students

L2 **AVERAGE** activities for average to above-average students

L3 **CHALLENGING** activities for above-average students

LEP **LIMITED ENGLISH PROFICIENCY** activities

 Block Scheduling

Block scheduling differs from traditional class scheduling in the amount of time allotted to each period. The extended timeframe provided by block scheduling affords you the opportunity to implement a greater number of research-oriented and activity-intense projects to motivate and involve your students. Activities that are particularly suited to use within the block scheduling framework are identified throughout this chapter by the following designation.

T E A C H E R ' S   C O R N E R

NATIONAL GEOGRAPHIC SOCIETY

NATIONAL GEOGRAPHIC SOCIETY PRODUCTS AVAILABLE FROM GLENCOE

To order the following products for use with this chapter, contact your local Glencoe sales representative or call Glencoe at 1-800-334-7344:

- *The Presidents: A Picture History of Our Nation* (CD-ROM)
- *GTV: A Geographic Perspective on American History* (Videodisc)
- *GTV: The American People: Fabric of a Nation* (Videodisc)

ADDITIONAL NATIONAL GEOGRAPHIC SOCIETY PRODUCTS

To order the following products for use with this chapter, call National Geographic Society at 1-800-368-2728:

- *The United States as a World Power: From the 1890s to the 1970s* (Filmstrip)
- *Building a Nation: The Story of Immigration* (Filmstrip)
- *Immigration: The Triumph of Hope* (Video)

Chapter Overview

Progressive reforms developed as a response to growing social problems such as child labor. The success of these reforms is reflected in the changes they brought to government.

Introducing the Chapter

Point out to students that certain traditions, values, and customs of the United States had been developed by 1880. Have students recall and list key events and themes from previous chapters, such as economic opportunity, a democratic government, and individualism. Discuss what forces might threaten these values—for example, political corruption could threaten a democratic government. Then have students read the opening vignette.

 Display the Chapter 8 Teaching Transparency and have students complete the activity sheet.

Extension Activity
Have students complete Beyond the Transparency on the activity sheet for Chapter 8 and present their projects after the class has completed the chapter.

History Journal

Have students research and write a report on the activism of Mary Harris Jones, also known as Mother Jones. Encourage students to consider how working full-time, beginning at the age of 10, and then doing additional handwork at home would prevent an individual from getting an education and a better-paying job.

CHAPTER
8

Progressive Reforms

JULY 7, 1903: WORKING CHILDREN MARCH TOWARD PRESIDENT'S MANSION

President Theodore Roosevelt faced a difficult decision. Should he meet with a handful of children who were marching 125 miles from Kensington, Pennsylvania, toward Oyster Bay, New York, to confront him at his home?

These marchers represented the thousands of children who worked in factories, mills, and mines. They were seeking the President's support for a law prohibiting child labor.

Though Roosevelt sympathized with the children, he feared supporting any demand voiced by their leader, radical organizer Mary Harris Jones, known as Mother Jones. President Roosevelt advocated reform, not revolution.

Finally, on July 27, after 20 days of marching, the children arrived. Through a representative, Roosevelt sent his reply: "No!" His fear outweighed his sympathy. Despite Roosevelt's refusal to meet with Jones and the children, the child labor debate did not go away.

The child labor debate was just one issue that Americans confronted between 1880 and 1920. Political corruption, labor unrest, and urban decay also plagued the United States during this period of rapid industrial and urban growth. By responding to these issues while avoiding radical upheaval, the American people fueled one of the greatest periods of reform in American history, the Progressive era. ∎

Write your reaction to the working conditions for children as depicted in this photograph. What reforms would you initiate to change this situation?

232

✚ EXTRA CREDIT PROJECT

Contemporary Child Labor Practices Ask students to research contemporary situations where children are employed. Suggest that they consider children whose parents are migrant workers, own a restaurant, or work in seasonal farming businesses. Prompt students to consider how children are able to help supplement the family's income and still attend school. Encourage students also to study child labor practices in other countries, particularly developing countries. Ask students to prepare a chart listing the countries and vital information about the affected industries, hours, wages, educational opportunities, and impact on home and society.

COURTESY GEORGE EASTMAN HOUSE

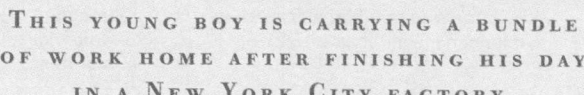

THIS YOUNG BOY IS CARRYING A BUNDLE
OF WORK HOME AFTER FINISHING HIS DAY
IN A NEW YORK CITY FACTORY.

233

**History and
the Humanities**

📖 Focus on American
Fine Art Prints, Print 14—
June by Ellen Day Hale

FYI

The Carpet Industry
Iqbal Masih was sold by
his poor parents to a carpet factory at the age of 4
and worked as an inden-
tured servant weaving
carpets for 6 years—
much of the time shack-
led to a loom. When he
escaped, Masih became a
crusader against child
slave labor, closing down
dozens of carpet factories
in his native Pakistan and
winning international
acclaim. In 1994 he
received the Reebok
"Youth in Action" human
rights award. Shortly after
his return to Pakistan, the
12-year-old, who wanted
to be "the Abraham
Lincoln of his people,"
was shot dead in his vil-
lage. A local man was
arrested for the crime, but
some suspect the carpet
industry was involved.

**Performance
Assessment**

Refer to page 232B for
performance assessment
activities for this chapter.

📂 Also see Activity 8 in
the Performance Assess-
ment Strategies and
Activities for an additional
activity as well as for suggested rubrics. 📇

Examining the Visual

Exploiting Children American photographer
Lewis W. Hines (1874–1940) used his art to
bring social ills to public attention. Trained as a
sociologist, Hines began to portray the immigrants who crowded onto Ellis Island in 1905.
He also photographed the tenements and
sweatshops where the immigrants were forced
to live and work. In 1909 Hines published "Child
Labor in the Carolinas" and "Day Laborers

Before Their Time," the first of his many photo-
essays documenting child labor. These photos
showed children as young as 8 years old working long hours in dangerous conditions. Hines
kept a careful record of his conversations with
the children by secretly taking notes inside his
coat pocket and photographing birth entries in
family Bibles. He measured the children's
heights by the buttons on his vest.

FOCUS

Section Objectives

1. Examine the growth of cities in the United States.
2. Analyze the impact of rapid urbanization on American life in the late 1800s.
3. Discuss the experiences of immigrants in the United States.
4. Describe the reaction of middle-class people to industrialization, urbanization, and immigration.

Bellringer Activity

 While taking attendance at the beginning of the class period, display **Section Focus Transparency 23,** and have students answer the questions. (Or use the blackline master.)

VISUAL INSTRUCTION

Baxter Street Court Immigrants often clustered where they could find familiar foods, churches, and common languages.

Ask: How did Riis describe tenement living conditions? *(dead air; rotting food; sickly, neglected children; no light)*

History and the Humanities

U.S. History and Art Transparency 19—*Cliff Dwellers* by George Bellows

American Music: Cultural Traditions—"Polka 'Wiesniaczka'" by Pawlo Humeniuk and band; "De Little Old Log Cabin in the Lane" by Carroll C. Clark

Facing a New Order

1890: LIFE AND DEATH IN A NEW YORK CITY APARTMENT

THE JACOB A RIIS COLLECTION, MUSEUM OF THE CITY OF NEW YORK

Baxter Street Court
Jacob Riis photographed this tenement alley in New York City in 1888.

PHOTOGRAPHER AND JOURNAL-IST JACOB RIIS HAD BREATHED ENOUGH STAGNANT AIR, SMELLED ENOUGH ROTTING FOOD, AND SEEN ENOUGH SICKLY CHILDREN TO KNOW HOW THE POOR OF NEW YORK CITY LIVED. In one of his writings he offered to take readers on a guided tour of an overcrowded apartment building:

Be a little careful, please! The hall is dark and you might stumble over the children pitching pennies back there. Not that it would hurt them; kicks and cuffs are their daily diet. They have little else.

Here where the hall turns and dives into utter darkness is a step, and another, another. A flight of stairs. You can feel your way, if you cannot see it. Close? Yes! What would you have? All the fresh air that ever enters these stairs comes from the hall-door that is forever slamming, and from the windows of dark bedrooms. . . .

Here is a door. Listen! That short hacking cough, that tiny, helpless wail—what do they mean? They mean that the soiled bow of white you saw on the door downstairs will have another story to tell—oh! a sadly familiar story—before the day is at an end. The child is dying with measles. With half a chance it might have lived; but it had none. The dark bedroom killed it.
—Jacob Riis, *How the Other Half Lives,* 1890

Between 1880 and 1920 people flocked to the cities from the countryside and abroad. While they often found opportunity, many also suffered from low wages, diseases, and wretched housing. How concerned citizens responded to these problems reshaped American government in the Progressive era.

AS YOU READ

Vocabulary

▶ tenement
▶ suburb
▶ urbanization
▶ immigrant
▶ political machine
▶ trust

Think About . . .

▶ the growth of cities in the United States.
▶ the impact of rapid urbanization on American life in the late 1800s.

▶ the experiences of immigrants in the United States.
▶ the reaction of middle-class people to industrialization, urbanization, and immigration.

234 CHAPTER 8 PROGRESSIVE REFORMS

Section 1 Resources

REPRODUCIBLE RESOURCES

Lesson Plan 8-1
Vocabulary and Guided Reading Activity 8-1
Cooperative Learning Activity 8
Unit 3 Great Debate
Section 1 Quiz

Unit 3 American Literature Reading
MULTIMEDIA RESOURCES
Section Focus Transparency 23
Map Transparency 8
Beginnings to 1900 Transparencies 30, 31, 32
Chapter Teaching Transparency 8

Chapter 8 Digest Audiocasette
The American People: Fabric of a Nation
U.S. History and Art Transparencies 15, 19
American Music: Cultural Traditions
Testmaker
Student Self-Test: A Software Review

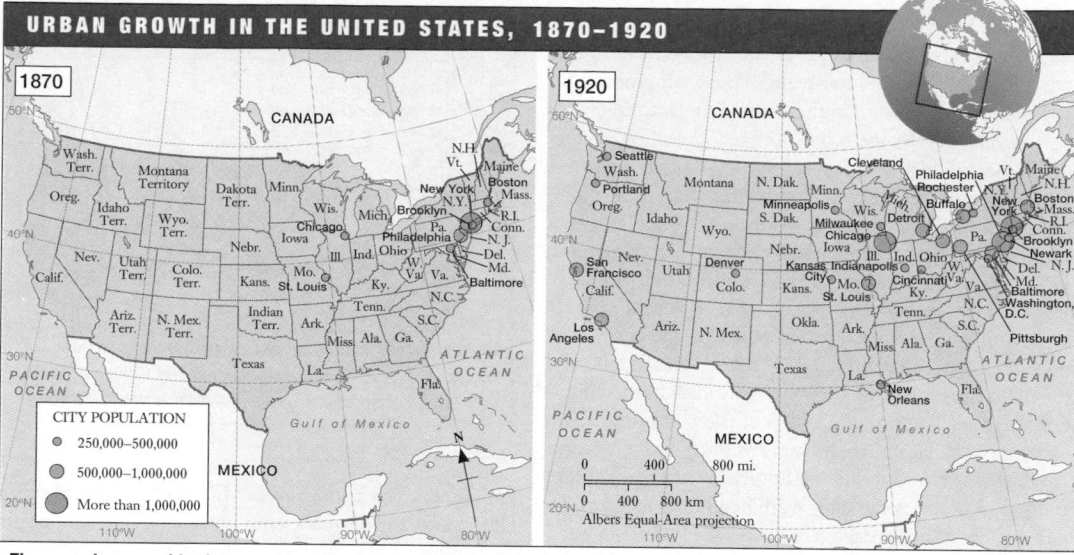

URBAN GROWTH IN THE UNITED STATES, 1870–1920

1870

1920

CITY POPULATION
- 250,000–500,000
- 500,000–1,000,000
- More than 1,000,000

The map shows rapid urban growth near the Great Lakes, a region with large coal deposits and good transportation. *What new cities with populations of 500,000–100,000 appeared in 1920?*

TEACH

Guided Practice

L1 Discussion Have students consider the impact of immigration and ethnic diversity on food, language, music, street names, and other aspects of everyday life in the United States today. Then create a class chart listing supporting evidence.

Show students Map Transparency 8 and have them complete the activity sheet.

Show students Beginnings to 1900 Transparencies 30, 31, 32, and have them complete the activity sheets.

MAP/CHART STUDY

Ask students to analyze the population shifts shown in the map and the chart. Point out that a similar trend was occurring throughout much of the world, and that it continues today. People are still moving to urban areas. Today, however, suburbs are growing faster than central cities.

Map Answer: *San Francisco, Los Angeles, St. Louis, Cleveland, Detroit, Buffalo, Baltimore, Pittsburgh, Boston*

Chart Answer: *It doubled.*

Shame of the Cities
Urban Growth Brings Problems

The substandard conditions that Riis described in the New York apartment building, or **tenement,** could be found in many cities around the nation. As these cities grew, so did their problems.

Urban Growth

Cities in the United States expanded rapidly in the late 1800s. In 1860 only 20 percent of the people in the United States lived in towns or cities with populations greater than 2,500. By 1900 this percentage had doubled.

As American cities grew and became overcrowded, people who could afford to moved to **suburbs.** These communities blossomed at the edges of big cities. New forms of mass transportation developed; that enabled suburban residents to commute more easily to their jobs in the center of the city. In addition, these improvements helped everyone move around the city more efficiently. In 1873 San Francisco began construction of cable-car lines. A large cable powered by a motor at one end of the rail line moved passenger cars along. In 1888 Richmond, Virginia, pioneered the use of the trolley car, a motorized train that was powered by electricity supplied through overhead cables. In 1897 Boston opened the nation's first subway, or underground railway.

Changes in transportation were just one advancement in technology that fostered **urbanization,** the growth of cities. Before the mid-1800s water power ran machinery; therefore, factories had to be near rivers. With the application of steam power in the mid-1800s, though, factories could be established anywhere that fuel, usually coal, was available. Factory owners sought locations where they had dependable access to coal for fueling their steam-driven machinery and to minerals, sand, or other materials they needed to run their factories. They prized sites where rail lines linked with water routes, such as New York, Chicago, and St. Louis.

The opening of a factory in a city was a magnet that pulled in new residents looking for jobs. Many of these people came from rural areas where they could find no work. New machines—reapers, threshers, binding machines, combines—were rapidly replacing manual labor

Urban Growth in the United States, 1870–1920

Population (in millions)

- Rural
- Urban

Year: 1870, 1880, 1890, 1900, 1910, 1920

Within 50 years, urban population had quintupled. *According to the chart, by how much did the rural population change between 1870 and 1920?*

Cooperative Learning

Research on Immigration Organize students into groups of 4 or 5 to research why people from a particular country or region left their homeland in the 1800s. Have students determine the tasks for individual members. Students may want to share stories about why their relatives may have moved to the United States. Encourage students to bring items from home that show their families' connections with other countries, states, or neighborhoods. Each group should report to the class, and the class should develop a hypothesis that explains why immigration to the United States increased dramatically in the late 1800s.

Independent Practice

L1 Making a Time Line

Have students construct a time line showing technological developments, ideas, or events that contributed to urbanization. Each entry could be illustrated with a picture and/or annotated with statistics or quotations.

☞ Have students complete the Chapter 8, Section 1 Vocabulary and Guided Reading Activity. (Also in Spanish.) **LEP**

☞ Have students complete the Chapter 8 Cooperative Learning Activity.

Block Scheduling

☞ Have students complete the Unit 3 Great Debate to enrich their understanding of child labor.

CHART STUDY

In 1900 total immigration was about 550,000; about 400,000, or 73 percent, came from southern and eastern Europe.
Answer: *1888 to 1908*

VISUAL INSTRUCTION

Steerage Passengers Anna Yezierska, a 16-year-old Jewish girl from Poland, remembered: "[We traveled in] steerage [the cheapest section of the ship] dirty bundles—foul odors— seasick humanity. . . ."
Answer: *availability of jobs*

---

on farms. One commentator noted in 1898 that "four men with improved agricultural implements now do the work formerly done by fourteen." Those who moved to cities often found work in the expanding factories.

Although jobs were the primary attraction of the cities, people also headed to cities for other reasons. Cities offered pleasures considered luxuries in rural areas—plays, concerts, and stores with fancy clothes. City dwellers got new technology, such as electricity and indoor plumbing, long before rural residents did. (See One Day in History, pages 240–241.) Finally, cities offered anonymity. In large urban areas people could easily disappear from the scrutiny of their friends and families.

The movement to the cities included both whites and African Americans. In 1865 at the end of the Civil War, most African Americans lived on farms and in small towns throughout the South. By the late 1800s, though, African Americans were beginning to move to cities. More than 40 percent of the people in Atlanta were African Americans. In most Northern cities, the African American population was increasing but did not exceed 3 percent in any given city in 1915.

Immigration

Like rural citizens of the United States, Europeans poured into American cities in the late 1800s and early 1900s. The United States had always been a land of **immigrants,** attracting people from other countries to live there. Beginning around 1880, however, the immigrant stream became a flood. Between 1880 and 1920 about 25 million immigrants entered the United States. That was half as many people as lived in the entire country in 1880.

Changing Sources of Immigrants

Chart: Immigrants (in thousands), Year 1820–1920

- Northern and Western Europe
- Southern and Eastern Europe
- Africa, Asia, Australia, South America, and North America

The numbers of immigrants from southern and eastern Europe increased dramatically in the early 1900s. *According to the chart, what range of years shows the greatest increase?*

Equally as important as the swelling tide of immigrants was the dramatic shift in their countries of origin, as shown on the chart on this page. Before 1890 most immigrants came from northern and western Europe—Great Britain, Ireland, Germany, and the Scandinavian countries. Many of these people spoke English, and most were Protestants. Between 1890 and 1920, though, about 80 percent of all immigrants came from southern and eastern Europe, from countries such as Italy, Greece, Poland, and Russia. They usually practiced the Roman Catholic, Eastern Orthodox, or Jewish faith. Most were poor, uneducated, and illiterate. The first sight of the United States for many of these newcomers was the Statue of Liberty and Ellis Island in New York Harbor. When Ellis Island opened in 1892, it marked the passage of processing immigrants from state to federal control.

Most immigrants arriving after 1880 settled in cities, because that was where jobs could be found. By 1920 nearly half of all urban dwellers were immigrants or the children of immigrants. The ethnic diversity of American cities impressed Danish immigrant Jacob Riis. Speaking of New York, he said, "A map of the city, colored to designate nationalities, would show more stripes than on the skin of a zebra, and more colors than any rainbow." One Polish immigrant found the large number of immigrants frustrating:

> I am polish man. I want be American citizen. . . . But my friends are polish people—I must live with them—I work in the shoe-shop with polish people—I stay all the time with them—at home—in the shop—anywhere. . . . when

Steerage Passengers Immigrants, such as those shown above arriving in New York in the early 1900s, often sailed on dangerously crowded ships. *Why did most immigrants to the United States settle in cities?*

236 CHAPTER 8 PROGRESSIVE REFORMS

Meeting Special Needs

Visual Learners This activity helps to address the particular needs of visual learners. On a map of Europe, help students identify the modern countries from which the largest numbers of immigrants came in the late 1800s and early 1900s: Italy, Greece, Poland, and Russia. Point out to students that many of these countries today have different borders than they did around 1900. Poland, for example, did not exist as an independent republic until 1918. Discuss the tremendous ethnic diversity that existed in southern and eastern Europe. Help students recognize that using maps is a good strategy for understanding the sources of immigration.

An Immigrant Apartment Jessie Tarbox Beals took this photo, "Room in a Tenement Flat," in New York City in 1910. In poor areas of New York, where political machines were strong, apartments housed an average of 1.9 people per room. *What other problems did city overcrowding create?*

I come home—I must speak polish and in the shop also. In this way I can live in your country many years—like my friends—and never speak—write well English—and never be good American citizen.
>—Polish immigrant, Commission on the Problem of Immigration, 1914

Social Problems

Others found the growth of cities frustrating as well. Many Americans agreed with Congregationalist minister Josiah Strong that cities were wicked places and indeed posed threats to the very core of their civilization:

The city has become a serious menace to our civilization. . . . Here [in the city] is heaped the social dynamite; here roughs, gamblers, thieves, robbers, lawless and desperate men of all sorts, congregate; men who are ready on any pretext to raise riots for the purpose of destruction and plunder; here gather foreigners and wage-workers; here skepticism and irreligion abound.
>—Josiah Strong, *Our Country,* 1885

Strong's attack on cities reflected his own dislike of immigrants. His views, however, also reflected the existence of real problems in cities. Many jobs paid so poorly that workers had to find other ways, sometimes illegal, to add to their income. Gambling, robbery, and extortion were widespread. In 1906 Chicago had an estimated 10,000 prostitutes, many of whom were

under the age of 19. The city also had about 7,000 cocaine addicts. As cities grew, so did violence. The murder rate increased from 1.2 per 100,000 people in 1900 to 6.8 per 100,000 in 1920. Gang fights between rival political groups often marred election days.

Cities were not equipped to respond to their growing problems. Without enough police officers, crime was rampant. Without enough firefighters, fires quickly raged out of control. Without adequate sanitation systems, garbage and sewage piled up in the streets and polluted the drinking water. Two of the most severe urban problems were poor housing and political corruption.

Many of the people pouring into the cities could not afford their own apartments—and not enough places existed even if they could—so frequently they doubled up. Landlords divided small apartments into two or more even smaller units. Property owners converted horse stables, garages, and storage shacks into apartments. They added new buildings in the backyards of existing ones.

As buildings were carved up or constructed ever closer together, many apartments had no source of fresh air. Architects tried to combat this problem by designing dumbbell apartments. These structures were narrower in the middle than on the ends, like the letter *I*. With this design vertical spaces called air shafts could be left between buildings to allow light and air into each apartment.

SECTION ONE **237**

NATIONAL GEOGRAPHIC SOCIETY

 Videodisc

GTV: The American People: Fabric of a Nation

Side 3, Chapter 1
Title: *The Golden Door*
Subject: The flood of immigration between 1880 and 1920
Ask: Why did so many immigrants want to come to the United States? *(They regarded it as the land of opportunity.)*

Side 3, Chapter 2
Title: *Going to Town!*
Subject: Migration to cities
Ask: Why did so many Americans move to cities? *(They hoped to find better jobs and more opportunities.)*

VISUAL INSTRUCTION

An Immigrant Apartment In 1905, journalist Eleanor McMain described a block of tenements in New Orleans's Italian district as "death traps." Only 35 of the 144 families on the block had separate toilets. Sometimes, 6 or 7 families shared only one. There were no bathtubs on the entire block.

Answer: *gambling, general lawlessness, poor housing, inadequate sanitation, poverty, robbery, extortion, drug addiction, gangs, fires, and vermin*

Portfolio Project

Interviewing Have students interview local merchants to find out about their relationship with the city government. Students should clearly identify three things: services the city provides the merchant, such as garbage collection; regulations the city imposes, such as

building codes; and the attitude of the merchant toward the government. In class, discuss ways that a corrupt politician could reward or punish businesses. Students may then file their interview notes in their portfolios.

ASSESS

The air shafts, though, became dangerous. Tenants threw garbage out of their windows into the shafts. The smell on a hot summer day could be so nauseating that tenants had to close their windows. Worse than the putrid smell were the rats, insects, and disease germs that thrived in the garbage.

Living conditions were bad for most newcomers to the city, but they were worse for African Americans. As a result of the racial prejudice of many whites, African Americans were restricted to living in only small parts of cities. As their population increased, the African American neighborhoods became even more overcrowded than the areas where immigrants lived.

Political Corruption

Politicians controlled the valuable contracts for building the new transportation lines, bridges, and firehouses that a growing city needed. Many showed more concern for filling their own pockets, however, than for solving the problems that Riis and others identified. A mayor could become wealthy overnight by accepting a bribe from a company trying to win a construction contract with the city. Businesses, then, usually added the cost of the bribe onto the contract with the city. Well-connected businesses prospered, and so did the politicians. Taxpayers paid the bill.

In order to keep the wealth flowing to themselves and their allies, politicians had to remain in office. They won the necessary votes by doing favors for people. The poor people of a city, especially immigrants and African Americans, often needed help—a job, a bag of coal, legal advice—that a wealthy politician could provide. All that the politician asked in return was a vote on Election Day. Some politicians developed and ran sophisticated organizations, known as **political machines,** to win votes. In each ward, or political district within a city, a machine representative controlled jobs, contracts, and favors. This person was the ward boss.

The most famous political machine in the country controlled life in New York City and was headquartered in Tammany Hall. George Washington Plunkitt, a member of the New York State Assembly, was a minor boss in the Tammany Hall machine.

By observing Plunkitt in action and reading his diaries, a newspaper reporter pieced together a typical workday for Plunkitt. At 6:00 A.M., Plunkitt followed a fire truck to the scene of a fire and provided food, clothes, and temporary shelter for tenants who had just been burned out. "Fires," the reporter noted, "are considered great vote-getters." Later that morning, Plunkitt "paid the rent of a poor family" about to be evicted and "gave them a dollar for food." Then he found jobs for four men who had just been fired.

In the afternoon Plunkitt attended two funerals, one Italian and one Jewish. At each, he sat in the very front so everyone would see him. After dinner Plunkitt went to a church fair, where he bought tickets at every single fund-raising booth, and bought ice cream for all the children, "kissed the little ones, flattered their mothers, and took their fathers out for something down at the corner." At 9:00 P.M., he returned to his office, where he pledged to donate money to help a church buy a new bell. Later that night he attended a wedding reception and gave a "handsome wedding present to the bride." Finally, at midnight, after 18 hours of making friends and winning votes, Plunkitt went to bed.

Plunkitt's long hours paid off handsomely. His Tammany Hall associates rewarded him for his ability to deliver a large number of votes to party candidates each Election Day. For example, when the park board was planning a new park, they slipped word to Plunkitt of the location long before any plans had been made public. Then, from the unsuspecting owners, Plunkitt bought the land where the park would be established. Weeks later, when the board announced its decision to construct a new park, Plunkitt resold the land to the park board at a much higher price than he paid for it. By the time of his death, Plunkitt was a millionaire.

THE BETTMANN ARCHIVE

Controlling City Hall This lithograph by Joseph Keppler shows the power of Tammany Hall. *In what ways were political machines corrupt?*

Industrial Disorder
Squeezing Small Businesses and Workers

Plunkitt was not the only person to prosper while others struggled just to survive. By 1910 the income of the wealthiest 2 percent of Americans accounted for almost 20 percent of the total income of all workers, double what it had accounted for in 1896.

Extending the Content

Vicious Cycle The conditions in the crowded city neighborhoods created a cycle of poverty and crime that was difficult to break. Poor children who worked long hours in the factories could not attend school. Hence, they could not receive the education that could help them escape from poverty. In addition, the slums and tenements were breeding grounds for disease.

Ask students how people disposed of their garbage without an adequate sanitation system. What effect did this method of disposal have on their lives? *(Tenement residents sometimes threw their garbage into the open spaces between apartment buildings. The rotting food stank, attracted rats and insects, and spread diseases.)*

The Oil Industry This cartoon entitled *NEXT!* published in the magazine *Puck* depicts the control of Standard Oil over government and suppliers. *How did a large company also provide benefits to consumers?*

One reason for this growing concentration of wealth was the rash of business mergers and buyouts in the 1890s. Such consolidations usually resulted in the formation of **trusts,** a combination of companies dominating an industry, usually created for the purpose of reducing competition in that industry. Often a small handful of people, or even a single individual, ruled a trust.

The size of these large companies accounted for some benefits to consumers. Large firms could afford to develop and use expensive new machinery that, in turn, lowered the cost of producing goods. Companies were so large that any small cost-cutting measure could save enormous amounts of money. For example, by reducing the cost of each oil storage can by only 15 cents, Standard Oil saved more than $5 million a year. Such production efficiency could lead to cheaper retail prices. Items that were once luxuries, such as glass bottles, were now commonly available and inexpensive. "Never in human history was the creation of material wealth so easy and so marvelously abundant," pointed out one United States senator.

The senator cautioned, however, "Here are dangers it will behoove us to gravely contemplate." The new, efficient companies exacted a heavy cost in human suffering. Though wages increased slowly between 1890 and 1910, most workers lived just outside the reach of financial ruin. Everyday expenses such as rent, food, and clothes absorbed virtually all of the income of typical workers.

In between the wealthy owners and the poorly paid laborers was a growing middle class. This group consisted of managers, clerks, small-business owners, college professors, members of the clergy, lawyers, and other professionals. The middle class, which was able to afford the

mass-produced goods, praised the technological triumphs that led to greater production efficiency. They felt threatened, however, by both the rich and the poor and blamed the growing problems of society on these groups:

N early all problems which vex society have their sources above or below the middle-class man. From above come the problems of predatory wealth. . . . From below come the problems of poverty and of pigheaded and brutish criminality.

—*California Weekly,*
December 18, 1908

To many educated, honest, middle-class Americans, the traditional values that they prized were under assault. Trusts, though efficient, threatened to squeeze small businesses out of existence. Workers, plagued by crime and poverty, seemed vulnerable to revolutionary calls for radical change. Middle-class Americans and their allies responded to these threats by calling for a return to traditional values—economic opportunity, religious morality, political honesty, and social stability. This effort to reform the United States and preserve its democratic values became known as the Progressive movement.

SECTION REVIEW

Vocabulary
1. Define: tenement, suburb, urbanization, immigrant, political machine, trust.

Checking Facts
2. What combination of factors attracted rural Americans as well as immigrants to cities in the United States?

3. What effect did urban and industrial growth have on life in American cities?

Critical Thinking
Determining Cause and Effect
4. How do you think the continuous flow of new workers into the cities affected the wages of all workers?

Linking Across Time
5. In what ways do the conditions in American cities of the late 1800s and early 1900s resemble those in cities today? In what ways do they differ?

SECTION ONE   **239**

Evaluate

Have students complete the Section Review.

📁 🖸 Assign the Section 1 Quiz or use the Testmaker to develop a customized quiz. (Also in Spanish.) **LEP**

Reteach

🎧 Have students listen to the Chapter 8, Section 1 Audiocassette. (Also in Spanish.) **LEP**

Enrich

📁 Have students complete the Unit 3 American Literature Reading.

VISUAL INSTRUCTION

The Oil Industry Puck, a mischievous spirit or elf in English folklore, tormented people, usually in fun.

Answer: *It used new machinery and more efficient practices that lowered retail prices.*

CLOSE

Have students exchange section time lines with a partner. The two students should compare the entries each has chosen, and discuss any differences. *(Answers will vary, but should include information about technological developments, ideas, or events that contributed to urbanization.)*

Section 1 Review Answers

1. tenement (235), **suburb** (235), **urbanization** (235), **immigrant** (236), **political machine** (238), **trust** (239)
2. People flocked to cities in search of work, entertainment, new technology, and anonymity.
3. Housing deteriorated, crime increased, and political machines developed.

4. With a steady stream of potential workers, employers could keep wages low.
5. Answers might include that cities still attract immigrants and rural residents and have tenements, crime, and corruption, but that today's cities provide more services.

TEACH

Making the Historical Connection

As the United States and the world began to inch toward a modern industrialized era, new discoveries and inventions were conducted by daring risk takers. Edison began his important research on electric lighting in 1878, but inventors worldwide were also investigating the process. On October 21, 1879, after thousands of experiments, Edison produced the first practical incandescent lightbulb. His experiments involved passing electricity through a wire filament, but that caused the filament to melt or burn. When he used scorched cotton thread—equivalent to carbon wire—in an evacuated glass bulb, he was able to successfully light a glass bulb for 40 hours.

FYI

Other Great Scientific Discoveries of 1880

• A French physician, Charles-Louis-Alphonse Laveran, isolated the microorganism that caused malaria.

• Henry Draper used dry plates—an advancement in the area of photography—and took the first photograph of the Orion nebula.

• The first modern seismograph was devised by a British geologist, John Milne.

240

One Day in History

Thursday, January 1, 1880

MARKET BASKET

Here is where a dollar will go:

Parasol . . . . 50¢
Perfumed kid gloves
  Two-button $1
  Four-button $1.50
Hat, trimmed $2.50

COURTESY THE OAKLAND MUSEUM HISTORY DEPARTMENT, OAKLAND, CA

Imitation-gold pocket
  watch $12
Corset $3
Muslin shirt $1
Neckwear—ties, bows,
  scarves . . . . 25¢
Baseball, by mail $1.50
Dental fee: vitalized or
  gas . . . . 25¢
Boys' short
  pantaloons . . . . 50¢
Walking skirt with
  ruffle . . . . 50¢
Black Elysian
  overcoat $4.50
Waterproof cape $8.25
Admission to
  New York circus . . . 25¢, 50¢
  Reserved . . . . 25¢ extra

UPI/BETTMANN

The Edison Lamp Inventor Thomas A. Edison stands in his laboratory holding the first incandescent vacuum light tube, which uses carbonized cotton thread as a filament.

Edison's New Lamp

An invention of great promise; Menlo Park illuminated

MENLO PARK—On New Year's Eve, the little hamlet of Menlo Park, New Jersey, was illuminated by 40 streetlamps lighted with electricity. Tonight the display will be repeated. In addition to the streetlamps, there were 100 electric burners in operation in machine buildings, private buildings, and Professor Edison's laboratory. The number of lights will be increased daily until there are 800. One of the lamps now in use has been lighted, day and night, for 17 days. The others have been used for 2 weeks. The Pennsylvania Railroad Company carried passengers to and from the park at a reduced fare, and as many as 3,000 people took the opportunity to witness the illumination.

Background Information

The Pirates of Penzance Both the American and British copyrights were established when this comic opera opened in New York and England. W.S. Gilbert, a dramatist, and Arthur Sullivan, a composer, teamed up with Richard D'Oyly Carte, the manager of the Royalty Theatre in Soho. The plot is based on a strange incident in Gilbert's childhood in which he was kidnapped and ransomed by Neapolitan brigands. In the opera a band of good-natured and inefficient Cornish pirates are celebrating the return of their young apprentice, Frederic, an orphan. Frederic, however, shocks the pirates by telling them that he intends to lead an honest life.

CULVER PICTURES

NATION: By an act of Congress, women have won the right to practice law and to argue cases before the United States Supreme Court.

Latimer Joins Hiram Maxim

BOSTON—After illustrating the workings of the telephone's components for Alexander Graham Bell's 1876 patent, Lewis Howard Latimer has become interested in the incandescent lightbulb invented by Thomas Edison. Latimer has agreed to join Hiram Maxim's United States Electric Lighting Company as a patent draftsman. He will work on patenting methods for manufacturing superior carbon filaments used in the new electric lamps, hoping to make the lamps last longer and cost less.

Master Draftsman Lewis Latimer earns recognition for creating technical drawings that illustrate patents.

PHOTOGRAPHS AND PRINTS DIVISION, SCHOMBURG CENTER FOR RESEARCH IN BLACK CULTURE, NEW YORK PUBLIC LIBRARY, ASTOR, LENOX AND TILDEN FOUNDATIONS.

THE PIERPONT MORGAN LIBRARY, NEW YORK, THE GILBERT AND SULLIVAN COLLECTION

Gilbert and Sullivan's New Opera Opens The *Pirates of Penzance*, direct from London, debuted last evening at the Fifth Avenue Theatre in New York City.

MUSIC

THIS YEAR'S HIT SONGS

"Oh! Dem Golden Slippers"

"In the Evening by the Moonlight"

"A Policeman's Lot Is Not a Happy One"

BOOKS

NEW AND SOON TO BE RELEASED

Ben-Hur by Lew Wallace

Daisy Miller by Henry James

Five Little Peppers and How They Grew by Margaret Sidney

The Brothers Karamazov by Fyodor Dostoyevsky

TIME CAPSULE
1880

AMERICAN LIFE

February 19: Gail Borden organizes *Houston Post* newspaper company.

March 24: The Salvation Army makes its debut.

May 30: Irish-American Paddy Ryan wins world heavyweight boxing title by knocking out England's Joe Goss.

June 2–8: The Republican National Convention, the first chaired by an African American, nominates Ohio's James Garfield for President.

June 3: Alexander Graham Bell sends the first wireless telephone message.

November 2: Susan B. Anthony and Elizabeth Cady Stanton try to vote for President; their ballots are refused.

November 8: French actress Sarah Bernhardt makes her American debut in Alexandre Dumas's *La Dame aux Camélias.*

November 17: Chinese Exclusion Treaty restricts entrance of immigrants.

December 20: One mile of Broadway is illuminated with arc lamps.

PORTFOLIO PROJECT

Oral History

Interviewing Risk Takers Ask students to interview an inventor, experimenter, writer, or entertainer. Encourage them to formulate a slate of questions about the individual's field of expertise. Suggest to students that they find out what kinds of problems had to be solved in order for the individual to achieve success in his or her chosen profession. Have students find out what has changed that makes the interviewee's job different. Students should also determine what personal qualities are required for pursuing a similar career. Invite volunteers to share the written summaries of their interviews before filing them in their portfolios.

CLOSE

Discuss January 1, 1880, with students and ask them what effect the discovery of electricity has had on their lives. *(Answers will vary but should review electric conveniences that make their lives less harsh.)*

FOCUS

Section Objectives

1. Identify the different types of people who became progressives.
2. Analyze the aspects of American society that were criticized by the progressives.
3. List the different ways progressives tried to address problems linked to urbanization and industrialization.

Bellringer Activity

While taking attendance at the beginning of the class period, display **Section Focus Transparency 24,** and have students answer the questions. (Or use the blackline master.)

VISUAL INSTRUCTION

Children's Advocate A social reformer and pacifist, Jane Addams was a co-winner (with Nicholas Murray Butler) of the Nobel Peace Prize in 1931. Hull House offered college-level courses in various subjects and training in the fine arts.

Ask: In what ways did Hull House serve the community? *(Neighborhood residents learned to speak English, discussed political events, and held celebrations; a day nursery for children of working parents was provided.)*

Facts on File

Landmark Documents in American History Have students review "Twenty Years at Hull House, Jane Addams, 1903" and write a paragraph about the intent of the document.

242

SECTION 2

A Generation of Reformers

EARLY 1890s: "SAINT JANE" OPENS NURSERY FOR THE POOR

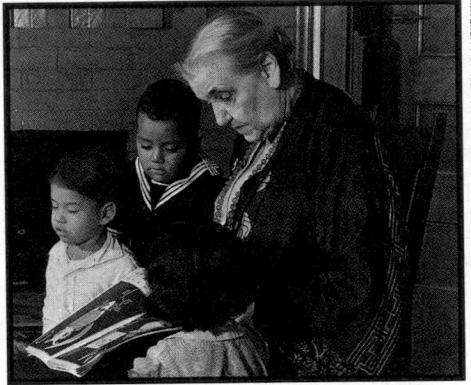

Children's Advocate
Jane Addams, founder of Hull House, reads a picture book to the young children in her nursery.

WITHIN A YEAR AFTER MOVING TO CHICAGO IN 1889, YOUNG, IDEALISTIC JANE ADDAMS MET THREE CHILDREN WHOM SHE NEVER FORGOT. "One had fallen out of a third-story window, another had been burned, and the third had a curved spine due to the fact that for three years he had been tied all day long to the leg of the kitchen table." The children had each been left alone, day after day, while their parents worked. Their parents earned so little money that they could not hire anyone to watch their children.

Addams, a quiet, dignified woman from a well-to-do family in a small Illinois town, had moved to Chicago because she wanted to help the poor. She and a friend had purchased a large, but run-down, old home known as Hull House in the midst of a densely populated immigrant neighborhood. They repaired the house and made it into a community center where neighborhood residents could learn to speak English, discuss political events, and hold celebrations. In addition, because of those three injured children, Addams opened a day nursery. Working parents no longer had to leave their young children unsupervised during the day. For her work, neighbors referred to her as Saint Jane.

Addams realized that the machines that had brought such great prosperity were also the engines of great

AS YOU READ

Vocabulary
▶ progressive
▶ muckraker
▶ social gospel movement
▶ settlement house

Think About . . .
▶ the different types of people who became progressives.
▶ the aspects of American society that were criticized by the progressives.

▶ the different ways progressives tried to address problems associated with urbanization and industrialization.

242 CHAPTER 8 PROGRESSIVE REFORMS

Section 2 Resources

REPRODUCIBLE RESOURCES
📁 Lesson Plan 8-2
📁 Vocabulary and Guided Reading 8-2
📁 Section 2 Quiz
📁 Skill Reinforcement Activity 8
📁 Geography in History Activity 8

MULTIMEDIA RESOURCES
🔦 Section Focus Transparency 24
🎧 Chapter 8 Digest Audiocassette
💿 Landmark Documents in American History
💿 Testmaker
💿 Student Self-Test: A Software Review

misery. Jane Addams was just one of many Americans who, at the turn of the century, advocated reforms to confront the problems caused by industrialization and urbanization. The efforts of these reformers, the **progressives,** dominated the political landscape of the early 1900s.

Progressive Ideals
Protecting the Public Interest

During Jane Addams's youth the United States consisted mostly of small towns, small businesses, and small-scale problems. As Addams grew up, though, she watched larger cities, larger businesses, and larger problems develop. Small-town politicians never practiced corruption on the scale of George Washington Plunkitt and his Tammany Hall cronies. Rural poor people did not live in concentrations of garbage and stagnant air as did city tenement dwellers. A village blacksmith could never control a town the way a large steel company could dominate the people of a city.

Like the populists of the 1880s and 1890s, progressives feared the concentration of power in the hands of the wealthy few. While hardworking immigrants could not afford to provide for their hungry and ill children, financiers like J.P. Morgan became millionaires by manipulating ownership of the companies for which these immigrants toiled. Through campaign contributions and bribes, corporate trusts bought influence with lawmakers. Progressives wanted reforms to protect the public interest.

Unlike the populists, who usually lived in rural areas, the progressives generally lived in cities. By the 1890s cities faced crippling problems: housing shortages, political corruption, and spiraling crime rates. In the chaotic cities, progressives wanted to reestablish order and stability.

Progressives were also unlike populists in their greater faith in experts. While populists emphasized the wisdom of average people, progressives focused on the ability of knowledgeable experts to analyze and solve problems. Just as Thomas Edison had conquered technological problems in developing the lightbulb, progressives believed that trained experts could analyze and conquer crime, alcoholism, and political corruption. Many progressives praised business owners for their expertise in solving the problems of producing and distributing goods and in running a store or a factory smoothly. Though fearing the power of big businesses, progressives often respected the efficient methods they used.

Progressive Analysts
Analyzing and Publicizing Society's Problems

Progressives looked to government to solve problems. Virtually all progressives shared the hope that a well-run government could protect the public interest and restore order to society. Beyond this hope, though, progressives differed widely in their beliefs, goals, and actions.

New Intellectuals

Changes in higher education influenced many progressives. Between 1870 and 1920 college enrollment increased more than tenfold, and many schools established separate social science departments, such as economics, political science, and sociology. These departments attempted to analyze human society with the same objectivity that scientists used to study nature. Their establishment reflected a growing faith in the ability of people to analyze society and solve human problems. Many social science professors and the students they influenced became progressives. For example, Columbia University historian Charles Beard applied his knowledge of American history to reforming corrupt city governments. Not all the new intellectuals, however, worked for universities. Mary Ritter Beard, wife of Charles, wrote extensively about how scholars had ignored the contributions of women in history.

One of the influential members of the new social science fraternity was Lester Ward. Much of Ward's childhood was spent "roaming over those boundless

THE BETTMANN ARCHIVE

Lester Ward Brown University appointed Lester Ward professor of sociology in 1906 at the age of 65. *What did the new college social science departments attempt to analyze and why?*

SECTION TWO **243**

TEACH

Guided Practice

L1 Debate Organize the class into two groups, one defending Lester Ward's view that government should "liberate the forces of society," the other opposing his view as one that might lead to a tyrannical government. Students should try to clarify the proper limits of government action and understand how the progressives influenced the way some people think today.

VISUAL INSTRUCTION

Lester Ward A sociologist who was instrumental in establishing sociology as an academic discipline in the United States, Ward worked for most of his life for the federal government, mainly in the fields of geology, paleontology, and botany. The original subject of *Dynamic Sociology,* Ward's most important book, was education. By 1876, he had shifted the focus of the work to sociology.

Answer: *They analyzed human society attempting to solve human problems with scientific objectivity.*

Cooperative Learning

Debating the Issue of Child Labor Organize the class into small groups to debate whether children under the age of 16 should be allowed to work. Students should assume they are holding their debate in the early 1900s. Each group should include 2 students who support a federal ban, 2 who oppose any governmental restrictions, and 2 who believe the issue should be decided by each state individually. Each pair of students should write an outline summarizing their viewpoint. Select 1 group at random to hold a debate for the class to watch.

Independent Practice

L2 **Research** Explain to students that Rockefeller's influence remains strong through the charitable foundation he set up in 1913. Today this organization has over $1.6 billion in assets and contributes money to medical, educational, and other humanitarian programs throughout the world. Have students choose another charitable foundation to research.

☛ Have students complete the Chapter 8, Section 2 Vocabulary and Guided Reading Activity. (Also in Spanish.) **LEP**

VISUAL INSTRUCTION

Exposing Unsanitary Conditions An idealistic socialist supporter, Sinclair wrote novels that impacted American political history. *Oil!* (1927) was based on the Teapot Dome Scandal and *Boston* (1928) detailed the Sacco-Vanzetti case.

Answer: *spent 7 weeks with Chicago stockyard workers*

FYI

Progressives and Populists Both groups wanted a stronger government to protect the rights of average citizens. Both also called for a federal income tax and greater regulation of railroads. The movements, however, responded to different concerns—populists to agricultural problems and progressives to urban ones.

---

prairies" of Illinois and Iowa in the mid-1800s "and admiring nature." After surviving three wounds as a Union army soldier in the Civil War, he got a job as a minor clerk in the United States Treasury Department. For the next 40 years, he held a variety of federal government jobs. For most of this period, he worked for the United States Geological Survey, studying rocks, plants, and animals in the lightly settled territories of the West.

In his free time, Ward taught himself Greek, Latin, French, and German, and participated in various book clubs, debating the latest ideas on science, history, and philosophy. In 1869 he began outlining his first book, *Dynamic Sociology,* which he completed in 1883. In this book and five others, Ward analyzed social concerns just as scientifically as he studied natural phenomena. He challenged the widely held belief that it was natural for the strong, such as the owners of large corporations, to prosper while the weak, the workers, suffered. What was natural, Ward argued, was for people to control and change their social environment—the laws, customs, and relationships among people—for their own benefit. "The day has come for society to take its affairs into its own hands and shape its own destinies."

Government's Job

The shaping of a society's destiny, according to Ward, was the job of the government. For example, if tenements were inadequate, then government should pass laws, spend money, or take other steps to improve housing. Ward believed that a larger role by government would improve the social environment and expand the options of individuals. "The true function of government," Ward proclaimed, "is not to fetter, but to liberate the forces of society, not to diminish but to increase their effectiveness."

In 1906 at age 65, Ward finally took his first full-time academic position. He became professor of sociology at Brown University. Social scientists such as Ward claimed that scientific study of human problems would provide better ways to run the cities. These new intellectuals often depended upon others, however, to motivate the public and to attack specific problems with specific solutions.

Angry Writers

Among those who motivated the public were many writers known as **muckrakers.** That label came from a character in a seventeenth-century book, *Pilgrim's Progress,* who spent all of his time raking up the dirt and filth, or muck, on the ground. The muckrakers combined careful research, vivid writing, and intense moral outrage. Most of these crusaders wrote long, investigative articles for popular magazines such as *McClure's, Collier's, Cosmopolitan,* and *American Magazine.* Writers attacked wealthy corporations that exploited child labor, corrupt police departments that protected prostitution rings, and prestigious churches that owned disease-ridden tenements. Ida Tarbell, a "conventional-minded lady, sweet and gracious," was one of the most famous of the muckrakers. She wrote a series of widely read articles detailing the rise of the Standard Oil Company. Tarbell exposed the ruthless methods used by its owner, John D. Rockefeller, to crush his competition—including Tarbell's father.

In addition to articles, some muckrakers, such as Upton Sinclair, wrote novels. Sinclair grew up in near-poverty in Baltimore. His father, a salesperson, suffered from alcoholism and was never very successful. By 1904 the 26-year-old Sinclair was a gentle, innocent-looking young writer. He had already completed four novels, each featuring a courageous individual who fought against social injustice. In that year a radical newspaper, *Appeal to Reason,* hired Sinclair to write a novel about the exploitation of workers in the United States.

To prepare for the contracted novel, Sinclair lived among the stockyard workers of Chicago for seven weeks. He later recalled how he sat "in their homes at night, and talked with them and then in the daytime they would lay off their work, and take me around, and show me whatever I wished to see. I studied every detail of their lives."

Based on his close observations of how workers lived, Sinclair wrote *The Jungle,* a novel about a Lithuanian immigrant who worked in the meatpacking

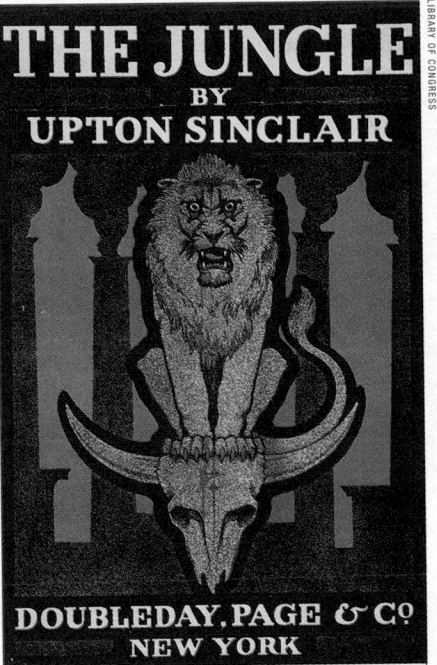

Exposing Unsanitary Conditions The publication of *The Jungle* led to the passage of the first federal food-inspection laws. *How did Sinclair prepare himself to write about exploited workers?*

Meeting Special Needs

Visual Learners This activity helps to address the particular needs of visual learners. Pair students to write anti-child labor slogans that could have been used in the early 1900s. Slogans should be brief and yet combine clarity with emotional appeal to attract the attention of a bystander. Then ask students to bring in contemporary magazines or books with pictures showing politicians, religious leaders, or protesters advocating some type of political, economic, or social reform. Discuss the motivations and tactics of people seeking change. Encourage pairs to write a slogan that could be used by one of these groups. Invite volunteers to share their slogans and explain their message.

BROWN BROTHERS

Preparing Meat for Consumers Complaints about unsafe meat preparation began in 1899, after United States soldiers got seriously ill from eating spoiled canned meat. *How would photos like this one of the Chicago stockyards around 1900 support the charges made by Upton Sinclair?*

Religious Reformers

Another group of progressives also appealed to the conscience of Americans. The **social gospel movement** included Christians who emphasized the role of the church in improving life on the earth rather than in helping individuals get into heaven.

One leader of the social gospel movement was Walter Rauschenbusch. Described by one journalist as "a tall, spare man, with a twinkle in his eyes," Rauschenbusch followed in the footsteps of six family generations and became a minister. After studying theology in Rochester, New York, and in Germany, he became pastor of the Second German Baptist Church in New York City.

industry. In focusing on one worker's life, Sinclair intended to arouse public sympathy for the common laborer. His graphic descriptions of the unsanitary conditions in the packing plant, however, sparked a reaction to the meat industry itself that completely overshadowed his intended focus. As Sinclair noted somewhat sadly, "I aimed at the public's heart, and by accident I hit it in the stomach." His book made consumers ill—and angry:

> There would come all the way back from Europe old sausage that had been rejected, and that was moldy and white—it would be dosed with borax and glycerine, and dumped into the hoppers, and made over again for home consumption. There would be meat that had tumbled out on the floor, in the dirt and sawdust, where the workers had tramped and spit uncounted billions of consumption germs. There would be meat stored in great piles in rooms; and the water from leaky roofs would drip over it, and thousands of rats would race about on it.
> —Upton Sinclair, *The Jungle*, 1906

Sinclair, like each of the muckrakers, had a vision of a just and orderly society. In Sinclair's society workers would receive adequate wages and consumers would purchase healthful food. The muckrakers' aim was to awaken people to the growing social, economic, and political evils and inequities in the nation.

Rauschenbusch's theological training did not prepare him for what he confronted in New York City. His church bordered a region aptly named Hell's Kitchen. Unemployment, alcoholism, and desperation plagued residents of this poverty-stricken neighborhood.

Rauschenbusch, as a devout Christian, turned to the Bible and his faith for a proper response to the new industrial system that made "the margin of life narrow in order to make the margin of profit wide." He concluded that the cause of many social ills was fierce competition. Owners and managers, many of whom were practicing Christians, believed they had to be ruthless or they would go out of business:

> Competitive commerce . . . makes men who are the gentlest and kindliest friends and neighbors, relentless taskmasters in their shops and stores, who will drain the strength of their men and pay their female employees wages on which no girl can live without supplementing them in some way.
> —Walter Rauschenbusch, *Christianity and the Social Crisis*, 1907

Rauschenbusch and other advocates of the social gospel believed that environmental conditions such as unemployment and poverty, and not an individual's personal depravity, caused the ills in society. Hence, they believed, every Christian should strive to better the economic and political conditions in the world.

SECTION TWO **245**

Curriculum Connection

Science In the late 1800s, Charles Darwin's theory of evolution through natural selection heavily influenced scientific thought. Some people applied the principle of "survival of the fittest" to human society and concluded that helping the poor live better was unnatural and thus wrong. Others pointed out that many animals survive by cooperation rather than aggressive competition. Students might be interested in a related controversy in the 1970s concerning the degree to which social organization is influenced by genetics, as detailed in *Sociobiology* by Edward O. Wilson and *Not in Our Genes* by Richard Lewontin.

Portfolio Project

Writing an Advertisement Discuss the reasons why Upton Sinclair focused on the life of a typical immigrant in *The Jungle*. In the early 1800s, writers usually detailed the lives of the wealthy and powerful. By the 1900s, Sinclair and other writers of realistic fiction began to scrutinize the daily life of common people. Like social scientists, these writers believed that close, detailed study of people would lead to greater understanding of human behavior. Using this information, have students write an advertisement for their portfolios announcing the publication of *The Jungle*. Encourage volunteers to share their products. 👏

IMPACT OF PROGRESSIVE REFORMS, 1889–1912

1889 Jane Addams starts Hull House.

1894 Ida B. Wells begins a national antilynching campaign.

1906 Upton Sinclair publishes *The Jungle*, an exposé of the meatpacking industry.

1912 Massachusetts becomes the first state to adopt a minimum wage.

1880 1885 1890 1895 1900 1905 1910 1915 1920 1925

1893 Florence Kelley helps pass a law in Illinois prohibiting child labor.

1899 National Consumers League forms to investigate conditions under which goods are made.

1908 The Supreme Court upholds an Oregon law limiting hours for women laundry workers.

Progressive Activists
Solving Society's Problems

Most progressives who analyzed problems took action to solve them as well. Sinclair ran for Congress three times and for governor of California once. Rauschenbusch skillfully helped his parish members cope with unemployment, alcoholism, and other social ills. Sinclair and Rauschenbusch, like Ward, however, were more influential as analysts who identified and publicized problems than as activists who solved them.

Other progressives were more influential as activists who successfully won reforms on specific issues rather than as analysts. Progressives usually focused their efforts on the problems they saw firsthand or felt personally. For example, Sinclair wrote about the meatpacking workers he lived with. Rauschenbusch confronted the problems of the urban poor. Similarly, many women who were progressives emphasized the problems faced by women and children. Many African American progressives stressed issues affecting African Americans.

Concerned Women

In most families, whether urban or rural, women had more responsibility for raising the children than did men. Consequently, women were particularly outraged about the problems of children who labored in factories.

One of the leaders in the battle against child labor was Florence Kelley. Her father, a member of the United States House of Representatives, opposed slavery and supported women's right to vote. He taught Florence to read at a young age and to value education. She graduated from Cornell University in New York and attended graduate school in Switzerland.

In 1891 she went to live and work at Jane Addams's Hull House. During her seven years there, she investigated and reported on the use of child labor. "In the stores on the West Side," Kelley reported in 1895, "large numbers of young girls are employed thirteen hours a day throughout the week, and fifteen hours on Saturday."

Kelley was, in the words of a friend, "explosive, hot-tempered, determined . . . a smoking volcano that at any moment would burst into flames." What she unearthed in her investigations, though, outraged even many mild-mannered people. Kelley charged that "children are found in greatest number where the conditions of labor are most dangerous to life and health." Children working in the tobacco industry suffered from nicotine poisoning. Children in paint factories suffered

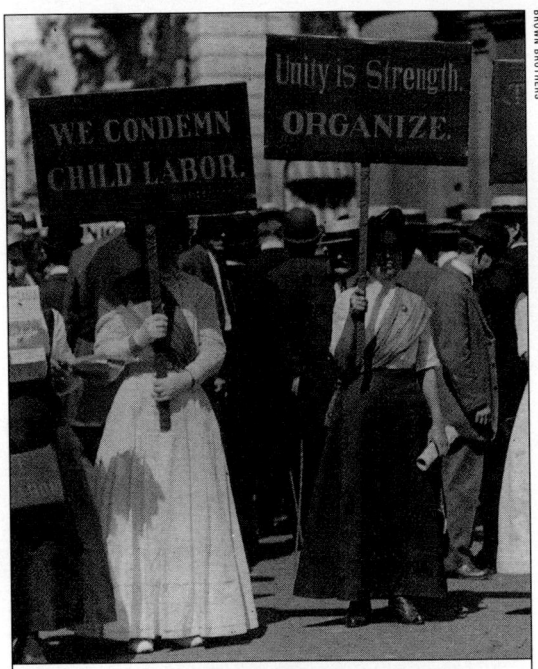

BROWN BROTHERS

WE CONDEMN CHILD LABOR.

Unity is Strength. ORGANIZE.

Child Labor Activists This photograph shows one of the many child labor protest marches held in the early 1900s. *Why are the women particularly upset about child labor?*

Extending the Content

Progressive Ideals Although the progressives desired to secure the common good, individually they were motivated by different forces and ideals. Some progressives felt they needed to experience for themselves the unjust treatment they wished to abolish. Others believed that such problems were best approached by carefully studying them in schools. The religious progressives undertook reform as part of their Christian duty to aid all people. Other progressives fought for reforms that would primarily help them and their own class, sex, or race. Ask students to identify an issue about which they have changed their minds and to analyze why they changed their viewpoint. Discuss whether people usually change their positions because of new information or because of new experiences.

from breathing in toxic arsenic fumes. Children in clothing factories suffered spinal curvature from hunching over sewing machines 48 hours each week.

Kelley pressed the federal government to outlaw the use of child labor. "Why," she thundered, "are seals, bears, reindeer, fish, wild game in the national parks, buffalo, [and] migratory birds all found suitable for federal protection, but not children?"

Kelley continued her battle against child labor after she left Hull House. As general secretary of the National Consumers League (NCL), she helped organize consumer boycotts of goods manufactured by children or by workers toiling in unsanitary or dangerous conditions.

The National Consumers League

Most members of the NCL were, like Kelley, middle-class or upper-class women concerned about problems such as exploitation of children in factories. Many NCL members also supported the work of **settlement houses,** institutions that provided educational and social services to poor people. Hull House was the best known of the 400 settlement houses established between 1886 and 1910. In addition to their work in settlement houses, women were very active in clubs that promoted the arts, education, and community health. By the early 1920s, almost 1 million women had joined such clubs. The NCL, the settlement houses, and the women's clubs indicate that women were taking a more active role in confronting political and economic problems than they had in the past.

Some of the reforms advocated by Kelley and other women were not supported by many of the men who were progressives. For example, Walter Rauschenbusch opposed granting women the vote, even though this was a vital issue to Kelley and many female reformers.

African American Activists

For the urban African American family, racism intensified such problems as high unemployment and inadequate housing. Many white factory owners refused to hire African Americans—except as strikebreakers. In most cities African Americans could live only in well-defined areas, which quickly became overcrowded as cities grew. Furthermore, racism remained firmly entrenched in the minds of most whites, including most

LIBRARY OF CONGRESS

NWTUL of Chicago The National Women's Trade Union League, like the National Consumers League, united workers and middle-class reformers. *How do its slogans reflect this?*

progressives. Many whites viewed African Americans as lazier, less intelligent, and more immoral than whites. In no other period of American history did state governments pass so many laws designed to restrict African Americans to a secondary role in society. African Americans working for reform often felt outside the Progressive movement.

The most dangerous problem for African Americans was lynching, murder by a mob without a trial, often by hanging. In 1892 about 230 people were lynched in the United States. Most of these people were African Americans, killed by groups of angry whites. Leading the antilynching movement was Ida B. Wells.

Born to enslaved parents in Holly Springs, Mississippi, in 1862, Wells remembered how much her parents emphasized education. "Our job," Wells recalled, "was to learn all we could."

When Wells was 14 her parents died in a yellow fever epidemic. Ida, the oldest of the 6 living children, refused to let her family be broken up. She lied about her age in order to get a job teaching school so that she could support her family.

In 1884 she got a better teaching job in Memphis and began writing for a local newspaper. Soon after arriving in Memphis, Wells became a controversial advocate of equality for African Americans because of an incident on a train. Upon taking a seat, she was told by the conductor that she was in a car reserved for whites and that she would have to move. Wells refused.

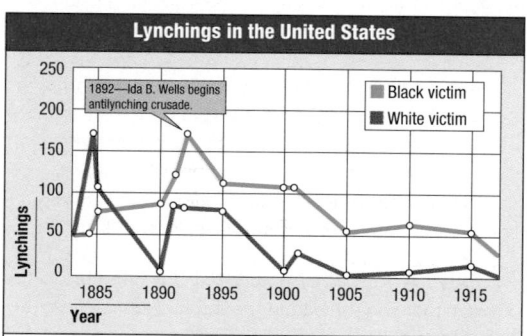

Lynchings in the United States

1892—Ida B. Wells begins antilynching crusade.

■ Black victim
■ White victim

Before 1886 most lynchings were done by whites to whites. After that date the victims of lynchings, most of which occurred in the South, were usually African American. *According to the chart, when did lynchings of African Americans peak?*

VISUAL INSTRUCTION

NWTUL of Chicago WTUL strikers pressed for higher wages to feed children.

Answer: *The first two slogans appealed to working women, while the third one appealed to middle-class reformers protecting women's traditional role in the home.*

CHART STUDY

In the early 1890s white Americans felt threatened by African American economic competition. Similar sentiments surfaced in the late 1890s when an anti-imperialist movement protested the extension of the Constitution to the Philippines, Puerto Rico, and Hawaii.

Answer: *These lynchings peaked in 1892.*

ASSESS

Meeting Lesson Objectives

Each section objective is tested by the section review question(s) that follows it in parentheses.

1. Identify the different types of people who became progressives. (1, 3, 4)
2. Analyze the aspects of American society that were criticized by the progressives. (4, 5)
3. List the different ways progressives tried to address problems linked to urbanization and industrialization. (2, 4)

Cultural Perspectives

Broadening Experiences Florence Kelley's values, like those of many progressives, were shaped by travel. While studying in Europe, she learned about economic reforms to deal with industrialization there. Jane Addams first thought of starting a settlement house after seeing one in London. Charles Beard's interest in reform was stimulated by a visit to Hull House while he was in college. Discuss with students what experiences they have had that have shaped their positions on various issues.

Lynching Protest The daughter of slaves, Wells was born in Holly Springs, Mississippi, in 1862. She was a teacher before turning to journalism in the 1880s. Wells argued that lynching stemmed not from the defense of white womanhood, but from whites' fear of economic competition from African Americans. The Alpha Suffrage Club she founded in Chicago may have been the first African American woman suffrage group.

Answer: *by writing newspaper editorials and giving speeches*

Evaluate

Have students complete the Section Review.

☛ ▣ Assign the Section 2 Quiz or use the Testmaker to develop a customized quiz. (Also in Spanish.) **LEP**

Reteach

🎧 Have students listen to the Chapter 8, Section 2 Audiocassette. (Also in Spanish.) **LEP**

Enrich

☛ Have students complete the Chapter 8 Geography in History Activity.

CLOSE

Ask students to discuss how the United States today shows the impact of progressive reforms. *(Answers may include that child labor laws and public education have given children more opportunities to continue their education.)*

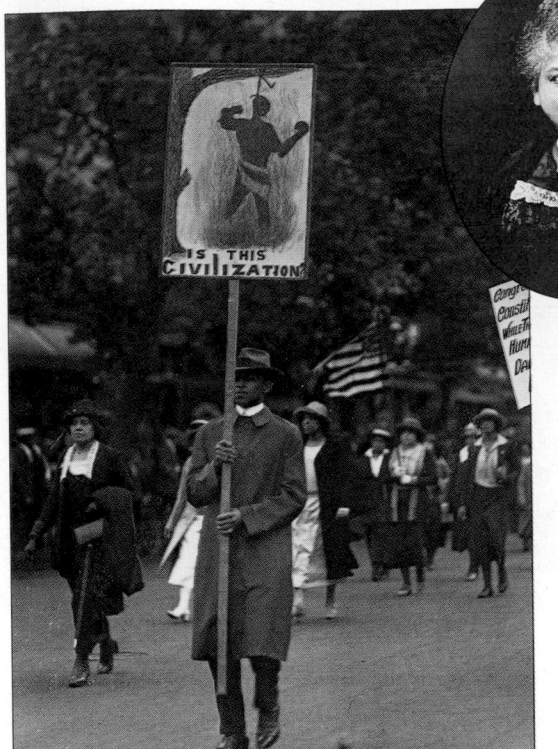

UPI/BETTMANN

NEW YORK PUBLIC LIBRARY

IS THIS CIVILIZATION?

Lynching Protest Opponents of lynching (above) appealed to national pride as one reason to end the murder of African Americans. Ida B. Wells (above right) led a national battle against lynchings. *How did Wells alert the public about the racism that motivated these mob murders?*

Though only about four and a half feet tall, Wells put up a fierce struggle:

> He tried to drag me out of the seat, but the moment he caught hold of my arm I fastened my teeth in the back of his hand. . . . He went forward and got the baggage-man and another man to help him and of course they succeeded in dragging me out. They were encouraged to do this by the attitude of the white ladies and gentlemen in the car. . . . I said I would get off the train rather than go in [to a segregated car]—which I did.
>
> —Ida B. Wells, *Crusade for Justice*

In her writing Wells expressed the same pride and courage that she showed in the train incident. Nevertheless, after writing articles criticizing the poor education that African Americans received in Memphis schools, she was fired from her teaching position. She became a full-time journalist, writing articles for several African American–owned newspapers.

248 CHAPTER 8 PROGRESSIVE REFORMS

The night of March 9, 1892, changed Ida Wells's life. That night a mob of angry whites lynched three African American men in Memphis. Wells wrote a scathing newspaper editorial attacking the lawless treatment of African Americans in Memphis. Moving to Chicago in 1894, Wells launched a national campaign to end lynching. From Chicago she wrote articles, gave speeches, and carried out investigations to expose the racism that motivated mob murderers. Within three years the number of lynchings went down by one-quarter.

Lynching was an extreme expression of the racism that Wells and other African Americans witnessed. Wells was not alone in fighting back, though. Racial oppression triggered the founding of the National Association for the Advancement of Colored People (NAACP) in 1909 and the National Urban League in 1910. Both organizations worked to help African Americans improve their living conditions.

As Wells and the progressives awakened the public to social ills and organized campaigns to remedy these ills, the number of people pressuring the government to respond increased. Progressives set out their agenda to reform the political structure, to modify the economic system, and to improve the moral climate of communities across the nation.

SECTION REVIEW

Vocabulary

1. Define: progressive, muckraker, social gospel movement, settlement house.

Checking Facts

2. Describe some of the different methods progressives used to combat social, political, and economic injustices.

3. How did the methods of the activists differ from those of the analysts? How were they similar?

Critical Thinking

Making Comparisons

4. In your opinion, which of the methods used by the progressives was most effective in combating injustices? Explain your answer, citing as examples the actions of two of the progressives discussed.

Linking Across Time

5. Explain whether or not you think modern-day journalists consider themselves muckrakers.

Section 2 Review Answers

1. **progressive** (243), **muckraker** (244), **social gospel movement** (245), **settlement house** (247)

2. Progressives wrote books, organized campaigns, and opened settlement houses.

3. Analysts mostly wrote while activists organized campaigns to pressure the government for reform. Both groups wanted to identify and solve social problems.

4. Students might argue that Wells's antilynching campaign was more effective than Ward's writings on sociology.

5. Some journalists continue to investigate corrupt and immoral actions.

Critical Thinking Skill

DETERMINING CAUSE AND EFFECT

Learning the Skill

When reading and studying historical information, it is important to determine cause-and-effect relationships in order to comprehend the significance of various events.

The skill of determining cause and effect requires considering why an event occurred. A *cause* is the action or situation that produces an event. An *effect* is the result or consequence of an action or a situation.

How to Determine Cause and Effect

Follow these steps to determine cause and effect:

a. Ask questions about why events occur.

b. Identify two or more events.

c. Look for vocabulary clues to help decide whether one event caused the other. Words or phrases such as *because*, *as a result of*, *for this reason*, *therefore*, *thus*, *as a consequence*, *as an outgrowth*, and *if . . . then* indicate cause-and-effect relationships.

d. Identify the outcomes of the events.

e. Look for relationships between the events. Check for other, more complex, connections beyond the immediate cause and effect.

For example, read the passage below:

> When Florence Kelley went to live and work at Hull House, she became an activist for outlawing child labor. Children's long working hours, detrimental health conditions, and poor factory environment were the causes of her activism. She helped organize consumer boycotts of goods manufactured by children and supported the work of settlement houses.

When studying the reform movement mentioned in the passage above, a graphic organizer such as the one below aids in understanding multiple causes and effects.

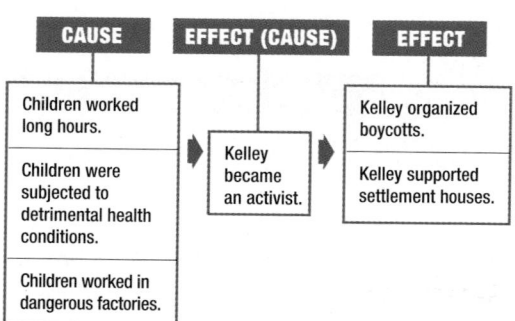

Practicing the Skill

On a separate piece of paper, make a cause-and-effect diagram for each statement below by writing the cause on the left and the effect on the right. Then connect the two parts of the statement with an arrow.

1. Not all immigrants stayed in the United States. Some became homesick and returned to the land of their birth.

2. As a result of meeting three neglected children, Jane Addams decided to open a day nursery to aid working parents.

3. If muckrakers wrote articles attacking wealthy corporations that exploited child labor, corrupt police departments that protected illegal activities, and prestigious churches that owned disease-ridden tenements, then the public would be alerted to these social ills.

4. As an outgrowth of Upton Sinclair's publication *The Jungle*, public sympathizers began to consider providing adequate wages for workers and improving sanitary conditions in the meatpacking industry.

5. Ida B. Wells launched a national campaign to end lynching by writing articles, giving speeches, and carrying out investigations to expose the racism that motivated mob murders. For this reason, the number of lynchings went down by one-quarter within three years.

Applying the Skill

Choose a contemporary reform movement—such as changing affirmative action policies, providing universal health insurance, or ensuring Social Security benefits for retirees—or select your own area of interest. Write a paragraph detailing the causes and possible effects of the reforms you might institute. Then use the information in your paragraph to construct a cause-and-effect diagram.

Additional Practice

For additional practice, see Reinforcing Skills on page 263.

CRITICAL THINKING SKILL **249**

TEACH

This lesson familiarizes students with the procedures to follow in order to determine cause and effect. Point out to students that asking questions about why an event occurs helps to determine the cause. Encourage students to look for clue words that signal whether one event caused another event, and then to determine the relationships between the events. A model of a cause-and-effect graphic organizer is provided to aid students in organizing information visually. Suggest to students that they use the graphic organizer when determining the relationships between multiple causes and/or effects.

 Videodisc

GTV: The American People: Fabric of a Nation

Side 3, Chapter 3
Title: Home Sweet Home?
Subject: The urban immigration experience
Ask: What was life like for the immigrants who settled in eastern cities? *(They often lived in poverty.)*

Additional Practice

☞ Have students complete the Chapter 8 Skill Reinforcement Activity.

Practicing the Skill Answers

1. Cause: Immigrants got homesick. Effect: They returned to the land of their birth.
2. Cause: Addams meets neglected children. Effect (Cause): She grows concerned about child welfare. Effect: Addams opens a day nursery.
3. Causes: Corporations exploit child labor; corrupt police protect illegal activities; prestigious churches own disease-ridden tenements. Effect (Cause): Angered journalists publish articles. Effect: The public is alerted to these social ills.
4. Cause: Upton Sinclair published *The Jungle*. Effect: Public sympathizers consider improved wages and sanitary conditions.
5. Cause: lynching; Effect (Cause): Ida B. Wells is moved to write articles and to give speeches to expose racism. Effect: The number of lynchings is reduced in three years.

249

250

FOCUS

Section Objectives

1. Identify the main elements of progressive reform at the state and local levels.
2. Identify the conflicting motives underlying progressive reforms.
3. Explain how progressives viewed the role of government, and how they worked to eliminate political corruption.
4. List reforms designed to help all workers, particularly women and children.

Bellringer Activity

While taking attendance at the beginning of the class period, display **Section Focus Transparency 25**, and have students answer the questions. (Or use the blackline master.)

VISUAL INSTRUCTION

Wisconsin Reforms This 1912 *Chicago Tribune* cartoon is entitled "Mr. La Follette's Strongest Card— His Wisconsin Record." La Follette later was the unsuccessful presidential candidate of the League for Progressive Political Action (the Progressive party) in 1924, winning almost 5 million votes, or about one-sixth of the total cast.

Ask: What would the railroad tycoons have to do if La Follette's bill passed? *(The railroad owners would have to pay a fair share of taxes.)*

SECTION 3

Progressive Agendas

SPRING 1901: WISCONSIN CHALLENGES THE RAILROADS

Wisconsin Reforms
La Follette fought to loosen the railroad's control of state government.

THE YOUNG LEGISLATOR LOOKED TERRIFIED AS HE WALKED INTO THE OFFICE OF WISCONSIN GOVERNOR ROBERT LA FOLLETTE. The governor, hoping to protect the legislator's identity, referred to him by a letter. "E., what's the matter?" With that, E. burst into tears.

As a progressive, La Follette was fighting to break the tight grip of the railroad tycoons and political bosses on the state government. He needed E.'s support for his bill requiring the railroads to pay a fair share of taxes.

"Governor, I can't help it. I've got to vote against the railroad taxation bill," E. explained sorrowfully. He went on, "I haven't slept any for two or three nights. I have walked the floor. I have thought of resigning and going home."

"Tell me all about it," La Follette said.

"Well," E. replied, "you know that all I have in the world I have put into that factory of mine. I have told you about how proud I was of the thing. Now," he said, "this railroad lobby [people who try to influence the legislature] tells me that if I vote for that railroad taxation bill they will ruin me. . . . I can't beggar my family. I have a wife and babies." He knew that the railroads could put his factory out of business easily. They simply had to charge his competitors slightly lower rates for transporting their goods than they charged him. His goods would then cost more, and his sales would quickly vanish.

La Follette and E. talked for a long time about their duty as elected officials to protect the public interest. Then E. returned to the legislative chamber. Just before casting his vote, E. confessed to the legislator next to him, "It is a question between my honor and my bread and butter, and I propose to vote for my bread and butter." He voted against the bill.

AS YOU READ

Vocabulary

► direct primary
► initiative
► referendum
► recall

Think About . . .

► the main elements of progressive reform at the state and local levels.
► the conflicting motives underlying progressive reforms.

► how progressives viewed the role of government, and how they worked to eliminate political corruption.
► reforms designed to help all workers, particularly women and children.

Section 3 Resources

REPRODUCIBLE RESOURCES

- Lesson Plan 8-3
- Vocabulary and Guided Reading Activity 8-3
- Section 3 Quiz
- Chapter 8 Test
- Performance Assessment Activity 8
- Reteaching Activity 8
- Enrichment Activity 8
- Political Cartoon 16

MULTIMEDIA RESOURCES

- Section Focus Transparency 25
- Landmark Documents in American History
- Chapter 8 Digest Audiocassette
- Testmaker
- Student Self-Test: A Software Review
- Vocabulary PuzzleMaker

E.'s dilemma over how to vote demonstrated the clout of the railroads in 1901. The wealth and power of the railroads undermined the democratic process in Wisconsin and in many other states and cities. La Follette, however, did not give up. In 1903 he triumphed. The Wisconsin legislature passed the railroad tax hike. The choice between serving the public interest and giving in to powerful private interests, though, made life difficult for many progressives.

Political Reform
Making Government More Responsive to Citizens

Hoping to make it easier for dedicated officials like La Follette and E. to serve the public, progressives fought to end the stranglehold that the railroads and other powerful special interests had on government. Political machines, declared Kansas newspaper editor William Allen White, had to "be reduced to mere political scrap iron by the rise of the people." Most progressives agreed with White, but few agreed on how to destroy and supplant the machines and the corruption that made them powerful. Reforms in government were the first steps.

Galveston: Model of Efficiency

A hurricane helped initiate one alternative to machine politics on the city level. On September 8, 1900, driving rains and a tidal wave devastated Galveston, Texas. The storm killed 6,000 people. Almost the entire city was between 7 and 17 feet underwater.

Galveston's mayor and city council members were effective politicians but poor administrators. The task of rebuilding the city overwhelmed the weak city government. Reformers, including many Galveston business leaders, convinced the state legislature to set up a new local government to replace the large, slow-moving city council with a smaller, more centralized government. In March 1901, the legislature approved a new charter for Galveston that placed the power of the city government into the hands of five commissioners. Of the five, two were elected and three were appointed by the governor. With power centralized in just five people, the city could move quickly to clean up the damage from the storm.

Changing the type of people serving as government leaders was as important as changing the structure of city government. Four of the five commissioners were prominent local business leaders rather than Plunkitt-style politicians. They applied their experience in running businesses efficiently to the operation of Galveston's government. Under the guidance of its new

TEACH

Guided Practice

L1 Discussion Some businesses benefited from machine politics, but many suffered, especially ones whose owners opposed the machine. Graft and corruption raised everybody's taxes. Consequently, small-business owners often led reform efforts. Ask students to find out the structure of their city government. They should point out any influences of progressive reforms.

CHART STUDY

City government manages and provides services for more than 60 percent of Americans. These services include education, health and welfare, police and fire protection, recreational facilities, and street maintenance. Municipalities vary greatly in size, the largest being New York City with more than 7 million people. The smallest municipalities may have only a few hundred residents. All city governments are organized into 3 branches: legislative, executive, and judicial.

Answer: *city council/city manager system*

FORMS OF MUNICIPAL GOVERNMENT IN THE UNITED STATES

COMMISSIONER SYSTEM
- Each department head is a specialist in their field
- Only about 50 cities with populations more than 25,000 use this governmental form

Voters Elect → Police / Fire / Public Works / Finance / Health and Welfare

The mayor/city council system with a strong mayor utilizes effective political leadership to balance the interest of varied cultural groups. Such a system works well for large and diversely populated cities. The chief weakness of both the commissioner and council/manager systems is the lack of a leader to effect coordination.

MAYOR/CITY COUNCIL SYSTEM
- Mayor has broad powers: proposes new legislation, can veto acts of the council, prepares the city budget
- City Council determines basic governmental policy and raises revenue for community

Voters Elect → Mayor / City Council
Strong-mayor plan *Mayor Appoints*
Weak-mayor plan *Council Appoints*
→ Police / Fire / Public Works / Finance / Health and Welfare

CITY COUNCIL/CITY MANAGER SYSTEM
- Modeled after business firms
- Most common in cities with populations more than 25,000
- Mayoral role mostly ceremonial
- "City Council" also called Board of Selectpersons

Voters Elect → City Council
One is the **Mayor,** who presides over the council, but usually has no more power than the others.
Council Appoints → City Manager
City managers are almost always professional administrators. Like a corporation's general manager, the city manager can be dismissed by the council for being ineffective.
City Manager Appoints → Police / Fire / Public Works / Finance / Health and Welfare

Municipalities—villages, towns, and cities—across the United States embody some form or variation of one of the three systems of local government detailed above. *Which governing system operates a city like a business firm?*

Cooperative Learning

Political, Economic, Social, and Moral Reforms Organize students into several small groups to find out about the current status of several of the progressive reforms mentioned in this section, such as the commissioner system, the direct primary, and temperance. After each group has reported on its findings, discuss how much the progressive movement has influenced the United States today.

Independent Practice

 Making a Time Line
Ask each student to make a time line showing the main events in the life of Robert La Follette. Interested students may want to consult other sources for further details about La Follette.

◤ Have students complete the Chapter 8, Section 3 Vocabulary and Guided Reading Activity. (Also in Spanish.) **LEP**

VISUAL INSTRUCTION

"Fighting Bob" One of La Follette's trademarks was his hair, which he combed straight up in the front. A short man, he hoped that this hairstyle would make him look taller and more forceful.

Answer: *through a series of reforms called the Wisconsin Plan that led to the use of direct primary, initiative, referendum, and recall in elections*

FYI

Local-Level Reforms
Point out that reforms often start at the local level and spread. In 1875 Nebraska established preferential primaries so voters could indicate their choices for senator. By 1912 more than one-half of the states had such primaries.

Cumberland, Wis. 1897

"Fighting Bob" Robert La Follette was an eloquent spokesperson for the popular causes of his constituents. *How was La Follette able to attack the power of the political bosses?*

government, Galveston soon began to rebuild ruined buildings, to fix its destroyed streets, and to get its finances in order.

Reformers around the nation noted Galveston's quick recovery under its commissioner system. By centralizing power in the hands of a few business-oriented managers, Galveston had developed an efficient city government. Within 20 years more than 500 cities across the United States adopted a commissioner system. Another 158 cities had adopted a city-manager system in which the city council hired a professional to manage all the daily affairs of the city.

Even cities that did not adopt the commissioner system or the city-manager system learned from the example of Galveston and reduced the power of machine politicians by streamlining their government. Cutting government spending reduced the number of padded contracts that politicians could dole out to their friends. Trimming the bloated government payrolls reduced the number of jobs a politician had available to pass out as favors. These reforms made government more efficient.

In addition many cities changed their election procedures. Electing city council members at large, rather than from each ward, reduced the power of each local ward boss. Holding nonpartisan elections, in which candidates ran as individuals rather than as party representatives, reduced the power of parties. By undercutting the power of ward bosses and parties, reformers hoped that well-qualified candidates would have better chances to win elections.

Some progressives, hoping to make government more efficient, advocated reforms to undercut the machines. Others, though, supported reforms because they feared the power of immigrants and the poor. These progressives wanted to reduce the influence of immigrants and other poor people whom they blamed for causing the crime, prostitution, and disorder in the cities.

Wisconsin: Laboratory of Democracy

Many progressives believed that the solution to political corruption lay in making government more responsive to citizens. Governor Robert La Follette made Wisconsin the premier example of a state in which citizens directed and controlled their government.

La Follette was born in a two-room log cabin on a Wisconsin farm in 1855. By the time he was a student at the University of Wisconsin, he already displayed the traits that would lead him to political success. One classmate called him "the chairman of the undergraduate greeters" because of his friendly, outgoing manner. La Follette opposed with righteous indignation, however, any system by which a minority received special privileges. He felt an "overmastering sense of anger and wrong and injustice" at the gap between poor students like himself and the wealthy fraternity members.

La Follette's anger propelled him into politics. He served six years in Congress before he ran for governor. After losing two races, "Fighting Bob" finally won in 1900. Shortly after La Follette took office, one political boss swaggered into his office to cut a deal and to boast about his power over members of the legislature. "I own them," he told the newly elected governor. "They're mine!" La Follette, fiery and moralistic, refused to compromise with the boss. As he declared in his autobiography, "In legislation, *no bread* is better than *half a loaf.*"

As governor, La Follette attacked the power of the bosses through a series of reforms known as the Wisconsin Idea. He opposed the conventions at which parties nominated candidates to run for office. Because machine bosses controlled the selection of delegates, the bosses effectively controlled whom the party nominated. Reform candidates had virtually no chance of being selected to run. In 1903 La Follette pressured the legislature to pass a law requiring each party to choose its candidates through a **direct primary,** an election open to all voters within the party. As a result of that law, the power to nominate and select candidates passed from the bosses to the electorate.

In Wisconsin, as in many states, bosses also controlled the introduction and passage of bills in the legislature. Legislators felt more accountable to the bosses than to the citizens who elected them. To work around the power of the bosses, La Follette introduced three reforms, each of which had been developed in other states.

Meeting Special Needs

Visual Learners This activity addresses the particular needs of visual learners. Have students discuss the similarities and differences between the 3 forms of government presented in the diagraphic on page 251. Students should note that the individuals who determine policy are elected by voters. In addition, all systems have some means of providing needed services to people who reside in a given municipality.

Ask students to explain which individuals have the most power, and how teamwork is important to effect the smooth functioning of local government. Then have students study their local government and find a matching system in the diagraphic. Encourage them to create a similar visual representation showing any differences or additions.

ARCHIVE PHOTOS

The Bosses of the Senate Locate the two doorways in this 1889 political cartoon by Joseph Keppler. *How does the difference between the doors show Keppler's view of the Senate?*

The **initiative** allowed citizens to introduce a bill into the legislature and required members to take a vote on it. The **referendum** established a procedure by which voters cast ballots for or against proposed laws. The **recall** gave citizens a chance to remove an elected official from office before the person's term ended. Wisconsin adopted all three of these proposals, thereby giving citizens power to bypass or to punish machine-controlled legislators. Other states under progressive leadership followed the example of Wisconsin and instituted similar reforms.

Attacking Corruption in the Senate

Another reform La Follette and progressives favored affected the federal government: the direct election of senators. According to the United States Constitution, each state legislature elected the two senators from that state. When a powerful political machine or large trust gained control of a state legislature, it also captured two Senate seats. Then senators repaid the machine or trust with federal contracts and jobs. By the early 1900s, muckraker Charles Edward Russell charged, the Senate had become "only a chamber of butlers for industrialists and financiers."

To counter Senate corruption, progressives called for direct election of senators by the voters of each state. In 1912 Congress proposed a direct-election amendment to the Constitution. In 1913 the states ratified the Seventeenth Amendment.

Expanding Voting Rights

Some progressives tried to increase not only the influence but also the number of citizens participating in government. After an 1848 women's rights conference in Seneca Falls, New York, women began organizing to win suffrage, the right to vote. By 1890 women had won at least partial suffrage in 19 states. In most of these states, women could vote in local or state elections, but they could not vote in presidential elections. Only Wyoming and Utah gave women full voting rights.

The suffrage movement gathered momentum in the 1890s. The National American Woman Suffrage Association grew from 13,000 members in 1893 to 75,000 members in 1910. By 1912, 9 states, all west of the Mississippi River, allowed women to vote in all elections. Suffrage advocates continued to push for a constitutional amendment to grant women full voting rights in all states. They would not achieve that goal, however, until the passage of the Nineteenth Amendment in 1920.

While women fought to win the vote, African Americans struggled to regain it. Beginning in Mississippi in 1890, state after state in the South revised its constitution and laws to prevent African Americans from voting. In Louisiana, for example, more than 130,000 African Americans voted in 1896. In 1900, after changes in the constitution and the laws, the number of African Americans registered to vote there plunged to 5,320.

SECTION THREE   **253**

Portfolio Project

Improving Workplace Safety Have students work in pairs to investigate the treatment today of workers injured on the job. They may want to look into the number of workers injured each year, government regulations to protect workers, the attitudes of business owners toward workplace injuries, the cost of insurance, and the steps taken in other countries to protect workers. Each pair can share its findings with the class and make specific proposals for changes to improve workplace safety. Pairs should support their written results with a visual such as a chart or graph before filing their written products in individual portfolios.

VISUAL INSTRUCTION

The Bosses of the Senate Joseph Keppler (1838–1894) was an Austrian-born caricaturist and founder of *Puck*, the first successful humorous weekly in the United States. Keppler drew cover cartoons for *Frank Leslie's Illustrated Newspaper* before starting *Puck* as a German-language weekly. In 1877 an English-language version was begun. Initially Keppler drew all the cartoons for *Puck*, focusing on political humor.

Answer: *The door for the common citizens is small and locked shut. The door for the wealthy trust owners is wide and open. Keppler thought that the Senate defended the interests of the wealthy while it ignored the needs of average citizens.*

 Curriculum Connection

Language Arts Have students write a new title for the cartoon on this page. The title should suggest the main point of the cartoon.

 Facts on File

Landmark Documents in American History Have students review "Declaration of Women's Rights (Seneca Falls Declaration and Resolutions, Declaration of Independence for Women), 1848" and write a paragraph about the intent of the document.

253

VISUAL INSTRUCTION

Woman Suffrage Supporters In 1916 suffragists also flew an airplane above President Wilson's yacht and dropped petitions supporting the Nineteenth Amendment.

Answer: *African Americans*

Curriculum Connection

Mathematics Josephine Goldmark's collection of data reflected the growing interest in statistics, the branch of mathematics that focuses on analyzing large amounts of numerical information. The development of statistical methods during the 1800s gave scientists and social scientists new tools to use in studying the world.

FYI

Spelling Reform While some people tried to change government, others tried to change spelling. In 1906 a committee including Mark Twain and several university presidents proposed reforming the spelling of 300 words. For example, they wanted to change *through* to *thru* and *mixed* to *mixt*. Though supported by the National Education Association and the American Association for the Advancement of Science, the movement was widely ridiculed and had little impact.

Woman Suffrage Supporters In 1916 these activists from Kentucky traveled to St. Louis to urge delegates at the Democratic National Convention to support equal rights for women. *What other Americans were denied the right to vote?*

The drive to win voting rights for African Americans made little progress before 1915. African American progressives won little support from white progressives for their cause.

Economic Reform
Using Government to Protect Citizens

Progressives hoped that political reform would pave the way for economic reform. Once the political system was rescued from controlling private interests, citizens could use government to protect the public interest.

Regulating Big Business

Government regulation proved to be one means of taming powerful special interests. In Wisconsin La Follette established a state railroad commission. This group of experts, many from the University of Wisconsin, oversaw the operation of all railroads in Wisconsin. They held the power to revise, overturn, and thereby regulate rates charged by the railroads. Thus the commission prevented the railroads from unfairly overcharging small farmers whose livelihoods depended on the railroads for shipping their grain to market. Under regulation, factories could no longer bribe the railroads into giving them an unfair rate advantage over other factories in the state. La Follette declared that his goal "was not to 'smash' corporations, but to drive them out of politics, and then to treat them exactly the same as other people are treated."

Other states followed Wisconsin's lead, establishing commissions to regulate railroads, electric power companies, and gas companies. Some cities went beyond mere regulation, setting up and running utilities as part of city government.

Caring for Injured Workers

Owners and workers clashed repeatedly over issues such as how companies should treat injured workers. Factories, coal mines, and railroads were particularly dangerous places to work. In 1914 about 35,000 people died on the job; another 700,000 were injured. Companies often fired seriously injured workers because they could no longer do their jobs. In a fiercely competitive business climate, no company could afford the expense of caring for its injured workers unless all of its competitors did the same.

Articles by muckrakers and protests by unions slowly roused public anger at the irresponsibility of big business. In 1902 Maryland passed the first state law requiring employers to buy insurance that would compensate workers injured on the job. By 1916, the year that Congress passed the Workmen's Compensation Law, about two-thirds of the states required companies to have some type of workers' compensation program.

Limiting the Workday

In 1900 about one-fifth of all people working outside their homes were women. Most progressives believed that women were naturally weaker than men and thus

---

Extending the Content

Regulating Big Business During the late 1800s, business leaders in several major industries formed powerful trusts and cut prices to eliminate their competition. Many companies then abused their power by raising prices and limiting production. To regulate these businesses, Congress passed the Sherman Antitrust Act of 1890. In 1911, after Ida Tarbell exposed the abuses committed by the Standard Oil Company, the government used the Sherman Act to break up that company into 33 separate firms. This act helped safeguard competition and protected the public interest. Today most of the large oil companies are descendants of the companies formed in the breakup of Rockefeller's trust.

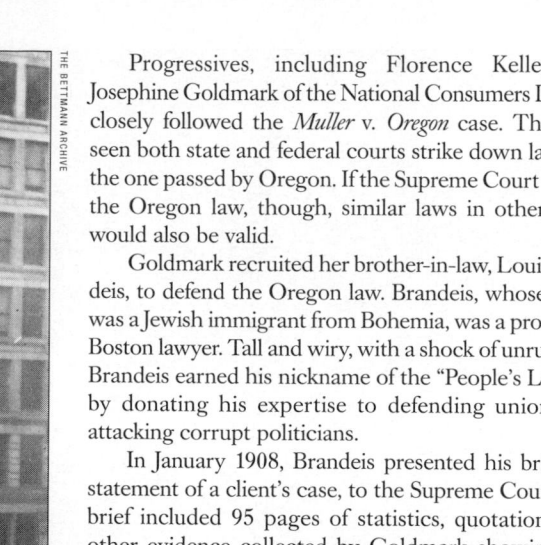

A Factory Tragedy On March 25, 1911, a fire at the Triangle Shirtwaist Factory killed 146 female workers. Because the company locked the doors from the outside to prevent workers from taking breaks, many had no chance to escape. Outrage at the deaths caused New York City to pass a strict building code. *What other laws were passed in the early 1900s to protect workers?*

Progressives, including Florence Kelley and Josephine Goldmark of the National Consumers League, closely followed the *Muller* v. *Oregon* case. They had seen both state and federal courts strike down laws like the one passed by Oregon. If the Supreme Court upheld the Oregon law, though, similar laws in other states would also be valid.

Goldmark recruited her brother-in-law, Louis Brandeis, to defend the Oregon law. Brandeis, whose father was a Jewish immigrant from Bohemia, was a prominent Boston lawyer. Tall and wiry, with a shock of unruly hair, Brandeis earned his nickname of the "People's Lawyer" by donating his expertise to defending unions and attacking corrupt politicians.

In January 1908, Brandeis presented his brief, the statement of a client's case, to the Supreme Court. The brief included 95 pages of statistics, quotations, and other evidence collected by Goldmark showing that long hours damaged the health of women and, in effect, threatened the public interest. "The overwork of future mothers," Brandeis wrote, "thus directly attacks the welfare of the nation."

Goldmark's evidence proved persuasive. In a unanimous decision, the Supreme Court upheld the Oregon law. They agreed that a state government, to protect the public interest, had a right to regulate the work of women. After the *Muller* decision, Illinois, Virginia, Michigan, Louisiana, and other states quickly passed similar laws.

more deserving of protection. Even a Tammany Hall boss, Big Tim Sullivan, worried about the ravages of work on young women: "I had seen me sister go out to work when she was only fourteen and I know we ought to help these gals by giving 'em a law which will prevent 'em from being broken down while they're still young."

In 1903 Oregon passed a law that prohibited employing women in a factory or a laundry for more than 10 hours a day. Portland laundry owner Curt Muller, fined $10 for breaking the law, challenged it. Muller, like other business owners, argued that the government had no right to interfere in a private contract between an owner and a worker. The Oregon Supreme Court disagreed with Muller and upheld the fine. Muller then appealed to the United States Supreme Court, which agreed to hear the case.

A Crusading Lawyer Louis Brandeis served as an associate justice of the United States Supreme Court from 1916 to 1939. *What nickname did Brandeis earn and why?*

SECTION THREE   **255**

VISUAL INSTRUCTION

A Factory Tragedy Female sewing machine operators employed in the shirtwaist industry led a series of strikes when they unionized as the International Ladies' Garment Workers' Union.
Answer: *1916 Workmen's Compensation Law; 1903 Oregon law prohibiting workdays of more than 10 hours for women in factories; laws passed in several states in the wake of Muller v. Oregon*

A Crusading Lawyer Louis Brandeis (1856–1941) was known for advocating economic, social, and political justice. In his judicial opinions, he mistrusted both the unlimited exercise of governmental power and the monopolization of economic activity by certain big businesses. Brandeis University, opened in Waltham, Mass., in 1948, was named for him.
Answer: *the "People's Lawyer" because he donated his expertise to defending unions and attacking corrupt politicians*

FYI

Labor Relations The question of labor relations was a central theme of one of the most popular books of the 1890s, Edward Bellamy's *Looking Backward, 2000–1887.* In this utopian novel, people worked in a national industrial army until they retired at age 45. The book sold more than 1 million copies and prompted the organization of clubs to discuss Bellamy's ideas.

Cultural Perspectives

International Woman Suffrage In 1902 the first International Woman Suffrage Conference was held in Washington, D.C. Subsequently, women in other countries received suffrage before those in the United States did. In 1918 women in Great Britain, Austria, Canada, Czechoslovakia, Germany, Hungary, Ireland, Poland, Scotland, and Wales were enfranchised. In 1919 women in Azerbaijan Republic, Belgium, British East Africa, Holland, Iceland, Luxembourg, Rhodesia, and Sweden obtained the right to vote. Ask students to research international suffrage, determining the extent to which it has been achieved and noting important events contributing to its attainment. Students may want to display information on a class chart.

ASSESS

A High School Classroom in 1900 Students are observing an experiment and taking notes in this science class. *How many high schools existed in 1900?*

Length of School Year, 1880–1920

In 1920, 311,000 people graduated from high school.

In 1880, 24,000 people graduated from high school.

Progressives supported laws requiring attendance at school. *How many more days on average did students attend school in 1920 than in 1880?*

Brandeis's use of Goldmark's data revolutionized legal thought. Previously courts evaluated laws only on narrow legal grounds. Beginning with the *Muller* decision, courts considered the law's impact on people's lives. Brandeis and Goldmark won a major victory in the progressives' battle to carve out a new role for government as protector of the public interest.

Social and Moral Reform
Convincing Government to Support Children and Women

The progressives' desire to protect the public interest included a broad range of social reforms. Many reforms were designed to help children. For example, progressives supported establishing separate courts that would be sensitive to the needs and problems of juveniles. They also backed laws providing financial assistance to children in homes with no father present. One of the key progressive reforms for children was the expansion of public education.

Educating Children

During the late 1800s, state after state passed laws requiring young people to go to school. The number of schools jumped sharply. Before the Civil War, only a few hundred high schools existed across the nation. By 1900 there were 6,000 high schools; by 1920, there were 14,000. The expansion of public education then led to a sharp decline in illiteracy. In 1870 approximately 20 percent of the people in the United States were illiterate. By 1920 only 6 percent could not read.

In addition to growing, public education was changing. Philosopher John Dewey criticized schools for overemphasizing memorization of knowledge. Instead,

Critical Thinking

The *Muller* Decision The *Muller* decision raised an issue that remains hotly debated today: the proper grounds upon which courts should make decisions. Brandeis believed that if the Supreme Court ruled strictly on precedent, it would overturn the Oregon law, as it and other courts had overturned other laws. He convinced the justices, however, that the Oregon legislature had acted properly to protect its citizens. Today, citizens continue to debate the extent to which courts should follow precedent and the extent to which they should adjust their interpretations to changing conditions. Discuss current issues in the news that involve court rulings. Point out that conflict over rulings is often based on different views of the Constitution rather than different views of the evidence.

Margaret Sanger As Mrs. Margaret Sanger (left) and her sister Mrs. Ethel Byrne leave the Court of Special Sessions in Brooklyn, New York, on January 8, 1917, they are greeted by an immigrant family. *What kind of crusade did Sanger undertake and what law did she break in the process?*

UPI/BETTMANN

charges against her were dropped in 1916, Sanger faced constant opposition to her work.

Another reform that aimed to protect women was the temperance movement, the drive to restrict or prohibit the use of alcohol. Intoxicated men sometimes beat their wives and children, and the temperance movement aimed to stop such abusive behavior at the source—alcohol. The largest temperance organization was the Women's Christian Temperance Union (WCTU), founded in 1874. By 1900 it had almost 300,000 members. One-fourth of the United States population lived in areas with some restrictions on alcohol purchase or consumption.

Frances Willard led the WCTU from 1879 until her death in 1898. She encouraged the organization to attack social ills other than the abuse of alcohol. The WCTU advocated voting rights for women, lobbied for prison reform, promoted world peace, and spoke out on various health issues. Willard's slogan was, Do everything.

The WCTU under Willard was typical of many progressive organizations. While it focused on one problem that seemed to be rampant in cities, it supported several other reform causes. Although the problem it confronted was nationwide, the organization won its first victories on the city and state levels. In order to achieve a nationwide solution, the temperance movement, like other progressive reforms, would have to convince Congress and the President to take a more active role in social reform. The progressives, then, needed to develop a new role for the federal government in the United States.

Dewey argued, schools should relate learning to the interests, problems, and concerns of students. He believed that the "true center" of a child's education was "not science, nor literature, nor history, nor geography, but the child's own social activities." Dewey wanted schools to teach students to be good citizens. "Education," he declared, "is the fundamental method of social progress and reform." Most progressives agreed with him.

Protecting Women

Just as some progressives emphasized reforms to protect children, others focused on reforms that primarily affected women. The most controversial of these reforms was the birth control movement. A New York nurse, Margaret Sanger, had seen many women die from poorly performed abortions. In 1914 she launched a drive to inform women about ways they could prevent pregnancy. Under New York's Comstock Act of 1873, though, information describing methods of birth control was considered obscene. Almost immediately after starting her crusade, Sanger was arrested for violating the Comstock Act. Though the

---

SECTION REVIEW

Vocabulary

1. Define: direct primary, initiative, referendum, recall.

Checking Facts

2. Explain the ruling in the case of *Muller* v. *Oregon*.

3. Describe the reforms that protected women and children.

Critical Thinking

Determining Cause and Effect

4. Why did the progressives believe that political reform was necessary before economic reform could be achieved?

Linking Across Time

5. Do big businesses have more or less influence on government today than they did around 1900? Give examples to support your viewpoint.

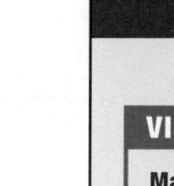

VISUAL INSTRUCTION

Margaret Sanger Sanger is credited with originating the term *birth control*.

Answer: *to inform women of ways to avoid pregnancy; New York's 1873 Comstock Act*

Evaluate

Have students complete the Section Review.

☞ 🖳 Assign the Section 3 Quiz or use the Testmaker to develop a customized quiz. (Also in Spanish.) **LEP**

☞ 🖳 Assign the Chapter 8 Test or use the Testmaker to develop a customized test.

☞ Have students complete the Chapter 8 Performance Assessment Activity. 🖱

Reteach

🎧 Have students listen to the Chapter 8, Section 3 Audiocassette. (Also in Spanish.) **LEP**

☞ Have students complete the Chapter 8 Reteaching Activity. (Also in Spanish.) **LEP**

Enrich

☞ Have students complete the Chapter 8 Enrichment Activity. (Also in Spanish.) **LEP**

☞ Have students complete Interpreting Political Cartoons 16.

CLOSE

Have students annotate their time lines on the life of La Follette to include the other events in this section.

Section 3 Review Answers

1. direct primary (252), **initiative** (253), **referendum** (253), **recall** (253)

2. The Supreme Court upheld a state's power to limit the hours women worked.

3. Some progressives advocated such reforms as banning child labor, limiting women's hours of labor, requiring school attendance, and outlawing alcohol.

4. They thought they had to change the political players and structure to end political corruption. Government could then reform the economy.

5. Answers may include that citizens nominate candidates and elect senators directly today but that most politicians still rely on contributions from wealthy individuals and businesses.

TEACH

Making the Historical Connection

Women were major players in the Progressive era, yet their involvement in reform movements dates back as far as the American Revolution. Often reformers were middle-class women taking the idea of charity a step further, sometimes even into the public sphere. Most of their efforts were aimed at helping others, however. In the 1840s the movement to abolish slavery absorbed many Northern women. In spite of their commitment and abilities, they were sometimes excluded from full participation in the movement solely because they were women. This made some of them realize it was time to start a drive for their own rights.

Turning Point

The Seneca Falls Convention was a turning point in the history of American women. For the first time women organized to enunciate demands to remedy inequalities based on sex. Within the convention itself, the passage of Resolution 9 was also a turning point. The decision to pursue voting rights changed the nature of women's struggle for equality for the next 70 years.

CASE STUDY Turning Point

Woman Suffrage

SENECA FALLS WOMEN'S RIGHTS CONVENTION, JULY 19–20, 1848

MEMORANDUM

For: Concerned Women and Men

Subject: Women's Rights

A convention to discuss the social, civil and religious condition and rights of woman will be held in the Wesleyan Chapel of Seneca Falls, New York, on Wednesday and Thursday, 19th and 20th July current; commencing at 10 A.M. During the first day the meeting will be exclusively for women who are earnestly invited to attend. The public generally are invited to be present on the second day when Lucretia Mott of Philadelphia and other ladies and gentlemen will address the convention.

Advertisement
Seneca Court Courier
July 13, 1848

The Case

Elizabeth Cady Stanton and Lucretia Mott were amazed when about 300 people, including African American abolitionist Frederick Douglass among the 40 men, responded to their call to meet in a small chapel in Seneca Falls, New York, to discuss women's rights.

On the morning of Wednesday, July 19, organizers presented what one scholar calls "the single most important document of the nineteenth-century American woman's movement." By paraphrasing the Declaration of Independence of 1776, Mott, Stanton, Mary Ann McClintock, Jane Hunt, and Mott's sister Martha Wright produced a document they called a Declaration of Sentiments.

It stated:

We hold these truths to be self-evident: that all men and women are created equal; that they are endowed by their Creator with certain inalienable rights; that among these are life, liberty, and the pursuit of happiness; that to secure these rights governments are instituted, deriving their just powers from the consent of the governed. Whenever any form of government becomes destructive of these ends, it is the right of those who suffer from it to refuse allegiance to it, and to insist upon the institution of a new government, laying its foundation on such principles, and organizing its powers in such form, as to them shall seem most likely to effect their safety and happiness.

Stanton had insisted on including in the declaration a resolution stating: "[I]t is the duty of the women of this country to secure to themselves their sacred right to the elective franchise"—a proposal considered unthinkable at the time. Even her husband, Henry Stanton, who was generally supportive of her views, was angry and embarrassed by her demand for entry into the white masculine domain of voting.

The Case at a Glance

| Female abolitionists are excluded from an antislavery convention. | → | Mott and Stanton determine to hold a convention on women's rights. | → | The Seneca Falls Convention on women's rights is called in 1848. | → | Conventioneers agree on demands, except for suffrage; debate rages. | → |

The Seneca Falls assembly unanimously adopted 11 resolutions, but Stanton's resolution on full voting rights for women—Resolution 9—met bitter resistance. Would it pass? More than that, what would happen when the convention was over?

The Background

In 1776, shortly before the drafting of the Declaration of Independence, Abigail Adams wrote to her husband, John: "If particular care and attention is not paid to the ladies, we are determined to foment a rebellion, and will not hold ourselves bound by any laws in which we have no voice or representation." Her strong words went unanswered. Only New Jersey allowed women the vote in its state constitution, and the privilege was revoked in 1806. Adams's idea was not dead, but it lay dormant for some 42 years until woman suffrage was again seriously addressed—at Seneca Falls.

Seneca Falls leader Elizabeth Cady Stanton's position as a women's rights activist took shape at the 1840 World's Anti-Slavery Convention in London, England. There she began a lifelong friendship with Quaker abolitionist Lucretia Mott. When Stanton, Mott, and all other female delegates were banned from convention debate because of their sex and only allowed to listen from behind a screen, the famous abolitionist William Lloyd Garrison joined the evicted women as a nonparticipant. He declared, "After battling so many long years for the liberties of African slaves, I can take no part in a convention that strikes down the most sacred rights of all women."

As a result of their exclusion, Stanton and Mott spent much of their time together in London discussing the plight of women. They determined to organize a convention on women's rights, but, busied by other demands, they did not pursue the idea for another eight years.

Back in the United States, Stanton later joined Ernestine Rose and Paulina Wright Davis in a huge petition drive to demolish laws that forced married women to surrender everything they owned to their husbands. That campaign helped achieve passage of the Married Women's Property Act of New York

"The family, and not the individual, has been the political unit, and the head of the family . . . has been the political representative of the rest. To give the suffrage to women would be to reject the principle that has thus far formed the basis of civilized government."

Historian Francis Parkman, "The Woman Question," *North American Review,* 1879

"Strange as it may seem to many, we now demand our right to vote according to the declaration of the government under which we live. . . . We have no objection to discuss the question of equality, for we feel that the weight of argument lies wholly with us, but we wish the question of equality kept distinct from the question of rights, for the proof of the one does not determine the truth of the other."

Elizabeth Cady Stanton, address delivered at Seneca Falls and Rochester, N.Y.

CULVER PICTURES

CULVER PICTURES

"All that distinguishes man as an intelligent and accountable being, is equally true of woman; and if that government only is just which governs by the free consent of the governed, there can be no reason in the world for denying to woman the exercise of the elective franchise, or a hand in making and administering the laws of the land."

Frederick Douglass, editorial, *North Star,* July 28, 1848

"The power of women is in her dependence, flowing from the consciousness of that weakness which God has given her for her protection, and which keeps her in those departments of life that form the character of individuals and of the nation."

Pastoral letter of the Congregational ministers of Massachusetts, 1837

CASE STUDY **259**

FYI

Catharine Beecher At the time of the Seneca Falls Convention, the prevailing attitude was that women belonged in the home and not in public life. One school of thought, credited to Catharine Beecher, agreed with this limited sphere for women but suggested that through their influence in the home, women could be powerful social agents. This philosophy is sometimes called "domestic feminism" or "the cult of domesticity." Beecher pushed hard for improving women's education, arguing that it was women, as mothers or teachers, who shape children's minds. Beecher wrote many books on the issue and on practical subjects. *A Treatise on Domestic Economy* was reprinted every year from 1840 to 1856. She wrote "The proper education of a man decides the welfare of an individual; but educate a woman, and the interests of a whole family are secured."

| Douglass and Stanton finally sway convention to approve demand for woman suffrage. | → | Women continue to organize. Fight for suffrage lasts until 1920, when the right is granted. |

Analyzing the Case

Ask students to read the Outcome section of the case study and discuss the following questions:

1. What was the immediate outcome of the convention? *(The women produced a Declaration of Sentiments, including the demand for the right to vote.)*
2. What actions did women take in the years that followed? *(They organized into groups to fight for women's rights, but the groups did not always agree.)*
3. Why did it take so long for woman suffrage to become a reality? *(Answers will vary but should reflect an understanding of the controversy of the issue at that time.)*

Notes

_____
_____
_____
_____
_____
_____
_____
_____
_____
_____
_____
_____
_____
_____
_____
_____
_____

260

CASE STUDY Turning Point

in 1848, which states in part: "The real and personal property of any female who may hereafter marry, and which she shall own at the time of her marriage . . . shall not be subject to the disposal of her husband." Promotion of this act marked the first time that women had run a campaign directed specifically at furthering their own rights, and it set the stage for the Seneca Falls Convention.

The Opinions

The opinions on the status of women excerpted on the previous page reflect the general spirit of the debate that emerged from Seneca Falls. The 1848 convention brought woman suffrage center stage. It remained a matter of fiercely divided opinion for the next 72 years.

The Outcome

The debate on suffrage divided the participants and the organizers of the Seneca Falls Convention. Stanton found support in Frederick Douglass, but many others opposed Resolution 9. Some feared that demanding suffrage at that point in time was too radical a step. Stanton's husband boycotted the convention (and even left town for the duration) because of Resolution 9. Even her dear friend Lucretia Mott told Stanton, "Thou will make us ridiculous. We must go slowly."

The convention broke temporarily and continued two weeks later in nearby Rochester, New York. There, with the influence of Stanton and Douglass, the resolution passed by a narrow margin. The demand for woman suffrage was officially added to the Declaration of Sentiments.

The Woman's Hour has Struck

WOMAN SUFFRAGE *is* COMING

Women's confidence about winning the vote increased with the victorious feeling that struck the nation at the end of World War I. This 1919 poster celebrates the passage of the Nineteenth Amendment. It was ratified by the states in 1920.

After the Convention As feared, the public and the press ridiculed the Seneca Falls Convention. Except for Douglass's *North Star* and Horace Greeley's *New York Tribune*, newspapers did not take the women or their meeting seriously.

260 CASE STUDY

Cooperative Learning

Classroom Convention Point out to students that in 1848 a "convention" was simply a meeting to discuss a particular topic. Invite students to convene such a meeting of their own. Solicit ideas for the subject of the meeting and a name for the convention. Have the whole class vote to determine the theme and title of its convention. Then organize the class into groups to carry out the convention. Groups will be needed to plan,

to moderate, and to record the convention's discussion. Encourage all students to voice an opinion during the discussion. Another group will work to draft a Declaration of Sentiments on the subject, based on the results of the convention. Still another group could work on publishing and distributing the Declaration of Sentiments to the class or to other classes.

The years following the convention, however, witnessed a growing number of women's meetings. These gatherings created widening public awareness of women's rights issues. For example, African American abolitionist leader Sojourner Truth attended the First National Woman's Rights Convention in Worcester, Massachusetts in 1850, and demanded the inclusion of African American women in the struggle for suffrage.

Civil War and Reconstruction When the Civil War erupted in 1861, women's rights activists put their own interests aside. Seneca Falls leaders and other women in the North worked long and hard for the Union cause. They consequently felt angry and betrayed when the Fourteenth Amendment, ratified in 1868, enfranchised African American men and omitted any reference to women. The abolitionist argument that African American male suffrage deserved precedence over women's issues resulted in a bitter rift between leaders of the woman suffrage movement and prominent abolitionists.

In the wake of the Fourteenth and Fifteenth Amendments, disagreements on how to proceed with the fight for suffrage plagued the women's rights movement. Some promoted a national amendment for woman suffrage; others promoted general reform, with suffrage in a list of demands. In 1890, however, Stanton and Susan B. Anthony merged their National Woman Suffrage Association with the rival (and more conservative) American Woman Suffrage Association, led by Lucy Stone and Julia Ward Howe. The resulting organization—the National American Woman Suffrage Association (NAWSA)—dampened the radical push for suffrage somewhat, but did restore unity to the movement.

The Twentieth Century The early years of the 1900s saw gradual advances in women's rights to education, employment, property ownership, and local election voting. Slowly the idea of women voting became slightly less terrifying or ludicrous to those in power.

Women continued to speak, march, hold meetings, and petition the government for suffrage. Finally, women's dramatic mobilization on the home front during World War I convinced many that it was wrong to withhold the vote from these citizens. One World War I era poster demanded: "We give our work, our men, our lives if need be. Will you give us the vote?"

In 1919 Congress at last voted to do just that. The states ratified the proposed amendment and it became the Nineteenth Amendment to the Constitution in 1920. That November the last surviving participant of the Seneca Falls Convention, Charlotte Woodward Pierce, voted for the President of the United States.

The Significance

The Seneca Falls Convention, though ridiculed at the time, now marks the birth of an organized women's movement for equality in the United States. The convention provided a precedent and model for women to speak publicly on their own behalf. The issues outlined in the Seneca Falls Declaration of Sentiments remained issues of concern for women well into the next century.

RESPONDING TO THE CASE

1. On passage of the 1848 Married Women's Property Act, Ernestine Rose said it was "not much . . . only for the favored few and not for the suffering many. But it was a beginning and an important step." How did the women's rights movement subsequently succeed in attracting less privileged people?

2. What impact did the Civil War years and postwar events have on the fight for woman suffrage?

3. Study the four opinions excerpted on page 259, and explain why they are said to "reflect the general spirit of the debate on woman suffrage."

4. Seneca Falls is often described as the birthplace of the woman suffrage movement. What was the turning point at that meeting?

5. Compare the original Declaration of Independence of 1776 to the adaptation for the Seneca Falls Declaration of Sentiments of 1848. Explain how language can generate enthusiasm for a cause.

Elizabeth Cady Stanton emerged as the leader at the Seneca Falls Convention, and she continued to be an activist for the rest of her life. Research one of the figures mentioned in this case study and write a brief biography of her or him to include in your portfolio.

 Block Scheduling

The Portfolio Project on this page provides an excellent opportunity to enrich and extend the key elements of this case study.

CLOSE

Invite students to discuss the significance of the Seneca Falls Convention. Ask these questions: How did women's expanded activism affect the country during the Progressive era? (*Women were instrumental in gaining reforms in child welfare and in labor conditions, and in influencing decisions through their investigative journalism.*) What effect did the focus on suffrage have on the struggle for women's rights? (*At first it divided women, who disagreed over tactics, but it finally united them with a common goal. In the process of working for the vote, women developed new leadership skills and strategies.*)

Responding to the Case Answers

1. It won support from African Americans, notably Frederick Douglass and Sojourner Truth; it drew a wider audience by campaigning and taking public action such as demonstrations.
2. The war effort and postwar emphasis on African American male suffrage slowed the fight for woman suffrage during those years.
3. Opinions ranged from those maintaining that certain areas of civic activity should be restricted to men to those advocating that men and women should be equal before the law.
4. The passage of Resolution 9.
5. The Declaration of Independence is a revered document in American history. By using the same phrases and cadences in their Declaration of Sentiments, the authors linked the ideas of national independence and women's rights.

Chapter ⑧ Review

Reviewing Key Terms

Answers will vary, but they should reflect students' understanding of the vocabulary words and their relationships.

Recalling Facts

1. Factory jobs, rural unemployment, and cultural opportunities attracted people to cities.

2. Companies operated by trusts could produce goods at lower cost.

3. Workers were paid very poorly.

4. They formed trusts that dominated certain industries.

5. Progressives were more likely to live in cities and to trust experts than were populists.

6. Intellectuals encouraged the scientific study of social problems.

7. Muckrakers were writers who exposed problems. *The Jungle* outraged the public.

8. The plan established a five-person commission to run the government.

9. Under La Follette, Wisconsin established direct primaries, initiatives, referendums, and recalls, and set up a commission to regulate the railroads.

10. Progressives supported public schools and opposed child labor.

Critical Thinking

1. Answers will vary. Many supporters of the Galveston system wanted government to be more efficient and less responsive to immigrants. La Follette wanted more direct citizen involvement.

2. Answers will vary, but students should note the ethnic diversity, the pushcarts selling fresh produce, the variety in styles of clothing, the lack of

---

Reviewing Key Terms

Imagine that you are a muckraker who is investigating the need for reform in your city. Use the following vocabulary words to write an article summarizing the corruption and stating your recommendations.

urbanization	referendum
recall	political machine
direct primary	initiative

Recalling Facts

1. Identify the major factors that contributed to the growth of cities in the late 1800s.

2. How did consumers benefit from the existence of large trusts?

3. Why did the average urban worker live on the edge of poverty?

4. How did men such as J.P. Morgan and John D. Rockefeller amass huge fortunes during this period?

5. How were the progressives different from the populists?

6. How did intellectuals such as Charles Beard, Mary Ritter Beard, and Lester Ward influence the thinking of the reformers?

7. Who were the muckrakers? How did the public react to Upton Sinclair's book *The Jungle*?

8. What were the principal features of the plan to rebuild Galveston?

9. What reforms did Robert La Follette bring about in Wisconsin?

10. How did progressive reforms benefit children?

Critical Thinking

1. Recognizing Ideologies Do you think progressives believed in democracy? In your answer clarify what you think democracy means. Then indicate whether the progressive view of democracy agrees with

---

your view. Use examples from among the progressive reformers to support your conclusion.

2. Making Inferences The photograph on this page shows Delancey Street in New York City in 1905. What aspects of urban life are shown in this picture?

3. Drawing Conclusions List and evaluate four changes caused by the growth of cities. Explain both the benefits and the costs of each change.

4. Making Comparisons How did the women's struggle to gain the vote parallel the struggle of African Americans for equal rights? How did it differ?

5. Making Generalizations Make a list of 10 progressive individuals described in this chapter. When possible, indicate whether each came from a poor family or a prosperous one. Use this information to write a sentence describing the background of these progressives.

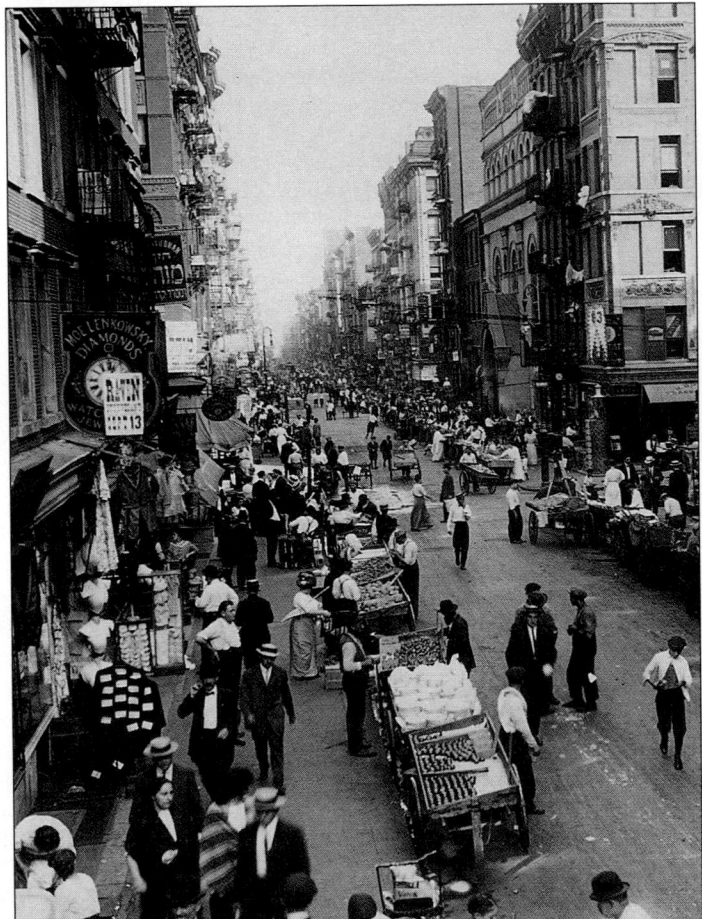

ARCHIVE PHOTOS

---

automobiles, the different signs, and the apartment buildings with their balconies.

3. Answers may include poor housing, crime, political corruption, ethnic diversity, and new forms of transportation.

4. Few progressives supported either group. Women

wanted to gain the vote; African Americans wanted to regain it.

5. Answers will vary. Many progressives, including Addams, Rauschenbusch, and Kelley, came from prosperous homes.

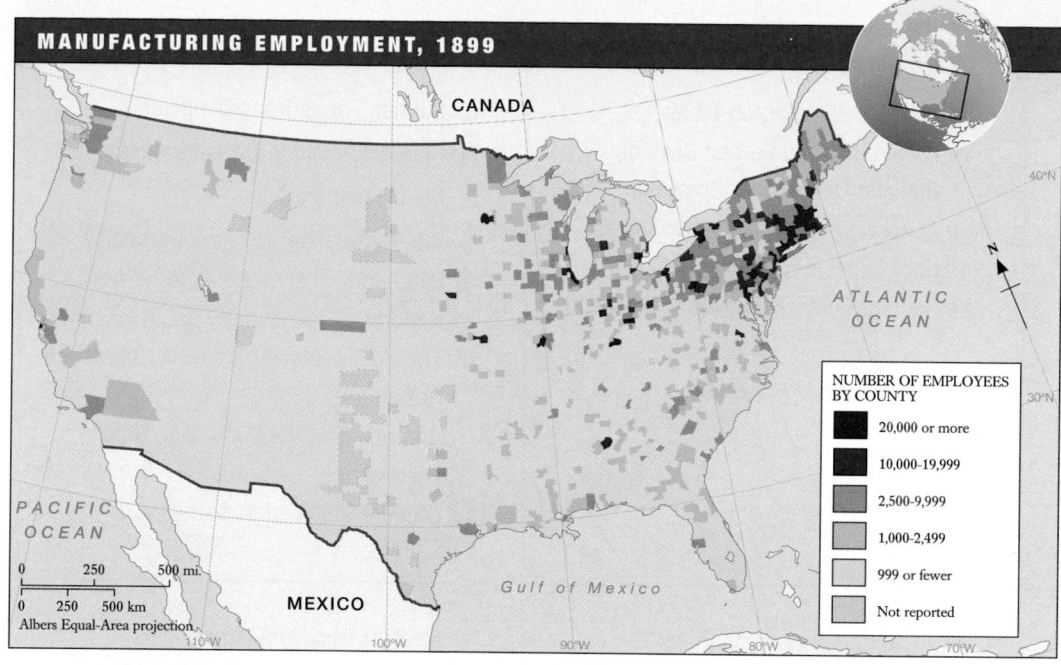

MANUFACTURING EMPLOYMENT, 1899

CANADA

ATLANTIC
OCEAN

PACIFIC
OCEAN

0   250   500 mi.

0   250   500 km

Albers Equal-Area projection

MEXICO

Gulf of Mexico

NUMBER OF EMPLOYEES
BY COUNTY

20,000 or more

10,000-19,999

2,500-9,999

1,000-2,499

999 or fewer

Not reported

Geography and History

1. The Northeastern region of the United States had the heaviest concentration of manufacturing employment.
2. The center of industry was shifting to the Midwestern region of the United States.
3. The densest employment areas were often located near water, which was used as a power source for factories.
4. Washington state; California, Montana
5. People moved to those areas where manufacturing jobs were available. As the population became more dense, larger cities and urban life developed.

Portfolio Project

What, in your opinion, is the major problem facing the United States today? Make a list of ways in which you could enlist people to work together to solve the problem. Choose a visual or graphic format to effectively display your ideas, and share them with your classmates. Then file your written list in your portfolio.

Cooperative Learning

The progressives identified a set of problems that needed correction 100 years ago. What are the major problems facing your community today? Work with a few of your classmates to create a list for class discussion. Then, work in small groups to choose one problem and prepare to participate in a round-table discussion to explore ways of solving that problem.

Reinforcing Skills

Determining Cause and Effect
How did politicians gain power in the cities during the Progressive Era? Why did this political power often lead to corruption?

Geography and History

Study the map on this page to answer the following questions:

1. Which region of the United States had the heaviest concentration of manufacturing employment?

2. In 1890 upstart Illinois passed venerable Massachusetts to take third place in the gross value of manufactured goods. It also passed Ohio to become the leader in agricultural machinery. In what direction was the center of industry shifting?

3. The densest areas of employment were often located geographically near what power source?

4. What areas in the West led manufacturing in 1899?

5. What correlation can you make between the growth of cities and the density of manufacturing employment?

HISTORY JOURNAL

This period of history from the late 1800s through the early 1900s showed great change in response to progressive action. What changes did you feel were the most powerful? What impact do these changes have on your life today? What changes can you initiate that will affect future generations? Write your responses to these questions in your journal.

History Journal

Student journals should include references to progressive reforms, such as instituting laws against child labor, improving factory working conditions for all, and changing city governments. After indicating how these reforms have affected their lives, students should suggest changes they would like to see for the future.

BONUS QUESTION

This question may be used for extra credit on the chapter test.

How did reforms force employers to act responsibly?

Answer: *Worker compensation laws were instituted.*

Portfolio Project

The list should reflect an understanding of the problem and appropriate avenues to take to reach a solution. Students should note individuals or groups that they might enlist. The visual or graphic format should support the student presentation.

Cooperative Learning

Criteria for the completion of the project will vary. Organize students into small groups and discuss your expectations. Students should complete necessary research before participating in the problem-solving discussion.

Reinforcing Skills

Politicians often gained support by providing services to the poor. To pay for this, some politicians took bribes and kickbacks from contractors in exchange for contracts with the city.

Progressivism Takes Hold

DAILY LESSON OBJECTIVES	REPRODUCIBLE RESOURCES	MULTIMEDIA RESOURCES
SECTION 1 Theodore Roosevelt and the Modern Presidency 1. Analyze how Theodore Roosevelt's background shaped his actions as a politician. 2. Identify examples of how Roosevelt expanded the power of the presidency. 3. Compare the actions of Roosevelt and Taft as Presidents.	📂 Reproducible Lesson Plans 📂 Vocabulary and Guided Reading Activities (English or Spanish) 📂 Cooperative Learning Activities 📂 Geography in History Activities 📂 Section Quizzes (English or Spanish)	📽 Section Focus Transparencies 📽 Chapter Teaching Transparencies 📽 Map Transparencies 📽 U.S. History and Art Transparencies 💿 Landmark Documents in American History 💿 The Presidents: A Picture History of Our Nation 🎧 American Music: Cultural Traditions 💿 Testmaker 💿 Student Self-Test: A Software Review
SECTION 2 Woodrow Wilson and the New Freedom 1. Analyze how Woodrow Wilson's background shaped his actions as a politician. 2. Compare the candidates in the 1912 presidential election. 3. Identify examples of how Woodrow Wilson expanded the power of the presidency.	📂 Reproducible Lesson Plans 📂 Vocabulary and Guided Reading Activities (English or Spanish) 📂 Skill Reinforcement Activities 📂 Section Quizzes (English or Spanish)	📽 Section Focus Transparencies 💿 Landmark Documents in American History 💿 Testmaker 💿 Student Self-Test: A Software Review
SECTION 3 Limits to Progressivism 1. Identify the obstacles to and shortcomings of the Progressive movement. 2. Describe the conflicts between progressives and immigrants. 3. Analyze the relationship between progressives and workers.	📂 Reproducible Lesson Plans 📂 Vocabulary and Guided Reading Activities (English or Spanish) 📂 Supreme Court Case Studies 📂 Enrichment Activities (English or Spanish) 📂 Reteaching Activities (English or Spanish) 📂 Section Quizzes (English or Spanish)	📽 Section Focus Transparencies 💿 Landmark Documents in American History 💿 Testmaker 💿 Student Self-Test: A Software Review
CHAPTER REVIEW AND EVALUATION	📂 Chapter 9 Test, Forms A and B 📂 Performance Assessment Strategies and Activities	💿 Student Self-Test: A Software Review 💿 Vocabulary PuzzleMaker 💿 Testmaker 🎧 Chapter Digests Audiocassettes

🕐 00:00 If time does not permit teaching the entire chapter, summarize using the Chapter 9 Digests Audiocassettes and the accompanying activities and tests. (Available in English or Spanish.)

Cooperative Project

Organize the class into 2 groups to debate and evaluate the Progressive era. In one group, each student should find 3 facts to support the idea that progressives improved society; similarly, students in the other group will show how progressives failed to improve society. Next ask each group to prepare and share 10 statements based on their facts. Then conduct a class debate about the success or failure of the Progressive movement. **LEP** 🔲

Suggested Rubric: An Issue Controversy. See Performance Assessment Strategies and Activities, p. 51.

Individual Project

Ask each student to take a paragraph from this chapter and research the event, peson, or theme it describes. The student should re-write the paragraph, adding details that expand the original ideas, in order to provide greater understanding of the topic.

Suggested Rubric: Self-Assessment. See Performance Assessment Strategies and Activities, p. 53.

Key to Ability Levels

Teaching strategies have been coded for varying learning styles and abilities.

L1 **BASIC** activities for all students

L2 **AVERAGE** activities for average to above-average students

L3 **CHALLENGING** activities for above-average students

LEP **LIMITED ENGLISH PROFICIENCY** activities

Block Scheduling

Block scheduling differs from traditional class scheduling in the amount of time allotted to each period. The extended timeframe provided by block scheduling affords you the opportunity to implement a greater number of research-oriented and activity-intense projects to motivate and involve your students. Activities that are particularly suited to use within the block scheduling framework are identified throughout this chapter by the following designation. 🔲

T E A C H E R ' S   C O R N E R

NATIONAL GEOGRAPHIC SOCIETY

Chapter Overview

This chapter recounts the expansion of the power of the federal government under Presidents Roosevelt, Taft, and Wilson. It further analyzes the complex relationships among progressives, African Americans, immigrants, and radicals.

Introducing the Chapter

Tell students that in this chapter they will learn about the expansion of the power of the presidency in the early 1900s. Have them read the vignette. Discuss the meaning of the cartoon about J.P. Morgan and how fear of Morgan could drive citizens to clamor for a stronger federal government.

 Display Map Transparency 9, National Forests, on the board and distribute copies of the activity sheet. Point out to students that the United States Forest Service was established in 1909.

Extension Activity

Have students complete Beyond the Transparency on the activity sheet for Chapter 9 and present their projects after the class has completed the chapter.

History Journal

Have students think about the impressions of Morgan that they noted in their journals. Ask them to read an encyclopedia article or book chapter on the life of Morgan. After they have done so, ask them again to record their impressions of the man.

CHAPTER

9

Progessivism Takes Hold

FEBRUARY 25, 1901: MORGAN CREATES THE FIRST BILLION DOLLAR CORPORATION

For J.P. Morgan, it was a day of triumph. In just 4 months of feverish activity, Morgan had master-minded the formation of the world's first billion dollar corporation, U.S. Steel. Through buying out leading steel companies, Morgan's steel trust won control of 60 percent of the nation's steel-making capacity.

For many people, though, Morgan's triumph was a frightening one. The 168,000 steelworkers, whose 12-hour days spent in dangerous mills made the steel industry so profitable, feared they would have no bargaining power with the giant new corporation. How low would Morgan drive wages? How high would he drive steel prices?

Only one institution seemed big enough to protect average citizens from Morgan: the federal government. Since the founding of the nation, however, the federal government had done far more to nurture corporations than to challenge them. In early 1901, with President McKinley in office, people had no reason to expect much change. Little did Americans realize that the role of the federal government in American life would soon change dramatically as progressives carried out their agenda. ■

HISTORY JOURNAL

After studying this cartoon, describe your impression of J.P. Morgan.

How do you think the federal government could protect "average citizens" from him?

264

EXTRA CREDIT PROJECT

Analyzing Cartoons The original title for the cartoon is *The Latest,* and the caption reads, "J.P. Morgan (through the megaphone to the Sun, Moon, and other planets)—'Say, if I could get you fellows together in a [bid] on the Light business, there ought to be a bunch of money in it for all of us, see!'"

Have students analyze what is happening and what is represented by symbols in the cartoon. Then invite them to find current cartoons that deal with business issues today, and analyze one or two of them in a similar way. Students should then compare the business issues at stake in Morgan's time and their own. ◔

CULVER PICTURES

THIS CARTOON SHOWS J.P. MORGAN ATTEMPTING
TO FORM A TRUST WITH THE SUN AND PLANETS
IN ORDER TO MONOPOLIZE THE LIGHT BUSINESS.

265

GLENCOE
TECHNOLOGY

 Videodisc

American History

Side 2, Chapter 9
Title: The Progressive
Era
Subject: Sequences con-
cerning the Progressive
Era
Ask: What was the major
goal of the progressive
reformers? *(to correct injus-
tices in American society)*

 **Performance
Assessment**

Refer to page 263B for
performance assessment
activities for this chapter.

 Also see Activity 9
in the Performance
Assessment Strategies
and Activities for an
additional activity as well
as for suggested rubrics.

Examining the Visual

Judge **Magazine** This cartoon ran in 1901 in
Judge magazine. Magazine critic John Tebbel
has called *Judge* "the best humor magazine
ever published in America." Started in 1881, the
16-page magazine ran cartoons, political satire,
humorous sketches, doggerel, and jokes.
Beyond politics the humor was gentle, but the
political humor could be vicious. In 1885 the
Judge Company reorganized with some financial help from the Republican party. The magazine reorganized again in 1910, and *Judge*
became tremendously popular before World
War I. In 1923, with something of an all-star
staff, *Judge*'s circulation rose to 250,000; each
copy sold for 15 cents. The magazine suffered
losses during the Depression, and it finally went
out of business just before World War II.

SECTION

1

Section Objectives

1. Analyze how Theodore Roosevelt's background shaped his actions as a politician.
2. Identify examples of how Roosevelt expanded the power of the presidency.
3. Compare the actions of Roosevelt and Taft as Presidents.

Bellringer Activity

 While taking attendance at the beginning of the class period, display the **Section Focus Transparency 26,** and have students answer the questions.

VISUAL INSTRUCTION

McKinley's Assassin
McKinley ultimately died from gangrene and infection of the gunshot wound to his stomach.

Ask: Was there anything suspicious about Czolgosz? *(Detective Ireland thought he looked innocent except for the handkerchief wrapped around his hand.)*

History and the Humanities

🎧 American Music: Cultural Traditions—"Whitehouse Blues" by Charlie Poole & the North Carolina Ramblers

---

Theodore Roosevelt and the Modern Presidency

SEPTEMBER 6, 1901: PRESIDENT MCKINLEY ASSASSINATED

McKinley's Assassin
Leon Czolgosz had a one-day trial and was executed a month later.

PRESIDENT MCKINLEY SHOOK HANDS WITH ADMIRERS AT THE PAN-AMERICAN EXHIBITION IN BUFFALO, NEW YORK, AS SECRET SERVICE DETECTIVE SAM IRELAND STOOD GUARD. Next in line to greet the President was a young man, anarchist Leon Czolgosz, who caught Ireland's eye:

W hen Czolgosz came up I noticed that he was a boyish-looking fellow, with an innocent face, perfectly calm, and I also noticed that his right hand was wrapped in what appeared to be a bandage. I watched him closely, but was interrupted by the man in front of him, who held on to the President's hand an unusually long time . . . and

it was necessary for me to push him along so that the others could reach the President. Just as he released the President's hand, and as the President was reaching for the hand of the assassin, there were two quick shots. Startled for a moment, I looked and saw the President draw his right hand up under his coat, straighten up, and, pressing his lips together, give Czolgosz the most scornful and contemptuous look possible to imagine.

—Detective Sam Ireland,
In Our Times by Mark Sullivan

The doctors who came to the hospital emergency room where McKinley was taken thought the President might survive Czolgosz's attack. Despite surgery and

---

AS YOU READ

Vocabulary

► resource management
► holding company
► arbitration

Think About . . .

► how the background of Theodore Roosevelt shaped his actions as a politician.
► how Roosevelt expanded the power of the presidency.

► the similarities and differences in actions that Roosevelt and Taft took when each was President.

Section 1 Resources

REPRODUCIBLE RESOURCES

📂 Lesson Plan 9-1
📂 Section 1 Quiz
📂 Vocabulary and Guided Reading Activity 9-1
📂 Cooperative Learning Activity 9
📂 Geography in History Activity 9

MULTIMEDIA RESOURCES

🔖 Section Focus Transparency 26
🎧 American Music: Cultural Traditions
🔖 Map Transparency 9
💿 Landmark Documents in American History
🔖 U.S. History and Art Transparency 12

🔖 Chapter Teaching Transparency 9
💿 The Presidents: A Picture History of Our Nation
💿 Testmaker
💿 Student Self-Test: A Software Review
🎧 Chapter 9 Digest Audiocassette

other efforts to save his life, President McKinley died 8 days later, on September 14. Czolgosz was later electrocuted, after admitting to a compulsion to kill a "great ruler."

Vice President Theodore Roosevelt was away on a hiking trip in the Adirondack Mountains at the time. He succeeded to the presidency shortly before his forty-third birthday. Upon taking the oath of office, Roosevelt became the nation's youngest President. This energetic young man soon changed the American people's idea of what the role of the President should be.

Early Political Career
Public Success, Personal Sorrow

Despite ridicule from his educated and respectable friends, Roosevelt entered politics immediately after graduating from Harvard College (and deciding against Columbia Law School) in 1880. Politics, his friends chided him, was for grasping, disreputable people, like the machine bosses whom they considered corrupt and uncultured. Roosevelt argued that "if this were so, it merely meant that the people I knew did not belong to the governing class, and that the other people did. . . . I intended to be one of the governing class." In 1881 Roosevelt showed the strength of his intention by winning election to the New York State Assembly.

He gained reelection twice before personal tragedy struck. On February 14, 1884, in a tragic coincidence, Roosevelt's young wife died in childbirth just hours after the death of his beloved mother. Emotionally shattered, Roosevelt left politics and fled New York for the Dakota Territory. There he ran a pair of cattle ranches in what he described as "a land of vast silent spaces, of lonely rivers, and of plains where the wild game stared at the passing horseman."

In 1886 after a disastrous winter demolished most of his cattle herd, Roosevelt returned to the East and to politics, his first love. For the next 12 years, he held various government positions, from civil service commissioner to assistant secretary of the navy. When the United States went to war against Spain in 1898, Roosevelt resigned and organized a group of volunteers called the Rough Riders. Their successful assault on San Juan Hill in Cuba made Roosevelt a national hero. He rode his new fame to victory in the 1898 race for governor of New York.

Roosevelt and McKinley
Balancing the Republican Ticket

When President McKinley prepared to run for reelection in 1900, he needed someone to replace Garret Hobart, his first Vice President, who had died in 1899. Roosevelt seemed a logical choice. After all, the governor of New York had earned public recognition as a war hero and was equally popular with ranchers in the West and reformers in the cities.

Basically a man of action, Roosevelt considered the vice presidency a do-nothing position leading to political oblivion. Political oblivion was exactly where New York's Republican party hoped to send the politician whose stubborn independence they found so irksome. The bosses schemed to kick Roosevelt out of New York to serve as McKinley's Vice President. After he and McKinley won the election, Roosevelt

TEACH

Guided Practice

L2 **Discussion** Have students analyze Roosevelt's geographic base of support. As a resident of New York City, he appealed to eastern urbanites. His years in the Dakota Territory reassured westerners. The South, mostly Democratic, had little influence in Republican party politics. Roosevelt had no ties to the Midwest, but McKinley was from Ohio.

 Show students Map Transparency 9 and have them complete the activity sheet.

FYI

The 0-Year Election Jinx From 1840 through 1960, every President elected in a year ending in 0 died in office: William Henry Harrison, Abraham Lincoln, James Garfield, William McKinley, Warren Harding, Franklin Roosevelt, and John Kennedy. The pattern was broken by Ronald Reagan, elected in 1980 and 1984.

NATIONAL GEOGRAPHIC SOCIETY

The Presidents: A Picture History of Our Nation

Have students view "Theodore Roosevelt" and use the information to write a brief biography to include in their portfolios.

| ★ ★ ★ | **GALLERY OF PRESIDENTS** | ★ ★ ★ |

Theodore Roosevelt

"Our relations with the other powers of the world are important; but still more important are our relations among ourselves. Such growth in wealth, in population, and in power as this nation has seen . . . is inevitably accompanied by a like growth in the problems which are ever before every nation that rises to greatness."

Inaugural Address, March 4, 1905

1 9 0 1 – 1 9 0 9

THE BETTMANN ARCHIVE

BACKGROUND
▶ Born 1858; Died 1919
▶ Republican, New York
▶ Elected Vice President 1900
▶ Assumed presidency 1901
▶ Elected President 1904

ACHIEVEMENTS IN OFFICE
▶ Panama Canal begun
▶ Meat Inspection and Pure Food and Drug Acts (1906)
▶ United States Forest Service started (1905)

SECTION ONE **267**

Cooperative Learning

Presidential Power Have students compare the power of the United States President with the power of the chief executive in other countries. Organize students into small groups, each of which should investigate another country. Together, groups should choose a country to research and plan the scope of their project, dividing the work equally. For example, some students may search for information in the library, some create outlines from their reading, others create a written or visual presentation, and others proofread and check facts. Groups should share their findings and discuss whether the United States President is a relatively powerful or a relatively weak head of state.

Independent Practice

L1 Writing Assign students to write a memo such as one Roosevelt may have written to a close friend explaining why he took the vice presidency, or his feelings upon assuming the presidency at McKinley's death. Students may emphasize Roosevelt's sense of duty to his country and his party.

☞ Have students complete the Chapter 9, Section 1 Vocabulary and Guided Reading Activity. (Also in Spanish.) **LEP**

☞ Have students complete the Chapter 9 Cooperative Learning Activity.

VISUAL INSTRUCTION

Roosevelt as Conservationist John Muir was born in 1838 in Scotland and came to the United States with his family when he was 11. In 1892 he founded the Sierra Club, a conservation organization that grew through the century, with about 540,000 members in the mid-1990s.

Answer: *to manage the nation's forests and prevent short-sighted lumbering practices*

History and the Humanities

📖 U.S. History and Art Transparency 12—*Merced River, Yosemite Valley* by Albert Bierstadt

---

sadly wrote to a friend, "I do not expect to go any further in politics."

The reserved and serious McKinley, a predictable, solid Republican, provided a sharp contrast to his impulsive Vice President. To one senator, the constantly moving Roosevelt resembled "a steam engine in trousers." Wherever Roosevelt went, he became the center of attention. "When Theodore attends a wedding he wants to be the bride," noted a relative, "and when he attends a funeral he wants to be the corpse."

Not all the Republican machine bosses had approved of Roosevelt's nomination as Vice President. When Ohio Senator Mark Hanna heard of the Roosevelt nomination, he shouted at his allies, "Don't any of you realize that there's only one life between that madman and the Presidency?"

Fifteen months later, that "one life" was gone. The "madman" was President. Though Roosevelt pledged to carry out McKinley's moderate policies, the new President's dramatic style transformed the presidency.

CULVER PICTURES

Roosevelt as Conservationist President Theodore Roosevelt and naturalist John Muir, right, survey Yosemite Valley. As a result of Muir's efforts, Yosemite became one of the nation's first national parks. *Why did Roosevelt start the Forest Service?*

Thanks in part to his energetic speeches, Americans perceived Roosevelt as a President who could take charge. For his part, Roosevelt saw the presidency as a "bully pulpit" from which to preach the ideas he advocated. The young President captivated audiences with his toothy grin, vigorous gestures, and somewhat squeaky voice.

Throughout his government career, Roosevelt supported progressive reform in strong language while in practice he pursued a more moderate course of action. In this way, Roosevelt persuaded the public that he was a reformer at the same time he reassured the business community of his basic conservatism. For example, as governor, Roosevelt had supported progressive labor legislation but repeatedly threatened to bring out armed troops to control strikers. "We Republicans," Roosevelt had written in 1896, "hold the just balance and set our faces as resolutely against the improper corporate influence on the one hand as against demagogy and mob rule on the other."

During the late 1800s, strong Congresses and relatively weak Presidents had predominated. Roosevelt reversed that traditional division of power. The new President employed the considerable powers of his office and his own personal magnetism to bypass congressional opposition. In doing so, Roosevelt became the first modern President.

Managing Natural Resources
New Ideas About the Environment

Roosevelt put his stamp on the presidency most clearly in the area of conservation. From his boyhood explorations, Roosevelt had viewed America's minerals, animals, and rugged terrain as priceless national resources. For the good of the nation, thought Roosevelt, these treasures must be protected from greedy private developers, eager to make a quick dollar. As President, Roosevelt eagerly assumed the role of protector. He argued that the government must distinguish "between the man who skins the land and the man who develops the country. I am going to work with, and only with, the man who develops the country."

Roosevelt quickly applied that philosophy in the dry Western states, where farmers and city dwellers competed for scarce water. To increase crop yields and to protect themselves from droughts, farmers demanded more water to expand their irrigation systems. Rapidly growing cities such as Los Angeles also thirsted for this precious resource. In 1902 Roosevelt

---

Meeting Special Needs

Visual Learners This activity helps address the particular needs of visual learners. Direct students' attention to the diagraphic on page 270 explaining monopolies. In small groups or with partners, ask them to discuss the image of the cord wrapping around the heads Raw Materials, Manufacturing, Distribution, and Price. What do they think this symbolizes?

Make sure students understand that monopolies can apply to many different kinds of industries or businesses. Elicit from students the main idea that if an industry can control all 4 factors outlined in the diagraphic, it is likely to hold a monopoly. Encourage students to create a graphic organizer of their own to express this idea.

NATIONAL PARK AND MONUMENT DESIGNATIONS, 1901–1909

1902 Crater Lake National Park, Oregon, is established.

1904 Sully Hill National Park (now a wildlife refuge), North Dakota, is established.

1906 Two national parks are established—Mesa Verde in Colorado and Platt in Oklahoma (now Chickasaw National Recreation Area).

1908 Eight national monuments, including Grand Canyon, are established.

1901 1902 1903 1904 1905 1906 1907 1908 1909

1901 Yellowstone, Yosemite, Sequoia, General Grant (now part of Kings Canyon), and Mt. Rainier parks already exist.

1903 Wind Cave National Park, South Dakota, is established.

1906 The first four national monuments, including Devil's Tower, are established.

1907 Five national monuments, including Chaco Canyon, are established.

1909 Mt. Olympus National Monument is established.

supported passage of the Newlands Reclamation Act, which authorized the use of federal funds from the sale of public lands to pay for irrigation and land development projects in the dry farms and cities of the West. Under the new law, Roosevelt supported the construction of 25 irrigation or reclamation projects.

Roosevelt also backed efforts to save the nation's forests by preventing shortsighted lumbering companies from overcutting. He appointed his close friend Gifford Pinchot to head the United States Forest Service. Like Roosevelt, Pinchot was a firm believer in **resource management,** the rational scientific management of natural resources such as timber or mineral deposits.

With the President's support, Pinchot's department drew up regulations controlling lumbering on federal lands. This position satisfied neither business nor environmental interests. Business leaders, hoping to profit from unlimited cutting, criticized restrictions instituted by Pinchot as unwarranted government interference in the workings of private business. On the other hand, veteran environmental activists like John Muir of California criticized Pinchot for supporting any cutting in the few remaining unspoiled forests. They argued that forests should be kept in a completely unspoiled condition for people to enjoy.

In addition to supporting Pinchot's moderate actions in lumbering, Roosevelt took other steps to provide for the managed use of the nation's resources. He added 150 million acres to the national forests, quadrupling the amount of land they contained. Roosevelt also established 5 new national parks, created 51 federal bird reservations, and started 4 national game preserves. These solid conservation accomplishments hardly put an end to private exploitation of the country's natural treasures, but they did initiate government protection of such resources. At the very least, Roosevelt's constant championing of the causes of conservation and resource management served to place the issue on the national agenda.

Supervising Big Business
"Speak Softly and Carry a Big Stick" Does Not Apply

Other issues were already on the national agenda when Roosevelt took office. One involved the growth of large trusts—giant firms that controlled whole areas of industry by buying up all the companies with which they did business. This concentration of wealth and economic power under the control of large trusts had dramatically reshaped the American economy. Buyouts, takeovers, and mergers reached a feverish pitch between 1897 and 1903. By 1899 an elite group of 6 companies controlled about 95 percent of the railroads in the country.

Most Americans were suspicious of the trusts. By lowering prices trusts drove smaller companies out of business. They then established monopolies and were able to fix high prices without fear of competition. In 1890 Congress passed the Sherman Antitrust Act, which was designed to prohibit such monopolies, but it had proven

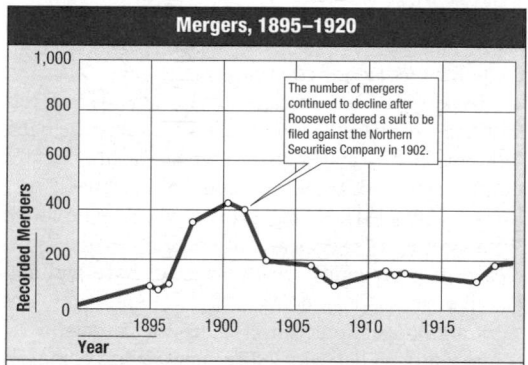

Mergers, 1895–1920

The number of mergers continued to decline after Roosevelt ordered a suit to be filed against the Northern Securities Company in 1902.

Recorded Mergers / Year

The Progressive era resembled the 1980s in terms of the large number of recorded mergers that occurred during that time. *According to the graph above, what effect did the Sherman Antitrust Act have on mergers?*

Ask: How many national parks existed when Roosevelt became President? How many national monuments?
Answer: *five, none*

GRAPH STUDY

The Sherman Act was named for sponsoring Senator John Sherman. His brother was William Tecumseh Sherman.
Answer: *little effect*

FYI

Teddy Bears A political cartoon once showed Roosevelt, a noted hunter, sparing a bear cub's life. Soon people called stuffed bears "teddy bears."

Notes

Portfolio Project

Propaganda Roosevelt often gave emotion-laden speeches to emphasize points, even if they overstated his actual beliefs. His attacks on the wealthy appealed to the emotions of many supporters. In practice, though, he defended big business interests. Most of his advisers were wealthy men with ties to big business. Have students find an advertisement, speech, or political cartoon that appeals to the emotions, and write a brief analysis of the piece, determining whether or not it is propaganda. Have them include both the piece and its analysis in their portfolios.

Facts on File

Landmark Documents in American History Have students review "*Northern Securities Company* v. *United States*, 1904" and write a paragraph about the intent of the document.

Curriculum Connection

Language Arts Finley Peter Dunne wrote a weekly newspaper column in which he used a character, Mr. Dooley, an Irish saloonkeeper in Chicago, to comment on news. Dunne's satirical comments on politicians made him a popular writer. His use of dialect followed in the traditions of writers such as Joel Chandler Harris, Bret Harte, and Mark Twain.

THE ANATOMY OF A MONOPOLY

Like other monopolies trying to achieve dominance in their industries, American Bell Telephone used aggressive business practices to gain control of the four most important aspects of its industry: raw materials, manufacturing, distribution, and price.

Raw Materials
- Bell cooperated with the copper trust and other trusts for a steady supply of raw materials, while its competitors had to seek their materials elsewhere and at higher prices.

Manufacturing
- American Telephone and Telegraph (a Bell holding company) controlled all the patents related to the phone.
- With its control of technology and with little competition, Bell made improvements only as needed to ensure continued success and control.

Distribution
- Bell withheld service from specific regions based on profitability.
- Because the telephone was not widely available, people often chose phone service from Bell or none at all.

Price
- Competitors were removed or absorbed into the monopoly through price wars.
- With no alternatives, the public paid what the monopoly demanded.

American Bell Telephone was one of several large trusts and monopolies that existed at the turn of the century. Like others of his time, Alexander Graham Bell was a shrewd businessperson whose company rose to the top of a lucrative new industry. *What elements of the industry did Bell control?*

---

hard to enforce. Industrialists simply devised substitute methods of retaining control—for example, the **holding company.** Holding companies bought controlling interests in the stock of other companies instead of purchasing the companies outright. While the "held" companies remained separate businesses on paper, in reality the holding company controlled them.

In public Roosevelt capitalized on the widespread mistrust of the wealthy industrialists. He called them the "criminal rich," "malefactors of great wealth," and "a miracle of timid and short-sighted selfishness," yet Roosevelt avoided breaking up trusts whenever he could. "I have let up in every case," he said in describing his record of prosecuting trusts, "where I have had any possible excuse for so doing."

Cautious actions offset Roosevelt's outspoken comments. This behavior led one newspaper columnist, Finley Peter Dunne, writing in a thick Irish dialect, to summarize Roosevelt's trust policies as mixed: "On wan hand I wud stamp thim undher fut; on th' other hand not so fast."

Battling Monopolies

Roosevelt combined dramatic public relations with moderate action in 1902. J.P. Morgan, a powerful Wall Street banker, had joined with a handful of the nation's wealthiest men to finance the Northern Securities Company. This holding company combined the stock of the Union Pacific, Northern Pacific, and Burlington railroads to dominate rail service from Chicago to the Pacific Ocean. Roosevelt, deciding that the company was a monopoly in violation of the Sherman Antitrust Act, ordered his attorney general to file suit against the Northern Securities Company in 1902.

In 1904 the Supreme Court, in a 5–4 vote, sided with Roosevelt, ruling that the Northern Securities Company had indeed violated the Sherman Antitrust Act. Roosevelt declared victory, claiming it as "one of the great achievements of my administration. . . . The most powerful men in the country were held to accountability before the law."

Much of the public hailed Roosevelt as a trustbuster who challenged and defeated the most powerful

Extending the Content

J.P. Morgan John Pierpont Morgan was born into a wealthy Connecticut family in 1837. He followed in his father's footsteps, going into banking after completing his education. His father had risen to the top of a London-based banking firm, renaming it after himself. After his father's death, J.P. Morgan changed the firm's name again—to J.P. Morgan & Company—and moved headquarters to Wall Street. It became the largest, most powerful financial house in the country, backing the federal treasury with $62 million in gold during the 1895 depression, and supporting banks to rein in the Panic of 1907. In addition to controlling some of the nation's largest industries, Morgan had an enormous art collection, most of which he bequeathed to New York's Metropolitan Museum.

financiers in the United States. The common, working people felt they had a fearless ally in the White House, one who would defend them from powerful corporations.

Despite the public praise, the Northern Securities case hardly changed the day-to-day operations of the railroads. The railroads west of Chicago continued to operate under the control of a few giant railroad firms, with little competition. None of the organizers of the trust went to jail or suffered significant financial loss for breaking the law. Instead they remained immensely powerful. Within a few months, Morgan would help Roosevelt further develop his image as a defender of the public interest.

Settling Strikes

In May 1902, the United Mine Workers (UMW) called a strike of the miners who dug the anthracite, or hard coal, that fired most of the furnaces in the United States. The UMW hoped to win a 20 percent pay increase and to reduce the miners' long workday to 8 hours, while at the same time securing the mine owners' recognition of the union. For their part, the mine owners firmly opposed a union that might force them to raise wages and improve mine safety conditions. They simply refused to negotiate with the striking workers.

The strike continued through the summer and into the fall. As the reality of a cold winter approached, the

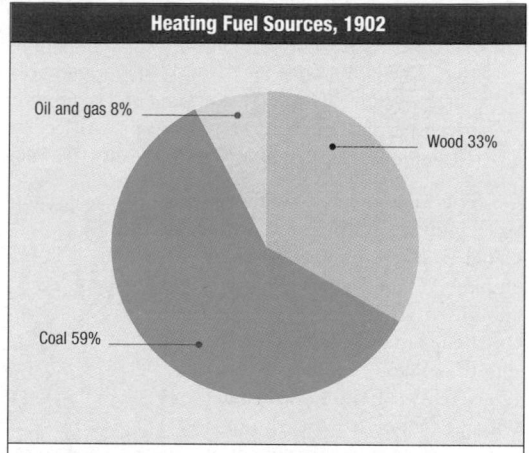

Heating Fuel Sources, 1902

Oil and gas 8%

Wood 33%

Coal 59%

Many Americans used coal for cooking fuel as well as for heating. *How important a role did coal play as a heating resource?*

shivering public demanded a settlement. President Roosevelt stepped in and urged the union and the owners to accept **arbitration,** a settlement imposed by an outside party.

Although the UMW agreed, the owners did not. They intended to destroy the union, regardless of the public interest. One of the owners, George Baer, claimed that workers did not need a union, that they should trust the selfless, conscientious owners:

CULVER PICTURES

Coal Strike of 1902 As the coal supply dwindled during the coal strike of 1902, the lines of people fearful of facing a winter without coal grew longer. *Why did mine owners initially resist an arbitrated settlement?*

GRAPH STUDY

Bituminous, or soft coal, tends to crumble when burned; anthracite burns from the inside out.

Answer: *Coal was a major heating fuel source, accounting for more than half the heating fuel used in 1902.*

FYI

Earthquake On April 18, 1906, San Francisco experienced the worst earthquake in its history. The land around the fault line shifted 21 inches (53 cm) and more than 500 people were killed. Jack London wrote in the May 5, 1906, issue of *Collier's Weekly:* "The earthquake shook down in San Francisco hundreds of thousands of dollars' worth of walls and chimneys. But the conflagration that followed burned up hundreds of millions of dollars' worth of property. . . . Not in history has a modern imperial city been so completely destroyed. San Francisco is gone!"

VISUAL INSTRUCTION

Coal Strike of 1902 Attorney Clarence Darrow presented the United Mine Workers' case to the President's commission. The settlement came in March 1903.

Answer: *They were determined to destroy the union.*

Cultural Perspectives

Reclamation Act of 1902 In 1902 the Newlands Reclamation Act became law in order to develop and irrigate the West. Although it resulted in impressive engineering and irrigation feats, the property rights of Americans of Mexican descent, guaranteed by the 1846 Treaty of Guadalupe Hidalgo, were ignored. The 1846 treaty allowed the people living on land ceded by Mexico to remain, retain their property, and become citizens. The 1902 law, however, dispossessed these people of their land (except in the state of New Mexico). The Reclamation Act has been called "among the most devastating pieces of legislation in history" for Hispanic Americans.

271

ASSESS

Meeting Lesson Objectives

Each section objective is tested by the section review question(s) that follows it in parentheses.

1. Analyze how Theodore Roosevelt's background shaped his actions as a politician. (1, 4)
2. Identify examples of how Roosevelt expanded the power of the presidency. (2, 3)
3. Compare the actions of Roosevelt and Taft as Presidents. (5)

VISUAL INSTRUCTION

Buyer Beware This ad merely claims its product is healthful; others promised to cure everything. One product label read: "Vitalizes and enriches the blood, tones up the system, builds up the broken-down, cures dyspepsia, debility, dropsy, chills and fevers . . . etc."

Answer: *Pure Food and Drug Act and Meat Inspection Act*

NATIONAL GEOGRAPHIC SOCIETY

The Presidents: A Picture History of Our Nation

Have students view "William H. Taft" and use the information to write a brief biography to include in their portfolios.

The rights and interests of the laboring man will be protected and cared for not by the labor agitators, but by the Christian men to whom God in His infinite wisdom has given the control of the property interests of the country.
—George F. Baer, *Letter to W.F. Clark*, July 17, 1902

The mine owners' stubbornness infuriated Roosevelt, who called Baer's comment "arrogant stupidity." If the owners refused to submit to arbitration, Roosevelt threatened to order federal troops into the mines. Then he sent Secretary of War Elihu Root to meet with J.P. Morgan to work out a settlement proposal. Fearing that Roosevelt would carry through on his threat and responding to the urging of the powerful Morgan, the mine owners finally accepted arbitration. The result was a compromise that gave each side part of what it had sought.

The miners won a 9-hour workday and a 10 percent pay increase, which was passed along to consumers in the form of higher coal prices. On the issue of union recognition, however, the owners won—they did not have to recognize the union.

In 1904, when Roosevelt ran for President in his own right, he coined a phrase that could have been used to describe his approach to the coal strike: "I shall see to it that every man has a square deal, no less and no more." Roosevelt saw himself standing above the battling classes, rendering to each a fair share of the spoils.

Despite the coal price hike, a relieved public felt it had been given a square deal. Americans hailed Roosevelt, whose powerful language shaped the public image of him as a fighter for their protection. Not since Abraham Lincoln had a President seemed to act so boldly on behalf of the public's interest.

Protecting Consumers

Roosevelt also defended the public interest on consumer issues. He was President when Upton Sinclair published *The Jungle* in 1906, exposing the unsanitary practices of the meatpacking industry. *The Jungle* provoked a massive crusade. Roosevelt jumped to the head of the crusade and pushed the Meat Inspection Act through Congress.

The Meat Inspection Act of 1906 outlawed misleading labels and dangerous chemical preservatives. It also showed Roosevelt's willingness to compromise with the trusts. For example, Roosevelt agreed that the government, rather than the packers, should pay for the inspection. In addition, he dropped the requirement that meat be dated, which would have informed consumers about the meat's age.

Buyer Beware Progressives were first to take action against false advertising claims by patent medicines and foods. *What legislation was passed to protect consumers?*

★ ★ ★ GALLERY OF PRESIDENTS ★ ★ ★

William Howard Taft

1909–1913

"I have had the honor to be one of the advisers of my distinguished predecessor, and, as such, to hold up his hands in the reforms he has initiated. I should be untrue to myself, to my promises, and to the declarations of the party platform upon which I was elected to office, if I did not make the . . . enforcement of those reforms a most important feature of my administration."

Inaugural Address, March 4, 1909

THE BETTMANN ARCHIVE

BACKGROUND
► Born 1857; Died 1930
► Republican, Ohio
► Governor of the Philippines 1901–1904
► Secretary of War 1904–1908
► Chief Justice of the United States 1921–1930

ACHIEVEMENTS IN OFFICE
► Postal Savings System (1910)
► Alaska given territorial government (1912)

Critical Thinking

Demonstrating Reasoned Judgment A single event, such as the coal strike settlement in 1902, often has many outcomes. For Roosevelt the settlement was a success because of the praise he received. For business owners it was a moderate success because it stopped a rising tide of public resentment against them. For union members the settlement was a mixed success, because the miners won a shorter workday and a pay increase but lost on the major issue of the strike. Historians often disagree about the outcome of a particular event. Ask students to evaluate the various outcomes of the 1902 coal strike and determine which result was most significant. *(Answers will vary but should focus on the outcomes mentioned in the text.)*

Though *The Jungle* focused specifically on meat, progressives worried about all of the foods and medicines that Americans consumed. Quack doctors sold concoctions of alcohol, cocaine, opium, and other drugs that claimed to heal everything from liver ailments to baldness. Many of these patent medicines, or nonprescription drugs, were worthless at best and addictive or dangerous at worst. On the same day that Congress passed the Meat Inspection Act, it also passed the Pure Food and Drug Act. This act prohibited the manufacture, sale, or shipment of impure or falsely labeled food and drugs in interstate commerce. The Food and Drug Administration (FDA) was not established until much later, in 1938. This agency broadly expanded the power of the federal government to protect consumers from fraudulent advertising claims by patent medicine dealers and from unsafe foods.

THE BETTMANN ARCHIVE

Taft's Style "There is no use trying to be William Howard Taft with Roosevelt's ways," Taft said. He was happiest as a lawyer outside politics. *What were Taft's strengths?*

Going Beyond Roosevelt
Taft Quietly Furthers Roosevelt's Work

No President before had ever served more than two terms. In keeping with that tradition, Roosevelt decided not to run for reelection in 1908. Instead Roosevelt chose his fellow Republican, William Howard Taft, an experienced diplomat and administrator, to run for President on the Republican ticket. Taft, a large, slow-moving, but extremely intelligent man, ran a mild-mannered campaign. Thanks to Roosevelt's energetic efforts on his behalf, however, Taft won the election.

In office Taft repeated the pattern he had established on the campaign trail. Instead of dashing about, making fiery speeches and remaining in the public eye, Taft remained calm, quiet, and often almost unnoticeable.

Although he had none of Roosevelt's flair, Taft carried out—and went beyond—many of his predecessor's policies. In dealing with trusts, he rejected accommodation in favor of prosecution. In only four years as President, Taft prosecuted almost twice as many trusts as did Roosevelt in his nearly eight years, including two of the most powerful, Standard Oil and the American Tobacco Company.

In other areas, Taft was at least as strong a progressive as Roosevelt. He expanded the number of acres of national forest. He supported laws requiring mine owners to improve safety. He established the Children's Bureau, a federal agency that protected the rights and interests of children.

Despite all of these achievements, Taft never received the public acclaim Roosevelt did. Taft did not view the presidency as a bully pulpit from which to lead moral crusades. Rather, he considered the presidency an adminis-

trative post, a job. He never had the eye for public relations opportunities that Roosevelt had. Nor did he have the ability to mobilize the nation with stirring speeches as Roosevelt had. By 1912 Roosevelt had become completely disillusioned with Taft; he was upset over Taft's failure to exert strong public leadership. With a new presidential election on the horizon, Roosevelt wondered if Taft was enough of a progressive activist to warrant his continued support.

SECTION REVIEW

Vocabulary

1. Define: resource management, holding company, arbitration.

Checking Facts

2. What were the highlights of Roosevelt's resource management plan? How did his background influence his actions?

3. How did Roosevelt's handling of the coal strike expand presidential power?

Critical Thinking

Determining Cause and Effect
4. What effect did Roosevelt have on the attitude of the public toward the use of natural resources?

Linking Across Time

5. Compare the ideas of Theodore Roosevelt and of William Taft regarding the use of government power.

VISUAL INSTRUCTION

Taft's Style Following his love for the law, Taft felt his highest achievement was his 1921 appointment as Chief Justice of the United States Supreme Court.

Answer: *He was intelligent and an excellent administrator.*

 Facts on File

Landmark Documents in American History Have students review "Meat Inspection Act, 1906," and "Pure Food and Drug Act, 1906," and write a paragraph about the intent of one of the documents.

Evaluate

Have students complete the Section Review.

☞ 🖵 Assign the Section 1 Quiz or use the Testmaker to develop a customized quiz. (Also in Spanish.) **LEP**

Reteach

🎧 Have students listen to the Chapter 9, Section 1 Audiocassette. (Also in Spanish.) **LEP**

Enrich

☞ Have students complete the Chapter 9 Geography in History Activity.

CLOSE

Discuss with students the main features of Theodore Roosevelt's administration. Encourage students to make an outline of the section, including one entry for each head in the section.

Section 1 Review Answers

1. **resource management** (269), **holding company** (270), **arbitration** (271)
2. parkland designation, creation of the United States Forest Service, and the Reclamation Act of 1902; background of exploration made him value the nation's resources
3. He used the power of the presidency to

threaten the mine owners, establishing a precedent for presidential participation in future labor disputes.
4. He placed the issue on the national agenda.
5. Both Presidents believed in expanding the power of the government.

SECTION 2

Woodrow Wilson and the New Freedom

SEPTEMBER 1910: BOSSES NOMINATE WILSON FOR GOVERNOR

WOODROW WILSON COLLECTION BOX 3 PRINCETON UNIVERSITY ARCHIVES. USED BY PERMISSION OF THE PRINCETON UNIVERSITY LIBRARIES

"LOOK AT THAT MAN'S JAW!" EXCLAIMED A DELEGATE TO THE NEW JERSEY DEMOCRATIC CONVENTION UPON SEEING THE TALL, SHARPLY DRESSED WOODROW WILSON FOR THE FIRST TIME. That long, strong jaw of the just-nominated candidate for governor suggested an unbending moralist, one solidly in the progressive mold. Wilson, however, was not the candidate of New Jersey progressives; he was the handpicked choice of machine boss James Smith, Jr. The New Jersey machine backed Wilson, the popular president of Princeton University, because he was both electable and, as a political novice, nonthreatening to the entrenched machine. When Wilson rose to give his acceptance speech, however, he expressed views

Thomas Woodrow Wilson
As an undergraduate, Wilson and his friends made a "compact" to become powerful and principled leaders.

that neither the bosses nor the reformers expected from him:

> I shall enter upon the duties of the office of governor, if elected, with absolutely no pledge of any kind to prevent me from serving the people of the state with singleness of purpose.
>
> —Woodrow Wilson, Acceptance Speech, 1910

With these words, Wilson declared his independence from the machine. From a reformer in the delegation came the cry, "Thank God, at last, a leader has come!" "Go on, go on," other delegates shouted. Wilson went on to pledge his support for almost every progressive cause desired by New Jersey reformers, from direct election of senators

AS YOU READ

Vocabulary
▸ regulatory commission
▸ socialism
▸ capitalism

Think About . . .
▸ how Woodrow Wilson's background shaped his actions as a politician.
▸ the similarities and differences among the presidential candidates in the 1912 election.
▸ examples of how Woodrow Wilson expanded the power of the presidency.

to the establishment of utility **regulatory commissions** to oversee the utilities' compliance with existing laws. At the end of his speech, the reformers, who had greeted him skeptically, applauded wildly. Some reformers ran up to the platform and tried to lift him to their shoulders, but Wilson would have none of that. His sponsors, figuring that the new politician was just playing to the crowd, assumed his backbone was not as strong as his jaw. They were wrong. Soon after election, Wilson began destroying the political machine that brought him to power.

Wilson's Rise to Power
From Professor to Progressive

Thomas Woodrow Wilson entered politics with a firm set of moral values that he had learned from his father, a Presbyterian minister, and his mother, the daughter of a Presbyterian minister. Wilson was born in Virginia in 1856 and grew up in Georgia and South Carolina. Although both of his parents were educated and avid readers, "Tommy" did not learn the alphabet until age 9 and could not read until age 11. Although he may have suffered from a learning disability, he persevered and became an excellent student. He attended law school, and eventually received a Ph.D. in political science from Johns Hopkins University in 1886. During his 16 years as a professor, he frequently won praise from students for his outstanding skills as a lecturer. In 1902 he was selected president of Princeton University, a post he held until he ran for governor.

When nominated, Wilson possessed no government experience. In dozens of articles and several books written during his academic career, however, he had expressed his political views. Wilson ridiculed Populists as "crude and ignorant" for their unquestioning trust in the wisdom of common citizens. He attacked Theodore Roosevelt and the Republicans for carrying political reforms to "radical lengths." The best model of government, he said, was the British system, which allowed for slow, orderly change under strong leadership from a well-educated elite. Because of his criticisms of most reformers and his praise for the British system, Wilson was generally branded a conservative rather than a progressive Democrat.

Once elected, however, Wilson proved that he was independent of the machine. Smith wanted to return to the seat he had once held in the United States Senate. Because the Seventeenth Amendment had not yet been ratified, the New Jersey legislature appointed the state's two senators. Smith, who had recruited Wilson to run for governor, expected Wilson's support in winning the

NEWARK EVENING NEWS

Boss Smith Wilson tried to dissuade Smith from running for senator and eventually backed Martine on principle. *How did Wilson's first actions as governor surprise people?*

votes of state legislators. In the Democratic primary, Smith had finished behind Thomas E. Martine. Wilson, calling machine bosses "warts upon the body politic," endorsed Martine. Without the governor's backing, an exasperated Smith and his machine lost. As one reporter put it, Wilson had "licked that gang to a frazzle."

From that battle onward, Wilson supported and won one progressive reform after another in New Jersey. He revamped election laws, established utility regulatory boards, and allowed cities to change to the commissioner form of government. To the embarrassment of the New Jersey machine, in less than two years as governor, Wilson transformed the state into a model of progressive reform.

The Election of 1912
Spoilers and Third Parties

Wilson's success in New Jersey attracted national attention. The Democratic party, which had elected only 1 President since the Civil War, needed a fresh new leader. The party met in Baltimore in June 1912, to choose its presidential nominee. The leading contenders were Wilson and Champ Clark, a Missouri representative and longtime reform activist. During a solid week of feverish politicking and 45 rounds of voting, the delegates could not reach agreement on a candidate. Finally the powerful Illinois machine threw its support to Wilson, and he won the nomination. In the 1912 election, as in 1910, Wilson owed his success to machine politicians.

SECTION TWO **275**

Cooperative Learning

Role Playing Organize the class into groups of 8 students. In each group, individuals should take the roles of Roosevelt, Taft, Wilson, and Debs, and their respective running mates. Assign each group an issue from the 1912

campaign to research. Each group should then hold a debate on their issue for the rest of the students. Possible issues are trusts, the environment, suffrage for women, child labor law, and consumer protection.

Socialist Candidate Debs Eugene Debs (in the train window, wearing a bow tie) takes time out from his busy whistle-stop campaign to pose with his campaign workers. *Why did some of Debs's supporters not vote for him?*

Independent Practice

L1 Time Line Have students make a time line of Woodrow Wilson's life. Include his birth, work, and accomplishments. Ask students to consider how Wilson's background might have influenced his actions.

✏ Have students complete Chapter 9, Section 2 Vocabulary and Guided Reading Activity. (Also in Spanish.) **LEP**

VISUAL INSTRUCTION

Socialist Candidate Debs Debs had also been the Socialist candidate in 1900 and 1904, polling 96,000 and 400,000 votes, respectively.

Answer: *They were afraid he could not win.*

Bull Moose Paraphernalia Senator Hiram Johnson was Roosevelt's running mate.

Answer: *TR said he was "fit as a bull moose" and ready to run for President.*

FYI

Eugene Victor Debs Debs went to work on the railroads at age 14. At 20, he helped organize a local branch of the Brotherhood of Locomotive Firemen, and remained devoted to the cause of labor. He was city clerk of Terre Haute and a member of the Indiana legislature. He spent 6 months in jail for his involvement in the Pullman Strike of 1894.

The Republicans

The Republicans were even more divided than the Democrats. Taft retained the support of most party officials, but few progressive Republicans stood by him. Widespread Democratic successes in the 1910 congressional elections convinced many Republicans that supporting Taft would cost them the White House in 1912. Progressive Republicans turned to the only person powerful enough to challenge an incumbent President: former President Roosevelt. Fearing that Taft was not progressive enough and that other leaders like Robert La Follette were too radical, Roosevelt entered the race. At the Republican Convention, though, Taft won the nomination.

The Bull Moose Party

Instead of quietly accepting defeat, Roosevelt bolted the Republican party. Declaring himself "fit as a bull moose," he created the Progressive party, often called the Bull Moose party. Social reformers, including Jane Addams, eagerly flocked to Roosevelt. "Roosevelt bit me and I went mad," confessed Kansas journalist William Allen White. The Progressive party platform included calls for many long-standing goals of the progressives:

THE BETTMANN ARCHIVE

Bull Moose Paraphernalia The Progressive party was loud, colorful, and often compared to a revival meeting. *How did the Progressive party get its nickname?*

a minimum-wage law for women; prohibition of child labor; workers' compensation laws; a federal trade commission to regulate business and industry; woman suffrage; and initiative, referendum, and recall.

In addition to Wilson, Taft, and Roosevelt, Eugene Debs ran for President. Debs, leader of the American Railway Union during the Pullman strike in 1894, had run in 1908 and received about 420,000 votes. Debs believed in **socialism,** an economic theory advocating collective, or social, ownership of factories, mines, and other businesses. As a response to the problems caused by private ownership of big business, socialism gained considerable support in the United States in the early 1900s. Debs rejected the moral and economic basis of **capitalism,** in which private individuals own the means of production and profit by their ownership. If trusts did not serve the public interest, Debs passionately argued, then the government should take them over and run them. His faith in people and his energy won Debs many followers. One supporter commented, "That old man with the burning eyes actually believes that there can be such a thing as the brotherhood of man. And that's not the funniest part of it. As long as he's around I believe it myself."

Meeting Special Needs

Learning Disability This activity will be particularly helpful for students needing extra work on the basic points. Ask students to bring in pictures, newspaper or magazine stories, or objects that portray or represent the United States President in action. Discuss the many roles of the President, such as proposing legislation, representing the United States overseas, and commanding the military.

POLITICAL MATHEMATICS.

CULVER PICTURES

Party Division The cartoon above was printed on September 4, 1912. Using political and mathematical symbols, the cartoonist reduced the election to its lowest common denominator. *Which party does each animal symbolize?*

The Front-runners

Debs, despite his powerful oratory, and Taft, despite his influence as the incumbent, soon realized that they could not win. Taft recognized that many voters opposed him because they thought he lacked leadership on progressive causes. "I might as well give up," he lamented, "there are so many people in the country who don't like me." Debs attracted large crowds wherever he went, but he could not convince many of his supporters that he had a chance to win. They gave their vote instead to one of the two front-runners, Wilson or Roosevelt.

Wilson and Roosevelt agreed on many basic issues, such as the need for a stronger federal government to influence the economy, but to win votes the candidates highlighted their differences, particularly on the great question of the day—the trusts.

The Trust Issue

Roosevelt believed that trusts must be accepted and regulated. Though known as a trustbuster while President, in 1912 he maintained that breaking up the trusts was "futile madness." Big companies, Roosevelt decided, were as necessary to modern life as big factories, big stores, and big cities. He ridiculed efforts to promote competition in a trust-dominated economy as "preposterous."

Instead, government must be big enough and powerful enough to protect the public interest by controlling the excesses of big business. Just as La Follette in Wisconsin tamed the railroads by setting up a commission of experts to oversee their operation, so Roosevelt proposed establishing a federal regulatory commission to oversee trade practices of big businesses. He labeled that regulatory program the New Nationalism.

Wilson criticized Roosevelt's program as one that supported "regulated monopoly." If big businesses were destroying competition, Wilson argued, then government must break up big businesses. He urged that a strong federal government should dismantle—not regulate—the trusts so that small businesses could once again compete freely. Wilson referred to his program of restoring competition as the New Freedom. He

PRESIDENTIAL ELECTION, 1912

CANADA

Wash. 7
Oregon 5
Idaho 4
Nevada 3
Calif. 13
Montana 4
Wyoming 3
Utah 4
Arizona 3
N. Dak. 5
S. Dak. 5
Nebraska 8
Colorado 6
New Mexico 3
Minn. 12
Iowa 13
Kansas 10
Okla. 10
Texas 20
Wis. 13
Ill. 29
Mo. 18
Ark. 9
La. 10
Mich. 15
Ind. 15
Ky. 13
Tenn. 12
Miss. 10
Ala. 12
Ga. 14
Ohio 24
W. Va. 8
Va. 12
N.C. 12
S.C. 9
Fla. 6
Vt. 4
Maine 6
N.H. 4
Mass. 18
N.Y. 45
R.I. 5
Conn. 7
N.J. 14
Pa. 38
Del. 3
Md. 8

Roosevelt 11
Wilson 2

PACIFIC OCEAN
ATLANTIC OCEAN
Gulf of Mexico
MEXICO

PARTY: CANDIDATE	ELECTORAL VOTE	POPULAR VOTE
Democratic: Woodrow Wilson	435	6,296,547
Progressive: Theodore Roosevelt	88	4,118,571
Republican: William Howard Taft	8	3,486,720
Socialist: Eugene V. Debs	0	900,672

0   300   600 mi.
0 300 600 km
Albers Equal-Area projection

In 1908 people had said that the name Taft stood for "Take advice from Teddy." By 1912, however, "Teddy" Roosevelt had abandoned the incumbent President Taft and formed a party to run against him. *Which states voted for President Taft?*

VISUAL INSTRUCTION

Party Division The donkey first symbolized the Democratic party when opponents called Andrew Jackson a "jackass" in 1828. Cartoonist Thomas Nast later popularized the symbol, and in 1874 created the elephant as the GOP symbol.

Answer: *The elephant represents the Republicans, the moose represents the Progressives, and the donkey represents the Democrats.*

MAP STUDY

Taft was hurt and disappointed at the attacks of Roosevelt, whom he had considered a friend.

Answer: *Utah and Vermont*

FYI

The *Titanic* In April 1912, the British luxury liner *Titanic* sank on its maiden voyage. The huge, double-hulled ship was declared unsinkable. It struck an iceberg in the dark, however, and sank 400 miles (640 km) off Newfoundland. The *Titanic* carried lifeboats for about half its 2,224 passengers. Only 705 survived. Due to this disaster, the first International Convention for the Safety of Life at Sea was held in 1913. Ships were then required to have lifeboats for every passenger and to keep radio watch around the clock.

Portfolio Project

PORTFOLIO PROJECT

Speech Writing Students should write a campaign speech for one of the 1912 presidential candidates. They should emphasize patriotic themes by showing how their candidate carries on in the tradition of other respected Americans, such as Jefferson or Lincoln. Suggest that students include their final speech in their portfolios.

ASSESS

Meeting Lesson Objectives

Each section objective is tested by the section review question(s) that follows it in parentheses.

1. Analyze how Woodrow Wilson's background shaped his actions as a politician. (2)
2. Compare the candidates in the 1912 presidential election. (1, 5)
3. Identify examples of how Woodrow Wilson expanded the power of the presidency. (3, 4)

Evaluate

Have students complete the Section Review.

☞ Assign the Section 2 Quiz or use the Testmaker to develop a customized quiz. (Also in Spanish.) **LEP**

VISUAL INSTRUCTION

Wilson in Action Wilson called a special session of Congress on April 7, 1913, in order to present his legislative request personally.

Answer: *opposed high tariffs*

💿 Facts on File

Landmark Documents in American History Have students review "Underwood-Simmons Tariff Act (Underwood Act, Tariff Act of 1913), 1913" and "Federal Reserve Act, 1913 (Glass-Own Act)" and write a paragraph about the intent of one of the documents.

pledged to make the nation safe for aggressive young entrepreneurs once again: "What this country needs above everything else is a body of laws which will look after the men who are on the make rather than the men who are already made."

The Campaign Trail

Wilson, with a smooth, analytical speaking style honed during years of lecturing as a professor, and Roosevelt, with his energetic personality, captivated audiences wherever they spoke. Crowds of 10,000 people, straining to hear, stood and listened to hour-long speeches from each candidate. In Milwaukee on October 14, less than a month before the election, a would-be assassin shot Roosevelt as he prepared to give a speech. Slowed by his glasses case and the bulky speech still in his coat pocket, the bullet did not stop Roosevelt. "Friends," he began, "I shall have to ask you to be as quiet as possible. I do not know whether you fully understand that I have just been shot, but it takes more than that to kill a Bull Moose." He gave his speech, at times nearly fainting, before going to the hospital for treatment. Wilson, in a show of fair play, suspended his campaign until Roosevelt recovered.

The intensive campaigning and brilliant oratory, though, did not inspire the citizens. On Election Day, only 59 percent of the voters went to the polls and they seemed to follow traditional party loyalties. The only surprise was Debs, who more than doubled his vote total from 1908. Democrats united behind Wilson, while Roosevelt and Taft split the Republican voters. The result: Wilson won a landslide in the electoral college, even though he got only 42 percent of the popular vote.

The New Freedom in Operation
Wilson Increases Federal Power

Once inaugurated Wilson immediately took charge of the government. "The president is at liberty, both in law and conscience, to be as big a man as he can," Wilson had once written. "His capacity will set the limit." Two weeks into his term, Wilson became the first President to hold regularly scheduled press conferences. Allowing reporters to question him directly, Wilson knew, would make him a more powerful leader in shaping legislation. During his eight years as President, Wilson demonstrated his power as he crafted reforms affecting the tariffs, the banking system, the trusts, and the rights of workers.

Wilson in Action Wilson broke a 113-year tradition by addressing Congress. *What was Wilson's view of tariffs?*

Reducing Tariffs

Five weeks after taking office, Wilson appeared before Congress—something no President had done since John Adams in 1800—to present his bill to reduce tariffs. High tariffs symbolized the special treatment government accorded big business. Adding taxes to the price of imported goods protected businesses from foreign competition. The consumers paid for this protection of big business in the form of higher prices. Progressives had long attacked high tariffs as an example of how government served the special interests at the expense of the public interest.

Wilson personally lobbied members of Congress to support the tariff reduction bill. Rarely had a President, even Roosevelt, taken such an active role in promoting specific legislation. Representatives for the trusts flooded Washington to defeat the tariff reduction bill. Wilson took the offensive. Charging that the nation's capital was so full of lobbyists for big business that "a brick couldn't be thrown without hitting one of them," he called on Congress to defend "the interests of the public." In 1913, with the attention of the voting public focused on it by Wilson's charges, Congress passed and Wilson signed into law the Underwood Tariff, which reduced the average tariff on imported goods to about 30 percent of the value of the goods, or about half the tariff rate in the 1890s.

Reforming Banks

Wilson's second major legislative initiative attempted to bolster the banking industry. The United States had not had a central bank since the 1830s, when President Andrew Jackson destroyed the Second Bank of the United States. During the economic depressions

Extending the Content

Tariffs Many economists who opposed other progressive reforms supported tariff reduction. They believed in laissez-faire economics. *Laissez faire* comes from a French phrase meaning "to leave alone." They believed that economies worked best when the government intervened the least; hence they opposed all regulations and tariffs. For other people, attitudes on tariffs often followed regional lines.

Representatives from agricultural regions generally opposed high tariffs because they increased the prices of manufactured goods. Representatives from industrial regions usually supported high tariffs to protect factories in their districts. Ask students how Wilson persuaded Congress to pass the tariff reduction bill. *(He personally lobbied members.)*

Bank Failures, 1880–1915

[Graph showing "Number of Suspended Banks" on the y-axis (0 to 600) and "Year" on the x-axis (1880 to 1915)]

Economic depression causes bank failures to skyrocket.

Rise in bank failures stimulates debate on banking reform.

In 1907, 91 banks failed in what became known as the Panic of 1907. In 1908 the number of bank failures rose to 155.
Which year in this 35-year period saw the most bank failures?

that had hit the United States periodically over the decades that followed, hundreds of small banks collapsed in bankruptcy, wiping out the life savings of many of their depositors. To restore public confidence in the banking system, Wilson proposed establishing a Federal Reserve System. Banks would have to keep a portion of their deposits in a reserve bank, which would provide a financial cushion against unanticipated losses. If banks prepared better for economic downturns, Wilson reasoned, fewer would go broke when depressions hit. In addition, a reserve system would serve as a central bank for the entire economy, controlling interest rates and the amount of money in circulation.

Advocates of a reserve system disagreed about who should control the reserve banks. Wealthy bank presidents and industrialists argued that the big banks should control the system because they had the expertise. Many progressives favored a government regulatory agency directly controlled by the President and Congress and thereby responsive to the public. Wilson proposed a compromise system composed of 12 regional banks that a board appointed by the President would oversee. Congress approved Wilson's proposal at the end of 1913, creating the Federal Reserve System.

Regulating Trusts

When he entered the White House, Wilson vowed to break up the trusts. In 1914 Congress passed the Clayton Antitrust Act, which broadened the Sherman Antitrust Act of 1890. For example, the Clayton Act promoted competition by prohibiting interlocking directorates, which allowed companies to work together to reduce competition. The Clayton Act also made corporate officers personally responsible for violations of antitrust laws.

Wilson also backed efforts to regulate trusts. In 1914 Congress established the Federal Trade Commission (FTC), which attempted to stop unfair trading and business practices among companies. For example, the FTC could prevent companies from working together in order to keep prices high. Fair trade, Wilson hoped, would give small companies better chances to compete with larger companies.

Protecting Workers

As President, Wilson supported a variety of progressive federal labor laws. For example, in 1916, Wilson signed the first federal law regulating the use of children as workers in factories and mines. The Supreme Court struck down the law in 1918, however, claiming that whether or not children could work was a matter for the state courts.

Wilson also supported laws requiring that all companies contracting with the government provide their workers with compensation for injuries on the job. These laws greatly strengthened the role of the federal government in protecting workers.

During his presidency Wilson built upon Roosevelt's foundation. He expanded the role of the federal government and of the President. Like Roosevelt, Wilson saw himself as a crusader, using federal power to protect common citizens. In Wilson's view (and that of most progressives), however, the common citizens were white, native-born, and capitalists. Other Americans, such as African Americans, immigrants, and socialists, often suffered during the Progressive era.

SECTION REVIEW

Vocabulary

1. Define: regulatory commission, socialism, capitalism.

Checking Facts

2. As governor of New Jersey, how did Wilson demonstrate his political independence? How did this independence shape his presidency?

3. How was the Clayton Antitrust Act an example of expanding presidential power?

Critical Thinking

Making Generalizations

4. Based on the actions of Roosevelt, Taft, and Wilson, what statement can you make about the value of public relations to politicians?

Linking Across Time

5. Roosevelt and Wilson's view of the presidency differed from McKinley and Taft's. Give examples to show the current President's view.

SECTION TWO **279**

Chapter 9
SECTION 2

GRAPH STUDY

The House of Morgan helped bail out banks during the Panic of 1907.
Answer: *1893*

 Facts on File

Landmark Documents in American History Have students review "Clayton Antitrust Act, 1914" and "Federal Trade Commission Act, 1914" and write a paragraph about the intent of one of the documents.

Reteach

Have students listen to the Chapter 9, Section 2 Audiocassette. (Also in Spanish.) **LEP**

Enrich

Have interested students research the 1912 election campaign and prepare a mock debate among the three candidates. Encourage students to prepare for the debate and stage it in period costumes for the rest of the class.

CLOSE

Ask students to review their time lines of Wilson's life. On the chalkboard, make a class time line that includes all of the entries used by the students.

Section 2 Review Answers

1. regulatory commission (275), **socialism** (276), **capitalism** (276)
2. by opposing the election of Boss Smith, the man who had recruited him to run for governor; he pursued policies he thought were right and said, "The president is at liberty . . . to be as big a man as he can."
3. It symbolized the President's ability to challenge commercial interests.

4. Politicians need to advertise their accomplishments in order to maintain their popularity.
5. Answers should reflect that students understand how activist Roosevelt and Wilson's views were different compared with Taft and McKinley's.

TEACH

This lesson reviews with students the procedures to follow in making comparisons, particularly regarding point of view. Have students practice the skill by comparing points of view on an event from Chapter 9. Encourage them to apply the skill by taking an opinion poll among students on a current issue and then summarizing the results. Explain that this skill is especially helpful in determining the many sides to an issue.

Additional Practice

☞ Have students complete the Chapter 9 Skill Reinforcement Activity.

Critical Thinking Skill

MAKING COMPARISONS

Learning the Skill

When you make comparisons, you determine similarities and differences between ideas, events, or objects. Knowing how to make comparisons will help you understand historical change. Differing points of view voiced by groups and individuals can influence the course of history. For example, environmentalists may advocate the preservation of national parks as a necessary and beneficial government action; the logging industry may oppose the same preservation issue as an interference in the pursuit of their business. Comparing the positions helps in understanding the issues.

Making comparisons can help you organize information in your writing or thinking. It is also a citizenship skill that will help you choose between alternative candidates or policies.

The Process

Follow these steps to make comparisons:

a. Identify or decide what will be compared.

b. Determine a common area or areas in which comparisons can be drawn, such as positions on a certain issue, reactions to a certain event, goals of certain groups, and so on.

c. Look for similarities and differences within these areas. For example, two politicians' positions on labor rights might be very similar, very different, or similar in some respects and different in others.

d. If possible, find information that explains the similarities and differences.

Practicing the Skill

1. Using the chart below, identify the groups that share the same position on the strike.

2. Do those groups have the same reasons for their positions? Explain.

3. On what common grounds can you compare the various groups?

4. Which two groups' positions and reasons conflict the most?

5. Which point of view is probably most similar to that of the United Mine Workers?

Applying the Skill

Take an opinion poll among your classmates about a current issue in the news. Summarize the opinions and write a paragraph comparing the different results. What reasons could explain the differences or similarities?

Additional Practice

For additional practice, see Reinforcing Skills on page 291.

COMPARISON CHART		
Who?	Position on the Coal Strike of 1902	Why?
United Mine Workers	Supports	They originated the strike, seeking an 8-hour workday and recognition of their union.
Mine owners	Oppose	They believe workers' demands are excessive and want to crush the union, keeping the industry free of regulation.
Coal-consuming public	Opposes	They suffer from the coal shortages and high prices that the strike engenders.
President Roosevelt	Officially neutral	He wants to halt the strike, but thinks owners are too selfish.
IWW	Supports	While not agreeing with the UMW on everything, the IWW promotes solidarity with all workers.

Practicing the Skill Answers

1. UMW and IWW both support the strike; mine owners and the coal-consuming public oppose the strike.

2. No, the strike's effects on owners and the public are different, but negative in both cases, causing the two groups to oppose the strike. IWW supports in principle; UMW supports for its own gain.

3. whether they support or oppose the coal strike

4. The United Mine Workers and the mine owners conflict the most.

5. The IWW point of view is probably most similar to that of the United Mine Workers.

Limits to Progressivism

NOVEMBER 1914: AFRICAN AMERICAN ACTIVIST CHALLENGES WILSON

William Monroe Trotter
In 1901 Trotter founded the *Guardian,* which reached a circulation of 2,500 within 8 months.

"Two years ago you were thought to be a second Lincoln," William Monroe Trotter angrily reminded President Wilson. Trotter, the outspoken editor of the Boston newspaper the *Guardian,* and four other African American leaders were meeting with Wilson to protest the segregation of African American and white workers in federal offices in Washington, D.C. These offices had been integrated for almost 50 years, since the end of the Civil War, and now the President had tried to change that. Wilson agreed to meet with the African American delegation, but he had little sympathy for their complaints. After nearly an hour of tense discussion, an exasperated Trotter challenged President Wilson, "Have you a New Freedom for white Americans and a new slavery for 'your Afro-American fellow citizens'? God forbid!"

Wilson resented anyone challenging his authority, particularly a defiant African American. "You have spoiled the whole cause for which you came!" barked Wilson, as he pointed to the door. The meeting was over, and the five men exited. Though unsuccessful in changing Wilson's policy, Trotter's final question did make his objective clear: he wanted progressives to address the needs of African Americans as well as white Americans.

Few white progressives thought to challenge the racism rampant in American society because they themselves had deeply negative attitudes toward all minority groups. As a result African Americans found themselves ignored by the mainstream of the Progressive movement. Two other groups—immigrants and radical workers—also found themselves battling progressives on many issues.

AS YOU READ

Vocabulary
▶ accommodation
▶ melting pot
▶ nativism
▶ eugenics

Think About . . .
▶ the obstacles to and shortcomings of the Progressive movement.
▶ what areas of conflict existed between progressives and immigrants.

▶ the relationship between progressives and workers.

Section 3 Resources

REPRODUCIBLE RESOURCES
📂 Lesson Plan 9-3
📂 Vocabulary and Guided Reading Activity 9-3
📂 Section 3 Quiz
📂 Chapter 9 Test

📂 Performance Assessment Activity 9
📂 Enrichment Activity 9
📂 Supreme Court Case 7
📂 Reteaching Activity 9

MULTIMEDIA RESOURCES
🎞 Section Focus Transparency 28
💿 Landmark Documents in American History
💿 Vocabulary PuzzleMaker
🎧 Chapter 9 Digest Audiocassette
💿 Student Self-Test: A Software Review
💿 Testmaker

FOCUS

Section Objectives

1. Identify the obstacles to and shortcomings of the Progressive movement.
2. Describe the conflicts between progressives and immigrants.
3. Analyze the relationship between progressives and workers.

Bellringer Activity

While taking attendance at the beginning of the class period, display the **Section Focus Transparency 28,** and have students answer the questions. (Or use the blackline master.)

VISUAL INSTRUCTION

William Monroe Trotter Trotter was class president in high school, graduated from Harvard, and worked in real estate before starting the Guardian. He was bold, radical, and sometimes cantankerous. He was sued by B.T. Washington, arrested for protesting the movie *The Birth of a Nation,* and had his passport revoked for planning a demonstration at the Versailles peace conference.

Ask: What specific issue brought Trotter's delegation to address the President? *(racial segregation of federal office workers)*

 Facts on File

Landmark Documents in American History Have students review *"Plessy* v. *Ferguson,* 1896" and write a paragraph about the intent of the document.

TEACH

Guided Practice

L1 Discussion Ask students to explain why some white people sympathized with African American demands for equality. For example, some may have interpreted the Declaration of Independence to mean that everyone was entitled to equal rights. Others may have supported equal rights because of religious beliefs. Still others, assuming that African Americans would eventually resume voting, may have sought African American political support. Discuss how patriotic, religious, and political views might reinforce one another.

VISUAL INSTRUCTION

Washington's Successes No longer limited to vocational training, the Institute became Tuskegee University in 1985, offering undergraduate and graduate degrees in academic and professional fields. About 3,700 students were enrolled in the mid-1990s.

Answer: *self-sufficiency and economic advancement for African Americans*

Washington's Successes Booker T. Washington (with Roosevelt, upper right) was the first African American invited to the White House for dinner. As founder and president of Tuskegee Institute (a vocational school, the print shop of which is shown above), Washington was the most admired African American leader in the beginning of the 1900s. *What did Washington and his school promote?*

African Americans and Equality

"Jim Crow" Entrenched

For African Americans, continuing poverty and discrimination marked the Progressive era. About two-thirds of African Americans scratched out livings in the rural South. Most were sharecroppers, farmers who traded a share of their crop in return for land to plant and money to buy seeds and tools. Sharecroppers generally found that the tobacco or cotton they raised barely covered their rent and the money they had borrowed, so they were almost always in debt.

African Americans who could leave their farms joined the flood of rural people moving to cities in search of opportunity. Though most went to Southern cities, an increasing number headed north, hoping to escape racism. In Northern cities, though, African Americans found much of the same discrimination and segregation that they had experienced in the South. In addition, in the North, African Americans competed with immigrants for jobs. This competition created tension and sometimes violence between the two groups.

In both the North and the South, segregation was a matter of custom. Beginning in the 1880s, however, Southern states and cities started passing laws requiring racial segregation. Taking their name from a character

in an old minstrel song, the Jim Crow laws required, for example, that trains have separate cars for African American and white passengers. They also mandated segregation in hotels, restaurants, parks, and every facility open to the public. Atlanta even required separate Bibles for African Americans and whites to swear upon when called as witnesses in court cases. In 1896, in *Plessy* v. *Ferguson,* the Supreme Court ruled that separate, segregated facilities were constitutional as long as they were equal. The only dissenter in the "separate but equal" decision was Justice John Harlan, a Southerner and former slaveholder. "Our Constitution is color-blind," protested Harlan fruitlessly.

Despite the requirements of the courts that separate facilities must be equal, they rarely if ever were. African American children received a second-class education compared to what white children received. For example, in 1900 in Adams County, Mississippi, the school system spent $22.25 per white student and only $2 per African American student.

Accommodating Racism

Leading one African American response to racism in the Progressive era was Booker T. Washington. The son of enslaved parents, Washington grew up in a log cabin with a dirt floor. He worked as a janitor to pay his way through Hampton Institute, a federally funded school in Virginia in 1868 established to educate African Americans freed from slavery. In 1881 the state of Alabama hired the mild-mannered but ambitious 25-year-old Washington to open a vocational school for African Americans in Tuskegee. Over the next 33 years, Washington molded Tuskegee Institute into a nationally prominent school where African American students could learn 38 trades and professions, including farming, forestry, plumbing, sewing, and nursing.

Cooperative Learning

Debate Organize a classroom debate around this statement: History shows that advocates of gradual change are more effective than those demanding immediate change. Form two groups of students, one supporting the statement and the other opposing it. Students should find examples from history that support their viewpoints. Students might use the American Revolution, the abolition movement, and other reform drives as evidence. Make sure all students play a role in the debate.

Washington believed that African Americans could achieve economic prosperity, independence, and the respect of whites through hard work as farmers, craft workers, and laborers. By succeeding at such jobs, African Americans would become valuable members of their communities without posing a threat to whites. Publicly Washington urged African Americans to bend to white racism by accepting without challenge Jim Crow laws, voting restrictions, and less desirable jobs. This policy, known as **accommodation,** emphasized economic success over racial equality.

Many African Americans, particularly poor farmers, agreed with Washington. Struggling to escape poverty, they believed that economic gains were more important than winning the vote, ending segregation, or directly challenging white domination.

Agitating for Equality

In spite of Washington's popularity, many African Americans opposed Washington's apparently meek acceptance of humiliating discrimination. The leading opponent of accommodation was W.E.B. Du Bois. Born in 1868 and raised in a free African American family in Massachusetts, Du Bois became the first African American to receive a Ph.D. from Harvard University. He taught history and social science at Atlanta University before helping found the National Association for the Advancement of Colored People (NAACP) in 1909. He served as that organization's director of publications for 24 years.

A proud and strong-willed man, Du Bois summoned African Americans to demand equality at once. "The way for a people to gain their reasonable rights," he pointed out, "is not by voluntarily throwing them away." Du Bois argued that the key to winning equality was not in developing vocational skills but in voting. With the vote African Americans would gain the political influence to end lynchings, to provide better schools for their children, and, in general, to challenge the white domination of society.

Reacting to African Americans

Most white people, including most progressives, ignored or actively opposed the efforts of Du Bois, Washington, and other African Americans to achieve equality. Many agreed with Theodore Roosevelt, who confided to a friend, "Now as to the Negroes! I entirely agree with

ARCHIVE PHOTOS

William Edward Burghardt Du Bois Both Du Bois and Trotter opposed Washington's views. *What idea did Du Bois reject?*

you that as a race and in the mass [they] are altogether inferior to the whites."

Some progressives—usually women—did support African American reformers. Jane Addams, for example, criticized racial discrimination and helped organize the NAACP. The alliance between white female reformers and African Americans reached back to the 1830s. Many white women continued to identify with the cause for racial equality because, like themselves, African Americans were caught in a web of discrimination.

Among sympathetic whites, Washington's ideas were more acceptable than those of Du Bois because Washington did not directly challenge white social and political domination. These people might have been less supportive had they known that Washington privately supported many of the same goals as Du Bois. He quietly provided money to pay for court cases challenging Jim Crow laws, to win back voting rights for African Americans, and to support antilynching campaigns.

The activism of Washington, Du Bois, and other African Americans led to some advances in spite of the lack of support from progressives. For example, the African American illiteracy rate was cut in half between 1900 and 1910, and the number of African Americans owning land increased by 10 percent.

Immigrants and the Melting Pot

American Anxiety Comes to a Boil

Like African Americans, immigrants struggled to find their place in American society. After the flood of newcomers from eastern and southern Europe between 1890 and 1914, immigrants and their children constituted about one-third of the American population. The United States became even more of a **melting pot**—a society in which various racial, ethnic, and cultural groups were blended together—than it had been before 1890. Each immigrant went through the assimilation process of absorbing a new culture. For most the first steps in assimilating the culture of the United States, or

W.E.B. Du Bois In 1905 Du Bois and Trotter organized the Niagara Movement, a radical forum promoting African American rights. Its 29 members planned to lobby for "just legislation for the colored people" and to educate and enhance public opinion.

Answer: *Washington's accommodation to white domination*

Independent Practice

L1 Biography Ask students to research and write a brief biography of one of the people mentioned in this section, such as William Monroe Trotter, Jane Addams, or "Big Bill" Haywood. Set aside time for students to share their finished work with the class.

 Have students complete the Chapter 9, Section 3 Vocabulary and Guided Reading Activity. (Also in Spanish.) **LEP**

Curriculum Connection

Literature In 1903 W.E.B. Du Bois published one of his most famous works, *The Souls of Black Folk,* a collection of 15 essays. In 1 essay Du Bois spelled out his differences with and his praise for Washington. "Manly self-respect," Du Bois claimed, was "worth more than lands and houses."

Curriculum Connection

Religion In 1054 a split over religious and political issues divided the western and eastern branches of Christianity. The western branch, the Roman Catholic Church, followed the teachings of the pope. The Eastern Orthodox branch included the Greek Orthodox, Russian Orthodox, and several other churches, mostly in eastern Europe or the Middle East.

Facts on File

Landmark Documents in American History Have students review "Gentlemen's Agreement, 1907" and "Root-Takahira Agreement ("Gentlemen's Agreement") on Japanese Immigration, 1908," and write a paragraph about the intent of one of the documents.

GRAPH STUDY

By 1890 the United States included more than 150 different religions or denominations. Most of these groups were Protestant.

Answer: *decreased by 1 percent*

Americanization, were learning English and understanding the laws and system of government of the United States.

Americanizing the Newcomers

Few progressives valued the cultural diversity that immigrants brought to the United States. Most, like Theodore Roosevelt, considered the cultures of all immigrant groups inferior to the culture of the United States. Americanization, to Roosevelt, was a process of stripping away an immigrant's old habits and replacing them with new, American ones. With his usual confidence, Roosevelt had no doubt that the American melting pot could assimilate as many European immigrants as wished to come to the United States.

Not everyone shared Roosevelt's optimism about the melting pot. Among those who feared that the flood of immigrants was destroying American culture were some progressives, as well as advocates of **nativism,** a policy of favoring native-born individuals over foreign-born ones.

Many nativists were Protestants who opposed immigration because of the large number of Roman Catholics, Eastern Orthodox Christians, and Jews who arrived between 1890 and 1920. As the chart on this page shows, the Protestant domination of the United States was facing a challenge. Other nativists feared that radical immigrants, though few in number, would undermine the economic system and the government of the United States.

Opposition to immigration existed throughout society. Woodrow Wilson, while a professor at Princeton, complained that countries such as Hungary and Poland were "disburdening themselves of the more sordid and hapless elements of their population." A sign in a restaurant in California read John's Restaurant. Pure

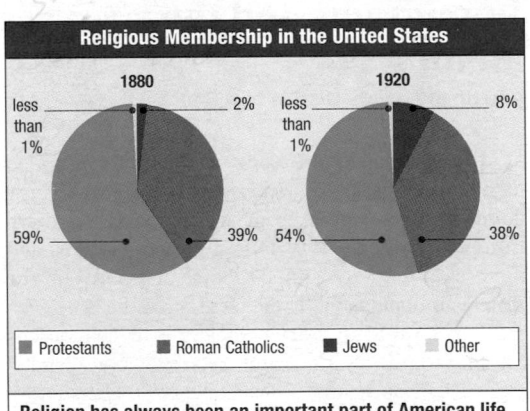

Religious Membership in the United States

1880
less than 1%
2%
59%
39%

1920
less than 1%
8%
54%
38%

■ Protestants ■ Roman Catholics ■ Jews ▫ Other

Religion has always been an important part of American life. *According to the graphs, how did the percentage of Americans who were Catholics change?*

American. No Rats. No Greeks. Job advertisements often included a footnote, "No Irish Need Apply."

Some opponents of immigration claimed to have scientific evidence proving that some racial or ethnic groups were superior to others. In particular they asserted that the Anglo-Saxon and Nordic peoples of northern and western Europe were smarter, stronger, and more moral than the Slavs and Mediterranean peoples of southern and eastern Europe. Jews, African Americans, and Asians, they claimed, were even more inferior. Based on these mistaken beliefs, some people advocated a **eugenics** movement, an effort to improve the human race by controlling breeding. The eugenics movement successfully convinced some state legislatures to allow forced sterilization of criminals and individuals who were diagnosed as having severe mental disabilities.

Imposing Restrictions

Nativists had begun calling for sweeping restrictions on immigration in the late 1840s. At that time about 150,000 Roman Catholics from Ireland were entering the United States each year because of a disastrous famine in their homeland.

As immigration swelled after 1880, reaching more than 1 million immigrants a year by 1905, the call for restriction became a loud chorus. The federal government began limiting Chinese immigration in 1882. In 1903 Congress prohibited individuals "dangerous to the public welfare," meaning political radicals, from immigrating. In 1907 Roosevelt worked out a "gentlemen's agreement" with Japan whereby the Japanese government limited the number of Japanese allowed to leave for the United States. All of these restrictions were targeted at specific groups. Still many Americans wanted much broader restrictions that would dramatically limit immigration from southern and eastern Europe.

In 1907, in response to the concerns of nativists, Congress established a commission to study how well immigrants were assimilating into American life. In its report issued in 1911, the Dillingham Commission concluded that the new immigrants from eastern and southern Europe were not assimilating as well as the older immigrants from western and northern Europe and that they never would. Hence, the commission recommended, Congress should restrict immigration, especially from eastern and southern Europe.

Some labor unions also called for immigration restrictions, hoping that a reduction in the number of people looking for work would help push wages upward. Ironically many labor union members were themselves recent immigrants.

Under these combined pressures, Congress adopted a wide-ranging restriction on immigration in 1917. This law refused entry to immigrants over the age of 16 who

---

Portfolio Project

Research Assign students to write a short article describing the American Federation of Labor today. The AFL, which merged with the Congress of Industrial Organizations in 1955 to form the AFL-CIO, remains the largest labor federation in the United States. The organization includes about 100 unions and about 14 million members. Point out that students can find out about the AFL-CIO through library books, periodicals, or by contacting a local union office. Students may want to include their articles on the American Federation of Labor in their portfolios.

Closing the Door Behind Them Forgetting they were once immigrants themselves, many Americans demanded immigration restrictions. *What were some of the fears of those opposed to open immigration?*

and pay their rent opposed progressives who wanted to ban child labor. Immigrants from cultures in which drinking wine or beer was a traditional social behavior often resented progressives who advocated temperance. These conflicts over economic, social, and political issues increased tensions between immigrants and progressives.

Workers and Radicals
Progressives Uneasy as Unions Gain Strength

Progressives also had tense relationships with many labor unions and were deeply opposed to radical labor leaders and ideologies. On one hand progressives sympathized with workers in factories, mines, and mills who suffered from low wages, dangerous working conditions, and the constant threat of unemployment. Most progressives recognized that workers needed protection. On the other hand, progressives firmly supported capitalism and rejected all other economic systems. Most were horrified by socialists such as Eugene Debs, who argued that workers or the government should own the factories and operate them in the public interest.

Supporting Unions

Among progressives, the strongest advocates of unions were those who had the most contact with laboring people—the settlement house reformers. Jane Addams and others saw how unions won fairer wages, safer working conditions, and greater job stability for workers.

could not pass a literacy test. Because schooling was limited in southern and eastern Europe, the literacy requirement affected immigration from these areas most sharply. More severe restrictions would come in the 1920s. (See Case Study, pages 404–407.)

Responding to Nativism

In a climate of restrictions and nativism, many immigrants relied upon one another for support. They formed mutual assistance societies, organizations that provided care for the sick and paid for funerals for members who died. Virtually every immigrant group had its own newspapers, its own athletic and social clubs, and its own theater groups. In many immigrant communities, churches and synagogues became centers of social as well as religious activity. There, new arrivals could meet people who spoke the same language and understood their customs.

Though old, ethnic hostilities frequently kept immigrant groups divided, they sometimes joined together for political battles, often in opposition to progressive reforms. For example, many immigrants supported the urban political machines that progressives tended to attack. Some poverty-stricken immigrant families who relied on the labor of their children to help them buy food

United in Labor These picketers at a New York garment workers' strike carry signs in English, Greek, Yiddish, and Italian. *Why did some progressives dislike labor unions?*

SECTION THREE **285**

VISUAL INSTRUCTION

Closing the Door Behind Them This cartoon uses stereotypical images of immigrants to simplify its message. The shadows cast on the wall behind the prosperous-looking Americans show their poor, immigrant backgrounds.

Answer: *Some feared a change in the religious make-up of the country; some feared radical political elements; some feared "American" culture and northern European genes would be diluted by "inferior" ethnic groups.*

United in Labor The years 1912–1913 saw textile workers striking in Massachusetts, New York, and Pennsylvania. This photo shows a 1913 strike.

Answer: *Some progressives felt unions were too radical.*

Global Connection

In 1910 the Union of South Africa was formed from several southern African British-controlled provinces. It did not protect the rights of nonwhite people living there. In response to debate over the Natives Land Act, the African National Congress (ANC) was formed to advocate equal rights for black people in South Africa. In spite of ANC pressure, the law was passed in 1913, setting aside 87 percent of the land for white ownership. In later years the ANC was outlawed at times, but remains South Africa's oldest political organization.

Extending the Content

Head of the AFL English-born Samuel Gompers was one of the most influential leaders in the history of United States labor. He came to New York in 1863 and became an American citizen 9 years later at age 22. An early member of the Cigar-Makers' International Union, he formed the AFL in 1886. He was the organization's president (except for one year) until his death in 1924. He was conservative in his approach and strove to make unionism respectable. He urged labor to remain outside partisan politics and ideology, wishing to focus on economic goals. Eventually he supported Democrats William Jennings Bryan and Woodrow Wilson. He labeled the Clayton Antitrust Act of 1914 "labor's Magna Carta."

ASSESS

In addition to backing unions, many progressives supported political reforms advocated by labor unions, such as limits on the length of the workday, a minimum wage for women, and an end to child labor. The largest labor organization was the American Federation of Labor (AFL), a coalition of unions that represented about 1.5 million workers by 1904. While the AFL called for these reforms, it trusted government less than did many progressives. The AFL realized that a government that could grant such reforms could also revoke them. The best protection for a worker, according to the AFL, was a strong union capable of negotiating with the owners.

AFL leaders also distrusted the government because they had frequently seen government side with owners to break strikes and crush unions. State governors or the President often sent in troops to reopen a plant shut down by striking workers. At other times courts ended strikes by declaring them illegal under the Sherman Antitrust Act, which banned all actions that restrained trade. Although this act was written to break up business monopolies, the courts used it to crack down on unions. Owners who knew that the courts or the troops would end a strike for them had almost no reason to negotiate with unions. Without that ability to strike, unions had little power.

Challenging Capitalism

Unions often included some socialists as members. While they envisioned radical changes in the long term, socialists often worked for short-term reforms that improved the lives of workers. They generally supported stronger unions that could fight for higher wages, shorter hours, and better working conditions. Socialists also called for public ownership of railroads, trolley lines, and utilities such as water and electricity. Most supported the right of women to vote.

Though the progressives shared many of the short-term goals of the socialists, the two groups analyzed problems differently and came up with different solutions. For example, when progressives saw a problem, such as the high number of workers killed on the job, they blamed insensitive owners and supported a factory safety law to solve the problem. Socialists seeing the same problem blamed the capitalist system of competition that forced owners to require workers to risk their lives so that the company could remain in business. Even if a law improved workplace safety, argued the socialists, the problems of workers would not go away until the competitive system that caused them was eliminated.

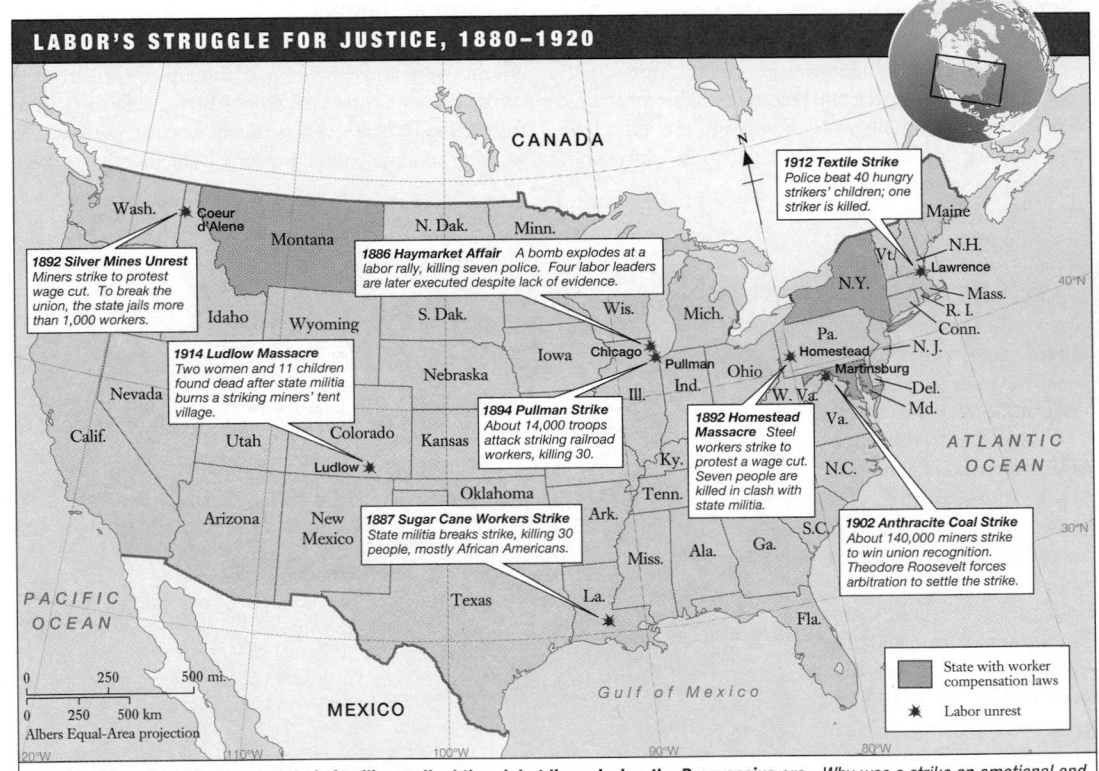

LABOR'S STRUGGLE FOR JUSTICE, 1880–1920

1912 Textile Strike Police beat 40 hungry strikers' children; one striker is killed.

1892 Silver Mines Unrest Miners strike to protest wage cut. To break the union, the state jails more than 1,000 workers.

1886 Haymarket Affair A bomb explodes at a labor rally, killing seven police. Four labor leaders are later executed despite lack of evidence.

1914 Ludlow Massacre Two women and 11 children found dead after state militia burns a striking miners' tent village.

1894 Pullman Strike About 14,000 troops attack striking railroad workers, killing 30.

1892 Homestead Massacre Steel workers strike to protest a wage cut. Seven people are killed in clash with state militia.

1887 Sugar Cane Workers Strike State militia breaks strike, killing 30 people, mostly African Americans.

1902 Anthracite Coal Strike About 140,000 miners strike to win union recognition. Theodore Roosevelt forces arbitration to settle the strike.

State with worker compensation laws

★ Labor unrest

0   250   500 mi.
0 250 500 km
Albers Equal-Area projection

Across the nation, workers and their families walked the picket lines during the Progressive era. *Why was a strike an emotional and often frightening experience for the men, women, and children involved?*

286 CHAPTER 9 PROGRESSIVISM TAKES HOLD

Cultural Perspectives

Native American Activist Gertrude Simmons Bonnin, a contemporary of W.E.B. Du Bois, held similar goals of advancement and equality for Native Americans. Born in 1876 on a Sioux reservation in South Dakota, Bonnin was educated in white schools but remained deeply connected to her traditional upbringing and knowledge. She named herself Zitkala-Sa, Lakota for "Red Bird." A teacher, writer, editor,

musician, and activist, she was a vocal critic of hypocrisy and paternalism in federal policy toward Native Americans. She promoted pan-Indianism (focusing on issues affecting all Native Americans, not specific tribes) and was an officer and longtime member of both the Society of American Indians and the National Council of American Indians.

Some radical labor organizations not only rejected capitalism, but they also rejected the willingness of socialists to run candidates for political office and to work with progressives. One such group was the Industrial Workers of the World (IWW), formed in Chicago in 1905. Wobblies, as IWW members were known, wanted a single union for all workers. They believed that workers should confront owners directly rather than through political battles. "Shall I tell you what direct action means?" one IWW pamphlet asked. "The worker on the job shall tell the boss when and where he shall work, how long and for what wages and under what conditions." Under the leadership of William D. ("Big Bill") Haywood, the IWW successfully organized unskilled workers that the AFL often ignored, such as miners, lumberjacks, and migrant farm laborers. In the most popular union song, sung to the tune of "Battle Hymn of the Republic," an IWW organizer and songwriter expressed the union's belief that workers needed to join together for their own protection:

IWW Organizes Strike Thousands of workers went on strike (sometimes called the Bread and Roses Strike) in Lawrence, Massachusetts, in 1912. One striker was killed and many others sent to prison. The union leader stated, "Bayonets cannot weave cloth." *What did he mean?*

When the union's inspiration through
the workers' blood shall run,
There can be no power greater anywhere
beneath the sun.
Yet what force on earth is weaker than the
feeble strength of one?
But the union makes us strong.

Solidarity forever!
Solidarity forever!
Solidarity forever!
For the union makes us strong.

They have taken untold millions
that they never toiled to earn,
But without our brain and muscle
not a single wheel could turn.
We can break their haughty power,
gain our freedom when we learn
That the union makes us strong.
—Ralph Chaplin, "Solidarity Forever," 1915

The members of the IWW, in addition to socialists, African Americans, and immigrants, often worked at cross-purposes to most progressives. Ironically these groups suffered the most from the poverty, corruption, and other social ills that motivated progressives. Despite this irony, the progressives did orchestrate an expansion of government power to meet the problems caused by urbanization and industrialization. That change in the role of government would have a significant and lasting effect on American life.

SECTION REVIEW

Vocabulary
1. Define: accommodation, melting pot, nativism, eugenics.

Checking Facts
2. What led to the immigration law of 1917? How did the 1917 immigration restrictions differ from those passed in 1882 and 1907?

3. How was the Sherman Antitrust Act of 1890 used against unions?

Critical Thinking
Making Comparisons
4. How were progressives and Wobblies similar? How were they different?

Linking Across Time
5. Do you think that the United States is more or less of a melting pot today than it was in the early 1900s? Provide evidence to support your viewpoint.

🎧 Have students listen to the Chapter 9, Section 3 Audiocassette. (Also in Spanish.) **LEP**

📁 Have students complete the Chapter 9 Reteaching Activity. **LEP**

Enrich

📁 Have students complete the Chapter 9 Enrichment Activity.

📁 Have students complete Supreme Court Case Study 7.

VISUAL INSTRUCTION

IWW Organizes Strike The average Lawrence mill-worker worked 56 hours a week for 16 cents an hour.

Answer: *Soldiers might have power, but it is the textile workers that get the factories' work done.*

 Curriculum Connection

Music The IWW used songs—both satirical and serious—to rally its members and promote its ideals. The IWW printed its first official song book in 1908.

CLOSE

Write on the chalkboard one to three words suggested by students to summarize each page of the section. Use the process of selecting these words as a review of the entire selection.

Section 3 Review Answers

1. **accommodation** (283), **melting pot** (283), **nativism** (284), **eugenics** (284)
2. fears held by nativists; they were more broad-based than earlier restrictions
3. Courts ended strikes, declaring them restraints of trade.

4. Both rejected capitalism; socialists ran candidates for public office, but Wobblies did not.
5. Answers may include that the immigration total is lower today than in the early 1900s, but more immigrants come from Asia and Central America.

CULTURE OF THE TIME

TEACH

Making the Historical Connection

Have students recall cultural aspects previously presented that drew people to cities. *(plays, concerts, stores with fancy clothes, and amusement parks)* Due to the city's concentrated population, new trends in fashion, music, theater, and leisure-time activities started and quickly spread. Ragtime's emergence in the 1890s also coincided with new technical means of mass music production—recordings and piano rolls—and an expanded publishing industry.

 Curriculum Connection

Music Ragtime was the musical style that immediately preceded jazz and consisted of a syncopated melody. Some consider its roots to be a blend of rural African American music and the piano music of European composers such as Chopin and Liszt. Scott Joplin, Louis Chauvin, Thomas M. Turpin, Jelly Roll Morton, James P. Johnson, and Fats Waller were some of the most well-known ragtime composers. Students may be interested to know that the theme song "The Entertainer," for the movie *The Sting* (1973), starring Paul Newman and Robert Redford, was composed by Scott Joplin. The Broadway musical *Ain't Misbehavin'* consists of songs written by Fats Waller.

Ragtime

The ragtime years, named for the sprightly music of African American composer Scott Joplin, were an extraordinary time in the nation's history. Industrialization and innovation transformed the way Americans worked and played. Newly discovered "free time" presented the challenge of what to do with it. The invention of the camera made it possible to record many scenes of people eager to meet this new challenge.

LIBRARY OF CONGRESS

WORLD TRAVELER

Ingenuity, determination, and achievement were some of the "American" virtues embodied by journalist **Nellie Bly.** Traveling around the world in 72 days (with one dress) in 1890, she outdid the record set in Jules Verne's popular novel *Around the World in 80 Days.*

THE BETTMANN ARCHIVE

POPULAR MUSIC

Sales of sheet music flourished when Scott Joplin began entertaining audiences with **ragtime piano music**—syncopated, high-stepping dance music born on the Mississippi Delta.

Background Information

A Time of Adventure Nellie Bly, an American journalist famous for her daring exposés, was the pen name of Elizabeth Cochrane Seaman (1867–1922). Her pen name came from the song "Nelly Bly" by Stephen Foster. She began her newspaper career at the age of 18 after writing a letter to the *Pittsburgh Dispatch* in support of women's rights. The editor liked her writing and hired her as a reporter. Other adventurers such as Robert E. Peary and Matthew Henson also typified the spirit of discovery evident in the early 1900s. Henson, an African American, was the only American with Peary at the end of his journey to the North Pole in 1909.

CULTURE OF THE TIME

LIVE THEATER

The **vaudeville act,** unique to American theater, gave many actors and comedians who later became stars their start, often as children. The curtain behind the performers displayed the first commercial messages. Vaudeville, minstrel, and variety troupes toured the country, influencing community groups who then created their own shows.

THE BETTMANN ARCHIVE

EXCITING RIDES

Amusement parks, such as Luna Park on New York's **Coney Island,** provided a **"bully"** time for everyone. They offered exciting rides and elaborate slides for the young and daring.

CULVER PICTURES

SIDEWALK ENTERTAINERS

Traveling **organ grinders** in urban areas provided entertainment and amusement for city dwellers. Often they sold peanuts or popcorn and had trained animals (usually monkeys) who performed for the audience. People who lived during this time period had a chance to laugh and take a break from their tough daily routine of trying to make ends meet.

THE BETTMANN ARCHIVE

CULTURE OF THE TIME **289**

History and the Humanities

American Music: Cultural Traditions— "Maple Leaf Rag" by Scott Joplin; "St. Louis Tickle" by Vess L. Ossman.

FYI

Vaudeville Vaudeville was the most popular form of entertainment in the United States from the 1880s to the early 1930s. The term *vaudeville* comes from a French word for a light play with music, popular in France during the 1800s. Some vaudeville theaters presented 20 or more acts on a single bill, or performance. The standard pattern, however, was 8–10 acts, consisting of magicians, acrobats, comedians, trained animals, jugglers, singers, and dancers. Many future stars, such as Jack Benny, George Burns, W.C. Fields, Sophie Tucker, Will Rogers, and Lillian Russell, developed their arts under the vaudeville system.

CLOSE

Ask students to examine each image and explain in what form the cultural phenomena shown still occurs today. *(space travel or similar adventures, a variety of types of amusement parks, live theater performances, buskers or other street performers, popular new music styles)*

Portfolio Project

Creating a Feature Have students collect images to create a contemporary collage that reflects their culture. Elements can focus on daring individuals, forms of entertainment, and music. Suggest to students that they list other images to include in addition to those activities pictured in this feature. Encourage students to search for images in magazines, newspapers, and other periodicals. They can draw, trace, or photocopy their choices. After students have written captions for their images, invite volunteers to share their completed "features." They can then file their products in their portfolios.

289

Reviewing Key Terms

1. socialism, capitalism
2. arbitration
3. accommodation
4. nativism, eugenics
5. holding company

Recalling Facts

1. He was Vice President when President McKinley was assassinated.
2. He broke up the Northern Securities Company and settled a coal strike.
3. Industrialists devised methods—such as forming holding companies—to maintain monopolies.
4. Taft supported mine safety laws, conservation (he expanded the national forest), and child welfare (he established the Children's Bureau).
5. Debs did not believe that private individuals should profit from the labor of others.
6. He took a direct role in shaping legislation, crafting reforms, and lobbying both the Congress and the press to support his goals.
7. Wilson proposed the Federal Reserve System.
8. The decision in the case upheld the constitutionality of Jim Crow laws.
9. Washington believed African Americans should accommodate white racism while Du Bois was in favor of confrontation.
10. According to socialism, workers, either directly or through the government, should own factories, mines, and other businesses. Progressives were not prepared for so radical a change.

Critical Thinking

1. Answers will vary but should be investigative in nature. Yes/no questions should be used sparingly.
2. Family background made

Reviewing Key Terms

Complete the sentences below with one of the vocabulary terms listed:

arbitration	eugenics
socialism	accommodation
capitalism	nativism
melting pot	holding company

1. _____ and _____ are two different economic systems.

2. Theodore Roosevelt helped resolve the coal miners' strike of 1902 when he imposed _____ by a third-party commission.

3. W.E.B. Du Bois opposed _____, Booker T. Washington's approach to racism.

4. One theory opposed to immigration was _____; another was the so-called science of _____.

5. A _____ can skirt antitrust laws by retaining controlling interests in companies or industries without owning them.

Recalling Facts

1. How did Theodore Roosevelt become President?

2. Give two examples of how Theodore Roosevelt expanded the power of the presidency.

3. Why was the Sherman Antitrust Act difficult to enforce?

4. Identify three progressive reforms President Taft supported.

5. Why did Eugene Debs reject capitalism?

6. How did Woodrow Wilson expand the power of the presidency?

7. How did President Wilson restore public confidence in the banking system?

8. What effect did the Supreme Court decision in *Plessy* v. *Ferguson* have on the Jim Crow laws?

9. How did the views of Booker T. Washington differ from those of W.E.B. Du Bois?

10. Briefly explain the concept of socialism. Why did it frighten the progressives?

Critical Thinking

1. **Formulating Questions** Assume the role of an arbitrator in the United Mine Workers strike of 1902. To settle this strike, you will need to understand the two sides' demands and recognize two opposing sets of values. Write at least three questions you would ask each side. Explain what you hope to learn from these questions.

2. **Determining Cause and Effect** Explain how Woodrow Wilson's family background, education, intellectualism, public speaking style, and previous leadership experience affected his actions as a politician.

3. **Demonstrating Reasoned Judgment** Imagine that you are a registered voter and a member of a trade union. The election of 1912 is one week away. Identify the candidates who are running for election and their platforms. Which candidate will get your vote? Give reasons to support your answer.

4. **Making Comparisons** Elizabeth Gurley Flynn (below) was a fiery speaker and organizer who joined the Industrial Workers of the World at age 16. Compare the main differences between the IWW's views on workers' rights and those of the progressives.

5. **Recognizing Bias** Reread the section entitled "Americanizing the Newcomers" on page 284. What examples of bias do you detect in the attitudes of the progressives toward the immigrants? How do their attitudes differ from those of the nativists?

BROWN BROTHERS

Wilson value intellect; education and work as a professor made him an excellent speaker. Political inexperience and high moral sensibilities may have made it hard for him to win over other politicians.
3. Candidates are Taft, Debs, Roosevelt, and Wilson. Answers will vary on which candidate gets the trade union vote, but Debs is a likely answer because he supported workers' rights.
4. Both sought reforms favoring workers. Progressives trusted government to enact gradual reforms; IWW sought direct worker involvement in industrial policy and profits.

5. They assumed foreign cultures were inferior to their own. Progressives felt immigrants could be improved by Americanization, nativists felt immigrants would destory the United States.

CHAPTER
9
REVIEW

UNITED STATES PARKLANDS, 1909

National park

National monument

Geography and History

1. It shows he contributed a great deal: Roosevelt established 5 national parks and 18 national monuments.

2. The West, especially near mountains, contained the most national parks.

3. Yellowstone and Yosemite were the largest parks; Grand Canyon was the largest monument.

4. There were more national monuments.

History Journal

Student journals should include references to the Presidents' attitudes and reforms on labor, race relations, and business.

? BONUS QUESTION

This question may be used for extra credit on the chapter test.

What was the "New Freedom"?

Answer: *Wilson's plan to promote business by dismantling trusts and restoring competition.*

Portfolio Project

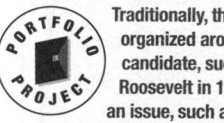

Traditionally, third parties have organized around a particular candidate, such as Theodore Roosevelt in 1912, or around an issue, such as prohibition.

Identify a recent or current "third party" and research its platform. What was or is its goal? What role did or does it have in nationwide events? Write a short paper examining this party and include it in your portfolio.

Cooperative Learning

Work in 5 groups to research the 5 tariffs that were passed between 1890 and 1913. Then regroup into teams containing a representative from each of the original 5 groups. Each new group should choose its own means of presenting its findings.

Reinforcing Skills

Making Comparisons Politicians who support contrasting solutions often share similar beliefs. For example, Roosevelt, an ardent capitalist, agreed with most Socialists in blaming competition as the source of employees' overwork and inadequate pay. What other beliefs did Roosevelt and Socialists share?

Geography and History

Study the map on this page to answer the following questions:

1. Given that there were 5 national parks and no national monuments when Roosevelt took office in 1901, what does this map show about his contributions to the preservation of the country's wilderness?

2. In 1909 which part of the country contained the most national parks?

3. Which were the largest parks and monuments in 1909?

4. Were there more national parks or national monuments in 1909?

HISTORY JOURNAL

Both Roosevelt and Wilson expanded the power of the presidency in the early 1900s. Do you think they promoted a progressive agenda? Explain. In what areas did progressivism fall short of its ideals?

Portfolio Project

One recent third-party campaign was H. Ross Perot's bid for President in 1992. His party, United We Stand America, rallied primarily around Perot's personality. Students may find examples of more local races as well.

Cooperative Learning

The five tariffs were passed in 1890, 1894, 1897, 1909, and 1913.

Reinforcing Skills

Roosevelt and many Socialists shared the belief that a return to a deregulated system would destroy progress made by larger companies in producing consumer goods at low cost. Both realized that as the economy evolved, so must the government.

Expansionism and World War I

DAILY LESSON OBJECTIVES	REPRODUCIBLE RESOURCES	MULTIMEDIA RESOURCES
SECTION 1 Becoming a World Power 1. Discuss the foreign policies of Roosevelt and Taft. 2. Describe opinions for expansionist policies of Roosevelt and Taft. 3. Explain the Open Door policy's importance for American trade. 4. Summarize American international political and economic growth.	☛ Reproducible Lesson Plans ☛ Vocabulary and Guided Reading Activities (English or Spanish) ☛ Cooperative Learning Activities ☛ Geography in History Activities ☛ Section Quizzes (English or Spanish)	🖰 Chapter Teaching Transparencies 🖰 Section Focus Transparencies 🖰 Map Transparencies 💽 Testmaker 💽 Student Self-Test: A Software Review
SECTION 2 Watching Europe's War 1. Discuss Wilson's actions in Mexico and the Caribbean. 2. Summarize the causes of World War I. 3. Describe American struggles to remain neutral during World War I. 4. Explain the decision to abandon neutrality in 1917.	☛ Reproducible Lesson Plans ☛ Vocabulary and Guided Reading Activities (English or Spanish) ☛ American Literature Readings and Activities ☛ Section Quizzes (English or Spanish)	🖰 Section Focus Transparencies 🖰 U.S. History and Art Transparencies 💿 Landmark Documents in American History 💿 Lessons of War 💽 Testmaker 💽 Student Self-Test: A Software Review
SECTION 3 World War I: There and Here 1. Describe the United State's mobilization efforts for World War I. 2. Describe United States military participation in World War I. 3. Discuss the negative effect the war had on civil liberties. 4. Explain how the home war effort furthered and hindered reform.	☛ Reproducible Lesson Plans ☛ Vocabulary and Guided Reading Activities (English or Spanish) ☛ Case Studies ☛ American Literature Readings and Activities ☛ Skill Reinforcement Activities ☛ Section Quizzes (English or Spanish)	🖰 Section Focus Transparencies 🖰 U.S. History and Art Transparencies 💿 Landmark Documents in American History 🎧 American Music: Cultural Traditions 💽 Testmaker 💽 Student Self-Test: A Software Review
SECTION 4 Reshaping the World 1. Summarize Wilson's Fourteen Points and European objections. 2. Describe events in Russia and their effect on other nations. 3. Describe the 1919 peace conference negotiations and treaty. 4. Explain why the Senate rejected the Treaty of Versailles.	☛ Reproducible Lesson Plans ☛ Vocabulary and Guided Reading Activities (English or Spanish) ☛ Reteaching Activities (English or Spanish) ☛ Enrichment Activities (English or Spanish) ☛ Section Quizzes (English or Spanish)	🖰 Section Focus Transparencies 💿 The Presidents: A Picture History of Our Nation 💿 Landmark Documents in American History 💽 Testmaker 💽 Student Self-Test: A Software Review
CHAPTER REVIEW AND EVALUATION	☛ Chapter 10 Test, Forms A and B ☛ Performance Assessment Strategies and Activities ☛ Unit 3 Test, Forms A and B	💽 Student Self-Test: A Software Review 💽 Vocabulary PuzzleMaker 💽 Testmaker 🎧 Chapter Digests Audiocassettes

`00:00` If time does not permit teaching the entire chapter, summarize using the Chapter 10 Digests Audiocassettes and the accompanying activities and tests. (Available in English or Spanish.)

Cooperative Project

Have students create a poster that shows the major literary, artistic, musical, and theatrical achievements from 1900 to 1920. Students should include the names of important figures in each field and a brief description of their most famous works. **LEP** 🔲

Suggested Rubric: A Poster. See Performance Assessment Strategies and Activities, p. 37.

Individual Project

Ask each student to imagine he or she is a native of one of the countries in whose affairs the United States intervened. Have students write letters to the President of the United States persuading him to stay out of their nation's affairs. Students should include reasons for their requests. 🔲

Suggested Rubric: Self-Assessment. See Performance Assessment Strategies and Activities, p. 53.

Key to Ability Levels

Teaching strategies have been coded for varying learning styles and abilities.

L1 **BASIC** activities for all students

L2 **AVERAGE** activities for average to above-average students

L3 **CHALLENGING** activities for above-average students

LEP **LIMITED ENGLISH PROFICIENCY** activities

Block Scheduling

Block scheduling differs from traditional class scheduling in the amount of time allotted to each period. The extended timeframe provided by block scheduling affords you the opportunity to implement a greater number of research-oriented and activity-intense projects to motivate and involve your students. Activities that are particularly suited to use within the block scheduling framework are identified throughout this chapter by the following designation. 🔲

TEACHER'S CORNER

NATIONAL GEOGRAPHIC SOCIETY

NATIONAL GEOGRAPHIC SOCIETY PRODUCTS AVAILABLE FROM GLENCOE

To order the following products for use with this chapter, contact your local Glencoe sales representative or call Glencoe at 1-800-334-7344:

- *The Presidents: A Picture History of Our Nation* (CD-ROM)
- *GTV: A Geographic Perspective on American History* (Videodisc)
- *GTV: The American People: Fabric of a Nation* (Videodisc)

ADDITIONAL NATIONAL GEOGRAPHIC SOCIETY PRODUCTS

To order the following products for use with this chapter, call National Geographic Society at 1-800-368-2728:

- *The United States as a World Power: From the 1890s to the 1970s* (Filmstrip)

Chapter Overview

The military presence of the United States in the Philippines, spurred mostly by economic interests, marked its desire for colonies. This story is a microcosm of American foreign diplomacy in the early 1900s, leading up to the involvement of the United States in World War I and the postwar peace conference.

Introducing the Chapter

Point out to students that the progressive reform movement went beyond the national boundaries as the United States became economically and politically involved with foreign nations. After students read the opening vignette, have them respond to the statement that McKinley wanted to "civilize" the Filipinos. Discuss how his words described the United States's sense of superiority and the progressive zeal to improve the lives of others.

 Display the Chapter 10 Teaching Transparency and have students complete the activity sheet.

Extension Activity
Have students complete Beyond the Transparency on the activity sheet for Chapter 10 and present their projects after the class has completed the chapter.

History Journal

Have students investigate Aguinaldo's capture and write a brief summary in their journals. Encourage students to comment on his status in Filipino history and the American government's decision not to support independence for the Philippines.

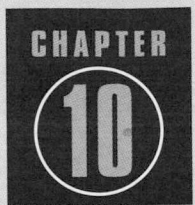

CHAPTER
10

Expansionism and World War I

MARCH 1901: GEORGE WASHINGTON OF THE PHILIPPINES CAPTURED

Senator George F. Hoar once called Emilio Aguinaldo the "George Washington of the Philippines" when Aguinaldo sought to liberate his country from foreign rule. When that rule was Spanish, Hoar and others had encouraged the Philippine liberation struggle.

Aguinaldo had responded in kind, shouting *"Viva los Americanos!"* This enthusiasm, however, did not last long. The United States had promised its support of Philippine independence if Aguinaldo joined the United States in its fight against Spain. After the war, that promise was not kept. President McKinley wanted to "civilize" the Filipinos before granting independence.

When the United States refused to accept Aguinaldo as the legitimate head of government, a struggle ensued. American officials no longer praised him as a founder of his country. Instead, they plotted his capture. Aguinaldo marked the United States as an enemy and led a guerrilla war to rid his country of American forces.

Aguinaldo's capture in 1901 did not end the Filipino struggle. The war lasted for another year.

How the United States became the enemy of Aguinaldo is only part of the larger story of American foreign policy under the progressives—a policy guided by an uneasy mixture of idealism and self-interest. ■

HISTORY JOURNAL

Study the illustration of this famous piece of sheet music, and write your reaction to the mood it creates.

Do you think American soldiers were always welcome in foreign countries? Why or why not?

✚ EXTRA CREDIT PROJECT

Letter Writing Have students write a series of letters between an American soldier fighting in World War I and someone at home. The letters should give a vivid, personal account of the war and the war effort at home. Suggest that students research periodicals, collected letters, or novels of the time for details that will make their letters interesting and accurate. Encourage students to choose a specific battle site involving American troops. In their letters, students may want to incorporate research about the country where the battle occurs.

CULVER PICTURES

Your Song—My Song—Our Boys' Song

OVER THERE

PHOTO © 1918
LIFE PUB. CO.

WORDS AND MUSIC BY
GEORGE M. COHAN

POPULAR LEO. FEIST INC. EDITION NEW YORK
HERMAN DAREWSKI MUSIC PUBLISHING CO. LONDON, ENG.

Norman Rockwell

THIS SPIRITED PATRIOTIC SONG GLORIFIED
THE ROLE OF THE UNITED STATES IN
WORLD WAR I.

293

GLENCOE
TECHNOLOGY

 Videodisc

American History

Side 1, Section G
Title: The Progressive Era and the First World War, 1901–1920
Subject: Overview of American history from symbols of the twentieth century to World War I
Ask: Why did the United States eventually enter the war? *(The government could not ignore the German U-boats, and most Americans supported the democracy that the Allies represented.)*

Side 2
Title: World War I
Subject: Sequences concerning World War I
Ask: Why was the American entry into the war so important for the Allies? *(The war had developed into a stalemate, and the American entry provided a new source of troops.)*

 Performance Assessment

Refer to page 292B for performance assessment activities for this chapter.

 Also see Activity 10 in the Performance Assessment Strategies and Activities for an additional activity as well as for suggested rubrics.

Examining the Visual

George M. Cohan A leading figure in the American theater during the early 1900s, Cohan (1878–1942) wrote more than 40 plays and musicals, and he produced, directed, and starred in most of them. His shows were noted for their high spirits and distinctive, often patriotic, American flavor. Born in Providence, R.I., he performed with his parents and sister in a popular vaudeville act called "The Four Cohans." He began to write songs and vaudeville sketches as a teenager. A movie of his life, *Yankee Doodle Dandy*, filmed in 1942, starred James Cagney. In addition to the title song, it included many of his best songs, such as "Give My Regards to Broadway," "You're a Grand Old Flag," "Harrigan," and "Over There." The illustration for the sheet music of "Over There" was done by a young Norman Rockwell (1894–1978).

FOCUS

Section Objectives

1. Discuss Roosevelt's Big Stick foreign policy and Taft's Dollar Diplomacy.
2. Describe the opinions behind the expansionist policies of Roosevelt and Taft.
3. Explain the importance of the Open Door policy for United States trade.
4. Summarize the growth of United States political and economic involvement in the Caribbean, Latin America, East Asia, the Pacific, and Europe.

Bellringer Activity

While taking attendance at the beginning of the class period, display **Section Focus Transparency 29**, and have students answer the questions. (Or use the blackline master.)

VISUAL INSTRUCTION

Coasting This political cartoon depicting a happy, daring Uncle Sam riding a bicycle was printed in 1898 by Arkell Publishing Company of New York. The wheels of the bike represent the Western and Eastern Hemispheres. The angry and annoyed people standing behind the fence are stylized to represent European countries, including Russia and Austria.

Ask: What did Senator Beveridge say most future wars would be about? *(conflicts for commerce)*

SECTION 1

Becoming a World Power

JANUARY 9, 1900: BEVERIDGE DEFENDS IMPERIALISM

ALBERT J. BEVERIDGE, SENATOR FROM INDIANA, STOOD UP BEFORE THE UNITED STATES SENATE AND SPOKE WITH CANDOR. "Most future wars will be conflicts for commerce," he declared. He argued that the United States must secure new markets. As the United States acquired new markets in the countries of Asia and of Latin America, it should be willing to send troops, if needed, to protect those markets. It should even be willing to **annex**, or put under the dominion of the United States, new territories, so that only the United States could control the markets.

As Beveridge argued his ideas, he recalled that the nation's Founders were not afraid to acquire the territo-

Coasting
The original caption states, "The old horse [Monroe Doctrine] was too slow for Uncle Sam."

ries of Louisiana and Florida and other continental territories farther west. "The founders of the nation were not provincial," he noted. "Theirs was the geography of the world. They were soldiers as well as landsmen, and they knew that where our ships should go our flag might follow."

A Special Destiny
Upholding Freedom Overseas

Progressives responded to the possibility of gaining foreign commercial markets and annexing new territories in vastly different ways. Some

---

AS YOU READ

Vocabulary
► annex
► imperialism
► corollary
► diplomacy
► territorial integrity

Think About . . .
► Roosevelt's Big Stick foreign policy and Taft's Dollar Diplomacy.
► the opinions behind the expansionist policies of Roosevelt and Taft.
► the importance of the Open Door

policy for United States trade.
► the growth of United States political and economic involvement in the Caribbean, Latin America, East Asia, the Pacific, and Europe.

---

294 CHAPTER 10 EXPANSIONISM AND WORLD WAR I

Section 1 Resources

REPRODUCIBLE RESOURCES

📁 Lesson Plan 10-1
📁 Vocabulary and Guided Reading Activity 10-1
📁 Cooperative Learning Activity 10
📁 Section 1 Quiz
📁 Geography in History Activity 10

MULTIMEDIA RESOURCES

🔋 Section Focus Transparency 29
🔋 Map Transparency 10
💿 Testmaker
🎧 Chapter 10 Digest Audiocassette
💿 Student Self-Test: A Software Review
🔋 Chapter Teaching Transparency 10

of them wanted to forge ahead; others did not. They all kept in mind, however, that the United States was different from the many countries of Europe. For decades the United States had a special destiny to uphold liberty and freedom. Some progressives agreed with Senator Beveridge that the people of the United States had a duty to spread the American way of life to lands recently acquired during the Spanish-American War of 1898.

To some extent the idea of exporting American capitalism and democracy to foreign lands overseas gained strength from the Progressive movement itself. The progressives had shown that Americans had the ability to organize and mobilize for social, political, economic, and even moral reform within the United States. The progressives reasoned that they could export their knowledge and products to less developed countries overseas.

Deeply ingrained racial attitudes added support to the American impulse to become involved in the affairs of other countries. Some Americans believed that the people of the Philippines, as well as the people of most of the Caribbean islands, were racially inferior and that they should succumb to the leadership of the United States.

Overseas Markets

Not only progressive ideas but also economic realities helped to spur the debate about the United States's engaging in commercial expansion around the world. Senator Beveridge touched upon the economic realities affecting industries and the workforce:

> Today we are making more than we can use. Today our industrial society is congested; there are more workers than there is work; there is more capital than there is investment. We do not need more money—we need more circulation, more employment. Therefore we must find new markets for our produce, new occupation for our capital, new work for our labor.
>
> —Albert J. Beveridge, in
> *The American Spirit*

Beveridge's cry for new markets struck a responsive chord in American farmers, manufacturers, and investors. As shown by the graph on this page, exports of American products rose dramatically in the early 1900s. Investors, as well as farmers and manufacturers, favored new markets.

Railroads offered a good example of an American industry that was seeking new opportunities for investment. By the turn of the century railroads already crisscrossed North America. Entrepreneurs eagerly looked overseas to lands where railroads had yet to be built. One railroad entrepreneur at the World's Fair Railway Conference spoke eloquently on his desire for commercial expansion:

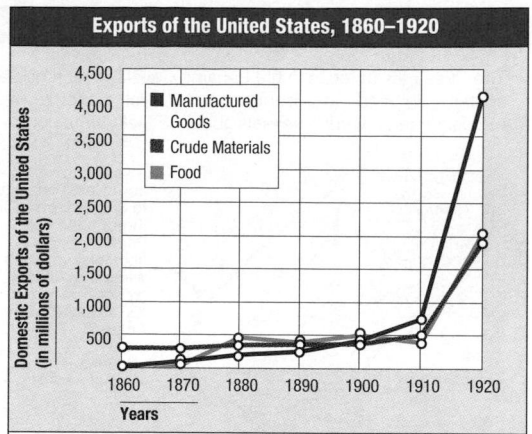

Exports of the United States, 1860–1920

The rise of exports from the United States led to even more demands for commercial overseas markets by American farmers, manufacturers, and investors. *What types of products yielded the greatest number of export dollars in 1910?*

We blow the whistle that's heard round the world, and all peoples stop to heed and welcome it. Its resonance is the diplomacy of peace. The locomotive bell is the true Liberty bell, proclaiming commercial freedom. Its boilers and the reservoirs are the forces of civilization. Its wheels are the wheels of progress, and its headlight is the illumination of dark countries.

> —Railway Conference Proceedings, in
> *Spreading the American Dream*

An Anti-imperialist Plea

Not all Americans favored expansion overseas. In 1902 the *Nation* magazine declared, "We made war on Spain four years ago for doing the very things of which we are now guilty ourselves." In this editorial the *Nation* pointed out that many Americans had previously opposed Spanish exploitation of local peoples, but now the government of the United States engaged in similar exploitation. Some Americans, like the author of the editorial, disapproved of **imperialism,** the policy of establishing economic, political, and military dominance over weaker nations, on humanitarian and moral grounds.

Other anti-imperialists prided themselves as Americans for being different from the Europeans, who were caught up in colonialism and militarism. They shared the sentiments of diplomat Carl Schurz, who lamented that extensive trading overseas would mean "wars and rumors of wars, and the time will be forever past when we could look down with condescending pity on the nations of the old world groaning under militarism and its burdens."

SECTION ONE **295**

TEACH

Guided Practice

L1 Discussion Have students discuss the role of the railroads in commercial expansion during the 1900s. Then ask them to consider how industries today are involved with new investment opportunities internationally.

Show students Map Transparency 10 and have them complete the activity sheet.

GRAPH STUDY

Ask students to explain what the graph shows. Encourage them to suggest reasons for the sudden increase in all three types of exports after 1910. Direct students to use the information here to draw conclusions about who might have been most interested in opening new markets overseas.

Answer: *manufactured goods*

FYI

American Attitudes The excerpt from the Railway Conference Proceedings reveals the sense of superiority many Americans had. They considered themselves to be superior to Asians, Africans, and Latin Americans and felt the United States could bring progress and civilization to other nations. This attitude influenced many foreign policy decisions.

Independent Practice

L1 Writing a Critical Response In 1978 the United States Senate agreed to turn over the Panama Canal to Panama on December 31, 1999. Ask students to write a short paper stating why they agree or disagree with this decision.

👉 Have students complete the Chapter 10, Section 1 Vocabulary and Guided Reading Activity. (Also in Spanish.) **LEP**

👉 Have students complete the Chapter 10 Cooperative Learning Activity.

CHART STUDY

Water flows in and out of the locks by gravity, so no pumps are needed. Locks are used to handle changes in elevation along the course of a canal and variations in tide level near a seacoast. *Cut* is an engineering term for an artificially created passageway or channel.

Answer: *85 feet (26 m)*

FYI

Panama Canal Philippe Bunau-Varilla, an engineer with the French company that had tried and failed to build a canal in Panama, finally negotiated a treaty on behalf of Panama with Secretary of State Hay. The new nation of Panama made Bunau-Varilla its first ambassador to the United States.

OPERATING THE LOCKS OF THE PANAMA CANAL

The three sets of locks in the Panama Canal are rectangular chambers, the largest concrete structures on earth, enabling ships to move from one water level to another by varying the amount of water in the locks. They are capable of raising and lowering vessels about 85 feet (26m), comparable to the height of a seven story building.

A vessel traveling from New York City to San Francisco through the Panama Canal is able to save 7,800 miles (12,600 km) by not having to sail around South America.

Before Panama Canal
After Panama Canal

5,200 miles / 8,370 km
13,000 miles / 20,900 km

The locks are operated by 700 ton (635 metric tons) watertight doors or gates situated at both ends which are perfectly balanced. They are 7 feet (2m) thick, 65 feet (20m) long, from 47 feet (14m) to 82 feet (25m) high, and weigh up to 730 tons (662 metric tons).

Upstream gates closed
Lock chambers
Control station
Downstream gates open
Downstream water level
Downstream water level
Upstream water level
Upstream water level
Power station

Gaillard Cut Pedro Miguel Lock Miraflores Lake
Gatun Locks *Gatun Lake* Miraflores Locks
Atlantic Ocean 85 ft. Pacific Ocean
Level of the Atlantic

1 To move a vessel upstream, where the water level is higher, the water level in the lock is lowered to that of the water just downstream. The downstream gates are opened and the ship moves slowly into the lock.

2 After the ship is secured to posts, the gates close and valves open to fill the lock with water from upstream.

3 As the lock fills, the ship rises to the level of the water upstream.

4 The upstream gates are then opened and the ship passes through.

To move a ship downstream, the process is reversed.

The opening of the Panama Canal reduced the average traveling time of early twentieth-century ships by 60 days. Today about 12,000 ships use its locks every year. *About how many feet can the locks raise or lower ships for passage through the canal?*

Policies in the Caribbean
Consolidating American Power

In spite of anti-imperialist arguments, the political and economic climate at the turn of the century favored commercial expansion, even if commercial expansion meant sending troops to keep order and defend markets. Such commercial and military endeavors suited the temperament of Theodore Roosevelt, who became President in 1901. "I have always been fond," Roosevelt explained, "of the West African proverb, Speak softly and carry a big stick; you will go far." Roosevelt preferred not to brag about American power, but rather to be so strong that other countries would bow to the United States. This philosophy came to be known as the Big Stick. Roo-sevelt's Big Stick policies in the Caribbean included the building of a canal in Panama and the extension of the Monroe Doctrine.

The Big Ditch

A canal across Central America linking the Pacific and Atlantic Oceans had been the dream of people of many different nationalities for years. The inset map above reveals the commercial and military advantages of such a canal. The reduction in travel time would save commercial fleets millions of dollars and increase the efficiency of naval fleets. The inefficiency of naval fleets during the Spanish-American War had underscored the need for a canal. When the war broke out in 1898, the battleship *Oregon* was sent from Seattle to Cuba. Because a canal did not exist at that time, the ship did not arrive until the war was nearly over.

296 CHAPTER 10 EXPANSIONISM AND WORLD WAR I

Meeting Special Needs

Reading Disability Students who have problems with reading comprehension will benefit from this activity, which furnishes practice in organizing information. In order to help students evaluate the policies of Roosevelt and Taft in the Caribbean and in Asia, students may find it helpful to create a chart. As they read the sec-tion, students can list in chart format each action that reflects the foreign policy of Roosevelt or Taft. Have students briefly describe the goal and result of each action. They can later use their charts to evaluate whether or not each action achieved the desired goal.

The United States went on to negotiate the Hay-Herrán Treaty with Colombia in 1903, offering $10 million outright and $250,000 annually for a canal zone 6 miles wide in Panama, which at the time belonged to Colombia. When the Colombian legislature held out for more money, Roosevelt responded angrily and plotted to support a revolution that would make Panama an independent country —one the United States could more easily control.

When the *Nashville,* a gunboat from the United States, arrived on November 2, 1903, the Panamanians began their rebellion. On November 4, 1903, the victorious rebels read a formal declaration of independence, and 2 days later the United States recognized the Republic of Panama. The new government had little choice but to accept the United States's terms for the building of a canal. The cutting of the canal began in 1904 and was completed 10 years later. Roosevelt took pride in having skillfully secured the canal, forging ahead in spite of reservations from Congress and legal advisers. He noted, "I took the Canal and let Congress debate."

Expansion of the Monroe Doctrine

Roosevelt had supported the revolution in Panama against Colombia to secure a canal for American interests. In general, though, he did not look kindly upon revolutions or any kind of disorder in the Caribbean. Striving to keep the region stable for American investment, he put down disorders in various Caribbean countries.

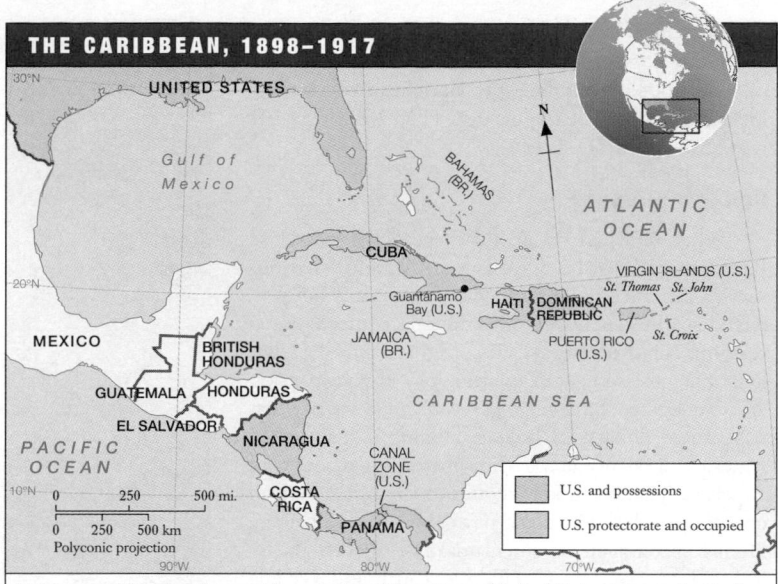

THE CARIBBEAN, 1898–1917

UNITED STATES
Gulf of Mexico
BAHAMAS (BR.)
ATLANTIC OCEAN
CUBA
VIRGIN ISLANDS (U.S.)
St. Thomas St. John
Guantánamo Bay (U.S.)
HAITI DOMINICAN REPUBLIC
JAMAICA (BR.)
PUERTO RICO (U.S.)
St. Croix
MEXICO
BRITISH HONDURAS
CARIBBEAN SEA
GUATEMALA HONDURAS
EL SALVADOR
PACIFIC OCEAN
NICARAGUA
CANAL ZONE (U.S.)
COSTA RICA
PANAMA

0   250   500 mi.
0   250   500 km
Polyconic projection

☐ U.S. and possessions
☐ U.S. protectorate and occupied

The map and the time line on this page show the pattern of United States intervention in the Caribbean from 1898 to 1917. *What islands became possessions of the United States?*

In 1904 and 1905 several European powers threatened the Dominican Republic. They wanted to collect money owed by Dominican customs, but could not do so peacefully because various factions in the Dominican Republic fought for control of customs revenues. Before Germany could send troops to collect the funds owed it, American troops seized Dominican customhouses and supervised the collection of customs fees and the repayment of debts. Roosevelt justified this action by issuing a **corollary,** or proposition, extending the Monroe Doctrine. His corollary asserted that "chronic wrongdoing" or "impotence" gave the United States the right to exercise "international police powers" in the Western Hemisphere. This changed the original intention of the Monroe Doctrine, which was to ward off European colonization. The United States now committed itself to

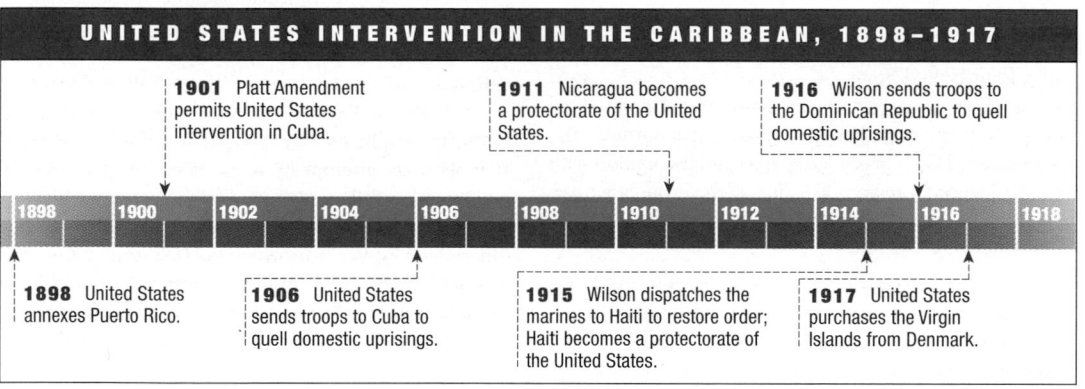

UNITED STATES INTERVENTION IN THE CARIBBEAN, 1898–1917

1901 Platt Amendment permits United States intervention in Cuba.

1911 Nicaragua becomes a protectorate of the United States.

1916 Wilson sends troops to the Dominican Republic to quell domestic uprisings.

1898 1900 1902 1904 1906 1908 1910 1912 1914 1916 1918

1898 United States annexes Puerto Rico.

1906 United States sends troops to Cuba to quell domestic uprisings.

1915 Wilson dispatches the marines to Haiti to restore order; Haiti becomes a protectorate of the United States.

1917 United States purchases the Virgin Islands from Denmark.

SECTION ONE   **297**

FYI

Roosevelt Corollary
Many U.S. legislators opposed Roosevelt's corollary and his actions toward making the Dominican Republic a protectorate. They claimed that his actions were unconstitutional because it was the Senate's right to make such decisions. Most Americans approved of the corollary, however, so the Senate agreed in 1907 to a treaty that maintained United States control of Dominican customs.

Portfolio Project

Writing an Editorial Is the United States still committed to maintaining stability in the Western Hemisphere? Ask students to search through current newspapers and journals for articles that substantiate or refute the policy set by Roosevelt's corollary to the Monroe Doctrine. Then have students share their findings in class.

Have each student research one time line event and write an editorial that either agrees or disagrees with the action. Some students may prefer to draw a political cartoon. Finished products should be placed in individual student portfolios.

CHART STUDY

Ask: What was the purpose of the Platt Amendment?

Answer: *to lay the groundwork for intervention in Cuba*

Missionary Influences
Manchuria is a region in northeastern China rich in natural resources, especially coal and iron. Of its approximately 91 million people, nearly all speak Northern Chinese (Mandarin), the official language of China. Its name derives from the Manchu warriors who conquered northern China in 1644.

Answer: *They built schools and hospitals to teach American educational and medical practices; introduced American goods and products; and displayed American symbols.*

At the Movies

Students may appreciate viewing Nicholas Ray's 1963 movie, *55 Days in Peking.* It portrays the Boxer Rebellion and stars Charlton Heston and Ava Gardner.

FYI

Boxer Rebellion The Boxers were members of a secret society opposed to foreign influence in China and known as the Righteous and Harmonious Fists. In June 1900, Boxers rioted in Beijing and laid siege to foreign legations. Diplomats, foreign civilians, and Chinese Christians were trapped behind barricades for nearly 60 days before an international rescue team came to end the uprising.

maintaining stability in the Western Hemisphere. The commitment would cause Roosevelt, Taft, and Wilson to send troops to a number of Caribbean countries—including Cuba, Nicaragua, and Haiti—during their respective terms of office.

Dollar Diplomacy

When William Howard Taft succeeded Roosevelt as President in 1909, he agreed with the spirit of Roosevelt's Big Stick policies, but not his tactics. Taft preferred a different form of conducting international relations, or **diplomacy.** His program, called Dollar Diplomacy—a somewhat milder approach to expansion and to interference in foreign governments—was one that substituted dollars for bullets. Hoping to gain more American influence in the hemisphere, Taft encouraged American bankers to lend money to Central American countries so that they could pay debts owed to Britain. He also encouraged entrepreneurial investment in the region. Investment in Central American mines, banana and coffee plantations, and railroads increased by $72 million from 1897 to 1914. Loans and investments had the effect of further impoverishing the fragile economies of Central American countries because most of their resources had to be used to pay back money, rather than to provide goods and services to their citizens. Throughout the 1900s, the United States State Department would use its power and influence in Latin America to protect American investors from loan defaults and unfriendly governments.

Missionary Influences In 1903 United States missionary Grace Roberts taught the Bible to Chinese women at a Manchurian outpost. *In what other ways did the missionaries try to spread American values, traditions, and the American way of life to the Chinese people?*

Policies in Eastern Asia
Establishing an American Presence

At the same time the United States consolidated its power in Latin America, it also turned to Asia to look for additional markets and to spread American values. Some Americans regarded Asia as a mysterious and alluring place. Others feared the growing Asian population, especially if it meant large numbers of Asians immigrating to the United States. The stereotypes that emerged in the 1800s lingered into the 1900s and characterized Asians as heathen and exotic—"the lawless hordes," "the yellow peril." Both prejudice against and fascination with Asia influenced foreign policy during the Progressive era.

The Chinese Market

While Americans at the turn of the century feared and discriminated against Chinese immigrants in the United States, the great numbers of people in China itself attracted them. The lure of souls, more than 400

million of them, to convert to Christianity inspired missionaries. The Student Volunteer Movement for Foreign Missions sprang up on college campuses all over the United States. During the 1890s the number of American missions in China doubled to more than 500.

Missionaries not only attempted to convert Chinese people to Christianity, but also built schools and hospitals and encouraged their converts to buy American products. As missionaries became more and more involved in China, they increasingly looked toward the American government for protection and help, especially when they confronted Chinese resentment and hostility. In 1900 missionaries asked for and received American military help in putting down the Boxer Rebellion, an attempt by a group of Chinese rebels to expel foreign influence from China.

Saving 400 million souls inspired missionaries, but 400 million bodies consuming goods inspired American businesspeople. The United States was not alone in its attraction to the Chinese market. China and its promise of wealth attracted Britain, France, Germany, Russia, and Japan as well.

Extending the Content

Comparing Foreign Policies Taft's approach to foreign policy was less aggressive than was Roosevelt's. Taft relied more on investment to secure American interests abroad and less on military intervention. Nevertheless, he did not hesitate to order the marines into action—in Nicaragua, for example—when he felt that American investments were threatened. Roose-velt employed military force in China to quell the Boxer Rebellion. Tell students that the Boxers, so called because they practiced gymnastics and boxing, killed missionaries during the rebellion. Ask why the Chinese might resent missionary activity. *(Missionaries considered the Chinese and their Buddhist beliefs as heathen.)*

By the latter half of the 1800s, these powers competed for influence in a China weakened by a decaying government, the Manchu dynasty. Each power vied for a chance to expand its interests in China. The United States wanted to share in these opportunities as well. Some Americans saw the possibility of building railroads, controlling ports, and selling manufactured products. At least two factors, however, put the United States at a distinct disadvantage: its geographical location, distant from China compared with Russia or Japan; and its navy, inferior to those of Japan, Germany, and Britain.

In 1899 and 1900 Secretary of State John Hay promoted a plan that would strengthen the American position in the scramble to gain control over specific regions of China. He sent notes to Japan and the key European powers asking them to accept the **territorial integrity** of China. In other words, Hay asked them not to control a specific part of China, but to leave the door open to trade for all nations in all parts of China. Because Russia, Japan, Britain, and France were jealous of one another's influence in China, they temporarily agreed with Hay's Open Door plan. The Open Door policy became a key concept in American foreign policy during the first decades of the 1900s. The hope of getting a share of the Chinese market continued to be the driving force in American policies in Asia and played a role in the American decision to annex the Philippines.

FOREIGN EXPANSION IN EASTERN ASIA

AREA OF CONTROL
- British
- French
- Japanese
- Portuguese
- Russian
- United States
- ★ Capital city

The map above shows foreign expansion in eastern Asia begining in 1842. The Philippine Islands provided a strategic location for the United States to establish commerce in eastern Asia. *How did the Open Door policy help the United States gain a foothold in eastern Asia?*

A War in the Philippines

As the United States celebrated its victory of 1898 against Spain, many wondered if the United States would allow the Philippines its independence. Before the Spanish-American War, the Filipinos had been waging a guerrilla war for independence from their colonial ruler, Spain. Filipino revolutionaries initially welcomed American forces into their country as liberators. The United States promised to support Philippine independence if the Filipino revolutionaries fought with the Americans against Spain. Moreover, the United States had drafted the Teller Amendment promising Cuba complete and unconditional freedom at the end of the war, and the Philippines expected similar treatment.

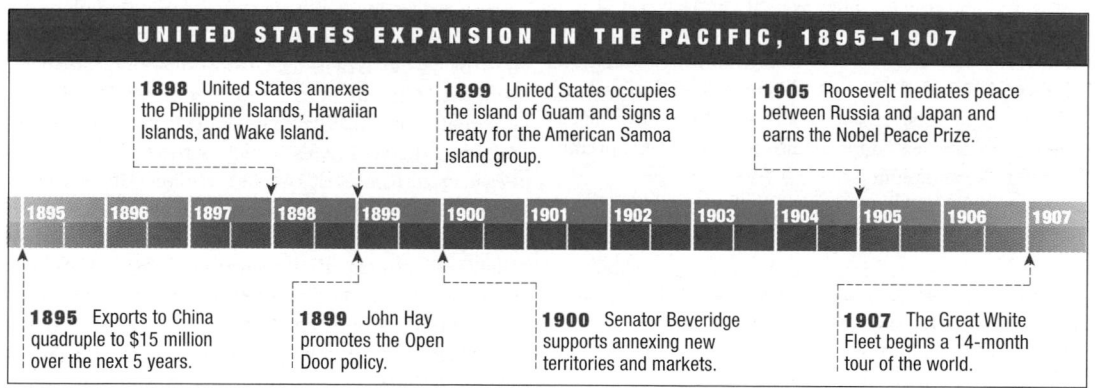

UNITED STATES EXPANSION IN THE PACIFIC, 1895–1907

1898 United States annexes the Philippine Islands, Hawaiian Islands, and Wake Island.

1899 United States occupies the island of Guam and signs a treaty for the American Samoa island group.

1905 Roosevelt mediates peace between Russia and Japan and earns the Nobel Peace Prize.

| 1895 | 1896 | 1897 | 1898 | 1899 | 1900 | 1901 | 1902 | 1903 | 1904 | 1905 | 1906 | 1907 |

1895 Exports to China quadruple to $15 million over the next 5 years.

1899 John Hay promotes the Open Door policy.

1900 Senator Beveridge supports annexing new territories and markets.

1907 The Great White Fleet begins a 14-month tour of the world.

SECTION ONE **299**

ASSESS

Meeting Lesson Objectives

Each section objective is tested by the section review question(s) that follows it in parentheses.

1. Discuss Roosevelt's Big Stick foreign policy and Taft's Dollar Diplomacy. (1, 2, 4, 5)
2. Describe the opinions behind the expansionist policies of Roosevelt and Taft. (2, 3, 4)
3. Explain the importance of the Open Door policy for United States trade. (4, 5)
4. Summarize the growth of U.S. political and economic involvement in the Caribbean, Latin America, East Asia, the Pacific, and Europe. (1, 4, 5)

VISUAL INSTRUCTION

The Great White Fleet The fleet received enthusiastic responses in Japan and other countries on its tour.

Answer: *It would provide a safe and convenient stop between the U.S. and the lucrative Chinese market.*

Curriculum Connection

Economics Discuss how possible investments and other financial gains influenced United States foreign policy decisions in both the Caribbean and eastern Asia.

THE BETTMANN ARCHIVE

The Great White Fleet Destroyers and battleships of the United States Navy were painted a dazzling white, giving the fleet its name. *What would be the advantage to the United States of having a port in Manila?*

To justify annexation of the Philippines, expansionists used the arguments first put forth by President McKinley, who feared "anarchy" and vowed to "educate," "uplift," and "civilize" the population. Not far behind these lofty intentions, other considerations lurked: the Philippines could provide a rich variety of natural resources, as well as a foothold in Asia—a naval stop on the way to China. McKinley decided to hoist the American flag and take control of the country.

Filipino revolutionaries, led by Emilio Aguinaldo, did not accept the American decision to annex the Philippines without a fight. They waged guerrilla war at full force in the Philippines until 1902 and at reduced levels until 1906. In total, 120,000 American troops fought in the war, 4,200 of whom died. Filipinos suffered far greater casualties: at least 15,000 rebels and 200,000 civilians died. The novelist Mark Twain depicted the supreme irony of the situation:

> There must be two Americas: one that sets the captive free, and one that takes a once-captive's new freedom away from him, and picks a quarrel with him with nothing to found it on; then kills him to get his land.
>
> —Mark Twain, "To the Person Sitting in Darkness," 1901

Balancing Russia and Japan

The port of Manila would be a stop on the way to the tempting Chinese market, and this in part explained the willingness of the United States to fight for the Philippines. As Albert Beveridge put it: "[J]ust beyond the Philippines are China's illimitable markets." This dream also shaped American policies with Japan. When Theodore Roosevelt assumed the presidency in 1901, Russia posed the greatest danger to the Open Door policy in China because it controlled the large Chinese province of Manchuria. Like Hay before him, Roosevelt attempted to change the situation through diplomacy.

In 1904 Japan launched an attack against Russia, destroying much of its fleet. Roosevelt opportunistically supported Japan because he regarded Russia as a greater enemy. In 1905 he mediated a peace agreement between the two rivals, which earned him the Nobel Peace Prize. Roosevelt's mediation of the Russo-Japanese War pleased Japan. It gained control over Korea, as well as key ports in China and the railroad in southern Manchuria. Roosevelt, however, made a point of checking Japanese power by negotiating rights for Russia in northern Manchuria and by having Japan agree to non-interference in the Philippines. His main interest was in seeing that no single power reigned supreme in Asia.

Critical Thinking

Demonstrating Reasoned Judgment Work with students to create a list of personal qualities and conditions that are essential for world leaders if they are to be successful mediators between antagonistic nations. Have students read about prominent world leaders, noting the tactics and negotiation strategies they have employed in order to resolve conflicts. Then brainstorm a class list of conflict resolution strategies that students can employ in daily situations.

The 14-month world tour of the Great White Fleet from 1907 to 1909 covered 46,000 miles (74,014 km). *What major canal was the fleet able to use to save mileage and time?*

Entanglement With Europe
Mediating Disputes

As the United States experimented in colonial and militaristic adventures overseas, its attitude toward Europe changed. For almost all of the 1800s, the United States had shunned entanglement with Europe. The democratic institutions of the United States set it apart from the colonial and militaristic ways of Europe—or so popular opinion believed. Nevertheless, when Hay shaped his Open Door policy and when Roosevelt mediated the Russo-Japanese War, they both participated in diplomacy that affected politics in Europe. They also showed that the United States could effectively resolve conflicts of interest in other parts of the world.

In the early 1900s the United States was often called upon to mediate disputes. In 1906 Roosevelt defused a crisis between Germany and France over Morocco. In 1911 Taft arbitrated a dispute between France and Great Britain over Liberia. In part, a desire for trading privileges in Africa motivated the efforts of Roosevelt and Taft in these cases. Far more than keeping an open door for American trade, the two Presidents hoped to keep peace in Europe. By 1900 the economy of the United States depended on markets all over the world. If tensions in Europe were to explode into war, American trade might suffer disastrously.

MAP STUDY

In order to call at as many ports in the Mediterranean as possible, the fleet broke up at Port Said. In separate groups, the ships visited Beirut, Smyrna, Athens, Salonika, Tripoli, Messina, Malta, Algiers, Naples, Villefranche, Marseilles, and Tangier. They rendezvoused at Gibraltar for the trip home.
Answer: *Suez Canal*

Evaluate

Have students complete the Section Review.

☛ ▣ Assign the Section 1 Quiz or use the Testmaker to develop a customized quiz. (Also in Spanish.) **LEP**

Reteach

∩ Have students listen to the Chapter 10, Section 1 Audiocassette. (Also in Spanish.) **LEP**

Enrich

☛ Have students complete the Chapter 10 Geography in History Activity.

CLOSE

Ask students to cite examples of how the United States government used the Big Stick policy, Dollar Diplomacy, and the Open Door policy in the Caribbean and Asia. *(Answers will vary, but should include information about the Panama Canal, loans and investments in Central America, the acquisition of the Philippines, and investments in eastern Asia.)*

Racial Politics

In addition to shifting the balance of power in China, the settlement of the Russo-Japanese War also had worldwide implications for racial politics. That an Asian people, the Japanese, had humiliated a white people, the Russians, kindled new national and racial pride in both the Chinese and the Japanese.

Japan reacted by protesting the 1906 segregation of Japanese children in San Francisco schools. A respected Japanese journal urged Japan to use its navy, if necessary, to end such humiliation:

> The whole world knows that the poorly equipped army and navy of the United States are no match for our efficient army and navy. It will be an easy work to awake the United States from her dream of obstinacy when one of our great admirals appears on the other side of the Pacific.
> —*Mainichi Shimbun*, 1906

Roosevelt soothed Japanese humiliation with "A Gentleman's Agreement" in 1907 that ended school segregation in San Francisco—while at the same time controlling Japanese immigration to California. As the controversy raged, Roosevelt began to calculate. Perhaps the delicate balance of power was shifting. Perhaps it was time for the United States to flex its muscles for the Japanese to see. Roosevelt had been building a stronger and more modern navy, and now he resolved to send the entire American fleet of 16 battleships around the world in a show of might. The Great White Fleet made a special stop in Japan in 1908.

SECTION REVIEW

Vocabulary

1. Define: annex, imperialism, corollary, diplomacy, territorial integrity.

Checking Facts

2. Give examples of how American feelings of superiority shaped United States expansion in the Western Hemisphere and overseas.

3. Give examples of antiexpansionist arguments.

Critical Thinking

Making Comparisons

4. Compare the interests of missionaries with those of investors regarding American involvement in China.

Linking Across Time

5. When Roosevelt felt that Russia might dominate Asia, he favored the Japanese. When Japan became mightier, he decided to demonstrate United States strength with the Great White Fleet. How does the United States today show both friendship toward and rivalry with the Japanese?

SECTION ONE   **301**

Section 1 Review Answers

1. **annex** (294), **imperialism** (295), **corollary** (297), **diplomacy** (298), **territorial integrity** (299)
2. Americans believed that people of the Caribbean and the Pacific were racially inferior and should succumb to American leadership. The United States became the international policeman of the Western Hemisphere and did not honor the independence of the Philippines.

3. disapproval based on humanitarian and moral grounds; the belief that overseas trading would lead to wars
4. The missionaries were inspired by the masses they could convert, while investors were interested in financial gains.
5. shows good relations through investments in and joint ventures with Japanese firms; shows rivalry through the competition in trade

TEACH

Making the Geography Connection

Since the Spanish-American War, a transoceanic canal had been considered essential. A Nicaraguan canal was part of the Republican party platform in the 1896 presidential campaign. In 1900 the Democratic party put building a canal on their platform, too. There was agreement about the need for a canal; the issue was where to locate it.

 ## Mapping Activity

Ask students to search in the library for a map that shows details of the Panama Canal. Have them sketch or trace the map and label Gatun Locks, Pedro Miguel Locks, Miraflores Locks, Gaillard (formerly Culebra) Cut, and the cities of Colón and Panama. Encourage them to put the map up in the classroom.

MAP STUDY

The Caribbean Sea is an arm of the Atlantic Ocean, lying between the West Indies, Central America, and North America.

Answer: *It is one of the narrowest pieces of land between the two oceans.*

Geography: Impact on History

Geography: Impact on History

LOCATION

The Panama Canal

Still considered one of the greatest engineering feats in the world, the Panama Canal cuts more than 50 miles (80.5 km) through the Isthmus of Panama. The story of how the only link between the Atlantic and Pacific Oceans came to be built on this site reads like a novel—full of suspense and intrigue.

A Race for the First Canal

When California entered the Union in 1850, the United States saw that a canal joining its 2 oceans would be a great military and commercial boon. Between 1870 and 1875, the United States Navy made official surveys of desirable locations. In 1881 a United States commission decided that a canal through Nicaragua would be the cheapest to build. It would need locks, but it would involve the least digging. Convinced that a transoceanic canal was in the best interests of the United States, the government bought a concession for a canal from Nicaragua.

About the same time, France obtained a grant to build a canal across the Isthmus of Panama. In a race with the Americans, French government officials persuaded Ferdinand de Lesseps, builder of the Suez Canal, to build it. Although he was 75, de Lesseps could not resist the offer. He formed a private company to raise money and drew up plans for a sea-level canal.

During the 6 years that de Lesseps worked on the canal, 2 out of 3 workers died of yellow fever or malaria. In 1898 de Lesseps had to admit that his plan for a sea-level canal would not work. Cutting through the continental divide was

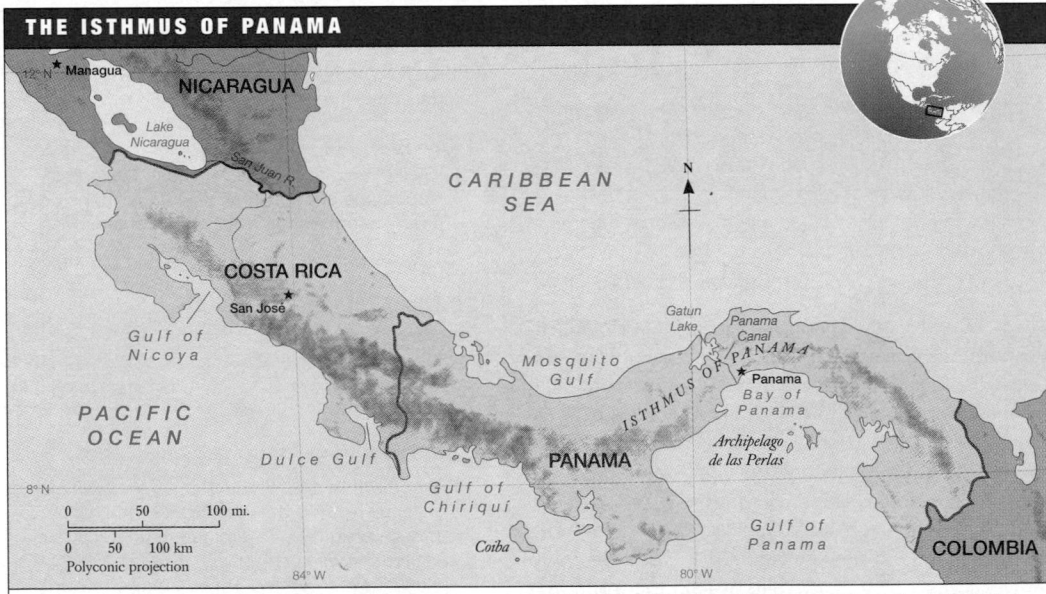

THE ISTHMUS OF PANAMA

Panama is shaped in a long, thin curve, with a roughly east-west orientation. Ships traveling the canal from the Atlantic to the Pacific travel from northwest to southeast. *Why was Panama a good place for a transoceanic canal?*

Geographic Themes

Location Panama is located in the tropics, which is the region that encompasses the equator and extends to about 23 degrees north and south latitude. The canal lies at approximately 9 degrees north latitude and 80 degrees west longitude. Discuss some facts about tropical regions: for example, temperatures at sea level in the tropics are warm year-round; days are long; some areas have rainy seasons or tropical rain forests. **Ask:** Why might tropical characteristics make a canal site more attractive? *(The water wouldn't freeze; there would be more daylight hours to use the canal.)*

not only extraordinarily expensive but almost impossible with the equipment he had. By then he had spent $320 million, at least 20,000 workers had died, and his company had gone bankrupt.

Panama or Nicaragua?

After the Spanish-American War, the United States renewed its interest in an American canal. Congress voted to build a canal in Nicaragua. Shortly afterward, the New Panama Canal Company (a French company that owned what was left of de Lesseps's canal in Panama) offered to sell the United States all of its canal rights and holdings for $40 million.

The United States would probably have stuck to its plan for a Nicaraguan canal, but a few days before Congress was to vote again on the canal's location, a volcano erupted in the French West Indies, killing 40,000 people. Philippe Bunau-Varilla, a representative of the French, seized the opportunity to remind Congress that potentially active volcanoes existed near the lake in Nicaragua where the approved canal was to be built. When Congress finally voted in 1902, Panama was in and Nicaragua was out as the site of the canal—by a margin of only 8 votes.

In the 1880s Nicaragua probably was the better choice for a canal; by the 1900s, Panama was a better site. The larger ships being built at that time would have had great difficulty negotiating the winding canal in Nicaragua. In hindsight, a Nicaraguan canal would have been a costly mistake because it soon would have become obsolete.

CULVER PICTURES

Miraflores Locks From the Pacific, the locks lift ships to Miraflores Lake and the next set of locks. *How long did it take to build the Panama Canal?*

Meanwhile, the intrigue continued. The Panama site depended upon the assent of Colombia, which controlled the isthmus. Colombia balked. Dissidents in Panama had long wanted to break with Colombia. Roosevelt spoke in favor of the rebels, who in turn favored an American canal. After Panama's successful revolt, it signed a treaty guaranteeing the United States the exclusive use and control of a canal zone 10 miles (16 km) wide across the isthmus, "in perpetuity."

Work Begins

In May 1904, a United States commission assumed the French property, and work began again on the Panama Canal. Colonel William C. Gorgas, an American physician who had wiped out yellow fever in Havana, Cuba, spent the first 2 years of construction clearing brush, draining swamps, and cutting out large areas of grass where

mosquitoes carrying malaria and yellow fever lived. At the height of the project, more than 40,000 workers were employed. In 1914 the cost for the completed project came to more than $380 million.

The Panama Canal Today

The Panama Canal remains a crucial commercial and military waterway. Its importance diminished somewhat with the advent of supertankers and large aircraft carriers too large to go through the canal. The high speeds and low operating costs of these ships have undercut the time-saving advantage of the canal. After World War II, the canal's military importance changed, too. The United States Navy decided to maintain fleets in both the Atlantic and Pacific Oceans. Still, an average of 34 oceangoing vessels travel through the Panama Canal each day—for a total of about 12,500 ships every year.

MAKING THE GEOGRAPHIC CONNECTION

1. What was one of the main problems preventing the French from completing the canal?

2. Was the decision to locate the canal in Panama a simple one? Explain.

3. **Location** Where is Panama, and why was a canal there important to an expanding United States?

Making the Geographic Connection Answers

1. Yellow fever and malaria killed most of the labor force; equipment was insufficient.
2. No, there were many variables and unpredictable factors involved in the decision, particularly political considerations and lobbying efforts from different parties.

3. Panama is in Central America. Having a canal there provides easy passage from the Caribbean Sea and Atlantic Ocean to the Pacific Ocean.

VISUAL INSTRUCTION

Miraflores Locks The mountain range near Culebra was 9 miles (14.5 k) wide and 550 feet (168 m) high. At one time 9,000 men worked at excavating the narrow cut, helped by steam shovels and substantial amounts of dynamite.

Answer: *About 22 years (1892–1914), dating back to de Lesseps's initial work.*

FYI

Labor Force Workers on the Panama Canal came from many countries, primarily the United States, Jamaica, Barbados, Spain, Italy, and India. Work crews were mostly segregated, as were housing and dining arrangements. Workers and their families made entire communities in the canal zone. Free but segregated schools were set up. Churches, hotels, laundries, and bakeries were established to support the "canal army."

CLOSE

Nicaragua was favored as a canal site in part because it is closer to the United States and having a canal there would shorten the distance from Boston to Los Angeles, for example. What factors dissuaded Americans from digging a canal in Nicaragua? *(volcanoes, political considerations)* What made Panama a better site over time? *(Today's larger ships could not have navigated a Nicaraguan canal; it would have become obsolete.)*

303

FOCUS

Section Objectives

1. Discuss the conflict between Wilson's belief in self-determination and his interventionist actions in Mexico and the Caribbean.
2. Summarize the events that caused World War I.
3. Describe the struggle of the United States to remain neutral during World War I.
4. Explain the decision of the United States to abandon neutrality and enter the war in 1917.

Bellringer Activity

While taking attendance at the beginning of the class period, display **Section Focus Transparency 30,** and have students answer the questions. (Or use the blackline master.)

VISUAL INSTRUCTION

Headlines Influence Public Opinion The *Lusitania* was a 32,000-ton (29,024 metric ton) Cunard liner. The captain had failed to zigzag his course as he had been instructed to do, and thus got in a German submarine's range.

Ask: What did some Americans demand as a result of this tragedy? *(a declaration of war)*

History and the Humanities

U.S. History and Art Transparency 21—*Allies Day, May 1917* by Childe Hassam

---

SECTION 2

Watching Europe's War

MAY 7, 1915: GERMANY SINKS *LUSITANIA*

Notice! Travellers intending to embark on the Atlantic voyage are reminded that a state of war exists between Germany and her allies and Great Britain and her allies; . . . and that travellers sailing in the war zone on ships of Great Britain or her allies do so at their own risk.
—*New York World*,
May 1, 1915

Headlines Influence Public Opinion
After reading this news report about the sinking of the *Lusitania* and the loss of life that resulted, Americans began to unify against Germany.

The passengers who sailed from New York on the British ship *Lusitania* that day seemingly ignored the warning that appeared in the newspaper. Bound for England, they enjoyed six days of dining and dancing on the luxury liner.

Early in the afternoon of May 7, in calm waters off the coast of Ireland, a German torpedo ripped into the side of the *Lusitania*. The huge ship sank within 18 minutes, taking with it the lives of nearly 1,200 men, women, and children, including 128 Americans.

Germany defended its action on the grounds that the *Lusitania* carried a shipment of arms. It also pointed out that passengers had been warned not to sail in the war zone. Americans, however, were outraged. Some demanded a declaration of war, although most wanted to keep the United States out of the conflict. President Wilson chose to apply diplomatic pressure on Germany and try to hold it accountable for its actions. During the next few months Wilson sent increasingly severe protests to Germany. He insisted that it abandon unrestricted submarine warfare. Americans could no longer merely watch Europe's war.

AS YOU READ

Vocabulary
► self-determination
► coup
► alliance
► neutrality
► dogfight
► emigrate

Think About . . .
► the conflict between Wilson's belief in self-determination and his interventionist actions in Mexico and the Caribbean.
► the events that caused World War I.

► the struggle of the United States to remain neutral during World War I.
► the decision of the United States to abandon neutrality and enter the war in 1917.

304   CHAPTER 10 EXPANSIONISM AND WORLD WAR I

Section 2 Resources

REPRODUCIBLE RESOURCES

📁 Lesson Plan 10-2

📁 Vocabulary and Guided Reading Activity 10-2

📁 Section 2 Quiz

📁 Unit 3 American Literature Reading

MULTIMEDIA RESOURCES

🔊 Section Focus Transparency 30

🎧 Chapter 10 Digest Audiocassette

🔊 U.S. History and Art Transparency 21

💿 Landmark Documents in American History

💿 Lessons of War

💻 Testmaker

💻 Student Self-Test: A Software Review

Mexican Citizens Revolt This is just a portion of a mural found in Chapultepec Castle near Mexico City. It was created by David Alfaro Siqueiros. *How does this mural depict the period of the Mexican Revolution?*

MUSEO NACIONAL DE HISTORIA, MEXICO

Wilson's Foreign Policy
Intervention in Mexico

President Wilson brought to foreign policy an element of idealism that contrasted with the pragmatism of Roosevelt and Taft. He strongly believed that all peoples of the world had a right to **self-determination,** the right to choose the form of government they live under and to control their internal affairs. Yet President Wilson intervened in the affairs of other countries more than any previous President.

Revolution in Mexico

President Wilson, like Roosevelt, upheld the principles of the corollary to the Monroe Doctrine. Wilson maintained stability in the Western Hemisphere for American investment by sending American troops to quell domestic uprisings in Haiti in 1915, in the Dominican Republic in 1916, and in Cuba in 1917. He also continued Taft's Dollar Diplomacy policies by encouraging investors to buy out British enterprises in Central America. Dealing with Mexico and Europe, however, proved problematic for Wilson.

For 30 years the powerful Porfirio Díaz ruled Mexico. The stability of his rule encouraged American, British, and German investors, so much so that they controlled 90 percent of Mexico's mines, railroads, and industry. In 1911, however, Díaz fell from power, toppled by angry peasants whose land had been taken and middle-class Mexicans who had been deprived of their civil and voting rights.

Foreign investors feared that Francisco Madero, who replaced Díaz, would confiscate their property. Foreign diplomats—including the ambassador of the United States—and businesspeople plotted with discontented elements of the Mexican army to overthrow Madero. They wanted to replace him with Victoriano Huerta.

By the time President Wilson took office on March 4, 1913, Huerta had seized power, overthrowing the government and killing Madero in a bloody **coup.** Wilson thought the violence repulsive. He refused to recognize Huerta's government, vowing not to interfere directly.

> We shall have no right at any time to intervene in Mexico to determine the way in which the Mexicans are to settle their own affairs. . . . Things may happen of which we do not approve and which could not happen in the United States, but I say very solemnly that that is no affair of ours.
> —Woodrow Wilson, letter, 1914

American Intervention

A few months after expressing these beliefs, Wilson changed his mind, declaring that he had to teach Mexico to elect good officials. A minor incident concerning American honor was one reason for his shift. In April 1914, Mexican officials arrested several sailors from an American naval vessel in the port of Tampico. Local Mexican officials, as well as Huerta, quickly apologized for the incident. The American admiral in charge demanded a 21-gun salute to the American flag. Huerta demanded the same salute to the Mexican flag. This infuriated Wilson, who used the Tampico incident as a pretext for sending marines to the port city of Veracruz.

SECTION TWO   **305**

TEACH

Guided Practice

L1 Discussion Discuss with students the sinking of the Lusitania. Ask why do you think the United States did not declare war when the liner was sunk?

Curriculum Connection

Language Arts Ask students to write a short paper that considers how the conflict between Wilson's words on page 305 and his later actions in Mexico might have affected his reputation as President and the reputation of the United States in the eyes of the world.

VISUAL INSTRUCTION

Mexican Citizens Revolt David Alfaro Siqueiros (1896–1974) was a Mexican painter and muralist whose art reflected his Marxist political ideology. His murals relate his opposition to tyranny and his sympathy with workers and victims of oppression. Most of his large murals are in government buildings.

Answer: *The mural suggests it was a period of action and even violence; it shows a mass movement of peasants and middle-class workers.*

Facts on File

Landmark Documents in American History Have students review "Treaty With Haiti, 1916" and write a paragraph about the intent of the document.

Cooperative Learning

Creating a Newsmagazine Have students create a special issue of a magazine that reports United States foreign policy from Wilson's inauguration on March 4, 1913, to his war message to Congress on April 2, 1917. Students might include news articles, news analyses, news features, editorials, and political cartoons. Advise students to determine specific tasks for each individual. Suggest that they elect an editor-in-chief to help organize the selection of topics so that the end product contains varied and accurate coverage of the foreign policy of the period.

Independent Practice

 Making a List Have students list ways that U.S. businesses might have helped the Allies economically.

☛ Have students complete the Chapter 10, Section 2 Vocabulary and Guided Reading Activity. (Also in Spanish.) **LEP**

Curriculum Connection

Economics Interested students may wish to research and prepare a short report on one aspect of current United States investment in Mexico.

VISUAL INSTRUCTION

Archduke Franz Ferdinand of Austria Hoping that his sympathy for Slavs would ease tensions between Austria-Hungary and the Balkans, Archduke Franz Ferdinand arranged to tour Bosnia-Herzegovina with his wife, Sophie. As the couple rode through Sarajevo on June 28, 1914, an assassin jumped on their automobile and fired two shots, killing the Duke and his wife almost instantly. The murderer, Gavrilo Princip, was linked to a Serbian terrrorist group called the Black Hand.

Answer: *because Balkan ethnic groups were struggling for independence from Austria-Hungary*

Another cause for Wilson's change of mind was a rumor that a German ship bound for Veracruz carried guns for Huerta's army. In spite of Mexico's ongoing revolution, the occupation of Veracruz outraged most Mexicans. Anti-American riots broke out in Mexico and throughout Latin America. The European press condemned the American military intervention, and so did many Americans. Shocked, Wilson backed off, and agreed to allow the ABC powers—Argentina, Brazil, and Chile—to mediate.

In 1915 Venustiano Carranza followed Huerta as president of Mexico. When Wilson backed Carranza, the rebel leader Pancho Villa struck back by killing 18 American mining engineers in Mexico. Villa's band then crossed the border and killed 17 Americans in the town of Columbus, New Mexico.

Wilson sent an expedition of 15,000 troops into Mexico under the command of John J. Pershing to find and capture Villa. Though they never found Villa, both Mexican and American lives were lost in battle.

Despite this military involvement, the United States failed to control events in Mexico. By late January 1917, Wilson decided to withdraw forces from Mexico. Another, much larger, war raged in Europe.

Archduke Franz Ferdinand of Austria The Archduke poses with his wife, Sophie, and their family. *Why were Franz Ferdinand and his wife assassinated?*

Origins of World War I
Assassination and Alliances

What set off World War I in Europe? The bullet that killed the heir to the throne of the Austro-Hungarian Empire, Archduke Franz Ferdinand, started World War I. Austria-Hungary ruled over a large part of the Balkans, a mountainous area of southeastern Europe where many ethnic groups struggled for their independence. When a Serbian who supported Balkan independence assassinated Franz Ferdinand and his wife, all of Europe held its breath.

Entangling Alliances

By June 1914, almost any troublesome event could have sparked a war in Europe. Russia vied with Austria-Hungary and the Ottoman Empire for control over the Balkans. France, Russia, Britain, and Germany wrangled with one another to control ports and colonies overseas. The new naval force of Germany challenged Britain's long-established naval supremacy. Similarly, Germany's disciplined army struck fear into the hearts of neighboring Russia and France.

To gain security, many European countries organized themselves into a number of formal **alliances,** or unions. Each country that was part of a particular alliance vowed to help the allied countries in case of war. The members of the Triple Entente—which came to be called the Allies—were Britain, France, and Russia. Opposing the Allied Powers were the Central Powers, which consisted of Germany, Austria-Hungary, and the Ottoman Empire.

Because of the alliances, leaders in Europe knew that the assassination of Archduke Franz Ferdinand might mean world war. Russia reacted first by coming to the defense of the Serbian nationalists, in hopes of gaining influence in the Balkans. Russia's move brought the countries of the Triple Entente into the dispute, but Austria-Hungary and Germany needed to protect their interests too. Soon all of Europe erupted into war.

Early Years of the War

Austria-Hungary declared war on Serbia on July 28, 1914, and Germany declared war on Russia and France in the next few days. To avoid the strong defenses on the Franco-German border, German troops stormed through neutral Belgium. As a result, Great Britain, which was committed to the **neutrality,** or impartiality, of Belgium, declared war on Germany on August 4, 1914. A year later France, Russia, and Great Britain lured Italy into World War I on their side by promising Italy territory from the Austro-Hungarian Empire after the war was over. The map of Europe on page 307

Meeting Special Needs

Visual Learners Creating a graphic organizer helps to address the particular needs of visual learners. Students should review the various factors contributing to World War I in order to determine interrelationships. Suggest to students that they create categories such as *Politics* and *Economics* and list specific events or conditions that led up to World War I under the appropriate category. Remind students to include people, places, and countries that were involved. Then help them organize the information into a flow chart to represent visually the interrelationships involved with World War I. Have students explain the connections orally using their flow chart. Explain that creating a graphic organizer is a good strategy for understanding and organizing complex information.

EUROPE DURING WORLD WAR I, 1914-1918

On the map above, find the countries of the Triple Entente and those that made up the Central Powers. Note their positions. Identify and locate the countries that were neutral during the war. *Where did the Central Powers gain the most territory?*

Map legend:
- Central Powers
- Allied Powers
- Neutral countries
- Eastern and Western Fronts
- ★ Capital cities
- German submarine warfare zone

shows that battle lines, or fronts, formed in two principal places: the Eastern Front in Russia and Germany and the Western Front in Belgium and France.

By November 1914, opposing troops on the Western Front faced each other in a deadlock. French troops stopped a German advance toward Paris, but at heavy cost. For more than three years thereafter, each side held the other in check.

On the Eastern Front, the Central Powers rapidly pushed back a disorganized and unprepared Russian army. They advanced across hundreds of miles of territory and took hundreds of thousands of prisoners early in the war. Later Russian successes were less decisive. Hardship among the Russian people, coupled with plummeting confidence in the czar's leadership, threatened Russia's ability to fight at all. Talk of mutiny sped through the troops.

The Fields of Death

World War I resulted in greater loss of life and property than in any previous war. In the Battle of Verdun (February to July 1916), for example, French casualties

Preparing for a Gas Attack During the war many soldiers and civilians were killed by new weapons never before used—submarines, machine guns, poisonous gases, and tanks. *How did the loss of life and property in World War I compare with losses in previous wars?*

LAMBERT/ARCHIVE PHOTOS

numbered about 315,000 and German casualties about 280,000. In the Battle of the Somme, Britain suffered 60,000 casualties in one day of fighting. That battle raged

ABCNEWS INTERACTIVE™

Videodisc

Lessons of War

Side 1, Chapter 5
Title: How Wars Begin—World War I
Subject: Exploration of the reasons behind war, specifically World War I
Ask: What were the major reasons for the outbreak of World War I? *(The system of alliances meant that a very minor incident could initiate war. Once started, it was impossible to stop.)*

See Lessons of War Guidebook page 8 for complete lesson plan.

MAP STUDY

Neutral countries were Albania, Denmark, Norway, Luxembourg, the Netherlands, Persia, Spain, Sweden, and Switzerland.

Answer: *Romania, Russia, Serbia, Poland—the Eastern Front*

VISUAL INSTRUCTION

Preparing for a Gas Attack The odd-looking rubber gas mask filtered out poisonous fumes that could suffocate or blind a soldier. It was also hot and uncomfortable.

Answer: *greater than in any previous war*

Portfolio Project

Achieving World Peace Have students brainstorm to analyze the United States's dilemma over whether to enter the war. They should consider the principles that guided the foreign policy of the time, moral and idealistic beliefs, and emotional and economic interests. Then

ask students to write a personal essay in response to the following question: Is it possible for a nation to become involved in war because it desires a peaceful world? Students should plan to include their final copy in their individual portfolios.

MAJOR EVENTS AND BATTLES OF WORLD WAR I, 1914–1917

November 1914 The Allies declare war on the Ottoman Empire.

April 1915–January 1916 A German-trained Ottoman army defeats combined British forces at the Battle of Gallipoli in Turkey.

March–April 1917 The "February Revolution" occurs in Russia resulting in the end of czarism. Lenin returns to Russia.

1914   1915   1916   1917   1918

August 1914 Germans defeat the Russians at Tannenberg, Germany.

July–August 1915 Massacres occur in Armenia. Russians lose Poland.

October–December 1916 The French regain positions around Verdun.

July 1917 British officer T.E. Lawrence and Emir Faisal lead the Arabs to take the port of Aqaba on the Red Sea.

CHART STUDY

Ask: When did the Ottoman Empire enter the war?

Answer: *November 1914*

VISUAL INSTRUCTION

Life in the Trenches American doughboys were issued a canvas field kit that carried necessary equipment for survival in the trenches. The field kit consisted of cartridge belt, shovel or wire cutters, gas mask, steel helmet, and mess kit. The mess kit contained an oval "meat can" that served as both a skillet and a plate. Two days' worth of rations were contained in metal containers, along with hard biscuits called hardtack and a separate bacon tin. A condiment can had compartments for coffee, sugar, and salt. Infantrymen also carried a tent, tent poles, a bayonet, a compass, and a flashlight.

Answer: *dirt, barbed wire, and a stretch of land called no-man's land*

Curriculum Connection

Literature Encourage students to read Erich Maria Remarque's novel *All Quiet on the Western Front* or other novels, short stories, or poems that were written during or about World War I. Ask each student to write a short paper describing the attitudes of the characters and the author about the war.

from July to November of 1916 and resulted in more than 1 million deaths. In the end, the Allies had advanced the front only about 7 miles. A battle at Tannenberg, in East Prussia, was so disastrous that the Russian general shot himself in despair over the defeat.

The terrible destruction of World War I resulted from a combination of old-fashioned strategies and new technology. Military commanders continued to order massive infantry offensives. The command "Over the top!" sent soldiers scrambling out of the trenches to dash across a field with fixed bayonets, hurling grenades into enemy trenches. The attackers, however, were no match for automatic machine guns that could fire hundreds of rounds in rapid succession. Defensive artillery kept each side pinned in the trenches.

Both sides developed new weapons designed to break the deadlock. In April 1915, the Germans first used poison gas in the Second Battle of Ypres. The fumes caused vomiting and suffocation. When the Allies also began using poison gas as a weapon, gas masks became a necessary part of a soldier's equipment. Flamethrowers that shot out streams of burning fuel and tanks that could roll over barbed wire and trenches added to the destruction.

The fields of battle in World War I extended to the seas and to the skies. Germany challenged Britain's sea power with its submarine blockade. The two navies squared off in a major encounter on May 31 and June 1, 1916, in the Battle of Jutland, off the west coast of Denmark. Both sides claimed victory, but Britain retained control of the seas.

Great advances in aviation came about during World War I. At first planes were used mainly to observe enemy activities. Then Germany developed a machine gun timed to fire between an airplane's propeller blades. This invention led to the use of airplanes for combat. **Dogfights,** the name given to clashes between enemy aircraft, proved deadly for pilots but had little effect on the ground war.

During 1917 France and Britain saw their hopes for victory diminish. A revolution in Russia made the situation seem even more hopeless. In March 1917 (February in old Russian calendar), an uprising in Russia resulted in the overthrow of the czar. In November, Bolshevik party leader Vladimir I. Lenin seized control of the government and began peace talks with Germany. Thus, the Russian Revolution led to the end of fighting on the Eastern Front, freeing Germany to concentrate all its forces on the Western Front. The Allies' only hope seemed to be the entry of the United States into the war.

In the Trenches

The soldiers on the Western Front spent most of their time in muddy trenches. Enemy troops were protected from one another only by dirt, barbed wire, and a stretch of land—called no-man's-land—no more than 30 yards wide in some places.

Life in the Trenches British troops in a 1917 frontline trench near St. Quentin, France, rest before the next military assault. *What stretched between the trenches of enemy troops?*

Extending the Content

Causes of World War I Discuss with students what caused the outbreak of World War I. Aside from the assassination of Archduke Franz Ferdinand, the economic interests and military alliances of the European countries made war probable. Because of the entangling treaties and continued colonial aspirations, Europe was poised for a war that could have been set off by any number of events. Ask students to explain how the Russian Revolution affected the war on the Western Front. *(Russia withdrew from the war, so Germany was free to concentrate its forces on the Western Front.)*

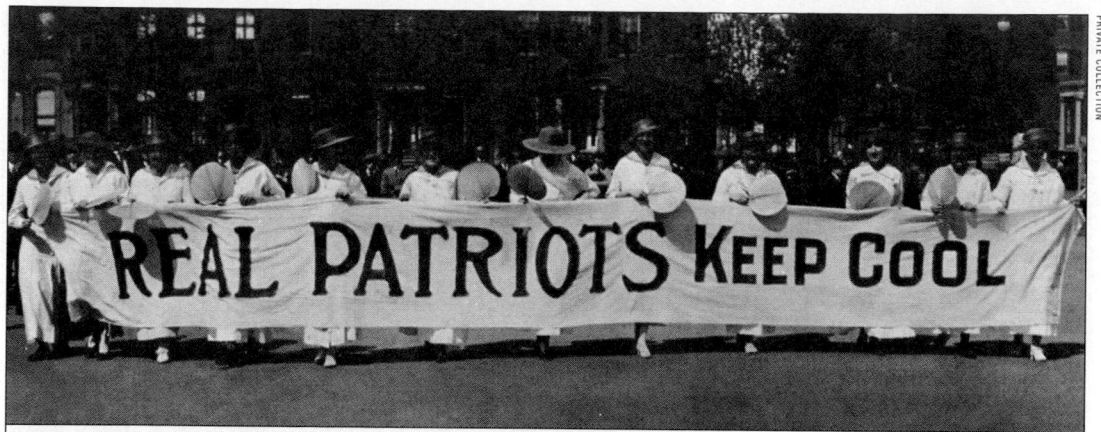

PRIVATE COLLECTION

Pacifists in World War I Early in 1915 several feminist leaders formed the Woman's Peace party to advocate peace. After the *Lusitania* disaster, they staged a protest parade to urge the President to work for peace despite German actions. *What was the myth of neutrality?*

Pacifists in World War I Leaders of the Woman's Peace party, such as Mrs. Henry Ford, organized a telegram campaign in 1915. On Thanksgiving Day President Wilson received hundreds of telegrams supporting peace from people all over the United States.

Answer: *Despite official neutrality political and business sympathies went to the Allies.*

At the Movies

Students may appreciate seeing the winner of the 1930 Academy Award for best picture, *All Quiet on the Western Front,* produced by Universal. The movie, based on Remarque's novel, starred Lew Ayres and was directed by Lewis Milestone.

Facts on File

Landmark Documents in American History Have students review "Appeal for Neutrality, Woodrow Wilson, 1914" and "*Lusitania* Notes, Woodrow Wilson, 1915" and write a paragraph about the intent of one of the documents.

When not shooting at the enemy, soldiers in trenches fought lice, rats, and the dampness and cold, as well as such diseases as dysentery, gangrene, and trench mouth. All understood the suffering they faced daily, if not the politics that created the trenches. By the end of World War I roughly 10 million soldiers and about 20 million civilians had died. Exact numbers were impossible to collect.

Many soldiers took the war as a personal challenge. Others became disillusioned. One German novelist portrayed a young German soldier crying out in protest:

> While they [government officials] continued to write and talk, we saw the wounded and dying. While they taught that duty to one's country is the greatest thing, we already knew that death-throes are stronger. . . . We loved our country as much as they; we went courageously into every action; but also we distinguished the false from true.
> —Erich Maria Remarque,
> *All Quiet on the Western Front,* 1929

Struggle for Neutrality
Evolving Events Lead to War

Woodrow Wilson longed to keep the United States out of World War I. In August 1914, he asked for neutrality, urging the American people not to take sides. He said, "We must be impartial in thought as well as in action." Neither side deserved America's support, thought the righteous Wilson. The American people, however, many of whom had recently **emigrated** from Europe, leaving one country to settle in another,

had their favorite sides. Millions had been born in Germany, England, Austria-Hungary, Russia, Ireland, or Italy; yet, for the most part, they too preferred to distance themselves from the bloodbath overseas.

Myth of Neutrality

While Wilson publicly proclaimed neutrality of the United States, American interests leaned toward the Allies. Although United States businesses traded with both sides in the European conflict, ties with the Allies were much stronger. A representative from the House of Morgan, the mighty New York financial institution, explained:

> Those were the days when American citizens were being urged to remain neutral in action, in word, and even in thought. But our firm had never for one moment been neutral: we didn't know how to be. From the very start we did everything that we could to contribute to the cause of the Allies.
> —Thomas W. Lamont,
> *Manchester Guardian,* January 27, 1920

American political and business sympathy pleased the Allies. They tried to sway popular support to their side too. One of the first things Britain did when war broke out was to cut the transatlantic cable to the United States, so all news had to come through Britain. The reports that arrived vilified the Germans. Soon many ordinary Americans favored the Allies in World War I.

Bryan and the Submarines

Although public sentiment was turning toward the Allies, Secretary of State William Jennings Bryan still favored neutrality—even after German submarines attacked ships on which American citizens traveled. The

---

Cultural Perspectives

Empire's End The last Ottoman sultan with any political and military power was Abdul Hamid. He was responsible for the massacres of Armenian men, women, and children living in Anatolia from 1894 to 1896. Although there was widespread condemnation in the West, the Ottomans did gain one friend among European nations—Germany. Hamid was overthrown in 1908 by the Committee of Union and Progress (CUP). Two important members of CUP, Enver Bey and Talaat Bey, forged the alliance with Germany that would carry into World War I. Abdul Hamid, with family and servants, returned to Constantinople, where he died peacefully in 1918. Ask students to research the Ottoman culture and its relation to the Armenian tragedy and to the subsequent involvement in World War I.

ASSESS

Meeting Lesson Objectives

Each section objective is tested by the section review question(s) that follows it in parentheses.

1. Discuss the conflict between Wilson's belief in self-determination and his interventionist actions in Mexico and the Caribbean. (1, 2, 5)
2. Summarize the events that caused World War I. (1, 3)
3. Describe the struggle of the United States to remain neutral during World War I. (1, 4)
4. Explain the decision of the United States to abandon neutrality and enter the war in 1917. (4, 5)

A German Submarine This camouflaged German submarine, or U-boat, was typical of those that operated from 1914 to 1918. *What strategy did the Germans employ to break the British blockade of Germany?*

Germans had developed this new weapon, the submarine, and they used it to surprise enemy merchant ships in the war zone Germany monitored around the British Isles. That strategy was in response to a British blockade of Germany that had effectively begun to starve the German people. Bryan could see that both sides had military reasons for acting as they did. He encouraged Wilson to forbid Americans from traveling in the submarine zones as a way of avoiding trouble with Germany. Wilson argued, however, that free and safe travel was a right of citizens of a neutral country.

The issue reached a crisis on May 7, 1915, when German submarines attacked the *Lusitania*, a British passenger ship. More than 1,000 passengers died, including 128 Americans, as the torpedoed ship quickly sank. Germany knew that the *Lusitania* secretly carried arms and had warned ahead of time that it might be a target for attack.

Nevertheless, Americans were outraged. "Damnable! Damnable! Absolutely hellish!" cried Billy Sunday, a fiery evangelist of the time. In spite of the tragedy, Wilson continued to believe that Americans should not be restricted from traveling the seas. In protest, Bryan resigned.

Reelection

The American people reelected Woodrow Wilson to the presidency in 1916 in a close race against Charles Evans Hughes. American voters responded to the Democratic campaign slogan: He kept us out of war! That slogan, however, made Wilson nervous. In spite of his neutrality efforts, he knew that the nation was edging closer to entering World War I.

The pressure on Wilson to enter the war came partly from his own moral commitment to the Allies; but it came also from American business leaders and

EVENTS LEADING UNITED STATES TO ENTER WORLD WAR I, 1914–1917

1915 Propaganda from the Allies, particularly regarding German atrocities in Belgium, influences U.S. citizens.

1916 Congress passes National Defense Act expanding the regular army, authorizing a national guard, and establishing the Reserve Officers Training Corps (ROTC).

1917 Germans sink U.S. supply ships *City of Memphis*, *Illinois*, and *Vigilante*.

1914 1915 1916 1917 1918

1914 U.S. floats loans and provides food and goods to the Allies.

1915 Bomb scares in the U.S. are linked to anarchism and the war in Europe.

1916 Allies suffer major losses in the war and look to the U.S. for support.

1917 After breaking off diplomatic relations with Germany, Wilson asks Congress to arm U.S. merchant ships.

310   CHAPTER 10   EXPANSIONISM AND WORLD WAR I

Critical Thinking

Making Inferences Remind students that to infer means to draw a conclusion based on facts and on what is known about the usual outcome of similar situations. Then ask students to make an inference about the Americans who wanted the United States to remain neutral. Discuss and list the various rea- sons these citizens had for not entering World War I. Ask students to write a paragraph giving their opinion about whether or not a nation should require citizens to fight in a war even if they do not understand its causes or they dis- agree with those causes.

Campaigning for Reelection This campaign van was used by supporters of President Wilson in 1916. *Why did President Wilson want to have a say in the peace settlement after World War I?*

investors. American companies had invested deeply in an Allied victory. By 1917 American loans to the Allies totaled $2.25 billion. If Wilson helped the Allies win, the money would be paid back. Even more important, his commitment to the Allies would ensure a place for American investment in postwar Europe.

In addition to these pragmatic motives, the idealistic Wilson truly wanted to have a say in a peace settlement. He longed to make sure that after World War I, no other war would ever threaten the world again. He felt that no one would listen seriously to his ideas unless the United States had actually proved itself in battle. Ironically, Wilson's desire for a peaceful world led him closer to war.

Closer to War

Several events led the United States to finally enter the war. In January 1917, a German official named Arthur Zimmermann cabled the German ambassador in Mexico instructing him to make an offer to the Mexican government. Zimmermann proposed that Mexico ally itself with Germany. In return, Germany would make sure that after the war Mexico would receive some of the region that it lost to the United States in 1848. A British official intercepted Zimmermann's telegram and spread the news to the United States. This incident occurred shortly after Wilson withdrew from the Pancho Villa chase, so the Zimmermann note made many Americans eager to humiliate both Mexico and Germany.

Another declaration from Germany led the United States even closer to war. On January 31, 1917, Germany announced an unrestricted submarine campaign. German people were starving, and the country was desperate to end the war. Because the United States was not truly neutral, the Germans felt they had nothing to lose by an onslaught. The Germans sank one ship after another, including the American supply ship *Illinois* on March 18, 1917.

By April 1, President Wilson was brooding and pacing the floor. "Once I lead these people into war," he confided to editor Frank Cobb, "they'll forget there was ever such a thing as tolerance. To fight you must be brutal and ruthless, and the spirit of ruthless brutality will enter into the very fabric of our national life." In spite of his doubt and anguish, on April 2, 1917, the President stood before the United States Congress and asked its members to declare war on Germany.

> It is a fearful thing to lead this great peaceful people into war, into the most terrible and disastrous of all wars, civilization itself seeming to be in the balance. But the right is more precious than peace, and we shall fight for the things which we have always carried nearest our hearts,—for democracy, for the right of those who submit to authority to have a voice in their own Governments, for the rights and liberties of small nations. . . . [W]e dedicate our lives and our fortunes, everything that we are and everything that we have, . . . America is privileged to spend her blood and her might for the principles that gave her birth and happiness and the peace which she has treasured.
>
> —Woodrow Wilson,
> War Message, April 1917

SECTION REVIEW

Vocabulary
1. Define: self-determination, coup, alliance, neutrality, dogfight, emigrate.

Checking Facts
2. How did Wilson continue the policies of Roosevelt and Taft?

3. What single act set off World War I? Why?

Critical Thinking
Drawing Conclusions
4. Why was the British government so eager to inform the United States of Germany's offer to Mexico? What did it hope to gain? How did this information affect Wilson's thinking on the war?

Linking Across Time
5. Wilson professed a belief in self-determination; however, he intervened in the affairs of other nations on several occasions. The United States sent troops to Grenada in 1983 and to Kuwait in 1991 to protect the interests of the United States. Do you think strong nations should have the right to intervene in the affairs of weaker nations? Why or why not?

Evaluate
Have students complete the Section Review.

Assign the Section 2 Quiz or use the Testmaker to develop a customized quiz. (Also in Spanish.) **LEP**

Reteach
Have students listen to the Chapter 10, Section 2 Audiocassette. (Also in Spanish.) **LEP**

Enrich
Have students complete the Unit 3 American Literature Reading.

VISUAL INSTRUCTION

Campaigning for Reelection The slogans on President Wilson's campaign van pledged preparedness and peace along with prosperity.

Answer: *to make sure that no other war would ever threaten the world again*

Facts on File
Landmark Documents in American History Have students review "Zimmermann Note, 1917" and "Declaration of War Against Germany ('Make the World Safe for Democracy'), Woodrow Wilson, 1917" and write a paragraph about the intent of one of the documents.

CLOSE

Have students discuss whether the United States should have entered World War I. *(Answers will vary but should mention the contributing factors reviewed in this chapter.)*

Section 2 Review Answers

1. self-determination (305), **coup** (305), **alliance** (306), **neutrality** (306), **dogfight** (308), **emigrate** (309)
2. He upheld Roosevelt's corollary by sending troops to the Caribbean. He continued Taft's Dollar Diplomacy by encouraging United States investors to buy out British enterprises.
3. Archduke Franz Ferdinand's murder;

because of the many alliances among European countries
4. At that time the United States was still neutral, and Great Britain hoped it would join the Allies. The information made Wilson decide to enter the war.
5. Answers will vary but should include information about humanitarian and world peace efforts.

311

Science, TECHNOLOGY, and Society

The Radio

With the invention of the radio, communication improved worldwide. The radio connected governments, as well as average citizens, providing information about international events and ending isolation across the globe. As a form of entertainment, the radio also impacted everyone's leisure time.

THE MARCONI COMPANY

GENERATING POWER

The use of wireless telegraphy during World War I affected the development of offensive and defensive fronts. This soldier is pedaling a stationary bike to generate the power needed to make radio contact between troops. The primary concern was communicating information between a fixed and a moving point.

IMPERIAL WAR MUSEUM

KDKA RADIO PHOTO, PITTSBURG, PA

THE "MUSIC BOX"

Frank Conrad, an engineer for Westinghouse, began broadcasting music from his garage after World War I. As interest in the broadcasts grew, Harry P. Davis, a Westinghouse vice president, launched the sale of the first commercial radio receiver in 1920 called the "music box" (above).

THE EVOLUTION OF RADIO BROADCASTING

Pre-1900s	1900s	1910s	1920s
ELECTROMAGNETIC WAVES, the precursor to radio, radar, and television, are demonstrated by James Maxwell in 1864.	**ELECTROMAGNETIC WAVES** first transmit sounds in a 1900 experiment by R. A. Fessenden.	**TRIODE VACUUM TUBE,** which allows for amplification of weak signals, is developed by Lee De Forest in 1906.	**BROADCASTING INDUSTRY,** including hundreds of radio stations and millions of receivers, is envisioned by David Sarnoff in 1916.

Background Information

Radio Broadcasting Evolves As wireless telegraphy (the wireless transmission of signals) changed to radio telephony (the wireless transmission of speech and music), the term *broadcasting* came into use. It referred to the transmission of sound to a small audience. People listened to the broadcasts by sharing headphones. With De Forest's invention of the triode vacuum tube, which amplified the signals, similar broadcasts reached more people. De Forest made several successful radio transmissions over a wide area, including a Caruso concert from the stage of the Metropolitan Opera House in New York City on January 12, 1910. He erected a transmitter on the roof of the opera house.

WESTINGHOUSE

TRANSMITTING SIGNALS

On November 2, 1920, KDKA of Pittsburgh conducted the world's first scheduled broadcast. By the mid-1920s, KDKA personnel were testing an experimental antenna, carried aloft by a big balloon (left). This was a far cry from the first mobile radio in 1901 (below), with its cylindrical aerial that allowed telegraphic transmissions around the country and to sailing vessels. Guglielmo Marconi, standing at the extreme right, is credited with the invention of wireless telegraphy.

THE MARCONI COMPANY

FYI

Radio and Radar Astronomy In 1932 American radio engineer Karl Jansky was investigating radio disturbances that interfered with transoceanic telephone service. He found that the disturbances were caused by cosmic "static," which he attributed to interaction between electrons and ions in space. This insight led to study of celestial bodies by examining the radio-frequency energy they emit or reflect. Radar reflections were first detected off the moon in 1946.

ENTERTAINMENT

Singing into an early microphone, Dame Nellie Melba's clear soprano soared across European and Atlantic airwaves on June 15, 1920, from the Marconi wireless factory in Chelmsford, England. This was the first advertised program of entertainment on the radio—until then the radio had been used mostly as a news service. Civilians were prohibited from using the wireless during the war.

THE CHANGING SHAPE OF RADIO

PORTFOLIO PROJECT

How has the radio changed since its inception in 1920? What impact has this form of communication had on other sectors of life? Make a collage labeling the different forms of radio technology available today.

Block Scheduling

The Portfolio Project on this page provides an excellent opportunity to enrich and extend the key elements of this feature.

| 1930s | 1940s | 1950s | 1960s–1990s |

FM RADIO becomes available in 1929.

TRANSISTOR RADIOS become commercially available in 1952.

STEREOPHONIC RADIO BROADCASTING begins in the 1960s. Sony introduces the first personal stereo, the Walkman, in 1979. By 1982 AM radio stations begin broadcasting in stereo.

SCIENCE, TECHNOLOGY, AND SOCIETY **313**

CLOSE

Discuss with students how advances in radio technology have affected their lives. Ask students to describe new models they have seen and recent changes in uses of radios. (*Answers will vary, but students should include information on the portability of radios, examples being boom boxes and Walkmans, and radio's cultural influences.*) Invite students to predict advances in radio for the future. (*Answers will vary, but students should support them with information they have learned from this feature and any research they have completed.*)

Portfolio Project

The Sinking of the _Titanic_ Have students research and write a summary about the role of wireless telegraphy during the sinking of the _Titanic_. Suggest that students also examine the connection to David Sarnoff, who eventually became president of RCA. Sarnoff became a leading figure in broadcast development in the United States, but at the time of the _Titanic_ disaster in 1912, he picked up the wireless message that the _Titanic_ had sunk. It was he who communicated this information to the press in New York City in time for the morning editions. Invite volunteers to share their projects, including visuals of the _Titanic_, before filing them in their portfolios.

PORTFOLIO PROJECT

FOCUS

Section Objectives

1. Describe the United States's mobilization efforts for World War I.
2. Describe American military participation in World War I.
3. Discuss the negative effect the war had on civil liberties.
4. Explain how the war effort at home both furthered and hindered the reform movement of the Progressive Era.

Bellringer Activity

 While taking attendance at the beginning of the class period, display **Section Focus Transparency 31,** and have students answer the questions. (Or use the blackline master.)

VISUAL INSTRUCTION

Patriotic Sales Print media played a pivotal role in shaping and managing public opinion about the war. Newspapers, posters, and magazines urged support of the war effort.

Ask: What is the threat behind this poster's plea? *(that American values like liberty will be lost if people don't buy bonds)*

Curriculum Connection

Literature American author Katherine Anne Porter (1890–1980) was best known for her short stories. She often set stories in the American South or Southwest. Porter wrote *Pale Horse, Pale Rider* in 1939.

SECTION 3

World War I: There and Here

FALL 1918: INFLUENZA AND BONDS SWEEP NATION

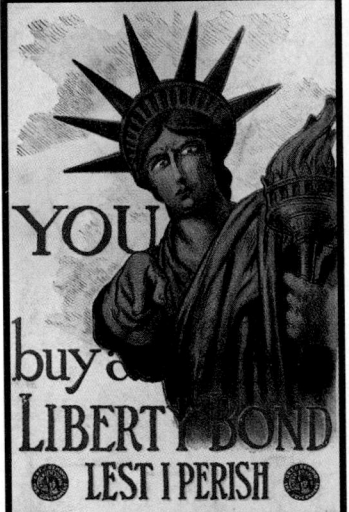

CULVER PICTURES

Patriotic Sales
Emotional appeals and celebrity endorsements characterized the sale of Liberty Bonds during World War I.

IN HER NOVELLA *PALE HORSE, PALE RIDER*, KATHERINE ANNE PORTER DESCRIBES LIFE ON THE HOME FRONT THROUGH THE EXPERIENCES OF A WOMAN NAMED MIRANDA. During 1918 Miranda's problems, like those of other young working women, were intimately linked to the war. One morning, she awakened with a headache and a queasy feeling in her stomach—symtoms of influenza. This disease had infected the people of Denver, where Miranda worked, and other cities across the nation. Thousands died. The deadly epidemic struck other countries too. It proved fatal to more American soldiers than did the war itself. About 57,000 American soldiers died from influenza while the United States was at war; about 53,500 died in battle.

Miranda tried to ignore her headache and the funeral processions that wound down the city's streets. She needed to concentrate on two other problems. She had fallen in love with a young man, Adam, who had to leave for the front in a few days. She also was being hounded to buy liberty bonds—loan certificates the government issued to help pay for the war. Bonds were sold at rallies throughout the country. Miranda could not afford a bond, but she was afraid she would lose her job if she refused to buy one.

That evening Miranda met Adam. The couple strolled to the theater. They could not, however, escape the hawking of the war. When the curtain rose for the third act, the audience beheld, not the actors, but an American flag draped

---

AS YOU READ

Vocabulary
► mobilization
► conscription
► doughboys
► propaganda

Think About . . .
► what efforts the United States made in mobilizing for World War I.
► the nature of American military participation in World War I.

► the negative effect the war had on civil liberties.
► how the war effort at home furthered and hindered the reform movement of the Progressive era.

314 CHAPTER 10 EXPANSIONISM AND WORLD WAR I

Section 3 Resources

REPRODUCIBLE RESOURCES

📁 Lesson Plan 10-3
📁 Vocabulary and Guided Reading Activity 10-3
📁 Unit 3 Case Study

📁 Section 3 Quiz
📁 Unit 3 American Literature Reading
📁 Skill Reinforcement Activity 10

MULTIMEDIA RESOURCES

🎞 Section Focus Transparency 31
💿 Landmark Documents in American History
🎞 U.S. History and Art Transparency 20
🎧 American Music: Cultural Traditions
📷 Testmaker
🎧 Chapter 10 Digest Audiocassette
💿 Student Self-Test: A Software Review

across a backdrop. In front of the flag, a middle-aged man began to sell Liberty Bonds. All of the words Miranda had ever heard about the war ran together in her mind:

> WAR to end WAR, war for Democracy, for humanity, a safe world forever and ever—and to prove our faith in Democracy to each other, and to the world, let everybody get together and buy Liberty Bonds and do without sugar and wool socks.
>
> —Katherine Anne Porter,
> *Pale Horse, Pale Rider,* 1939

Mobilization
Military Draft and Civilian Pressure

The pressures Miranda felt to back the war effort were typical for her generation. When President Wilson asked Congress to declare war, he knew that he needed the support of all Americans. War, he said, would involve **mobilization,** or preparation, by citizens and business enterprises. Wilson warned that any disloyalty would be met "with a firm hand." Support in Congress for the war resolution was very strong. To fund the war, Wilson raised income taxes and organized a vigorous Liberty Bond campaign. Secretary of the Treasury William Gibbs McAdoo also pressed the public for financing. "A man who can't lend his government $1.25 per week at the rate of 4 percent interest," he said, "is not entitled to be an American citizen."

Drafting an Army

In addition to raising money, the President initiated **conscription,** or compulsory enrollment in military service. The United States had not enforced a draft since the Civil War, and some Americans spoke out against it. "I feel it is my sacred duty to keep the stalwart young men of today out of a barbarous war 3,500 miles away," said Congressman Isaac Sherwood. Jeannette Rankin of Montana, the first woman elected to Congress, also opposed both conscription and the war declaration.

Many progressives, however, supported the war and the draft. They argued that the draft might prove to be a great equalizer. Young men from upper and lower classes and from many ethnic origins would serve side by side, learning to live together as brothers. This equality might then translate into reforms at home.

Secretary of War Newton D. Baker called June 5, 1917, the official day of registration for the draft, "a festival and patriotic occasion." Draft registration proceeded in the midst of local fairs and picnics. Men aged 21 to 30 (later the draft age was extended from 18 to 45) registered by the millions. A lottery decided those to be actually inducted into the military. About 11,000 women also volunteered as nurses, clerical workers, and telephone operators.

Segregating African Americans

The military was not an equalizer for African Americans, who were strictly segregated. The National Association for the Advancement of Colored People (NAACP) demanded that African Americans be allowed to become officers. Its persistence paid off, when more than 600 African Americans graduated from an officer-training program at Fort Des Moines. The military, however, did not give high rank to any of these officers. White officers commanded the African American Ninety-Second Division. Some African American troops were integrated with white French troops once they arrived in Europe. This tolerance abroad added to African Americans' discontent with prejudice back home.

Segregated Military The Fifteenth Negro Regiment shown above was made up of New Yorkers and nicknamed "the Buffalos." *How did the experience of African Americans in the war spur the desire for equal rights at home?*

Fighting Over There
American "Pep" and Strength in Numbers

Under the command of General John J. Pershing, the United States infantry—nicknamed **doughboys** after a cake traditionally baked for sailors—began coming ashore in France in late June 1917. The Allies

TEACH

Guided Practice

L1 Discussion The issue of whether or not to enter World War I was a very emotional one. Have students predict how the American public would participate in the war effort once the United States had officially committed itself.

Independent Practice

L1 Writing Have students write a short analysis of why the progressives' hope that the draft would be "a great equalizer" became meaningless in regard to the treatment of African Americans.

📁 Have students complete the Chapter 10, Section 3 Vocabulary and Guided Reading Activity. (Also in Spanish.) **LEP**

VISUAL INSTRUCTION

Segregated Military These soldiers were part of the 369th Infantry Regiment that served in the trenches for 191 days without losing ground to the Germans, giving it the best record of any United States Army infantry regiment in World War I.

Answer: *They had sacrificed just as other Americans had; interracial tolerance in France made American segregation harsher by comparison.*

Facts on File

Landmark Documents in American History Have students review "Selective Service Act of 1917" and write a paragraph about the intent of the document.

Cooperative Learning

Planning Promotional Campaigns Organize students into four groups. Have one group create a plan to promote conscription; another group plan to promote food conservation; a third group a plan to rouse support for the war effort from business and labor organizations; and a fourth group a plan to promote pacifism or opposition to the war. Have each group research its topic and then choose a spokesperson to present the plan. Make sure students find an appropriate way to divide and complete the work. 👐

History and the Humanities

U.S. History and Art Transparency 20—*I Want You for the U.S. Army* by James Montgomery Flagg

American Music: Cultural Traditions— "War Song Hits" ("For Your Country and My Country," "Goodbye Broadway, Hello France," "I Don't Know Where I'm Going But I'm on My Way," "Over There") by the Columbia Quartette.

VISUAL INSTRUCTION

Preparing for Battle Most of the artillery used by the A.E.F. was British or French ordnance. Of 3,499 pieces of artillery, only 477 were American-made, and only 130 of those were used in combat.

Answer: *the Western Front*

Block Scheduling

Have students complete the Unit 3 Case Study to enrich their understanding of pacifist protest during World War I.

---

desperately needed "men, men, men," as one French officer put it. Although most Americans fought separately from the European units, the Allies welcomed the relief the American Expeditionary Force (A.E.F.) offered.

The doughboys arrived in France singing "Pack Up Your Troubles in an Old Kit Bag" and "It's a Grand Old Flag." Aside from their confident air, the doughboys were unprepared for war. Pershing, known for his unbending will and a personality embittered by the death of his wife and children in a fire, described the problem: "A large percentage of them [American troops] were ignorant of practically everything pertaining to the business of the soldier in war." By late 1917, about 200,000 had arrived. Though they lacked training, American soldiers gained a reputation for courage and "pep."

The Eastern Front

The A.E.F. filled a breach left by heavy Allied losses on the Western Front and Russia's pullout from the war. Russia had suffered huge losses on the Eastern Front. Its new revolutionary government wanted no part of what they considered to be the czar's imperialistic—and now unwinnable—war. Russia signed a peace treaty with Germany on March 3, 1918, and gave up large amounts of territory, including Finland, Poland, Ukraine, and the Baltic states.

Yet Germany's strength was waning. American troops and military hardware added punch to the Allied attack in the west, and the military position of all of the Central Powers deteriorated rapidly in the fall of 1918. Bulgaria surrendered on September 29. British forces caused the surrender of the Ottoman Empire on October 30. Italy, with the help of France and Britain, brought about the surrender of Austria-Hungary in November.

World War I Casualties*		
Country	Killed	Wounded
Russia	1,700,000	4,950,0000
France	1,358,000	4,266,000
British Empire	908,400	2,090,000
Italy	650,000	947,000
Romania	335,700	120,000
United States	116,500	234,400
Germany	1,773,000	4,216,000
Austria-Hungary	1,200,000	3,620,000
Turkey	325,000	400,000
Bulgaria	87,500	152,400

*Figures are approximate. Not all countries are listed.

World War I devastated many countries. *Which three countries suffered most of the casualties?*

The Expeditionary Force's Role

More than 2 million American soldiers went to France during the war, the peak arriving in July 1918. Of these troops, nearly 1.4 million took part in active combat. Most were in the army or marines, but 50,000 United States naval forces, under the command of William S. Sims, were indispensable too. They convoyed troop transports and helped the British fleet chase submarines and keep German ships out of the North Sea.

Beginning in March 1918, the Germans launched a last desperate series of offensives on the Western Front. In June United States troops helped the French forces block a German advance at Château-Thierry. American troops then captured the town of Cantigny. The turning point of the war was at the Second Battle of the Marne in July. About 85,000 American troops helped end the German offensive. After that, the Allies advanced steadily.

Britain and France attacked the Germans near Amiens, and General Pershing led United States troops to a major victory at St.-Mihiel. The last major offensive of the war took place between the Meuse River and the Argonne Forest, beginning in September 1918. More than 1 million

Preparing for Battle At the end of the St.-Mihiel offensive, about 600,000 American troops moved northeast to the Meuse-Argonne region. Bad roads and tired horses slowed movement of supplies to 2 miles (3.22 km) an hour. *On which front were American troops concentrated?*

Meeting Special Needs

Reading Disability To help improve reading comprehension for students with reading difficulties, help students create a list of key terms for this section. Student pairs might quiz each other about the meaning and importance of each term on the list.

American troops took part in a campaign that finally convinced the Germans they could not overcome the superior strength of the Allies. Germany signed the armistice on November 11, 1918, and World War I came to an end.

Americans had fought in Europe for just over a year. They felt neither the despair nor the suffering of their European counterparts. Many doughboys, never away from home before, regarded the "Great War" as a dashing adventure, a romantic scene from movies they had seen in boot camp.

Not all soldiers, however, could romanticize the war. They had witnessed sobering scenes such as this one described in the diary of an American draftee:

> Many dead Germans along the road. One heap on a manure pile. . . . Devastation everywhere. Our barrage has rooted up the entire territory like a ploughed field. Dead horses galore, many of them have a hind quarter cut off—the Huns need food. Dead men here and there.
>
> —Battlefield diary, November 3, 1918, in *The American Spirit*

The War Effort at Home
Adversaries United—or Arrested

Unity, cooperation, conformity—these words described the war effort at home. **Propaganda**, a form of public information used to mold public opinion, became the tool by which business, labor, government, and American opinion would be molded to fight and win the war. Secretary of the Treasury McAdoo relentlessly pitched patriotism in his Liberty Bond campaigns. Herbert Hoover, food administrator, used slogans to urge housewives to conserve: Food will win the war, Use all leftovers, and Serve just enough. George Creel, who headed Wilson's Committee on Public Information, also relied on emotion and peer pressure to mold public opinion. To those who regarded his numerous flyers, movies, conferences, speeches, posters, news bulletins, tracts, pictures, headlines, and exhibits as heavy-handed, he defended his mission without apology. He called his work "the world's greatest adventure in advertising."

Response From the Heartland

The patriotism campaigns of McAdoo, Hoover, and Creel reached every city, town, and rural area of the United States. In Geneva, Illinois, for example, women formed the Women's Council of Defense to conserve food for the war effort. Because the Allies desperately needed food, many crops were shipped overseas and

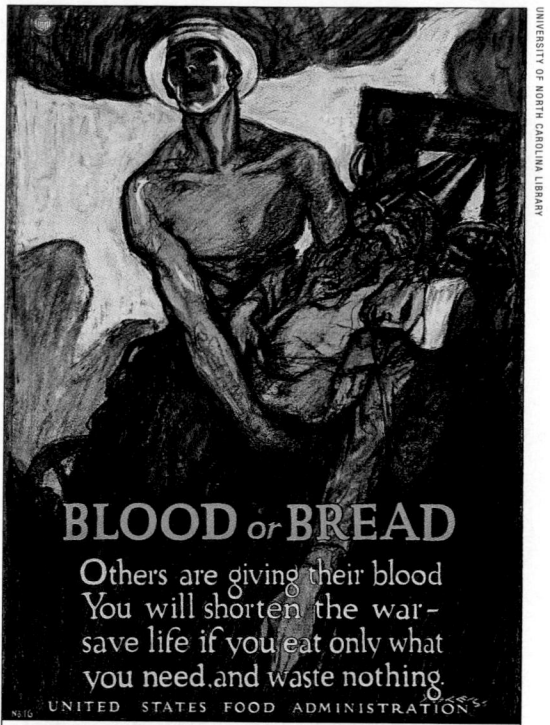

UNIVERSITY OF NORTH CAROLINA LIBRARY

BLOOD or BREAD

Others are giving their blood
You will shorten the war—
save life if you eat only what
you need, and waste nothing.
UNITED STATES FOOD ADMINISTRATION

Propaganda This poster by Henry Raleigh influenced public opinion in the United States during 1917 and 1918. *What message did this poster attempt to send to the American public?*

Americans at home were asked to conserve. Besides conserving food, women, along with adolescent girls and boys, pitched in to plow fields and plant and harvest corn while young men fought in France. The corn crops of the Midwest fed the whole nation.

Women and teenagers in Geneva also worked at the Burgess-Norton Company, a factory booming with war business. In 1916 the government awarded the factory a contract to produce ammunition. Burgess-Norton later received contracts to produce fuses for navy shells, as well as meat cleavers, saws, and brush axes for the army.

Cooperation of Business

The Burgess-Norton Company, like thousands of small companies across the country, willingly cooperated with the government's war mobilization. In doing their part for the war effort, they were also seizing an opportunity to grow and increase profits. For large corporations, the war promised still greater rewards.

In the name of unity (and expecting abundant profit), big businesses joined with the government in forming cooperative committees. They supervised the purchasing of war supplies and the granting of contracts. Progressives who lauded efficiency and cooperation

SECTION THREE **317**

VISUAL INSTRUCTION

Propaganda The Food Administration encouraged "Meatless Tuesdays" and "Wheatless Wednesdays" in order to conserve food.

Answer: *It urged people to join the war effort by conserving food.*

FYI

Selling the War To stir up enthusiasm for the war effort, the United States government printed posters containing highly charged language and images. One showed two German soldiers robbing a house after shooting the owner; the soldiers were labeled "Hindenburglers." Another entitled "Halt the Hun" showed an American soldier preventing a German soldier from bayoneting a defenseless woman and her baby.

FYI

Armistice In early October, the Germans notified the Associated Command that they wished to hear terms for an armistice based on Wilson's Fourteen Points. As armistice conditions were planned, a date rich with symbolism was set: the eleventh hour of the eleventh day of the eleventh month of the year. Meanwhile, in spite of the negotiators' date for peace, troops were kept in the field fighting and dying.

Portfolio Project

Position Paper In 1919 Congress passed the Nineteenth Amendment, which gave women voting rights. Have students respond to this statement by the president of the National American Woman Suffrage Association: "The greatest thing that came out of the war was the emancipation of women, for which no man fought. War subjected women and war liberated them." Students may want to include their response (along with a copy of the quote) in their portfolios.

smiled upon this centralized regulation, forgetting, in the heat of the moment, their former distrust of big business. Corporate profits tripled between 1914 and 1919.

Cooperation of Labor

Would labor cooperate with government and big business in the effort to win the war? In 1917 that question did not have a ready or immediate answer. Antiwar sentiment among ordinary workers had soared since 1914, and labor leadership was sharply divided. The American Federation of Labor and the Women's Trade Union League supported the war, while Socialists (members of the American Socialist party and the Industrial Workers of the World) opposed it as an imperialist ploy to make the world safe only for the profits of big business. Likewise, some women suffragists in the labor movement opposed the war, questioning Wilson's commitment to democracy. After all, women still could not vote in most states.

Samuel Gompers, who headed the American Federation of Labor, became a key figure in labor's support of the war. He easily shed his earlier pacifist ideals as he calculated the opportunities war might bring to the labor movement. If he cooperated with government by supporting mobilization, Gompers believed he could surely gain concessions from company leaders: higher pay and better working conditions; the right to organize and bargain collectively.

Even before the country entered the war, Gompers had pledged support to Wilson. In return, the government's Committee of Public Information secretly channeled money to Gompers's American Alliance for Labor and Democracy, a group organized to discredit Socialists in the labor movement.

The American Federation of Labor did attract thousands of workers to its ranks during the war years. By 1918, with its membership swelled to nearly 3 million, labor had won important concessions such as an 8-hour workday in many industries previously opposed to it.

These gains came at a price. For example, during the war workers labored under no-strike contracts. Later, women of all races and African American and Hispanic men quickly lost their

jobs when soldiers returned home to claim them. The labor movement itself lost some of its diversity as Gompers, in cooperation with the government, muzzled Socialist opponents. Thus weakened, the labor movement was unable to effectively face the backlash that would come after the war.

War and Civil Liberties

The lack of diversity in the labor movement reflected a similar pattern in society as a whole as the government passed legislation to unify everyone behind the war effort. The Espionage Act of 1917 and the Sedition Amendment of 1918 made any obstruction of the war effort illegal and curbed the civil liberties, or democratic rights, of those who spoke against the war. Government agencies broadly interpreted the new laws. Loyalty Leagues, organized by George Creel, encouraged Americans to spy and report on those who might be "disloyal." The Post Office withdrew circulation privileges from Socialist and antiwar newspapers such as the *Masses* and the *Milwaukee Leader,* and it even hired college professors to translate foreign periodicals to find out if they contained antiwar messages. As officials pressed for efficiency and absolute conformity in order to win the war, Wilson's fears of April 1, 1917, seemed prophetic. Just before he declared war, Wilson had expressed concern that the war would result in widespread intolerance.

During the war, freedom of speech took a severe beating. Socialist Rose Pastor Stokes was punished for a letter she sent to the *Kansas City Star* stating that

THE BETTMAN ARCHIVE

War Protesters Those against the war risked official punishment and often the ridicule of their fellow citizens. *Which groups tended to oppose American involvement in the war?*

Extending the Content

Dealing With Pacifists A young Socialist from Wisconsin named Ernest Meyer was drafted in April 1918. He was thrown in prison in Fort Leavenworth, Kansas, after refusing to put on a uniform. His companions in prison, besides criminals, were other conscientious objectors, mostly of the nonviolent Mennonite religion. In a letter he wrote, "I told you, comrade, I would

cling to my humor whatever befell, and I find material for laughter in this: these non-resisting Christians who would not harm a hair of their enemy's head or break a cherry crate to escape their persecutors, are locked behind iron bars with the murderer, the degenerate, and the insane, as if their prayers could topple kingdoms and their limbs contaminate a world."

EUGENE V. DEBS FOUNDATION

Courage of Convictions Before his arrest and 10-year sentence, Eugene Debs proclaimed to a crowd, "The master class has always declared the wars. The subject class has always fought the battles." *What law curtailed free speech?*

free speech. Senator Robert La Follette and Professor Zechariah Chafee, Jr., of the Harvard Law School openly defended Americans' rights to exercise their freedom of speech with regard to war. Groups formed to protect the rights of antiwar protesters. The Civil Liberties Union assisted pacifists and conscientious objectors who had been subjected to ridicule and abuse. Most Americans, however, gave little thought to restrictions of speech and supported the war without questioning the rights they were giving up.

After the war Supreme Court Justice Oliver Wendell Holmes, Jr., ruled that a citizen's freedom of speech should only be curbed when the words uttered constitute a "clear and present danger." He used yelling a false alarm of "Fire!" in a crowded theater as an example of a situation in which freedom of speech would be superseded by others' right to safety. The question remained whether critics of the war constituted a "clear and present danger" to the United States.

"no government which is for the profiteers can also be for the people, and I am for the people, while the Government is for the profiteers." For her words, a local court sentenced her to 10 years in prison. That decision was later reversed through a higher court. Socialist leader Eugene Debs served time in prison for telling his followers to "resist militarism, wherever found."

This atmosphere of legal repression, or official restriction of dissent, soon led to mindless crowd reaction. One night in Tulsa, Oklahoma, "gowned and masked gunmen" terrorized members of the Industrial Workers of the World. One member remembered the ordeal: "After each one [of us] was whipped another man applied the tar with a large brush, from the head to the seat. Then a brute smeared feathers over and rubbed them in."

Americans of German descent, like Socialists, suffered wartime harassment. All things German became suspect. Advertisers began to call sauerkraut "liberty cabbage" and hamburgers "liberty sausage" because they wanted to avoid German names. Many schools dropped German language classes from their curricula. In some small towns, anti-German feeling turned into violence. A mob numbering 500 in Collinsville, Illinois, lynched a young German-born man whom they suspected of disloyalty. When a jury found the mob leaders innocent, they shouted, "Nobody can say we aren't loyal now!"

Defending Free Speech

Not all Americans were caught up in the wartime frenzy. Some spoke out against the espionage and sedition laws and what they considered to be violations of

---

SECTION REVIEW

Vocabulary
1. Define: mobilization, conscription, doughboys, propaganda.

Checking Facts
2. How did United States troops help turn the tide of the war?

3. What was the purpose of the espionage and sedition laws?

Critical Thinking
Recognizing Bias
4. Look at the posters on pages 314 and 317. Explain how language and images can stir up enthusiasm for war.

Linking Across Time
5. As the United States mobilized for war, government and business joined forces as never before. Today, cooperation between government and business is common. Which industries are most closely connected with government? Why?

SECTION THREE **319**

Evaluate

Have students complete the Section Review.

☞ 🖳 Assign the Section 3 Quiz or use the Testmaker to develop a customized quiz. (Also in Spanish.) **LEP**

Reteach

🎧 Have students listen to the Chapter 10, Section 3 Audiocassette. (Also in Spanish.) **LEP**

Enrich

☞ Have students complete the Unit 3 American Literature Reading.

CLOSE

Ask students to briefly summarize the mobilization for war, the controversy over conscription, and the abridgement of civil liberties during World War I. Students may wish to put their information together in a time line.

Section 3 Review Answers

1. mobilization (315), **conscription** (315), **doughboys** (315), **propaganda** (317)

2. Their energy and overwhelming numbers gave a surge to Allied forces, convincing the Germans that they could no longer win the war.

3. They were designed to combat any efforts to obstruct the war effort.

4. Students may answer that mass media can use persuasive language, images, and peer pressure tactics to shape behavior and evoke emotions.

5. Students should support their answers with reasons and research. Possible answers may include the defense and space industries.

TEACH

Tell students that in this lesson they will learn about important reference materials and the types of information they contain. Discuss with students the fact that a single textbook or history book cannot include all of the information that is known about a particular topic. Many times our reading leaves us with further questions. Explain that libraries contain many reference materials that are useful sources of specific information. Students will practice using reference materials to answer questions and to prepare a plan for further research.

Additional Practice

👉 Have students complete the Chapter 10 Skill Reinforcement Activity.

Social Studies Skill

USING REFERENCE MATERIALS

Learning the Skill

If you want to write a paper on a topic related to World War I, you will need to use a variety of reference materials for research. Familiarity with such materials sharpens your research skills and helps you decide where to look for information. Try to locate the following types of reference sources in a library's reference department:

Encyclopedias

Encyclopedia articles give an overview of a topic. Most offer suggestions for further research at the end of an article, including a bibliography, list of related articles in the encyclopedia, or additional sources of information.

Indexes of Periodicals

Periodicals from the past reflect the culture, events, and concerns of their time; current periodicals provide the most recent research on a given topic. Several indexes can help you find information in periodicals. The *Readers' Guide to Periodical Literature* is a popular set of reference books that lists magazine articles by topic.

Historical Atlases

These contain maps with information about people and events of the past, and may also have articles and time lines. National Geographic's *Historical Atlas of the United States* is one source for United States history.

Statistical Sources

For information about the United States, the *Statistical Abstract of the United States* is a good place to start. Compiled by the Bureau of the Census, it contains data on more than 30 topics. The information dates back to 1790, the year the first census was taken.

Biographical Dictionaries

These tell about the life or achievements of noteworthy people. Webster's *American Biographies* and the *Dictionary of American Biography* are good sources.

Practicing the Skill

Study the chart below, then answer the following questions.

1. For each source, make up your own research question based on material in Chapter 10.

2. Find answers to the questions you wrote in question 1 in the appropriate reference materials.

3. Write a short report about a key figure in this chapter. Tell what sources you used.

4. Where would you look to find out more about World War I battlefields?

5. Look up the Philippines in two sources, and list two facts from each source.

Applying the Skill

Check today's newspaper for a story that interests you; where would you look for more information on the subject?

Additional Practice

For additional practice, see Reinforcing Skills on page 329.

ORGANIZATIONAL PATTERNS		
Source of Information	Uses	Sample Research Questions
Encyclopedias	Provide topic overviews; suggest further research	What were the main provisions of the Versailles Treaty
Periodicals	Reflect the past; supply current research on a topic	How did journalists react to the November Revolution?
Historical Atlases	Provide geographic context for historical information	Locate the Eastern and Western fronts during World War I.
Statistical Sources	Convey statistical information	What was the estimated total cost of World War I to the United States?
Biographical Dictionaries	Describe the backgounds and achievements of historical figures	Who were Emilio Aguinaldo, V.I. Lenin, and Georges Clemenceau?

Practicing the Skill Answers

1. Answers will vary, but students should prepare questions that can be answered from the source cited.
2. Answers will depend on the answers to Question 1.
3. Report subjects will vary. Likely sources are encyclopedias and biographical dictionaries.

4. Answers may vary, but a likely answer would be historical atlases.
5. Two facts about the Philippines should be different and should reflect information characteristic of different sources.

Reshaping the World

DECEMBER 1918: EUROPEANS CHEER WILSON

"WE WANT WILSON," THE WAR-WEARY CROWD ROARED. "Long live Dr. Wilson!" "Honor to Wilson the just!" British students with American flags smiled, tossing flowers in the President's path. Everywhere in Europe the Wilsons visited—Paris, Rome, Milan—the reception was jubilant. An Italian laborer spoke for millions when he said of Wilson:

> They say he thinks of us—the poor people; that he wants us all to have a fair chance; that he is going to do something when he gets here that will make it impossible for our government to send us to war again. If he had only come sooner! I have already lost my two sons. Do you believe he is strong enough to stop all wars?
>
> —Overheard conversation, 1918,
> *My Diplomatic Education*

NATIONAL ARCHIVES

Celebrating Wilson and Peace
Jubilant crowds greet President Wilson and British officials on Wilson's arrival in London.

Europeans had lost about 10 million soldiers in the war and twice as many civilians. Soldiers still suffered from wounds in crowded hospitals. French towns had been obliterated from the map. Ordinary Europeans had sacrificed, scrimping on food, often going cold and hungry. No wonder they looked for a savior—someone to end such brutality forever. They hailed Wilson hopefully because of his plan for a just and lasting peace. The President had outlined the plan in a 14-point document; his ideas came to be known simply as the Fourteen Points.

European leaders, however, regarded Wilson with skepticism. French Premier Georges Clemenceau observed, "God has given man Ten Commandments. He broke every one. President Wilson has his Fourteen Points. We shall see."

AS YOU READ

Vocabulary
► bolshevism
► irreconcilables
► reservationist

Think About . . .
► Wilson's Fourteen Points and the objections European leaders had to them.
► how events in Russia affected other nations.

► the 1919 Paris Peace Conference negotiations and resulting Treaty of Versailles.
► why the Senate rejected the Treaty of Versailles.

SECTION FOUR   **321**

Section 4 Resources

REPRODUCIBLE RESOURCES
📁 Lesson Plan 10-4
📁 Vocabulary and Guided Reading Activity 10-4
📁 Section 4 Quiz
📁 Chapter 10 Test
📁 Performance Assessment Activity 10
📁 Reteaching Activity 10
📁 Enrichment Activity 10
📁 Unit 3 Test

MULTIMEDIA RESOURCES
🎬 Section Focus Transparency 32
💿 The Presidents: A Picture History of Our Nation
💿 Landmark Documents in American History
🎧 Chapter 10 Digest Audiocassette
💻 Testmaker

FOCUS

Section Objectives

1. Summarize Wilson's Fourteen Points and the objections European leaders had to them.
2. Describe events in Russia and their effect on other nations.
3. Describe the 1919 peace conference negotiations and resulting Treaty of Versailles.
4. Explain why the Senate rejected the Treaty of Versailles.

Bellringer Activity

While taking attendance at the beginning of the class period, display **Section Focus Transparency 32**, and have students answer the questions. (Or use the blackline master.)

VISUAL INSTRUCTION

Celebrating Wilson and Peace When Wilson traveled to Europe at the end of the war, he was the first American president to leave the United States while in office.

Ask: What did Wilson represent to the European people? *(hope for peace)*

TEACH

Guided Practice

L1 Responding Ask students to respond to this comment Wilson made while campaigning to win support for the peace treaty: "Some people call me an idealist. Well, that is the only way I know I am an American. America is the only idealist nation in the world."

Independent Practice

L1 Research Encourage students to find out what happened to Wilson's League of Nations after the Treaty of Versailles and include their findings in a report.

🎧 Have students complete the Chapter 10, Section 4 Vocabulary and Guided Reading Activity. (Also in Spanish.) **LEP**

VISUAL INSTRUCTION

Early Soviet Art Russian artist El Lissitsky was an influential force in nonrepresentational art. He left the Soviet Union in 1921—when the government rejected modern art—but he returned in 1929.

Answer: *It shows the Bolsheviks (the triangle) assaulting the Whites (the circle).*

Points for Peace
Fear and Hope for the Postwar World

Wilson's Fourteen Points for peace had been a brilliant propaganda ploy as well as an earnest effort to steer a middle course between a radical peace settlement and a conservative, opportunistic peace settlement. Wilson gave his Fourteen Points speech to Congress on January 8, 1918, 10 months before the end of World War I. George Creel chose the most lyrical phrases from the speech to print in leaflets—about 60 million of them. He eagerly distributed them around the world, even dropping them from the air above Central Power countries.

Why had Wilson outlined his terms for peace so long before the war was over? The answer lay in the momentous events of the war years. Wilson believed that if he did not act quickly, he might lose the initiative to the Bolsheviks in Russia, who had powerful ideas of their own about reshaping the world.

Impact of Bolshevism

Russia had dealt a hard blow to the Allied cause when it withdrew from the war in early 1918. On March 3, 1918, Vladimir Ilyich Lenin, the new leader in Russia, signed the Treaty of Brest-Litovsk with Germany, formally ending Russian-German conflict. Lenin gave up large areas of land to the Germans because he needed peace to concentrate on domestic reform and on internal opposition by czarist forces, called the Whites. Events in Russia during the war help explain why **bolshevism,** a radical socialist ideology, posed such a threat to President Wilson.

Early Soviet Art The translated title of this El Lissitsky poster is *Beat the Whites With the Red Wedge.* It was created in 1920 to dramatize abstractly the social revolution in Russia. *How does this piece illustrate the conflict?*

When World War I began, an autocratic czar ruled Russia. Wilson's initial hesitation to enter the war stemmed, in part, from his distaste for associating with the absolute monarchy of the czarist rulers. By July 1917, the czar had already surrendered his power, and the Russian parliament had set up a provisional government led by moderate Socialist Aleksandr Kerensky. His liberal policies and commitment to keep Russia in the war made Kerensky very popular with the Allies.

At home, however, domestic problems overwhelmed Kerensky. Chief among them was the war's unpopularity and the disintegration of the Russian army. In the midst of chaotic discontent, the Bolsheviks, led by Lenin, seized power from Kerensky in November 1917

★ ★ ★ GALLERY OF PRESIDENTS ★ ★ ★

Woodrow Wilson
1913–1921

"The world must be made safe for democracy. Its peace must be planted upon the tested foundations of political liberty. We have no selfish ends to serve. We desire no conquest, no dominion. We seek no indemnities for ourselves, no material compensation for the sacrifices we shall freely make. We are but one of the champions of the rights of mankind."

War Message, April 2, 1917

BROWN BROTHERS

BACKGROUND
▶ Born 1856; Died 1924
▶ Democrat, New Jersey
▶ President of Princeton University 1902–1910
▶ Governor of New Jersey 1911–1913

ACHIEVEMENTS IN OFFICE
▶ Underwood Tariff Act (1913)
▶ Federal Reserve Act (1913)
▶ Clayton Antitrust Act (1914)
▶ Child Labor Act (1916)

Cooperative Learning

Negotiating Have students hold a peace conference. Organize the class into four groups. Each group should participate as one of the Big Four nations. Structure the negotiations around a copy of Wilson's Fourteen Points. Students have the power to accept, amend, or reject each point and should confer within their group before negotiating with the other groups' members. 📖

(October in old Russian calendar). All of Europe, as well as the rest of the world, watched the tumultuous events in Russia. American journalist John Reed described the "October Revolution" in *Ten Days That Shook the World*.

This revolution frightened world leaders. They knew that bolshevism could potentially attract millions of discontented, war-weary workers to its ranks. Lenin's beliefs were rooted in the Communist ideology of philosopher Karl Marx, who called for class war between workers and capitalists rather than world war between capitalist governments. Lenin blamed the war on capitalism and named workers of all nationalities as its hapless victims.

Wilson and other world leaders feared the Bolsheviks' radical message. They were embarrassed when Lenin published copies of secret pacts made between allied European powers early in the war. The pacts revealed that the Allies were not simply fighting for democracy but also hoped to divide the world among themselves. The publication of the pacts put Wilson in a difficult position. He did not want to be associated with them, nor did he want to support the Bolsheviks. His answer to this dilemma emerged as the Fourteen Points. Wilson hoped that his plan for lasting peace would attract the attention of common people, distracting them from bolshevism.

Wilson's Fourteen Points

The Fourteen Points promised that all countries signing the peace treaty would enjoy equality of trade and "removal, as far as possible, of all economic barriers" in the postwar world. This provision reassured Germany, who feared harsh reprisals. The points stressed the importance of territorial integrity and self-determination for countries invaded during the war, including Russia, Belgium, France, and Italy. They outlined specific recommendations for adjusting borders after the war, so that the Austro-Hungarian Empire would be divided into several new states based on nationality.

The Fourteen Points also suggested new forms of international conduct: freedom of ocean travel and trade, open agreements instead of secret pacts, and arms reductions. One point called for "impartial adjustment" of colonial claims, with a voice for both the colonial populations and the foreign governments claiming dominion over them.

Wilson believed the most important point to be the establishment of a League of Nations, an international mediating body "affording mutual guarantees of political independence and territorial integrity to great and small states alike." He thought that such a league could bond all nations of the world together. If the League provided for the security of each individual state, then the ancient dream of peace among nations might succeed.

Reaction to the Fourteen Points

While the European masses greeted the Fourteen Points with great enthusiasm, British and French leaders were more restrained. They did not have time to sit down with Wilson and discuss his grand ideas. The war needed their attention. Nonetheless, David Lloyd George, the pragmatic prime minister of Great Britain, knew that he could never agree to freedom of the seas, thus giving up British naval dominance. Likewise, Georges Clemenceau knew that France would never concede to ignoring the damage inflicted by Germany. From the outset the Fourteen Points were no match for the fierce determination of France to punish Germany.

One of the Fourteen Points was ignored seven months after the points were announced—the right of Russia to have "institutions of her own choosing." Yielding to pressure from the Allies, Wilson sent American battalions to the Russian ports of Vladivostok and Murmansk. He did so under the pretense of helping Czech troops stranded there after Russia pulled out of the war. In reality the intervention gave aid to the White Army that was engaged in a civil war against the Bolsheviks.

CULVER PICTURES

Program for the Peace of the World
By PRESIDENT WILSON January 8, 1918

I. Open covenants of peace, openly arrived at, after which there shall be no private international understandings of any kind, but diplomacy shall proceed always frankly and in the public view.

II. Absolute freedom of navigation upon the seas, outside territorial waters, alike in peace and in war, except as the seas may be closed in whole or in part by international action for the enforcement of international covenants.

III. The removal, so far as possible, of all economic barriers and the establishment of an equality of trade conditions among all the nations consenting to the peace and associating themselves for its maintenance.

IV. Adequate guarantees given and taken that national armaments will reduce to the lowest point consistent with domestic safety.

V. Free, open-minded, and absolutely impartial adjustment of all colonial claims, based upon a strict observance of the principle that in determining all such questions of sovereignty the interests of the population concerned must have equal weight with the equitable claims of the government whose title is to be determined.

VI. The evacuation of all Russian territory and such a settlement of all questions affecting Russia as will secure the best and freest cooperation of the other nations of the world in obtaining for her an unhampered and unembarrassed opportunity for the independent determination of her own political development and national policy, and assure her of a sincere welcome into the society of free nations under institutions of her own choosing; and, more than a welcome, assistance also of every kind that she may need and may herself desire. The treatment accorded Russia by her sister nations in the months to come will be the acid test of their goodwill, of their comprehension of her needs as distinguished from their own interests, and of their intelligent and unselfish sympathy.

VII. Belgium, the whole world will agree, must be evacuated and restored, without any attempt to limit the sovereignty which she enjoys in common with all other free nations. No other single act will serve as this will serve to restore confidence among the nations in the law which they have themselves set and determined for the government of their relations with one another. Without this healing act the whole structure and validity of international law is forever impaired.

VIII. All French territory should be freed and the invaded portions restored, and the wrong done to France by Prussia in 1871 in the matter of Alsace-Lorraine, which has unsettled the peace of the world for nearly fifty years, should be righted, in order that peace may once more be made secure in the interest of all.

IX. A readjustment of the frontiers of Italy should be effected along clearly recognizable lines of nationality.

X. The people of Austria-Hungary, whose place among the nations we wish to see safeguarded and assured, should be accorded the freest opportunity of autonomous development.

XI. Rumania, Serbia and Montenegro should be evacuated; occupied territories restored; Serbia accorded free and secure access to the sea; and the relations of the several Balkan States to one another determined by friendly counsel along historically established lines of allegiance and nationality; and international guarantees of the political and economic independence and territorial integrity of the several Balkan States should be entered into.

XII. The Turkish portions of the present Ottoman Empire should be assured a secure sovereignty, but the other nationalities which are now under Turkish rule should be assured an undoubted security of life and an absolutely unmolested opportunity of autonomous development, and the Dardanelles should be permanently opened as a free passage to the ships and commerce of all nations under international guarantees.

XIII. An independent Polish State should be erected which should include the territories inhabited by indisputably Polish populations, which should be assured a free and secure access to the sea, and whose political and economic independence and territorial integrity should be guaranteed by international covenant.

XIV. A general association of nations must be formed under specific covenants for the purpose of affording mutual guarantees of political independence and territorial integrity to great and small States alike.

Wilson's Hope The Fourteen Points were brief but influential, condensing Wilson's plan for peace to one page. *How did other world leaders react to Wilson's plan?*

VISUAL INSTRUCTION

Wilson's Hope Eight points concern territorial and political settlements, five aim to prevent future wars, the last proposes the League of Nations.

Answer: *Many thought it was too idealistic.*

FYI

John Reed Reed was an eyewitness to the 1917 revolution in Russia. Back in the United States, he wrote *Ten Days That Shook the World* and helped lead the Communist Labor Party. For his Communist activities, Reed was indicted for sedition. In 1919 he returned to Russia and was elected to the Second Congress of the Communist International.

 Facts on File

Landmark Documents in American History Have students review "Fourteen Points, Woodrow Wilson, 1918" and write a paragraph about the intent of the document.

 NATIONAL GEOGRAPHIC SOCIETY

 The Presidents: A Picture History of Our Nation

Have students view "Woodrow Wilson" and use the information to write a brief biography to include in their portfolios.

Meeting Special Needs

Attention Deficit Disorder This activity will help students having difficulty focusing on the content of the section. Point out that these seven pages are essentially about three topics: Wilson's peace plan, the peace negotiations and final treaty, and the reaction to the treaty in the United States. The topics are introduced by the main heads Points for Peace, A Troubling Treaty, and Rejection at Home. Read and discuss with students the first page of the section, which sets the stage for the rest of the section. Then ask students to read Points for Peace. When they finish, they should write down the subheads from the text and a topic summary sentence. They can then go on to the next topic in the section.

323

Wilson also unwittingly endangered his Fourteen Points with a political move at home. As the midterm congressional elections of 1918 drew near, Wilson issued an appeal urging Americans to vote Democratic. This appeal enraged Republicans, who took it as an affront to their patriotism. When voters later elected Republican majorities to Congress, Wilson lost credibility at the negotiating table with European leaders.

A Troubling Treaty
Vision and Vengeance Clash

Woodrow Wilson walked into the Paris Peace Conference at the Palace of Versailles in January 1919 with the cheers of the European crowds still ringing in his ears, but he was in a very weak bargaining position. As the conference dragged on for five long months, he would give up more and more of his Fourteen Points as well as his own good spirits and health. By April he appeared thinner, grayer, grimmer, and more nervous. His face twitched as he spoke, and he expressed greater moral rigidity than ever before. This irritated the European leaders around him. "I never knew anyone to talk more like Jesus Christ," said Clemenceau in exasperation.

An Atmosphere of Exclusion

One of the Fourteen Points promised that international negotiations and agreements would be made in the open, eliminating secret pacts. From early on, however, this principle was ignored. The press was kept away from the negotiations. The Allied Powers also pared down the number of countries actually shaping the final outcome to the "Big Four"—the United States, Great Britain, France, and Italy. Germany and Russia—two countries whose futures hinged on the outcome of the treaty—were completely shut out of negotiations.

Great Britain, Italy, and France insisted on the exclusion of a German representative. France even refused Germany the right to have observers at the proceedings. Wilson had argued for peace among equals, but now he deferred to the wishes of his three wartime allies. Before the conference concluded, France obtained concessions to occupy an industrial region of Germany for 15 years, won back its northeastern territories of Lorraine and Alsace, and established a reparations commission to assess money Germany would pay for French losses.

The exclusion of Russia at the conference stemmed from confusion and fear. In 1919 Europe seemed on the brink of revolution. Bolshevik forces had not fallen to the White Russian opposition, in spite of American and Japanese intervention. In Germany radical groups threatened to overthrow the newly established Social Democratic government. Communists gained power in Hungary. Leaders of the Western democracies at Versailles were worried about the revolutionary movements sweeping Europe.

The Big Four vacillated and disagreed. Should they include Russia to try to soften its impact, or should they use direct military action to subdue the Bolsheviks? Neither extreme won the day. Instead, they simply excluded Russia from the conference, but as a contemporary observer noted, "the black cloud" of Russia remained, "threatening to overwhelm and swallow up the world."

An Atmosphere of Self-Interest

The Fourteen Points dwindled to even fewer as the Big Four debated what to do about German and Turkish colonies in Asia and Africa. In Wilson's original plan, all colonies would have a say in their own destiny. Colonies of Allied Powers hoped this principle would include them. To victorious France and Great Britain, however, the self-determination of their colonies was completely unacceptable. Rather than losing their own colonies, they were eager to enjoy the spoils of war by absorbing the colonies of their defeated enemies.

The final compromise did little to honor Wilson's call for "impartial adjustment of all colonial claims." Allied Powers would retain their own colonies and the League of Nations would give them control over Central

THE BETTMANN ARCHIVE

Germany Impoverished Germany's huge postwar debt helped bankrupt its economy and made it fertile ground for the rise of fascism. Some poorer citizens turned to rummaging through refuse heaps in hopes of finding everyday necessities. *How was Germany treated at the Paris Peace Conference?*

Portfolio Project

Essay Writing Have students write an essay examining the similarities and differences between being a good national citizen and being a good world citizen. Are the two mutually dependent or exclusive? Once students are satisfied with their final essays, encourage them to include them in their portfolios.

NEGOTIATION OF THE TREATY OF VERSAILLES

Japanese Delegates Like the Big Four, Japan sent 5 delegates to Versailles; 22 other nations had 1 to 3 delegates each. *What did Japan request at the peace conference?*

Power colonies. These mandated colonies, however, would be ruled in the name of the League.

Italy presented another challenge to the Fourteen Points. It, too, wanted some of the spoils of war—parts of the Austro-Hungarian Empire including the ports of Fiume and Trieste. Wilson resisted Italy's expansion because his plan advocated forming Balkan states from the land of Austria-Hungary. Much of what Italy wanted would go to the newly created state of Yugoslavia (shown on the map on page 326). Soon Italians would turn to Benito Mussolini, who vowed to avenge their humiliation.

Japan, the mighty force of the Pacific, also came to Versailles to make its demands as the world shifted and realigned. Japan wanted full recognition of its rights in the Shandong Province of China, which Germany had controlled before the war. During the heat of the war, world powers had little time to protect their stake in China, leaving Japan to consolidate its interests there. Japan's demand to control the province directly opposed the self-determination provisions of the Fourteen Points.

Nonetheless, Japan devised a scheme to secure its control of Shandong. Japanese delegates asked that an article formally declaring the equality of all races be attached to the peace agreement. This request exposed the limitations of Wilson's progressive approach. Much of progressive foreign policy, especially in the Caribbean, had been based on the assumption that white people knew best. While the Fourteen Points provided for a degree of self-determination, Wilson was

not ready to change the power structure of the world so radically. The Japanese proposal directly challenged not only Wilson, but all of the colonial powers at the conference who held dominion over people of color in Asia and Africa. Rather than deal with this troubling situation, the conference let Japan expand its influence in China, provided it drop its racial equality proposal. Thus, by cleverly manipulating the issue of race, Japan gained power in China. The Japanese victory enraged student radicals in China, who rioted in protest through the streets of Beijing.

By June 28, 1919, when the Treaty of Versailles was signed, a beleaguered and ill Woodrow Wilson had only one consolation left: the provision for the League of Nations had not been rejected, even though most of his original Fourteen Points had vanished. He returned to the United States driven by the idea that the League of Nations must not fail. Only an international league could deal with the injustices built into the Treaty of Versailles.

Rejection at Home
Political and Personal Obstacles

Woodrow Wilson's long stay in Europe took its toll on his health. Moreover, his rivals in Congress had united against him. Approval for the League of Nations now hinged on ratification of the Treaty of Versailles by the United States Senate.

Opposition in Congress

Opposition to the League was consolidated in two camps in Congress. One camp, the **irreconcilables,** was mostly progressive Republicans, many of whom had been in elected office since the turn of the century. They included Robert La Follette, William Borah, Hiram Johnson, and a handful of others. They called themselves irreconcilables because under no circumstances would they be reconciled to voting for the League of Nations.

SECTION FOUR   **325**

VISUAL INSTRUCTION

Japanese Delegates Japan also agreed to support other nations' claims to former German colonies in return for a favorable decision on Shandong.

Answer: *control of the Shandong Province of China*

 Facts on File

Landmark Documents in American History Have students review "Treaty of Versailles, 1919," "Lodge Reservations, 1919," "League of Nations Covenant, 1919," "League of Nations Mandates, 1919," and "Expositions of the League of Nations, Woodrow Wilson, 1919" and write a paragraph about the intent of one of the documents.

Curriculum Connection

Geography The treaty was concerned with disposition of the Balkans, as the area had been the site of internal wars even before World War I. The area called the Balkan Peninsula is bordered by the Sava and Danube Rivers to the north, the Black Sea and the Bosporus to the east, the Sea of Marmara, the Dardanelles, and the Aegean Sea to the south, and the Adriatic and Ionian seas to the west. It covers roughly 184,000 square miles (477,000 square km).

Extending the Content

Seeds of War The treaty that ended World War I may have sown the seeds of World War II. Think about these points as you consider that hypothesis: the humiliation of Germany and Italy; the division of Austria-Hungary into many nationalistic states; the exclusion of Russia and Germany from the treaty process; Allied rule over the Central Powers' colonies; and the revolutionary movements sweeping Europe. Some say that the Treaty of Versailles ensured another war as much as it resolved the problems that caused World War I.

ASSESS

Meeting Lesson Objectives

Each section objective is tested by the section review question(s) that follows it in parentheses.

1. Summarize Wilson's Fourteen Points and the objections European leaders had to them. (3, 5)

2. Describe events in Russia and their effect on other nations. (2)

3. Describe the 1919 peace conference negotiations and resulting Treaty of Versailles. (4)

4. Explain why the Senate rejected the Treaty of Versailles. (1)

MAP STUDY

One goal of the new borders was to unite Slavic Serbs, Croats, and Slovenes. The name of the resulting country, Yugoslavia, means "Land of the South Slavs."

Answer: *The new countries of Hungary, Czechoslovakia, and Austria, and parts of Yugoslavia, Romania, and Poland were once Austria-Hungary; Germany, East Prussia, and parts of Poland were once the German Empire; Finland, Russia (the Soviet Union by 1922), Estonia, Latvia, Lithuania, and parts of Poland and Romania were once the Russian Empire.*

EUROPE AFTER WORLD WAR I, 1920–1922

BOUNDARIES OF FORMER EMPIRES
- Austria-Hungary
- Germany
- Russia
- ★ Capital cities
- National boundary

After the war the European empires were divided into smaller countries. Compare this map of Europe to the map of Europe during World War I on page 307. *Which new countries make up what were once Austria-Hungary and the German and Russian Empires?*

Irreconcilables clung to the old argument that the United States was better off steering clear of the corrupting influence of Europe. They were mainly anti-imperialists and feared that if the United States joined the League of Nations, it would be put in the immoral position of defending the colonial activities of European powers. They preferred to focus attention on reform at home rather than on politics abroad. Nevertheless, they did not completely favor isolationism—a policy that supported indifference in affairs outside the United States.

The **reservationists,** on the other hand, approved of the idea of the League of Nations but wished to modify Wilson's particular proposal. They disliked the article specifying that the League preserve "the territorial integrity and existing political independence of all Members of the League." Vague wording described how such an obligation would be fulfilled. Both reservationists and irreconcilables feared that this article —Article 10—could involve the United States in armed conflict. It also seemed to suggest that the League itself would have the authority to decide if and when the United States, or any League members, would enter a conflict in defense of a member nation's independence. If this were so, the power of the League superseded the power of Congress to declare war.

By late summer 1919, anti–League of Nations sentiment spread from Washington throughout the country. An advertisement in the *Boston Herald* on July 8, 1919, for an anti-League meeting warned: "AMERICANS, AWAKE! Shall We Bind Ourselves to the War Breeding Covenant? It Impairs American Sovereignty! Surrenders the Monroe Doctrine! . . . Entangles us in European and Asiatic Intrigues!"

Besides the reservationists' concern about Article 10, they also objected to the League for other reasons. Led by Senator Henry Cabot Lodge, they hoped to embarrass the President. Lodge, like Wilson, had formerly been a scholar. Though Lodge often acted in an aristocratic manner, he resented the same behavior in Wilson. He seethed with anger at the thought of Wilson getting full credit for the League when he himself had often suggested an international peacekeeping body. Motivated by anger as well as genuine misgivings, Lodge fought to attach his amendments to the original proposal for the League. Wilson refused to consider a compromise.

326 CHAPTER 10 EXPANSIONISM AND WORLD WAR I

Cultural Perspectives

Ottoman Empire The Ottoman Empire began its rule in the 1300s, and over the next 200 years it became the most powerful empire in the world. Its conquests spread its territory over what is now Turkey, and parts of southwestern Asia, southeastern Europe, and northern Africa. The Ottomans were Muslims, though the empire encompassed people of many religions within its borders. For the most part the Ottomans allowed different religious groups to practice freely, and a leader from each group would represent its members before the government. The empire had been declining for a few centuries before World War I and covered only Asia Minor, parts of southwestern Asia, and part of the Balkans. Defeated in war, it ceased to exist in 1922.

ME IDEA IS TO HIT TH' LAD WITHOUT TOUCHIN' THE APPLE

WILLIAM TELL, REVERSED.
—Harding in the Brooklyn *Eagle*.

Wilson Shot Down This cartoon characterizes the partisan opposition to the Treaty of Versailles. *How can personal opinions about an individual color one's decisions to support or not support that individual's policies?*

Speaking to the People

Growing impatient with senators and critics, Wilson decided to take his case to the American people. If he had their overwhelming support, the Senate would not dare defy him. In September 1919, President Wilson organized a grueling 9,000-mile (14,481-km) cross-country speaking tour by train: 26 different stops in 27 days.

As in Europe, cheering crowds greeted Woodrow Wilson during his tour. In spite of his failing health, he often spoke eloquently:

> For the first time in the history of a civilized society, a great international convention, made up of the leading statesmen of the world, has proposed a settlement which is for the benefit of the weak and not the benefit of the strong.
>
> —Woodrow Wilson, speech in Los Angeles, September 1919

Crowds gathered and cheered. The President waved and rallied. His dream, though, was not to be. On September 25, 1919, as he spoke in Pueblo, Colorado, he fell violently ill and was rushed back to Washington, D.C. A few days later, he suffered a paralytic stroke. For weeks Wilson could not function as President. When finally he was able to make decisions, he refused to modify any of his ideas. As both Lodge and Wilson remained

entrenched in their positions, the Senate voted to reject the Treaty of Versailles with its League of Nations.

Wilson refused to give up. He looked forward to the presidential election of 1920. The Democratic party did not seriously consider renominating President Wilson because of his illness. Wilson, however, pinned his hopes on the party's nominee, Governor James M. Cox from Ohio. Woodrow Wilson saw the election of 1920 as a "solemn referendum" on the League of Nations.

Most of the country, however, was not listening. Other concerns captured their attention. The Red Scare—a fear of bolshevism—spread throughout the United States. Wilson himself had contributed to this hysteria during the war by supporting the Espionage Act of 1917 and the 1918 Sedition Amendment that had led to the arrest of several Socialist labor leaders.

In the election of 1920, the country responded to this fear by isolating itself, turning away from Europe and the world's troubling revolutions. Repudiating the League of Nations and the idea of internationalism, the American people opted for a promise of "normalcy" by electing the Republican Warren G. Harding to the presidency. Woodrow Wilson lived for three years after leaving office, but he never regained his health. He died on February 3, 1924, shortly after telling some of his friends that he was "tired of swimming upstream."

SECTION REVIEW

Vocabulary
1. Define: bolshevism, irreconcilables, reservationist.

Checking Facts
2. How did Russia's withdrawal from World War I and its separate peace with Germany affect other nations?

3. Why was the League of Nations so important to Wilson? Why did the Senate oppose it?

Critical Thinking
Drawing Conclusions
4. Rather than dealing with the concept of racial equality as Japan requested, the Versailles conference bargained to let Japan expand its influence in China. Why did Wilson and other leaders accept Japan's proposal?

Linking Across Time
5. Consider Wilson's efforts to implement his peace plan and how other leaders reacted. How have American leaders tried to affect peace in other situations (e.g. Haiti, Bosnia, or the Middle East in the 1990s) and how were their efforts received?

VISUAL INSTRUCTION

Wilson Shot Down The legendary William Tell shot an apple off his son's head, with unerring skill. The Republican elephant tries to save the apple (League of Nations) and hit Wilson.

Answer: *One might oppose a policy one would normally favor, as Lodge did.*

Evaluate

Have students complete the Section Review.

☞ ◙ Assign the Section 4 Quiz or use the Testmaker to develop a customized quiz. (Also in Spanish.) **LEP**

☞ ◙ Assign the Chapter 10 Test or use the Testmaker to develop a customized test. (Also in Spanish.) **LEP**

☞ Have students complete the Chapter 10 Performance Assessment Activity. 📼

Reteach

🎧 Have students listen to the Chapter 10, Section 4 Audiocassette. (Also in Spanish.) **LEP**

☞ Have students complete the Chapter 10 Reteaching Activity. (Also in Spanish.) **LEP**

Enrich

☞ Have students complete the Chapter 10 Enrichment Activity. (Also in Spanish.) **LEP**

CLOSE

Have students recall the Fourteen Points. List them on the board. Discuss what became of each point at the conference and at home.

Section 4 Review Answers

1. bolshevism (322), **irreconcilable** (325), **reservationist** (326)
2. It allowed Germany to focus all its strength on fighting the Allies. It made it easier for the United States to join the Allies.
3. He believed that an international mediating body would bond the world's nations together. The Senate feared the country would lose power to other countries.

4. The proposal challenged the colonial powers who held dominion over people of color in Asia and Africa. Progressive foreign policy was based on the belief that white people knew best. The Big Four were not ready to change the world's power structure.
5. Students should give reasons to support their answers.

327

Chapter ⑩ Review

Reviewing Key Terms

Answers will vary, but they should reflect students' understanding of the vocabulary words and events during World War I.

Recalling Facts

1. New markets would bring profits; extensive trading overseas might lead to war.
2. Roosevelt's Big Stick policy was based on the idea that the United States was stronger than other countries. Taft's Dollar Diplomacy was a milder approach to expansion and influencing foreign nations. By asking American businesses to invest in Central American countries, Taft hoped to gain influence in the hemisphere.
3. the right of all people to govern themselves and to control their own interests; intervention in Haiti, the Dominican Republic, Cuba, Mexico, and later in Europe
4. the Tampico arrests, Veracruz, the changing support of Mexican rebel leaders, and the Villa chase
5. because he thought neither side deserved United States support; to stay out of the war
6. newspapers, magazines, books, advertisements, and posters
7. African American soldiers were segregated from other American troops, denied high rank, and commanded by white officers.
8. food conservation; bond purchases; women and children filling jobs; companies producing goods for the war
9. He used parts of Wilson's speech to create leaflets for worldwide distribution.
10. Bolshevism was a radical socialist ideology that could potentially attract millions of discontented, war-weary workers.

Reviewing Key Terms

Imagine that you have kept a diary of events covering the outbreak of World War I and the United States involvement in the war. Write headlines for 10 diary entries, using each of the following terms in a headline:

alliance
neutrality
dogfight
mobilization
conscription

doughboys
propaganda
bolshevism
irreconcilable
reservationist

Recalling Facts

1. Why did overseas markets appeal to many Americans? Why did some oppose commercial expansion overseas?

2. What policies did Roosevelt and Taft implement in the Caribbean?

3. What is self-determination? What actions did Wilson take that were not consistent with his belief in self-determination?

4. Describe the United States's involvement in Mexico during the first 2 decades of the 1900s.

5. Why did Wilson claim neutrality before World War I?

6. Give examples of print media that historians might use to study public opinion during World War I.

7. Describe the racial bias that existed in the United States military during World War I.

8. What actions were taken to support the war on the home front during World War I?

9. How did George Creel help spread Wilson's ideas about peace?

10. Why did bolshevism frighten President Wilson and other world leaders?

Critical Thinking

1. Recognizing Bias When Roosevelt negotiated peace between Russia and Japan, he claimed neutrality. What evidence suggests that he actually favored one side? Why would it be to his advantage to pretend he was unbiased?

2. Determining Cause and Effect President Woodrow Wilson did not want to involve the United States in World War I. Instead he wished to remain neutral, supporting neither Germany nor Russia. The President wanted the people of the United States to be "impartial in thought as well as in action." On April 2, 1917, however, the President asked the members of Congress to declare war on Germany. What factors or international incidents involving the United States caused President Wilson to reverse his position?

3. Predicting Consequences Think about the convictions of Eugene Debs and Rose Pastor Stokes and the terrorization of IWW members in Oklahoma. In what ways might the abridgement of civil liberties lead to mob rule?

4. Making Generalizations The photo below depicts the devastation and ruins of the Arras Cathedral in France after a German offensive. How would people who suffered in World War I have gone about rebuilding their nations? Make a list of priorities to follow in the aftermath of a disaster of this magnitude. How did President Wilson's Fourteen Points hope to address the international efforts of postwar rebuilding?

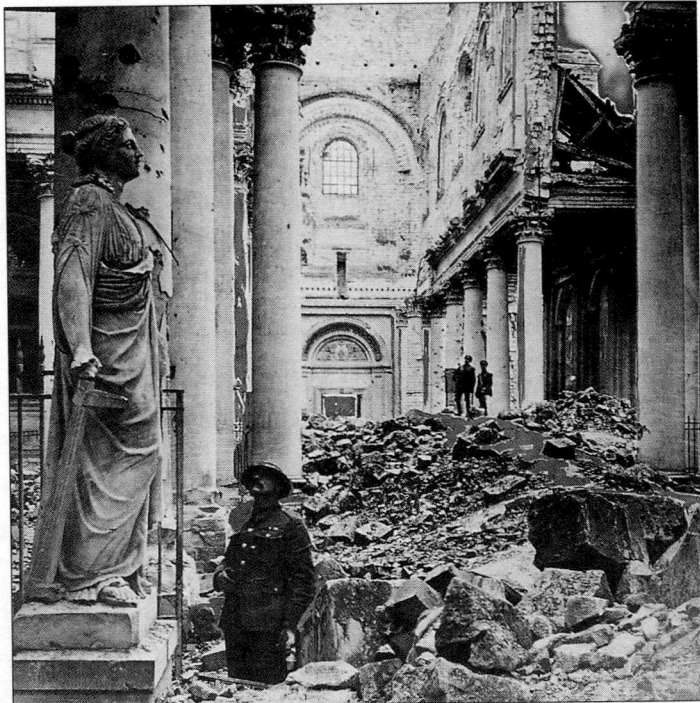

ARCHIVE PHOTOS/POPPERFOTO

Critical Thinking

1. Since Russia posed the greater danger to the Open Door policy, Roosevelt favored Japan; because of racial issues, it was best for him to appear unbiased.
2. German ships transporting guns to Huerta's army; American economic ties with the Allies; submarine attacks; the Zimmermann note
3. Answers will vary, but students should give reasons to support their responses using examples of mob action from this section.
4. Answers will vary, but lists should focus on providing the basic necessities such as food, water, clothing, and shelter. The Fourteen Points promised equality of trade for all countries, supported territorial integrity, suggested new forms of international conduct, and recommended a League of Nations.

CHAPTER 10 REVIEW

Portfolio Project

Select a country in Europe that was involved in World War I. Research what life was like for the citizens of that country during the war. Try to locate and review primary sources to supplement textbook and other secondary source materials. Primary sources might include letters, diaries, personal memoirs, and legal documents such as wills and titles. Prepare a written report about "life during World War I." You may want to support your report with appropriate visuals—pictures from newspapers and magazines, photographs, paintings, and drawings. Share your report orally with your classmates before filing your written account in your portfolio.

Cooperative Learning

With a small group, stage the debate over the selective exclusion that occurred during the 1919 Paris Peace Conference. Use information from Section 4, as well as additional research, to represent the Big Four countries. Try to identify the reasons the Big Four finally excluded Germany and Russia from the peace negotiations.

Reinforcing Skills

Using Reference Materials

Imagine that you are a reporter who was assigned a feature story commemorating Theodore Roosevelt. Think about the various reference materials that could be sources of information about his family, his accomplishments, and his career. Refer to the Tools of Reference chart on page 320 as you list the various reference materials you could use. Explain the type of information that you expect to learn from each source.

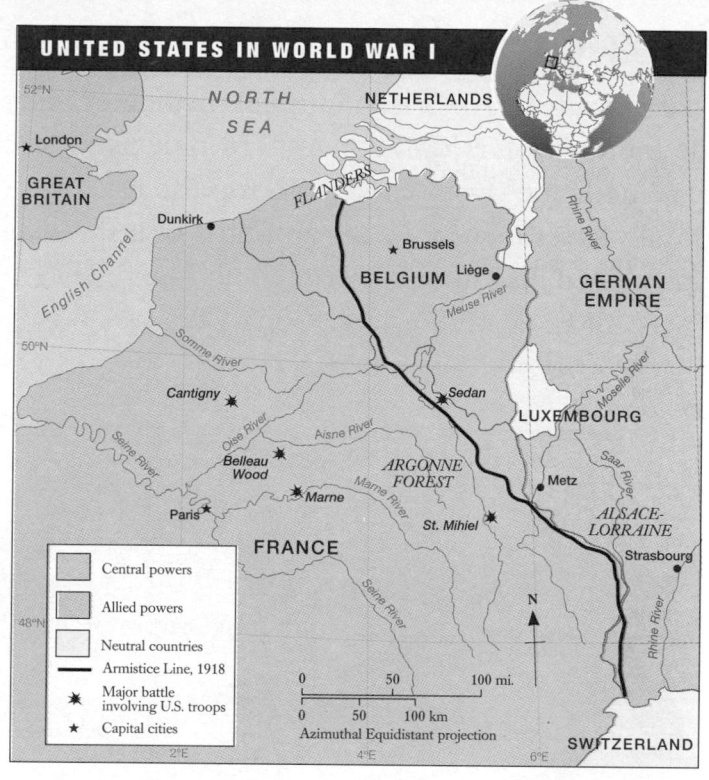

UNITED STATES IN WORLD WAR I

Central powers
Allied powers
Neutral countries
— Armistice Line, 1918
✳ Major battle involving U.S. troops
★ Capital cities

0   50   100 mi.
0   50   100 km
Azimuthal Equidistant projection

Geography and History

Study the map on this page to answer the following questions:

1. Name two important World War I battles involving United States troops. In what country did the fighting occur?

2. Which French city was an important naval landing site for British and Allied replacement troops? Why?

3. Which capital city of western Europe was most threatened by nearby warfare? How did this affect the way the war was fought?

4. Through what countries did the Armistice Line extend? Were these countries primarily Allied Powers or Central Powers?

HISTORY JOURNAL

Through the era of expansionism and World War I, the United States established itself as a world leader and entered the international political arena. How did the emergence of the United States as a world power affect the lives of returning soldiers and their families? Write your response in your journal. Compare your new entry to your original prediction in your journal response to page 292. Underline any new information that you have learned after reading this chapter.

Geography and History

1. Answers will vary, but should include any two of the following: Cantigny, Belleau Wood, Marne, and St. Mihiel are all in France; Sedan is on the France-Belgium border.
2. Dunkirk. It was an important naval landing site because of its proximity to England.
3. Paris was almost surrounded by fighting. Its defense was a major Allied objective.
4. The Armistice Line extended through Belgium and France. Both countries were Allied Powers.

History Journal

Student journals should include references to the aftermath of war, such as changes in the economy and job opportunities, new attitudes about ethnic and racial discrimination, feelings about the status of the United States as a world power, and accompanying fear of international radical movements. Students should also compare these responses to those for page 292.

? BONUS QUESTION

This question may be used for extra credit on the chapter test.
What did many progressives see as a positive side to conscription? *(promoting domestic reforms and equalizing social classes)*

Portfolio Project

Written reports should reflect research of a European country using a variety of primary and secondary sources. Encourage students to use visual displays to extend their findings in order to show the reality of destruction and the hardships that war causes.

Cooperative Learning

Answers will vary, but students may mention such reasons as France did not want to include Germany because of the damage it had inflicted upon France, or that Russia was excluded because of its growing revolutionary movement.

Reinforcing Skills

Students should demonstrate their knowledge of the different types of reference materials available and the purpose each reference source serves.

Making the Historical Connection

Heavily advertised cure-all medicines and soda fountains were 2 distinguishing features of American life in the late 1880s. The popularity of these 2 items inspired an Atlanta pharmacist to create a "medicine" that would taste good enough to top the long list of soda flavors available in local drugstores.

FYI

Patent Medicines Before the Civil War, nearly half of all advertising was for medicines and drugs. Everywhere, but particularly in Western settlements where doctors were scarce, people turned to patent medicines in hopes of warding off a variety of ills. The term *patent medicine* did not mean there were patents on the product. The term was a holdover of an old British phrase. When the king or queen chose specific purveyors of products, the product was given a "patent of royal favor." Most American patent medicines had alcohol as a main ingredient, flavored with roots, herbs, and extracts. As competition increased, these medicines made increasingly outlandish claims about their powers, eventually leading to regulations on advertising.

Then...

Coca-Cola: Symbol of America

In the heyday of American cure-all medicines and soda fountains, Dr. John S. Pemberton decided to create a "medicine" tasty enough to top the lists of soda fountain flavors. In 1886, after months of taste-testing, he produced his famous "nerve tonic"—actually 99 percent sugar water—and Coca-Cola was born.

① Pemberton's partner Frank Robinson created the product's name and its flowing script. His adjectives "delicious and refreshing" became almost synonymous with the drink. Bottles, advertising, and recipes changed, but the Coca-Cola script remained the same.

PRINTS SUPPLIED BY THE COCA COLA COMPANY

Fun Facts

FOR LOVE OF TRADITION
When the Coca-Cola Company tried altering its recipe in 1985, the popular uproar forced a reintroduction of "Coke Classic" within 3 months.

ADVERTISING AT ITS BEST
Some say that "Coca-Cola" is the second most recognized term on the earth, after "OK."

Background Information

Ownership of Coca-Cola Within a few years of creating Coca-Cola, Pemberton died. Asa Candler, another pharmacist in Atlanta, Georgia, paid a total of $2,300 for the business in 1891, and he incorporated it the next year. The company grew dramatically in the next decade. In 1890 it sold about 9,000 gallons (34,100 liters) of Coca-Cola syrup; in 1900 it sold 370,877 gallons (1,404,882 liters). Soon after that Candler established Coca-Cola plants outside of Atlanta. In 1919 a group of investors led by Ernest Woodruff purchased the company for $25,000,000. Woodruff's son Robert served as company president from 1923 to 1955.

2 Pemberton spent $150 in advertising during the first year—at a time when a streetcar sign cost a penny and 1,000 free-sample coupons could be printed for a dollar. Soon the Coca-Cola name was visible on all kinds of items, such as the 1910 baseball score-card, below.

DRINK
Coca-Cola
DELICIOUS   REFRESHING

5¢

THE STRENUOUS LIFE
On the street or curb or any phase of endeavor loses much of its nerve racking and physically exhausting terrors if you drink
Coca-Cola
Refreshes!   Invigorates!
Sustains!
5¢ Sold Everywhere 5¢

HOME TEAM / VISITING TEAM
RUNS
9   8
Coca-Cola
HOME TEAM / VISITING TEAM
HITS
11   13
PERPETUAL COUNTER
HOME TEAM / VISITING TEAM
ERRORS
2   1

PRINTS SUPPLIED BY THE COCA COLA COMPANY

PRINTS SUPPLIED BY THE COCA COLA COMPANY

Stats

PRODUCT DEVELOPMENT

	Originated	Patent Registered
Coca-Cola name	1886	1893
Coke name	1941	1945
Contoured bottle	1916	1960

ORIGINAL RECIPE

Water, sugar, lime juice, coco, citric acid, vanilla, caffeine, orange, lemon, nutmeg, cinnamon, coriander, neroli, alcohol

THE COMPETITION

- Before Pepsi Cola became a threatening competitor, Coca-Cola refused two offers to buy out the nearly bankrupt company.

- Hire's Root Beer and Dr. Pepper were already on many soda fountain menus by the time Coca-Cola arrived.

- Dr. Pemberton originally called his concoction "my temperance drink," in response to the growing temperance movement of the day.

3 At soda fountains, Coca-Cola syrup was often stored in urns like this one. It was mixed with carbonated water at soda fountains and served in a glass for 5 cents. Many soda fountains were inside drugstores, emphasizing the belief (popular since Roman times) that carbonated water had healing properties.

...Now

PORTFOLIO PROJECT

ANALYZING ADVERTISING

Coca-Cola is one of the best advertised products in the country. From the start, the product name has appeared on matchbooks, blotters, clocks, calendars, lamps, serving trays, and playing cards, among other things. In what ways do you see Coca-Cola advertised today? How are today's approaches similar to and different from those of the past? What do you consider to be the most effective forms of advertisement today? Why? Compile examples and explanations for your portfolio.

EVOLUTION OF DISTRIBUTION

Bottles of ready-to-drink Coca-Cola were not widely distributed until the turn of the century when the crimped-crown bottle cap became the industry standard.

THEN AND NOW   **331**

PRINTS SUPPLIED BY THE COCA COLA COMPANY

Then & Now

 FYI

Secret Formula Sometimes called "7X," Coca-Cola's recipe is the "most jealously guarded trade secret in the world," according to commercial historians. Many people believe the syrup contained cocaine in its earliest incarnation. In the late 1800s, before its addictive and debilitating effects were well known, cocaine was considered a wonder drug and included in many patent medicines. Some sources say the cocaine was removed from the recipe in 1905. Official Coca-Cola sources say cocaine was never part of the formula. In the 1900s, Coca-Cola positioned itself in the market as a refreshing drink, not as a health tonic.

 Block Scheduling

The Portfolio Project on this page provides an excellent opportunity to enrich and extend the key elements of this feature.

CLOSE

Encourage a class discussion about the images on these pages. Which of the images appear familiar? Can students relate any of them to things they might see today? Ask students to discuss what factors might make a product successful over time.

PORTFOLIO PROJECT

Portfolio Project

Corporate History Have students research the history of the Coca-Cola Corporation or another company they are interested in. Point out that the encyclopedia may have information on bigger corporations; for smaller companies, students may need to conduct interviews or review periodicals. Companies may supply information on request, but remind students that although this is a good source for basic facts, it is also promotional material and so they will need to use additional sources. Students can finalize their work in a written summary, an oral report (with written notes), or a visual presentation.

The Unit at a Glance

Chapter 11

Although at times the early 1920s were troubled with repression, strikes, and race riots, the primary mood was one of optimism and prosperity. The United States had emerged from World War I as the world's greatest creditor nation and a dominant economic power. Businesses flourished, corporations grew and merged, and the labor force swelled as new industries met the voracious appetite of consumers.

Chapter 12

The 1920s also witnessed an avalanche of new mass-produced goods—from the electric iron to the refrigerator to the automobile. The United States became a nation on wheels during this heady era of jazz, speakeasies, and installment buying. While the good life seemed to be the standard for the decade, not all Americans participated in it. Many continued to struggle in poverty and debt as the 1920s roared on.

00:00 Out of Time?

If time does not permit teaching every chapter in this unit, use the Chapter Digest Audiocassettes and the accompanying student activities and tests. The Chapter Digest Audiocassettes are available in Spanish.

UNIT
4

The New Era of the Twenties

CHAPTER 11
Getting on With Business

CHAPTER 12
A Prospering Society

332

Portfolio Project

Create a 1920s Poster Have students create a poster showing images that represent society during the 1920s. Have students select from the following areas that you can list on the board or on a chart: advertising for automobiles and new middle-class products; fads and fashions of youth; professional sports; music (jazz) and dance (the Charleston); movies; books and magazines; and social changes such as restricting immigration and prohibition. Students can draw images, or select them from magazines. After writing captions on their posters, invite volunteers to share their completed products before filing them in their portfolios.

333

Introducing the Unit

 Show students the Unit 4 Time Line Transparency and/or assign the accompanying activity sheet. Tell students that they will learn about postwar turmoil which was followed by a period of thriving economy and major changes in the workplace. Students will also examine 1920s cultural developments of the prospering United States.

GLENCOE TECHNOLOGY

 Videodisc

American History

Side 1, Section H
Title: The Twenties and the Great Depression, 1920–1940
Subject: Overview of American history from life in the 1920s to the beginnings of World War II.
Ask: In what ways were the 1920s different from preceding eras? *(rapidly changing society and technology, along with prosperous business)*

Side 2
Title: The Roaring Twenties and the Great Depression
Subject: Sequences concerning the Roaring Twenties and the Great Depression
Ask: What type of music became popular during the Roaring Twenties? *(jazz)*

Examining the Visual

Art Deco As the industrialization of the 1900s gathered pace, the sensuous flowing lines of Art Nouveau gave way to the jagged rhythms of Art Deco. This photograph entitled *Illumination*, courtesy of the Niagara Mohawk Power Company in West Syracuse, New York, depicts a vitrolite panel created by an unknown artist. The panel is located in the Niagara Hudson Building and is constructed with shaded and tinted glass. The colors of the panel are illuminated by light entering from behind. The Art Deco style confidently celebrated the machine age with emphatic geometrical lines and shapes, vibrant color schemes, and the use of modern, man-made material such as plastic. The skyscraper deco with its streamline style created the feeling of rushing headlong toward the future.

TEACH

Making the Historical Connection

After World War I, many Americans wanted to forget about world problems and just have fun. As F. Scott Fitzgerald illustrated in this selection from *The Great Gatsby,* however, the Jazz Age's illusion of unending prosperity often resulted in empty, morally bankrupt lives. In contrast, not everyone in the 1920s had the means to live it up the way Gatsby and his acquaintances did. Students may want to read poet Langston Hughes's "The Weary Blues" for another view of the era.

 At the Movies

Jack Clayton's 1974 film version of *The Great Gatsby,* shot in Rhode Island, starred Mia Farrow, and Robert Redford as Jay Gatsby. Another Fitzgerald novel, *The Last Tycoon,* was made into a movie of the same name in 1976. Directed by Elia Kazan, it starred Robert DeNiro and Ingrid Boulting.

Block Scheduling

Team Teaching This excerpt from *The Great Gatsby* can be presented in a team teaching context, in conjunction with English or Language Arts.

The Great Gatsby

BY F. SCOTT FITZGERALD

In this excerpt from F. Scott Fitzgerald's novel The Great Gatsby, *the narrator describes a party at a mansion on Long Island. Music, dancing, and carefree parties—with a hint of emptiness—typified the Jazz Age of the 1920s.*

There was music from my neighbor's house through the summer nights. In his blue gardens men and girls came and went like moths among the whisperings and the champagne and the stars. At high tide in the afternoon I watched his guests diving from the tower of his raft, or taking the sun on the hot sand of his beach while his two motor-boats slit the waters of the Sound, drawing aquaplanes over cataracts of foam. On weekends his Rolls-Royce became an omnibus, bearing parties to and from the city between nine in the morning and long past midnight, while his station wagon scampered like a brisk yellow bug to meet all trains. And on Mondays eight servants, including an extra gardener, toiled all day with mops and scrubbing-brushes and hammers and garden-shears, repairing the ravages of the night before.

Every Friday five crates of oranges and lemons arrived from a fruiterer in New York—every Monday

The Spirit of '26 Illustrator John Held, Jr., captured the jazzy verve of the 1920s in this 1926 *Life* magazine cover.

these same oranges and lemons left his back door in a pyramid of pulpless halves. There was a machine in the kitchen which could extract the juice of two hundred oranges in half an hour if a little button was pressed two hundred times by a butler's thumb.

At least once a fortnight a corps of caterers came down with several hundred feet of canvas and enough colored lights to make a Christmas tree of Gatsby's enormous garden. On buffet tables, garnished with glistening hors-d'oeuvre, spiced baked hams crowded against salads of harlequin designs and pastry pigs and turkeys bewitched to a dark gold. In the main hall a bar with a real brass rail was set up, and stocked with gins and liquors and with cordials so long forgotten that most of his female guests were too young to know one from another.

By seven o'clock the orchestra has arrived, no thin five-piece affair, but a whole pit full of oboes and trom-

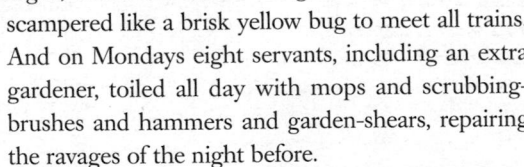
Background Information

Literary Movements of the 1920s F. Scott Fitzgerald belonged to the "lost generation," a group of restless young writers who lived mostly in Paris after World War I. Always searching for something to believe in, Fitzgerald's lavish, rootless lifestyle was emblematic of the lost generation. Other lost-generation writers include Ernest Hemingway and John Dos Passos. A parallel literary movement of the 1920s was the Harlem Renaissance. It encouraged self-respect among African Americans. Its members, including writers Langston Hughes, Zora Neale Hurston, and Claude McKay, gathered in Harlem to explore and encourage African American culture.

bones and saxophones and viols and cornets and piccolos, and low and high drums. The last swimmers have come in from the beach now and are dressing upstairs; the cars from New York are parked five deep in the drive, and already the halls and salons and verandas are gaudy with primary colors, and hair shorn in strange new ways, and shawls beyond the dreams of Castile. The bar is in full swing, and floating rounds of cocktails permeate the garden outside, until the air is alive with chatter and laughter, and casual innuendo and introductions forgotten on the spot, and enthusiastic meetings between women who never knew each other's names.

> **THERE IS A BURST OF CHATTER AS THE ERRONEOUS NEWS GOES AROUND THAT SHE IS GILDA GRAY'S UNDERSTUDY.**

The lights grow brighter as the earth lurches away from the sun, and now the orchestra is playing yellow cocktail music, and the opera of voices pitches a key higher. Laughter is easier minute by minute, spilled with prodigality, tipped out at a cheerful word. The groups change more swiftly, swell with new arrivals, dissolve and form in the same breath; already there are wanderers, confident girls who weave here and there among the stouter and more stable, become for a sharp, joyous moment the center of a group, and then, excited with triumph, glide on through the sea-change of faces and voices and color under the constantly changing light.

Suddenly one of these gypsies, in trembling opal, seizes a cocktail out of the air, dumps it down for courage and, moving her hands like Frisco, dances out alone on the canvas platform. A momentary hush; the orchestra leader varies his rhythm obligingly for her, and there is a burst of chatter as the erroneous news goes around that she is Gilda Gray's understudy from the *Follies*. The party has begun.

I believe that on the first night I went to Gatsby's house I was one of the few guests who had actually been invited. People were not invited—they went there. They got into automobiles which bore them out to Long Island, and somehow they ended up at Gatsby's door. Once there they were introduced by somebody who knew Gatsby, and after that they conducted themselves according to the rules of behavior associated with amusement parks. Sometimes they came and went without having met Gatsby at all, came for the party with a simplicity of heart that was its own ticket of admission. . . .

Dressed up in white flannels I went over to his lawn a little after seven, and wandered around rather ill at ease among swirls and eddies of people I didn't know—though here and there was a face I had noticed on the commuting train. I was immediately struck by the number of young Englishmen dotted about; all well dressed, all looking a little hungry, and all talking in low, earnest voices to solid and prosperous Americans. I was sure that they were selling something: bonds or insurance or automobiles. They were at least agonizingly aware of the easy money in the vicinity and convinced that it was theirs for a few words in the right key.

As soon as I arrived I made an attempt to find my host, but the two or three people of whom I asked his whereabouts stared at me in such an amazed way, and denied so vehemently any knowledge of his movements, that I slunk off in the direction of the cocktail table—the only place in the garden where a single man could linger without looking purposeless and alone.

RESPONDING TO LITERATURE

1. Fitzgerald has been called the "chronicler of the Jazz Age." Based on this excerpt, how would you define the era?

2. What is the narrator's attitude toward the lifestyle and values of the wealthy? Explain.

CLOSE

Discuss the piece with students. Point out that Gatsby, the main character, does not appear. The reader's opinion of him is based only on bits of gossip and descriptions of his excessive parties. Ask the students if they think the information supplied is sufficient to understand his character. What do students think the narrator's detached attitude contributes to the overall mood? Ask students how they would describe Fitzgerald's prose and why. Do they like it? Is it effective or unusual?

Responding to Literature Answers

1. Answers will vary, but students may describe the era as one of excess, of superficiality, gaiety, and wealth. The writer portrays people being very self-conscious while acting very uninhibitedly.

2. Answers will vary, but students should mention that the narrator is attracted by the lifestyle of the wealthy yet aware that their lives are empty and meaningless.

Getting On With Business

DAILY LESSON OBJECTIVES	REPRODUCIBLE RESOURCES	MULTIMEDIA RESOURCES
SECTION 1 Postwar Turmoil 1. Identify the factors that led to the Red Scare. 2. Explain the causes and effects of the Great Migration. 3. Identify how the Progressive movement endured in the 1920s. 4. List the reasons that progressivism declined during the 1920s.	📁 Reproducible Lesson Plans 📁 Vocabulary and Guided Reading Activities (English or Spanish) 📁 Cooperative Learning Activities 📁 Case Studies 📁 Great Debates in American History 📁 Geography in History Activities 📁 Supreme Court Case Studies 📁 Section Quizzes (English or Spanish)	🖌 Chapter Teaching Transparencies 🖌 Section Focus Transparencies 🖌 Map Transparencies 💿 Landmark Documents in American History 💿 Powers of the Supreme Court 💻 Testmaker 💻 Student Self-Test: A Software Review
SECTION 2 The Republican Influence 1. Explain how the policies of Harding, Coolidge, and Hoover supported big business. 2. Describe how Republican foreign policy fostered the international expansion of big business. 3. Explain the reasons for American involvement in Latin America.	📁 Reproducible Lesson Plans 📁 Vocabulary and Guided Reading Activities (English or Spanish) 📁 Section Quizzes (English or Spanish)	🖌 Section Focus Transparencies 💿 The Presidents: A Picture History of Our Nation 💿 Landmark Documents in American History 💻 Testmaker 💻 Student Self-Test: A Software Review
SECTION 3 Prosperity and American Business 1. Explain the reasons for prosperity. 2. Describe attitudes toward business. 3. Identify changes in the structure and management of businesses. 4. Explain how corporate policies reduced the appeal of unions.	📁 Reproducible Lesson Plans 📁 Vocabulary and Guided Reading Activities (English or Spanish) 📁 Section Quizzes (English or Spanish)	🖌 Section Focus Transparencies 🖌 U. S. History and Art Transparencies 📖 Focus on American Fine Art Prints 💻 Testmaker 💻 Student Self-Test: A Software Review
SECTION 4 The Changing Nature of Work 1. Identify how scientific management changed the workplace. 2. Explain white-collar job growth. 3. Identify the kinds of white-collar jobs that most women held. 4. Describe the office environment.	📁 Reproducible Lesson Plans 📁 Vocabulary and Guided Reading Activities (English or Spanish) 📁 Reteaching Activities (English or Spanish) 📁 Enrichment Activities (English or Spanish) 📁 Skill Reinforcement Activities 📁 Section Quizzes (English or Spanish)	🖌 Section Focus Transparencies 💻 Testmaker 💻 Student Self-Test: A Software Review
CHAPTER REVIEW AND EVALUATION	📁 Chapter 11 Test, Forms A and B 📁 Performance Assessment Strategies and Activities	💻 Student Self-Test: A Software Review 💻 Vocabulary PuzzleMaker 💻 Testmaker 🎧 Chapter Digests Audiocassettes

⏱ **00:00** If time does not permit teaching the entire chapter, summarize using the Chapter 11 Digests Audiocassettes and the accompanying activities and tests. (Available in English or Spanish.)

Cooperative Project

Organize students in heterogeneous groups of four or five to research and report on an industry that was unionized during the 1920s. Students may want to consider whether there have been any recent strikes of its workers; and if so, what the causes were and the effects on the families of the workers. Encourage students to note the gains that have been made in working conditions and benefits. 🔲

Suggested Rubric: A Research Report. See Performance Assessment Strategies and Activities, p. 39.

Individual Project

Have students imagine that they are living during the 1920s and their homes have just been wired for electricity. Ask them to write a letter to a friend explaining the changes that electricity will make in their home life. Encourage students to include the electrical appliances that they expect to buy now that electricity is available. **LEP** 🔲

Suggested Rubric: A Self-Assessment. See Performance Assessment Strategies and Activities, p. 53.

Key to Ability Levels

Teaching strategies have been coded for varying learning styles and abilities.

L1 **BASIC** activities for all students

L2 **AVERAGE** activities for average to above-average students

L3 **CHALLENGING** activities for above-average students

LEP **LIMITED ENGLISH PROFICIENCY** activities

Block Scheduling

Block scheduling differs from traditional class scheduling in the amount of time allotted to each period. The extended timeframe provided by block scheduling affords you the opportunity to implement a greater number of research-oriented and activity-intense projects to motivate and involve your students. Activities that are particularly suited to use within the block scheduling framework are identified throughout this chapter by the following designation. 🔲

TEACHER'S CORNER

NATIONAL GEOGRAPHIC SOCIETY

NATIONAL GEOGRAPHIC SOCIETY PRODUCTS AVAILABLE FROM GLENCOE

To order the following products for use with this chapter, contact your local Glencoe sales representative or call Glencoe at 1-800-334-7344:

- *The Presidents: A Picture History of Our Nation* (CD-ROM)
- *GTV: A Geographic Perspective on American History* (Videodisc)
- *GTV: The American People: Fabric of a Nation* (Videodisc)

ADDITIONAL NATIONAL GEOGRAPHIC SOCIETY PRODUCTS

To order the following products for use with this chapter, call National Geographic Society at 1-800-368-2728:

- *The United States as a World Power: From the 1890s to the 1970s* (Filmstrip)
- *Decades of History: The 20th Century–The Early Years* (Filmstrip)

Chapter Overview

This chapter looks at how postwar turmoil led to the decline of progressivism. It covers the three Presidents who fostered a pro-business climate that eventually changed the nature of the workplace.

Introducing the Chapter

Remind students that in 1919 the nation was just emerging from World War I. Explain that after the war Americans craved what President Harding called "normalcy," and that after a period of turmoil this desire would evolve into a general belief that what was good for American business was good for Americans. Have students read the vignette on this page and think about how it illustrates the American climate in general.

Display Chapter Teaching Transparency 11 on the board and distribute copies of the activity sheet for students to complete.

Extension Activity
Have students complete Beyond the Transparency on the activity sheet for Chapter 11 and present their projects after the class has completed the chapter.

History Journal

Have students select one element from the photo and describe it in detail (e.g. a streetcar, a sign, gas lamp, clothing, car). Ask them to find some historical background about it and write a brief descriptive paragraph.

CHAPTER 11

Getting on With Business

OCTOBER 28, 1925: MISSING EPISODE OF *ANNIE* PUBLISHED

From the moment the orphan with the frizzy curls appeared in American homes on August 5, 1924, she found her way into the hearts of all.

On October 27, 1925, the *Chicago Tribune* accidentally left *Little Orphan Annie* out of the newspaper. Reader response was so strong that an apology, along with 2 *Annie* comic strips, was seen in the next day's paper.

How could a comic strip capture so much attention? In part, Annie's innocent strength seemed to reflect the self-image of the United States in the era following World War I. Annie's creator, Harold Gray, had left her without relatives or entanglements. This gave Annie the freedom to do what she wanted and go where she pleased.

Annie's foster father, Daddy Warbucks, was a weapons tycoon who showered Annie with kindness, gifts, and love. His character sent a resounding message that businesspeople could be honest and decent. In the big business era of the 1920s, millions of people seemed to agree. ■

HISTORY JOURNAL

How does the image on the opposite page illustrate the bustle of business that characterized the 1920s? Identify details from the photograph to support your response.

336

EXTRA CREDIT PROJECT

Tracking Reforms Ask students to write a paragraph recalling the progressive reforms of earlier decades. Have students share their paragraphs and try to predict what types of progressive reforms occurred in the 1920s.

THIS 1922 PHOTO OF NEW YORK CITY'S TIMES
SQUARE CAPTURES THE HIGH ENERGY THAT
FILLED THE COUNTRY AFTER WORLD WAR I.

337

Performance Assessment

Refer to page 335B for performance assessment activities for this chapter.

 Also see Activity 11 in the Performance Assessment Strategies and Activities for an additional activity as well as for suggested rubrics.

Notes

Examining the Visual

Times Square Located just below Central Park in Manhattan, near the intersection of Broadway and 42nd Street, Times Square has long been New York's theater district. In this photo, marquees for movie and vaudeville theaters—the Criterion, Loews, Capitol, and the New Amsterdam—seem to dominate the cityscape. In the foreground is an entrance to the city's subway system. The city now has three subway systems, the first of which (the Interborough Rapid Transit, or IRT) opened in 1904. Signs of a bustling economy in this single scene are the many people pursuing their particular errands, the moving truck in the lower left, the packed sidewalks in the distance, the customers and interested browsers at the newsstand, and the steady stream of streetcars and private vehicles in the streets.

FOCUS

Section Objectives

1. Identify the factors that led to the Red Scare.
2. Explain the causes and effects of the Great Migration.
3. Identify ways in which the progressive movement continued during the 1920s.
4. List the reasons that progressivism declined during the 1920s.

Bellringer Activity

 While taking attendance at the beginning of the class period, display **Section Focus Transparency 33,** and have students answer the questions. (Or use the blackline master.)

VISUAL INSTRUCTION

Vanzetti and Sacco Today, many historians believe that Sacco may have been guilty, and that Vanzetti was probably innocent. Regardless, historians think that the evidence against them was insufficient.

Ask: What factors led to the indictment of Sacco and Vanzetti? *(fear of immigrants, whose ways were different, and fear of radical politics)*

Facts on File

Landmark Documents in American History Have students review "Bartolomeo Vanzetti, statement to the court, 1917" and write a paragraph about the intent of the document.

SECTION
1

Postwar Turmoil

AUGUST 23, 1927: SACCO AND VANZETTI EXECUTED; WORLDWIDE RIOTS

Vanzetti (left) and Sacco (right)
The pair arrive for trial at the Dedham Courthouse in Massachusetts.

IN 1921 NICOLA SACCO AND BARTOLOMEO VANZETTI HAD BEEN CONVICTED OF MURDERING A PAYMASTER AND A SHOE FACTORY GUARD DURING A ROBBERY IN SOUTH BRAINTREE, MASSACHUSETTS. Many people believed that the men had been found guilty only because they were immigrants and **radicals,** advocating political and social revolution. By 1927 Sacco and Vanzetti had exhausted every legal appeal. Now they were about to be executed.

In his final defiant words to Judge Thayer, Vanzetti declared that he was innocent of the murders but unshakable in his unpopular beliefs:

I am suffering because I am a radical and indeed I am a radical; I have suffered because I was an Italian, and indeed I am an Italian; I have suffered

more for my family and for my beloved than for myself; but I am so convinced to be right that if you could execute me two times, and if I could be reborn two other times, I would live again to do what I have done already.

—Bartolomeo Vanzetti, speech to Judge Thayer, 1927

The years of the trial of Sacco and Vanzetti showed the United States desperately struggling to defend itself against the dangers following World War I. Many Americans feared immigrants whose ways appeared different and threatening. For a time, many Americans also believed that the radical politics of the 1917 Russian Revolution might overtake this country. Sacco and Vanzetti seemed to represent all the fears of the United States during the turbulent postwar years.

As You Read

Vocabulary
► radical
► anarchism
► prohibition

Think About . . .
► factors that led to the Red Scare.
► the causes and effects of the Great Migration.
► ways in which the Progressive movement continued during the 1920s.
► the reasons that progressivism declined during the 1920s.

338 CHAPTER 11 GETTING ON WITH BUSINESS

Section 1 Resources

REPRODUCIBLE RESOURCES

📂 Lesson Plan 11-1
📂 Section 1 Quiz
📂 Vocabulary and Guided Reading Activity 11-1
📂 Cooperative Learning Activity 11

📂 Unit 4 Case Study
📂 Unit 4 Great Debate
📂 Geography in History Activity 11
📂 Supreme Court Case 9

MULTIMEDIA RESOURCES

📽 Section Focus Transparency 33
📽 Chapter Teaching Transparency 11
💿 Landmark Documents in American History
📽 Map Transparency 11
🔊 Powers of the Supreme Court
💻 Testmaker

Sacco and Vanzetti
A Miscarriage of Justice

Some criminal evidence linked Sacco, a shoemaker, and Vanzetti, a fish peddler, to the murders. Neither man had ever been accused of a crime before his arrest, and none of the money from the robbery was ever traced to the men.

Their trial, too, was marked by serious breaches of fairness. The judge, Webster Thayer, had repeatedly denounced Sacco and Vanzetti for their immigrant backgrounds and for their belief in a radical political theory called **anarchism.** Anarchists believe that the restraint of one person by another is evil, and they do not recognize the authority of any government.

During the six years the men stayed in jail, Judge Thayer refused repeated motions for a new trial. Finally, the Massachusetts governor appointed a special committee to review the case one more time. The committee included Abbott Lawrence Lowell, president of Harvard, and Dr. Samuel W. Stratton, president of the Massachusetts Institute of Technology.

One witness told the committee that, even before the trial, the foreman of the jury had declared, "They ought to hang anyway." The committee agreed that the judge had not behaved properly when he had referred to Sacco and Vanzetti as "dagos" and worse. The committee, however, still backed Judge Thayer's decision to execute the prisoners.

Prominent Americans, including future justice of the Supreme Court Felix Frankfurter, protested the scheduled executions. Sacco and Vanzetti, Frankfurter argued, were being punished for their "alien blood and abhorrent philosophy," rather than for murder.

Americans were not the only protesters. During the six years of appeals, the Sacco and Vanzetti case had be-

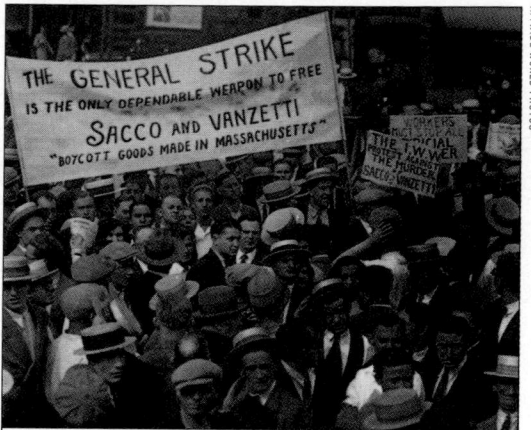

Sympathizers Protest Supporters of organized labor protest the Sacco and Vanzetti guilty verdict. *How widespread was support for Sacco and Vanzetti?*

come world famous. When Sacco and Vanzetti were executed, riots broke out from Japan to Warsaw, from Paris to Buenos Aires. Crowds menaced the United States Embassy in Rome, and workers went on strike in France, Italy, and the United States.

Sacco's last words were "Long live anarchy!" Before he died, Vanzetti gave an interview to a reporter. In broken but eloquent English, he said:

> If it had not been for these thing, I might have live out my life, talking at street corners to scorning men. I might have die, unmarked, unknown, a failure. Now we are not a failure. This is our career and our triumph. Never in our full life can we hope to do such work for tolerance, for joostice [justice], for man's onderstanding [understanding] of man, as now we do by an accident.
>
> —Bartolomeo Vanzetti,
> *New York World*, May 13, 1927

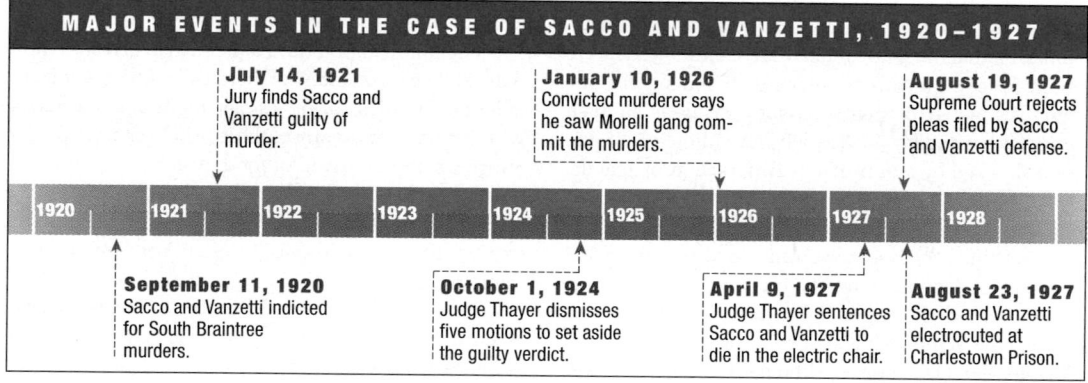

MAJOR EVENTS IN THE CASE OF SACCO AND VANZETTI, 1920–1927

July 14, 1921
Jury finds Sacco and Vanzetti guilty of murder.

January 10, 1926
Convicted murderer says he saw Morelli gang commit the murders.

August 19, 1927
Supreme Court rejects pleas filed by Sacco and Vanzetti defense.

1920 | 1921 | 1922 | 1923 | 1924 | 1925 | 1926 | 1927 | 1928

September 11, 1920
Sacco and Vanzetti indicted for South Braintree murders.

October 1, 1924
Judge Thayer dismisses five motions to set aside the guilty verdict.

April 9, 1927
Judge Thayer sentences Sacco and Vanzetti to die in the electric chair.

August 23, 1927
Sacco and Vanzetti electrocuted at Charlestown Prison.

SECTION ONE **339**

Cooperative Learning

Planning a Political Campaign Have student groups plan mini-campaigns for a governor's election in 1924. Students will belong to either the Democratic or the Republican party and will have a specific responsibility within their group. Tasks might include conducting further research on issues, drawing up a party platform, and creating campaign slogans. Platforms must include suggestions for dealing with the Red Scare. Invite each group to select a candidate who will give a speech based on the platform, issues, and slogans the group creates.

TEACH

Guided Practice

L1 Recognizing Bias
Explain to students that the United States criminal justice system is based on the presumption of innocence. The judge and the foreman of the jury that convicted Sacco and Vanzetti presumed that the defendants were guilty before the evidence was heard. Have students discuss instances of bias in decision making that occur today and how such decisions affect people's lives.

Show students Map Transparency 11 and have them complete the activity sheet.

VISUAL INSTRUCTION

Sympathizers Protest The term *boycott* in the slogan came from Charles Boycott, a retired British army captain. In 1873 he became an estate manager in Ireland, serving writs of eviction on tenants who could not pay their rents due to the bad harvests. The Irish leader Charles Parnell urged that, without violence, the tenants should avoid any communication with those who refused their demand for lower rents.

Answer: *Support was worldwide; riots broke out from Japan to Warsaw, from Paris to Buenos Aires when they were executed.*

CHART STUDY

Ask: What court rejected pleas filed by the Sacco and Vanzetti defense? *(Supreme Court)*

339

Independent Practice

 Map Study Have students locate on a world map some of the places where protests of the Sacco and Vanzetti trial took place and note its far-reaching effects.

 Have students complete the Chapter 11, Section 1 Vocabulary and Guided Reading Activity. (Also in Spanish.) 340 **LEP**

 Have students complete the Chapter 11 Cooperative Learning Activity.

Curriculum Connection

Civics/Language Arts
Have students read the Bill of Rights and then write an analysis of some of the ways in which the Palmer raids violated the rights of individuals.

FYI

William Allen White
William Allen White turned the *Emporia Gazette* from a small-town newspaper into a nationally famous one. White won the Pulitzer Prize for editorial writing in 1923.

VISUAL INSTRUCTION

"Put Them Out and Keep Them Out" The word *bolshevism* comes from the Russian word *bolshinstvo,* which means "majority."

Answer: *a violent wave of anti-Communist panic*

Fifty years to the day of their execution, August 23, 1977, Massachusetts governor Michael Dukakis cleared the names of Sacco and Vanzetti. Their trial, Dukakis said, had been "permeated with prejudice."

The Red Scare
Anti-Communist Panic

Judge Felix Frankfurter described the atmosphere in Boston during the Sacco and Vanzetti trial. He said that outside the courtroom "the Red hysteria was rampant; it was allowed to dominate within."

Indeed, Boston had become one of the centers for the Red Scare, a violent wave of anti-Communist panic that swept through the United States in 1919 and 1920. In November 1917, the Bolshevik Revolution had installed a Communist government in Russia. Communist uprisings in Hungary and Bavaria made it seem as though communism were spreading rapidly.

Two small Communist parties had formed in the United States in 1919. Their total membership never exceeded 70,000, just one-tenth of 1 percent of the adult population. Even so, many people began to fear that a Communist revolution like the one in Russia was brewing in this country.

During World War I, George Creel's Committee on Public Information had whipped up public hatred of Germans. After the war many Americans transferred this hatred to anyone who had been born in another country. Foreigners were especially vulnerable to attack when, like Sacco and Vanzetti, they favored radical politics.

Public officials, business leaders, and the press all contributed to the Red Scare. More than any other person, President Wilson's attorney general, A. Mitchell Palmer, directed the Red Scare.

A Climate of Fear

A progressive lawyer and politician from Pennsylvania, Palmer had no doubt that Communists were about to take over his country's government. For one thing, Palmer had spent the war serving as an alien property custodian. In this job he had collected and been shocked by reams of anti-American propaganda. As a pacifist Quaker, Palmer despised the Bolshevik theory that promoted violent revolution.

To Palmer the Bolshevik plan to take over the world seemed to become a reality on June 2, 1919, when bombs exploded in eight cities throughout the United States. One of the bombs shattered the front of Palmer's Washington, D.C., home. Although the bomb thrower

"Put Them Out and Keep Them Out" The title of this political cartoon expressed the sentiments of those who were influenced by the Red Scare. *What was the Red Scare?*

was killed in the blast, evidence suggested he was an Italian immigrant and anarchist.

After the bombings, Palmer asked for and got an appropriation of $500,000 from Congress to launch a campaign to "tear out the radical seeds that have entangled American ideas in their poisonous theories." Within the Justice Department's Bureau of Investigation, Palmer established the General Intelligence—or antiradical—division. Under the direction of J. Edgar Hoover, this division began to gather information about domestic radical activities.

The Palmer Raids

In November 1919, Palmer's men staged raids on the Union of Russian Workers in 12 cities. In December, 249 aliens were deported to Russia on a ship the popular press nicknamed "The Soviet Ark." Most of the deportees had never participated in any terrorist or criminal activity but merely favored nonviolent radical causes.

The following month Palmer's men arrested more than 4,000 people, many of them United States citizens, in 33 major cities during a single night of raids. Seized without warrants, many of these prisoners were denied attorneys and deprived of food, water, heat, and even bathroom facilities. In Boston one detainee leaped 5 stories to his death, 2 prisoners died of pneumonia, and another went insane. In New York guards beat many prisoners.

Some critics challenged Palmer's methods. William Allen White, newspaper editor, called Palmer's raids "un-American." He went on to argue:

Meeting Special Needs

Visual Learners This activity helps to address the particular needs of visual learners. As students read this section, lead them through the photographs, charts, and other graphics as a way of informally telling the story of the section. Have students use the time lines to summarize events and also to discuss the length of time it can take to bring about change. They may want to add other important dates creating master time lines to display in the classroom.

And if a man desires to preach any doctrine under the shining sun, and to advocate the realization of his vision by lawful, orderly, constitutional means—let him alone. If he is Socialist, anarchist, or Mormon, and merely preaches his creed and does not preach violence, he can do no harm. For the folly of his doctrine will be its answer. The deportation business is going to make martyrs of a lot of idiots whose cause is not worth it.

—William Allen White, *Emporia* (Kansas) *Gazette*, January 8, 1920

The public, however, generally applauded Palmer's January raids. Even though most of the prisoners eventually were released because they had nothing to do with radical politics, the *Washington Post* proclaimed that this was "no time to waste on hairsplitting over infringement of liberty." Six hundred radicals were expelled from the country before the Department of Labor, in charge of aliens, halted the deportations.

By midsummer the height of the Red Scare seemed to be over. The raids and deportations had demoralized American radicals. Businesses had broken a rash of strikes. Bolshevism had failed to spread beyond Russia.

In September 1920, a bomb exploded at the corner of Broad and Wall Streets, the center of New York City's financial district, killing more than 30 people and injuring hundreds more. If the bombing had occurred the year before, Americans might have interpreted it as part of a plot to overthrow the government. Now the United States seemed to be determined not to give way to panic. One newspaper reported:

The public is merely shocked, not terrorized, much less converted to the merits of anarchism. Business and life as usual. Society, government, industry functioning precisely as if nothing had happened.

—*Cleveland Plain Dealer*, September 18, 1920

Labor Unrest

In the middle of the Red Scare, an outbreak of strikes brought the threat of revolution uncomfortably close to home. The cost of living had more than doubled from pre-war levels. When their wages lagged far behind, angry workers went on strike.

Of the 3,600 strikes during 1919, the Seattle general strike, the police strike in Boston, the steel strike, and the coal strike proved the most disruptive. Each major strike further inflamed an already fearful public. During the Boston police strike, all the Boston newspapers called the strike "Bolshevistic." When labor leader Samuel Gompers asked Massachusetts governor Calvin Coolidge to help settle the strike, Coolidge wired back the refusal that launched his national political career: "There is no right to strike against the public safety by anybody, anywhere, anytime."

The 350,000 steelworkers who went on strike in September 1919 worked a 12-hour day, 7 days a week. Each time they changed between the day and the night shift, they had to work 24 hours straight, risking injury and death. Elbert Gary, the head of United States Steel, denied their simple demand—one day's rest out of the week. At first the public sympathized with the strikers. Supported by the press, however, the steel companies portrayed the strike as a radical outbreak and dangerous uprising. As public opinion began to turn against them, the strikers had little chance.

The steel owners provoked riots, broke up union meetings, and employed police and soldiers to end the strike. African Americans recruited from the impoverished South to replace the striking workers also helped break the strikes. In the end, 18 strikers were killed, and the steelworkers' union won none of its demands.

The coal strike lasted for a month in the late fall of 1919 and threatened to paralyze a country that depended on coal to heat its homes and run its factories. When the 394,000 striking miners finally obeyed a presidential order to go back to work, they went back to the same working conditions.

All the major strikes of 1919 were portrayed in the press as anti-American actions that threatened the United States government. The issues of long hours and poor working conditions got lost in the shuffle.

The Great Migration
Opportunities in the North

Between 1916 and 1920, half a million African Americans left the South for new jobs in the North. Many of these migrants were World War I veterans. These

Urban African American Population

City	1920	1930	Increase
Atlanta	62,831	90,119	43%
Birmingham	70,256	99,127	41%
Chicago	109,458	233,903	114%
Cleveland	34,815	73,339	111%
Detroit	40,838	120,066	194%
Los Angeles	15,579	38,894	150%
New York	152,467	327,706	115%
Philadelphia	134,229	219,599	64%
Washington, D.C.	110,701	132,955	20%

African American populations increased in urban areas across the United States from 1920 to 1930. *What two cities had the largest increases?*

FYI

Opposing Points of View During the Red Scare, many Americans believed that people who promoted radical causes should be treated without regard for their rights. Others, such as journalist William Allen White, argued that the arrests and deportations of alleged Communists gave radical causes more publicity than they deserved. Preserving freedom of speech would allow Americans to consider various theories of government without being swayed by pity or fear.

Curriculum Connection

Mathematics To visualize the increase in urban African American populations, students can convert the data in the chart to a bar graph, showing the 1920 and the 1930 figures for each city. They might also research the total populations for each city in 1920 and 1930 and find what percentage of each total was African American.

CHART STUDY

Help students realize that urban growth occurred in other parts of the United States besides the North by citing cities from the chart in the South and West.

Answer: *Detroit and Los Angeles*

Portfolio Project

A Letter Home Lead students in a discussion of what daily life must have been like for a steelworker. Have them also talk about the effect a steel strike might have on business leaders and their companies, and on the public. Help them recognize that each major strike caused elements of the public to be less tolerant of strikers, and to lay blame more heavily on Communist influences. Even though the strikers only wanted safer working conditions, public fear of violence and revolution overrode the real strike issues. Then have students write a letter from a young steelworker to a parent, filing their completed products in their portfolios.

FYI

Differing Views While Booker T. Washington advocated separate development in the U.S. for African Americans, and Marcus Garvey promoted the "Back to Africa Movement," W.E.B. Du Bois argued that African Americans should fight for equal rights in the U.S., including the right to vote and to have equal opportunities. Du Bois was the first African American to graduate from Harvard with a Ph.D.

Block Scheduling

☞ Have students complete the Unit 4 Case Study to enrich their understanding of the Seattle General Strike.

Block Scheduling

☞ Have students complete the Unit 4 Great Debate to enrich their understanding of Prohibition.

Firefighter Recruits Service workers such as these firefighter recruits were part of growing African American communities in the North. *What other salaried jobs did African Americans perform in Northern communities?*

soldiers bitterly resented the discrimination they had experienced in the war. No longer satisfied to struggle on Southern farms, African Americans began to seek better opportunities in the North.

Many African Americans corresponded with a newspaper, the *Chicago Defender,* a key source of information about jobs and conditions in the North. One man wrote to the *Defender* to explain why so many African Americans were migrating north. In the South, he wrote, the wages of a grown man were 50 to 75 cents a day for all labor. "He is compelled to go where there is better wages and sociable conditions, . . . many places here in this state the only thing that the black man gets is a peck of meal and from three to four lbs. of bacon per week, and he is treated as a slave."

African Americans Find Better Pay

In the North, African Americans took jobs as meatpackers, metalworkers, and autoworkers, all for more pay than they could have made in the South. A migrant to Chicago who had found employment in the sausage department of a meatpacking plant wrote: "We get $1.50 a day and we pack so many sausages we don't have much time to play but it is a matter of a dollar with me. . . ."

Only 50 African Americans worked for the Ford Motor Company in 1916. By 1920 Ford had 2,500 African American employees. Six years later their numbers had quadrupled to 10,000.

Between 1910 and 1930, the Great Migration swelled Chicago's African American population from 44,000 to almost 234,000. Cleveland, the home of 8,500 African Americans in 1910, sheltered 68,000 by the end of the 1920s.

Northern whites, however, were no more eager than Southern whites had been to share power and opportunity with African Americans. Many Northern whites reacted violently to this Northern migration.

Racial Unrest

In 1917 race riots erupted in 26 Northern cities. Racial conflicts escalated even further after the war. Riots broke out in many cities, including the nation's capital, during the hot summer of 1919.

Southern African Americans who had migrated to Washington, D.C., during the war had been competing for jobs in an atmosphere of mounting racial tension. Newspaper reports of rumored African American violence against whites contributed to the tension.

Following one such newspaper story, 200 sailors and marines marched into the city, beating African American men and women. A group of whites also tried to break through military barriers to attack African Americans in their homes. Determined to fight back, a group of African Americans boarded a streetcar and attacked the motorman and the conductors. African Americans also exchanged gunfire with whites who drove or walked through their neighborhoods.

President Wilson had to call in federal troops to control the crowds, which finally dispersed in a driving rain. When the Washington riot ended, 4 days after it began, 4 men had been killed, 11 had suffered serious wounds, and dozens more had been injured. Three hundred people were arrested for rioting or for carrying weapons.

Few cities escaped racial violence during the early 1920s. Knoxville, Omaha, and Tulsa all experienced deadly struggles between African Americans and whites. Several radical African American groups sprang out of this ferment. Marcus Garvey's "Back to Africa" movement became the most famous.

The Garvey Movement

A black man from Jamaica, Marcus Garvey had grown up at the very bottom of Jamaican society. Black Jamaicans had no economic or political voice in this white-controlled British colony.

Educated as a journalist and filled with ambition, Garvey arrived in New York City at the age of 28. There

Extending the Content

Determining Causes and Effects of Racial Unrest When President Wilson brought Southern whites into government jobs, they demanded the segregation of African American civil service workers. As a result, many African Americans left government service for private jobs, where some earned more than white civil service workers. Jealous of the African Americans' advancement, some angry whites wanted to keep African Americans "in their place." African Americans, however, especially those who had fought in the war, were determined to fight for their rights. Newspapers further stirred up these racial resentments, which culminated in the Washington, D.C., race riot. Have students discuss the influence of the media on contemporary race relations.

he found an enthusiastic audience for his particular version of Booker T. Washington's African American self-help doctrine.

Where Washington advocated separate development in the United States, Garvey encouraged African Americans to return to Africa "to establish a country and a government absolutely on their own." To this end, Garvey founded the Universal Negro Improvement Association, which peaked at a membership of 250,000. With its program of African American pride and power, Garvey's "Back to Africa" movement foreshadowed the Black Muslim movement of the 1960s.

Garvey's message encouraged poor African Americans, who were his most fervent supporters. A member of the NAACP's board of directors said:

> The sweeper in the subway, the elevator boy eternally carrying fat office men and perky girls up and down a shaft, knew that when night came he might march with the African army and bear a wonderful banner to be raised some day in a distant, beautiful land.
>
> —Mary White Ovington, *Portraits in Color,* 1927

Thousands invested in Garvey's Black Star Line of ships that would take back African Americans to their "home" in Africa. The Black Star Line collapsed, however, partly because unscrupulous white business dealers sold Garvey leaky ships and faulty equipment. Arrested and charged with mail fraud, Garvey was deported as an undesirable alien.

ARCHIVE PHOTOS

A Master Showman Marcus Garvey dressed in a hat with a white plume and a fancy colorful uniform, declaring himself president of the African empire. *What did Marcus Garvey advocate?*

Whites called Garvey the "Moses of the Negroes," but some African American leaders, particularly W.E.B. Du Bois, criticized his unconventional methods and personal flamboyance. Marcus Garvey, however, gave African Americans pride and hope for the future.

Progressivism Endures
New Social Reforms Enacted

Even during this period of labor unrest and social tension, the reform impulse endured. For example, Senator George Norris of Nebraska successfully resisted efforts to turn over the government power plant at Muscle Shoals to business interests. The Women's Joint Congressional Committee lobbied for social reforms throughout the 1920s. On the state level, reformers also succeeded in instituting such programs as old-age pensions, workers' compensation, and city planning.

The postwar decade began with two important reforms whose roots were firmly planted in the Progressive Era. The Eighteenth Amendment established national Prohibition in 1919, and the Nineteenth Amendment gave women the right to vote in 1920.

Prohibition

Between 1906 and 1919, 26 states had passed laws limiting the sale of liquor. Progressives supported **prohibition,** or a ban on alcohol. They championed national Prohibition, a law that would forbid the manufacturing, transporting, and selling of liquor, arguing that an outright ban on drinking would be a great boon to society. In the House of Representatives debate on the Prohibition amendment, Congressman Richard Austin from Tennessee predicted that "a [prohibition] law which has emptied the jails in Tennessee and virtually wiped out the criminal side of the dockets of the courts will do the same in every State."

During the war, antisaloon advocates successfully linked Prohibition with patriotism. Conserving the grain that would have gone into liquor became part of the war effort. The antisaloon league also stirred up the country's anti-German hysteria, blaming German brewers for making American soldiers unfit.

By 1918, three-quarters of the population lived in "dry" states or counties. The cities, with their large immigrant populations, however, remained "wet" until the national amendment was ratified in 1919. This amendment was enforced by the Volstead Act, a law passed in 1919 declaring beverages containing one-half of 1 percent of alcohol intoxicating. When the Volstead Act took effect in January 1920, many Americans had high hopes that the new law would reduce poverty and wipe out

SECTION ONE **343**

**ABCNEWS
iNTERACTiVE**™

  Videodisc

***Powers of the
Supreme Court***

Side 1, Chapter 25
Title: Amendment 18 (1919): Prohibition of Liquor
Subject: Problems during Prohibition
Ask: What was the major problem facing the government during Prohibition? *(People refused to obey the law.)*

See Powers of the Supreme Court Guidebook page 41 for complete lesson plan.

VISUAL INSTRUCTION

A Master Showman Marcus Garvey reached the height of his power in 1920 when he presided at an international convention with delegates from 25 countries followed by a parade of 50,000 through the streets of Harlem. He taught that African Americans would be respected only when they were economically strong, and he preached an independent African American economy within the framework of white capitalism.

Answer: *the return of African Americans to Africa to establish their own country and government; African American pride and power*

Cultural Perspectives

"Back to Africa" Movement Tell students that Garvey's "Back to Africa" movement was not the first such movement. Modern Liberia was founded in 1822 by freed slaves from the United States. Ask students to do research either on what life is like in Liberia today for the Americo-Liberians (descendants of the original founders), who make up about 5 percent of the total Liberian population, or on how the founding of Liberia took place.

ASSESS

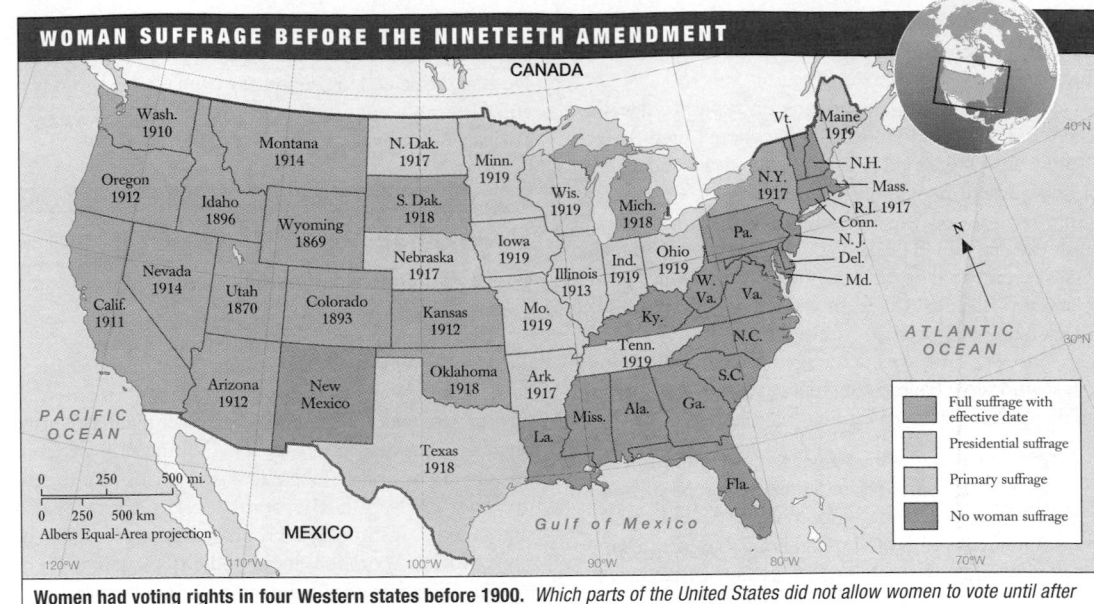

WOMAN SUFFRAGE BEFORE THE NINETEENTH AMENDMENT

Full suffrage with effective date
Presidential suffrage
Primary suffrage
No woman suffrage

Women had voting rights in four Western states before 1900. *Which parts of the United States did not allow women to vote until after the passage of the Nineteenth Amendment?*

prostitution and crime. John Kramer, the first Prohibition Commissioner of the United States, enthusiastically proclaimed: "We shall see that it [liquor] is not manufactured. Nor sold, nor given away, nor hauled in anything on the surface of the earth or under the earth or in the air."

Suffrage

Like the fight for Prohibition, women's struggle for voting rights got its final push from the war experience. Women had begun pursuing the right to vote in 1848, but the fight died down in the decades before the Progressive Era.

Progressives supported suffrage because they believed women's votes could help pass a variety of reforms, especially those that protected women and children. A new period of activism, beginning around 1910,

won rewards when several states—mostly in the West—approved suffrage.

Agnes Geelan, who later became mayor of her town and state senator from North Dakota, remembered: "We were allowed to vote in state elections . . . but there were restrictions. Women could only vote for women candidates. Men could vote for either men or women, and I didn't like that discrimination."

The campaign for national suffrage gathered steam in 1916, thanks to Carrie Chapman Catt's National American Woman Suffrage Association (NAWSA) and Alice Paul's Congressional Union, later the National Woman's party. The two groups argued intensely over tactics. The Woman's party favored radical actions, such as picketing the White House and going on hunger strikes when arrested. In a somewhat less radical way, NAWSA

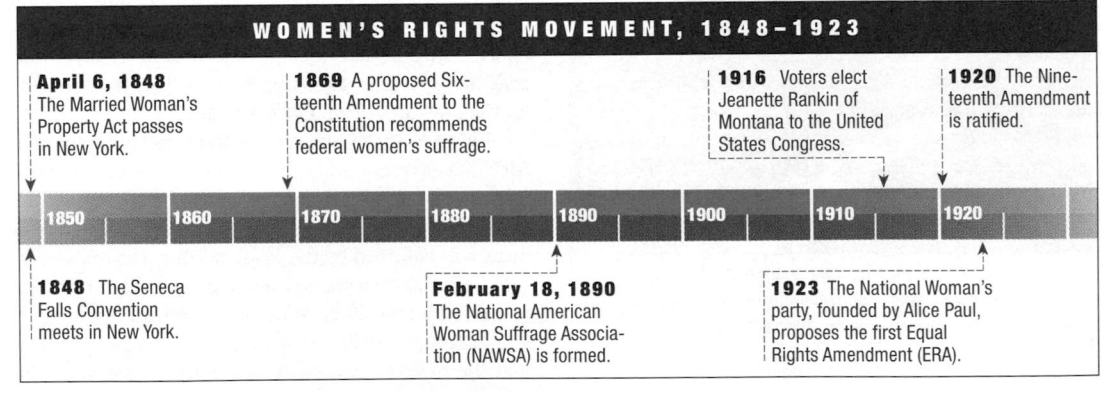

WOMEN'S RIGHTS MOVEMENT, 1848–1923

April 6, 1848 The Married Woman's Property Act passes in New York.

1869 A proposed Sixteenth Amendment to the Constitution recommends federal women's suffrage.

1916 Voters elect Jeanette Rankin of Montana to the United States Congress.

1920 The Nineteenth Amendment is ratified.

1850　1860　1870　1880　1890　1900　1910　1920

1848 The Seneca Falls Convention meets in New York.

February 18, 1890 The National American Woman Suffrage Association (NAWSA) is formed.

1923 The National Woman's party, founded by Alice Paul, proposes the first Equal Rights Amendment (ERA).

Critical Thinking

Making Generalizations Ask what sorts of attempts have been made to limit alcohol consumption in the 1980s and 1990s, such as bans on hard liquor advertisements on television, warning labels on alcohol products, and higher liquor taxes. Encourage students to discuss the influences of the media, advertising, and peer pressure upon the success and failure of these attempts. Then have students consider organi-

zations such as MADD (Mothers Against Drunk Driving) and SADD (Students Against Drunk Driving), which promote an awareness of the dangers of alcohol abuse. Invite them to discuss whether these organizations have been effective and to think of other ways to foster awareness in their communities and schools of the dangers of alcohol abuse.

CULVER PICTURES

Carrie Chapman Catt Catt waves to supporters in New York City in 1920. *What group did Catt lead and what suffrage tactics did she support?*

publicized women's contributions to the war effort, an argument President Wilson used in urging Congress to approve suffrage. Ratification of the national suffrage amendment finally came on August 26, 1920.

The right to vote did not grant women full equality. In many states, a woman still could not serve on juries, hold office, enter business, or sign contracts without her husband's permission. Despite the years of hard work that went into gaining the right to vote, two out of three women who had the vote failed to use it in the 1920 election.

After winning the vote, women united to support one important piece of legislation, the Sheppard-Towner Maternity Act of 1921. Stimulated by high rates of maternal and infant mortality, the act provided funds for states to employ public health nurses, hold child-care conferences, and educate new mothers. The Sheppard-Towner Act was the first allocation of federal funds for welfare purposes. It had faced opposition from the American Medical Association. Other opponents argued that the bill was "inspired by foreign experiments in communism." Even so, Congress passed the Sheppard-Towner Act almost unanimously. It stayed in effect until 1929 when Congress failed to renew it.

Decline of Progressivism

Despite the passage of Sheppard-Towner, the 1920s hardly provided a friendly environment for reform. Progressive legislation that survived Congress or state legislatures frequently perished as a victim of a hostile Supreme Court.

For example, in 1916 Congress had passed a Child Labor Act, controlling the employment of children. Two years later the Court declared the act unconstitutional on the grounds that Congress could not use its commerce power to regulate labor conditions. To make it uneconomical for businesses to hire children, Congress passed a new law establishing a prohibitive tax on child-manufactured products. The Court found the new law unconstitutional as well.

Progressive legislation to benefit working women fared little better. In 1923 the Court struck down a Washington, D.C., law enacting a minimum wage for women.

Progressivism declined for other reasons besides a hostile Supreme Court. After the brutality of World War I, many reformers had lost faith in finding political solutions to social problems. The turmoil of the postwar years also helped to weaken the Progressive movement. Many progressives were middle-class property owners. Shocked by the violence of the strikes and fearful of radical political ideas, many of these progressives found their sympathies shift more firmly to the side of big business.

SECTION REVIEW

Vocabulary

1. Define: radical, anarchism, prohibition.

Checking Facts

2. How did Sacco and Vanzetti symbolize the fears of many Americans in the postwar era?

3. Identify some of the reforms that continued in the 1920s as a result of the Progressive movement.

Critical Thinking

Determining Cause and Effect

4. List the factors that led many African Americans to seek better employment opportunities in the North.

Linking Across Time

5. Progressive legislation, particularly that dealing with working conditions, was often defeated by a hostile Supreme Court during this time period. Are laws to protect workers still needed today? Why or why not?

Evaluate

Have students complete the Section Review.

📁 🔲 Assign the Section 1 Quiz or use the Testmaker to develop a customized quiz. (Also in Spanish.) **LEP**

Reteach

🎧 Have students listen to the Chapter 11, Section 1 Audiocassette. **LEP**

Enrich

📁 Have students complete the Chapter 11 Geography in History Activity.

📁 Have students complete Supreme Court Case Study 9.

VISUAL INSTRUCTION

Carrie Chapman Catt After the adoption of the Nineteenth Amendment, Catt reorganized her suffrage association—2 million strong—into the League of Women Voters to work for continuing national progressive legislation.

Answer: *National American Woman Suffrage Association (NAWSA); less radical tactics, such as publicizing women's contributions to the war effort*

CLOSE

Have students work in small groups to create a list of factors that contributed to the decline of progressivism. Invite groups to present their results to the class. *(the Supreme Court overturned progressive legislation; reformers lost faith after the war; fear of violent strikes and radical political ideas; political and social turmoil)*

Section 1 Review Answers

1. **radical** (338), **anarchism** (339), **prohibition** (343)
2. They were immigrants and radicals—groups that many Americans believed were stirring up a Communist revolution.
3. social reforms such as old-age pensions, workers' compensation, and city planning; prohibition; woman suffrage

4. dismal job opportunities and low wages in the South; discrimination experienced in the war
5. Answers will vary, but may include information about worker's rights today, such as affirmative action, basic working conditions, insurance benefits, and so on.

FOCUS

Section Objectives

1. Explain how the policies of Harding, Coolidge, and Hoover supported business.
2. Describe how foreign policy in the 1920s fostered international expansion of big business and moved away from military and political involvement in Europe.
3. Explain the reasons for United States economic and military involvement in Latin America.

Bellringer Activity

 While taking attendance at the beginning of the class period, display **Section Focus Transparency 34**, and have students answer the questions. (Or use the blackline master.)

VISUAL INSTRUCTION

Campaign Buttons The 1920 election was the first in which women could vote and the first to have returns broadcast on radio.

Ask: How did each of these Presidents handle the press? *(According to Strout, Harding shrugged them off, Coolidge was stiff and controlling, and Hoover impressed them with his responses.)*

Facts on File

Landmark Documents in American History Have students review "Inaugural Address, Warren G. Harding, 1921" and write a paragraph about the intent of the document.

SECTION 2

The Republican Influence

NOVEMBER 2, 1920: HARDING DEFEATS COX

RICHARD STROUT BEGAN RE-PORTING FOR THE *CHRISTIAN SCIENCE MONITOR* IN 1922 AND CONTINUED FOR 62 YEARS. The first three Presidents he covered—Warren Harding, Calvin Coolidge, and Herbert Hoover—could not have been more different.

Richard Strout said that Warren Gamaliel Harding, a fun-loving man who was elected in a landslide in 1920, did not have the answers. "He was furthermore aware of his inadequacies, and he was pathetic. . . . He said, 'Gentlemen, gentlemen, go easy on me. I just want to go out on the golf course today and shoot a round.'"

Calvin Coolidge, Harding's stern Vice President, succeeded to the presidency when Harding died. Coolidge then handily won the 1924 election. In an interview con-

FILE PHOTO BY RALPH J. BRUNKE

Campaign Buttons
Republicans held the White House through the 1920s.

cerning the thirtieth United States President, Strout said:

Calvin Coolidge only answered written questions from the press, and so, one time, we all got together and wrote down the same question. We wanted to know if he was going to run for re-election in 1928. So Coolidge looked at the first question and put it aside. Then he looked at the second and did the same thing. He went through all the slips of papers, I think there were a total of twelve, and on the last one he paused, read it to himself, and went on dryly: "I have a question about the condition of the children in Poland." We all smiled. He may have smiled too. And that concluded the press conference.
—As told to Tom Tiede, *American Tapestry*, 1988

AS YOU READ

Vocabulary
► internationalism
► disarmament

Think About . . .
► how the policies of Harding, Coolidge, and Hoover supported big business.
► how Republican foreign policy in the 1920s fostered the international expansion of big business and moved away from military and political involvement in Europe.
► the reasons for United States economic and military involvement in Latin America in the 1920s.

346 CHAPTER 11 GETTING ON WITH BUSINESS

Section 2 Resources

REPRODUCIBLE RESOURCES
📂 Lesson Plan 11-2
📂 Vocabulary and Guided Reading Activity 11-2
📂 Section 2 Quiz

MULTIMEDIA RESOURCES
🔦 Section Focus Transparency 34
💿 The Presidents: A Picture History of Our Nation
💿 Landmark Documents in American History
💾 Testmaker
💾 Student Self-Test: A Software Review
🎧 Chapter 11 Digest Audiocassette

Herbert Hoover, the engineer who had performed brilliantly as secretary of commerce under Harding and Coolidge, easily won the presidency in 1928 after Coolidge declined to run. In the same interview, Strout said:

> Herbert Hoover was the first great man in my life. I thought he was going to be the greatest president we ever had. . . . He had each of us ask our questions, and then he would remember all of the questions and answer them one by one. It was remarkable. "As for your question, Mr. Strout, blah, blah, blah." He did it perfectly. I always thought he had a great mind, and he did.
> —As told to Tom Tiede, *American Tapestry*, 1988

Although their personalities were strikingly different, the three Republican Presidents pursued similar policies in the 1920s. Rejecting the social reforms of the Progressive Era, the Republican Presidents—Harding, Coolidge, and Hoover—put their faith in big business, both at home and abroad. If government allowed business to prosper, all Americans would reap the rewards.

Harding and the Teapot Dome
Scandals Strike the Administration

In 1920 Warren G. Harding trounced Democrat James M. Cox in the general election. Many observers saw this as a rejection of Woodrow Wilson's brand of **internationalism**, his policy of cooperation and

THE BETTMAN ARCHIVE

Harding's Style Harding (third from left) enjoys an outing in 1922 with Henry Ford and Thomas Edison. *Who was Harding's opponent in the 1920 presidential election?*

involvement with other countries. As a senator, Harding had fought against joining Wilson's League of Nations. Now he promised, "We do not mean to be entangled."

Harding owed his success to Americans' exhaustion with the war years, with progressivism, and with the turbulence of 1919. Tired of reformers' attacks and President Wilson's demands for self-sacrifice, the country longed for a rest.

Return to Normalcy

Harding reassured the American people. In a campaign speech in 1920 he said, "America's present need is not heroics, but healing; not nostrums, but normalcy; not revolution, but restoration; not agitation, but adjustment; not surgery, but serenity."

★ ★ ★ **GALLERY OF PRESIDENTS** ★ ★ ★

Warren G. Harding

1 9 2 1 – 1 9 2 3

"Our supreme task is the resumption of our onward normal way. Reconstruction, readjustment, restoration—all these must follow. If it will lighten the spirit and add to the resolution with which we take up the task, let me repeat for our nation we shall give no people just cause to make war upon us. We hold no national prejudice; we entertain no spirit of revenge."

Inaugural Address, March 4, 1921

CULVER PICTURES

BACKGROUND
► Born 1865; Died 1923
► Republican, Ohio
► Elected lieutenant governor of Ohio 1903
► Elected to the Senate 1914
► Elected President 1920

ACHIEVEMENTS IN OFFICE
► Washington Disarmament Conference (1921)
► Signing of peace treaties with Austria and Germany (1921)

SECTION TWO **347**

TEACH

Guided Practice

L2 Discussion Have students summarize the reasons for Harding's success in 1920.

Independent Practice

L2 Creating a Time Line Ask students to make a time line of significant events between Harding's and Hoover's elections. Students who are learning English can work in pairs with students who are proficient in English. **LEP**

 Have students complete the Chapter 11, Section 2 Vocabulary and Guided Reading Activity. (Also available in Spanish.) **LEP**

VISUAL INSTRUCTION

Harding's Style In the photo Secretary of the Interior Albert Fall is seated to the right of Harding.
Answer: *James M. Fox*

NATIONAL GEOGRAPHIC SOCIETY

 The Presidents: A Picture History of Our Nation

Have students view "Warren G. Harding" and use the information to write a brief biography to include in their portfolios.

Cooperative Learning

Biographical Research Organize the class into three groups. Each group should research the life of one of the three Presidents—Harding, Coolidge, or Hoover. The research should focus on the years before the man became President and the experiences that would shape his policies and conduct in office. Students may divide the work among themselves in a variety of ways: by using different sources; by focusing on different times in their subject's life; or by researching an element of his life, such as education, family, or business experiences. Make sure each student takes part in the research. Set aside a time for groups to share with the class what they have learned about the Presidents. 👝

Teapot Dome Affair This 1923 cartoon depicts the fall of public officials as the oil scandal was revealed. *Why did people not blame Harding when scandals during his administration came to light?*

People were not always sure exactly what the word *normalcy* meant—it was not even in the dictionary. Harding sounded presidential, however, and he most certainly looked presidential—tall, handsome, and stately.

Harding's first two years in office began well. He called a presidential conference to consider the problem of unemployment. Well aware of his own limitations, Harding named some bright and able officers to his cabinet: Secretary of State Charles Evans Hughes, Secretary of the Treasury Andrew Mellon, and Secretary of Commerce Herbert Hoover.

Harding also surrounded himself with his old friends from Ohio. People called these friends "The Poker Cabinet" or "The Ohio Gang." Alice Roosevelt Longworth described the White House atmosphere under Harding: "the air heavy with tobacco smoke, . . . cards and poker chips at hand—a general atmosphere of waistcoat unbuttoned, feet on desk, and spittoons alongside."

Some of Harding's poker buddies used their positions to line their pockets with money. The head of the Veterans Bureau was fined and sent to jail for selling off veterans hospital supplies for a personal profit. Eventually, another adviser resigned in disgrace and another narrowly avoided going to prison. Two of Harding's other advisers committed suicide rather than face public humiliation.

Teapot Dome Affair

Of the many scandalous situations that occurred during Harding's administration, the Teapot Dome Affair became the most famous. Harding's secretary of the interior, Albert Fall, leased government oil fields—one at Teapot Dome, Wyoming—to wealthy friends in exchange for hundreds of thousands of dollars in bribes. Eventually, Fall made history by being the first cabinet officer to go to prison, but the wealthy businesspeople who bribed him were never punished. A popular joke at the time quipped, "In America, everyone is assumed guilty until proved rich."

Upon hearing the news of a Senate investigation of oil leases, Harding grew depressed and distraught over his friends' betrayal. He became ill in Seattle, contracted pneumonia, and died in San Francisco on August 2, 1923, before the press began to reveal news of his administration's corruption. Americans mourned Harding, whom they had loved. Indeed the public seemed less angry at the corrupt government officials than they did at the exposers of the scandals. Senators Thomas J. Walsh and Burton K. Wheeler, who attempted to bring the crimes to light, were labeled "the Montana scandalmongers" by the *New York Tribune* and "assassins of character" by the *New York Times.* After decades of exposure, the American public had tired of muckraking and truly wanted a return to "normalcy." They got it when Harding's Vice President, Calvin Coolidge, succeeded to the presidency.

Silent Cal and Big Business
Business Prospers Under Republicans

Coolidge had a dry personality that symbolized the old-fashioned virtues of the New England in which he had been raised. The journalist William Allen White once remarked that Coolidge had the expression of one "looking down his nose to locate that evil smell which seemed forever to affront him." Alice Roosevelt Longworth said he looked as if he had been "weaned on a pickle."

Yankee Background

Born on a Vermont farm that his family had worked for five generations, Coolidge attended a one-room schoolhouse. After Harding's death, Coolidge's father, a justice of the peace, administered the presidential oath to his son by the light of a kerosene lamp. With his upright Yankee background and unquestioned reputation for complete honesty, Coolidge soon erased any damage the Harding scandals had caused the Republican administration.

Although he lacked Harding's personal warmth, Coolidge carried out Harding's programs. Both administrations rejected government programs to help ordinary citizens. When the victims of a Mississippi River

Meeting Special Needs

Visual Learners This activity is especially helpful to students who use visual techniques for effective learning. Have students discuss the elements of the cartoon. If necessary, help them recognize the visual pun of the teapot and understand that the steamroller of the oil scandal is going to flatten some politicians, possibly all the way to the White House. Invite them to draw their own cartoon or image to suggest the scandal and repercussions of the Teapot Dome Affair.

flood appealed to the government for help, for example, President Coolidge replied, "The government is not an insurer of its citizens against the hazards of the elements." (See One Day in History, pages 394–395 for more on the 1927 flood.)

Policies Toward Business

Big business was another matter. The *Wall Street Journal* could justly brag that "Never before, here or anywhere else, has a government been so completely fused with business." The Harding and Coolidge administrations gave big business a boost in three ways. They appointed businesspeople to commissions that were supposed to regulate business. They selected Supreme Court justices who ruled against progressive legislation. Finally, they named conservatives to powerful cabinet positions.

Harding and Coolidge appointed to regulatory commissions people who opposed regulation. The Interstate Commerce Commission, the Federal Trade Commission, and the Bureau of Corporations soon began to overlook business's violations of antitrust laws.

Harding and Coolidge made 5 conservative appointments to the Supreme Court. From its origin in 1789 until 1925, the Supreme Court had struck down only 53 acts of Congress. During the 1920s the Supreme Court found 12 progressive laws unconstitutional, including the child labor law and the Washington, D.C., minimum wage law for women.

Cabinet positions in the Republican administrations went to wealthy business leaders who used their positions to protect big business interests. Andrew Mellon—secretary of the treasury under Harding, Coolidge, and Hoover—showed where the heart of 1920s politics lay. The third wealthiest person in the United States, Mellon immediately set out to cut government spending and reduce taxes on corporations and on people with high incomes.

Andrew Mellon's Influence

Mellon feared that if high taxes deprived a business person of too much earnings, "he will no longer exert himself and the country will be deprived of the energy on which its continued greatness depends." The multimillionaire with the straggly bow tie almost completely overturned the progressive tax policies of the Wilson years. Thanks to Mellon's efforts, a person making a million dollars a year in 1926 paid less than one-third of the taxes a millionaire had paid in 1921.

Coolidge agreed with Mellon; government should interfere with big business as little as possible. "Four-fifths of all our troubles in this life would disappear if we would only sit down and keep still," said Silent Cal. When Coolidge chose not to run in 1928, America's beloved humorist, Will Rogers, commented that Coolidge retired a hero "not only because he hadent [sic] done anything, but because he had done it better than anyone."

Herbert Hoover, The Wonder Boy
From Engineer to President

As secretary of commerce under both Harding and Coolidge, Herbert Hoover was a key architect of the Republican era. An intelligent and dedicated President, Hoover inherited the blame when the Republican prosperity later came crashing down.

GALLERY OF PRESIDENTS

Calvin Coolidge
1923–1929

AP/WIDE WORLD PHOTOS

"I favor the policy of economy, not because I wish to save money, but because I wish to save people. The men and women of this country who toil are the ones who bear the cost of the Government. Every dollar that we carelessly waste means that their life will be so much the more meager. Every dollar that we prudently save means that their life will be so much the more abundant."

Inaugural Address, March 4, 1925

BACKGROUND
► Born 1872; Died 1933
► Republican, Massachusetts
► Elected governor of Massachusetts 1918
► Elected Vice President in 1920
► Assumed presidency 1923
► Elected President 1924

ACHIEVEMENTS IN OFFICE
► Kellogg-Briand Pact (1928)
► Improved relations with Mexico
► Support of American business

 Global Connection

In November 1923, Adolf Hitler attempted a coup d'état, later called the Beer Hall Putsch, against the German government. Hitler and his men stormed into a beer hall where a right-wing political group was meeting and convinced the group to join their "revolution." The next day, about 3,000 Nazis marched on Munich, but the government stopped the putsch with force. Hitler served only 8 months of a 5-year treason sentence but in that time determined to take power legally.

 NATIONAL GEOGRAPHIC SOCIETY

 The Presidents: A Picture History of Our Nation

Have students view "Calvin Coolidge" and use the information to write a brief biography to include in their portfolios.

Portfolio Project

Outlining a Position Ask students to read the excerpt from Coolidge's Inaugural Address in the Gallery of Presidents. Do they agree or disagree with Coolidge's philosophy? Have them each write a brief position statement, including reasons why they favor or reject Coolidge's idea. Recommend to students that they include this activity in their portfolios.

Hoover, a successful mining engineer (once chief engineer for the Chinese Imperial Bureau of Mines), had brilliantly managed the United States Food Administration during World War I. As director of the Belgian Relief Committee, which provided food to starving Europeans, Hoover's name was a household word in the United States years before he became President.

Secretary of Commerce

Coolidge, who prided himself on restraint, sneered at Hoover's optimistic energy and called his secretary of commerce the "Wonder Boy." Indeed, during the 1920s, it seemed there was nothing the "Wonder Boy" could not do.

Hoover expanded the Commerce Department to control and regulate airlines, radio, and other new industries. He helped organize trade associations—groups of firms in the same line of business—to minimize price competition, which Hoover thought inefficient. Hoover also pushed the Bureau of Standards to standardize everything manufactured in the nation from nuts and bolts to tires, mattresses, and electrical fixtures.

Hoover supported zoning regulations, eight-hour workdays in major industries, improved nutrition for children, and conservation of natural resources. He even pushed through the Pollution Act of 1924, the first effort to control coastline oil pollution.

Attitudes Toward Business

Hoover believed above all in volunteer effort and free enterprise. As secretary of commerce, Hoover had argued that American business was entering a new era. With the growth of trade associations, Hoover hoped businesses would show a new spirit of public service.

In 1928 many Americans agreed with Will Rogers, who said, "I always did want to see [Hoover] elected. I wanted to see how far a competent man could go in politics. It has never been tried before."

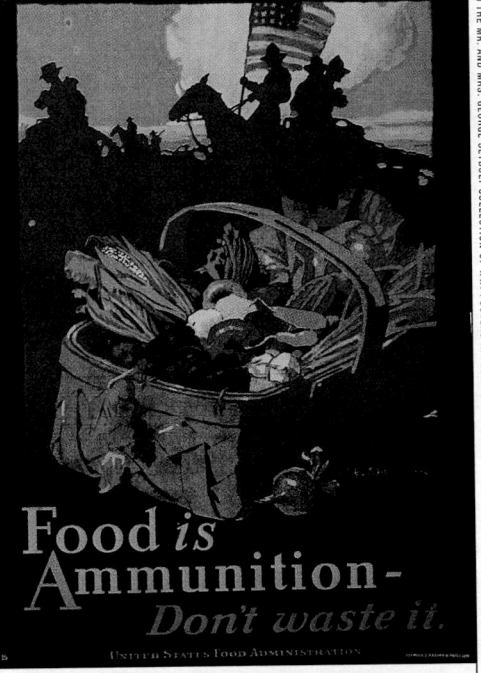

Food is Ammunition—
Don't waste it.
UNITED STATES FOOD ADMINISTRATION

FROM THE MR. AND MRS. GEORGE SEYBOLT COLLECTION OF WWI POSTERS IN THE BOSTON ATHENAEUM

Hoover's Achievements Herbert Hoover gained a reputation for competence during World War I. *How did Hoover's view of big business differ from his predecessors'?*

Republican Foreign Policy
Business Ties Replace Political Ties

After World War I, the United States shied away from political involvement in Europe. Nevertheless, all three Republican administrations increased the country's economic ties to Europe and the rest of the world. During the 1920s military assistance gave way to economic expansion and control. Herbert Feis, who was an influential historian of United States policy, wrote, "The soldiers and sailors had done their part, [and now] the dollar was counted on to carry on their work. It was regarded as a kind of universal balm."

In the 1920s the government encouraged United States firms to dramatically expand their international business. During this decade, American businesses came to dominate world markets in cars, tractors, electrical equipment, and farm machinery. "World peace through world trade" was how business leaders like Thomas J. Watson of International Business Machines (IBM) put it.

The Dawes Plan

Although the United States government did not direct this worldwide economic expansion, its policies fostered the international expansion of big business. The Dawes Plan showed how the United States influenced European economics without direct government intervention.

After World War I, the Allies owed $10 billion in war debts to the United States. Americans insisted on repayment, but the Allies could not pay unless they got the $33 billion Germany owed them in war reparations.

When Germany defaulted on its payments in December 1922 and January 1923, French soldiers marched into Germany's Ruhr Valley. To avert another war, the United States stepped in. The United States sent a business leader instead of an army. Charles G. Dawes, a wealthy Chicago banker, negotiated loans from

Extending the Content

Biography As a result of arranging the Dawes Plan, Charles G. Dawes won the 1925 Nobel Peace Prize. He became Coolidge's Vice President in 1925. He had been named the first federal budget director in 1921 and later served as ambassador to Great Britain for 4 years. After 1932 he was chairman of the board of City National Bank and Trust Company in Chicago.

STEPS LEADING TO THE DAWES PLAN

1. European Allies sell their holdings in the United States to help finance war.

2. The United States provides loans, war materials, and farm products to the Allies during the war.

3. Britain, France, Belgium, and other Allies demand reparations from Germany after the war.

4. The United States demands payments of war debts from France, Britain, and Belgium, 1922.

5. Germany experiences catastrophic inflation and defaults on its reparations payments.

6. The Dawes Plan makes loan to Germany and establishes an annual reparations schedule.

ATLANTIC OCEAN

GREAT BRITAIN
GERMANY
BELGIUM
FRANCE
UNITED STATES

N

0   500   1,000 mi.
0   500   1,000 km
Mercator projection

During World War I, the United States provided the Allies with loans and supplies. The Dawes Plan was set up to help recover the debt. *Which countries were paying war debts to the United States?*

---

private American banks to Germany and set up a new payment schedule.

These negotiations took shape as the Dawes Plan, a way for Germany to meet its financial obligations and avoid war. United States banks loaned Germany $2.5 billion so that Germany could make war reparations to the Allies. In turn, the Allies repaid this money to the United States government. Even though this money represented only a fraction of what the Allies and the United States were actually owed, the Dawes Plan restored payments that otherwise would not have been made. As a result, the potential for war on that score was reduced.

The most powerful nation in the world during the 1920s, the United States proved to be a reluctant giant. To stay clear of Europe's power struggles, the United States embarked on a twofold policy. The United States attempted to destroy the weapons of war through the Washington Conference. The United States also signed the Kellogg-Briand Pact to outlaw armed struggle.

The Washington Conference

In November 1921, Charles E. Hughes addressed the nine nations meeting at the Washington Naval Conference to discuss **disarmament**, the limitation or reduction of weapons. The delegates knew they were to discuss specifically the limitation of naval arms. Hughes, United States secretary of state, shocked his fellow world leaders when he asked them to destroy their battleships. Eventually, three major

treaties emerged—making this the first successful disarmament conference in modern history.

After much controversy, the United States, Great Britain, Japan, France, and Italy pledged to limit the number of their largest ships and to stop constructing new ships. Great Britain and the United States got to keep 500,000 tons of ships each; Japan, 300,000 tons; and France and Italy, 167,000 tons each. The Japanese ambassador complained that the ratio of 5:5:3 sounded like "Rolls-Royce, Rolls-Royce, Ford." Japan agreed only after winning concessions that prohibited new American, British, and Japanese naval bases on the western Pacific islands.

For its part, Japan promised to respect China's sovereignty and independence. Despite this pledge, which kept the China market open to American business, the United States was concerned about Japanese power and ambitions in the Pacific.

The Kellogg-Briand Pact

The United States's second attempt to free itself from involvement in Europe, the Kellogg-Briand Pact, began as a two-nation pact initiated by France's foreign minister, Aristide Briand, to outlaw war and ensure France's security. Secretary of State Frank Kellogg, however, wanted a world treaty to outlaw war.

Fourteen nations initially signed the Kellogg-Briand Pact of 1928. Although the treaty declared war illegal, it failed to include punishments for future attackers.

ASSESS

Meeting Lesson Objectives

Each section objective is tested by the section review question(s) that follows it in parentheses.

1. Explain how the policies of Harding, Coolidge, and Hoover supported business. (1, 4)

2. Describe how foreign policy in the 1920s fostered international expansion of big business and moved away from military and political involvement in Europe. (2, 5)

3. Explain the reasons for United States economic and military involvement in Latin America. (3)

MAP STUDY

The Dawes Plan did not decrease German debt but made the payment schedule more attainable. Still, Germany defaulted on its payments in 1929.

Answer: *France, Great Britain, Belgium*

 Facts on File

Landmark Documents in American History Have students review "Four Power Pacific Treaty (Treaty of Washington), 1921–1922," "Nine Power Pacts, (Washington Conference Treaties), 1921, 1922," "Five Power Naval Treaty, 1922–1923," and "Kellogg-Briand Peace Pact, 1928 (Pact of Paris)" and write a paragraph on the intent of one of the documents.

Cultural Perspectives

Nicaragua Before the arrival of Europeans, the area of modern Nicaragua was inhabited mainly by the Niquirano and Chorotegano (probably of Aztec origin) in the west and the Bawihka in eastern coastal areas. In 1522 the Spanish launched a military expedition against them under Gil González de Avila. The Spanish controlled the area, and all of Central America,

until the United Provinces of Central America organized against Spain in 1823. The federation eventually dissolved, and in 1838 Nicaragua became an independent nation. Ask students, in what ways are Nicaraguan and the United States's national origins similar? *(original populations invaded by Europeans, early colonization, rebellion for independence)*

Evaluate

Have students complete the Section Review.

📧 📱 Assign the Section 2 Quiz or use the Testmaker to develop a customized quiz. (Also in Spanish.) **LEP**

Reteach

🎧 Have students listen to the Chapter 11, Section 2 Audiocassette. (Also in Spanish.) **LEP**

Enrich

📧 Have students choose one of the countries of Central America or the Carribbean and report on the current status of the country.

CLOSE

Use the time lines students made at the beginning of this section. To focus discussion ask students which President they felt was most effective. *(Hoover is a likely answer, but students should support any answer with facts from the text.)*

VISUAL INSTRUCTION

César Augusto Sardino Sandino was assassinated by the Nicaraguan National Guard in 1934.

Answer: *The marines were officially in Nicaragua to protect American business interests. They helped maintain governments favorable to American interests.*

LIBRARY OF CONGRESS

César Augusto Sandino Sandino opposed the United States Marines and was a hero in his country. *Why were United States troops in Nicaragua?*

Many people scorned it as a "parchment peace," but the pact demonstrated Americans' high hopes for an end to military entanglements with Europe.

Relations with Latin America

Although the United States wanted to avoid political involvement in Europe, it chose to protect its interests in Latin America. During the 1920s, American business firms continued their long-standing expansion to the south, searching for markets and raw materials. By 1924 the United States controlled the financial policies of 14 out of 20 Latin American countries.

United States control of Latin America represented more than an extension of business-government cooperation. The United States felt it had the right and the duty to extend its civilization south of the border. Little had changed since the turn of the century.

Though the United States government had begun to reduce its military presence in Latin America after

World War I, it still did not hesitate to use soldiers to protect its business interests. From 1909 to 1933, United States Marines were present almost continuously in Nicaragua, where American bankers and policymakers essentially controlled the economy. Coolidge withdrew troops from Nicaragua briefly in 1925, but sent them back in 1926 when factional fighting threatened to destabilize the country.

United States authorities mediated a peace agreement between the factions, but some of the players on the liberal side refused to sign. Among them was liberal nationalist César Augusto Sandino. At first fighting to restore the Nicaraguan constitutional government, he kept his grassroots army together to fight the United States forces until they withdrew from the country.

Congress criticized Coolidge's military action, but he argued that the United States was "not making war on Nicaragua any more than a policeman on the street is making war on passersby." Yet congressional resistance and popular opposition to Coolidge's use of troops in Nicaragua hinted at a shift in United States policy toward Latin America. By 1929 American policymakers had finally begun to recognize that United States troops in Latin America created resentment abroad and criticism at home.

Domestically and internationally the Harding, Coolidge, and Hoover administrations showed a firm commitment to promoting the country's business interests. Most Americans shared the firm belief that United States business could spread peace and prosperity to the nation and to the world at large.

SECTION REVIEW

Vocabulary
1. Define: internationalism, disarmament.

Checking Facts
2. How did the Dawes Plan show the Republicans' belief that the interests of big business and government were the same?

3. What were American businesses looking for in Latin America?

Critical Thinking
Making Comparisons
4. Briefly characterize Harding, Coolidge, and Hoover to show their differences and similarities.

Linking Across Time
5. Do you think a treaty such as the Kellogg-Briand Pact could have helped prevent World War I? Why or why not?

Section 2 Review Answers

1. **internationalism** (347), **disarmament** (351)
2. A government-sponsored financial plan was used to facilitate the repayment of loans made by private United States banks.
3. new markets and raw materials

4. Harding was more likable than Coolidge. Hoover was probably the most energetic and intelligent. All three supported big business, but Hoover was more balanced in his approach.
5. Students may answer yes or no but should support their answers.

SECTION 3

Prosperity and American Business

1925: *THE MAN NOBODY KNOWS* IS BEST-SELLER

Best-selling Author Bruce Barton
Barton stressed the human life of Jesus with perky prose and chapter titles such as "The Sociable Man" and "His Advertisements."

BRUCE BARTON'S SUBJECT—BIG BUSINESS—AND HIS HERO—JESUS—SEEMED AN UNLIKELY COMBINATION FOR A BOOK. Surprisingly, Barton's *The Man Nobody Knows* became America's best-seller during 1925 and 1926. A one-time journalist and the founder of a large advertising agency, Barton told Americans that Jesus had been the first modern business leader. After all, he wrote, Jesus "picked up twelve men from the bottom ranks of business and forged them into an organization that conquered the world."

Barton explained that when Jesus said he must be about his father's business, he had meant more than simply religion. Barton wrote:

Ask any ten people what Jesus meant by his "Father's business," and nine of them will answer "preaching." To interpret the words in this narrow sense is to lose the real significance of his life. It was not to preach that he came into the world; nor to teach; nor to heal. These are all departments of his Father's business, but the business itself is far larger, more inclusive. For if human life has any significance it is this—that God has set going here an experiment to which all His resources are committed. He seeks to develop perfect human beings, superior to circumstance, victorious over Fate. No single kind of human talent or effort can be spared if the experiment is to

AS YOU READ

Vocabulary
▶ industrial productivity
▶ capital
▶ corporation
▶ oligopoly
▶ welfare capitalism

Think About . . .
▶ the causes of the prosperity of the 1920s.
▶ what the prevailing attitudes toward big business were in the 1920s.
▶ changes that occurred in the structure and management of American businesses during the 1920s.
▶ how corporate policies of the 1920s reduced the appeal of the unions.

SECTION THREE **353**

THE BETTMANN ARCHIVE

Guided Practice

 Responding Write on the board *People Who Rule the United States: Big Business Leaders*. Beneath this line, write these statements from the text: *These men rule by virtue of their ability. They determine who shall hold office.* Ask students to write their reactions to these statements. Do they approve or disapprove? Why? Collect their reactions and read several aloud. Encourage debate about the merits and drawbacks of such a situation. 🔲

Global Connection

The postwar boom the United States experienced was not universal. Battlefield countries had lost economic infrastructure and still owed large debts. Germany was hit especially hard; rampant inflation sometimes made currency worthless in a matter of hours. In 1927 Germany's economy collapsed. In the late 1920s, other economies followed suit. Brazil, for example, suffered a crash when coffee prices fell.

---

succeed. The race must be fed and clothed and housed and transported, as well as preached to, and taught and healed. Thus all business is his Father's business. All work is worship; all useful service prayer.

—Bruce Barton, *The Man Nobody Knows*, 1925

The Glorification of Business
Business Grows in Power and Prestige

The America that made Bruce Barton's book a bestseller changed business almost into a religion and elevated the successful businessperson to the status of a religious hero. In 1921, after touring and examining 12 of the country's biggest businesses, writer Edward Earl Purinton published an article idolizing big business. He praised the business manager of Gary, Indiana, the world's largest one-industry city, saying that successful business leaders were naturally suited to be powerful religious leaders:

> He is called upon by the pastors and priests of churches of a dozen different faiths and nationalities, whose members are employees of the U.S. Steel Corporation, to address the congregations in some helpful, appropriate way. Because he is a fine business man, with power, skill and money back of him, the men of the city want to hear what he has to say. And because he is a gentleman, kind, thoughtful, and sympathetic, the women of the church listen gladly to his lay sermons.
>
> —Edward Earl Purinton, "Big Ideas from Big Business," *The Independent*, April 16, 1921

Not only wealthy Americans revered business. After all, President Coolidge had said, "The man who builds a factory builds a temple—the man who works there worships there." As profits, salaries, dividends, and industrial wages rose during this decade, the gospel of big business became a national creed. Popular magazines printed articles praising corporate leaders, such as Walter Chrysler, *Time* magazine's Man of the Year in 1929.

A list of 59 people who "ruled" the United States appeared in newspapers in the 1920s. The list omitted all elected officials but included John D. Rockefeller, J.P. Morgan, a number of Du Ponts, and Treasury Secretary Andrew Mellon. The person who had compiled the list explained, "These men rule by virtue of their ability." Too busy to hold public office themselves, "they determine who shall hold such office."

Even universities, traditionally hostile to business matters, joined in the admiration for business leaders. In 1925 the Princeton University newspaper asked:

> What class of men is it that keeps governments, businesses, families, solidly on their feet? What class of men is it that endows universities, hospitals, Foundations? . . . What class of men are the fathers of most of us—fathers who provide decently for their families, who educate their children, who believe in order and justice, who pay taxes to support jails, insane asylums and poor houses, which neither they nor theirs are likely to occupy?
>
> —*Daily Princetonian*, January 7, 1925

Predictably, the one answer to all the questions was *business*men.

A Booming Economy
Industry on the Go

Americans thanked big business for the prosperity the country enjoyed during the 1920s. The United States had emerged from World War I in a splendid economic

Increased Productivity The development of assembly lines and the use of electric generators boosted industrial productivity. *How did new technology contribute to the expanding economy?*

Cooperative Learning

Creating a Magazine Students might prepare a short business magazine of the 1920s, containing reports on such topics as the status of the economy, the increase in mergers, the managerial revolution, and changes in labor policies. Organize students into groups and have each group choose a topic and prepare a report for the magazine. Each student in the group should be given a specific job, such as researching, writing, or editing. Students might produce the magazine using desktop publishing equipment, if available. 🔲

position. At the beginning of the war, the United States had owed other countries money. Now the United States was a creditor nation, collecting debts from war-torn Europe.

In contrast to other major powers whose farms and factories had been devastated by the war, America's productive capacity had expanded. Following a short period of social and economic unrest immediately after the war, the United States bounded into several years of record-breaking prosperity.

Between 1922 and 1928, **industrial productivity**—the amount of goods each hour of labor produced—rose by 70 percent. Corporate investors reaped the largest rewards, but many ordinary Americans also benefited. Workers earned higher wages than at any previous time in the history of the United States.

America's productivity soared as new technology and techniques introduced greater efficiency into manufacturing. Electrical motors powered 70 percent of machines in 1929, compared with only 30 percent in 1914. The assembly line that revolutionized the auto industry in 1914 soon moved into other industries as well.

When American business boomed, companies needed bigger and better offices. A growing urban population required new apartment buildings, and a spreading suburban population demanded new roads and houses. As a result, building and road construction took off during the decade.

New Industry

New industries also sprang up, adding to the rapid growth of the decade. The manufacturing of light metals, such as aluminum; a brand-new synthetics industry; motion picture production; and radio manufacturing all provided new jobs and products for the American public.

Automobile manufacturing ranked as the most important of all the new industries. Henry Ford was one of several automobile makers, but it was his name that became a synonym for the booming new industry. In 1923 a public opinion poll declared Henry Ford would be a more popular candidate for President than President Harding. In another contest, college students voted Ford the third greatest figure of all time. Only Napoleon and Jesus got more votes.

In 1907 Ford had declared:

I will build a motor car for the great multitude. It will be large enough for the family but small enough for the individual to run and care for. It will be constructed of the best materials, by the best men to be hired, after the simplest designs that modern engineering can devise. But it will be so low in price

The Radiator Building, Night, New York The skyscraper, represented here in a 1927 painting by Georgia O'Keeffe, was an architectural glorification of business. *Where were skyscrapers built? Why?*

that no man making a good salary will be unable to own one—and enjoy with his family the blessing of hours of pleasure in God's great open spaces.
—Henry Ford, quoted in *American Civilization in the First Machine Age: 1890–1940*, 1970

During 1913 and 1914, Ford introduced the moving production line, an innovation that made it possible to assemble his car in 93 minutes instead of the 14 hours it had taken a year before. By 1925 a completed auto rolled off the Ford assembly lines every 10 seconds. The auto industry's dramatic expansion in the 1920s gave birth to a host of related industries: steel, rubber, petroleum, machine tools, and road building.

The New Commercial Downtowns

As roads and automobiles remade the horizontal landscape of the United States, skyscrapers began to revolutionize the country's vertical landscape. During the

SECTION THREE **355**

 History and the Humanities

U.S. History and Art Transparency 22— *Yellow Cactus Flower* by Georgia O'Keeffe

Focus on American Fine Art Prints, Print 15— *The Voice of the City of New York Interpreted* by Joseph Stella

VISUAL INSTRUCTION

The Radiator Building, Night, New York In its original size of 48 x 30 in. (121.9 x 76.2 cm), the red bar on the left is seen to be a misty neon sign bearing the name of O'Keeffe's husband, photographer Alfred Stieglitz.

Answer: *in big and small cities; to provide space for growing urban populations*

Curriculum Connection

Art One of the era's best-known skyscrapers is New York's Chrysler Building, considered a premier example of art deco architecture. The term *art deco* was coined in the 1960s in reference to a 1925 Paris exhibition of industrial and decorative art. An amalgam of both classical and modern influences, the style uses repeated motifs, graduated shapes, and parallel lines, resulting in elegant ornamentation, classical proportions, and an aerodynamic, streamlined look.

Meeting Special Needs

Learning Disability This activity will help learners who have difficulty with abstract concepts. Review the idea of industrial productivity with students using a concrete example. For example, if a baker can make 4 cakes in an hour mixing the batter by hand, and then makes 6 cakes in an hour using an electric beater, his

or her productivity has increased by 50 percent. If 8 cakes were made per hour, it would be a 100 percent increase in productivity. Point out that industrial productivity measures this kind of increase in output across all industries or types of industries.

Independent Practice

L3 **Research** Remind students that "the urge to merge" also flourished in the 1980s. Ask students to check business or news magazines for articles written in the early 1980s about leveraged buyouts. Students might note other similarities between the decades. Have volunteers report to the class about what their research revealed.

✏ Have students complete the Chapter 11, Section 3 Vocabulary and Guided Reading Activity. (Also in Spanish.) **LEP**

VISUAL INSTRUCTION

Growth of Chain Stores Chain stores were able to cut costs by purchasing in greater volume and by instituting greater efficiency than traditional corner stores. For example, Woolworth needed just 36 buyers for 1,500 stores. If each store were individually owned, every store would need a buyer.

Answer: *One person could probably not manage a chain of stores in the old-fashioned hands-on fashion; upper management would become more remote, and new levels of middle management would be needed to oversee the day-to-day work.*

---

war, construction had been abruptly halted. Now it seemed Americans were reaching for the sky as they made up for lost time.

In 1910 European travelers to New York City had been surprised by 20-story skyscrapers. By 1930 they found themselves in the shadows of 60-story buildings. On May 1, 1931, the new Empire State Building dwarfed even the Bank of Manhattan's 71 stories and the Chrysler Building's 77 stories. At 102 stories, topped by a slender mast, the Empire State Building had become the tallest building in the world.

If New York had its skyscrapers, the rest of the United States would have theirs, too. Houston had its Petroleum Building, Chicago its Tribune Tower, and Cleveland its Terminal Tower. Even prairie towns raised the giant buildings. Tulsa and Oklahoma City had not even existed when the first skyscraper was completed in 1885. By the end of the 1920s, these cities, too, celebrated their own new skylines.

The Corporate Revolution
New Ideas in Business Management

During the 1920s American industry produced new products and constructed soaring new monuments. In this decade the United States also witnessed the culmination of the corporate revolution that had begun in the late 1800s. Many family-run firms could no longer raise enough **capital**—an accumulation of money—to invest in research and development. Unable to purchase the new technology or to afford national advertising, small

companies could not compete. American business became big business, as thousands of small firms went out of business or were absorbed into larger companies or **corporations**—businesses owned by multiple stockholders, whose personal rights and responsibilities are legally separate from the organization's.

The Urge to Merge

Between 1920 and 1928, more than 5,000 mergers joined firms together in larger and more powerful entities that could then buy out smaller companies. Thus the total number of firms dropped by hundreds. The Federal Trade Commission (FTC) had been created to protect small businesses against such takeovers. The person President Coolidge appointed to the chairmanship of the FTC, however, scorned the commission as a "publicity bureau to spread socialistic propaganda" and "an instrument of oppression and disturbance and injury instead of help to business." Under William E. Humphrey, the FTC soon began to encourage instead of to prosecute trade associations and business mergers.

Some of the most obvious examples of business mergers were seen among utility companies. Many local electric companies were absorbed into huge regional systems and utility empires. From 1919 to 1927, 3,700 local power companies turned their lights off for good. By 1930, 10 holding companies supplied 72 percent of the nation's power.

Four meatpackers, 3 major baked goods companies, and 4 tobacco producers dominated their industries during the 1920s. Such a situation, in which a few major producers influence an entire industry, is called an **oligopoly**. Oligopoly prevailed in banking,

Growth of Chain Stores Chinese American Joe Shoong founded National Dollar Stores, Inc., with one small store in 1903. It had grown into a chain of stores by the 1920s. *How might management of a group of chain stores differ from that of a single store?*

Portfolio Project

Survey Have students survey grocery stores in their area and determine if the stores are chain stores or independently owned and operated. Students should then write a summary of their findings, reporting any similarities or differences they noted between stores or types of stores. Suggest that students add their survey and summary to their portfolios. 📁

Growth of Business Associations Booker T. Washington (seated, second from left) founded The National Negro Business League. The League encouraged African American enterprises in the 1920s. *How do you think such associations could help prevent small businesses from takeovers?*

too, as large banks swallowed smaller ones. By 1929, 1 percent of the banks controlled more than 46 percent of the country's banking resources.

A smaller and smaller number of American businesses began to wield unmatched economic power. By 1929 half of America's corporate wealth belonged to its 200 largest corporations.

As small firms went out of business, chain stores and other large companies thrived. The Great Atlantic and Pacific Tea Company (A & P) expanded from 400 stores in 1912 to 15,500 stores by 1932. A single strong leader could no longer run big businesses like the A & P. The new companies demanded a new type of leadership.

The Managerial Revolution

Everyone knew who Henry Ford was, but during the 1920s, the average American could no longer identify the chairperson of the board of directors of any other large corporation. Anonymous, replaceable managers rather than the strong personalities of the past now directed big firms.

Colleges stepped in to train the new leaders for the large corporations. Indeed, during the 1920s, almost every leading university established its own business school. In 1924 the Harvard Graduate School of Business Administration dedicated 23 elegant new buildings on a site across the Charles River from the university. The president of the First National Bank of New York had given $6 million toward the building of Harvard's business school.

During the 1927–1928 school year, Northwestern University offered more than 30 courses on business, from "Bank Practice and Policy" to "Psychology of Business

Relations." New York University students could even take a course in "Restaurant, Tea Room, and Cafeteria Organization."

Smaller businesses that had grown more complicated also required a more specialized kind of managerial know-how. New college-trained business managers soon began to replace the company-trained general managers of an earlier generation.

By 1924 in Muncie, Indiana, for example, the old job of general manager of the glass factory had been divided into five new jobs: production manager, sales manager, advertising manager, personnel manager, and office manager. Companies grew by adding laborers. To supervise these larger workforces, however, they now seemed to need more layers of management.

Another plant in the same city had employed 200 workers in 1890 and supervised them with a small staff: a president, a vice president who was also general manager, a secretary, treasurer, and two foremen. By 1924 the same plant had 6 times as many workers, but now required 15 times as many foremen, as well as the addition of 2 superintendents, an auditor, and assistants to the secretary and treasurer.

Industry's Labor Policies
Suppressing Union Organization

Big corporations with specialized managerial staffs had almost complete control over the workforce during the 1920s. Immediately after the war, the Red Scare had struck a crushing blow to labor by associating unions with Communists. For the rest of the decade, corporations kept labor submissive with an effective combination of punishment and reward. The American Plan was the punishment, and welfare capitalism was the reward.

The American Plan

The American Plan was made up of a variety of activities companies used after the war to demoralize and destroy unions. Corporations called it the "American Plan" to give it the ring of patriotism. One of the plan measures, open-shop associations, allowed employers to stick together in blacklisting union members.

SECTION THREE **357**

VISUAL INSTRUCTION

Growth of Business Associations This photograph was taken in the early 1900s.

Answer: *They might pool their financial resources to ward off buyouts.*

FYI

Prestige of Science During the 1920s one of the few rivals of big business and the business executive in terms of public prestige was science and the scientist. The theories of physicist Alfred Einstein and psychologist Sigmund Freud captivated the public. Sales managers aided the promotion of new products or techniques by calling them "scientific."

Curriculum Connection

Sociology The changing demands of the workplace were accompanied by a rise in college enrollments. The percentage of 18- to 24-year-olds enrolled in college rose from 2.9 percent in 1910 to 7.2 percent in 1930. Enrollments had risen steadily, however, since statistics were first compiled in 1870. At that time, only 1.1 percent of 18- to 24-year-olds were enrolled in college.

Extending the Content

Economics Ask students to read the description in the text of the Muncie, Indiana, plant. Then call attention to the description of another plant in the same city. This plant employed 200 workers in 1890 and rapidly expanded due to technological advances. Then have students figure out the ratio of workers to foremen in 1890 and in 1924. Explain that foremen are supervisors. In 1890 there were 200 workers and 2 foremen, or 100 workers per foreman. In 1924 there were 1,200 workers and 30 foremen, or 40 workers per foreman. Ask for some possible reasons for the changing ratio. Note that as work is broken down into smaller tasks, more supervisors may be needed for the different tasks.

LIMITING LABOR UNIONS, 1917–1929

1917 *Hitchman Coal Co. v. Mitchell* reinforces "yellow dog contracts"; virtually decrees nonunion shop.

1921 *Duplex Printing Press Co. v. Deering* revokes rights to boycott, organize strikes.

1925 *Coronado Coal Co. v. United Mine Workers* applies Antitrust Act to labor.

| 1917 | 1918 | 1919 | 1920 | 1921 | 1922 | 1923 | 1924 | 1925 | 1926 | 1927 | 1928 | 1929 | 1930 | 1931 |

1920 5,047,800 union members

1923 3,622,000 union members

1926 3,502,000 union members

1929 3,461,000 union members

Meeting Lesson Objectives

Each section objective is tested by the section review question(s) that follows it in parentheses.

1. Explain the reasons for the prosperity of the 1920s. (1)

2. Describe the prevailing attitudes toward big business in the 1920s. (2, 4)

3. Identify the changes that occurred in the structure and management of American businesses during the 1920s. (1, 3)

4. Explain how corporate policies of the 1920s reduced the appeal of unions. (5)

CHART STUDY

Ask: How many members did unions lose from 1920 to 1929? *(1,586,800)*

Evaluate

Have students complete the Section Review.

📁 🔲 Assign the Section 3 Quiz or use the Testmaker to develop a customized quiz. (Also in Spanish.) **LEP**

Reteach

🎧 Have students listen to the Chapter 11, Section 3 Audiocassette. (Also in Spanish.) **LEP**

Companies also employed spies who joined unions and then informed employers about labor discontent and identified labor organizers.

As part of the American Plan, many companies offered their workers only "yellow-dog" contracts. With a yellow-dog contract as a condition of employment, an employee agreed not to become a member of a union or to organize fellow employees.

Big business, of course, tried to make it sound as though the American Plan was in the worker's best interest. Elbert H. Gary, head of U.S. Steel, wrote:

> The principle of the "open shop" is vital to the greatest industrial progress and prosperity. It is of equal benefit to employer and employee. It means that every man may engage in any line of employment that he selects and under such terms as he and the employer may agree upon; that he may arrange for the kind and character of work which he believes will bring to him the largest compensation and the most satisfactory conditions, depending upon his own merit and disposition.
>
> —Elbert H. Gary, *New York Times*, September 18, 1919

The Supreme Court favored management over labor with several key rulings. In 1915 the Court had upheld the yellow-dog contract. In 1921 it declared a union boycott illegal and drastically limited workers' rights to picket. In the 1925 *Coronado* case, the same Court that so carefully guarded the rights of big businesses ruled that unions could be sued for damages under antitrust rules.

Between 1921 and 1929, union membership dropped from about 5 million to about 3.5 million. Phil Bart, a lifelong union organizer, recalled how difficult it was to organize strikes in the auto industry in 1928:

> There were no laws to protect strikers then, and there wasn't much public sympathy either. We had to struggle against the place and time. The authorities were intolerant, and when we set up a line the police might come right in and knock hell out of us. The strikers could try to protect themselves by putting up a fight or something, but you could not go to the courts, you could not go to the government; they didn't care. . . . We never forced management to bargain, but working conditions did get better.
>
> —Phil Bart, quoted in *American Tapestry*, 1988

Welfare Capitalism

Working conditions got better partly because employers sought to reduce the appeal of independent unions. The combination of programs employers adopted in order to convince workers they did not need unions became known as **welfare capitalism**.

During the 1920s most employers improved plant conditions, hired company doctors and nurses, and provided a variety of activities from glee clubs to sports teams. For example, the Hammermill Paper Company sold its workers cheap gasoline, while Bausch and Lomb established dental and eye care clinics for its employees.

In 1922 the president of General Electric Company, Gerard Swope, had told a group of foremen in Schenectady, New York, "You are constantly being hounded to increase your output. One of the ways of getting it is to have your men cooperate with you." American business leaders heeded this message and began practicing welfare capitalism in their own companies.

During the 1920s most United States companies offered safety programs and group insurance. A few of the largest corporations instituted stock purchase opportunities and pension plans. In the 1920s U.S. Steel alone paid out more than $10 million a year in worker benefits. Even Elbert Gary, the head of U.S. Steel, had come to believe that such generosity to workers actually profited his company. In 1923 he told his stockholders, "It pays to treat men in that way."

Cultural Perspectives

Union Diversity The early labor movement weakened itself by not including minorities in its ranks. White workers viewed African Americans as job competitors instead. A few labor groups did try to organize both white and African American workers in the late 1860s. The Knights of Labor was the most successful, but by the 1900s it had lost influence to organizations of craft and trade unions, such as the American Federation of Labor. The AFL did not have an official racist policy, but it could not control its federated trade unions, some of which did. In the 1920s, A. Philip Randolph promoted biracial cooperation in unions. He formed the Brotherhood of Sleeping Car Porters in 1925. Ironically, this turned out to be an all–African American union, because the occupation came to be held exclusively by African Americans.

LIBRARY OF CONGRESS

Keeping the Workforce Content A company-sponsored basketball team was a benefit these employees received under welfare capitalism. *What other benefits did welfare capitalism offer, and why?*

Many companies also began programs in which workers could elect representatives to speak to management. Employers called this "industrial democracy" and boasted that it would erase the differences between workers and bosses. Edward Purinton wrote that by providing employee representation on the board of directors, "owners of a business now give the manual workers a chance to think and feel in unison with [the bosses]. All enmity is between strangers. Those who really know each other cannot fight."

Employers may have believed that the interests of worker and employer were identical and that company unions were a form of democracy. The workers knew that the company unions had no real power and called them "Kiss Me Clubs." In the absence of worker-led unions, welfare capitalism maintained the power inequalities that gave management full authority over labor. Indeed, Charles M. Schwab, the head of Bethlehem Steel Corporation, made the owners' position very clear: "I will not permit myself to be in a position of having labor dictate to management."

Welfare capitalism may not have done away with the vast inequities between employer and employed, but by the 1920s, worker-led unions were in a serious decline. By 1929 only about 1 in 12 workers belonged to a union.

While the United States was prosperous, welfare capitalism seemed to keep the workforce content. In January 1929, the head of the Chicago and Alton Railroad boasted, "In our shops since the strike of 1922, the shop employees have been very quiet. The

employee is much happier. . . . He is a peaceful worker and a peaceful citizen."

As employee well-being increased efficiency and profits, welfare capitalism paid off for big business. Corporations also used welfare capitalism to restore their public image after the muckraking scandals of the Progressive Era.

During the 1920s, professional public relations experts promoted the idea of humane businesses that not only looked to the welfare of their employees but also acted in the service of society. The Western Electric Company, for example, offered to send literature teaching household management to women.

> The science of managing a home indicates the use of electrical appliances, but the company wants to teach the science whether it sells the goods or not. This is "good business" because [it is] genuine service.
>
> —Edward Earl Purinton, "Big Ideas from Big Business," *The Independent*, April 16, 1921

The idea of public service became an ideal for big business during the 1920s. Business leaders joined service groups such as the Rotary Club, whose motto became "He profits most who serves best." According to the Rotarians, "the businessman was no longer a profit-maker or even a bread-winner, he was a public servant."

SECTION REVIEW

Vocabulary
1. Define: industrial productivity, capital, corporation, oligopoly, welfare capitalism.

Checking Facts
2. List three examples that illustrate the new admiration Americans had for big business during the 1920s.

3. What two methods did corporations use to manage labor in the 1920s?

Critical Thinking
Recognizing Ideologies
4. Why would Coolidge appoint someone opposed to the activities of the FTC to be its chairperson?

Linking Across Time
5. The names "American Plan" and "open shop" cast opponents in a negative light because no one should want to support an "un-American Plan" or a "closed shop." What groups today have names that suggest nonmembers oppose something highly valued?

Enrich

Have students interview someone in the community who belongs to a union. Have students ask about the functions of the union as well as why the person belongs. Have students share their findings with the class.

VISUAL INSTRUCTION

Keeping the Workforce Content Women's basketball originally had six players on a team; each team member played either offense or defense and could not cross the center line.

Answer: *Benefits included safety programs, group insurance, stock purchase opportunities, and pension plans; benefits were offered to combat the appeal of unions.*

CLOSE

When the economy boomed in the 1920s, big business encouraged Americans to consume, enjoy, and spend. This was in contrast to traditional values and the government's recent promotion of frugality during World War I. Ask students what influences helped bridge the gap between these competing values. What role did advertising play? How did working conditions change when employers like Ford started viewing workers as potential consumers? (*Advertising convinced Americans that it was good or necessary to spend; when viewed as consumers, workers were paid more liberally.*)

Section 3 Review Answers

1. industrial productivity (355), **capital** (356), **corporation** (356), **oligopoly** (356), **welfare capitalism** (358)
2. *The Man Nobody Knows* was a best-seller; popular magazines and newspapers praised "businessmen"; newspapers listed business leaders among the 59 people who "ruled" the country.

3. the American Plan and welfare capitalism
4. Coolidge opposed government regulation of business.
5. Possibilities include Morality in the Media and People for the American Way.

TEACH

Making the Historical Connection

The 1920s were the beginning of what has been called "The Machine Age," and the automobile was its defining element. Historian Richard Guy Wilson wrote, "The machine age meant new processes—mass production, 'Fordism,'—factories, great corporations, and new ways of hiring. . . . The machine age encompassed the vast new skyscraper city, with its transportation systems compacted one on top of the other, and the new horizon city composed of filling stations, drive-ins, and super highways."

FYI

Packard James Packard's first car hit the road in 1899. Shortly thereafter, in 1902, the Packard Motor Car Company came into being. The Packard was soon called "America's Rolls Royce." A 1910 Packard limousine cost $5,450—about 16 times the average per capita income. High costs came from low production: in 1913 Packard's Detroit plant employed 4,525 workers to produce 2,984 cars. Developing cheaper models later helped Packard survive hard times, but the company ultimately closed down in 1958.

Science, TECHNOLOGY, and Society

The Automobile

By the 1920s Ford, General Motors, and Chrysler dominated auto manufacturing, and gasoline-burning internal combustion replaced the once wide array of power sources. Gasoline and automobile industries and related businesses drastically changed the look, pace, and values of the country.

AUTOMOTIVE STATUS

Even as more people could afford automobiles, cars remained symbols of status and glamour, such as this 1929 Packard Roadster. Many independent auto makers did not survive the depression of 1920–1921, but Packard survived to become the leading luxury car of the decade. Sales of luxury cars peaked in 1928 and 1929.

PHOTOGRAPH: BENJAMIN MAGRO.COURTESY OF THE SEAL COVE AUTO MUSEUM

AUTOMOBILE DEVELOPMENTS

1920s	1930s	1940s	1950s
POST–WORLD WAR I The industry adopts wartime technology with superchargers for greater speed and shock absorbers for a better ride.	**NEW FEATURES** By 1930 balloon tires are widely used for a smoother ride; electric lights become standard.	**POST–WORLD WAR II** Wartime gas rationing ends and pleasure driving returns, with bigger, more powerful cars.	**STYLE** Decorative tail fins inspired by Lockheed P-38 fighter planes dominate styling.

Background Information

Decline and Development While the automobile helped boost some industries and activities, it led to decline or even obsolescence in other areas. Railroads, for example, declined as personal cars and the burgeoning trucking industry brought more flexibility to both personal and commercial transport. Some thriving towns on railroad lines shrank to the point of ghost towns as railway travel fell out of favor. City streets and downtown areas suffered, too. New road design and layout catered to auto circulation and speed; the results were rarely pedestrian-friendly. The premium on parking turned many downtown buildings into lifeless parking lots and garages. Businesses moved to the outskirts of town for lower rent, free parking, and proximity to growing suburbs. City streets were losing their role as focal points for human interaction.

PUBLIC SERVICES

Motorization of public services gave increased speed and efficiency to police and fire departments, the post office, even library bookmobiles. The United States Postal Service's rural free delivery (RFD) reduced rural people's isolation, and door-to-door package delivery boosted mail-order sales of companies such as Sears, Roebuck and Montgomery Ward.

THE BETTMANN ARCHIVE

THE WORLD THAT CARS MADE

PORTFOLIO PROJECT

How have cars affected your environment? Look around your neighborhood and identify and describe features that are there only because of cars. How would it look if electricity were the primary car fuel?

ROADSIDE SIGNS

Mass auto travel prompted businesses to advertise in big, loud signs that would catch the eye of passing motorists. In the 1920s, Elizabeth Boyd Lawton led a movement to reform what she saw as a threat to outdoor beauty. She formed the Committee for the Restriction of Outdoor Advertising in 1923. One Lawton supporter lamented, "Where highways run, where the motor car goes [one sees an] eruption of filling stations, hot-dog stands, Tumble Inns, garages, vegetable booths, scarifying field and forest for rods around."

PHOTO BY DECIO GRASSI

GASOLINE

Originally a little-used waste product of kerosene production, gasoline was an essential commodity by the 1920s. It was sold on city street corners and on country roads. The "pump" evolved from a hand-operated tank with a measurement container to a self-measuring, price-calculating machine.

Block Scheduling

The portfolio project on this page provides an excellent opportunity to enrich and extend the key elements of this feature.

FYI

Burma Shave One of the most famous roadside ads from this era was the Burma Shave campaign. In 1925 businessman Allan Odell created the ads, consisting of 6 little red signs placed along the road 100 paces apart. Each bore a few words of a silly rhyme. First in Minneapolis, then all over the country, a collection of "poems" sprang up. For example "Every shaver/now can snore/six more minutes/than before/by using/Burma Shave."

1960s	1970s	1980s	1990s
IMPORTS American small cars first compete with imports.	**OIL** The Volkswagen Beetle surpasses the Model T as the best-selling car ever. After the 1973 oil crisis, government mandates high mileage standards.	**NEW METHODS** Computer-aided design, computer-aided engineering, and factory robots replace traditional design and manufacturing processes.	**OLD IDEAS** Environmental concerns and limited oil resources renew interest in electric cars and nongasoline power sources.

SCIENCE, TECHNOLOGY, AND SOCIETY **361**

CLOSE

Discuss with students the effect of automotive technology on American society. Ask: How did cars affect the physical environment? *(Businesses and signs appeared wherever cars went; students might also mention pollution as a later effect.)* What other industries grew in relation to the growing automobile industry? *(petroleum and mail-order industries, and travelers' services, among others)*

Portfolio Project

Research Invite students to focus on one of the elements related to automobiles on this page and research a business in that area. They might choose a particular car company, an oil drilling and refining company, or a delivery system such as the U.S. Postal Service or a more recently developed private carrier. Suggest that they take a historical perspective on the business they choose, noting what caused its development or how it changed over time. Provide time for students to present their findings to the class, and recommend that they include a copy of their written work in their portfolios.

SECTION
4

FOCUS

Section Objectives

1. Identify how scientific management changed the workplace.
2. Explain the growth of white-collar work.
3. Identify the kinds of white-collar jobs that most women held.
4. Describe the office environment of the 1920s.

Bellringer Activity

While taking attendance at the beginning of the class period, display **Section Focus Transparency 36**, and have students answer the questions. (Or use the blackline master.)

VISUAL INSTRUCTION

Early Ford Assembly Line
Ford employed many immigrants who spoke a variety of languages and knew little English. In order to create a cohesive production unit, Ford instituted compulsory English-language classes based on the Berlitz method.

Ask: What were the benefits of the assembly line? *(It sped up manufacturing and reduced costs; workers were able to purchase the products they produced.)*

The Changing Nature of Work

1924: ASSEMBLY LINE BOOSTS SALES AND EARNINGS

BROWN BROTHERS

Early Ford Assembly Line
Workers place tires and steering wheels on the Model T.

IN 1924 THE TYPICAL FACTORY WORKER WORKED ON AN ASSEMBLY LINE, REPEATING ONE SMALL TASK. Sociologists Robert and Helen Lynd wrote of one such worker: "The worker is drilling metal joint rings for the front of a well-known automobile. He stands all day in front of his multiple drill-press, undrilled rings being brought constantly to his elbow and his product carted away."

The man described above drilled a pair of joint rings 3 times each minute, over and over again. In a 9-hour day, he performed his job 1,620 times.

Although a worker's contribution to making an automobile usually involved tedious work, many factory laborers could still hop into their own cars and drive home at the end of the workday. In that sense, Henry Ford's dream of 1907 had come true. The assembly line sped up car manufacturing and reduced the cost of producing automobiles. Ford passed that savings on to his customers by slashing the prices of his cars.

Henry Ford
Workers' Lives Change

Henry Ford was one of the first **industrialists,** people who dealt with the commercial production and sale of goods and services, to act on the realization that

---

AS YOU READ

Vocabulary
▶ industrialist
▶ scientific management
▶ white-collar worker

Think About . . .
▶ how scientific management changed the workplace.
▶ what caused the growth of white-collar work.
▶ the kinds of white-collar jobs most women held.
▶ the office environment of the 1920s.

Section 4 Resources

REPRODUCIBLE RESOURCES

- Lesson Plan 11-4
- Vocabulary and Guided Reading Activity 11-4
- Section 4 Quiz
- Chapter 11 Test
- Performance Assessment Activity 11
- Reteaching Activity 11
- Enrichment Activity 11
- Skill Reinforcement Activity 11

MULTIMEDIA RESOURCES

- Section Focus Transparency 36
- Testmaker
- Vocabulary PuzzleMaker
- Student Self-Test: A Software Review
- Chapter 11 Digest Audiocassette

each worker is also a consumer. If workers had more money, Ford reasoned, they could purchase more of his cars. So in 1914 Ford took the revolutionary action of doubling the wages of the workers at his plant in Highland Park, Michigan.

Working for Henry Ford

In an era when $2 a day was considered a generous wage, Ford offered $5 a day to workers of "thrifty habits." Workers who refused to learn English, rejected the company detective's advice, gambled, drank, or pursued "any malicious practice derogatory to . . . moral behavior" did not get the raise. In 2 years, three-quarters of Ford's workers made $5 a day.

Other industrialists called Ford a "traitor to his class" because his actions defied the conventional wisdom of keeping wages low and prices high. Ford, however, reasoned that well-paid workers would be less likely to seek other jobs and more likely to do their boring jobs willingly. In 1926 Ford again delighted the workers and shocked the business world by reducing the workweek at his plant from a 48-hour, 6-day week to a 40-hour, 5-day week.

Ford could easily afford to cut back his workers' hours and increase their pay beyond the standards of the time. The assembly line methods that permitted mass production made tremendous profits for Ford, whose company earned an estimated $264,000 per day in 1922.

In addition to their increased wages, Ford's workers gained some other benefits from the new assembly line work. Because the jobs required no skills and little training, laborers could master their work quickly. Almost anyone who wanted to work could do the new jobs.

Henry Ford employed ex-convicts, as well as the physically and mentally challenged. He believed a worker to be "equally acceptable whether he has been

TEACH

Guided Practice

L1 Discussion Check to see that students understand the reference to Ford as a "traitor to his class." Ask students if there are still class distinctions in society today. Then have them discuss Ford's view that the worker is also a consumer and the ways policies Ford initiated affected production. How does Ford's view still apply? **LEP**

GRAPH STUDY

Explain to students that before mass production, an artisan approach encouraged pride in products and continual honing of skills. The laborer controlled the speed and rhythm of the work. Mass production meant endless repetition of a few easily learned, segmented tasks at a pace set by the machine. This discouraged the improvement of skills and any attachment to the completed product.
Answer: *$450*

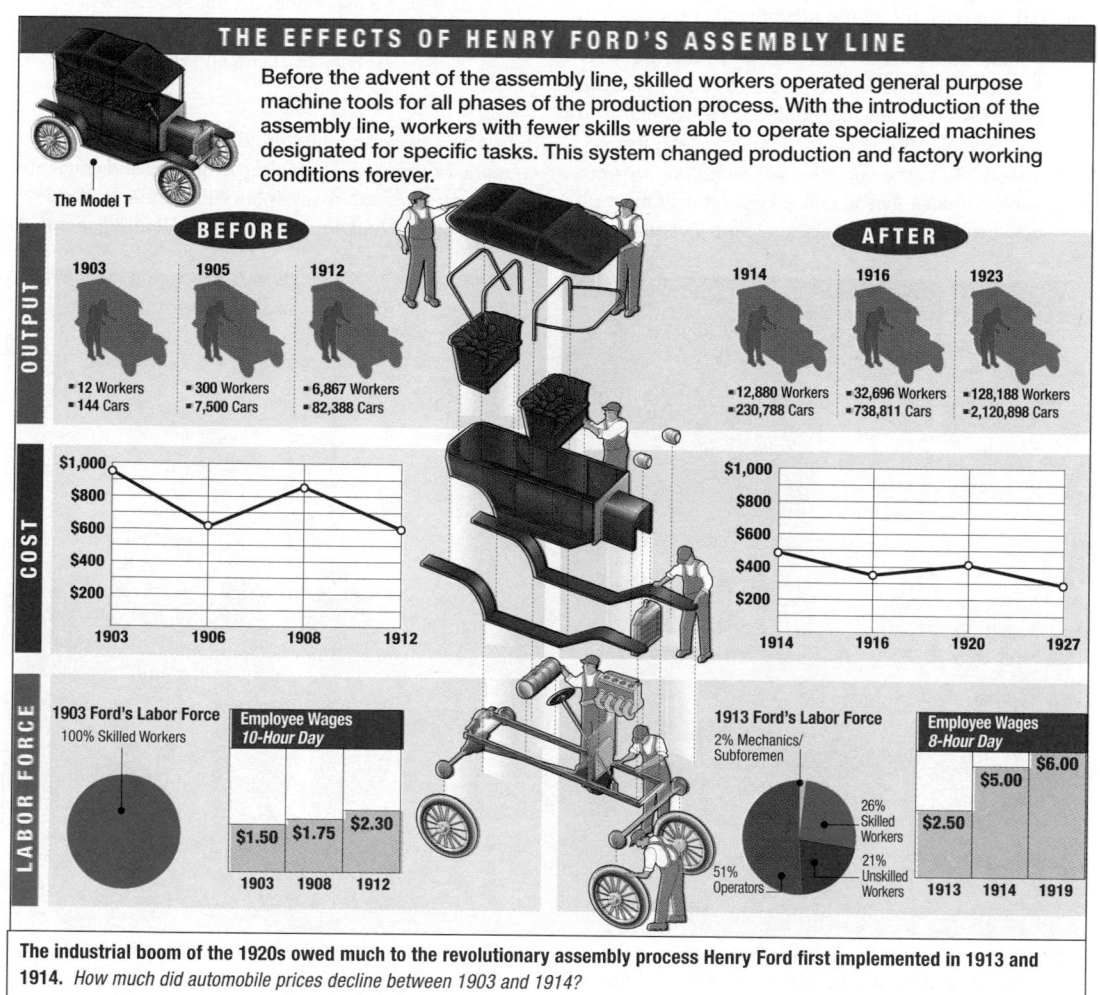

THE EFFECTS OF HENRY FORD'S ASSEMBLY LINE

Before the advent of the assembly line, skilled workers operated general purpose machine tools for all phases of the production process. With the introduction of the assembly line, workers with fewer skills were able to operate specialized machines designated for specific tasks. This system changed production and factory working conditions forever.

The Model T

BEFORE

OUTPUT

1903
- 12 Workers
- 144 Cars

1905
- 300 Workers
- 7,500 Cars

1912
- 6,867 Workers
- 82,388 Cars

AFTER

1914
- 12,880 Workers
- 230,788 Cars

1916
- 32,696 Workers
- 738,811 Cars

1923
- 128,188 Workers
- 2,120,898 Cars

COST

(graph: $1,000 / $800 / $600 / $400 / $200 — 1903, 1906, 1908, 1912)

(graph: $1,000 / $800 / $600 / $400 / $200 — 1914, 1916, 1920, 1927)

LABOR FORCE

1903 Ford's Labor Force
100% Skilled Workers

Employee Wages
10-Hour Day
$1.50 | $1.75 | $2.30
1903 | 1908 | 1912

1913 Ford's Labor Force
2% Mechanics/Subforemen
26% Skilled Workers
21% Unskilled Workers
51% Operators

Employee Wages
8-Hour Day
$2.50 | $5.00 | $6.00
1913 | 1914 | 1919

The industrial boom of the 1920s owed much to the revolutionary assembly process Henry Ford first implemented in 1913 and 1914. *How much did automobile prices decline between 1903 and 1914?*

SECTION FOUR **363**

Cooperative Learning

Simulations of Assembly Lines As an approach to this section, students might prepare classroom simulations of assembly lines of the 1920s, such as a factory assembly line or a cafeteria line. Organize students into groups that include members of varying abilities. Each student should have a role in planning and acting out the simulations. The members of the group should first decide what their assembly line will do. Then they can set up the order and sequence of the assembly, create stations for each stage of production, and provide information at each station concerning the number of people involved and the amount of time needed to do the job. Students should also determine the daily productivity of their line.

in Sing Sing or at Harvard and we do not even inquire from which place he has graduated. All that he needs is the desire to work." Henry Ford prided himself on hiring thousands of immigrants and members of minority groups who might not otherwise have had good job opportunities.

Man or Machine?

The Czech immigrants who worked for Henry Ford and in other factories brought a new word to the United States during the 1920s. The word *robot* came to mean a machine that acts like a person or a person who acts like a machine. In the new factories, it began to be difficult to tell where the worker ended and the machine began.

Typically, a mechanized assembly line delivered the material to workers at waist level, so they did not have to waste valuable time walking, stooping, reaching, or bending. Each worker, doing a tiny part of the total job, worked at a pace set by the machine:

> There were presses that punched sheet steel. All that the worker had to do was to insert the steel before the press descended and withdraw his hands quickly. But some men became fatigued, or surrendered to the numbness or monotony, or were simply careless. The machines cut off their hands.
> —Geoffrey Perrett, *America in the Twenties*, 1982

The steel company prevented these accidents by chaining the workers' hands to their machines. All day, the men's hands jerked back and forth, even when they were out of material. As one visitor to a model steel plant wrote, "There they work, chained to their machines, as galley slaves were chained to their oars."

Mass production meant skilled jobs got broken down into their most basic operations, to be repeated without pause almost all day long. Many workers, not just those who worked in Ford plants, held these repetitive jobs on assembly lines. Skills that had taken a lifetime to master soon became unnecessary. In 1924 a steelworker lamented:

> You had to know how to use the old carbon steel to keep it from gettin' hot and spoilin' the edge. But this "high speed steel" and this new "stelite" don't absorb the heat and are harder than carbon steel. You can take a boy fresh from the farm and in three days he can manage a machine as well as I can, and I've been at it twenty-seven years.
> —Robert S. Lynd and Helen Merrell Lynd, *Middletown*, 1929

The new simple factory jobs did not require much training or thought. To do the job quickly and efficiently, however, demanded discipline. Foremen at the Ford plant prohibited the workers from leaning on their

MOVIE STILL ARCHIVES

Downtrodden Workers The owner exploits factory workers in this image from the classic movie *Metropolis* filmed in 1925. *What words would you use to describe how these workers seem like robots?*

Meeting Special Needs

Visual Learners This activity helps to address the particular needs of visual learners. Have students use the diagraphic on page 363 to interpret information related to the assembly line. Discuss the three levels of information provided in the output level, students may want to figure out the average number of automobiles produced per worker. In the cost level, lead students to note the slight rise in 1920 due to postwar inflation. Likewise, students should note that information in the third level three relating to real wages in 1914 and 1919 needs to be considered in light of inflation. Encourage students to discuss the relationships between all three levels of data in any applicable year. They may also want to compare data before and after the advent of the assembly line.

machines, sitting, squatting, singing, talking, whistling, smoking, or smiling on the job. Laborers had to talk like ventriloquists, not moving their lips, in what they called the "Ford whisper." They set their faces in frozen grimaces that became known as "Fordization of the face." Describing the atmosphere in his auto plant, Ford explained, "There is not much personal contact. The men do their work and go home."

Breaking down skilled work into tiny jobs increased production and profits, raised the wages of laborers, and provided jobs for thousands of people in need of work. It also, however, threatened to turn the workers into machines. Although Henry Ford was the first to use the assembly line for large-scale mass production, the blessings and the curses of the new mass production stemmed from the theories of Frederick Taylor.

Scientific Management
Efficiency Equals Profits

Born into an upper-class family in Pennsylvania, Frederick Taylor joined the Midvale Steel Works in Philadelphia as a laborer in 1878 at the age of 22. Within 6 years, the young man had become chief engineer and a careful observer of his coworkers.

For himself, Taylor appreciated the virtue of hard work, calling it "the real monotonous grind which trains character." The wealthy young man concluded, however, that most of his fellow factory workers were lazy and sloppy in performing their jobs. Taylor argued that developing more efficient working methods would heighten the workers' productivity, raise their wages, and profit the company.

Taylor's theory, which came to be known as **scientific management**, suggested that efficiency, or time-study, experts analyze each work operation and find ways to minimize the time necessary to do a job. Breaking each job into its simplest operations, time-study experts would train workers to carry out their simplified tasks and then time them to see if they could meet the new standards. Taylor advised management to offer cash incentives to workers who produced more than the standard quantities that had been established for their jobs.

Taylor successfully tested scientific management at Midvale Steel. At first both management and labor criticized Taylor's ideas. The bosses at Midvale opposed scientific management because it disrupted their long-established routines. For their part, the workers remained unimpressed by the money incentives. They suspected scientific management of being simply the "scientific sweating of labor."

One new industry, however, had no traditional routines to be upset by Taylor's revolutionary new methods. The auto industry adapted Taylor's ideas from the very beginning.

In 1911 Taylor published his major work, *The Principles of Scientific Management.* That same year, the Taylor Society was founded to spread Taylor's ideas. Four years later, Taylor's book had been translated into eight European languages and Japanese.

By the 1920s many established industries had gotten the message that saving time meant greater profits. Scientific management truly came into its own during the antiunion era that followed the post-World War I strikes. In the 1920s the Taylor Society boasted new members from some of the country's biggest corporations: General Electric, Du Pont, and American Telephone and Telegraph Company (AT&T).

Workers in Manufacturing, 1899–1925			
Year	Blue-Collar Workers	White-Collar Workers	Ratio of Blue: White
1899	4,496,000	349,000	11.4 : 1
1904	5,173,000	546,000	9.5 : 1
1909	6,256,000	750,000	8.3 : 1
1914	6,592,000	911,000	7.2 : 1
1919	8,482,000	1,384,000	6.1 : 1
1921	6,487,000	1,087,000	5.8 : 1
1925	7,873,000	1,270,000	6.2 : 1

The ratio of blue-collar wage earners to salaried white-collar workers decreased from 1899 to 1925. *What was the ratio of blue-collar to white-collar workers in 1925?*

The New White-Collar Workers
Business Occupations Surge

Frederick Taylor's ideas about the organization of the workplace influenced these new workers. During the 1920s even the physical layout of offices began to resemble factories with their assembly lines. Papers passed from worker to worker along a moving belt. A writer described one such firm in 1929:

> Orders are passed along by means of a belt and lights from a chief clerk to a series of checkers and typists, each of whom does one operation. The girl at the head of the line interprets the order, puts down the number and indicates the trade discount;

FYI

Frederick Taylor
Frederick Taylor wanted not only to control completely the way workers spent their time but also to keep them from having any voice at all in the production process. He said he wanted to take away "all possible brain work" from the factory floor.

CHART STUDY

Explain to students that the term *blue-collar* indicates that jobs were performed in work clothes and often involved manual labor. Help them recognize that an increase in white-collar workers arose from the demands of advanced industrialization. This was related to the increase in commercialization of industrial firms, and the increase in administrative and supervisory tasks. Have students note that the number of salaried employees increased almost twice as fast as the number of industrial wage earners from 1899 to 1914.
Answer: *6.2:1*

Portfolio Project

Consumer Goods Probe to see if students know what is meant by *consumer goods.* Ask them to name products available in the 1990s, such as microwaves, televisions, compact discs, and computer games. Point out that electricity became widely available in the 1920s, and for the first time, people could buy electric irons, washing machines, refrigerators, and radios. Have students make a collage or drawing of advertisements for various consumer goods. They may want to settle on one product line such as radios, televisions, or CDs. Have them share their products in small groups and then file the collages or drawings in their portfolios.

the second girl prices the order, takes off the discount, adds carriage charges and totals; the third girl gives the order and number and makes a daily record; the fourth girl puts this information on an alphabetical index; the fifth girl time-stamps it: it next goes along the belt to one of several typists, who makes a copy in sextuplicate and puts on address labels; the seventh girl checks it and sends it to the storeroom.

—C. Wright Mills, *White Collar,* 1951

During the 1920s more new workers than ever before were going to work each day dressed in business clothes. Although women were among their ranks, these workers—professionals, wholesale and retail salespeople, and clerks—became known as **white-collar workers** because of the white shirts and ties uniformly worn by the men.

As corporations grew larger and more complex, the industrial transformation of the early twentieth century gave rise to a host of new occupations—from typist, clerk, and stenographer to junior manager. Thriving insurance and banking industries added to the growing need for still more white-collar jobs.

Scientific Management Creates New Jobs

Moreover, between 1920 and 1930, the ranks of white-collar workers swelled by 36 percent, from 10.5

million people to 14.3 million people. During the same decade, the number of manual workers increased only 13 percent, from 16.9 million to 19.2 million.

White-collar work got another boost from thriving United States factories. By 1929, led by the supercharged automobile industry, 9 of the 20 biggest United States corporations were turning out consumer goods. Exploding with new products, businesses now needed to persuade consumers to buy these new goods. Two growing white-collar professions—sales and advertising—proved indispensable to big business.

The Lure of Sales

Popular magazines in the 1920s advertised, "Don't envy successful salesmen—be one!" Descriptions of salespeople making $5,000 to $30,000 a year, at a time when even autoworkers were earning less than $2,000 a year, lured thousands of young people into the profession.

If they showed brashness and drive, salespeople could make a lot of money. The pressure to succeed, however, could be devastating. Many companies used the quota system in which, to keep the job, each salesperson had to sell 20 percent or 25 percent more every year.

To make a quota, a salesperson needed to learn and apply sales psychology taught in a variety of books. According to a 1925 essay by famed lawyer Clarence Darrow, a leading sales textbook of the time even compared selling to hunting for prey: "The expert fisherman tries out the fish—if one kind of bait doesn't get the strike, he changes . . . He carefully lays his snares, places his bait and then the unsuspecting Prospect falls into the trap."

Sometimes a salesperson simply could not wait for a prospect to fall into the trap. A more aggressive approach was in order. *Selling News,* a magazine for salespeople, awarded a cash prize for this winning entry to a "sales ideas" contest. An electric cleaner salesperson who had seen a woman shaking a rug out of a second-story window told the following story. Because the door to her upstairs rooms was open, the salesperson walked right in, pretending to have an appointment to clean the woman's house. In the words of the salesperson, the woman was "very much surprised, assuring me that I had the wrong number. But during my very courteous apologies I had managed to get my cleaner connected and in action. The result was that I walked out minus the cleaner, plus her contract and check."

The salespeople who could succeed, using whatever methods, won the biggest rewards. One company gave a yearly banquet at which the best salesperson feasted on oysters, roast turkey, and ice-cream dessert. The runner-up was served the same feast, but without the oysters. So it went, down to the one with the worst sales record. This poor person's humiliation was served

Lining Up the Salesforce As electricity became available to all, salespeople like these found a ready market for their wares. *What kind of tactics might these salespeople use to be successful?*

Extending the Content

Advertising Cosmetics One category of consumer goods that grew at an incredible pace during the 1920s was cosmetics. In 1919 no "lady" was supposed to use cosmetics. In 1929 it was calculated that more than a pound of face powder and 8 rouge compacts were sold for every woman in the country. There were 1,500 brands of face cream and 2,500 brands of lipstick to choose from. Have students make a list of contemporary cosmetic products and companies and compare them to those that existed in the past. Students may also be interested in noting the growth of cosmetic products for males.

up before the group on a small plate of boiled beans and crackers.

The Advertising Worker

If the salesperson sold Americans what they needed and wanted, it was the advertising worker who persuaded Americans to need and want what was being offered for sale. Certainly, by 1925, United States corporations spent more than $1 billion a year on advertising. In the 1920s advertiser and author Bruce Barton argued, "Advertising is the spark plug on the cylinder of mass production . . . and sustains a system that has made us leaders of the free world." The advertising company Barton began started with a $10,000 loan in 1919 and eventually became a multimillion-dollar business.

Who worked for a typical large advertising company? Most advertising workers were young, white college graduates or former newspaper writers. Advertising companies hired women for the special knowledge only they could provide about the types of products women used and wanted. In the largest ad agencies, however, male employees outnumbered females by 10 to 1. As in many other businesses, men in advertising occupied almost all the positions that carried executive authority. Even the best-paid women copywriters earned far less than men who performed the same jobs.

Advertising workers got used to producing at a hectic pace. One ad copywriter later recalled, "If you have never wrapped a cold towel around your head at three o'clock in the morning in an effort to get a piece of copy ready for delivery before nine, you have never given it your all." The job turnover was high: More than 1 out of 3 advertising workers switched employers each year. Yet, if an advertising worker could stand the exhausting pace, he or she could make an annual salary exceeding $5,000, more than 3 times what an automobile worker earned. Advertisers prided themselves on knowing what Americans wanted. Indeed, they liked to consider themselves not advertising workers but "consumption engineers." Great business leaders, a 1920s advertising magazine boasted, might someday "learn almost as much about what the people

THE BETTMANN ARCHIVE

Skilled Labor in the 1920s Office In the 1920s many young women spent their working hours in large typing "pools" like this one. *What skills did a typist need to possess?*

of the United States really know about and are interested in as does the junior copywriter of a fourth rate advertising agency."

Women in the Workforce
From Factories to Offices

At the turn of the century, less than 1 in 5 women workers held clerical, managerial, sales, and professional positions. When women began to flood the workforce during the 1920s, however, many left their houses dressed in black skirts and starched white blouses. These women workers were heading for offices and stores, not factories. By 1930, 44 percent of employed women worked at white-collar jobs.

Typecasting Women

It all started with the typewriter. E. Remington and Sons sold the first typewriting machines in 1874. Almost all the new typists were middle class, high-school educated, and female. Why? To do the job, a worker needed to be a good speller and possess a knowledge of grammar, capitalization, and punctuation. Most lower-class men and women lacked these skills; a middle-class man with a high-school diploma could find a much better-paying job.

For female high-school graduates, however, the story was different. Before the typewriter an educated working woman had few choices: she could become a teacher or a nurse or take a factory job for which she

ASSESS

Meeting Lesson Objectives

Each section objective is tested by the section review question(s) that follows it in parentheses.

1. Identify how scientific management changed the workplace. (1, 2)
2. Explain the growth of white-collar work. (1, 4)
3. Identify the kinds of white-collar jobs that most women held. (1, 3)
4. Describe the office environment of the 1920s. (5)

VISUAL INSTRUCTION

Skilled Labor in the 1920s Office Young women began to work in new white-collar professions such as this large mail-order-house typing pool. Jobs such as typist, stenographer, and cashier became known as woman's work. Employers assumed that women worked only for luxuries or worked only until they got married. Therefore, these jobs paid far less than jobs of similar responsibility performed by men.

Answer: *be a good speller and have a knowledge of grammar, capitalization, and punctuation*

Cultural Perspectives

Overseas Automobile Manufacturing

James Flink states in *The Automobile Age* that although the credit for the first gasoline-driven motor vehicle was given to the Duryea brothers from the United States in 1893, the internal combustion engine was first perfected in Germany and France. These countries were 10 years ahead of their British and American counterparts in the technological development of the gasoline auto. The credit for being "first" is generally given to Etienne Lenoir of France because his engine was commercially successful in 1860. Other European developers included the Germans Otto in 1876 and Daimler and Benz in 1885. Ask students to find out how Ford's assembly line allowed him to surpass the initial advances of the Europeans.

Evaluate

Have students complete the Section Review.

📼 💿 Assign the Section 4 Quiz or use the Testmaker. (Also in Spanish.) **LEP**

📼 💿 Assign the Chapter 11 Test or use the Testmaker.

📼 Have students complete the Chapter 11 Performance Assessment Activity.

Reteach

🎧 Have students listen to the Chapter 11, Section 4 Audiocassette. (Also in Spanish.) **LEP**

📼 Have students complete the Chapter 11 Reteaching Activity. (Also in Spanish.) **LEP**

Enrich

📼 Have students complete the Chapter 11 Enrichment Activity. (Also in Spanish.) **LEP**

VISUAL INSTRUCTION

Switchboards These telephone operators operated a long-distance and transcontinental phone exchange.

Answer: *less manual labor; not as tiring; cleaner environment; better pay*

CLOSE

Write these headings on the board: *New Ways of Doing Jobs* and *New Jobs.* Ask students to list information from this section under the headings. *(Doing Jobs: assembly line; scientific management; New Jobs: automobile workers; advertisers; clerks)*

ARCHIVE PHOTOS

Operating the Switchboards Ever-growing communications systems provided employment opportunities for women of the 1920s. *Why did women choose this kind of work?*

was overqualified. Even if typing paid no better than operating a machine in a factory, the new office work allowed an educated young woman to work in a clean, attractive environment.

Previously, one man or a small group of male clerks, who could expect eventual promotion to managerial positions, had done the clerical work in a typical office. Women, who did not command high wages or look forward to advancement, could operate all the new office technology—typewriters, dictaphones, telephones.

Because any of the new jobs could be performed as easily at one firm as another, the stenographer or typist found herself in a large "pool" of similarly skilled workers. In a book called *The Job,* Sinclair Lewis described such a pool in which an "unrecognized horde of girls . . . merely copied or took the bright young men's dictation." He added, "They were expected to keep clean and be quick-moving; beyond that they were as unimportant to the larger phases of office politics as frogs to a summer hotel."

Shop Clerks and Telephone Operators

In the same way that secretarial work provided an alternative to nursing or teaching for female high-school graduates, telephone companies and the new department stores offered women without a high-school diploma a pleasant alternative to factory work or domestic service. By 1930, 736,000 women had gone to work as shop clerks, cash girls, wrappers, stock clerks, cashiers, or switchboard operators.

Women employees eagerly accepted the challenges of their new job situations. Shop work involved less manual labor than factory work, and the environment was cleaner. The pay equaled or exceeded what women

workers could earn performing unskilled labor. The jobs were important, too. It was up to the salesclerk, for example, to see that people's new needs and wants were satisfied.

Men and Women in the Office

By the 1920s offices and stores had two distinct cultures, neatly divided by sex. Women dominated in the clerical, unskilled occupations. There neatness, orderliness, and courtesy played a big role, but job responsibility involved simple, repetitive routines. Women's jobs provided little chance for advancement except to the positions of cashier or executive secretary, or perhaps to marriage. Secretarial work taught a woman endurance, modesty, and obedience, so many people considered it perfect preparation for marriage.

Men, on the other hand, found jobs as managers, senior cashiers, chief clerks, head bookkeepers, floorwalkers, salespeople, or advertising workers. In these jobs energy, initiative, and creativity paid off and could lead to a better position in the company.

Though the new work environment of the 1920s clearly defined the separate jobs of each gender, it also provided for the first time an opportunity for educated men and women to meet and share the workplace. These new coworkers would soon become consumers of a host of new products thriving United States factories produced.

SECTION REVIEW

Vocabulary

1. Define: industrialist, scientific management, white-collar worker.

Checking Facts

2. Why did management and labor at Midvale Steel oppose scientific management at first? Why did the auto industry adopt the new methods from the beginning?

3. List three white-collar jobs men held in the 1920s. Compare these with white-collar jobs women held, in terms of qualifications, salary, and opportunity for advancement.

Critical Thinking

Determining Cause and Effect
4. Why were there suddenly so many new white-collar workers during the 1920s?

Linking Across Time

5. Compare the office environment of today with that of the 1920s. Are any jobs today thought to be primarily for men or for women?

Section 4 Review Answers

1. industrialist (362), **scientific management** (365), **white-collar worker** (366)
2. Management did not want to disrupt long-established work routines. Workers were suspicious of being exploited. The auto industry had no traditional routines to be upset by Taylor's methods.
3. Men were managers, senior cashiers, and chief clerks. Women were usually typists, tele-

phone operators, or sometimes salesclerks. Qualifications were the same, but men's salaries and opportunities for advancement were greater.
4. Corporations grew larger and more complex.
5. Answers will vary, but may include information about new technology and improved working conditions, and any jobs thought to be specific for men or women.

Study and Writing Skill

IDENTIFYING TEXT PATTERNS

Learning the Skill

A clear organizational pattern helps a writer communicate an idea. Recognizing organizational patterns and identifying the intent of each can aid reading comprehension and writing effectiveness. Historical writing is often organized chronologically, telling events in the order that they occur. Look for other patterns as you read.

Cause-and-Effect Pattern

The cause-and-effect pattern shows which events caused others to happen. Key words can make the relationship explicit, as in the sentence *About 2,000 mergers took place, resulting in the loss of hundreds of firms.* Read the passage on scientific management on page 365. Here, the causal relationship is implicit, not stated outright. Note that the cause is stated first: "time-study experts analyze each work operation." Sometimes an effect will be stated first, followed by its cause or causes.

Compare-and-Contrast Pattern

The compare-and-contrast pattern highlights similarities or differences. This can show how ideas or methods change over time. Read the passage on page 368 describing office positions held by men and women. Words and phrases such as *distinct* and *on the other hand* suggest a compare-and-contrast pattern.

Spatial Pattern

A spatial pattern explains how places, people, objects, or events relate to one another in terms of location. Examine the description of the assembly line on page 362. Find the key words that show place relationships, such as *in front of* and *away.*

Other Patterns

The chart below outlines a variety of text patterns.

Practicing the Skill

1. Refer back to the chapter to find examples of at least four organizational patterns shown below.

2. Find magazine articles that discuss the relationship between business and government today. Identify any organizational patterns.

3. Which text pattern would be most appropriate for an explanation of a science experiment? A description of a battlefield? A biographical account?

4. Write a sentence about the Great Migration using any of the text clues below.

5. Check your portfolio; which pattern or text clues do you use most often in your own writing?

Applying the Skill

Use one of the patterns listed in the chart to describe a social effect of the automobile today.

Additional Practice

For additional practice, see Reinforcing Skills on page 373.

ORGANIZATIONAL TEXT PATTERNS

Organization	Description	Text Clues
Cause-and-effect	Clarifies causal relationships	*because, consequently, led to, resulted in, therefore*
Compare-and-contrast	Highlights similarities or differences	*although, by comparison, however, in contrast, similarly, unlike*
Chronological	Describes events in order of occurrence	*in 1917, at 10 A.M., after, as, before, finally, first, second, last, next, when*
Pro-and-con	Juxtaposes arguments in favor of and against an idea, proposal, or action	*in favor of, in support of, on the plus side, the case against, the downside is, the disadvantages are*
Problem-and-solution	States problems and discusses actual or possible solutions	*the problem is, the challenge we face, the difficulty is, the trouble was, answered, resolved, solved, the answer is, the solution was*
Spatial	Explains locational relationships	*above, beside, near, north, south, east, west*; place names: *Tokyo, Ohio*
Question-and-answer	Links questions and answers	*how, why, when, where, what, who; clearly, undoubtedly, the answer is*

TEACH

This skill teaches students how to recognize organizational patterns in writing. Point out that the skill involves examining textbook models of various patterns, noting text clues that point to a particular pattern. Students will then practice the skill by locating samples of different organizational patterns in the textbook and other written sources.

 Curriculum Connection

Language Arts Many of the text patterns outlined here can also be used in spoken language. Oratory, or formal public speaking, has text patterns of its own. Oratorical skill was equated with power in ancient Greece, where most male citizens represented themselves or served as jurors in court. Oratory was formalized into a five-part structure: introduction, narrative, arguments, subsidiary remarks, and summary. Later Romans refined the study of oratory, identifying three ways to sway an audience: appealing to the audience's character, its emotions, or its logic.

Additional Practice

☞ Have students complete the Chapter 11 Skill Reinforcement Activity.

Practicing the Skill Answers

1. Answers will vary, but students should identify which paragraphs on which pages fit into a particular text pattern.

2. Answers will vary. Encourage students to attach the articles or photocopies to their answer.

3. Answers may vary but likely answers are: science experiment: either cause-and-effect or chronological; battlefield description: spatial; biographical account: chronological.

4. Sentences about the Great Migration should make sense with the use of chosen text clues.

5. Answers will vary. Students should explain their answer with examples or reasons.

369

TEACH

Making the Historical Connection

An attitude of "Eat, drink, and be merry" prevailed in the aftermath of World War I. Jazz gained nationwide popularity and came to define the decade. More Americans had money to spend and free time to enjoy. They pursued leisure-time activities with an enthusiasm that earned the era the nickname "the Roaring Twenties."

Currriculum Connection

Music Influenced by African American folk songs, European harmonies, spirituals, and ragtime, jazz was born in the American South around 1900. As the nation grew more mobile, jazz spread to every region. Chicago and New York became jazz hotspots. Improvisation and syncopation made the music novel and unpredictable. In the 1920s jazz styles favored dancing, but were often played to accompany the classic blues vocalists.

History and the Humanities

🎧 *American Music: Cultural Traditions*—"Muskrat Ramble" by Louis Armstrong and His Hot Five; "Downhearted Blues" by Bessie Smith.

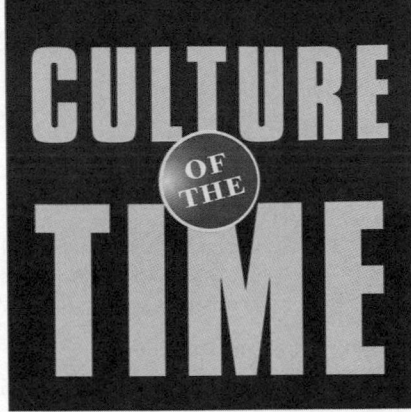

CULTURE
OF
THE
TIME

The Roaring Twenties

During the 1920s—the golden age of jazz—Americans danced to the decade's joyous music at a frantic and ever accelerating pace. Inspired by jazz, Americans began to improvise leisure time activities that had no purpose other than having fun. People roared through the decade intent on enjoying every exciting moment of it, as though everyone shared an unspoken premonition that it could not last.

COMIC HERO
Charlie Chaplin's comic film character, "the Tramp," captured the country's imagination. His mustache, derby hat, bamboo cane, and outsize shoes were recognized around the world—and often imitated, as these young fans attest.

ARCHIVE PHOTOS

The One and Only

Charlie Chaplin
In his First Million Dollar Picture
"A DOG'S LIFE"
A 'First National' Attraction

#203, J. WILBUR SANDISON COLLECTION, WHATCOM MUSEUM OF HISTORY AND ART, BELLINGHAM, WA

LIBERTY

LADIES & GENT'S SHOE SHINE

370 CULTURE OF THE TIME

Background Information

The Movie Business By the beginning of the 1920s, the film industry was the fifth largest in the United States. It was dominated by several studio companies, including Paramount Pictures, Fox, Universal, and Metro-Goldwyn-Mayer (MGM, formed from a merger of three important film companies). Actors signed contracts binding them to one company or another, and the stars' images were carefully cultivated by the company. Movie houses, too, were usually associated with one film studio and therefore showed films that came out of that studio. The studios' dependence on star attraction allowed popular actors to demand high salaries and in some cases—such as Mary Pickford and Charlie Chaplin—become independent producers of their own films.

CULTURE OF THE TIME

DAREDEVILS IN THE AIR

A passion for flying possessed the nation, and novelty-crazed audiences were not satisfied by planes simply flying in straight lines. At almost any open field, **stunt flyers** looped, spiraled, and even played airborne tennis for thrilled spectators.

GULF COAST BLUES

By CLARENCE WILLIAMS

BESSIE SMITH

Exclusive Columbia Phonograph Artist

CLARENCE WILLIAMS
MUSIC PUBLISHING CO. INC.
1547 BROADWAY · NEW YORK

PRINTED IN U.S.A.

SINGING THE BLUES

In the flourishing world of African American music, arts, and letters in the Jazz Age, singer **Bessie Smith** reigned as "Empress of the Blues." Guitarist Danny Barker said, "She could bring about mass hypnotism."

FAD FEVER

Of the fads that roared in and out of the 1920s, **flagpole-sitting** may have been the oddest. Started as a publicity stunt by "Shipwreck" Kelly in 1924, the idea took off. In Baltimore, Maryland, flagpole fervor reached epic proportions after Avon Foreman set an endurance record there. One week in 1929, as many as 20 people perched on poles at various points around the city.

DANCE CRAZES

The **Charleston** and the **tango** were the hot dances of the decade. The mania for dance-until-you-drop marathons branched out to other wacky dance endeavors, such as this couple's tango from Santa Monica to Los Angeles.

FYI

Barnstormers Stunt flyers (sometimes called barnstormers) often flew war surplus planes, especially the JN-4D training planes. Many of these, affectionately called "Jennies," were built too late for World War I use and were therefore very inexpensive. Most of the pilots were skilled aviators and ran few risks, in spite of the dangerous appearance of their acts (for example, the tennis players in this photo are attached to the wing by cables). One pilot commented wryly on his profession: "The most dangerous thing about flying is the risk of starving to death."

CLOSE

Ask: How do you think jazz music reflected the feelings and spirit of Americans in the 1920s? *(It was new, daring, and full of energy.)*

Portfolio Project

Research Students might research the life of Bessie Smith, Louis Armstrong, or another jazz musician of the time. In particular, students might investigate whether the famous African American jazz musicians of the 1920s were able to escape the widespread racial prejudice of the time. Invite students to give an oral report to the class, and prepare a written report to include in their portfolio.

Reviewing Key Terms

1. Sacco and Vanzetti
2. Woodrow Wilson
3. industry-dominating businesses
4. large employers
5. Frederick Taylor and Henry Ford

Recalling Facts

1. the Bolshevik Revolution and Communist government in Russia; Communist uprisings in Hungary and Bavaria; two Communist parties formed in the United States
2. to find better-paying jobs
3. The Supreme Court overturned progressive legislation; reformers lost faith after the war; many were fearful of violent strikes and radical political ideas.
4. ordinary life, free from concerns of war or political strife
5. He thought high taxes would discourage the wealthy from investing their money in business.
6. It increased productivity.
7. Mergers and the demise of small, family-run businesses
8. company doctors and nurses, glee clubs, sports teams
9. so they could afford to buy a Ford car, would not look for other jobs, and would do their boring jobs more willingly
10. by breaking down production stages to small, robot-like jobs on the assembly line

Critical Thinking

1. Factors may include women's determination and persistence, tactics including demonstrations and speeches, and the role of women during the war. These factors kept the issue alive and put women's capability to handle the responsibility of suffrage beyond doubt.

Reviewing Key Terms

On a separate sheet of paper, identify the person, people, or group from the following list who was associated with each concept in the numbered list below.

• Frederick Taylor and Henry Ford
• large employers
• César Augusto Sandino
• Woodrow Wilson
• industry-dominating businesses
• Sacco and Vanzetti

1. anarchism
2. internationalism
3. oligopoly
4. welfare capitalism
5. scientific management

Recalling Facts

1. What were some of the causes of the Red Scare? Name at least three contributing factors.

2. Why did so many African Americans migrate from the South to the North from 1916 to 1920?

3. List three factors that contributed to the decline of progressivism in the 1920s.

4. What do you think Harding meant by *normalcy*?

5. Why did Andrew Mellon believe millionaires should not pay taxes?

6. How did technology affect productivity in the 1920s?

7. Name two factors that contributed to the development of oligopolies in the 1920s.

8. List three types of welfare capitalism programs.

9. Give three reasons why Henry Ford doubled his workers' wages in 1914.

10. How did Henry Ford apply the theory of scientific management?

Critical Thinking

1. **Determining Relevance** In the photo below, a woman carries the American flag down New York's Fifth Avenue in a parade for woman suffrage. Women and men had been organizing, marching, and asking for the vote for women for 72 years. What factors were most important in the final push for woman suffrage, and why?

2. **Synthesizing Information** The Republican Presidents of the 1920s supported big business and rejected programs for the public welfare. How did the government's support of big business affect ordinary citizens both positively and negatively?

3. **Determining Cause and Effect** The idolization of business and business leaders created a national climate that benefited big business. What do you think might have been some negative effects of the glorification of business?

4. **Making Comparisons** Compare the careers of women and men in white-collar professions in the 1920s.

THE BETTMANN ARCHIVE

2. Government support helped businesses prosper, so there were more jobs and workers earned higher wages. Many smaller firms were forced out of business. Many businesses discouraged the formation of unions, so workers did not have a forum in which to voice complaints. Often work-

ers' needs were ignored until companies learned that contented workers were less likely to form unions.
3. Business people involved in corrupt activities would be less likely to be caught. It became more difficult for employees to gain better working conditions.

4. Women received less pay and were mostly limited to clerical or unskilled jobs with little chance of advancement. Men held higher-paying jobs, as head bookkeepers or chief clerks, which often led to even better positions.

CHAPTER
11
REVIEW

Portfolio Project

Research the requirements for setting up a small business in your community. Investigate areas such as government regulations, financing, and the costs of leasing space and buying equipment. The local chamber of commerce might direct you in your research. Write a report on your findings, and include your final report in your portfolio.

Cooperative Learning

Work in small groups to research and report on one of the following industries between 1919 and 1929: textiles, railroads, shipping, farming, aviation, or chemistry. As part of your research, find out whether the industry did well or had problems, and describe the causes of the success or struggle. As a group, choose a medium for presenting your findings, such as a newspaper article, skit, or collage, and share your project with the rest of the class.

Reinforcing Skills

Identifying Text Patterns Use one of the text patterns outlined on page 369 to summarize what you have learned about one of the following subjects: the Harlem Renaissance, Prohibition, President Hoover, or business in the 1920s. Use the text clues listed in the chart on page 369 to get started.

Geography and History

Study the map on this page to answer the following questions:

1. Which cities in the United States had more than 1 million residents in 1930?

2. Which regions of the country had the densest urban population? Which had the sparsest? What might explain this population distribution?

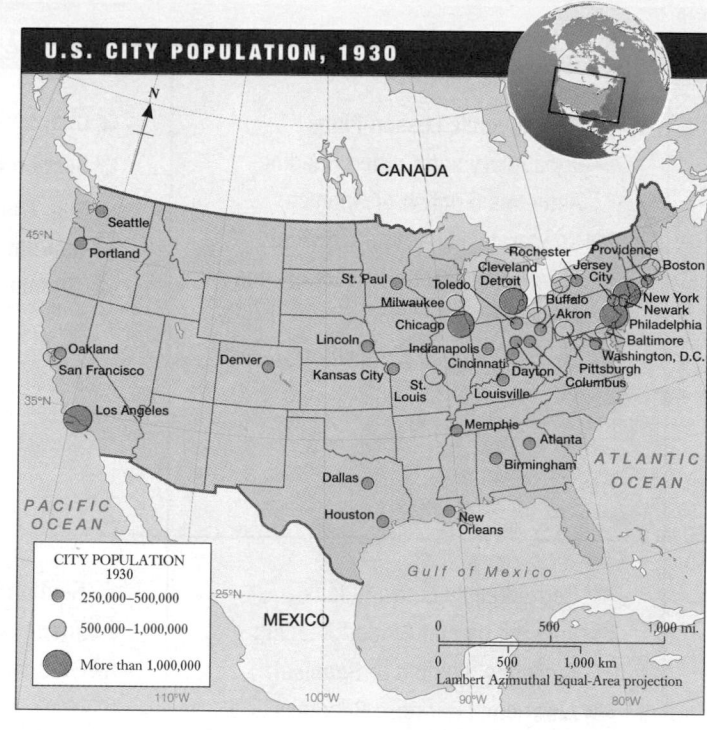

U.S. CITY POPULATION, 1930

CANADA

Seattle
Portland
Oakland
San Francisco
Los Angeles
Denver
Lincoln
Kansas City
St. Paul
Milwaukee
Chicago
Indianapolis
St. Louis
Toledo
Cincinnati
Dayton
Louisville
Columbus
Cleveland
Detroit
Akron
Pittsburgh
Rochester
Buffalo
Providence
Jersey City
Boston
New York
Newark
Philadelphia
Baltimore
Washington, D.C.
Memphis
Atlanta
Birmingham
Dallas
Houston
New Orleans

PACIFIC OCEAN
ATLANTIC OCEAN
Gulf of Mexico
MEXICO

CITY POPULATION 1930
● 250,000–500,000
● 500,000–1,000,000
● More than 1,000,000

0   500   1,000 mi.
0   500   1,000 km
Lambert Azimuthal Equal-Area projection

3. How does this population map from 1930 reflect the Great Migration of African Americans from the South?

4. How does the location of the nation's five largest cities show the importance of geography in determining where large population centers are located?

5. Note that few states in the West had large population centers in 1930. How do you account for this?

HISTORY JOURNAL

The 1920s were a time of great innovation and excitement, yet also a conservative time. Can these two conditions peacefully coexist? Write a brief description identifying aspects of the 1920s where innovation dominated and those where conservatism dominated. You might consider who did well in the period and who struggled. How would you summarize the overall climate of the 1920s?

Geography and History

1. Los Angeles, Chicago, Detroit, Philadelphia, and New York

2. The Northeast and Midwest were densest; Central Plains and Western states (except the coast) were sparsest. Nearness to waterways and financial systems led to industrial growth; industry attracted more people.

3. The concentration of large urban areas in the industrial North, in contrast to the fewer big cities of the South, suggests that population was redistributed northward.

4. These cities experienced a large population increase, including African Americans and others coming from the South. Business and industry there expanded rapidly.

5. Automobiles gave the population mobility; it was easier to move greater distances. Many Easterners and Southerners could drive to the West Coast in search of new opportunities.

History Journal

Students should show the 1920s to be innovative in technology, art, music, and in some ways lifestyle, but conservative in business, religion, politics, and social welfare.

Portfolio Project

Remind students to use resources such as business directories, the Yellow Pages, and people they know who are involved in business. The final project should reflect multiple sources, as well as an understanding of the demands of a start-up business.

Cooperative Learning

Students' work should show evidence of research in the chosen subject; each member of the group should contribute to the project. The final piece should be presented clearly to the class.

Reinforcing Skills

Students' summaries should employ one of the outlined text patterns. The use of the chosen pattern should make sense with the subjects students choose.

? BONUS QUESTION

This question may be used for extra credit on the chapter test.
Why did John Scopes volunteer to break the law?
Answer: *To bring to trial a law he thought unjust*

A Prospering Society

DAILY LESSON OBJECTIVES	REPRODUCIBLE RESOURCES	MULTIMEDIA RESOURCES
SECTION 1 Growth of the Middle Class 1. Identify how and why the standard of living of many, though not all, Americans rose during the 1920s. 2. Describe the effects of the automobile on the economy and culture of the 1920s. 3. Tell how advertising and mass media affected American buying habits and fashions in the 1920s.	Reproducible Lesson Plans Vocabulary and Guided Reading Activities (English or Spanish) Cooperative Learning Activities American Literature Readings and Activities Section Quizzes (English or Spanish)	Chapter Teaching Transparencies Section Focus Transparencies Map Transparencies Testmaker Student Self-Test: A Software Review
SECTION 2 The Jazz Age 1. Identify the leisure-time activities of Americans during the 1920s. 2. Describe the musical and literary contributions of the 1920s. 3. Explain how the writers of the Lost Generation and the Harlem Renaissance reacted to American society of the 1920s.	Reproducible Lesson Plans Vocabulary and Guided Reading Activities (English or Spanish) American Literature Readings and Activities Skill Reinforcement Activities Section Quizzes (English or Spanish)	Section Focus Transparencies Testmaker Student Self-Test: A Software Review
SECTION 3 Cultural Conflicts 1. Explain how 1920s social changes caused conflicts among various groups in the United States. 2. Identify some reasons for and effects of the widespread disregard for Prohibition. 3. Describe the resurgence of the Ku Klux Klan in the 1920s. 4. Explain how the election of 1928 reflected the cultural conflicts of the decade.	Reproducible Lesson Plans Vocabulary and Guided Reading Activities (English or Spanish) Geography in History Activities Supreme Court Case Studies Reteaching Activities (English or Spanish) Enrichment Activities (English or Spanish) Section Quizzes (English or Spanish)	Section Focus Transparencies Landmark Documents in American History Testmaker Student Self-Test: A Software Review
CHAPTER REVIEW AND EVALUATION	Chapter 12 Test, Forms A and B Performance Assessment Strategies and Activities Unit 4 Test, Forms A and B	Student Self-Test: A Software Review Vocabulary PuzzleMaker Testmaker Chapter Digests Audiocassettes

00:00 If time does not permit teaching the entire chapter, summarize using the Chapter 12 Digests Audiocassettes and the accompanying activities and tests. (Available in English or Spanish.)

Cooperative Project

Organize students in small groups to study the role of mass media in society today. During the 1920s society and mass media emphasized youth and beauty. Discuss traits that are emphasized today. Provide students with current newspapers and magazines, amd ask students to identify examples of materials that emphasize those traits. Then have them list the positive and negative aspects of that emphasis. **LEP**

Suggested Rubric: A Self-Assessment. See Performance Assessment Strategies and Activities, p. 53.

Individual Project

Section 2 describes writers of the Lost Generation and the Harlem Renaissance. Have each student choose a short piece by a writer from one of these groups and carefully read it. Then have students write a description of the author's point of view for a local newspaper.

Suggested Rubric: A Newspaper Article. See Performance Assessment Strategies and Activities, p. 31.

Key to Ability Levels

Teaching strategies have been coded for varying learning styles and abilities.

L1 **BASIC** activities for all students

L2 **AVERAGE** activities for average to above-average students

L3 **CHALLENGING** activities for above-average students

LEP **LIMITED ENGLISH PROFICIENCY** activities

Block Scheduling

Block scheduling differs from traditional class scheduling in the amount of time allotted to each period. The extended timeframe provided by block scheduling affords you the opportunity to implement a greater number of research-oriented and activity-intense projects to motivate and involve your students. Activities that are particularly suited to use within the block scheduling framework are identified throughout this chapter by the following designation.

TEACHER'S CORNER

NATIONAL GEOGRAPHIC SOCIETY

INDEX TO NATIONAL GEOGRAPHIC MAGAZINE

The following articles may be used for research relating to this chapter:

- "Immigration Today: New York's New Immigrants," by Alice J. Hall, September 1990.
- "New Life for Ellis Island," by Alice J. Hall, September 1990.

NATIONAL GEOGRAPHIC SOCIETY PRODUCTS AVAILABLE FROM GLENCOE

To order the following products for use with this chapter, contact your local Glencoe sales representative or call Glencoe at 1-800-334-7344:

- *The Presidents: A Picture History of Our Nation* (CD-ROM)
- *GTV: A Geographic Perspective on American History* (Videodisc)
- *GTV: The American People: Fabric of a Nation* (Videodisc)

ADDITIONAL NATIONAL GEOGRAPHIC SOCIETY PRODUCTS

To order the following products for use with this chapter, call National Geographic Society at 1-800-368-2728:

- *The United States as a World Power: From the 1890s to the 1970s* (Filmstrip)
- *Decades of History: The 20th Century—The Early Years* (Filmstrip)
- *Building a Nation: The Story of Immigration* (Filmstrip)
- *Immigration: The Triumph of Hope* (Video)

Chapter Overview

The prosperity of the 1920s brought leisure time and new national pastimes such as baseball and movies. George Herman "Babe" Ruth, one of the most famous home run hitters ever, was a hero to sports fans of all ages.

Introducing the Chapter

Point out to students that Chapter 12 covers the same time period as Chapter 11 but from a different perspective–that of the social and cultural events of the 1920s. Have students recall that this decade was a period of national prosperity with an emphasis on youth, fun, and material possessions. Then have students read the opening vignette.

 Display Map Transparency 12 on the board and distribute copies of the activity sheet. After students have completed the activities, point out that the desire to restrict immigration was accentuated during the postwar turmoil and increased in the early 1920s.

Extension Activity

Have students complete Beyond the Transparency on the activity sheet for Chapter 12 and present their projects after the class has completed the chapter.

History Journal

Have students investigate Babe Ruth's career during the 1920s and the records he achieved. Encourage students to study other famous baseball players including those players who performed in the Negro Baseball League.

CHAPTER 12

A Prospering Society

In St. Louis, Missouri, 40,000 fans witnessed the fourth game of baseball's World Series. Millions more enthusiastic fans were listening to popular radio announcer Graham McNamee as Babe Ruth came to bat.

McNamee reported, "The Babe is waving that wand of his over the plate. Bell is loosening up his arm. The Babe hits it clear into the center-field bleachers for a home run! For a home run! Did you hear what I said? Oh, what a shot! . . . Oh, boy! Wow! That is a World Series record, three home runs in one series game, and what a home run!"

No one better symbolized the period of the 1920s than home run hitter Babe Ruth. He was a contradictory man with an amazing athletic talent, a gigantic appetite for pleasure, and a casual disregard for rules.

Like its baseball hero, the United States also exhibited some basic contradictions during the 1920s. At the same time most of the country was plunging breathlessly into the new era, many Americans sought to return to a simpler past. Deep conflicts in the United States over religion and immigration added turmoil to the excitement of this decade, which was rapidly becoming full of radios, newspapers, movies, and advertising.

Babe Ruth was a perfect hero for a country undergoing vast change in a bold, hungry, and lawless era. ■

HISTORY JOURNAL

Before you read the rest of this chapter, write any other information you know about the history of baseball. Then write what societal changes you think took place in the 1920s.

374

✚ EXTRA CREDIT PROJECT

A Personality From the 1920s Have students skim through Chapter 12 and look at the photographs, caption descriptions, and subheads to help them choose one of the figures from this era to study in depth. Remind students to focus on this personality's impact in social and cultural areas during this era. Have students read novels, newspapers, magazines, and primary source material about their person. Then based on their notes and recollections, ask students to create a biographical sketch of their personality. Students may also want to include supporting visuals before filing their completed product in their portfolios.

NATIONAL BASEBALL LIBRARY, COOPERSTOWN, N.Y.

THE EMERGENCE OF MASS COMMUNICATION
IN THE 1920S MADE SPORTS STARS LIKE
BABE RUTH FAMOUS WORLDWIDE.

375

 At the Movies

Two movies were filmed about Babe Ruth's life. *The Babe Ruth Story,* an overly sentimental biography filmed in 1948, starred William Bendix and included actual film clips of the Babe. More recently, John Goodman starred in *The Babe,* filmed in 1992. Critics found Goodman's fine performance marred by a lackluster script in which Ruth is portrayed as a sloppy drunkard with an excessive appetite for pleasure. In addition there are several documentary films available including *Babe Ruth* (1983, WGBH Boston), *Babe Ruth: The Fence Buster* (1954, Fox Movietone News), and *Babe Ruth: The Man, the Myth, the Legend* (1989).

 Performance Assessment

Refer to page 374B for performance assessment activities for this chapter.

 Also see Activity 12 in the Performance Assessment Strategies and Activities for an additional activity as well as for suggested rubrics.

Examining the Visual

The Sultan of Swat Babe Ruth (1895–1948) was the first great home run hitter in baseball history. He attracted so many fans that Yankee Stadium, which opened in 1923, was nicknamed *The House That Ruth Built.* Born in Baltimore, he began his baseball career in 1914 with the Baltimore Orioles, a minor league team at the time. Later that same year he joined the Boston Red Sox as a pitcher. In 1920 the Red Sox sold Ruth to the New York Yankees for $125,000. A left-handed hitter who stood 6 feet 2 inches and weighed 215 pounds, Ruth hit a record 60 home runs in 1927 in a 154-game season. In 1961 Roger Maris of the Yankees set another record by hitting 61 home runs in a 162-game season. Ruth's lifetime total of 714 home runs remained a major league record until Hank Aaron hit his 715th home run in 1974.

FOCUS

Section Objectives

1. Identify how and why the standard of living of many, though not all, Americans rose during the 1920s.
2. Describe the effects of the automobile on the economy and culture of the 1920s.
3. Tell how advertising and mass media affected American buying habits and fashions in the 1920s.

Bellringer Activity

While taking attendance at the beginning of the class period, display **Section Focus Transparency 37,** and have students answer the questions. (Or use the blackline master.)

VISUAL INSTRUCTION

A New Era of Consumer Goods The advent of more and larger grocery stores eventually replaced the street peddlers and door-to-door delivery services that had supplied households in the past.

Ask: What effect did new food packaging techniques have on American eating habits? *(People could buy produce out of season and food that was already partly prepared, such as sliced bread.)*

SECTION 1

Growth of the Middle Class

1922: SINCLAIR LEWIS PUBLISHES *BABBITT*

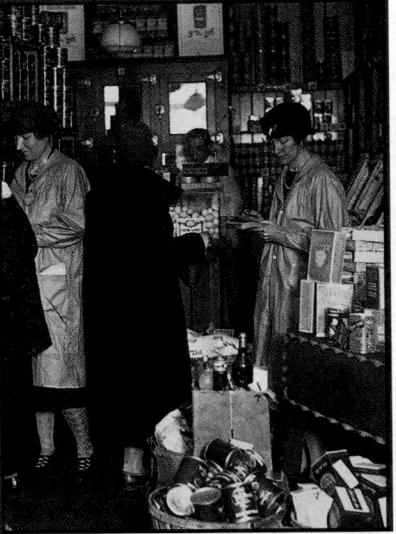

WRITER SINCLAIR LEWIS INVENTED THE BOOMING TOWN OF ZENITH IN 1922 FOR HIS NOVEL *BABBITT*. It could have been any one of many American cities in the 1920s. The novel's main character, George Babbitt, declared:

> Zenith manufactures more condensed milk and evaporated cream, more paper boxes, and more lighting-fixtures, than any other city in the United States, if not in the world. But it is not so universally known that we also stand second in the manufacture of package-butter, sixth in the giant realm of motors

A New Era of Consumer Goods
Self-service was an innovation in retail shopping.

and automobiles, and somewhere about third in cheese, leather bindings, tar roofing, breakfast food, and overalls!

... When I add that we have an unparalleled number of miles of paved streets, bathrooms, vacuum cleaners, and all the other signs of civilization; that our library and art museum are well supported and housed in convenient and roomy buildings; that our park-system is more than up to par, with its handsome driveways adorned with grass, shrubs, and statuary, then I give but a hint of the all-round unlimited greatness of Zenith!

—Sinclair Lewis, *Babbitt,* 1922

AS YOU READ

Vocabulary
► standard of living
► credit
► mass media
► flapper

Think About . . .
► how and why the standard of living of many, though not all, Americans rose during the 1920s.
► the effects of the automobile on the economy and the culture of the 1920s.
► how advertising and mass media affected American buying habits and fashions in the 1920s.

376 CHAPTER 12 A PROSPERING SOCIETY

Section 1 Resources

REPRODUCIBLE RESOURCES

- Lesson Plan 12-1
- Vocabulary and Guided Reading Activity 12-1
- Cooperative Learning Activity 12
- Performance Assessment Activity 12
- Section 1 Quiz
- Unit 4 American Literature Reading

MULTIMEDIA RESOURCES

- Chapter Teaching Transparency 12
- Testmaker
- Section Focus Transparency 37
- Map Transparency 12
- Chapter 12 Digest Audiocassette
- Student Self-Test: A Software Review

Americans as Consumers
Buying Power Increases for Most

The industrialization of the late 1800s was finally beginning to offer real rewards to residents of towns like Zenith. Between 1923 and 1929, American workers saw their real income rise 11 percent. With more than just enough money to live on, many American workers could buy more of the goods they produced. They began to feel that they were part of a growing middle class.

In the 1920s many middle-class American consumers improved their **standard of living.** That is, necessities and luxuries were more available—and affordable. Compared to people overseas, Americans like George Babbitt could afford to buy more goods and, compared to people overseas, Americans like George Babbitt had a higher standard of living.

New Consumer Products

Thanks to refrigeration, Americans ate fresh fruits and vegetables, that were available in stores year-round. Thanks to improved packaging, they bought a wider variety of packaged food, including that great invention, sliced bread. They now purchased ready-made clothes, which replaced home-sewn or tailored garments.

Some regional differences between Americans began to blur as clothing and other mass-produced goods became cheaper and more popular. In most parts of the country, people bought identical vacuum cleaners, electric irons, toasters, washing machines, and refrigerators.

These marvelous machines reduced the time it took to do housework. In their newfound leisure time, Americans could now listen to radios and phonographs or talk to each other on the telephone.

Without electricity, all these machines would have stayed on their inventors' drawing boards. During the 1920s electrical current needed to run machines became more widely available, not just in the houses of the wealthy but also in the homes of many average Americans.

Not all American homes had electricity. Many parts of rural America, especially in the South, were not electrified for many years. Even without electricity, some working-class homes showed an improvement in their standard of living during this decade. Many poor people traded wood fuel for coal, walked on linoleum floors instead of wooden ones, and retired their water buckets when fresh water began to gush from indoor faucets.

Poverty in the Midst of Plenty

Not all Americans were able to improve their standard of living during this period. Low wages and unemployment combined to drive many American families into poverty. Farmers and other workers suffered when the goods they produced dropped in price.

For example, thousands of farmers had replaced their workhorses with Ford's Fordson tractors. With this efficient machine farmers produced more wheat and corn than the country could consume. In a market economy, when supply exceeds demand, prices tend to drop.

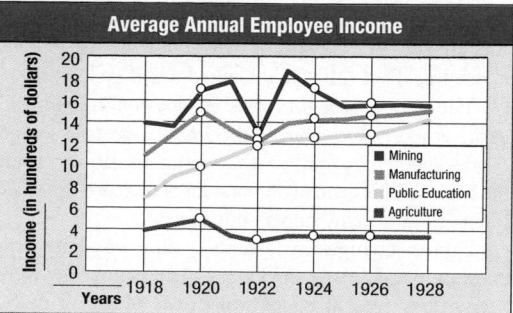

Average Annual Employee Income

Income (in hundreds of dollars) — Years 1918, 1920, 1922, 1924, 1926, 1928

- Mining
- Manufacturing
- Public Education
- Agriculture

Not all workers' wages increased during the 1920s. *In which area did income decrease?*

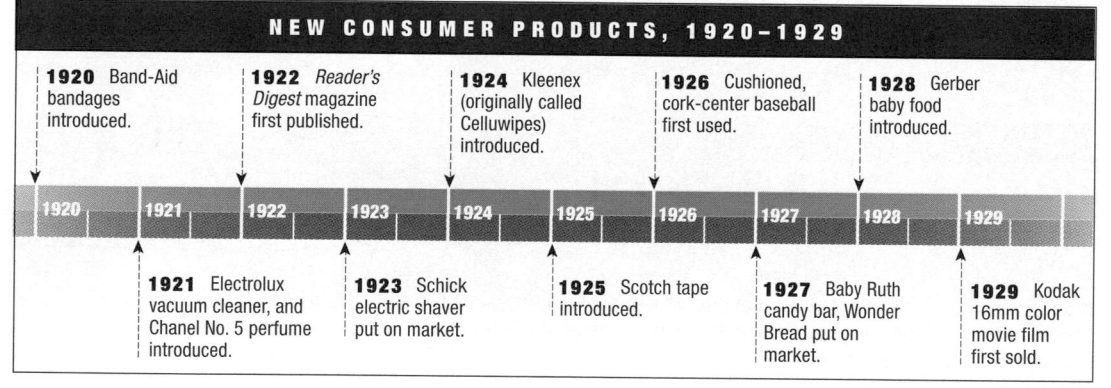

NEW CONSUMER PRODUCTS, 1920–1929

1920 Band-Aid bandages introduced.

1922 *Reader's Digest* magazine first published.

1924 Kleenex (originally called Celluwipes) introduced.

1926 Cushioned, cork-center baseball first used.

1928 Gerber baby food introduced.

1920 · 1921 · 1922 · 1923 · 1924 · 1925 · 1926 · 1927 · 1928 · 1929

1921 Electrolux vacuum cleaner, and Chanel No. 5 perfume introduced.

1923 Schick electric shaver put on market.

1925 Scotch tape introduced.

1927 Baby Ruth candy bar, Wonder Bread put on market.

1929 Kodak 16mm color movie film first sold.

TEACH

Guided Practice

L1 Discussion Read aloud this quote from *Babbitt:* "To George F. Babbitt, as to most prosperous citizens of Zenith, his motor car was poetry and tragedy, love and heroism." Have students discuss and vote on a product that symbolizes the present age as the car did the 1920s.

Show students Map Transparency 12 and have them complete the activity sheet.

GRAPH STUDY

The decade began with a short but sharp economic depression in 1921. Unemployment that year reached 5.73 million. For the rest of the decade, it hovered around 2.5 million.

Answer: *Income decreased. in mining and agriculture.*

CHART STUDY

Have students choose one of the new products and explain how it made life easier.

Cooperative Learning

Role Play As an approach to this section, have students work in groups to prepare short skits portraying the lifestyles of the 1920s. Possible characters include a middle-class family, a car salesperson with customers, shoppers at a newly opened chain store, or a group of college students. The dialogue should reflect what students have learned about the culture of the decade.

Independent Practice

L2 **Research** Have students find out how much buying on credit adds to the price of automobiles today. Ask students to share their findings with the class.

📁 Have students complete the Chapter 12, Section 1 Vocabulary and Guided Reading Activity. (Also in Spanish.) **LEP**

📁 Have students complete the Chapter 12 Cooperative Learning Activity.

VISUAL INSTRUCTION

Cars for Fun Fast-moving cars brought new traffic and parking problems to cities. Manual and automatic traffic lights appeared in big cities such as New York, Cleveland, and Philadelphia by the early 1920s. The first parking fee was charged in Boston, but parking meters did not appear until 1932, when Oklahoma City installed the first.

Answer: *Many Americans could afford an automobile and had leisure and resources enough to use them for recreation.*

During the 1920s a glut of produce sent farm prices into a decline. In 1919 a bushel of corn could buy five gallons of gasoline. By 1921 it only fetched a half gallon.

The period brought hardships for coal miners and textile workers, too. During the 1920s industries began to use electricity rather than coal to power their machinery. This drop in demand for coal drove the price down and put many miners out of work.

Due to changes in fashion—rising hemlines and a new demand for silk stockings—Americans now were buying less cotton. As cotton prices plunged, many textile factories in the Northeast and South were forced to shut down. For the first time in a century, overall factory employment decreased.

By some estimates, a third of American families lived below minimum levels for a decent life. Their inability to buy what the United States produced would contribute to the unraveling of the booming economy by the end of the decade. Despite the plight of farmers and workers in depressed industries, however, most Americans in the 1920s shared George Babbitt's satisfaction. The automobile was beginning to give even ordinary Americans a share in the United States's plenty.

America Hits the Road
Automobiles Redefine the Country

More than any other single consumer item, the automobile defined the United States of the 1920s. In 1927 Americans owned 4 out of 5 of the world's cars, averaging 1 motor vehicle for every 5.3 persons. The Model T car Henry Ford introduced in 1908 transformed the automobile from a high-priced item to one many moderate-income families could afford. On May 27, 1927, when the last of 15 million Model T's rolled off the line, the average American family made $2,000 a year and could buy a new car for less than $300.

Cars for Fun Automobiles crowd Nantasket Beach, Massachusetts, on a Fourth of July in the early 1920s. *How does this photo illustrate Americans' rising standard of living?*

Meeting Special Needs

Reading Disability To help address the needs of students who have difficulty reading, have students create an outline using the subheadings in this section. Once they have done this, encourage them to listen to the Chapter Digest Audiotape and highlight or circle the topics in their outline as they are discussed.

CREATING A SYSTEM FOR ROADWAYS

As the American passion for driving accelerated, getting around in cars proved increasingly challenging. In 1920 there were about 8 million cars on the road, but fewer than 36,000 miles of paved roads. Few roads had names, numbers, or signs to warn drivers of imminent danger. From 1920 to 1930 about 100,000 miles of road were paved—the government's second highest expense. Meanwhile, states implemented traffic rules, uniform road signs, and qualifications for the licensing of drivers.

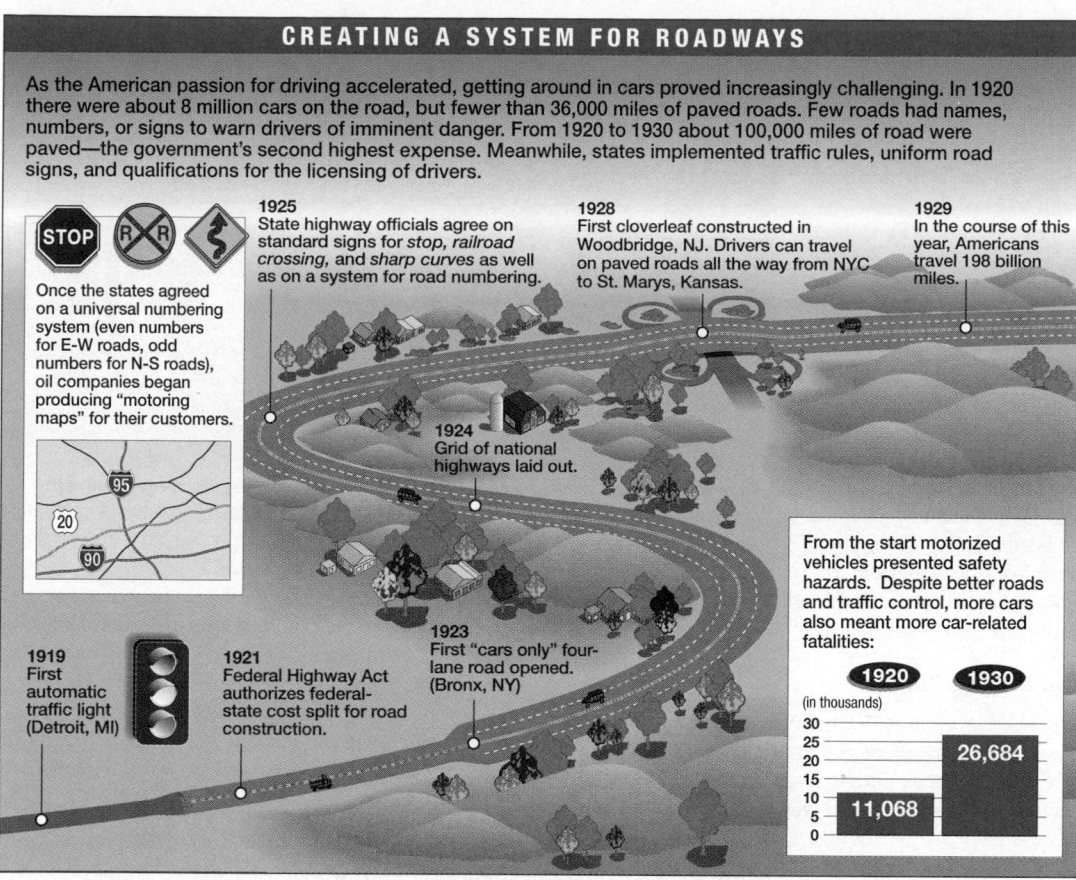

1925 State highway officials agree on standard signs for *stop, railroad crossing,* and *sharp curves* as well as on a system for road numbering.

Once the states agreed on a universal numbering system (even numbers for E-W roads, odd numbers for N-S roads), oil companies began producing "motoring maps" for their customers.

1928 First cloverleaf constructed in Woodbridge, NJ. Drivers can travel on paved roads all the way from NYC to St. Marys, Kansas.

1929 In the course of this year, Americans travel 198 billion miles.

1924 Grid of national highways laid out.

1919 First automatic traffic light (Detroit, MI)

1921 Federal Highway Act authorizes federal-state cost split for road construction.

1923 First "cars only" four-lane road opened. (Bronx, NY)

From the start motorized vehicles presented safety hazards. Despite better roads and traffic control, more cars also meant more car-related fatalities:

1920 **1930**

(in thousands)

1920	11,068
1930	26,684

The automobile industry boomed in the United States during the 1920s. *How many more traffic fatalities were there in the United States in 1930 than in 1920? What steps did state and federal agencies take to bring order to crowded roadways?*

Curriculum Connection

Geography Mexico was a booming oil region early in the century, but American companies had difficulty doing business there after the Mexican Revolution. The new republic tried to control or at least profit from the oil industry on its territory. Texas and Oklahoma were also big oil-producing states, but in the 1920s Californian oil took center stage. Around 1920 worldwide demand for oil exceeded supply; in California gasoline was rationed at 3 gallons per week for a car owner. By 1923 the state was producing one-fourth of the world's oil.

Sharing so visibly in the wealth of society, more and more Americans came to feel that the booming Coolidge economy was working for them. They enthusiastically entered a new era, the age of the automobile. In turn, the age of the automobile would revolutionize American life for decades to come.

Shifting the Economy

Automobile manufacturing became America's biggest industry during the 1920s and soon boosted the entire economy. Cars required vast quantities of steel, lead, nickel, and gasoline. Workers in all these industries thrived. Another 5 million Americans worked to produce glass and rubber that automobile making demanded.

Businesses flourished to serve the needs of a newly mobile nation. Garages, filling stations, hot dog stands, restaurants, tearooms, tourists' roadside camps—all sprang into existence only after the automobile drove onto the American scene.

Besides boosting industry, the automobile radically changed the face of the country. Villages along the new automobile routes thrived, while villages along the railroad lines began to disappear.

At the end of World War I, the United States had just 7,000 miles (11,263 km) of concrete roads. By 1927 a network of 50,000 miles (80,450 km) was growing at the rate of 10,000 miles (16,090 km) each year. Even-numbered highways like Route 66 ran east-west; odd-numbered highways ran north-south. Few Americans minded that states paid for these roads by taxing gasoline. (See Geography, pages 384–385.)

The Romance of the Automobile

The automobile was more than just a convenient way to get from one place to another. It soon became an integral part of the American dream. Henry Ford boasted that his customers could have a Model T in any color "so long as it is black." By the middle 1920s though, Americans wanted their

Portfolio Project

Creating an Advertisement Have students write a 1926 magazine advertisement for one of the new automobiles that came in a variety of colors. (Refer students to page 381 for an example of 1920s advertising.) Invite students to include their finished advertisement in their portfolios.

cars to make a fashion statement. With the invention of lacquer finishes, automobiles of 1925 and 1926 delighted buyers with bold new shades from Arabian Sand to Versailles Violet.

Even Henry Ford had to give in. At the end of May 1927 he shut down the plant that had produced the Model T—America's first real car. Ford's announcement of the brand-new Model A was a major event of 1927. Beginning at 3:00 A.M. on December 2, almost 1 million people lined up in front of Ford Motor Company's New York headquarters, eagerly trying to catch the first glimpse of Ford's colorful new cars.

Automotive Leisure Autocamping became a favorite vacation; car owners could buy special tents to attach to their cars. *Did people have mixed feelings about cars? What were they?*

The Driving Culture

The car changed American culture in countless ways. Dating habits of young people, Sunday outings of families, places people lived and vacationed, and ways people shopped—all were affected by the automobile.

By 1927, 4 out of 5 cars had closed tops, compared with only 1 in 10 in 1919. The new, closed car was a room on wheels. Now protected from the weather, teenagers especially enjoyed the privacy of closed cars.

On Sundays many families hopped into their cars for short day trips. With "auto-mobility," many city workers moved to houses in the new suburbs. Car owners now traveled easily to once distant places.

One such traveler described his stay at a roadside camp in North Carolina. The tourists had come from as far away as Washington state:

> There were fourteen cars in the camp, ranging all the way from dusty Fords to big and glittering limousines with balloon tires and tremendous horsepower. . . . And for the first time in history, the common, ordinary "fo'kes" of the North and South are meeting one another on a really large scale, mostly by means of the National chariot—the Ford car.
>
> —C.P. Russell, "The Pneumatic Hegira," *The Outlook,* December 9, 1925

In addition to bringing far-flung Americans together for the first time, the automobile also saddled many people with their first debt. Eager to own a car, a person

could now put a deposit down, drive a new car away, and pay off the balance, plus interest, in installments. By 1927, two out of three cars were purchased on the installment, or time-payment, plan.

A banker who loaned money to prospective car buyers bemoaned the change in American habits of thrift, including his own, in an essay written in 1925:

> The ease with which a car can be purchased on the time-payment plan is all too easy a road to ruin. The habit of thrift can never be acquired through so wasteful a medium as an automobile. Instead, the habit of spending must be acquired, for with the constant demand for fuel, oil, and repairs, together with the heavy depreciation, the automobile stands unique as the most extravagant piece of machinery ever devised for the pleasure of man. But—I still drive one myself. I must keep up with the procession.
>
> —William Ashdown, "Confessions of an Automobilist," *Atlantic Monthly*, June 1925

Selling America
New Ways to Buy

Even thrifty Americans such as William Ashdown felt pressured to buy cars on the installment plan. One reason was the brash salesmanship the dealers practiced.

A Ford dealer speaking with reporter Jesse Rainsford Sprague said his boss had instructed him to sell 20 cars a month in a depressed rural area. In speaking of one customer, the dealer said:

Extending the Content

Statistics Point out to students that generalizations based on statistical data are more reliable than those based on opinion. The generalization that advertising became big business in the 1920s is based on statistics such as these: In 1929 corporations spent $1.8 billion on ads; advertising agencies in the 1920s employed 600,000 people; in 1927 Henry Ford spent $1.3 million on newspaper ads for his new Model A Ford. Ask students to make some generalizations about what they have read about consumerism in the 1920s. For example, what are 2 ways American buying habits changed during the 1920s? *(buying on credit; shopping at chain stores)*

The man was a poor devil of a renter seven or eight miles out of town who never had enough cash ahead to buy a wheelbarrow, but Burke insisted that one of my salesmen go out there with him to try and land a sale. When they got there a couple of the children were down with whooping cough and a hailstorm had laid out his bean crop, but Burke came back and told me he would expect me to put over a Ford on the fellow before he came on his next trip.

—Jesse Rainsford Sprague, "Confessions of a Ford Dealer," *Harper's Monthly Magazine*, June 1927

Buying on Time

Automobiles were not the only product Americans were buying on **credit**—putting money down and paying the balance in installments. In 1928, 85 percent of furniture, 80 percent of phonographs, 75 percent of washing machines and radios, and 70 percent of refrigerators were also bought on credit.

Buying on time could add as much as 40 percent to the price consumers eventually paid; but for the first time, buyers could have an item without saving the money to pay for it. That $43.50 phonograph became irresistible when the price read, "$5 down and $5 a month."

Most Americans no longer looked at debt as shameful. They began to regard installment buying as an easy way to raise their standard of living.

Chain Stores

If Americans were buying more and buying on the installment plan, they were also shopping in a different type of store. In the 1920s Americans flocked to the new chain stores that began to spring up all over the country—grocery stores such as A&P, Safeway, and Piggly Wiggly and department stores such as J.C. Penney and Sears, Roebuck. In 1918 there were 29,000 such stores. By 1929 there were 160,000.

Now that customers could hop into their cars and drive to a chain store, the owners of the traditional corner stores lost their main advantage—convenience. Besides being convenient, the chain stores also offered lower prices, greater reliability, better service, and wider choice. At F.W. Woolworth, for example, a shopper with 10 cents or less could buy anything from Rosh Hashanah cards to Venetian Night incense, from an ice cream sundae to a packet of gumdrops or foreign stamps.

Advertising

Americans' buying habits changed most of all because of the sudden growth of advertising. Advertising itself was not new, of course. Since colonial times, American retailers had used newspapers to inform the public about products and prices. What revolutionized advertising in the 1920s was the idea of using it to create consumer demand.

Even tight-lipped and thrifty Calvin Coolidge acknowledged the power of advertising to make "new thoughts, new desires and new actions" seem attractive to an impressionable public. He added, "It is the most potent influence in adopting, and changing the habits and modes of life, affecting what we eat, what we wear, and the work and play of the whole nation."

Advertising suddenly sprang into prominence because Americans' purchases could barely keep pace with the factories' explosion of new goods. Advertisers helped sell their clients' products.

The new **mass media** (a term first used in 1923 to refer to modes of communication that reached large numbers of people) gave advertisers a huge audience of potential consumers. Newspapers, radio stations, billboards, and national magazines all bombarded consumers with one message: Buy, buy, buy!

Advertising became big business in the 1920s. Critics complained that for every dollar spent to educate consumers in what to buy, a mere 70 cents went to pay for schools.

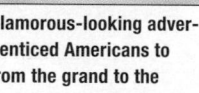

"I FOUND NO REPRODUCING PIANO ITS EQUAL -- THATS WHY I BOUGHT IT"

Welte-Mignon
LICENSEE
REPRODUCING PIANO

THE MASTER'S FINGERS ON YOUR PIANO

OFFERED BY 115 LEADING PIANO MANUFACTURERS. SEND FOR OUR BOOK OF FAMOUS ARTISTS.

THE AUTO PNEUMATIC ACTION CO., W. C. HEATON, PRESIDENT, 653 WEST 51st STREET, NEW YORK

The Advertising Industry Glamorous-looking advertisements such as this one enticed Americans to buy all kinds of products, from the grand to the mundane. The ads often featured well-known artists' work, and tended toward flowery language. *How did advertisements create consumer demand?*

Cultural Perspectives

Mah-jongg The game of mah-jongg was wildly popular in the 1920s. It developed in China in the 1800s and is thought to be based on Chinese games in existence since about 500 B.C. Usually played by 4 players, mah-jongg consists of 144 tiles engraved with symbols, which are picked and discarded until 1 player gets a winning combination. Specific rules vary, but the game is similar to the card game rummy.

ASSESS

Meeting Lesson Objectives

Each section objective is tested by the section review question that follows it in parentheses.

1. Identify how and why the standard of living of many, though not all, Americans rose during the 1920s. (4, 3)
2. Describe the effects of the automobile on the economy and culture of the 1920s. (2)
3. Tell how advertising and mass media affected American buying habits and fashions in the 1920s. (1, 5)

Youth Sets the Scene
Creating the "Roaring Twenties"

During this decade advertisers took advantage of the nation's growing fascination with youth to sell products that promised youthful vitality or style. Never before had American culture idolized the young as it did in the 1920s. The loss of so many young men in World War I seemed to place a special premium on youth. Now, instead of young people modeling themselves on their elders, adults tried to act like children.

Fashions and Fads

As youth came to mean stylishness, young people became the models for fashion, dress, music, and language. Styles that began on college campuses spread quickly to the public, thanks to cheap mass production and advertising in the national mass media. Women everywhere wore yellow rain slickers and multicolored bandanas at the waist. Men sported raccoon coats and golf stockings.

Other fads spread equally quick. The 1920s could be called the age of the fad—a sudden explosion of interest in some product or activity. In Baltimore, for example, 15-year-old Avon Foreman sat on a flagpole for 10 days, 10 hours, 10 minutes, and 10 seconds in 1929. For months Americans everywhere tried to do the same. Then they turned their attention elsewhere. Like the automobile, mass-produced items, and national advertising, the fads of the 1920s helped establish a common culture.

New Ideals of Beauty

The Gibson Girl, an ideal of feminine beauty before World War I, had long, flowing hair. Her dress emphasized her womanly figure, highlighted her tiny waist, and covered her legs.

The 1920s girl—at least the one promoted in advertising and movies—turned this modest image upside down and inside out and emerged as a **flapper.**

BROWN BROTHERS

The Influential Young Revealing bathing suits, as seen on this beach in the late 1920s, were part of the daring attire of both men and women. *In what way was the obsession with youth a reaction to World War I?*

382 CHAPTER 12 A PROSPERING SOCIETY

THE BETTMANN ARCHIVE

Flappers Flaunt Tradition Dashing flappers were sometimes called shebas; their male counterparts sheiks. *How did the flapper differ from the Gibson Girl?*

School Days

If American teenagers were taking to the road in the evening, they were spending more time at school during the day. Most Americans could afford to keep their children in school longer now because many were finally prosperous enough not to need the children's wages. By 1930, 51 percent of all high-school-age youths were in school, compared with less than 6 percent in 1890.

The schools Americans built to accommodate their students looked nothing like the little red schoolhouses of earlier years. In the 1920s the new high school building, with its huge gym and gleaming laboratory was the pride of the neighborhood.

Only one out of eight young people went to college in 1930, but that was three times the number who had attended college at the turn of the century. Both high school and college students were eager consumers who helped set trends for fashion and amusement. The mass media helped to make youth the best-selling image of the 1920s.

Named for the open galoshes she flapped around in, the flapper bound her chest to flatten it, loosened her blouse and dropped its waist, lifted her hemline, and rolled down her stockings. She bobbed her hair short and crowned the shorn locks with a close-fitting hat.

In 1928 the *Journal of Commerce* estimated that in the previous 15 years the average woman had stripped away 12 ¼ yards (11.2 m) of material from her outfit, leaving only a scant 7 yards (6.4 m) of cloth in addition to her rolled-down stockings. These were now silk or the new rayon, no longer the practical cotton or wool ones of the past.

The flapper may have looked like a little girl or even a little boy, but she applied makeup with a bold hand. So did her mother.

Women's New Freedoms

Before World War I, women had been arrested for smoking or using profanity in public. Appearing at the beach without stockings or going without a corset was considered indecent exposure, even in cities as large and sophisticated as Chicago. Ten years later, flappers smoked, drank, left corsets in the cloakroom at the dance, and went joyriding in automobiles. Society, far from curbing women's new behavior, seemed to encourage it.

For one thing, the women's movement and new laws gave women a greater measure of economic and intellectual independence than they had been allowed before the war. In addition, the automobile gave the young a new and exciting independence from their families.

SECTION REVIEW

Vocabulary
1. Define: standard of living, credit, mass media, flapper.

Checking Facts
2. How did the automobile change dating patterns of the young and the vacation habits of families?

3. How did the increasing school attendance of young people show that most Americans were more prosperous during the 1920s?

Critical Thinking
Determining Cause and Effect
4. How did changes in women's fashion affect the cotton industry?

Linking Across Time
5. The practice of buying products on time still exists today with the use of charge cards or payment plans. List at least two benefits and two drawbacks of this practice.

SECTION ONE **383**

Evaluate
Have students complete the Section Review.

📁 💿 Assign the Section 1 Quiz or use the Testmaker to develop a customized quiz. (Also in Spanish.) **LEP**

Reteach
🎧 Have students listen to the Chapter 12, Section 1 audiocassette. (Also in Spanish.) **LEP**

Enrich
📁 Have students complete the Unit 4 American Literature Reading.

VISUAL INSTRUCTION

Flappers Flaunt Tradition Make-up had been considered disreputable in preceding generations, but flappers used it freely, even rouging their newly revealed knees.

Answer: *The flapper wore short skirts, short hair, and had a boyish figure; the Gibson Girl wore long hair and long skirts with small waists.*

CLOSE

Ask students to identify the changes that industrialization, the automobile, advertising, and the new youth culture brought to American life.

Section 1 Review Answers

1. standard of living (377), **credit** (381), **mass media** (381), **flapper** (383)
2. Young daters could escape adults in cars, and families could vacation far from home.
3. Families no longer depended upon children's wages or work to get by.

4. The use of silk stockings and short skirts reduced demand for cotton. Prices then declined and many textile factories closed.
5. Benefits: buyers need not carry cash and can pay for items over time. Drawbacks: buyers may pay more for items, go into debt, and not save.

Geography: Impact on History

TEACH

Making the Geography Connection

Have students recall that Henry Ford started the moving production line to make automobiles in 1913–1914. Point out that the number of cars registered in the United States rose from 8,000 in 1900 to about 8,000,000 in 1920 (see diagraphic on page 379) and to more than 17,000,000 in 1925. By 1925 an auto rolled off the Ford assembly lines every 10 seconds. The birth of industrialized cities made it important to be able to move from place to place, but there were only about 369,000 miles of paved roads in 1920. Increases in automobile ownership created a demand for good roads.

MAP STUDY

Most new national highways followed a major historic route that had already been widely used by travelers such as the Santa Fe Trail. U.S. Route 66 was an exception. A joint board of state and federal highway officials designated and numbered a national system of highways. Cyrus Avery from Tulsa, Oklahoma, along with two other Midwestern board members, routed U.S. Route 66 through Tulsa, because Avery thought Oklahoma needed a major U.S. highway.

Answer: *Abraham Lincoln's Tomb, Petrified Forest, Painted Desert, and the Ozark Mountains*

384

MOVEMENT

Route 66

The construction of U.S. Route 66 provided Americans with a main artery for travel that linked the Midwest with the Far West. The ensuing movement of people and goods had dramatic effects on the nation's culture and economy.

Building a Spirit of Travel

Pulitzer Prize–winning author James Agee described the American story as having five main characters: the continent, the people, the automobile, the road, and the roadside. According to Agee, these five characters met because of the restless nature of Americans:

> The twenties made him [the American] rich and more restive still and he found the automobile not merely good but better and better. It was good because continually it satisfied and at the same time greatly sharpened his hunger for movement.
>
> —James Agee,
> *Fortune,* September 1934

Cars alone could not satisfy the American hunger for movement. Only the construction of a vast network of highways would finally enable Americans to travel freely. This increased movement of people and goods contributed to the reduction of regional differences.

One famous highway, U.S. Route 66, allowed Americans to fulfill their desire to take to the road. How did the United States high-way system, including roads such as Route 66, develop?

Building the Roadway

Americans enjoyed driving their cars and soon wanted better roads. People were interested in what Americans in other parts of the country were doing and how they lived.

Car owners and manufacturers were not the only ones demanding new roads. Since the early 1900s, farmers in the Midwest and the Southwest had cried out for roads on which to transport their products

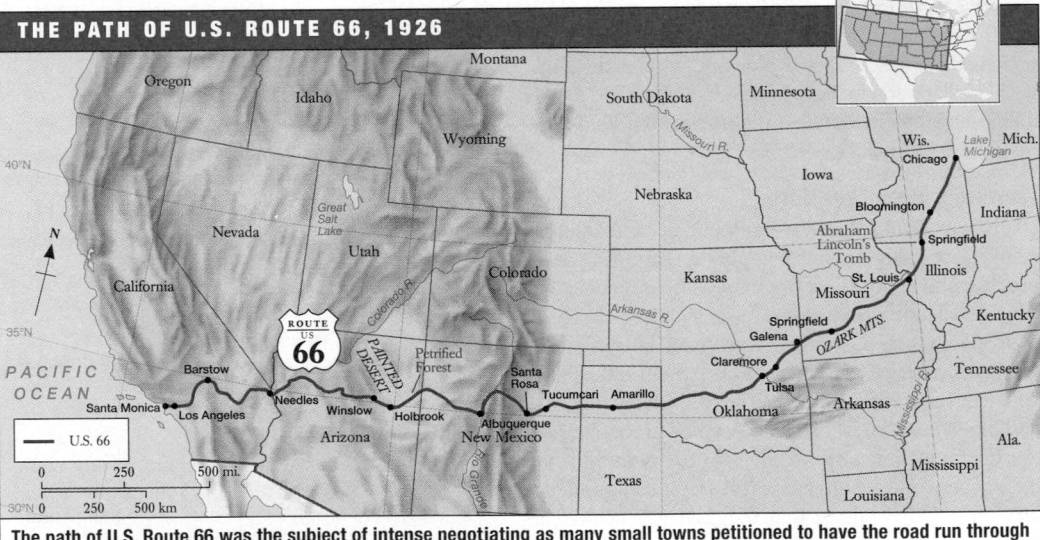

THE PATH OF U.S. ROUTE 66, 1926

The path of U.S. Route 66 was the subject of intense negotiating as many small towns petitioned to have the road run through their community. *What other points of interest besides towns were located on Route 66?*

384 GEOGRAPHY: IMPACT ON HISTORY

Geographic Themes

Movement The highway system was not the first example of interstate transportation in the United States. From 1790 to 1840 more than 3,000 miles of canals were dug to move goods inland from the Eastern seaboard. From 1840 to 1900 many railroads were built and became the major form of transportation for goods and people until the 1950s. With the launching of air travel, the number of airline passengers grew from 6,000 in 1926 to more than 450,000,000 in 1990. When the Interstate Highway Act was passed in 1956, old highways such as Route 66 were eventually bypassed. Invite students to discuss how improvements in transportation affect movement across the country. What trend is apparent with each improvement in transportation? *(People can travel more often and greater distances, and arrive more quickly.)*

to market. Farmers had been dependent on trains to freight their produce at whatever rate the railroad monopoly set.

Local political-action groups pressed Congress to legislate highway building and to break the railroad's stranglehold over transportation. In 1916 the Federal Aid Road Act responded to the pleas of these groups. The Road Act provided federal aid for half of the construction costs of any rural highway intended to carry mail. The new state highway departments were to plan the routes of the new roads. A second federal provision in 1921 granted money to states that would connect their roads to the roads of other states, forming a main thoroughfare. These acts set the basis for a national highway system.

When U.S. Route 66 officially opened on November 11, 1926, it became one of the main arteries of the national highway system. This "great diagonal highway" between Chicago and Los Angeles cut through the Middle West, straddled the Great Plains, crossed the deserts of the Southwest, and reached to the very edge of the Pacific Ocean. Route 66 spanned 8 states and ran through 200 towns, covering 2,400 miles (38,616 km). In the late 1920s, Route 66 was an autotourist's vacationland.

During the Depression of the 1930s, Route 66 became famous as the road that migrants in search of jobs in California followed. John Steinbeck once wrote, "66 is the mother road, the road of flight."

BROWN BROTHERS

A Roadside Autocamp Americans enjoyed the fresh air and fellowship found at roadside autocamps. *What goods and services did these autotourists require?*

Building the Roadside

The car and the highways provided Americans with a new form of recreation and business in the 1920s: autocamping. Millions of Americans packed tents and headed for the countryside. Car dealers even advertised autotourism as a way to strengthen the family. They pictured the prosperous middle-class family traveling down Route 66 exploring the United States.

Much of the land Route 66 crossed had not experienced the same prosperity as the rest of the nation in the 1920s. The same technology that brought cars and highways also revolutionized farming with new machinery. When the overproduction of grains glutted the market, however, prices fell. Many farmers went bust, losing their farms as well as their jobs.

The unemployed farmers and other people who lived in rural areas throughout the western states were not quite sure what the new highways were, nor what businesses the highways could bring to their communities. When Route 66 opened, though, they soon found out.

Many unemployed farmers enthusiastically joined the retail petroleum business selling gasoline, oil, and other services to passing tourists. After these new entrepreneurs opened gas stations, they went on to build tourist courts and cafes where tourists could rest and try local foods. Billboards began advertising such roadside attractions as man-eating pythons. In those days any promise became fair in the battle to get the tourist to stop and spend money.

Geography: Impact on History

VISUAL INSTRUCTION

A Roadside Autocamp This family from Colorado is enjoying dinner in Camp New York in the 1920s.

Answer: *gasoline and oil for their cars, food, water, lodging, camping supplies, amusements, and entertainment*

Mapping Activity

Ask students to compare a contemporary map of U.S. Route 66 with the 1926 version in their text and create a list of changes. Encourage them to note differences in the number and size of cities and towns along U.S. Route 66, and new highways that have appeared.

CLOSE

Ask students to examine the concept of franchised service stations and restaurants that line the interstates of the United States from coast to coast. How has this standardization contributed to the reduction of regional differences? *(Local color, unique restaurants, and "mom and pop" gas stations were lost. Uniformity in restaurants and service stations was gained.)*

MAKING THE GEOGRAPHIC CONNECTION

1. What did Americans want to learn as they drove to other parts of the United States?

2. What events led to the establishment of a national highway system?

3. **Movement** As Americans traveled along roads such as Route 66, what impact did they have on the economy of local cities and towns?

GEOGRAPHY: IMPACT ON HISTORY **385**

Making the Geographic Connection Answers

1. Americans wanted to learn what other Americans were doing in other parts of the country and how they lived.

2. In addition to car owners and manufacturers who wanted new roads, farmers wanted roads to transport their products to market. Local political groups wanted to break the transportation rates set by the railroad monopoly. The Federal Aid Road Act of 1916 and a second federal provision in 1921 supported the development of a national highway system.

3. Unemployed farmers joined the retail petroleum business selling gasoline, oil, and other services such as tourist courts and cafes. Forms of amusement and entertainment were also created to attract tourists. Citizens were exposed to the varied cultures of the different areas of the United States.

FOCUS

SECTION 2

The Jazz Age

OCTOBER 6, 1927: FIRST TALKING MOTION PICTURE RELEASED

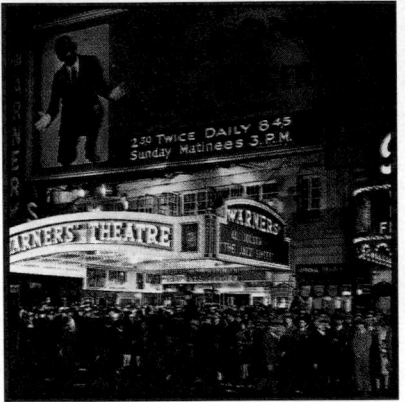

The Jazz Singer **Opens in New York**
Crowds gather at Warners' Theatre to view the first film using the Vitaphone sound system.

TEENAGERS ENTERED THE HUSHED THEATER AS THOUGH IT WERE THE PALACE IT LOOKED LIKE. Furniture, statues, and rugs from all over the world filled the lobby. One couple stopped in surprise as they caught sight of themselves in the huge mirrors that covered every wall. For just a moment, they thought they had become their favorite movie stars. Like guests at a grand ball, the girl and her date got ready to ascend the marble staircase. Inside the huge auditorium with its painted ceiling, the couple rested back in their plush seats. Fans blowing over ice cooled the summer air. The movie started!

More than any other entertainment, movies defined and helped create American culture in the 1920s. Glamorous settings like the movie house described above showed that many Americans in the 1920s had new-found leisure as well as the wealth to enjoy it. By the millions, Americans were now discovering the pleasures of movies, sports, live music, dancing, radio, and an abundance of newspapers, magazines, and books. (See Then and Now, pages 410–411.)

At the Movies
Connecting Americans

In the 1920s Americans went to the movies about once a week. Sociologists Robert S. Lynd and Helen Merrell Lynd profiled an average American city—Muncie, Indiana—in their 1929 book *Middletown*. In the 1920s Muncie boasted 9 motion picture theaters for a town of 35,000. The movies at these theaters operated from 1:00 P.M. to 11:00 P.M. every day of the year.

AS YOU READ

Vocabulary
▶ syndicate
▶ tabloid
▶ materialism

Think About . . .
▶ ways people used their leisure time during the Jazz Age.
▶ the musical and literary contributions of the 1920s.
▶ how the writers of the Lost Generation and the Harlem Renaissance reacted to American society of the 1920s and the prevailing atmosphere of materialism.

Silent Film Stars Rudolph Valentino, a famous silent film actor, and Agnes Ayres starred in *The Sheik* (1921). *What kind of role made Rudolph Valentino so popular with women?*

publicize stories that kept fans attached to "their" stars' loves, marriages, and divorces. When the romantic leading man Rudolph Valentino died at age 31 in 1926, nearly 30,000 tearful women thronged his funeral.

Through the fans' identification with stars, movies transformed Americans' tastes and behaviors. When stars like Mary Pickford or Gloria Swanson appeared in a new dress style or hairstyle, millions of women suddenly began to demand the same look.

New American Heroes
Sports and Individual Triumphs

Now that so many Americans had the time, the energy, and the money to play, they took to sports almost as avidly as they had embraced the movies. Before this decade, 300 private clubs and a handful of public courts easily served the few people who played tennis. By the late 1920s, the United States boasted nearly 1,000 tennis clubs and enough municipal courts to accommodate more than 1 million players, who swatted at 300,000 new tennis balls each month.

Golf, too, became widely popular during the 1920s. Before the war, golf had been a game for the wealthy. By 1927, 2 million players were putting away on 5,000 courses, many of them open to working-class people. Cities also constructed swimming pools, baseball diamonds, summer camps, playgrounds, and recreation centers.

Sports Stars

Hard-playing Americans also provided huge audiences for professional sports. The era's popular sports heroes—baseball's Babe Ruth and Oscar Charleston, boxing's Jack Dempsey, tennis's Helen Wills, football's Red Grange, golf's Bobby Jones—became as newsworthy off the field as movie stars. Explaining America's fascination with sports heroes, the historian George Mowry wrote:

Jack Dempsey Heavyweight boxing champion Jack Dempsey was a hero to millions of Americans. *What other professional sports provided heroes for Americans?*

Escaping Together

At the movies, Americans escaped to a different world, both on and off the screen. The movies—silent until *The Jazz Singer* in 1927—spoke powerfully to their audiences. A *Saturday Evening Post* ad encouraged Americans to "Go to a movie . . . and let yourself go." Each week, Americans of all ages, but especially high school and college students, paid as little as 10 cents for a few hours of fantasy.

Because every seat in the movie palace cost exactly the same admission price, going to the movies helped level the differences among Americans. A team of white-gloved ushers treated modest workers with the same courtesy they showed to rich businesspeople.

Even more important, because many of the major movie studios had chains of outlets, people in Muncie were now watching exactly the same stories people watched in California. The movies quickly became more popular than regional forms of entertainment.

Some people worried that the movies promoted immoral behavior. The ads for a movie called *Flaming Youth*, for example, promised "neckers, petters, white kisses, red kisses, pleasure-mad daughters, sensation-craving mothers, . . . the truth—bold, naked, sensational." In 1922 the Motion Picture Producers and Distributors Association tacked a moral message onto the end of each movie. Yet the movies themselves stayed as suggestive as ever.

Wishing on Stars

Seated in the dark, audiences could easily imagine themselves on the screen. Americans also relished reading about the stars' private lives in gossip columns by Louella Parsons and Hedda Hopper. The major movie studios hired publicity departments to make up and

TEACH

Guided Practice

L1 Discussion Ask students which characteristics that make stars attractive to fans have changed or remained the same. Do Americans still idolize movie stars and sports figures? Ask students for examples and reasons.

VISUAL INSTRUCTION

Silent Film Stars Valentino, whose real name was Rodolfo d'Antonguolla, played a desert warrior in *The Sheik*. This was followed by a sequel, *Son of the Sheik* (1926).
Answer: *He played a romantic leading man.*

Jack Dempsey In 1927 Jack Dempsey's second fight with Gene Tunney featured the famous "long count." Dempsey knocked Tunney down in the seventh round but did not go to a neutral corner immediately. The referee delayed starting the count and gave Tunney 14 seconds to get up. Tunney won the fight.
Answer: *baseball, tennis, football, and golf*

Cooperative Learning

Personalities of the 1920s As an approach to this section, students might form research groups to explore one of the following topics: movie stars, sports heroes, musicians, or writers of the 1920s. Within groups, each student or a pair of students should choose a particular person to research and share the findings with the group. Then each group should decide how to present its findings to the class (oral reports, displays, skits, and so on). Encourage students to support their presentations with visuals and recordings where appropriate.

387

FPG INTERNATIONAL CORP

Independent Practice

L1 Research Ask students to research other stars of the Negro Baseball League such as Satchel Paige, Smoky Joe Williams, and Josh Gibson. The National Baseball Hall of Fame in Cooperstown, New York, is a source for data.

 Have students complete the Chapter 12, Section 2 Vocabulary and Guided Reading Activity. (Also in Spanish.) **LEP**

Curriculum Connection

Geography Have students find the English Channel on a map and use the map scale to estimate the width of the channel. It took Ederle 14 hours and 31 minutes to swim across the channel.

VISUAL INSTRUCTION

Sports Heroes Gertrude Ederle's record for the 35-mile (56-kilometer) distance stood as the women's record for 35 years. After her channel triumph, in which her hearing was permanently impaired, she taught swimming to deaf children.

Oscar Charleston, the phenomenal Indiana outfielder, was nicknamed the Hoosier Comet. He was involved in professional baseball from 1915–1941.

Answer: *Ederle became the first woman to swim the English Channel; Charleston led the Negro Leagues in home runs 6 times between 1921 and 1933.*

On the battlefield, in the factory production line, at home in a city apartment, and increasingly even in the business world the individual was becoming lost in a welter of the hive. The sporting field was one of the few remaining areas of pure individual expression where success or failure depended precisely upon individual physical and intellectual prowess. And if the masses themselves could not or would not participate directly they could at least, by a process of identification, salute the old virtues.

—George E. Mowry, *The Twenties: Fords, Flappers, & Fanatics*, 1963

Americans learned about their heroes by watching them perform. They also devoured newspaper and magazine articles about them. In 1926 Jack Dempsey, the "Manassa Mauler," lost his heavyweight boxing title to Gene Tunney. Sports fans all over the country chuckled at the aging fighter's answer when his wife asked him what had happened. "Honey," Dempsey answered, "I forgot to duck."

In 1926 a 19-year-old girl named Gertrude Ederle, popularly known as "Our Trudy," became the first woman to swim the English Channel, beating the fastest man's record by a full two hours. Before her swim, W. O. McGeehan wrote in the *New York Herald Tribune*, "If there is one woman who can make the swim, it is this girl, with the shoulders and back of Jack Dempsey and the frankest and bravest pair of eyes that ever looked into a face." After swimming the English Channel, Gertrude Ederle said simply, "I just knew if it could be done it had to be done, and I did it." A huge ticker tape parade greeted her return to New York City.

One of the greats in baseball's Negro League, Oscar Charleston led the league in home runs six times between 1921 and 1933. Regarded as one of the greatest players of all time, Charleston was never allowed to play in the major leagues because of the color of his skin.

The Lone Eagle

No American hero of the 1920s equaled Charles Lindbergh, whose solo flight across the Atlantic in 1927 excited more enthusiasm than any single event before, or perhaps since. The modest young man in his flying machine served to join America's pioneer past with an optimistic view of the country's technological future.

NATIONAL BASEBALL LIBRARY & ARCHIVE, COOPERSTOWN, NEW YORK

Sports Heroes Assisted by her coach, Gertrude Ederle (above) trains for her English Channel swim off the coast of France. Oscar Charleston (left) was inducted into the National Baseball Hall of Fame in 1976. *What did these sports figures accomplish?*

Lindbergh's flight and the public response to it never could have taken place without modern machinery and the combined efforts of thousands of people. Still, many Americans preferred to regard their hero as a traditional pioneer, "the lone eagle." To them, Lindbergh's accomplishment seemed to demonstrate the triumph of individual American heroism in a bewildering new age of machines. Amelia Earhart, who became the first woman to fly across the Atlantic Ocean, matched his feat in 1928.

New Rhythms in the Air
Blues, Jazz, and the Charleston

During the 1920s Americans entertained themselves at movies and sports events. They also began to listen to two exciting new types of music: soulful blues and frantic jazz that would give its name to the entire era.

Meeting Special Needs

Oral Learners To address the particular needs of oral learners, pair students to review the people and events noted on the entertainment time line. Encourage them to discuss the events in an organized and chronological fashion, including the year, month, and day where applicable. Ask pairs to review their text, adding other key figures and their accomplishments to the appropriate place on the time line. Then invite students to create similar time lines for the most recent 10 years. Remind pairs to include significant people and events. Newspapers, magazines, almanacs, encyclopedias, and other reference materials can be useful aids. Have volunteers share their products with the class.

King Oliver's Creole Jazz Band Louis Armstrong played the cornet, and his wife, Lil Hardin, played the piano in this Chicago band later known as King Oliver's Dixieland Jazz Band. *How did jazz make its way to Northern cities?*

Imitating African American jazz bands, white bands, such as those of Paul Whiteman and Bix Beiderbecke, performed widely at dances for young people. Supper clubs and country clubs provided settings for the slow dancing and the Charleston that young people so enjoyed and that older people declared immoral, shocking, and scandalous.

The Charleston was by no means the only dance of the 1920s, an era that has been called "The Dance Age" as well as "The Jazz Age." With its flying beads, knocking knees, and crossing hands, however, the Charleston will forever represent the 1920s. The Charleston first appeared in an African American revue called "Runnin' Wild" in 1924. Although initially considered too difficult for amateurs to master, within a year this whirlwind had swept the country.

While live music defined the 1920s, recorded music became part of the mainstream only after electricity made the phonograph and radio possible. Commercial radio had a modest start when stations in Detroit and Pittsburgh broadcast the 1920 presidential election returns. By the middle of the decade, few people found themselves out of earshot of a radio speaker. In the late 1920s, the roof of practically every tenement house on the Lower East Side of New York City looked like a forest of radio antennae. Radio brought entertainment and advertising to a mass market and helped spur the explosive growth of the mass-market economy.

The blues grew out of work songs and field chants of enslaved African Americans. In the 1920s African American singers, such as Bessie Smith and Gertrude "Ma" Rainey, sang their sad songs to huge audiences in clubs on Chicago's South Side and recorded them on African American labels for major record companies.

Jazz began in New Orleans and moved north when African Americans migrated there during World War I. Not a single note was written down, but the musicians all seemed to know what to play.

Singing of joy in the face of oppression, jazz contains strands of music from many European countries. Nevertheless, jazz is above all an African American creation, and it could have developed only in a city in the United States. In 1925 J.A. Rogers wrote, "With its cowbells, auto horns, calliopes, rattles, dinner gongs, kitchen utensils, cymbals, screams, crashes, clankings and monotonous rhythm [jazz] bears all the marks of a nerve-strung, strident, mechanized civilization."

When it moved to Chicago in 1920, Joseph "King" Oliver's Creole Jazz Band found a ready audience of urban African Americans. In 1922 King Oliver invited his talented former cornet student to join the band. When the student, Louis Armstrong, later switched to the trumpet, he became perhaps the most famous jazz musician of all time.

Time to Read

The Rise of Print Media

With time on their hands and with more education than any previous generation, more Americans in the 1920s read. During the 1920s scores of new magazines came into existence. At least 20 magazines boasted circulations of a million readers. *Reader's Digest* debuted in 1922, *Time* in 1923, and *The New Yorker* in 1925.

SECTION TWO **389**

King Oliver's Creole Jazz Band Armstrong's first recorded solo appeared on the band's recording of *Chimes Blues* (1923). Lil Hardin, a classically trained pianist, coached him. He played the cornet and switched to the trumpet in 1925. In a 1932 London performance, he acquired the nickname "Satchmo."

Answer: *African Americans from New Orleans took jazz with them when they migrated north after World War I.*

FYI

The Power of the Radio In the 1920s radio played the role television plays in today's culture. People from every income group listened to the same programs and advertisements. The voices of popular radio announcers reached the entire country. Some people even put ads in the newspaper to tell their friends not to call them while their favorite programs were on! The first television transmission took place during the height of this age of radio. In April 1927, a hand-sized screen showed a grainy image of Herbert Hoover, transmitted from Washington, D.C. to New York City.

Portfolio Project

Critical Review Organize small groups and have students find and listen to some of the blues and jazz music of the 1920s. Then have each student write a music review of a 1920s blues or jazz recording. It can be one they have listened to in class or another selection by a singer or composer of the time period. Suggest that students collect sample reviews from newspapers and magazines to use as models. You may want to consider the elements that make an effective review with the class before they begin writing. Invite students to share their reviews and then file their written products in their portfolios.

Curriculum Connection

Art Have students research the work of some of the famous painters of the period, such as Pablo Picasso, Henri Matisse, George Wesley Bellows, and Thomas Hart Benton. Students might bring books of paintings to share with the class.

FYI

Fitzgerald and Hemingway F. Scott Fitzgerald and Ernest Hemingway lived the lifestyles of their characters. Fitzgerald and his wife, Zelda, threw lavish jazz parties. Hemingway hunted and fished. While Hemingway promoted these traditional masculine values in his writing, Fitzgerald's writing evoked nostalgia for the solid midwestern values his Jazz Age characters scorned.

VISUAL INSTRUCTION

A Painting of Gertrude Stein Gertrude Stein's best-known book is *The Autobiography of Alice B. Toklas* (1933). She wrote about herself from the viewpoint of Alice B. Toklas, her friend and secretary. She settled in Paris in 1903, and her apartment became a gathering place for many writers, musicians, and painters.

Answer: *She called them the lost generation.*

More people were reading newspapers as well, although the number of newspapers dropped as papers gathered into **syndicates**—chains of newspapers under centralized direction. The contents of the newspapers began to look more similar as the syndicates provided editorials, sports, gossip, and Sunday features for a national audience.

With their small pages and large type, **tabloid** newspapers made ideal reading for crowded, rocking subway cars. Tabloids swept the country in the 1920s. New York alone had 3, with a combined circulation of 1.6 million readers. The tabloids battled each other, attempting to sell papers by publicizing scandals or fads, such as dance marathons in which young people danced until they dropped.

Most of the fads reported in the tabloids grew old very quickly. One fad though thrived long enough to launch a publishing empire. Two young men, Richard Simon and Lincoln Schuster, began their publishing company by bringing out a crossword puzzle book that eventually sold two million copies.

Americans were hungry for books and the 1920s saw the birth of several major publishing houses, including Simon and Schuster, Morrow, Viking, and Harcourt, Brace. The Book-of-the-Month Club and the Literary Guild began mass distribution of books within months of each other in 1926.

The Lost Generation
Attacking Materialism

While ordinary Americans happily pursued new leisure activities—movies, radio, music, dance, and reading—some writers began to attack America's **materialism.** They questioned a society that placed more importance on money and material goods than it did on intellectual, spiritual, and artistic concerns.

Leaving the United States Behind

During the 1920s some prominent American writers and artists moved to Europe, partly because they felt the United States was "the enemy of the artist, of the man who cannot produce something tangible when the five o'clock whistle blows." The expatriates also felt that it was cheaper to live in Europe than it was to stay at home.

The dollar was especially strong in Paris where writers Gertrude Stein, Ernest Hemingway, and F. Scott Fitzgerald took up residence in the 1920s. Gertrude Stein made bold experiments with language in her plays, operas, and books. She also gave the literary era its name when she told her friend Hemingway, "You are all a lost generation."

Ernest Hemingway set most of his novels in Europe and portrayed the ruined innocence of his postwar generation. His masterpiece *The Sun Also Rises,* published in 1926, quoted Gertrude Stein's comment on its title page. The book tells of Jake, an expatriate American who bears physical and psychological wounds from the war. It ends on a note of quiet despair.

F. Scott Fitzgerald's earliest novels and stories were set in the United States where he wrote about daring college students. *The Great Gatsby,* published in 1925 and considered Fitzgerald's greatest work, explored the empty lives of Americans with too much money. Daisy, the main female character, feels purposeless and lost.

Criticizing the United States From Within

Many of the most significant writers of the 1920s never left the United States or left for only brief periods. Like the expatriates, American writers who stayed home took up their pens to expose what they considered the shallow and money-centered culture of their nation.

In his trilogy, *U.S.A.,* John Dos Passos suggested the United States had become two nations, one rich and one poor. Experimenting with free-form writing and leaving punctuation behind, Dos Passos wrote,

A Painting of Gertrude Stein The Spanish artist Pablo Picasso painted Gertrude Stein in 1906. Stein encouraged experimental painters such as Picasso and Henri Matisse. *What phrase did Stein create that described the 1920s literary era?*

THE METROPOLITAN MUSEUM OF ART, BEQUEST OF GERTRUDE STEIN, 1946

Extending the Content

Publishing Talk about some of the publishing developments of the 1920s, such as national magazines, syndicated newspapers, tabloids, and such book clubs as Book-of-the-Month and Literary Guild. Ask students how those developments affect their world today. Students should note that many of those ideas, and even some of the companies, still exist. Encourage students to brainstorm for each category a list of contemporary print materials that have had a strong influence on their lives. Then invite students to note the impact of evolving technology on published products such as CD-ROM, audio books, and publications on the Internet.

"...on the streets you see only the downcast faces of the beaten the streets belong to the beaten nation ... we stand defeated America."

Sinclair Lewis attacked the materialism of small-town America in satiric novels such as *Main Street*, which was a best-seller in 1920, and *Babbitt*, which was equally popular two years later. The term *Babbitt* is still used to refer to the ordinary 1920s American—a narrow-minded, obsessed businessperson whose deepest desires are determined by advertising.

Ironically, just as intellectuals were complaining that art could not possibly flourish in the United States, American writers were publishing some of the country's best literature ever.

The wittiest critic of the United States during this period was H.L. Mencken. His targets often richly deserved his nasty insults. When Mencken labeled the South the "Sahara of the Bozart," or wasteland of the fine arts, however, he could not have been more mistaken. From his home in Oxford, Mississippi, William Faulkner was crafting the brilliant and difficult works that would eventually win him a Nobel Prize in literature.

DENVER CENTER THEATRE COMPANY

Emperor Jones The plays of Eugene O'Neill such as *Emperor Jones* (1920) brought serious themes to Broadway in the 1920s and still affect audiences today. *What issues did writers of the 1920s address?*

The Harlem Renaissance
A Literary and Artistic Movement

At the same time the Lost Generation of white writers was questioning materialistic American culture, African American writers who had migrated to the nation's Northern cities began to express their own identity and a rising anger at Northern racism. Bustling with nightclubs and cafes and alive with blues and jazz, a section of New York City called Harlem lured African American and white intellectuals. The African American literary and artistic movement that resulted became known as the Harlem Renaissance.

Alain Locke was a professor of literature at Howard University, a graduate of Harvard, and the first African American Rhodes scholar. Locke urged his fellow African Americans to create a new literature. In *The New Negro,* Locke wrote that the younger genertion of African Americans is "vibrant with a new psychology ... the new spirit is awake in the masses."

Inspired by Locke, writers like Langston Hughes and Claude McKay spoke out in the strongest voices of the

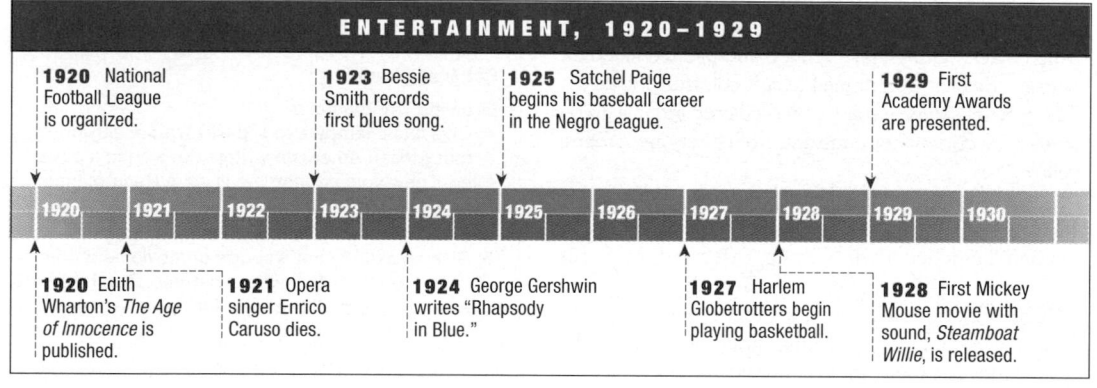

ENTERTAINMENT, 1920–1929

1920 National Football League is organized.

1923 Bessie Smith records first blues song.

1925 Satchel Paige begins his baseball career in the Negro League.

1929 First Academy Awards are presented.

1920 1921 1922 1923 1924 1925 1926 1927 1928 1929 1930

1920 Edith Wharton's *The Age of Innocence* is published.

1921 Opera singer Enrico Caruso dies.

1924 George Gershwin writes "Rhapsody in Blue."

1927 Harlem Globetrotters begin playing basketball.

1928 First Mickey Mouse movie with sound, *Steamboat Willie*, is released.

SECTION TWO **391**

ASSESS

Meeting Lesson Objectives

Each section objective is tested by the section review question(s) that follows it in parentheses.

1. Identify the leisure-time activities of Americans during the 1920s. (1, 2, 5)
2. Describe the musical and literary contributions of the 1920s. (2,3)
3. Explain how the writers of the Lost Generation and the Harlem Renaissance reacted to American society of the 1920s. (1, 3, 4)

VISUAL INSTRUCTION

Emperor Jones In the early 1920s, O'Neill rejected realism and tried to capture on stage the "force behind" human life. *Emperor Jones* is an expressionistic play that traces the personal and racial past of a black porter who becomes a Caribbean dictator.

Answer: *materialistic American culture, northern racism*

CHART STUDY

Ask: Who recorded the first blues song?
Answer: *(Bessie Smith)*

Cultural Perspectives

Storytelling During the 1920s writers' themes reflected their different experiences in the United States. Zora Neale Hurston left New York City in 1927 to travel the back roads of the South. The folklore she collected evolved from a rich tradition of storytelling that existed for centuries in West Africa. As part of an effort to make sense of their new environment, African

Americans continued this tradition. Stories of exaggeration, sometimes called "lies," include humorous beginnings, for example "why" the possum has no hair on its tail. Encourage students to read some of this folklore in Zora Neale Hurston's *Mules and Men* (1935). This was the first book of African American folklore published by an African American.

Langston Hughes The sketches Hughes wrote about an African American called "Simple" were well known. Most of these sketches have no plot, but Simple expresses his opinions about current issues, relating what an intelligent, but uneducated proud African American might say if given the chance.

Answer: *jazz/blues themes and rhythms; the culture of the poorest African Americans*

Evaluate

Have students complete the Section Review.

🖝 ⬛ Assign the Section 2 Quiz or use the Testmaker to develop a customized quiz. (Also in Spanish.) **LEP**

Reteach

🎧 Have students listen to the Chapter 12, Section 2 Audiocassette. (Also in Spanish.) **LEP**

Enrich

🖝 Have students complete the Unit 4 American Literature Reading.

CLOSE

Have students compare contemporary leisure-time activities and musical and literary contributions with those of the 1920s. Which are the same? What new trends have emerged? *(Answers will vary, but should note the continued popularity of listening to music and dancing; reading; attending plays, movies, and sports events.)*

Langston Hughes A pioneer of modern African American literature, Hughes was descended from a prominent family of abolitionists. *What themes did Hughes use in his poetry?*

I have sown beside all waters in my day.
I planted deep, within my heart the fear
That wind or fowl would take the grain away.
I planted safe against this stark, lean year.

I scattered seed enough to plant the land
In rows from Canada to Mexico
But for my reaping only what the hand
Can hold at once is all that I can show.

Yet what I sowed and what the orchard yields
My brother's sons are gathering stalk and root,
Small wonder then my children glean in fields
They have not sown, and feed on bitter fruit.

—Arna Bontemps, "A Black Man
Talks of Reaping," 1927

Harlem Renaissance. Hughes, a gifted poet, was one of the first African American writers to use jazz and blues themes and rhythms in his poetry. In a 1926 essay called "The Negro Artist and the Racial Mountain," Hughes argued that what was truly worth expressing would be found in the culture of the poorest African American people: "If white people are pleased we are glad. If they are not, it doesn't matter. We know we are beautiful. And ugly too. The tom tom cries and the tom tom laughs."

Claude McKay migrated from his native Jamaica to Harlem. There he wrote poems such as "If We Must Die" and "The White City" that challenged African Americans to fight for their rights. McKay's autobiographical novel, *Home to Harlem,* published in 1928, expressed his fascination with all the shades of people who could be called black: "Brown girls rouged and painted like dark pansies. Brown flesh draped in soft colorful clothes . . . The cabaret singer, a shiny coffee-colored girl in a green frock . . . chocolate, chestnut, coffee, ebony, cream, yellow. . . ."

In addition to Langston Hughes and Claude McKay, many other talented African American men and women launched their writing careers during this exciting period. For example, Arna Bontemps, a poet and a friend of Langston Hughes, wrote the following poem in which the images of planting grain pointed out the inequalities between African Americans and whites:

Of the many gifted African American women involved in the movement, a young anthropologist named Zora Neale Hurston eventually became the best known. Hurston's plays, short stories, and articles began to appear in the 1920s, and featured the African American folklore she had listened to as a child. Her 1937 masterpiece, *Their Eyes Were Watching God,* portrayed the first heroic African American woman in American literature.

In the 1920s African Americans began to find their own unique voices in new and exciting literature. The writers of the Harlem Renaissance proclaimed that blacks would no longer accept second-class citizenship in any area of American life.

SECTION REVIEW

Vocabulary

1. Define: syndicate, tabloid, materialism.

Checking Facts

2. How did movies and radio increase the similarities between Americans in different parts of the country?

3. Why did so many American writers criticize American values during the postwar period?

Critical Thinking

Drawing Conclusions

4. Give two examples to support the conclusion that African American writers developed a powerful new voice during the Harlem Renaissance.

Linking Across Time

5. Give an example of a sports or movie hero from the 1920s and of a modern hero. Explain how each hero helped to shape American fashions and/or values.

Section 2 Review Answers

1. syndicate (390), **tabloid** (390), **materialism** (390)

2. Movies and radio influenced behavior and tastes. Americans all over the country adopted similar fashions and bought similar products.

3. They considered American culture shallow and money-centered.

4. Langston Hughes and Arna Bontemps were among many African American writers who wrote about the experiences of African Americans.

5. Answers might include information such as: in the 1920s people admired Gertrude Ederle for her youthful determination and in the 1990s they admire skating star Kristi Yamaguchi for the same quality.

Critical Thinking Skill

SYNTHESIZING INFORMATION

Learning the Skill

The author of this book gathered information from many sources to present a story of how Americans lived in the 1900s. To integrate all the evidence into a cohesive story, the author used a process called synthesis.

The skill of synthesizing involves combining and analyzing information obtained from separate sources or at different times to make logical connections.

Follow these three basic steps to synthesize data:

a. Select relevant information.

b. Analyze information and build connections.

c. Reinforce or modify connections as you acquire new information.

Being able to synthesize can be a useful skill for you as a student. Suppose you needed to write a research paper on the status of women in the 1920s. You would need to synthesize what you learn to inform others.

Organizing Existing Ideas and Adding New Data

Begin by detailing the ideas you already have about the status of women in the 1920s. A graphic organizer such as the one below aids in categorizing facts.

SYNTHESIZING	
Women's Status in the 1920s	
Economic	Many women worked in factories and offices at low-level, low-paying jobs.
Political	Women gained the right to vote in 1920.
Social	Women had new social freedoms—smoking, drinking, freer clothing styles.
Educational	Many women had a high school education.

Then select an article about women in the 1920s such as the following:

In 1923 the National Woman's party first proposed an equal rights amendment to the Constitution. This amendment stated that "men and women shall have equal rights throughout the United States and every place subject to its jurisdiction." The National Woman's party pointed out that legislation discriminating against women existed in every state. For example, in some states, the law gave husbands control over the earnings of their wives and prevented women from sitting on juries. Women could not attend some of the best schools, and they were delegated to the lower levels of professions.

Some progressive women reformers, however, opposed the goals of the National Woman's party. These progressives favored protective legislation, which had brought shorter hours and better working conditions for many women. The progressives succeeded in their efforts to defeat the amendment.

Practicing the Skill

1. On a sheet of paper, revise the graphic organizer to incorporate relevant information in the article by verifying and modifying the original ideas.

2. Using only your existing knowledge, write a paragraph about how the automobile affected Americans in the 1920s. Next, review Section 1 of this chapter to rewrite your paragraph, integrating ideas from the text and illustrations.

3. Create a visual display that includes relevant information about baseball today. Support your design with text that will help viewers synthesize the message you are presenting.

4. In Section 2 of this chapter, Gertrude Stein described the literary era of the 1920s in her statement, "You are all a lost generation." Write a response to this assertion.

5. Find three different newspaper or magazine reviews of the same movie and synthesize the information in a single critique.

Applying the Skill

Discuss and list with a partner ideals of the 1920s, synthesizing information from Chapter 11 and Sections 1 and 2 of Chapter 12. Highlight those ideals that exist today and discuss which ones have changed. Then make a list of present-day ideals, incorporating those from the 1920s that still exist and adding any new ones.

Additional Practice

For additional practice, see Reinforcing Skills on page 409.

TEACH

This skill familiarizes students with the procedures to follow in order to synthesize information. Point out that the skill will help students learn that synthesizing is the process of combining information gathered from different sources or at different times. They are taught a three-step process of synthesizing. Students are shown how to organize what they already know and then add the new information to that schema. Students are also encouraged to use a graphic organizer as they categorize the material. An example of a graphic organizer is provided.

Additional Practice

☛ Have students complete the Chapter 12 Skill Reinforcement Activity.

Practicing the Skill Answers

Answers will vary

1. Additions to revised graphic organizers:
Economic—husband controlled wife's earnings
Political—laws discriminated against women, ERA defeated
Social—protective legislation brought shorter hours and better working conditions for women
Educational—unable to attend best schools
2. Impact of automobile: boosted the economy; caused borrowing on time; changed dating and vacation habits; enabled cross-country travel
3. Contemporary baseball topics and statistics with supporting visuals should be included.
4. Information should include the literary era of the 1920s attacking America's materialism and society as the enemy of the artist.
5. The basic steps for synthesizing data should be incorporated in the new critique.

TEACH

Making the Historical Connection

In the spring of 1927 Calvin Coolidge was President, movies were silent, and business was booming. Aviation was the industry of adventure and romance in the 1920s, so when the charming Captain Charles Lindbergh made his record-breaking flight, newspapers devoted pages to the story, including every lofty gesture and mundane detail.

FYI

Charles Lindbergh Born in 1902, Lindbergh grew up in MInnesota. After 2 years at the University of Wisconsin, he started flying as a stunt pilot. He completed flight training to become an Army Air Service Reserve pilot. Later he flew mail between Chicago and St. Louis. An offer of $25,000 to the first pilot to fly nonstop from New York to Paris inspired Lindbergh's famous flight. He continued to work in aviation for the rest of his life. In 1929 he married the poet Anne Morrow. The couple suffered unwanted fame when their infant son was kidnapped and killed. In the 1960s Lindbergh became an active spokesman for conservation.

SPORTS: Princeton crew beats Yale in rowing regatta; Yale's first loss in 5 years

One Day in History

Saturday, May 21, 1927

MARKET BASKET

Here is where a dollar will go:

Mobil oil . . . . 30¢/quart
Memorial wreath for
  Memorial Day . . . . 89¢
Men's cotton broadcloth
  pajamas $1.69
Gallon-size Auto Vacuum
  jug (keeps hot drinks
  hot in the car) $1.89

Wrigley's chewing gum . . . 5¢
Cotton fabric . . . . . . 39¢/yard
Silk and rayon hose . . 50¢/pair
Hatbox $2.69
6-volt battery for all
  small cars $5.99
2-car garage, built $350
Electric waffle iron $5
Hy-Dyve swimsuit . . . . $4–$5
Balloon-cord car tire . . . $7.98
Apartment: 5 rooms, gas,
  set tubs, stove $28/mo
White Mountain icebox
  . . . . $27.50
  . . . . . . ($5 down, $1 weekly)
Kelvinator refrigerator
  (installment plan available)
  . . . . $210

Lindbergh Crosses the Atlantic

"Lone Eagle" Lands—World Sighs in Relief

PARIS—Just 33 hours and 29 minutes after he took off from New York, Captain Charles E. Lindbergh landed at Le Bourget airfield in Paris. The 25-year-old "Lone Eagle" became the first person to survive a nonstop flight across the Atlantic. "No man before me had commanded such freedom of movement over the earth," said Lindbergh. "For me the *Spirit of St. Louis* was a lens focused on the future, a forerunner of mechanisms that would conquer time and space."

The *New York Times* reported from Paris:

> *Lindbergh did it. Twenty minutes after 10 o'clock tonight suddenly and softly there slipped out of the darkness a gray-white airplane as 25,000 pairs of eyes strained toward it. At 10:24 the* Spirit of St. Louis *landed and lines of soldiers, ranks of policemen and stout steel fences went down before a mad rush as irresistible as the tides in the ocean.*

"The Lone Eagle," Charles Lindbergh, becomes the first to fly across the Atlantic from New York (not Newfoundland) to Paris, and the first to do it alone.

Background Information

Saudi Arabia In the late 1800s, the Saud family, which had ruled most of the area now called Saudi Arabia, lost land to the Ottoman Empire and smaller, tribal groups. The Saud family was in exile, but in 1902 a young leader in the family, Abd al-Aziz Ibn Saud led an army to recover territory his ancestors had controlled. Within a few years he regained control of the Najd region of Central Arabia, and eventually took over several other regions, including the western coastal area of Hejaz. In 1915 Great Britain claimed Saudi lands as a protectorate. Though Ibn Saud had unified the regions of Arabia under his control by around 1925, the British did not recognize the kingdom's sovereign or independent status until 1927. In 1932 Ibn Saud officially proclaimed the area the Kingdom of Saudi Arabia.

WORLD: Yesterday Great Britain recognized Saudia Arabian independence and sovereignty in the Treaty of Jeddah.

Deluge Devastates Louisiana

NEW ORLEANS—The Associated Press reports, "The restless gurgle of muddy water echoed from the northern boundary of Louisiana tonight to within 50 miles (80.5 km) of the Gulf of Mexico." About 100,000 people have taken refuge in LaFayette; more are still fleeing the water. The flood has cut a path 150 miles (241 km) long and 50 miles (80.5 km) wide across the state.

Secretary of Commerce Herbert Hoover says, "There has never been a calamity such as this flood."

The flood threatened weak points along the Atchafalaya River 140 miles (225 km) north of New Orleans. The current was tearing the embankment to pieces in McCrea, where more than 200 workers fought in the mud and rain to keep the flood off the sugar plantations of 5 parishes.

Clara Bow, "the 'It' Girl" of the 1920s, is a huge box office draw.

MUSIC

Popular Songs of 1927:

"Ol' Man River"

"Let a Smile Be Your Umbrella"

"My Blue Heaven"

BOOKS

This Week's Best-Sellers:

Twilight Sleep by Edith Wharton

Revolt in the Desert by T.E. Lawrence

MOVIES

- *Rough House Rosie,* with Clara Bow
- *Mr. Wu,* starring Lon Chaney
- *Slide, Kelly, Slide,* starring William Haines, a Metro-Goldwyn Mayer picture
- Cecil B. DeMille's *King of Kings,* which premiered last Thursday at the grand opening of Graumann's Chinese Theater in Hollywood, California

---

CLOSE

Discuss May 21, 1927 with students. To spark discussion, ask why aviation was so popular in the 1920s. What do the Market Basket objects and their prices say about society of the day?

Oral History

Memoir Point out that the 1927 flood in Mississippi did not get the news coverage it might have because of excitement over Lindbergh. Similarly, the Northeast's hurricane of 1938 was little known outside the region because news was focused on the start of war in Europe. Ask students if they ever witnessed or were part of a newsworthy event that was not covered because of another dramatic story. Have students describe the event, and discuss the other events happening at the same time. If possible, students should tape-record their recollections first, then transcribe their oral description and include the transcript in their portfolio.

SECTION

3

FOCUS

Section Objectives

1. Explain how social changes of the 1920s caused conflicts among various groups of people in the United States.
2. Identify some reasons for and effects of the widespread disregard for Prohibition.
3. Describe the resurgence of the Ku Klux Klan in the 1920s.
4. Explain how the election of 1928 reflected the cultural conflicts of the decade.

Bellringer Activity

While taking attendance at the beginning of the class period, display **Section Focus Transparency 39,** and have students answer the questions.

VISUAL INSTRUCTION

Celebrities in the Scopes Trial *Inherit the Wind,* a play by Jerome Lawrence and Robert E. Lee, is a dramatization of the Scopes trial.

Ask: What did Darrow and Bryan each represent, even before the trial? *(Darrow represented the urban intellectual; Bryan the rural faithful.)*

Cultural Conflicts

JULY 10, 1925: SCOPES TRIAL BEGINS, DAYTON, TENNESSEE

Celebrities in the Scopes Trial
Clarence Darrow (left) and William Jennings Bryan (right) were said to have respected each other, in spite of their differences.

DURING A SIZZLING HOT JULY IN 1925, A SIMPLE TRIAL IN THE SMALL TOWN OF DAYTON, TENNESSEE, TURNED INTO A SHOWDOWN BETWEEN RELIGION AND SCIENCE. A local science teacher, John Scopes, was on trial for teaching evolution. Scopes and all the other teachers who used the state-approved textbook had broken the Butler Act, a new state law against teaching "any theory that denies the story of the Divine Creation of man as taught in the Bible."

When the Butler Act was passed in 1925, Tennessee's governor had signed it reluctantly, commenting, "Nobody believes that it is going to be an active statute." He was wrong. When a small item about the law appeared in the *New York Times,* the American Civil Liberties Union (ACLU) raised money to test the law in court. All it needed was a Tennessee teacher to volunteer to be arrested for breaking the Butler Act.

In 1925 John Scopes agreed to go on trial to test the legality of the Butler Act. Clarence Darrow, an urban liberal, volunteered as defense lawyer for Scopes. William Jennings Bryan, three times a candidate for President and a hero to rural America, joined the prosecution to testify as an expert on the Bible.

Broadcast over the radio and reported in hundreds of newspapers, the Scopes trial symbolized many of the bitter conflicts that rocked the United States during the 1920s. In this decade, struggles between Americans erupted over religion, over drinking, and even over who was considered an American.

AS YOU READ

Vocabulary
► fundamentalism
► evangelist
► speakeasy
► bootlegger
► quota

Think About . . .
► how the social changes of the 1920s caused conflicts among various groups of people in the United States.
► possible reasons for and effects of the widespread disregard for Prohibition.
► the nature of the resurgence of the Ku Klux Klan in the 1920s.
► how the election of 1928 reflected the cultural conflicts of the decade.

Section 3 Resources

REPRODUCIBLE RESOURCES

📁 Lesson Plan 12-3
📁 Vocabulary and Guided Reading Activity 12-3
📁 Section 3 Quiz
📁 Chapter 12 Test
📁 Performance Assessment Activity 12
📁 Reteaching Activity 12
📁 Supreme Court Case 10
📁 Unit 3 Test

MULTIMEDIA RESOURCES

🔦 Section Focus Transparency 39
💿 Landmark Documents in American History
🖥 Testmaker
🎧 Chapter 12 Digest Audiocassette
🖥 Student Self-Test: A Software Review
🖥 Vocabulary PuzzleMaker

Charismatic Preacher Aimee Semple McPherson Some 1920s evangelists mixed religion and show business. Here Aimee Semple McPherson dramatically pleads with her Los Angeles congregation for contributions. *In which regions of the country was fundamentalism strongest?*

The Power of Religion
Something Familiar in Changing Times

The turning point of the Scopes trial came on the last day, when Darrow put Bryan on the stand and questioned him at length about the Bible's account of creation, which Bryan claimed to believe literally. Darrow, who saw the case as an important constitutional issue, asked Bryan if he thought the earth had been made in 6 days, and Bryan had to admit, "Not 6 days of 24 hours." The judge finally halted the questioning when the 2 adversaries ended up shaking their fists at each other.

When the trial was over, both sides claimed victory: the jury had taken less than 10 minutes to find John Scopes guilty and fine him $100, but the Tennessee Supreme Court later acquitted him on a technicality. Although some biology teachers continued to teach evolution, the Butler Act remained the law in Tennessee (until 1967, when it was repealed). To many it seemed that **fundamentalism**—a movement that affirmed the literal truth of the Bible—had won.

Nonetheless, Darrow's piercing questions disturbed Bryan, who had been forced to admit that a "day" in the Bible might be a million years or more. Because Bryan had based his position on the idea that the Bible must be read literally and not interpreted, he was aware of contradicting himself. The elderly statesman died less than a week later and was mourned by millions.

The Scopes case may have dealt fundamentalism a blow, but the movement continued to thrive in the United States. Rural people, especially in the South and Midwest, remained faithful to their churches. When large numbers of farmers migrated to cities during the 1920s, they brought fundamentalism with them. The familiar religion helped them make sense of their new lives.

At the same time, however, the traditional religions began to take on some modern aspects. In Southern California several fundamentalist preachers, or **evangelists,** used radio to reach many people.

Aimee Semple McPherson used show business techniques to attract a radio following to her "Foursquare Gospel." McPherson barnstormed the country in 1921 and 1922, raising $1.5 million for the construction of her Angelus Temple. After the temple was completed in 1923, McPherson kept it filled every night.

SECTION THREE   **397**

TEACH

Guided Practice

L2 **Debate** Have students debate the pros and cons of laws such as the Volstead Act. Pose the following questions: Should the law attempt to control such potentially harmful behavior as drinking alcohol? If the majority of people disobey a law, should it be repealed regardless of its merit?

VISUAL INSTRUCTION

Charismatic Preacher Aimee Semple McPherson "Sister Aimee" McPherson gained added notoriety for a 5-week disappearance in 1926, which she claimed was a kidnapping, and for many lawsuits against her in the following years, often over libel or slander charges.

Answer: *South and Midwest*

Cooperative Learning

Panel Discussion Have students prepare panel discussions on various aspects of the following general topic: Great Social Changes of the 1920s Sparked Intense Reactions. Organize students into groups, each having students with varying abilities and strengths. Each group should decide on a focus for its discussion. Remind students that each person should contribute to the discussion.

THE BETTMANN ARCHIVE

Independent Practice

L3 Research Some students might research when, how, and why national Prohibition was ended in the United States. *(It ended in 1933 when the Twenty-first Amendment was ratified, repealing the Eighteenth Amendment. Prohibition had been difficult to enforce, it increased gangland crime, and the struggling economy could benefit from taxes on the legal sale of alcohol.)*

📁 Have students complete Chapter 12, Section 3 Vocabulary and Guided Reading Activity. (Also in Spanish.) **LEP**

VISUAL INSTRUCTION

Ordinary Criminals Prohibition and drinking provided material for endless jokes. *College Humor,* a popular magazine in the 1920s, ran this one: "Whiskey kills more people than bullets." "That's because bullets don't drink."

Answer: *buying from boats in international waters or smuggling from Canada*

The Failure of Prohibition
Gangsters and Citizens Ignore the Law

Like the battle over whether fundamentalism belonged in schools, the struggle to enforce Prohibition, enacted by an amendment in 1919, pitted small-town residents and farmers against a newer, more urban America. Most fundamentalists stood firmly in favor of Prohibition, claiming that strict laws could and should control people's behavior. Opponents of Prohibition, on the other hand, preferred more tolerance.

Prohibition succeeded in eradicating the saloon. The demise of the saloon decreased alcohol consumption among people who could not afford to go to the new **speakeasies,** clubs where liquor was sold in violation of the law. Most middle-class people, however, simply refused to obey the Volstead Act, which was passed to enforce Prohibition. This widespread refusal gave the 1920s its well-deserved reputation as a lawless decade.

Enforcement Problems

Prohibition was hard to enforce for many reasons. For one thing the United States had more than 10,000 miles (16,090 km) of coastlines and land borders where smugglers were all too happy to sneak in the alcohol that many Americans refused to give up. People who made, sold, or transported illegal liquor were known as **bootleggers.** A former bootlegger from Barre, Vermont, later recalled, "We ran mostly ale. We got it in Canada for five bucks a case and sold it here for fifteen or twenty. You could load a lot of ale into those big crates we had. We kept five or six cars on the road at the time."

In 1924 the Department of Commerce estimated the value of liquor smuggled into the country at $40 million. In addition, hundreds of ships that anchored in international waters dispensed legal liquor to anyone who came out by boat.

Thousands of druggists sold alcohol quite legally on doctors' prescriptions. During the 1920s some doctors began to prescribe alcohol for a variety of real and imagined complaints. Women who had not been able to drink in saloons went to the new speakeasies, where both men and women eagerly gulped down Prohibition's new drink, the cocktail.

Illegal distilling could and did take place anywhere. An industrious bootlegger could make his own home brew with a portable still that sold for six or seven dollars. Between 1919 and 1929, the production of corn sugar increased sixfold, and most of it ended up in illegal liquor.

Prohibition had other ill effects. Americans came to have a casual attitude about disobeying the law. A tiny

Ordinary Criminals During Prohibition, many Americans devised creative ways to carry illegal alcohol, such as these strap-on containers. *What were other ways people avoided the Prohibition laws?*

Meeting Special Needs

Attention Deficit Disorder This activity helps to address the particular needs of students with attention deficit disorder. Have students read the subsection entitled "The Failure of Prohibition" (pp. 398–399). Working alone or with a partner, students should record in their notes three examples of Prohibition's failure. *(e.g., the Vermont bootlegger smuggling, speakeasies selling drinks, courts overwhelmed by liquor cases)* force of Prohibition agents received very little pay for the thankless job of enforcing a law many Americans hated. In 1923 one Prohibition agent toured several American cities to see how difficult it would be to purchase an illegal drink. It took him only 3 minutes in Detroit; in New Orleans, a drink could be had in a mere 35 seconds.

Many people simply refused to take the law seriously. One San Francisco jury in a Prohibition case drank up liquor that had been used in court as evidence!

Big City Crime

As federal courts choked on too many liquor cases, many government officials took part in the bribery and corruption that accompanied the unenforceable law. Fiorello La Guardia, a member of Congress from New York who would later become a reform-minded mayor of New York City, estimated it would take a police force of 250,000 to enforce Prohibition in New York, and another 200,000 agents to police the police.

Perhaps the worst effect of Prohibition was its contribution to the explosive growth of big-city crime. Gangsters had been around before Prohibition, but when they took over bootlegging, crime soared to new heights.

The gangs bought out hundreds of breweries and transported illegal beer in armored trucks. They stationed "soldiers" to hijack other gangs' shipments, and killed their rivals in a series of gruesome slayings. Al Capone, the head of a gang of Chicago bootleggers, became a multimillionaire driving through the streets in an armored car with bulletproof windows.

Celebrity Criminals Chicago gangster Al Capone broke laws flagrantly but was eventually convicted of income tax evasion. *How did Prohibition contribute to a soaring crime rate in the 1920s?*

Organized Intolerance Ku Klux Klan members share their values with the next generation. *Did the Klan generally support or oppose Prohibition?*

Crosses in the Night
Klan Terrorism Surges and Subsides

The forces favoring Prohibition centered in rural areas and small towns where fundamentalist preachers warned their congregations against the sinful ways of the big city. The Ku Klux Klan, which suddenly blazed back onto the American scene in the 1920s, also flourished in small towns, and it fought some of its fiercest battles with the liquor interests. The rebirth of the Klan pointed up many of the conflicts that divided American society during this period.

Like the hooded secret order of Reconstruction days, the new Klan began in the South under a burning cross, sparking some Southern whites' hatred for African Americans. When the Klan spread from Georgia in the 1920s, however, it added new enemies to its list. In Texas

SECTION THREE **399**

VISUAL INSTRUCTION

Celebrity Criminals The most powerful criminal of the era, Capone headed a gang of 700 men. By the end of the 1920s he controlled Chicago's 10,000 speakeasies and ran the bootlegging business from Canada to Florida.

Answer: *It created an illegal market for alcohol, which was soon run by criminal gangs.*

Organized Intolerance The origin of the name "Ku Klux Klan" is uncertain but is thought to come from an illiterate spelling of the Greek word *kuklos,* which means circle or ring, plus the English word *clan.*

Answer: *The Klan appealed to some white people's prejudices, insecurities, and fears of social change.*

 At the Movies

The Klan began its twentieth-century resurgence in 1915, when a former Methodist minister organized a "fraternal order" in Atlanta. That same year, the hugely successful silent film *The Birth of a Nation* debuted. It was a 3-hour epic about the Civil War and Reconstruction, featuring a derogatory portrayal of African Americans and a prominent "heroic" role for the Ku Klux Klan. Although many African Americans and white liberals boycotted the film, it went on to gross $10 million, the record for a silent film.

Portfolio Project

Write a Newspaper Story Direct students to write a headline and news story about the resurgence of the Ku Klux Klan in the United States during the 1920s. Remind students to open their stories by telling what, where, when, and who. In the following paragraphs they should try to support their story with why and how statements. Suggest that students include their completed story in their portfolios.

FYI

Resistance to the KKK
On September 15, 1923, J.C. Walton, the governor of Oklahoma, declared martial law in the state. He called out more than 6,000 National Guard troops and declared that anyone who helped the Klan carry out its program would be considered enemies of the state and dealt with by the military.

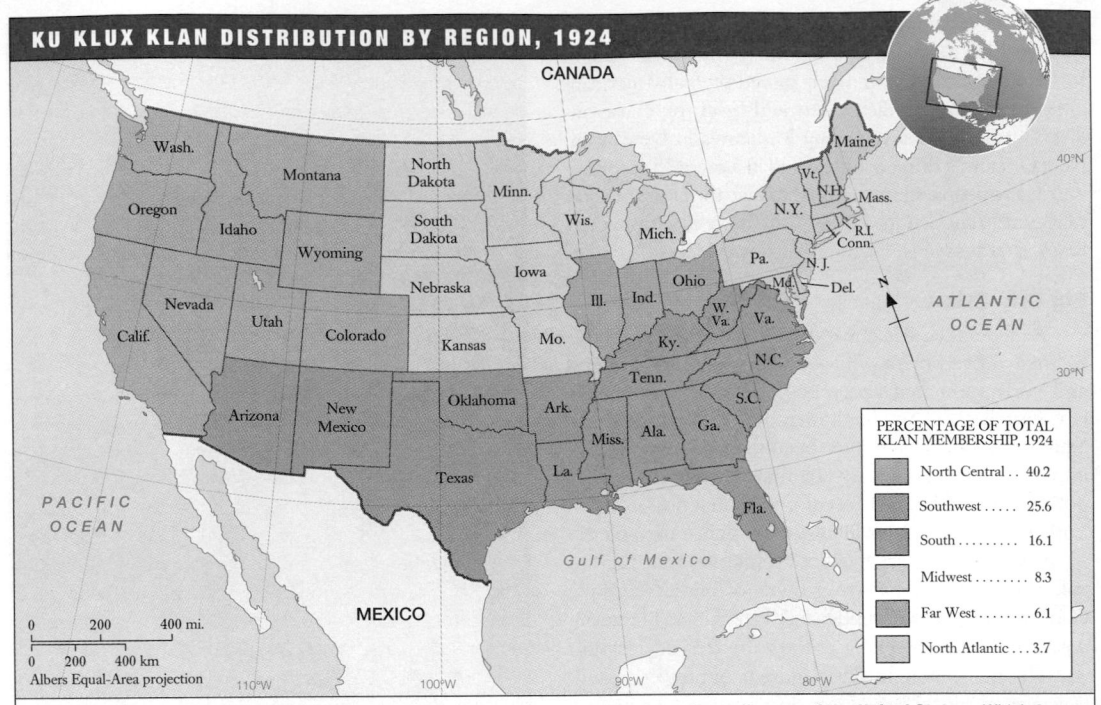

KU KLUX KLAN DISTRIBUTION BY REGION, 1924

PERCENTAGE OF TOTAL KLAN MEMBERSHIP, 1924	
North Central . .	40.2
Southwest	25.6
South	16.1
Midwest	8.3
Far West	6.1
North Atlantic . . .	3.7

While the Ku Klux Klan thrived during the 1920s, it was not equally popular throughout all areas of the United States. *Which 3 regions of the country accounted for more than 80 percent of Klan membership?*

the Klan attacked Mexican Americans; in California it fought Japanese immigrants; in New York the Klan's targets were Jews and European immigrants; and in New England, it stirred up hatred of French Canadians.

All over the country, Klan members participated in violent activities—tarring and feathering, flogging, and lynching. The Southwest saw some of the worst terror. In a single year, Oklahoma's Klan was responsible for no less than 2,500 floggings.

With its secret initiation rites, hooded robes, and burning crosses, the Klan mainly provided a fellowship of prejudice for ill-educated men whose lives offered few other satisfactions. It soon became strong in Northern cities such as Detroit, Pittsburgh, and Indianapolis, where many African Americans had recently migrated.

The Ku Klux Klan claimed its greatest strength in Indiana where almost half a million men had joined. David Stephenson, state head of the Klan in Indiana, bragged with some truth, "I am the law in Indiana." On parade night in Kokomo, the police disappeared and white-sheeted figures directed traffic.

The new Klan even gained a foothold in the industrial Northeast and in California. In 1923, 10,000 New Jersey Klan members burned a cross in New Brunswick, New Jersey, almost in sight of Manhattan. Similar scenes took place in Anaheim, California.

Klan members believed that as "pure" Americans, they should be the guardians of society's behavior and morals. In America's cities, Klan members enjoyed a feeling of superiority in their common hatred for whichever group they thought was beneath them.

Under Hiram Wesley Evans, a Texas dentist and the Klan's Imperial Wizard and Emperor, the secret society's rolls swelled to almost 5 million members. Evans believed the Klan represented "the great mass of Americans of the old pioneer stock." By this, he meant "a blend of various peoples of the so-called Nordic race, the race which, with all its faults, has given the world almost the whole of modern civilization."

Evans and his followers felt modern America had forced them to become strangers in their own land:

> One by one all our traditional moral standards went by the boards, or were so disregarded that they ceased to be binding. The sacredness of our Sabbath, of our homes, of chastity, and finally even of our right to teach our own children in our own schools fundamental facts and truths were torn away from us.
>
> —Hiram Wesley Evans,
> "The Klan's Fight for Americanism,"
> *The North American Review,* March–May, 1926

Extending the Content

Klan's Decline In the 1920s Ku Klux Klan prejudice erupted in violence against the Klan's traditional enemy, African Americans. The new Klan was as likely to attack Catholics, bootleggers, political opponents, or people Klan members believed to be immoral. For example, in Alabama in 1927 the Klan beat a white woman who had been divorced. A Catholic teenager who grew up in Indiana recalled that word spread that "the Pope was finally pulling into town on the south-bound from Chicago to take over. A mob formed and stoned the train."

Evans expected to win "a return of power into the hands of the everyday, not highly cultured, not overly intellectualized, but entirely unspoiled and not de-Americanized, average citizen of the old stock."

The Klan prided itself on its pure-blooded Americanism, but it shared many similarities with German and Italian movements of this period. Like the European groups, the Klan stressed nationalism and racial purity, attacked alien minority groups, disapproved of the urban culture, and called for a return to the past.

The Ku Klux Klan began to sink back into obscurity in 1925 when David Stephenson, who had insisted he was the law in Indiana, went to jail for the second-degree murder of a woman he had kidnapped and brutally abused. Klan members who had believed in its stated ideals of chastity and morality deserted the organization in large numbers.

In 1928 the Klan could not prevent the nomination of Al Smith, a Catholic, for President of the United States. Although Smith could see crosses burning in the fields as his campaign train crossed Oklahoma, the Klan itself was almost burned out.

Closing the Doors
Popular Pressure Against Immigration

The Ku Klux Klan's drive for "pure Americanism," if not their methods, found a sympathetic echo in mainstream America. Many Americans associated immigrants with radicalism and disloyalty. These fears had fueled the Red Scare, the Palmer raids, and the case against Sacco and Vanzetti. Rural Americans in particular believed that immigrants had somehow caused erosion of old-fashioned American values.

An immigration act in 1921 attached the force of law to bigotry when it reversed the century-long tradition of open immigration from Europe. The law limited the number of immigrants by applying a **quota** system, in which the number of immigrants from any country in a year could not exceed 3 percent of the number of people in the United States from that country according to the 1910 census. That favored immigrants from northern and western Europe because most of the immigrants from these areas had arrived by this time.

In 1924 the National Origins Act reduced the number of immigrants and excluded Asians altogether. It also decreased the quota percentage from 3 to 2. Congress also changed the census year used as the basis for the quotas from 1910 to 1890. By using the 1890 census instead of the 1910 census, the law slashed the number of immigrants allowed in from eastern and southern Europe because the large immigrations after 1890 came from these areas.

In the debate on the bill, members of Congress vented their hatred of immigrants, especially immigrants who lived in New York. One representative from Kansas contrasted the "beer, bolshevism, unassimilating settlements and perhaps many flags" to his idealized view of the United States: "constitutional government; one flag, stars and stripes."

The law attempted to maintain the ethnic mixture that the United States had in 1890 in order to ensure that the country would stay "American." The authors of the law assumed that Asians, Italians, and Poles were less American than were Irish and Germans who had come in large numbers in the 1800s and therefore had a larger quota in the law.

The National Origins Act made it exceptionally difficult for people from countries with low quotas to immigrate to the United States. In the 1930s immigration to the United States dwindled to a trickle. (See the Case Study on pages 404–407.)

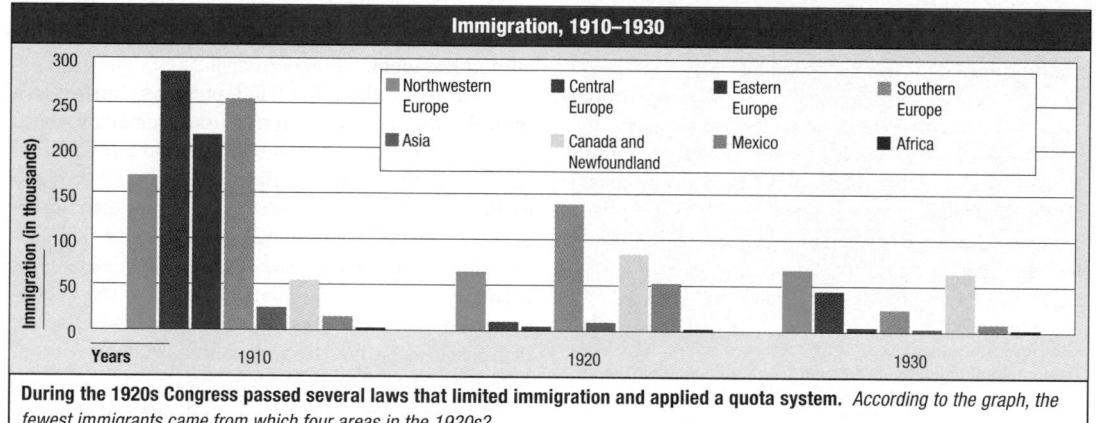

Immigration, 1910–1930

Northwestern Europe · Central Europe · Eastern Europe · Southern Europe · Asia · Canada and Newfoundland · Mexico · Africa

Immigration (in thousands) — Years: 1910, 1920, 1930

During the 1920s Congress passed several laws that limited immigration and applied a quota system. *According to the graph, the fewest immigrants came from which four areas in the 1920s?*

Global Connection

On July 17, 1928, Mexico's president-elect, Álvaro Obregón, was assassinated. Though not directly involved in the Mexican Revolution, Obregón had been active in politics since 1912. He was elected president in 1920 and implemented many reforms in Mexico's education system, land policy, and church relations. The United States considered his government too radical and did not recognize it until 1923. After a brief retirement, Obregón re-entered politics, feeling the Constitution's reforms were being abandoned.

 Facts on File

Landmark Documents in American History Have students review the "Immigration Quota Act of 1924 (National Origins Act)" and write a paragraph about the intent of the document.

GRAPH STUDY

The National Association of Manufacturers opposed the National Origins Act of 1924, fearing their supply of cheap labor would be cut off.

Answer: *Africa, Asia, Eastern Europe, and Central Europe*

Cultural Perspectives

Immigration Forces Economic hardship after World War I was not the only force inspiring immigration to the United States. After civil war and revolution in Russia, the government established a secret police organization that arrested around 90,000 people and executed more than 11,000 with its campaign against counter-revolution. When Lenin died in 1924, a struggle for power ensued, causing more political chaos in the country. In Italy in the early 1920s, Benito Mussolini and his Fascist party strove for power with similar ruthlessness. A nationwide campaign of intimidation, violence, and murder gave the Fascists 65 percent of the vote in 1924. Many would-be immigrants who hoped to escape political repression were prevented from coming to the United States because of policies based on prejudice against their nationality.

ASSESS

Meeting Lesson Objectives

Each section objective is tested by the section review question that follows it in parentheses.

1. Explain how the social changes of the 1920s caused conflicts among various groups of people in the United States. (1, 5)
2. Identify reasons for and effects of widespread disregard for Prohibition. (4)
3. Describe the resurgence of the Ku Klux Klan in the 1920s. (2)
4. Explain how the 1928 election reflected cultural conflicts of the decade. (3)

Evaluate

Have students complete the Section Review.

✎ 🔲 Assign the Section 3 Quiz or use the Testmaker to develop a customized quiz. (Also in Spanish.) **LEP**

✎ 🔲 Assign the Chapter 12 Test or use the Testmaker to develop a customized test.

✎ Have students complete the Chapter 12 Performance Assessment Activity.

The Challenge of Change
Conflict Personified in the 1928 Election

During the 1920s Americans found themselves suddenly thrust, sometimes unwillingly, into a modern, urban world. In 1910 more than half of all Americans lived in villages of less than 2,500 people. During the 1920s, 6 million people left the farm for the city, and by 1930 only 44 percent of Americans still lived in rural areas.

Hostility and Fear

The battles fought in the 1920s over religion, over drinking, and over who could be considered an American shared a common thread of fear and hostility to everything an urban society seemed to represent. At best, the laws passed to try to stop change merely postponed it.

Democratic Candidate for President, Al Smith Smith inspired supporters and frightened others. *How might radio have hurt his presidential campaign?*

For example, Tennessee's law to prevent the teaching of evolution received world attention in the Scopes trial. The Eighteenth Amendment to curb Americans' thirst for liquor was often ignored before its repeal in 1933. After the late 1920s, the Ku Klux Klan and the values it represented had all but disappeared, except in the South. While the National Origins Act stemmed the tide of eastern European immigration, it did not stop immigrants from the Western Hemisphere. After the 1920s Mexicans, French Canadians, and Puerto Ricans became the new American immigrants.

City Versus Country

Tensions between the city and the country erupted into national election politics for the first time in 1928 when New York Governor Al Smith made his bid for national power. Probably no Democrat could have defeated Republican Herbert Hoover in the middle of this prosperous decade. Smith, furthermore, seemed to stand for everything small-town Americans feared most: the big city with sinful and foreign ways.

For example, the governor had been born in a tenement house near the East River in New York City. Fearful voters saw Smith as a voice for immigrants. He openly opposed Prohibition, which small-town Americans supported.

Rural voters and city voters who held traditional values gaped at Smith's brown derby hat, his expensive tailor-made suits, and his ever-present cigar. Even the accent with which Smith pronounced "radio" as "raddio" or said "foist" for "first" made the candidate seem un-American. Most important of all, many Americans wondered whether the devout Catholic governor could remain independent of the pope if he were to be elected President.

Hoover, on the other hand, presented himself as a typical Iowa farm boy, who recalled diving in the swimming hole under the willow branches and trapping rabbits in the woods. Of course, he had since become a millionaire mining engineer. Hoover had also spearheaded relief efforts after World War I and had successfully served under two Republican Presidents as secretary of commerce. When he accepted the Republican nomination for President, however, Hoover spoke of himself as "a boy from a country village, without inheritance or influential friends."

The popular vote of 1928 reflected Americans' intense interest in the election. Only half the eligible

Critical Thinking

Recognizing Bias An anti-Catholic bias existed among many people not associated with extreme groups such as the Klan. These people, like Klan members, suspected that church came before country for Catholics and were thus nervous about electing them to office. In addition to anti-Catholic feeling, other biases also worked against Al Smith's bid for President. Ask: Why did small-town Americans fear his candidacy in 1928? *(They saw him as a spokesperson for immigrants; he opposed Prohibition; his style was brassy and loud, emblematic of people from big cities, who were often associated with corruption.)*

Hoover Triumphant Herbert Hoover won the 1928 race for President with a pro-business platform. *How did he present himself to Americans in his campaign?*

ARCHIVE PHOTOS

voters had cast ballots in the 1924 contest. In 1928 more than two-thirds of the eligible voters turned out. Many of the new voters in 1928 were Catholic women, casting ballots for the first time.

To no one's surprise, Hoover won in a landslide. Lost in the excitement of Hoover's victory was the fact that for the first time in a decade of Republican prosperity, a President had failed to win the 12 largest cities in the United States. In 1924 the Republicans had carried these big cities by 1.3 million votes. Political change was clearly in the wind.

The 1920s, a time of rapid social change in the United States, was an exciting and troubling decade. The promise of an easier, more bountiful and modern life existed side by side with old suspicions, fears, and hatreds. The change that thrilled some people threatened others who tried unsuccessfully to cling to older ways. The people in power—white, Protestant, and male—still gave lip service to the small-town virtues of the past, but in the 1920s the United States was changing rapidly into a modern, urban society. It would change even more with the Great Crash in 1929.

SECTION REVIEW

Vocabulary
1. Define: fundamentalism, evangelist, speakeasy, bootlegger, quota.

Checking Facts
2. Why were so many people attracted to the Ku Klux Klan during the 1920s? Why did the Klan's popularity die out so suddenly?

3. Why was the presidential election of 1928 seen as a contest between rural and urban values?

Critical Thinking
Making Inferences
4. Why do you think so many Americans disobeyed the Prohibition amendment?

Linking Across Time
5. Do racial and ethnic biases still exist in the United States today? Give evidence to support your claim.

SECTION THREE   **403**

VISUAL INSTRUCTION

Hoover Triumphant In his campaign, Hoover promised Americans continued prosperity, predicting "a chicken in every pot and a car in every garage."

Answer: *as someone from middle America who had made it on his own*

Reteach

🎧 Have students listen to the Chapter 12, Section 3 audiocassette. (Also in Spanish.) **LEP**

📁 Have students complete the Chapter 12 Reteaching Activity.

Enrich

📁 Have students complete the Chapter 12 Enrichment Activity. (Also in Spanish.) **LEP**

📁 Have students complete the Chapter 12 Geography in History activity.

📁 Have students complete Supreme Court Case Study 10.

CLOSE

Discuss how social changes in the 1920s increased conflict among different groups and led to new legislation. How did fundamentalism help many Americans make sense of the bewildering changes that were taking place? *(the religion's certainty was reassuring when everything else was shifting and new)*

Section 3 Review Answers

1. **fundamentalism** (397), **evangelist** (397), **speakeasy** (398), **bootlegger** (398), **quota** (401)
2. The Klan appealed to some people's fears, insecurities, and prejudices. Members fell away when a leader was convicted of murder.

3. Smith dressed and talked like a New Yorker. Hoover claimed he was a midwestern farm boy.
4. They disliked it controlling personal behavior.
5. Yes. The Ku Klux Klan and other racist groups still exist, as do discrimination, hostility, and racial and ethnic slurs.

403

TEACH

Making the Historical Connection

Shortly after the United States became an independent nation, the issue of immigration became a topic of debate—a debate that persists to this day. In the 1920s societal change, new patterns of immigration, and a general postwar desire for security made immigration a hot issue. Many blamed new immigrants for changes that they found distressing, and they felt the best way to keep the United States safe and "American" was to keep foreign-born people out. Others disagreed, but the result of the debate was the National Origins Act of 1924.

Turning Point

The National Origins Act of 1924 was a turning point in the long story of American immigration. It was the final push on a door that had been gradually closing over the preceding decades. Before 1924 immigration had been relatively open. Afterwards it was very restrictive and remained so in the decades that followed.

 Turning Point

The National Origins Act

MAY 26, 1924

MEMORANDUM

"American institutions rest solely on good citizenship. They were created by people who had a background of self-government. New arrivals should be limited to our capacity to absorb them into the ranks of good citizenship. America must be kept American. For this purpose, it is necessary to continue a policy of restricted immigration. . . . I am convinced that our present economic and social conditions warrant a limitation of those to be admitted. . . . Those who do not want to be partakers of the American spirit ought not to settle in America."

President Calvin Coolidge,
State of the Union Address,
December 6, 1923

The Case

A few months after Coolidge's speech, Congress took him at his word. Led by Representative Albert Johnson of Washington and Senators Henry Cabot Lodge of Massachusetts and Hiram Johnson of California, Congress passed the Immigration Act of 1924, also called the National Origins Act.

The act strictly limited immigration from every country outside the Western Hemisphere by imposing quotas. Until 1929, quotas would be based on the national origins of the United States population using the 1890 census. After that, quotas would be set using the 1920 census. The bill limited total immigration to about 150,000 people per year starting in 1929, a drastic reduction from the almost 1 million that arrived each year from 1900 to 1914.

For a nation founded by immigrants, the National Origins Act seemed a complete reversal of its traditional policy. For a nation worried about its future, the act seemed a promise to keep America for Americans. What did it mean to be an American? Who was able, or qualified, to become one? Should the country continue its relatively open policy, or were tighter restrictions needed? These questions were central to the debate over the National Origins Act.

Despite certain objections, President Coolidge signed the bill into law on May 26, 1924.

The Background

Before the Civil War, most Americans agreed that an open immigration policy was essential to the country's growth. Immigration provided settlers for the territories and workers for expanding industry. Most immigrants of the time—like most Americans—had

404 CASE STUDY

The Case at a Glance

| Immigrants to the United States start coming from "new" countries. | → | Anti-immigrant feeling grows, partly out of fear of these unfamiliar people. | → | World War I confirms many Americans' fears that foreign ties bring foreign wars. | → | A first restrictive law in 1921 introduces the idea of a nation-based quota. | → |

roots in northern and western Europe. That did not mean all new arrivals were equally welcomed: early Irish and German immigrants, for example, often faced a hostile reception. Nonetheless, because most early immigrants and Americans shared similar roots, few saw immigration as a threat to the country's values, and most viewed it as an integral part of the national character and tradition. While the United States had a surplus of land and a shortage of labor, an open policy seemed to serve its needs.

Changing Views This view had changed dramatically by the late 1800s. Regional and national economies experienced a frightening series of depressions. The Western frontier was disappearing; the South was in transition. Urban problems of overcrowding, disease, and labor unrest worried many Americans. Newcomers were blamed for these problems—especially the "new" immigrants who came from Asia and southern and eastern Europe.

Prejudice and anti-immigrant feelings grew in the late 1800s, as did calls to limit immigration. In California, Chinese immigrants were unfairly blamed for many social and economic ills. Riding the wave of anti-Chinese feelings, Congress passed the Chinese Exclusion Act of 1882, preventing Chinese immigrants from becoming United States citizens. For the first time, the United States had restricted immigration based solely on national origin. Prior restrictions were based on keeping criminals or those with contagious diseases out of the country.

Eugenics In arguing for the exclusion of new immigrants, restrictionists promoted eugenics, the idea that heredity, or genetics, determined who was "fit" or "unfit," and thus superior or inferior. Eugenics suggested that persons from northern or western European stock could be true Americans because they were "fit"—intelligent, strong, and self-reliant. People from southern and eastern Europe, Asians, Africans, and Jews were deemed "unfit" and therefore unable to become Americans.

Evidence for eugenics came from biased studies, but Americans increasingly believed in it. Senator William Dillingham's 1911 commission published a report stating that the new immigrants were a threat to the nation and that certain ethnic groups should be considered undesirable. Madison Grant's widely read book, *The Passing of the Great Race* (1916),

> "Unless the U.S. adopts this biologic principle [of racial differences] they will be flooded over by people of inferior stock because of their greater fecundity [birth rate]."
>
> Dr. Harry H. Laughlin, speaking for the United States secretary of labor in support of the National Origins Act

> "I felt confident that the President would sign the Immigration bill, for I know he sympathizes with the general purposes of the legislation and realizes fully its great importance. It is a very great measure, one of the most important if not the most important, that Congress has ever passed. It reaches far into the future."
>
> Senator Henry Cabot Lodge (right)

> "Immigrants have contributed greatly to the industrial development of this country; contributed not alone by their numbers but also by their age, sex and training."
>
> Constantine Panunzio (left) in his 1927 book, *Immigration Crossroads*, in defense of open immigration

> "This association protests against the enactment of said measures as . . . intolerant in purpose and effect, unfounded upon any fair, useful or logical test for fitness for American citizenship, and unjust to race stocks which have proved pre-eminently loyal in peace time and in war, law abiding and productive. . . ."
>
> Emily S. Bernheim, Executive Secretary of the United Neighborhood Houses of New York, in a letter to President Coolidge opposing the act

CASE STUDY   405

Turning Point

Videodisc

GTV: A Geographic Perspective on American History

Side 3, Chapter 5
Title: Making a Mark
Subject: The impact of immigration, 1870–1910
Ask: How did immigration affect the growth of industry in the United States? (*It provided a constant source of labor.*)

FYI

Henry Cabot Lodge
Born in Massachusetts in 1850, Henry Cabot Lodge received the first Ph.D. in political science granted by Harvard University. A scholarly man, he edited the influential *North American Review* in the mid-1870s. He started his political career in the state legislature in 1880. He was elected to the United States House of Representatives in 1887, and in 1893 began his 31-year tenure in the Senate. Lodge is most famous for masterminding the opposition to the Treaty of Versailles and the League of Nations. Supporting the National Origins Act was one of his last efforts as a senator; he died in 1924.

| The 1921 law is deemed ineffective and a new, harsher bill is introduced in 1924. | → | Debate is fierce over the bill, but in the end the National Origins Act of 1924 becomes law. |

Analyzing the Case

Ask students to read the memorandum on page 404 and the opinions on page 405 to get an idea of the range of feeling on the issue of immigration.

1. What factors did Coolidge claim justified restricting immigration? *("present economic and social conditions")*
2. Whose opinions (other than Coolidge's) favored restrictive immigration policies? *(Laughlin's and Lodge's)*
3. What reasons did supporters of more open immigration give for their stance? *(Immigrants have contributed to the development of the country; arbitrary quotas for immigration are unfair.)*

Notes

Turning Point

supported this view. Grant claimed that heredity was the key factor in all human progress. These works seemed to "prove" that the new immigrants were inferior and an "alien menace."

World War I convinced many that the open immigration tradition had failed, since foreign ties had involved the country in a horrible war. The 1917 revolution of the Bolsheviks in Russia linked fears of communism with foreigners in American minds. Labor unrest and domestic terrorism inspired dread that the United States might collapse from internal strife.

Congress passed the first widely restrictive immigration law in 1921, with a limit of 357,000 people per year based on a national quota system. Many felt the 1921 law did not do enough. It failed to decrease southern and eastern European immigration. Representative Albert Johnson and Senators Lodge and Hiram Johnson pressed for an even stronger law. With the National Origins Act of 1924, restrictionists won the debate over immigration. This law would govern immigration until 1965.

The Opinions

Since the nation's founding, opinions have been split between open and restrictive immigration policy. Restrictionists were dominating the debate by the early 1900s, but many Americans held firm to the belief that immigration was one of the country's greatest strengths. They championed a more open policy. The quotes on the preceding page reveal the conflict in opinions on immigration and the National Origins Act.

The Outcome

The Response Many foreign governments reacted angrily to the new immigration policy. Japanese Lieutenant General Bunjiro Horinouchi stated, "We must be determined to undergo whatever hardships are necessary in avenging the insult which America has done our country." Another Japanese leader said, "If history teaches anything, an eventual collision between Japan and America on the Pacific is inevitable." Some Americans felt the act would harm all foreign relations.

Public opinion and newspaper editorials in the United States, though, reflected widespread support for the National Origins Act. The *Cleveland Plain Dealer* stated in an editorial, "Immigration is a domestic problem. The Japanese are neither as unsophisticated nor so domineering as to try to override the clearly expressed will of friendly America."

Congress soon moved to strengthen immigration restrictions even more. It created a border patrol to prevent illegal immigration—not by Mexicans or Canadians, but by Europeans trying to get around quota restrictions. It also gave immigration officers more power to arrest suspected illegal residents.

Border Patrol In 1926 these Border Patrol officers in Laredo, Texas, show off their equipment and personnel for a photo portrait by Eugene Goldbeck. They hoped to prevent Europeans from evading quotas by coming in through Mexico.

Cooperative Learning

Debate In 1963 President Kennedy wrote that the National Origins Act "is at complete variance with American traditions and principles that the qualifications of the immigrant do not depend upon his country of birth, and [it] violates the spirit expressed in the Declaration of Independence that 'all men are created equal.'" Share and discuss this quote with students. Point out that even in recent times immigration issues have aroused controversy, as was the case with California's Proposition 187 in 1994. Form the class into groups and assign each group a pro- or anti-immigration stance. Students should work together to find support for their position and to develop a proposal for change in immigration policy. Make sure each student works on his or her group's project. Finally, hold a class debate about immigration.

Immediate Effects The act had immediate effects on immigration. For the most part, it ended legal Chinese and Japanese immigration. The goal of encouraging more immigrants from northern and western Europe and restricting the number from other areas was achieved. The Quota Board set up by the act raised the British quota from 34,007 under the 1921 law to 65,721, while setting the Italian quota at 5,802, Poland's at 6,524, and Greece's at 307.

The National Origins Act was the main catalyst for changes in the character of United States immigration. First, total immigration fell sharply. From 1906 to 1915, 9.4 million people had immigrated to the United States. Less than 2 million immigrated to the United States from 1925 to 1948.

More notably, the national origins of immigrants changed dramatically, just as restrictionists had desired. From 1900 to 1910, northern and western Europe had sent 21.7 percent of all United States immigrants; southern and eastern Europe, 70.8 percent; Canada and Mexico, 2.6 percent; and all other countries, 4.9 percent. From 1924 to 1946, northern and western Europe sent 43.1 percent of immigrants; southern and eastern Europe, 18.9 percent; Canada and Mexico, 33 percent; and all others, 5 percent.

People scrambled to get the required visas before their country's annual quota was filled. Irma Busch from Germany recalled, "I went to Hamburg in 1924, and it was one year before I finally got my quota number. . . . At the consulate, they said to me, that if I had been born a little bit further down in Silesia, in the Polish sector, I couldn't have come here, because that would have been under a different quota. There were always more people applied from that part than there was a quota for."

Later Effects Even before and during World War II, the quotas held fast. Thousands desperate to flee the terror of fascism were shut out, including many Jews. Boats of hopeful immigrants were turned away. In 1938, as anti-Jewish violence erupted in Germany, Congress rejected a proposal to admit about 20,000 German children, most of them Jews. Congress claimed that it might draw the nation into war—and would violate the quota system. Yet in 1940 Congress admitted 15,000 English children to the United States.

As a result of the National Origins Act, the United States suffered a labor shortage, especially agricultural workers, during World War II. The

United States asked Mexico to help ease the shortage. The resulting bracero program allowed Mexicans to enter the United States as short-term farmworkers. More than 4 million Mexicans served as braceros in the United States until Congress ended the program in 1964.

The Significance

For more than 40 years, the National Origins Act remained in force. Americans continued to support it, but as the early 1960s civil rights movement grew, President Kennedy and others questioned whether the act truly reflected American values. In 1965 Congress passed a new immigration law, ending the National Origins Act. The 1965 law seemed to return the United States to its former, more open status. While limiting open immigration to 200,000, it allowed in any number of relatives of United States citizens. It gave each country the same quota, 20,000, but did not end the quota system.

The main results of the National Origins Act—limits on total immigration and the use of a quota system—remained unaffected. More than 70 years after the act, its restrictive principles continue to dominate United States immigration policy.

RESPONDING TO THE CASE

1. Why did the restrictionists support a quota system for immigration? What did they hope such a system would accomplish?

2. One of the effects of the National Origins Act was that immigration from Canada and Mexico increased greatly. Would supporters of the act have welcomed these immigrants? Explain.

3. Did the National Origins Act achieve the goals of its supporters? Explain.

PORTFOLIO PROJECT Suppose you are an opponent of the National Origins Act in the 1920s. You have the opportunity to address Congress before they decide on the bill. What would you say to them to convince them of your argument? Write a brief address you could give to the House of Representatives and the Senate explaining your views.

Block Scheduling

The Portfolio Project on this page provides an excellent opportunity to enrich and extend the key elements of this case study.

CLOSE

Discuss the case with the class. Ask students how World War I helped foster anti-immigration feeling. *(People felt that American involvement in the war came from connections to Europe.)* Many of those arguing for restrictions on immigration were descendants of immigrants themselves. What was one factor that made many of them reverse a policy they had benefited from? *(The new immigrants were coming from different countries than their forebears had come from.)*

Responding to the Case Answers

1. Restrictionists thought the quota system would help decrease immigration, particularly from certain countries. They hoped to cut the proportion of immigrants that came from southern and eastern Europe, Asia, and Africa.

2. Answers may vary but should reflect the fact that supporters of the National Origins Act were concerned that newcomers to the country be "similar" to those who already lived here. Thus, for example, they might welcome English-speaking Canadians but not French-speaking Canadians or Spanish-speaking Mexicans.

3. The National Origins Act essentially achieved the goals of its supporters. Immigration from places other than western Europe fell. See the sixth paragraph under Outcome for figures.

407

Chapter ⑫ Review

Reviewing Key Terms

Answers will vary, but should reflect student's understanding of the vocabulary words and their relationships.

Recalling Facts

1. 11 percent; their standard of living rose.
2. Occupations in agriculture, mining, textiles
3. Advertising in the 1920s created consumer desires for new styles and new products. This preoccupation with possessions contributed to, as well as reflected, the materialism of the decade.
4. Items of clothing, sports equipment or activities, games, or dances
5. Examples: Babe Ruth, Jack Dempsey, Helen Willis, Red Grange, Bobby Jones, Oscar Charleston, Gertrude Ederle; physical skill, individual accomplishment
6. By flying alone, he represented the pioneer past. By flying a plane, he represented the technological future.
7. Alain Locke; examples: Langston Hughes, "The Negro Artist and the Racial Mountain"; Claude McKay, *Home to Harlem;* Arna Bontemps, "A Black Man Talks of Reaping"; Zora Neale Hurston, *Their Eyes Were Watching God*
8. During the trial the defense forced the prosecution to admit to "interpreting" the Bible. Although John Scopes was found guilty and the teaching of evolution was still illegal, the validity of fundamentalism, which professed to take the Bible literally, was probably questioned by many.
9. His murder conviction caused members to leave.
10. Bigotry and fear of bolshevism motivated the restrictions; the immigration of Asians was stopped.

Reviewing Key Terms

In each of the following lines, the two terms are related in some way. On a separate piece of paper, write a sentence for each pair that clearly explains the relationship between the two terms.

credit   standard of living
tabloid   syndicate
evangelist   fundamentalism
speakeasy   bootlegger
mass media   materialism

Recalling Facts

1. How much did the real income of American workers increase between 1923 and 1929? How did this increase affect their standard of living?

2. Give examples of some occupations that the prosperity of the 1920s adversely affected.

3. How did advertising reflect the materialism of the 1920s?

4. Compare a fad of the 1920s with a fad of today.

5. Identify three sports heroes of the 1920s. What ideals of the age did these people represent?

6. How did Charles Lindbergh's accomplishment link the values of the nation's past and future?

7. Who inspired the Harlem Renaissance? Identify three writers of this literary movement and a work of each.

8. How did the Scopes trial test fundamentalism?

9. How was David Stephenson responsible in part for the decline of the Ku Klux Klan?

10. Why did many Americans seek to restrict immigration during the 1920s? How did the National Origins Act of 1924 affect Asian immigration to the United States?

Critical Thinking

1. Drawing Conclusions How did the Model T and chain stores such as F.W. Woolworth and J.C. Penney diminish the differences between city and country life? What other 1920s innovations had a similar influence?

2. Determining Cause and Effect What were some effects of mass-media advertising and high-pressure sales in the 1920s?

3. Making Generalizations This chapter discusses the work of writers such as Sinclair Lewis, Alain Locke, Langston Hughes, Gertrude Stein, and Zora Neale Hurston. What generalization can you make about the topics these writers selected?

4. Recognizing Ideologies Philadelphia Public Safety Director "Duckboards" Butler smashes beer kegs at the edge of the Schuylkill River in 1924 in the photograph below. Support for and opposition to the Volstead Act marked opposing sets of values in different segments of the population. Identify each group's values. What contemporary issues are actively debated by people with opposing sets of values?

CULVER PICTURES

Critical Thinking

1. The Model T and goods from chain stores were available in cities and rural areas. Movies, records, and radio promoted common tastes.
2. Business growth; expansion of some industries; idealizing youth; the spread of fashion; increased buying on time

3. Students may generalize that writers from both groups criticized American society for different reasons: the Lost Generation, for materialism; the Harlem Renaissance, for racial discrimination.
4. Those who favored prohibition believed that people's

behavior should be controlled for the welfare of the state; those opposed believed that individual freedom demands tolerance of behavior not harmful to society. Current examples could include extent of people's right to privacy and legalization of drugs.

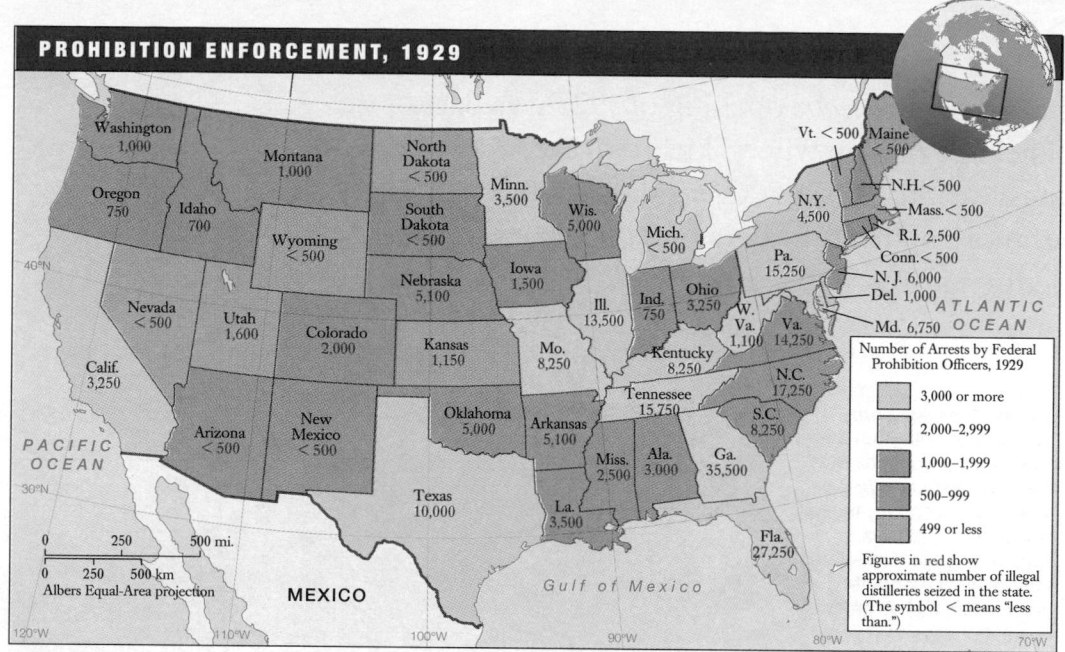

PROHIBITION ENFORCEMENT, 1929

Washington 1,000
Oregon 750
Idaho 700
Montana 1,000
North Dakota <500
Minn. 3,500
Wis. 5,000
Mich. <500
Vt. <500
Maine <500
N.H. <500
Mass. <500
R.I. 2,500
Conn. <500
N.Y. 4,500
Pa. 15,250
N.J. 6,000
Del. 1,000
Md. 6,750
Nevada <500
Utah 1,600
Wyoming <500
South Dakota <500
Nebraska 5,100
Iowa 1,500
Ill. 13,500
Ind. 750
Ohio 3,250
W. Va. 1,100
Va. 14,250
Calif. 3,250
Colorado 2,000
Kansas 1,150
Mo. 8,250
Kentucky 8,250
N.C. 17,250
Arizona <500
New Mexico <500
Oklahoma 5,000
Arkansas 5,100
Tennessee 15,750
S.C. 8,250
Texas 10,000
La. 3,500
Miss. 2,500
Ala. 3,000
Ga. 35,500
Fla. 27,250

PACIFIC OCEAN

ATLANTIC OCEAN

MEXICO

Gulf of Mexico

0   250   500 mi.
0   250   500 km
Albers Equal-Area projection

40°N
30°N
120°W   110°W   100°W   90°W   80°W   70°W

Number of Arrests by Federal Prohibition Officers, 1929

- 3,000 or more
- 2,000–2,999
- 1,000–1,999
- 500–999
- 499 or less

Figures in red show approximate number of illegal distilleries seized in the state. (The symbol < means "less than.")

Portfolio Project

Research the lives of people who were teenagers during the 1920s. Your local history museum or back issues of newspapers may be helpful. Try to learn about some of the following topics: education, styles of clothing, forms of recreation, and music. You may wish to explore family albums. Look for pictures that record styles of clothing, hairdos, and social events of that period. Report your findings orally to the class. You may also want to share a display of any supporting visuals you discovered. Then file your written summary in your portfolio.

Cooperative Learning

In small groups discuss why organizations such as the Ku Klux Klan use violent means to obtain their ends and often violate the civil rights of other citizens. To what extent are such organizations protected by the Constitution? What laws protect citizens from the threats and intimidation practiced by such groups?

Reinforcing Skills

Synthesizing Information Imagine that you are living in the 1920s. Decide whether you are a city or a farm dweller. Select material from each section of Chapter 12, and synthesize the material into a written account of a day in your life.

Geography and History

Study the map on this page to answer the following questions:

1. The 1920s have sometimes been called "the lawless decade." How does this map's information reinforce that nickname and connect to the geographic theme of movement?

2. In which states did federal Prohibition officers make the most arrests?

3. Name the two states where the most illegal distilleries and equipment were seized?

4. Assuming that the number of arrests and seizures reflects illegal activity in a given place, what region or regions had the fewest arrests? Why might this be so?

HISTORY JOURNAL

In many ways the 1920s were delightful yet troubled. What events did you learn about in this chapter that support this conclusion? Did any of these events match the changes you predicted in your journal response to page 374? Write your responses to these questions in your journal.

Geography and History

1. By the large number of arrests and the numbers of illegal distilleries found in every state; the arrests occurred across the country, indicating the movement of liquor throughout the United States
2. Illinois, Kentucky, Pennsylvania, New York, Texas, California, Delaware
3. Georgia and Florida
4. The less populated Far West; the puritanical traditions of residents of the New England states; Rhode Island was an exception because of its proximity to New York City and ocean access

History Journal

Student journals should include references to the fun fads and fashion, music, and literature of the 1920s, and at the same time note the dramatic social changes such as the growth of fundamentalism, prohibition, and immigration restriction.

BONUS QUESTION

This question may be used for extra credit on the chapter test.

Why did tabloid newspapers become popular during the 1920s?

Answer: *Their small pages and large type made ideal reading for crowded, rocking subways and streetcars.*

Portfolio Project

Written summaries should reflect research of any 1920s topics including a review of primary resources. Encourage visual displays that support written findings. These do not have to be permanently filed in individual portfolios.

Cooperative Learning

Most states have laws that protect individuals from assault, threats to commit a felony, foul language, and anonymous or repeated phone calls.

Reinforcing Skills

Evaluate the accounts for use of chapter details and evidence of relating the details coherently.

Making the Historical Connection

The movie theaters of the 1920s evolved from Edison's arcades of the mid-1890s, promoted under the name Kinetoscope, and the nickelodeons of the early 1900s. By the early 1910s, filmmakers began to produce photoplays that supplemented vaudeville acts and had more developed narratives. The interest in these shows peaked between 1909 and 1921, requiring the construction of larger theaters. Theaters built after World War I primarily showcased silent motion pictures. Vaudeville remained popular, but the theater marquees of the day showed that the "silents" had gained equal billing or better.

FYI

Theater Facts Silent films made heavy use of caption cards to tell the audience what was going on. Simple captions explained the passing of time, but cards also carried long speeches. Those who could not read had to go with someone who could.

At least 20 other brands of theater organs existed even though most people called them all by the generic name of Wurlitzer. Robert Hope-Jones invented the organ that was built by the Rudolph Wurlitzer Company.

Then...
Old Movie Houses

The *Alabama Theatre* opening of 1927 was part of the golden age of film, when films portrayed a glittering fantasy world. To show these films, architects designed ever more opulent theaters that people nicknamed "picture palaces."

1 A local newspaper proclaimed, "Birmingham Gets a $1,500,000 Christmas Gift" when the *Alabama Theatre* opened in 1927. This movie palace has 2,500 seats spread over the three-tiered interior. Above a giant proscenium arch is an oval dome that caps the room.

Fun Facts

BROWN BROTHERS

RIGHT THIS WAY
Being an usher often required the talents of a police officer, diplomat, and valet. During a formalized training program, ushers were drilled in the proper and polite treatment of the public, including learning a variety of hand signals.

Background Information

Nickelodeons and Cinemas Tiny halls and converted shops where motion pictures were projected on a screen were first called nickelodeons because they charged audiences an entrance fee of five cents. By 1907 it was estimated that there were 3,000 in the United States alone. As the larger cinemas were built, the old and ill-equipped nickelodeons were replaced. By the mid-1920s the picture palace, with all its trappings, was an accepted and cherished part of American life. Theater openings and movie premieres drew crowds. By the late 1920s the number of cinemas had grown from about 15,000 in 1915 to more than 20,000. The introduction of sound caused an immediate reduction in the number of buildings, for it proved uneconomic to convert many of the older and more dilapidated silent cinemas.

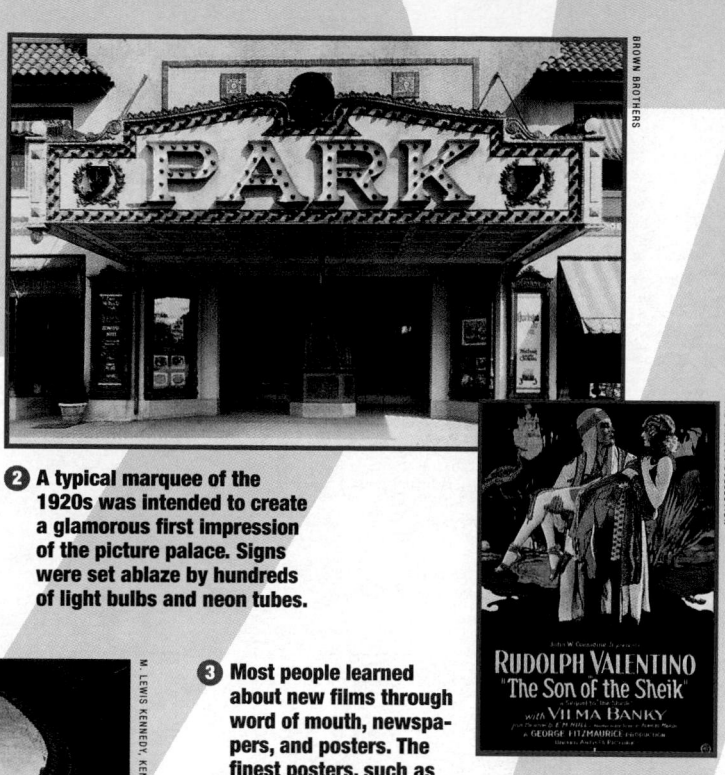

BROWN BROTHERS

THE CARSON COLLECTION

RUDOLPH VALENTINO
"The Son of the Sheik"
with VILMA BANKY

M. LEWIS KENNEDY, KENNEDY STUDIOS

2 A typical marquee of the 1920s was intended to create a glamorous first impression of the picture palace. Signs were set ablaze by hundreds of light bulbs and neon tubes.

3 Most people learned about new films through word of mouth, newspapers, and posters. The finest posters, such as this one advertising the posthumous release of Rudolph Valentino's last feature in 1926, were as powerful as the films they promoted.

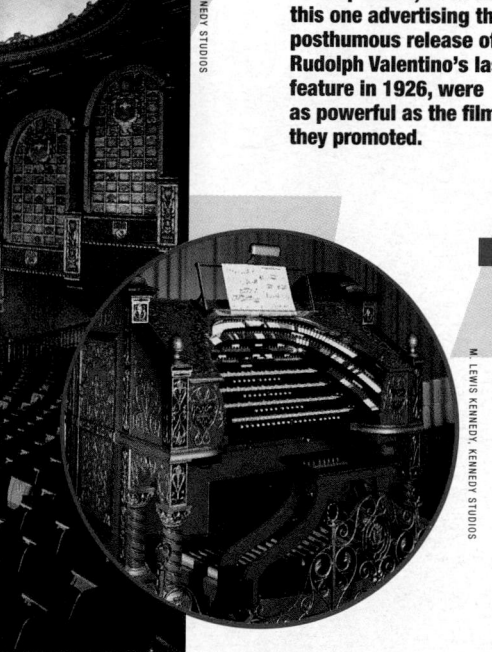

M. LEWIS KENNEDY, KENNEDY STUDIOS

Stats

ATTENDANCE

By 1922 average weekly theater admissions totaled 40 million. By 1929 theater admissions totaled 80 million. In May 1924, there were reported to be 578 cinemas in New York City alone, with seating for 428,926.

TICKET PRICES

Ticket prices were never less than 10 cents, and at first-run theaters they were often more than 75 cents.

STAR SALARIES

In June 1927, Louis B. Mayer renewed Greta Garbo's MGM contract at a salary of $5,000 per week.

SOUND PRICES

- According to a 1929 article in *Variety*, equipping cinemas with sound systems would cost close to $3 million.

- *Broadway* (1929) was one of the first sound films to use a movie camera mounted on a special crane that was built for Universal Studios at a cost of $75,000.

...Now

MOVIE HOUSE COMPARISON

PORTFOLIO PROJECT

How do the cinemas of today compare with the 1920s movie houses? Select one contemporary theater and create a booklet for your portfolio that includes pertinent information and visuals. Be sure to include any data you can think of that would help someone make a Then and Now kind of comparison in the future.

THE MIGHTY WURLITZER

To the average moviegoer, any pipe organ that accompanied a silent movie was a "Wurlitzer." The organ often rose high above the stage floor on a lift, sometimes reaching balcony level. On several occasions, organists had to be rescued when the lift became stuck in the highest position.

THEN AND NOW **411**

 Block Scheduling

The portfolio project on this page provides an excellent opportunity to enrich and extend the key elements of this feature.

 FYI

Movie Snacks During the 1920s shops adjacent to these majestic theaters sold food and drink that patrons consumed before or after the show. The white-gloved ushers leading the way to plush velvet seats inspired awed reverence. Smacking of burlesque and the carnival, food within the picture palace was most definitely not allowed.

CLOSE

Ask: How is going to the movies the same or different from the 1920s? *(In the 1920s moviegoers saw mostly silent films and theaters were much more elaborate than today. There are no organs playing music in theaters today. Snacks are sold inside the theaters.)*

PORTFOLIO PROJECT

Portfolio Project

Moving to Hollywood Ask students to research information on the development and growth of Hollywood as the site for the moviemaking industry. Students should note that filmmakers moved to the West Coast because of the constant sunshine, moderate temperatures, and varied landscapes available for filming. In addition, land was cheap and wages were low. Encourage students to select a movie studio such as MGM, RKO, Universal, or Paramount, and gather data on its growth. Have students prepare a booklet or poster about producers, directors, stars, and movies. Invite volunteers to share their products before filing them in their portfolios.

The Unit at a Glance

Chapter 13

The stock market crash of 1929 signaled the beginning of a severe economic downturn. In the early 1930s, manufacturing sputtered, unemployment skyrocketed, banks and businesses failed, farms dried up, and farmers were uprooted. For many the harsh realities of bread lines, soup kitchens, and abandoned farms shattered the American dream.

Chapter 14

In 1933 newly elected President Franklin D. Roosevelt launched the New Deal—a program dedicated to economic recovery, relief, and reform. The New Deal also ushered in an enlarged and more influential federal government.

00:00 Out of Time?

If time does not permit teaching every chapter in this unit, use the Chapter Digest Audiocassettes and the accompanying student activities and test. The Chapter Digest Audiocassettes are available in Spanish.

 History and the Humanities

U.S. History and Art Transparency 24— *Migrant Mother, 1936* by Dorothea Lange

UNIT 5

Economic Crisis and the New Deal

CHAPTER 13
The Great Depression

CHAPTER 14
The New Deal

412

 Portfolio Project

Biographical Sketch Ask students to examine the photograph and note how Lange's portrait of one woman embodies the predicament of the entire nation during the Depression. Lange's career also reveals many of the important ideals of the New Deal as well as trends in the world of fine art. Ask students to use an encyclopedia or materials in the school library to research and write a one-page biographical sketch of a Depression era painter, writer, or photographer such as Lange. They should focus on details of how the person coped with hard times and how their artwork reflected aspects of the Depression.

Introducing the Unit

Show Students the Unit 5 Time Line Transparency and/or assign the accompanying activity sheet. No two decades in United States history contrast as starkly as the 1920s and the 1930s. Ask students to suggest words and phrases that characterize the 1920s, such as optimism, prosperity, celebration, Jazz Age, credit, and mobility. Then have students study the image and read the titles on this page. Discuss what they imply about the 1930s.

NATIONAL GEOGRAPHIC SOCIETY

Videodisc

GTV: A Geographic Perspective on American History

Side 4, Chapter 3
Title: Thinking Big
Subject: Depression, Dust Bowl, New Deal
Ask: What was the New Deal? *(government programs designed to end the Depression)*

413

Examining the Visual

Migrant Mother Under Roosevelt's New Deal, the Resettlement Administration (later the Farm Securities Administration, or FSA) sought to help the 'one third poor' who had lost their homes, jobs, and land. The Historical Section of the Administration relied on photographers and writers to inspire public support. In 1935 the agency hired Dorothea Lange to help document the plight of migrant families. A year later Lange snapped this image, in Nipomo, California, and jotted the following: "Migrant agricultural worker's family. Seven hungry children. Mother age 32. . . . These people had just sold their tires in order to buy food." Published in the San Francisco *News*, "Migrant Mother" inspired readers to send food to this FSA camp.

LITERATURE

The Grapes of Wrath

BY JOHN STEINBECK

At the height of the Depression, drought gripped the Great Plains. In this excerpt from The Grapes of Wrath, *novelist John Steinbeck conveys the Oklahoma farmers' frustration at the prospect of losing their farms.*

On the Road Dorothea Lange's portrait, "Homeless Family," tells a Depression story of uprooting.

Some of the owner men were kind because they hated what they had to do, and some of them were angry because they hated to be cruel, and some of them were cold because they had long ago found that one could not be an owner unless one were cold. And all of them were caught in something larger than themselves. Some of them hated the mathematics that drove them, and some were afraid, and some worshiped the mathematics because it provided a refuge from thought and from feeling. If a bank or a finance company owned the land, the owner man said, the Bank—or the Company—needs—wants—insists—must have—as though the Bank or the Company were a monster, with thought and feeling, which had ensnared them. These last would take no responsibility for the banks or the companies because they were men and slaves, while the banks were machines and masters all at the same time. Some of the owner men were a little proud to be slaves to such cold and powerful masters. The owner men sat in the cars and explained. You know the land is poor. You've scrabbled at it long enough, God knows.

The squatting tenant men nodded and wondered and drew figures in the dust, and yes, they knew, God knows. If the dust only wouldn't fly. If the top would only stay on the soil, it might not be so bad.

The owner men went on leading to their point: You know the land's getting poorer. You know what cotton does to the land; robs it, sucks all the blood out of it.

The squatters nodded—they knew, God knew. If they could only rotate the crops they might pump blood back into the land.

Well, it's too late. And the owner men explained the workings and the thinkings of the monster that

---

Background Information

The Dust Bowl Thousands of farm families were forced to leave their homes as a result of the terrible dust storms that swept the Great Plains during the 1930s. Many of these people migrated to California and found low-paying jobs in the state's fertile agricultural areas. The migrant families lived in crowded shacks or camped outdoors. In *The Grapes of Wrath,* John Steinbeck narrates the experiences of one such family—the Joads—who learn that in order to survive, the poor must work together. This 1939 novel won a Pulitzer Prize.

---

was stronger than they were. A man can hold land if he can just eat and pay taxes; he can do that.

Yes, he can do that until his crops fail one day and he has to borrow money from the bank.

But—you see, a bank or a company can't do that, because those creatures don't breathe air, don't eat side-meat. They breathe profits; they eat the interest on money. If they don't get it, they die the way you die without air, without side-meat. It is a sad thing, but it is so. It is just so. . . .

The squatting men looked down again. What do you want us to do? We can't take less share of the crop—we're half starved now. The kids are hungry all the time. We got no clothes, torn an' ragged. If all the neighbors weren't the same, we'd be ashamed to go to meeting.

And at last the owner men came to the point. The tenant system won't work any more. One man on a tractor can take the place of twelve or fourteen families. Pay him a wage and take all the crop. We have to do it. We don't like to do it. But the monster's sick. Something's happened to the monster.

But you'll kill the land with cotton.

We know. We've got to take cotton quick before the land dies. Then we'll sell the land. Lots of families in the East would like to own a piece of land.

The tenant men looked up alarmed. But what'll happen to us? How'll we eat?

You'll have to get off the land. The plows'll go through the dooryard.

And now the squatting men stood up angrily. Grampa took up the land, and he had to kill the Indians and drive them away. And Pa was born here, and he killed weeds and snakes. Then a bad year came and he had to borrow a little money. An' we was born here. There in the door—our children born here. And Pa had to borrow money. The bank owned the land then, but we stayed and we got a little bit of what we raised.

> IT'S NOT US. IT'S THE
> MONSTER. THE BANK
> ISN'T LIKE A MAN.

We know that—all that. It's not us, it's the bank. A bank isn't like a man. Or an owner with fifty thousand acres, he isn't like a man either. That's the monster.

Sure, cried the tenant men, but it's our land. We measured it and broke it up. We were born on it, and we got killed on it, died on it. Even if it's no good, it's still ours. That's what makes it ours—being born on it, working it, dying on it. That makes ownership, not a paper with numbers on it.

We're sorry. It's not us. It's the monster. The bank isn't like a man.

Yes, but the bank is only made of men.

No, you're wrong there—quite wrong there. The bank is something else than men. It happens that every man in a bank hates what the bank does, and yet the bank does it. The bank is something more than men, I tell you. It's the monster. Men made it, but they can't control it.

The tenants cried, Grampa killed Indians, Pa killed snakes for the land. Maybe we can kill banks—they're worse than Indians and snakes. Maybe we got to fight to keep our land, like Pa and Grampa did.

And now the owner men grew angry. You'll have to go.

But it's ours, the tenant men cried. We——

No. The bank, the monster owns it. You'll have to go. . . . And the owner men started their cars and rolled away.

RESPONDING TO LITERATURE

1. The tenants say about the land, "That's what makes it ours—being born on it, working it, dying on it." Do you agree or disagree? Explain.

2. Who do you think Steinbeck believes is ultimately responsible for the tenants' loss of their land? Explain.

Responding to Literature Answers

1. Answers will vary. Students who agree may claim that the land belonged to the tenant farmer because it was a part of him and therefore priceless. Those who disagree could argue that land, like any other possession, only belongs to those who can afford it.

2. Answers will vary. Students should notice that Steinbeck is on the side of the tenants rather than of the bank, but he also seems to suggest that the tenants should unite: "Maybe we got to fight to keep our land."

The Great Depression

DAILY LESSON OBJECTIVES	REPRODUCIBLE RESOURCES	MULTIMEDIA RESOURCES
SECTION 1 The Crash and Its Aftermath 1. Describe the stock market crash of 1929 and explain why it occurred. 2. Explain how the crash led to the Depression and describe some underlying causes of this downturn. 3. Discuss Hoover's response to the Depression and how the failure of his policies led to his defeat in the election of 1932.	Reproducible Lesson Plans Vocabulary and Guided Reading Activities (English or Spanish) Cooperative Learning Activities Geography in History Activities Great Debates in American History Section Quizzes (English or Spanish)	Chapter Teaching Transparencies Section Focus Transparencies Map Transparencies Time Line Transparencies The Presidents: A Picture History of Our Nation Student Self-Test: A Software Review Testmaker
SECTION 2 The Dream on Hold 1. Tell how the Depression affected rural and urban families differently. 2. Describe how communities responded to hardship. 3. Explain upheaval in the family during the Depression.	Reproducible Lesson Plans Vocabulary and Guided Reading Activities (English or Spanish) Skill Reinforcement Activities American Literature Readings and Activities Section Quizzes (English or Spanish)	Section Focus Transparencies and Activities Student Self-Test: A Software Review Testmaker
SECTION 3 Life During the Depression 1. Explain how people coped with the sacrifices and hardships of the Depression. 2. Describe innovations and methods of escape that changed people's lifestyles in the 1930s. 3. Describe art and literature movements that highlighted themes of social reform.	Reproducible Lesson Plans Vocabulary and Guided Reading Activities (English or Spanish) Reteaching Activities (English or Spanish) Enrichment Activities (English or Spanish) Section Quizzes (English or Spanish)	Section Focus Transparencies American Music: Cultural Traditions Focus on American Fine Art Prints Student Self-Test: A Software Review Testmaker
CHAPTER REVIEW AND EVALUATION	Chapter 13 Test, Forms A and B. Performance Assessment Strategies and Activities Mid-Book Test	Student Self-Test: A Software Review Testmaker Vocabulary PuzzleMaker Chapter Digests Audiocassettes

00:00 If time does not permit teaching the entire chapter, summarize using the Chapter 13 Digests Audiocassettes and the accompanying activities and tests. (Available in English or Spanish.)

Cooperative Project

Have students work in heterogeneous discussion groups of three. In each group students can take turns playing the roles of a farm worker, a city dweller, and a government official. Have the farm worker and the city dweller each try to persuade the government official that he or she has the greater need for help. **LEP**

Suggested Rubric: A Skit. See Performance Assessment Strategies and Activities, p. 41.

Individual Project

Have students look at examples of primary sources in this chapter in which people describe their hardships during the 1930s. Ask students to use the primary sources as a model for writing a letter to President Hoover from a person affected by the Depression. Ask them to use the letter to persuade Hoover to take a specific action that would help ease the hard times.

Suggested Rubric: A Self-Assessment. See Performance Assessment Strategies and Activities, p. 53.

Key to Ability Levels

Teaching strategies have been coded for varying learning styles and abilities.

L1 BASIC activities for all students

L2 AVERAGE activities for average to above-average students

L3 CHALLENGING activities for above-average students

LEP LIMITED ENGLISH PROFICIENCY activities

Block Scheduling

Block scheduling differs from traditional class scheduling in the amount of time allotted to each period. The extended timeframe provided by block scheduling affords you the opportunity to implement a greater number of research-oriented and activity-intense projects to motivate and involve your students. Activities that are particularly suited to use within the block scheduling framework are identified throughout this chapter by the following designation.

TEACHER'S CORNER

NATIONAL GEOGRAPHIC SOCIETY

NATIONAL GEOGRAPHIC SOCIETY PRODUCTS AVAILABLE FROM GLENCOE

To order the following products for use with this chapter, contact your local Glencoe sales representative or call Glencoe at 1-800-334-7344:

- *The Presidents: A Picture History of Our Nation* (CD-ROM)
- *GTV: A Geographic Perspective on American History* (Videodisc)
- *GTV: The American People: Fabric of a Nation* (Videodisc)

ADDITIONAL NATIONAL GEOGRAPHIC SOCIETY PRODUCTS

To order the following products for use with this chapter, call National Geographic Society at 1-800-368-2728:

- *1929-1941: The Great Depression* (Video)
- *Decades of History: The 20th Century—The Early Years* (Filmstrip)

Chapter Overview

Suddenly in 1929 the mood in the United States changed. The stock market crash and the Depression that followed altered daily life and social consciousness. Decline in business, agriculture, and foreign trade left many people without hope.

Introducing the Chapter

Ask students what would happen if 25 percent of the people in their town lost their jobs. What if, on top of that, the banks lost most people's savings, and there was no relief or help from the government? What would they do? Point out that this is what many Americans faced in the beginning of the 1930s.

 Display the Chapter 13 Teaching Transparency and distribute copies of the activity sheet. After students have completed the activities, point out that most people were unprepared for the Depression because of the rise of prosperity in the late 1920s. Ask students to recall examples of this.

Extension Activity
Have students complete Beyond the Transparency on the activity sheet for Chapter 13 and present their projects after the class has completed the chapter.

 History Journal

Have students review their responses to the opening story and photograph. Have them write about people's views on charity and work during the Depression. What are their own views?

CHAPTER

13

The Great Depression

DECEMBER 1932: NEW YORK RESPONDS TO ITS NEEDIEST CASES

Daily stories in the *New York Times* in 1932 described the city's neediest families and asked readers to contribute to a fund to help them. One story described an unemployed plasterer, Mr. C., who had starved himself so that his 2-year-old could have enough food.

One morning Mr. C. "fell to the floor and could not rise. A doctor said he had injured himself so seriously by voluntarily starving himself that an operation was imperative. Help is asked to keep the family in food and shelter until Mr. C. is able to work."

Mr. C. was only one of millions of people who had enjoyed prosperity during the 1920s but whose fortunes fell in the early 1930s. Between 1929 and 1932 millions of hardworking men and women lost their jobs. Most of these people were proud and used to providing for their own families. They felt ashamed to take charity.

The 1930s witnessed one of the longest, deepest, and most devastating economic depressions ever experienced by the United States. After a decade of high living, the abrupt financial breakdown came as a severe shock. The affluence enjoyed by many Americans during the Roaring Twenties began to evaporate in the fall of 1929. ■

HISTORY JOURNAL

Before you read the rest of this chapter, write what you think the Great Depression was like and what you think the chapter will be about.

416

EXTRA CREDIT PROJECT

Planning a Budget Help students grasp the dire straits facing a family provider during the Depression years by trying to allocate a limited amount of funds. Each student should figure one week's salary, their final paycheck, based on the minimum hourly wage, a 40-hour week, and a family of 3. Ask them to write down what they would purchase with this amount, and deduct each purchase from the total. For how many days does the money last? What monthly bills go unpaid?

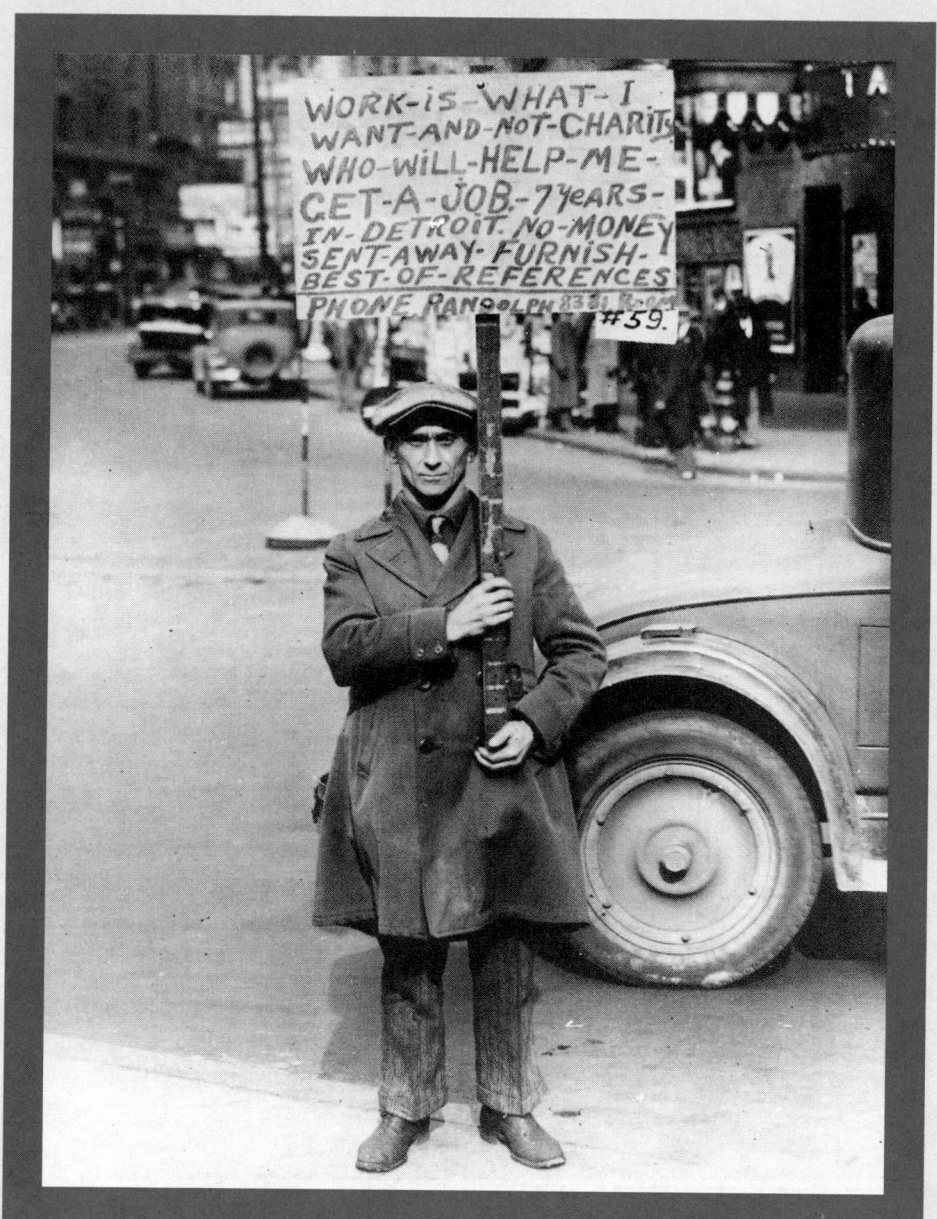

AN UNEMPLOYED WORKER
GETS HIS MESSAGE ACROSS.

© 1995, THE DETROIT NEWS. PHOTO BY THE DETROIT NEWS COLLECTION

417

Examining the Visual

Unemployed Worker Ask students to read
the text of the worker's sign in this photograph.
The sign appears to be constructed from available scrap materials, cardboard, and a guitar
neck. Begin a discussion about the emotions
expressed in the man's facial expression and
choice of words. How is he presenting himself
to the world? What means of free advertising
would be available today that were not available
during the Depression? Ask students to compose a few lines for such an announcement, as
if they were out of work and needed money.
How would they describe themselves?

FOCUS

Section Objectives

1. Describe the stock market crash of 1929 and explain why it occurred.
2. Explain how the crash led to the Depression and describe some underlying causes of this downturn.
3. Discuss Hoover's response to the Depression and how the failure of his policies led to his defeat in the election of 1932.

Bellringer Activity

While taking attendance at the beginning of the class period, display **Section Focus Transparency 40,** and have students answer the questions. (Or use the black-line master.)

VISUAL INSTRUCTION

Gloomy Investors Business cycles have always been a part of United States history. Economic crises in the 1820s, 1870s, and 1890s led to widespread business and bank failures.

Ask: How did a group of bankers attempt to stop the panic? *(They bought large blocks of stock in a futile effort to increase investor confidence, stabilize prices, and stop the panic selling.)*

The Crash and Its Aftermath

OCTOBER 24, 1929: NEW YORK STOCK EXCHANGE CRASHES

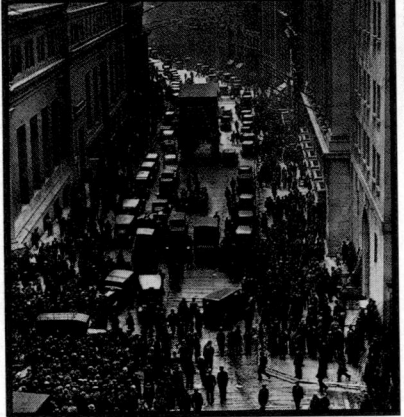

Gloomy Investors
Crowds of stockholders gather on Wall Street as they prepare to sell at a loss.

THURSDAY MORNING AT 10:00, WALL STREET WAS JAMMED. A crowd of thousands gathered outside the New York Stock Exchange, waiting for news. The rumble of loud voices hinted to spectators of the bedlam inside. Traders shouted out their orders to sell, sell, sell. Few were willing to buy the **stocks,** shares in business ownership whose price and value constantly fluctuate, so prices plunged steeply in the stampede.

At noon, five of the nation's leading bankers met in the building across the street from the stock exchange. In an effort to stabilize the plummeting market, these men pledged to pump undisclosed millions into the stock market. By buying stocks, they hoped to make prices rise. Rumors of the meeting had a calming effect on the stock market. Selling slowed and the panic began to subside. When the bankers' representative, Richard Whitney, strode across the floor later that afternoon to deliver his orders for large blocks of stock above asking prices, the stock market had already begun to rally. At closing time stock prices started to rebound from the morning's slump.

The stock market's recovery was short-lived. The following Monday the stock exchange opened with a rush of sales that wiped out all the gains of the preceding week. The bankers met again and decided they could do nothing

---

AS YOU READ

Vocabulary
► stock
► speculation
► margin
► depression
► unemployment

Think About . . .
► the causes of the stock market crash.
► other factors that contributed to the country's economic decline.
► the nature and effectiveness of President Hoover's response to the Depression.

Section 1 Resources

REPRODUCIBLE RESOURCES

📁 Lesson Plan 13-1
📁 Vocabulary and Guided Reading Activity 13-1
📁 Cooperative Learning Activity 13
📁 Unit 5 Great Debate
📁 Section 1 Quiz
📁 Geography in History Activity 13

MULTIMEDIA RESOURCES

📀 Section Focus Transparency 40
🔵 The Presidents: A Picture History of Our Nation
🎧 Chapter 13 Digest Audiocassette
📀 Map Transparency 13
💾 Testmaker
💾 Student Self-Test: A Software Review
📀 Chapter Teaching Transparency 13

Driven to Ruin Forced to pay off debts for stocks that were suddenly worthless, people such as this man made drastic adjustments. *Why had so many people invested so heavily in the stock market?*

Why Did the Crash Occur?
Margin Buying Fuels Speculation

According to economists and politicians of the late 1920s, the United States had entered a new era in which everyone could be rich. Many people agreed with the words of a leading politician:

If a man saves $15 a week, and invests in good common stocks, and allows the dividends and rights to accumulate, at the end of twenty years he will have at least $80,000 and an income from investments of around $400 a month. He will be rich.
—John J. Raskob, Democratic National Committee chairman, 1929

Stock Market Speculation

Such advice inspired thousands of people to pour their savings into stocks. Many investors, however, wanted to make their fortunes immediately. Hoping that heavy financial risks would pay off quickly, people in the late 1920s speculated in the stock market. **Speculation** was a way of gambling with short-term investments. Speculators would buy stocks they thought would quickly rise in price. After the price of their stocks went up, they would sell the stocks for a profit.

Stocks made large gains between 1927 and 1929. A speculator who bought stock in Hershey Chocolate in August 1928, for example, and sold it in September 1929, made more than 100 percent profit on the investment. Banks at the time commonly paid an annual rate of under 7 percent on savings accounts. The

to check the decline. On Tuesday, October 29, the flood of sales continued. Historians have called this "the most devastating day in the history of markets." A gloomy quiet pervaded the trading floor. The week before, traders ran across the floor in panic, trying to submit their orders before prices dropped further. That day, however, the stock exchange was as dour as a funeral parlor. A reporter from the *New York Times* described the somber scene: "Orderly crowds lined up before each [selling] post, talking in subdued tones, without any pushing." In that last week in October 1929, the stock market began a momentous decline that came to be known as the great crash. During that time $30 billion in stock value—about the same amount of money the United States had spent in World War I—evaporated completely along with people's dreams of achieving permanent prosperity.

Selected Stock Prices, 1927–1929

Stock	Aug. 31, 1927	Aug. 31, 1928	Sept. 3, 1929	Oct. 29, 1929	Nov. 15, 1929
American and Foreign Power	$23.86	$38.00	$167.75	$73.00	$67.86
American Telephone and Telegraph (AT&T)	$169.00	$182.00	$304.00	$230.00	$222.00
Detroit Edison Co.	$151.00	$205.00	$350.00	not listed	$195.00
General Electric Co.	$142.00	$168.13	$396.25	$210.00	$201.00
Hershey Chocolate	not listed	$53.25	$128.00	$108.00	$68.00
International Business Machines (IBM)	$93.00	$130.86	$241.75	not listed	$129.86
People's Gas Chicago	$147.13	$182.86	$374.75	not listed	$230.00

Stock values peaked just before the crash, and then tumbled sharply. *If you had bought 10 shares of AT&T in August 1927 and sold them in September 1929, how much would you have profited? If you had bought them in September 1929 and sold them in November 1929, how much would you have lost?*

SECTION ONE **419**

VISUAL INSTRUCTION

Driven to Ruin If an investor could not repay borrowed money, the broker became the owner of the depreciated or even worthless stock. Thus brokers and clients both lost.

Answer: *Economists and politicians had encouraged speculation as a way of getting rich.*

TEACH

Guided Practice

L2 **Hypothesizing** Ask students to imagine how a crash might affect the business of a toy company and the business of a dairy company. Point out that the company's financial soundness would be important, as well as the need of the public for its products.

Show students Map Transparency 13 and have them complete the activity sheet.

CHART STUDY

Producers of essential goods and services, such as those in the table, survived the crash in a reduced state, but thousands of other companies were wiped out. By 1932 the nation's manufacturing output stood at 54 percent of its 1929 level.
Answers: *$1,350; $820*

Cooperative Learning

Coping With a Crisis Have students sit in heterogeneous groups of four or five and consider how they would economize if suddenly their families' incomes were lost and no welfare aid was available. What would they give up first? How would they cut back? Discuss what are the basic essentials of daily life and how a person gets them with no income.

Independent Practice

L3 Researching

Encourage interested students to research and write brief reports on the first depression in American history, brought on by the Embargo Act of 1807 (see page 117). Have them include a comparison of the effects of that depression on the general public with the effects of the Great Depression. Volunteers can share their reports with the class.

✎ Have students complete the Chapter 13, Section 1 Vocabulary and Guided Reading Activity. (Also in Spanish.) **LEP**

✎ Have students complete the Chapter 13 Cooperative Learning Activity.

NATIONAL MUSEUM OF AMERICAN ART, SMITHSONIAN INSTITUTION. MUSEUM PURCHASE

Black Tuesday The Latin words *Dies Irae* literally mean "Day of Wrath," but colloquially the expression means "Judgment Day." *What do you see in the picture that shows how the artist feels about the date October 29?*

100 shares, in effect buying $10,000 worth of stock. As long as the price of the stock continued to rise, the buyer could sell later, pay back what had been borrowed, and realize a tidy profit.

In the boom years of the late 1920s, savvy margin buyers made fortunes. Buying stocks at low prices, they watched gleefully as stock values soared. When they thought a stock had reached its peak price, they sold it, paying off the stockbroker with the money they made from the sale.

As long as stock prices kept going up, brokers were happy to lend money to speculators. After all, they received up to 20 percent interest on their loans. As soon as prices began to slide, brokers had to protect their loans. Because the stocks were their only collateral, when stock prices began to decline, brokers called in their margins. In other words, they asked investors who had borrowed money from them to put down more cash. If the customer could not pay, the broker sold the stock, keeping the proceeds as repayment for the loan.

The Beginning of the End

By the summer of 1929, brokers had lent out more than $6 billion in margin loans to their customers. Realizing that the huge number of people investing in the stock market meant the market was saturated, a few investors began to sell, and stock prices slowly declined in the autumn of 1929. Brokers began calling in their margins. Many investors did not have cash to pay for their stocks, so brokers were forced to sell. Enforced selling pushed prices down further. Noticing the downturn, other investors began selling their stock in panic. Amid the flood of unmet margin calls and the deluge of panic selling, the crash gained speed and force.

By the last week in October, the bottom fell out of the stock market. Stocks tumbled even further in November. In a few months the prices of major stocks fell 75 percent. People who had been millionaires suddenly were deep in debt.

Stock market investors, however, were not the only people brought down by the crash. Many banks had lent their cash reserves to stockbrokers. The brokers lost the

dramatic difference between the return on a savings account and the return on stock speculation made the stock market an attractive gamble for thousands of Americans.

The common practice of buying on **margin** involved paying only a fraction of a stock's dollar value. In such a transaction, an investor put down as little as 5 percent of the stock price and borrowed the rest of the money from a stockbroker. The stock itself was collateral for the loan. In other words, if the investor could not repay the loan, the broker gained ownership of the stock. Investors buying on margin could buy more stock with their money than investors who did not borrow from brokers. For example, an investor with $500 could buy 5 shares of a stock costing $100 per share. Buying on margin, however, the investor could use the $500 to buy

Meeting Special Needs

Reading Disability For students who have reading difficulties, you may wish to have them outline this rather long and complex section. Ask them to copy the main heads and subheads in their notebooks, leaving space after each head for their notes about key events and concepts.

money when their customers could not respond to the margin calls and failed to repay their loans. Because savings deposits were not federally insured, people who had prudently tucked their money in banks found their savings had vanished. Thus, the stock market crash caught millions of innocent bystanders in the financial crunch.

The Onset of the Depression

In the first few months after the crash, business leaders and economists spoke confidently, predicting a quick recovery. In December 1929, Secretary of the Treasury Andrew Mellon announced, "I see nothing in the present situation that is either menacing or warrants pessimism." As the new decade dawned, however, the United States fell into a deep business depression.

A period of severely reduced economic activity, known as a **depression,** is characterized by a sharp rise in **unemployment** as people lose their jobs and are unable to find new ones. The depression that began in October 1929 was the most devastating economic down-

turn in the nation's history. Raging through most of the 1930s, this sickening decline became known as the Great Depression.

The Causes of the Great Depression
Weaknesses in the Economy

After that disastrous week in October 1929, the economy began unraveling. Economists then saw flaws few had noticed during the get-rich-quick era of the mid-1920s.

Depressed Farms and Industries

The shiny glow of prosperity had not rubbed off on all Americans in the 1920s. Farmers' incomes fell throughout the decade. The textile, lumber, mining, and railroad industries also declined. In the months preceding the crash, the automobile and construction industries suffered from a decrease in orders. As a result, wages

A DEPRESSED ECONOMY

It is tempting to see a landmark event like the stock market crash as the cause of the Great Depression. In reality, however, trends, decisions, technology, and foreign relations all contributed to the slump that, by 1932, had driven the country's manufacturing output down to 54 percent of its 1929 level.

Finance
In the late 1920s, investors speculated in overvalued stocks. They borrowed from brokers, who borrowed from banks, who loaned out the savings of depositors. After the crash, the Federal Reserve restricted the money supply, making recovery difficult.

Foreign Trade
After the crash, the United States was unable to lend money to other nations; their American crops and import goods declined. Higher tariffs at home and abroad also hurt trade.

Agriculture
In the 1920s new technology had increased productivity, leading to crop surpluses, lower prices, and hard times. In the 1930s many farmers lost their farms as banks foreclosed on mortgages.

Industry
Overproduction and underconsumption had been developing before 1929. When the crash came, shaky businesses failed. By 1933 unemployment reached 25 percent.

Business Activity in the United States, 1915-1940
Percent change in business activity; 0 represents the long-term trend

Conditions in industry, finance, agriculture, and trade contributed to the economic climate of the Great Depression. *How might the decline in industrial production have affected the agricultural surplus? How might the decline in the amount of money in circulation have affected industrial production?*

SECTION ONE   **421**

Portfolio Project

Mathematics Ask students to make their own graph of unemployment in the 1930s using the following data:

Year	%
1930	9%
1931	16%
1932	24%
1933	25%
1934	22%
1935	21%
1936	17%
1937	15%
1938	19%
1939	17%

Include the graphs in students' portfolios.

dropped and employers laid off workers. With their incomes cut, many farmers and workers could not afford the manufactured goods that the nation's industries had been churning out at impressive rates in the 1920s. This underconsumption became a major weakness in the economy.

Wealth Distribution

Another factor contributing to the underconsumption that fueled the Depression was the growing gap in wealth between rich people and Americans of more ordinary means. Although business profits in many industries rose throughout the 1920s, not all workers received a proportionate share of these profits. This meant that there was not enough consumer buying power to keep up with all the goods being produced. By the late 1920s, radios, telephones, refrigerators, washing machines, and other goods were piling up in warehouses across the country.

Monetary Policy

Errors in monetary policy also contributed to the crash. After the crash the Federal Reserve System, charged with regulating the amount of money in circulation, followed a restrictive policy that dried up credit. This policy left the country with a supply of money in circulation that was not large enough to allow the economy to bounce back after the stock market bubble burst.

Decline in Foreign Trade

Weaknesses in the American economy also sapped the strength of foreign economies, some of which were already unstable. Throughout the 1920s the United States served as a bank for other nations, lending money to aid foreign industries and speed recovery from the Great War. During the late 1920s, however, as Americans began pouring borrowed money into the stock market, bank funds for loans to other nations dried up. International trade slowed down because, without American loans, other nations had less money to spend on our nation's goods. High tariffs—taxes on imported products—further blocked international trade. This decline fed into the cycle of underconsumption, further weakening the American economy.

After the stock market crash, all these problems with the economy began to take their toll. The economic slowdown frightened everyone, from East Coast executives to Midwestern store owners, from Utah miners to the President of the United States.

Hoover's Response
Voluntary and Local Action Fail

Herbert C. Hoover occupied the White House when the Depression began. Nicknamed the Great Engineer, Hoover was elected President by a wide margin in 1928. Orphaned at age 8, he left his Iowa home to move in with relatives in Oregon. Although his early childhood was sad, in young adulthood Hoover buried unhappiness with driving ambition. He graduated from Stanford University in 1895 with an engineering degree. For the next 18 years he worked on engineering projects all over the world, building an unshakable reputation for solving technical problems and amassing a personal fortune.

Hoover's Quaker upbringing gave him a strong desire to serve humanity. After the outbreak of World War I, he coordinated war relief efforts in Europe and

★ ★ ★ **GALLERY OF PRESIDENTS** ★ ★ ★

Herbert C. Hoover
1 9 2 9 – 1 9 3 3

"Ours is a land rich in resources; stimulating in its glorious beauty; filled with millions of happy homes; blessed with comfort and opportunity. . . . No country is more loved by its people. I have an abiding faith in their capacity, integrity, and high purpose. I have no fears for the future of our country. It is bright with hope."

Inaugural Address, March 4, 1929

HERBERT HOOVER PRESIDENTIAL LIBRARY-MUSEUM

BACKGROUND
▶ Born 1874; Died 1964
▶ Republican, Iowa
▶ Headed the Commission for Relief in Belgium 1914–1917
▶ Secretary of Commerce 1921–1928

ACHIEVEMENTS IN OFFICE
▶ Federal Farm Board (1929)
▶ Smoot-Hawley Tariff Act (1930)
▶ Reconstruction Finance Corporation (1923)

Extending the Content

Protectionism By raising the tariff on foreign imports, Hoover hoped to protect American industry. The Smoot-Hawley Tariff Act of 1930, opposed by many economists, was welcomed by protectionists who believed that high tariffs would make the United States "self-contained and self-sustaining." Nevertheless, the Depression continued. Protectionism is still debated today. Ask students to discuss the pros and cons of high tariffs on, for example, foreign automobiles.

food production in the United States. Efficient and successful, Hoover inspired confidence. He quickly rose as an important political figure. President Harding appointed him secretary of commerce in 1921.

From this influential post, Hoover tried to put into practice his vision for the United States. He encouraged voluntary associations of business leaders to eliminate inefficiency in industry. He suggested that federal, state, and local governments coordinate efforts to dampen harmful swings in the business cycle. With these and other measures, Hoover was sure that the United States in 1928 was "nearer to the final triumph over poverty than ever before in the history of any land." His optimism and confidence matched the mood of the country and won him the presidency.

Initial Reaction to the Depression

Only months after Hoover made that prediction, the stock market crashed. Realizing that people's plummeting faith in the economy hindered chances of recovery, Hoover tried to bolster confidence. "We have now passed the worst," he told Americans in May 1930, "and . . . shall rapidly recover."

Even with his optimistic pronouncements, the President took immediate action to try to arrest the economic downturn. Following his own faith in voluntary action, he called a meeting of business leaders and asked them to pledge not to cut wages or production of goods. He suggested that city and state governments stimulate their local economies by funding building projects to provide new jobs.

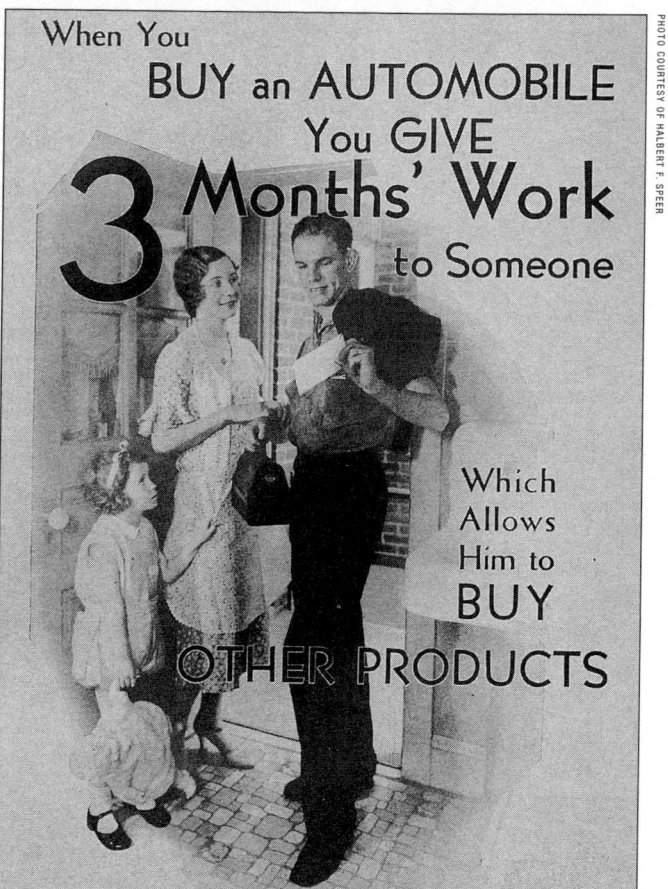

When You
BUY an AUTOMOBILE
You GIVE
3 Months' Work
to Someone

Which Allows Him to BUY OTHER PRODUCTS

PHOTO COURTESY OF HALBERT F. SPEER

Wishful Thinking Auto companies urged Americans to help the economy by spending money—money that most Americans did not have. *In what ways did Hoover's efforts to end the Depression fall short?*

Hoover also funneled aid to farmers through the Agricultural Marketing Act, which Congress had passed even before the economy began to weaken in the

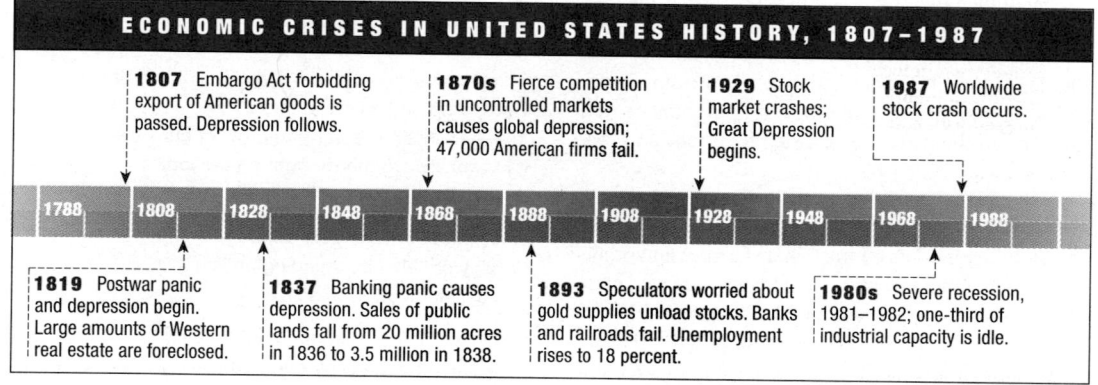

ECONOMIC CRISES IN UNITED STATES HISTORY, 1807–1987

1807 Embargo Act forbidding export of American goods is passed. Depression follows.

1870s Fierce competition in uncontrolled markets causes global depression; 47,000 American firms fail.

1929 Stock market crashes; Great Depression begins.

1987 Worldwide stock crash occurs.

1788 | 1808 | 1828 | 1848 | 1868 | 1888 | 1908 | 1928 | 1948 | 1968 | 1988

1819 Postwar panic and depression begin. Large amounts of Western real estate are foreclosed.

1837 Banking panic causes depression. Sales of public lands fall from 20 million acres in 1836 to 3.5 million in 1838.

1893 Speculators worried about gold supplies unload stocks. Banks and railroads fail. Unemployment rises to 18 percent.

1980s Severe recession, 1981–1982; one-third of industrial capacity is idle.

VISUAL INSTRUCTION

Wishful Thinking On reading this poster one worker asked, "How'd they expect us to buy autos when we can't buy food?"
Answer: *Hoover relied too much on encouraging voluntary action by business leaders and local governments. Farmers and others needed more immediate, concrete aid.*

FYI

Early Depressions The depressions of 1807 and 1819 shown on the time line did not affect most citizens as directly as later depressions did. Most people in the early years of the nation lived on self-sufficient farms and dealt in a "cash economy." The depression that followed the Embargo Act did affect textile producers in New England as it shut off the supply of raw materials from abroad.

CHART STUDY

Ask: When was the most recent stock market crash?
Answer: *1987*

Cultural Perspectives

Immigration Decline Immigration quotas based on national origin, which favored immigrants from northern and western Europe, remained in force during the Depression. Relatively few Europeans wanted to immigrate to a country in the grip of massive unemployment, however. About 350,000 Europeans came to the United States during the decade of the Depression, but almost as many people returned to Europe in the same period. Ask students to find out which countries in Europe were hardest hit by the worldwide Depression. *(Those most deeply in debt to the United States—Great Britain and Germany)*

WORLD'S HIGHEST STANDARD OF LIVING

There's no way like the American Way

Natural Disaster Margaret Bourke-White was one of the four original staff photographers for Life magazine. This photograph, probably the most famous of her career, was taken at a flood relief station in Louisville, Kentucky, in 1937. *What examples of irony do you see in this photo?*

aftermath of the crash. Through this legislation, the federal government established the Farm Board, which lent money to farmers to help them set up cooperative marketing associations. Farmers who joined these associations agreed to sell their crops as a group. If they could not get the prices they wanted at the time of the harvest, they would store their crops until prices rose.

Voluntary marketing associations might, in time, have raised crop prices. Many farmers, however, needed immediate help paying the mortgages on their land. The Farm Board was not authorized to lend money to individual farmers, so thousands of farm families went bankrupt in the early 1930s, losing their jobs and their homes.

The Depression Deepens

Despite Hoover's efforts to help farmers and others, business conditions in the United States worsened in the 2 years after the crash. About 23,000 businesses failed in 1929. In 1932, 32,000 businesses went under. The average family's annual income dropped from $2,300 in

1929 to $1,600 in 1935. Unemployment rose from about 5 percent in 1929 to almost 25 percent in 1932.

The early 1930s saw mounting poverty and destitution. In major cities bread lines stretched for blocks, as people waited for one scant meal a day.

E.Y. (Yip) Harburg, a song lyricist, captured the prevailing mood of desperation and shock at the time. Harburg wrote the words to the most famous song of the Depression era, "Brother, Can You Spare a Dime?"

They used to tell me I was building a dream,
And so I followed the mob—
When there was earth to plow or guns to bear
I was always there—right on the job.

They used to tell me I was building a dream
With peace and glory ahead—
Why should I be standing on line
Just waiting for bread?

Once I built a railroad, made it run,
Made it run against time.

Critical Thinking

Making Inferences Yip Harburg found a bright side to the Depression in a return to the use of imagination. Tell students that library use surged during the 1930s; one Indiana town, for example, found that circulation of books rose 145 percent between 1929 and 1933. Ask students to make inferences about the causes of this rise, based on what they know about the times. *(They may mention, among other things, that both the lack of funds for other entertainment and the leisure time suddenly available to the jobless contributed to the increase in library use.)*

Once I built a railroad,
Now it's done—
Brother, can you spare a dime?

Once I built a tower, to the sun.
Brick and rivet and lime,
Once I built a tower,
Now it's done—
Brother, can you spare a dime?

Once in khaki suits,
Gee we looked swell,
Full of that Yankee Doodle-de-dum
Half a million boots went sloggin' through Hell,
I was the kid with the drum.

Say don't you remember, they called me Al—
It was Al all of the time.
Say don't you remember I'm your pal—
Buddy, can you spare a dime?

—E.Y. Harburg,
"Brother, Can You Spare a Dime?"

The bands of the time were playing this song in 1930 and 1931. During the 1932 presidential campaign, the Republicans tried to discourage the radio networks from playing the song, but it had already impressed voters.

Ironically, Harburg also wrote one of the most optimistic songs of the decade, "Somewhere Over the Rainbow." He himself saw the Depression as a time of release from the business world. With the downward economic trend came a change of ideals that he deemed positive:

> With the Crash, I realized that the greatest fantasy of all was business. The only realistic way of making a living was versifying. Living off your imagination.
>
> We thought American business was the Rock of Gibraltar. We were the prosperous nation, and nothing could stop us now. A brownstone house was forever. You gave it to your kids and they put marble fronts on it. There was a feeling of continuity. If you made it, it was there forever. Suddenly the big dream exploded. The impact was unbelievable.
>
> —E.Y. Harburg, in *Hard Times* by Studs Terkel

With the number of unemployed growing every month, charity funds soon proved completely inadequate. Toledo, Ohio, could afford to spend only 2 cents per relief meal per day. New York City gave only $2.39 per week to each family on relief. Thousands of people were turned away.

With poverty pressing down on them, some people wrote President Hoover in anger and frustration:

> Why should we hafto . . . have foodless days . . . and our children have Schoolless days and Shoeless days and the land full of plenty and Banks bursting with money? Why does Every Thing have Exceptional Value Except the Human being? Why are we reduced to poverty and starving and anxiety and Sorrow So quickly under your administration?
>
> —Robert S. .McElvaine,
> *Down & Out in the Great Depression*

Too Little Too Late
Discontent Continues to Rise

Facing such harsh criticism, Hoover reluctantly introduced new government programs to deal with the economic crisis. He still insisted that voluntary action and local programs were the best ways to relieve the Depression. By early 1932, however, he had to admit that these measures had failed.

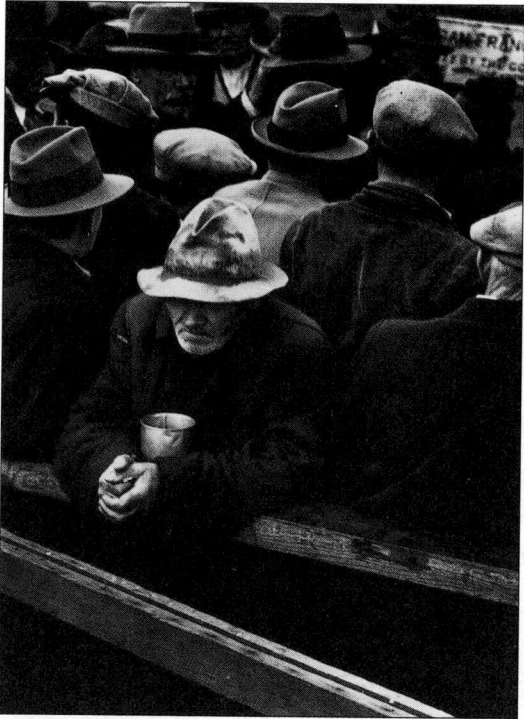

"Why should I be standing on line?" Dorothea Lange described "White Angel Bread Line" as her most famous photograph and added that life for people in 1932 had begun to crumble on the edges. *According to Yip Harburg's lyrics, what might some of these men have done before the Depression?*

VISUAL INSTRUCTION

"Why should I be standing on line?" Lange was known for the exceptional naturalness of her photos. She said, "I have this gray coat that I put on, and I just disappear and don't even look anybody in the eye, and am just concerned with the camera and not with the people and they let me go ahead and I do what I want."

Answer: *Some of the men might have been farmers, soldiers, railroad workers, or construction workers.*

FYI

Insured Savings
Students may not realize that bank failures on the scale of those that occurred during the Depression are no longer feared. The Federal Deposit Insurance Corporation (established in 1933) now insures accounts up to $100,000 in banks that are members of the Federal Reserve System.

Critical Thinking

Demonstrating Reasoned Judgment
Discuss with students whether the government has an obligation to control the way banks and savings and loans invest their money if the government is going to insure these financial organizations. Does government insurance mean that there should also be government regulation?

ASSESS

Trying to respond to the deepening economic crisis, Hoover obtained congressional approval for a federal relief agency called the Reconstruction Finance Corporation (RFC) in February 1932. The RFC was the largest federal program of economic aid that any President had ever proposed. The agency was authorized to dispense $2 billion in loans to faltering banks, insurance companies, and railroads. Hoover hoped that the RFC would inspire confidence in business. The theory was that funding such institutions would stimulate industry and eventually create more jobs.

The trickle-down measure, however, could not relieve the immediate suffering of the unemployed. The Emergency Relief Act, passed in July 1932, enabled the RFC to distribute an additional $300 million in loans to state governments for unemployment relief. These governments did not qualify for RFC loans, however, unless they were on the verge of bankruptcy. By the end of the year, the RFC had distributed only half of its available money.

Mounting Protests

With wages dropping, unemployment growing, and so little money trickling into relief measures, resentment grew among people beaten down by the Depression. One group, veterans of the Great War, organized a massive lobbying effort to get aid for themselves and their families. The government had promised these veterans a bonus for serving in the war, payable in 1945. Organizing themselves into disciplined companies, a group of jobless veterans from Portland, Oregon, traveled to Washington, D.C., in May 1932 to try to persuade Congress to grant them their bonus 13 years early. The bonus army, as this group was called, enforced strict rules to keep the movement united and respectable. Among these rules were "no panhandling, no drinking, and no radicalism."

The group from Portland started with 1,000 veterans. By the time Congress was to vote on the bonus in June, the ranks of the bonus army had swelled to 17,000. Setting up camp in abandoned buildings in Washington, D.C., and on the marshy flats along the shores of the Anacostia River, the veterans remained orderly. Many veterans had brought their families with them. Wives set up housekeeping while the children made new friends from all over the country.

On June 17, the day the Senate was slated to vote on the bonus bill, the veterans marched to the Capitol steps to await the outcome. Late in the afternoon, Senator Elmer Thomas of Oklahoma appeared on the Capitol steps and told the leader of the group, Walter W. Waters, that the bill had been defeated. As the men began to hiss and boo, Waters took charge: "Let us show them that we can take it on the chin. Let us show them that we are patriotic Americans. I call on you to sing 'America.'" Thousands of the men joined in singing and then formed ranks and marched back to their camps.

With the bonus bill dead, several thousand veterans left Washington. About 2,000 remained throughout the month, however, hoping that the bill would be revived before the congressional session ended in July. After Congress again refused to approve the bonus bill, the veterans slowly began to disperse. They did not leave quickly enough for Hoover, however, who saw the bonus army as a hostile force. On July 28, Hoover dispatched Army Chief of Staff Douglas MacArthur and his aide

AP/WIDE WORLD PHOTOS

The Bonus Army Led by Walter W. Waters, veterans of World War I marched peacefully from Portland, Oregon, to Washington, D.C., to lobby for early payment of their promised benefits. *How was the military training of these men reflected in their protest?*

Hostile Reception Bonus-seeking veterans were attacked by soldiers near the veterans' makeshift shacks in the Anacostia Flats, approximately three miles from the White House. *How did Hoover respond to the bonus army?*

VISUAL INSTRUCTION

Hostile Reception After Congress had adjourned without action on the bonus bill, the mood of the remaining veterans grew angry. They picketed the White House and occupied vacant federal buildings, increasing tension within the Hoover administration.

Answer: *He was afraid they might be hostile. He sent federal troops to remove them.*

Dwight D. Eisenhower to clear the veterans from the federal buildings. Cavalry units, tanks, infantry with fixed bayonets, and a machine-gun detachment marched on the unarmed veterans. Fleeing in terror, the veterans crossed the Anacostia River to the bonus army encampments. MacArthur pursued the veterans and torched the camp. More than 100 people were injured and a baby died, asphyxiated by tear gas. The press, appalled at the brutal attack, commented: "What a pitiful spectacle is that of the great American Government, mightiest in the world, chasing unarmed men, women, and children with Army tanks."

The Election of 1932

The routing of the bonus army was the last nail in Hoover's political coffin. The public, which already considered the President cold and unfeeling because he refused to pay for unemployment relief, now saw him also as a vicious bully. On hearing about the attack on the veterans at Anacostia by MacArthur's troops, Democratic presidential candidate Franklin D. Roosevelt turned to his friend Felix Frankfurter and said, "Well, Felix, this will elect me."

Roosevelt's prediction proved correct. Hoover stayed in Washington through most of the campaign. When he did make public appearances, he was often booed into retreat. On Election Day, on his way to vote, people hurling stink bombs attacked his car. Roosevelt won the presidency by a landslide. Herbert Hoover, for all of his early optimism and organizational skills, was defeated by the Depression and its crushing economic problems.

SECTION REVIEW

Vocabulary

1. Define: stock, speculation, margin, depression, unemployment.

Checking Facts

2. Describe weaknesses within the system of stock market investing prior to the Depression.

3. Describe Hoover's efforts to deal with the Depression.

Critical Thinking

Determining Cause and Effect
4. Discuss the major causes of the Depression.

Linking Across Time

5. Today investors can buy securities on 50 percent margin if they can guarantee that they have collateral or property equal in value to the remaining 50 percent. How might this practice have prevented some of the problems that led to the stock market crash?

Section 1 Review Answers

1. stock (418), **speculation** (419), **margin** (420), **depression** (421), **unemployment** (421)
2. investments based on borrowed funds and extension of credit; no collateral or insurance required
3. urged voluntary action and local programs; RFC; Emergency Relief Act

4. speculation; farm and industrial overproduction and underconsumption; unequal distribution of wealth; flawed monetary policy; decline in foreign trade
5. Higher margin and collateral requirements would have made default less likely.

Evaluate

Have students complete the Section Review.

📁 📀 Assign the Section 1 Quiz or use the Testmaker to develop a customized quiz. (Also in Spanish.) **LEP**

Reteach

🎧 Have students listen to the Chapter 13, Section 1 Audiocassette. **LEP**

Enrich

📁 Have students complete the Chapter 13 Geography in History Activity.

CLOSE

As you discuss the section with students, ask: How did the stock market crash cause unemployment? What factors other than the crash contributed to the Depression? To help students answer these questions, have them review the graphic on page 421.

TEACH

Making the Historical Connection

Although there had been signs of economic trouble brewing, much of the United States was thriving and optimistic during the 1920s. The crash meant the end of high spirits and high hopes. Comedian Harpo Marx, who went broke in the crash, remarked: "Life would no longer be, ever again, all fun and games. The bam-bang-sock-and-pow part was over, and so was the permanent, floating New Year's Eve party."

FYI

Saving the Market
Some of the country's leading financiers had tried to avert the crash by pumping money into the market, but others seemed to be more interested in profiting from the panic. The president of Chase National Bank sold 42,506 shares of his own bank, bought them back later in the year at a lower price, and made a profit of $4 million.

SPORTS: Babe Ruth of the New York Yankees hits 500th home run.

One Day in History

Tuesday, October 29, 1929

MARKET BASKET

Here is where a dollar will go:

Average cost to produce a
  Hollywood film . . . $360,000
One-year subscription to a
  survey of best stocks .. $65
Double room at the
  Lexington Hotel, N.Y.C. .. $5
Dinner at a Hollywood
  restaurant $1.50

W.L. HAMILTON/SUPERSTOCK

Studebaker automobile . . . . .
  . . . . $1,185–$2,350
Boston to New York one way
  via rail or boat $4
Movie ticket . . . . 25¢–75¢
Phonograph record . . . . . 50¢
Bottle of Moxie . . . . . 9¢ small
  . . . . 15¢ large
Daily local newspaper . . . . 2¢

ARCHIVE PHOTOS

Pair of shoes . . . . $2–$5
One dozen oranges . . . . . . 39¢
Loaf of bread . . . . 9¢
One pound of ham . . . . . . 50¢

Panic Looms Large: Today's stock market activity caused so much chaos and confusion that analysts are already calling the day "Black Tuesday."

Stocks Hit the Skids

Market sees biggest losses yet

NEW YORK—Trading in record numbers today on the New York Stock Exchange, investors rushed to sell. Despite last week's optimism and the efforts of bankers to pump money into the market, today's activity brought the panic that everyone had feared since Thursday's crash. On the brink of ruin, investors collectively unloaded 16,338,000 shares. By the end of the day, prices had plummeted $14 billion.

One man on the street was overheard muttering to himself, "Don't tell me it's going up. It's down and it's going down. It will never go up again." A New York drugstore owner reports leaving his store because of "hysterical demands for sleeping potions, sedatives, and other nerve potions." On Broadway, a young marketeer was seen unsuccessfully hawking his $12,000 Duesenberg automobile for $1,500 in cash.

Meanwhile, rumors say that John D. Rockefeller, Jr., has been quietly liquidating his stocks for weeks.

Background Information

That's Entertainment It would take time for the full effects of the crash to be felt. In the meantime, it was business as usual in the entertainment industry. The show business periodical *Variety*, in its characteristically irreverent style, ran the headline WALL ST. LAYS AN EGG, then went on, under the headline WORLD'S SAPPIEST CITY, to claim that community entertainers in Brooklyn's theaters—"the world's premiere laboratory of hokum"—were unmatched for "gusto, unanimity, endurance, insatiability and dumbness."

One Day in History, Tuesday, October 29, 1929

One Day in History

NATION: Madame Curie visits White House to receive America's gift of $50,000. The money will buy a gram of radium for cancer research.

Byrd Explores the South Pole

LITTLE AMERICA, Antarctica—Commander Richard E. Byrd has built an air base at his Little America camp on the Ross Ice Shelf. From here he plans to fly over the South Pole, matching his feat of being the first to fly over the North Pole. His party is currently exploring by snowmobile, and fighting frostbite.

Commander Richard E. Byrd

Happy Days?

HOLLYWOOD—By bizarre coincidence, the Casa Loma Orchestra recorded a new tune today heralding cheerful times. The song, "Happy Days Are Here Again," couldn't have come at a more needed time, but the lyrics just don't ring true on this unhappy day. Milton Ager and Jack Yellen wrote the tune for the film *Chasing Rainbows.*

MUSIC

Popular Songs of 1929:

"Stardust" by Hoagy Carmichael, Mitchell Parish

"St. James Infirmary" by Joe Primrose

"Honeysuckle Rose" by Fats Waller, Andy Razaf

"Ain't Misbehavin'" by Fats Waller

RADIO

Premieres:

- *The Back Home Hour*
- *The Fleischmann Hour* (with Rudy Vallee)
- *The Rise of the Goldbergs*
- *The Hour of Charm* (with Phil Spitalny and his all-girl orchestra)

Wisecracking, roughhousing Marx Brothers complete their first film, *The Cocoanuts.* Filming takes place between performances of their current Broadway hit, *Animal Crackers.*

$5 Down! 52 Weeks to Pay! **Trade in your old radio or Victrola for $20–$75 toward a *NEW* Jackson-Bell radio!**

"Peter Pan" model: $85.00

ONE DAY IN HISTORY **429**

TIME CAPSULE

1929

AMERICAN LIFE

January 15: Kellogg-Briand Pact outlaws war; Frank Billings Kellogg, U.S. secretary of state, later wins Nobel Peace Prize.

February 14: Seven of the "Bugs" Moran gang are gunned down in "St. Valentine's Day Massacre" in Chicago.

July–August: Helen Wills wins Wimbledon and U.S. Open tennis titles, each for the third consecutive time.

September 24: Lt. James H. Doolittle makes first flight using instruments only.

October 8–14: Philadelphia Athletics win World Series.

October 23: First transcontinental all-air flight, New York to Los Angeles, takes 36 hours with overnight stop.

Publishing: Ernest Hemingway's *A Farewell to Arms,* Thomas Wolfe's *Look Homeward, Angel,* and William Faulkner's *Sartoris* are published.

Broadcasting: William S. Paley founds CBS.

CLOSE

Discuss "Black Tuesday." Ask: Would a stock market crash today have as great an effect on national life? *(Probably not; the market is better regulated.)* What are some modern explorations akin to Byrd's? *(space; deep-sea)*

Oral History

Interview Show students examples of oral history such as the work of Studs Terkel, including his recent *Coming of Age.* Have them interview an older person, asking what that person remembers from earlier years about some crisis or turning point in American life. (Students are unlikely to find anyone who recalls the 1929 crash, but they may find someone who recalls hearing a firsthand account from a parent.) Students should write up their interview notes, including a description of the person being interviewed. Volunteers can share their notes with the class before putting them in their portfolios.

429

SECTION
2

FOCUS

Section Objectives

1. Tell how the Depression affected rural and urban families differently.
2. Describe how communities responded to hardship.
3. Explain upheaval in the family during the Depression.

Bellringer Activity

While taking attendance at the beginning of the class period, display **Section Focus Transparency 41,** and have students answer the questions.(Or use the blackline master.)

VISUAL INSTRUCTION

Black Blizzard Dry, hot weather, and depletion of plant life are the two biggest causes of dust storms. Cutting plants and trees can stimulate loss of soil because roots hold topsoil in place.

Ask: What were some of the short- and long-term effects of the dust storms? *(Dust storms lifted topsoil, buried fields, roads, and equipment, and, in the long run, destroyed crops and ruined farmers.)*

The Dream on Hold

APRIL 14, 1935: DUST STORM SOCKS MEADE COUNTY, KANSAS

Black Blizzard
Lifting topsoil from a farmer's wheat fields, this dust storm obscures the sun's light.

ONE PERSON THOUGHT THAT LIFE ITSELF WAS COMING TO AN END. Another was sure that Judgment Day had arrived. A third simply brought her rocking chair to the center of her living room and waited out the storm. She was content because the tape over her window frames was blocking out almost every particle of dust. She boasted that under such conditions "almost any housewife could have died happily."

On Sunday, April 14, 1935, one of the biggest dust storms of this century swept over the Great Plains of the United States. Huge black clouds of dust, more than 1,000 feet (304.8 m) high, formed a wall miles wide. Birds flew frantically trying to escape suffocation in the roiling storm. Motorists were stranded for hours along the highway, totally blinded by the impenetrable cloud. The rain sent mud balls splattering to the ground. Dust from the "black blizzard" piled up on railroad lines, and it took snowplows several days to clear off the tracks.

Dust storms like these plagued the Great Plains during the drought years of 1932 to 1939. Especially hard hit were the Dakotas, Nebraska, Kansas, Oklahoma, eastern Colorado and New Mexico, and the Texas Panhandle. Burying crops and killing livestock, the natural disasters of dust storms and drought worked in tandem with the economic disaster of the Depression to bring thousands of farmers to financial ruin. Although Dust Bowl farmers were among the hardest hit, farmers throughout the country suffered severe hardship during the Depression.

AS YOU READ

Vocabulary
► foreclosure
► penny auction
► repatriation

Think About . . .
► how the Depression affected people differently in rural and urban areas.
► the ways communities responded to the sudden arrival of hard times.
► how men, women, and families were each affected differently by the economy.

430 CHAPTER 13 THE GREAT DEPRESSION

Section 2 Resources

REPRODUCIBLE RESOURCES
📁 Lesson Plan 13-2
📁 Vocabulary and Guided Reading Activity 13-2
📁 Section 2 Quiz
📁 Unit 5 American Literature Reading
📁 Skill Reinforcement Activity 13

MULTIMEDIA RESOURCES
💡 Section Focus Transparency 41
💿 Testmaker
💿 Student Self-Test: A Software Review
🎧 Chapter 13 Digest Audiocassette

On the Farms
From Foreclosures to Migration

Heading into their second decade of economic depression, farmers received severely low prices for their crops. Falling incomes made it impossible for many to pay their mortgages. A bank that held an unpaid farm loan would have a **foreclosure,** whereby it would take back ownership of the property without letting the farmer pay off the rest of the mortgage. In the early years of the Depression, thousands of farmers lost their land. As the Depression deepened, however, some of the farmers thought of their own inventive ways to get around their financial problems. One Iowan recalled how farmers connived to resist the foreclosures by the banks, saying, "[The] mortgaging of farms was getting home to us. . . . [The bankers would] put up a farmer's property and have a sale." He continued:

A ll the neighbors'd come in, and they got the idea of spending twenty-five cents for a horse. They was paying ten cents for a plow. And when it was all over, they'd all give it [the property] back to him [the farmer being foreclosed upon]. It was legal and anybody that bid against that thing, that was trying to get that man's land, they would be dealt with seriously, as it were.

—Harry Terrell, in *Hard Times*

Penny auctions—staged sales of property for pennies to friends, who simply returned it later—helped some farmers stay on their land. Borrowing money from relatives saved the farms of others. On the drought-ridden plains, however, where for seven successive years crops were pulverized, thousands of farmers had no choice but to abandon their fields. The Okies, as these Great Plains farmers were called, headed west in search of a better life for themselves and their families.

Migration of the Okies

The plight of the Okies dramatized that of the desperately unemployed throughout the United States. They exhausted any savings they had. They sacrificed everything they owned except what they could carry with them. Uprooted, the Okies drifted anywhere they thought they might have a chance to find work. California, with its huge farms, lured many. Leaflets advertising jobs for seasonal work drew them onward, across the highways. A writer late in the 1930s described it this way:

T hey came along U.S. Highway 30 through the Idaho hills, along Highway 66 across New Mexico and Arizona, along the Old Spanish Trail through El Paso, along all the other westward trails. They came in decrepit, square-shouldered 1925 Dodges and 1927 La Salles; in battered 1923 Model-T Fords that looked like relics of some antique culture; in trucks piled high with mattresses and cooking utensils and children, with suitcases, jugs, and sacks strapped to the running boards.

—Frederick Lewis Allen,
Since Yesterday

When they reached California, the Okies were in for even more hard times. Although a few jobs were

MIGRATIONS OF THE OKIES

The Okies traveled two major routes to reach California. Both the Rockies and the Sierra Nevadas lay between the Dust Bowl and the West Coast. *At what points did these routes diverge or connect?*

TEACH

Guided Practice

L2 **Role Play** To help students anticipate how the Depression would affect people on farms and in cities, have them role-play different responses. Have students choose an occupation in a rural or urban area such as: a Hollywood writer, a New York stockbroker, a Tennessee sharecropper. Several students can improvise a scene in a highway diner. Start the scene by playing the role of a radio announcer, broadcasting news about the stock market crash, and ask students to play out their responses in character. Suggest that they include discussion of impending events that might worsen or improve their conditions. **LEP**

MAP STUDY

Have students name the states they would pass through on the way from Albuquerque to Seattle. *(Arizona, California, Oregon)* Discuss with students why highways 30 and 66 followed northern and southern routes to the West Coast *(The highest mountain peaks and driest desert are in the middle latitudes.)*

Answer: *intersection at Portland, Oregon; divergence in Southern California*

Cooperative Learning

Readers' Theater Have different groups of students select passages from Steinbeck's *The Grapes of Wrath* to read aloud in readers' theater productions. Ask them to rehearse a few times through, perform the passage for the class, and finish by telling why they chose the selected passage.

Independent Practice

L2 Writing an Argument
Have students imagine they are defending a Mexican American family faced with deportation. They should write an opening statement to be presented in court. Some students may wish to write counterarguments representing the hostile sentiments of some farmworkers.

☞ Have students complete Chapter 13, Section 2 Vocabulary and Guided Reading Activity. (Also in Spanish.) **LEP**

available, competition for those jobs was fierce. With Okies entering the state by the hundreds daily, the number of unemployed in the labor market quickly skyrocketed. Yet, bouncing down rutted roads, driven by hope and false rumor, the Okies still kept coming. For the California farm owners, the migration of the Okies was a boon. The owners could lower wages nearly to starvation levels and still find takers for the most wretched of jobs. Huddled on the outskirts of farm towns, luckless Okies without employment set up temporary camps. People living within the towns often saw these unemployed as dirty, ignorant outsiders and sent the police to dislodge them. Bitter and dispirited, the Okies continued their migration, wandering up and down the West Coast, searching for a lucky break.

Tenant Farmers

The farm crisis of the 1930s also hit tenant farmers, most of whom lived in the South. Tenant farmers did not own the land that they farmed. Therefore they were extremely vulnerable to changes in the farm economy during the thirties.

As the Depression dragged on, the government began to pay landowners to let some of their land lie fallow, or go unplanted. This reduced surplus crops, causing prices for those remaining crops to rise. Most landowners decided to take out of production the land their tenant farmers used rather than the land they used. Tenant farmers lost their jobs and were also thrown off the land where some had worked and lived for many years. Also, as landowners used their government checks to buy farm equipment such as tractors and cultivators, they no longer needed year-round farmhands. Instead, they would hire a few day laborers on a temporary basis for the essential seasonal work.

The following letter, from a Georgia farmer to a government relief official, highlights the tenant farmers' situation:

> I have Bin farming all my life. But the man I live with Has Turned me loose taking my mule [and] all my feed. . . . I have 7 in my family. I ploud up cotton last yeare. I can rent 9 acres and plant. . . . But I haven't got a mule [or] no feed.
> —From a letter to Harry Hopkins

Sharecroppers These former farmers of Caruthersville, Missouri, have been evicted and are forced to move on. *What made a tenant farmer so vulnerable?*

Evicted from the farms, with little hope of finding work with other landowners, tenant farmers and their families took to the roads to look for work, often leaving behind many possessions of a lifetime. Since most of the African Americans living in the South had been tenant farmers, they suffered disproportionately from the upheaval in agriculture. However, white tenant farmers suffered severe hardship as well.

Mexican American Workers

The tenant farmers were not the only group who faced discrimination during the Depression. Mexican Americans, many of whose families had been in this country for several generations, found themselves branded illegal aliens, foreigners who had no right to live and work in the United States.

Although farm owners in California welcomed a surplus of Mexican and Mexican American migrant workers to help keep wages low during the harvest season, city officials wanted to send all people of Mexican descent back to Mexico. For example, between 1931 and 1934, Los Angeles officials rounded up more than 12,000 people of Mexican descent and forced them to return to Mexico. A number were United States citizens. Nevertheless, they were denied their legal rights and threatened with deportation if they refused to leave on their own. With no choice in the matter, many Mexican Americans gathered their belongings and boarded the government-sponsored trains that dumped them across the border.

Mexicans and Mexican Americans living in the Southwest and Texas also faced increased discrimination and threats of deportation during the Depression years. Many were agricultural workers caught in the crunch of the depressed farm economy of the United States. Out of work, they fled to the cities to apply for relief. Here, they were easy prey for immigration officials, who denied them fair hearings and summarily deported them. Seeing the hopelessness of the situation, many Mexican Americans decided to seek **repatriation,** or return to a former homeland, and they applied to the Mexican consulate for permission to return. In Austin, Texas, for example, 60 percent of all people of Mexican descent had returned to Mexico by January 1931.

In the City
Jobless, Homeless, and Penniless

The prospect for people without jobs was just as bleak in the cities as on the farms. By 1933 one of every four people was out of work. In some cities, however, the jobless rate soared above the national level. Unemployment ran 30 percent in Buffalo, 50 percent in Chicago and Cleveland, and 80 percent in Toledo.

Evidence of the economic crisis was clearly visible in most cities. "For Rent" notices festooned closed-down shop windows. Apple sellers hawked their wares on street corners. These unemployed men and women had bought

AP/WIDE WORLD PHOTOS

On Every Corner Fred Bell, known as "Champagne Fred" in San Francisco, had inherited a fortune in the 1920s, but in 1931 he joined the ranks selling apples on the street. *How did many people who had no money acquire bushels of produce to sell?*

SECTION TWO **433**

Portfolio Project

Mapping Migrations Have students create maps indicating one migration pattern of the Depression. A pattern might show movement from farms to cities, from Southeastern regions to Northern ones, from the Southwestern states to Mexico, or from the Midwest to the West. Students can research the routes by using historical atlases and texts, or by interviewing older community members. They can accompany the maps with one-page first-person narratives, describing one part of the trip as if they were undergoing the journey themselves. After sharing their maps and stories, students should add these pieces to their portfolios.

surplus apples on credit from Pacific Coast apple growers and hoped to sell the fruit to passersby at a small profit. Those with less of an entrepreneurial spirit turned to panhandling. Beggars roved the sidewalks in most cities, accosting better-off citizens for spare change.

The most telling sign of the Depression, however, was the absence of activity. In the most depressed areas, factory smokestacks spewed no smoke. Loading docks received no deliveries. Construction sites were eerily silent, the skeletons of half-finished buildings rusting in the rain. Pedestrians slowed their pace. Time seemed to dawdle during the Depression years. This was especially true for the unemployed who had little but time on their hands.

Unemployed Workers

Despite promises to President Hoover to keep factories running full tilt, many factory owners began to lay off workers after a year or two of economic decline. The layoffs followed a pattern. African Americans and members of other minorities were usually the first to lose their jobs. Next, full-time employees were asked to share their jobs with others. Then, even these scaled-down jobs were cut.

With wage reductions many working people were no better off than people who qualified for relief. In many cities the jobless and those with jobs became economic equals.

To reduce living expenses, people moved in with relatives. As many as 15 people would crowd into an apartment built for a couple or a family of 3. Evictions of renters who could not make their monthly payments were so common in some neighborhoods that children invented a new game based on their own experience:

They would pile all the doll furniture up first in one corner and then in another. "We ain't got no money for the rent, so we's moved into a new house," a tot explained to the teacher. "Then we got the constable on us, so we's moving again."
—Caroline Bird, *The Invisible Scar*

Just as these children adapted to their transient situation by making a game out of it, people from all levels of society had to adapt to immense changes and learn how to do without. People lost their jobs, their homes, most of their possessions, but still they survived. Among the saddest and most touching testaments to hu-

Living in Hoovervilles People called shantytown slums Hoovervilles, newspapers became Hoover blankets, and empty pockets turned inside out were Hoover flags. *What other makeshift plans did people devise when they faced losing their homes?*

434   CHAPTER 13 THE GREAT DEPRESSION

man adaptability and survival were the makeshift cities that sprang up on the fringes of metropolitan areas. People sarcastically nicknamed these communities Hoovervilles.

Hoovervilles and the Homeless

During the early years of the Depression, the number of homeless people in the United States skyrocketed. Although no one ever took an official census, it was estimated that by 1932 about 2 million people were on the road, job seekers and their families looking for work and a place to settle. At least that many had constructed temporary or not-so-temporary shelters in Hoovervilles. One woman described her amazement when she first saw the sprawling Hooverville in Oklahoma City:

H ere were all these people living in old, rusted-out car bodies. I mean that was their home. There were people living in shacks made of orange crates. One family with a whole lot of kids were living in a piano box. This wasn't just a little section, this was maybe ten-miles wide and ten-miles long. People living in what ever they could junk together.

—Peggy Terry, in *Hard Times*

For some, life on the Hooverville streets was squalid beyond belief. Garbage scraps were all these poor people could scrounge for food. For other people life was simple and pleasant. They kept their homes, however humble, sparkling clean and shared food with neighbors.

Helping others became a way of life, even among people who had not previously known each other. Those who did know each other often developed a trust that transcended the hard times. A young girl, orphaned during the Depression, remembered her friendship with the owners of a local grocery store.

L ouise was a Bohemian girl. Her mother had a grocery store that they lived behind. Louise used to do the books, and there was always owing. You never said to the people: "Do you have the money to pay me?" They would say, "Write it in the book." And you wrote it in the book, because this was their family food, and they had to have it. It wasn't that you were giving it away. Eventually, you'd be paid.

—Dorothe Bernstein, in *Hard Times*

The Better-Off

Even relatively well-to-do people sometimes had to depend on the aid and charity of their neighbors during the Depression. For example, people who owned rental property did not qualify for food supplements in most city relief programs. Unable to collect rents, some landlords let their unemployed tenants stay on for free, and the tenants shared their food with the landlord.

Nevertheless, people who were wealthy before the Depression had much greater chances of weathering the economic storm and coming out with minimal financial damage. Such people might have had to sell a summer home or give up a vacation trip. They might have had to postpone buying a new car or forgo the latest fashions. Most were able to make ends meet, however, and live a comfortable, if less luxurious, life.

A handful of people took advantage of the rock-bottom prices brought on by the Depression to increase their wealth. For example, J. Paul Getty eventually became one of the richest men in the world by buying up oil companies at bargain prices during the 1930s. Such people were the exception.

For most Americans the loss of money and material possessions was not nearly as damaging as the sense of lost hope and pride brought on by years of unemployment or underemployment. These losses, along with changing roles and expectations, were most apparent within families.

In the Family
Making Do With Less

In many families the father—the traditional provider—lost status and self-esteem during the Depression. With loss of income, many men were no longer able to support their families or maintain their former lifestyles. Some hid out at home, discouraged, listless, and cranky. Others hit the pavement every day, hoping against hope to land a new job. Still others set themselves daily tasks to keep busy. One person remembered:

M y father spent two years painting his father's house. He painted it twice. It gave him something to do. It prevented him from losing all his—well, I wouldn't say self-respect, because there were many, many people who were also out of work. He wasn't alone.

—Bob Leary, in *Hard Times*

The Woman's World

Women, traditionally taking the role of homemakers, suffered less upheaval throughout the Depression years. Their families came to depend on them even more during those lean years, because their efforts at economizing kept many families from starvation. Many

ASSESS

Meeting Lesson Objectives

Each section objective is tested by the section review question(s) that follows it in parentheses.

1. Tell how the Depression affected rural and urban families differently. (1, 2)
2. Describe how communities responded to hardship. (1, 2, 3, 5)
3. Explain upheaval in the family during the Depression. (3, 4)

Evaluate

Have students complete the Section Review.

☞ 🖳 Assign the Section 2 Quiz or use the Testmaker to develop a customized quiz. (Also in Spanish.) **LEP**

Reteach

🎧 Have students listen to the Chapter 13, Section 2 Audiocassette. **LEP**

Enrich

☞ Have students complete the Unit 5 American Literature Reading.

Cultural Perspectives

Cooperating to Survive Acting selflessly is a survival mechanism for groups as a whole. Often the most selfless people are those who have the least. In *The Grapes of Wrath,* Ma Joad says, "If you're in trouble or hurt or need—go to poor people. They're the only ones that'll help." Students can discuss or write about why they feel acting selflessly might be a group survival mechanism. Does it work for minorities within larger groups? Have students use examples to support their analysis.

435

ARCHIVE PHOTOS

Women on the Job In spite of rising unemployment, the number of women in the workforce increased. *How did unemployment for men and women contribute to domestic upheaval?*

CLOSE

From farms to cities, some of the same effects of hard times that were felt in the 1930s still exist today. For example, the controversy caused by some people being willing to work for lower wages still continues. The fear that immigrants will work for lower wages still causes immigration restrictions. Ask students to discuss other ways that hard times now are similar to those of the Depression years. *(Answers will vary. Students may suggest high levels of unemployment, current farming problems in the Great Plains, homelessness, and the debate over relief programs.)*

eled in search of work, and Hope herself worked in town in exchange for board.

On weekends and holidays, I'd go traipsin' up to grandma's and we'd all be together, the whole family; and everybody played an instrument and we sang. We just got closer as a family during that time.

—Hope Moat, in *Making Do: How Women Survived the '30s* by Jeane Westin

Although some people came away from the Depression with an increased sense of inner strength or with stronger bonds to their family, for most the Depression was aptly named. It was a time of psychological and spiritual as well as economic depression. People stayed home and avoided socializing, ashamed of their worn clothes or their decline in fortune. Young people put off getting married, and married couples avoided having children. Undernourishment in children was common throughout the country. Milk consumption dropped in state after state. Economic factors shaped these choices, but so did a deep lack of hope and faith in the future. Everywhere, health officials reported that at the city and state levels child welfare and public nursing were usually the first services to be cut. During the 1930s deep despair entered the grain of American life. Some have called the Depression an invisible scar, one that, though unseen, would take many years to heal.

women revived traditional home crafts, such as canning vegetables, drying food, and sewing clothes. They started home industries, such as taking in laundry, selling baked goods, or renting out rooms to boarders. In many families not only did women run the household, but they also held a job outside the home.

During the Depression women faced increasing discrimination in professional fields. Jobs that traditionally went to women, however, such as clerical work and retail sales, did not decline as extensively as professional and manufacturing jobs that traditionally went to men. Therefore, many employment opportunities were open to women during the 1930s. Throughout the Depression the number of working women grew in the United States.

Growing Up in the Thirties

Domestic upheaval, with many fathers unemployed and many mothers working long hours for low wages, took its toll on families. The Depression tore some families apart. Many of the hoboes who hitchhiked across the country on freight trains were unemployed men who had at first set out in search of work in other parts of the country. Unsuccessful and ashamed to return home, they deserted their families and lived together in hobo camps along the side of the railroad tracks.

With other families hard times actually brought family members closer. Hope Moat's family, from Cincinnati, Ohio, lost everything during the Depression, and they had to split up. Hope's mother and brother went to live with her grandparents on their farm. Her father trav-

SECTION REVIEW

Vocabulary

1. Define: foreclosure, penny auction, repatriation.

Checking Facts

2. What conditions led to the establishment of Hoovervilles?

3. Discuss three ways the Depression affected women's roles in the family.

Critical Thinking

Predicting Consequences

4. Discuss both the economic and the psychological effects of the Depression on a typical American family.

Linking Across Time

5. Although the current economic picture differs greatly from that of the Great Depression, there are still people who are unemployed. Suggest reasons for unemployment in the United States today. In your opinion what, if anything, should the government be doing about current unemployment?

Social Studies Skill

DRAWING INFERENCES FROM MAPS

Learning the Skill

A logical conclusion derived from facts is called an inference. Maps present facts in a visual format; the map on this page shows precipitation and temperature from 1932 through 1939, years when dust storms swept across the Great Plains. From this information you can make inferences about the causes of those storms.

How to Make an Inference

To make an inference, follow these steps:

a. Study the map key, which explains what the colored numerals mean. Plus and minus symbols tell whether the deviation was above or below normal.

b. Note the location of the Dust Bowl. You can see that every weather station in the Dust Bowl area and most stations in the surrounding area recorded decreased precipitation and increased temperatures.

c. From this data you might infer that drastically decreased precipitation and increased temperatures contributed to the dust storms. This inference is correct.

d. Examine the map for other possible inferences.

Practicing the Skill

1. Which was a more important cause of the dust storms—low precipitation or high temperatures?

2. Would you expect to find worse crop damage in North Dakota or in Oklahoma?

3. What would you infer about how well California agriculture fared during the decade?

4. What would you infer about farming conditions in South Carolina at the time?

5. What facts suggest that rainfall and temperature were not the only causes of the Dust Bowl?

Applying the Skill

Find a map in one of your textbooks and make an inference from it, using the facts shown in the map to support your inference.

Additional Practice

For additional practice, see Reinforcing Skills on page 449.

TEACH

In this feature students learn to make logical inferences based on the facts shown on a map. Students will look at a United States map with data about temperature and precipitation levels in the 1930s and make inferences related to the Dust Bowl.

Point out that the Dust Bowl was one of the most cataclysmic events in the history of American agriculture. Studying this map will help students understand some of the underlying causes.

MAP STUDY

Point out to students that the map contains no data about winds or farming practices, other causes of Dust Bowl conditions that they can read about on pages 438–439.

Answer: *eight: Texas, New Mexico, Colorado, Wyoming, South Dakota, Nebraska, Kansas, and Oklahoma*

Additional Practice

Have students complete the Chapter 13 Skill Reinforcement Activity.

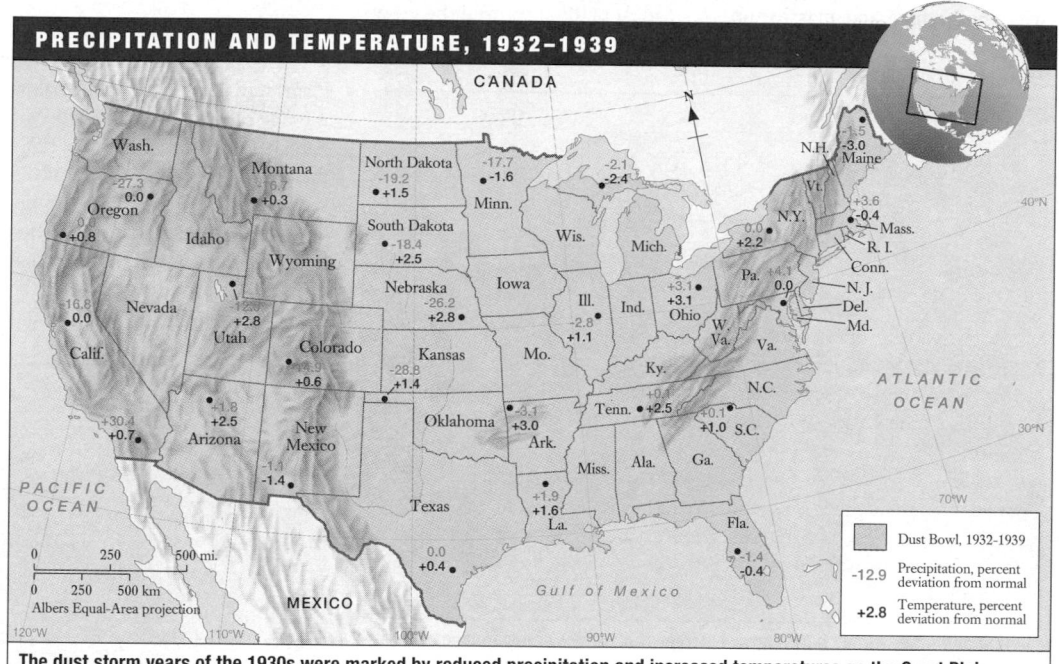

PRECIPITATION AND TEMPERATURE, 1932–1939

The dust storm years of the 1930s were marked by reduced precipitation and increased temperatures on the Great Plains. *How many states were affected by Dust Bowl conditions?*

Practicing the Skill Answers

1. The unusually low precipitation seems to have been a more important cause of the dust storms.

2. Crop damage would be worse in Oklahoma.

3. California would have fared relatively well. Although northern California had less precipitation than usual, southern California had more than usual; temperatures were normal.

4. Farming conditions would have been normal in South Carolina; temperature and precipitation were close to normal.

5. Some states such as Oregon and Minnesota had below-normal precipitation but did not experience Dust Bowl conditions.

Making the Geography Connection

During the Depression a natural disaster could be unusually devastating, causing total property damage to people who had no means to recover financially. For farmers in the Dust Bowl, natural cycles of dry, hot weather, started a chain of catastrophe: crop failures, wind storms, soil erosion, loss of land, and a long hard journey West. Ask students why soil erosion could cause a farm to be worthless to its owner.

VISUAL INSTRUCTION

Before and After The barns on this Beadle County farm were drifted with dust up to 6-feet deep in 1935. The same farm 2 years later shows a healthy growth of Sudan grass and cane, planted in cooperation with the Soil Conservation Service. The new growth prevented further wind erosion and made reoccupation of the farm possible.

Answer: *periods of dry hot weather; the flat, semi-arid features of plains*

Geography: Impact on History

REGION

The Dust Bowl

With Manifest Destiny achieved, Americans thought that they had conquered the continent. The Dust Bowl of the 1930s proved them wrong. The devastation of the Dust Bowl taught people that nature cannot simply be conquered—it must be adapted to and protected.

The Prairie Ecosystem and the Prairie Farms

The Great Plains is a semidesert region lying in the "rain shadow" of the Rocky Mountains. The rain shadow is the lee side of a mountain barrier, which receives much less precipitation than the windward side. Weather systems moving up from the Gulf of Mexico and down from the Arctic collide over the prairie, causing storms with high winds and massive updrafts.

The native grasses of the Great Plains grew deep roots, which enabled them to survive fires and to hold moisture in the soil. These grasses formed a thick, dense sod that sheltered the soil from wind and rain erosion. Thus the soil and the grasses protected each other.

After the Louisiana Purchase (1803), Americans began to settle west of the Mississippi. The Homestead Act (1862) spurred the growing movement to "conquer" the prairie. The "sodbusters" plowed up the sod and planted wheat to sell for a profit. In the early part of the twentieth century, especially during World War I, world demand for wheat grew sharply. Tens of thousands of square miles of prairie were converted to wheat fields. The plowing continued after the war, as falling prices put pressure on farmers to produce more, and huge tractors increased productivity.

Portrait of a Dust Storm

The problems in the Great Plains remained hidden until below-average rains fell from 1930 to 1933. After the severe drought of 1934, the prairie grasses were so frail and withered that even the remaining grasslands were in danger. Where the grasses had been plowed, however, the land did not stand a chance.

NATIONAL ARCHIVES, STILL PICTURES BRANCH (CN-3641)

NATIONAL ARCHIVES, STILL PICTURES BRANCH (CN-3640)

Before and After At this ruined farm, emergency plantings of sugar cane, shown at right, reduced wind erosion and added organic matter to the soil. *Which causes of Dust Bowl conditions are not subject to human control?*

Geographic Themes

Region A dust storm can begin with a gentle wind, or simply with warm air rising and picking up smooth fine soil. Farmers today often break dry soil into clumps that the wind cannot lift. Other techniques for preserving soil include leaving crops in the field, using crops with strong roots, and planting legumes and grains together.

Recent reports from the United States Geologic Survey indicate that a series of dust storms within the past 1,000 years turned the Great Plains into an area of desert-like sand dunes. Scientists worry that with current models of global warming, rising temperatures and dry weather may cause the return of devastating storms to semi-arid areas. What effect might dust storms have on the Great Plains today?

THE SHELTERBELT, 1940

In response to the Dust Bowl disaster, the government expanded its role in aiding agriculture. Government workers planted trees in shelterbelts to fight the effects of windstorms. By 1940 more than 40 million trees had been planted. *What agricultural practices contributed to Dust Bowl conditions?*

When the winds came in the spring of 1934, the dust rose in great black clouds, forming swirling masses that darkened the sky. Folksinger Woody Guthrie reported, "The storm was as black as tar and as big as an ocean. It looked like we was done for." Once the strong winds subsided, the topsoil—reduced to dust—was blown in drifts that made farms, homes, and businesses literally worthless. People left the region in droves to find work and food and to escape the ravaged land.

Protecting the Heartland

Nothing could bring back six feet of lost topsoil, but Dust Bowl farmers welcomed New Deal efforts to rehabilitate the land and to protect it from drought, wind erosion, and water erosion.

The Soil Conservation Service, created in 1935, encouraged farmers to use contour plowing and terracing, practices that reduce runoff, water loss, and soil erosion. The service taught farmers not to plow fields under after a harvest, but to leave the stubble to protect the soil, and it taught them about crops that offered better soil protection.

The Forest Service planted strips of trees to make shelterbelts, or windscreens (see map). It also provided saplings to individual farmers.

These measures were successful in returning the land to production. Once the worst was over, though, many farmers returned to their old practices. The climate and landforms of the Great Plains, however, have not changed, and soil erosion remains a great danger.

MAKING THE GEOGRAPHIC CONNECTION

1. What geologic and climatic features define the Great Plains region? How did each of these features contribute to the dust storms of 1934?

2. What change did the farmers of the Great Plains make to their environment? How did this change contribute to the dust storms?

3. Region What changes did the government introduce to rehabilitate and protect the land?

Making the Geographic Connection Answers

1. Answers will vary. The Great Plains are flat prairie lands that lie east of the Rocky Mountains. The weather is often dry and windy. Because the area is so flat, winds can travel over wide areas picking up speed. Because of dry weather the plant growth can suffer and the soil become easy for the winds to pick up. Mountains often break rain clouds and absorb the rain before it can fall on the prairies.

2. Answers will vary. Farmers cleared trees and plants on the prairies for farming, planted fields with one crop, and removed all crops after harvest, leaving the soil vulnerable to wind.

3. Answers will vary. The government passed the Soil Conservation Act, giving farmers saplings and paying them to learn techniques such as terrace farming and crop rotation. The government also planted trees in a shelter belt.

Mapping Activity

Have students use an atlas to research weather in the Great Plains. Ask them to write a paragraph explaining why each shelterbelt planting formed a north-south line. *(Wind and weather move from west to east. Trees break the force of the wind, retain moisture, and hold soil in place.)*

MAP STUDY

Have students identify states that the government chose for shelterbelt plantings. What were the northern and southern boundaries of the shelterbelt? *(North Dakota, Texas)*

Answer: *clearing native foliage; one crop farming, plowing old crops under*

FYI

New Crops The prairie naturally grows a thick mixture of grasses (grains) and legumes. Some native plants, such as Eastern gamagrass, Johnsongrass, and Illinois bundleflower may cross with corn, wheat, rye, and soy to create new food crops.

CLOSE

Create a flow chart of the dust storms of the 1930s. Write the headings *Causes, Results, Effects,* and *Responses* on the board, and ask students to suggest items for each heading. *(Examples: causes: dryness, heat; results: crop failure, storms; effects: dust buries farms; responses: soil protection, people leave)*

FOCUS

Section Objectives

1. Explain how people coped with the sacrifices and hardships of the Depression.
2. Describe innovations and methods of escape that changed people's lifestyles in the 1930s.
3. Describe art and literature movements that highlighted themes of social reform.

Bellringer Activity

While taking attendance at the beginning of the class period, display **Section Focus Transparency 42,** and have students answer the questions. (Or use the blackline master.)

VISUAL INSTRUCTION

Story of Triumph *Gone With the Wind* heralded the success and widespread use of color films. Three-strip Technicolor was developed in 1933, but studios were slow to adopt its use because the 50% increase in production costs rarely paid off. *Snow White and the Seven Dwarfs* (1937) and *Gone With the Wind* (1939), the top 2 films of the decade, were the notable exceptions. By the end of the 1940s about half of all films were made in color.

Ask: Why would this story appeal to Depression-era audiences? *(Loss of wealth was a universal experience. Lavish scenes and romance helped to transport audiences away from harsh everyday reality.)*

Life During the Depression

JUNE 30, 1936: *GONE WITH THE WIND* SMASHES SALES RECORDS

COURTESY OF THE ACADEMY OF MOTION PICTURE ARTS AND SCIENCES

A Story of Triumph
Margaret Mitchell's novel went on to break box office records as a film in 1939.

PENNED BY AN UNKNOWN JOURNALIST WHO HAD NEVER WRITTEN A FULL BOOK BEFORE, MARGARET MITCHELL'S NOVEL, *GONE WITH THE WIND,* BECAME AN INSTANT SUCCESS DURING THE DEPRESSION. Through its pages readers stepped back in time to the world of Scarlett O'Hara and Rhett Butler in plantation Georgia, during and after the Civil War. Vivid with description, the book told of plantation life in a land only recently tamed:

It was a savagely red land, blood-colored after rains, brick dust in droughts, the best cotton land in the world. It was a pleasant land of white houses, peaceful plowed fields and sluggish yellow rivers, but a land of contrasts, of brightest sun glare and densest shade. The plantation clearings and miles of cotton fields smiled up to a warm sun, placid, complacent. At their edges rose the virgin forests, dark and cool even in the hottest noons, mysterious, a little sinister, the soughing pines seeming to wait with an age-old patience, to threaten with soft sighs: "Be careful! Be careful! We had you once. We can take you back again."

—Margaret Mitchell,
Gone With the Wind, 1936

The outbreak of the Civil War brought upheaval to this peaceful world. Readers were caught in the flames of Atlanta burning and dragged through the decimated

---

AS YOU READ

Vocabulary
► status symbol
► mass media

Think About . . .
► how people lived, coped, and even escaped during the Depression era.
► forms of escape that people sought or created in the thirties.
► themes that were prominent in art, literature, and entertainment of the period.

Section 3 Resources

REPRODUCIBLE RESOURCES

- Lesson Plan 13-3
- Vocabulary and Guided Reading Activity 13-3
- Performance Assessment Activity 13
- Chapter 13 Test
- Mid-Book Test
- Reteaching Activity 13
- Enrichment Activity 13

MULTIMEDIA RESOURCES

- Section Focus Transparency 42
- Chapter 13 Digest Audiocassette
- Testmaker
- American Music: Cultural Traditions
- Focus on American Fine Art Prints, Print 16
- Student Self-Test: A Software Review

fields of the O'Hara family's plantation, Tara. Lost in this broken world of postwar Reconstruction, millions of readers momentarily escaped from their own troubled time. They put aside their worries as they experienced the epic drama, defeat, and triumphs of Margaret Mitchell's memorable cast of characters.

Gone With the Wind won the 1937 Pulitzer Prize for fiction and in 1939 was made into one of the most popular movies of all time. During the Depression fans had the fun of reading the book and anticipating the casting of the movie before finally seeing the characters come to life on the big screen. Other works of historical fiction also enjoyed immense popularity, transporting readers to another era and allowing them to forget the ordeals of the Depression.

The Car Craze Continues
The United States Hits the Highway

Just as reading books provided an emotional escape from the dire circumstances of the Depression, owning an automobile gave people the sense that they could physically escape their problems. America's romance with cars, which began in the prosperous years of the 1920s, continued through the poverty-ridden 1930s. Auto shows drew tens of thousands. Then, as now, a new car was a **status symbol**, a sign of wealth or great prestige.

Cars for Show

The Depression highlighted the status value of the automobile. Even people who could not afford the fuel to drive considered their cars among their most prized possessions. One person recalled his grandfather's car:

> My grandfather owned a car [during the Depression] but it never left the garage. He had it jacked up for two years. Gasoline was just too expensive. He told how he polished the car once a week. How he took good care of it, but he never drove it. Couldn't afford it.
> —Ben, in *Hard Times*

Whether they could afford their cars or not, many Americans kept the autos and continued to drive them despite the expense. A restless spirit lured thousands to the highways during the Depression.

THE BETTMANN ARCHIVE

Year of the Auto The year 1935 was a banner year for the American automobile. Auto show attendance zoomed, and car sales dramatically increased. *What did automobiles symbolize to their owners in the 1930s?*

TEACH

Guided Practice

L1 Making Predictions
Ask students to recall some of the compromises and sacrifices that American families made during the Depression. Discuss different regions of the country and the different effects of the Depression on rural and urban lifestyles. Then have students predict or imagine ways that people could relieve the stress of economic hardship through arts and entertainment.

VISUAL INSTRUCTION

Year of the Auto In 1935 New York City police had to open the doors early at the auto show to prevent the excited crowds from obstructing traffic. Discuss with students how the popularity of cars could affect the economy in a positive way. A saying of the time was, "Buy a car now—help bring back prosperity." How could money generated by car sales affect other areas of employment?

Answer: *People took long car trips as affordable vacations, because they were seeking work, for adventure, or simply as an escape from trouble at home.*

Cooperative Learning

Brainstorming Have students work in groups to prepare a visual display of all the occupations that are positively affected when car sales increase. The display should show visually how each industry is affected by the automobile sales and should indicate why car sales are a good barometer of the economy's health. Students should work with group members cooperatively to brainstorm, to plan and complete their displays, and to delegate tasks.

Independent Practice

L2 Analyzing Trends
Have students research ways that film technology has evolved from the first motion pictures up until today. Students might include innovations such as 3-D viewing, stereo sound, and computer effects. Ask students to write a 3-paragraph essay beginning with the highlights of their research, then telling why the technology continues to change, and concluding with predictions for how it may change in the future.

📁 Have students complete the Chapter 13, Section 3 Vocabulary and Guided Reading Activity. (Also in Spanish.) **LEP**

On the Move

By the mid-1930s a maze of two-lane roads crisscrossed the United States. Heading down these bumpy byways, people took off for parts unknown. Some were searching for work. Others were seeking adventure. Many were pioneering what would soon become an American institution: the driving trip as a family vacation.

During the 1930s tourism grew to be the third largest industry in the United States. Thirty-five million vacationers took to the roads in 1935 alone. One woman recalled a yearlong journey she took with her husband and son in the middle of the decade:

> The roads in those days were not the way they are now, and there weren't many motels, although in the East they had what they called auto courts; sometimes these were little better than primitive log cabins. We camped beside the road when we couldn't find a tourist home or a hotel. . . .
>
> This country was so different for families traveling in the thirties. You stayed with local people and ate the food the region was famous for. For instance, in the South there were antebellum houses that were turned into tourist homes, and I think it only cost about $1.50 a night—for the three of us—with an absolutely gigantic dinner and breakfast thrown in.
> —Marion Conrad, in *Making Do: How Women Survived the '30s*

Light Work Electrical appliances manufactured in the 1930s were making housework lighter and easier. *What messages about housework are shown in this ad?*

Trailers—mobile homes that could be hitched to the back of a car—became popular in the 1930s. Ideal for vacations in isolated areas or for rent-free accommodations in a city, trailers tapped into the American dream, promoting freedom and opportunity. The trailer fad peaked in the summer of 1937, when a Florida observer reported that an average of 25 trailers entered his state each hour.

The automobile industry itself just kept growing. The number of registered automobiles in the United States jumped from 24 million in 1933 to 32 million in 1940. Even in the early 1930s, more than half of the families in the United States owned a car.

Escape From Household Drudgery
Electricity Transforms the Home

The car was the ultimate escape machine for the Depression decade. It was not the only machine prized for its powers. The appliance revolution that began in the 1920s continued into the 1930s. As more and more houses were wired with electricity, the market for remarkable new household appliances grew. In the late 1930s, government programs helped bring electricity to many isolated regions of the country, such as the mountains of Arkansas.

The refrigerator was, by far, the most sought after of the new appliances. Even during the worst years of the Depression, refrigerator sales continued to climb. Replacing the clunky old icebox, the refrigerator promised a cleaner, safer way to store food. Gone was the incessant drip-drop of melting ice and the creeping puddle of water that always seemed to spill over the edge of the icebox's collecting pan. With the hum of the refrigerator's whirring motor, families could rest assured that their food would stay fresh. The spread of electrification also eased burdensome household chores such as washing and ironing clothes. Doing laundry had traditionally involved a whole day of bending over tubs full of scalding water and another full day of heating and reheating a heavy iron for pressing. Simple washing machines and the electric iron transformed this work from a weekly ritual of torture. With modern appliances, doing laundry became a set of relatively painless tasks to be squeezed in between other household chores.

For some people electrical power seemed no less than a miracle. An Arkansas congressman remembered the day it miraculously appeared:

I wanted to be at my parents' house when electricity came. It was in 1940. We'd all go around flipping the switch to make sure it hadn't come on yet. We didn't want to miss it. When they finally came on, the lights just barely glowed. I remember my mother smiling. When they came on full, tears started to run down her cheeks.

—Clyde T. Ellis, in *Hard Times*

People in these regions welcomed the escape from drudgery that new appliances afforded them.

Escape Through Entertainment
Song, Spectacle, and Fantasy

For a child in the 1930s, a dime would buy a round-trip fare on a streetcar, two apples from a corner vendor, a malt at the drugstore fountain, or an afternoon at the movies. Faced with these choices, many adults as well as children did without afternoon snacks and saved their pennies in order to claim a seat in the local theater for a Saturday double-feature matinee.

The Silver Screen

Movies changed dramatically as "talkies"—movies with sound—became more common in the early 1930s. At first, all sound was taped live in the studio at the same

MOVIE STILL ARCHIVES

Dynamic Duo Ginger Rogers and Fred Astaire set the standard for lighter-than-air dance steps with nine Hollywood hits. *Why were dance numbers especially popular in the 1930s?*

time the movie was being filmed. Any editing of the movie threw the sound track out of sync with the picture. As a result the actors looked as if they were mouthing their lines, but the words did not match up. Immobile microphones also stunted acting and directing styles. When speaking, the actors and actresses had to stand in place in front of the microphones. They could not change positions or even turn their heads for fear of spoiling the sound. For these reasons, early talkies had a stiffness to them that contrasted with the smooth pace of the old silent movies.

Continued improvement of sound technology ushered in the era of musicals. Watching such gems as *Flying Down to Rio* and *42nd Street*, audiences swooned at the sensuous steps of Fred Astaire and Ginger Rogers. They thrilled at the spectacle of rows of high-stepping dancers. So far removed from the dreariness of the Depression, these sumptuous pageants transported people to a world of glitz and glamour.

Color-film technology added another appealing dimension to 1930s movies. Over the decade more and more movie theaters bought the equipment to project the full-color films the studios began making. The release of the movie version of *Gone With the Wind* in 1939 converted any diehards who preferred black and white. The searing scenes of Atlanta under Union General William Sherman's torch had some viewers shielding their eyes from the imagined heat of dancing flames.

Gone With the Wind was the epitome of a Depression era film. It drew viewers into a romantic, faraway world. It engaged them with a twisting, dramatic plot.

LANDMARKS IN POPULAR ENTERTAINMENT, 1930–1939

1930 *The Lone Ranger* airs from WXYZ in Detroit over a four-station radio network.

1935 Clifford Odets's play *Waiting for Lefty* celebrates the worker, as does Chaplin's film *Modern Times* the following year.

1938 Orson Welles's radio play *The War of the Worlds* causes panic. *Superman* comic strip first appears.

| 1925 | 1927 | 1929 | 1931 | 1933 | 1935 | 1937 | 1939 | 1941 | 1943 | 1945 |

1933 Radio soap opera *Ma Perkins* begins a 27-year run. *Flying Down to Rio* is first Astaire and Rogers film.

1937 Walt Disney's first animated feature is *Snow White and the Seven Dwarfs*.

1939 MGM's *Gone With the Wind* tops profit records and remains unsurpassed.

SECTION THREE **443**

History and the Humanities

🎧 American Music: Cultural Traditions— "Wildwood Flower" by The Carter Family; "Talking Dust Bowl" by Woody Guthrie.

📖 Focus on American Fine Art Prints, Print 16: *New York, New Haven, and Hartford* by Edward Hopper

VISUAL INSTRUCTION

Dynamic Duo Astaire and Rogers went their separate ways in 1939. Fred danced on to partners Eleanor Powell, Rita Hayworth, Anne Miller, Cyd Charisse, and Judy Garland; meanwhile Ginger pursued dramatic roles.

Answer: *Upbeat dance routines helped create a fantasy. Synchronized sound made the effect of song and dance more spectacular.*

 ## At the Movies

Students may wish to view *Gone With the Wind*, the decade's most popular film, or *Top Hat*, the most successful of the Astaire-Rogers musicals. These movies will show the contrast between popular culture and real events during the Depression.

CHART STUDY

Ask: What was the most profitable Hollywood film?
Answer: Gone With the Wind.

Portfolio Project

Designing an Ad Campaign Ask students to create an advertisement with pictures and text advertising a refrigerator, radio, or labor-saving device that was new in the 1930s. Students will have to research these developments, think about a potential market for one product, and create some copy that rings true for both product and audience. They may also want to research period illustration and design styles as they create the pictures. After displaying their projects, students should include them in their portfolios. 📽️

ASSESS

Meeting Lesson Objectives

Each section objective is tested by the section review question(s) that follows it in parentheses.

1. Explain how people coped with the sacrifices and hardships of the Depression. (1, 3, 4)

2. Describe innovations and methods of escape that changed people's lifestyles in the 1930s. (1, 2, 3, 4)

3. Describe art and literature movements that highlighted themes of social reform. (3, 4, 5)

VISUAL INSTRUCTION

Entertainment Center
Radio transported audiences so far into fantasy that popular acts included the ventriloquist Edgar Bergen, and two white comics playing wildly stereotyped African Americans, *Amos 'N' Andy*. In 1938 Orson Welles's terrifying broadcast, *War of the Worlds*, jokingly reported a Martian invasion that thousands of listeners believed to be true.

Answer: *Daytime: soap operas and quiz shows; afternoons: children's shows; evenings: news, followed by variety, drama, music, and comedy*

It tugged at all the emotions—love, anger, fear, pity, and hope. Best of all, it lasted for nearly four hours, not including an intermission for a meal. A more satisfying afternoon of entertainment could not be had for the price of just one thin dime.

During an average week in the mid-1930s, between 60 million and 90 million people flocked to the movies. For their daily entertainment, however, most people turned on the radio.

The Golden Age of Radio

Unlike today's compact radio that can be carried in the palm of the hand, the radio of the 1930s was a substantial piece of furniture. Granted an honored place in the living room, the radio, with its rich wood cabinet, often served as a visual focus, the mantel for family photographs and mementos. It also served as a social focus, the gathering place for hours of spirit-lifting amusement.

More than 10 million households owned radios in 1929. A decade later that number had almost tripled. Like television today, radio served many purposes. It was the family's communication link to the outside world. It was the housewife's companion as she did her daily chores. It gave the unemployed the comfort of company. It occupied young children when they returned home from school. Radio enlivened long winter evenings with engrossing family entertainment.

Radio programming in the 1930s set a pattern that television would follow for years. Daytime radio included soap operas, panel discussions, and quiz shows designed to appeal to women working at home. During the

Entertainment Center The radio was a piece of furniture that became the entertainment center and focal point of the living room in many homes. *What sorts of shows were broadcast in the mornings, afternoons, and evenings?*

late afternoon, children's programs came on. Adventure stories, such as *The Lone Ranger* and *Superman*, originated in the 1930s and captured young audiences well into the 1950s. The evening was reserved for news programs, variety shows, comedy hours, dramatic presentations of plays, and live musical performances.

Sponsored by big-name corporations, radio programs tended to avoid controversial issues. Audiences of the **mass media**—movies, radio, and other large networks of communication—were most often seeking a means of escape. A few used it as a forum to discuss difficult questions or controversial views.

Voices That Would Not Be Stilled
Bleak Visions of Reality

Despite many Americans' obsession with escape, quite a few people took an interest in defining the nation's problems and exploring solutions. Angry at injustices, they spoke out candidly. Many were artists—writers, painters, photographers, playwrights—whose works still inspire social awareness and empathy today.

The Mirror of Literature

During the 1930s many serious writers shifted their focus from the anxiety of the individual to the mass struggles of people caught in a system that robbed them of their vitality. John Steinbeck and John Dos Passos, two writers acclaimed during this turbulent decade, stressed the struggles of individuals in society. In addition, both writers evaluated the effectiveness of society in upholding the rights of people of different classes. They intended that their writing serve as a mirror in which society could see itself. These writers wanted their readers to take a long, hard look at the evils and injustices of society. They wanted to inspire their readers to fight for social change.

The Grapes of Wrath by Steinbeck was one of the most famous and influential novels of the 1930s. This American classic focused on an Okie family driven from their land:

> Pa borrowed money from the bank, and now the bank wants the land—wants tractors, not families on the land. Is a tractor bad? Is the power that turns the long furrows wrong? If this tractor were ours it would be good—not mine, but ours. If our tractor turned the long furrows of our land, it would be good. Not my land, but ours. We could love that tractor then as we have loved this land when it was ours. But this tractor does two things—it turns the land and turns us off the land. There is little differ-

Extending the Content

Art and Politics You may want to refer to the Case Study "Art and Politics at Rockefeller Center" on pages 472 through 475 as another example of art that attempted to make a political statement during the 1930s. Students can examine the work of other political artists of the time such as the murals of Jose Orozco, or the cartoons of William Gropper.

Regionalism Grant Wood's *American Gothic* hung with works by Thomas Hart Benton and John Steuart Curry in 1933. The models for the painting, Wood's sister Nan and his dentist, Dr. McKeeby, are shown in the photo above right. *What sentiments does Wood's painting convey?*

ence between this tractor and a tank. The people are driven, intimidated, hurt by both. We must think about this.

—John Steinbeck, *The Grapes of Wrath,* 1939

Statements in the Arts

No less insistent than the 1930s writers were the artists of the time who clamored for social change. They sought to show the United States in all its Depression era bleakness. Thomas Hart Benton, Edward Hopper, and Grant Wood each focused on a particular region of the country and tried to convey the flavor of life there as they saw it. Through these works of art, viewers perceived the trials of poor farmers, unemployed workers, and others struggling to hold on to their ideals during years of hardship.

Playwrights and theater directors also used their works to make statements about society. Emphasizing the struggle of labor against exploitative factory owners, the play *Waiting for Lefty* by Clifford Odets glorified the

Depression era worker. This and other plays promoted the visions of playwrights for a just world.

In contrast, documentary photography showed the United States of the Depression era stripped of hopes and dreams. Staring into the faces of destitute migrant workers from Alabama, the evicted wheat farmers from the Dust Bowl, and the hungry children in Hoovervilles, few viewers could avoid sensing these people's anger, shame, and misery. The photographs immediately convey the scope of the Depression, which shattered the lives of so many Americans.

SECTION REVIEW

Vocabulary
1. Define: status symbol, mass media.

Checking Facts
2. Other than automobiles, what three machines of the 1930s changed people's lives? Explain how.

3. Explain why escapist films and realistic fiction were both popular during the 1930s.

Critical Thinking
Drawing Conclusions
4. Unemployment remained high during the 1930s, but movie attendance and sales of cars and radios rose. Decide if you feel the 1930s constituted a depressing time to be a teenager. Explain why or why not.

Linking Across Time
5. Explain why so much of the art, music, literature, and film of the 1930s is still popular today.

Section 3 Review Answers

1. status symbol (441), **mass media** (444)
2. Answers will vary. Students might mention that the radio made entertainment cheaper; the refrigerator made food safer; the vacuum cleaner made housework easier.
3. Films offered escape from the Depression; others wanted to think more about causes, effects, and solutions of the Depression.

4. Answers will vary. Students might say that radio, movies, and cars made the 1930s less depressing, but not as carefree as the culture of the 1920s.
5. Culture of the 1930s aimed at escape, so the media provided a spectacle that is still fun today. The first talkies made use of classic literature—the appeal of which stands the test of time.

VISUAL INSTRUCTION

Regionalism The painting *American Gothic* has been the subject of many spoofs over the years.

Answer: *They portray a bleak view of life and a respect for the people who endure it.*

Evaluate

Have students complete the Section Review.

📁 💿 Assign the Section 3 Quiz or use the Testmaker to develop a customized quiz. (Also in Spanish.) **LEP**

📁 💿 Assign the Chapter 13 Test or use the Testmaker to develop a customized test.

📁 Have students Complete the Chapter 13 Performance Assessment Activity.

Reteach

🎧 Have students listen to the Chapter 13, Section 3 Audiocassette. (Also in Spanish.) **LEP**

📁 Have students complete the Chapter 13 Reteaching Activity (Also in Spanish.) **LEP**

Enrich

📁 Have students complete the Chapter 13 Enrichment Activity (Also in Spanish.) **LEP**

CLOSE

Play the song "Somewhere over the Rainbow." Discuss how it relates to the mood of the 1930s.

TEACH

Making the Historical Connection

In the midst of the Depression, works of fantasy often provided respite for the human imagination. Point out that because they reached millions simultaneously, movies and radio programs created a feeling of solidarity and closeness with others, as well as the possibility of realms where life was easier and more exciting.

446

CULTURE OF THE TIME

Hard Times

The harsh reality of the Great Depression was something that Americans faced every day. Most people could hope for only a few hours a week of escape into a fantasy world where life was beautiful and problems could be easily solved. Movies, radio, comics, and new novelty games provided that escape.

"THE GREAT ZIEGFELD", 1936, MGM/MOTION PICTURE & TELEVISION PHOTO ARCHIVE

MUSICAL SPECTACLE

In sharp contrast to daily life during the Depression, musicals such as **The Great Ziegfeld** sparkled with lavish sets and cascades of smiling dancers. This tribute to theatrical producer Florenz Ziegfeld won Academy Awards for best picture and best director in 1936.

446   CULTURE OF THE TIME

© PARKER BROTHERS/NATIONAL GEOGRAPHIC S

FANTASY TYCOONS

Players of **Monopoly** could pretend to own railroads and luxury hotels. Even though the game had many rules, it became an instant success in 1935, sending its unemployed inventor, Charles Darrow, into six-figure wealth.

FILE PHOTO BY DOUG MINDELL/
PERMISSION COURTESY OF PARKER
BROTHERS

Background Information

New Technologies and Novelties Point out that films with sound, national radio networks, and three-strip Technicolor were all new technologies developed during the Depression. Branches of the media—radio, comics, and film competed with each other for most inexpensive and spectacular, spurring the development of both technology and gimmicks. Theaters commonly offered door prizes, for example. Explain that the game Monopoly broke into a market in which novelty games like miniature golf, and backgammon had already swept the nation. Bingo, Lotto, and dance marathons became fads at the same time. Discuss how novelty was one element that compelled audiences to keep luxuries such as entertainment in their tight budgets. What were other elements? (*Fantasy, giveaways, cash prizes.*)

THRILLS AND CHILLS

Monsters in films such as *Dracula, Frankenstein,* and **King Kong** could make people forget about ordinary troubles. In 1933 Kong's battle atop the **Empire State Building** also gave moviegoers the chance to see "the world's tallest building," built just two years earlier.

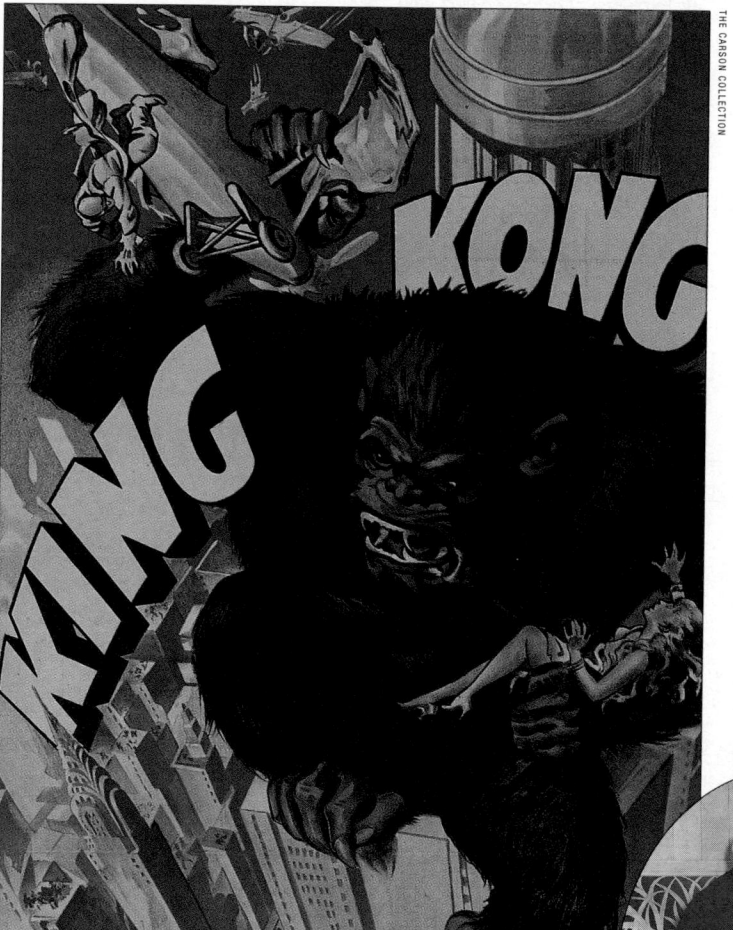

THE CARSON COLLECTION

REPRINTED BY PERMISSION: TRIBUNE MEDIA SERVICES, INC., 2-13-38

SUPERHEROES

As real gangsters ran wild, Chester Gould's **Dick Tracy** upheld law and order in the daily comics. Flash Gordon, Tarzan, Buck Rogers, and Superman kept the universe safe from other cartoon villains.

"TUNE IN TOMORROW . . ."

Heard but not seen, these **actors at NBC** played realistic murder victims. Soap operas and serials such as *Ma Perkins, One Man's Family,* and *Our Gal Sunday* kept listeners riveted to the radio.

THE BETTMANN ARCHIVE

CULTURE OF THE TIME **447**

Portfolio Project

Reviewing Key Terms

1. repatriation
2. status symbol
3. speculation
4. foreclosure
5. margin

Recalling Facts

1. When prices began to fall and brokers called in margins, investors who bought on margin could not repay what they had borrowed.
2. The stock market crashed; wealth was unequally distributed, and workers could not afford to buy what they produced; dust storms destroyed farms; overproduction and underconsumption weakened agriculture and industry.
3. Congress passed and Hoover carried out the Agricultural Marketing Act, the Reconstruction Finance Corporation, and the Emergency Relief Act, but the money did not reach the unemployed.
4. The song reinforced the idea that working people were suffering hard times.
5. Dust storms drove people from the land; new farm machinery made small farms impractical; the government paid to have land lie fallow, so tenant farmers were evicted.
6. Homeless people lived in shantytowns built from scrap.
7. Prairie grasses that protected the soil from erosion had been replaced with wheat; fall plowing left the soil exposed.
8. The automobile provided a way to escape the Depression physically.
9. People were interested in lifestyles that they could not afford.
10. Answers will vary. Steinbeck's realistic writing and Lange's photography depicted the Depression as it was.

Reviewing Key Terms

Choose the vocabulary term that best completes the sentences below. Write your answers on a separate sheet of paper.

speculation	repatriation
margin	status symbol
foreclosure	mass media

1. Because of the depressed farm economy in the Southwest and Texas, many Mexican American workers were deported, and others voluntarily sought _____ to Mexico.

2. Even during the Depression people continued to take pride in auto-mobile ownership. Their automobile, whether they could afford to drive it or not, was a _____ that established their position in the community.

3. One of the causes of the stock market crash of 1929 was reckless _____ in overvalued stocks, as people gambled by making short-term investments.

4. As farmers fell behind in making their farm mortgage payments, they feared a _____ by the bank that held the mortgage.

5. Often investors paid only part of a stock's value and borrowed the rest; such buying on _____ hastened the crash.

Recalling Facts

1. Why did the stock market crash of 1929 occur?

2. Identify several causes of the Depression.

3. State two steps President Hoover took to end the Depression. Why were these steps unsuccessful?

4. Why did the Republican party try to discourage radio stations from playing "Brother, Can You Spare a Dime?"

5. State three reasons why many farmers were out of work during the Depression.

6. Explain what Hoovervilles were.

7. What farming practices contributed to Dust Bowl conditions?

8. Explain why automobiles were so popular during the Depression.

9. During the Depression why was so much of the entertainment extravagant and unrealistic?

10. Give examples of a realistic approach in literature and art that highlighted social problems in the Depression.

Critical Thinking

1. **Making Inferences** This photo of Hoover and FDR in an open limousine records a special occasion. Using your knowledge of history, and evidence from the photo, identify the occasion.

2. **Predicting Consequences** Suppose a factory produced mass-market goods such as small cars that were too expensive for workers to buy. What would the consequences be for the factory owners? What would the consequences be for the workers? What could be done to address this problem?

3. **Making Comparisons** Compare the ways that people in the cities and people in rural areas helped one another during the Depression.

4. **Drawing Conclusions** Mexican Americans and African Americans were among the first to lose their jobs during the Depression. Why did this occur?

5. **Making Generalizations** Why did sales of refrigerators and other electrical appliances continue to rise throughout the 1930s in spite of hard times?

UPI/BETTMANN

Critical Thinking

1. It is probably the day of Franklin Roosevelt's first inauguration.
2. If workers could not afford the product, the market would be limited to the upper and middle classes; falling demand would mean falling employment. A solution would be to pay the workers more so they could afford the product.
3. Some rural people held penny auctions; some urban people shared apartments.
4. Many Mexican Americans and African Americans were tenant farmers. They were evicted after the government began to pay landowners to let fields lie fallow.
5. Answers will vary. People sought escape from drudgery; the government extended electrification to rural areas, making appliances possible; advertising created a demand.

CHAPTER 13 REVIEW

Portfolio Project

The Depression of the 1930s was a worldwide event. Investigate and write a report on how another country handled the hard times and unemployment of the Depression. You might choose Great Britain or Germany or any country in which you have a special interest. Keep your report in your portfolio.

Cooperative Learning

Form a film-review group and divide up the responsibility for analyzing videotapes of some of the film classics of the 1930s, such as *King Kong*, *Gone With the Wind*, or one of the films starring Fred Astaire and Ginger Rogers. Present a panel discussion on these films, evaluating them and comparing them with some of the popular films of the 1990s.

Reinforcing Skills

Drawing Inferences From Maps
Look at the map on page 431 showing the migration routes of the Dust Bowl farmers between 1930 and 1939. What can you infer about why these migrants chose to go to California? Write a paragraph explaining what facts in the map support your inference.

Geography and History

Study the map on this page to answer the following questions:

1. What does the red line on the map signify? Would Dust Bowl farmers traveling west be more likely to settle in areas west and south of the red line or in areas east and north of it? Why?

2. What special opportunities for farming would California's growing season offer?

3. If migrant wheat farmers from Dust Bowl states hoped to grow wheat again, which West Coast

states would offer them the best prospects?

4. In which states were forest products a major crop? What other crops were grown in those states?

5. What crops were grown in Idaho? What natural feature is associated with the growing areas in that state?

WEST COAST CROPS, 1936

CANADA

0   100   200 mi.
0 100 200 km
Albers Equal-Area projection

N

Washington

Columbia R.

Oregon

Montana

Missouri R.

Idaho

Snake R.

Wyoming

Great Salt Lake

Nevada

Utah

40°N

Colorado

50°N

Sacramento R.

PACIFIC OCEAN

Less than 150-day growing season

San Joaquin R.

120°W

California

More than 150-day growing season

Colorado R.

Arizona

New Mexico

Rio Grande

MEXICO

110°W   30°N

AREAS OF MAJOR AGRICULTURAL PRODUCTION, 1936

Fruits
Wheat and other grains
Other

Limits of 150-day growing season

CROPS
● Apples
◉ Citrus fruits

Vegetables
Potatoes
Cotton
Grapes

Sugar beets
Forest products

HISTORY JOURNAL

Write a brief account of what you learned in this chapter. What information about the Depression did you find most interesting or affecting?

Geography and History

1. The red line marks the limits of the 150-day growing season. They would be more likely to settle west and south of the line to take advantage of the longer growing season.
2. It would permit the growing of citrus fruits. Quickly grown crops might be harvested more than once.
3. Oregon, Washington, and California
4. Forest products were a major crop in Washington and Oregon. Apples, grapes, and other fruits also grew in these states, along with wheat and other grains.
5. Sugar beets, grapes, other fruits, potatoes, and wheat grew in Idaho. Many growing areas appear to lie along the Snake River valleys.

History Journal

Invite volunteers to share parts of their history journals with the class.

BONUS QUESTION

This question may be used for extra credit on the chapter test.
Ask: What opportunities did cross-country highways provide for people during the Depression? *(People could take driving trips; they could look for work in other states)*

Portfolio Project

Invite volunteers to share their research reports with the class. Include at least one report on each country that students have investigated.

Cooperative Learning

Students may wish to illustrate the points they make in the panel discussion by using a few clips from videotapes of the movies they review.

Reinforcing Skills

Students might point out that going west was a way of getting out of the Dust Bowl. The map shows that both major highways, 30 and 66, led to California; migrants would have reason to hope that farmworkers would be needed there.

The New Deal

DAILY LESSON OBJECTIVES	REPRODUCIBLE RESOURCES	MULTIMEDIA RESOURCES
SECTION 1 FDR and the First New Deal **1.** Cite issues and events that persuaded voters to choose FDR as President. **2.** Detail the legislation of the Hundred Days. **3.** Discuss FDR's relationship with the public during the Hundred Days.	📂 Reproducible Lesson Plans 📂 Vocabulary and Guided Reading Activities (English or Spanish) 📂 Cooperative Learning Activities (English or Spanish) 📂 Geography in History Activities 📂 Enrichment Activities (English or Spanish) 📂 Section Quizzes (English or Spanish)	🖐 Chapter Teaching Transparencies 🖐 Section Focus Transparencies 🖐 Map Transparencies 🌐 The Presidents: A Picture History of Our Nation 🌐 Landmark Documents in American History 💿 Student Self-Test: A Software Review 💿 Testmaker
SECTION 2 Criticism and Reformulation **1.** Discuss the objections of tenant farmers, labor unions, radicals, conservatives, and the Supreme Court to the New Deal. **2.** Identify some of the legislation of the Second New Deal. **3.** Describe the impact that Roosevelt's proposed change in the Supreme Court had on the momentum of the Second New Deal.	📂 Reproducible Lesson Plans 📂 Vocabulary and Guided Reading Activities (English or Spanish) 📂 Case Studies 📂 American Literature Readings and Activities 📂 Section Quizzes (English or Spanish)	🖐 Section Focus Transparencies 🌐 A Geographic Perspective on American History 💿 Student Self-Test: A Software Review 💿 Testmaker
SECTION 3 The Impact of the New Deal **1.** Describe how women, African Americans, and Native Americans were affected by New Deal legislation and attitudes. **2.** Discuss the new role that the government began to take in ensuring the welfare of its citizens.	📂 Reproducible Lesson Plans 📂 Vocabulary and Guided Reading Activities (English or Spanish) 📂 Supreme Court Case Studies 📂 Reteaching Activities (English or Spanish) 📂 Section Quizzes (English or Spanish)	🖐 Section Focus Transparencies 🌐 Landmark Documents in American History 💿 Student Self-Test: A Software Review 💿 Testmaker
CHAPTER REVIEW AND EVALUATION	📂 Chapter 14 Test, Forms A and B 📂 Performance Assessment Strategies and Activities 📂 Unit 5 Test, Forms A and B	💿 Student Self-Test: A Software Review 💿 Testmaker 💿 Vocabulary PuzzleMaker 🎧 Chapter Digests Audiocassettes

 If time does not permit teaching the entire chapter, summarize using the Chapter 14 Digests Audiocassettes and the accompanying activities and tests. (Available in English or Spanish.)

Cooperative Project

Have students work in groups of four or five. One student can prepare interview questions, while one serves as a recorder taking notes during an interview. Ask the remaining students to each choose a person that they have read about from the 1930s. Students can work in pairs to interview each other, or work in small groups to field questions as a panel. **LEP** 💿

Suggested Rubric: Group Work and the Individual. See Performance Assessment Strategies and Activities, p. 37.

Individual Project

Have students create their own posters of New Deal successes and failures. Encourage students to experiment with ways of presenting information in posters. You might, for example, recommend that they create icons for parts of the poster, or that they present hard statistics in one format and analytical statements in another. Students might also choose to create a computer-generated poster. 💿

Suggested Rubric: A Poster. See Performance Assessment Strategies and Activities, p. 37.

Key to Ability Levels

Teaching strategies have been coded for varying learning styles and abilities.

L1 **BASIC** activities for all students

L2 **AVERAGE** activities for average to above-average students

L3 **CHALLENGING** activities for above-average students

LEP **LIMITED ENGLISH PROFICIENCY** activities

 Block Scheduling

Block scheduling differs from traditional class scheduling in the amount of time allotted to each period. The extended timeframe provided by block scheduling affords you the opportunity to implement a greater number of research-oriented and activity-intense projects to motivate and involve your students. Activities that are particularly suited to use within the block scheduling framework are identified throughout this chapter by the following designation. 💿

T E A C H E R ' S   C O R N E R

 NATIONAL GEOGRAPHIC SOCIETY

NATIONAL GEOGRAPHIC SOCIETY PRODUCTS AVAILABLE FROM GLENCOE

To order the following products for use with this chapter, contact your local Glencoe sales representative or call Glencoe at 1-800-334-7344:

- *The Presidents: A Picture History of Our Nation* (CD-ROM)
- *GTV: A Geographic Perspective on American History* (Videodisc)
- *GTV: The American People: Fabric of a Nation* (Videodisc)

ADDITIONAL NATIONAL GEOGRAPHIC SOCIETY PRODUCTS

To order the following products for use with this chapter, call National Geographic Society at 1-800-368-2728:

- *The American Presidency* (Filmstrip)
- *Decades of History: The 20th Century—The Early Years* (Filmstrip)
- *1929-1941: The Great Depression* (Video)

Chapter Overview

President Roosevelt, and First Lady Eleanor Roosevelt gave Americans new hope. The First Lady brought compassion and accessibility to her role, linking the people and the President. FDR's New Deal created millions of jobs and changed the role of government.

Introducing the Chapter

Have students read the chapter opener. Ask them to describe some ways that the Roosevelts interacted with the public. Ask students to infer how this approach might have helped change the mood of the nation.

Display the Chapter 14 Teaching Transparency and distribute copies of the activity sheet. After students have completed the activities, point out that Roosevelt's New Deal programs focused on the three R's—relief, recovery, and reform. Ask students the meaning of each.

Extension Activity

Have students complete Beyond the Transparency on the activity sheet for Chapter 14 and present their projects after the class has completed the chapter.

History Journal

Have students review their impressions of why Americans needed a "new deal." Ask them to write in what ways Americans today would want to change the way government operates.

CHAPTER

14

The New Deal

MAY 27, 1938: ELEANOR ROOSEVELT VISITS ARTHURDALE, WEST VIRGINIA

First Lady Eleanor Roosevelt and her square dance partner promenaded down the aisle of clapping onlookers in the Arthurdale High School auditorium.

Five years had passed since Mrs. Roosevelt helped to establish the resettlement community of Arthurdale, West Virginia, and she wanted to be on hand to celebrate the graduation of its first high school senior class.

In 1933 in the midst of the Depression, the federal government persuaded a number of families to move from Morgantown, West Virginia, where most farm families could barely eke out a living, to Arthurdale. Residents there would ideally be able to remain employed and self-sufficient during the year by combining subsistence farming with small industry. To encourage people to make the move

to Arthurdale, the federal government promised that each family would have a house with plumbing and electricity, a plot of land, and a job in a nearby factory.

Arthurdale was the first of the government-sponsored communities established by the Resettlement Administration, one of President Roosevelt's New Deal programs. These communities gave hope to people mired in the Depression. Under the President's leadership, the United States government assumed a new responsibility for the welfare of the American people and for the future of the nation's economy. ■

HISTORY JOURNAL

Consider the problems people were facing as the Hoover administration ended. In what ways did people need a "new deal"? Write your ideas in your journal.

450

➕ EXTRA CREDIT PROJECT

Planning a "New Deal" Point out that, as the President faced with a national depression, Roosevelt took on a monumental challenge, to create jobs, provide emergency relief, and to bolster economic institutions such as businesses and banks. Before students learn about actual New Deal programs, have them design

programs of their own. Ask each student to propose, in writing, three government actions that might help solve some of the problems during the Depression. The proposal should explain what is helpful about each action, as well as what difficulties or obstacles the country might encounter in implementing it.

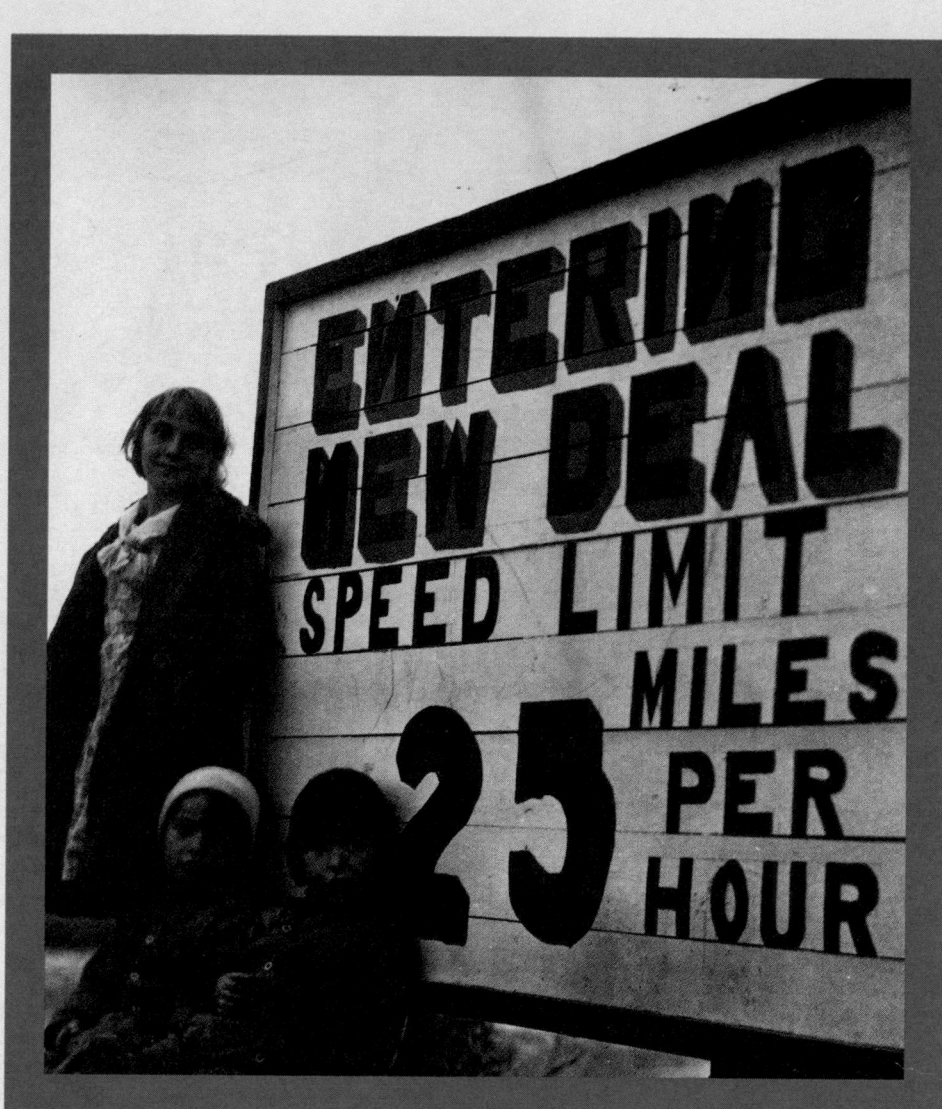

MARGARET BOURKE-WHITE/LIFE MAGAZINE © TIME WARNER INC.

THIS WESTERN TOWN TOOK ITS NAME
FROM ROOSEVELT'S PROMISE TO
GIVE AMERICANS A NEW DEAL.

451

History and the Humanities

🎧 American Music: Cultural Traditions—"Franklin D. Roosevelt's Back Again" by Bill Cox and Cliff Hobbs.

Curriculum Connection

Architecture The International Style emerged during the 1930s, emphasizing simplicity and barrenness through use of concrete and glass. Walter Gropius and Charles Edouard Jenneret (Le Corbusier) influenced American architecture using this style.

Performance Assessment

Refer to page 450B for performance assessment activities for this chapter.

📁 Also see Activity 14 in the Performance Assessment Strategies and Activities for an additional activity as well as for suggested rubrics.

Examining the Visual

Two Photographers Margaret Bourke-White established herself as an industrial and architectural photographer, but, like Dorothea Lange, she became interested in photography as a means for social action. She and Lange showed America the human side of economic crisis. She published a book of 70 photographs of poverty-stricken Americans, entitled *You Have Seen Their Faces*, with text by Erskine Caldwell. In 1936 a Bourke-White photograph appeared on the first cover of *Life* magazine. In 1941 she became the first woman photographer attached to the armed forces. Students might draw comparisons between the photograph on this page and Dorothea Lange's "Migrant Mother" on page 413.

Section Objectives

1. Cite issues and events that persuaded voters to choose FDR as President.
2. Detail the legislation of the Hundred Days.
3. Discuss FDR's relationship with the public during the Hundred Days.

Bellringer Activity

While taking attendance at the beginning of the class period, display **Section Focus Transparency 43,** and have students answer the questions. (Or use the blackline master.)

VISUAL INSTRUCTION

New Leader Roosevelt's confidence contrasted with Hoover's moodiness. During the ride to his inauguration, FDR tried to chat with the unresponsive Hoover. Finally he gave up and began waving to the cheering crowds.

Ask: What did FDR consider to be his first major task? *(to restore people's faith in the government and the economy)*

Global Connection

In the 1932 elections in Germany, Hindenburg won 18 million votes; Hitler, 11 million; and the Communist party, 5 million. The Nazi party held a plurality of seats in the German Reichstag. Hitler was confident enough to turn Hindenburg down when asked to be his Vice Chancellor.

FDR and the First New Deal

MARCH 4, 1933: FRANKLIN D. ROOSEVELT TAKES PRESIDENTIAL OATH

FRANKLIN D. ROOSEVELT LIBRARY

New Leader
Roosevelt's inauguration was the result of a landslide win.

DULL, GRAY SKIES HUNG OVER WASHINGTON. An icy wind gusted down the city's broad boulevards, chilling the crowd that packed the walk in front of the Capitol steps. Suddenly the high, clear notes of a bugle sounded out a fanfare. Franklin Delano Roosevelt, partially paralyzed from polio, leaning on the arm of his son, mounted the inaugural platform. As he walked up the steps to the podium, the band began playing "Hail to the Chief."

After Roosevelt took the oath of the office of the President, he turned to face the crowd. He had planned his first words as President carefully, because he knew that the nation would be listening closely to find out just what kind of President he would be.

Three and a half years of economic depression had left millions unemployed, hungry, and homeless. Thousands of banks had closed. Assembly lines had ground to a halt while breadlines stretched for blocks down city streets. Farmland lay fallow, abandoned by angry farmers unable to recover even the costs of planting. Americans had lost faith in their country. Roosevelt considered his first major task was to restore that faith.

His voice echoing over the public-address system, Roosevelt declared the following:

AS YOU READ

Vocabulary
► moratorium
► dole
► subsidy

Think About . . .
► issues and events that persuaded voters to elect FDR.
► the legislation of the Hundred Days.

► FDR's relationship with the public during the Hundred Days.

Section 1 Resources

REPRODUCIBLE RESOURCES

- Lesson Plan 14-1
- Vocabulary and Guided Reading Activity 14
- Cooperative Learning Activity 14
- Section 1 Quiz
- Enrichment Activity 14
- Geography in History Activity 14

MULTIMEDIA RESOURCES

- Section Focus Transparency 43
- The Presidents: A Picture History of Our Nation
- Map Transparency 14

- Landmark Documents in American History
- Testmaker
- Chapter 14 Digest Audiocassette
- Student Self-Test: A Software Review
- Chapter Teaching Transparency 14

This great Nation will endure as it has endured, will revive and will prosper. So, first of all, let me assert my firm belief that the only thing we have to fear is fear itself—nameless, unreasoning, unjustified terror which paralyzes needed efforts to convert retreat into advance.

—Inaugural Address, March 4, 1933

Cheers and roaring applause burst from the crowd at the end of the President's address. For the first time that day, Roosevelt grinned. Then he descended the steps, determined to lead this country out of its prolonged economic depression.

FDR Takes the Helm
Personal and Political Victories

Franklin Delano Roosevelt was born on January 30, 1882, into a wealthy, well-connected family. As a child Roosevelt was popular with his classmates and received good grades in school. Nevertheless, the future President showed no signs of distinction.

A classmate described Roosevelt as "nice but colorless." Several decades later, when Roosevelt was running for office, a political analyst would confirm the classmate's opinion:

> Franklin Roosevelt is no crusader. He is no tribune of the people. He is no enemy of entrenched privilege. He is a pleasant man who, without any important qualifications for the office, would very much like to be President.
> —Walter Lippmann, 1932

Marriage to Eleanor Roosevelt

Franklin's distant cousin Eleanor introduced him to a world he had not seen in his sheltered youth. At the age of 20, Eleanor had volunteered at a settlement house in the slums of New York City. Franklin, accompanying Eleanor to the home of one of her students, exclaimed, "I didn't know people lived like that!"

On March 17, 1905, Franklin and Eleanor were joined in marriage. Republican President Theodore Roosevelt, Franklin's distant cousin and Eleanor's uncle, led Eleanor down the aisle. A few years later, Franklin followed in Theodore Roosevelt's footsteps, launching a political career.

An Emerging Politician

In 1910 FDR, as Franklin Roosevelt came to be known, was elected as a Democrat to the New York state legislature. In 1913 President Wilson appointed him assistant secretary of the navy. He served in this post for 7 years until 1920, when, at the age of 38, he gained the Democratic nomination for Vice President. Roosevelt did not become Vice President, however, because the Democratic presidential candidate lost the election.

In 1921, while vacationing at his family's summer home, FDR suffered an attack of poliomyelitis that left his legs completely paralyzed. Nevertheless, Roosevelt was determined to return to an active political life.

FRANKLIN D. ROOSEVELT LIBRARY

Two Visions Joined In this 1905 photograph, newlyweds Eleanor and Franklin Roosevelt pose on the steps of their Hyde Park home. Eleanor's volunteer activities helped expand Franklin's awareness of social issues. *What qualities of Franklin and Eleanor Roosevelt prepared them for leadership?*

TEACH

Guided Practice

L2 Making Comparisons Discuss how the contrast in personalities between Hoover and FDR helped Roosevelt win the presidency during an economic depression. Have students read Lippmann's assessment of FDR. Discuss what they feel are personal qualities that make a good president.

Show students Map Transparency 14 and have them complete the activity sheet.

VISUAL INSTRUCTION

Two Visions Joined Raised in the utmost of comfort, Franklin Roosevelt nevertheless developed a strong social conscience and will partly due to his struggle with polio. In 1926 he purchased a spa and farm in Warm Springs, Georgia, which he made available to others afflicted with polio.

Answer: *Eleanor and Franklin were both well-connected people. They also had compassion, determination, and strong social consciousness.*

Cooperative Learning

Creating a Visual Aid Ask teams of students to create visual presentations about FDR's life. Each team member should complete one of the following tasks: collect photocopied or drawn images relating to FDR, create a list of FDR's accomplishments while in office, choose excerpts from FDR's speeches, or create a time line of the events in FDR's personal life. Then each team should compile the information on a large poster.

Independent Practice

 Researching Banking Have students consult encyclopedia articles and economics texts to find out what happens when millions of people withdraw their money from banks at the same time. Students can write a description of why this event would cause a problem for the banks and ultimately for the economy at large.

📁 Have students complete the Chapter 14, Section 1 Vocabulary and Guided Reading Activity. (Also in Spanish.) **LEP**

📁 Have students complete the Chapter 14 Cooperative Learning Activity.

Curriculum Connection

Civics Ask students to discuss whether the duty of American citizenship includes following a presidential request, such as Roosevelt's, to redeposit money in a bank. Students can discuss the extents and limits of a citizen's financial duties.

NATIONAL GEOGRAPHIC SOCIETY

The Presidents: A Picture History of Our Nation

Have students view "Franklin D. Roosevelt" and use the information to write a brief biography to include in their portfolios.

Years of treatment never did restore the use of his legs, but the experience increased his ability to empathize with others and strengthened his spirit. As he remarked, "If you have spent two years in bed trying to wiggle your big toe, everything else seems easy."

At the Democratic convention in 1924, Roosevelt made his first public political appearance since having been stricken with polio. From that appearance on, Roosevelt's political career skyrocketed. Twice he won the governorship of New York—in 1928 by a slim margin and in 1930 by a landslide. His innovative relief measures, including a statewide relief program, won him national praise. Then in 1932 he accepted the Democratic nomination for President.

The Roosevelt Victory

Both Roosevelt and Hoover promoted conservative measures to end the Depression. President Hoover, however, was reluctant to institute direct relief measures, and he projected a grim attitude. Both of these things made him widely unpopular. Roosevelt, on the other hand, possessed a buoyant spirit and a warm smile and promised direct action. These were enough to sweep him into office and to get a wide Democratic majority elected to both houses of Congress.

An experimenter at heart, Roosevelt was open to all ideas. He employed Republicans as well as Democrats, conservatives as well as liberals, university intellectuals as well as experienced politicians.

The day Roosevelt took office a flurry of activity began that did not let up for more than three months. This time of intensive legislation and policy setting came to be called the Hundred Days.

The Hundred Days
Drastic Reform Measures

Months before Roosevelt's inauguration, thousands of panicky Michigan residents had begun flocking to their local banks to withdraw cash from savings accounts. This activity depleted bank funds to such an extent that many banks actually closed. In mid-February 1933, the governor of Michigan declared a banking **moratorium,** a temporary shutdown of operations, in effect closing all state banks. He hoped that this would give the banks enough time to replenish their supplies of ready cash and, thus, restore depositors' confidence. The moratorium, however, actually had the opposite effect: It caused the panic to spread and intensify. Overnight, people throughout the nation began to panic. By Inauguration Day, 38 states had closed their banks, and the remaining 10 states had sharply restricted banking operations. The majority of Americans, having lost faith in their financial institutions, were hoarding money, hiding cash under mattresses, and storing gold in pillowcases.

Stemming the Bank Crisis

Even before the inauguration, Roosevelt had directed his future secretary of the treasury, William Woodin, to develop a plan for dealing with the bank crisis. Woodin proposed that Roosevelt call a special session of Congress and declare a partial bank holiday for all financial institutions until after Congress met on March 9. The President announced the plan on the afternoon of March 5, directing the banks to accept all deposits and make emergency loans for food and animal

---

★ ★ ★ **GALLERY OF PRESIDENTS** ★ ★ ★

Franklin Delano Roosevelt
1933–1945

"There is a mysterious cycle in human events. To some generations much is given. Of other generations much is expected. This generation of Americans has a rendezvous with destiny."

Nomination acceptance speech, Democratic National Convention, 1936

FRANKLIN D. ROOSEVELT LIBRARY

BACKGROUND
▶ Born 1882; Died 1945
▶ Assistant secretary of the navy 1913–1920
▶ New York governor 1929–1932
▶ Elected President in 1932, 1936, 1940, and 1944

ACHIEVEMENTS IN OFFICE
▶ Agricultural Adjustment Act
▶ National Industrial Recovery Act
▶ The Social Security Act of 1935
▶ Yalta Conference (1945)

454 CHAPTER 14 THE NEW DEAL

Meeting Special Needs

Visual Learners To help visual learners, have students begin a diagram of the banking system of savings deposits with a picture of a bank, a person, and a $100 bill. They can expand the diagram as they research, alone or in teams, and create a visual representation of what effects sudden massive withdrawals would have on the banks and depositors.

Attention Deficit Disorder If your class includes students with attention deficit disorder, have them outline the section on the board by using the heads. Have them look for clues in the heads to identify how Roosevelt dealt with the economic crisis.

feed over the course of the next four days but to refrain from conducting any other business.

From March 5 to noon on March 9, Secretary Woodin and his advisers worked around the clock to hammer out legislation that would end the banking crisis. When Congress met on the afternoon of March 9, the President's representative read the bill aloud. It stated that banks in sound financial shape would be reopened immediately. Those lacking assets would remain closed until the government could develop a way to open them safely. Congress promptly passed the bill, and Roosevelt signed it that evening.

FDR reassured people that their money would be safer in the newly reopened banks than hidden in their homes. Within a few days, deposits exceeded withdrawals. The banking crisis was over.

A New Deal

When Roosevelt accepted the Democratic nomination for President, he had pledged "a new deal for the American people." Now that he had taken office, it was time to fulfill that promise and put the rest of his legislative program, the New Deal, into effect.

The overwhelming approval that the Democrat-controlled Congress gave his banking bill persuaded Roosevelt to extend the special session to work on other New Deal legislation. The bills Roosevelt introduced—some of which actually had been first proposed by the Hoover administration—addressed the three R's: relief for the unemployed, recovery measures to stimulate the economy, and reform laws to help lessen the threat of another economic disaster.

Emergency Relief

By 1933 many of the millions of people who had been unemployed for more than three years had no choice left to them but to apply for public aid. Local relief agencies, however, could not meet the growing demand for aid. In response, FDR asked Congress to appropriate $500 million that a new agency, the Federal Emergency Relief Administration (FERA), would distribute to state and local relief agencies. The bill passed on May 12.

Eight days later the FERA swung into action. Headed by experienced administrator and social worker Harry Hopkins, the agency distributed $5 million in its first 2 hours of operation. One government official, worried about this fast pace of spending, suggested that a slower, more conservative distribution of funds might work out better in the long run. Hopkins responded, "People don't eat in the long run—they [have to] eat every day."

Although Hopkins disbursed the millions allotted to FERA quite freely, he disliked the **dole,** which is what

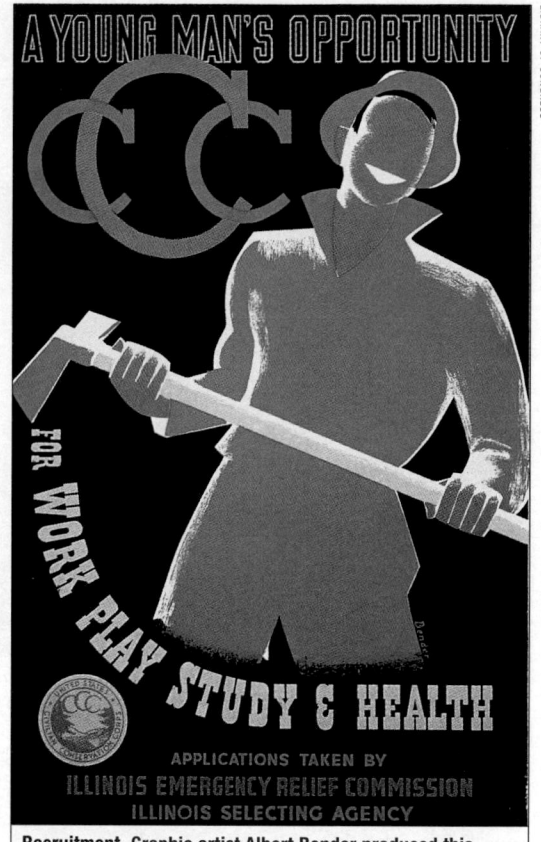

A YOUNG MAN'S OPPORTUNITY

CCC

FOR WORK PLAY STUDY & HEALTH

APPLICATIONS TAKEN BY
ILLINOIS EMERGENCY RELIEF COMMISSION
ILLINOIS SELECTING AGENCY

LIBRARY OF CONGRESS

Recruitment Graphic artist Albert Bender produced this energetic design to promote the CCC. *What did the CCC offer to its recruits that the dole did not?*

government charity was called. He, along with Roosevelt, felt that giving money to people broke down their self-respect and their will to work. To combat this weakening of morale, Roosevelt proposed relief programs that would put people back to work.

Civilian Conservation Corps

One of these programs was the Civilian Conservation Corps (CCC). The CCC put hundreds of thousands of unemployed men to work each season on environmental projects. The CCC constructed many of the facilities in the state and national parks.

Roosevelt hoped the CCC would create "a mass exodus of unemployed to the forests." Instead of going on relief, unmarried men between the ages of 18 and 25 would work in the corps to preserve the environment. According to Roosevelt's plan, the Labor Department would recruit the workers, the War Department would run the camps, and the Interior Department would supervise the work projects.

SECTION ONE **455**

Portfolio Project

Speech Writing Have students write a persuasive speech that FDR could have used during the Hundred Days to promote his solutions to the banking crisis or to defend his emergency relief measures. Students should keep in mind the audience for the speech and identify its characteristics, then address issues that would be persuasive to the listeners. The written speeches can be kept in students' portfolios, while a performance of each speech can be recorded and evaluated.

Work and Happiness William Gropper painted the mural *Construction of the Dam* in 1939. In it Gropper depicts the energy and productivity New Deal programs engendered. He also conveys a sense of harmony among the construction workers. *How does Gropper achieve this effect?*

NATIONAL MUSEUM OF AMERICAN ART, WASHINGTON, DC/ART RESOURCE, NY

Curriculum Connection

Language Arts Ask students to review the conditions surrounding Roosevelt's presidency and the measures he implemented during the Hundred Days. Then ask them to consider what Roosevelt meant when he said in his acceptance speech that his generation had a "rendezvous with destiny." Have students write a description of a rendezvous with destiny that their own generation faces.

CCC members lived in barracks, ate together in mess halls, and followed a strict schedule. Room and board and a salary of $30 a month were provided to each man in exchange for his labor. The workers sent most of their salaries back to their families.

All told, by 1942 when the CCC was disbanded, 2,650 camps had been built and a total of 2.5 million men had served in them. The CCC excluded women and limited the numbers of African Americans, Hispanic Americans, and Native Americans it accepted into its ranks. Furthermore, the minorities who were permitted to join the corps were segregated from the white workers. So, although the CCC helped many people, it still discriminated against minorities and women—some of the people hardest hit by the Depression.

Among the first recruits to the CCC were several thousand members of the bonus army. This army had returned to Washington, D.C., in the spring of 1933 to lobby again for early payment on the bonus certificates they had received as veterans of World War I. Roosevelt, like Hoover, was reluctant to grant them the money. Instead of sending in troops to run the veterans out of Washington as Hoover had done, however, Roosevelt had coffee served to the veterans and then arranged for them to meet with his aides. These aides first gave the veterans the idea of seeking employment in the CCC.

Public Works Administration

The Public Works Administration (PWA) was another New Deal program that helped provide jobs for the unemployed. With a grant of $3.3 billion to carry out public projects, the PWA put people back to work building schools and dams, refurbishing government buildings, planning sewage systems, improving highways, and generally modernizing the nation. The PWA's massive spending on wages, materials, and supplies for projects nationwide was intended to stimulate industry and spur economic recovery.

National Recovery Administration

Another of Roosevelt's goals was to increase the productivity of industry. Between 1929 and 1933, America's factories had decreased their production levels by about 40 percent. To help factories recover, Roosevelt sponsored the National Industrial Recovery Act (NIRA). After its passage on June 16, 1933, the NIRA established the National Recovery Administration (NRA) to carry out the new law.

The NIRA relaxed the antitrust laws of the early 1900s and called for business leaders to confer and establish codes to set quality standards, production levels, prices, maximum work hours, and minimum wages. The NIRA also declared that workers should be allowed to

Extending the Content

Recovery Projects Besides working at a national level, the PWA revitalized local economies throughout the United States. For example, in 1934 the PWA granted New York Mills, a small town in Minnesota, money to build a village water system. All the town's unemployed men went back to work during this construction project. In addition engineering contractors, plumbing and electrical companies, and materials suppliers gained new business from the project. Students can analyze the economic impact that construction of a new school, hospital, transportation, or public works project might have on their community. Is such a project currently underway in their community? Encourage them to brainstorm the far-reaching effects on business, employment, and reduced social costs of one such construction project.

Working Eagle Hired by the Works Progress Administration, Charles Coiner created the best-known symbol of the New Deal. *What was the function of a blue-eagle poster?*

CULVER PICTURES

policies had controversial results. Owners of large companies established codes that put small businesses at such a disadvantage that many small-business owners felt that they were being forced into bankruptcy, and for this they blamed the NRA.

Agricultural Adjustment Administration

The Agricultural Adjustment Administration (AAA) was equally controversial. This agency was established to help farmers who had been hard hit by the Depression. The AAA paid farmers a **subsidy,** or financial assistance, to reduce the production of crops and the number of animals they raised. Such cutbacks would help bring the supply of agricultural products more in line with the demand for them, causing prices to rise.

Although the plan was sound in theory, problems developed as it was put into practice. For example, by the time the AAA was established in the spring of 1933, farmers had already planted their fields and farm animals had already produced many young. Therefore, in order to meet the AAA's guidelines, farmers had to plow under portions of their crops and kill the newborn animals. At a time when thousands of people were suffering from malnutrition, this action struck many as immoral and wasteful.

In response, Roosevelt authorized the FERA to buy some of the crops and livestock before they were destroyed and to distribute them to the needy. Yet not all the farm products could be redistributed. For example, most of the animals that were slaughtered were too young to be used as food. To explain the apparent waste, Secretary of Agriculture Henry A. Wallace stated, "Agriculture cannot survive in a capitalistic society as a philanthropic enterprise." His explanation did little to appease the people who were distressed by the AAA's policies.

Tennessee Valley Authority

Another New Deal recovery program was the Tennessee Valley Authority (TVA). The TVA built dams in the Tennessee River to turn the river's water

organize labor unions and to bargain collectively. Shortening individual workers' hours forced businesses to hire more people, which, in turn, created 2 million additional jobs.

The NRA could not effectively penalize business leaders who decided not to adhere to the industry-set standards. So to encourage business leaders to comply voluntarily with the codes, the NRA launched a huge publicity campaign. It adopted as its symbol a dark blue eagle and asked businesses that followed the codes to prominently display a blue-eagle poster. Then the NRA asked people to buy their goods only from businesses displaying the blue eagle.

The public rallied in support of businesses displaying the eagle. Despite the public's enthusiasm, the NRA's

TENNESSEE VALLEY AUTHORITY, 1917–1980

1917–1918 During WWI, U.S. Army Corps builds power plant in Tennessee Valley.	1933 FDR creates the Tennessee Valley Authority.	1939 The TVA completes three major dams; four new ones are under way.		

1900	1910	1920	1930	1940	1950	1960	1970	1980	1990

1920s Senator Norris and Ford Company dispute public v. private ownership.	1936 TVA brings electricity to farms, and REA brings loans to farmers' cooperatives.	1940s Wartime needs spur further construction, including a 28-story dam.	1970s The TVA constructs nuclear power facilities.

SECTION ONE **457**

Cultural Perspectives

Evaluating Policies The CCC's enlistment policies illustrate how discrimination can intensify during hard times. The enlistment first of young white males, followed by limited and segregated enrollment of minorities, reflected a philosophy that placed primary importance on employing white males. The exclusion of women reflected the belief that families and the nation's economy depended on male employment. Have students take part in a letter-writing campaign aimed at Franklin or Eleanor Roosevelt or at Harold Hopkins, giving arguments for expanding enrollment in the CCC.

Curriculum Connection

Civics In a 1932 campaign speech, Hoover referred to Roosevelt's proposals as the "philosophy of stagnation, of despair . . . the end of hope." Many business leaders and others felt that the New Deal constituted a Socialist government, a threat to liberty. Have students compare Roosevelt's New Deal with Hoover's proposed solutions. Ask them whether or not the New Deal represented a departure from democracy.

power into electricity. A reporter outlined the TVA's plan as follows:

> First, says the TVA, you fill up your gullies, terrace your land, strip-plow your slopes, and let the water flow down as slowly as possible. You collect the water behind dams and produce power. You use part of this power to make phosphate fertilizer, and with the fertilizer you grow legumes which enrich and hold your soil. You use some of the rest of the power on the farm itself.
>
> —"A Dream Takes Form in TVA's Domain," *New York Times Magazine*, April 19, 1936

The TVA aimed to do much more than just generate electricity. It was also intended to enrich the land, to create fish-filled lakes that would, in turn, increase tourism, and to provide jobs for the residents of the Tennessee Valley. Although the TVA achieved some of these goals, it was not well received by everyone. Farmers whose lands were permanently flooded by backwaters the dams created were certainly not pleased by the project. Also, some business leaders considered the government-sponsored agency an unfair competitor, resenting the rock-bottom rates the TVA charged. They lobbied to prevent similar programs from being approved for other regions of the country.

Reform Laws

In addition to providing relief and stimulating recovery, the New Deal legislation enacted reform measures. Among the most important reform measures were the Truth-in-Securities Act and the Glass-Steagall Banking Act.

The Truth-in-Securities Act was designed to eliminate fraud in the stock market. Under this law, a company that deliberately deceived investors about its financial status could be sued. The Glass-Steagall Banking Act prohibited banks from investing savings deposits in the stock market, which was too unpredictable to assure the safety of these funds. It also established the Federal Deposit Insurance Corporation (FDIC) to insure bank deposits in all member banks. With this insurance people regained confidence that their money would be safe in FDIC banks.

THE TENNESSEE VALLEY AUTHORITY, 1930s

Plotted on this map are the sites at which major TVA dams were located. Also shown is the area receiving TVA power. Locate these sites and identify the area that receives TVA power. *In what other states besides Tennessee are there TVA dams? Besides Tennessee, what other states benefit from TVA power?*

Critical Thinking

Demonstrating Reasoned Judgment Ask each student to list what they feel are the rights and responsibilities of citizenship. Have students share and discuss their lists with the class. Then ask the class to consider whether or not relief—or the dole—should be a right of citizenship. Should citizens be responsible for contributing to the welfare of others? What should be the limits to citizens' rights and responsibilities for general welfare?

The President and the People
Access to the White House

President Roosevelt's positive, vigorous style was reflected not only in his legislative programs but also in life at the White House, where glumness had reigned during the last few months of the Hoover administration. On Inauguration Day the head of the secret service, Colonel Edmund Starling, drove the brooding former President and his wife to the train station. When Starling returned, he reported that the White House was "transformed during my absence into a gay place, full of people who oozed confidence." The friendly informality of the White House made many Americans feel personally connected to the President.

Fireside Chats

FDR promoted this feeling by informally addressing the American public in frequent radio broadcasts known as fireside chats. In these chats, Roosevelt explained the legislation of the New Deal in simple, straightforward terms. Humorist Will Rogers quipped that in Roosevelt's first fireside chat, on March 12, 1933, the President explained the complex subject of banking in terms that even bankers could understand. His steady, relaxed voice reassured people across the nation that their problems would be solved and, more importantly, that they could participate in solving them. In his broadcast about the NRA, Roosevelt said the following:

T he essence of the plan is a universal limitation of hours of work per week for any individual by common consent, and a universal payment of wages above a minimum, also by common consent. I cannot guarantee the success of this nation-wide plan, but the people of this country can guarantee its success. . . . [I] do have faith, and retain faith, in the strength of common purpose, and in the strength of unified action taken by the American people.
—Franklin D. Roosevelt, Fireside Chat, July 24, 1933

FDR's skillful handling of the press matched his masterful management of radio publicity. Hoover had met infrequently with reporters and only answered questions that had been written out beforehand. Roosevelt, on the other hand, held weekly press conferences in which he was willing to answer all questions. This made him very popular with reporters—a relationship that often worked to his advantage.

Electricity for Farms Under the Rural Electrification Act, low-interest, 20-year loans were granted to farmers' cooperatives to help connect rural homes to cheap power sources such as the TVA. *Why were some business leaders opposed to the TVA? Why did some farmers oppose it?*

During the Hundred Days between March 9 and June 16, President Roosevelt proposed 15 bills. These came to be known collectively as the First New Deal. Congress, with only minor changes, passed all 15 of his proposals. For a President to be able to collaborate so successfully with a Congress was a major victory. FDR, however, was a Democrat at a time when Democrats controlled Congress, a fact that greatly facilitated the passage of FDR's legislative programs.

SECTION ONE **459**

ASSESS

Meeting Lesson Objectives

Each section objective is tested by the section review question(s) that follows it in parentheses.

1. Cite issues and events that persuaded voters to choose FDR as President. (2)
2. Detail the legislation of the Hundred Days. (1, 3, 4)
3. Discuss FDR's relationship with the public during the Hundred Days. (2, 5)

VISUAL INSTRUCTION

Electricity for Farms People often look to technology for answers to pressing social problems. The REA, for example, focused on using electrical networking to help solve economic depression in farming areas. Have students discuss plausible technological solutions to one of today's social problems, such as homelessness, low academic achievement, or damage to the environment.

Answer: *Some business leaders felt that the government control and low prices unfairly shut out private industry. Some farmers' lands were flooded by backwaters from the new dams.*

Portfolio Project

Making Maps Have students do research in the library on deforestation. Then have students create before-and-after maps showing deforestation and reforestation. The "before" map can show details of the effects of deforestation on a particular area such as the Tennessee River Valley. The "after" map should show how building dams, planting trees, and other measures have helped to restore woodlands, wildlife, and forest-related industry in the chosen area. Students should keep the finished maps on file in their portfolios.

Evaluate

Have students complete the Section Review.

📁 💿 Assign the Section 1 Quiz or use the Testmaker to develop a customized quiz. (Also in Spanish.) **LEP**

Reteach

🎧 Have students listen to the Chapter 14, Section 1 Audiocassette. (Also in Spanish.) **LEP**

Enrich

📁 Have students complete the Chapter 14 Enrichment Activity. (Also in Spanish.) **LEP**

📁 Have students complete the Chapter 14 Geography in History Activity.

CLOSE

Ask students to list legislation of the First New Deal. For each item, ask whether recovery, relief, reform, or a combination of these describes the act. (Refer students to section heads for specific legislation.)

460

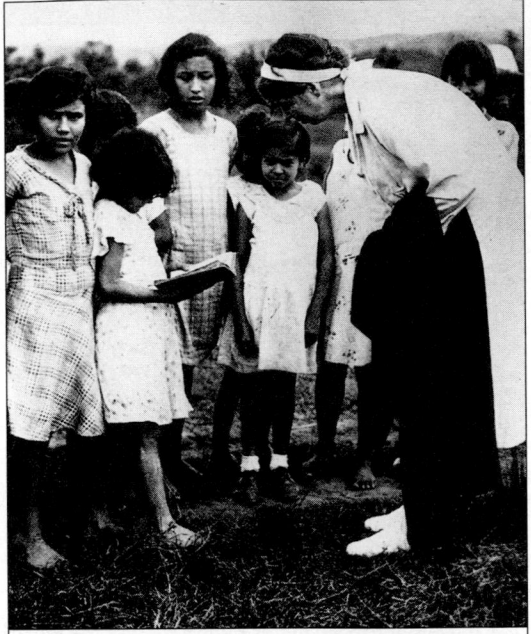

AP/WIDE WORLD PHOTOS

Woman of Action While touring Puerto Rico in 1934, Mrs. Roosevelt listens to a young girl read from her schoolbook. In addition to speaking English, the First Lady spoke Spanish, French, and German. *In what ways did Eleanor Roosevelt affect the presidency?*

Eleanor's Influence

Eleanor Roosevelt first became involved in politics during her husband's battle with polio. Hoping to keep FDR's name before the public, Eleanor became active in the Democratic party. She soon took up other causes, joining the Women's Trade Union League and the League of Women Voters. When FDR returned to politics, Eleanor did not give up her own political activities. Instead, she lobbied for laws to end child labor, worked for better conditions in state hospitals, discussed with her husband the appalling plight of people stranded by the Depression, and used her influence to help relieve their suffering.

Eleanor gave people throughout the nation the sense that they had access to the President. Hundreds of thousands of people wrote to her each year, seeking help and offering solutions to the nation's problems.

This letter comes to you from the . . . lead and zinc field of southeastern Kansas. Thirty-eight percent of the entire world supply of lead and zinc ore is produced in this district. We have here health hazards known as "lead poisoning" in the smelters and silicosis, the most dreaded industrial disease known to medical science. . . . These health hazards can be eliminated if the mining trusts will install air

---

cleaning devices. This, of course, costs money and the greedy, grasping employers apparently haven't any extra. . . . Why [doesn't] the labor department make a health and hygiene survey of this district? Will you add your voice to ours in requesting this be done[?]

—Letter from the Cherokee County Central Labor Body, Columbus, Kansas, 1938

Eleanor saw to it that all the letters that she received were answered. Those letters that were of special concern to her, like the one reprinted above, she showed to the President, often persuading him to take action.

She held her own press conferences regularly and traveled across the country giving lectures on a variety of topics that were of great concern to her and the American people. According to her friend Adlai Stevenson, "What rendered this unforgettable woman so extraordinary was not merely her response to suffering; it was her comprehension of the complexity of the human condition." Showing concern for everyone she met, the First Lady symbolized the energy, empathy, and responsiveness of the Roosevelt administration.

The Roosevelts' warm public images aligned the majority of Americans behind President Roosevelt and his New Deal. Throughout 1934, however, the country remained mired in economic depression. Critics quickly arose to attack Roosevelt and the New Deal.

SECTION REVIEW

Vocabulary
1. Define: moratorium, dole, subsidy.

Checking Facts
2. What are some of the reasons why Roosevelt won the election of 1932?

3. How did the CCC and the PWA differ?

Critical Thinking
Predicting Consequences
4. What might have happened if Roosevelt's legislation had failed to address any one of the three R's?

Linking Across Time
5. Roosevelt's decision to talk frequently with reporters, answer all correspondence, and broadcast fireside chats were all examples of his approachable style. Compare the leadership styles of President Coolidge and President Roosevelt.

Section 1 Review Answers

1. moratorium (454), **dole** (455), **subsidy** (457)
2. He promised to take direct relief measures and expressed confidence and concern.
3. The CCC addressed environmental projects, while the PWA addressed construction projects.
4. Without recovery, people would continue on relief; without relief, many could not contribute

to recovery; and without reform, recovery and relief could slip away.
5. Coolidge: cold, reserved, believed government should not be involved in citizens' personal needs
Roosevelt: warm, charming, believed government should be involved in people's lives.

Social Studies Skill

INTERPRETING IMAGES

Learning the Skill

Many painters and photographers have documented American life. You can learn about a period from their works; you can get an idea of how people dressed, what technology they used, and where they lived and worked. Paintings and photographs are artists' impressions, however, and not objective records of the subjects they portray. To interpret an image, therefore, you must understand how it reflects the views of the person who created it. Both painter and photographer make choices about what to include and how to show it. These choices affect the impressions their works give.

Interpreting a Painting or Photograph

When you look at an image, ask yourself the following questions:

a. What has the painter or photographer chosen to portray? The artist might have represented only a small segment of society or symbolized the subject rather than documenting it precisely. What has been left out?

b. What is the central impression created by the image? Through the use of form and color, the artist might have idealized the subject, for example, or made it frightening.

c. How is the impression communicated? Photographers can control what the lens "sees" just as painters can control what appears on a canvas. Photographers can pose people and can exclude elements that do not support the impression they want to convey.

Practicing the Skill

1. Look below at the section of Thomas Hart Benton's mural *America Today*. How has Benton idealized the steelworkers and the industry?

2. Study the photograph below. What impression does it convey about the steelworkers' relationship to the city? How has the photographer communicated this impression?

3. Examine the mural on page 456. What can you learn about the New Deal from this image?

4. Review the two photographs of Eleanor Roosevelt on pages 453 and 460. How does each photograph give a different impression of her?

5. Look at the poster on page 455. How does the artist use the drawing to support the text on the poster?

Applying the Skill

Find a painting or photograph that interests you in a book or magazine. Apply what you have learned about interpreting images.

Additional Practice

For additional practice, see Reinforcing Skills on page 483.

America Today Thomas Hart Benton depicts steelworkers in this section from a large mural. *How does Benton convey the atmosphere of a steel mill?*

High Above New York This 1912 photograph shows men at work on the Woolworth Building, then the world's tallest building. *How does the photographer capture the danger?*

SOCIAL STUDIES SKILL **461**

TEACH

This feature helps students develop the skill of interpreting images. Point out that artists and photographers make choices when they determine what an image will look like. Learning this skill will help students recognize those choices and decide what they as viewers can learn from the image.

VISUAL INSTRUCTION

America Today Thomas Hart Benton the best-known muralist of his time, specialized in dramatization of American themes. He painted this scene in 1930.

Answer: *He conveys an atmosphere of heat, danger, and exertion by his use of fiery colors lighting up the darkness and by the strenuous postures of the workers.*

High Above New York Ask students to imagine where the photographer might be situated. *(above the workers, perhaps in a less breathtaking spot)*

Answer: *The photographer has emphasized the danger of the ironworkers' position by showing so little of the structure on which they are working and so much of the city and river far below.*

Additional Practice

☞ Have students complete the Chapter 14 Skill Reinforcement Activity.

Practicing the Skill Answers

1. Benton has created an impression of hard work and harmony by making the workers extremely muscular and by having them work in close proximity, sharing some of the same tools.
2. By showing the workers high above the city and in the foreground, the photographer has emphasized the importance, creativity, and daring of their relationship to the city.

3. The mural gives the impression that the New Deal inspired hard work and cooperation.
4. In the somewhat self-conscious pose of the first photograph, she appears unassertive and quiet. The second photograph shows her unselfconsciously absorbed in her work.
5. He depicts a healthy young man who seems delighted with the opportunity to wield an axe.

TEACH

Making the Historical Connection

TEACH

Making the Historical Connection

The percentage of American households with telephones grew from 35 percent in 1920 to 44 percent in 1930. During the Depression decade this number declined by a few percentage points before resuming its rise. Today 93 percent of the nation's households have telephone service, each making or receiving an average of 3,516 calls per year.

FYI

Ma Bell During the Depression, AT&T, Bell's parent company, laid off some 20 percent of its workers. Nevertheless, the company maintained full payment of shareholders' dividends, a decision that was very unpopular with labor. The passage of the Wagner Act in 1935 led to the formation of the National Federation of Telephone Workers, which supplanted the Bell System's company-sponsored unions.

Science, TECHNOLOGY, and Society

The Telephone

Although the telephone industry shared in the hard times of the 1930s, technical development went forward. Replacement of operator-assisted calling with dial telephones continued; one operator at the switchboard could now do the work of six. By the end of 1935, 48 percent of telephones were dial operated.

FRANKLIN D. ROOSEVELT LIBRARY

HELLO GIRL
FDR had a special switchboard installed in the White House with Louise Hachmeister ("Hacky") as operator. He called her the phone detective and the hello girl. Eleanor Roosevelt said, "I doubt that there is a more consistently courteous group in America than telephone operators."

A TELEPHONE HISTORY

1870s	1880s	1890s	1900s	1910s	1920s	1930s

ALEXANDER GRAHAM BELL patents the first operational telephone in 1876; this patent was probably the most valuable patent ever issued.

FIRST COAST-TO-COAST CALL connects Bell and his assistant, Watson, in 1915. Dial phones are in use by 1919, and the work of the operator grows more mechanical.

SHORTWAVE RADIO helps make the first transatlantic telephone transmission possible in 1927. A handheld unit containing both earpiece and mouthpiece comes into use in the 1930s.

Background Information

Down on the Farm The number of farm telephones dropped steeply during the 1920s and 1930s. This decline reflects the long period of hard times in the farming economy. In addition major telephone companies considered it unprofitable to subsidize rural service.

The government was also unwilling to help. Although the New Deal funded rural electrification, rural telephone systems usually had to be capitalized by the users themselves. Such capital was hard to come by in farming areas at that time.

THE LAST WORD

The 1930s model, at left, was one of the earliest to combine the receiver and transmitter in a handheld, dial-operated instrument. This model and its later variations were standard for decades.

PHONE LOG

PORTFOLIO PROJECT

Keep a personal record for one week of your incoming and outgoing calls, both local and long-distance. Classify the calls as family, school-related, or social. Then assess the impact of the telephone on your life. How might you have sent or received each message without using a telephone?

Block Scheduling

The Portfolio Project on this page provides an excellent opportunity to enrich and extend the key elements of this feature.

FYI

Clouded Crystal Ball
When Alexander Graham Bell demonstrated his brand new invention for the leading telegraph company, Western Union, its executives wrote to him saying that the telephone had "no commercial possibilities"; they saw no future, they said, for "an electrical toy." Twenty years later stock in Bell's company was worth $1,000 a share.

JAMES McMULLAN INC.

THE FRONT PAGE
HECHT & MacARTHUR'S
LINCOLN CENTER THEATER at the VIVIAN BEAUMONT

BROOKLYN MUSEUM

TELEPHONE

GET THAT STORY

By the 1930s the telephone was as essential to the reporter as the notepad and pencil—as vital to newspapering as it was to almost every other kind of business.

CLOSE

Ask students what adjuncts to the telephone they find useful. *(They may mention answering machines, beepers, faxes.)* Ask them to assess the relative importance of the telephone and television in their lives. Which would they rather do without? *(They should cite reasons for their answers.)*

THE PAY PHONE

During the Depression years, the pay phone was a blessing to those who had to defer their dream of a household telephone. This telephone booth, called the Yin-Yang, was designed for the 1939 New York World's Fair.

1940s	1950s	1960s	1970s	1980s	1990s

DIRECT DIAL connects domestic long-distance calls by 1951. An undersea cable with long-life amplifiers and polyethylene insulation improves transatlantic calls in 1956.

SATELLITE TRANSMISSION and Touch-Tone phones help handle high volumes of calls by the early 1960s. International direct dialing begins in 1970.

MOBILE TELEPHONES make use of cellular radio technology in 1982. The Department of Justice ends the Bell monopoly in 1984. The 1990s introduce widespread use of conference calls, fiber optics, faxes, voice mail, and videoconferences.

PORTFOLIO PROJECT

Portfolio Project

Telephone Etiquette Have students create a telephone etiquette handbook. Suggest that they include instructions for answering the telephone, for taking or leaving messages, for opening and closing a conversation, for dealing with unsolicited commercial calls, and other matters they think are important. They may wish to include advice on efficient and courteous ways to use answering machines as well. Have them keep their handbooks in their portfolios.

FOCUS

Section Objectives

1. Discuss the objections of tenant farmers, labor unions, radicals, conservatives, and the Supreme Court to the New Deal.
2. Identify some of the legislation of the Second New Deal.
3. Describe the impact that Roosevelt's proposed change in the Supreme Court had on the momentum of the Second New Deal.

Bellringer Activity

While taking attendance at the beginning of the class period, display **Section Focus Transparency 44,** and have students answer the questions. (Or use the blackline master.)

VISUAL INSTRUCTION

Rage for Reform
Townsend's plan was regarded as unrealistic because it would have required a sum equal to one-half the 1934 national income to finance it.

Ask: What did Townsend believe his program could accomplish? *(He believed that it would rescue the elderly from poverty and end the Depression.)*

Criticism and Reformulation

SEPTEMBER 1933: DOCTOR LAUNCHES CRUSADE TO AID THE ELDERLY

Rage for Reform
The popularity of Townsend's pension program influenced the passage of the 1935 Social Security Act, even though economists considered his plan to be unworkable.

ONE DAY IN 1933, DR. FRANCIS E. TOWNSEND, A 66-YEAR-OLD RETIRED PHYSICIAN, WITNESSED SOMETHING THAT CHANGED HIS LIFE. While standing at his bathroom window shaving, he saw "three very haggard old women, stooped with great age, bending over the [trash] barrels, clawing into the contents." That these elderly people should be reduced to such poverty and degradation infuriated him.

Townsend channeled his fury into formulating a plan to aid America's aged and, at the same time, to stimulate the economy. According to his plan, every person over age 60 would be asked to retire, freeing up jobs for younger people. Each retired person would receive a pension of $200 per month on the condition that the person spend the entire sum in 30 days. Townsend claimed that the pension would rescue the elderly from poverty, and the enforced spending would act as a transfusion of cash into the economy. Furthermore, it would create a demand for products, which, in turn, would result in a demand for more workers to produce them. Townsend believed that his social security program would bring about an immediate end to the Depression.

In the southern California community where Townsend lived, the idea gained widespread appeal. To publicize the plan, Townsend began circulating petitions, speaking at meetings, and organizing

AS YOU READ

Vocabulary
► unionization
► demagogue

Think About . . .
► the objections of tenant farmers, labor unions, radicals, conservatives, and the Supreme Court to the New Deal.

► the legislation of the Second New Deal.
► the impact of Roosevelt's proposed change in the Supreme Court on the momentum of the Second New Deal.

464 CHAPTER 14 THE NEW DEAL

Section 2 Resources

REPRODUCIBLE RESOURCES
📁 Lesson Plan 14-2
📁 Vocabulary and Guided Reading Activity 14-2
📁 Unit 5 Case Study
📁 Unit 5 American Literature Reading

MULTIMEDIA RESOURCES
🔊 Section Focus Transparency 44
🎧 Chapter 14 Digest Audiocassette
💻 Student Self-Test: A Software Review
💻 Testmaker
💿 A Geographic Perspective on American History

clubs. Within a few years, Townsend clubs had sprung up throughout the nation.

The success of Dr. Townsend's movement indicated the level of discontent many elderly people felt during Roosevelt's first term. Older people, however, were not the only ones to find fault with Roosevelt. By the end of 1934, people from all walks of life were attacking Roosevelt's policies.

New Deal: Big Deal!
Discontent With the Pace of Recovery

Under Roosevelt's New Deal, the economy had begun to recover. Between 1933 and 1934, the national income rose 25 percent. By 1934 hundreds of factories that had closed in the early 1930s were again producing goods. Many farmers had refinanced their mortgages with government assistance. Millions of people who had been unemployed were receiving relief or holding federally funded jobs.

Nevertheless, the recovery was incomplete. Although by 1934 incomes had risen substantially, they were still far below precrash levels. On average, workers in the cities made 13 percent less than they had made in 1929. Farm prices lagged 28 percent behind 1929 prices. More than 20 percent of the working population were still unemployed. For many farmers, factory workers, and unemployed citizens, the New Deal had taken too long to accomplish too little.

Protests of Tenant Farmers

The New Deal's agricultural program, the AAA, actually did some farmers more harm than good. To reduce the amount of crops that would be produced, the AAA paid landowners to let some of their land lie unused. Technically, the landowners were supposed to divide their AAA checks with their tenant farmers. In reality, however, few landowners complied with this

AP/WIDE WORLD PHOTOS

Common Cause Although African Americans and whites were segregated in most work and social situations, in the Southern Tenant Farmers' Union (STFU), African American and white tenant farmers joined forces to fight the landowners who had unjustly evicted them. *What did the AAA require of landowners?*

SECTION TWO **465**

TEACH

Guided Practice
L2 Making the Connection Have students help you list criticisms of the current President and the sectors of society from which they come. FDR was increasingly criticized toward the end of his first term. Ask students what those criticisms might have been and from whom they might have come.

VISUAL INSTRUCTION

Common Cause In its first few months, the STFU signed up 1,400 members in Arkansas. By the end of 1935, membership had grown to 30,000 in several states, and the AAA could no longer ignore the STFU's protests.

Answer: *to divide their AAA checks with their tenant farmers*

NATIONAL GEOGRAPHIC SOCIETY

 Videodisc

GTV: A Geographic Perspective on American History

Side 4, Chapter 3
Title: Thinking Big
Subject: Depression, Dust Bowl, New Deal
Ask: What was the New Deal? *(government programs designed to end the Depression)*

Cooperative Learning

Role-Playing Organize the class into discussion groups. Each group member should play one of the following roles: farm laborer, factory worker, unemployed person, business leader, older person, or FDR. Have the groups read the section to find out what each person's criticism of FDR would be and how FDR would respond to that criticism. Then have each group role-play a meeting between citizens and FDR.

Independent Practice

L3 Research Have students consult almanacs to find the latest unemployment statistics. Have them compare the current rate of unemployment with the rate in 1934. Then they should compare the actual number of people who were unemployed in 1934 with the number unemployed today.

✎ Have students complete Chapter 14, Section 2 Vocabulary and Guided Reading Activity. (Also available in Spanish.) **LEP**

GRAPH STUDY

In order to circumvent the NIRA provision that guaranteed workers the right to join unions, many employers formed company-sponsored unions. The workers' most important goal in many strikes during the 1930s was to win the right to organize their own unions and have them recognized.

Answer: *between 1935 and 1937*

Union organizing efforts in the mid-1930s focused on the auto industry, where the United Automobile Workers (UAW) pioneered the sit-down, a work stoppage in which workers refuse to leave their place of employment until their demands are met.

Inside the Plant: Most of the strikers are orderly and disciplined. They organize an orchestra and chorus, games, sports, and classes in labor history and other subjects.

LIBRARY OF CONGRESS

UPI/BETTMANN NEWSPHOTOS

June 1936 UAW tries to organize autoworkers. Spies hired by General Motors (GM) infiltrate meetings. Union activists are fired. GM refuses to recognize the union.

January 11 GM cuts off heat to the plant and blocks delivery of food. Police attack with tear gas; strikers fight back with firehoses and improvised projectiles; 13 strikers are wounded by gunfire.

1 Day   10 Days   20 Days   30 Days   40 Days

December 30 Workers at GM's Fisher Body #1 plant in Flint, Michigan, begin a sit-down strike.

January 6 An injunction against the strike is voided when the judge is found to own GM stock. Strikers ignore a later injunction.

Strike spreads: Soon 18 other GM plants in 10 cities are closed. Public opinion turns against GM.

Cars Produced in a Week

53,000 Before Strike

1,500 During Strike

Support: John L. Lewis, head of the CIO, and Governor Frank Murphy of Michigan, support the strikers. A local restaurant offers its facilities; a Women's Emergency Brigade prepares food and marches in picket lines.

A watershed in labor history was the push by the Congress of Industrial Organizations (CIO) to organize workers on an industry-wide basis rather than on a craft basis, as in the older American Federation of Labor (AFL). *Judging from the membership graph, when did industrial unions begin to take hold?*

---

requirement. Instead, they tended to reduce the number of acres planted by evicting their tenant farmers and did not even share with them the AAA subsidy. Poverty-stricken before the New Deal, tenant farmers were then also homeless and jobless.

A group of Southern tenant farmers who were outraged by this situation organized the interracial Southern Tenant Farmers' Union (STFU). They went on strike to obtain raises for working tenant farmers and day laborers. They petitioned the Department of Agriculture to give them a guarantee that tenant farmers would get their fair share of AAA payments. They also promoted nonviolent protest and showed that African Americans and whites could work together effectively.

The STFU met with strong opposition. Landowners worked with law enforcement agents to harass STFU leaders, threaten union members, and break up STFU meetings. Desperate for help, the STFU appealed to Roosevelt for aid. Roosevelt responded with promises but no action. Bitterly disappointed, one STFU leader wrote, "Too often he [Roosevelt] has talked like a cropper [tenant farmer] and acted like a planter [landowner]."

Voices of Labor

The National Industrial Recovery Act (NIRA) of 1933 had permitted all workers to join unions of their choice, bargain collectively for wage increases and other work benefits, and go on strike to try to force employers to meet their demands. The NIRA thus renewed most workers' hopes for change. In just the first 2 years following its passage, unions added about 1 million new workers to their ranks.

Although unions organized workers' efforts and provided them with leaders who could negotiate with owners and managers, some workers believed that unions were not as effective as worker-organized strikes and protests. Unions tended to dissipate revolutionary energy by focusing on contracts and negotiations rather than on rebellion.

Meeting Special Needs

Reading Disability To help students with reading disabilities, have them list the headings of the section. Then have them scan the information under each heading to find out what sectors of society leveled criticism at FDR and to find out how FDR reacted. Ask them to list this information under each heading on their outlines as they study the section.

"When Mr. Knudsen put his name to a piece of paper and says that General Motors recognizes the UAW-CIO—until that moment, we were non-people, we didn't even exist. [Laughs] That was the big one. [His eyes are moist.]"
Bob Stinson, a striker
quoted in *Hard Times* by Studs Terkel

The End [February 11] GM agrees to negotiate. The union wins recognition and a six-month contract. Workers are no longer afraid to join the union.

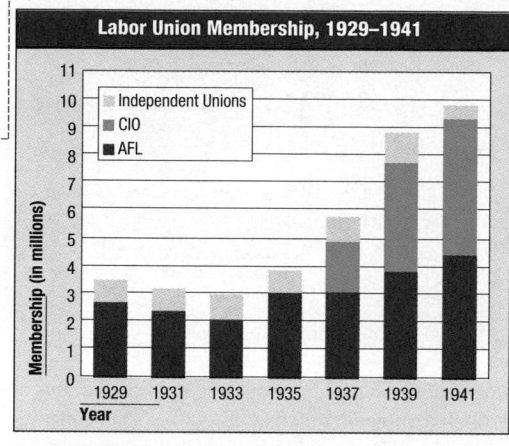

Labor Union Membership, 1929–1941

Unionization, or the formation of unions, did not generally ease the conflict between workers and management, however. The number and intensity of such conflicts increased after passage of the NIRA. An especially heated conflict occurred in 1934 when Minneapolis truck drivers tried to get local business representatives to negotiate with their union. Business leaders responded by banding together to break the strike. Then, on July 16, the police opened fire on unarmed picketers, shooting 67 people and killing 2. One hundred thousand Minneapolis citizens marched in the funeral procession for the slain workers. Confronted by such strong union sympathy, business leaders agreed to negotiate with unions.

During 1934 similarly bitter strikes took place throughout the nation. Textile workers from Georgia to Massachusetts staged a massive strike, while San Francisco workers from various unions struck together. That year more than 1.5 million workers staged 1,800 strikes.

Because unionization tended to increase the number of strikes and protests, business leaders and factory owners generally tried to prevent workers from unionizing. Although it was illegal, many employers fired or intimidated workers who tried to start unions. Even

Roosevelt, who had supported the NIRA, worried more about labor's power to halt economic recovery with strikes than he did about protecting the rights the bill supposedly ensured.

Reactionary and Radical Voices

Frustrated with the slowness and the limited scope of Roosevelt's New Deal, many Americans turned to leaders who promised simple and sometimes radical solutions to the nation's pressing problems. These leaders gained huge followings during the mid-1930s.

Dr. Townsend, who organized more than 5 million supporters for his pension plan, was one such leader. Townsend focused on getting Congress to approve his plan. In 1935, however, Townsend's plan was soundly defeated in Congress.

Another popular leader was Father Charles E. Coughlin, a Roman Catholic priest with his own weekly radio show. Coughlin was a **demagogue,** a leader who gains power by appealing to people's prejudices and fears rather than by appealing to reason.

In 1933 and 1934, Coughlin supported Roosevelt because he thought the President agreed with his ideas, such as nationalizing the banks and running them as a federal business like the post office. By 1935, Coughlin realized that Roosevelt had no intention of changing the nation's financial system. At that point he began calling the President a "great betrayer and a liar."

FDR was not the only person Coughlin attacked. He also spoke out against powerful bankers and later extended his hatred of particular bankers who happened to be Jewish to hatred of all Jews. Although the Jewish people were clearly not responsible for the economic plight of the nation, Coughlin's anti-Semitism gave his

Police and Strikers Clash During the 1934 strike, truckers fought with police in an attempt to prevent loaded vehicles from leaving a warehouse. *How did Minneapolis citizens react to the violence?*

AP/WIDE WORLD PHOTOS

Curriculum Connection

Mathematics Have students use the information in the sit-down strike graphic to solve the following problem. The strike lasted approximately six weeks. What was GM's approximate production loss, reckoned in numbers of cars, during the strike?

VISUAL INSTRUCTION

Police and Strikers Clash In Minneapolis, as in other cities, business leaders and conservatives formed a Citizens' Alliance to try to break the strike.

Answer: *Sympathy for the strikers was strong, although business leaders were opposed.*

Portfolio Project

Reporting a Strike Ask students to research one of the strikes of the 1930s and prepare a newspaper report about it. You may wish to consider the following possibilities:
Davidson-Wilder Coal Strike, Tennessee, 1932
Ford Hunger March, Detroit, 1932
Meat-Packing Strike, Hormel, Iowa, 1933

Jobs-for-Negroes Boycott, N.Y.C., 1934
Longshoremen's Strike, San Francisco, 1934
Pacific Northwest Lumber Strike, 1935

Have volunteers read their reports to the class. Students can keep the reports in their portfolios.

Curriculum Connection

Global Connection

Two of a Kind Father Charles Coughlin, above, claimed approximately 9 million supporters before the church ordered him to step out of the public spotlight. Huey P. Long, right, also had an enormous following. *How did Long maintain control of Louisiana while he was a member of the United States Senate?*

followers a group of people to blame for their troubles. Coughlin also preached that the wealth of the few should be redistributed among the many, an idea that appealed to many in the working class.

Coughlin's impassioned speeches increased his following. In the mid-1930s he commanded a radio audience of 30 million. Superiors in the church, however, embarrassed by Coughlin's behavior, finally imposed silence upon the priest in 1942.

A contemporary of Coughlin, Senator Huey P. Long of Louisiana was equally popular and just as opposed to FDR's programs. Long had achieved almost instant popularity when, as governor of Louisiana, he had pushed through new taxes to raise funds for schools and hospitals that would serve the poor. Long had seen to it that roads were improved and bridges were built in previously neglected areas of the state.

While still governor, Long was elected to the United States Senate in 1930. Just before he left the office of governor to take his seat in the Senate, he replaced the lieutenant governor with two successors who would follow his commands while he was in Washington, D.C. Then, as senator, he abolished local Louisiana governments, putting himself in control of all appointments to government offices such as those of the police and fire departments.

As senator he also launched his Share Our Wealth campaign with the slogan: Every man a king, but no one wears a crown. According to Long's proposal, all in-

comes above $5 million would be confiscated and redistributed, providing each family with a $5,000 income. Long's plan, like Coughlin's, appealed to many in the working class, helping him to gain widespread support.

Having taken complete control of the Louisiana government, Long then set his sights on controlling the United States government. In September 1935, however, Long was assassinated, putting an end to his plans.

New Deal: No Deal!
Conservatives and Courts Oppose FDR

Roosevelt not only faced opposition from people who demanded that the government do more for the needy, but also from people who demanded it do less. Among his greatest enemies were bankers and politicians with whom he had worked so successfully when he first took office.

Attack From the Conservatives

Many business leaders charged that Roosevelt was interfering too much with private businesses and spending an excessive amount of money on relief. They attacked the President's top advisers for lacking the political and business experience necessary to address adequately the needs of businesses. Most claimed that

Extending the Content

American Liberty League Conservative opponents of the New Deal stated that the Liberty League's two objectives were to teach respect for the rights of persons and property, and to teach the duty of government to encourage private enterprise and protect property. FDR commented: "An organization that only advocates two or three out of the Ten Commandments . . . would have certain shortcomings in having failed to advocate the other seven or eight Commandments." Ask students what other "commandments" for good government Roosevelt might have had in mind.

Roosevelt had created an unmanageable bureaucracy and was leading the nation toward socialism.

In 1934 a number of unhappy politicians and businesspeople formed the American Liberty League, an organization dedicated to "upholding the Constitution." This stated goal masked the league's real purpose: to destroy the New Deal. By waging a propaganda war, league members hoped to force Roosevelt supporters out of office. The Liberty League, described by one reporter as "the largest collection of millionaires ever assembled under the same roof," never gained much support.

Attack From the Courts

The courts were more successful in attacking the New Deal than were the millionaires. In the mid-1930s the Supreme Court overturned two key pieces of New Deal legislation, the NIRA and the AAA, on the grounds that they were both unconstitutional. It objected to the multitude of NIRA codes the executive branch had helped design and found that the NIRA's regulation of all industries—from dog food to shoulder pads—gave the executive branch too much power over small local businesses. In addition, the Court faulted NIRA codes that regulated intrastate as well as interstate business, arguing that the Constitution gave the federal government power only to regulate commerce between states—not within states.

The Court also objected to the means by which the AAA funded its agricultural subsidies: by levying a processing tax on businesses that bought the agricultural products. The Court deemed taxation was an improper method of regulating agricultural production.

Faced with attacks by radicals, liberals, and conservatives and hampered by the Supreme Court, Roosevelt revamped his recovery and reform policies. In 1935 he launched his new program—the Second New Deal.

The Second New Deal
Extending Relief and Reform

Like the First New Deal, the Second New Deal included sweeping legislation in many different areas. The new laws expanded relief programs, aided farmers and workers, and provided economic reforms.

Expanding Relief

Despite the success of the First New Deal, 10 million people remained unemployed in 1934. To put more people back to work, Roosevelt proposed a $4.8 billion relief program, the Works Progress Administration (WPA), in his Second New Deal.

Congress approved the proposed WPA in April 1935. Headed by Harry Hopkins, the administrator who had so forcefully taken charge of the FERA, the WPA then began processing the applications it received for projects nationwide. Building projects, including construction of hospitals, schools, airports, and playgrounds, were the mainstay of the program. The WPA also put unemployed teachers, artists, writers, and actors back to work. Teachers taught people to read. Painters designed murals for public buildings. Writers wrote guidebooks describing America's historical and cultural heritage. Actors traveled the country, bringing live theater to people who had never seen a play before.

A single WPA project might benefit a community in a variety of ways. For example, in San Antonio, Texas, in 1939

NATIONAL MUSEUM OF AMERICAN ART, WASHINGTON, DC/ART RESOURCE, NY

Jobs for Artists This 1935 Moses Soyer painting, *Artists on WPA*, depicts painters preparing works to be hung in public buildings. *How does Soyer convey the effect that WPA projects had on the morale of artists?*

Cultural Perspectives

Cultural Exodus Even before Hitler began to step up the persecution of Europe's Jews in 1938, German and Austrian artists and scientists—many of them Jews—sensed the temper of the times. They began to emigrate in large numbers—often coming to the United States. Scientists Albert Einstein and Leo Szilard, thinkers Hannah Arendt and Erik Erikson, artist Joseph Albers, writer Thomas Mann, architect Walter Groplus, and composer Paul Hindemith were among the hundreds of refugees who enriched America's cultural and scientific life as a result of Hitler's rise to power.

Block Scheduling

📁 Have students complete the Unit 5 Case Study to enrich their understanding of FDR's attempt to "pack" the Supreme Court.

VISUAL INSTRUCTION

A Powerful Project In 1936 only about 14.5 percent of the 6,800,000 farms in the country had electric power.

Answer: *It stimulated local economies and provided millions of jobs.*

ASSESS

Meeting Lesson Objectives

Each section objective is tested by the section review question(s) that follows it in parentheses.

1. Discuss the objections of tenant farmers, labor unions, radicals, conservatives, and the Supreme Court to the New Deal. (1, 2, 4)

2. Identify some of the legislation of the Second New Deal. (3)

3. Describe the impact that Roosevelt's proposed change in the Supreme Court had on the momentum of the Second New Deal. (5)

the WPA sponsored a $300,000 project that included building a scenic walkway along the San Antonio River, deepening the river channel to permit small-craft navigation, landscaping the riverfront, and building an outdoor theater. This project stimulated the local economy and beautified the city.

Both directly and indirectly, the WPA improved the quality of life in communities across the nation. In all, during its 5 years of operation, the WPA gave jobs to more than 8 million people.

In August 1935 another program, the Social Security Act, was passed. With its passage, the government accepted direct responsibility for meeting the basic needs of its citizens. This program instituted pension and survivors' benefits for the elderly and the orphaned and aid to individuals injured in industrial accidents. Monthly Social Security payments ranged from $12 to $85. Millions of people, however, did not even qualify for the program. Many of those who did not qualify were members of minority groups.

Aiding Recovery

Roosevelt further aided recovery by restoring to workers and farmers the rights and privileges that the Supreme Court had revoked. When the Supreme Court declared the NIRA unconstitutional in May 1935, workers lost their right to join unions of their choice and to bargain collectively. The July 1935 Wagner Act, however, restored those rights. It also set up a federal agency, the National Labor Relations Board (NLRB), to ensure that employers followed the new law.

After the Supreme Court struck down the AAA, Roosevelt proposed the Soil Conservation Act of 1936, which required farmers to reduce the acreage of the same crops the AAA had previously paid them not to plant. Under this act, the money for farm subsidies would not come from a processing tax—as it had under the AAA—but from the treasury.

The Rural Electrification Act (REA) of 1935 lent money to groups of farmers who organized to build power plants. For years utility companies had refused to extend service to isolated rural areas, arguing that it was not profitable. As a result, before the REA, fewer than 1 in 10 American farms had electricity. By the late 1940s, however, electricity had been extended to 90 percent of all farms.

Pushing for New Reforms

The REA indirectly attacked utility companies by enabling people to obtain electricity without them. Roosevelt also attacked these huge conglomerates directly with the Public Utility Holding Company Act, passed in June 1935. This act, which pared down the holding

CULVER PICTURES

A Powerful Project In this 1938 photograph, a skilled WPA employee works on intricate wiring. *In what ways did the WPA improve the quality of life during the Second New Deal?*

Critical Thinking

Demonstrating Reasoned Judgment
Although President Roosevelt was not entirely in sympathy with the Wagner Act, he believed that the Supreme Court's invalidation of the NIRA made it imperative to restore labor's rights. The NLRB, which the Wagner Act established, was pro-labor and pro-union. Organize students into groups. Have half the groups develop arguments in support of unionization; have the other half develop arguments against unionization. Ask each group to present its view. Bring the groups together to discuss their stands and offer arguments supporting their views.

companies, helped eliminate corruption and inefficiency in the utility industries and reduced consumers' costs.

The legislation regulating the utility companies enraged many business leaders who believed that the government was assuming too much power over businesses. These people became even angrier when the President proposed increased taxes on the incomes of wealthy corporations and individuals. This revenue bill passed Congress in 1935.

The Revenue Act of 1935 as well as other Second New Deal legislation convinced millions of Americans that the President was on their side. Roosevelt's popularity soared as the 1936 election season began.

Reelection and Redirection
Victory Won and Momentum Lost

Roosevelt geared his campaign toward the lower and middle classes, who had been hardest hit by the Depression, promising legislation that was not only charitable but that helped people to help themselves. The Republican candidate, Kansas's Governor Alfred Landon, supported most of Roosevelt's New Deal programs but said that he would run them more efficiently. Nevertheless, Landon gave people little reason to switch to him. In the most lopsided election since 1820, FDR won the majority of votes in every state but Maine and Vermont. Backed by 60 percent of the voters, Roosevelt believed the American people had endorsed his New Deal.

Conflict Over the Judicial Branch

Forging ahead, in February 1937 Roosevelt introduced a bill to increase the number of justices on the Supreme Court. Having been distressed by the Court's rulings against New Deal legislation, FDR wanted to appoint additional judges sympathetic to his programs. Publicly, however, Roosevelt insisted that he was merely trying to ease the workload of the aging justices. People reacted negatively to his tampering with the delicately balanced judicial system. Republican critics accused Roosevelt of wanting to become a dictator.

Although even some Democrats eventually criticized him, Roosevelt stuck to his proposal. Then, in the middle of the fight, the Supreme Court upheld several key New Deal programs. At this point, FDR backed down. To save face, he eventually signed a watered-down bill enacting measures to speed up judicial processes.

Fair Labor Standards Act

Opposition to Roosevelt's proposed judicial system changes and an economic recession that began in 1937 slowed down his political momentum. In 1937 and 1938,

An Unpopular Proposal When FDR proposed adding seats to the Supreme Court, most people thought he meant to "pack the court" with justices who would sustain his New Deal legislation. *How did this controversy end?*

Roosevelt proposed numerous other programs. He only secured passage of one New Deal law in 1938, the Fair Labor Standards Act, which regulated wages and working hours. Then, as tensions in Europe and Asia grew, the President began to concentrate on international issues and the New Deal slowly ground to a halt.

SECTION REVIEW

Vocabulary
1. Define: unionization, demagogue.

Checking Facts
2. Why did some people, particularly bankers and conservative politicians, oppose the New Deal?

3. How did the Second New Deal meet some of the criticisms of the First New Deal?

Critical Thinking
Recognizing Bias
4. Why might the views of tenant farmers and landowners on the question of who should get AAA reimbursement be different?

Linking Across Time
5. Compare FDR's "court-packing" effort with attempts made by recent administrations to change the direction of the Supreme Court. How do they differ?

VISUAL INSTRUCTION

An Unpopular Proposal Roosevelt's doomed effort was not unprecedented. Over the years, Congress had often been persuaded to change the number of justices for political reasons.

Answer: *FDR backed down.*

Evaluate

Have students complete the Section Review.

☞ 🖵 Assign the Section 2 Quiz or use the Testmaker to develop a customized quiz. (Also in Spanish.) **LEP**

Reteach

∩ Have students listen to the Chapter 14, Section 2 Audiocassette. **LEP**

Enrich

☞ Have students complete American Literature Reading 5.

CLOSE

Discuss with the class how Roosevelt's second term as President differed from his first term. What do students think were the most serious criticisms of the First New Deal? *(pages 465–469)* How did Roosevelt address these criticisms in his Second New Deal? *(WPA, Social Security Act, NLRB, REA, public utilities legislation, taxes on wealthy corporations and individuals)*

Section 2 Review Answers

1. unionization (467), **demagogue** (467)
2. Their profit interests were threatened by such measures as the NIRA, REA, Public Utilities Holding Company Act, and 1935 revenue bill.
3. WPA and Social Security expanded relief; NLRB, Soil Conservation Act, and REA helped workers and farmers; public utilities were regulated; wealthy were taxed.

4. Tenants thought they deserved the subsidy because they had been evicted; owners thought they deserved it because they owned the land.
5. FDR tried to restructure the Court; recent Presidents try only to appoint justices who favor their policies.

TEACH

Making the Historical Connection

Much of the art of the 1930s helped people escape the doldrums of the Depression, but some artists used their works to reflect on problems or to make suggestions about the future of the United States. Diego Rivera used his art both to record problems of the United States and to suggest solutions.

Turning Point

Diego Rivera and Nelson Rockefeller were on a collision course from the beginning. The turning point came when Rockefeller delivered his polite ultimatum—the head of Lenin must go—and Rivera refused to comply. Both parties won and both lost. Rockefeller destroyed the mural; Rivera painted another. Each pleased his loyal supporters, but the general public criticized and ridiculed them both.

CASE STUDY · Turning Point

Art and Politics at Rockefeller Center

SPRING 1933

> May 4, 1933
>
> Dear Mr. Rivera,
>
> While I was in the No. 1 building at Rockefeller Center yesterday viewing the progress of your thrilling mural, I noticed that in the most recent portion of the painting you had included a portrait of Lenin. This piece is beautifully painted but it seems to me that his portrait, appearing in this mural, might very easily seriously offend a great many people. . . . As much as I dislike to do so I am afraid we must ask you to substitute the face of some unknown man where Lenin's face now appears. . . .
>
> With best wishes, I remain sincerely,
> Nelson A. Rockefeller

The Case

Nelson Rockefeller, grandson of oil magnate John D. Rockefeller, Sr., commissioned Mexican muralist Diego Rivera to paint a fresco mural into the fresh plaster of the RCA Building's grand hall in Rockefeller Center. The mural's middle panel was nearly 41 feet by 19 feet (12.5 m by 5.8 m). The mural's proposed title was *Man at the Crossroads Looking with Hope and High Vision to the Choosing of a New and Better Future*. The Rockefeller family approved a preliminary sketch by Rivera that showed man standing between the bad times of the past and the good times of the future. A faceless leader united the people and brought order out of chaos.

Rivera began painting the mural in March 1933. On May Day (May 1), an international day in honor of workers, Rivera painted a portrait of the late Russian Communist ruler V.I. Lenin in place of the faceless leader. Rivera described his mural:

> On the left . . . I showed a night club scene of the debauched rich, a battlefield with men in the holocaust of war, and unemployed workers in a demonstration being clubbed by the police. On the right, I painted corresponding scenes of life in a socialist country: a May Day demonstration of marching, singing workers; an athletic stadium filled with girls exercising their bodies; and a figure of Lenin, symbolically clasping the hands of a black American and a white Russian soldier and worker, as allies of the future.

When Rockefeller asked Rivera to alter the design by eliminating the image of Lenin, Rivera responded:

> I am sure that that class of person who is capable of being offended by the portrait of a deceased great man, would feel offended, given such a men-

The Case at a Glance

Rockefeller family hires Rivera to paint mural for Rockefeller Center.	The theme is agreed upon: man at the crossroads looking toward a better future.	Rivera makes sketch of mural with faceless leader uniting the workers.	On May Day, Rivera gives the leader the face of Lenin.

Diego Rivera, above, painted a controversial mural in Rockefeller Center, New York, left. Nelson Rockefeller is shown at upper left.

The Background

The Rockefeller family developed Rockefeller Center between 1929 and 1939. When 64 percent of the workers in the building trades were unemployed, 75,000 men were employed in constructing Rockefeller Center. John D. Rockefeller, Jr., was the epitome of the successful American capitalist. While all around him workers were losing faith in an economy that could not employ them, Rockefeller provided meaningful, profitable work.

Mrs. John D. Rockefeller, Jr., was a founder of the Museum of Modern Art in New York City. In 1931 she brought Rivera to the United States, where he gave a show the next year. Some of the images in that show had realistically depicted starving workers and idle mills in the United States. She was also aware that in his Mexico City murals Rivera had painted a mocking caricature of John D. Rockefeller, Sr., the founder of the family's fortune.

Rivera regarded Lenin as the father of a unified and successful working class. Lenin provided the rallying point for what Rivera thought

tality, by the entire conception of my painting. Therefore, rather than mutilate the conception, I should prefer the physical destruction of the conception in its entirety, but conserving, at least, its integrity. . . . I could change the sector which shows society people playing bridge and dancing, and put in its place, in perfect balance with the Lenin portion, a figure of some great American historical leader, such as Lincoln, who symbolizes the unification of the country and the abolition of slavery.

The next move was up to Rockefeller. If he insisted that Rivera change the portrait of Lenin to an unknown man, would that constitute censorship? Who owns a work of art—the artist who creates it, the person who buys it, or the public?

CASE STUDY **473**

Rockefellers demand that an unknown leader replace Lenin, but Rivera refuses.	→	Rockefellers pay Rivera and destroy the mural.

Turning Point

Analyzing the Case

After students read The Opinions section of this case, have them discuss the following questions:

1. Rivera saw this issue as a choice between the individual's rights and the group's rights. Explain his point of view. *(He believed that his mural belonged to all humanity rather than to Rockefeller.)*

2. The *New York Times* saw the dispute as one over what type of art was most appropriate for an office building. Why might some people consider Rivera's mural an inappropriate choice for Rockefeller Center? *(Rockefeller Center was a capitalist enterprise; Rivera's mural was a socialist statement)*

3. What would have been the most likely outcome if the Rockefellers had allowed Rivera's mural to be seen as he had painted it? *(Answers will vary. The Rockefellers would have been criticized.)*

Notes

When Diego Rivera could not complete his mural for Rockefeller Center, he asked the Mexican government for a duplicate space and was given a wall on the third floor of the Palacio de Bellas Artes (Palace of Fine Arts) in Mexico City.

was an impending world revolution. Rivera explained the use of Lenin in the mural in this way:

> If the United States wished to preserve its democratic forms, it would ally itself with Russia against [Nazi] fascism. Since Lenin was the preeminent founder of the Soviet Union and also the first and most altruistic theorist of modern communism, I used him as the center of the inevitable alliance between the Russian and the American [against fascism].

The Opinions

To Rivera this dispute was between individual ownership as championed by capitalism and collective ownership as advocated by communism. He stated:

> There are only two real points of view from which to choose: the point of view of capitalist economy and morality . . . the right of individual property . . . and the point of view of socialist economy and morality . . . the rights of the human collectivity.
>
> —quoted in Bertram Wolfe, *Diego Rivera: His Life and Times*, 1939

Many artists saw the issue of censorship at the heart of the dispute, claiming that the Rockefellers were attempting to suppress Rivera's free speech.

To refute this view, a newspaper editorial expressed the opinion that it was not censorship that was at issue but rather logic. It was illogical to have a communistic mural in a capitalist building:

> The issue between Rivera and Rockefeller Center would thus have nothing to do with the right of the artist to represent the world as he sees it. The mural painter is not concerned with visions and intuitions but with telling a story and inculcating a lesson. His message must therefore make sense. There is no sense in making a monumental wall-painting cry "Liar" to the wall on which it is spread.
>
> —*New York Times,* May 11, 1933

The Decision

On May 9 Rockefeller ordered Rivera to stop work on the mural, and the carpenters covered it with large frames of stretched canvas. After the guards drove Rivera from his scaffold, the building manager paid off the artist's $21,000 contract and gave him a letter of dismissal.

474 CASE STUDY

Cooperative Learning

Debate This feature concerns both the political statement Diego Rivera made in his mural and his right to make this statement in a privately commissioned work of art. The question that runs through this feature as an underlying theme is "Who owns a work of art: the artist, the person who buys it, or the public?" After students have had an opportunity to become familiar with Rivera's and Rockefeller's positions, have them form two teams to debate whether Rivera's mural should have been allowed to remain on the walls of Rockefeller Center.

Nearly 100 admirers of Rivera's art paraded in front of the RCA Building, carrying signs that read Save Rivera's Art and We Want Rivera. There was a great uproar; committees of artists agitated for and against the mural.

Rockefeller was eager to avoid controversy and said in a letter to his father, "We are hoping that the disagreeable public criticism which has been leveled at us this past week will be turned to sympathetic understanding of our position." On May 12, 1933, the *World-Telegram* reported Rockefeller's assurance that the "uncompleted fresco of Diego Rivera will not be destroyed or in any way mutilated, but . . . will be covered, to remain hidden for an indefinite time."

The Rockefellers allowed the mural to remain covered until February 9, 1934. At midnight, just as the weekend was beginning, workers rolled wheelbarrows into the building and crumbled the fresco into powder, which was wheeled away.

The Significance

When Rivera learned that his painting had been smashed, he made his goal clear: "My object was attained when the painting was destroyed. I thank the Rockefellers for its destruction because the act will advance the cause of the labor revolution."

In Mexico City, Rivera applied to the Mexican government for a wall at the Palace of Fine Arts where he could let people see what kind of painting it was that these "patrons of the arts" had chosen to destroy. He introduced into the new mural's nightclub scene a portrait of John D. Rockefeller, Jr., drinking champagne. Rockefeller actually did not drink alcohol.

To Rivera the significance of the dispute lay in the distinction between the individual's rights (as represented by capitalism) and the rights of the group (as represented by communism):

Let us take, as an example, an American millionaire who buys the Sistine Chapel, which contains the work of Michelangelo. . . . Would that millionaire have the right to destroy the Sistine Chapel? . . . In human creation there is something which belongs to humanity at large, and . . . no individual owner has the right to destroy it or keep it solely for his own enjoyment.

—Diego Rivera

The lawyers of Rockefeller Center completely deflated the protests that were planned by the artistic community. They made public the year-old letter in which Rivera told the Rockefellers that he would prefer to see the whole mural destroyed rather than change Lenin's portrait.

 Block Scheduling

The Portfolio Project on this page provides an excellent opportunity to enrich and extend the key elements of this case study.

RESPONDING TO THE CASE

1. Make two columns on a sheet of paper. On one side list the arguments made by Rivera and on the other side list the arguments made by Nelson Rockefeller on behalf of his family. Explain which side appears to have the stronger position.

2. Discuss whether a person who owns a work of art but does not let it be seen is guilty of censorship. For example, could a newspaper publisher/owner who stopped an objectionable story from being printed be considered guilty of censorship?

3. Which, if any, of Rockefeller's responses constituted censorship: his request that Lenin's portrait be changed, his covering the mural with canvas for nine months, or his chiseling it off the wall? Defend your answer.

4. Discuss whether a painting is owned by the painter who created it, the person who bought it, or the general public.

PORTFOLIO PROJECT

Write a letter to the editor of the *New York Times* either defending or opposing Rivera's position, Rockefeller's position, or the *Times*'s position. In your letter, begin by stating fairly the view you are discussing, and then present your best arguments either for or against it. Conclude with a clear statement summarizing your own position.

CASE STUDY **475**

 Curriculum Connection

Literature Students may know E.B. White as the author of such children's classics as *Charlotte's Web.* They might also enjoy getting acquainted with White's essays and light verse. Bring to class White's poem "I Paint What I See" (available in *Poems and Sketches of E.B. White* or in the *Norton Book of Light Verse,* ed. Russell Baker). This poem has fun with the Rockefeller-Rivera clash. Read it aloud or have students read it responsively. Ask students whether they can determine the poet's attitude.

CLOSE

Review with the class the reasons Rivera's work was destroyed. *(His ideology conflicted with Rockefeller's values.)* Discuss with students their feelings about public art in their school and hometown. Do they approve of all this art? What do they think should be done about art they dislike?

Responding to the Case Answers

1. Rivera's points: the Rockefellers had approved his preliminary sketch; his Communist sympathies were well known. Rockefeller's points: in his notes and sketch, Rivera never identified the "leader" as Lenin; he was hired to glorify workers, not communism.
2. Censorship usually means stopping people from seeing something created by another and not something created or owned by you.

3. If students believe that Rockefeller owned the painting and could do anything he wanted with it, none of his actions constitute censorship; if students believe that Rivera or the public owned it, all of his actions are censorship.
4. Answers will vary but might include: the Rockefellers believed the buyer owned a painting; Rivera believed the painter and the public owned it.

SECTION

3

FOCUS

Section Objectives

1. Describe how women, African Americans, and Native Americans were affected by New Deal legislation and attitudes.

2. Discuss the new role that the government began to take in ensuring the welfare of its citizens.

Bellringer Activity

While taking attendance at the beginning of the class period, display **Section Focus Transparency 45**, and have students answer the questions. (Or use the blackline master.)

VISUAL INSTRUCTION

Open-Air Concert In 1955 Marian Anderson became the first African American singer to perform at the Metropolitan Opera. In 1958 she was named a delegate to the United Nations.

Ask: What part did Eleanor Roosevelt play in arranging the concert? *(She arranged for the use of the Lincoln Memorial when the use of the DAR's hall was denied; she also resigned from the DAR.)*

The Impact of the New Deal

EASTER 1939: MARIAN ANDERSON DAZZLES CROWD AT LINCOLN MEMORIAL

Open-Air Concert
Contralto Marian Anderson, celebrated in the concert halls of Europe, sings on the steps of the Lincoln Memorial.

THE WHITE MARBLE OF THE LINCOLN MEMORIAL GLEAMED IN THE SUNSHINE. A crowd of 75,000 people gathered in front of it on the grassy hill and beside the reflecting pool. At the dedication ceremony 10 years earlier, African Americans had been assigned seats in a separate, roped-off section across the road. This Sunday, however, African Americans and whites sat together, awaiting the appearance of the famous opera singer Marian Anderson.

The crowd hushed as Anderson appeared at the foot of the monument and turned to face the crowd. She began singing, "My country 'tis of thee, sweet land of liberty." She sang slowly as if singing a solemn hymn.

It was an inspiring moment because plans for the concert had almost had to be abandoned. There was no concert hall in the capital large enough to seat the enormous crowd expected to attend her performance other than Constitution Hall. The Daughters of the American Revolution (DAR), which owned the hall, had refused Anderson the right to sing there, however, simply because she was an African American. Dismayed, Anderson had turned to the Roosevelts for help.

When Eleanor Roosevelt heard about the DAR's refusal to

AS YOU READ

Vocabulary
► discrimination
► federal regulation

Think About . . .
► the impact that New Deal legislation had on women, African Americans, and Native Americans.

► the new responsibility the government began to take for the welfare of its citizens.

Section 3 Resources

REPRODUCIBLE RESOURCES

- Lesson Plan 14-3
- Vocabulary and Guided Reading Activity 14-3
- Performance Assessment Activity 14
- Section 2 Quiz
- Chapter 14 Test
- Unit 5 Test
- Reteaching Activity 14
- Supreme Court Case Study 11

MULTIMEDIA RESOURCES

- Section Focus Transparency 45
- Landmark Documents in American History
- Testmaker
- Chapter 14 Digest Audiocassette
- Vocabulary PuzzleMaker
- Student Self-Test: A Software Review

host the famous singer, she not only resigned from the organization but also encouraged Anderson to apply for permission to give a free concert on the steps of the Lincoln Memorial. Almost immediately Anderson's request was approved. Thus, with help from the White House, Anderson's thousands of fans were not disappointed, and the concert was a majestic success.

Although the Roosevelt administration's record on gender and race was mixed, to the nation's women and minority groups it was the most accessible and sympathetic administration in the nation's history. The Roosevelt administration passed legislation, created programs, and made other significant changes that benefited African Americans, Native Americans, and women. Such changes were among the most important legacies of FDR's New Deal.

Women Gain Political Recognition
New Deal Furthers Women's Rights

On March 6, 1933, 2 days after President Roosevelt's inauguration, approximately 35 reporters gathered in the Red Room of the White House to wait for the First Lady. The scene looked like any other press conference—reporters quietly talking and reviewing their lists of questions—except that all of the reporters were women. This was the first of what Eleanor Roosevelt promised would be weekly press conferences.

In addition to what the First Lady had to say to the press, the mere fact that she had decided to hold weekly press conferences made news in Washington. Mrs. Hoover had met with reporters just once in her four-year tenure as First Lady—and then only reluctantly. Eleanor Roosevelt had been politically active even before she came to the White House, and, as First Lady, she increased her political activities. One of her causes was helping women gain economic and political power. She restricted her press conferences to women reporters to help them keep their jobs. During the Depression many newspapers cut back their staffs, and women were often the first to be let go. Eleanor Roosevelt felt that if she would only meet with women reporters, at least these women would be retained by their employers.

Partly because of Eleanor's influence, women gained political recognition. Women, she felt, were in the best position to promote child welfare, education, fair labor standards, and even world peace. To this end, in addition to publicizing these causes, the First Lady worked to get women appointed to political posts. Women's roles in government expanded substantially during the Roosevelt years.

Women in Power

In his first term as President, Roosevelt appointed the first woman in United States history to a cabinet post: Frances Perkins, a former social worker, who had served as industrial commissioner for New York State. As secretary of labor, Perkins pushed hard to obtain a social security program and a minimum-wage law that would boost the pay of thousands of poorly paid women in the workforce.

Roosevelt also appointed the first woman to the federal appeals court, the first women ambassadors, and a woman as director of the mint. Women were asked to serve as advisers in many

HISTORICAL PICTURES SERVICE, CHICAGO

Meet the Press The candid and informal way the Roosevelts addressed reporters won the press over completely. Here Eleanor Roosevelt (center) is holding one of her regular press conferences to which only women were admitted. *Why did the First Lady restrict her press conferences to women reporters?*

TEACH

Guided Practice

L2 Women's Roles
Have students discuss why Eleanor Roosevelt believed that women were in the best position to promote child welfare, education, fair labor standards, and world peace. Then ask if it follows that men were also in the best position to promote certain issues. What might those issues have been?

VISUAL INSTRUCTION

Meet the Press The idea for Eleanor Roosevelt's all-women press conferences came from Lorena Hickock, the highest-paid woman reporter with the Associated Press. Hickok and Mrs. Roosevelt had befriended each other along the campaign trail, becoming so close that Eleanor granted her an exclusive interview after the inauguration.

Answer: *She wanted to help women reporters keep their jobs at a time when newspapers were cutting staff.*

Cooperative Learning

Affirmative Action Debate Use the issue of Eleanor Roosevelt's all-female press conferences to initiate a class discussion of affirmative action. Do students think that special action is necessary to redress past inequality in hiring practices? Education? Do they think the government should promote such action? Using a simplified debate format, have students address these questions. Organize the class into two groups—one to assemble the best arguments in favor of affirmative action, the other the best arguments against it. Let each group appoint one student to record the group's arguments, another to present them to the class, and a third to offer rebuttals to the opposing group's arguments. Students may wish to vote on the outcome.

Independent Practice

 Research Ask students to investigate the life of Frances Perkins, Mary McLeod Bethune, Henry Roe Cloud, or Gertrude Bonnin. Make sure they find out how the individual worked to meet the needs of a particular segment of American society. Have them present their research visually, such as in a sculpture, a play, a poster, or a videotape.

✏️ Have students complete the Chapter 14, Section 3 Vocabulary and Guided Reading Activity. (Also in Spanish.) **LEP**

FYI

Olympic Champion
African American Jesse Owens won four gold medals in the 1936 Olympics in Berlin. His victories were an embarrassment to Hitler, who presided over the games. Hitler believed that fair-skinned Germans were superior to all other races.

VISUAL INSTRUCTION

African American Concerns Mary McLeod Bethune, a college president, founded the National Council of Negro Women.

Answer: *The black cabinet was a forward step because it addressed African American concerns, but its members held secondary posts and had only indirect influence.*

New Deal agencies. In all, more than 100 women held senior positions in the federal government during FDR's administration. This was still only a fraction of the number of such positions held by men.

Facing Discrimination

Even though a greater number of women entered public life during Roosevelt's administration, in general they still faced **discrimination,** or prejudicial treatment. For example, although Roosevelt was a strong supporter of women's rights, he tended to appoint women to government posts that would be least likely to lead to conflicts with men. Thus the women in his administration had more limited influence than it might seem.

Therefore, despite the fact that there were women in government, these women could not prevent women in the workforce from experiencing unfair treatment. NRA codes often granted women lower pay than men, even for the same jobs. Many businesses refused to hire married women during the Depression, and married women whose husbands worked were often forced to resign from their jobs.

The reasons for these severe practices were twofold. First, most people believed that unless a woman's wages were essential for family survival, the woman should not work but should stay at home. Second, the majority of Americans thought that because jobs were so scarce, working wives should give up their jobs so that men could take their places. People believed in these arguments even in the face of logical contradictions. For example, many men would not have taken the jobs vacated by women anyway because they were jobs thought to be inappropriate for men, such as secretarial work, nursing, and teaching.

African Americans Gain a Voice
Change Comes Slowly

The year 1934 was a dramatic one in United States political history. In the congressional elections, most African Americans switched their allegiance from the Republican party to the Democratic party. Although they had voted overwhelmingly for Republicans since Reconstruction, they changed allegiance mainly to support Roosevelt and the New Deal.

FRANKLIN D. ROOSEVELT LIBRARY

African American Concerns Seen here with actress Hattie McDaniel, Mary McLeod Bethune (right), led meetings of the black cabinet. *How did the black cabinet reflect Roosevelt's progressive yet cautious civil rights policies?*

At the urging of Eleanor Roosevelt and other key political advisers, FDR kept himself informed about issues important to African Americans. Much of his information came from a group of about 50 African American appointees who served in various branches of his administration. This group came to be known as the black cabinet.

The Black Cabinet

Although most African Americans in the Roosevelt administration were appointed to secondary posts, they nevertheless exerted influence collectively as the black cabinet. Mary McLeod Bethune, head of the Negro Affairs Division of the National Youth Administration, was the most influential member of the black cabinet. A personal friend of Eleanor Roosevelt's, Bethune often shared the black cabinet's ideas with her. The First Lady then discussed them with FDR.

Harold Ickes, secretary of the interior, also worked closely with African Americans to improve race relations, and he passed along their concerns to FDR. He integrated his department, appointing several prominent African Americans to key positions. Under Ickes, the PWA allocated funds for the construction of African American hospitals, universities, and housing projects. PWA building contracts also contained a clause requiring that the number of African Americans hired be at least equal in proportion to their number in the local population. This practice would become a basis for civil rights legislation in the 1960s and the 1970s.

Meeting Special Needs

Visual Learners Students who learn best visually can benefit by examining the images and the four main heads of this section. What do they notice about the images and the heads? *(Diverse groups of people are meeting and negotiating; it seems that women, African Americans, and Native Americans make some gains.)* Have students predict what some of FDR's specific legacies were. *(He might have promoted laws and organizations that gave more power to women and people of color.)*

Other New Deal agencies also greatly aided civil rights during the Depression. The WPA gave jobs to hundreds of thousands of African Americans. The FERA and other relief agencies granted aid to 30 percent of all African American families.

Failure to Stand for Justice

The Roosevelt administration exceeded all previous administrations in the number of African Americans that it appointed to government positions and in the amount of federal aid that it provided African Americans. The President, however, failed to take a strong stand on civil rights issues.

Roosevelt did little to eliminate unfair hiring practices and discriminatory job conditions. Some government agencies, such as the TVA, often refused to hire African American workers. Most of the government agencies that did hire African Americans, including the CCC and the armed forces, segregated African Americans and whites. In addition, African American workers often received lower wages and were prevented from obtaining many jobs by stiff hiring restrictions.

Roosevelt also failed to push for a federal anti-lynching law. Acts of mob violence, such as lynching, increased during the early years of the Depression. Unlike Hoover, Roosevelt publicly condemned what he called "that vile form of collective murder." Roosevelt, however, hesitated to support antilynching legislation because he was afraid that he would alienate the Southern white leaders who strongly opposed such laws.

Roosevelt's desire to maintain the support of Southern whites also kept him from abolishing the poll tax. Election officials levied this tax to prevent poor African Americans and whites from voting in elections.

Roosevelt expressed the views of many liberal Americans at the time about race relations. He advocated only slow, cautious change, a stand that exasperated racial and ethnic minorities. Nevertheless, the President recognized the vital importance of working toward social equality. During a meeting with black cabinet member Mary McLeod Bethune, FDR said the following:

> **P**eople like you and me are fighting and must continue to fight for the day when a man will be regarded as a man regardless of his race or faith or country. That day will come, but we must pass through perilous times before we realize it.
>
> —Franklin D. Roosevelt

Native Americans Gain an Ally
Preserving Tribal Ownership

Native Americans, like African Americans, had long been subject to discrimination, deprivation, and degrading policies. Earning an average annual income of $48, Native American families were the poorest in the nation. New Deal agencies and policies provided many Native Americans with jobs and aid.

The most significant New Deal program to aid Native Americans was the Indian Reorganization Act of 1934, authored by John Collier, the commissioner of Indian affairs. Collier had been involved in Native

AP/WIDE WORLD PHOTOS

Navajo Meet With Collier Showing one of the woolen products by which they make their living, Navajo protest a government limit on the number of sheep they may raise. Left to right: Dan Phillipe, interpreter; John Collier, commissioner; Johnnie Chief and Slim Salt, Navajo representatives. *What was the average annual income of Native American families at the start of the New Deal?*

 Curriculum Connection

Mathematics FDR favored a stronger role for federal government in improving the lives of all Americans. These improvements cost money. Under FDR the public debt increased more than it had in the nation's history, reaching $43 billion in 1940 compared with $16.5 billion in 1930. In 1993 the public debt reached $4,351 billion. Have students calculate what percentage of the 1993 debt is reflected in the 1940 debt. *(less than 1 percent)*

VISUAL INSTRUCTION

Navajo Meet with Collier The Navajo are the largest of all Native American groups in the United States, with a population of about 100,000. Navajo lands cover more than 24,000 square miles (64,000 square km) in New Mexico, Arizona, and Utah.

Answer: *$48*

Portfolio Project

Writing a Position Statement Tell students to imagine they are members of the black cabinet and to write a statement expressing the cabinet's view on FDR's failure to address numerous civil rights issues. Students should focus on a specific issue, such as unequal hiring practices within federal agencies or failure to abolish poll taxes. After presenting their statements to the class, students can add them to their portfolios.

479

ASSESS

VISUAL INSTRUCTION

Harvest In all of his works, Jones depicted farmers as craftspeople.

Answer: *The farmers in the foreground cut and stack the wheat while those in the background operate threshing machines.*

 Facts on File

Landmark Documents in American History Refer students to "Social Security Act, 1935," "National Labor Relations Act, 1935," "Soil Conservation Act, 1936," "Wagner-Steagall Act, 1937," and the "Fair Labor Standards Act of 1938." Have them write a paragraph about the intent of one of the documents.

CHART STUDY

Ask: When did the federal government begin urging Native Americans to leave reservations and relocate in cities? *(1953)*

Harvest by Joe Jones In this work, painted about 1935, and in similar works, Jones wanted "the working people, the people producing useful things with their hands" to enjoy seeing themselves portrayed with understanding. *What aspects of the painting depict skills needed for farmwork?*

American politics since 1923, when he had founded the American Indian Defense Association. In this and the Indian Reorganization Act of 1934, Collier built upon the ideas and initiatives of Winnebago teacher Henry Roe Cloud and Sioux writer Gertrude Bonnin. The goals of both the association and the Reorganization Act were to promote Native American cultures and to preserve tribal ownership of reservation lands.

Collier's Indian Reorganization Act furthered these goals by preventing the government from seizing unclaimed reservation land and selling it to people who were not Native American. Government seizure of reservation territory, which had been going on since the late 1800s, had deprived Native Americans of their most valuable lands and reduced the reservations to one-third of their original sizes. With the Indian Reorganization Act, Native Americans gained control of their reservations and could decide how their lands would be used and managed.

The Indian Reorganization Act also encouraged Native Americans to establish their own governments on reservations. Once these governments had been established, the Indian Bureau was authorized to provide the funds needed to build schools and hospitals, to establish businesses, and to start arts and crafts cooperatives.

An Expanded Government Role
The Government Takes on New Tasks

By including the excluded—women, African Americans, Native Americans, farmers, common laborers, the poor—the New Deal brought government closer to all

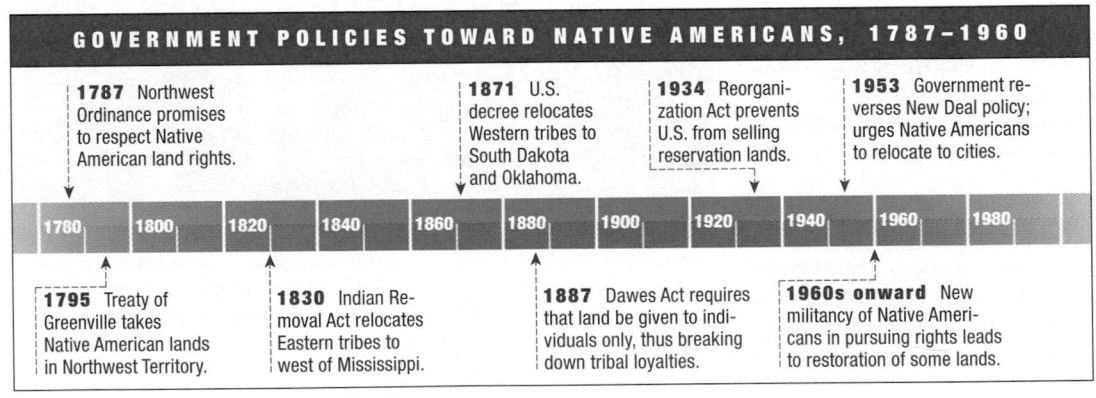

GOVERNMENT POLICIES TOWARD NATIVE AMERICANS, 1787–1960

1787 Northwest Ordinance promises to respect Native American land rights.

1871 U.S. decree relocates Western tribes to South Dakota and Oklahoma.

1934 Reorganization Act prevents U.S. from selling reservation lands.

1953 Government reverses New Deal policy; urges Native Americans to relocate to cities.

1780 | 1800 | 1820 | 1840 | 1860 | 1880 | 1900 | 1920 | 1940 | 1960 | 1980

1795 Treaty of Greenville takes Native American lands in Northwest Territory.

1830 Indian Removal Act relocates Eastern tribes to west of Mississippi.

1887 Dawes Act requires that land be given to individuals only, thus breaking down tribal loyalties.

1960s onward New militancy of Native Americans in pursuing rights leads to restoration of some lands.

480 CHAPTER 14 THE NEW DEAL

Extending the Content

Keynesian Economics Influential British economist John Maynard Keynes suggested in the 1930s that government intervention could best control economic investments, employment, and consumer consumption. The United States and several other nations put his theories to work by instituting public works programs to combat the Depression. More recent thinkers, such as American economist Milton Friedman, have taken a conservative view, repudiating the idea of government intervention. Ask students how they think the country would have fared in the Depression without the government spending programs that were part of the New Deal.

New Deal Legislation and Agencies, 1933–1938

Year	Name and Purpose	Year	Name and Purpose
1933	**Emergency Banking Act:** Reopened banks under government supervision	1935	**Resettlement Administration (RA):** Helped resettle destitute farmers on better land and unemployed workers in planned communities
	Civilian Conservation Corps (CCC): Employed young men in environmental projects		**Works Progress Administration (WPA):** Employed people for construction, maintenance, education, and creative projects
	Federal Emergency Relief Act: Provided funds for local and state relief organizations		**Social Security Act:** Instituted pension and survivors' benefits for the elderly and the orphaned and provided aid to people injured in industrial accidents
	Agricultural Adjustment Act (AAA): Subsidized farmers to reduce crop and livestock production		**National Labor Relations Board (NLRB):** Guaranteed workers the right to join labor unions of their choice, bargain collectively, and call strikes
	Emergency Farm Mortgage Act: Provided funds for the refinancing of farm mortgages		**Rural Electrification Act (REA):** Lent money to rural cooperatives for the building of power plants
	Tennessee Valley Authority (TVA): Provided funds for the development and electrification of the Tennessee River Authority		**Public Utility Holding Company Act:** Allowed a maximum of only two holding companies to control any one utility company
	Truth-in-Securities Act: Required full disclosure of information about stocks and bonds	1936	**Soil Conservation Act:** Subsidized farmers to reduce soil-depleting crops and to employ soil conservation measures
	Home Owners' Loan Act: Provided funds for the refinancing of home mortgages	1937	**National Housing Act:** Authorized low-rent public housing projects
	National Industrial Recovery Act (NIRA): Created work codes and industry standards		**Farm Security Administration (FSA):** Lent money to sharecroppers and tenant farmers to help them buy their own farms; established camps for migrant workers
	Public Works Administration (PWA): Funded projects to revive industry and fight unemployment	1938	**Fair Labor Standards Act:** Established minimum wages and maximum hours for all employees of businesses engaged in interstate commerce
	Glass-Steagall Banking Act: Guaranteed bank deposits with the Federal Deposit Insurance Corporation (FDIC)		
1934	**Federal Housing Administration (FHA):** Insured bank loans for the construction and rehabilitation of homes		
	Indian Reorganization Act: Restored tribal ownership of reservation land to Native Americans		

Examine the legislation of Roosevelt's New Deal shown on the chart. List each piece of legislation under one or more of the following heads, as appropriate: housing, agriculture, labor, civil rights, relief, unemployment, banking, industry, utilities. *Judging from your list, what issues concerned FDR most? What issues concerned him least?*

the people. During the Roosevelt administration, 14 percent of all families obtained aid or relief from the federal government. Millions were able to stay off of relief because of government jobs with the CCC, the PWA, and the WPA. Other New Deal agencies helped people hold on to their farms, keep their homes, stay in business, and bargain with employers for better pay.

Federal regulation, or the expansion of the federal government into almost all aspects of people's lives, was a direct legacy of the New Deal. Under President Roosevelt, for the first time, the federal government assumed responsibility for the economic welfare of individuals as well as for the health of the nation's economy at large. In taking on such obligations, FDR's New Deal proved to be a turning point in the country's history.

The New Deal increased many people's confidence in the nation's political and economic systems. The government programs of the New Deal, however, neither eliminated individual poverty nor ended the Depression. The economy did not completely recover from the Depression until World War II was well under way.

SECTION REVIEW

Vocabulary

1. Define: discrimination, federal regulation.

Checking Facts

2. How did the PWA, the WPA, and the FERA work to end discrimination against African Americans?

3. What new responsibilities did the government acknowledge during FDR's administration?

Critical Thinking

Identifying Assumptions

4. The Indian Reorganization Act aimed at promoting Native American cultures and preserving tribal ownership of reservation lands. What assumptions about Native American cultures underlie these goals?

Linking Across Time

5. How is the position of women in the workforce today different from what it was in the 1930s? How is it similar?

SECTION THREE **481**

Evaluate

Have students complete the Section Review.

📁 💿 Assign the Section 3 Quiz or use the Testmaker to develop a customized quiz.

📁 💿 Assign the Chapter 14 Test or use the Testmaker to develop a customized test.

📁 💿 Assign the Unit 5 Test or use the Testmaker to develop a customized test.

📁 Have students complete the Chapter 14 Performance Assessment Activity.

Reteach

🎧 Have students listen to the Chapter 14, Section 3 Audiocassette. **LEP**

📁 Have students complete the Chapter 14 Reteaching Activity. (Also in Spanish.) **LEP**

Enrich

📁 Have students complete Supreme Court Case Study 11.

CLOSE

List New Deal measures, and ask students to fill in the purpose for each one.

Section 3 Review Answers

1. discrimination (478), **federal regulation** (481)

2. PWA: racially integrated; constructed African American hospitals, universities, housing; WPA: hired African Americans; FERA: provided aid to 30 percent of all African American families

3. including all citizens; providing aid and relief

4. that Native American cultures are valuable and should be preserved, not assimilated; that tribal ownership, rather than private ownership, is integral to Native American cultures

5. much more numerous today and their presence is accepted; still experience discrimination, especially in rates of pay

Reviewing Key Terms

1. demagogue
2. discrimination
3. moratorium
4. subsidy
5. unionization

Recalling Facts

1. unemployment, a bank crisis, hunger, homelessness, and a farming crisis
2. the period of legislation in the first three months of FDR's administration
3. CCC members lived in an army-like setting, working on environmental preservation and recreational projects.
4. Small businesses believed it let large businesses establish codes that put them at a disadvantage. Large businesses resented regulation.
5. the AAA; by setting up a situation in which tenant farmers were driven off the land by landowners
6. Business opposed regulation of industry, unionization, and increased taxes. The Court overturned key pieces of New Deal legislation.
7. The Rockefellers had provided many jobs for working people in the construction of Rockefeller Center; they resented the implication that communism was the wave of the future and that capitalism had failed.
8. by being politically active herself and by encouraging her husband to appoint women to political posts
9. It integrated some government agencies, provided relief, allocated funds for African American and Native American interests, appointed African Americans to government jobs, and passed laws to promote Native American culture and preserve tribal ownership of lands.
10. NIRA, NLRB, Fair Labor Standards Act

Reviewing Key Terms

Match the sentences below to the vocabulary term they define or describe. Write your answers on a separate sheet of paper.

moratorium	unionization
dole	demagogue
subsidy	discrimination

1. A certain kind of leader gains power by appealing to the public's fears and prejudices rather than to their reason.

2. Although women and minority groups made some advances during the New Deal administrations, they still faced many barriers based on prejudice.

3. When he first came to office, Franklin Roosevelt declared a temporary shutdown of most banking operations.

4. In order to bring supply in line with demand, the Agricultural Adjustment Administration gave farmers financial assistance in return for their agreement to reduce crop production.

5. Workers joined together and chose their own leaders to negotiate wages and working conditions with factory owners and managers.

Recalling Facts

1. What major problems did President Roosevelt face as he began his first term of office in 1933?

2. What were the Hundred Days?

3. Describe the life and work of a member of the Civilian Conservation Corps.

4. In what ways was the National Recovery Administration (NRA) controversial?

5. What New Deal legislation created problems for farmers? What were those problems?

6. What opposition did Roosevelt meet from business leaders? From the Supreme Court?

7. Why was the Rockefeller family so concerned about Diego Rivera's painting of Lenin during this time of economic depression?

8. How did Eleanor Roosevelt help to advance the cause of women in politics?

9. What did the Roosevelt administration do to improve conditions for African Americans? What did it do for Native Americans?

10. What legislation benefited organized labor during the 1930s?

Critical Thinking

1. **Synthesizing Information** The photograph on this page shows President Roosevelt delivering one of the regular radio addresses that he called fireside chats. How did these addresses reflect his personal style?

2. **Making Comparisons** In what ways did Roosevelt's solutions to Depression problems differ from those that Hoover offered? How did the two men differ in temperament, and how was that difference reflected in their approaches to economic conditions?

3. **Determining Cause and Effect** How might the circumstances of FDR's earlier years have contributed to making him the kind of President he became?

4. **Demonstrating Reasoned Judgment** What conditions of the times made some Americans willing to listen to the messages of demagogues such as Father Coughlin and Huey Long?

5. **Drawing Conclusions** What kinds of political recognition did women and minority groups achieve during the New Deal administrations? What barriers still remained?

FRANKLIN D. ROOSEVELT LIBRARY

Critical Thinking

1. FDR's manner was relaxed and friendly. He expressed his charm through fireside chats.
2. Hoover was cautious and conservative; he was reluctant to provide direct relief. FDR was daring and experimental; he instituted direct relief.
3. His experience with polio taught him to endure and overcome difficulties. Eleanor helped open his eyes to the plight of the less fortunate.
4. Frustration with the slowness and limitations of the government led many people to turn to demagogues who promised easy solutions.
5. They received some political appointments, mostly minor, and were sometimes consulted, usually unofficially. FDR failed to take a strong stand against poll taxes, unfair hiring practices, and discriminatory job conditions.

Portfolio Project

Interview a friend or relative who is a senior citizen. Ask for that person's opinions about the present Social Security program. Report your findings in a letter to an imaginary newspaper editor. In your letter urge people to support legislation that will either leave Social Security as it is, modify it, or abolish it. Be sure to include the reasons for your opinion. Keep the letter in your portfolio.

Cooperative Learning

Work with two or three other students to research the life of one person prominent during the Roosevelt years. For example, you could look up Frances Perkins, the first woman to serve in a President's cabinet, or John Collier, the innovative commissioner of Indian affairs. Each group member might find out about a different aspect of the person's life, such as his or her childhood, education, or early career. Then, as a group, prepare a presentation of your material for the rest of the class.

Reinforcing Skills

Interpreting Images Turn to page 471. Examine the cartoon and read the caption. How does the artist convey the unpopularity of FDR's proposal to add several justices to the Supreme Court? What detail in the cartoon shows that the President's own party disliked his proposal? What seems to be FDR's reaction to the criticism?

Geography and History

Study the map on this page to answer the following questions:

1. Which states voted Republican in all three of the elections shown? In what part of the country are they located?

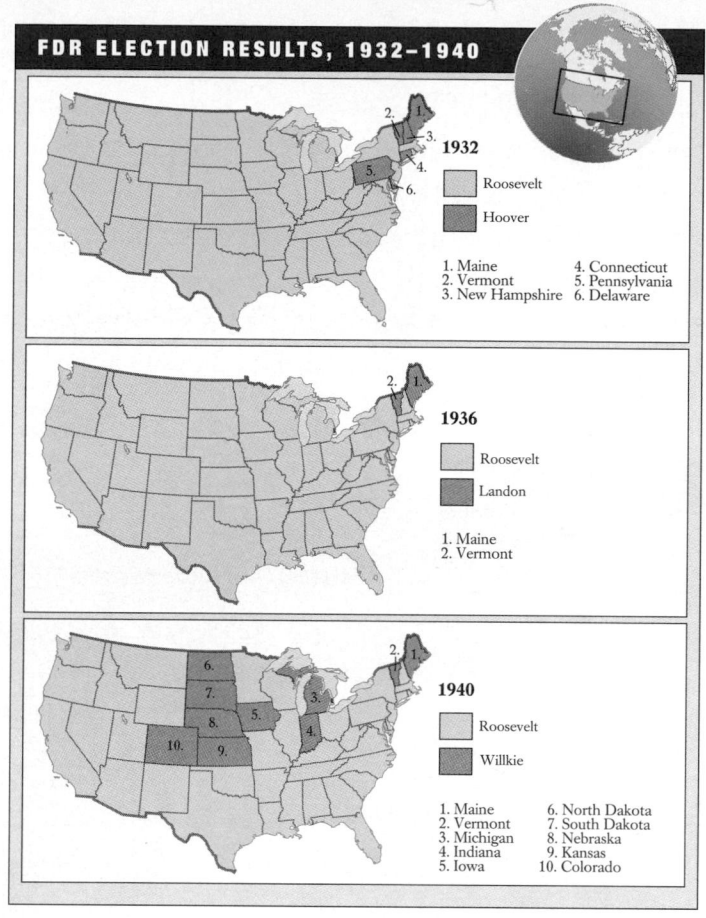

FDR ELECTION RESULTS, 1932–1940

1932
- Roosevelt
- Hoover

1. Maine
2. Vermont
3. New Hampshire
4. Connecticut
5. Pennsylvania
6. Delaware

1936
- Roosevelt
- Landon

1. Maine
2. Vermont

1940
- Roosevelt
- Willkie

1. Maine
2. Vermont
3. Michigan
4. Indiana
5. Iowa
6. North Dakota
7. South Dakota
8. Nebraska
9. Kansas
10. Colorado

2. Compare the 1932 and 1936 maps. What does the comparison show you about the popular appeal of Roosevelt's policies during the First New Deal?

3. Compare the 1936 and 1940 maps. How many more states did Roosevelt lose in the election of 1940?

4. In what regions of the country did the Republicans make gains in 1940?

HISTORY JOURNAL

Look back at your journal entry for this chapter. Do you think that people received the kind of "new deal" they needed from the Roosevelt administration? Why or why not? Write your response in your journal.

Geography and History

1. Maine and Vermont voted Republican in all three elections; they are in the Northeast.
2. Roosevelt's landslide was even more complete in 1936, reflecting popular approval of New Deal policies. Several states that had voted Republican in 1932—New Hampshire, Connecticut, Pennsylvania, and Delaware—voted Democratic in 1936.
3. Roosevelt lost eight more states in 1940 than he did in 1936—Michigan, Indiana, Iowa, North Dakota, South Dakota, Nebraska, Kansas, and Colorado.
4. Republicans made gains in the Great Plains and in the Midwest.

History Journal

Ask for volunteers to share their journal entries with the class. Discuss whether they have supported their opinions with persuasive reasons.

? BONUS QUESTION

This question may be used for extra credit on the chapter test.

Ask: What New Deal projects brought electricity to rural Alabama? *(the TVA and REA)*

Portfolio Project

Discuss with students the criteria for a good letter to the editor. It should be clear, courteous, persuasive, and brief. Encourage students to edit the first drafts of their letters with the above criteria in mind.

Cooperative Learning

As groups begin their work, make sure that each group member has a clear assignment and knows how to go about completing it.

Reinforcing Skills

The President looks glum as objects are hurled at him. The peace dove has lost its olive branch and is in full flight. Among the President's attackers is a donkey, the symbol of his own party.

Making the Historical Connection

At the Depression's height almost no passengers were interested in air travel. Cars and trains made the outrageous expense of air travel unthinkable. Flying did not appeal to most people's ideas of safety either. Once technological improvements brought down prices and ensured safety, however, Americans took to the sky.

FYI

Wings of the World The DC-3 quickly became the world's most popular airplane, carrying 90 percent of all air passengers in 1939. During World War II, Douglas modified the plane to create military versions. The official military names were C-47, C-53, C-117, and R4D, but pilots affectionately called them "Doug" or "Gooney Bird." When production halted in 1946, 803 commercial models and 10,123 military versions had rolled out the door. These planes continued to fly worldwide, carrying a total of 600 million passengers by 1960. A few "Gooney Birds" still fly today.

Then...

The DC-3 Passenger Plane

In the early 1930s, TWA adviser Charles Lindbergh asked that the new Douglas passenger plane be able to cross the Rockies with only one engine running. By 1935 the DC-3 not only passed this test, but, according to American Airlines president C.R. Smith, was the first plane to "make money just by hauling passengers."

PHOTO BY BOB SHANE

❶ The all-metal body was easy to maintain and clean. Cowl flaps and engine mounts made service speedy.

❷ The multicellular wings survived pressure tests with lead weights and even a steamroller.

UNITED AIRLINES/PHOTO COURTESY OF ED DAVIES

❸ The soundproof cabin could accommodate 21 seats or 14 sleeping berths.

UNITED AIRLINES/PHOTO COURTESY OF ED DAVIES

Fun Facts

ATTENDANTS OF THE AIR

A nurse from Iowa, Ellen Church, proposed adding attendants to passenger flights and became the first American stewardess in 1930. The nursing background of early flight attendants reassured passengers.

Background Information

Looking for Profits In the 1920s airlines attracted an elite group of travelers. Forced to compete with comfortable, affordable rail service and highway travel, early airlines survived on mail delivery, splitting up a few lucrative government contracts. The airmail boom of the early 1930s led to improved airstrips and air traffic control. The search began for a plane large enough, safe enough, and comfortable enough to attract a profitable number of passengers. The plane would also have to be inexpensive to run and maintain. Donald Douglas set his designers to work on a large, two engine plane that would fly even if an engine, set of instruments, or landing gear failed. The result was the DC-1 in 1932, the improved DC-2 in 1933, and finally the first profitable plane, the DC-3, in 1935.

④ Automatic pilot and dual controls provided safety, and meant that pilots no longer had to reach across each other while flying the plane.

⑤ Strong retractable landing gear made use of a new "pork chop" joint.

Stats

PERFORMANCE
- Maximum speed:
  230 miles per hour (370 kmph)
  Average speed:
  180 miles per hour (257.4 kmph)

- Average range:
  1,500 miles (2,413.5 km)

SIZE
- Weight: 25,200 pounds
  (11,440.8 kg)

- Height: 16 feet 11 inches (5.2 m)

- Length: 64 feet 6 inches (19.7 m)

PROFITS
- The DC-3 was the first American passenger plane to turn a profit; it earned the Douglas Aircraft Company more than $1 billion.

- With space for 21 passengers, the DC-3 provided 50 percent more space than its predecessors, and only increased operating costs by 3 percent.

- Sample fares: $18.95, one way, Los Angeles to San Francisco; $288, round trip, New York to the West Coast

...Now

MODERN AIR TRAVEL

Find pictures and information about a modern passenger plane in books or brochures. What features of this new plane represent improvements over its forerunners?

Using a photo or your own drawing of the plane, create a diagram with call-out lines highlighting some of the plane's features. Include service, performance, and profitability as well as physical characteristics.

IN-FLIGHT SERVICE
Amenities included lavatories with running water, electric razors, heating and cooling systems, and meals served on tables with linens, silverware, and china.

Portfolio Project

Industry Changes Students can create descriptions of travel aboard the DC-3 in the 1930s. Point out that Ellen Church, the first stewardess, spoke of inconveniences before the DC-3 such as emergency fuel stops, faulty heating, and air sickness caused by very bumpy flights. Church said, "In looking back, I wonder why anyone rode at all." Have students use the images and captions on pages 484 and 485 to imagine what a flight on the DC-3 might be like in comparison to rail travel, automobile travel, or early air travel. Students should write a description of their "first" flight and include these pieces in their portfolios.

Then & Now

Block Scheduling

The Portfolio Project on this page provides an excellent opportunity to enrich and extend the key elements of this feature.

CLOSE

Ask students to discuss what obstacles the airlines faced in their quest to develop passenger service? *(passengers had very little money during the time of the depression; people weren't used to the idea of flying)*

Notes

The Unit at a Glance

Chapter 15

World War II began in Europe. Japan attacked Pearl Harbor, and the United States was drawn into the war. Hitler advanced through Europe, and the Allies banded together to defeat Hitler. War in the Pacific culminated in dropping atomic bombs on Hiroshima and Nagasaki.

Chapter 16

As the United States mobilized for war, just about everyone was affected. The chapter focuses on the effects of social change due to the war effort and examines how civil rights were addressed or denied.

00:00 Out of Time?

If time does not permit teaching every chapter in this unit, use the Chapter Digest Audiocassettes and the accompanying student activities and tests. The Chapter Digest Audiocassettes are available in Spanish.

UNIT

6

The United States Transformed

CHAPTER 15
World War II

CHAPTER 16
The Home Front

486

Portfolio Project

Diverse Contributions Have students research how African Americans, Native Americans, and Hispanic Americans contributed to the war effort. Students should examine war workers at home as well as armed service organizations. Suggest that students analyze and write a report comparing minority contributions in the war in Europe to their treatment at home in the United States.

Introducing the Unit

Show students the Unit 6 Time Line Transparency and/or assign the accompanying activity sheet. Unit 6 begins with the start of World War II in 1939 and progresses through the end of the war in 1945.

GLENCOE
TECHNOLOGY

Videodisc

American History

Side 1, Section 1
Title: World War II and the Beginning of the Cold War, 1941–1960
Subject: Overview of American history from entry into World War II to postwar American Life.
Ask: What event brought the United States into World War II? *(the Japanese attack on Pearl Harbor)*

© PHILIP MAKANNA

487

Examining the Visual

Building to Victory United States involvement in World War II sparked a production miracle as planes, ships, bombs, and tanks rapidly rolled off the assembly lines. From 1940 to 1945 the United States built 299,293 aircraft. In comparison, Germany built 113,514 aircraft and Japan 58,834. Airplane design also played an important role. Japanese Zero fighters were among the planes that attacked Pearl Harbor and gave the Japanese air superiority early in the war. The Zero could climb faster, fly higher, and outmaneuver United States planes of the time. Two United States planes that proved effective against the Zero were the Wildcat (above, foreground) and the Hellcat (above, rear). The Hellcat alone was responsible for destroying about 5,000 enemy planes.

TEACH

Making the Historical Connection

Before he worked as a war correspondent, Ernie Pyle wrote a column about his daily experiences that appeared in as many as 200 newspapers. In 1944 he won a Pulitzer Prize for his reporting on the war campaigns in North Africa, France, Sicily, and Italy. Pyle died of injuries from Japanese machine-gun fire on the Pacific Island of Ie Shima on April 18, 1945.

VISUAL INSTRUCTION

At the Front This photograph, taken en route to the invasion of Okinawa, shows Ernie Pyle talking with soldiers below decks on a Navy transport.

Ask: How was Pyle able to write such accurate and compelling accounts of the war? *(He experienced the war alongside the soldiers who fought it and listened to their stories.)*

Dispatches From the Front

PERSONALIZING THE WAR

BY ERNIE PYLE

Popular World War II correspondent Ernie Pyle brought the war home by writing about the experiences, thoughts, and feelings of army soldiers at the front lines of combat. The following excerpt from one of Pyle's columns recounts the Ninth Infantry Division's fight to recapture a French town from the Germans.

At the Front Ernie Pyle accompanied Allied forces in the invasions of North Africa, Italy, and Okinawa, in addition to Normandy.

In Normandy, July 17, 1944—Tank Commander Martin Kennelly wanted to show me just where his tank had been hit. As a matter of fact he hadn't seen it for himself yet, for he came running up the street the moment he jumped out of the tank.

So when the firing died down a little we sneaked up the street until we were almost even with the disabled tank. But we were careful not to get our heads around the corner of the side street, for that was where the Germans had fired from.

The first shell had hit the heavy steel brace that the tread runs on, and then plunged on through the side of the tank, very low.

"Say!" Kennelly said in amazement. "It went right through our lower ammunition storage box!

I don't know what kept the ammunition from going off. We'd have been a mess if it had. Boy, it sure would have got hot in there in a hurry!"

The street was still empty. Beyond the tank about two blocks was a German truck, sitting all alone in the middle of the street. It had been blown up, and its tires had burned off. This truck was the only thing you could see. There wasn't a human being in sight anywhere.

Then an American soldier came running up the street shouting for somebody to send up a medic. He said a man was badly wounded just ahead. He was extremely excited, yelling, and getting madder because there was no medic in sight.

Background Information

Dangerous Work War correspondents and photographers have often been killed or injured while covering battles. They are usually unarmed and often risk their lives to provide coverage of action on the front lines. While indi-

vidual reasons for assuming this risk vary, war correspondents have provided important historical documentation of the nature and particulars of war.

Word was passed down the line, and pretty soon a medic came out of a doorway and started up the street. The excited soldier yelled at him and began cussing, and the medic broke into a run. They ran past the tanks together, and up the street a way they ducked into a doorway.

On the corner just across the street from where we were standing was a smashed pillbox. It was in a cut-away corner like the entrances to some of our corner drugstores at home, except that instead of there being a door there was a pillbox of reinforced concrete, with gun slits.

The tank boys had shot it to extinction and then moved their tank up even with it to get the range of the next pillbox. That one was about a block ahead, set in a niche in the wall of a building. That's what the boys had been shooting at when their tank was hit. They knocked it out, however, before being knocked out themselves.

For an hour there was a lull in the fighting. Nobody did anything about a third pillbox, around the corner. Our second tank pulled back a little and just waited. Infantrymen worked their way up to second-story windows and fired their rifles up the side street without actually seeing anything to shoot at.

Now and then blasts from a 20-mm gun would splatter the buildings around us. Then our second tank would blast back in that general direction, over the low roofs, with its machine gun. There was a lot of dangerous-sounding noise, but I don't think anybody on either side got hit.

Then we saw coming up the street, past the wrecked German truck I spoke of, a group of German soldiers. An officer walked in front, carrying a Red Cross flag on a stick. Bob Capa, the photographer, braved the dangerous funnel at the end of the side street where the damaged tank stood, leapfrogging past it and on down the street to meet the Germans.

> **NOW AND THEN BLASTS FROM A 20-MM GUN WOULD SPLATTER THE BUILDINGS AROUND US.**

First he snapped some pictures of them. Then, since he speaks German, he led them on back to our side of the invisible fence of battle. Eight of them were carrying two litters bearing two wounded German soldiers. The others walked behind with their hands up. They went on past us to the hospital. We assumed they were from the second knocked-out pillbox.

I didn't stay to see how the remaining pillbox was knocked out. But I suppose our second tank eventually pulled up to the corner, turned, and let the pillbox have it. After that the area would be clear of everything but snipers.

The infantry, who up till then had been forced to keep in doorways, would now continue up the street and poke into the side streets into the houses until everything was clear.

That's how a strong point in a city is taken. At least that's how ours was taken. You don't always have tanks to help, and you don't always do it with so little shedding of blood.

But the city was already crumbling when we started in on this strong point, which was one of the last, and they didn't hold on too bitterly. But we didn't know that when we started.

I hope this has given you a faint idea of what street fighting is like. If you got out of it much more than a headful of confusion, then you've got out of it exactly the same thing as the soldiers who do it.

RESPONDING TO LITERATURE

1. If you had been a teenager during World War II, how might Ernie Pyle's dispatches from the front have influenced you?

2. Does Pyle's writing make you feel as if you are an eyewitness to the war? Explain.

At the Movies

The 1945 movie *G.I. Joe* portrayed Ernie Pyle's coverage of the war in Italy. Other films about World War II include *Back to Bataan* (1945), *A Bridge Too Far* (1977), *Das Boot* (1981), and *30 Seconds Over Tokyo* (1944).

Block Scheduling

Team Teaching This excerpt from *Ernie's War: The Best of Ernie Pyle's World War II Dispatches* can be presented in a team teaching context, in conjunction with English or Language Arts.

CLOSE

Ask: How might eyewitness coverage differ from reports gathered from official government or military sources? Why might people prefer to read or view eyewitness accounts of a war? *(Answers will vary. Some students may say that eyewitness accounts are more likely to be honest about both positive and negative aspects of a war, while official reports may be slanted for political reasons. People may prefer to read eyewitness accounts because they picture day-by-day events in vivid detail.)*

Responding to Literature Answers

1. Students who think they would have read Ernie Pyle's columns might express interest in the close-up approach to covering the war, or say that they might have read the columns because of concern for loved ones in battle. Students who say they wouldn't read Pyle's columns might express discomfort about reading such a detailed account of the horrors of war. Students might state that the columns might have influenced them to aid the war effort, oppose the war, or become a journalist like Ernie Pyle.

2. Ernie Pyle provides the eyewitness feeling by quoting participants, explaining situations from the perspective of the participant, and providing detailed descriptions of action.

World War II

DAILY LESSON OBJECTIVES	REPRODUCIBLE RESOURCES	MULTIMEDIA RESOURCES
SECTION 1 The Road to War 1. Describe the rise of totalitarianism in Europe and its impact on world events. 2. Explain the motives behind Japan's policy of territorial expansion and why Americans were opposed to it. 3. Explain why at first the United States adopted a policy of neutrality toward escalating world tensions.	• Reproducible Lesson Plans • Vocabulary and Guided Reading Activities (English or Spanish) • Great Debates in American History • Cooperative Learning Activities • Skill Reinforcement Activities • Geography in History Activities • Section Quizzes (English or Spanish)	• Chapter Teaching Transparencies • Section Focus Transparencies • Map Transparencies • Lessons of War • Student Self-Test: A Software Review • Testmaker
SECTION 2 The War Begins 1. Describe Hitler's conquest of Europe. 2. Compare the views of American isolationists and interventionists and explain how this division in public opinion shaped the American response to events in Europe and Asia. 3. Explain how the increasing American economic pressure was one factor that led to Japan's attack on Pearl Harbor.	• Reproducible Lesson Plans • Vocabulary and Guided Reading Activities (English or Spanish) • Section Quizzes (English or Spanish)	• Section Focus Transparencies • U.S. History and Art Transparencies • Great Speeches • Landmark Documents in American History • Student Self-Test: A Software Review • Testmaker
SECTION 3 United States at War 1. Describe the roles of women and minorities in the war. 2. Explain the overall military strategies of the Allied Powers in Europe and the Pacific. 3. Explain the social impact of the war on the people and countries involved.	• Reproducible Lesson Plans • Vocabulary and Guided Reading Activities (English or Spanish) • Enrichment Activities (English or Spanish) • Reteaching Activities (English or Spanish) • Section Quizzes (English or Spanish)	• Section Focus Transparencies • Landmark Documents in American History • Life Unworthy of Life: A Holocaust Curriculum • Lessons of War • Powers of the Congress • A Geographic Perspective on American History • Student Self-Test: A Software Review • Testmaker
CHAPTER REVIEW AND EVALUATION	• Chapter 15 Test, Forms A and B • Performance Assessment Strategies and Activities	• Student Self-Test: A Software Review • Vocabulary PuzzleMaker • Testmaker • Chapter Digests Audiocassettes

 If time does not permit teaching the entire chapter, summarize using the Chapter 15 Digests Audiocassettes and the accompanying activities and tests. (Available in English or Spanish.)

Cooperative Project

Churchill, Roosevelt, Stalin, Hitler, and Mussolini were all strong leaders, but they did not fight the war alone. Divide the class into research teams and have students identify the key people behind each leader, including their roles before and during the war. **LEP** 🎞️

Suggested Rubric: A Research Report. See Performance Strategies and Activities, p. 39.

Individual Project

Have students interview people who remember World War II, asking them questions about specific experiences such as their reactions when they heard about Pearl Harbor or the dropping of the atomic bomb. If possible, have students ask permission to record the interview on audio or video tape. Have them share the results of their interiew with the class. 🎞️

Suggested Rubric: A Slide Show or Photo Essay. See Performance Strategies and Activities, p. 55.

Key to Ability Levels

Teaching strategies have been coded for varying learning styles and abilities.

L1 **BASIC** activities for all students

L2 **AVERAGE** activities for average to above-average students

L3 **CHALLENGING** activities for above-average students

LEP **LIMITED ENGLISH PROFICIENCY** activities

Block Scheduling

Block scheduling differs from traditional class scheduling in the amount of time allotted to each period. The extended timeframe provided by block scheduling affords you the opportunity to implement a greater number of research-oriented and activity-intense projects to motivate and involve your students. Activities that are particularly suited to use within the block scheduling framework are identified throughout this chapter by the following designation. 🎞️

TEACHER'S CORNER

NATIONAL
GEOGRAPHIC
SOCIETY

INDEX TO NATIONAL GEOGRAPHIC MAGAZINE

The following articles may be used for research relating to this chapter:

- "Blueprints for Victory," by John F. Shupe, May 1995.
- "The Wings of War," by Thomas B. Allen, March 1994.
- "Douglas MacArthur: An American Soldier," by Geoffrey C. Ward, March 1992.
- "Pearl Harbor: A Return to the Day of Infamy," by Thomas B. Allen, December 1991.

- "Remembering the Blitz," by Cameron Thomas, July 1991.
- "The Bismarck Found," by Robert D. Ballard, November 1989.
- "Living With Radiation," by Charles E. Cobb, Jr., April 1989.
- "Ghosts of War in the South Pacific," by Peter Benchley, April 1988.
- "Corregidor Revisited," by William Graves, July 1986.

NATIONAL GEOGRAPHIC SOCIETY PRODUCTS AVAILABLE FROM GLENCOE

To order the following products for use with this chapter, contact your local Glencoe sales representative or call Glencoe at 1-800-334-7344:

- *The Presidents: A Picture History of Our Nation* (CD-ROM)
- *GTV: A Geographic Perspective on American History* (Videodisc)

- *GTV: The American People: Fabric of a Nation* (Videodisc)

ADDITIONAL NATIONAL GEOGRAPHIC SOCIETY PRODUCTS

To order the following products for use with this chapter, call National Geographic Society at 1-800-368-2728:

- *Lost Fleet of Guadalcanal* (Video)
- *Decades of History: The 20th Century—The Early Years* (Filmstrip)

- *The United States as a World Power: From the 1890s to the 1970s* (Filmstrip)

Chapter Overview

War began in Europe as Hitler rose to power. The United States gradually became more involved and mobilized for war with Germany. Japan attacked Pearl Harbor, and the United States found itself at war on two fronts.

Introducing the Chapter

Have students read page 490. Ask students to list some reasons that countries go to war. Then ask why Roosevelt or the United States should have been concerned about what was happening in Europe.

Display the Chapter Teaching Transparency for students and have them complete the activity sheet for Chapter 15.

Extension Activity

Have students complete Beyond the Transparency on the activity sheet for Chapter 15 and present their projects after the class has completed the chapter.

History Journal

Have students review the impressions of World War II they wrote in their journals. Then ask them to write down several questions related to World War II that they are curious about or would like to investigate. If their questions are not answered after they have read the chapter, encourage them to explore the topic further.

CHAPTER
15

World War II

SEPTEMBER 1, 1939: GERMANY INVADES POLAND

President Franklin Roosevelt was awakened by a telephone call at 2:30 A.M. on September 1, 1939. Bill Bullitt, United States ambassador to France, reported an urgent call from Tony Biddle in Warsaw.

"Several German divisions are deep in Polish territory, and fighting is heavy. Tony said there were reports of bombers over the city. Then he was cut off."

"Well, Bill," Roosevelt said, "it's come at last. God help us all."

"It" was war in Europe. Only 21 years after the end of World War I, war had begun again. In response to Germany's invasion of Poland, Great Britain began mobilizing troops. Two days later Great Britain and France declared war on Germany.

Bringing the United States out of the Great Depression was Roosevelt's most pressing con-

cern, but growing political unrest in Europe and Asia also demanded his attention. The invasion of Poland was only the latest international crisis of the 1930s.

Looking back, Roosevelt could see the roots of the crisis in Europe in the rise to power of Benito Mussolini and Adolf Hitler. He had also watched as Japan flexed its military might. It was clear to him that these events could hurl the United States into global conflict. He could not know that the war to come would be the most devastating in history, or that it would make the United States the richest and most powerful nation in the world. ■

HISTORY JOURNAL

Before you read the rest of this chapter, write down what you know
about World War II and what you think this chapter will be about.

490

EXTRA CREDIT PROJECT

Costs of War Have students research charts, graphs, and photographs for information about the casualties during World War II. Students can then analyze and report about the costs of war in terms of human lives.

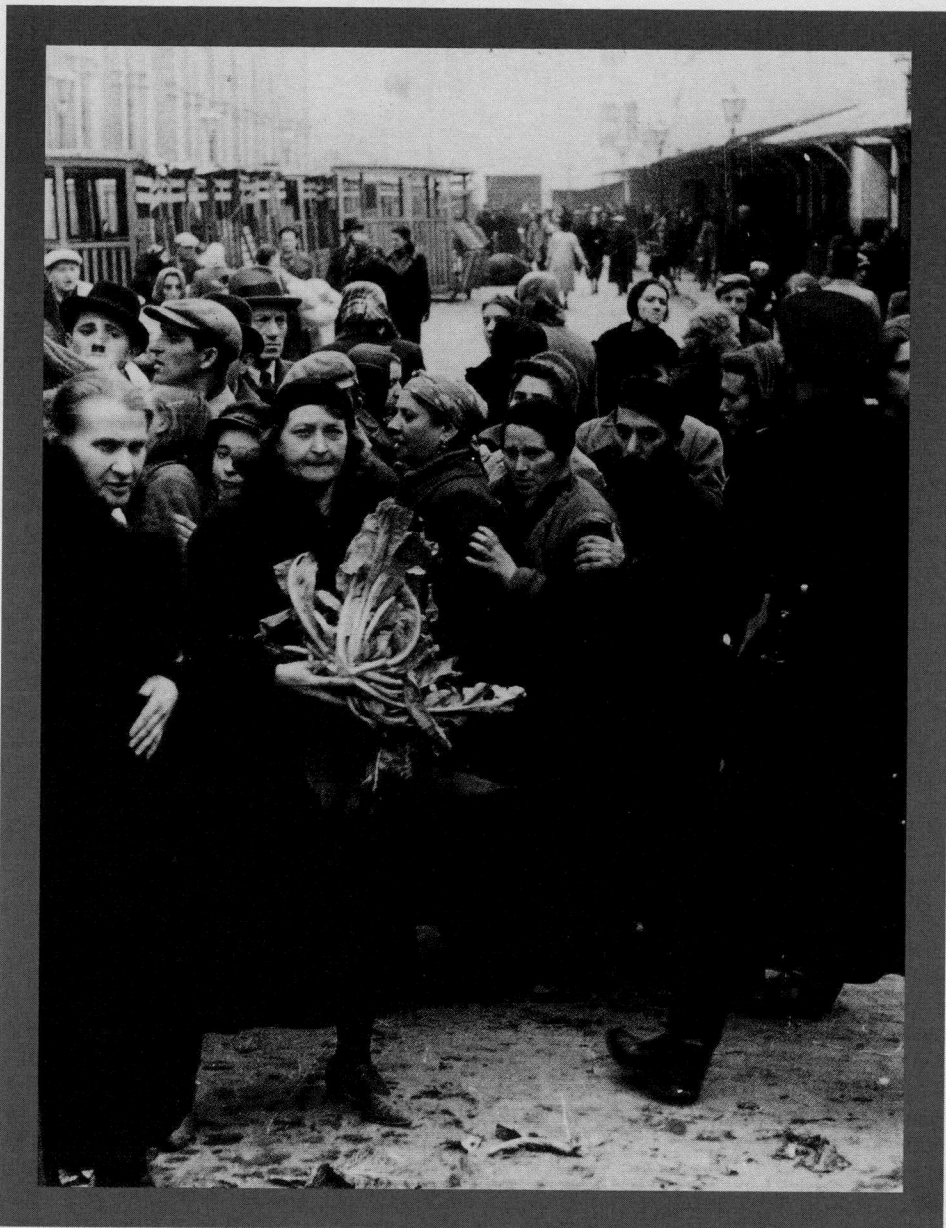

BUNDESARCHIV

THE DAY AFTER GERMANY DEFEATED POLAND,
MEMBERS OF HITLER'S SS BEGAN ROUNDING
UP GROUPS OF POLISH JEWS IN KRAKÓW.

491

 GLENCOE
TECHNOLOGY

 Videodisc

American History

Side 2
Title: World War II
Subject: Sequences concerning World War II
Ask: What were the major Allied Powers during World War II? *(United States, France, Britain)*

 Performance Assessment

Refer to page 490B for performance assessment activities for this chapter.

Also see Activity 15 in the Performance Assessment Strategies and Activities for an additional activity as well as for suggested rubrics.

 Curriculum Connection

English "The Woman With the Lettuce," a work by American poet Sharon Olds, was inspired by the photograph on p. 491. Olds describes the woman in the picture like this: "She stares directly/at the camera, the vast, delicate/plant in her grip like an argument—/its glowing throats reaching out/from the center. Furious, she stands and takes her/last chance to look right at us."

Examining the Visual

Deportation Jews and other Poles deemed to be undesirable were segregated, deported as prisoners to work in Germany, or shot. Jews in Warsaw were forbidden to leave a walled section of the city, known as the Warsaw ghetto.

Half a million Jews were crammed into an area that should have housed 10,000 people. The faces of the people in the photograph show the emotional impact of having to give up homes, families, and possessions.

FOCUS

Section Objectives

1. Describe the rise of totalitarianism in Europe and its impact on world events.
2. Explain the motives behind Japan's policy of territorial expansion and why Americans were opposed to it.
3. Explain why at first the United States adopted a policy of neutrality toward escalating world tensions.

Bellringer Activity

While taking attendance at the beginning of the class period, display **Section Focus Transparency 46,** and have students answer the questions. (Or use the blackline master.)

VISUAL INSTRUCTION

Hitler Hitler's emotional speeches had a hypnotic effect on his audiences, who cheered "Heil Hitler!" ("Hail Hitler!") in response.

Ask: How did the rest of the world react? *(His speeches warned the world about the threat of the German Reich.)*

SECTION 1

The Road to War

JULY 13, 1934: HITLER ADDRESSES THE REICHSTAG

THE BETTMANN ARCHIVE

ADOLF HITLER RECOGNIZED AND MADE USE OF THE POWER OF THE SPOKEN WORD. "Every great movement on this globe owes its rise to the great speakers," he had said. As he stood before the Reichstag, the German house of representatives, on July 13, 1934, Hitler sensed that the moment for a powerful speech was at hand. Two weeks before, he had ruthlessly eliminated those members of his own political party who stood in the way of his rise to absolute power. In a night of blood and terror, Hitler's storm troopers had shot or stabbed hundreds of Hitler's political enemies.

Though he began speaking in a hoarse whisper, Hitler's voice soon rose to a screech. Stabbing the air with his hands, he spat out words such as *traitor, poison,* and *blood.* As Reichstag members sat in stunned silence, Hitler took full responsibility for the murders. He had

Hitler
Speaking with power and emotion, Hitler tried to sway the minds of his people.

killed, he declared, from the highest of motives—his love for the German people and the German state:

I gave the order to shoot those who were the ringleaders in this treason, and I further gave the order to burn out down to the raw flesh the ulcers of this poisoning of the wells in our domestic life and of the poisoning of the outside world. And I further ordered that if any of the mutineers should attempt to resist arrest, they were immediately to be struck down with armed force. . . . I am ready to undertake the responsibility at the bar of history for the twenty-four hours in which the bitterest decisions of my life were made . . . to hold fast to the dearest thing that has been given us in this world—the German people and the German Reich!
—Adolf Hitler, 1934

AS YOU READ

Vocabulary
► fascist
► totalitarian
► appeasement
► blitzkrieg

Think About . . .
► the rise of totalitarianism in Europe and its impact on world events.
► the motives behind Japan's policy of territorial expansion and why Americans were opposed to it.

► why the United States at first adopted a policy of neutrality toward escalating world tensions.

492 CHAPTER 15 WORLD WAR II

Section 1 Resources

REPRODUCIBLE RESOURCES

📂 Lesson Plan 15-1
📂 Section 1 Quiz
📂 Vocabulary and Guided Reading Activity 15-1
📂 Cooperative Learning Activity 15

📂 Unit 6 Great Debate
📂 Geography in History Activity 15
📂 Skill Reinforcement Activity 15

MULTIMEDIA RESOURCES

🖥 Section Focus Transparency 46
💿 Lessons of War
📀 Testmaker
🎧 Chapter 15 Digest Audiocassette
🖥 Map Transparency 15
💻 Student Self-Test: A Software Review
🖥 Chapter Teaching Transparency 15

Hitler's bold justification of the murders swept millions of Germans off their feet and united them behind his government. It also frightened into silence those Germans who still opposed his rule. Hitler's speech warned the rest of the world that this new German Reich was a force not to be ignored.

The Rise of Dictators
Mussolini and Hitler on the Move

Before 1934 Americans had been too preoccupied with their own problems to take Hitler's emotional speeches seriously. The suffering the Great Depression caused convinced most people in the United States that their first priority lay at home, not overseas. The enormous cost of victory in World War I—both in money and in lives—convinced many that the nation should stay out of Europe's troubles.

Keeping with public sentiment, President Roosevelt's foreign policy concentrated at first on making the United States a "good neighbor" to the countries in this hemisphere. At his inauguration in 1933, he announced the Good Neighbor policy. This policy supported the idea of nonintervention among nations. Roosevelt pledged that the United States would not interfere in the internal affairs of its Latin American neighbors. Events in Italy and Germany, however, would soon make it impossible for the United States to avoid intervention in Europe.

Mussolini's Rise in Italy

The events that brought Italy to the center of the world stage began after World War I. Although Italy had fought on the victorious Allied side, the war had left the country in economic chaos. Thousands of soldiers returning to civilian life could not find jobs.

A wounded veteran himself, Benito Mussolini burst onto the Italian political scene with a threat and a

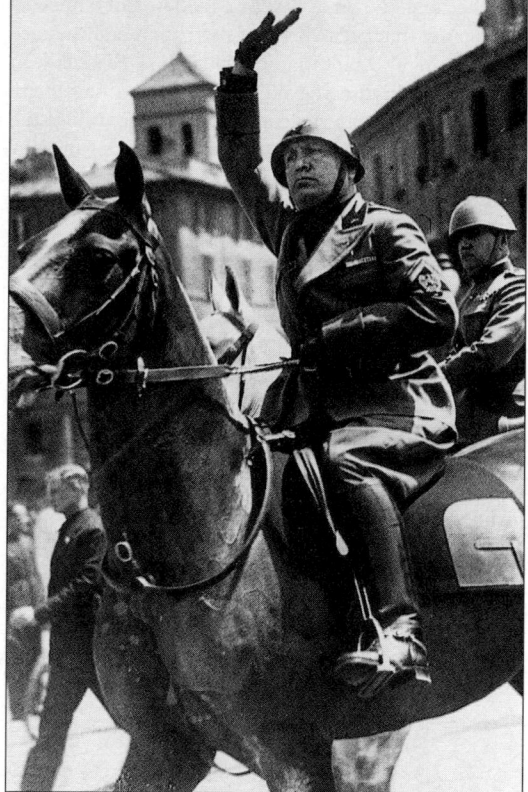

AP/WIDE WORLD PHOTOS

Il Duce on Horseback Mussolini, shown here in 1933 reviewing troops in Rome, ruled Italy for almost 21 years. *How did economic conditions in Italy after World War I make his rise to power easier?*

promise of change. Painting himself as a modernizer and as a champion of order and efficiency, *Il Duce* (the leader), as he called himself, challenged Italians to join with him in rebuilding their shattered economy and in restoring Italy's power in the Mediterranean region. Mussolini gained a following of political demonstrators

THE SPREAD OF DICTATORSHIP, 1929–1939

1929 Hitler denounces Treaty of Versailles.

1933 Hitler becomes chancellor of the Nazi party. Hitler empowered to make laws.

1936 Mussolini and Hitler both send troops to Spain to fight for General Franco.

1938 Hitler occupies Austria and the Sudetenland in Czechoslovakia.

1929 | 1930 | 1931 | 1932 | 1933 | 1934 | 1935 | 1936 | 1937 | 1938 | 1939

1932 Nazi party becomes most powerful in Germany.

1934 Hitler abolishes office of president, declares himself the führer.

1935 Mussolini's troops invade Ethiopia.

1939 Germany and Soviet Union sign nonagression pact. Hitler invades Poland.

SECTION ONE **493**

TEACH

Independent Practice

L2 **Writing** Have students describe a current example of persons coming to the aid of a cause in a country other than their own. Include reasons the individuals were motivated to aid the cause.

📁 Have students complete the Chapter 15, Section 1 Vocabulary and Guided Reading Activity. (Also in Spanish.) **LEP**

📁 Have students complete Cooperative Learning Activity 15.

MAP STUDY

Use the map on this page to list the areas of totalitarian expansion. Compare the expansionist movements based on the map. Discuss how Hitler's strategy in the quest for new territories contrasted with Mussolini's.

Answer: *1938*

Block Scheduling

📁 Have students complete the Unit 6 Great Debate to enrich their understanding of World War II: Isolationism vs. Interventionism.

---

who became known as **fascists,** followers of a political philosophy that preached that the nation and the race were more important than the individual. Fascists won elections by frightening people into supporting them. Black-shirted gangs roamed the streets smashing the offices of opposing political parties and breaking up their meetings. As the leader of the Fascist party, Mussolini became a **totalitarian** dictator, completely controlling all aspects of Italian life.

In spite of these ruthless tactics, many Italians, and even some Americans, saw Mussolini as a model of strength and determination. Once in power, he succeeded in bringing energy and discipline to Italian society with a flood of new government economic and social programs. Under Mussolini, for example, Italian trains ran on time, and engineers built 400 new bridges and 4,000 miles (6,436 km) of roads.

Mussolini also kept his promise to restore Italy's power in the Mediterranean. In October 1935, his armies invaded the African nation of Ethiopia. Ethiopian soldiers on horseback, armed with outdated guns and spears, were no match for the bombers and machine guns of the modern Italian army. By May 1936, Mussolini controlled Ethiopia.

Hitler Founds the Nazi Party

As Mussolini did, Adolf Hitler rose to power in Germany during the troubled times after World War I. Wounded and gassed during the war, Hitler nursed his bitterness by transforming a tiny workers' party into the mighty National Socialist German Workers' party, which became known as the Nazi party. In a series of speeches during the 1920s, Hitler spelled out the Nazi program. The German people, he said, had been divided into warring social classes for too long. By eliminating the differences between rich and poor, the Nazis would make the German people strong and united. Moreover, Hitler said, Jews and others who were not blond, blue-eyed members of what he called the "Aryan" or Germanic race had betrayed Germany in World War I. The Jews, Hitler said, were to blame for Germany's economic problems.

THE EXPANSION OF EUROPEAN TOTALITARIANISM, 1900–1939

Germany
Areas of German expansion
Italy
Areas of Italian expansion
★ Capital city
← German expansion
← Italian expansion

Once in power, the totalitarian regimes of Mussolini and Hitler moved across Europe and parts of Africa, conquering every small and weak country in their paths. *When did Germany take over Austria?*

Meeting Special Needs

Reading Disability To meet the needs of students with reading disabilities, have students with reading comprehension problems skim the visuals and section heads before reading the section.

Protest Through Art Pablo Picasso's famous painting *Guernica* is a masterpiece of protest against the bombing of the town of Guernica during the Spanish civil war. *How does his unconventional portrayal of this event contribute to its overall effect as a protest statement against war?*

Building the Third Reich

When the Depression struck Germany in 1929, the German government was unable to find jobs for 6 million unemployed workers. Hitler took advantage of the discontent to appeal to the German people to rebuild their economy and to revive their honor by bringing him to power. He denounced the Treaty of Versailles, which dismantled the German military and required Germany to pay huge sums of money to the Allies. In an election held in July 1932, the Nazi party became the most powerful in Germany, though it failed to win a clear majority. Nevertheless, Hitler held out for full powers as chancellor, which he got in January 1933.

Once in power Hitler moved to eliminate opposition. In February 1933, he persuaded German president Paul von Hindenberg to suspend most German civil rights. A month later, by false promises and threats of violence, Hitler convinced the Reichstag to give him the power to make laws without its consent. In June 1934, Hitler demanded that members of the military swear personal allegiance to him. After Hindenberg's death in August 1934, Hitler abolished the office of president and declared himself the führer, or supreme leader of the Third Reich, the German Empire. Thus, Hitler also became a totalitarian dictator.

With all power concentrated in his hands, Hitler defied the Treaty of Versailles by rebuilding the German military. In 1936 he took his defiance a step further and sent troops into Germany's Rhineland. This put German soldiers on the eastern border of France. When Great Britain and France did not resist the action, Hitler's plans grew even more ambitious.

The Axis Tests Its Strength
Mussolini and Hitler Join Forces

Hitler and Mussolini were two powerful leaders who had dreams of expanding their borders, and both were building armies mighty enough to seize new lands at will. When these two dictators formed an alliance in 1936, dubbed the Axis Powers, fear struck the hearts of many Europeans, including the Soviets whose communism clashed with fascism.

Fighting the Spanish Civil War

The outbreak of a bitter and bloody civil war in Spain complicated the situation in Europe. In 1931 a parliamentary government under a democratic constitution replaced the Spanish monarchy. Led by Spanish army General Francisco Franco, conservative and pro-monarchy rebel troops attempted to overthrow the Spanish government in 1936. The war quickly grew into an international struggle. Because Franco, like Mussolini, strongly opposed communism, Mussolini felt compelled to aid Franco's cause. He sent airplanes and thousands of soldiers from the Italian army. Hitler also sent Franco bombers and troops.

On the other side, the Soviet Union supported the Republicans who fought for the elected government. Though the governments of Great Britain, France, and the United States were officially neutral, many citizens in these countries backed the Republicans. Some 3,000 Americans who opposed Franco's political stance formed the Abraham Lincoln Brigade and fought in Spain for

SECTION ONE **495**

Portfolio Project

Summaries Have students use the material in this section to write a brief summary of the events on "the road to war," emphasizing the rise of totalitarianism and Japanese aggression.

Have them use section heads as their summary outline guide. Ask them to add these summaries to their portfolio.

Cha...
SEC...

VIS...
Ret...
bro...
in N...
wh...
Cze...
Ans...
avo...

FYI

Invasion of Poland At the time of the invasion, the Polish military consisted of outdated infantry and horse cavalry. They were ineffectual against the 1,500 planes, including Stuka dive bombers, and the panzers, or German tanks. Also, they were not prepared for their invaders, whom Hitler had instructed to "close their hearts to pity."

 Curriculum Connection

Literature Many great writers found ample fodder for their works in the events preceding and during World War II. Ernest Hemingway served as a war correspondent in Spain during the Spanish Civil War. Readings might include: *For Whom the Bell Tolls; Byline: Ernest Hemingway;* and *Ernest Hemingway: Selected Letters 1917–1961.*

...cause. Many were far-left supporters of ...the Americans who volunteered felt that ...Italy could come to the aid of Franco ...democracy in Spain, nothing would stop ...ving on to France. "And after France?" ...the end, Franco's fascist forces prevailed.

...itler in Munich

...in the Spanish civil war did not satisfy ...increase German power. In March 1938, ...that Austria was part of Germany, and ...olled into Vienna, Austria's capital, to seal ...rriage between the two countries. Six ...itler's armies occupied the Sudetenland ...hoslovakia, an area with a large ethnic ...tion. To justify his aggression, Hitler ex- ...had taken the Sudetenland to satisfy the ...ns living there to become part of Ger- ...goal, he said, was to defend the German-speaking people of Czechoslovakia against political oppression by the Czechs.

Eager to avoid another war, the leaders of Great Britain and France adopted a policy of **appeasement** toward Hitler, in which they gave in to his demands in an attempt to keep the peace. At a conference in Munich in September 1938, British Prime Minister Neville Chamberlain and French Premier Edouard Daladier agreed not to oppose Hitler's move against the Sudetenland. Describing this crisis as a family affair, Hitler promised that he would respect the rest of Czechoslovakia and make no new territorial demands in Europe. A joyful Chamberlain, supported by President Roosevelt, told a jittery world that war had been averted and that the Munich Pact meant "peace for our time." Not all British politicians agreed. Winston Churchill, who would soon replace Chamberlain as prime minister, remarked, "Britain and France had to choose between war and dishonor. They chose dishonor. They will have war."

Invading Poland Leads to War

When Hitler seized the rest of Czechoslovakia just five and a half months later, Churchill's words proved prophetic. Any remaining hope that Hitler could be stopped short of waging all-out war was shattered on August 23, 1939, when Germany signed a nonaggression pact with the Soviet Union. The agreement pledged that neither country would attack the other. By securing his eastern border against Soviet attack, Hitler freed himself to direct his forces against the rest of Europe.

The suspense concerning where Hitler would strike next was short-lived. Poland, a country historically beset by its stronger neighbors, was once again the fuse igniting the powder keg. In a secret section of their nonaggression treaty, Germany and the Soviet Union

Returning to London On September 30, 1938, Prime Minister Neville Chamberlain, home from the Munich Conference, speaks to a crowd. *What did he believe he had accomplished?*

had already agreed to divide Poland between them. With Soviet approval, Hitler's tanks rumbled across the border into Poland at dawn on September 1, 1939, while his *Luftwaffe* (air force) bombarded Polish cities. This swift, all-out style of attack, known as **blitzkrieg** (lightning war), was devastatingly effective. Two days later, Great Britain and France, who had pledged to defend Poland against outside aggression, declared war on Germany. World War II had begun.

The Rise of Militarism
Japan Flexes Its Muscles

Japan was as aggressive a nation in Asia as Hitler's Germany was in Europe. During the 1930s ambitious Japanese military leaders began a policy of territorial expansion. Confined to a chain of small islands and Korea, Japan's growing population strained its resources. Though rich in industrial know-how, Japan was poor in land for agriculture and in raw materials for its industries. It depended on imports from the United States and other countries for such essential commodities as wheat, petroleum, rubber, coal, iron, and timber. Japanese military leaders resented this dependence on foreign suppliers, which made them vulnerable to economic and military pressure from abroad. To make Japan secure and self-sufficient, these leaders pushed to expand Japan's borders beyond its home islands onto the Asian mainland.

Extending the Content

Japan's Military Attitude Point out to students that at the time of the Japanese aggression in China in the mid-1930s, the Japanese military regarded conquest as honorable. They also saw it as a way to solve the country's problems of limited land and natural resources along with a growing population. Because this approach worked in 1905 in Manchuria and Korea, Japan's military leaders continued to

seek expansion. The Japanese also counted on the United States to allow their expansion to continue. Ask: Why would the Japanese think that the United States was not a threat? *(President Roosevelt had signed the Neutrality Acts and American public opinion was strongly against involvement in another war after World War I.)*

ARCHIVE PHOTOS

Military leaders occupied a special place in Japanese society. The chiefs of the Imperial Army and Navy were independent of the civilian government and answered only to the emperor in matters of national defense. These leaders regarded foreign conquest as a badge of personal honor. They had already savored the sweetness of victory when Japan won the large and potentially productive island of Taiwan in a war with China in 1895. Ten years later, they tasted conquest again when Japan won footholds in Manchuria and Korea on the Asian mainland by defeating Russia in the Russo-Japanese War in 1904 and 1905. Now they looked to the rest of Manchuria and East Asia for new lands to add to their empire.

Japan Invades Manchuria

The most tempting target for Japanese expansion was Manchuria, in northern China. This vast region was poorly defended, and it had abundant resources. Japanese military leaders hoped that Manchuria would provide living space for Japan's surplus population and enough raw materials, food, and manufactured goods to make Japan self-sufficient. In September 1931, Japan launched an attack on Manchuria. Within a few months, the Japanese army had overpowered the province. In September 1932, Japan installed a Japanese-controlled puppet government and renamed the region "Manchukuo."

UPI/BETTMANN NEWSPHOTOS

Symbol of Power Emperor Hirohito, shown above right in 1934, was emperor of Japan from 1926 until he died in 1989. *Why was the Japanese military so powerful?*

The League of Nations, of which Japan was a key member, condemned Japan for its aggression. In contempt, Japan merely withdrew from the League. Meanwhile, Japan argued that its military actions in Manchuria were essential to its long-term security. The world remained unconvinced.

Shutting the Open Door

The United States protested Japan's expansion into China but did little more. Roosevelt refused to recognize Japan's puppet government in Manchuria. Later, when Japan used its base in Manchuria to launch a full-scale assault on China, Roosevelt authorized small loans to the government of China to help them buy military supplies. He also urged Americans to boycott Japanese silk.

Perhaps the strongest critics of Japanese aggression against China were the American people. Many Americans felt a special sympathy and kinship with the Chinese. Fiction such as *The Good Earth* by Pearl Buck painted a picture of Chinese peasants as noble and long-suffering. Chiang Kai-shek (Jiang Jieshi), the leader of China, and Soong Meiling, his American-educated wife, were popular figures in the United States, even appearing on the cover of *Time* magazine. American missionaries had long been active in China, and many Americans saw themselves as China's protectors. Some Americans even believed that, in time, China would come to resemble the United States.

The most important reason for Americans' alarm at the invasion of China, however, was economic. The American business community saw China as a boundless market for American goods. To protect this market, the United States had long asserted its Open Door policy, assuring all countries equal access to China's markets. If Japan succeeded in conquering China and in closing that open door, the United States stood to lose close to $100 million in annual cotton sales. As Japan grew stronger and gained control of more natural resources, its industries would be better able to compete with American businesses for world sales. For these reasons, many feared Japan's continued aggression in China.

The "China Incident"

By 1937 Japanese forces moved south from Manchuria against Shanghai and Nanjing, major Chinese cities. Japanese soldiers killed tens of thousands of Chinese civilians. Leaders in Tokyo tried to play down the military actions in China, referring to them as the "China Incident." In reality the "China Incident" was a full-scale war.

The Japanese attacks on Shanghai and Nanjing alarmed already anxious Americans. Even such a strong opponent of American involvement in foreign conflicts as Senator George Norris condemned the Japanese actions as "disgraceful" and "barbarous." The United States, however, leveled nothing stronger than words at the Japanese.

SECTION ONE   **497**

VISUAL INSTRUCTION

Symbol of Power Hirohito's reign was called "Showa," or "Enlightened Peace." Although the constitution of Japan gave him supreme authority, Hirohito's role was merely to ratify the policies of his ministers and advisers.

Answer: *The military leaders were especially honored in Japanese society and Japan had a long tradition of aggressive territorial expansion.*

ASSESS

Meeting Lesson Objectives

Each section objective is tested by the section review question(s) that follows it in parentheses.

1. Describe the rise of totalitarianism in Europe and its impact on world events. (1, 2)
2. Explain the motives behind Japan's policy of territorial expansion and why Americans were opposed to it. (3, 4)
3. Explain why at first the United States adopted a policy of neutrality toward escalating world tensions. (5)

Cultural Perspectives

State Shinto and the Emperor Shinto, the oldest religion of Japan, involves worshiping many gods, called *kami*, which are found in parts of nature—in mountains and trees, for example. It also involves ancestor worship. From 1868 through World War II, the government recognized State Shinto as Japan's official religion. Key elements of State Shinto were patriotism and the belief that the emperor of Japan must be worshiped as a divine being. After World War II, however, the Japanese government, under United States pressure, abolished State Shinto. The nation's 1947 constitution states that the real power is in the will of the people; the duties of the emperor, who inherits the throne, are entirely ceremonial.

BUNDESARCHIV

Assault on Nanjing Japanese invaders march behind one of their tanks in 1937 during the violent assault on the Chinese capital that claimed the lives of about 200,000 citizens. *What was the American sentiment toward the Chinese?*

Evaluate

Have students complete the Section Review.

✏ 🖵 Assign the Section 1 Quiz or use the Testmaker to develop a customized quiz. (Also in Spanish) **LEP**

Reteach

🎧 Have students listen to the Chapter 15, Section 1 Audiocassette. (Also in Spanish) **LEP**

Enrich

✏ Have students complete the Chapter 15 Geography in History Activity.

CLOSE

Summarize with the class the content of the section by creating a time line of the major events.

America's Nonneutral Neutrality
Resistance to Another War

With hostilities spreading in Europe and Asia, Congress took action to try to keep the United States from becoming involved. After Italy's invasion of Ethiopia in 1935, and again after the outbreak of the Spanish civil war in 1936, Congress passed a series of laws called the Neutrality Acts. These laws prohibited the sale of American weapons to nations at war and tried to keep citizens of the United States from traveling on ships belonging to warring countries. The laws also required that countries at war pay cash for nonmilitary trade goods like cotton or wheat.

Roosevelt reluctantly signed the Neutrality Acts. In doing so he bowed to strong public sentiment against American involvement in another war. A 1937 Gallup poll found that nearly two-thirds of Americans thought that the nation's participation in World War I had been a mistake. Although Roosevelt regarded both Germany and Japan as serious threats to the nation's security, he faced an uphill battle in preparing the United States for the possibility of another war.

Roosevelt knew that to fight a war, the United States would need tanks, planes, guns, and other supplies. To this end, he asked Congress in 1938 for $300 million in additional spending. By 1939 Roosevelt was asking

Congress for a $1.3 billion military budget. He had decided that Hitler and Mussolini were "two madmen," who "respect force and force alone." History would prove Roosevelt correct.

SECTION REVIEW

Vocabulary

1. Define: fascist, totalitarian, appeasement, blitzkrieg.

Checking Facts

2. What similarities existed between the rise of totalitarianism in Italy under Mussolini and in Germany under Hitler?

3. Why were Americans alarmed by Japan's aggressiveness in China?

Critical Thinking

Recognizing Ideologies

4. Many Americans condemned the "China Incident." Why did the United States respond with only words?

Linking Across Time

5. Today many Americans have taken an antiwar position, believing that war is immoral. Compare today's antiwar feelings with the antiwar feelings of people in the 1930s that led to the policy of neutrality.

Section 1 Review Answers

1. fascist (494), **totalitarian** (494), **appeasement** (496), **blitzkrieg** (496)
2. In both situations, one strong individual controlled all aspects of society and rose to power in the economic chaos left after World War I.
3. They were afraid Japan would not honor the Open Door policy, threatening American interests there.

4. Most Americans wanted to avoid entry into another war.
5. Students may answer that isolationists were in favor of avoiding war for economic and political reasons; today, many wish to avoid war strictly on moral grounds.

Critical Thinking Skill

RECOGNIZING IDEOLOGIES

Learning the Skill

Ideology is a basic set of beliefs about freedom and equality, life, culture, and the desired role of the state and government. Recognizing ideology in a speech or statement can help you to identify a person's political beliefs.

The lists below show the ideologies characteristic of a totalitarian dictatorship and of a democracy.

Totalitarian Dictatorship

• The leader has total and absolute power.

• People have no power to limit their leaders.

• Government is not accountable for its actions.

• Power is gained by military force.

Democracy

• People hold the power to rule.

• People have individual liberty and equal opportunity.

• Majority rule combines with respect for minority rights.

• People choose their leaders.

How to Recognize Ideologies

To recognize ideologies in written passages, follow these steps:

a. Read the passage and state it in your own words.

b. Identify the important or key words in the passage.

c. Identify unstated beliefs, ideas, facts, or opinions.

d. Compare this to what you know about the characteristics of specific ideologies.

Read this sentence once spoken by John F. Kennedy:

A sk not what your country can do for you; ask what you can do for your country.

The first step is to restate the sentence in your own words; for example, "People should help their country instead of expecting the country to do things for them."

Next, identify key words such as "what you can do." Then look for any unstated ideas, such as, "people have a responsibility to make changes in their country."

Finally, use what you know about political ideologies to make a statement about the author's political beliefs; for example, "In this statement, the author wants people to take action, so the passage reflects a democratic ideology."

Political Rally Hitler staged spectacular political shows to highlight his speeches, such as at this rally at Bückeberg in 1934. *How does this scene reflect the ideology behind Hitler's rise to power as a dictator?*

Practicing the Skill

Now read the following passage by Adolf Hitler and use what you have learned about recognizing ideologies to answer the questions.

T here must be no decisions by majority, but only responsible persons, and the word *council* is once more reduced to its original meaning. At every man's side there stand councilors, indeed, but one man decides.

1. What does "no decisions by majority" mean?

2. State the main idea of the passage in your own words.

3. Note the key words and important ideas in the passage.

4. What do you think are the unstated ideas or beliefs in this passage?

5. In your opinion, what political ideology does this passage reflect? Explain your answer.

Applying the Skill

Find a passage from a political statement or speech. Analyze the passage and write what it tells you about the author's political ideology.

Additional Practice

For additional practice, see Reinforcing Skills on page 521.

CRITICAL THINKING SKILL **499**

TEACH

Tell students it is often difficult to determine ideologies by looking at words alone; it is often helpful to look at related actions. During Hitler's rule, for example, young Germans were indoctrinated in Nazi ideology through groups like the Hitler Youth, for boys, and the League of German Girls. Boys were taught the importance of physical fitness, courage in battle, and unswerving loyalty to their Führer. Under the Third Reich, women were legally barred from holding high party offices, university professorships, or judicial posts. German girls were taught early that their destiny and contribution to Hitler's cause was to bear and rear "proper" German children.

Additional Practice

☞ Have students complete the Chapter 15 Skill Reinforcement Activity.

VISUAL INSTRUCTION

Political Rally **After Hitler assumed command of the German armed forces, officers and enlisted men swore an oath of allegiance to Hitler.**

Answer: *The scene shows Hitler's belief that all Germans should think and act identically and that Hitler himself should lead them.*

Practicing the Skill Answers

1. Decisions are not made based on what the majority of people think or feel.

2. Answers will vary. Students might suggest that there should be only one person who makes decisions.

3. key words and ideas: no decisions by majority, one man decides

4. When he says one man, Hitler means himself. He should be the "responsible person" that makes all the decisions.

5. It reflects a totalitarian dictatorship because the leader has all the power; the majority of people have no power to make decisions.

FOCUS

Section Objectives

1. Describe Hitler's conquest of Europe.
2. Compare the views of American isolationists and interventionists and explain how this division in public opinion shaped the American response to events in Europe and Asia.
3. Explain how the increasing American economic pressure was one factor that led to Japan's attack on Pearl Harbor.

GLENCOE
TECHNOLOGY

**Great
Speeches**

Volume V–Franklin D. Roosevelt (first Inaugural and Declaration of War)

VISUAL INSTRUCTION

Surrender of Paris In 1806 Napoleon began the *Arc de Triomphe* as a monument to his troops, and King Louis Philippe completed it in 1836. After World War I, the Allied governments realized that many soldiers killed in battle could not be identified. Each government chose an unknown soldier as a representative and buried the soldier in a monument. France buried its unknown soldier beneath the *Arc de Triomphe.*

Ask: What caused the French forces to be demoralized? *(The Germans stormed around the defensive bunkers of the Maginot Line and successfully attacked them from the rear.)*

SECTION

2

The War Begins

JUNE 14, 1940: GERMAN TROOPS OCCUPY PARIS

Surrender of Paris
The French surrender Paris to the Germans.

PARIS WAS SILENT AND OMINOUSLY DESERTED AS DAWN BROKE ON FRIDAY, JUNE 14, 1940. The shutters over house and shop windows were closed and barred. The Metro was not running. No cars, trucks, or bicycles moved down the magnificent boulevards or along the narrow, twisting streets. Three million of the nearly 5 million people who lived in Paris and its surrounding neighborhoods had already fled. The rest stayed indoors and waited.

The night before, under a flag of truce, French officers had met with German officials near Paris. The French knew Paris would fall under a German assault. Rather than see their beautiful city destroyed, they handed it over to the Germans.

By 5 A.M. on Friday morning, columns of German infantry were marching three abreast toward railroad stations and other key points inside Paris. Roger Langeron, chief of the Paris police, watched as German soldiers entered the city. Writing in his diary for that fateful Friday, Langeron described the "terrible thing" that had befallen France. He mourned the "interminable defile of motorized troops" that made its way through Paris from Saint-Denis toward Montrouge. He recorded in his diary the dark parade of leather-clad motorcyclists and armored tanks that moved down empty streets before "shuttered" houses.

In the midafternoon, Langeron was summoned to meet the new German military governor at the Crillon Hotel. By then swastika flags were already flying over the public buildings of Paris.

AS YOU READ

Vocabulary
▶ interventionism
▶ isolationism

Think About . . .
▶ Hitler's conquest of Europe.
▶ the views of American isolationists and interventionists, and how this division in public opinion shaped

the American response to events in Europe and Asia.
▶ how the increasing American economic pressure was one factor in Japan's attack on Pearl Harbor.

Section 2 Resources

REPRODUCIBLE RESOURCES
📁 Lesson Plan 15-2
📁 Vocabulary and Guided Reading Activity 15-2
📁 Section 2 Quiz

MULTIMEDIA RESOURCES
💿 Section Focus Transparency 47
💿 Landmark Documents in American History
💿 Testmaker
🎧 Chapter 15 Digest Audiocassette

📺 Great Speeches
💿 Student Self-Test: A Software Review
📖 U.S. History and Art Transparency 23

Hitler Crushes Europe
The Continent Gives Up

The unopposed German occupation of Paris was a triumph for Hitler's forces, which in two months had conquered most of Western Europe. On April 9, 1940, more than seven months after invading Poland, Hitler unleashed an air and sea assault against Denmark and Norway. A few weeks later, German tanks and bombers drove the Netherlands, Belgium, and Luxembourg to their knees. "The small countries are smashed up, one by one, like matchwood," England's new prime minister, Winston Churchill, complained.

France Surrenders

Despite Germany's victories, the French had prepared to make a stand. About a million French soldiers held positions along the Maginot Line, a system of heavily armed steel and concrete bunkers built after World War I and stretching hundreds of miles along the German border, from Belgium to Switzerland. In addition, England had sent troops and supplies to aid in the defense of France.

In early May 1940, German tanks stormed across the French border from Belgium, swept around the north end of the Maginot Line, and attacked French positions from the rear. Fixed firmly in concrete and pointing toward Germany, the heavy artillery pieces of the Maginot Line were never fired.

France had placed its faith in the strength of the Maginot Line, and its failure demoralized the French. Within a few short weeks, France's fate was sealed. The pulverizing attacks of the German tank corps, supported by massive air power, sent the French and British armies reeling backward. By the end of May, French soldiers were throwing down their weapons in the face of the German advance, and the British forces had retreated to the French seacoast town of Dunkirk on the English Channel. A fleet of military and private vessels saved the British army from destruction by evacuating 338,000 French and British troops from Dunkirk between May 28 and June 4, 1940. French forces were left to face the German invaders alone.

Britain in the War In the photo above, British destroyers loaded with troops that had been stranded at Dunkirk arrive safely at a British port. The photo at the left shows civilians huddled in a cramped subway tunnel during the London blitz. *Why did Germany begin to strike Great Britain after dark?*

French resistance lasted only a few weeks more. On June 3, German bombers had attacked Paris airports. A week later Italy declared war on France, and Mussolini's forces attacked from the south. On June 14, German troops marched into Paris. Finally, in a railway car on June 22, a jubilant Hitler personally accepted the French surrender.

The Battle of Britain

With France secure, Hitler began an all-out attack on Great Britain in the summer of 1940. Great Britain, however, was not as easily conquered. Although badly outnumbered, Britain's Royal Air Force had excellent fighter planes and highly dedicated pilots. So many German planes were shot down by British fighter pilots that Germany had to abandon daylight attacks. A proud Prime Minister Churchill declared that "never in the field of human conflict was so much owed by so many to so few."

Hoping to avoid further defeat, Hitler sought the cover of darkness. From September 1940 to May 1941, German aircraft dropped tons of bombs on London almost every night. The blitz, as the British called the bombing raids, killed more than 20,000 Londoners alone. The entire city of Coventry and large parts of London

TEACH

Bellringer Activity

While taking attendance at the beginning of the class period, display **Section Focus Transparency 47,** and have students answer the questions. (Or use the blackline master.)

Guided Practice

L2 **Linking Past and Present** The Lend-Lease Act provided aid to the USSR, which many Americans denounced. Today the United States is on friendlier terms with Russia and other former Soviet Union countries. Discuss current public opinion on giving economic aid to these countries.

VISUAL INSTRUCTION

Britain in the War The town of Dunkirk has an excellent harbor, so it was able to accommodate the fleet of more than 800 vessels that evacuated the troops. The fleet included military vessels such as cruisers, destroyers, gunboats, and minesweepers, as well as private vessels such as fishing boats, motorboats, and yachts.

Answer: *So many German planes were shot down by British fighter pilots that Hitler sought the cover of darkness to minimize his losses.*

Cooperative Learning

Debate War-related Issues Establish several topics for debate. (For example, a President should always abide by public opinion. The United States should enter a war only in self-defense.) Students should work in debate teams to prepare their arguments. Help the teams to assign the various duties.

were reduced to smoking rubble. In the face of this assault, Churchill pleaded for more American aid. The future course of the United States at this point, however, was far from clear.

The Americans Respond
A Conflict of Attitudes

The rapid fall of France stunned people in the United States, but Americans still disagreed about what should be done. Some who supported **interventionism** believed the United States should give all possible support to Britain short of declaring war on Germany. Others who supported **isolationism** thought the United States should stay out of the war.

One influential interventionist was William Allen White, a Kansas City journalist. He formed the Committee to Defend America by Aiding the Allies. With more than 600 local branches, the group promoted vigorous American support of Britain, short of active participation in the war.

Isolationists banded together to form the Committee to Defend America First. Its members thought the United States should keep out of Europe's business. America First drew support from a broad range of Americans, including pacifists and socialists, Democrats and Republicans. Former President Herbert Hoover, union activist John L. Lewis, and architect Frank Lloyd Wright belonged, as did representatives from German and Italian ethnic groups. Robert E. Wood, the chairman of Sears, Roebuck and Co., headed the governing committee. The most famous speaker for the group was aviator Charles Lindbergh. He argued that the United States was strong enough to stand alone, despite Hitler's victories. Within a few months of its founding, America First had about 60,000 members.

Selective Service

Aware of the split in public opinion and mindful of the upcoming presidential election, Roosevelt continued on a cautious course of aid to the Allies. In September 1940, Roosevelt arranged the transfer of 50 overage American destroyers to Britain. In return, the United States was given the right to establish naval and air bases on British territory in Newfoundland, Bermuda, and British Guiana (now Guyana). The same month the President signed the Selective Training and Service Act, which established the first peacetime draft in United States history. The law applied to all men between 21 and 35. More than 1 million men were to serve in the military for 1 year, but they were

To Help or Not to Help Many Americans were indecisive about involvement in World War II. *Does this cartoon support interventionism or isolationism?*

authorized to serve only in the Western Hemisphere. The Selective Service Act laid the groundwork for a United States military capable of fighting a global war.

On the surface, these moves brought the United States closer to involvement. Yet Roosevelt explained them as strengthening United States defenses and keeping the nation out of the war. Roosevelt took a similar stance during the 1940 election campaign: "Your President says this country is not going to war!" Approving voters returned him to the presidency for a third term.

Lend-Lease

With the election won, Roosevelt moved to support the Allies openly. In January 1941, he proposed the Lend-Lease bill. This bill gave the President the right to sell, lend, or lease military supplies to any nation deemed "vital to the defense of the United States." Roosevelt defended this plan by explaining that Britain did not have the money to purchase arms. If a neighbor's house were on fire, Roosevelt argued, you would loan that person your garden hose without worrying about the price. The United States, the President declared, must become the "great arsenal of democracy."

Polls indicated that most Americans agreed with Roosevelt. Nearly 80 percent of those questioned in one poll favored the Lend-Lease plan. Given these results,

502 CHAPTER 15 WORLD WAR II

Congress approved the Lend-Lease Act in March 1941, providing an initial budget of $7 billion. Before Lend-Lease ended, more than $50 billion in weapons, vehicles, and other supplies would go to support the Allied war effort. Shipments to Britain began at once. Economically, at least, the United States was at war with Germany.

Lend-Lease heated up the United States's involvement in the war in another way. During the spring and summer of 1941, German submarines patrolling in "wolf packs" sent tens of thousands of tons of British and American supply ships to the bottom of the Atlantic every week. To make sure that Lend-Lease supplies arrived safely in Britain, in April Roosevelt ordered the United States Navy to help the British track German U-boats. By summer the navy had orders to guard British ships as they traveled across the Atlantic and to destroy enemy submarines that threatened their passage.

The undeclared war between German and American ships worsened in the fall of 1941. In September a German submarine fired on the *Greer,* an American destroyer. Calling the Germans "the rattlesnakes of the Atlantic," Roosevelt ordered the navy to shoot Axis vessels on sight. In October German U-boats torpedoed the destroyer *Kearny* and sank the destroyer *Reuben James,*

killing about 100 Americans. Congress revised the Neutrality Acts to allow armed American merchant ships to carry munitions directly to England.

Though Lend-Lease aid to the Allied Powers seemed to be pulling the United States into the war, most citizens supported it in principle. When Germany suddenly attacked the Soviet Union in June 1941, however, the United States extended Lend-Lease aid to the USSR. Some people in the United States were outraged at the idea of sending Lend-Lease aid to a Communist country. Isolationist Charles Lindbergh said he would prefer an alliance with Nazi Germany, with all its faults, to an alliance with "the godlessness and barbarism that exist in the Soviet Union."

Churchill, who had criticized the Communists for years, however, cheered the United States aid to the Soviets. "I have only one purpose," Churchill remarked, "the destruction of Hitler. . . . If Hitler invaded Hell I would at least make a favorable reference to the Devil in the House of Commons." Churchill was aware that Germany's opening of an eastern front would take some pressure off Britain. Battles against the Soviets in the east tied up 200 German divisions that might otherwise have been used in an invasion of Britain.

History and the Humanities

 U.S. History and Art Transparency 23— *Fallingwater* (Kaufmann House) by Frank Lloyd Wright

 Facts on File

Landmark Documents in American History Have students review "Radio Address on Selective Service Registration Day, Franklin D. Roosevelt, 1940," "Fireside Chat on National Defense, Franklin D. Roosevelt, 1940," "Destroyers-for-Bases Agreement, 1940," Burke-Wadsworth Act (Selective Training and Service Act), 1940," "'Four Freedoms' Speech, Franklin Roosevelt, 1941," "Lend-Lease Act, 1941," and "Atlantic Charter, 1941." Ask students to write a paragraph about the intent of one of the documents.

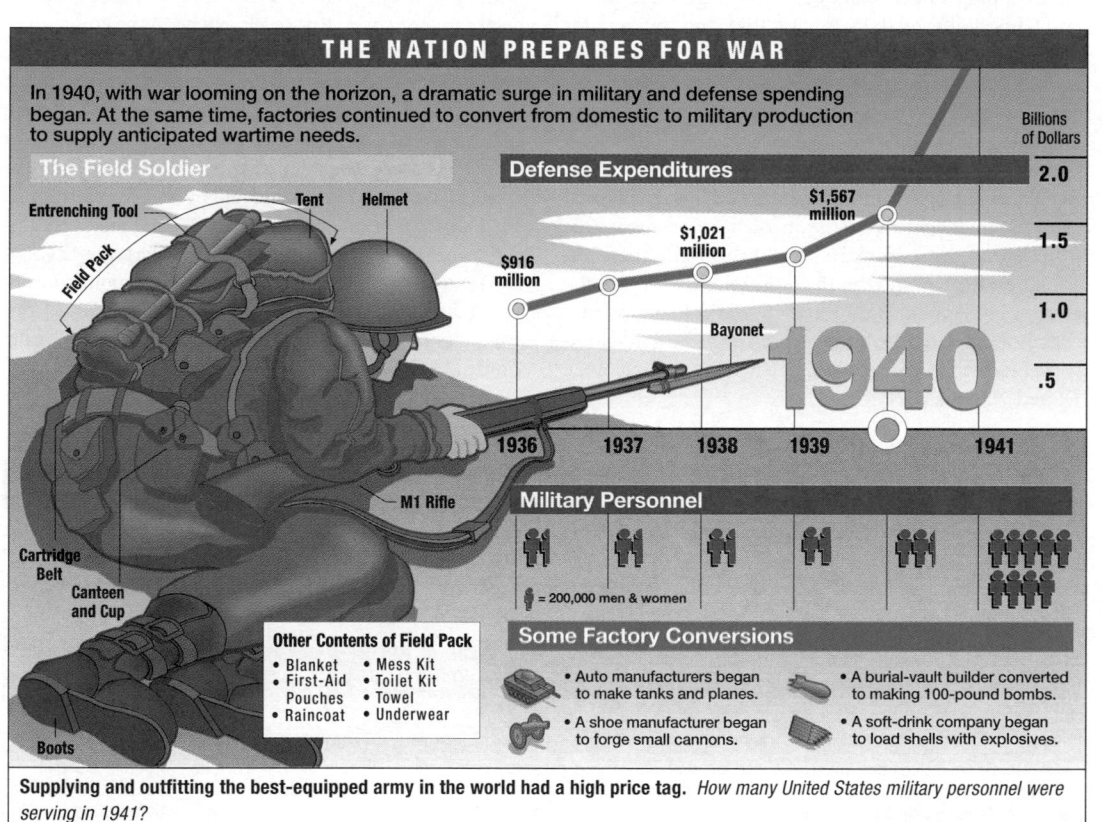

THE NATION PREPARES FOR WAR

In 1940, with war looming on the horizon, a dramatic surge in military and defense spending began. At the same time, factories continued to convert from domestic to military production to supply anticipated wartime needs.

The Field Soldier

Entrenching Tool · Tent · Helmet
Field Pack
M1 Rifle
Cartridge Belt
Canteen and Cup
Boots

Other Contents of Field Pack
- Blanket
- First-Aid Pouches
- Raincoat
- Mess Kit
- Toilet Kit
- Towel
- Underwear

Defense Expenditures

Billions of Dollars
2.0
1.5
1.0
.5

$916 million
$1,021 million
$1,567 million
Bayonet
1940

1936 1937 1938 1939 1941

Military Personnel

= 200,000 men & women

Some Factory Conversions
- Auto manufacturers began to make tanks and planes.
- A shoe manufacturer began to forge small cannons.
- A burial-vault builder converted to making 100-pound bombs.
- A soft-drink company began to load shells with explosives.

Supplying and outfitting the best-equipped army in the world had a high price tag. *How many United States military personnel were serving in 1941?*

Portfolio Project

Interviewing Have students interview at least three people of various ages about World War II. Students can ask whether the United States should have fought the war, how important the war was, and what results it produced here and elsewhere. Encourage students to interview one

person who lived through the war. Urge them to explain whether they can make any generalizations about their results based on the age of the persons interviewed. Suggest that, as appropriate, students use charts or graphs to present their findings.

ASSESS

Meeting Lesson Objectives

Each section objective is tested by the section review question(s) that follow it in parentheses.

1. Describe Hitler's conquest of Europe. (2)
2. Compare the views of American isolationists and interventionists, and explain how this division in public opinion shaped the American response to events in Europe and Asia. (4)
3. Explain how the increasing American economic pressure was one factor that led to Japan's attack on Pearl Harbor. (3)

LIBRARY OF CONGRESS

Roosevelt and Cordell Hull Cordell Hull, above right, served as secretary of state from 1933 to 1944. He was a leader in the drive to create the United Nations. *What goal prompted the formation of the United Nations?*

The Atlantic Charter

Stopping Hitler was not the only goal Roosevelt and Churchill shared. In August 1941, the two met for four days on a warship off the coast of Newfoundland. In addition to discussing military strategy, Roosevelt and Churchill agreed on a set of common principles establishing their goals for a postwar world. Their joint public statement was known as the Atlantic Charter. Recalling Wilson's Fourteen Points, the Charter affirmed each nation's right to choose its own government, free from fear of aggression. To protect this right, the United States, Britain, and the 15 others who had signed the charter by September 24 resolved to create an international organization to protect the security of all countries. Later, this dream took shape in the founding of the United Nations (UN).

The Japanese Threat Increases
Rome–Berlin–Tokyo Axis Formed

In the Pacific, Japan's continued aggression clearly violated the principles that Roosevelt and Churchill supported in the Atlantic Charter. In July 1940, Japan announced a plan for the future of Asia called the Greater East Asia Co-Prosperity Sphere. The sphere was in reality a Japanese empire, to include much of China, Southeast Asia, and the western Pacific. On September 27, Japan made an alliance with Germany and Italy, the Rome-Berlin-Tokyo Axis, which promised that each would defend the other if they were attacked by the United States.

The United States Responds

The United States responded to Japan's aggressive stance by applying economic pressure. Roosevelt's goal was to limit Japanese expansion by cutting off supplies, without provoking Japan to war. He placed an embargo on the sale of scrap metal to Japan. In September 1940, when Japan occupied French colonial possessions in northern Indochina, Roosevelt extended the embargo to include aviation fuel, all metals, chemicals, machine parts, and other products with military uses to Japan. This game of check and countercheck continued into 1941. When, in July of that year, Japan seized control of the rest of Indochina, Roosevelt retaliated by freezing all Japanese assets in the United States and ending all trade with Japan.

Despite mounting tensions, the United States continued to negotiate with the Japanese. In part, the negotiations were an attempt to buy time for the nation to fortify the Philippines and to build the "two-ocean navy" Congress authorized in 1940. Roosevelt's secretary of state, Cordell Hull, however, did not budge from his principles. He refused to meet with General Hideki Tojo in October

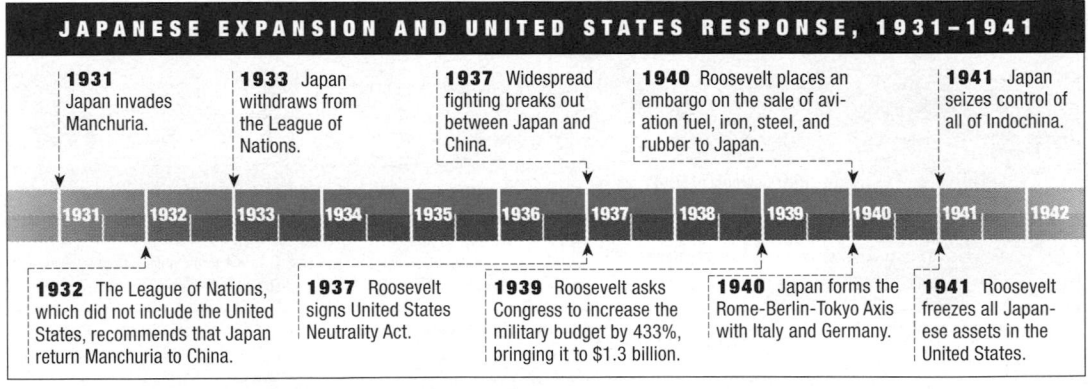

JAPANESE EXPANSION AND UNITED STATES RESPONSE, 1931–1941

1931 Japan invades Manchuria.

1933 Japan withdraws from the League of Nations.

1937 Widespread fighting breaks out between Japan and China.

1940 Roosevelt places an embargo on the sale of aviation fuel, iron, steel, and rubber to Japan.

1941 Japan seizes control of all of Indochina.

1931 1932 1933 1934 1935 1936 1937 1938 1939 1940 1941 1942

1932 The League of Nations, which did not include the United States, recommends that Japan return Manchuria to China.

1937 Roosevelt signs United States Neutrality Act.

1939 Roosevelt asks Congress to increase the military budget by 433%, bringing it to $1.3 billion.

1940 Japan forms the Rome-Berlin-Tokyo Axis with Italy and Germany.

1941 Roosevelt freezes all Japanese assets in the United States.

504 CHAPTER 15 WORLD WAR II

Extending the Content

Japanese Leadership During the 1930s, military officers began to hold political office in Japan. By 1936 the military gained control of the government, and in October 1941, General Hideki Tojo became prime minister. When talks between the United States and Japan failed to end the embargo, Tojo decided to wage war. The early Japanese victories made Tojo popular in Japan, but he was forced to resign as prime minister in 1944 after Japan suffered a series of major defeats. After the war, the Allies tried 25 top Japanese leaders for war crimes. Tojo and 6 others were executed and the rest received prison sentences. Explain that war crimes, such as an attack without a declaration of war, are violations of the international rules of war.

THE EXPANSION OF THE JAPANESE EMPIRE, 1931–1942

■	Japan before 1931
▨	Expansion 1931–1933
▨	Expansion 1933–1941
▨	Expansion 1941–1942
—	Farthest extent of Japanese control
←	Japanese advance
✳	Battle site and date
★	Capital city

From 1931 to 1941 Japan's expansionism led to its control of most of East Asia. When Japan decided to attack the United States, Pearl Harbor was the chosen target. *Geographically, what might have influenced this decision?*

1941 and insisted that Japan honor the Open Door policy with China and that it stop its expansionism. The United States would resume trade with Japan, Hull said, only if Japan withdrew from China and Indochina.

Yamamoto's Plan

By November 1941, the United States government knew that war with Japan would come. With negotiations deadlocked and its oil supplies dwindling, the Japanese decided to take the offensive. Some Americans suspected an attack on Malaya or the Philippines. The Japanese, however, had accepted the plan of Admiral Isoroku Yamamoto, who advised striking the United States closer to home. An attack on the American naval base at Pearl Harbor offered Japan the possibility of delivering a knockout blow to the American fleet. Yamamoto, however, was far from optimistic about Japan's long-range prospects. "In the first six months to a year of war with the United States and England I will run wild," Yamamoto told his government prophetically. "I will show you an uninterrupted succession of victories, but if the war is prolonged for two or three years I have no confidence in the ultimate victory."

SECTION REVIEW

Vocabulary

1. Define: interventionism, isolationism.

Checking Facts

2. What are the major events that led to France's surrender to Hitler?

3. Why did Roosevelt cut off trade with Japan on products with a military use?

Critical Thinking

Making Inferences

4. After war broke out, Roosevelt said, "This nation will remain a neutral nation, but I cannot ask that every American remain neutral in thought as well." What can you infer from these words?

Linking Across Time

5. Choose one goal of the Atlantic Charter. Was it realized? Can the results still be seen today?

SECTION TWO **505**

Evaluate

Have students complete the Section Review.

Assign the Section 2 Quiz or use the Testmaker to develop a customized quiz. (Also in Spanish.) **LEP**

Reteach

Have students listen to the Chapter 15, Section 2 Audiocassette. (Also in Spanish.) **LEP**

Enrich

Have interested students view the film *Tora! Tora! Tora!*, which details the Japanese attack on Pearl Harbor. Ask students to prepare a film review for the class.

CLOSE

Ask: How did President Roosevelt prepare the United States for war before his reelection? How did he change after his reelection? *(Before his reelection, Roosevelt began to build up the military, claiming the buildup was for defensive purposes. After his reelection, he was more supportive of the Allies through the Lend-Lease bill. He also ordered the navy to protect Lend-Lease shipments and to help destroy German submarines.)*

Section 2 Review Answers

1. **interventionism** (502), **isolationism** (502)
2. The Germans moved behind the Maginot Line, rendering the Line's artillery useless. Germany continued attacks by air and on the ground, and Italy joined in the offensive.
3. Roosevelt wanted to limit Japan's ongoing military expansion.

4. Answers will vary. Students might suggest that Roosevelt himself was against the Axis Powers but could not yet say so publicly.
5. Answers will vary. Students might point out that one goal was to protect countries' security. The current United Nations has had mixed success in achieving this goal.

TEACH

Making the Historical Connection

By late 1941 Japan had taken control of Indochina and Manchuria. Japan had formally aligned itself with the Axis. The U.S. had placed an embargo on the sale of scrap metal, fuel, and other military supplies to Japan and had frozen Japanese assets. Efforts to reach a diplomatic solution seemed destined to fail.

FYI

Declaring War The United States officially declared war against Japan on December 8, 1941. In the Senate, the vote was 82 to 0 in favor of declaring war; in the House of Representatives, it was 388 to 1. Representative Jeanette Rankin, Republican of Montana, voted against the declaration. She had also voted against the resolution declaring war on Germany in 1917.

At the Movies

The film *Tora! Tora! Tora!* depicts the battle at Pearl Harbor. You may wish to have students watch this movie on video and discuss the bombing of Pearl Harbor.

506

One Day in History

Sunday, December 7, 1941

MARKET BASKET

Here is where a dollar will go:

Movie ticket . . . . 40¢
Eastman Brownie
   camera $2.56
Chevrolet
   Aerosedan $880.00
Wool sports jacket . . . $15.00
Boy's haircut . . . . 50¢
Flashlight battery . . . . 4¢

THE BETTMANN ARCHIVE

Coffee (1 lb.) . . . . 24¢
Chicken (1 lb.) . . . . 23¢
Frozen shrimp (1 lb.) . . . . 15¢
Salad dressing (1 qt.) . . . . 33¢
Coca-Cola (6-pack) . . . . . 25¢
Milk (1 qt.) . . . . 14¢

NATIONAL ARCHIVES

Unprovoked Attack: Set aflame by Japanese bombs, United States battleships burn in their moorings at Pearl Harbor. The first attack occurred at 7:55 in the morning, local time, and most of the damage to the fleet occurred during the first 30 minutes of the sneak attack.

Japan Attacks Fleet

Japanese forces attack the United States Pacific Fleet in Pearl Harbor, Hawaii

NEW YORK—Sudden and unexpected attacks by the Japanese air force and navy on Pearl Harbor, Honolulu, and other United States possessions in the Pacific have plunged the nation into World War II.

The initial attack on the United States Pacific Fleet at Pearl Harbor, Hawaii, apparently launched by Japanese submarines and bombers carrying torpedoes, caused widespread damage and death. United States military casualties totaled more than 3,400. Of these, more than 2,300 were killed. The major targets of the Pearl Harbor attack were the 8 United States battleships moored there. The battleship *Arizona* was completely destroyed. The *California, Nevada,* and *West Virginia* sank, and the *Oklahoma* capsized. More than 180 United States aircraft were also destroyed.

Although radar indicated a large number of incoming planes, military personnel thought they were United States B-17s that were due to arrive.

Background Information

Unmet Objectives The Japanese did not succeed in their attempt to destroy the Pacific Fleet. No aircraft carriers were at Pearl Harbor at the time. Of the eight battleships hit, all but two were repaired. The oil storage facilities at Pearl Harbor remained intact.

NATION: Yale, Harvard, and Princeton Universities cut their programs from four to three years by staying in session all year.

War Fashions

NEW YORK—Reflecting the military influence of the day, a "Sentry Duty" cape is modeled at a benefit for the British-American Ambulance Corps held at the Rainbow Room. The show also previewed air-raid fashion.

"Sentry Duty" Cape

First Lady at Radcliffe

CAMBRIDGE, MA—On December 12, Eleanor Roosevelt will be initiated into the Radcliffe College chapter of Phi Beta Kappa at its annual dinner. Her speaking topic will be "Women—Nazi, Fascist, and Democratic."

The Maltese Falcon premieres, starring Humphrey Bogart.

MOVIES

- **How Green Was My Valley,** starring Walter Pidgeon and Maureen O'Hara
- **Citizen Kane,** starring Orson Welles
- **Dr. Jekyll and Mr. Hyde,** starring Spencer Tracy and Ingrid Bergman

Martha Graham's New York City dance company performs *Letter to the World*.

MUSIC

Hit songs: "Deep in the Heart of Texas," "I'll Remember April," "The Anniversary Waltz"

Top records: "Chattanooga Choo Choo" by Glenn Miller, "Buckle Down, Winsocki" by Benny Goodman

Color with a miniature camera
At last—a Kodak that makes full-color "stills"
When you buy Kodachrome film, the cost of your slides is included.
unbelievable at $14.50

REPRINTED COURTESY EASTMAN KODAK COMPANY

ONE DAY IN HISTORY   507

CLOSE

Ask: How might the attack on Pearl Harbor have convinced isolationists to change their positions? *(They might have been angered by the attack and have realized that the U.S. could no longer remain neutral.)* How might the attack have strengthened the resolve of Americans to resist fascism? *(Americans experienced aggression firsthand and became more determined to resist.)*

Oral History

Vivid Memories Many Americans who were alive on December 7, 1941, remember the attack on Pearl Harbor. Have students interview three residents of the community who remember the day of the attack. Have students record information such as where the interview sub-jects were and what they were doing when they heard the news of Pearl Harbor, how they reacted, and how the event affected their lives. Have students put written transcripts of the interviews in their portfolios.

507

FOCUS

Section Objectives

1. Describe the roles of women and minorities in the war.
2. Explain the overall military strategies of the Allied Powers in Europe and the Pacific.
3. Explain the social impact of the war on the people and countries involved.

Bellringer Activity

When taking attendance at the beginning of the class period, display **Section Focus Transparency 48,** and have students answer the questions. (or use the blackline master.)

VISUAL INSTRUCTION

Declaring War All but one member of Congress voted to declare war.

Ask: What caused the nation to unite and rally behind Roosevelt? *(The country was incensed at the surprise attack on Pearl Harbor that killed more than 2,400 Americans.)*

TEACH

Guided Practice

L2 **Discussion** Many citizens felt it was their duty to join the armed forces. Discuss whether patriotism would be a motivating force today if the United States were to enter a war.

SECTION 3

The United States at War

DECEMBER 7, 1941: JAPANESE ATTACK PEARL HARBOR

Declaring War
On December 8, 1941, President Franklin Roosevelt asked for and received a declaration of war on Japan from a joint session of Congress.

WITHOUT WARNING, JAPANESE DIVE BOMBERS AND TORPEDO PLANES SWOOPED OUT OF THE CLEAR, BLUE HAWAIIAN SKY AND RAINED DEATH AND DEVASTATION ON AMERICAN SHIPS ANCHORED IN THE HARBOR AND ON AMERICAN PLANES AT NEARBY AIR BASES. John Garcia, like others who witnessed the attack on Pearl Harbor, never forgot it:

I was sixteen years old, employed as a pipe fitter apprentice at Pearl Harbor Navy Yard. On December 7, 1941, oh, around 8:00 a.m., my grandmother woke me. She informed me that the Japanese were bombing Pearl Harbor. I said, "They're just practicing." She said, no, it was real and the announcer is requesting that all Pearl Harbor workers report to work. I went out on the porch and I could see the anti-aircraft fire up in the sky. . . . I was asked . . . to go into the water and get sailors out that had been blown off the ships. Some were unconscious, some were dead. So I spent the rest of the day swimming inside the harbor, along with some other Hawaiians. . . . We worked all day at that.

—As told to Studs Terkel, *"The Good War,"* 1984

In less than 3 hours, the Japanese destroyed 19 ships, including 5 battleships, and 188 planes. More than 2,400 Americans were killed. It was the worst defeat by a foreign power in United States military history. Yet Pearl Harbor aroused and united Americans as nothing else could have done. It hurled the nation into war, bent on revenge and committed to victory.

AS YOU READ

Vocabulary
▶ unconditional surrender
▶ sonar technology

Think About . . .
▶ the roles of women and minorities in the war.
▶ the overall military strategies of the Allied Powers in Europe and the Pacific.
▶ the social impact of the war on the people and the countries involved.

508 CHAPTER 15 WORLD WAR II

Section 3 Resources

REPRODUCIBLE RESOURCES
📁 Lesson Plan 15-3
📁 Section 3 Quiz
📁 Vocabulary and Guided Reading Activity 15-3
📁 Enrichment Activity 15
📁 Reteaching Activity 15
📁 Performance Assessment Activity 15

📁 Chapter 15 Test

MULTIMEDIA RESOURCES
🔖 Section Focus Transparency 48
⚙ Powers of the Congress
⚙ Lessons of War
⚙ A Geographic Perspective on American History

💿 Landmark Documents in American History
💾 Life Unworthy of Life: A Holocaust Curriculum
💿 Student Self-Test: A Software Review
💿 Testmaker and Vocabulary PuzzleMaker
🎧 Chapter 15 Digest Audiocassette

Mobilizing at Home
Organizing the Fighting Forces

On December 8, President Roosevelt asked Congress to declare war on Japan to avenge what he called a "date which will live in infamy." Because the United States had not attacked first, the pact between the Axis Powers did not require Hitler and Mussolini to follow Japan into war against the United States. Nevertheless, Germany and Italy declared war a few days later. Now the United States had to prepare quickly for global war on two fronts.

Boosting the Number of Troops

The Selective Service Act had been in force for more than a year, but United States armed forces had only 1.8 million men when war was declared. Increased draft calls soon began to fill the ranks, as thousands of men and women enlisted.

Their reasons for signing up varied from one person to the next. Patriotism, anger toward the Axis, a desire for adventure, and joblessness all played parts in decisions to join the military. By 1942 nearly 3.9 million Americans were in uniform. The number more than doubled by 1943, and in 1945 it peaked at more than 12 million. By the end of the war, more than 15 million men and nearly 216,000 women had served.

Minorities in Uniform

The armed forces included about 1 million African Americans. Their experiences differed from those of white personnel. Like much of the rest of United States society, the military was officially segregated. When African Americans enlisted, they were assigned to all-African American units, usually commanded by white officers. African Americans were often given jobs as cooks or laborers. Many white commanders would not send African American units into combat.

Those African American units that did fight, however, performed with distinction. In late 1944 General Dwight D. Eisenhower called for African American service troops to volunteer for combat in integrated units. Many did so, and Eisenhower and other generals became convinced that racially integrated combat units were more successful than segregated units.

Other minority groups also enlisted. Nearly 350,000 Hispanic Americans served, and they suffered many of the same kinds of discrimination as African Americans. Hispanics were the most decorated of American ethnic groups, while the Japanese American 442nd Regiment was the most decorated unit. Japanese American soldiers fought loyally during the war in spite of the severe discrimination suffered by their families back home. Many

Combat Skills African American troops in France during 1944 proved their skill in field artillery units. *By serving in combat, how did African American soldiers begin to alter the United States military's attitude toward minorities?*

Native Americans also joined the war effort. One group of Navajo became part of the Marine Signal Corps. They outwitted the Japanese by sending messages in a code based on the Navajo language.

The European Front
The Struggle to Defeat Germany

As the military geared up for combat, Allied political leaders met to determine overall strategy for the war. Shortly after Pearl Harbor, Roosevelt and Churchill decided that defeating Germany would be their first priority. Later, in 1943 at the Casablanca Conference in Morocco, at which Stalin was not present, the Allied leaders agreed to wage war until the Axis Powers accepted an **unconditional surrender**—a surrender without any concessions. The United States would fight a defensive war against Japan in the Pacific while the Allies concentrated their joint offensive efforts on defeating Nazi Germany.

Invasion of the Soviet Union

Although the Soviets and the Nazis had signed a nonaggression pact in 1939, Soviet leader Joseph Stalin distrusted Hitler. The German invasion of the Soviet Union on June 22, 1941, however, shocked the Soviets.

SECTION THREE   **509**

Cooperative Learning

World War II: Key Players Assign pairs of students to research and report on a group or an individual prominent during the war. Have them find out background, characteristics, involvement in the war, and contributions during the war. Subjects may include: Roosevelt, Churchill, Stalin, Patton, Eisenhower, MacArthur, WACs, Navajo, and African Americans. Encourage the use of visuals and have the pairs give oral presentations of their reports to the class.

Independent Practice

L2 **Research** Have students research women's and minorities' roles in the United States military today. Have them prepare a report detailing how these roles have changed since World War II and discussing whether discrimination against these groups still exists.

⊲ Have students complete the Chapter 15, Section 3 Vocabulary and Guided Reading Activity. (Also in Spanish.) **LEP**

VISUAL INSTRUCTION

After the Battle General Friedrich von Paulus led the German forces in the attempt to take Stalingrad. As winter approached, Hitler denied Paulus's request to pull back from the city. Few of the supplies that the German *Luftwaffe* was to drop by air ever arrived.

Answer: *Stalin felt that the Allies should have directed more military support to help the Russians.*

Global Connection

In 1943 two Frenchmen, Jacques-Yves Cousteau (then a French naval engineer) and Emile Gagnan, developed scuba gear, enabling divers to stay under deeper water longer because it controls the flow of air at different depths.

After the Battle The Soviet defense of Stalingrad gave the Allies an advantage in Europe. *Why was Stalin angry with the Allies after the battle of Stalingrad?*

Using blitzkrieg tactics on a vast scale now, German troops surged north toward Leningrad and south toward the Crimean peninsula. By November they had begun to encircle Moscow. An unusually severe winter and the determination of Soviet troops and civilians drove back the attackers. In the north, German troops surrounded Leningrad for almost 900 days, starving to death more than half a million residents.

In the spring of 1942, the Germans launched a new attack on the Soviet oil fields in southwestern Russia. By September, 300,000 Nazi troops had begun a major assault on the city of Stalingrad. The battle continued for five months amid the ruins and rubble of the city, until the Germans surrendered in February 1943. As many as 250,000 German troops, and many more Soviets, were killed or they froze to death. The Battle of Stalingrad halted Germany's eastward advance, but Stalin never forgave the Allies for failing to help defend the Soviets. His country had suffered more casualties at Stalingrad than the United States did during the entire war. After the war, United States General George C. Marshall called the refusal of the British and Soviet people to accept defeat "the great factor in the salvage of our civilization."

Allied Offensives

Rather than face a winter deep within Russia, the Allies decided on a less risky assault. In November 1942, American and British troops landed in North Africa, advancing into Morocco and Algeria against a German

tank division led by General Erwin Rommel, dubbed "the Desert Fox." The British gained an important victory in Egypt at El Alamein. This battle, like Stalingrad, marked a turning point in the war. Although 5,000 Americans died in a German counterattack in Tunisia, the Allies were victorious in North Africa by May 1943.

The Allies used bases in North Africa to launch an invasion of southern Europe, landing in Sicily in July 1943. They battled German troops for more than a month before driving them out of Sicily. Meanwhile, Mussolini's Fascist government fell from power. British forces invaded Italy from Sicily. On September 8, Italy announced its unconditional surrender to the Allies.

Germany, however, was determined to fight the Allies for control of Italy. Some of the most bitter fighting of the war occurred at Anzio beach and at Cassino Pass in central Italy. It was this kind of fighting—months of bombing, destruction, and death—that led cartoonist Bill Mauldin to write one of his darker captions: "Look at an infantryman's eyes and you can tell how much war he has seen." The Allies finally broke through German defenses in May, and Rome was liberated on June 4, 1944.

D-Day

The spotlight on the victory in Italy quickly shifted west. On June 6, 1944, General Eisenhower directed the largest combined land-sea-air invasion in history. The code name for the offensive was Operation Overlord, but most Americans remember the assault as D-Day. The D-Day invasion was, according to Churchill, "the most difficult and complicated that has ever taken place." Some 175,000 Allied soldiers began to come ashore before dawn along a 60-mile (96.5-km) stretch of the coast of Normandy in France. Once they had established a beachhead, at a cost of 2,245 killed and 1,670 wounded, the Allied forces had a base from which they would try to sweep the Germans out of France.

The success of D-Day also hinged on American industry. For months before the invasion, United States and British planes had dropped thousands of tons of bombs on German railroad lines, factories, and cities. Moreover, the huge Allied invasion force had been carried by American transports of all kinds. Without the industrial workers who had made this equipment, the Allied forces could not have landed in or retaken France.

The Beginning of the End

As the war progressed, the Allies gradually proved their dominance in the skies. Both experienced and new pilots flew fighters, bombers, and spy planes. That done, ground troops could advance cautiously eastward toward Germany. On August 25, 1944, American and French forces liberated Paris to great rejoicing by most inhabi-

Meeting Special Needs

Reading Disability To help students organize events, have them make four columns on a sheet of paper and label them Allied Powers, Axis Powers, Axis-controlled Countries, and Neutral Countries. Students can then use the text and the map on page 511 to identify and list the countries under appropriate headings. Next, let small groups of students talk about the events in the section, using their charts as a supporting reference.

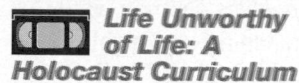

The European phase of World War II lasted five years, eight months, and seven days. Civilians suffered heavy losses in life and property from bombings, forced evacuations, and starvation. *What countries shown on the map were not directly affected by World War II? Why?*

GLENCOE TECHNOLOGY

Life Unworthy of Life: A Holocaust Curriculum

The Holocaust Curriculum includes videotaped interviews with Holocaust survivors and a variety of blackline masters. You may use the curriculum to enrich student understanding of the Holocaust.

MAP STUDY

Ask students to examine the map to propose possibilities of attacks by sea by both Allied and Axis Powers. Have them consider factors such as mountain barriers that attack forces would face.
Answer: *Ireland, Portugal, Saudi Arabia, Spain, Sweden, and Turkey*

NATIONAL GEOGRAPHIC SOCIETY

 Videodisc

GTV: A Geographic Perspective on American History

Side 4, Chapter 6
Title: Echoes of War
Subject: Effects of World War II on America
Ask: How did the role of the U.S. in world affairs change after World War II? *(The U.S. emerged as the most powerful nation on Earth.)*

---

tants. In the meantime, Allied forces had launched an invasion of France's Rhône Valley from the south. By summer's end France, Belgium, and Luxembourg were in Allied hands. Soviet troops advanced on Germany from the east.

Sea power was also crucial to Allied planning. Before the United States had entered the war, German U-boats had preyed on North Atlantic shipping, even briefly threatening cities on the east coast of the United States. While at sea sailors faced the triple peril of attack from above, from the surface, and from below—from planes, battleships, and U-boats. By late 1943 advances in **sonar technology**—technology allowing detection of submerged objects by means of sound waves—had given the Allies an edge in locating and sinking U-boats. More and more Allied naval convoys were safely crossing the Atlantic, keeping the Allies' enormous armies well provisioned. This lifeline made possible an offensive, not just a defensive, strategy.

While the Allies prepared for an invasion of Germany itself, Hitler launched a last desperate strike. In December Germany mounted a counteroffensive in the Ardennes Forest of Belgium. Hitler's tanks drove a bulge of troops and artillery 80 miles (128.7 km) long and 50 miles (80.5 km) deep into the Allied lines. After weeks of heavy fighting, during which 76,000 Allied soldiers were killed or wounded, the Germans were pushed back. The so-called Battle of the Bulge was the final German offensive of the war. The road into Germany, blocked for 6 weeks, was now open. As the Allied armies advanced, however, they had to confront the horrors committed by Hitler's government.

The Holocaust

When Allied soldiers entered Germany in 1945, they found the terrible consequences of Hitler's fanatical hatred of Jews and other peoples. In early 1942 Hitler had put into action what he called "the final solution" to his "Jewish problem." Nazi soldiers rounded up Jews from all over Europe and shipped them to concentration camps. In these camps Jews were used for slave labor, subjected to medical experiments and other atrocities,

SECTION THREE **511**

Portfolio Project

Summarizing Have students research and write a summary about one aspect of Operation Overlord (e.g., weather conditions; intelligence operations; individual beaches; American, Canadian, and British troops; German preparedness). Make and distribute copies of the summaries, and have students assess the complexity of the invasion. Then give students an opportunity to revise their summaries if they wish before they place the summaries in their portfolios.

FYI

Kristallnacht *Kristallnacht,* a German word meaning the "night of broken glass," is the name given to November 9, 1938. This is the night when many historians believe the Holocaust began. Starting that night and continuing for about 48 hours, the Nazis killed dozens of Jews, sent tens of thousands of others to concentration camps, and destroyed more than 2,000 synagogues. They also destroyed about 7,500 Jewish businesses in the country during that time period.

VISUAL INSTRUCTION

Nazi Atrocities Those in the concentration camps who were not able to work, including the aged and the sick, usually died in the gas chambers and many other people literally were worked to death.

Answer: *Slavs, Gypsies, Communists, and homosexuals*

AP/WIDE WORLD PHOTOS

Nazi Atrocities The horror of Nazi persecution is evident in the photo above of emaciated survivors of one of the concentration camps at Evensee, Austria. In the photo at the left, Nazi troops take Jewish people in Warsaw, Poland, from their homes. *What other civilian groups in Europe did the Nazis persecute and kill?*

FYI

Pacific Commanders The United States commander in chief of the Pacific fleet was Admiral Chester W. Nimitz, and his Japanese counterpart was Admiral Isorokued Yamamoto, the man who planned the attack on Pearl Habor.

starved, beaten, shot, and put to death in gas chambers. Their bodies were buried in mass graves or incinerated in fiendishly efficient crematoriums.

Reports about these horrors were circulating as early as 1942. Only when the Allies liberated the death camps in 1945, however, did the world learn for certain the ghastly extent of Hitler's plan to wipe out the Jews of Europe. Walter Rosenblum, an American soldier, helped liberate Dachau, a concentration camp in southern Germany. He recalled:

> The first thing I saw as I went down this road to Dachau were about forty boxcars on a railroad siding. . . . I looked into these boxcars and they were full of emaciated bodies, loaded all the way to the top. Forty boxcars full of dead people.
> —As told to Studs Terkel, *"The Good War,"* 1984

Hitler's henchmen, along with thousands of Nazi collaborators, massacred about 6 million Jewish men, women, and children. More than two-thirds of the total Jewish population in Europe was destroyed. They also

killed some 6 million Slavs, Gypsies, Communists, homosexuals, and others, most of them civilians. This mass extermination lives in infamy as the Holocaust, which has come to mean the "great destruction."

Some critics have charged that Roosevelt could have lessened the extent of this tragedy, pointing out that only 21,000 Jewish refugees were admitted to the United States in the early 1940s. This was a small fraction of the number permitted under existing immigration quotas. Moreover, some people thought Roosevelt was indifferent to the mass suffering of European Jews. In 1944 the United States War Department resisted proposals to bomb the gas chambers at the Auschwitz concentration camp. Roosevelt countered that his policy was to defeat Germany quickly and thus save all Hitler's victims from further persecution.

Victory in Europe

After turning back the Nazi onslaught on their homeland, Soviet troops moved west. They ousted Nazi governments or aided anti-German forces throughout eastern and central Europe in 1944 and 1945. They encircled Vienna and Prague, prize capitals of central Europe, and warned off the western Allies from challenging their control. Residents of the formerly Nazi-occupied countries,

Extending the Content

Concentration Camps Journalist and author C. L. Sulzberger reports that after General Eisenhower first visited a concentration camp, "he cabled Washington and London to send journalists and members of Congress and Parliament to Germany as soon as possible." Eisenhower wanted no one to doubt the extent of the atrocities that had been committed. His

fears have been partly justified, for today some individuals inside and outside of Germany insist that the Holocaust did not take place. Have students research who has tried to deny the Holocaust and how their denials have been received. Urge students to describe the kinds of evidence that are available to determine the truth of what actually happened in the camps.

fearing new foreign armies, were not always sure which army to surrender to. Already it was clear to the world that the Soviet Union and the United States were replacing Germany as superpowers in Europe.

Allied forces began their final assault on Germany early in 1945. Soviet troops crossed Poland, as British and American troops swept into northern Germany from the Netherlands. Crossing rivers was among the gravest dangers, as retreating Nazis often tried to mine the bridges. By the end of March, American forces had crossed the Rhine River and were advancing steadily toward Berlin, Germany's capital.

In the midst of Allied successes in Europe a tragedy occurred in the United States. On April 12, Franklin Roosevelt died, after 12 years in office. Vice President Harry S Truman took the oath of office and assumed leadership of the country. Roosevelt's death did not halt the Allied advance. By late April Soviet troops had surrounded the city of Berlin. On April 30, Hitler committed suicide.

Berlin fell on May 2, and Germany surrendered unconditionally on May 7. War-weary Allied soldiers could look forward to being sent home. Sergeant Harold Murphy of Decatur, Illinois, expressed the feelings of thousands of other fathers in a postcard mailed to his baby daughter that day: "The War ended today, honey, and I hope to see you soon." The Allies declared May 8, 1945, V-E Day, or Victory in Europe Day.

The Pacific Front
To Japan Through the Islands

The war in Europe was over, but the United States continued to fight a very different kind of war in the Pacific. After its brutal attack on Pearl Harbor, the Japanese army swept to victory after victory. In early 1942 Japanese forces captured the Dutch East Indies, which were rich in oil and other natural resources. Then they took Burma, Wake Island, and Guam and forced the surrender of 12,000 American soldiers in the Philippines.

By May 1942, United States forces in the Pacific began to reverse the tide that had been flowing against them. In the battle of the Coral Sea, American carrier-based planes bombarded the Japanese fleet, stopping the Japanese advance toward Australia. A month later at the Battle of Midway, American planes sank 4 Japanese aircraft carriers and destroyed more than 300 planes. This was the first major Japanese defeat, and it greatly reduced the threat to Hawaii.

Despite these setbacks, Japan still held many fortified Pacific islands. To counter this advantage, American military planners adopted an "island hopping"

strategy. Hoping to surround Japanese strongholds and cut them off from supplies, United States Marines captured key islands, building bases from which to attack the Philippines and eventually Japan itself.

Guadalcanal

A typical United States offensive in the Pacific was the attack on Guadalcanal in the Solomon Islands. During the summer of 1942, the Japanese began building an airfield on the island, preparing for an invasion of Australia. To keep the Japanese from finishing the airfield, 10,000 marines waded ashore to seize the island on August 7, 1942.

Once on land, the marines battled both the enemy and the steaming jungle environment. Scorching heat, relentless humidity, rotting gear, poisonous insects, and tropical fevers, such as malaria and dysentery, were the everyday conditions of jungle warfare.

The battle for Guadalcanal continued over six grueling months, as Japanese soldiers were ordered to fight to the death to hold the island. Even after the United States Navy destroyed Japanese ships in the area, isolating the enemy remaining on the island, it took three months to drive off the Japanese.

Guadalcanal was the first territory Japan lost in the war. In their unsuccessful attempt to hold the island, the Japanese lost 25,000 men. Americans learned that every Pacific battle would be bloody and hard fought and that the Japanese could be beaten.

Battles for islands like Guadalcanal cost thousands of American lives from 1942 to 1945. In a 6-week battle for Iwo Jima in early 1945, for example, the marines

Mobile Rocket Unit A barrage of explosives are launched from a United States Marine rocket unit during a 1945 assault on the Japanese on an island in the Pacific. *What advantage would a unit on wheels provide?*

UPI/BETTMANN NEWSPHOTOS

VISUAL INSTRUCTION

Mobile Rocket Unit These armed vehicles enabled United States soldiers to fight the hidden Japanese wherever they surfaced.

Answer: *Quick repositioning and escape from the enemy*

Facts on File

Landmark Documents in American History Have students review "Germany's Surrender in World War II, 1945" and write a paragraph about the intent of the document.

ABCNEWS INTERACTIVE™

 Videodisc

Lessons of War

Side 1, Chapter 6
Title: Can a Battle Change History?
Subject: The Battle of Midway
Ask: Who won the Battle of Midway? *(the United States)*

See Lessons of War Guidebook page 10 for complete lesson plan.

Cultural Perspectives

Discussion During the war, the Japanese assumed that Americans were ignorant of the Japanese language. Nisei units, however, formed of Japanese American citizens born in the United States, translated and decoded Japanese battle plans. Discuss why these Nisei might have chosen to perform this work and why it was valuable to the United States.

513

MAP STUDY

American soldiers were so isolated on islands in the Pacific that when the war ended in 1945, some soldiers did not know until weeks later.

Answer: *Students should identify Japanese-controlled areas and locate major battles noted on the map, including Iwo Jima, Tarawa, Okinawa, Saipan, and Guadalcanal.*

 Facts on File

Landmark Documents in American History Have students review Truman's "Announcement of the Atomic Bombing of Hiroshima, 1945" and "Japan's Surrender in World War II, 1945" and write a paragraph about the intent of one of the documents.

ASSESS

Meeting Lesson Objectives

Each section objective is tested by the section review question(s) that follow it in parentheses.

1. Describe the roles of women and minorities in the war. (5)
2. Explain the overall military strategies of the Allied Powers in Europe and the Pacific. (1, 2, 4)
3. Explain the social impact of the war on the people and countries involved. (3)

THE ALLIED ADVANCE IN THE PACIFIC, 1942–1945

Legend:
- Japan before 1931
- Japanese-controlled
- Farthest extent of Japanese control
- Allied advance
- Battle site and date
- Atomic bombing
- Capital city

0   750   1,500 mi.
0   750   1,500 km
Mercator projection

Allied forces retook areas in the Pacific captured by the Japanese army between 1942 and 1945. *What areas fell to the Japanese during these years? What major battles occurred during their recapture?*

suffered about 20,000 casualties to secure this tiny island 700 miles (1,126.3 km) from Japan. At about the same time, the United States achieved another objective when General Douglas MacArthur directed the American recapture of the Philippines. The strategy of inching island by island toward an eventual invasion of Japan was working. The United States and its allies agreed, however, that it might take years and up to a million deaths to conquer the Japanese home islands.

To step up the pressure on Japan, American long-range B-29 bombers began sustained strikes on the Japanese mainland in June 1944. By November they were bombing Tokyo itself. In one raid on Tokyo in March 1945, napalm bombs caused a firestorm in the city, incinerating 83,000 Japanese citizens. Despite casualties like these and the near total destruction of Japanese sea and air power, Japanese military leaders refused to accept the unconditional surrender that the United States demanded.

The Atomic Bomb

With little hope of forcing a Japanese surrender, President Truman scheduled an invasion of Japan for late 1945 and early 1946. Then on July 16, 1945, American

scientists, led by physicist J. Robert Oppenheimer, gave Truman another choice when they successfully detonated the first atomic bomb in the desert near Alamogordo, New Mexico. Truman chose to use the bomb on Japan with the hope of ending the war without an invasion. (See page 516.) On August 6, 1945, the *Enola Gay,* an American B-29, dropped a single atomic bomb code-named Little Boy on the Japanese city of Hiroshima. A Japanese journalist described the bomb's devastating effects:

> Suddenly a glaring whitish pinkish light appeared in the sky accompanied by an unnatural tremor. . . . Within a few seconds the thousands of people in the streets . . . and in the gardens in the center of town were scorched by a wave of searing heat. . . .
>
> By the evening the fire began to burn down and then it went out. There was nothing left to burn. Hiroshima had ceased to exist.
>
> —Barrington Boardman,
> *From Harding to Hiroshima,* 1987

514 CHAPTER 15 WORLD WAR II

Critical Thinking

Analyzing Information Encourage students to think about the issues that a nation considers as it decides what kinds of weapons to develop and use. For example, napalm is an incendiary bomb filled with jellied gasoline. When released, it ignites everything it touches, setting fires that are hard to extinguish. A neutron bomb is a type of hydrogen bomb that gives off large amounts of radiation but little blast or heat. Neutron bombs are designed to kill people without destroying property. Guide students in discussing the moral, military, and social issues involved when a nation decides to use a particular type of weapon.

World War II Deaths*		
Country	**Military Deaths**	**Civilian Deaths**
United States	405,000	2,000
Great Britain	271,000	60,600
Germany	2,850,000	2,300,000
France	210,700	173,300
USSR	14,500,000	7,000,000
Poland	850,000	5,778,000
Italy	279,800	93,000
China	1,324,000	10,000,000
Japan	1,506,000	300,000
Spain	12,000	10,000

*approximate

The United States suffered approximately 2,000 civilian deaths during World War II. *What factors account for this comparatively low estimate?*

The atomic blast killed 100,000 people instantly, and another 100,000 men, women, and children died later from burns, radiation, or other wounds caused by the blast. The bomb destroyed more than 4 square miles of the city. On August 8, the Soviet Union entered the war against Japan as it had promised. When the Japanese still did not surrender, the United States dropped a second atomic bomb on the city of Nagasaki on August 9. The bomb killed 40,000 more Japanese citizens. Five days later, on August 14, the Japanese government surrendered. After 6 years of fighting, World War II was over.

The Impact of War
A Changed World

For the Axis Powers as well as for the Allies, World War II was the most devastating war in history and the first to bring mass civilian deaths. Grigori Baklanov, who served in the Soviet military, expressed in stark terms the tragedy these numbers represent: "Of my generation, out of one hundred who went to fight, three came back. Three percent." Baklanov noted with despair, "I was the only one from our class of all the boys who went to the front who remained alive after the war. What else is there to say?"

Beyond the tragic loss of life, the war also devastated thousands of cities and villages throughout Europe and Asia. Capitals like Berlin, Tokyo, London, and Manila suffered heavy damage. Everywhere, transportation systems were mangled, factories were destroyed, and economies were left in shambles.

As the chart on this page indicates, the United States suffered fewer deaths than many other nations, and it had less destruction of property. Fewer than 1 percent of United States citizens were killed or wounded in the war. By contrast, the Soviet Union lost more than 8 percent of its population. Also, the demand for war supplies pulled the American economy out of the Great Depression and made it more productive and prosperous.

The war changed the lives of the men and women who served in it. Many left their homes for the first time to travel across the country and around the world. They were exposed to new ideas and opinions. Anne Bosanko Green described life in the WACs (Women's Army Corps):

> We suddenly left our humdrum lives, our jobs, and schools and were moved all around the vast United States or across the Atlantic and Pacific oceans to lands we had never thought we would see. We did not have to worry about our families and homelands being destroyed while we were off seeing the world. We were learning new skills, [and] meeting new people. . . .
> —Anne Bosanko Green, *One Woman's War,* 1989

In addition to its effects on returning servicemen and servicewomen, the war transformed the lives of millions of Americans on the home front. In all areas of United States society—business, agriculture, labor, and government—the war brought varied and lasting changes.

SECTION REVIEW

Vocabulary

1. Define: unconditional surrender, sonar technology.

Checking Facts

2. What was the overall military strategy of the Allied Powers?

3. What was the social impact on the people and the countries involved in World War II?

Critical Thinking

Determining Cause and Effect

4. How did the application of advanced technology make World War II the most devastating war in history?

Linking Across Time

5. How have conditions in society changed for women and ethnic minorities since World War II? How might the war have contributed to these changes?

CHART STUDY

These deaths left thousands of orphans of war. **Answer:** *Conflicts were not waged on U.S. soil.*

Evaluate

Have students complete the Section Review.

📁 💿 Assign the Section 3 Quiz or use the Testmaker to develop a customized quiz. (Also in Spanish.) **LEP**

📁 💿 Assign the Chapter 15 Test or use the Testmaker to develop a customized test.

📁 Have students complete the Chapter 15 Performance Assessment Activity.

Reteach

🎧 Have students listen to the Chapter 15, Section 3 Audiocassette. (Also in Spanish.) **LEP**

📁 Have students complete the Chapter 15 Reteaching Activity. (Also in Spanish.) **LEP**

Enrich

📁 Have students complete the Chapter 15 Enrichment Activity. (Also in Spanish.) **LEP**

CLOSE

Ask: What forced Japan to accept unconditional surrender? (*The dropping of two atomic bombs on Japan in August 1945.*)

Section 3 Review Answers

1. unconditional surrender (509), **sonar technology** (511)
2. Overall strategy: to defeat the Axis Powers first and then to attack Japan
3. In many countries, thousands or even millions were killed. For survivors, many moved to new places and were exposed to new ideas. All areas of life were changed by the war.

4. Students may answer that the war produced weapons that could quickly and indiscriminately annihilate population centers.
5. Students may answer that, although they continue to struggle for equality, women and ethnic minorities generally found greater acceptance in the workplace after World War II.

515

TEACH

Making the Historical Connection

Ask students to summarize the war against Japan up to 1945. Review the success or failure of the United States island-hopping strategy and of the sustained air strikes on the Japanese mainland. Include in the discussion the perspective of hindsight in evaluating decisions made during the war. Does the perspective of time help to make an issue clearer, or does it add other elements to make the issue more complex?

Turning Point

The course of history hinged on Truman's decision to use the bomb on Japan. Years of research by some of the best scientists and physicists in the world gave the United States the capability of using an atomic bomb. The possibility of extended war with Japan and loss of many more American lives motivated Truman to make a quick decision. After meeting with his advisers and weighing the options, Truman decided to drop the bomb on Hiroshima, Japan.

CASE STUDY — Turning Point

Dropping the Bomb

AUGUST 6, 1945

> **MEMORANDUM**
>
> For: The President
>
> Subject: Dropping the Bomb
>
> I think it is very important that I should have a talk with you as soon as possible on a highly secret matter.
>
> I mentioned it to you shortly after you took office, but have not urged it since on account of the pressure you have been under. It, however, has such a bearing on our present foreign relations and has such an important effect upon all my thinking in this field that I think you ought to know about it without much further delay.
>
> Secretary of War Henry L. Stimson
> April 24, 1945

The Case

When Truman received Stimson's note on April 24, 1945, he had been President for only 12 days. Stimson wanted to talk with Truman about the atomic bomb. The war in Europe was drawing to a close, and the President was turning his attention to ending the war with Japan and to the negotiations that would shape the postwar world. Truman met with Stimson the next day, and the information Stimson shared would significantly influence Truman's strategy for ending the war.

Truman faced a critical question: Now that the atomic bomb was almost ready, would the United States use this fearsome new weapon against Japan? Truman later insisted that he "regarded the bomb as a military weapon and never had any doubt that it should be used." Some others did have doubts, but the evidence available today indicates that Truman and other leading policy makers did not. The decisions they made about when and how to use the weapon, however, had major military, political, and ethical consequences for the postwar world.

The Background

Truman's meeting with Stimson gave him his first knowledge of the atomic bomb; Stimson informed him that the bomb would probably be ready within four months. Although Stimson supported using the bomb to end the war, he also pointed out serious problems that the bomb would pose for the world after the war. Chief among these were a possible atomic arms race and the danger of an atomic war. To address these challenges, Stimson proposed that Truman appoint a committee to advise him on policy regarding atomic weapons. The President took Stimson's advice, and the Interim Committee, as it was called, met in Washington on May 31.

516   CASE STUDY

The Case at a Glance

| Roosevelt dies; Truman becomes President. | → | Truman faces the end of the war in Europe and the need to end the war in Asia. | → | Stimson informs Truman of the availability of the atomic bomb. | → | Truman appoints an Interim Committee to advise on atomic policy. | → |

The goal of Truman and the Interim Committee appears to have been to find the most effective way to use the bomb to shock Japan into surrendering. Even though the Russians had promised to enter the war against Japan by August 8, many American military leaders assumed that an amphibious landing on the Japanese mainland would be necessary to end the war. The cost in American lives would be high, and many believed that using the bomb could end the war without an invasion.

The Opinions

The quotes on this page represent the range of opinions about using the atomic bomb that were expressed during the summer of 1945. Stimson's statement expresses the majority opinion—that the bomb had to be used to end the war quickly and to save American lives. The other statements question the use of this new weapon.

The Options

The opinions you have read indicate that Truman had these options to consider:

1. Drop the bomb on Japanese cities to force an immediate end to the war.

2. Carry out a demonstration of the weapon to persuade Japan to surrender.

3. Launch an invasion of Japan.

4. Rely on Japan's deteriorating military situation and the entry of the Soviet Union into the war to force Japanese surrender.

5. Negotiate surrender terms acceptable to Japan and the United States.

The Decision

The Interim Committee made its decision and gave it to Truman on June 1:

> The present view of the Committee was that the bomb should be used against Japan as soon as possible; that it be used on a war plant surrounded by workers' homes; and that it be used without prior warning.

> —Recording Secretary R. Gordon Arneson, from minutes taken on May 31

"In the light of the alternatives which, on a fair estimate, were open to us I believe that no man, in our position and subject to our responsibilities, holding in his hands a weapon of such possibilities for accomplishing this purpose and saving those lives, could have failed to use it and afterwards looked his countrymen in the face."

Henry L. Stimson
Secretary of War

"I told him [Stimson] I was against it on two counts. First, the Japanese were ready to surrender and it wasn't necessary to hit them with that awful thing. Second, I hated to see our country be the first to use such a weapon."

General Dwight D. Eisenhower
Supreme Allied Commander

"I have had a feeling that before the bomb is actually used against Japan that Japan should have some preliminary warning of say two or three days in advance. . . . The position of the United States as a great humanitarian nation and the fair play attitude of our people generally is responsible in the main for this feeling."

Ralph A. Bard
Undersecretary of the Navy

"If the United States were to be the first to release this new means of indiscriminate destruction upon mankind, she would sacrifice public support throughout the world, precipitate the race for armaments, and prejudice the possibility of reaching an international agreement on the future control of such weapons."

James Franck
University of Chicago

ABCNEWS INTERACTIVE™

⊙ **Videodisc**

Communism and the Cold War

Side 1, Chapter 5
Title: The Bomb
Subject: Discussions about the bombing of Hiroshima and Nagasaki and the results
Ask: Why was dropping the atomic bomb on Hiroshima and Nagasaki so controversial? *(Hundreds of thousands of civilians were killed.)*

See Communism and the Cold War Guidebook page 9 for complete lesson plan.

CASE STUDY   **517**

| The Soviet Union promises to enter the war against Japan by August. | → | Predicted outcome of an invasion of the Japanese mainland indicates an unacceptable cost in time and lives. | → | Truman decides to use the atomic bomb against Japan. |

Analyzing the Case

Have students read through the opinions and the options. Discuss with students what considerations were important for ending the war in the Pacific as quickly as possible.

1. Which opinions were based on an assumption of the Japanese readiness to surrender? What evidence existed to support or refute those opinions? *(Both Bard and Eisenhower assumed the Japanese would surrender soon. The tenacity of the Japanese military, especially of the kamikaze pilots, and the military force of over 5 million men refuted the assumption.)*
2. Which opinion predicts effects beyond the end of the war that dropping the bomb would cause? *(Franck's opinion outlines the postwar results of the action, some of which proved to be true.)*
3. In your opinion, if a decision or action solves an immediate problem, how heavily should future effects of the action be weighed? *(Students might suggest that the circumstances surrounding a decision sometimes outweigh the effects an action will have in the future.)*

Turning Point

Above, a column of smoke billows 20,000 feet over Hiroshima, Japan, after the first atomic bomb strike. The aftermath is shown on the left.

Secretary of State Byrnes informed the President of the Interim Committee's decision. Later, he said that "with reluctance [Truman] had to agree that he could think of no alternative and found himself in accord with what I told him the Committee was going to recommend." Why did Truman choose Option 1?

Apparently Truman rejected Option 2, a demonstration, for reasons offered by the Interim Committee and its scientific panel. A demonstration would not help to end the war. The committee did not offer evidence to support this judgment. They knew, however, that a successful test would not necessarily cause the Japanese to surrender unconditionally. An unsuccessful test, they believed, would be worse than none.

Truman placed the highest value on ending the war with the loss of as few American lives as possible. Both Options 3 and 4 would cost countless American lives and bring an indefinite extension of the war with no certain outcome. The Japanese might never surrender. They seemed prepared to fight to the end, whatever that would mean, even the

loss of many Japanese lives. Option 4 had an added disadvantage. If the Soviets entered the fighting, they would gain an advantage in postwar negotiations about new governments in Eastern Europe. Truman and other United States leaders preferred not to be indebted to the Soviets for any help in ending the war with Japan.

Truman probably never viewed Option 5 as a real possibility. The only surrender acceptable to American leaders would be unconditional. The only surrender acceptable to the Japanese would include at least one condition: that they be allowed to keep their emperor. Truman saw the bomb as just another weapon—legitimate in wartime, when the goal was to win.

The Outcome

The bomb was successfully tested on July 16, 1945, at a remote desert site near Alamogordo, New Mexico. On August 6, 1945, the United States dropped an atomic bomb carrying more power than 20,000 tons of TNT on Hiroshima, Japan, an

518 CASE STUDY

Cooperative Learning

Testing Other Options Have students work in small groups to discuss the other options. Have each group choose one of the options besides the first and discuss whether or not it might have achieved the same goal of ending

the war with Japan. After students have discussed the issues, have them create an imaginary scenario of what might have happened had Truman chosen that option. Each group should then present their findings to the class.

Turning Point

important military center. The next day President Truman gave a statement that included the following: "Let there be no mistake: we shall completely destroy Japan's power to make war. Only a Japanese surrender will stop us."

Most Americans and their allies breathed a sigh of relief, knowing that the war would soon end. Yet they also recognized that, as the *London Daily Express* put it, "The world has changed overnight."

The Interpretations

More than half a century has passed since that summer in 1945. The years have brought knowledge and perspectives unavailable to Truman and other decision makers of that time. During these years three main interpretations have emerged.

One is that Truman and Stimson were correct in their idea that the bombings were necessary to end the war and save lives. According to this view, these were the only significant motives of those who ordered the bombing of Hiroshima and, three days later, Nagasaki.

Another interpretation is that dropping the bomb was unnecessary, even immoral. People holding this view argued that while Truman and the others were honest, they were also naive; they failed to take into account the long-term effects of dropping the bomb, such as the arms race and the cold war.

A third group also saw the bombings as unnecessary and unwise. In addition, they said that Truman and the other policy makers had ulterior motives, that they engaged in "atomic diplomacy." They used the bombings to try to intimidate the Soviets. As a result, said this group, they failed to consider seriously alternatives to dropping the bomb.

Today controversy over the decision to drop the atomic bomb continues. As time passes new evidence becomes available. For example, the first viewpoint found support in later evidence from Japan that seemed to show that without the bombings the war might have continued for many months. Such findings support the often repeated but much challenged idea that the bombings saved as many as 1 million American lives.

Another source of new evidence has been medical reports about those who survived the bombings at Hiroshima and Nagasaki. Many sickened and

A Japanese prisoner of war weeps at the news of Japan's surrender.

died soon afterward. Over the years more evidence has emerged about long-term effects of atomic radiation. Today, for example, survivors of the bombings have a higher than average incidence of leukemia and thyroid cancer. Thus medical reports about survivors add to the evidence used by those who raise ethical questions about the bomb.

RESPONDING TO THE CASE

1. Look again at the opinions of Henry L. Stimson and James Franck and contrast their predictions of the consequences of using the bomb. Why do you think they differed so much?

2. Which consequences of using the bomb did Truman predict correctly? Which were different from what he might have expected?

3. Some scientists were more likely than political leaders to oppose the use of the atomic bomb. What could account for these differences?

4. What conflicts in values did you discover as you read the quotations on page 517? Have our values as Americans changed over time, giving new meanings to the events of the 1940s?

PORTFOLIO PROJECT

In 1995, 50 years after the bombing of Hiroshima, many people discussed whether the bombing should have taken place. Write down your opinion and your reasoning, and place your work in your portfolio.

CASE STUDY **519**

Curriculum Connection

Language Arts
Discuss the interpretations of the decision to drop the bomb. Have students choose one interpretation with which they disagree and write a persuasive essay detailing their reasons.

Block Scheduling

The Portfolio Project on this page provides an excellent opportunity to enrich and extend the key elements of this case study.

CLOSE

Write The Case at a Glance flowchart on the chalkboard. Work with students to continue the chart through the dropping of the bomb and the postwar effects. What was the Interim Committee's advice to Truman? *(The bomb should be used against Japan as soon as possible on a war plant surrounded by workers' homes, and that it be used without prior warning.)* Why did Truman feel he had no alternative to dropping the bomb? *(He believed that defeating Japan by means of conventional warfare would cost too many American lives.)* What were the arguments opposing the bombings? *(That Japan would soon surrender on its own, that a demonstration of the bomb would convince Japan to surrender, and that the use of the bomb against a civilian population was inhumane and unjustifiable.)*

Responding to the Case Answers

1. Answers might include the difference of perspective. Stimson was concerned with the immediate problem of ending the war and saving American lives. Franck concentrated on the future effects dropping the bomb might have.
2. Truman predicted that the bomb would end the war quickly; it did. The long-term effects, such as the arms race, were probably different from what he expected.

3. Answers might include scientists' better understanding of the force and effects of the bomb and politicians' views that it was just another weapon.
4. Values cited might include believing the United States should be a defender, not an aggressor, or the conflict between the American sense of fair play and the strategic advantage needed in war.

519

Chapter Review

Reviewing Key Terms

1. unconditional surrender
2. appeasement
3. totalitarian
4. isolationism
5. blitzkrieg

Recalling Facts

1. He said he killed out of concern for Germany and its people. Many rallied behind him; others were silenced by fear.
2. The Axis helped Franco's regime win the war.
3. to acquire land and natural resources
4. denied supplies and credit to nations at war; discouraged Americans from travel on warring countries' ships
5. British pilots were better skilled and had better planes; he attacked British cities by night with rockets.
6. It allowed the U.S. to sell, lend, or lease military supplies to nations deemed "vital to the defense of the United States." It committed the U.S. economically to the war against Germany.
7. Allies invaded North Africa instead of coming to Stalingrad.
8. Normandy invasion; by a massive Allied offensive
9. It means "great destruction."
10. Cities and villages suffered heavy damage, as did transportation systems, factories, and economies.

Critical Thinking

1. Many Americans felt the way to keep democracy safe in the United States was to stop fascism in Europe.
2. Japanese soldiers would fight relentlessly in the first year of battle, but a lengthy war would have eventually depleted Japan's supplies.

Reviewing Key Terms

Match the vocabulary term from the list below to the sentence that describes it. Write your answers on a separate sheet of paper.

blitzkrieg   interventionism
totalitarian   isolationism
unconditional   appeasement
surrender

1. The United States insisted upon _____ in negotiations with the Japanese.

2. Early in the war, the policy of _____ enabled Hitler to occupy the Sudetenland region of Czechoslovakia without any official opposition from Great Britain or France.

3. A _____ type of government demands complete control over the lives of its citizens.

4. Those people who supported a policy of _____ thought the United States should not become involved in the war.

5. _____ was a rapid and devastating style of attack that helped Hitler to gain control of Poland quickly.

Recalling Facts

1. In his speech before the Reichstag, how did Hitler justify his orders to murder those who stood in his way to political power? What effect did his words have on the German people?

2. Germany and Italy formed an alliance in 1936 known as the Axis Powers. How did this alliance affect the outcome of the Spanish civil war?

3. Why did Japan wish to expand its territory during the 1930s and 1940s?

4. What was the function of the Neutrality Acts?

5. Why was the Battle of Britain an initial failure for Germany? What strategy did Hitler try in his "blitz" of London to ward off further failure?

6. Describe the Lend-Lease Act. How did its passage signify a deeper American commitment to the war?

7. Why did the Battle of Stalingrad cause Stalin to resent Great Britain and the United States?

8. What famous battle led to the liberation of France? How was liberation accomplished?

9. Why is the name Holocaust used to describe Hitler's atrocities against Jews in Europe during World War II?

10. What was the effect of the war on the cities of Asia and Europe?

Critical Thinking

1. Identifying Assumptions Many people in the United States supported the Republican cause in Spain. Some even volunteered to fight in the Spanish civil war. What assumptions might they have made about the expansion of totalitarian governments in Europe that led them to become involved in what could have been seen as strictly Spain's problem?

2. Determining Cause and Effect Admiral Isoroku Yamamoto promised Japan a series of victories for the first year of a war with the United States and Great Britain if Japan took his advice to strike the United States close to home. He also said, however, that unless

3. anger at the Axis, patriotism, and a desire for adventure
4. Questions and reasons should indicate an understanding of, for example, the injustice of the situation, the horrors witnessed, the loss the children felt, or the elation of the liberated.
5. Students might cite the impact of economics on political stability, the risks of appeasing aggressive nations, the ability of people to work together for a common cause, and the damaging nature of war.

Japan won the war quickly victory would be impossible. Considering what you now know about Japan during this time period, identify the cause and effect relationship that caused Yamamoto to hold this view.

3. Making Inferences Once Japan attacked Pearl Harbor and the United States entered the war, many men and women volunteered for duty. What reasons did they give for enlisting? Why do you think these reasons were important to them?

4. Formulating Questions The young people in the photograph were liberated from a concentration camp at the end of the war. If you could ask them any questions about their experience, what would you ask them? Why?

5. Determining Relevance World War II was the most destructive war ever waged in terms of lives lost and property destroyed. What can people of today learn from this period in history?

Portfolio Project

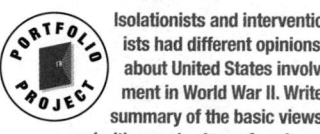

Isolationists and interventionists had different opinions about United States involvement in World War II. Write a summary of the basic views, priorities, and values of each group. Explain your own position on this issue and give reasons for taking that position. Place your finished work in your portfolio.

Cooperative Learning

Working in small groups, analyze the various types of propaganda used during World War II by the Axis Powers and by the Allies. Assign group members specific tasks of gathering information, writing descriptions and summaries of what you find, analyzing the propaganda, and then making a presentation to the class. Try to include some visuals in your presentation.

D-DAY INVASION, JUNE 6, 1944

GREAT BRITAIN

London

Dover

Southampton Portsmouth Shoreham

Portland Calais

Dartmouth

Strait of Dover

Utah (U.S.)
Omaha (U.S.)
Gold (British)
Juno (Canadian)
Sword (British)

English Channel

Cherbourg

Dieppe N

Le Havre

Seine River

Territory controlled by Allies one week after D-Day invasion

St-Lô Caen

Axis territory

NORMANDY

Allied territory

0 25 50 mi.
0 25 50 km
Lambert's Conformal
Conic projection

FRANCE

Allied invasion force

2° W 0° 2° E

Reinforcing Skills

Recognizing Ideologies Research a political slogan or choose one that you already know. Write out the slogan and explain what it reveals about the ideology of the person or group who holds that ideology.

Geography and History

Study the map on this page to answer the following questions:

1. The map shows the Allied invasion routes from Great Britain to Normandy beginning June 6, 1944. Utah, Omaha, Gold, Juno, and Sword were code names for the Normandy beaches. Write an explanation of the Allied attack.

2. Why do you think the invasion was launched from five sites rather than from one?

3. The Nazis were fooled into thinking the D-Day invasion would come near Calais. Why do you think the Allies chose to land on the Normandy peninsula instead?

4. What evidence from the map suggests that the plan for the D-Day invasion was an effective one?

HISTORY JOURNAL

Write down at least two new ideas you learned about World War II. Explain whether or not those ideas help you to understand international events in today's world.

Geography and History

1. U.S. troops left Dartmouth, struck Utah beach; U.S. left Portland, struck Omaha beach; British left Southampton, struck Gold beach; Canadians left Portsmouth, struck Juno beach; British left Shoreham, struck Sword beach
2. Multiple attacks could fracture German resistance.
3. Normandy beachheads were closer to Paris and to the main ports of departure.
4. Just one week after the battle, the Allies had advanced as much as 20 miles inland.

History Journal

Student journals should include references to the political causes and the military solutions of the war. They might also include their ideas concerning today's political and military issues.

BONUS QUESTION

This question may be used for extra credit on the chapter test.
What geographic and environmental features made the Pacific islands a difficult battlefield for U.S. troops?
Answer: *The number of islands, their isolation, the heat and humidity, and the prevalence of diseases made the islands difficult battlefields.*

Portfolio Project

Isolationists supported nonintervention, believing the cost of war would be too great. Interventionists believed the Axis represented too much danger to freedom and could not be ignored.

Cooperative Learning

Group presentations can include information on specific pieces of propaganda and also on themes used in propaganda campaigns by either side.

Reinforcing Skills

Student responses should reveal an ability to interpret accurately the political slogan they choose.

521

The Home Front

DAILY LESSON OBJECTIVES	REPRODUCIBLE RESOURCES	MULTIMEDIA RESOURCES
SECTION 1 Mobilizing the Home Front 1. Describe the problems the government of the United States faced in maintaining morale and mobilizing the economy. 2. List two major tasks of converting the economy of the United States to war production. 3. Explain the purposes of rationing. 4. List two ways the war affected labor in the United States.	☛ Reproducible Lesson Plans ☛ Vocabulary and Guided Reading Activities (English or Spanish) ☛ Cooperative Learning Activities ☛ Supreme Court Case Studies ☛ Section Quizzes (English or Spanish)	♟ Chapter Teaching Transparencies ♟ Section Focus Transparencies ♟ Map Transparencies ◉ Landmark Documents in American History ▣ Student Self-Test: A Software Review ▣ Testmaker
SECTION 2 The War and Social Change 1. Describe the population shifts in the United States during World War II, and explain the relationship between mobility, overcrowding, and social stress. 2. Explain the origins and effects of some of the social problems that surfaced during the war years. 3. Evaluate the status of New Deal social programs during the war.	☛ Reproducible Lesson Plans ☛ Vocabulary and Guided Reading Activities (English or Spanish) ☛ Section Quizzes (English or Spanish)	♟ Section Focus Transparencies ♟ U.S. History and Art Transparencies ▣ Student Self-Test: A Software Review ▣ Testmaker
SECTION 3 The War and Civil Rights 1. Define racism and explain how African Americans fought racism during World War II. 2. Identify A. Philip Randolph and explain the purpose and effect of the March on Washington Movement. 3. Describe the violations of Japanese Americans' civil liberties during World War II.	☛ Reproducible Lesson Plans ☛ Vocabulary and Guided Reading Activities (English or Spanish) ☛ Geography in History Activities ☛ American Literature Readings and Activities ☛ Interpreting Political Cartoons ☛ Supreme Court Case Studies ☛ Reteaching Activities (English or Spanish) ☛ Section Quizzes (English or Spanish) ☛ Skill Reinforcement Activities ☛ Enrichment Activities (English or Spanish)	♟ Section Focus Transparencies ◉ Lessons of War ◉ Landmark Documents in American History ◉ The American People: Fabric of a Nation ▣ Student Self-Test: A Software Review ▣ Testmaker
CHAPTER REVIEW AND EVALUATION	☛ Chapter 16 Test, Forms A and B ☛ Performance Assessment Strategies and Activities	▣ Student Self-Test: A Software Review ▣ Vocabulary PuzzleMaker ▣ Testmaker ∩ Chapter Digests Audiocassettes

 If time does not permit teaching the entire chapter, summarize using the Chapter 16 Digests Audiocassettes and the accompanying activities and tests. (Available in English or Spanish.)

Performance Assessment

Cooperative Project

Have students work in small groups to create two or three newspaper front pages with war news and domestic events of the times. Students will need to research newspapers of the World War II period to find these events.
LEP

Suggested Rubric: A Newspaper Article. See Performance Assessment Strategies and Activities, p. 31.

Individual Project

Have students use the information in the chapter to write a letter from a woman with a job in a defense industry to a friend in the armed sevices overseas. Have them include the woman's opinion of her job as well as some details about daily life on the home front during wartime.

Suggested Rubric: A Self-Assessment. See Performance Assessment Strategies and Activities, p. 53.

Key to Ability Levels

Teaching strategies have been coded for varying learning styles and abilities.

L1 **BASIC** activities for all students

L2 **AVERAGE** activities for average to above-average students

L3 **CHALLENGING** activities for above-average students

LEP **LIMITED ENGLISH PROFICIENCY** activities

Block Scheduling

Block scheduling differs from traditional class scheduling in the amount of time allotted to each period. The extended timeframe provided by block scheduling affords you the opportunity to implement a greater number of research-oriented and activity-intense projects to motivate and involve your students. Activities that are particularly suited to use within the block scheduling framework are identified throughout this chapter by the following designation.

T E A C H E R ' S   C O R N E R

 NATIONAL GEOGRAPHIC SOCIETY

INDEX TO NATIONAL GEOGRAPHIC MAGAZINE

The following articles may be used for research relating to this chapter:

- "Pearl Harbor: A Return to the Day of Infamy," by Thomas B. Allen, December 1991.
- "Japanese Americans: Home at Last," by Arthur Zich, April 1986.

NATIONAL GEOGRAPHIC SOCIETY PRODUCTS AVAILABLE FROM GLENCOE

To order the following products for use with this chapter, contact your local Glencoe sales representative or call Glencoe at 1-800-334-7344:

- *The Presidents: A Picture History of Our Nation* (CD-ROM)
- *GTV: A Geographic Perspective on American History* (Videodisc)
- *GTV: The American People: Fabric of a Nation* (Videodisc)

ADDITIONAL NATIONAL GEOGRAPHIC SOCIETY PRODUCTS

To order the following products for use with this chapter, call National Geographic Society at 1-800-368-2728:

- *Decades of History: The 20th Century—The Early Years* (Filmstrip)
- *The United States as a World Power: From the 1890s to the 1970s* (Filmstrip)

Chapter Overview

As the United States is drawn into war, the nation focuses on mobilizing people, goods, and services for the war effort. The resulting social changes lead to a growing awareness of civil rights and a broadening of the acceptable roles of all Americans.

Introducing the Chapter

After students have read page 522, discuss with them how war can sometimes unify the people of a nation. Ask students what Americans believed to be the purpose or goal of the war. Explore why people felt motivated to work together toward this goal. How might this have affected the sense of prosperity that prevailed during and after the war?

Display the Chapter Teaching Transparency for students. Have students complete the activity sheet for Chapter 16.

Extension Activity
Have students complete Beyond the Transparency on the activity sheet for Chapter 16 and present their projects after the class has completed the chapter.

History Journal

Some students may have read or know about *The Diary of Anne Frank*. Have students compare their impressions of what life was like for Americans on the home front to what life was like for people who lived in war-torn Europe.

CHAPTER 16

The Home Front

1942: AMERICANS PULL TOGETHER

World War II jolted the American people—who were still troubled by a depressed economy—with an electric sense of purpose. After a decade of severe job shortages, thousands of American men and women willingly served in the armed forces.

Others worked on farms and in factories to produce the food and weapons needed to win the war. During the war years, the United States became a country on the move. Many of the new recruits had never before left their hometowns.

The war disrupted the homes, families, and lives of all Americans. Many women followed their husbands to military bases. Both men and women went in search of high-paying jobs in the defense industry. Many African Americans traveled north and west hoping to escape poverty and discrimination.

This mingling of people from different backgrounds altered the way Americans looked at themselves. The American people began to recognize some of the political, social, and economic consequences of living in such a diverse society. The prosperity that Americans experienced from a full-employment economy during the war years enabled them to live better after the war. ■

HISTORY JOURNAL

Before you read the rest of this chapter, write your reactions to the above description of the home front. What do you think life was like for Americans at home during the war years?

522

✚ EXTRA CREDIT PROJECT

Technology Have students explore how the rapid technological changes that took place during World War II affected jobs, life at home, recreation, and strategies for war. Students can choose one area to look into, searching newspapers and magazines of the period for examples of new products, technological improvements, and the conversion of wartime technology to peacetime technology. Areas to look into are computers, weaponry, mass media and communications, transportation, and home appliances.

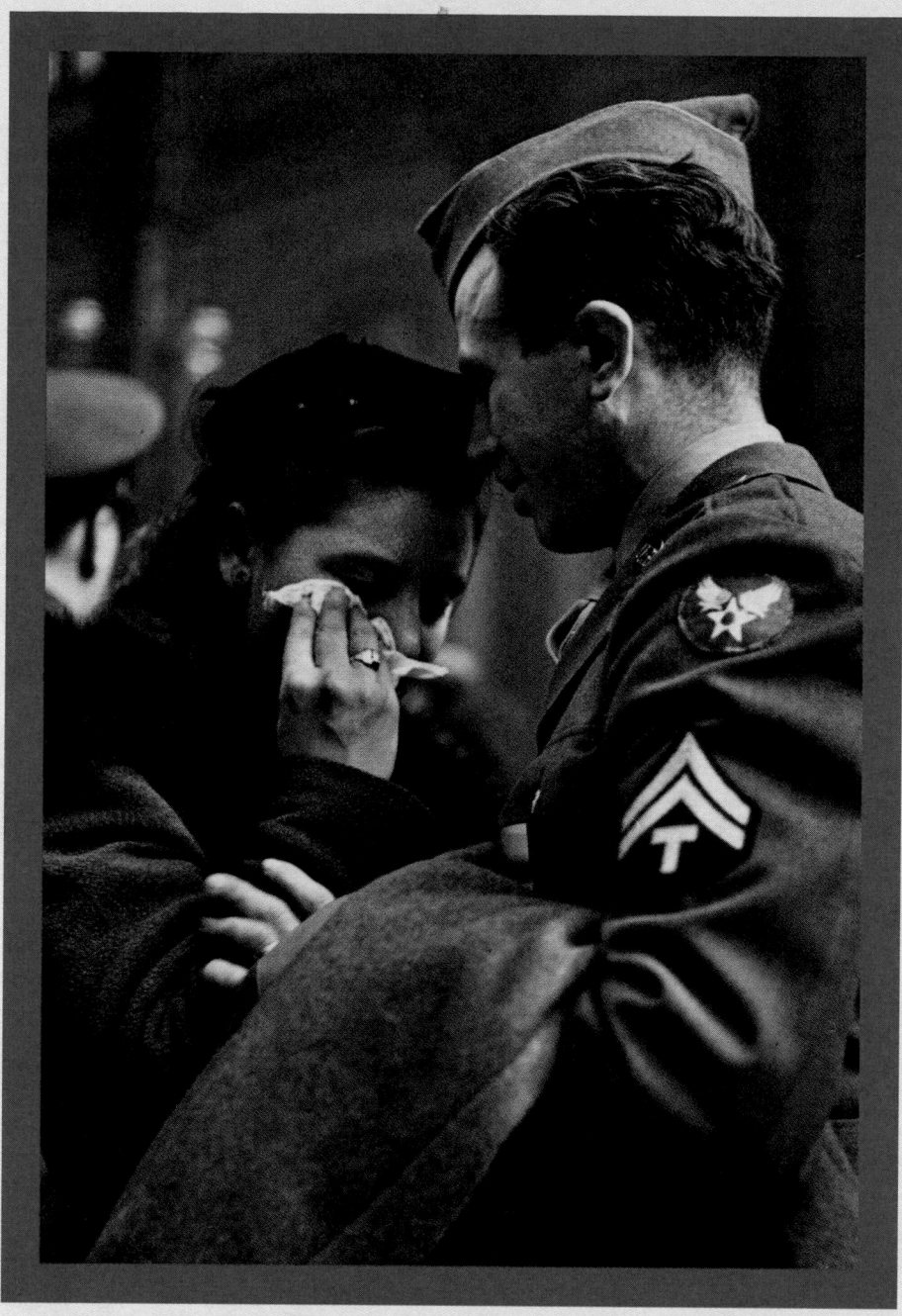

ALFRED EISENSTAT/LIFE MAGAZINE ©TIME INC.

THE WAR BROUGHT SADNESS
AND ANGUISH TO SEPARATED FAMILIES
AND FRIENDS.

523

 **History and
the Humanities**

American Music:
Cultural Traditions—
"Take Me Back to Tulsa":
by Bob Wills and his
Texas Playboys; "Boogie
Woogie Bugle Boy" by
the Andrews Sisters; and
"Jersey Bounce" by
Benny Goodman and his
orchestra.

 **Performance
Assessment**

Refer to page 522B for
performance assessment
activities for this chapter.

Also see Activity 16
in the Performance
Assessment Strategies
and Activities for an
additional activity as well
as for suggested rubrics.

Examining the Visual

Leaving Home The number of military personnel on active duty jumped from 458,000 in 1940 to more than 12 million in 1945. How did families and friends keep in touch? People at home wrote letters called V-mail (V for Victory) and sent packages with food and warm clothing. War marriages took place whenever a furlough could be arranged. By the war's end, more than 16 million people had served in the United States armed forces.

SECTION
1

FOCUS

Section Objectives

1. Describe the problems the government of the United States faced in maintaining morale and mobilizing the economy.
2. List two major tasks of converting the economy of the United States to war production.
3. Explain the purposes of rationing.
4. List two ways the war affected labor in the United States.

Bellringer Activity

While taking attendance at the beginning of the class period, display **Section Focus Transparency 49,** and have students answer the questions. (Or use the blackline master.)

VISUAL INSTRUCTION

Gearing Up Donald M. Nelson, a Sears, Roebuck executive who was named head of the War Production Board (WPB), led the enormous task of gearing up production levels in order to supply war needs. By spring 1942, thousands of new plants were operating and thousands of older factories had converted to war production under Nelson's direction.

Ask: How did celebrities also help to boost the war effort? *(by boosting morale at home and abroad)*

Mobilizing the Home Front

DECEMBER 7, 1941: JAPANESE BOMB PEARL HARBOR

CULVER PICTURES

AT THE BEGINNING OF DECEMBER 1941, THE UNITED STATES WAS AT PEACE, AND MOST AMERICANS WERE PREPARING FOR THE HOLIDAYS. The Japanese attack on Pearl Harbor on December 7 stunned Americans and permanently changed their lives. Everyone had a story to tell about how he or she first heard the startling news. Maxine Andrews, one of the famous Andrews Sisters singing trio, remembers that day:

B ut oh, I remember the day war was declared. We were in Cincinnati. It looked like we were gonna break the house record in the theater. It didn't matter how cold it was or how high the snow, people were

lined up for blocks. . . . This Sunday morning, I walked over and there were no lines. I thought, "Now, this is funny." I walked onto the stage, which was very dark. The doorman and the stagehands were sitting around the radio. They had just one light on. They were talking about Pearl Harbor being bombed. I asked the doorman, "Where is Pearl Harbor?"
—As told to Studs Terkel, *"The Good War,"* 1984

The Andrews Sisters, like other stars and celebrities, bolstered the morale of Americans both at home and abroad. In small towns and big cities, on army posts and navy ships, entertainers lifted spirits and helped unify the country.

Gearing Up
Posters like this one encouraged Americans to increase their wartime efforts at home.

AS YOU READ

Vocabulary
► gross national product
► inflation
► consumer price index
► bond

Think About . . .
► the problems the government of the United States faced in maintaining morale and mobilizing the economy.
► the two major tasks of converting the economy to war production.
► the purposes of rationing.
► ways in which the war affected labor in the United States.

Section 1 Resources

REPRODUCIBLE RESOURCES
📁 Lesson Plan 16-1
📁 Vocabulary and Guided Reading Activity 16-1
📁 Cooperative Learning Activity 16
📁 Section 1 Quiz
📁 Supreme Court Cases 13, 15

MULTIMEDIA RESOURCES
💿 Chapter Teaching Transparency 16
💿 Section Focus Transparency 49
💿 Map Transparency 16
💿 Landmark Documents in American History

💿 Student Self-Test: A Software Review
💿 Testmaker
🎧 Chapter 16 Digest Audiocassette

Building National Morale
Motivating Citizen Efforts

Japan's surprise attack on Pearl Harbor ended the bitter argument between isolationists and those who favored intervention in the war. Shocked and angered by the attack, Americans rallied to support their government. Most believed they were fighting for what President Roosevelt called the Four Freedoms: freedom of speech and expression, freedom of worship, freedom from want, and freedom from fear.

Calling All Volunteers

To raise and maintain the country's morale, the government created the Office of Civilian Defense (OCD). Citizens were asked to contribute "an hour a day for the U.S.A." They could choose from a number of civil defense projects. For example, volunteer air-raid wardens enforced blackouts while spotters scanned the skies for enemy planes.

Many other Americans helped the war effort by growing their own vegetables. In 1941 the secretary of agriculture suggested that because farmers were busy feeding the army, people who wanted fresh vegetables should plant "victory gardens." A few months later, backyards, vacant lots, and such unlikely places as zoos, racetracks, and jails sprouted colorful arrays of vegetables planted by conscientious citizens. Victory gardens eventually produced 40 percent of all the vegetables grown in the country during the war.

Volunteers also collected materials for the war effort. Newspapers, rubber, scrap metal, aluminum pots, tin cans, box springs—anything that could be turned into armaments—were deposited on designated street corners. Students brought these materials to collection centers. By June 1942, the Boy Scouts had salvaged so much wastepaper that paper collection was temporarily called off. Eventually these efforts supplied much of the steel, half of the tin, and half of the paper that was needed to fight the war.

Salvage for Victory Stores posted signs such as the one above to show they were supporting the war effort. Neighborhood children such as these in New York City, who are members of a recycling group called the Tin Can Club Number One, cut, washed, and flattened cans for war use. *How did salvaging scrap materials help the war effort?*

The Media Go to War

To keep Americans informed about the war, the government established the Office of War Information. Its function was to coordinate war news from various federal agencies. The office also encouraged newspapers, radio stations, and the movie industry to help Americans understand the progress of the war and the government's policies.

The entertainment industry, however, needed no encouragement from the government. Hollywood rushed to copyright titles such as *Bombing of Honolulu, Yellow Peril, My Four Years in Japan,* and *V for Victory.* A month after Pearl Harbor, filmmakers were hard at work

SECTION ONE **525**

Cooperative Learning

Role Playing Organize the class into small groups. Have each group create a skit about how the war affected families in the United States. Each student in a group should take the part of a family member. The groups should show how their "families" responded to the need to ration, do war work, and conduct scrap drives. Encourage students to be creative and look for ways to personalize their skits. For example, they might play music of the time or refer to household products that were common during the war years.

TEACH

Guided Practice

L2 Simulation To give students a sense of the frustrations felt by consumers in a time of high inflation, allot each student $5.00 and tell them they are going shopping. Write these prices on the chalkboard: apples, $1.00 per lb.; potatoes, 25 cents per lb.; chicken, 50 cents per lb.; cereals, $1.00 per box. Have students "spend" their money by writing out a shopping order. Then tell them that after one month each item now costs 25 cents more. Change prices on the chalkboard, ask them to shop again and discuss how their buying power changed.

Show students Map Transparency 16 and have them complete the activity sheet.

VISUAL INSTRUCTION

Salvage for Victory The Tin Can Club Number One, located on East 103rd Street, was the first of its kind in New York City. It was sponsored by the New York Salvage Committee.

Answer: *Salvaging and recycling provided raw materials for war weapons, vehicles, and other war items.*

Facts on File

Landmark Documents in American History Have students review "Radio Appeal on the Scrap Rubber Campaign, Franklin D. Roosevelt, 1942" and write a paragraph about the intent of the document.

Independent Practice

L2 Linking Past and Present Have students review pages 314–319 of their text. Ask them to write a comparison of the methods used to maintain morale in World War I and World War II.

▱ Have students complete the Chapter 16, Section 1 Vocabulary and Guided Reading Activity. (Also in Spanish.) **LEP**

▱ Have students complete the Chapter 16 Cooperative Learning Activity.

VISUAL INSTRUCTION

The Plane Production Push The plant workers in this photo include women; they are working on the production line at the Curtiss-Wright Corporation, building P-40 Warhawks.

Answer: *In 1944, at the height of production, there were more than 90,000 military aircraft being produced.*

---

on their versions of the war. The heroes were gallant Americans played by actors such as John Wayne. The villains—all stereotypes—were sadistic Germans, bumbling Italians, and sneaky Japanese.

Comic strip characters also went to war. Terry of *Terry and the Pirates* fought the Japanese instead of pirates. Little Orphan Annie called on readers to collect scrap metal, and her father, Daddy Warbucks, served as a general. Superman promoted the Red Cross and war bonds. New comic strips with titles such as *G.I. Joe, War,* and *Don Winslow of the Navy* appeared.

Songwriters, too, joined in. A popular song told how the war changed one musician's life:

He was a famous trumpet man from out Chicago way,
He had a boogie sound that no one else could play,
He was top man at his craft.
But then his number came up and he
    was called in the draft.
He's in the army now ablowin' reveille.
He's the boogie woogie bugle boy of Company B.
—Hughie Price and Don Raye, "The Boogie
    Woogie Bugle Boy of Company B," 1941

Patriotic songs such as "This Is the Army Mister Jones," and "American Patrol" were popular at the beginning of the war. After 1942, though, patriotism gave way to more sentimental songs such as "I Left My Heart at the Stage Door Canteen" and "You'd Be So Nice to Come Home To."

Advertisements in magazines and newspapers and on billboards and radio shows also stimulated national unity. Advertisers reversed their usual emphasis on selling goods and instead urged Americans to use less rather than buy more. The popular slogan was "Use it up, wear it out, make it do or do without." The materials and energy that ordinarily went into producing consumer goods would now be needed to make the instruments of war.

Military Plane Production, 1941–1945

The Plane Production Push At defense plants and converted factories throughout the nation, mechanized assembly lines doubled the daily output and reduced production hours. As the graph on the right shows, production had not yet reached peak capacity by 1943. *At the peak in 1944, approximately how many planes were produced?*

526 CHAPTER 16 THE HOME FRONT

Meeting Special Needs

Attention Deficit Disorder To help students with attention deficit disorder, discuss the meaning of the word *morale*—the feelings of an individual or group with regard to confidence, courage, discipline, and willingness to endure hardship. Have students write the word *morale* in their notebook. Then as they study the section, they can write down phrases to describe how the United States government attempted to maintain the morale of the people on the home front. Encourage them to look for evidence that the government's efforts were successful.

Staging a Production Miracle
Manufacturing War Machines

Although the Roosevelt administration had taken steps to prepare the country for war before Pearl Harbor, much remained to be done. In 1941 only 15 percent of industrial production was going to military needs. To help United States industry convert to war production, President Roosevelt created the War Production Board (WPB) in January 1942. The WPB's job was to "exercise general responsibility" over the nation's economy.

First came the task of getting industrialists to convert their factories from civilian to military production. To accomplish this the WPB issued orders limiting the production of materials not essential to the war effort. Manufacturers switched from making consumer goods such as shirts, toys, and cars to making uniforms, bombs, tanks, and aircraft.

Next came the job of convincing businesses to build new plants to increase production. The government often paid for the new plants and equipment and also agreed to grant relief from antitrust laws to war-related industries. To eliminate the risk for businesses, military contractors were reimbursed for their costs and guaranteed a fixed and generous profit. "If you . . . go to war . . . in a capitalist country, you have to let business make money out of the process or business won't work," said Secretary of War Henry Stimson.

The WPB's plan succeeded, and industrial production nearly doubled. This was accomplished with the help of people like Henry Kaiser, the genius of ship construction. His Richmond, California, shipyard cut the time needed to build merchant ships from 105 days to 46, then to 29, then to 14 days from start to finish! By 1944 the United States had created such a surplus of armaments that the government ordered some defense plants to stop hiring and to cut back on items like anti-tank guns and trainer planes.

At a meeting between Roosevelt, Churchill, and Stalin in Tehran, late in 1943, the Soviet leader offered a toast: "To American production, without which this war would have been lost."

Directing a Wartime Economy
Controls, Rationing, and Taxes

The United States economy grew at a staggering rate during the war. The **gross national product (GNP),** the dollar value of all goods and services produced annually, increased in the United States from $90.5 billion in 1939 to $211.9 billion in 1945.

The war created 17 million new jobs, and many workers put in long hours of overtime. Farmers shared in the prosperity as crop prices doubled between 1940 and 1945. As people made more money, they sought more of the consumer goods that were in short supply. This increased demand pushed prices up. By the spring of 1942, the cost of living had risen 15 percent above 1939 levels.

Roosevelt worried about the effects of this **inflation,** or general rise in wages and prices. The first step he took to control inflation was to freeze wages. Trade unions, however, opposed a wage freeze. Because they were enthusiastic political supporters of FDR, the administration moved slowly and cautiously.

Controlling Wages and Prices

The administration set up the National War Labor Board (NWLB) to control wages and monitor inflation. In July 1942, the NWLB adopted a wage formula that allowed wage increases up to 15 percent over January 1,

CHART STUDY

Ask: The United States declared war on Japan in December 1941. How many months later did the United States government impose the Victory Tax?

Answer: *10 months later*

MAJOR WARTIME ECONOMIC LEGISLATION, 1941–1943

JANUARY 1941 The Office of Production Management (OPM) is created.

AUGUST 1941 The Supply Priorities and Allocations Board (SPAB) is established.

JANUARY 1942 The War Production Board (WPB) is created to help convert industry to war production.

OCTOBER 1942 The Revenue Act imposes Victory Tax—a 5 percent gross income tax on all annual incomes of more than $624.

1941   1942   1943   1944

APRIL 1941 The Office of Price Administration (OPA) is established to oversee marketplace and rationing system.

JANUARY 1942 The Emergency Price Control Act (EPCA) passes, authorizing price ceilings on consumer goods.

OCTOBER 1942 The Office of Economic Stabilization (OES) is established to oversee entire economy.

JULY 1943 The Current Tax Payment Act requires employers to deduct federal taxes from employees' checks.

SECTION ONE   **527**

Portfolio Project

Eliminating Luxuries During the war, the War Production Board identified products that it considered unnecessary and stopped their production so that raw materials could go into the war effort instead. Those unnecessary products included beer mugs, asparagus tongs, corn poppers, lobster forks, and hair curlers. If students had to make a choice today, what products would they consider unnecessary? Have them each write a list and explain their reasoning in making their selections. Ask them to add their lists to their portfolios.

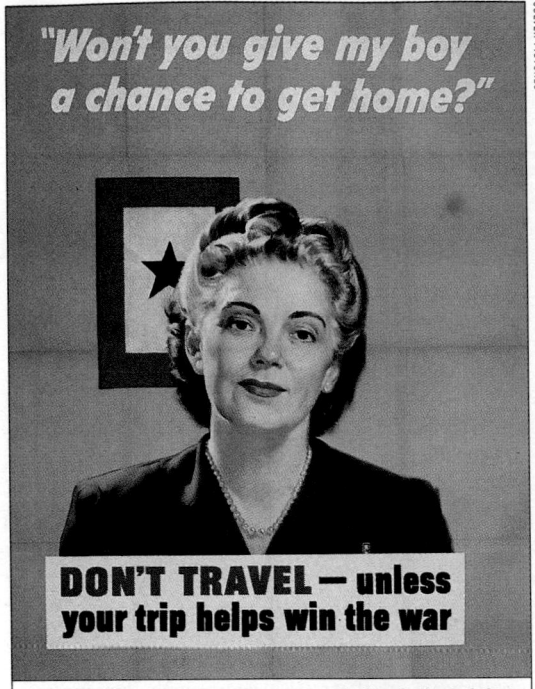

CULVER PICTURES

"Won't you give my boy a chance to get home?"

DON'T TRAVEL — unless your trip helps win the war

Motivating Sacrifice The blue star on the flag indicated that a family member was serving in the military. A gold star would indicate that an individual had been killed. *How does this flag strengthen the poster's image?*

1941, levels—the amount the NWLB had estimated living costs had risen.

In April 1943, faced with continued inflation, the government issued a "hold the line" order. Restrictions, however, applied to hourly wages, not to weekly earnings. By working overtime, workers could still earn a good deal more money. Consequently, while wage rates rose by a relatively modest 24 percent during the war, weekly earnings rose by a tremendous 70 percent.

If wages were to be limited, workers wanted prices controlled as well. Early in 1942 Congress let the Office of Price Administration (OPA) fix maximum prices. The OPA soon set a ceiling on all prices.

Overall, however, a reasonable balance existed between wages and prices throughout the war. The **consumer price index (CPI)**, a statistic showing the price change of selected goods and services, rose about the same percentage as wages between 1939 and 1945.

Reducing Demand Through Rationing

One method the OPA used in hopes of keeping prices down was rationing, a way of distributing limited goods fairly. Rationing reduced demand because ration coupons were needed to purchase many goods, such as meat and butter. The OPA set up local rationing boards that set quotas for each family's coupons. Families received ration coupons based on the number of people in a household and their needs. They presented coupons when buying rationed items. Merchants, in turn, gave these coupons to suppliers in order to restock their shelves. In this way the government controlled demand and kept prices from rising.

Rationing was one of the most controversial elements of the war effort. Although Americans were earning more, government restrictions limited their spending. They could afford automobiles and gasoline, but Detroit was producing tanks, not cars, and gasoline was limited. Because they found gasoline rationing so irritating, some Americans learned to bend the rules.

I was a certified ski instructor and was with the National Ski Patrol, so the army hired me to certify skiers and mountaineers for the mountain troops that were trained in Leadville, Colorado. They gave me a 'C' card for an unlimited amount of gasoline to go skiing on the weekends. . . .

But you'd better believe I had a long waiting list of people to ride up to the mountains with me every weekend. One of the guys who went with me owned a small butcher shop and had a contract to supply a hotel, and he seemed to be able to get unlimited quantities of meat. So every month I turned my meat stamps over to him and was able to get meat anytime I wanted it. You had to work the angles— good old American ingenuity I guess—and it didn't hurt anything.

—As quoted by Archie Satterfield,
The Home Front, 1981

Paying for a Costly War

World War II cost the United States 10 times more than World War I did. From 1941 to 1945, the government's operating budget was $321 billion, nearly twice as much as its total spending in the preceding 150 years. Taxes met about 40 percent of the war costs; the government borrowed the rest.

Before the war began, many Americans did not pay any federal income tax. Only about 26 million tax returns were filed in 1941. In 1942 Congress passed a Revenue Act that FDR called "the greatest tax bill in American history." This legislation increased corporate taxes and required nearly all Americans to pay income taxes.

In 1943 Congress approved a system for withholding taxes through monthly payroll deductions. Now the modern tax structure, begun in 1913 when Congress instituted a direct tax on income, was completed.

Extending the Content

More About Rationing According to "Rationing Why and How," a publication put out by the Office of Price Administration in 1942, there were 2 chief methods, or basic rules, applied in the United States to ration goods. These rules were developed because the supply and demand varied for each item and so all rationed goods could not be distributed in the same way.

First, when the supply was large enough to distribute some of an item to all, everybody got a share, and more of that item might be supplied to those with special needs—the elderly, for example.

Second, when the supply of an item was not large enough to distribute some to all, the item went only to those who needed it in connection with the war effort or the public welfare.

While taxes provided for 40 percent of the cost of the war, borrowing, mostly from Americans, paid for the remaining 60 percent. To borrow money, the government sold **bonds,** certificates that promised that the government would pay the holder the amount borrowed plus interest. The bonds also controlled inflation by reducing the money consumers had to spend and they helped sell the war to the American public.

The Treasury Department recruited both Madison Avenue advertisers and Hollywood stars to help sell bonds. Creative public relations stunts boosted sales. The publishers of *Batman* comic books devoted a cover to a picture of their hero urging the purchase of war bonds. Hollywood stars trav-

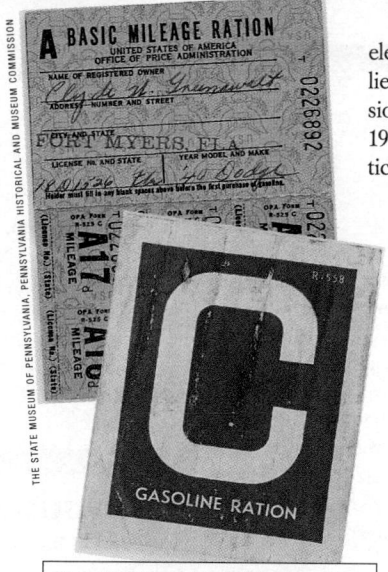

THE STATE MUSEUM OF PENNSYLVANIA, PENNSYLVANIA HISTORICAL AND MUSEUM COMMISSION

Rationing Every World War II family in the United States was familiar with ration coupons like these. *Do you agree with the principle of rationing? Why or why not?*

eled across the country to perform at rallies and auctioned their personal possessions. In the first big war bond sale in 1942, some 337 actors and actresses participated, working 18 hours a day.

Even children helped pay for the war. At the post office, they bought war stamps that they pasted into albums. When their stamps totaled $18.75, they received a war bond redeemable for $25 10 years later. Adult Americans bought bonds to help family members in the armed services, to invest their money safely, to preserve "the American way of life," to combat inflation, and to save for postwar purchases. When the war ended, Americans had saved $129 billion that they could spend on homes, appliances, and goods they were unable to buy during the war.

DISTRIBUTING RATIONED GOODS

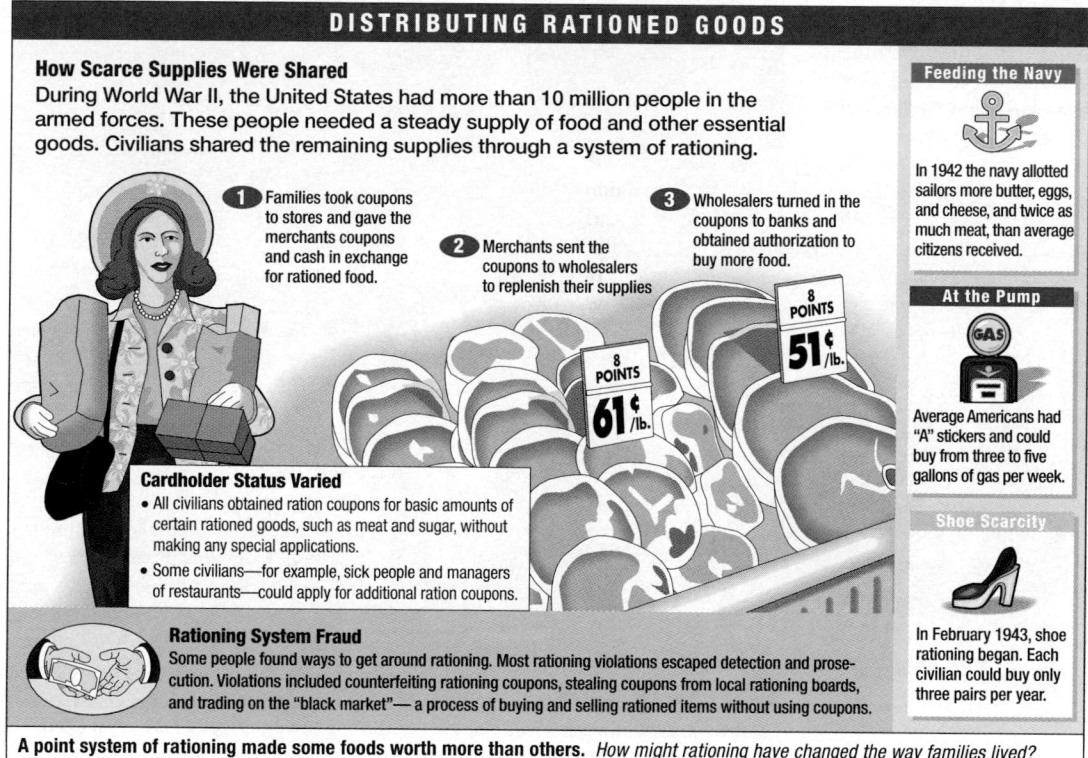

How Scarce Supplies Were Shared
During World War II, the United States had more than 10 million people in the armed forces. These people needed a steady supply of food and other essential goods. Civilians shared the remaining supplies through a system of rationing.

1 Families took coupons to stores and gave the merchants coupons and cash in exchange for rationed food.

2 Merchants sent the coupons to wholesalers to replenish their supplies

3 Wholesalers turned in the coupons to banks and obtained authorization to buy more food.

Feeding the Navy
In 1942 the navy allotted sailors more butter, eggs, and cheese, and twice as much meat, than average citizens received.

At the Pump
Average Americans had "A" stickers and could buy from three to five gallons of gas per week.

Shoe Scarcity
In February 1943, shoe rationing began. Each civilian could buy only three pairs per year.

Cardholder Status Varied
• All civilians obtained ration coupons for basic amounts of certain rationed goods, such as meat and sugar, without making any special applications.
• Some civilians—for example, sick people and managers of restaurants—could apply for additional ration coupons.

Rationing System Fraud
Some people found ways to get around rationing. Most rationing violations escaped detection and prosecution. Violations included counterfeiting rationing coupons, stealing coupons from local rationing boards, and trading on the "black market"— a process of buying and selling rationed items without using coupons.

A point system of rationing made some foods worth more than others. *How might rationing have changed the way families lived?*

Cultural Perspectives

Discrimination Against African Americans Although wartime employment helped African Americans to make economic gains during World War II, they were blatantly excluded from living in better neighborhoods. During the war years in San Francisco, for example, public housing authorities segregated the races. Other cities, including Seattle and

Chicago, did not segregate the housing of racial groups, but the opposition of white residents was strong and limited the success of housing integration efforts. In the armed services, separate training and housing for African Americans also existed. The United States military did not desegregate until several years after the end of World War II.

ASSESS

Meeting Lesson Objectives

Each section objective is tested by the section review question(s) that follows it in parentheses.

1. Describe the problems the government of the United States faced in maintaining morale and mobilizing the economy. (1, 2, 3)
2. List two major tasks of converting the economy of the United States to war production. (1, 3)
3. Explain the purposes of rationing. (4)
4. List two ways the war affected labor in the United States. (5)

Trying to Uphold a No-Strike Pledge
Labor's Wartime Efforts

While the wages of many Americans increased dramatically during the war, not everyone shared in this prosperity. The major labor unions, however, had issued a pledge that, as long as the war continued, their workers would not strike for higher salaries and better working conditions.

In return, the NWLB enforced settlements between companies and their workers on hours, wages, and working conditions. It also had authority to seize plants whose owners refused to cooperate. The no-strike pledge, however, was not legally binding, and more than 3 million workers went on strike in 1943.

The most serious strikes occurred in the coalfields. Wages had been frozen in 1942, but prices and profits had continued to rise, and miners thought they were entitled to a raise. United Mine Workers president John L. Lewis, a miner himself, led nearly 450,000 coal miners out on strike in 1943 when the NWLB denied them a raise. At congressional hearings, when Lewis was reminded that the government was trying to hold down wages to control inflation, he replied, "Do you mind first inflating the stomachs of my members?"

After his pleas to miners to return to work failed, President Roosevelt took over the mines. When FDR was urged to put striking miners in jail, however, one adviser cautioned: "There are not enough jails in the country to hold these men, and, if there were, I must point out that a jailed miner produces no more coal than a striking miner." Eventually Lewis, the mine operators, and the administration agreed on a raise.

Workers in the coal, steel, and railroad industries went out on strike during the war. Despite these strikes, labor largely lived up to the no-strike pledge.

Recruiting New Workers
Women Fill the Gap

More than 15 million Americans left work to serve in the armed forces during the war. Many of the remaining adults, as well as adolescents, assumed those positions. As new war-related plants were built, the need for civilian workers increased dramatically.

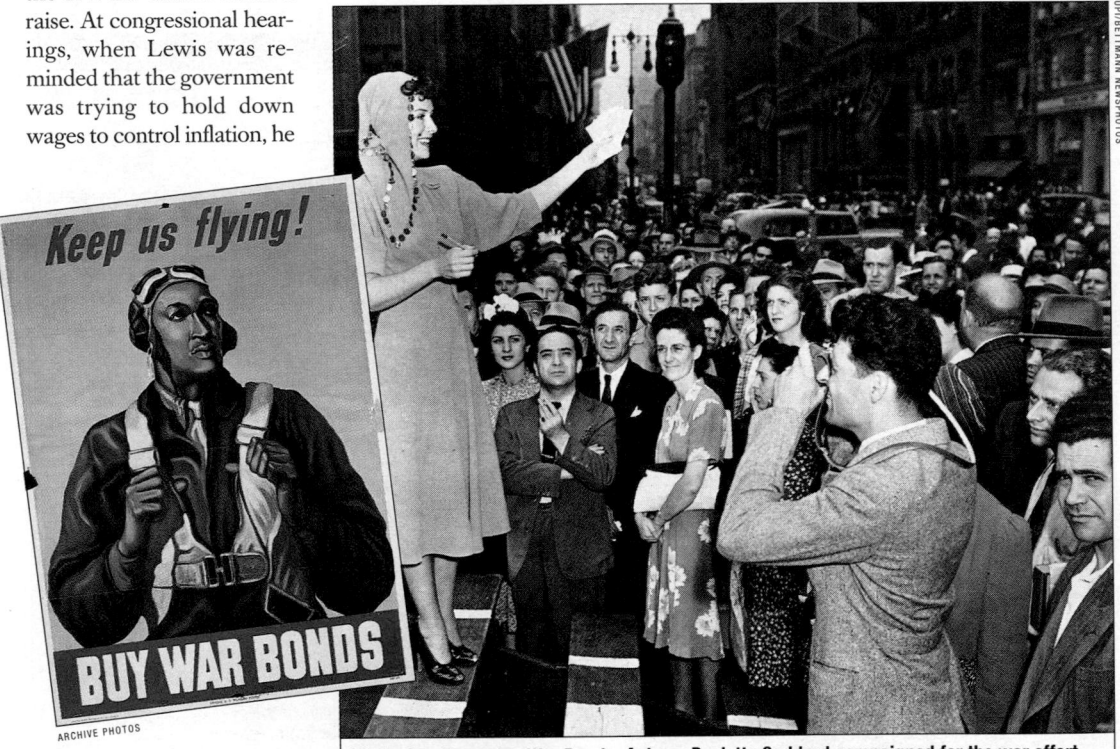

UPI/BETTMANN NEWSPHOTOS

Keep us flying!

BUY WAR BONDS

ARCHIVE PHOTOS

Movie Star Promotes War Bonds Actress Paulette Goddard campaigned for the war effort. *How much do you think celebrity appearances influence people's decisions?*

Critical Thinking

Making Inferences Read this quotation to students: "When the war ended, Americans had saved $129 billion that they could spend on homes, appliances, and goods that they were unable to buy during the war." Ask students to work in pairs to research economic consequences that are likely to follow in such a situation, including a possible postwar spending spree followed by a period of inflation as prices increase because of heavy product demand. Have them present their findings in the form of an oral report.

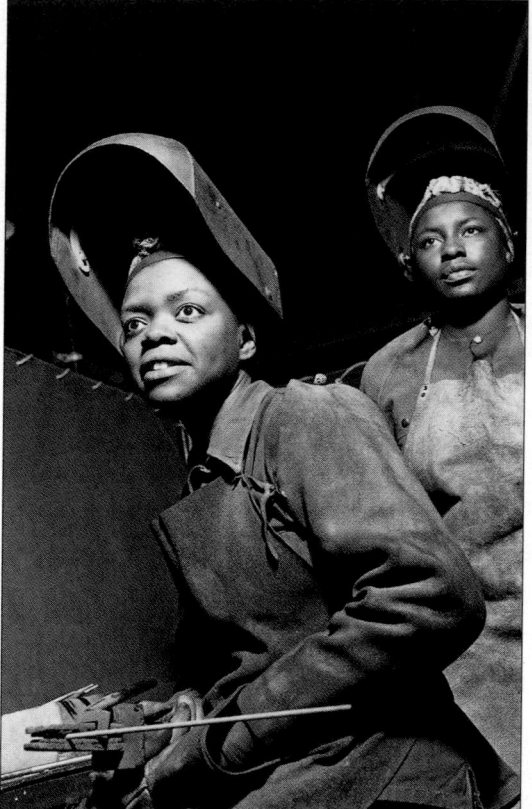
LIBRARY OF CONGRESS

A New Workforce Women already working in domestic service or in textile-related jobs were among the first to be hired for wartime defense jobs. As the need grew, recent high school graduates were also recruited. *How did these workers help to change society's opinion of women's capabilities?*

At first, jobs were easily filled by the unemployed. Wartime labor demands wiped out the unemployment of the Depression years and created other opportunities. Between 1940 and 1945, about 6 million women joined the civilian labor force. The proportion of women who worked rose from 27 percent to 37 percent as women replaced the men who were at war.

The labor shortage opened up doors for women in many occupations. The most startling increase in numbers of working women occurred in defense industries, such as airplane manufacturing and shipbuilding, where female employment jumped by 460 percent. In plants and shipyards, women worked on assembly lines as welders, riveters, and mechanics. Although "Rosie the Riveter" transformed the nature of the labor force, women generally had a hard time gaining acceptance by male workers. Helen Studer, a riveter at Douglas Aircraft in Los Angeles during the war, told her story:

The men really resented the women very much, and in the beginning it was a little bit rough. . . . The men that you worked with, after a while, they realized that it was essential that the women worked there, 'cause there wasn't enough men and the women were doing a pretty good job. So the resentment eased. However, I always felt that they thought it wasn't your place to be there.

—As reported by Sherna B. Gluck,
Rosie the Riveter Revisited, 1987

Three of every four new women workers were married. All women, however, suffered two disadvantages. They received 60 percent less pay than men, and they had little job security. The NWLB called for equal pay for equal work, but women were often placed in lower job classifications, so the gap between men's and women's earnings increased.

For the most part, women found that wartime opportunities were only temporary. As the war ended, so did their jobs. Between 1944 and 1946, about 4 million women either lost their jobs or left them.

Faced with mobilizing for the greatest international conflict in their history, American workers performed production miracles. They were rewarded with full employment and a higher standard of living. Yet fighting the war on the home front created new problems. The elimination of women from the postwar workforce was only one of these problems. The war also strained the American family and society in new ways.

SECTION REVIEW

Vocabulary
1. Define: gross national product, inflation, consumer price index, bond.

Checking Facts
2. What problems did the United States confront in maintaining morale at home during the war?

3. What were two major tasks that the United States faced in converting the economy to producing products for war?

Critical Thinking
Expressing Problems Clearly
4. What problem was the process of rationing designed to solve?

Linking Across Time
5. Describe two ways in which World War II affected labor in the United States. Do any of these conditions exist here today?

VISUAL INSTRUCTION

A New Workforce Sonya Jason, who worked coating glider wings in a Pittsburgh factory during the war, described the growing need for female workers: "By late 1943, acute labor shortages meant that even a short, skinny 16-year-old with an eighth-grade education was employable."

Answer: *Their work proved that women could be successful at jobs outside the home in a wide variety of fields.*

Evaluate

Have students complete the Section Review.

📠 🖸 Assign the Section 1 Quiz or use the Testmaker to develop a customized quiz. (Also in Spanish.) **LEP**

Reteach

🎧 Have students listen to the Chapter 16, Section 1 Audiocassette. (Also in Spanish.) **LEP**

Enrich

📠 Have students complete Supreme Court Case Studies 13, 15.

CLOSE

Ask students to write down one important economic event that happened between 1941 and 1945. What effect(s) did that event cause? *(The gross national product of the United States increased from $90.5 billion in 1939 to $211.9 billion in 1945. People made more money and wanted more consumer goods, bringing about inflation.)*

Section 1 Review Answers

1. **gross national product** (527), **inflation** (527), **consumer price index** (528), **bond** (529)
2. The problems included scarce services, food, material, and money; the government responded by inspiring people to volunteer their services, grow vegetables, collect material for the war effort, and buy savings bonds.

3. The United States had to convert industry to war production, and it had to direct the economy to avoid inflation.
4. Rationing was designed to distribute limited goods fairly and keep prices down.
5. Initially, the number of workers dropped until women joined the workforce. Most women stopped working after the war, but today many women work full-time or part-time.

CULTURE
OF THE
TIME

TEACH

Making the Historical Connection

Fletcher Henderson, the first jazz bandleader to effectively use orchestral arrangements, formed his first big band in 1923. Benny Goodman's band gained national recognition in about 1935, and the Big Band era began. By the time the United States entered the war, Americans had made jitterbugging to big band sounds a national craze.

FYI

Music While live music experienced a wartime boom, the music recording industry declined. War rationing severely limited the use of shellac, the raw material from which records were made.

 History and the Humanities

 American Music: Cultural Traditions— "Jersey Bounce" by Benny Goodman; "Muskrat Ramble" by Louis Armstrong.

The Big Band Era

Thousands of families bid tearful farewells as loved ones left for war. Newspaper headlines screamed of battles and bombings. Paychecks hit an all-time high, but goods were few because everything from silk to steel was needed to fuel the war. No wonder people turned to entertainment for escape.

THE CROONER
The idol of millions of fans, singer **Frank Sinatra** put some members of his adoring audiences into a swoon, or faint, as he sang his romantic lyrics. Although during wartime many of his fans were teenagers, his tunes were popular with all generations.

3-D MANIA
After the seriousness of war, fads in the later 1940s reflected the need for pure fun. These boys, members of New York's Madison Square Boys' Club, wear special glasses to read their **3-D comics**.

532 CULTURE OF THE TIME

Background Information

Origins of Jazz African Americans originated jazz music and dance. Jazz drew on the harmonic structures of European music and the vocal and percussive rhythms of African music. Many of the early jazz musicians grew up on the plantations of the South. The work songs and spiritual songs of enslaved African Americans strongly influenced early jazz. Dances such as the jitterbug descended from nineteenth- and twentieth-century stage dancing, as well as from the dances of enslaved African Americans and the dances of the people of the Caribbean and Africa.

SOOTHING SOUNDS

Big-name bands like Duke Ellington's played the music of the day on stage and even in the movies. **The Duke** and his band are shown here in a scene from the movie *Reveille With Beverly*.

A DANCING CRAZE

Jitterbuggers went wild in the war years with routines that demanded rhythm and stamina. Couples jived to both live bands and jukebox recordings.

A GI SIGNATURE

The name and image of the whimsical character **Kilroy** was scribbled on walls, bunkers, and in other locations. Kilroy left the message that GI Joe had been there.

PATRIOTIC LEGWEAR

When silk and nylon were needed to make parachutes, women improvised by painting their legs with makeup to create **simulated stockings.** They even used devices to draw seams— with some difficulty, of course.

Curriculum Connection

Music You might invite students to listen to recordings of the big bands, including those featuring Count Basie, Duke Ellington, Benny Goodman, Billie Holiday, Artie Shaw, and Glenn Miller. Have students compare this music to the music they enjoy. What are the similarities? The differences?

CLOSE

Ask students what they think drew many Americans to music and dance during such a time of strife and sadness? *(Music and dance provided an outlet that would help people forget their troubles.)* Do they think that Big Band music would have become so popular without the war? Why or why not? *(The pressures of the war helped fuel the Big Band craze. Without those pressures, the phenomenon might never have occurred.)* How did the entertainment offered by the big bands help Americans to survive a national crisis? *(Entertainment helped Americans to feel positive and gave them hope.)*

Portfolio Project

Big Band Who's Who Have students create biographical profiles, including discographies— or listings of recordings—for prominent performers of the Big Band era. Students might start by asking members of the community who were alive during that time to recall their own favorite performers. Students can then look in libraries, music stores, or video stores for resources. When they finish their profiles, students can put them in their portfolios. 📁

FOCUS

Section Objectives

1. Describe the population shifts in the United States during World War II, and explain the relationship between mobility, overcrowding, and social stress.
2. Explain the origins and effects of some of the social problems that surfaced during the war years.
3. Evaluate the status of New Deal social programs during the war.

Bellringer Activity

✍ While taking attendance at the beginning of the class period, display **Section Focus Transparency 50,** and have students answer the questions. (Or use the blackline master.)

VISUAL INSTRUCTION

Moving In 1940 about 48 percent of African Americans lived in cities, compared to more than 77 percent in 1950.

Ask: How were these families' motives similar to those of immigrants to the United States? *(Students may reply that the basic motive of trying to find a better life has been the same for centuries.)*

SECTION

The War and Social Change

1941–1945: AMERICANS MIGRATE

Moving
Many families moved to cities for freedom from prejudice and for economic opportunity.

BETWEEN 1941 AND 1945, ONE IN EVERY FIVE AMERICANS MOVED FROM ONE AREA OF THE COUNTRY TO ANOTHER. Among them were more than 700,000 African Americans. Since the end of Reconstruction, African Americans had faced grueling hardships. As the economy boomed during the war, many African Americans sought opportunities outside the South. Most hoped to escape grueling working hours, poverty, and demeaning segregation. Sybil Lewis was one of these Americans. This is what she said about leaving Oklahoma and heading west:

I had always been told that California was a liberal state and there was no segregation there. "Go west," that was the theme. "Everything is great in California, all doors are open, no prejudice, good jobs, plenty of money." . . . When I arrived, though, I found it wasn't quite the way I had imagined. . . .

In many ways California was no different from Oklahoma or the South, because people brought their feelings with them.
—As told to Mark Jonathan Harris, Franklin D. Mitchell, and Steven J. Schechter, *The Homefront*, 1984

AS YOU READ

Vocabulary
▶ migration
▶ deficit spending

Think About . . .
▶ the population shifts in the United States during World War II and the relationship between mobility, overcrowding, and social stress.

▶ the origins and effects of some of the social problems that surfaced during the war years.
▶ the status of New Deal social programs during the war.

534 CHAPTER 16 THE HOME FRONT

Section 2 Resources

REPRODUCIBLE RESOURCES
📁 Lesson Plan 16-2
📁 Vocabulary and Guided Reading Activity 16-2
📁 Section 2 Quiz

MULTIMEDIA RESOURCES
📽 Section Focus Transparency 50
📽 U.S. History and Art Transparency 25
💿 Student Self-Test: A Software Review

🖥 Testmaker
🎧 Chapter 16 Digest Audiocassette

Americans on the Move
A Population Reshuffled

When more than 15 million Americans left civilian jobs to join the military, African Americans and whites who remained at home sought jobs that opened up in shipyards, aircraft plants, munitions factories, and military bases. This reshuffling made up the greatest short-term **migration,** or movement, of people in American history.

In general, Americans migrated from rural areas to urban areas, from the East to the West, and from the North to the South. The largest gains were in the Far West, which included California, Washington, and Oregon. Much of the wartime shipbuilding and airplane manufacturing took place there. More than 1.4 million Americans migrated to California alone. Next in population gain were Texas and the three South Atlantic states of Maryland, Florida, and Virginia.

Other areas of the country also grew. Big war contracts went to the auto manufacturers of Detroit and the arms manufacturers of New England. New arsenals, new steel and other metal plants, and new military bases sprang up in both rural and urban areas.

The movement of Americans from farms to cities reflected both the wartime demand for workers and the changes in American agriculture. Between 1940 and 1945, the number of farm workers fell by 11 percent while farm output increased by more than 15 percent. By using more fertilizer and more machinery and by consolidating small farms into larger ones, fewer farmers were able to grow more crops.

It seemed that almost everyone in the United States was moving. Migrants drove their cars until the tires were worn smooth. Others stood on crowded trains and buses. Young wives with babies joined their husbands at defense jobs or in army camps. Old men and young boys went west and south for jobs.

African Americans made up a large part of this migrating stream. In areas where the most wartime

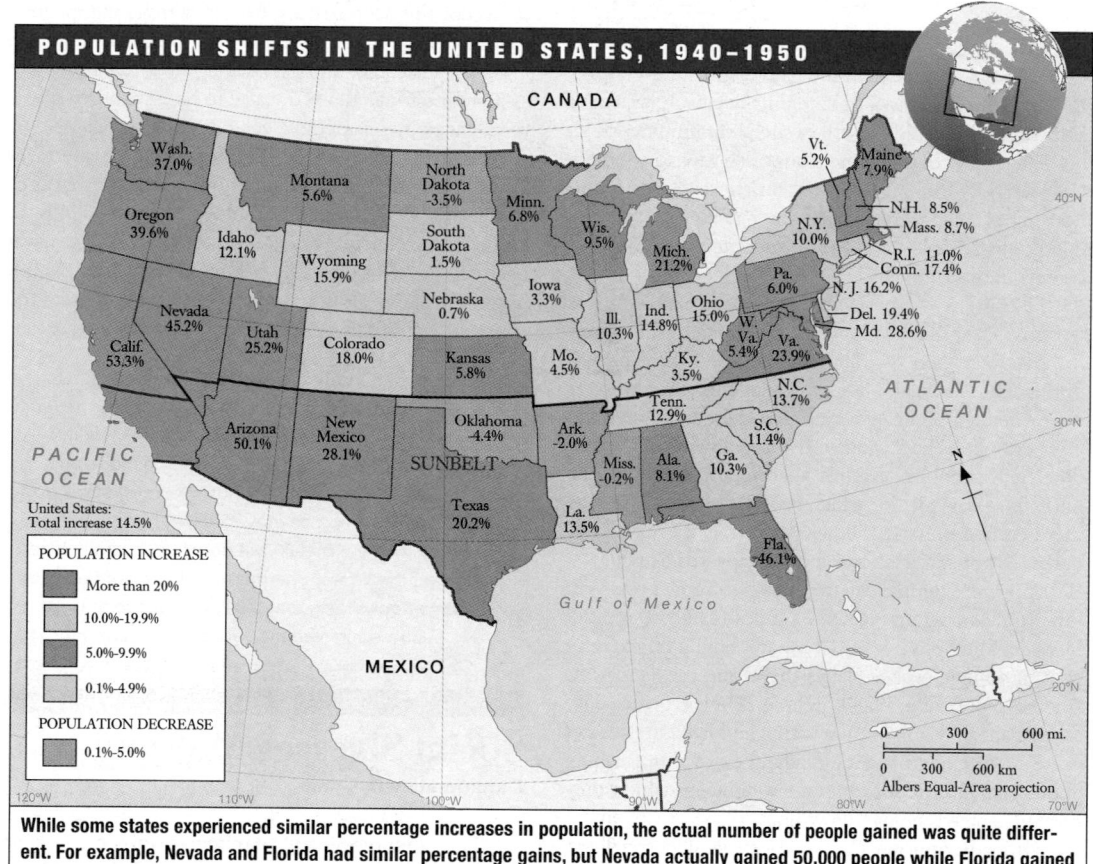

POPULATION SHIFTS IN THE UNITED STATES, 1940–1950

Wash. 37.0%
Oregon 39.6%
Idaho 12.1%
Montana 5.6%
North Dakota -3.5%
Minn. 6.8%
Wis. 9.5%
Mich. 21.2%
Vt. 5.2%
Maine 7.9%
N.H. 8.5%
Mass. 8.7%
N.Y. 10.0%
R.I. 11.0%
Conn. 17.4%
N.J. 16.2%
Pa. 6.0%
South Dakota 1.5%
Wyoming 15.9%
Nevada 45.2%
Utah 25.2%
Colorado 18.0%
Nebraska 0.7%
Iowa 3.3%
Ill. 10.3%
Ind. 14.8%
Ohio 15.0%
W. Va. 5.4%
Del. 19.4%
Md. 28.6%
Calif. 53.3%
Kansas 5.8%
Mo. 4.5%
Ky. 3.5%
Va. 23.9%
N.C. 13.7%
Arizona 50.1%
New Mexico 28.1%
Oklahoma -4.4%
Ark. -2.0%
Tenn. 12.9%
S.C. 11.4%
Ga. 10.3%
Miss. -0.2%
Ala. 8.1%
SUNBELT
Texas 20.2%
La. 13.5%
Fla. 46.1%
CANADA
ATLANTIC OCEAN
PACIFIC OCEAN
Gulf of Mexico
MEXICO

United States: Total increase 14.5%

POPULATION INCREASE
More than 20%
10.0%–19.9%
5.0%–9.9%
0.1%–4.9%
POPULATION DECREASE
0.1%–5.0%

0   300   600 mi.
0   300   600 km
Albers Equal-Area projection

While some states experienced similar percentage increases in population, the actual number of people gained was quite different. For example, Nevada and Florida had similar percentage gains, but Nevada actually gained 50,000 people while Florida gained 874,000 people. *Which states experienced actual population losses?*

Cooperative Learning

Effects of Mobility Organize the class into small groups. Have each group conduct a panel discussion on the topic of mobility and its effects on a population. Encourage students to consider both the positive and negative effects, as well as the values implied by those who move. For example, while the intermingling of cultures may foster understanding, it also may cause overcrowding and racial tensions; but while family and cultural traditions may be disrupted in a new locale, there also may be an implied faith in a better future.

TEACH

Guided Practice

L2 Using an Analogy
Discuss this scenario: Four high schools from different parts of a city have to merge into one school. Ask: What problems might occur? How can this scenario illuminate problems associated with wartime population moves? *(Students may say there would be trouble because people would not know each other.)*

Independent Practice

L2 Geography Themes
Have students identify the geography theme that is most exemplified in Section 2 and give examples to support their choice.

Have students complete the Chapter 16, Section 2 Vocabulary and Guided Reading Activity. (Also in Spanish.) **LEP**

MAP STUDY

Have students write one or more sentences describing the general changes in population for the main areas of the country. *(The South and West grew. The North and Midwest diminished in importance.)*

Answer: *Oklahoma, North Dakota, Arkansas, Mississippi*

FYI

Social Concerns of the First Lady Realizing the strains and changes that women working during wartime would be experiencing, Eleanor Roosevelt was the driving force behind the Community Facilities Act, later called the Lanham Act. Under its provisions, the first government-sponsored child-care center was established in the summer of 1942.

Global Connection

Looking ahead to the task of rebuilding Europe after the war, England and the United States set up the International Monetary Fund and the International Bank for Reconstruction and Development. As Averell Harriman, ambassador to Russia, stated in early 1944, "Economic assistance is one of the most effective weapons at our disposal to influence European political events in the direction we desire. . . ."

---

production took place, the African American population almost doubled. In contrast to other groups who stayed only temporarily, African Americans tended to remain in their new homes.

One of the most congested areas was Mobile, Alabama. From 1940 to 1943, Mobile's population climbed by 61 percent. The novelist John Dos Passos described the impact of this massive population growth on Mobile:

> Sidewalks are crowded. Gutters are stacked with litter that drifts back and forth in the brisk spring wind. . . . Cues [lines] wait outside of movies and lunchrooms. The trailer army has filled all the open lots with its regular ranks. In cluttered backyards people camp out in tents and chickenhouses and shelters tacked together out of packingcases.
> —John Dos Passos, *State of the Nation*, 1944

Boomtowns Emerge
Coping with Overcrowding

Many migrants headed for large industrial cities. Others went to the small towns that grew into boomtowns in the shadows of smoking defense plants and shipyards. The rapid growth of such communities overburdened services that Americans often took for granted. New arrivals looking for work in these places found housing scarce, medical facilities inadequate, sanitary conditions terrible, schools overcrowded, and day-care centers almost nonexistent.

Housing was a problem for almost all migrant war workers. The National Housing Agency figured that it had to house 9 million migrating workers and their families during the war years. Thus, lodgings for new workers were often temporary—barracks, trailers, and even tents.

Schools lacked money, teachers, and equipment. One high school in Mobile accommodated twice the number of students for which it was designed. Teachers there earned only $1,150 per year while a typist could make $1,440 and a laborer in the shipyards $2,600.

A prime example of a troubled boomtown was Willow Run, Michigan, located 27 miles (43.4 km) west of Detroit. The Ford Motor Company built a huge factory to produce bomber planes there, and the factory attracted more than 32,000 people. They crowded into small trailers, drank impure water, and lived in dread of a fire or an epidemic. Eventually, the government built about 10,000 units of temporary housing, which only partially solved the overcrowding.

Other boomtowns experienced similar problems, though on a smaller scale. Pascagoula, Mississippi, a small town with a fine shipyard, nearly quadrupled its

Race Riots An explosion showers burning gasoline on a passenger-packed trolley car during the Detroit race riots of **June 21, 1943.** *What conditions contributed to the race riots of 1943?*

population during the war. Older residents often refused to accept the new arrivals. Recent arrivals complained that they were made to feel inferior because they lived in trailers instead of houses. Lacking an adequate sewage system, the town allowed waste to be discharged into a river, causing considerable ecological damage.

San Diego, California, was once a quiet waterfront town, but an aircraft factory there grew from a workforce of 6 in the 1930s to more than 50,000 in the 1940s. In addition, San Diego was the home of the largest naval base on the West Coast as well as a thriving shipbuilding center. One longtime resident remembered the changes brought about by this population increase:

> We used to go to bed by ten, or anyway, by eleven. Now some theaters and cafes never close! I remember it was like that in the Klondike. Now when boatloads of sailors hurry ashore, and all those soldiers from Fort Rosecrans and Camp Callan swarm in on payday, this town goes crazy. In one day they eat 50,000 hot dogs! Even shoe shine boys get the jitters. Sherman's Cafe has ten bars, and a dance floor so big that 5,000 can dance at once.
> —Quoted in *National Geographic*, January 1942

Social Stresses Multiply
Communities in Crisis

The rapid movement of migrants into new regions and cities created severe social stresses. Native residents of cities such as Los Angeles, San Diego, and Detroit

---

Meeting Special Needs

Reading Disability Help students with reading disabilities talk about some of the events described in the text, such as the Detroit riots, as they might be described in a television news story. Encourage students to use the section heads to identify the main ideas, and remind them to try to answer the questions *who, what, when, where, why,* and *how.* Then have them prepare a brief television news story about the event to present to the class. Stress that their news stories should be factual and should avoid personal opinions.

often resented the newcomers. Midwesterners labeled the migrants from Arkansas, Oklahoma, Tennessee, and Kentucky "hillbillies" and stereotyped them as poor and lazy. Workers in the shipyards and factories discriminated against African Americans who came in search of jobs. The situation was especially tense in Detroit.

Racial Tensions Explode

By 1943 Detroit was home to about half a million migrants, including many Southern whites and 60,000 African Americans. As a result, housing, transportation, and recreational facilities were over-crowded. Most African Americans, both the newly arrived and the native Detroiters, were wedged into an area called Paradise Valley. There, according to the Detroit Housing Commission, more than half the dwellings were substan-dard. Bottled-up racial tensions finally erupted in violence on a hot summer night in June 1943. Pic-nickers, most of them African Americans, were returning home from a Sunday outing when a fight broke out. Nobody remembered why. Apparently some African American teenagers had bumped a white sailor and his girlfriend. Sailors from the navy arsenal nearby joined the fray. As rumors spread of sexual assaults and murders, rioters smashed windows and stoned cars. African American crowds attacked white workers returning from the night shift. The overworked police force, shorthanded because many experienced officers had joined the military, could not control the violence.

The next day, Bloody Mon-day, large crowds of whites roamed up and down Detroit's main street in search of African Americans to beat or kill. Whites dragged African Americans off trolley cars and beat them; police shot looters and battled with rooftop snipers. After a day of violence, the governor of Michigan requested federal assistance. Six thousand soldiers moved into Detroit to control the crowds and restore order. In the 36 hours of rioting, 25 African Americans and 9 whites lost their lives, and nearly 700 people were injured. Also, $2 million worth of property was destroyed.

Zoot Suits Some people objected to the roomy zoot suits because the amount of wool cloth used in men's suits was sup-posed to be rationed after March 1942. *Why did some men wear zoot suits and defy the rule on rationing?*

Discrimination led to other race riots in 1943. African American soldiers, who resented unfair treat-ment, inferior housing, and the brutality of military po-lice, were involved in riots at 9 army training camps, mostly in the South. In August 1943, Harlem exploded when rumors circulated that a white New York City police officer had killed an African American soldier. Unlike the Detroit riot, the Harlem riot did not see pitched battles; however, 5 African Americans were killed and 410 people were injured before the police restored order.

The Zoot Suit Riots

African Americans were not the only minority group involved in violent clashes in the summer of 1943. Op-portunities for farmworkers in the Southwest brought thousands of Mex-icans illegally to the United States. At the same time, many Americans of Mexican descent shifted from agricul-tural work to industrial and manufac-turing jobs. They worked at factories in and around Los Angeles. There, as elsewhere, they suffered discrimination and prejudice. They were segregated from other Americans, insulted by po-lice, and given only the lowest-paying jobs.

In Los Angeles this prejudice turned into hatred of Hispanic Ameri-can teenagers, many of whom wore zoot suits. A zoot suit included a long jacket that reached to the fingertips and had heavily padded shoulders and pleat-ed trousers tightly tapered at the cuffs.

Mexican Americans did not have a monopoly on zoot suits, however. On the whole, zoot-suit-ers were young people seeking es-cape from the burdens of life in the slums. The zoot suit set them apart from the rest of society and served as a badge of independence. In Los Angeles, many of the zoot-suiters were underemployed teenagers, many of whom were caught between two cultures.

For several months, zoot-suiters and white sailors had clashed in Los Angeles. Sailors stationed at the nearby Chavez Ravine Naval Base blamed zoot-suiters for stabbing and robbing military personnel. In June they cruised the Mexican American sections of Los Angeles in cars, beating up people they found wearing zoot suits. Even though the sailors had started the trouble,

SECTION TWO **537**

 Curriculum Connection

Civics Ask students to identify the civil rights (rights that belong to all citizens) that were violat-ed during the zoot suit riots. The list should include the rights of zoot-suiters, naval personnel, and others, including the right to security of person and property and the right to be treated fairly by individuals, groups, and the government.

VISUAL INSTRUCTION

Zoot Suits Just as zoot suits were becoming increasingly popular among young Mexican American and African American men, the War Production Board ruled that the wool in men's suits had to be reduced by 26%. Some men defied the ruling and continued wear-ing zoot suits, which became a symbol of ethnic identity and were especially popular with jazz musi-cians.

Answer: *Sharing a distinctive clothing style was a way for men to show unity with others of their ethnic group.*

 History and the Humanities

U.S. History and Art Transparency 25—*The Red Stairway* by Ben Shahn.

Portfolio Project

Comparing Past and Present Ask students to make a list of the major social stresses in the United States today. Have them write a compar-ison showing which modern stresses are the same as those that people at home suffered during World War II and which are different. Give students a chance to share their ideas with others in small groups, and then encourage them to revise their work. Suggest that they label their work with an identifier for the chapter and section. They can then place the compar-isons in their history portfolios. As they learn more history later in the year, they may want to add to the comparisons or revise them.

VISUAL INSTRUCTION

Teens at Work Many teens—including Roy Popp, the boy shown in this photo—worked to fill gaps left by men serving in the war. The nation's first peace-time draft law, initiated in September 1940, required all men aged 21 through 35 to register for military service. When the draft was later extended to men aged 18 through 44, the number of males in the workforce decreased further.

Answer: *Students may answer that teens benefited by getting paid and learning certain work skills, but some dropped out of school and thus may have limited their future job options.*

ASSESS

Meeting Lesson Objectives

Each section objective is tested by the section review question(s) that follows it in parentheses.

1. Describe the population shifts in the United States during World War II, and explain the relationship between mobility, overcrowding, and social stress. (1, 4)

2. Explain the origins and effects of some of the social problems that surfaced during the war years. (2, 5)

3. Evaluate the status of New Deal social programs during the war. (3)

---

the police arrested only the zoot-suiters. To end the violence, the city had to be declared off-limits to naval personnel. When the city council outlawed zoot suits, the situation cooled.

The violence in Los Angeles and other cities prompted Philip Murray, president of the Congress of Industrial Organizations (CIO), to write President Roosevelt. He urged the administration to prepare an educational campaign "to eradicate the misconceptions and prejudices" that had contributed to the riots. The President replied in a short note that read in part, "I join you and all true Americans in condemning mob violence, whatever form it takes and whoever its victims."

One idealistic African American student had expected that Roosevelt would stand behind the demands of minorities for fair treatment. After Roosevelt's reply to Murray, she expressed her feelings of hopelessness in this poem entitled "Mr. Roosevelt Regrets."

> What'd you get, black boy,
>   When they knocked you down in the gutter,
> And they kicked your teeth out,
> And they broke your skull with clubs,
> And they bashed your stomach in?
> What'd you get when the police
>   shot you in the back,
> And they chained you to the beds
> While they wiped the blood off?
> What'd you get when you cried
>   out to the Top Man?
> When you called the man next to God,
>   as you thought,
> And you asked him to speak out to save you?
> What'd the Top Man say, black boy?
> Mr. Roosevelt regrets. . . .
> —Pauli Murray, as printed in *The Crisis*, August 1943

Wartime Family Stresses
Children on Their Own

Other stresses caused by the war itself fell on both whites and African Americans. As families migrated, children and adolescents were moved from familiar neighborhoods to strange surroundings. Men and women worked long hours of overtime at their defense jobs, sometimes leaving children unattended. Single-parent families became common as men went into the armed forces, leaving their wives and children behind.

As more mothers of young children took jobs, newspapers and magazines complained about "latchkey children" and "eight-hour orphans." Agnes Meyer, the wife of the publisher of the *Washington Post*, traveled around

the country investigating social conditions in boom-towns. She wrote:

> In the San Fernando Valley, in the city limits of Los Angeles, where several war plants are located, a social worker counted 45 infants locked in cars of a single parking space [lot]. In Vallejo, the children sit in the movies, seeing the same film over and over again until mother comes off the swing shift and picks them up. Some children of working parents are locked in their homes, others locked out.
> —Agnes E. Meyer, *Journey Through Chaos*, 1943

Teenagers were often left to care for themselves. Unlike younger children, they could get jobs. From 1940 to 1944, the number of teenage workers nearly tripled to 2.9 million. More than 1 million teenagers dropped out of school. Although child labor laws governed the kind of work they did and the number of hours they could work, these laws were often ignored. Because of the widespread disregard for these laws, 19 states extended the number of hours teenagers could work.

With teenagers left to fend for themselves in society, it was not surprising that juvenile delinquency increased. During the war years, a widely viewed documentary film, *Youth in Crisis*, aroused public concern. The film described how adolescents, abandoned by their parents and subjected to wartime stress, picked up a "spirit of recklessness and violence." To help curb rising juvenile delinquency, some communities enforced curfews.

Teens at Work This 16-year-old worked on a transport plane's fuselage on an assembly line at a West Coast aircraft plant. *What advantages and disadvantages might working teens have experienced?*

Extending the Content

Riots and Freedom of Speech The United States Constitution guarantees everyone the right to assemble in peace, to petition the government for grievances, and to express dissent, or disagreement, as an individual or in a group. This dissent may take the form of a demonstration where public policy is being protested. If disruption of order occurs, however, accompanied by violence that injures others or causes property damage, then the action is called a riot. Riots are illegal in all states of the United States, although the precise definition of a riot varies from place to place.

A Fourth Win Citizens visit Roosevelt after his reelection. *Why do you think Roosevelt was reelected?*

Even though the war caused new problems for American children, many later remembered this period as the most exciting time of their lives. Memories include collecting scrap, watching war movies in which the "good guys" always won, and being intensely interested in news of the war.

The End of the New Deal
Military Objectives Take Over

In December 1943, President Roosevelt announced that "Dr. New Deal" had outlived his usefulness and would have to make way for "Dr. Win-the-War." This was simply a way of saying that military objectives needed to take priority over social reform. Many of the New Deal programs, such as Social Security, unemployment compensation, old-age benefits, and the Tennessee Valley Authority (TVA), however, had become, and would remain, a permanent part of American life. Even the generally conservative Republican party had, by 1944, incorporated most New Deal programs into its platform.

Both liberals and conservatives, however, agreed with the President that they should shelve any reforms that could interfere with war production. For example, bringing electricity to rural areas had to be postponed since copper wire was needed for military purposes. The workweek was lengthened from 40 to 48 hours in order to boost industrial output. Many antitrust prosecutions were suspended to avoid interfering with efficiently run businesses. Child labor laws were changed to permit teenagers to join the labor force. "Progressives should understand that programs which do not forward

the war must be given up or drastically curtailed," wrote David Lilienthal, head of the TVA.

The war made it possible to phase out a number of New Deal agencies. These included the Civilian Conservation Corps, the Works Progress Administration, and the National Youth Administration. Congress had created these agencies to ease unemployment. With full employment during the war, they were no longer needed.

World War II, however, extended the New Deal in some respects by continuing the role of government in economic planning. Wartime economic growth convinced many people that government spending could ensure full employment and prosperity. In the future the government would resort to **deficit spending**, using borrowed money, to counteract economic downturns.

The war also made possible the election of Franklin D. Roosevelt to an unprecedented fourth term as President in 1944. His margin of victory over Republican Thomas E. Dewey, however, was the narrowest in all of his four campaigns.

Americans on the home front suffered from housing shortages, overcrowding, a breakdown of law and order, and juvenile delinquency during the war years. At the same time, most people reaped the financial rewards of a wartime, full-employment economy. Although minority groups did not yet enjoy many benefits, the war did provide new opportunities in employment and enabled them to make some headway in their struggle for civil rights. Some of the New Deal reform measures had to be set aside during the war but were not forgotten. They would be taken up again when the war ended.

SECTION REVIEW

Vocabulary
1. Define: migration, deficit spending.

Checking Facts
2. What were the origins of some of the social problems that came about during the war years?

3. What effect did the war have on New Deal agencies and reforms?

Critical Thinking
Synthesizing Information
4. How did the migration of Americans during the war affect industrial cities in the short and long run?

Linking Across Time
5. Compare the problems of working mothers during the war with those of today's working mothers.

VISUAL INSTRUCTION

A Fourth Win The town supervisor of Hyde Park, New York, is shown with his son as they congratulate President Franklin Roosevelt on his reelection. They marched with other citizens in a victory torchlight parade to the President's home.

Answer: *Answers will vary. Voters may have wanted to maintain a stability of leadership during the war.*

Evaluate
Have students complete the Section Review.

📀 Assign the Section 2 Quiz or use the Testmaker to develop a customized quiz. (Also in Spanish.) **LEP**

Reteach
🎧 Have students listen to the Chapter 16, Section 2 Audiocassette. (Also in Spanish.) **LEP**

Enrich
Have interested students prepare a report on the status of deficit spending today and present their report to the class.

CLOSE

Ask students to write a one-sentence summary for each main head in this section. Then write some of the sentences on the chalkboard, and challenge the class to fill in supporting details. *(Answers will vary. For example, during the war, millions of Americans moved either to join the military or to find work or improved conditions at home.)*

Section 2 Review Answers

1. migration (535), **deficit spending** (539)
2. mobility, overcrowding, lack of housing, antagonism between old and new residents, pressures on families due to work schedules
3. Some programs, such as the CCC, were discontinued. Others, such as Social Security, were left in place.

4. Students may say that in the short run, industrial cities suffered problems from rapid population growth; today some areas have improved, but run-down areas still remain.
5. Students may state that there is more day care available now, but working mothers often do most or all of the child rearing.

539

Geography: Impact on History

TEACH

Making the Geography Connection

The movement of industrial workers during World War II dramatically changed the social and economic landscape of the U.S. People traveled and moved to parts of the country they had never seen, and worked side by side with people of different races and genders. Housing, schools, retail stores, places of worship, and systems of transportation and communication expanded to meet the influx of new workers.

Mapping Activity

Have students examine the railroad tracks and describe the routes that led to and from the various industries. Encourage them to infer why there was a route going to and from the hills. *(possibly for lumber)*

MAP STUDY

Point out the hillside and swamp areas, and discuss why there might be no businesses or residences there at this time.

Answer: *Other industries shown on the map are oil refining, motor vehicle assembly, and rail transportation.*

PLACE

Richmond, California: A War Boomtown

Located in California on San Francisco Bay, Richmond was transformed almost overnight during World War II. Between 1940 and 1943, Richmond's population grew nearly 400 percent, from 23,642 to 93,738. Like other suburban towns in California, Richmond had large tracts of undeveloped land, a major rail line, and a deepwater harbor—a perfect mixture for shipbuilding.

Kaiser's Role in Richmond

After being awarded major contracts to build Liberty ships, huge merchant ships used to supply troops with jeeps, tanks, and rations, industrialist Henry J. Kaiser located four of his shipyards in Richmond. Resolved to beat his deadlines and to lower his costs, he applied mass-production methods to his shipbuilding operations. Like other industrialists, however, Kaiser soon faced a severe shortage of workers.

To attract and keep good workers, Kaiser raised his wages to some of the highest in the country, instituted a company health plan, and—prompted by First Lady Eleanor Roosevelt—organized one of the first day-care centers for children of working women.

Kaiser's efforts paid off. At their peak, his Richmond shipyards employed more than 90,000 workers, including significant numbers of whites and African Americans from the South, Chinese Americans, Native Americans, women, and teenagers. Although only 240 African Americans called Richmond home in 1940, more than 10,000 worked at Kaiser's shipyards there during the war. Kaiser's employees succeeded in transforming the nation's entire shipbuilding industry, and their accomplishments earned Kaiser the nickname "Sir Launchalot."

RICHMOND, CALIFORNIA, 1943

San Pablo Bay

San Pablo

North Richmond

San Francisco Bay

Oil Refineries

Richmond

El Cerrito

Shipyard No. 1

Shipyard No. 4

Ford Motor Co.

Shipyard No. 2

Shipyard No. 3

Richmond Inner Harbor

37°55'N

- - - - - - Old coastline
———— Street
———— New street
– ∙ – ∙ – City boundary
+–+–+ Railroad

■ War housing
■ Shipyards
▣ Swamp
■ Other residential
■ Industry
■ Hillsides

0   1   2 mi.
0   1   2 km
Polyconic projection

N

122°25'W   122°20'W

Wartime housing was constructed as close as possible to the shipyards. *What industries other than shipbuilding are indicated on the map?*

Geographic Themes

Movement In general, people who migrated during the war moved from rural to urban areas, from East to West, and from North to South. In what ways did the wartime migration differ from the arrival of early colonists or the great westward expansion in the United States of the 1800s?

Social Strains

Richmond's rapid growth strained social relations. The first migrants, or "newcomers," often arrived to find public housing in short supply. Racial quotas limited any available public housing slots, forcing most African Americans to live in overcrowded rooming houses in the segregated part of Richmond.

Longtime residents, or "old-timers," resented the presence of the newcomers, many of whom lived in tents, cars, and homemade shanties because of the lack of housing. In the workplace, union leaders, most of whom were old-timers, pressured the newcomers to join their unions. Unions then restricted these new members from skilled-job classes, thus preserving the best-paying jobs for the old-timers. African Americans and women faced extra burdens in the workplace. Often employers tried to keep them in menial, low-paying jobs, and coworkers regularly harassed them. At first many unions also tried to exclude them from their ranks. As the war neared its end, African Americans, women, and other newcomers were usually the first ones to be laid off.

The Boomtown Legacy

The wartime boom permanently changed Richmond. After the war many migrant workers remained and settled there. By 1950 Richmond's population had stabilized at about 100,000 people—compared to about 24,000 in 1940. It now housed a greater diversity of

COURTESY OF THE BANCROFT LIBRARY, KAISER PICTORIAL COLLECTION

Richmond Shipyard No. 2 Celebrates Hundreds of Kaiser workers gather for the launch of the Liberty ship *Robert E. Peary*—built in a record-breaking 4 days, 15 hours, and 29 minutes. *Where did many of these workers live?*

people than ever before. Before the war, for example, African Americans made up only about 1 percent of Richmond's population. By 1950 more than 13 percent of the city's residents were African American.

As urban areas like Richmond became more diverse, outer suburbs expanded, largely due to "white flight." Developers quickly built subdivisions and tract housing in response. Although many African Americans also desired to live in these suburbs, discrimination by real estate brokers and others limited their opportunities.

Boomtowns also contributed to a lasting shift in the relationships of work, community, and home in the United States. More and more Americans now lived in one place,

worked in another, and maintained family roots in yet another part of the country. Changing jobs and homes became more common as people tried to advance in corporate positions.

Ultimately, millions of workers who remained on the home front during World War II, including many African Americans, gained valuable skills and made economic gains. Steady work in boomtowns like Richmond enabled them to support their families, pay off debt incurred during the Great Depression, and save money for new cars and homes. In turn, their new economic wealth and political power would help fuel the vast economic growth and social change of the 1950s and 1960s.

MAKING THE GEOGRAPHIC CONNECTION

1. What geographical features of Richmond made it suitable for shipbuilding?

2. What were some of the social tensions that occurred in Richmond? Describe their causes.

3. **Place** How did the large increase in Richmond's population during World War II have a lasting effect on life there? How did the growing population of Richmond affect the surrounding landscape?

VISUAL INSTRUCTION

Richmond Shipyard No. 2 Celebrates The Richmond shipyards built more than 700 cargo ships during the war.

A few workers lived in public housing, but many had to live in tents, cars, and homemade shanties.

FYI

Henry Kaiser Before setting up his shipbuilding plant at Richmond, Henry Kaiser ran companies that built roads and bridges, levees, and highways. He helped organize the construction of the Hoover, Bonneville, and Grand Coulee dams. During the war, he ran seven shipyards. Workers at his shipyards could build a ship in as little as $4\frac{1}{2}$ days.

CLOSE

Ask: What attracted Americans to boom towns like Richmond? *(the opportunity to find well-paying jobs)* How did the influx of new workers increase the diversity of urban areas? *(Many African Americans sought jobs in boom towns. After the war many of these newcomers remained.)*

Making the Geographic Connection Answers

1. Richmond's large tracts of undeveloped land, major rail line, and deep-water harbor made it suitable for shipbuilding.

2. Long-time residents of Richmond resented these newcomers, who competed for living space. Migrants, particularly African Americans, faced housing shortages caused by racial quotas in housing and segregation. Many migrants lived in homemade dwellings or tents. African Americans and women faced job discrimination. They worked at lower-paying and more menial jobs. Unions tried to exclude African Americans from their ranks. Unions pressured other workers to join their organizations.

3. Many migrant workers settled in Richmond, increasing the community's diversity. Outer suburbs expanded. Developers bought up land and built subdivisions.

541

FOCUS

Section Objectives

1. Define racism and explain how African Americans fought racism during World War II.
2. Identify A. Philip Randolph and explain the purpose and effect of the March on Washington Movement.
3. Describe the violations of Japanese Americans' civil liberties during World War II.

VISUAL INSTRUCTION

Protesting for Fair Employment This man carried on his protest outside a dairy in Chicago.

Ask: Why is job discrimination damaging to individuals? *(It leaves people without enough money to support themselves and contributes to feelings of hopelessness.)*

ABCNEWS INTERACTIVE™

Videodisc

Lessons of War

Side 2, Chapter 8
Title: At the Front
Subject: Contributions of minorities in World War II
Ask: What type of discrimination did minority troops encounter in World War II? *(They fought in segregated units.)*

See Lessons of War Guidebook page 47 for complete lesson plan.

542

SECTION 3

The War and Civil Rights

1941: RACIST HIRING PRACTICES MEET WITH RESISTANCE

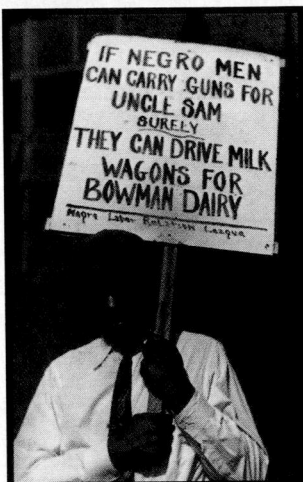

Protesting for Fair Employment This sign reflects one form of racial injustice that occurred during the war.

ALTHOUGH AFRICAN AMERICANS FOUGHT AND DIED FOR THE UNITED STATES IN BOTH WORLD WARS, THEY FACED DISCRIMINATION AS THEY SEARCHED FOR JOBS AT HOME. The hiring policy of North American Aviation, one of the nation's largest aircraft manufacturers, was typical of the discrimination many companies practiced. The president of North American Aviation publicly stated its policy in 1941:

> While we are in complete sympathy with the Negro, it is against company policy to employ them as aircraft workers or mechanics . . . regardless of their training, but there will be some jobs as janitors for Negroes.
> —As quoted by Daniel S. Davis, *Mr. Black Labor,* 1972

Other executives shared this view. As one steel company head said in 1941, "We haven't had a Negro worker in twenty-five years and do not plan to start now."

Civil Rights Movement Grows
Fighting Racism

During World War II, the demands of African Americans for equal treatment grew louder. Many whites as well as African Americans came to recognize the uncomfortable similarity between racial tensions in the United States and Hitler's belief in a superior race. A leading African

AS YOU READ

Vocabulary
► racism
► civil liberties

Think About . . .
► how African Americans fought racism during World War II.
► the purpose and effect of the March on Washington Movement organized by A. Philip Randolph.
► the violations of Japanese Americans' civil liberties during World War II.

542 CHAPTER 16 THE HOME FRONT

Section 3 Resources

REPRODUCIBLE RESOURCES
📁 Lesson Plan 16-3
📁 Vocabulary and Guided Reading Activity 16-3
📁 Section 3 Quiz
📁 Chapter 16 Test
📁 Unit 6 Test
📁 Performance Assessment Activity 16

📁 Reteaching Activity 16
📁 Enrichment Activity 16
📁 Unit 6 American Literature Reading
📁 Geography in History Activity 16
📁 Political Cartoon 27
📁 Supreme Court Case 16

MULTIMEDIA RESOURCES
🔵 Lessons of War
📖 Section Focus Transparency 51
🔵 Landmark Documents in American History
🔵 The American People: Fabric of a Nation
💻 Student Self-Test: A Software Review
💻 Vocabulary PuzzleMaker and Testmaker
🎧 Chapter 16 Digest Audiocassette

American newspaper, the *Amsterdam News,* deplored the "race discrimination and segregation, mob brutality—the entire Nazi pattern of U.S. racial conditions."

Racism is the belief that race determines human capacities and that some races are superior to others. Racism was the basis for the system of segregation and discrimination that existed in law and in fact throughout most of the United States. For many years anthropologists had been challenging the once popular idea that certain races were superior. By the 1940s scholars considered doctrines of racial supremacy to be unscientific and false. The differences that mattered, they said, were not between races but between individuals. Racial traits or characteristics were really a product of environmental influences, they concluded. White Americans who continued to justify segregation felt increasingly uncomfortable with comparisons of discrimination in the United States and Hitler's theories of racial superiority. One Southern politician conceded in 1944 that the Nazis "have wrecked the theories of the master race with which we were so contented so long."

African Americans responded to this heightened awareness of racism with a new militancy. As they moved from the South, where they could not vote, to the North and the West, African Americans began to flex their political muscles. They became more vocal, insisting on opportunities that they had long been denied. Some picketed factories with signs such as: Hitler Must Own This Plant, Negroes Can't Work Here. If We Must Fight, Why Can't We Work?

The African American press pushed a "Double V" campaign—victory at home as well as abroad. They insisted that fighting the war should not diminish the struggle for equality; on the contrary, progress toward equality should help win the war.

Civil Rights Gains
The March on Washington Movement

In the South, African Americans were legally segregated from whites in all public facilities. In much of the rest of the country, trains, buses, restaurants, and movie theaters were segregated, too. Throughout the nation, poverty kept most African Americans confined to slums and ghettos, and those who could afford better housing faced exclusion by homeowners and real estate salespeople in middle-class neighborhoods.

The war led civil rights groups to develop new forms of protest against these injustices. In the summer of 1941, A. Philip Randolph led the movement for African American equality. The son of a minister, he had grown up in the South where the Ku Klux Klan terrorized African Americans to keep them in line. After arriving in New York in 1906 at the age of 17, Randolph attended college at night and worked at various jobs during the day.

Quiet but determined, Randolph became a respected leader of African Americans. By following his goal of "creating unrest among the Negroes," Randolph

AP/WIDE WORLD PHOTOS

Testifying for Civil Rights A. Philip Randolph, on the right, is shown before the Senate Armed Services Committee testifying that millions of African Americans would refuse to register for or to be drafted into the military unless racial segregation and discrimination ended. *How did the war serve to attract attention to the unjust treatment of minority groups?*

Bellringer Activity
While taking attendance at the beginning of the class period, display **Section Focus Transparency 51,** and have students answer the questions. (Or use the blackline master.)

TEACH

Guided Practice
L1 Discussion A. Philip Randolph encouraged African Americans to participate in mass marches, protest rallies, boycotts, and acts of civil disobedience. Have students discuss the effectiveness of these forms of protest and then have them suggest other methods available to citizens who wish to call attention to important issues.

VISUAL INSTRUCTION

Testifying for Civil Rights Even during World War I, Randolph was calling for more positions for African Americans in the United States military and in the war industry. In 1917 he cofounded a magazine, *The Messenger* (known as *Black Worker* after 1929) to promote his goals.

Answer: *It became increasingly obvious that African Americans and other minority groups serving and dying for their country during the war deserved more civil rights at home.*

Cooperative Learning

Debate Ask students to research an African American leader such as Booker T. Washington, Mary McLeod Bethune, W.E.B. Du Bois, Ida B. Wells, Fanny Lou Hamer, Malcolm X, Martin Luther King, Jr., or Jesse Jackson. Have pairs of students role-play a debate between two of these leaders on the following topic: Education is one of the most important tools for winning equality.

Independent Practice

L2 Writing Have students write a letter to President Roosevelt or an editorial to a newspaper from the point of view of an African American experiencing job discrimination during World War II. Ask them to request constructive change and to give reasons why in their letter or editorial.

☛ Have students complete the Chapter 16, Section 3 Vocabulary and Guided Reading Activity. (Also in Spanish.) **LEP**

CHART STUDY

Point out to students that the losses in job distribution for African Americans between 1940 and 1944 took place in these categories: agriculture; business, repair, and recreation; construction; and domestic services. Ask students if they think that the lower percentages in those categories indicate that most African Americans serving in the war left jobs in those categories to do so.

Answer: *domestic services*

---

eventually became known as the Father of the Civil Rights Movement.

Randolph's leadership qualities first surfaced in 1925 when he led a movement to organize the porters who worked on the sleeping cars of the nation's trains. The Brotherhood of Sleeping Car Porters, which Randolph organized, worked to obtain higher wages and better working conditions for its members. New Deal reforms before the war, such as the Wagner Act, helped the organization win its fight to bargain as a union.

By May 1941, Randolph had turned his energies to battles in the national political arena. He was appalled by discrimination in the armed forces, in which African Americans had already fought for their country during World War I. The exclusion of African Americans from well-paying jobs in war industries to which billions of federal dollars were flowing also angered him. To help right these wrongs, Randolph organized a March on Washington Movement (MOWM). Supporters rallied behind the slogan: We loyal American citizens demand the right to work and fight for our country.

Randolph's approach differed from the mainstream civil rights organization of the time, the National Association for the Advancement of Colored People (NAACP). The NAACP, the largest organization fighting for equal treatment for African Americans, urged African Americans to "persuade, embarrass, compel and shame our government and our nation" to end discrimination. In contrast to the NAACP, Randolph called for direct action, a "thundering march" on Washington rather than

African American Jobs: 1940, 1944		
Occupation	Percentage of Workforce	
	1940	1944
Agriculture	32.1%	21%
Business, repair, and recreation	1.5%	1.2%
Construction	2.5%	1.9%
Domestic services	36.5%	29.3%
Government	1.2%	3.5%
Manufacturing	9.5%	18.3%
Mining	0.9%	2.1%
Professional services	4.3%	5.3%
Trade and finance	8.1%	11.9%
Transportation and utilities	3.4%	5.5%

African Americans experienced both gains and losses in nonagricultural jobs during World War II. *Despite the gains, what field continued to account for the highest percentage of African American workers?*

the use of cumbersome political and legal processes. In addition, Randolph demanded changes that would benefit Northern urban African Americans as well as those living in the South. Finally, he excluded white people from the MOWM because he maintained that the victims of discrimination must assume responsibility for abolishing it. "No one will fight as hard to remove and relieve pain as he who suffers from it," Randolph counseled.

Roosevelt and Randolph Compromise

As preparations for the March on Washington moved ahead, government officials began to worry. Roosevelt wanted to prevent the march, which would embarrass the government. He was also afraid that a march that brought 50,000 to 100,000 people to Washington might end in violence. The President sent his wife, Eleanor, as well as government officials, to persuade Randolph to call off the march. To show his sympathy, Roosevelt publicly condemned job discrimination and ordered his defense chiefs to do something about it.

When Randolph refused to call off the march, Roosevelt finally met with him. Randolph demanded three key changes in government policy, all of which an executive order of the President could bring about. First, he wanted defense contracts denied to employers who practiced discrimination. Next, he asked that job segregation in federal agencies be abolished. Finally, he asked for the desegregation of the armed forces.

Randolph did not get all he demanded, but his threat of a mass demonstration in the nation's capital marked a real breakthrough in equal treatment and opportunities for African Americans. Roosevelt's Executive Order 8802, issued on June 25, 1941, stipulated that government agencies, job training programs, and defense contractors put an end to discrimination. It also created the Fair Employment Practices Committee (FEPC) to investigate violations of the order. The President, however, did not agree to integrate the armed forces.

As Randolph canceled the march, African American leaders hailed the executive order as a major step forward. The MOWM, however, did not disband. Randolph continued to urge mass marches and protest rallies to focus attention on discrimination. He also encouraged boycotts of segregated facilities and acts of civil disobedience to show nonviolent opposition to government laws or policies. African American protesters willingly accepted punishment for such illegal actions.

Other Victories

Encouraged by Randolph's success in protesting discrimination, other African American civil rights leaders organized the Congress of Racial Equality (CORE) in 1942. CORE continued the strategy of mobilizing mass resistance to discrimination and employed acts of

---

Meeting Special Needs

Reading Disability Have students with reading comprehension problems skim the section and use the section heads and subheads to create an outline. Have them also preview the visuals before they begin reading the section.

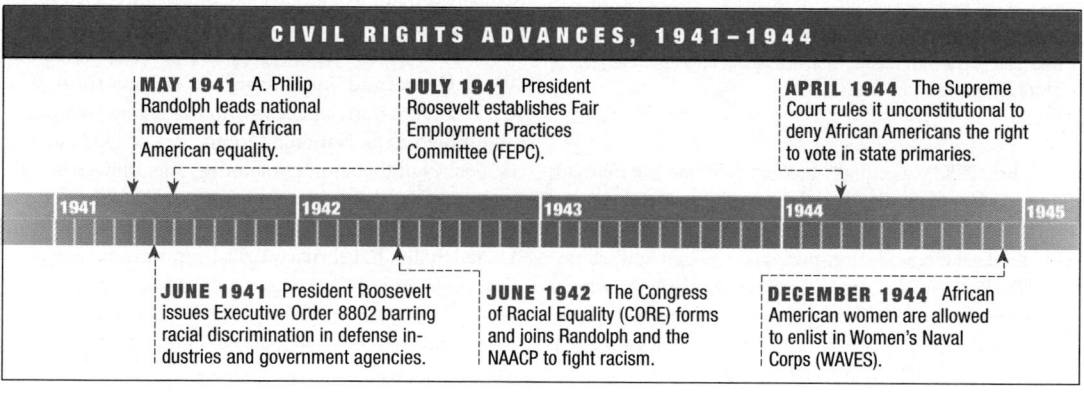

UPI/BETTMANN

Meanwhile, the membership of the NAACP grew. By 1946 it had risen to 450,000, almost 10 times the membership in 1940. The NAACP continued to rely on traditional, noncontroversial means of protesting, such as education, political pressure, and legal action. The organization won an important victory in 1944 when the Supreme Court ruled that it was unconstitutional to bar African Americans from voting in Democratic primaries in eight Southern states. In *Smith* v. *Allwright,* the Court held that political parties were agents of the state and they could not nullify the right to vote by practicing racial discrimination.

The FEPC Fights Discrimination
Obstacles to Success

Through the efforts of the NAACP, CORE, and MOWM, but mainly due to the critical labor shortage during the war, the share of jobs African Americans held in war industries grew. In addition, the FEPC helped open up some jobs in the federal government for African Americans and Hispanic Americans.

The FEPC faced major obstacles, however, in battling racial discrimination. The committee could act only on formal complaints about hiring practices or discrimination on the job, but many people were afraid to file complaints. Moreover, the committee's authority was severely limited. The FEPC was given no power to enforce its orders but had to rely on support from other federal agencies. For example, the only action the FEPC could take against defense contractors who discriminated against minorities was to recommend that their government contracts be canceled. Because canceling defense contracts would jeopardize military production, however, the cancellation was unlikely to occur.

Skilled Labor Some African Americans held skilled-labor jobs during the war, while others were excluded. *How did African Americans work to lessen discriminatory labor practices?*

nonviolent civil disobedience such as sit-ins at movie theaters and restaurants. Through the use of such tactics, shunned by more conservative organizations, CORE helped end segregation in public accommodations in several Northern cities.

CIVIL RIGHTS ADVANCES, 1941–1944

MAY 1941 A. Philip Randolph leads national movement for African American equality.

JULY 1941 President Roosevelt establishes Fair Employment Practices Committee (FEPC).

APRIL 1944 The Supreme Court rules it unconstitutional to deny African Americans the right to vote in state primaries.

1941   1942   1943   1944   1945

JUNE 1941 President Roosevelt issues Executive Order 8802 barring racial discrimination in defense industries and government agencies.

JUNE 1942 The Congress of Racial Equality (CORE) forms and joins Randolph and the NAACP to fight racism.

DECEMBER 1944 African American women are allowed to enlist in Women's Naval Corps (WAVES).

SECTION THREE   **545**

Portfolio Project

Time Lines Have students skim the section looking for important dates. Ask them to create a Chapter 16, Section 3 time line and add it to the other time lines in their portfolios.

Facts on File

Landmark Documents in American History Have students review "Executive Order 9066 (Japanese Relocation Order, 1942)" and *Korematsu* v. *United States* (1944) and write a paragraph about the intent of one of the documents.

Videodisc

GTV: The American People: Fabric of a Nation

Side 4, Chapter 2
Title: United We Stand?
Subject: Japanese internment during World War II
Ask: Why were Japanese Americans interned during World War II? (*The government feared sabotage.*)

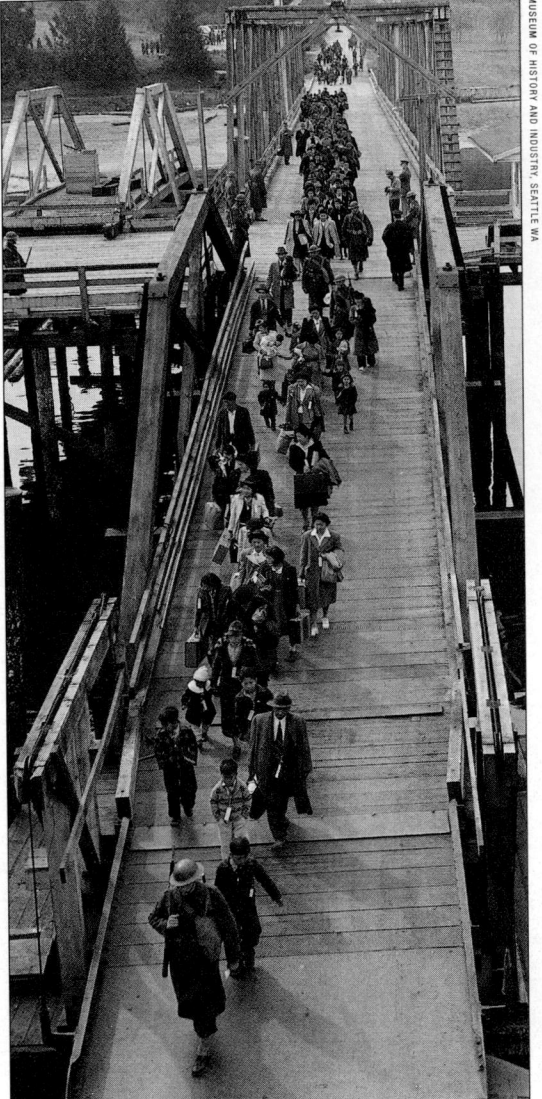

Internment On March 30, 1942, Japanese American evacuees are led from their homes on Bainbridge Island, Washington. According to regulations, they are taking only what they can carry with them. *What does the armed escort suggest about the nature of the relocation?*

MUSEUM OF HISTORY AND INDUSTRY, SEATTLE WA

The FEPC was equally ineffective when the railroad unions ignored its order to end discrimination. Other government agencies reasoned that the United States could not afford a nationwide transportation walkout in wartime.

The committee also fought public opinion, which was prejudiced against it. Members of Congress, especially Southern Democrats, claimed the agency fostered racial discord and saw it as a first step toward commu-

nism. The FEPC withstood a congressional investigation, but it had to fight with Congress for every scarce dollar that it received.

Far from being a radical organization, the FEPC was led by moderates who moved slowly and cautiously. Significantly, the FEPC did not consider segregation, as opposed to discrimination, a cause for action. In several instances, the FEPC approved the creation of separate facilities for African American and white workers.

In all, the FEPC received 8,000 complaints, only one-third of which were resolved successfully. More often than not, employers defied its directives. In the summer of 1945, just before the war ended, Congress slashed the FEPC's budget in half and shortly thereafter dissolved the agency.

Internment of Japanese Americans
Fear Leads to Relocation

Generally, World War II brought about few restrictions on **civil liberties,** or rights guaranteed to all citizens. Almost no one vocally opposed the war after Pearl Harbor, and little danger existed of an attack on the United States. As a result, there was not a repetition of the hysteria and pressure to conform that had occurred during World War I. Most Americans showed tolerance toward persons of foreign ancestry, including citizens of German and Italian descent. The treatment of Japanese Americans, however, became the exception.

Relocation

Spring 1942 brought events that are burned into the memories of Japanese Americans. Even though they showed no evidence of disloyalty, more than 100,000 Japanese Americans were moved from their homes to relocation camps. One evacuee, Helen Murao, explained why. "We looked like them [the enemy]. That was our sin."

Of the 110,000 Japanese Americans who lived on the West Coast and in Hawaii, about one-third were Issei—foreign-born Japanese who had entered the United States before the National Origins Act of 1924 had dramatically cut the number of immigrants allowed into the country. Two-thirds were Nisei—mainly children of Issei who were citizens because they had been born in the United States. In February 1942, the government decided that all Japanese Americans, citizens as well as aliens, would be relocated from their homes and confined in internment camps located in Arkansas and the Western states.

Extending the Content

The Internment Experience The Japanese Americans arrived at control centers where each family was given a number. Family members had to put tags with that number on themselves and their few possessions. Next they went to assembly centers where they were housed in terrible conditions—at stockyards, fairgrounds, and racetracks. After that they were sorted onto

trains that took them to 10 separate internment camps in isolated areas of Utah, Arizona, Colorado, Arkansas, Idaho, California, and Wyoming. They lived in barracks with an army cot and a blanket for each person. Barbed wire fences with guard towers constantly reminded the displaced Japanese Americans that they were no longer free.

Japanese Americans were vulnerable because they could easily be singled out and they lacked political power. In addition, they had little economic influence.

Popular sentiment against Japanese Americans on the West Coast grew intense after the bombing of Pearl Harbor. The *San Francisco Chronicle* pushed to have Japanese Americans interned. Individuals, including Earl Warren, attorney general of California, (later chief justice of the United States), and several members of Congress, supported relocating Japanese Americans. Finally, on February 19, 1942, President Roosevelt signed Executive Order 9066 authorizing the removal of Japanese Americans from the West Coast.

Economic Hardship

The executive order subjected Japanese Americans to extreme economic hardship. Because they were permitted to take only a few belongings with them to the camps, they were forced to sell most of their possessions. Bargain hunters descended on their farms and businesses to take advantage of the evacuees. Signs began to appear reading Evacuation Sale—Furniture Must All Be Sold. In the end most Japanese American families received about 5 cents for every dollar's worth of their possessions. Property not immediately sold was either stored or left with friends. Much of this was stolen, vandalized, or sold through legal loopholes. Even more devastating was the loss of farms, houses, and places of business. Estimates of this loss hover around $500 million.

Over the course of several months, the Japanese Americans were ordered to report to relocation centers. The military justified this action on the basis that Japanese Americans would commit sabotage to aid Japan in an attack on the West Coast. General John DeWitt, head of the Western Defense Command argued: "The very fact that no sabotage to aid Japan has taken place to date is a disturbing and confirming indication that such action will be taken."

Other motives were equally important. Farmers and business associations thought they would gain from eliminating Japanese American competitors. Politicians believed they would increase their popular support by favoring relocation. General DeWitt expressed the commonly held view, "the Japanese race is an enemy race."

Life in the Camps

From the relocation centers, Japanese Americans were moved to 1 of 10 armed and guarded internment camps located in sparsely settled areas. For example, Topaz, a camp in Utah, was 4,600 feet (1,402.08 m) above sea level. Here inmates endured temperatures ranging from 106° F (41.1° C) in summer to −30° F (−34.5° C) in winter. They also lived in a constant whirlwind of dust.

The other camps were similarly barren. Japanese Americans taken to Heart Mountain, Wyoming, also suffered from winter temperatures as low as −30° F (−34.5° C). For those from the mild California valleys, the camps were tolerable at best. One camp resident wrote a poem in the camp newspaper, the *Sentinel*.

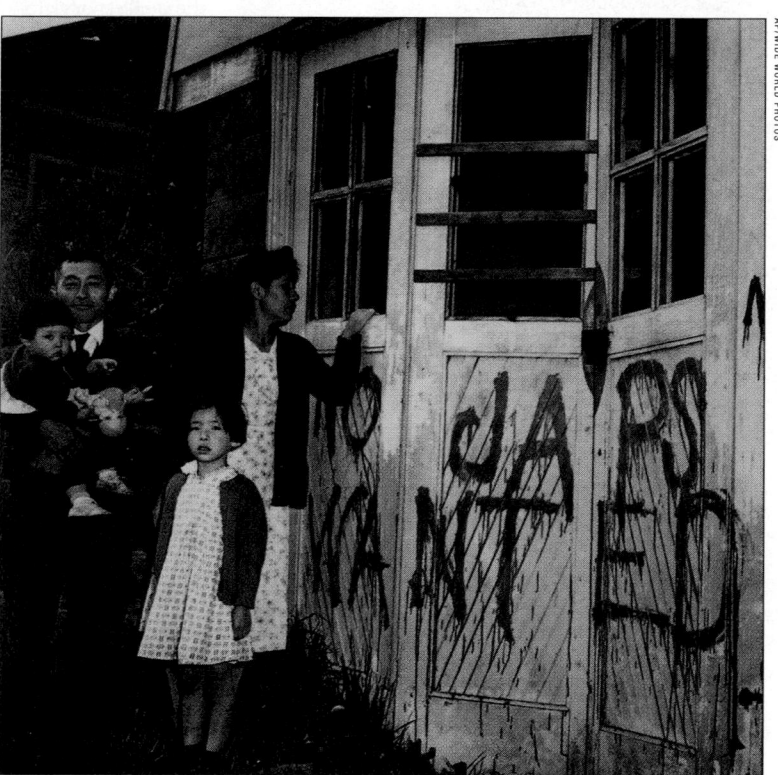

AP/WIDE WORLD PHOTOS

Internees Return Shigeo Nagaishi and his Nisei family find broken windows in their home and garage when they return to Seattle, Washington, from the relocation center in Hunt, Idaho, on May 10, 1945. *Why was this treatment of Japanese Americans unfair?*

SECTION THREE   **547**

 Curriculum Connection

Art Photographer Ansel Adams recorded life at an internment camp. He published his photo-essay in a book called *Born Free and Equal.* Outraged citizens who did not think Japanese Americans should be "free and equal" burned copies of the book.

VISUAL INSTRUCTION

Internees Return Many of the Japanese American internees returned to damaged homes and ruined fields. They also faced continued prejudice.
Answer: *They had committed no crime.*

ASSESS

Meeting Lesson Objectives

Each section objective is tested by the section review question(s) that follows it in parentheses.

1. Define racism and explain how African Americans fought racism during World War II. (1, 2, 4)
2. Identify A. Philip Randolph and explain the purpose and effect of the March on Washington Movement. (3)
3. Describe the violations of Japanese Americans' civil liberties during World War II. (5)

Cultural Perspectives

Bias Against Japanese Immigrants Before the outbreak of World War II, Japanese people had immigrated to California in large numbers (12,000 in 1900 alone). Although they were hardworking, productive citizens, many Americans resented their presence and their economic successes. When World War II began, about 93,000 Japanese Americans were living in California, and Los Angeles was the center of the nation's Japanese community. The attack on Pearl Harbor fueled the racial bias against the Japanese that was already smoldering. Support for the internment of these basically loyal citizens was based on this preexisting bias and on fear.

Evaluate

Have students complete the Section Review.

📁 💾 Assign the Section 3 Quiz. (Also in Spanish.) **LEP**

📁 💾 Assign the Chapter 16 Test or use the Testmaker. (Also in Spanish.) **LEP**

📁 Have students complete the Chapter 16 Performance Assessment Activity.

Reteach

🎧 Have students listen to the Chapter 16, Section 3 Audiocassette. **LEP**

📁 Have students complete the Chapter 16 Reteaching Activity. (Also in Spanish.) **LEP**

Enrich

📁 Have students complete the Chapter 16 Enrichment Activity. (Also in Spanish.) **LEP**

📁 Have students complete the Unit 6 American Literature Reading.

📁 Have students complete the Chapter 16 Geography in History Activity.

📁 Have students complete Interpreting Political Cartoons 27.

📁 Have students complete Supreme Court Case Study 16.

CLOSE

Ask: How might African Americans or Japanese Americans have felt about fighting for the U.S.? *(angry)*

AP/WIDE WORLD PHOTOS

Compensation for Internees On August 10, 1988, President Ronald Reagan signed Public Law 100-383. Among other things, this law makes apologies and restitution to individuals of Japanese ancestry who were interned during World War II. Each eligible person received $20,000 in tax-free payments over a 10-year period. *Do you think that this compensation was adequate? Why or why not?*

> Snow upon the rooftop
> Snow upon the coal;
> Winter in Wyoming—
> Winter in my soul.

One evacuee, Peter Ota, recalled the camp where he was interned:

> It's a desolate, flat, barren area. The barracks was all there was. There were no trees, no kind of landscaping. It was like a prison camp. Coming from our environment, it was just devastating.
> —As told to Studs Terkel, *"The Good War,"* 1984

This was no exaggeration. Entire families lived in a single room in the barracks, sparsely furnished with cots, makeshift dressers, and bare lightbulbs.

Despite the stark surroundings, the evacuees created a number of alternative communities to serve their cultural needs. The Japanese Americans published newspapers; started schools, churches, bands, Boy Scout groups, and softball leagues; built tennis courts; landscaped flower and vegetable gardens; and gave trumpet and tap dancing lessons. They were determined to replenish their lives with the dignity and the resources that they and their children would need when the war ended.

Some of the evacuees were released to work at jobs in the interior of the United States before the end of the war. They were allowed to resettle in the East or the Midwest. Most, however, remained in the camps for the duration of the war.

Judicial Rulings Support Relocation

The Supreme Court upheld the wartime policies that deprived Japanese Americans of their civil rights. In 1943, in *Hirabayashi* v. *United States,* the Court unanimously decided that a curfew order affecting only Japanese Americans did not violate their constitutional rights. Chief Justice Harlan Fiske Stone wrote: "In time of war residents having ethnic affiliations with an invading enemy may be a greater source of danger than those of a different ancestry."

In December 1944, in *Korematsu* v. *United States,* the Court upheld the order providing for the relocation of Japanese Americans. It based its decision largely on the grounds that the judiciary could not second-guess military decisions. One of the dissenting justices, however, termed the decision a "legalization of racism." Nevertheless, the Court also ruled that citizens could not be held in relocation centers once their loyalty had been established. By then, however, the camps were being closed down.

The United States recorded both gains and losses in the areas of civil rights and civil liberties during the war years. While African Americans fought hard to win the smallest of victories, Japanese Americans found themselves regarded as enemies of the United States and suffered humiliation and loss of their liberties. As the war ended, however, all Americans looked ahead and hoped for prosperity and justice in a peaceful postwar world.

SECTION REVIEW

Vocabulary

1. Define: racism, civil liberties.

Checking Facts

2. How did African Americans fight racism during World War II?

3. Using the example of the March on Washington Movement, how did A. Philip Randolph's approach to protest differ from that of the National Association for the Advancement of Colored People?

Critical Thinking

Recognizing Bias

4. What obstacles hampered the effectiveness of the Fair Employment Practices Committee?

Linking Across Time

5. Do you think the violations of Japanese Americans' civil liberties that occurred during World War II could happen again to others in the United States? Why?

Section 3 Review Answers

1. racism (543), **civil liberties** (546)

2. Organizations including the NAACP and CORE gave a voice to the protests of African Americans, and acts of civil disobedience increased.

3. The March on Washington Movement typified the active nature of Randolph's approach.

The NAACP urged persuasive rather than active methods.

4. It had no authority to enforce its orders and could only act on formal complaints.

5. Answers will vary. Students may reply that it could happen again, especially in a war situation with irrational fears.

Social Studies Skill

READING ECONOMIC GRAPHS

Learning the Skill

During the 1940s dramatic economic changes affected many Americans. In the early 1940s, government spending on war materials boosted production. To meet rising production, manufacturers hired more workers, who then had more money to spend, further increasing demand and production. Then in 1942 thousands of American men left their jobs to serve in the armed forces. Production dropped. Soon other Americans filled the open positions, stopping the decline in production. Patterns of this kind—in prices, interest rates, or wages—form what is called a business cycle. Business cycle graphs can help you visualize the direction and extent of economic change.

Line graphs illustrate change over time. A business cycle graph, such as the one below, is a type of line graph that shows changes in economic activity, as measured by the value of goods and services produced. In the graph below, the horizontal line in the center represents the trend line of economic activity over the period. The data points show how the value of goods and services produced at a given time varies above (+) or below (–) the trend line.

Patterns of Economic Activity

To interpret this type of graph, follow these steps:

a. First compare each data point to the trend line. It tells you how much economic production increased or decreased in a given year.

b. Next determine if the line connecting a group of data points has a downward or upward slope. A downward slope shows falling production and an upward slope shows rising production.

c. Identify the business cycle of which a given year is a part. Look for a pattern of rising production, peak, declining production, and bottom. A given year may belong to a business cycle that began in an earlier year; for example, the business cycle that includes 1923 begins with rising production in 1922.

Practicing the Skill

1. Look at the graph below. How much did production vary from the trend line in 1941?

2. How much did production decline during the period 1930–1931?

3. Find the business cycle that began with rising production during 1942. When did this cycle end?

4. The 1920s and the 1940s were both periods of economic prosperity, yet their business cycles appear quite different. How do you explain this?

5. During which Depression years might Americans have felt most hopeful? Explain.

Applying the Skill

Find several economic graphs in news-magazines or in the business sections of newspapers. Select one that shows a trend in economic activity, and write a brief description of the graph's content. Explain what trend the graph shows and how you determined that trend.

Additional Practice

For additional practice, see Reinforcing Skills on page 553.

TEACH

This skill familiarizes students with reading economic graphs. Point out that brief declines in economic activity are called recessions. A depression occurs when there are lengthy and large drops in economic activity. Periods with above average activity are called booms. During a boom, total spending increases. If the supply of goods and services becomes smaller than the demand for them, there is likely to be inflation, or rapidly rising prices.

Additional Practice

☛ Have students complete the Chapter 16 Skill Reinforcement Activity.

CHART STUDY

A business graph shows changes in economic activity. Other ways of calculating the relative health of the economy might include measuring the Gross National Product, consumer spending, or new housing starts.

Answer: *After the war, the economy experienced a dramatic decline.*

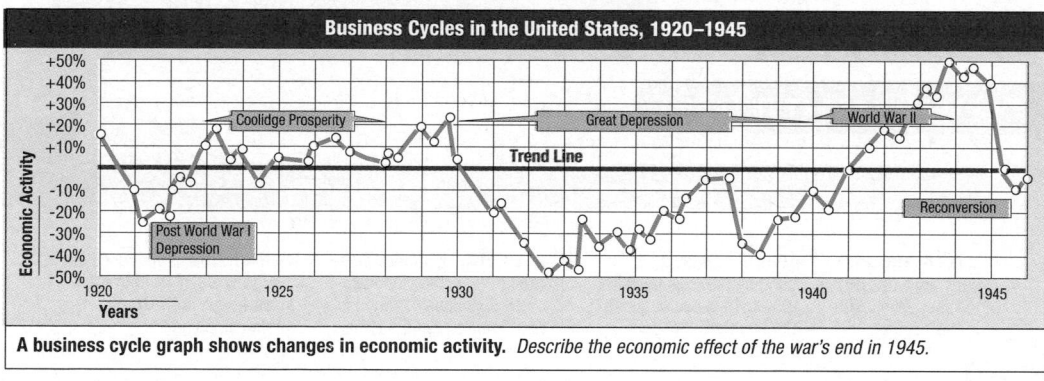

Business Cycles in the United States, 1920–1945

A business cycle graph shows changes in economic activity. *Describe the economic effect of the war's end in 1945.*

Practicing the Skill Answers

1. Production remained the same as the average.

2. Production declined by 20 percent.

3. The cycle ended in 1943.

4. In the 1920s economic activity remained steadily above the average, but in the 1940s there was a rapid change in prosperity due to World War II.

5. In 1933 there was a sharp rise in economic activity, but in 1936 there was a steady rise almost to the average.

TEACH

Making the Historical Connection

The tremendous numbers of casualties incurred from the very start of World War II pushed scientists to discover new ways to save lives on the battlefield. When World War II began, blood storage and transfusion techniques had not been perfected. Penicillin had not been prepared for human use. Battlefield doctors often amputated infected limbs. Many wounded soldiers died from bacterial infections.

FYI

Blood Segregation At American Red Cross blood banks during the war, technicians segregated donated blood by race.

Curriculum Connection

Sociology Charles Richard Drew, an African American surgeon and professor of medicine in the 1940s, studied new techniques in blood transfusion. He served as director of the American Red Cross Blood Bank during World War II. In 1950, after an automobile accident, Drew arrived at a hospital in desperate need of a blood transfusion. The hospital turned Drew away because of his race. Drew died en route to another hospital.

Science, TECHNOLOGY, and Society

Medical Breakthroughs

Medical advances reduced the overall mortality rate of the wounded in World War II to 3 percent, down from 6 percent in World War I. The innovations of wartime surgeons and researchers, aided by government funding, greatly enriched civilian medicine after the war.

HELP FOR INJURED VETERANS

Vast numbers of soldiers lost limbs in World War II, encouraging the development of lighter, better-functioning prostheses and increasing social acceptance of their use. This veteran is wearing an artificial arm developed at the United States Army Prosthetic Research Laboratory after the war. The wearer's muscle contractions activate electrodes that generate the electric currents that control the limb.

UPI/BETTMANN

MEDICAL BREAKTHROUGHS

Pre-1938	1940	1942
SULFA DRUGS, early antibiotics, are first developed in the 1930s.	**BLOOD PLASMA** is found by U.S. scientists in 1939 to be a useful substitute for whole blood in transfusions.	**PENICILLIN** is first used on a large scale in 1943 to treat Allied troops in the North Africa campaign.
	ALBUMIN, a protein separated from whole blood using a new technique, is found in 1940 to be a useful alternative to plasma.	

Background Information

Defeating Disease Medical advances significantly improved a soldier's chance of surviving a war. Care of wounds was not the only important advance. In the Civil War, for example, diseases like typhoid, malaria, and dysentery killed more than twice as many soldiers as did battlefield wounds. Though soldiers in World War II still died of disease, the percentage of disease-related casualties was much lower than in earlier wars.

PLASMA, THE LIFE GIVER

One of the most important medical breakthroughs was the use of blood plasma to prevent shock, a life-threatening condition resulting from blood loss that caused arteries to collapse, cutting off circulation to vital organs. Plasma, the liquid part of the blood, was easier to preserve than whole blood and caused far fewer allergic reactions. When transfused, plasma kept arteries open and helped the wounded live long enough to be evacuated and to undergo surgery. Plasma, General George Patton said, "saves more lives than you could believe."

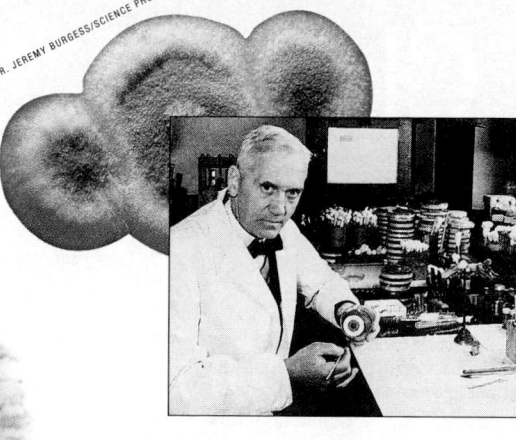

DR. JEREMY BURGESS/SCIENCE PHOTO LIBRARY

BROWN BROTHERS

© FPG INTERNATIONAL CORP.

MIRACLE DRUG

Penicillin replaced sulfa drugs as the antibiotic of choice because it actually killed bacteria instead of just stopping their growth and it had fewer side effects. The strange story of the discovery of penicillin dates back to 1928, when British physician Alexander Fleming, above, accidentally grew a new variety of mold that killed all nearby bacteria. The significance of Fleming's discovery was not recognized until the early 1940s.

HOW ARE DISCOVERIES MADE?

PORTFOLIO PROJECT

What factors account for the large number of medical advances made during World War II? Which factor do you think was most important? Explain your reasoning in a paragraph.

1944	1946	1948 to 1990s

ALEXANDER FLEMING, Howard Florey, and Ernst Chain receive the Nobel Prize in 1945 for the discovery of penicillin.

U.S. ARMY SURGICAL RESEARCH UNIT is founded in 1945, the forerunner of the specialized burn treatment centers of today.

GENES responsible for hereditary breast, colon, and kidney cancers are isolated in the early 1990s; giving hope for new tests and treatments in the future.

SCIENCE, TECHNOLOGY, AND SOCIETY   **551**

 Science, Technology, and Society

Block Scheduling

The Portfolio Project on this page provides an excellent opportunity to enrich and extend key elements of this feature.

CLOSE

Ask: How did the war serve as a catalyst for significant advances in medicine? *(Armies attempting to lower casualty rates worked assiduously to develop new technologies.)* How might the war have differed without these medical advances? *(Students may answer that more soldiers might have died and that it might have been more difficult to win the war.)*

Notes

_____
_____
_____
_____
_____
_____
_____
_____
_____
_____
_____
_____
_____
_____
_____
_____
_____
_____
_____
_____
_____

 PORTFOLIO PROJECT

Portfolio Project

Effects of a Wonder Drug Invite students to interview a doctor, nurse, or pharmacist who practiced both before and after the invention of penicillin. How did the invention of this new drug change the way they worked? How did they feel about this new invention? What thoughts do they have about current or future medical treatment techniques? Students can put transcripts of their interviews in their portfolios.

Chapter ⑯ Review

Reviewing Key Terms

1. inflation
2. civil liberties
3. gross national product
4. racism
5. deficit spending

Recalling Facts

1. victory gardens, recycling, manufacturing, war bonds and taxes, and OCD
2. cause: increased earnings and demand for consumer goods. OPA set price ceilings.
3. It ensured food and fuel for the military.
4. Citizens paid income taxes; corporate taxes increased; government sold war bonds and stamps.
5. President of the UMW
6. defense plant welders, riveters, and mechanics
7. rural to urban, East to West, and North to South
8. Housing became scarce and day care, schools, medical facilities overcrowded; sanitation was often poor.
9. often resented newcomers
10. Women gained skills and respect; industry boomed; children were often left alone.
11. Social Security, unemployment compensation, old-age benefits, and the TVA
12. He helped African Americans organize for better wages and working conditions.
13. It threatened mass march on Washington; Roosevelt ordered an end to job discrimination.
14. nonviolent resistance to unfair laws; African Americans; fairer employment, decline in segregation, and increased political access
15. People worked together; many reexamined their beliefs about race.
16. They lived under guard in crowded conditions; started churches, schools, and newspapers, played sports, and gardened.

Reviewing Key Terms

Match each of the following sentences with the vocabulary term that best defines or describes it. Write your answers on a separate sheet of paper.

inflation   deficit spending
migration   racism
gross national civil liberties
  product

1. By 1942 the annual cost of living had rapidly increased by 15 percent.

2. In relocating and interning Japanese Americans, the United States denied them these rights.

3. This total value of all goods and services produced annually in the United States more than doubled during the war years.

4. This doctrine has caused the segregation and discrimination that African Americans have experienced.

5. During the wartime economic growth, the government used borrowed money to ensure full employment and prosperity.

Recalling Facts

1. How did civilians contribute to the war effort?

2. Explain why inflation occurred during the war and how the government tried to fight it.

3. How did rationing help the war effort?

4. The United States government spent $321 billion between 1941 and 1945, nearly twice as much as it had spent in the preceding 150 years. How did the government raise the money to finance World War II?

5. Who was John L. Lewis?

6. What kind of work did women do during the war?

7. Describe migration patterns in the United States during World War II.

8. What happened to the cities when large numbers of migrant war workers arrived?

9. How did the native residents of the boomtowns feel about the newcomers?

10. What are some of the advantages and disadvantages that society experienced as a result of having women enter the workforce during World War II?

11. What aspects of the New Deal became a permanent part of United States political policy?

12. Who was A. Philip Randolph, and what did he accomplish?

13. Explain the March on Washington Movement, and tell what this movement accomplished.

14. What is civil disobedience? Who used civil disobedience between 1941 and 1945, and what did they accomplish?

15. Give examples of how the war furthered the cause of racial equality.

16. Describe what life was like for those held in the Japanese internment camps.

Critical Thinking

1. **Making Generalizations** Movies like the one advertised by this poster (right) were very popular during the war years. How did the entertainment industry help with the war effort in the United States?

2. **Recognizing Bias** Navy personnel roamed the streets of Los Angeles in 1943 beating zoot-suiters, but only the zoot-suiters were arrested. What can you infer about the attitudes of the arresting police officers?

3. **Identifying Assumptions** How did the military justify the relocation of Japanese Americans? On what assumptions was the justification based?

4. **Making Comparisons** A. Philip Randolph and members of the NAACP had differing philosophies about how to bring about social change. Compare Randolph's methods of civil disobedience with the less controversial tactics of the NAACP. Which do you think are more effective?

THE CARSON COLLECTION

Critical Thinking

1. Patriotic movies and music helped convince Americans their cause was just and the war was winnable. Entertainment helped people to temporarily forget bad feelings about the war. Entertainers sold war bonds.
2. Racial prejudice was a strong factor in the arrests.
3. Japanese Americans were suspected of planning sabotage and espionage. Assumptions were based mostly on West-Coast Japanese Americans' proximity to Japan.
4. Randolph favored direct action: boycotts, protests, and civil disobedience. NAACP favored using publicity to shame the government into granting civil rights. Student answers as to which method was most effective will vary, but should include logical or factual support.

Portfolio Project

Write an essay that discusses ways in which an individual can cope with and ease racial tensions today. You might relate incidents or comments that you may have witnessed. Conclude by making recommendations that you can apply to everyday social situations. (An example might be speaking out among peers when racial comments or jokes are made.)

Cooperative Learning

In small groups plan an oral history project. Interview family members or older neighbors who lived at home during World War II. Find out about their memories of social changes and the importance of entertainment. Write down their stories. You might bring to class examples of some of the music they listened and danced to.

Reinforcing Skills

Reading Economic Graphs Use what you know about economic graphs to answer the following questions.

1. What kinds of information might be represented on a business cycle graph?

2. What kinds of events or activities might have an effect on the business cycle?

3. Why might an economic graph include significant events or activities?

4. Why is it helpful to include a long-term average on an economic graph?

Geography and History

Study the map on this page to answer the following questions:

1. Which states experienced a decrease in their African American populations?

AFRICAN AMERICAN POPULATION, 1940–1950

CANADA

POPULATION SHIFTS
- More than 70% increase
- 40%-70% increase
- 10%-40% increase
- 0%-10% increase
- Decrease
- → Migration routes

0   200   400 mi.
0 200 400 km
Albers Equal-Area projection

2. Which states experienced the greatest increase in their African American populations?

3. Which states experienced the smallest increase in their African American populations?

4. Use the map to summarize the migration routes of African Americans in the East from 1940 to 1950.

5. Use what you have learned in this chapter to explain the causes of the population changes shown on the map. What were some of the effects of the population changes?

HISTORY JOURNAL

Look back at your journal response to page 522. Do you think that people's attitudes can change as a result of experiencing a war? Using what you have learned in this chapter, write your response in your journal.

some of the causes of economic fluctuation.

4. A long-term average shows whether economic changes are minor or severe.

Geography and History

1. Mississippi, Alabama, and Georgia

2. New Hampshire, Michigan, and Wisconsin

3. Tennessee, North Carolina, and South Carolina

4. African Americans generally moved from Southern states to Northern states, except for those who moved from Georgia and South Carolina south to Florida.

5. The population changes were caused largely by the desire for jobs available in the industrial centers of the wartime north. The changes provided African Americans with many opportunities and helped to integrate many areas. The migration also left some areas overcrowded and taxed social services.

History Journal

Student journals should include references to World War II and how it might have changed people's attitudes about war.

BONUS QUESTION

This question may be used for extra credit on the chapter test:

At the end of the war, how much money did Americans have available to spend on consumer goods they could not purchase during the war?

Answer: *$129 billion*

Portfolio Project

Student responses might include references to specific situations involving racial tension and general suggestions to remedy racism.

Cooperative Learning

Group responses might include a presentation that sheds light on the social history of World War II. Students should use excerpts from interviews to support their presentations.

Reinforcing Skills

1. Economic activity, dates, long-term averages, and events might be included on a business cycle graph.

2. Wars, political administration, and industrial activities may have an effect.

3. Including events on an economic graph helps explain

TEACH

Making the Historical Connection

A total of more than 15 million men served in the military during the war. Women ably filled the jobs the men left behind and worked at new jobs created by the war. In defense industries, female employment increased by 460 percent.

FYI

Big Payoff Players in the All-American Girls Baseball League earned at least $55 per week, an outstanding salary for women of the time. Women in offices or factories made between $10 and $20 per week.

At the Movies

Renewed interest in the All-American Girls Baseball League followed the 1992 release of the Hollywood movie *A League of Their Own,* which fictionalized the story of the league.

Then...

Women's Baseball

In 1943, when half of the male professional baseball players were serving in World War II, Philip Wrigley, owner of the Chicago Cubs, organized the All-American Girls Baseball League. The league's athletes thrilled and entertained thousands of war-weary fans with their skill and left a lasting mark on the history of baseball.

 The Muskegon Lassies played from 1946 through 1950, managed by Ralph "Buzz" Boyle. All league managers were men.

GREATER MUSKEGON GIRLS PROFESSIONAL BALL CLUB

MUSKEGON LASSIES

21503

OFFICIAL 10¢ SCORE CARD

A-A-GBL

"Watch the girls play ball"

All American Girls PROFESSIONAL BALL LEAGUE MARSH FIELD

NATIONAL BASEBALL LIBRARY HALL OF FAME, COOPERSTOWN, NEW YORK

❷ The league's skirted uniforms left legs unprotected. Scrapes, or "strawberries," were continually created as skin met the ground when players slid into bases.

Fun Facts

KEEPING UP APPEARANCES
In the early years of the league, players were required to attend "charm school," where they learned how to apply makeup and act in social situations. They were also fined $50 if they appeared "unkempt" in public.

Background Information

Major League Recognition The National Baseball Hall of Fame was founded in 1936. For decades this institution recognized only players from the National and American Leagues, so only white male players were selected for recognition. In 1962 Jackie Robinson was inducted into The Hall of Fame. In 1971 the Hall of Fame began to consider and elect players from the Negro Leagues. No women have been elected, but in 1988 the Hall of Fame installed an exhibit to recognize women's accomplishments in baseball.

Stats

PLAY-OFF CHAMPIONS, 1943–1945
- 1943, Racine Belles
- 1944, Milwaukee Chicks
- 1945, Rockford Peaches

STARTING SALARY
- $55 per week

LEAGUE BATTING CHAMPS, 1943–1945
- 1943, Gladys Davis
- 1944, Betsy Jochum
- 1945, Mary Crews

3 The 1945 Rockford Peaches, above, won the team's first league pennant. Between 1943 and 1954, when the league's last teams disbanded, more than 550 women played on a total of 15 teams.

4 Dorothy "Kammie" Kamenshek of the Rockford Peaches, the league batting champion in 1946 and 1947, was offered a contract by a men's professional baseball team.

...NOW

A SPORTS REPORT

PORTFOLIO PROJECT

Create a report about any sport that women participated in 50 years ago and continue to participate in today.

Collect facts about past and current individual female athletes, including records they have set, and money they have earned. In your report describe if and how the status of women in the sport has changed.

FAN HOSPITALITY

Fans housed the teams as they traveled, raised money to pay injured players' medical expenses, and hosted celebrations. One family in Racine, Wisconsin, gave the Racine Belles a yearly picnic, serving each player's favorite food.

THEN AND NOW   **555**

Curriculum Connection

Mathematics Statistics pervade the world of professional sports. Invite students to explore sports statistics and the ways in which they are calculated. Students might wish to keep statistics for a player or team to see how these statistics work in practice.

Block Scheduling

The Portfolio Project on this page provides an excellent opportunity to enrich and extend the key elements of this feature.

CLOSE

Ask: How have opportunities changed for the female athletes of today? *(Answers will vary. Students may say that compared to the 1940s, today's women are able to find more opportunities in Olympic sports, college basketball and volleyball, and professional bowling, tennis, golf, and marathon runs. Some may say, however, that women's opportunities and financial rewards still lag behind those of male athletes.)*

Portfolio Project

Sports Story Invite each student to create a written profile of a contemporary female athlete. Students might interview a local athlete or research a prominent national or international sports figure. Encourage students to find out how the athlete became interested in her sport, what her biggest challenges as an athlete have been, and what her goals for the future are. Students can put their profiles in their portfolio.

The Unit at a Glance

Chapter 17

The cold war originated in the post–World War II period. It extended into Asia and Latin America, and finally it initiated a dangerous nuclear arms race.

Chapter 18

Social and domestic concerns in the United States, where Americans were entering a period of extraordinary prosperity, mobility, and technological change, are the focus of this chapter.

Chapter 19

McCarthyism and the fear that Americans felt as communism spread through Eastern Europe and Asia dominated the 1950s; not even the United States Army was safe from charges of harboring Communist conspirators.

[00:00] Out of Time?

If time does not permit teaching every chapter in this unit, use the Chapter Digests Audiocassettes and the accompanying student activities and tests. The Chapter Digests Audiocassettes are available in Spanish.

UNIT

1

1945
1963

The Postwar World

CHAPTER 17
The Uneasy Peace

CHAPTER 18
The Postwar Era

CHAPTER 19
Cold War Politics

556

Portfolio Project

Research Television Have students research how life changed in the United States after television became common in American homes. Students should note the rise of televisions in homes in the United States, and they may also want to investigate the quality of the reception and the types of shows people typically watched. In the Norman Rockwell painting on this spread, a worker installs a television antenna on a house. Ask students what the purpose of such an antenna was. Why do few homes today have such antennas? Students can file their reports in their portfolios.

PHOTO COURTESY OF THE NORMAN ROCKWELL MUSEUM AT STOCKBRIDGE

557

Introducing
the Unit

Show students the Unit 7 Time Line Transparency and/or assign the accompanying activity sheet. Explain that this unit is about the period of time following the end of World War II.

GLENCOE
TECHNOLOGY

Videodisc

American History

Side 1, Section 1
Title: World War II and the Beginning of the Cold War, 1941–1960
Subject: Overview of American history from entry into World War II to postwar American life
Ask: What was the cold war? *(war of words between the Soviet Union and the United States)*

Examining the Visual

Norman Rockwell The Norman Rockwell painting on this page, *New Television Antenna*, was painted in 1949. In that year the installation of such an antenna was a new and remarkable event. To many Americans Norman Rockwell is the best-known illustrator who ever lived. He painted 321 cover illustrations for the *Saturday Evening Post,* the most popular magazine of its day. Rockwell's themes are rooted in American values and pride in those values. He chose to accentuate the positive in the American character. For 70 years Rockwell's paintings covered the significant events of the 1900s in the United States. During World War II, he created Rosie the Riveter. He portrayed the civil rights movement of the 1960s and public personalities from Harry Truman to John Wayne.

TEACH

Making the Historical Connection

After World War II, some leaders within the government instituted cold war repression against anyone suspected of Communist leanings. E.L. Doctorow shows how some people, many of whom had suffered fascist persecution during the war, were subjected to an insidious form of terror calculated to break them.

VISUAL INSTRUCTION

The Postwar Era An art movement known as abstract expressionism flourished in the United States from the mid-1940s to the mid-1950s. Abstract expressionists emphasized color and shapes in their paintings. By rejecting recognizable forms, these artists expressed their opposition to society's values, which they considered to be shallow and false. They believed that abstract methods were better suited to express their attitudes toward life. Franz Kline at first painted city scenes; then he switched to abstract compositions that he felt reflected the patterns of the urban landscape.

The Book
OF
Daniel

BY E.L. DOCTOROW

E.L. Doctorow captures anti-Communist paranoia in this excerpt from the novel The Book of Daniel. *The FBI, who suspects Daniel's parents of Communist espionage, visits Daniel's home.*

Early the next morning, as I was leaving for school, the doorbell rang and I opened the door and two men were standing on the porch. They were dressed neatly, and did not appear to be of the neighborhood. They had thin, neat faces and small noses, and crew-cut hair. They held their hats in their hands and wore nice overcoats. I thought maybe they were from one of those Christian religions that sent people from door to door to sell their religious magazines.

"Sonny," said one, "is your mother or father home?"

"Yes," I said. "They're both home."

My mother did not allow me to delay going to school just because the FBI had come to the door. I don't know what happened on that first visit. The

NATIONAL MUSEUM OF AMERICAN ART, WASHINGTON DC/ART RESOURCE, NY

The Postwar Era After reading the literature selection, consider how this 1959 Franz Kline painting reflects a mood of menace or foreboding.

men went inside and, going down the splintery front steps, I turned and caught a glimpse of Paul coming out of the kitchen to meet them just as the door closed. My mother was holding the door and my father was coming forward in his ribbed undershirt, looking much skinnier than the two men who rang the bell.

When the FBI knocks on your door and wants only to ask a few questions, you do not have to consent to be asked questions. You are not required to talk to them just because they would like to talk to you. You don't have to go with them to their office. You don't have to do anything if you are not subpoenaed or arrested. But you only learn the law as you go along.

Background Information

Communism in the United States The worldwide appeal of communism after World War II made many Americans uneasy. Some people even believed that Communist agents were attempting to infiltrate the United States government. As a result, conservative politicians conducted widespread investigations to determine the extent of communism in the United States. Many Americans supported these investigations, which they believed would help safeguard them from the threat of Communist expansion.

"They don't know what they want," Paul says to Rochelle. "It's routine. If you don't talk to them, they have nothing to pin their lies on. They are clumsy, obvious people."

"I'm frightened," my mother says. "*Polizei* don't have to be smart."

"Don't worry," Paul says. "Mindish won't suffer from anything we said." He is walking back and forth in the kitchen and he is pounding his fist into his palm. "We have done nothing wrong. There is nothing to be afraid of."

It develops that all of Mindish's friends are being questioned. Nobody knows what he is being held for. There has been no announcement on the radio, there has been no story in the newspaper. Sadie Mindish is in a state of hysterical collapse. Her apartment has been searched. Her daughter has stayed home from school. Nobody knows if they even have a lawyer.

The next day the same two FBI men come back again, this time in the early evening. They sit on the stuffed, sprung couch in the living room parlor with their knees together and their hats in their hands. They are very soft-spoken and friendly. Their strange names are Tom Davis and John Bradley. They smile at me while my mother goes to the phone to call my father.

"What grade are you in, young fellow?"

I don't answer. I have never seen a real FBI man this close before. I peer at them, looking for superhuman powers, but there is no evidence that they have any. They look neither as handsome as in the movies nor as ugly as my parents' revulsion makes them. I search their faces for a clue to their real nature. But their faces do not give clues.

When Paul comes home, he is very nervous.

"My lawyer has advised me that I don't have to talk to you if I don't want to," my father said. "That particular fact you neglected yesterday to mention."

> ### WHEN THE FBI KNOCKS ON YOUR DOOR AND WANTS ONLY TO ASK A FEW QUESTIONS, YOU DO NOT HAVE TO CONSENT.

"Well, yes sir, Mr. Isaacson, but we were hoping you would be cooperative. We're only looking for information. It's nothing mysterious. We thought you were a friend of Doctor Mindish. As his friend, you may be in a position to help him."

"I will be glad to answer any questions in a court of law."

"Do you deny now that you know him?"

"I will answer any questions in a court of law."

The two men leave after a few minutes, and then they sit in their car, double-parked in front of the house, for ten or fifteen minutes more. They appear to be writing on clipboards or on pads, I can't tell exactly. It is dark and they have turned on the interior car light. I am reminded of a patrol man writing a parking ticket. But the sense is of serious and irrevocable paperwork, and I find it frightening. There is some small, grey light in the dark sky over the schoolyard. The wind is making whistling noises at the edges of the window.

"Danny!" Rochelle says sharply. "Get away from there."

My father takes my place at the curtains. "That is outrageous," he says. "Don't you see, it is part of the treatment. They are trying to shake us up. But we're too smart for them. We're onto them. They can sit out there all night for all I care."

> ### RESPONDING TO LITERATURE
>
> 1. What kind of view of the postwar United States does this passage suggest?
>
> 2. Daniel later likens the FBI investigation to a searchlight in a Nazi concentration camp. Why is this ironic in the 1950s?

Block Scheduling

Team Teaching This excerpt from *The Book of Daniel* can be presented in a team teaching context, in conjunction with English or Language Arts.

CLOSE

To close the section, conduct a discussion with students. Remind them that the constant presence of the FBI agent unnerves the family in the selection. Discuss how the tension created by the FBI infiltrates every aspect of the family's life. Point out that the FBI agents are always polite and never threaten the family. Why then is the family so frightened? *(because they are afraid that they are up against an entire government and they do not know what to expect)* Finally, have students consider how the bland FBI agents symbolize the postwar period. (*The postwar period was a time of conformity.*)

Responding to Literature Answers

1. The passage is told from the viewpoint of a child, but it nonetheless presents a frightening view of a world in which anyone can become a suspect of the government for unknown reasons.

2. Answers may vary, but students should note that one reason the United States entered World War II was to help defeat the fascists. In this passage, the American government appears to be using Nazi scare tactics.

The Uneasy Peace

DAILY LESSON OBJECTIVES	REPRODUCIBLE RESOURCES	MULTIMEDIA RESOURCES
SECTION 1 The Cold War Begins 1. Describe events that led to Soviet dominance in Eastern Europe. 2. Explain how differences between the United States and Soviet Union helped fuel the cold war. 3. Explain how the Truman Doctrine and Marshall Plan further defined and deepened the cold war.	📁 Reproducible Lesson Plans 📁 Vocabulary and Guided Reading Activities (English or Spanish) 📁 Cooperative Learning Activities 📁 American Literature Readings and Activities 📁 Section Quizzes (English or Spanish)	Chapter Teaching Transparencies Section Focus Transparencies Landmark Documents in American History Communism and the Cold War The Presidents: A Picture History of Our Nation Student Self-Test: A Software Review
SECTION 2 The Cold War Deepens 1. Explain the causes of the Berlin blockade and how the blockade affected the arms race. 2. Analyze factors that led to a Communist victory in China. 3. Review the Korean War.	📁 Reproducible Lesson Plans 📁 Vocabulary and Guided Reading Activities (English or Spanish) 📁 American Literature Readings and Activities 📁 Section Quizzes (English or Spanish)	Section Focus Transparencies Landmark Documents in American History Communism and the Cold War Great Speeches Testmaker Student Self-Test: A Software Review
SECTION 3 Cold War in the Atomic Age 1. Explain how a Soviet atomic bomb affected society and the arms race. 2. Explain Eisenhower's massive retaliation strategy. 3. Explain the disarmament movement. 4. Analyze the effects of *Sputnik* on the United States.	📁 Reproducible Lesson Plans 📁 Vocabulary and Guided Reading Activities (English or Spanish) 📁 Skill Reinforcement Activities 📁 Case Studies 📁 Geography in History Activities 📁 Section Quizzes (English or Spanish)	Section Focus Transparencies Landmark Documents in American History Communism and the Cold War The Presidents: A Picture History of Our Nation Great Speeches Testmaker Student Self-Test: A Software Review
SECTION 4 A New Battleground 1. Analyze why Americans and Soviets competed for the loyalty of emerging nations. 2. Explain CIA involvement in emerging nations. 3. Review American policy in the Middle East. 4. Review U.S. policy in Cuba.	📁 Reproducible Lesson Plans 📁 Vocabulary and Guided Reading Activities (English or Spanish) 📁 Reteaching Activities (English or Spanish) 📁 Enrichment Activities (English or Spanish) 📁 Section Quizzes (English or Spanish)	Section Focus Transparencies Landmark Documents in American History Communism and the Cold War Testmaker Student Self-Test: A Software Review
CHAPTER REVIEW AND EVALUATION	📁 Chapter 17 Test, Form A and B 📁 Performance Assessment Strategies and Activities	Student Self-Test: A Software Review Vocabulary PuzzleMaker Chapter Digests Audiocassettes

 If time does not permit teaching the entire chapter, summarize using the Chapter 17 Digests Audiocassettes and the accompanying activities and tests. (Available in English or Spanish.)

Cooperative Project

Organize students into groups of four or five to make a time line of political events explained in the chapter. Have students include major works of the time in literature, art, music, architecture, and other cultural areas. Each person within the group should be responsible for one section. Then the students could regroup by sections, compare information, and decide how to execute the time line for the section in the clearest and most interesting way. **LEP** 🎞

Suggested Rubric: Group Work and the Individual. See Performance Assessment Strategies and Activities, p. 49.

Individual Project

Use this activity after Section 1. Have the students imagine that they are advisors who are expected to provide input to President Roosevelt in February 1945 on plans being made for the Yalta Conference. They should write a paper persuading Roosevelt to take a firm stance safeguarding the rights of countries not represented at the conference. 🎞

Suggested Rubrics: An Issue Controversy, A Research Report. See Performance Assessment Strategies and Activities, pp. 39 and 51.

Key to Ability Levels

Teaching strategies have been coded for varying learning styles and abilities.

L1 **BASIC** activities for all students

L2 **AVERAGE** activities for average to above-average students

L3 **CHALLENGING** activities for above-average students

LEP **LIMITED ENGLISH PROFICIENCY** activities

 Block Scheduling

Block scheduling differs from traditional class scheduling in the amount of time allotted to each period. The extended timeframe provided by block scheduling affords you the opportunity to implement a greater number of research-oriented and activity-intense projects to motivate and involve your students. Activities that are particularly suited to use within the block scheduling framework are identified throughout this chapter by the following designation. 🎞

TEACHER'S CORNER

NATIONAL GEOGRAPHIC SOCIETY

Chapter Overview

The postwar world plunged into the cold war as the Allies disagreed about the fate of a conquered Germany. Soon, two superpowers, the Soviet Union and the United States dominated world affairs.

Introducing the Chapter

Have students read the narrative on this page about the Cuban missile crisis. Ask them to think about how they would feel if they knew nuclear missiles were aimed at this nation from an island only 90 miles away.

🗄 Display Chapter Teaching Transparency 17 and distribute copies of the corresponding activity sheet for students to complete.

Extension Activity
Have students complete Beyond the Transparency on the activity sheet for Chapter 17 and present their projects after the class has completed the chapter. 📼

History Journal

Suggest that students interview a parent or other adult who remembers the Cuban missile crisis and file their reports in their journals.

CHAPTER

17

The Uneasy Peace

OCTOBER 22, 1962: THE WHITE HOUSE

President John F. Kennedy walked into the Oval Office at 6:59 P.M., stepping over TV cables on the way to his desk. He was about to deliver some frightening news to the American people—news of a mounting Soviet threat in Cuba.

In a controlled, almost dull tone, Kennedy explained what the United States would do in response to the threat caused by the Russians installing missiles in Cuba. It would ask for a United Nations meeting. It would blockade Cuban shipping lanes with American destroyers to keep more weapons from reaching the island, and it would put the United States military on full alert. If even one missile were fired from Cuba toward any nation in the Western Hemisphere, the United States would launch a nuclear attack on the Soviet Union. Suddenly the world teetered on the brink of disaster.

What had happened? Just 17 years before, people of the United States and the Soviet Union embraced and toasted their stunning World War II victory. Franklin Roosevelt's warmth and diplomacy in dealing with the Soviets near the end of the war had raised hopes of cooperation between the two powers. Now, however, the wartime alliance had soured into a bitter and dangerous rivalry—a cold war—affecting the entire world. ■

HISTORY JOURNAL

Think about what you have heard or know about the Cuban missile crisis or the early cold war.

What do you think it would have been like to live through those events?

560

EXTRA CREDIT PROJECT

Cuban Missile Crisis Have students conduct research to find out more about the Cuban missile crisis. To help them focus their research, you many want to suggest that they concentrate on one of the following people or terms and write a brief report on his/its part in the Cuban missile crisis: Bay of Plgs, La Brigada, Nikita Krushchev, Fidel Castro, John F. Kennedy, the CIA. 📼

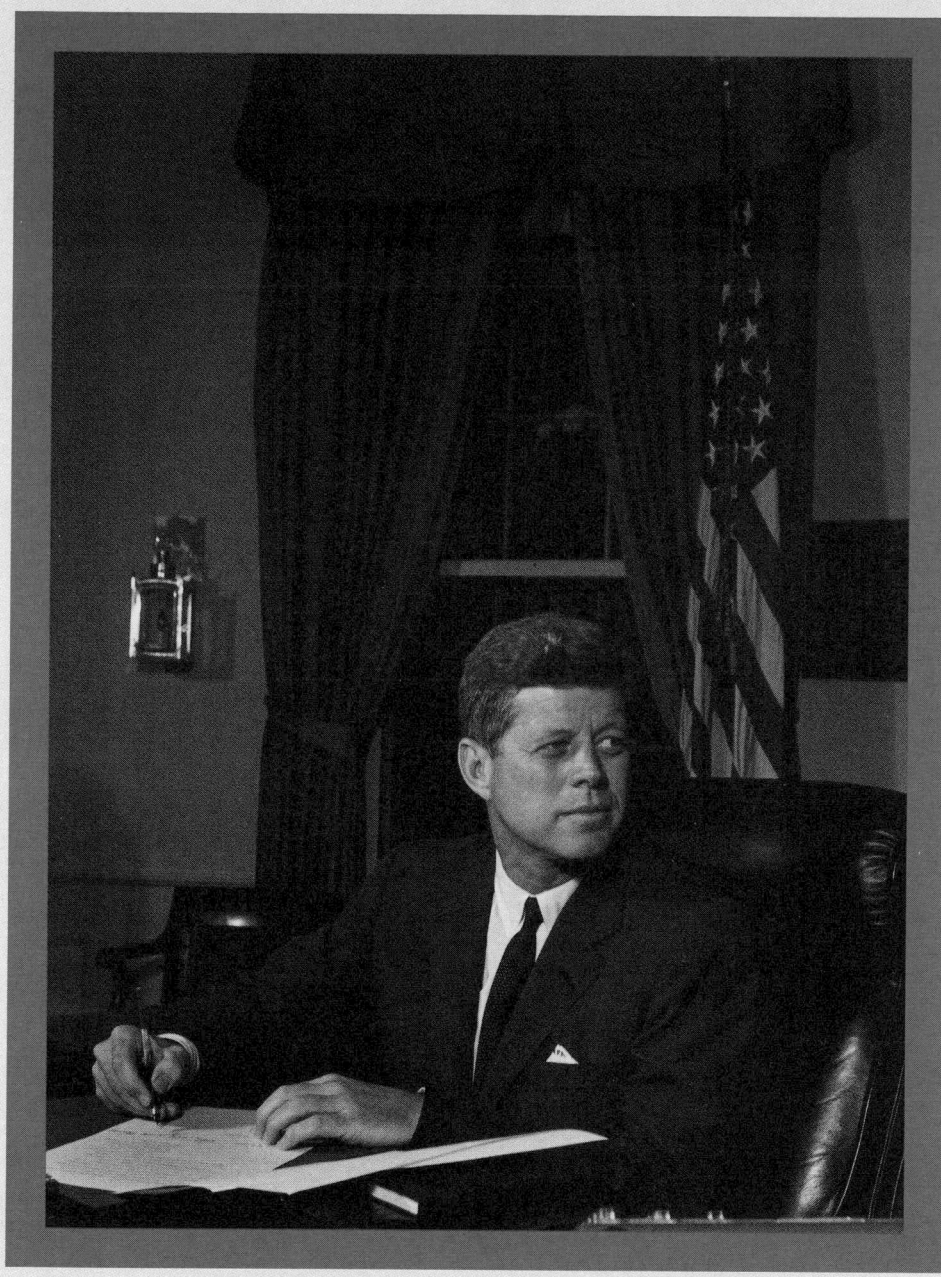

CECIL STOUGHTON/LIFE MAGAZINE © TIME WARNER, INC.

PRESIDENT JOHN F. KENNEDY PAUSES TO
REFLECT DURING THE CUBAN MISSLE CRISIS.

561

History and
the Humanities

U.S. History and Art
Transparencies 29 and
30—*Day of the Fair* by
Andrew Wyeth; *Forward*
by Jacob Lawrence

American Music:
Cultural Traditions—"We
Shall Not Be Moved" by
the Freedom Singers

Performance
Assessment

Refer to page 560B for
performance assessment
activities for this chapter.

Also see Activity 17
in the Performance
Assessment Strategies
and Activities for an
additional activity as well
as for suggested rubrics.

Examining the Visual

John F. Kennedy The Cuban missile crisis
was one of the most important international
confrontations of John F. Kennedy's presidency.
This photo catches the President during a
reflective moment at the height of the emergency. The way he resolved the Cuban missile
conflict would have implications for the United
States and for the world. Draw students' attention to Kennedy's contemplative facial expression. Encourage them to discuss the scope of
his responsibility to the nation and to the world.
Have students consider the depth and complexity of feelings such an event might evoke in
a leader. Be sure students have some understanding of what it must be like to be alone in
the seat of power.

FOCUS

Section Objectives

1. Describe the events that led to Soviet dominance in Eastern Europe, the Truman Doctrine, and the cold war.
2. Explain how the ideological differences between the Soviet Union and the United States helped to fuel the cold war.
3. Explain how the Truman Doctrine and the Marshall Plan further defined and deepened the cold war.

Bellringer Activity

While taking attendance at the beginning of the class period, display **Section Focus Transparency 52,** and have students answer the questions. (Or use the blackline master.)

VISUAL INSTRUCTION

War's End Have students skim the page and notice that the photograph shows what is described in the quotation from Andy Rooney. Students will probably identify Rooney as the whimsical commentator on the newsmagazine show *Sixty Minutes.*

Ask: Where did the American and Soviet armies meet? *(near the Elbe River south of Berlin)*

The Cold War Begins

APRIL 25, 1945: GIs MEET SOVIET TROOPS

War's End
American and Soviet soldiers congratulate each other on the fall of Nazi Germany.

LILACS BLOOMED AND THE SUN SHONE ON APRIL 25, 1945, AS AMERICAN SOLDIERS BATTLING THE GERMANS FROM THE WEST APPROACHED THEIR SOVIET ALLIES FIGHTING FROM THE EAST. Victory was in the air, and as the armies neared the Elbe River south of Berlin, small patrols of Americans drove out in jeeps to meet their Soviet comrades-in-arms. Throughout the day Soviet and American soldiers embraced for the first time. Andy Rooney, staff writer for the armed forces newspaper, *Stars & Stripes,* caught the moment:

There was a mad scene of jubilation on the east and west banks of the Elbe at Torgau as infantrymen of Lieutenant General Courtney H. Hodges . . . swapped K

rations for a vodka with soldiers of Marshal Kornian's Ukrainian Army, congratulating each other . . . on the linkup.

Men of the 69th Division sat on the banks of the Elbe in warm sunshine today with no enemy in front of them or behind them and . . . watched their new Russian friends and listened to them as they played accordions and sang Russian songs.

The Russian soldiers are the most carefree bunch . . . that ever came together in an army. They would best be described as exactly like Americans, only twice as much. . . . You get the feeling of exuberance, a great new world opening up.

—Andy Rooney, "Good Soldiers Meet," *Stars & Stripes,* April 28, 1945

AS YOU READ

Vocabulary
► containment
► cold war

Think About . . .
► the events that led to Soviet dominance in Eastern Europe, the Truman Doctrine, and the cold war.
► how the ideological differences between the Soviet Union and the

United States helped to fuel the cold war.
► how the Truman Doctrine and the Marshall Plan further defined and deepened the cold war.

562 CHAPTER 17 THE UNEASY PEACE

Section 1 Resources

REPRODUCIBLE RESOURCES

Lesson Plan 17-1
Vocabulary and Guided Reading Activity 17-1
Cooperative Learning Activity 17
Section 1 Quiz
Unit 7 American Literature Reading

MULTIMEDIA RESOURCES

📖 Section Focus Transparency 52
🎞 Landmark Documents in American History
📷 Map Transparency 17
💿 Focus on Government
📖 Chapter Teaching Transparency 17

🔵 Communism and the Cold War
🔵 The Presidents: A Picture History of Our Nation
🎧 Chapter 17 Digest Audiocassette
💻 Testmaker
💻 Student Self-Test: A Software Review

An Iron Curtain Falls

Soviets Break With Allied Nations

The possibility of the opening of that "great new world" evaporated quickly. The war left the United States and the Soviet Union as the world's dominant powers. Cautious allies during the struggle, the two nations emerged from the war with misgivings about one another. Each viewed the other with deep mistrust. Each had special interests to protect. Each carried the weight of its own history to the moment.

An Uneasy Alliance

During the war, Britain, the Soviet Union, the United States, and 23 other nations had joined forces as the Allied Powers. Having pooled their military might, the 26 set out to crush the Axis Powers in Europe and Asia.

The organization was a strong, but uneasy, alliance. Among its members were nations with old hatreds and misunderstandings of one another, bound together by a common enemy. At the heart of the alliance stood the United States and the Soviet Union.

While the Soviets praised the courage of American soldiers and the leadership of President Roosevelt, old hostilities simmered beneath the surface. The Soviets resented that American troops, along with British and French forces, had tried to undo their revolution of 1917. When that attempt failed, the United States still refused to recognize the Soviet government until 1933. Furthermore, Soviet propaganda stirred up popular fears of American capitalism with its divisions between rich and poor and its swings between prosperity and depression.

The Allies' delay in launching a second front also made Stalin suspicious. He had counted on an invasion of France in 1942 to divert German forces from his country. The United States and Britain delayed the attack for two years, making Stalin think that the Americans secretly wanted a weakened Soviet Union.

Americans also harbored fears of the Soviet Union. Communism, with its emphasis on world revolution, had always frightened Americans. Furthermore, past Soviet agreements with Germany rankled Americans. In 1918 the Soviets struck a separate peace with Germany, forcing the West to fight Germany without Soviet help. In 1939 Stalin signed a short-lived nonaggression pact with Hitler. Adding to American fears were memories of Stalin's bloody attacks on his internal enemies in the 1930s.

During the war Roosevelt struggled to keep the Allies focused on military issues—the common problem—and off the areas of disagreement. As the war came to an end, the United States and the Soviet Union faced their greatest challenge.

Victory in Europe After World War II, victory celebrations took place in both American and Soviet cities. *What effects of the war are evident in this picture?*

Two Views of the World

At the end of the war, the western Soviet Union was a scene of awful destruction. More than 20 million Soviets had died in the struggle. Ground fighting and air bombing had destroyed more than 4.7 million homes, nearly 2,000 towns, and 70,000 villages. Through the ruins wandered the hungry and homeless—25 million of them—seeking a place to settle.

Nothing was more important to Soviet leaders than protecting themselves from a rearmed Germany and rebuilding their shattered economy. One key to their security, they believed, was a permanently weakened Germany. Another was a ring of pro-Soviet nations protecting their western border. From Napoleon's attack on Moscow in 1812 through the German invasions of World Wars I and II, enemy armies had always swept in from the west.

Unlike the Soviets, the Americans emerged from the war more powerful than when they entered it. American deaths of 405,000 were tragic, but the number was small compared with the millions of Soviet dead. A booming American economy controlled nearly 50 percent of the world's wealth, and most Americans felt proud of their successful fight for democracy.

American leaders envisioned a future of international peace and prosperity. They imagined a world patterned after the United States—democratic, open to business expansion and free trade. In this world free nations would solve their differences by talking, not by fighting. Like the Puritans and the believers in Manifest Destiny before them, many Americans felt they had a mission: to build a free world with the United States leading the way.

SECTION ONE **563**

Cooperative Learning

Debate One approach to using this section is for students to prepare a debate. Explain that each student will participate on one side or the other in a debate on the topic "The Marshall Plan helped to keep world peace." Organize students into two groups. Each student should research one aspect of the plan. Remind students that each person should have a role in planning the debating points.

VISUAL INSTRUCTION

Victory in Europe A victory celebration takes place in Stalingrad, May 1945.

Answer: *In the background are buildings damaged in the war.*

TEACH

Guided Practice

L1 Discussion Ask for students' definitions of *cold war*. Discuss whether students feel a cold war is in progress at the present time. Ask students to recall conditions that existed at the end of World War II. Remind them of the political alliances that existed at the time and how they had developed.

Show students Map Transparency 17 and have them complete the activity sheet.

Independent Practice

L1 Ethics Encourage students to research and write about whether Truman could have or should have renegotiated the Yalta agreements after he knew that the United States had the advantage of having successfully exploded an atom bomb.

Have students complete the Chapter 17, Section 1 Vocabulary and Guided Reading Activity. (Also in Spanish.) **LEP**

Have students complete the Chapter 17 Cooperative Learning Activity.

Turning Point at Yalta
Soviets Take Power in Eastern Europe

In February 1945, near the end of the war, the Big Three—Roosevelt, Churchill, and Stalin—met in the Soviet city of Yalta to work out control of the postwar world. The three men and their advisers arrived at a moment when victorious Soviet armies were sweeping across Eastern Europe.

Each leader brought his own concerns to the table. Churchill hoped to save the British Empire; Stalin intended to protect his borders and rebuild his country. Unlike Churchill and Stalin, who believed in great powers controlling spheres of influence, Roosevelt sought the worldwide spread of democracy and free trade. The American President, however, also needed Soviet aid in the war against Japan. All agreed, ultimately, that working out these interests together was the only path to peace.

Every day for a week, the Big Three met in the ballroom of the former czar's palace along the Black Sea. They talked, debated, and compromised.

The meeting at Yalta marked a high point of cooperation among the Big Three. It also became a turning point in the relationship between the major powers, and in many ways it determined the form the postwar world would take.

Big Three Agreements

Many key agreements came out of the Yalta talks. Much to Roosevelt's relief, Stalin agreed to join the fight against Japan "two or three" months after Germany

The Big Three Meet At Yalta, Churchill, Roosevelt, and Stalin reached a number of historic agreements. *Which of these agreements affected the future of Germany?*

surrendered. In return, Stalin would receive territories in Asia. Stalin also pledged Soviet support for the United Nations (UN), an international body that would be formed to help keep world peace.

Agreement broke down over Germany and Eastern Europe. Even though all three leaders feared a rearmed Germany, they disagreed on how to keep Germany under control. Stalin wanted to punish Germany by demanding $20 billion in war payments. Half of the money would go to the Soviet Union to help rebuild its shattered economy. Roosevelt and Churchill knew that Germany could not afford the payments without their help; they feared having to support Germany so it could pay Stalin.

Rather than debate the issue, the three agreed that each nation would control the part of Germany its troops held at the end of the war. Later a commission would solve the problem of war payments.

Control in Eastern Europe

Eastern Europe and Poland were even touchier issues. Stalin demanded recognition of Soviet power in Poland, Romania, Bulgaria, Austria, Hungary, and Czechoslovakia to protect his western border. Soviet forces already occupied much of Eastern Europe, and Stalin had installed a government in Poland. Roosevelt and Churchill protested strongly. Britain went to war "so that Poland should be free," Churchill exclaimed.

In the end, however, Roosevelt and Churchill had little choice but to give in. With the Pacific war still raging, they had no means of forcing Stalin to back down. Reluctantly they agreed to Soviet influence in Eastern Europe but insisted that Stalin hold "free and unfettered elections" at an "early date."

In the weeks after the conference at Yalta, Roosevelt worried as the Soviets installed Communist governments in country after country. Still, he had faith in his ability to win Stalin's trust of the West. Newly elected to a fourth term, Roosevelt believed he could persuade Stalin that the Soviets had nothing to fear and could relax their iron grip on Eastern Europe. Any such hopes were dashed, however, when Roosevelt died suddenly on April 12, 1945.

Truman Comes to Power
Truman Gets Tough With Stalin

"I don't know whether you fellows ever had a load of hay or a bull fall on you, but last night the moon, stars, and all the planets fell on me." Harry S Truman could well feel overwhelmed on his first day as President—April 13, 1945. Nations were still battling, and the world had reached a turning point in its history: The old system of

---

EUROPE AT THE END OF WORLD WAR II

BERLIN

Tegel

Gatow

Tempelhof

ATLANTIC OCEAN

NORWAY

SWEDEN

FINLAND

NORTH SEA

BALTIC SEA

IRELAND

GREAT BRITAIN

London ★

DENMARK

ESTONIA

LATVIA

LITH.

E. PRUSSIA (GER.)

Moscow ★

SOVIET UNION

NETH.

Berlin ★

GERMANY

BELG.

Torgau

POLAND

Paris ★

LUX.

FRANCE

SWITZ.

AUSTRIA

HUNGARY

CZECH.

Trieste

ROMANIA

BLACK SEA

PORTUGAL

SPAIN

ITALY

YUGOSLAVIA

BULGARIA

ALB.

MEDITERRANEAN SEA

GREECE

TURKEY

0   300   600 mi.

0   300   600 km

Azimuthal Equal-Area projection

British, French, and U.S. controlled, May 1945

Soviet controlled, May 1945

Occupied zones of Germany:

American   French

British   Soviet

——— National boundaries, 1937

★ Capital city   ✈ Airport

At the close of World War II, the political map of Europe underwent massive changes. *Which European nations fell under the control of the Soviet Union at the end of the war?*

MAP STUDY

Stalin wanted control of Eastern Europe to protect the western border of the Soviet Union from invasion.

Answer: *Eastern Europe: Estonia, Latvia, Lithuania, East Prussia, East Germany, Czechoslovakia, Hungary, Romania, Yugoslavia, Bulgaria, Poland, Albania*

ABCNEWS INTERACTIVE™

 Videodisc

Communism and the Cold War

Side 2, Chapter 3
Title: United Nations
Subject: The development of the United Nations and the organization's assistance to developing countries
Ask: Why was the UN formed? *(to promote world peace and cooperation)*

See Communism and the Cold War Guidebook page 48 for complete lesson plan.

---

power was crumbling and a new, unknown system remained to be built.

Truman stepped into the presidency unprepared. Raised in a small Missouri town with little chance for an education, the gritty, intelligent Truman worked his way up from the farm to business and finally to the United States Senate. Nominated as Roosevelt's running mate in 1944, he spent only 12 weeks as Vice President before Roosevelt's death.

During those 83 days, Truman got little information from Roosevelt. The President shared no details of key military or foreign policies with him, and Truman received only two short foreign relations briefings. According to Roosevelt's key adviser, Harry Hopkins, Truman himself knew "absolutely nothing of world affairs." Yet only 10 days after Truman assumed the presidency, international events took center stage.

Formation of the United Nations

At Yalta, the Big Three had agreed in principle to an international peacekeeping organization. On April 25, 1945, 50 countries met in San Francisco to draft the charter for the United Nations. United States support was voiced in Truman's address to the conference: "We must build a new world, a far better world—one in which the eternal dignity of man is respected."

The first article of the charter stated that the purpose of the United Nations was to maintain international peace and security. By October 1945, a majority of the participating nations had ratified the charter, and the United Nations officially came into existence.

The United States hoped that the United Nations would help to bring about a world in which every country would be free to run its own government. The Soviet Union—and to a lesser extent Great Britain—believed, however, that self-determination applied only to those countries that did not have strategic value to Soviet, or British, interests. In particular, the Soviets were determined to control Eastern Europe as a protection against future aggression from the West.

Truman's advisers urged him to get tough with the Soviets, and Truman exhibited his hard-line approach during the visit of Soviet ambassador V.M. Molotov. Truman sharply criticized Molotov for failing to support the Yalta agreements. Specifically, Truman demanded to know why the Soviets had not held free elections in Poland.

SECTION ONE   **565**

 Facts on File

Landmark Documents in American History Have students review "United Nations Charter, 1945" and write a paragraph about the intent of the document.

Portfolio Project

Constructing a Graph To calculate the relative influence of the United States, Great Britain, and the Soviet Union, students should consult an atlas to find the number of square miles in the countries under the control of the United States, Great Britain, and the Soviet Union in 1945. Students can then make a graph of the results to put in their portfolios.

Mapping Have students find out what the geographic conditions were in areas of Europe in which World War II was fought. They should consider the season of the year and the probable effects of weather and terrain on battle action. Then have students draw a map that shows the influence of geography on one battle. Have students put their maps in their portfolios.

FYI

Harry S Truman The middle initial in Harry S Truman's name does not stand for anything. It is an initial and nothing more. According to the Truman Library, the President himself sometimes included and sometimes omitted the period after the *S.*

 Facts on File

Landmark Documents in American History Have students review "Potsdam Agreement, 1945"; "'Iron Curtain Speech,' Sir Winston Churchill, 1946"; "Truman Doctrine, 1947"; "Recovery Program, 1947" and write about the intent of one of the documents.

 The Presidents: A Picture History of Our Nation

Have students view "Harry S Truman" and use the information to write a brief biography to include in their portfolios.

Accustomed to Roosevelt's friendly, patient style, Molotov was shaken. "I have never been talked to like that in my life," he reportedly said to Truman.

"Carry out your agreements and you won't get talked to like that," Truman snapped.

Meetings at Potsdam

In this mood of growing hostility, Truman, Stalin, and Churchill met in Potsdam, a suburb of Berlin, in July 1945. Germany had surrendered in May, but the fight with Japan wore on. At this final wartime meeting, the three leaders tried to tie up some loose ends from Yalta, especially the future of Germany.

Truman and Stalin were meeting for the first time, and Truman was determined to be hard-nosed. A few days into the sessions, the already determined Truman learned that American scientists had successfully exploded the atomic bomb. He kept the news to himself, but it was soon clear that something had happened. Churchill recalled, "When he [Truman] got to the meeting after having read the report he was a changed man. He told the Russians just where they got off and generally bossed the whole meeting."

In spite of Truman's attitude, the three leaders reached agreement on Germany. The country would be completely disarmed and its war industries dismantled. Each occupying nation would be allowed to take war payments from its zone.

With this decision the three leaders began moving down the path to a divided Germany. The western half of Germany would remain under British, French, and United States control. The eastern half would stay in Soviet hands. The capital city of Berlin, 110 miles (177 km) deep in the Soviet zone, would also be carved up among the four nations.

All too quickly the world was dividing into two camps. The United States dominated one. The Soviet Union dominated the other.

The Idea of Containment

Over the next seven months, Truman's and Stalin's mistrust of one another grew. Stalin continued to oppress most of Eastern Europe, forcing loyalty to the Soviet Union through phony trials and executions. In the Middle East, Stalin kept his troops in Iran long after United States and British troops had pulled out. Iran complained before the United Nations, and Truman protested as well. In early 1946 the United States gave Britain a $3.5 billion loan but ignored a Soviet request for help.

On February 9, 1946, Stalin added to the growing tension with an important speech in which he declared that capitalism was a danger to world peace. Capitalism and communism, he said, would eventually clash. Because of that danger, he would protect Soviet security by stopping trade with the West and developing modern weaponry no matter how high the cost. In the United States, Supreme Court Justice William Douglas said the speech sounded like "a declaration of World War III."

Truman then received a momentous 16-page telegram from George Kennan, a brilliant young diplomat at the American embassy in Moscow. An expert in Soviet history and culture, Kennan advised Truman that the United States needed to pursue "long-term, patient, but firm and vigilant containment of Russian expansive tendencies." **Containment**—the restriction of communism to its current borders—was the only way to secure the peace.

A few weeks later, in March 1946, Winston Churchill supported this view in a famous speech at Westminster College in Fulton, Missouri. Somberly he warned that "from Stettin in the Baltic to Trieste in the Adriatic, an

---

GALLERY OF PRESIDENTS

Harry S Truman
1945–1953

"The American people desire, and are determined to work for, a world in which all nations and all peoples are free to govern themselves as they see fit. . . . Democracy alone can supply the vitalizing force to stir the peoples of the world into triumphant action, not only against their human oppressors, but also against their ancient enemies—hunger, misery, and despair."

Inaugural Address, January 20, 1949

THE HARRY S TRUMAN LIBRARY

BACKGROUND
► Born 1884; Died 1972
► Democrat, Missouri
► Served in the Senate 1935–1944
► Elected Vice President 1944
► Assumed presidency 1945
► Elected to full term 1948

ACHIEVEMENTS IN OFFICE
► United Nations founded (1945)
► Marshall Plan (1947)
► North Atlantic Treaty Organization (1949)

Extending the Content

The Berlin Wall The Berlin Wall was built in 1961 to separate Communist East Berlin from non-Communist West Berlin. The wall was 26 miles (42 km) of massive concrete slabs. Pipes, barbed wire, armed guards, guard dogs, electric alarms, mines, and trenches fortified the wall. In November 1989, East Berliners gained the freedom to travel to West Berlin. Elated Germans began to tear down the wall. By 1992 most of the wall had been removed, although several sections remain as memorials. Parts of the wall were also sold to museums and private individuals. Discuss with students the significance of the physical destruction of the wall. *(It symbolized the collapse of communism.)*

iron curtain has descended across the continent." Furthermore, Churchill warned, English-speaking people should join forces against the Soviet threat. "There is nothing the Communists admire so much as strength and nothing for which they have less respect than for military weakness."

Cold War Is Declared
Foreign Aid Blocks Communism

Churchill's speech gave the world a clear picture of the future: The West, led by the United States, would resist any Soviet attempts to expand its influence in the world. The **cold war** had begun—a United States–Soviet conflict in which the two powers would avoid fighting each other directly but would block each other's goals around the world.

The Truman Doctrine

In February 1947, the British gave the United States a chance to put containment to work. Nearly bankrupt at the end of the war, the British asked the United States government to take over support of the Greek and Turkish governments. The Soviet Union was trying to force the Turks to share control of a key shipping channel between the Black Sea and the Mediterranean. In Greece the government was fighting Communist rebels, although the Soviet Union was not directly involved.

Truman talked to his advisers, who convinced him that the United States had to act. Otherwise, they believed, the Communists might succeed, and that would "open three continents to Soviet penetration."

Truman agreed but knew he had to convince a Congress that wanted to reduce taxes—not raise them. He would have to "scare the American people" and Congress into supporting the plan.

UPI/BETTMANN

Iron Curtain Speech Winston Churchill speaks at Westminster College. *What was Churchill's famous speech about?*

On March 12, 1947, Truman called a joint session of Congress. In his speech he grimly pictured a threatening world:

At the present moment, nearly every nation must choose between alternative ways of life. The choice is too often not a free one.

One way of life is based upon the will of the majority and is distinguished by free institutions, representative government, free elections, guarantees of individual liberty, freedom of speech and religion, and freedom from political oppression.

The second way of life is based upon the will of a minority forcibly imposed upon the majority. It relies

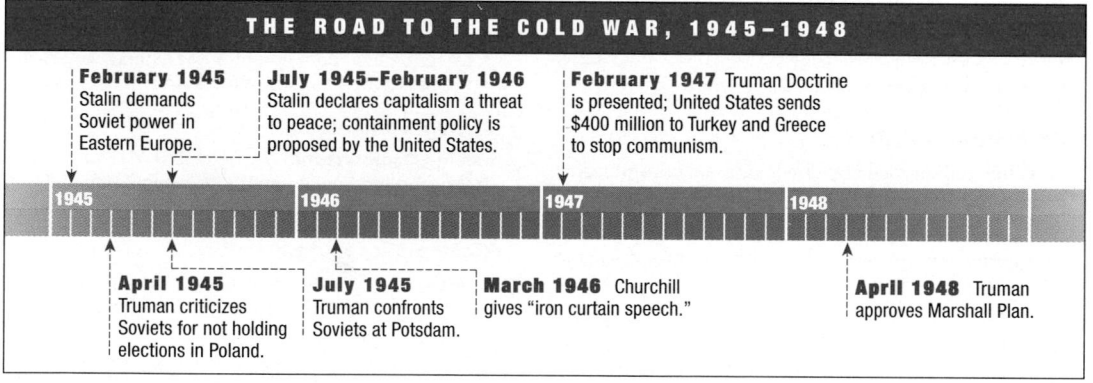

THE ROAD TO THE COLD WAR, 1945–1948

February 1945 Stalin demands Soviet power in Eastern Europe.

July 1945–February 1946 Stalin declares capitalism a threat to peace; containment policy is proposed by the United States.

February 1947 Truman Doctrine is presented; United States sends $400 million to Turkey and Greece to stop communism.

1945   1946   1947   1948

April 1945 Truman criticizes Soviets for not holding elections in Poland.

July 1945 Truman confronts Soviets at Potsdam.

March 1946 Churchill gives "iron curtain speech."

April 1948 Truman approves Marshall Plan.

SECTION ONE   **567**

VISUAL INSTRUCTION

Iron Curtain Speech Churchill called for an Anglo-American alliance.

Answer: *It urged English-speaking people to unite against the Soviet threat.*

ASSESS

Meeting Lesson Objectives

Each section objective is tested by the section review question(s) that follows it in parentheses.

1. Describe the events that led to Soviet dominance in Eastern Europe, the Truman Doctrine, and the cold war. (1, 2, 3)
2. Explain how the ideological differences between the Soviet Union and the United States helped to fuel the cold war. (1, 2, 3)
3. Explain how the Truman Doctrine and the Marshall Plan further defined and deepened the cold war. (1, 3, 4, 5)

CHART STUDY

Ask: What nations did the Truman Doctrine aid? *(Greece and Turkey)*

Cultural Perspectives

The Future of Europe At Yalta major differences of opinion arose over the political future of post war Europe. Discuss the American, British, and Soviet perspectives. Roosevelt's vision, for example, was influenced by economic considerations. A free, democratic Europe would represent fertile new markets for American business and trade. Churchill was driven by security considerations. Stalin wanted to protect his western border. Each nation had suffered through two world wars during the previous three decades, and all of the leaders wanted a postwar Europe over which they could exert influence and control.

Facts on File

Landmark Documents in American History Have students review "Marshall Plan (European Recovery Program), 1947" and write a paragraph about the intent of the document.

VISUAL INSTRUCTION

Marshall Plan The French in this poster translates as "New Growth, Better Life, Inter-European Cooperation."

Answer: *Nations had to agree to spend the aid money on American goods.*

Evaluate

Have students complete the Section Review.

Assign the Section 1 Quiz or use the Testmaker to develop a customized quiz. (Also in Spanish.) **LEP**

Reteach

Have students listen to the Chapter 17, Section 1 Audiocassette. (Also in Spanish.) **LEP**

Enrich

Have students complete the Unit 7 American Literature Reading.

CLOSE

To wrap up the section, ask: Over which Eastern European nations did Stalin demand control at Yalta? *(Poland, Romania, Bulgaria, Austria, Hungary, and Czechoslovakia)*

sève nouvelle   vie meilleure

coopération inter-européenne

Marshall Plan A poster urges European cooperation with the Marshall Plan, which is seen as an opportunity for new growth and new life. *How did nations qualify for Marshall Plan aid?*

upon terror and oppression, a controlled press and radio, fixed elections, and the suppression of personal freedoms.

—Harry S Truman, Speech to Joint Session of Congress, March 12, 1947

Truman went on to state that the United States must help all free people who were "resisting attempted subjugation by armed minorities or outside pressures." Then he asked for $400 million in military and economic aid to support the Greek and Turkish governments. Although many observers felt that Truman painted too harsh a picture, his dramatic appeal worked. Congress approved the request about one month later.

This view, which came to be known as the Truman Doctrine, defined United States foreign policy for the next 20 years. From this moment on, most Americans would view communism as a worldwide threat to democracy that they had a duty to resist. The cold war would become not just a struggle for territory but a fight between two opposing views of the world.

The Marshall Plan

While military aid could help contain communism, Truman and his advisers knew it was only part of the answer. In June 1947, Secretary of State George Marshall suggested another way to bolster freedom—a plan for helping Europe rebuild.

The war had been over for two years, but Europeans were still struggling to survive. Cities and towns had been bombed into ruins. Roads and canals were destroyed.

Worst of all, millions of people were sick, homeless, and hungry. In May 1947, Churchill lamented that Europe was "a rubble heap . . . a breeding ground of pestilence [disease] and hate."

Conditions like these were not only heartbreaking but also dangerous. Such terrible suffering provided ideal conditions for communism to grow, and already Communist parties were gathering strength in France and Italy. A ruined, starving Europe would drain the American economy—and American businesses desperately depended on European markets.

Marshall's plan involved spending billions of dollars to help put Europe, including the USSR, back on its feet. To qualify for the aid, nations had to agree to spend the dollars on goods from the United States. At first many conservatives in Congress disagreed with the plan, but events in Eastern Europe soon changed their minds. The Soviets refused to take part in the plan, criticizing it as the United States's way of taking over Europe. In February 1948, the Communist party seized control of Czechoslovakia, completing the Soviet domination of Eastern Europe.

Two months later Truman approved Congress's bill for $17 billion in aid to Europe over 5 years. Sixteen nations participated in the plan, and by 1952 it was more successful than anyone had dreamed. The Communist party in Western Europe was severely weakened. Western European industries had increased their output by 64 percent, and the prosperity of the United States was ensured. At the same time, however, tensions with the Soviet Union continued to grow.

SECTION REVIEW

Vocabulary
1. Define: containment, cold war.

Checking Facts
2. What was the toll taken in Russian life and property during World War II? Which six Eastern European nations did Stalin demand control over at Yalta?

3. Describe the commitment of the United States to rebuild Europe as part of the Marshall Plan.

Critical Thinking
Making Comparisons
4. Why did the Soviets prefer Roosevelt's style of diplomacy to Truman's?

Linking Across Time
5. What was the political status of Eastern Europe at the start of the cold war? How has that status changed today?

Section 1 Review Answers

1. **containment** (566), **cold war** (567)
2. More than 20 million died, and 25 million lost their homes and livelihood. Stalin demanded control over Poland, Romania, Bulgaria, Austria, Hungary, and Czechoslovakia.
3. The United States pledged billions of dollars to European reconstruction.

4. Truman, blunt and impatient, dealt with the Soviets from a position of distrust. Roosevelt wanted to work with the Soviets and their interests to build peace.
5. At the start of the cold war, Eastern Europe was under Soviet control. Today, all of these nations have asserted their independence.

The Cold War Deepens

JUNE 1948: UNITED STATES AIR FORCE HEADS FOR BERLIN

Berlin Airlift
Young Berliners are glad to see cargo planes arrive with much-needed supplies.

ON A LAZY SATURDAY MORNING IN 1948, LIEUTENANT COLONEL GUY B. DUNN, JR., HEADED FOR A GOLF GAME NEAR BROOKLEY AIR FORCE BASE IN ALABAMA. Before he could get to the course, though, Colonel George S. Cassidy told him they had to get to work—fast. They had to organize 12 aircraft, 3 crews per aircraft, and 62 maintenance people to start a squadron of planes. Their destination—Berlin.

Dunn and his group got under way quickly. Once airborne and droning over the Atlantic, Dunn's colleague Lieutenant Colonel Jim Haun got on the radio. From the air he organized the rest of the squadron, calling on crews from Travis Air Force Base in California and Great Falls Air Force Base in Montana.

The 12 planes heading to Berlin were cargo planes on a mission of mercy—not bombers. Just two weeks later, though, the UN Security Council ordered 60 B-29 bombers—the "atomic bombers"—to bases in Great Britain. There they would be within easy striking range of Moscow.

Berlin Crisis
Soviets in Germany

Not since the cold war began had the United States and the Soviet Union inched so close to war. Threatening speeches and hostile policies had deepened the two countries' fear of each other. Now they had a powder keg on their hands—Berlin.

Since the end of the war, Soviet and American plans for Germany had put the two nations on a collision course. The United States wanted a strong Germany to promote the recovery of Western Europe and to help contain communism. The Soviets demanded a powerless Germany that could never attack the Soviet Union again.

AS YOU READ

Vocabulary
► land reform
► arms race
► limited war

Think About . . .
► the causes of the Berlin blockade and how the blockade affected the arms race.
► factors that led to a Communist victory in China and the effect of China's government on the United States foreign policy.
► how the Korean War helped define the powers of the presidency and the growth of the United States military.

SECTION TWO **569**

Section 2 Resources

REPRODUCIBLE RESOURCES
📁 Lesson Plan 17-2
📁 Vocabulary and Guided Reading Activity 17-2
📁 Section 2 Quiz
📁 Unit 7 American Literature Reading

MULTIMEDIA RESOURCES
💾 Section Focus Transparency 53
💿 Landmark Documents in American History
💿 Communism and the Cold War
📼 Great Speeches

💿 Testmaker
🎧 Chapter 17 Digest Audiocassette
💿 Student Self-Test: A Software Review

Section Objectives

1. Explain the causes of the Berlin blockade and its effect on the division of Europe and the arms race.
2. Analyze why communism succeeded in China and how that change affected United States foreign policy.
3. Review events in the Korean War and their effect on presidential power and military growth.

Bellringer Activity

While taking attendance at the beginning of the class period, display **Section Focus Transparency 53,** and have students answer the questions. (Or use the blackline master.)

VISUAL INSTRUCTION

Berlin Airlift Identify the photo as one of German children waving to a plane during the airlift. Discuss implications of the airlift.

Ask: What issues precipitated the Berlin blockade? *(Soviet leaders declared a new currency for all of Berlin, blockaded highways and railroads, and shut off West Berlin's electric power.)*

Facts on File

Landmark Documents in American History Have students review "Note on Berlin Blockade and Airlift, 1948" and "North Atlantic Treaty (North Atlantic Pact), 1949" and write a paragraph about the intent of one of the documents.

TEACH

Guided Practice

L2 **Citizenship** Discuss Truman's foreign policy. What obligations do citizens have to influence government policies? *(tell their representatives and senators about policies they support)* In what way can they fulfill these obligations? *(learn as much as possible)*

Independent Practice

L1 **Making a Time Line** Have students make a time line from 1948 to 1953. Let them skim to find out where to place events. Then have students expand the time line as they read on.

☞ Have students complete the Chapter 17, Section 2 Vocabulary and Guided Reading Activity. (Also in Spanish.) **LEP**

VISUAL INSTRUCTION

Help Arrives By the time the blockade ended, Berlin was completely split. West and East Berlin each had its own police, currency, and public utilities systems.

Answer: *Truman chose an airlift rather than troops to force open the roads because he did not want to provoke World War III.*

Unable to find a common solution, the two powers pursued their own aims in the zones of Germany and Berlin that they controlled. The United States, Britain, and France hammered out plans to rebuild the three western zones, tie their economies to the rest of Europe, and lay the groundwork for a free West German state. The Soviets viewed these plans with growing anger and alarm.

On June 18, 1948, tensions reached a breaking point when the United States, Britain, and France announced a new currency for the three western zones and West Berlin. Outraged, the Soviet government angrily reminded the Western powers that at Potsdam they had agreed to treat Germany as one country. The Soviets warned them to scrap their currency plan or accept a Soviet currency system for the eastern zone and *all* of Berlin.

Over the next three days, tempers flared. Western leaders reminded the Soviets they had no authority in West Berlin. The Soviets insisted on seeing Berlin as a part of their territory. At meetings on June 22, the powers searched for a compromise but gave up at 10:00 P.M. with no solution.

Showdown in Berlin

In a surprise announcement the next morning, Soviet leaders declared that their currency would start circulating the following day. It would be the official currency in the Soviet zone and all four zones of Berlin. At the same time, Soviet troops blockaded the highways and railroads crossing the eastern zone to West Berlin. Finally, the Soviets shut off West Berlin's electric power.

Suddenly 2 million West Berliners became hostages. Sealed off from the outside world, they had no way to import the 4,000 tons (3,628 t) of food, fuel, and clothes they needed every day. By isolating West Berlin, Stalin hoped to force the Allies into giving up their plans for West Germany or surrendering Berlin—a key Allied listening point—to the Communists.

At this point Truman seemingly faced two terrible choices. He could order American troops to force open the roads and railroads and risk provoking World War

Help Arrives This plane carries the first shipment of coal to Berlin. *Why did Truman choose an airlift rather than troops to open the roads to Berlin?*

III, or he could hand Berlin over to Stalin. Truman's advisers had another idea, though, and after he heard them out, he declared, "We are going to stay—period."

Taking advantage of a 1945 agreement to keep three air corridors open to Berlin, Truman launched an airlift to the trapped city. More than 50 C-54 and 80 C-47 cargo planes, all war-weary and badly in need of repair, were pressed into service. A lifeline to the West, they would fly everything from milk, potatoes, blankets, and coal to clothing and vitamin pills into West Berlin's Templehof and Gatow airports.

Airlift Saves Berlin

For 11 months American and British pilots worked to exhaustion, flying through summer thunderstorms and the dangerous fog and rain of Berlin's winter. At first they landed every 3 minutes, carrying in 2,400 pounds (1,089.6 kg) of supplies a day. At the peak of the airlift, the planes set down on makeshift runways every 45 seconds, day and night. Feverishly, crews unloaded some 13,000 tons (11,791 t) of supplies a day and sent the planes on their way.

The effort—some 277,000 flights delivering 2 million tons (1.8 million t) of supplies—melted the hatred between former American and German enemies.

Before long West Berliners by the hundreds were traveling out to Templehof to thank the pilots. They brought whatever gifts they had—flowers, hand-knitted sweaters, treasured family heirlooms. "An old man, so

---

Cooperative Learning

Map Study Students should work in groups to produce a presentation of the geographic features of Korea, including temperature, terrain, and precipitation. Each group should divide up the tasks fairly so that every member contributes. They should also decide on a medium through which to present the information they find. The result may be a relief map with annotations, a series of maps representing each of the elements listed above, or any other type of map that will supply the geographic background for an understanding of the Korean conflict.

thin you could see through him showed up with a watch that would have fed him for months on the black market," recalled the American public affairs officer. "He insisted on giving it to an American. He called it 'a little token from an old and grateful heart.' "

The blockade was a complete disaster for Stalin. World opinion turned against the Soviet Union and its tactic of starving innocent people to achieve its ends. The United States, however, emerged a resourceful hero, and Berlin quickly became a symbol of America's fight against communism.

In May 1949, Stalin lifted the blockade, but the strong West Germany he had tried to prevent now became a reality. Late in May the United States, Britain, and France agreed to form the Federal Republic of Germany, sealing tight the once loose border between the eastern and western zones. In October 1949, Stalin countered by declaring the German Democratic Republic of Eastern Germany. With those decisions Europe lay divided in half, and the Allied Powers saw that a new alliance was needed.

Allies Form NATO

The Berlin blockade convinced the Allies that Western Europe needed military as well as economic support to remain free. In April 1949, a month before Stalin lifted the blockade, the United States, Canada, and 10 European

nations formed the North Atlantic Treaty Organization (NATO). Not since the Revolutionary War had the United States joined a military alliance with Europe.

In Truman's mind, NATO would work like a "trip-wire." If the Soviet Union dared to invade Western Europe, it would "trip the wire" and set off an American military response. Said Truman, "An armed attack against one or more [nations] in Europe or North America shall be considered an attack against them all." NATO knit Western Europe together as a force and discouraged individual countries from staying uncommitted to the rest.

Truman also persuaded Congress to spend $1.5 billion for military aid to NATO countries, beginning a military buildup in the United States. A few years later, in 1955, the Soviet Union matched NATO with the Warsaw Pact, a Soviet–Eastern Europe alliance planted squarely across the iron curtain.

The Cold War in Asia
Changes Rock the Far East

While the cold war unfolded in Europe, massive changes rocked the Far East. Throughout Asia, British, French, and Dutch colonies began demanding their

DIVIDED EUROPE, 1955

In 1955 NATO and the Warsaw Pact divided Europe into two sections as shown. *What correlation existed between NATO members and participants in the Marshall Plan?*

ABCNEWS INTERACTIVE™

Videodisc

Communism and the Cold War

Side 1, Chapter 4
Title: Spheres of Influence: NATO and the Warsaw Pact
Subject: Creation of alliances
Ask: What was the purpose of NATO? *(to protect Western Europe from Communist takeovers)*

See Communism and the Cold War Guidebook page 7 for complete lesson plan.

MAP STUDY

NATO nations united to prevent the Soviets from attacking Western Europe. The Warsaw Pact nations united to prevent attack from Western Europe.

Answer: *NATO members received Marshall Plan aid while Warsaw Pact nations did not.*

Meeting Special Needs

Limited English Proficiency Pair each student with limited English proficiency with a student fluent in English for discussion and study. Encourage students to use the visuals to help them understand the text. Then have pairs listen to the Chapter 17, Section 2 portion of the chapter audiocassettes after they have read the section. The audiocassettes are also available in Spanish. **LEP**

VISUAL INSTRUCTION

Mao Inspects the Red Army After Jiang Jieshi moved to Taiwan, with the help of generous American aid over two decades, he set Taiwan on the road to modern development. In 1979, however, the United States broke diplomatic relations with Taiwan in order to establish full relations with the People's Republic of China.

Answer: *They united to defeat the Japanese.*

FYI

Pinyin The spelling of the leaders' names given in parentheses is the Wade-Giles spelling, a system used in older books. Chinese names are now spelled according to a system called Pinyin.

Mao Inspects the Red Army Mao Zedong reviews his troops as they prepare to march behind enemy lines. *Why did Chinese Communist and Nationalist forces unite during World War II?*

freedom. Stretched thin by the job of rebuilding at home, the European powers had little choice but to give in. In 1947 Britain granted freedom to India and to Pakistan—which later split into Pakistan and Bangladesh—and in 1949 the Dutch gave up control of Indonesia.

Civil War in China

At the end of World War II, revolution was also raging in China, one of the key allies of the United States. There, Jiang Jieshi (Chiang Kai-shek), leader of the Nationalist government, was fighting a civil war with Mao Zedong (Mao Tse-tung), leader of the Communist forces.

To most Americans, Jiang's success seemed essential to world peace. They believed a strong anti-Communist government in China, the most populous country in the world, would block Soviet expansion and give the United States an important trading partner. Mao's success, many feared, could open Asia to Soviet control.

Yet this view of China was too simple. For one thing, Americans did not understand the Soviets' mistrust of Mao. A brilliant leader, Mao described himself as part tiger and part monkey—part ruthless and part clever. Stalin did not trust Mao or his brand of communism, saying once that "the Chinese Communists are not

really Communists. They are 'margarine' Communists." A weak China, like a weak Germany, would have pleased Stalin more. Likewise, Americans failed to understand a major cause of the Chinese civil war—the oppression by a landlord class of millions of peasant farmers.

In the early 1910s, the Nationalist party swept into power, promising to rid China of foreign powers and to institute **land reform**—redistribution of property to the land-hungry peasants. Once in power, however, the Nationalists ignored the needs of the peasants and put up with corruption at all levels of government. Furthermore, Jiang forced the Communists who helped put him in power out of the government. By the late 1920s, the Communists and the Nationalists were locked in battle.

When the Japanese invaded China in 1937, the Nationalists and the Communists joined forces to defeat the Japanese. As the fighting wore on, however, the fortunes of the Nationalists and the Communists changed dramatically.

Within a year Japanese forces crushed the Nationalist armies and conquered China's coast and river valleys—the industrial and farming heart of the country. With this defeat, the Nationalists lost much of their military strength and their power base.

Portfolio Project

Writing After the Revolutionary War, George Washington warned against foreign entanglements. Have students write a brief essay explaining how conditions changed to justify United States involvement in organizations such as NATO and the UN. Students can place their essays in their portfolios.

By contrast, the Communists took advantage of the war to expand their control in the countryside. Stepping in where the Japanese had destroyed normal life, the Communists set up governments and small police forces. They gave peasants their own plots of land. In time, more and more people felt Mao's Communists protected and took care of them.

By the end of World War II, Communist forces had grown from about 100,000 in 1937 to more than 900,000. As their shoestring army attracted more followers, they began to fight Jiang. Soon they welcomed deserters from Jiang's poorly fed, sickly army into their own ranks.

Truman Steps In

Late in 1945 Truman sent George Marshall to meet with Jiang and Mao and find a way for the two leaders to share control. The idea, however good, was doomed. Both Mao and Jiang wanted to control China alone.

At this point, Truman had to choose a side, and he chose Jiang's. To fuel the Nationalist cause, the United States sent more than $3 billion to help solve China's problems. In return Truman told Jiang to stop his friends from helping themselves to the treasury, to take care of his tattered army, and to answer the cry for land reforms by dividing the land more fairly among the people.

Jiang continued to ignore these problems, while Mao's forces began winning battles. By January 1949, Jiang's forces abandoned Beijing. In May Mao seized Shanghai; in October he took Guangzhou and declared the People's Republic of China. Jiang fled to the offshore island of Taiwan in December, and in the American view, 500 million Chinese were "lost" to communism.

The Response of the United States

To many Americans, Mao's victory represented a frightening failure of containment. The most populous nation on the earth had fallen into the enemy camp. "Who lost China?" many demanded to know.

Republican leaders blamed Truman and the State Department. They believed more military support would have stopped Mao.

Truman responded that China was not America's to lose. Jiang, Truman said, lost because he refused to solve his nation's problems. The United States already had expensive programs to pay for in Europe. A full-scale war in China would have been too costly.

Still, the failure of containment was disturbing. To anchor freedom in Asia, the National Security Council urged the President to support the remaining friendly nations in Asia. Jiang's government was one. Another was Bao Dai's regime in Vietnam.

The Arms Race Begins

As hard as the Truman administration tried to keep people calm, events in Berlin and China unnerved everybody—including Truman himself. In January 1950, he ordered a high-level study of the defenses of the United States. The outcome of that study—the top secret National Security Council Report NSC-68—suggested beginning a massive buildup of weapons to stay ahead of the Soviets. The subsequent competition between the United States and the Soviet Union for greater military strength became known as the **arms race.**

According to NSC-68, the Soviet Union should be considered an enemy with a "design for world domination." As the leader of the "free world," only the United States could be expected to lead the fight against Soviet expansion. That job, however, required a huge army and navy and the best weapons that money could buy. To pay for such a massive defense system would require more than three times the $13 billion defense budget.

Truman and his advisers agreed with the report, but they worried about persuading Congress and the public to support a huge increase in taxes. "We were sweating over it," said a State Department aide, "and then, thank God, Korea came along."

THE COMMUNIST TAKEOVER OF CHINA, 1911–1949

1911 Nationalists form the new Republic of China.

1934 Mao and his followers begin Long March.

1946 Chinese civil war resumes.

1910　1920　1930　1940　1950

1921 Chinese Communist party forms.

1937 Nationalists and Communists join forces against Japan.

1949 Communists declare People's Republic of China; Nationalists flee to Taiwan.

ABCNEWS INTERACTIVE™

⊙ **Videodisc**

Communism and the Cold War

Side 2, Chapter 7
Title: Korean War
Subject: Images of the Korean War, including newsreel footage
Ask: Who led the American forces in Korea? *(General MacArthur)*

See Communism and the Cold War Guidebook page 55 for complete lesson plan.

Side 1, Chapter 6
Title: The Arms Race
Subject: Development of the arms race between the United States and the Soviet Union
Ask: What was the purpose of the arms race? *(to ensure that each nation could defend itself against attack)*

See Communism and the Cold War Guidebook page 11 for complete lesson plan.

CHART STUDY

Ask: When did the Nationalists flee to Taiwan? *(1949)*

Extending the Content

Mao The young Mao was a Nationalist and strongly anti-Western. His nationalism combined with his combativeness made him admire the military, which supported him in conflicts with his party in the 1950s and 1960s. Mao at first regarded the Chinese peasants as incapable of revolution. Yet gradually he decided that the power of hundreds of millions of peasant farmers would be useful to him. In 1955 Mao speeded up collectivization of farms. Then came the Great Leap Forward, an effort to create small-scale industry throughout China. The experiment faltered through waste, confusion, and inefficient management. In 1966 the party launched the Cultural Revolution to supress intellectuals and bureaucrats. This too failed.

GLENCOE
TECHNOLOGY

Great Speeches

Volume I—General Douglas MacArthur—Soviet Union

Ask: Why did the arms race occur? *(to ensure national defense)*

ASSESS

Meeting Lesson Objectives

Each section objective is tested by the section review question(s) that follows it in parentheses.

1. Explain the causes of the Berlin blockade and its effect on the division of Europe and the arms race. (2, 5)

2. Analyze why communism succeeded in China and how that change affected United States foreign policy. (1, 4)

3. Review events in the Korean War and their effect on presidential power and military growth. (1, 3)

Hot War Flares in Korea
North Korean Communists Invade South

About 4:00 A.M. on a rainy June 25, 1950, some 75,000 North Korean troops following Soviet-made tanks poured across the 38th parallel into South Korea. They "struck like a cobra," recalled General Douglas MacArthur. While the attack took everyone by surprise, it followed years of squabbling.

At the end of World War II, Korea suffered a fate much like Germany's. The victors divided Korea along the 38th parallel, leaving a Communist government with a powerful army in the north and a pro-Western government in the south. Both governments wanted to reunify Korea on their own terms. Now the North Koreans had made the first move.

KOREAN WAR, 1950-53

→ UN forces
→ Chinese Communist and N. Korean forces
→ N. Korean forces
— Truce line, July 1953
★ Capital city

PEOPLE'S REPUBLIC OF CHINA

SOVIET UNION

3. Farthest advance of UN forces Nov. 1950

SEA OF JAPAN

Pyongyang ★

NORTH KOREA

38th Parallel (Int'l. boundary 1950)

Panmunjom
Seoul ★
Inchon

2. UN landing Sept. 1950

4. Farthest advance of North Koreans and Chinese Jan. 1951

1. Farthest advance of North Koreans Sept. 1950

YELLOW SEA

SOUTH KOREA

Pusan

Korea Strait

JAPAN

0   50   100 mi.
0 50 100 km
Conic projection 126° E   129° E

The Korean War raged along the Korean peninsula. *What city is located near the 38th parallel?*

Truman Responds

Truman decided to fight back, viewing the assault as a test of containment. Without seeking approval from Congress, Truman ordered air and naval forces to Korea on June 27. The same day, he sought the help of the United Nations.

In a strange twist of fate, the Soviet delegate to the UN Security Council was not present to block Truman's request. He had walked out of the United Nations to protest the council's unwillingness to seat a representative from Mao's China. With little debate, the Security Council condemned the Korean invasion and voted to provide money to help South Korean, American, and supporting UN forces repel the attack.

Through the summer the North Korean army swept southward, cornering UN forces in the southeast around Pusan. On September 15, however, MacArthur launched a brilliant naval invasion behind enemy lines at Inchon, a port city near Seoul. With 18,000 marines and tanks, he rolled east and freed Seoul. From there the UN forces drove the North Koreans back to the 38th parallel.

MacArthur smelled victory, and he persuaded Truman to let him fight on to free all of Korea. Through the autumn MacArthur's troops pushed the North Korean army deeper into their own territory. By November MacArthur had them backed against the Chinese border at the Yalu River.

As MacArthur's troops approached the Yalu River and aircraft began bombing bridges crossing into China, Mao warned MacArthur to back off. Stubborn and overconfident, MacArthur paid no attention to Mao. Instead, he launched another attack to the north. In late November, however, huge numbers of Chinese troops surged across the Yalu and attacked the UN forces, taking MacArthur by surprise. Through the bitterly cold Korean winter, Chinese forces drove the UN troops back across the 38th parallel. There the war ground to a brutal stalemate, with both Chinese and UN troops fighting and dying over small snow-covered hills.

Truman Fires MacArthur

After Chinese troops had joined the fight, Truman decided to give up the idea of freeing all of Korea and to seek a peace settlement. Outraged and anxious to win the war, MacArthur demanded permission to attack China, using nuclear weapons if necessary. "In war there is no substitute for victory," he insisted.

"We are trying to prevent a world war—not start one," Truman shot back. MacArthur, however, was bent on victory. He publicly criticized Truman's policy of **limited war**—keeping the fight confined to one area and avoiding the use of nuclear weapons. Finally, in April 1951, Truman fired MacArthur.

Cultural Perspectives

The Chinese Civil War The civil war between the Chinese Nationalists and the Chinese Communists might have been avoided had the Nationalists kept their promises to the people. By denying peasants the land they were promised, by forcing friendly Communists out of the government, and by ignoring corruption, however, the Nationalists practically guaranteed their unpopularity and a bitter struggle for

power with the Communists. Some students might research and make a report on Chinese farmers of this era. Was there anything about their society or culture that would make them support one leader over another? Students should try to obtain statistics or information on improvements made under the rule of Mao Zedong.

"Who does Truman think he is — the PRESIDENT?"

MacArthur Fired Truman's firing of General Douglas MacArthur was the beginning of a decline in the President's popularity. *Why was Truman criticized throughout his second term?*

The Korean War's Impact
Support Grows for a Stronger Military

The Korean War settled little in Asia. When it ended in 1953, the official border was set at the cease-fire line, not far from where the fighting began. Korea continued to be divided in half with a Communist regime in the north and a pro-Western government in the south. Still, the conflict had far-reaching effects.

First, the Korean War convinced Americans that a huge military buildup was a good idea. Moving faster than NSC-68 suggested, Congress increased defense spending from $22.3 billion in 1951 to $50.4 billion in 1953. The United States emerged from the Korean War with an army of 3.5 million as well as overseas military bases and powerful new weapons like the long-range B-52 bomber. Moreover, the country now had a stockpile of 750 nuclear warheads, an increase of 600 in 2 years.

The public also supported Truman's decisive actions in Korea, overlooking the fact that he never sought or received a declaration of war from Congress. Truman's independent action enhanced the power of the presidency and laid the foundation for later undeclared wars.

President Truman's action ignited a storm of public fury. After all, Americans had just won a world war. Why not let MacArthur, a warrior and a hero, rid Asia of communism? Truman's popularity took a nosedive; only 29 percent of the public agreed with the action he had taken. Returning to the United States for the first time since World War II, MacArthur at first received widespread public support.

Many government officials supported Harry Truman, however. They knew that the United States could not afford to provoke the Soviet Union into open warfare. Nor could the United States expend all of its resources in Asia, leaving the continent of Europe unprotected. After a much-publicized United States Senate investigation of Douglas MacArthur's dismissal, however, popular support for his position declined sharply.

In July 1951, shortly after General MacArthur's firing, United Nations representatives and North Koreans met to begin peace talks. The fighting and the talks dragged on for two more years. The peace talks were finally settled by the next President of the United States, Dwight D. Eisenhower.

SECTION REVIEW

Vocabulary
1. Define: land reform, arms race, limited war.

Checking Facts
2. What does the acronym NATO stand for? What is the name of NATO's Soviet counterpart?

3. Why did President Truman relieve General Douglas MacArthur of his command in Korea?

Critical Thinking
Drawing Conclusions
4. How might a Nationalist victory in the Chinese civil war have affected the outcome of the Korean conflict?

Linking Across Time
5. The reunification of East and West Germany took place in 1990. At that time newly independent Poland expressed strong reservations about a reunified Germany and even asked that Soviet troops stationed in Poland remain to buttress Poland's defenses. How did Poland's concerns in 1990 mirror Soviet concerns about Germany immediately after World War II?

Evaluate

Have students complete the Section Review.

☛ 🖸 Assign the Section 2 Quiz or use the Testmaker to develop a customized quiz. (Also in Spanish.) **LEP**

Reteach

🎧 Have students listen to the Chapter 17, Section 2 Audiocassette. (Also in Spanish.) **LEP**

Enrich

☛ Have students complete the Unit 7 American Literature Reading.

CLOSE

Have students discuss the items included on their time lines. Have them decide on the three or four most significant events. You might want to ask questions such as: What caused the Allies to form NATO? *(to guard against Soviet invasion of Western Europe; in response, the Warsaw Pact was formed by the Soviet Union and the Contries of Eastern Europe);* What was NSC-68? *(a report that suggested the United States should lead the fight against Soviet expansion);* Where did Jiang Jieshi retreat to after the defeat of his forces? *(Taiwan)*

Section 2 Review Answers

1. land reform (572), **arms race** (573), **limited war** (574)
2. NATO: North Atlantic Treaty Organization. Its counterpart was the Warsaw Pact.
3. MacArthur publicly criticized Truman's policy of limited war.
4. If Chinese Nationalists had won, the United States might have fought an offensive war supporting South Korea instead of a defensive one against North Korea.
5. After World War II, the Soviets wanted to prevent a German attack; Poland feared Germany because it had encroached on Polish territory in two wars.

FOCUS

Section Objectives

1. Explain the effect of the Soviet atomic bomb on American society and the arms race.

2. Explain the causes and effects of Eisenhower's massive retaliation strategy and how it changed American foreign policy.

3. Explain the reasons for a growing disarmament movement and the outcomes of that movement.

4. Analyze the effects of *Sputnik* on the United States's military, its schools, and its industry.

Bellringer Activity

While taking attendance at the beginning of the class period, display **Section Focus Transparency 54,** and have students answer the questions. (Or use the blackline master.)

VISUAL INSTRUCTION

Atomic Scare American troops had not yet begun fighting in the Korean conflict when the United States learned that the Soviet Union had exploded an atomic bomb. Ask students to predict what the United States's response would be to this situation.

Ask: What did Truman do to calm the public's jangled nerves? *(He organized the Federal Civil Defense Administration.)*

Cold War in the Atomic Age

AUGUST 1949: THE SOVIET UNION JOINS THE NUCLEAR CLUB

THUNDER BOOMED OMI-NOUSLY, AND HAIL CLAT-TERED DOWN ON THE WHITE HOUSE ROOF THE MORNING OF SEPTEMBER 23, 1949. Just after 10:30 A.M., White House reporters finished a routine meeting with Charles Ross, President Harry S Truman's press secretary. On their way out, however, Ross's secretary, Myrtle Bergheim, told the reporters to stick around. She called them out of the nearby pressroom and back into Ross's office just seconds before 11:00 A.M. None of them knew what was coming, and none of them realized how perfectly the storm outside would fit the news.

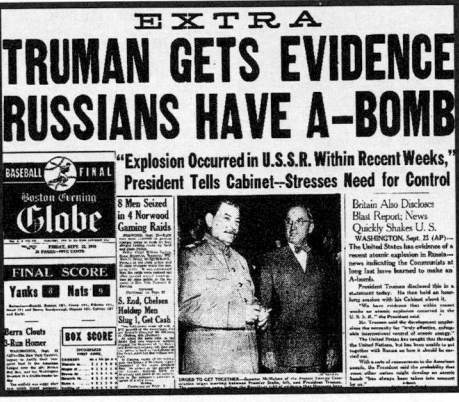

Atomic Scare
The world became a more frightening place for many Americans when they learned that the USSR had exploded an atomic bomb.

As the last reporter filed in, Ross said, "Close the door. Nobody is leaving until everybody has this statement."

Ross handed each reporter a short statement by Truman. The first reporter to scan the copy gasped; in seconds the whole group tore out of Ross's office and down the hall for the pressroom phones. In the mad rush, somebody crashed into a stuffed deer head and broke off its nose.

When the presidential statement hit the papers, it stunned the nation. "We have evidence," Truman announced, "that within recent weeks an atomic explosion occurred in the USSR."

AS YOU READ

Vocabulary
► massive retaliation
► brinksmanship
► military-industrial complex

Think About . . .
► how the Soviet atomic bomb affected American society and the arms race.
► why Eisenhower favored a policy of massive retaliation and how it changed American foreign policy.

► what caused the growth of the disarmament movement and its influence.
► the effects *Sputnik* had on the military, schools, and industry of the United States.

Section 3 Resources

REPRODUCIBLE RESOURCES
- Lesson Plan 17-3
- Vocabulary and Guided Reading Activity 17-3
- Section 3 Quiz
- Geography in History Activity 17
- Skill Reinforcement Activity 17
- Unit 7 Case Study

MULTIMEDIA RESOURCES
- Section Focus Transparency 54
- Communism and the Cold War
- Landmark Documents in American History
- The Presidents: A Picture History of our Nation
- Great Speeches
- Chapter 17 Digest Audiocassette
- American Music: Cultural Traditions

Living With Fear
Two Nuclear Powers

With this chilling announcement, the United States's sense of security went up in a cloud of smoke—a dark, fearsome mushroom-shaped cloud. The world now had two nuclear powers, and what happened to Hiroshima and Nagasaki could just as easily happen to New York or Chicago or Los Angeles.

Public Worry

When the atomic age burst into history at Hiroshima in 1945, Americans were shocked, confused, and terrified. Like children whistling in the dark, they also joked about the bomb. Stores had atomic sales, bars sold atomic cocktails, musicians wrote ballads and polkas about the bomb, but under the surface laughter ran a deep current of fear. Months passed before Americans got used to the idea of life with the bomb.

With Truman's announcement America's fears surged back to the surface. The media jumped on the story, both soothing the panic with helpful advice and intensifying fears with hair-raising descriptions. One radio show broadcast the following account of a make-believe nuclear attack on Chicago:

> Most of those in the center of the city were violently killed by the blast or by the following vacuum, which explosively burst their stomachs. . . . Those few who escaped the blast, but not the gamma rays, died slowly after they had left the ruined city. No attempt at identification of the bodies or burial ever took place. Chicago was simply closed.
>
> —NBC radio program, August 1949

To help calm the public's jangled nerves, Truman organized the Federal Civil Defense Administration (FCDA). Within months the agency flooded the country with posters and booklets telling people they *could* survive a nuclear war—if they were prepared.

How should Americans prepare? Best of all, they could build some kind of underground bomb shelter. A simple one could be a trench covered with dirt. They could also take shelter in the family car or a well-stocked basement protected with piles of dirt around the outside walls.

If a shelter was not handy when an attack came, people learned to "jump in any . . . ditch or gutter" and "bury their faces in their arms." Grade schools instructed children in these procedures. To keep from panicking during an attack, people were encouraged to use "little tricks to help steady their nerves—reciting jingles or the multiplication tables."

Once again, all of America seemed preoccupied with nuclear war. Real estate agents offered houses in "safe locations." Doctors and ministers took courses on coping with radiation injuries and panic. Entrepreneurs tried to sell every product they could dream up—burn medicine, ready-made bomb shelters, dog tags, even radiation-proof clothing for dad, mom, kids, and the dog.

The Game Gets Deadlier

Scary as nuclear bombs were, most Americans thought the best way to prevent nuclear war was to have more and better bombs than the Soviets. Truman agreed. In January 1950, after a heated debate with his advisers, the President ordered scientists to develop a deadly hydrogen bomb, a superbomb. By late 1952, the scientists were ready to test the first H-bomb–nicknamed Mike—on a coral island in the South Pacific.

No one who saw the explosion after the bomb was dropped ever forgot it. Out of a blast of white heat, 5

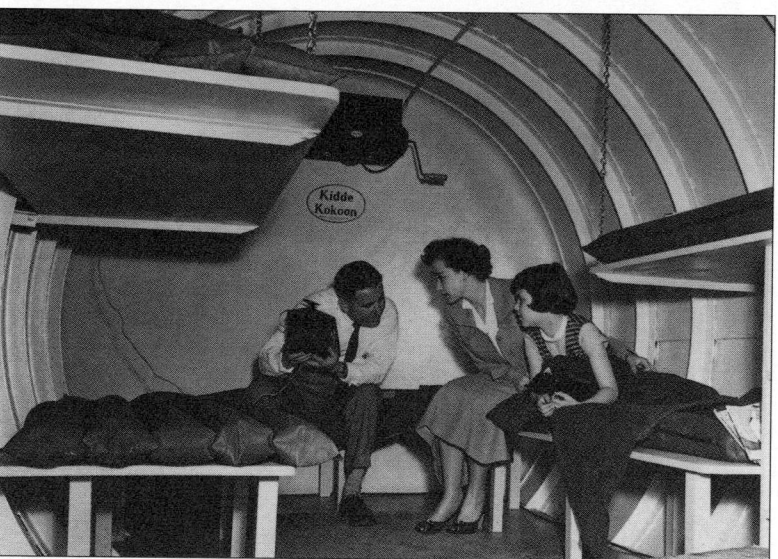

UPI/BETTMANN NEWSPHOTOS

Bomb Shelter Public fear of nuclear attack resulted in the building of backyard bomb shelters and numerous publications from the Federal Civil Defense Administration. *What caused Americans to become so fearful during the 1950s?*

SECTION THREE   **577**

Cooperative Learning

Presenting Information From the Time
Students might collect newspaper clippings, magazine articles, sheet music, or other artifacts from the years 1949 to 1961. You might organize the class into several groups, each of which can concentrate on one three-year period. Have group members divide the work fairly and assign roles. When the work is complete, the groups can reassemble and brainstorm ideas for organizing the information and presenting it as a culminating activity.

Independent Practice

 Citizenship Have students consider how they feel about today's relationship between the United States and the former Soviet Union. How have conditions surrounding this relationship changed? Have students write a letter to their state or federal representatives expressing their concerns.

📼 Have students complete the Chapter 17, Section 3 Vocabulary and Guided Reading Activity. (Also in Spanish.) **LEP**

💿 **Facts on File**

Landmark Documents in American History Have students review "'I Shall Go to Korea' speech, Dwight D. Eisenhower, 1952" and write a paragraph about the intent of the document.

VISUAL INSTRUCTION

The First Family Mamie Dowd Eisenhower shared Ike's roving military life. When she settled in as First Lady, she proved a gregarious, gracious hostess, unlike Bess Truman, her shy predecessor. Ike himself was tough but likable, well-traveled, and acquainted with world leaders.

Answer: *Eisenhower portrayed an image of success, competence, and confidence.*

---

times hotter than the center of the sun, billowed a monstrous mushroom-shaped cloud. Purple, gray, and yellow and nearly 100 miles (160.9 km) wide, it climbed 25 miles (40.2 km) into the sky. The blast carved a mile-long (1.6 km) crater in the bottom of the ocean and spilled radioactive dust over thousands of square miles. Nuclear scientists had let a terrible genie out of the bottle, and now there was no way to put it back.

Eisenhower Elected
A War Hero in the White House

Three days after the H-bomb Mike blew a coral island to smithereens, Republican Dwight D. Eisenhower won the 1952 presidential election. The World War II hero stepped into the White House at the height of the cold war. China had fallen. United States troops were bogged down in Korea. Growing stockpiles of atomic bombs had Americans on edge. In the midst of mounting danger, Ike seemed like the perfect leader.

Raised on the Kansas frontier and honed into a tough army officer by West Point and World War II, Eisenhower was both a seasoned soldier and a grandfather figure. He had an instinct for people, and his homespun charm won hearts instantly. Said one of Eisenhower's World War II compatriots: "He has the power of drawing the hearts of men towards him as a magnet attracts bits of metal. He merely has to smile at you, and you trust him at once." People, as the campaign buttons said, liked Ike.

Eisenhower in Korea

Americans found President Eisenhower's upbeat outlook and his practicality comforting in dangerous times. They also liked his determination to settle the Korean War.

Before the election in 1952, Eisenhower had accused the Democrats of "mishandling the war," and vowed that his first job as President would be "to bring the Korean war to an early and honorable end. If that job requires a personal trip to Korea," Eisenhower had declared, "I shall make that trip."

True to his word, three weeks after the election, Eisenhower toured the Korean front and confirmed his hunch that peace talks offered the only way out. "Small attacks on small hills would not end this war." Still, Eisenhower took time to review other ways of ending the war, including full-scale war against China and nuclear attacks on Korea. Finally, though, he decided to demand peace talks backed up by a veiled threat to use nuclear weapons.

The First Family Mamie and Ike's eight years in the White House was the longest they had lived in one place. *What qualities did Eisenhower project to Americans?*

The death of Joseph Stalin in March 1953 aided Eisenhower's search for peace. Communist leaders in China and North Korea could no longer be sure of Soviet help; nor could they be sure whether Eisenhower was bluffing or telling the truth about a nuclear attack. With little choice but to settle the fight, United Nations and Communist delegates finally signed an agreement in July 1953 dividing Korea into two parts at the truce line.

Eisenhower and Dulles

With the Korean War behind him, Eisenhower could focus on the cold war and the arms race. Like Truman, Eisenhower was a passionate anti-Communist. Unlike Truman, however, Eisenhower stepped into office with a solid grasp of world affairs. He had lived in Latin America, Europe, and Asia. As a World War II general and, later, the commander of NATO, he had mingled with heads of state. Even so, Eisenhower wanted a secretary of state who would hold the line on communism and advise him on areas like the Middle East and Asia.

John Foster Dulles fit the bill. A polished international attorney, Dulles had spent more than 40 years in foreign relations. The son of a Presbyterian minister, white-haired Dulles was also deeply religious and fiercely anti-Communist. Many Americans found Dulles humorless and argumentative. Churchill once said that Dulles was the only "bull he knew who carried his own china shop with

---

Meeting Special Needs

Learning Disability This activity helps address the particular needs of students with learning problems. Have students listen to Chapter 17, Section 3 on the chapter audiocassettes and follow along in their text as they listen. The audiocassettes are also available in Spanish. Then have students work in pairs to summarize out loud the most important events in the section. Students may want to review the heads and visuals in the section as prompts. **LEP**

him." Premier Nikita Khrushchev of the Soviet Union would later say of Dulles that he "knew how far he could push us and he never pushed us too far."

A New Strategy
Cold War Questions

Together, Eisenhower and Dulles took a fresh look at the cold war game board. Problems and unknowns were everywhere. Who would replace Stalin in the Soviet Union? How long could the United States afford to build bigger armies and navies and bombs? Was containment the best defense against communism? How did nuclear weapons figure into all of this?

In May 1953, Eisenhower assigned three top-level groups to study the situation, while he worked with defense officials to cut military costs. Out of these studies emerged a new containment policy.

Massive Retaliation

Instead of depending on costly armies and navies to fight limited wars as Truman did, Eisenhower decided to rely on cheaper air power and nuclear weapons. This program, called the New Look, would retire 500,000 soldiers and 100,000 sailors but would increase the air force by 30,000 men. The new defense plan would save about $4 billion a year, thereby providing "a bigger bang for the buck."

Smaller armies and navies required a different way to fight communism, so Eisenhower and Dulles proposed a new policy. If the Soviet Union attacked any nation, the United States would launch **massive retaliation**—an instant nuclear attack "by means and at places of our own

John Foster Dulles Dulles speaks before the United Nations. *What policy did Eisenhower and Dulles propose to fight communism?*

choosing." Such a vague threat, Eisenhower believed, would force the Communists to think twice before attacking because they could not be sure where the United States might strike.

Critics called this tough stance **brinkmanship**—the art of never backing down from a crisis, even if it meant pushing the nation to the brink of war. By keeping the Communists from testing every weak spot along their borders, the United States could stay out of small, limited wars that cost huge amounts of money.

To back up this tough stance, Eisenhower and Dulles also circled the Soviet Union and China with more American military bases and allies. By the end of the decade, Dulles had worked out mutual defense treaties with 43 countries around the globe.

★ ★ ★ **GALLERY OF PRESIDENTS** ★ ★ ★

Dwight David Eisenhower

1953–1961

THE BETTMAN ARCHIVE

"We must be ready to dare all for our country. For history does not long entrust the care of freedom to the weak or the timid. We must acquire proficiency in defense and display stamina in purpose. We must be willing, individually and as a Nation, to accept whatever sacrifices may be required of us. A people that values its privileges above its principles soon loses both."

Inaugural Address, January 20, 1953

BACKGROUND
► Born 1890; Died 1969
► Republican, Kansas
► Graduated West Point 1915
► Commanding general of United States forces in Europe 1942
► Supreme commander of the Allied Expeditionary Force in Europe 1943

ACHIEVEMENTS IN OFFICE
► Southeast Asia Treaty Organization formed (1954)
► NASA formed (1958)

Portfolio Project

Writing One reason for Eisenhower's popularity with the American people was his record as a successful general in World War II. Students should identify two or more earlier presidents who were war heroes before they embarked on a political career. Have students write an essay comparing the success of each man in warfare with his ability as chief executive. Have students explain the qualities of a military person that may equip him or her for the position of president. Students can place their essay in their portfolios.

Facts on File

 History and the Humanities

Policy Dangers

The policy of massive retaliation had two dangerous results. First, it gave the United States only two extreme ways of responding to a Communist attack: either fight a nuclear battle or do nothing. The middle ground, using armies to fight small wars, virtually disappeared. The United States had to gamble on threats and Soviet insecurity to keep the peace.

Second, the Soviets did not sit idly by and let the United States sprint ahead in the arms race. Heavy spending by the United States for nuclear weapons spurred the Soviets to step up their own research, and in July 1953, they exploded an H-bomb in Siberia. "The U.S. and Soviet Union are like two scorpions in a bottle, each capable of killing the other but only at the risk of his own life," observed J. Robert Oppenheimer, father of the atomic bomb. The world had reached, in Churchill's words, a new "balance of terror."

H-bomb Test A mushroom-shaped cloud from a nuclear test looms over the Marshall Islands in the fall of 1952. *What was the name of the biggest H-bomb the United States tested?*

Eisenhower Wages Peace
A Plan for Nuclear Disarmament

Eisenhower was a realist. He knew he had to be tough with the Soviets, so he kept the war machine working. Like Oppenheimer, he understood that nuclear war was pointless. From the early days of his presidency, Eisenhower searched for ways to disarm atomic weapons.

A few weeks after Stalin's death, Eisenhower made his famous "Chance for Peace" speech before a group of newspaper editors. "An era ended with the death of Joseph Stalin," Eisenhower said, inviting friendlier relations with the Soviet Union. He went on to spell out the high costs of cold war. "Every gun that is made, every warship launched, every rocket fired signifies . . . a theft from those who hunger and are not fed, those who are cold and not clothed." Eisenhower closed with an appeal for nuclear disarmament.

In December 1953, Eisenhower carried his appeal to the United Nations. There he proposed an "atoms for peace" plan in which Soviets and Americans would contribute radioactive materials to a stockpile for peaceful uses.

Nuclear Fallout from Bravo H Bomb Test, 1954

Hours after explosion
0   6   7   8   9   10   11   12   13   14   15   16 17

Wind Direction

Pacific coral islands

Heaviest fallout — Lightest fallout

0 20 40 60 80 100 120 140 160 180 200 220 240 260 280 300 320 340
Miles from center of explosion

The radioactive fallout from Bravo affected 239 of the inhabitants of the Marshall Islands and 28 American service personnel. *How far did the heaviest fallout travel? The lightest fallout?*

Extending the Content

Massive Retaliation The American policy of massive retaliation and its later counterpart, mutually assured destruction (MAD), were based on the assumption that sane leaders would never risk the annihilation of their countries' people for any reason. Discuss with students the assumptions that led to the location of the H-bomb test. Ask: Were the dire effects of nuclear fallout anticipated? Was the testing morally justified? Why or why not?

Fallout Fears

As Eisenhower worked for peace, arms research continued. On March 1, 1954, the United States set off the biggest H-bomb it had ever tested—the equivalent of 15 million tons (13.6 million metric tons) of TNT, nicknamed Bravo.

The massive explosion in the South Pacific created a radioactive cloud that rained deadly silver ash on 7,000 square miles (18,130 sq km) of ocean waters and islands. Worst of all, radioactive ash fell on 23 Japanese fishers aboard the *Lucky Dragon*, some 80 miles (128.7 km) from the blast. By the time the fishers got back to Japan, all 23 were sick with radiation poisoning. A few months later, Aikichi Kuboyama, the radioman, died.

Suddenly people had something new to worry about—radioactive fallout. It was possible to live hundreds of miles from a nuclear blast and still be killed. Around the world, concern grew about nuclear tests and the effects of their deadly radioactive clouds.

Talks in Geneva

By the autumn of 1954, international voices were clamoring for a halt to the arms race. Late that year Soviet and Western leaders finally agreed to meet the following summer—their first face-to-face talk since 1945.

Eisenhower flew to the meeting in Geneva, Switzerland, with high hopes of improving relations between the United States and the Soviet Union. The first few days of meetings went poorly, however. The Soviet leaders—Nikolay Bulganin and Nikita Khrushchev, the real power—"drank little and smiled much," Eisenhower commented. Their actions seemed unnatural, rehearsed.

After several days, Eisenhower decided to loosen things up. Speaking earnestly to the Soviet leaders, he proposed the "open skies" idea in which the two nations would inspect each other's military sites from the air. Bulganin agreed to think about the idea, but Khrushchev dismissed the plan as an obvious spying ploy. Ten years

Nuclear Arms, 1945–1965

The arms race led to a dramatic rise in the number of nuclear warheads. *How does the number of Soviet warheads in 1960 compare with the number of American warheads that year?*

of bitter mistrust stood in the way of the idea, and in the end the Soviets let it die. Even so, the Geneva conference did end on an upbeat note—the powers had begun to talk again.

The Deep Freeze Returns

Soviet Power in Hungary

Through the rest of 1955 and into 1956, the cold war seemed to be thawing. The talks in Geneva had broken the ice, and back home Khrushchev made some astounding statements. In a momentous speech before the Party Congress in February 1956, he openly condemned Stalin's crimes against the Soviet people. Moreover, he

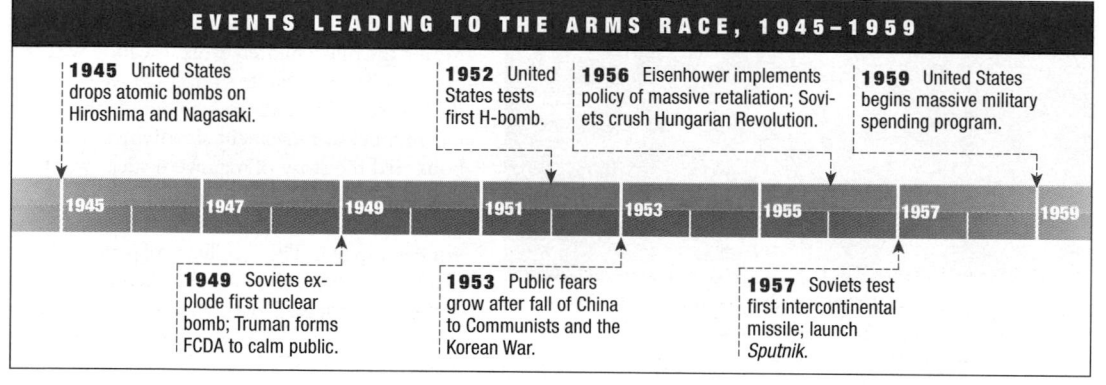

EVENTS LEADING TO THE ARMS RACE, 1945–1959

1945 United States drops atomic bombs on Hiroshima and Nagasaki.

1952 United States tests first H-bomb.

1956 Eisenhower implements policy of massive retaliation; Soviets crush Hungarian Revolution.

1959 United States begins massive military spending program.

1949 Soviets explode first nuclear bomb; Truman forms FCDA to calm public.

1953 Public fears grow after fall of China to Communists and the Korean War.

1957 Soviets test first intercontinental missile; launch *Sputnik*.

SECTION THREE   **581**

GRAPH STUDY

The success of nuclear weapons depends on their being undetectable. The Hiro-shima and Nagasaki bombs were carried on large airplanes. Since then nuclear wea-pons have been miniaturized and put inside missiles that can be launched from silos, submarines, or mobile launchers.

Answer: *The Soviets had far fewer warheads than the Americans in 1960.*

ABCNEWS INTERACTIVE ™

 Videodisc

Communism and the Cold War

Side 1, Chapter 18
Title: Civil Defense
Subject: 1954 film on civil defense and fallout
Ask: What was the purpose of fallout shelters? *(protection from radiation)*

See Communism and the Cold War Guidebook page 29 for complete lesson plan.

Cultural Perspectives

The Hungarian Uprising In November 1956 fierce opposition to the pro-Soviet government broke out in Hungary, but the Soviets suppressed it with military force. Afterward, however, Communist Hungary, with liberal economic and cultural spheres, became the most tolerant of the Soviet-bloc nations. Have students work in groups to find out more about the Hungarian uprising. What social, cultural, and historical factors affected how the Hungarians reacted? Students may also want to consider how Hungary's liberal economic and cultural spheres helped it in the 1980s when communism in the region collapsed. How did Hungary avoid the unrest so prominent in neighboring nations like Czechoslovakia and Romania?

CHART STUDY

Fear was the major motivation behind the arms race. Each side feared its opponent's destructive capabilities.

Ask: When did the Soviets explode their first nuclear bomb? *(1949)*

ASSESS

Meeting Lesson Objectives

Each section objective is tested by the section review question(s) that follows it in parentheses.

1. Explain the effect of the Soviet atomic bomb on American society and the arms race. (1, 4)

2. Explain the causes and effects of Eisenhower's massive retaliation strategy and how it changed American foreign policy. (1, 4)

3. Explain the reasons for a growing disarmament movement and the outcomes of that movement. (1, 2, 3, 5)

4. Analyze the effects of *Sputnik* on the United States's military, its schools, and its industry. (3)

---

stated that Communists and capitalists might be able to live together peacefully and even declared that the Soviets might tolerate different kinds of communism.

All over Eastern Europe, Khrushchev's words inspired people to seek more freedom. In Hungary a new government announced that the country would leave the Warsaw Pact and remain neutral. The Soviets responded with force. On November 4, 1956, Khrushchev sent 200,000 troops and 2,500 tanks into Budapest to put down an uprising of poorly armed students and workers. Khrushchev, the "bare-knuckle slugger" who was taking control, had revealed another side. Clearly, the cold war was far from over.

Sputnik Fires the Arms Race

If any hopes remained of slowing the arms race, they fizzled completely in the fall of 1957. On August 1, the Soviets tested their first successful intercontinental missile, a long-range missile carrying a nuclear warhead. On October 4, the Soviets jolted Americans when they launched *Sputnik*, a 184-pound (83.5 kg) satellite, into orbit around the earth.

People read the news with awe and fear: the United States was running second in the survival race. Critics accused Eisenhower of "permitting a technological Pearl Harbor." A missile gap had developed, they cried, and now the United States was threatened by satellites they feared were capable of carrying weapons!

Sputnik shifted the arms race into high gear. Almost immediately Eisenhower increased the funding for missile development from $4.3 billion in 1958 to $5.3 billion in 1959. He launched the National Aeronautics and Space Administration (NASA), which worked feverishly to close the missile gap. With large new congressional appropriations, the Defense Department expanded the B-52 bomber fleet, built submarines outfitted with nuclear missiles, and installed a ring of short-range missiles in Europe.

To make sure the United States would not be caught short again, the government poured money into education to train scientists and engineers. Billions of dollars also went to universities; nearly one-third of all university scientists and engineers directed their energies to full-time weapons research. A powerful military-educational-industrial combination was taking shape.

Protests Slow Testing

In spite of the Soviets' military achievements and the United States's headlong race to keep up, strong pressure was still building for arms control. The nuclear fallout scare of 1954 continued into 1955 when radioactive rain fell in Chicago. Scientists and doctors began to warn of fallout dangers like bone cancer and leukemia.

In 1957, the same year that *Sputnik* roared into orbit, a group of business, scientific, and publishing leaders established SANE, the Committee for a Sane Nuclear Policy. Within a year its membership grew to 25,000, and SANE began pressuring for change with powerful newspaper ads: "We must stop the contamination of the air, the milk children drink, the food we eat."

In 1957 Nevil Shute's novel *On the Beach* hit the best-seller list, adding its strength to the growing antinuclear movement. Terrifyingly real, the book told the story of massive nuclear war that destroyed the Northern Hemisphere and sent clouds of radioactive dust swirling into the Southern Hemisphere. There, millions of people talked, planned, worried, cried—and waited for the end. In the book, Moira Davidson, a young Australian woman, rages at her friend, submarine commander Dwight Towers:

The Space Race Begins Technicians prepare *Explorer I*, the United States's first artificial earth satellite, for launch. *Why did Eisenhower increase funding for missile development?*

Critical Thinking

Analyzing Consequences *Sputnik* and the missile gap led to huge increases in military spending on both sides during the next three decades. Have students work together to examine the consequences of such enormous military spending. By the time arms reduction treaties were signed in the late 1980s and early 1990s, the Soviet economy was faltering. Most observers were amazed that Soviet President Mikhail Gorbachev was able to restructure his nation's economy. Some groups can examine the problems in the Soviet economy and how defense spending contributed to them. Other groups may want to examine the American economy over the same period and how defense spending affected social programs.

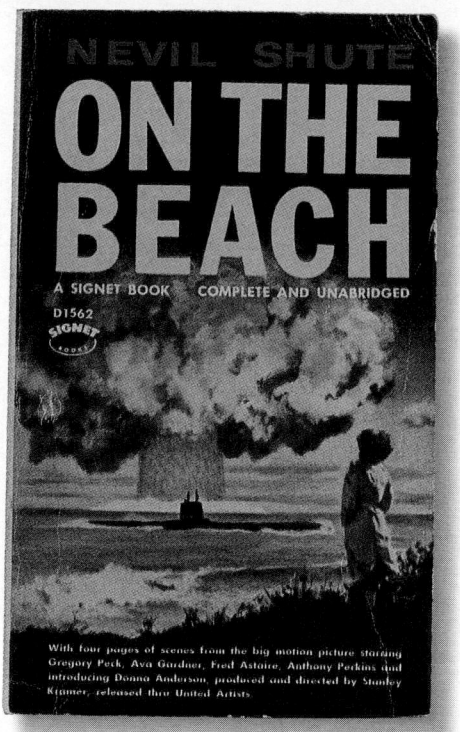

COURTESY, SIGNET BOOKS/PHOTO BY DOUG MINDELL

People Fear Nuclear Fallout Nevil Shute's novel helped galvanize public opinion against nuclear testing. *What percentage of Americans in 1957 wanted the United States to stop H-bomb testing?*

It's not fair. No one in the Southern Hemisphere ever dropped a bomb. . . . We had nothing to do with it. Why should we have to die because other countries nine or ten thousand miles away from us wanted to have a war? . . ."

There was a pause, and then she said angrily, "It's not that I'm afraid of dying, Dwight. We've all got to do that sometime. It's all the things I'm going to have to miss. . . . All my life I've wanted to see the Rue de Rivoli. I suppose it's the romantic name. It's silly, because I suppose it's just a street like any other street. But that's what I've wanted, and I'm never going to see it. Because there isn't any Paris now, or London, or New York."

—Nevil Shute, *On the Beach*, 1957

Forty newspapers serialized *On the Beach,* and eventually the book was made into a movie. The book contributed its weight to shifting public opinion. In 1957 a Gallup Poll found that 63 percent of Americans wanted the government to halt H-bomb tests.

In response to a growing worldwide outcry, the United States and the Soviet Union agreed to stop nuclear testing in the atmosphere. That agreement held until the Soviets set off another bomb in 1961. In 1963 the nuclear powers finally signed a test-ban treaty that outlawed nuclear tests in the atmosphere but permitted them underground and in outer space.

The Military-Industrial Threat

Changes in nuclear testing solved the immediate problem. Yet the United States and the Soviet Union continued to invent new doomsday weapons and build huge stockpiles. In the process, a new threat was growing in the United States—the vast, interwoven military establishment and arms industry. At the end of his presidency, Eisenhower alerted the nation to the danger of this **military-industrial complex** that could threaten freedom in the United States:

In the councils of government we must guard against the acquisition of unwarranted influence . . . by the military-industrial complex. The potential for the disastrous rise of misplaced power exists and will persist.

We must never let the weight of this combination endanger our liberties or democratic processes.

—President Dwight Eisenhower,
Farewell Speech, 1961

SECTION REVIEW

Vocabulary

1. Define: massive retaliation, brinkmanship, military-industrial complex.

Checking Facts

2. Why did Eisenhower appoint Dulles as his secretary of state?

3. What steps did the United States take to close the missile gap after the launching of *Sputnik*?

Critical Thinking

Predicting Consequences
4. Just before he left office, President Eisenhower predicted the rise of a military-industrial complex in the United States. What are some possible consequences of an alliance between industry and the military?

Linking Across Time

5. During the Geneva convention in 1955, President Eisenhower proposed an "open skies" policy. Although neither nation agreed to it, it is practiced today. How?

SECTION THREE **583**

TEACH

Making the Historical Connection

The announcement of the Soviets' first step into space came close on the heels of the International Geophysical Year's first major scientific project—the firing of a rocket into space to study the effects of the sun's radiation on communications. United States scientists, who were cooperating with the Russians and other nations in the IGY, congratulated the Soviets, but the political ramifications had many officials more worried than they had been since the beginning of the cold war. The big concern was the effect the event might have on developing nations' choosing between the two powers. The United States responded to *Sputnik* by launching its own artificial satellite, *Explorer I,* in the spring of 1958.

ABCNEWS INTERACTIVE™

 Videodisc

Communism and the Cold War

Side 1, Chapter 14
Title: Sputnik Launches the Space Race
Subject: The beginning of the space race
Ask: Why did *Sputnik* launch a space race? *(Each side feared that the other would control space.)*

584

One Day in History

Friday, October 4, 1957

MARKET BASKET

Here is where a dollar will go:

8-oz. bottle of Coca-Cola . . 5¢
Loaf of bread . . . . 19¢
Roll of film . . . . 42¢
Hotel room, per night $5
Men's leather shoes . . $19.95

Bicycle $64.95
Record $9.98
Steak, per pound $1
Phonograph $28.50

Magazine . . . . 25¢
Movie projector $89.95
Television set $550
Ford sedan $2,272
4-bedroom house . . . $19,500

Sputnik I Soviet students look at a model of the Soviet Union's artificial satellite. The name *Sputnik* means "fellow traveler," a reference to its companion satellite, Earth.

Soviet "Moon" Circles Earth

Reds Win Race Into Outer Space

MOSCOW, OCTOBER 4—The Soviet Union today launched the first manufactured "moon." Named *Sputnik*, the Soviet satellite is now spinning around Earth at a speed of five miles a second.

Weighing 185 pounds and measuring 23 inches in diameter, the artificial moon was launched by an intercontinental ballistic missile, which gave the satellite the necessary spin to circle the world in 1 hour and 35 minutes.

Background Information

Revolutionary Food Trend The popularity of frozen dinners, which were derived from the rations developed for fliers during the war, rose as the number of households with televisions rose. The association between the two was no accident: Swanson's, the first big distributor of frozen dinners, called them TV dinners and even designed the packaging to look like a television set. Special "TV trays"—trays that folded out to a standing position—were developed so the whole family could watch their favorite TV show as they ate. The dinners were relatively expensive—98 cents per meal. A chicken dinner at a restaurant during the time period cost about $1.25.

THE CAT IN THE HAT introduces Thing One and Thing Two in Dr. Seuss's new series of Beginner Books. *Cat* nets $8 million.

Hoffa to Head Teamsters

WASHINGTON—James R. Hoffa was elected president of the giant Teamsters Union last night in open defiance of the AFL-CIO order that the union clean its house of corrupt elements like Hoffa. His election is certain to spur support for federal legislation to crack down on labor racketeering. The AFL-CIO has warned the Teamsters that it faces expulsion if it doesn't rid itself of corruption and those responsible for it.

Beaver and Wally Cleaver

Leave It to Beaver Debuts

NEW YORK—The Cleaver family, with Beaver and big brother Wally, makes its first television appearance. In the first episode, Beaver tried to avoid being "spelled from school."

Althea Gibson (right) and Darlene Hard

New Champion Honored

NEW YORK—A ticker-tape parade welcomed home tennis champion Althea Gibson after her dual victory at Wimbledon. Gibson first won the women's singles title and then won the women's doubles.

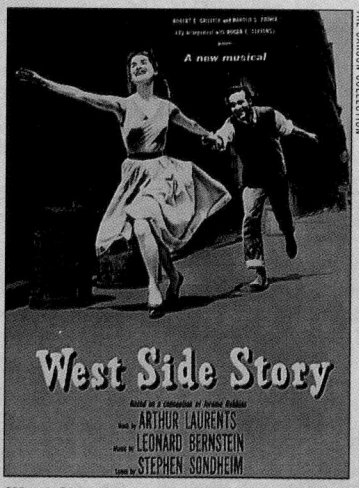

***West Side Story*, based on *Romeo and Juliet*, with music by Leonard Bernstein, opens on Broadway.**

MUSIC

DETROIT—Entrepreneur Berry Gordy, Jr., invests $700 to start Motown, a new record company that promotes African American rock musicians such as Stevie Wonder and Diana Ross and the Supremes.

TIME CAPSULE
1957

AMERICAN LIFE

January: Survey shows 51 percent of high school seniors will not attend college because they lack money or the personal goals.

February: The Southern Christian Leadership Conference is formed.

March 30: United States commissions second atomic submarine.

May 6: Senator John F. Kennedy wins Pulitzer Prize for *Profiles in Courage.*

July 12: Surgeon general reports a direct relationship between lung cancer and smoking.

August 1: Nation's first solar-heated commercial building opens in Albuquerque, New Mexico.

August 30: A filibuster record of 24 hours, 27 minutes is set by Senator Strom Thurmond, against civil rights legislation.

September 19: The first underground atomic explosion is set off near Las Vegas, Nevada.

December 18: First atomic power plant opens in Shippingport, Pennsylvania.

Oral History

"Where Were You . . ." Just as many Americans can say what they were doing the day John F. Kennedy was shot, most know where they were when they heard that *Sputnik* had been launched. Ask students to interview someone who remembers that day. What was that person's reaction to the news? How did it affect his or her attitude about the Soviet Union? Was he or she afraid of war? Explain that the International Geophysical Year, a study of the sun and the earth by scientists of 67 nations, was in progress at the time. How might the future have been different if the United States and the Soviet Union had kept up the cooperative effort of space study? Have students write a report for their portfolios.

CLOSE

Ask: What effect did the Soviets' launch of *Sputnik* have on United States leaders? Scientists? Individual citizens? *(leaders—worry; scientists—guarded congratulations; citizens—fear)*

585

Study and Writing Skill

ANALYZING SECONDARY SOURCES

Have students recall the quotation by Andy Rooney at the beginning of the chapter. Explain that this quotation is a primary source because it was written by Rooney at the time of the events.

Point out that this history text is a secondary source because, like the book by Newhouse, it contains quotations from many primary sources. Primary sources provide firsthand information.

Explain that when students write research papers, they nearly always research a topic using secondary sources. This lesson will help them evaluate those sources.

VISUAL INSTRUCTION

Secondary Sources *War and Peace in the Nuclear Age* **may still be available in libraries. Encourage students to check it out and summarize some events.**

Answer: *Some sources might be talks, speeches, or televised coverage of events involving leaders, such as Kennedy or Eisenhower. Other sources might be photos or excerpts from the public television series mentioned on the cover.*

Additional Practice

☞ Have students complete the Chapter 17 Skill Reinforcement Activity.

Learning the Skill

A source created at or near the time of the events it reports is a primary source. Historians often use primary sources such as letters, original documents, speeches, and photographs as the basis for their descriptions or analyses of events. Books or other materials that draw from primary sources to explain a topic are secondary sources. Most history books are secondary sources.

The book *War and Peace in the Nuclear Age,* by John Newhouse, is a secondary source that analyzes the cold war events described in this chapter. The value and accuracy of a secondary source depend on how its author uses primary sources.

To determine whether an author uses primary sources effectively, ask these questions:

a. Are there references to primary sources in the acknowledgments, footnotes, or text?

b. Who are the authors of the primary sources? What insights or biases might these people have?

c. Is the information from the primary sources interwoven effectively to support or describe an event?

d. Are different kinds of primary sources considered? Do they represent varied testimony?

e. Is the interpretation of the primary sources sound?

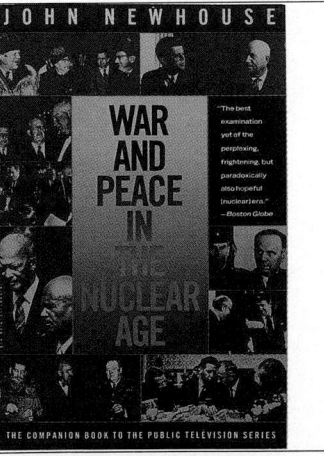

Vertical text along image: FROM "WAR AND PEACE IN THE NUCLEAR AGE" BY J. NEWHOUSE. REPRINTED WITH PERMISSION OF RANDOM

Secondary Sources Good secondary sources synthesize information from primary sources to give a full picture of events. *Judging from the information on the book's cover, what do you think are some of the sources it analyzes?*

Practicing the Skill

Read the following excerpt from *War and Peace in the Nuclear Age*. Identify the primary source Newhouse uses. Then answer the questions that follow.

Eisenhower was very taken with the Open Skies idea. . . . Eisenhower described in his memoirs the . . . [reaction] of Soviet Prime Minister Bulganin, who said it had real merit and would be studied sympathetically. "The tone of his talk seemed as encouraging as his words," wrote Eisenhower. A few minutes later, walking toward the bar with Khrushchev, he was disabused but enlightened. " 'I don't agree with the Chairman,' Khrushchev said, smiling—but there was no smile in his voice. I saw clearly then . . . the identity of the real boss of the Soviet delegation." "From then on," said Eisenhower, "I . . . devoted myself exclusively to an attempt to persuade Mr. Khrushchev of the merits of the Open Skies plan."

1. What primary source does Newhouse quote?

2. Why is Eisenhower an excellent primary source to explore the topic?

3. How well has Newhouse used the excerpt to convey Eisenhower's feelings? To create a sense of immediacy?

4. Is the information from the primary source interwoven effectively into the text?

5. What other primary sources could you use to explore the cold war years?

Applying the Skill

Find and read an in-depth article in a newspaper or magazine today. Then analyze how reliable you think the primary sources are. How effectively does the author interweave information from the primary sources? List the primary sources the writer used.

Additional Practice

For additional practice, see Reinforcing Skills on page 595.

Practicing the Skill Answers

1. Eisenhower's memoirs
2. Not only was he present, he was also knowledgeable about world affairs and could interpret events well.
3. He relays Eisenhower's feelings well. He says that Eisenhower was in turn encouraged, enlightened, understood clearly, and then changed his strategy by speaking only to Khrushchev about the Open Skies plan.

Newhouse also creates a sense of immediacy by making readers feel as if they are at the scene.
4. Yes. Quotations from Eisenhower are interwoven with the narrative.
5. Letters from world leaders to others, documents about the Open Skies plan, memos from White House staffers, speeches by world leaders, and photographs from the era

A New Battleground

MIDNIGHT, AUGUST 2, 1953: CIA PLOTS THE TAKEOVER OF IRAN

L ATE IN THE SUMMER OF 1953, TROUBLE WAS BREWING IN IRAN, AND EISENHOWER WAS WORRIED. This Middle Eastern country was important to the United States for two reasons: Iran bordered the Soviet Union, and it had some of the richest reserves of oil in the world.

Eisenhower worried about Iran's troubled economy and its increasing reliance on the Soviet Union. If the Communists seized Iran's government, yet another country—and one with a huge supply of valuable oil—would join the Soviet bloc. Something had to be done quickly. That something began this way:

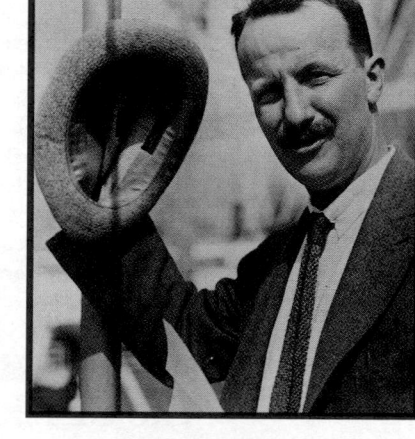

Kermit Roosevelt
This dapper-looking man was actually a spy for the United States.

A large, ornate garden in Teheran [Iran's capital]. A medium-sized, medium-height, rather nondescript American wearing a dark turtleneck shirt, Oxford gray slacks, and Persian sandals, opens the gate to the garden, slips out, glances up and down the street, and silently climbs into the back seat of an ordinary-looking black sedan. Without a backward glance, the driver pulls away slowly, smoothly and heads toward the royal palace. In the back seat, the American huddles down on the floor and pulls a blanket over him.

At the palace gate, the sentry flashes a light in the driver's face, grunts, and waves the car through. Halfway between the gate and the palace steps, the driver parks, gets out, and walks away. A slim, nervous man walks down the drive, glancing left and right as he approaches. The American pulls the blanket out of the way and sits up as the man enters the car. . . .

AS YOU READ

Vocabulary
► emerging nation
► covert operation
► nationalization

Think About . . .
► the rivalry between the Americans and the Soviets for the loyalty of emerging nations.
► the methods by which the CIA became involved with emerging nations.
► the goal of American policy in the Middle East and the area's importance to the United States.
► United States involvement in Cuba and the effects of the missile crisis.

SECTION FOUR **587**

FOCUS

Section Objectives

1. Analyze the rivalry between the Americans and the Soviets for the loyalty of emerging nations.
2. Explain CIA involvement in emerging nations.
3. Review American policy in the Middle East and explain the area's importance to the United States.
4. Review the United States's involvement in Cuba and the effects of the Cuban missile crisis.

Bellringer Activity

While taking attendance at the beginning of the class period, display **Section Focus Transparency 55,** and have students answer the questions. (Or use the blackline master.)

VISUAL INSTRUCTION

Kermit Roosevelt Have students recall what they know of recent United States relations with Iran. Have them note the date and title of Kermit Roosevelt's book on Iran.

Ask: With whom did Roosevelt meet in Iran? *(the Shah of Iran)*

Section 4 Resources

REPRODUCIBLE RESOURCES

📂 Lesson Plan 17-4
📂 Vocabulary and Guided Reading Activity 17-4
📂 Section 4 Quiz
📂 Chapter 17 Test
📂 Performance Assessment Activity 17
📂 Enrichment Activity 17

MULTIMEDIA RESOURCES

📦 Section Focus Transparency 55
💿 Communism and the Cold War
🔘 Landmark Documents in American History
🎧 Chapter 17 Digest Audiocassette
💻 Testmaker
💻 Student Self-Test: A Software Review
💻 Vocabulary PuzzleMaker

TEACH

Guided Practice

L1 Discussion Discuss the importance of Middle Eastern oil to the United States economy. Have students find out how much oil was used in the United States in the late 1940s, what it was used for, and how much oil was supplied by the Middle East. Discuss the effects on businesses if the supply of oil is cut.

VISUAL INSTRUCTION

The CIA The American eagle is the national bird and a symbol of strength. The radiating spokes of the compass rose depict the gathering of intelligence data from all areas of the world to a central point.

Answer: *The CIA conducted undercover missions of all kinds to win the loyalty of emerging nations.*

They look at each other. Then His Imperial Majesty, Mohammed Reza Shah Pahlavi, Shahanshah of Iran, Light of the Aryans, allows himself to relax and even smile.

—Kermit Roosevelt, *Countercoup: The Struggle for Control of Iran,* 1979

The American hiding under the blanket in the backseat that night was Kermit (Kim) Roosevelt, the grandson of President Theodore Roosevelt and a cousin of Franklin Delano Roosevelt. A top United States spy, Roosevelt had entered Iran under a phony name to meet secretly with Iran's 34-year-old Shah, or ruler.

Why were Roosevelt and the Shah sneaking around in the middle of the night? What was going on?

New Worlds to Conquer
Movements for National Independence

Iran, like many developing countries, found itself in turmoil after World War II. These **emerging nations**—developing countries in Asia, Latin America, and Africa—were shaking off colonial rule and taking charge of their futures. So widespread and powerful were these movements for national independence that between 1946 and 1960 alone 37 new countries emerged. Loyal to neither the United States and its democratic allies nor the Soviet Union and the Communist bloc, these newly independent nations became a new cold war battleground.

United States Interests

Winning the loyalty of emerging nations was crucial to Eisenhower. The United States depended on rich stores of rubber, oil, and other natural resources from developing countries and on their vast markets for American products. Just as important, emerging nations that were allied with the United States could help defend against Communist expansion.

Eisenhower and Dulles believed they needed to act decisively. They assumed that struggles for self-determination in the developing world were really revolutions directed by the Soviet Union. Left unopposed, these revolutions could result in neutral states or, worse, Communist ones throughout the Southern Hemisphere. If the Soviets managed to increase their influence in these regions, said Dulles, the scales would tip decisively against the Western democracies.

The Views of Emerging Nations

Drawing emerging nations into the American camp was difficult, however. Many newly independent countries, such as India and Egypt, wanted no part of outside control—United States or Soviet. Having just gotten rid of one foreign ruler, they had no desire for another.

Even establishing friendships with emerging nations proved difficult. For the millions of poor people in developing nations, life was a grim daily struggle to stay alive. They resented the United States's wealth, which they glimpsed in the luxurious lifestyles of American tourists and diplomats. Likewise, Soviet propagandists pointed to America's troubled race relations and asked nonwhite people in these nations: If the United States does not treat its fellow citizens equally, how will it treat you? Finally, in the struggles of emerging nations, the United States often sided with the wealthy, not the common, people. Even though America itself was born of revolution, the United States now worried about protecting its overseas investments and military bases. To people struggling for freedom, the United States seemed like just another threat.

Facing resistance from emerging nations, the United States used many methods to win friends and wage cold war. Massive amounts of foreign aid—the primary method—helped improve farming, schools, and medical care in developing countries. When Eisenhower became President, he relied increasingly on the Central Intelligence Agency, the CIA, to promote the allegiance of newly independent nations. The CIA spied and conducted **covert operations,** or undercover missions, of all kinds.

The CIA Joins the Fight
Agents Spy on the Soviet Union

The CIA was not Eisenhower's idea but rather a government agency President Truman created. After World War II, Truman decided that peacetime America no

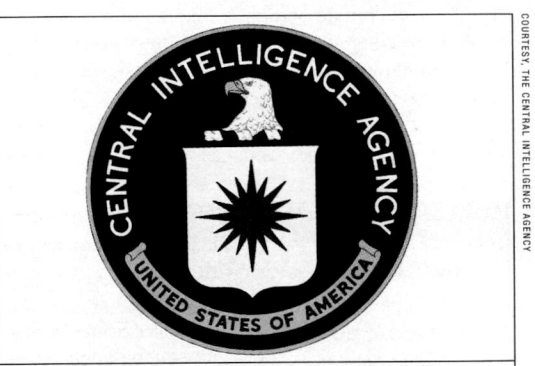

COURTESY, THE CENTRAL INTELLIGENCE AGENCY

The CIA President Truman approved the seal of the CIA on February 17, 1950. *What actions did the CIA take during Truman's administration?*

Cooperative Learning

Producing a Newspaper Have students work together to produce a newspaper about the cold war in Egypt and in Latin America. Some may want to write an editorial stating opinions about Castro's ideas for reform and his method of seizing power. Others might consult an almanac to find out the tolls paid for passage through the Suez Canal for the 10 years from 1946 to 1956. They can construct a graph to show this information. Still others might want to locate Cuba's Bay of Pigs. They can research the conditions in the bay that contributed to the failure of the planned invasion and write an article about their findings. 🔖

CIA ACTIONS IN THE WORLD, 1950–1962

East Asia
6) Supported friendly governments in Laos and South Vietnam, after 1954;
7) Attempted overthrow of Indonesian government, 1957 (unsuccessful)

Central America
Attempted to overthrow governments: 1) Guatemala, 1954 (successful); 2) Cuba, 1961 (unsuccessful); 3) Dominican Republic, 1960 (successful)

Africa/Middle East
4) Attempted assassination of Congo leader, 1961; 5) Overthrow of Iranian government, 1953

0   1,500   3,000 mi.
0   1,500 3,000 km
Robinson projection

The green areas of the map represent regions of the world with emerging nations. In these countries the CIA exerted extensive covert powers. *How did the United States justify the interference of the CIA in foreign governments?*

longer needed a network of spies. By 1946, however, Truman changed his mind as United States–Soviet relations soured and intelligence gathering began to seem necessary again.

CIA Powers

In 1947 Congress passed the historic National Security Act, which streamlined the defense system and created the CIA and the National Security Council (NSC). The newly created NSC and CIA reported directly to the President.

The act also gave the CIA sweeping powers with this loose definition of its job: The CIA shall perform "functions and duties related to intelligence affecting national security as the National Security Council will direct." This language left the CIA free to spy and to carry on covert operations. Used with care, the CIA enabled the President to take quick, controversial action in foreign trouble spots without waiting for congressional or public approval. This resource gave the White House virtual control of foreign policy.

In its early years, the CIA carried out few covert operations. Its main job was to spy on the Soviet military and prop up European democracies by secretly funding democratic political parties, labor unions, and other pro-Western groups.

The CIA was so successful that in 1949 Congress gave that agency the right to spend unlimited amounts of money without telling anyone except the director where the money went and what it was used for. This authority gave the President and the CIA a free hand. In time they would bribe overseas politicians, hire secret armies, and plot the assassinations of troublesome leaders.

The CIA Grows Powerful

With its increase in power and funding, the CIA mushroomed. In 1949 the agency had about 300 employees and spent $4.7 million. Just 3 years later, the CIA had grown to 20 times its original size. It employed nearly 6,000 people all over the world and spent nearly $82 million.

As the CIA grew, more Americans saw it as "the good way to fight communism." Exciting, glamorous, and challenging, the agency attracted talented young graduates from Harvard, Yale, and other top universities. Eventually the CIA would have an important role, instead of just a hand, in shaping events all over the world. As the map above shows, CIA agents worked behind the scenes worldwide to overthrow neutral or pro-Soviet governments and to prop up pro-Western ones.

SECTION FOUR   **589**

Independent Practice

L2 Citizenship Have groups of students assume the roles of talented young people attracted to a career in the CIA. Members should discuss their patriotic motives and identify the area of the world in which they would like to work and the nature of the work they would like to do.

Have students complete the Chapter 17, Section 4 Vocabulary and Guided Reading Activity. (Also in Spanish.) **LEP**

Meeting Special Needs

Reading Disability This activity helps to address the particular needs of learners with reading comprehension problems. Have students skim the section to find the vocabulary words that are introduced. Be certain that they understand each term before they read the section. Then have students listen to the Chapter 17, Section 4 Audiocassette after they have read the section. The audiocassettes are also available in Spanish.

The CIA and the Shah
The CIA Attempts an Overthrow

The CIA's first attempt to overthrow a government took place in Iran. At the end of World War II, a monarch and a two-house parliament ruled oil-rich Iran. The Shah (king), Mohammad Reza Pahlavi, was a dark, handsome man who looked dashing and powerful but was actually young and insecure.

After the war the Shah faced a tough problem—Iranian hatred of the British-owned Anglo-Persian Oil Company. Through Anglo-Persian Oil, the British controlled most of Iran's oil industry and drained the country of great wealth. Angry Iranians wanted to take control of their oil, but they needed a leader.

The man who stepped forward to lead the Iranians was not the Shah but wealthy 70-year-old Dr. Mohammad Mossadeg. On the surface Mossadeg seemed harmless. He was small, thin, and often emotional. He appeared to be no threat to the Shah. Beneath the surface, however, the rich landowner was a masterful politician.

In 1951 the popular Mossadeg had become prime minister and pushed through the legislature a bill authorizing **nationalization** of the oil fields—that is, declaring them the property of Iran. Outraged, the British refused to accept the payment Mossadeg offered. Instead, the British shut down their refineries, stopped buying Iranian oil, and convinced other countries to do the same. As Iran's oil market dried up, its economy slipped toward bankruptcy.

Eisenhower Steps In

By the time Eisenhower took office, Iran was in serious trouble. In Eisenhower's mind the situation was a perfect breeding ground for communism. The best way to protect Iran's oil supply for the West, Eisenhower thought, was to keep the Shah and get rid of Mossadeg.

Eisenhower ordered CIA agent Kim Roosevelt, who was in a "safe house" in Tehran, to engineer Mossadeg's overthrow. In a plan nicknamed AJAX, Roosevelt would organize military and public support for the Shah. Then the Shah would sign a royal decree deposing Mossadeg.

The CIA Operation

AJAX got off to a bad start in August 1953 when the Shah grew nervous about the plot and fled Tehran without signing the decree. It took Roosevelt four days to find the Shah, get the signed document, and deliver it to Mossadeg. By that time, though, the prime minister had discovered the plot. Mossadeg announced the attempted takeover on the radio and demanded the arrest of the Shah's supporters. In response, mobs of Iranians, including Communist supporters, ran wild in the streets, rioting, looting, and searching for enemies. Mossadeg called a stop to the violence only after the United States ambassador threatened to order all Americans out of Iran. Mossadeg knew that his government would look like a failure if the Americans pulled out.

With the mobs under control, Roosevelt sent his Iranian agents into action. On August 19, 200 Zirkaneh giants—huge, frightening-looking weight lifters—marched through Tehran's bazaars chanting, "Long live the Shah!" Other agents ran alongside, passing out money and gathering a crowd of artisans, students, police, and professionals. As the crowd headed for Mossadeg's house, Roosevelt rounded up the Shah's military supporters, who set off with tanks and guns.

The CIA agents and the Shah's men met and clashed with Mossadeg's supporters near Mossadeg's house. The battle lasted several hours and left 400 dead or injured. When Mossadeg's forces ran out of ammunition, the resistance ran out of steam. On the following day Mossadeg surrendered, and the Shah's supporters begged the Shah to return.

The Shah returned victorious. Soon after, Mossadeg was jailed. With the Shah in power, a group of Western oil companies was able to sign an agreement to buy and sell Iranian oil and share the profits with the Shah. AJAX had ensured the CIA's future. It had also planted the seeds of Iranian hatred of the United States.

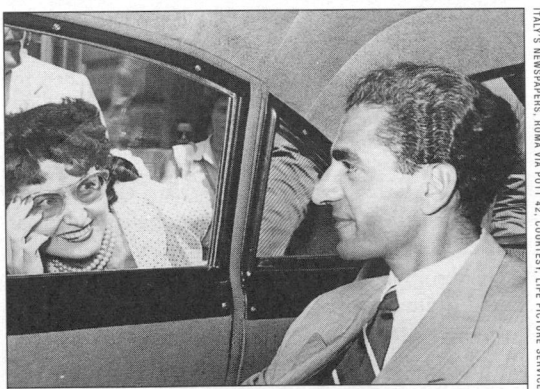
The Shah Flees Tehran A woman in Rome peers into the Shah's Buick. *Why did the Shah flee Tehran?*

War in Egypt
A Suez Canal Crisis

Three years later another hot spot ignited in the Middle East. This time the CIA was not involved, but the event showed Eisenhower that the developing coun-

Portfolio Project

Writing Direct students to research how the Shah, who was supported by the CIA, gained power. How does the policy of Mohammad Reza Pahlavi compare with that of his father? Have students write about their findings and add their paper to their portfolios.

Letter Writing Have students write a letter that might have been received from an Iranian pen pal in 1953. How does the writer feel about events that are transpiring in Iran? Have students add their finished letters to their portfolios.

Suez Canal Sunken ships obstruct the canal in Port Said.
Who sank the ships and why?

tries of the world presented difficult and dangerous problems.

In 1953 Egypt declared itself an independent republic, and in 1954 the passionate Arab nationalist General Gamal Abdel Nasser demanded that Britain give up control of the Suez Canal, which cut through his country. More than 75 percent of Western Europe's oil imports were shipped through the Suez Canal, a key link between the Persian Gulf and the Mediterranean Sea. Nasser wanted to collect the $25 million in annual profits from tolls. As part of his plan for modernizing Egypt, Nasser also wanted to build a dam on the Nile River to provide electric power and irrigation water for farms.

To help draw Egypt into the United States camp, Dulles had offered to help Nasser build his dam. Soon afterward, though, the independent Nasser made an arms deal with the Soviets, and Dulles angrily canceled the loan. In July 1956, Nasser fought back by seizing the Suez Canal. With the millions in tolls from the canal, Egypt would finance the Nile River dam itself.

In October 1956, before Eisenhower could work out a solution to the crisis, Israel, Britain, and France invaded Egypt to seize the canal. Eisenhower and Dulles were appalled, fearing the action would drive the Middle East into the Soviet camp and threaten vital oil resources. Eisenhower called for a UN resolution condemning the

actions of the three American allies. Without United States support, they pulled out, and the canal was returned to Egypt—full of sunken ships.

While Eisenhower managed to head off a full-scale war, the incident had serious consequences. It opened the Middle East to the Soviets, who appeared to side with Egyptian nationalists and eventually built Nasser's dam. The conflict also revealed weaknesses in the Western camp and pulled the United States deeper into Middle Eastern affairs. Afraid of growing Soviet influence in the oil-rich Middle East, Eisenhower promised aid, both economic and military, to pro-Western governments in the region. This policy, known as the Eisenhower Doctrine, would soon involve fighting communism and the Arab governments that did not join the Western camp.

Latin America
The Cold War Arrives

The spirit of nationalism fired up people in Central and South America during this period, too. For decades the United States had invested in the region's economies, and by the mid-1950s, United States companies controlled more than $7 billion of oil, mineral, and agricultural resources in Latin America. These firms enjoyed rich profits from their investments in the region, but little wealth trickled down to the masses of people who lived in poverty. Nationalistic leaders knew they had to loosen the grip of the United States firms on their economies. Revolution was simmering.

Revolution in Cuba

By the early 1950s, United States corporations virtually controlled the island nation of Cuba. Nearly 90 percent of Cuba's mines, ranches, and oil, half of its sugar crop, and 3 million acres of its land belonged to Americans. Only a few high-level Cubans lived well. Most suffered in grinding poverty.

In 1952 Fulgencio Batista overthrew the government and installed himself as dictator, friendly to the United States. He did little to improve life for the Cuban people, however, and in 1958 a young lawyer named Fidel Castro led a group of peasants and middle-class Cubans in a successful revolt against Batista.

Once in power, Castro moved quickly to solve Cuba's problems by demanding control of American properties. When the United States refused to discuss the matter, Castro turned to the Soviets for economic help. Soon after, Eisenhower ordered the CIA to train a secret force of anti-Castro Cubans called La Brigada, which could be used to overthrow Castro. Before

SECTION FOUR **591**

**ABCNEWS
INTERACTIVE**™

 Videodisc

Communism and the Cold War

Side 2, Chapter 13
Title: Bay of Pigs
Subject: 1961 invasion of Cuba
Ask: Why was the invasion an embarrassment? *(The U.S. supported the invasion, but it failed.)*

See Communism and the Cold War Guidebook page 64 for complete lesson plan.

Side 1, Chapter 16
Title: Cuban Missile Crisis
Subject: the missile crisis
Ask: How was the crisis resolved? *(The Soviets withdrew the missiles.)*

See Communism and the Cold War Guidebook page 64 for complete lesson plan.

Extending the Content

Suez Canal Economic warfare became an important cold war tactic. When Iran seized Anglo-Persian oil, Great Britain organized a multinational boycott of Iranian oil. When Egypt's Nasser signed an arms deal with the Soviets, the United States canceled an important loan to Egypt. When Great Britain refused to give up the Suez Canal, Nasser seized it.

Britain and France were then afraid that Nasser might close the canal altogether and cut off oil shipments from the Persian Gulf. Their subsequent seizure of the canal eventually led to a loss of British and French influence in the Middle East. Ask: What happened to the United States's influence in the region? *(The United States became more deeply involved.)*

Facts on File

Landmark Documents in American History Have students review "Letter to Khrushchev on the Cuban Missile Crisis, 1962, and write a paragraph about the intent of the document.

ASSESS

Meeting Lesson Objectives

Each section objective is tested by the section review question(s) that follows it in parentheses.

1. Analyze the rivalry between the Americans and the Soviets for the loyalty of emerging nations. (1, 3, 4)
2. Explain CIA involvement in emerging nations. (1, 5)
3. Review American policy in the Middle East and explain the area's importance to the United States. (2, 5)
4. Review the United States's involvement in Cuba and the effects of the Cuban missile crisis. (3, 4)

Eisenhower left office in 1961, Castro had seized all American businesses and signed a trade agreement with Moscow. The United States and Cuba had broken diplomatic relations.

Kennedy and Cuba

In 1961 John F. Kennedy became President and faced, in his words, the problem of a "Communist satellite on our very doorstep." With Castro's success in Cuba and growing crises in Africa and Southeast Asia, Kennedy feared a Soviet upper hand in the cold war. Before leaving office Eisenhower had urged Kennedy to step up the training of La Brigada. Now in office, Kennedy took the advice of CIA operatives and ordered La Brigada to land secretly in Cuba, inspire a popular uprising, and sweep Castro out of power.

The invasion on April 17, 1961, failed miserably. When the 1,500 commandos tried to land at the Bay of Pigs on Cuba's southern coast, they met disaster at every turn. Their boats ran aground on coral reefs, Kennedy canceled their air support to keep United States involvement secret, and the promised uprising of the Cuban people never happened. Within 2 days Castro's forces killed several hundred members of La Brigada and captured nearly all the rest.

The Bay of Pigs was a dark moment for Kennedy. The action exposed an American plot to overthrow a neighbor's government, and the clumsy affair made the United States look weak, like a paper tiger.

To the Brink of War

To assert the United States's strength, Kennedy searched for other ways to unseat Castro. Using the CIA in a plan called Operation Mongoose, he interrupted Cuban trade, ordered more raids by exiles, and even plotted Castro's assassination.

For Castro and Khrushchev, these activities were outrageous. Khrushchev did not want to lose his foothold in the Western Hemisphere, and Castro did not want to lose his freedom from United States influence. "We had

---

THE CUBAN MISSILE CRISIS: JULY – OCTOBER, 1962

Citing Fidel Castro's fear of an American invasion of Cuba, the Soviet Union transformed the island into an enormous military base during the summer of 1962. It was a stunning move that put the Soviet threat less than 100 miles from American shores. The standoff that ensued between the two cold war leaders placed the world close to its first nuclear war.

SOVIET MILITARY BUILDUP IN CUBA

July–October, 1962

- 3 intermediate-range ballistic missile sites in progress
- 42 medium-range ballistic missiles
- 432 surface-to-air missiles
- 82 high-speed Soviet jet bombers (MIG-15s, MIG-17s, and MIG-21s)
- 12 missile patrol boats
- 22,000 Soviet soldiers
- 4 separate military installations

RANGE OF CUBAN-BASED AIR POWER

intermediate ballistic missile range = 2,532 miles
medium ballistic missile range = 1,151 miles
MIG jet bomber range = 806 miles

UNITED STATES — Chicago, Los Angeles, New York City, Washington, D.C., Miami, CUBA, South America

THE EVENTS UNFOLD

July (last two weeks)	September 11	October 14	October 24	October 28
Soviets begin missile and other military shipments to Cuba.	Soviets warn United States that an attack on Cuba would mean war.	Photos from U.S. surveillance pilots show Soviet missiles in Cuba.	Kennedy imposes naval blockade of Cuba.	Khrushchev agrees to remove missiles from Cuba.

Enemy nuclear warheads positioned close to the United States posed an immediate danger to the country and raised the specter of all-out nuclear war between the United States and the Soviet Union. *Which United States cities are not in range of Cuban missiles?*

592 CHAPTER 17 THE UNEASY PEACE

Cultural Perspectives

Views From Cuba Castro's policies were controversial. On the one hand, all education and health-care services were free, and every citizen was guaranteed a job. However, the government owned most means of production, permitted no competing political parties, and controlled all mass media. Castro also supported violent revolutions in South and Central America. Have students conduct additional research and prepare a panel discussion. Some panel members should represent Cuban citizens, such as farmers or formerly unemployed workers, who support Castro. Others should represent businesspeople or freedom-seeking citizens who oppose Castro's policies. Panel members should support their viewpoints with facts.

The March to Havana Fidel Castro addresses a crowd of Cuban people. *How did Castro ascend to power?*

to think of some way of confronting America with more than words," Khrushchev recalled. Their solution was to install Soviet nuclear missiles and bombers near Havana, Cuba's capital, as a warning to the United States.

On October 14, 1962, a United States spy plane flying over Cuba got clear photos of crews installing Soviet missiles. Afraid that the Soviets were taking advantage of American weakness, Kennedy called a meeting of his closest advisers to decide what to do.

For a solid, nerve-racking week, the group thrashed out every possible response. Negotiations were ruled out at once; the group feared that drawn-out talks would give the Soviets time to install the missiles. Bombing the missile sites and invading Cuba were both proposed, but Kennedy feared that either could ignite a nuclear war. Finally, Kennedy agreed to block Cuban shipping lanes to halt further deliveries of nuclear weapons, then quietly push Khrushchev to remove the missiles.

On the evening of October 22, Kennedy announced this decision on national television. Within 2 days 180 warships were sailing to Cuba, B-52 bombers loaded with nuclear weapons were in the air, and military forces worldwide were on full alert—more than 200,000 in Florida alone. For the next 2 days, Soviet ships steamed toward Cuba, and the world waited to see what would happen. It was a time when "the smell of burning hung in the air," Khrushchev remembered later. The United States and the Soviet Union had edged to the brink of nuclear war.

On October 26, Khrushchev agreed to remove the missiles if the United States vowed never to attack Cuba. The next day he demanded the removal of United States missiles from Turkey. After frantic meetings, Kennedy

agreed to the first demand but ignored the second. He also ordered Khrushchev to get the missiles out of Cuba—or the United States would take them out. Finally, on October 28, Khrushchev backed down and the crisis ended.

After the Crisis

As the missiles left Cuba, the world stepped back from the brink and breathed a huge sigh of relief. War had been averted.

The standoff also changed the character of the cold war. At last the United States and the Soviet Union accepted each other's power and admitted the importance of negotiation. In this spirit, American and Soviet leaders installed a hot line, a Teletype link for communication when future crises arose.

The brush with nuclear war did nothing to slow the arms race, however. For the Soviet Union, the missile crisis had ended in public humiliation. The Soviets vowed, in the words of one official, "never [to] be caught like this again." Back home they launched a huge military buildup.

The United States's victory in the missile crisis renewed the nation's pride and its belief in containment. Through the rest of Kennedy's administration, the United States continued to stockpile nuclear weapons and serve as the world's police force. Before long, though, America's beliefs would be put to the test in the small Asian country of Vietnam.

SECTION REVIEW

Vocabulary

1. Define: emerging nation, covert operation, nationalization.

Checking Facts

2. What sparked the controversy between Iran and Great Britain in 1951?

3. Why was Castro's revolution politically worrisome to the United States? Why was it economically worrisome?

Critical Thinking

Predicting Consequences

4. Why was the United States so interested in seeing Castro's revolution fail?

Linking Across Time

5. In 1979 the Iranian people overthrew the Shah, an event that inaugurated a period of extreme anti-Americanism. What might account for the Iranian hatred of the United States?

The March to Havana Fidel Castro was born in Cuba in 1926. His father, who owned a small plantation, had emigrated from Spain.

Answer: *The dictator Batista did little to help the Cuban people, most of whom lived in poverty, enabling Castro to lead a successful revolt.*

Evaluate

Have students complete the Section Review.

☞ 🖥 Assign the Section 4 Quiz or use the Testmaker to develop a customized quiz. (Also in Spanish.) **LEP**

☞ 🖥 Assign the Chapter 17 Test or use the Testmaker to develop a customized test.

☞ Have students complete the Chapter 17 Performance Assessment Activity.

Reteach

🎧 Have students listen to the Chapter 17, Section 4 Audiocassette. (Also in Spanish.) **LEP**

☞ Have students complete Reteaching Activity 17. (Also in Spanish.) **LEP**

Enrich

☞ Have students complete the Chapter 17 Enrichment Activity. (Also in Spanish.) **LEP**

CLOSE

Ask: What might life be like for most Cubans if the Bay of Pigs invasion had succeeded? *(People might have greater personal freedom; Marxism has relieved some poverty at the expense of individual freedom.)*

Section 4 Review Answers

1. emerging nation (588), **covert operation** (588), **nationalization** (590)
2. the nationalization of the oil industry in Iran, which affected British refineries there
3. Politically, it created a Communist presence close to the United States. Economically, it destroyed American business interests in Cuba.

4. A Communist outpost 90 miles off the coast of Florida and Castro's attempts to export revolution in the hemisphere were principal worries.
5. the United States's support of the Shah, whom the Iranian people felt was unresponsive to their needs, and the defeat of Mossadeg's plan to nationalize the oil industry

Reviewing Key Terms

1. containment
2. limited war
3. massive retaliation
4. brinksmanship
5. cold war

Recalling Facts

1. The United States emerged from the war more powerful than when it entered. It controlled 50 percent of the world's wealth. By war's end 70,000 villages were destroyed in the western Soviet Union.
2. Stalin oppressed Eastern Europe. He declared capitalism a danger to world peace. Truman pursued a policy of long-term containment of Soviet expansion.
3. Marshall Plan aid to Europe helped cities rebuild, but the aid also was intended to prevent conditions from getting so bad that communism would flourish in Europe.
4. Americans believed a strong anti-Communist position in China would block Soviet expansion.
5. The Chinese Communists set up governments and small police forces. They gave peasants land. More and more Chinese people felt taken care of by Mao's Communists.
6. If Communist North Korea succeeded in overcoming South Korea, communism would spread.
7. It kept the peace but generated an arms race between the United States and the Soviet Union.
8. Krushchev distrusted the United States and rejected the "open skies" policy.
9. United States supplied aid to emerging nations; CIA tried to undermine leaders hostile to the United States.
10. Many Cubans lived in dire poverty. Batista (pro-United States) did little to improve life for the Cuban people.

594

Reviewing Key Terms

Match each vocabulary word to its definition below. Write your answers on a separate sheet of paper.

containment

cold war

limited war

brinksmanship

massive retaliation

land reform

1. confining war to one area without letting it spread to a global confrontation

2. securing peace by restricting communism to its current borders

3. a policy in which the United States would launch a nuclear strike against the Soviet Union if it attacked any ally

4. keeping peace by not backing down

5. blocking other nations' political and economic goals

Recalling Facts

1. How did the United States's position at the end of World War II compare with the Soviet Union's position?

2. Describe the events that prompted the United States to adopt the containment policy of keeping communism confined within its current borders.

3. How did the Marshall Plan help the United States implement its foreign policy following World War II?

4. Why did most Americans hope for a Nationalist victory in China?

5. How did Mao and the Communists win the support of the Chinese people?

6. Why did Harry S Truman view the invasion of South Korea as a test of containment?

7. What were some advantages and some dangers of a policy of massive retaliation?

8. Why did Nikita Khrushchev refuse to agree to Dwight Eisenhower's proposal to inspect each other's military sites?

9. What methods did the United States use to gain the friendship of emerging nations? How was the CIA involved?

10. What conditions in Cuba helped prepare the way for Fidel Castro's takeover?

Critical Thinking

1. Making Comparisons Compare the concerns of Franklin Roosevelt, Winston Churchill, and Joseph Stalin when they met at Yalta. How were their differences settled?

2. Determining Cause and Effect What caused the mistrust between Harry S Truman and Joseph Stalin? How did this mistrust affect the way in which each nation handled its foreign affairs?

3. Identifying Assumptions In 1956 Nikita Khrushchev spoke of tolerating different kinds of communism throughout the world. What did Eastern European nations assume this statement meant? How were these assumptions proven false in Hungary?

4. Making Inferences What is the message that Fidel Castro and Nikita Khrushchev may have wanted to deliver by posing for the photograph below on September 20, 1960? Do you think the photo effectively communicates this message? Why or why not?

5. Recognizing Ideologies How might a nation's view on testing nuclear weapons depend on its size and its power? How might a nation that is a member of the nuclear club feel about nuclear testing? How might a nation that is not a member of the nuclear club feel?

WIDE WORLD PHOTOS

Critical Thinking

1. Churchill wanted to save the British empire; Stalin wanted to protect and rebuild the Soviet Union; Roosevelt wanted free world trade. All three agreed that cooperation was necessary for peace.
2. Truman distrusted Stalin because Stalin oppressed Eastern Europe and wanted to develop modern weapons. Truman took a hard-line approach.
3. Eastern European nations assumed Khrushchev would tolerate self-determination, but when Hungary moved toward independence, it met with Soviet military oppression.
4. They may have wanted to show that the two nations were united and were friends.
5. Large powers might approve of testing in order to test their weapons. Small powers might worry about the hazards of testing.

NATO MILITARY BASES, 1950s

MEXICO

UNITED STATES

CUBA

Guantánamo Bay (U.S.)

Puerto Rico (U.S.)

Bermuda (U.K.)

CANADA

ALASKA (U.S.)

Johnston I. (U.S.)

Midway Is. (U.S.)

PACIFIC OCEAN

Marshall Is. (U.S.)

Guam (U.S.)

JAPAN

Okinawa (JAPAN)

SOUTH KOREA

PHILIPPINES

HONG KONG (U.K.)

North Pole

Greenland (DEN.)

ATLANTIC OCEAN

ICELAND

Azores (PORT.)

NORWAY

UNITED KINGDOM

NETH.
DEN.
BEL.
FRANCE GER.
W. GER.
POLAND
CZECH.
HUN.
ROM.
BULG.
GREECE
TURKEY
Crete (GR.)

PORTUGAL

SPAIN

ITALY

UNION OF SOVIET SOCIALIST REPUBLICS

MONGOLIA

CHINA

THAILAND

INDIA

INDIAN OCEAN

Equator

EGYPT

SAUDI ARABIA

OMAN

SRI LANKA

Legend:
- ■ U.S. military bases or ports
- NATO members
- Warsaw Pact members

0   500   1,000 mi.

0 500 1,000 km

Polar Stereographic projection

Portfolio Project

Interview someone who lived through the Cuban missile crisis. Ask the person to describe what it was like living through the crisis. Write a summary of your findings, and keep it in your portfolio.

Cooperative Learning

Work with others to create a newspaper about a topic from this chapter, such as the Cuban missile crisis or events in China. Include editorials, political cartoons, and feature articles.

Reinforcing Skills

Analyzing Secondary Sources The photo at left is a primary source that catches Castro and Khrushchev at a jovial moment. Write a paragraph for a secondary source explaining how the friendship between these two men created a world crisis.

Geography and History

Study the map on this page to answer the following questions:

1. How many military bases are on the map?

2. Near what part of the Soviet Union do you see the most bases?

3. Where are the Soviet Union and the United States closest together?

4. Which NATO bases may have been the most serious threat to the Soviets?

HISTORY JOURNAL

Write about how Americans felt during the Cuban missile crisis. Why did nuclear war seem imminent? How might it feel to live within range of a nuclear missile?

Geography and History

1. almost 50
2. near its western border
3. where Alaska is across Bering Strait from Soviet Union
4. Because more people lived in the western part of the Soviet Union, the bases near its western border were probably considered the most serious threat.

History Journal

Students may mention that war seemed imminent because missiles in Cuba were only 90 miles from the United States and that the Soviet Union was threatening the United States.

? BONUS QUESTION

This question may be used for extra credit on the chapter test.

Identify the strategy used in fighting the cold war. How was it different from strategies used in previous struggles? Where were the battlefields?

Answer: *The Soviets worked to install Communist governments while the United States worked to contain communism where it already existed. Opposing powers took sides in civil wars and disputes between smaller nations throughout the world.*

Porfolio Project

Students may want to ask the person what his or her strongest memory of the time is, or what they were doing when they heard about the missiles. What feelings seemed pervasive at the time?

Cooperative Learning

You may want to suggest to students additional topics, such as Truman's dealings with the Soviet Union, the Berlin airlift, the Marshall Plan, or CIA actions in the world.

Reinforcing Skills

Students should note that when Castro took control of U.S. businesses in Cuba, he sought help from the Soviets. Cuba's friendship with the Soviets led to Soviet military installations in Cuba, which precipitated a standoff between the two superpowers.

The Postwar Era

DAILY LESSON OBJECTIVES	REPRODUCIBLE RESOURCES	MULTIMEDIA RESOURCES
SECTION 1 Postwar Economy Booms 1. Explain how economic prosperity was maintained or increased as the nation converted from wartime to peacetime production. 2. Identify ways in which returning GIs received help as they reentered society. 3. Explain the relationship between the consumer culture and economic growth in the postwar period.	☞ Reproducible Lesson Plans ☞ Vocabulary and Guided Reading Activities (English or Spanish) ☞ Cooperative Learning Activities ☞ American Literature Readings and Activities ☞ Section Quizzes (English or Spanish)	🖥 Chapter Teaching Transparencies 🖥 Section Focus Transparencies 🖥 Map Transparencies 🖥 Unit Time Line Transparencies 💿 Landmark Documents in American History 💻 Testmaker 💻 Student Self-Test: A Software Review
SECTION 2 Suburban Lifestyles 1. Explain population movements following World War II and tell why they took place. 2. Demonstrate the impact of postwar population growth on American society. 3. Describe suburban values of the 1950s. 4. Describe the status of women and children during the 1950s.	☞ Reproducible Lesson Plans ☞ Vocabulary and Guided Reading Activities (English or Spanish) ☞ Geography in History Activities ☞ Supreme Court Case Studies ☞ Section Quizzes (English or Spanish)	🖥 Section Focus Transparencies 💻 Testmaker 💻 Student Self-Test: A Software Review
SECTION 3 Poverty and Plenty 1. Explain why the poor were "invisible" during the 1950s. 2. Explain how various groups of people, young and old, rural and urban, became caught in a cycle of poverty. 3. Describe the unique hardships that the poor of various minority groups experienced amid a generally affluent society.	☞ Reproducible Lesson Plans ☞ Vocabulary and Guided Reading Activities (English or Spanish) ☞ Reteaching Activities (English or Spanish) ☞ Supreme Court Case Studies ☞ Skill Reinforcement Activities ☞ Enrichment Activities (English or Spanish) ☞ Section Quizzes (English or Spanish)	🖥 Section Focus Transparencies 🖥 U.S. History and Art Transparencies 💻 Testmaker 💻 Student Self-Test: A Software Review
CHAPTER REVIEW AND EVALUATION	☞ Chapter 18 Test, Forms A and B ☞ Performance Assessment Strategies and Activities	💻 Student Self-Test: A Software Review 💻 Vocabulary PuzzleMaker 💻 Testmaker 🎧 Chapter Digests Audiocassettes

 If time does not permit teaching the entire chapter, summarize using the Chapter 18 Digests Audiocassettes and the accompanying activities and tests. (Available in English or Spanish.)

Cooperative Project

Organize students into groups of four or five to prepare a pictorial essay on the lives of Americans who lived in suburban, rural, and urban areas in the postwar era. The project should include art, diagrams, charts, and other appropriate graphics accompanied by written text. **LEP**

Suggested Rubrics: A Booklet or Pamphlet, A Cartoon, A Display, Group Work and the Individual, A Poster, A Slide Show or Photo Essay. See Performance Assessment Strategies and Activities, pp. 37, 44, 47, 50, 55, and 57.

Individual Project

Have interested students read and report on *The Organization Man* (William H. Whyte, Jr.), *The Lonely Crowd* (David Riesman), or *The Invisible Man* (Ralph Ellison). Each provides a thoughtful view of American society in the postwar era.

Suggested Rubrics: A Research Report, An Oral Presentation. See Performance Assessment Strategies and Activities, pp. 33 and 39.

Key to Ability Levels

Teaching strategies have been coded for varying learning styles and abilities.

L1 **BASIC** activities for all students

L2 **AVERAGE** activities for average to above-average students

L3 **CHALLENGING** activities for above-average students

LEP **LIMITED ENGLISH PROFICIENCY** activities

 Block Scheduling

Block scheduling differs from traditional class scheduling in the amount of time allotted to each period. The extended timeframe provided by block scheduling affords you the opportunity to implement a greater number of research-oriented and activity-intense projects to motivate and involve your students. Activities that are particularly suited to use within the block scheduling framework are identified throughout this chapter by the following designation.

TEACHER'S CORNER

 NATIONAL GEOGRAPHIC SOCIETY

NATIONAL GEOGRAPHIC SOCIETY PRODUCTS AVAILABLE FROM GLENCOE

To order the following products for use with this chapter, contact your local Glencoe sales representative or call Glencoe at 1-800-334-7344:

- *The Presidents: A Picture History of Our Nation* (CD-ROM)
- *GTV: A Geographic Perspective on American History* (Videodisc)
- *GTV: The American People: Fabric of a Nation* (Videodisc)

ADDITIONAL NATIONAL GEOGRAPHIC SOCIETY PRODUCTS

To order the following products for use with this chapter, call National Geographic Society at 1-800-368-2728:

- *Decades of History: The 20th Century—The Middle Years* (Filmstrip)
- *The United States as a World Power: From the 1890s to the 1970s* (Filmstrip)

Chapter Overview

After 15 years of depression and war, the United States entered a period of extraordinary prosperity, mobility, and technological change.

Introducing the Chapter

Have students read the vignette on this page. Encourage students to think about how shifting from war to peace might affect the economy, the movement of people from place to place, and the kinds of technology developed.

 Display Map Transparency 18 and distribute copies of the activity sheet for students to complete.

Extension Activity

Have students complete Beyond the Transparency on the activity sheet for Chapter 18 and present their projects after the class has completed the chapter.

History Journal

Have students notice the automobile and family in the photograph. Ask them to write about how they think life might have been different in the postwar era from life today.

CHAPTER
18

The Postwar Era

1955: MIDDLE-CLASS SUBURBANITES BLIND TO URBAN POVERTY

The sun glinted off the tail fins and chrome bumpers of the new Buick in the driveway as the Wilsons piled into the car for their weekly ritual—the Sunday afternoon drive. After a brief struggle over who would get the window seats, Sally, Tom, and Susan settled themselves in the backseat.

The car turned onto one of Chicago's newly completed expressways, and shortly the Wilsons were driving north on Michigan Avenue with its exclusive shops and fine restaurants. They parked to window-shop a bit, and when the children clamored for ice cream, the family stopped at an ice-cream parlor. Then they headed home to the tree-lined streets of their comfortable suburb of Morton Grove.

The Wilsons were a lucky family. Exactly 10 years ago, John Wilson was one of thousands of exhausted GIs marching on the road to Berlin.

Now John and Julie had 3 great kids with a fourth on the way and a beautiful home in the suburbs. Thanks to the GI Bill, John had a college degree (something his parents had never achieved) and a promising future with a large company.

On their drive the Wilsons never saw the not-so-lucky Americans who lived on Chicago's West Side: women talking on the steps of decaying buildings; men slumped in doorways; children playing ball on a sidewalk strewn with broken glass. ∎

HISTORY JOURNAL

Before you read the rest of this chapter, write what you know or understand about the 1950s and what you think this chapter will be about.

596

✚ EXTRA CREDIT PROJECT

The Postwar Era Have students conduct research about the postwar era. They may want to interview family friends or relatives about the time, or they may want to read newspaper or magazine articles published at the time. Topics they might want to focus on should include advertising and consumerism of the era, the impact of the GI Bill, farming, automobiles and mobility, or migration to the suburbs. Students can present important findings to the class, and then file their reports in their portfolios.

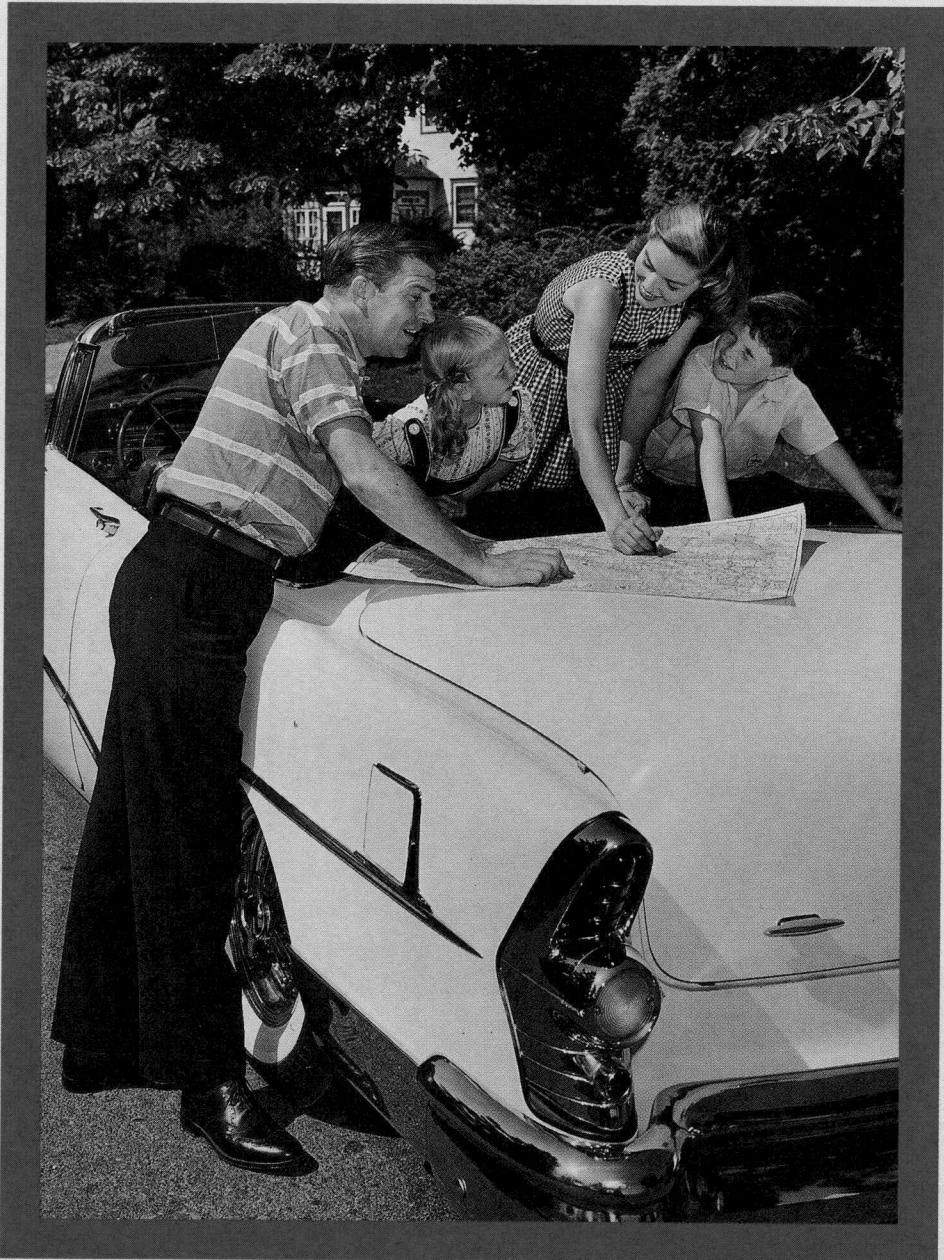

© SUPERSTOCK

THE SUBURBAN VALUES OF THE 1950S
STRESSED TOGETHERNESS, FAMILY,
AND THE "GOOD LIFE."

597

Performance Assessment

Refer to page 596B for performance assessment activities for this chapter.

 Also see Activity 18 in the Performance Assessment Strategies and Activities for an additional activity as well as for suggested rubrics.

Notes

Examining the Visual

The Invisible Poor The life of middle-class citizens in the United States was very different from that of the poor. Middle-class families in the suburbs needed (and could afford) automobiles. Family vacations often revolved around driving to national parks or amusement centers across the country. Many of the poor, on the other hand, had to rely on public transportation systems for mobility. This often meant that poor families could not get to jobs on the outskirts of cities. They also could not drive to the most inexpensive grocery stores and markets, so they were forced to pay whatever prices nearby stores charged.

SECTION
1

FOCUS

Section Objectives

1. Explain how economic prosperity was maintained (or increased) as the nation converted from wartime to peacetime production.
2. Identify ways in which returning GIs received help as they reentered society.
3. Explain the relationship between the consumer culture and economic growth in the postwar period.

Bellringer Activity

While taking attendance at the beginning of the class period, display **Section Focus Transparency 56,** and have students answer the questions. (Or use the blackline master.)

VISUAL INSTRUCTION

GI Housing The GI Bill promoted economic growth by encouraging spending. Unemployment benefits were paid to veterans who could not find jobs, and low-interest loans were offered to veterans starting businesses or buying homes or farms.

Ask: What was Veterans' Village? *(a University of Minnesota community for ex-GIs)*

Facts on File

Landmark Documents in American History Have students review "GI Bill of Rights (Servicemen's Readjustment Act), 1944" and write a paragraph about the intent of the document.

Postwar Economy Booms

FALL 1947: VETS ENROLL IN COLLEGE ON GI BILL

UNIVERSITY OF MINNESOTA

GI Housing
Veterans flooded college campuses after the war. Some ex-GIs and their families at the University of Minnesota lived in quonset units.

WORLD WAR II VETERAN KEN-NETH BAKER, HIS WIFE, LAURA, AND THEIR BABY DAUGHTER AR-RIVED ON THE CAMPUS OF THE UNIVERSITY OF MINNESOTA ON A COOL SEPTEMBER MORNING IN 1947. Ken was one of 6,000 married "vets" on campus ready to begin the fall semester. His family was assigned to one of the 674 housing units in Veterans' Village, a university community for ex-GIs, where rents were based on each vet's ability to pay. Veterans who had the most seniority were assigned to the best units—converted steel barracks with gas heat and indoor bathrooms. As newcomers, Kenneth and Laura would be living in a trailer with no plumbing. That meant that they would have to use the public bathhouse and the public laundry.

Nevertheless, the Bakers considered themselves lucky. As Ken observed, "Even a hovel in Veterans' Village is heaven compared to the way I lived in the service." Living in Veterans' Village meant that Ken and Laura could get by on their monthly government allowance of $90.

Life in Veterans' Village fostered a spirit of cooperation. With more than 900 babies among the village population, every adult became a guardian to every child. The Bakers shopped in the village grocery store, which the veterans' campus community owned and operated. Ken and several of his buddies joined the veterans'

AS YOU READ

Vocabulary
► demobilization
► real income
► discretionary income
► conglomerate

Think About . . .
► how economic prosperity was maintained or increased as the nation converted from wartime to peacetime production.

► those programs that helped returning GIs reenter society.
► how the consumer culture that developed following the war spurred economic growth.

598 CHAPTER 18 THE POSTWAR ERA

Section 1 Resources

REPRODUCIBLE RESOURCES

Lesson Plan 18-1

Vocabulary and Guided Reading Activity 18-1

Cooperative Learning Activity 18-1

Section 1 Quiz

Unit 7 American Literature Reading

MULTIMEDIA RESOURCES

Chapter Teaching Transparency 18

Section Focus Transparency 56

Landmark Documents in American History

Map Transparency 18

Student Self-Test: A Software Review

Testmaker

Chapter 18 Digest Audiocassette

bowling league. Laura took special classes in sewing, cooking, and child care. On Friday nights, Laura and Ken joined other residents of Veterans' Village in the recreation center to dance to the recorded music of popular big bands of the day.

Similar veterans' communities could be found on most large college campuses in the postwar United States, thanks to the GI Bill of Rights. The GI Bill was designed to ease the transition from military to civilian life by providing veterans with financial aid for education and housing and to begin small businesses. Nearly 8 million veterans took advantage of educational assistance. Armed with college degrees or technical training, the vets contributed their energy and talent to what would become the nation's longest unbroken period of prosperity.

From War to Peace
Returning GIs Spur Economy

More than 16 million Americans had served in the armed forces during World War II. **Demobilization,** the dismantling of the huge United States war machine, was a daunting task, somewhat like trying to reverse the direction of a river's flow. After peace was achieved in 1945, war-weary soldiers stationed around the world waited eagerly to come home. After thousands of citizens appealed to their congressional representatives to speed up the process, the number of soldiers on active duty dropped from 12 million in 1945 to 1.6 million by mid-1947. This rapid demobilization provided much-needed workers for United States industry, which was in the process of converting from wartime to peacetime production.

Economic Growth

After years of "going without" during the Great Depression and the war, Americans hungered for new cars, electronics, appliances, and gadgets. Industry set out to fill the growing demand for consumer goods. The automobile industry produced 2 million cars in 1946 and nearly 2 times that many by 1955. Americans bought 975,000 television sets in 1948, and 2 years later they bought 7.5 million sets. By 1960 about 75 percent of all American families owned at least 1 automobile, and 87 percent owned at least 1 television set. Consumers also purchased more refrigerators, washing machines, vacuum cleaners, and cameras than ever before. Electric can openers, electric garage door openers, and electric pencil sharpeners appeared on the market and quickly became part of the new American way of life.

The GNP, or gross national product (the total value of a country's goods and services), rose rapidly—

NOW, for the first time anywhere

Motorola Color TV

THE GREATEST DEVELOPMENT OF THE ELECTRONIC AGE

Now, you can take your choice of three beautiful Motorola color TV sets. Their superb craftsmanship, outstanding design and lovely woods will earn them a place among the finest furnishings. Without a doubt, they are worthy cabinets for Motorola color TV—the finest in color television.

A 1950s Spending Spree During the 1950s, electricity consumption more than doubled, due in large part to the purchases of electrical appliances and televisions. *Why did Americans have so much money to spend?*

from just more than $100 billion in 1940 to about $300 billion in 1950 and then to $500 billion by 1960. This increase in goods and services that characterized the postwar period gave Americans the highest standard of living the world had ever known. People lived more comfortably than ever before. The United States, home to just 6 percent of the world's population, produced and consumed nearly half the world's goods.

Wage and Price Issues

The reconversion to a peacetime economy brought problems, too. During the war, civilian paychecks included plenty of overtime pay. In addition, government policies had kept a lid on prices. When postwar wages failed to keep up with now-rising prices, blue-collar workers launched a wave of strikes and work stoppages, refusing to work until their demands were met.

Despite rising prices, most American workers continued to prosper. Average annual earnings for factory workers rose from $3,302 in 1950 to $5,352 in 1960. **Real income,** the amount of income earned taking into account an increase in prices, increased more than 20 percent during the same period. Working-class Americans began to accumulate **discretionary income**—money to buy what they wanted as well as what they

TEACH

Guided Practice

L2 Discussion Ask why Americans' daily lives would have been affected less by the cold war than by World War II. Have students speculate about how peace affected such areas as jobs, business, and agriculture.

Show students Map Transparency 18 and have them complete the activity sheet.

Independent Practice

L2 Research Have volunteers examine magazines of the 1950s. Others can locate videotapes of TV programs from the 1950s. Ask the researchers to explain the ways of life portrayed and the messages in ads and commercials.

Have students complete the Chapter 18, Section 1 Vocabulary and Guided Reading Activity. (Also in Spanish.) **LEP**

Have students complete the Chapter 18 Cooperative Learning Activity.

VISUAL INSTRUCTION

A 1950s Spending Spree The message of many advertisements in the 1950s—and today as well—is that you will be a happier and better person if you buy the product.

Answer: *They had saved during the war, government policies kept prices low, and most American workers' incomes increased faster than inflation.*

Cooperative Learning

Dramatization Have the class work in groups of five. Each member of a group should role-play one of the following: a GI returning to college, a manager in a large corporation, a farmer, a teenager who has just moved to the suburbs, or a homemaker. Group members will take turns describing their lives (work, leisure, family life). In their preparation, students should work together to help one another define the roles they are to play.

Curriculum Connection

Civics Call attention to the last sentence in Nelson Poynter's quotation. Ask students to write an essay on why democracy is strengthened when educational opportunities increase and how democracy depends on educated citizens.

FYI

Color Television The first commercial color telecast was presented in 1953 by Columbia Broadcasting System in New York City. Throughout the 1950s, however, color television remained too expensive for widespread use.

---

needed. This increased purchasing power further fueled the rapid economic growth.

Persuading the Consumer

Advertising became the fastest growing industry in the postwar United States. Manufacturers employed new marketing techniques. These techniques were carefully planned to whet the consumer's appetite. It was also the purpose of these advertisers to influence choices among brands of goods that were essentially the same. In his 1957 best-seller, *The Hidden Persuaders,* Vance Packard described the role of advertisers:

> These motivational analysts . . . are adding depth to the selling of ideas and products. They are learning, for example, to offer us considerably more than the actual item involved. A Milwaukee advertising executive commented to colleagues in print on the fact that women will pay two dollars and a half for skin cream but no more than twenty-five cents for a cake of soap. Why? Soap, he explained, only promises to make them clean. The cream promises to make them beautiful.
>
> —Vance Packard, *The Hidden Persuaders,* 1957

According to these hidden messages, a freezer became a promise of plenty, a second car became a symbol of status, and a mouthwash became the key to immediate social success.

The increased popularity of television played a major role in the development of the advertising industry and the gospel of consumerism. Television networks depended on advertising revenues to pay for the programs they produced. At the same time, advertisers found television a perfect medium for reaching consumers. Television, after all, was still a novelty for most people in the United States during the early 1950s, and they watched the television commercials just as avidly as the television programs.

Television ads became something of an art form in themselves. They not only sold products, they also entertained the viewers with showy dramatizations and catchy jingles. As the decade progressed, the presence and influence of television advertising became pervasive, and acquiring material goods like those shown on TV became a goal of the growing, status-conscious middle class.

TV Commercials Advertisers discovered that television was a good way to reach consumers. Advertising was the fastest growing industry in the postwar United States. *What techniques did advertisers use?*

Impact of the GI Bill
A Boom for Colleges and Housing

More than any other factor, the GI Bill of Rights, Congress passed in 1944, shaped American society in the postwar period. One veteran concurred:

> The GI Bill of Rights, of course, had more to do with thrusting us into a new era than anything else. Millions of people whose parents or grandparents had never dreamed of going to college saw that they could go. . . . Essentially I think it made us a far more democratic people.
>
> —Nelson Poynter, in *Americans Remember the Home Front*

As a result of the GI Bill, the greatest wave of college building in the nation's history took place during the postwar years. Many states vastly increased their support of higher education. For example, during the postwar period California State University opened campuses at Sacramento, Los Angeles, Long Beach, Fullerton, Hayward, Northridge, and San Bernardino.

In addition to educational benefits, the GI Bill offered low-interest mortgages to veterans who wanted to purchase homes. This spurred a huge demand for housing after the war, creating a construction boom and fostering a trend toward mass production. Using mass production methods, the housing industry built 13 million

---

Meeting Special Needs

Reading Disability To address the particular needs of students with reading disabilities, have students look at the visuals in the section to answer oral questions about the postwar period: Were there many goods for Americans to buy? Were automobiles important? What was happening in business and farming?

Visual Learners To address the particular needs of visual learners, ask students to think about how postwar Americans were a "people on the move." Then have them create a visual essay with collected or drawn pictures showing increased mobility.

new homes during the 1950s. Home ownership had always been a part of the American dream. The rate of home ownership increased between 1940 and 1960 from 44 to 62 percent of American households. The GI Bill allowed millions of Americans to achieve a standard of living that was generally better than that of their parents.

The New World of Business
Corporate Values Stress Conformity

During the postwar years, the motto of major corporations became "bigger is better." Business mergers, the combining of several companies, created **conglomerates**—firms that had holdings in a variety of unrelated industries. Many of the nation's biggest corporations grew even bigger during the postwar years. The net sales of IBM jumped from $119.4 million in 1946 to $1.7 billion in 1961. General Motors doubled its net assets during the 1950s from $1.5 billion in 1951 to $2.8 billion in 1960.

Up the Corporate Ladder

Rapid corporate growth during the 1950s gave rise to new employment opportunities and a new lifestyle for the nation's white-collar workers (clerical and professional workers) who viewed the corporate life as a secure career. Major corporations provided their employees

Corporate Image Large corporations encouraged conformity and offered training programs that helped develop the "corporate image." At some companies, holding the proper beliefs was just as important as wearing the proper necktie. *What might be the benefits and disadvantages of working for a large corporation?*

with everything from company neckties to memberships in exclusive country clubs. Training programs encouraged employees to adopt the company point of view. Companies such as IBM sent their managers to schools to learn not only management techniques, but company beliefs as well.

Critics charged corporations with destroying individuality by expecting employees to conform to company standards of thinking, dressing, and behaving. As sociologist C. Wright Mills commented, "When white-collar people get jobs, they sell not only their time and energy but their personalities as well."

Major corporations greatly influenced American life and values in the 1950s. To those climbing the corporate ladder—that is, being promoted to higher and higher levels of responsibility—wages were but one concern. Equally important were benefits such as a pension plan, medical insurance, a performance bonus, an expense account, a paid vacation, and a company car. For employees who dedicated themselves to the corporate lifestyle and successfully met the expectations of their superiors, the rewards of corporate life were further proof that the United States was a land of opportunity—at least for some Americans.

During the 1950s positions of power and authority within the corporate world belonged mostly to white males. Minority representation was very rare. Women were expected to fill different roles in the postwar American workforce. The widely read *Life* magazine explained women's roles one way:

Household skills take her into the garment trades; neat and personable, she becomes office worker and saleslady; patient and dexterous, she does well on repetitive, detailed factory work; compassionate, she becomes teacher and nurse.

—*Life,* 1956

The Service Sector

The nation's public and private service industries enjoyed tremendous expansion during the postwar years. Government jobs at the national, state, city, and county levels included social workers, teachers, and civil servants. In private business, there was a big growth in the number of secretarial and clerical workers, bank tellers, and telephone operators, as well as service workers in the insurance, transportation, and retail sales areas. Hospitality and recreation industries needed more service workers

SECTION ONE **601**

ASSESS

Meeting Lesson Objectives

Each section objective is tested by the section review questions that follow it in parentheses.

1. Explain how economic prosperity was maintained (or increased) as the nation converted from wartime to peacetime production. (1, 2, 3, 4)
2. Identify ways in which returning GIs received help as they reentered society. (2, 4)
3. Explain the relationship between the consumer culture and economic growth in the postwar period. (2, 3, 4, 5)

GRAPH STUDY

After the war, farms grew larger and more efficient. As corporations bought up small farms, fewer people owned farms. With more machinery, as well as advances in water and soil management, fewer people produced more goods. Some small farmers could not compete with large farms.

Answer: *The number rose.*

---

with the increased number of bowling alleys, skating rinks, movie theaters, hotels, and restaurants. The unprecedented number of cars, appliances, radios, and television sets purchased by consumers created a need for skilled mechanics and repairpeople. For the first time in United States history, workers who performed services began to outnumber those who manufactured products.

Farms Become Big Business
Small Farmers Leave for the City

The postwar years also saw a transformation in agriculture from family business to corporate enterprise. Two studies conducted of Plainville, a pseudonym for a small rural community in southeast Missouri, told a large story. The first study, conducted in 1939, revealed a community of small farms. Here, farmers grew a variety of small crops, raised a few chickens, and bred a few cows. Fifteen years later, Plainville had been transformed. Farming had become big business. As incomes doubled, or even tripled, residents joined the consumer society. Nearly every home had a television set. The way of life in rural Plainville was almost indistinguishable from that in suburban areas.

Plainville was typical of the changing nature of farming throughout the postwar United States. The size of farms increased. Farmers learned that large-scale farming lowered the cost of production. For example, in 1960 the average cost of corn production was $61 per acre when grown on 160 acres (64.8 ha); the cost dropped to $54 per acre on 640 acres (259.2 ha). As the size of farms grew, the value of fertile farmland rose rapidly.

Farm Auction A farmer, defeated by weather and economic conditions, must auction off his Nebraska farm. *Why were small farms unable to compete with large farms?*

Farming Becomes Big Business

30.5 / 13.5	297 / 175	25.8 / 10.7
1940 1960	1940 1960	1940 1960
Farm population (in millions)	Average acreage per farm	Persons supplied per farm

As farms grew larger, the number of people needed to work on them dropped. *What happened to the number of people supplied per farm?*

While a few farmers benefited from these changes, others suffered. Because small farms could not compete with large farms, many small-farm families sold their land and migrated to urban areas. As farm size doubled, the total number of farms dropped from more than 6 million in 1940 to fewer than 4 million in 1960, and the farm population fell from about 30 million to about 13 million. By 1960 only 8 percent of the population lived on farms.

An Automobile Culture
The 1950s' Fascination With Cars

The migration of farm families to the city was characteristic of the population as a whole. Americans were on the move, and the automobile became indispensable to their way of life. Auto dealers sold a record 58 million cars during the 1950s. Car manufacturers kept the public buying by changing body styles and adding more options, which made the previous year's models obsolete, at least in style. Turning out large, high-powered, steel-and-chrome fantasies in every color of the rainbow, the automakers provided sparkling steel chariots for every taste and income level.

Curb Service and Drive-ins

Americans practically lived in their automobiles. "Come as you are, eat in your car" became a popular slogan of fast-food drive-ins that provided curb service. Traveling on roller skates, waitresses and waiters, called carhops,

---

Drive-in Restaurant Hamburgers, french fries, and Cokes were drive-in favorites during the 1950s. *What encouraged automobile travel?*

Americans began to head to the West and the Southwest. Houston, Dallas, Phoenix, and Albuquerque were some of the cities whose populations soared. The greatest growth phenomenon, however, took place in California, which accounted for one-fifth of the nation's population growth in the 1950s. By 1963 California had surpassed New York as the nation's most populous state.

The most significant population shift was the migration of white Americans from cities to suburbs. The greater availability of automobiles, the expansion of the highway system, and the affordability of mass-produced suburban housing spurred the movement. By the end of the 1950s, more than one-fifth of all Americans lived in the suburbs. Suburbanization changed the landscape of the nation and the lifestyle of middle-class Americans.

took orders and delivered food directly to the customer's car window. Drive-in theaters showed movies on large outdoor screens that the audience watched from the privacy of their own cars.

Ribbons of Highway

The development of an extensive interstate highway system encouraged automobile travel. The Highway Act of 1956 authorized $32 billion for the construction of more than 40,000 miles of federal highways across the United States. President Eisenhower proudly described his administration's commitment to the interstate highway system:

> The amount of concrete poured to form these roadways would build . . . six sidewalks to the moon. . . . More than any single action by the government since the end of the war, this one would change the face of America.
>
> —President Dwight D. Eisenhower

Migration to the Suburbs

The moving van became the symbol of American mobility in the postwar period. During each year of the 1950s, nearly one-fifth of the population changed residences. Attracted by warm climates and plentiful jobs,

---

SECTION REVIEW

Vocabulary

1. Define: demobilization, real income, discretionary income, conglomerate.

Checking Facts

2. What kinds of benefits did the GI Bill of Rights offer to veterans?

3. What caused the heavy demand for consumer goods after the war?

Critical Thinking

Analyzing Information

4. How did the return of the GIs change the job market for women? Were any of the changes positive? In what way?

Linking Across Time

5. What trend in business today is an extension of the "bigger is better" trend of the postwar years?

SECTION ONE **603**

VISUAL INSTRUCTION

Drive-in Restaurant Some types of drive-ins still exist today: drive-ins in which customers drive up to a window, place an order, and pick up the food. Drive-ins in which a waitress brings food to a customer's car are not so common today.

Answer: *the development of an extensive interstate highway system*

Evaluate

Have students complete the Section Review.

☛ ▣ Assign the Section 1 Quiz or use the Testmaker to develop a customized quiz. (Also in Spanish.) **LEP**

Reteach

🎧 Have students listen to the Chapter 18, Section 1 Audiocassette. (Also in Spanish.) **LEP**

Enrich

☛ Have students complete the Unit 7 American Literature Reading.

CLOSE

Ask students questions such as the following: What made television attractive to advertisers? *(Many watched, and they viewed the commercials as closely as the programs.)* How did Americans show their attachment to the automobile after the war? *(They bought record numbers of cars and created drive-in businesses.)*

Section 1 Review Answers

1. demobilization (599), **real income** (599), **discretionary income** (599), **conglomerate** (601)
2. The bill provided money for education and low-interest loans for homes, farms, and businesses.
3. Overtime pay for wartime production, a lack of goods for years, and policies that kept prices fixed made workers anxious to buy.

4. Women's roles in the job market changed as they left manufacturing jobs and returned home to traditional roles. Some changes were positive: they had more time to spend with families.
5. Many companies today continue to buy other companies and form conglomerates.

Geography: Impact on History

TEACH

Making the Geography Connection

The population of the United States has shifted many times in the course of its history. After World War II, the population shifted from the cities to the suburbs. The American way of life—for white middle-class Americans at least—changed with this shift.

Mapping Activity

Have students use the scale to determine the distance between each Levittown and its nearest major city. Ask: How did the distance between Levittown and the major city affect people who worked in the city?

MOVEMENT

New American Landscape: Suburbia

By 1945 a severe housing shortage had developed in the United States. During the war new housing starts had slowed to a standstill. Then hundreds of thousands of GIs came home, got married, and began looking for homes. The nation needed 5 million new housing units—the sooner, the better.

The Suburbs

The construction industry in the United States had to meet quite a challenge. Cities were too crowded for new construction to occur, and relocating millions of people to remote, sparsely populated areas of the country would be expensive and impractical. The builders' solution was to create a new addition to the country's landscape—planned communities on the outskirts of cities. This decision would transform not only the landscape of the country but also the lifestyles of the mostly white, middle-class Americans who began migrating from crowded cities to the open, quieter environment of the suburbs. Following World War II, several planned communities were constructed just outside many of the nation's big cities.

Levittown, U.S.A.

The first and most famous postwar planned community was begun in 1946 on Long Island, New York, about 30 miles (48.2 km) from midtown Manhattan. The community, called Levittown, was named for the company that built it, Levitt & Sons, and was constructed on 1,200 acres (486 ha) of potato farmland.

Levittown's design included single-family homes, parks, playgrounds, shopping centers, swimming pools, baseball diamonds, handball courts, and clubhouses for fraternal and veterans organizations. Each home was exactly the same and sold for the same price: $7,990.

The homes at Levittown were mass-produced. Specialized construction crews hurried from one

home site to the next, digging foundations, pouring concrete, erecting walls and roofs, and installing plumbing and electrical fixtures. During the height of the construction at Levittown, workers finished a new home every 15 minutes.

Levittown was an immediate success. Just 3 years after construction began, 10,600 houses had been built, and Levittown's population

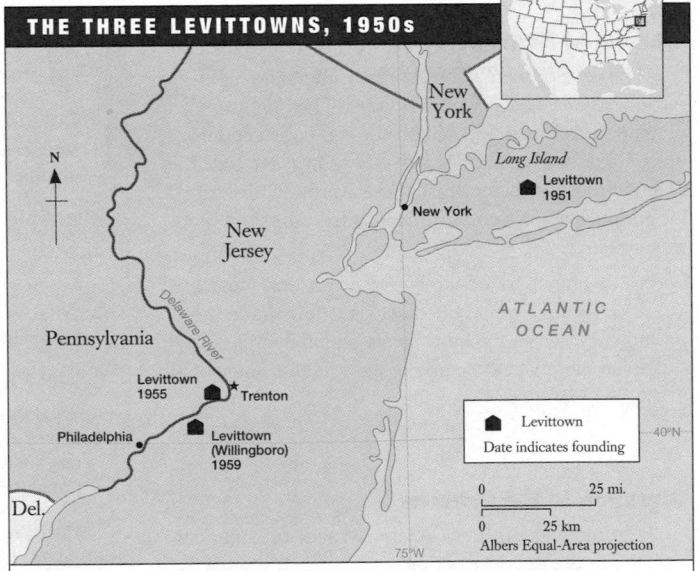

THE THREE LEVITTOWNS, 1950s

The first Levittown was so successful that its builders constructed two more—one in Pennsylvania and one in New Jersey. *What cities were they near?*

Geographic Themes

Movement Compare the movement of people to planned communities such as Levittown to other time periods of American history. What are the reasons people moved to the suburbs in the 1950s? *(They were looking for a better quality of life.)* In other time periods, what were the reasons Americans moved? *(Pilgrims in 1600s—to gain religious freedom; Easterners in mid-1800s—to get land; Oklahoma residents during 1920s and 1930s—to find jobs and food.)*

had swelled to more than 40,000. The residents loved their new community. One former GI who had moved to Levittown with his wife and another relative from a 1-bedroom apartment in Brooklyn said, "That was so awful I'd rather not talk about it. Getting into this house was like being emancipated."

A New Landscape

The construction of planned communities such as the three Levittowns accounted for several important changes in the landscape. First, these types of planned communities, or subdivisions, had never existed before. They combined elements of city life with features of rural living, blurring the distinctions that had once existed between these two ways of life.

Second, the new communities were an attractive alternative to the increasingly crowded, dirty cities in which most Americans lived. People who could afford to move did so, resulting in a migration of white middle-class Americans from the cities to surrounding suburbs.

Finally, the suburbs created a new way of life for many Americans. Long daily commutes to and from jobs in the cities became more and more common. New local governments were created to administer the affairs of these fledgling communities and new school systems were needed to educate the children of the suburbs. In short, the postwar housing shortage led to a transformation in the way the nation looked and in the way many Americans lived.

Suburban Living All the streets in Levittown curved at exactly the same angle, and trees were planted along them, 1 every 28 feet (8.5 m). Despite such rigid conformity, residents from the city loved the openness and country feel of this new suburb. *How many homes were constructed in the first Levittown?*

Modern Conveniences Homes in Levittown had a living room with a fireplace, two bedrooms, and a large attic that could be converted into two additional bedrooms. They also had the latest conveniences: radiant heat, an electric kitchen, an automatic washing machine, and a built-in television. *How much did these homes cost when they were first built?*

MAKING THE GEOGRAPHIC CONNECTION

1. Where was the first Levittown built, and what major city was it near? Where do you think many of the Levittown residents had lived before they moved to Levittown?

2. How were the homes in Levittown mass-produced? During the height of construction at the Levittown on Long Island, how often was a new home completed?

3. Movement After a decade of middle-class migration to the suburbs, the quality of life in most big cities began to decline. What were possible reasons for this decline?

Making the Geographic Connection Answers

1. The first Levittown was built on Long Island, near New York City. Many residents probably came from New York City.
2. Specialized construction crews worked on only one part of the project. For instance, one crew would only pour foundations, another would just put on roofs, and so forth. A house was completed every 15 minutes.

3. The cities were deserted by middle-class whites, who took their tax money with them to the suburbs. Just poor people remained in the cities, and they did not have enough money to improve things.

VISUAL INSTRUCTION

Suburban Living The houses in Levittown were built by the same crews within a short period of time.
Answer: *10,600 homes*

Modern Conveniences Residents had conveniences that many other Americans would not have for decades.
Answer: *$7,990*

NATIONAL GEOGRAPHIC SOCIETY

Videodisc

GTV: The American People: Fabric of a Nation

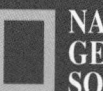

Side 4, Chapter 4
Title: Greener Pastures
Subject: Suburbs
Ask: Why did people move to the suburbs? *(crowded cities, dirt, crime)*

GTV: A Geographic Perspective on American History

Side 4, Chapter 8
Title: Shifting Winds
Subject: Population movements
Ask: How have the populations of cities changed since the 1940s? *(Many moved to the suburbs.)*

CLOSE

Ask students what kinds of planned communities exist today. *(condominiums, subdevelopments)*

605

FOCUS

Section Objectives

1. Explain population movements following World War II and tell why they took place.
2. Demonstrate the impact of postwar population growth on American society.
3. Describe suburban values of the 1950s.
4. Describe the status of women and children during the 1950s.

Bellringer Activity

While taking attendance at the beginning of the class period, display **Section Focus Transparency 57,** and have students answer the questions. (Or use the blackline master.)

VISUAL INSTRUCTION

Family Values Suburbs changed landscapes and lifestyles. Ask students to notice in this photo how suburban life is different from what they know of city life.

Ask: How many white Americans lived in the suburbs? *(60 million)*

SECTION
2

Suburban Lifestyles

1950s: AMERICANS MIGRATE TO SUBURBS

JILL JOHNSON PARKED THE GREEN AND WHITE STATION WAGON NEXT TO A NUMBER OF OTHER SIMILAR VEHICLES AT THE TRAIN STATION. As Bob Johnson joined the crowd waiting for the 8:22 A.M. commuter into the city, the Johnson children waved and blew kisses to their dad. Jill Johnson's next stop was Eisenhower Elementary School where Bill, a fourth grader, and Susan, a second grader, spent their day. Mary Ann, age four, and baby Jimmy then accompanied their mom to the shopping center.

The Village Market Mall provided ample parking for its 30 or more stores and offices. Shoppers had access to a large department store, a bank, a beauty salon and a barber shop, a drugstore, a dry cleaner, and a supermarket. Physicians, dentists, and attorneys occupied offices on the

Family Values
Following World War II, many families moved to the suburbs in search of the good life.

second floors of the two-story buildings in the shopping center.

Jill dropped off Bob's suits at the dry cleaner and then stopped at the supermarket to pick up cookies for the Cub Scout meeting and steaks to barbecue on Sunday. She also picked out frozen TV dinners so that the family could eat while they watched *The Adventures of Ozzie and Harriet* on Friday night.

With the morning errands completed, Jill Johnson and her children headed for home, a neat one-story frame house with a picture window and an attached garage, located on a street with many similar houses. The neighborhood's well-kept lawns and newly planted flowers and trees reflected pride of ownership. The Johnsons, along with 60 million other white Americans, were enjoying the comfortable lifestyle of the suburbs.

AS YOU READ

Vocabulary
► suburbia
► baby boom

Think About . . .
► the population movements that took place following World War II and why they occurred.
► how the postwar population growth impacted American society.
► the suburban values of the 1950s.
► the status of women and children during the 1950s.

Section 2 Resources

REPRODUCIBLE RESOURCES
📁 Lesson Plan 18-2
📁 Vocabulary and Guided Reading Activity 18-2
📁 Section 2 Quiz
📁 Geography in History Activity 18

📁 Supreme Court Case Studies 17, 18

MULTIMEDIA RESOURCES
🔖 Section Focus Transparency 57
💿 Student Selt-Test: A Software Review
💿 Testmaker
🎧 Chapter 18 Digest Audiocassette

Growth of Suburbia
Cities Lag Behind as Suburbs Grow

During the 1950s, 85 percent of new home construction took place in **suburbia**—residential areas outside the city. The number of suburban dwellers doubled, while the population of central cities rose only 10 percent. Reasons for the rapid growth of suburbia varied. Some whites wanted to escape the crime and the congestion of city neighborhoods. Others fled because of their prejudices against African Americans and Hispanic Americans who were moving to cities in growing numbers. Generally, middle-class white Americans considered migration to the suburbs a move upward to a better life for themselves and their children.

In contrast to city life, suburbia offered a retreat to the picturesque countryside. As developers in earlier periods had done, the developers of the 1950s attracted home buyers with promises of fresh air, green lawns, and trees. Many suburbs had "park," "forest," "woods," "grove," or "hill" as part of their names.

The new suburbs were usually located on the fringes of major cities. Farmland or vacant wooded areas became

African American Suburbs In Richmond, California, a group of African American community leaders developed a planned community, named Parchester Village, for middle-class African Americans. *Why was suburban life denied to many Americans in the 1950s?*

LOS ANGELES

0   10   20 mi.

0   10   20 km
Polyconic projection

Los Angeles County

SAN FERNANDO VALLEY

SAN GABRIEL MOUNTAINS

34°N

Burbank
162.6%

Glendale
44.6%

Beverly Hills
14.9%

Santa Monica
55.6%

Pasadena
42.2%

Los Angeles
64.8%

Inglewood
110.5%

Compton
343.3%

Redondo Beach
258.9%

Torrance
915.0%

Whittier
108.9%

Pomona
185.3%

118°30'W

Ontario
228.4%

San Bernardino County

PACIFIC OCEAN

Long Beach
109.5%

Anaheim
844.5%

116°W

Santa Ana
214.4%

Riverside County

Orange County

33°30'N

117°30'W

- Populated area in 1940
- Populated area in 1960
- County boundary
- **109.5%** Percent change in population

The Los Angeles area was one of the most rapidly growing parts of California between 1940 and 1960. *Which counties experienced the most growth between 1940 and 1960?*

sites for new subdivisions. In southern California, development of the San Fernando Valley, formerly sprinkled with orange groves, helped make Los Angeles the fastest growing area in the postwar period.

Suburbs had low population densities compared with cities. Single-family homes on large plots of land, wide streets, and open spaces gave suburbs the "country" feeling that new middle-class homeowners craved. They could enjoy this openness because residents owned automobiles, which allowed them to travel to jobs, schools, and shopping facilities.

Affordability became a key factor in attracting home buyers to the suburbs. Because the GI Bill offered low-interest loans, new housing was more affordable during the postwar period than at any other time in American history. Equally attractive was the government's offer of income tax deductions for home mortgage interest payments and property taxes.

Though affordable, the suburbs did not offer opportunities for homeownership to everyone. Many American cities had small but growing populations of middle-class minorities, particularly African Americans and Hispanic Americans, who also longed to escape the noise, the dirt, and the crime of the cities. By and large, however, the developers of the nation's postwar suburbs refused to sell homes to minorities. By 1960, for example, Levittown, Long Island, had a population of more than 65,000, but it had not a single African American resident. Despite having achieved a measure of financial success, America's middle-class minorities were still denied full access to the American dream.

SECTION TWO   **607**

TEACH

Guided Practice

L1 **Discussion** In 1951 *Time* magazine said of college students: "The most startling thing about the younger generation is its silence." Discuss the meaning of the quotation and the information it gives about the 1950s.

Independent Practice

L1 **Identifying Characteristics** Have students study the As You Read box. Then have them write *Life in the Suburbs* and the subheads *Positive Aspects* and *Negative Aspects* on a sheet of paper. Suggest that they make notes under the subheadings as they read the section.

Have students complete the Chapter 18, Section 2 Vocabulary and Guided Reading Activity. (Also in Spanish.) **LEP**

MAP STUDY

As highways were built out from cities, new suburbs grew up along them. This growth in turn led to a need for more highways.

Answer: *Los Angeles and Orange Counties*

VISUAL INSTRUCTION

African American Suburbs The first families moved into Parchester Village in the spring of 1950.

Answer: *Some people were excluded from the suburbs by prejudice.*

Cooperative Learning

Report Have students work with one another in heterogeneous groups of 5 or 6 to prepare a report on the lives of families in the suburbs of the United States in the 1950s. The reports should include both written material and visuals (pictures, graphs, charts). Before they begin the project, have groups divide tasks among members. Some students may do additional research, others may write text, while others may prepare visuals or collect memorabilia from the 1950s.

607

Suburban Ideal Togetherness was an important value during the 1950s. *What criticisms were leveled at the suburban dream?*

The American Dream
Community Spirit in the Suburbs

Low-income and minority groups were largely excluded from suburban society. Millions of white, middle-class Americans, however, shared a lifestyle that represented to them the American dream. They owned their homes, sent their children to good schools, lived in safe communities, and were economically secure. Such were the dreams of the immigrants who had sailed into New York Harbor half a century before, and now those dreams finally had been realized by many of their children.

Nevertheless, some Americans found fault with the "dream." Social critics of the 1950s deplored the conformity of suburban life. They mocked what they regarded as the sameness of the "cookie-cutter" houses, the lack of privacy, and the decline of individuality. Folksinger Malvina Reynolds satirized the middle-class suburbanites in a popular song titled "Little Boxes":

And they all play on the golf course
And drink their martinis dry,
And they all have pretty children
And the children go to school,
And the children go to summer camp
And then to the university,

Where they are put
in boxes
And they come out all
the same.

—Malvina Reynolds,
"Little Boxes"

Such criticism would not have rung true with most suburbanites. Emerging from an era of depression and a world war, the residents of suburbia during the 1950s saw themselves creating thousands of new communities built on a common desire for a decent existence. They prized the informality and togetherness of suburban life. The Welcome Wagon, a community organization that provided information and offered gifts and coupons from local stores, greeted new families. Most newcomers moved easily into the social life of the neighborhood by joining a bowling league, a bridge club, or a church group. One suburban resident observed: "Before we came here, we used to live pretty much to ourselves. . . . Now we stop around and visit with people or they visit with us. I really think [suburban living] has broadened us."

Cooperation and group participation helped forge community spirit in the suburbs. This spirit extended to church membership, which increased from 48 percent

"Cookie-cutter" Houses A cartoonist pokes fun at the sameness of suburban life. *Why did suburbanites like the suburbs?*

Meeting Special Needs

Reading Disability To address the particular needs of students with reading disabilities, let students imagine talking to someone from a nation where most people are farmers. Have them write six words or phrases to help this person understand suburban life. Examples might be *car pool, baby-sitting,* or *commuter.*

Visual Learners To address the particular needs of visual learners, have students work with the map of Los Angeles to point out the suburbs and the city center. Discuss how suburbs changed the landscape and the lifestyles of people.

ARCHIVE PHOTOS

Billy Graham An ordained Southern Baptist minister, Graham first gained recognition through his radio broadcasts, tent revivals, and appearances at "Youth for Christ" rallies. During the 1950s, many considered him fundamentalism's chief voice. *How did religion help shape the values of the people living during the 1950s?*

of the population in 1940 to 63 percent in 1960. The resurgence of religion became evident in all areas of life, from movies to politics. Hollywood's hit films included such religious extravaganzas as *The Robe, The Ten Commandments,* and *Ben Hur.* Congress added "under God" to the Pledge of Allegiance and "In God We Trust" to all United States currency. President Eisenhower told Americans, "Everybody should have a religious faith, and I don't care what it is."

Religious leaders helped spread religious commitment with the aid of modern communications. They had their own radio and television programs, best-selling books, and newspaper columns. Billy Graham, a popular Protestant minister and preacher, attracted thousands of people throughout the United States and in other parts of the world with his large-scale evangelical campaigns. Fulton J. Sheen, a Roman Catholic bishop, became a television personality through his weekly program optimistically titled *Life Is Worth Living.* Protestant minister Norman Vincent Peale attracted many thousands of followers with his message of "positive thinking."

Critics claimed that churches downplayed faith and emphasized comfort and security. Instead of searching for God, the critics said, most Americans turned to religion for peace of mind and a sense of belonging. For whatever reasons, American families flocked to their churches and synagogues throughout the 1950s. Billboards and television commercials proclaimed: "Bring the whole family to church" and "The family that prays together stays together." Messages like these clearly indicated that postwar society was focused on the family.

Baby Boom
A Child-centered Culture

Like the economy, the family enjoyed unprecedented growth in the postwar years. The nation's population increased by 19 million in the 1940s and by almost 30 million in the 1950s. The fertility rate—the number of births per thousand women—peaked at 123 in 1957, up about 20 percent from the Depression years of the 1930s. That meant that a baby was born in the United States every 7 seconds! This phenomenal population growth, known as the **baby boom,** continued until the mid-1960s.

SECTION TWO   **609**

Portfolio Project

Research Have students investigate and write about why middle-class minorities could not buy homes in the suburbs in the 1950s. Have students find out whether this practice still holds true today and, if so, what actions are being taken to rectify the situation. Students can place their finished work in their portfolios.

Creative Writing Have students use the Malvina Reynolds song as a model to write a song or poem about their era. They should use details that characterize the time. Have them include their songs or poems in their portfolios.

Curriculum Connection

Mathematics Have students use the Bureau of Census statistical abstracts or almanacs to research the distribution of population by age for the decades 1930 to 1990. Then have them graph their results, clearly indicating baby boomer years.

FYI

The Baby Boom Parents of baby boomers seized the opportunity to give their children what they themselves never had. Their enthusiasm for activities such as music lessons, scouting, and Little League was often fueled by memories of rationing and limited supplies during the Great Depression and World War II.

Like the resurgence of religion in the 1950s, the emphasis on family reflected a desire for close social and emotional ties. A *McCall's* magazine article in 1954 coined the term "togetherness" to describe young married couples whose lives centered on raising large families. Americans in the 1950s married at an earlier age and had more babies than their parents. Between 1940 and 1960, the birthrate for third and fourth children in a family more than doubled.

The baby boom further fueled the economy and helped sustain prosperity. Growing families needed larger houses, so the construction industry prospered. As the baby boomers progressed from diapers to school classrooms to college diplomas, industries and institutions grew to satisfy their needs. During the 1950s, school enrollments increased by 13 million. School districts struggled to erect new buildings and temporary classrooms to accommodate the nation's children. In California a new school was completed every 7 days throughout the 1950s, and still the state faced a shortage of classrooms.

Catering to the Kids

Many baby-boom kids enjoyed a lifestyle of unprecedented privilege. Schools became not only institutions of learning but also centers of social activity. After-school programs included an endless variety of lessons and sports events. Parents, who wanted to give their children all the advantages their new prosperity allowed, enthusiastically supported these activities. Music lessons in the schools drove up the sale of musical instruments from $86 million in 1950 to $149 million in 1960. The number of Girl Scouts and Brownies doubled, and the number of Little Leagues grew from about 800 to nearly 6,000 during the 1950s.

The Lone Ranger In this very popular television western, the Lone Ranger and his Native American friend, Tonto, set out to bring law and order to the West. *Who were some of the other television heroes of the 1950s?*

School Enrollment, 1910–1970, Grades K–8

(bar graph showing Population in millions on y-axis from 0 to 35, Years on x-axis)

Year	Population (in millions)
1910	~17
1920	~19.5
1930	~21.5
1940	~19.5
1950	~19.5
1960	~28
1970	~33

School enrollments skyrocketed in the 1950s. *How many students were enrolled in schools in 1910? In 1970?*

Baby boomers were the nation's first generation raised on television from their earliest years. Programming for children included everything from puppet shows to tales of the Old West. Young viewers gathered around the television to watch Buffalo Bob and his freckle-faced marionette, and when the youngsters heard the familiar opening line, "Say kids, what time is it?" they responded in unison, "It's Howdy Doody time!" At its height the popular *Kukla, Fran, and Ollie* puppet show attracted an audience of 10 million viewers. Kukla (a clown), Ollie (a snaggle-toothed dragon), and several other Kuklapolitan puppets visited with Fran Allison in an unrehearsed weekly program that charmed adults as well as children.

Television heroes included the Lone Ranger, Hopalong Cassidy, and Captain Video (Guardian of the Universe). Also popular were shows featuring heroic dogs and horses—*Lassie, Rin-Tin-Tin,* and *My Friend Flicka.* On *Ding Dong School,* kindly Miss Frances led her television audience in constructive preschool activities and songs. Millions of viewers joined Annette, Cubby, Karen, and the other Mouseketeers on *The Mickey Mouse Club.* Captain Kangaroo, Mr. Green Jeans, and a collection of puppet friends entertained more than one generation of youngsters.

Extending the Content

Economics Discuss the impact of population growth on resources, the landscape, and other aspects of the environment. Students may consider changes in residential neighborhoods and school campuses. Also discuss whether a growing population always leads to economic prosperity or whether it can lead to economic problems. It may be necessary to help students recall that a central idea of economics is scarcity, or limited resources.

First Polio Vaccination Some polio victims (above) needed an iron lung to breathe; others suffered paralysis and had to use crutches. A massive vaccination program (right) began after the Salk vaccine was approved for use in 1955. *How did Dr. Albert Sabin contribute to eliminating the polio threat?*

UPI/BETTMANN NEWSPHOTOS

MARCH OF DIMES BIRTH DEFECTS FOUNDATION

Advertisers and toymakers jumped on the television bandwagon. Products aimed at the growing market of 5- to 14-year-olds rang up big sales. In 1954 a popular Walt Disney television program introduced folk hero Davy Crockett, portrayed by Fess Parker. The resulting Davy Crockett "cult" created a $100 million market for coonskin caps and dozens of other items with Davy's picture on them. The show's theme song, "The Ballad of Davy Crockett," sold 4 million records.

Critics argued that television produced passive children. Children's programming, they claimed, was boring, mindless, and often violent. Still, some programs carried positive messages. Good triumphed over evil. Gentleness, kindness, and truthfulness prevailed. The joy and wonder of childhood were encouraged and celebrated.

Healthier, Happier Children

By the 1950s medical science had made great strides toward combating childhood diseases. Antibiotics and vaccines helped control diseases such as diphtheria, influenza, and typhoid fever. Polio, however, continued to baffle the medical profession. In 1952 a record number of 58,000 cases of polio was reported in the United States. Those who survived were often permanently paralyzed. The most severe cases were confined to iron lungs—large metal tanks with pumps that helped patients breathe. Polio became the most feared disease of the postwar period.

Dr. Jonas Salk finally developed an effective vaccine against polio and in doing so became the medical hero of the 1950s. Salk first tested the vaccine on himself, his wife, and their three sons. In 1954, 2 million schoolchildren took part in a mass testing program. The test, which was the largest effort of its kind in history, utilized the services of thousands of physicians and millions of volunteers. On April 12, 1955, the Salk vaccine was declared a safe and effective weapon against polio. Through the work of Dr. Salk, who became a hero to people throughout the world, and Dr. Albert Sabin, who developed an oral version of the vaccine, the threat of polio was virtually eliminated.

SECTION TWO **611**

First Polio Vaccination
Iron lungs withdraw air 15 to 30 times a minute from a tank in which a person is enclosed. When air is withdrawn, the person's chest rises. Then the air is forced back in, causing the person to exhale.

More than 80 percent of people who contracted polio recovered without permanent effects. In some, however, the disease destroyed nerve cells in the spinal cord, causing paralysis or difficulty in talking, breathing, or swallowing.

Answer: *He developed an oral version of the polio vaccine.*

FYI

Nobel Prize The 1952 Nobel Prize for Medicine and Physiology was given to Dr. Selman A. Waksman, a Russian-born American, for his discovery (with others) of streptomycin, an antibiotic used to treat bacterial diseases like tuberculosis.

 Curriculum Connection

Science Discuss infectious diseases that people today fear, such as AIDS. Ask students how people might react to a vaccine against AIDS and how the reaction would be like or unlike the reaction to a polio vaccine. Remind students that polio was a disease most often contracted by children.

Cultural Perspectives

Vaccines An inoculation is the injection of dead or weakened viruses or other germs into the body to cause a mild form of a disease in order to produce immunity. The first people to do this were residents of ancient China, India, and other places. Shibasaburo Kitasato of Japan in 1889 produced the first pure culture of a tetanus virus, which is used to make tetanus vaccine. He was also one of the discoverers of the bubonic plague germ, which he used to develop a vaccine. Have students conduct research to find out more about vaccines and inoculations around the world. What disease has been eliminated worldwide in recent years because of a vaccine? *(smallpox)*

VISUAL INSTRUCTION

Dr. Benjamin Spock Dr. Spock's famous baby book reinforced an idea that the feminist movement later took issue with: that a woman's place is in the home. Dr. Spock's book is still popular, however, and some of his ideas are still widely accepted. One such idea is that early childhood experiences influence a person's entire life.

Answer: *Dr. Spock's book discouraged spanking and encouraged mothers to create an atmosphere of warmth and trust for their children.*

Curriculum Connection

Literature Have students read the story "Profession: Housewife" by Sally Benson and explain how it reflects women's attitudes and problems in the postwar era. (The story, first published in 1940 in the *New Yorker*, is available in anthologies of the *New Yorker* stories and in anthologies of short stories.)

Dr. Benjamin Spock The famous doctor visits the Anderson quintuplets. *How did his books influence the rearing of children?*

Dr. Salk's fame was paralleled by that of another medical person, Dr. Benjamin Spock. During the 1950s only the Bible sold more copies than Spock's book *Baby and Child Care*. Spock popularized the theory that early childhood experiences influence an individual's entire life. He urged mothers to spare the rod and to devote themselves to creating an atmosphere of warmth and trust for their children so that they would grow into happy, well-adjusted adults. "You can think of it this way: useful, well-adjusted citizens are the most valuable possessions a country has, and good mother care during early childhood is the surest way to produce them." Dr. Spock suggested that the government should pay mothers so that they would not have to seek outside employment. This idea failed to gain popular support, and opponents even suggested that it smacked of socialism.

A Woman's Place
Back Into the Labor Force

Spock's theories helped reinforce the concept of motherhood as a profession in itself and strengthened the old idea that a woman's place was in the home. "No job is more exacting, more necessary, or more rewarding than that of housewife and mother," stated an article in the *Atlantic* in 1950. Statistics indicated that American women agreed. The median age of marriage for women fell from 21.5 in 1940 to 20.1 in 1956. By 1950 nearly 60 percent of all women between the ages of 18 and 24 were married.

Mother and Homemaker

In the 1950s women were discouraged from attending college. A high-school textbook on family living counseled young women that "Men are not interested in college degrees, but in the warmth and humanness of the girls they marry." Many women who did graduate from college concentrated their studies in such fields as home economics or child development. A survey found that most college women believed "it is natural for a woman to be satisfied with her husband's success and not crave personal achievement."

The suburban lifestyle strengthened the distinctions between male and female roles. Fathers often left home early in the morning to commute to jobs in the city. When they returned home in the evening, the children had been fed, bathed, and dressed for bed. Most mothers assumed responsibility for the daily routine of child rearing in addition to cooking, cleaning, shopping, washing clothes, and participating in school and community activities. John Cheever, who set many of his novels and short stories in the suburbs of New York, described one such woman:

She gets up at seven and turns the radio on. After she is dressed, she rouses the children and cooks the breakfast. Our son has to be walked to the school bus at eight o'clock. When Ethel returns from this trip, Carol's hair has to be braided. I leave the house at eight-thirty, but I know that every move that Ethel makes for the rest of the day will be determined by the housework, the cooking, the shopping, and the demands of the children. I know that on Tuesdays and Thursdays she will be at the A & P between eleven and noon, that on every clear afternoon she will be on a certain bench in a playground from three until five, that she cleans the house on Mondays, Wednesdays, and Fridays, and polishes the silver when it rains. When I return at six, she is usually cleaning the vegetables or making some other preparation for dinner. Then when the children have been fed and bathed, when the dinner is ready, when the table in the living room is set with food and china, she stands in the middle of the room as if she has lost or forgotten something, and this moment of reflection is so deep that she will not hear me if I speak to her, or the children if they call. Then it is over. She lights the four white candles in their silver sticks, and we sit down to a supper of corned-beef hash or some other modest fare.

—John Cheever, "The Season of Divorce" from *The Stories of John Cheever*

Critical Thinking

Comparing and Contrasting Women who grew up in the 1950s often had a narrow view of job possibilities. Many expected that if they ever worked, they would be waitresses, store clerks, or factory workers. Those who planned careers usually prepared to become secretaries, nurses, or schoolteachers. Because of the feminist movement of the 1960s and 1970s, young women now feel encouraged to pursue any career that interests them and for which they have some aptitude. Today, nearly all careers are open to both women and men. Research and report on whether women today work outside the home for the same reasons they did in the 1950s. Then discuss continuing barriers to women in the workplace, such as the "glass ceiling."

Popular culture reinforced the image of women as cute and perky rather than intelligent or career-minded. Actresses such as Doris Day, Debbie Reynolds, and Sandra Dee became role models for white women of the 1950s. Each portrayed the sweet, funny, innocent, wholesome, blond girl-next-door in popular box-office hits of the decade. Television situation comedies (sitcoms) emphasized the role of woman as wife and mother. In such shows as *Father Knows Best* and *Leave It to Beaver,* Dad dispensed wisdom and advice while apron-clad Mom tended to domestic matters. In programs such as *Our Miss Brooks* and *Private Secretary,* the main character was an unmarried career woman whose goal in life was simply to find a husband.

The educational system often encouraged schoolgirls of the 1950s to follow in their mothers' footsteps. While boys studied woodworking, auto mechanics, or courses preparing them for college, girls learned typing, cooking, and etiquette. However, a Gallup Poll in 1962 showed that 90 percent of the mothers surveyed hoped that their daughters would not lead the same lives as they had.

LAMBERT/ARCHIVE PHOTOS

Housework In the 1950s, hanging the laundry outside to dry was common. *What did Dr. Spock think was the most rewarding profession?*

Women Question Their Role in Society

Despite the apparent happiness of the middle-class American woman, something was amiss. Many of these women did not feel the complete fulfillment that devotion to their homes and families was supposed to provide. Yet many considered women who were dissatisfied with this role to be either mentally disordered, unfeminine, or both. For example, psychiatrist Helene Deutsch declared that truly feminine women related to the outside world only through identification with their husbands and children.

In 1957 Smith College graduates of the class of 1942 answered an alumnae questionnaire prepared by Betty Friedan that raised the issue of a woman's role in society. Years of such research and interviews with women led to Friedan's landmark book, *The Feminine Mystique,* published in 1963. Friedan described the situation:

CHANGING ROLE OF WOMEN, 1940–1963

1940 Only 1.5 million married women work.

1950s Women are discouraged from pursuing careers.

1956 Average age of marriage for women falls to 20.1.

1962 92% of mothers in Gallup Poll hope daughters lead lives different from theirs.

1940 1942 1944 1946 1948 1950 1952 1954 1956 1958 1960 1962

1946 Dr. Spock reinforces idea that women's place is in the home.

1957 Baby boom peaks.

1960 Number of working mothers jumps to 6.6 million.

1963 *The Feminine Mystique* is published.

SECTION TWO **613**

VISUAL INSTRUCTION

Housework In the 1950s, suburban women often stayed home during the day caring for children and completing household chores.

Answer: *housewife and mother*

 Curriculum Connection

Sociology Ask students for names of female role models today. Write the names on the chalkboard and discuss why each is admired and respected. Then discuss how and why these women might be different from role models of the 1950s. What traits were admired during the 1950s?

 At the Movies

Students may want to look for Doris Day movies at their local video store. Doris Day starred in many Warner Brothers movies of the 1950s because of her sunny personality and girl-next-door image. Her movies include *The Pajama Game* (1957), *Pillow Talk* (1959), *Lover Come Back* (1961).

CHART STUDY

Ask: How many married Women worked outside the home in 1940? *(1.5 million)*

Meeting Special Needs

Reading Disability To address the particular needs of students with reading disabilities, have students work in small groups to list the jobs they think they might have as adults. Ask them to discuss which jobs most people would have considered inappropriate for women in the 1950s.

Visual Learners To address the particular needs of visual learners, have students examine magazines from both today and the 1950s. What differences in lifestyles do they notice? How are women's roles portrayed? Do men's roles seem the same or different? What consumer goods are people encouraged to buy? What issues are people concerned about?

Betty Friedan After Betty Friedan discovered that her unhappiness was shared by other women, she wrote *The Feminine Mystique*, which explored causes for the frustrations of modern women in traditional roles. Friedan went on to cofound the National Organization for Women.

Answer: *the social pressures that women felt*

Women at Work Female factory workers run machinery at a company in Illinois.

Answer: *4 times faster*

ASSESS

Meeting Lesson Objectives

Each section objective is tested by the section review question(s) that follows it in parentheses.

1. Explain population movements following World War II and tell why they took place. (1)
2. Demonstrate the impact of postwar population growth on American society. (1, 2, 3, 5)
3. Describe suburban values of the 1950s. (2, 3, 4, 5)
4. Describe the status of women and children during the 1950s. (2, 4, 5)

The problem lay buried, unspoken, for many years in the minds of American women. It was a strange stirring, a sense of dissatisfaction, a yearning that women suffered in the middle of the twentieth century in the United States. Each suburban wife struggled with it alone. As she made the beds, shopped for groceries, matched slipcover material, ate peanut butter sandwiches with her children, chauffeured Cub Scouts and Brownies . . . she was afraid to ask even of herself the silent question—"Is this all?"

—Betty Friedan, *The Feminine Mystique*, 1963

Betty Friedan After the publication of *The Feminine Mystique*, Friedan organized the National Organization of Women. *What was Friedan's book about?*

Friedan had finally identified the "problem that had no name." While many American women were happy with their roles as housewives and mothers, many others felt social pressures had relegated them to roles as lifelong domestics.

Women in the Workforce

At the end of World War II, the government and industries urged women to "go back home" and "give your job to a vet." Women, who were largely excluded from important jobs in the corporate world, were also squeezed out of the manufacturing jobs they had held during the war.

Whether by pressure or by choice, many women who had taken on nontraditional jobs during the war returned to the familiar roles of full-time homemakers and mothers. For women in the lower economic ranks, however, staying at home was not an option. Millions of such women continued to enter the job market while still maintaining their roles as housewives and mothers. During the 1950s the rate of female employment increased 4 times faster than that of males. The number of working wives nearly doubled from 17 percent in 1940 to 32 percent in 1960. The number of working mothers leaped from 1.5 million to 6.6 million. By 1960 nearly 40 percent of women with children between the ages of 6 and 17 had jobs outside the home.

Married women over 35 represented the greatest

increase in female employment in the 1950s. Many of these women had worked outside the home before having a family. They then had stayed home to raise their children, who were now either married or off to school. These women filled the millions of clerical and secretarial positions created in the postwar period that the relatively small number of young single women who were entering the job market could not fill.

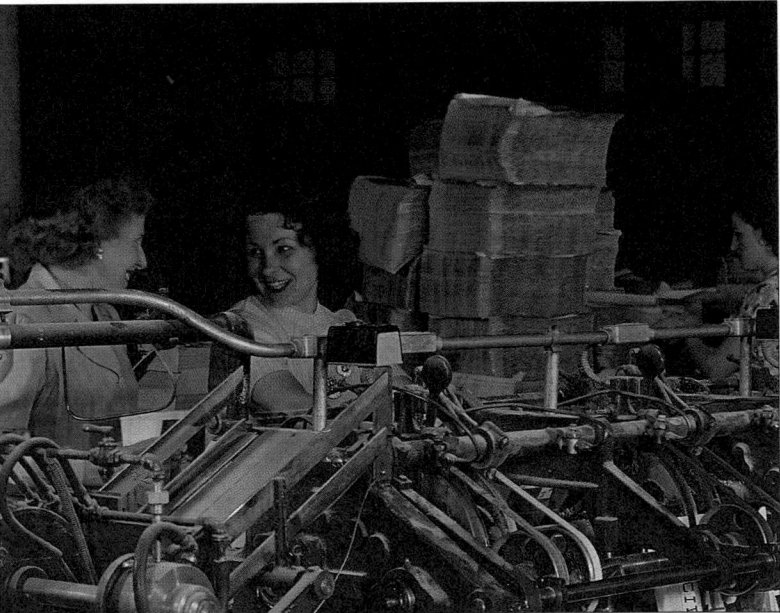

Women at Work Women run folding machines at this plant in Chicago. *How much faster did the rate of female employment increase than that of males in the 1950s?*

Cooperative Learning

Report Have groups of students work together to compare opportunities for workers today and in the 1950s. Students should work together to divide the work fairly and to decide how they want to present their findings. Students will want to consider opportunities for women, minorities, and the poor as well as opportunities for college-educated and middle-class workers. In what ways have opportunities changed? In what ways have they not changed? What fields seem to offer the greatest potential for workers today? What fields are most difficult for women and minorities to enter today? In the 1950s?

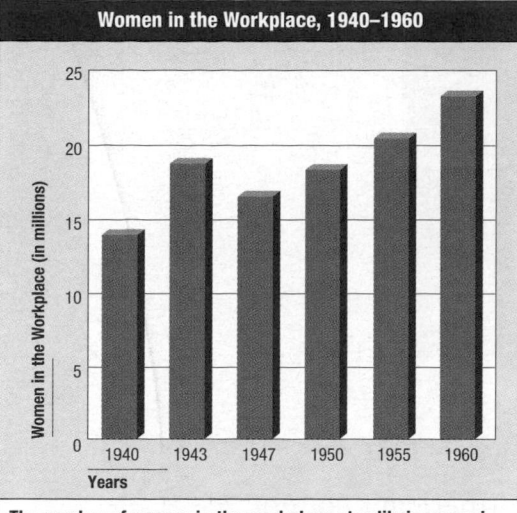

Women in the Workplace, 1940–1960

Women in the Workplace (in millions)

Years: 1940, 1943, 1947, 1950, 1955, 1960

The number of women in the workplace steadily increased from 1940 to 1960. *How many women worked in 1940? In 1960?*

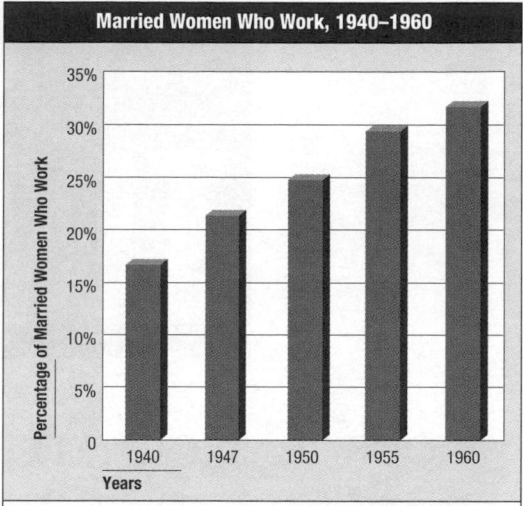

Married Women Who Work, 1940–1960

Percentage of Married Women Who Work

Years: 1940, 1947, 1950, 1955, 1960

The percentage of married women who work also steadily increased. *What percentage of married women worked in 1940? In 1960?*

CHART STUDY

Even today, women often do not earn as much as men. Encourage students to discuss solutions to this inequity.

Answer: *In 1940, about 14 million women worked; in 1960 about 23 million. In 1940 about 17 percent of married women worked; in 1960 about 32 percent.*

When surveyed about why they worked, married women no longer talked about professional advancement or job satisfaction. They claimed their motives for working were to make money for the children's education or the mortgage or a second car or a vacation—in other words, to get a piece of the American dream. In households where the husband earned between $7,000 and $10,000 a year, the rate of women's employment increased from 7 percent in 1950 to 25 percent in 1960. The 1960 United States census indicated that the number of households earning $15,000 or more would be cut in half if women's earnings were excluded. Women thus faced a dilemma. Economic pressures to maintain a comfortable lifestyle forced them into the workplace in record numbers, but social pressures led them to believe their proper place was at home taking care of their children and husbands.

Most women's jobs, however, were low-paying and were either temporary, part-time, or held no opportunity for advancement. In areas such as insurance and banking, for example, women made up 50 percent or more of the workforce, but they held 20 percent or less of higher-level managerial positions. Many women in these industries worked as bank tellers or secretaries. High-level positions were reserved for men.

Stereotyped images of women's roles erected barriers to women's equal treatment. After World War II, the salary gap between full-time male and full-time female wage earners widened. In 1955 women earned 64 percent of average male wages; in 1963 they earned only 60 percent as much as men. A 1959 study concluded that women could not expect a professional career. Men simply would not take women's professional aspirations seriously.

Women were not alone in their plight. Despite the prosperity of postwar society, many Americans—victims of racial prejudice and discrimination, neglect, and cultural differences—were denied full participation in the American dream.

Evaluate

Have students complete the Section Review.

☛ 🖥 Assign the Section 2 Quiz or use the Testmaker to develop a customized quiz. (Also in Spanish.) **LEP**

Reteach

🎧 Have students listen to the Chapter 18, Section 2 Audiocassette. (Also in Spanish.) **LEP**

Enrich

☛ Have students complete the Chapter 18 Geography in History Activity.

☛ Have students complete Supreme Court Case Studies 17, 18.

CLOSE

Ask: What happened after World War II to make a home in the suburbs affordable for many Americans? *(the GI Bill)* How did TV promote and maintain postwar consumerism? *(TV promoted consumer goods.)* Who did not share in the lifestyle of postwar suburbia, and why? *(Minority groups were excluded from the suburbs because of prejudice.)*

SECTION REVIEW

Vocabulary

1. Define: suburbia, baby boom.

Checking Facts

2. How and why did baby-boom kids enjoy privileges not available to their parents?

3. Why was there a resurgence of religion during the postwar years?

Critical Thinking

Recognizing Bias

4. In 1955 women earned only 64 percent of the average wages men earned. What values does this statistic reflect?

Linking Across Time

5. Compare children's television programs today with those of the 1950s. How are they similar? Different? What can you conclude about the values of both periods?

SECTION TWO   **615**

Section 2 Review Answers

1. suburbia (607), **baby boom** (609)

2. Thanks to postwar prosperity, parents who had grown up during the Depression and had experienced wartime shortages could now give their children things they never had, such as music lessons, scouting, and sports programs.

3. Among other reasons, people wanted social and emotional ties after the war.

4. Men discouraged the professional aspirations of women; women's work is worth less

5. Similarities include marketing products associated with particular programs and stars. One difference is that today's programs are more sophisticated. Values include educational enrichment for children and consumerism.

CULTURE
OF
THE
TIME

TEACH

Making the Historical Connection

Discuss with students the idea that rock music may have developed rapidly because of the prosperity of the times. Teens had more money to purchase records and more time to listen to music on the radio because they did not have to work—unlike their counterparts of 10 years earlier. Teens became a distinctive subculture, with their own music, clothes, and attitudes. Advertisers soon learned to sell to this large group of consumers.

Curriculum Connection

Music Explain that rock and roll music developed from the blues and country rhythms and lyrics that came from Southern African American musicians. Chuck Berry, an African American singer from St. Louis, is usually credited with being the first rock and roll songwriter and singer. His lyrics appealed to teenagers because they expressed the feelings and problems of young people. Some white gospel singers, such as Pat Boone and Elvis Presley, liked the new sound and started recording the songs of African American songwriters and singers. Rock and roll immediately became immensely popular with white teenagers, who up to that point had not heard this kind of music.

Rock 'n' Roll Arrives

After the upheaval of World War II, Americans sought security in an uncertain world. Many women left wartime jobs to become full-time housewives. Veterans returned to a pumped-up economy full of opportunity. Parents who had experienced the Depression lavished their newly acquired affluence on their children.

MOVIE STILL ARCHIVES

UNIVERSAL APPEAL

Little Richard (Richard Wayne Penniman) started his career as a gospel singer. In the mid-1950s, however, his single "Tutti Frutti" became a hit. Pat Boone's rendition of the song made it popular among white teenagers and introduced them to the rock music already popular among African Americans. Until the record company Motown began releasing the records of African American artists, most of these musicians were relatively unknown to white audiences.

© SID AVERY, 1956/MOTION PICTURE & TELEVISION PHOTO ARCHIVE

POPULAR ICON

With the popularity of the Mouseketeers on the *Mickey Mouse Club* television show and the opening of Disneyland in Southern California, Walt Disney became one of the most well-known and beloved figures in the United States.

FILE PHOTO BY RALPH BRUNKE

616 CULTURE OF THE TIME

Background Information

Rock 'n' Roll and the Radio Radio played an important role in the spread of rock music. Soap operas and dramas, once so popular on radio, had moved to television. To capture a new audience, radio stations began to play rock and roll music. Disc jockeys became powerful forces in promoting the popularity of rock performers. Dick Clark acted as a disc jockey, albeit on television, on *American Bandstand* and helped to further the careers of many rock stars.

ROCK 'N' ROLL IS HERE TO STAY

On *American Bandstand*, hosted by the youthful-looking Dick Clark, teen fans danced in front of the TV camera to the live music of hit singers. From its studio in Philadelphia, *Bandstand* helped spread the urban rock scene throughout the country and tapped into a growing market for records.

ARCHIVE PHOTOS

DANGER
BE CAREFUL
WHEN BELT
IS IN MOTION.

PAUL SCHUTZER/LIFE MAGAZINE. © TIME, INC.

PHOTOPLAY ARCHIVES/LGI

LOVABLE LUCY

I Love Lucy was television's first smash-hit situation comedy. Lucy (Lucille Ball) was always concocting harebrained schemes and getting into funny scrapes as a result. Everything got back to "normal" when Lucy obeyed her husband and went home. The show mirrored and reinforced the prevailing attitudes about male and female roles.

"THE KING"

In 1956 **Elvis Presley** skyrocketed to rock 'n' roll stardom—despite the objections of parents all over the country, who deplored his suggestive onstage antics. Nicknamed "Elvis the Pelvis," the country singer from Tennessee was the most popular rock star in history.

C   O   O   L

DANCE WITH ME, BABY

Dancing became extremely popular among teenagers in the 1950s. Teenagers continued to dance the jitterbug that their parents had originated, in addition to their own creations—**line dances, the twist, the bop, the Watusi, the stroll, the slide, the pony, and the monkey.**

© SID AVERY, 1956/MOTION PICTURE & TELEVISION PHOTO ARCHIVE

History and the Humanities

🎧 American Music: Cultural Traditions—"It's Mighty Dark to Travel" by Bill Monroe & the Blue Grass Boys; "Rocket 88" by Jackie Brenston & His Delta Kings; "Rock Around the Clock" by Bill Haley & his Comets

At the Movies

Suggest that groups of students pick a movie video that depicts the 1950s (for example, *Back to the Future, American Graffiti, Grease*) or a rerun of a television program that depicts, or was popular during the time (for example, M*A*S*H, *I Love Lucy, Happy Days, Laverne and Shirley, Dobie Gillis*). Ask them to view the show and make a list of the styles, slang expressions, attitudes, and behaviors that are different from those of today. Have groups share their lists.

CLOSE

Ask students to draw on their own knowledge either to explain what has happened to rock music since the 1950s or to discuss what current rock music is like. (*Students could discuss the British invasion—Beatles, Rolling Stones; folk protest singers during the 1960s [folk rock]; progressive rock; soul music; country rock; jazz rock; heavy metal; disco; punk rock; rap music; alternative rock.*)

PORTFOLIO PROJECT

Portfolio project

Make a Rock 'n' Roll Album Ask each student to pick a different rock and roll star to research. (Suggest that they ask a parent or another adult who his or her favorite rock singer was and why.) Tell students to find out how the singer got into the rock and roll business, what his or her most popular songs were, and what contributions the singer made to the 1950s musical scene. Have students write the results of their research and include it in their portfolios. A compilation of all the reports can be made into a class book entitled "1950s Rock Stars."

SECTION

3

FOCUS

Section Objectives

1. Explain why the poor were "invisible" during the 1950s.
2. Explain how various groups of people, young and old, rural and urban, became caught in the cycle of poverty.
3. Describe the unique hardships that the poor of various minority groups experienced amid a generally affluent society.

Bellringer Activity

While taking attendance at the beginning of the class period, display **Section Focus Transparency 58,** and have students answer the questions. (Or use the blackline master.)

VISUAL INSTRUCTION

El Barrio In the 1950s, as today, some people who worked long hours were paid so little that it was almost impossible to lift their families out of poverty.

Ask: Why were the urban poor of the 1950s "invisible"? *(Many prosperous Americans lived in the suburbs and did not see the poverty in other places. Others ignored it. Also, the poor were not well represented in government.)*

Poverty and Plenty

1955: FAMILIES STRUGGLE IN EL BARRIO

El Barrio
Families like the Lopezes worked hard but struggled to make ends meet. The urban poor, who flooded cities after World War II, had little or no political representation.

PEDRO AND MARIA LOPEZ AND THEIR FIVE CHILDREN LIVED IN AN UNFURNISHED APARTMENT IN EAST HARLEM. El Barrio, as this section of New York City was called, had become one of the most densely populated places in the world, with nearly 300,000 people per square mile.

The Lopez family paid $40 a week in rent for their fourth-floor walk-up, which consisted of a living room, a bathroom, a kitchen, and one bedroom. Despite Maria's scrupulous housekeeping, the apartment was infested with rats and roaches.

Six days a week, Pedro got up at 4:30 A.M. to commute to his job as a die cutter, for which he earned $75 weekly. Maria earned another $60 weekly by working part-time and weekends in a supermarket, which was a 45-minute trip from home.

When Pedro had to miss work because of a stomach ulcer, Maria applied for temporary aid from the Department of Social Services. The application was denied because her son Anthony had been suspended from school for truancy.

Because of additional medical expenses, Pedro and Maria came up $5 short that month when the rent was due. Their landlord promptly issued an eviction notice. In desperation, Pedro ignored his doctor's orders and returned to his job and even took a second job evenings and Sundays. Ten-year-old Manuel dropped out of school and found a job to help pay his family's bills.

Like many American families in the 1950s, the Lopezes were dedicated to the values of thrift, hard work, and a good education. The American dream, however, seemed always beyond

---

AS YOU READ

Vocabulary
► culture of poverty
► termination policy

Think About . . .
► why the poor felt as if they were invisible during the 1950s.
► how groups of people, young and old, rural and urban, were caught in the cycle of poverty.

► the hardships that the poor of all groups experienced in a generally affluent society.

---

618 CHAPTER 18 THE POSTWAR ERA

Section 3 Resources

REPRODUCIBLE RESOURCES

📂 Lesson Plan 18-3
📂 Vocabulary and Guided Reading Activity 18-3
📂 Section 3 Quiz
📂 Chapter 18 Test
📂 Reteaching Activity 18
📂 Enrichment Activity 18
📂 Supreme Court Case Study 20
📂 Skill Reinforcement Activity 18

MULTIMEDIA RESOURCES

🔊 Section Focus Transparency 58
🔊 United States History Fine Art Transparency 17
💿 Student Self-Test: A Software Review
💿 Vocabulary PuzzleMaker
💿 Testmaker
🎧 Chapter 18 Digest Audiocassette

their grasp. Pedro, Maria, and their children belonged to a class of Americans whose dreams rarely came true and whose problems went largely unnoticed by the rest of society. The Lopezes were unfortunate members of the nation's **culture of poverty,** the poor—largely invisible—members of a generally affluent American society.

The Invisible Poor
The Causes of Poverty

Picture postcards of New York City in the 1950s reflected the glory of the postwar United States. Skyscrapers soared heavenward; the waters swarmed with commercial traffic; sleek passenger jets cruised a cloudless sky; and in the harbor, Madame Liberty beckoned with promises of freedom, equality, and opportunity.

Hidden Poverty

Hidden behind the tall buildings, away from the bustling harbor, was a very different United States. It was a nation of crumbling streets and tenements, of hungry and sometimes homeless people; a nation not of freedom and equality but of prejudice and discrimination; a nation not of plenty but of desperate need.

The "invisible poor" were so well hidden that many Americans believed that poverty in the United States had been nearly eliminated. In 1956 historian Arthur Schlesinger stated that "the central problems of our times are no longer problems of want and privation." Four years later *Fortune* magazine declared that there were fewer than 1 million poor people left in the United States and predicted that by 1970 there would be none at all.

Reasons for Invisibility

Social and political factors combined to make the poor invisible. Prosperous Americans, for example, simply closed their eyes to the poverty around them because the postwar popular culture glorified the "good life."

As the middle class moved to the suburbs after World War II, they left the poor behind. The inner cities became isolated islands of poverty—out of sight and out of mind. The population of midtown Manhattan dropped from 1.5 million during the day to 2,000 at night. Writer John Brooks noted that midtown Manhattan was "tidally swamped with bustling humanity every weekday morning . . . and abandoned again at nightfall when the wave sucked back." Working in midtown Manhattan, the suburbanites rarely saw the hundreds of thousands of poor families who lived in the Bronx, Brooklyn, and Queens.

Michael Harrington When Harrington published *The Other America,* many denied that poverty was a problem in the United States. *What was Harrington's definition of poverty?*

The lack of any effective political voice also kept the poor invisible. In the past the urban poor had included large numbers of European immigrants who were aided by big-city political bosses, most of whom had European backgrounds themselves. With such aid the immigrants and their children often struggled out of poverty and fled the noisy, dirty cities for the calm and quiet of the suburbs. Progressive urban reforms of the 1900s and the increase in federal programs in the 1930s, however, helped undermine the political-boss system's monopoly on social services. The urban poor of the 1950s, who flooded the cities during and after World War II, included displaced white people from Appalachia, African Americans, Hispanic Americans, and Native Americans.

In 1962 author Michael Harrington shocked prosperous Americans by revealing the extent of poverty in their midst. In his book, *The Other America,* Harrington wrote that 50 million Americans lived in poverty. He explained that poverty was defined not only by a lack of money but also by the absence of hope:

> The poor live in a culture of poverty . . . [and] for reasons beyond their control, cannot help themselves. . . . The poor get sick more than anyone else in the society. . . . When they become sick, they are sick longer than any other group in the society. Because they are sick more often and longer than anyone else, they lose wages and work, and find it difficult to hold a steady job. And because of this, they cannot pay for good housing, for a nutritious diet, for doctors . . . [and] their prospect is to move to an even lower level . . . toward even more suffering.
> —Michael Harrington, *The Other America,* 1962

SECTION THREE   **619**

VISUAL INSTRUCTION

Michael Harrington While researching *The Other America,* Harrington lived with the people he studied. He noticed that poverty passes from one generation to the next in an unbroken cycle. He concluded that poverty had become a part of the culture of the people he cared about.

Answer: *Harrington defined poverty as not only a lack of money but also a lack of hope for the future.*

TEACH

Guided Practice

L2 Discussion Refer to Harrington's definition of poverty as both a lack of money and a lack of hope. Have students discuss how a democracy is affected when its citizens lack hope.

Independent Practice

L2 Writing Have students write about reasons for poverty in the 1950s. Ask them to include these categories: movement of people, political change, and social attitudes.

📁 Have students complete the Chapter 18, Section 3 Vocabulary and Guided Reading Activity. (Also in Spanish.) **LEP**

Cooperative Learning

Dramatization Have groups of three or four discuss what life was like for those who lived in poverty during the 1950s. Then have each group role-play testifying before a congressional committee on poverty. Each member of the group should represent one of the social groups discussed in the section. Ask students to help one another define their roles. 🗣

Curriculum Connection

Economics Have students research how the United States government defines poverty and how it calculates the number of poor people in the nation. Student findings should include information about poverty level or the poverty line.

History and the Humanities

Focus on United States History Fine Art Transparency 17—*Children at Play* by Jacob Lawrence.

The Culture of Poverty
The Downside of Government Programs

Harrington and others pointed out that the poverty of the 1950s was a "new" poverty. The poverty of the Depression era was a general condition that affected large parts of society. Nationally organized, large-scale social welfare programs and labor organizations had responded with work programs and relief payments. When the economy began to recover, so too did the people. In contrast, the poor in the postwar era had no such massive social welfare programs to enable them to break out of poverty.

Additional studies supported Harrington's findings. One study concluded that 40 percent of the American people were ill-housed, ill-clothed, and ill-fed. Another study found that 34.5 million Americans lived on less than $2.10 a day. Americans could no longer deny that poverty was a major social problem.

The reasons for poverty in the United States were varied. Some of the poor, particularly African Americans

The Elderly Harrington estimated that there were more than 8 million elderly poor in the United States. *What contributed to the poverty of elderly people?*

and Hispanic Americans, faced long-standing racial and ethnic prejudice and discrimination. The poor also included jobless Appalachian whites, who moved to the cities because of the lack of opportunity in the hills, and Native Americans, who lived both in the cities and on reservations. Finally, there were the growing numbers of elderly Americans who were not covered by Social Security and had never received pensions from their employers. Whatever the reasons for the existence of poverty, the problem was not limited by age, race, or ethnic heritage.

The Young and the Old

Almost half of the poor were children under the age of 18. By the early 1960s, many of the nation's poor children were the third generation in their families to have been raised on welfare. A depressing cycle of poverty was born—generation after generation totally dependent on government aid for their sustenance, knowing no other way of life.

While many children were born into poverty, many elderly Americans simply grew into it. Approximately 8 million Americans over the age of 65 had incomes of less than $1,000 a year. The following testimony details the problems afflicting the elderly during the 1950s and 1960s:

> Louise W_____, age 73, lives by herself in a single furnished room on the third floor of a rooming house located in a substandard section of the city. In this one room, she cooks, eats, and sleeps. . . . Widowed at 64, she has few friends remaining from her younger years. Those who do remain do not live near her, and it is difficult for her to see them. . . . And so she stays confined to her one room and the bathroom shared by nine other people. When the weather is warm enough, she ventures down the long flight of stairs about once a week for a walk to the corner and back.
> —Testimony at the 1960 Senate hearing on the aged

The plight of the nation's elderly citizens was, ironically, partly the result of scientific and technological progress. Modern medicine prolonged their lives, while modern technology often left them unemployed. Mechanization wiped out the farm chores and factory jobs formerly available to older workers. Thus, many elderly Americans spent their final years without work and without dignity.

Rural and Urban Poverty

At least a third of the poor worked on farms or lived in depressed rural areas. Changes in modern farming created deep pockets of rural poverty. As corporate farms and large-farm owners came to dominate production, many small independent farmers found it difficult to

---

Meeting Special Needs

Reading Disability LEP To address the needs of students with reading disabilities, show the movie *The Blackboard Jungle* or *West Side Story*. Have students identify social problems that existed in the 1950s. To what extent do these movies romanticize the problems?

Visual Learners To address the needs of visual learners, call attention to the diagraphic on page 621. Have students make their own graphic displays that show information about poverty in the 1950s, such as regions where poverty was great, what kind of jobs people held, and so on. Students should draw conclusions from the information they present.

HARD TIMES IN APPALACHIA

Mining companies in Appalachia determined and controlled every aspect of a miner's life. Companies provided "cradle to grave" benefits: housing, utilities, meals, transportation, hospital care, and even funerals. As shown in the deductions column on the pay slip below, miners paid exorbitantly high fees for "mandatory benefits." Consequently, a work-related dispute meant a miner lost not only his job, but housing and food for his family as well.

Coal Miner's Pay Slip (2-week period)

DEDUCTIONS

Powder ($5.67): Miners usually owned the equipment to mine coal, but purchased blasting powder from the mining company.

Scrip ($44.00): A mining-company purchasing system that had worth only within a particular company camp.

Rent ($4.50): Fee charged to workers for company-built housing.

Burial Fund ($1.00): A deduction to provide proper burials for those killed in mining accidents.

Doctor (.80): Miners were required to pay for a camp physician selected by the mining company.

Due Company: It was possible for a miner to work all month, yet *owe* the mining company money because his deductions exceeded his wages.

TOTAL DEDUCTIONS: ($69.45)

CREDITS

Overtime ($8.94): Miners worked 6 days a week, 10 hours a day, but many exhausted themselves by working several shifts in a row to earn more.

Shift Differential ($2.60): The difference, usually an increase, in wage rates for different shifts or types of work performed.

Pinch: A charge for coal deducted from a miner's haul because pieces were too small or were of poor quality.

Total Amount Due Miner ($35.84): After deductions, the miner might receive a small salary.

Bottom Line
Total Earnings: $105.29
Total Deductions: $ 69.45

TOTAL DUE MINER: $ 35.84

KINGSTON-POCAHONTAS COAL (Inc.)

Few workers were able to save enough money to enable them to leave a mining company; so it was not unusual to see three generations of a single family working the same mine, side by side. It was difficult, if not impossible, to rise above the cycle of debt created in a mining camp. *What put 70 percent of Appalachia's coal miners out of work by 1960?*

CHART STUDY

In rural areas, changing farming methods displaced impoverished small farmers. In Appalachia, modernization of coal mines and a drop in demand left thousands without jobs. In both farming and mining, economic or technological changes displaced groups from their traditional roles. This was often the first step in the cycle of poverty.

Answer: *a drop in demand for coal and increased use of machinery*

Notes

---

compete and slipped into poverty. Across the Southern United States, thousands of small-farm families lacked adequate diets in the midst of the world's most productive agricultural system.

Residents of Appalachia, a region covering 80,000 square miles (207,200 sq. km) and parts of 9 states, suffered severely. In 1960 about three-fourths of Appalachia's 8 million people had a median family income of about $2,000 a year. A drop in the demand for coal coupled with the increased use of machinery put almost 70 percent of the region's coal miners out of work.

Rural poverty drove thousands of people to the cities, straining already inadequate housing, school systems, and transportation facilities. Governmental efforts to provide low-cost housing often did more harm than good. Slum clearance merely shoved the poor from one part of the city to another. The projects—low-rent public housing complexes—imposed harsh restrictions on tenants. Large families with low incomes had priority. A family could be evicted if the marriage broke up or the family income exceeded the limits set by the housing authority. Housing projects often actually contributed to the cycle of poverty.

The African American Experience
Overcoming Racial Roadblocks

The poverty of African Americans had a unique quality that other groups did not share. African Americans, unlike many of the other poor, had to contend with deep-seated racial prejudice. While Southern African American farmers suffered the same poverty as their

SECTION THREE **621**

Portfolio Project

Interview Have each student interview someone who lived during the 1950s. Students can tape their interviews or take notes. Does the person remember attention being paid to issues of poverty? What are the person's memories of life then? Have students summarize their interviews in writing and add them to their portfolios.

Harlem in the 1950s Harlem was the home of a great African American literary circle in the 1920s. After the Depression, however, overcrowding, the deterioration of old buildings, and high unemployment had their effect on the area. *How did James Baldwin describe the problems facing the people of Harlem?*

with which, in my childhood, we awaited winter: it is coming and it will be hard; there is nothing anyone can do about it.
—James Baldwin,
Notes of a Native Son, 1955

In New York City in 1955, 50 percent of African American families had incomes under $4,000 a year (compared with 20 percent of the white families), and 40 percent of all New York's welfare recipients were African American. Unemployment among African American workers was double that of white workers, and average wages were about half of what white workers earned.

Racial prejudice formed a barrier to economic as well as social advancement. Many African American workers, because of their color, were denied access to all but the lowest-paying jobs. Many African American students lacked opportunities in a segregated school system. African American doctors and lawyers often found it difficult to practice anywhere but in African American neighborhoods where they would never earn as much as their white colleagues.

white counterparts, the rural South harbored that force of racial terrorism, the Ku Klux Klan. The Klan used physical violence, including many instances of torture and lynchings, to intimidate African Americans and keep them "in their place."

African Americans carried this fear of white terrorism with them when they migrated to Northern cities. By the mid-1950s, nearly half of the African American population lived in cities. Atlanta, Los Angeles, Detroit, Chicago, New York—each had its ghetto. James Baldwin, African American novelist, essayist, and activist, described Harlem in the postwar period:

H arlem, physically at least, has changed very little in my parents' lifetime or in mine. Now as then the buildings are old and in desperate need of repair, the streets are crowded and dirty, there are too many human beings per square block. Rents are 10 to 58 percent higher than anywhere else in the city; food, expensive everywhere, is more expensive here and of an inferior quality; and now that the war is over and money is dwindling, clothes are carefully shopped for and seldom bought. Negroes, traditionally the last to be hired and the first to be fired, are finding jobs harder to get, and, while prices are rising implacably, wages are going down. All over Harlem now there is felt the same bitter expectancy

Hispanic Hardships
The Search for Migrant Farmwork

Spanish-speaking Americans made up the nation's second largest minority group. Puerto Ricans, like Pedro and Maria Lopez, who were described earlier, flocked to the United States in the 1950s, drawn by stories of abundance and a desire to escape the poverty of their island homeland. During the decade, the Puerto Rican population of the United States grew from 300,000 to nearly 1 million. Many of these immigrants crowded into the slum neighborhoods of New York City.

Puerto Rican immigrants faced other difficulties in addition to their poverty. The language barrier slowed their assimilation into United States society. Native culture and strong family traditions were slowly lost as young Puerto Ricans adopted American ways. Women found jobs more easily than men did, which strained the traditional husband–wife relationship.

Mexican Americans suffered from the same discriminations that Puerto Ricans faced, with an added burden—they rarely felt politically secure. Because Puerto Rico is a commonwealth of the United States, Puerto Ricans are United States citizens, free to travel, work,

Extending the Content

Unemployment During the 1930s the unemployment rate reached 25 percent. In 1944, the unemployment rate was 1.2 percent. In the 1950s and 1960s unemployment was more than 6 percent. Some economists believe that unemployment rates below 3 to 4 percent should no longer be expected now that more women and young people (2 groups with higher rates of unemployment than the rest of the population) have entered the labor force.

and live within the country. Mexico, however, is a sovereign foreign state, and Mexican immigrants are legally defined as aliens. Officers of the Immigration and Naturalization Service were charged with tracking down immigrants who were in this country illegally. In the process, they could stop any Mexican American on the street and demand proof of citizenship.

Agricultural Workers

Many Mexican American families had been citizens of the United States for generations. Many lived in urban centers, especially in California, Texas, and the Midwest. They were less noticed than the migrant farmworkers, however. While Mexican Americans made up the largest group of migrant farmworkers, African Americans, Puerto Ricans, and poor whites lived and worked under the same oppressive conditions. Migrant workers followed the crops from state to state for 7 or 8 months a year, from harvesting spring vegetables in Texas to picking fall apples in Washington. They slept in shacks or in labor camps and worked 10 or 12 hours a day in the

Living Conditions A 1960 television documentary titled *Harvest of Shame* revealed the shocking living conditions of the nation's 2 million migrant workers. *What was the* bracero *program?*

fields. Some migrant workers worked for piece rates; others received an hourly wage of 50 cents. Migrant workers toiled outside the protection of labor laws. Children worked the fields with their parents, often on ladders or using hazardous machinery. Injured farmworkers received no workers' compensation.

Some Mexicans illegally entered the United States to work in the fields. Others entered this country legally, under the *bracero* program—an agreement forged with the Mexican government during World War II to permit seasonal immigration of farmworkers. State employment officials recruited Mexican braceros, or temporary workers, to harvest crops. Braceros were expected to return to Mexico after the harvest, but many stayed on illegally.

In 1953 the government launched a deportation program that became known as Operation Wetback. Illegal Mexican aliens were called wetbacks—a derogatory term—because thousands of them entered the United States by swimming across the Rio Grande. In 3 years, Operation Wetback deported more than 3 million people.

Field Work Agriculture depended heavily on migrant workers to do the stoop labor associated with harvesting crops such as tomatoes and beans. *What is the work and travel cycle of a typical migrant family?*

SECTION THREE   **623**

Cultural Perspectives

Migrant Life Have students conduct research to find out what life as a migrant laborer is like today. Students may want to focus on workers in a specific region of the country, such as the Southwest or Southeast. Students may want to write about what daily life is like for a typical family during a growing season, or they may want to focus on one aspect of life, such as education, housing, travel routes, or crops picked. Newspaper or magazine articles about migrant workers may help students find out about the lives of specific people.

Evaluate

Have students complete the Section Review.

📁 ⦿ Assign the Section 3 Quiz or use the Testmaker to develop a customized quiz. (Also in Spanish.) **LEP**

📁 ⦿ Assign the Chapter 18 Test or use the Testmaker to develop a customized test.

📁 Have students complete the Chapter 18 Performance Assessment Activity.

Reteach

🎧 Have students listen to the Chapter 18, Section 3 Audiocassette. (Also in Spanish.) **LEP**

📁 Have students complete the Chapter 18 Reteaching Activity. (Also in Spanish.) **LEP**

Enrich

📁 Have students complete the Chapter 18 Enrichment Activity. (Also in Spanish.) **LEP**

📁 Have students complete Supreme Court Case Study 20.

CLOSE

Ask: What caused poverty in postwar America? *(prejudice, changes in industry, growing numbers of elderly, lack of aid)*

624

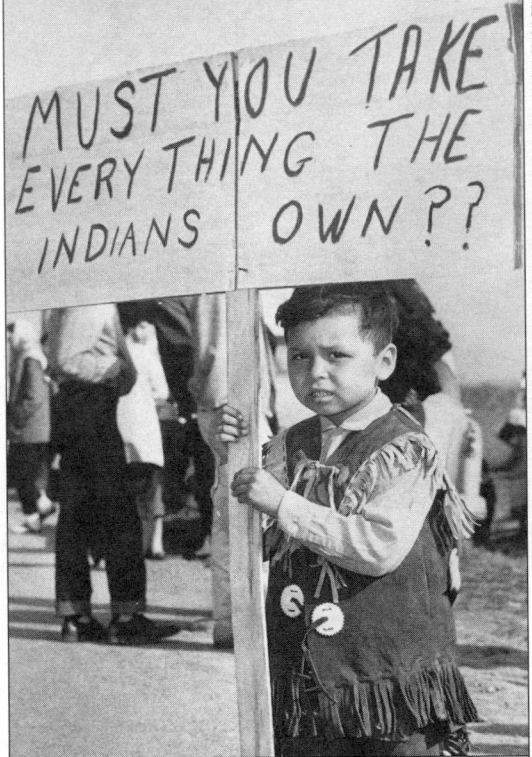

Relocation Under the Voluntary Relocation Program, more than 60,000 Native Americans moved to cities. Nearly one-third, however, decided to return to be with their people.
Why did the United States government encourage Native Americans to leave their reservations?

Displaced Native Americans
The Government's Termination Policy

One of America's smallest minorities—Native Americans—continued to be its poorest, most ignored group. By 1960 almost two-thirds of the nation's 600,000 Native Americans lived on reservations. Unemployment rates were staggering—more than 70 percent among the Blackfeet of Montana and the Hopi of Arizona; 86 percent among the Choctaw of Mississippi. Many Native Americans migrated to the cities where they encountered much of the same discrimination and poverty that African Americans and Hispanic Americans endured.

In 1953 the federal government adopted a new Native American policy called "termination." The Indian Reorganization Act of 1934 had attempted to restore lands to Native American ownership; however, the purpose of this new policy was to end the reservation

system and terminate all federal services to Native American nations. The result of the **termination policy** was the loss of hundreds of thousands of acres of Native American lands to agricultural, lumber, and mining interests.

As an incentive to leave the reservations, the government helped Native Americans relocate to cities through the Voluntary Relocation Program. Relocation offices provided moving expenses, help in finding housing and jobs, and temporary living expenses. Relocating to the cities, however, proved to be disorienting and culturally wrenching for thousands of Native Americans who left their Native American groups. A Seminole petition to President Eisenhower sounded the cry of all Native American groups who struggled for identity in the 1950s:

> We do not say that we are superior or inferior to the White Man and we do not say that the White Man is superior or inferior to us. We do say that we are not White Men . . . do not wish to become White Men but wish to . . . have an outlook on all things different from the outlook of the White Man.
> —Seminole Petition to President Eisenhower

The termination policy of the 1950s, like nearly every Native American policy before it, ended up victimizing Native Americans. Individual Native American nations and organizations of Native Americans officially protested termination. Lacking political representation, their protests went unanswered, and Native Americans remained the most "invisible" of all minority groups.

SECTION REVIEW

Vocabulary
1. Define: culture of poverty, termination policy.

Checking Facts
2. How was the poverty of the 1950s different from the poverty of the Great Depression?

3. Why did Mexican Americans rarely feel politically secure in the United States?

Critical Thinking
Identifying Assumptions
4. Keeping in mind that during the 1950s the poor were "invisible," what do you think many middle-class Americans of the 1950s assumed about the poor?

Linking Across Time
5. What are the characteristics of poverty today? Is poverty still hidden? Have different groups become impoverished?

Critical Thinking Skill

RECOGNIZING BIAS

Learning the Skill

Father Knows Best was one of the most popular sit-coms in the years 1954–1962. Robert Young played Jim Anderson, the bumbling but wise traditional head of this ideal all-American, middle-class family. Jane Wyatt played his wife, Margaret; the children's names were Betty (nick-named "Princess" by her father), Jim, Jr. ("Bud"), and Kathy ("Kitten"). The show exemplified the prevailing attitudes of what a family should be: white, attractive, with a comfortable lifestyle and minimal problems, up-holding family values and middle-class morals. In each half-hour plot, one family member got into an innocent scrape that was resolved only when the father stepped in and proved once again that he "knew best."

That many Americans thought *Father Knows Best* represented the ideal family shows their bias toward this kind of family. A bias is a personal outlook that inhibits impartial judgment. Everyone has some biases—for example, thinking that cats make better pets than dogs without ever having owned dogs is a bias.

Television programs reflect the biases of a society or certain groups within the society. Through the selections they make, the people who control the content of a program—writers, producers, and advertising spon-sors—reveal their own biases or the biases that they expect will appeal to their audiences.

The way a character is depicted can convey a posi-tive or negative attitude toward particular groups and is-sues. Being aware of this can help prevent you from accepting a biased point of view as the truth. Accepting a biased view as the truth may indicate that you have similar biases.

How to Recognize Bias

When checking for bias, ask yourself the following questions:

a. What clues in costume, setting, and dialogue might make you think that the character's lifestyle is desirable or undesirable?

b. What image is the character projecting, and how closely does it represent real life?

c. Does the character have ideas or attitudes that he or she thinks (by inference, body language, or outright statement) that all people either have or should have?

d. What do your reactions to the character indicate about your own biases?

Recognizing Bias *Father Knows Best* was a popular televi-sion show in the 1950s. *What does this picture show about the "ideal American family"?*

Practicing the Skill

Look at the picture of the Anderson family and answer the following questions:

1. Is the family dressed the way most families you know dress for dinner?

2. What do the children's nicknames suggest?

3. What does the role of the mother seem to be?

4. Who seems to be the central figure in the pic-ture? What message does this give?

5. Does the portrayal of the Anderson family make you angry? Wishful? Amused? Amazed? What does this say about your own biases?

Applying the Skill

Compare the family in a current television pro-gram with the Anderson family. What clues indicate the biases of the show's writers? Does the family seem "typical"? What ideas or ideals does the fam-ily espouse? Are they ones you accept?

Look for examples of bias in other television shows, advertisements, newspaper or magazine articles, or current fiction. Focus on a particular subject, such as women's roles or attitudes about government, in your investigation.

Additional Practice

For additional practice, see Reinforcing Skills on page 627.

This skill feature presents ways of recognizing bias. Students will learn to look for clues in costume, setting, and vocabulary. Then students will apply these methods to photographs and television shows. This feature will teach students the importance of applying these methods in their everyday lives.

VISUAL INSTRUCTION

Recognizing Bias *Father Knows Best* was a 1950s comedy. In 1977, NBC showed a movie, *The Father Knows Best Reunion.* In this movie the family had under-gone changes typical of the 1970s: the parents suffered from empty-nest syndrome, Betty was a widow with children and a career, Bud had a troubled marriage, and Kathy was dating a divorced man. Students may want to consider what biases the 1977 movie had.

Answer: *It presents the ideal family as a happy, well-dressed, middle-class group gathered around the dinner table. Mother brings in the meal; daughter, the plates. Other family members smiling-ly watch and wait for the food.*

Additional Practice

📁 Have students complete the Chapter 18 Skill Reinforcement Activity.

Practicing the Skill Answers

1. No. Families today do not often get dressed up for dinner unless it is a special occasion.

2. The girls have feminine and submissive nick-names (Princess, Kitten) rather than nicknames suggesting leadership or action. "Bud" suggests a pal, perhaps a boy who is active in sports or other male-bonding activities.

3. perhaps that of housekeeper and cook

4. The father is the central figure. This suggests that the family revolves around him, that he is the leader and others obey his requests.

5. How students feel will reflect their biases. If they feel angry, it may mean that they think the images portrayed are not accurate and may even be harmful. If they feel wishful, it may mean they would like real life to be as simple and as pleas-ant as it is portrayed in television of the 1950s.

Reviewing Key Terms

1. baby boom
2. suburbia
3. demobilization
4. conglomerates
5. termination policy

Recalling Facts

1. A Veterans' Village was a university community where ex-GIs could find affordable housing; nearly 8 million
2. The demand for products grew, causing the GNP to triple from 1940 to 1950.
3. It helped feed the growing hunger for material goods.
4. Most new houses were built in the suburbs.
5. Financially stable, middle-class, white Americans seeking a better life lived there.
6. Teenagers developed their own subculture and spent money on clothes, movies, and especially records.
7. that not all women were content as homemakers
8. Because they had no voice, no one addressed their needs.
9. Because the Depression affected a large segment of the population, the government provided relief. In the 1950s, the poor were isolated and not offered as much aid.
10. Migrant farmworkers traveled from place to place 8 months of the year, slept in shacks or labor camps, and worked 10–12 hours a day for substandard wages

Critical Thinking

1. Employees got good salaries, training, and benefits; conformity to company standards—values, dress, and behavior.
2. Suburbs grew; people traveled; shopping, dining, entertainment were accessible.
3. Renovate buildings, more jobs, more crime prevention, less prejudice toward minorities.

626

Reviewing Key Terms

Choose the vocabulary term that best completes the sentences below. Write your answers on a separate sheet of paper.

demobilization   conglomerates
suburbia   baby boom
culture of   termination
   poverty   policy

1. The rapid population growth after World War II is referred to as a _____ .

2. This population increase fueled the growth of _____ , communities on the outskirts of cities.

3. Shifting people and business back to peacetime pursuits was called _____ .

4. The "bigger is better" philosophy of the postwar years led to the formation of huge _____.

5. The _____ resulted in the loss of hundreds of thousands of acres of Native American lands to agricultural, mining, and lumber interests.

Recalling Facts

1. Describe a Veterans' Village. How many veterans took advantage of the educational assistance offered by the GI Bill?

2. What happened to the economy as working-class Americans accumulated discretionary income?

3. How did advertising affect the demand for consumer goods?

4. Where were most new homes built in the 1950s?

5. What kind of people lived in suburbia? Describe their lifestyle.

6. Many teenagers shared in the affluence of the 1950s. As their parents' discretionary income increased, teenagers had more money to spend as well. How did this affluence affect the culture of the 1950s?

7. What was the problem Betty Friedan identified in *The Feminine Mystique*?

8. How did poor people's lack of an effective political voice contribute to the cycle of poverty?

9. How was the poverty of the 1950s different from the poverty of the Depression era?

10. Describe some of the hardships in the lives of most migrant farmworkers.

Critical Thinking

1. **Synthesizing Information** What were some of the advantages and disadvantages inherent in corporate life in the 1950s?

2. **Synthesizing Information** In what ways did the lifestyle of Americans in the 1950s revolve around the automobile?

3. **Drawing Conclusions** The "white flight" that began in the postwar period is still happening. What factors might help reverse this trend? What social and economic conditions would persuade people to move back to the cities?

4. **Determining Cause and Effect** How did the baby boom affect the economy?

5. **Making Comparisons** Compare the position of women during World War II with their position in the postwar era.

6. **Distinguishing Fact From Opinion** List 5 facts and 5 related commonly held opinions people had about women in the 1950s. Discuss the difference between the facts and opinions.

7. **Making Inferences** In 1960 *Fortune* magazine claimed that there were fewer than 1 million poor in the United States and that poverty

They have everything...

Oshkosh B'gosh

BRONKS

smart style... swell fit... super value!

would be completely eliminated by 1970. How could people of the time have been so blind to the problem of poverty?

8. **Making Comparisons** The growth of suburbia in the 1950s affected the quality of life in urban areas. Compare suburban life of the 1950s with city life during that period.

9. **Analyzing Information** Look at the information about Appalachia on page 621. Why did this region suffer so much during the 1950s?

10. **Making Comparisons** Look at the advertisement pictured above. Why would advertisers in the 1950s market directly to teens? Do they do so today? Compare the affluence of teenagers today with that of teenagers of the 1950s.

---

4. Child-oriented activities increased; TV programs developed for children; direct marketing toward children.
5. World War II: women worked for the war effort; after the war, they were told the jobs were needed for the soldiers.
6. Answers will vary but might include that woman's

place is in the home. A sample fact would be that many women were dissatisfied with their roles as homemakers.
7. Students may suggest: the poor were isolated in the cities.
8. Answers will vary. Students might say that in the suburbs people had money for material goods; housing and shop-

ping areas were new. Cities were crowded; housing and income were poor; and more minorities were present.
9. A drop in demand for coal led to the poverty in Appalachia.
10. Many teenagers, like those today, had money of their own.

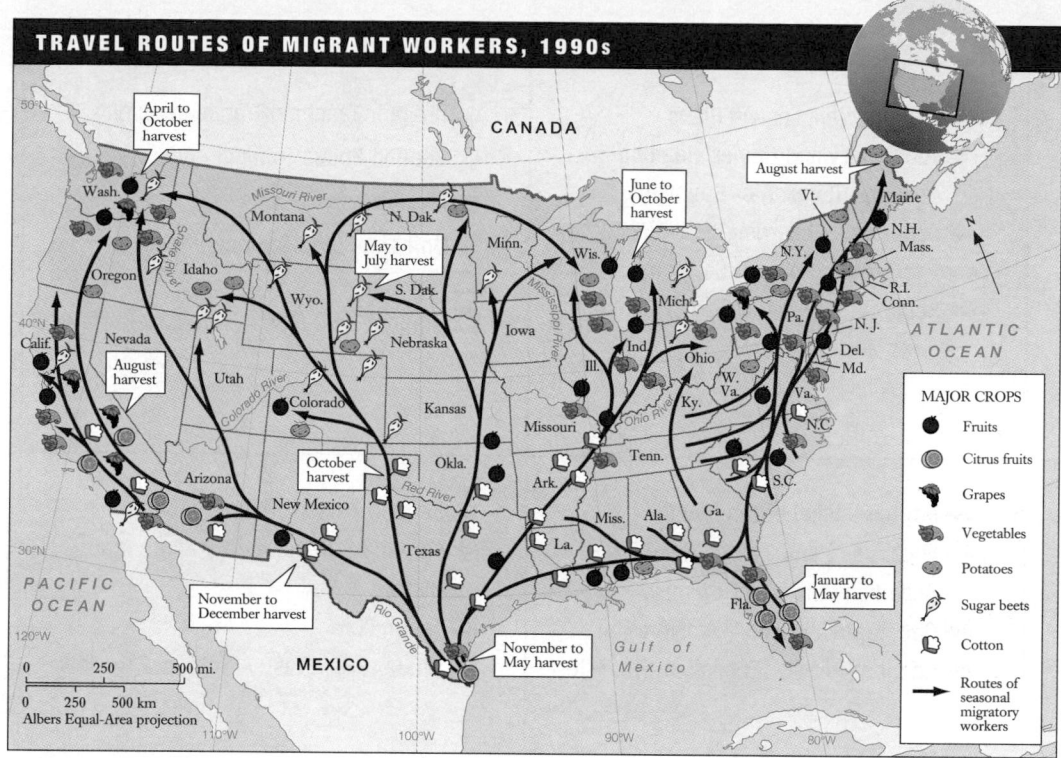

TRAVEL ROUTES OF MIGRANT WORKERS, 1990s

April to October harvest

August harvest

Wash.
Montana
N. Dak.
June to October harvest
Vt.
Maine

Oregon
Idaho
May to July harvest
Minn.
Wis.
N.Y.
N.H.
Mass.

S. Dak.
Wyo.
Iowa
Mich.
R.I.
Conn.

Calif.
Nevada
Nebraska
Ill.
Ind.
Ohio
Pa.
N.J.
ATLANTIC OCEAN

August harvest
Utah
Colorado
Kansas
Missouri
Ky.
W. Va.
Del.
Md.
N

Arizona
October harvest
New Mexico
Okla.
Tenn.
Ark.
Va.
N.C.

PACIFIC OCEAN
Texas
Miss.
Ala.
Ga.
S.C.

November to December harvest
La.
January to May harvest

November to May harvest
MEXICO
Gulf of Mexico
Fla.

CANADA

Missouri River

Snake River

Colorado River

Red River

Mississippi River

Ohio River

Rio Grande

50°N
40°N
30°N
120°W
110°W
100°W
90°W
80°W

0   250   500 mi.
0   250   500 km
Albers Equal-Area projection

MAJOR CROPS

Fruits
Citrus fruits
Grapes
Vegetables
Potatoes
Sugar beets
Cotton

Routes of seasonal migratory workers

Portfolio Project

Talk to a friend or relative who is a baby boomer. What does he or she think are the advantages and disadvantages of being a baby boomer? How is life different for people of your generation? What do you think baby boomers' effect on society will be when they retire? Write a report that focuses on these questions. Place it in your portfolio.

Cooperative Learning

Form groups to research the special hardships placed on one of the following groups: displaced Native Americans, Hispanics (one group can discuss Mexicans and another Puerto Ricans), and Southern African Americans. Share your findings.

Reinforcing Skills

Recognizing Bias Choose a group in society, such as the elderly, teenagers, the visually impaired, or motorcycle riders. Collect information about how the group is portrayed in television programs, commercials, movies, newspaper and magazine articles, and so on. Then decide what bias society has toward the group. Do you think society's bias about the group has any basis in fact? Why or why not?

Geography and History

Study the map on this page to answer the following questions:

1. To which states do migrant workers travel to harvest citrus fruits?

2. Which parts of the country do migrant workers go to in winter?

3. In how many states do migrant workers pick cotton?

4. Which states have August harvests?

5. Which areas of the country have the longest harvests?

HISTORY JOURNAL

Are the poor still invisible today? How do you think conditions have or have not changed for the working poor today? What, if anything, is being done to combat poverty in your community?

Geography and History

1. California, Arizona, Texas, Florida
2. southern regions—Southwest, Florida
3. 15
4. California and Maine (Washington and Michigan have harvest months that include August)
5. Texas and Washington

History Journal

Suggest that students think of such issues as homelessness, problems associated with welfare, and current legislation dealing with poverty before they begin writing.

BONUS QUESTION

This question may be used for extra credit on the Chapter Test.

Explain the plight of the farmer in the 1950s. How did corporate farming contribute to farmers' problems?

Answer: *Many farmers could not keep up with modernization in farming. They were unable to compete with those who managed corporate farms and had the money to modernize. Many independent farmers fell into poverty or moved to the cities.*

Portfolio Project

Encourage students to think carefully about the effect the baby boomers are going to have on their own generation. Suggest that they research issues dealing with Social Security, Medicare and Medicaid, and rising health costs.

Cooperative Learning

Suggest that groups assign a specific topic to each group member. Ask the librarian to put helpful books on reserve, show students where they might look for information on their topics, or provide some books in the classroom.

Reinforcing Skills

Suggest that students use the same groups as in the Cooperative Learning exercise to discuss bias against the group they chose and then share their results with the class. Or students may wish to write up their findings on the group they chose.

627

Cold War Politics

DAILY LESSON OBJECTIVES	REPRODUCIBLE RESOURCES	MULTIMEDIA RESOURCES
SECTION 1 Retreat From the New Deal 1. Identify causes of the conservative backlash that followed World War II. 2. Describe Truman's struggle to implement the Fair Deal.	📂 Reproducible Lesson Plans 📂 Vocabulary and Guided Reading Activities (English or Spanish) 📂 Cooperative Learning Activities 📂 Interpreting Political Cartoons 📂 Section Quizzes (English or Spanish)	🔦 Chapter Teaching Transparencies 🔦 Section Focus Transparencies 🔦 Map Transparencies 🔦 Unit Time Line Transparencies 💿 Testmaker 💿 Student Self-Test: A Software Review
SECTION 2 The Cold War at Home 1. Analyze the causes and effects surrounding the rise of anti-Communist sentiment and the phenomenon of McCarthyism. 2. Describe how blacklisting affected American society.	📂 Reproducible Lesson Plans 📂 Vocabulary and Guided Reading Activities (English or Spanish) 📂 Geography in History Activities 📂 Section Quizzes (English or Spanish)	🔦 Section Focus Transparencies 💿 Landmark Documents in American History 💿 Testmaker 💿 Student Self-Test: A Software Review
SECTION 3 The Eisenhower Years 1. Explain Eisenhower's policy of consensus decision-making. 2. Analyze the growing role of electronic media in politics.	📂 Reproducible Lesson Plans 📂 Vocabulary and Guided Reading Activities (English or Spanish) 📂 Reteaching Activities (English or Spanish) 📂 Enrichment Activities (English or Spanish) 📂 Supreme Court Case Studies 📂 Skill Reinforcement Activities 📂 Section Quizzes (English or Spanish)	🔦 Section Focus Transparencies 📼 Great Speeches 💿 Landmark Documents in American History 💿 Testmaker 💿 Student Self-Test: A Software Review
CHAPTER REVIEW AND EVALUATION	📂 Chapter 19 Test, Forms A and B 📂 Performance Assessment Strategies and Activities	💿 Student Self-Test: A Software Review 💿 Vocabulary PuzzleMaker 💿 Testmaker 🎧 Chapter Digests Audiocassettes

🕐 If time does not permit teaching the entire chapter, summarize using the Chapter 19 Digests Audiocassettes and the accompanying activities and tests. (Available in English or Spanish.)

Cooperative Project

Have students bring to class editorials or letters to the editor about subjects that relate to topics discussed in the chapter: nuclear power, communism, Soviet-American relations, campaign tactics, or the mood of the nation. Organize the class into small groups, and assign each group two or more articles. Have groups mount the articles on poster board, identify the facts and opinions, and explain how they can distinguish one from the other. 🔲

Suggested Rubric: Group Work and the Individual. See Performance Assessment Strategies and Activities, p. 49.

Individual Project

Ask students to choose one of the major figures introduced in this chapter. Have them conduct research to discover additional information about the person and then give a speech to the class about the figure. In addition to library research, some students may want to interview grandparents, older relatives, or neighbors about their memories of the figure during the late 1940s and early 1950s. **LEP** 🔲

Suggested Rubrics: An Oral Presentation, A Research Report. See Performance Assessment Strategies and Activities, pp. 33 and 39.

Key to Ability Levels

Teaching strategies have been coded for varying learning styles and abilities.

L1 **BASIC** activities for all students

L2 **AVERAGE** activities for average to above-average students

L3 **CHALLENGING** activities for above-average students

LEP **LIMITED ENGLISH PROFICIENCY** activities

Block Scheduling

Block scheduling differs from traditional class scheduling in the amount of time allotted to each period. The extended timeframe provided by block scheduling affords you the opportunity to implement a greater number of research-oriented and activity-intense projects to motivate and involve your students. Activities that are particularly suited to use within the block scheduling framework are identified throughout this chapter by the following designation. 🔲

T E A C H E R ' S   C O R N E R

NATIONAL GEOGRAPHIC SOCIETY

NATIONAL GEOGRAPHIC SOCIETY PRODUCTS AVAILABLE FROM GLENCOE

To order the following products for use with this chapter, contact your local Glencoe sales representative or call Glencoe at 1-800-334-7344:

- *The Presidents: A Picture History of Our Nation* (CD-ROM)
- *GTV: A Geographic Perspective on American History* (Videodisc)
- *GTV: The American People: Fabric of a Nation* (Videodisc)

ADDITIONAL NATIONAL GEOGRAPHIC SOCIETY PRODUCTS

To order the following products for use with this chapter, call National Geographic Society at 1-800-368-2728:

- *Decades of History: The 20th Century—The Middle Years* (Filmstrip)
- *The United States as a World Power: From the 1890s to the 1970s* (Filmstrip)
- *1945-1989: The Cold War* (Video)
- *The Rise and Fall of the Soviet Union* (Video)

Chapter Overview

McCarthyism, an extreme form of anticommunism, grew out of the mood of fear that people in the United States felt as communism spread through Eastern Europe and Asia. Not even the United States Army was safe from unfounded charges that gained publicity for the accusers.

Introducing the Chapter

Have students read the vignette on this page. Then review United States–Soviet relations in the late 1940s and 1950s. Remind students of the growing fear of communism, the failure of containment in China, and the fear of the atomic bomb.

Display Chapter Teaching Transparency 19 and distribute copies of the activity sheet. After students have completed the activities, point out that court cases and hearings can capture and personalize the broad controversies within a society during a particular period.

Extension Activity

Have students complete Beyond the Transparency on the activity sheet for Chapter 19 and present their projects after the class has completed the chapter. 📦

History Journal

Have students write about how accusations of disloyalty to the United States might affect what kinds of jobs were available to an individual.

CHAPTER
19

Cold War Politics

JUNE 9, 1954: McCARTHY VERSUS THE ARMY

Joseph Welch was one of many people caught up in the controversy surrounding congressional hearings on Communists. Dozens of people, under questioning, had helplessly watched their careers and their reputations slip away. They left the hearings branded "Communists," "spies," or "subversives."

Welch faced his questioner, Senator Joseph McCarthy, the nation's self-appointed Communist hunter of the early 1950s. He was a dreaded man who was determined to prove that Communists were lurking in every office and department of the United States government.

McCarthy rarely offered any evidence against people he accused, but in the cold war atmosphere of the 1950s, proof did not matter. Fear, rather than reason, ruled.

The McCarthy hearings were an example of the extreme conservatism that dominated the politics of the time. His campaign of intimidation went unchecked for nearly four years. Few people were willing or able to confront McCarthy effectively.

Welch, a Boston attorney, appeared before McCarthy to defend the United States Army against allegations that it was harboring Communists. Under the glare of hot lights and with the nation closely watching on TV, Welch, weary of McCarthy's slander, replied calmly and firmly. His famous rebuttal challenged the senator. "I think I never really gauged your cruelty or your recklessness, . . ." Welch said. "Have you no sense of decency, sir, at long last? Have you left no sense of decency?" ■

HISTORY JOURNAL

Think about what you know about Joseph McCarthy, communism, blacklisting, or the Red Scare.
Write what you think happened to people accused of being Communists in the 1950s.

✚ **EXTRA CREDIT PROJECT**

Research Have students conduct in-depth research about a person or topic covered in this chapter. You may want to suggest such topics as Joseph McCarthy, McCarthyism, blacklisting, the Red Scare, the Rosenbergs, Alger Hiss, or the Hollywood Ten. Students may want to present their findings to the class. Have them file their reports in their portfolios. 📦

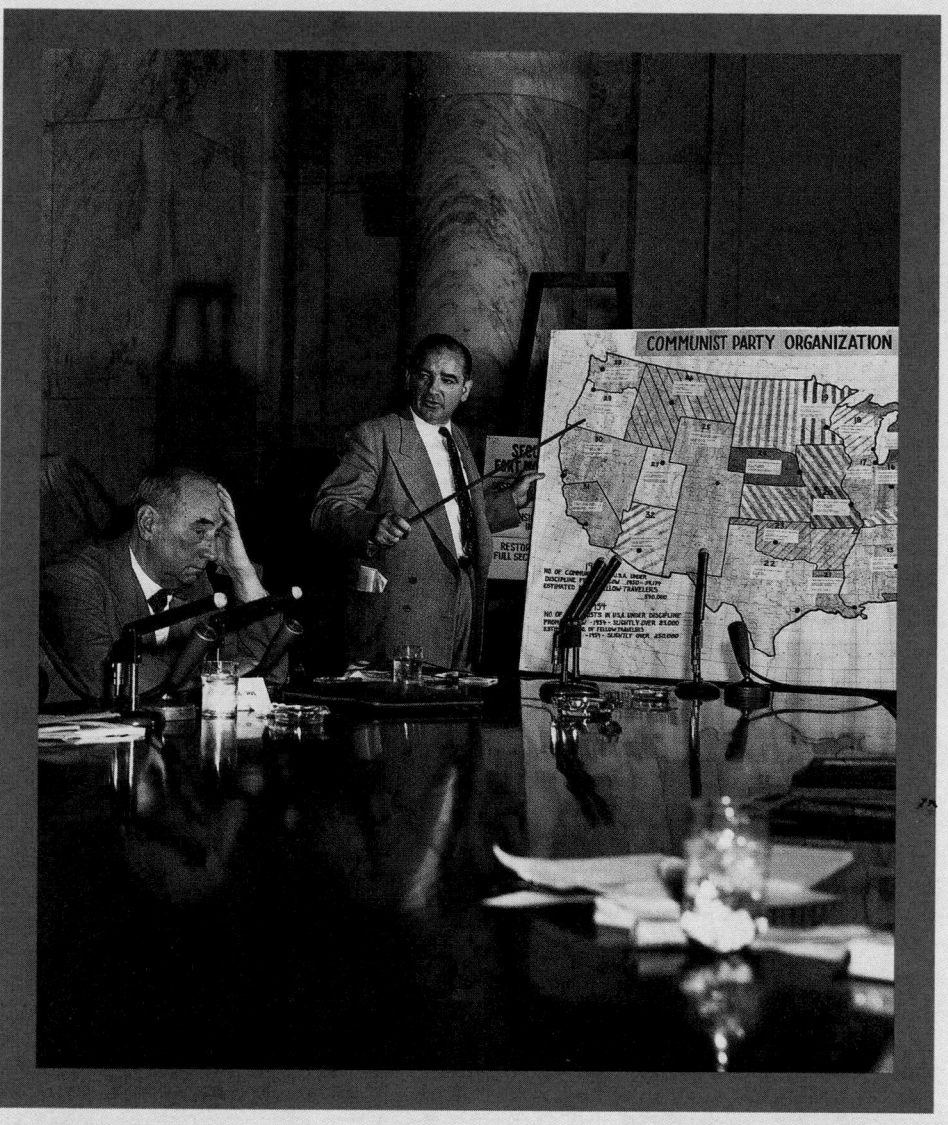

UPI/BETTMANN

SENATOR JOSEPH McCARTHY TESTIFIES ON
COMMUNIST PARTY ORGANIZATION IN THE UNITED
STATES AS A WEARY JOSEPH WELCH LISTENS.

629

ABC NEWS
INTERACTIVE™

Videodisc

*Communism and
the Cold War*

Side 1, Chapter 11
Title: Communists in our
Midst: McCarthyism
Subject: McCarthyism
Ask: Who was Mc-
Carthy? *(a senator who
hunted Communists)*

**See Communism and
the Cold War Guide-
book page 19 for com-
plete lesson plan.**

GLENCOE
TECHNOLOGY

Videodisc

American History

Side 2
Title: The Cold War
Subject: The cold war
Ask: What were Ameri-
cans most fearful of during
this time? *(nuclear war)*

Examining the Visual

McCarthy Testifies The angriest clash of the 30-day Army-McCarthy hearings came June 9, 1954, when McCarthy accused Welch of trying to "foist on the committee" a lawyer with former Communist affiliations. He stated that Welch's attorney had been a member of the National Lawyer's Guild after it had been declared subversive by the House Un-American Activities Committee. Joseph Welch in return denounced McCarthy as a "cruelly reckless character assassin." He went on to declare: "If there is a God in heaven, it will do neither you nor your cause any good." Welch's expression indicates his dejection over the harsh exchange between the two that had just taken place.

**Performance
Assessment**

Refer to page 628B for performance assessment activities for this chapter.

☞ Also see Activity 19 in the Performance Assessment Strategies and Activities for an additional activity as well as for suggested rubrics. ☞

FOCUS

Section Objectives

1. Identify causes of the conservative backlash that followed World War II.
2. Describe Truman's struggle to implement the Fair Deal.

Bellringer Activity

While taking attendance at the beginning of the class period, display **Section Focus Transparency 59,** and have students answer the questions. (Or use the blackline master.)

VISUAL INSTRUCTION

A Changing Country After the war ex-GI Joe Heinrich and his wife were unable to find housing in San Francisco. So Heinrich hitchhiked 100 miles every day to and from college in San Francisco. He left daily at 6:15 A.M. and returned at 6:30 P.M.

Ask: How do you think this great influx of veterans looking for work affected the job market? *(Returning veterans all looked for jobs and housing at the same time. There was, at first, a great deal of turmoil in both the job and housing markets.)*

SECTION 1

Retreat From the New Deal

1946: VETERANS RETURN TO A CHANGING COUNTRY AFTER WORLD WAR II

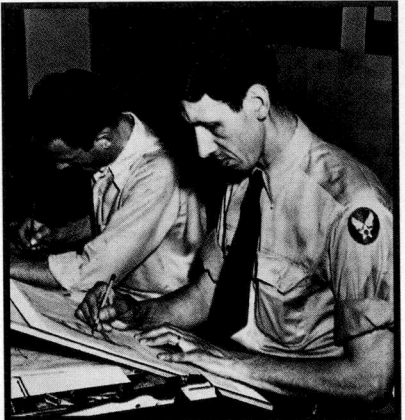

A Changing Country
After the war, thousands of veterans returned to a country in flux. Americans now wanted to put the war behind them and enjoy the freedoms for which they had sacrificed and fought.

THE NEWSREELS SHOWED THOUSANDS OF CHEERING SAILORS, SOLDIERS, AND AIRMEN CROWDING INTO TIMES SQUARE OR POURING OFF TROOP SHIPS. Their families and girlfriends and wives leaped into their arms, shedding tears of joy. They flung caps into the air. They kissed the ground. When the homecomings were over, however, World War II veterans faced the task of rebuilding their lives and careers in a very uncertain time.

Many men were able to pick up their jobs more or less where they had left off before the war. Others, however, had put education and career decisions on hold to serve in the military. There was at first a great deal of turmoil in the job market, as the economy adjusted to peacetime production and to the flood of returning workers.

The 1946 movie *The Best Years of Our Lives* dramatized the difficulties of veterans during the first weeks of their return. In the following scene, a drugstore manager, Mr. Thorpe, is talking to Fred Derry, a much-decorated bombardier:

Thorpe: I can see that you had a splendid war record, Derry.

Derry: Just average, Mr. Thorpe.

Thorpe: But you'll understand that since this business changed hands we're

AS YOU READ

Vocabulary
▶ closed shop
▶ right-to-work law
▶ union shop
▶ whistle-stop tour

Think About . . .
▶ the factors and conditions in the United States after World War II that contributed to a conservative backlash against New Deal policies.
▶ the struggle Truman faced in his attempt to implement the Fair Deal.

630 CHAPTER 19 COLD WAR POLITICS

Section 1 Resources

REPRODUCIBLE RESOURCES

📁 Lesson Plan 19-1
📁 Vocabulary and Guided Reading Activity 19-1
📁 Cooperative Learning Activity 19
📁 Section 1 Quiz
📁 Political Cartoon 12

MULTIMEDIA RESOURCES

📽 Chapter Teaching Transparency 19
📽 Section Focus Transparency 59
📽 Map Transparency 19
🎧 Chapter 19 Digest Audiocassette
💾 Testmaker
💿 Student Self-Test: A Software Review

under no legal obligation to give you your old job back.

Derry: I wasn't thinking of getting my old job back, Mr. Thorpe. I'm looking for a better one.

Thorpe: What are your qualifications, your experience?

Derry: Two years behind a soda fountain, and three years behind a Norden bomb sight. . . . I was only responsible for getting the bombs on the target. I didn't command anybody.

Thorpe: I see; I'm sure that work required great skill. But unfortunately, we've no opportunities for that with Midway Drugs.
— RKO Pictures, *The Best Years of Our Lives,* 1946

Not everybody faced what Fred Derry did, going back to the drugstore where he once worked. One of Derry's compatriots resumed his prestigious work as a bank manager. The nation as a whole was looking in a new direction. People wanted to put wartime sacrifices behind them, put veterans back to work, and enjoy the prosperity and freedom for which they had fought.

A Conservative Turn
Shortages Create Demand for Change

Richard M. Nixon carried a law degree and a modest war record with him when he came home. Like thousands of other veterans, he was looking for a job. Within two years he would begin to work the levers of power in Washington.

Nixon's quick political climb began when a group of California business leaders backed him as a candidate for Congress in 1946. Nixon was part of the conservative backlash, or opposition, to the New Deal. He was also an outspoken anti-Communist who would soon become a prominent figure in the cold war politics of the 1950s.

The Twelfth Congressional District in southern California in many ways mirrored the political makeup of the nation. There were slightly more Democrats than Republicans registered in the voting rolls, but that advantage was vanishing because of a growing resentment among voters over postwar shortages in jobs, goods, and housing. Business leaders, farmers, and bankers were generally hopeful but nervous about the nation's economic outlook.

Often in times of uncertainty, voters look with suspicion at the policies of the party in power. In 1946 many voters turned against the Democrats and the New Deal.

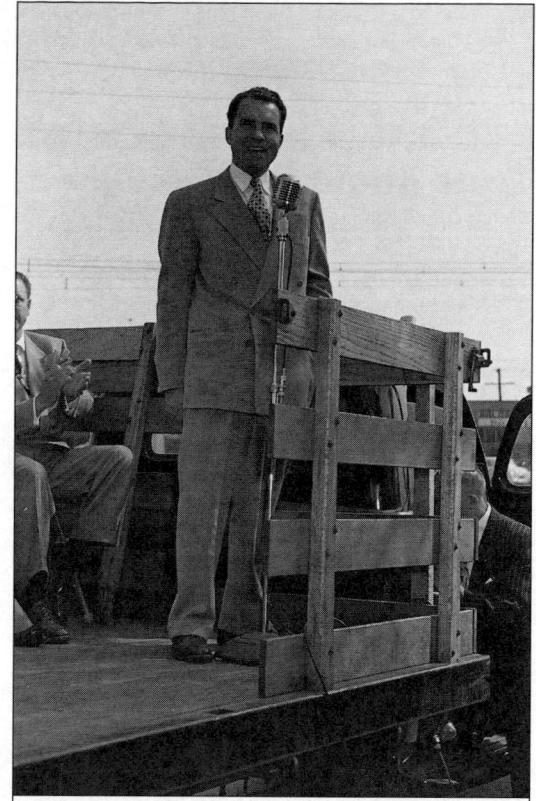

ARCHIVE PHOTOS

Nixon **The congressman speaks on the campaign trail.** *Why did many voters turn against the Democrats in 1946?*

There were "two definite opinions on the American system," Nixon told a group of prominent people in his congressional district. "One advocated by the New Deal is government control regulating our lives. The other calls for individual freedom and all that initiative can produce." He was talking to a handful of California Republicans, but he might as well have been addressing disaffected voters in many states who would soon sweep Republicans into Congress.

In congressional districts throughout the country, growing fears about communism resulted in particularly nasty campaign battles. Candidates whipped up anti-Communist rhetoric, publicly and subtly accusing their opponents of being "Red," the slang term for Communists and Communist sympathizers. The accusations, even if unfounded, were often hard to erase from the minds of voters.

When the Eightieth Congress convened in January 1947, many incumbents had been replaced. The conservative shift brought a new group of Republicans to Washington and gave the Republican party control of Congress. They came ready to correct what they saw

SECTION ONE   **631**

TEACH

Guided Practice

L1 **Discussion** Have volunteers interview someone who served in the armed forces during wartime. Then have the volunteers describe what it was like for that person to reenter the labor force after being away for a few years.

 Show students Map Transparency 19 and have them complete the activity sheet.

FYI

Economic Worries After World War II, people were uncertain about how the economy would react when the wartime defense industry shut down. Shortages of jobs, goods, and housing were accompanied by soaring prices for consumer goods. Business leaders, bankers, and farmers were nervous about whether the economy would rebound or decline.

VISUAL INSTRUCTION

Nixon **Richard Nixon campaigns for Congress from California.**

Answer: *They resented shortages in jobs, goods, and housing.*

Cooperative Learning

Recognizing Propaganda Explain that the word *propaganda* often suggests the use of false or distorted information to further the interests of a group or person. Some of the 1946 campaigns for Congress involved the use of such propaganda. The campaign attacks were characterized by broad accusations of wrong-

doing with little or no evidence to support them. Assign small groups of students to find recent examples of political propaganda. Each group should divide up the work fairly, assign roles, and prepare a presentation comparing political propaganda today with that of the 1940s.

Independent Practice

L1 Making a Time Line

Have students construct a time line for one of the following topics: African American civil rights, economic changes, or labor issues. Suggest that students use information from previous chapters to begin their time lines and then add new information from this section.

📋 Have students complete the Chapter 19, Section 1 Vocabulary and Guided Reading Activity. (Also in Spanish.) **LEP**

📋 Have students complete the Chapter 19 Cooperative Learning Activity.

VISUAL INSTRUCTION

A Typical Grocery Store Merchants like Guido cut prices in response to President Truman's pleas to help keep inflation under control. Their efforts, however, did not prevent prices from soaring when wartime controls were lifted.

Answer: *Some blamed the unions for rising prices because strikes stopped production, which contributed to shortages.*

CHART STUDY

When wartime controls were lifted, the prices of goods soared. In the 26 months between June 1946 and August 1948, the wholesale price index rose 45 percent.

Answer: *The price of a pound of butter went up the fastest.*

---

as a threat to the nation's peacetime economy: the New Deal. That meant taking on the man who now embodied the spirit of the New Deal—President Harry Truman.

Fears About the Economy
Rising Costs Blamed on Unions

While Nixon and the other 1946 congressional hopefuls were campaigning, the nation's economy had been following a precarious path. Business leaders and conservatives were pressuring Truman to lift the government's wartime limits on prices. Finally he gave in and prices for basic goods immediately shot up.

The President called on businesses to keep prices down voluntarily as a patriotic measure to help stabilize the economy. Nevertheless, the inflation rate climbed to about 25 percent in mid-1946. The price hikes did little to dampen the spending desires of more prosperous Americans, who eagerly snatched up items, such as refrigerators, that were now beginning to return to stores after wartime shortages. Many workers watched the purchasing power of their wages shrink. They began to protest. Labor union membership had been growing during the war, but the unions generally had neither asked for nor received wage increases. After the war unions grew restless and began to make more and more demands on employers.

Rising Food Prices, 1946			
Month	A Loaf of Bread	A Pound of Butter	A Dozen Eggs
March	$0.09	$0.55	$0.48
June	$0.11	$0.61	$0.51
September	$0.12	$0.83	$0.67
December	$0.12	$0.92	$0.70

Rising Food Prices The price of basic goods skyrocketed after price controls were lifted. *For which of the three types of food shown on the chart did the price rise the most?*

Americans started their days with a full breakfast of news about strikes in their morning papers. Unions were stopping production in industries across the nation. There were more strikes, measured in lost work hours, than at any other time in American history.

In 1946 and 1947 many people were getting fed up with rising prices and with lingering shortages in basics such as beef and gasoline. Many targeted their frustrations at the unions. They felt that the unions had become greedy in their demands, forcing up the cost of goods. Critics accused the Truman administration of not having the courage, or the alertness, to confront the economic problems.

Backlash Against the New Deal

The Republicans in the Eightieth Congress had been elected, by and large, on the promise to "clean up the mess in Washington." Senator Robert Taft of Ohio observed that their task was "the restoration of freedom and the elimination or reduction of constantly increasing interference with family life and with business" by the government. His comment was reflected in two of the Republicans' goals: to cut back New Deal spending and to rein in labor. The

A Typical Grocery Store Tedaldo Guido stands in front of his grocery store in North Tonawanda, New York, in 1947. *Why did some people blame the unions for the rising cost of goods?*

Meeting Special Needs

Reading Disability To address the needs of students with reading comprehension problems, have students work in pairs to look at the photographs and other visuals in this section. Then have pairs read the captions and the boldface heads to each other, discussing the meaning.

Ask pairs to then create an outline for the section using the heads as a guideline. Students can then listen to the Chapter 19, Section 1 portion of the Chapter Audiocassettes. The audiocassettes are also available in Spanish.

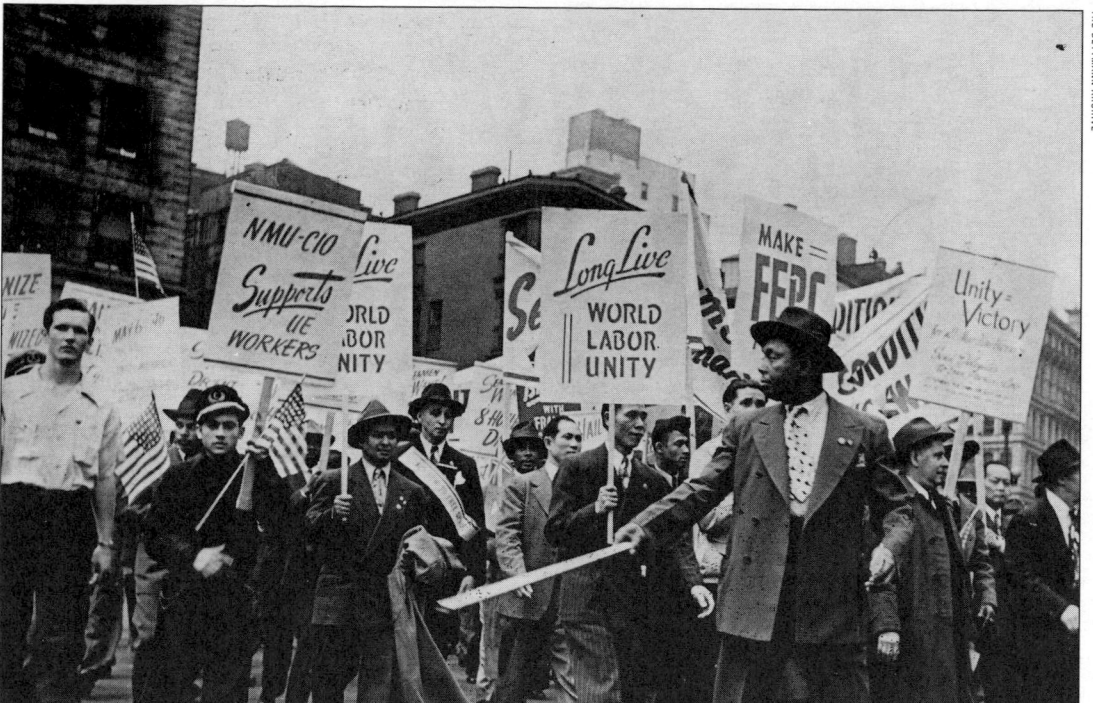

THE BETTMANN ARCHIVE

Labor Strikes Begin Workers march through New York City in a 1946 labor parade. Truman's sour relations with labor turned sweeter after his veto of the Taft-Hartley bill. *Why was labor unhappy with Truman? What did Truman do that improved his relationship with organized labor?*

controversy over labor quickly became focused on a single issue: the Taft-Hartley bill.

The 1935 National Labor Relations Act, a major New Deal protection for workers, had recognized the unions' right to bargain collectively. Employers complained that the act had given unions too much power. Companies cited crippling strikes and agreements broken by unions and complained that they had lost the ability to manage their employees. Conservative members of Congress thought the time had come to strengthen the management position.

The Taft-Hartley bill sought to ban the **closed shop,** a workplace where only union members could be hired. The bill also allowed states to pass **right-to-work laws,** which outlawed **union shops** (shops in which new workers were required to join the union).

The bill tipped the balance of power in other ways as well. It allowed employers to sue if the unions did not live up to their contracts. It provided for "cooling off" periods during which labor and management would resume bargaining. The bill also enabled the President to intervene in strikes that endangered national health and safety by ordering workers back to their jobs for 80 days.

Truman Fights the Taft-Hartley Bill

Truman and the Congress went to war over the Taft-Hartley bill, which the President called "a slave labor bill." The President shared the public concern about union power. He had on some occasions locked horns with union leaders and forced them to back down in their demands, but he felt that the new bill threatened important worker protections. Congress passed the bill, Truman vetoed it, and Congress voted to override the veto.

The bill proved to be less of a threat to labor than was feared, but it had an important side effect. Truman's strong opposition to the measure gave him a new political ally—labor. After months of souring relations with the unions, Truman had in a single stroke become a friend of the worker. "I don't give a hang what the unions say about me, or do to me politically: that isn't my job," Truman had growled to his aides after tangling with striking mine and railroad workers. "But when they run a balance sheet on Harry Truman, they'll realize they got a fine fair shake."

Truman's balance sheet got plenty of credit from his veto of the Taft-Hartley bill. It gave Truman labor support—a formidable weapon he would carry into the 1948 presidential election. He would need all the help he could get in this election.

SECTION ONE **633**

Curriculum Connection

Communications Assign students to write and deliver the first paragraph of a speech by Henry Wallace or Strom Thurmond explaining why they are running for President.

Curriculum Connection

Economics Review with students the basic theories regarding supply and demand in a free market. Increases in demand should drive up prices, increases in supply should push down prices, and increases in prices should cause supplies to increase and demand to decrease. During the war, controls kept both the supply of goods and prices low. After the war, the country allowed market forces to regulate supplies and prices.

The Uphill Race in '48
Truman Defends Civil Rights Program

Harry Truman never wanted to be President. Over and over again, he wished out loud that someone else would take the dubious honor of toiling away in the big drafty house he and his family referred to as the "Great White Jail."

Yet a strange paradox resided in this outwardly simple man. He knew he lacked the understanding of foreign policy and the passion for domestic reform of his predecessor, but he had one quality in himself that he trusted supremely: the determination to do the right thing. In the end Harry Truman trusted his ability to do the right thing more than he trusted anybody else he saw looming on the presidential horizon. The man who as senator had called himself "just a country jake who works at the job" liked being Just Plain Harry and thought a "country jake" could run the country just fine.

Daunting Prospects

Political experts and members of Truman's own Democratic party thought he should let someone else run for President in 1948. Only 36 percent of the voters approved of his administration. His public image floundered. Many saw him as soft on labor and on communism.

Prices had doubled since 1939, and Truman was blamed. In many opinion columns, news stories, and cartoons, he was portrayed as weak and incompetent. A popular quip of the time was, "To err is Truman." One of his campaign jingles, "We're just wild about Harry," was mockingly rendered as "We're just mild about Harry."

Before confronting the Republicans, Truman first had to face attacks from his own party that promised to rob him of votes from conservative and liberal Democrats. Henry Wallace, a former member of Truman's cabinet, split from the Democratic party to form the Progressive party and took many liberals with him. Wallace advocated stronger civil rights legislation, more federal spending for social programs, and a less confrontational stance toward the Soviet Union. The latter position gained him the support of the Communist party, which he did not reject. Wallace's refusal to take an anti-Communist stand proved disastrous to his candidacy. For a time, however, the Progressive party appeared to be a serious political contender that could spoil Truman's chances for reelection.

Civil Rights

The other threat to Truman's campaign came over the issue of civil rights. The President was a longtime supporter of equal rights for African Americans. He had begun the desegregation of the armed forces and had urged the Justice Department to prosecute cases in which African Americans were deprived of their civil rights. Before the 1948 Democratic convention he had unveiled a civil rights plan that included an antilynching bill and a ban on poll taxes, which had previously blocked poor people from voting.

Civil rights issues shattered the Democratic national convention. Liberals managed to insert into the Democratic platform a mildly worded plank affirming the party's commitment to eliminate "racial, religious, and economic discrimination." It also commended Truman's "courageous stand" on civil rights.

A group of conservative Southern Democrats, the so-called Dixiecrats, broke from the party to form a States' Rights Democratic party. It nominated South Carolina governor Strom Thurmond as its candidate. The party attracted some conservatives who wanted a repeal of New Deal measures, but the Dixiecrats' main issue was their own support of racial segregation and

Civil Rights Legislation Truman received the Robert S. Abbott Award for making the most significant contribution to democracy in 1948. Truman's civil rights plans earned him the respect of many African Americans. *How did the Southern congressional delegation react to Truman's civil rights program?*

Extending the Content

The 1948 Elections Southern Democrats who opposed Truman's civil rights legislation formed the States' Rights Democratic party (also known as the Dixiecrat party). They nominated Strom Thurmond, governor of South Carolina, as their presidential candidate. Thurmond carried 4 states and received 39 electoral votes. Thurmond felt that the federal government was taking over duties that belonged to the states. At one time he favored racial segregation but later changed his views and supported some civil rights legislation. He was elected to the Senate in 1954 as a write-in candidate and is still a senator today. Have students read newspapers or magazines to find out about Strom Thurmond's views today.

UPI/BETTMANN

Running on the Rails Truman won the support of thousands of Americans as he crossed the country on his whistle-stop campaign tour. *What did Truman claim about the Republicans?*

VISUAL INSTRUCTION

Running on the Rails Truman campaigns in Richmond, Indiana. His tireless effort to reach thousands of voters conveyed his straightforward style. Dewey's cool, reserved manner failed to reach voters and helped seal his fate.

Answer: *Truman claimed the Republicans were not serious about solving the nation's problems because Congress had failed to pass a single one of Truman's proposals.*

their opposition to federal government action on civil rights—action they insisted violated the authority of states. Asked why Southern members of Congress revolted against Truman's civil rights proposals when Roosevelt had advocated virtually the same measures, Dixiecrat Strom Thurmond replied, "Yeah, but he means it."

During the campaign friends warned Truman to soften his stand so as not to offend Southern conservative Democrats. To one such friend Truman wrote:

I am not asking for social equality, because no such thing exists, but I am asking for equality of opportunity for all human beings and, as long as I stay here, I am going to continue that fight. When the mob gangs can take four people out and shoot them in the back, and everybody in the country is acquainted with who did the shooting and nothing is done about it, that country is in a pretty bad fix from a law enforcement standpoint. . . . I am going to try to remedy it and if that ends up in my failure to be reelected, that failure will be in a good cause.
—Harry S Truman, August 18, 1948

Truman indeed faced failure. With the Democrats in disarray and their candidate weakened, the Republicans believed that anyone they nominated could crush Truman in November.

The Republican nomination went to the man FDR had trounced in 1944, New York governor Thomas E. Dewey. He presented a sharp contrast to Truman's feisty, freewheeling style: Dewey was reserved and meticulous. He was known as an intelligent and efficient administrator.

Although dapper and confident, Dewey was not going to sweep the nation off its feet with charisma. The Republicans, however, were not worried. In his speeches, Dewey never even referred to Truman; he campaigned like a man who had already won the election. It seemed that the race was Dewey's to win.

Running on the Rails

Although Truman's campaign staff was pessimistic about his chances, the President remained confident. In a particularly shrewd move, Truman waited until the end of the Republican national convention and then called a special session of Congress. He challenged Republicans to make good on their platform promises. He handed Congress a string of his own proposals, including his civil rights legislation. When Congress failed to pass a single bill, Truman was able to claim that the Republicans were not serious about solving the nation's problems.

Truman could now point to a whole menu of New Deal–style measures that the Eightieth Congress rejected: aid to farmers, a minimum-wage hike from 40 to 75 cents, a housing bill, increased Social Security coverage, and new price controls. This gave him the

Curriculum Connection

History Have students research and write a brief summary of an earlier controversy over states' rights and then share their information with the class. For example, students could research the Kentucky and Virginia Resolutions of 1798–1799, the Hartford Convention of 1814–1815, the nullification controversy of 1832–1833, or the secession crisis of 1860–1861.

SECTION ONE   **635**

Cultural Perspectives

Panel Discussion Have panels of 4 or 6 students compare the views of Southern white Democrats who feared Truman's civil rights plan with the views of civil rights leaders, such as those who presented Truman with the Robert S. Abbott Award for making the most significant contribution to democracy in 1948. Have groups consider how each of these groups might feel about Truman's reelection campaign, and why. Groups may want to conduct additional research to find out which viewpoints have over time become more prevalent.

ASSESS

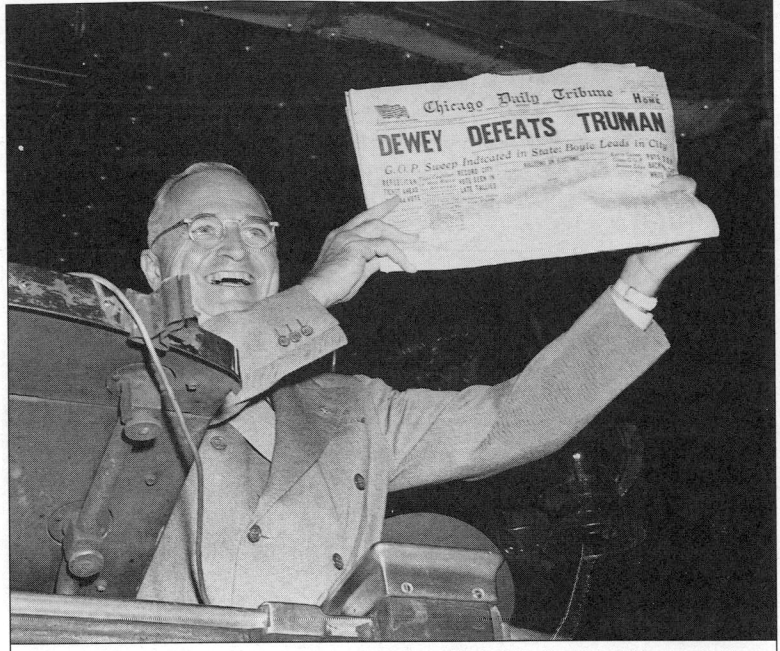

Election Results In one of the most famous photos in United States history, Truman holds up the *Chicago Daily Tribune* with its headline erroneously announcing the 1948 election results. *Why did people think Dewey was sure to win the presidential election?*

UPI/BETTMANN

Stopping in town after town, he spoke to enthusiastic crowds from the rear platform of the train. To people who had only seen pictures of the President and heard him speak on the radio, the impression was strong. Truman told his listeners about the troubles in Washington. He ticked off the failures of "that do-nothing Eightieth Congress." After that he asked the crowd if they wanted to meet his family. They did, of course. His wife, Bess, and daughter, Margaret, joined him on the platform. The crowds ate it up.

Still, few people believed Truman could win. In the last weeks before the election, polls showed him trailing by up to 10 percentage points. *Newsweek* polled 50 experts from across the country; not one gave Truman a chance. When one of his aides hand-ed the magazine to Truman, he looked at it, grinned, and said, "Forget it, they're always wrong."

On Election Day, Truman went home to Independence, Missouri, where he voted, took a Turkish bath, and confidently awaited the results. He went to bed early and was awakened at midnight and again at 4:00 A.M. by aides telling him he was winning. Radio commentators kept predicting that Dewey would come on strong as new precincts reported in. The *Chicago Daily Tribune* went to press with the historic and later embarrassing banner headline, "Dewey Defeats Truman." Nothing of the sort happened. Truman won big.

ammunition he needed against the Republicans in an unprecedented national campaign tour.

Many past Presidents had stayed put in the White House during their campaigns—to do otherwise was thought undignified. Truman, however, wanted to take his case to the people, so he took the White House on the road. From Labor Day to Election Day, Truman conducted his famous train trip, or **whistle-stop tour,** of the country in the Ferdinand Magellan, an ornately appointed suite of railroad cars that once belonged to FDR. More than 20 staff members and dozens of reporters accompanied the President on his 32,000-mile (51,488km) trip.

EVENTS OF THE TRUMAN YEARS, 1945–1949

1945 Truman becomes President. World War II ends.

1946 Price controls are lifted. Inflation soars. Eightieth Congress is elected.

1948 Truman defeats Dewey.

1945 | 1946 | 1947 | 1948 | 1949

1947 Taft-Hartley labor bill passes. Truman Doctrine is announced. Marshall Plan is implemented.

1949 Fair Deal programs are proposed, including low-income housing and increases in Social Security and the minimum wage.

The Fair Deal
Roosevelt's New Deal Revisited

The romantic view of the 1948 election is that of the underdog overcoming the odds through grit and determination. In recent times, historians have noted that President Truman's reelection victory was really due to the resilience of FDR's Democratic party, which was sufficient to overcome even Truman's unpopularity. The vote to reelect Truman was, in effect, a vote for Franklin Roosevelt's fifth term. The strength of the party was also evident because the Democrats regained the majority in both houses of Congress in the 1948 election.

For nearly four years, the Republican-controlled Congress had thwarted President Truman's hopes of continuing and expanding the New Deal. Now, fresh from his victory, Truman marched into the Democrat-controlled Congress with a State of the Union message that unveiled the Fair Deal, his new lease on life for the New Deal. It called for legislation favoring such causes as national medical insurance, extension of Social Security, new public power projects, public housing, and repeal of the Taft-Hartley Act. It was bold, ambitious, and liberal.

The Fair Deal registered its successes. The Social Security system was broadened to cover 10 million more people than it had before. The minimum wage rose from 40 to 75 cents per hour. The Housing Act of 1949 authorized the construction of about 800,000 low-income units.

In many ways the Fair Deal was doomed. Republicans and conservative Dixiecrats often voted as a bloc to defeat many of Truman's legislative proposals, especially in the area of civil rights. Events in the country, and in the world, also helped to undermine the Fair Deal. The fresh wave of support Truman gained in the election gradually faded as charges of corruption riddled his administration.

In addition, President Truman was blamed for not taking stronger action to prevent the Communist takeover of China. The United States became bogged down in a costly and stalemated war in Korea. As military spending again soared, Congress had little interest in funding social programs.

Truman's presidency fell victim to these changes. By the end of his term, when he decided not to run for reelection, his popularity had sunk to a new low. Events inside and outside of Washington contributed to Truman's fall. Another factor was the nation's fear of communism—a fear that Truman himself had helped to create.

The Fair Deal Truman's struggle with Dixiecrats over the Fair Deal is exemplified in the cartoon. *How did Republicans and conservative Southern Democrats help to defeat Truman's legislative proposals?*

SECTION REVIEW

Vocabulary
1. Define: closed shop, right-to-work law, union shop, whistle-stop tour.

Checking Facts
2. What issue did Richard M. Nixon and other Republican candidates try to use in the election of 1946? How successful or unsuccessful was it? Why?

3. How successful was Harry Truman's Fair Deal legislation after the 1948 election? What accounts for its success or lack of success? Explain your answer.

Critical Thinking
Recognizing Ideologies
4. In what ways did President Truman's values help and hurt him? List examples and explain.

Linking Across Time
5. Which of Truman's Fair Deal programs are still hot political issues today? Why do you think this is so?

VISUAL INSTRUCTION

The Fair Deal This cartoon plays off the saying "You can lead a horse to water, but you can't make it drink" to make a statement about Truman's Fair Deal.

Answer: *They voted as a bloc to defeat his proposals.*

Evaluate

Have students complete the Section Review.

📁 ◎ Assign the Section 1 Quiz or use the Testmaker to develop a customized quiz. (Also in Spanish.) **LEP**

Reteach

🎧 Have students listen to the Chapter 19, Section 1 Audiocassette. (Also in Spanish.) **LEP**

Enrich

📁 Have students complete Interpreting Political Cartoon 12.

CLOSE

Ask students questions such as these: Why was inflation a problem after the war? (*The war caused shortages, and businesses raised prices when controls were lifted.*) Why did Truman's chances seem slim in the 1948 election? (*The Democrats were divided over Truman's policies on civil rights and labor.*) What effect did the confrontational actions of the 80th Congress have on Truman? (*Truman's fight over the Taft-Hartley Act won him union support.*)

Section 1 Review Answers

1. closed shop (633), **right-to-work law** (633), **union shop** (633), **whistle-stop tour** (636)
2. the nation's fear of communism; the Republicans gained control of Congress; many feared a Communist takeover
3. It was moderately successful: Truman won on social security, the minimum wage, and low-income housing, but he lost on civil rights.

4. Voters liked Truman's aggressive style, but many white Democrats were angered by his civil rights stance.
5. National medical insurance, extension of Social Security, public housing. These are all expensive programs.

TEACH

Making the Historical Connection

In 1869 John Hyatt invented celluloid, the first synthetic plastic to receive wide commercial use. Celluloid could be sawed, carved, and made into sheets. Common celluloid items were combs, dentures, clock cases, and photographic film. Early celluloid caught fire easily and was hard to mold. Soon after celluloid was invented, other scientists invented rayon (the first manufactured fiber) and cellophane.

FYI

Plastics Production The United States leads the world in the production of plastics, which depends on plentiful supplies of coal and petroleum. The plastics industry is growing rapidly in Canada, Mexico, and South America. Texas manufactures more raw plastics than any other state.

Science, TECHNOLOGY, and Society

FILE PHOTO BY DOUG MINDEL

Plastics

Plastics are human-made materials that can be shaped into many forms. They can be as hard as steel or as soft as a pillow. A shortage of raw materials during World War II led to both the development of new plastics and the use of old plastics in new ways. Mass production helped plastics come into common use in American homes and businesses.

© DAN MCCOY/RAINBOW

NEW PLASTICS

New types of plastics invented during World War II led to new ways of using them in medicine, including this plastic heart valve.

POPPERFOTO

NEW USES FOR OLD MATERIALS

Nylon, once used mostly for women's hosiery, is used to make parachutes for the war effort, May 1944.

THE HISTORY OF PLASTICS

1930s	1940s	1950s	1960s
LUCITE AND PLEXIGLAS are used in airplane windows; nylon for hosiery; vinyl for garden hoses and raincoats; polystyrene for food containers, tiles, and electrical equipment.	**POLYESTER** is used in car bodies, luggage, and magnetic tape. Polyethylene, silicone, and epoxy are developed but are not in widespread use.	**POLYETHYLENE** is inexpensive to produce and is used for plastic bags, plates, and cups. Silicones are used for lubricants and heart valves. Epoxy is a strong adhesive.	**HIGH-TEMPERATURE** plastics are developed and used for electronics and missiles.

638 SCIENCE, TECHNOLOGY, AND SOCIETY

Background Information

Plastics in Medicine Certain plastics are important in medicine because they have no adverse effect on the body and are not affected by chemicals produced by the body. For example, doctors use plastic screws and plates to fix broken bones. They sew up wounds with plastic thread. Surgeons can replace parts of the intestines with sections made of plastic. They put plastic devices into the heart to replace faulty heart valves. Lightweight plastics can be used to make artificial limbs; the plastic is made to match the skin color of the patient. Some artificial hands even have plastic skin with fingerprints.

HULTON DEUTSCH COLLECTION LIMITED

AIRCRAFT WINDOWS

Plexiglas, a light, transparent, weather-resistant thermoplastic, was used for windows in World War II planes.

© GREG ANTHONY/LIGHT SOURCES

JUKEBOXES

After the war, plastics found their way into products used for entertainment (such as this jukebox), products used in nuclear and space research and architecture, as well as toys, automobiles, and household items.

PLASTICS EVERYWHERE

PORTFOLIO PROJECT

To better understand the effect plastics have had on people's lives, keep a list for one day of everything you use that is made of plastic. Are the lenses of your glasses made of plastic? What about your sneakers? How pervasive are plastics? Write down the results of your inquiry and keep a copy in your portfolio.

FILE PHOTO BY DOUG MINDEL

1970s	1980s	1990s
PLASTIC microwave cookware, computer housing, and CDs are developed. Biodegradable plastics are introduced.	**HEAT-RESISTANT** plastic foam covers space-shuttle fuel tanks. Photodegradable plastics are introduced.	**PLASTICS** that carry an electric current are developed for batteries, wiring, and static-resistant fabrics.

SCIENCE, TECHNOLOGY, AND SOCIETY   **639**

Portfolio Project

PORTFOLIO PROJECT

Research Have students research something having to do with plastics. They may want to focus on the use of plastics in one field of interest to them, such as in industry, architecture, medicine, or science. Or they may want to focus on how plastics are manufactured, focusing on one or more of the following processes: molding, casting, laminating, extrusion, or calendaring. Have students share their findings with the class, and then file their work in their portfolios.

639

SECTION

2

FOCUS

Section Objectives

1. Analyze the causes and effects surrounding the rise of anti-Communist sentiment and the phenomenon of McCarthyism.
2. Describe how blacklisting affected American society.

Bellringer Activity

While taking attendance at the beginning of the class period, display **Section Focus Transparency 60,** and have students answer the questions. (Or use the blackline master.)

VISUAL INSTRUCTION

The Spread of Anticommunism After 21 years in the United States Senate, Robert M. La Follette, Jr., of Wisconsin, lost the 1946 primary to Republican Joseph R. McCarthy. McCarthy was elected to the Senate later that year, and by 1950, when this Wisconsin newspaper was published, he was one of the most feared figures in American politics.

Ask: What caused anti-Communist sentiment? *(the Soviet development of the atomic bomb, the spread of communism in China and other places, politicians who used fear to propel themselves into the limelight)*

The Cold War at Home

MAY 1, 1950: WISCONSIN TOWN FALLS TO THE "COMMUNISTS"

The Spread of Anticommunism Mosinee, Wisconsin, like many American towns, thought the threat of communism a serious problem. This newspaper depicts what life would be like under Communist rule.

MOSINEE, WISCONSIN, WAS A TYPICAL QUIET AMERICAN TOWN—UNTIL THE DAY THE "COMMUNISTS" TOOK OVER. On May 1, 1950, armed soldiers stormed into Mosinee, seizing Mayor Ralph Kronenwetter. The mayor and Police Chief Carl Gewiss were arrested and taken to city hall, where the Soviet hammer-and-sickle flag was raised high. When Gewiss refused to cooperate with the invaders, he was "liquidated."

The Communist forces circled the town and set up roadblocks to prevent escape. Red guards took over the Mosinee power plant; they arrested the local newspaper editor and began converting his printing presses to publish the new propaganda paper, *The Red Star*.

Soldiers then raided the public library and private homes to "purge" them of anti-Communist literature.

Members of the clergy and business leaders were rounded up and put in concentration camps.

Meanwhile, at the high school, Communist party workers organized a parade to celebrate the new regime. They marched down Main Street and gathered for a rally in the center of town—newly dubbed "Red Square."

Then, at 7:00 P.M., the soldiers put down their weapons, the prisoners were freed, and Mosinee residents held a good old-fashioned picnic to celebrate the joys of freedom and democracy. They raised the American flag as the high school band played "The Star-Spangled Banner." An American Legion commander addressed the crowd about the virtues of the American way of life.

The takeover was a hoax, of course. The armed subversives were actually patriotic United States sol-

---

AS YOU READ

Vocabulary
► vigilante
► blacklisting

Think About . . .
► the causes and effects surrounding the rise of anti-Communist sentiment and the phenomenon of McCarthyism.

► how blacklisting affected various aspects of American society.

---

640 CHAPTER 19 COLD WAR POLITICS

Section 2 Resources

REPRODUCIBLE RESOURCES

📁 Lesson Plan 19-2

📁 Vocabulary and Guided Reading Activity 19-2

📁 Section 2 Quiz

📁 Geography in History Activity 19

MULTIMEDIA RESOURCES

🎛 Section Focus Transparency 60

🎧 Chapter 19 Digest Audiocassette

💿 Landmark Documents in American History

💿 Testmaker

💿 Student Self-Test: A Software Review

diers; the leader of the "coup" was an ex-Communist. Project organizers, including the American Legion, chose May Day as their date because in the Soviet Union it was a major holiday celebrating communism. The Mosinee event received nationwide news coverage.

Although the takeover seems rather humorous now, it reflected a pervasive fear. Mayor Kronenwetter died the next day of a heart attack; a clergyman died days later. Town historians said the deaths were associated with the stress of the event. The Mosinee story is an extreme example of a wave of anticommunism that swept the country during the late 1940s and early 1950s. Watching the spread of communism around the world, and listening to the rhetoric of politicians and commentators, millions of Americans feared that seemingly friendly citizens—the local PTA president, a bank secretary, the railroad worker next door—were working feverishly for the Communist takeover of the United States government.

The menace of Communist traitors poisoning the life of small-town America was very real to many people. Some of them felt that their fellow citizens were not taking the threat seriously enough.

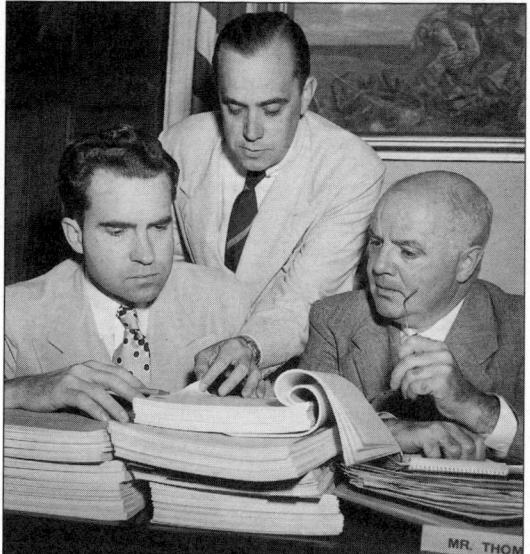

The House Un-American Activities Committee Richard Nixon looks over testimony in the trial of Alger Hiss. *Why was Nixon considered the voice of reason during the hearings?*

The Hunt for Communist Sympathizers
Fear Tactics and Intimidation

The fear of communism did not start with the cold war. It grew, explosively, in the climate produced by the development of the Soviet atomic bomb, the spread of communism in the world, and the efforts of some unscrupulous Americans to use fear as a way to defeat their enemies and to propel themselves to positions of political power.

Long after the Red Scare of 1919 and well before the heyday of anticommunism in the 1950s, conservatives in Congress had looked for a way to discredit President Roosevelt and his New Deal administration. The House Un-American Activities Committee, or HUAC, held hearings that explored the issue of Communist influence in the New Deal. Little came of the hearings, largely because World War II intervened and the country rallied behind its President. Concern about communism was put aside as Stalin's Soviet government became a temporary ally.

Almost immediately after the war, the mood began to change. Stalin turned more openly belligerent toward the United States. Winston Churchill delivered his famous "iron curtain" speech. The cold war was launched. After the war the HUAC hearings resumed. For months the

committee loudly declared the existence of Communists in the Truman administration but failed to find any. In 1947, however, the committee got a new cast of characters, most notably a young congressman with a keen mind and an ability to skewer a reluctant witness during cross-examination. The postwar history of the HUAC quickly became the story of Richard Nixon and Alger Hiss. It was a case that made one man and broke another.

The American Communist Party

Surrounded by men who were at times emotional, vindictive, and racist, Congressman Nixon became the voice of reason on the HUAC. Some committee members resorted to demagoguery—stirring people up by appealing to their emotions—and to character assassination. Nixon, by contrast, spoke quietly, usually from a brief of carefully gathered facts.

To be sure, there were Communists and Communist sympathizers to be found, but there were far more former Communists. The American Communist party was in its heyday during the Depression, when much of the nation was suffering and out of work. Marxist and Leninist writings and the speeches of Stalin—touting the rights of the working class and criticizing the failures of capitalism—appealed to many liberals in the United States. The party drew workers, intellectuals, artists, and college students to its ranks. Interest in communism became a chic intellectual trend. In a time of extensive poverty, racial injustice, and the abuse of workers by powerful corporations, communism seemed to promise

SECTION TWO **641**

VISUAL INSTRUCTION

The House Un-American Activities Committee Representative Richard Nixon, Robert Stripling, and Representative J. Parnell Thomas look over testimony in the HUAC spy inquiry on August 26, 1948, before turning it over to the Justice Department.

Answer: *Nixon, unlike others who were emotional, vindictive, or racist, spoke quietly using carefully gathered facts.*

TEACH

Guided Practice

L1 Discuss List words that students associate with communism. Discuss any positive or negative connotations. Then review the relationship between the United States and the Soviet Union during World War II. Remind students that the two countries were allies during the war, despite having earlier disagreements.

Independent Practice

L2 Making a Time Line Have students make time lines showing actions taken by key people in this section. The first time a person is listed on the time line, have students describe the person.

☞ Have students complete the Chapter 19, Section 2 Vocabulary and Guided Reading Activity. (Also in Spanish.) **LEP**

Cooperative Learning

Classroom Debate Set up a class debate based on the Alger Hiss case. Half of the students should prepare to defend Hiss; the other half should prepare to prosecute him. Encourage students to divide work fairly and to get information about the case from books, magazine articles, and newspaper accounts of the time. 📖

Analyzing Media Have groups of students bring in newspaper or newsmagazine accounts of foreign leaders or U.S. leaders who hold unpopular opinions and who are vilified by the press. Have groups discuss whether these individuals are stereotyped, and if so, how. Groups can present their findings to the class. 📖

relief. The ideology had not yet acquired an association with evil and repression.

This association came in the late 1930s, when Stalin stepped up his campaign of terror against his enemies and tightened internal security in the Soviet Union. His strong-arm tactics caused many sympathizers in the United States to become disillusioned with communism. By World War II, public interest in communism in the United States had virtually died.

The rise of the cold war, however, caused changes that brought the HUAC's activities into the spotlight once again. The cold war resulted in increased espionage activity by Stalin against the United States. That legitimized fears that the Soviet Union was trying to undermine the United States government.

The Case of Alger Hiss

Politicians and voters wanted to see a strong case brought against the spies they thought had infiltrated the government. That case came along in 1948 when Nixon met Whittaker Chambers, a senior editor at *Time* magazine. Like many intellectuals, Chambers had been attracted to the Communist party in the 1930s, but unlike most intellectuals, he had become deeply involved in Communist espionage activities. He later joined the ranks of those disillusioned with the party and became as staunch an anti-Communist as he had been a fervent Communist.

Chambers told Nixon and the HUAC that during his Communist days he had become closely involved with a man named Alger Hiss. Hiss was the spy suspect

Alger Hiss Hiss listens to a question during his trial. *What made Hiss a perfect villain for Communist-hunting politicians?*

Red hunters dreamed of catching. He had served in influential positions in government and society. If it could be proved that Hiss was a Communist, it would support the allegations that the HUAC had been making for years.

Alger Hiss was a graduate of Harvard Law School who had gained a coveted spot as clerk for Supreme Court Justice Oliver Wendell Holmes. He had served as a New Dealer under Roosevelt and had even gone to Yalta as a member of FDR's staff.

Many conservative Republicans believed that Roosevelt had sold out to the Soviet Union at Yalta, and the Hiss connection made that argument even more plausible. At the time of his arrest, Hiss was president of the Carnegie Endowment for International Peace. Peace organizations in general were highly suspect as instruments for "softening" the United States, so the Soviets could take over the nation by surprise. Hiss was the perfect target for the HUAC.

The Role of Whittaker Chambers

Chambers had been seeking an audience for his accusations against Hiss for almost a decade by the time he was introduced to Nixon. The FBI had investigated the case and had been unable to make much of the charges by Chambers. FDR heard about the allegations and dismissed them. A New York grand jury failed to bring an indictment against Alger Hiss.

Now Chambers told Nixon that Hiss had been, and probably still was, a high-ranking Communist party operative. In highly publicized hearings, Nixon staked his personal career on the guilt of Hiss and the integrity of Chambers. Showing talents honed as a high school and college debater and as an experienced lawyer, Nixon bore down on Hiss and discredited him with a style of questioning that observers called both brilliant and ruthless. At first Hiss denied ever knowing Chambers. Then, confronted with Chambers in person, Hiss lost his composure and admitted having known Chambers under another name.

Although the FBI continued its investigation of Hiss, the attorney general's office did not yet have sufficient evidence from Chambers to press its case against Hiss in the hearings. The story seemed to end there, with Hiss's reputation smeared but with nothing proven.

Proof in a Pumpkin Patch?

It was at this point that the case took its most bizarre turn. Late in 1948 two investigators visited Chambers's farm in Maryland, and Chambers, who had not

POSTWAR ANTICOMMUNISM, 1947–1954

March 1947
Federal Employee Loyalty Program established.

January 1950
Hiss is convicted of perjury.

August 1950
Rosenbergs are arrested for espionage.

May–June 1954
Army/McCarthy hearings are held.

| 1947 | 1948 | 1949 | 1950 | 1951 | 1952 | 1953 | 1954 |

August 1948
HUAC takes on Hiss case.

June 1950 War breaks out in Korea.

September 1950
McCarran Act is passed.

June 1953
Rosenbergs are executed.

December 1954
McCarthy is censured.

previously accused Hiss of engaging in espionage, suddenly said: "I think I have what you're looking for." Taking the investigators out to a pumpkin patch, he rummaged through the pumpkins, finally finding the one for which he was looking. As his guests watched in amazement, Chambers dramatically pulled off the top, reached into the pumpkin, and pulled out a roll of microfilm.

The microfilm showed copies of secret State Department documents that became known in national headlines as the Pumpkin Papers. Some documents had been copied on a typewriter that was eventually traced to Alger Hiss.

This was the bombshell Nixon and the HUAC had been looking for. The committee hearings led the courts to take up the case against Alger Hiss again. He could no longer be tried for espionage, since the alleged spying had taken place so long before. Hiss was convicted in 1950 on two counts of perjury and sentenced to five years in prison.

Many books have been written debating Hiss's guilt or innocence. In many he is portrayed as a man who destroyed himself, partly with statements like: "Until the day I die, I shall wonder how Whittaker Chambers got into my house to use my typewriter." When he made the statement in court, laughter erupted in the room. Alger Hiss was a ruined man.

Richard Nixon emerged the real victor in the case. The press, which initially supported Hiss, wound up running dramatic pictures of Nixon scrutinizing the microfilm and making tough public statements about the case. He became identified as a relentless pursuer of Communist subversion. In his memoirs Nixon explains, regarding his later decision to run for the Senate, "I recognized the worth of the nationwide publicity that the Hiss case had given me—publicity on a scale that most congressmen only dream of achieving."

Truman Joins the Red Hunt

Compared with FDR, Harry Truman had a far greater suspicion and dislike of Communists. His own rhetoric about "the enemy within" contributed to the fears of subversion, but he was forced into taking an even stronger, highly public stand on the subject to defend himself against the accusations of headline-hunting congressmen.

Responding to the label of being "soft," Truman in 1947 instituted the Federal Employee Loyalty Program,

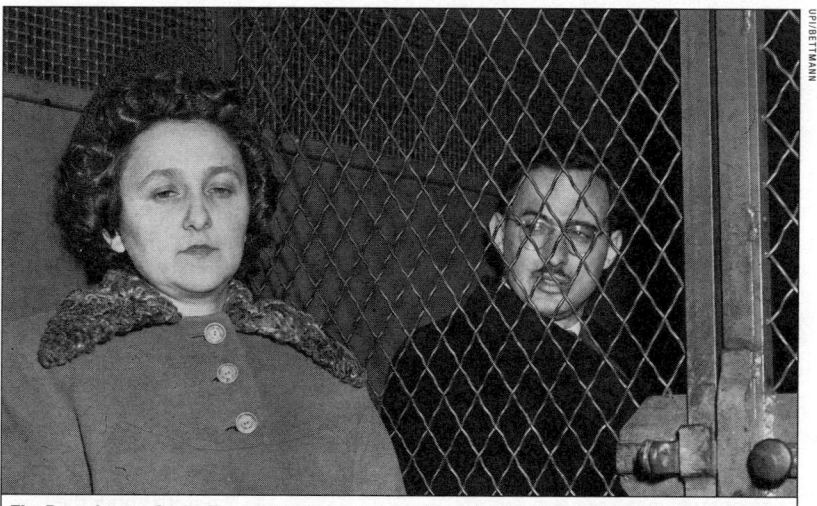

UPI/BETTMANN

The Rosenbergs On April 5, 1951, Ethel and Julius Rosenberg were convicted of spying for the Soviet Union. *Why did Truman join the Red Hunt?*

Portfolio Project

Writing Ask students to prepare questions they would like to ask Alger Hiss and Richard Nixon about their statements and actions toward each other between 1948 and 1950.

Encourage students to make their questions precise and detailed. When students are finished, ask them to place their work in their portfolios.

Facts on File

Landmark Documents in American History Have students review "McCarran Act (Internal Security Act of 1950, Subversive Activities Control Act), 1950," and "Senate Censure of Joseph McCarthy, 1954" and write a paragraph about the intent of one of the documents.

Nuclear Fission The first nuclear weapons produced energy through fission, in which an atomic nucleus splits into fragments. In 1952 the United States began making more powerful weapons that produced energy through fusion, in which nuclei combine to form more massive nuclei.

The Red Scare Women demonstrate against the conviction of Ethel and Julius Rosenberg. *What message do these demonstrators want to send?*

designed to evaluate the loyalty of government employees. Although the program had checks meant to protect individuals' rights, it was often abused by ambitious officials.

Under the program, even the slightest suspicion of disloyalty or the slimmest connection to a Communist party member was enough to put a government worker out of a job. Employees were suspect for openly criticizing American foreign policy, advocating equal rights for women, owning books on socialism, and attending foreign films. Others lost jobs because of associations or former associations with radicals, or because they belonged to a group classified as dangerous. From 1947 to 1951 a "loyalty board" investigated more than 3 million government employees; nearly 3,000 were forced to resign, and 212 were fired. Yet the probes uncovered no positive proof of subversion or espionage.

To many in Congress, Truman's anti-Communist measures were not enough. So in 1950 Congress passed its own tough law, the McCarran Act. This act did not directly outlaw the Communist party but made it illegal for Americans to engage in activities that would create a Communist government. It required Communist organizations to register with the federal government. Communists were not allowed to work in defense plants or to obtain United States passports.

Truman vetoed the McCarran Act, declaring, "In a free country, we punish men for crimes they commit, but never for the opinions they hold." Congress easily overrode the veto.

Seeking United States Secrets

On the heels of the Hiss conviction, a new case broke into the headlines and served to heighten people's fears of Communist espionage. In 1950 a young British scientist, Klaus Fuchs, admitted he had handed over to the Soviets American government specifications for the manufacture of the atomic bomb. A bizarre series of circumstances led investigators to Ethel and Julius Rosenberg, a New York City couple who had likely been members of the Communist party.

The government charged the Rosenbergs with conspiracy in a plot that prosecutors said was intended to transmit top secret bomb specifications to the Soviets. Ethel's brother, a soldier stationed at the Manhattan Project in New Mexico, accused the Rosenbergs of recruiting him to collect the information. The couple were convicted and sentenced to death.

On June 19, 1953, at 8:06 P.M., Julius Rosenberg walked calmly into the electric chair chamber at Sing Sing prison in New York State. Moments later, his wife Ethel followed him. A reporter who witnessed the executions said of Ethel afterward that she had "gone to meet her maker, and would have a lot of explaining to do."

Ethel and Julius Rosenberg died protesting their innocence. Appeals and worldwide protests failed to save them. Ethel's brother served 10 years of a 15-year sentence.

The Rosenbergs had frequently been offered a deal: Testify against others and avoid the death penalty. "Since we are guilty of no crime, we will not be party to the nefarious plot to bear false witness against other innocent progressives to heighten hysteria in our land," Julius wrote.

Ever since, in books, movies, and magazine and newspaper articles, people have been trying to uncover the truth about the Rosenbergs. Arguments abound on both sides, but recently released Soviet documents seem to confirm the Rosenbergs' guilt.

Extending the Content

The Rosenbergs Julius Rosenberg, an electrical engineer, was an active member of the Communist party in 1939. In 1940 he began working for the United States Army. In 1945 the Army fired him for being a Communist. Ethel Rosenberg's brother worked for the Army on the atomic bomb project at Los Alamos, New Mexico, and is said to have given the Rosenbergs secret information. Recent documents released in Russia seem to support the evidence that the Rosenbergs delivered atomic secrets to the Soviets.

The McCarthy Era
Unfounded Accusations Ruin Many

Even before Ethel and Julius Rosenberg had been arrested and charged with spying for the Soviet Union in July 1950, Senator Joseph McCarthy took up the anti-Communist cause. McCarthy had impressed few people in his first three years in Congress, which began in 1947. The congressional press corps sized him up as a small-time politician. He drank too much and could get offensive and even violent at times. He was not well liked; but he learned how to be feared.

On February 9, 1950, McCarthy stood up at a Republican women's club meeting in Wheeling, West Virginia, waved some papers in the air, and announced he had a list of 205 Communists working in the State Department. In follow-up investigations of McCarthy's claim, he wavered on the exact number—from 205 to 81 to 57 to "a lot." His basic theme, however, remained the same: Communists thrived in Truman's administration. They had to be rooted out. Joe McCarthy was the one to do it.

McCarthy never produced a shred of credible evidence; however, in hearings and public statements, he attacked and ruined official after official of the United States government. Almost nobody was safe from his accusations. The accused either resigned under a cloud of suspicion or were fired as security risks.

These accusatory, anti-Communist times were named after the Wisconsin senator. They became known as "the McCarthy era." He gave a new word, *McCarthyism,* to the language. It referred to the use of intimidation and often unfounded accusations in the name of fighting communism.

Despite his tactics, McCarthy won considerable public support, at least at first. Millions of Americans believed that he was fighting a lonely battle—that he was a patriot challenging traitors and subversives. He was making the country safe for democracy.

FYI

Unsubstantiated Claims McCarthy's source for his accusations against the State Department were lists that he claimed contained the names of Communists and Communist sympathizers. Yet McCarthy was unable or unwilling to clarify the sources and contents of his lists, which called into question the validity of his charges.

Global Connection

In 1945 the United States exploded the first atomic bomb in New Mexico. The Soviet Union tested its first atomic bomb in 1949. China, France, Great Britain, and India have also exploded nuclear weapons.

TELEVISION AND SENATOR McCARTHY

Joseph McCarthy came to power just as television began to appear in the American home. During the decade following McCarthy's first election to the United States Senate, TV began to usurp radio and newspapers as the country's essential transmitter of news and information. By 1956, 8 out of 10 American families owned a television.

Number of TVs Purchased (in millions)

1946: McCarthy Elected to United States Senate
In the midst of a nationwide postwar Red Scare, McCarthy arrives in Washington. By the end of the term, he will have masterfully united the new medium of television and the country's fear of communism.

1948: Presidential Election Returns Broadcast on TV
As Harry Truman is reelected, a Gallup Poll reports that 73% of all Americans expect a war against the Communists.

1950: McCarthy Alleges "205 Communists in the State Department"
In February the previously unknown senator waves papers that he claims name Communists inside the United States government. Although the list never materializes, many Americans take the senator's claims seriously.

1953: Murrow Confronts McCarthy
Edward R. Murrow, one of the nation's most respected news commentators, launches the documentary series *See It Now.* More than 2 million households watch Murrow devote 4 programs to McCarthy's investigations; calls and letters run 8-to-1 against the senator.

1954: McCarthy vs. the Army
Television broadcasts 36 days of hearings as Senator McCarthy charges the United States Army with subversion. Such exposure of his tactics turns public sentiment against him, and by year's end his colleagues censure him for conduct "contrary to Senate traditions."

1946 | 1947 | 1948 | 1949 | 1950 | 1951 | 1952 | 1953 | 1954 | 1955 | 1956

McCarthy's media savvy helped him take advantage of the new medium of television. *How many televisions did Americans own in 1954?*

GRAPH STUDY

Television and Senator McCarthy McCarthy used the new medium of television to spread his message effectively during numerous hearings and public statements.

Answer: *Approximately 30 million televisions were purchased in 1954.*

Cultural Perspectives

Debate Patrick McCarran, who sponsored the McCarran Act in 1950, sponsored in 1952 the *Immigration and Nationality Act.* This act tightened controls over aliens and immigrants in the United States. Controversy still exists today over United States policies regarding aliens and immigrants. Organize the class into two teams to debate this issue. One team, assuming the role of a recent immigrant, should research and support reasons for relaxing immigration controls. The other team should research and support reasons for tightening controls. Teams should divide up the work, plan their arguments and counterarguments, and then conduct the debate.

VISUAL INSTRUCTION

McCarthyism A capacity crowd heard Senator McCarthy criticize American participation in the United Nations, NATO, and other foreign alliances (1956). **Answer:** *the United States Army*

Curriculum Connection

Psychology Have students research and write about the mass hysteria that contributed to the hunt for Communists in the United States in the 1950s. What fears did people have that made them so worried about Communist infiltration?

ASSESS

Meeting Lesson Objectives

Each section objective is tested by the section review question(s) that follows it in parentheses.

1. Analyze the causes and effects surrounding the rise of anti-Communist sentiment and the phenomenon of McCarthyism. (1, 2, 3, 4, 5)
2. Describe how blacklisting affected American society. (1, 2, 3)

The Senate subcommittee on investigations, of which McCarthy became chairman in 1953, provided him with an official forum from which to launch public attacks on government employees. His was not the only show in town. Numerous other congressmen conducted their own hearings and investigations, and the HUAC's activities continued as well.

For Republicans, McCarthy was a loose cannon, and his conservative colleagues often distanced themselves from him, except when it suited their own purposes. Although few people liked him, some took advantage of his talent for keeping himself and his issue in the spotlight.

In his highly public role, the senator accumulated enormous power. At the height of his power, he could make politicians, bank presidents, network executives, and average citizens quake. For a long time, few people dared challenge him. Harry Truman, in his retirement, acknowledged the extent of McCarthy's hold on the nation's affairs:

> M cCarthyism . . . the meaning of the word is the corruption of truth, the abandonment of our historical devotion to fair play. It is the abandonment of 'due process' of law. It is the use of the big lie and the unfounded accusation against any citizen in the name of Americanism and security. . . .
>
> This horrible cancer is eating at the vitals of America and it can destroy the great edifice of freedom.
> —Harry S Truman, radio and TV address,
> November 17, 1953

McCarthy's rise to power was swift and heady. The senator eventually grew reckless with it, throwing accusations around fearlessly—but also, many noted, with a growing sense that if he ever ran out of names to smear, his bubble would burst.

McCarthy Goes Too Far

That is just what happened. McCarthy went too far. When President Eisenhower took office in 1953, he decided to ignore the senator as much as possible, hoping McCarthy would do himself in. In addition, Eisenhower did not want to offend conservatives in his own party by engaging in a risky battle with one of their own.

Hunting for ever more sensational targets, McCarthy hurled his next accusations against the United States Army in 1954; and the army was ready. Meeting the senator's unsupported allegations with a quiet presentation of the facts, army attorney Joseph Welch calmly shredded McCarthy's charges of a Communist conspiracy in the United States Army. To a nation watching the subcommittee hearings on TV, Welch presented an intelligent contrast to McCarthy's sensational theatrics. McCarthy sealed his own fate.

A political cartoon of the time showed McCarthy trapped in a spider's web, crying, "I can't do this to me!" He did, though, along with a growing number of opponents who broke their silence to take a public stand against him. In 1954 the Senate voted to condemn McCarthy.

When the senator died in 1957, sickened from alcohol and exhaustion, few people mourned. Many hoped an era had died with him—but it had not.

AP/WIDE WOLRD PHOTOS

McCarthyism Joseph McCarthy acknowledges the cheers of a flag-waving crowd at New York's Carnegie Hall. *Who did McCarthy accuse in 1954?*

Critical Thinking

Assessing Outcomes The McCarthy era officially ended with McCarthy's death in 1957. In the end, few spies were purged from the United States government. Yet for many people the impact of McCarthy was felt for a lifetime. During the 1950s, thousands of workers in hundreds of industries lost their jobs because of false accusations of Communist sympathies. Why do students think even McCarthy's fellow conservatives kept their distance from McCarthy? *(because he was a volatile, sometimes irrational person, who they feared could as easily accuse them of being a Communist as he accused others)*

The Red Hunt Goes On
Spying on Neighbors Encouraged

Just as Red hunting did not begin with McCarthy, it did not end with him, either. The business of spying on neighbors, friends, teachers, even clergy had spread throughout the society. Government films and brochures urged citizens to expose anyone they suspected of having Communist leanings.

The McCarthy era spawned hundreds of watchdog groups run by private citizens. The motives and methods of these **vigilantes**—self-appointed doers of justice—could be vicious and were often illegal. John Henry Faulk found this out the hard way in 1957, the year of McCarthy's death.

A Texan with a quick mind and an affection for radical ideas, Faulk had a radio program in New York City in which he dispensed his own brand of whimsy and humor. In the mid-1950s Faulk was elected vice president of a local chapter of the American Federation of Television and Radio Actors. He won partly because of his stand against **blacklisting,** the effort by conservative groups to brand people as Communists and prevent them from holding jobs. One such group, called AWARE, had ruined the careers of many performers, and Faulk and others sought to stem the group's influence. AWARE responded with a nasty campaign to associate Faulk with communism. It then pressured the advertisers on Faulk's radio show to cancel their ads. Faced with negative publicity and the loss of advertising dollars, CBS fired Faulk.

Faulk countered with a lawsuit against AWARE that took 6 years to settle. In 1963 a jury awarded him $3.5 million in damages, although the award was reduced to $550,000 on appeal. In the meantime, Faulk could find no work for years. His career had been effectively ruined. Ironically, years later CBS made a highly successful television movie sympathetically dramatizing the Faulk story.

The legacy of the Red hunters had by then faded—but did not disappear completely. There remained the living memory of the thousands of people who had been smeared, blacklisted, and ostracized. In 1963 when Faulk's name was finally cleared, the memory of such things was still very fresh.

As late as 1960, for instance, city and state employees all over the country were forced to swear to and sign an oath of loyalty. In Massachusetts, teachers had to make the following promise:

> I do solemnly swear or affirm that I will uphold and defend the Constitution of the United States of America and the Commonwealth of Massachusetts and that I will oppose the overthrow of the govern-

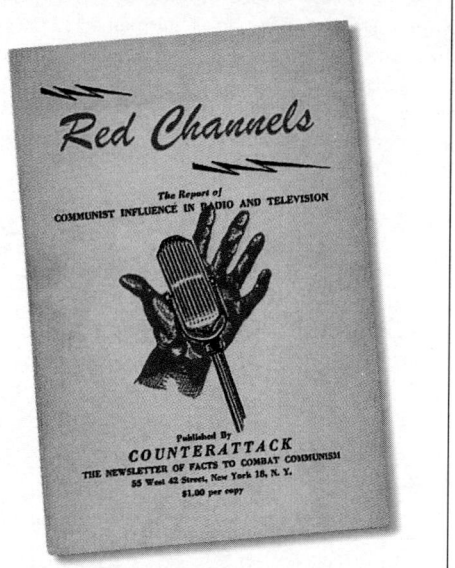

The Red Hunt Vigilante groups published brochures such as this to expose suspected Communists. *Why was John Henry Faulk accused of being a Communist?*

ment of the United States of America or of the Commonwealth by force or violence or any illegal or unconstitutional method: I am not a member of the Communist party.

> Subscribed by me under penalty of perjury, this ___ day of _____ , 1960.

SECTION REVIEW

Vocabulary

1. Define: vigilante, blacklisting.

Checking Facts

2. Give two examples of the government's response to growing fears of communism.

3. In what ways did Communist-hunting continue after McCarthy?

Critical Thinking

Distinguishing Fact From Opinion

4. Given the nation's preoccupation with communism, what can you conclude about the stereotype of Communists prevalent at the time?

Linking Across Time

5. How did Richard Nixon's career benefit from the fear of communism before the Alger Hiss case?

SECTION TWO **647**

VISUAL INSTRUCTION

The Red Hunt Conservative groups tried to brand people as Communists and sway public opinion by distributing anti-Communist literature such as *Red Channels.*

Answer: *because of his stand against blacklisting.*

Evaluate

Have students complete the Section Review.

Assign the Section 2 Quiz or use the Testmaker to develop a customized quiz. (Also in Spanish.) **LEP**

Reteach

Have students listen to the Chapter 19, Section 2 Audiocassette. (Also in Spanish.) **LEP**

Enrich

Have students complete the Chapter 19 Geography in History Activity.

CLOSE

Ask students these questions: What was the significance of the Hiss case? *(It showed how frightened government officials were of spies, and it made Nixon well known.)* What evidence did McCarthy have to support his charges? *(none that he produced)* How did politicians show they were not soft on communism? *(by passing the McCarran Act and the Federal Employee Loyalty Program).*

Section 2 Review Answers

1. vigilante (647), **blacklisting** (647)
2. reactivating the House Un-American Activities Committee and beginning the Federal Employee Loyalty Program in 1947
3. Vigilante groups remained active, and the government produced anti-Communist films and brochures.

4. People thought liberal intellectuals were possibly Communists.
5. In his congressional campaign of 1946, Nixon claimed there were Communists within the Democratic administration.

TEACH

Making the Historical Connection

Review with students the causes and effects of postwar anti-Communism. *(Causes: the Soviet development of the atomic bomb, the spread of communism worldwide, the scare tactics of some politicians; Effects: reactivating the House Un-American Activities Committee, beginning the Federal Employee Loyalty Program)* Then briefly discuss with students the cases of Alger Hiss, the Rosenbergs, and John Henry Faulk. Ask students what, if anything, these people could have done to protect themselves from the charges against them.

Turning Point

The Hollywood Ten pleaded the First Amendment and remained silent as a protest against questions they believed the HUAC had no right to ask (such as whether or not they had ever been members of the Communist party). The Ten were jailed for contempt of Congress.

Turning Point
The Hollywood Ten

OCTOBER, 1947

TRANSCRIPT

Robert Stripling [Chief Investigator]: Mr. Lawson, are you now or have you ever been a member of the Communist party of the United States?

John Howard Lawson [Screenwriter #1]: The question of Communism is in no way related to this inquiry, which is an attempt to get control of the screen and to invade the basic rights of American citizens in all fields.

Ring Lardner, Jr. [Screenwriter #2]: I could answer that question, but I'd hate myself in the morning.

J. Parnell Thomas [Committee Chairman]: Any real American would be proud to answer that question.

The Case

Congress formed the House Un-American Activities Committee (HUAC) in the late 1930s to combat extremist movements. Following World War II, the committee became concerned about Communists in Hollywood. In 1947 the committee obtained membership files of the Communist party in Hollywood and subpoenaed prominent writers and directors on the list to ask them what the committee already knew—whether they had ever been members of the Communist party. During the committee hearings, the following witnesses became known in the press as the Hollywood Ten:

- Alvah Bessie, screenwriter
- Herbert Biberman, screenwriter and director
- Lester Cole, screenwriter
- Edward Dmytryk, director
- Ring Lardner, Jr., screenwriter
- John Howard Lawson, screenwriter
- Albert Maltz, screenwriter
- Samuel Ornitz, screenwriter
- Adrian Scott, screenwriter and producer
- Dalton Trumbo, screenwriter

The committee had no legal power to prosecute, and it was not illegal to belong to the Communist party. In the words of Chairman J. Parnell Thomas, the committee's goal was to "uncover the truth and let Hollywood and the American public do the rest."

The Background

From the mid-1930s to the mid-1950s, about 300 film directors, actors, writers, and designers, along with many people in other walks of life, joined the Communist party. Interest in Communist philosophy grew among people who had doubts about

The Case at a Glance

| In the 1930s communism grows in popularity in the United States. | After World War II, the fear of communism increases dramatically. | The HUAC obtains the files of the Hollywood Communist party. | The HUAC subpoenas 10 Hollywood writers and directors. |

capitalism and felt that it led to the exploitation of workers. Communism seemed to promise improved conditions for workers and equity for people of all races. Joining the party was popular in the 1930s, when being a Communist often meant being concerned about workers' rights and about racism. By the late 1930s, many craft unions in the film industry were formed, and the Communist party was involved in a struggle for workers' benefits. During World War II, the Communists in the Soviet Union were allies of the United States against Nazi Germany. Before and during World War II, the federal government encouraged Hollywood movie moguls to make upbeat movies about the Soviet Union so that Americans would support the fight against the Nazis.

With the defeat of Germany and the end of World War II, however, attitudes toward the Soviet Union began to shift. Americans became increasingly fearful of Soviet leader Joseph Stalin and his interest in the spread of communism worldwide. As the cold war heightened, tolerance of communism dissolved. Stalin's repressive tactics against his people caused many party members to quit. Although membership in the Communist party was never illegal, the party lost popularity.

People became worried that Communists were influencing many aspects of American society. They suspected that Communists in Hollywood were not just working to secure the rights of workers, but also to control the content of films. The federal government now encouraged movies showing Communists in a bad light and depicting the Soviet Union as an enemy. In this atmosphere, the House Un-American Activities Committee decided to turn a spotlight on Hollywood and investigate Communists in the movie business. The probe was a way to influence the movie industry and gain publicity for the HUAC.

The Opinions

People in Hollywood were divided on whether to cooperate with the HUAC. Some Hollywood witnesses who appeared before the committee were people who saw evidence of Communist activity around them. The committee responded favorably to these "friendly witnesses." Those less willing to cooperate with the committee received less cordial treatment. These people were termed "unfriendly witnesses."

There has been a small group within the Screen Actors Guild which has consistently opposed the policy of the Guild board and officers of the Guild. . . . That small clique . . . has been suspected of more or less following the tactics that we associate with the Communist Party.

Ronald Reagan, president of the Screen Actors Guild

I am convinced that these Hollywood Commies are agents of a foreign country. If I have any doubt that they are [Communists], then I haven't any mind.

Sam Wood, producer and director

Today J. Parnell Thomas is engaged in a personally conducted smear campaign of the motion picture industry. . . . Silence the artist and you have silenced the most articulate voice the people have.

Katharine Hepburn, movie star

You [the committee] are using the old technique . . . to create a scare . . . in order that you can smear the motion picture industry . . . . The Bill of Rights was established . . . to prevent the operation of any committee which could invade the basic rights of Americans.

John Howard Lawson, screenwriter

CASE STUDY **649**

FYI

The HUAC The House Un-American Activities Committee gained fame in 1948 during its investigation of Communists in the Department of State, which led to the conviction of Alger Hiss. Later, the HUAC looked into Communist influence in almost all areas of life. As a result, many employees had to take loyalty oaths, and some were blacklisted.

The committee's critics charged that it abused its power and violated the constitutional rights of witnesses. They thought witnesses should have the right to cross-examine their accusers. Others believed that looking for Communist conspirators was the responsibility of the police, the FBI, or the courts. Supreme Court rulings in the 1950s and 1960s curbed the committee's activities. For example, the Court ruled that witnesses may refuse to answer questions unrelated to matters under investigation.

| The Ten plead the First Amendment and refuse to answer questions. | → | The Ten are jailed for contempt of Congress. |

Turning Point

Analyzing the Case

Have students read the case study up to and including The Options.

1. What were the benefits and costs of cooperating with the HUAC? *(If they answered yes, they would be at the mercy of the committee. They might have to reveal names of others. If they answered no, they could be charged with perjury if it were proven that they did not tell the truth.)*

2. In light of the history of the United States, is the statement by John Howard Lawson accurate? How have interpretations of the Bill of Rights differed over time? *(The Supreme Court has ruled that freedom of speech may be limited when its expression creates a clear and present danger to society. What is dangerous to society is open to interpretation.)*

3. Which of the four options presented was likely to have the most serious legal consequences? Moral consequences? Career consequences? *(Answering no could open a person up to a charge of perjury, which carried the greatest penalty; answering yes might open a person up to revealing information about other writers; pleading the Fifth Amendment might be seen as an admission of guilt and destroy a writer's career.)*

Notes

_____
_____
_____
_____
_____
_____
_____
_____

The press reported on the witnesses and committee members alike and publicized the time the HUAC Chairman Thomas smashed a gavel to splinters while calling for order. On the editorial page of the *New York Times*, the hearings themselves were deplored:

> Finally, an investigation of this kind, once begun, has no ready stopping-place. One of the Government's witnesses has already declared that Broadway is worse than Hollywood in the matter of Communist penetration, and that the reading departments of the publishing houses are "very, very heavily infiltrated with Communists." Are we now to go on from Hollywood to Broadway, and then from Broadway to the publishing houses, searching for suspects all along the line, and after that carry the hunt into the radio and then into the . . . press?
>
> —*New York Times*

The Options

Witnesses who appeared before the HUAC were asked, "Are you now or have you ever been a member of the Communist party?" When responding, the witnesses had several options.

1. Refuse to answer on the grounds that Congress has no authority to investigate behavior protected by the First Amendment, the right to freedom of speech and thought. The witnesses' lawyers warned that this response might bring a charge of contempt of Congress because the Supreme Court had established Congress's right to inquire. The Hollywood Ten maintained that Congress could not legislate away the First Amendment of the Bill of Rights and, therefore, had no right to investigate where they could not legislate.

2. Refuse to answer, pleading the Fifth Amendment, which gives people the right not to testify against themselves. Using this tactic was assumed by many to be an admission of Communist party membership.

3. Answer yes and place themselves at the mercy of the committee. This tactic would make them

Nine of the Hollywood Ten await fingerprinting after their surrender.

HISTORICAL PICTURES SERVICE, CHICAGO

subject to more questions, such as requests for the names of other people in the Communist party.

4. Answer no and risk being charged with perjury if the committee proved they were not telling the truth. Perjury carried a greater penalty than contempt of Congress.

The Outcome

In October 1947 the Hollywood Ten agreed among themselves to plead the First Amendment and remain silent as a protest against questions they believed the HUAC had no right to ask.

The Ten were held in contempt of Congress for refusing to testify. In December 1947 a grand jury indicted them and found them guilty of contempt. The appeals process ran until 1950, when the Supreme Court refused to hear the case and let the verdict stand. The Ten served jail terms of about one year.

In one of the ironies of history, some of the Hollywood Ten and Chairman Thomas would meet again. A newspaper columnist discovered that Thomas had raised the salaries of his staff members in return for payments, or kickbacks, from the grateful employees. Thomas was indicted for fraud and pleaded no contest. He was fined $10,000 and served a 9-month sentence in the same prison in which some of the Hollywood Ten were confined.

Cooperative Learning

Research Organize students into small groups. Each group should identify and answer one broad question about the Hollywood Ten case and share its answer with the class. Possible questions include the following: Was communism really a threat in the 1940s? Can movies influence public attitudes enough to make them a threat? Does the government have the right to influence the arts? Within each group, individual students should be responsible for finding particular information to help answer the group's question. 📖

Hollywood celebrities protest the tactics of the HUAC's investigation into alleged Hollywood communism.

HISTORICAL PICTURES SERVICE, CHICAGO

In December 1947, one week after the Hollywood Ten were cited for contempt, the film industry fired them. The industry, facing a serious economic crisis, desperately needed favorable publicity. Industry officials hoped that firing the Ten would boost Hollywood's image.

Fifty top film executives met at the Waldorf-Astoria Hotel in New York City. After two days of conferences, they fired the Hollywood Ten and released a statement saying, "We will not knowingly employ a Communist."

In addition to the jail sentences and firings, the Hollywood Ten were blacklisted. Many were unable to find any work in the film industry for the next 10 years. Others, like Ring Lardner, Jr., could work only under pseudonyms. The Hollywood Ten were not the only ones to be penalized, however.

Some of the Ten's colleagues stood up for them. Famous actors, such as Gene Kelly, Judy Garland, and Humphrey Bogart, took part in benefits and speeches on behalf of the Ten. Because of their support, these actors' reputations were also tainted. MGM Studios received so many letters criticizing Katharine Hepburn that they told the famous actress they could not use her in films again until public opinion of her improved.

The Significance

The HUAC hearings on communism in Hollywood ended a few days after the Ten refused to testify. Four years later in 1951, the HUAC again investigated communism in the film industry. This time witnesses pleaded the Fifth Amendment to avoid contempt charges. The committee sent no one to jail, but the industry again responded by denying work to 250 actors, writers, and directors.

Following the HUAC hearings, there was a noticeable increase in the number of movies with an anti-Communist point of view. By some estimates, between 1947 and 1954 more than 50 films were released preaching the view that Communists were the enemies of the United States.

The Hollywood Ten decided to go to prison rather than submit to questioning from the HUAC. They believed that the United States Constitution protected them from having to answer to the committee. Screenwriter Dalton Trumbo expressed his feelings about the experience in this poem, which he wrote to his family from prison:

> **S**ay then but this of me:
> Preferring not to crawl on his knees
> In freedom to a bowl of buttered slops
> Set out for him by some contemptuous clown,
> He walked to jail on his feet.

RESPONDING TO THE CASE

1. List reasons the House Un-American Activities Committee felt it needed to investigate communism in the Hollywood film industry. List the arguments of the Hollywood Ten for not answering the committee's questions. Explain which side appears to have the stronger position.

2. How might the Hollywood Ten have responded to the committee's questions without showing contempt but at the same time remain true to their beliefs in the freedom of thought guaranteed in the Bill of Rights?

3. What might have happened if the Hollywood Ten had testified at the HUAC hearings?

 PORTFOLIO PROJECT

The First Amendment of the Bill of Rights guarantees a person's freedom of speech and thought. Do you think the Hollywood Ten's First Amendment rights were violated by the HUAC? Explain your reasoning. What dangers or benefits do you see in clamping down on unpopular opinions?

CASE STUDY **651**

 Turning Point CASE STUDY

 Curriculum Connection

Art The government's role in the arts is still being debated. In 1990 United States senator Orrin Hatch headed a movement in Congress to stop government funding of the National Endowment for the Arts (NEA). Some of the artists being supported by the NEA were criticized for producing works that many thought were obscene.

Block Scheduling

The Portfolio Project on this page provides an excellent opportunity to enrich and extend the key elements of this case study.

CLOSE

Hold a class discussion about blacklisting. What are some reasons people give to justify blacklisting? *(to prevent information or ideas dangerous to the public from being presented)* What are reasons people are opposed to blacklisting? *(It is unfair to prejudge people who have not done anything harmful, simply because of their political or religious beliefs.)*

Responding to the Case Answers

1. HUAC wanted assurances that Hollywood would produce movies that depicted communism unfavorably, and the hearings would give the HUAC added publicity. Members of the Hollywood Ten said that the HUAC was unlawfully investigating matters protected by the Bill of Rights. Students' answers should show understanding of both sides of the issue.

2. They could have pleaded the Fifth Amendment, but many considered that doing so would be an implicit admission of Communist party membership.

3. The Hollywood Ten might have been asked to renounce any affiliation that they had with the Communist party. This act may have prevented jail terms and assured steady work in Hollywood, but the artists would have compromised their personal integrity.

SECTION

3

The Eisenhower Years

APRIL 5, 1954: PRESIDENT EISENHOWER ADDRESSES THE NATION

HIS WAS A VOICE OF REASON IN AN UNREASONABLE AGE. He had the inner assurance and five-star strength of a man who had met the enemy and won. When he spoke, people felt that things might come out all right, if they would all pull together, as they had on the battlefields of Europe during World War II.

Dwight David Eisenhower won the confidence of the American people. Maybe it had something to do with the innocent smile he wore when he held up a big fish he had just caught; or the commanding presence one saw in his eyes; or his baldish dome, which made him appear taller than he was. Maybe it was his halting speech, which seemed to hold six decades of experience and caution in each pause.

Dwight Eisenhower was not a fist-pounding speech maker. He did not have the flair for dropping verbal bombs on an audience the way General Douglas

We Like Ike
These campaigners in San Francisco show their support for Dwight David Eisenhower, who won the confidence of the nation in the 1950s.

MacArthur and General George Patton did. Eisenhower counseled calmly, like the family doctor. He spoke to a generation of Americans who were uneasily watching communism advance on the world's continents, who built bomb shelters in their backyards and bought lead-lined suits in the naive hope of surviving a nuclear holocaust. Both his words and his tone had a soothing effect:

No one can say to you that there are no dangers. Of course there are risks, if we are not vigilant. But we do not have to be hysterical. . . . We can stand up and hold up our heads and say, "America is the greatest force that God has ever allowed to exist on his footstool." As such it is up to us to lead this world to a peaceful and secure existence.

—President Eisenhower,
radio and TV address, April 5, 1954

AS YOU READ

Vocabulary
► consensus decision making
► electronic media

Think About . . .
► the process by which Eisenhower's policy of consensus decison making worked.

► the growing role of the electronic media in politics during the 1950s.

Warrior in the White House

An Efficient Campaigner and President

The United States's favorite patriot, the supreme allied commander in Europe, had never voted in his life when the Republicans began urging him to run for the presidency in 1952. Living in Paris, General Eisenhower began reading United States history books and studying economics, but he was not quick to commit himself to a run for the White House. In fact, he even refused an offer of $40,000 from *McCall's* magazine just to say whether he was a Republican. Ike was not a man of haste. In 1952, however, he answered the call of duty to his country.

A New Kind of Campaign

Given Eisenhower's popularity and lack of involvement in political controversy, the outcome of the election was never much in doubt. The Democratic candidate, Governor Adlai E. Stevenson of Illinois, conducted a respectable, even admirable, race. The governor was a witty, eloquent speaker who appealed to liberal intellectuals, but the country as a whole was not in a liberal frame of mind in 1952.

For every voter who found Stevenson sophisticated, there were two who dubbed him and his followers eggheads. He was articulate and sophisticated, not a man who could win the average voter with a folksy style. Stevenson's greatest obstacle, however, was that he belonged to the same party as Harry Truman.

Although new to politics, Eisenhower did not lack political instincts, as shown by his choice of Senator Nixon as his running mate. By adding an experienced politician and champion of anticommunism to his ticket, Ike clinched the conservative vote and eased the fears of those who wondered about his grasp of domestic issues.

At first, however, the choice of Nixon threatened to blow up in Ike's face. Early in the campaign, a newspaper revealed the existence of a "secret fund" of contributions from citizens, which it said was used to support Nixon in an extravagant lifestyle. Some party members called for Nixon to quit the ticket.

Nixon, the prosecutor, went on the offensive. At Ike's suggestion, he took his case to the voters in a live TV broadcast on September 23, 1952. In quiet tones Nixon gave a lengthy and thorough accounting of all his financial holdings, which were quite modest. The fund, he said, was used for travel from his Washington home to California, and it was neither illegal nor immoral.

In this politically shrewd talk, he clearly implied that those who attacked him were those who opposed

Richard and Pat Nixon In his "Checkers" speech, Nixon introduced his wife, Pat, to the viewers and emphasized his family values. *How did Nixon portray his critics in his Checkers speech?*

his efforts to fight communism. Nixon did admit to one contribution for his personal use. An admirer had sent his family a dog. His young daughters loved that dog, which they named Checkers, and he was not going to give it back.

The emotional appeal from Nixon won him a wave of support from viewers. The broadcast became known as the Checkers speech. As in the Hiss case, Nixon came out on top. Calling him "my boy," Ike embraced Nixon, and the campaign rolled on.

Ike's election campaign resembled his military campaigns: It was organized, efficient, and determined. His speeches offered little in the way of specifics—he promised to "clean up the mess in Washington." Adlai Stevenson warned that the Republican platform was "as slippery as a bunch of eels—you can't stand on it." It did not matter. The Republicans hammered away at the themes of Truman-era weakness and incompetence—with Nixon slamming the "scandal-a-day administration," and Ike promising to go to Korea himself to put an end to the war. This was what voters wanted to hear. "We like Ike" echoed in the auditoriums of the country, and the Republicans marched on to victory. The 1952 election was not so much a win for the Republican party as it was a measure of the personal popularity of the smiling hero of World War II.

A New Command

A seasoned soldier knows that in battle lives depend not only on good generals but also on the cooperative efforts of every fighter. It is no surprise, then, that

SECTION THREE **653**

GLENCOE
TECHNOLOGY

Great Speeches

Volume II–Richard Nixon ("Checkers" Speech)

 Facts on File

Landmark Documents in American History Have students review "Checkers Speech, Richard Nixon, 1952" and write a paragraph about the intent of the document.

VISUAL INSTRUCTION

Richard and Pat Nixon In his "Checkers" speech, Richard Nixon told stories that underscored frugality and plainness. At one point, Nixon said about his wife, Pat: "Pat doesn't have a mink coat. But she does have a respectable Republican cloth coat, and I always tell her that she would look good in anything."

Answer: *Nixon portrayed his critics as opposing his efforts to fight communism.*

TEACH

Guided Practice

L2 **Recalling Facts** Ask students what they remember about Eisenhower and his role in World War II. List this information on the chalkboard, and ask students to evaluate whether they would expect him to be successful as a President.

Cooperative Learning

Dramatization Organize the class into pairs of students. In each pair, one student should assume the role of Richard Nixon and one should assume the role of a reporter. They can conduct an interview that could have taken place during the 1952 presidential campaign.

Choose a few pairs of students to present their interviews to the class. Then have the class discuss the interviews as you list on the chalkboard issues that were important to voters in the 1952 campaign.

653

President Eisenhower used **consensus decision making,** a management style based on group efforts, to solve problems. "No one has a monopoly on the truth," he declared.

Eisenhower had a clear vision of what he thought was right, and he was comfortable in an administrative role. He focused on major issues only, delegating other matters to his advisers. Everything moved through proper channels in the new administration.

The President had great respect for successful business leaders, and he was convinced that the country would function best on proven business principles. In fact, he named corporate executives to most key posts in his administration. To the government's regulatory agencies, he appointed business leaders friendly to the industries they were supposed to regulate.

One of President Eisenhower's major initiatives during his first term in office was to encourage private development of hydroelectric and nuclear power plants. He unsuccessfully urged Congress to turn over to private companies the operation of one New Deal program, the Tennessee Valley Authority. He did, however, approve the Atomic Energy Act of 1954, which allowed private companies to operate nuclear power plants. The first nuclear-powered generator to produce electricity for public use began operation in Arco, Idaho, in 1955.

Ike unwaveringly followed "middle of the road" policies. Political observers increasingly criticized his emphasis on consensus decision making as cumbersome and ineffective. As a columnist noted in 1959, however, "The public loves Ike. The less he does, the more they love him. That, probably, is the secret. Here is a man who doesn't rock the boat."

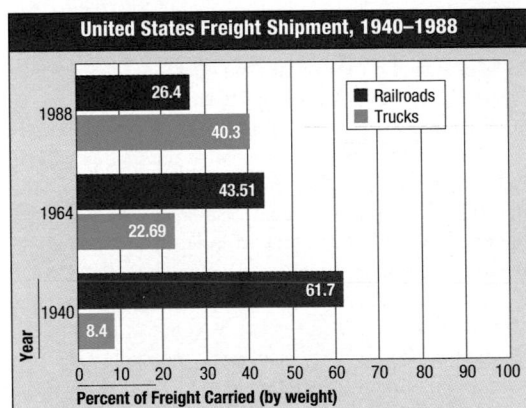

United States Freight Shipment, 1940–1988

Year	Railroads	Trucks
1988	26.4	40.3
1964	43.51	22.69
1940	61.7	8.4

Percent of Freight Carried (by weight)

From 1940 to 1988, the amount of freight that trucks carried rose. The amount that trains carried decreased. Trains, however, remained an important means of transporting freight. *How much freight was carried by trains in 1940 and in 1988?*

654 CHAPTER 19 COLD WAR POLITICS

A Second Term
Ike Builds Interstate System as Cold War Deepens

This "secret" was the strategy that successfully carried him through a second presidential race in 1956. The race was practically a rerun of 1952. Once again Eisenhower squared off against Adlai Stevenson and won.

Although the outcome of the two campaigns was the same, the tone was different. Eisenhower had suffered a heart attack in 1955 and was running a less energetic campaign on his record of "peace, progress, and prosperity." The nation still liked Ike but was lukewarm to his party. Democrats retained control of Congress in 1956.

Eisenhower's second term was notable for decisions both made and postponed. As in his first term, domestic problems took a backseat to foreign policy. Trouble threatened when Castro came to power in Cuba. Although the President had ended the Korean War, the cold war grew icier. In 1957 the Soviets shocked the United States by sending up *Sputnik I,* the first space satellite.

The United States hurried to catch up in the space race, although Eisenhower was not eager to spend too much money to do it. *Explorer I,* the country's answer to *Sputnik I,* went up less than four months later, on January 31, 1958. Later that year, Congress created the National Aeronautics and Space Administration (NASA).

Paving America

Ike was less concerned with blazing a path into space than he was with paving new roads across the nation. The second Eisenhower term witnessed the most ambitious and expensive public works program in American history: construction of the federal interstate highway system.

Eisenhower's pet program, launched in 1956, was a departure from his generally conservative approach to spending. The President believed the country needed a network of highways to increase road safety, promote commerce, and preserve the nation's unity.

Besides Ike's personal support, the program had the backing of a powerful coalition that included oil companies, automobile and rubber manufacturers, letter carriers, bakers, truckers, and other groups. All stood to benefit from the road building.

Congress appropriated $32 billion to build 41,000 miles (65,969 km) of highways. Ten years later, cars and trucks crisscrossed the nation along the world's finest highway system. The final cost was more than $80 billion.

Ike's Legacy

Ike described himself as "conservative when it comes to money and liberal when it comes to human beings." During his terms, Congress extended Social Security to cover another 7 million people and unemployment compensation to cover another 4 million people. The minimum wage increased from 75 cents per hour to $1, and federally financed housing for low-income families increased. The President also approved building the St. Lawrence Seaway, connecting the Great Lakes to the Atlantic Ocean.

By 1960 the Eisenhower administration was stalled. Lack of progress in easing the cold war was crushing to Ike. The President's health, mirroring the prestige of the nation, sank. It was an opportunity tailor-made for a young political hopeful from Massachusetts, John F. Kennedy.

In With the New
Television Gives Kennedy a Victory Over Nixon

The 1960 presidential contest between Richard Nixon, son of a California shopkeeper, and John F. Kennedy, son of a Massachusetts millionaire, pitted against each other two men and two political philosophies that seemed to offer the country a real choice.

On the surface, Kennedy versus Nixon meant Catholic versus Protestant, a member of the Harvard elite facing a self-styled middle American. It was Kennedy the spender against Nixon the fiscal conservative, the Kennedy style and wit versus the proven Nixon experience.

In reality many of these much-celebrated differences mattered little. The two men had similar opinions on foreign and domestic issues. When Nixon ran for the Senate in 1950 against Helen Gahagan Douglas, Kennedy showed up at his office with a $1,000 contribution from his father for Nixon's campaign. The Kennedys thought Douglas just as dangerously left-leaning as Nixon did.

When Kennedy advocated an armed invasion of Cuba during the campaign, he was taking just the position Nixon had privately urged under Eisenhower. Ironically, Nixon had to disagree publicly with Kennedy because he had to support his administration's view. In 1960 Kennedy was not a vigorous advocate of civil rights, and Nixon had long been a moderate on the issue.

Facts on File
Landmark Documents in American History Have students review "Kennedy-Nixon Debates, 1960" and write a paragraph about the intent of the document.

MAP STUDY
The interstate highway system committed the nation to a transportation system based primarily on motor vehicles. The highways were a boon for many industries. Yet they also led to increases in oil consumption and pollution.

Answer: *east of the Mississippi*

ASSESS

Meeting Lesson Objectives
Each section objective is tested by the section review question(s) that follows it in parentheses.

1. Explain Eisenhower's policy of consensus decision-making. (1, 2, 4)
2. Analyze the growing role of electronic media in politics. (1, 3, 5)

INTERSTATE HIGHWAYS, 1950s TO PRESENT

The construction of the present interstate highway system began under the Eisenhower administration in the 1950s. *In which regions of the United States were the most interstate highways built?*

SECTION THREE **655**

Portfolio Project

Economics Have students conduct research to identify several effects of raising the minimum wage (for example, increasing the minimum wage might increase wages for those who work, but it might also reduce the number of jobs for low-income workers). Then have students write about and support their reasons for whether the minimum wage today should be increased. Students can place their completed essays in their portfolios.

The Nixon-Kennedy Debates During the 1960 televised debates between Nixon and Kennedy, the public was influenced by Kennedy's wit and youthful appearance. *How did Nixon's whistle-stop campaign strategy hurt him in his run for the presidency?*

VISUAL INSTRUCTION

The Nixon-Kennedy Debates Kennedy and Nixon appear with moderator Howard K. Smith on a studio monitor moments before their debate on September 26, 1960.

Answer: *Nixon's whistle-stopping left him looking haggard.*

Evaluate

Have students complete the Section Review.

📁 📀 Assign the Section 3 Quiz or use the Testmaker to develop a customized quiz. (Also in Spanish.) **LEP**

📁 📀 Assign the Chapter 19 Test or use the Testmaker to develop a customized test. **LEP**

📁 Have students complete the Chapter 19 Performance Assessment Activity.

Reteach

🎧 Have students listen to the Chapter 19, Section 3 Audiocassette. (Also in Spanish.) **LEP**

📁 Have students complete the Chapter 19 Reteaching Activity. (Also in Spanish.) **LEP**

Enrich

📁 Have students complete the Chapter 19 Enrichment Activity. (Also in Spanish.) **LEP**

📁 Have students complete Supreme Court Case Study 32.

CLOSE

Ask: Why did Eisenhower choose Nixon as his running mate? *(experience; anti-Communist)*

656

Campaign Issues

Actually, the 1960 campaign provided something much more interesting than the stereotypes of the two men. It was a political battle waged over issues of national and international importance. Cuba, just off the tip of Florida, was fast becoming a perceived Communist threat. The United States had been left behind again when the Soviets sent a dog—the papers nicknamed it "mutnik"—into space. Violent Communist movements in Asia had not ended with the Korean War but were only shifting to Southeast Asia in a little country called Vietnam.

The 1960 campaign for the presidency was fought over such issues to a virtual standoff—a result that indicates how closely the two young candidates resembled each other. Of the two, Kennedy was younger by several years, but that did not seem to cost him many votes. He was a Roman Catholic, and surveys indicated that cost him 1.5 million votes. Nixon had far more experience in foreign affairs: He had confronted violent anti-American crowds in Venezuela, met Khrushchev in a debate in Moscow, and talked with leaders around the world.

It was the choice that Nixon made to adopt the whistle-stop campaign strategy of Harry Truman, however, that helped to cause his own defeat. Truman's recipe for victory turned out to be Richard Nixon's recipe for defeat. The **electronic media**—TV and radio—for the first time were becoming a big factor in a presidential campaign, something that Kennedy exploited with his boyish good looks and infectious humor. The televised debate between Nixon and Kennedy in 1960 became a contest between a weary campaigner who was being squeezed dry by his grueling campaign schedule and a candidate whose aides knew how to help him work smarter, not harder.

The candidates met in a tide-turning televised debate on September 26, 1960. Viewers saw in Nixon a man stretched to his limits. Early in the whistle-stop campaign, Nixon had injured his knee. For weeks it continued to jolt him with pain, but he had carried on, racking up mile after mile in a desperate push to keep his promise to campaign in every state. He lost weight and looked haggard and drawn.

Kennedy, meanwhile, arrived for the debate tan and fit from a rest in Florida. It did not matter that radio listeners scored the debate for Nixon on the strength of his arguments. Television conveyed Kennedy's warmth and ease to 70 million viewers.

The Election

The election returns were the closest in history. Kennedy took 49.7 percent of the popular vote to 49.5 percent for Nixon, although the difference in electoral votes (303 to 219, respectively) proved more substantial. Many Republicans and some independent observers cried foul, claiming election fraud in Texas and Illinois, where a single county might have wiped out Kennedy's victory of just over 100,000 votes out of the 69 million that were cast.

A *New York Herald Tribune* writer, Earl Mazo, who had long been friendly to Nixon, started a journalistic investigation of vote fraud. Nixon, however, called him off, telling him that such an investigation was pointless. "Earl," he said, "no one steals the presidency of the United States."

SECTION REVIEW

Vocabulary

1. Define: consensus decision making, electronic media.

Checking Facts

2. List three characteristics that made Eisenhower an attractive candidate to voters.

3. How did television influence the election of 1960?

Critical Thinking

Recognizing Ideologies

4. What does Eisenhower's emphasis on consensus decision making tell you about his values?

Linking Across Time

5. Find an example of a recent event that demonstrates the importance of electronic media in national affairs.

Section 3 Review Answers

1. consensus decision making (654), **electronic media** (656)
2. Eisenhower was calm, a Republican, and a war hero.
3. by showing voters a youthful Kennedy debating a tired Nixon
4. that he was willing to share responsibility and that he trusted the people he appointed
5. for example, presidential use of television addresses

Critical Thinking Skill

DISTINGUISHING FACT FROM OPINION

Learning the Skill

Distinguishing fact from opinion is often not easy. Senator Joseph McCarthy convinced many Americans that Communists thrived in Truman's administration. Yet he never produced credible evidence.

Learning to distinguish fact from opinion can help you make reasonable judgments about what others say. A fact is a statement that can be proven by evidence such as records, documents, government statistics, or historical sources. An opinion is a statement that may contain some truth but also contains a personal view or judgment.

The following steps will help you to sift facts from opinions and to judge the reliability of what you read or hear.

a. Identify the facts. Ask yourself the following: Can these statements be proved? Where can I find information to verify them?

b. Check the sources for the facts. Reliable sources include almanacs, encyclopedias, the *Congressional Record,* and so on. Often statistics sound impressive but they come from an unreliable source such as an interest group trying to gain support for its programs.

c. Identify the opinions. Sometimes opinions contain phrases such as *in my view, I believe, it is my conviction, I think.*

d. Identify the purpose. What does the speaker or author want you to believe or do?

UPI/BETTMANN

Recognizing Opinion Senator McCarthy waves a report that he says proves presidential candidate Adlai Stevenson's associations with groups promoting "the suicidal Kremlin-based policies" of the Soviet Union. *What do you think was McCarthy's purpose in making such allegations?*

Practicing the Skill

During the presidential race in 1960, John F. Kennedy and Richard M. Nixon met in a series of debates. The following is from Kennedy's opening remarks on September 26.

This is a great country, but I think it could be a greater country; and this is a powerful country, but I think it could be a more powerful country. I'm not satisfied to have 50 percent of our steel mill capacity unused. I'm not satisfied when the United States had last year the lowest rate of economic growth of any major industrialized society in the world, because economic growth means strength and vitality; it means we're able to sustain our defenses; it means we're able to meet our commitments abroad.

1. Identify the facts. Is there a way to prove that 50 percent of the steel mill capacity was unused or that economic growth was slow? What could you do to check these facts?

2. Notice the opinions. What phrases does Kennedy sometimes use to signal his opinions?

3. What opinions does Kennedy state that do not use signal words?

4. What is the purpose of Kennedy's statement? What does Kennedy want listeners to do?

5. How does knowing this purpose help you listen more objectively?

Applying the Skill

Record or take notes on a television interview. List three facts and three opinions that were stated. Then answer the following questions.

Do the facts seem reliable? Why or why not? How could you verify the facts? What opinions were stated? Were signal words used? If so, what were they? Was the person being interviewed trying to convince viewers of some position? Explain that position. Does knowing the position help you to listen more effectively? How?

Additional Practice

For additional practice, see Reinforcing Skills on page 659.

CRITICAL THINKING SKILL **657**

TEACH

This skill feature explains that knowing how to differentiate facts from opinions can help one determine the reliability and usefulness of information. Students will read a quotation from John F. Kennedy's opening remarks in his first debate with Richard M. Nixon. They will use the quotation to learn techniques for distinguishing facts from opinions.

VISUAL INSTRUCTION

Recognizing Opinion Addressing a dinner audience of 1,400 in Chicago, McCarthy charged that Stevenson had a record of associations with allegedly subversive groups.

Answer: *His purpose was probably to discredit Stevenson and to frighten people away from voting for Stevenson.*

Additional Practice

☞ Have students complete the Chapter 19 Skill Reinforcement Activity.

Practicing the Skill Answers

1. Facts are that 50 percent of steel mill capacity is unused and that the United States had the lowest rate of economic growth of any major industrial society. These can both be proven.

2. He uses phrases such as *I think* to introduce opinions, such as that the United States could be a greater and more powerful country.

3. Economic growth means strength and vitality; it means we are able to sustain our defenses and meet our commitments abroad.

4. Kennedy wants to convince voters that he can make the nation greater and more powerful. Kennedy wants listeners to vote for him.

5. Knowing that Kennedy is trying to persuade voters, listeners can be more objective.

Chapter ⑲ Review

Reviewing Key Terms

1. electronic media
2. whistle-stop tour
3. closed shop
4. blacklisting
5. consensus decision making

Recalling Facts

1. During the war, most factories shifted to making war equipment, so cars and appliance production was reduced.
2. The Dixiecrats included conservative Southern Democrats who blocked civil rights legislation in Congress.
3. It helped him gain popularity with ordinary people.
4. It was designed to eliminate government workers who might be Communists or subversives.
5. In the 1940s the Soviets developed the atomic bomb, Chinese Communists came to power, and Stalin expanded Russia's espionage activities. In the 1950s the threat of Communists taking over Korea instigated the Korean War, the Soviets launched *Sputnik*, and communism spread in southeast Asia.
6. McCarthy's hysterical behavior on television helped to discredit him.
7. Encourage students to organize their paragraphs around a central theme or topic and keep events in chronological order.
8. The pejorative term referred to Stevenson's intellectual prowess. Voters wanted someone with whom they could identify.
9. The space race became an extension of the cold war.
10. The public saw Hiss as a traitor, Eisenhower as a father figure, Stevenson as a liberal intellectual, Nixon as a staunch anti-Communist, Dewey as a staid career politician, and McCarthy first as a champion but then as a hysterical and accusatory person.

Reviewing Key Terms

Choose the vocabulary word that best completes the sentences below. Write your answers on a separate sheet of paper.

closed shop   blacklisting
vigilante   electronic media
consensus   whistle-stop tour
  decision making

1. During the Nixon-Kennedy presidential campaign, TV and radio, also known as the _____, for the first time became an important factor.

2. Truman took his campaign to the people by conducting his famous 32,000-mile (51,500-km) _____.

3. A workplace at which only union members can be hired is called a _____.

4. Efforts to brand people as Communists and prevent them from working by placing them on a list of suspected Communists is called _____.

5. Dwight Eisenhower practiced a management style based on group agreement called _____.

Recalling Facts

1. Why were consumers eager to purchase new cars and appliances following the war?

2. Who were the Dixiecrats, and how did they influence politics?

3. What was the significance of Truman's whistle-stop tactic in the 1948 presidential election?

4. Briefly describe the Federal Employee Loyalty Program.

5. Name 3 international events that contributed to cold war fears at home in the 1940s; then name 3 events from the 1950s.

6. How did television affect the outcome of the Army-McCarthy hearings?

7. Describe the anti-communism of the 1950s. Include major figures and their significance.

8. Adlai Stevenson's critics referred to him as an egghead. Why? What does the use of this term suggest about the American ideal for political leadership in the 1950s?

9. Explain the impact of *Sputnik I* on the mood of the United States.

10. The chapter describes the appearance and personality of various figures of the era. From the following list, choose two and describe how the public perception of them affected their careers: Alger Hiss, Dwight Eisenhower, Adlai Stevenson, Richard Nixon, Thomas Dewey, Joseph McCarthy, and Harry Truman.

Critical Thinking

1. Analyzing Information This chapter deals largely with perceptions—how an idea, event, or person is accurately or inaccurately perceived by the public. Give one example from the chapter of the public perception of an event, idea, or person. Then discuss whether you think the perception was accurate and why you think so.

2. Making Generalizations Identify a trend regarding the role of government during the cold war?

3. Synthesizing Information The photograph below exemplifies how many people felt at the time about the Rosenbergs. Why was the nation so concerned about the spread of communism from the Soviet Union to the United States? Why were people worried about war with the Soviets?

4. Recognizing Ideologies Identify ways in which the methods of Joseph McCarthy ran counter to American political ideals and constitutional protections.

5. Evaluating Information The McCarthy hearings were broadcast, showing the senator attacking the witnesses. How might McCarthy's performance have affected public perception of him?

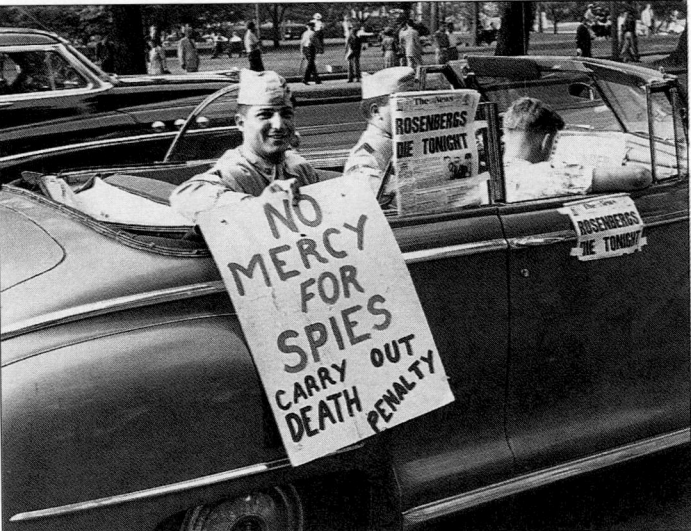

© ELLIOTT ERWITT/MAGNUM PHOTOS

Critical Thinking

1. Encourage students to give details from the text that support their statements.
2. Answers will vary, but might include that the government played the watchdog role, preparing against a perceived threat of communism.
3. Americans felt that communism curtailed freedom and other democratic ideals. Because it was spreading in other parts of the world, they felt Russia might try to take over the United States by force or infiltration.
4. McCarthy violated individuals' First Amendment rights to free speech and association and refused to make specific charges.
5. Radio and TV listeners could hear and see McCarthy's irrational accusations and theatrical behavior and judge for themselves that he had perhaps gone too far.

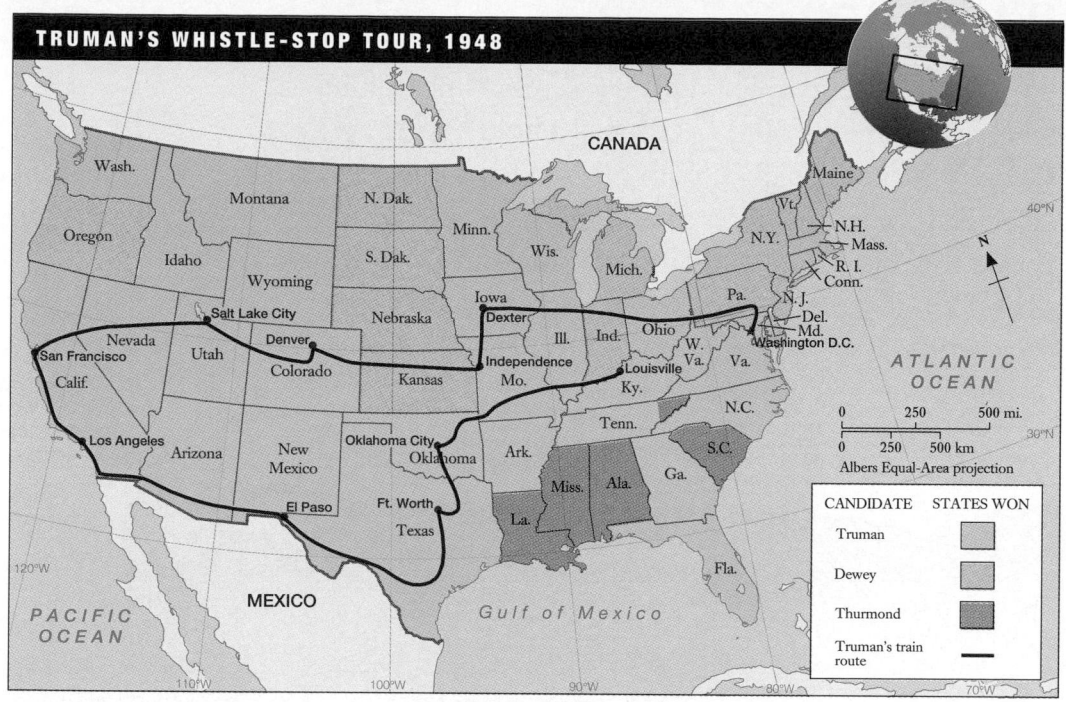

TRUMAN'S WHISTLE-STOP TOUR, 1948

CANADA

ATLANTIC
OCEAN

PACIFIC
OCEAN

MEXICO

Gulf of Mexico

0   250   500 mi.
0   250   500 km
Albers Equal-Area projection

CANDIDATE	STATES WON
Truman	
Dewey	
Thurmond	
Truman's train route	

Geography and History

1. They voted for Truman.
2. 17
3. Louisiana, Mississippi, Alabama, South Carolina, eastern Tennessee
4. The Northeast and some of the Midwest
5. 4

History Journal

Be sure students back up their examples with information from the book. You might have them think about the current feeling in America about communism, as well as about other kinds of groups, such as militia organizations, before they begin writing.

? BONUS QUESTION

This question may be used for extra credit on the Chapter Test.

Name five of President Eisenhower's accomplishments.

Answer: *He built the interstate highway system; he encouraged the private development of hydroelectric and nuclear power; he increased the minimum wage; he extended the Social Security system; he increased low-income housing; he approved the building of the St. Lawrence Seaway.*

Portfolio Project

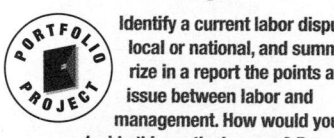

Identify a current labor dispute, local or national, and summarize in a report the points at issue between labor and management. How would you decide this particular case? Does the Taft-Hartley Act apply? Keep your report in your portfolio.

Cooperative Learning

Form two groups. One group should portray supporters of Senator McCarthy. The other group should portray his critics. Select spokespersons to conduct a debate on the following topic: Senator McCarthy's attacks on Communists were justified, although he went too far. Some innocent people had to suffer to protect the nation.

Reinforcing Skills

Distinguishing Fact From Opinion Read the excerpt on page 646 from Truman's 1953 speech on McCarthyism. Which statements are opinions, and which are facts? How can you tell? Are there facts in the lesson text on pages 644–645 that support or dispute the opinions? If so, list them.

Geography and History

Study the map on this page to answer the following questions:

1. Notice the states that Truman visited. Which way did most of these states vote?

2. According to the map, through how many states did Truman travel on his whistle-stop campaign?

3. Conservative Southern Democrats nominated Strom Thurmond as their presidential candidate. According to the map, where was Dixiecrat support strongest?

4. In which regions of the country was support for Dewey strongest?

5. Of the states Truman visited on his tour, how many voted for Dewey?

HISTORY JOURNAL

Write what you learned about the fears and attitudes of Americans during the cold war. What caused those fears? Do you think they could return? Record your thoughts in your journal.

CHAPTER 19 REVIEW **659**

Portfolio Project

Direct students by listing as examples some strikes, such as the 1994–95 baseball strike or a local strike involving teachers or government employees. Give suggestions for research material. Encourage them to explain what facts motivated their decision.

Cooperative Learning

Have students point out specific things McCarthy said to back up their assertions about how he was perceived. Have them discuss whether public opinion would have turned against him without the radio and TV exposure.

Reinforcing Skills

Answers will vary, but might include: Truman's opinions are in loaded phrases, such as "this horrible cancer . . . can destroy . . . freedom" and "McCarthyism . . . is the corruption of truth." The facts he uses are that McCarthy's accusations were unfounded and due process was abandoned.

TEACH

Making the Historical Connection

The Corvette was a product of the postwar era; it was the first plastic car. The entire body of the Corvette weighed only 411 pounds, 300 pounds less than if it had been made of steel. By using plastic, Chevrolet went into production years earlier than if they had used traditional materials. The tooling cost was only $500,000 (compared with a cost of $4,500,000 for steel). The plastic used was thicker than steel and much sturdier. A hammer blow that could dent a steel car body bounced harmlessly off the Corvette. If the plastic body did break, damage could be repaired in an hour. The only metal body part on the Corvette was the gas tank flap.

FYI

The Early Years The first Corvettes were more showboat than sports car, and terrible sales the first two years of production nearly killed the Corvette. Only 300 Corvettes were produced the first year. At the end of the second year, 1,100 cars, out of the 3,400 produced, remained unsold. It was the introduction of the V-8 engine that saved the Corvette, and the car rapidly grew into a true world-class sports machine.

Then...
The 1955 Corvette

The first Corvette rolled off the assembly line in Flint, Michigan, on June 30, 1953. It was a bold experiment for General Motors officials, who wanted to compete with sleek European sports cars. GM produced only 300 of the 1953 Corvettes—in white only. In 1955 GM introduced 2 new colors—Gypsy red and Corvette copper.

1 The revolutionary fiberglass body is still a Corvette trademark.

2 Imitation knock-on hubcaps looked like race car hubcaps.

Fun Facts

© RON KIMBALL

THE FIRST CORVETTES
Most of the 300 Corvettes made in 1953 went to GM employees. Of these 300 Corvettes, 225 can be accounted for today. A 1953 Corvette in good condition could be worth as much as $500,000 today.

660   THEN AND NOW

Background Information

The Postwar Years After World War II, people across the nation were ready to have fun once again. Many became interested in driving cars just for the fun of it. At about this time, Chevrolet began working on a sports car—the Corvette. GM made a few mistakes, but eventually the Corvette caught on. The first mistake was an automatic transmission (a dream feature for most drivers back then but not right for sports car drivers). GM also quickly replaced the Corvette's six-cylinder engine with its V-8. GM's most daring concept was a fiberglass body.

3 The Corvette's logo was two crossed flags that looked like those used at racetracks.

© RON KIMBALL

© NICKY WRIGHT

© RON KIMBALL

4 Wire mesh guarded the headlights from bouncing rocks.

Stats

PRODUCTION

The 1955 Corvette came with either a 6-cylinder (V-6) or a V-8 engine. The V-8 also had an enlarged gold "V" in the word *Chevrolet* on the front fenders. The overwhelming majority of 1955 Corvettes were V-8 powered. Like other Corvettes, the 1955s had a fiberglass body, a chrome-framed grille, no side windows or outside door handles, and a wraparound windshield.

PERFORMANCE

- 0 to 60 mph in 8.7 seconds
- Top speed of 106 mph
- V-8 (12-volt electrical system)

Standard equipment: Powerglide automatic transmission with floor shift, whitewall tires, clock, cigarette lighter, driver's side mirror

PRICE

Base Price:	$2,934.00
Heater:	$91.40
AM Radio:	$145.15
V-8	$135.00
Total:	**$3,305.55**

...Now

© RON KIMBALL

CORVETTE COMPARISON

PORTFOLIO PROJECT

How does the 1955 Corvette compare with Corvettes today? Research newspapers and magazines for advertisements and articles about Corvettes. If possible, interview a Chevrolet dealer and get a price list. What do today's options say about how people use their cars? Create a brochure from the information you gather.

THE PLASTIC CAR

The Corvette was the first of several mass-produced "plastic" cars popular in the 1950s. Fiberglass was much cheaper to use for car bodies than steel.

FAIR-WEATHER FRIEND

The number one owner complaint was rain leaking in. As one owner put it, "Strictly a dry-weather car. Floor can hold 4 gallons of water."

 Block Scheduling

The Portfolio Project on this page provides an excellent opportunity to enrich and extend the key elements of this feature.

CLOSE

In the 1950s *Consumer Reports* recommended the VW Beetle as an alternative to the Corvette for the man who wanted sports car performance with family convenience. Do your students think consumers took this advice? (*They may answer no, because they think Beetles are not sporty, or they may feel that people of the era found the Beetle to be a fun car.*) Discuss with students which features of the Corvette may have appealed to drivers of the time. (*Its revolutionary fiberglass body, its sportiness, its speed, its uniqueness, and so on.*)

 PORTFOLIO PROJECT

Portfolio Project

1950s Technology Have students research technology gains that occurred during World War II and that became available in the postwar era. Then have students design their own cars using as much of the postwar technology as possible. Students should explain each new technology and how they could incorporate it into a car. Some technologies they may want to explore include plastics of the time, manufacturing techniques, engines, even computers. Students can keep their car designs in their portfolios.

The Unit at a Glance

Chapter 20

The civil rights struggle of the 1950s and 1960s reflected a change in consciousness about treatment of African Americans and other minorities. The struggle involved grassroots movements, nonviolent and militant groups, the courts, the federal government, and the media.

Chapter 21

Presidents Kennedy and Johnson and the Supreme Court furthered social reform in the 1960s. Kennedy laid the groundwork for a civil rights act as part of his New Frontier. Johnson enacted the civil rights act and many more social reform programs under his Great Society. The Supreme Court of Earl Warren passed many social reform decisions.

Chapter 22

In the 1960s and 1970s, more groups fought for their civil rights. Women sought to gain equality with men. Hispanic Americans organized for political power. Native Americans used protests and the court system to regain lost lands. Young people created a counterculture to protest the Establishment.

UNIT 8

Toward Equality and Social Reform

CHAPTER 20
The Civil Rights Struggle

CHAPTER 21
The Kennedy and Johnson Years

CHAPTER 22
Voices of Protest

662

⏲ Out of Time?

If time does not permit teaching every chapter in this unit, use the Chapter Digest Audiocassettes and the accompanying student activities and tests. Both the Chapter Digest Audiocassettes are available in Spanish.

Portfolio Project

Interview Invite students to interview people who took part in the social reform movements of the 1960s and 1970s. Student interviewers should try to find out what it was like to be part of this era of reform and what the specific movements were about. They should augment the interview whenever possible with photographs, news articles, and so on. After students have prepared transcripts of the interviews, have them create a cover sheet entitled Profiles of an Era of Reform. Students can file their Profiles packets in their portfolios.

Introducing the Unit

 Show students the Unit 8 Time Line Transparency and assign the accompanying activity sheet. Remind students that the main beneficiaries of the prosperity of the 1950s were upper- and middle-class white people. From the late 1950s through the 1970s, several other groups began to gain equality and institute social reform.

GLENCOE
TECHNOLOGY

Videodisc

American History

Side 1, Section J
Title: Contemporary America, 1960–1990s
Subject: Overview of American history from the Kennedy years to the end of the 20th century.
Ask: Under what circumstances did Lyndon Johnson assume the presidency? *(He was John F. Kennedy's Vice President and became President when Kennedy was assassinated.)*

663

Examining the Visual

About the Orator Dr. Martin Luther King, Jr., speaking at the march on Washington, August 28, 1963, declared, ". . . There are those who are asking the devotees of civil rights, 'when will you be satisfied?' We can never be satisfied as long as the Negro is the victim of the unspeakable horrors of police brutality[,] . . . our bodies . . . cannot gain lodging[,] . . . the Negro's basic mobility is from a smaller ghetto to a larger one[,] . . . our children are stripped of their self-hood and robbed of their dignity by signs reading 'For Whites Only'[,] . . . a Negro in Mississippi cannot vote and a Negro in New York believes he has nothing for which to vote."

TEACH

Making the Historical Connection

Many people in the United States did not share in the postwar prosperity. Millions continued to live in poverty, particularly African Americans and other people of color. The injustice of this situation inspired a period of active social protest across the nation.

 At the Movies

Films about the civil rights movement include *Mississippi Burning*, 1988; *The Long Walk Home*, 1989; *Malcolm X: El Hajj Malik El Shabazz*, 1991.

 Block Scheduling

Team Teaching
These poems can be presented in a team teaching context, in conjunction with English or Language Arts.

Voices of Change

During the 1960s and 1970s, women and people of color began to challenge predominant ethnic, racial, and gender stereotypes and worked to overturn laws that restricted their rights and freedoms. The authors of the following poems assert their identities by linking personal experiences to a broader understanding of culture, gender, tradition, and family. They represent the diversity of American culture during this period.

To Be of Use
by Marge Piercy

The people I love the best
jump into work head first
without dallying in the shallows
and swim off with sure strokes almost out
    of sight.
They seem to become natives of that element.
the black sleek heads of seals
bouncing like half-submerged balls.

I love people who harness themselves, an ox to a
    heavy cart.
who pull like the water buffalo, with massive
    patience,
who strain in the mud and the muck to move
    things forward,
who do what has to be done, again and again.

I want to be with people who submerge
in the task, who go into the fields to harvest
and work in a row and pass the bags along,
who stand in the line and haul in their places,
who are not parlor generals and field deserters
but move in common rhythm
when the food must come in or the fire be put out.

Women
by Alice Walker

They were women then
My mama's generation
Husky of voice—Stout of
Step
With fists as well as
Hands
How they battered down
Doors
And ironed
Starched white
Shirts
How they led
Armies
Headragged Generals
Across mined
Fields
Booby-trapped
Ditches
To discover books
Desks
A place for us
How they knew what we
Must know
Without knowing a page
Of it
Themselves.

664   LITERATURE

Background Information

Protest Writers Writers belonging to the social protest movement were all pioneers whose voices echoed the experience of millions. As a result of the protest movements, departments and centers specializing in the study of women, African Americans, Hispanics, Asian Americans and Native Americans were established in universities all over the United States. Fittingly, many of the poets represented in this unit are currently professors in those departments.

© FAITH RINGGOLD INC.

Dinner Quilt Faith Ringgold's "soft" quilt art tells of growing up as an African American in Harlem. *Dinner Quilt* tells about Christmas dinners with Aunt Connie, who would embroider place mats with names of famous African American women, such as Fannie Lou Hamer.

The Immigrant Experience
by Richard Olivias

I'm sitting in my history class,
The instructor commences rapping,
I'm in my U.S. History class,
And I'm on the verge of napping.

The Mayflower landed on Plymouth Rock.
Tell me more! Tell me more!
Thirteen colonies were settled.
I've heard it all before.

What did he say?
Dare I ask him to reiterate?
Oh, why bother,
It sounded like he said,
George Washington's my father.

I'm reluctant to believe it,
I suddenly raise my *mano*.
If George Washington's my father,
Why wasn't he Chicano?

RESPONDING TO LITERATURE

1. Why does Alice Walker admire the women of her mother's generation? What does she mean by "Headragged Generals"?

2. In what ways do you think Richard Olivas would change the way American history is taught in high school?

VISUAL INSTRUCTION

Dinner Quilt Many women in Faith Ringgold's family had worked in cloth—her great-great-grandmother had sewn quilts. It almost seemed natural for Faith to begin to work in "soft art," using cloth to create soft sculpture and quilts that told stories of African Americans and their life experiences.

Ask: What is *Dinner Quilt* about? *(Christmas dinners at Faith Ringgold's Aunt Connie's house.)*

Writing Activity

Have students briefly describe one of the poems in their own words, reflecting the degree to which they were able to "step into the shoes" of this character. Evaluate the writing based on the student's choice of words and use of descriptive writing.

CLOSE

Ask students to brainstorm some words and phrases that evoke the experiences of the characters depicted in the poems. *(frightened, confused, injured, dazed, committed, shocked, shaken, weary, enlightened, sad)*

Responding to Literature Answers

1. Answers will vary, but students will probably mention that the women always worked hard and imparted their values to their children. She refers to servants.

2. Answers will vary, but students might say that he would emphasize the role minorities have played.

665

The Civil Rights Struggle

DAILY LESSON OBJECTIVES	REPRODUCIBLE RESOURCES	MULTIMEDIA RESOURCES
SECTION 1 Challenging Segregation 1. Describe the legal assault on school segregation that culminated in *Brown* v. *Board of Education* in 1954. 2. Describe the resistance by whites in South to school desegregation. 3. Explain President Eisenhower's reluctance to support school desegregation.	📂 Reproducible Lesson Plans 📂 Supreme Court Case Studies 📂 Vocabulary and Guided Reading Activities (English or Spanish) 📂 Geography in History Activities 📂 Case Studies 📂 Cooperative Learning Activities 📂 Skill Reinforcement Activities 📂 Section Quizzes (English or Spanish)	🖌 Chapter Teaching Transparencies 🖌 Section Focus Transparencies 🖌 Map Transparencies 💿 Powers of the Supreme Court 💿 Set on Freedom 💿 Landmark Documents in American History 💿 Student Self-Test: A Software Review 💿 Testmaker
SECTION 2 Freedom Now 1. Describe the strategies used by SCLC to counter segregation in the South. 2. Describe the role the SNCC played in the civil rights movement.	📂 Reproducible Lesson Plans 📂 Vocabulary and Guided Reading Activities (English or Spanish) 📂 Supreme Court Case Studies 📂 Interpreting Political Cartoons 📂 Section Quizzes (English or Spanish)	🖌 Section Focus Transparencies 💿 Powers of the Supreme Court 💿 Martin Luther King, Jr. 💿 Landmark Documents in American History 💿 Student Self-Test: A Software Review 💿 Testmaker
SECTION 3 Government Response 1. Describe how politics shaped President Kennedy's civil rights policy. 2. Explain how militants on both sides of the civil rights issue forced Kennedy to side with Martin Luther King, Jr. 2. Describe the successes of the civil rights movement during Lyndon Johnson's presidency.	📂 Reproducible Lesson Plans 📂 Vocabulary and Guided Reading Activities (English or Spanish) 📂 American Literature Readings and Activities 📂 Section Quizzes (English or Spanish)	🖌 Section Focus Transparencies 📼 Great Speeches 💿 Powers of the Supreme Court 💿 Landmark Documents in American History 💿 Student Self-Test: A Software Review 💿 Testmaker
SECTION 4 Disappointed Hopes 1. Explain the conflict of opinions on appropriate strategies and attitudes within the civil rights movement. 2. Describe black power, black pride, and the black separatist movement. 3. Explain the causes of the riots in Northern cities during the summers of 1965 to 1967.	📂 Reproducible Lesson Plans 📂 Supreme Court Case Studies 📂 Vocabulary and Guided Reading Activities (English or Spanish) 📂 Reteaching Activities (English or Spanish) 📂 Enrichment Activities (English or Spanish) 📂 Section Quizzes (English or Spanish)	🖌 Section Focus Transparencies 💿 Landmark Documents in American History 💿 Set on Freedom 💿 Student Self-Test: A Software Review 💿 Testmaker
CHAPTER REVIEW AND EVALUATION	📂 Chapter 20 Test, Forms A and B 📂 Performance Assessment Strategies and Activities	💿 Student Self-Test and Software Review 💿 Vocabulary PuzzleMaker 💿 Testmaker 🎧 Chapter Digests Audiocassettes

🕛 If time does not permit teaching the entire chapter, summarize using the Chapter 20 Digests Audiocassettes and the accompanying activities and tests. (Available in English or Spanish.)

Cooperative Project

Have students prepare and present a debate between the followers of Martin Luther King, Jr., and the followers of Malcolm X. Make sure they cover these two issues: non-violent protest strategies and violent protest strategies, the integration of whites and African Americans and the separation of the two races, i.e. black separatism. **LEP** 📼

Suggested Rubric: An Oral Presentation. See Performance Assessment Strategies and Activities, p. 33.

Individual Project

Many college students were jailed in the South for taking part in nonviolent demonstrations. If students were experiencing this, what might they want to say to President Kennedy regarding their goals and the necessity for government assistance? What might President Kennedy's response be, in light of his belief at that time in the political necessity of not alienating segregationists? Have students write their plea to Kennedy and his possible response. 📼

Suggested Rubric: A Journal. See Performance Assessment Strategies and Activities, p. 29.

Key to Ability Levels

Teaching strategies have been coded for varying learning styles and abilities.

L1 **BASIC** activities for all students

L2 **AVERAGE** activities for average to above-average students

L3 **CHALLENGING** activities for above-average students

LEP **LIMITED ENGLISH PROFICIENCY** activities

Block Scheduling

Block scheduling differs from traditional class scheduling in the amount of time allotted to each period. The extended timeframe provided by block scheduling affords you the opportunity to implement a greater number of research-oriented and activity-intense projects to motivate and involve your students. Activities that are particularly suited to use within the block scheduling framework are identified throughout this chapter by the following designation.

T E A C H E R ' S   C O R N E R

NATIONAL
GEOGRAPHIC
SOCIETY

INDEX TO NATIONAL GEOGRAPHIC MAGAZINE

The following articles may be used for research relating to this chapter:

- "Philadelphia's African Americans," by Roland L. Freeman, August 1990.
- *I Dream a World: America's Black Women* (A Special Edition), August 1989.

NATIONAL GEOGRAPHIC SOCIETY PRODUCTS AVAILABLE FROM GLENCOE

To order the following products for use with this chapter, contact your local Glencoe sales representative or call Glencoe at 1-800-334-7344:

- *The Presidents: A Picture History of Our Nation* (CD-ROM)
- *GTV: A Geographic Perspective on American History* (Videodisc)
- *GTV: The American People: Fabric of a Nation* (Videodisc)

ADDITIONAL NATIONAL GEOGRAPHIC SOCIETY PRODUCTS

To order the following products for use with this chapter, call National Geographic Society at 1-800-368-2728:

- *Decades of History: The 20th Century—The Middle Years* (Filmstrip)

Chapter Overview

In the mid-1950s, African Americans fought to be represented in the mainstream of United States society.

Introducing the Chapter

There was considerable resistance to school integration in the South in the 1950s. African American students such as Elizabeth Ann Eckford encountered violence when trying to integrate. Have students read the narrative, which tells about such resistance.

 Display the Chapter Teaching Transparency and distribute the corresponding activity sheet.

Extension Activity

Have students complete "Beyond the Transparency" on the activity sheet for Chapter 20 and present their projects after the class has completed the chapter. 📦

 History Journal

After students have read the vignette and studied the photograph, have them write an account of Elizabeth Eckford's experience in their own words.

☑ **Performance Assessment**

Refer to page 666B for performance assessment activities for this chapter.

👈 Also see Activity 20 in the Performance Assessment Strategies and Activities for an additional activity as well as for suggested rubrics. 📦

CHAPTER
20

The Civil Rights Struggle

SEPTEMBER 4, 1957: SCHOOL OPENS AT LITTLE ROCK CENTRAL HIGH

Elizabeth Ann Eckford and her mother made a crisp black and white dress for Elizabeth to wear her first day in the new school. The eight other African American students arranged to go to school together, but Elizabeth never got the message.

She went instead by bus, and when she arrived at Little Rock Central High School, she headed for the front door. To her surprise, she found the way blocked by an angry crowd of white townspeople and hundreds of armed soldiers, members of the Arkansas National Guard sent by the governor.

Elizabeth tried to follow a white student through the door but was stopped by a soldier. "When I tried to squeeze past him," she recalled later, "he raised his bayonet, and then the other guards moved in and raised their bayonets.... Somebody started yelling, 'Lynch her! Lynch her!'"

Elizabeth and the 8 other students never made it into Central High that day. It took 3 more weeks, intervention by the President, 1,000 paratroopers, and 10,000 members of the Arkansas National Guard to integrate the school.

It was a pattern repeated often in the years to come. Legislation and court orders were not enough. Grassroots efforts by the local African American community and nonviolent demonstrations were not enough. It took all of these efforts together to bring the Constitution's promise of equality for all closer to reality. ■

 HISTORY JOURNAL

Before you read the rest of this chapter, write your understanding of the kinds of problems African Americans faced in their struggle for civil rights.

666

➕ **EXTRA CREDIT PROJECT**

Recording the Experience Have students use school or public library resources to find out more about the Little Rock Nine. Ask them to use what they learn to write a diary entry, a short story, or a poem about the Little Rock integration experience. They can write from the point of view of an integrating African American student, a white student at Little Rock Central, or a soldier. Before students begin, discuss the process of adopting a point of view. Encourage students to attach photocopies of newspaper or magazine accounts to enrich their final product. 📦

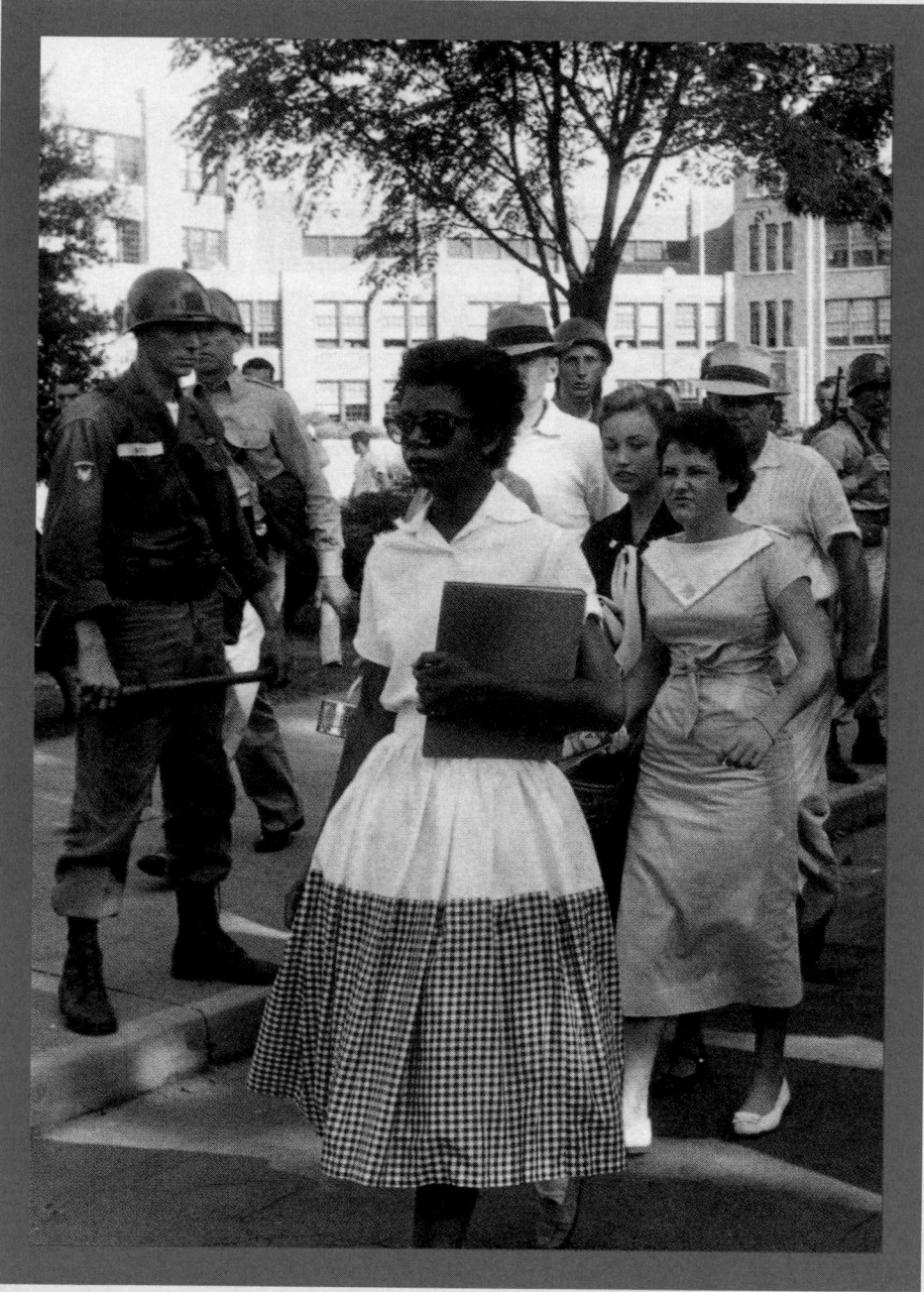

STATE TROOPS HAD DEFENDED SEGREGATION;
LATER FEDERALIZED TROOPS ENABLED
INTEGRATION.

667

 ABCNEWS INTERACTIVE™

◉ **Videodisc**

Martin Luther King, Jr.

Side 1, Chapter 3
Title: Ted Koppel: MLK Overview
Subject: Overview of the life of Dr. Martin Luther King, Jr.
Ask: When did Martin Luther King, Jr., first gain national attention? *(the Montgomery bus boycott)*

See Martin Luther King, Jr., Guidebook page 4 for complete lesson plan.

GLENCOE TECHNOLOGY

 ◉ **Videodisc**

American History

Side 2
Title: Civil Rights
Subject: Civil rights
Ask: What event in Montgomery brought the civil rights movement to national attention? *(Montgomery bus boycott)*

Examining the Visual

The People and the Event Invite students to look closely at the facial expressions and "body language" of the individuals in the photograph. Discuss how Elizabeth seems to exude grace under pressure; she looks determined, yet not aggressive. Several others in the crowd look aggressive; the soldiers appear ready for action. Then inform students that, after this first day, Elizabeth Eckford was escorted to Central High School, along with the 8 other African American students, by Daisy Bates, Arkansas president of the NAACP. On September 25, Bates and the students were finally able to enter and stay in the school, protected by 1,000 federalized paratroopers.

FOCUS

Section Objectives

1. Describe the legal assault on school segregation in various parts of the country that culminated in *Brown* v. *Board of Education* in 1954.

2. Describe the resistance by whites in the South to school desegregation.

3. Explain President Eisenhower's reluctance to support school desegregation.

Bellringer Activity

While taking attendance at the beginning of the class period, display **Section Focus Transparency 62**, and have students answer the questions. (Or use the blackline master.)

VISUAL INSTRUCTION

Two Americas Though slavery had been prohibited by the Thirteenth Amendment, so-called "Jim Crow" laws (see Chapter 9, Section 3) allowed situations like the one depicted on this page to exist.

Ask: What other kinds of segregation did African Americans face? *(African Americans had to enter through the back door of public buses, sit in separate train waiting rooms, eat in separate restaurants, and attend separate schools.)*

SECTION 1

Challenging Segregation

EARLY 1950s: THE UNITED STATES

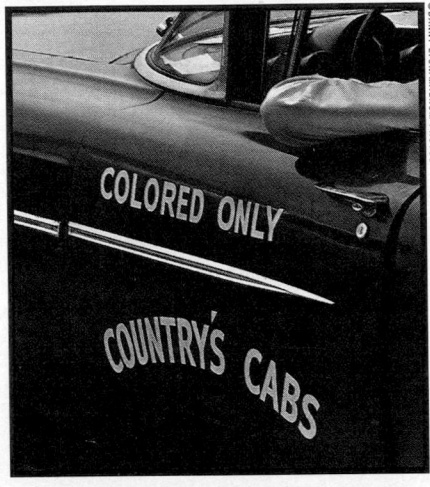

Two Americas
African Americans were not allowed to ride in the same cabs as white patrons.

AFRICAN AMERICANS MADE GAINS DURING WORLD WAR II. Yet they did not share in the promise and prosperity that followed, and most white Americans seemed unaware of this. Novelist Ralph Ellison wrote:

> I am an invisible man. . . . I am invisible, understand, simply because people refuse to see me. . . . When they approach me they see only my surroundings, themselves, or figments of their imagination—indeed everything and anything except me.
>
> —Ralph Ellison,
> *Invisible Man,* 1952

In the South, laws that ensured **segregation** enforced this invisibility. Indeed, separation of blacks and whites formed a fundamental part of southern culture. All across the region, African Americans had to enter public buses by the back door, sit in separate waiting rooms at train stations, eat in separate restaurants, and attend separate schools. The power to vote was regularly withheld.

In the North, the pattern of urban life often resulted in *de facto* segregation—segregation in fact though not by law. As African Americans migrated to Northern cities, white people moved out to the suburbs.

AS YOU READ

Vocabulary
► segregation
► civil rights

Think About . . .
► the issues surrounding school segregation that culminated in *Brown* v. *Board of Education* in 1954.
► the resistance by many whites in the South to school desegregation.

► why President Eisenhower was reluctant to support school desegregation.

668 CHAPTER 20 THE CIVIL RIGHTS STRUGGLE

Section 1 Resources

REPRODUCIBLE RESOURCES
- 📁 Lesson Plan 20-1
- 📁 Section 1 Quiz
- 📁 Supreme Court Case Study 21
- 📁 Vocabulary and Guided Reading Activity 20-1
- 📁 Geography in History Activity 20
- 📁 Unit 8 Case Study
- 📁 Cooperative Learning Activity 20
- 📁 Skill Reinforcement Activity 20

MULTIMEDIA RESOURCES
- 📷 Section Focus Transparency 62
- 💿 Powers of the Supreme Court
- 🎬 Set on Freedom
- 💿 Landmark Documents in American History
- 💿 Student Self-Test: A Software Review
- 💻 Testmaker
- 🗺 Map Transparency 20
- 🎧 Chapter 21 Digest Audiocassette

Other, more subtle, means of separating whites and African Americans emerged. For example, school districts were carefully drawn so that they included only black neighborhoods or only white ones.

The country had two societies, one white and one black. The invisible world of the African Americans, however, was about to make its presence known.

The Segregation System
The North Eases, the South Intensifies

While the American people struggled to adjust to post-World War II life, they faced a number of troubling social issues. Among these issues was the question of what place African Americans would occupy in the country they had bravely helped to defend. In the North, African Americans began achieving modest gains in fair housing and fair employment protections. In much of the South, however, there was widespread resistance to changing the rights of African Americans.

The issue that most inflamed both segregationists and integrationists was public education. The reason was that public schools placed children from the age of six on in daily social situations of playing and learning. Attitudes learned in the classroom could be expected to influence the students for the rest of their lives.

In the early 1950s, 17 states and the District of Columbia prohibited African American and white children from attending school together. Only 16 states required their public schools to be integrated, and individual school districts often violated these requirements.

Then in 1950 three Supreme Court decisions handed down on a single day gave a new direction to those who were fighting for **civil rights,** the rights of all citizens. First, the Court ruled that railroad dining cars operating in the South must provide equal service to all travelers, regardless of race. Second, the Court ruled that African American students could not be segregated within a school also attended by whites. Third, the Court recognized that "intangible factors," not just buildings or books, had to be considered when comparing the education provided for African Americans and whites.

The Challenge of the Courts
Supreme Court Rules Against Segregation

For more than 50 years, *Plessy* v. *Ferguson* had stood as the legal precedent for the "separate but equal" doctrine. This 1896 Supreme Court opinion held that if separate accommodations provided in railroad cars were equal for African American and white passengers, then

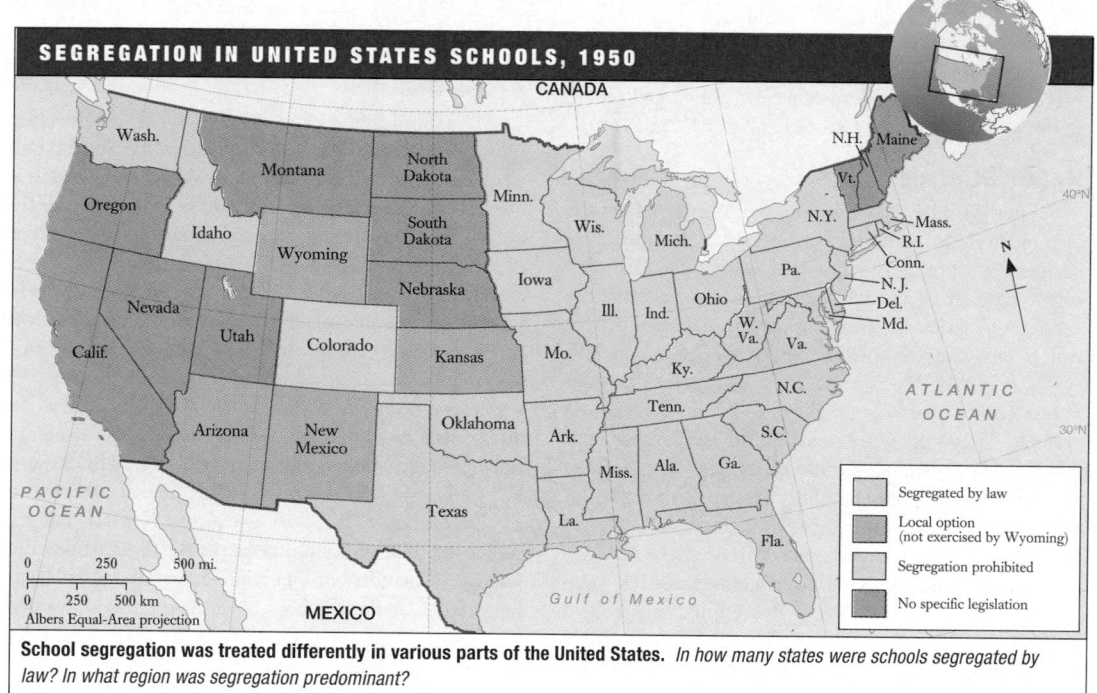

SEGREGATION IN UNITED STATES SCHOOLS, 1950

Segregated by law

Local option (not exercised by Wyoming)

Segregation prohibited

No specific legislation

School segregation was treated differently in various parts of the United States. *In how many states were schools segregated by law? In what region was segregation predominant?*

TEACH

Guided Practice

L2 Discussion Discuss the NAACP's decision to challenge the broad concept of school segregation rather than approach it case by case. Why was this an important move? What might have happened if the NAACP had lost the case?

Show students Chapter 20 Map Transparency and have them complete the activity sheet.

ABCNEWS INTERACTIVE™

 Videodisc

Powers of the Supreme Court

Side 2, Chapter 22
Title: *Brown* v. *Board of Education of Topeka* (KS)
Subject: Case that ended school segregation
Ask: How did *Brown* affect public education? *(ruled segregation unconstitutional)*

See Powers of the Supreme Court Guidebook page 87 for complete lesson plan.

Cooperative Learning

Separate but Equal Organize the class in two groups to research the "separate but equal" doctrine. One group should research the *Plessy* v. *Ferguson* case, which set the legal precedent for "separate but equal" schools. The other group should research the *Brown* v. *Board of Education* case, which overturned the "separate but equal" doctrine. Groups should then come together for a class discussion of their findings—or group spokespersons may be selected for class presentations.

MAP STUDY

Many states that were segregated by law were states of the old Confederacy (see Chapter 6).

Answer: *17; the South*

©UPI/BETTMANN

Fighting Segregation Through the System Thurgood Marshall and Mrs. L.C. Bates, president of the NAACP, talk with Arkansas students outside the Supreme Court. *In what way was the* Brown *case different from previous segregation cases?*

the resulting segregation was constitutional. Soon the "separate but equal" principle was being used to justify segregation in housing, restaurants, public swimming pools, and other public facilities.

NAACP Strategy

After World War II, the National Association for the Advancement of Colored People (NAACP) initiated a series of court cases that chipped away at the *Plessy* ruling. In case after case, the Supreme Court held that the separate facilities provided for African Americans were not, in fact, equal to those provided for white people.

The NAACP had worked out a strategy that concentrated first on desegregating graduate and specialized schools. They hoped to prove that the facilities for non-whites were not equal to those of whites. Then, instead of building new school buildings for use by only a handful of African American students, states would be forced to integrate. After succeeding on this level, the NAACP planned to attack segregation in elementary and high schools. In 1950 the NAACP weighed the recent actions of the Supreme Court and made a bold decision. Rather than trying to prove case by case that the "separate but equal" doctrine was unworkable, they agreed

to fight segregation head-on. They would challenge the courts that segregation itself was illegal.

Leading this effort for the NAACP was Thurgood Marshall, who later became the first African American justice on the Supreme Court. Marshall was extremely popular among Southern African Americans. As one supporter explained, Marshall was "of the people. He knew how to get through to them. Out in Texas or Oklahoma or down the street here in Washington at the Baptist Church, he would make these rousing speeches that would have them all jumping out of their seats."

Then the NAACP began to decide which among the nation's segregated school districts to bring before the Supreme Court. A suitable case required parents courageous enough to sign a court petition despite pressure from local officials. It also required patience. The NAACP expected to lose when the suits were first tried. This would allow for an appeal to the Supreme Court.

Brown Decision

The Supreme Court case that helped overturn school segregation did not originate in the South at all. The case was called *Brown* v. *the Board of Education of Topeka, Kansas*. By selecting a case from outside the South, the Court hoped to emphasize that the question of school segregation was a national one.

The "separate but equal" school facilities in Topeka were of comparable quality. Seven-year-old Linda Brown, however, had to cross through a railroad switching yard to catch the bus to her all-black elementary school, which was miles away. Why, her father insisted, couldn't she attend the all-white school just a few blocks from her home instead of riding a bus to a school located miles away?

Oral arguments before the Supreme Court were set for December 9, 1952. As usual, the NAACP lawyers rehearsed their presentation before the mostly nonwhite faculty and students of Howard Law School in Washington, D.C. After the hearing came months of waiting. The Court then asked for some more information, but before arguments were heard again, Chief Justice Fred M. Vinson died suddenly. President Eisenhower

Meeting Special Needs

Visual Learners This activity helps to address the particular needs of visual learners. Have students look at the visuals and, if appropriate, have them read the heads in this section. They can use this information to summarize the major points of the section in their own words.

appointed in Vinson's place the former governor of California, Earl Warren.

Warren felt that such a sensitive decision required a unanimous decision. Such a decision would send a clear message to all parts of the country. Again, weeks of negotiations went on before the Court announced its decision. That historic moment came on May 17, 1954. Chief Justice Warren, in delivering the opinion, said:

> **D**oes segregation of children in public schools solely on the basis of race, even though the physical facilities and other tangible factors may be equal, deprive children of the minority group of equal educational opportunities? We believe it does. . . . To separate them from others of similar age and qualifications solely because of their race generates a feeling of inferiority as to their status in the community that may affect their hearts and minds in a way very unlikely ever to be undone.
>
> We conclude that in the field of public education the doctrine of 'separate but equal' has no place. Separate educational facilities are inherently unequal.
> —*Brown v. Board of Education*, 1954

Resistance to *Brown*
The South Resists Integration

When the Supreme Court declared in 1954 that school segregation was illegal, they said nothing about how integration was to be carried out. That announcement came a year later. The rather vague ruling of the Court, pronounced in May 1955, was that integration should take place "with all deliberate speed" and "at the earliest possible date." The reluctance to give definite guidelines for ending segregation may have been the price that Chief Justice Warren had to pay for his justices' unanimous decision. After all, the integration decision was not a popular one among many groups. Polls showed that 80 percent of Southern whites opposed the *Brown* decision.

Some of the nation's school districts took steps to comply with the ruling. Other districts, particularly in the South, devised plans to resist the decision.

Massive Resistance

In Southern districts where resistance was strong, white students, encouraged by parents, refused to attend integrated schools. The Ku Klux Klan reemerged, while other white Southerners joined the less militant White Citizens' Councils.

Resistance often received encouragement from those in high offices. Virginia's governor, Thomas Stanley, declared, "I shall use every legal means at my command to continue segregated schools in Virginia." Southern state legislatures passed more than 450 laws and resolutions aimed at preventing enforcement of the *Brown* decision. In 1956 the Virginia state legislature passed a massive resistance measure that cut off state aid to all desegregated schools.

In the same year, 100 Southern members of Congress signed what came to be called the Southern Manifesto, praising "the motives of those states which have declared their intention to resist forced integration by any lawful means." One of the three Southern representatives who refused to sign was Lyndon B. Johnson of Texas, future President of the United States.

Eisenhower and *Brown*

When elected President in 1952, Dwight Eisenhower carried 4 of the 11 states of the old Confederacy, only the second time the Republicans had made inroads in the solidly Democratic South since Reconstruction. Out of personal conviction, and out of loyalty to his Southern constituents, Eisenhower attempted to be neutral toward desegregation. He neither endorsed nor refuted the Supreme Court decision, saying instead, "I don't believe you can change the hearts of men with laws or decisions." Privately, he called his appointment of Earl Warren to the Supreme Court his biggest mistake.

In 1956 the African American student Autherine Lucy was suspended and then expelled from the University of Alabama after whites rioted to prevent her from remaining. Eisenhower said, "I would certainly hope that we could avoid any interference with anybody as long as that state, from its governor down, will do its best to straighten it out." The university continued to exclude African Americans for the next seven years.

Crisis at Little Rock
Desegregation Meets Violent Resistance

Little Rock, Arkansas, seemed an unlikely place for a showdown on school segregation. Just 5 days after the *Brown* decision, the Little Rock school board announced its willingness to obey the new law. The school district superintendent worked out a careful plan that consisted in its first stage of placing 9 African American students in Central High School, a school with approximately 2,000 white students. Then on September 2, 1957—the night before the first day of school—Arkansas governor, Orval Faubus, appeared on statewide television. The

SECTION ONE   **671**

Independent Practice

L2 **Citizenship** Point out that President Eisenhower claimed that you cannot "change the hearts of men with laws or decisions." Have students write a one-page essay detailing why they agree or disagree.

📂 Have students complete the Chapter 20, Section 1 Vocabulary and Guided Reading Activity. (Also in Spanish.) **LEP**

📂 Have students complete the Chapter 20 Cooperative Learning Activity.

GLENCOE
TECHNOLOGY

 Videodisc

Set on Freedom: The American Civil Rights Movement

Side A, Chapter 8
Title: Integration of Central High School, Little Rock, Arkansas, 1957
Subject: Federal government, desegregation
Ask: What role did the federal government play in the integration of Central High School? *(used troops to protect students and keep school open)*

Portfolio Project

Report Have students research the Ku Klux Klan and write about its activities, telling why it became stronger after the *Brown* v. *Board of* *Education* ruling. Suggest that students file their reports in their portfolios. 📂

ASSESS

Meeting Lesson Objectives

1. Describe the legal assault on school segregation in various parts of the country that culminated in *Brown* v. *Board of Education* in 1954. (1, 2, 5)
2. Describe the resistance by whites in the South to school desegregation. (3)
3. Explain President Eisenhower's reluctance to support school desegregation. (4)

VISUAL INSTRUCTION

Answer: *Little Rock Central High was integrated.*

Evaluate

Have students complete the Section Review.

Reteach

🎧 Have students listen to the Chapter 20, Section 1 audiocassette. (Also in Spanish.) **LEP**

Enrich

👉 Have students complete the Chapter 20 Geography in History Activity.

👉 Have students complete Supreme Court Case Study 21.

CLOSE

Ask: What problem faced African Americans in the early 1950s? *(segregation)*

672

UPI/BETTMANN NEWSPHOTOS

State and Federal Authorities Struggle Opposition to school desegregation by white citizens of Arkansas was so strong that armed soldiers had to protect African American students. *What were the results of this military intervention?*

governor announced that he had ordered state National Guard soldiers to surround Central High School the next morning. This move was necessary, the governor claimed, because of "evidence of disorder and threats of disorder."

The nine new students stayed away from school the next day, as school plans to delay and federal court orders to desegregate followed one another in quick succession. Many saw the issue as a fight between federal and state authority, but President Eisenhower was reluctant to intervene. Finally Governor Faubus met with Eisenhower. Faubus asked for but was denied a one-year delay in implementing desegregation. The meeting ended with the President thinking he had persuaded Faubus to allow integration of the school.

Chaos Erupts

Then, in a surprising show of defiance, Faubus removed the National Guard and left Little Rock. The result was chaos, as an angry crowd of nearly 1,000 white people gathered at the school the next day, September 4. The "Little Rock Nine," as the students had been dubbed, were forced to leave school at midday under police protection.

President Eisenhower was forced to intervene. Reluctantly he ordered federal troops into Little Rock and nationalized the Arkansas National Guard, to protect the students. For the first time since Reconstruction, a President had sent federal troops into the South to enforce the United States Constitution. On September 25, the day after the President's action, hundreds of paratroopers lined the route to the high school. The nine students arrived in a military convoy and were escorted by armed federal soldiers.

The paratroopers left at the end of the month, but the federalized National Guard remained for the rest of the school year. The next year, Little Rock public schools closed entirely.

White students attended private schools, schools outside the city, or none at all. Most African American students had no school to attend. Finally, in August 1959, following another Supreme Court ruling, the Little Rock school board reopened and integrated its public schools.

SECTION REVIEW

Vocabulary
1. Define: segregation, civil rights.

Checking Facts
2. What did *Brown* v. *Board of Education* say about the "separate but equal" doctrine?

3. In what way did many white Southerners react to the *Brown* decision, and what were some results of this reaction?

Critical Thinking
Making Inferences
4. Why did President Eisenhower feel that appointing Earl Warren to be chief justice of the United States was his worst mistake?

Linking Across Time
5. What events over the course of the first half of the 1900s might have been important in leading the Supreme Court to reconsider the *Plessy* v. *Ferguson* decision?

---

672 CHAPTER 20 THE CIVIL RIGHTS STRUGGLE

Section 1 Review Answers

1. segregation (668), **civil rights** (669)
2. It said that separate public education facilities are inherently unequal.
3. White Southerners resisted it; violence and federal intervention preceded integration.
4. Warren pushed for a unanimous decision in the *Brown* case, supporting integration; Eisenhower preferred a neutral stance.

5. Students might suggest that Americans felt that segregation was similar to Hitler's racial ideology. Contending for influence in developing countries in Africa, the United States looked bad supporting segregation. There were vigorous African American protests against discrimination.

Study and Writing Skill

PRESENTING STATISTICAL DATA

Learning the Skill

Effectively presented statistical data can strengthen and clarify oral and written material. NAACP lawyers, for example, used statistical data to present each of the cases brought against segregated school systems.

Understanding how to show statistical data in graph or chart form allows you to present information clearly and effectively, often focusing on a specific aspect of a broad topic. Data thus presented can be used to answer specific questions or to draw conclusions.

Below is a list of four visual-presentation formats and the main features of each.

Statistical Data Presentation Formats	
Format	**Characteristics**
Bar graphs	Compare data using colored bars
Charts	Show various aspects of data, using columns and rows
Circle graphs	Show percentages of a whole using a segmented circle
Line graphs	Show changes or trends over time using lines on a grid

To present statistical data, follow these steps:

a. Define the topic you want to cover.

b. Collect data about the topic (you can ask a reference librarian for assistance).

c. Decide which aspect(s) of the data to highlight.

d. Organize and present the data, highlighting the aspects you selected.

Practicing the Skill

Analyze the presentation of the data in the bar graph, the chart, and the circle graph below, Segregated Professional Schools,1945.

1. The bar graph uses labeled, colored bars to present information. What does the bar graph show? What do the divided bars indicate?

2. The chart presents data in labeled rows and columns. What does the chart show? Does it present more or less data than the bar graph?

3. The circle graph uses a circle to represent the total number of schools (74). What percentage accepted only white students, and what percentage accepted only African American students?

4. Which seems most effective to you—the bar graph, the chart, or the circle graph? Why?

5. You could also use a line graph to show a trend such as the number of law schools open to African American students over a specified period of time. What is another trend you could show with a line graph, using the data on this page?

Applying the Skill

Choose a chart or graph in a current newspaper or magazine. Analyze the information it presents. How else might this data be visually presented? Would it be more or less effective? Why?

Additional Practice

For additional practice, see Reinforcing Skills on page 697.

TEACH

This skill teaches students how to present statistical data clearly and concisely. Students study and discuss charts and graphs, referring to specific examples of a chart, a bar graph, and a circle graph. Students then explain how a line graph could be used to present similar kinds of data. Point out to students that how they choose to present statistical data depends upon what aspects of the data they wish to emphasize.

Additional Practice

☞ Have students complete the Chapter 20 Skill Reinforcement Activity.

Notes

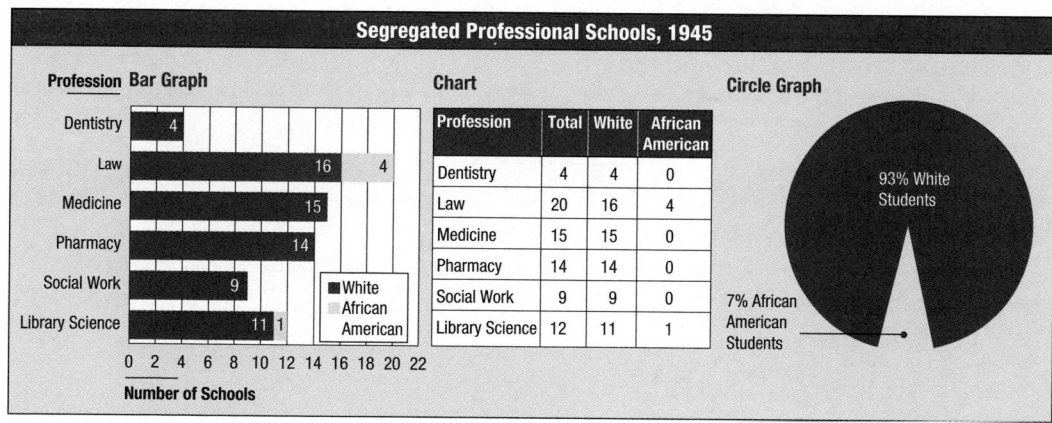

Segregated Professional Schools, 1945

Bar Graph — Number of Schools; White, African American

Profession	Total	White	African American
Dentistry	4	4	0
Law	20	16	4
Medicine	15	15	0
Pharmacy	14	14	0
Social Work	9	9	0
Library Science	12	11	1

Circle Graph: 93% White Students; 7% African American Students

Practicing the Skill Answers

1. in 1945, the number of six kinds of professional schools open to white students, to African American students; schools of law and of library science open to both

2. same kind of information as the bar graph but presented in a different format; more, lists number of schools open to African Americans, even when number is 0

3. whites: 93%; African Americans: 7%

4. Answers will vary: bar graph, visually cleaner; chart, presents more information; circle graph, less specific information but whole picture at a glance.

5. Answers will vary: the number of schools of library science open to African American students and the number open to white students over a specific period of time.

SECTION

2

FOCUS

Section Objectives

1. Describe the strategies used by the Southern Christian Leadership Conference to counter segregation in the South.
2. Describe the role the Student Nonviolent Coordinating Committee played in the civil rights movement.

Bellringer Activity

 While taking attendance at the beginning of the class period, display **Section Focus Transparency 63,** and have students answer the questions. (Or use the blackline master.)

FYI

Backlash Rosa Parks and her husband lost their jobs as a result of taking part in the boycott.

VISUAL INSTRUCTION

Simple Refusal Stirs Boycott Rosa Parks was fingerprinted by Deputy Sheriff D. H. Lackey. Fingerprinting is a reliable method of identification because no two people's prints are identical.

Ask: What happened as a result of Rosa Parks's actions? *(African American citizens conducted a successful boycott of Montgomery buses.)*

Freedom Now

DECEMBER 1, 1955: MONTGOMERY, ALABAMA—BUS BOYCOTT BEGINS

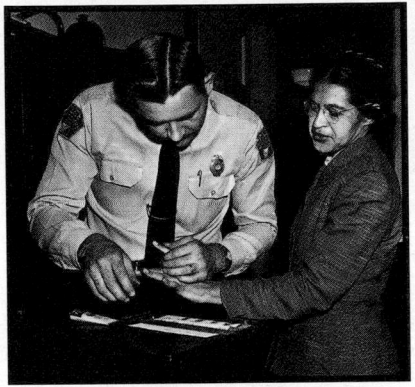

**Simple Refusal Stirs Boycott
Rosa Parks was prepared to fight for her civil rights.**

ROSA PARKS WAS TIRED. It was the Christmas shopping season, and the 43-year-old bespectacled woman worked hard as a tailor's assistant in a Montgomery, Alabama, store.

When Parks boarded the Cleveland Avenue bus, she was pleased to find a seat in the middle section. In Montgomery, African American riders could occupy the middle section seats unless the front seats reserved for whites were fully occupied. Then, in order to provide more seats for white riders, African American passengers had to move to seats farther back in the bus or stand.

By the third stop, the seats reserved for whites had filled up, and one white man was standing. The other African American passengers in Parks's row of seats got up and stood in the back, but she did not move.

The bus driver, James Blake, called out, "If you don't stand up, I'm going to have to call the police and have you arrested." "You may do that," Rosa Parks replied.

The Bus Boycott in Montgomery
Economic Means to Attain Goals

Rosa Parks's simple decision not to give up her seat set in motion a series of events with far-reaching consequences for the whole country. Later, many people came to regard her action as the true beginning of the civil rights movement of the 1950s and the 1960s. Out of Montgomery emerged the courage, leadership, and strategies for an entire movement.

The news of Parks's arrest soon spread through Montgomery's African American community. Protests like Parks's were not new, but hers was the kind of case community leaders had been waiting for. Parks was dignified, soft-spoken, well liked. She was a former secretary of the local NAACP chapter and was active in her church. The previous summer she had attended an

---

AS YOU READ

Vocabulary
► boycott
► nonviolent resistance
► civil disobedience

Think About . . .
► the strategies that the Southern Christian Leadership Conference used to counter segregation in the South.

► the role that the Student Nonviolent Coordinating Committee played in the civil rights movement.

674   CHAPTER 20   THE CIVIL RIGHTS STRUGGLE

Section 2 Resources

REPRODUCIBLE RESOURCES

📁 Lesson Plan 20-2
📁 Section 2 Quiz
📁 Vocabulary and Guided Reading Activity 20-2
📁 Supreme Court Case Study 35
📁 Interpreting Political Cartoons 24

MULTIMEDIA RESOURCES

📷 Section Focus Transparency 63
🌐 Powers of the Supreme Court
⊙ Martin Luther King, Jr.
🌐 Landmark Documents in American History
💾 Student Self-Test: Software Review
💾 Testmaker
🎧 Chapter 20 Digest Audiocassette

interracial workshop at the Highlander Folk School in Tennessee. Now, local civil rights leaders asked if she would be willing to fight her case for as long as it took to win. Despite her mother's and husband's fears, she said yes.

The Boycott

Immediately the call went out for a **boycott** of the Montgomery bus system. By refusing to use the services of the bus company, African Americans would exert economic pressure on the company. Jo Ann Robinson, an English professor at Alabama State College, worked through the night writing and mimeographing 35,000 leaflets that instructed, "Don't ride the buses to work, to town, to school, or anywhere on Monday."

Meanwhile, ministers and community leaders met and pledged their support of the one-day boycott. They agreed to a second meeting at Holt Street Baptist Church on Monday evening to decide whether to continue the boycott for more than one day.

Dr. Martin Luther King, Jr., the new minister of the Dexter Avenue Baptist Church, announced the boycott during his Sunday morning services, asking for the congregation's support. So did other ministers, including the white minister of the Trinity Lutheran Church.

A Successful Strategy

On Monday, nearly empty buses rolled through Montgomery. Although Rosa Parks was found guilty and fined $10 plus $4 in court charges, the boycott was a success. Of the 52,000 passengers who normally rode the bus every day, 40,000 were African American, and they had stayed away in droves. That afternoon the ministers and community leaders met again to organize. They named themselves the Montgomery Improvement Association and selected a president—Dr. King.

That evening some 5,000 people packed into the Holt Street Baptist Church. Loudspeakers were hastily set up for the thousands more who gathered outside. King told the crowd:

> There comes a time when people get tired. We are here this evening to say to those who have mistreated us so long that we are tired—tired of being segregated and humiliated, tired of being kicked about by the brutal feet of oppression . . .
>
> If you will protest courageously and yet with dignity and Christian love, in the history books that are

Supporting the Movement Dr. Martin Luther King, Jr., was a powerful communicator. *How did King use his communication abilities to promote civil rights?*

> written in future generations, historians will have to pause and say "there lived a great people—a black people—who injected a new meaning and dignity into the veins of civilization." This is our challenge and our overwhelming responsibility.
>
> —Dr. Martin Luther King, Jr., 1955

The Montgomery bus boycott lasted nearly 400 days. At first the city's 18 African American–owned cab companies filled in by agreeing to accept African American passengers for 10 cents, the price of bus fare. Then the city threatened to fine the taxi companies for not charging the full 45-cent taxi fare.

Next, boycott leaders worked out an elaborate plan of car pooling. Station wagons picked up riders at 42 separate locations. Funds to buy and operate the station wagons—called "rolling churches" because they were painted with the names of churches—came from white and African American supporters of the boycott in Montgomery and throughout the nation. When city officials countered by preventing the "rolling churches" from getting the necessary insurance, King arranged coverage with Lloyd's of London, an insurer known for covering almost any risk.

City officials had not expected such strong resistance from the African American community. As the bus company continued to lose money day after day, the segregationists in power became increasingly frustrated. The mayor, the city commissioners, the police commissioner, and the city council all publicly joined the White Citizens' Council. King's house was bombed. King and 88 other African American leaders were arrested and fined for conspiring to boycott.

TEACH

Guided Practice

L1 Discussion With students discuss why Rosa Parks's action was considered successful even though she was found guilty and fined.

VISUAL INSTRUCTION

Supporting the Movement Dr. Martin Luther King, Jr., would remain faithful to his insistence on nonviolence and in 1964 would be awarded the Nobel Peace Prize.

Answer: *He spoke effectively to his congregation, encouraging their support of civil rights protest activities.*

Facts on File

Landmark Documents in American History Have students review "'The Montgomery Story,' Martin Luther King, Jr., 1956" and write a paragraph about the intent of the document.

Cooperative Learning

Newspaper Reports Organize the class into three heterogeneous groups. Each group should research and write a news report on one of these topics: Rosa Parks's refusal to give up her seat, the bus boycott, or the emergence of a coordinated civil rights movement. Remind students to keep two perspectives in mind—that of the African American citizens and that of the Montgomery officials. Groups can then combine their reports into a news booklet covering the series of events.

VISUAL INSTRUCTION

Impact of Boycott Felt
Montgomery lost about
$18,000 a day during the
boycott (40,000 x 45 cents).

Answer: *The Supreme Court ruled that segregation on Montgomery buses was unconstitutional.*

ABCNEWS
iNTERACTiVE™

Videodisc

Powers of the Supreme Court

Side 1, Chapter 21
Title: Amendment 14
(1868): Civil Rights
Subject: The beginnings
of the bus boycott
Ask: What led to the
boycott? *(Rosa Parks's arrest)*

**See Powers of the
Supreme Court Guide-
book page 33 for com-
plete lesson plan.**

*Martin Luther
King, Jr.*

Side 1, Chapter 10
Title: 1956 Montgomery
Bus Boycott: Rosa Parks
Subject: Rosa Parks
describes what happened.
Ask: Who was Rosa
Parks? *(African American
who refused to give up seat)*

**See Martin Luther King,
Jr. Guidebook page 13
for complete lesson
plan.**

DAN WEINER, COURTESY SANDRA WEINER

Impact of Boycott Felt Although African Americans enjoyed few rights in the South, their numbers gave them economic power. *What finally ended the Montgomery bus boycott?*

The end of the boycott finally came when the United States Supreme Court ruled that segregation on Montgomery buses was unconstitutional. City officials challenged this ruling on the grounds that it violated states' rights. When the Court's written order was received on December 20, 1956, however, the segregationists gave up. All riders sat where they pleased on buses that rolled through Montgomery.

> A in't gonna ride them buses no more,
> Ain't gonna ride no more.
> Why don't all the white folk know
> That I ain't gonna ride no more.
> —Sung by Montgomery boycotters,
> 1955–1956

Martin Luther King, Jr.
An African American Leader Emerges

After the Montgomery boycott, Dr. Martin Luther King, Jr., emerged as the unchallenged leader of the African American protest movement. Short in stature and gentle in manner, King was at that time only 27 years old. What had propelled him into this demanding role in history?

The son of a Baptist minister, King, like his father, was named after Martin Luther, the founder of the Protes-

tant branch of Christianity. The younger King grew up in a comfortable, middle-class home in Atlanta. He attended Morehouse College there and when he was 18 years old decided on a career in the ministry. He already showed a gift for the eloquent, emotion-arousing art of speaking popular in Southern churches. After a trial sermon in his father's Ebenezer Baptist Church, he was ordained a Baptist minister.

King then went north for more schooling—to Crozer Theological Seminary in Pennsylvania and then to Boston University for a Ph.D. in religion. By the time he first arrived in Montgomery in September 1954 as pastor of the Dexter Avenue Baptist Church, he had also met and married Coretta Scott.

The Creation of SCLC

Following the success of the Montgomery bus boycott, King faced the issue of how to extend the lessons learned there to other cities and other civil rights arenas. In January 1957, King called a meeting in Atlanta of 60 Southern ministers to discuss nonviolent integration.

The news that the home and the church of King's friend and fellow minister Ralph Abernathy had been bombed marred the beginning of the conference. After a hurried trip back to Montgomery to survey the damage, King returned to Atlanta to assume the presidency of the newly formed Southern Christian Leadership Conference (SCLC).

Nonviolence

From the beginning of the Montgomery boycott, King encouraged his followers to use **nonviolent resistance.** This meant that those who carried out the demonstrations should not fight with authorities, even if provoked to do so.

The SCLC and the Fellowship of Reconciliation (FOR), the latter an interracial organization founded in 1914, conducted workshops in nonviolent methods of resistance for civil rights activists. Those attending learned how to sit quietly while others jeered at them, called them names, and even spat on them. Workshop participants also learned how to guard themselves against blows and how to protect one another by forming a circle of bodies around someone under attack.

676 CHAPTER 20 THE CIVIL RIGHTS STRUGGLE

Meeting Special Needs

Learning Disabled This activity helps to address the particular needs of learning disabled students. Provide for students an audio or video recording of a speech by Dr. Martin Luther King, Jr. (available at most public libraries).

Have students discuss King's method of delivering a speech. Ask students why they think people listened so intently to what Dr. King had to say.

King's use of nonviolent tactics has often been compared to those Mohandas Gandhi used in India's struggle for independence from Great Britain. In both cases the final victory depended on using moral arguments to change the minds of the oppressors. King linked nonviolence to the Christian theme of loving one's enemy. He was certainly familiar with Gandhi's teachings, however, and in 1959 traveled to India to talk with some of Gandhi's followers.

The Gandhian strategy of nonviolence involved four steps: investigation, negotiation, publicity, and demonstration. Applied to civil rights actions, this meant that the activists ought first to look into a situation and gather the facts. Next, the activists should attempt to negotiate with the party responsible for the segregation. Failing that, others should be made aware of the situation and what the activists intended to do. Only then should action, such as a march or a demonstration, be carried out.

Soon after the victory in Montgomery, nonviolent methods began to be applied in a startlingly fresh way. Students in universities and colleges all over the country were tired of waiting for change. They vowed to integrate the nation's segregated lunch counters, hotels, and entertainment facilities by a simple new strategy of nonviolent resistence—sitting.

A Season of Sit-ins
Students Sit to Protest

The first sit-in was not elaborately planned. The four African American freshmen from North Carolina Agricultural and Technical College had never attended a workshop on nonviolence, but late one night they began to talk about what they could do to fight segregation. Earlier in the day Joseph McNeil, one of the four, had tried to get something to eat at the local bus station but had been turned down. He was hurt and resentful.

"We should just sit at the counter and refuse to go until they serve us," one suggested.

"You really mean it?" his friend asked.

"Sure I mean it," the first replied.

The next day, February 1, 1960, the four walked into a local store. Nervous, they first tested the waters to see if their business was welcome. One bought a tube of toothpaste, another some school supplies. Then the four sat down at the whites-only lunch counter and asked for coffee and doughnuts.

"I'm sorry but we don't serve colored here," the waitress said.

STATE HISTORICAL SOCIETY OF WISCONSIN

Sit-ins: A Powerful Instrument of Integration Employing nonviolent tactics brought abuse not only from authorities but also from people who disagreed with the protesters. *Who started the sit-ins?*

SECTION TWO **677**

ABCNEWS INTERACTIVE™

 Videodisc

Martin Luther King, Jr.

Side 1, Chapter 11
Title: 1956 Montgomery Bus Boycott: Street Scenes
Subject: Street scenes in Montgomery during bus boycott
Ask: What made the boycott so successful? *(bus companies lost revenue)*

See Martin Luther King, Jr. Guidebook page 15 for complete lesson plan.

Side 1, Chapter 12
Title: 1956 Montgomery Bus Boycott: the Ku Klux Klan
Subject: Ku Klux Klan members, Montgomery
Ask: What was the Ku Klux Klan? *(prosegregration white supremacist group)*

See Martin Luther King, Jr., Guidebook page 16 for complete lesson plan.

VISUAL INSTRUCTION

Sit-ins: A Powerful Instrument of Integration Northern students picketed chain stores such as Woolworth's to support Southern students' sit-ins.

Answer: *four African American students who sat at a whites-only lunch counter*

Portfolio Project

Report Martin Luther King, Jr., was heavily influenced by Mohandas Gandhi's tactics of nonviolent resistance. Gandhi, in turn, had been influenced by Henry David Thoreau's essay, "Civil Disobedience." Have students research and write a brief report on Gandhi or Thoreau, explaining the philosophy of nonviolent resistance or of civil disobedience. Suggest that they file the reports in their portfolios.

Independent Practice

L2 **History** Martin Luther King, Jr., was named after Martin Luther, a sixteenth-century clergyman. Have students research and write a brief report on Martin Luther. In the report, have students discuss ways in which Martin Luther King, Jr., could be compared with Martin Luther.

✎ Have students complete the Chapter 20 Section 2 Vocabulary and Guided Reading Activity. (Also in Spanish.) **LEP**

ASSESS

Meeting Lesson Objectives

Each section objective is tested by the section review questions that follow it in parentheses.

1. Describe the strategies used by the Southern Christian Leadership Conference to counter segregation in the South. (1, 2, 5)
2. Describe the role the Student Nonviolent Coordinating Committee played in the civil rights movement. (1, 3, 4)

CHART STUDY

Ask: When was segregation declared illegal?
Answer: *May 1954*

"I beg your pardon," Franklin McCain said. "You just served me at a counter two feet away. Why is it that you serve me at one counter and [not] at another?"

The 4 continued to sit at the counter until it closed about half an hour later. The next day they came back, accompanied by 27 other students. The third day, 63 students sat down at the lunch counter. They were not served, so they just sat. On the fourth day, 3 white students from the Women's College of the University of North Carolina joined them. By Friday, the fifth day, the number of demonstrators had grown to about 300. They sat in shifts. If some students had to leave to attend class, other students who stood waiting behind them took their place at the lunch counter.

On Saturday evening 1,600 students attended a victory rally, exhilarated by the announcement that the company was ready to negotiate. They soon discovered that the celebration was premature, however, for the company was willing to make only token changes in its segregation policy.

Two months later students resumed their lunch-counter sit-ins. Adopting a new hard line, the city arrested 45 students and charged them with trespassing. This in turn so enraged the students and their supporters that they launched a massive boycott of stores with segregated lunch counters. As sales dropped by a third, the merchants reluctantly gave in. Six months after the 4 freshmen had first sat down and asked for coffee, they were finally served.

The Sit-ins Spread

Meanwhile, the spontaneous grassroots movement started a reaction that spread like a brushfire throughout the border states and the upper South. By April 1960, college and high school students in 78 communities had staged sit-ins, and 2,000 protesters had been arrested. A year later those numbers had nearly doubled. By September 1961, 70,000 African American and white students were sitting in for social change.

The targets of many sit-ins were Southern stores that were part of national chains. In some Northern cities, however, students picketed stores of the same chains, carrying signs that read We Walk So They May Sit. As more lunch counters integrated under the pressure of sit-ins, variations of the technique emerged. Students held "kneel-ins" to integrate churches, "read-ins" in libraries, "wade-ins" at beaches, and "sleep-ins" in motel lobbies.

A Student Movement

The driving center of the civil rights movement had spread from the legal committees of the NAACP and African American churches to college campuses. The students were impatient. As schoolchildren in 1954 when the Supreme Court ruled on the *Brown* decision, they had expected immediate results, but progress had been slow. In 1957 African Americans had shared in the excitement of Ghana's independence from Great Britain. During 1960 alone, 11 African countries threw off the shackles of colonialism. "All of Africa will be free before we can get a lousy cup of coffee," writer James Baldwin complained.

The nonviolence of the students provoked increasingly hostile reactions from those who opposed them. In Nashville, after four students had successfully desegregated a bus terminal, they were badly beaten. In other cities white teenagers poked students in the ribs, ground cigarettes out on their backs, or threw ketchup on them as they ate.

The Creation of SNCC

Ella J. Baker, executive secretary of King's SCLC, was impressed with the students' commitment and courage, but she was concerned about their lack of coordination and leadership. She invited 100 student leaders of the sit-ins to a conference at Shaw University in Raleigh, North Carolina, over Easter weekend in April 1960. To her surprise, some 300 students showed up,

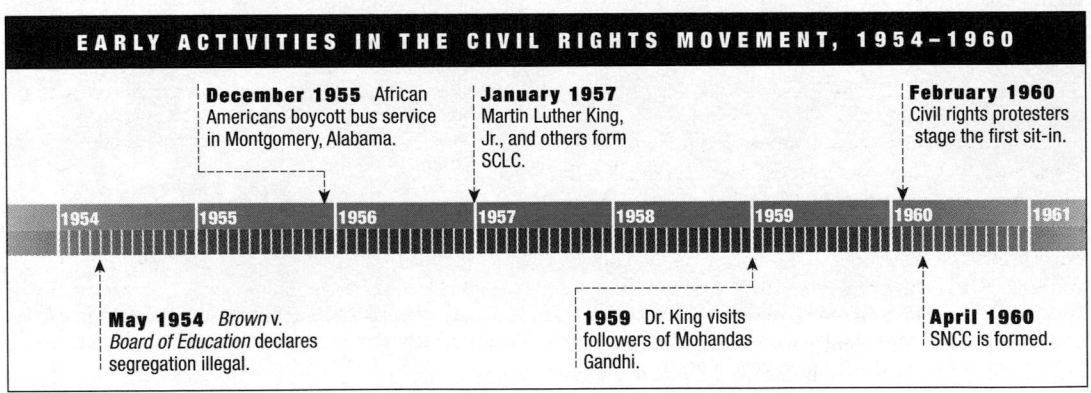

EARLY ACTIVITIES IN THE CIVIL RIGHTS MOVEMENT, 1954–1960

December 1955 African Americans boycott bus service in Montgomery, Alabama.

January 1957 Martin Luther King, Jr., and others form SCLC.

February 1960 Civil rights protesters stage the first sit-in.

1954 | 1955 | 1956 | 1957 | 1958 | 1959 | 1960 | 1961

May 1954 *Brown v. Board of Education* declares segregation illegal.

1959 Dr. King visits followers of Mohandas Gandhi.

April 1960 SNCC is formed.

678 CHAPTER 20 THE CIVIL RIGHTS STRUGGLE

Extending the Content

Commitment to Nonviolence Ralph Abernathy's church and home were bombed shortly after King had organized the Atlanta conference on nonviolent resistance. In the face of this and many other acts of violence, King and his followers stuck to their commitment of nonviolence. Discuss with students why they think so many people were willing to resist using violence, even when faced with continued violence. Some students may wish to share their findings about Gandhi and Thoreau from the Portfolio Project on page 677.

most from Southern African American communities, but a few also from Northern colleges. Out of that meeting came a new civil rights organization, the Student Nonviolent Coordinating Committee (SNCC, pronounced *snihk*).

King addressed the students that weekend. He stressed the moral power of nonviolence, saying, "The tactics of nonviolence without the spirit of nonviolence may become a new kind of violence."

One of the slogans students warmly applauded at the conference was "jail not bail." The decision to refuse bail and to remain in jail came about for practical as well as philosophical reasons. Supporters of the sit-ins throughout the country had been contributing bail money so that students who were arrested could be quickly released on bail. As the number of arrests grew, the bail money became a heavy drain on the treasuries of civil rights organizations. Philosophically, opting for jail placed the burden of supporting the arrested protesters onto the police and local officials. Also, through press coverage, jail service kept the eyes of the nation focused on the protesters and their conflicts with the authorities.

In adopting "jail not bail," SNCC followed an American tradition of **civil disobedience,** or nonviolent resistance of unfair laws. Henry David Thoreau, for example, had spent a night in jail in 1846 for refusing to pay his poll tax as a protest against slavery and the Mexican War. He wrote in his essay "Civil Disobedience":

> How does it become a man to behave toward this American government today? I answer, that he cannot without disgrace be associated with it. I cannot for an instant recognize that political organization as my government which is the slave's government also.
>
> —Henry David Thoreau, "Civil Disobedience," 1849

Within a year SNCC evolved from an activity that students engaged in between classes to a full-time commitment. The most active students postponed their studies, dropping out of college to work for the movement. In the fall of 1961, SNCC sent 16 "field secretaries" to areas most resistant to integration. By early 1964 that number had grown to 150.

A field secretary could count on only about $10 a week from SNCC, so most roomed and boarded with local African American residents. This arrangement could mean considerable hardship to many Southern African Americans who lived constantly on the edge of poverty. SNCC workers and their hosts were also subject to physical harassment, even danger.

Yet, more than federal court decisions and civil disobedience would be required before the segregation system of 100 years would finally break down. The active commitment of the nation's President and the force of the executive branch also would be needed. The year that the sit-ins erupted and SNCC was formed, John F. Kennedy became the presidential nominee of the Democratic party.

come let us build a new world together
STUDENT NONVIOLENT COORDINATING COMMITTEE

Student Activism Grows Student activism powered SNCC, an organization that helped bring the civil rights movement out of the courtroom and into the segregated communities of the South. *How did the policy of "jail not bail" focus public attention on civil rights issues?*

SECTION REVIEW

Vocabulary
1. Define: boycott, nonviolent resistance, civil disobedience.

Checking Facts
2. What was the major goal and the primary tactic of SCLC?
3. Why did SNCC members adopt the policy of "jail not bail"?

Critical Thinking
Determining Cause and Effect
4. How successful were the student sit-ins? Did they have a major effect on the integration of public facilities in the South? Do you think they have had a lasting effect on attitudes in the South?

Linking Across Time
5. What were the goals of the abolitionists of the 1850s? How were the goals of people such as Dr. Martin Luther King, Jr., and Ralph Abernathy similar to and different from those of the abolitionists?

SECTION TWO   **679**

VISUAL INSTRUCTION

Student Activism Grows Birmingham's "Bull" Connor felt that SNCC members were publicity-hungry, "upstart" students who were damaging the Southern economy and disturbing the peace.

Answer: *The TV and press coverage of jailed civil rights protesters focused public attention on the issues of the movement.*

Evaluate

Have students complete the Section Review.

☞ 💿 Assign the Section 2 Quiz or use the Testmaker to develop a customized quiz.

Reteach

🎧 Have students listen to the Chapter 20, Section 2 audiocassette. (Also in Spanish.) **LEP**

Enrich

🗀 Have students complete Interpreting Political Cartoons 24.

🗀 Have students complete Supreme Court Case Study 35.

CLOSE

Ask: What were the two groups that emerged as major forces for civil rights, and what were some of their activities? *(SCLC and SNCC; nonviolent protests, marches, boycotts, sit-ins)*

SECTION

3

FOCUS

Section Objectives

1. Describe how politics shaped President Kennedy's civil rights policy.
2. Explain how militants on both sides of the civil rights issue forced Kennedy to side with Martin Luther King, Jr.
3. Describe the successes of the civil rights movement during Lyndon Johnson's presidency.

Bellringer Activity

 While taking attendance at the beginning of the class period, display **Section Focus Transparency 64,** and have students answer the questions. (Or use the black-line master.)

VISUAL INSTRUCTION

Freedom Riders Face Violence The Fellowship of Reconciliation (FOR), a non-violent, interracial organization founded in 1914, had sponsored a biracial "freedom ride" in 1947. The photo on this page is of a Freedom Ride in 1961.

Ask: What dangers did Freedom Riders face? *(firebombings, beatings)*

At the Movies

The 1988 movie *Mississippi Burning* is a fictionalized account of three civil rights workers (Andrew Goodman, Michael Schwerner, and James Chaney) murdered in Mississippi in 1964.

Government Response

MAY 21, 1961: FREEDOM RIDERS MOBBED IN MONTGOMERY, ALABAMA

Freedom Riders Face Violence
Soldiers guard a bus carrying Freedom Riders.

THE PASSENGERS WERE EXPECTING TROUBLE. On the way to Birmingham, Alabama, from Atlanta, Georgia, one of their buses had been firebombed, burned to an iron skeleton. An angry, violent mob had met the second bus as it limped into the Birmingham terminal. After that the bus drivers, all white, refused to go on. For two days the "Freedom Riders," as the passengers were called, waited for the bus company to find other drivers. Others of their group recuperated in hospital beds. Finally, frustrated, they left the city by plane.

Some thought the Freedom Rides were over then. However, a group of students fresh from sit-ins in Nashville, Tennessee, flew to Birmingham intent on continuing the integrated journey. United States Attorney General Robert Kennedy asked for, and thought he had received, a pledge from the governor of Alabama to protect the bus and its passengers.

The ride was calm during the first leg of the journey to Montgomery, Alabama. Alabama state patrol cars were seen at intervals. When the bus pulled into the Montgomery terminal, however, an angry mob of about 1,000 white people quickly surrounded the bus. No police were present.

John Doar, a Justice Department lawyer on the scene, placed a call to the attorney general's office as the bus rolled into the station. "Now the passengers are coming off," Doar reported. "They're standing on a corner of the platform. Oh, there are fists, punching. A bunch of men led by a guy with a bleeding face are beating them," Doar continued. "There are no cops. It's terrible. It's terrible. There's not a cop in sight. People are yelling, 'Get 'em, get 'em.' It's awful."

The mob violence and the city's indifference became front-page news throughout the world. Deeply disturbed and faced with international embarrassment,

AS YOU READ

Vocabulary
▶ enfranchisement
▶ militant
▶ filibuster

Think About . . .
▶ the ways in which politics shaped President Kennedy's civil rights policy.
▶ how militants forced President Kennedy to side with Dr. Martin Luther King, Jr.

▶ the successes of the civil rights movement that came about during Lyndon Johnson's presidency.

Section 3 Resources

REPRODUCIBLE RESOURCES
📋 Lesson Plan 20-3
📋 Section 3 Quiz
📋 Unit 8 American Literature Reading
📋 Vocabulary and Guided Reading Activity 20-3

MULTIMEDIA RESOURCES
📋 Section Focus Transparency 64
📼 Great Speeches
💿 Powers of the Supreme Court
💿 Landmark Documents in American History

💾 Student Self-Test: Software Review
💾 Testmaker
🎧 Chapter 20 Digest Audiocassette

President Kennedy and his brother Robert sent federal marshals to keep order in Alabama. The segregationists would never forgive them for that move.

The next night Robert Kennedy called Governor John Patterson and pleaded with him to reinforce the marshals protecting Martin Luther King, Jr., and a group of his followers who were trapped inside a church by a crowd of several thousand whites. At the last minute, Patterson did send in Alabama National Guard troops to assist the marshals, but not until after the following exchange:

"You are destroying us politically," Patterson told Kennedy.

Kennedy replied, "It's more important that the people in the church survive physically than for us to survive politically."

JFK and Civil Rights
Kennedy Supports Civil Rights

John F. Kennedy had not demonstrated a strong commitment to civil rights when he had become a candidate for the presidency in 1960. Like many other politicians on the state and national scene, his views on the civil rights issue reflected mainly its political importance to him. The question to him was how his stand would help him defeat his Republican opponent, Richard Nixon.

On the Campaign Trail

The dilemma Kennedy faced was this: To win, he needed both the segregationists' vote in the South and the African Americans' vote in the North. Kennedy relied upon his vice-presidential running mate, Texas Senator Lyndon Johnson, to bring the Southern white vote. Republican Eisenhower had attracted significant African American support in the 1956 election, and Kennedy expected that Nixon would make a bid for that support by endorsing civil rights.

Kennedy decided to make an all-out effort for the African Americans' vote. He endorsed the sit-ins and promised to sponsor a civil rights bill during the next congressional session. He also pledged—"with a stroke of the presidential pen," he said—to end racial discrimination in federally supported public housing.

In the closing days of the campaign, King's arrest during a sit-in at an Atlanta department store put both presidential candidates to the test. The other protesters were quickly released, but not King. The judge had ruled that King's sit-in arrest was a violation of his probation, which King had received as a result of an earlier con-

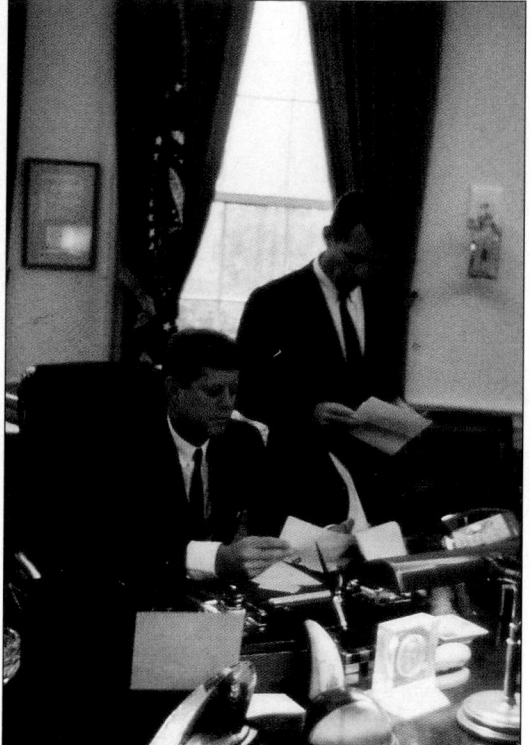

Politics and Civil Rights **The Kennedys were politicians who understood the political significance of the civil rights issue.** *What was John Kennedy's position on civil rights during the presidential campaign?*

viction for driving without a valid driver's license. King was sentenced to four months of hard labor on a Georgia road gang. He was led off in handcuffs and shackles to a rural state prison.

Coretta King and other King supporters feared that King might not come out of that prison alive. There followed a flurry of phone calls to whomever the civil rights leaders thought might be able to help.

Nixon did nothing. John Kennedy, however, telephoned Coretta King and expressed to her his concern, and Robert Kennedy phoned the judge on King's behalf. When King was released a day later, the Kennedys were given much of the credit. "It's time for all of us to take off our Nixon button," Martin Luther King, Sr., exclaimed gratefully.

John Kennedy won the election by the narrowest margin of popular votes in any presidential election in the twentieth century. His ability to carry 7 of the 11 states of the old Confederacy and 70 percent of the African American vote was a major factor in his political success at that time.

TEACH

Guided Practice

L3 Discussion Lead students in a discussion of Kennedy's failure to keep his campaign promises on civil rights. Are Presidents obliged to keep campaign promises? Have recent Presidents kept their campaign promises? Explain.

 Curriculum Connection

Literature Have students discuss their interpretation of how the following words of Victor Hugo relate to the civil rights movement of the 1960s: "No army can withstand the strength of an idea whose time has come."

VISUAL INSTRUCTION

Politics and Civil Rights JFK valued RFK's opinions and support. The brothers talked with each other several times each day.

Answer: *Kennedy decided during the campaign that, to get the African American vote, he would endorse civil rights protests and promise to sponsor a civil rights bill.*

Cooperative Learning

Registering to Vote Organize the class into 2 groups to research the ease or difficulty of registering to vote, then and now. One group can research the tactics used in the South before 1965 to keep African Americans from registering to vote. The other group can contact the local election board to find out how to register to vote in their community. If possible, have students obtain a copy of a voter registration form. Together, students can complete the form and compare the earlier voter registration process in the South with that of today.

VISUAL INSTRUCTION

The Push for Voter Participation The photo was taken in 1964—the same year that three voter registration workers were shot in Mississippi. (See At the Movies, page 680.)

Answer: *Suing for voting rights was often unsuccessful, as many federal judges, some appointed by President Kennedy, were unsympathetic to civil rights issues.*

 Facts on File

Landmark Documents in American History Have students review "'Freedom Riders' statement, John F. Kennedy, 1961" and write a paragraph about the intent of the document.

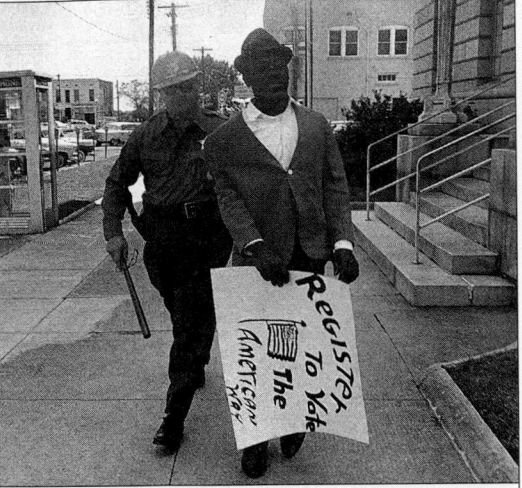

The Push for Voter Participation In Selma, an African American man carrying a voter registration sign is arrested by an Alabama State Trooper. *Why was the initial attempt at enfranchisement unsuccessful?*

Kennedy's Civil Rights Strategy

Despite his campaign promises, Kennedy made no mention of civil rights in his Inaugural Address. Instead, during his first two years in office he tried to avoid losing either Southern white or African American support. He failed to back the promised civil rights bill, which would have required Southern school districts to submit desegregation plans by 1963. When he finally did issue an executive order on housing discrimination in late 1962, it was so weak that it had little effect.

Rather than attacking segregation, Kennedy sought to keep black support by promising African Americans jobs and votes. To find more jobs, Kennedy created a presidential committee, headed by Vice President Johnson. The committee was charged with ending job discrimination in federal government departments and businesses that contracted with the federal government. Johnson chose to rely on voluntary efforts instead of using strict measures such as canceling contracts. The result was that during Kennedy's term the committee accomplished little.

Kennedy was not any more successful in helping African Americans obtain voting rights. In 100 counties of the Deep South, only 5 percent of voting-age African Americans were registered to vote. The civil rights acts passed in 1957 and in 1960 gave the attorney general power to sue in federal courts on behalf of African Americans denied the right to vote because of their race. Accordingly, Robert Kennedy had sent a group of lawyers to the South, to sue when necessary. In 3 years the Justice Department had filed 50 voting-rights cases.

The results of this effort at **enfranchisement,** or obtaining the rights of citizenship, for African Americans through the courts was, however, largely unsuccessful. This was so in part because President Kennedy himself had appointed a number of federal judges who were unsympathetic to civil rights.

Although President Kennedy could produce neither the jobs nor the votes he promised, he did appoint a number of African Americans to his administration. He invited prominent African Americans to social events at the White House and made other symbolic gestures that the African American community applauded. At the same time, many politicians appreciated his reluctance to address segregation issues head-on. His efforts to appeal to both sides of the civil rights issue might have continued if **militants**—activists who would not tolerate any compromise—on both sides had not forced his hand.

Kennedy and the Militants
Kennedy Sides With Civil Rights Protesters

Civil rights demonstrators demanded "Freedom now!" and white segregationists cried "Segregation forever!" If violent whites attacked nonviolent demonstrators, Kennedy would have to make a choice. Either he would have to stay aloof, losing the support of those aligned with the civil rights movement, or he would have to intervene, alienating segregationists. This presented Kennedy with a difficult political dilemma.

The Freedom Riders

The first crisis occurred with the arrival on the scene of the Freedom Riders. James Farmer, executive director of the Congress of Racial Equality (CORE), organized these carefully selected interracial groups of bus passengers. In December 1960, the Supreme Court had ruled that all bus stations and terminals serving interstate travelers should be integrated. The purpose of the Freedom Rides was to test the execution of that decision.

On May 4, 1961, the first busload of 13 CORE volunteers rolled out of the Washington, D.C., bus terminal, bound for New Orleans. On the bus, whites sat in the back, and African American volunteers sat in the front. At each stop, African American volunteers got off the bus and entered the whites-only waiting rooms to test whether the facilities were integrated.

The first leg of the journey went well. Violence, however, soon caught up with the Freedom Riders at Anniston, Alabama, where one of the buses was firebombed. When Robert Kennedy finally intervened in Montgomery, he appealed to the Freedom Riders to wait for

Meeting Special Needs

Attention Deficit Disorder Have students with attention deficit disorder work with partners to study the diagraphic about the Freedom Riders. Encourage partners to tell each other the story of the Freedom Riders in their own words.

the situation to calm down before continuing. They insisted, however, on moving on to Jackson, Mississippi, and potentially more danger. Each of the 26 African Americans and 2 whites aboard the bus wrote out the names and addresses of persons to be notified in case they were killed. "Everyone on the bus was prepared to die," one Freedom Rider recalled.

Kennedy made a deal with Mississippi Senator James O. Eastland. Kennedy would not interfere by sending in federal marshals if Eastland would guarantee there would be no mob violence.

There were no mobs waiting for the Freedom Riders in Jackson; however, police, state troopers, and Mississippi National Guard soldiers were everywhere. As the Riders stepped off the bus and tried to enter the whites-only waiting room, they were quickly arrested for trespassing and taken to jail.

Despite the violence and the jail sentences, more Freedom Riders kept coming all summer. More than 300 were jailed in Jackson alone. Finally, the attorney general petitioned the Interstate Commerce Commission to issue a ruling against segregation of interstate facilities. The ICC made such an announcement on September 22; CORE's victory was secured.

The Voter Education Project

In an effort to steer the civil rights organizations away from violent confrontations with Southern segregationists, Robert Kennedy began to stress the importance of African American voter registration. He reasoned that if more

THE FREEDOM RIDE, MONTGOMERY, ALABAMA, MAY 20, 1961

At Birmingham on May 14, 1961, the Freedom Riders had been savagely attacked. Bus drivers refused to take the group farther. The governor refused to guarantee their safe passage. Finally, however, on the morning of May 20, they set out on the 90-mile trip from Birmingham to Montgomery.

8:30 A.M., May 20: Bus leaves Birmingham with protection of police patrol cars and planes.

9:50 A.M.: Planes fly away as bus crosses Montgomery city line.

Route of the Freedom Rides

Dep. May 4, 1961
Arr. May 14 Dep. May 20
Arr. May 24 and 25
Arr. May 20 Dep. May 24

10:00 A.M.: As bus arrives, patrol cars disappear. The terminal seems empty.

10:00 A.M.: A group of up to 1,000 whites advance with lead pipes, bottles, baseball bats—setting upon the Freedom Riders as they emerge from the bus.

2:30 P.M.: Governor Patterson, at the State Capitol, orders the arrest of the Freedom Riders.

10:05 A.M.: As mob slams into them, riders are forced to flee, but their way is blocked. Some find shelter in post office.

10:10 A.M.: Police arrive, but mob reign continues for 2 hours.

Despite serious injuries, ambulances are forced away.

The Freedom Riders put their lives on the line to ensure desegregation. *How did the danger increase for these Freedom Riders when they crossed the line from Montgomery to Birmingham?*

SECTION THREE **683**

GRAPH STUDY

Presidential aide John Seigenthaler recounted the mob scene at the bus terminal: "The Freedom Riders emerging from the bus were being mauled. It looked like two hundred, three hundred people all over them. There were screams and shouts. . . ."

The one white man aboard the bus, Jim Zwerg, was viciously attacked—as if the mob was furious that he would side with African Americans.

Answer: *The police patrol cars and the airplanes left, leaving the riders unprotected.*

Portfolio Project

Photo Essay Have students research and develop a photo essay about the Freedom Riders. Students may photocopy pictures from library sources, asking for librarian assistance as necessary. Have them write a brief caption for each picture. Encourage them to include the photo essays in their portfolios.

 Facts on File

Landmark Documents in American History Have students review and write a paragraph about the intent of the document.

VISUAL INSTRUCTION

Protest Leaders March for Equality King and Abernathy led the protesters in Birmingham, knowing that this would probably lead to their arrest.

Answer: *They were protesting Birmingham's closing of public facilities such as parks, playgrounds, swimming pools, and golf courses in order to avoid desegregating those areas.*

Facts on File

Landmark Documents in American History Have students review "Address on Birmingham racial strife, John Kennedy, 1963," "Radio and Television Remarks following Renewal of Racial Strife in Birmingham, John F. Kennedy, 1963," "Statement on the Sunday Bombing in Birmingham, John F. Kennedy, 1963," "Second Statement on the Sunday Bombing in Birmingham, John F. Kennedy, 1963," "Statement on meetings with civic leaders and members of the clergy of Birmingham, John F. Kennedy, 1963," "Telegram to George Wallace, John F. Kennedy, 1963," and "Statement on March on Washington for Jobs and Freedom, John Kennedy, 1963" and write a paragraph about the intent of one of the documents.

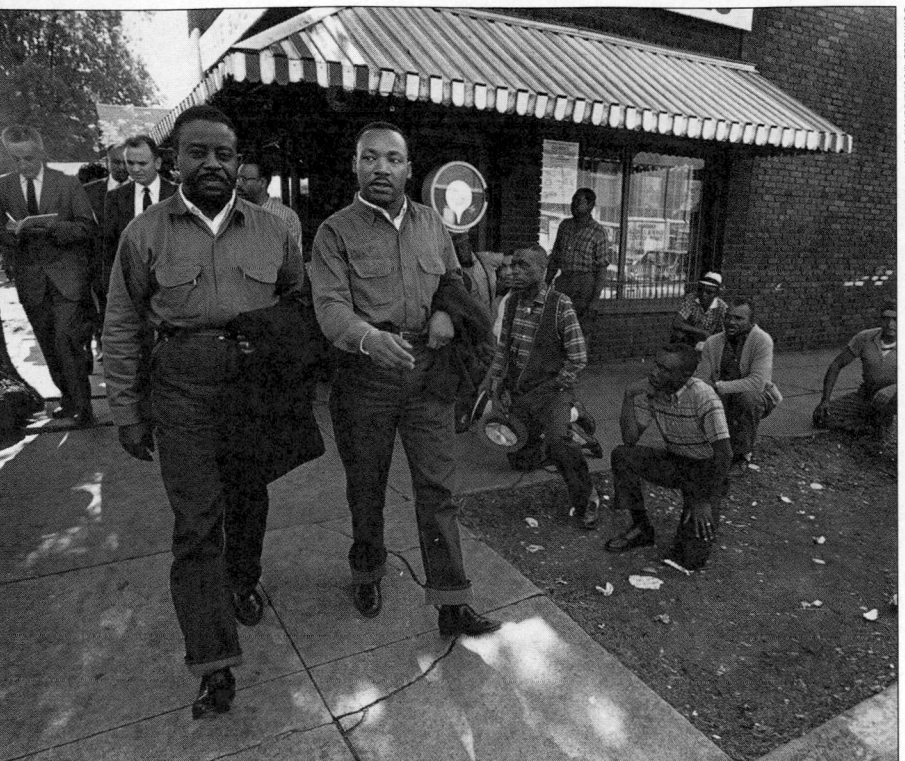

©CHARLES MOORE/BLACK STAR

Protest Leaders March for Equality Ralph Abernathy and Martin Luther King, Jr., lead a group of demonstrators in Birmingham, Alabama. *What were civil rights demonstrators protesting in Birmingham?*

African Americans voted in elections, they would be able to wield some power on important issues, such as housing and education.

Of course, the idea of encouraging voter registration of African Americans was not a new idea. Groups such as SNCC had been working to increase African American registration for some time. To encourage collaboration on voter registration, Kennedy called for a meeting in June 1961 of representatives of SCLC, SNCC, CORE, and NAACP. The result was the Voter Education Project, staffed mainly by SNCC workers. An umbrella group called the Council of Federated Organizations, or COFO, carried out voter registration in Mississippi.

To increase the number of African Americans on voting rolls, SNCC workers held workshops. They explained the sometimes lengthy application forms and accompanied eligible voters to the registration offices.

Few of the eligible voters were able to get their names on the rolls. They were turned away because the registration dates were changed, or they made spelling mistakes, or they failed outrageously difficult tests on the state constitutions. "Sometimes out of 20 or 25 Negroes who went to register, only one or two would pass the test," SNCC worker Anne Moody recalled. "Some of them were flunked because they used a title (Mr. or Mrs.) on the application blank; others because they didn't."

The presence of so many SNCC workers and their effectiveness in organizing local African American communities brought terrorist responses from some white segregationists. In Georgia four churches that had been used to register African American voters were bombed. Workers were beaten, assaulted, and shot. African Americans who dared to vote were evicted from their land, fired from their jobs, and cut off from their credit.

At the organizational meeting, Robert Kennedy's representatives had seemed to pledge money and protection for the workers. Although some private foundation funds were made available, the Justice Department failed to protect the civil rights volunteers it had encouraged to work in the South. The department reasoned that maintaining law and order was the responsibility of local governments. The result was that the militants in the civil rights movement became as alienated from the Kennedy administration as the white segregationists. Then, on September 30, 1962, President Kennedy had to send the United States Army to enforce a court order to enroll James Meredith in the University of Mississippi. It had become clear that Kennedy was losing control of the segregation issue.

Decision at Birmingham

In the spring of 1963, President Kennedy finally chose sides in the segregation struggle. It happened during King's campaign of massive civil disobedience in Birmingham, Alabama.

In 1962 Birmingham had closed parks, playgrounds, swimming pools, and golf courses to avoid desegregating

Extending the Content

Using the Media Remind students that Martin Luther King, Jr., and other civil rights leaders often used the media to keep their issues in the public eye. Refer students to Science, Technology, and Society on pages 710–711. Discuss with students why King, with the media in mind, might have chosen Good Friday as the day on which he was to be arrested in Birmingham. Continue a discussion about the overall effect of media on the movement. You may want to provide, or have students look up, press coverage in library files.

them. "We believed that while a campaign in Birmingham would surely be the toughest fight of our civil rights careers," King wrote later, "it could, if successful, break the back of segregation all over the nation."

The Demonstrations

Civil rights leaders planned the demonstrations to gradually increase in frequency and size. The effect was to keep the attention of newspaper and television reporters focused on the streets of Birmingham.

The conflict was dramatic. Representing one side was the police commissioner, Eugene "Bull" Connor. Thickset and heavily jowled, Connor took pride in the toughness with which he handled integrationists. People around the world watched in horror as he set snarling police dogs on demonstrators or washed small children across streets with the powerful impact of fire hoses.

Representing the opposition was King, who timed the demonstrations to include his arrest on Good Friday, the Christian holy day marking the death of Jesus. During King's two weeks in jail, he wrote the eloquent "Letter from Birmingham Jail." King began the letter on the margins of a full-page newspaper ad that a group of white ministers had taken out. The ad called for an end to the demonstrations. King's letter from jail attempted to explain his use of civil disobedience:

> We know through painful experience that freedom is never voluntarily given by the oppressor; it must be demanded by the oppressed. Frankly, I have yet to engage in a direct-action campaign that was "well-timed" in the view of those who have not suffered unduly from the disease of segregation. For years now I have heard the word "Wait!" It rings in the ear of every Negro with piercing familiarity. This "Wait" has almost always meant "Never." We must come to see, with one of our distinguished jurists, that "justice too long delayed is justice denied."
>
> —Martin Luther King, Jr.
> "Letter From Birmingham Jail," 1963

After his release from jail, King began a new tactic of using African American schoolchildren in the demonstrations. To those who protested that the children, who ranged in age from 6 to 18, were too young, King replied, "Children face the stinging darts of segregation as well as adults."

On the first day, about 1,000 singing children marched out from the church headquarters and in small groups headed toward the city's downtown. They were quickly arrested. The next day the police cast aside all restraint and set upon the child marchers with dogs, clubs, and fire hoses. At one point more than 2,000 children and adults were in jail.

The police tactics swung public opinion squarely around in favor of the protesters. Adult demonstrators came out into the streets in record numbers. King described the scene on May 27, 1963, when white business leaders were meeting privately to work out a settlement:

> On that day several thousand Negroes had marched on the town, the jails were so full that police could only arrest a handful. There were Negroes on the sidewalks, in the streets, standing, sitting in the aisles of downtown stores. There were square blocks of Negroes, a veritable sea of black faces. They were committing no violence; they were just present and singing. Downtown Birmingham echoed to the strains of freedom songs.
> —Martin Luther King, Jr., *Why We Can't Wait,* 1964

Local business leaders gave in and agreed to desegregate the big department stores. King called off the demonstrations; but shortly after, on May 11, 1963, bombs exploded at King's motel and at his brother's home, and rioting erupted. Alarmed that the protest might turn violent, President Kennedy decided to cast his lot with Martin Luther King, Jr.

©STEVE SCHAPIRO/BLACK STAR

Power Through Song Civil rights workers often sang together in nonviolent protest. *What was the result of police violence against nonviolent protesters in Birmingham?*

FYI

The Freedom Singers
The Freedom Singers was a chorus that performed around the country, spreading inspiration through freedom songs and raising money for the civil rights movement. Bernice Johnson Reagon, one of the original Freedom Singers, now sings with the inspirational women's a cappella group, Sweet Honey in the Rock.

VISUAL INSTRUCTION

Power Through Song Protesters sang songs such as "Ain't Gonna Let Nobody," with lyrics such as these: "Ain't gonna let (nobody, no segregation, no despair, no police, etc.) turn me around, Turn me around! . . ."

Answer: *The public, informed through the media, reacted negatively to violence used against nonviolent protesters; the public turned in favor of the protesters.*

SECTION THREE   **685**

Cultural Perspectives

African American Freedom Songs Music was an important part of the civil rights movement and the African American culture. You may wish to bring to class and play for students some recordings of "freedom songs" popular during the civil rights movement (most public libraries have such songs in their collections). If practical, invite a music teacher or a musician to teach one of the songs to the class, to be accompanied by rhythmic clapping.

ABCNEWS
INTERACTIVE™

Videodisc

Powers of the Supreme Court

Side 1, Chapter 22
Title: Amendment 15 (1870): Black Suffrage
Subject: Events leading to passage of the Voting Rights Act of 1965
Ask: Which President was responsible for passage of the Voting Rights Act? *(Lyndon Johnson)*

See Powers of the Supreme Court Guidebook page 35 for complete lesson plan.

 Facts on File

Landmark Documents in American History Have students review "Civil Rights Act, 1964," "Voting Rights Bill address to Congress, Lyndon Johnson, 1965," etc. and write a paragraph about the intent of one of the documents.

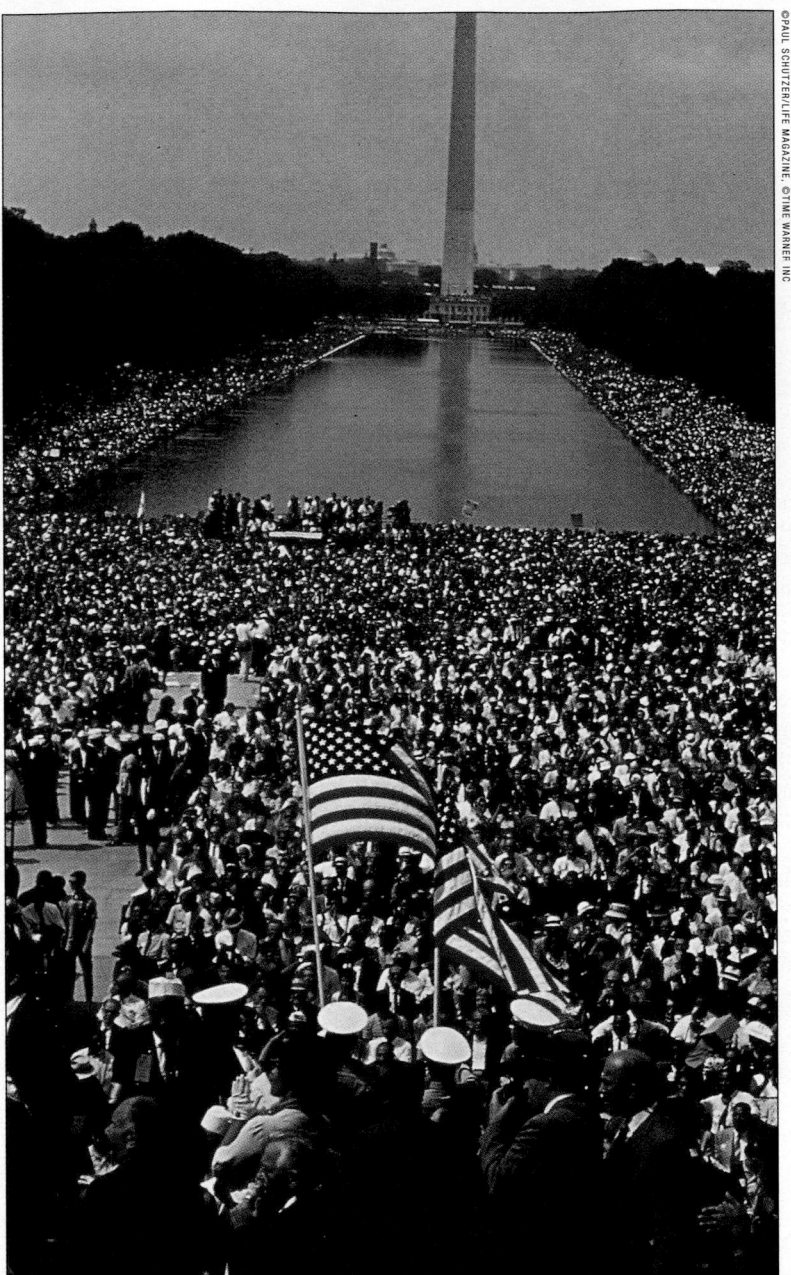

The People March More than 200,000 gathered at the Lincoln Memorial to call for civil rights reforms. *Who were the organizers of the march?*

the President appeared on national television. "We are confronted primarily with a moral issue," he said. "It is as old as the Scriptures and is as clear as the American Constitution." He then announced that he would send Congress a civil rights bill, which, it turned out, would deliver crushing blows to segregation.

Later that night in Jackson, Mississippi, a white sniper killed Medgar Evers, head of the state NAACP. By the time President Kennedy was assassinated in November 1963, his civil rights bill was moving toward passage in the House.

The March on Washington

The massive protest march on the nation's capital on August 28, 1963, began as a cry for jobs. As planning went on, however, the goals of the march grew to embrace the entire civil rights movement. A key demand was support for passage of Kennedy's civil rights bill. The march's organizers were a coalition of labor leaders, clergy, liberals, and grassroots workers.

Trains and buses brought in thousands of demonstrators from all over the country. It was the largest crowd ever to attend a civil rights demonstration. There were two highlights, most agreed, in a day of memorable songs, speeches, and appearances: Mahalia Jackson's singing of the spiritual "I Been 'Buked

June 11, 1963, was a historic day for the civil rights movement. In the afternoon President Kennedy federalized the Alabama National Guard to enforce a court order requiring the admission of two African American students to the University of Alabama. That evening and I Been Scorned" and King's delivery of a speech, in which he cried, "I have a dream that one day this nation will rise up and live out the true meaning of its creed: 'We hold these truths to be self-evident, that all men are created equal.' "

Critical Thinking

Analyzing Decisions President Kennedy decided to support the civil rights movement in the summer of 1963. The country had watched with revulsion as the drama at Birmingham had played itself out. The mood of the country was changing, and Kennedy was running as fast as he could to get out in front of a movement that was gaining momentum with each day. Discuss with students their opinions about Kennedy's decision and the timing of the decision, especially in light of the march on Washington.

The Triumph of Civil Rights
Johnson Signs Civil Rights Act

Following President Kennedy's assassination on November 22, 1963, presidential leadership of civil rights efforts fell on Lyndon B. Johnson. Born and raised in the South, Johnson had removed himself from the segregationist ranks in 1956 when he refused to sign the Southern Manifesto. In addition, Johnson had overseen the passage of a limited civil rights act in 1957.

LBJ Carries On

Johnson was determined to overcome liberal doubts about his presidency by achieving passage of Kennedy's civil rights bill without compromising any of its most important elements. The bill passed the House in February 1964 but faced an uncertain future in the Senate.

The Southerners in the Senate intended to prevent a vote by launching a **filibuster**—that is, they would debate the bill nonstop to keep it from coming to a vote. According to Senate rules, a motion to end debate could carry only if it had the support of two-thirds of those present and voting. With Southern Democrats solidly behind the filibuster, 26 of the 33 Republicans in the Senate would have to vote with Northern Democrats in order to end it.

The one man who could deliver these votes was the Senate minority leader, Everett McKinley Dirksen. A conservative Republican from Illinois, he was not known as a friend of civil rights. Yet Dirksen ended months of suspense by lining up the Republican votes to end debate and to pass the bill. Dirksen explained his decision with a quote from Victor Hugo: "No army can withstand the strength of an idea whose time has come."

On July 2, 1964, President Johnson signed into law the most comprehensive civil rights legislation enacted up to that time. It met the demands of the civil rights activists in several key ways. For example, the civil rights movement had protested the forced exclusion or separation of African Americans and whites in public places. Title II of the 1964 Civil Rights Act forbade segregation in hotels, motels, restaurants, lunch counters, theaters, and sporting arenas that did business in interstate commerce. As a result, most businesses in Southern cities and large towns desegregated immediately after passage of the Civil Rights Act. The act also relieved individuals of the responsibility for bringing discrimination complaints to court. The act made bringing discrimination cases the job of the federal government.

Protest in Selma

The passage of the Civil Rights Act did not mean that the work of the civil rights movement was over. Legislation still did not exist to enforce the Fifteenth Amendment, which forbids any state from depriving citizens of the right to vote because of race. King decided to force this issue by mounting another campaign of nonviolent resistance, this time in Selma, Alabama. At the start of King's campaign there, only 383 African American citizens out of a possible 15,000 were registered.

Selma was an excellent choice for another reason as well. After Birmingham, King had begun to rely increasingly on the power of television and newspapers to reach the conscience of America. Selma had in the person of its sheriff, Jim Clark, a civil rights antagonist who rivaled Birmingham's Bull Connor for ruthlessness.

After 2 months of beatings, arrests, and 1 murder, civil rights leaders in Selma announced a climactic protest march from Selma to the state capital in Montgomery, 54 miles (87 km) away. Though Governor George Wallace banned the march, Hosea Williams, who was King's chief aide in Selma, and John Lewis, a SNCC leader, decided to defy Wallace and march anyway.

THE CIVIL RIGHTS MOVEMENT PROGRESSES, 1961–1965

May 1961 A busload of CORE workers takes the first Freedom Ride to test the recent integration ruling.

June 1963 Kennedy federalizes the Alabama National Guard to enforce integration at the University of Alabama.

July 1964 A comprehensive Civil Rights Act is signed into law.

September 1962 James Meredith requires federal protection to enroll at the University of Mississippi.

August 1963 Thousands march on Washington in civil rights protest.

August 1965 The Voting Rights Act is signed into law.

SECTION THREE **687**

Independent Practice

L2 **Citizenship** Have students write a paragraph responding to one idea in the excerpt from King's "Letter from Birmingham Jail," page 685.

📁 Have students complete the Chapter 20 Section 3 Vocabulary and Guided Reading Activity. (Also in Spanish.) **LEP**

GLENCOE
TECHNOLOGY

 Great Speeches

Volume I—Martin Luther King, Jr. ("I Have a Dream")
Volume V—Lyndon B. Johnson (1965 Voting Rights Act)

CHART STUDY

Ask: Why did President Kennedy federalize the Alabama National Guard in June 1963?

Answer: *to enforce integration at the University of Alabama*

Cooperative Learning

Marches and Rallies Point out that many groups have marched or rallied in Washington, D.C., to gain the attention of government officials and of the public. Organize the class into 4 or more groups, each to research and write a brief report on a march or rally in Washington, D.C. Each report should include the date, the name of the group (if appropriate), its major cause, and what it hoped to gain. You may suggest these: Poor People's Campaign (Resurrection City), 1968; ERA, 1978; Earth Day, 1970 or 1990; Anti-Nuclear, 1980; Animal Rights 1990; Anti-Apartheid, 1984; Civil Rights Anniversary, 1993. Arrange for a class presentation of each group's report. 🖑

ASSESS

Meeting Lesson Objectives

Each section objective is tested by the section review question(s) that follows it in parentheses.

1. Describe how politics shaped President Kennedy's civil rights policy. (1, 2, 4)

2. Explain how militants on both sides of the civil rights issue forced Kennedy to side with Martin Luther King, Jr. (1, 2)

3. Describe the successs of the civil rights movement during Lyndon Johnson's presidency. (3, 5)

VISUAL INSTRUCTION

Push for Enforcement of the Fifteenth Amendment SNCC leaders had tried to talk the SCLC out of the march, feeling it was too dangerous. SCLC staged the march anyway; individual SNCC members participated.

Answer: *On horseback, with gas masks on, troopers used tear gas, clubs, whips, and ropes against marchers.*

UPI/BETTMANN

Push for Enforcement of the Fifteenth Amendment At Edmund Pettus Bridge civil rights activists in Alabama met violence—and won sympathy for their cause. *How did the troopers drive the marchers back?*

On March 7, 1965, Williams and Lewis led 600 demonstrators onto the Edmund Pettus Bridge outside Selma on the way to Mongtomery. Sheriff Clark's deputies lined both sides of the bridge, and 100 state troopers blocked the opposite end.

The leader of the troopers gave the marchers two minutes to disperse, then set upon them with tear gas and clubs, driving them back to Selma and into the reach of Sheriff Clark's men.

Sheyann Webb remembered her experience as an eight-year-old marcher:

I saw those horsemen coming toward me and they had those awful masks on; they rode right through the cloud of tear gas. Some of them had clubs, others had ropes or whips, which they swung about them like they were driving cattle. . . .

I began running and not seeing where I was going. I remember being scared that I might fall over the railing and into the water. . . . I heard more horses and I turned back and saw two of them and the riders were leaning over to one side. It was like a

nightmare seeing it through the tears. I just knew then that I was going to die. . . .

—Sheyann Webb, from *Selma, Lord, Selma: Girlhood Memories of the Civil Rights Days,* by Sheyann Webb and Rachel West Nelson, as told to Frank Sikora

Governor George Wallace had different memories:

As Major Cloud tells the story, he gave no orders to attack, and because of the noise of the melee it was almost impossible to hear commands. When it was over, there were mercifully no serious injuries—and no deaths. But this was not at all the way I had wanted things to turn out. I was saddened and angry.
—George C. Wallace, *Stand Up for America*

King, who had been out of town for the Sunday march, returned to lead a second one on March 9. When he reached the middle of the bridge, he halted, led the marchers in prayer, and sang "We Shall Overcome." Then, to the astonishment of his followers, he wheeled around and led the marchers back to Selma.

Meeting Special Needs

Learning Disabled This activity helps to address the particular needs of students who are learning disabled. In a small group, have volunteers take turns reading the quoted material by Sheyann Webb and George Wallace. Discuss with students the two different perspectives on the same incident.

No one knew that King had reluctantly agreed, at the request of the Johnson administration, not to complete the march. King needed the support of the President. In addition, he felt that the first bloody march had accomplished its purpose.

Once again public opinion in the North rallied to King's cause, and once again a President moved to join him. On March 15, 1965, in an emotional televised speech to Congress, Johnson promised to send a bill to Congress that would guarantee African Americans the most basic right of citizenship—the right to vote. Finally on March 21, the march from Selma to Montgomery, already twice turned back, proceeded peacefully under the protection of the federalized Alabama National Guard.

The Voting Rights Act of 1965

At Selma the civil rights movement protested laws designed to prevent African Americans from voting. Of special concern were literacy tests, which were used to deny African Americans the right to vote in Alabama, Mississippi, Louisiana, South Carolina, Georgia, Virginia, and 39 counties of North Carolina.

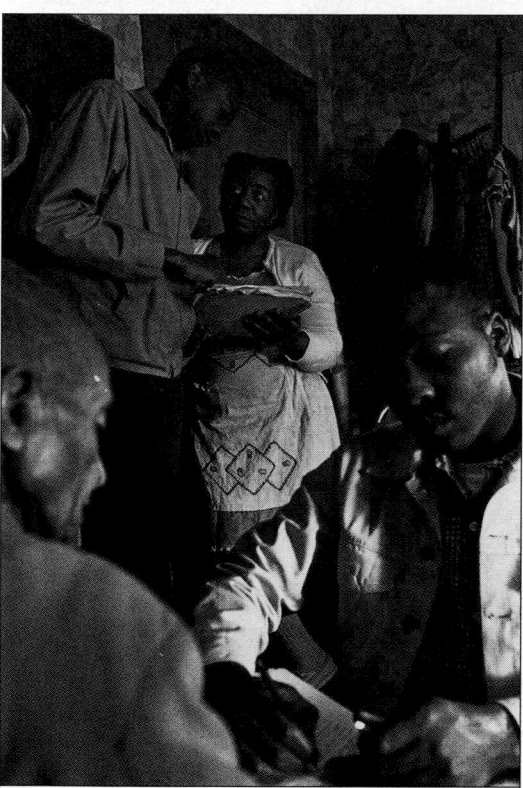

©CHARLES MOORE/BLACK STAR

Voter Registration These Mississippi residents get help registering to vote. *How did African Americans use their new political power?*

African American Voting Power, 1970–1976

African American Elected Officials in Mississippi

Year	Number
1970	81
1972	129
1974	191
1976	210

Expanded voting rights meant success at the polls. *Between which two time periods were there the greatest number of increases in African American elected officials?*

The 1965 Voting Rights Act provided that if literacy or other similar tests were used, and if less than 50 percent of the voting-age citizens were registered, then racial discrimination could be presumed. In such cases literacy tests were automatically suspended, and eligible African American citizens were allowed to enroll whether or not they could read. The act further provided that if local registrars would not enroll African Americans, the President could send federal examiners who would.

As a result of the act, 740,000 African American voters registered to vote in 3 years. They used their new political power to help win elections for hundreds of African American officials. African Americans also used their power to help defeat Selma Sheriff Jim Clark, who lost his reelection campaign to a racial moderate.

SECTION REVIEW

Vocabulary

1. Define: enfranchisement, militant, filibuster.

Checking Facts

2. What role did politics play in shaping President Kennedy's civil rights policies? What role did militants play?

3. In what ways did President Johnson exert leadership in the civil rights struggle after Kennedy's death?

Critical Thinking

Determining Cause and Effect

4. In what ways do you think the media and public opinion affected Kennedy's decision to take action on civil rights issues?

Linking Across Time

5. With the passage of the 1964 and 1965 civil rights bills, President Johnson felt that African Americans had all the tools they needed to achieve the rights of full citizenship. Explain whether he was right or wrong.

Section 3 Review Answers

1. **enfranchisement** (682), **militant** (682), **filibuster** (687)
2. Kennedy had tried to keep Southern white and African American support; but then militants endangered protesters and federal intervention became necessary.
3. Johnson got major civil rights legislation passed in 1964 and 1965 and got the Voting Rights Act passed in 1965.

4. The media brought the issue to the public's attention; when the public stood behind civil rights, so did Kennedy.
5. Sample answer: Many gains were made after 1965, but people have been slow to change their attitudes. Sample: Yes, they have rights; no, there is still discrimination.

VISUAL INSTRUCTION

Voter Registration Most applicants welcomed the workers, but many felt somewhat apprehensive about voter registration.

Answer: *They elected African Americans to public office.*

GRAPH STUDY

These represent African Americans elected to legislatures (U.S. and state combined):
1970: 182, 1980: 326, 1990: 447, 1993: 571
Answer: *1972 to 1974*

Evaluate

Have students complete the Section Review.

📂 🔲 Assign the Section 3 Quiz or use the Testmaker to develop a customized quiz. (Also in Spanish.) **LEP**

Reteach

🎧 Have students listen to the Chapter 20, Section 3 audiocassette. (Also in Spanish.) **LEP**

Enrich

📂 Have students complete the Unit 8 American Literature Reading.

CLOSE

Ask: How did Lyndon Johnson proceed with civil rights issues after John Kennedy's assassination? *(enacted the proposed Civil Rights Act; enacted the Voting Rights Act)*

FOCUS

Section Objectives

1. Explain the conflict of opinions on appropriate strategies and attitudes within the civil rights movement.
2. Describe black power, black pride, and the black separatist movement.
3. Explain the causes of the riots in Northern cities during the summers of 1965 to 1967.

Bellringer Activity

While taking attendance at the beginning of the class period, display **Section Focus Transparency 65,** and have students answer the questions. (Or use the blackline master.)

VISUAL INSTRUCTION

Split Emerges Stokely Carmichael turned down scholarships to white colleges in order to attend Howard University, where he joined CORE in its fight for integration of public accommodations. Again turning down scholarships, this time for graduate school, Carmichael went South to work with SNCC, to which he was elected chairman in 1966. He resigned in 1967, as many in SNCC considered his beliefs about black power to be too radical.

Ask: What replaced the cry "We Shall Overcome"? *(We Shall Overrun)*

SECTION 4

Disappointed Hopes

JUNE 1966: KING AND SNCC MARCH TOGETHER ONE LAST TIME

©BOB FITCH/BLACK STAR

Split Emerges
Stokely Carmichael speaks out.

WHAT BEGAN IN JUNE 1966 AS A SOLO MARCH THROUGH MISSISSIPPI IN DEMONSTRATION OF AFRICAN AMERICANS' RIGHT TO VOTE TURNED INTO ONE LAST MARCH IN UNITY. After that the civil rights movement disintegrated into separate factions with radically different goals, ideals, and strategies.

James Meredith, who in 1962 became the first African American to attend the University of Mississippi, undertook the 220-mile (354-km) walk to demonstrate African Americans' right to vote and their right to move without fear through the state. When he fell wounded on the roadside, his back full of buckshot, civil rights workers rushed to Mississippi to complete his march.

During the day they trudged down U.S. Highway 51 arm in arm: Martin Luther King, Jr., of SCLC; Floyd McKissick, of CORE; and Stokely Carmichael, of SNCC.

As they stopped to speak in courthouse squares, King and Carmichael preached two separate gospels.

King, despite the increasing numbers of killings and assaults, continued to call on his followers to answer violence with nonviolence. The SNCC and CORE marchers, however, had given up on nonviolence and sang a new tune. When King and his supporters began their theme song, "We Shall Overcome," they were often drowned out by the militants' new version, "We Shall Overrun."

The climactic moment came in Greenwood. Carmichael, just released from a few hours in jail for erecting a tent against a state trooper's orders, leaped onto a flatbed truck and raised his hand in a clenched-fist salute. "This is the twenty-seventh time I have been arrested—and I ain't going to jail no more," he shouted.

AS YOU READ

Vocabulary
► martyr
► black separatism
► black pride
► black power

Think About . . .
► the conflicting opinions within the civil rights movement regarding strategies and attitudes.

► the concepts of black power and black pride and the ideals of the black separatist movement.
► the causes of the summer riots of 1965–1967 in Northern cities.

690   CHAPTER 20 THE CIVIL RIGHTS STRUGGLE

Section 4 Resources

REPRODUCIBLE RESOURCES

📂 Lesson Plan 20-4
📂 Section 4 Quiz
📂 Supreme Court Case Study 36
📂 Vocabulary and Guided Reading Activity 20-4
📂 Chapter 20 Test

📂 Performance Assessment Activity 20
📂 Reteaching Activity 20
📂 Enrichment Activity 20

MULTIMEDIA RESOURCES

📠 Section Focus Transparency 65
💿 Landmark Documents in American History
💿 Set on Freedom
💿 Student Self-Test: A Software Review
💿 Testmaker
💿 Vocabulary PuzzleMaker
🎧 Chapter 20 Digest Audiocassette

"We been saying freedom for six years and we ain't got nothin'. What we gonna start saying now is Black Power!" King tried to calm the crowd, but the new cry of "Black Power" drowned out his call of "Freedom Now!" By the time the march reached Jackson, Mississippi, the new call had replaced the old one.

New Directions in Civil Rights

I.A

African Americans Turn to Radical Protest

The change in direction in SNCC had been in the making for a long time. In the early 1960s the students shared in the ideal of a new, better American society. After the 1964 and 1965 civil rights acts, when the new laws were not immediately enforced, SNCC volunteers became disillusioned. Indeed, the progress that did occur seemed to come at enormous cost. One **martyr,** or person who dies in the name of an important cause, followed another: the four young girls killed when their church was bombed in Birmingham in 1963; the three civil rights workers shot in Mississippi in 1964; and on and on. As time went on, SNCC leaders began to discuss

©UPI/BETTMANN

Seeking Political Support Fannie Lou Hamer (center) and two other MFDP candidates visit the Capitol. *What was the result of their efforts?*

three key issues: the role that white volunteers should play within the organization; a growing movement among some African Americans toward **black separatism,** or the separation of the races in America; and the continued use of nonviolence as a strategy for change.

SNCC's efforts to work within the political system also left members disillusioned. In 1964 the Mississippi Freedom Democratic Party (MFDP), a grassroots group that SNCC supported, asked to be recognized at the national Democratic party convention as the legitimate Democratic party in the state. They challenged the regular Democratic party principally on the grounds that fewer than 5 percent of the African American population in the state was allowed to vote.

President Johnson, however, was not sympathetic to the MFDP. He did not want the convention distracted from its main job of enthusiastically supporting his policies. Also, he did not want to risk sending white Southern Democrats in flight to the Republican party. Johnson assigned Minnesota senator Hubert Humphrey the job of sidetracking the MFDP challenge, suggesting that at stake might be the vice-presidential nomination that Humphrey was hoping for.

The compromise Humphrey pushed through gave the MFDP only 2 of the 40 Mississippi seats. SNCC and MFDP members, who had risked their lives by openly challenging the local regular Democrats, felt the white liberals at the convention had let them down. Fannie Lou Hamer, sharecropper and member of the MFDP, summed it up by exclaiming, "We didn't come all this way for no two votes."

Black Pride

The success of the civil rights movements in the early 1960s gave rise to **black pride,** a pride in being African American. Ralph Bunche, famous for his skills as a diplomat, wrote in 1961, "I am confident that I reflect accurately the views of virtually all Negro Americans when I say that I am proud of my ancestry, just as I am proud of my nationality." Other African American leaders also recognized the importance of black pride, as well as the harm done by the feelings of inferiority that had long afflicted African Americans. Malcolm X, a strong African American leader, bitterly recalled his youthful efforts at straightening his hair in order to look more like a white person:

> This was my first big step toward self-degradation: when I endured all of that pain, literally burning my flesh to have it look like a white man's hair. I had joined that multitude of Negro men and women in America who are brainwashed into believing that the black people are "inferior"—and white people "superior."
>
> —Malcolm X, *Autobiography of Malcolm X*, 1965

TEACH

Guided Practice

L2 Discussion Have students read over the excerpt from *Autobiography of Malcolm X* on this page. Invite them to discuss what it might actually have felt like to have burned one's flesh in order to look like a white person. Might this give rise to feelings of anger at a later time?

FYI

New Term In 1989 Jesse Jackson proposed the term *African American* to replace the term *black.*

VISUAL INSTRUCTION

Seeking Political Support Annie Devine, Fannie Lou Hamer, and Victoria Grey (shown in photo) of the MFDP challenged the seating at the 1964 Democratic National Convention. Hamer was among the first African American delegates to the 1968 convention.

Answer: *MFDP gained 2 of the 40 Mississippi seats.*

SECTION FOUR **691**

Cooperative Learning

Civil Rights Strategies Organize the class into 3 heterogeneous groups. Have students conduct group panel discussions, with 1 student in each group acting as moderator. The other students should choose 1 of the following questions to research and discuss in a panel, from the perspective of the 1960s: Can black separatism work in the United States? Is violence in self-defense, or in response to violence, justifiable? Is nonviolent civil disobedience an effective strategy for attaining full equality? 📖

Curriculum Connection

Art Many African American artists used African motifs in their creations, which often expressed outrage with society or portrayed scenes from African American history. An example is *Wall of Love* by William Walker. Have students research African American art and, if possible, bring some pictures to share with the class.

VISUAL INSTRUCTION

Differences Deepen
Malcolm X's father, a Baptist preacher, had been a follower of Marcus Garvey. Garvey had promoted black separatism in the 1920s and had preached that African Americans should resettle in Africa. The photo on this page shows Malcolm X in 1963 addressing an integration rally in Birmingham.

Answer: *African Americans should return to Africa or should occupy an exclusive area in the United States.*

 Facts on File

Landmark Documents in American History Have students review "Death of Malcolm X statement, Martin Luther King, Jr., 1965" and write a paragraph about the intent of the document.

©UPI/BETTMANN

Differences Deepen The growing movement for black separatism and militancy, led by people such as Malcolm X, unsettled many white people. *What did black separatists propose as the best way of achieving their goal of black separatism?*

As the 1960s progressed, younger and more race-conscious African Americans adopted natural "Afro" haircuts and put on African-inspired dashikis in place of shirts and ties. The new pride was reflected also in language, music, lifestyle, and many other aspects of African American culture. Even the words that African Americans used to describe themselves changed. The term *Negro*, used for years by many prominent leaders, was abandoned because of its evocation of the slave trade. The word *colored* was rejected as not being sufficiently precise. The new preferred term was the simple adjective *black*, turned into a noun.

Sometimes the powerful desire of African Americans to proclaim their own self-worth was expressed in anti-white feelings. This was part of the reason that some SNCC workers raised in their planning group the troublesome question of the role of white volunteers.

Some within SNCC argued that white college-trained workers thoughtlessly took over the jobs that African Americans with little schooling were just learning to do. Moreover, some accused white volunteers of being insensitive to the local conditions under which African Americans lived. "Let the whites go fight racism in their own communities," they said. Others, however, pointed out the sacrifices and efforts that white SNCC workers made. Some activists protested that by exclud-

ing whites, SNCC itself could be accused of racism. Ultimately, the new view won, and the white workers were asked to give up leadership positions in SNCC.

Malcolm X and Black Separatism

Emerging African American pride was one factor in the move toward black separatism. According to the promoters of black separatism, this could best be achieved by African Americans returning to Africa or by their occupying an exclusive area within the United States on land that the federal government supplied to them.

Black separatism was the antithesis of the civil rights movement's goal of racial integration. It was a view promoted by, among others, the Nation of Islam, a sub-group of the Islamic religion commonly known as the Black Muslims.

The most vocal Black Muslim was Malcolm X. A brilliant and bold orator, Malcolm X preached a message that included religious justification for black separatism. He was ousted from the Nation of Islam in a fight over leadership and went on a pilgrimage to the Islamic holy city of Makkah. There he was exposed to more traditional Islamic religious teachings, which do not include racial separatism. On his return to the United States, he softened his views on the separation of blacks and whites. On February 21, 1965, three members of the Nation of Islam assassinated Malcolm X as he spoke in Harlem.

Though Malcolm X's views on separatism gradually softened toward the end of his life, he never supported King's nonviolent methods. Instead, he advocated the use of weapons for self-defense, believing that African American nonviolence simply emboldened violent white racists. Shortly before his death, Malcolm X pointed out in a speech at Selma, "The white people should thank Dr. King for holding black people in check."

SNCC's New Leadership

The rhetoric of Malcolm X lived on long after his death and influenced SNCC members and other young militants. The final turnaround in SNCC's orientation came in 1966 with the election of Stokely Carmichael as chairman.

Carmichael was arrested many times during Freedom Rides, sit-ins, and marches. Jailers were happy to see him go because he was never reluctant to argue with them over the condition of mattresses and other jail comforts. Once, when six other Riders were put in solitary confinement, he banged on his cell door asking for equal treatment, which he finally received.

One of Carmichael's projects during his leadership of SNCC was the formation of an African American political party in Lowndes County in Alabama. The party failed to put any of its candidates into office in the

Meeting Special Needs

Visual Learners This activity helps to address the particular needs of students who are visual learners. Invite students to study the photos in this section. Discuss with them the emotions expressed in or evoked by the images. What do the images tell them about "disappointed hopes"?

1966 election. It was, however, a bold attempt to seize political power, or **black power** as it was called. The symbol used for the Lowndes County Freedom Organization was a black panther about to spring.

The Long, Hot Summers
Riots Erupt in Northern Cities

Although civil rights activists fought their major campaigns in the South, the pattern of segregation was not confined to states that belonged to the former Confederacy. It was a growing frustration among African Americans over conditions in the North that led to some of the most dramatic and tragic confrontations of the 1960s.

The migration to Northern cities that began in the early 1900s had by 1965 resulted in the relocation of some 3 million Southern African Americans. More than two-thirds of the total African American population were now urban dwellers. Of these, more than half were concentrated in just 12 cities.

Perhaps more than in the South, life in Northern cities bred frustration among many African Americans. Problems of poverty, unemployment, and racial discrimination followed the migrants as they fled the South. The empty promise of racial equality in the North ignited a smoldering fire of rage in many African American communities. The following poem by Langston Hughes, written in 1951, captures the emotions of many city-dwelling African Americans of the mid-1960s:

What happens to a dream deferred?
    Does it dry up
like a raisin in the sun?
Or fester like a sore—
And then run?
Does it stink like rotten meat?
Or crust and sugar over—
like a syrupy sweet?

Maybe it just sags
like a heavy load.

Or does it explode?
      —Langston Hughes, "Harlem," 1951

Watts, First of a Series

The arrest for a traffic violation of the young African American in the Los Angeles ghetto should have been routine. Perhaps it was the warm, humid August weather that drew people onto the streets. Or perhaps it was the time,

7:00 P.M., still early enough in the evening to attract a restless crowd.

For whatever reason, that simple arrest in Watts on August 11, 1965, exploded into a major riot that lasted 6 days. Before it was over, 34 people were dead, 1,072 were injured, and 4,000 had been arrested. Close to 1,000 buildings were damaged or destroyed, with a property loss that totaled nearly $40 million.

The Watts riot was the first, but not the most destructive, of a series of racial disorders that hit cities throughout the United States in the summers of 1965, 1966, and 1967. Like some kind of seasonal plague, a fever of rage, looting, and arson seemed to erupt in one crowded city after another.

Many of the riots began in similar ways, with an arrest or a police raid that was followed by rumors of resistance and police brutality. The numbers of men, women, and children involved were immense: there were 30,000 rioters in Watts, while another 60,000 milled about in the streets; in the 1967 Detroit, Michigan, riot, 7,000 people were arrested.

Typically, looters headed for white-owned businesses, stripping them clean of merchandise, then setting fire to the buildings. Some stores escaped destruction by putting up signs that read Negro Owned or Blood (meaning African American). Nevertheless, African American–owned businesses were often destroyed. As the fires burned, snipers prevented firefighters from

© DECLAN HAUN, BLACK STAR

Violence Erupts The riots in the Watts section of Los Angeles in 1965 were the first of many to break out in cities in the United States. *What sparked the riots in Watts?*

VISUAL INSTRUCTION

Violence Erupts The population of the Watts district of Los Angeles was approximately 98 percent African American.

Answer: *generally: frustration; specifically: the arrest of a young African American for a traffic violation*

 GLENCOE **TECHNOLOGY**

 Videodisc

Set on Freedom: The American Civil Rights Movement

Side A, Chapter 27
Title: The Watts Riots, 1965
Subject: Riots in Watts section of Los Angeles
Ask: What sparked the Watts riots? (*African American arrested for traffic violation*)

 Facts on File

Landmark Documents in American History Have students review "King assassination remarks, Lyndon Johnson, 1968," "King assassination announcement, Robert F. Kennedy, 1968," and "Mourning proclamation for Martin Luther King, Lyndon Johnson, 1968" and write a paragraph about the intent of one of the documents.

Portfolio Project

Newspaper Reports Have students research the Watts riot, then write a headline and a brief newspaper article describing the riot. Or, they may research and write about the Watts riot and the riots in Northern cities, comparing the various riots that took place from 1965 to 1967. Have students file the reports in their portfolios.

693

VISUAL INSTRUCTION

The Panthers Black Panthers wore black leather jackets and berets.

Answer: *used weapons for self-defense and retaliation*

Independent Practice

L2 Citizenship Have students read about the Black Panther party and write an article such as might appear as an encyclopedia entry under "Black Panther Party."

👉 Have students complete the Chapter 20 Section 4 Vocabulary and Guided Reading Activity. (Also in Spanish.) **LEP**

ASSESS

Meeting Lesson Objectives

Each section objective is tested by the section review question(s) that follows it in parentheses.

1. Explain the conflict of opinions on appropriate strategies and attitudes within the civil rights movement. (1, 2, 4, 5)
2. Describe black power, black pride, and the black separatist movement. (1, 2)
3. Explain the causes of the riots in Northern cities during the summers of 1965 to 1967. (3)

The Panthers Members of the Black Panther party attend the funeral of one of their members in Seattle, Washington. *In what way did the Black Panthers differ from other groups of African Americans at the time?*

doing their work. As a result, whole blocks were left to burn. In Watts in 1965, and again in Detroit in 1967, National Guard troops were sent in to help local police. While the riots were raging, a new African American political group appeared. In 1966 the Black Panther party was formed in Oakland, California. Its goals included protecting African American communities from police harassment and assuming neighborhood control of police, schools, and other services. The Black Panthers differed significantly from other African American groups in that they supported the use of weapons for self-defense and retaliation.

Reasons Why

During the first 9 months of 1967, more than 150 cities in the United States reported incidents of racial disorders. In Newark, New Jersey, and in Detroit, Michigan, the incidents erupted into full-scale riots.

To identify and address the causes of the riots, President Johnson appointed a National Advisory Commission on Civil Disorders, headed by Governor Otto Kerner of Illinois. The Kerner Report, as the commission's findings came to be known, was released in March 1968. As a basic cause of the rioting, the Kerner Report pointed to the "racial attitude and behavior of white Americans toward black Americans." This could be visible, the report said, in patterns of racial discrimination and prejudice, in African American migration to the cities followed by white flight to the suburbs, and in the existence of African American ghettos. The report cited three triggers for the racial violence: frustrated hopes of African Americans; the approval and encouragement of violence, both by white terrorists and by some African American protest groups; and the sense many African Americans had of being powerless in a society dominated by whites.

The Kerner Report concluded that "the nation is rapidly moving toward two increasingly separate Americas." To divert that move, the report recommended the elimination of all racial barriers in jobs, education, and housing; greater public response to problems of racial minorities; and increased communication across racial lines.

One More Assassination
The Death of King

The Kerner Report did not end race riots in the United States. One more outburst of rage swept through nearly 130 ghettos following the April 4, 1968, death of Dr. Martin Luther King, Jr., at the hands of a white assassin. The 39-year-old minister was shot while stand-

Extending the Content

Assassinations Robert Kennedy was assassinated on June 6, 1968, while campaigning in California for the Democratic presidential nomination. Kennedy was shot to death by a young Arab from Jordan, Sirhan Sirhan, who objected to Kennedy's pro-Israeli views. Discuss with students the kinds of issues and situations that have sometimes led to extreme violence, such as assassinations.

ing on a balcony with friends in Memphis, Tennessee.

The acceptance of violence as a means of social protest continued to concern King up until his death. Protesters against the war in Vietnam had long been pressing him to come out with an antiwar statement. The issue was not only the war itself but also its financial cost, which was at the expense, many thought, of the war against poverty at home.

King was reluctant to oppose the Johnson government, a stand he knew would be unpopular among many of his supporters. The logic of his commitment to nonviolence, however, demanded it. Finally, in 1967 he began to make speeches denouncing the war. He declared that "the promises of the Great Society," the name given Johnson's social program, "have been shot down on the battlefield of Vietnam."

King did lose many supporters because of his anti-war statements. Partly in an effort to rebuild his political strength, he turned toward organizing an interracial coalition of the poor. His final trip to Memphis was to rally support for the mostly African American garbage collectors who were attempting to unionize.

The night before his death King spoke at a church rally. He might have had a premonition when he said, "We've got some difficult days ahead. But it doesn't matter with me now. Because I've been to the mountaintop." King went on to say, "I may not get there with you, but I want you to know tonight . . . that we as a people will get to the promised land!"

The Movement Appraised
Civil Rights Gains

Without strong leadership in the years following King's death, the civil rights movement floundered. Middle-class Americans, both African American and white, tired of the violence and the struggle. The war in Vietnam and crime in the streets at home became the new issues at the forefront of the nation's consciousness.

In retrospect, the 14 years between the Supreme Court's momentous *Brown* decision and King's death were years of great progress in civil rights. Not since the passage of the Thirteenth, Fourteenth, and Fifteenth Amendments during Reconstruction had so many gains been made. It is for this reason that these years are sometimes called the Second Reconstruction. The fear among some civil rights leaders today is that, as in the original Reconstruction, a gradual slipping away of hard-won victories

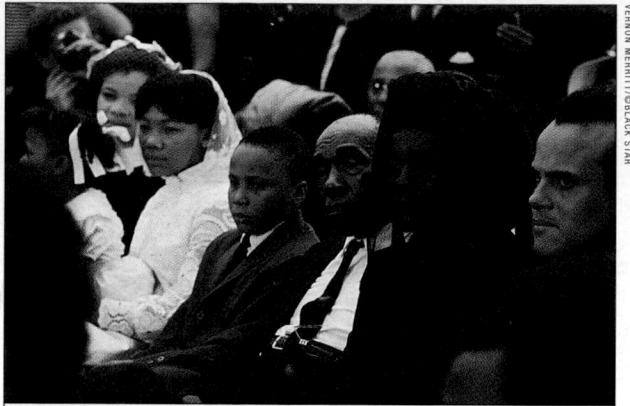

VERNON MERRITT/©BLACK STAR

Leadership Void Coretta Scott King mourns the death of her husband. *How did King's death affect the civil rights movement?*

will mark the ensuing years. To guard against this, civil rights groups remain vigilant in their quest for progress.

Because of the combined efforts of state and federal legislatures, the courts, and the people themselves, some measure of political power was given to African Americans. The next gains would have to come through the political process. Meanwhile, other minorities who also thought of themselves as disenfranchised looked to the civil rights movement of the 1950s and the 1960s as a model for their own efforts.

SECTION REVIEW

Vocabulary
1. Define: martyr, black separatism, black pride, black power.

Checking Facts
2. In what ways did the militant civil rights groups disagree with the strategies and attitudes of Martin Luther King, Jr.?

3. Describe the racial unrest that spread to major cities in the North during the summers of 1965–1967.

Critical Thinking
Predicting Consequences
4. What do you think would have happened in the civil rights movement had King not been assassinated?

Linking Across Time
5. Do you think the comparison of the civil rights movement of the 1950s and 1960s to Reconstruction is an appropriate one? Support your answer.

Evaluate

Have students complete the Section Review.

☛ 💿 Assign the Section 4 Quiz or use the Testmaker to develop a customized quiz. (Also in Spanish.) **LEP**

☛ 💿 Assign the Chapter 20 Test or use the Testmaker to develop a customized test. (Also in Spanish.) **LEP**

☛ Have students complete the Chapter 20 Performance Assessment Activity.

Reteach

🎧 Have students listen to the Chapter 20, Section 4 audiocassette. (Also in Spanish.) **LEP**

☛ Have students complete the Chapter 20 Reteaching Activity. (Also in Spanish.) **LEP**

Enrich

☛ Have students complete the Chapter 20 Enrichment Activity. (Also in Spanish.) **LEP**

☛ Have students complete Supreme Court Case Study 36.

CLOSE

Ask: How did African Americans' attitudes change? *(became proud of heritage and culture; became more assertive)*

Section 4 Review Answers

1. martyr (691), **black separatism** (691), **black pride** (691), **black power** (693)
2. They believed in violent response to violence; many believed in the separation of African Americans and whites.
3. African Americans continued to experience racial discrimination and prejudice, even after moving North. Their sense of frustration and powerlessness led to rioting.

4. Answers will vary. King might have regained power as a leader, and the movement might have become more focused and less violent.
5. During Reconstruction the South shifted away from a slave-based economy. During the 1960s the South had to change to an integrated society. Both eras involved adjusting social and political habits and attitudes.

695

Chapter ⑳ Review

Reviewing Key Terms

1. enfranchisement
2. civil rights
3. segregation
4. militant
5. boycott

Recalling Facts

1. segregation in schools
2. school districts designed for African Americans; whites moved from cities to suburbs; "separate but equal" laws
3. "separate but equal," segregated schools
4. Segregation negates equal education, instills inferiority
5. had to protect integrating students, uphold Constitution
6. National Association for the Advancement of Colored People, Student Nonviolent Coordinating Committee, Congress of Racial Equality, Southern Christian Leadership Conference; African American civil rights
7. complicated forms and tests, literacy tests, poll taxes
8. endorsed; nothing; to assuage opposing factions
9. bus riders testing integration of interstate bus facilities
10. Little Rock Nine, school integration; bus boycott, attack on Freedom Riders; protest march announced; riot; demonstrations, media, King jailed; massive march
11. against Southern Manifesto; signed 1964 Civil Rights Act, 1965 Voting Rights Act
12. political power for African Americans; political groups formed
13. valuing African American culture; led to idea of separation from whites
14. a study of causes of race riots; racial prejudice and discrimination; end discrimination, promote public awareness of plight of minorities
15. weakened because of militants and his antiwar stance

696

Reviewing Key Terms

On a separate sheet of paper, write the number of each phrase and the term it describes.

segregation   civil rights
boycott   militant
sit-in   enfranchisement

1. the attainment of the rights of citizenship, especially the right to vote

2. the political, economic, and social rights of a citizen

3. the enforced separation of races in schools, housing, and public facilities

4. one who aggressively pursues or defends a cause

5. an organized agreement not to use certain goods or services in order to exert pressure for change

Recalling Facts

1. What was the major issue in the early days of the civil rights movement?

2. What practices were used to enforce segregation before 1964?

3. What principle did the Supreme Court case *Plessy* v. *Ferguson* endorse? The case of *Brown* v. *Board of Education*?

4. According to the Supreme Court, why were separate facilities for whites and African Americans unconstitutional even when the facilities were physically equal?

5. What forced Eisenhower to order federalized National Guard troops to Little Rock, Arkansas, in September 1957?

6. What do the acronyms NAACP, SNCC, CORE, and SCLC stand for? What kinds of groups were these?

7. What kinds of "rules" or techniques were used to keep African American citizens from registering to vote?

8. What did John Kennedy say about civil rights during his campaign for the presidency? What did he say at his inauguration? Why did he change his mind?

9. Who were the Freedom Riders, and what was the purpose of the Freedom Rides?

10. Briefly explain the significance of each of the following places in the civil rights movement: Little Rock, Montgomery, Selma, Watts, Birmingham, and Washington, D.C.

11. How did Lyndon Johnson show support of civil rights issues both before and during his presidency?

12. What is black power, and how was it related to the civil rights movement?

13. What is black pride, and how was it related to black separatism during the 1960s and 1970s?

14. What was the Kerner Report? What did it identify as the causes of urban violence? What recommendations did it make?

15. How had Martin Luther King, Jr.'s, position as a leader in the civil rights movement changed in the late 1960s?

Critical Thinking

1. Predicting Consequences If the Supreme Court had given definite guidelines for carrying out school desegregation early on and if President Eisenhower had taken an early stand for desegregation, how do you think desegregation might have progressed? Explain.

2. Making Inferences Why, do you think, young people, especially students, took a more active role in the civil rights movement than adults?

3. Determining Cause and Effect In the mid-1960s, most people in the United States watched the evening news on television. Why was this custom significant to the civil rights movement?

4. Making Comparisons Compare the methods that Martin Luther King, Jr., used with those that Malcolm X and Stokely Carmichael used. What were the reasons behind each approach? Which proved most successful? Why?

5. Synthesizing Information How were trends in population movement (to Northern cities) reflected in the methods that civil rights protesters used?

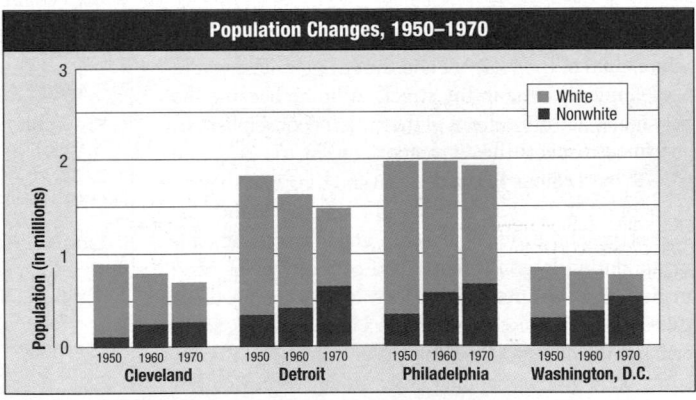

Population Changes, 1950–1970

■ White
■ Nonwhite

Population (in millions)

3

2

1

0

| 1950 1960 1970 | 1950 1960 1970 | 1950 1960 1970 | 1950 1960 1970 |
| Cleveland | Detroit | Philadelphia | Washington, D.C. |

Critical Thinking

1. Answers will vary. Integration might have been smooth, nonviolent; or, still opposition from Southerners
2. Students might point out that they believed change possible in their lifetimes; inspired by recent independence of African countries

3. Viewers witnessing racism and brutal treatment became sympathetic to movement.
4. King was for nonviolent peaceful protest; Malcolm X and Carmichael wanted militant confrontation. Both felt their methods would be more effective. Answers will vary.

5. As African Americans migrated North, they became more discontented with the pace of reform.

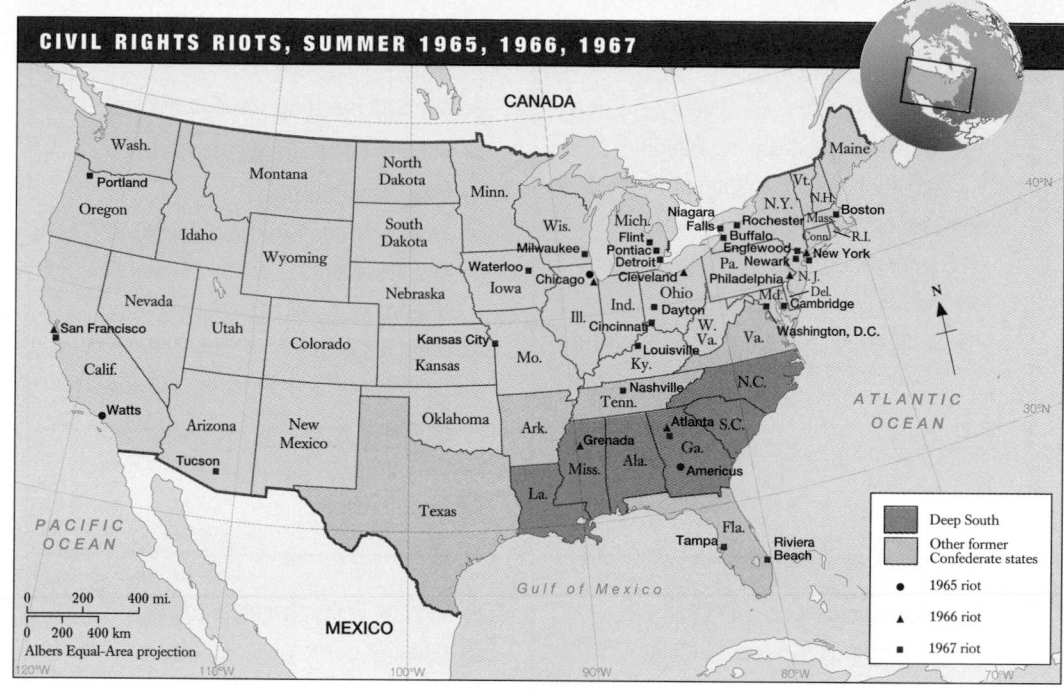

CIVIL RIGHTS RIOTS, SUMMER 1965, 1966, 1967

	Deep South
	Other former Confederate states
•	1965 riot
▲	1966 riot
■	1967 riot

Portfolio Project

Choose a civil rights figure such as Martin Luther King, Jr., Rosa Parks, Fannie Lou Hamer, Mahalia Jackson, Malcolm X, or Stokely Carmichael. Research this person, and write a personal profile. Include copies of photographs, speeches, and so on, as appropriate.

Cooperative Learning

In *Brown* v. *Board of Education,* the Supreme Court handed down a unanimous decision. In some recent civil rights cases, however, the Court has been divided. With a few other students, consult newspapers and periodicals to identify some of these cases. Choose one, research it, and create a chart that lists the arguments on both sides. Share your findings with other groups in the class.

Reinforcing Skills

Presenting Statistical Data

Study the bar graph on page 696. What information does the graph give you? Use the graph to write a brief statement about population trends in the cities of Cleveland, Detroit, Philadelphia, and Washington, D.C. from 1950 to 1970.

Geography and History

Study the map on this page to answer the following questions:

1. Which cities had civil rights riots in 1965? In what regions of the country are these cities located?

2. In what 2 regions of the country did most of the 1966 and 1967 riots take place?

3. What geographical differences do you see between the locations of

the civil rights protests of the early 1960s and the riots of 1965–1967? What might have caused this shift?

4. Which cities had more than one riot? Why might this have happened?

5. Which areas of the country experienced few or no riots? What might be a reason for this?

HISTORY JOURNAL

Look back at your journal response to page 666. Having read this chapter, what are your new understandings about strivings for equality and social reform from 1954 to 1976?

Geography and History

1. Watts, California; Chicago, Illinois; Americus, Georgia; West, Midwest, South
2. Midwest and Northeast
3. The civil rights protests of the early 1960s took place in the South; the riots of 1965 to 1967 took place mainly in the Midwest and Northeast, where many African Americans had recently migrated and had begun to feel anger and frustration at the lack of change that had taken place.
4. Chicago, New York, Atlanta, and San Francisco; these cities had large African American populations, perhaps feeling anger and frustration
5. There were few or no riots in the Rocky Mountains and Great Plains areas of the country; perhaps few African Americans had settled there.

History Journal

Students' responses should reflect an expanded understanding of the civil rights struggle in the 1950s and 1960s.

? BONUS QUESTION

This question may be used for extra credit on the chapter test.

How did the nature of actions for civil rights change over the period 1950 to 1970? Summarize the trend.

Answer: *Actions went from nonviolent protest to civil disobedience, to violent protest and resistance, to ideas of black separatism.*

Portfolio Project

Students' reports should give details on the contributions of the individual and perhaps on the individual's personal and philosophical motivations.

Cooperative Learning

Tasks can be divided: half the group can identify recent decisions and choose one; the other half can research the chosen decision. The entire group should create the chart listing the arguments. The chart should show both sides clearly.

Reinforcing Skills

The graph shows white and nonwhite population figures in four cities in 1950, 1960, and 1970. The number of whites decreased or stayed the same in all four cities from 1950 to 1970; the number of nonwhites increased in the cities during that time.

The Kennedy and Johnson Years

DAILY LESSON OBJECTIVES	REPRODUCIBLE RESOURCES	MULTIMEDIA RESOURCES
SECTION 1 New Frontier and Great Society 1. Compare the styles, goals, and accomplishments of the Kennedy and Johnson presidencies. 2. Identify and evaluate some of the major reform programs of the 1960s.	☛ Reproducible Lesson Plans ☛ Vocabulary and Guided Reading Activity (English or Spanish) ☛ Geography in History Activities ☛ Cooperative Learning Activities ☛ Skill Reinforcement Activities ☛ Section Quizzes (English or Spanish)	🖳 Chapter Teaching Transparencies 🖳 Section Focus Transparencies 🖳 Map Transparencies ● Powers of the Supreme Court ◍ The Presidents: A Picture History of Our Nation ▭ Great Speeches ◍ Landmark Documents in American History ◉ Student Self-Test: A Software Review ◉ Testmaker
SECTION 2 The Supreme Court and Civil Liberties 1. Explain how reapportionment helped ensure equal representation. 2. Explain why the Supreme Court ruled against prayer in public schools. 3. Analyze the Supreme Court decisions protecting the rights of accused offenders to due process.	☛ Reproducible Lesson Plans ☛ Supreme Court Case Studies ☛ Interpreting Political Cartoons ☛ Vocabulary and Guided Reading Activity (English or Spanish) ☛ Reteaching Activities (English or Spanish) ☛ Enrichment Activities (English or Spanish) ☛ Section Quizzes (English or Spanish)	🖳 Section Focus Transparencies ● Powers of the Supreme Court ◍ Landmark Documents in American History ◉ Student Self-Test: A Software Review ◉ Testmaker
CHAPTER REVIEW AND EVALUATION	☛ Chapter 21 Test, Forms A and B ☛ Performance Assessment Strategies and Activities	◉ Student Self-Test: A Software Review ◉ Vocabulary PuzzleMaker ◉ Testmaker ⌢ Chapter Digests Audiocassettes

`00:00` If time does not permit teaching the entire chapter, summarize using the Chapter 21 Digests Audiocassettes and the accompanying activities and tests. (Available in English or Spanish.)

Cooperative Project

Organize the class into heterogenous groups of four or five to make a time line of important events covered in the chapter. Have them include the presidencies, the Supreme Court decisions, and the major scientific and cultural events of the time. Groups may illustrate their time lines if they wish. **LEP**

Suggested Rubric: A Poster. A Display. See Performance Assessment Strategies and Activities, pp. 38 and 57.

Individual Project

Have students write a brief biographical sketch of President Kennedy and of President Johnson. The sketches need not compare the two Presidents but should include information on the style, goals, and achievements of each President. ▭

Suggested Rubric: A Research Report. See Performance Assessment Strategies and Activities, p. 39.

Key to Ability Levels

Teaching strategies have been coded for varying learning styles and abilities.

L1 **BASIC** activities for all students

L2 **AVERAGE** activities for average to above-average students

L3 **CHALLENGING** activities for above-average students

LEP **LIMITED ENGLISH PROFICIENCY** activities

Block Scheduling

Block scheduling differs from traditional class scheduling in the amount of time allotted to each period. The extended timeframe provided by block scheduling affords you the opportunity to implement a greater number of research-oriented and activity-intense projects to motivate and involve your students. Activities that are particularly suited to use within the block scheduling framework are identified throughout this chapter by the following designation. ▭

TEACHER'S CORNER

NATIONAL GEOGRAPHIC SOCIETY

NATIONAL GEOGRAPHIC SOCIETY PRODUCTS AVAILABLE FROM GLENCOE

To order the following products for use with this chapter, contact your local Glencoe sales representative or call Glencoe at 1-800-334-7344:

- *The Presidents: A Picture History of Our Nation* (CD-ROM)
- *GTV: The American People: Fabric of a Nation* (Videodisc)
- *GTV: A Geographic Perspective on American History* (Videodisc)

ADDITIONAL NATIONAL GEOGRAPHIC SOCIETY PRODUCTS

To order the following products for use with this chapter, call National Geographic Society at 1-800-368-2728:

- *Decades of History: The 20th Century—The Middle Years* (Filmstrip)
- *The American Presidency* (Filmstrip)
- *The Vietnam War* (Filmstrip)
- *Government in the United States* (Filmstrip)
- *The United States as a World Power: From the 1890s to the 1970s* (Filmstrip)
- *1945-1989: The Cold War* (Video)
- *Branches of Government Series:* The Judicial Branch. (Video)
- *In the Eyes of the Law* (Video)

Chapter Overview

In the 1960s President Kennedy gave the nation new hope through his vision of a New Frontier. President Johnson went on to carry out massive reform through his Great Society programs. Chief Justice Earl Warren steered the Supreme Court in a new direction—that of social reform.

Introducing the Chapter

Explain to students that many early Peace Corps volunteers, drawn to President Kennedy's vision and promise, felt that they were about to take part in something that would make a positive difference in the world. Invite students to read on this page the narrative about one volunteer's expectations.

 Display the Chapter Teaching Transparency and distribute the corresponding activity sheet.

Extension Activity

Have students complete "Beyond the Transparency" on the activity sheet for Chapter 21 and present their projects after the class has completed the chapter.

History Journal

Have students study the photograph on page 699 and write a paragraph describing their interpretation of the relationship between the Peace Corps volunteer and the people with whom she is working.

CHAPTER
21

The Kennedy and Johnson Years

1961: THE BIRTH OF THE PEACE CORPS

In his Inaugural Address, President Kennedy proclaimed the purpose of the Peace Corps: "To those people in the huts and villages of half the globe struggling to break the bonds of mass misery, we pledge our best efforts to help them help themselves. . . ."

Kennedy and his vision deeply inspired many Americans, as Roger Landrum, volunteer to Nigeria from 1961 to 1963, remembers:

". . . when he [Kennedy] announced the Peace Corps idea, I wrote him a letter saying, 'If you will do it, I will volunteer.'"

"I grew up in rural Michigan and I'd never been overseas before. I was at my mother's house when the telegram came inviting me to train for Nigeria. I remember my hands were shaking as I opened it. I had never heard of Nigeria but I defi-

nitely felt I was participating in history. This was a new era of American participation in the world. Peace Corps volunteers were the front-line people making fresh contact with a whole bunch of newly independent nations. There was a sense of exhilaration about maybe carrying forth democracy and establishing new relations with Asia, Africa, and South America."

Landrum and thousands of other volunteers went on to make Kennedy's dream a reality, symbolizing the best of the "New Frontier." ■

HISTORY JOURNAL

Before you read the rest of this chapter, write your impressions of the Kennedy and Johnson years and what you think this chapter will be about.

698

➕ **EXTRA CREDIT PROJECT**

Clarifying Methods Ask students to think about the photograph for a while, focusing on how this volunteer is helping people help themselves—which was President Kennedy's pledge for the Peace Corps. Have students write and place in their portfolios a comparison of these two concepts: "helping people," and "helping

people help themselves." Encourage students to give examples of both methods from current local or national events and situations. Also, set aside time for a class discussion in which students can present their ideas, making sure to point out the merits of both types of aid.

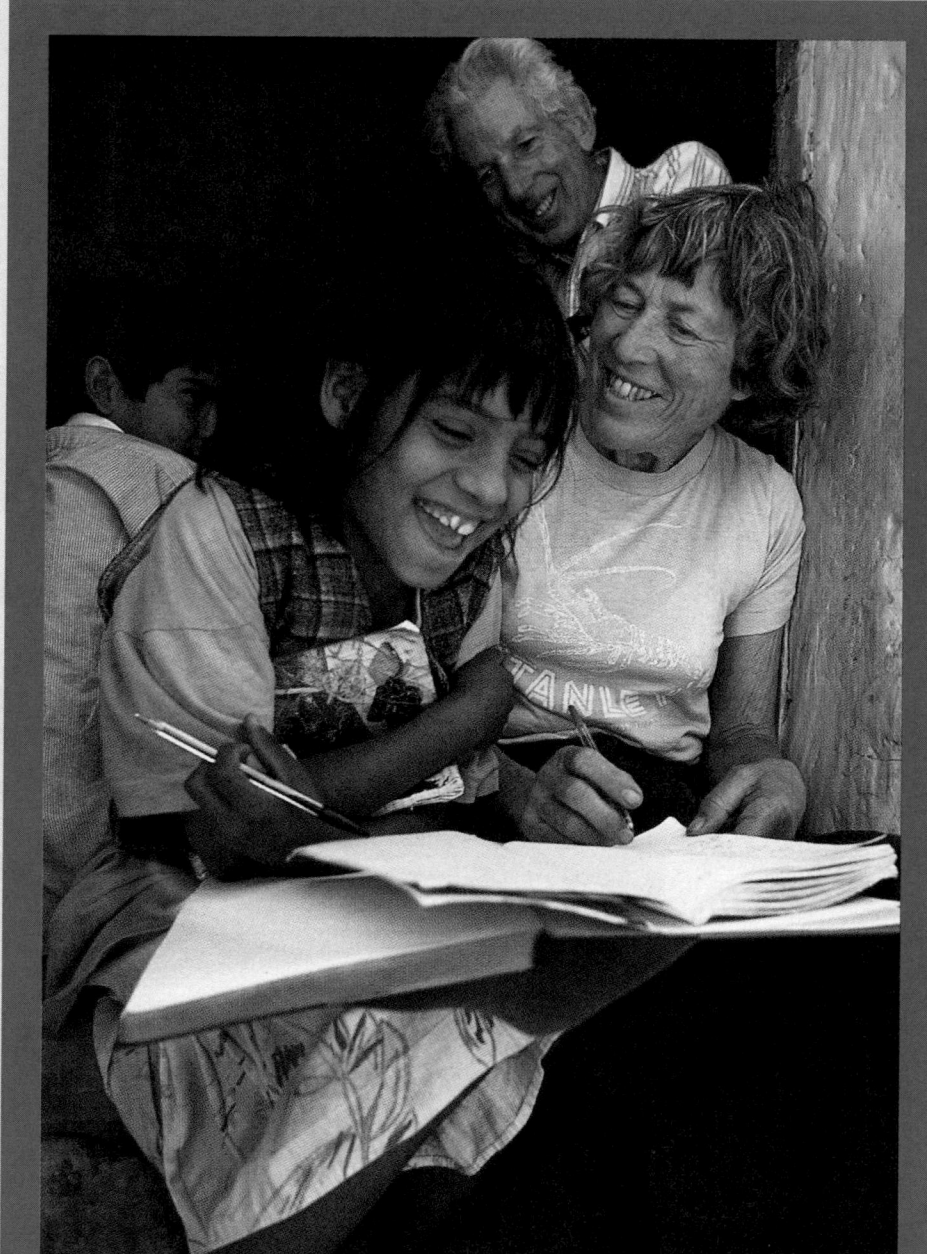

© DAEMRICH/THE IMAGE WORKS

PEACE CORPS VOLUNTEERS
IN HONDURAS

699

FYI

VISTA As part of his Great Society's war on poverty, Lyndon Johnson initiated Volunteers in Service to America (VISTA) in 1964. The goal of VISTA, something like a domestic Peace Corps, is to help low-income communities in the United States develop local resources to achieve local goals. Cooperating with local organizing groups, VISTA volunteers live and work in the communities they serve, phasing out when the communities have become more self-reliant. Typical VISTA projects include: setting up health clinics and women's crisis centers and working on programs involved with youth recreation, hot lunches for senior citizens, rural transportation systems, urban housing rehabilitation, drug abuse counseling, and alternative education.

 Performance Assessment

Refer to page 698B for performance assessment activities for this chapter.

Also see Activity 21 in the Performance Assessment Strategies and Activities for an additional activity as well as for suggested rubrics.

Examining the Visual

Corps Goals The official legislation authorizing the Peace Corps cited these three goals: 1. To help the people of interested countries and areas in meeting their needs for trained manpower 2. To help promote a better understanding of Americans on the part of the peoples served 3. To help promote a better understanding of other peoples on the part of Americans. The volunteer in the photo is helping people in Honduras learn English. Have students evaluate the achievement of the three listed goals in light of what they can infer from the photo.

New Frontier and Great Society

JANUARY 20, 1961: JOHN F. KENNEDY SWORN IN AS PRESIDENT

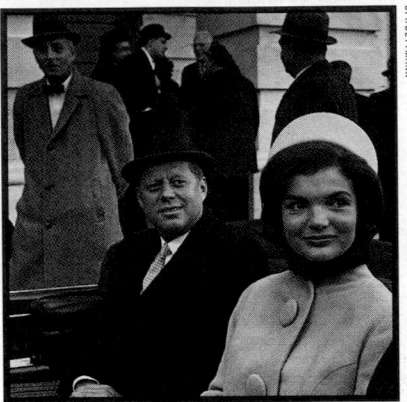

Camelot Begins
President Kennedy inspired a spirit of optimism.

THEY STOOD TOGETHER ON THE INAUGURAL PLATFORM: THE 43-YEAR-OLD JOHN F. KENNEDY, TANNED, VIGOROUS, AND COATLESS DESPITE THE SUBFREEZING WEATHER, AND 70-YEAR-OLD DWIGHT D. EISENHOWER, WEARING A MUFFLER, LOOKING LIKE A TIRED GENERAL. The appearances of the two men, a generation apart in age, symbolized the change of leadership. Kennedy, many voters believed, would get the United States moving again.

Behind Kennedy on the platform were other members of his glamorous family: his beautiful wife, Jackie; his younger brother Robert, soon to be attorney general of the United States; and his parents, Rose and Joseph P.

Kennedy, founders of a political dynasty. As Kennedy began his Inaugural Address, his hands chopped at the air in the style that was familiar to those who had seen his campaign appearances on television. His speech promised so much:

> Let the word go forth . . . that the torch has been passed to a new generation of Americans—born in this century, tempered by war, disciplined by a hard and bitter peace. . . .
>
> Let every nation know, whether it wishes us well or ill, that we shall pay any price, bear any burden, meet any hardship, support any friend, oppose any foe to assure the survival

AS YOU READ

Vocabulary
► mandate
► coalition
► pragmatist

Think About . . .
► the differences in styles, goals, and accomplishments of the Kennedy and Johnson presidencies.
► some of the major reform programs of the 1960s.

Section 1 Resources

The President and Helpers President Kennedy's two children, Caroline and John, Jr., were frequent visitors to the oval office. *What did Kennedy ask of his fellow Americans in his Inaugural Address?*

January 1961 to the funeral procession through the grief-soaked streets of Washington, D.C., in 1963, what survives is a strong impression of the Kennedy spirit. It was a force that propelled the nation into a new political era.

The Kennedy Years

Kennedy Pursues a New Frontier

In the eyes of most historians, the scattered accomplishments of Kennedy's abruptly ended term hardly amounted to a finished political record. Compared to the hard-driving presidencies of FDR and Lyndon Johnson, whose first years were packed with new initiatives, Kennedy's young administration moved slowly. He came into office with the narrowest margin of victory of any modern President—not enough to claim a **mandate** (a clear endorsement of his ideas) from the American public. In Congress, Kennedy faced a powerful conservative **coalition,** or temporary alliance with a common purpose. He, therefore, pursued his course with more caution than boldness.

He grew into the job. His days were long, hard, and fast-paced. As his term progressed, his initiatives became bolder, and his handling of Congress became more aggressive and assured.

and the success of liberty. . . . All this will not be finished in the first 100 days. Nor will it be finished in the first 1,000 days. . . . But let us begin. . . . And so, my fellow Americans—ask not what your country can do for you—ask what you can do for your country.
—John F. Kennedy, Inaugural Address, 1961

The promise John Fitzgerald Kennedy gave the United States was never realized. JFK had scarcely more than 1,000 days himself—1,036 to be exact—before an assassin's bullet cut him down. Looking back at his brief presidency, from the buoyant, wintry inaugural in

★ ★ ★ GALLERY OF PRESIDENTS ★ ★ ★

John Fitzgerald Kennedy

1 9 6 1 – 1 9 6 3

"Now the trumpet summons us again—not as a call to bear arms, though arms we need—not as a call to battle, though embattled we are—but a call to bear the burden of a long twilight struggle . . . against the common enemies of man: tyranny, poverty, disease, and war itself."

Inaugural Address,
January 20, 1961

UPI/BETTMANN

BACKGROUND
► Born 1917; Died 1963
► Democrat, Massachusetts
► Served in the navy 1941–1945
► Elected to the House of Representatives 1946
► Elected to the Senate 1952
► Assassinated, November 1963

ACHIEVEMENTS IN OFFICE
► United States Peace Corps (1961)
► Trade Expansion Act (1961)
► Nuclear Test Ban Treaty (1963)

SECTION ONE **701**

Cooperative Learning

Early Influences Students will understand Kennedy and Johnson better if they know something about their early lives. Organize the class into two groups, one for each President. In groups, members can investigate topics such

as home town, home life, family social position, family members, favorite sports and hobbies, schooling, and so on. Each group can share its findings with the class, including visuals as appropriate.

TEACH

Guided Practice

L2 Discussion The Kennedy-Nixon election of 1960 was the first in which TV helped to make history. Radio listeners thought Nixon had won the debates. TV viewers believed that the more dynamic-appearing Kennedy won. Have students share their opinions about this kind of media influence.

Show students Map Transparency 21 and have them complete the activity sheet.

NATIONAL GEOGRAPHIC SOCIETY

 The Presidents: A Picture History of Our Nation

Have students view "John F. Kennedy" and use what they learn to write a biography for their portfolios.

VISUAL INSTRUCTION

The President and Helpers Caroline and John, Jr., remain in the public eye as adults.

Answer: *"Ask not what your country can do for you—ask what you can do for your country."*

 Facts on File

Landmark Documents in American History Have students review "Inaugural Address, John F. Kennedy, 1961" etc. and write a paragraph about the intent of one of the documents.

701

The New Frontier

Kennedy may not be remembered as a President who accomplished a great deal in terms of domestic legislation. He may stand, however, as one who effected a great change of thinking among the American people. His idealism rang out in this speech:

> We stand today on the edge of a new frontier—the frontier of the 1960s, a frontier of unknown opportunities and paths, a frontier of unfulfilled hopes and threats. . . . The new frontier of which I speak is not a set of promises—it is a set of challenges.
>
> —John F. Kennedy, Presidential nomination acceptance speech, 1960

The New Frontier became the label for Kennedy's vision of progress at home. It was not an organized set of legislative initiatives for economic change, like Roosevelt's New Deal or Johnson's Great Society, which was yet to come. Kennedy was often in a position of reacting to events—such as civil rights disturbances and the Cuban missile crisis—instead of blazing new trails. The New Frontier, then, was more a personal vision of Kennedy's, a progressive ideology but by no means a radical one.

As Kennedy began the campaign that had ushered him into office, many liberals had become complacent. Although in 1960 the economy was sluggish, the country still enjoyed the prosperity that followed on the heels of World War II. Issues that had consumed the liberals of the New Deal era—economic inequalities and the overhaul of large corporations—no longer seemed so critical. As economist John Kenneth Galbraith, in a 1958 study of the United States, summarized, "[Capitalism] works, and in the years since World War II, quite brilliantly."

Liberals in the 1960s reasoned that if the country maintained its current progress, those at the bottom of the economic heap would in time better themselves. According to this view, the two major issues still to be resolved in the 1960s were civil rights and civil liberties. Other problems, such as inner-city slums, inadequate education, and poverty, could be solved by fine tuning.

The Kennedy Aura

Jack Kennedy cultivated a stylish, charismatic image that moved people to very strong views of him, both positive and negative. "Since the thirty-fifth president and his wife are about the most physically attractive people to have lived in the White House, the urge of the publicists, magazines, networks, and photographers to fuse two American dreams and reveal the White House as the ultimate movie set is irresistible," Alistair Cooke wrote in 1963. "To put it mildly, the president has yielded to this urge and has manipulated it."

Many considered JFK a hero. Others distrusted him. Their reasons ranged from dislike of his wealthy father

Success in Space In the spacecraft *Friendship*, John Glenn became the first American to orbit the earth—and the country celebrated! *Space was part of the New Frontier; how did Kennedy define the New Frontier in his acceptance speech?*

JOHN F. KENNEDY LIBRARY, BOSTON

A Warm Send-off JFK greets early Peace Corps volunteers and wishes them well.
What was the main function of Peace Corps volunteers?

The Space Race

During the early 1960s, a nation's accomplishments in space became a test of leadership in technology and defense. The Soviet Union gained an edge in the so-called space race when cosmonaut Yuri Gagarin orbited the earth in April 1961. The following month, in a message to Congress, President Kennedy asked for a commitment to the goal of "landing a man on the moon and returning him safely to earth" before 1970.

The challenge caught the imagination of the public and ensured the dedication of American astronauts. The space agency, National Aeronautics and Space Administration (NASA), developed a three-stage program to put Americans in space. The first stage, Project Mercury, consisted of a series of test flights between 1961 and 1963. John H. Glenn, Jr., became the first American to orbit the earth during a Mercury flight in February 1962. During 1965 and 1966 Project Gemini launched a second series of flights in which two-man teams practiced maneuvering and docking spacecraft while orbiting the earth. The Apollo program, which would accomplish the moon-landing goal that Kennedy had established, began in 1968.

Programs at Home and Abroad

Kennedy's efforts to perk up the economy were among his successes. Increased spending for defense and for the space program poured billions of dollars into government contracts that would increase employment. The Area Redevelopment Act channeled federal funds into needy regions. Congress raised the minimum wage from $1 to $1.25 an hour. These measures contributed to a general economic upswing that lasted until the early 1970s.

During his administration Kennedy initiated several programs for international development. The Alliance for Progress was a series of aid projects undertaken cooperatively with Latin American countries that agreed to democratic reform. The Peace Corps sent volunteers to developing countries, where they lived among the local people and assisted in education and rural development projects. Among the most popular of the Kennedy programs, the Peace Corps continues today. In its first 34 years, the Peace Corps sent 140,000 volunteers to 100 countries.

and the threat of a family dynasty to anti-Catholic and anti-Eastern biases. "All that Mozart string music and ballet dancing down there, and all that fox hunting and London clothes," one congressman said. "He's too elegant for me."

Kennedy's Working Style

The team that Kennedy gathered around him in his administration were, as one journalist noted, "the best and the brightest" of the President's generation. Most were educated at top Eastern schools, and many were recruited from the executive rooms of big business.

Kennedy and his team were content, on the domestic front, to nudge along economic growth and to strengthen public programs. This is what he meant by "getting the country moving again" and restoring United States prestige abroad. The President's interests were centered on foreign policy—the cold war and the containment of communism.

In August 1961, Communists built a wall between East Berlin and West Berlin to prevent East Germans from fleeing to the West. Kennedy reaffirmed his support for West Berliners in a speech delivered near the Berlin Wall in 1963. He said, "All free men, wherever they may live, are citizens of Berlin, and, therefore, as a free man, I take pride in the words, 'Ich bin ein Berliner.'"

Kennedy considered himself more a **pragmatist,** someone interested in practical solutions to problems, than a liberal. Most of the United States's problems "are technical . . . administrative problems," he explained. "They [involve] sophisticated judgments which do not lend themselves to the great sort of 'passionate movements' which have stirred this country so often in the past."

Independent Practice

L3 **History** John F. Kennedy won a Pulitzer Prize in biography for his book *Profiles in Courage,* which recounts the exploits of several people whom Kennedy regarded as especially courageous. Encourage students to find the book in the library, read one or more of the profiles, and report to the class.

📁 Have students complete the Chapter 21, Section 1 Vocabulary and Guided Reading Activity. (Also in Spanish.) **LEP**

📁 Have students complete the Chapter 21 Cooperative Learning Activity.

VISUAL INSTRUCTION

A Warm Sendoff Peace Corps facts: In 1995, there were 6,500 volunteers. The largest program year was 1966 (15,556 volunteers); the smallest was 1987 (5,169 volunteers). The average age of volunteers is 30 years (the oldest volunteer is 81); 92% are single; 79% have bachelor's degrees.

Answer: *to assist developing countries with education and rural development projects*

Portfolio Project

Reviewing Literature Kennedy was very interested in the arts. At his inauguration, the poet Robert Frost read the poem "The Gift Outright." Have students find and read a copy of Frost's poem. They can then write a summary of the poem in their own words and write a commentary on why they think Frost chose this particular poem to read at Kennedy's inauguration. Suggest that they file their summaries in their portfolios. 📁

FYI

Assassination Theories
There have been many books written about JFK assassination theories. Some recent titles are: *Plausible Denial* by Mark Lane, *The Man Who Knew Too Much* by Dick Russell, *Case Open* by Harold Weisberg, and *Deep Politics and the Death of JFK* by Peter Dale Scott.

 Facts on File

Landmark Documents in American History Have students review "Undelivered speech, John F. Kennedy, 1963," "Remarks upon arrival at Andrews Air Force Base, Lyndon Johnson, 1963," and "Mourning Proclamation, Lyndon Johnson, 1963" and write a paragraph about the intent of one of the documents.

Highlights of the Kennedy Presidency

1961	1962	1963
January • John F. Kennedy is inaugurated on January 20. **March** • Peace Corps is assembled. • Committee on Equal Employment Opportunity is established. • Twenty-third Amendment grants the right to vote to District of Columbia. **May** • Alan Shepard, Jr., is the first United States astronaut in space. • Minimum wage is raised from $1.00 to $1.25. **August** • Alliance for Progress is initiated. • Communist East Germany builds the Berlin Wall.	**February** • John Glenn, Jr., is the first United States astronaut to orbit the earth. **May** • United States naval forces and ground troops are sent to Laos. **June** • Supreme Court declares school prayer unconstitutional. **September** • Race riots erupt at University of Mississippi. **October** • JFK "quarantines" Cuba; Soviets remove missiles. **November** • JFK lifts quarantine of Cuba.	**May** • Telstar II communications satellite is launched. **June** • National Guard assists with integration of University of Alabama. • President's Advisory Council on the Arts is created. • JFK recommends strong civil rights legislation. **August** • "Hot line" is established between United States and USSR. • Civil rights protesters march on Washington. **September** • United States treaty is ratified banning nuclear testing in the atmosphere, outer space, and under water.

The Kennedy administration was a time of new frontiers—at home, around the world, and in space. *When did the first American orbit the earth?*

Kennedy's efforts to pass an education aid bill showed the obstacles he faced in Congress. The coalition of Republicans and Southern Democrats feared that increased federal support for education might mean less state control. The issue of aid to parochial schools was a further complication. Kennedy felt that supporting such aid would expose him to the accusation that as a Catholic he favored parochial schools. As negotiations wore on, both Protestants and Catholics became displeased with him. Kennedy was unable to push the education bill through Congress, something that Lyndon Johnson, a Protestant, later managed to do.

Hopes Cut Off
Assassin Kills Kennedy

Many people expected more than they were getting from Kennedy on issues such as civil rights. "I was furious with the administration's civil rights posture," recalled Roger Wilkins, a lawyer with the Agency for International Development. "I thought it was slow, lethargic, and unresponsive."

Arthur Schlesinger, Jr., who served as special assistant to Kennedy, however, notes that the President "was soon educated by events...." Later in his term, Kennedy seemed to be seizing control of events. He called for a thawing of the cold war with the Soviet Union. Two months later the two nations signed a treaty limiting nuclear testing. As one of his last efforts, Kennedy requested his economic advisers to prepare a plan directed at poverty in the United States. He also promised action on civil rights.

Kennedy's hope was to achieve a greater mandate for his programs in the 1964 election. With this in mind, in late November 1963 he took a trip to Dallas, Texas, to smooth over party differences and gather electoral support.

Tragedy in Dallas

CBS television news anchor Walter Cronkite cried as he gave the nation the news: President Kennedy had been fatally shot in Dallas while riding in a motorcade. For four days people across the United States sat hunched in front of their television sets, as images of violence and of mourning were etched forever into their minds. They pored over newspaper accounts of the grisly shooting, trying to understand why or how the tragedy could have happened.

They saw the pictures of Kennedy waving to cheering crowds as his open limousine wove through the streets of Dallas shortly before noon on November 22. As the motorcade approached an expressway, shots rang out and Kennedy slumped forward in his seat. Jackie Kennedy cradled her dying husband's head in her lap as the limousine raced to nearby Parkland Hospital. Kennedy was pronounced dead at 1:00 P.M. Vice President Lyndon Johnson was sworn in almost immediately as President.

Extending the Content

Checking Predictions President Kennedy's family played a major role in his political success. Tell students that as a young Massachusetts senator, Kennedy once said, "Just as I went into politics because Joe [his older brother] died, if anything happens to me tomorrow, my brother Bobby would run for my seat in the Senate. And if Bobby died, Teddy would take over for him." Discuss with students the degree to which JFK's prediction came true.

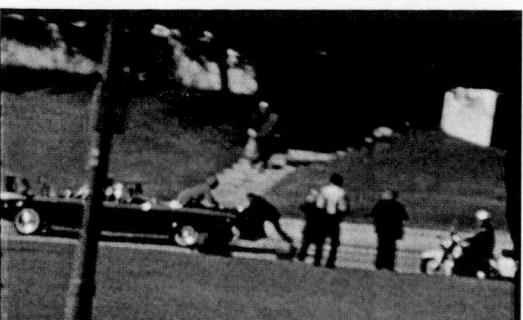

Tragedy Strikes Jacqueline Kennedy reacts to her husband's being shot. *Whom did police charge with the murder of the President?*

Police determined that the shots had been fired from a warehouse that overlooked the route of the motorcade. They arrested Lee Harvey Oswald, a 24-year-old warehouse worker, and charged him with the murder. Two days later Oswald was transferred from the city jail to the county jail. Television cameras covered the event live. As viewers across the country watched in disbelief, a Dallas nightclub owner, Jack Ruby, pushed through a circle of police officers and journalists and shot and killed Oswald at point-blank range.

The death of Oswald hampered investigations of the assassination. The Warren Commission, headed by Chief Justice Earl Warren, however, concluded in 1964 that Oswald had acted alone and not in a conspiracy of any kind. Critics of the Warren Commission maintain that the investigations were hastily concluded and that some group whose identity is as yet unknown most likely aided Oswald.

The Nation Mourns

The answer to the question, "Where were you when Kennedy was shot?" became frozen in people's memories. "I was in social studies class at Woodlands High School," said Bonnie Steinboch of White Plains, New York. "In the corridor, I saw Mr. Courtney, the art teacher, sobbing against the wall, and I was astonished that a grown-up, a teacher, would be so openly upset. Kennedy was the most important person in my life to die.... Months after he died, I realized one night in bed that I would never hear his voice again, and I sobbed for a long time."

Americans cried as they saw three-year-old John F. Kennedy, Jr., salute his father's funeral procession, and they stared at the riderless horse in the procession, a symbol of the fallen hero. The nation grieved as much for the President that John F. Kennedy might have become had he lived, as for the leader he had been. Commentator

JOHN F. KENNEDY LIBRARY, BOSTON

A Change of Leaders Vice President Lyndon Johnson takes the oath of office aboard *Air Force One* almost immediately after the assassination of President Kennedy. *What part did Jack Ruby play in the events surrounding the Kennedy assassination?*

SECTION ONE **705**

VISUAL INSTRUCTION

Tragedy Strikes Mrs. Kennedy reacts, as does the Secret Service. Vice President Lyndon Johnson, uninjured, was put under protective custody by the Secret Service almost immediately.
Answer: *Lee Harvey Oswald*

A Change of Leaders Onboard the presidential jet *Air Force One* on the runway at Love Field, LBJ took the presidential oath, administered by Judge Sarah T. Hughes, appointed by Kennedy in 1961.
Answer: *Ruby killed Oswald.*

FYI

Camelot In the legendary Camelot, leaders sat at a round table. With no head of the table, it was implied that rule was by all, not just by one.

Cultural Perspectives

Peruvian Village Reacts to Kennedy's Death From the Peruvian village of Huarocondo, Peace Corps worker Nancy Norton wrote to her parents regarding President Kennedy's death: "The paper said the whole world is in mourning. I don't know about the whole world, only about Huarocondo. Huarocondo is mourning. Everyone knows the president of the United States. They would be stricken if we weren't here. But they know we are here because of John Kennedy. They know we are sad because he is dead. They love us, so they are sad, too. Were I not here, I would never have believed that the world really cared." Discuss with students whether they believe that, generally, "the world cares." Invite them to back their opinions with examples.

VISUAL INSTRUCTION

Federal Support for the Arts In this Benny Andrews painting, the flag represents the U. S. Constitution, and the clenched fists represent Americans denied constitutional rights. The painting is entitled *Did the Bear*.

Answer: *Students will individually interpret the symbols.*

NATIONAL GEOGRAPHIC SOCIETY

The Presidents: A Picture History of Our Nation

Have students view "Lyndon B. Johnson" and use the information to write a brief biography to include in their portfolios.

Richard Neustadt wrote, "He left a broken promise, that 'the torch has been passed to a new generation,' and the youngsters who identified with him felt cheated as the promise, like the glamour, disappeared."

His widow compared the Kennedy years in the White House to Camelot, the site of the legendary King Arthur's court, about which a popular musical was written in the 1960s. The romantic hero and heroine, the battle between good and evil, a time of great happiness forever lost—all these images were more commonly applied to ballads and to myths than to political figures.

Johnson's Great Society
Johnson Pushes Social Reform

Johnson's administration began in the tragedy of Kennedy's assassination and ended in the tragedy of the disastrous war in Vietnam. In between Johnson carried forward Kennedy's dream of a New Frontier, then went beyond Kennedy's domestic programs to launch his own vision of the Great Society.

In the days following Kennedy's assassination, Johnson took several steps to reassure the world that he would carry on in the same tradition as Kennedy. In his first speech following his succession to office, he said, "All I have, I would have given gladly not to be standing here today," and asked for the nation's prayers and support. Looking back on those days, Johnson told his biographer, Doris Kearns Goodwin:

We were all spinning around and around, trying to come to grips with what had happened, but the more we tried to understand it, the more confused we got. We were like a bunch of cattle caught in the swamp, unable to move in either direction, simply circling 'round and 'round. I understood that; I knew what had to be done. There is but one way to get the cattle out of the swamp. And that is for the man on the horse to take the lead, to assume command, to provide direction. In the period of confusion after the assassination, I was that man.

—Doris Kearns Goodwin, *Lyndon Johnson and the American Dream*, 1976

The differences between the two men, Kennedy and Johnson, were striking. Whereas Kennedy was handsome, sophisticated, and well-educated, Johnson could be crude and intimidating. Politeness and polish were not

COURTESY BENNY ANDREWS

Federal Support for the Arts In 1965 Congress established a funding program for artists and arts organizations. This 1969 painting uses strong images to comment on African Americans' fight for civil rights in the United States. *What do you think the symbols represent?*

★ ★ ★ GALLERY OF PRESIDENTS ★ ★ ★

Lyndon Baines Johnson
1963–1969

LYNDON BAYNES JOHNSON LIBRARY

"Let us now join reason to faith and action to experience, to transform our unity of interest into a unity of purpose. For the hour and the day and the time are here to achieve progress without strife, to achieve change without hatred—not without difference of opinion, but without the deep and abiding divisions which scar the union for generations."

Inaugural Address, January 20, 1965

BACKGROUND

► Born 1908; Died 1973
► Democrat, Texas
► Representative, 1937–1948
► Served in the Senate 1949–1960
► Assumed the presidency 1963; elected to full term 1964

ACHIEVEMENTS IN OFFICE

► Civil Rights Act (1964)
► Voting Rights Act (1965)
► Medicare (1965)

Critical Thinking

Making Comparisons Most people in the United States alive at the time of President Kennedy's assassination remember what they were doing when they heard the terrible news. Ask students to try to relate this kind of impact on their own lives. In small groups they can discuss a public event—a natural disaster, the death of a favorite entertainer or leader, a tragic accident, for example—that affected them in a way somewhat similar to the way that Kennedy's death affected so many people.

among Johnson's attributes; but he was, as he said, the man for the job. He had been an apt student of politics. A member of the House in 1937 at age 29, he advanced to the Senate in 1949 and rose quickly to the powerful position of Senate majority leader in 1955.

Johnson was a genius at building coalitions. "Let us reason together," he would say, with a touch of understatement. He then used what those who received it called "the Treatment."

Johnson's method was to find out everything he could about the person he was talking to—family, friends, strengths, weaknesses, special interests. Then Johnson would proceed to flatter, cajole, promise, threaten, all the while suggesting that the other person's decision was going to make the difference between success or failure. "Lyndon got me by the lapels and put his face on top of mine and he talked and talked," a colleague said. "I figured [the choice] was getting drowned or joining."

Fashioning a Legacy

President Johnson had boundless confidence in himself, and he knew what he wanted to do. He promised to realize the Kennedy vision, and he did—perhaps better than Kennedy ever could have.

In 1963 Kennedy's program for social change was only an emerging vision. His liberalism was cautious and uncertain. Johnson had no such uncertainties. He was a man determined to do great things, and now he had the power to change the country. What then needed changing?

The answer depended on where you looked. In the suburban shopping malls that were springing up around

THE GREAT SOCIETY

The domestic programs of President Johnson's Great Society brought improvement to many areas of life, especially for the disadvantaged.

$ WAGES

The minimum wage goes from $1.25 to $1.40 per hour, an increase of about $6.00 a week for a full-time worker.

Percent of total population below poverty level

22% 1960

12% 1975

HOUSING

Federal funding makes possible new and subsidized low-income housing to replace substandard urban dwellings.

SCHOOLING

The government aids elementary, secondary, and college students. Young children get a boost from Head Start.

Total school expenditures in billions

$25 (1960) | $45 (1966) | $70 (1970) | $108 (1975)

✓ VOTING

All citizens are guaranteed the right and the liberty to vote, along with federally monitored voter registration.

+ MEDICAL CARE

The elderly receive federally funded health care through Medicare; younger, needy recipients receive it through Medicaid.

Infant mortality rate

Deaths/1,000 live births: 30, 20, 10, 0 — 1960 '65 '70 '75

MAJOR GREAT SOCIETY PROGRAMS, 1964–1966

1964
- Civil Rights Act
- Economic Opportunity Act
- Wilderness Preservation Act

1965
- Elementary and Secondary Education Act
- Medical Care Act
- Voting Rights Act
- Omnibus Housing Act
- National endowments for the arts and for the humanities
- Water Quality Act
- Immigration Act
- Higher Education Act

1966
- Traffic and Motor Vehicle Safety Act
- Minimum wage law
- Truth in Packaging Act
- Model Cities Act

During Lyndon Johnson's presidency, great strides were made in programs for social change. *What were some areas of life affected by Great Society programs? What age groups were affected?*

The Elementary and Secondary Education Act was the first major federal aid package for education in U.S. history.

Answer: *wages, housing, schooling, voting, medical care; all age groups*

ABCNEWS INTERACTIVE™

Videodisc

Powers of the Supreme Court

Side 1, Chapter 28
Title: Amendment 24 (1964): Poll Taxes
Subject: excerpt from Johnson's speech on why poll taxes should be outlawed
Ask: Why did Johnson oppose poll taxes? *(used to prevent African Americans from voting)*

See Powers of the Supreme Court Guidebook page 44 for complete lesson plan.

 Facts on File

Landmark Documents in American History Have students review "Great Society speech, Lyndon Johnson, 1965," etc., and write a paragraph about the intent of one of the documents.

Critical Thinking

Making Inferences A President reveals his values in the kinds of programs he tries to push through Congress. Discuss with the class the major legislative initiatives of the Johnson years—better education for the young, housing for the poor, medical care for the elderly, voting rights for all. What do these initiatives say about Johnson's values?

Meeting Lesson Objectives

Each section objective is tested by the section review questions that follow it in parentheses.

1. Compare the styles, goals, and accomplishments of the Kennedy and Johnson presidencies. (1, 2, 3, 4)

2. Identify and evaluate some of the major reform programs of the 1960s. (3, 4, 5)

VISUAL INSTRUCTION

A Head Start It began as a summer program; by the end of the 1970s, most programs were full-year. The enrollment in 1995 reached approximately 740,000.

Answer: *to give preschool children from disadvantaged families assistance toward their elementary education*

Global Connection

In the 1960s the Scandinavian countries of Sweden, Norway, and Denmark had extensive social welfare programs—covering areas such as health, employment, housing, and leisure.

---

the country, the United States looked robust. Measured in auto sales and economic indicators, the country hummed with prosperity. This was the nation that television viewers watched on *The Lucy Show* and other situation comedies, where everyday problems were solvable within a 22-minute show.

There was, of course, another America, as Michael Harrington revealed in his book, *The Other America*. He described a country within a country, where people were hungry when they went to bed, if in fact they had a bed. Chronic joblessness, unbudged by the New Deal or the postwar economic boom, was set like cement in rural towns and big-city slums. During the 1960s a vision of this other America slowly revealed itself to public consciousness. Strangely enough, it was Lyndon Baines Johnson (LBJ), the wheeling-dealing politician and friend of the rich, who understood the problem.

Johnson's homespun tales of his rag-poor past may have stretched the truth a bit, but he certainly knew hard times as a child growing up in central Texas. Later, as a

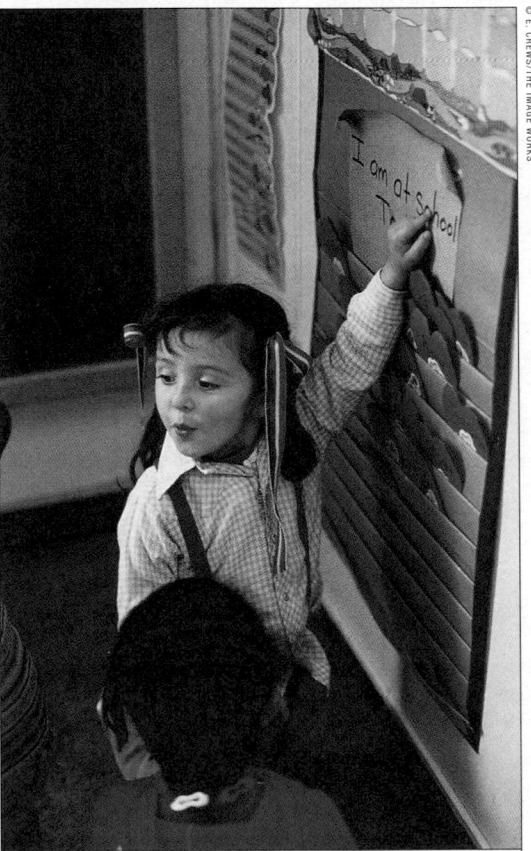

© E. CREWS/THE IMAGE WORKS

A Head Start This 3-year-old Hispanic girl is "reading" in a Head Start program. *What was the purpose of these programs?*

teacher of the rural poor in his home state, he felt a great empathy for people living in grinding, persistent poverty.

LBJ cared about the poor, and he cared about his place in history. He felt he could become the first President to create a just society that all but eliminated chronic poverty and hardship in the United States.

Johnson told Congress on March 16, 1964, that "in the past we have often been called upon to wage war against foreign enemies which threaten our freedom today. Now, we are asked to declare a war on a domestic enemy which threatens the strength of our nation and the welfare of our people."

That enemy, of course, was poverty. LBJ's ambitious war on poverty would be the cornerstone of his Great Society.

The Great Society

Johnson moved quickly to push Kennedy initiatives, including the Civil Rights Act, through Congress. He launched his war on poverty with the Economic Opportunity Act, the most ambitious attempt to aid the poor in the nation's history. It established Volunteers in Service to America (VISTA), a kind of domestic peace corps of citizens working in poor neighborhoods. The act also funded Project Head Start, to give preschoolers from disadvantaged families a leg up on elementary education.

The mood of the country, still affected by the shock of Kennedy's assassination, worked in Johnson's favor during the 1964 presidential election. Johnson overwhelmingly defeated Arizona senator Barry Goldwater and seized the mandate to introduce his own program of reform.

The Great Society rests on abundance and liberty for all. It demands an end to poverty and racial injustice . . . [It] is a place where every child can find knowledge to enrich his mind . . . where the city of man serves not only the needs of the body and the demands for commerce, but the desire for beauty and the hunger for community.
—Lyndon B. Johnson, University of Michigan commencement address, 1964

The President knew that what he called the "honeymoon" of his election would not last for long. "You've got to give it all you can that first year," he said. The result was the most comprehensive reform package to pass through Congress since the New Deal reforms of 1935.

Among the most significant pieces of legislation were Medicare, federally funded health care for the elderly, and Medicaid, its companion program for the needy who were too young to qualify for Medicare. These programs were the first to make health care available to those who could not afford it. The Voting Rights

---

Cooperative Learning

Poverty, Past and Present Lyndon Johnson had an unrealized dream of eliminating poverty. Organize the class in three or four groups. Each group can investigate a present-day problem linked in some way to issues of poverty— homelessness, unemployment, or crime, for example. Make sure all group members take an active part. After researching their issue, each group can present their findings to the class.

Transformed Living Spaces Improved urban housing was one of the many benefits of the Great Society programs. *What new housing department was created as part of Johnson's Great Society?*

VISUAL INSTRUCTION

Transformed Living Spaces LBJ'S initial plan for Model Cities was to improve housing, employment, schools, police, transportation, health care, and recreation; the plan was later modified.

Answer: *department of Housing and Urban Development*

Act of 1965 put teeth into the Fifteenth Amendment by providing for federal supervision of voter registration. Cities benefited from the Model Cities Act, which encouraged slum rehabilitation. A new department of Housing and Urban Development was created; its secretary, Robert Weaver, became the first African American to serve in a presidential cabinet.

Immigration legislation did away with a quota system that had existed for more than 50 years. As a result, people from a variety of cultures entered the United States, creating considerable variety in the ethnic mix of the population.

Successes and Limitations

Johnson's Great Society program of social and political reform is often compared with FDR's New Deal. The goals of the two were somewhat different. The New Deal sought social reforms in some areas—the creation of the Social Security system is an example. Its main goals, however, were to provide relief for the unemployed and the poor and to stimulate economic recovery.

The Great Society was more successful in creating legislative programs than in implementing them. It was underfunded, partly because the financing of the Vietnam War claimed a greater and greater proportion of the tax dollar. Still, the percentage of impoverished Americans, as measured by government standards, dropped from 22 percent in 1959 to 12 percent in 1969. The civil rights acts of 1964 and 1965 were landmark

achievements of the Johnson presidency. Perhaps the greatest weakness in the Great Society program was that it promised so much that, despite its successes, critics could always point to problems yet unresolved.

SECTION REVIEW

Vocabulary

1. Define: mandate, coalition, pragmatist.

Checking Facts

2. How was Kennedy's pragmatism reflected in his approach to legislative reforms?

3. What were the major legislative reforms launched in Johnson's administration?

Critical Thinking

Making Comparisons

4. How did Kennedy and Johnson differ in the way they worked with Congress?

Linking Across Time

5. How do the legislative achievements of the Great Society compare with the achievements of the New Deal? Which do you think will have a more lasting impact on society?

Evaluate

Have students complete the Section Review.

⬛ Assign the Section 1 Quiz or use the Testmaker to develop a customized quiz. (Also in Spanish.) **LEP**

Reteach

🎧 Have students listen to the Chapter 21, Section 1 audiocassette. (Also in Spanish.) **LEP**

Enrich

Have students complete the Chapter 21 Geography in History

**GLENCOE
TECHNOLOGY**

 Great Speeches

Volume I–John F. Kennedy (Inaugural Address)

CLOSE

Ask: How would you summarize Kennedy's presidency? Johnson's? (Kennedy: defense, space race, plans for social reform; Johnson: major social reform)

Section 1 Review Answers

1. **mandate** (701), **coalition** (701), **pragmatist** (703)
2. in his cautious, case-by-case approach to legislative reforms
3. civil rights, economic opportunity, VISTA, Head Start, Job Corps, wilderness preservation, and elementary and secondary education.

4. Kennedy worked cautiously with an often hostile Congress; Johnson worked confidently, boldly, and effectively.
5. New Deal responded to economic problems; Great Society responded to social problems; both impacted society long-term; students' opinons will vary.

Making the Historical Connection

As technology became more sophisticated and middle-class families continued to enjoy postwar prosperity, television came to play an integral part in the everyday lives of people in the United States. Not only did television provide instant entertainment, it also provided instant access to news—civil rights protests as well as the assassinated President's funeral were immediately accessible to the public.

FYI

Remote Control Early devices were often unstable, easily set in motion by sunlight, ringing phones, or clanking pet chains. Users of early remote controls often used them to change channels and avoid commercials. Today, in addition to commercial skipping, remotes are often used for channel browsing, or surfing.

Science, TECHNOLOGY, and Society

Television

For decades people in the United States had learned about the world through newspapers, radio, or newsreels. That changed, however, when television came on the scene—bringing comedy, education, social issues, politics, and violence right into viewers' living rooms. By 1960 more than 45 million households had TV sets.

COMEDY
The 1962–63 top-rated comedy, *The Beverly Hillbillies,* featured a mountain family that struck oil and moved to Beverly Hills, yet remained unaffected by the posh surroundings.

© JOE BARNELL/SUPERSTOCK
© GABI RONA/MOTION PICTURE & TV PHOTO ARCHIVE

TELEVISION HIGHLIGHTS

1920s	1940s	1950s
PHILO FARNSWORTH invents the first electronic television system.	**COLOR TELEVISION** is demonstrated in the United States for the first time in 1940. Today 90 percent of households have a color set.	**REMOTE CONTROL** is invented by Robert Adler and introduced by Zenith in 1955. Today at least 66 million households have remote-control devices.

Background Information

Turning Tide Television, as an "action" medium, required dramatic movement to capture viewers', attention. During the early and mid-1960s, white leaders such as Eugene "Bull" Connor encouraged violence as a response to nonviolent protesters. Television cameras tuned in to these dramas and brought them to the eyes of the public, whose sympathy turned quickly in favor of the protesters. Later in the movement, however, as African Americans became more militant, the TV cameras captured other kinds of drama—shouts of "Black power!" and "Burn, baby, burn!" accompanying images of cities being ravaged by race riots. This kind of drama tended to frighten and confuse white viewers, and their sympathy began to shift away from the protest movement.

VIOLENCE AND MOURNING

Across the nation viewers watched in profound sadness and near-disbelief as John F. Kennedy, Jr., saluted the casket carrying his assassinated father, President John F. Kennedy.

AP/WIDE WORLD PHOTOS

RACIAL UNREST

The often violent treatment of nonviolent civil rights protesters in the 1960s was brought to the public eye. Coverage such as this of a protester taking part in a 1963 sit-in in Greensboro, North Carolina, swung public sympathy to the side of the civil rights movement.

TELEVISION PROGRESS

PORTFOLIO PROJECT

Research one of the developments in television listed on the time line. Describe the innovation and explain its effect on society. Include photographs and other graphic aids. Share your findings with your classmates, and place your written report in your portfolio.

© SWERSEY/GAMMA LIAISON

EDUCATIONAL INROADS

Since its debut in 1969, *Sesame Street* has demonstrated the power of television as an educational tool—with characters such as Big Bird helping with the lessons.

1960s	1980s	1990s

TELSTAR, a communications satellite, launches international television broadcasting in 1962 by linking the United States and Europe for up to 20 minutes.

CABLE SYSTEMS are connected to 30 percent of homes in the United States. By 1987, half of United States households have cable.

PORTABLE VIDEO CAMERAS and videotapes let families record their own activities to play back on television. *America's Funniest Home Videos* is a hit.

SCIENCE, TECHNOLOGY, AND SOCIETY   **711**

Portfolio Project

Discussion Television brought viewers virtually face-to-face with current events. Have students talk with people who watched some of the dramatic events that received television coverage in the 1960s—violence against civil rights protesters at Birmingham or Pettus Bridge, the civil rights march on Washington, D.C., the funeral of John F. Kennedy, or the shooting of Lee Harvey Oswald, for example. Encourage students to find out what kinds of effects TV coverage had on these viewers. Did such coverage change their opinions or lives? In what ways? Students can write a summary of their discussions and add the summaries to their portfolios.

Science, Technology, and Society

FYI

Sesame Street Before *Sesame Street* appeared on the scene in 1963, most children's TV shows, such as *Captain Kangaroo,* moved at a predictably paced tempo. *Sesame Street,* in contrast, moved at a rapid pace, and children of all socioeconomic levels were spellbound. Additionally, research studies showed that preschoolers who watched six weeks of *Sesame Street* were substantially ahead of nonviewers in terms of recognizing letters, associating sounds with letters, and recognizing and sorting geometric forms.

CLOSE

Ask: How did television affect people in the 1960s? *(brought instant entertainment, education, and news into homes)* What were some innovations in TV technology? *(color, remote control, satellites, cable, videocassette recorders and tapes)*

TEACH

This skill helps students recognize that without clear communication, groups often make faulty assumptions about one another, and this leads to conflict. Students consider the basis of faulty assumptions between a group of Peace Corps volunteers and the Filipino people with whom they worked. Point out to students that local, national, and international problems can often be traced to faulty assumptions—which can be eliminated when basic beliefs and values are clarified.

Additional Practice

☞ Have students complete the Chapter 21 Skill Reinforcement Activity.

Notes

_____
_____
_____
_____
_____
_____
_____
_____
_____
_____
_____
_____
_____
_____
_____
_____
_____
_____

712

Critical Thinking Skill

IDENTIFYING ASSUMPTIONS

Learning the Skill

Conflict occurs when one group makes assumptions about the beliefs or values of another group. Assumptions are unquestioned suppositions of truth. To identify assumptions, follow these steps:

a. Identify the groups involved.

b. Define any conflicts that exist between the groups.

c. Identify the behaviors or attitudes causing the conflicts.

d. Analyze the behaviors or attitudes to find and validate the actual, not assumed, beliefs or values of the groups.

One example of conflict resulting from faulty assumptions took place between Filipino authorities and Peace Corps volunteers from the United States who arrived in the Philippines in the fall of 1961. The conflicts between these 2 groups were the result of assumptions made in the process of trying to carry out business dealings.

Study the chart below. It compares people from the United States and people from the Philippines in terms of what their cultures value in business relations, how business interactions are usually structured, and how business interactions are often carried out in terms of values and priorities.

Business Behaviors	
Philippine Culture	**United States Culture**
• Business relations tend to be long-term. • Business interactions are based on mutual assistance alliances involving reciprocal obligations. • Alliances sometimes interfere with the performance of business tasks.	• Business relations tend to be short-term. • Business interactions are based on formally or contractually defined job responsibilities. • Task-oriented business organization usually aids the performance of business tasks.

↓ ↓

Interaction in a business setting

↓

Filipinos make assumptions about people from the United States and vice versa, and conflicts occur.

Practicing the Skill

Use the chart and the text to answer these questions.

1. What are the major differences between Filipino and United States business practices?

David L. Szanton, a former Peace Corps volunteer and author of *Cultural Frontiers of the Peace Corps*, explains that the Philippine culture values "smooth interpersonal relations." Filipinos usually handle disagreements by "ignoring them, by pretending they do not exist, or by designating intermediaries to conduct negotiations between the parties involved." People from the United States, on the other hand, come from a culture that values open discussion, and they tend to handle conflicts directly.

2. How do Filipino and American values differ in terms of handling conflicts?

Szanton reports that the following kind of conflict would typically occur. Peace Corps volunteers would recommend solutions to problems and, not receiving any negative response, would believe that their recommendations had been accepted. Often, however, the Filipinos would not take action on the proposed solutions and when questioned would blame their inactivity on unforeseen circumstances.

3. What assumptions caused the misunderstandings between the Peace Corps volunteers and the Filipino authorities?

4. What might the Peace Corps volunteers have done to avoid such conflicts?

5. What might the Filipino authorities have done to avoid such conflicts?

Applying the Skill

Choose a local, national, or international conflict currently in the news. Define the conflict and the assumptions involved. What information might help the groups end the conflict?

Additional Practice

For additional practice, see Reinforcing Skills on page 721.

Practicing the Skill Answers

1. Filipino practices are long-term and alliance oriented; United States practices are short-term and based on defined tasks.

2. Filipinos avoid direct confrontation, whereas people in the United States value it.

3. The volunteers assumed that the Filipinos would communicate their disagreements directly; the Filipinos assumed their lack of response would make the disagreement "go away."

4. The volunteers might have asked directly whether their recommendations had been accepted, letting the Filipinos know that disagreement was acceptable.

5. The Filipinos might have let the volunteers know at the start that they did not agree with the recommendations, understanding that such directness would be appreciated.

SECTION 2

The Supreme Court and Civil Liberties

JANUARY 8, 1962: GIDEON PETITIONS THE SUPREME COURT

CLARENCE EARL GIDEON WAS A MAN BEATEN DOWN BY LIFE'S CIRCUMSTANCES AND BY HIS OWN FOOLISH MISTAKES. In 1962 he was an inmate of the Florida state prison, serving time for breaking into a poolroom and stealing money. He was a frail man, 51 years old, though he looked 10 years older. His face was gray and wrinkled and his lower lip continually trembled.

Prison life was not new to Gideon. He had served 4 previous jail terms. Poverty was also no stranger, since he had been a runaway at age 14; but now he wanted out. He worried about his family; his wife had started drinking, and his children were in foster homes.

Civil Liberties Strengthened
The Clarence Earl Gideon case was one of many landmark decisions made by the Warren Court.

He insisted he was convicted in an unfair trial for a crime he did not commit.

So Gideon wrote the Supreme Court a letter. In pencil, on lined prison paper, he petitioned the Court to release him on the grounds that the state had denied him his rights. At the time of his trial, with no money for a lawyer, he had asked the lower court to provide him with one, but the court had refused. Gideon had conducted his own defense.

Fourteen months after Gideon mailed off his plea to the Supreme Court, his conviction was overturned. The *Gideon* v. *Wainwright* ruling reversed an earlier

AS YOU READ

Vocabulary
▶ reapportionment
▶ due process

Think About . . .
▶ how reapportionment related to equal representation.
▶ why the Supreme Court ruled against prayer in public schools.
▶ the Supreme Court decisions aimed at protecting accused citizens' rights to due process.

SECTION TWO   **713**

Section 2 Resources

REPRODUCIBLE RESOURCES
📁 Lesson Plan 21-2
📁 Section 2 Quiz
📁 Vocabulary and Guided Reading Activity 21-2
📁 Enrichment Activity 21
📁 Reteaching Activity 21

📁 Supreme Court Cases 23-31, 33, 34
📁 Political Cartoons 18, 20, 21
📁 Performance Assessment Activity 21
📁 Chapter 21 Test

MULTIMEDIA RESOURCES
🔖 Section Focus Transparency 67
⬤ Powers of the Supreme Court
⬤ Landmark Documents in American History
⬤ Student Self-Test: A Software Review
⬤ Testmaker
⬤ Vocabulary PuzzleMaker
🎧 Chapter 21 Digest Audiocassette

DEPARTMENT OF CORRECTIONS OF THE STATE OF FLORIDA

FOCUS

Section Objectives

1. Explain how reapportionment helped ensure equal representation.
2. Explain why the Supreme Court ruled against prayer in public schools.
3. Analyze the Supreme Court decisions protecting the rights of accused offenders to due process.

Bellringer Activity

While taking attendance at the beginning of the class period, display **Section Focus Transparency 67,** and have students answer the questions. (Or use the blackline master.)

VISUAL INSTRUCTION

Civil Liberties Strengthened A mug shot is taken when police book, or register, a suspect.
Ask: Why did Gideon petition the Supreme Court? (*state would not provide a lawyer*)

FYI

Acquittal in Gideon
After the Court ruled in his favor, Clarence Earl Gideon had a new trial. Although he had fought for the right to legal representation, he chose to represent himself. The judge refused, however, and appointed a lawyer, who won his acquittal.

TEACH

Guided Practice

L2 Discussion Have students compare Earl Warren's view on reapportionment—as governor of California and as a Supreme Court justice (which is an appointed, not an elected, position).

Independent Practice

L2 Citizenship Invite students to further research a ruling made by the Warren Court. They can write a summary of the ruling and perhaps file it in their portfolios.

📁 Have students complete the Chapter 21, Section 2 Vocabulary and Guided Reading Activity. (Also in Spanish.) **LEP**

VISUAL INSTRUCTION

The Warren Court, 1965 Nominations: Roosevelt (Black, Douglas), Truman (Clark),Eisenhower (Harlan, Warren, Brennan, Stewart), Kennedy (White), Johnson (Fortas)

Answer: *that it stepped beyond its limits, infringed on state and local governments, intruded on family life, threatened national moral fabric* .

1. Byron R. White, 1962–1993
2. William J. Brennan, Jr., 1956–1990
3. Potter Stewart, 1958–1981
4. Abe Fortas, 1965–1969
5. Tom C. Clark, 1949–1967
6. Hugo C. Black, 1937–1971
7. Earl Warren, 1953–1969
8. William O. Douglas, 1939–1975
9. John M. Harlan, 1955–1971

The Warren Court, 1965 These Supreme Court justices were instrumental in one of the most extensive periods of social reform the country had ever known. *What did critics say about this reform-minded Court?*

decision and declared that, according to the Sixth Amendment, if a defendant cannot afford a lawyer, the court must supply one. The appeal to the Supreme Court by Gideon, a poor man with few resources, made legal history.

The Court's Authority
The Supreme Court Expands Its Boundaries

The Supreme Court, the branch of government that Alexander Hamilton called "the weakest of the three departments of power," has become mighty throughout its history. In its earliest days, the Court simply ruled on whether laws had been broken. In 1803 the Court expanded its powers by taking on the role of judging the validity, or constitutionality, of laws. That step sent shock waves through the young government. Presidents from Jefferson to Lincoln bridled at the expansion of judicial power that followed—but there was much more to come.

A further question remained, and it was one that would touch the lives of politicians, families, minorities, and children in modern times: Should the Court have a hand in making the country a better, safer, fairer place? That is, when legislatures are failing to bring about reform in social, economic, and political systems, should

the Court step in? At issue was whether Court rulings should merely take into account precedents and laws, or consider the needs of the country.

Dwight Eisenhower did not realize it, but when he appointed Earl Warren as chief justice of the United States, he was answering these questions for some time to come. No Supreme Court in United States history went further in making reform its business than the Warren Court of the 1950s and the 1960s.

The Warren Court
The Warren Court Supports Social Reform

When Earl Warren came to Washington, D.C., in 1953, most Americans saw their country as a place of prosperity, liberty, and justice. The Warren Court, however, saw a place where equal justice under the law was elusive if you happened to be an African American, a poor person, an accused criminal, an immigrant, or a city dweller. When Warren finished his historic 16-year term as chief justice in 1969, the Court had taken direct, far-reaching action to correct what it saw as the nation's social ills. In doing so, the reform-minded Court wielded more power and made a bigger impact on the country than had many Presidents.

President Eisenhower appointed Warren to head the nation's highest court, following Warren's years as a crime-fighting district attorney and then as governor of California. Despite his conservative image, Warren's beliefs grew more liberal over the years. The chief justice's written opinions were sometimes a reversal of positions he had taken as a governor.

The Warren Court era of liberal activism was launched with the 1954 *Brown* v. *Board of Education* decision on school desegregation. Critics from Joseph McCarthy to more moderate thinkers said the Court was stepping far beyond its limits—infringing on the rights of state and local governments, intruding on family life, and threatening the moral fabric of the United States.

Calls for the chief justice's impeachment were heard periodically throughout his tenure. "Impeach Earl Warren" billboards and pamphlets appeared throughout the South and even at Earl Warren High School in Downey, California. The movement, to which Warren gave little heed, heated up when the Court entered its most active period of reform in the early 1960s.

Cooperative Learning

School Prayer The school prayer issue aroused strong feelings in the 1960s, and it still does. Read to the class the First Amendment of the United States Constitution, and discuss the meaning of the section relating to religion. Invite students to discuss in small groups the issue of prayer in public schools. To prepare, they may

wish to research the 2 cases cited on the chart on page 715. Point out that the discussions should be based on sharing opinions or viewpoints, not on deciding what is right or wrong. Groups can share their findings and opinions in a whole-class discussion. ✍

In 1962 changes in the makeup of the Supreme Court gave Warren a clear majority of judges who were likely to side with him on most issues. In the 1960s the Court handed down a series of historic decisions affecting the nation's political process, the civil liberties of individuals, and the operation of the criminal justice system. The chart on this page highlights some of those decisions.

One Person, One Vote

Warren called *Baker* v. *Carr* "the most important case of my tenure on the Court." He was referring to one of a series of cases from 1962 to 1964 that redistributed political power in the United States.

The old methods by which states carved up voting districts were devised when this was a nation of country dwellers. When twentieth-century industrialization drew more and more people to cities, however, the size and shape of districts did not change to reflect the shifts in population.

For example, 6 million people lived in Los Angeles County in 1960. Yet, 1 state legislator, whose vote carried the same weight as the legislator from a rural district of 14,000 people, represented the city.

This, in effect, made the vote of each citizen in Los Angeles County worth less than the vote of a resident of that rural district. Farm groups and others who wished to preserve their voting power opposed a **reapportionment** proposal—a plan changing the number of legislative seats assigned to each district. The plan

was defeated with the help of the governor of California at the time, Earl Warren.

In 1962, however, Chief Justice Earl Warren had a new constituency—the nation. In many places legislative districts were drawn in ways that favored a particular political party, a practice known as gerrymandering. Throughout the nation, there was a need for a redrawing of political districts according to a "one person, one vote" principle of equal representation.

In Florida, for example, one-fifth of the population lived in Dade County, where Miami is located, but Dade County residents elected only 4 of Florida's 133 state legislators. Traditionally, the Supreme Court had left such political matters as apportionment up to the state legislatures. Some citizens, however, frustrated when the legislatures did not take action, brought suits against state officials. In time, these suits came before the Supreme Court on appeal.

In the *Baker* v. *Carr* suit, the residents of Memphis, Tennessee, complained that their votes were worth less than the votes of rural residents. The Supreme Court ruled that the federal courts, which had originally declined to hear the case, should decide it. The Court's 1962 decision opened the door for the lower courts to involve themselves with reapportionment. "Never in American history has a single judicial decision opened the gates for such a massive change in the nation's political structure," printed the *Washington Post*.

Subsequent cases went further in forcing states to reorganize their voting systems. In 1964 the Court

Warren Court Decisions on Key Issues of the 1960s	
Reapportionment	**School Prayer**
Gomillion v. *Lightfoot,* 1960 Outlawed racial gerrymandering in case involving the city limits of Tuskegee, Alabama	*Engel* v. *Vitale,* 1962 Ruled unconstitutional a nondenominational prayer drafted by the State of New York and read voluntarily in school classrooms; the decision banned prayer in public schools
Baker v. *Carr,* 1962 Established federal authority to oversee that state voting districts ensure equal representation for all citizens; the ruling opened the door to Supreme Court involvement in what previously had been seen as a "political" issue outside the Court's jurisdiction	*Abington* v. *Schempp,* 1963 Banned Bible reading and other religious exercises in public schools, saying this constituted the government establishment of religion
Wesberry v. *Sanders,* 1964 Required that states redraw their voting districts for the United States Congress according to population; each district had to have roughly the same number of people, so every citizen's vote carried the same weight, according to the "one person, one vote" principle	**Rights of the Accused**
	Gideon v. *Wainwright,* 1963 Established that people accused of a crime have the right to a lawyer, even if they cannot afford one
Reynolds v. *Sims,* 1964 Applied the "one person, one vote" standard to their state legislatures, requiring state elective districts to be reapportioned; the ruling also demanded the apportionment by population of both houses of a bicameral state legislature	*Escobedo* v. *Illinois,* 1964 Ruled that people have the right to a lawyer from the time of arrest or when they become the subject of a criminal investigation
	Miranda v. *Arizona,* 1966 Required that accused people be informed of their right to a lawyer and their right not to testify against themselves

The Warren Court extended the reach of the Supreme Court. *What were some areas the Warren Court dealt with in its historic decisions of the 1960s?*

Videodisc

Powers of the Supreme Court

Side 2, Chapter 23
Title: *Miranda* v. *Arizona*
Subject: *Miranda* v. *Arizona* case
Ask: Whose rights did *Miranda* safeguard? *(the accused)*

See Powers of the Supreme Court Guidebook page 89 for complete lesson plan.

CHART STUDY

The Supreme Court, as a court of appeals, reviews verdicts of lower courts.
Answer: *Warren Court dealt with the U.S. political process, the civil liberties of individuals, the operation of the criminal justice system*

Facts on File

Landmark Documents in American History Have students review "*Baker* v. *Carr, 1962,*" "*Gideon* v. *Wainwright, 1963,*" "*Escobedo* v. *Illinois, 1964,*" "*Reynolds* v. *Sims, 1964,*" and "*Miranda* v. *Arizona, 1966*" and write a paragraph about the intent of one of the documents.

Meeting Special Needs

Attention Deficit Disorder To help students with attention deficit disorder, have students read the section opener and the information under each of the main heads (The Court's Authority, The Warren Court, The Reform Achievements). After they have completed each of the four segments, assist them in summarizing in their own words what they have read before they go on.

715

Meeting Lesson Objectives

Each section objective is tested by the section review question(s) that follows it in parentheses.

1. Explain how reapportionment helped ensure equal representation.(1, 4)
2. Explain why the Supreme Court ruled against prayer in public schools. (2)
3. Analyze the Supreme Court decisions protecting the rights of accused offenders to due process. (1, 3, 5)

VISUAL INSTRUCTION

Prayer in the Classroom These first graders in South Carolina in 1966 are taking part in school prayer, even after the *Engel* v. *Vitale* decision. Many school districts left the issue of prayer up to individual teachers.

Answer: *Government should play no part in composing prayers to be recited by the public.*

demanded that states redraw their voting districts—for representation to state legislatures as well as to Congress—to make them roughly equal in population. The Court also directed that in state legislatures with two houses, both should be apportioned according to population. Warren wrote the majority opinion:

> Legislators represent people, not trees or acres. Legislators are elected by voters, not farms or cities or economic interests. As long as ours is a representative form of government, and our legislatures are those instruments of government elected directly by and directly representative of the people, the right to elect legislators in a free and unimpaired fashion is a bedrock of our political system.
> —*Reynolds* v. *Sims*, 1964

The 1964 reapportionment rulings and the cases grouped with them affected one-third of the nation's states. In time all 50 states reshaped their legislatures.

Prayer in Schools

People knew Earl Warren to be a very religious man who read the Bible regularly. Justice Hugo Black had been a Sunday school teacher for 20 years. Yet in 1962 these two justices led the Court in banning prayer in public schools, a decision that was shocking to many Americans.

At issue in *Engel* v. *Vitale* was a 22-word nondenominational prayer drafted by the state of New York and recommended to be recited daily by public school children. The prayer read: "Almighty God, we acknowledge our dependence upon Thee, and we beg Thy blessings upon us, our parents, our teachers, and our country."

Parents of 10 students in Hyde Park, New York, objected to the voluntary readings. The Court agreed

Prayer in the Classroom *Engel* v. *Vitale* raised the issue of prayer in public schools. *According to Justice Black's written opinion, what part should government play in issues relating to religion?*

with them, saying that even voluntary prayer subjected religious minorities or nonbelievers to "indirect coercive pressure." Citing the First Amendment provision that "Congress shall make no law respecting an establishment of religion," Justice Black wrote in the majority opinion that this "must at least mean that in this country it is no part of the business of government to compose official prayers for any group of the American people to recite as a part of a religious program carried on by government."

In later decisions, the Court also prohibited Bible reading and other religious exercises in the classroom. The rulings disturbed some parents and clergy. Others, including some teachers, atheists, and religious people, were relieved. Legislators tried, and failed, to pass a constitutional amendment permitting school prayer.

The Rights of the Accused

When police arrested Ernesto Miranda at his home on charges of kidnapping and rape, he had no idea that his name would become a shorthand term for the rights of accused criminals and that his case would be a required course of study for every police recruit and law student. In *Miranda* and other key cases, however, the Warren Court handed down decisions that revolutionized how criminal justice is exercised in this country.

Warren, a former prosecutor, personally showed a great deal of concern for the rights of accused criminals and the conduct of police during the arrest and interrogation of suspects. The Court's rulings reinforced the right of accused citizens to **due process,** or the established legal rules and procedures.

The last major criminal justice ruling had come in 1936, when police were barred from torturing suspects in order to obtain confessions from them. The new wave of reform rulings began in 1963 when Clarence Earl Gideon won his appeal to the Supreme Court. The ruling upheld the right of an accused to have an attorney, even when the accused could not afford one. The decision resulted in a new trial for Gideon, in which he was represented by a local attorney and was acquitted.

In the 1964 case of *Escobedo* v. *Illinois,* the Court ruled that the right to legal counsel begins at the moment of arrest or as soon as someone becomes the subject of police suspicion. Warren felt, however, that the Court needed to take stronger action to protect accused criminals. This led to one of the most controversial rulings in the Supreme Court's history.

The case was *Miranda* v. *Arizona,* which came before the Court in 1966. Police had ar-

Portfolio Project

Summary Ask students to research one of the reapportionment decisions listed on the chart on page 715, or a more recent decision. Have them use what they learn to write a summary of the decision and the issues involved. Encourage them to file their summaries in their portfolios.

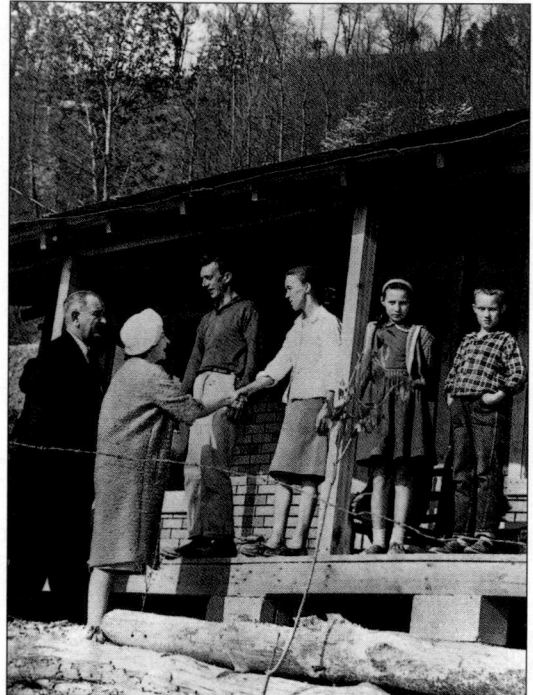

Extending a Helping Hand President and Mrs. Johnson visit with the Fletcher family in Inez, Kentucky. *What three groups benefited greatly from LBJ's reform programs?*

The Reform Achievements
Far-reaching Reforms Require Follow-up

The Supreme Court, Congress, and the President did not always speak with one voice on the subject of social reform. Controversies marked the reform period from 1954 to 1969. Decisions made during this time are still being argued about and fought in the courts. Congress today faces tough decisions about how to pay for aid programs launched with such promise 30 years ago.

Nevertheless, the efforts of the 3 branches of government combined to bring about the greatest package of reform measures since FDR's New Deal. One measure of the change is to recall how, in 1948, civil rights proposals by President Truman splintered the Democratic party. Some 20 years later, a Democratic President, Lyndon Johnson, worked with Congress in providing for minorities, the poor, and the elderly. The Supreme Court upheld much of this legislation and extended individual liberties.

Yet some groups still remained in the shadows in regard to reform. One group was women, who were not a minority in terms of their numbers, but who frequently played a secondary role to men. Women watched the changes of the Kennedy–Johnson era with interest and planned their own strategies for reform, which would extend into the next decade.

rested Ernesto Miranda for kidnapping and rape. After the police interrogated him for 2 hours, Miranda signed a confession. In a divided 5–4 ruling, the Court set aside his conviction.

Chief Justice Warren gave specific instructions that would sound familiar to anyone who has watched police shows on television: "Prior to any questioning, the person must be warned that he has a right to remain silent, that any statement he does make may be used as evidence against him, and that he has a right to the presence of an attorney, either retained or appointed."

The "Miranda card" that police departments use today lists instructions to read to suspects at the time of their arrest. Arresting officers must prove that a defendant has waived the right to legal counsel.

Police departments were disturbed by the *Miranda* ruling, saying it restricted them in performing their duties. Richard Nixon used the ruling to boost the "crime in the streets" issue during the 1968 presidential race. On the other hand, a supporter of the ruling quoted Winston Churchill: "The quality of a nation's civilization can be largely measured by the methods it uses in the enforcement of its criminal law."

SECTION REVIEW

Vocabulary
1. Define: reapportionment, due process.

Checking Facts
2. Why did the Supreme Court rule that prayer in the public schools was unconstitutional?

3. What were the main Supreme Court decisions protecting the rights of the accused, and what rights were involved?

Critical Thinking
Determining Cause and Effect
4. Why did Chief Justice Warren consider the reapportionment decisions the most significant actions taken by the Court during his tenure?

Linking Across Time
5. The 1950s and the 1960s saw advances in the achievement of civil rights for several minority groups. What minority groups are pressing for full civil rights today?

SECTION TWO   **717**

TEACH

Making the Historical Connection

Many people in the United States felt inspired by the vision and promise of their young President, John F. Kennedy. Kennedy had begun to bring his vision to fruition when on November 22, 1963, he was shot and killed by an assassin. The nation was in shock.

FYI

Motorcade Vice President Johnson, Mrs. Johnson, and Secret Service agents traveled in the third car. None of them was injured.

ABCNEWS INTERACTIVE™

◉ Videodisc

Powers of the President

Side 1, Chapter 15
Title: Presidential Vacancy
Subject: Kennedy's assassination and Johnson's swearing in—in Dallas
Ask: Who became President when Kennedy was killed? *(Lyndon Johnson)*

See Powers of the President Guidebook page 20 for complete lesson plan.

SPORTS: The Harvard/Yale football game is canceled

One Day in History

Friday, November 22, 1963

IN MEMORIAM

- Broadway theaters closed and musical events were canceled.
- Memorial programs preempted regular shows on television networks.
- Holiday lighting was turned off.
- The lights in Times Square were turned off.
- Wall Street stopped business early.
- The conductor of the Boston Symphony Orchestra led the orchestra in the funeral march from Beethoven's third symphony. More than 2,600 people stood solemnly with bowed heads.

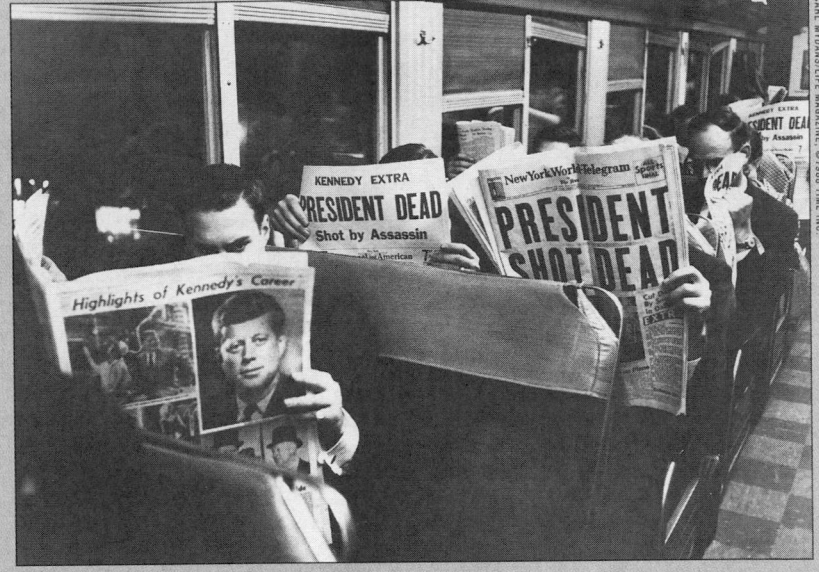
Heads Bowed These commuters, like most people across the nation, are solemnly focused on details of the Kennedy assassination.

Two women outside Parkland Hospital react to news of Kennedy's death. Much came to a standstill as a result of this tragic event.

Kennedy Assassinated

The President is shot and killed as he rides in a motorcade in downtown Dallas

DALLAS—President John F. Kennedy was shot and killed shortly after 12:30 P.M. today as he rode in an open Lincoln Continental in a motorcade through downtown Dallas. Kennedy was rushed to Parkland Memorial Hospital. He did not regain consciousness and was declared dead 30 minutes later. Mrs. Kennedy was near her husband at the hospital when he died.

With Kennedy in the limousine were his wife, Jacqueline, and Texas governor and Mrs. John Connally. The governor sustained serious injuries.

Ninety-nine minutes after Kennedy was declared dead, District Judge Sarah T. Hughes, on board *Air Force One* at Love Field, swore in Vice President Lyndon B. Johnson as the thirty-sixth President of the United States.

Background Information

The Secret Service This federal law enforcement agency, under the jurisdiction of the Department of the Treasury, is charged with the personal protection of the President, the Vice President, and other high government officials and their families. The agency had taken special security precautions for President Kennedy's motorcade through Dallas, but to no avail. After Kennedy's assassination, the Secret Service underwent a major overhaul—the budget and staff expanded, and the agency began using more modern and sophisticated information-gathering techniques and computer technologies.

One Day in History, Friday, November 22, 1963

NATION: Lee Harvey Oswald, a worker in the Texas School Book Depository, has been charged with the murder of President Kennedy.

AP/WIDE WORLD PHOTOS

Top TV Shows

1. *The Beverly Hillbillies*
2. *Bonanza*
3. *The Dick Van Dyke Show*
4. *Petticoat Junction*
5. *The Andy Griffith Show*
6. *The Lucy Show*
7. *Candid Camera*
8. *The Ed Sullivan Show*
9. *The Danny Thomas Show*
10. *My Favorite Martian*

POPULAR FILMS

- *Lilies of the Field*
- *Hud*
- *The V.I.P.s*
- *Tom Jones*

ARCHIVE PHOTOS

DANCE

The Limbo Rock This acrobatic dance became popular in 1963, introduced by Chubby Checker, father of the original twist.

© MICHAEL OCHS ARCHIVES

MUSIC

Beach Boys This clean-cut group from Southern California, with their melodic songs about hot rods and surfing, had 5 hit songs in 1963.

MARKET BASKET

Here is where a dollar will go:

First-class stamp . . . . 5¢

FILE PHOTO BY DOUG MINDELL

Eggs, one dozen . . . . 55¢
Bacon, one pound . . . . 69¢
Bread, one loaf . . . . 19¢
Coffee, one pound . . . . 38¢
Kodak Brownie camera $22

FILE PHOTO BY DOUG MINDELL

Royalite portable
  typewriter $49.95
Woman's cardigan
  sweater $7.99
Man's chambray shirt $1.47
Movie ticket . . . . 75¢
Flashlight battery . . . . 32¢
Schoolbag $3
New York subway
  token . . . . 15¢
Bicycle $47.95
Ford Fastback Coupe $3,095

TIME CAPSULE
1963

AMERICAN LIFE

January 24: A cold wave causes the death of 150 people across the nation.

February 7: Boeing conducts initial flight of 727 aircraft.

February 22: Inventor patents first steel-frame tennis racket.

March 21: Last prisoners leave Alcatraz Island; the prison closes.

April 24: Boston Celtics are National Basketball Association (NBA) champions for fifth straight time.

June 12: *Cleopatra,* starring Elizabeth Taylor and Richard Burton, opens; it is the most expensive movie made to date.

July 1: U.S. Postmaster General inaugurates zip code system.

July 22: Sonny Liston knocks out Floyd Patterson and retains world heavyweight boxing title.

December 10: Linus Pauling wins Nobel Peace Prize.

December 24: New York's Idlewild Airport is renamed John F. Kennedy Airport.

Oral History

Interview Most people were deeply affected by the assassination of President Kennedy. Ask students to interview one or two people who remember the assassination. Student interviewers should ask how the interviewees found out about the assassination (TV, radio, newspaper, word of mouth) and what their initial reaction was. How did it affect their immediate lives? Was work or school canceled? Did they also see the shooting of Oswald and the Kennedy funeral on TV? How did these affect them? Students can write up transcripts of their interviews and keep them in their portfolios.

PORTFOLIO PROJECT

CLOSE

What effect did President Kennedy's assassination have on the nation? *(shock, mourning, nation came to virtual standstill)*

719

Reviewing Key Terms

1. pragmatist
2. due process
3. coalition
4. reapportionment
5. mandate

Recalling Facts

1. interested in practical solutions to problems; came out in support of civil rights when militants had put protesters in danger and when public sympathy had swung in favor of the movement
2. reaching past boundaries to new frontiers; international cooperation and development; promoting democracy
3. education, poverty, civil rights
4. Oswald had acted alone in killing the President; the investigations were hasty; Oswald probably acted in a conspiracy
5. a clear endorsement; Kennedy's narrow victory meant less support for his programs; Johnson's mandate meant he could boldly pursue his programs
6. New Frontier dealt with ideals; Great Society translated ideals into reforms; Great Society, produced programs
7. more successful in creating programs than in implementing them; many programs were underfunded
8. gerrymandering violated "one person, one vote"; Court required states to redraw their districts according to population
9. The Court reasoned school prayer violated the First Amendment: "Congress shall make no law respecting the establishment of religion."
10. *Gideon:* right to a lawyer, retained or assigned; *Escobedo:* right to counsel begins at first suspicion; *Miranda:* suspects informed of rights at time of arrest

Reviewing Key Terms

On a separate sheet of paper, write the vocabulary term that best completes each sentence below.

mandate	reapportionment
coalition	due process
pragmatist	liberalism

1. A _____ comes up with practical solutions to individual situations.

2. Through _____ the rights of the accused are protected.

3. People united by a common purpose form a strong _____.

4. Voting power was put in proportion to population by _____.

5. Winning an election by a large margin would indicate a clear _____ from the people.

Recalling Facts

1. Why did John Kennedy call himself a pragmatist, not a liberal? Cite an example of his pragmatism.

2. What ideals of the Kennedy years does the establishment of the Peace Corps reflect?

3. What kinds of reforms had Kennedy begun to take action on when he was assassinated?

4. What was the conclusion of the Warren Commission related to the assassination of Kennedy? What have critics said about the commission's findings?

5. What is a mandate? How were Kennedy's and Johnson's abilities to carry out their programs affected by their respective electoral mandates?

6. Explain how the New Frontier differed from the Great Society. Which was more effective? Why?

7. What was the ultimate limitation to many Great Society programs?

8. How did gerrymandering affect voters' rights? How did the Supreme Court address this in the 1960s?

9. What was the Supreme Court's reasoning for banning prayer and religious exercises in public schools?

10. How were the rights of accused people expanded during the 1960s?

Critical Thinking

1. **Making Generalizations** Identify a common theme in the various laws and Supreme Court decisions described in this chapter.

2. **Making Comparisons** Compare the public images of Kennedy and Johnson. How do you think public image affected each of them politically?

3. **Demonstrating Reasoned Judgment** Some have argued that expanding the rights of the accused has made it more difficult to prosecute criminals and has been responsible for an increase in crime. Write an essay giving your opinion.

4. **Evaluating Information** When Johnson became President, he initially kept all of Kennedy's cabinet appointees—even though there were political differences, and Johnson knew that Kennedy's appointees might resent him. Why do you think Johnson retained these officials?

5. **Making Inferences** The cold war was based on fear, mistrust, and the attempts of the Soviet Union and the United States to curtail each other's influence in the world. In the photo below, JFK and John Glenn ride in a victory parade, celebrating Glenn's success in space. How was the space race related to the cold war?

MICHAEL ROUGIER/LIFE MAGAZINE. © TIME, INC.

Critical Thinking

1. upholding rights guaranteed to all U.S. citizens
2. Kennedy: young, handsome, charismatic; first TV President; support from idealists; lost support because of Catholicism, East Coast upbringing. Johnson: brash, intimidating, unpolished; common man, made good; confidence, drive; reform programs
3. Answers will vary. Students might suggest: yes, criminals escape through "loopholes"; no, the legal system works
4. Answers will vary. Students might suggest: Johnson wanted to push through the Kennedy initiatives, capitalizing on and aligning with the idealism ignited by New Frontier.
5. The United States and the Soviet Union each feared the other would gain control of space and, thus, military superiority.

Portfolio Project

In *Baker* v. *Carr* and subsequent rulings, the Supreme Court made decisions that led to the reapportionment of state electoral districts. Do library research (books, newspaper stories, magazine articles) to find out how reapportionment, including recent Supreme Court rulings, has affected your state. Write a summary, and place it in your portfolio.

Cooperative Learning

With a small group, research one of the Kennedy or Johnson reform programs—the Peace Corps, the Alliance for Progress, Project Head Start, or the Job Corps, for example. In addition to using library reference sources, you may also find listings of local program offices in the government listings of your telephone directory. Use your research to answer questions such as these: Did the program achieve its goals? Is it still in existence? Has it expanded or contracted? What problems has it faced or is it facing? Share what you learn with your class. Display visual aids if appropriate.

Reinforcing Skills

Identifying Assumptions Write a brief essay identifying some assumptions that civil rights workers identified and sought to clarify. Then explain why the identification and clarification of assumptions is important socially and politically.

Geography and History

Study the map on this page to answer the following questions:

1. How many congressional districts did Georgia have before reapportionment in 1964? After reapportionment?

2. Before reapportionment, how many state legislative districts were

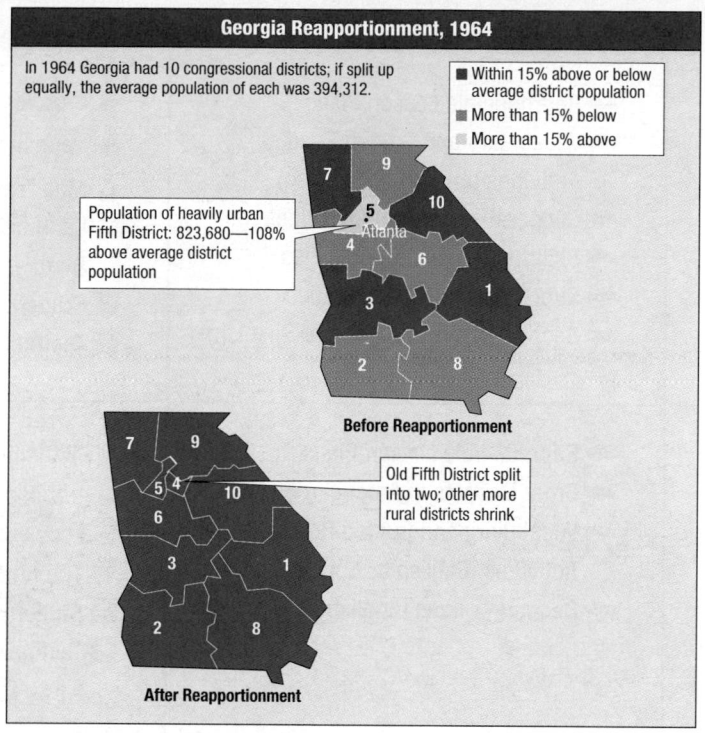

Georgia Reapportionment, 1964

In 1964 Georgia had 10 congressional districts; if split up equally, the average population of each was 394,312.

- ■ Within 15% above or below average district population
- ■ More than 15% below
- ▨ More than 15% above

Population of heavily urban Fifth District: 823,680—108% above average district population

Before Reapportionment

Old Fifth District split into two; other more rural districts shrink

After Reapportionment

more than 15 percent below average in population? How far above average was the Fifth District?

3. Legislative seats were tied to districts, regardless of the population of the districts. What, therefore, was the political significance of the population differences among districts before reapportionment?

4. What happened to the old Fifth District after reapportionment?

5. After reapportionment, how many districts fell above or below the average in population?

HISTORY JOURNAL

Your journal response to the photograph on page 699 indicates your previous understanding of the social reforms that took place during the Kennedy and Johnson years. Having read this chapter, what is your new understanding? Write your response in your journal.

Geography and History

1. 10, 10
2. 5, more than 15 percent
3. A person's vote had more influence in lightly populated districts than in heavily populated districts—voters did not have to "compete" with so many others.
4. It was split into two districts (more voting power).
5. none; all were in the average range

History Journal

Students' responses should reflect a deeper understanding of the New Frontier, the Great Society, and the Warren Court decisions.

? BONUS QUESTION

This question may be used for extra credit on the chapter test.

Describe each of the following with a brief phrase: New Frontier, Great Society, Warren Court.

Answer: *international and domestic ideals; social reform programs; protecting citizens' rights*

Portfolio Project

Students' summaries should cite the Court ruling(s) and give specific examples of the effects on the state.

Cooperative Learning

Students should choose the program as a group. Half the group can conduct library research, the other half can research local program offices. Make sure all students take part. The group's final report can be oral or written, presented or displayed.

Reinforcing Skills

Sample: assumptions about race, rights, abilities, needs; to identify inequities and clear the way for equality

Voices of Protest

DAILY LESSON OBJECTIVES	REPRODUCIBLE RESOURCES	MULTIMEDIA RESOURCES
SECTION 1 The Revival of Feminism 1. Understand the origin of the women's movement in the 1960s. 2. Analyze the economic, political, and social issues involving women. 3. Analyze the role of Congress and the Supreme Court in bringing about reform. 4. Describe the battle for the ERA.	Reproducible Lesson Plans Vocabulary and Guided Reading Activities (English or Spanish) Cooperative Learning Activities Skill Reinforcement Activities Supreme Court Case Studies Section Quizzes (English or Spanish)	Chapter Teaching Transparencies Section Focus Transparencies Map Transparencies Landmark Documents in American History Student Self-Test: A Software Review Testmaker
SECTION 2 Hispanic Americans Organize 1. Describe the history and culture of the five major Hispanic American groups. 2. Recognize the major problems facing Hispanic Americans in the 1960s and 1970s and what Hispanic Americans did to address the issues.	Reproducible Lesson Plans Great Debates in American History Vocabulary and Guided Reading Activities (English or Spanish) Section Quizzes (English or Spanish)	Section Focus Transparencies U.S. History and Art Transparencies Focus on Fine Art Prints The American People: Fabric of a Nation Student Self-Test: A Software Review Testmaker
SECTION 3 Land Claims of Native Americans 1. Understand the history of the relationship between Native Americans and the United States government. 2. Identify the problems facing Native Americans in the 1960s and 1970s and what they did to address the issues.	Reproducible Lesson Plans American Literature Readings and Activities Vocabulary and Guided Reading Activities (English or Spanish) Section Quizzes (English or Spanish)	Section Focus Transparencies Student Self-Test: A Software Review Testmaker
SECTION 4 The Counterculture 1. Review the beliefs and values of the counterculture movement. 2. Compare communal living in the United States in the past with that of the counterculture in the 1960s and 1970s. 3. Explain the cultural aspects of the counterculture that the rest of society adopted.	Reproducible Lesson Plans Vocabulary and Guided Reading Activities (English or Spanish) Reteaching Activities (English or Spanish) Enrichment Activities (English or Spanish) Section Quizzes (English or Spanish)	Section Focus Transparencies Student Self-Test: A Software Review Testmaker
CHAPTER REVIEW AND EVALUATION	Chapter 22 Test, Forms A and B Performance Assessment Strategies and Activities	Student Self-Test: A Software Review Vocabulary PuzzleMaker Testmaker Chapter Digests Audiocassettes

00:00 If time does not permit teaching the entire chapter, summarize using the Chapter 22 Digests Audiocassettes and the accompanying activities and tests. (Available in English or Spanish.)

Cooperative Project

Organize students into four groups. Have each group choose one of these minorities: women, Hispanic Americans, Native Americans, the counterculture. Have groups research their minority and then choose one of their own group members to be on a panel representing their minority. Lead a panel discussion about the problems and reactions of each minority in the 1960s and 1970s. **LEP** 🖫

Suggested Rubric: An Oral Presentation. See Performance Assessment Strategies and Activities, p. 33.

Individual Project

Invite students to choose a rock musician or group of the 1960s or 1970s. Have students do research and write a report on the history and achievements of the group and and how the music affected the youth of the period. 🖫

Suggested Rubric: A Research Report. See Performance Assessment Strategies and Activities, p. 39.

Key to Ability Levels

Teaching strategies have been coded for varying learning styles and abilities.

L1 **BASIC** activities for all students

L2 **AVERAGE** activities for average to above-average students

L3 **CHALLENGING** activities for above-average students

LEP **LIMITED ENGLISH PROFICIENCY** activities

 Block Scheduling

Block scheduling differs from traditional class scheduling in the amount of time allotted to each period. The extended timeframe provided by block scheduling affords you the opportunity to implement a greater number of research-oriented and activity-intense projects to motivate and involve your students. Activities that are particularly suited to use within the block scheduling framework are identified throughout this chapter by the following designation. 🖫

TEACHER'S CORNER

 NATIONAL GEOGRAPHIC SOCIETY

INDEX TO NATIONAL GEOGRAPHIC MAGAZINE

The following articles may be used for research relating to this chapter:

• "Who Owns Our Past?" by Harvey Arden, March 1989.

NATIONAL GEOGRAPHIC SOCIETY PRODUCTS AVAILABLE FROM GLENCOE

To order the following products for use with this chapter, contact your local Glencoe sales representative or call Glencoe at 1-800-334-7344:

• *The Presidents: A Picture History of Our Nation* (CD-ROM)
• *GTV: The American People: Fabric of a Nation* (Videodisc)

• *GTV: A Geographic Perspective on American History* (Videodisc)

ADDITIONAL NATIONAL GEOGRAPHIC SOCIETY PRODUCTS

To order the following products for use with this chapter, call National Geographic Society at 1-800-368-2728:

• *Decades of History: The 20th Century—The Middle Years* (Filmstrip)
• *The American Presidency* (Filmstrip)
• *The Vietnam War* (Filmstrip)

• *The United States as a World Power: From the 1890s to the 1970s* (Filmstrip)
• *1945-1989: The Cold War* (Video)

Chapter Overview

Women, Hispanic Americans, Native Americans, and young people protested the limits that had been placed on them. The power of these protests helped turn the whole country in a new direction.

Introducing the Chapter

As various groups began to push against the limits imposed on them, some strong leaders emerged to organize the resulting protest efforts. Have students read the narrative on this page, which tells about two leaders who helped Hispanic Americans organize for workers' rights.

Display the Chapter Teaching Transparency and distribute the corresponding activity sheet.

Extension Activity
Have students complete "Beyond the Transparency" on the activity sheet for Chapter 22 and present their projects after the class has completed the chapter.

History Journal

Ask students to review the history of women, Hispanic Americans, Native Americans, and youth in the United States up until the mid-1950s. Have students record why this might or might not have been the right time for these groups to protest.

CHAPTER
22

Voices of Protest

1966: GRAPE GROWERS AND WORKERS MEET

Picking grapes in the California fields was hot, dirty, difficult work. When thirsty, workers had to go for their own water, costing them valuable picking time. To remedy such conditions, a new union, the United Farm Workers (UFW), headed by César Chávez, sent its best negotiator to talk with the ranch owner.

Cofounder of the UFW with César Chávez, Dolores Huerta was a tough negotiator. She demanded protective clothing for the workers and a pollution-reduction device for the tractors. She insisted that each crew receive a can of drinking water. She demanded better wages for the grape pickers.

"Sister, it sounds to me like you're asking for the moon for these people," said one of the rancher's lawyers.

"Brother, I'm not asking for the moon for the farmworkers. All we want is just a little ray of sunshine for them," Huerta replied.

Huerta and her fellow Mexican Americans, like members of other minority groups, followed the civil rights movement with great interest. They hoped the time was right for them to achieve progress in their own struggle for equality.

Meanwhile, the nation itself faced social turbulence that turned into a social revolution. White, middle-class women began questioning their traditional role in society. Many young people began to reject the values of their parents. Some attempted to establish their own culture, a counterculture to the one they had known before. ■

HISTORY JOURNAL

Write what you understand about the protest movements in the 1950s, 1960s, and 1970s of Hispanic Americans and others such as Native Americans, women, and members of the counterculture.

722

EXTRA CREDIT PROJECT

Create a Leader Profile Invite students to choose one of the minority groups in this chapter (women, Hispanic Americans, Native Americans), or the counterculture. Have them skim the heads and captions in the chapter or use library resource books to get an idea of the activities of the group from the mid-1950s to the present. They should then choose a person who was influential in promoting the interests of the group and create a profile of this person—in written form or in a web-style graphic organizer. Students may report their findings to the class, or you may display the profiles on a Leaders bulletin board.

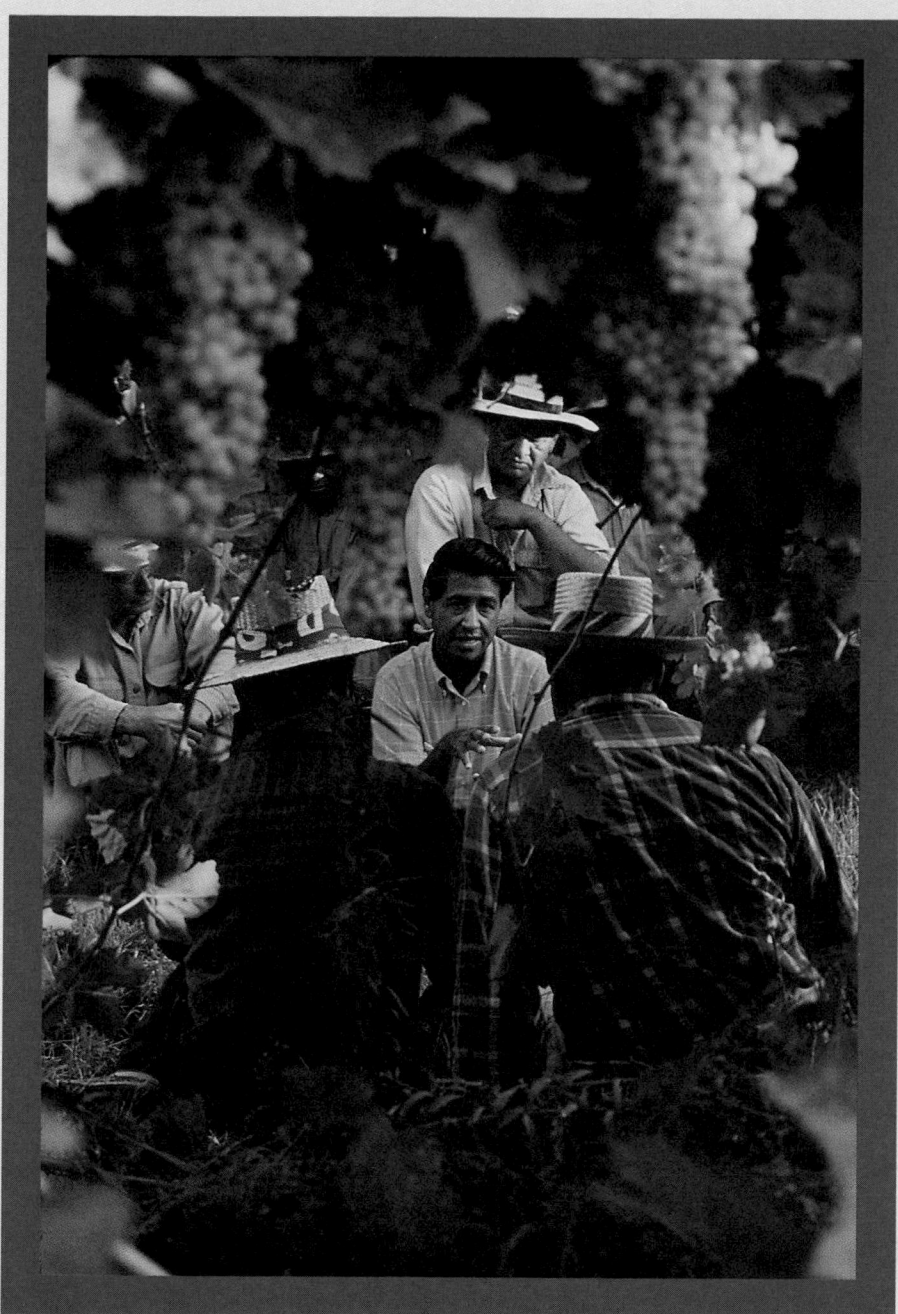

ARTHUR SCHATZ/LIFE MAGAZINE. ©TIME, INC.

LEADERS SUCH AS CÉSAR CHÁVEZ HELPED
MINORITY GROUPS FIGHT FOR CIVIL RIGHTS.

723

FYI

Native American Protest Leaders Dennis Banks and Russell Means were early leaders of the Native American protest movement. Banks and Means cofounded the American Indian Movement (AIM) in 1968. The movement was established to protect the traditional ways of Native Americans; to engage in legal cases protecting Native American treaty rights; to improve federal, state, and local social services to urban neighborhoods; and to prevent harassment of Native Americans by police. Sometimes confrontational in method, the movement was nonetheless successful in bringing Native American issues to the public eye.

 Performance Assessment

Refer to page 722B for performance assessment activities for this chapter.

 Also see Activity 22 in the Performance Assessment Strategies and Activities for an additional activity as well as for suggested rubrics.

Examining the Visual

Committed Leaders The photo on page 723 was taken in 1968 as César Chávez continued the work that he and Dolores Huerta had begun earlier. Point out to students that Chávez is sitting among the farmworkers he represented. Chávez had come from a family of migrant workers and had been a migrant farmworker himself. From his own experience, he was very aware of farmworkers' sufferings, and he felt that they had to organize in order to protect themselves and improve their condition. Mention that most of the leaders of minority groups protesting at this time acted as a result of their own experiences with oppression.

FOCUS

Section Objectives

1. Understand the origins of the women's movement in the 1960s.
2. Analyze the economic, political, and social issues involving women.
3. Analyze the role of Congress and the Supreme Court in bringing about reform.
4. Describe the battle for the ERA.

Bellringer Activity

While taking attendance at the beginning of the class period, display **Section Focus Transparency 68,** and have students answer the questions. (Or use the blackline master.)

VISUAL INSTRUCTION

Second-Class Citizens Casey Hayden and other women in SNCC helped students such as those in the photo, who were headed for Mississippi to help with voter registration.

Ask: What did women like Casey Hayden and Mary King conclude about the roles of women in SNCC? *(They concluded that women were treated as second-class citizens; women did not have leadership roles in SNCC and were often confined to lesser tasks. SNCC men seemed to make an assumption of male superiority.)*

SECTION 1

The Revival of Feminism

NOVEMBER 1964: WOMEN SPEAK OUT AGAINST OPPRESSION

AP/WIDE WORLD PHOTOS

Second-Class Citizens
Casey Hayden checks students' credentials.

DURING THE SUMMER OF 1964, CASEY HAYDEN *AND* MARY KING SHARED WITH OTHER STUDENT NONVIOLENT COORDINATING COMMITTEE (SNCC) MEMBERS THE DANGERS OF WORKING FOR CIVIL RIGHTS IN THE SOUTH. Tear gas, water from fire hoses, snarling dogs, and police clubs did not distinguish between women or men, but hit both with equal force. Hayden and King, both white women, learned about bravery by seeing their African American "sisters" beaten so badly they could only whisper the word *freedom.* They learned about commitment from Fannie Lou Hamer, who was evicted from her home when she tried to register to vote, but who never gave up.

Hayden and King also gained insight from working for SNCC that summer. They concluded that as white, middle-class women, they too were second-class citizens.

In the early 1960s nearly half the students sitting in at the lunch counters and riding the freedom buses were women. Yet few women had leadership roles within SNCC itself. Ironically, "women's work" was to type memos, make sandwiches, take minutes at meetings, and perform other menial tasks, but not to make decisions. Finally, Hayden and King wrote an unsigned memo protesting the men's attitude:

Assumptions of male superiority [among SNCC men] are as widespread and deep-rooted and every much as crippling to the woman as the assumptions of white supremacy are to the Negro. . . . [We need to] stop the discrimination and start the slow process of changing values and ideas so that all of us gradually come to understand that this is no more a man's world than it is a white world.

—SNCC Position Paper, 1964

AS YOU READ

Vocabulary
▶ women's liberation
▶ feminist

Think About . . .
▶ the basis for the women's movement in the 1960s.
▶ the economic, political, and social issues involving women in the 1960s.
▶ how Congress and the Supreme Court brought about civil rights reform.
▶ the battle for the ERA and why the amendment was defeated.

724 CHAPTER 22 VOICES OF PROTEST

Section 1 Resources

REPRODUCIBLE RESOURCES

- Lesson Plan 22-1
- Section 1 Quiz
- Vocabulary and Guided Reading Activity 22-1
- Cooperative Learning Activity 22
- Skill Reinforcement Activity 22
- Supreme Court Case 40

MULTIMEDIA RESOURCES

- Section Focus Transparency 68
- Chapter Teaching Transparency
- Map Transparency 22
- Landmark Documents in American History
- Chapter 22 Digest Audiocassette
- Student Self-Test: A Software Review

The response to the memo was laughter and scorn. The next fall the two women tried again, this time in a signed memo addressed to other SNCC women. "Perhaps we can start to talk with each other more openly than in the past," they wrote, "and create a community of support for each other." The time was not right for such an appeal, though. Then, a few months later, the pressures of black separatism pushed whites of both sexes out of SNCC.

Hayden and King concluded that the fight for **women's liberation**—freedom from the limits of traditionally female roles—was a separate fight. The women's experience in the civil rights movement provided them with some strategies, but equality for women would require its own organization and its own movement.

Origins of the Women's Movement
Women Express Growing Discontent

The women's movement that sprang up in the 1960s had multiple origins, which perhaps accounts for how quickly it swept the country. One wing of the women's movement, founded on the experiences of women like Hayden and King, grew out of the civil rights struggle. Another got its start with Betty Friedan, who first identified the "problem that had no name." In addition, President Kennedy in 1961 appointed a Presidential Commission on the Status of Women, chaired at first by Eleanor Roosevelt and later by Esther Peterson.

Although the movement began primarily among white, middle-class women, by the 1970s it had spread across all racial, social, and economic lines. The movement did not achieve all its legislative goals. Nevertheless, it accomplished major changes in the status of women at home, in school, at work, and in professional and personal relationships.

The Early History

In the 1800s the struggle for women's rights was a parallel movement to the antislavery crusade and involved many of the same people. Susan B. Anthony and Elizabeth Cady Stanton, for example, were reformers who were active in both struggles. For a time, achieving both objectives seemed possible. An 1838 issue of the abolitionist newspaper *The Liberator* stated, "As our object is universal emancipation, to redeem women as well as men from a servile to an equal condition—we shall go for the rights of women to their utmost extent." The women, however, eventually split with the abolitionist

men, who worried that the issue of women's equality might weaken support for the fight against slavery.

Women gained the right to vote only after a long struggle. As late as 1910 only Wyoming, Colorado, Utah, and Idaho had given women full voting rights. Then in 1919 Congress finally passed the Nineteenth Amendment, guaranteeing these rights to all women. The amendment was ratified the following year. After the voting rights victory, little happened in the women's movement. Although more and more women joined the labor force, most of them were steered into low-paying categories of so-called women's work, such as clerical, teaching, and factory jobs.

Such was the situation when Betty Friedan published her landmark book *The Feminine Mystique* in 1963. The book ridiculed the notions that women were only suited for low-paying jobs and that achievement for women could be measured only by their success as wives and mothers. Her ideas struck a chord with many women across the country, and they began to consider alternatives to marriage, childbearing, and homemaking. Yet at the same time, the book inspired strong opposition among many women who rejected Friedan's ideas as an attack on traditional roles.

Women's Roles Until the women's movement of the 1960s, it was believed that women's fulfillment came only through the roles of wife and mother. *What person challenged that belief?*

TEACH

Guided Practice

L2 Discussion Explain that in the 1950s most women who planned a career considered these options: teacher, secretary, and nurse. Discuss with students the situation today. Do their parents, teachers, counselors, and others who talk with them about career choices make distinctions between options for male and female students? Encourage volunteers to give examples.

VISUAL INSTRUCTION

Women's Roles Shopping, as depicted in the photo, was part of a woman's role as a homemaker.

Answer: *Betty Friedan, in* The Feminine Mystique

Show students Map Transparency 22 and have them complete the activity sheet.

Cooperative Learning

Equal Pay? Organize the class into 5 or 6 groups. Each group can choose a profession or area of work and research and graph the average salaries of male workers and female workers in that profession at these or other points in time: 1955, 1965, 1975, 1985, and 1995. Groups can compare their graphs and discuss their findings and conclusions.

Independent Practice

L2 Encourage students to learn about the roles of women in other countries (Saudi Arabia, Sweden, Sri Lanka, for example) in the 1960s and 1970s. They can begin their research by looking up the topic "Women" in *World Book Encyclopedia.* They can then create a chart comparing the roles of women in the countries they have chosen with those of women in the United States.

📋 Have students complete Chapter 22, Section 1 Vocabulary and Guided Reading Activity. (Also in Spanish.) **LEP**

📋 Have students complete the Chapter 22 Cooperative Learning Activity.

GRAPH STUDY

In the 104th Congress, 1995, the gender distribution of the Senate was 92 percent male, 8 percent female; the House was 89.2 percent male, 10.8 percent female.

Answer: *Women generally have come to have more jobs at the executive/managerial level and more training at the undergraduate and graduate level; they have also held more political positions (with the exception of Chief Executive).*

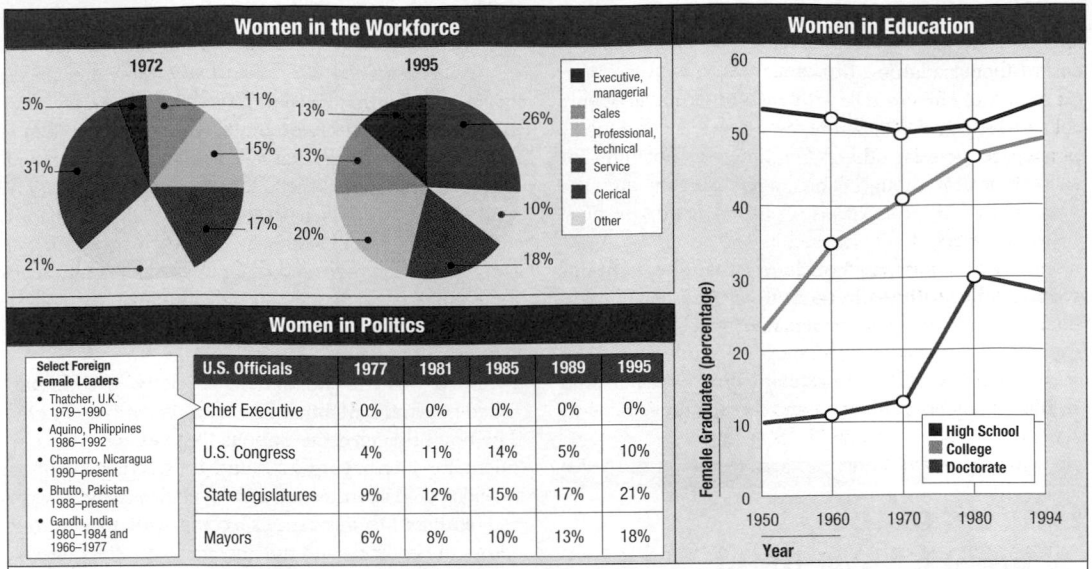

Statistics reveal that women have made strides in the areas of work, schooling, and politics—although obstacles to equal opportunity still exist. *What story do the graphs and charts above tell you about the progress of women in the last half of this century?*

The Woman's Dilemma

Minority women faced a special problem in that they encountered both sexual and racial discrimination. They experienced sexual discrimination by men, both white and African American; and they faced racial discrimination by whites, men, and other women. In describing that period, author Toni Morrison explains how African American women "look at white women and see the enemy, for they know that racism is not confined to white men and that there are more white women than men in this country."

Many African American, Hispanic American, Native American, and Asian American women chose to delay their fight for equality in one sphere while they struggled for recognition in the other. Because priorities needed to be established, many women chose to seek full civil liberties for their ethnic group as their first objective. Equality between men and women would have to come later.

Women's Issues in the 1960s
Women Demand Equal Rights

When the President's Commission on the Status of Women issued its report in October 1963, relatively few people noticed. The civil rights struggle at home and the Vietnam War abroad claimed much more public attention. As a follow-up to the commission, however, a permanent Citizens' Advisory Council on the Status of Women was formed, and 32 states set up their own commissions. These actions produced a strong network for the future of **feminists,** or activists for women's equal rights.

The commission's report identified many of the issues that would occupy feminists over the next decades. It presented statistics on how women fared in employment, in education, and in government.

Economic Rights

In 1960 women made up one-third of the nation's workforce. Most of their jobs, however, offered less pay and prestige than the positions held by men. For example, women made up only 5 percent of the nation's managers and administrators and 12 percent of all professional and technical workers.

On average, for every dollar that a man earned on a job in the 1960s, a woman with the same job earned only 59 cents. The Equal Pay Act of 1963 required employers to pay women the same as men for the same work. This act provided a remedy for thousands of women. It did not, however, address the discrimination women faced in actually getting jobs.

More important gains came through the inclusion of women in Title VII of the Civil Rights Act of 1964, which prohibited discrimination in employment on the basis of sex as well as of race.

Meeting Special Needs

Learning Disability To help students with learning disabilities pick out the most important points of this section, have them create a study outline, using the heads in this section. As they complete each subhead, have them write notes about the important points. They can discuss their outlines with partners if appropriate.

Still, women would need to receive equal education and training, or laws alone would never be able to ensure them equal job opportunities. In 1960 women made up only 37 percent of the nation's undergraduate college students and received just 10 percent of the doctoral degrees conferred.

Political Rights

By the early 1960s women had been voting for 40 years, but they had achieved little success in obtaining political office, either elected or appointed. In 1963, for example, 351 women served in state legislatures, holding only 5 percent of the total legislative seats. Thirteen women held seats in Congress, down from a record number of 19 in 1961. The chart on page 726 gives information about the number of women holding high office in the United States and in other nations.

Reproductive Rights

At the same time that women were growing more aware of the limits on their economic and political freedoms, many also began demanding more personal freedoms. The right to control their own sexuality and reproductivity became a rallying cry of many feminists.

In 1960 the Food and Drug Administration approved the sale of the birth control pill, ushering in a period of new sexual freedom. Married and unmarried women became more knowledgeable about their own health and their bodies. Many women felt that the pill gave them the freedom to be sexually active without the risk of pregnancy. The pill gave these women more opportunity to make their own decisions about their bodies.

Meanwhile, many women had been making these decisions another way—through abortion. Because abortions were illegal, finding a qualified physician who was willing to perform the procedure was difficult and costly. Many who could not afford to have a safe abortion resorted to procedures performed by unqualified people. Many women suffered injury, sterility, or death because of unsafe abortions.

Some women took this risk because they did not want to be mothers; others chose abortion because they felt they were too poor or otherwise unfit to care for a baby. Still others were terrified of being pregnant and unmarried, a condition that carried a heavy social stigma at the time.

The push for reform of existing abortion laws came first from some doctors and lawyers, who were acutely aware of the dangers of illegal abortions. Many feminists

soon joined them. Many other people, however, believed that abortions should not be allowed. By the time of the 1972 Democratic party convention, abortion had become an explosive political issue. Although feminists were not successful in including a plank on abortion in the 1972 Democratic platform, the issue has refused to fade and is still bitterly contested today.

Social and Gender Relationships

As women reexamined their roles in society, old ways of relating to family members, husbands, friends, bosses, and fellow workers all came under question. Women postponed marriages as they prepared themselves for careers, and the divorce rate climbed as more and more women chose to exercise their options rather than remain in unsatisfactory marriages.

Many men willingly examined and adjusted their attitudes in response to the evolving consciousness of women. For other men, understanding their changing roles proved frustrating; many found it difficult to get beyond the most trivial issues. "It's getting so you don't know what to do when you come to a door," one man complained. "Open it and a women's libber comes through, you get a dirty look. Don't open it and you feel like an unmannered slob who just kicked his grandmother in the shins."

Women's Responses to the Issues
Feminists and Antifeminists Organize

Two types of women's rights organizations had sprung up in the United States by the mid-1960s, and both were made up primarily of white, middle-class, college-educated women. The organizations differed in the age groups they represented and in their organizational structures. Both groups, however, frequently worked together on legislative and political issues, exchanging ideas and strategies.

The Founding of NOW

It started as a statement scribbled on Betty Friedan's luncheon napkin. It became a large and powerful national organization that has helped elect politicians, that has helped correct inequality in women's employment, and that wields considerable lobbying power today in the halls of government in Washington, D.C.

Hot Buttons NOW quickly became a leader in the fight for women's rights. *What kinds of issues does NOW deal with?*

VISUAL INSTRUCTION

Hot Buttons The buttons in the image relate to women's issues in the 1960s and 1970s. At present, women also focus on issues such as elections and Supreme Court appointments.

Answer: *elected officials, women's employment, government lobbying*

Facts on File

Landmark Documents in American History Have students review "NOW Statement of Purpose, 1966," "NOW Invitation to Join, 1966," and "Bill of Rights for Women, 1968" and write a paragraph about the intent of one of the documents.

Global Connection

In the 1990s the United States has been far from a world leader in terms of the percentage of women lawmakers, as the following 1991 figures for selected countries show: United States, 6.4 percent; Bangladesh, 10.3 percent; China, 21.3 percent; Finland, 38.5 percent; Germany, 20.4 percent; India, 7.1 percent; Japan, 2.3 percent; Mexico, 12.4 percent; Syria, 8.4 percent; Venezuela, 9.9 percent; Zimbabwe, 12.0 percent

Portfolio Project

Interview To find out more about women's issues, have students interview three women from three different generations. They might ask questions such as these: How do you feel about the education and employment opportunities you faced as a young person? Were any of your important life choices made on the basis of others' ideas about women's roles? Were you encouraged to go to college? Were you encouraged to vote and be politically active? Ask students to use the notes from their interviews to write summaries. Have them file the summaries in their portfolios.

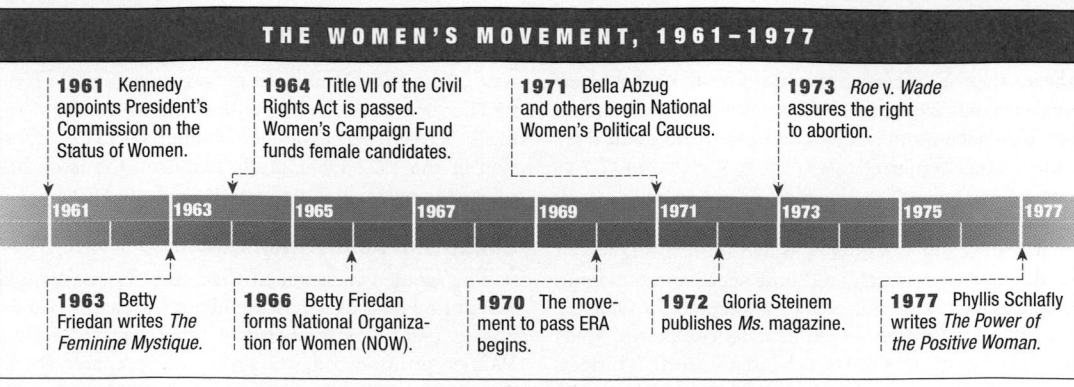

THE WOMEN'S MOVEMENT, 1961–1977

1961 Kennedy appoints President's Commission on the Status of Women.

1964 Title VII of the Civil Rights Act is passed. Women's Campaign Fund funds female candidates.

1971 Bella Abzug and others begin National Women's Political Caucus.

1973 *Roe* v. *Wade* assures the right to abortion.

| 1961 | 1963 | 1965 | 1967 | 1969 | 1971 | 1973 | 1975 | 1977 |

1963 Betty Friedan writes *The Feminine Mystique.*

1966 Betty Friedan forms National Organization for Women (NOW).

1970 The movement to pass ERA begins.

1972 Gloria Steinem publishes *Ms.* magazine.

1977 Phyllis Schlafly writes *The Power of the Positive Woman.*

The National Organization for Women (NOW) began in 1966 at a conference on the status of women. The women were concerned that complaints of sex discrimination before the Equal Employment Opportunity Commission (EEOC) were not being given serious consideration. Whereas cases of racial discrimination were filed by organizations or government agencies, cases of sex discrimination were filed by individuals and, therefore, received less attention. Conference participants, therefore, decided to form a civil rights organization for women.

During lunch the following day, 28 women and men each contributed $5 for expenses, and Friedan scribbled on a paper napkin the name of the new organization and its purpose. The statement of purpose was accepted virtually unchanged 4 months later at the first formal meeting of the organization, which named Friedan president. The statement of purpose read:

Momentum Grows Bella Abzug, left, represented New York in Congress and helped found the National Women's Political Caucus. Gloria Steinem, right, helped Abzug establish the caucus; she also founded *Ms.* magazine. *How did NWPC help the women's movement make progress?*

© ADAM SCULL/GLOBE PHOTOS

To take action to bring women into full participation in the mainstream of American society now, assuming all the privileges and responsibilities thereof in truly equal partnership with men.
—NOW, Statement of Purpose, 1966

Eight years later NOW's membership had soared to 40,000 people in 1,000 chapters. By 1995 its membership had reached 250,000, and the organization had an approximate annual budget of $7 million. At its first national conference, NOW outlined its goals: passage of a constitutional amendment guaranteeing equal rights for all, enforcement of Title VII of the Civil Rights Act, maternity leave benefits, better child care, equal and unsegregated education, equal job training opportunities, and abortion rights.

NOW's success has helped inspire the creation of several other women's organizations. The National Women's Political Caucus (NWPC), founded in 1971, worked to put women in public office and also supported political candidates of both sexes who were sympathetic to feminist issues. In 1974 the Women's Campaign Fund began to raise money for female candidates. Two women achieved important political breakthroughs that year. Ella Grasso was elected governor of Connecticut, the first woman to head a state in her own right, not as a successor to her husband. Voters in San Jose, California, elected Janet Gray Hayes as mayor, the first woman to head a large city.

Minority women also formed separate organizations. These included the North American Indian Women's Association in 1970, a conference of Mexican American women in 1971, the Conference of Puerto Rican Women in 1972, and the National Black Feminist Organization in 1972.

The growing momentum of the women's movement was evident by July 1972, when *Ms.,* a feminist magazine, published its first issue. A preview edition of 300,000 copies completely sold out in eight days. The magazine

Extending the Content

Other Views The July 1972 issue of *Good Housekeeping* included articles such as "On Being a Woman: A Child's Interest in Sex" and "It's More Fun if You Make It in Gingham!" One *GH* short story, entitled "A Man of My Own," carried this introduction: "I was always happy to let Bonnie get me blind dates with her 'extra' men, but then I began to wonder: Would I ever find a knight-in-shining-armor, just for me?"

Cosmopolitan, July 1972, contained features such as "Flirtation, Seduction, or Rapport?" and a quiz entitled "Are You a Threat to Men?" *Ladies' Home Journal* for July 1972 included the regular feature "Can This Marriage Be Saved?" and regular specialty departments such as Food, Patterns and Beauty, and Decorating.

took up issues that up until then had never found their way into the pages of more traditional women's magazines such as *Good Housekeeping* and *Cosmopolitan*. *Ms.* also helped popularize the title "Ms." as an alternative to "Miss" or "Mrs." when a woman's marital status was unknown or irrelevant. Women's studies courses appeared at universities, and several men's colleges began opening their doors to women. By 1980 women made up 51 percent of all college undergraduates and received 30 percent of all doctorates.

Radical Feminism

Because to many women in the United States equality of the sexes was a revolutionary idea, NOW was by definition a radical organization. To some women, however, it was not radical enough. These more radical women were mostly white and well educated but generally younger than their counterparts in NOW. Many of them had learned about social reform through their civil rights and student protest activities.

The younger feminists lacked the national network of NOW but excelled in grassroots organization. The women practiced participatory democracy—every woman had a voice in discussions and a chance to develop her own skills and talents.

Small, informal discussion groups met regularly at participants' homes for "consciousness-raising" sessions. Women talked openly about their experiences in childhood, school, families, marriages, and careers. They analyzed issues of common concern to all women and tried to identify those for which political changes seemed most attainable.

The radical feminists tended to favor more dramatic protests than their NOW sisters. They ridiculed the 1968 Miss America contest by crowning a sheep as the winner. In one widely reported episode, they threw girdles, bras, hair curlers, false eyelashes, and other symbols of what they called feminine enslavement into a "freedom trash can." Such events resulted in a great deal of media attention and often produced negative reaction from the public.

The Opposition

Not all women embraced the new ideas of women's liberation with equal enthusiasm. A great many women accepted certain feminist ideas but rejected others. Some disagreed with the radical feminists' methods. Some were adamantly opposed to the movement's general support of a woman's right to abortion. Still other women viewed feminism as an attack on traditional values, which included the subordination of women to men and the importance of a full-time commitment to family.

Among the most prominent of the antifeminists was author and attorney Phyllis Schlafly. Schlafly had long

Women's Issues *Ms.* magazine articles addressed issues important to feminists. *What were some traditional women's magazines in 1972?*

been active in Illinois and national politics where she was a strong voice for conservative causes. As the feminist movement gained strength, Schlafly directed her energies against it. In her 1977 book, *The Power of the Positive Woman*, she argued that a woman's most important and satisfying role was in the home and that the primary duty of women was to uphold the traditional values of the church, family, and country. Schlafly asserted that feminist organizations did not represent the views of all women. Her leadership offered a powerful choice for many women.

Response of Congress and the Courts
Strides and Conflicts

Despite the opposition of the antifeminists, the accumulated effect of the women's movement began to be visible in the responses of Congress and the courts. In 1970 the Labor Department issued an order calling for all federal contracts to require the employment of a

VISUAL INSTRUCTION

Women's Issues The July 1972 issue of *Ms.* magazine had articles and features such as these: "Woman's Body, Woman's Mind: A Guide to Consciousness-Raising"; "Populist Mechanics: Demystifying Your Car"; "On Getting Angry"; "Competing with Women"; "The Equal Rights Amendment: What's in It for You?"; "A Marriage of Equals."

Answer: Good Housekeeping, Cosmopolitan

Global Connection

In March 1969, 71-year-old Golda Meir assumed the position of interim prime minister of Israel. She won the position officially in the October elections of that year and served until her resignation in 1974. Meir, born in Kiev, Ukraine, had been active in politics since the late 1920s.

Cultural Perspectives

Native American Women Organize The North American Indian Women's Association, founded in 1970, worked to enhance a sense of well-being among Native Americans through unity of purpose. The organization also sought to improve communication among Native American groups, enhance awareness of Native American culture, and improve family life, health, and education among Native American people.

ASSESS

Meeting Lesson Objectives

Each section objective is tested by the section review question(s) that follows it in parentheses.

1. Understand the origins of the women's movement in the 1960s. (5)
2. Analyze the economic, political, and social issues involving women. (2, 4, 5)
3. Analyze the role of Congress and the Supreme Court in bringing about reform. (4, 5)
4. Learn the story of the battle for the ERA. (1, 2, 3)

VISUAL INSTRUCTION

Opposing Sides In the photos, anti-ERA activist Phyllis Schlafly is leading a group called the "baby buggy brigade," protesting a federal day-care bill. The ERA supporters are observing the 60th anniversary of woman suffrage in the U.S.

Answer: *Equality of rights under the law shall not be denied or abridged by the United States or by any state on account of sex.*

---

certain percentage of women. In 1972 the Education Amendments Act outlawed sex discrimination in education. On the local level, that meant that school boards had to rewrite policies that limited cooking classes to girls and shop classes to boys. It also obliged schools to increase their support of girls' athletics. The United States armed forces relaxed some restrictions against women in 1973 and in 1976 opened up the military academies of Annapolis and West Point to women.

In the 1970s, however, two legislative and court issues divided American society into opposing camps. These were the proposed Equal Rights Amendment (ERA) and the Supreme Court's decision on abortion. These two issues galvanized the opposition—which until that time had been somewhat dispersed—and gave it a new focus and sense of purpose.

The Fight for ERA

The idea of a constitutional amendment specifically addressing the issue of women's equality was not a new one. The National Woman's party had first proposed an Equal Rights Amendment in 1923 and reintroduced it in every subsequent session of Congress.

As late as 1962, the President's Commission on the Status of Women did not favor the passage of the amendment. This view was shared by many women's groups, including the League of Women Voters, who were concerned that passage of the ERA would cancel legal protections women already enjoyed. In the late 1960s, however, the courts began to strike down these protective laws because they were in conflict with Title VII of the Civil Rights Act of 1964. As a result, the League withdrew its objection to the amendment.

The proposed amendment was a simple one. It read: "Equality of rights un-

der the law shall not be denied or abridged by the United States or by any State on account of sex." Two other brief clauses provided Congress with enforcement power and established that the amendment would go into effect two years after ratification.

The proponents of the amendment felt that in 1970 the time was right for its passage. That year the amendment flew through the House of Representatives on a voice vote of 350 to 15. Two years later, it carried the Senate by a vote of 84 to 8. To become law, however, the amendment needed to be ratified, or approved, by three-fourths of the state legislatures within the next seven years.

Opposing Sides Pro-ERA activists and anti-ERA activists such as Phyllis Schlafly, with loudspeaker above, felt strongly about their positions. *What did the ERA propose?*

Critical Thinking

Identifying Assumptions Feminists and antifeminists hotly debated the issue of women in relation to "home and family." With students, discuss both sides of this issue. As part of the discussion, encourage them to identify the underlying assumptions, beliefs, and values of both sides.

Thirty states quickly approved the amendment by 1973; then the drive for ratification stalled. NOW, which had taken over leadership of the drive for ratification after a short power struggle among women's groups, was taken by surprise.

The feminists had underestimated the opposition to the amendment and the ability of conservative women's groups to mobilize opinion against women's liberation. Although opinion polls showed that the majority of Americans favored the concept of equality between men and women, the same polls also indicated that an even larger percentage of the population did not wish to change men's and women's social and family roles. For these concerned people, the ERA represented too radical a change. They vowed to kill the amendment.

The Defeat of ERA

Schlafly and her supporters charged that passage of the ERA would lead directly to women in combat in wartime, the breakdown of the family, government funding of abortion, and elimination of separate public bathrooms for men and women. The "Stop ERA" forces dramatized their concerns in California by presenting state senators with live mice and asking, "Do you want to be a man or a mouse?" In Illinois they handed out apple pies in the state legislature as symbols of traditional homemaking values, and they brought in baby girls bearing signs that read Don't Draft Me.

As the original ratification period ran out, supporters of ERA managed to obtain a 3-year extension from Congress. They failed, however, to add a single state during that period, and by the 1982 deadline, they were still 3 short of the 38 state approvals required. The amendment was never added to the Constitution.

Roe v. Wade

In 1973 the Supreme Court announced its decision in *Roe* v. *Wade,* which established a woman's right to have an abortion. Even before the Court's historic pronouncement, several states had modified their laws to permit abortion under specific conditions. Many feminists, however, wanted all abortion limits repealed on the grounds that women should have absolute control over their own bodies. Many other people, however, including some feminists, were against abortion. These people believed that life begins at conception and that abortion at any time during pregnancy constitutes

FILE PHOTO BY RALPH J. BRUNKE

STOP ABORTION NOW

KEEP ABORTION LEGAL

An Issue Divided Much of today's women's rights debate focuses on the issue of abortion. *Why do some people oppose abortion?*

murder. Therefore, they opposed abortion on moral grounds.

The Supreme Court's decision set forth the manner in which states could limit the right to abortion. The decision established that no limitations could be imposed by the states during the first trimester, or first three months, of pregnancy. State law could legalize abortions during the second trimester in situations that were potentially dangerous to a woman's health. The state could choose to restrict abortion during the third trimester to protect the life of an unborn child capable of sustaining life outside the womb.

A Shift in Focus

In the process of moving through the Supreme Court, the abortion issue shifted in focus from the rights of the mother to the rights of the unborn child. Rather than settling the issue of abortion, however, the Supreme Court decision intensified controversy.

The political and moral battle between the "pro-choice" supporters (those favoring the individual's right to abortion) and the "pro-life" forces (those opposed to abortion) dominated many political contests. The debate has continued no less passionately in the 1990s.

SECTION REVIEW

Vocabulary

1. Define: women's liberation, feminist.

Checking Facts

2. What were some major issues facing women in the 1960s?

3. Why did the Equal Rights Amendment provoke such controversy?

Critical Thinking

Expressing Problems Clearly

4. In what way did the Supreme Court decision in *Roe* v. *Wade* clarify the focus of the women's movement?

Linking Across Time

5. What were the major changes that the women's movement caused in this country? How is life for a young woman growing up in the United States today different from that of a young woman in the 1950s?

VISUAL INSTRUCTION

An Issue Divided Controversy continues in the 1990s.

Answer: *believe life begins at conception, so believe that abortion is murder*

🔘 **Facts on File**

Landmark Documents in American History Have students review "*Roe* v. *Wade, Doe* v. *Bolton,* 1973" and write a paragraph about the intent of the document.

Evaluate

Have students complete the Section Review.

📁 🔲 Assign the Section 1 Quiz or use the Testmaker to develop a customized quiz. (Also in Spanish.) **LEP**

Reteach

🎧 Have students listen to the Chapter 22, Section 1 Audiocassette. (Also in Spanish.) **LEP**

Enrich

📁 Have students complete Supreme Court Case Study 40.

CLOSE

What strides did women make in the 1960s and 1970s? *(equal pay, employment, educational opportunities; more political positions, right to abortion)*

Section 1 Review Answers

1. women's liberation (725), **feminist** (726)

2. political representation; job and educational opportunities; reproductive rights; social and gender relationships

3. Some saw it as stopping discrimination; others saw it as causing the breakdown of the family and leading to government-funded abortions.

4. It dealt with abortion, a controversial issue; women took stands on the issue.

5. The movement changed the nation's perception of women; today's women have more choices.

731

TEACH

This skill familiarizes students with the steps to follow in conducting a successful interview. Students prepare for an interview with Betty Friedan, including writing questions that they might ask during the interview. Point out that interviews enable interviewers to gather information first-hand from people involved in interesting events or situations. Interviews become primary sources.

Additional Practice

☛ Have students complete the Chapter 22 Skill Reinforcement Activity.

Notes

_____
_____
_____
_____
_____
_____
_____
_____
_____
_____
_____
_____
_____
_____
_____
_____
_____
_____
_____
_____
_____
_____
_____
_____

Social Studies Skill
CONDUCTING INTERVIEWS

Learning the Skill

Interviews allow you to gather information about interesting people such as Betty Friedan, the founder and first president of the National Organization for Women (NOW). Friedan (pictured right) became a leader in the struggle for women's rights. In 1970 Friedan made the following assessment of the barriers facing women.

W e are beginning to know that no woman can achieve a real breakthrough alone, as long as sex discrimination exists in employment, under the law, in education, in mores, and in denigration of the image of women.

Even those of us who have managed to achieve a precarious success in a given field still walk as freaks in a "man's world" since every profession—politics, the church, teaching—is still structured as a man's world.
—Betty Friedan, *Voices of the New Feminism,* 1970

To interview Betty Friedan or anyone else, you would want to follow these steps.

a. Make an appointment. Contact the person, and explain why you want the interview, what kinds of things you hope to learn, and how you will use the information. Discuss where and when you will conduct the interview, and ask if you may use a tape recorder.

b. Gather background information. Find out about the early life, education, career, and other accomplishments of the person you will interview. Familiarize yourself with books or articles the interviewee has published. Then do research on the topics you will discuss.

c. Prepare questions. Group questions into subject categories, beginning each category with general questions and moving toward more specific questions. Formulate each question carefully, phrasing it in a way that encourages a well-developed answer. If the answer could be simply yes or no, rephrase the question.

d. Conduct the interview. Introduce yourself and restate the purpose of the interview. Ask questions and record responses accurately. Ask follow-up questions to fill gaps in information.

e. Transcribe the interview. Convert your written or tape-recorded notes into a transcript, a written record of the interview presented in a question-and-answer format.

© SAGA/ARCHIVE PHOTOS

A Powerful Leader Betty Friedan, founder of NOW, has been very influential in the women's liberation movement.

Practicing the Skill

If you were to interview Betty Friedan:

1. What kind of background information might you gather?

2. What are some broad categories of questions you might ask based on the quotation to the left?

3. What are some specific questions you might ask, based on the quotation?

4. What would you do if you ran out of prepared questions and there was a lull in the interview?

5. What might you do with information gathered in an interview with Friedan?

Applying the Skill

The women's movement probably included some women you know—your mother, aunts, grandmothers, neighbors. All these women have had to find their own answers in a society in which gender does make a difference. Interview one or more women of three different generations. Ask about their experiences as women in the United States. Ask about their attitudes toward feminist issues, past and present. As you transcribe the interviews, be aware of any common themes or surprising differences. You may want to summarize your findings or create a comparison chart.

Additional Practice

For additional practice, see Reinforcing Skills on page 759.

Practicing the Skill Answers

1. Answers will vary: her interests as a young person; where she went to school; her achievements to date; her publications.
2. Answers will vary: categories such as sex discrimination, "a man's world."
3. Answers will vary: What examples can you give of sex discrimination in employment? Under the law? In education? In mores? Related to the denigration of the image of women?

4. Answers will vary: express an interest in what has been said so far and ask related questions; ask if there is some information that she would like people to have.
5. Answers will vary: prepare a report for class; contribute to a class project on feminism; make the transcript an entry in a journal about women's issues.

SECTION 2

Hispanic Americans Organize

1966: SUPPORT GROWS NATIONWIDE FOR UFW GRAPE BOYCOTT

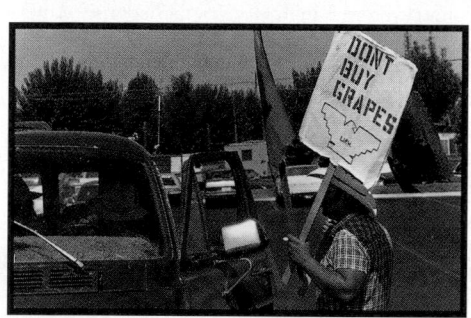

Powerful New Strategy
Consumers make decisions.

DURING THE LATE 1960s IT WAS A SCENE REPEATED IN MANY SUPERMARKETS AND NEIGHBORHOOD GROCERY STORES THROUGHOUT THE UNITED STATES. Grapes were on sale—green and purple, luscious, full of juice, appealing to the sight and to the taste. If you were doing the family shopping, you might be tempted to reach for a bunch—until you remembered what you had seen on TV or read in the newspapers about the California grape industry. The industry's problems were reaching consumers. Some grocers even posted this sign above the fruit as a reminder:

Notice: California Grape Boycott United Farm Workers led by César Chávez are calling for a boycott of California table grapes. . . . It is this grocer's current policy to inform consumers of the boycott request so that each consumer can make his or her own purchase decision. It's your decision—to boycott or not.
—Table grape boycott notice, 1966

Shoppers did decide, and many put the grapes back into the bin. By appealing to the nation's consumers, César Chávez, founder of the United Farm Workers (UFW) of America, gained the support he needed to win recognition of his union among California farm owners. The union used the new strategy of a nationwide boycott alongside the more familiar tactics of strikes, pickets, and demonstrations. Chávez would use it successfully again, when bargaining with the owners of vineyards and lettuce fields.

AS YOU READ

Vocabulary
► extended family
► undocumented immigrant
► representation
► bilingualism
► assimilation

Think About . . .
► the history and culture of the five major Hispanic American groups.

► the issues facing Hispanic Americans in the 1960s and 1970s and how Hispanic Americans addressed these issues.

SECTION TWO **733**

ARTHUR SCHATZ/LIFE MAGAZINE. ©TIME, INC.

Section Objectives

1. Describe the history and culture of the five major Hispanic American groups.
2. Recognize the major problematic issues facing Hispanic Americans in the 1960s and 1970s and what Hispanic Americans did to address the issues.

Bellringer Activity

While taking attendance at the beginning of the class period, display **Section Focus Transparency 69,** and have students answer the questions. (Or use the blackline master.)

VISUAL INSTRUCTION

Powerful New Strategy
The aim of the boycott was to help farmworkers gain rights, such as a living wage, sanitary facilities in the fields, and the right to work and live with dignity.

Ask: How was the boycott successful? *(made farm owners recognize farmworkers' union and hear workers' requests)*

Section 2 Resources

REPRODUCIBLE RESOURCES
📁 Lesson Plan 22-2
📁 Section 2 Quiz
📁 Unit 8 Great Debate
📁 Vocabulary and Guided Reading 22-2

MULTIMEDIA RESOURCES
🔦 Section Focus Transparency 69
🔦 U.S. Art and History Transparency 32
📖 Focus on Fine Art Prints, Prints 18 and 19
💿 The American People: Fabric of a Nation

🎧 Chapter 22 Digest Audiocassette
💿 Student Self-Test: A Software Review
💿 Testmaker

NATIONAL GEOGRAPHIC SOCIETY

 Videodisc

GTV: The American People: Fabric of a Nation

Side 4, Chapter 6
Title: Look Again
Subject: Hispanic American diversity
Ask: From what countries do most Hispanic Americans trace their roots? *(Mexico, Cuba)*

MAP STUDY

Today, the proportional distribution of Hispanic Americans remains much the same.
Answer: *Southwest, Northeast, Florida*

TEACH

Guided Practice

L2 **Discussion** Invite students to discuss the advantages and disadvantages of assimilation. Discuss the extent to which assimilation opens doors to better education, jobs, housing, and political power. Remind students that assimilation can also erode a people's attachment to their cultural heritage.

Recent Hispanic American History
Diverse Yet Similar

Look at a map of the United States. Read out the names of places in the Southwest and Southeast: San Francisco, Los Angeles, Santa Fe, San Antonio, Rio Grande, Ponce de Leon Bay. These names all suggest the long history of Hispanic culture in North America. From the first explorers in the 1500s to the most recent immigrants, Hispanic Americans have added a distinctive element to the language and culture of the United States.

The term *Hispanic American* refers to those Americans who have come, or are descended from others who came, from Spanish-speaking lands such as Mexico, Puerto Rico, and Cuba. Hispanic Americans are the fastest-growing minority in the country. From 3 million in 1960, the Hispanic population rose to 15 million in 1980 and approximately 27 million in 1995. As many feminists began to demand their rights in the 1960s and 1970s, many Hispanic Americans did as well. Both groups were characterized by diversity: their members came from many different places and had varying interests.

Similarities and Differences

Regardless of their country of origin, Hispanic Americans shared the Spanish language and culture and a strong loyalty to family and community. The majority were Roman Catholic. They maintained close ties with their **extended families,** which included grandparents, aunts, uncles, and cousins as well as parents, brothers, and sisters. Economic and social pressures forced many urban Hispanic Americans to live in mostly Hispanic neighborhoods, or barrios.

In other ways Hispanic Americans were and are a diverse group. The successful Cuban American banker in Miami, the Puerto Rican teenager in New York City's South Bronx, and the Mexican American field-worker in California's San Joaquin Valley all faced different political and economic issues.

Five Major Groups

Hispanic Americans may be divided into five major subgroups: Mexican Americans, Puerto Ricans, Cuban Americans, those from Central America, and those from South America. Each group has its own history and settlement pattern.

Many Mexican Americans were grandchildren or great grandchildren of the 1 million people who fled

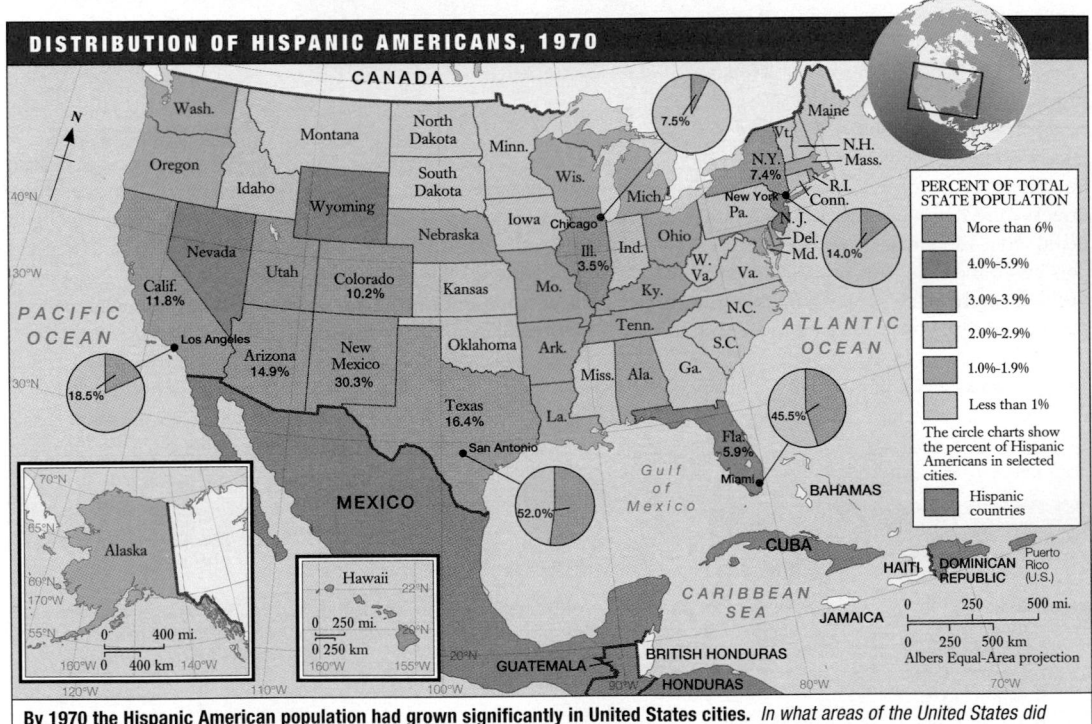

DISTRIBUTION OF HISPANIC AMERICANS, 1970

By 1970 the Hispanic American population had grown significantly in United States cities. *In what areas of the United States did Hispanic Americans tend to settle?*

Cooperative Learning

Bilingual Education Have students research the controversial topic of bilingual education. Organize the class into two groups. One group can concentrate on the pros of bilingual education; the other group can concentrate on the cons. For background, they can look up the topic of bilingual education in the *World Book* *Encyclopedia.* They can look for magazine articles in the *Readers' Guide to Periodical Literature,* and they may find individual books listed in the library catalog system. Set aside class time for the groups to present both points of view. A discussion can follow but need not lead to a right/wrong conclusion.

Enrichment Celebrations such as this Puerto Rican Day parade add to the cultural diversity of the United States. *What is one of the main reasons that many Puerto Ricans came to the United States?*

Mexico in the 20 years following Mexico's 1910 revolution. Others traced their origins to families who lived in Mexican territories that were incorporated into the United States after the Mexican War. Others first came to this country as *braceros,* farmworkers who were issued temporary work permits by the United States government during World War II and after. Still others were **undocumented immigrants**—people who lacked legal papers for residing in the United States. Many Mexican Americans maintained ties with relatives and friends in Mexico through frequent visits or moves back and forth.

Because Puerto Rico is a possession of the United States, Puerto Ricans may enter this country as citizens. After World War II, 1 out of every 6 Puerto Ricans came to this country seeking economic opportunities not available in Puerto Rico. In the 1960s, of the 1 million Puerto Ricans in the United States, 600,000 lived in New York City. Most were unskilled, poorly educated, and stuck in low-paying jobs.

Cubans began arriving in this country in large numbers after Fidel Castro's revolutionary movement overthrew the dictator Fulgencio Batista in 1959. One great migration began following the Cuban missile crisis of 1962, when 3,000 people a week arrived for several months. A second migration took place between 1965 and 1970, when 368,000 Cubans immigrated to the United States. In 1980, 130,000 Cubans left their homes for this country in what is known as the Mariel Boatlift. A great number of this nation's Cuban Americans settled in and around Miami; large Cuban communities also grew up in New York City and in New Jersey. Many of these immigrants left Cuba for political, not economic, reasons and had little difficulty establishing themselves in the United States.

Two other groups of Hispanic Americans are those with roots in Central America and South America.

Civil war caused tens of thousands of Salvadorans, Guatemalans, and Nicaraguans to seek asylum here. Economic changes and chronic poverty led many of South Americans to enter this country. The largest number of these are from Colombia. More than 100,000 Colombians immigrated between 1966 and 1979. Most settled in New York City, Miami, and Los Angeles.

Hispanic Americans Respond
Hispanic Americans Organize

While the numbers of Hispanic Americans increased dramatically during the 1960s and 1970s, their development as a political force occurred more slowly. Because of the Hispanic Americans' diversity, it was difficult for any one leader to unite all the segments into a single force.

Political Issues

For Hispanic Americans, as for other minorities, a major political issue was **representation,** which would result from electing to public office people to represent their views. In some border towns such as El Paso, Texas, Hispanic American voters outnumbered other voters two to one, but few Hispanic American candidates were nominated or elected to office. Gerrymandering in other cities, such as Los Angeles, helped to keep Hispanic Americans from massing their votes. Gradually, with changes such as reapportionment, a few Hispanic American candidates were elected. For example, in 1961 voters in San Antonio, Texas, elected Democrat Henry B. González to the House of Representatives. In 1964 Texans elected E. "Kika" de la Garza to represent the Lower Rio Grande Valley in the House.

Gradually, Hispanic Americans began to organize politically. La Raza Unida, which translates roughly as "the people united," resulted from an effort to organize a national political party that would unite the sometimes divided Hispanic American elements. José Angel Gutiérrez, a 25-year-old Texan, formed the party early in 1970 to give Mexican Americans political control over some 20 southern Texas counties in which they made up the majority of the population. In September of that year, Rodolfo "Corky" González, an activist and poet from Colorado, formed the Colorado La Raza Unida. Two years later a national convention drew 3,000 Chicanos, the ethnic label adopted by many Mexican Americans.

Another pressing political issue concerned the *bracero* program. In periods of labor shortage such as occurred during World War II, American growers pressed the United States government to allow farm laborers to enter

SECTION TWO **735**

VISUAL INSTRUCTION

Enrichment The spectators in the photograph are watching a Puerto Rican Day parade in New York City in 1991.

Answer: *seeking economic opportunities not available in Puerto Rico*

Independent Practice

L2 Geography Have students research one of the five major Hispanic American groups. Have them write a short paper explaining why that group left their homeland, where they settled in the U. S., what their problems and successes have been, and what contributions they have made to U.S. culture.

Have students complete Chapter 22, Section 2 Vocabulary and Guided Activity. (Also in Spanish.) **LEP**

Block Scheduling

Have students complete the Unit 8 Great Debate to enrich their understanding of the relationship between bilingualism and assimilation.

Meeting Special Needs

Attention Deficit Disorder To assist students with attention deficit disorder, divide the section into segments, based on heads and subheads. Invite students to read one segment at a time, summarizing it in their own words before they move on to the next segment, at a later time.

ASSESS

Meeting Lesson Objectives

Each section objective is tested by the section review question(s) that follows it in parentheses.

1. Describe the history and culture of the five major Hispanic American groups. (1, 2, 3, 5)

2. Recognize the major problematic issues facing Hispanic Americans in the 1960s and 1970s and what Hispanic Americans did to address the issues. (1, 3, 4, 5)

VISUAL INSTRUCTION

Hard Work The average annual earnings for migrant workers in the nation in the late 1960s was $1,307.

Answer: *poor working conditions for farm laborers, employment discrimination, limited or no social services*

History and the Humanities

U.S. History and Art Transparency 32—*Still Life with Red Car 1986* by Frank Romero.

Focus on American Fine Art Prints, Prints 18 and 19—*Jar, San Idelfonso Pueblo, New Mexico,* by Maria Montoya Martinez; *Valley of the Bluebonnets* by Porfirio Salinas.

Hard Work Hispanic Americans often toiled in grape and lettuce fields like these. *What problems did Hispanic Americans face?*

on temporary, restricted permits. Although Mexico disliked the program, fearing that the workers would face ethnic discrimination, it reluctantly consented to accept it. The program was scrapped in 1965 when Mexican Americans complained about the poor working conditions that the workers suffered.

The plight of the undocumented immigrant and the related problem of controlling the United States–Mexico border were other troublesome issues. Poverty in Mexico was the source of much illegal immigration. No one really could be sure how many people had crossed over the 2,000-mile (3,218-km) border without proper documents.

The journey to the United States was a difficult and dangerous one for these undocumented immigrants. They were vulnerable to exploitation—first by "coyotes," often unscrupulous guides who demanded large sums of money for transporting the immigrants across the border. Coyotes frequently robbed the immigrants, sometimes abandoning them in the wilderness. Immigrants who successfully reached the United States also often faced exploitation—by employers. Because the workers were in the country illegally, they had no place to turn for protection, and they were often forced to work under poor conditions for little pay.

Other challenges awaited undocumented immigrants once they reached this country. Communities generally provided education and emergency health care to anyone who needed it, but undocumented immigrants were often denied other social services, such as unemployment insurance and food stamps, even though most

of them paid taxes. In addition, families in need often would not apply for aid for fear of being deported—that is, sent back to their native land.

Undocumented immigrants were not the only ones who suffered. Many Hispanic Americans who were in this country legally faced discrimination from employers as the federal government's Immigration and Naturalization Service (INS) pressured businesses not to hire undocumented immigrants. Many employers, in order to avoid attracting the attention of the INS, simply stopped hiring people of color or those with Hispanic-sounding names, regardless of the workers' legal status.

Economic Issues

Among minorities, economic subjects such as wages and working conditions were not easily distinguished from broader political and social issues. César Chávez believed that they all must be treated as a single issue.

Partly as a result of Chávez's leadership, farmworkers became unionized for the first time. Chávez, a soft-spoken, patient man, has been called a "quiet explosion." Much of his work centered on the grape-growing area around Delano, in California's San Joaquin Valley. There he faced bitter opposition from the growers as well as from the Teamsters Union, which had received permission from the growers to represent the workers even though the workers had not been consulted.

In his union work, Chávez followed the nonviolent philosophy of India's Mohandas K. Gandhi and our own country's Martin Luther King, Jr. Chávez explains:

Portfolio Project

Creative Writing Provide students with a list of Hispanic Americans who have made achievements in literature, science, politics, and other fields. Ask each student to choose a person (or they may choose a Hispanic person they know personally) to write about. They may write a biographical sketch, a news article, a short story, or a poem. Whatever the format, encourage them to portray their subject as a real person, with believable individual traits. Have them include their sketches in their portfolios.

I f someone commits violence against us, it is much better—if we can—not to react against the violence, but to react in such a way as to get closer to our goal. People don't like to see a nonviolent movement subjected to violence. . . . That's the key point we have going for us. . . . By some strange chemistry, every time the opposition commits an unjust act against our hopes and aspirations, we get tenfold paid back in benefits.

—César Chávez, *Labor Leaders in America,* 1987

Realizing the limits of his resources in Delano, Chávez hit upon the idea of organizing national and international boycotts of farm products. He first used the boycott tactic when negotiating with the growers of table grapes. He then later called successfully for boycotts of wine grapes and of lettuce.

Social and Cultural Issues

All Hispanic Americans share some social and cultural problems. As people of color, most have been subject to some degree to the pervasive racial and ethnic prejudices in United States society.

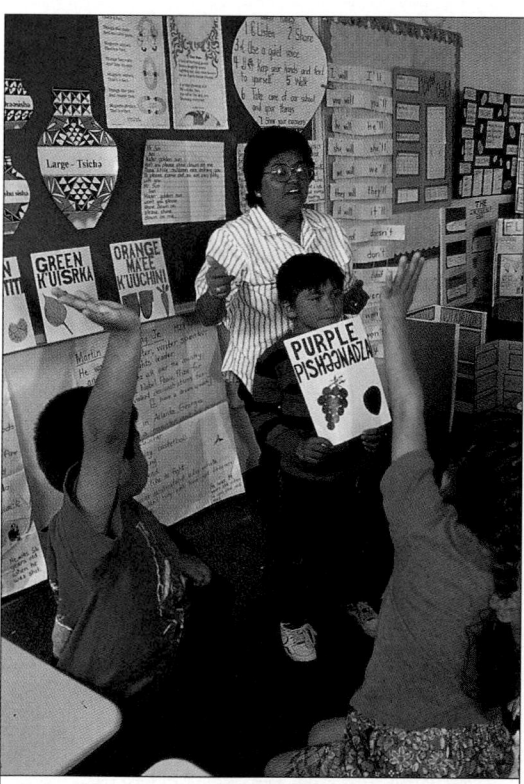

Bilingual Education These first graders of Acoma Pueblo in New Mexico enjoy the benefits of a bilingual classroom. *What were the arguments against bilingual education?*

Social reforms brought about through the civil rights movement did not immediately benefit Hispanic Americans. Hispanic Americans were regarded as white, and therefore they did not receive many of the legal protections granted other minorities. Not until 1970 did a federal district court rule that Mexican Americans constituted an "identifiable ethnic minority with a pattern of discrimination."

In the 1970s **bilingualism,** the use of two languages, became a center of stormy controversy. The proponents of bilingualism claimed that educating children in their native tongue as well as in English was the only way to ensure that minority students would receive an education equal to that of English-speaking classmates. Those who objected to bilingualism felt it delayed the successful **assimilation,** or incorporation, of minorities into the mainstream of society. A small group of opponents expressed fears that the United States would become a bilingual country.

In 1968 the Bilingual Education Act had provided federal assistance to school districts for developing bilingual education programs. In 1974 the legal issues were decided in favor of bilingual education, when the Supreme Court ruled that schools had to meet the needs of those children who had a limited knowledge of English. Nevertheless, the issues of bilingualism and assimilation remain contentious ones in communities across the nation.

SECTION REVIEW

Vocabulary

1. Define: extended family, undocumented immigrant, representation, bilingualism, assimilation.

Checking Facts

2. What are the five major Hispanic American groups and what attitudes do they share about family and community?

3. What were some major problems facing Hispanic Americans in the 1960s and 1970s?

Critical Thinking

Making Comparisons

4. Compare what César Chávez said about the gains made through nonviolent resistance to the actual experiences of Martin Luther King, Jr., and civil rights protesters in Birmingham and Selma, Alabama.

Linking Across Time

5. How was the experience of Mexican Americans in the West in the late 1800s different from that of Hispanic American groups in general in the 1960s and 1970s?

VISUAL INSTRUCTION

Bilingual Education In transitional programs, native language decreases as proficiency in English increases; in developmental programs, native language continues even as English proficiency increases.

Answer: *it would slow assimilation; the United States would become bilingual*

Evaluate

Have students complete the Section Review.

☞ ⊙ Assign the Section 2 Quiz or use the Testmaker to develop a customized quiz. (Also in Spanish.) **LEP**

Reteach

⌒ Have students listen to the Chapter 22, Section 2 Audiocassette. (Also in Spanish.) **LEP**

Enrich

☞ Have students complete the Chapter 22 Geography in History Activity.

CLOSE

Ask students to recount the experience of Hispanic Americans in the United States in the 1960s and 1970s. *(grew in numbers; diverse groups shared common traits, lacked organization and representation; immigrants faced discrimination; workers united; groups joined politically to gain rights and improve living and working conditions)*

Section 2 Review Answers

1. extended family (734), **undocumented immigrant** (735), **bilingualism** (737), **assimilation** (737)
2. Mexican Americans, Puerto Ricans, Cuban Americans, Central Americans, South Americans; loyalty to family and community
3. low-paying jobs; racial and ethnic prejudice; inadequate political representation, social services, and conditions for immigrant workers

4. Both knew that public sympathy is aroused when nonviolence is met with violence.
5. In the late 1800s, Mexican American land in the West was taken over by white settlers; yet Mexican American culture had already been established in the West. In the 1960s and 1970s, many Hispanic Americans settled in other parts of the country and were newcomers to the United States.

737

TEACH

Making the Historical Connection

Many California farmworkers were migrants who suffered racial discrimination and lived and worked under extremely poor conditions. César Chávez, Dolores Huerta, and other labor organizers felt that unionization was essential to guarantee fair treatment of these workers.

Turning Point

Where strikes and limited boycotts had failed, the broadly supported, industry-wide table-grape boycott proved successful in 1970, when national grape sales fell significantly and growers allowed farmworkers to unionize.

Turning Point

The United Farm Workers and the Grape Boycott

JANUARY, 1968

MEMORANDUM

Mr. President, in September the United Farm Workers Organizing Committee, AFL-CIO—UFWOC— began the third year of their strike and boycott against California growers of fresh table grapes. They are solemnly dedicated to non-violent, direct action as a tactic to obtain human dignity, and to guarantee by contract improved living and working conditions through collective bargaining with their employers.

Senator Harrison Williams, D-N.J.
Chair, Subcommittee on Migratory Labor
Congressional Record, October 11, 1968

The Case

In January 1968, labor organizer Dolores Huerta and 60 other members of the United Farm Workers Organizing Committee (UFWOC) set off from California on a cross-country bus trip. They were headed for New York City, the biggest market for West Coast grapes, to kick off UFWOC's latest campaign in its struggle for farmworkers' rights— a boycott of California table grapes. As they crossed the United States, the farmworkers set up boycott committees in dozens of communities. At each stop, they spoke in churches, schools, and homes, urging people to support their efforts to unionize farmworkers by not buying grapes.

The grape boycott grew out of earlier efforts to force grape growers to let their workers join the union. When those pickets, strikes, and negotiations failed, UFWOC turned to the boycott.

The growers insisted that the boycott was illegal and that most farmworkers did not want a union. In the months and years that followed, the growers and the farmworkers would each try to win consumers to their side. The boycott would be won or lost in supermarket aisles across the country.

The Background

California's farmworkers—mainly Mexican Americans, but also whites, African Americans, Filipino Americans, and others—were among the poorest of the poor. Many were migrants, following the harvest up and down California's Central Val-

738   CASE STUDY

The Case at a Glance

| Labor organizers ask grape growers to let workers unionize; growers refuse. | → | UFWOC strikes and boycotts Giumarra Vineyard Corporation. | → | Giumarra Vineyard finds alternative ways to get grapes sold. | → | UFWOC boycotts all grape growers. | → |

ley, picking grapes, lettuce, and other crops. Even though the entire family, including the children, worked long hours in the fields, the average yearly income for a migrant farmworker's family was well below the poverty level of $3,000. Exposed to pesticides in the fields and with little access to health care, the average migrant worker could expect to live only 49 years compared with 70 years for the average United States citizen.

Farmworkers had never been able to organize an effective union. They had been excluded from the National Labor Relations Act (NLRA), passed in 1935, which guaranteed other workers the right to join unions and to bargain collectively with their employers.

Organizing Workers In the 1960s, however, farmworkers in California were beginning to build a union. One of the leaders of this new movement was César Chávez. Chávez, a Mexican American, grew up in a migrant farmworker family in California. Like many other farmworker children, Chávez left school at 14 to work full-time in the fields. In the 1950s Chávez began working with a group that was helping Mexican American communities in California organize to fight discrimination.

In 1962 Chávez set off on his own to organize agricultural workers in Delano, California, the heart of California's grape-growing empire. He called his organization the Farm Workers Association (FWA). Within 3 years the FWA had more than 1,000 members and had begun to use traditional labor tactics, including strikes, to win wage increases. In 1966 the FWA joined with the Agricultural Workers Organizing Committee (AWOC), another farmworker organization, to form the United Farm Workers Organizing Committee (UFWOC). The new organization was headed by Chávez and other FWA leaders along with Larry Itliong and Philip Vera Cruz, Filipino American labor organizers from AWOC.

Building Support UFWOC members went from vineyard to vineyard talking to workers about the union and pressing growers to allow elections so that workers could choose a union to represent them. Once workers had a union, UFWOC argued, they could use collective bargaining to win contracts that would guarantee higher wages, better working conditions, and benefits.

"Gandhi taught that the boycott is the most nearly perfect instrument of non-violent change, allowing masses of people to participate actively in a cause. . . . Even if people cannot picket with us or contribute money or food, they can take part in our struggle by not buying certain products."

César Chávez

Farmworker

"Employer importation and use of strikebreakers, presence of Mexican alien greencarders, and court injunctions severely limiting the union's right to picket, left no recourse for the workers but to seek public support through a consumer boycott of grapes."

Senator Harrison Williams

César Chávez

"If we, as farmers and employers, accept the union as bargaining agent, we are taking away the individual laborer's right of choice—his right to freedom of work. This is a struggle for the right of a farmer to deal directly with his employees—a stand for free enterprise."

Louis Rozzoni, president, California Farm Bureau

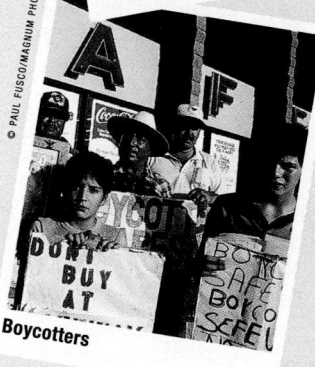
Boycotters

"When we tried to fight back in the past, we found the grower was too strong, too rich, and we had to give up. César Chávez has shown us we can fight back."

Farmworker

FYI

The National Labor Relations Act of 1935
This act guaranteed the right to unionize and prohibited employers from interfering with union efforts to bring workers into unions. In guaranteeing collective bargaining, it required employers to negotiate with representatives elected by workers. The agricultural industry, however, was not covered by this act, and therefore farmworkers could not benefit from its protections.

Notes

Grape sales drop at markets. → Growers give in and allow workers to unionize.

739

Analyzing the Case

After students have read The Background, The Opinions, and The Significance, discuss the following.

1. Why did UFWOC want farmworkers to join a union? *(Workers could collectively bargain for higher wages and better working conditions and benefits.)*
2. According to UFWOC, why would raising workers' wages mean only a slight increase in the price of grapes? *(Workers' wages accounted for only a small part of the cost of grape production.)*
3. In what ways was the boycott a landmark event? *(Farmworkers gained the right to unionize and got better pay and working conditions; the event showed the power of grassroots groups and boycotts.)*

Notes

Turning Point

César Chávez leads marches for farmworkers' rights.

In 1967 UFWOC targeted the Giumarra Vineyard Corporation, the largest table-grape grower in California. Giumarra, however, refused to allow union elections, and the vineyard's workers voted to strike. Giumarra then brought in other workers in an attempt to break the strike. To force Giumarra to negotiate, UFWOC called on consumers to boycott Giumarra grapes. To evade the boycott, Giumarra began shipping its grapes under other companies' labels. UFWOC decided that the only way to make the boycott work was to expand it to all table grapes. Chávez later explained, "It was the only way we could do it. We had to take on the whole industry. The grape itself had to become a label."

The Opinions

The growers insisted that most farmworkers did not want a union. They claimed that California farmworkers were the highest paid of any American farmworkers and that they were already adequately protected by labor laws. The growers argued that they could not afford to pay higher wages and warned that increased farmworker wages would mean higher prices for consumers. The growers also maintained that the boycott was illegal—prohibited by the NLRA.

Many conservative politicians, including California Governor Ronald Reagan and President Richard Nixon, supported the growers. Nixon said the boycott should be condemned "with the same firmness we condemn . . . any other form of lawbreaking."

Many supermarkets also supported the growers, claiming to do so under the banner of consumer rights. They argued that they should continue to stock grapes so that consumers could choose for themselves whether or not to support the boycott.

Chávez and UFWOC argued that the growers should at least allow the workers themselves to decide whether or not they wanted a union by letting them hold elections. UFWOC pointed out that they had always offered growers the option of holding elections before calling for strikes or boycotts. At the few vineyards where elections were held, workers overwhelmingly voted to join UFWOC.

UFWOC maintained that farmworkers' wages were unfairly low. Raising these wages would mean only a slight increase in the price of grapes at the supermarket, they said, since United States Department of Labor records showed that only 2 cents to 5 cents of every dollar invested in grape production went to the workers. Furthermore, UFWOC claimed the consumer boycott was legal because the provisions of the NLRA that restricted the use of boycotts did not cover farmworkers.

People across the United States and Canada supported the boycott. They set up more than 400 boycott committees and raised more than $20,000 a month for UFWOC. Boycott supporters picketed supermarkets, calling on store managers to stop selling grapes and shoppers to stop buying them. Students demanded that school cafeterias stop serving grapes. In Boston, one group dumped grapes into the harbor in a protest reminiscent of the Boston Tea Party. Religious leaders, including California's Catholic bishops, defended the farmworkers' right to unionize. Politicians, too, began to stand up for

740 CASE STUDY

Cooperative Learning

Point-of-View Scenarios Organize the class into five groups. Each group should choose one of these parties: farmworkers, growers, union representatives, supermarkets, consumers. Have groups research the position of their party. They can use information in the case study as well as information from library resources. Each group should then prepare a "grape boycott scenario" (one segment or the entire story) from the point of view of their party. Provide class time for all scenarios to be presented by group representatives. Join students in a follow-up discussion of the various points of view.

the farmworkers. All the major Democratic presidential candidates and the mayors of three dozen cities, including New York, declared their support for the boycott.

The Players

César Chávez Director of UFWOC. Chávez was a firm believer in nonviolence as a means of bringing about social change. To make this point and to draw public attention to the boycott, Chávez fasted for 25 days. He said, "Social justice for the dignity of man cannot be won at the price of human life."

Growers Just 30 growers grew 85 percent of California table grapes. Giumarra alone had 10 percent of the market. Many growers were suspicious of Chávez's motives. Some even called him a Communist.

Consumers The farmworkers called on shoppers to stop buying grapes, and many did. *New York* magazine reported that many Americans "would rather eat a cyanide pellet than a California grape these days."

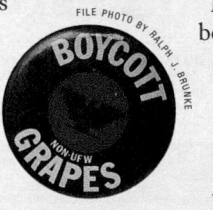
Boycott Button

The Outcome

The grape boycott turned out to be one of the most successful consumer boycotts in United States history. In New York City, sales of grapes declined by 90 percent during the summer of 1968. National grape sales fell by 12 percent. Prices for grapes dropped too. One grower admitted, "It is costing us more to produce and sell our grapes than we are getting paid for them. . . ."

Finally, in the summer of 1970, most growers gave in and signed agreements with UFWOC. The new contracts called for pay increases, employer contributions to worker health and welfare funds, union control over hiring, and joint worker-grower committees to regulate pesticide use.

The Significance

Most historians consider the grape boycott to be a landmark in twentieth-century American labor history. For the first time, United States farmwork-

ers gained the right to unionize. The contracts negotiated by the union led to increased pay and better working conditions for many farmworkers.

The grape boycott also demonstrated the power of grassroots organizing and of the boycott as a tool for social change. Other groups would later adopt these same tactics to bring about change in other areas, such as the environment.

Perhaps most importantly, the grape boycott heralded the emerging political power of Hispanic Americans and others who took part in the struggle. In the years that followed, Hispanic Americans would join together in the National Council of La Raza Unida to lobby Washington on behalf of Hispanic Americans. They would use their newfound political muscle to oppose discrimination, to fight for bilingual education and changes in immigration law, and to elect Hispanics to government posts.

RESPONDING TO THE CASE

1. Make a chart in which you list the growers arguments against the boycott and UFWOC's responses. Which arguments do you find most convincing?

2. In your opinion, why was the boycott successful?

3. What are some of the advantages and disadvantages of a boycott as a strategy for bringing about change? Should groups involve consumers in disputes through boycotts?

PORTFOLIO PROJECT Imagine you are in charge of a public relations campaign for the grape growers. Write a newspaper ad in which you try to persuade shoppers not to boycott grapes. Then take the position of a supporter of the grape boycott, picketing a grocery store. How would you convince a shopper not to buy grapes? Write a script of a conversation you might have with a shopper. Also, design a poster to carry while picketing. Place the ad, the script, and the poster design in your portfolio.

CASE STUDY **741**

Responding to the Case Answers

1. growers: farmworkers did not want a union, California farmworkers were highly paid, increased wages would mean higher consumer prices, boycott was illegal; UFWOC: growers should have allowed workers to decide if they wanted to unionize, wages were unfairly low, increased wages would not increase prices significantly, boycott was legal; students' responses will reflect individual opinions

2. Answers will vary; highly supported; forced grape sales down, affecting growers economically; growers let workers unionize

3. Answers will vary; brings issue to consumers, hits at economic level; involves large number of people, takes time; yes: consumers are ultimate recipients of product; no: it should be between the parties immediately involved, should not influence consumer buying patterns

SECTION

3

FOCUS

Section Objectives

1. Understand the history of the relationship between Native Americans and the United States government.
2. Identify the problematic issues facing Native Americans in the 1960s and 1970s and what they did to address the issues.

Bellringer Activity

While taking attendance at the beginning of the class period, display **Section Focus Transparency 70,** and have students answer the questions. (Or use the blackline master.)

VISUAL INSTRUCTION

Sacred Lands Water from Blue Lake irrigates corn fields and pastures and provides water for the pueblo.

Ask: What is the main reason that Blue Lake is important to the Taos Pueblo people? *(It is sacred to them.)*

Land Claims of Native Americans

DECEMBER 15, 1970: TAOS PUEBLO PEOPLE REGAIN SACRED BLUE LAKE

Sacred Lands
The Taos Pueblo people fight for their sacred lands.

BLUE LAKE HAS ALWAYS BEEN SACRED TO THE TAOS PUEBLO PEOPLE. Physically, Blue Lake is a small body of water in the Sangre de Christo range of the Rocky Mountains in northern New Mexico. In 1966 Pueblo governor John C. Reyna tried to explain the deeper importance of the lake to the Taos people. "The lake," he said,

Is as blue as turquoise. It is surrounded by evergreens. In the summer there are millions of wildflowers. Springs are all around. We have no buildings there, no steeples. There is nothing the human hand has made. The lake is our church. . . . We pray to the water, the sun, the clouds, the sky, the deer. Without them we could not exist."

—John C. Reyna

Reyna was speaking for the Taos Pueblo people, who were working to regain control of Blue Lake and the surrounding land. Control had been stripped from them in 1906 when the United States government made the area part of the Carson National Forest. The Taos Pueblo had used the land for centuries, yet the United States government never gave them title or **compensation,** money or something else in return for a loss.

What ultimately turned the tide for the Taos Pueblo was the fact that President Nixon looked favorably on their cause. The Native Americans' desire to avoid integration dovetailed neatly with Nixon's belief that peoples should not be forced together if they wanted to remain independent. Nixon's administration had been

---

AS YOU READ

Vocabulary
► compensation
► liberate

Think About . . .
► the nature of the relationship betweeen Native Americans and the United States government.

► the problems facing Native Americans in the 1960s and 1970s and the methods used by Native Americans to solve the problems.

Section 3 Resources

REPRODUCIBLE RESOURCES
- Lesson Plan 22-3
- Section 3 Quiz
- Vocabulary and Guided Reading 22-3
- Unit 8 American Literature Reading

MULTIMEDIA RESOURCES
- Section Focus Transparency 70
- Chapter 22 Digest Audiocassette
- Student Self-Test: A Software Review
- Testmaker
- Vocabulary PuzzleMaker

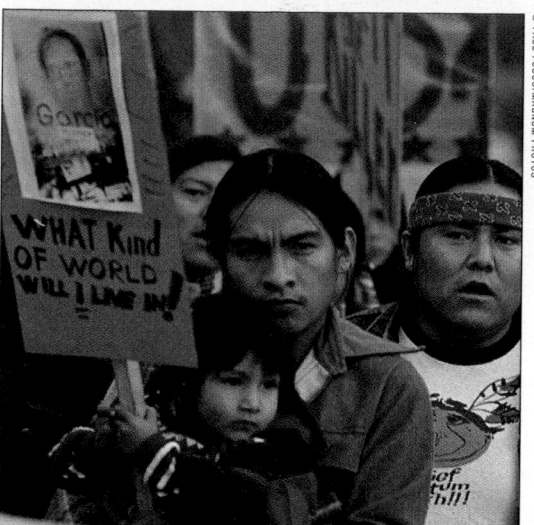

© PAUL FUSCO/MAGNUM PHOTOS

Demonstrations Native Americans in New Mexico take part in a civil rights protest. *What are some other methods Native Americans have used to regain control of thier lives?*

American was still threatened as the 1960s began. From 1960 to 1970, their population soared from 551,500 to 792,730, a rate of increase four times the national average. About two-thirds of all Native Americans lived off the reservations. Most were in large cities such as Los Angeles and Chicago. The federal government's Bureau of Indian Affairs managed the 285 reservations, mostly west of the Mississippi River, with little input from the Native Americans themselves.

During this time, on and off the reservations, Native Americans were the most disadvantaged of this nation's racial and ethnic minorities. More than 38 percent lived below the poverty line, as compared to 33 percent of African Americans and only 12 percent of the United States as a whole. Unemployment was widespread, frequently as high as 50 percent. With a school dropout rate of 50 percent, many Native Americans were unprepared to compete. Life expectancy was lower than the national average. The rates of tuberculosis and alcoholism were the highest in the nation, while the suicide rate among Native Americans was double that of the rest of the country.

seeking a way to gain credibility in the eyes of the Native American nations in order to help them move toward desired independence. Furthermore, it was evident that the Taos Pueblo had been seriously wronged when control of Blue Lake had been taken from them. Their victory, decades in coming, was realized on December 15, 1970, when President Nixon signed into law legislation to return the sacred site of Blue Lake to the Taos Pueblo.

Recent History of Native Americans
United States Controls Native Americans

As with Hispanic Americans, assimilation was an issue among Native Americans and a factor in government decisions for several decades. Unlike other minorities, Native Americans had never been immigrants, for they were already here when Europeans first colonized the country. Nevertheless, starting in the late 1880s, Native Americans became virtual wards of the state—powerless, with little voice in their own affairs. FDR's administration returned a limited amount of control to Native Americans living on reservations. Eisenhower's administration, however, reversed Roosevelt's New Deal policy on Native Americans.

In spite of the changing federal policy between the 1930s and the 1950s, the cultural identity of the Native

Native American Responses
A Fight to Regain Control

During the 1960s and 1970s, Native Americans began to organize in order to combat these problems. They met on and off their reservations, on college campuses, in tribal powwows, and in conferences. They negotiated with museums and universities to regain sacred objects that had been removed from Native American lands. They sued to reclaim land, water, and other rights lost when treaties were broken. Some of the younger activists formed militant groups, such as the American Indian Movement (AIM), and tried to achieve social reform by force.

Many Native Americans did not want to blend their traditional cultures with the American mainstream. They wanted self-determination, the opportunity to participate themselves in the political and economic decisions that affected their lives.

Radical Movements

Frustrated by what they saw as their failure to achieve justice through legal channels, a group of Oglala Sioux decided to take matters into their own hands. On the evening of February 27, 1973, a caravan of 54 cars rolled into a small, quiet town just after dusk. Many of the cars' occupants were armed. First they shot out streetlights; then they seized ammunition and rifles from a trading post. All the town's white people were herded into one house. Roadblocks were set up on all the roads

SECTION THREE **743**

**Chapter 22
SECTION 3**

VISUAL INSTRUCTION

Demonstrations In August 1974, the year of the photo, the U.S. Civil Rights Commission heard complaints of mistreatment of Native Americans by whites in New Mexico and nearby states. A 1975 study upheld the complaints' validity.

Answer: *They organized, held tribal powwows, negotiated to reclaim sacred objects, used the courts to reclaim lost lands, and staged occupations to capture public attention.*

TEACH

Guided Practice

L2 Discussion With students, compare the problems of Native Americans with the problems of other minorities. Why do Native Americans perceive themselves as having legitimate claims that other minorities do not have? *(They are indigenous.)* Encourage students to speculate on why some Native Americans have chosen to operate outside the legal system for their rights.

FYI

Wounded Knee *Bury My Heart at Wounded Knee* (1970) by Dee Brown tells the history of Native Americans in the West. Tracing white conquest of Native Americans, the book ends with the symbolic termination of Native American freedom at Wounded Knee, South Dakota.

Cooperative Learning

Native Americans Organize the class into two groups; each group is to identify and research a recent event or situation involving Native Americans in your area or across the nation. Set aside class time for groups to report their findings and compare present-day situations to those of the 1960s and 1970s.

Independent Practice

L2 **Researching** Have students research and summarize the Native American occupation of Alcatraz Island in 1969 or of the Bureau of Indian Affairs in 1972.

☞ Have students complete the Chapter 22, Section 3 Vocabulary and Guided Reading Activity. (Also in Spanish.) **LEP**

CHART STUDY

The government initially refused to represent the tribes because they were not federally recognized.
Answer: *the United States Court of Claims*

ASSESS

Meeting Lesson Objectives

Each section objective is tested by the section review questions that follow it in parentheses.

1. Understand the history of the relationship between Native Americans and the United States government. (4, 5)
2. Identify the problematic issues facing Native Americans in the 1960s and 1970s and what they did to address the issues. (1, 2, 3)

---

leading into the town, which the Sioux then declared **liberated,** or freed from outside control.

The liberated town was Wounded Knee, little more than a fork in the road on the Pine Ridge reservation in southwestern South Dakota. To its liberators Wounded Knee was significant as the site of a massacre more than 80 years earlier where United States troops had killed almost 300 Sioux men, women, and children. Responding to the present-day Sioux militancy, United States marshals began a 71-day siege of the town to starve out

LAND RECOVERY, 1950s–1970s

Land Saga, 1794–1980

1794 Passamaquoddy and other local Native American groups sign treaty with the state of Massachusetts.

1820 The territory that is now Maine breaks away from Massachusetts. Native American lands are now part of Maine.

1957 Passamaquoddy leader John Stevens discovers a copy of the 1794 treaty. Stevens tries to get compensation for lands lost to white settlers over the years.

1975 Eastern Native American groups win protection under the 1790 Trade and Non-Intercourse Act, which had required congressional approval of all treaties.

1977 Carter administration steps in to help negotiate an out-of-court settlement.

1980 Maine Indian Claims Settlement Act provides more than $80 million for Native Americans to buy back land lost under the treaty. Native Americans begin to buy back huge tracts of tribal land.

The Passamaquoddy and Penobscot people used the courts to fight for lands they had lost to white settlers. *What group took over the work of the ICC after it was dissolved in 1978?*

---

the captors. Members of AIM and other sympathetic Native Americans from across the nation soon joined the captors at Wounded Knee.

When the siege lifted, two Native Americans had been killed and one marshal wounded. The issues cited—alleged corruption in the white-sponsored government on the reservation, broken treaties, and lack of self-determination—were not resolved.

What the demonstration did achieve was to focus the nation's attention on the deplorable living conditions of Native Americans. Like earlier dramatic occupations of United States property—at Alcatraz Island in 1969 and the Bureau of Indian Affairs building in Washington, D.C., in 1972—the occupation of Wounded Knee brought into the open a problem that had been ignored for almost a century.

Challenges Through the Courts

In spite of their frustrations, Native Americans did have some success in the courts. In 1946 President Truman created the Indian Claims Commission (ICC) to hear and settle all outstanding land claims that Native Americans brought against the government. When the commission was dissolved in 1978, the United States Court of Claims continued its work. During its lifetime the ICC heard 670 cases and awarded about $775 to each claimant. Most of the claims stemmed from broken treaties and seizures of Native American land without agreement or compensation. Many Native Americans were not satisfied with the results of the settlements. They would have preferred to have had their lands restored to them instead of receiving cash payments. The act setting up the ICC, however, had provided that compensation could be made only with money.

As time went on, though, some land restorations were made in addition to cash settlements. The claims of Native American peoples in Alaska, who include Aleut and Inuit, had not been dealt with since the purchase of the Alaskan territory from Russia in 1867. The Alaska Native Land Claims Settlement Act of 1971 gave more than 40 million acres (16,200,000 ha) to native peoples and paid out $962.5 million in cash. The act established 12 regional corporations to manage these resources. This action helped fulfill the Alaskan natives' desire for self-determination but created many difficulties. Few Alaskan natives were experienced in managing large corporations. Also, the regional division tended to weaken the traditional pattern of organization important in Native American societies.

In 1980 the Sioux were awarded $106 million for lands in South Dakota that had been taken from them illegally. In 1988 the Puyallup people of Washington received $162 million in settlement of claims from a treaty signed in the 1850s.

Meeting Special Needs

Visual Learners To help students who are visual learners, join students in analyzing the visuals in this section. Discuss what they can learn about Native Americans from the photos and graphics. 📖

Cultural Pride Native Americans have taken part in powwows such as this one to keep in touch with their cultural traditions. *What Native American issues have United States courts dealt with?*

VISUAL INSTRUCTION

Cultural Pride These Native Americans on Cheyenne River Reservation are in traditional dress for a powwow.

Answer: *Native American land claims, disputes among Native American nations, disagreements over reservation borders, disputes over water, timber, oil, mineral, hunting, and fishing rights.*

Evaluate

Have students complete the Section Review.

☞ 🔘 Assign the Section 3 Quiz or use the Testmaker to develop a customized quiz. (Also in Spanish.) **LEP**

Reteach

🎧 Have students listen to the Chapter 22, Section 3 Audiocassette. (Also in Spanish.) **LEP**

Enrich

☞ Have students complete the Unit 8 American Literature Reading.

CLOSE

Ask: Why have Native Americans resisted assimilation? *(They value their culture, land, and traditions; they do not want to lose them.)*

Sacred Lands

Congress also addressed the issue of lands sacred to Native Americans. The Taos Pueblo people of New Mexico, for example, struggled for decades to regain possession of their sacred Blue Lake. After the ICC finally acknowledged the Taos title to the land, Congress passed an act in 1970 approving a return of a portion of the national forest and the lake area to the Taos people. In exchange, the Taos gave up their claims to the Taos township.

The courts of the United States have also helped resolve long-standing disputes among Native American nations. For example, disagreements between the Hopi and the Navajo stemmed from the government's establishment of reservation borders in 1882. The Hopi claimed that these borders favored the Navajo. The court's 1962 ruling restored some of the disputed land to the Hopi and provided joint use of a larger area. The ruling, however, required the relocation of some 13,000 Navajo. Also at issue were water and timber rights, oil and mineral rights, and hunting and fishing rights. Many of these cases were not completely resolved by the ICC and continue to be fought in the United States courts.

SECTION REVIEW

Vocabulary
1. Define: compensation, liberate.

Checking Facts
2. What were the major problems facing Native Americans during the 1960s and 1970s?

3. What are some steps Native Americans took to address the problems?

Critical Thinking
Making Inferences
4. Native Americans have expressed a preference for regaining control of their traditional homelands rather than receiving cash settlements. What does this tell you about the values of these Native Americans?

Linking Across Time
5. How has Native American resistance to domination by the United States government changed since the early 1800s? Are the new Native American strategies more or less successful than the old ones?

Section 3 Review Answers

1. **compensation** (742), **liberate** (744)
2. lack of power over their own lives, lack of ownership of land
3. They organized themselves, negotiated, used the legal system, protested, and conducted militant occupations.
4. They value their culture over monetary gain; they feel a strong connection to the land.

5. The resistance has changed from passive resistance to legislative pressure and sometimes to active resistance. The new strategies have been more successful because some gains have been made, and the public has been made more aware of issues facing Native Americans.

Geography: Impact on History

TEACH

Making the Geography Connection

When Native Americans left rural areas and moved to cities, they often faced lives of poverty and cultural lack. In response they established urban cultural centers and set up community service programs. Often they maintained ties to relatives and friends still on rural reservations.

Mapping Activity

After students have studied the maps on pages 746 and 747, invite them to tell the story that the maps depict in their own words. (*Native Americans moved from rural lands to urban areas over time, yet seemed to stay in many of the same general regions of the country*)

MAP STUDY

The symbols on this map represent types of population concentration, not actual population figures.

Answer: *Oklahoma, New Mexico, Arizona, Washington, Montana, North Dakota, South Dakota, Nebraska, North Carolina*

MOVEMENT
Native American Urban Settlement

Beginning in the 1950s, large numbers of Native Americans left the reservations and moved to cities. This urban migration brought many changes to Native American individuals and communities.

Living on Reservations

In the nineteenth century, the United States government implemented the reservation policy, primarily during two major removal periods. This policy forced Native Americans to move from traditional lands to prescribed reservation areas, which were ultimately broken down further into individual parcels of land. Deprived of large expanses of land on which to hunt and gather and unable to support themselves by farming or ranching, Native Americans faced lives of poverty.

Moving to the Cities

Before the 1950s most Native Americans lived rural lives—on reservations or on traditional lands. During the 1950s, however, the federal government began to push for the assimilation of Native Americans into mainstream culture. Toward this goal the government sought to move Native Americans off reservations and into cities, where it seemed jobs were plentiful and assimilation would be rapid.

To hasten the process even more, the government adopted a policy known as termination. Under this policy the federal government began to cut off aid to Native American nations. Without this aid many nations could not survive on the reservations. Federal officials hoped

this policy would eventually allow the government to abolish the reservations altogether.

To further encourage Native Americans to move to cities, the Bureau of Indian Affairs (BIA) set up the Voluntary Relocation Program. BIA offices provided money and services to help Native American families relocate. Many Native

Americans took advantage of the program and moved to cities such as Minneapolis, Chicago, Denver, Oklahoma City, Seattle, San Francisco, and Los Angeles.

Such government policies and programs brought many Native Americans to cities. Other Native Americans, however, moved on their own. Opportunities for edu-

NATIVE AMERICAN U.S. DISTRIBUTION, 1910

NATIVE AMERICAN POPULATION
Density per sq. mile
- Greater than 1.0
- 0.25 to 1.0
- Less than 0.25

Native American population concentrations, counties
- 10,000
- 5,000
- 2,500

0   250   500 mi.
0   250   500 km
Albers Equal-Area projection

Before World War II, most Native Americans lived on reservations or in areas that had once been tribal lands. *In what areas of the country was most of the Native American population located?*

Geographic Themes

Movement Living on ancestral lands, Native Americans tended to be hunters and gatherers, using, but not depleting, natural resources. On reservations, Native Americans attempted to farm, but with little success. A few were successful at ranching, and some were able to take advantage of timber and mineral resources. With the move to urban areas, many hoped they would be able to make a better living. The skills that Native Americans had built up over the centuries, however, were for the most part unusable in white society. In urban settings, Native Americans were often employed in low-paying jobs, though some found success in white-collar positions.

cation and employment were limited on most reservations, and many Native Americans came to cities in search of better schools and jobs. Still others came to join family members and friends.

The urban migration that began in the 1950s brought tens of thousands of the Native American population to United States cities. In 1930 less than 10 percent of the Native American population lived in urban areas. By 1970 that figure had climbed to 45 percent, and still the migration continued. By 1990 nearly 67 percent of Native Americans lived in cities.

Urban Life

Despite the help offered by relocation programs, Native Americans who moved to cities faced many problems. Moving from rural to urban environments, surrounded by non-Native American culture and discrimination, many Native Americans wrestled with painful questions about their cultural identities. How could they live in two worlds at once?

One young Native American man who had grown up in a city said, "What is an Indian? I don't know. Perhaps that is because I have been raised in white society. My mother was raised on the reservation so perhaps I should know what an Indian is. People say, 'It doesn't matter how much Indian you are if you feel Indian.' I don't 'feel' Indian. . . . Perhaps this feeling of Indian is feeling kinship for people with Indian blood. . . . I search for something to validate myself as an Indian. I know Indians are sharing and giving people, they lack ma-

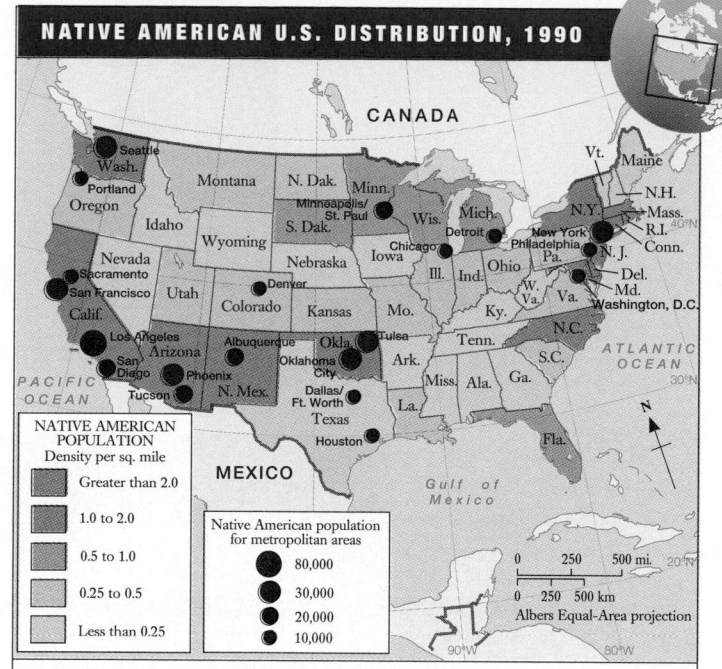

NATIVE AMERICAN U.S. DISTRIBUTION, 1990

By 1990 more Native Americans lived in cities than in rural areas. *What states included cities with more than 30,000 Native American residents?*

terialism—but that's a hard way to live in the city. . . ."

Some urban Native Americans built successful careers in law, medicine, and education. For many Native Americans, however, city life proved to be a life of poverty. At the time of the 1980 census, one-quarter of all urban Native Americans were living below the federal poverty level. Often these urban newcomers lacked education and thus found it hard to get jobs that paid well. Without a decent income, they could not afford adequate housing, food, or health care.

Urban Native Americans also had to deal with unaccustomed necessities such as rent, transportation, and child care. On the

reservations these services had been unnecessary or had been provided by the federal government.

Faced with the challenges of urban life, some Native Americans found strength in their traditional values. They began to establish cultural centers to keep their traditions alive. They set up community programs and clinics to meet their own needs for social services and health care. Many urban Native Americans also maintained close ties to the reservations (those that had not been destroyed by termination), trying to maintain a balance between a rural life that no longer sustained them and an urban life that was not yet comfortable.

CLOSE

Have students trace the movement of Native Americans from the 1800s to the present day. *(forced by U.S. government to leave tribal lands and move to reservations in the 1800s, then pushed by government to leave reservations and move to cities from the 1950s on)* What has been the experience of most Native Americans in cities? *(poverty and discrimination, feeling cut off from culture, roots; difficulty finding mainstream success)*

MAKING THE GEOGRAPHIC CONNECTION

1. What did the United States government do to get Native Americans to leave the reservations? Why?

2. What were some problems Native Americans faced when they moved to cities?

3. Movement Why did Native Americans begin moving to cities during the 1950s?

GEOGRAPHY: IMPACT ON HISTORY **747**

Making the Geographic Connection Answers

1. the government, under the termination policy, encouraged Native Americans to move to cities; the BIA offered money and other services to urge families to relocate; the government adopted this policy to hasten Native American assimilation into mainstream society—once assimilation had taken place, the government would cut off federal aid to Native American reservations

2. poverty; discrimination; lack of education and jobs; inadequate housing, food, health care; sense of being cut off from cultural roots
3. the government encouraged and assisted such moves, presuming cities would offer better job opportunities; individuals went in search of better schools and jobs; others joined friends already in cities

748

FOCUS

Section Objectives

1. Review the beliefs and values of the counterculture movement.
2. Compare communal living in the United States in the past with that of the counterculture in the 1960s and 1970s.
3. Explain the cultural aspects of the counterculture that the rest of society adopted.

Bellringer Activity

 While taking attendance at the beginning of the class period, display **Section Focus Transparency 71,** and have students answer the questions. (Or use the blackline master.)

VISUAL INSTRUCTION

Music Icon "The Times, They Are a-Changin,'" another Dylan song, became an anthem of the times.

Ask: What issues did Dylan's music address? *(issues such as racism, war, pollution, apathy)*

Curriculum Connection

Music The change in musical styles included groups that began in the late 1950s, such as the Kingston Trio.

SECTION 4

The Counterculture

1965: ROCK MUSIC PROVIDES A VOICE FOR THE COUNTERCULTURE

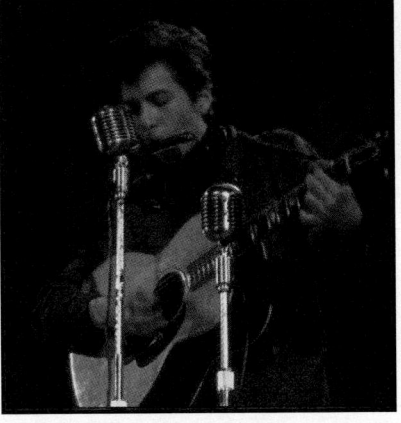

© JOHN LAUNOIS/BLACK STAR

Music Icon
Bob Dylan's music caught the mind, heart, and beat of a generation.

THE YOUNG PEOPLE WHO STRUGGLED FOR SOCIAL REFORM IN THE 1960S HAILED BOB DYLAN AS THEIR GUERRILLA MINSTREL. He fought for social justice with a guitar and a song. More than any other musician of the time, Dylan gave popular music a social consciousness. Many agreed that he was the spokesperson for his generation. In a 1962 song, Dylan asked one question after another about racism, war, pollution, apathy—the major issues of the day:

How many roads must a
man walk down
Before you call him a man? yes, 'n'
How many seas must a white dove sail
Before she sleeps in the sand? yes 'n'
How many times must the cannon balls fly
Before they're forever banned?
The answer, my friend, is blowin' in the wind,
The answer is blowin' in the wind.
—Bob Dylan, "Blowing in the Wind," 1962

Then in 1965 Dylan changed his tune. In albums such as *Bringing It All Back Home* and in an appearance at the Newport Folk Festival he signaled that change by playing half his music on an acoustic guitar and half on an electric guitar backed up by a rock group. The reaction was electrifying. Where had the old Dylan gone? Who was this new hard-driving musician with tousled hair who sounded so sarcastic, so sneering, so accusing:

How does it feel,
To be without a home,
Like a complete unknown,
Like a rolling stone?
—Bob Dylan, "Like a Rolling Stone," 1965

Once again Bob Dylan had caught the heartbeat of American youth, even before they felt the beat themselves. His unbridled energy, explosive anger, and rejection of what had gone before were signs of the arrival of

AS YOU READ

Vocabulary
► counterculture
► generation gap
► hippie
► commune
► cultural diffusion
► entrepreneur

Think About . . .
► the beliefs and values of the counterculture.
► how communes prior to the 1960s were similar to or different from the counterculture communes.

► the cultural aspects of the counterculture that were adopted by society at large, such as diet, fashion, music, and pop art.

748 CHAPTER 22 VOICES OF PROTEST

Section 4 Resources

REPRODUCIBLE RESOURCES

📋 Lesson Plan 22-4

📋 Section 4 Quiz

📋 Vocabulary and Guided Reading 22-4

📋 Performance Assessment Activity 22

📋 Reteaching Activity 22

📋 Enrichment Activity 22

📋 Chapter 22 Test

MULTIMEDIA RESOURCES

🖥 Section Focus Transparency 71

🎧 Chapter 22 Digest Audiocassette

💻 Student Self-Test: A Software Review

💻 Testmaker

💻 Vocabulary PuzzleMaker

the **counterculture,** a culture of young people with values that ran counter to those of the established culture.

Profile of a Generation
Youth Reacts to Tradition

The 1950s had been a turbulent time politically. The majority of American youth, however, did not seriously challenge the social order of the time. Of course, that age had its social critics, writers such as Jack Kerouac and Allen Ginsberg, who turned their backs on the social and cultural values of their time. These critics, however, were few in number and did not gain many followers.

In the 1960s the first of the baby boomers became teenagers. Having grown up during the cold war, many of these young people felt they were living on the edge of disaster. The threat of nuclear war was ever present as was the possibility of fighting in a faraway jungle war. Many blamed their elders, who included not only their parents but everyone over the age of 30, for creating the world in which they lived. The differences in attitudes between people of different age groups, or the **generation gap,** became a divisive force in society.

Music was perhaps the main instrument of communication within the young generation. Listening to and discussing the new music—rock and roll—was the way these young people identified one another as members of the same group. The affluence that carried over from the 1950s and the availability of small, cheap, portable radios and of record players meant that teenagers could listen to their own music while parents were tuned in to something completely different.

Beliefs and Values

Not all the young people of the 1960s hopped on the counterculture bandwagon. For that matter, a few of those who did could no longer be considered young. There was no such thing as a typical member of the movement, and different counterculture groups had different goals. What the members of the counterculture did have in common was a rejection of the prevailing middle-class values, the attitudes and beliefs of what they called the "Establishment"—people and institutions that represented power, authority, and the status quo.

In the counterculture's way of thinking, the older generation was inhibited, so the young placed a premium on "doing your own thing." The Establishment was materialistic, so the youth culture attempted to break from habits of regular employment and consumerism. Better, so the thinking went, to make what you need, share what you have with others, and

© CHARLES GATEWOOD/THE IMAGE WORKS

Questioning Authority The generation gap was not unique to the 1960s. Conflict between young and old is a common theme in history. *Why did young people in the 1960s feel they were living in danger?*

not want what you do not have. Science, technology, and the emphasis on reason were blamed for bringing the world to the brink of nuclear disaster, so the counterculture stressed intuition and inner feelings over intellect.

New Views

Hippies, as members of the counterculture came to be called, searched for peak moments, or emotional highs, in sex and drugs. Their rejection of more conservative morals against premarital sex, plus the availability of the birth control pill, opened the door to a new era of sexual freedom. These new views attempted to separate sex from love. Some of the flaunting of the new sexuality, such as explicit song lyrics or public nudity, were self-indulgences meant to shock the older generation; however, there was a price to be paid. For example, venereal disease climbed at an alarming rate among young people during the 1960s.

The self-appointed guru, or spiritual leader, of many drug users was Timothy Leary, an academic dropout who experimented with the mind-altering drug lysergic acid diethylamide (LSD). He was fired by Harvard University for violating a pledge not to involve undergraduates in his experiments. Leary then became an advocate of drug use and coined the slogan: Turn on, tune in, drop out.

The use of LSD declined when word got around about its unpleasant side effects, "bad trips," and possible genetic effects. Meanwhile, the smoking of marijuana, also known as grass or pot, increased. In the absence

SECTION FOUR **749**

TEACH

Guided Practice

L1 Discussion During the 1960s many older people saw the United States as a land of opportunity, but many young people felt alienated from society. This resulted in a generation gap. Discuss with students present-day generation-gap issues—about what do they and their parents disagree?

VISUAL INSTRUCTION

Questioning Authority The sunglasses, headbands, beads, long hair, sandals, and flowers popular to the counterculture were in sharp contrast with the more traditional styles of the Establishment—as depicted in the photograph.

Answer: *They grew up during the cold war and felt the world was on the brink of disaster.*

Curriculum Connection

Mathematics In 1955 there were 11,185,000 young people age 15 to 19 in the United States out of a total population of 165,248,000. In 1965, there were 17,052,000 young people in that age group out of a total population of 194,583,000. Ask students to calculate the percentage of young people to the whole population for 1955 (7 percent) and 1965 (9 percent). Then have them discuss the increased influence of young people on society in the 1960s.

Cooperative Learning

Aspects of the Counterculture Organize the class into heterogenous groups. Ask each group to choose and research an aspect of the counterculture such as music, art, fashion, or food. Groups can then gather illustrations, photographs, graphics, artifacts, and so on, to depict their topic—make sure each student takes part. Provide space for a display entitled "The Counterculture."

FYI

Moonie Weddings

Moonies were married in mass wedding ceremonies (for as many as 5,800 couples), known as Blessings. Rev. Moon and his wife presided over the ceremonies. Moonies believed that Blessed couples would have sinless children. The couples and their children would be leaders in a new world order and would be able to enter the Kingdom of Heaven.

VISUAL INSTRUCTION

Age of Aquarius Hippies of the 1960s liked to paint their vehicles with colorful designs, as in the photograph.
Answer: *spirituality*

Sharing Jointly tended gardens and livestock played an important part in many rural communes. Meal preparation was usually rotated among communards—though women often ended up doing food preparation while men tended the gardens and livestock.
Answer: *more than 2,000 rural communes*

of today's scientific evidence of marijuana's dangers, its proponents favorably compared the use of the drug to the older generation's use of alcohol and tobacco. Some marijuana users moved on later to more powerful and more harmful drugs.

New Religious Movements

In their rejection of materialism, many members of the counterculture embraced spirituality. This included a broad range of beliefs, from astrology and magic to Eastern religions and new forms of Christianity. Many of the religious groups centered around charismatic leaders, individuals who possessed remarkable personal appeal. Some of the religious groups had strict rules against drug use and premarital sex. Their centers, therefore, were frequently refuges to young people searching to recapture their lives from drug abuse.

Although not all religious groups were authoritarian in structure, some were. In these groups, the leader dominated others and controlled their lives, sometimes to the point of arranging marriages between members. Religion became the central experience in the believer's life. The authoritarian figure was a sort of parent figure, and believers formed an extended family that took the place of the family into which a member had been born. Some followers seemed to reject many aspects of their previous lives when they entered these groups. This could lead to painful conflicts. Parents accused religious sects of using mind-control methods; some attempted to recapture and deprogram their children. Also at issue was the right to choose one's own religion, even when that religion was at odds with widely held beliefs about individual free will.

Sharing In this New Mexico commune, as in others, members shared food and eating space. *About how many communes existed in 1970?*

Age of Aquarius Counterculture youth often went beyond the boundaries of customary behavior. The use of drugs was one development that troubled older people. *What did many members of the counterculture use to replace materialism?*

Two examples of authoritarian, mind-controlling religious groups that attracted considerable attention beginning in the 1960s were the Unification Church and the Hare Krishna movement. Both were the offspring of established religions, and both were imports from abroad. Members of the Unification Church were popularly known as "Moonies," after their Korean-born founder, the Reverend Sun Myung Moon. He claimed to have had a vision in which Jesus told him that he, Moon, was the next messiah and was charged with restoring the Kingdom of God on Earth. The Hare Krishnas traced their spiritual lineage through Swami Bhaktivedanta, founder of the American sect, to a Hindu sect that began in fifteenth-century India and that worshiped the god Krishna. In dress, diet, worship, and general style of living they tried to emulate Hindu practitioners of another time and place.

Living Arrangements
Young People Live in Groups

Looking at American society in 1967, author Joan Didion wrote:

A dolescents drifted from city to torn city sloughing off both the past and the future as snakes shed their skins, children who were never taught and would never now learn the games that had held the society together.

—Joan Didion,
Slouching Towards Bethlehem, 1967

Meeting Special Needs

Visual Learners Help students who are visual learners determine the main idea of the section by having them look at and think about all the visuals. They should consider the overall impression they get, and they should study details. In pairs, students can discuss what the visuals tell them about the counterculture.

In San Francisco such adolescents gravitated to Haight-Ashbury, a district near Golden Gate Park. In New York City they concentrated in the East Village.

City Hangouts

A common practice was for individuals to organize into groups that shared living quarters, without regard to sex or marital status. Many coffeehouses had a "pad"—a room with a few mattresses on the floor or horizontal space sufficient at least to roll out a sleeping bag—where anyone who wished could "crash" for a night. The Diggers, a loosely formed group in San Francisco, operated a "free store" of used clothing. Something was always happening in the street—a performance by a free theater or an unplanned concert. Drugs were readily available.

Thousands of young people converged on the cities during the summer; some of them were disturbed runaways. City hangouts became crowded. In the fall of 1967 some particularly violent murders shook up everyone. Small groups began retreating to the country, where they formed **communes,** communities that shared property in common.

Rural Communes

The practice of people with similar religious, political, or cultural ideals retreating into the countryside to create their own utopian community has a long tradition in American society. Two highly successful examples were the Shakers, a religious order founded in the 1700s, and the Harmony Society, which lasted from 1804 to 1906.

At the height of the modern commune movement in 1970, the *New York Times* estimated the number of rural communes at more than 2,000, though few of them had more than 30 members. Some held meetings, wrote out bylaws, and discussed the ideal community. Communes such as Twin Oaks near Louisa, Virginia, for example, responded to the new women's liberation movement by eliminating distinctions between women's work and men's work. Any member was as likely to work in the kitchen as in the fields.

Other communes, as one observer noted, searched for "Eden rather than Utopia."

They sought out secluded spots of natural beauty where commune members could act as they wished without disturbing their neighbors. They also praised spontaneity and resisted making decisions, imposing order, or doing anything else that resembled planning or organization.

Community relationships were prized. One member of a Vermont commune described her experience:

> The things that make up community are terribly subtle; it's the little things . . . someone getting his hair cut on the porch, the children around sweeping up the hair, each taking a turn snipping . . . making dinner with a crew once a week, remembering who's a vegetarian and needs a special meal. Expanded consciousness of others . . . nothing big and spectacular. The scenes that move me are the little things about our life together.
>
> —Rosabeth Moss Kanter, *Commitment and Community,* 1971

The problems that arose on the Edenlike communes often stemmed from lack of organization. Without rules regarding visitors and new members, the communes were often overrun by the curious or the "weekend hipster." Privacy was in short supply. So was money, and without an economic base such as a home industry, some residents were forced to work outside the commune to raise cash. Despite the counterculture rhetoric of equality, women were often assigned traditional cooking and child-rearing roles. Nearly all of the communes were short-lived, or changed members frequently.

Marching to a New Beat Drama, color, and public display were important elements of the counterculture. *What kinds of entertainment took place on city streets?*

© GREGG MANCUSO/STOCK BOSTON

VISUAL INSTRUCTION

Marching to a New Beat Young people such as those in the photograph were members of what was known as the "love generation," celebrating love, drama, free thinking, and community.

Answer: *performances by free theaters, concerts*

Independent Practice

L2 **Responding to Music** Encourage students to find and listen to musical recordings by, for example, Bob Dylan, Janis Joplin, Jimi Hendrix, or Jefferson Airplane. Have them write down their impressions.

 Have students complete the Chapter 22, Section 4 Vocabulary and Guided Reading Activity. (Also in Spanish.) **LEP**

FYI

Haight-Ashbury This hippie haven of the late 1960s was known for its ornate Victorian architecture, an easy availability of psychedelic drugs such as marijuana and LSD, and a prevailing mood of love and community. By 1968, however, drug "busts," an influx of outsiders, and increasing heroin use marked the end of the love-in heyday.

Portfolio Project

Interview Have students interview an older grocery-store owner or supermarket manager about the changes in the kinds of foods they have begun to sell in recent years. How might these trends be related to the health food movement that began in the 1960s? Students can write up the results of their interviews and their opinions or reflections and file them in their portfolios. 📓

Notes

_____
_____
_____
_____
_____
_____
_____
_____
_____
_____
_____
_____
_____
_____
_____
_____

Counterculture and the Mainstream
Counterculture Affects the Mainstream

Those whom the counterculture influenced responded in various ways. The radicals rejected mainstream American culture and dropped out for a few years or permanently. The moderates enjoyed aspects of the counterculture such as the music, yet managed to hold down demanding jobs. In cities across the nation some young professionals in the 1960s lived together in familylike urban communes. During the day they practiced law or accounting, and in the evening returned to the house or apartment they shared with like-minded professionals who sought an alternative lifestyle.

While many, if not most, members of the counterculture generation eventually returned to more conventional lifestyles, the mainstream adopted some aspects of the counterculture in a process called **cultural diffusion.** Examples of cultural diffusion can be seen in aspects of the mainstream's diet, fashion, music, and art.

Diet

The rapid growth of health food stores and of vegetarian restaurants across the nation, along with the availability of many new food products, can be credited partly to the counterculture's interest in diet and food production. The back-to-the-land movement made consumers aware of the advantages of stone-ground cereals and organically grown produce. New items in the American diet, such as yogurt and ranch-fed chicken, became available in supermarkets. Environmental concerns prompted people to analyze the economics of feeding a nation on beef as opposed to fish, poultry, or vegetables. Some adopted an exclusively vegetarian diet.

Fashion

The counterculture generation, as one observer of the 1960s noted, dressed in costumes rather than in occupational or class uniforms. The colorful, beaded, braided, patched, and fringed garments that both men

Psychedelic This colorful poster advertises The Yardbirds, The Doors, and others. *What effect did counterculture musicians hope their music would have?*

and women wore turned the fashion industry upside down. The international world of high fashion took its cues from young men and women on the street. Men's clothing became more colorful and women's clothing became more comfortable.

Protest often expressed itself in clothing. The counterculture adopted military surplus attire not only because it was inexpensive, but also because it expressed rejection of materialist values and blurred the lines of social class. For the same reasons, clothing of another age was recycled, and worn-out clothing repaired with patches. A mark of high distinction was to wear a patch that had been patched.

Ethnic clothing was popular for similar reasons. Beads and fringes imitated Native American costumes; tie-dyed shirts borrowed techniques from India and Africa. Ideally, each person created his or her own costume, but specialists became **entrepreneurs**—small-business owners—and sold their products at street fairs and rock concerts.

Perhaps the most potent symbol of the era was hair; a popular 1967 musical about the period was titled, fittingly, *Hair.* Long hair on a young man was the ultimate symbol of defiance. Slogans appeared, such as, Make America beautiful—give a hippie a haircut. School officials debated the acceptable length of a student's hair—could it curl over the collar or not? Once the initial shock wore off, longer hair on men and more individual clothes for both men and women became generally accepted. What was once anti-Establishment clothing was soon mainstream.

Music and Dance

Counterculture musicians hoped that their music—rock and roll—would be the means of toppling the Establishment and reforming society. It did not succeed because rock stars and their music were absorbed into the mainstream where the music brought material success worth billions of dollars to performers, promoters, and record companies.

Rock and roll was an international phenomenon that combined African American music with elements of popular white music. In the early 1950s only African American musicians played rhythm and blues (R & B), a high-energy music that emphasized the beat over the lyrics. When a few African American singers such as

Extending the Content

Communes Brook Farm, a community living project in Massachusetts from 1841 to 1847, had among its members the social reformer Margaret Fuller and the authors Ralph Waldo Emerson and Nathaniel Hawthorne. Hawthorne, in fact, used Brook Farm as a setting for one of his most popular novels, *The Blithedale Romance.* Another kind of collective community is the kibbutzim of Israel. Begun in 1909, there are more than 250 functioning today. Under this system, property is collectively owned and the community is collectively run. Members work in exchange for goods and services such as housing, food, education, and child and medical care.

Chuck Berry and Little Richard began to add lyrics that spoke to the trials and tribulations of adolescents, they created a whole new audience.

Sam Phillips, a Memphis recording engineer, said in 1951, "If I could find a white man who had the Negro sound and the Negro feel, I could make a billion dollars." A few years later he found that man in Elvis Presley. Not only did Presley have the sound and the feel, he also put on an electrifying show, dancing wildly while singing and playing his guitar. Other white performers such as Buddy Holly soon joined Presley in stardom.

Meanwhile, in England, four young men from Liverpool with working-class backgrounds began learning popular music by listening to the recordings of African American musicians. Calling themselves the Beatles, they took England by storm in 1963 and a year later made their American debut on the Ed Sullivan TV show. "Beatlemania" soon swept the country, inspiring many rock and roll imitators.

The final ingredient in the rock and roll mix was the addition of lyrics that spoke to the fears and hopes of the new generation and to the widening rift between the young and their parents. Bob Dylan provided these lyrics, as did the Beatles and many other musicians; while spirited performers like Janis Joplin made songs seem to come alive.

The use of electrically amplified instruments also drastically changed the sound and feel of the new music. One master of this new guitar sound was Jimi Hendrix, a musician from Seattle who lived overseas and achieved stardom only after returning to the United States with the influx of musicians from Great Britain.

At rock festivals such as Woodstock, in August 1969, and Altamont, in December of that same year, hundreds

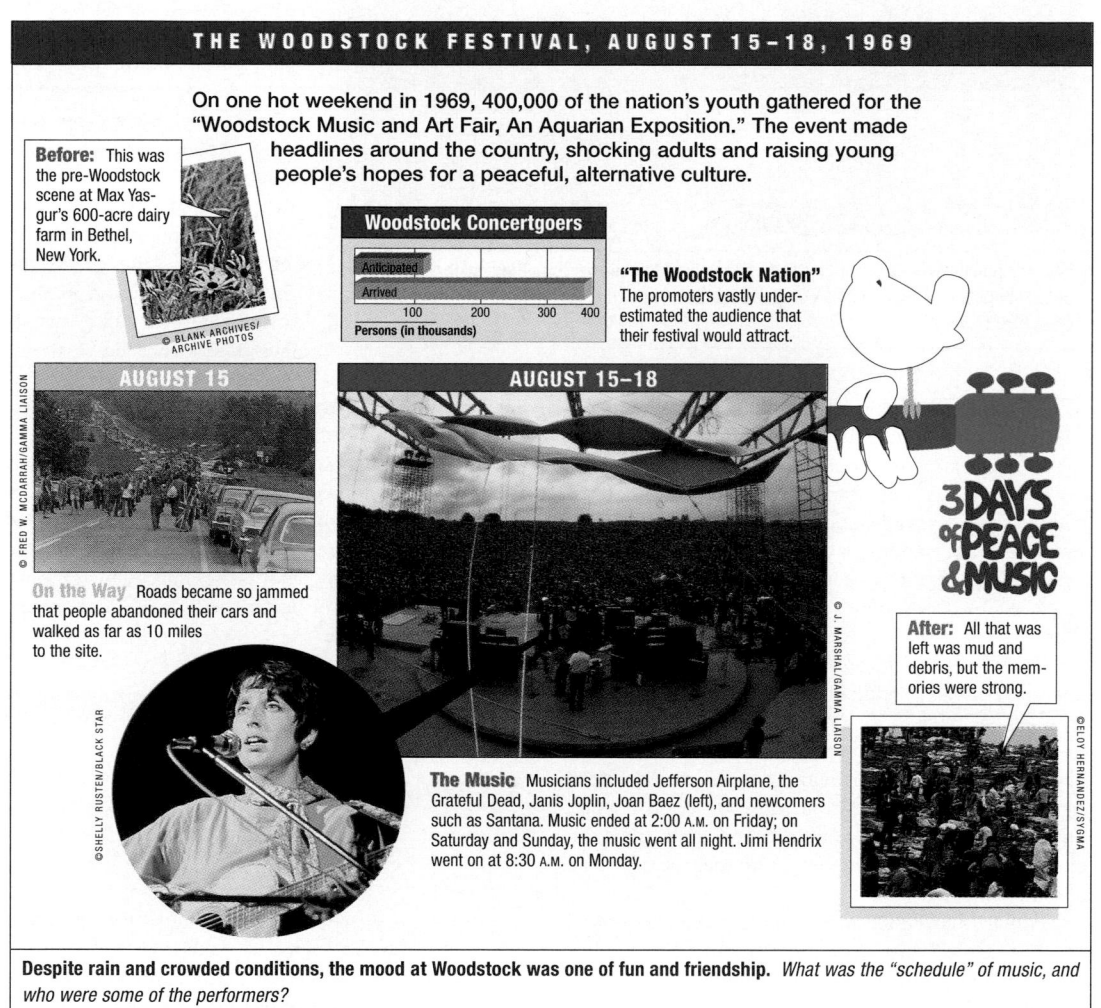

THE WOODSTOCK FESTIVAL, AUGUST 15–18, 1969

On one hot weekend in 1969, 400,000 of the nation's youth gathered for the "Woodstock Music and Art Fair, An Aquarian Exposition." The event made headlines around the country, shocking adults and raising young people's hopes for a peaceful, alternative culture.

Before: This was the pre-Woodstock scene at Max Yasgur's 600-acre dairy farm in Bethel, New York.

Woodstock Concertgoers

"**The Woodstock Nation**" The promoters vastly underestimated the audience that their festival would attract.

AUGUST 15

On the Way Roads became so jammed that people abandoned their cars and walked as far as 10 miles to the site.

AUGUST 15–18

3 DAYS OF PEACE & MUSIC

After: All that was left was mud and debris, but the memories were strong.

The Music Musicians included Jefferson Airplane, the Grateful Dead, Janis Joplin, Joan Baez (left), and newcomers such as Santana. Music ended at 2:00 A.M. on Friday; on Saturday and Sunday, the music went all night. Jimi Hendrix went on at 8:30 A.M. on Monday.

Despite rain and crowded conditions, the mood at Woodstock was one of fun and friendship. *What was the "schedule" of music, and who were some of the performers?*

SECTION FOUR   **753**

GRAPH STUDY

Woodstock Tidbits:
• Most Woodstock festival-goers were white, middle-and upper-middle-class, and between 16 and 30 years old.
• Residents of nearby Monticello made 30,000 sandwiches for festival-goers.
• Musicians stayed in a motel and were flown to and from the concert in helicopters.

Answer: *Schedule: until 2 A.M. Friday; all night Saturday, Sunday; last act, 8:30 A.M. Monday. Performers: Jefferson Airplane, the Grateful Dead, Janis Joplin, Joan Baez, Santana, Jimi Hendrix*

FYI

Beatles In the mid-1960s, the Beatles added a new sense of melody to the strong beat of rock music. They sang and wrote meaningful lyrics that often reflected the social concerns of the time, for example, the 1965 tune "Nowhere Man."

Cultural Perspectives

Ethnic and Period Clothing Counterculture youth liked to borrow clothing styles from other cultures and historical periods. They were especially fond of clothing from cultures that were less involved with mass industry than the United States. In style were colorfully patterned pullover shirts, or dashikis, from Africa; shirts, robes, and full pants with tie-dye, batik, or paisley designs from India and Persia; and clothing with beads, fringes, and feathers, such as Native Americans might wear. Also popular were elegant and opulent designs reflecting the Victorian and Edwardian periods.

ASSESS

Meeting Lesson Objectives

Each section objective is tested by the section review question(s) that follows it in parentheses.

1. Review the beliefs and values of the counterculture movement. (1, 2, 3, 5)

2. Compare communal living in the United States in the past with that of the counterculture in the 1960s and 1970s. (1, 3)

3. Explain the cultural aspects of the counterculture that the rest of society adopted. (1, 4, 5)

VISUAL INSTRUCTION

Pop Art Warhol's art expressed his disdain for materialistic culture.
Answer: *give meaning to, become part of the art*

At the Movies

The Rose, 1979, starring Bette Midler, was loosely based on the personal and professional life and the drug-related death of rock singer Janis Joplin.

History and the Humanities

U.S. History and Art Transparency 26—*Map* by Jasper Johns

Pop Art Andy Warhol's reproductions of images of famous personalities, such as this one of Elizabeth Taylor, made icons out of the familiar. *What role did many pop artists want observers to take?*

such as Marilyn Monroe and Elizabeth Taylor, and repeated them over and over. Warhol also reproduced items such as boxes of household cleaning products, making the pictures as realistic as possible. Roy Lichtenstein used as his inspiration frames from comic strips. He employed the bold primary colors of red, yellow, and black, and in comic book fashion put words like *blam* and *pow* into his paintings.

Robert Rauschenberg incorporated actual objects into his art to break down the distinction between art and reality. A 1955 composition titled "Bed" included a real quilt and pillow. Claes Oldenburg reproduced common, everyday objects such as a three-way electric plug or a toilet bowl in giant scale.

Pop artists expected these symbols of popular culture to carry, as art, some of the same meaning as they did in their original form. The artists sometimes referred to themselves as only the "agents" of

of thousands of people got together to celebrate the new music. Though the fast-paced, energetic beat of rock and roll was made for dancing, the style of dancing had changed dramatically. Each individual danced without a partner, surrounded by others who also danced alone—a perfect metaphor for the counterculture, which stressed individuality within the group.

Art

During the 1960s, one art critic observed, the distinctions between traditional art and popular art, or pop art, dissolved. The primary purpose of pop art seemed to be to entertain. The entertainment, however, had a bite to it—a bite that for many gave the art enormous significance. In poking fun at the established culture, pop artists selected many of the same targets as did the counterculture—for example, a consumer society's love of material possessions.

Pop art derived its subject matter from elements of the popular culture, such as photographs, comics, advertisements, and brand-name products. Artist Andy Warhol, for example, used images of famous people,

the art and said it was up to the observer to give meaning to the work and thus become part of it.

An outgrowth of this philosophy was a new kind of theater staged by pop artists in the 1960s, called a "happening." An artist would set a scene, which differed at each performance, and allow each observer to express his or her reaction to what was presented. The response of the audience became part of the drama, and each performance was unique.

The Counterculture Appraised

Counterculture Expands Consciousness but Takes a Toll

When the music faded away and the crowds at the corner of Haight and Ashbury packed up and returned home, what remained? The young people of the 1960s had forced people all across the country to take a look

Critical Thinking

Making Comparisons With students, discuss today's hairstyles and clothing fashions. Do they reflect a continuation of any of the trends of the 1960s? What messages do today's styles send?

An Inner Adventure

In the last analysis, was the counterculture a real movement? Not in the sense of the other modern efforts at social reform. These other efforts generally worked within the established social system and advocated organized political, legislative, and economic measures to accomplish concrete goals.

Although there were many in the counterculture who chose to effect change by working within the existing social system, there were also those who completely rejected this strategy. Commune members, for example, hoped that their success in establishing new ways for people to live together would encourage others to do the same. Some people were primarily interested in economic reforms, such as better wages and improved working conditions for the poor. Still others were dissatisfied with their lives and found in the symbols of the counterculture—long hair, peace signs, unconventional dress—the security and status of belonging to a group. All in all, many members of the counterculture were more concerned about their own inner adventures than social reform.

There was one issue, however, that had the power to draw together different elements from the counterculture and beyond. This issue was the war in Vietnam. The war itself, in turn, became the dominant issue on the social and political landscape of the United States, an issue that would reshape the nation's self-image in the decades to come.

Feeling the Music Janis Joplin and others used music as a form of self-expression. *In what ways was the counterculture an expression of inner adventure?*

inside themselves for a brief moment and to question some fundamental values about the individual and society. Musical sounds were never the same again; colors were forever brighter.

Dangers and Divisions

On the other hand, casual sex and the use of drugs took their toll. Many plans for social change were never achieved. People learned the hard way that ideals, such as love not war and sharing versus possessing, are not effective unless there is a plan to put them into action. Planning required organization and careful thought, which many rejected as characteristic of the Establishment.

The complications and contradictions in the movement were also apparent in the diversity of its members. Although there were those who were sincerely dedicated to specific goals of social justice for African Americans, women, Native Americans, and Hispanic Americans, even within these groups there were differences in thought and strategy that often undermined their efforts at social change.

SECTION REVIEW

Vocabulary

1. Define: counterculture, generation gap, hippie, commune, cultural diffusion, entrepreneur.

Checking Facts

2. What were the major beliefs and values of the counterculture?

3. Why did urban and rural communal living fail in the counterculture?

Critical Thinking

Synthesizing Information

4. In what ways did the counterculture itself become an "establishment"?

Linking Across Time

5. How did the counterculture help change the way Americans today think about food and diet?

VISUAL INSTRUCTION

Feeling the Music Janis Joplin seemed to express music with her whole body.

Answer: *many youth mostly interested in personal change and changes in consciousness*

Evaluate

Have students complete the Section Review.

☞ 🔘 Assign the Section 4 Quiz or use the Testmaker to develop a customized quiz. (Also in Spanish.) **LEP**

☞ Assign the Chapter 22 Test or use the Testmaker to develop a customized test.

☞ Have students complete the Chapter 22 Performance Assessment Activity.

Reteach

🎧 Have students listen to the Chapter 22, Section 4 Audiocassettes. (Also in Spanish.) **LEP**

Have students complete the Chapter 22 Reteaching Activity. (Also in Spanish.) **LEP**

Enrich

☞ Have students complete the Chapter 22 Enrichment Activity. (Also in Spanish.) **LEP**

CLOSE

Ask: What is your opinion of the effects of the counterculture? *(positive: affected consciousness, clothing, food, music, values; negative: sex, drugs)*

Section 4 Review Answers

1. **counterculture** (749), **generation gap** (749), **hippie** (749), **commune** (751), **cultural diffusion** (752), **entrepreneur** (752)
2. antimaterialism, "doing own thing," feelings over intellect, healthy foods, casual sex, expanded spirituality, more relaxed attitudes
3. violence in the city; lack of organization in rural centers

4. facets of the counterculture became established in the mainstream; the counterculture became part of established culture
5. The focus of the counterculture on healthy foods and diet made the public aware of nutrition and exercise, which has continued to the present.

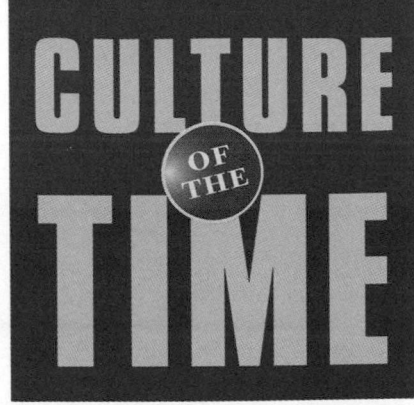

CULTURE
OF
THE
TIME

TEACH

Making the Historical Connection

The movement toward breaking barriers and fighting for equality and reform in the 1960s formed the backdrop for the bright, fast-paced, groundbreaking nature of music and other forms of entertainment. The innovative and flamboyant styles of musicians such as the Beatles and Jimi Hendrix both prompted and reflected the trends of 1960s youth.

Curriculum Connection

Music The early music of the Beatles was influenced by rock artists such as Chuck Berry, Buddy Holly, and the Everly Brothers; the lyrics were often those of simple love songs. The Beatles' later music, however, incorporated complex chord progressions, and the lyrics were relevant to social and cultural issues of the time.

At the Movies

The Beatles starred in two movies: *A Hard Day's Night* (1964) and *Help!* (1965). The full-length cartoon *Yellow Submarine* (1968) featured the Beatles and their music.

756

The Beat of the Sixties

The youth of the 1960s marched to a new beat. The Beatles, Jimi Hendrix, Janis Joplin, the Doors, and others revolutionized music. A nonconformist, optimistic attitude prevailed. Bright colors, flamboyant designs, and long hair decorated the scene. Fast-paced comedy with a political bite sharpened entertainment.

THE GRADUATE
This topical movie comedy reflected both the vulnerability of youth and the **anything-goes attitude** that was prevalent in the 1960s.

THE BEATLES
In the mid-1960s, 4 British rock singers took the United States by storm. Their melodies were complex and their lyrics socially relevant. Millions of youth listened to their music and imitated their optimistic, flamboyant style—**Beatlemania** was born.

756 CULTURE OF THE TIME

Background Information

Jimi Hendrix This talented singer, guitarist, and songwriter was born in 1942 in Seattle, Washington. In his early teens he was very enthused by rhythm and blues and would listen at length to recordings of blues greats such as Muddy Waters. Whenever possible, Hendrix would sit on his back porch with an old guitar and try to play along with the musicians on the recordings. After a stint as an army paratrooper, he moved seriously into music, touring as an instrumentalist with R & B shows. In 1966 Hendrix, now singing as well as playing, moved to England and organized the very successful Jimi Hendrix Experience. In 1967 Hendrix returned to the United States, where he appeared at the Monterey Pop Festival. His highly amplified musicianship and dramatic antics brought him immediate celebrity.

CULTURE OF THE TIME

LAUGH-IN

This **innovative, fast-paced TV comedy** combined sketches, one-liners, and celebrity cameo appearances with sight gags and catch phrases ("Sock it to me," "You bet your bippy") in a loosely structured frenetic whole that was highly appealing to viewers in the late 1960s.

REPRINTED WITH PERMISSION FROM TV GUIDE/1965 ©, NEWS AMERICA PUBLICATIONS, INC.

JIMI HENDRIX

The electric guitar revolutionized music, and Jimi Hendrix revolutionized the electric guitar. His hyper-amplified, magnetic performances of **heavy rock** and **psychedelic blues** were embellished by his flashy outfits and outrageous stage antics—such as smashing or burning his guitar. Hendrix was a gifted rock musician—one of the most innovative of the 1960s.

© ALLAN KOSS/THE IMAGE WORKS

CULTURE OF THE TIME **757**

Portfolio Project

Research Movies such as the Beatles' *A Hard Day's Night* inaugurated new film techniques that became identified with the counterculture of the 1960s (quick cuts, surreal scene changes, slapstick comedy, political humor). Ask students to watch a video of this movie or, if possible, a video including clips from the TV series *Laugh-In*. Have them write a description of the production's unique film style and tell how they think it relates to the beat of the sixties. They can save their descriptions in their portfolios.

Reviewing Key Terms

1. feminist
2. undocumented immigrant
3. compensation
4. generation gap
5. cultural diffusion

Recalling Facts

1. civil rights movement, Friedan's identification of "the problem that had no name," Presidential Commission on the Status of Women
2. Schlafly opposed feminists, ERA; *The Feminine Mystique*, Friedan, identified feminist issues; *Roe* v. *Wade*, abortion rights; ERA, proposed constitutional amendment, equal rights for women
3. constitutional amendment for equal rights; enforcement, Title VII; maternity leave, child care; equal education, job training; abortion rights
4. political, economic reasons; incorporated territories; farm workers, were immigrants
5. took time to unite groups
6. similar: a minority group suffering discrimination; different: on land before white settlers, wanted land back
7. the site of massacre more than 80 years earlier where U.S. troops had killed almost 300 Sioux; in 1973, they gained public attention
8. general: middle-class values and attitudes; specific: inhibitions, materialism, science, technology, reason and intellect, conservative morals
9. sought: idyllic, natural surroundings; unstructured, shared living situations; community; found: little privacy, lack of organization and money, disruption by outside visitors
10. long hair: identification and defiance; rock and roll: spoke to personal, social issues; dance: individuals within group; pop art: criticism of established culture

Reviewing Key Terms

On a separate sheet of paper, write the vocabulary term that best completes each sentence.

generation gap	amendment
compensation	feminist
undocumented immigrant	cultural diffusion

1. Each _____ in the women's liberation movement was striving for equal rights with men.

2. An _____ comes to the United States without paper documents.

3. Native Americans wanted _____ for lands they had lost to the United States government.

4. Differences in opinion between youth and their elders resulted in a _____.

5. Through _____, many aspects of the counterculture became incorporated into the mainstream.

Recalling Facts

1. What were 3 origins of the women's movement of the 1960s?

2. How does each of the following relate to the women's movement: Phyllis Schlafly, *The Feminine Mystique, Roe* v. *Wade*, the ERA?

3. What goals were set for NOW at its first national conference?

4. For what reasons did Hispanic Americans come to the United States?

5. Hispanic Americans are not a single group. How has this diversity affected their attaining civil rights?

6. In what ways were Native American issues similar to and different from the issues of other groups seeking civil rights?

7. Why did Native Americans seize the town of Wounded Knee in 1973? Explain whether their goals were met or not.

8. What general and specific aspects of traditional culture did the counterculture reject?

9. What were people seeking in rural communal living in the 1960s and 1970s? What did they find?

10. What role did the following play in the counterculture: hair style, rock and roll, dance, pop art?

Critical Thinking

1. **Synthesizing Information** In what ways did the civil rights movement affect the women's movement?

2. **Making Generalizations** How does bilingualism for Hispanic Americans relate to self-determination for Native Americans?

3. **Making Comparisons** Below, a Native American woman stands with AIM's Dennis Banks and Clyde Bellecourt. They were involved in the 1973 occupation of Wounded Knee. Compare the methods used by Native Americans, women, and Hispanic Americans to achieve equality.

4. **Recognizing Ideologies** How were the values and goals of the counterculture different from those of women, Hispanic Americans, and Native Americans? In what ways were they similar?

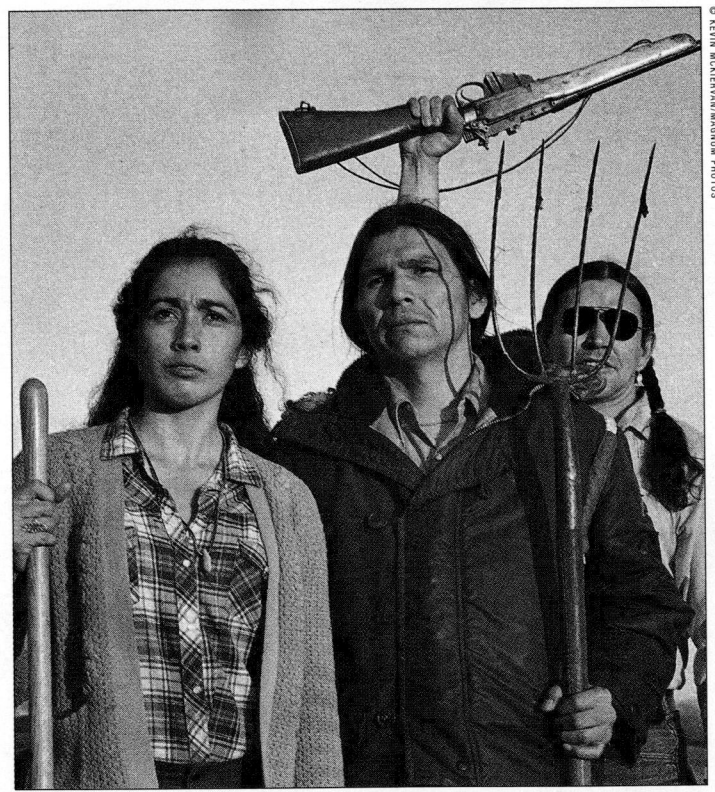

© KEVIN MCKIERNAN/MAGNUM PHOTOS

Critical Thinking

1. encouraged by successes of African Americans; made more aware of own inequality; learned from methods
2. bilingualism can help Hispanic Americans in school; can slow assimilation, which, however, can help preserve own culture; self-determination allows Native Americans control over own lives, not assimilating, preserving cultural values
3. Native Americans used political system, engaged in violent protest; women and Hispanic Americans organized, used political system, engaged in nonviolent protest
4. different: wanted to change, not share in, culture; weren't organized; didn't make economic, political gains; different goals; focus on individual experience within group; similar: wanted to do own thing

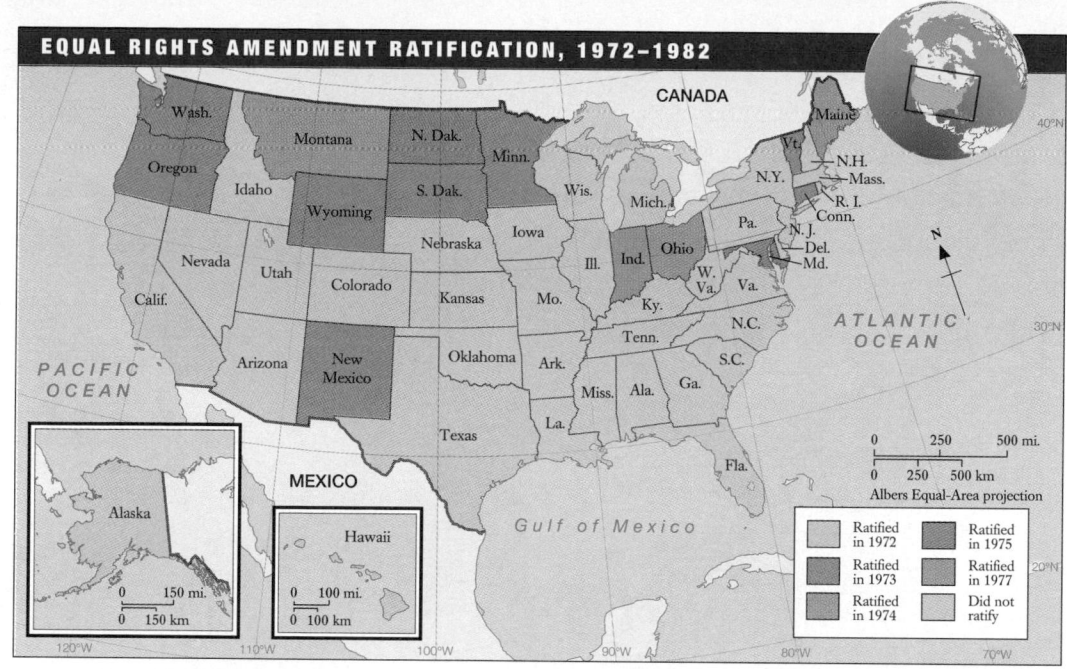

EQUAL RIGHTS AMENDMENT RATIFICATION, 1972–1982

CANADA

PACIFIC OCEAN

ATLANTIC OCEAN

MEXICO

Gulf of Mexico

Alaska

Hawaii

Albers Equal-Area projection

Ratified in 1972
Ratified in 1973
Ratified in 1974
Ratified in 1975
Ratified in 1977
Did not ratify

Portfolio Project

Choose and research one of the reform groups covered in this chapter (women, Hispanic Americans, Native Americans—perhaps even members of the counterculture). What have been the group's successes and failures over the years? Is the group still active today? How has it changed? Does its membership still reflect the same type of people (age, social and economic status, and so on)? What are the group's current problems, issues, or goals? Write a report based on your findings, including copies of photographs, articles, or graphics, if possible. Place the results in your portfolio.

Cooperative Learning

With three or four other students, choose and research one controversial issue mentioned in this chapter—feminism, ERA, abortion, assimilation, bilingualism, restoration of land/sacred sites, for example.

Look at both sides of the issue, and conduct an informal debate within your group, with two or more students representing each point of view.

Reinforcing Skills

Conducting Interviews Gather biographical information that would help you prepare for an interview with Phyllis Schlafly. Use what you find, along with material from the chapter, to develop a list of 10 questions to ask her. The results of your interview might be used as part of a report on feminism and antifeminism in the women's liberation movement of the 1960s and 1970s.

Geography and History

Study the map on this page to answer the following questions:

1. How many states ratified the ERA early, in 1972? In 1973?

2. How many states ratified the ERA from 1974 to 1977?

3. How many states never ratified the ERA?

4. Did your home state ratify the ERA? If so, when?

5. What regional trends do you notice in terms of ratification?

HISTORY JOURNAL

Review your journal response to the photograph on page 723. What new information do you have about the voices of protest of the 1960s and 1970s? Write your response in your journal.

Geography and History

1. 22, 8
2. 5
3. 15
4. Answers will vary.
5. sample: many states in South never ratified; Northeast ratified early; other regions mixed

History Journal

Students' responses should reflect an understanding of the goals and methods of the four groups discussed in this chapter: women, Hispanic Americans, Native Americans, and counterculture youth.

? BONUS QUESTION

This question may be used for extra credit on the chapter test.

For what was each of these groups voicing protest: women, Hispanic Americans, Native Americans, counterculture youth?

Answer: *(equality with men; political and economic rights; civil rights and compensation for lost land; a change in traditional culture)*

Portfolio Project

Students' reports should include specific examples of the group's activities. Reports may be presented orally.

Cooperative Learning

Students should choose the issue as a group. Group members can then split into two teams to research and debate the two sides of the issue. Make sure each group has a moderator to structure the debate. All students should play some part.

Reinforcing Skills

Students' questions should incorporate the information listed and suggestions given in items b and c on page 732.

TEACH

Making the Historical Connection

The postwar prosperity of the 1950s set the stage for the popularity of fast-food restaurants, with their promise of immediate gratification and reasonably high quality food. McDonald's was one of the first and most popular fast-food chains.

FYI

Ronald McDonald Houses McDonald's does more than just serve food. Ronald McDonald Houses are homes away from home for families of children being treated for serious illnesses at nearby hospitals. The houses are supported by local McDonald franchisees, hospital administrators, doctors, and parent volunteer groups. There are approximately 150 Ronald McDonald Houses across the United States.

Then...

The First McDonald's

In 1955 Ray Kroc, a 53-year-old milkshake-mixer salesman, acquired franchising rights from Maurice and Richard McDonald, owners of a successful hamburger restaurant franchise. The detail-oriented Kroc followed the menu and the food-processing method of the original McDonald's—and created an empire.

2 McDonald's employees follow set procedures for food preparation and presentation, established by the McDonald brothers and refined over the years.

1 This restaurant, with the now-famous golden arches, was typical of McDonald's in the 1950s.

Fun Facts

© McDONALD'S CORPORATION

RONALD McDONALD
Ronald McDonald made his first public appearance in 1963 in Washington, D.C. Ronald was played by Willard Scott, who later became the weatherperson on NBC's *Today Show*.

Background Information

A Family Restaurant Early on Ray Kroc designed his restaurants specifically to attract middle-class families and to discourage youthful loitering. Unlike some restaurants that encouraged hanging out, the clean and well-lit McDonald's restaurants had no jukeboxes, telephone booths, pinball machines, cigarette machines, or newsstands.

3 McDonald's Original Menu Items and Prices

Hamburger	15¢
Cheeseburger	19¢
French Fries	10¢
Milk	10¢
Milk Shake	10¢
Root Beer	10¢
Orangeade	10¢
Coca-Cola	10¢
Coffee	10¢

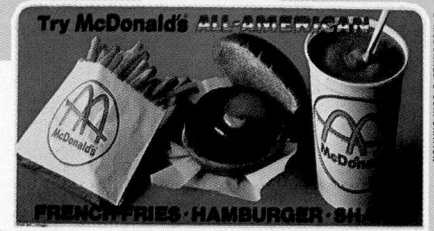

© MCDONALD'S CORPORATION

4 This cheerful, winking fellow is Speedee, an early McDonald's symbol.

© MCDONALD'S CORPORATION

© MCDONALD'S CORPORATION

...Now

McFacts

1955 Ray Kroc acquires franchising rights to McDonald's

1955 "Speedee" becomes company symbol

1961 Ray Kroc buys McDonald's name for $2.7 million

1963 Ronald McDonald makes his debut

1967 First McDonald's restaurants outside U.S. open, in Canada and Puerto Rico

1968 Big Mac is introduced

1972 McDonald's becomes a billion-dollar corporation

1973 McDonald's makes the cover of *Time* magazine

1975 First drive-through opens, in Oklahoma City, Oklahoma

1986 Complete food product ingredient listing is introduced

1990 Foam packaging is phased out

1993 McDonald's is in 69 countries; 95 billion+ hamburgers sold

1995 McDonald's opens franchises in Estonia, Romania, Malta, Colombia, Jamaica, and Slovakia

IMPACT OF FAST FOOD

PORTFOLIO PROJECT

Write a one-page magazine article on how fast-food restaurants such as McDonald's affect what and how teenagers eat today. Gather information from library resources, from your own experiences, and from talking with others. You may want to include suggestions for future fast-food establishments. Place the article in your portfolio.

RONALD'S FRIENDS

Ronald has many friends in McDonaldland, all of whom like and respect him. Some of Ronald's friends are Hamburglar, Grimace, Birdie the Early Bird, The Fry Kids, The Happy Meal Guys, CosMc, McNugget Buddies, Mayor McCheese, The Professor, The Captain, and Uncle O'Grimacy.

© MCDONALD'S CORPORATION

 Block Scheduling

The Portfolio Project on this page provides an excellent opportunity to enrich and extend the key elements of this feature.

FYI

Updating the Menu
Though the McDonald's menu remains relatively constant, items have been added over the years in response to changing customer tastes. Menu additions include Filet-O-Fish, 1963; Big Mac, 1968; Quarter Pounder, 1972; Egg McMuffin, 1973; complete breakfast line, 1977; Chicken McNuggets, 1983; salads, 1987; McChicken, 1989; low-fat frozen yogurt, 1990; McLean Deluxe, 1991; McGrilled Chicken, 1995.

CLOSE

Ask: Who was Ray Kroc? *(bought, expanded McDonald's)* Name some McDonald's symbols. *(Speedee, arches, Ronald McDonald)* How many countries have McDonald's? *(69+)*

PORTFOLIO PROJECT

Portfolio Project

The Story Behind the Business This feature gives a broad overview of the growth of McDonald's under Ray Kroc's leadership. Invite students to research in depth the story of McDonald's or of another business—local, national, or international. They can prepare a report, telling the story of the company from inception to the present day, including charts, graphs, photographs, and illustrations, if possible. Allow class time for presentations, and invite students to file their written reports in their portfolios.

The Unit at a Glance

Chapter 23
The United States escalated its role in Vietnam from economic supporter to military combatant. As losses in the Vietnam War mounted, disillusionment grew and antiwar protest flamed.

Chapter 24
In the 1968 election, conservatives overwhelmed liberals. President Nixon pursued a policy of détente and eventually withdrew all troops from Vietnam by 1973. The Watergate scandal led to his resignation in 1974. The remaining years of the decade brought a dimming of United States economic power and status and strength abroad.

Introducing the Unit

Show students the Unit 9 Time Line Transparency and/or assign the accompanying activity sheet. Tell students that the time frame of Unit 9 overlaps that of Unit 8, since both include the 1960s through the 1970s. Ask them to recall major themes and events from Unit 8 and discuss how they relate to the title of Unit 9—The Troubled Years.

Out of Time?

If time does not permit teaching every chapter in this unit, use the Chapter Digest Audiocassettes and the accompanying student activities and tests. The Chapter Digest Audiocassettes are available in Spanish.

UNIT

9

The Troubled Years

CHAPTER 23
The Vietnam War

CHAPTER 24
From Nixon to Carter

762

Portfolio Project

Interview Have students interview someone who was growing up or was an adult during the late 1960s and 1970s. Interviews should center on finding out why this era is often known as the troubled years. Students should ask about their respondents' impressions of the decade and prepare a transcript of the interview to include in their portfolios. Encourage students who have access to a cassette recorder or video camera to tape the interview and include the tape in their portfolios.

ABCNEWS INTERACTIVE™

 Videodisc

Powers of the President

Side 1, Chapter 36
Title: Military Buildup
Subject: Using the Vietnam War as an example of the President's role as commander in chief of the military
Ask: What power does the President have over the military *(commander in chief)*

See Powers of the President Guidebook page 44 for complete lesson plan.

GLENCOE TECHNOLOGY

 Videodisc

The American History Videodisc

Side 2
Title: Vietnam
Subject: Sequences concerning Vietnam
Ask: Why did the United States become involved in Vietnam? *(to protect the area from communism)*

Examining the Visual

A Young Soldier Private First Class Phillip Wilson carries a rocket launcher across a stream in the demilitarized zone in 1966. He was killed a few days later. The five-mile-wide zone was established between North and South Vietnam as an area where no military action was to be permitted.

LITERATURE

TEACH

Making the Historical Connection

The social protests of the early 1960s empowered many Americans. When the United States became involved in the Vietnam War, therefore, people readily expressed their opposition. The war became an issue that involved all Americans, deeply dividing the country. As a result, everyone who lived through the period became a veteran of the war. The literature selection presents the viewpoint of one such veteran.

VISUAL INSTRUCTION

Three Flags In its use of the American flag as an icon, *Three Flags* (1958) heralds the transition to pop art, in which familiar items are treated as aesthetic objects. Later, during the 1960s, some artists used national symbols, such as the flag and war medals, to question why people had to die to defend them. Ask students where else they may have seen familiar items used as aesthetic objects.

Born
ON THE
Fourth of July

BY RON KOVIC

Some Americans tried to end the Vietnam War by protesting at home. Others went to fight in Vietnam. After being shot and permanently paralyzed in Vietnam, Ron Kovic began to question the war effort. This excerpt from his personal narrative shows how Kovic's experience at a peace rally in Washington, D.C., helped him decide to join the antiwar movement.

A young girl sat down next to me and handed me a canteen of cool water. "Here," she said, "have a drink." I drank it down and passed it to Skip who passed it to someone else. That was the feeling that day. We all seemed to be sharing everything.

We listened as the speakers one after another denounced the invasion of Cambodia and the slaying of the students at Kent State. The sun was getting very hot and Skip and I decided to move around. We wanted to get to the White House where Nixon was holed up, probably watching television. We were in a great sea of people, thousands and thousands all around us. We

Three Flags Jasper Johns and other pop artists incorporated everyday objects into their paintings and sculptures. Johns's *Three Flags* (1958) invites viewers to question their feelings about the American flag.

COLLECTION OF WHITNEY MUSEUM OF AMERICAN ART, NY. PHOTOGRAPHY BY GEOFFREY CLEMENTS, NY.

finally made it to Lafayette Park. On the other side of the avenue the government had lined up thirty or forty buses, making a huge wall between the people and the White House. I remember wondering back then why they had to put all those buses in front of the president. Was the government so afraid of its own people that it needed such a gigantic barricade? I'll always remember those buses lined up that day and not being able to see the White House from my wheelchair.

We went back to the rally for a while, then went on down to the Reflecting Pool. Hundreds of people had taken off their clothes. They were jumping up and

Background Information

Vietnam Remembered Celebrations and parades marked the end of World War II. Because most Americans wished to forget about the Vietnam War, no such festivities were held at its conclusion. As a result, many Vietnam veterans felt that their experience had been denied by the nation. Finally, nearly nine years after the end of the war, the Vietnam Veteran's Memorial was constructed. This monument helped Americans come to terms with the war and grieve for their dead. Some veterans felt able to describe their experiences for the first time. Among them was veteran Ron Kovic, whose autobiography, *Born on the Fourth of July,* became a major motion picture.

down to the beat of bongo drums and metal cans. A man in his fifties had stripped completely naked. Wearing only a crazy-looking hat and a pair of enormous black glasses, he was dancing on a platform in the middle of hundreds of naked people. The crowd was clapping wildly. Skip hesitated for a moment, then stripped all his clothes off, jumping into the pool and joining the rest of the people. I didn't know what all of this had to do with the invasion of Cambodia or the students slain at Kent State, but it was total freedom. As I sat there in my wheelchair at the edge of the Reflecting Pool with everyone running naked all around me and the clapping and the drums resounding in my ears, I wanted to join them. I wanted to take off my clothes like Skip and the rest of them and wade into the pool and rub my body with all those others. Everything seemed to be hitting me all at once. One part of me was upset that people were swimming naked in the national monument and the other part of me completely understood that now it was their pool, and what good is a pool if you can't swim in it.

> ## I WANTED TO SHOUT BACK AT THE CHARGING POLICE, TELL THEM I WAS A VETERAN.

I remember how the police came later that day, very suddenly, when we were watching the sun go down—a blue legion of police in cars and on motorcycles and others with angry faces on big horses. A tall cop walked into the crowd near the Reflecting Pool and read something into a bullhorn no one could make out. The drums stopped and a few of the naked people began to put their clothes back on. It was almost evening and with most of the invading army's forces heading back along the Jersey Turnpike, the blue legion had decided to attack. And they did—wading their horses into the pool, flailing their clubs, smashing skulls. People were running everywhere as gas canisters began to pop. I couldn't understand why this was happening, why the police would attack the people, running them into the grass with their horses and beating them with their

clubs. Two or three horses charged into the crowd at full gallop, driving the invading army into retreat toward the Lincoln Memorial. A girl was crying and screaming, trying to help her bleeding friend. She was yelling something about the pigs and kept stepping backward away from the horses and the flying clubs. For the first time that day I felt anger surge up inside me. I was no longer an observer, sitting in my car at the edge of a demonstration. I was right in the middle of it and it was ugly. Skip started pushing the chair as fast as he could up the path toward the Lincoln Memorial. I kept turning, looking back. I wanted to shout back at the charging police, tell them I was a veteran. When we got to the memorial, I remember looking at Lincoln's face and reading the words carved on the walls in back of him. I felt certain that if he were alive he would be there with us.

I told Skip that I was never going to be the same. The demonstration had stirred something in my mind that would be there from now on. It was so very different from boot camp and fighting in the war. There was a togetherness, just as there had been in Vietnam, but it was a togetherness of a different kind of people and for a much different reason. In the war we were killing and maiming people. In Washington on that Saturday afternoon in May we were trying to heal them and set them free.

RESPONDING TO LITERATURE

1. **What do you think contributed most to changing Ron Kovic's attitude about the Vietnam War?**

2. **If you had been a teenager during the Vietnam War, what do you think your attitudes toward the war and war protesters might have been? Why?**

At the Movies

The film version of *Born on the Fourth of July* starred Tom Cruise. Its director, Oliver Stone, won the 1989 Academy Award for best director. Other films about Vietnam include *Platoon, Good Morning Vietnam, Coming Home, Apocalypse Now,* and *The Deer Hunter.*

Block Scheduling

Team Teaching This excerpt from *Born on the Fourth of July* can be presented in a team teaching context, in conjunction with English or Language Arts.

CLOSE

Ask students to imagine that they had been American soldiers in Vietnam. How would they have felt about the war protesters? If they had been antiwar demonstrators, how would they have felt about the veterans? *(Either group could feel sympathy, or anger and resentment.)*

Responding to Literature Answers

1. The feeling of togetherness generated by the people who had gathered in Washington, D.C., to help heal people and set them free from the pain of the war.

2. Answers will vary. Some students may believe the war was necessary and that it should have been fought to victory. Others may believe the cost was too great and that the Vietnamese should have fought their own war. Some students may claim that the war protesters betrayed their country. Others may argue that the protesters were patriots, striving to uphold American ideals.

The Vietnam War

DAILY LESSON OBJECTIVES	REPRODUCIBLE RESOURCES	MULTIMEDIA RESOURCES
SECTION 1 War in Southeast Asia 1. Understand why the Vietnamese wanted a Communist government. 2. Explain why the United States feared communism in Asia. 3. Analyze why the United States sent the military into Vietnam. 4. Describe why the United States did not defeat the Vietcong guerrillas	Reproducible Lesson Plans Vocabulary and Guided Reading Activities (English or Spanish) Cooperative Learning Activities Great Debates in American History American Literature Readings and Activities Geography in History Activities Section Quizzes (English or Spanish)	Chapter Teaching Transparencies Section Focus Transparencies Map Tranparencies Powers of the President Landmark Documents in American History Student Self-Test: A Software Review Testmaker
SECTION 2 1968: A Year of Crises 1. Demonstrate what made the Tet offensive a turning point. 2. Demonstrate the domestic trauma caused by the assassinations of King and Kennedy 3. Discuss how 1968 was a pivotal years in American politics.	Reproducible Lesson Plans Vocabulary and Guided Reading Activities (English or Spanish) Case Studies American Literature Readings and Activities Section Quizzes (English or Spanish)	Section Focus Transparencies Landmark Documents in American History Student Self-Test: A Software Review Testmaker
SECTION 3 The War at Home 1. Explain the origins and evolution of the student protest movement. 2. Describe the emergence of the antiwar movement from the student movement. 3. Analyze the role of the media in shaping public opinion about the war in Vietnam.	Reproducible Lesson Plans Vocabulary and Guided Reading Activities (English or Spanish) Skill Reinforcement Activities Supreme Court Case Studies Section Quizzes (English or Spanish)	Section Focus Transparencies Powers of the President Landmark Documents in American History Powers of the Supreme Court. Student Self-Test: A Software Review Testmaker
SECTION 4 Ending the War 1. Identify the steps Nixon took to end the war in Vietnam. 2. Examine the results of Nixon's war strategy. 3. Understand the reactions in the United States as the war went on. 4. Understand the real costs of the Vietnam War.	Reproducible Lesson Plans Vocabulary and Guided Reading Activities (English or Spanish) Reteaching Activities (English or Spanish) Enrichment Activities (English or Spanish) Supreme Court Case Studies Section Quizzes (English or Spanish)	Section Focus Transparencies Landmark Documents in American History Student Self-Test: A Software Review Testmaker
CHAPTER REVIEW AND EVALUATION	Chapter 23 Test, Forms A and B Performance Assessment Strategies and Activities	Student Self-Test: A Software Review Testmaker Vocabulary PuzzleMaker Chapter Digests Audiocassettes

 If time does not permit teaching the entire chapter, summarize using the Chapter 23 Digests Audiocassettes and the accompanying activities and tests. (Available in English or Spanish.)

Cooperative Project

Organize the class into small groups. Have each group use tracing paper to make a map of Indochina showing Laos, Cambodia, and Vietnam. Have students label the map using the map of Inchochina on page 769 as a guide. Post the maps around the classroom and have students refer to them as they study this chapter. **LEP** 🔲

Suggested Rubric: A Map. See Performance Assessment Strategies and Activities, p. 27.

Individual Project

Have students use the descriptions in Section 1 The Ground War and the Endless War, as the basis for writing a letter home from an imaginery person in the United States military to his or her family or friends. Make it clear to students that while they make include their opinions of the war in the letter, they should be accurate in their use of details found in the chapter. 🔲

Suggested Rubric: A Journal. See Performance Assessment Strategies and Activities, p. 29.

Key to Ability Levels

Teaching strategies have been coded for varying learning styles and abilities.

L1 **BASIC** activities for all students

L2 **AVERAGE** activities for average to above-average students

L3 **CHALLENGING** activities for above-average students

LEP **LIMITED ENGLISH PROFICIENCY** activities

Block Scheduling

Block scheduling differs from traditional class scheduling in the amount of time allotted to each period. The extended timeframe provided by block scheduling affords you the opportunity to implement a greater number of research-oriented and activity-intense projects to motivate and involve your students. Activities that are particularly suited to use within the block scheduling framework are identified throughout this chapter by the following designation. 🔲

TEACHER'S CORNER

NATIONAL GEOGRAPHIC SOCIETY

INDEX TO NATIONAL GEOGRAPHIC MAGAZINE

The following articles may be used for research relating to this chapter:

- "The Mekong," by Thomas O'Neill, February 1993.
- "Hong Kong—Plight of the Boat People," by Larry Kohl, February 1991.
- *Vietnam: The Hard Road to Peace* (A Special Edition), November 1989.

NATIONAL GEOGRAPHIC SOCIETY PRODUCTS AVAILABLE FROM GLENCOE

To order the following products for use with this chapter, contact your local Glencoe sales representative or call Glencoe at 1-800-334-7344:

- *The Presidents: A Picture History of Our Nation* (CD-ROM)
- *GTV: The American People: Fabric of a Nation* (Videodisc)
- *GTV: A Geographic Perspective on American History* (Videodisc)

ADDITIONAL NATIONAL GEOGRAPHIC SOCIETY PRODUCTS

To order the following products for use with this chapter, call National Geographic Society at 1-800-368-2728:

- *Decades of History: The 20th Century—The Middle Years* (Filmstrip)
- *The American Presidency* (Filmstrip)
- *The Vietnam War* (Filmstrip)
- *The Changing Faces of Communism Series:* Vietnam. (Filmstrip)
- *The United States as a World Power: From the 1890s to the 1970s* (Filmstrip)
- *1945-1989: The Cold War* (Video)

Chapter Overview

United States involvement in the war in Vietnam was the result of applying cold war policies and ideas to a war of national liberation. Involvement in the war greatly changed the spirit and mood of the United States.

Introducing the Chapter

Point out to students that the Vietnam War was one of the most divisive in the history of the United States. One of the most significant assaults of the war was the Tet offensive in 1968. Have students read the narrative on this page about the offensive.

Display the Chapter Teaching Transparency, and distribute copies of the activity sheet. After students have completed the activities, explain that Tet was a turning point because Americans began to doubt whether the United States could win the war.

Extension Activity

Have students complete Beyond the Transparency on the activity sheet for Chapter 23 and present their projects after the class has completed the chapter.

History Journal

Have students investigate an incident of domestic turmoil connected with the war and write a brief synopsis in their journals.

CHAPTER
23

The Vietnam War

It was nearly 3 A.M. on the first night of Tet, the Vietnamese New Year. A small truck and a taxicab filled with Vietcong guerrillas rolled through the quiet city streets. As they turned onto Thong Nhut Boulevard, a broad, tree-lined avenue that ran past the American embassy, the guerrillas opened fire.

Two United States soldiers inside the embassy grounds returned the fire. One soldier, 23-year-old Charles Daniel, shouted: "They're coming in! They're coming in! Help me! Help me!" Moments later Daniel and his companion, 20-year-old William Sebast, lay dead.

Thus began a bloody 6-hour assault on the United States embassy in Saigon, the capital of South Vietnam. When the fighting was over, 19 guerrillas and 5 American soldiers had lost their lives. According to one reporter, the embassy grounds looked like "a butcher shop in Eden."

By 1968 United States troops had been fighting for 3 years. Policy makers saw Vietnam as a battle to prevent the spread of communism in Southeast Asia. In pursuing this policy of containment, the United States had become entangled in a tragic war thousands of miles from its shore.

This would be the nation's longest war, claiming the lives of more than 58,000 United States soldiers and more than 2 million Vietnamese. It would leave Southeast Asia in ruins and divide American society as had no other issue since the Civil War. ■

HISTORY JOURNAL

Before you read the rest of this chapter, write briefly what you know about the domestic turmoil caused by the war in Vietnam and what you think this chapter will tell you about the war.

766

 EXTRA CREDIT PROJECT

Create a Map Have students construct a detailed map of one of the military campaigns of the Vietnam War. Suggest that they use one of these campaigns: Dien Bien Phu, the Tet offensive, or Operation Rolling Thunder. Remind students that useful maps have clear labels and keys. Encourage them to use color to make distinctions clear.

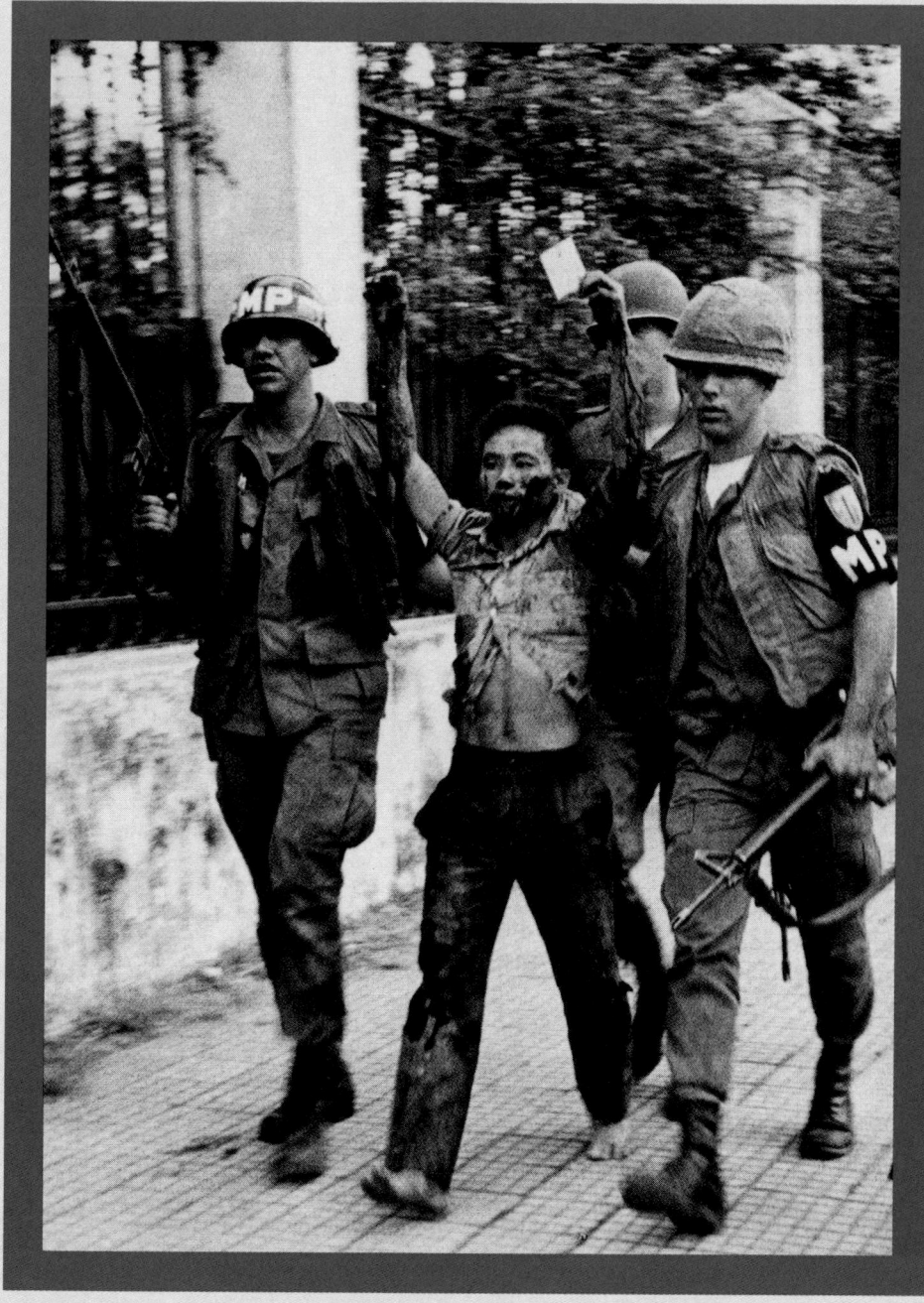

A SURVIVING MEMBER OF THE GUERRILLA
TEAM THAT ATTACKED THE UNITED STATES
EMBASSY IN SAIGON IS LED AWAY.

767

 Videodisc

*Communism and
the Cold War*

Side 2, Chapter 8
Title: The Vietnam War
Subject: Summary of
the Vietnam War
Ask: How was Vietnam
divided after 1954? *(into
North Vietnam and South
Vietnam)*

**See Communism and
the Cold War Guide-
book page 56 for com-
plete lesson plan.**

 **Performance
Assessment**

Refer to page 766B for
performance assessment
activities for this chapter.

☞ Also see Activity 23
in the Performance
Assessment Strategies
and Activities for an
additional activity as well
as for suggested rubrics.
📁

Examining the Visual

Embassy Attack The Communists used
thirty-five battalions in their attack against
Saigon and the surrounding area during the Tet
offensive. The highly trained Vietcong C-10
Sapper Battalion attacked the presidential
palace, the ARVN Joint General Staff headquarters, the national radio station, and the
United States embassy compound. A 10-man
sapper squad occupied the embassy grounds
for 6 hours that night. They were later killed or
captured by an assault force of United States
paratroopers.

SECTION
1

FOCUS

Section Objectives

1. Understand why most of the Vietnamese wanted a Communist government.
2. Explain what the United States feared would happen if Communists took control of Vietnam.
3. Analyze the reasons why the United States brought military forces into Vietnam.
4. Describe why the United States was unable to defeat the Vietcong guerrillas.

Bellringer Activity

While taking attendance at the beginning of the class period, display **Section Focus Transparency 72**, and have students answer the questions. (Or use the blackline master.)

VISUAL INSTRUCTION

Independence Ho Chi MInh, real name Nguyen That Thanh, was born in central Vietnam in 1892. As a revolutionary leader, he often had to assume aliases and disguises to evade his enemies. *Ho Chi MInh* means "he who enlightens."

Ask: From whom did Ho declare independence? *(The Vietminh were declaring their independence from the French.)*

War in Southeast Asia

SEPTEMBER 2, 1945: VIETNAM DECLARES ITS INDEPENDENCE

Independence
Ho Chi Minh makes an appeal to the United States for support.

HALF A MILLION VIETNAMESE FILLED BA DINH SQUARE IN CENTRAL HANOI. Peasants in straw hats, many of whom had come on foot from distant villages, mingled with Hanoi residents on the grassy square. At noon a frail figure with piercing black eyes and a wispy black beard climbed onto a wooden platform set up at one end of the square. He was Ho Chi Minh, the 55-year-old leader of the Vietnamese nationalist force known as the Vietminh. The crowd began chanting, "Doc-Lap, Doc-Lap" ("independence, independence"). For several minutes Ho stood there smiling, buoyed by the crowd's enthusiasm. Finally he raised his hands, and the crowd grew still.

"We hold these truths to be self-evident, that all men are created equal, that they are endowed by their creator with certain unalienable rights, among them life, liberty, and the pursuit of happiness." With those words borrowed from the American Declaration of Independence, Ho proclaimed the independence of Vietnam from French colonial rule. The crowd roared its approval.

Later in the day, United States Army officers joined Vietnamese leaders to celebrate Vietnam's liberation. During World War II Japan had occupied Vietnam. The Americans and the Vietminh had fought side by side to drive out the Japanese. When the Japanese surrendered in August 1945, the Vietminh took over the capital of Hanoi and declared Vietnam independent.

Yet the warm friendship of that September day soon chilled, as Vietnam became a battleground in the cold war that followed World War II. In just 20 years, Vietnamese nationalists and the United States would become bitter enemies, embroiled in war.

AS YOU READ

Vocabulary
► national liberation
► containment
► domino theory
► guerrilla warfare
► pacification program

Think About . . .
► why most Vietnamese wanted a Communist form of government.
► what the United States feared would happen if Communists took control of Vietnam.
► why the United States introduced military forces into Vietnam.
► why the United States was unable to defeat the Vietcong guerrillas.

768 CHAPTER 23 THE VIETNAM WAR

Section 1 Resources

REPRODUCIBLE RESOURCES

📁 Lesson Plan 23-1
📁 Vocabulary and Guided Reading Activity 23-1
📁 Cooperative Learning Activity 23
📁 Unit 9 Great Debate
📁 Section 1 Quiz

📁 Unit 9 American Literature Reading
📁 Geography in History Activity 23

MULTIMEDIA RESOURCES

📖 Section Focus Transparency 72
📖 Map Transparency 23
📖 Chapter Teaching Transparency 23

🔵 Landmark Documents in American History
🔵 Powers of the President
🔲 Testmaker
🎧 Chapter 23 Digest Audiocassette
💿 Student Self-Test: A Software Review

The French War in Indochina

Ho Chi Minh Leads Vietminh Against the French

Although the Vietnamese had declared their independence, the French were unwilling to give up the empire they had ruled for more than 60 years. The colonies in Indochina—the present-day nations of Cambodia, Laos, and Vietnam—were among the richest of France's overseas colonies, supplying such valuable resources as rice, rubber, and tin.

The French, however, faced a powerful foe in Ho Chi Minh. Ho was a staunch, and at times ruthless, revolutionary committed to the struggle for Vietnamese independence. Ho founded the Vietminh in 1941 to drive the French from Vietnam. Like Ho, most Vietminh leaders were committed Communists. Their primary goals were extensive land reform and the creation of an independent unified Vietnam. They were waging a war of **national liberation** to free their country from foreign control.

By 1945 the Vietminh army numbered 5,000 and had a firm base of support in northern Vietnam. The French, meanwhile, tried to regain control of southern Vietnam as the Japanese withdrew. Tensions mounted, and fighting broke out between the French and the Vietminh. In November 1946, a French ship shelled the city of Haiphong, setting off a full-scale war.

The French entered the war confident of victory. Ho, however, predicted a different outcome. "If ever the tiger [the Vietminh] pauses," he said, "the elephant [France] will impale him on his mighty tusks. But the tiger will not pause, and the elephant will die of exhaustion and loss of blood."

The French soon controlled the major cities and towns, while the Vietminh retreated into the countryside. There they waged a relentless war—avoiding major battles, ambushing French troops, and staging hit-and-run raids on French outposts—while building support among the peasants.

United States Support for the French

In 1950 the French, unable to crush the Vietminh, appealed to Washington, D.C., for aid. President Truman was not eager to support France's colonial ambitions. Yet the cold war had increased tensions in Europe. Truman was afraid to lose France as an ally against the Soviets, who in August 1949 had exploded their first atomic bomb.

Also Indochina had assumed a new importance. The Communist victory in China in 1949 fed American fears of Communist takeovers elsewhere in Asia.

If the United States failed to stop communism in Indochina, Truman believed, it would sweep across the rest of Asia. The United States policy of **containment**—opposing communism wherever it appeared in an effort to "contain" its spread—would pull the United States closer to war in Southeast Asia.

In 1950, just before the outbreak of the Korean War, Truman agreed to send $20 million in direct military aid to the French. Over the next 4 years, the United States paid for most of the French war effort, pumping more than $2.6 billion into the French attempt to "save" Vietnam from communism.

VIETNAM, 1954–1967

The division of Vietnam left the North without its main source of rice in the South. Emergency imports from Burma prevented a famine. *What United States military base is located near the partition line between North and South Vietnam?*

SECTION ONE **769**

TEACH

Guided Practice

L2 Discussion Have a student read the excerpt from Ho Chi Minh's speech on page 768. Ask students why they think he used words borrowed from the American Declaration of Independence in the Vietnamese Declaration of Independence.

Show students Map Transparency 23 and have them complete the activity sheet.

FYI

Dien Bien Phu The battle of Dien Bien Phu was a disastrous defeat for the French. The 12,000 French forces greatly underestimated the strength of the Vietminh.

MAP STUDY

Ask students to analyze the map of Vietnam. Point out how close Vietnam is to Communist China and how that influenced the decision of the United States to support the French.
Answer: *Khesanh*

Cooperative Learning

Peace Conference Organize the class into 8 groups. Inform the groups that they are to represent countries that met in Geneva in 1954 to draft a peace agreement between the French and the Vietminh. One group should represent each of the following: Great Britain, the United States, France, the Soviet Union, China, Laos, Cambodia, and the Vietminh. Have each group research its position. Groups should present their findings as if they were at the peace conference.

Facts on File

Landmark Documents in American History Have students review "Letter to Ngo Dinh Diem, John F. Kennedy, 1961" and write a paragraph about the intent of the document.

VISUAL INSTRUCTION

An Isolated Leader Diem was born into a family that had long served as mandarins (high-ranking civil servants) to the imperial court in Hue. Once imprisoned by the Vietminh, Diem was set free by Ho Chi Minh.

Answer: *He was a nationalist and a fierce anti-Communist.*

Curriculum Connection

English Ask students to consider the description of Vietnamese peasants: "like a mound of straw ready to be ignited." Point out that the phrase is a simile. The power of the phrase comes from its simplicity and vividness. Remind students to watch for other similes used to describe the war in Vietnam.

The End of French Rule

Despite American aid, France was losing the war. When in May 1954 the Vietminh overran Dien Bien Phu, a French outpost in northwestern Vietnam, it signaled the end of French control of Vietnam.

The day after the French surrendered at Dien Bien Phu, representatives of the United States, Great Britain, France, the Soviet Union, China, Laos, Cambodia, and the Vietminh met in Geneva to hammer out a peace agreement. According to its terms, Vietnam would be temporarily divided along the 17th parallel. The Vietminh would withdraw north of that line, and the French would withdraw to the south. Vietnam would be reunified in 1956 after national elections. The Vietminh agreed, confident that they would win the promised elections.

The United States Enters the War

Fear of the Spread of Communism Spurs Action

Fearful of just such a Communist victory, the United States refused to sign the agreement. President Eisenhower believed that the loss of South Vietnam would deny the United States access to the resources and markets of all Southeast Asia. In 1954 Eisenhower explained the **domino theory** to a group of reporters. "You have a row of dominoes set up," he said. "You knock over the first one, and what will happen to the last one is a certainty that it will go over very quickly." If South Vietnam fell to communism, the other nations of Southeast Asia would fall in turn, just like dominoes.

The Diem Regime

Years of war and colonial rule had left South Vietnam in disarray. A tiny ruling class controlled the wealth, while millions of landless peasants toiled in poverty. Political and economic reforms were desperately needed. The United States pinned its hopes on Ngo Dinh Diem, a nationalist and fierce anti-Communist. From 1954 to 1961, the United States pumped more than $1 billion into South Vietnam, but $4 out of every $5 of the aid was spent on the military, leaving only a fraction of the aid for economic development.

An aloof man who always dressed in white, Diem was an aristocratic Catholic who had little in common with the people he ruled, most of whom were Buddhist peasants. He ran the country as if it were a personal empire. Half his cabinet members were relatives, and he imprisoned anyone who dared to speak out against his autocratic rule.

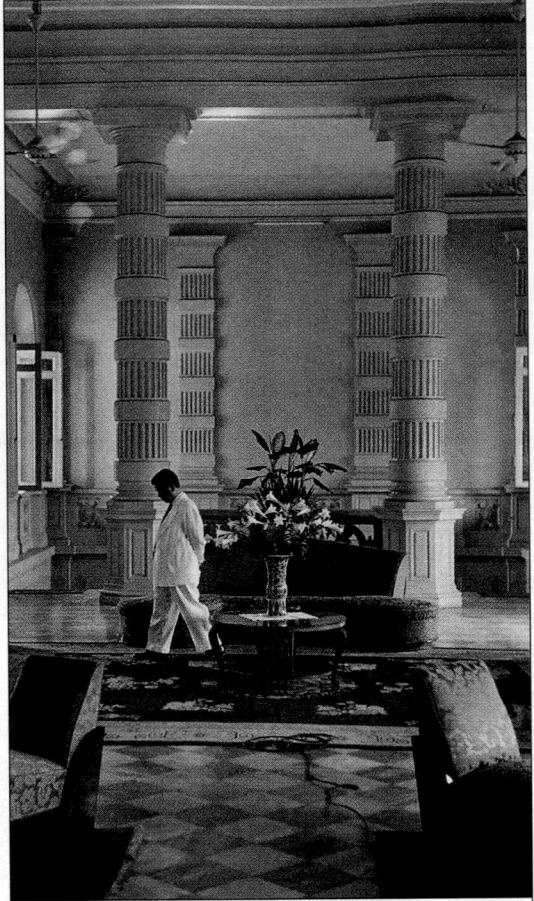

An Isolated Leader Diem did not understand the concerns and needs of his people. *Why did the United States support Diem?*

United States advisers urged Diem to try to win peasant support by breaking up the huge estates of wealthy landowners and handing out farming plots to the landless peasants. Diem, however, rejected any reforms that would weaken the ruling class.

Civil War

In 1957, with American support, Diem canceled the elections promised by the Geneva Accords. As even Eisenhower admitted, if the elections had been held, Ho Chi Minh would have won.

Instead of elections Diem held a "referendum" to prove he had the support of the people in South Vietnam. American advisers assured Diem that they would be satisfied if he had 60 percent approval, but he rigged the vote so that he won by a whopping 98 percent. In Saigon, for example, he claimed 605,000 votes even though the city had only 405,000 registered voters.

Meeting Special Needs

Attention Deficit Disorder This activity should help those students who have difficulty paying attention for long periods of time to become familiar with the primary topics in this section. Ask students to preview the photographs, maps, headings, and charts. Encourage them also to pay close attention to the expressions on the faces of the people in the photographs on these pages.

EVENTS LEADING TO UNITED STATES INVOLVEMENT IN VIETNAM, 1945–1964

1946 War between France and Vietminh begins.

1950 Truman sends $20 million to aid French war effort.

1954 French surrender at Dien Bien Phu. Geneva Accords divide Vietnam.

1963 Diem killed as South Vietnamese army assumes power.

1944 1946 1948 1950 1952 1954 1956 1958 1960 1962 1964

1945 Ho Chi Minh declares Vietnamese independence from France.

1949 China becomes Communist.

1954 Diem assumes power.

1957 Diem cancels elections promised by Geneva Accords.

1964 North Vietnamese attack the American destroyer the *Maddox*. Gulf of Tonkin Resolution passes in Congress.

Diem's brutal policies and his refusal to hold elections angered many Vietnamese. Their discontent proved fertile ground for the Vietminh. As one Vietminh soldier later said, the peasants were "like a mound of straw ready to be ignited."

In late 1960 the Vietminh and other groups opposed to Diem united in South Vietnam to form the National Liberation Front (NLF). Like the Vietminh, most of the NLF leaders were Communists. They promised economic reform, reunification with the North, and genuine independence. They also waged a campaign of terror, assassinating 2,000 government officials in 1960. The NLF, also known as the Vietcong, had close ties to the government of Ho Chi Minh. Over the years the NLF would get increasing support from North Vietnam and, indirectly, from China and the Soviet Union as well. The new President of the United States, John F. Kennedy, faced a difficult choice: abandon Diem or deepen American involvement in Vietnam.

The Kennedy Years

Like Truman and Eisenhower, President Kennedy saw Vietnam as part of the global struggle in the fight against communism. "Vietnam represents the cornerstone of the Free World in Southeast Asia," he declared. Despite some misgivings, Kennedy greatly expanded the United States's role in Vietnam. Kennedy's plan was twofold. The first part was to strengthen the South Vietnamese army with United States technology and military advisers to help them win the war against the Vietcong. The second was to pressure Diem to make political and economic reforms to eliminate the conditions that had allowed communism to take root in the first place. By 1963 Kennedy had tripled the amount of aid and increased the number of United States military advisers to 16,000.

Once again, however, Diem refused to go along. Instead of paying for new schools, health clinics, or land reform, American funds often ended up in the pockets of corrupt Saigon officials. Despite United States aid, the ineffective South Vietnamese army failed to score major victories against the Vietcong.

The Overthrow of Diem

The crisis in Vietnam deepened in the spring of 1963. As a crowd of Buddhists gathered in the city of Hue on May 8 to protest a government ruling forbidding the display of Buddhist flags, government troops fired on them. The attack stirred new and powerful protests.

A month after the attack at Hue, a Buddhist monk set himself on fire as a protest against the Diem regime. Other monks soon followed his example. A horrifying photograph of a monk engulfed in flames appeared in newspapers and on television screens around the world. Almost overnight, world opinion turned against Diem.

Ultimate Protest The Buddhist monk Thich Quang Duc sacrificed himself to protest the government persecution of Buddhists. Other monks lay in front of nearby fire trucks to prevent their moving to assist Duc. *What caused the crisis in Vietnam to deepen?*

SECTION ONE **771**

Portfolio Project

Editorials Have students write a hypothetical editorial about the Diem regime for a newspaper. Students may choose to argue in favor of or in opposition to United States support of his regime.

Remind them that an editorial should clearly state an opinion and provide sufficient facts to support that position. Students should place their sample editorials in their portfolios.

Videodisc

Powers of the President

Side 2, Chapter 16
Title: Use of Force
Subject: Gulf of Tonkin
Resolution
Ask: Why did the President request the Gulf of Tonkin Resolution? *(The Vietnamese had attacked.)*

See Powers of the President Guidebook page 78 for complete lesson plan.

Side 2, Chapter 17
Title: Gulf of Tonkin
Resolution
Subject: Leaders discuss
resolution
Ask: What was the Gulf of Tonkin Resolution? *(It allowed the President power to conduct war in Vietnam.)*

See Powers of the President Guidebook page 79 for complete lesson plan.

VISUAL INSTRUCTION

The Pain of War Bombs and napalm were used to blast a path so that troops could continue to move through the jungle.

Answer: *He ordered the first bombing of North Vietnam.*

By early August the Diem regime teetered on the brink of collapse; yet Kennedy feared he had no alternative to Diem. In late August, however, a group of South Vietnamese army generals met secretly with United States officials to propose the overthrow of Diem. With United States support, the plan went forward.

On the night of November 1, 1963, South Vietnamese army officers seized control of the government. In the confusion surrounding the takeover, Diem was killed. Just three weeks later, Kennedy himself was assassinated, and the war in Vietnam now troubled his successor, President Lyndon B. Johnson.

Johnson's War
Involvement Expands in 1964

Like his predecessors, President Johnson believed that Vietnam was a key battle in the cold war. He rejected any settlement of the war that did not guarantee a non-Communist government in South Vietnam.

Also like Truman, Johnson was haunted by the loss of China. "I am not going to be the president who saw Southeast Asia go the way China went," he vowed. Johnson also believed he had to take a strong anti-Communist stand to fend off the 1964 election challenge by conservative Republican Barry Goldwater.

Also like Truman, Johnson took over the presidency with little experience in international affairs. He surrounded himself with the same team that had guided Kennedy's foreign policies—Secretary of State Dean Rusk, Secretary of Defense Robert McNamara, and National Security Adviser McGeorge Bundy—the architects of the United States war in Vietnam. Johnson, like Kennedy, hoped to keep the Vietcong from overrunning South Vietnam. By 1964, however, Diem's successors had proved just as unsuccessful in waging the war and just as unpopular with the South Vietnamese. Only massive economic and military aid from the United States would keep the regime from toppling.

Johnson did not want to lose Vietnam, but he did not want to be seen as recklessly plunging the nation deeper into war. He needed the support of Congress and of the American public to expand United States involvement. He got it in August 1964.

The Gulf of Tonkin Resolution

In early August Johnson announced that North Vietnamese torpedo boats had attacked two United States destroyers patrolling in the Gulf of Tonkin off the coast of North Vietnam. Johnson angrily declared that Americans had been the victims of "unprovoked" attacks. He urged Congress to pass a resolution giving him authority to "take all necessary measures to repel any armed attack against the forces of the United States and to prevent further aggression." An alarmed Congress almost unanimously passed the Gulf of Tonkin Resolution. The resolution was not a declaration of war, but it authorized Johnson to widen the war. The resolution, he said, "was like grandma's nightshirt—it covered everything."

Few Americans questioned the President's account of the incident. Years later, however, it was revealed that Johnson had withheld the truth from the public and Congress. The American warships had been helping South Vietnamese commandos raid two North Vietnamese islands the night of the attacks.

Operation Rolling Thunder

Six months later a second incident provided another excuse for deeper involvement. In February 1965 Vietcong forces attacked a United States military base at Pleiku, South Vietnam, and killed eight Americans. Johnson retaliated by ordering the first American bombing of North Vietnam. Code-named Operation Rolling Thunder, the bombing would continue almost nonstop for three years.

In addition to bases, roads, and railways in North Vietnam, the air attacks targeted the so-called Ho Chi Minh

The Pain of War The sheer horror of the fighting is captured in this photo taken during Operation Prairie. *How did President Johnson respond to the attack on Pleiku?*

Extending the Content

Domino Theory Point out to students that the emphasis the United States placed on a military solution to the war in Vietnam had its roots in the domino theory. As early as 1953, for example, the National Security Council decided that "under present conditions any negotiated settlement would mean the eventual loss to communism not only of Indochina but of the whole of Southeast Asia." Ask: How did the domino theory prove to be wrong? *(Vietnam fell to the Communists, but many countries in the region maintained democratic governments.)*

Trail, a tangled network of dirt roads and muddy trails along which soldiers and supplies flowed from North Vietnam through Laos and Cambodia into South Vietnam. Yet the raids failed to cut off North Vietnamese aid to the NLF. The South Vietnamese army continued to suffer heavy losses at the hands of the Vietcong.

Meanwhile in 1967 a new regime had taken power in South Vietnam under General Nguyen Van Thieu. Like Diem, Thieu lacked popular support. As a result, the NLF continued to grow, soon controlling the majority of villages in the countryside. Johnson believed that the Saigon government would fall without direct American support. In March of 1965, he made a fateful decision.

United States Troops in Vietnam

One month after the attack on Pleiku, two battalions of American Marines waded ashore at Da Nang, South Vietnam. General William Westmoreland, the commander of United States forces in Vietnam, had asked Johnson to send the troops to guard the United States air base at Da Nang. Johnson agreed, assuring Americans that peace was on the horizon.

The trickle of United States troops soon swelled to a torrent. By the end of 1965, more than 180,000 American troops were fighting in South Vietnam. By the end of 1966, that number had doubled; and by the end of 1967, nearly 500,000 soldiers had been sent to Vietnam—more than all the United States troops in Korea at the height of that conflict.

Fighting the War
Early Optimism Turns to Frustration

The first United States troops to land in Vietnam shared the optimism of policy makers at home. As Marine Lieutenant Philip Caputo wrote, "When we marched into the rice paddies on that damp March afternoon, we carried, along with our packs and rifles, the . . . conviction that the Vietcong would be quickly beaten." Within just two years, however, that optimism had turned to bitter frustration.

Through relentless bombing and combat, the United States hoped to destroy the Vietcong's will to fight in order to force them to the bargaining table. The measure of the United States's success in the war was not territory gained but body counts—a tally of the number of enemy killed. Optimistic reports of body counts from the field led many at home to believe the United States was winning the war.

American officials, however, underestimated the Vietcong and their North Vietnamese allies. As Ho Chi

Vital Supply Line The North Vietnamese kept the Vietcong in the South resupplied by sending men, equipment, and ammunition down the Ho Chi Minh Trail. *Why did the United States bomb this trail?*

Minh had warned the French, "You can kill ten of my men for every one I kill of yours, but even at those odds, you will lose and I will win." Although United States forces claimed to have killed 220,000 Communists by the end of 1967, the war raged on.

The Air War

Because bombing cost fewer American lives than ground combat, the United States relied more and more on air power. Once Johnson unleashed Operation Rolling Thunder, the air war over Vietnam escalated dramatically—from 25,000 bombing raids in 1965 to more than 108,000 in 1967.

At first the attacks were limited to military targets and supply routes in North Vietnam, but soon the B-52s hammered roads, railways, factories, and homes in South

SECTION ONE **773**

VISUAL INSTRUCTION

Vital Supply Line The Ho Chi Minh Trail was not a single path, but a network of jungle paths that wound through Laos and Cambodia into the highlands of South Vietnam.

Answer: *They wanted to stop the movement of men and supplies that was helping the enemy fight in South Vietnam.*

Independent Practice

L3 Research Have students research novels written about the war in Vietnam. You may want to ask them to prepare a bibliography to share with the class or have them prepare a short oral report about one of the novels.

📁 Have students complete Chapter 23, Section 1 Vocabulary and Guided Reading Activity. (Also in Spanish.) **LEP**

📁 Have students complete the Chapter 23 Cooperative Learning Activity.

 Block Scheduling

📁 Have students complete the Unit 9 Great Debate to enrich their understanding of the war in Vietnam.

Cultural Perspectives

Asian Immigrants The United States has accepted more than 1 million refugees from war-torn Laos, Cambodia, and Vietnam since the 1970s. These refugees have contributed much to American society, but some Americans favor restrictions on immigration. Discuss with students the pros and cons of limiting immigration—not only from Asian nations, but from any nation in the world. Ask: How would the United States be different today if immigration had been forbidden in the 1800s? *(Our cultural heritage would not be as diverse.)*

ASSESS

Meeting Lesson Objectives

Each section objective is tested by the section review question(s) that follows it in parentheses.

1. Understand why most of the Vietnamese wanted a Communist government. (1)

2. Explain what the United States feared would happen if Communists took control of Vietnam. (1, 2, 3)

3. Analyze the reasons why the United States brought military forces into Vietnam. (2, 5)

4. Describe why the United States was unable to defeat the Vietcong guerrillas. (1, 4)

VISUAL INSTRUCTION

Routing Out the Enemy Agent Orange was a mixture of herbicides that the military sprayed in Vietnam from 1962 to 1970. It received its name from the orange band that was painted on each barrel. Agent Orange also contained small amounts of dioxin—a substance that is highly toxic, even in minute quantities.

Answer: *Much of it was destroyed.*

Vietnam and neighboring Laos and Cambodia. By 1967 the United States had dropped more bombs on Vietnam than the Allies dropped during all of World War II. The air raids leveled dozens of cities, killed thousands of civilians, and turned the once lush rice fields and forests into a moonscape pitted with craters.

Yet the immense firepower of the United States Air Force failed to rout the Vietcong. To evade the bombers, the Vietcong used and expanded a vast network of underground tunnels dug during the conflict with the French in the 1940s. Soldiers and supplies continued to flow south from North Vietnam through more than 30,000 miles of tunnels.

The Ground War

While United States bombers rained terror on Vietnam from above, United States ground forces attempted to wipe out the Vietcong through "search-

Routing Out the Enemy A chemical defoliant, Agent Orange, was used to eliminate Vietcong staging areas. The top photo shows a forest before spraying in 1965; the lower photo shows the same area in 1970. *What happened to the vegetation?*

774 CHAPTER 23 THE VIETNAM WAR

and-destroy" missions. To the inexperienced United States troops, the first challenge was simply finding the enemy in these unfamiliar jungles. Flying into Vietnam for the first time, Philip Caputo described the terrain:

> An unbroken mass of green stretched westward, one ridgeline and mountain range after another, some more than a mile high and covered with forests that looked solid enough to walk on. It had no end. It just went on to the horizon.
>
> I could see neither villages, nor fields, roads, or anything but endless rain forests the color of old moss. . . . "Out there" they called that humid wilderness where the Bengal tiger stalked and the cobra coiled beneath its rock and the Viet Cong lurked in ambush.
>
> —Philip Caputo, *A Rumor of War,* 1977

Once on the ground, the troops slogged through the countryside on endless patrols—plagued by suffocating heat, clouds of mosquitoes, razor-sharp jungle grasses, and hungry leeches. Soaked in sweat and weighed down by 50 to 70 pounds of equipment, United States soldiers waded knee-deep along muddy trails and through flooded rice fields. Cautiously they inched along. Each rock, each clump of weeds, might hide a mine that would cripple or kill in an instant. American soldiers called one especially lethal booby trap a "Bouncing Betty." It leaped out of the ground just before it exploded.

All South Vietnam became a war zone, as United States troops searched the fields, forests, and villages for Vietcong. Yet how could they be sure whether a peasant was friend or enemy? They were all Vietnamese. As one soldier explained, "The Vietcong would be the farmer you waved to from your jeep in the day who would be the guy with the gun out looking for you at night." The enemy was everywhere and nowhere.

Guerilla Tactics

The Vietcong employed **guerrilla warfare** tactics, using small bands of fighters to harass United States troops. Unlike conventional forces, guerrilla fighters avoid open battles. Instead they try to wear down the enemy—with ambushes, hit-and-run raids, and sabotage—and force them to withdraw. As one observer noted, "The guerrilla wins if he does not lose; the conventional army loses if it does not win." By that definition, the United States was losing the war.

The Vietcong guerrillas had two advantages over the United States forces. First, they knew the terrain and could move unseen through the mountains and jungles. Second, through a combination of terrorism and the genuine appeal of their nationalist struggle, they had the support of many peasants who supplied food and

---

Critical Thinking

Identifying Assumptions In a guerrilla war, the mobility of a single soldier is as important as the mobility of an army. The United States mistakenly assumed that it could fight the Vietcong in the rice fields and jungles of Vietnam with troops trained to fight on the battlefields of Western Europe. Discuss with students other assumptions of American leaders that proved incorrect.

shelter and kept them informed of American troop movements.

To deprive the Vietcong of their peasant support, United States troops undertook a **pacification program,** uprooting entire villages and forcing the people to move to cities or refugee camps surrounded by barbed wire. Then the army burned the fields and empty villages.

The program, however, failed to stop the Vietcong, who simply moved elsewhere. Instead the pacification program created new enemies for the Americans—the peasants who were forced to leave the beloved land of their ancestors. "I have to stay behind to look after this piece of garden," one grandfather pleaded with Americans evacuating his village. "Of all the property handed down to me by my ancestors, only this garden now remains.... If I leave, the graves of my ancestors, too, will become forests. How can I have the heart to leave?"

Despite these policies, the United States also tried to win friends among the Vietnamese peasants through development projects. Teams of volunteers visited villages offering medical care and farming advice. United States bombs and bullets, however, undermined these efforts to win Vietnamese "hearts and minds."

Meanwhile American losses in Vietnam continued to mount. By 1967 more than 14,000 United States soldiers had been killed. Yet United States military power still failed to crush the Vietcong. As one reporter observed, every powerful blow from the American war machine "was like a sledgehammer on a floating cork.... Somehow the cork refused to stay down."

The Endless War

For Americans fighting a seemingly unwinnable war, Vietnam was a frustrating and terrifying nightmare. Nurses working in mobile army surgical hospital (MASH) units near the front and on hospital ships off the coast probably had a better feeling for the Vietnam tragedy than anyone. They saw the wounded every day, day after day. Ruth Sidisin of the Air Force Nurse Corps said: "Vietnam was not John Wayne. In Vietnam, every day was disaster day." Most of the United States troops were young and inexperienced; the average soldier was just 19 years old, 7 years younger than the average soldier in World War II. These young people were miles from home in a steamy jungle filled with daily horrors—mud, heat, booby traps, and an invisible enemy. They fought bravely, but the war seemed endless. Some turned to drugs to escape. Some snapped under pressure, no

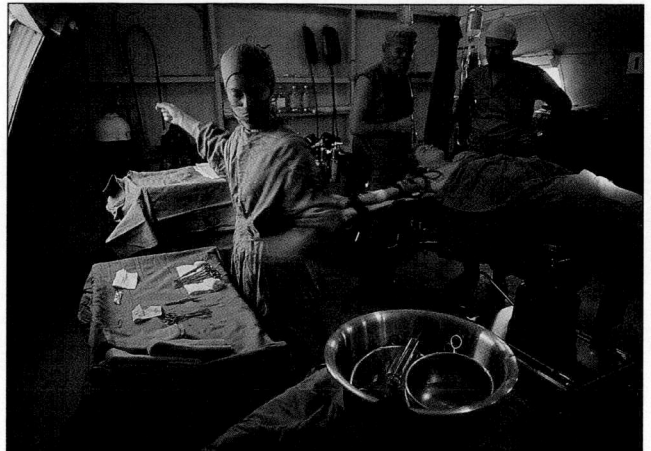

© RAY CRANBOURNE, EMPIRE/BLACK STAR

Nurses Battle More than 7,500 nurses served during the war in Vietnam. *What is a MASH unit?*

longer able to tell friend from foe. David Ross, a 19-year-old army medic, had volunteered to fight in Vietnam, but 2 years of war had shaken his faith in his country's goals.

> I volunteered, you know. Ever since the American Revolution my family had people in all the different wars, and that was always the thing—when your country needs you, you go. You don't ask a lot of questions, because the country's always right. This time it didn't turn out that way.
> —David Ross, in *Everything We Had,* 1981

SECTION REVIEW

Vocabulary

1. Define: national liberation, containment, domino theory, guerrilla warfare, pacification program.

Checking Facts

2. Why did the United States support the French war effort in Vietnam?

3. Why did the war escalate under President Johnson?

Critical Thinking

Recognizing Biases

4. In what ways did the United States military planners fail to understand the Vietnamese culture? How did this affect pacification programs in South Vietnam?

Linking Across Time

5. Does the United States continue to be concerned with cold war issues today? Explain why or why not.

VISUAL INSTRUCTION

Nurses Battle More than 11,500 women served in Vietnam, many as nurses. In 1993 a statue was erected in Washington, D.C., in their honor. It depicts women attending a wounded soldier.

Answer: *mobile army surgical hospital*

Evaluate

Have students complete the Section Review.

📁 🔲 Assign the Section 1 Quiz or use the Testmaker to develop a customized quiz. (Also in Spanish.) **LEP**

Reteach

🎧 Have students listen to the Chapter 23, Section 1 Audiocassette. (Also in Spanish.) **LEP**

Enrich

📂 Have students complete the Unit 9 American Literature Reading.

📂 Have students complete the Chapter 23 Geography in History Activity.

CLOSE

Ask small groups to draft a summary of this section. Have groups present their results orally to the class. *(The United States became involved in war because it feared the spread of communism; the United States was unprepared for a guerrilla war.)*

Section 1 Review Answers

1. national liberation (769), **containment** (769), **domino theory** (770), **guerilla warfare** (774), **pacification program** (775)
2. The United States did not want to lose France as an ally. Also, most policy makers viewed the war as a cold war battle to contain communism.

3. Johnson followed the policies of his predecessors and expanded the war as a natural result of the domino theory.
4. They underestimated the nationalist spirit of the Vietnamese. They created enemies by relocating peasants away from their ancestral land.
5. No, it has developed better economic and political relations with the few Communist countries that remain.

FOCUS

Section Objectives

1. Demonstrate how and why the Tet offensive was a turning point in United States involvement in the war in Vietnam.
2. Demonstrate the domestic trauma the assassinations of Martin Luther King, Jr., and Robert F. Kennedy caused.
3. Discuss how the events of 1968 changed the direction of politics in the United States.

Bellringer Activity

While taking attendance at the beginning of the class period, display **Section Focus Transparency 73,** and have students answer the questions. (Or use the blackline master.)

VISUAL INSTRUCTION

The War's General West-moreland was a West Point graduate and a decorated veteran of World War II and the Korean War. He later became chief of staff of the army. In 1972 he retired from the military.

Ask: Why did Westmoreland claim Tet as a victory for the United States? *(United States military forces had killed more than 33,000 enemy troops. Westmoreland felt this would weaken them, and the enemy would surrender.)*

1968: A Year of Crises

NOVEMBER 21, 1967: GENERAL WESTMORELAND REPORTS END IS NEAR

The War's General
General William Westmoreland was an architect of United States military action in Vietnam from 1964 to 1968.

FACED WITH GROWING OPPOSITION TO THE WAR AT HOME, PRESIDENT JOHNSON BROUGHT GENERAL WILLIAM WESTMORELAND BACK FROM SAIGON TO REASSURE THE AMERICAN PUBLIC ABOUT THE WAR. On November 21, 1967, in an address to the National Press Club in Washington, D.C., Westmoreland delivered an upbeat report: "I am absolutely certain that whereas in 1965 the enemy was winning, today he is certainly losing," he said. "There are indications that the Vietcong and even Hanoi know this. . . . We have reached an important point when the end begins to come into view."

Just 10 weeks later, however, General Westmoreland's words rang hollow. On January 30, 1968, the first day of the Vietnamese New Year, or Tet, Communist forces launched a massive attack, striking without warning at civilian and military targets throughout South Vietnam. Within 24 hours about 84,000 Communist soldiers had stormed more than 100 South Vietnamese cities and towns, a dozen United States military bases, and even the United States embassy in Saigon.

Tet Offensive: A Turning Point
Losses High on Both Sides

Though United States and South Vietnamese forces retook most of the targets within hours or days, a bitter battle over the ancient city of Hue raged for nearly three weeks. To recapture the city, United States forces hammered its streets with bombs and artillery fire. The fighting left the beautiful city of old temples and palaces a "shattered, stinking hulk, its streets choked with rubble and rotting bodies."

AS YOU READ

Vocabulary
► conservative era
► liberal era

Think About . . .
► what made the Tet offensive a turning point in United States involvement in the war in Vietnam.
► the effects the assassinations of Dr. Martin Luther King, Jr., and Robert F.

Kennedy had on subsequent political and social events.
► how events of 1968 altered the political direction of the United States.

Section 2 Resources

REPRODUCIBLE RESOURCES
- Lesson Plan 23-2
- Vocabulary and Guided Reading Activity 23-2
- Unit 9 Case Study
- Section 2 Quiz
- Unit 9 American Literature Reading

MULTIMEDIA RESOURCES
- Section Focus Transparency 73
- Landmark Documents in American History
- Testmaker
- Student Self-Test: A Software Review
- Chapter 23 Digest Audiocassette

United States forces routed the Vietcong, killing an estimated 33,000 enemy troops in the first 2 weeks of the month-long Tet offensive. The cost was high, however. More than 1,100 American soldiers, 2,300 South Vietnamese troops, and 12,500 Vietnamese civilians were killed. More than 1 million Vietnamese became refugees. Dozens of towns and villages lay in ruins. As one American army officer said of the battle for the village of Ben Tre, "We had to destroy the town to save it."

General William Westmoreland quickly claimed Tet as a victory for the United States and boasted that "the enemy is on the ropes." Even the Communists admitted that Tet had not achieved their major goal, "to spur uprisings throughout the South." Tet also marked a turning point in the war. It showed that no place in South Vietnam—not even the American embassy—was safe from attack. It shattered American confidence and raised grave doubts about Johnson's policies in Vietnam.

Critics of United States Policy

"What the hell is going on?" asked Walter Cronkite, the respected CBS newscaster. "I thought we were winning the war!" After returning from a trip to Saigon after the Tet offensive, Cronkite reported that "it seems now more certain than ever that the bloody experience in Vietnam is to end in a stale-mate . . . [and] that the only rational way out . . . will be to negotiate."

"If I've lost Walter," lamented President Johnson, "then it's over. I've lost Mr. Average Citizen." Editorials in *Newsweek, Time,* and the *Wall Street Journal* also called for a negotiated settlement of the war and a prompt withdrawal of American troops.

Televised reports challenged official statements and brought home the brutality and hopelessness of the war. The desperate struggle to regain the United States embassy and the destruction of Hue stunned Americans. The brutality of the United States's ally shocked millions

as they watched a South Vietnamese police chief draw his revolver, place it against the head of a young Vietcong prisoner, and pull the trigger. Such images prompted Americans to question United States policy: Was the United States really defending democracy in Vietnam? If so, at what cost?

The horrifying images of Tet contradicted the rosy picture of the war Westmoreland had painted the previous fall. Public opinion polls showed that in the 6 weeks after the Tet offensive, the percentage of Americans who approved of Johnson's handling of the war plunged from 40 to 26; Johnson's overall approval ratings dropped from 48 to 36 percent. The massive antiwar protests of the previous year grew even larger. Crowds of angry demonstrators chanted, "Hey, hey, LBJ. How many kids did you kill today?"

SECTION TWO   **777**

VIETNAM WAR, 1968–1973

The United States depended heavily on the use of air power in the war in Vietnam because it cost fewer American lives. *Why did the United States stage so many bombing raids in Laos and Cambodia, just west of Vietnam?*

TEACH

Guided Practice

L2 Discussion Walter Cronkite was a respected television news anchor during the Vietnam War. His views on the war had a great impact on the American public. Ask students to identify a television journalist whom they especially respect. What impact might this person have on their opinions of a military or social crisis?

MAP STUDY

The United States brought in heavy equipment and engineers and contractors who built roads, bridges, helipads, and airfields; dug six deep draft harbors; and linked Saigon and Washington with an efficient communications system.

Answer: *to destroy supply lines, hiding places, and villages of those who supported the enemy*

FYI

Tet Offensive The Tet offensive caught the United States military completely off guard. In the words of a West Point textbook published after the war Tet was an "intelligence failure ranking with Pearl Harbor."

Cooperative Learning

Research Arrange the class into small groups to research one of the following topics: movie stars, sports heroes, musicians, or writers of the late 1960s. Each student should pick a topic related to the group's theme and share his or her findings with the group. Each group should then decide how to present its findings to the whole class. They may choose to create a video or a display or make an oral presentation.

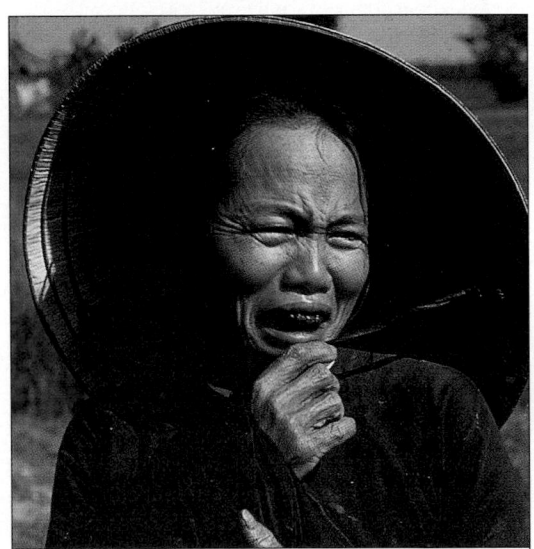

The Horror of War Three marines in flak jackets drag a sniper victim out of the line of fire during the battle of Hue. *What effect did Tet have on the 1968 presidential campaign?*

Democratic Challengers

As President Johnson's popularity took a nosedive, he faced another crisis. The liberal Minnesota Senator Eugene McCarthy had entered the New Hampshire Democratic primary. Running on an antiwar platform, McCarthy challenged Johnson for the presidential nomination.

Since the summer of 1967, antiwar Democrats had been searching for a candidate to replace President Johnson. They first tried to recruit New York Senator Robert Kennedy, a vocal critic of the war and the brother of slain President John Kennedy. Reluctant to challenge the President and split the party, Kennedy at first refused. The antiwar Democrats then turned to McCarthy.

At the beginning of January, with support from just 17 percent of the Democratic party, McCarthy had seemed to pose little threat to Johnson's reelection bid. Then came Tet.

McCarthy's antiwar stand attracted thousands of college students. With the motto Be clean for Gene, the students trimmed their hair, dressed in suits and ties, and

swarmed across New Hampshire, knocking on doors and urging residents to vote for McCarthy. On March 12 McCarthy surprised everyone by winning nearly half the popular vote as well as 20 out of 24 state delegates to the national nominating convention.

Not all of those who voted for McCarthy favored United States withdrawal from Vietnam; many favored stepping up the United States effort to win the war. Whatever their politics, New Hampshire voters agreed that Johnson's policies had failed.

On March 16 another antiwar candidate entered the race—Robert Kennedy. His challenge, however, embittered many of McCarthy's supporters, who feared that McCarthy and Kennedy would split the antiwar vote. With a promise to carry on the goals of his brother's New Frontier, Kennedy attracted widespread support from minorities, the poor, and the working class, as well as wealthier mainstream Democrats. As the Vietnam War drained more and more money from social reform at home, the ranks of Kennedy's supporters swelled.

Johnson's Decision

Shaken by Tet, McCarthy's success in New Hampshire, and Kennedy's entry into the presidential race, President Johnson faced a further dilemma. Following the Tet offensive, General Westmoreland and the Joint Chiefs of Staff had requested an additional 206,000 American troops—a 40 percent increase. Westmoreland claimed that Tet losses had weakened the Vietcong. With additional troops, he argued, the United States

The War Touches Both Sides The Tet offensive brought widespread destruction and affected thousands of civilians. *What did Westmoreland want to do to follow up the Tet offensive?*

could take advantage of their weakness and score a military victory. Uneasy about the request for additional troops, Johnson asked his new secretary of defense, Clark Clifford, to make a recommendation.

After questioning the Joint Chiefs of Staff, Clifford became convinced that "the military course we were pursuing was not only endless but hopeless." The top military commanders could give him no reason to believe the Communists could be beaten by "an additional 200,000 American troops, or double or triple that quantity."

As a result Clifford recommended that the President reject Westmoreland's request and instead encourage the South Vietnamese to do more of the fighting. Bitterly Johnson accepted Clifford's recommendation—he would send only a few thousand additional troops to Vietnam. For the first time in three years of war, Johnson refused to support Westmoreland.

On March 31, three years after the first American troops landed in Vietnam, Johnson made a televised speech. He announced that the United States would limit the bombing of North Vietnam, and he appealed to Ho Chi Minh for a negotiated settlement to the war. Then Johnson dropped his own bombshell: "I have decided that I shall not seek and I will not accept the nomination of my party for another term as your president."

Unable to build a Great Society at home and wage a war at the same time, Johnson got out of the race. He later confided to his biographer Doris Kearns Goodwin the reasons why:

> On one side, the American people were stampeding me to do something about Vietnam. On the other side, the inflationary economy was booming out of control. Up ahead were dozens of dangerous signs pointing to another summer of riots in the cities. . . . And then the final straw. The thing I feared from the first day of my presidency was actually coming true. Robert Kennedy had openly announced his intention to reclaim the throne in the memory of his brother. . . . The whole situation was unbearable to me.
>
> —Doris Kearns Goodwin, *Lyndon Johnson and the American Dream*, 1976

Two days later, McCarthy swept the Wisconsin Democratic primary.

A Surprise Announcement The day before Johnson withdrew from the presidential race, his eldest daughter, Lynda, sent her husband, Charles Robb, off to Vietnam. *Why did Johnson decide not to run for reelection?*

Tragedy and Turmoil
Bloodshed and Political Upheaval Dominate 1968

According to Vietnamese tradition, the first guest through the door during the Tet holiday serves as a sign of the year to come. The Vietcong commandos who burst into the United States embassy in the early morning hours of Tet ushered in a troubled year for Americans, a year of turmoil, frustrated hopes, and shattered dreams.

Tensions over the war in Vietnam and the civil rights struggle at home had been building for years. Now they exploded. The troubling events of 1968 would lead many Americans to reject the liberalism of the 1960s and embrace a new conservatism in hopes of bringing an end to the war and restoring peace at home.

King's Assassination

A nation still reeling from the shock of Tet and Johnson's refusal to run for reelection suffered another blow in April—the assassination of civil rights leader Martin Luther King, Jr. One of the earliest critics of United States involvement in Vietnam, King had linked the struggle for racial equality and economic justice to the struggle for peace. "The black revolution is much more than a struggle for the rights of Negroes," he declared. "It is forcing America to face all its interrelated flaws—racism, poverty, militarism, and materialism."

The news of King's murder stunned the nation. Thousands of his admirers took part in peaceful marches and

VISUAL INSTRUCTION

A Surprise Announcement Lyndon Johnson used President Truman's statement of withdrawal from the Democratic race in 1952 as a model for his own speech.

Answer: *He could not build a Great Society at home and wage a war at the same time.*

Curriculum Connection

Sociology Refer students to the quotation from Martin Luther King, Jr., linking the struggle for racial equality and economic justice to the struggle for peace: "The black revolution is much more than a struggle for the rights of Negroes. It is forcing America to face all its interrelated flaws—racism, poverty, militarism, and materialism." Ask students if they think King's statement applies to American society today.

Portfolio Project

Front Page Have students select one event from this section and create a front page newspaper article telling about the event. It should include a headline, a main or lead story, and a photo with a caption. Remind students that the first paragraph in the story should answer the questions *who, what, when, where,* and *why.* Students should place this front page in their portfolios.

Chapter 23
SECTION 2

Curriculum Connection

Civics Ask students why they think the war continued to go on even though there was so much opposition to it.

VISUAL INSTRUCTION

The Last Farewell The 21-car funeral train was occupied by guests and the press in all but the last 5 cars, which were reserved for the Kennedy family and friends. The casket was placed in a special observation car with a rear platform trimmed in garlands of fresh green leaves.

Answer: *Kennedy appealed to minorities, the poor, and young protesters.*

Notes

---

memorial services, but the shock and grief soon turned to rage. Within hours many African Americans stormed through the streets of cities around the country. Their anger and frustration exploded in rioting, looting, and burning. In Chicago fires raged through a 20-block area of the city's heavily African American West Side. In Washington, D.C., soldiers armed with rifles and machine guns stood guard outside the White House and the Capitol as African Americans looted and burned.

The Democratic Primaries

While the nation agonized over unrest at home and war abroad, the presidential race picked up speed. Three candidates now scrambled for the Democratic nomination: Eugene McCarthy, Robert Kennedy, and Vice President Hubert Humphrey.

Although Humphrey championed civil rights and social reform, his ties to Johnson's Vietnam policies repelled the antiwar liberals. To line up convention support, Humphrey avoided the primaries and courted the Democratic party bosses, who in some states chose the delegates.

McCarthy waged a spirited crusade against the war and social injustice, but his low-key, intellectual style appealed mainly to educated middle-class liberals. "He

has wit, charm, and grace," columnist I.F. Stone observed, "but he seems to lack heart and guts."

Robert Kennedy, on the other hand, made passionate appeals on behalf of the have-nots of American society. Campaigning against poverty, racism, and the war, Kennedy reached out to African Americans, Native Americans, Hispanic Americans, and young protesters. With Johnson out of the race, Kennedy quickly became the front-runner.

Kennedy won early primary victories in Indiana and Nebraska, but McCarthy rebounded and scored a victory in the Oregon primary. California, the nation's most populous state, was next. Both candidates campaigned energetically, but when the polls closed on June 4, Kennedy had won 46 percent of the popular vote and McCarthy just 41 percent. California was a winner-take-all state, so Kennedy claimed all the convention delegates.

Kennedy's Assassination

That evening, moments after the victorious Kennedy spoke to cheering supporters at a Los Angeles hotel, he lay dying, the victim of an assassin's bullet. The nation reeled in shock. Within two months two liberal leaders—both critics of the war and advocates of civil rights—had been killed. The deaths of King and

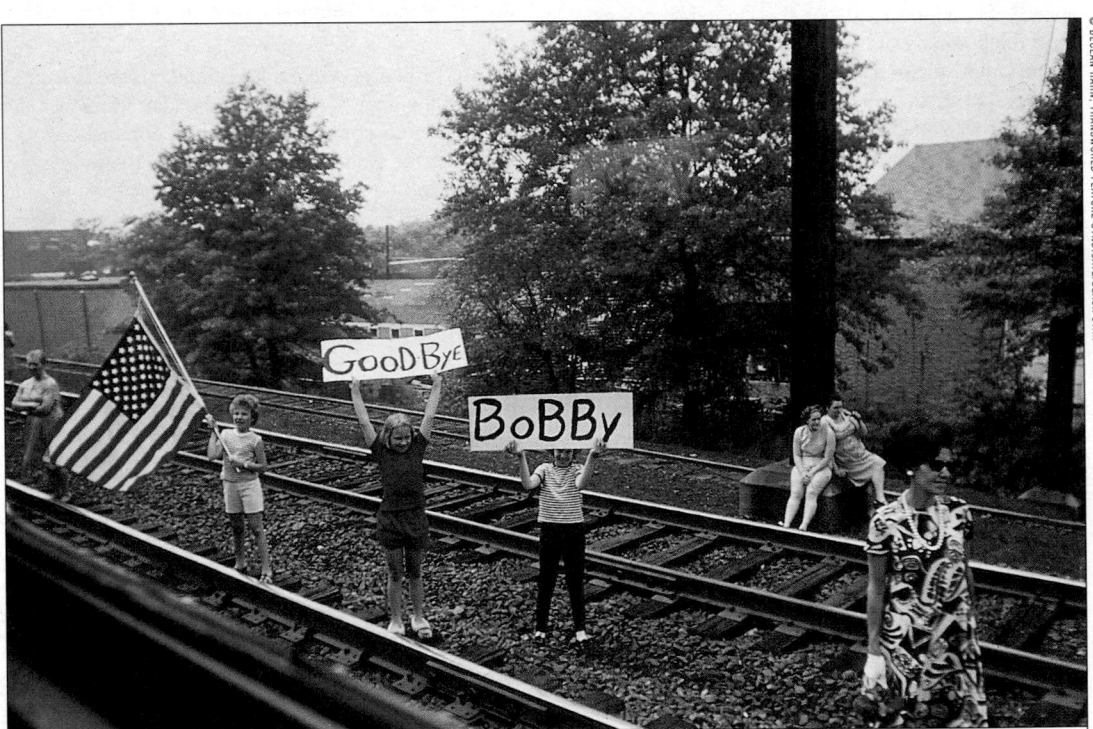

The Last Farewell Mourners lined the route as a special funeral train carrying the body of Robert F. Kennedy traveled from New York City to Washington, D.C., for burial in Arlington National Cemetery. *To what groups did the Kennedy campaign appeal?*

780 CHAPTER 23 THE VIETNAM WAR

Extending the Content

Democratic Candidates On the chalkboard make a list of the Democratic candidates for the 1968 presidential election. Under each name write some attributes of the candidate, such as politics, personality, and opinions on the issues of the day. Ask students to contribute to the list and discuss the merits of each candidate.

780

Kennedy shattered the hopes of antiwar and civil rights activists who had sought to work within the political system. Many despaired that politics would ever be an effective way to enact change. "I won't vote," one young African American from New York declared. "Every good man we get they kill."

The Election of 1968
National Politics Become More Conservative

The simmering anger and frustration many Americans felt over the deaths of King and Kennedy would boil over in the August heat, as Democrats met in Chicago to nominate a candidate for President. The resulting convention turmoil would shock the nation and splinter the Democratic party. In the process, it would help pave the way for a new **conservative era** in presidential politics in which the role of government would be limited and individuals would depend less on the government for assistance.

The Democratic Convention

With Kennedy dead and McCarthy unable to rally more than a few convention delegates, Hubert Humphrey looked like a sure winner of the Democratic nomination. Humphrey's support for Johnson's Vietnam policies, however, angered many antiwar activists. Nearly 10,000 of them flocked to Chicago to protest, if they could not prevent, Humphrey's nomination.

Most of the demonstrators had come to pressure delegates to adopt an antiwar platform. Some, however, hoped to provoke violence that would discredit the Democrats. With memories of the riots after King's death still fresh, Chicago Mayor Richard Daley mobilized 12,000 Chicago police officers and put 5,000 members of the National Guard on call. "As long as I am mayor," he vowed, "there will be law and order."

Daley's forces ringed the convention hall with barbed wire. On August 28, as convention delegates cast their ballots for Hubert Humphrey, helmeted police savagely clubbed demonstrators and bystanders in downtown Chicago. The protesters chanted, "The whole world is watching." As television cameras broadcast the brutal scene to homes across the nation, the image of the Democrats as the party of disorder was etched in the minds of millions of Americans.

Nixon and the Republicans

The Republicans presented themselves as the party of stability. According to writer Norman Mailer, the Republican convention in Miami was a "convention

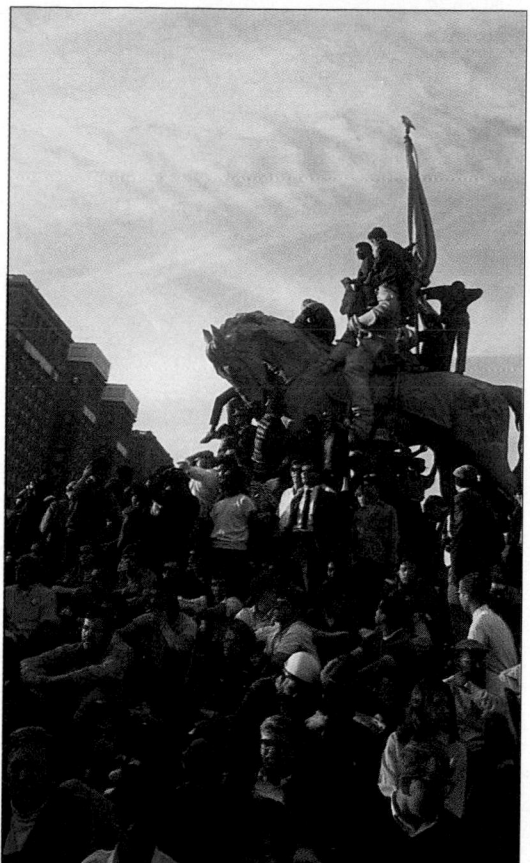
© DENNIS BRACK/BLACK STAR

The Whole World Watched Democratic delegates, reporters, and ordinary citizens, as well as demonstrators, were attacked by police and members of the National Guard. *What effect did the violence in Chicago have on Humphrey's chances in the coming presidential election?*

of the clean, the brisk, the orderly, the efficient"— a marked contrast to the Democratic convention. Republican delegates quickly picked Richard Nixon, the former Vice President, to once again be their candidate for President.

Just six years earlier, Nixon's political career seemed dead. In 1962 after losing the race for governor of California, Nixon had announced that he was retiring from politics, telling reporters, "You won't have Nixon to kick around anymore." Richard Nixon was a fighter, not a quitter. Now he was making a comeback.

A shrewd politician, Richard Nixon saw that the disorder and violence of the 1960s frightened many Americans. They were impatient with urban violence and campus unrest, and they resented the counterculture's challenge to traditional values. Nixon would try to appeal to those who, as one reporter put it, yearned for

SECTION TWO **781**

Cultural Perspectives

Tet Tet is the Vietnamese celebration of the lunar new year. Families make a special effort to be together at this time. Decorations, fireworks, special cakes with meat and beans, candied fruits, and certain kinds of flowers and plants are all part of the celebration. The first day of Tet sets the tone for the year, so effort is made to make it the very best day possible. The first visitor on the New Year is also believed to influence the happiness or well-being of the family during the rest of the year. Discuss with students new year traditions from their own cultures and how they compare to those of Tet.

ASSESS

Meeting Lesson Objectives

Each section objective is tested by the section review question(s) that follows it in parentheses.

1. Demonstrate how and why the Tet offensive was a turning point in the United States involvement in the war in Vietnam. (2, 4)

2. Demonstrate the domestic trauma assassinations of Martin Luther King, Jr., and Robert F. Kennedy caused. (3)

3. Discuss how the events of 1968 changed the direction of politics in the United States. (1, 5)

VISUAL INSTRUCTION

Nixon's the One Nixon announced his candidacy for the presidency in February 1968. His chief rivals were Governors Nelson Rockefeller of New York and Ronald Reagan of California.

Answer: *He promised to end the domestic turmoil, reduce spending on failing social programs, and end the war in Vietnam.*

"a kind of Eisenhowerian calm, after the pains and shocks and tragedies of the Democratic years."

In his acceptance speech at the Republican convention, Nixon echoed that deep yearning:

> As we look at America, we see cities enveloped in smoke and flame. We hear sirens in the night. We see Americans hating each other; killing each other at home. And as we see and hear these things millions of Americans cry out in anger: Did we come all this way for this?
>
> —Richard M. Nixon, Republican convention, 1968

Nixon promised to end the turmoil and to protect the "first civil right of every American . . . to be free from

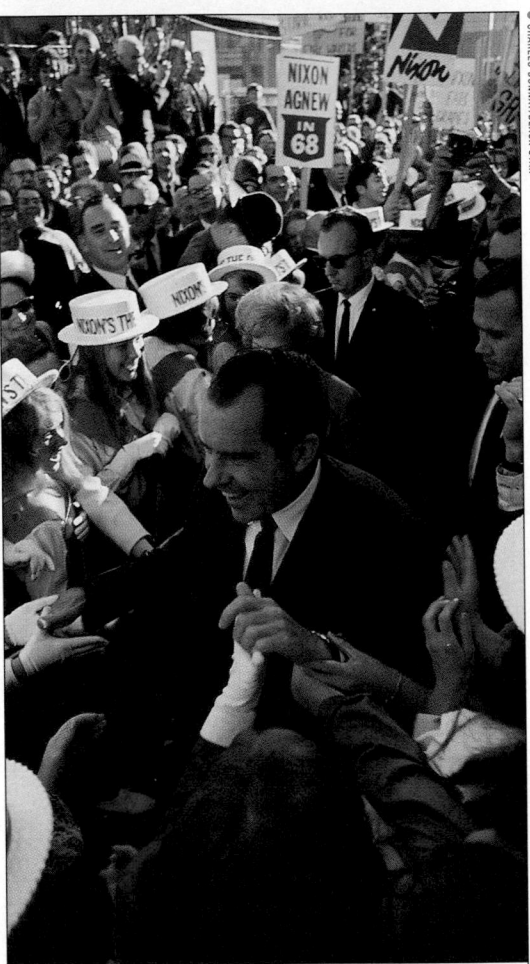

Nixon's the One Sensing victory as Election Day drew near, Nixon supporters were jubilant as their candidate arrived to speak at a campaign rally. *What did Nixon pledge to do if he was elected?*

domestic violence." He attacked Johnson's Great Society, declaring that it was "time to quit pouring billions of dollars into programs that have failed." To Americans weary of the Vietnam War, he promised "peace with honor."

The Wallace Campaign

The only threat to Nixon's presidential campaign came from further right. The conservative governor of Alabama, George Wallace, was running as the candidate of the American Independent party. In his campaign for the presidency, Wallace was attempting to capture the same conservative voters that Nixon sought—those who feared school integration, resented the Great Society's antipoverty programs, and despised antiwar protesters.

As governor of Alabama, Wallace had once pledged to enforce "segregation now . . . segregation tomorrow . . . segregation forever." As a presidential candidate, he tried to appeal to the fears and prejudices of blue-collar workers around the country by lashing out at the "brief-case-totin' bureaucrats, ivory-tower guideline writers, bearded anarchists, smart-aleck editorial writers, and pointy-headed professors looking down their noses at us."

Wallace called for victory in Vietnam, and he denounced the antiwar protesters. "If any demonstrator ever lays down in front of my car," he pledged to his supporters, "it will be the last car he will ever lay down in front of."

Wallace's popularity climbed as his attacks grew more shrill. By mid-September, polls showed that he had won the support of 21 percent of the voters. His campaign suffered a setback, however, when he picked Curtis LeMay, a retired air force general, as his running mate. LeMay frightened even devoted Wallace supporters when he argued that the United States should "drop nukes on Vietnam."

The Election

By the end of September, polls showed Humphrey trailing Nixon by 15 percentage points and leading Wallace by only 7 points. Crippled by his loyalty to Johnson's Vietnam policy, Humphrey was falling further and further behind. In mid-October he tried to salvage his campaign by calling for a halt to the bombing of North Vietnam. Johnson tried to help by ordering a complete halt to the bombing on October 31.

Humphrey managed to close in on Nixon, but it was too late. On Election Day Nixon won 43.4 percent of the popular vote, edging out Humphrey by less than 1 percent. Nearly 14 percent of the voters rejected both the Republican and Democratic parties and cast their votes for Wallace.

The 57 percent of voters who supported Nixon or Wallace signaled the rise of a new conservative major-

---

Critical Thinking

Making Comparisons Have students discuss why Martin Luther King, Jr., and Robert F. Kennedy were so widely viewed as leaders who could bridge the social and poltical problems of the 1960s. Ask students if they think there are leaders today who are regarded with the same admiration and respect as King and Kennedy.

PRESIDENTIAL ELECTION RESULTS, 1968

PARTY	ELECTORAL VOTE	POPULAR VOTE
Republican: Nixon-Agnew	301	31,785,480
Democratic: Humphrey-Muskie	191	31,275,166
American Independent: Wallace-LeMay	46	9,906,473

Nixon defeated Humphrey by half a million votes, ushering in a new era of conservative presidential politics. "In city after city," one observer noted, "racial conflicts had destroyed the old alliance. The New Deal had unraveled block by block." *Where did Nixon obtain most of his support? Where was Wallace particularly strong?*

ity. Since the election of 1964, the Democrats had lost nearly 12 million voters, including many in the once solidly Democratic South. The New Deal **coalition**, or alliance, of liberals, African Americans, and Southern whites was finally shattered over two divisive issues—civil rights and the war in Vietnam. Many of those who abandoned the Democrats felt that the party's social reforms—particularly the push for civil rights—had gone too far and that the Democrats had failed in Vietnam.

Some observers interpreted the election as a sign that the American political system was still alive and healthy. One British journalist noted, "The enormous power of the presidency passed peacefully from one man to another [despite] the fear that the country was coming apart."

The outcome of the 1968 election, however, disheartened others. For them, Nixon's election signaled more than just the end of a **liberal era,** a time when government power was used to promote social progress. It marked a defeat for those who had tried to work within the American political system to bring about racial equality, economic justice, and an end to the war in Southeast Asia.

SECTION REVIEW

Vocabulary

1. Define: conservative era, liberal era.

Checking Facts

2. Why was the Tet offensive a turning point in the war in Vietnam?

3. How did the deaths of Dr. Martin Luther King, Jr., and Robert F. Kennedy affect the momentum of the antiwar and the civil rights movements?

Critical Thinking

Synthesizing Information

4. Why did Johnson deny the request by General Westmoreland for an additional 206,000 troops?

Linking Across Time

5. In 1968 a liberal era ended and a conservative era began. Since your birth, has the United States tended to have conservative or liberal Presidents? Do you predict a change in the political orientation of the country in your lifetime? Why or why not?

SECTION TWO **783**

Evaluate

Have students complete the Section Review.

Assign the Section 2 Quiz or use the Testmaker to develop a customized quiz. (Also in Spanish.) **LEP**

Reteach

Have students listen to the Chapter 23, Section 2 Audiocassette. (Also in Spanish.) **LEP**

Enrich

Have students complete the Unit 9 American Literature Reading.

CLOSE

Ask students to describe the political climate just before the 1968 election and how it was divided on the issues of race, the war, and poverty.

Section 2 Review Answers

1. conservative era (781), **liberal era** (783)
2. The horrible images of Tet conflicted with the public's perception of the war. After Tet, support of the war began to decline.
3. Workers in the movement who had believed change could occur within the system became disheartened and could not work with the same dedication.

4. Clark Clifford, Johnson's secretary of defense, convinced him the war could not be won with the use of additional troops.
5. Conservative. Answers will depend on students' assessment of the nation's mood.

CULTURE
OF
THE
TIME

TEACH

Making the Historical Connection

The war in Vietnam was ever-present in Americans' minds during the early 1970s. Nightly television reports and symbols of protest on clothing, buttons, and bumper stickers "brought the war home," and it was nearly impossible for citizens not to take sides.

FYI

New Television Reality
All in the Family premiered in January 1971. The show's title was changed in 1979 to *Archie's Place* and was aired until September 1983. The show had one basic set, a small cast, and little reliance on guest stars. *All in the Family* was the first sitcom to be videotaped before a live audience.

The show broke new ground in story development and character treatment; hot topics were handled successfully on the show, and "taboo" words were uttered. *All in the Family* showed that Americans were sophisticated enough to appreciate a well-written, well-produced, and well-acted topical comedy.

EXPRESS YOURSELF
Wearing buttons or patches and attaching bumper stickers to one's car were popular and visual ways to express opinions on issues of the day.

FILE PHOTO BY JEFF WILLS

FILE PHOTO BY DOUG MINDELL

An Era of Consciousness

By the early 1970s, millions of Americans—especially those on college campuses—were protesting the ills of society. Attitudes concerning authority, politics, the environment, and many traditional American values shifted dramatically during this period. The entire society, it seemed, was under siege.

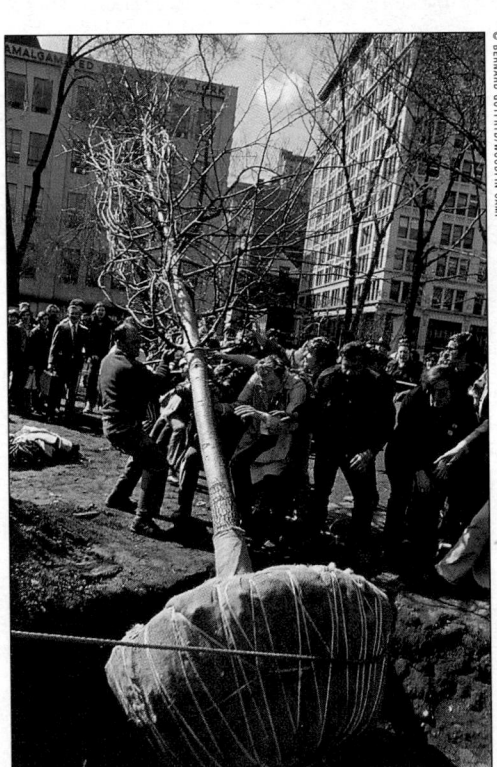

© BERNARD GOTFRYD/WOODFIN CAMP

© BILL PIERCE/SYGMA

MUSIC AND POLITICS
The lyrics of many songs revealed strong anti-war and antiestablishment sentiments. "I-Feel-Like-I'm-Fixin'-To-Die Rag," sung by **Country Joe and the Fish,** described the threat of the draft and service in Vietnam.

EARTH DAY
A new **awareness of the environment** and the limits of our natural resources was emerging. The first Earth Day on April 20, 1970, celebrated this new national consciousness and brought environmental concerns into the political mainstream.

784 CULTURE OF THE TIME

Background Information

Environmental Legislation During the 1970s Congress passed much far-reaching environmental legislation. Amendments to the Clean Air Act of 1963 were passed in 1970, which gave the government authority to set air standards. The Environmental Protection Agency (EPA) was also established in 1970. Other important bills of the 1970s were the Clean Water Act; the Endangered Species Act; and statutes to limit factory pollution, to protect seacoasts, and to remove scars left by strip mining. More than 100 million acres of virgin land were also set aside for national parks, wildlife refuges, and wilderness areas. In all, some 35 environmental laws took effect during this decade.

PROM NIGHT
While thousands of students protested on campuses and in the streets, many other young men and women were more concerned about **less political issues** such as going to school, getting a job, and finding a date for the prom.

THE SMALL SCREEN
In 1971 a brash new series, *All in the Family,* debuted. Many of the period's conflicts were highlighted by the show's characters: outspoken, bigoted Archie Bunker, the husband; conservative, peacemaking Edith, his wife; and their daughter, Gloria, and liberal son-in-law, Michael.

MOVIE STILL ARCHIVES

CULTURE OF THE TIME   **785**

 Curriculum Connection

Science Many new areas of study and career opportunities have developed as a result of the environmental movement of the 1970s. Have students research careers in air pollution, water pollution, or solid waste management. Ask them to identify what courses and areas of study are necessary to pursue such a career.

CLOSE

Ask students to identify the political and social issues presented on these pages. What do they have in common? Are any of them still issues today? *(the war in Vietnam, pollution and the environment, traditional values, individuality)*

Portfolio Project

Objects of Expression Protest buttons and, later, message T-shirts grew out of the American tradition of campaign buttons. Ask students to identify an issue about which they would like to express their opinion. Have them create a button, patch, or T-shirt that conveys their message. Students can combine a slogan and art work, create a logo or icon, or write a slogan. Encourage students to include this design in their portfolios.

FOCUS

Section Objectives

1. Explain the origins and evolution of the student protest movement.
2. Describe the emergence of the antiwar movement from the student movement.
3. Analyze the role of the media in shaping public opinion about the war in Vietnam.

Bellringer Activity

While taking attendance at the beginning of the class period, display **Section Focus Transparency 74,** and have students answer the questions. (Or use the blackline master.)

VISUAL INSTRUCTION

Student Movement Launched Mario Savio was a philosophy major transfer student from New York City and chairman of the University Friends of SNCC. It was as a leader of several civil rights groups that he fought for free speech.

Ask: Why did Mario Savio found the Berkeley Free Speech Movement? (*to protest the university ban of on-campus recruitment for off-campus organizations*)

SECTION

3

The War at Home

FALL 1964: BERKELEY STUDENTS DEMAND RIGHT TO FREE SPEECH

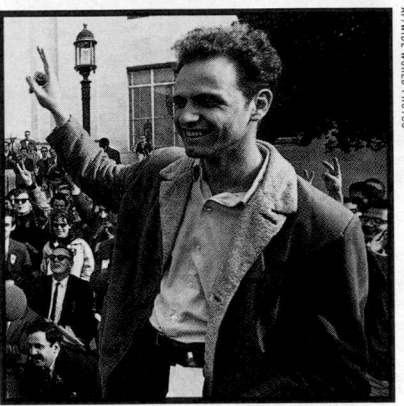

Student Movement Launched
Mario Savio was suspended from school for organizing student protests.

MARIO SAVIO, A 21-YEAR-OLD STUDENT AT THE BERKELEY CAMPUS OF THE UNIVERSITY OF CALIFORNIA, SENT A LETTER TO A FRIEND IN AUGUST OF 1964. "I'm tired of reading about history," he wrote. "I want to make it." Savio got his chance that fall when he returned to Berkeley. Uneasy about student activism, university officials had banned on-campus recruitment for off-campus political activities. Led by Savio, a group of students founded the Berkeley Free Speech Movement (FSM) to protest the ban.

On December 2, nearly 6,000 students rallied on the steps of Sproul Hall, the administration building of the university. Folksinger Joan Baez joined the throng, singing the civil rights anthem, "We Shall Overcome." Savio stirred the students to action with a fiery speech. Universities, he claimed, had become vast knowledge factories serving only the interests of United States corporations. Students were treated not as human beings but as products rolling off an assembly line, diploma in hand. He called on his fellow students to resist:

> There is a time when the operation of the machine becomes so odious, makes you so sick to heart, that . . . you've got to put your bodies upon the gears and upon the wheels . . . and you've got to make it stop.
> —Mario Savio, December 2, 1964

Inspired by Savio's speech, more than 1,000 students marched into Sproul Hall and staged a sit-in. This was the first, but by no means the last, time students would use civil disobedience to press their demands on campus. Just after 3:00 A.M., police began clearing the building, arresting nearly 800 demonstrators.

AS YOU READ		
Vocabulary	**Think About . . .**	
▶ draft	▶ the reasons for the growth and development of the student movement.	▶ the role the media played in determining public opinion about the war.
▶ deferment		
▶ conscientious objector	▶ the social and political conditions that led to student protests against the war in Vietnam.	
▶ hawk		
▶ dove		

Section 3 Resources

REPRODUCIBLE RESOURCES

📁 Lesson Plan 23-3
📁 Vocabulary and Guided Reading Activity 23-3
📁 Section 3 Quiz
📁 Skill Reinforcement Activity 23
📁 Supreme Court Case Study 37

MULTIMEDIA RESOURCES

📼 Section Focus Transparency 74
🔘 Powers of the President
🔘 Landmark Documents in American History
🔘 Powers of the Supreme Court
💾 Testmaker
💾 Student Self-Test: A Software Review
🎧 Chapter 23 Digest Audiocassette

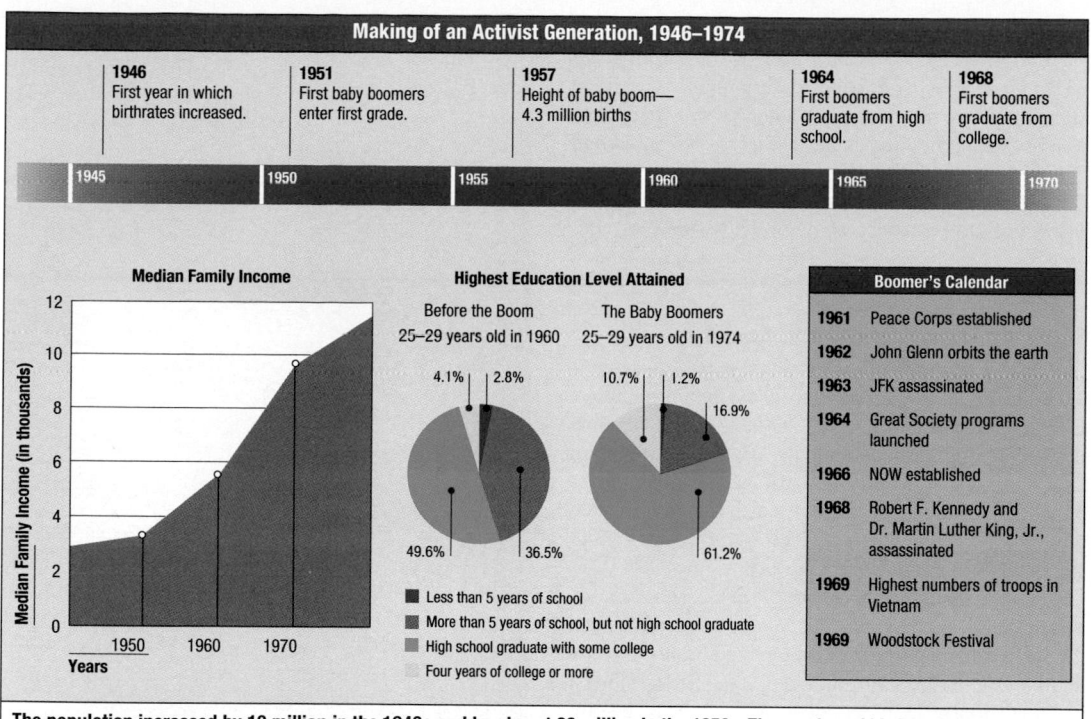

Making of an Activist Generation, 1946–1974

1946	1951	1957	1964	1968
First year in which birthrates increased.	First baby boomers enter first grade.	Height of baby boom—4.3 million births	First boomers graduate from high school.	First boomers graduate from college.

1945   1950   1955   1960   1965   1970

Median Family Income

(graph: Median Family Income in thousands, 0 to 12; Years 1950, 1960, 1970)

Highest Education Level Attained

Before the Boom
25–29 years old in 1960

4.1% 2.8%
49.6% 36.5%

The Baby Boomers
25–29 years old in 1974

10.7% 1.2%
16.9%
61.2%

- Less than 5 years of school
- More than 5 years of school, but not high school graduate
- High school graduate with some college
- Four years of college or more

Boomer's Calendar

1961	Peace Corps established
1962	John Glenn orbits the earth
1963	JFK assassinated
1964	Great Society programs launched
1966	NOW established
1968	Robert F. Kennedy and Dr. Martin Luther King, Jr., assassinated
1969	Highest numbers of troops in Vietnam
1969	Woodstock Festival

The population increased by 19 million in the 1940s and by almost 30 million in the 1950s. The number of births per thousand women peaked in 1957. *How many babies were born in 1957?*

In the days following the arrests, nearly 70 percent of Berkeley students protested. They picketed administration buildings brandishing signs that read Shut This Factory Down and I Am a U.C. Student: Do Not Fold, Bend, or Mutilate.

University officials eventually backed down. In early 1965 they lifted the ban on campus political activity. By 1965, however, student protests had spread like wildfire across the nation's campuses. Unlike the "silent generation" of the 1950s, the rebellious students of the 1960s became outspoken critics of American society. At first, their protests focused on students' rights. Soon a new issue would arise to fuel student passions—the war in Vietnam.

The Student Movement
Student Activism Emerges in the Early 1960s

The students who protested at Berkeley were children of the post–World War II baby boom. Having grown up in the 1950s, they were now attending college in unprecedented numbers. In 1950 only 1 million young Americans attended college. By 1960 that number had jumped to 4 million. By the end of the decade, nearly 8 million students flooded the nation's campuses.

Raised in the prosperity of the postwar years, the college students of the 1960s had grown up in economic security, free of the worries that had troubled their Depression-era parents. Seventy-five percent of them came from families with incomes above the national average. Mostly white and middle class, student activists could afford to be idealistic and rebellious.

A youthful President Kennedy, who appealed to young Americans in 1961 to "ask not what your country can do for you—ask what you can do for your country," stirred their idealism. Thousands responded, joining the Peace Corps and VISTA, its domestic counterpart.

Others, like Mario Savio, joined the civil rights movement. Inspired by African Americans who risked their lives in the struggle for racial equality, nearly 1,000 Northern white students volunteered for SNCC's Mississippi Freedom Summer Project in 1964. As the white volunteers journeyed south, they got a firsthand look at racism and poverty in the United States. They returned to their Northern campuses that fall schooled in the techniques of nonviolent civil disobedience and determined to fight injustice.

Only a minority of American college students joined the protest movement. At the height of campus unrest in 1970, only 12 percent identified themselves as part of the radical New Left. The majority of students joined

SECTION THREE   **787**

ABCNEWS INTERACTIVE™

Videodisc

Powers of the President

||||||||||||||||||||||||||

Side 2, Chapter 18
Title: Vietnam Protests
Subject: Sights and sounds of antiwar protests
Ask: Why did so many people oppose the war? *(They thought the war was unjust and unwinnable.)*

See Powers of the President Guidebook page 81 for complete lesson plan.

Facts on File

Landmark Documents in American History Have students review "The Port Huron Statement of the Students for a Democratic Society, 1962" and write a paragraph about the intent of the document.

fraternities and sororities, cheered at football games, and majored in subjects that they hoped would help them earn a good living after college. Although they rejected radical politics, many of these students still shared the activists' concerns about students' rights, civil rights, and the war in Vietnam.

Although the student rebels were a minority, they were vocal and attended some of the nation's top universities. Their protests would draw increasing attention as the decade progressed.

Students for a Democratic Society

One of the earliest radical student groups was the Students for a Democratic Society (SDS). Formed by a small group of students at the University of Michigan in 1960, SDS formed the core of the New Left, a rebirth of radical American politics. Disillusioned with liberalism, members of the New Left believed that problems such as racism and war could only be solved through sweeping changes in American society.

In June 1962, 60 members of SDS from a dozen campuses met at Port Huron, Michigan, to draft what they called an agenda for a generation. It began: "We are people of this generation, bred in at least modest comfort, housed now in universities, looking uncomfortably to the world we inherit."

Written for the most part by Tom Hayden, a 22-year-old student from the University of Michigan, the document went on to spell out the ills afflicting the United States. The United States, Hayden argued, was controlled by massive government, corporate, and educational bureaucracies that left individuals powerless. As a cure SDS envisioned a radical movement to bring about "participatory democracy," in which citizens would seize control over decisions affecting their lives.

The Port Huron Statement signaled the political awakening of a generation of students and the beginning of an era of student activism. As SDS member Sharon Jeffrey recalled, "It was exalting. We felt that we were different, and that we were going to do things differently. . . . It felt like the dawn of a new age."

Protesting the War

At first SDS tackled domestic issues. In the summer of 1964, SDS volunteers moved into poor urban neighborhoods and organized residents to fight for jobs, better housing, schools, and community services.

By the fall of 1964, SDS had organized chapters on nearly 50 campuses around the country. Then a new issue loomed—the war in Vietnam. At its December 1964 national convention, SDS members voted to protest the war by organizing a march on Washington for the following April. Because United States involvement in Vietnam was still limited to military advisers and aid,

© P. JONES GRIFFITHS/MAGNUM PHOTOS

A National Organization SDS members at Yale University mobilized antiwar activities on campus. *How many members did SDS have in 1965?*

opposition to the war remained muted. No one expected more than a few thousand marchers. Then President Johnson began to escalate the United States commitment to South Vietnam.

When Johnson ordered the large-scale bombing of North Vietnam in 1965 and sent in the first combat troops, the antiwar movement mushroomed. Some Americans felt betrayed by Johnson, whom they had considered a peace candidate in 1964. SDS now led a crusade to end the war in Vietnam. Within a single year, the ranks of SDS had swollen to more than 150 chapters with 10,000 members.

On April 17, more than 20,000 people crowded around the Washington Monument for the SDS antiwar march—the first of increasingly massive, and eventually more militant, protests. Folksinger Judy Collins sang

"The Times They Are A-Changin'." The words seemed prophetic:

Come senators, congressmen
Please heed the call
Don't stand in the doorway
Don't block up the hall.
For he that gets hurt
Will be he who has stalled.
There's a battle
Outside and it's ragin'
It'll soon shake your windows
And rattle your walls
For the times they are a-changin'.

—Bob Dylan,
"The Times They Are A-Changin'," 1963

That spring SDS also helped organize several university teach-ins. The first teach-ins took place at the University of Michigan at Ann Arbor. On March 24, 1965, shortly after the first United States ground combat troops landed in South Vietnam, more than 3,500 students and professors jammed into 4 lecture halls. They sang folk songs, analyzed United States foreign policy, and debated the war until dawn. In the following weeks, similar teach-ins sprang up at campuses across the nation.

Resisting the Draft

Opposition to the war led some students to resist the **draft**, a system of selecting individuals for military service. Since the early 1950s, all 18-year-old men had been required to register for the draft. In theory all those who registered were eligible to serve in the armed forces if needed. Individuals could be given **deferments**, or postponements of military service, however, due to their health or occupation. College students were among those who received deferments in large numbers during the Vietnam War.

Critics of the draft pointed out that, partly because of college deferments, the burden of the war fell unfairly on the poor, the working class, and minorities. Poor and working-class men were twice as likely to be drafted and, if drafted, twice as likely to fight as men from the middle class. African Americans made up 18 percent of those drafted to fight in Vietnam, although they were only 10 percent of the nation's population.

During the Vietnam War, thousands of defiant young men challenged the idea that citizens have a military obligation to their country. "The war in Vietnam is criminal and we must act together, at great individual risk, to stop it," the resisters declared. They argued that without a draft, the government could not continue to wage the war.

Some became **conscientious objectors,** claiming that their moral or religious beliefs prevented them from fighting in the war. Others, in defiance of federal law, refused to register for the draft or burned their draft cards. Protesters harassed campus recruiters for the military and disrupted campus Reserve Officers' Training Corps (ROTC) classes. Some went to jail for refusing to be drafted. Thousands more fled the country.

As the number of young men called up by the draft increased from 5,000 per month in 1965 to 50,000 per month in 1967, the ranks of draft resisters swelled. By the fall of 1966, more than 3 dozen draft resistance groups had sprung up on college campuses around the country.

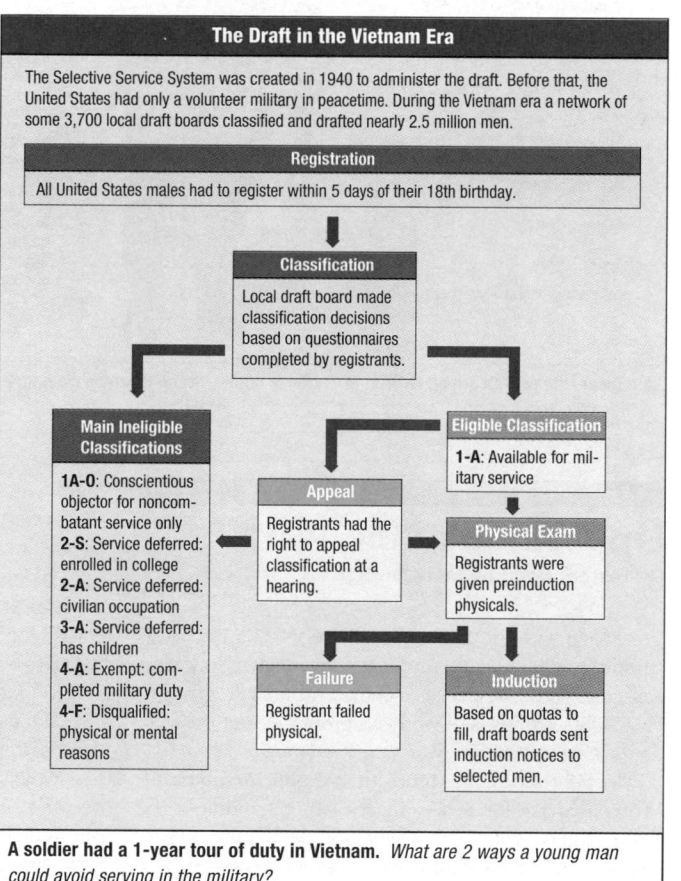

The Draft in the Vietnam Era

The Selective Service System was created in 1940 to administer the draft. Before that, the United States had only a volunteer military in peacetime. During the Vietnam era a network of some 3,700 local draft boards classified and drafted nearly 2.5 million men.

Registration

All United States males had to register within 5 days of their 18th birthday.

Classification

Local draft board made classification decisions based on questionnaires completed by registrants.

Main Ineligible Classifications

1A-O: Conscientious objector for noncombatant service only
2-S: Service deferred: enrolled in college
2-A: Service deferred: civilian occupation
3-A: Service deferred: has children
4-A: Exempt: completed military duty
4-F: Disqualified: physical or mental reasons

Eligible Classification

1-A: Available for military service

Appeal

Registrants had the right to appeal classification at a hearing.

Physical Exam

Registrants were given preinduction physicals.

Failure

Registrant failed physical.

Induction

Based on quotas to fill, draft boards sent induction notices to selected men.

A soldier had a 1-year tour of duty in Vietnam. *What are 2 ways a young man could avoid serving in the military?*

 Curriculum Connection

Civics Ask students how people protest today. Students should compare and contrast these methods with the ones used by students in the 1960s.

FYI

Draft Resistance The draft resistance movement chose the Greek letter *omega* as its symbol. Omega is also the symbol of ohm, the unit of measure for the resistance of electric current. During the war period, more than 200,000 draft-age men were accused of draft offenses, although only about 4,000 served time in prison.

CHART STUDY

The Selective Service was created in 1940 to administer the draft. Before that the United States had only a volunteer military in peacetime.

Answer: *A draftee could fail the preinduction physical or obtain a deferment.*

Portfolio Project

Position Paper Ask students to imagine they were of draft age during the Vietnam War. Have them write several paragraphs stating their position on the draft. Suggest they do some additional reading or interview family members or people from the community to help them define their position. Students should include this paper in their portfolios.

ABCNEWS
INTERACTIVE™

Videodisc

Powers of the Supreme Court

Side 1, Chapter 8
Title: Amendment 1 (1791): Freedom of Speech
Subject: People exercising their right of free speech
Ask: Why is freedom of speech important in a democracy? *(People need to freely express themselves so that the government can respond.)*

See Powers of the Supreme Court Guidebook page 11 for complete lesson plan.

Curriculum Connection

Mathematics Some 4,854 helicopters were lost during the war, each costing about $250,000.

VIETNAM TOUR OF DUTY

The largest generation in American history came of age during the Vietnam era. Many young men enlisted in the military, while others sought to avoid service through deferments or draft evasion. Most of those in the military were drafted through the Selective Service System.

- 28 million males came of draft age
- = 1 million men
- Approximately 8 million served in the military
- Approximately 2.1 million served in Vietnam
- 1.6 million served in combat
- 57,000 were killed
- 270,000 were wounded

TRAINING

Day 1
Arrive at Fort Dix, N.J., one of the army's 6 basic training centers, for 8 weeks.

Week 1
Orientation. Receive supplies, physical, inoculations, haircut. Learn how to salute, make bed to military specifications. Some physical training.

Weeks 2–4
Continue military and physical training. Begin drilling.

Weeks 5–6
Rifle-range training.

Weeks 7–8
Combat squad assignment for final drills and testing. Graduation.

Weeks 8–16
Advanced combat training at a site such as Fort Jackson, S.C.
30-day leave. Report to assigned air force base.

- Camouflaged helmet or "pot"
- Smoke grenade
- Flak jacket
- Canteen
- Antipersonnel mine
- Personal items: photos, letters, mementos, etc.
- M16 rifle
- **Total: 50 pounds or more of gear, ammunition, food, and water**

COMBAT DUTY

Day 1
Military or charter flight to Cam Ranh Bay, Vietnam. Assignment to combat or other division.

Week 1
Orientation. Assignment to company or battalion within the division.

Weeks 2–52
Active combat (patrol, search and destroy, reconnaissance) for several weeks followed by short rest periods, security operations, or training. One week rest and recreation near end of tour.

End of week 52
Sign up for additional 6-month tour followed by stateside leave or ship out. If 2-year military commitment is up, return home. If not, assignment to other duties, but not Vietnam.

A typical soldier was armed with an M16 rifle, a smoke grenade, and a claymore—an antipersonnel mine. *How many men were sent to Vietnam?*

Opposition to the War
Protesters Become More Diverse

Along with the increasing number of United States troops in Vietnam, the antiwar movement also grew. Religious groups, peace groups, antinuclear groups, civil rights groups, and women's groups joined the students in protesting the war.

In February 1967, more than 2,500 members of Women Strike for Peace, most of them middle-class homemakers, stormed the Pentagon demanding to see "the generals who send our sons to Vietnam." When refused entrance, the women began pounding on the doors with their shoes. Secretary of Defense Robert McNamara eventually ordered that the women be allowed to enter and present their petition to an aide.

Huge antiwar rallies in the spring of 1967 drew hundreds of thousands of protesters to New York City and San Francisco. Marching alongside the students were Americans from all walks of life: priests, businesspeople, and mothers pushing children in strollers.

Antiwar protests grew as more and more Americans demonstrated a willingness to risk arrest in acts of civil disobedience protesting the war. The SDS rallying cry became "From Protest to Resistance." Thousands responded in what organizers called a dramatic confrontation between the "people" and the "warmakers," the March on the Pentagon. On October 21, 1967, more

790 CHAPTER 23 THE VIETNAM WAR

Extending the Content

News Censorship Ask students to discuss the issue of news censorship. You may want to give examples of past censorship—for example, the military censorship imposed during World War II (1939–1945). The United States Congress enacted laws prohibiting the publication of any information that would interfere with the war effort or endanger national security. Other examples involve nondemocratic countries that routinely censor the news media, such as Iran or China. Ask students to develop some guidelines for media censorship, especially during wartime.

than 50,000 protesters crowded onto the Pentagon steps where armed troops awaited. Scores of young men burned their draft cards as supporters chanted, "Burn cards, not people!" Some protesters, pleading with the troops to join them, placed flowers in the barrels of the rifles. Hundreds of protesters were arrested, and many were beaten.

Key leaders, too, began to criticize the war in 1967. Senator William Fulbright, once a supporter of the war, held a series of televised hearings in which critics of the war analyzed United States policy. Martin Luther King, Jr., pointed out that each dollar spent in Vietnam was one dollar less for social reform at home. By early 1966 the federal government was pouring nearly $2 billion a month into Vietnam—more than the Johnson administration ever spent in a single year on the war on poverty.

FILE PHOTO BY RALPH J. BRUNKE

A Soldier's Voice Opinions on the war were visible at home and on the battlefield. *What message was this soldier trying to convey with his helmet sticker?*

War Divides the Nation

By 1967 the United States was deeply divided over the war. **Hawks,** those who supported the war, urged stepping up the war effort to win a military victory. **Doves,** those who supported the withdrawal of United States troops and a negotiated end to the war, questioned both the cost and the morality of the war.

Many Americans were neither hawks nor doves but were disturbed both by the war and the protests against it. A December 1967 poll showed that 70 percent of Americans believed the protests were "acts of disloyalty" to the soldiers fighting the war. As the war raged on, however, many became convinced that the United States was hopelessly bogged down in an unwinnable war. That frustration could be heard in the words of one Iowa homemaker: "I want to get out, but I don't want to give up."

Bringing the War Home

In the aftermath of the Tet offensive, public opinion on the war shifted dramatically. In early January 1968, hawks outnumbered doves by 62 to 22 percent. By March the number of hawks had fallen to 41 percent, while the number of doves had climbed to 42 percent.

Antiwar protests increased in size and number on the nation's campuses. From January to June 1968, nearly 40,000 students at more than 100 colleges staged protests. Though most protests were peaceful, violence occasionally erupted.

The most violent uprising took place that spring at Columbia University in New York City and reflected the growing militancy of SDS. The protest at Columbia linked two potent issues—civil rights and the Vietnam War. At noon on Tuesday, April 23, more than 600 stu-

dents rallied to protest university ties to military research. They also objected to a university plan to build a gym on public parkland in a nearby Harlem neighborhood.

When university officials refused to listen to student demands, the protest escalated. Led by the SDS and the students' Afro-American Society, the protesters took over five university buildings, including the office of the university president. "We are fighting to recapture a school from business and war," wrote student James Kunen, "and rededicate it to learning and life." A week later New York City police officers stormed the buildings to arrest the students and drag them off to waiting police vans.

The Media and the War
Coverage Sways Public Opinion

The antiwar protesters gained a powerful ally as the war continued on—the mass media. Television, especially, played an important role in molding public opinion. Satellite technology meant that the war could be broadcast at home almost as it happened. The scenes of brutal fighting, desperate refugees, and dying United States soldiers shocked the more than 60 million Americans who tuned in to the nightly news.

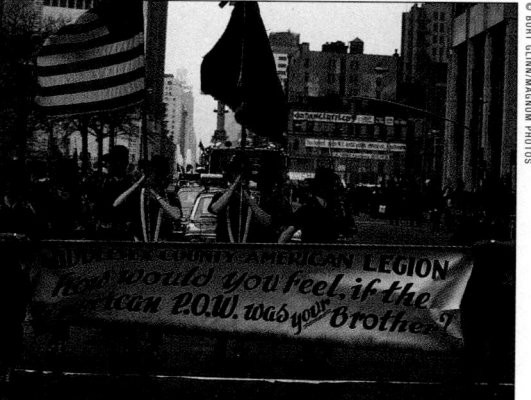

© BURT GLINN/MAGNUM PHOTOS

Support for the War The message on the banner in this photo captures the sentiment that war protests were "acts of disloyalty" to the fighting soldier. *How do you think you would feel about antiwar protesters if you knew someone who was a POW?*

VISUAL INSTRUCTION

A Soldier's Voice In June 1967, 448,000 soldiers were in Vietnam.

Answer: *He is concerned about his safety in Vietnam.*

Support for the War POW stands for the words *prisoner of war.*

Answer: *Answers will vary, but most students will say they would be supportive because their actions might help to end the war and bring home the POWs more quickly. Students might express anger at the protesters whose actions might be jeopardizing the POWs.*

Cultural Perspectives

Navajo Warriors Navajos conduct rituals for purifying warriors returning home after they have fought in battle. They pay homage to their enemies and reconcile with their spirits. Native American veterans in World War II, for example, participated in such rituals. Have students research or discuss from personal knowlege or experience how soldiers are brought back into the community in their culture after a war.

791

Independent Practice

L3 Writing Have students write a brief essay on how the media shaped public opinion about the Vietnam War.

☞ Have students complete the Chapter 23, Section 3 Vocabulary and Guided Reading Activity. (Also in Spanish.) **LEP**

VISUAL INSTRUCTION

The War Touches Home In 1966, the year this photo was taken, 5,008 draftees were killed in Vietnam.

Answer: *In June 1969,* Life *magazine published the photos of 242 Americans who had been killed in 1 week in Vietnam.*

In contrast with earlier wars, the military did not censor the press in Vietnam. Reporters and photographers easily got press passes and tramped through the muddy jungle, side by side with American patrols. In 1968, at the height of United States involvement, 800 reporters covered the Vietnam War.

Early Reporting on the War

During the early years of the war, most reporters agreed that the United States was fighting the spread of communism and that South Vietnam deserved and needed American support. They applauded South Vietnamese leader Diem. In June 1960, *Newsweek* called him "one of Asia's ablest leaders."

A More Critical Press

After the Tet offensive in early 1968, however, respected reporters such as Walter Cronkite began to raise serious questions about the war. After a trip to Saigon in 1968, Cronkite told viewers, "To say we are closer to victory today is to believe, in the face of the evidence, the optimists who have been wrong in the past." Such reports undercut official optimism and eroded public support for the war.

Reporters not only questioned official reports that the war could be won but also raised more fundamental questions: Should the United States be in Vietnam? Was Vietnam worth the cost? In the wake of Tet, James Reston, a columnist for the *New York Times*, asked: "What is the end that justified this slaughter? How will we save Vietnam if we destroy it in the battle?"

The media also brought home the immense tragedy of the war—its cost in human lives. In June 1969, *Life* magazine published the photos of 242 Americans who had been killed in 1 week in Vietnam. Their young faces served as a reminder that the nightly casualty figures represented real people—the sons, brothers, husbands, and fathers of those at home.

The My Lai Massacre

One of the most shocking incidents of the war surfaced in November 1969. Journalist Seymour Hersh discovered that, in March 1968, United States forces under the command of Lieutenant William L. Calley, Jr., had massacred nearly 350 Vietnamese civilians in the village of My Lai. Americans read the account of 22-year-old Private Paul Meadlo: "We huddled them up. We made them squat down. . . . I poured about four clips into the group. . . . The mothers was hugging their children. . . . Well, we kept right on firing."

Lieutenant Calley was court-martialed and sentenced to life im-

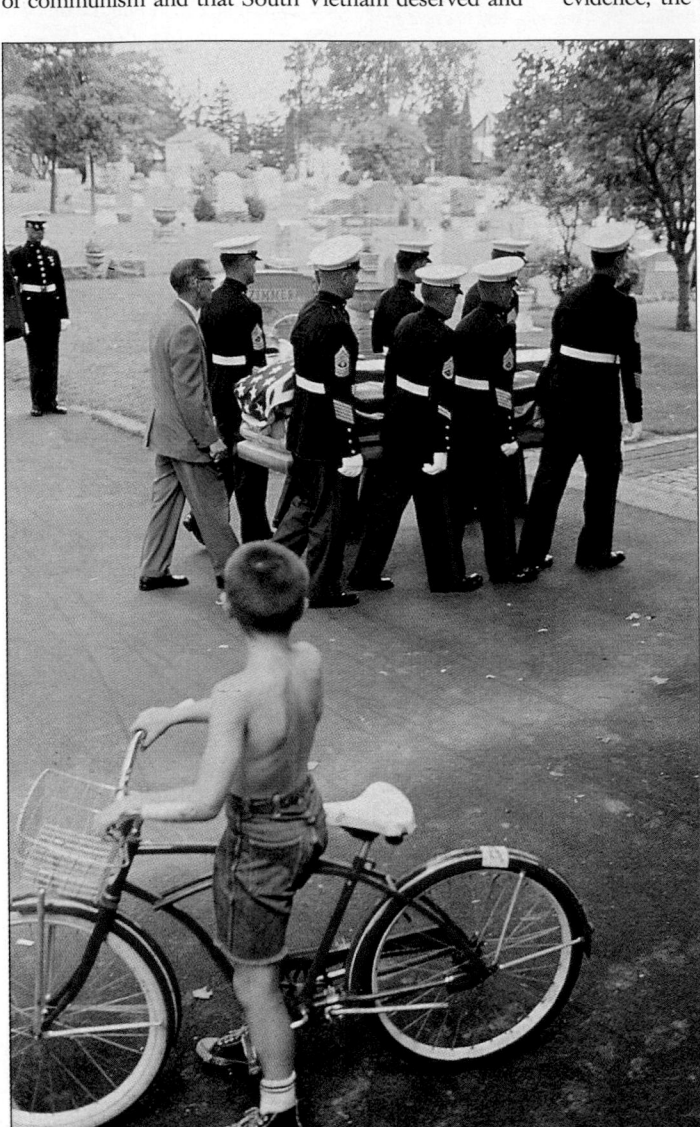

The War Touches Home A boy stops to watch the funeral of Private First Class Robert Damian Wuertz, Jr., the first casualty of war from Massillon, Ohio. *Give an example of how the media brought home the personal cost of the war.*

Critical Thinking

Recognizing Bias Ask students if they think the news media are ever completely objective. Ask them to comment on the inherent conflict between objectivity and self-interest on the part of reporters and editors. Have students identify the kinds of pressures that could be placed on members or media organizations to slant how the news is presented.

prisonment. Though the actions of the United States forces shocked Americans everywhere, some felt a certain amount of sympathy for Calley, who claimed he was "following a direct order." The military eventually reduced Calley's sentence.

Nixon and the Antiwar Movement

Nixon Seeks to Silence Protesters

Public pressure had made the Vietnam War a key issue during the 1968 election. President Johnson had been forced out of the race for his failed Vietnam policies. Johnson realized that the unpopularity of the war overshadowed his other accomplishments. Richard Nixon had been elected President in part because he promised an end to the unpopular war.

In June 1969, President Nixon announced that he would start bringing United States troops home as part of his plan to "Vietnamize" the war. The fighting continued, however, and so did the protests. On October 1, nearly 2 million Americans across the nation demonstrated for peace in Vietnam. One month later more than 300,000 protesters flooded Washington, D.C., taking their plea for peace to the White House. By the end of the year, doves outnumbered hawks on college campuses by 3 to 1.

To rally support for his policies, President Nixon appealed to what he called the silent majority. In a November 3 speech, Nixon declared that a minority was threatening America's security "by mounting demonstrations in the streets. . . . North Vietnam cannot defeat or humiliate the United States," the President insisted. "Only Americans can do that." To fend off this "enemy" at home, Nixon appealed "to you, the great silent majority of my fellow Americans—I ask for your support."

Conflict over the war would come to a head the following spring. A new wave of demonstrations and violence would rock the country and cause many on both sides of the issue to fear for the nation's future.

The War Comes Home

On April 30, 1970, President Nixon announced that he had ordered United States troops to invade Vietnam's neutral neighbor, Cambodia, to clean out Communist bases there. His expansion of the war soon led to massive protests across the country.

The Cambodian invasion outraged students at Ohio's Kent State University. Two days after the President's announcement, they surrounded the campus

A Different Kind of Violence A shocked young woman kneels beside the body of a Kent State student killed by a National Guard member's bullet. *What prompted the student protest at Kent State?*

ROTC building, pelting it with firecrackers and rocks. Then they burned it to the ground. In response Ohio Governor James Rhodes called members of the National Guard to Kent State on May 3.

The next day at noon, about 600 students held a peaceful protest on the Kent State campus commons. A campus police officer bellowed through a bullhorn: "This assembly is unlawful! This is an order—disperse immediately!"

The students refused to leave. Some lobbed stones and sticks at the soldiers, shouting, "Pigs off campus!" In reply the troops hurled tear gas at the students. Then their commander ordered, "Prepare to move out and disperse this mob."

The members of the National Guard, many as young and nervous as the students they confronted, pointed their bayonets at the demonstrators and marched toward them. Choking and weeping from the tear gas, dozens of students fled. A group of soldiers retreated to the top of a nearby hill. Suddenly they turned, raised their rifles, and fired into the crowd.

"My God," a girl screamed, "they're killing us!" Seconds later, nine students had been wounded, and four students were dead. None of them were radical activists. One was an ROTC student, and two had simply been crossing the campus on their way to lunch.

The soldiers claimed they had fired in self-defense. A later investigation found otherwise, declaring the action of the National Guard "unwarranted and inexcusable."

Public reaction following the shootings revealed just how deeply divided the country was during the 1960s. Some Americans blamed the students for the violence at Kent State. They resented the college students for

VISUAL INSTRUCTION

A Different Kind of Violence Students, not knowing that Ohio (unlike most states) permitted its National Guard to use live ammunition, kept pelting troops with sticks and stones even when the soldiers aimed their rifles.

Answer: *They were outraged that Nixon would order the bombing of neutral Cambodia.*

Facts on File

Landmark Documents in American History Have students review "Kent State Shootings Address, Richard Nixon, 1970" and "The President's News Conference of May 8, 1970, Richard Nixon, 1970" and write a paragraph about the intent of one of the documents.

ASSESS

Meeting Lesson Objectives

Each section objective is tested by the section review question(s) that follows it in parentheses.

1. Explain the origins and evolution of the student protest movement. (1, 2, 4)
2. Describe the emergence of the antiwar movement from the student movement. (1, 2, 4)
3. Analyze the role of the media in shaping public opinion about the war in Vietnam. (3, 5)

Extending the Content

Cabinet Dissension After the Kent State shootings, Walter Hinkel, secretary of the interior and former governor of Alaska, wrote an impassioned letter to the President urging him to open up lines of communication with young people. He also suggested Nixon urge Vice President Agnew to reduce his attacks on students and their motives for antiwar actions.

He felt Agnew's verbal attacks further distanced students from the government. Hinkel's letter was leaked to the press. President Nixon was outraged and felt betrayed by a member of his own cabinet. Nixon later met with a small group of college presidents who had earlier sought to discuss the student issue with him.

Evaluate

Have students complete the Section Review.

📁 💿 Assign the Section 3 Quiz or use the Testmaker to develop a customized quiz. (Also in Spanish.) **LEP**

Reteach

🎧 Have students listen to the Chapter 23, Section 3 Audiocassette. (Also in Spanish.) **LEP**

Enrich

📁 Have students complete Supreme Court Case Study 37.

CLOSE

Discuss the role of the press during wartime. Ask students if their allegiance should be to rules of their profession or to their country. Ask if they would compromise their ethics as journalists to support a war. *(Some may feel a duty to patriotism first; others to the need to present the facts.)*

---

their privileges, their countercultural values, and their rebelliousness. Other people condemned the government. The grief-stricken father of Allison Krause, one of the slain students, asked, "Is this dissent a crime? Is this a reason for killing her?"

Jackson State

Violence flared again a week later at the nearly all-African American college of Jackson State in Mississippi. An outbreak of vandalism in downtown Jackson prompted local officials to call in 500 National Guard troops to back up 80 state highway patrol officers and 125 city police officers.

On the evening of May 14, rocks and bottles began to fly in downtown Jackson, and a city truck was set on fire. At 10:30 P.M., police, highway patrol officers, and National Guard troops approached the nearby campus where students had gathered. Suddenly a bottle crashed near an officer. Without warning, police and highway patrol officers opened fire. The hail of bullets lasted nearly 30 seconds; 12 students were wounded, and 2 were killed, both innocent bystanders.

The End of a Decade

The protests after the Cambodian invasion marked the climax of a decade of student protest. Although some protests would continue until the war ended in 1973, the massive demonstrations of the 1960s were over. Their failure to end the war frustrated many students. One of the pioneers of the student movement, SDS, splintered into smaller extremist groups such as the militant Weathermen. Other students gave up political action altogether.

Government harassment of the New Left also took a toll. Although prohibited by law from spying on American citizens, the Central Intelligence Agency collected files on 7,200 Americans. Federal Bureau of Investigation agents secretly joined leftist groups and triggered feuds between members or instigated violent encounters with the police. Racked by internal dissent and weakened by government crackdowns, the New Left fell apart as the war in Vietnam wound down and United States troops returned home.

Although the student movement failed in its goal of radically transforming United States society, it did succeed in effecting change. The antiwar protests helped to force a shift in United States policy. The campus demonstrations brought about reforms in how universities were governed and enlarged students' role in campus life.

The radicalism of students during the 1960s alarmed many Americans and fueled growing conservatism. Along with inner-city riots, assassinations, and the Vietnam War, widespread campus unrest seemed to be a sign that something was deeply wrong with the country.

The Aftermath of Violence The morning after the shooting, 230 bullet holes were counted in the walls of Alexander Hall, a women's dormitory at Jackson State College. *Why do you think the authorities reacted so violently to student unrest?*

SECTION REVIEW

Vocabulary

1. Define: draft, deferment, conscientious objector, hawk, dove.

Checking Facts

2. What events prompted SDS and other student groups to shift their attention from domestic issues to antiwar activities?

3. Why was the Vietnam War a "living room war"? How was media coverage different from that of earlier wars?

Critical Thinking

Determining Relevance

4. How did the lyrics of "The Times They Are A-Changin'" reflect the goals of New Left groups like SDS?

Linking Across Time

5. Describe your generation. Do you identify with your generation as much as students did during the 1960s? Explain why or why not.

Section 3 Review Answers

1. draft (789), **deferment** (789), **conscientious objector** (789) **hawk** (791), **dove** (791)
2. The escalation of the war and the increase in the draft call brought about the shift in focus.
3. It was covered by television; there was no censorship.

4. The lyrics expressed the hope and urgency for change in American society that SDS felt.
5. Answers will vary. No, students are focused on individual concerns. Yes, students are concerned about the environment, violence, poverty, and racism.

Social Studies Skill

UNDERSTANDING PUBLIC OPINION POLLS

Learning the Skill

Public opinion polls have become a major factor in political life. For example, eroding public support for the war in Vietnam was a key factor in President Johnson's decision not to seek reelection in 1968. Polls, however, can only offer a snapshot of public opinion at one point in time, and only about the specific questions asked.

A public opinion poll should collect information in an objective and scientific way. Pollsters often use "random sampling," a method that employs the mathematical rules of probability, to obtain a representative segment of the population for questioning—called a "sample."

Sampling allows pollsters to infer something about a whole group by looking closely at a small part of it. Before pollsters can make inferences from their data, however, they must account for a "margin of error" in their sampling.

Questions must be written so the pollsters will find out what they want to know without influencing the results. Questions should be phrased to be as neutral as possible.

Knowing how to read and understand data from a public opinion poll will help you judge what other citizens are thinking and feeling about people, issues, and events of the day.

Use these steps to analyze a public opinion poll:

a. Look at the date and title for the overall context of the poll.

b. Look to see who was questioned. How large was the sample?

c. Read the questions carefully and decide whether they were phrased in an unbiased way.

d. State the numerical results in sentence form.

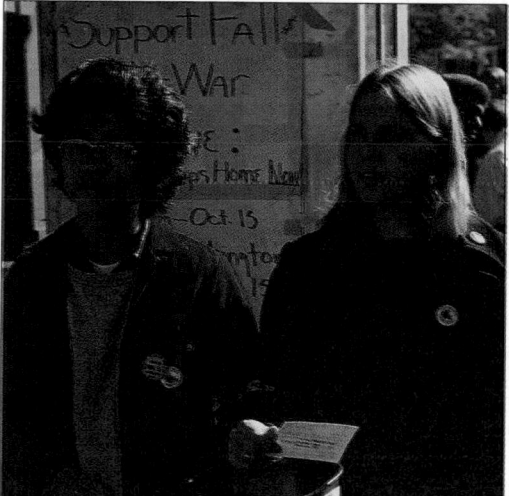

Rallying Support Opinions about the war varied among students. *What is the opinion of these students about the war?*

Public Opinion Poll, March 1969

What do you think the United States should do next in regard to the Vietnam War situation?	
Margin of error: 3–4 percentage points	Sample size: 1,500*
Escalate war (go all-out)	32%
Pull out (let South Vietnamese take over)	26%
Continue present policy (work for cease-fire at Paris, stay in Vietnam as long as necessary)	19%
End the war as soon as possible	19%
Other	4%

*Twenty-one percent expressed no opinion.

Practicing the Skill

Look carefully at the poll results shown on this page and answer the following questions:

1. What is this poll about?

2. Is the question phrased objectively?

3. What is the sample size?

4. What is the margin of error?

5. State the numerical results in sentence form.

Look for published public opinion polls in newspapers and magazines. Use the questions above to help you analyze the poll results.

Applying the Skill

Select an issue of concern to you and other students in your school and decide what you want to know about it. Develop a nonbiased question to poll that issue. Randomly select a sample group from the population you have decided to poll. Record answers. Present your results in a chart. Include your sample size and a brief summary.

Additional Practice

For additional practice, see Reinforcing Skills on page 805.

TEACH

This skill lesson familiarizes students with how public opinion polls are developed and how the information collected is evaluated. Students develop their own poll to collect information on topical issues. Point out to students that they should be careful in interpreting the results of public opinion polls—they should consider the objectivity of the questions and the size of the sample.

VISUAL INSTRUCTION

Rallying Support Americans largely approved of every aggressive United States initiative in Vietnam, from Rolling Thunder to the Christmas bombings in 1972, but only insofar as they believed these actions would hasten the end of the conflict. Public opinion tended to ebb and flow with the success or failure of presidential actions.

Answer: *They supported the President's actions on the war.*

Additional Practice

☞ Have students complete the Chapter 23 Skill Reinforcement Activity.

Practicing the Skill Answers

1. The poll is about what people think should be done next in Vietnam.

2. Yes

3. The sample size is 1,500 people.

4. Margin of error is 3–4 percentage points.

5. No one strong opinion about what should be done next was indicated in the poll results, although 32% of the respondents were in favor of escalating the war.

FOCUS

Section Objectives

1. Identify the steps Nixon took to end the war in Vietnam.
2. Examine the results of Nixon's war strategy.
3. Understand the reactions in the United States as the war continued.
4. Understand the real costs of the Vietnam War.

Bellringer Activity

While taking attendance at the beginning of the class period, display **Section Focus Transparency 75**, and have students answer the questions. (Or use the blackline master.)

VISUAL INSTRUCTION

A Solemn Moment In the fall of 1969, a series of moratoriums were held in communities throughout the country. On October 15, hundreds of thousands of middle-class Americans held prayer vigils and candlelight marches and sang the antiwar chant, "Give Peace a Chance." On November 14, a San Francisco protest drew 100,000 participants.

Ask: How had the makeup of the groups of protesters changed with these marches? *(They now included more people of all ages and people from the the middle class.)*

SECTION 4

Ending the War

NOVEMBER 13–15, 1969: PROTESTERS DEMAND AN END TO WAR

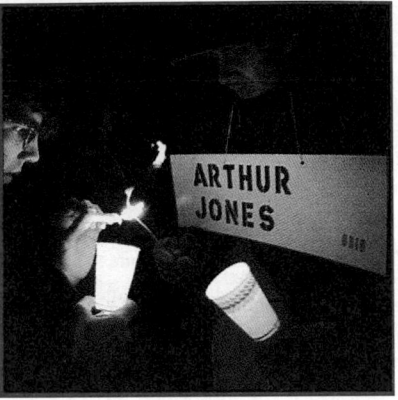

A Solemn Moment
Each soldier killed in Vietnam is honored.

DURING THE EVENING OF THURSDAY, NOVEMBER 13, THOUSANDS OF PEOPLE ASSEMBLED OUTSIDE THE GATES OF VIRGINIA'S ARLINGTON NATIONAL CEMETERY. Across the Potomac River lay Washington, D.C. The lights of the capital twinkled in the distance as the group stood in the darkness and biting cold.

In single file the protesters set off to walk the four miles (6.4 km) across the river to the White House. Each marcher carried a lighted candle and a placard bearing the name of a United States soldier killed in Vietnam or of a Vietnamese village destroyed by the war. Six drummers beating out a funeral march led the way. Just outside the gates of the White House, each marcher paused for a moment and spoke aloud the name on the placard.

The first marcher was Judy Droz, a 23-year-old widow and the mother of a 10-month-old child. Softly she spoke the name of her husband, Lieutenant Donald G. Droz, who had been killed in Vietnam the previous April. Behind her, in turn, another woman angrily shouted out her dead brother's name. Hour by hour, 1 by 1, they came. Forty-five thousand marchers, 45,000 names—through 2 nights and days, the March Against Death continued.

On Saturday, November 15, 2 hours after the last marcher filed past the White House, nearly 300,000 Americans swarmed around the Washington Monument. They had journeyed to Washington, D.C., from all over the nation to protest United States involvement in the Vietnam War. This November mobilization, which was the largest demonstration in the nation's history, reflected the mushrooming opposition to the war. The protesters were no longer just long-haired student radicals but ordinary Americans like Judy Droz.

AS YOU READ

Vocabulary
► negotiate
► nationalist movement

Think About . . .
► the steps Nixon took to end the war in Vietnam.
► the result of Nixon's war strategy.
► the reactions in the United States as the war continued.
► the costs of the Vietnam War.

796 CHAPTER 23 THE VIETNAM WAR

Section 4 Resources

REPRODUCIBLE RESOURCES

- Lesson Plan 23-4
- Vocabulary and Guided Reading Activity 23-4
- Section 4 Quiz
- Chapter 23 Test
- Performance Assessment Activity 23
- Reteaching Activity 23
- Enrichment Activity 23
- Supreme Court Case Study 38

MULTIMEDIA RESOURCES

- Section Focus Transparency 75
- Landmark Documents in American History
- Testmaker
- Chapter 23 Digest Audiocassette
- Student Self-Test: A Software Review
- Vocabulary PuzzleMaker

Working Toward Peace
Four Years of Struggle

By the end of the 1960s, Vietnam had become, in the words of one Nixon aide, "a bone in the nation's throat." By 1969, about 15 years after United States advisers were first sent to Vietnam, more than 36,000 Americans had come home in flag-draped coffins.

Nixon knew he had to end this unpopular war. During the 1968 campaign, he had claimed to have a secret plan for ending the war quickly and achieving peace with honor in Vietnam. The war would drag on, however, for four more years. In the end the settlement would bring neither peace to Vietnam nor honor to the United States.

Vietnamization

Despite pressure to end the war quickly, Nixon was determined to keep an independent pro–United States government in South Vietnam and to preserve the prestige of the United States as the leader of the free world.

Even the most optimistic military advisers estimated that it would take eight more years for the United States to win the war in Vietnam. The President realized that the American people would never accept eight more years of war. Public pressure was increasing to bring American troops home—now.

In May 1969, Nixon unveiled his secret plan: South Vietnamese soldiers would be trained and equipped to take the place of American troops, a process that came to be known as Vietnamization. As the South Vietnamese took over more of the fighting, United States troops would start coming home.

Vietnamization was part of a larger shift in foreign policy, known as the Nixon Doctrine. On an Asian tour in 1969, Nixon redefined the United States's role in Southeast Asia and the rest of the developing nations. The United States would no longer step in militarily to protect its Asian allies from Communist threats. Although the United States would continue to provide weapons and financial aid to Asian nations, in the future they would have to fight their own wars.

In November 1969, Nixon announced the withdrawal of 60,000 troops from Vietnam. Over the next 3 years, the number of American troops in Vietnam dropped from more than 500,000 to less than 25,000. The troop withdrawals, Nixon believed, would help silence antiwar protesters and buy him time to pursue a more favorable settlement on the battlefield and in the Paris peace talks.

The Paris Peace Talks

Peace talks had begun in Paris in 1968 but had yielded few results. Around the table sat representatives of the United States; its ally, the Thieu government of South Vietnam; North Vietnam; and its ally, the South Vietnamese Communists, known as the Vietcong. Each side had interests to protect; neither the Communists nor the anti-Communists were willing to compromise.

The United States and South Vietnam insisted that all North Vietnamese forces withdraw from South Vietnam and that the Thieu regime remain in power. The North Vietnamese and the Vietcong demanded that United States troops withdraw from South Vietnam and that a coalition government that included the Vietcong would replace the Thieu regime.

Nixon sought to continue the peace talks by sending his national security adviser, Henry Kissinger, to

Vietnamization United States military officers train South Vietnamese soldiers to take over more of the fighting in the war. *Why did the concept of Vietnamization become politically necessary for President Nixon?*

TEACH

Guided Practice

L3 Discussion Discuss the Nixon Doctrine. Ask students to determine how the Nixon Doctrine has influenced American foreign policy since 1969. You may open the discussion by asking whether or not the Nixon Doctrine was a good policy for the country to adopt.

Global Connection

Ho Chi Minh died on September 2, 1969, at the age of 79.

VISUAL INSTRUCTION

Vietnamization The first major test of this policy was an attempt to cut the Ho Chi Minh Trail in Laos. The failure of the mission showed the weaknesses of the South Vietnamese army.

Answer: *It allowed the beginning of the withdrawal of American troops from Vietnam.*

Cooperative Learning

Research Organize the class into small groups to research one of the four groups that met at the Paris peace talks that began in 1968.

Each student group should share their findings orally with the rest of the class.

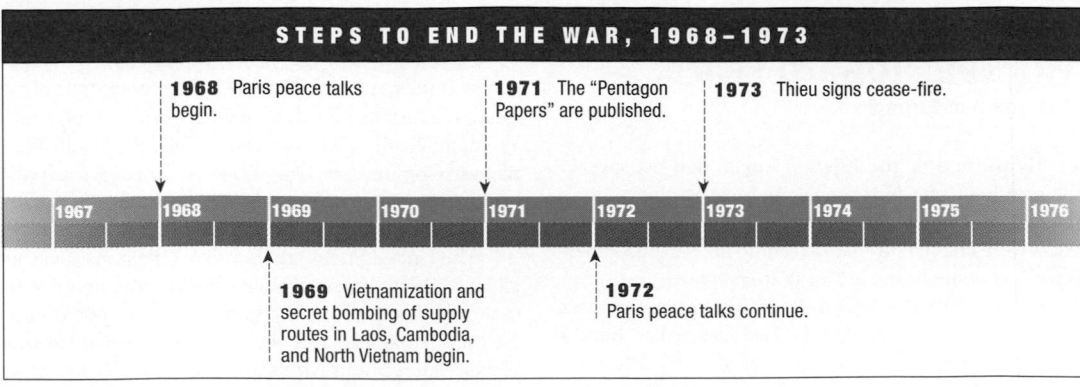

STEPS TO END THE WAR, 1968–1973

1968 Paris peace talks begin.

1971 The "Pentagon Papers" are published.

1973 Thieu signs cease-fire.

| 1967 | 1968 | 1969 | 1970 | 1971 | 1972 | 1973 | 1974 | 1975 | 1976 |

1969 Vietnamization and secret bombing of supply routes in Laos, Cambodia, and North Vietnam begin.

1972 Paris peace talks continue.

CHART STUDY

Ask: When did President Nixon institute the policy of Vietnamization?

Answer: *(1969)*

Independent Practice

L1 Statistics Have students research statistics to compare them with the cost of the war. For example, have them find communities with a population close to the number killed in Vietnam, or items that add up to the dollar expenditure of the war.

☛ Have students complete the Chapter 23, Section 4 Vocabulary and Guided Reading Activity. (Also in Spanish.) **LEP**

VISUAL INSTRUCTION

United States Fire Power Cambodia became independent in 1953 and declared itself neutral in the struggle between the Communist and non-Communist countries. Communists took over the country in 1975.

Answer: *He hoped to force the North Vietnamese to negotiate.*

negotiate secretly with North Vietnam's foreign minister, Le Duc Tho. Kissinger, a Jewish refugee who had escaped Nazi Germany, was a respected professor of international relations at Harvard University when Nixon tapped him for government service. Kissinger, a skilled negotiator, was also ambitious. "What interests me," he once said in an interview, "is what you can do with power."

Nixon shared that interest. Over the years he relied more and more on Kissinger alone to help him carry out foreign policy, eventually appointing him secretary of state. Convinced that debate would weaken their ability to negotiate, Kissinger and Nixon kept their foreign policy moves hidden from the American press, the public, and even from Nixon's own cabinet.

The Secret War

One such hidden policy lay at the core of Nixon's strategy for winning the war in Vietnam. To force the North Vietnamese to negotiate as American forces

United States Fire Power Bombing brought death and destruction to the neutral countries of Laos and Cambodia. *Why did Nixon begin the secret bombing of Laos and Cambodia?*

withdrew, Nixon ordered the secret bombing of enemy supply routes and bases in Cambodia, Laos, and North Vietnam in March 1969. As Nixon confided to aide H. R. Haldeman:

> I call it the madman theory, Bob. I want the North Vietnamese to believe I've reached the point where I might do anything to stop the war. We'll just slip the word to them that "for God's sake, you know Nixon is obsessed about communism. We can't restrain him when he's angry—and he has his hand on the nuclear button"—and Ho Chi Minh himself will be in Paris in two days begging for peace.
>
> —H. R. Haldeman, *The Ends of Power,* 1978

The bombing raids failed to cut completely the supply lines or bring the North Vietnamese to the bargaining table. Instead the attacks spread the war to Cambodia and Laos. Despite the failure of the air attacks, Nixon and Kissinger believed that eventually their strategy would work. For the next four years the United States would pursue the same carrot-and-stick policy—tempting North Vietnam with the carrot of negotiations, and then threatening them with the stick of escalating war.

A Bigger Stick

More than 3,600 secret bombing missions and 110,000 tons of bombs had failed to wipe out Communist bases in Cambodia. Nixon decided he needed a bigger stick. On April 30, 1970, he went on television to announce that he was sending United States troops across the border into Cambodia to attack North Vietnamese bases.

Secretary of Defense Melvin Laird and Secretary of State William Rogers opposed Nixon's decision. Both men feared the reaction of the American public. Nixon insisted, convinced that his bold move would stun the North Vietnamese and force them to negotiate.

Meeting Special Needs

Reading Disability Have pairs of students scan a topic or topics from this section, being careful to look at maps, charts, and images and their captions. Let one student read the segment aloud. Ask the second student to retell the information in his or her own words. Students should be sure to include the main ideas and events in their account. This activity should help students with reading disabilities comprehend information in this section.

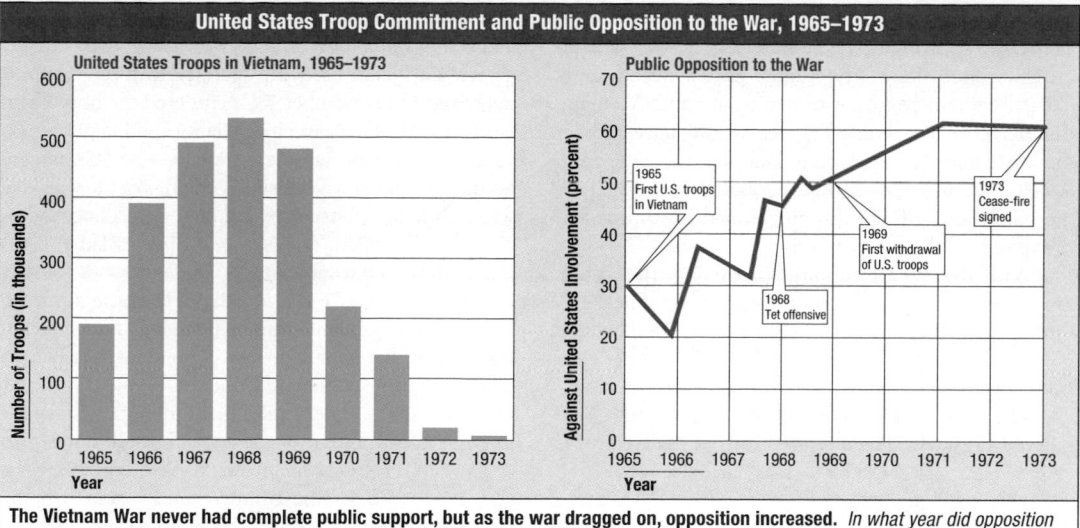

United States Troop Commitment and Public Opposition to the War, 1965–1973

United States Troops in Vietnam, 1965–1973

Public Opposition to the War

1965 First U.S. troops in Vietnam

1968 Tet offensive

1969 First withdrawal of U.S. troops

1973 Cease-fire signed

The Vietnam War never had complete public support, but as the war dragged on, opposition increased. *In what year did opposition peak?*

The Home Front
Growing Opposition

Nixon hoped to rally support for his policy by making it public. Instead the news provoked widespread protests. College campuses exploded in demonstrations and violence as the National Guard fired on and killed antiwar protesters at Kent State. Local police did the same at Jackson State.

Despite the public outcry, Nixon and Kissinger insisted that their strategy would bring the war to an honorable end. Others disagreed. An editorial in a respected Midwest newspaper argued:

> In asking the American people to support the expansion of the Vietnam war to Cambodia, as he has already expanded it to Laos, [Nixon] asks them to believe the same false promises which have repeatedly betrayed them against their will into ever deeper involvement on the mainland of Asia.
>
> They are asked to seek peace by making war; to seek withdrawal of our troops by enlarging the arena of combat; to diminish American casualties by sending more young men to their death.
> —*St. Louis Post-Dispatch,* May 3, 1970

Further damage to the government's credibility came in June 1971, when the *New York Times* published the "Pentagon Papers," a secret Defense Department study of United States involvement in Vietnam prepared during the Johnson administration. Leaked to the press by a former Defense Department analyst, Daniel Ellsberg, the report offered evidence that in the past the government had lied to the public about the war. Publicly, American Presidents had insisted that the United States was fighting to keep South Vietnam free from communism. According to the "Pentagon Papers," the real reason for pouring troops into Vietnam was to "avoid a humiliating defeat." Although there was nothing in the work damaging to the Nixon administration, the White House tried to block publication of the report. The Supreme Court upheld the right of the *New York Times* to print the "Pentagon Papers."

The Final Years of War
The Agony Continues

Despite United States training and billions of dollars in military aid, the South Vietnamese troops proved unable to defeat the Communist forces. In a disastrous test of Vietnamization in February 1971, South Vietnamese troops invaded neighboring Laos to cut off the flow of supplies from North Vietnam to South Vietnam. Alerted to South Vietnamese battle plans by Vietcong agents, the North Vietnamese troops crushed the South Vietnamese forces in just 6 weeks.

Renewed Peace Talks

Finally, in October 1972, talks reopened in Paris. For the first time in nearly 10 years of war, peace seemed within reach. The North Vietnamese agreed to drop

SECTION FOUR **799**

Portfolio Project

War Images Have students research images of the war in Vietnam in books and magazines. Students should select one that reflects their perception of the war and write an expla- nation about why they chose it. The image and explanation should be included in the student's portfolio.

Facts on File

Landmark Documents in American History Have students review "Agreement on Vietnam, 1973" and write a paragraph about the intent of the document.

VISUAL INSTRUCTION

Fleeing to Safety The helicopter lift out of Saigon continued for about 21 hours. Pilots flew continuously for 10–15 hours. Each trip took a total of 45 minutes: 10–15 minutes to load and 40 minutes in the air.

Answer: *He accepted the offer of $1 billion in military equipment and assurance that the United States would respond if North Vietnamese violated the settlement.*

ASSESS

Meeting Lesson Objectives

Each section objective is tested by the section review question(s) that follows it in parentheses.

1. Identify the steps Nixon took to end the war in Vietnam. (1, 2)
2. Examine the results of Nixon's war strategy. (3, 4)
3. Understand the reactions in the United States as the war continued. (2, 3)
4. Understand the real costs of the Vietnam War. (3, 4, 5)

---

their demand that a coalition government replace South Vietnam's President Thieu. Kissinger, too, offered critical concessions. The United States would allow North Vietnamese troops to remain in South Vietnam. Furthermore the United States would agree to let the Vietcong play a role in a final political settlement. A cease-fire agreement was negotiated that called for the withdrawal of all remaining American troops and the return of all American prisoners of war.

With the 1972 election approaching, the White House was eager to reach a firm agreement of peace. A settlement of the festering war in Vietnam would assure Nixon's reelection. Just days before the November election, a beaming Kissinger announced, "Peace is at hand."

The settlement fell apart, however, when South Vietnamese President Thieu refused to sign the treaty. He knew he was doomed if North Vietnamese troops were allowed to remain in the South.

Again Nixon used the military to force Hanoi to negotiate. On December 18, he ordered the bombing of North Vietnam's major cities, Hanoi and Haiphong. For 12 days bombers hammered away. The "Christmas" bombings—the most massive bombings of the war—laid waste to homes, hospitals, and factories. Thousands of civilians were killed. The *New York Times* called it "diplomacy through terror."

In January 1973, the North Vietnamese agreed to return to the bargaining table. It took just one week to **negotiate,** that is, to reach an agreement, nearly identical to the one hammered out the previous October. What broke the stalemate? The bombing had taken its toll, but even more important was United States pressure on Thieu. Nixon promised that the United States would "respond with full force should the settlement be violated by North Vietnam" and sent $1 billion in military equipment to the South Vietnamese. Reassured, Thieu signed the cease-fire.

Although Nixon claimed he had achieved peace with honor, many Americans believed that the agreement brought neither. These critics pointed out that the same peace agreement could have been reached 4 years earlier. In those 4 years approximately 107,000 South Vietnamese, 500,000 North Vietnamese, and 21,000 more American troops had been killed.

The Fall of Saigon

The peace accords failed to bring peace to Vietnam. Issues unresolved by the treaty would be settled by soldiers on the battlefield, not politicians in Paris.

Shortly after the last American troops left in March 1973, the cease-fire collapsed. Fighting broke out not only in Vietnam but also in Laos and Cambodia. In March 1975, North Vietnam launched an offensive against the weakened forces of South Vietnam. Thieu turned to Washington for aid, and Congress refused to grant it.

In April 1975, Communist troops marched into Saigon. American television audiences watched

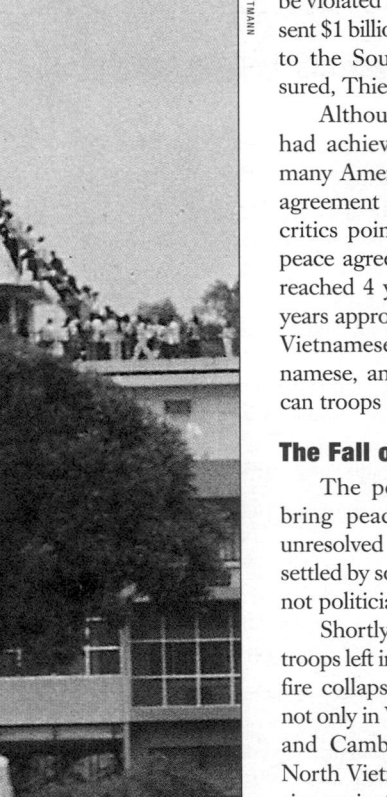

Fleeing to Safety In the 19 hours before the collapse of the capital, United States helicopters evacuated more than 7,000 American personnel and selected South Vietnamese citizens. *Why did President Thieu eventually agree to the cease-fire?*

Extending the Content

Relations with Vietnam In February 1994, President Bill Clinton lifted the 19-year trade embargo on Vietnam. In January 1995, the two countries agreed to establish diplomatic relations. One reason given for resuming relations with Vietnam was to encourage the flow of information on American POWs and MIAs. Ask students their opinions on whether the United States and Vietnam should have reestablished official channels.

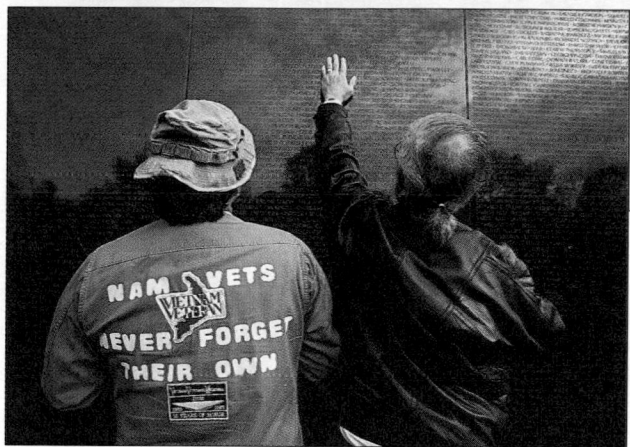

©LES STONE/SYGMA

A Sacred Place The Vietnam Veterans Memorial in Washington, D.C., is made of black granite panels that carry the names of 58,000 Americans who died in Vietnam. Visitors come and touch the names of those they knew and often make a rubbing of a soldier's name. *Why do you think this memorial has had such an impact on those who have come to visit it?*

as desperate South Vietnamese, many of whom had supported the Americans, scrambled to escape. A United States Army medic described the turmoil on an aircraft carrier offshore:

> There were people coming out in boats, half-sinking boats. . . . There were all these choppers we had left there; they were using these to fly out, the Vietnamese. This flight deck was so full of choppers that we had to push them overboard because there was no room, we couldn't get our own choppers in. . . . It was total chaos.
>
> —Al Santoli, *Everything We Had*, 1981

In the dawn hours of April 30, 1975, Saigon fell to the Communists; soon after, South Vietnam surrendered to North Vietnam.

The Costs of the War

Thousands of Lives and Billions of Dollars

The nation paid a high price to end the war in Vietnam. More than 58,000 Americans were dead; 300,000 were wounded, many of them permanently disabled. More than $150 billion had been poured into the war, while social programs at home went underfunded.

For the first time in history, the United States had lost a war. The extreme optimism and self-confidence that Americans felt following World War II had been shattered. Despite every advantage in wealth and technology, the United States had been unable to defeat a **nationalist movement,** the desire of a group of people to be free of any foreign influence.

The people of Southeast Asia also paid a great price for the war in Vietnam. In the course of the war, more than 8 million tons of bombs—the equivalent of 640 Hiroshimas—had been dropped on Southeast Asia. Two million Vietnamese and uncounted Cambodians and Laotians were dead. Their land lay in ruins; their villages—to the Vietnamese the heart of their ancient culture—had been destroyed.

SECTION REVIEW

Vocabulary

1. Define: negotiate, nationalist movement.

Checking Facts

2. Explain the steps Nixon took to end the war.

3. Explain the costs of the war in Vietnam from the perspective of the United States and that of the people of Southeast Asia.

Critical Thinking

Predicting Consequences

4. Why was the Thieu government unwilling to sign a peace treaty that allowed North Vietnamese troops to remain in South Vietnam? What were some of the consequences for South Vietnam by agreeing to the cease-fire in 1973?

Linking Across Time

5. United States involvement in Vietnam officially ended in 1973. What effects of the war are still part of American life?

SECTION FOUR   **801**

TEACH

Making the Historical Connection

President John F. Kennedy made the pledge in 1961 to put a man on the moon before the end of the decade. The Apollo program, which would reach this goal, began in 1968. At the time of the moon landing, the country was embroiled in controversy over the war in Vietnam and was pushing forward with President Johnson's Great Society social programs.

FYI

Voting Power Three-quarters of Fayette, Mississippi's 1,700 residents were African Americans, but until the Voting Rights Act of 1968, they were unable to get enough names on the registration books to elect any African American officials. The new mayor is the brother of slain civil rights leader Medgar Evers.

SPORTS: Baseball's centennial year is one of many changes.

One Day in History

Sunday, July 20, 1969

MARKET BASKET

Here is where a dollar will go:

Minimum wage
  per hour $1.60
Transistor radio $29.95
1 gallon regular gas . . . . . 33¢

Body paint kit $6
Deodorant . . . . 69¢
Box of cereal . . . . 27¢
Concert ticket for Newport
  Jazz Festival $3.50
One-bedroom apartment
  at the Watergate,
  Washington, D.C. . . $28,000
Hairdryer $35

Explorer Edwin Aldrin "Beautiful! Beautiful!" exclaimed the astronaut. About seven hours after landing, both *Apollo* astronauts began their exploration of the moon.

The *Eagle* Has Landed!

Man steps on the moon for the first time in history

HOUSTON—At 10:56 P.M. astronaut Neil Armstrong declared, "That's one small step for man, one giant leap for mankind," when he took his first cautious steps on the lunar surface. Television cameras mounted on the outside of the *Eagle* landing craft recorded Armstrong's movements live for the whole world to watch.

Edwin "Buzz" Aldrin joined Armstrong 15 minutes later for a 2-hour tour of the moon. They collected samples, took photographs, performed experiments, and radioed their feelings and findings back to the earth. They also spoke via telephone link with President Nixon.

Astronaut Michael Collins was in the *Apollo 11* mother ship in lunar orbit 70 miles (113 km) above the surface.

Landing on the moon was not easy. The astronauts had to manually fly their ship over the rocky surface to find a level site for their craft in the plain known as the Sea of Tranquility.

Background Information

Activating the Landing Craft As the three astronauts began their 11th orbit of the moon, Aldrin got into the *Eagle* for the first time to power it up, start the oxygen flowing into the spacecraft, and make sure everything was in working order. Forty-five minutes later, Armstrong joined him. On the 13th orbit, *Eagle* undocked from *Columbia*, leaving Collins to pilot the spacecraft around the moon alone.

NATION: Charles Evers was sworn in as the first African American mayor of Fayette, Mississippi.

Packaged Politics

NEW YORK—*The Selling of the President (1968)*, written by 26-year-old reporter Joe McGinniss, is a shocking, often funny, insider's account of how Nixon's team of technicians, ghostwriters, and pollsters helped him capture the presidency from Hubert H. Humphrey.

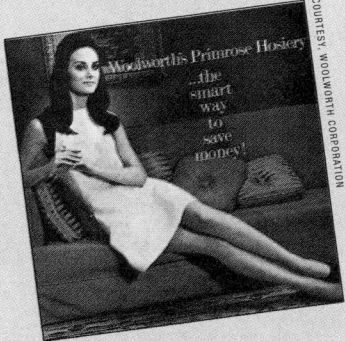

Pantyhose find an eager market.

Hosiery Revolution

NEW YORK—More women are making the switch from nylon stockings to panty hose. Spurred by the popularity of the miniskirt, panty hose have found a place in fashion. Lively designs, colors, and better fit have also fueled phenomenal growth. Sales rose this year to 624 million pairs, up from 200 million last year.

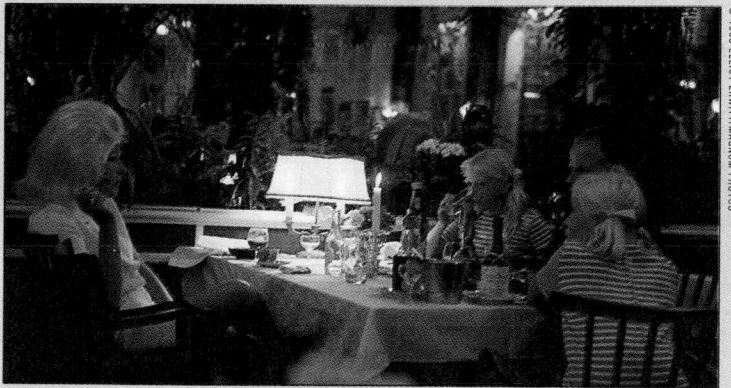

Spending is up as Americans engage in more leisure activities.

LIFESTYLE

Cash registers at restaurants, movie theaters, concert halls, and clothing stores are ringing across the United States. Per capita spending on clothing this year was $189.96. More surprising was the increase in entertainment expenditures—$198.86 per person, up $58.93 from 1965.

Americans Are Talking

More than one-half of the 225 million telephones in service all over the world are used in the United States.

ENTERTAINMENT

Easy Rider, starring Peter Fonda and Dennis Hopper, is one of the most popular and controversial movies of the year. Some moviegoers think the film reflects the fears and concerns of today's youth about national problems; others feel the movie glorifies drug use and escapism. Many believe it will capture an academy award for Fonda, son of movie legend Henry Fonda.

The hip heroes of *Easy Rider* find violence and bigotry on their cross-country journey.

January 28: An offshore oil-well blowout in the Santa Barbara, California channel covers a 30-mile stretch of shoreline with 235,000 gallons of oil.

February 8: Boeing 747, the largest commercial airplane, makes first flight.

March 17: Golda Meir, 70, is sworn in as Israel's fourth prime minister.

April 17: The Ford Maverick compact car is introduced to compete with the Volkswagen.

May 22: California governor Ronald Reagan sends the National Guard to Berkeley after students clash with authorities.

June 22: Actress and singer Judy Garland dies.

July 8: The National Association of Broadcasters announces a plan to phase out cigarette advertising on radio and television.

October 16: The New York Mets win their first World Series.

December 1: The first draft lottery since 1942 is held.

Oral History

Interview Have each student interview a member of the community who recalls the moon landing, saw the movie *Easy Rider*, read the book *The Selling of the President*, or purchased any of the items listed in the market basket. Have students write a summary of their interview. Encourage students to include this work in their portfolios.

CLOSE

Ask students to select one item from the page about which they were most surprised or interested. Have them explain why.

803

Chapter ㉓ Review

Reviewing Key Terms

1. deferment
2. guerrilla warfare
3. hawk
4. conservative era
5. domino theory

Recalling Facts

1. leader of the North Vietnamese nationalists; land reforms and an independent Vietnam
2. Vietnam, Cambodia, Laos
3. The Vietminh defeated the French and ended its control.
4. He was a fierce nationalist and an anti-Communist.
5. He repressed the Buddhists and refused reforms.
6. It authorized President Johnson to widen the war.
7. ambush, hit and run techniques, and sabotage
8. paths for supplies from North to South Vietnam
9. commander of United States forces in Vietnam
10. shattered public confidence
11. Westmoreland wanted 206,000 more troops; Clifford wanted the Vietnamese to assume more of the fighting.
12. failure to win the war in Vietnam or war on poverty
13. Resources to fight were taken from social programs.
14. More voted Republican.
15. He appealed to the fear of disorder and violence.
16. have more personal control over government policies
17. registration and classification of 18-year-old males
18. They gave uncensored information about the war.
19. Some blamed students; others, the government.
20. Foreign policy and university governance changed.
21. Average citizens protested.
22. South Vietnamese given training and supplies to fight
23. to avoid a defeat
24. North Vietnamese could remain in the South; Thieu did not need to be replaced.
25. It fell to the Communists.

Reviewing Key Terms

Choose the vocabulary term that best completes each sentence below. Write your answers on a separate sheet of paper.

dove	guerrilla warfare
deferment	domino theory
hawk	conservative era

1. One way to avoid military service was to obtain a _____ .

2. The Vietnamese used _____ to their advantage in fighting the Americans.

3. Someone who supported the war and wanted a military victory was called a _____ .

4. By the late 1960s, the nation had entered the _____, in which many Americans favored limiting government.

5. The _____ was an accepted concept during the cold war.

Recalling Facts

1. Identify Ho Chi Minh, his goals, and his role in the Vietnam War.

2. What nations made up Indochina?

3. What happened at Dien Bien Phu?

4. Why did the United States support Ngo Dinh Diem?

5. Why was the Diem government overthrown?

6. What was the Gulf of Tonkin Resolution?

7. List some of the guerrilla warfare tactics the Vietcong used.

8. What was the Ho Chi Minh Trail? Why was it important?

9. Who was General William Westmoreland?

10. Explain why the Tet offensive was a turning point in the war.

11. On what issue did Westmoreland and Clark Clifford disagree?

12. Why did Johnson decide not to run for reelection?

13. How did Dr. Martin Luther King, Jr., link the civil rights movement to his opposition of United States policy in Vietnam?

14. How did the events of the Democratic convention affect the outcome of the election in 1968?

15. What was Richard Nixon's strategy for winning the presidency in 1968?

16. What were some of the goals of Students for a Democratic Society?

17. Explain how the draft system worked during the Vietnam era.

18. Explain how the media influenced public opinion during the war.

19. What was public reaction to the shootings at Kent State?

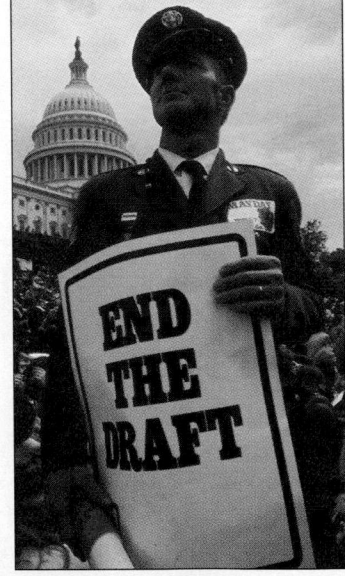

© SHELLY RUSTEN/BLACK STAR

20. What impact did student and other antiwar protest groups have on government policies both domestically and in Vietnam?

21. What was the significance of the November 1969 march to Washington, D.C.?

22. Explain the process of Vietnamization.

23. What did the Pentagon Papers reveal about the government's motivation for fighting in Vietnam?

24. What concessions did the United States and the North Vietnamese make at the Paris peace talks that finally ended the war?

25. What happened in Vietnam after the last American troops left?

Critical Thinking

1. **Determining Cause and Effect** Explain why Ngo Dinh Diem's attitudes toward his people ultimately led to his overthrow and assassination.

2. **Demonstrating Reasoned Judgment** President Johnson made the decision not to run for re-election in 1968. Determine whether you believe that President Johnson's decision was a good one or a bad one for him and the country. Write at least three reasons to support your decision.

3. **Identifying Alternatives** Imagine that you are a student during the Vietnam era and you are going to be drafted into the military. List several choices you could make in response to the draft. Explain the advantages and disadvantages of each possible decision.

4. **Making Comparisons** Presidents Johnson and Nixon had different plans to fight and win in Vietnam. Compare each of their major war strategies.

Critical Thinking

1. He did not understand his people, was intolerant of their religion, and did not allow any dissent.
2. Good decision: the country was divided and did not support him. Bad decision: he understood best what the issues were; the country needed continuity.
3. seek deferment (allow time for the war to end; be seen as unpatriotic); go to Canada (start new life; be away from family and friends); accept draft (do what government asks; be killed or injured); apply to be conscientious objector; resist draft (go to jail).
4. Johnson poured money and men into Vietnam. Nixon made South Vietnamese take more responsibility. Both were aggressive.

Portfolio Project

Use books, periodicals, and newspapers to learn about the plight of American POWs (prisoners of war) and MIAs (soldiers missing in action) in Vietnam. Make a time line to show what the government and private citizens have done on their behalf. Explain at least two courses of action that one might take to further the cause of verifying that prisoners are in Vietnam and promoting their return.

Cooperative Learning

Work with your classmates to organize the class into two groups. One group should contact friends, relatives, or veterans groups to locate two Vietnam veterans and arrange to have the veterans visit the class. The other group should create a list of questions to ask the veterans. It will be useful to think about questions that will help you learn about how the veterans joined the military, their combat or other training, their experiences in Vietnam, and their adjustment to civilian life after their return.

Reinforcing Skills

Understanding Public Opinion Polls Write a brief explanation of how public opinion polls can impact government decisions or public policy. Include at least one example from either the period discussed in this chapter or the present.

Geography and History

Study the map on this page to answer the following questions:

1. Do the countries that border Vietnam share any of the same physical characteristics? Explain.

2. What are the two principal river deltas in Vietnam?

3. What countries share the Northern Highlands?

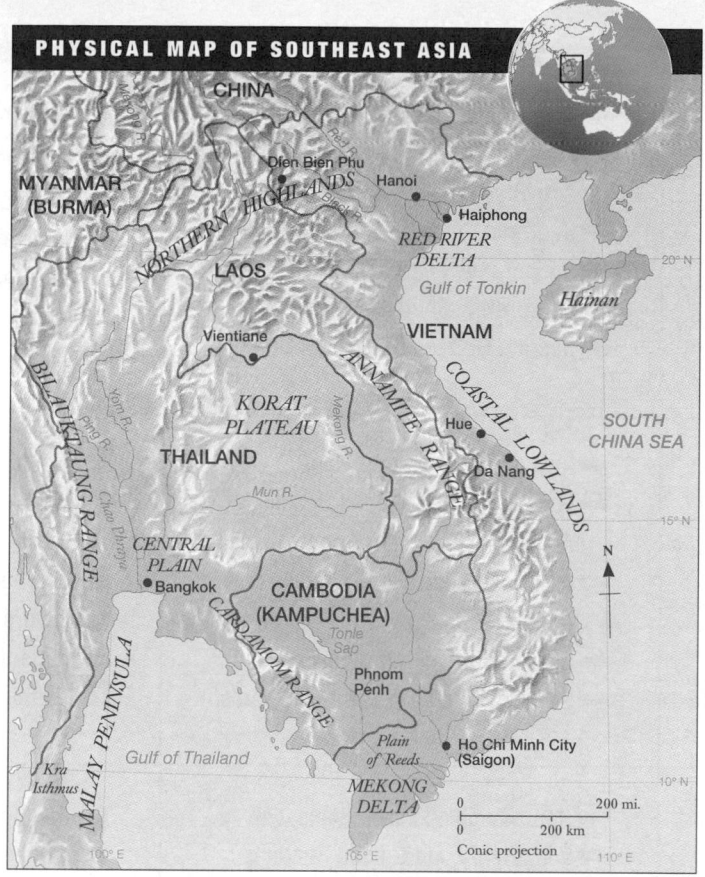

PHYSICAL MAP OF SOUTHEAST ASIA

CHINA
MYANMAR (BURMA)
NORTHERN HIGHLANDS
Dien Bien Phu
Hanoi
Haiphong
RED RIVER DELTA
20° N
Gulf of Tonkin
Hainan
LAOS
Vientiane
VIETNAM
KORAT PLATEAU
THAILAND
Mun R.
ANNAMITE RANGE
COASTAL LOWLANDS
Hue
Da Nang
SOUTH CHINA SEA
15° N
BILAUKTAUNG RANGE
CENTRAL PLAIN
Bangkok
CAMBODIA (KAMPUCHEA)
Tonle Sap
CARDAMOM RANGE
Phnom Penh
N
MALAY PENINSULA
Gulf of Thailand
Plain of Reeds
Ho Chi Minh City (Saigon)
10° N
Kra Isthmus
MEKONG DELTA
0   200 mi.
0   200 km
Conic projection
100° E
105° E
110° E

4. How did the shape of Vietnam affect the kind of battles that were fought during the war?

5. What clues does the latitude of Vietnam give you about its climate? How would the climate affect how the war was fought?

HISTORY JOURNAL

Look back at your journal response in the chapter opener. What new understandings about the Vietnam War do you have after reading this chapter? Write your response in your journal.

Geography and History

1. Yes, Laos and Cambodia share the Annamite Mountains.
2. Mekong Delta and Red River Delta
3. Laos, Myanmar (Burma), China
4. There are not large expanses of flat, dry land where United States troops could effectively use their machinery and equipment. The dense jungles and mountains made it difficult to conduct a conventional war.
5. Vietnam is near the equator; the mountains are not high, contributing to a warm climate. Warm temperatures would be difficult for unacclimated soldiers to fight in.

History Journal

Students should include references to what they learned about the domestic turmoil of this period and how the Vietnam War was conducted.

? BONUS QUESTION

This question may be used for extra credit on the chapter test.
What resources were used to fight the war?
Answer: *money, men and women, faith in government leadership and policies*

Portfolio Project

One might become a member of an MIA or POW organization or write to a Congressional delegation, urging action and support.

Cooperative Learning

Students should seek additional information from their guests about a soldier's experience in Vietnam other than what is provided in the text.

Reinforcing Skills

Public opinion polls are taken by polling companies, media agencies, and the government to measure response to events as well as opinions on issues. Government officials can use this information to plan legislation or weigh in on policy decisions. Public opinion forced Johnson not to seek reelection.

From Nixon to Carter

DAILY LESSON OBJECTIVES	REPRODUCIBLE RESOURCES	MULTIMEDIA RESOURCES
SECTION 1 A New Majority 1. Describe the appeal of Nixon's conservatism. 2. Present the strategies Nixon used to build a new conservative coalition. 3. Identify the ways in which the policies of the new conservatism affected society.	Reproducible Lesson Plans Vocabulary and Guided Reading Activities (English or Spanish) Supreme Court Case Studies Cooperative Learning Activities Interpreting Political Cartoons Section Quizzes (English or Spanish)	Chapter Teaching Transparencies Section Focus Transparencies Map Transparencies Landmark Documents in American History The Presidents: A Picture History of Our Nation Student Self-Test: A Software Review
SECTION 2 Nixon Foreign Policy 1. Describe how relations with China and the Soviet Union changed. 2. Discuss how Nixon and Kissinger used the dynamics of the Sino-Soviet relationship to advantage. 3. Analyze United States and Latin American relationships since 1945. 4. Evaluate Nixon's 1972 victory.	Reproducible Lesson Plans Vocabulary and Guided Reading Activities (English or Spanish) American Literature Readings and Activities Skill Reinforcement Activities Section Quizzes (English or Spanish)	Section Focus Transparencies Landmark Documents in American History Communism and the Cold War Powers of the President Student Self-Test: A Software Review Testmaker
SECTION 3 The Watergate Crisis 1. Describe how President Nixon abused the powers of his office. 2. Discuss how a free press reigned in the executive branch. 3. Describe how the system of separation of powers succeeded in preserving the government.	Reproducible Lesson Plans Vocabulary and Guided Reading Activities (English or Spanish) Supreme Court Case Studies Interpreting Political Cartoons Section Quizzes (English or Spanish)	Section Focus Transparencies Landmark Documents in American History Powers of the President Powers of the Congress Powers of the Supreme Court Student Self-Test: A Software Review Testmaker
SECTION 4 Ford and Carter 1. Explain the causes of the economic stagflation of the mid-1970s. 2. Describe the effects of the 1973 oil embargo. 3. Identify the results of President Ford's economic policies. 4. Describe Carter's foreign policy. 5. Describe the new environmental awareness of the late 1970s	Reproducible Lesson Plans Vocabulary and Guided Reading Activities (English or Spanish) Supreme Court Case Studies Geography in History Activities Interpreting Political Cartoons Reteaching Activities Enrichment Activities (English or Spanish)	Section Focus Transparencies Powers of the President Landmark Documents in American History The Presidents: A Picture History of Our Nation Lessons of War Student Self-Test: A Software Review
CHAPTER REVIEW AND EVALUATION	Chapter 23 Test, Forms A and B Performance Assessment Strategies and Activities Unit 9 Test, Forms A and B	Student Self Test: A Software Review Vocabulary PuzzleMaker Testmaker Chapter Digests Audiocassettes

`00:00` If time does not permit teaching the entire chapter, summarize using the Chapter 24 Digests Audiocassettes and the accompanying activities and tests. (Available in English or Spanish.)

✔ Performance Assessment

Cooperative Project

Organize the class into small groups. Have each group make a short list of what they consider to be traditional American values. Have groups present their lists to the class orally. As a class, make a composite list that represents the most frequently mentioned values. **LEP**

Suggested Rubric: An Oral Presentation. See Performance Assessment Strategies and Activities, p. 33.

Individual Project

Have students arrange to interview an elected official of your city, town, or school. Ask students to create a list of questions prior to the interview. You may suggest that students focus on why the official decided to run for office and how the campaign was run. Have students present their findings to the class. ▭

Suggested Rubric: An Oral Presentation. See Performance Assessment Strategies and Activities, p. 33.

Key to Ability Levels

Teaching strategies have been coded for varying learning styles and abilities.

L1 **BASIC** activities for all students

L2 **AVERAGE** activities for average to above-average students

L3 **CHALLENGING** activities for above-average students

LEP **LIMITED ENGLISH PROFICIENCY** activities

Block Scheduling

Block scheduling differs from traditional class scheduling in the amount of time allotted to each period. The extended timeframe provided by block scheduling affords you the opportunity to implement a greater number of research-oriented and activity-intense projects to motivate and involve your students. Activities that are particularly suited to use within the block scheduling framework are identified throughout this chapter by the following designation. ▭

T E A C H E R ' S   C O R N E R

NATIONAL GEOGRAPHIC SOCIETY

INDEX TO NATIONAL GEOGRAPHIC MAGAZINE

The following articles may be used for research relating to this chapter:

- "New Eyes on the Universe," by Bradford A. Smith, January 1994.
- "Venus Revealed," by William Newcott, February 1993.
- "Satellite Rescue," by Thomas Y. Canby, November 1991.
- "Neptune: Voyager's Last Picture Show," by Rick Gore, August 1990.
- "San Diego—Where Two Californias Meet," by Neil Morgan, August 1989.
- "High Tech: The Future is Now," by Michael E. Long, July 1989.

NATIONAL GEOGRAPHIC SOCIETY PRODUCTS AVAILABLE FROM GLENCOE

To order the following products for use with this chapter, contact your local Glencoe sales representative or call Glencoe at 1-800-334-7344:

- *The Presidents: A Picture History of Our Nation* (CD-ROM)
- *GTV: The American People: Fabric of a Nation* (Videodisc)
- *GTV: A Geographic Perspective on American History* (Videodisc)

ADDITIONAL NATIONAL GEOGRAPHIC SOCIETY PRODUCTS

To order the following products for use with this chapter, call National Geographic Society at 1-800-368-2728:

- *Decades of History: The 20th Century—The Middle Years* (Filmstrip)
- *The American Presidency* (Filmstrip)
- *The Vietnam War* (Filmstrip)
- *The United States as a World Power: From the 1890s to the 1970s* (Filmstrip)
- *1945-1989: The Cold War* (Video)

Chapter Overview

The Nixon presidency began in triumph and ended in disgrace. The country was plagued with economic woes and a dimming of its image abroad. The events of this decade—the end of the war, the thawing of the cold war, Watergate, and the waning of national optimism—are as complex as they are controversial.

Introducing the Chapter

Ask students what they know about President Nixon, his administration, and the Watergate scandal. It may be useful to write student impressions on the chalkboard. Remind students that it is important to understand the details of these subjects in order to understand fully the history of those years and that judgments should be withheld until the facts are learned.

Display the Chapter Teaching Transparency and distribute copies of the activity sheet.

Extension Activity

Have students complete Beyond the Transparency on the activity sheet for Chapter 24 and present their projects after the class has completed the chapter.

History Journal

Ask students to investigate an economic, political or environmental crises of this period and write a brief summary in their journals.

CHAPTER 24

From Nixon to Carter

AUGUST 8, 1974: THE PRESIDENT DECIDES

After a week of sleepless nights, an exhausted, pale President Nixon walked into the Oval Office of the White House and sat down behind his desk. He was alone except for a few television technicians and the White House photographer, Ollie Atkins. His voice cracked as he joked nervously with the crew.

At 9 P.M. the television crew signaled Nixon to begin. The President gazed into the camera: "Good evening. This is the thirty-seventh time I have spoken to you from this office in which so many decisions have been made that shape the history of this nation." Then came the moment that so many people had anticipated. For the first time in the nation's history, a President resigned from office.

Less than two years before, a beaming, triumphant President Nixon had addressed the nation, fresh from a landslide reelection victory. He had forged a new conservative coalition and was widely hailed for his bold foreign policy moves.

Yet he had overstepped the limits of the presidency and had broken the laws he had sworn to uphold. Richard Nixon had defied the American constitutional system, and now that system had taught him that no one is above the law, not even the President of the United States. ■

HISTORY JOURNAL

Before you read this chapter, write briefly what you know about any of the political, economic, and environmental crises this country faced during the 1970s.

806

✚ EXTRA CREDIT PROJECT

Persuasive Writing Ask students to write brief essays on the topic "The Importance of Free Elections to Democracy." You may wish to approach the topic by asking students to consider what happens in countries when free elections do not take place.

AFTER RESIGNING THE PRESIDENCY, RICHARD NIXON BOARDED A HELICOPTER TO BEGIN HIS RETURN TO PRIVATE LIFE IN CALIFORNIA.

807

Performance Assessment

Refer to page 806 for performance assessment activities for this chapter.

Also see Activity 24 in the Performance Assessment Strategies and Activities for an additional activity as well as for suggested rubrics.

Notes

Examining the Visual

A Drama Concludes The outstretched arms and fingers, held in a V-shape, is a classic pose of Richard Nixon and reminiscent of his greatest political victories. In this photo, however, the President is leaving the White House for the last time, having announced his resignation from office the night before.

FOCUS

Section Objectives

1. Describe the appeal of Nixon's conservatism.
2. Present the strategies by which Nixon hoped to build a new conservative coalition.
3. Identify the ways in which the policies of the new conservatism affected society.

Bellringer Activity

While taking attendance at the beginning of the class period, display **Section Focus Transparency 76,** and have students answer the questions. (Or use the blackline master.)

VISUAL INSTRUCTION

A Need to Be Heard Mayor John Lindsay ordered the flag at city hall in New York to fly at half-staff to honor the students killed at Kent State, and workers stormed student demonstrators.

Ask: What prompted the construction workers to march? *(They were tired of hearing from only those who opposed Nixon and the war.)*

SECTION 1

A New Majority

MAY 8, 1970: WORKERS BATTLE ANTIWAR PROTESTERS

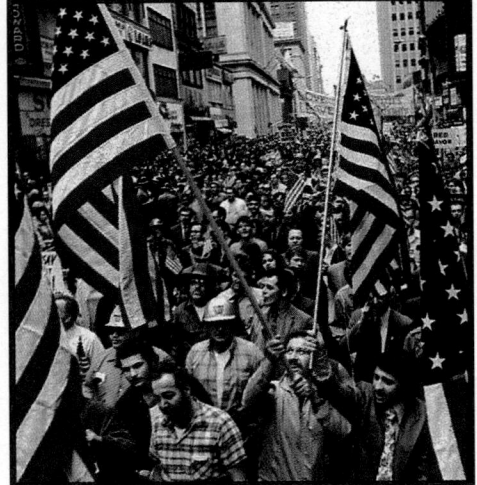

A Need to Be Heard
Working-class Americans take to the streets in support of President Nixon and his policies.

"WHEN YOU WERE STILL UP ON BROADWAY YOU COULD HEAR THE RUCKUS, THE HOLLERING. The peace demonstrators trying to outshout the construction workers. The construction workers hollering, 'U.S.A., all the way' and 'We're Number One.' And the peace demonstrators screaming up there that the war was unjust and everything else."

Thirty-one-year-old Joe Kelly, construction worker and family man, was one of several hundred workers who battled peace demonstrators in New York City that day. Wearing a yellow construction helmet bearing the message For God and Country, Kelly joined in, hurling insults and throwing punches.

The violent noon-hour rampage marked the beginning of two weeks of flag-waving marches in support of the Nixon administration and its Southeast Asia policies. The marchers were fed up with those they called flag-burning radicals who opposed the war.

Although other workers joined in, the construction workers led the way. Their hard hats soon became a symbol of traditional American values. Many, like Joe Kelly, were demonstrating for the first time in their lives.

Their message found a sympathetic ear at the White House. A few days after the Wall Street riots, President Nixon himself was awarded his own hard hat inscribed Commander in Chief.

AS YOU READ

Vocabulary
► backlash
► silent majority
► revenue sharing
► Southern strategy

Think About . . .
► why Nixon's conservatism appealed to so many Americans at the time.
► the strategies Nixon used to build a new conservative coalition.
► what effect Nixon's conservatism had on the life of an average citizen.

Section 1 Resources

REPRODUCIBLE RESOURCES
📖 Lesson Plan 24-1
📖 Vocabulary and Guided Reading Activity 24-1
📖 Cooperative Learning Activity 24
📖 Section 1 Quiz
📖 Political Cartoons 8, 9
📖 Supreme Court Cases 39, 43

MULTIMEDIA RESOURCES
📷 Section Focus Transparency 76
📷 Map Transparency 24
📷 Chapter Teaching Transparency 24

📀 Landmark Documents in American History
📀 The Presidents: A Picture History of Our Nation
📀 Testmaker
🎧 Chapter 24 Digest Audiocassette
📀 Student Self-Test: A Software Review
📀 Vocabulary PuzzleMaker

The War Within
Conflicts Set the Stage for Change

Like the workers and demonstrators who came to blows on Wall Street, American society at the end of the 1960s was divided into hostile camps. A decade of war and social change had ripped the nation apart. Not since the Civil War had the country seemed so divided—with conservatives pitted against liberals, workers against students, whites against African Americans, old against young.

As the 1960s drew to a close, the United States seemed to be at war with itself. Riots rocked 125 American cities following the assassination of Dr. Martin Luther King, Jr., in April 1968. In August of that year, police battled protesters at the Democratic National Convention in Chicago. Then, in October 1969, nearly 300 members of the Weather Underground, a militant wing of the Students for a Democratic Society (SDS), swept through the streets of Chicago smashing windows and shouting, "Long live the victory of the people's war!" Scenes of these so-called days of rage filled the television news, fueling the fears of millions of Americans.

The Conservative Backlash

Like construction worker Joe Kelly, a growing number of Americans became fed up with the social protests of the 1960s. The result was a conservative **backlash,** a sudden reaction against the liberalism of the 1960s. Mostly white working-class and middle-class Americans, these people saw the protests as an unprincipled attack on traditional values: hard work, family, religion, patriotism, and respect for law and order. They feared that unchecked violence and social disorder would destroy the country.

In part, they blamed the liberal policies of the Johnson years for the unrest of the decade. They resented the Warren Court for "meddling" in social issues and for "coddling" criminals. According to one poll, by 1968, 3 out of 5 Americans disagreed with the Warren Court's decisions.

They also resented paying taxes to support federal programs that they believed benefited only the poor and minorities. As one middle-class Chicagoan put it, "We are the forgotten men. We don't get one cent from the government." The cost of living rose steadily during the 1960s (by more than 7 percent in 1969), and income failed to keep pace. Many Americans saw the good life slipping away from them, and they resented it. They yearned for a return to traditional values and an end to the turmoil.

Nixon and the Silent Majority

In his 1968 campaign for President, Richard Nixon shrewdly tapped the deep well of discontent felt by these Americans, whom he called the **silent majority.** He promised to listen to "the great majority of Americans, the forgotten Americans, the non-shouters, the non-demonstrators."

Raised in a hard-working middle-class family, Nixon seemed to share the silent majority's values. He campaigned against the Great Society's "welfare mess" and pledged to "quit pouring billions of dollars into programs that have failed." He railed against Supreme Court decisions that he claimed had "tipped the balance against the peace forces in this country and strengthened the criminal forces." He promised to end the Vietnam War honorably and to restore law and order.

His appeal to what one writer called "the unblack, the unyoung, and the unpoor" paid off. In his victory speech after defeating Hubert Humphrey, Nixon promised to end the years of turmoil and unite the country: "We want to bridge the generation gap. We want to bridge the gap between the races. We want to bring America together."

Nixon at the Wheel Nixon is driving backwards—in effect driving to reverse 1960s civil rights gains. *What groups were divided against one another during the late 1960s?*

TEACH

Guided Practice

L3 **Discussion** Discuss the issue of civil liberties versus the power of the police. Ask students to identify the civil liberties granted under the Constitution and the legal powers of the police. Have students come to consensus on the proper relationship between the two. Ask them to compare the 1970s with the present in terms of this issue.

Show students Map Transparency 24 and have them complete the activity sheet.

VISUAL INSTRUCTION

Nixon at the Wheel This political cartoon uses caricature to exaggerate two of Nixon's features—his eyebrows and nose.

Answer: *Conservatives were against liberals, workers against students, whites against African Americans, and old against young.*

 Facts on File

Landmark Documents in American History Have students review "Inaugural Address, Richard Nixon, 1969" and "Silent Majority Speech, Richard Nixon, 1969" and write a paragraph about the intent of one of the documents.

Cooperative Learning

Supreme Court Assign small groups of students to research an aspect of the Supreme Court. For example, you may want to assign groups to study the authority of the Court, landmark decisions by the Court, or how the Court is organized. Encourage each student to offer information for the group report. Have each group report its findings to the class by an oral presentation, charts, or skits.

Notes

Despite his promises of unity, Nixon divided Americans even further. Intent on holding onto power, he took to heart the advice of one of his aides who claimed that the art of politics was the art of discovering who hated whom. Nixon played on the anger and fears of the silent majority as he set about building a new conservative coalition.

Nixon's New Conservatism
A Policy Born of Anger and Resentment

Once in office, Nixon sought to address the two major concerns of the silent majority—resentment of the federal government and fear of social disorder. A powerful civil rights movement, a broad antiwar coalition, and a Congress controlled by Democrats, however, would limit his attempts to advance conservative legislation. A practical man as well as a fighter, President Nixon compromised when necessary and pursued his conservative agenda whenever possible. Thus, in his first term, Nixon accepted many liberal programs and signed bills to boost Social Security benefits, expand the Job Corps, and build low-cost housing. He approved Democrat-sponsored legislation to lower the voting age to 18 and established the Environmental Protection Agency (EPA) and the Occupational Safety and Health Administration (OSHA).

Nixon's New Federalism

Even as he signed these liberal bills, Nixon began to steer a more conservative course. He introduced what he called the New Federalism—a series of programs that would "reverse the flow of power and resources from the states and communities to Washington and start power and resources flowing back . . . to the people."

To shift power back to the states, Nixon established a program of **revenue sharing** through which the federal government returned some of its tax money to local governments. He and his supporters hoped that more conservative state and local governments would use the money for law enforcement and civic projects instead of liberal programs to create jobs for the unemployed.

In one of his most controversial moves, Nixon sought to reduce the federal government's role in the nation's welfare system. In August 1969, the President introduced the Family Assistance Plan (FAP), an attempt to streamline the massive federal welfare bureaucracy and reduce welfare cheating. Instead of piecemeal handouts and a maze of federal agencies, regulations, and caseworkers, the FAP was a simple plan designed to give poor families a minimum annual income and then let them take responsibility for themselves. The FAP proposed a guaranteed minimum yearly income of $1,600 for a family of 4. To qualify for aid, heads of households had to sign up for job training.

The FAP quickly came under fire from both conservative and liberal camps. Conservative critics rejected the idea of a guaranteed annual income and insisted that the new program would only increase the number of people on the welfare rolls. Liberals denounced the plan, claiming that the payments were inadequate and that the job training program prepared trainees for low-paying jobs that held little chance for advancement. Although the plan passed in the House, it died in the Senate.

Despite his failure to overhaul the welfare system, Nixon successfully chipped away at the Great Society's base by cutting off federal grants for urban renewal, job

★ ★ ★ **GALLERY OF PRESIDENTS** ★ ★ ★

Richard Milhous Nixon
1 9 6 9 – 1 9 7 4

"The greatest honor history can bestow is the title of peacemaker. This honor now beckons America—the chance to help lead the world . . . onto that high ground of peace that man has dreamed of since the dawn of civilization. If we succeed, generations to come will say of us now living that we helped make the world safe for mankind."

Inaugural Address, January 20, 1969

BACKGROUND
- Born 1913; Died 1994
- Republican, California
- Served in the navy 1942–1946
- Elected to the Senate 1950
- Resigned as President 1974

ACHIEVEMENTS IN OFFICE
- Environmental Protection Agency (1970)
- First United States President to visit China (1972)

© J.P. LAFONT/SYGMA

810 CHAPTER 24 FROM NIXON TO CARTER

Meeting Special Needs

Reading Disability Have students who have difficulty in reading work in pairs or small groups and create word webs for the important vocabulary words in this section. They also may want to include other terms that they are having difficulty understanding. Some words they might use are *backlash, silent majority, new federalism,* and *Southern strategy.*

training, and education. In 1973 he abolished the Office of Economic Opportunity, a cornerstone of Johnson's anti-poverty program.

When the Democratic majority in Congress opposed his bids to reduce funding for certain programs, Nixon defied them by impounding, or refusing to spend, the funds. By 1973 Nixon had impounded nearly $15 billion in funds, crippling more than 100 federal programs. Programs in the areas of health, housing, education, and the environment were the hardest hit.

The courts eventually ruled that impoundment was illegal because it gave the President a veto power not granted in the Constitution. Only Congress, they ruled, had the authority to decide how federal funds should be spent.

Under Arrest Black Panther leader Bobby Seale and police come face-to-face in this 1971 photo. *What kind of actions did FBI undercover agents promote in the Black Panthers?*

Law and Order

To combat crime and social unrest, Nixon appointed his former law partner, John Mitchell, attorney general. A steely-eyed political veteran, Mitchell was an archconservative. He boasted, "This country is going so far right you won't recognize it."

As head of the Justice Department, Mitchell promoted measures to strengthen police powers—even at the cost of civil liberties. For example, he supported the use of wiretaps without a court order and the detention of criminal suspects without bail.

To silence antiwar and civil rights protesters and other critics, Nixon and Mitchell marshaled the forces of several federal agencies. The President used the Internal Revenue Service to harass enemies by auditing their tax returns. The Federal Bureau of Investigation (FBI) illegally tapped their phones and broke into their homes and offices, searching for information to embarrass and discredit them.

In addition undercover FBI agents joined the ranks of SDS and African American militant groups such as the Black Panthers. In some cases the agents deliberately set up violent clashes between these groups and the police. In 1969, for example, when the FBI targeted the Black Panther party, police killed an estimated 28 Panthers. Hundreds more were arrested.

Building a New Majority
Nixon Woos Disaffected Democrats

While shifting the national agenda toward more conservative programs, Nixon was also looking ahead to 1972 elections. He had been elected in 1968 by a slim plurality—less that 1 percent of the popular vote. Congress remained in Democratic hands. Nixon realized that to regain Republican control of Congress and to be reelected he would need to forge a new majority.

Shortly after the 1968 election, Nixon adopted a strategy that would guide his policies for the remainder of his presidency. In a report entitled "The Emergence of a Republican Majority," Kevin Phillips, a Nixon campaign aide, analyzed the results of the 1968 election. He claimed that conservative Democrats—primarily white ethnic voters, Southern whites, suburbanites, and blue-collar workers—were tired of the liberals who had come to control the Democratic party. He argued that these voters were ready to leave the Democrats and join the Republicans to form a new conservative majority under Nixon's leadership.

An Appeal to the South

According to Phillips's report, a growing number of conservative Americans lived in the Sunbelt—the Southern states, plus Texas, California, New Mexico, Oklahoma, and Arizona. Since the end of World War II, these states had more than doubled in population.

SECTION ONE **811**

Independent Practice

L2 **Writing** Ask students to write a brief essay on domestic surveillance. In particular, ask students to address the use of federal agencies like the FBI and IRS for such activities.

📁 Have students complete the Chapter 24, Section 1 Vocabulary and Guided Reading Activity. (Also in Spanish.) **LEP**

📁 Have students complete the Chapter 24 Cooperative Learning Activity.

VISUAL INSTRUCTION

Under Arrest Huey P. Newton and Bobby Seale founded the Black Panther Party for Self-Defense in Oakland, California. Its goal was to protect the African American community from brutal and racially motivated police action. By the late 1960s, the Panthers were drawing criticism from other African American groups who saw the African American struggle as fundamentally racial, not economic. By the late 1970s, the party had ceased to exist.

Answer: *They sometimes deliberately set up violent clashes between the Black Panthers and the police.*

Portfolio Project

Supreme Court Decisions Ask students to review some recent Supreme Court decisions and evaluate them according to the Court's interpretation of the law along a conservative-liberal continuum. Have students select one decision and explain why they feel it was a conservative or liberal one. Students should include this essay in their portfolios. 📁

VISUAL INSTRUCTION

Wallace Supporters Wallace's goal in the 1968 election was to deadlock the electoral college. This would have given him bargaining power to help select the next President.

Answer: *His platform stressed patriotism.*

ASSESS

Meeting Lesson Objectives

Each section objective is tested by the section review question(s) that follows it in parentheses.

1. Describe the appeal of Nixon's conservatism. (1, 2)

2. Present the strategies by which Nixon hoped to build a new conservative coalition.(1, 3)

3. Identify the ways in which the policies of the new conservatism affected society. (4, 5)

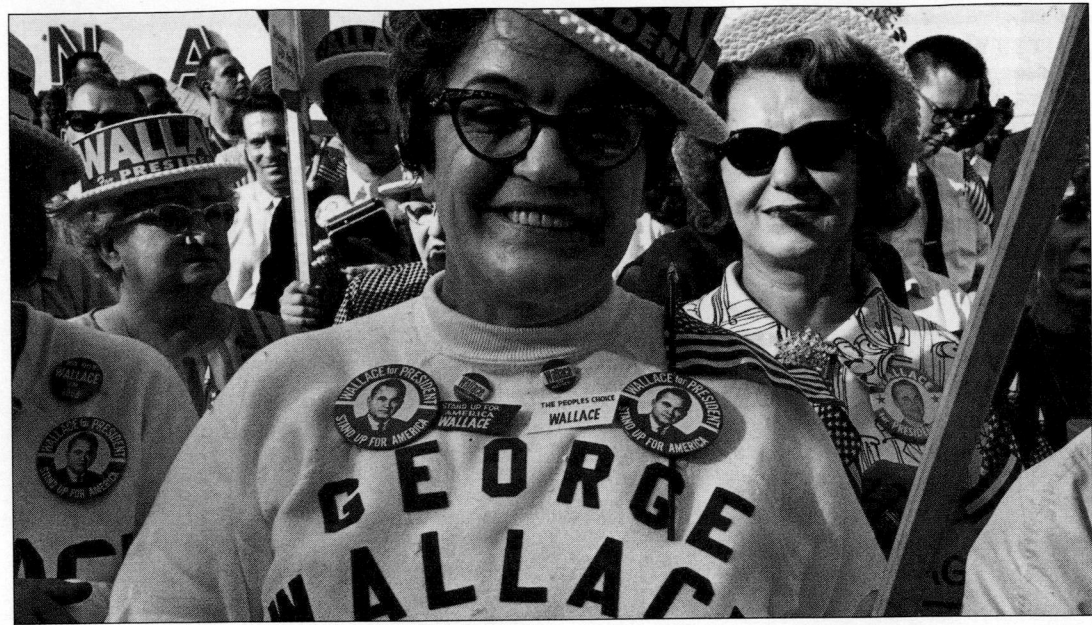

Wallace Supporters Nixon's Southern strategy was designed to lure voters like this one away from George Wallace. *What does the slogan on the woman's button tell you about Wallace's political platform?*

The South had long been a Democratic stronghold, but many white Southern Democrats believed that the party had become too liberal. As a result some of them had left the party and supported the conservative segregationist George Wallace in the 1968 presidential election. These conservative Democrats had helped Wallace—the former governor of Alabama—win 13.5 percent of the popular vote and carry 5 Southern states. Nixon planned to lure these voters away from Wallace with his conservative agenda. By adding the Wallace voters and other discontented Democrats to the 43.4 percent of Americans who had voted for Nixon in 1968, the Republicans hoped to build a powerful new majority that would help them recapture Congress and hold on to the White House.

Nixon adopted a **Southern strategy**—a plan designed to appeal directly to Southern white conservatives. To bring these voters into the Republican camp, the President appealed to their discontent with racial integration, a liberal Supreme Court, and Eastern liberals.

Attacks on Civil Rights

In the 1968 election, Nixon won barely 13 percent of the African American vote, and he knew he was unlikely to attract more African American voters in 1972. To gain votes in the South, Nixon believed he could afford to alienate African Americans on civil rights issues. He made his position clear in a September 1968 press conference when he stated: "There are those who want instant integration and those who want segregation forever. I believe we need to have a middle course between those two extremes." In effect Nixon sided with those who wanted to delay desegregation and told African Americans seeking their rights that they were extremists.

Once in office Nixon used the Department of Health, Education and Welfare (HEW) to carry out his strategy. In 1969 HEW stepped in to delay desegregation plans for school districts in South Carolina and Mississippi, despite a Supreme Court ruling that school desegregation begin at once. Shocked by the turnaround in federal policy, the NAACP responded, "For the first time since Woodrow Wilson we have a national administration that can be rightly characterized as anti-Negro."

Two years later the Supreme Court ruled that courts could order the desegregation of school systems by busing if necessary. Nixon went on television to denounce the ruling and to urge Congress to prohibit forced busing. Although Congress did not heed his call, Southern segregationists got the message—President Nixon was on their side. The message also reached those in Northern cities—including many Democrats—who opposed busing.

Nixon further angered civil rights supporters by opposing the extension of the Voting Rights Act of 1965. This act had added 1 million African Americans to the

Extending the Content

School Desegregation Review the issue of school desegregation. Discuss with students why busing was thought by some to be a solution to the problem. Also ask students to consider why many people thought that busing caused more problems than it solved.

voting rolls, greatly increasing African American political power. Despite the President's opposition, Congress voted to extend the act.

The Nixon Court

Many conservatives also resented the liberalism of the Warren Court. In their eyes recent Supreme Court rulings on questions such as integration and school prayer were an attack on traditional values.

To reverse the liberal decisions of the Warren Court, Nixon sought to fill vacancies on the Court with conservative judges. When Chief Justice Earl Warren resigned in 1969, Nixon nominated conservative federal judge Warren Burger to head the court. Later that year Nixon selected a conservative Southerner, South Carolina federal circuit judge Clement F. Haynsworth, Jr., to fill another opening. He hoped this appointment would help solidify his support among white Southerners.

Haynsworth, however, quickly came under fire for his record of antilabor and anti–civil rights rulings, and the Senate rejected his appointment. Furious at the defeat, Nixon chose another conservative Southern judge, though one much less qualified than Haynsworth—Florida federal appeals court judge G. Harrold Carswell. Civil rights groups were outraged. During a state election campaign in 1948, Carswell had affirmed his belief in white supremacy. Even more damaging was his poor record as a federal judge; higher courts had overturned many of his rulings. Even Carswell's promoters were half hearted in their support.

When the Senate rejected Carswell's nomination, Nixon claimed the votes against Haynsworth and Carswell reflected the Democratic Senate's prejudice against the South. He used the defeat to further align himself with Southern conservatives. "I understand the bitter feelings of millions of Americans who live in the South," Nixon declared.

Nixon's subsequent choices to fill seats on the Supreme Court—Harry A. Blackmun, Lewis F. Powell, Jr., and William H. Rehnquist—were all well qualified and conservative. The Senate confirmed these nominations with little opposition.

Although Nixon appointed four conservative justices to the Supreme Court, the Court did not always rule conservatively. On issues such as abortion, desegregation, and the death penalty, it took a liberal stance. On other issues, such as civil liberties, police power, and censorship, however, the Court's rulings reflected a shift to the right.

Attacks on Liberals

In his bid to capture the Wallace vote, Nixon launched shrill attacks on his liberal opponents—the press, the liberal Democrats, and the student protesters.

To carry out the broadsides, he enlisted the aid of his outspoken Vice President, Spiro Agnew. In speeches across the country, Agnew used his license from the administration and a knack for colorful language to characterize the administration's opponents. He called liberal Democrats "sniveling hand-wringers." The television news media drew Agnew's scorn for what he saw as a liberal bias.

The Nixon administration also had a fear of what they saw as the Eastern establishment. As a result Agnew called media executives "curled-lip boys in eastern ivory towers." While Nixon insisted his goal was to bring Americans together, Agnew revealed a different strategy: "If in challenging, we polarize the American people, I say it is time . . . to rip away the rhetoric and to divide on authentic lines."

Nixon's Southern strategy failed to yield major Republican victories in the 1970 state and congressional elections. The Southern strategy did, however, lay the groundwork for Nixon's own reelection campaign in 1972. Coupled with the policy of New Federalism, the Southern strategy helped shift the national agenda to the right. While the policies of Johnson's Great Society had promised to protect the rights of the poor and minorities, Nixon's new conservatism promised to look out for the middle class. Yet even as Nixon was reshaping the political landscape at home, a far more pressing issue demanded his attention abroad—the Vietnam War.

SECTION REVIEW

Vocabulary

1. Define: backlash, silent majority, revenue sharing, Southern strategy.

Checking Facts

2. What were the concerns of those whom Nixon sought as supporters?

3. What steps did Nixon take to build a new coalition of voters?

Critical Thinking

Evaluating Information

4. Evaluate the Nixon law-and-order campaign. What groups did he feel threatened security? What kinds of tactics did he support to ensure law and order?

Linking Across Time

5. Do you think there is a new silent majority today? If so, give examples of their political and social concerns.

FYI

Nominees Blocked Not since Grover Cleveland was President had Congress rejected two Supreme Court nominees.

Evaluate

Have students complete the Section Review.

Assign the Section 1 Quiz or use the Testmaker to develop a customized quiz. (Also in Spanish.) **LEP**

Reteach

Have students listen to the Chapter 24, Section 1 Audiocassette. (Also in Spanish.) **LEP**

Enrich

Have students complete Interpreting Political Cartoons 8, 9.

Have students complete Supreme Court Case Studies 39, 43.

CLOSE

Ask students to give the main ideas from this section. Write their suggestions on the board to create a summary of this section. *(A backlash by conservatives against antiwar activities and liberal government policies emerged. Nixon ushered in a period of conservatism in legislation, judicial decisions, and economics.)*

Section 1 Review Answers

1. backlash (809), **silent majority** (809), **revenue sharing** (810), **Southern strategy** (812)

2. They were concerned that there was lack of support for the government and that traditional values were under attack.

3. He appointed four conservative justices and undermined advances in civil rights and social programs.

4. He hoped to suppress protesters, critics, and black militants by using wiretaps, detaining criminals without bail, and having the FBI and IRS harass dissidents.

5. Answers may vary. Yes, some still have the same concerns. No, concerned groups speak out.

TEACH

Making the Geography Connection

Remind students that part of Nixon's 1972 election strategy targeted voters from Southern states. This was an indication of the emerging growth and power of the Sunbelt states.

FYI

Center of Population If identical weights, each representing the location of one person on the date of the census, were placed on an imaginary, flat, weightless, and rigid map of the United States, the point of perfect balance between weights would be the center of population. At each census since 1790, this point has been moving steadily westward. The 1990 census placed the center of population 9.7 miles (15.61 km) southeast of Steelville, Missouri.

MAP STUDY

The states of the Sunbelt had widespread growth soon after air conditioning became affordable. Before then, people hesitated to settle in an area with such stifling summers.

Answer: *Florida*

Geography: Impact on History

REGION
The Rise of the Sunbelt

Regions can be defined by many different criteria—climate, vegetation, geographic features, or industrial characteristics, for example. Since the 1970s a new region has emerged with its own distinctive political and economic characteristics—the Sunbelt, the fastest growing area in the United States.

The Sunbelt

This region includes 15 states, each with a generally mild and sunny climate, and extends from Virginia on the East Coast to Southern California in the West. The states are Virginia, North Carolina, South Carolina, Tennessee, Georgia, Florida, Alabama, Mississippi, Arkansas, Texas, Louisiana, New Mexico, Arizona, and the southern part of California.

Why the Region Grew

During World War II, the United States military established scores of training bases in the South. Thousands of civilians followed military personnel south to take advantage of the business opportunities the bases provided. Cities such as San Diego, California; Mobile, Alabama; and Norfolk, Virginia, had huge increases in population. In

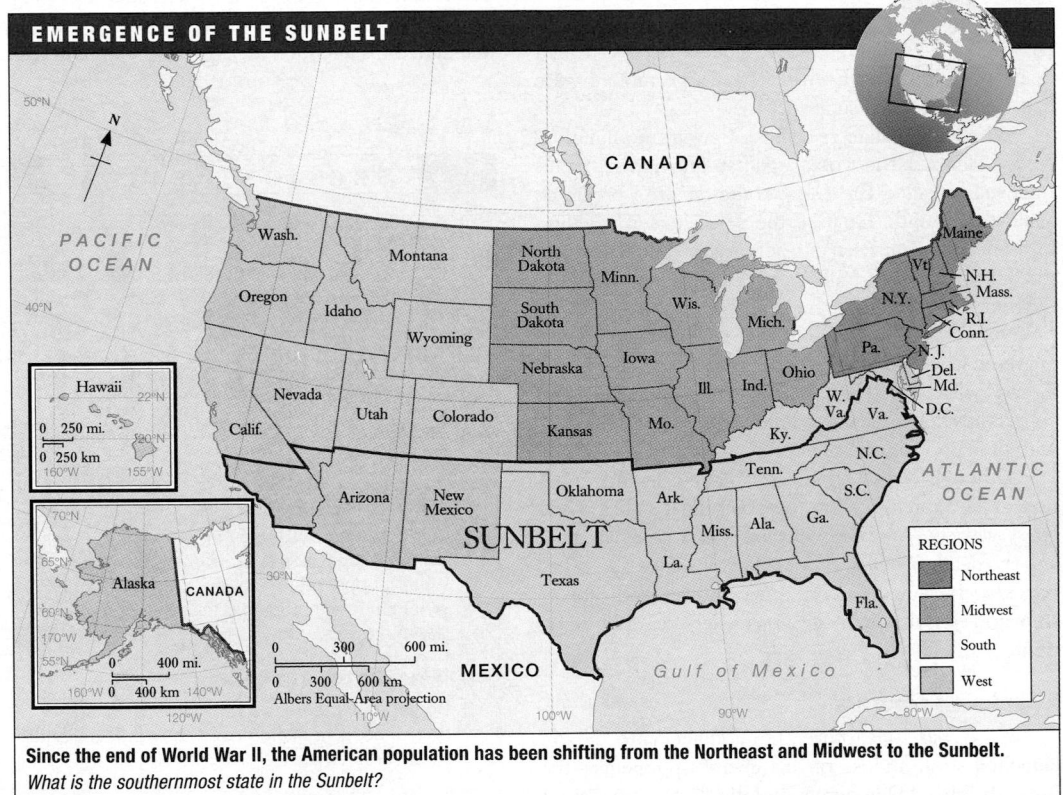

EMERGENCE OF THE SUNBELT

REGIONS
- Northeast
- Midwest
- South
- West

Since the end of World War II, the American population has been shifting from the Northeast and Midwest to the Sunbelt. *What is the southernmost state in the Sunbelt?*

Geographic Themes

Movement Between 1970 and 1976, the elderly population nationwide increased 14.8 percent. The South and West had gains of 22.1 and 20.5 percent, respectively, in persons aged 65 and over. In contrast, the elderly population in the Northeast and North Central regions grew by a smaller percentage than the national average. The difference was probably the result of net out-migration of elderly persons from the North. Arizona, New Mexico, and Florida showed increases greater than 30 percent in the number of persons 65 and over. Ask the following: What are some businesses and services a community with a large number of senior citizens might need to provide? (*medical and recreation facilities, public transportation, restaurants, stores, support and social organizations*) the 1950s the testing and development of rockets, missiles, space vehicles, and military aircraft often took place on or near military facilities and brought still more jobs and people to the area.

The economic climate of the late 1970s forced many changes on businesses and individuals. New government policies and a severe drought created a crisis for American farmers, for example. Between 1979 and 1988, nearly 1 million jobs on farms and in related businesses disappeared. As a result, many people from farming regions were forced to look for work elsewhere.

The recession of the late 1970s and early 1980s deeply affected the auto and steel industries of the Northeast and Midwest. Factory after factory in these states closed, leaving unemployed workers little choice but to leave the area.

States began to compete with each other to lure new business to their area. Offers of tax incentives and the lenient labor laws in the South and West drew companies to the region. Some industries that moved were new (such as the computer industry), but many others were not.

There were other attractions to the Sunbelt. Lower cost of living, lower taxes, available energy sources, and inexpensive land all prompted business growth. Several large dams provided sources of water and abundant, cheap electricity. New air and highway transportation networks also helped the Sunbelt to grow.

Finally, air conditioning—no longer a luxury affordable only to

Urban Growth Sun City businesses and neighborhoods spill into the Arizona desert. *Why have retirees moved to the Sunbelt?*

the rich—made working in the Sunbelt's stifling summer heat more bearable and the region more attractive to potential employers.

The Attraction of Prosperity

On the heels of corporate moves to the South and West came service, entertainment, and retail industries. As the population exploded, once quiet residential communities began to look more like cities, with malls, industrial parks, and large housing developments replacing open fields and wooded areas.

The warm climate and sandy beaches along the Gulf of Mexico and the southern Atlantic fueled growth in the tourist industry. Warm weather, planned retirement communities, and the lower cost of living also lured many retirees to

the Sunbelt states. Sun City, Arizona, is an example of an area whose growth has been largely the result of the interregional migration of retirees.

Increased Political Power

As the population has shifted to the South and West, the political importance of the Sunbelt has also increased. According to 1990 census reports, some of the Sunbelt states have grown by as much as 20 percent since 1980. As a result, Sunbelt states have gained 11 seats (excluding California, which had a total state gain of 7 seats) in the House of Representatives. Northern and Midwestern states have lost 21 seats in the House during the same period. Current Census Bureau estimates indicate that this trend will continue into the 2000s.

Mapping Activity

Have students select one state from the Sunbelt and research its growth (population, industry, congressional representation) in the last 10 years and write a brief report. Students should include a map of the state with their reports.

VISUAL INSTRUCTION

Urban Growth Florida and Texas also attract large numbers of retirees.

Answer: *The warm climate, planned communities, and relatively low cost of living lure retirees.*

CLOSE

Discuss with students some effects of increased movement of people to the Sunbelt region. (*increased political power; need for more roads, schools, stores; demand for natural resources; need for regional planning; possible pollution*)

MAKING THE GEOGRAPHIC CONNECTION

1. What have been some of the political consequences of the growth of the Sunbelt region?

2. What kinds of businesses and industries have moved to the Sunbelt?

3. **Region** What has made the Sunbelt so attractive to people and companies since the end of World War II?

Making the Geographic Connection Answers

1. Sunbelt states have increased their representation in Congress. This has increased their political power and ability to lobby more effectively for their needs.

2. computer companies, service industries, recreational and retail businesses, space and military, entertainment, manufacturing

3. lower taxes and cost of living, lenient labor laws, inexpensive land, energy and water sources, mild climate, improved transportation systems, ready availability of air conditioning

FOCUS

Section Objectives

1. Describe how Nixon changed the United States's political relationships with the Soviet Union and China.
2. Discuss how Nixon and Kissinger used the dynamics of the Chinese and Soviet relationship to American advantage.
3. Analyze the changes in the relationship between the United States and Latin America since World War II.
4. Evaluate the reasons for Nixon's landslide victory in the election of 1972.

Bellringer Activity

While taking attendance at the beginning of the period, display **Section Focus Transparency 77,** and have students answer the questions. (Or use the blackline master.)

VISUAL INSTRUCTION

A Step Toward Détente Kissinger's family fled Nazi Germany in 1939 when he was 15 years old. He studied at Harvard and later became a professor there. In 1973 he shared the Nobel Peace Prize with North Vietnamese Premier Le Duc Tho—the premier refused to accept the prize.

Ask: What government position did Henry Kissinger hold at the time of his trip? *(He was security adviser to President Nixon.)*

SECTION 2

Nixon Foreign Policy

JULY 1971: KISSINGER MAKES TOP-SECRET CHINA TRIP

A Step Toward Détente
The secrecy of Kissinger's trip was nearly revealed by a newspaper reporter.

IN THE EARLY-MORNING DARKNESS, UNITED STATES SECURITY ADVISER HENRY KISSINGER BOARDED A PAKISTANI JET FOR A SECRET FLIGHT INTO MAINLAND CHINA. His mission, code-named Polo after Marco Polo, another trailblazing China traveler, was to arrange a presidential visit to the People's Republic of China. His cover was a "stomach indisposition" he had supposedly developed during a stopover in Pakistan. To help Kissinger's plane evade Soviet and Indian radar, Chinese navigators teamed with the Pakistani crew to guide the plane on a special route over the Himalayas. According to the plan, Kissinger would not contact the United States until he returned to Pakistan; if successful, he was simply to send the code word *Eureka.*

Kissinger's trip to mainland China was in itself a major breakthrough; he was the first high-level United States official to visit that country in more than 20 years. Now, after months of careful diplomatic moves and secret messages relayed by third parties, Kissinger was meeting China's leaders face-to-face.

Back in the United States, Nixon and a few trusted aides waited anxiously for news from Kissinger. On July 11, Kissinger cabled his deputy at the White House, Alexander Haig, who then put a call through to Nixon's home in San Clemente, California.

"What's the message?" Nixon asked.

"Eureka," Haig replied.

Four days later, on network television, Nixon told the world of Kissinger's mission. The news amazed many in Nixon's audience because Republicans had adamantly opposed recognition of the People's Republic of China and had barred the country's admission to the United Nations.

AS YOU READ

Vocabulary
▶ détente
▶ realpolitik
▶ balance of power
▶ liberation theology

Think About . . .
▶ how Nixon changed the United States's political relationships with the Soviet Union and China.
▶ how Nixon and Kissinger used the dynamics of the Chinese and Soviet relationship to American advantage.
▶ changes in the relationship between Latin America and the United States since 1945.
▶ why Nixon won the 1972 election.

Section 2 Resources

REPRODUCIBLE RESOURCES
📄 Lesson Plan 24-2
📄 Vocabulary and Guided Reading Activity 24-2
📄 Section 2 Quiz
📄 Unit 9 American Literature Reading
📄 Skill Reinforcement Activity 24

MULTIMEDIA RESOURCES
🖐 Section Focus Transparency 77
💿 Landmark Documents in American History
💿 Communism and the Cold War
💿 Powers of the President

💻 Student Self-Test: A Software Review
💻 Vocabulary PuzzleMaker
💻 Testmaker
🎧 Chapter 24 Digest Audiocassette

Détente

A Shift in Foreign Policy

Although President Nixon's policy in Vietnam provoked fierce criticism, he was widely hailed for a series of bold moves in other parts of the world. Envisioning a new world order, Nixon abandoned the cold war policy of confrontation and initiated a policy of **détente,** an attempt to repair strained relations between the United States and the Communist powers. In a dramatic reversal of nearly 25 years of cold war politics, Nixon sought better relations with both China and the Soviet Union.

A New World View

The world in 1970 little resembled the world of the 1950s, when the cold war policy of containment was forged. Five economic superpowers—the United States, the Soviet Union, Japan, China, and the European Economic Community, a coalition of the nations of Western Europe—had replaced the 2 superpowers, the United States and the Soviet Union. President Nixon believed that economic power was the key to political power and that these 5 superpowers would determine the political future.

Nor was the Communist world united in 1970. Tensions between the Soviet Union and China had erupted in the 1960s, resulting in armed clashes between the two former allies in 1969. By playing one Communist power against the other, Nixon and Kissinger hoped to gain concessions from both.

Nixon and Kissinger shared a belief in **realpolitik,** practical politics. According to this view, a nation should pursue policies and make alliances based on its national interests rather than on any particular view of the world. Thus, if improved relations with China and the Soviet Union would benefit the United States, then the United States should set aside its bias against communism and pursue those relations.

An Official Review Premier Zhou Enlai and President Nixon inspect troops during Nixon's 1972 visit to China. *Why did the United States initiate a policy of détente?*

Kissinger and Nixon promoted a foreign policy based on a **balance of power** among nations. "It will be a safer world and a better world," the President declared in 1971, "if we have a strong, healthy United States, Europe, Soviet Union, China, Japan—each balancing the other."

Nixon and Kissinger believed that détente was the key to this balance. Détente would limit Communist expansion and curb the nuclear arms race through negotiation rather than armed conflict.

Détente made sense economically, too. The United States was not eager to pour billions of dollars into another regional conflict like Vietnam. In addition trade with the Soviet Union and China would open up new markets for American products.

Nixon was able to undertake this bold shift in foreign policy in part because of his reputation as a cold warrior. Elected to Congress in 1946 on an anti-Communist platform, he gained fame in the 1940s as a member of the House Un-American Activities Committee. Certainly no one could question Nixon's genuine commitment to anti-communism.

Kissinger: The Master Player

Kissinger and Nixon's shared love of secrecy and personal power also contributed to Nixon's success in international relations. As national security adviser and later as secretary of state, Kissinger reported directly to Nixon, devised policy with him, and often conducted secret negotiations on his behalf. This working style frequently excluded other government officials and avoided public debate. In dealing with China, however, Nixon and Kissinger's system of secrecy helped them achieve a foreign policy breakthrough.

The People's Republic of China

Since the Communist takeover of China in 1949, the United States had refused to recognize the People's Republic of China, the most populous nation on the earth. Diplomatic relations between the 2 nations had been cut off. Instead the United States recognized the anti-Communist Chinese government in exile on the island of Taiwan.

SECTION TWO **817**

TEACH

Guided Practice

L3 Discussion Discuss with students the link between anti-Communist thinking and cold war policies. Ask students to explain how President Nixon's policy of détente represented a shift from past United States relations with the Communists.

VISUAL INSTRUCTION

An Official Review Zhou was the most influential spokesperson for China in international affairs after the Communists took control in 1949.

Answer: *He was trying to improve our strained relations with the Communist powers.*

Facts on File

Landmark Documents in American History Have students review "Announcement on China, Richard Nixon, 1971," "Toasts During China Visit," "U.S. Chinese-Communiqué of 1972 (Shanghai Communiqué)," and "Remarks on Return From China, Richard Nixon, 1972" and write a paragraph about the intent of one of the documents.

Cooperative Learning

Map Skills Organize students into five work groups. Using a world map, have them locate the countries identified as economic superpowers on page 817. Have each group research essential facts about one superpower, including the European Economic Community in 1971 (Belgium, France, Italy, Luxembourg, the Netherlands, and West Germany). Suggested areas to research could include geography, size, population, type of government, and major industries and products. Have each group share their findings by creating an annotated map of the superpower they selected to research.

VISUAL INSTRUCTION

The Cold War Begins to Warm Nixon was the first President to be received at the Kremlin. He would visit with Brezhnev again in 1973 and 1974.

Answer: *It wanted to prevent a Chinese-American alliance, slow the arms race, and increase trade with the United States.*

Global Connection

Lon Nol named himself president and took control of the Cambodian government. He had earlier overthrown Prince Sihanouk and proclaimed Cambodia a republic.

Videodisc

Communism and the Cold War

Side 1, Chapter 20
Title: Détente
Subject: Overview of détente between United States and the Soviet Union
Ask: Why was détente welcomed? *(It lessened the chances of a nuclear war.)*

The United States had treated the People's Republic as an outlaw nation; it had cut off trade and vetoed the country's admission to the United Nations. To the cold war policy makers, the People's Republic was a "red menace" threatening to gobble up its Asian neighbors.

By the time Nixon became President, however, each side had good reasons for wanting to heal the rift. After years of border disputes and the Soviet invasion of Czechoslovakia, China distrusted and feared the Soviet Union. The United States hoped that recognition of China would help end the war in Vietnam, drive a deeper wedge between the two Communist superpowers, and pressure the Soviet Union into making greater negotiating concessions on limiting nuclear arms.

The winds of change began to blow in the fall of 1970 when Nixon confided to a *Time* magazine reporter that he wanted to go to China. Then, in April 1971, a ping-pong ball made headline news when the Chinese hosted an American table tennis team in the first official contact between the 2 nations in more than 2 decades. Only 1 week later the United States announced the end of the trade embargo against China.

In July 1971, Nixon sent Kissinger on a secret mission to Beijing. Soon afterward Nixon stunned the world with the announcement that he would travel to China to normalize relations between the 2 countries. That fall, after the United States abandoned its opposition, China was admitted to the United Nations.

In February 1972, Nixon arrived in China for a week-long visit. Accompanied by reporters and television camera crews, the President visited the Great Wall and met with Chinese leaders Mao Zedong and Zhou Enlai. Friendly gestures abounded. Chinese musicians played

Cold War Begins to Warm Soviet Premier Leonid Brezhnev and President Nixon share a lighter moment during Nixon's trip to Moscow in 1972. *Why was the Soviet Union anxious to meet with the United States?*

"America the Beautiful," and Nixon quoted lines from Mao's poetry.

The United States and China agreed to allow greater scientific and cultural exchange and to resume trade. Although formal diplomatic relations were not established until 1979, Nixon's trip marked the first formal contact with China in more than 25 years.

The Soviet Union

In a second dramatic foreign policy move, Nixon visited Moscow only three months after his trip to China. The Soviets eagerly welcomed the thaw in cold war politics. They wanted to prevent a Chinese-American alliance and to slow the costly arms race. They also hoped to gain access to United States technology and to buy badly needed American grain.

During his visit Nixon met with Soviet leader Leonid Brezhnev and signed agreements on trade and technological exchange. Even more important, Nixon signed a landmark arms agreement, the result of negotiations known as the Strategic Arms Limitation Talks (SALT). The economic and military pacts were linked: the United States promised to allow the Soviets to buy wheat and corn and other consumer goods if the Soviets agreed to make arms concessions.

The SALT Agreement

SALT made history with the openness of the negotiations and the limits it placed on specific nuclear missiles. It limited the number of missile defense systems in each country to one system for the capital city and one system for the main missile launching center. It allowed the addition of certain weapons only if others were dismantled. SALT had weaknesses: it did not limit long-range bombers or missiles loaded with multiple independently targeted warheads; it did not prohibit the development of new nuclear weapons systems. Even so, by restricting the number of some nuclear weapons, it eased tensions between the United States and the Soviet Union and put a brake on the expensive and perilous nuclear arms race. It also laid the groundwork for the more substantive SALT II negotiations.

Middle East
Kissinger and Shuttle Diplomacy

By 1973 Nixon foreign policy stood at a turning point. Nixon and Kissinger's major theories—realpolitik, maintenance of an equilibrium of power among nations, and détente—had worked well in relations with China and the Soviet Union. Their foreign policy approach was soon to be tested severely in the Middle East.

Meeting Special Needs

Learning Disability Pair a student who has learning disabilities with another member of the class and have them work together to create an outline of the events and concepts of this section.

Encourage students to use the section captions as a guide to structure their outline. This activity can help students with learning disabilities divide the section into manageable parts. **LEP**

Occupied Golan Heights Israeli Defense Minister Moshe Dayan looks out from an observation post in Syria. *What prompted the Yom Kippur War?*

The Yom Kippur War

Armed and advised by the Soviet Union, Egypt and Syria attacked Israel on October 6, 1973, the Jewish holy day of Yom Kippur. They were attempting to regain territories lost to Israel in the 1967 Six-Day War. Almost immediately, Nixon and Kissinger saw this conflict as an opportunity for the United States to assume a peace-making role in the Middle East and thus gain an edge over the Soviet Union in the region.

To make their plan work, Kissinger, now secretary of state, tried to determine the war's outcome by alternately withholding and granting supplies to Israel. The stakes rose when the Arab oil-producing countries stopped shipments to the United States to protest its aid to Israel. Fuel prices skyrocketed and so did United States inflation. Nixon and Kissinger now had an urgent economic need to establish better relations with Arab countries, even at the expense of Israel. When the Israelis violated a cease-fire, Kissinger forced them to back down by cutting off supplies. On October 26, a new cease-fire took effect.

Searching for Lasting Peace

During the next two years, Kissinger shuttled back and forth between Middle Eastern cities, trying to resolve the oil crisis and broker a lasting peace. Arab nations ended the oil embargo in March 1974, and in September 1975, Egypt and Israel signed a historic peace agreement: Egypt officially recognized Israel for the first time, and the Israelis gave up part of the Sinai Peninsula, their first-ever withdrawal from occupied lands. As part

of the settlement, the United States promised massive military aid to both parties.

Pleased by Kissinger's negotiations and the United States's promises of aid, Egypt abandoned the Soviet Union in favor of the United States. With Kissinger's help, Arabs and Israelis met to talk about long-term peace for the first time. Kissinger also carefully staked out a more neutral territory for the United States in Arab-Israeli affairs, thus reducing the likelihood of future oil embargoes.

Nonetheless shuttle diplomacy had its costs. By shutting the Soviets and the Palestinians out of Middle East negotiations, Nixon and Kissinger endangered détente and encouraged the Soviet Union to arm radical Arab factions such as the Palestinian Liberation Organization (PLO). Kissinger's shuttle diplomacy also created suspicions among the negotiating parties that the United States was playing one country against another.

Latin America Since 1945
The Region Undergoes Many Changes

The years following World War II brought sweeping changes to Latin America. Economies grew rapidly, and democracy flourished. Yet by the 1970s, 2 shadows loomed over Latin America—deepening economic crises and the rise of military dictatorships.

Economic Growth

In the postwar prosperity of the 1950s, the rapidly growing economies of North America and Western Europe clamored for Latin American exports such as oil, minerals, coffee, bananas, and sugar. As the world economy grew, Latin America prospered.

Export income and loans helped fund Latin America's own industrial development. In 1950 Latin America produced just $11 billion worth of manufactured goods. By 1974 that total had climbed to $66 billion.

Foreign investment mounted too. By the mid-1960s, United States investment in Latin America reached $9 billion, and in 1980 it topped $35 billion.

The Growing Debt

As industrial production grew, Latin American nations began borrowing from banks in the United States and Western Europe to finance their economic growth. Bankers flocked to Latin America. Latin American countries sank even deeper in debt when oil prices rose in 1974 and 1979.

The ability of these borrowers to repay their loans, however, depended on an expanding international market for products from Latin America and stable interest rates. In the 1980s the demand for Latin American oil

 Videodisc

Powers of the President

Side 2, Chapter 9
Title: World Leader
Subject: Role of President as a world leader, includes Nixon in China
Ask: How did Nixon help establish diplomatic ties with China? *(He was the first President to visit China since the Communists took over.)*

See Powers of the President Guidebook page 68 for complete lesson plan.

VISUAL INSTRUCTION

Occupied Golan Heights Israeli General Moshe Dayan served as the country's defense minister in 1967 and became a symbol of Israeli courage for his victory in the Six-Day War.

Answer: *Egypt and Syria were attempting to regain territory they lost to Israel in the 1967 Six-Day War.*

Portfolio Project

Biography Ask each student to select one of the major figures mentioned in this section (Kissinger, Zhou, Brezhnev, Allende, Pinochet, McGovern, or Wallace). Have students research the life of the person they have identified and write a brief biography of him. Students should include the reports in their portfolios.

Independent Practice

 L2 Writing Ask students to write a brief essay to describe and defend détente. Have students include specific examples of how the policy benefits the United States and other countries.

✎ Have students complete the Chapter 24, Section 2 Vocabulary and Guided Reading Activity. (Also in Spanish.) **LEP**

⚡ Curriculum Connection

Geography Have students work in teams to prepare maps of Latin America. Each team should focus on one subject such as dates of independence, principal products, natural resources and features, population, or languages.

VISUAL INSTRUCTION

Government Target Archbishop Oscar Arnulfo Romero of El Salvador supported land reforms and jobs for the poor. His assassination in 1980 touched off widespread rioting.

Answer: *They sided with the poor for social change and were a threat to the status quo.*

UPI/BETTMANN

Government Target Archbishop Romero greets his parishoners after a Sunday mass at the San Salvador Basilica. *Why were left-leaning clergy often targets of government repression?*

fell when Western industrial nations suffered a recession. As their export earnings declined, Latin American nations were also hit by rising interest rates. The results were disastrous. The debt consumed most of Latin America's export earnings. Once eager to make loans, bankers now closed their doors to the struggling debtors. One despairing manager of a Mexican oil company lamented in September 1982, "Six months ago, there were so many bankers in [my office] you couldn't walk across the room. Now they don't even answer my telephone calls."

The Rise of Democracy

The victory of democracy over dictatorship during World War II led many Latin Americans to demand democracy at home. A group of Brazilians opposed to the dictator ruling their country in the 1940s declared, "If we fight against fascism at the side of the United Nations so that liberty and democracy may be restored to all people, certainly we are not asking too much in demanding for ourselves such rights and guarantees."

In addition postwar prosperity was creating an emerging middle class that believed that its interests would be best served by democracy. By 1946 dictators had been forced out of Peru, Cuba, El Salvador, Guatemala, Colombia, Venezuela, and Brazil. New political parties sprouted, and women gained the right to vote. By 1959 only 4 military governments remained.

The new democracies faced serious challenges—poverty, illiteracy, and hunger. Often their attempts at eco-

nomic change, such as land reform, disturbed the upper classes, who feared the loss of their wealth and power. The elite turned to their traditional allies, the military, to halt the reforms. From 1962 to 1964, democratic governments in 8 countries fell to military dictatorships.

An Era of Change
Governments Topple

The failure of Latin American democracies and the rise of repressive military governments led some Latin Americans to choose more radical means of bringing about change. During the 1960s, left-wing revolutionary guerrilla movements sprang up throughout Latin America. Revolutionaries were willing to postpone democratic reforms such as free elections and a free press until basic social reforms had been achieved.

The Catholic Church, which served 80 percent of the population, added its voice to those clamoring for reform in Latin America. The church had long been an ally of the rich and powerful. In the 1960s, however, thousands of young priests and nuns began to speak out, asserting that the church must side with the poor in the struggle for social justice. This doctrine, known as **liberation theology,** led many religious leaders to call for Socialist reforms. As Mexican Bishop Sergio Mendes declared in 1970, "Only socialism can give Latin America a true development. . . . I believe that a socialist system best conforms to Christian principles of true brotherhood, justice, and peace."

A Troubled Era

By 1970 the military ruled most of Latin America. Only Costa Rica, Uruguay, Chile, Mexico, Colombia, and Venezuela enjoyed democracies. Chile and Uruguay fell to dictators during the 1970s. Economic crises in the 1970s and massive opposition to repression, however, led to the fall of many military governments during the 1980s.

United States-Latin American Relations

After World War II, the United States wanted democratic governments and the free enterprise system to flourish in Latin America so that these nations would be good allies and trading partners. It also wanted to protect United States investments and to prevent the

Extending the Content

Literature and Movies Isabel Allende, niece of Chile's assassinated president, Salvador Allende, published a best-selling novel, *House of the Spirits.* The novel, set in Chile, recounts the saga of the Trueba family from the turn of the century to the time of Allende's overthrow in 1973. In 1994 the novel was made into a motion picture. Discuss with students other novels, stories, poems, or movies they know that are based on any events or individuals mentioned in this section or period.

spread of communism. On occasion these foreign policy goals conflicted with each other and with the aims of the Latin American countries involved.

Mexico in particular had a love-hate relationship with the United States. It welcomed United States investments and wanted its northern neighbor to allow millions of Mexicans to cross the border to find work, yet it fought to stay clear of United States-sponsored trade agreements. Although the United States still offered many advantages that Mexico depended on—jobs for migrant workers, large oil markets, technology, and investments—Mexico, along with the rest of Latin America, was beginning to challenge the United States's domination of its economic development.

To break the American grip on their economies, many Latin American countries wanted to create their own industries rather than just supply raw materials and cheap labor for United States businesses. Some reform-minded politicians also wanted to break up large plantations and redistribute land to small farmers. Some wanted to nationalize certain industries—to take them from private owners and run them as national government businesses. The United States government joined major landowners and businesspeople in opposing such socialist reforms.

A Policy of Intervention

To protect United States business interests and to prevent leftist politicians from achieving successes in Latin America, the United States government often supported the region's right-wing dictators. Interventionism, government interference in the political or economic affairs of another country, had been prac-

ticed by the United States in Latin America for nearly 100 years. After World War II, intervention came to mean anything from providing weapons and training for Latin American armies to economic sanctions and invasions.

Allende Pushes for Change

In 1970 a Socialist named Salvador Allende ran for the presidency of Chile, promising land reform and nationalization of foreign industries. Although Nixon and Kissinger discounted the importance of most of South America, they saw Allende's candidacy as a major threat to the United States. Both Nixon and Kissinger feared that a Socialist Chile would ally with Cuba and the Soviet Union and perhaps start a Communist "domino effect" in South America. An undercover campaign to defeat Allende thus began. Nixon authorized the CIA to try to "fix" the election with bribes, propaganda, and other "dirty tricks." When Allende won, Nixon ordered the CIA to incite a military coup before Allende actually took office. CIA operatives even conspired with right-wing groups to assassinate Allende. Those tactics also failed, but Nixon and Kissinger did not give up.

By now, with the CIA's reputation on the line, the secret war against Allende intensified. While the United States cut off all aid to Chile, the CIA spent millions of dollars financing antigovernment media and military opposition. Finally in 1973 a military force headed by General Augusto Pinochet seized the government and killed Allende. Even though Pinochet's government abolished civil liberties, executed thousands, and ended economic reforms, the United States quickly resumed trade and economic relations with Chile.

Congress later investigated the involvement of the United States in the overthrow of Chile's elected government and condemned Nixon and Kissinger's maneuvers against Allende. This episode also weakened détente, because it was a clear violation of an earlier United States-Soviet pledge to use negotiations rather than force in dealing with regional crises.

MICHAEL MAUNEY/LIFE MAGAZINE © TIME INC.

Physician Turned Politician Salvador Allende tried to build a socialist society within a parliamentary democracy. *Why did Nixon and Kissinger fear Allende's presidency?*

The Election of 1972
A Republican Triumph

Nixon's trips to China and the Soviet Union boosted his popularity at home. In the summer of 1971, following the invasion of Laos, only 31 percent of the American public supported Nixon's policies. By the summer of 1972, however, after his well-publicized visits abroad, his approval rating soared to nearly 62 percent. As Election Day neared, a Republican victory seemed certain.

SECTION TWO **821**

VISUAL INSTRUCTION

Physician Turned Politician Allende helped to organize Chile's Socialist party shortly after receiving his medical degree in 1932.

Answer: *They feared his links to communism.*

ASSESS

Meeting Lesson Objectives

Each section objective is tested by the section review question(s) that follows it in parentheses.

1. Describe how Nixon changed the United States's political relationships with the Soviet Union and China. (1, 5)

2. Discuss how Nixon and Kissinger used the dynamics of the Chinese and Soviet relationship to American advantage. (1, 2, 5)

3. Analyze the changes in the relationship between the United States and Latin America since World War II. (1, 4)

4. Evaluate the reasons for Nixon's landslide victory in the election of 1972. (2, 3)

FYI

Allende Victory Allende received 36.3 percent of the vote, a plurality, not a majority as required by law. Thus, the Chilean Congress had to declare the new president on October 24 and so named Allende.

Cultural Perspectives

Mestizos Latin America includes the diverse countries of Central and South America. Before the Europeans arrived, this was all Native American land. Most of the early Spanish and Portuguese came without wives and families. They were more interested in obtaining wealth and power than in developing a continent. These men married local women, and a new mestizo group emerged, integrating Native American and European ancestry. Discuss with students how intermarriage affected the culture of Latin America.

821

GRAPH STUDY

John Hospers of California and Theodora Nathan of Oregon received one vote from an elector in Virginia. **Answer:** *approximately 95 percent*

Evaluate

Have students complete the Section Review.

☞ 🔲 Assign the Section 2 Quiz or use the Testmaker to develop a customized quiz. (Also in Spanish.) **LEP**

Reteach

🎧 Have students listen to the Chapter 24, Section 2 Audiocassette. (Also in Spanish.) **LEP**

Enrich

☞ Have students complete the Unit 9 American Literature Reading.

CLOSE

Ask students how Nixon's foreign policy decisions affected events at home. *(Nixon's trips to China and the Soviet Union and the withdrawal of troops in Vietnam boosted his popularity. This helped Nixon win the 1972 election.)*

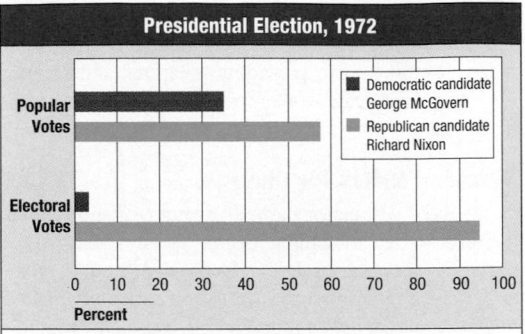

Presidential Election, 1972

A Sweeping Victory Nixon captured approximately 47 million votes and McGovern nearly 30 million. *What percentage of the electoral vote did Nixon obtain?*

The Divided Democrats

The Democratic party was hopelessly split. Four major candidates competed for the presidential nomination: former Vice President Hubert Humphrey, Maine Senator Edmund Muskie, South Dakota Senator George McGovern, and former governor of Alabama George Wallace.

Humphrey, who had lost to Nixon in 1968, was unable to muster support for a rematch. The moderate Muskie started strong, but the liberal McGovern soon overtook him. McGovern's opposition to the Vietnam War gave voters a clear alternative to Nixon's war policies.

Wallace posed the greatest threat to Nixon. Wallace had galvanized many conservative voters with his attacks on busing, criminals, protesters, and "pointy-headed intellectuals." As a Democratic nominee or a third-party candidate, Wallace could pull these voters away from Nixon. Wallace won a string of Southern primaries and came in a close second in some Northern states. His campaign was cut short in May 1972 by the bullet of a would-be assassin. The attack left Wallace paralyzed for life and forced him to withdraw from the campaign.

An early opponent of the Vietnam War and a social reformer, McGovern won a number of key primaries. Recent reforms in Democratic party rules had increased the number of women, minority group members, and young persons among the delegates at the convention, assuring McGovern's nomination. McGovern was not a middle-of-the-road candidate. He called for a $30 billion cut in defense spending, immediate withdrawal from Vietnam, and pardons for Vietnam draft resisters.

Many traditional Democratic supporters were unhappy with the party's drift to the left. Denied a seat at the convention, AFL-CIO President George Meany ordered union members—traditionally staunch Democrats—to withhold support from McGovern.

The Republican Campaign

Nixon's campaign suffered no setbacks. His trips to the People's Republic of China and the Soviet Union and his withdrawal of United States troops from Vietnam helped silence his foreign policy critics. An upturn in the economy further bolstered his popularity. He easily won over voters who had previously supported Wallace with promises to fight busing and end "the age of permissiveness."

Nixon also capitalized on the Democrats' disarray and their choice of the liberal McGovern. He called them the party of "hooligans, hippies, and radical liberals." Many conservative Democrats agreed and voted Republican on Election Day.

Nixon won the 1972 election in a landslide, carrying every state but Massachusetts. He won 60.8 percent of the popular vote. The electoral vote margin was even greater, 520 to 17. The Southern strategy had paid off.

Yet a shadow loomed over Nixon's victory. He had been accused of authorizing a "dirty tricks" campaign against the Democrats. Shortly before the election, burglars hired by the Committee to Re-Elect the President had been caught breaking into Democratic national headquarters in Washington. Nixon and his aides denied any involvement in the break-in, and for the time being at least the public believed them. As Nixon began his second term, however, the tangled story behind the burglary began to unravel.

SECTION REVIEW

Vocabulary

1. Define: détente, realpolitik, balance of power, liberation theology, interventionism.

Checking Facts

2. Why were both the Soviet Union and China receptive to visits by President Nixon?

3. Why was Nixon's popularity so high just before the election in 1972?

Critical Thinking

Analyzing Information

4. Give several examples of how the relationship between the United States and Latin America has changed since 1945.

Linking Across Time

5. Give specific examples of the impact of the United States's new relationships with China and the Soviet Union.

Section 2 Review Answers

1. **détente** (817), **realpolitik** (817), **balance of power** (817), **liberation theology** (820)
2. The Chinese distrusted the Soviet Union and wanted improved relations with the United States to counter Soviet power. The Soviets hoped to prevent a Chinese-American alliance, slow the arms race, and gain access to American technology.
3. Nixon's trips to China and the Soviet Union increased his popularity.
4. The United States wanted democracy to flourish there and to have Latin America be a good ally and trading partner. These goals included opposing socialist reforms that Latin American governments wanted to institute. Latin Americans often opposed United States interference.
5. increased travel, cultural exchanges, trade activity

Social Studies Skill
INTERPRETING POLITICAL CARTOONS

Learning the Skill

For more than 200 years, American newspapers and magazines have published political cartoons. Reading political cartoons from the past can help you appreciate how people of other times felt about important issues. Interpreting current political cartoons can increase your awareness of differing views on today's important issues.

A cartoon is meant to entertain, usually by using a play on words or by creating amusing images. A political cartoon also makes a comment on a current political issue by using caricatures, symbols, and analogies.

To help you interpret a political cartoon, study the use of each of the visual techniques described below. Then combine the individual messages to determine what impression the cartoonist wants to leave with the reader.

Caricature

A caricature is an exaggerated picture. By deliberately exaggerating unusual or distinctive features of a well-known subject, the cartoonist produces a comic image and also helps the reader to recognize the subject. The cartoon on this page, for example, exaggerates two of President Nixon's most recognizable facial features—the size of his nose and the dark circles around his eyes.

Symbol

A symbol is an idea, image, or object that stands for or suggests something else. Some symbols are widely used and need no explanation. For example, a dove as a symbol of peace is recognized almost anywhere. In the cartoon on this page, the person labeled Congress symbolizes the father figure in the story of George Washington and the cherry tree. The axe behind Nixon's back is a symbol of his guilt. The cartoonist in this case expects the reader to be familiar with the cherry tree story and to recognize these symbols.

Analogy

An analogy compares two related things or ideas by using one as a reference for illustrating the other. For example, an analogy might be drawn between the benefits of walking and the benefits of reading, as follows: reading is to the mind as walking is to the body.

In this cartoon, evidence of President Nixon's actions is compared to George Washington's axe. The analogy is that the evidence in the Watergate affair was to Con-

I claim executive privilege

gress what the axe was to George Washington's father—proof of his involvement. In this unfavorable comparison, Nixon does not admit his offense as young Washington did. Instead he uses his privilege as the nation's Chief Executive to try to hide the evidence of his actions.

Practicing the Skill

1. Look at the political cartoon on page 825 of your textbook. What does the crown in the cartoon represent?

2. What feature of John Ehrlichman is exaggerated in this cartoon?

3. Using as a clue what you know about the Nixon administration, determine why the cartoonist chose this setting for his drawing.

4. What is the message shown by having Nixon with his hand in the mouth of Arthur Burns?

5. What does it mean that Kissinger and Ehrlichman also have headwear?

Applying the Skill

Find a cartoon in a newspaper or magazine. Write a brief summary of the cartoon's message.

Additional Practice

For additional practice, see Reinforcing Skills on page 847.

SOCIAL STUDIES SKILL   **823**

© BILL MAULDIN/CHICAGO SUN-TIMES

TEACH

This skill demonstrates how political cartoons can express points of view. By interpreting a political cartoon from the 1970s, students will discover that cartoonists use humor both to entertain and to influence. They will see how three features of a cartoon—caricature, symbol, and analogy—can be combined to convey a political message.

Additional Practice

☞ Have students complete the Chapter 24 Skill Reinforcement Activity.

Practicing the Skill Answers

1. Nixon's strong sense of power as President
2. his eyebrows
3. Nixon surrounded himself with a small group of advisers, much like a king's court.

4. He did not want to hear what Burns had to say.
5. They both had positions of higher influence than the others.

FOCUS

Section Objectives

1. Describe how President Nixon abused the powers of his office.
2. Discuss how a free press functioned to rein in the executive branch.
3. Discuss how the constitutional system of separation of powers worked to preserve the integrity of the government.

Bellringer Activity

 While taking attendance at the beginning of the period, display **Section Foucs Transparency 78,** and have students answer the questions. (Or use the black-line master.)

VISUAL INSTRUCTION

**A Turn in the Presidency
The Watergate burglars were Eugenio R. Martinez, Virgilio R. Gonzalez, Frank A. Sturgis, James McCord, Jr., and Bernard L. Barker.**

Ask: How were the burglars caught? *(The night watchman noticed tape over the lock on the garage door and called the police.)*

Facts on File

Landmark Documents in American History Have students review "Watergate Investigations Address, Richard Nixon, 1973" and "Statement on Haldeman, Ehrlichman Resignations, Dean's Dismissal, Richard Nixon, 1973" and write a paragraph about the intent of one of the documents.

The Watergate Crisis

JUNE 17, 1972: BURGLARS BREAK INTO DEMOCRATIC PARTY HEADQUARTERS

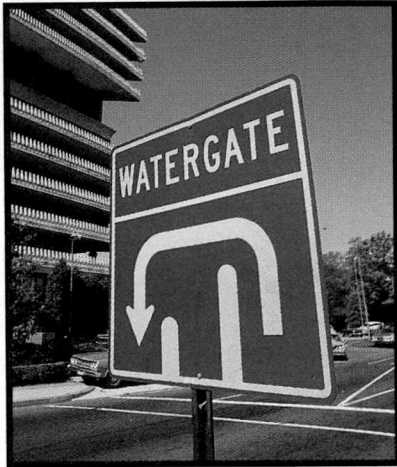

© DENNIS BRACK/BLACK STAR

**A Turn in the Presidency
The Watergate burglary was one of several "dirty tricks" in a larger plan called Gemstone.**

SHORTLY AFTER MIDNIGHT ON JUNE 17, 1972, SECURITY GUARD FRANK WILLS WAS MAKING HIS ROUNDS OF THE WATERGATE BUILDING, A VAST OFFICE-APART-MENT COMPLEX IN WASHING-TON, D.C. As he checked the doors connecting the building to an underground parking garage, the 24-year-old Wills noticed something odd. The locks on the doors had been taped to keep them from locking. "I took the tape off, but I didn't think any-thing of it," he said later. "I thought maybe the building en-gineer had done it." Wills finished his rounds and then strolled across the street to a diner for a cheeseburger, french fries, and a shake.

An hour later Wills was back at work. Once again he checked the garage doors. They had been retaped! This time Wills called the police.

The police found more taped doors on the building's sixth floor, headquarters of the Democratic National Commit-tee (DNC). They cautiously be-gan to search the DNC offices one by one.

Suddenly, behind a glass and wood partition, one of the police officers spotted an arm. "Hold it!" he shouted. "Come out!" A moment later, not 2 but 10 hands shot up. Five men dressed in business suits emerged. On the floor lay lock picks, 40 rolls of film, 2 cameras, 2 "bugs"—tiny electronic devices for listening—and $1,754 in cash.

When police returned the next day, they found more elec-tronic equipment, several suitcases, and $3,566.58 in cash. They also found a tiny black address book. In it, next to the name Howard Hunt, were a telephone num-ber and the phrase: *W. House.*

AS YOU READ

Vocabulary
▶ impeachment
▶ pardon

Think About . . .
▶ how President Nixon abused the powers of his office.
▶ how a free press worked to help keep members of the government in check.

▶ how constitutional checks and bal-ances functioned to preserve the integrity of the government.

---

824 CHAPTER 24 FROM NIXON TO CARTER

Section 3 Resources

REPRODUCIBLE RESOURCES
📂 Lesson Plan 24-3
📂 Vocabulary and Guided Reading Activity 24-3
📂 Section 3 Quiz
📂 Political Cartoon 4
📂 Supreme Court Case 42

MULTIMEDIA RESOURCES
🖥 Section Focus Transparency 78
💿 Landmark Documents in American History
🔵 Powers of the President
🟦 Student Self-Test: A Software Review

🔵 Testmaker
🎧 Chapter 24 Digest Audiocassette
📂 Powers of the Congress
📂 Powers of the Supreme Court

It would take 22 months and the combined efforts of Congress, the press, and the courts to bring the Watergate story to light. What emerged was not just the story of a burglary but a tale of crimes committed by the man sworn to uphold the Constitution and the nation's laws—the President of the United States.

The Nixon White House

An Imperial Presidency

When Richard Nixon first took office in 1969, the White House was already the seat of considerable power. Since the outbreak of World War II, United States Presidents had gradually assumed powers in foreign policy making that the Constitution seemed to reserve for Congress. During the war President Roosevelt had, in effect, made treaties with foreign nations without the advice or consent of the Senate. Both Truman and Johnson had sent troops into combat without a congressional declaration of war. When national security was at stake, they argued, the President had to be able to respond quickly—even if that meant Congress was not consulted.

Nixon, however, outdid his predecessors in ignoring constitutional checks on presidential powers. He impounded funds for federal programs he opposed, defying the constitutional mandate that Congress control spending. He ordered United States troops to invade Cambodia without seeking congressional approval. As the executive branch flexed its muscles, the legislative branch weakened, and the balance of powers set forth in the Constitution tipped in favor of a more powerful presidency. By the 1970s the constitutional presidency had become what some critics called the imperial presidency.

President Nixon

Richard Nixon reached the White House after nearly 25 years in politics. A skilled lawyer and a shrewd politician, Nixon loved public life and hoped to be remembered as a great statesman.

He greatly admired former Presidents Woodrow Wilson and Teddy Roosevelt.

Yet Nixon had a darker side. At times mean-spirited and suspicious, he made his reputation in the late 1940s by hounding alleged Communists in the United States government. This was the Nixon who thrived on the power of the imperial presidency and whom his critics dubbed King Richard.

The Inner Circle

Nixon surrounded himself with a small group of trusted and loyal aides. At the head of what some critics called the palace guard stood Harry Robins "H. R." Haldeman, the President's chief of staff, and John Ehrlichman.

Haldeman was Nixon's closest aide. A former advertising executive, Haldeman first worked for Nixon in 1956 when Nixon was campaigning for Vice President. The uncomplaining Haldeman described his role: "I get done what he wants done, and I take the heat for it." Ehrlichman, a former Seattle lawyer, handled domestic policies. Together with Henry Kissinger, Haldeman and Ehrlichman formed an inner circle that wielded more power than the President's cabinet.

The Enemies List

By surrounding himself with aides who almost always agreed with him, Nixon created his own house of mirrors, where all opinions reflected his own. Protected from criticism, Nixon grew increasingly isolated.

All the President's Men This cartoon shows how those who wanted to be heard by the President had to press hard to do so. His most powerful assistants are positioned closest to him.
Whom does Nixon seem most willing to listen to here?

Cooperative Learning

Research Organize the class into small groups to research the activities of the Nixon administration before the Watergate scandal. Groups should decide among themselves how to divide the research responsibilities so that everyone makes a contribution. Groups can then report their findings to the class.

TEACH

Guided Practice

L2 Discussion Presidents are often accused of being isolated from the public. Discuss the meaning of the phrase "a house of mirrors." Have students evaluate the phrase in terms of elected officials they are familiar with today.

VISUAL INSTRUCTION

All the President's Men An editorial cartoon tells the artist's view about an issue using few words. It should convey its point at a glance.
Answer: *Henry Kissinger*

ABCNEWS INTERACTIVE™

 Videodisc

Powers of the President

Side 2, Chapter 23
Title: Watergate Scandal
Subject: News reports about the scandal
Ask: What was the Watergate scandal? *(Someone had broken into the Democratic National Headquarters)*

See Powers of the President Guidebook page 88 for complete lesson plan.

ABCNEWS
iNTERACTiVE™

Videodisc

Powers of the President

Side 2, Chapter 24
Title: Presidential Denials
Subject: Nixon denies involvement in Watergate
Ask: Why did many people believe that the President was involved? *(The break-in had occurred during the election campaign, and some of the President's advisers were implicated.)*

See Powers of the President Guidebook page 90 for complete lesson plan.

Side 2, Chapter 25
Title: Watergate Committee Hearings
Subject: Montage of statements
Ask: What was the purpose of the hearings? *(to determine whether there had been any official wrongdoing)*

See Powers of the President Guidebook page 91 for complete lesson plan.

One Nixon aide recalled: "You were either for us or against us, and if you were against us we were against you." In 1971 Nixon ordered his special counsel, Chuck Colson, to put together an enemies list. Colson, who described himself as a "flag-waving . . . anti-press, anti-liberal, Nixon fanatic," eagerly set about his task.

Colson drew up a list of more than 200 individuals and 18 organizations that the administration regarded as enemies. The list included many notable liberal Americans. Among them were politicians such as Senators Edward Kennedy and George McGovern, Representatives Bella Abzug and Shirley Chisholm, and the entire African American leadership of the House; college presidents, such as Kingman Brewster of Yale University; Hollywood stars, such as Steve McQueen, Paul Newman, and Jane Fonda; and 57 members of the media.

Once the list was complete, Nixon asked the FBI to spy on these individuals and try to discredit them. He also ordered the IRS to harass them with tax audits.

The Huston Plan

A concern that the antiwar movement might undo him as it had toppled Johnson in 1968 fed Nixon's fears. The massive public outcry following the announcement of the Cambodian invasion in April 1970 had shaken the President. He believed he had to silence his critics or face defeat at the polls in 1972.

In June 1970, White House aide Tom Huston submitted a plan for a secret police operation to combat the antiwar movement. The Huston plan would expand and unify the work of the FBI, the CIA, the National Security Agency, and the Defense Intelligence Agency. The entire operation would be run out of the White House. To defend what the White House considered to be national security, agents would infiltrate antiwar groups, open people's mail, and tap telephones. They would break into homes and offices in search of information that could be used to discredit or even blackmail Nixon's critics.

Although Huston admitted that much of the plan was illegal and would violate the rights of United States citizens, President Nixon approved it. FBI Director J. Edgar Hoover, however, feared that the plan would reduce the FBI's power and blocked it.

CREEP

As the 1972 presidential election neared, Nixon's worries mounted. The Republican party had failed to regain control of either the House or the Senate in the congressional elections of 1970. Past campaign losses, to John F. Kennedy for President in 1960 and to Pat Brown for governor of California in 1962, haunted Nixon. He wanted 4 more years in the White House.

In early 1971, Nixon looked like a loser. A poll in February showed Democratic presidential hopeful Edmund

Muskie out in front of Nixon, 43 to 40 percent. By March Muskie was ahead 44 to 39 percent, and by May he led Nixon by a still greater margin at 47 to 39 percent.

Taking no chances with his reelection campaign, the President put his trusted friend John Mitchell in charge. In March 1971, Mitchell resigned as attorney general and set up the Committee to Re-Elect the President (CREEP). The burly, pipe-smoking Mitchell soon launched a massive illegal fund-raising campaign. Of the nearly $60 million collected, more than $350,000 was squirreled away in a special fund to pay for "dirty tricks" operations against Nixon's Democratic foes.

The Plumbers

Nixon feared that the press might expose his illegal campaign activities. Those fears deepened that summer when the *New York Times* published the "Pentagon Papers." Although the papers dealt with Vietnam policy before the Nixon administration, Nixon feared their publication would lead to leaks of classified documents damaging to his administration. To prevent such a disaster, CREEP created a special investigations unit, nicknamed "the plumbers," to stop security leaks.

The plumbers' first target was Daniel Ellsberg, the Defense Department analyst who had leaked the Pentagon Papers to the press. In an attempt to uncover embarrassing details about Ellsberg's personal life, the plumbers broke into the office of Ellsberg's psychiatrist. They found nothing they could use against Ellsberg.

Then, in January 1972, CREEP aide G. Gordon Liddy came up with a daring plan. A team of plumbers would break into Democratic National Committee headquarters, copy documents, and wiretap the phones. By doing so the White House could keep tabs on Democratic election strategies. The plan, okayed by John Mitchell, was set in motion on the morning of June 17, 1972, at the Democratic party offices in the Watergate complex.

Unraveling Watergate
The Press, the Courts, and Congress at Work

Later, on the morning of June 17, *Washington Post* reporters Bob Woodward and Carl Bernstein got a call about the Watergate break-in. Woodward, a 29-year-old Yale graduate, and Bernstein, a 28-year-old college dropout, were an unlikely team. Inexperienced but ambitious, the 2 young reporters worked tirelessly to uncover the entire story.

Their investigations soon revealed that two of the Watergate conspirators—G. Gordon Liddy and E. Howard Hunt—were employees of CREEP. They also learned that the burglars had been paid from a CREEP

Meeting Special Needs

Visual Learners Ask students to scan the images in this section to help them identify its main themes. Have students tell you or write the themes in their journals. This activity should help students who are visual learners navigate this material more effectively by using the images to give meaning to the text. **LEP**

fund the White House staff controlled. The deeper the two reporters dug, the more evidence they found that the Watergate break-in was one of many illegal activities planned and paid for by the President's advisers.

Eager to put a lid on the investigation, Nixon held a press conference that August. He assured the public that White House counsel John Dean had conducted an investigation of the incident and found that "no one on the White House staff was involved in this very bizarre incident." At the same time Nixon secretly authorized the payment of more than $460,000 in CREEP funds to keep the Watergate burglars quiet about White House involvement.

Woodward and Bernstein kept digging. In a front-page story on October 10, the 2 reporters pulled together the evidence they had unearthed that summer.

F BI agents have established that the Watergate bugging incident stemmed from a massive campaign of political spying and sabotage conducted on behalf of President Nixon's re-election and directed by officials of the White House and the Committee for the Re-election of the President.

—Bob Woodward and Carl Bernstein,
Washington Post, October 10, 1972

THE WATERGATE SCANDAL

As individuals one by one decided on a course of action, the truth concerning the Watergate scandal began to reveal itself. The national media followed and sustained the drama from the beginning of the scandal to its historical conclusion.

THE JUDGE

John J. Sirica
Chief Judge
U.S. District Court
He thrust Watergate into the midst of the Senate Select Committee proceedings by reading McCord's letter publicly.

© THE WASHINGTON POST

THE SENATOR

Mike Mansfield
Senate Majority Leader
In order to maintain public confidence in the political process, he urged the Senate to examine the recent campaign and how it was waged.

© THE WASHINGTON POST

The media profiled the men in the Watergate spotlight.

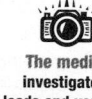

The media investigated leads and verified leaks.

THE COUNSEL

John Dean
White House Counsel
While still working at the White House, he created a legal safety net for himself before giving his Senate testimony.

© THE WASHINGTON POST

THE PRESIDENT

President Nixon resisted all efforts to reveal information to Congress or the courts about his administration and his involvement in Watergate. Only upon the collapse of his political base did Nixon offer his resignation.

THE AIDE

Alexander Butterfield
White House Aide
Only when threatened with arrest by the Senate sergeant-at-arms did he testify publicly about the existence of the White House taping system.

© THE WASHINGTON POST

The media uncovered the link between the White House and the Watergate break-in.

THE SUPREME COURT

Warren Burger
Chief Justice
The Supreme Court upheld the lower courts' rulings about the tapes and reaffirmed that the Court, not the executive branch, had the power to define the law.

© THE WASHINGTON POST

THE PROSECUTOR

Archibald Cox
Special Prosecutor
He rejected the White House offer of tape summaries and limited access to further evidence believing it would compromise his investigation.

© THE WASHINGTON POST

The media kept the public informed about the proceedings.

The truth about Watergate emerged as a result of the investigatory activities of the courts, Congress, and the media. *Why did Senator Mansfield assemble a Senate committee to investigate the 1972 presidential election?*

SECTION THREE **827**

Portfolio Project

Time Line Have students research other important current events that took place between June 1972 and August 1974 and create their own time line of the events they determine to be most significant. They may include national or international news as well as sports and cultural events. Students should include this time line in their portfolios. 📷

Independent Practice

L2 Writing Have students write a brief essay or create a graphic about the impeachment process. Explain that it is important to understand the process because of what it tells us about how the constitutional system should work.

📕 Have students complete the Chapter 24, Section 3 Vocabulary and Guided Reading Activity. (Also in Spanish.) **LEP**

VISUAL INSTRUCTION

Headline News The *Washington Post* won the 1972 Pulitzer Prize for Distinguished Public Service for its investigation of Watergate.

Answer: *Sirica's reading McCord's letter in court*

ABCNEWS INTERACTIVE™

Videodisc

Powers of the Congress

Side 1, Chapter 39
Title: Impeachment
Subject: Process of impeachment and Nixon
Ask: Why did the House consider impeaching Nixon? *(He had covered up his participation in the Watergate scandal.)*

See Powers of the Congress Guidebook page 43 for complete lesson plan.

It was sensational news. The White House fought back, calling the *Post's* story "a senseless pack of lies" put together by the liberal paper to discredit the administration. As the 1972 election neared, Nixon worked to bury the Watergate story.

For a time the President's strategy seemed to work. Few other journalists picked up the story. Just before the 1972 election, polls showed that only 48 percent of Americans had even heard of Watergate.

The Watergate Trial

The Watergate story might have remained just a bizarre incident, but early in 1973, shortly after Nixon began his second term, the Watergate burglars went on trial before federal judge John J. Sirica. Nicknamed Maximum John because of his reputation for handing out long prison terms, Sirica was a no-nonsense judge who warned the Watergate defendants, "Don't pull any punches—you give me straight answers." Angered by the Watergate scandal, Sirica was determined to use his courtroom to search for the real story behind the Watergate break-in.

Afraid of a lengthy prison sentence, one of the Watergate burglars, James W. McCord, agreed to cooperate. In a letter to Judge Sirica, McCord alleged that White House officials had lied about their involvement in the affair and had pressured the defendants "to plead guilty and remain silent." McCord's letter blew the lid off the case.

The Senate Hearings

While Judge Sirica pursued the case in a Washington courtroom, the Senate began its own investigation of Watergate. From May to November in 1973, the Senate Select Committee on Presidential Campaign Practices heard testimony from a parade of White House officials.

Sam J. Ervin, the 76-year-old senator from North Carolina, chaired the committee. Ervin was a Harvard Law School graduate who had earned the respect of his colleagues during his 18-year Senate career.

Ervin was known to be a staunch defender of First Amendment rights. He called the Constitution "the finest thing to come out of the mind of man." Ervin steered the hearings with a commanding wit and down-to-earth common sense.

On April 30, 1973, Nixon made another attempt to shield the White House from the gathering storm by announcing the resignations of Dean, Haldeman, and Ehrlichman. All 3 men had been involved in Watergate. Speaking on television, the President denied any attempt at a cover-up and vowed: "There can be no whitewash at the White House." Polls, however, showed that half of those watching believed the President had taken part in a cover-up.

Under pressure from Congress and the public, Nixon ordered Attorney General Elliot Richardson to appoint a special prosecutor to investigate Watergate. Richardson chose Harvard law professor Archibald Cox and promised the Senate that Cox would have complete independence from the White House and broad powers of investigation.

Public interest in the case grew that summer as the Senate committee began televised hearings. Each day millions of Americans watched—fascinated—as the story unfolded.

The most damaging testimony came from John Dean, the White House counsel. Dean testified for nearly 30 hours. He claimed that there had been a cover-up and charged that the President himself had directed it.

Then, in July, another bombshell exploded. White House aide Alexander Butterfield told the Senate

Headline News By the spring of 1973, Watergate was big news, and the byline of Woodward and Bernstein was familiar to readers following the story. *What event brought the Watergate burglary back into the news in 1973?*

Extending the Content

Impeachment Trial The Vice President usually presides over the activities of the Senate. However, if the Senate is hearing impeachment charges against the President, the chief justice of the United States presides. If Nixon's impeachment had come to trial, Chief Justice Warren Burger, a Nixon appointee, would have presided.

The Constitution at Work The Watergate committee, above, was chaired by Sam J. Ervin, shown at the top right. Among those questioned were H. R. Haldeman, second photo right, John Ehrlichman, third photo right, and John Mitchell, bottom right. *In what branch of government did Ervin serve?*

committee that early in 1971 Nixon had installed a tape recording system in the White House. The news that the President had bugged his own office was electrifying. Here was proof of Nixon's guilt or innocence.

By August the hearings were the top-rated daytime television show. Democrat Sam Ervin became a national hero as he grilled Mitchell, Haldeman, Ehrlichman, and other White House figures about Watergate. Republican Senator Howard Baker asked each witness the question to which all Americans wanted the answer: "What did the President know and when did he know it?"

The Tapes

Both the Senate committee and Special Prosecutor Cox called on Nixon to surrender tapes of conversations that might pertain to the Watergate break-in. Nixon refused and claimed executive privilege, insisting that the release of the tapes would endanger national security. Cox and Ervin persisted. Cox declared, "There is no exception for the president from the guiding principle that the public, in the pursuit of justice, has a right to every man's evidence." He sought a court order to force Nixon to hand over the tapes.

Nixon again tried to shift attention away from the scandal. On August 15 he urged Americans to put Watergate behind them. He felt that after 12 weeks and 2 million words of televised testimony, it was time to get

on with the "urgent business of our nation." Few Americans agreed.

Finally Nixon ordered Attorney General Richardson to fire Cox. Richardson, remembering his promise to the Senate, refused and resigned. When Richardson resigned, Nixon ordered the deputy attorney general, William Ruckelshaus, to fire Cox. Ruckelshaus refused and was himself fired. Finally Solicitor General Robert Bork fired Cox. Public outcry over what came to be known as the Saturday Night Massacre forced Nixon to appoint another special prosecutor, attorney Leon Jaworski. Jaworski renewed the demand for the tapes. Nixon balked, and Jaworski took the case to court.

The crisis was deepening. Already nearly 50 Nixon administration officials, including Mitchell, Haldeman, and Ehrlichman, faced criminal charges.

That fall Nixon's troubles multiplied. In October 1973, Vice President Spiro Agnew pleaded no contest to charges of income tax evasion and accepting bribes while governor of Maryland and resigned. Nixon nominated Gerald R. Ford, a popular, conservative member

SECTION THREE **829**

Cultural Perspectives

Anti-Castro Cubans Eugenio Martinez, one of the five Watergate burglars, was a veteran of the Bay of Pigs invasion of Cuba. He had also taken part in a variety of CIA-funded anti-Castro campaigns. Discuss with students the conditions at the time in Cuba under Castro. Ask them why they think Cubans would seek to overthrow Castro's Communist government.

VISUAL INSTRUCTION

The Constitution at Work Majority Leader Mike Mansfield suggested a low-profile senator, Sam J. Ervin, to chair an investigation examining the way the 1972 election campaign had been conducted.

Answer: *legislative*

ABCNEWS INTERACTIVE™

Videodisc

Powers of the Supreme Court

Side 2, Chapter 24
Title: *United States* v. *Nixon*
Subject: Discussion of *United States* v. *Nixon* case
Ask: How did the Court rule in *United States* v. *Nixon?* *(Nixon had to release the tapes.)*

See Powers of the Supreme Court Guidebook page 91 for complete lesson plan.

 Facts on File

Landmark Documents in American History Have students review "*United States* v. *Nixon,* 1974," "Articles of Impeachment for Richard Nixon, 1974," "Resignation Speech, Richard Nixon, 1974," "White House Departure Speech, Richard Nixon, 1974," and "Letter of Resignation, Richard Nixon, 1974" and write a paragraph about the intent of one of the documents.

WATERGATE CHRONOLOGY, 1972–1974

JUNE 1972 Watergate break-in is reported.

JANUARY 1973 McCord alleges White House involvement.

JUNE 1973 John Dean implicates Nixon in cover-up.

OCTOBER 1973 House Judiciary Committee launches impeachment inquiry.

AUGUST 1974 Nixon releases tapes and resigns.

1972   1973   1974   1975

AUGUST 1972 Nixon denies involvement.

NOVEMBER 1972 Nixon reelected.

MAY 1973 Senate hearings begin.

JULY 1973 Butterfield testifies conversations were taped. Nixon refuses to release tapes.

JULY 1974 Supreme Court orders surrender of tapes. House committee recommends impeachment.

ASSESS

Meeting Lesson Objectives

Each section objective is tested by the section review question(s) that follows it in parentheses.

1. Describe how President Nixon abused the powers of his office. (2, 5)

2. Discuss how a free press functioned to rein in the executive branch. (5)

3. Discuss how the constitutional system of separation of powers worked to preserve the integrity of the government. (1, 3, 4)

---

of Congress from Michigan, to fill the post. Congress quickly confirmed the nomination.

Then, in December, Nixon's own finances came under fire. Federal investigators reported that in 1970 and 1971 the President had paid only about $800 a year in federal taxes on an annual salary of $200,000. Since 1969 he had paid no state income tax even though he was still a legal resident of California.

Pressure for the tapes was also mounting. In April 1974, the President released edited transcripts of some of the tapes in question. Although his aides had cut the most incriminating comments, the profanity, pettiness, and ethnic insults that peppered the President's conversations shocked many people.

Even more revealing was what was missing from the tapes. Gaps in the tapes indicated the President was not telling the public the whole truth. When Nixon again refused to release the unedited tapes, Jaworski took the case to the Supreme Court. On July 24, in *United States v. Nixon*, the Supreme Court unanimously ruled that President Nixon had to release the tapes.

The Move for Impeachment

Also in July the House Judiciary Committee began to draft articles of **impeachment,** or charges of misconduct, against the President. The impeachment process allows Congress to check the power of officials in the executive and judicial branches. Impeachable offenses include criminal activity, but are not limited to acts that are illegal.

Under the Constitution the House of Representatives determines whether impeachment charges are justified. If so, the Senate then serves as the jury for the trial. Only one President, Andrew Johnson, had ever been impeached.

On July 30, following several days of televised debate, the House committee voted to recommend impeachment of President Nixon on 3 counts: obstructing justice by trying to cover up the role of the White House in the Watergate burglary; violating the rights of United States citizens by using the FBI, the CIA, and the

IRS to harass critics; and defying congressional authority by refusing to turn over the tapes. The articles of impeachment would now go to the House of Representatives for a vote.

Nixon was trapped. On August 5, he handed over the tapes, confessing that they were "at variance with some of my earlier statements." The tapes revealed that just days after the Watergate break-in, the President had ordered the CIA to halt the FBI investigation of the case: "Don't go any further into this case, period." Impeachment charges seemed certain.

The Final Days

For three days Nixon paced, brooded, and conferred with his few remaining friends in Congress. No matter how he counted the votes in the House and Senate, they added up to certain impeachment and probable conviction in the Senate.

By Wednesday, August 7, key Republican leaders had joined the chorus demanding the President's resignation. Nixon made his decision. That evening Nixon met with

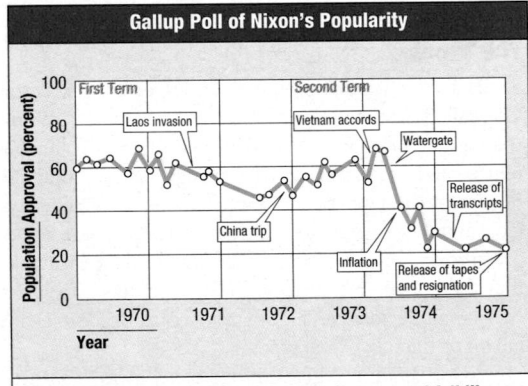

Gallup Poll of Nixon's Popularity

With changing events, Nixon's popularity rose and fell like a roller coaster. *What was Nixon's approval rating when he resigned?*

Critical Thinking

Expressing Problems Clearly Ask students to identify the options President Nixon faced after the House voted to recommend impeachment. Have them discuss the advantages and disadvantages of each option. Ask students whether they agree or disagree with Nixon's decision and have them explain why.

You Be the Judge In their work, cartoonists made use of the personalities, attitudes, and actions of those involved in the Watergate scandal. *What kind of attitude about cover-ups and lies is suggested by the White House dialogue in this cartoon?*

a group of 46 loyal congressional leaders. In a long, rambling speech, he thanked them for their years of support. Twenty minutes later he would address the nation—the first American President ever to resign from office.

The following day Nixon and his family flew back to California, and Gerald Ford was sworn in as President. President Ford declared, "Our long national nightmare is over." A President had fallen, but the American political system had survived.

The Aftermath
A Pardon, New Laws, and Continuing Doubts

A month later President Ford **pardoned,** or excused, Nixon for any crimes he had committed or might have committed while in the White House. Many Americans felt Nixon had escaped justice. Others, however, believed it was time to put Watergate to rest and to look to the future.

To counter the trend toward greater presidential power and curb future abuses, Congress enacted a series of laws. The War Powers Act of 1973 required the President to consult with Congress before sending American troops into prolonged action. In 1974 Congress passed the Congressional Budget and Impoundment Control Act, which prohibited the impounding of federal money by the President.

Also in 1974 Congress strengthened the Federal Election Campaign Act of 1972, setting limits on campaign contributions. Finally Congress extended the Freedom of Information Act by passing the Privacy Act, allowing citizens to have access to the files that the government may have gathered on them.

The Nixon White House had threatened the foundation of American democracy—constitutional law. Yet, as many pointed out, the system worked. The legislative and judicial branches reasserted their powers to rein in the executive branch. Congress investigated the charges, and the independent judiciary forced the President to release evidence. Eventually 31 Nixon administration officials were convicted and went to prison for Watergate-related offenses.

At the same time, Watergate was deeply disquieting. The nation's leaders had committed serious crimes. Then the new President had pardoned the most important offender. Had a deal been made? How could Americans continue to trust their government? Coming on the heels of the war in Vietnam, Watergate further undermined the nation's self-confidence.

SECTION REVIEW

Vocabulary
1. Define: impeachment, pardon.

Checking Facts
2. Identify examples of President Nixon's abuse of power.

3. List laws that Congress passed after Watergate in an attempt to curb presidential power and the potential for abuses.

Critical Thinking

Drawing Conclusions
4. President Gerald Ford pardoned Richard Nixon for his actions in Watergate. What were some of the consequences of this decision?

Linking Across Time
5. How has the Watergate scandal influenced the way the press exercises its responsibility today as the citizens' watchdog?

SECTION THREE **831**

VISUAL INSTRUCTION

You Be the Judge Thirty-one Nixon administration officials were sent to prison for Watergate-related offenses.

Answer: *They accepted them as a normal part of conducting government; they lied about their reactions to the public.*

Evaluate

Have students complete the Section Review.

☛ Assign the Section 3 Quiz or use the Testmaker to develop a customized quiz. (Also in Spanish.) **LEP**

Reteach

☊ Have students listen to the Chapter 24, Section 3 Audiocassette. (Also in Spanish.) **LEP**

Enrich

☞ Have students complete Interpreting Political Cartoons 4.

☞ Have students complete Supreme Court Case Study 42.

CLOSE

Have students use the time line to identify connections between events in the Watergate incident. *(See pages 827–831.)*

Section 3 Review Answers

1. impeachment (830), **pardon** (831)
2. He impounded funds for programs he opposed, sent troops into Cambodia without Congress's knowledge, used the IRS and FBI to harass "enemies," and set up an illegal fund-raising campaign.
3. the War Powers Act, the Congressional Budget and Impoundment Control Act, the Federal Election Campaign Act, and the Privacy Act
4. Americans questioned whether they could trust the government; the nation's self-confidence was further undermined.
5. It watches government actions more closely and has done more investigative reporting.

TEACH

Making the Historical Connection

Review the events of the Watergate crisis with students, beginning with the break-in and ending with Nixon's final release of the tapes. Discuss with students what other actions Congress and the courts had taken to seek information about the conduct of the 1972 presidential campaign and the Watergate break-in.

Remind students that the Constitution outlines the process for the removal of government officials who have committed crimes. Point out that that President Nixon had several opportunities to cooperate with the Watergate investigation and did not.

Turning Point

Congressional supporters of President Nixon felt betrayed when they read transcripts of some of the released tapes. They were now faced with sufficient evidence to vote for impeachment. Without their support Nixon would most probably have faced removal from office.

Turning Point

The Attempted Impeachment of Nixon

SUMMER 1974

MEMORANDUM

For: Judiciary Committee of the House of Representatives

Subject: Impeachment of Richard M. Nixon

Richard M. Nixon has acted in a manner contrary to his trust as President and subversive of constitutional government, to the great prejudice of the cause of law and justice, and to the manifest injury of the people of the United States.

Wherefore Richard M. Nixon, by such conduct, warrants impeachment and trial, and removal from office.

The articles of impeachment voted by the Judiciary Committee of the House of Representatives, July 27–30, 1974

The Case

The impeachment proceedings against President Richard Nixon in 1974 revolved around 4 words in the United States Constitution—"high Crimes and Misdemeanors." Article II, Section 4, grants Congress the power of impeachment:

> The President, Vice President and all civil Officers of the United States, shall be removed from Office on Impeachment for, and Conviction of, Treason, Bribery, or other high Crimes and Misdemeanors.

The Constitution, however, does not define "high Crimes and Misdemeanors." In the summer of 1974, the members of the Ninety-third Congress faced the difficult task of deciding for themselves what that definition was.

These four words served as the constitutional battleground for the impeachment case against Nixon. This battle would involve all three branches of government, as well as the "fourth estate"—the press. It would challenge the fundamental political will of the American people and their leaders—and put the Constitution to one of its greatest tests.

The Background

In late July 1974, more than 2 years after the Watergate break-in, the House Judiciary Committee voted for 3 articles of impeachment against President Richard Nixon based on his actions in the Watergate affair:

- Article I—that the President "prevented, obstructed, and impeded the administration of justice" (obstruction of justice)—passed 27 to 11.

The Case at a Glance

| The House Judiciary Committee meets to consider articles of impeachment. | → | The House struggles with the definition of "high Crimes and Misdemeanors." | → | The House committee determines that impeachable offenses have been committed. | → | Nixon's supporters read transcripts of some of the released tapes. | → |

- Article II—that the President "repeatedly engaged in conduct violating the constitutional rights of citizens. . . ." (abuse of presidential powers)—passed 28 to 10.
- Article III—that the President "failed without lawful cause or excuse to produce papers and things as directed by duly authorized subpoenas. . . ." (contempt of Congress)—passed 21 to 17.

The chairman of the House Judiciary Committee, Representative Peter W. Rodino, Jr., a Democrat from New Jersey, hoped to bring these articles before a full vote of the House, the next step in the impeachment process, on August 19. If the House voted for any one of these articles, Nixon would be brought to trial before the Senate sometime that fall. Lastly, if the Senate convicted Nixon, he would be removed from office.

Charting a New Course History provided little guidance for members of the Ninety-third Congress as they moved through the process. Before 1974 the House had voted to impeach only 13 officials, including 1 President, Andrew Johnson, in 1868. To many in Congress, however, the evidence against Nixon seemed overwhelming, and there was no need to consider historical precedent. In addition, the Senate Watergate Committee, Special Prosecutor Leon Jaworski and his staff, and the press all compiled their own evidence. Representative Jack Brooks of Texas, a Democratic member of the House Judiciary Committee, listed Nixon's offenses: "The cover-up of crimes, obstructing the prosecution of criminals, surreptitious entries, wiretapping for political purposes, suspension of civil liberties of every American, tax violations and personal enrichment at public expense, bribery and blackmail; flagrant misuse of the FBI, the CIA and the IRS."

Support for the President Still, the President's supporters in Congress—most of them fellow Republicans—remained convinced that the evidence failed to prove Nixon had committed an impeachable offense. Ten Republican members of the House Judiciary Committee, led by Charles Wiggins of California, stayed firm in their support of Nixon. Each had voted against all three articles of impeachment.

Nixon hoped that his congressional supporters could slow down or even stop the impeachment

"I have revered all Presidents and I have searched within my heart and my conscience and searched out the facts, and when I test the facts I find that the President of the United States . . . must be found wanting."

Peter Rodino, chairman of the House Judiciary Committee (HJC)

AP/WIDE WORLD PHOTOS

". . . My faith in the Constitution is whole, it is complete, it is total, and I am not going to sit here and be an idle spectator to the diminution of the Constitution. . . . The framers confided in the Constitution the power if need be to remove . . . a President swollen with power and grown tyrannical."

Barbara Jordan, Democrat from Texas, member of the HJC

UPI/BETTMAN

"For those who are looking for the smoking pistol, I am just afraid they are not going to find it, because the room is too full of smoke."

Hamilton Fish, Republican from New York, member of the HJC

© DENNIS BRACK/BLACK STAR

"It's a . . . weak circumstantial case. . . . The committee has avoided any kind of standard on what is an impeachable offense."

Charles Wiggins, Republican from California, member of the HJC

UPI/BETTMAN

CASE STUDY   **833**

The House committee votes for three articles of impeachment.	→	Nixon resigns from office.

Analyzing the Case

After students read the Opinions and the Decision, discuss the following questions with them.

1. How did Nixon's supporters view the moves for impeachment by the House committee? *(They thought it was a political move, not a constitutional one.)*

2. Why did Nixon's opponents dislike the impeachment process? *(If the proceedings stopped, it would be a serious threat to the constitutional system.)*

3. What prompted Nixon's decision to resign? *(He finally realized he had little support left.)*

ABCNEWS INTERACTIVE™

  Videodisc

Powers of the Congress

Side 1, Chapter 39
Title: Impeachment
Subject: Explanation of the process of impeachment, specifically deals with Nixon

Ask: Why did the House consider impeaching Nixon? *(He had covered up his participation in the Watergate scandal.)*

See Powers of the Congress Guidebook page 43 for complete lesson plan.

Turning Point

House Judiciary Committee members (left to right): Harold D. Donohue, D-Massachusetts, John Doar, chief counsel, Chairman Peter Rodino, D-New Jersey, Edward Hutchinson, R-Michigan, and Albert Jenner, minority counsel.

process. After the Judiciary Committee's vote in late July, however, hope waned that there would be enough votes to stop the momentum. Nixon's presidency depended on keeping the support of at least 34 senators. Nixon felt he could count on 36 senators—8 Democrats and 28 Republicans. To convict the President of impeachment took a two-thirds majority in the 100-member Senate. As long as Nixon could count on these 36 senators, he could complete his term.

The Opinions

Nixon's supporters viewed the House Judiciary Committee's vote and the continuing momentum for impeachment as a political act, not a constitutional one. Some Republicans even believed that the "liberal" Democrats hoped to overturn the national election results of 1972 that had swept Nixon into office. Like Nixon, his supporters held an intense dislike and distrust for members of the press, which they felt had prejudiced the country against the President. More importantly to them, no "smoking gun" that proved the President had directly com-

mitted a crime had yet been found—after more than 2 years of investigations. Without this evidence, his supporters believed no grounds for his impeachment existed.

Nixon's opponents, both Democrats and Republicans, also did not like the impeachment process, but for vastly different reasons. To them, evidence clearly showed that Nixon had abused the power of the presidency. If impeachment proceedings stopped, a serious injustice would be committed against the constitutional system of checks and balances.

The Decision

After the House Judiciary Committee's vote, members of Congress felt a grave sense of urgency. It was August of an election year. Could Congress avoid a prolonged impeachment battle with Nixon? Could it persuade him to resign and avoid a brutal fight?

Rodino, House Speaker Carl Albert, and House Majority Leader Thomas "Tip" O'Neill, resolved to move the impeachment process forward. They

834 CASE STUDY

Cooperative Learning

Role Playing Organize the class into four groups. Assign each group one of the following roles:
1. Representative Peter Rodino
2. Representative Charles Wiggins
3. Chief of Staff Alexander Haig
4. President Richard Nixon

Give each group time to research their roles in the impeachment process. Have the groups convene and present the events as they occurred.

cleared the House's calendar and set a firm date of August 19 for impeachment proceedings. Wiggins and other Nixon supporters tried to delay the process with procedural matters. Although the President's supporters knew they might lack the votes to delay, they were determined to remain loyal to Nixon. Then, in the midst of all the activity, Wiggins learned of the existence of a "smoking gun"—and of his betrayal by the President.

The "Smoking Gun" On July 24, the Supreme Court had voted 8 to 0 that Nixon must turn over 64 unedited tape recordings to Special Prosecutor Jaworski. Although no President had ever disobeyed a Supreme Court decision, Nixon delayed handing over the tapes until early August. Nixon realized that if he did not comply with the Court's order, the House would consider that a high crime. In turning over the tapes, however, Nixon worried that he was giving evidence to both his supporters and opponents that would reveal that he had directed a cover-up attempt soon after the Watergate break-in and had lied about it—the tapes would become the "smoking gun."

Alarmed by Nixon's hesitation and his deteriorating health, the President's chief of staff, Alexander Haig, asked Wiggins to meet with him and James St. Clair, the special counsel to the President, on August 2. Having just learned the contents of the transcripts of the tapes, Haig and St. Clair let Wiggins read 5 or 6 key pages before the documents were made public. Once Wiggins read the transcript pages he felt betrayed and could no longer defend the President. On August 5, Wiggins made public his change of mind: ". . . I am prepared to conclude that the significant career of public service of Richard Nixon must be terminated involuntarily."

Nixon's White House staff continued to try to convince the President that efforts to fight were hopeless—that the country would be best served by his resignation. Nixon, however, still resolved to carry the fight, mistakenly believing he continued to have enough support in the Senate to block his conviction.

The Decision to Resign The country was approaching a crisis. Finally, in a face-to-face meeting with Senator Barry Goldwater and a few other supporters on August 7, Nixon realized he had only 2 choices: have the Senate remove him from office, or resign.

On August 9, Nixon turned in his resignation, by Constitutional requirement, to the Secretary of State: "I hereby resign the Office of President of the United States." This one-sentence letter made Nixon the first President in United States history to resign. His resignation ended the impeachment process, but ensured a smooth and peaceful transition of power from Nixon to Vice President Gerald R. Ford, who became the thirty-eighth President.

The Significance

Although Nixon resigned from office without seeming to admit his guilt, the constitutional system of checks and balances did its work. Some Americans believed that Nixon's resignation merely revealed that corruption existed at even the highest level of government, but most agreed that it proved that Article II, Section 4, of the United States Constitution worked as intended.

RESPONDING TO THE CASE

1. Why did some in Congress support the President in his fight against impeachment? Why did others want him removed from office?

2. In your opinion, did Nixon commit "high Crimes and Misdemeanors"? Defend your viewpoint.

3. Do you agree or disagree that Nixon's resignation proved that the constitutional system worked? Defend your viewpoint.

4. The Ninety-third Congress never defined "high Crimes and Misdemeanors" during the impeachment process. Should the Constitution be amended to define this term? Why or why not?

 The media, both print and electronic, played an important role in keeping the public informed throughout the Watergate saga. President Nixon's resignation was the culmination of more than two years of investigation and litigation. Write a news story about Nixon's resignation and the immediate events that led up to it. Be sure to include this story in your portfolio.

CASE STUDY **835**

Responding to Case Answers

1. Some believed only circumstantial evidence had been collected, and it was a political, not constitutional, fight. Others believed there was sufficient evidence that he had acted illegally.

2. Some students may believe that he had abused his presidential powers in campaign activities, the cover-up, and misuse of federal agencies, and that this was sufficient grounds; others may believe the President needs to have the power to maintain law and order and to accomplish goals that have been set.

3. Agree: the process allowed the House to force him to a decision—face impeachment proceedings or resign; disagree: the process allowed him not to have to stand trial.

4. No, the Constitution has to allow for circumstances to change. Yes, it would help to promote more rapid movement in the process.

SECTION

4

FOCUS

Section Objectives

1. Explain the causes of stag-flation in the economy of the mid-1970s.
2. Describe the effects of the 1973 oil embargo.
3. Identify the results of President Ford's economic policies.
4. Describe Carter's foreign policy initiatives and problems.
5. Explain how environmental problems of the late 1970s led to Americans' new awareness.

Bellringer Activity

While taking attendance at the beginning of the class period, display **Section Focus Transparency 79,** and have students answer the questions. (Or use the blackline master.)

VISUAL INSTRUCTION

A Scarce Commodity To help meet demand for gasoline, the government allowed increased oil imports and encouraged refiners to increase their capacity.

Ask: How would a gasoline shortage today affect your daily activities and mobility? *(Answers may vary. Students might mention that it would be difficult to get to school, work, or social events; fewer people in the family could use the car.)*

Ford and Carter

WINTER 1973: OIL EMBARGO FUELS GAS PANIC

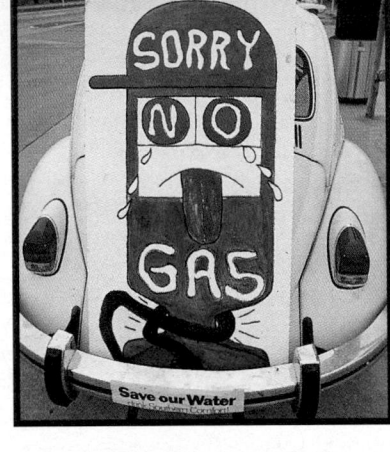

A Scarce Commodity
Many Americans had to rearrange their lives around the availability of gasoline.

DURING THE WINTER OF 1973–1974, AN UNFAMILIAR DRAMA WAS ENACTED AT GAS STATIONS ALL ACROSS THE UNITED STATES. From dawn to dusk, cars queued up at the gas pumps, forming lines that often snaked down the street for blocks. Panicky motorists rushed to any gas station that had a supply, and they often had to wait for 2 hours or more. When they finally did reach the pump, they were often limited to buying only a few gallons of gas—and at a higher price! Even after the oil embargo was over, gas prices continued to rise. Another round of sharp increases occurred during the energy crisis of 1979. By 1980 the price of gasoline was more than $1 a gallon, more than twice the 1973 price.

The competition for fuel frayed people's nerves and rattled their tempers. Drivers fought with one another, waved guns at harried service station employees, and sometimes even smashed gas pumps in rage and frustration. "These people are like animals foraging for food," said the owner of a station in Miami. "If you can't sell them gas, they'll threaten to beat you up, wreck your station, run over you with a car."

A feeling of powerlessness intensified the motorists' anger. Political and trade decisions made halfway around the globe hindered their freedom to drive to work or the shopping center. The forces at work at the gas pumps would continue to overshadow American life throughout most of the 1970s: religious fervor and political unrest in North Africa and Southwest Asia, the unstable politics that governed the international flow of oil, and a runaway United States economy.

AS YOU READ

Vocabulary
▶ inflation
▶ stagflation
▶ embargo
▶ recession
▶ human rights
▶ dissident

Think About . . .
▶ the causes of stagflation in the mid-1970s.
▶ the effects of the oil embargo.
▶ the results of President Ford's economic policies.

▶ President Carter's foreign policy initiatives.
▶ why Americans developed a new environmental awareness.

Section 4 Resources

REPRODUCIBLE RESOURCES
📂 Lesson Plan 24-4
📂 Vocabulary and Guided Reading Activity 24-4
📂 Section 4 Quiz
📂 Chapter 24 Test
📂 Performance Assessment Activity 24
📂 Reteaching Activity 24

📂 Enrichment Activity 24
📂 Geography in History Activity 24
📂 Political Cartoons 7, 17
📂 Supreme Court Cases 47, 48
📂 Unit 9 Test

MULTIMEDIA RESOURCES
📖 Section Focus Transparency 79
⚙ Powers of the President

💿 Landmark Documents in American History
💿 Lessons of War
💿 The Presidents: A Picture History of Our Nation
💿 Vocabulary PuzzleMaker
💿 Testmaker
🎧 Chapter 24 Digest Audiocassette

Ford Follows Nixon

Ford Faces Many Challenges

When Richard Nixon resigned the presidency in disgrace, he left to his successor, Vice President Gerald R. Ford, a nation in crisis. A humiliating defeat in Vietnam had battered American prestige, and the Watergate scandal had left the American people deeply shaken.

Ford tried to pull the country together. On September 8, 1974, in an effort to consign the Watergate scandal to history, Gerald Ford pardoned Richard Nixon for any federal crimes he might have committed as part of the Watergate break-in and cover-up. The pardon outraged many Americans who strongly believed that all citizens, even the President, must be accountable to the Constitution and the laws of the land. Despite Ford's best intentions, the United States remained a troubled and divided nation.

The Stagflation Dilemma

Perhaps the greatest obstacle to President Ford's effort to restore public faith in government was his inability to control the economy. Since the end of World War II in 1945, most Americans had become used to a rising standard of living. Now, however, two economic conditions that rarely occur at the same time shattered American prosperity: slowing productivity and rising **inflation**—or the steady increase of prices.

Industry had begun stagnating, or slowing down. During the 1970s industrial productivity—the rate of goods produced per hour—had slowed, causing the cost of producing goods to rise. At the same time, foreign firms, especially those in Japan and West Germany, were able to manufacture high-quality goods quickly and inexpensively and to market them successfully in the United States. American consumers spent more on these high-quality, less expensive products, causing United States productivity to slow down even more.

The second cause of the American economic dilemma

was rising inflation. As a result of inflation, the dollar fell in value against foreign currencies, and its purchasing power at home and abroad fell dramatically. A pair of gloves that once sold for $5 might now sell for $10. The annual inflation rate, which had been 3.3 percent in 1972, soared to 11 percent by 1974. Economists referred to this combination of stagnating growth and spiraling inflation as **stagflation.**

An Energy Crisis Is Born

The major cause of the United States's inflationary spiral was an international oil crisis with roots in the turbulent politics of North Africa and Southwest Asia. The United States economic machine demanded huge amounts of oil. Foreign oil suppliers—principally Arab nations—met nearly one-third of that demand.

Since 1960 many oil-rich nations in Africa, Southwest Asia, and South America had sold their oil as part of the Organization of Petroleum Exporting Countries (OPEC). OPEC countries set common prices and regulated production quotas and ceilings. These trade practices allowed them to control both the price and availability of oil throughout the world.

During the Yom Kippur War in 1973, in which Israel fought Syria and Egypt, Saudi Arabia imposed an **embargo,** or a restriction of trade, on oil shipped to Israel's allies, including the United States. At the same

THE MIDDLE EAST, 1973

OPEC member

★ Capital city

OPEC oil price increases sent a message to the United States and the Soviet Union: Developing countries would no longer cater to the needs of the superpowers. *What Southwest Asian nations belong to OPEC?*

Cooperative Learning

Role Play Have students role-play a meeting between representatives from OPEC, Israel, the United States, Japan, and West Germany to discuss economic concerns. Assign students to groups composed of individuals with varying abilities. Have each group prepare and stage a meeting for the class.

FYI

New Vice President President Ford chose the former governor of New York, Nelson Rockefeller, to be his Vice President. This was the first time in United States history that there was an unelected President and Vice President in office.

TEACH

Guided Practice

L2 Analysis Direct students' attention to the top graph on page 839, and ask them whether there appears to be a statistical correlation between consumer prices and unemployment. Have students explain their answers.

MAP STUDY

Saudi Arabia exports more oil than any other country in the world.

Answer: *Iran, Iraq, Kuwait, Qatar, Saudi Arabia, the United Arab Emirates, Bahrain*

Facts on File

Landmark Documents in American History Have students review "Remarks on Taking the Oath of Office, Gerald R. Ford, 1974," "Pardon of Richard Nixon Remarks, Gerald Ford, 1974," and "Proclamation 4311, Granting Pardon to Richard Nixon, 1974" and write a paragraph about the intent of one of the documents.

Videodisc

Lessons of War

Side 2, Chapter 4
Title: Diplomacy: Camp David Accords
Subject: The 1978 meeting between Israeli Prime Minister Begin and Egyptian President Sadat
Ask: Why were the Camp David Accords so historic? *(It was the first agreement between an Arab nation and Israel.)*

See Lessons of War Guidebook page 38 for complete lesson plan.

The Presidents: A Picture History of Our Nation

Have students view "Gerald R. Ford" and use the information to write a brief biography to include in their portfolios.

838

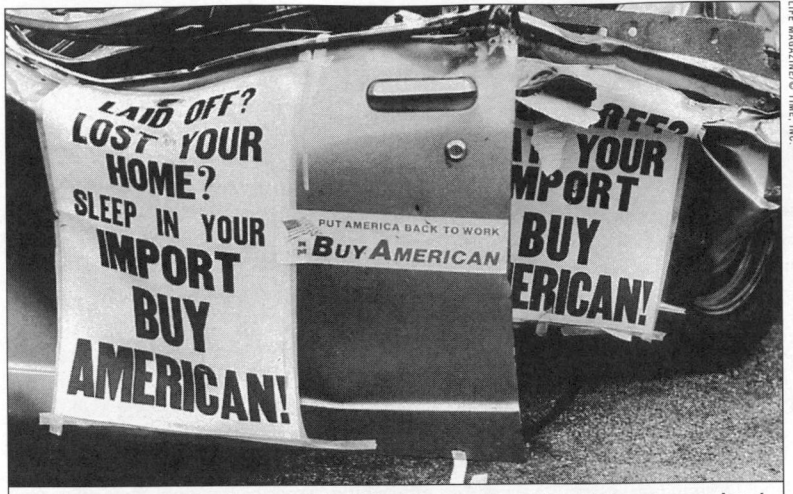

Steel Industry in Decline Angry at the rapidly rising numbers of imported cars, unemployed steelworkers in Fairfield, Alabama, vented their frustration by bashing this Toyota. *Why were Americans buying so many Japanese cars during the 1970s?*

When the Arab oil embargo and OPEC price increases hit the United States economy in 1973, most American car buyers wanted nothing to do with Detroit's oversized "gas-guzzlers." Many consumers switched to foreign cars, especially those manufactured in Japan. Imported autos, which held only a 17 percent share of the United States market in 1970, captured a whopping 37 percent by 1980. By that year, a dozen American auto plants had closed, and 300,000 autoworkers had lost their jobs.

The steel industry came close to a complete collapse. In 1946 the United States provided 60 percent of the world's steel. By 1980 that figure had fallen to 14 percent, and steel executives questioned whether their industry could survive.

time, other OPEC countries nearly quadrupled their prices. Although the embargo was lifted in 1974, its economic effects continued through the end of the decade.

Wheels and Steel

The oil embargo had a profound effect on United States auto and steel industries. The big, gleaming cars produced in Detroit had long represented American know-how around the world. Now, more than any other product, they symbolized the United States's industrial decline.

Again foreign steel manufacturers presented stiff competition. Because of their computerized and automated production facilities, they were able to keep production costs down. United States steel companies, whose plants were old-fashioned by foreign standards, saw their costs rise 10 percent a year, forcing them to raise the price of American steel. As a result American manufacturers began buying nearly one-fifth of their steel from foreign producers. The steel industry appealed

---

★ ★ ★ **GALLERY OF PRESIDENTS** ★ ★ ★

Gerald R. Ford

1974–1977

"I have not sought this enormous responsibility, but I will not shirk it. Those who nominated me and confirmed me as Vice President were my friends. . . . They were of both parties, elected by all the people and acting under the Constitution in their name. It is only fitting then that I should pledge to them and to you that I will be the President of all the people."

August 9, 1974

COURTESY GERALD FORD LIBRARY

BACKGROUND
▶ Born 1913
▶ Republican, Michigan
▶ Served in the navy 1942–1946
▶ Elected to House of Representatives 1948
▶ Succeeded to presidency 1974

ACHIEVEMENTS IN OFFICE
▶ Amnesty program for Vietnam War draft dodgers
▶ Council on Wage and Price Stability (1974)

838 CHAPTER 24 FROM NIXON TO CARTER

Meeting Special Needs

Limited English Proficiency Focus attention on the way in which new words are created by combining parts of two or more existing words. Such new words are called blends. *Stagflation*, for example, is a blend formed from *stagnation* and *inflation*. This activity should help students with reading disabilities unlock the meaning of some of the technical vocabulary in this section. **LEP**

to Congress to use stiff quotas, tariffs, and other international agreements to set limits on imports. Congress refused, fearing retaliation by foreign governments against American trade.

The President Responds

President Ford decided that the economy could best be revived by attacking inflation. At press conferences, he wore a red and white lapel button emblazoned with the letters WIN, the acronym for "Whip Inflation Now." In addition he supported high interest rates, which made money more expensive for everyone to borrow, including the government. By tightening credit Ford hoped to reduce spending, which would result in an oversupply of goods and thus lower prices. Ford also clamped down on government spending by vetoing new health, housing, and education legislation.

The measures Ford took helped to cool inflation, which fell to 6 percent by 1976. As a result of Ford's restrictions, however, industrial production plummeted and unemployment rose. Before long, almost 1 out of every 10 people was out of work. During 1974 and 1975, the country plunged into its worst **recession,** or economic slowdown, since the Great Depression.

Carter Takes Charge
Recession: An Election Issue

The struggling economy was the key issue as Americans went to the polls in 1976 to elect a President. Although Americans liked Gerald Ford well enough as a person, they rejected his leadership, especially his economic policies. James Earl Carter, a peanut farmer and former governor of Georgia, was elected the nation's thirty-ninth President.

Jimmy Carter knew that he had to cure the economic ills that were draining the nation's vitality. He tried to jolt the economy out of recession by increasing government spending and cutting taxes. Both measures were meant to stimulate economic growth. Unemployment came down, but inflation took off. For 2 years the annual inflation rate hovered above 10 percent.

Further fueling inflation was a dramatic OPEC price increase in 1979. The cost of a barrel of OPEC oil zoomed to $30, and another oil shortage ensued. Businesses, industries, and homeowners faced energy shortages, and once again motorists lined up at gas stations to buy expensive fuel.

Carter asked Americans to turn down their thermostats to 68 degrees in the winter, switch off unnecessary lights, and go "gasless" on Sundays. Businesses

reduced their operating hours and schools extended vacations, all in an effort to conserve energy. As a result of these dramatic lifestyle changes, Carter's approval rating fell to 26 percent, almost as low as Nixon's had been at the darkest moments of his presidency. Americans were weary of want and sacrifice, and they directed their anger and frustration at Washington.

Human Rights and Foreign Policy
Fostering Peace and Respect for Sovereignty

Standing up for **human rights** at home and abroad was the cornerstone of Jimmy Carter's foreign policy. A devout man, Carter tried to apply the religious principles that governed his private life to the conduct of

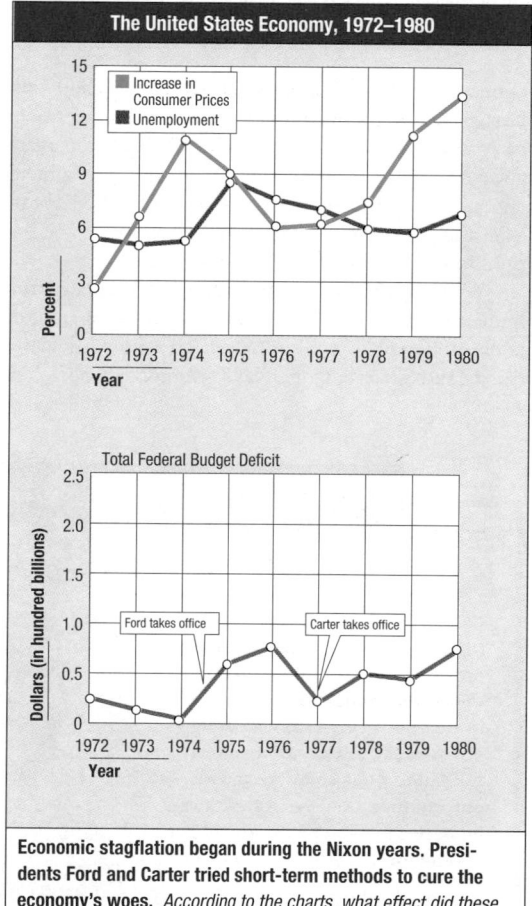

The United States Economy, 1972–1980

Economic stagflation began during the Nixon years. Presidents Ford and Carter tried short-term methods to cure the economy's woes. *According to the charts, what effect did these methods have on the United States economy?*

Portfolio Project

Interviews Have students interview members of their family or the community to find out how the recession of 1974–1975 affected their lives. Students might also ask about the effects of the rising oil prices. Have students create a report of the results of the interviews for their portfolios. The report may be a video, a chart, or a summary of the text of their interviews.

**Independent
Practice**

L1 Writing Have students imagine that they are Olympians for the 1980 Olympic Games in Moscow. Tell them to write President Carter explaining why they disagree with the boycott.

 Have students complete the Chapter 24 Vocabulary and Guided Reading Activity. (Also in Spanish.) **LEP**

VISUAL INSTRUCTION

Resistance Fighters Afghanistan took no sides during the Cold War. It used aid from both the United States and the Soviet Union to build roads, factories, and so on.

Answer: *The United States refused to participate in the 1980 Olympics; he imposed a grain embargo on the Soviet Union.*

NATIONAL GEOGRAPHIC SOCIETY

 The Presidents: A Picture History of Our Nation

Have students view "James E. Carter, Jr." and use the information to write a brief biography to include in their portfolios.

Resistance Fighters The Afghan rebels used guerrilla tactics to overcome the superior equipment of the Soviets. *What was Carter's response to the Soviet attack of Afghanistan?*

© MICHAEL PHILIPPOT/SYGMA

dissidents, those who openly criticized Soviet policies. When Carter offered imprisoned or exiled dissidents his moral support, Soviet leaders accused him of meddling in their internal affairs.

In 1979 the Soviet Union invaded Afghanistan. Outraged at what he considered to be interference in the affairs of a sovereign nation, Carter ordered sanctions against the Soviet Union. The United States and other nations refused to participate in the 1980 Olympic Games in Moscow; in addition the United States government imposed a grain embargo on the Soviet Union.

Playing the Peacemaker

Carter's stand on human rights was reflected in other areas of his foreign policy. His primary goals were to foster peace and respect for other nations' sovereignty.

public affairs. Like Woodrow Wilson early in the 1900s, Carter crafted a foreign policy based on the defense of basic rights and freedoms he believed should be available to all people throughout the world: the right to choose leaders in fair and honest elections, the right to a fair trial, the right to worship and travel freely, and the right to free expression.

When Carter thought a nation had violated the human rights of its own citizens or citizens of another country, he spoke out strongly. This was particularly true of the Soviet Union. The Kremlin often punished

For example, Carter sought to slow down the arms race between the United States and the Soviet Union. American and Soviet negotiators worked hard to draft a treaty limiting the number of missiles, bombers, and nuclear warheads each side could stockpile. Finally, in June 1979, Carter and Soviet leader Leonid Brezhnev signed the second Strategic Arms Limitation Treaty (SALT II), expanding the first agreement negotiated during President Nixon's administration.

★ ★ ★ **GALLERY OF PRESIDENTS** ★ ★ ★

James Earl Carter, Jr.
1977–1981

"Let us learn together and laugh together and work together and pray together, confident that in the end we will triumph together in the right. The American dream endures. We must once again have full faith in our country—and in one another. I believe America can be better. We can be even stronger than before."

Inaugural Address, January 20, 1977

COURTESY JIMMY CARTER LIBRARY

BACKGROUND
▶ Born 1929
▶ Democrat, Georgia
▶ Graduated naval academy 1946
▶ Served in the navy 1946–1953
▶ Elected state senator 1962
▶ Elected governor 1970

ACHIEVEMENTS IN OFFICE
▶ Negotiated Israeli-Egyptian peace treaty (1978)
▶ Negotiated SALT II (1979)

Extending the Content

The China Syndrome This 1979 motion picture dramatizes a modern nightmare, the near-core meltdown of a nuclear reactor. Ask if any students have seen or heard of this movie and discuss their reactions to it. If no one in the class has seen the movie, you may want to generate a discussion by asking any of the following questions.

Do students think there are any nuclear power plants operating today with faulty equipment? Ill-trained operators? Any that are poorly built? That have insufficient evacuation plans? That are not monitored closely enough by federal agencies?

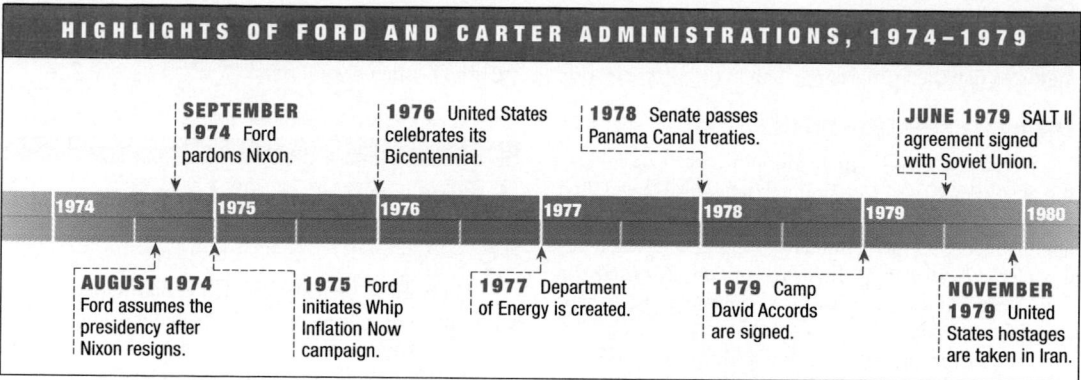

HIGHLIGHTS OF FORD AND CARTER ADMINISTRATIONS, 1974–1979

SEPTEMBER 1974 Ford pardons Nixon.

1976 United States celebrates its Bicentennial.

1978 Senate passes Panama Canal treaties.

JUNE 1979 SALT II agreement signed with Soviet Union.

1974　1975　1976　1977　1978　1979　1980

AUGUST 1974 Ford assumes the presidency after Nixon resigns.

1975 Ford initiates Whip Inflation Now campaign.

1977 Department of Energy is created.

1979 Camp David Accords are signed.

NOVEMBER 1979 United States hostages are taken in Iran.

Continuing Nixon's policy of détente, Carter hoped to reduce the "balance of terror" between the United States and the Soviet Union. Strong opposition to the SALT II agreement surfaced in the United States. Congress did not believe the limits set forth by the treaty could be verified. The treaty languished in the Senate. In response to the Soviet invasion of Afghanistan, Carter asked the Senate to delay consideration of the pact. In the end SALT II was never ratified.

Continuing President Nixon's efforts, Carter established normal diplomatic relations with the People's Republic of China. In doing so, he cleared the way for valuable technical and commercial exchanges between the two formerly hostile nations.

The Panama Canal

Carter also tried to encourage peace and sovereignty in Latin America and to develop a more favorable image of the United States in that region. His administration cut back military aid to South and Central American dictators and negotiated an agreement to give control of the Panama Canal to that nation by the year 2000. Despite strong conservative opposition, the United States Senate ratified this agreement in 1978, along with a second treaty that gave the United States the right to defend the neutrality of the canal.

The Camp David Accords

President Carter's most successful foreign policy initiative was to assist in forging a peace treaty between Israel and Egypt. These age-old enemies had fought four wars since the creation of Israel in 1948. When their most recent conflict ended in 1973, a tense, bitter diplomatic stand-off ensued between the victorious Israelis and the defeated Egyptians.

In 1978 President Anwar el-Sadat of Egypt told American news reporter Walter Cronkite that he would do whatever he could to make peace with Israel. Carter then seized what he knew was a unique opportunity. In

Former Enemies Begin (left) and Sadat (right) celebrate their efforts toward peace. *Why was Carter able to bring the two men together?*

September of that year, Carter invited Israeli Prime Minister Menachem Begin and President Sadat to Camp David. For two weeks, Carter, Secretary of State Cyrus Vance, and others patiently talked the 2 leaders through their differences and tried to reconcile them. Finally Carter was able to make the historic announcement

SECTION FOUR **841**

© DIRCK HALSTEAD/GAMMA LIAISON

Cultural Perspectives

African American Ambassador Former civil rights activist Andrew Young of Georgia served as United States ambassador to the United Nations during the Carter administration. He was a controversial figure there, primarily because of his outspoken criticism of apartheid and his concern for developing nations. He resigned in 1979.

ASSESS

Meeting Lesson Objectives

Each section objective is tested by the section review question(s) that follows it in parentheses.

1. Explain the causes of stagflation in the economy of the mid-1970s. (1, 2)
2. Describe the effects of the 1973 oil embargo. (2)
3. Identify the results of President Ford's economic policies. (1, 3, 4)
4. Describe Carter's foreign policy initiatives and problems. (1, 5)
5. Explain how environmental problems of the late 1970s led to Americans' new awareness. (2)

Evaluate

Have students complete the Section Review.

☞ 🖳 Assign the Section 4 Quiz and Chapter 24 Test or use the Testmaker. (Also in Spanish.) **LEP**

☞ Have students complete the Chapter 24 Performance Assessment Activity.

842

---

that the two leaders had constructed a "framework for peace." In March 1979, Begin and Sadat flew to Washington to sign the formal agreement in the White House.

The Iranian Hostage Crisis

In February 1979, Shah Mohammad Reza Pahlavi, the absolute ruler of Iran and a close ally of the United States, was deposed in a revolution sparked by extreme liberal and conservative Iranians. Iran's new leader, Muslim cleric Ayatollah Ruholla Khomeini, despised the United States for its political, financial, and military support of the Shah.

On November 4, an armed mob stormed the United States embassy in Tehran, the capital of Iran, and seized diplomats and military personnel. Angry and frustrated, Americans stared helplessly at their television screens while an angry, chanting Iranian mob set up a giant poster that defiantly proclaimed in English: U. S. Can Not Do Anything.

For many months, it seemed that the message on the Iranian poster told the truth. Finally, in April 1980, President Carter authorized a daring commando raid to rescue the hostages. The raid was a disaster for the United States. Encountering a violent dust storm over southern Iran, several of the helicopters ferrying the commandos to Tehran suffered mechanical failures. The raiders landed to assess the situation and decided to scrub the mission. As the commandos beat a hasty retreat from the Iranian desert, a helicopter collided with a cargo plane, killing 8 men and wounding 5.

Months later Carter agreed to release $8 billion in Iranian assets he had ordered "frozen" in the United States at the start of the crisis. It was not until January 20, 1981, President Ronald Reagan's Inauguration Day, that the hostages were freed.

A New Sense of Limits
Foreign Affairs and Economy Questioned

The United States's troubled economy and apparent weakening of power and influence in foreign affairs left many Americans worried and pessimistic about the future. Throughout the 1970s, Americans faced change in nearly every facet of their lives. The nation that had sent men to the moon, the nation where everything had seemed attainable, was developing an unfamiliar sense of limits.

The Polluting of America

A newly urgent concern for the environment typified this sense. Environmentalists warned that two forces were abusing and destroying the United States's natural resources. The first was governmental reluctance to curb unrestricted industrial growth and commercial development. The second was the greed of businesses that some claimed placed profit before responsibility. Environmental horror stories became front-page news. Birds hatched chicks deformed by severe genetic abnormalities. Commercial fishing crews returned from the deep oceans with catches contaminated by mercury and a wide variety of industrial chemicals. Oil spills fouled stretches of coastline with heavy crude that destroyed scenic beauty and sometimes killed the local wildlife.

Then in 1978 the problem hit home. The soil and groundwater of Love Canal, New York, a community near Niagara Falls, was found to be so polluted by poisonous chemicals from nearby industries that the Environmental Protection Agency (EPA) declared the entire town unfit for human habitation. The residents of Love Canal were evacuated, their homes boarded up, and the community sealed off by a tall, chain-link fence. The United States had its first toxic-waste ghost town.

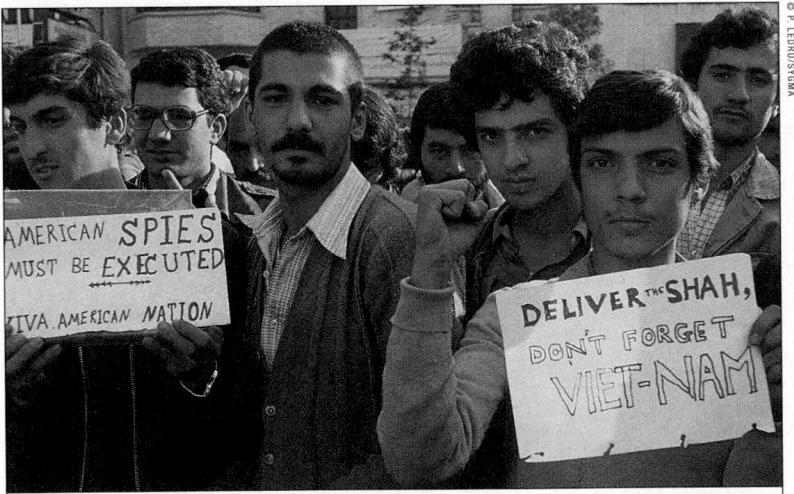

Anti-American Fervor These young men wanted the Shah, who was in the United States seeking medical treatment, returned to Iran. *Why was there anti-American feeling in Iran?*

Critical Thinking

Recognizing Ideologies Have students research other examples of foreign policy decisions made by President Carter that reflected his belief in human rights. Then have students select a decision and defend or reject its human rights basis.

© NEAL PALUMBO/GAMMA LIAISON

The Nuclear Power Dilemma

Environmentalists also objected to the spread of nuclear power plants throughout the United States. Well-organized protesters appeared in every part of the country to condemn the construction and operation of nuclear power plants. Although the protesters filed legal challenges, waged spirited public information campaigns, and sometimes resorted to civil disobedience, their concerns went largely unheeded—that is, until one fateful day in March 1979.

On that day a series of human and mechanical errors in the Unit 2 reactor of the Three Mile Island nuclear power station near Harrisburg, Pennsylvania, combined to produce the worst nuclear power accident in United States history. The nuclear reactor core overheated and released a wave of radioactive water and steam. Fearing a massive release of radiation, officials evacuated 100,000 nearby residents. The disaster never came, but the Unit 2 reactor, littered with radioactive debris, had to be shut down.

The nuclear dilemma typified the difficult 1970s, a decade in which every advance harbored a setback and every promise included a threat. Looking back, some observers believe the decade forced a fundamental change in the American outlook, described by economist Robert Lekachman as "a shift from the easy politics of growth to the era of limits."

A Near Miss The cooling towers of Three Mile Island loom large in this downtown scene of Goldsboro, Pennsylvania. *What happened to the Unit 2 reactor during the nuclear accident?*

Throughout the 1970s, legislation was proposed to protect the environment. Congress toughened air pollution standards and imposed strict regulations on the logging industry. In 1972 the government told business and industry that the release of toxic waste into United States waterways must stop by 1985. To further improve water quality, the EPA distributed $19 million to local governments for the construction of waste treatment plants. In 1978 Interior Secretary Cecil Andrus extended for 2 decades restrictions against development on 40 million acres of federal lands in Alaska. In addition President Carter placed more than 100 million acres of Alaskan land under the federal government's protection as national parks, national forests, and wildlife refuges.

SECTION REVIEW

Vocabulary
1. Define: inflation, stagflation, embargo, recession, human rights, dissident.

Checking Facts
2. What happened during the OPEC oil embargo?

3. What happened to the economy during the Ford administration?

Critical Thinking
Determining Cause and Effect
4. Why were Americans developing a sense of limitations about the power and stature of the United States?

Linking Across Time
5. In 1936 President Franklin Roosevelt said, "The truth is found when men are free to pursue it." How does this statement help to explain the fundamental basis for President Jimmy Carter's foreign policy some 40 years later?

VISUAL INSTRUCTION

A Near Miss Mechanical and human error at the site forced 100,000 people to evacuate.

Answer: *The core overheated and released radioactive steam and water.*

Reteach

🎧 Have students listen to the Chapter 24, Section 4 Audiocassette. (Also in Spanish.) **LEP**

🗂 Have students complete the Chapter 24 Reteaching Activity. (Also in Spanish.) **LEP**

Enrich

🗂 Have students complete the Chapter 24 Enrichment Activity. (Also in Spanish.) **LEP**

🗂 Have students complete the Chapter 24 Geography in History Activity.

🗂 Have students complete Interpreting Political Cartoons 7, 17.

🗂 Have students complete Supreme Court Case Studies 47, 48.

CLOSE

Draw a time line on the board. Have students provide entries of significant events, such as: 1973 Oil embargo; 1974 Nixon pardoned; 1976 Carter elected; 1978 Camp David Accord; 1979 Hostages taken in Iran; 1980 Three Mile Island.

Section 4 Review Answers

1. inflation (837), **stagflation** (837), **embargo** (837), **recession** (839), **human rights** (839), **dissident** (840)
2. There were gasoline shortages and many attempts to conserve energy by individuals, businesses, and government.
3. Inflation and industry stagnation (stagflation) resulted in a recession.

4. The economy and the failure to resolve the hostage crisis made people feel vulnerable.
5. Carter believed that if all people were free, they would choose governments that were good for them and for the world community.

TEACH

Making the Historical Connection

The Soviet Union led the way in achievement during the early years of the space race, due in large part to its superiority in rocket technology. The United States was never far behind, however. It led in the areas of communication and weather-satellite technology.

FYI

Earth Technology
Synthetic soil is made from zeolites, a common group of minerals found across the United States. Components of synthetic soil have been found to provide a very precise timed release of plant nutrients that could provide a garden or field with the potential for years of fertility with minimal risk of pollution.

Science, TECHNOLOGY, and Society

Outer Space to the Kitchen

After the Soviet Union launched *Sputnik,* the first artificial satellite, politics drove the space race. As scientists overcame technological barriers, and political tensions between the United States and the Soviets eased, much of what was learned from space research began to make its way into our everyday lives. Scientists continue working to make outer space more habitable.

SPACE FOOD
The need for lightweight, nutritious food for astronauts led to the development of the freeze-drying process and to the improved packaging and processing methods for many of our foods today.

STEPS INTO SPACE

1950s	1960s	1970s
SPACE RACE BEGINS The Soviets launch *Sputnik* and put the first animal into orbit. National Aeronautics and Space Administration is established.	**MEN IN SPACE** Soviet Yuri Gagarin is first human in space; Alan Shepard is the first American in space; *Apollo 11* lands men on the moon.	**SPACE EXPLORATION** First U.S. space station, *Skylab,* launched. *Viking* space probes reach Mars. First U.S.-Soviet mission, *Apollo-Soyuz,* launched.

Background Information

Space Pen A special rubberlike ink was also developed for use in space. The ink is almost solid; only when the ballpoint revolves does friction liquify just enough ink for smooth writing. The pen design and ink create a pen with many advantages for use on Earth—uniform ink flow with no skipping, long pen life, and the ability to write on many surfaces. This pen has also been purchased by the Soviet Union and used by its cosmonauts in space.

FIRST SPACE WALK

Edward H. White, the first American to walk in space, floats outside his *Gemini 4* spacecraft. He had to fire a maneuvering gun to move around in the zero gravity during this 1965 mission.

SYNTHETIC SOIL

Researchers are developing synthetic soil to use in growing plants as part of a recyclable life support system in a future spacecraft.

NASA

SPACE RACE SPINOFFS

PORTFOLIO PROJECT

Research other applications of space technology that have made their way into workplaces, homes, hospitals, or the entertainment industry. Try to include illustrations in the report. Be sure to place this work in your portfolio.

© KEVIN WILSON PHOTOGRAPHY

WRITING UNDER WATER

The pen used here was originally developed for NASA astronaut record keeping on Apollo missions. Its special cartridge allows ink to flow regardless of gravity or atmospheric pressure.

NASA

1980s	1990s
WORKSHOPS IN SPACE The first United States reusable spacecraft, the shuttle *Columbia,* orbits the earth for the first time. Sally Ride becomes the first American woman in space.	**EXPANDING FRONTIERS** Hubble Space Telescope, an orbiting observatory, is launched with a 15-year lifetime in space. Expected launch of the space probe *Cassini* to Saturn.

SCIENCE, TECHNOLOGY, AND SOCIETY **845**

Portfolio Project

Time Line Have students conduct further research into milestones in the United States space program in order to create their own time lines. Encourage students to include recent events and discoveries. Students should be sure to add this work to their portfolios.

845

Chapter 24 Review

Reviewing Key Terms

1. impeachment
2. revenue sharing
3. silent majority
4. détente
5. recession

Recalling Facts

1. marches, campus shootings, and the social programs
2. making the voting age 18, starting the EPA and OSHA
3. New Federalism and closing the OEO
4. Burger, Blackmun, Powell, and Rehnquist
5. foreign policy advisor, national security advisor, and secretary of state
6. to limit the nuclear arms race; open foreign markets
7. It eased threats of Soviet aggression toward China.
8. It controlled missile defense systems.
9. He resolved the oil embargo and brokered a peace.
10. It protected U.S. interests and blocked Communist politicians; the overthrow of Allende
11. He impounded funds, secretly invaded Cambodia, and illegally used federal agencies.
12. He read McCord's letter.
13. Dean—White House counsel, Haldeman—chief of staff, and Erhlichman—domestic policy. All took part.
14. firings and resignations of White House staff; Cox, Richardson, Ruckelshaus, and Bork
15. Impeachment begins in the House; a trial held in the Senate.
16. Organization of Petroleum Exporting Countries; raised oil prices, making American products less competitive.
17. the right to honest elections, a fair trial, to worship and express oneself freely.
18. Egypt, Israel, and the U.S.; it was a first step toward a peace treaty between Israel and Egypt.
19. The U.S. appeared weak, Carter did not appear strong.
20. Love Canal and Three Mile Island

Reviewing Key Terms

Match the key term below with the phrase that best defines its meaning. Write the word and the appropriate phrase on a separate sheet of paper.

détente   realpolitik
recession   revenue sharing
impeachment   silent majority

1. an accusation, a charge against
2. a plan where the federal government returns some tax money back to the states
3. "forgotten" Americans, nonprotesters
4. an attempt to repair relations with China and the Soviet Union
5. an economic slowdown

Recalling Facts

1. Identify some events and policies that helped bring about the conservative backlash of the late 1960s.
2. Name two Democratic-sponsored pieces of legislation that Nixon supported and signed into law.
3. Give two examples of conservative policies Nixon implemented.
4. Name the four Supreme Court justices President Nixon appointed.
5. Identify Henry Kissinger. Describe the various roles he held in the Nixon administration.
6. Explain why President Nixon was eager to implement a policy of détente with the People's Republic of China and the Soviet Union.
7. How did better relations between the United States and the People's Republic of China affect the balance of power in the world?
8. What were the basic elements of the SALT Agreement?
9. What were two successes of Kissinger's shuttle diplomacy?

10. Briefly explain the United States policy of interventionism in Latin America. Give an example.
11. Give three examples of Nixon's unlawful exercise of the power of his office.
12. What happened in Judge Sirica's court that first linked the White House to the Watergate break-in?
13. Identify John Dean, H. R. Haldeman, and John Ehrlichman. Describe their roles in Watergate.
14. Describe what happened in the Saturday Night Massacre. Who was involved?
15. Briefly explain how the impeachment process works according to the Constitution.
16. What is OPEC? Describe how it contributed to the economic problems of the United States in the 1970s.
17. What were some of the basic beliefs that drove President Carter's foreign policy?
18. What countries were involved in the Camp David Accords? Explain why the Camp David Accords were so important?

19. How did the Iranian hostage crisis hurt the Carter administration?
20. Name two environmental crises that took place during the Carter administration.

Critical Thinking

1. **Making Generalizations** President Nixon impounded funds that were to be used for federal programs, supported wiretapping without a court order, and authorized secret bombings. What generalization can you make about the methods he used to accomplish his goals?

2. **Making Comparisons** Two segments of society with different values disagreed over the Vietnam War. Compare how the silent majority and social protesters felt about the issues of patriotism and law and order.

3. **Determining Cause and Effect** What were two effects of President Nixon's trip to the People's Republic of China?

4. **Analyzing Decisions** How did Nixon's belief in realpolitik influence decisions he made about the Soviet Union and the People's Republic of China?

Critical Thinking

1. He often worked secretly, and outside the law, to achieve his goals.
2. The silent majority believed that citizens should support government decisions; the protesters believed in questioning government. Both felt they were right.
3. It eased tensions between the United States and China and raised Nixon's popularity.
4. He was able to overlook his ideological differences with the two countries.
5. secretly sending troops to Cambodia and Laos and impounding federal funds

5. Determining Cause and Effect
What actions of the Nixon administration caused Congress to enact the War Powers Act and the Congressional Budget and Impoundment Act?

Portfolio Project

PORTFOLIO PROJECT

List five qualities you think a United States President should possess. If you were able to vote tomorrow, what three domestic issues would concern you the most? What three global issues would concern you? If no candidate held your views on all issues, write an essay to explain how you would determine your choice.

Cooperative Learning

The Vietnam War polarized citizens of the United States. Work in small groups. Each group should identify a social or political issue today that deeply divides people. Each group should then report their issue to the class. Try not to duplicate any issues another group has worked on. The groups should also research each side of their selected topic and prepare a report to share with the class. As you prepare your reports, be sure to give each side of the issue equal conviction.

Reinforcing Skills

Interpreting Political Cartoons
Thomas Curtis has a national reputation as the author of cartoons with a conservative viewpoint. He penned the cartoon on page 846 in 1973 while working for the *Milwaukee Sentinel*. Identify the symbols the author uses to convey his message. How do you interpret the cartoon? For example, what does he use to portray the Soviet Union? What message is the cartoonist trying to convey?

PHOENIX, ARIZONA, 1950–1994

PHOENIX CITY LIMITS	AREA (sq. mi.)	POPULATION
1950	16.9	106,818
1994	345	1,051,515

– – Intermittent river

0 3 6 mi.
0 3 6 km
Polyconic projection

Geography and History

Study the map on this page to answer the following questions. You will need to write your answers on a separate sheet of paper.

1. How large was the growth in square miles in the Phoenix area between 1950 and 1994?

2. How much did the population of Phoenix increase from 1950 to 1994?

3. In which direction did the city undergo the largest area of growth?

4. Beyond the city limits of Phoenix, where do you think population will increase?

HISTORY JOURNAL

Look back at your journal response in the chapter opener. What have you learned about how the government responded to the economic, political, and environmental crises of the 1970s?

Geography and History

1. Between 1950 and 1994 it grew by 328.1 square miles.
2. Between 1950 and 1994 the population grew by 944,697 people.
3. north
4. near the major highways, 10, 17, 60, and 89

History Journal

Students should include references to the responsibilities and powers of the presidency.

? BONUS QUESTION

This question may be used for extra credit on the chapter test:
What did the impeachment process test?
Answer: *the constitutional process of checks and balances*

Portfolio Project

Students may suggest qualities such as honesty, experience in foreign affairs, knowledge of economic and environmental issues, definition of what the government can and cannot do, ability to work with Congress, and so on. Students should also include three domestic and three global issues of concern to them.

Cooperative Learning

The groups should present a variety of issues, and each member should assume some responsibility for the report. Opinions should be supported by research and facts.

Reinforcing Skills

The shark represents the Soviet Union. The blood in the water, the injury to Nixon's presidency. Students may suggest that the shark is interested in following the blood to a potential prey. The cartoonist believes the Soviet Union may still be our enemy and will take advantage of a potential weakness.

TEACH

Making the Historical Connection

A new form of popular music—rock and roll—evolved in the 1950s and 1960s. Rock lovers liked the music loud and with plenty of percussion effects. Both of these qualities helped to drive the demand for high-quality stereophonic sound.

FYI

Small Size, Big Sound
The size of the spiral track on a compact disc (CD) is only about 1.5 millionths of a meter wide. That is about the same size as a wavelength of infrared light or 3 thousandths of the diameter of a human hair.

Then...

The Stereo

The popularity of rock 'n' roll, the development of stereo records, and the introduction of stereo sound in radio broadcasting all fueled the demand for consumer products that could produce quality and higher volume sound. A new industry—home entertainment—was born during the 1960s.

❶ A component stereo system in the 1960s had at least 6 separate units, which made it bulky, heavy, potentially confusing to assemble, and often visually unattractive.

© ROY DOTY, COURTESY POPULAR SCIENCE

Fun Facts

MUSIC MAKES MONEY
By the 1980s the recording industry employed nearly 31,990 men and women and had total annual sales of nearly $4 billion.

FILE PHOTO BY RALPH J. BRUNKE

Background Information

Compact Discs To make a laser recording, the sound signal has to be digitized (stored in numerical code). This new signal then modulates a very sharp laser beam that is focused on photosensitive masters to record a pattern of dots. The playback disc has a shiny, reflecting surface, and the dot pattern on the master is transferred to it as a series of nonreflecting pits.

To play back the sound, the process is reversed. A laser beam is focused on the disc to track the spiral path of the recording. As the laser beam is reflected, the pits break it up into pulses of light. These light pulses are then converted into electric signals. The electric signals are decoded and strengthened before they reach the speakers.

2 A 1960s turntable (shown right) was one unit of a component stereo system. Its parts were the drive system, the stylus, the cartridge, and the tonearm. Other components of a stereo included an amplifier and speakers or headphones.

FILE PHOTO BY DOUG MINDELL

DR. JEREMY BURGESS/SCIENCE PHOTO LIBRARY

Stats

RECORDS

A long-playing vinyl record (LP) is 12 inches in diameter.

An LP plays at 33⅓ rpm (revolutions per minute) and has about 30 minutes of sound on each side.

There are about 250 grooves per inch on an LP.

COSTS

In 1968 a stereo LP cost $4.98; a monaural LP cost $3.98.

The average price for a stereo component system in 1969 was about $200.

SALES

Record sales for 1968 were $1.1 billion.

In 1975 there were 73 million phonographs in the United States.

3 The waves in the grooves of a record make the stylus, or needle, vibrate. An enlarged image of this part is shown above. The vibrations then become electric signals that the speakers or headphones change into sound.

...Now

MUSIC TO YOUR EARS

PORTFOLIO PROJECT

Write a brief report on the different ways music can be played in the home. Compare contemporary systems with those available during the years covered in this unit. Compare them in terms of cost, technology, quality, and portability. Be sure to include this report in your portfolio.

SUPERSTOCK

SOUND IN EVERY SHAPE AND SIZE

A console stereo system was available in a variety of shapes and designs—it could look like a fireplace, a cube, a grandfather clock, a tea cart, or a chest. Some were even shaped like hexagons!

ARCHIVE PHOTOS

THEN AND NOW   849

  Block Scheduling

The Portfolio Project on this page provides an excellent opportunity to enrich and extend the key elements of this feature.

FYI

Recording Achievements Several organizations present awards for artistic and commercial achievement. The Grammy Awards are given by the National Academy of Recording Arts and Sciences (NARAS) for artistic achievements. The Grammy winners are determined by the academy members, who include musicians, engineers, and producers. The Recording Industry Association of America (RIAA) presents awards to artists who sell a specific number of records. When 500,000 copies of an album have been sold, an artist receives a gold record. A platinum record is given for sales of 1 million copies. Multiplatinum indicates sales of 2 million or more.

CLOSE

Ask students where and in what form (radio, tape, CD) they play music during the day. What qualities do they want from the sound? *(clarity, balance)* What do they think will be the next step in sound technology? *(smaller systems, less distortion at high volume)*

Portfolio Project

PORTFOLIO PROJECT

Music Survey Have students conduct a survey of classmates, friends, or members of the community to determine their music listening habits. For example, students might ask respondents how many hours they spend listening to music, and how many tapes, CDs, and records they own. It might be interesting for students to survey two different groups (older people and teenagers, middleschool students and high schoolers) and compare and contrast their findings. Students should include the results of their surveys in their portfolios.

⏱ Out of Time?

If time does not permit teaching every chapter in this unit, use the Chapter Digest Audiocassettes and the accompanying student activities and tests. The Chapter Digest Audiocassettes are available in Spanish.

UNIT
10

1980

New Challenges

PRESENT

CHAPTER 25
The Reagan and Bush Years

CHAPTER 26
A Changing Nation in a Changing World

850

Portfolio Project

Current Events Have students select one of the topics dealt with in this unit, such as health-care reform, neoconservatism, the budget deficit, affirmative action, or right-wing militia organizations. For the duration of the unit, students can read newspaper and newsmagazine articles having to do with their topic and clip out or photocopy the articles. Then have them write a report of their findings that updates the information in the book. Students can then file their reports in their portfolios. 📁

Introducing
the Unit

 Show students the Unit 10 Time Line Transparency and/or assign the accompanying activity sheet. Explain that this unit deals with events that occurred in the 1980s and 1990s. Ask students to recall major events from this period. Help them place the events on the time line, if possible. Before you begin, you may want to allow students a short period of time for research.

History and the Humanities

U.S. History and Art Transparency 31—*Ocean Park #124* by Richard Diebenkorn

851

Examining the Visual

Earth From Space Taken from space, this photograph of North America and South America was computer enhanced to add color and to sharpen lines, creating a more powerful image. With the fast growth of new technology, especially computers, artists now create new pieces of artwork with different colors, shapes, text treatment, and meaning.

"Double Face"

FROM *THE JOY LUCK CLUB* BY AMY TAN

The United States is a nation of immigrants who came in search of new opportunities. Throughout our history immigrants have faced the same dilemma: how to preserve their language and culture in the face of pressure to adapt to a new society. The narrator in the following selection explores differences between her Chinese culture and the culture of her new country.

It's hard to keep your Chinese face in America. At the beginning, before I even arrived, I had to hide my true self. I paid an American-raised Chinese girl in Peking to show me how.

"In America," she said, "you cannot say you want to live there forever. If you are Chinese, you must say you admire their schools, their ways of thinking. You must say you want to be a scholar and come back to teach Chinese people what you have learned."

"What should I say I want to learn?" I asked. . . .

"Religion, you must say you want to study religion," said this smart girl. "Americans all have different ideas about religion, so there are no right and wrong answers. Say to them, I'm going for God's sake, and they will respect you."

For another sum of money, this girl gave me a form filled out with English words. I had to copy these words

Mothers and Daughters These characters in the movie *The Joy Luck Club* face problems related to preserving their heritage and adapting to American ways.

over and over again as if they were English words formed from my own head. Next to the word NAME, I wrote *Lindo Sun.* Next to the word BIRTHDATE, I wrote *May 11, 1918,* which this girl insisted was the same as three months after the Chinese lunar new year. Next to the word BIRTHPLACE, I put down *Taiyuan, China.* And next to the word OCCUPATION, I wrote *student of theology.*

I gave the girl even more money for a list of addresses in San Francisco, people with big connections. And finally, this girl gave me, free of charge, instructions for changing my circumstances. "First," she said, "you must find a husband. An American citizen is best."

She saw my surprise and quickly added, "Chinese! Of course, he must be Chinese. 'Citizen' does not mean Caucasian. But if he is not a citizen, you should immediately do number two. See here, you should have

---

TEACH

Making the Historical Connection

During the 1970s and 1980s, many people became interested in tracing their roots. It is often difficult, however, for immigrants in the United States to practice traditional customs and preserve their heritage in the face of the dominant American culture. As this literature selection suggests, this loss of identity is particularly difficult for immigrant parents to deal with. The mother in Amy Tan's "Double Face" is distressed by the inability of her American-born daughter to understand the Chinese character.

VISUAL INSTRUCTION

Mothers and Daughters
Amy Tan's book *The Joy Luck Club* was published in 1989. It was a phenomenal best-seller and won many awards. Like the character in this excerpt, Tan describes herself as having two personalities: one public, one private. She puts on the public personality when she is playing the role of celebrity, a role that she is uneasy with. She says she is most comfortable wearing grungy clothes, being silly, and boring her husband while he is trying to read the newspaper.

Background Information

Amy Tan's Influences The series of stories in *The Joy Luck Club* are based on Amy Tan's relationship with her mother. Like the daughter in "Double Face," Tan rejected the Chinese part of herself and cultivated the American. When Tan's mother became ill, however, Tan recalled something her mother had once asked her: "If I die, what would you remember?" *The Joy Luck Club* is the result of Tan's decision to remember everything she could about her mother.

a baby. Boy or girl, it doesn't matter in the United States. Neither will take care of you in your old age, isn't that true?" And we both laughed.

"Be careful, though," she said. "The authorities there will ask you if you have children now or if you are thinking of having some. You must say no. You should look sincere and say you are not married, you are religious, you know it is wrong to have a baby."

I must have looked puzzled, because she explained further: "Look here now, how can an unborn baby know what it is not supposed to do? And once it has arrived, it is an American citizen and can do anything it wants. It can ask its mother to stay. Isn't that true?"

But that is not the reason I was puzzled. I wondered why she said I should look sincere. How could I look any other way when telling the truth?

> **"SAVE TODAY FOR TOMORROW, AT BANK OF AMERICA."**
> **I THOUGHT TO MYSELF, THIS IS WHERE AMERICANS WORSHIP.**

See how truthful my face still looks. Why didn't I give this look to you? Why do you always tell your friends that I arrived in the United States on a slow boat from China? This is not true. I was not that poor. I took a plane. I had saved the money my first husband's family gave me when they sent me away. And I had saved money from my twelve years' work as a telephone operator. But it is true I did not take the fastest plane. The plane took three weeks. It stopped everywhere: Hong Kong, Vietnam, the Philippines, Hawaii. So by the time I arrived, I did not look sincerely glad to be here.

Why do you always tell people that I met your father in the Cathay House, that I broke open a fortune cookie and it said I would marry a dark, handsome stranger, and that when I looked up, there he was, the waiter, your father. Why do you make this joke? This is not sincere. This was not true! Your father was not a waiter, I never ate in that restaurant. The Cathay House had a sign that said "Chinese Food," so only Americans went there before it was torn down. Now it is a McDonald's restaurant with a big Chinese sign

that says *mai dong lou*–"wheat," "east," "building." All nonsense. Why are you attracted only to Chinese nonsense? You must understand my real circumstances, how I arrived, how I married, how I lost my Chinese face, why you are the way you are.

When I arrived, nobody asked me questions. The authorities looked at my papers and stamped me in. I decided to go first to a San Francisco address given to me by this girl in Peking. The bus put me down on a wide street with cable cars. This was California Street. I walked up this hill and then I saw a tall building. This was Old St. Mary's. Under the church sign, in handwritten Chinese characters, someone had added: "A Chinese Ceremony to Save Ghosts from Spiritual Unrest 7 A.M. and 8:30 A.M." I memorized this information in case the authorities asked me where I worshipped my religion. And then I saw another sign across the street. It was painted on the outside of a short building: "Save Today for Tomorrow, at Bank of America." And I thought to myself, This is where American people worship. See, even then I was not so dumb! Today that church is the same size, but where that short bank used to be, now there is a tall building, fifty stories high, where you and your husband-to-be work and look down on everybody.

My daughter laughed when I said this. Her mother can make a good joke.

Block Scheduling

Team Teaching This excerpt from *The Joy Luck Club* can be presented in a team teaching context, in conjunction with English or Language Arts.

 At the Movies
Encourage interested students to rent the movie *The Joy Luck Club*, which is available at most video stores.

CLOSE

To close the section, conduct a discussion with students. The mother used the term "Chinese face" to indicate aspects of Chinese culture and the term "American face" to indicate American culture. Ask students why they think it is necessary for the mother to preserve her Chinese face. *(because it reflects her culture, her sense of self, and her ways of viewing the world)* Why does she sometimes hide her Chinese face behind her American face? *(to fit in better to American culture)* Is her American face genuine or simply learned? *(It is her representation of what she thinks Americans are like; it is not genuine in the sense that it doesn't come naturally.)*

The Reagan and Bush Years

DAILY LESSON OBJECTIVES	REPRODUCIBLE RESOURCES	MULTIMEDIA RESOURCES
SECTION 1 The Reagan Revolution 1. Describe the political and religious coalition than took Reagan to the presidency. 2. Explain how Reaganomics affected the economy. 3. Identify the successes and shortcomings of the Reagan revolution. 4. List changes that occurred in the Supreme Court during Reagan's terms.	Reproducible Lesson Plans Vocabulary and Guided Reading Activities (English or Spanish) Cooperative Learning Activities Interpreting Political Cartoons Supreme Court Case Studies Skill Reinforcement Activities Section Quizzes (English or Spanish)	Chapter Teaching Transparencies Section Focus Transparencies Map Transparencies Powers of the President Landmark Documents in American History Economics in Action Powers of the Supreme Court Student Self-Test: A Software Review Testmaker
SECTION 2 The Collapse of Communism 1. Explain how changes in Soviet and United States foreign policy led to arms reductions. 2. Identify the causes for the breakup of the Soviet Union in the 1980s. 3. Think about how the cold war's end changed United States foreign policy. 4. Notice ways in which the arms race changed during the Reagan-Bush years.	Reproducible Lesson Plans Vocabulary and Guided Reading Activities (English or Spanish) Interpreting Political Cartoons Section Quizzes (English or Spanish)	Section Focus Transparencies Communism and the Cold War Lessons of War Student Self-Test: A Software Review Testmaker
SECTION 3 The Bush Presidency 1. Explain what happened as a result of military cutbacks in the United States. 2. Explain the origins and outcome of the Persian Gulf War. 3. Explain how the changing economy affected the way Americans lived and worked in the 1980s and 1990s.	Reproducible Lesson Plans Vocabulary and Guided Reading Activities (English or Spanish) Geography in History Activities Interpreting Political Cartoons Supreme Court Case Studies Reteaching Activities (English or Spanish) Enrichment Activities (English or Spanish) Section Quizzes (English or Spanish)	Section Focus Transparencies The Presidents: A Picture History of Our Nation Powers of the President Powers of the Congress Landmark Documents in American History Student Self-Test: A Software Review Testmaker
CHAPTER REVIEW AND EVALUATION	Chapter 25 Test, Forms A and B Performance Assessment Strategies and Activities	Student Self-Test: A Software Review Vocabulary PuzzleMaker Testmaker Chapter Digests Audiocassettes

`00:00` If time does not permit teaching the entire chapter, summarize using the Chapter 25 Digests Audiocassettes and the accompanying activities and tests. (Available in English or Spanish.)

✔ Performance Assessment

Cooperative Project

Organize students into groups of four or five. Have the groups investigate the economic aspects of the arms buildup. Students might create a line graph showing the growth of the defense budget and pie graphs showing the defense budgets as a percentage of the federal budget. Have the groups present their results to the class. **LEP** 📋

Suggested Rubrics: An Oral Presentation, Group Work and the Individual. See Performance Assessment Strategies and Activites, pp. 33 and 49.

Individual Project

Before students read about the end of the cold war, point out that reduced tensions between the superpowers led to reduced military spending. Have students identify which problems in United States society most deserve the government funds spent on the military. Have them write up their ideas in a report or present them to the class orally. 📋

Suggested Rubric: An Oral Presentation. See Performance Assessment Strategies and Activites, pp. 33 and 49.

Key to Ability Levels

Teaching strategies have been coded for varying learning styles and abilities.

L1 `BASIC` activities for all students

L2 `AVERAGE` activities for average to above-average students

L3 `CHALLENGING` activities for above-average students

LEP `LIMITED ENGLISH PROFICIENCY` activities

Block Scheduling

Block scheduling differs from traditional class scheduling in the amount of time allotted to each period. The extended timeframe provided by block scheduling affords you the opportunity to implement a greater number of research-oriented and activity-intense projects to motivate and involve your students. Activities that are particularly suited to use within the block scheduling framework are identified throughout this chapter by the following designation. 📋

TEACHER'S CORNER

NATIONAL GEOGRAPHIC SOCIETY

INDEX TO NATIONAL GEOGRAPHIC MAGAZINE

The following articles may be used for research relating to this chapter:

- "Information Revolution," by Joel L. Swerdlow, October 1995.
- "Russia: Playing by New Rules," by Mike Edwards, March 1993.
- "The Bolshevik Revolution," By Dusko Doder, October 1992
- "East Europe's Dark Dawn," by Jon Thompson, June 1991.
- "Computer Rebuilds the Ancient Sphinx," by Mark Lehner, April 1991.
- "Dispatches From Eastern Europe," by Tad Szulc, March 1991.

- "Mother Russia on a New Course," by Mike Edwards, February 1991.
- "Berlin's Ode to Joy," by Priit J. Vesilind, April 1990.
- "Advanced Materials—Reshaping Our Lives " by Thomas Y. Canby, December 1989.
- "High Tech: The Future is Now," by Michael E. Long, July 1989.

NATIONAL GEOGRAPHIC SOCIETY PRODUCTS AVAILABLE FROM GLENCOE

To order the following products for use with this chapter, contact your local Glencoe sales representative or call Glencoe at 1-800-334-7344:

- *The Presidents: A Picture History of Our Nation* (CD-ROM)
- *GTV: The American People: Fabric of a Nation* (Videodisc)
- *GTV: A Geographic Perspective on American History* (Videodisc)

ADDITIONAL NATIONAL GEOGRAPHIC SOCIETY PRODUCTS

To order the following products for use with this chapter, call National Geographic Society at 1-800-368-2728:

- *The Changing Faces of Communism Series:* Poland. (Video)
- *The Rise and Fall of the Soviet Union* (Video)
- *Russia: After the U.S.S.R.* (Video)
- *The Soviet World in Transition* (Filmstrip)
- *The American Presidency* (Filmstrip)
- *Miniature Miracle: The Computer Chip* (Video)

Chapter Overview

During the late 1980s and early 1990s, Americans faced much uncertainty in the post–cold war world, as well as many difficult social, economic, and environmental problems at home. In addition, the United States had to position itself to deal with countless changes in other countries of the world—changes thought impossible a mere decade before.

Introducing the Chapter

Point out that Ronald Reagan was an extremely popular President. Ask students to read the narrative on this page and think about why his appeal was so universal. As they read the chapter, have them look for other reasons for his popularity and think about how his image matched his presidency.

 Display the Chapter 25 Teaching Transparency and distribute copies of the activity sheet.

Extension Activity

Have students complete Beyond the Transparency on the activity sheet for Chapter 25 and present their projects after the class has completed the chapter. 🖿

History Journal

Suggest that students interview a parent or another adult about Reagan's popularity, using the following questions: How did Reagan's career as a movie actor enhance his popularity? How did people feel about his term as governor of California?

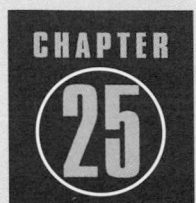

CHAPTER

25

The Reagan and Bush Years

The New York Hilton banquet hall glittered with diamonds at the $500-per-plate dinner that launched Ronald Reagan's third try for the presidency. Far from California where he had been an actor and governor, Reagan wanted to prove that he appealed to the entire nation.

Throughout his campaign, Reagan implied that life had been better in an earlier time. People were good. They believed in family and trusted in God. They stood on their own two feet. People might have been poor, as Reagan had been, but with hard work and a bit of luck, a person could still achieve the American dream.

Such a simple, sturdy United States was part myth, part reality. The future President's poignant picture of it, though oversimplified, tapped into a deep longing in Americans who were weary of the turmoil of the 1960s and 1970s and frightened by declining economic fortunes at home and reduced political and military influence abroad. ■

HISTORY JOURNAL

Why do you think Ronald Reagan had so much appeal for people? Predict whether this initial popularity would last throughout his presidency.

854

 EXTRA CREDIT PROJECT

The American Dream Have students use what they learned in previous chapters to compare life in the United States in the 1940s and 1950s with life in the 1960s and 1970s. Ask students to write a report on the two periods and analyze the picture of the United States that Reagan presented to voters as an ideal. Have them answer these questions in their reports: How accurate was Reagan's depiction of the United States? What was there about the 1960s and 1970s that would make Americans desire Reagan's picture of the United States? 🖿

UPI/BETTMANN

RONALD AND NANCY REAGAN WALTZ DURING
THE DINNER AT WHICH REAGAN DECLARED
HIMSELF A CANDIDATE FOR PRESIDENT.

855

Curriculum Connection

Geography Note that Reagan's rise to the presidency coincided with the rise of the Sunbelt. Have students research the changes in the geographic distribution of the American population in the 1970s. Display the results of their research on an outline map.

Performance Assessment

Refer to page 854B for performance assessment activities for this chapter.

 Also see Activity 25 in the Performance Assessment Strategies and Activities for an additional activity as well as for suggested rubrics.

Examining the Visual

The All-American Couple Ronald Reagan's experience as a movie actor put him at ease in front of the camera as no other President had been. Ask students what elements of the photograph on this page look like a movie set from the 1940s. (Students may need to ask an adult about 1940s movies or think of movies they have seen from that era to help them with this question.) Note the big band, Fred Astaire–Ginger Rogers look of the picture. Ask students how this nostalgic return to the 1940s would have appealed to voters.

FOCUS

Section Objectives

1. Describe the political and religious coalition that took Reagan to the presidency.
2. Explain how Reaganomics affected the economy.
3. Identify the successes and shortcomings of the Reagan revolution.
4. List changes that occurred in the Supreme Court during Reagan's terms.

Bellringer Activity

While taking attendance at the beginning of the period, display **Section Focus Transparency 80,** and have students answer the questions. (Or use the blackline master.)

VISUAL INSTRUCTION

Released! A parade celebrating the return of hostages occurs in New York. In October 1979, Carter allowed the deposed Shah of Iran into the United States for medical treatment. Later, Iranians seized the United States Embassy in Iran and demanded the Shah's return. Carter refused. The hostages were not freed until after the 1980 elections.

Ask: What effect did the freeing of the hostages and the inauguration of Reagan have on the American people? *(Many Americans hoped they were entering a new era or "morning in America" again.)*

856

The Reagan Revolution

JANUARY 20, 1981: AMERICAN HOSTAGES LEAVE TEHRAN

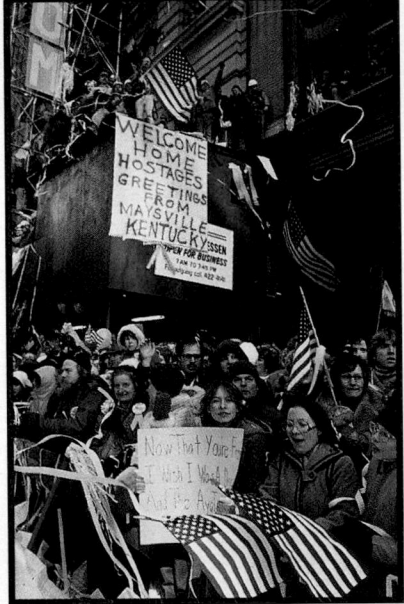

Released!
Jubilant crowds welcome the released hostages home.

YOUNG ISLAMIC MILITANTS CALLED OUT INSULTS AS AMERICAN HOSTAGES, STILL BLINDFOLDED, WERE LED OUT ONTO THE TARMAC AT THE TEHRAN AIRPORT. The 52 captives climbed into an Algerian 727 that waited there to carry them on the first leg of a journey that would return them to the United States after 444 days in captivity.

After what seemed like endless delays, the plane rose into the blue desert sky above Iran. Bill Belk, one of the captives, remembers, "When the wheels lifted off the runway there was a great shout of rejoicing. 'We are off! We are free!' I think lifting off of that runway was the greatest thrill of my entire life. It was a moment of pure joy." The time was 12:25 P.M. Eastern Standard Time.

The sequence of events could not have been better for Ronald Reagan. At the exact moment the plane became airborne, the newly elected President was concluding his Inaugural Address in Washington, D.C. One hour later, when he was sure the plane had cleared Iranian airspace, the new President announced the happy news that the nation had waited so long to hear.

The freeing of the hostages and the swearing in of the fortieth President marked an important shift for the nation. Many hoped the United States was leaving behind the self-doubt and indecisiveness of the post-Vietnam years and entering a new era. To them it looked as though it would be "morning in America" again as candidate Reagan had promised.

AS YOU READ

Vocabulary
► mandate
► neoconservatism
► supply-side economics
► deregulate

Think About . . .
► the political and religious coalition that brought Reagan to the presidency.
► how Reaganomics affected the economy.
► the successes and shortcomings of the Reagan revolution.
► the changes that occurred in the Supreme Court during Reagan's administration.

Section 1 Resources

REPRODUCIBLE RESOURCES
- Lesson Plan 25-1
- Vocabulary and Guided Reading Activity 25-1
- Cooperative Learning Activity 25
- Section 1 Quiz
- Political Cartoons 10, 11, 19, 30–34
- Supreme Court Cases 49, 50, 51
- Skill Reinforcement Activity 25

MULTIMEDIA RESOURCES
- Section Focus Transparency 80
- Map Transparency 25
- Chapter 25 Digest Audiocassette
- The Presidents: A Picture History of Our Nation

- Economics in Action
- Powers of the Supreme Court
- Landmark Documents in American History
- Testmaker
- Student Self-Test: A Software Review
- Chapter Teaching Transparency 25

A Broad New Coalition
Neoconservatives, the Religious Right, and Reagan

Reagan's race for the presidency came at a time when the country's mood was changing. Many Americans were unsympathetic to the protest movements and boisterous freedoms of the 1960s and the expensive social programs of the 1970s. A powerful conservative groundswell had been building momentum for years.

The changing mood of the country found its voice in Reagan. He received support from nearly all segments of American society: Democrats and Republicans, the rich and the poor, insiders as well as outsiders. This broad-based support swept Reagan into office with a **mandate**—an order from the voters—to make changes in the way the nation was run. The people were eager for Reagan to deliver on his promise to "get the government off people's backs" and restore the old-fashioned virtues of the heartland.

A New Conservatism

As the 1980s began, many conservative Americans believed that government had grown too large in the 1960s and 1970s. They challenged the central beliefs of liberalism: that a fair and equal society can be achieved and that government ought to play a major role in guaranteeing and regulating it. These conservatives believed that the government had spent too much of the taxpayers' money; created bloated, inefficient bureaucracies; and kept the economy from flourishing on its own.

Reagan's appeal most attracted those Americans who were convinced that some problems just could not be solved by the government and must simply be accepted. Government, they believed, should withdraw from most areas of American life, and people should behave with more restraint. Businesses, in particular, should be freed from government restraint so they could become more profitable and thus strengthen the country. This was **neoconservatism**, a new type of conservatism. It signaled a return to the type of conservative thinking that was popular in the early years of the 1900s.

The Religious Right

Neoconservatism was not the only new doctrine to gain favor during the 1970s. When President Carter proclaimed himself "born-again," he spotlighted a major trend in American culture—the emergence of evangelical Christianity as a powerful religious and political force.

The most recent wave of evangelism began in the 1950s with the spiritual crusades of the Reverend Billy Graham. The movement grew rapidly in the 1960s and 1970s with the advent of television ministers—dubbed

The Religious Right The Reverend Jerry Falwell, leader of the Moral Majority, becomes a force in national elections. *What beliefs did Falwell and other members of the Moral Majority favor that influenced the election of 1980?*

televangelists—who preached to huge home audiences via television. By the middle of the 1970s, as many as 70 million Americans identified themselves as born-again.

In contrast to Jimmy Carter, a moderate political liberal, many evangelicals saw their religious zeal reflected in political conservatism. Like conservatives, they were morally opposed to drugs, pornography, and abortion. They firmly rejected liberal social policies and strongly favored free enterprise and a foreign policy backed up by a strong military.

During the 1980 presidential campaign, a California-based group called Christian Voice flooded the Midwest and the South with political literature. Their candidate was Ronald Reagan. Through Reagan, the evangelicals believed, biblical principles could become law.

One of the most effective political organizations of the religious right was the Moral Majority, founded in 1979 by another televangelist, the Reverend Jerry Falwell. In a little over a year, the Moral Majority registered between 2 and 3 million new voters. Falwell and his associates enjoyed the confidence of President Reagan and exerted powerful political influence—that is, until the organization was disbanded in 1989. This followed a series of scandals and financial wrongdoings within other groups of the religious right that, in the minds of many Americans, had discredited the moral force of the entire movement.

SECTION ONE   **857**

VISUAL INSTRUCTION

The Religious Right Baptist Minister Jerry Falwell founded the Moral Majority, an organization that tried to influence lawmakers, in 1979.

Answer: *Evangelical Christians were conservatives. They favored free enterprise and a strong military.*

TEACH

Guided Practice

L1 The 1980s Ask students what they know about the 1980s and Ronald Reagan. List their responses. Tell students that this section covers what became known as the Reagan revolution, or Reaganomics.

Show students Map Transparency 25 and have them complete the activity sheet.

Independent Practice

L2 Public Opinion Ford and Carter were the first incumbent Presidents since Hoover not to be reelected. Have students read newsmagazines from the time to find out how Americans felt and report their findings to the class.

Have students complete the Chapter 25, Section 1 Vocabulary and Guided Reading. (Also in Spanish.)
LEP

Have students complete the Chapter 25 Cooperative Learning Activity.

Cooperative Learning

Reaganomics Posters Organize students into five or six groups. Have students prepare posters that explain the assumptions and the results of Reaganomics. Remind the groups that each person should have a part in the project. Group members will need to plan the poster, divide the work fairly, and complete the project. Posters might include charts, graphs, or other visual aids. Some groups may want to explain their posters to the rest of the class. Display all posters in the classroom.

Shifting Political Allegiance

Ronald Reagan's triumph over President Carter was much more than a victory for neoconservatism and the religious right. It also represented a reshuffling of many historic voting patterns in the United States.

Reagan captured 44 of the 50 states, giving him 489 electoral votes to Carter's 49. The Republicans also captured the Senate. This landslide was primarily due to the force of Reagan's personality. Many voters simply liked him as a person, and they had enormous confidence in Reagan's ability to cure the nation's ills.

Reagan ran strongly in the West and the Southwest, where Republicans usually do well. He also captured the industrial states around the Great Lakes and in the Northeast, which had become Democratic strongholds. In those states, his supporters were mostly blue-collar and ethnic voters who responded to his pledges to revive the economy, fight communism, and oppose abortion. The South was another Democratic stronghold. Yet Reagan, boosted by his support from the religious right, won every Southern state except Carter's home state of Georgia. Many older voters also viewed the 69-year-old Reagan as a politician who would be sensitive to their needs.

Reagan + Economics = Reaganomics

Balanced Budget Pledge Not Achieved

Ever since the 1930s, most American Presidents had subscribed to the ideas of British economist John Maynard Keynes. Keynes believed that the key to stimulating an economy was government spending, which often required higher taxes.

President Ronald Reagan and his economic advisers replaced this approach with what was called **supply-side economics.** According to this theory, the key to economic vitality was reducing taxes, especially those on wealthy individuals and large corporations. Lower taxes would encourage more saving and investment, which would lead to business expansion and more jobs. The result would be a larger supply of goods for consumers who, thanks to tax cuts, now had more money to spend.

Within months of taking office, Reagan got Congress to approve one of his biggest campaign promises: a major reduction of income taxes that favored, above all, the wealthiest Americans. That raised a tough question. Lower taxes meant less money flowing into the Treasury, but Reagan was also sharply increasing military spending. How was he going to balance the budget, as he had also promised voters?

His answer was to chip away at domestic programs. Welfare benefits were cut, and a million recipients of food stamps were removed from the government rolls. Fewer government programs were available to revitalize big cities and pay for children's meals in the nation's public schools. Medicare benefits were slashed, requiring the elderly to pay more for health care, and unemployment compensation was reduced.

Most of the scaled-down programs had grown out of the liberal social agenda that had dominated presidential and congressional politics for decades. Cutting them back fit Reagan's conservative view that the government should be less involved in the lives of its people, even those people who needed help.

⭐ ⭐ ⭐ **GALLERY OF PRESIDENTS** ⭐ ⭐ ⭐

 Ronald Reagan

1 9 8 1 – 1 9 8 9

"We are a nation that has a government—not the other way around. And this makes us special among the nations of the Earth. Our government has no power except that granted it by the people. It is time to check and reverse the growth of government which shows signs of having grown beyond the consent of the governed."

Inaugural Address, January 20, 1981

AP/WIDE WORLD PHOTOS

BACKGROUND
▶ Born 1911
▶ Republican, California
▶ Governor of California, 1967–1975

ACHIEVEMENTS IN OFFICE
▶ Economic Recovery Tax Act (1981)
▶ Proposal for SDI (1983)
▶ INF Treaty with the Soviet Union (1987)
▶ Three appointments to the Supreme Court

858 CHAPTER 25 THE REAGAN AND BUSH YEARS

Meeting Special Needs

Limited English Proficiency Preview the key vocabulary words and any other words that might pose difficulties with students whose first language is not English. Then preview the main ideas of the section by explaining the basic features of neoconser-vatism and Reaganomics. Some students may benefit from listening to Chapter 25, Section 1 on the Chapter Audiocassettes. The audiocassettes are also available in Spanish. **LEP**

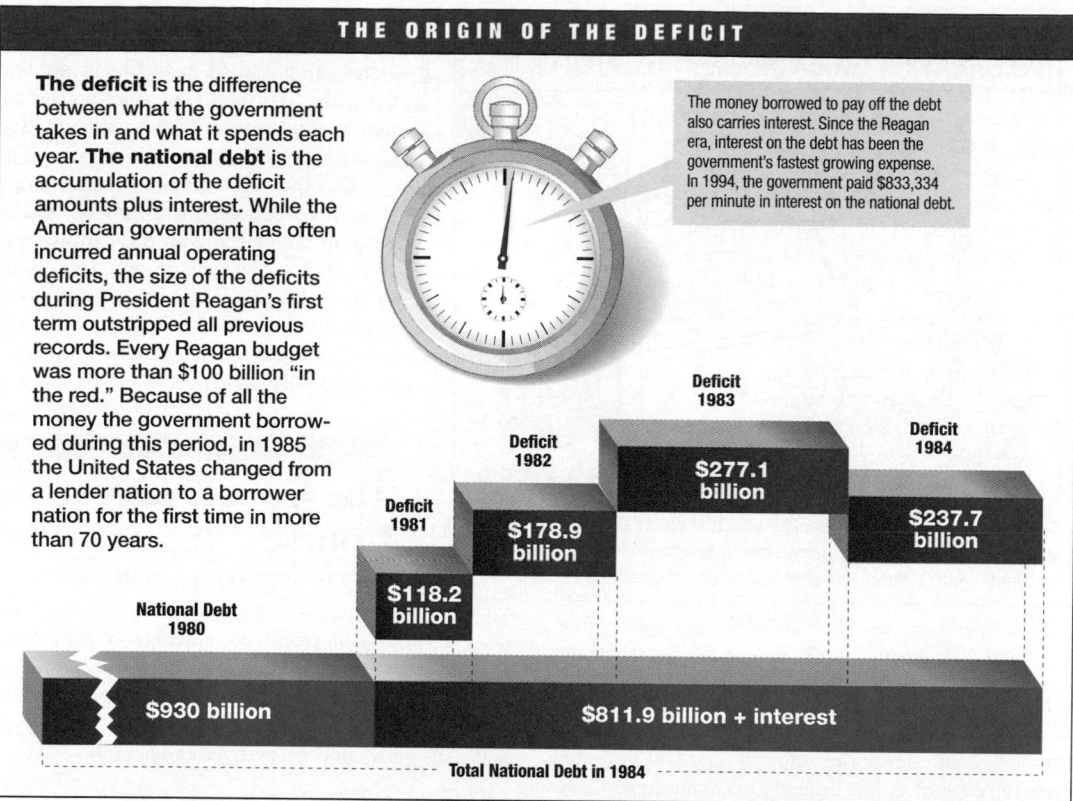

THE ORIGIN OF THE DEFICIT

The deficit is the difference between what the government takes in and what it spends each year. **The national debt** is the accumulation of the deficit amounts plus interest. While the American government has often incurred annual operating deficits, the size of the deficits during President Reagan's first term outstripped all previous records. Every Reagan budget was more than $100 billion "in the red." Because of all the money the government borrowed during this period, in 1985 the United States changed from a lender nation to a borrower nation for the first time in more than 70 years.

The money borrowed to pay off the debt also carries interest. Since the Reagan era, interest on the debt has been the government's fastest growing expense. In 1994, the government paid $833,334 per minute in interest on the national debt.

National Debt 1980

$930 billion

Deficit 1981
$118.2 billion

Deficit 1982
$178.9 billion

Deficit 1983
$277.1 billion

Deficit 1984
$237.7 billion

$811.9 billion + interest

----- Total National Debt in 1984 -----

Reagan's economic policies halted runaway inflation and unemployment. At the same time, government spending (mostly on defense) outpaced revenues. The resulting deficit made people wonder if the prosperity of the Reagan years was built on borrowed money. *When did consumers see the benefits of Reaganomics?*

Recession and Recovery

Reagan's economic policies, dubbed Reaganomics, sparked a radical change in government fiscal policy. The policies succeeded in controlling the double-digit inflation of the Carter years. High interest rates, however, prevented many Americans from borrowing the money to make major purchases or expand businesses.

The nation slumped into another severe 2-year recession as productivity declined. A third of the nation's factories and mines stood idle. Detroit's auto sales plunged to their lowest levels in 2 decades. By late 1982, 10 percent of the labor force, or about 11 million people, were out of work—the greatest number since 1940.

Many farmers and businesspeople were caught in a bind. They had taken out loans at high interest rates during the 1970s, when prices were high. Now, with income down, they could not make their payments.

Many farmers lost their farms, and business bankruptcies skyrocketed. During a single week in August 1982, a record 572 businesses failed, the highest weekly total since the Great Depression.

By the end of 1982, the tide turned. Interest rates dropped to about half of the all-time high of 21.5 percent that they had hit in 1981. With interest rates falling, companies could afford to invest again. With inflation edging down, people could keep more of their tax cuts and buy houses, cars, and smaller consumer items.

Unemployment was still above 9 percent in 1983, but increased business activity did create more jobs. Productivity turned upward. A cycle of growth was restored. In 1984 the gross national product increased by more than 9 percent, the biggest 1-year gain since 1951.

The Drive to Deregulate

In Reagan's view government red tape hamstrung business and industry, kept companies less profitable, and ultimately weakened the American economy.

Reagan signaled that his administration would **deregulate**, giving companies more leeway to operate freely. He set up a task force to advise him on how to ease regulations and to find appropriate people to work in the federal agencies that watched over various industries.

GRAPH STUDY

Answer: *Consumers saw the benefits of Reaganomics by the end of 1982 as double-digit inflation eased, interest rates dropped, and productivity rose.*

 FYI

Reagan the Actor
Reagan was a popular President. His experience as a Hollywood actor contributed to his successful public appearances. Reagan paid a great deal of attention to his public appearances. Some observers noted that he devoted more hours to fine-tuning his speeches and public addresses than any other President.

 FYI

James Watt Watt's appointment as secretary of the interior was controversial because of his position on issues involving land, water rights, and the environment. He had been the president of a Denver-based law foundation that worked to loosen controls on the use of public lands. Watt resigned in 1983 after making a speech that contained an offensive remark about African Americans, women, Jews, and the disabled.

Portfolio Project

Research Have students conduct research on the current status of the federal budget deficit to find out why it is such a big problem. Students may want to create visuals to help explain the problem. Have students file their research results in their portfolios.

Newspaper Article In 1981 Reagan survived an assassination attempt. Suggest that interested students investigate the incident by reading newsmagazine accounts from the time. Then have students write a news story about the event. Students can place their work in their portfolios.

VISUAL INSTRUCTION

Answer: *Jimmy Carter*

ASSESS

Meeting Lesson Objectives

Each objective is tested by the section review questions that follow in parentheses.

1. Describe the political and religious coalition that took Reagan to the presidency. (1, 2, 3)
2. Explain how Reaganomics affected the economy. (1, 2, 3, 5)
3. Identify successes and shortcomings of the Reagan revolution. (all)
4. List changes that occurred in the Supreme Court during Reagan's terms. (2, 4)

**ABCNEWS
INTERACTIVE**™

Videodisc

*Powers of the
Supreme Court*

Side 2, Chapter 19
Title: Vision of the Court
Subject: Rehnquist
Ask: Define judicial activist. *(the Court should formulate policies)*

**See Powers of the
Supreme Court Guidebook page 82 for complete lesson plan.**

DEREGULATION GIVES CONSUMERS GREATER CHOICES

... AND WOULD YOU FOLKS LIKE MAINTENANCE OR NO MAINTENANCE?

ROULETTE AIR
LET US TAKE YOU FOR A SPIN

Airline Deregulation Some people feared that airline deregulation would lead to cost cutting and lax safety standards; others welcomed lower prices on popular routes. *Which President first began deregulating the airlines?*

porations could use for oil drilling, mining, and logging. The EPA eased the safety checks required on new chemicals and pesticides and relaxed its rules on the expensive pollution-control equipment that companies had to use.

On the issue of the environment, Reagan's economic philosophy seemed to put him out of step with most Americans. In a 1985 public opinion poll, two-thirds of the public rejected Reagan's approach, saying they would be willing to pay higher prices and even sacrifice some jobs in return for tighter limits on pollution.

The Conservative Course

Unemployment Drops as Deficit Grows

Soon the new approach took effect. The National Highway Traffic Safety Administration slowed its demands for air bags and tighter fuel-efficiency standards for cars, requirements the auto industry had protested were too expensive. The Federal Communications Commission took a hands-off attitude toward cable television, allowing almost unrestricted growth in that new field.

At the direction of President Carter, Congress had begun to free the airline industry of regulations controlling its fares and routes. The Reagan administration encouraged the process. Passengers reaped a bonanza of additional flights and cheaper fares as the airlines cut into one another's territory and waged bruising price wars. Away from the big cities, however, the effect was that some small communities lost service altogether.

The Environmental Rearguard

The restrictions that Reagan lifted from American industry were not all just red tape. Many laws tried to prevent companies from polluting the air or water and attempted to regulate the disposal of dangerous wastes. Thus Reagan's deregulation policy ran up against the environmental movement that had made major gains in the 1970s.

To the environmentalists' dismay, Reagan often sided with business. He suggested that some risk or damage to the environment was the price the country had to pay if it wanted companies to provide jobs, build up profits, and strengthen the economy.

Reagan's first secretary of the interior, James Watt, sharply increased the amount of public land that cor-

In many ways Reagan's leadership and popularity unified the nation. Many of his policies, however, increased long-standing divisions. Strains were showing between different economic and racial groups as well as between conservatives and liberals.

Successes of the Revolution

Although some people opposed President Reagan's proposals, he had personal qualities that helped to promote his positions: a great ability to communicate with his audience and a sense of humor. For many people he represented a restored faith in the American way of life.

As the economy recovered from the 1982 recession, the President's popularity soared. The inflation rate dropped just as the 25 percent cut in income taxes was putting more money into the hands of consumers. Feeling new confidence in the economy, Americans made purchases they had put off during the recession. Sales of every type of goods and service shot upward, and industries hired back workers who had been laid off. By the end of Reagan's second term in 1988, unemployment had dropped to 5.5 percent—the lowest in 14 years.

To celebrate, President Reagan went before Congress in 1984 saying, "America is back—standing tall, looking to the '80s with courage, confidence, and hope. . . . Send away the hand-wringers and doubting Thomases."

Shortcomings of the Revolution

The Reagan revolution, however, did not benefit all Americans equally. Although the tax cuts benefited everybody, they benefited the rich most of all. At the

Cultural Perspectives

Understanding Cultures Millions of Asians have immigrated to the United States since 1965. Many of these people have come from China, India, the Philippines, and South Korea. Numerous Vietnamese, Cambodians, and Laotians came to the United States after United States troops withdrew from Vietnam in 1973. Have students choose one of the Asian nations mentioned and conduct research to find out more about the social and cultural aspects of these societies. (For example, in the Vietnamese culture, people owe loyalty to their family before all else and hold their families' interests above their own. Men share responsibility with women for raising, caring for, and disciplining children.)

same time, the cuts in social programs drove some of those at the bottom of the economy deeper into poverty, creating what social scientists called a new urban underclass.

Reagan's pro-family philosophy had appealed to many women voters in the 1980 election. Increasingly, however, Reagan's seeming lack of concern for women's issues alienated many women. In 1983 the *New York Times* identified a "gender gap" in attitudes toward Reagan, as more women opposed him.

Reagan's supporters and opponents alike worried about one notable failure of Reaganomics: its inability to produce a balanced budget. During the 1980 campaign, Reagan had attacked the Carter administration for spending $73.8 billion more than it took in that year. By 1985, however, the deficit had zoomed to more than $212 billion. By the following year, the Reagan administration had run up a greater total deficit than all the administrations in American history combined.

A New Orientation on the Supreme Court

Reagan's conservative philosophy included passionate opposition to two major Supreme Court decisions—that prayer in public schools is unconstitutional and that women have a constitutional right to abortion. On both of these deeply emotional issues, Reagan sought constitutional amendments that would reverse the Court's decisions. Meanwhile, he waited for his chance to appoint justices who would leave policy making to the legislative and executive branches of government.

Reagan's first Supreme Court appointment was a historic one. In 1981 he named Sandra Day O'Connor the first woman justice in the Court's history. Later he appointed other conservative justices.

The Supreme Court began to hand down some conservative decisions that pleased the President. For example, the Court curtailed affirmative action and limited the rights of criminal suspects.

Nevertheless, the Court's direction proved to be a slow drift toward conservatism, not a sharp turn. At the conclusion of Reagan's presidency in 1989, the existing decisions about abortion and prayer in public schools were still the law of the land.

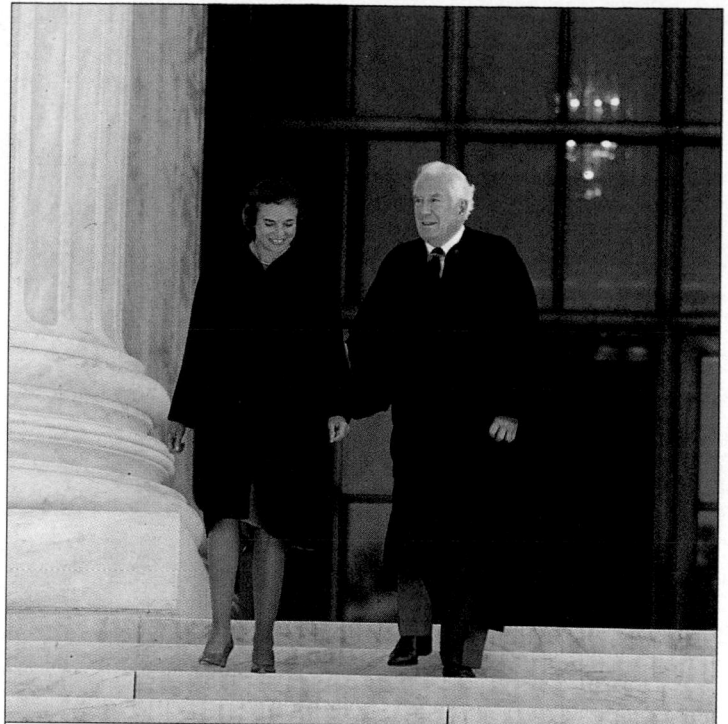

© OWEN FRANKEN/SYGMA

The Supreme Court In 1981 Arizona judge Sandra Day O'Connor became the first woman to serve on the Supreme Court. Reagan nominated her in part because of her conservative views. *What Supreme Court decisions did Reagan oppose?*

SECTION REVIEW

Vocabulary

1. Define: mandate, neoconservatism, supply-side economics, deregulate.

Checking Facts

2. How did Reagan's election reshuffle traditional American political patterns? How did Reaganomics differ from Keynesian economics?

3. What policies did the Reagan economic plan propose to bring the nation out of the recession?

Critical Thinking

Predicting Consequences

4. What might the long-term consequences be of having a conservative Supreme Court?

Linking Across Time

5. How might Reagan's environmental policies affect Americans today and people around the world in the future?

VISUAL INSTRUCTION

The Supreme Court Sandra Day O'Connor has generally sided with conservative Court members, but she has been sympathetic to liberal views on a few issues, including affirmative action.

Answer: *Reagan was especially opposed to women's right to abortion and to banning prayer in public schools.*

Evaluate

Have students complete the Section Review.

☞ 🖳 Assign the Section 1 Quiz or use the Testmaker to develop a customized quiz. (Also in Spanish.) **LEP**

Reteach

🎧 Have students listen to the Chapter 25, Section 1 Audiocassette. (Also in Spanish.) **LEP**

Enrich

☞ Have students complete Interpreting Political Cartoons 10, 11, 19, 30–34.

☞ Have students complete Supreme Court Case Studies 49, 50, 51.

CLOSE

Ask students questions such as the following: What is neoconservatism? *(a belief that government should withdraw from people's lives and leave people and businesses to run their own affairs)* How did deregulation affect the airline industry? *(Prices came down and the number of flights increased, but many small communities lost service.)*

Section 1 Review Answers

1. **mandate** (857), **neoconservatism** (857), **supply-side economics** (858), **deregulate** (859)

2. Reagan won the industrial states and the South, both traditional Democratic strongholds. Reaganomics emphasized reducing taxes to stimulate growth rather than increasing spending.

3. reducing taxes to encourage saving and investment, to increase business expansion and jobs, and to create more consumer goods

4. Since Supreme Court justices are appointed for life, conservative justices may take a conservative stance on laws for many years to come.

5. His environmental policies helped American businesses but risked damaging the environment for future generations.

TEACH

Making the Historical Connection

In the 1830s Charles Babbage developed the idea for a mechanical computer, an idea that he refined for almost 40 years. When performing calculations, Babbage's machine could store completed sets of punched cards for use in later operations. This machine contained all the elements of a modern computer: storage, a working memory, a system for moving between the two, and an input device. The technology of Babbage's time, however, was not sophisticated enough to create the precision parts he needed to construct his machine, and Babbage lacked funding for his project. In addition, Babbage, like others of his time, did not understand electricity.

FYI

Calculators The first true calculating machines were developed in the 1600s. Blaise Pascal in 1642 invented the first automatic calculator. It performed addition and subtraction by means of a set of wheels linked by gears. The first wheel represented the numbers 1 to 10, the second wheel represented 10's, the third 100's, and so on. When the first wheel was turned 10 notches, a gear moved the second wheel forward one notch.

Science, TECHNOLOGY, and Society

Personal Computers

Before their workings could fit on miniature chips, computers were huge machines in back rooms of offices. Hundreds of people could log on at work, but they had no access to computers at home or at school. Once personal computers (PCs) became easily available in the 1980s, their use soared. By the end of the 1980s, PCs sat on desks nationwide.

UPI/BETTMANN NEWSPHOTOS

© DAN McCOY/RAINBOW

ENIAC
The University of Pennsylvania's ENIAC computer cost $500,000. It could carry out operations at electronic speed, but it had no memory. Scientists had to rewire the computer for each new problem it tackled. Six full-time technicians scurried about replacing any of the 17,000 vacuum tubes that randomly blew out.

HISTORY OF PERSONAL COMPUTERS

1940s	1950s	1960s
In 1946 **ENIAC,** the first general-purpose electronic digital computer, fills a huge room. It weighs 30 tons.	In 1951 **UNIAC,** the first commercially available computer, accurately predicts Eisenhower's election 45 minutes after the polls closed. It is the first computer to use letters as well as numbers. First **TRANSISTORIZED COMPUTERS** introduced in 1958.	**COMPUTER** circuits are placed on chips. More than 10,000 computers are in use worldwide by 1961.

Background Information

Early Personal Computers The first personal computer, the Altair, was introduced in 1975. It cost $400, and came in a hard-to-assemble kit. Only hobbyists bought this computer, which did not work that well. It had no external memory, no printer, and no keyboard. Limited programming and data entry could be done by flipping toggle switches on the front. Despite this, the Altair was a big hit with hobbyists, who sensed that they were on the front line of a technological revolution.

In 1977 Steven Jobs and Stephen Wozniak founded the Apple Computer Company. They introduced the Apple II personal computer. It was much less expensive than a mainframe, and so, for the first time, computers became available to people other than technicians and computer specialists.

NOTEBOOK COMPUTERS

Some notebook computers today weigh less than 3 pounds. The first "portable" notebook computer weighed 30 pounds and needed an electrical outlet. It was not until 1985 that rechargeable batteries and LCD screens made computers truly portable.

© TOM McCARTHY/RAINBOW

FILE PHOTO BY DOUG MINDELL

© T.J. FLORIAN/RAINBOW

SMALLER AND SMALLER

Transistors, such as the one on the left, replaced the much larger vacuum tubes. Today computers can contain thousands or millions of transistors and related circuitry on a chip smaller than a fingernail (above).

PCs DO EVERYTHING

Modern computers have made typewriters (still common in the 1980s) virtually obsolete. They can replace many other office items as well, including adding machines, erasers, and carbon paper. Computers can send letters, fax documents, and create artwork. They can analyze volumes of data or provide access to libraries of information around the world. A modern desktop computer has more computing power than the huge room-filling computers of the early 1960s.

COMPUTERS TODAY

Think about how computers affect you. Keep a list for one day or one week detailing every use you make of a computer. How would someone have performed these activities a decade ago? How pervasive are computers in your life? Keep your results in your portfolio.

1970s	1980s	1990s
Entire workings of computers can now be placed on **CHIPS.** More than 100,000 computers in use in 1971. **APPLE** personal computer introduced in 1977.	**IBM** personal computer is introduced in 1981. In 1984 Apple introduces the first Macintosh powerful enough to support a mouse, windows, and elaborate software.	**MORE THAN 145,000,000** personal computers are in use in the United States.

Block Scheduling

The Portfolio Project on this page provides an excellent opportunity to enrich and extend the key elements of this feature.

FYI

Supercomputers Mainframes are powerful computers used to solve very complicated problems and manage huge quantities of information. Most take up the space of several large filing cabinets. The fastest mainframes are called supercomputers. They are used to model weather systems, to design cars and aircraft, and to solve complicated mathematical problems for scientists and engineers. Supercomputers are rare because they are very expensive. The fastest supercomputers have many processors that work at the same time. Each processor can work on a separate piece of a program.

CLOSE

To wrap up this feature, ask students questions such as the following: What was ENIAC like? *(It filled a room, had 17,000 vacuum tubes, weighed 30 tons, and required 6 technicians to run it.)* What has allowed modern computers to become so small? *(Miniaturization allows chips today to hold millions of transistors and other circuitry, which used to fill an entire room.)*

863

Portfolio Project

Research Have students research computers. They may want to focus on uses for computers in a field of interest or computers of the future. Topics to explore include optical processors (which use laser light rather than electric currents), virtual reality programs that provide realistic simulations, artificial intelligence (which helps computers make decisions), biological computers that are grown rather than manufactured, molecular storage systems (which could contain all the knowledge of the human race in a space smaller than a paperback book), computer animation, and multimedia. Have students file their reports in their portfolios.

864

TEACH

This feature deals with the skill of making accurate predictions. Students will follow steps to see how political leaders might have predicted the success of Ronald Reagan's presidential campaign. In the process students will learn the procedures for combining reliable facts with observations of similar patterns and situations to make realistic predictions.

VISUAL INSTRUCTION

Protesters In this photograph, American students protest United States involvement in Nicaraguan affairs during the Reagan years. Have students consider how demonstrations such as this one may influence public opinion about Central America. How might political rivals use demonstrations to garner support for their candidates? *(by having the candidates state their agreement with the demonstrators)* Based on experiences that they know about (such as demonstrations against the Vietnam War), what effect do students predict these types of protests make? *(They raise public awareness and can influence public and political opinions, especially if enough people become involved.)*

Answer: *that some voters are worried, frustrated, or angry about certain government policies or issues*

Additional Practice

☞ Have students complete the Chapter 25 Skill Reinforcement Activity.

Critical Thinking Skill

PREDICTING CONSEQUENCES

Learning the Skill

Making accurate predictions depends both on gathering reliable facts and observing past behaviors in similar situations. Use the following steps to make predictions:

a. Review what you already know by listing facts, events, and people's responses. The list will help you recall important events and how they affected people.

b. Define and analyze patterns. Try to determine what the patterns show.

c. Incorporate your knowledge and observations of similar situations.

d. Make a prediction.

Practicing the Skill

By his election to the presidency, Ronald Reagan proved that his personality and brand of politics were what Americans wanted in 1980. Candidates for public office, however, often make decisions and define policies based on how they think voters will respond.

Use the information in the chart to help you apply the events of the 1970s described in the first column to the Republicans' decision to choose Ronald Reagan as their 1980 presidential candidate.

1. Review the facts and events listed on the chart.

2. Do you notice any patterns? What do the facts tell you about the 1970s? How did people feel?

3. Recall similar situations in which voters suffered through hard times. How would they feel about a President who promised to "restore America's strength and pride"?

4. Based on this information, what kind of candidate might Republican leaders choose, and why?

5. Now use this information to make a prediction about an upcoming election.

Applying the Skill

Read newspapers and think about an event that affects your community, such as local land uses or construction of a new sports complex. Using the steps described, make an educated prediction about what will happen. Explain your reasoning.

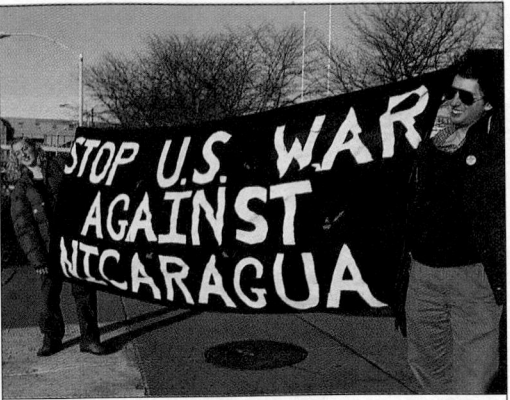

Protesters Americans protest United States involvement in Nicaragua. *What can demonstrations such as these tell observers about the mood of voters?*

RECOGNIZING PATTERNS	
Facts/Events of the 1970s	**Results/Reactions**
The OPEC oil embargo caused inflation and a shortage of fuel.	Americans felt helpless and angry.
President Ford vetoed programs in health, housing, and education to reduce government spending and fight inflation.	Many people lost jobs; Americans suffered the worst recession in 40 years.
President Carter increased government spending and cut taxes, ending the recession and reducing unemployment.	Americans lost spending power as inflation rose.
Carter called on Americans to conserve energy and work toward energy self-sufficiency.	Americans felt frustrated at being asked to bear such a great burden.
To conserve energy, Americans bought smaller, imported cars. United States automakers lost sales to Japanese and German automakers.	American workers suffered unemployment as several automobile plants closed and their suppliers of materials lost business.
Americans were taken hostage by Iranians. A rescue attempt 5 months later failed. The hostages were released after 14 months only when Carter unfroze Iranian assets.	Americans saw their leaders forced to give in to terrorists' demands.

Additional Practice

For additional practice, see Reinforcing Skills on page 889.

Practicing the Skill Answers

Answers will vary.

1. Answers should accurately reflect the facts and events listed on the chart.

2. In the 1970s many people felt helpless, angry, and frustrated because they had lost jobs, inflation rose dramatically, and overseas nations seemed to be pushing the United States around.

3. During the Depression and the early postwar years, Americans struggled. They wanted a leader to restore the nation's economic strength and role overseas.

4. They might choose a leader who seemed to embody strength, confidence, and pride in America.

5. Students should use the process detailed on this page to make a realistic prediction about an upcoming election.

SECTION 2

The Collapse of Communism

MAY 6, 1992: GORBACHEV COMES TO FULTON, MISSOURI

Mikhail Gorbachev
Addressing the students of Westminster College, Gorbachev announces that the cold war has at last come to an end.

THE SPRING SUN SHONE DOWN ON THE CAMPUS OF WESTMINSTER COLLEGE IN FULTON, MISSOURI, WHERE MORE THAN 10,000 PEOPLE HAD GATHERED. They had come to hear a speech by Mikhail Gorbachev, the former president of the Soviet Union.

Carolyn O'Donley, a college student, basked in the thrill of seeing a major historical figure on her campus of just 750 students. "Gorbachev and his wife, Raisa, walked through the crowd shaking people's hands," she said. "Everyone was very excited—it was a very positive feeling to have them here." She added, "I think there were reporters from every country in the world, too."

The reporters were there to cover more than a speech, for Gorbachev was only the second major historical figure to visit the school. In 1946—before any of the students present on that day were born—Winston Churchill, prime minister of Great Britain during World War II, had spoken at Westminster. In a famous speech, Churchill warned of the onset of the cold war and of Soviet oppression in Europe. "From Stettin in the Baltic to Trieste in the Adriatic, an iron curtain has descended across the continent," Churchill had said.

Now Gorbachev—who did more than any other person to end the cold war and lift the iron curtain from Europe—looked out on the sea of

---

AS YOU READ

Vocabulary
- ▶ mutual deterrence
- ▶ glasnost
- ▶ perestroika

Think About . . .
- ▶ how changes in Soviet and United States relations led to arms reductions.
- ▶ the causes for the breakup of the Soviet Union in the late 1980s.

- ▶ how the cold war's end changed the foreign policy of the United States.
- ▶ the ways in which the arms race changed during the Reagan-Bush years.

SECTION TWO   **865**

Section 2 Resources

REPRODUCIBLE RESOURCES
- 📁 Lesson Plan 25-2
- 📁 Vocabulary and Guided Reading Activity 25-2
- 📁 Section 2 Quiz
- 📁 Political Cartoons 40–49

MULTIMEDIA RESOURCES
- 🔊 Section Focus Transparency 81
- 🎧 Chapter 25 Digest Audiocassette
- 💿 Communism and the Cold War
- 💻 Testmaker
- 💿 Student Self-Test: A Software Review
- 💿 Lessons of War

FOCUS

Section Objectives
1. Explain how changes in Soviet and United States foreign policy led to arms reductions.
2. Identify the causes for the breakup of the Soviet Union in the late 1980s.
3. Think about how the cold war's end changed United States foreign policy.
4. Notice ways in which the arms race changed during the Reagan-Bush years.

Bellringer Activity
✏️ While taking attendance at the beginning of the class period, display **Section Focus Transparency 81**, and have students answer the questions. (Or use the blackline master.)

VISUAL INSTRUCTION

Mikhail Gorbachev
Gorbachev was the leader of the Soviet Union from 1985 to 1991. He gained worldwide fame for his efforts to make changes in what was then the Soviet Union and for his efforts to improve relations with other nations. In 1990 Gorbachev received the Nobel Peace Prize.

Ask: What did Churchill's speech warn of, and how did Gorbachev's visit relate to this speech? *(Churchill foresaw the beginning of the cold war and warned people of the descending iron curtain. Gorbachev's visit signaled the end of both the cold war and the iron curtain.)*

VISUAL INSTRUCTION

East Meets West Although President Reagan was a staunch anti-Communist, he welcomed the opportunity to open a dialogue with the Soviets and thus promote world peace.

Answer: *Ronald Reagan had always been a fervent anti-Communist.*

TEACH

Guided Practice

L1 The Cold War Discuss why, with Reagan's emphasis on military strength and military solutions, it was not surprising that the cold war would "reheat."

ABCNEWS
INTERACTIVE™

Videodisc

Communism and the Cold War

Side 1, Chapter 24
Title: Germany: United Once More
Subject: Unified Germany
Ask: What challenges faced the newly united Germany? *(The East lagged far behind the West.)*

See Communism and the Cold War Guidebook page 38 for complete lesson plan.

faces assembled. He picked up on Churchill's theme when he said that the world was no longer divided between East and West, but "between the rich and the poor countries, between the North and the South."

People in the crowd applauded enthusiastically, as they did throughout his speech, for this was an amazing moment. Many that day recalled that little more than 10 years earlier, President Reagan had called the Soviet Union an "evil empire." Now they were listening to a speech by the man in charge when that empire collapsed. It was remarkable evidence of the changes that had occurred in the world and in the United States since the beginning of the Reagan administration.

A Challenge to the Soviets
Strong Military Gives Reagan Negotiating Power

When Ronald Reagan was a young film actor in Hollywood, he played the part of a Wild West hero in such films as *Santa Fe Trail* (1940) and *Law and Order* (1953). When he arrived in Washington in 1981, he brought with him some of the swagger and steely resolve of the Western heroes he had portrayed on the screen.

Ever since his days as president of the Screen Actors Guild, from 1947 to 1952 and again in 1959, Reagan had been a fervent anti-Communist. During congressional investigations into Communist activity in the movie industry in the late 1940s and early 1950s, Reagan worked to expose suspected Communists.

In 1982 Reagan told an audience that the Soviet Union was the "focus of evil in the modern world." The President served notice on the Soviets that he intended to confront them whenever possible.

The Arms Buildup

Since the dawn of the nuclear age, the United States and the Soviet Union had maintained a nuclear balance called **mutual deterrence.** This theory held that as long as accurate missiles capable of complete destruction targeted both countries, neither nation would ever start a nuclear war. In their efforts to prevent each other from tipping that balance, both superpowers engaged in an ever-escalating arms race.

East Meets West Soviet President Mikhail Gorbachev stands with President Ronald Reagan during White House ceremonies. *Explain the irony in this picture.*

Although Reagan preached economy in government and cut many domestic programs, he proposed the biggest arms buildup in American history. Reagan wanted to develop new weapons systems and enlarge the fleet. He urged Congress to vote funds for an untried system of orbiting satellites that could fire laser beams to shoot down any Soviet missiles launched toward the United States. Reagan called the system the Strategic Defense Initiative (SDI). The press quickly dubbed it "Star Wars," and critics assailed its feasibility.

The President said that military power would make the nation feel good again about itself and its place in the world. "America is back, standing tall," he said. The cost was a breathtaking $1.5 trillion over a 5-year period.

While Reagan pressed for more planes, missiles, and ships, Soviet foreign policy strengthened his hand. The Soviet war in Afghanistan raged on, and Soviet support for Communist guerrilla activity in Central America, Africa, and the Philippines remained active.

Two incidents in 1983 confirmed Reagan's worst fears about the Soviet Union. The first occurred in Poland, where the Soviets installed a new, repressive government and jailed members of a popular democratic revolution. Some analysts think that only the intervention of Pope John Paul II, himself a Pole, prevented Soviet military intervention.

In a second incident, the Soviets earned worldwide condemnation in 1983 for shooting down a Korean Airlines passenger jet that had accidentally entered Soviet airspace. The jet, attacked by a MIG fighter, plunged into the Pacific, killing all 269 passengers and crew.

Negotiation Through Strength

While building up American military strength, Reagan offered the Soviets numerous proposals for controlling or reducing nuclear and conventional arms. The President believed that by making the United States strong and taking a hard line, he could intimidate the Soviets into concessions at the bargaining table.

For example, Reagan made a blunt offer to the Soviets. If they would agree to destroy some of their missiles aimed at Western Europe, then the United States would call off the placement in Western

Cooperative Learning

Debate As an approach to this section, students might debate the pros and cons of the arms buildup and the use of military strength to fight communism. Assign students to two groups. Remind students that each person should have a role in planning the debate. Have groups plan their arguments and counter-arguments. Then stage the debate.

Europe of additional missiles targeted at the USSR. Talks on this question began in 1981. Dissatisfied with their progress, Reagan ordered the installation of more missiles in 1983. The talks collapsed, and it became clear to the Soviets that Reagan was a tough negotiator.

Reagan's refusal to consider any unilateral, or one-sided, reduction of the American nuclear stockpile prompted an intense debate throughout the country during 1982 and 1983. Politicians, scientists, and church leaders formed a nuclear freeze movement, calling for a halt to the production and placement of nuclear weapons. In June 1982, 1 million Americans marched in support of the movement. The march was the largest peacetime protest ever staged by Americans.

Gorbymania Fascinated by Gorbachev, Americans were eager to buy souvenirs—such as these Gorby dolls—of his visit. *Why did Gorbachev's proposals surprise Reagan?*

A Thaw in the Cold War
Superpowers Agree to Reduce Nuclear Arms

A remarkable transformation in Soviet-American relations began to take shape at the beginning of Ronald Reagan's second term as President. The impetus for change came in part from the two leaders of the superpowers. One was Mikhail Gorbachev, a dynamic leader committed to reforming his country's collapsing economy and establishing productive ties with the West. The other was Ronald Reagan, whose every action in foreign policy had, according to Donald Regan, his chief of staff, "been carried out with the idea of one day sitting down at the negotiating table with the leader of the USSR and banning weapons of mass destruction from the planet."

Ice Breaking

The setting for this transformation was a series of summit meetings between the two leaders. In 1985 at the first one in Geneva, Switzerland, the two leaders sized each other up. Their exchanges were direct. Gorbachev held to his view that outer space should be weapon free. Reagan stood firm, reserving the right of the United States to implement SDI as protection against Soviet missiles.

In October 1986, the two leaders met in Reykjavik, Iceland. At this meeting, Gorbachev unveiled a broad range of new arms control proposals covering topics such as long-range missiles and the Strategic Defense Initiative. The sweep of Gorbachev's proposals stunned President Reagan and his advisers. In an attempt to capture a historic opportunity, both sides worked long beyond the scheduled close of the meetings. Neither Reagan nor Gorbachev, however, would compromise on the issue of weapons in space. In the end, this second meeting produced no agreement.

Arms Cuts

Reagan and Gorbachev met twice more to discuss arms control. In December 1987, Gorbachev and his wife, Raisa, visited Washington, D. C. In the spring of 1988 the Soviets hosted the Reagans. At both meetings, style overshadowed substance. Americans caught "Gorbymania"; Soviets marveled at Ron and Nancy in Red Square.

In the midst of the social activities, the Intermediate-Range Nuclear Forces (INF) treaty went into effect in June 1988. The treaty was the first agreement of its kind; it aimed to reduce the number of nuclear missiles in each superpower's arsenal. Although covering only one type of missile, the treaty cleared the way for later arms pacts.

The INF treaty was perhaps the greatest foreign policy triumph of Reagan's presidency. After escalating the arms race and increasing tensions between the superpowers, Reagan ended his presidency on much friendlier terms with the Soviets. During the Reagan years, the United States had gone further than in any previous presidency to stabilize Soviet-American relations.

Further Arms Reduction

George Bush, Reagan's successor, continued to press the merits of democratic capitalism and to speak out vigorously against communism. Bush, too, believed in bargaining from a position of military strength.

By late 1989 the Reagan and Bush strategy produced results. Bush and Gorbachev met aboard a ship in the Mediterranean Sea to discuss ending the arms race. Less than a year later, the superpowers agreed to limit their troops and conventional weapons in Europe and Asia. Bush also ordered the Strategic Air Command to relax its 24-hour-a-day combat-ready status. Gorbachev called Bush's order a "great event." Then he ordered the

Independent Practice

L1 Making a Time Line Have students make a time line for the previous section and then add the events of the Reagan administration described in this section.

📂 Have students complete the Chapter 25, Section 2 Vocabulary and Guided Reading Activity. (Also in Spanish.) **LEP**

VISUAL INSTRUCTION

Gorbymania Gorbachev worked to improve relations with Western nations and to reduce tensions and conflicts worldwide. Before its breakup, the Soviet Union was the largest nation in the world in area. It covered more than half of Europe and nearly two-fifths of Asia. It had the third largest population in the world, after China and India.

Answer: *because of their sweeping range*

Meeting Special Needs

Visual Learners To help students who learn best visually, have them compare the map Divided Europe, 1955 (page 571) with the map Europe in 1995 (page 870). Ask them to list the differences they see. Have students refer to these maps and lists as they read the chapter.

867

ABCNEWS INTERACTIVE™

💿 Videodisc

Communism and the Cold War

Side 1, Chapter 21
Title: A New Soviet Union: Communist Rule Ends
Subject: The end of the Soviet Union
Ask: What replaced the USSR? *(The Commonwealth of Independent States)*

See Communism and the Cold War Guidebook page 33 for complete lesson plan.

VISUAL INSTRUCTION

Lech Walesa Walesa began his career as an electrician in the shipyards of Gdansk. He took part in the workers' rights movement and won the 1983 Nobel Peace Prize for preventing violence while gaining workers' rights. In 1980 Walesa headed Solidarity, an organization composed of 50 trade unions.

Answer: *Solidarity*

Lech Walesa After seeing protesters shot down in a 1970 demonstration, Walesa became a leader in Poland's trade union movement. Despite arrest and harassment for his political activism, Walesa continued to fight for democracy. *What was the name of Walesa's labor union?*

Eastern Europe Changes

By 1989 no Communist leader in Eastern Europe could count on Soviet tanks to suppress his opponents. The first country to loosen communism's grip was Poland. Lech Walesa, a shipyard worker in the Baltic port of Gdansk, led the labor union Solidarity in the 1980s as it won concessions from the government. Even after Solidarity was banned, Walesa's character inspired the antigovernment movement. Pope John Paul II, a fellow Pole, also lent inspiration from afar to the forces of democracy. Under growing public protest, the Communist president was obliged to step aside. Walesa was elected president of Poland in a December 1990 landslide.

Czechoslovakia's relatively smooth passage to democracy resulted in the election in 1989 of playwright Vaclav Havel as president. Slovaks in the eastern portion of the country, however, wanted a separate nation, and Czechs in the western portion were obliged to concede. Havel, a Czech, lost office in 1992 in a democratic vote mainly because few Slovaks would vote for him. He reluctantly agreed to the nation's split into the Czech Republic and Slovakia in 1993.

Europe's worst violence since World War II began in June 1991 in Yugoslavia. Throughout the early 1990s, the world watched helplessly as ethnic groups that had lived side by side for generations turned on each other. Secretary-General Boutros Boutros-Ghali of the UN termed the bloodbath "tragic, dangerous, violent, and confused."

A New Germany

The USSR's declining influence in the late 1980s set off a political chain reaction. Unification of the two Germanies, divided since 1949, came swiftly on the heels of Gorbachev's sweeping reforms.

Months of protests in East Germany, for 40 years a Soviet ally, led to the ouster of Communist leader Erich Honecker in October 1989. All summer East Germans had been fleeing their country through Hungary, and now the trickle became a flood. On November 9, 1989, the government capitulated and said it would issue exit visas to anyone who asked. Hordes of citizens immediately began to break through the Berlin Wall, a symbol of Germany's division, built on Soviet orders in 1961.

Plans for unifying the 2 countries began immediately. On October 3, 1990, far sooner than anyone had predicted, the 2 nations joined as the Federal Republic of Germany. Overnight the 62 million West Germans and 16 million East Germans became

destruction of all Soviet short-range nuclear missiles and halted nuclear testing for 1 year. In October 1991, NATO responded by cutting its nuclear forces in Europe by 80 percent. Such cutbacks offered relief to both sides after a decade of unprecedented arms buildup.

The Soviet Breakup
Eastern Bloc Countries Declare Independence

Relief from defense spending came too late, however, to save the faltering Soviet economy. When Gorbachev took office in March 1985, he spoke of **glasnost,** opening up Soviet society to new ideas. He hoped to improve everyday life for Soviet citizens and to get more consumer goods into stores by easing the government's near-total control over the economy. This restructuring of the way Soviets did business was called **perestroika.**

Perestroika and glasnost extended into the realm of politics as well. In 1989 Soviet citizens were allowed to vote for non-Communists for the first time, breaking down the USSR's one-party system.

Portfolio Project

Writing an Editorial Ask students to imagine the Soviet reaction to the United States arms buildup and the Star Wars proposal. Suggest that students write a newspaper editorial from the Soviet perspective. Students can place their editorials in their portfolios after they share them.

Star Wars Report Suggest that students conduct research on the technology of Star Wars, its feasibility, and its potential effectiveness. Students might give oral reports to the class, using diagrams or other visual aids. Students can file their reports in their portfolios.

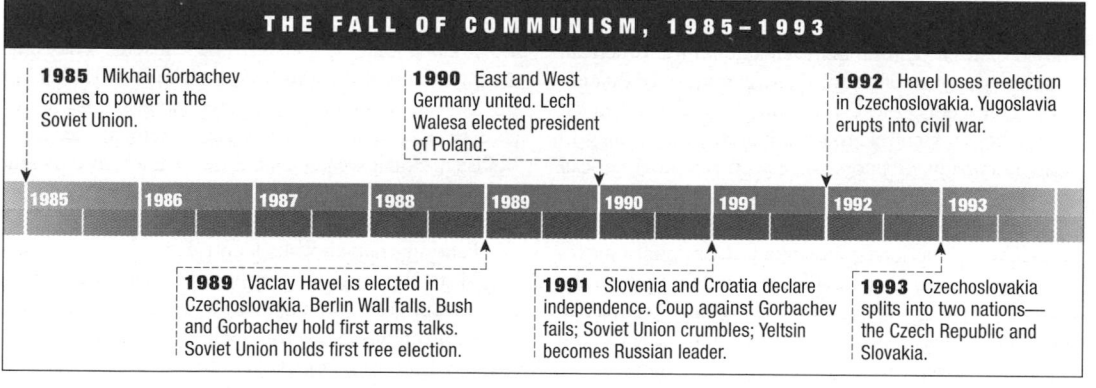

A New Russia Soviet citizens dismantle a giant statue of Lenin to signify their dissatisfaction with the old regime. *In what other ways did people in the former Soviet Union indicate they wanted change?*

recover. Terrorist attacks abated, though they continued to cause grave concern among the majority of the nation's citizens. The international community remained firm in its opposition to such violence.

The Attempted Gorbachev Coup

In the Soviet Union, Gorbachev's policies of glasnost and perestroika led Communist party loyalists to fear for their jobs and privileges. It was this faction—the Soviet Union's political elite—that plotted a coup against Gorbachev in August 1991.

The coup attempt was met with condemnation from world leaders as well as Soviet citizens. Defiantly opposing the coup was Boris Yeltsin, president of the Russian Federation, the largest republic in the USSR. From his office in Moscow, Yeltsin rallied a fearful but growing crowd to oppose the coup, at times speaking from a balcony to thousands gathered in the streets. His effort succeeded, and the coup instigators ended their attempt to take over the government.

The Collapse of the Soviet Union

Mikhail Gorbachev resigned as Communist party leader and banned any party involvement in government affairs. With these moves, the party's 73-year monopoly on political power came to an end, and with the loss of centralized control, the Soviet Union began to break up.

People living in many of the USSR's 15 republics agitated for autonomy. The first to break from the union were the peoples of Lithuania, Latvia, and Estonia. They had voted to secede in early 1991. Ukraine, breadbasket

a European powerhouse with a combined economy worth $1 trillion a year.

The excitement of reunification soon faded, though, as Germans faced the difficult task of raising the living standard of the former East Germans. Adding to the instability of reunification was the arrival of thousands of refugees from other eastern European countries. Right-wing groups called neo-Nazis, disturbed by the changes, launched violent attacks on the foreigners. By the mid-1990s, however, the German economy was beginning to

THE FALL OF COMMUNISM, 1985–1993

1985 Mikhail Gorbachev comes to power in the Soviet Union.

1990 East and West Germany united. Lech Walesa elected president of Poland.

1992 Havel loses reelection in Czechoslovakia. Yugoslavia erupts into civil war.

| 1985 | 1986 | 1987 | 1988 | 1989 | 1990 | 1991 | 1992 | 1993 | |

1989 Vaclav Havel is elected in Czechoslovakia. Berlin Wall falls. Bush and Gorbachev hold first arms talks. Soviet Union holds first free election.

1991 Slovenia and Croatia declare independence. Coup against Gorbachev fails; Soviet Union crumbles; Yeltsin becomes Russian leader.

1993 Czechoslovakia splits into two nations—the Czech Republic and Slovakia.

SECTION TWO **869**

Extending the Content

The Soviet Economy The Soviet Union, despite its vast size and resources, could not keep up with the United States in cold-war spending on troops and weapons. After 1989 arms reductions helped each nation attend to neglected domestic problems, but laying off hundreds of thousands of soldiers posed its own problems. Unemployment afflicted both nations' economies, and housing shortages compounded Russia's crisis. Ask students whether each government should gradually or rapidly make further defense cuts.

MAP STUDY

Estonia, one of the first Soviet republics to declare its independence from the Soviet Union, had endured more than 50 years of forced annexation to the Soviet Union.

Answer: *Estonia, Latvia, Lithuania, Belarus, Ukraine, Moldova, Armenia, Azerbaijan, Georgia, Russia, Kazakhstan, Uzbekistan, Turkmenistan, Kyrgyzstan, and Tajikistan*

 Videodisc

Communism and the Cold War

Side 2, Chapter 16
Title: El Salvador
Subject: Different perspectives on the leftist rebellion in El Salvador and images of El Salvador
Ask: Why was the United States worried about a Communist regime in El Salvador? *(The United States did not want another Communist ally that might try to spread revolution to other countries.)*

See Communism and the Cold War Guidebook page 69 for complete lesson plan.

EUROPE, 1995

A dizzying series of political and economic changes swept the former Soviet Union and its allies in Eastern Europe after 1989. By 1995 the region had fragmented into many independent nations. *Which of the countries shown above used to be a part of the Soviet Union?*

of the Soviet Union, declared its independence just days after the August coup, as did 9 other republics. The USSR no longer existed.

Central America
United States Involvement Creates Controversy

The United States's strong military stance in the early 1980s and the subsequent end to the cold war had a profound effect on relations with Central America. For many decades the United States had treated the nations of that region with casual disdain. When the United States thought that invading a Central American country was in its interest, there was little that nation could do except protest. The United States encouraged democracy in Central America but was also willing to support corrupt dictators there who served American interests.

Partly in response to American support for repressive Central American governments, Communist movements and guerrilla resistance flourished throughout the region. Pointing to Soviet and Cuban involvement in these rebel movements, President Reagan made Central America a priority in his war against communism.

"The national security of all the Americas is at stake in Central America," Reagan told a joint session of Congress in 1983. "If we cannot defend ourselves there, we cannot expect to prevail elsewhere." During his first administration, Reagan demonstrated this point dramatically. In October 1983, leftists on the tiny Caribbean island of Grenada staged an uprising. Uneasy over reported Cuban and Soviet influence in the area, Reagan dispatched an invasion force to oust the leftists and install a prodemocracy government.

El Salvador

Soon after taking office, Reagan became concerned about the instability of the government in El Salvador, a country about the size of Massachusetts. The right-wing government, controlled by military officers and a small group of landowners, had come to power in a coup two years earlier. Now this government was shaky. Leftist guerrillas were attacking government forces in the countryside, where peasant people had struggled in poverty for decades.

Fearing that another Central American country would go the way of Communist Cuba, Reagan persuaded Congress to send military aid to El Salvador and American "advisers" to train Salvadoran soldiers. Some 1,600 Salvadoran troops were brought to the United

870 CHAPTER 25 THE REAGAN AND BUSH YEARS

Cultural Perspectives

Revolution and Refugees The following sign appeared in Prague, Czechoslovakia, in 1989 to recap the fall of communism in Eastern Europe: "Poland—10 Years; Hungary—10 Months; East Germany—10 Weeks; Czechoslovakia—10 Days; Romania—10 Hours." The collapse of communism gave people the freedom to move, but it also gave them the freedom to attack minorities. By 1992 half a million Gypsies had fled from Romania. Yugoslavia's civil war forced 2 million Muslims to flee Bosnia-Herzegovina; many others were killed. Have students read news magazines to find out about the social and cultural life of Bosnian Muslims or Romanian Gypsies and how the world community has responded to their persecution.

States for training. The United States had to act, the administration felt, because the Salvadoran guerrillas had the backing of Cuba and Nicaragua, and ultimately of the Soviet Union.

Opponents of Reagan's policy claimed that poverty and government oppression were the real causes of the rebellion. The Reagan administration pressed the government of El Salvador to speed up its land reform and to outlaw the military "death squads" that roamed the country killing anyone suspected of sympathizing with the guerrillas. In 1983 these right-wing squads killed as many as 200 people a week.

Throughout the rest of the 1980s, the civil war continued. By the end of 1988 the fighting had cost the lives of between 65,000 and 70,000 Salvadorans. The United States had contributed $3 billion to the government during that time.

It was not until the ending of the cold war that real progress toward a peaceful settlement was possible. In 1991 the United States and the Soviet Union urged UN Secretary-General Javier Pérez de Cuéllar to intervene in the peace negotiations between the government and the guerrillas. At a meeting between the 2 sides in New York, plans for a new peace initiative were announced. The next year, some 1,000 UN peacekeeping troops were dispatched to El Salvador,

and within days a formal peace accord was ratified as the United States secretary of state, James Baker, looked on.

Nicaragua

In Nicaragua, as in El Salvador, the Reagan administration decided to fight communism with military aid. The Nicaraguan government was made up of Marxist revolutionaries who called themselves Sandinistas. In 1979 the Sandinistas, after years of guerrilla warfare, had overthrown the brutal Nicaraguan dictator Anastasio Somoza. The Somoza family had ruled the country with iron fists and American support since the 1930s.

Now the Sandinistas found themselves opposed by right-wing guerrillas, including some former officers of Somoza's despised paramilitary National Guard. Not unexpectedly, President Reagan backed the right-wing guerrillas, called *contras*, after the Spanish word *contra*, meaning "against." As part of a cover operation, the CIA trained and armed approximately 10,000 *contras*, at bases in Honduras and Costa Rica.

Reagan justified these actions by portraying Nicaragua as "a Soviet ally on the American mainland only two hours' flying time from our own borders." Cuban military advisers, medical experts, and teachers were aiding the Sandinistas. In addition, the Soviet Union

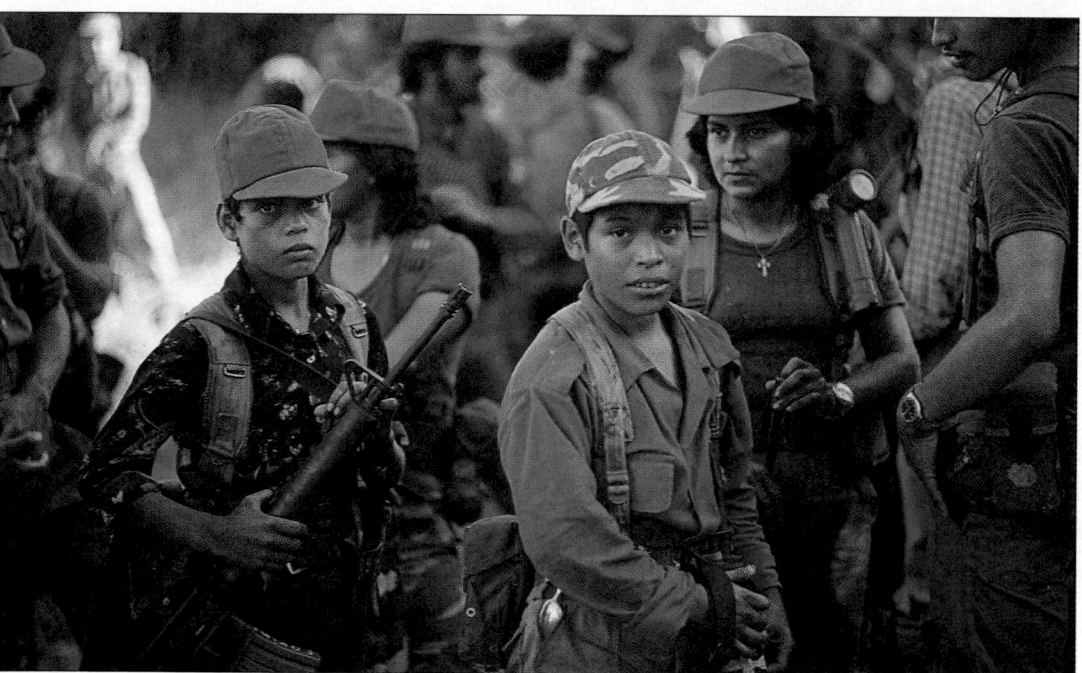

© S. CHALATENANGO/SYGMA

Guerrilla Warfare in El Salvador **Young boys and girls joined the guerrillas to fight Salvadoran soldiers.** *Why did the Reagan administration support the right-wing government of El Salvador?*

SECTION TWO **871**

VISUAL INSTRUCTION

Guerrilla Warfare in El Salvador El Salvador has more than twice as many people per square mile as does China. Ownership of scarce fertile land has caused much conflict. In 1979 civil war broke out. Boys and girls as young as 12 (or even younger) sometimes took part in the fighting.

Answer: *because it did not want other South or Central American nations falling to communism*

ABCNEWS INTERACTIVE ™

 Videodisc

Lessons of War

‖‖‖‖‖‖‖‖‖‖‖‖‖‖

Side 2, Chapter 5
Title: Compromise: El Salvador
Subject: The El Salvador Peace Agreement illustrates ways of peacefully resolving differences
Ask: Why did the United States want peace in El Salvador? *(The United States feared that instability in the nation would lead to a Communist regime.)*

See Lessons of War Guidebook page 40 for complete lesson plan.

Critical Thinking

Drawing Conclusions Point out that the United States considered the countries of Central America to be in the United States's "backyard." Ask how this attitude might make the people in those countries feel. Ask also how American support of corrupt dictators might have affected other nations' perceptions of the United States. Do students think the United States has a legitimate need for covert operations in the conduct of foreign policy? Why or why not? Have students defend their opinions with examples or facts.

ABCNEWS INTERACTIVE™

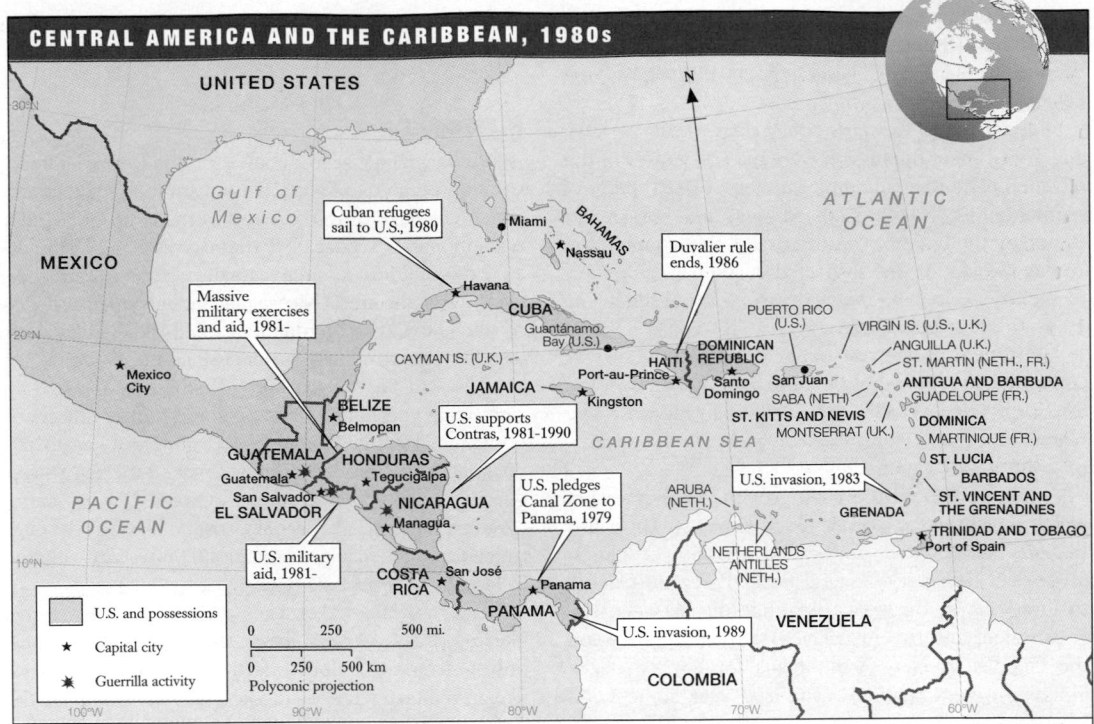

CENTRAL AMERICA AND THE CARIBBEAN, 1980s

The central role that Communist Cuba played in the Caribbean and in Central America made political instability in the region a major concern of President Reagan. He feared the domino effect: one nation after another falling to communism. Use this map to describe the role of the United States in the Caribbean and Central America.

was also sending military aid, including fighter planes and attack helicopters. Intelligence reports also indicated that the Sandinistas were sending military aid to the leftist rebels in El Salvador.

As the CIA role in Nicaragua became more widely known, heated debate erupted in the United States. News emerged early in 1984 that the CIA had placed mines in the harbors of Nicaraguan ports and trained the *contras* to incite mob violence and to murder their political opponents. An angry Congress forbade any more military aid to Nicaragua. Congress relaxed its ban in 1986. By that time, however, allegations that Reagan and his aides had broken the law in their efforts to support the *contra* resistance were undermining the President's Nicaraguan policy.

The Iran-*contra* Scandal

Throughout the summer of 1987, millions of Americans sat riveted to their TV screens, following 1 of those rare congressional hearings that achieve major importance and high drama. The hearings reminded many of the Watergate hearings 14 years earlier.

Once again, as with Watergate, Congress was looking into wrongdoing by officials in the administration,

including some close to the President. Once again, the abuses concerned officials taking the law into their own hands. Once again, the key questions were: Who authorized the illegal activities? Was the President involved?

According to Hawaii senator Daniel K. Inouye, cochairperson of the congressional committee, the Iran-*contra* scandal was "much more serious than Watergate, not because of who was (or was not) involved but because of what was involved: the formulation and conduct of American foreign policy."

The details of the Iran-*contra* scandal were complicated and murky. In essence, United States officials privately arranged arms sales to Iran, presumably with the hope that Iran would use its influence to free American hostages being held by pro-Iranian groups in Lebanon. This was at a time—the mid-1980s—when Washington was publicly condemning Iran as a terrorist nation and insisting that the United States would make no deals for the hostages' release. To make matters worse, profits from the arms sales were secretly funneled to the Nicaraguan *contras* to help finance their guerrilla war against the Sandinistas. Congress had specifically forbidden any military aid to the *contras*.

Portfolio Project

Research Suggest that students choose one Central American nation and research the history of that country's relations with the United States. Have students summarize their findings in written reports, which they can include in their portfolios. 📎

Letter Writing Have students read about life in El Salvador, Nicaragua, or Haiti in the 1970s or 1980s. Then have students imagine living in one of these nations. They can write to a pen pal in the United States, describing reactions to events. Students can place their letters in their portfolios. 📎

The President's National Security Council (NSC), which was supposed to be a research and advisory body, carried out these activities. An NSC aide, Colonel Oliver North of the Marine Corps, and his boss, Admiral John Poindexter, ran the secret operation.

The report of the congressional committees stopped short of accusing the President of wrongdoing, but it took a dim view of his hands-off management style. Reagan was portrayed as "fuzzy" on specific details and out of touch with important activities within his administration.

The scandal made the President look bad either way. If he did not know what Poindexter and North were doing in his name, then, his critics contended, he must be incompetent. If he did know, then he was guilty of breaking the law forbidding military aid to the *contras*—a law that he himself had signed.

North and Poindexter were tried and convicted of offenses relating to the scandal. North was sentenced to perform community service, but his sentence was subsequently set aside on appeal. Poindexter received a six-month jail term.

Overall, the scandal seemed to have little effect on the American public's regard for President Reagan, however, leading some to dub him the "Teflon" President. He appeared to have a nonstick surface to which bad news would not adhere. At the end of Reagan's second administration, polls showed that two-thirds of the American public approved of his conduct in office.

The Caribbean
Moving Toward Democracy

Oppressive dictatorship had long been the norm in the island nation of Haiti. In 1957 Dr. François Duvalier was elected president. The popular leader soon established himself as a dictator, maintained in power by an intimidating private army called the *Tontons Macoutes*. On the eve of his death in 1971, Duvalier appointed his son, Jean-Claude Duvalier, as his successor. Repression, grinding poverty, and corruption continued.

It was not until late 1986 that Jean-Claude and his family were forced to flee the island. Euphoria over his overthrow was short-lived, however. Rioting and repeated coups d'état threatened the stability of the nation.

In 1990 voters in Haiti elected Father Jean-Bertrand Aristide, a left-wing Catholic priest, as president. Unfortunately, the Aristide government proved no more stable than its predecessors. Within eight months, a military junta overthrew the government in a violent coup. Aristide fled to exile in the United States.

Following the coup, thousands of Haitians attempted to flee the country in makeshift boats. Most headed for the

United States, where instead of welcoming them, the Bush administration attempted to return them to Haiti.

During the campaign for the presidential election of 1992, candidate Bill Clinton promised to reverse this policy. Yet when he became President, fearing a mass exodus of Haitians seeking refuge, he ordered the repatriation continued. He promised the Haitian people that he would continue to work on their behalf to secure a democratic solution to their island's turmoil.

Perhaps no country in the Western Hemisphere was more profoundly affected by the changes in the Soviet Union than Cuba. Ever since Fidel Castro aligned himself with the Soviet bloc in the early 1960s, Cuba was perceived as a threat to the United States and to the security of the region.

In 1989 President Gorbachev visited Fidel Castro. Although the two leaders signed a treaty of friendship, serious rifts had developed in their relationship. The meeting signaled a reduction of Soviet financial aid that had long kept the Cuban economy afloat. To counter the effects of the cutbacks, Castro moved to reduce government spending by making deep cuts in the Cuban bureaucracy. He expanded rationing to include all consumer products. These measures, however, were not sufficient to revitalize the economy.

In 1992 President Bush increased the pressure on the Castro regime by ordering a ban that prevented any ship doing business with Cuba from entering American ports. By 1993 Castro had begun to allow some free enterprise in an effort to bolster Cuba's sinking economy.

SECTION REVIEW

Vocabulary

1. Define: mutual deterrence, glasnost, perestroika.

Checking Facts

2. List the ways in which Mikhail Gorbachev helped to bring about an end to the cold war.

3. Summarize United States policy toward each of these countries: El Salvador, Nicaragua, Haiti, and Cuba.

Critical Thinking

Drawing Conclusions

4. What were some of the factors that contributed to the breakup of the Soviet Union?

Linking Across Time

5. Think about how the arms race changed during the Reagan-Bush years. Do you think these trends will continue? Why or why not?

ASSESS

Meeting Lesson Objectives

Each section objective is tested by the section review question(s) that follows it in parentheses.

1. Explain how changes in Soviet and U.S. foreign policy led to arms reductions. (1, 2)

2. Identify causes for the breakup of the Soviet Union. (1, 2, 4, 5)

3. Explain how the cold war's end changed foreign policy. (1, 2, 3, 4, 5)

4. Notice how the arms race changed during the Reagan years. (1, 2, 5)

Evaluate

Have students complete the Section Review.

☛ ⊙ Assign the Section 2 Quiz or use the Testmaker to develop a customized quiz. (Also in Spanish.) **LEP**

Reteach

⌒ Have students listen to the Chapter 25, Section 2 Audiocassette. (Also in Spanish.) **LEP**

Enrich

☛ Have students complete Interpreting Political Cartoons 40–49.

CLOSE

What effect did Gorbachev's policies have on the Soviet Union? *(It broke up into 15 republics when he eased centralized control.)*

Section 2 Review Answers

1. mutual deterrence (866), **glasnost** (868), **perestroika** (868)

2. He discussed ending the arms race, agreed to limit troops and weapons in Europe and Asia, destroyed Soviet short-range nuclear missiles, and halted nuclear testing for one year.

3. United States policy in these nations was intended to prevent the spread of communism.

4. Soviets were allowed to vote, a coup against Gorbachev occured, Communist party lost power, and people agitated for autonomy

5. Possible answer: Yes, arms reductions will continue because nations cannot afford a huge military, and the fear of Communist domination has passed.

TEACH

Making the Historical Connection

The fall of the Berlin Wall was an opening in the dike that led to a flood of Communist nations regaining their freedom.

ABCNEWS INTERACTIVE™

Videodisc

Communism and the Cold War

Side 1, Chapter 23
Title: Fall of the Wall
Subject: Berlin Wall
Ask: What did the fall of the Berlin Wall symbolize? *(the end of communism)*

See Communism and the Cold War Guidebook page 37 for complete lesson plan.

One Day in History

November 9, 1989

MARKET BASKET

Here is where a dollar will go:

Loaf of bread	65¢
Movie ticket	$4
1-liter soft drink	$1
Velour shirt	$14.95
Theater ticket	$20
CD player	$229.95

FILE PHOTO BY DOUG MINDELL

Cellular phone	$995
Microwave oven	$219.99
19-inch color TV	$209
Apple II computer	$795
Dodge Medallion	$8,995

FILE PHOTO BY DOUG MINDELL

Pizza	$7.95
Camcorder	$893
4-bedroom house	$73,900

© ANTHONY SUAU/GAMMA LIAISON

Jubilation: East and West Berliners celebrate atop the infamous Berlin Wall near the Brandenburg Gate after East Germany announces the opening of its borders.

Berlin Wall Falls

East Berliners rush through Berlin Wall—symbol of the cold war—as travel limits are lifted

WEST BERLIN—Today East Germany lifted its 28-year-old restrictions on travel to the West. Within hours, thousands of East Berliners swarmed across the infamous Berlin Wall for a boisterous celebration.

East Berliners walked, biked, or drove to crossing points (including the notorious Checkpoint Charlie) to enter the other half of their city, a place they could only gaze at just hours before. Cheers, champagne, flowers, and applause greeted their arrival. Border guards, who formerly had orders to fire on any escape attempts, smiled and took snapshots. "This is what we have dreamed of all these years," asserted an elderly East Berlin woman.

Background Information

How the Wall Fell The following events led to the opening of East Germany's borders: East Germany celebrated its fortieth anniversary in October with a 2-day visit by Mikhail Gorbachev. After Gorbachev left, the government arrested demonstrators protesting economic problems and lack of democractic freedoms. More than 170,000 East Germans had already emigrated to the West, first through Hungary (which permitted East German holiday visitors to cross into Austria), and then through Czechoslovakia. President Erich Honecker, a hard-line Communist who had ruled East Germany since its inception, was forced to resign. In November the government opened its borders in an attempt to turn the tide of escaping citizens and convince them that leaving the country was unnecessary.

NATION: By a narrow margin, Douglas Wilder is the first African American elected governor.

The Big One?

SAN FRANCISCO—North America's most destructive earthquake since 1906 hits the Bay Area minutes before the beginning of the 3rd World Series game between the Oakland Athletics and the San Francisco Giants. Measuring 7.1 on the Richter scale, the 15-second tremor kills 90 people, buckles highways and the Bay Bridge, and causes $6 million in damages.

Earthquake Damage

Market Plunges

NEW YORK—Wall Street's Dow Jones Industrial Average drops 190.58 points in 1 day as confidence weakens in "junk" bond financing of company mergers and acquisitions, marking the most drastic 1-day slide in the market since the stock market crash of 1929.

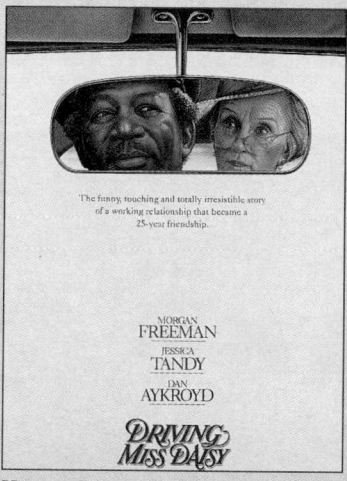

The funny, touching and totally irresistible story of a working relationship that became a 25-year friendship.

MORGAN FREEMAN
JESSICA TANDY
DAN AYKROYD

DRIVING MISS DAISY

Morgan Freeman and Jessica Tandy (best actress) star in Oscar winner.

MOVIES

Popular Movies: *Field of Dreams* ("If you build it, he will come"), *When Harry Met Sally, Glory, Dead Poet's Society, Batman, The Little Mermaid, Indiana Jones and the Last Crusade, My Left Foot, Born on the Fourth of July, Do the Right Thing*

The new "typical American family": *The Cosby Show* garners an Emmy.

TELEVISION

- **Top Ten shows:** *The Golden Girls, A Different World, The Cosby Show, Cheers, Roseanne, Dear John, 60 Minutes, The Wonder Years, L.A. Law, Empty Nest*
- **Specials:** *Lonesome Dove, Billy Crystal, War and Remembrance*

LPs Become History

An era comes to an end when almost all music stores stop carrying records and begin selling CDs and audiocassettes exclusively. It's good that Thomas Edison is not around to see his invention replaced by the new technology.

AMERICAN LIFE

February: Soviets withdraw troops from Afghanistan.

June 4: Iran's Ayatollah Khomeini dies at age 86.

July 3: United States Supreme Court rules that states can limit abortion.

August 23: Latvians, Lithuanians, and Estonians form human chain stretching across the three republics to protest USSR.

September 26: Vietnamese troops leave Cambodia after 11 years of occupation. Civil war ensues.

November: President Bush signs act that awards $20,000 to each surviving Japanese American internment–camp victim.

November 16: The murder of six Jesuit priests brings demands that Congress stop supporting the El Salvadoran government.

December 25: Romanian President Nicolae Ceausescu and wife are executed after being convicted of genocide and theft.

CLOSE

Ask: What did the Brandenburg Gate symbolize? Why was it so important? *(It symbolized East Germans' lack of freedom and served as a reminder of East and West Germany's joint past and a hope for their future reunification.)*

PORTFOLIO PROJECT

Oral History

Personalizing History If possible, have students interview someone of Eastern European heritage about the Berlin Wall—preferably someone who lived in Europe during the Communist era. Alternatively, they can interview an adult who remembers those two time periods. Suggest that students ask: What did you think when the wall went up? How did Eastern and Western Europe differ during the years the wall was there? What were your reactions when the wall came down? What could East Germans do that they had been unable to do while the wall was there? Have students write up the results of their interviews and put them in their portfolios.

FOCUS

Section Objectives

1. Explain what happened as a result of military cutbacks in the United States.
2. Explain the origins and outcome of the Persian Gulf War.
3. Explain how the changing economy affected the way Americans lived and worked in the 1980s and 1990s.

Bellringer Activity

While taking attendance at the beginning of the class period, display **Section Focus Transparency 82,** and have students answer the questions. (Or use the blackline master.)

TEACH

Guided Practice

L2 Discussion Read several current headlines from a local newspaper to the class. Choose stories that deal with conditions in China, South Africa, the Persian Gulf, Mexico, and Canada or that discuss significant demographic changes in the United States. Ask students how these developments might affect their lives.

VISUAL INSTRUCTION

The Democrats Jackson is one of the most effective orators in the United States.

Ask: What was the rainbow coalition? *(people from many backgrounds who supported Jesse Jackson and civil rights)*

876

The Bush Presidency

JULY 18, 1988: JESSE JACKSON ADDRESSES THE DEMOCRATIC NATIONAL CONVENTION

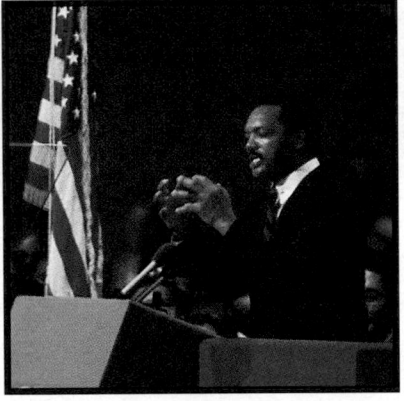

© DENNIS BROCK/BLACK STAR

The Democrats
During the 1988 primaries, Jesse Jackson and Michael Dukakis competed for the Democratic nomination.

THE REVEREND JESSE JACKSON STOOD BEFORE THE THOUSANDS OF NOISY DELEGATES WHO HAD COME TO ATLANTA, GEORGIA, TO NOMINATE THE DEMOCRATIC CANDIDATE FOR PRESIDENT. His mission that night, as it had been throughout the primary campaigns, was to give voice to those people who had been termed forgotten Americans. In a rich Southern accent he intoned, "They catch the early bus. . . . They raise other people's children. . . . They drive dangerous cabs. . . . They work in hospitals. . . . No job is beneath them and yet when they get sick they cannot lie in the bed they made up every day. America, that is not right. We are a better nation than that."

Jackson was one of several candidates vying for the Democratic nomination that year. During the 1960s he had worked in the civil rights movement with Martin Luther King, Jr. With the support of many African Americans, Jackson attracted a "rainbow coalition" of supporters from various ethnic and racial groups. Jackson's supporters believed that he addressed problems that other major party candidates generally avoided, such as homelessness, unemployment, and inequality.

1988 Election
Bush Versus Dukakis

As Ronald Reagan's second term drew to a close, the election campaign for his successor heated up. The Republicans' clear choice to follow him was his Vice President, George Bush.

On the Democratic side, Jackson won several primaries, but he did not gain enough votes to win the

---

AS YOU READ

Vocabulary
► apartheid
► trade deficit
► global economy
► working poor

Think About . . .
► what Americans hoped would result from military cutbacks and whether these hopes materialized.
► what actions by Iraq triggered the Persian Gulf War, and how United

States and UN forces responded to Iraq's actions.
► the effects the changing economy had on the way Americans lived and worked in the 1980s and 1990s.

Section 3 Resources

REPRODUCIBLE RESOURCES
📖 Lesson Plan 25-3
📖 Vocabulary and Guided Reading Activity 25-3
📖 Section 3 Quiz
📖 Chapter 25 Test
📖 Performance Assessment Activity 25
📖 Reteaching Activity 25

📖 Enrichment Activity 25
📖 Geography in History Activity 25
📖 Political Cartoons 6, 14, 15, 22, 23, 25, 28, 50
📖 Supreme Court Cases 52–57

MULTIMEDIA RESOURCES
💾 Section Focus Transparency 82

💿 The Presidents: A Picture History of Our Nation
💿 Powers of the President
💿 Powers of the Congress
💿 Landmark Documents in American History
🎧 Chapter 25 Digest Audiocassette
💾 Testmaker and Vocabulary PuzzleMaker
💾 Student Self-Test: A Software Review

nomination. Ultimately the Democrats nominated Michael Dukakis, governor of Massachusetts. Dukakis was credited with having brought his home state out of a deep recession with the so-called Massachusetts Miracle of the early 1980s.

Electronic Campaigning

In 1988 both Bush and Dukakis relied heavily on expert consultants to produce expensive, carefully scripted television commercials and promotional materials for their campaigns. The candidates were packaged and promoted as if they were consumer products like laundry detergent or breakfast cereal. Instead of concentrating on the issues, TV ads were often personal attacks on the opposing candidate. The ads themselves became the topic of news coverage.

When the votes were counted, Bush carried 40 states, giving him 426 electoral votes to 112 for Dukakis. Polling results showed that 85 percent of those who had supported Ronald Reagan voted for Bush. Voters seemed to be saying not only that they wanted Bush for President, but also that they wanted him to continue Reagan's policies.

Bush Faces New Problems

When George Bush took the oath of office, he looked out on a world far different from the one his predecessor faced. As Communist governments in Eastern Europe fell, the United States had to reevaluate its diplomatic and military goals. Now free of the burden of containing communism, the nation could commit a greater share of its resources to domestic matters: revitalizing the cities, restoring respect for public schools, and building a domestic economy that could compete internationally.

The public consensus that both the military force and the defense budget should be reduced touched off arguments about how much and how fast. In early 1992

Campaigning In the 1988 election, George Bush won the votes of most Reagan supporters. *What kind of policies did the voters want Bush to follow?*

★ ★ ★ **GALLERY OF PRESIDENTS** ★ ★ ★

George Bush
1989–1993

AP/WIDE WORLD

"Some see leadership as high drama, and the sound of trumpets calling, and sometimes it is that. But I see history as a book with many pages, and each day we fill a page with acts of hopefulness and meaning. The new breeze blows, a page turns, and the story unfolds. And so today a chapter begins, a . . . story of unity, diversity, and generosity— shared, and written, together."

Inaugural Address, January 20, 1989

BACKGROUND
▶ Born 1924
▶ Republican, Texas
▶ Elected to the House of Representatives 1966
▶ Elected Vice President 1980, 1984

ACHIEVEMENTS IN OFFICE
▶ Americans with Disabilities Act (1990)
▶ Clean Air Act (1990)
▶ START Treaty (1991)

SECTION THREE **877**

Cooperative Learning

Debate Have students conduct a debate on this question: Should media personnel be allowed to remain behind enemy lines during wartime? Elements of the debate should include the public's need to know, the military's need for secrecy, and a reporter's need to do his or her job. Mention the case of Peter Arnett, a reporter for Cable News Network who stayed in Baghdad during the Persian Gulf War. Teams of students should divide up the work, conduct the research, and prepare arguments and counterarguments. Stage the debate.

Independent Practice

 Have students write about the efforts of black South Africans to gain rights.

☛ Have students complete the Chapter 25, Section 3 Vocabulary and Guided Reading Activity. (Also in Spanish.) **LEP**

● **Videodisc**

Powers of the Congress

Side 2, Chapter 42
Title: Persian Gulf Crisis: U.S. Reaction
Subject: The President's decision to send troops overseas
Ask: What power allowed the President to send troops? *(his power as commander in chief)*

See Powers of the Congress Guidebook page 118 for complete lesson plan.

The Persian Gulf As they fled the country, Saddam Hussein's troops set fire to hundreds of Kuwaiti oil wells. The dense smoke polluted skies over many parts of Southwest Asia and Northeast Africa. *Why did Hussein try to pull Israel into the war?*

the Pentagon ordered personnel cuts and other cuts that would save $103 billion over 5 years. Ironically, these cutbacks were announced just weeks after fighting men and women had proved their effectiveness by winning a war on a Southwest Asia battleground.

The Persian Gulf War
A Battle Over Oil

In early August 1990, news reached the White House that Iraqi forces had invaded neighboring Kuwait and taken over its capital. In the view of President Bush, Iraq's dangerous dictator, Saddam Hussein, had threatened half the world's oil supply and was thumbing his nose at the United States. The attack seemed to threaten the post–cold war order, and the President and his secretary of state, James Baker, were quick to respond.

The two men devoted themselves to putting together a coalition of countries to fight Iraq. Bush promised Saudi Arabia, an Iraqi neighbor, that he would commit American military forces to defend that country from Hussein's aggression. "I will see this through with you," he told the Saudi ambassador.

Twenty-eight nations joined the effort, including several Arab states. The most personnel came from the United States—half a million troops. Additional military support came from Saudi Arabia, Egypt, Great Britain, Syria, and France.

A Quick Victory

On January 17, 1991, a United States–led military force launched air strikes against Iraqi military targets in Baghdad, the capital, and other Iraqi cities. For 5 weeks Allied aircraft flew more than 40,000 sorties, demolishing Iraqi industrial and military sites and draining the fighting spirit of Iraqi troops. Many Iraqi civilians were killed also. The ground war began on February 24, 1991, when Allied tanks and personnel advanced against Iraqi troops in Kuwait.

Hussein had tried to draw Israel into the war in a desperate ploy to detach the Arab members from the coalition. Here too his efforts failed. Israel, although hit by numerous "Scud" missiles launched from Iraq, stayed out of the war at the urging of the American government.

The Allies pressed forward to a quick victory. When the 1,000-hour air battle and 100-hour ground blitz ended, about 100,000 Iraqi soldiers lay dead, and Kuwait was liberated. Fewer than 300 Allied troops died as a result of the war. When it ended, more than 90 percent of the American public approved of how President Bush had handled the war.

While fleeing Kuwait, Hussein's forces set fire to Kuwait's oil fields, filling the skies with thick black smoke and coating both sea and land with oily sludge. Scientists could not gauge the long-term effects of this environmental sabotage.

A New World Order

The return of American troops from the Persian Gulf War was a time of national celebration. Yellow ribbons, the nation's sign of remembrance, fluttered from tree trunks. After weeks of being glued to their televisions, people were glad to see the war over.

At the time few noticed that the celebration at the end of this small war was bigger than any held to honor the end of more than 40 years of cold war. The Gulf War probably could not have happened during the cold war. The United States would not have risked a confrontation with the Soviets. By 1991 that risk had disappeared.

Meeting Individual Needs

Reading Disability To meet the needs of students with reading disabilities, have them watch the ABC News videos relating to the Persian Gulf War. Then have students prepare their own news report summarizing the causes and results of the war. Students may want to videotape and play their news reports for the class.

The Gulf War seemed to help the United States regain the prestige it had lost in Vietnam. It also boosted American influence in the Arab world and set the stage for new peace talks in Southwest Asia. These held the most promise yet that Israel and its Arab neighbors would come to terms. The war also brought new respect to the United Nations (UN), which had unanimously condemned Iraqi aggression and sponsored the Allied military effort.

New Role for the United Nations

The Persian Gulf War signaled the UN's changing role in world affairs. Created in 1945 the UN was often ignored by the superpowers or their allies. Yet it contributed to world peace as UN negotiators arranged cease-fire agreements in dozens of conflicts. These conflicts ranged from the 1949 Arab-Israeli war to the 1988 end of hostilities between Morocco and the Polisario Front in a battle over the Western Sahara.

When Iraq invaded Kuwait, the United Nations took on new importance in battling aggression. For the first time, United States and Soviet leaders, cooperating with the UN, worked together to end a world crisis. In addition, between 1988 and 1992, UN forces, wearing blue helmets or berets, continued to police the world's hot spots and attempted to bring order to troubled lands. Altogether, it was engaged in 13 actions during that time—as many as it had undertaken in the previous 42 years of its existence. These actions took place all over the world.

In Cambodia the United Nations organized elections and provided materials for new homes for the country's 370,000 refugees. UN troops monitored the civil war in the former Yugoslavia and attempted to enforce sanctions against government forces. In Somalia UN peacekeepers tried to safeguard supply lines carrying food to the starving people of the nation. Many of the UN's efforts were thwarted, however, because sanctions failed to halt conflict, and rebels carried off food, clothing, and medicine intended for victims.

International Politics
New Nations, New Governments

With the end of the cold war came both new hope and new challenges to maintain a peaceful world. After Gorbachev's landmark steps to open Soviet society to democracy and a free-market economy, optimism blossomed worldwide. Cooperation extended even to Antarctica, as 25 leading nations signed an accord in October 1991 to protect that frozen continent's environment from exploitation.

China proved an exception in at least one important way. Although its aging leaders allowed some free enterprise to take root, they generally clamped down on political freedom. In June 1989, China's rulers ordered troops to crush a democracy movement in Beijing. Television carried pictures to the United States of Chinese tanks rolling into a peaceful crowd of some 5,000 student demonstrators in Tiananmen Square. Two images in particular were imprinted on the public mind. One was of a replica of the Statue of Liberty called the Goddess of Democracy, which the students erected as a symbol of their desire for freedom. The other was of a lone protester facing a row of oncoming tanks—an unarmed youth standing against the military might of a repressive regime. The Chinese government never released casualty figures for the massacre at Tiananmen Square, and estimates vary widely, from 700 to 5,000.

© BALDEV/SYGMA

Tiananmen Square This demonstration by students in Tiananmen Square occurred on the day of Mikhail Gorbachev's arrival. *How did the world community react to China's crackdown on the pro-democracy activists?*

ABCNEWS
INTERACTIVE™

● Videodisc

Powers of the Congress

Side 2, Chapter 43
Title: Persian Gulf Crisis: Hostages
Subject: The President's need to respond to Americans abroad
Ask: What dangers did Americans overseas face during the crisis? *(kidnapping or terrorist attack; being considered enemy aliens)*

See Powers of the Congress Guidebook page 119 for complete lesson plan.

VISUAL INSTRUCTION

Tiananmen Square Chinese students held demonstrations calling for democracy and an end to corruption in government. The military crushed the demonstrations, large numbers of students were arrested, and some were executed.

Answer: *The United States and other members of the world community continued their trade with China.*

Portfolio Project

Freedom Fighters Crushing the democracy movement in 1989 had many consequences for China's rulers. Some of the movement's leaders escaped to the United States and other nations, where they carried on their struggle. World opinion turned against Communist regimes. In addition, free-market reforms allowed the Chinese to prosper. Invite interested students to research and write a report on one activist who is working for freedom, either in China, South Africa, or another nation. They may want to consider such people as Harry Wu in China or Nelson Mandela in South Africa. Students can place their reports in their portfolios. 📖

Facts on File

Landmark Documents in American History Have students review "Persian Gulf War Resolution, 1991" and "Persian Gulf War Cessation Address, George Bush, 1991" and write about the intent of either document.

VISUAL INSTRUCTION

Mandela Freed! While imprisoned from 1962 to 1990, Mandela became a symbol of the struggle for racial justice.

Answer: *It signified the beginning of the end of apartheid.*

CHART STUDY

Ask: How long was Nelson Mandela in prison?

Answer: *27 years*

Videodisc

Powers of the Congress

Side 2, Chapter 44
Title: Persian Gulf Crisis: World Reaction
Subject: The role of the executive branch in responding to threats
Ask: What did the United States want from other nations? *(It wanted them to ally against Iraq.)*

See Powers of the Congress Guidebook page 120 for complete lesson plan.

The power of the images set off a debate in the United States. President Bush, drawing on his diplomatic experience in China as the head of the United States Liaison Office in Beijing from 1974 to 1975, attempted to dampen the moral outrage many Americans felt because he feared a breakdown in Chinese-American relations. A majority in Congress, on the other hand, wanted to impose stiff sanctions on the Chinese. It was later revealed that Bush, ignoring the wishes of Congress, had sent a secret mission to China to discuss relations between the two countries. Despite concerns over human rights violations, the United States continued to pursue trade relations with China.

Mandela Freed! After Nelson Mandela was freed from a South African prison, anti-apartheid groups all over the world rejoiced. *What did the release of Mandela signify?*

Peaceful Revolution in South Africa

At the end of a century that had seen almost every African country throw off the yoke of colonial government, racism was still the law of the land in South Africa. Whites clung to the system of **apartheid,** a policy of racial segregation, which excluded black South Africans from meaningful participation in the government.

For decades the world community had treated the nation as an outcast. In 1968 the Olympic committee banned South African participation in the games. In 1977 the United Nations imposed an arms embargo. In 1986 the United States Congress, over President Reagan's veto, imposed economic sanctions. Most American companies stopped doing business with South Africa, and the nation began to slip into recession. Even white South Africans began to realize that apartheid was a dead-end street.

The 1990s saw an enormous transformation take place in South Africa. Credit for the change goes largely to two remarkable leaders: Nelson Mandela and F.W. de Klerk. Nelson Mandela was the leader of the African National Congress (ANC), the outlawed organization that struggled to win rights for blacks in South Africa. In 1964 the white government sentenced Mandela to life imprisonment for treason, yet he continued to be an international symbol of the struggle against apartheid in South Africa.

De Klerk was elected president of South Africa in 1989. Recognizing that his nation could no longer survive under apartheid, he announced that he was going to release Nelson Mandela from jail and to legalize the ANC. Following that dramatic moment, he began the tough negotiations with the ANC that resulted in the first-ever multiracial election in his country.

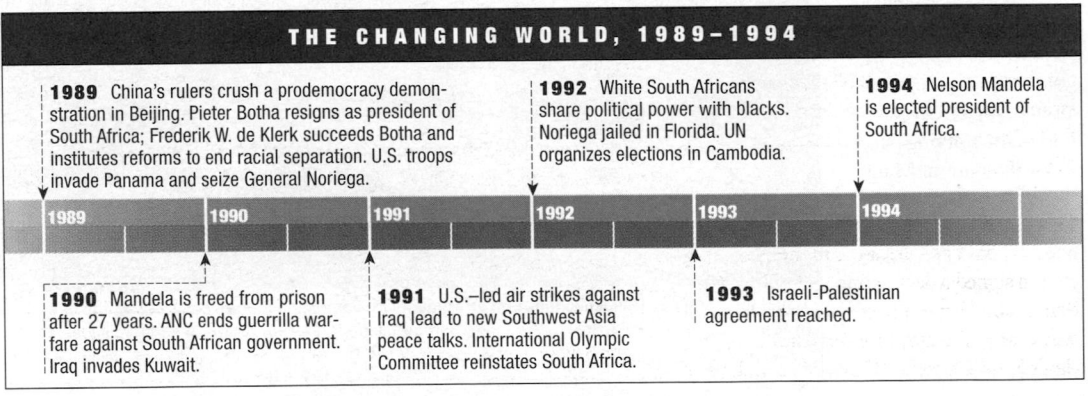

THE CHANGING WORLD, 1989–1994

1989 China's rulers crush a prodemocracy demonstration in Beijing. Pieter Botha resigns as president of South Africa; Frederik W. de Klerk succeeds Botha and institutes reforms to end racial separation. U.S. troops invade Panama and seize General Noriega.

1992 White South Africans share political power with blacks. Noriega jailed in Florida. UN organizes elections in Cambodia.

1994 Nelson Mandela is elected president of South Africa.

1990 Mandela is freed from prison after 27 years. ANC ends guerrilla warfare against South African government. Iraq invades Kuwait.

1991 U.S.–led air strikes against Iraq lead to new Southwest Asia peace talks. International Olympic Committee reinstates South Africa.

1993 Israeli-Palestinian agreement reached.

880 CHAPTER 25 THE REAGAN AND BUSH YEARS

Extending the Content

Dome of the Rock Although Israelis and Arabs contest several pieces of land in the Middle East, the Dome of the Rock in Jerusalem epitomizes their dispute. Two of the holiest sites in Jerusalem are located under this building's roof. Inside lies the spot where Muslims believe Muhammad ascended into heaven in A.D. 632. Jews believe the Dome of the Rock is built on the site of their Second Temple, which was destroyed by the Romans in A.D. 70. The two groups have passionate attachments to the same place. Ask students to discuss how a fair and peaceful agreement over the Dome of the Rock might be worked out.

On April 27, 1994, lines of voters—black and white—stretched across the South African landscape. Many waited for hours in pouring rain. Observed white playwright, Athol Fugard, "White South Africans should consider themselves one of the luckiest groups of people on the face of the earth. In spite of our terrible history, we weren't torn apart by the violence disemboweling countries like Yugoslavia."

When the votes were counted, 75-year-old Nelson Mandela was president of South Africa, and F.W. de Klerk was deputy president. The nation entered the new era with hopes high.

American Troops in Panama

In the Western Hemisphere, the United States once more used military force to achieve its aims. In February 1988, a United States federal grand jury indicted Panamanian leader Manuel Antonio Noriega on drug-dealing charges. American troops stormed the Central American nation in December 1989 to overthrow Noriega and bring him to trial. The United States alleged that he had turned Panama into a depot to launder illicit money and channel drugs between Colombian drug cartels and American dealers. In April 1992, a jury in Florida convicted him of these crimes.

Middle East Peace Talks

The Persian Gulf War prodded many Arabs and Israelis to try again to bury their ancient hostilities and live in peace. Using diplomatic influence gained in the war, Secretary of State James Baker brought together negotiators from many countries and factions in late 1991.

The massive changes Gorbachev had unleashed also had a ripple effect in Israel. Almost 400,000 Soviet Jews were allowed to immigrate to Israel in the late 1980s and early 1990s. Israel asked for a $10 billion loan from the United States to help resettle the immigrants. In return, Israeli leaders agreed to come to the negotiating table in Washington, D.C. The talks held out the most promise in years for a resolution of the Arab-Israeli conflict. After months of intense negotiations, in 1993 Palestinians and Israelis signed an agreement for limited Palestinian self-rule in Gaza and in the West Bank.

The next year saw the United States play a pivotal role in another historic accord. In 1994 Israel and neighboring Jordan signed a declaration in the Rose Garden of the White House, ending a state of war that had existed for 46 years. Said Jordan's King Hussein, "Out of all the days of my life, I do not believe there is one such as this." It seemed clear that the two leaders hoped to leave a legacy of peace in the long-troubled region. The road to peace, however, was anything but smooth. In November 1995, an assassin's bullets killed Israeli Prime Minister Yitzhak Rabin. The attack cast a pall over the peace negotiations.

Battles for Markets
United States, Canada, and Mexico Open Trade Doors

Although the cold war had ended, competition and even conflict over trade continued. Through most of the 1980s, the United States led the world in exporting goods to other nations. Beginning in the late 1980s, however, Americans imported more than they exported each year, creating a costly **trade deficit.** The country was losing ground to its main competitors, including the European Union (EU)—formerly called the European Community—a 12-nation trade bloc, and the Asian nations of Japan, Taiwan, South Korea, and China.

One response to global economic competition was to form a United States–led trade bloc. In 1988 the United States signed an agreement with Canada to gradually remove tariffs and other obstacles to trade on everything from lumber to cassettes to cars. Then, in a momentous event, the two nations joined with Mexico to sign the North American Free Trade Agreement (NAFTA) in August 1992.

Homage to a Leader Jordan's King Hussein traveled to Israel to speak at Prime Minister Rabin's funeral. *Why was this speech such a historic event?*

VISUAL INSTRUCTION

Homage to a Leader King Hussein of Jordan speaks at Yitzhak Rabin's funeral, November 1995. The blue hats many wear were distributed because of the extremely hot sun.

Answer: *because Israel and the Arab nation of Jordan had long been enemies and only recently had the two nations cooperated for peace*

ABC**NEWS**
INTERACTIVE™

 Videodisc

Powers of the Congress

Side 2, Chapter 45
Title: Persian Gulf Crisis: Congress Debate
Subject: The role of Congress in using the military overseas
Ask: Why was Congress reluctant to send troops? *(It feared another Vietnam.)*

See Powers of the Congress Guidebook page 121 for complete lesson plan.

Cultural Perspectives

Extended Families Mexican households contain, on average, between five and six people. Often, several generations of a family live together. Many women (as well as men) in cities have jobs. Women in farm areas often help in the fields. Many young people in the cities have part-time or full-time jobs. During the 1980s, however, far more people entered the labor force than retired, but the economy did not grow much. In addition, thousands of refugees from El Salvador, Guatemala, and Nicaragua entered Mexico. Unemployment became worse. Ask: Considering that 70 percent of Mexico's exports are to the United States, what could the United States do to aid Mexico? What would be the consequences of these actions?

ABCNEWS
INTERACTIVE™

● Videodisc

Powers of the Congress

Side 2, Chapter 46
Title: Persian Gulf Crisis: Congress Votes
Subject: The ways in which Congress can support the use of military force
Ask: What did Congress finally agree to do? *(Congress agreed to back the President.)*

See Powers of the Congress Guidebook page 122 for complete lesson plan.

The Recession This defense-related shipyard in Bath, Maine, once employed thousands of people, but as defense spending was cut, so were jobs. As the 1990s began, Americans were buying more imported goods. *Who did defense cuts affect?*

drastically. The economy and the nation needed to readjust.

The Arms Build-Down

Americans realized the economy was in serious trouble as the effects of military budget cuts spread across the country. The terms of treaties signed with the Soviet Union in the late 1980s called for major troop reductions. The Pentagon moved to eliminate 500,000 active duty military personnel by 1997. Army, navy, marine, and air force reserve units throughout the country also felt the budget cutters' axe. The 1990 cuts, affecting about one-fourth of the American military facilities in Europe, touched airfields, barracks, and even remote weather stations. These first cuts set the pace for those to follow. "General Motors is eliminating seventy-four thousand employees over three years," said General Colin Powell, chairman of the Joint Chiefs of Staff. "We're doing that many alone from January to September [of 1992]."

The defense cuts also affected American civilians. An estimated 1.35 million defense industry workers would lose their jobs by 1997. Demand was dropping for everything from soldiers' socks to billion-dollar B-2 bombers. Following the cancellation of the Seawolf nuclear submarine program, General Dynamics, Connecticut's second largest employer, planned to lay off nearly a quarter of its 17,000 workers. Smaller companies serving the defense industry were particularly hard hit. In Dallas-Fort Worth half the manufacturing jobs lost were defense related. In San Diego similar defense-related positions accounted for one-third of all lost jobs. Across the country, two-thirds of the 190,000 manufacturing jobs lost in 1990 were in military-related industries.

Military contracts from foreign governments saved some defense-related jobs. Workers at the McDonnell-Douglas complex in St. Louis, for example, prepared to supply Saudi Arabia with 72 new F-15 fighters. Nevertheless, cuts in defense spending cost defense contractors

The pact offered two main benefits. It would end most cross-border tariffs and quotas on goods and services by the year 2000, and it would give the NAFTA members greater leverage in negotiating with the EU and the Asian powers. With this leverage, businesses could nurture potential new markets while maintaining old ones. American and Canadian labor unions and some corporate leaders opposed NAFTA. Their main fear was that manufacturing jobs would move to lower-wage plants in Mexico and thus hurt American and Canadian workers. Environmentalists also worried about pollution controls.

Recession Adjustments
Defense and Automobile Industries Lose Markets

By early 1991 the American economy was fraught with problems: economic growth had halted; unemployment was rising; and the after-tax income for most workers was falling. Defense spending, still the single largest allocation of the federal budget, had been cut

Critical Thinking

Economic Consequences The 1992 defense budget of the United States was close to $300 billion. Some have suggested that instead of producing costly weapons, regardless of need, the government should support research and put off producing weapons until a need becomes clear and cost controls are assured. Others feel that when orders to a defense plant decrease, it affects the local economy. The plant orders fewer raw materials from suppliers, and the truckers who deliver goods also lose business. Individual workers lose their jobs or work fewer hours. Discuss with students the pros and cons of decreasing or increasing defense spending for the American economy.

a major portion of their business. To make matters worse, the recession limited the industry's ability to retool factories and retrain employees to work in other high-tech fields, such as environmental protection or the construction of power plants or high-speed trains. Companies and workers began looking to the government to help pay for transforming the factories. "Priming the pump is the way to go," said John O'Brien, chairman of Grumman Corporation, a leading defense contractor.

Economic Woes The budget deficit caused George Bush problems during his presidency. *What weakened the nation's economy?*

The Stubborn Recession

Defense was not the only industry caught in a changing world. Automobile makers, like many manufacturers, found themselves losing out to worldwide competition. In 1988 American automakers earned a record $11 billion in profits. Three years later they lost a record $7.5 billion. Falling revenue was only a symptom of their economic ills: the United States's share of worldwide automobile sales fell from 75 percent in 1950 to just 19 percent in 1991. American industry had come face-to-face with the realities of a **global economy.** This new system of worldwide trade was evident in the variety of inexpensive, foreign-made goods that American consumers found in local stores. The popularity of those foreign products upset the balance of trade between the United States and other countries. By the 1990s, each year the total value of goods the United States bought from other countries was about $100 billion more than the total value of goods it sold to other countries. This trade deficit, weakened the nation's economy and hurt the ability of American companies to compete with foreign companies.

The nation's inability to compete hit home in the nation's industrial towns and cities. In the video documentary *Roger and Me,* filmmaker Michael Moore recorded what happened to his hometown of Flint, Michigan, as General Motors closed its facilities there. Once a thriving middle-class community, Flint began to resemble a ghost town. Unemployed autoworkers left town to seek jobs elsewhere, and local businesses quickly lost most of their customers. Deputies evicted people from their homes because they could not pay their rent or meet their mortgages. Along Flint's main street, boards covered the windows and doors of stores, restaurants, movie theaters, and offices.

Meanwhile, in Washington, D.C., the Bush administration and Congress struggled to find ways to jump-start the economy. Bush proposed a cut in the capital gains tax that he said would stimulate new investment. Calling the proposal a tax break for the rich, the Democrats in Congress defeated it. Faced with an ever-growing deficit, Bush broke his "no new taxes" campaign pledge. After a series of budget summits with congressional leaders, Bush agreed to a tax increase that fell mostly on those with low and average incomes. The Federal Reserve System carried out another recession-fighting strategy, cutting interest rates 18 times between 1989 and the end of 1992. Lower interest rates had spurred the economy out of every recession since 1948 by fueling consumer spending and increasing demand for manufactured goods. The recession of the early 1990s, however, proved unyielding. Interest rates on savings accounts went down as well, driving investors to the stock market, where they hoped for greater returns. For retirees who depended on the interest income from their savings accounts, lower interest rates often meant real hardships.

The recession persisted, and by late 1992 the United States economy stood trapped in the longest stagnant period since World War II. Sales at major corporations and neighborhood shops alike kept declining, forcing more layoffs—of white-collar workers as well as blue-collar. Government, businesses, and consumers found themselves with little cash to promote economic growth.

Ballooning Debt

Many economists believed that the recession's stubbornness was due in part to the nation's enormous debt. For years the federal government had operated with a budget deficit, spending more money each year than it collected in taxes and revenues. In 1992 the deficit reached $333 billion. Some economists estimated that the deficit could soar to $500 billion, 5 percent of the nation's income, by the year 2002. The government financed the deficit by selling billions of dollars worth of bonds each month, often to overseas investors. Paying the interest on those bonds reduced the government's

VISUAL INSTRUCTION

Economic Woes Some people believe that the government should become the employer of last resort if industry cannot use a nation's total labor force. Although many European nations have such a policy, the idea has received little support in the United States, where federal budget deficits are seen as a major problem.

Answer: *the trade deficit*

ABCNEWS INTERACTIVE

Videodisc

Powers of the Congress

Side 2, Chapter 47
Title: Persian Gulf Crisis: War
Subject: The air war against Baghdad
Ask: How did the war end? *(Iraq was defeated.)*

See Powers of the Congress Guidebook page 124 for complete lesson plan.

Portfolio Project

Creating Charts Have students create charts showing the cyclical nature of unemployment and economic depression in a community. Suggest that students begin their charts with initial layoffs at a local manufacturing plant. Students can explain their charts to the class and then file them in their portfolios.

Writing Ask students to research some problems faced by the unemployed. They may wish to interview a friend or family member who was unemployed sometime between 1989 and 1993. Have students write an essay highlighting the concerns and hopes of the unemployed. Students can place completed essays in their portfolios.

ASSESS

Meeting Lesson Objectives

Each section objective is tested by the section review question(s) that follows it in parentheses.

1. Explain what happened as a result of military cutbacks in the United States. (1, 2)
2. Explain the origins and outcome of the Persian Gulf War. (3)
3. Explain how the changing economy affected the way Americans lived and worked in the 1980s and 1990s. (1, 2, 4, 5)

VISUAL INSTRUCTION

Banks Close Depositors line up to retrieve their money from a closed United Savings Bank in Paterson, New Jersey.

Answer: *Banking executives and borrowers benefited; the taxpayers got the bill.*

Evaluate

Have students complete the Section Review.

☞ 🖥 Assign the Section 3 Quiz or use the Testmaker to develop a customized quiz. (Also in Spanish.) **LEP**

☞ 🖥 Assign the Chapter 25 Test or use the Testmaker to develop a customized test.

☞ Have students complete the Chapter 25 Performance Assessment Activity.

resources for combatting the recession. In addition, interest payments diverted spending away from programs to improve education, end drug abuse, rebuild the nation's roads and railways, and fight urban decay. Government economists kept predicting that the economy would rebound by mid-1992, but high levels of personal and corporate debt worked against recovery. Like the government, individuals and corporations were paying interest on their own debts.

Wealth and Poverty
Stock and Banking Scandals Hurt Working Class

The recession and the economic policies that resulted from it touched people at all income levels. The effects on the wealthy, the middle class, and the poor were vastly different. In 1989 the richest 1 percent of American households owned 36 percent of the country's total private wealth. This represented a 5 percent increase in the wealthy elite's share since 1983. At the same time, the number of people living in poverty rose from about 11 percent of the population in the 1970s to about 15 percent in 1991.

The Income Gap

The rich got richer for a number of reasons. Top corporate executives commanded ever-higher salaries. Even during the layoffs and plant closings of the late 1980s and early 1990s, pay for top executives continued to rise, soaring to 160 times the pay of an average worker. Many well-off people also benefited from tax law changes. The Reagan administration argued that giving the wealthy more capital to invest would expand business. The effects would "trickle-down" to the middle and lower classes. In 1986 tax reform decreased taxes on the wealthy from 70 percent to 30 percent of their taxable income, but the "trickle down" effect did not occur for everyone.

Others became rich through elaborate and sometimes illegal business deals. In the 1980s a wave of corporate takeovers swept the country. One of the largest was Chevron's takeover of Gulf Oil at a cost of $13.4 billion. The 2 brokerage houses involved in the merger together received $45 million. Corporate mergers offered great profits to some merger specialists while extracting a high price from the nation's economy. Corporations that might be takeover targets often sacrificed long-term performance in favor of short-term profits. This practice weakened the economy.

The deregulation of the banking industry opened another avenue for enrichment. Officers in institutions such as Lincoln Savings and Loan in California made large loans to businesses that had little chance of succeeding. Often, the bankers knew or were related to the businesses' top executives. The borrowers paid themselves huge salaries; the banking executives pocketed fat commissions. When the businesses failed, the bank often failed as well. There was no money to repay the investors or to cover the deposits of the customers. Taxpayers got the bill for more than 1,000 bank or savings-and-loan failures, at an estimated cost of $500 billion.

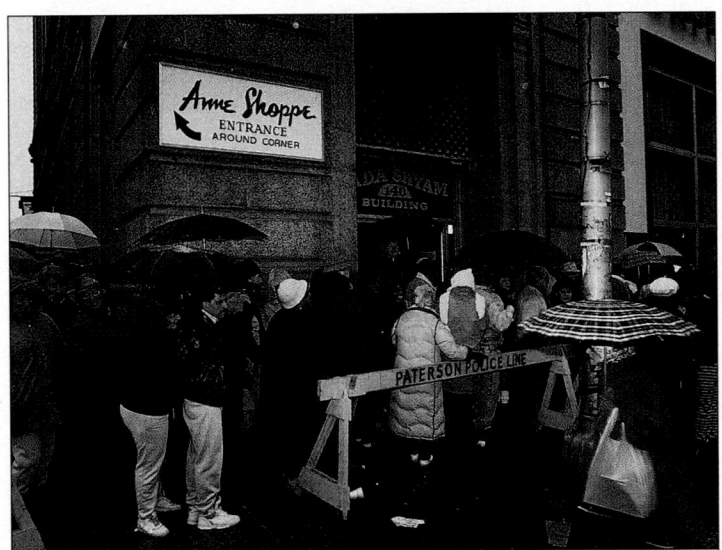

© PETER BYRON/BLACK STAR

Banks Close Many banks failed in the 1980s because of their irresponsible lending practices. *Who benefited most from these loans? Who ended up paying for the failed loans?*

Pressures on the Middle Class

American taxpayers shouldered the bulk of the tax burden for the failed savings-and-loan institutions. In the late 1980s and early 1990s, working people coped with stagnant incomes and a declining quality of life. More and more businesses were moving factories and jobs to cheaper, less regulated foreign labor markets; and changing technologies were making many blue-collar jobs obsolete. For Americans in the middle and the lower classes, affordable health care became increasingly difficult to find. Some retirees learned that their union pension plans had been mismanaged. Most of all, they

Meeting Special Needs

Visual Learners To meet the needs of students who learn best visually, have them create a graph showing how quickly debt can grow if a lender charges 1.5 percent interest per month on a $10,000 loan. The amount owed is given at right.

January	$10,000		January	$11,957
March	$10,302		March	$12,318
May	$10,614		May	$12,691
July	$10,935		July	$13,074
September	$11,265			
November	$11,606			

watched their children's opportunities for a better future dwindle.

Unlike previous downturns, the recession of the early 1990s also barreled through the suburban United States. Forty percent of the jobs lost in the recession of the early 1990s were white-collar jobs. Hardworking members of the middle class, like Ben D'Cruz, saw the American dream evaporate before their eyes. In 1991 D'Cruz was laid off from a $48,000-a-year job at Norden Systems in New York. He looked in vain for a comparable position; he applied for jobs paying as little as $19,000 without success. After spending most of his retirement savings, D'Cruz relied on unemployment compensation and his wife's earnings to make ends meet. "It's very tough out there," he said. "Even if you go out of Long Island, it's happening all over." Many of the white-collar layoffs turned out to be permanent, as global competition forced companies to cut costs aggressively.

Otherwise encouraging economic developments failed to make a difference for hard-pressed middle-class Americans in the early 1990s. Home mortgage rates fell to their lowest levels in two decades, while prices dropped for numerous consumer goods, such as television sets and personal computers. Nevertheless, consumer purchases did not increase because consumers found that their incomes had not kept pace with rising costs. The increased taxes on the middle class had left them with less money to spend than they had had a decade earlier.

The Frayed Safety Net

As the recession deepened, the people with the least money to spend lost the most economic ground. Half the adults living in poverty, 14 million people, were classified as **working poor.** These adults earned less than $12,195 a year, too little to pull a family of 4 out of poverty. The nation's poorest people had been left out of the business boom of the 1980s. Like the middle class, the working poor lost jobs to foreign labor and automation. Workers fortunate enough to hold on to basic jobs watched their earning power plummet.

The Urban Poor A young mother in a San Francisco homeless shelter feeds her toddler son. *How many children lived in poverty in 1989?*

These circumstances affected some more than others. Between 1983 and 1989 the net worth of white families fell 8 percent. During the same period, the net worth of African American and Hispanic families fell 42 percent. Women and children were now the poorest of the poor; the number of poor single-parent families increased. By 1989, nearly 1 of every 5 children was living in poverty; 14 percent of these children were white, 35 percent were Hispanic, and 43 percent were African American.

The economic losses of African Americans and Hispanic Americans were mainly felt in cities. City revenues fell, and urban dwellers began to see crumbling streets, leaking sewers, and broken bridges. Some cities closed schools and eliminated educational programs due to decreased revenues for education. While city problems multiplied, cities found that their share of federal dollars fell. Federal aid to cities in 1992 was 64 percent less than it had been in 1980.

SECTION REVIEW

Vocabulary

1. Define: apartheid, trade deficit, global economy, working poor.

Checking Facts

2. What effects did cuts in defense spending have on civilians in the United States?

3. What triggered the Persian Gulf War, and what were the results of the war?

Critical Thinking

Predicting Consequences

4. How is global economic competition changing relations between the United States and its neighbors Canada and Mexico?

Linking Across Time

5. What similarities existed between the economy of the United States in the 1930s and the economy of the United States in the early 1990s?

VISUAL INSTRUCTION

The Urban Poor Since the mid-1970s, the homeless population in the United States has grown. Many are men and women who cannot find jobs or afford housing. The number of homeless families has also increased.

Answer: *nearly 1 of every 5*

Reteach

🎧 Have students listen to the Chapter 25, Section 3 Audiocassette. (Also in Spanish.) **LEP**

📁 Have students complete the Chapter 25 Reteaching Activity.

Enrich

📁 Have students complete the Chapter 25 Enrichment Activity. (Also in Spanish.) **LEP**

📁 Have students complete the Chapter 25 Geography in History Activity.

📁 Have students complete Interpreting Political Cartoons 6, 14, 15, 22, 23, 25, 28, 50.

📁 Have students complete Supreme Court Case Studies 52–57.

CLOSE

What were the effects of defense cutbacks? *(Cutbacks accounted for two-thirds of lost manufacturing jobs.)* How did the wealthy increase their personal wealth in the 1980s? *(high salaries, favorable tax changes)*

Section 3 Review Answers

1. apartheid (880), **trade deficit** (881), **global economy** (883), **working poor** (885)

2. Civilians who worked in manufacturing jobs for defense contractors lost their jobs.

3. Iraq invaded Kuwait. This threatened the world's oil supplies. The United States launched air strikes against Iraq, quickly ending the war.

4. Global competition is forcing the United States to form its own trade bloc (NAFTA) with Mexico and Canada.

5. widespread unemployment, greater welfare needs, depleted savings

Making the Historical Connection

This quotation from Ronald Reagan's farewell address sums up the 1980s: "And how stands the city on the winter night? More prosperous, more secure and happier than it was eight years ago. . . ." It was an era of technological toys and of a nation wanting to acquire.

Curriculum Connection

Science In 1986 health officials predicted that the number of deaths caused by AIDS (acquired immunodeficiency syndrome) would increase more than tenfold in 5 years, causing 179,000 deaths at a health cost of up to $16 billion. This nearly always fatal disease was largely ignored until the mid-1980s, when people finally saw its epidemic potential. Money was then allotted to AIDS research in greater proportion. In 1987, AZT, a drug used not as a cure but to extend the lives of victims and relieve some symptoms, won FDA approval.

CULTURE
OF THE
TIME

© STEVE SCHAPIRO/SYGMA

The Rap on the Eighties

In the 1980s many Americans focused on comfort and appearance, trying to live well and look good. Technology changed, too. Compact discs (CDs), juice boxes, and cordless telephones appeared. A new movie rating, PG-13, was invented. New words, such as *couch potato* and *yuppie,* entered our language.

APPEARANCE COUNTS

Baby boomers placed low-fat, high-fiber foods, designer clothes, and health clubs high on their agendas. **Jane Fonda workout** books and videos sold well.

© J.L. ATLAN/SYGMA

A DEADLY DISEASE

In 1981 medical experts identified a mysterious disease that came to be called AIDS. Rock Hudson raised public awareness of the disease when he acknowledged in 1985 that he was battling AIDS. On October 11, 1987, thousands of people gathered in Washington, D.C., to display an **AIDS quilt.** Each square of the quilt represented someone who had died of the disease.

Background Information

What the Eighties Were Like Have students research a topic on some aspect of the 1980s. Suggest the following topics: AIDS; music and musicians; technology (and subsequent technological "toys"); medicine (MRI machines, rising health-care costs); space research (*Voyager II*'s findings, the *Challenger* explosion, the first *Columbia* space shuttle, or Sally Ride); astronomy (discovery of a new galaxy); the murder of John Lennon; the break-up of the AT&T telephone monopoly; the Cabbage Patch doll phenomenon; double-digit inflation; Japanese automobile production; the air traffic controller strike; and the new fitness trend. Have students write their findings in a report. Encourage them to include visual representations of their subject. Display their reports, and then have students put them in their portfolios.

CABLE TV ARRIVES

MTV, which began the rock video business, was one of many new cable television stations that originated during the 1980s. Others included CNN, the Disney Channel, the Discovery Channel, A&E, and TNT. VCRs also became popular during this period, increasing 72 percent in sales from 1980 to 1981.

MUSICIANS COME TOGETHER

In 1985 musicians from around the world performed to raise money for drought-stricken Africa. The concert, called **Live Aid,** was staged in both Philadelphia and London, and almost 2 billion people watched it. It grossed $70 million. The "We Are the World" (the concert's theme song) record and video raised another $50 million.

© BENSON/GAMMA LIAISON

THE MATERIAL GIRL

One of many musicians to appear at Live Aid, **Madonna** had 5 best-selling albums in the 1980s. Her stage shows, along with clever promotion, helped ensure her success in the 1980s.

RAPPERS ROAR

Its syncopated, rhythmic beat and its chanted, rhyming lyrics made **rap music** a form of expression almost anyone could enjoy. The most popular rappers projected an image of power, independence, and arrogance that appealed to their fans.

PHOTO OF ALBUMS BY DOUG MINDELL

© TOM MIHALEK/SYGMA

CULTURE OF THE TIME   **887**

FYI

New Technology When VCRs and videocassettes became popular, the movie industry suffered a drop in ticket sales. So that they could be seen as well as heard, rock stars soon started making videocassettes to accompany their music. MTV quickly provided the market for these cassettes. Michael Jackson's album *Thriller*, which sold more than 20 million copies worldwide in 1983 and 1984, was made into a video and displayed the dancing and moon walking, as well as the singing, of the top recording artist of the year. ("Beat It" was given a Grammy for best record, *Thriller* for best album, and Jackson himself for best male pop vocalist.)

CLOSE

Have students characterize the 1980s. *(It was a time of technological advances. People rushed to buy the new gadgetry. People were interested in comfort and entertainment. Some concern was given to altruistic endeavors, such as those involving AIDS.)*

Portfolio Project

A Scandalous Time The 1980s were full of juicy scandals. After Zsa Zsa Gabor was convicted of slapping a Beverly Hills police officer, she was sentenced to 3 days in jail and asked to reveal her age. Hotel queen Leona Helmsley was convicted of income tax evasion and sentenced to 4 years in jail. ("We don't pay taxes," she once said. "The little people pay taxes.") Televangelist Jim Bakker was sentenced to 45 years for selling bogus vacations. A scandal at the Department of Housing and Urban Development revealed $2 billion in losses, including money stolen by "Robin HUD," who "gave" $5 million to the poor.

Chapter ㉕ Review

Reviewing Key Terms

1. trade deficit
2. glasnost
3. apartheid
4. global economy

Recalling Facts

1. religious right, Democrats, Republicans, rich, poor who wanted to downsize government
2. Reaganomics favored lower taxes over government spending.
3. The wealthy benefited from reduced taxes; the poor lost welfare benefits.
4. Air and water pollution standards were eased, allowing for environmental abuses.
5. INF treaty; reduction of nuclear missiles
6. Gorbachev instituted reforms and resigned as head of the Communist party, which ended centralized control.
7. threat of Soviet attack ended, allowing defense cutbacks
8. Marxists in El Salvador; trained the *contras,* the right-wing guerillas trying to regain control from the Sandinistas.
9. He lost some credibility, but his popularity remained.
10. to show Hussein that aggression against oil-field countries would not be tolerated
11. economic sanctions from other countries; de Klerk's release of Mandela and legalization of ANC
12. A larger market for free trade could increase sales; some feared job loss because of lower Mexican wages.
13. Tighter government budgets and the end of the cold war led to military cutbacks.
14. It hurt the United States's ability to compete with foreign companies.
15. suburbia—white-collar workers lost jobs; urban—blue-collar workers lost jobs and social and housing programs

Reviewing Key Terms

Choose the vocabulary term that best completes each sentence below. Write your answers on a separate sheet of paper.

trade deficit   glasnost
global economy   perestroika
apartheid

1. A _____ is created when a country imports more than it exports.

2. Gorbachev's policy of _____ encouraged Soviet citizens to look beyond communism to new ways of doing things.

3. South Africa used _____ to keep blacks separated from whites and out of the government.

4. Economic competition among nations is a feature of the _____ .

Recalling Facts

1. What forces combined to sweep Ronald Reagan into office in 1980?

2. How did Reaganomics differ from Keynesian economic theories?

3. How did Reagan and Bush tax policies affect wealthy Americans? Poor Americans?

4. How did Reagan's deregulation policies affect the environment?

5. What was Reagan's greatest achievement in foreign policy? Why was it so important?

6. What led to the collapse of communism in the Soviet Union? How was Gorbachev himself instrumental in bringing about the collapse?

7. How did the focus of United States foreign policy shift after the end of the cold war?

8. Who were the Sandinistas? What was the United States's role in the Nicaraguan civil war?

9. How did the Iran-*contra* scandal affect Ronald Reagan's presidency?

10. Why did President Bush and Secretary of State Baker seek to involve a large number of nations in the coalition against Iraq in the Persian Gulf War?

11. Explain the steps by which apartheid was abolished in South Africa.

12. What were the advantages of the NAFTA pact? Why were some people so opposed to it?

13. What prompted the military cutbacks in the United States in the early 1990s?

14. How did the trade deficit weaken the nation's economy?

15. In what ways did the recession of the early 1990s change both the suburban and urban United States?

Critical Thinking

1. **Making Comparisons** Compare the end of communism in East Germany to its end in Poland.

2. **Making Inferences** The picture below shows Muscovites rallying behind Yeltsin's brave stand against the coup attempt by Communist party loyalists. How did the coup attempt actually speed up the Soviet collapse?

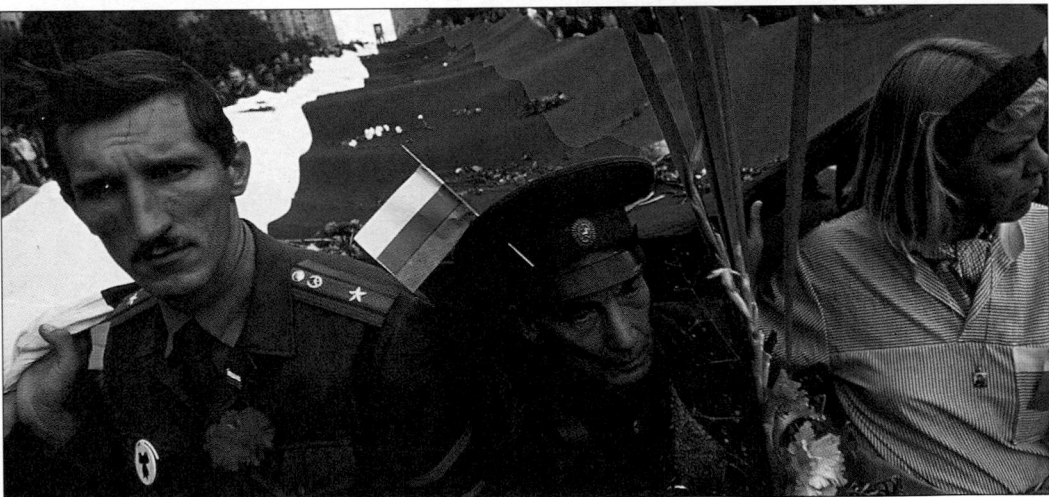

© KLAUS REISINGER/BLACK STAR

Critical Thinking

1. Poland—public protest; influence of Solidarity, Lech Walesa, Pope John Paul II; East Germany—opened borders to keep citizens from leaving for other countries
2. Angered by the attempt and backed by citizens who had supported Yeltsin, Gorbachev resigned as party head and banned party involvement in government affairs.
3. assumes that the same jobs will be done in each country and that American workers will accept low-paying jobs
4. Answers should show an understanding that economic strength takes into account GDP and exports as well as levels of unemployment, inflation, and debt.
5. White-collar workers lost job security and put off buying houses. Because of defaults, banks granted few new mortgages.

3. Identifying Assumptions Some critics of NAFTA argued that free trade would drive down Americans' wages to Mexican levels. What assumptions does this argument make?

4. Making Comparisons How was the recession of the early 1990s similar to the Great Depression of the 1930s? How were the two eras different?

5. Determining Cause and Effect In the early 1990s, home mortgage rates were lower than they had been in 20 years, and yet sales of new homes rose slowly. What caused the slow sales?

Portfolio Project

Imagine that you are a resident of East Berlin the day the Wall goes down. Write down what you think your reactions to that event might be. What would you now be able to do that you could not do before November 9, 1989? If possible, read some newspapers or newsmagazines from that period to learn the actual reactions of Berliners. Keep the results of your research in your portfolio.

Cooperative Learning

Form small groups and take turns explaining the following economic terms and concepts and describing how they work: the deficit, the national debt, supply-side economics, balanced budget, global economy, recession, trade deficit, and trickle-down economics.

Reinforcing Skills

Predicting Consequences
Dubbed "The Great Communicator" because he seemed to reach people so well, Ronald Reagan was a tremendously popular President. How do you think he will be regarded in future years? For instance, how will the success of his foreign policy be rated? His fiscal policies? How

PERSIAN GULF WAR, 1991

Legend	
Iraq and occupied territory	Allied ground attack
Nations sympathetic to Iraq	U.S. warships
Nations contributing forces against Iraq	U.S. bombers or missiles
Oil fields	Capital city

0   150   300 mi.
0 150 300 km
Mercator projection

will he be rated politically? Personally? Back up your predictions with solid evidence from the text.

Geography and History

Study the map on this page to answer the following questions:

1. In which countries were United States bombers located?

2. Which countries were sympathetic to Iraq?

3. Where did the Allied ground attack take place?

4. Locate the oil fields in Southwest Asia.

5. Which nations helped in the Allied invasion?

HISTORY JOURNAL

Use the following questions to help you record your ideas about President Reagan's image at the time of his presidency and in the future: How did his strong anti-Communist stance affect his popularity? Did the growth in the national debt affect Reagan's popularity? How does your generation view the policies and decisions made in the 1980s? Use current newsmagazines to help you with your answers.

Geography and History

1. Turkey and Saudi Arabia
2. Lebanon and Jordan
3. in the southern part of Iraq near Kuwait; in Kuwait itself
4. They are in Saudi Arabia, the Persian Gulf, Iran, Iraq, and Syria.
5. Egypt, Saudi Arabia, United Arab Emirates, Bahrain, Syria, Qatar (and the United States)

History Journal

Students' journals should show that they know that the responsibility for the debt will end up on their shoulders and that Reagan's strong anti-Communist stance helped end the cold war.

? BONUS QUESTION

This question may be used for extra credit on the chapter test.
Explain the importance of the declaration signed in the White House Rose Garden in 1994.
Answer: *Israel and Jordan signed a declaration that ended a 46-year state of war and was a symbol of future peace in Southwest Asia.*

Portfolio Project

Students' projects should reflect what it would be like to lack the freedom to go where they wanted to go, say what they wanted to say, and visit people they wanted to see. After the opening of the wall, citizens had all those freedoms.

Cooperative Learning

Students may wish to make a game of this assignment, using, for example, a Trivial Pursuit game board or a point system.

Reinforcing Skills

Students' answers should reflect their knowledge of Reagan's actual decisions regarding foreign policy, economics, and politics. You might suggest that they consult newsmagazines from the time period.

A Changing Nation in a Changing World

DAILY LESSON OBJECTIVES	REPRODUCIBLE RESOURCES	MULTIMEDIA RESOURCES
SECTION 1 The Clinton Agenda 1. Explain the 1992 presidential campaign and the election results. 2. Describe the successful and unsuccessful legislation of the Clinton administration. 3. Explain the reasons behind the Balkan crisis and the responses to the crisis worldwide.	📁 Reproducible Lesson Plans 📁 Vocabulary and Guided Reading Activities (English or Spanish) 📁 Cooperative Learning Activities 📁 Interpreting Political Cartoons 📁 Supreme Court Case Studies 📁 Section Quizzes (English or Spanish)	🔦 Chapter Teaching Transparencies 🔦 Section Focus Transparencies 🔦 Map Transparencies 💿 The Presidents: A Picture History of Our Nation ⬛ Testmaker ⬛ Student Self-Test: A Software Review
SECTION 2 The New Conservatism 1. Explain the factors that led the Republicans to sweep the 1994 midterm elections. 2. List important figures in the 104th Congress and their roles. 3. Discuss the goals of the Contract With America. 4. Explain why Congress has such a difficult time passing a balanced budget.	📁 Reproducible Lesson Plans 📁 Vocabulary and Guided Reading Activities (English or Spanish) 📁 Interpreting Political Cartoons 📁 Supreme Court Case Studies 📁 Great Debates in American History 📁 Section Quizzes (English or Spanish)	🔦 Section Focus Transparencies 💿 Landmark Documents in American History ⬛ Testmaker ⬛ Student Self-Test: A Software Review
SECTION 3 Toward a New Century 1. List arguments for and against gerrymandering. 2. Explain the changing nature of work in an increasingly technological society. 3. Describe the financial and educational challenges facing schools and educators as the United States moves toward the twenty-first century.	📁 Reproducible Lesson Plans 📁 Vocabulary and Guided Reading Activities (English or Spanish) 📁 Reteaching Activities (English or Spanish) 📁 Enrichment Activities (English or Spanish) 📁 Geography in History Activities 📁 Interpreting Political Cartoons 📁 Supreme Court Case Studies 📁 Skill Reinforcement Activities 📁 Section Quizzes (English or Spanish)	🔦 Section Focus Transparencies 💿 Economics in Action 💿 Focus on Government ⬛ Testmaker ⬛ Student Self-Test: A Software Review
CHAPTER REVIEW AND EVALUATION	📁 Chapter 26 Test, Forms A and B 📁 Performance Assessment Strategies and Activities 📁 Unit 10 Test, Forms A and B	⬛ Student Self-Test: A Software Review ⬛ Vocabulary PuzzleMaker ⬛ Testmaker 🎧 Chapter Digests Audiocassettes

[00:00] If time does not permit teaching the entire chapter, summarize using the Chapter 26 Digests Audiocassettes and the accompanying activities and tests. (Available in English or Spanish.)

Cooperative Project

Organize students into groups of four. Each student should assume the role of one of the following: a government official, advocates for environmental protection, day care, and health care for the elderly. Have each advocate explain his or her need for federal funds to the official. Have the government official work out a compromise with the three advocates. **LEP** 📇

Suggested Rubrics: Group Work and the Individual, An Oral Presentation. See Performance Assessment Strategies and Activities, pp. 34, 50.

Individual Project

After students have examined the United States in a global economy, ask them to research and write about the effects of the North American Free Trade Agreement on the job market and the environment in the United States, Canada, and Mexico. Tell them to focus their research on whether the trade bloc is making the three nations' economies more alike or less alike. 📇

Suggested Rubric: A Research Report. See Performance Assessment Strategies and Activities, pp. 39.

Key to Ability Levels

Teaching strategies have been coded for varying learning styles and abilities.

L1 **BASIC** activities for all students

L2 **AVERAGE** activities for average to above-average students

L3 **CHALLENGING** activities for above-average students

LEP **LIMITED ENGLISH PROFICIENCY** activities

 Block Scheduling

Block scheduling differs from traditional class scheduling in the amount of time allotted to each period. The extended timeframe provided by block scheduling affords you the opportunity to implement a greater number of research-oriented and activity-intense projects to motivate and involve your students. Activities that are particularly suited to use within the block scheduling framework are identified throughout this chapter by the following designation. 📇

TEACHER'S CORNER

NATIONAL
GEOGRAPHIC
SOCIETY

INDEX TO NATIONAL GEOGRAPHIC MAGAZINE

The following articles may be used for research relating to this chapter:

- "Earth Day: 25 Years Old," by Frank Graham, Jr., April 1995.
- "The Endangered Species Act," by Douglas H. Chadwick, March 1995.
- "Hawaii's Vanishing Species," by Elizabeth Royte, September 1995.
- "Silence of the Songbirds," by Les Line, June 1993.
- "Our Disappearing Wetlands," by John G. Mitchell, October 1992.
- "Dolphins in Crisis," by Kenneth S. Norris, September 1992.
- "Endangered Old-Growth Forests," by Rowe Findley, September 1990.

NATIONAL GEOGRAPHIC SOCIETY PRODUCTS AVAILABLE FROM GLENCOE

To order the following products for use with this chapter, contact your local Glencoe sales representative or call Glencoe at 1-800-334-7344:

- *The Presidents: A Picture History of Our Nation* (CD-ROM)
- *GTV: A Geographic Perspective on American History* (Videodisc)
- *GTV: The American People: Fabric of a Nation* (Videodisc)

ADDITIONAL NATIONAL GEOGRAPHIC SOCIETY PRODUCTS

To order the following products for use with this chapter, call National Geographic Society at 1-800-368-2728:

- *Hawaii: Strangers in Paradise* (Video)
- *Energy: The Problems and the Future* (Video)
- *The Right Whale: An Endangered Species* (Video)

Chapter Overview

In 1992 voters elected William Jefferson Clinton President of the United States, the first Democrat to hold that office since Jimmy Carter. Two years later, however, the nation's voters took a conservative turn, and Republicans won the largest midterm victory in 70 years.

Introducing the Chapter

Have students read the narrative on this page about Ross Perot. Ask them to think about what may have appealed to voters about Ross Perot.

Display Chapter Teaching Transparency 26 and distribute copies of the corresponding activity sheet for students to complete.

Extension Activity

Have students complete Beyond the Transparency on the activity sheet for Chapter 26 and present their projects after the class has completed the chapter.

History Journal

Have students review what they wrote about Ross Perot, Bill Clinton, George Bush, or another presidential candidate. Then have them write about what issues might be important to presidential candidates today.

A Changing Nation in a Changing World

OCTOBER 1992: ROSS PEROT'S INFOMERCIAL DRAWS A WIDE AUDIENCE

Ross Perot rarely spoke in public. He bought time on television instead. On these "infomercials," he sat before charts that plotted the economic decline of the United States, told the American people that the engine of government was "broke," and declared that he was ready to get under the hood and fix it.

For half an hour Texas billionaire Ross Perot lectured on the United States economy. Surprisingly, his show drew a larger audience than the baseball play-off game that aired right after it.

During the 1992 presidential campaign, thousands of volunteers formed a grassroots movement to place Perot on the ballot in all 50 states. One volunteer was Jack Gates, a retired lawyer living in Santee, South Carolina. Gates explained to his son why he supported Perot: "I feel sorry for your children and your children's children, to whom we have left a legacy of a debt which currently is four trillion dollars...."

Perot presented himself as a successful business leader who could not be bought by special-interest groups. Perot felt he could end the gridlock that gripped the nation's capital and get the country's finances in order. He spent $60 million of his own money on his campaign and won more than 18 percent of the popular vote in the election. ■

HISTORY JOURNAL

What do you think Perot's candidacy and his high percentage of the popular vote revealed about the American people?

890

✚ EXTRA CREDIT PROJECT

The 1992 Election Ross Perot spent his own money trying to convince voters in 1992 to elect him President of the United States. Have students research Perot's platform in depth. What problems did Perot see with the United States economy, and what were his proposals to fix them? Encourage students to investigate the debates in which he participated. How did Perot fare, and what might explain his performance? What do they think of Perot's solutions to American economic woes? Do his answers seem feasible? Why or why not? Have students present interesting findings to the class and then file their reports in their portfolios.

© MATTHEW McVAY/TONY STONE IMAGES, INC.

ROSS PEROT SPEAKS TO HIS
SUPPORTERS DURING HIS 1992
PRESIDENTIAL CAMPAIGN.

891

 Videodisc

*GTV: The American
People: Fabric of a
Nation*

Side 4, Chapter 1
Title: America's Choir
Subject: A profile of
Americans in the 1990s
Ask: In what way is the
United States a multicul-
tural society? *(People from
all cultural backgrounds
have become citizens and
have contributed to the
American way of life.)*

 **History and
the Humanities**

🎧 American Music:
Cultural Traditions—
"Crossfire" by Stevie Ray
Vaughan and Double
Trouble

 **Performance
Assessment**

Refer to page 890B for
performance assessment
activities for this chapter.

📁 Also see Activity 26
in the Performance
Assessment Strategies
and Activities for an
additional activity as well
as for suggested rubrics.

Examining the Visual

Ross Perot Many voters supported Perot's candidacy for President because they thought he was a political outsider with no commitments to powerful interest groups. Some voters thought Perot's business background would make him an effective President. Perot began his business career in 1957 as a computer salesperson. In 1962 he founded Electronic Data Systems (EDC), a company that provided computer services. This company made huge profits, and Perot became a billionaire. Perot said he decided to enter the 1992 presidential election because Clinton and Bush had failed to adequately address such issues as the large national deficit. After the election Perot formed an organization called United We Stand America to push for political reforms and reduction of the deficit.

The Clinton Agenda

AUGUST 1992: CLINTON BUS TOUR ON THE ROAD

The Clinton Campaign
Presidential candidate Bill Clinton takes his bus tour to North Carolina.

THE CAMPAIGN BUS ROLLED THROUGH FARM COUNTRY THAT LAY ALONG THE BANKS OF THE MISSISSIPPI RIVER. On board were Democratic presidential candidate Bill Clinton, his wife, Hillary Rodham Clinton, vice-presidential candidate Al Gore, and his wife, Tipper Gore. About 150 reporters trailed along as the bus made its way from St. Louis to Minneapolis. During the day, the candidates gave radio and television interviews, met with local politicians, and visited factories and coffee shops.

Working men and women, their jobs done for the day, appeared at the roadside. There were women in lawn chairs, kids on a trampoline, a farmer sitting atop his combine holding a homemade sign: Clinton-Gore in '92. One night people lined the highway holding lit candles. Wherever 500 or more people were gathered, the bus stopped. Up went the lights, on went the sound system, and the country crossroads would become an in-

stant rally. The candidates made speeches, but they also listened. They heard about people losing jobs, concerns about dry weather and low crop prices, and fears about wages not covering medical expenses. What the candidates heard were individual stories that collectively would determine the focus of the next election.

1992 Election
The Economy

Hard hit by recession, American voters approached the 1992 presidential election with one chief concern: the economy. The Democratic and Republican parties brought their fundamental disagreement concerning how best to invigorate the economy into the heart of the campaign. Republicans favored increasing the incentives available to big and small businesses in order to help

AS YOU READ

Vocabulary
► universal coverage
► family leave
► crime bill

Think About . . .
► the 1992 presidential campaign and the election results.
► the successful and unsuccessful legislation of the Clinton administration.

► the reasons behind the fighting in the Balkans and how the world responded to the crisis.

892 CHAPTER 26 A CHANGING NATION IN A CHANGING WORLD

PRESIDENTIAL ELECTION, 1992

Party	Electoral Vote	% of Popular Vote
Democratic: Clinton - Gore	370	43.2%
Republican: Bush - Quayle	168	37.7%
Independent: Perot - Stockdale	0	19.0%
Turnout: 55% of eligible voters		(About 0.1% cast votes for other candidates.)

In 1988 electors in 40 states cast their votes for George Bush. In 1992 Bush's reelection bid garnered electoral votes in only 18 states, many of them small. *In what areas of the country was Bush's support the strongest? The weakest?*

them expand and create more jobs. Democrats preferred higher taxes on the wealthy, more funds for job retraining, and increased investment in the nation's transportation and communication networks and in its educational system.

The weak economy overshadowed the fact that, for the first time in more than 40 years, the nation was free from the threat of nuclear war with the Soviets. The chief concerns in this election were domestic: skyrocketing health-care costs, the increase in violent and drug-related crimes, the need for improved education—and how to finance solutions to these problems.

Three-Way Race

After defeating opponents in Democratic primaries, 45-year-old Arkansas Governor Bill Clinton received his party's nomination for President. Clinton challenged the Republican candidate, President George Bush, by focusing on the faltering economy. Clinton chose Tennessee Senator Albert Gore, Jr., a well-known environmentalist, as his running mate. Bush retained Vice President Dan Quayle as his running mate.

The third person in the race was Ross Perot, who capitalized on voter discontent with the gridlock between the Republican President and a Congress controlled by the Democrats. He outlined a program to cut

the federal budget deficit in five years, a plan that asked all Americans to "share the pain" of fixing the problems.

Voters' discontent with elected officials also changed the complexion of many congressional races. A record number of legislators either chose not to run again or were defeated. A record 164 women stepped forward to run for Congress, and another 8 women sought governorships.

Voter Appeals

In the presidential race Bush offered a long career of government service and his first-term successes in foreign affairs. Democratic challenger Bill Clinton brought 12 years of experience as governor of Arkansas and a reputation as a reformer. With no government experience, Ross Perot ran on his business success. To a large extent the campaign centered on voters' convictions about which candidate could lead the nation out of economic decline.

Bush painted Clinton as a "tax-and-spend" Democrat. Clinton attacked Bush's emphasis on foreign policy and his neglect of domestic concerns, especially the economy, health care, education, and crime. Bush cast shadows on Clinton's character, citing his avoidance of military service and his participation as a young man in demonstrations against the Vietnam War. Democrats tried to capitalize on reports that Bush took part in

SECTION ONE **893**

TEACH

Guided Practice

L1 **Discussion** On the chalkboard, list the presidential candidates who ran in the 1992 campaign. Under each name write a few attributes of that candidate's campaign and philosophy.

Show students Map Transparency 26 and have them complete the activity sheet.

MAP STUDY

Clinton took advantage of many Americans' perceptions that Bush was unconcerned about domestic issues and that the gap between rich and poor had grown during Bush's presidency.

Answer: *the South and West; the Northeast, Far West, and Midwest*

FYI

The Perot Factor Presidential candidates without support from the two major parties rarely fare well. In 1924 Robert La Follette won 16.6 percent of the vote, most of it in the North. In 1968 George Wallace won 13.5 percent, most of it in the South. But Ross Perot won 19 percent, with at least 10 percent in almost every state. Partly because of Perot, Clinton won only 2 million more votes than Democrat Michael Dukakis did in his broad defeat in 1988.

Cooperative Learning

The 1992 Elections Organize the class into cooperative groups. Remind students that as a result of the 1992 election, almost 1 in every 4 members of Congress was newly elected. The numbers of minorities and women increased significantly. Have groups research reasons for

the dramatic changes. Ask teams to investigate how scandals, voter registration and turnout, and prevailing economic conditions may have contributed to the changes. Let teams plan the research to be done and decide how to present their findings to the rest of the class.

Curriculum Connection

Civics President Clinton nominated Ruth Bader Ginsberg to fill a vacancy on the Supreme Court. The Senate approved her in August 1993, and she became the second woman to serve as a justice of the Court.

FYI

Bill Clinton In high school, Bill Clinton was active in a variety of clubs and held many offices. A schoolmate later recalled that Bill was "always running for something." Clinton also played tenor saxophone in the school band. At the age of 17, Clinton met John F. Kennedy on a visit to Washington, D.C. It was then that Clinton decided to pursue a political career.

The Presidents: A Picture History of Our Nation

Have students view "William J. Clinton" and use the information to write a brief biography to include in their portfolios.

secret, illegal arms shipments to Iran in the 1980s. The campaign grew complicated with Perot's witty participation in the televised presidential debates and his 30-minute campaign commercials.

In the end a frustrated electorate, concerned about a government that they saw as expensive and inefficient, voted for change, ousting Bush after one term. Clinton became the first Democrat elected to the White House since Jimmy Carter in 1976. Although Clinton's margin in electoral votes was 2 to 1, his margin in popular votes was only 5 percent. Clinton got 43 percent of the popular vote, compared to Bush's 38 percent and Perot's 19 percent (more than any independent candidate in 80 years).

Voters' desire for change rippled through the nation. In California voters sent 2 women to the Senate and elected the first person of Korean heritage—Jay C. Kim—to serve in Congress. In Colorado Ben Nighthorse Campbell became the first Native American in the Senate. In Illinois Carol Moseley Braun became the first African American woman to hold a Senate seat. Across the country 14 more African Americans, 9 more Hispanics, and 23 more women won seats in Congress. These historic changes made Congress a more representative body than ever before.

Health-Care Reform
Attempts to Make Health Care Accessible to All

As Inauguration Day approached, Clinton and his advisers met in Little Rock, Arkansas, to select members of the new administration. He held a nationally televised economic summit aimed at developing a consensus on the direction of economic policy for the next four years.

Out of that meeting came a surprising and dramatic call for health-care reform. In an impassioned, table-pounding speech, President Clinton asserted that the cost of health care was "going to bankrupt the country."

Health-Care Issues

There could be no question that medical costs were rising faster than any other segment of the economy. By 1993 nearly 14 percent of the gross domestic product—$2.7 billion a day—was spent on health care. Costs for doctors, nurses, hospitals, medicines, and a vast array of high-tech equipment were skyrocketing. Just the paperwork alone cost close to $100 billion per year. Meanwhile dissatisfaction with a system that looked at the bottom line rather than at the concerns of the sick seemed to be growing almost as fast as costs.

High costs were only part of the problem. Across the nation an estimated 39 million people had no health insurance. Many claimed they were too rich for Medicaid and too poor to afford private health insurance. About 10 million of the uninsured were children who, without regular medical checkups, risked developing chronic illnesses. Nor did the health-care crisis affect only the uninsured. Millions of others worried about losing coverage. If they lost their jobs—and many did during the recession—they lost their health insurance. What the public wanted, the Clinton administration thought, was security. People wanted assurance that they would have health care when they needed it.

Reform Plans

Within days of his inauguration, Clinton established a task force on health care. The huge 500-member group, chaired by Hillary Rodham Clinton, met in secret to hammer out proposals that would both reduce health-

---

GALLERY OF PRESIDENTS

William Jefferson Clinton

1993–

© M. REINSTEIN/FPG INTERNATIONAL

"America has called upon me to be our next president. But our forebears call on all of us at this moment to honor their efforts, their sacrifices, their ideals, and their lives, by working hard and working together to improve this good and great nation. . . . They call on us to take our dreams and our hopes, and make them real. Thank you, and God bless America."

Address to media, November 4, 1992

BACKGROUND
▸ Born 1946
▸ Elected attorney general of Arkansas 1976
▸ Elected governor of Arkansas 1978, 1982, 1984, 1986, 1990

ACHIEVEMENTS IN OFFICE
▸ Family Leave Bill (1993)
▸ Brady Bill (1993)
▸ Crime Bill (1993)
▸ NAFTA (1993)

Meeting Special Needs

Limited English Proficiency To help students whose first language is not English, have them examine the map on page 893. Let them identify what each color on the map stands for. Then have them explain how many votes each candidate received. What regions of the country voted for Clinton? What regions voted for Bush? You may want to have students listen to the Chapter 26 Audiocassettes for Section 1. The audiocassettes are also available in Spanish. **LEP**

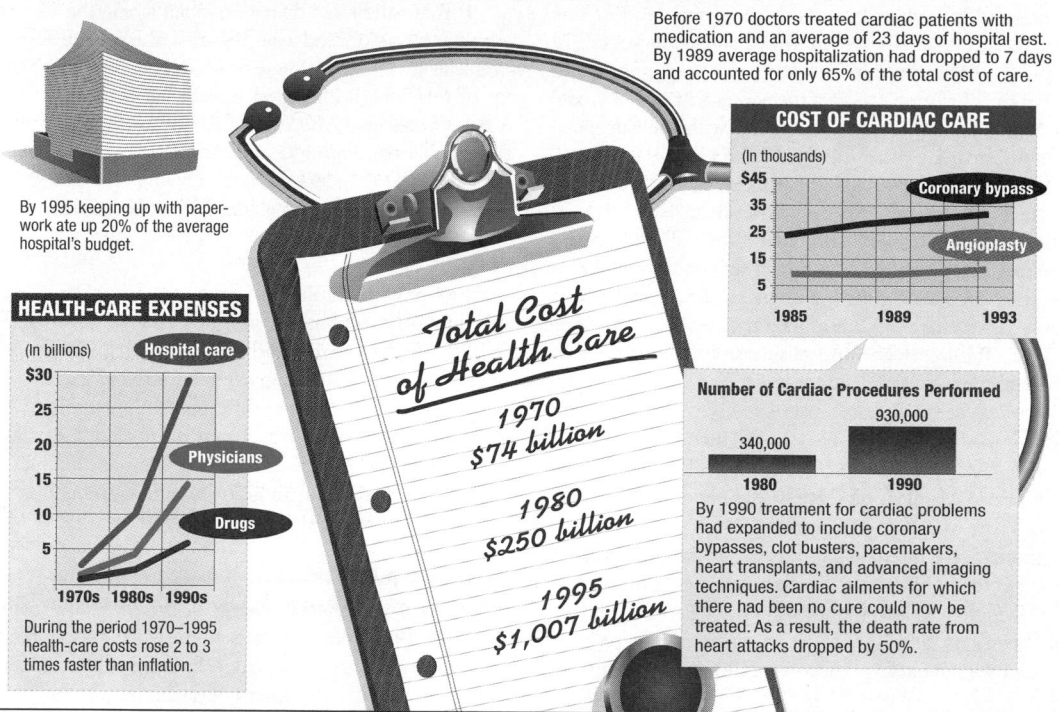

THE RISING COST OF HEALTH CARE

The total cost of health care has risen dramatically in the United States. In 1972 the average American's health-care costs were $387 per year. By 1992 that number had risen almost 10 times to $3,098. Contributing reasons for this rise include (1) an exploding bureaucracy of regulators and insurers and the subsequent expansion of hospital billing departments; (2) rising hospital costs and doctors' fees; and (3) new technology, drugs, and medical procedures.

Before 1970 doctors treated cardiac patients with medication and an average of 23 days of hospital rest. By 1989 average hospitalization had dropped to 7 days and accounted for only 65% of the total cost of care.

By 1995 keeping up with paper-work ate up 20% of the average hospital's budget.

COST OF CARDIAC CARE
(In thousands)

Coronary bypass

Angioplasty

1985   1989   1993

HEALTH-CARE EXPENSES
(In billions)

Hospital care

Physicians

Drugs

1970s   1980s   1990s

During the period 1970–1995 health-care costs rose 2 to 3 times faster than inflation.

Total Cost of Health Care

1970
$74 billion

1980
$250 billion

1995
$1,007 billion

Number of Cardiac Procedures Performed

340,000   930,000

1980   1990

By 1990 treatment for cardiac problems had expanded to include coronary bypasses, clot busters, pacemakers, heart transplants, and advanced imaging techniques. Cardiac ailments for which there had been no cure could now be treated. As a result, the death rate from heart attacks dropped by 50%.

Along with huge increases in the cost of health care in recent years, attributable to advances in technology and bureaucratic red tape, come benefits such as lower death rates. *What happened to Clinton's health-care reform bill?*

care costs and guarantee **universal coverage,** or health insurance for all. It was a complex job. The administration wanted to build on the existing principle of employer-provided health insurance, making it mandatory instead of voluntary, and to put more discipline into health costs by cutting out waste and fraud. All of this was to be accomplished without new taxes, with a minimal increase in costs to employers or people already insured, and without any reduction of medical services.

After months of hearings, public debate, and discussions, the Clinton administration submitted a health-care reform bill to Congress on October 27, 1993. It was 1,342 pages long. Few people understood it all. Lobbying surrounding the measure was intense. Many groups, including the American Medical Association, pharmaceutical companies, insurers, and business associations, spent millions of dollars on advertisements aimed at raising doubts about the plan. They claimed the plan was expensive and would result in rationed care. Meanwhile

both Democrats and Republicans introduced competing and generally more modest proposals.

The debate seesawed back and forth for almost a year, with no single plan gaining enough support to pass. Finally in August 1994, the Senate recessed without bringing a health-care bill to the floor. Most involved felt that reform on the scale imagined by Clinton was not possible at the time.

International Concerns
Post-Cold War Policies

Even as the nation struggled with domestic issues, international matters created divisions. Although the issues varied widely, the common concern for American policy makers was how to define the role of the United States now that it was the only remaining superpower.

SECTION ONE   **895**

Portfolio Project

Canada's Health-Care System Ask students to research Canada's health-care system. Suggest that they find out how the system works, what coverage it provides, and how it is paid for. Have students give their ideas on whether or not Canada's system would work in the United States. Students can file their reports in their portfolios.

Global Connection

In 1993 the name for the economic agreement between 12 European nations was changed from the European Community to the European Union (EU). In 1994 the EU expanded its membership to include 16 nations, accepting Austria, Finland, Norway, and Sweden. Six other nations—Poland, Slovakia, the Czech Republic, Hungary, Romania, and Bulgaria—have been invited to apply for membership. The European Central Bank (which hopes to issue a single European currency) is located in Frankfurt, Germany. Europol (an international police force) is located in The Hague. The European environmental agency will be in Copenhagen. The trademark office and health and safety office will be in Madrid. London became the home of the Medicine Evaluation Agency.

Independent Practice

L2 Have students do research to find out about the most recent developments in the Balkans. Ask them to discuss their results. List students' findings on the chalkboard to refer to as they read this section.

✏ Have students complete the Chapter 26, Section 1 Vocabulary and Guided Reading Activity. (Also in Spanish.) **LEP**

✏ Have students complete the Chapter 26 Cooperative Learning Activity.

VISUAL INSTRUCTION

Civil War in Bosnia Before its civil war, Bosnia had good roads linking Croatia and Serbia, but Serbian forces destroyed the bridges on these roads during the war. Sarajevo and Mostar have airports, but during the war there were no commercial flights landing and taking off from these airports. In June 1992, the United Nations reopened the airport in Sarajevo to planes carrying food and medicine to Bosnia's people.

Answer: *The Serb minority attacked the Muslim-dominated government in Bosnia-Herzegovina.*

North American Free Trade Agreement

One of the first foreign policy issues to confront the Clinton administration involved trade with Canada and Mexico. Under President Bush the United States had signed the North American Free Trade Agreement (NAFTA), which called for the gradual elimination of tariffs and trade barriers among the three nations. The goal was to make these countries a single market of 370 million people producing and consuming goods and services. The hope was that the agreement would create an entity that would be competitive with the European Union (formerly called the European Community).

In 1993 both Canada and Mexico ratified the treaty. In the United States, however, proponents faced opposition from labor unions and environmentalists. Business groups praised the treaty, saying it would create jobs, lower the cost of goods, and make the United States more competitive. Labor argued that workers would be hurt by the treaty because businesses would move jobs to Mexico where wages were lower. With no export duties to pay, Mexican businesses could send their products back into the United States without incurring any additional costs. Farmers also feared NAFTA, saying that low-priced Mexican produce would undercut American goods. Environmentalists joined the fray with their contention that United States businesses would move to Mexico to avoid strict antipollution laws at home.

President Clinton lobbied hard for Senate approval of the treaty and agreed to many compromises that made the final package more appealing to its opponents.

In the end the treaty won support from both Democrats and Republicans and passed both houses of Congress with comfortable majorities. Most provisions of the treaty were due to be phased in over 15 years.

Balkan Crisis

Perhaps the most difficult conflict facing the Clinton administration abroad was the civil war in the former Yugoslavia. The one-time Communist nation was made up of 6 republics inhabited mostly by 3 major groups: Serbs, Croats, and Muslims. In the early 1990s several of the republics, including Croatia and Bosnia-Herzegovina, declared their independence, leaving the Yugoslav government—and its army—in the hands of Serbs.

Croatia

Fighting first broke out in Croatia, where the Croatian majority established an independent government in 1991. Minority Serbs, fearing domination by the Croats, seized control with backing from the Serbs of Yugoslavia. After 6 months of brutal fighting, NATO nations declared an embargo on arms shipments to all of the Balkan republics, and the UN sent peacekeepers to the area to monitor a cease-fire. Although sporadic fighting continued, Croatia remained generally quiet for several years.

Bosnia-Herzegovina

A similar conflict flared up in Bosnia-Herzegovina. There the Serb minority attacked the Muslim-dominated government. As in Croatia, Yugoslav arms supported Serb forces, and the outgunned Muslims were forced to call on the international community for help. In 1992 the UN responded by delivering bread and medical supplies to victims of the fighting. This did nothing to end the conflict, however. Night after night terrifying images from the besieged capital, Sarajevo, appeared on the news: women in babushkas dodging gunfire as they filled water containers at the public well, children hit by snipers while playing, wounded soldiers treated in makeshift hospitals, old people without heat or food trying to survive the winter. Then the images grew more horrifying, and a new term entered the language: *ethnic cleansing*. Word began to reach the West that Bosnian Serbs were killing thousands of Bosnian Muslims in a manner that evoked

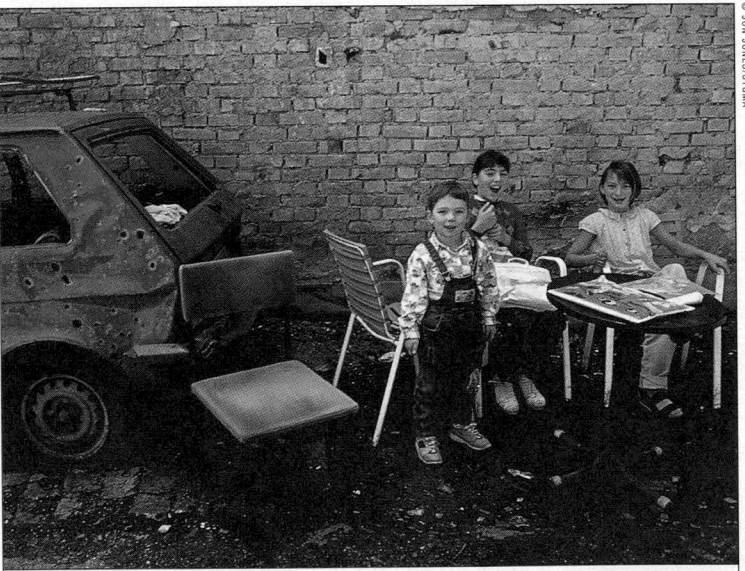

Civil War in Bosnia Children play beside a bullet-ridden car in the streets of Sarajevo. *What caused the fighting in Bosnia-Herzegovina?*

Extending the Content

The Balkan Crisis Bosnia-Herzegovina has always been a potential site for conflict because of the cultural and religious differences between its groups of people. In the late 1980s, relations between the groups steadily worsened, especially between Serbs and non-Serbs. In 1991 most Croats and Muslims voted for independence for Bosnia-Herzegovina. Most Serbs opposed independence and began a war against non-Serbs. The Serbs sought to remove all non-Serbs from the Bosnian territories they claimed. In 1992, the UN imposed an oil and trade embargo in an attempt to stop the war. During the war, thousands of people were killed. Hundreds of thousands were forced from their homes.

memories of Adolf Hitler's death camps. In 1993 the UN stepped up its involvement, setting up safe areas to protect Muslim civilians.

Debate Over an Arms Embargo

In 1995 these safe areas began to fall. The Serb military first overran Srebrenica and then Zepa, setting off an intense policy debate in Washington. At issue was whether to lift the arms embargo and encourage the Muslims to fight back. Congress, in a move spearheaded by Senator Robert Dole of Kansas, passed a resolution to abolish the embargo. To protect UN troops from being caught in the crossfire, however, the resolution would not take effect until all UN troops were out of the area. Dole reasoned that "the principle at the heart of this debate is simple: giving a small, war-torn country the right to self-defense against the most brutal and genocidal aggression on the European continent since the Second World War." Whether the United States finally leads the international community to reverse the embargo will have significant implications, not only for Bosnia, but for America's place in the world.

President Clinton, who had favored the repeal of the arms embargo as a presidential candidate, now spoke against repeal. It would, he said, cause a serious breach between the United States and its NATO allies, especially Great Britain and France. Furthermore it would certainly result in intensified fighting that could lead to wider conflict. "In short," he concluded, "unilateral lift means unilateral American responsibility." His plan was to work with the allies in protecting the safe areas, ensuring supply routes, and encouraging a settlement. NATO, he said, would contribute to air strikes aimed at bringing about these ends. On this issue Clinton saw the United States not as a leader of the NATO alliance but as a cooperating partner. While the two sides disagreed over how to proceed, both were of one mind in their reluctance to commit ground troops.

THE BALKANS, 1991–1995

Yugoslavia population groups in 1992 (before war)
- 4% Others
- 2% Hungarians
- 3% Montenegrins
- 6% Macedonians
- 8% Albanians
- 8% Slovenes
- 10% Muslims
- 21% Croats
- 38% Serbs

Legend:
- Limit of Serb control, November 1992
- Limit of Serb control, October 1995
- Migration of Serbs from Croatia
- ■ UN 'safe zone'
- ★ Capital city

0   50   100 mi.
0   50   100 km
Conic projection

Besides Serbs, Croats, and Muslims, Yugoslavia was also home to Slovenes, Albanians, Macedonians, Montenegrins, and Hungarians in 1992. *What two safe areas were overrun by Serbs in 1995?*

New Leadership

By midsummer 1995 the United States was beginning to see that it must take the lead in the search for peace in the Balkans. After nearly 3 years of following the lead of the Europeans, Clinton was ready for a new initiative. On August 7, he approved a plan for Bosnia that offered rewards to the combatants if they signed a peace accord and threatened punishments for all sides if they chose to fight on. Bosnia then signed a United Nations-sponsored peace treaty.

Invasion of Haiti

The Caribbean nation of Haiti, which shares an island with the Dominican Republic, has had a turbulent history of instability and repression. In one of the first democratic elections ever held there, people chose Jean Bertrand Aristide as their president. The former priest and champion of the poor was greeted as a herald of decency and fair play.

His administration did not last long, however. He was soon overthrown by a military junta and fled to the

---

MAP STUDY

Bosnia-Herzegovina consists of two regions: the wooded, mountainous northern region, and the flat southern farmland. Bosnia-Herzegovina has exceptionally cold and snowy winters. Before the war, many people visited the region for its excellent ski slopes.

Answer: *Srebrenica and Zepa*

FYI

The Bosnian Government From 1945 to 1990, Communists held power in all of Yugoslavia, including Bosnia. In 1990, in Bosnia's first free elections since the Communists took over, non-Communists gained a majority of seats in the government. A 7-member collective presidency heads Bosnia. It consists of 2 Croats, 2 Bosnian Muslims, 2 Serbs, and 1 other person. Voters elect these 7 members. The members then elect a president.

Cultural Perspectives

Bosnia Forty-four percent of the people in Bosnia-Herzegovina are Muslims, 32 percent are Serbs, and 17 percent are Croats. Most people speak Serbo-Croatian. Serbs, however, write the language with the Cyrillic alphabet (the alphabet used to write Russian), while Muslims and Croats use the Roman alphabet. Bosnian Muslims practice the Islamic faith, while Croats practice the Roman Catholic faith, and Serbs practice the Serbian Orthodox faith. Organize the class into 3 groups, assigning each group 1 of these 3 cultures and societies to investigate further. Groups will want to present their findings to the class, explaining their culture's view of the civil war and how the culture and values of each group have affected that group's attitudes and responses to the war.

ASSESS

Meeting Lesson Objectives

Each section objective is tested by the section review question(s) that follows it in parentheses.

1. Explain the 1992 presidential campaign and the election results. (2, 5)
2. Describe the successful and unsuccessful legislation of the Clinton administration. (1, 2, 5)
3. Explain the reasons behind the Balkan crisis and the responses to the crisis worldwide. (3, 4)

United States. The international community responded to the coup by imposing economic sanctions. Soon the already poor nation was in desperate shape. Faced with a repressive and often brutal government and confronted by severe food shortages, hordes of Haitians took to the sea in makeshift boats, heading for what they hoped was freedom and economic security in the United States.

The refugees' departure put the United States in a difficult position. It did not want to encourage people to undertake a dangerous trip in which many might drown, and it did not want to encourage mass illegal immigration. On the other hand in a land that preached the virtues of democracy and freedom, Americans had a hard time turning away such desperate people.

President Clinton was soon caught up in the dilemma. During his campaign, he chastised the Bush administration for refusing to admit Haitian refugees into the United States. Upon taking office, however, fearing a huge migration, Clinton continued the Bush policy. Political pressures against this stand mounted, and finally Clinton offered the refugees a safe haven at the Guantánamo Bay Naval Base in Cuba. This policy too was flawed. No one anticipated the huge numbers who poured out of Haiti: as many as 2,000 to 3,000 people per day. The only recourse, many felt, was for the United States military to invade Haiti and return Aristide as president.

In the fall of 1994, Clinton sent troops to the nation. Aristide was returned to power, and for a time troops maintained order. In April of the next year, at Haiti's National Palace, Clinton turned over the United States's peacekeeping role to the United Nations. Despite earlier doubts many Americans considered the Haitian policy a success. Only 1 United States soldier had died, and the flow of refugees was stopped.

Ups and Downs
Hits and Misses

From the beginning Clinton's management of domestic as well as foreign policy seemed to bump along from crisis to crisis. This erratic style was reflected in wild swings in his popular standing. A mere 2 days after his inauguration, television viewers were told that "the Clinton White House looked like the Not-Ready-for-Prime-Time Players." Yet by the end of 1993, with the economy recovering from the

recession and unemployment at its lowest point since 1991, a national poll showed that 63 percent of those surveyed thought Clinton was a President who could get things done.

The Budget

Clinton's struggle to pass his budget was a cliffhanger. The President entered office intending to reverse Reaganomics and redirect the nation's resources from consumption to investment in transportation, schools, and industry. He proposed a "stimulus package" aimed at revitalizing industry and creating jobs throughout the nation. Cutbacks in wasteful or unnecessary federal programs, a modest reduction in defense spending, and some higher taxes and fees, primarily on the most affluent 1 percent of taxpayers, would offset these spending increases.

Two major obstacles lay in the way. One was the deficit, which in the public's mind loomed as a major threat to the nation's economic well-being. The other was entitlement programs, such as Social Security, Medicare, and veterans' benefits. By 1992 these programs consumed almost half of the budget and were rising. The President's budget made only minor cuts in entitlements.

The Clinton economic plan aimed to reduce federal deficits through fiscal 1998 by $496 billion. Many felt the budget was not bold enough—though it included cuts in 150 programs, it eliminated only 6. One of these was a subsidy for beekeepers that Clinton often referred to in speeches. As it turned out, even the beekeepers were spared.

Boat People Haitian refugees crowd a small boat. Boats like this frequently capsized when the seas became rough. *What conditions in Haiti caused people to flee that country?*

898   CHAPTER 26   A CHANGING NATION IN A CHANGING WORLD

Critical Thinking

Synthesizing Information Encourage interested students to research the issues surrounding the arrival by boat of thousands of Haitians to the United States in the early 1990s. Students will want to examine why the Haitians fled their country and what happened to them on their return. What do students think are the obligations of the United States concerning people who enter the country illegally in search of a better life, better economic conditions, or freedom from persecution? Can the United States open its doors to all such people? What policies do students think the United States should follow in these matters? Students should support their arguments with facts.

The Brady Bill President Clinton shakes hands with James Brady, sponsor of the Brady Bill, which placed a waiting period on handgun purchases. *When was the Brady Bill passed?*

sions that would put more police on the streets, build prisons, add new applications of the death penalty, and ban 19 assault weapons. It also included money for crime prevention, such as creating midnight basketball leagues that allowed people to participate in sports programs at night. The bill had opponents on both sides. Conservative Republicans and Democrats, under pressure from the National Rifle Association, opposed the weapons ban and argued that the bill spent too much on crime prevention. The Black Caucus opposed an increased use of the death penalty. Many felt provisions for police and prisons were too expensive. In the end, however, few wanted to vote against crime legislation, and the bill passed.

A Weakened President

Questions about Whitewater (a complicated and questionable real estate deal that Clinton was involved in as governor of Arkansas) and criticism for erratic leadership during the first half of his term fed voter discontent. Clinton's appearing on a Monday night football broadcast, where he talked foreign policy in his jogging clothes, and his performing on MTV may have made him one of the nation's most accessible Presidents. At the same time, he may have risked losing the authority that the Executive Office of President conveys. As the 1994 midterm elections approached, Republicans positioned themselves to take advantage of Clinton's vulnerability.

After many amendments the final budget squeaked through Congress without a single vote of support from Republicans. Historians noted this was the first time that a budget plan had ever won in Congress without support from the minority party. While Clinton claimed the bill's passage as a victory, few saw it as sweeping reform. Many feared that the timid performance by Congress and the President only added to the frustration of voters, who wanted dramatic cuts and tax reductions.

Legislative Successes

The first bill on the Clinton agenda to pass Congress gave workers up to 12 weeks per year of unpaid **family leave** for the birth or adoption of a child or the illness of a family member. The Family Leave Bill had come up twice during Bush's administration, and twice Bush vetoed it. Now Clinton could claim a solid victory.

Another piece of legislation was the Brady Bill, named after President Reagan's press secretary, who was permanently injured as a result of a 1981 assassination attempt on Reagan. The Brady Bill required a waiting period for the purchase of handguns to allow police time to check criminal records. Vigorously opposed by the National Rifle Association (NRA), the bill nonetheless gained support across the nation as fear grew about crimes committed with guns. In 1993, despite a filibuster attempt by a group of Senate Republicans, the bill was finally passed. Clinton signed it into law in November.

Gun control also played a major role in the debate over a third piece of legislation that the Clinton administration fought hard to win, the **crime bill.** This bill had provi-

SECTION REVIEW

Vocabulary

1. Define: universal coverage, family leave, crime bill.

Checking Facts

2. What were the most important issues of the 1992 presidential campaign?

3. Summarize the events that occurred during the Balkan crisis.

Critical Thinking

Predicting Consequences

4. Explain the reasons behind the argument to lift the arms embargo on the Muslims in the Balkans. Why was President Clinton opposed to lifting the arms embargo? What are the ramifications of either solution?

Linking Across Time

5. In the 1992 election, nearly 1 out of every 4 members of Congress was newly elected. How do the reasons behind this voter dissatisfaction compare with the voter dissatisfaction following the end of World War II?

VISUAL INSTRUCTION

The Brady Bill Many police departments endorsed the Brady Bill because they saw the use of handguns as an increasing threat to public safety.
Answer: *November 1993*

Evaluate

Have students complete the Section Review.

🖿 🖸 Assign the Section 1 Quiz or use the Testmaker to develop a customized quiz. (Also in Spanish.) **LEP**

Reteach

🎧 Have students listen to the Chapter 26, Section 1 Audiocassette. (Also in Spanish.) **LEP**

Enrich

🖿 Have students complete Interpreting Political Cartoons 13, 29.

🖿 Have students complete Supreme Court Case Studies 58, 59, 60, 66.

CLOSE

What did NAFTA do? *(It eliminated tariffs and trade barriers among the United States, Mexico, and Canada.)* What were some of Clinton's successes? *(the Family Leave Bill, the Brady Bill, the crime bill)*

Section 1 Review Answers

1. **universal coverage** (895), **family leave** (899), **crime bill** (899)
2. the economy, health-care costs, drugs and violence, the need for improved education
3. The Serbs seized control of Croatia, and then moved into Bosnia-Herzegovina, where they killed thousands of Bosnian Muslims.

4. Some suggested lifting the arms embargo so the Bosnian Muslims could defend themselves. Clinton was opposed because he felt it would result in intensified fighting. Neither solution committed United States ground troops.
5. In both periods, voters were concerned about the economy and their futures.

Geography: Impact on History

TEACH

Making the Geography Connection

Where to put the nation's garbage has become a critical problem in the United States. Although recycling has become more widespread in recent years, the United States still produces more garbage per capita than any other nation in the world.

Mapping Activity

Use a map to point out places to which New York City ships its garbage. Then have students consider what alternatives there might be to shipping trash to landfills across the nation. *(incinerating, recycling)* What are the disadvantages and advantages of these alternatives? *(Incineration can pollute the air; it's difficult to recycle everything.)*

MAP STUDY

New York ships its trash to 17 different states.

Answer: *Students should list all the states to which the arrows on the map lead; Missourri; Connecticut*

HUMAN/ENVIRONMENT INTERACTION

America's Landfills

A typical American generates 4 pounds of garbage a day. This adds up to about 180 million tons of solid waste each year. Some of the trash is recycled or incinerated, but about 70 to 80 percent of the solid waste is put into sanitary landfills, where it is buried between layers of dirt.

The Need for Landfills

In the early days of the nation, people threw trash wherever they wanted. As cities grew, however, disposing of trash did become a problem. In 1930, New York City became one of the first cities to send its trash to sanitary landfills. Now many communities have municipal landfills to take care of their own waste. Densely populated areas such as New York State, however, have less space available for landfills. They have to ship their garbage out to other areas of the country.

Despite the fact that moving trash from one area of the country to another has created conflict, huge loads of garbage are still sent out daily by truck or by train. The problem came to a head during a 1992 rail strike. Trainloads of East Coast garbage were stranded in the Midwest and people got an eyeful (and noseful) of the trash. Then, as now, no one wants a landfill nearby, but the garbage must go somewhere.

Environmental Impact

Many people are worried that landfills will harm the environment because of problems with surface and groundwater pollution, dangerous gas emissions, and noxious fumes. Landfills work by biodegrading, or breaking down, plants and animal products by bacterial action. This process produces an oozing liquid called leachate, as well as highly flammable methane gas.

New landfills are being built to be more environmentally sound. The landfill site is lined with clay and plastic to prevent leakage, and the methane gas is piped out and used as a fuel.

Reclaiming the Land

When landfills are full, they are covered over with earth, and the land is "reclaimed." Newark and JFK International Airports were

WHERE NEW YORK'S TRASH GOES

100,000 tons (half of what New York City throws out weekly) goes to Staten Island's Fresh Kills landfill, the largest in the world.

Movement of garbage

0   200   400 mi.

0   200   400 km
Albers Equal-Area projection

New York City ships 200,000 tons of garbage to landfills each week. *Where else does New York City ship its garbage? What is the most distant state to which New York City ships its garbage? The closest?*

Geographic Themes

Human/Environment Interaction As wonderful as the idea of recycling trash is, it is also creating new problems. New York, for example, expects to recycle 1 million tons a year, but it is now facing a burgeoning problem: how to process and market the resulting tons of paper, glass, metal, and plastic. If it fails to come up with a solution, the city may be forced to dump the waste at the Fresh Kills landfill—which is precisely what the recycling program was created to avoid. Private companies sort and resell the recycled items, but there is no assurance that enough private processors will be found to absorb the huge amount of recycled items that New York has to look forward to. Have students discuss how they think recycling might work. Ask what other alternatives to waste disposal they can think of.

© PHILIP JON BAILEY/STOCK BOSTON

Landfills This landfill in Massachusetts is a repository for trash from all over the state. The largest landfill in the world is Fresh Kills in New York. It receives 17,000 tons of garbage each day. The landfill covers 3,000 acres and takes up 2.4 billion cubic feet of space. Contents of the landfill include: paper (50%), miscellaneous (20%), organic (13%), metal (6%), glass (1%), and plastic (less than 1%). *When was Fresh Kills built? Where was it built?*

built on top of landfills. Hospitals, golf courses, and community parks have all been built on top of land that has been reclaimed.

Fresh Kills landfill in New York is the largest in the world. As parts of it become full, they are covered over with earth. Trees and wildflowers are then planted to help them revert back to their natural state. Fresh Kills landfill, however, was begun in 1948 on top of a salt marsh

before people were environmentally conscious. Although it was eventually cleaned up, for many years it leaked more than a million gallons of leachate (waste percolated into a liquid state) into the water.

Long-range Plans

How will the United States deal with its waste problems? Other methods of disposal include incineration, waste-to-energy programs,

and recycling. These methods account for a relatively small percentage of waste disposal, however. The use of sanitary landfills puts an ever-increasing burden on rural and less heavily populated areas, whose residents often resent their urban neighbors. The best answer may be to decrease the amount of solid waste being generated and by reusing and recycling goods.

MAKING THE GEOGRAPHIC CONNECTION

1. What are some of the problems that landfills create for the environment? How are these problems being solved today? How does land reclamation fit into these solutions?

2. What methods of waste disposal other than landfills are being used today? Which method is used most often? What are some solutions currently being considered to alleviate the problem?

3. **Human/Environment Interaction** What impact do you think the recycling of paper, plastic, metal, and glass could have on future landfills?

Making the Geographic Connection Answers

1. There are problems with surface and ground-water pollution, dangerous gas emissions, and noxious fumes. Now landfills are lined with clay and plastic to prevent leakage. Methane gas is piped out to be used as a fuel. Reclaiming land-fills to use as parks or as constructions sites is a creative solution to the problem of what to do with ugly landfills.

2. Other methods of waste disposal are incineration, waste-to-energy programs, and recycling. Landfills, however, are the most common method of waste disposal. Recycling and solid waste reduction are solutions to the waste disposal problem being considered today.

3. The landfills will not be so full, especially of nonbiodegradable items.

CLOSE

Ask: Why do we need land-fills? *(Each American generates 4 pounds of trash per day. The trash needs to go somewhere, and landfills, especially if they are environmentally sound, are an effective solution to this waste problem.)* What happens to landfills when they are full? *(They are covered with earth, and the land is reclaimed.)*

Notes

FOCUS

Section Objectives

1. Explain the factors that led the Republicans to sweep the 1994 midterm elections.
2. List important figures in the 104th Congress and their roles.
3. Discuss the goals of the Contract With America.
4. Explain why Congress has such a difficult time passing a balanced budget.

Bellringer Activity

While taking attendance at the beginning of the class period, display **Section Focus Transparency 84,** and have students answer the questions. (Or use the blackline master.)

VISUAL INSTRUCTION

The Contract With America
On September 27, 1994, House Minority Whip Newt Gingrich of Georgia leads a rally where Republican Congressional candidates pledge a "Contract With America."

Ask: For how long had the Democrats controlled the House in 1994? *(40 years)*

SECTION 2

The New Conservatism

SEPTEMBER 27, 1994: REPUBLICANS UNVEIL CONTRACT WITH AMERICA

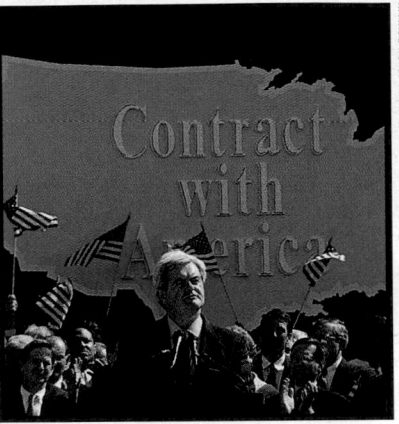

The Contract With America
Newt Gingrich calls for a Contract With America that cuts taxes, sets term limits, and creates a balanced budget amendment.

IT WAS AN UNUSUALLY WARM DAY IN WASHINGTON AS MORE THAN 300 REPUBLICAN CANDIDATES FOR THE UNITED STATES HOUSE OF REPRESENTATIVES STOOD ON THE WEST FRONT OF THE CAPITOL. Led by Representative Newt Gingrich of Georgia, the group was launching an all-out drive to gain a majority in the House, which had been controlled by the Democratic party for 40 years. This public signing of a document they called the Republican Contract With America was the kick-off event of the campaign.

One by one, the candidates stepped forward to sign the contract, which contained 11 categories that listed 34 pieces of legislation they promised to try to pass within the first 100 days of the 104th Congress. It was, in the words of Republican National Committee member Dan Lungren, an attempt to "nationalize this election." "Incumbent members of Congress," he continued, "have so many advantages in terms of constituent services and local issues, the only way you can turn a sufficient number of them out is to base the campaign on overarching national issues."

The Contract With America proclaimed that government had become "too big, too intrusive, and too easy with the public's money." It said that a new Republican majority would "be the beginning of a Congress that respects the values and shares the faith of the American family." To achieve their goals, the contract called for a carefully honed and tested list of items that had the approval of a majority of voters: tax cuts, reduced spending on everything but Social Security and defense, a balanced budget amendment to the Constitution, term limits for members of Congress. Divisive issues, such as abortion rights and gun control, received no mention in the contract.

AS YOU READ

Vocabulary
▶ bipartisan coalition
▶ unfunded mandate
▶ pork barrel legislation

Think About . . .
▶ factors that led to the Republican sweep of the 1994 midterm elections.
▶ the important figures in the 104th Congress and their roles.
▶ the goals of the Contract With America.
▶ why Congress has such a difficult time passing a balanced budget.

Section 2 Resources

REPRODUCIBLE RESOURCES
- Lesson Plan 26-2
- Vocabulary and Guided Reading Activity 26-2
- Section 2 Quiz
- Political Cartoons 35–39
- Supreme Court Case 65
- Unit 10 Great Debate

MULTIMEDIA RESOURCES
- Section Focus Transparency 84
- Landmark Documents in American History
- Chapter 26 Digest Audiocassette
- Testmaker
- Student Self-Test: A Software Review

A Desire For Change **People vote in Iowa, where a Republican governor and an all-Republican House were elected in November 1994.** *How big a victory did Republicans garner nationwide?*

The Midterm Election

A Desire for Change

Early in the campaign, many Democrats—including President Clinton—were gleeful. They felt that the United States was once again number one in productivity, the economy was growing, employment was rising, inflation was low, and the deficit was shrinking.

What many people failed to realize, however, was that even if people had jobs, those jobs were often lower-paying than their previous ones and offered fewer benefits. Workers saw friends and neighbors get laid off and then forced to take temporary or part-time jobs. Democrats seriously underestimated the extent to which this middle-class stagnation fed a hunger for change, leading voters into the Republican camp. Many blamed welfare cheats and high taxes for their failure to get ahead.

Election Results

When the results of exit polls began to come in on November 8, 1994, pollsters did not believe what they showed. Statisticians checked the figures again, but there was no mistake. Republicans had garnered the biggest midterm victory of the century, overthrowing 40 years of Democratic dominance in Congress.

Before the election, Democrats had a 56 to 44 majority in the Senate; after the votes were counted, that majority had been reversed to favor the Republicans 52 to 48. In the House the election of 53 new Republicans, who now controlled that body by a margin of 230 to 204, shattered the old Democratic majority of 256 to 178. As if to add insult to injury, some Democrats, including Senator Richard Shelby of Alabama, switched their party affiliation to the Republican side.

Not one incumbent Republican senator, representative, or governor lost a race, but many leading Democrats, including House Speaker Tom Foley of Washington State, did. Foley's defeat was the first for a sitting speaker since before the Civil War. The Republican sweep extended to the state level, where the GOP captured 11 new governorships and 9 new state legislatures. Many called the election results a revolution.

Looking for Reasons

Few were surprised that the Republicans gained congressional seats in 1994 because it is usual for the incumbent party to experience some setbacks in midterm elections. What was astonishing was the breadth and scope of the victory. Much of it, of course, could be attributed to voter frustration with the failure of the Clinton administration and the Democratic Congress to make the changes they had promised. As one former

SECTION TWO **903**

Cooperative Learning

Voting Blocs During the 1970s, 1980s, and 1990s, about 55 percent of all qualified voters voted in presidential elections. More women voted than men, and there were more voters in the 55-to-75 age range than in any other age group. Organize the class into cooperative groups, and have them research why some groups of people vote more than others. How does being from a group that is likely to vote affect a person's clout with politicians (for example, are politicians careful not to anger elderly voters because they vote in such large numbers?) Students will want to divide up the work fairly and decide on a method of presentation. They may also want to create charts to show differences in voting patterns by region, age, education level, income, and so on.

Guided Practice

L1 **Discuss** Review with students some of the issues that are important to Americans. How do the politicians who are elected reflect the importance of these issues? *(Politicians who say they will solve problems that people are concerned about are more likely to be elected than politicians who focus on issues that people do not care about very much.)*

VISUAL INSTRUCTION

A Desire for Change Voters in 1994 voted Republican because they were dissatisfied with incumbents and Washington insiders. One senior White House official said of the election, "What the people have said is, 'We're going to make you folks [the Republicans] co-CEOs. We know you don't like [the Democrats]. But if you don't get together and do the job, we may just fire both of you.'"

Answer: *the biggest midterm victory of the century*

Facts on File

Landmark Documents in American History Have students review "Contract With America, 1994" and "First Speech as Speaker, Newt Gingrich, 1995" and write a paragraph about the intent of one of the documents.

Independent Practice

L2 **Election Results**
Have students find information similar to that provided on the chart on this page pertaining to another election. Students may want to graphically organize their information and then share their findings with the class.

📁 Have students complete the Chapter 26, Section 2 Vocabulary and Guided Reading Activity. (Also in Spanish.) **LEP**

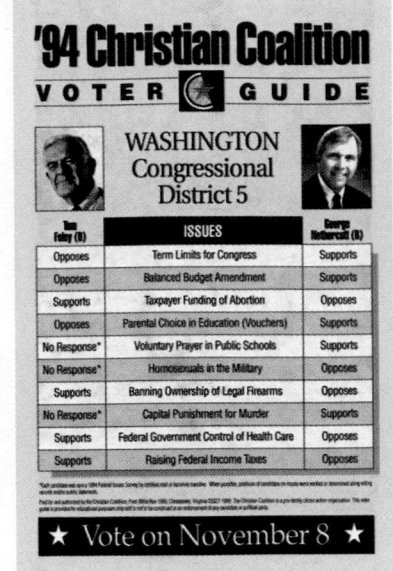

COURTESY OF CHRISTIAN COALITION

Voter Guide Lists such as this one published by the Christian Coalition compared candidates' records. *How much did the Coalition spend distributing such guides?*

While these groups did not endorse any candidates, they used a strategy termed voter education to publish voter guides that compared candidates' positions on issues important to their organization. The Christian Coalition distributed a list in Tom Foley's district in Washington State, for example, that included candidates' voting records on such issues as term limits for Congress, a balanced budget amendment, taxpayer funding for abortion, and voluntary prayer in public schools. After the election, the coalition claimed to have spent $2 million distributing 33 million voter guides to 60,000 churches nationwide.

Another factor in the Republican sweep may have been a white male backlash against one of the tenets of the Clinton agenda. Two years earlier Bill Clinton had told voters he would create a multicultural administration staffed by women and men who "looked like America." The newly elected representatives reflected voter dissatisfaction with that vision of the nation. A profile of the average Republican voter showed him to be a white, male, high school or college graduate who was a talk radio listener and a gun owner. He might also have

Democrat who voted Republican said, "We always vote for change and we never get it."

There were other factors at work as well. Some observers credited the win to the way the Republicans used new methods of communication that completely bypassed such traditional media as newspapers and television. To keep congressional candidates around the country informed of the issues and abreast of new ideas, Newt Gingrich and his political operation sent out 700,000 videotapes preceding the 1994 election. Conservative Republicans funded a cable TV network called National Empowerment Television that carried their message to millions of viewers. The boom in talk radio shows, hosted by conservatives such as Rush Limbaugh, allowed the public to listen in on around-the-clock discussions of issues important to the right wing of the party. Computer networks, with more than 30 million subscribers, offered yet another channel of communication. In addition Gingrich, as part of his strategy of nationalizing the election, used C-Span, the cable television network that featured gavel-to-gavel coverage of Congress, to promote the party message.

The Effect of Conservative Groups

Other powerful influences in the 1994 election were the political activities of conservative groups such as the Christian Coalition and Americans for Term Limits.

How Americans Voted in 1994

Exit polls: How Americans voted in the race for the House	Republican	Democratic
All	51%	49%
Males	57%	43%
Females	46%	54%
Whites	58%	42%
African Americans	8%	92%
Non-high school graduates	40%	60%
High school graduates	52%	48%
College graduates	55%	45%
Postgraduate study	42%	58%
Talk radio listeners	64%	36%
Gun owners	69%	31%
Crime victims	53%	47%
Contributors to Perot's United We Stand	69%	31%
Do you want the President and the Congress to be of the same party?		
Yes		54%
No		34%

The Republicans convinced most categories of voters to vote for their party. *Which groups voted most heavily Democratic? Republican?*

Meeting Special Needs

Reading Disability To help students with reading comprehension difficulties, list on the chalkboard the important people from this section: Bill Clinton, Newt Gingrich, Bob Dole, and any others you feel are important. Under each name, list ideas and laws that each person supports. Help students to see that because these people support different types of legislation, they may disagree with each other. Then have students read the section (or listen to it on the Chapter 26 Audiocassette) to see how these issues were finally resolved. Add this information to the list on the chalkboard.

contributed to United We Stand America, the organization of presidential candidate Ross Perot, because a majority of Perot's supporters also voted Republican. The Congress these voters elected was largely white and male, suburban or rural, and socially traditional. Many new members were baby boomers between the ages of 32 and 48. If 1992 was the year of the woman in American politics, 1994 might have been called the year of the young white man.

With the retirement of many moderate members of Congress in both parties, the coalition of New Deal Democrats and moderate Republicans that had held sway in American politics since Franklin Delano Roosevelt was President seemed to have collapsed. No one doubted that the Democratic party had been rebuffed. The nation now turned its attention to the new, more conservative legislature to see if Republicans could deliver on their promises any better than their predecessors.

HENG
LIANHE ZAOBAO
SINGAPORE

New Leaders in Congress The Republicans controlled both houses of Congress for the first time in decades. *Who was the new speaker of the House?*

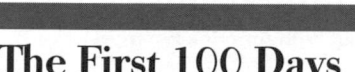

The First 100 Days
Gingrich and Dole Lead Congress

In the days following the election, jubilant Republicans paraded the Contract With America before television cameras and promised to enact its main provisions in the first 100 days of the 104th Congress. So confident were Republicans that they distributed a "citizen's scorecard" on which voters could keep track

of their performance. "Hold your elected officials accountable for the promises they've made!" they said.

A New Leadership Team

New majorities in both houses of Congress meant new leadership at all levels. Not only were the speaker of the House and the majority leader of the Senate Republicans for the first time in decades, but every committee in both houses of Congress—long run by Democrats—now had a Republican chairperson.

In the House

Newt Gingrich of Georgia became the new speaker of the House. Briefly a college professor, the nine-term member of Congress emerged as the most outspoken and

THE FIRST FIVE MONTHS: JANUARY 23, 1995–MAY 22, 1995

January 23, 1995 Congressional Accountability Act is signed.

March 23, 1995 Unfunded Mandate Reform is signed into law.

April 4–5, 1995 House and Senate pass Crimes Against Children Act.

28 other pieces of legislation of the Contract With America pass the House but not the Senate.

January | February | March | April | May

February 6, 1995 Line-Item Veto Act passes House. It passes the Senate on March 23.

March 10, 1995 House passes Common Sense Product Liability and Legal Reform Act. Senate passes the act two months later.

May 22, 1995 Paperwork Reduction Act is signed into law.

SECTION TWO   **905**

VISUAL INSTRUCTION

New Leaders in Congress This cartoon portrays a Republican stampede, although in reality the Republicans' margins of victory in many races were not huge.
Answer: *Newt Gingrich*

 FYI

The Republicans When the Republicans gained control of Congress after the 1994 midterm election, it marked the sixth time in seven elections that the voters had divided the government between the parties.

The Republicans often call their party the GOP (which stands for Grand Old Party). They gave their party this nickname in the 1880s. When the Republican party was first formed in the mid-1800s, its candidates got most of their support from people opposed to slavery. To broaden their support, the party passed legislation that appealed to farmers. During the 1920s, the Republican party became known as the party of prosperity.

CHART STUDY

Ask: Which item on the contract was the first to become law?
Answer: *Congressional Accountability Act*

PORTFOLIO PROJECT

Portfolio Project

The Contract With America Have interested students research the 34 pieces of legislation in the Contract With America, focusing especially on term limits, balancing the budget, health-care reform, and welfare reform. How do today's politicians or political candidates stand on each of these issues? Which of these issues

are still being debated today, and why? How do voters feel about these issues? Then have students summarize their findings and explain their stand on each of these issues and the reasons behind their opinions. Students can file their work in their portfolios.

VISUAL INSTRUCTION

New Senate Leadership Robert Dole has served in the United States Senate since 1969. He also has served as Chairman of the Republican party, was his party's nominee for Vice President in 1976, and was a candidate for President in 1980, 1988, and 1996.

Answer: *early in 1995*

Block Scheduling

☞ Have students complete the Unit 10 Great Debate to enrich their understanding of term limits.

FYI

Dole's Influences
Robert J. Dole (born in 1923) was a star high school basketball player when he was young. He hoped to attend medical school at the University of Kansas on a basketball scholarship, but in 1943 he enlisted in the United States Army and was severely wounded during combat in Italy. Dole returned to the United States weighing only 90 pounds and in a complete body cast. He was hospitalized for three years and decided during this time to pursue a law degree. Dole entered politics in 1950, beginning an illustrious political career.

colorful leader of the party. Many commentators noted the many parallels between his background and that of the President. Both were Southerners of about the same age; both had received deferments during the Vietnam War; and both were very effective politicians. Gingrich had devoted most of his career in the House to breaking the Democratic hold on Congress.

The new second-in-command in the House was also a college professor before entering politics. Majority Leader Richard Armey was first elected to Congress in 1984. He hailed from Flower Mound, Texas, where he developed a reputation as a plain-living conservative. Though he started out as a loner—at one time he even advocated the abolition of Social Security—Armey learned to bring Republicans and Democrats together in **bipartisan coalitions** to work on issues important to him. One of his efforts was aimed at closing military bases around the country, a sensitive political issue because so many civilian jobs were at stake. Armey proposed a commission able to work without congressional interference, and its recommendations led to the closing of many surplus military installations after 1987. In 1994 Armey and his staff wrote most of the Contract With America.

In the Senate

A third member of the Republican leadership to receive increased national attention after the 1994 sweep was new Senate Majority Leader Robert Dole of Kansas. A long-time minority leader, Dole had his roots in the moderate wing of the Republican party where he was known as conservative on economic and defense issues but more liberal on social issues. Along with the newer Republican leadership, for example, he supported easing restrictions on business and cutting capital gains taxes, but he backed regulatory measures favored by Democrats that provided for inspection of meat and drinking water to ensure public safety. Early in 1995 the 71-year-old Dole announced that he would run for President, and polls showed him to be the early leader for the Republican nomination.

New Senate Leadership Robert Dole became Senate majority leader when the Republicans took control of the Senate in 1995. *When did Dole announce that he would run for President of the United States?*

Fulfilling the Promises
A Meeker Contract With America Emerges

The new Congress opened with a bustle of activity. As part of its promise to reduce the size of government, the House eliminated several committees and cut its staff by a third. By the end of their first 100 days in office, members of the Republican-controlled House had passed all of the 34 bills in the Contract With America. Two of these bills—with substantial Democratic support—were then approved by the Senate and signed into law. Five of the bills were passed by both the House and the Senate but not made into law. Twenty-eight other bills were passed by the House but not the Senate. Many questioned whether this flurry of activity resulted in the fundamental change that the newly elected lawmakers had vowed to provide.

The first law Congress passed was the first precept in the Contract With America. It required that all laws that apply to the nation also apply to Congress. This action would bring both houses of Congress into compliance with civil rights and equal employment regulations. The new bill was similar to one that the 103rd Congress had worked out. The sticking point in such legislation had always been the separation of powers: Does the Justice Department or the executive branch police the legisla-

906 CHAPTER 26 A CHANGING NATION IN A CHANGING WORLD

Extending the Content

Unfunded Mandates The Americans with Disabilities Act of 1990 protected people with disabilities from discrimination in employment. It also required that public buildings, trains, and buses be accessible to people with disabilities. This act was an unfunded mandate. No money was given to states or businesses to implement the changes by the deadlines. Many small-business owners complained they couldn't afford to make the extensive changes required by the law. Although this law was not affected by the Contract With America, have students discuss the pros and cons of unfunded mandates.

ture? To resolve this issue, the new law established an Office of Compliance outside the executive branch to see that Congress observed workplace laws.

The second law restricted the federal government's ability to pass **unfunded mandates,** or laws that states or businesses must comply with but for which Congress supplies no money. The Congressional Budget Office estimated that such regulations had cost state and local governments about $10 billion between 1983 and 1990.

The legislation did not eliminate such mandates, however. What it did was make legislators aware of unfunded mandates within a bill, and then have them vote on such mandates separately. There were many exemptions, however. Most unfunded mandates deal with discrimination based on race, color, religion, sex, national origin, age, or disability, and the new law did not affect discrimination laws. Also exempted were bills dealing with constitutional rights such as voting or those relating to Social Security, and bills "necessary to national security."

In other areas the pressures of leadership began to temper campaign promises. After many years out of power, congressional Republicans were not quick to give up the perquisites such power conveys. Gingrich and other Republicans had, for example, long complained that party ratios were stacked against them in Congress. The Rules Committee, which has the vital task of deciding which bills make it to the House floor, had long been weighted in favor of the Democrats by a ratio of 9 to 4. Once Gingrich came to power he was quick to change the ratio—not, however, to make it more fair. The new ratio became 9 to 4 in favor of the Republicans. "That's the way it's always been done," he explained.

Wrestling With Tough Issues
Roadblocks to Term Limits and a Balanced Budget

After the flurry of activity in the House, many elements of the Contract With America stalled in the Senate, where moderate Republicans and Democrats, regarding them as unwise, prevented their passage.

Waste in Government Clinton and Gore stand by reams of federal rules and regulations. The two jumped on the waste-in-government bandwagon by revealing plans to cut, consolidate, and reshape government, saving taxpayers $108 billion by the year 2000. *Why did many elements of the Contract With America stall in the Senate?*

Term Limits

During the 1990s the movement to limit the terms of members of Congress gained momentum, riding the hope that in keeping members from having a lifetime job, Congress would become a "citizen legislature" that was more in touch with "middle America." Because the Supreme Court had declared that state laws limiting the terms of House and Senate members were unconstitutional, only a constitutional amendment could limit lawmakers' terms. The Republicans had made such an amendment part of their contract. In the House several versions of the bill failed to win the two-thirds approval needed to pass an amendment. A majority in Congress, unwilling to limit their own terms, rejected a related bill to make the law retroactive.

While self-interest may have motivated some legislators, the issue of term limits also brought up matters of constitutional balance between the legislative and executive branches of government. Some theorized that a less experienced legislature would become more—not less—susceptible to pressures from lobbyists. Not only would newer members of Congress rely more on the expertise of lobbyists, they might also vote to please those lobbyists to get jobs after their terms expired.

Balanced Budget Amendment

For years politicians of both parties had railed against a government that did not, in the words of the Contract With America, "live under the same budget constraints

VISUAL INSTRUCTION

Waste in Government Two forklifts carry reams of federal rules and regulations, which Clinton and Gore vow to revamp.

Answer: *Moderates regarded them as unwise.*

FYI

Laws Congress and state legislatures pass thousands of laws per year. These laws are added to the hundreds of volumes of laws already in existence. Today federal laws alone fill 125,000 pages. As the number of laws increases, it is more difficult to know what the laws are in a given case and impossible to enforce them all.

The Contract With America The Contract With America contained 11 parts. The first section had 8 reforms that the 104th Congress wanted to pass on the first day. These included the Congressional Accountability Act, passed into law January 23, 1995, and 7 other bills that passed only in the House. These bills advocated cutting committee staffs by one-third, a truth-in-budgeting reform, term limits, banning proxy voting in committees, opening committee meetings to the public, auditing the House books, and tax cuts. Ten other acts contained 26 bills some Republicans wanted to pass in the first 100 days.

Cultural Perspectives

Small-Business Owners The number of businesses owned by African Americans increased from about 190,000 to about 425,000 between 1970 and 1990. Approximately 95 percent of these businesses, however, were owned and managed by only one person. Have students consider how a small-business owner might feel about some of the issues discussed in this chapter, such as health-care reform, welfare reform, unfunded mandates, and environmental issues.

as families and businesses." A proposed constitutional amendment that would have required the federal government to balance its budget easily passed the House and failed in the Senate by only one vote.

While balancing the budget seemed a prudent idea, especially in the face of spiraling national debt, the issue was complex. Those who complained about government's lack of fiscal responsibility failed to note the extent to which individuals and businesses engage in deficit financing when they take out a mortgage or charge purchases to their credit card. While many states and cities have laws requiring them to balance their budgets, these laws do not take into account bond issues, which invoke long-term debt used to finance projects such as building a school or constructing a highway.

Another stumbling block in the way of balancing the federal budget was that the cry for a balanced budget was counterbalanced by equally loud demands for tax cuts and increased spending. As one writer pointed out, President Clinton in 1995 asked for an additional $25 billion in defense spending while at the same time calling for tax cuts for the middle class.

Once Republicans gained control of Congress, many of them proved to be as hungry for "pork" as the Democrats had been. "Pork" is short for **pork barrel legislation,** which usually advocates projects of questionable necessity that bring jobs and money into a legislator's district. In 1995 much of the pork was in the defense budget. Congress appropriated $7 billion more than the Defense Department requested—for projects such as repairing housing on military bases, constructing a physical fitness center at a naval shipyard, and building two B2 bombers at a cost of $1 billion each.

The extravagance led some House members to set up a bipartisan coalition consisting of Democrats and Republicans, called "pork busters," to curb such excesses. Said Representative David Minge, cochair of the group, "The resolve we have as a nation to accept the sacrifice necessary to balance the budget is undermined when certain members of Congress and certain communities get prizes while other people are trying to tighten their belts."

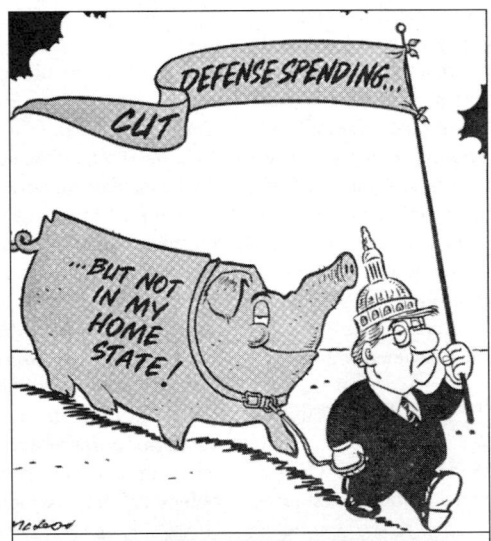

Pork Barrel Legislation Critics believed that much of the pork in the 1995 budget was in defense spending. *How much more did Congress appropriate for the Defense Department than they requested?*

Following the fight over the constitutional amendment, Republicans in Congress proposed a plan that would lead to a balanced budget by the year 2002 while at the same time providing tax cuts. President Clinton countered with his own proposal, one that he said would balance the budget in 10 years and would cause less pain than the Republican plan. One of the chief hurdles for both plans was that only a small percentage of federal expenditure is discretionary. Much of what the United States government spends goes to pay the national debt and to fund Social Security, Medicare, and other entitlement programs.

Reforming National Health Care

In 1995, 30 years after Lyndon Johnson signed the law creating Medicare, nearly everyone agreed that this program that insured the nation's elderly was working. They also agreed that with costs for Medicare rising at 10 percent per year, something had to be done to control expenses before the aging baby boomers bankrupted the program.

That is where the agreement ended. Deciding how to change Medicare, and how fast, proved difficult. President Clinton, exhausted after his protracted health-care initiatives failed in 1993, advocated only minor cutbacks that left Medicare virtually intact. He maintained that no overhaul of Medicare was possible without first reforming the entire health-care delivery system.

Republicans, anxious to deliver on their promises of a balanced budget and tax cuts, were hinting at major changes in the way Medicare delivered services, changes that they argued would provide more options for senior citizens and at the same time curtail spending. When the debate opened, the government was acting as the insurer, paying doctors and hospitals for services rendered. The Republican plan would have the government provide a "defined contribution," a fixed amount of money, or voucher, that a person could use to purchase coverage from any of a number of health insurance plans.

Many saw the struggle over Medicare as critical to the outcome of the 1996 election. Faced with opposition from powerful interest

Critical Thinking

Demonstrating Reasoned Judgment

Some people believe that every desire of society can be met by passing a law. This belief has led legislatures to make more and more laws to satisfy more and more special-interest groups. American courts, too, can affect laws, but the courts are not accountable to the public the way legislatures are. Some changes decreed by the courts (such as busing to achieve desegregation) have been extremely unpopular. Have students discuss whether the courts should defend the constitutional rights of every American regardless of popular opinion, or whether questions of great social importance should be settled by legislation. Have students support their ideas with reasons and examples.

groups, such as the American Association of Retired People (AARP) and the American Hospital Association, Republicans would have to convince voters, especially elderly people who vote in great numbers, that the program was good for them.

In many ways the debate over Medicare was a part of the broader debate over the role of the federal government. Speaker Newt Gingrich in his book *To Renew America* called Medicare "a government monopoly and therefore inefficient, wasteful, and slow to adapt to innovations in technology and management." Would the private sector do a better job? Or are there simply some jobs that only the government can do?

Welfare Reform

For many Americans, the idea of people receiving money without working for it was repugnant. They wanted, in the words of the Contract With America, to "discourage illegitimacy and teen pregnancy by prohibiting welfare to minor mothers and denying increased AFDC (Aid to Families with Dependent Children) for additional children while on welfare." As with so many measures in the contract, this one passed the House with ease and later stalled in the Senate, where members on both sides were concerned for children who would suffer from cutbacks. In September 1995 Democrats and moderate Republicans voted to eliminate provisions that cut funding for new children of mothers already on welfare.

In related matters the Senate also balked at proposed House cuts that would severely affect the poor. The Low Income Home Energy Assistance Program, which helps low-income people pay their heating bills, was eliminated by the House but restored by a Senate committee. That committee also recommended providing $1.9 billion more for education, job training, and health programs than the House's version of the bill had allowed. This amount was still far short of current spending, and $9.2 billion less than Clinton had requested.

The Role of Government
Cuts for the Arts, Humanities, and Environment

In the mid-1990s, as Republican budget cuts began to make themselves felt, few remained unaffected. More than half the people in the United States receive some kind of direct government assistance, ranging from college loans to welfare payments to Social Security. While some of the budget battles were part of an effort to cut government spending, others were symbolic of the Republicans' desire to reduce the reach of the federal government.

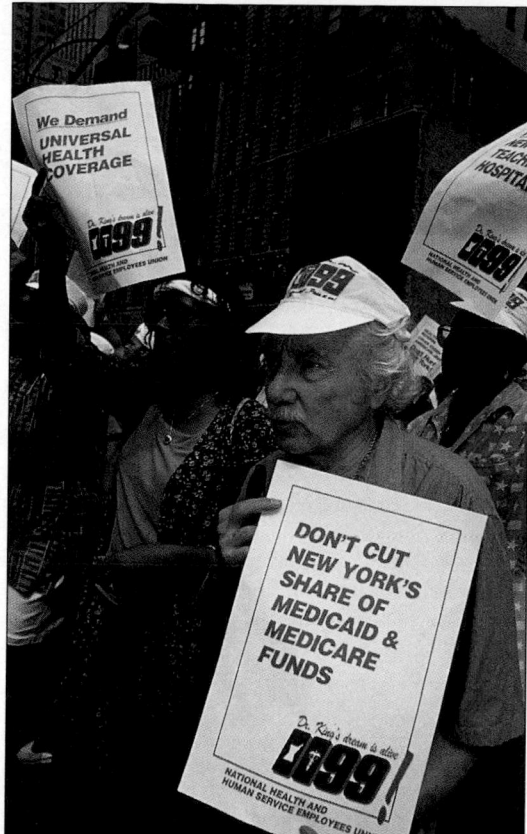

Health-Care Reform Citizens in New York demonstrate to show their support for federally funded health-care programs. *What did Newt Gingrich call Medicare?*

Funding the Arts and Humanities

One of the prime targets of the Republican right was the arts and humanities. Conservatives believed that the National Endowment for the Arts (NEA), the National Endowment for the Humanities (NEH), and other such agencies too often funded liberal or even obscene works. They wanted to abolish such programs because they felt that funding for music, theater, museums, libraries, and public broadcasting was best left to generous individuals and corporations.

Others believed, however, that since the United States supports arts and humanities far less than any other industrialized nation, support should not be reduced. They argued that a great nation without arts and humanities loses its greatness. In the end neither side got what it wanted. The National Endowment for the Arts and the National Endowment for the Humanities were not abolished, but they took cuts in government funding of nearly 40 percent.

SECTION TWO **909**

VISUAL INSTRUCTION

Health-Care Reform The American Association of Retired Persons and other organizations that advocate for the elderly supported keeping Medicare the way it was. Other groups, including many Republicans, felt Medicare would be more effective if it were privatized rather than run by the federal government.

Answer: *He called Medicare "a government monopoly . . . inefficient, wasteful, and slow to adapt to innovations in technology and management."*

FYI

Advocates for the Elderly The Gray Panthers is a national organization that fights age discrimination in employment and housing. It also works to end negative portrayals of older people by the media. It supports a national health-care plan and programs to increase the supply of affordable housing for all. The Gray Panthers publish a newspaper called *The Network.* They have about 85 chapters and 70,000 members in the United States.

Portfolio Project

Health-Care Reform Have students research various plans for health-care reform and briefly summarize their differences. Then have students explain which plan, if any, they support and why. Students can file their reports in their portfolios.

Welfare Reform Some states want the freedom to decide how welfare will be administered. Some advocates worry, however, that if too much leeway is given the states, people (especially children) may suffer. Let students research this issue, decide on a solution, and file their results in their portfolios.

ASSESS

Meeting Lesson Objectives

Each section objective is tested by the section review question(s) that follows it in parentheses.

1. Explain the factors that led the Republicans to sweep the 1994 midterm elections. (1, 2, 4)
2. List important figures in the 104th Congress and their roles. (2, 3)
3. Discuss the goals of the Contract With America. (2, 4, 5)
4. Explain why Congress has such a difficult time passing a balanced budget. (1, 4)

Environmental Protection

Environmental issues often spur bitter and passionate disagreement between conservationists and businesspeople. Conservationists criticize government for doing too little to protect the environment. Businesses complain that they cannot make a profit or compete with foreign firms if forced to meet strict pollution or waste-disposal standards. Most environmental programs try to compromise between these competing interests.

The Republican father of conservation was Theodore Roosevelt, the first President to make conservation a national goal. Roosevelt felt that our nation's forests and wilderness belong to all citizens, not just powerful interests. Roosevelt also believed, however, that a person could love nature but still cut down trees and hunt buffalo. People ever since have attempted to find the right balance between unfettered free enterprise on the one hand and government regulation of the nation's limited resources on the other.

Laws controlling pollution, for example, required compromises from both businesspeople and environmentalists. For many decades automobiles and factories

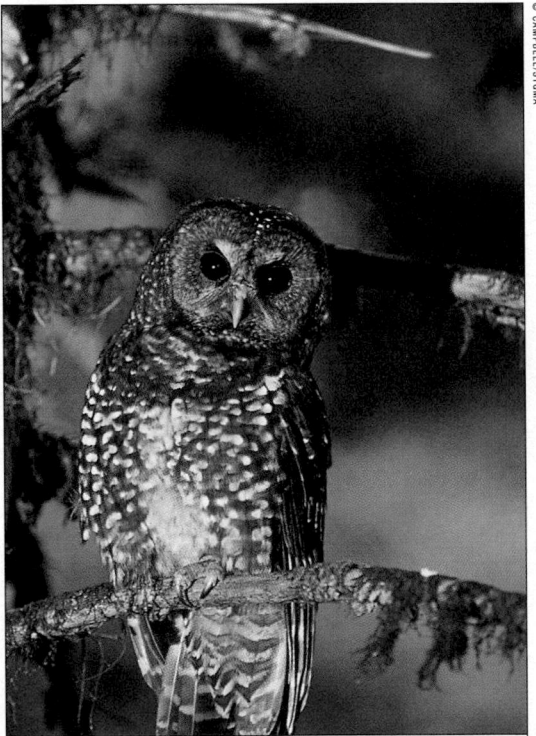

Spotted Owls An endangered species, the spotted owl became a symbol in a debate between environmentalists who wanted to preserve old-growth forests and loggers who wanted to work. *How did the Supreme Court rule on this issue?*

spewed pollutants into the air. In 1990 the Environmental Protection Agency (EPA) reported that nearly 150 million Americans lived in areas where the air was considered unhealthy. After much debate, Congress finally passed the Clean Air Act in 1990. The bill set pollution standards and deadlines for factories, oil refiners, and automakers.

The Clean Air Act did not deliver clean air as soon as environmentalists had hoped that it would. This was partly because Representative John D. Dingell from Detroit, chairman of the House Energy and Commerce Committee, won concessions for automakers. Automakers asserted that the costs of some requirements exceeded the benefits and that some changes were unrealistic.

Another environmental controversy of the 1990s pitted the logging industry against environmentalists. In Oregon the spotted owl was placed on the endangered species list, a move that would have prevented cutting timber from the forests the bird inhabited. Some of the land was on federal property. During the Bush administration, Secretary of the Interior Manuel Lujan, Jr., sided with the timber industry in voting to exempt from the Endangered Species Act timber sales on some federal lands in that state. He claimed that preventing the timber sales would cost 32,000 jobs. The Sierra Club and other environmental groups challenged the decision in federal court, eventually bringing the case to the Supreme Court, which in 1995 ruled that even on private lands, the habitat of the spotted owl must be preserved in order to keep the bird from becoming extinct.

The Conservative Agenda

For years many conservatives in the United States had seen regulations aimed at protecting the environment as intrusive and unfair. In their view such legislation saved endangered species at the expense of jobs for hardworking people, and cost businesses billions of dollars without providing any measurable benefit to the average taxpayer. Once in power Republicans launched what many saw as an all-out assault on measures designed to ensure a clean environment.

According to their plan, the budget of the Environmental Protection Agency would have been cut 34 percent. Republican legislation would have also strengthened the hold of ranchers, loggers, and miners on federal land while at the same time limiting the rights of others to use the land or prevent its misuse. It also eliminated funding for some EPA programs, such as regulation of sewage spills and toxic air pollution at oil refineries.

Even for some Republicans, these changes were too drastic. Democrats and 51 Republicans, the vast majority from the East, voted against this legislation. Some Republicans believe that a hard line on these issues might backfire at the polls.

Extending the Content

Environmental Protection This nation's chief source of air pollution is the automobile. In almost every American city, automobiles are used more than trains or buses. People find it more convenient to drive than to wait for a bus that may take too long to reach their destination or take them a little out of their way. If enough people rode buses or trains, air pollution could be greatly reduced.

Discuss with students what they as individuals can do to help reduce pollution in their community. Do they think more laws should be enacted (such as laws requiring carpool lanes on highways or bike paths beside new roads), or do they think other methods would be more effective? Encourage students to share their ideas.

© JEFF GREENBERG/RAINBOW

Liberty The Statue of Liberty, a symbol of the United States and a beacon of freedom for immigrants, stands on Liberty Island in New York Harbor. *How many such sites risked closure?*

Even national parks were not exempt from budget cuts. A proposal before Congress would have set up a park closure commission modeled after the one that closed military bases. At risk would be 314 of 368 national parks and historical sites, including Mount Rushmore, the Statue of Liberty, and the Washington Monument. Republicans in favor of the plan argued that since the government did not have enough money to maintain the parks properly, the lands would be better off in private hands where they could be run as efficient businesses. After much wrangling, however, the closure commission was defeated.

Shifting Obligations to the States

Federal Cuts Cause Cutbacks at Local Level

One writer referred to it as a boomerang: Congress cuts spending in Washington and the effects of those cuts rebound to the states, counties, and municipalities. In 1995 such effects were felt most strongly in California where state and county governments had been limiting taxation and spending for years. Until then many of these budgetary cutbacks had only minor effects on services, especially in the area of public health and welfare, because expanding federal government programs made up the difference.

With the new cost cutting in Washington, however, Los Angeles County was faced with the possibility of closing 40 walk-in clinics, slashing many social programs, and firing as many as 15,000 social workers. Education, too, suffered under the budget cutbacks. Test scores dropped, and dropout rates rose. Many people saw the California experience as a precursor to that of the nation.

Some in Washington applauded this trend toward local responsibility. They said it allowed people who use the programs to be closer to those who manage them. On the other hand local officials, who found themselves with nowhere to turn for funding, disagreed. To them it seemed as if the federal government was evading its responsibility to the people. As one frustrated local official stated, "We're the ones who have to close the hospitals."

After the health-care initiatives of the Clinton administration failed in Congress, the President looked to the states for innovative models that he hoped would serve as examples. After conservative gains in many state legislatures resulted in budget tightening, however, many of those new plans had to be shelved. Nationwide, the number of Americans without health insurance continued to increase.

Many experts saw a trend developing, and they wondered what its effect on communities would be. No one could predict whether taxpayers, once they saw their public library close, their museum cut back its hours, or their school building crumble, would reinstitute spending or if they would refuse to pay more taxes. The debate continues to exert a strong influence on political campaigns.

SECTION REVIEW

Vocabulary

1. Define: bipartisan coalition, unfunded mandate, pork barrel legislation.

Checking Facts

2. List some of the reasons that the Republicans swept the 1994 midterm elections.

3. Identify the following people and the role they played in the 104th Congress: Newt Gingrich, Robert Dole.

Critical Thinking

Predicting Consequences

4. For which programs did the Republicans want to cut funding? What were the arguments for and against these cuts?

Linking Across Time

5. Which of the Contract With America proposals are still being debated today? How, if at all, have attitudes toward these issues changed?

SECTION TWO   **911**

Evaluate

Have students complete the Section Review.

📁 🔲 Assign the Section 2 Quiz or use the Testmaker to develop a customized quiz. (Also in Spanish.) **LEP**

Reteach

🎧 Have students listen to the Chapter 26, Section 2 Audiocassette. (Also in Spanish.) **LEP**

Enrich

📁 Have students complete Interpreting Political Cartoons 35–39.

📁 Have students complete Supreme Court Case Study 65.

CLOSE

Ask: What are some pros and cons of term limits? *(pro: people with lifetime jobs in Congress lose touch with the average citizen; con: inexperienced legislators would be elected)* Why would it be difficult for any politician to make cuts in Medicare? *(Elderly people vote in great numbers, and they would most likely be opposed to cuts in Medicare.)* Who did the Republican right think should fund the arts and humanities? *(individuals and corporations)*

Section 2 Review Answers

1. **bipartisan coalition** (906), **unfunded mandate** (907), **pork barrel legislation** (908)
2. The Republicans used new outlets of communication; conservative groups published voter guides; there was a backlash against Clinton.
3. Gingrich: speaker of the House; Dole: Senate majority leader

4. Medicare, welfare, the National Endowment for the Arts, the National Endowment for the Humanities, environmental protection regulations, national parks, and others
5. Almost all of the proposals are still being debated today.

TEACH

Making the Historical Connection

Review with students arguments for and against affirmative action. *(For: it helps make up for past discrimination; it gives women and minorities an opportunity to break into areas they have been kept out of. Against: it leapfrogs women and minorities over qualified white males.)* Then discuss with students the apparent mood of the nation in 1992 when Clinton was elected, and how the mood had changed two years later as evidenced by the 1994 midterm election results. *(In 1992 voters desired change and sent more women and minorities to Congress than ever before. In 1994 there seemed to be a conservative backlash that favored white males.)*

 Block Scheduling

☞ Have students complete the Unit 10 Case Study to enrich their understanding of affirmative action.

Turning Point

This case went to the Supreme Court. The Court's decision was a compromise between two extreme positions (doing away with affirmative action altogether or leaving it as it is). The Court ruled that programs that use racial preferences must be be reviewed individually to decide whether there is a compelling need for the preferences.

Turning Point
Affirmative Action

SPRING 1995

MEMORANDUM

For: People of the Court

Subject: racial classifications

Any individual suffers an injury when he or she is disadvantaged by the government because of his or her race. . . . We hold today that all racial classifications, imposed by whatever federal, state, or local governmental actor, must be analyzed by a reviewing court under strict scrutiny. In other words, such classifications are constitutional only if they are narrowly tailored measures that further compelling governmental interests. . . .

Justice Sandra Day O'Connor
Supreme Court, June 12, 1995

The Case

In 1990 the state of Colorado was rebuilding a stretch of highway in the San Juan National Forest. The prime contractor on the job, Mountain Gravel and Construction, invited subcontractors to bid on the installation of guardrails along the 4.5-mile (7.24-km) road.

Randy Pech, the white owner of Adarand Constructors, was one of the bidders. Adarand's sole business was guardrail installation, and he had been in business for 14 years. Adarand did about $2.5 million of business per year.

Frank Gonzales, a Hispanic man who owned Gonzales Construction, was a second bidder. Gonzales Construction was a 10-year-old company engaged in environmental cleanup, demolition work, and road building as well as guardrail installation. Gonzales's company did about $3 million of business per year.

Both bids were in the $100,000 range. Of the two, however, Adarand's was lower. Adarand agreed to do the work for $1,700 less than Gonzales Construction.

Adarand, however, did not get the job. Instead the contract went to Gonzales. Mountain Gravel and Construction hired the company because it was minority-owned. Under a federal program, administered by the United States Department of Transportation, the prime contractor would receive a bonus of about 1.5 percent for hiring what was called a Disadvantaged Business Enterprise.

Randy Pech claimed that the policy discriminated against him because he was a white owner of a company. Of the five companies in Colorado that installed guardrails, three were minority-owned, and one was owned by a woman. Pech said his company was the only one adversely affected by the set-aside—the percentage of federal contracts set aside for minority firms.

Pech sued the Department of Transportation, which was headed by Federico Pena. Although two

The Case at a Glance

Randy Pech, a white owner of a company, submits the low bid on a federal project.	Frank Gonzales, a Hispanic owner, submits a slightly higher bid on the same project.	Because of a federal program that promotes minority firms, Gonzales gets the contract.	Pech sues, claiming he is being discriminated against because he is white.

lower courts rejected Adarand's claims, Pech's lawyers persisted, arguing that race-based set-asides violate the equal protection component of the Fifth Amendment's due process clause. They took the case all the way to the Supreme Court, which in 1994 agreed to hear the case.

The Background

By the mid-1990s, the United States had spent more than 30 years implementing the Civil Rights Act of 1964. In this effort, hundreds of regulations and thousands of lawsuits had opened jobs to groups who for generations had suffered from discrimination and unequal treatment. These groups included women, African Americans, Hispanic Americans, Native Americans, Asians, and the disabled.

One powerful tool used to win job equality was a policy called "affirmative action." President Kennedy instituted the policy in 1961 to encourage government managers and contractors to "take affirmative action" to ensure that all workers and applicants were treated without discrimination on the basis of race, religion, sex, or ethnic background.

President Johnson continued to support the policy after Kennedy's death. In the beginning employers were required to seek out minority applicants, but when it came time to hire, they could hire without regard to race or sex. In 1969, however, President Nixon tightened the rules. Through the "Philadelphia Plan," he opened Philadelphia's construction unions to minority apprentices.

Companies now had to hire minorities in proportion to their numbers in the local workforce. This rule led to more widespread quotas, which forced companies to hire a certain percentage of women and minorities, due to set-asides. By 1995 the effect of 162 federal affirmative action regulations was felt in the nation's private businesses, universities, hospitals, and thousands of other public institutions across the nation.

The Debate

During the late 1980s and early 1990s, increasing numbers of people, mostly white males, began to chafe under affirmative action regulations, saying the regulations had gone too far. They contended

"Government cannot make us equal; it can only recognize, respect and protect us as equal before the law . . . As far as the Constitution is concerned, it is irrelevant whether a government's racial classifications are drawn by those who wish to oppress a race or by those who have a sincere desire to help those thought to be disadvantaged."

Clarence Thomas,
Supreme Court Justice

". . . Discrimination's lingering effects, . . . reflective of a system of racial caste only recently ended, are evident in our work places, markets and neighborhoods. Job applicants with identical resumes, qualifications and interview styles still experience different reception, depending on their race."

Ruth Bader Ginsburg,
Supreme Court Justice

"We should reaffirm the principle of affirmative action. . . . We should have a simple slogan: 'Mend it but don't end it.'"

William Clinton,
President of the United States

"The only time they get a break is when it's against me. When I'm the low bidder they get a break."

Randy Pech,
Owner, Adarand Constructors

FYI

The Ruling The ruling issued by the Supreme Court in *Adarand* v. *Pena* put federal affirmative action programs on a far more tenuous legal footing than ever before. After the ruling, such programs were subject to the most rigorous level of court review, a test that has often proved difficult to pass.

Republicans, encouraged by the Supreme Court decision, have begun preparing a legislative assault. Their targets include scores of congressional initiatives that offer special consideration for women and minorities.

This attack may not be as easy as hoped, however, for all but two of the Supreme Court justices indicated that affirmative action is sometimes appropriate to address ongoing problems of discrimination.

| Two lower courts reject Pech's claims. The case goes to the Supreme Court. | → | The Supreme Court strikes a compromise: each case must be decided individually. |

Analyzing the Case

Have students read the Case Study through the section titled "The Precedents."

1. Summarize Pech's arguments. *(Pech claimed he was discriminated against because he was denied a federal construction contract even though he was the low bidder.)*

2. How did lower courts rule on Pech's claims? *(Two lower courts disagreed with Pech's claims, saying set-asides for minority-owned firms were legal.)*

3. Have students describe the precedents established by the Supreme Court. *(In 1980 the Supreme Court upheld a set-aside program, but in 1989 the Court ruled that governments had to prove that discrimination existed before set-asides were legal.)*

Notes

Turning Point

that jobs should not be awarded to anyone because of race or gender. After the Republicans won control of Congress in 1994, opponents of affirmative action gained a stronger voice in the debate. Supporters of affirmative action stood their ground. They insisted that few white males suffered any substantial losses, while women and minorities, long deprived, were given a chance to prosper. They pointed out, for example, that only 266,000 African American families belonged to the middle class in 1967, while more than 1 million African American families were middle class in 1989. They added that affirmative action programs were still needed to fight ongoing discrimination.

Critics of affirmative action called the policies undemocratic because they gave preferential treatment to women and minorities and discriminated against white males. These critics also claimed that affirmative action policies helped well-off minorities, but were useless weapons for fighting inner-city poverty.

The Precedents

In 1980 the Supreme Court upheld the public works set-aside program in a ruling on the *Fullilove* v. *Klutznick* case. By the end of the decade, however, a more conservative Supreme Court, with 3 Reagan-appointed justices and a new chief justice, weighed into the debate with a series of decisions that made substantial inroads into affirmative action regulations.

In one important 1989 case, *Richmond* v. *Croson*, the Court ruled that state and local governments had to prove that discrimination existed before they could set quotas for minority contractors. This proof was called "strict judicial scrutiny." Wrote Justice Sandra Day O'Connor, "An amorphous claim that there has been past discrimination in a particular industry cannot justify the use of an unyielding racial quota." Further, the Court ruled, affirmative action programs must be "narrowly tailored" to address specific cases of discrimination. Liberal justice Thurgood Marshall, writing in dissent, called the decision "a deliberate and giant step backward in this court's affirmative-action jurisprudence."

For a number of years after the *Richmond* decision, a two-tiered system remained in place. Local and state programs were subject to "strict scrutiny," while federal programs were held to a more relaxed standard, a standard that Randy Pech's attorneys argued against before the Supreme Court.

The Decision

The decision the Court rendered in *Adarand* v. *Pena* was in part a compromise between two extreme positions. Justices Antonin Scalia and Clarence Thomas, while concurring with the majority opinion, nevertheless issued separate opinions, which expressed their conclusion that all affirmative action programs were inherently unconstitutional. Wrote Scalia: "To pursue the concept of racial entitlement even for the most admirable and benign of purposes is to reinforce and preserve for future mischief the way of thinking that produced race slavery, race privilege, and race hatred."

On the other side, three of four justices, Ruth Bader Ginsberg, David A. Souter, and John Paul Stevens, filed dissenting opinions. They claimed that the Court should follow the precedent it set in *Fullilove* v. *Klutznick* and continue to allow federal set-asides for minorities. "There is no moral equivalence or constitutional equivalence between a policy that is designed to perpetuate a caste system and one that seeks to eradicate racial subordination," wrote Justice Stevens. "Remedial race-based preferences reflect . . . a desire to foster equality in society." In the minority's judgment, an interest in "consistency" did not justify treating differences as though they were similarities.

The Response

In the wake of the decision, both sides tried to put a positive spin on the news. Supporters of affirmative action claimed that the ruling was, in the words of Penda Hair, a senior attorney at the National Association for the Advancement of Colored People (NAACP), "a setback but not a disaster." She asserted that NAACP research showed "federal contracting programs would survive strict scrutiny be-

---

Cooperative Learning

Debate Organize students into two groups to debate whether set-asides to make up for past discrimination should be legal. One side will argue that set-asides should be legal, the other that set-asides should not be legal. Have members of each team assign responsibilities. Students will need to list their arguments and counterarguments and explain their supporting reasons. They may need to conduct additional research on this case or others. Then have two students from each group stage the debate. The audience should listen critically to decide whether each side provides adequate evidence to support its arguments (not which side they most agree with).

A man demonstrates at an affirmative action rally in San Francisco in July 1995.

That should not be surprising. We had slavery for centuries before the passage of the 13th, 14th, and 15th Amendments. We waited another 100 years for the civil rights legislation. Women have had the vote less than 100 years."

On June 13, 1995, Clinton remarked, "The court has approved affirmative action that is narrowly tailored to achieve a compelling interest. The constitutional test is now tougher than it was, but I am confident the test can be met in many cases."

Toward Resolution

Opinion polls taken after the *Adarand* decision have suggested a path toward resolution. They show that most Americans disapprove of preferential treatment, regardless of how any group was once treated. Most Americans, however, approve of compensatory actions, such as Head Start, college aid, job training, and other programs that help disadvantaged people catch up. Ideally these programs give everyone an equal opportunity to compete, but they do not guarantee who will win the race.

cause there's a very compelling reason for them. Right now, women- and minority-owned businesses are getting less than 6 percent of all federal contracts."

Opponents of affirmative action also saw reason to be optimistic about the decision. Clint Bolick of the Institute for Justice was quoted as saying, "The era of racial preferences is finally coming to an end. The Court said it had erred in creating one standard for government, another for everyone else. It's really the Court saying, 'Enough is enough'."

President Clinton, whose administration had vowed to study the controversy, issued a response the next month. The President outlined a compromise position. Affirmative action, he said, has not always been perfect. He looked forward to a day when it would have succeeded to the point where it would no longer be necessary: "I am resolved that that day will come, but the evidence suggests, indeed screams, that that day has not come. The job of ending discrimination in this country is not over.

RESPONDING TO THE CASE

1. Why did Randy Pech decide to sue the United States Department of Transportation?

2. Why did supporters of affirmative action feel that the programs should be kept in place?

3. Sandra Day O'Connor's opinion in *Adarand* v. *Pena* was seen as a compromise by some on the Supreme Court. Who took more extreme positions, and what did they say?

4. Why do you think most Americans support compensatory actions rather than affirmative action policies that give preferential treatment to minorities and women?

PORTFOLIO PROJECT

Consider both sides of the affirmative action debate. Collect newspaper and magazine articles presenting both sides as well as solutions to the conflict. Prepare a paper describing what you believe is the best way to resolve the affirmative action debate. Support your position with strong factual arguments.

CASE STUDY **915**

FOCUS

Section Objectives

1. List arguments for and against gerrymandering.
2. Explain the changing nature of work in an increasingly technological society.
3. Describe the financial and educational challenges facing schools and educators as the United States moves toward the twenty-first century.

Bellringer Activity

While taking attendance at the beginning of the class period, display **Section Focus Transparency 85,** and have students answer the questions. (Or use the blackline master.)

VISUAL INSTRUCTION

Atlantis and ***Mir*** **Hook Up**
This historic handshake took place two and one-half weeks before the twentieth anniversary of a similar in-space greeting between cosmonauts and astronauts: the *Apollo-Soyuz* Test Project in 1975.

Ask: When was the Russian space station *Mir* launched?
(in 1986)

Toward a New Century

JULY 6, 1995: RUSSIANS AND AMERICANS LINK UP IN SPACE

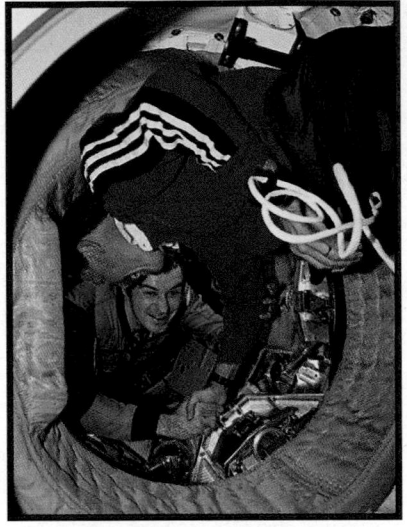

Atlantis and ***Mir*** Hook Up
American astronaut Robert L. Gibson shakes hands with *Mir* cosmonaut Vladimir N. Dezhurov in 1995.

NEARLY 240 MILES (386 KM) ABOVE THE EARTH, THE SPACE SHUTTLE *ATLANTIS* MOVED INTO ORBIT WITH *MIR* (MEANING *PEACE*), THE RUSSIAN SPACE STATION LAUNCHED IN 1986, SLOWLY CLOSING THE 4,000-MILE (6,436-KM) GAP BETWEEN THEM. By the next day, only 250 feet (76 m) separated the 2 crafts, which were circling at 17,500 miles (28,158 km) per hour. Tension increased as American astronauts Hoot Gibson and Charles Precourt continued the delicate maneuvers necessary to link the 2 ships. Inch by inch, they guided *Atlantis* until they had jockeyed the 100-ton spacecraft to within 3 inches of the Russian station. Soon the 2 were linked, soaring through space together. Russian cosmonauts and American astronauts swung open the hatches, and the 2 crews grasped each others' hands in joyous greeting. The moment was symbolic of the huge changes that had reshaped the map of the planet below.

Both the Russians and the Americans, faced with cutbacks in funding for their space programs, envisioned a future of cooperation. Plans are under way for a new space station, with modules supplied and assembled by both nations. Once it is in place, the plan is to invite the European Space Agency, Canada, and Japan to participate in and expand the facility. While questions remained about the commitment of the American and Russian governments to such an ambitious project, the fact that cosmonauts and astronauts were cruising above the earth in the summer of 1995 seemed to most observers a reason for optimism.

At its inception, the space program was an arm of the cold war. For both the USSR and the United States, the goal had been to beat the other in the space race. Winning meant setting records: first to orbit the earth, first to walk in space, first to set foot on the moon. Today in a new

AS YOU READ

Vocabulary
► militia group
► community policing

Think About . . .
► arguments for and against gerrymandering.
► the changing nature of work in an increasingly technological society.
► the financial and educational challenges facing schools and educators as the United States moves toward the twenty-first century.

Section 3 Resources

REPRODUCIBLE RESOURCES
- Lesson Plan 26-3
- Vocabulary and Guided Reading Activity 26-3
- Section 3 Quiz
- Chapter 26 Test
- Performance Assessment Activity 26
- Reteaching Activity 26
- Enrichment Activity 26
- Geography in History Activity 26
- Political Cartoons 5, 26, 51–55
- Supreme Court Cases 41, 61, 62
- Skill Reinforcement Activity 26
- Unit 10 Test
- End-of-the Book Test

MULTIMEDIA RESOURCES
- Section Focus Transparency 85
- Economics in Action
- Focus on Government
- Chapter 26 Digest Audiocassette
- Testmaker
- Vocabulary PuzzleMaker
- Student Self-Test: A Software Review

spirit of international cooperation, astronauts from different nations, both men and women, work together in spacecrafts that have become serious laboratories, where scientists conduct experiments in the microgravity, or weightlessness of space.

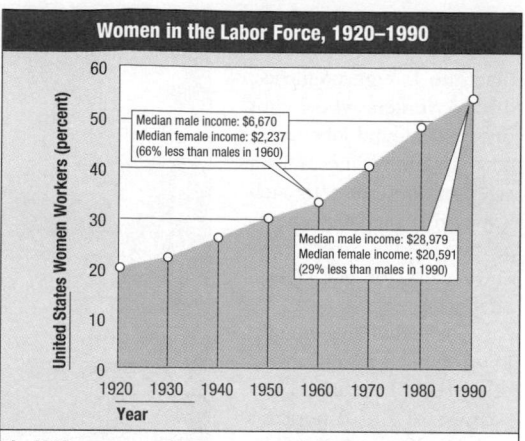

Women in the Labor Force, 1920–1990

Median male income: $6,670
Median female income: $2,237
(66% less than males in 1960)

Median male income: $28,979
Median female income: $20,591
(29% less than males in 1990)

In 1990 women made up more than half of the labor force.
How did the median salary of a woman in 1990 compare with that of a man?

New Roles, New Faces
Changes in the Workforce

Women astronauts' presence in space reflects a change that has been gradually taking place in the American workforce throughout the 1900s: increasing numbers of women with jobs outside the home. By the 1990s, more than half of American workers were women.

Women's Concerns

As the 1980s ended, women's pay still lagged far behind that of men. Women earned just $0.71 for every $1 earned by full-time male workers. Three of every 5 working women still held low-paying "pink-collar" jobs, such as secretary, waitress, salesclerk, and hairdresser. Women who earned yearly salaries of $30,000 or more made up just 13 percent of working women, versus 40 percent of working men at that salary level. African American, Hispanic, and Native American women lagged even further behind the national average. For example, African American women with college degrees earned 10 percent less than their white counterparts. The average Hispanic woman earned almost 20 percent less than the average white American woman.

Technology Changes Our Lives

Technological advances and changes in the global economy after 1980 dramatically changed the nature of work and the composition of the workforce in the United States. Factories made use of new technologies to lower costs and improve production. Computers and industrial robots helped streamline manufacturing methods. In some factories computers regulated every step of the manufacturing process—from the selection of raw materials to processing, packaging, and inventory control. Fewer and fewer factory workers were needed in automated plants, and those employees who remained required specialized skills.

Farming continued to change as well. Many farmers now ran their farms like corporations with high-tech equipment to help them oversee large operations. Such large farms are called "agribusinesses." One Illinois farmer uses a computer to keep track of how much corn each of his 5,000 steers eats. Computers and new types of farm machinery allowed fewer farmers to produce

more food, reducing the number of jobs in agriculture and speeding the movement of people from rural areas to cities and suburbs. In 1990 less than 2 percent of all Americans lived on farms. Around the country some small farmers, concerned about human health risks from the chemical pesticides, artificial hormones, antibiotics, and genetic manipulation involved in modern farming, began to raise food organically. Produce sections of most supermarkets contained a selection of fruits and vegetables grown without chemicals.

The Changing Job Market

As jobs in agriculture and manufacturing disappeared, many American workers found jobs in the service industry. Service positions accounted for 90 percent of the 42.6 million new jobs in the United States by the early 1990s. That number represents an increase of more than 15 percent since 1960. These businesses provide services rather than products to their customers. Retail stores, restaurants, hotels, banks, computer software companies, insurance firms, stock brokerages, and accounting firms are all service businesses.

One reason service businesses have grown so fast is that consumers are now spending their money in a different way than they once did. As incomes grew during the past two decades, people were able to satisfy their basic needs with a smaller proportion of their income. They then began to spend what was left on meals in restaurants, trips to Disneyland and the local mall, investment advice, massages, and health-club memberships.

The small number of jobs in the service industry that pay handsome salaries generally require specialized skills and training. Most service jobs pay far less than manufacturing jobs, which are fast disappearing because

SECTION THREE **917**

TEACH

Guided Practice

L1 Discussion In 1971 Gloria Steinem and several other women founded *Ms.* magazine to publicize women's issues. The magazine folded in 1989. In the summer of 1990, however, Steinem revived the magazine in an unprecedented manner: she launched it with no paid advertising because she thought advertising might compromise the degree of objective reporting. Discuss reasons Steinem might have chosen this course of action.

CHART STUDY

Have students study the chart on this page. Point out how the percentage of women in the workforce has changed over the years.

Answer: *In 1990 the median salary of a woman was 71 percent that of a man.*

FYI

Immigrants The immigration laws of the 1920s favored people from western Europe. The number of people allowed to immigrate each year from any one country was based on the number of people of that nationality already living in the United States, and most Americans at the time were of western European descent.

Cooperative Learning

Successful Women Organize the class into several heterogeneous groups, and ask each group to research experiences and qualities that have enabled one individual woman to succeed. Encourage students to use interviewing techniques and library research of biographies to uncover this information. Each group can present a brief report on one woman. All the reports can then be bound into a class booklet of successful women.

917

Independent Practice

L2 **Research** Barely one-half of one percent of top executives are women. Even the few women who make it into such top positions as vice president or higher are paid 42 percent less than their male counterparts. Have students find out more about obstacles to women in the workforce and report their findings to the class.

Have students complete the Chapter 26, Section 3 Vocabulary and Guided Reading Activity. (Also in Spanish.) **LEP**

VISUAL INSTRUCTION

Newcomers Many naturalization ceremonies occur on Citizenship Day, September 17. Applicants for naturalization must have lived for a certain time in the United States and be eighteen. They must know facts about the United States's political system, history, and government and speak some English.

Answer: *raised and revised immigration quotas gave preference to skilled workers.*

CHART STUDY

Few Europeans now immigrate to the United States.

Answer: *More people arrive from the Americas and Asia.*

of automation, corporate downsizing, and relocation of plants to foreign countries. Today workers who might once have found jobs on an auto assembly line or in a steel mill now turn to such low-paying service positions as fast-food worker, data-entry clerk, or gas station attendant.

The early 1990s brought improvements for one group of workers because of the passage of the Americans with Disabilities Act (ADA). The act bans discrimination in the hiring, promoting, and firing of handicapped persons. Included are those who are hearing or visually impaired, mentally handicapped, physically impaired, those who test positive for the human immunodeficiency virus (HIV), and those who have cancer or epilepsy.

Newcomers New American citizens are sworn in under a tent in Washington, D.C. *What did the amendments to the Immigration and Nationality Act do?*

The New Immigration
Easing Immigration Requirements

Like women, ethnic groups continue to seek a greater voice and greater political power. The increasing ethnic diversity of the United States dates back to 1965. At that time President Johnson and Congress reopened the gates to immigrants and ended the bias against newcomers from Asian and Hispanic countries. The Immigration Act of 1965, wrote one observer, created "a stampede, almost an invasion" of people "who hungered to enter."

Changes in Immigration Law

In 1990 amendments to the Immigration and Nationality Act increased the number of immigrants allowed into the United States. The amendments fixed the ceiling at 700,000 persons per year for the years 1992 through 1994 and at 675,000 persons per year beginning in 1995. The amendments placed no limit on the immigration of immediate family members of United States citizens. They did give preference, however, to people from nations that have sent few immigrants to the United States in recent years, including many European and African nations. The amendments also strengthened preferences for skilled workers.

During the 1970s, 1980s, and 1990s poverty and political conflicts in several parts of the world drove people toward the United States. Devastating wars in Southeast Asia created waves of political refugees, and the United States accepted more than 500,000 Asian refugees between 1975 and 1990. Even more entered the United States from the Philippines, China, Taiwan, South Korea, India, and Pakistan.

The chance for economic success that attracted legal immigrants also attracted undocumented immigrants—people living in the United States without

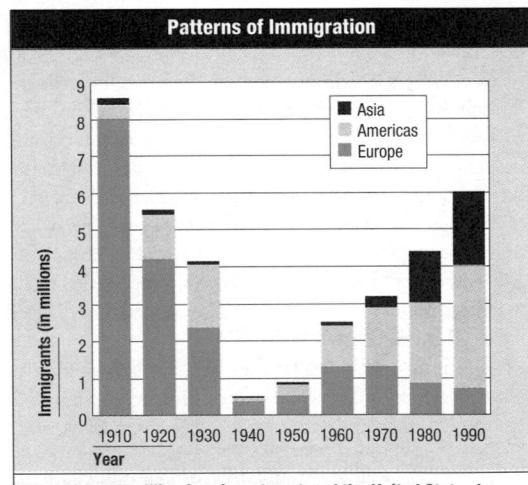

Patterns of Immigration

More than 11 million immigrants entered the United States between 1965 and 1995. *What immigration patterns can you identify?*

Meeting Special Needs

Limited English Proficiency To help students whose first language is not English, ask them to study the chart on this page. Have them explain how patterns of immigration differed in 1910 and 1990. You may want to have students use a globe or map to help them explain where most immigrants to the United States came from during different periods. **LEP**

proper visas. In 1986 Congress passed the Immigration Reform and Control Act. The law offered un-documented immigrants who had lived in the United States since 1981 a chance to become legal residents. More than 1 million immigrants took advantage of the law during its first year. As one Mexican-born housekeeper said:

> I am so happy. I prayed and prayed the INS [Immigration and Naturalization Service] wouldn't find me. I never knew what the next month would bring. Now I'll be able to make plans for the future. I already feel like it's my country.
> —Yolanda Perezin "Out of the Shadows," *Time*, May 4, 1987

The Effects of Immigration

The effects of such extensive immigration concerned many Americans. Some state governors complained that immigrants were competing with un-employed United States citizens for the limited number of available jobs. In 1981, however, a congressional com-mittee reported that immigrants "work hard, save and invest, and create more jobs than they take." Other crit-ics, forgetting America's immigrant past, wondered how so many new people, with their different customs, foods, and languages, would fit into American culture.

Despite these concerns, most observers predict that the United States will be as enriched and stimu-lated by its modern immigrants as it has been through-out its history. Cultural and ethnic differences conceived as problems in earlier times have usually come to be treasured for adding richness and diversity to American culture.

Race and Gender Issues
Equality for Minorities

At the beginning of the 1990s, African Americans found they had gained scant political power, and their lives had changed little during the preceding 10 years. Many African Americans lived in middle-class areas, but far more continued to live in inner city neighborhoods, where many remained trapped by drugs, crime, gangs, high unemployment, widespread poverty, and substan-dard schools. One such area erupted in riots in the

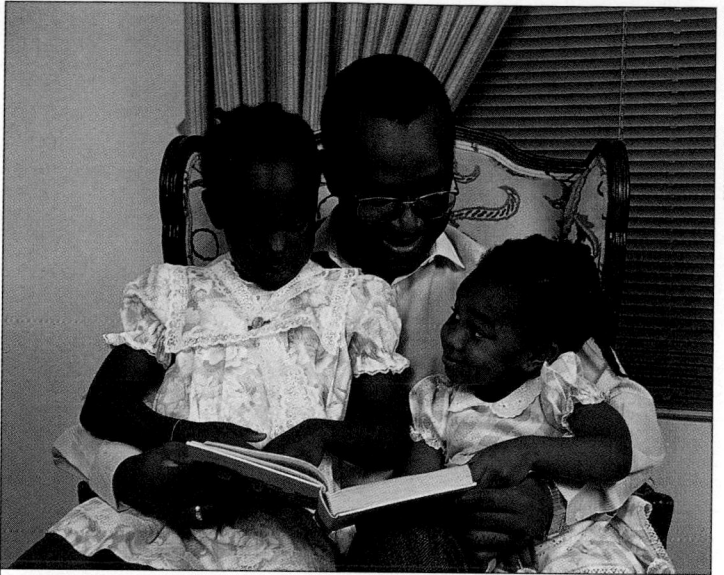

The Middle Class More African American families than ever before are part of the middle class. *How did affirmative action help African Americans leave inner city neigh-borhoods?*

summer of 1992 as residents of depressed South Central Los Angeles took to the streets to vent their anger.

The riot began in reaction to a not-guilty verdict in the widely publicized trial of four white police officers who were videotaped savagely beating a speeding African American motorist. African Americans focused on the trial as a way to redress the police brutality that many believed plagued their community. After the riots, com-munity residents, people from other neighborhoods, and business owners came together to rebuild. In doing so African Americans took an active part in addressing long-standing issues, such as getting a fair share of build-ing contracts and access to loan money and property insurance.

Affirmative Action

A series of executive orders and laws aimed at mak-ing sure racial minorities received help in their quest for equality had been in place since the 1960s. The original order, issued by President Lyndon Johnson, required employers to search aggressively for minority job appli-cants by such methods as placing ads in minority newspapers or advertising jobs in minority neighbor-hoods. Even more significant was President Nixon's order to admit members of minority groups into craft unions, where they would receive training. Secretary of Labor George Shultz pointed out to Nixon that of the 3.3 million construction workers in the United States, only 106,000 were African American, and 80 percent

SECTION THREE **919**

Portfolio Project

The Importance of Education In 1987 more than 15 percent of all African Americans had completed one to three years of college, and more than 10 percent had finished college. Have students conduct research to find out more about earnings in relation to education. Students can file their results in their portfolios.

Reporting Have students conduct research to find out what some cities have done to improve deteriorating neighborhoods. Than ask them to write a short essay on the approach to rejuve-nating old neighborhoods that they consider to be most effective. Students can place their essays in their portfolios.

919

GLENCOE
TECHNOLOGY

Videodisc

Economics in Action

Disc 2, Side 2, Chapter 30
Title: Technological and Social Change and the Economy
Subject: Focus on impact of social and technological changes on the American workforce
Ask: How has technology changed the American workforce? *(It is very difficult to get a good job without sophisticated technological training.)*

CHART STUDY

Between 1970 and 1990, approximately 1,200,000 new African American families became middle class.
Answer: *2,848,000*

---

of those were in the lowest-paying jobs.

In a groundbreaking action, Nixon required federal contractors to show evidence of "affirmative action" taken to meet the goal of increased minority employment. This plan, known as the Philadelphia Plan, set the stage for subsequent regulations and court rulings that expanded the scope of the original vision to include women and various other minorities in addition to African Americans. Affirmative action entailed creating outreach programs, preparing minority high school students for college admissions, and in some cases establishing quotas that defined how many female or minority places were available in schools or companies. Thirty years later the effects of these programs, collectively grouped under the label affirmative action, were beginning to make themselves felt.

The Federal Glass Ceiling Commission report, released in the spring of 1995, said that few women had managed to win top posts in major corporations. Yet in the rest of the economy, female workers seemed to be thriving. Nationwide in 1994, 43 percent of managers were women, leading experts to believe that many women were on their way up the corporate ladder. Close to 6.5 million women owned businesses, which collectively employed more people than all of the Fortune 500 companies combined. Another study showed that in nearly half of United States households in which both husband and wife worked, the women earned half or more than half of the total household income.

African Americans and Hispanic Americans profited, but slowly, in the years after affirmative action was implemented. The percentage of African Americans in professional and technical jobs had increased to 6.6 percent by 1995. In 1960, 1.3 percent of lawyers were African American. In 1995 that figure stood at 2.7 percent.

In some, mostly blue-collar, fields affirmative action has had a more significant impact. For example, the number of African American police officers rose from 24,000 in 1960 to 46,000 in 1990, out of a total of 457,000 police officers nationwide, and the number of African American electricians during this same period rose from 14,000 to 36,000, out of 619,000 electricians nationwide. While affirmative action programs have neither eliminated all barriers for all people, nor resolved the special problems of inner-city youth, many observers feel that overall affirmative action has helped many deserving

African Americans in the Middle Class

Year	Households (in millions)
1970	1,656,000
1980	2,212,000
1990	2,848,000

Households earning $25,000–$50,000 in 1990 dollars

During the 1980s more than 1.8 million African Americans became managers and professionals. *How many African American households were middle class in 1990?*

applicants gain access to education and jobs.

As Donald Clark, an African American longshoreman in Los Angeles who works to help African Americans advance within his union, said, "No, we have not arrived and we're not where we want to be, but thank God we're not where we used to be, either."

The Future of Affirmative Action

As the United States moved toward the twenty-first century, many people questioned affirmative action programs. Proponents of affirmative action said that these policies broaden the pool for jobs and college admissions to encompass a wide range of qualified people. Opponents argued that affirmative action policies leapfrog less-qualified women or minority applicants over better-qualified white males. Both proponents and opponents of affirmative action, however, seemed to be united over one issue: they both felt that establishing quotas is unfair.

The United States Supreme Court moved to narrow the scope of many affirmative action programs by declaring that they must "serve a compelling government interest . . . and be narrowly tailored to their goals." Meanwhile President Clinton, in a major address delivered in 1995, came out squarely in support of affirmative action. His message was, "Mend it, don't end it."

Political Shifts
The Changing Electorate

Throughout the 1980s and 1990s the population of the United States increased. It also moved. Millions of Americans swarmed to the South and the West in search of jobs and a warm climate. With changes in population came political changes. Using 1990 census information, state lawmakers began readjusting congressional, state, and local legislative district lines to conform to shifts in population. This redistricting would have wide effects, including the awarding of government contracts and the election of people of color to local, state, and national offices.

Redistricting

Gerrymandering—redrawing congressional districts to give one ethnic group or political party an electoral majority—went on as usual. For many Democrats

---

Extending the Content

Glass Ceiling The "glass ceiling" is a phrase that describes the barriers that prevent women from advancing in organizations. As of 1995, fewer than 5 percent of women held managerial positions in the 1,000 largest companies in the United States. Deterrents to women being able to break the glass ceiling are: (1) failure to recruit women, (2) women relegated to support positions, (3) women's lack of access to the old-boy network of information exchange, (4) lack of role models. The Equal Remedies Act of 1991 provides economic incentives for companies to eliminate discriminatory policies and set up glass ceiling committees to study gender-based discrimination. Have students discuss what, if anything, should be done to eliminate the glass ceiling, and why.

POPULATION SHIFTS 1980–1995

Wash. 24.7%
Montana 15.1%
North Dakota 0.6%
Minn. 10.3%
Vt. 5.2%
N.H. 5.0%
Maine 1.0%
Oregon 19.8%
Idaho 28.1%
Wyoming 15.0%
South Dakota 10.6%
Wis. 10.0%
Mich. 5.0%
Mass. –1.1%
N.Y. 1.4%
R.I. –0.5%
Conn. –0.5%
Nevada 40.7%
Utah 24.7%
Colorado 23.2%
Nebraska 8.0%
Iowa 5.5%
Ill. 6.4%
Ind. 9.0%
Ohio 5.6%
Pa. 3.5%
N. J. 5.2%
Del. 14.0%
Calif. 17.2%
Kansas 9.8%
Mo. 6.3%
Ky. 8.2%
W. Va. 2.6%
Va. 13.9%
Md. 11.3%
D.C. –13.0%
Hawaii 19.8%
Arizona 21.1%
New Mexico 20.3%
Oklahoma 7.5%
Ark. 9.7%
Tenn. 13.6%
N.C. 14.9%
S.C. 12.8%
Miss. 6.9%
Ala. 10.0%
Ga. 17.9%
Alaska 27.1%
Texas 18.0%
La. 6.1%
Fla. 18.4%
United States: Total increase 11.1%
SUNBELT

POPULATION INCREASE
More than 20%
10.0%–19.9%
5.0%–9.9%
0.1%–4.9%

POPULATION DECREASE
0.1%–13.0%

Albers Equal-Area projection

In the 1980s many Americans moved to the South and West in search of good jobs and warm climates. *Which states had the greatest percentage increases in population? The least percentage increases in population?*

---

the goal was to create districts in which African American and Hispanic American candidates would win elections. For many Republicans the goal was to pack minorities into compact districts and leave white majorities in surrounding districts. This type of redistricting raised the likelihood that increased numbers of white Republicans would offset any African American and Hispanic gains.

Opponents of gerrymandering complained that it removed the need to negotiate compromises and form coalitions, the normal work of politics. Critics pointed out that Asian Americans in California have substantial political power, which they got the old-fashioned way—by winning the votes of other groups rather than forming districts composed almost exclusively of a single group.

The Court Rules

In July 1995, the United States Supreme Court ruled on the side of those who opposed drawing congressional districts along predominantly racial lines. Race could still be a factor, ruled the high court, but not the "predominant" one. The ruling would affect not only Congress; by implication, it would also apply to electoral districts for everything from school boards to state legislatures.

While no one could gauge the long-term effects of the ruling, minorities had reason to be concerned. From 1990 to 1992 they had gained 24 seats in the House of Representatives, increasing their numbers from 45 to 69. Jesse Jackson, leader of the Rainbow Coalition and former presidential candidate, called the decision "devastating." He and others were also concerned that even with gerrymandering, ethnic minority groups remained underrepresented nationwide. The problem was attributed to a number of factors: many minority individuals were not yet citizens, they failed to vote, or they lived in predominantly white areas.

Emotional Issues
Americans React

On the surface the United States seemed at peace as the year 2000 approached. The country was not at war. The economy was humming along at a modest pace. Yet below the apparent calm lay some disturbing fears.

SECTION THREE   **921**

Cultural Perspectives

A Changing Nation Hispanic Americans make up the fastest-growing ethnic group in the United States and comprise 7 percent of the population. Because the term *Hispanic* is used to describe Spanish-speaking people or people of Latin American descent, the group is diverse. Hispanic Americans include people of Mexican, Puerto Rican, Caribbean, Cuban, Central American, or South American origin.

Various Hispanic groups lobby locally in support of issues such as bilingual education or better health care and housing. Invite students to investigate where many of the Spanish-speaking residents of their community have come from. Then students can interview or research to find out more about the social and cultural views of this local group.

GLENCOE TECHNOLOGY

 Videodisc

Focus on Government

Side 3, Chapter 58
Title: Lecture Launcher, Our Interdependent World
Subject: Growing international cooperation
Ask: How has the United Nations helped foster international cooperation? *(It provides a forum to discuss common concerns.)*

 Focus on Government is also available on videotape.

MAP STUDY

Between 1970 and 1986, the population of the southeastern part of the United States increased by 32 percent and the southwestern part by 40 percent. The population growth was due to both a sustained high birth rate and a high rate of immigration. The latter has been attributed to the area's inviting climate, good transportation and communication systems, and the ubiquitous air conditioning. The population growth has in turn increased manufacturing and other jobs in the area.

Answer: *Alaska, Arizona, Florida, and Nevada posted the biggest percentage gains; Iowa, North Dakota, West Virginia, and Wyoming decreased.*

VISUAL INSTRUCTION

The Oklahoma City Bombing Hundreds of paid rescue workers as well as volunteers from across Oklahoma and the nation turned out to help clear the rubble left after the bombing. Work progressed slowly, however, because the building was dangerously close to collapse and rescue workers had to be evacuated several times.

Answer: *because the suspects were Americans, not foreign terrorists*

Curriculum Connection

Sociology Militias are loosely organized, extremist paramilitary groups that are united by their distrust of the federal government and their opposition to gun control. To militia members, the Brady Bill and the 1994 ban on assault weapons exemplify the oppressive tactics of the federal government. Militia groups exist in 30 states. Their members are often men who feel disenfranchised and angry. Although some reports estimate that up to 100,000 people identify with militias, only about 10,000 people have actually joined them. Militia movements are probably the first national movements organized and directed on the information superhighway: public-access TV and computer bulletin boards.

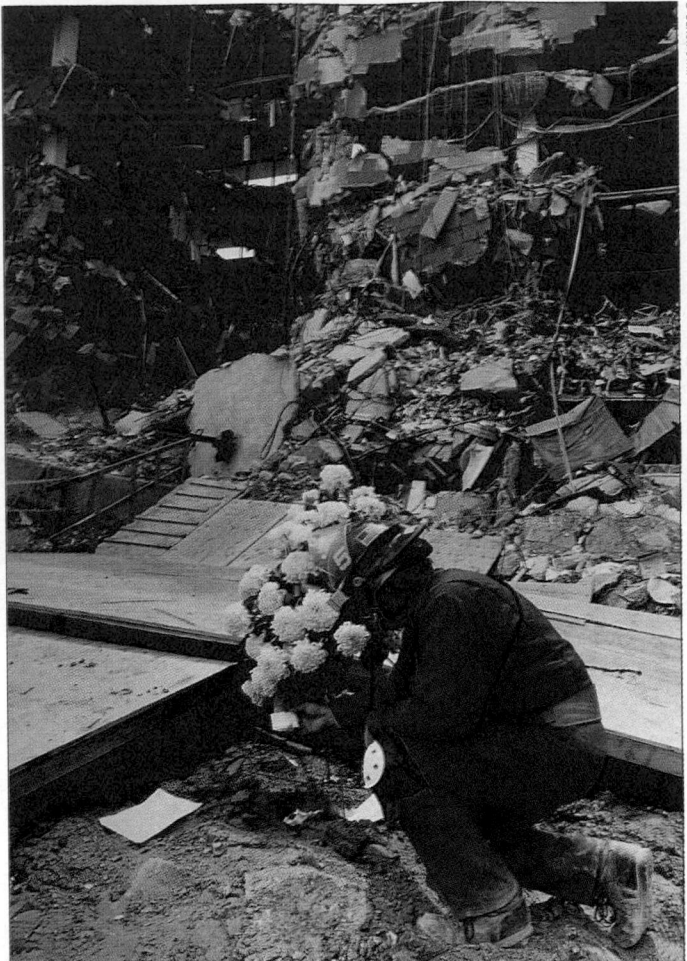

The Oklahoma City Bombing A worker at the site of the Oklahoma City bombing stops to read a card on a bouquet of flowers placed at the wreckage. *Why were Americans so upset to learn who the leading suspects in the bombing were?*

In the hours right after the bombing, many in the media speculated that the bombers were foreign terrorists. Soon, however, police and FBI agents suspected a right-wing fanatic, perhaps from a **militia group.** Americans learned to their horror that the leading suspects in the bombing were middle-American, clean-cut white men who were born and raised in the United States. Members of militia groups go far beyond simply wanting to reform government. For them, government itself is the enemy. While no one knew for certain why the Oklahoma building was singled out as the site for the bombing, experts believed that the site indicated an act of rebellion against the federal government for its actions against a religious group in Waco, Texas.

Street Violence

Despite the movement's high profile, the number of militia group members was small compared with the number of teenagers who randomly used guns to commit violent crimes. While the overall murder rate did not increase, the number of juveniles arrested for homicide increased by 117 percent. Most observers believed that guns—high-powered automatic weapons—were the chief reason for the increase.

The principal victims of the violence were young African American men living in the nation's cities. One out of every 20 African American and Latino men was killed before the age of 20. It was estimated that their death rate exceeded the rate of soldiers killed in World War II, which was one out of every 40.

The Militia Movement

Out of the mainstream of American politics, an angry—often clandestine—movement had been gathering force for a number of years. A little after 9 A.M. on the morning of April 19, 1995, it struck. A 2-ton homemade bomb packed in a rented truck tore apart the Alfred P. Murrah Federal Building in Oklahoma City. The explosion killed at least 168 people, including 15 children who were in the building's day-care center. It was the worst act of terrorism ever perpetrated in the United States. The father of a little boy who was severely wounded in the blast angrily led a television crew to his son's bedside. "This is America," he said. "We shouldn't have to run scared. We shouldn't be afraid to take a 2- or 3-year-old to the day-care center."

Many reasons were put forth for the violence. They ranged from the use of crack cocaine to the absence of stable families. Whatever the reason, the effect of so many random and meaningless killings was to increase feelings of fear and distrust among the citizenry.

As in many cities, the police chief of Bridgeport, Connecticut, decided to take action. Police Chief Thomas J. Sweeney helped to pioneer a new method of police patrolling known as **community policing,** which involves sending more foot patrols into neighborhoods and establishing better relationships between the police and the public. Sweeney and others are quick to point out, however, that the police cannot do it all. "You've got

Critical Thinking

Reasoned Judgment In the 1980s and 1990s, racist groups surfaced on many college campuses, spreading hateful messages through graffiti and pamphlets. In a nation where free speech is guaranteed to all, citizens voice their opinions. What do students think might be an effective solution to the problems associated with hate groups? Is it better to ignore such groups, hoping lack of publicity will discourage them, or is it better to take an active stance against them? Encourage students to offer any solutions they can think of.

Communities Fight Back People in this Detroit neighborhood worked together to form a Neighborhood Watch group to keep their community safe. *What happened to the homicide rate in Detroit in the mid-1990s?*

to stand together," he warns. "You've got to redevelop a sense of neighborhoods." He adds, this is "not something you're going to change in a presidency or the two-year term of a mayor. You need long-range focus."

By the mid-1990s it seemed that cities were beginning to make progress against crime. In New York, Detroit, and many other urban areas where the homicide rate had soared, the number of killings dropped sharply. While officials can neither agree on the reasons for the decline nor predict that the trend will continue, a nervous public continues to be relieved when it receives the good news.

The Debate Continues
The Abortion Controversy

Violence of another sort marked the controversy over abortion. On one side were pro-choice advocates who believed that every woman had the right to choose for herself whether to have an abortion. On the other side

were people who held a pro-life position and who wanted to overturn *Roe* v. *Wade*, the Supreme Court decision which in 1973 legalized abortion.

Since 1989 when the United States Supreme Court, in *Webster* v. *Reproductive Health Services*, upheld a state's right to restrict abortions, pro-life supporters had chipped away at legalized abortion through increasingly restrictive state laws. In 1995 they succeeded in defeating President Clinton's nomination of Henry Foster to be surgeon general after he acknowledged performing 39 abortions during his 38-year medical career. At times the dispute turned especially ugly, as radical opponents of abortion attacked and even killed doctors and other workers at women's health-care centers across the nation.

Educating the Workers of Tomorrow
Schools Face New Challenges

As jobs in all fields become more high tech and demanding, workers need to be better prepared and better educated. In 1983 a presidential commission warned that American students lagged behind students in other industrialized nations. In a report entitled *A Nation at Risk*, the commission recommended more homework, longer school days, a longer school year, higher salaries for teachers, and an emphasis on such basic subjects as English, math, science, history, and computer science.

Educational Goals

That the goals set in 1983 had not been met was evident in the "education summit" called by President Bush in 1989. He and the nation's governors agreed on 6 broad, national goals. These goals included making sure all children are healthy and intellectually stimulated enough to start school and raising the academic level of American students from near the bottom among industrialized nations to the top in mathematics and science achievement. These goals would raise the high school graduation rate from about 75 percent to 90 percent, erase illiteracy, and make schools once again safe and drug free.

Education reformers and politicians, however, cannot agree on how to achieve these goals. Some believe more funds are needed. Others point out that unless parents and communities encourage academic excellence, merely increasing spending will not be enough. Conservative Republicans want to dismantle the federal Department of Education, arguing that all public education ought to be funded and controlled at the state and local levels.

SECTION THREE **923**

Communities Fight Back Some communities form Neighborhood Watch groups by working together with the local police to implement a procedure for neighborhood residents to follow that helps prevent crime. One of the tenets of Neighborhood Watch programs is that neighborhood residents learn who their neighbors are and note strangers behaving suspiciously.

Answer: *The homicide rate in Detroit in the mid-1990s dropped sharply.*

ASSESS

Meeting Lesson Objectives

Each section objective is tested by the section review question(s) that follows it in parentheses.

1. List arguments for and against gerrymandering. (1, 3)
2. Explain the changing nature of work in an increasingly technological society. (2, 5)
3. Describe the financial and educational challenges facing schools and educators as the United States moves toward the twenty-first century. (4, 5)

PORTFOLIO PROJECT

Portfolio Project

School Reform Have students do research in recent issues of newsmagazines by reading articles on schools that are trying innovative methods to improve student learning. Have students then choose one or two approaches

that appeal to them. Let them summarize the methodology and present their findings to the class. Then students can file their reports in their portfolios.

Evaluate

Have students complete the Section Review.

👉 🖥 Assign the Section 3 Quiz or use the Testmaker to develop a customized quiz. (Also in Spanish.) **LEP**

👉 🖥 Assign the Chapter 26 Test or use the Testmaker to develop a customized test.

👉 Have students complete the Chapter 26 Performance Assessment Activity. 📼

Reteach

🎧 Have students listen to the Chapter 26, Section 3 Audiocassette. (Also in Spanish.) **LEP**

👉 Have students complete the Chapter 26 Reteaching Activity. (Also in Spanish.) **LEP**

Enrich

👉 Have students complete the Chapter 26 Enrichment Activity. (Also in Spanish.) **LEP**

👉 Have students complete the Chapter 26 Geography in History Activity.

👉 Have students complete Interpreting Political Cartoons 5, 26, 51–55.

👉 Have students complete Supreme Court Case Studies 41, 61, 62.

CLOSE

Does the United States have an obligation to keep its borders open to immigrants? *(Some students might feel that all immigrants should be allowed to enter; others might feel that the United States has finite resources and must set limits.)*

924

Coming Together Up to one million African American men gathered in Washington, D.C., in October 1995 to pledge themselves to family and community values. *What did leaders urge all Americans to do?*

Prospects for School Reform

During the 1980s and 1990s schools throughout the nation tried to improve their educational systems. Some yielded encouraging results. The School of Education at Boston University began managing all of the public schools in Chelsea, Massachusetts, in 1990. Milwaukee, Wisconsin, gave some public school students vouchers to attend private schools. Iowa, Arkansas, Utah, Ohio, and other states experimented with school-choice programs.

Not one of these plans tackled school funding. All schools are not created equal. Many communities fund schools through property taxes. As a result affluent communities can spend far more to educate their children than poor or working-class communities. The federal and state governments tried to equalize school systems by distributing more tax money to poorer districts but with little success. State legislatures in the 1990s used the courts to determine whether they can equalize funding by increasing state or sales taxes rather than property taxes.

The cry for school reform grew weaker in the 1990s as Americans, concerned about the deficit and taxes, used their limited resources to satisfy other priorities. Many school districts cut or reduced programs such as foreign languages, music, and sports. In many communities class sizes expanded and the school year was shortened.

In contrast to these negative trends, an innovative experiment called Microsociety shows promising results. For the program's five elementary schools—two in Massachusetts and three in New York—the school day is split in half. In the morning students attend history, science, English, and math classes. In the afternoon they simulate

real-life experiences such as holding jobs, paying taxes, and owning businesses. Results are dramatic. After six years, the mostly African American students at City Magnet School in Lowell, Massachusetts, scored an average of two years above the national norms in reading and math.

Finding Common Ground
Uniting All Americans

In the mid-1990s Clinton noted the rancor of political debate in the nation. It seemed that the United States was becoming a country divided not only between rich and poor, but also along racial, religious, and ethnic lines, and between government and the governed. Government leaders called on citizens to be mindful of the traditions of freedom and hope that have attracted people all over the world to the United States. Leaders urged Americans to renew their sense of community and purpose—to find the common ground that unites us all.

Some people did just that. In neighborhoods around Washington, D.C., residents formed orange-hat patrols. Wearing orange caps, the neighbors pick up litter, note license plate numbers of suspicious cars, and chat with passersby. They have made a difference. Crime is down and a sense of community has developed.

This idea and others like it, initiated by citizens themselves, may ultimately have more effect on the immediate world we live in than laws handed down by Congress.

SECTION REVIEW

Vocabulary

1. Define: militia group, community policing.

Checking Facts

2. As the 1980s ended, how much money did women make compared with the amount earned by men?

3. Why did some Democrats favor gerrymandering? Why did some Republicans favor it?

Critical Thinking

Recognizing Bias

4. Some education reformers believe that many problems in education can be solved if more money is spent on schools. Is this point of view biased?

Linking Across Time

5. How may the jobs that many Americans hold be different in the next century?

Section 3 Review Answers

1. militia group (922), **community policing** (922)

2. Women made 71 cents for every dollar made by men.

3. Democrats wanted to create districts in which African Americans and Hispanic Americans could win. Republicans wanted to leave white majorities in as many districts as possible.

4. This viewpoint disregards other problems in education that are not related to money.

5. Jobs will make more use of modern technology. Most new jobs are occurring in the service sector rather than in manufacturing or agriculture as in the past.

Social Studies Skill

ANALYZING NEWS MEDIA

Learning the Skill

Every citizen needs to understand current events in order to make decisions about election issues, causes, and career choices. To stay informed, people use a variety of news sources, from broadcast media (television and radio) to print media (newspapers and newsmagazines).

How to Analyze the News

To get an accurate profile of current events, you must learn to think critically about the news you hear or read:

a. First, think about the source of the news story: reports that reveal sources are more reliable than those that don't because if you know the sources, you can evaluate them. Can all facts be verified?

b. Second, many news stories also analyze and interpret events. Such analyses may be more detailed than other reports, but they also reflect a reporter's biases. See if you can identify biases as you read or listen.

c. Finally, ask yourself whether the news is even-handed and thorough. Is it reported on the scene or secondhand? Does it fairly represent both sides of an issue? How many sources are used? The more sources cited for a fact, the more reliable it is.

Broadcast Media

Visual impact and immediacy are television's main strengths. Both television and radio replace a written account with an oral presentation. Both are up-to-the-minute. Stories can be edited and updated almost until airtime. Reporters can even interrupt their broadcasts to include new information.

Print Media

Print media carry a greater variety of news stories, as well as features and editorials, than broadcast media do. Reader comment and opinion sections offer interaction with subscribers. Print news is less immediate than broadcast news and becomes out-of-date more quickly.

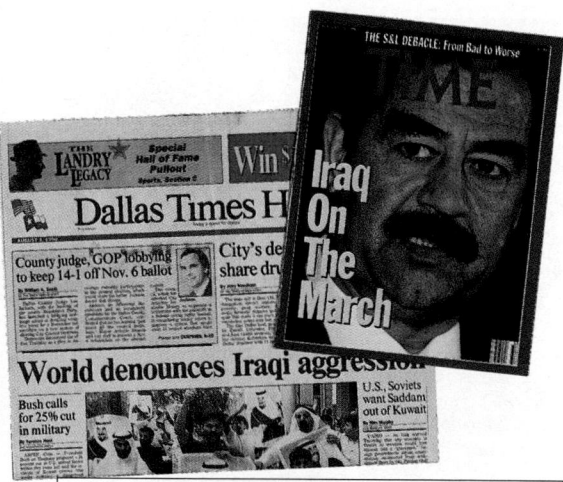

Media Representations Iraq's invasion of Kuwait in August 1990 immediately dominated news in the United States. *How do the headlines in the newspaper and the newsmagazine shown here emphasize different aspects of the event?*

Practicing the Skill

1. Find two articles, one in a current newspaper and the other in a newsmagazine, on a topic involving Latin America. Which article provided more in-depth coverage?

2. What points were the articles trying to make? Were the articles successful? Can the facts be verified?

3. Did either of the articles reflect bias? List any unsupported statements.

4. Was the news reported on the scene or secondhand? Do the articles seem to represent both sides fairly?

5. How many sources can you identify in the articles? List them.

Applying the Skill

Think of an issue in your community on which public opinion is divided. Read newspaper features and editorials about the issue and listen to television reports. Can you identify biases? Which reports most fairly represent the issue and the solutions? Why? Which reports are the most reliable? The least reliable? Why?

Additional Practice

For additional practice, see Reinforcing Skills on page 927.

SOCIAL STUDIES SKILL **925**

This feature deals with the skill of analyzing news media. Have students follow a series of steps to think critically about the news they hear or read. During the process point out to students the procedures for identifying biases, noticing the evenhandedness or fairness of news stories, and comparing sources of news stories.

VISUAL INSTRUCTION

Media Representations The typical newspaper story is written only hours before it reaches the reader. Newsmagazines, however, have deadlines as much as a week before printing.

Newsmagazines can carry longer articles and more elaborate photographs and illustrations than newspapers. The booklike format of newsmagazines allows in-depth treatment of topics, so often their stories are more analytical than those in some daily newspapers.

Answer: *The newsmagazine emphasizes Iraq's actions; the newspaper emphasizes worldwide responses. The newsmagazine may contain background information and possibly an in-depth analysis. The newspaper deals with the most recent developments.*

Practicing the Skill Answers

1. Answers should be supported by examples to explain why one coverage was more in-depth than the other.
2. Students should list points and the facts that can be verified.

3. Students should explain any bias that they find and list unsupported statements.
4. Answers should be supported by facts and reasons.
5. Students should list the sources they identify.

Additional Practice

☞ Have students complete the Chapter 26 Skill Reinforcement Activity.

Reviewing Key Terms

1. unfunded mandate
2. community policing
3. bipartisan coalition
4. pork barrel legislation
5. universal coverage

Recalling Facts

1. George Bush, William Clinton, and Ross Perot; Bush—successes in foreign affairs, tax-and-spend Democrats; Clinton—Bush's neglect of domestic concerns; Perot—federal budget deficit
2. Health care is expensive and growing more so, but reform is difficult because there are so many competing interests.
3. They thought the United States would provide a safe haven. Clinton sent troops to return Aristide to power.
4. Successes: budget reduction, Family Leave Bill, Brady Bill, crime bill; Disappointments: health-care reform, retaining voter confidence
5. Government assistance programs were cut; money for education, the arts, and the environment was cut.
6. the biggest midterm victory of the century; voter frustration, new communication outlets, a conservative swing
7. They promised to enact the provisions of the Contract With America. The House passed all 34 pieces of legislation, but only 2 were signed into law.
8. Clinton was opposed to major changes in Medicare; Republicans hinted at drastic cutbacks.
9. the service industry
10. Money for many schools comes from property taxes, which means more affluent areas have more money for schools. Future money might come from state or sales taxes, which would help to equalize school funding.

926

Reviewing Key Terms

Match each vocabulary word to its definition below. Write your answers on a separate sheet of paper.

bipartisan coalition	unfunded mandate
pork barrel legislation	community policing
universal coverage	militia group

1. laws that require states to take action without providing any money to the states to implement the action

2. sending more foot patrols into neighborhoods and establishing a better relationship between residents and police

3. a group consisting of both Republicans and Democrats

4. laws that usually involve spending money on projects of questionable necessity in order to bring money into a legislator's home district

5. health insurance or other programs that grant coverage to everyone regardless of ability to pay

Recalling Facts

1. What 3 candidates ran in the 1992 presidential campaign? On what issues did each candidate focus?

2. What are some of the problems with the current health-care system? Why is it so difficult to pass health-care reforms?

3. Why did Haitian refugees leave Haiti for the United States after Clinton became President? How was this issue resolved?

4. What were some of Clinton's successes and disappointments in office?

5. What are the effects of federal spending cuts on states, counties, and cities?

6. How big a victory did the Republicans achieve in the 1994 midterm elections? What accounted for their success?

7. What did the Republicans promise to do during the first 100 days of the 104th Congress? How successful were they?

8. Bill Clinton and Newt Gingrich talked to elderly voters in New Hampshire about health-care issues (see photo below). Where does each man stand on health-care issues?

9. As new jobs in agriculture and manufacturing disappear, in what industry do more and more Americans find new jobs?

10. Where does money for schools come from? From where might schools of the future receive funding?

Critical Thinking

1. **Making Comparisons** Explain why organized labor, farmers, and environmentalists feared NAFTA, while the Bush and Clinton administrations pushed for it.

2. **Identifying Central Issues** Explain the arguments that were used for and against arming the Bosnian Muslims.

3. **Drawing Conclusions** What did conservative groups do to influence the 1994 midterm elections? How successful were they?

4. **Expressing Problems Clearly** President Clinton supported affirmative action when he said, "Mend it, don't end it." Analyze the arguments for and against continuing affirmative action policies. Then explain which arguments you support and why.

5. **Determining Cause and Effect** What were some reasons that waves of political refugees entered the United States during the 1970s and the 1980s? What are some of the possible effects of extensive immigration to the United States?

© WALLY MCNAMEE/SYGMA

Critical Thinking

1. because jobs might move to Mexico, foreign produce could undercut U.S. prices, and pollution control would be lax in Mexico
2. Some favored arming the Muslims so they could defend themselves. Others felt that this would lead to escalated violence and killing.
3. Conservative groups published voter guides to influence voters. They were highly successful; the Republicans swept the midterm elections.
4. Proponents say these policies broaden the pool of qualified applicants. Opponents argue that less-qualified applicants are leapfrogged over better-qualified people.
5. wars, poverty, and political conflict, changes in immigration laws; more competition for jobs, more richness and diversity to American culture

926

RECENT IMMIGRATION TO THE UNITED STATES, 1990–1995

CANADA

Seattle (O,F,I)
Wash.
Portland (O,I,F)
Oregon
Montana
North Dakota
Minn.
Minneapolis (I)
Wis.
Mich.
Detroit (O,F,M)
Vt.
Maine
N.H.
Boston (O,I,W,E)
Mass.
Conn.
R.I.
N.Y.

Idaho
Wyoming
South Dakota
Iowa
Chicago (M,F,A,O,E,R,C,I)
Ill.
Cleveland (O,I,E)
Ohio
Philadelphia (I,U)
Pa.
N.J.
New York (W,O,A,F,R,E)

San Francisco (M,F,O,A,I)
Calif.
Nevada
Salt Lake City (M,D)
Utah
Denver (M,A)
Colorado
Nebraska
Kansas
Mo.
St. Louis (C,I)
Ind.
W. Va.
Va.
Del.
Md.
Washington, D.C. (A,O,I,F)

Las Vegas (M,F,A)
Los Angeles (M,A,F,O,I,C)
Arizona
New Mexico
Oklahoma
Ark.
Tenn.
Ky.
N.C.

San Diego (M,O,F,A,I)
Phoenix (M,A)
El Paso (M,A)
Dallas (M,I,A)
Texas
La.
Miss.
Ala.
Ga.
Atlanta (W,C)
S.C.

PACIFIC OCEAN
Hawaii (F,I,O)

San Antonio (M,A)
Houston (M,A,I)
New Orleans (M,I,O)
Fla.
Tampa (C,W,M)
ATLANTIC OCEAN

MEXICO
Gulf of Mexico
Miami (C,W,A,M)

IMMIGRANT GROUP
M Mexican
A Central American
C Cuban
W Other West Indian
I Indochinese
F Filipino
O Chinese and other Asian
R Russian and E. European
E Irish and W. European

FLOW OF IMMIGRATION
→ From Latin America
→ From Europe
→ From Asia

REGIONS
Northeast
Midwest
South Atlantic
Pacific
Mountain
South Central

0   250   500 mi.
0 250 500 km
Albers Equal-Area projection

DOMINICAN REPUBLIC
CUBA
HAITI
JAMAICA

Portfolio Project

Interview or read newspaper or newsmagazine accounts of someone who recently immigrated to this country. Write about his or her reasons for coming and the challenges and successes that they have had in a new country. Keep your report in your portfolio.

Cooperative Learning

Work with several of your classmates in a small group to conduct research to find out more about the changing electorate or the changing demographics of this nation. Each group should analyze information to make some predictions about the future. Groups might want to compile

their reports into a classroom book entitled *The Future of the United States*.

Reinforcing Skills

Analyzing News Media Choose one current issue and compare its coverage in two different media. Which medium supplies the most facts? Is the information accurate? What are the advantages and disadvantages of each medium?

Geography and History

Study the map on this page to answer the following questions:

1. In what regions of the United States do most immigrants from Asia settle?

2. Where do many immigrants from the Caribbean settle?

3. What immigrant groups have settled in Los Angeles?

4. What immigrant groups have settled in Atlanta?

5. How does Chicago's location help explain why it gets immigrants from so many parts of the world?

HISTORY JOURNAL

What did Ross Perot suggest in his infomercials to solve the country's problems? Why were his ideas so appealing to so many Americans?

Geography and History

1. The West Coast, the Northeast, the Midwest, and the South Central United States
2. Florida and the Northeast
3. Mexicans, Central Americans, Filipinos, Asians, Indochinese, and Cubans
4. West Indians and Cubans
5. Chicago is a large centrally located city, so it stands to reason that it would be a major stopping-off point or place through which people would travel.

History Journal

Ross Perot suggested getting the nation's finances in order. Americans liked his ideas because he presented solutions to the nation's economic problems that sounded as if they would work.

? BONUS QUESTION

This question may be used for extra credit on the chapter test.

Was the Endangered Species Act effective in protecting the habitat of the northern spotted owl in Oregon? Explain.

Answer: *Secretary of the Interior Manuel Lujan, Jr., exempted the timberlands where the owl lived from the Endangered Species Act. The Supreme Court, however, ruled in 1995 that even on private lands the habitat of the spotted owl must be preserved to prevent the owl from becoming extinct.*

Portfolio Project

If any students are fluent in a language other than English, they may want to conduct the interview in that language and then translate their findings into English for classmates.

Cooperative Learning

You might suggest that each group analyze demographic patterns in a different region of the United States. Then each group's information can be combined with that of other groups to form an analysis of the entire United States.

Reinforcing Skills

You may want to help focus students by suggesting the current issue to be analyzed. You may also want to suggest that students compare the issue's coverage in a newsmagazine, in a newspaper, or on a television news program.

927

TEACH

Making the Historical Connection

The United States boom in home video games began in 1979 when Atari, Midway, and other companies introduced games more challenging than Pong, such as Pac-Man, Galaxian, and Space Invaders. By 1982 books were published on video games, and consumers were spending more on video games than on movies and records.

FYI

Home Entertainment In the mid-1980s, a glut of poorly designed video games caused sales to plunge. Video games seemed dead. It was at this time that Nintendo introduced its home video game system in Japan. It was such an enormous success that Nintendo came to the United States to revive the video game craze here. Within five years Nintendo controlled 80 percent of the United States market. By the end of 1990, one of every three homes in the United States had a Nintendo system.

Then...

The Nintendo Entertainment System®

In 1985 video game sales in the United States plummeted. The nation seemed to have reached its saturation point. Then Nintendo introduced its Nintendo Entertainment System (NES), which revolutionized video games. No longer found only in arcades, Nintendo games could now be played on a home television set.

❷ In Super Mario Bros., Luigi and Mario® help the peaceful Mushroom People in their battle against the Koopa turtle tribe.

NINTENDO OF AMERICA, INC.

❶ The Nintendo Entertainment System used a control pad or joystick to control the action on the television screen. Nintendo released a new game, Super Mario Bros.®, for play on its new system.

NINTENDO OF AMERICA, INC.

Fun Facts

IN THE BEGINNING WAS PONG
The first successful totally electronic video game in the United States was Pong, a video Ping-Pong game. The three young engineers who invented Pong formed a company called Atari in 1974 to distribute the game.

928   THEN AND NOW

Background Information

A Home Networking Terminal Nintendo has its sights set on a goal that IBM and others have long assumed will be theirs: the first universal home computer. By the end of 1990, in United States homes there were 30 million Nintendo sets, 6 million Macintosh sets, and 18 million IBMs and compatibles. Thanks to a computer cable connector built into every Nintendo set, the system can be connected to a modem, a keyboard, and storage devices. When connected, the Nintendo system becomes a networking terminal. By plugging in a phone line, users can shop, research, make airline reservations, obtain stock quotations, and send E-mail.

FILE PHOTO BY DOUG MINDELL

④ Super Mario Bros. sold over 2.5 million copies in its first 4 months. It generated numerous sequels, television shows, magazines, fan clubs, and tie-ins.

Stats

MARIO TRIVIA

- Mario first appeared in Donkey Kong® in 1981. Mario was named Jumpman in this game.
- Mario was named after Mario Segali, the landlord of Nintendo's first warehouse in the United States.

VIDEO GAME FACTS

- In the United States, consumers spend more on video games than on any other form of entertainment, including movies and CDs.
- If Nintendo were a country, it would be more prosperous than many nations of the world.
- If all the Nintendo game paks sold around the world were laid end to end, they would stretch for about 82,860 miles (133, 322 km) —three and one-half times around the earth's equator.

...Now

③ Mario untiringly attempts to rescue Princess Toadstool from Bowser, the King of the Koopas.

NINTENDO OF AMERICA, INC.

VIDEO GAMES

PORTFOLIO PROJECT

Some people think that eventually the video game boxes that sit near the TV will link to a worldwide network. You might compete with a player overseas, order a pizza, or transfer money. Compare the video games of today with the video games of 1985, and then make predictions about the games of the future. Keep your report in your portfolio.

MARIO'S FIRST APPEARANCE

Donkey Kong derived its name from *donkey*, a stubborn, wily creature, and the mighty ape *King Kong*. To American video game salespeople, who were used to names with words such as *destroy* and *annihilate*, the name made no sense. Donkey Kong, however, was a huge success despite its name.

NINTENDO OF AMERICA, INC.

THEN AND NOW   **929**

Curriculum Connection

Economics Nintendo used a strategy called the razor marketing theory, which was first introduced by the toy industry in 1959 with Mattel's Barbie doll. This strategy focuses on developing and selling items to go with the original product (such as a Barbie outfit, a game cartridge, or a razor blade). Nintendo's game system is purposely kept inexpensive to entice consumers to buy it and to generate continuing sales of the software that is used with it.

Block Scheduling

The Portfolio Project on this page provides an excellent opportunity to enrich and extend the key elements of this feature.

CLOSE

Discuss with students the features of the Nintendo Entertainment System that made it so popular in the United States. *(Games could be played at home rather than in arcades; the games were fun.)*

Portfolio Project

The Future of Home Networking Have students investigate and formulate an opinion about the home networking system of the future. Do they think computers, televisions with cable lines, video game systems, or telephones will form the basis of this new technology? Do they foresee one piece of home equipment that incorporates televisions, telephones, personal computers, and video game systems, or do they think consumers will continue purchasing these items separately? Have students conduct research and explain their predictions to the class. They can file their results in their portfolios.

Appendix

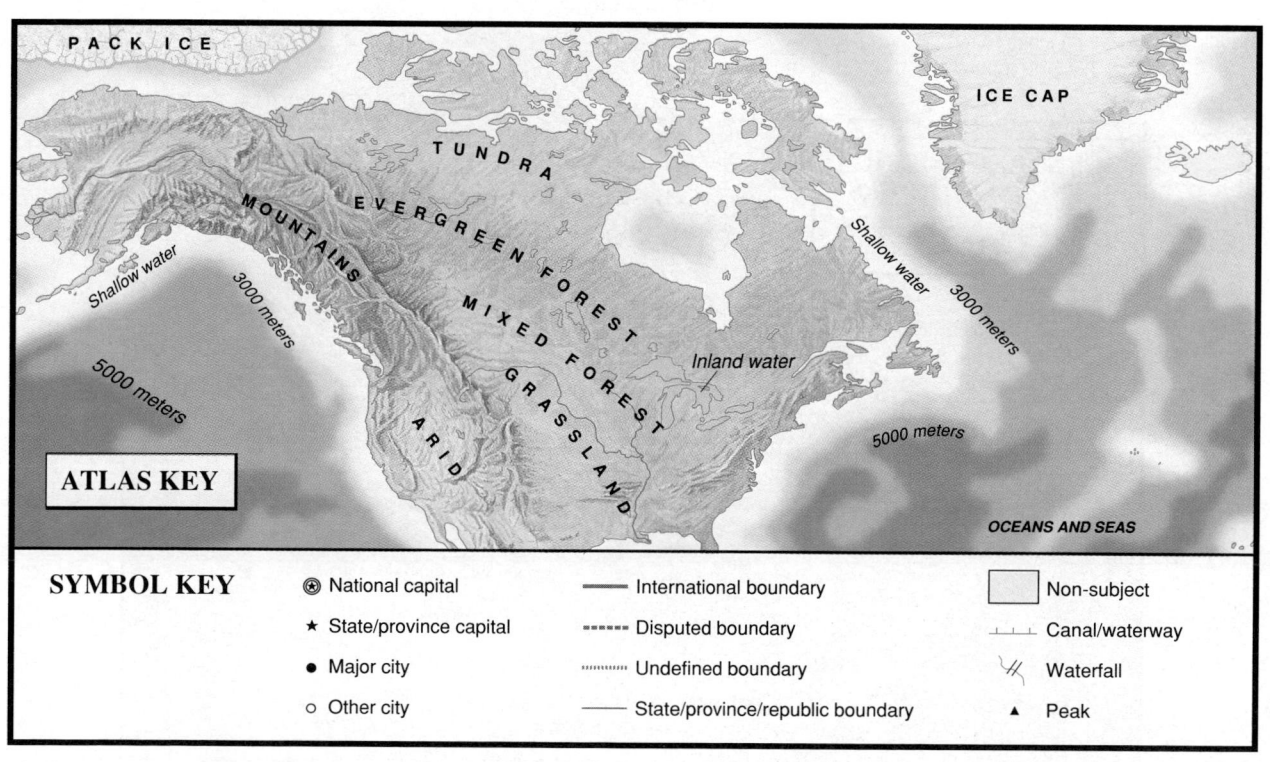

ATLAS KEY

SYMBOL KEY

⊛	National capital	——	International boundary	▢	Non-subject
★	State/province capital	- - - -	Disputed boundary	⊥⊥⊥	Canal/waterway
●	Major city	··········	Undefined boundary	⋉	Waterfall
○	Other city	——	State/province/republic boundary	▲	Peak

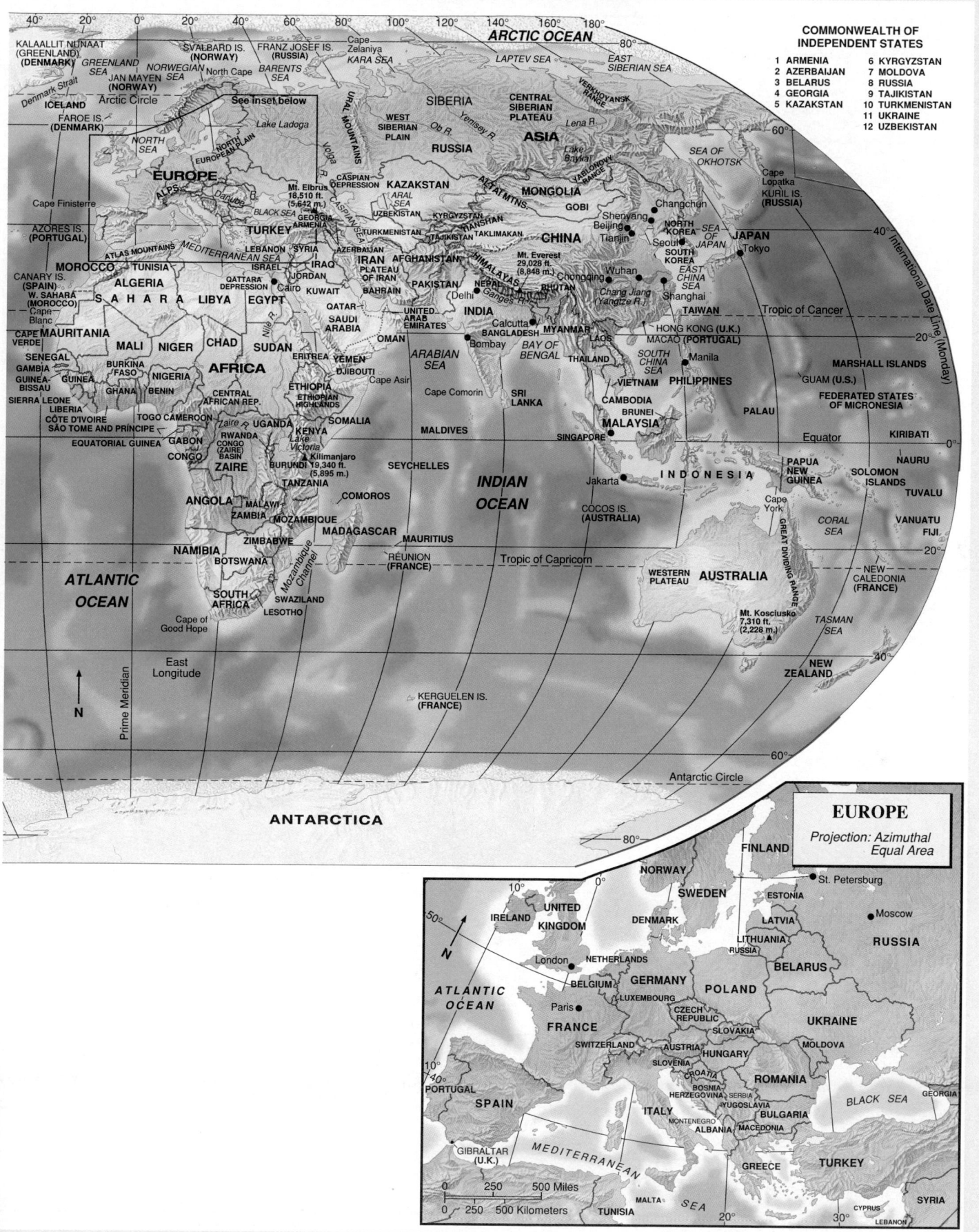

THE WORLD

ARCTIC OCEAN

COMMONWEALTH OF INDEPENDENT STATES

1	ARMENIA	6	KYRGYZSTAN
2	AZERBAIJAN	7	MOLDOVA
3	BELARUS	8	RUSSIA
4	GEORGIA	9	TAJIKISTAN
5	KAZAKSTAN	10	TURKMENISTAN
		11	UKRAINE
		12	UZBEKISTAN

EUROPE

Projection: Azimuthal Equal Area

0   250   500 Miles

0   250   500 Kilometers

Cape Flattery
Bellingham
Juan de Fuca Strait
Puget Sound
Seattle
Tacoma
Olympia
Mt. Rainier 14,410 ft. (4,392 m.)
F.D. Roosevelt Lake
Spokane
COLUMBIA PLATEAU
Pend Oreille Lake
Flathead Lake
Missouri River
Fort Peck Lake
Great Falls
Minot
Lake Sakakawea
Grand Forks
Fargo

WASHINGTON
Portland
Columbia River
Salem
Mt. Hood 11,235 ft. (3,424 m.)
Corvallis
Eugene
Lewiston
BITTERROOT
ROCKY
Helena
Butte
MONTANA
Billings
Yellowstone R.
NORTH DAKOTA
Bismarck

OREGON
Medford
Mt. Shasta 14,162 ft. (4,316 m.)
Goose Lake
Borah Peak 12,662 ft. (3,859 m.)
Boise
IDAHO
RANGE
Grand Teton Peak 13,770 ft. (4,197 m.)
Idaho Falls
BIGHORN MTN.
Powder River
SOUTH DAKOTA
BLACK HILLS
Rapid City
Pierre
Sioux Falls
Lake Oahe
Aberdeen

Eureka
Cape Mendocino
River
Sacramento
Twin Falls
Snake River
Pocatello
Great Salt Lake
WYOMING
Casper
North Platte River
NEBRASKA
GREAT PLAINS

Pyramid Lake
GREAT BASIN
GREAT SALT LAKE DESERT
RANGE
Salt Lake City
Ogden
Utah Lake
Orem
Provo
Rock Springs
Continental Divide
MOUNTAINS
Laramie
Cheyenne
Fort Collins
Greeley
North Platte
Grand Island
Platte
Republican River

Lake Tahoe
Reno
Carson City
NEVADA
Mono Lake
WASATCH
Green River
Boulder
Mt. Elbert 14,433 ft. (4,399 m.)
Denver
South Platte River
KANSAS
Salina
Hutchinson

Sacramento
Stockton
San Francisco
Oakland
San Jose
SIERRA NEVADA
Fresno
Mt. Whitney 14,494 ft. (4,418 m.)
Death Valley –282 ft. (–89 m.)
Las Vegas
Lake Mead
Lake Powell
COLORADO
Pikes Peak 14,110 ft. (4,301 m.)
Colorado Springs
Pueblo
SANGRE DE CRISTO MTNS.
Arkansas River
Wichita

CALIFORNIA
Bakersfield
Point Conception
MOJAVE DESERT
River
COLORADO PLATEAU
PAINTED DESERT
Grand Canyon
Flagstaff
Continental Divide
Santa Fe
Albuquerque
Canadian River
Enid
OKLAHOMA
Oklahoma City
Amarillo
Norman
Lawton

PACIFIC OCEAN
Los Angeles
San Bernardino
Riverside
Long Beach
Salton Sea
San Diego
Colorado River
Yuma
ARIZONA
Glendale
Phoenix
Mesa
Gila River
Tucson
Rio Grande
NEW MEXICO
Roswell
Las Cruces
El Paso
LLANO ESTACADO
Lubbock
Red River
Brazos River

GULF OF CALIFORNIA
Pecos River
TEXAS
Fort Worth
EDWARDS PLATEAU
Austin
San Antonio
Rio Grande
Corpus Christi
MEXICO
Brownsville

160° 155°
Kauai Channel
Kailua
Honolulu
HAWAII
PACIFIC OCEAN
Alenuihaha Channel
Mauna Kea 13,796 ft. (4,205 m.)
Hilo
0 100 Miles
0 100 Kilometers

180° 170° 160° 150°
RUSSIA
Arctic Circle
Pt. Barrow
BROOKS RANGE
Bering Strait
SEWARD PEN.
ALASKA
Yukon River
Fairbanks
Tanana River
Mt. McKinley 20,320 ft. (6,194 m.)
ALASKA RANGE
CANADA
Bethel
Iliamna Lake
Anchorage
Juneau
Sitka
BERING SEA
BRISTOL BAY
ALASKA PENINSULA
Shelikof Str.
Kodiak
GULF OF ALASKA
ALEUTIAN ISLANDS
0 250 500 Miles
0 250 500 Kilometers

95° 90° 85° 80° 75° 50° 70° 65°

CANADA

MAINE
Moosehead Lake
St. Lawrence River
Lake of the Woods 45°
Bangor

Red Lake
Lake Superior
Duluth
MINNESOTA

Lake Champlain
Mt. Washington 6,288 ft. (1,905 m.) ▲
Augusta
Burlington
Montpelier ★
Lewiston
Portland
N.H.
VT.
65°

WISCONSIN
Concord ★
Manchester
Green Bay
Appleton

Lake Michigan
Lake Huron
ADIRONDACK MTNS.
Hudson R.
Boston
MASS.
Cape Cod

Minneapolis ● St. Paul ★
Mississippi River
Lake Ontario
Utica
Albany ★
Worcester
Springfield
Rochester ○

Rochester
Syracuse
New Haven
Providence ★
R.I.

MICHIGAN
Niagara Falls
Buffalo
Binghamton
Hartford ★
CONN.
40°

Madison ★
Milwaukee
Racine
Grand Rapids
Flint
Lansing
Detroit
NEW YORK
Newark
Yonkers
New York
Allentown
N.J.

Sioux City ●
Dubuque
Rockford ○
Chicago
South Bend
Toledo
Erie
Lake Erie
Cleveland
Youngstown
Philadelphia ●
Trenton ★
Camden
Wilmington
Dover ★

IOWA
Aurora
Gary
Hammond
Fort Wayne
Akron
Canton
PENNSYLVANIA
Harrisburg ★
Pittsburgh
Wheeling
MD.
Baltimore
DEL.
DELAWARE BAY

Omaha ●
Council Bluffs ○
Des Moines ★
Joliet
Peoria
OHIO
Columbus ★
Dayton
Parkersburg
Arlington
Annapolis ★
Washington ⊛
D.C.

Lincoln ★
ILLINOIS
CENTRAL
LOWLAND
Springfield ★
Decatur
Muncie
Indianapolis ★
Cincinnati
WEST VIRGINIA
Ohio River
Charleston ★
Richmond ★
Newport News
ATLANTIC

Kansas City
Independence
East St. Louis
St. Louis
Wabash R.
INDIANA
Evansville
Louisville
Frankfort ★
Lexington
Huntington
Roanoke
VIRGINIA
Norfolk
CHESAPEAKE BAY
OCEAN
35°

Topeka ★
Lawrence
Kansas City
Jefferson City ★
Harry S. Truman Res.
KENTUCKY
Owensboro
Cumberland River
APPALACHIAN MOUNTAINS
Roanoke River
Cape Hatteras

MISSOURI
Springfield
OZARK PLATEAU
Durham
Greensboro
Raleigh ★
Nashville ★
Knoxville
Mt. Mitchell 6,684 ft. (2,037 m.) ▲
Winston-Salem

Tulsa ●
OZARK PLATEAU
ARKANSAS
Mississippi River
Memphis
Chattanooga
Huntsville
TENNESSEE
Tennessee River
PLATEAU
CUMBERLAND
Charlotte
Greenville
NORTH CAROLINA
70°

R.S. Kerr Res.
Fort Smith
North Little Rock
Little Rock ★
Hot Springs
Spartanburg
Columbia ★
SOUTH CAROLINA

Lake Eufaula
Pine Bluff
Greenville
Birmingham
Chattahoochee R.
Atlanta ★
Augusta
Charleston

Lake Texoma
Dallas ●
Shreveport
Meridian
Jackson ★
ALABAMA
Tuscaloosa
Montgomery ★
GEORGIA
Macon
30°

LOUISIANA
Hattiesburg
Alabama R.
Columbus
Albany
Savannah
COASTAL PLAIN

Sam Rayburn Reservoir
MISSISSIPPI
Mobile
Pensacola
Jacksonville

Baton Rouge ★
Lake Pontchartrain
Biloxi
Tallahassee ★
FLORIDA

Houston ●
Lafayette
Lake Charles
New Orleans
Cape Canaveral
Orlando

GULF OF MEXICO
Tampa
St. Petersburg
Lake Okeechobee
Palm Beach
25°

N ↑
Miami
Miami Beach
Cape Sable

Key West
Straits of Florida
THE BAHAMAS

CUBA
80°
75°

95° 90° 85°

UNITED STATES

⊛ National capital
★ State capital
● Major city
━ International boundary
─ State boundary

0   150   300 Miles
0 150 300 Kilometers

Projection: Albers Equal Area

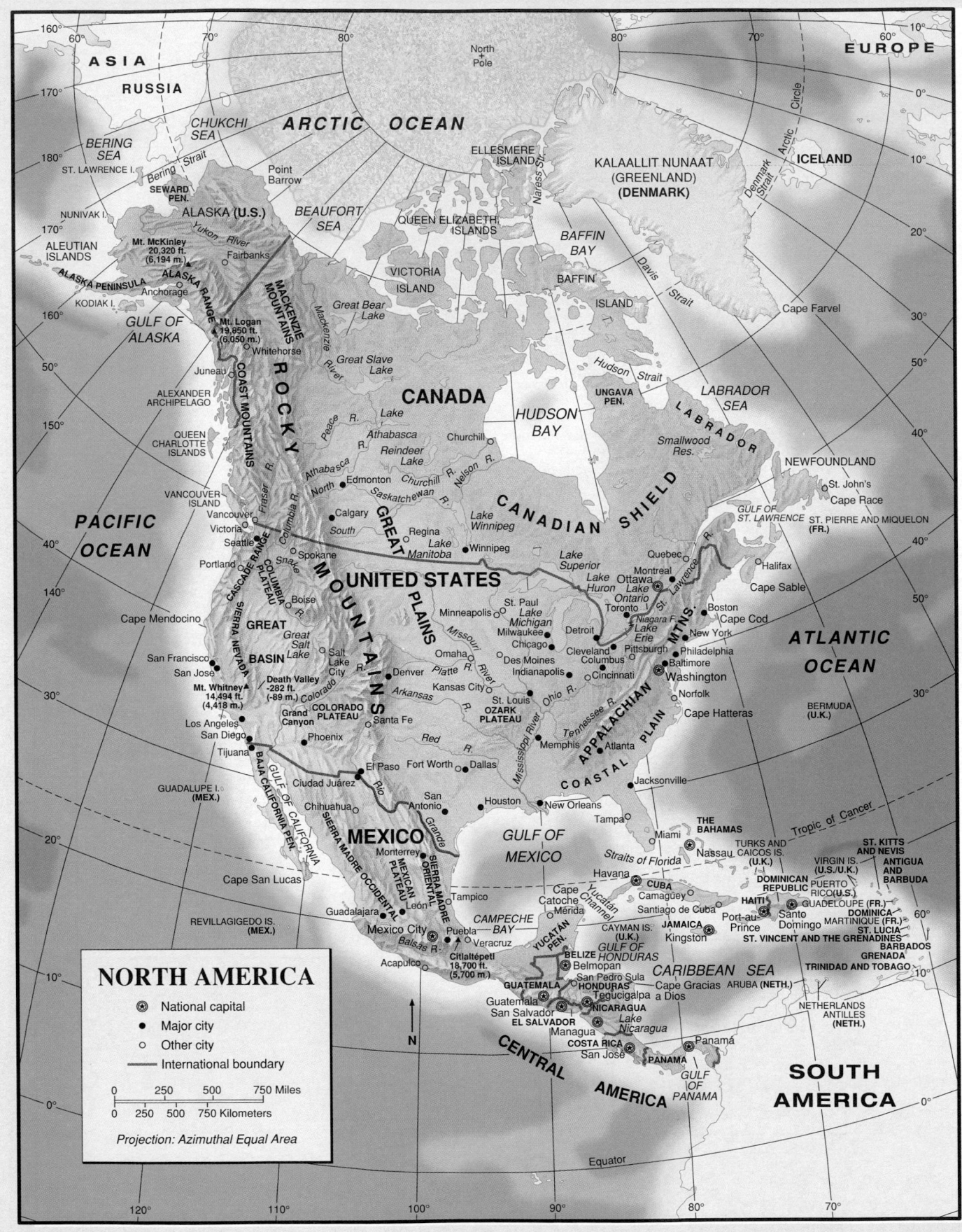

160° 60° 70° 80° 80° 70° 60° 10°
10°
ASIA
RUSSIA
EUROPE
170°
North + Pole
10°
CHUKCHI SEA
BERING SEA
180°
ST. LAWRENCE I.
Bering Strait
ARCTIC OCEAN
ELLESMERE ISLAND
KALAALLIT NUNAAT (GREENLAND) (DENMARK)
Arctic Circle
ICELAND
10°
Point Barrow
SEWARD PEN.
170°
NUNIVAK I.
ALASKA (U.S.)
BEAUFORT SEA
QUEEN ELIZABETH ISLANDS
Denmark Strait
20°
ALEUTIAN ISLANDS
Mt. McKinley 20,320 ft. (6,194 m.)
Yukon River
Fairbanks
30°
170°
ALASKA PENINSULA
ALASKA RANGE
Anchorage
MACKENZIE MOUNTAINS
VICTORIA ISLAND
BAFFIN BAY
Cape Farvel
KODIAK I.
GULF OF ALASKA
Mt. Logan 19,850 ft. (6,050 m.)
Whitehorse
Great Bear Lake
BAFFIN ISLAND
160°
50°
Juneau
Mackenzie River
Great Slave Lake
Hudson Strait
LABRADOR SEA
50°
ALEXANDER ARCHIPELAGO
ROCKY
CANADA
HUDSON BAY
UNGAVA PEN.
LABRADOR
150°
QUEEN CHARLOTTE ISLANDS
Lake
Peace R.
Athabasca R.
Reindeer Lake
Churchill
Smallwood Res.
NEWFOUNDLAND
40°
VANCOUVER ISLAND
Athabasca
North
Edmonton
Churchill R.
Nelson R.
CANADIAN SHIELD
St. John's
Cape Race
PACIFIC OCEAN
COAST MOUNTAINS
Vancouver
Calgary
Saskatchewan R.
Lake Winnipeg
GULF OF ST. LAWRENCE
ST. PIERRE AND MIQUELON (FR.)
40°
Victoria
South
Regina
Winnipeg
Quebec
Halifax
140°
Seattle
GREAT
Lake Manitoba
Lake Superior
Montreal
St. Lawrence R.
Cape Sable
Portland
CASCADE RANGE
COLUMBIA PLATEAU
Spokane
Columbia R.
Snake R.
UNITED STATES
PLAINS
Lake Huron
Ottawa
Toronto
Lake Ontario
Boston
Cape Cod
New York
50°
Cape Mendocino
Boise
MOUNTAINS
Minneapolis
St. Paul
Lake Michigan
Niagara Falls
Lake Erie
Detroit
ADIRONDACK MTNS.
Philadelphia
ATLANTIC OCEAN
GREAT
Great Salt Lake
Missouri R.
Milwaukee
Chicago
Cleveland
Pittsburgh
Baltimore
San Francisco
BASIN
Salt Lake City
Omaha
Des Moines
Columbus
Cincinnati
Washington
San Jose
Mt. Whitney 14,494 ft. (4,418 m.)
Death Valley -282 ft. (-89 m.)
Denver
Platte R.
Kansas City
St. Louis
Ohio R.
Norfolk
SIERRA NEVADA
Colorado R.
Arkansas R.
OZARK PLATEAU
APPALACHIAN
Cape Hatteras
BERMUDA (U.K.)
30°
Los Angeles
Grand Canyon
COLORADO PLATEAU
Santa Fe
Tennessee R.
San Diego
Phoenix
Red R.
Memphis
Atlanta
COASTAL PLAIN
Tijuana
BAJA CALIFORNIA
El Paso
Fort Worth
Dallas
Mississippi River
GUADALUPE I. (MEX.)
GULF OF CALIFORNIA
Ciudad Juárez
Rio Grande
San Antonio
Houston
Jacksonville
Chihuahua
New Orleans
THE BAHAMAS
Tropic of Cancer
ST. KITTS AND NEVIS
20°
MEXICO
Tampa
Miami
TURKS AND CAICOS IS. (U.K.)
VIRGIN IS. (U.S./U.K.)
ANTIGUA AND BARBUDA
Cape San Lucas
SIERRA MADRE OCCIDENTAL
Monterrey
SIERRA MADRE ORIENTAL
GULF OF MEXICO
Straits of Florida
Nassau
Havana
DOMINICAN REPUBLIC
PUERTO RICO (U.S.)
MEXICAN PLATEAU
CUBA
Camagüey
GUADELOUPE (FR.)
REVILLAGIGEDO IS. (MEX.)
León
Tampico
Cape Catoche
Santiago de Cuba
Port-au-Prince
HAITI
Santo Domingo
DOMINICA
MARTINIQUE (FR.)
Guadalajara
Mérida
Yucatán Channel
CAYMAN IS. (U.K.)
JAMAICA
ST. LUCIA
ST. VINCENT AND THE GRENADINES
Mexico City
Puebla
CAMPECHE BAY
YUCATÁN PEN.
Kingston
BARBADOS
Balsas R.
Veracruz
GULF OF HONDURAS
GRENADA
Citlaltépetl 18,700 ft. (5,700 m.)
BELIZE
Belmopan
San Pedro Sula
CARIBBEAN SEA
TRINIDAD AND TOBAGO
10°
Acapulco
GUATEMALA
Cape Gracias a Dios
ARUBA (NETH.)
Guatemala
Tegucigalpa
HONDURAS
NETHERLANDS ANTILLES (NETH.)
San Salvador
NICARAGUA
EL SALVADOR
Managua
Lake Nicaragua
N
COSTA RICA
San José
PANAMA
Panamá
SOUTH AMERICA
CENTRAL AMERICA
GULF OF PANAMA
0°
0°
Equator
120° 110° 100° 90° 80° 70°

NORTH AMERICA

- ⊛ National capital
- ● Major city
- ○ Other city
- —— International boundary

0   250   500   750 Miles
0   250   500   750 Kilometers

Projection: Azimuthal Equal Area

LATIN AMERICA

⊛ National capital
● Major city
○ Other city
— International boundary

0   500   1000 Miles
0 500 1000 Kilometers

Projection: Miller Cylindrical

EURASIA

⊛ National capital
● Major city
○ Other city
—— International boundary
----- Disputed boundary
········· Undefined boundary

0	500	1000 Miles
0	500	1000 Kilometers

Projection: Robinson

ALBAN. —Albania
BAH. —Bahrain
B.H. —Bosnia and Herzegovina
CR. —Croatia
ISR. —Israel
KUW. —Kuwait
LIECH. —Liechtenstein
LITH. —Lithuania
LUX. —Luxembourg
MACE. —Macedonia
MON. —Monaco
MONT. —Montenegro
S.M. —San Marino
SL. —Slovenia
SWITZ. —Switzerland
U.A.E. —United Arab Emirates

75° 90° 105° 120° 135° 150° 165° 180° 165° 150° 135°

SEVERNAYA ZEMLYA

TAYMYR PEN.
• Noril'sk
Yenisey

LAPTEV SEA

NEW SIBERIAN ISLANDS

EAST SIBERIAN SEA 75°

WRANGEL ISLAND

CENTRAL SIBERIAN
PLATEAU

KOLYMA
PLAIN

CHUKOTSK
PEN.

Bering Strait

Lower Tunguska R.
River
RUSSIA
Angara R.
Krasnoyarsk •
Bratsk Res.
• Novosibirsk
Novosibirsk Res.
Semipalatinsk •
Lake Zaysan

LENA PLATEAU
Lena River
Yakutsk •

SIBERIA

STANOVOY RANGE

VERKHOYANSK RANGE

Kolyma

KOLYMA RANGE

Anadyr R.
Magadan •

Cape Navarin

Mt. Klyuchevsk
15,584 ft.
(4,750 m.) ▲

SEA OF
OKHOTSK

KAMCHATKA
PEN.

BERING SEA 60°

KOMANDORSKIY IS.

SAYAN MTNS.
Lake Baykal
YABLONOVY RANGE

DA HINGGAN LING

Amur
Komsomol'sk •

Khabarovsk •

Cape Lopatka

ALTAI MTNS.
MONGOLIA
• Ulaanbaatar
DZUNGARIAN
BASIN
Ürümqi •
TIANSHAN
TURFAN
Tarim Depression
TAKLIMAKAN

MONGOLIAN
PLATEAU GOBI
ASIA

Songhua Jiang
NORTHEAST
(MANCHURIAN)
Harbin •
Changchun •
PLAIN
Shenyang •
Anshan •
N.
KOREA
Pyongyang •

L. Khanka
• Vladivostok

KURIL ISLANDS

La Pérouse Strait

Sapporo •

SEA OF
JAPAN

45°

CHINA
KUNLUN SHANBAYAN HAR
SHAN
HIMALAYAS
Annapurns Pk.
26,502 ft. PLATEAU OF
(8,078 m.) XIZANG
Mt. Everest Lhasa •
29,028 ft.
(8,848 m.) Mt. Kangchenjunga
28,208 ft. (8,598 m.)
NEPAL
Kathmandu Thimphu
BHUTAN
Ganges R.
Vārānasi • BANGLADESH
GANGES Dhaka •
PLAIN Khulna •
Calcutta •

Huang He
Beijing •
Tianjin •
NORTH
CHINA
PLAIN

Seoul •
Inchon • S. Taegu •
YELLOW KOREA
SEA
Kitakyūshū •

JAPAN
Kyōto • Tokyo •
Kawasaki •
Osaka • Yokohama •

PACIFIC

Wei He He
Xi'an •

Nanjing •
Chang Jiang
Chengdu • L. Tai
Hangzhou •
Chang L. Poyang
Changsha • Nanchang
Fuzhou •
Guiyang •
YUNGUI
PLATEAU
Kunming •

Shanghai •

EAST CHINA
SEA

RYUKYU IS.
(JAP.)

30°

OCEAN

MYANMAR
Chittagong •
Mandalay •
Chiang Mai •
ANNAMESE CORD.
BAY OF
BENGAL
Bassein •
Preparis
Channel
ANDAMAN IS.
(IND.)
CEYLON
NICOBAR IS.
(IND.)

Jiang
Guangzhou •
Macao • Victoria •
HONG KONG
MACAO (U.K.)
(PORT.)

Taipei •
TAIWAN
Kaohsiung •

Tropic of Cancer

Formosa Strait
Luzon Strait

Hanoi •
Haiphong •
LAOS
Vientiane
KHORAT
PLATEAU
Yangon • THAILAND Ubon •
Ratchathani •
Thonburi • CAMBODIA
Krung Thep VIETNAM
(Bangkok)
Tonle Sap Phnom Penh •
Ho Chi Minh City •

Savannakhet •
Da Nang •
INDOCHINA
SOUTH
CHINA

Cape Engaño
LUZON
Quezon City •
Manila •
MINDORO

PHILIPPINE
SEA

15°

ANDAMAN
SEA

SEA

PALAWAN

PHILIPPINES
Cebu •
MINDANAO
Davao •

George Town •
Ipoh •
MALAY
PEN.
Medan • Kuala Lumpur •
Strait of Malacca
MALAYSIA
SUMATRA SINGAPORE
Singapore •
Jambi •
BARISAN MTNS.
Palembang •
JAVA SEA
Bandung • Jakarta •
JAVA Surabaya •

Bandar Seri
Begawan
BRUNEI
SULU ARCH.
(PHIL.) Point Tinaca

BORNEO HIGHLANDS
BORNEO
Pontianak •
Banjarmasin •
CELEBES
Ujung Pandang •

HALMAHERA

Equator 0°

BANDA SEA

Cape d'Urville
Jayapura •
Jaya Pk.
16,499 ft.
(5,029 m.) ▲
NEW GUINEA

INDONESIA

90° 105° 120° 135° 150° 165°
15°

EUROPE

BLACK SEA

PONTUS MTS.

Istanbul
Bosporus
SEA OF MARMARA
Dardanelles
AEGEAN SEA
Bursa
Izmir
Denizli

Samsun

ANATOLIAN
ASIA MINOR
TURKEY
Ankara
Eskisehir
Kayseri
PLATEAU
Erciyes Dagi
12,369 ft.
(3,770 m.)
Konya

Antalya
TAURUS MTS.
Adana
Latakia
Nicosia
CYPRUS
Tripoli
Beirut
LEBANON
GOLAN HEIGHTS
Haifa
Nābulus
Tel Aviv-Yafo
Jerusalem
ISRAEL
WEST
BANK
GAZA
STRIP
DEAD SEA DEPRESSION
SINAI
PEN.
Al Aqabah
GULF OF AQABA

Bizerte
Cape Bon
Tunis
Sfax
GULF OF GABÈS
TUNISIA

Tripoli
Misrātah

MEDITERRANEAN SEA

Cape Hilāl
Banghāzī
GULF OF SIDRA

CYRENAICA

Matrūh

QATTARA DEPRESSION

Alexandria
Damanhūr
Delta of the Nile
Port Said
Tanta
Suez Canal
Ismailia
El Giza
Cairo
Faiyūm
Beni Suéf
El Minya
Suez

ARABIAN DESERT

LIBYAN DESERT

LIBYA

Sardalas

LIBYAN PLATEAU

Tropic of Cancer

EGYPT

Al Jawf

Qena
Luxor

Aswān

Lake Nasser

AFRICA

Nile River

Blue Nile R.
White Nile R.

40°
10°
20°
30°
30°
20°
10°

Inset map

Antayla
TAURUS MTS.
Adana
Gaziantep
Aleppo
Latakia
Euphrates River
Nicosia
CYPRUS
Hamāh
Deir-ez-Zor
Tripoli
Beirut
LEBANON
Hims
SYRIA
Damascus
MEDITERRANEAN SEA
Haifa
GOLAN HEIGHTS
ISRAELI-OCCUPIED
SYRIAN
Nābulus
ISRAEL
Tel Aviv-Yafo
WEST
Zarqa
Jerusalem
GAZA
STRIP
BANK
Amman
DESERT
Delta of the Nile
Port Said
Damanhūr
Ismailia
DEAD SEA DEPRESSION
JORDAN
Tanta
Suez Canal
El Giza
Cairo
Suez
SINAI
Faiyūm
PEN.
AN NAFUD DESERT
Beni Suéf
Al Aqabah
EGYPT
ARABIAN DESERT
Tabūk
El Minya
GULF OF SUEZ
GULF OF AQABA
Nile River

20°
20°

0   50   100 Miles
0 50 100 Kilometers

MIDDLE EAST

- ⊛ National capital
- ● Major city
- ○ Other city
- —— International boundary
- ----- Disputed boundary
- ·········· Undefined boundary

0   100   200   300 Miles
0   100   200   300 Kilometers

Projection: Azimuthal Equal Area

N

40° 50° 60° 40°

Trabzon

Erzurum Mt. Ararat 16,945 ft. (5,165 m.)

Lake Van

Malatya Diyarbakir Ardabil Tabriz *Lake Urmia* ASIA

Gaziantep Urmia Rasht ELBURZ MTNS. Mashhad

Aleppo Mosul Irbil Qazvin Mt. Demavend 18,386 ft. (5,604 m.)

ZAGROS

Hamâh Deir-ez-Zor Kirkuk Tehran

SYRIA Hims *Tigris R.* IRAQ Hamadân Qom GREAT SALT DESERT

Damascus SYRIAN MOUNTAINS Bâkhtarân Arâk I R A N PLATEAU OF IRAN Birjand

ISRAELI-OCCUPIED Baghdad Esfahân

JORDAN *Euphrates R.* Karbalâ Al Hillah

Zarqa DESERT Al Najaf Ahvâz Kermân

Amman An Nâsirîyah Abadan Shîrâz Zâhedân 30°

AN NAFUD Al Basrah KUWAIT Bûshehr

Tabûk DESERT Hawalli Kuwait Al Ahmadî

See inset below PERSIAN Bandar 'Abbâs

Ha'il *Strait of Hormuz*

NAJD PLATEAU Buraydah Ad Dammâm Manama GULF Dubai GULF OF OMAN

Madinah BAHRAIN QATAR Abu Dhabi

Yanbu al Bahr Al Hufûf Doha

RED TUWAYQ MTS. Riyadh UNITED ARAB EMIRATES Muscat Tropic of Cancer

SAUDI ARABIA Cape Al Hadd

SEA ARABIAN PENINSULA OMAN 20°

Jiddah Makkah RUB AL KHALI Duqm

ASIR MOUNTAINS At Ta'if

Mt. Nabî Shu'ayb 12,336 ft. (3,760 m.) San'a Al Ghaydah

Lake Tana Al Hudaydah YEMEN Al Mukallâ ARABIAN SEA

Bab el Mandeb Ta'izz

Aden GULF OF ADEN Cape Asir SOCOTRA (YEMEN)

40° 50° 60°

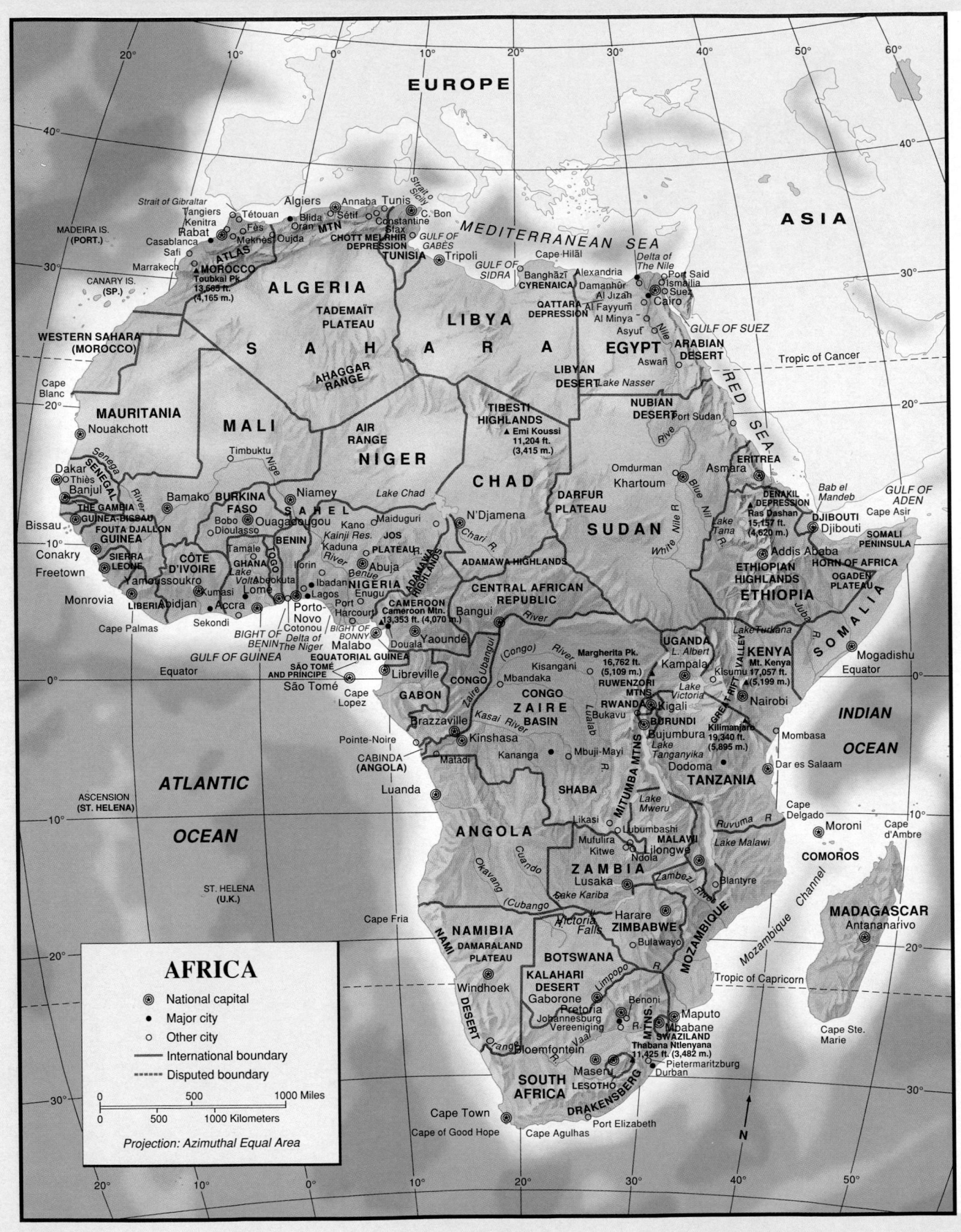

AFRICA

- ⊚ National capital
- • Major city
- ○ Other city
- —— International boundary
- ------ Disputed boundary

0   500   1000 Miles

0   500   1000 Kilometers

Projection: Azimuthal Equal Area

NEPAL

BHUTAN

BANGLADESH

CHINA

Tropic of Cancer

INDIA

90°

100°

110°

Chindwin R.

Mandalay
Myingyan

MYANMAR

Irrawaddy R.

ARAKAN MTNS.

20°

Salween

Henzada

River

Pegu

Bassein

C. Negrais

Yangon

Moulmein

GULF OF
MARTABAN

Preparis
Channel

Tavoy

Coco Channel

ANDAMAN
ISLANDS

ANDAMAN
SEA

Chiang Mai

Vientiane

LAOS

KHORAT
PLATEAU

THAILAND

Nakhon
Ratchasima

Nan

Ping R.

Chao Phraya R.

Krung Thep
(Bangkok)

Thonburi

Mekong River

Red R.

Black R.

Hanoi

Haiphong

GULF OF
TONKIN

INDOCHINA

ANNAMESE CORD.

Hue

Da Nang

Savannakhet

Ubon
Ratchathani

VIETNAM

Qui-Nhon

CAMBODIA

Tonle Sap

Nha-Trang

GULF OF
THAILAND

Phnom
Penh

Ho Chi Minh City

10°

ISTHMUS
OF
KRA

Long Xuyen

Pt. Bai Bung

SRI LANKA

NICOBAR
ISLANDS

N

Great
Channel

Hat Yai

SOUTH CHINA

SEA

INDIAN
OCEAN

George Town

MALAY

Ipoh

PENINSULA

Medan

Kuala
Lumpur

Strait of Malacca

MALAYSIA

ANAMBAS
IS.

NATUNA
ISLANDS

C. Datu

L. Toba

Johor Baharu

SINGAPORE
Singapore

Kapuas R.

Equator

0°

SUMATRA

Pekanbaru

Pontianak

Karimata Strait

Padang

Jambi

BARISAN

Palembang

MTNS.

JAVA SEA

MAINLAND
SOUTHEAST ASIA

⊚ National capital
● Major city
○ Other city
── International boundary

0   200   400 Miles
0   200   400 Kilometers

Projection: Mercator

Sunda Strait

Jakarta

Bandung

JAVA

Surakarta

Semarang

Yogyakarta

10°

90°

100°

110°

TERRITORIAL EXPANSION OF THE UNITED STATES

Alaska
1959

CANADA

0   400 mi.
0   400 km

175°W   155°W   135°W
70°N
60°N

C A

Washington
1889

Lewis and Clark 1804-1806

Columbia River

Portland

Montana
1889

Missouri River

North
Dakota
1889

Minnesota
1858

Pike 1805-1806

Oregon
1859

Oregon Trail

Idaho
1890

Snake River

ROCKY

Wyoming
1890

South Dakota
1889

BLACK
HILLS

Fremont 1842

Nebraska
1867

Iowa
1846

Fremont 1845

Salt Lake
City

Fort Bridger

Oregon Trail and Pony Express

St. Joseph

SIERRA

COAST

Pony Express

Nevada
1864

Utah
1896

MOUNTAINS

Colorado
1876

Fremont 1845

Kansas
1861

Independence

Missouri
1821

San Francisco

Sacramento

NEVADA

Old Spanish Trail

Powell 1869-1872

Colorado River

Santa Fe Trail

Arkansas River

Pike 1806-1807

OZARK
MTS.

RANGES

California
1850

Oklahoma
1907

Arkansas
1836

PACIFIC
OCEAN

Los Angeles

Arizona
1912

Santa Fe

New Mexico
1912

Texas
1845

Red River

Natchitoches

N

—— Explorer route
—— Settler trail
1912 Date of Statehood

Rio Grande

Pike 1805-1806

Houston

San Antonio

MEXICO

160°W   155°W
Hawaii
1959
22°N
20°N

0   150 mi.
0   150 km

0   150   300 mi.
0   150   300 km
Albers Equal-Area projection

120°W   110°W   100°W

Lewis and Clark 1804–1806
William Clark and Merriweather Lewis,
guided by the Shoshone princess
Sacajawea and the enslaved York,
crossed the Rockies and reached the
mouth of the Columbia River.

Zebulon Pike 1806–1807
Pike not only explored the Arkansas and
Red Rivers of the Southwest but also
entered Spanish territory. His reports on
the rich overland trade with Mexico and
on Spanish military weakness helped stimulate American expansion into Texas.

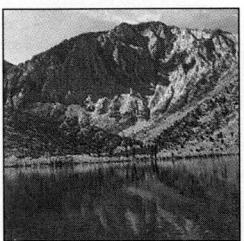

John Charles Fremont 1842–1844
Fremont's love of the wilderness
inspired him to undertake expeditions
to Wyoming, the Northwest, and
California. His surveys charted
America's westward expansion.

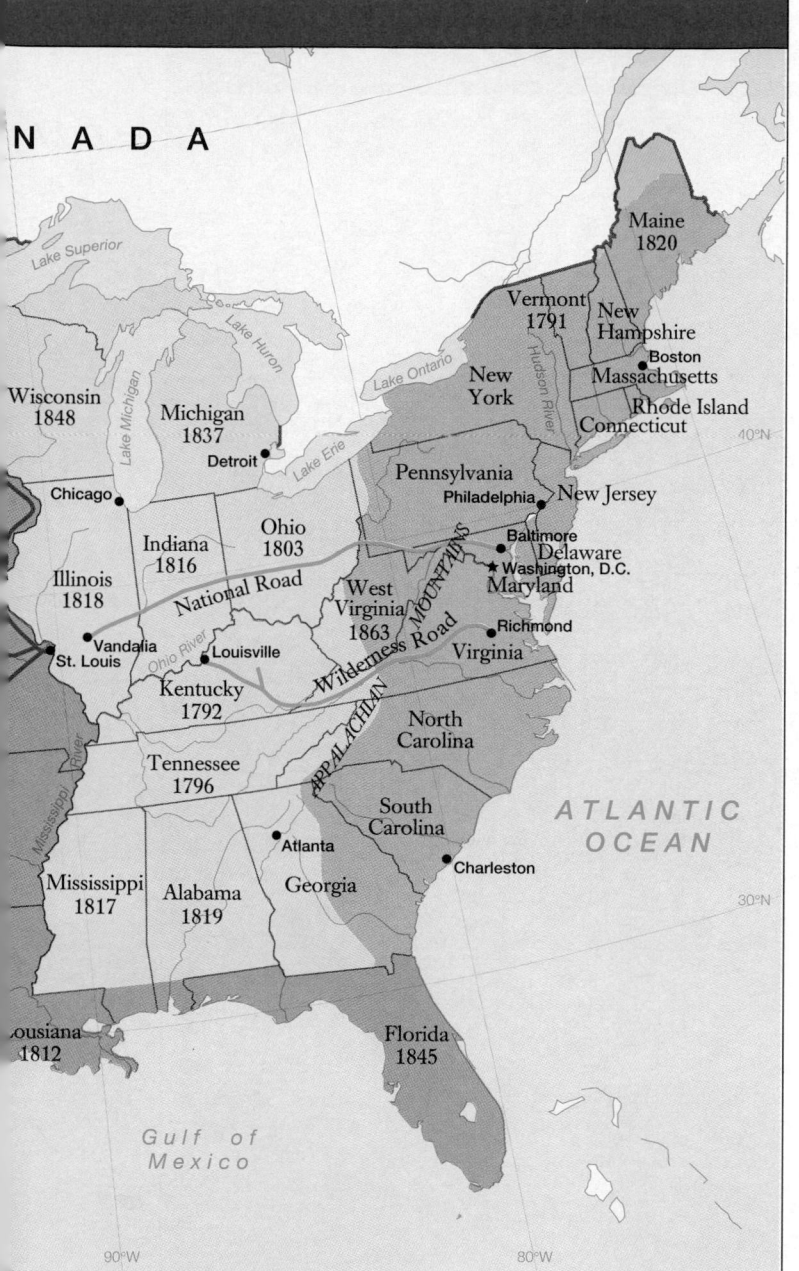

CANADA

Lake Superior

Lake Michigan

Lake Huron

Wisconsin
1848

Michigan
1837

Detroit

Chicago

Lake Ontario

Lake Erie

Maine
1820

Vermont
1791

New
Hampshire

Boston

Massachusetts

New
York

Rhode Island

Connecticut

40°N

Illinois
1818

Indiana
1816

Ohio
1803

National Road

Pennsylvania

Philadelphia

New Jersey

Baltimore

Delaware

Washington, D.C.

Maryland

Vandalia

St. Louis

Ohio River

Louisville

Wilderness Road

West
Virginia
1863

APPALACHIAN MOUNTAINS

Richmond

Virginia

Kentucky
1792

Mississippi River

Tennessee
1796

North
Carolina

ATLANTIC
OCEAN

Atlanta

South
Carolina

Charleston

Mississippi
1817

Alabama
1819

Georgia

30°N

Louisiana
1812

Florida
1845

Gulf of
Mexico

90°W

80°W

Territorial Expansion of the U.S.

1815

1818 Ceded by Britain

1819 Ceded by Spain

1820

1825

1830

1835

1840

1845

1850

1842 Ceded by Britain

1845 Texas Annexation

1846 Oregon Country

1848 Mexico Cession

1853 Gadsden Purchase

1765

1775 Original thirteen colonies

1780

1783 Treaty of Paris

1795

1803 Louisiana Purchase

1810

1825

1840

1855

1867 Treaty with Russia

1870

1885

1898 Hawaiian Annexation

1900

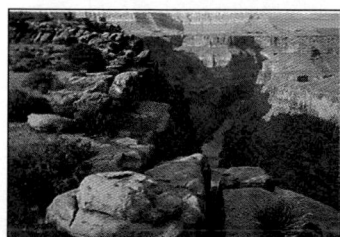

John Wesley Powell 1869
The Spanish explorer Coronado first discovered the Grand Canyon in 1540, but a party led by geologist and Native American scholar John Wesley Powell first saw the canyon from the Colorado River. The canyon extends for about 280 miles (451 km) and ranges in width from 4 to 18 miles (6.4 to 29 km).

Oregon Trail 1840s
Fur traders and missionaries opened this route stretching 2,000 miles (3,218 km) to Oregon. Pioneers undertook the difficult six months' journey in Conestoga wagons.

Promontory Point, Utah Territory, 1869
A golden spike marked the completion of the first transcontinental railroad linking the West Coast with the rest of the nation. The frontier steadily grew smaller as Americans settled in the vast empty spaces.

UNITED STATES CLIMATE REGIONS

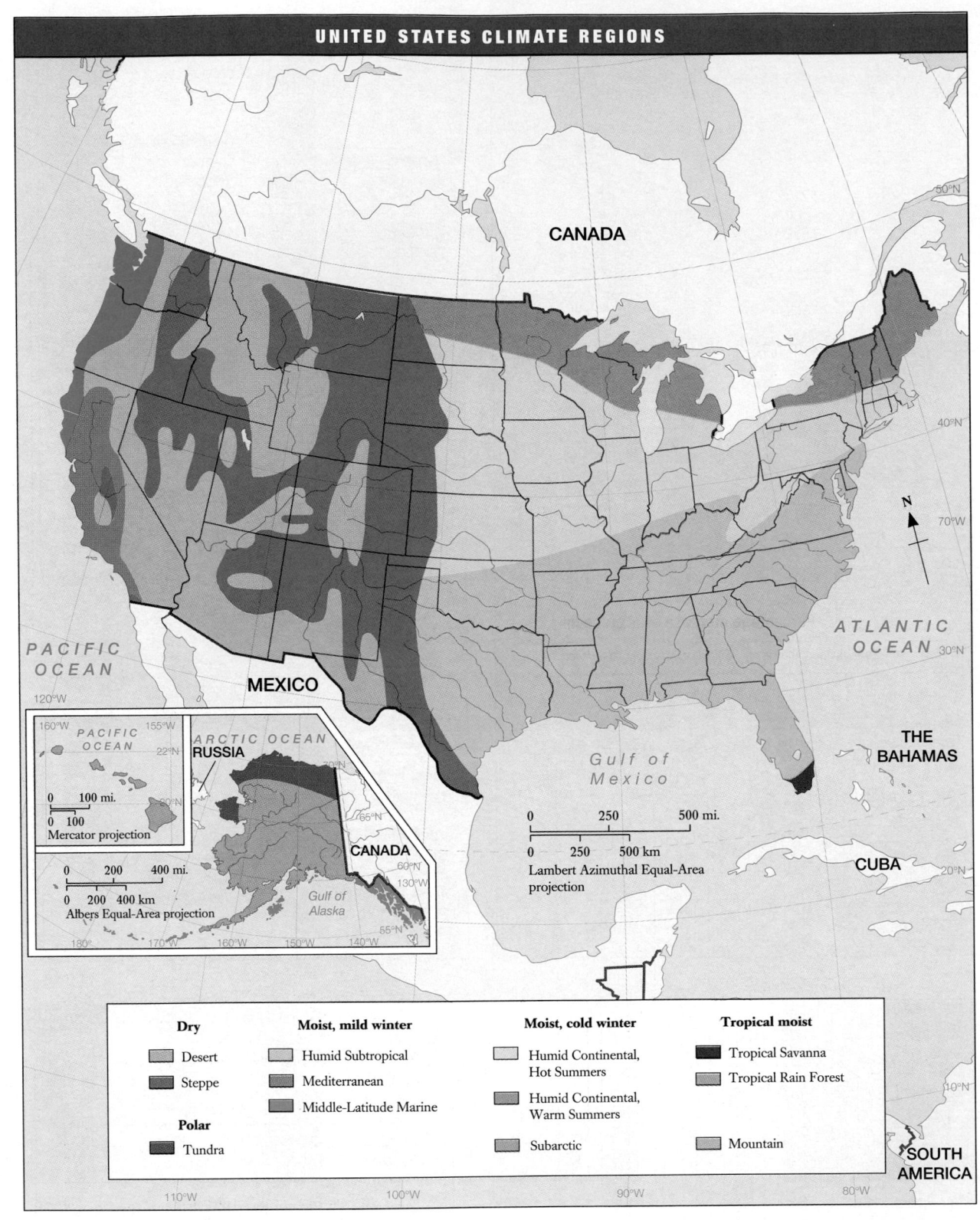

CANADA

PACIFIC
OCEAN

MEXICO

PACIFIC
OCEAN

ARCTIC OCEAN

RUSSIA

CANADA

Gulf of
Alaska

0   100 mi.
0   100
Mercator projection

0   200   400 mi.
0   200   400 km
Albers Equal-Area projection

Gulf of
Mexico

ATLANTIC
OCEAN

THE
BAHAMAS

CUBA

0   250   500 mi.
0   250   500 km
Lambert Azimuthal Equal-Area
projection

SOUTH
AMERICA

50°N
40°N
30°N
20°N
10°N
70°W
80°W
90°W
100°W
110°W
120°W

N

Dry

| | Desert |
| | Steppe |

Polar

| | Tundra |

Moist, mild winter

	Humid Subtropical
	Mediterranean
	Middle-Latitude Marine

Moist, cold winter

	Humid Continental, Hot Summers
	Humid Continental, Warm Summers
	Subarctic

Tropical moist

	Tropical Savanna
	Tropical Rain Forest
	Mountain

Population of the United States

Year	Population (in thousands)			Year	Population (in thousands)		
1790	3,929,214	4.5	–	1900	76,212,168	21.5	21.0
1800	5,308,483	6.1	35.1	1910	92,228,496	26.0	21.0
1810	7,239,881	4.3	36.4	1920	106,021,537	29.9	15.0
1820	9,638,453	5.5	33.1	1930	123,202,624	34.7	16.2
1830	12,866,020	7.4	33.5	1940	132,164,569	37.2	7.3
1840	17,069,453	9.8	32.7	1950	151,325,798	42.6	14.5
1850	23,191,876	7.9	35.9	1960	179,323,175	50.6	18.5
1860	31,443,321	10.6	35.6	1970	203,302,031	57.5	13.4
1870	38,558,371	10.9	22.6	1980	226,542,203	64.0	11.4
1880	50,189,209	14.2	30.2	1990	248,709,873	70.3	9.8
1890	62,979,766	17.8	25.5	2000*	276,242,000	78.1	11.1

Key:

☐ Population per square mile of land

▨ Percentage increase over preceding census

*estimated

Source: U.S. Department of the Census; *Statistical Abstract of the United States*, 1994.

Population Distribution by Age

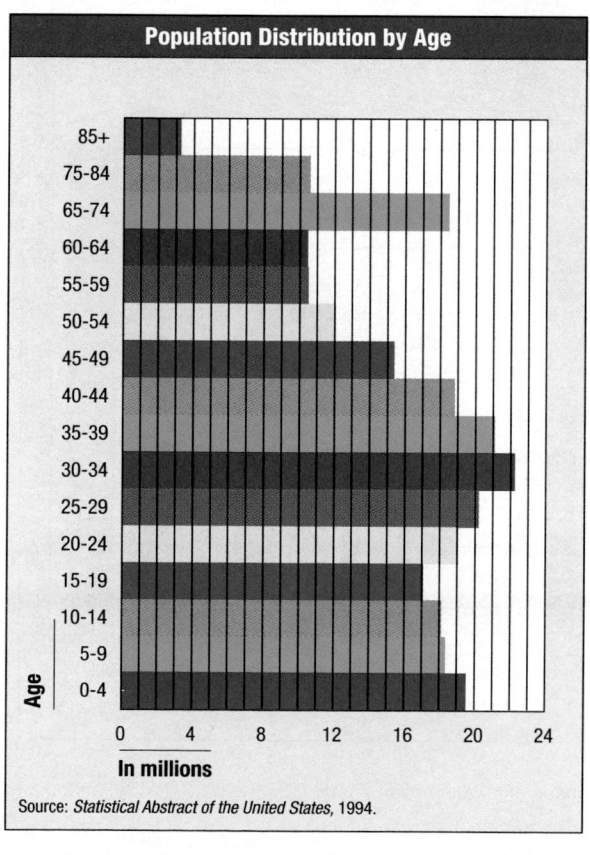

In millions

Source: *Statistical Abstract of the United States*, 1994.

Major Religions in the United States

Roman Catholic Church	58,267
Southern Baptist Convention	15,232
United Methodist Church	8,785
National Baptist Convention	3,500
Muslims	6,000
Jews	5,981
Evangelical Lutheran Church	5,245
Church of Jesus Christ of Latter-Day Saints (Mormon)	4,336
Church of God in Christ (Pentecostal)	3,710
Presbyterian Church (U.S.A.)	3,778
National Baptist Convention of America	3,500
Lutheran Church (Missouri Synod)	2,607
Episcopal Church	2,472
African Methodist Episcopal Church	3,500
Assemblies of God	2,235
Greek Orthodox Archdiocese of North and South America	1,950
United Church of Christ	1,584
Churches of Christ	1,690
American Baptist Churches in the U.S.A.	1,528
African Methodist Episcopal Zion Church	1,200
Christian Churches and Churches of Christ	1,071
Christian Church (Disciples of Christ)	1,023
Orthodox Church in America	1,030

In thousands

Source: *Statistical Abstract of the United States*, 1994; *Time* magazine (November 19, 1990).

Political Parties in Power in the Executive Branch

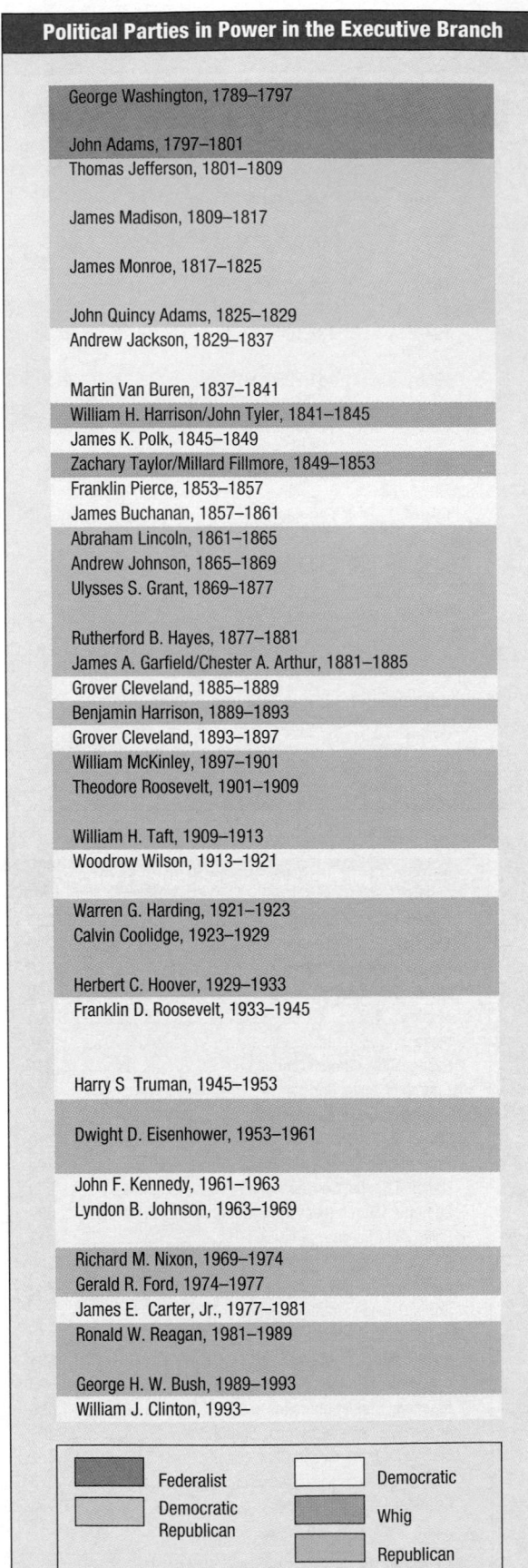

George Washington, 1789–1797

John Adams, 1797–1801
Thomas Jefferson, 1801–1809

James Madison, 1809–1817

James Monroe, 1817–1825

John Quincy Adams, 1825–1829
Andrew Jackson, 1829–1837

Martin Van Buren, 1837–1841
William H. Harrison/John Tyler, 1841–1845
James K. Polk, 1845–1849
Zachary Taylor/Millard Fillmore, 1849–1853
Franklin Pierce, 1853–1857
James Buchanan, 1857–1861
Abraham Lincoln, 1861–1865
Andrew Johnson, 1865–1869
Ulysses S. Grant, 1869–1877

Rutherford B. Hayes, 1877–1881
James A. Garfield/Chester A. Arthur, 1881–1885
Grover Cleveland, 1885–1889
Benjamin Harrison, 1889–1893
Grover Cleveland, 1893–1897
William McKinley, 1897–1901
Theodore Roosevelt, 1901–1909

William H. Taft, 1909–1913
Woodrow Wilson, 1913–1921

Warren G. Harding, 1921–1923
Calvin Coolidge, 1923–1929

Herbert C. Hoover, 1929–1933
Franklin D. Roosevelt, 1933–1945

Harry S Truman, 1945–1953

Dwight D. Eisenhower, 1953–1961

John F. Kennedy, 1961–1963
Lyndon B. Johnson, 1963–1969

Richard M. Nixon, 1969–1974
Gerald R. Ford, 1974–1977
James E. Carter, Jr., 1977–1981
Ronald W. Reagan, 1981–1989

George H. W. Bush, 1989–1993
William J. Clinton, 1993–

Federalist

Democratic Republican

Democratic

Whig

Republican

Graduation Rates

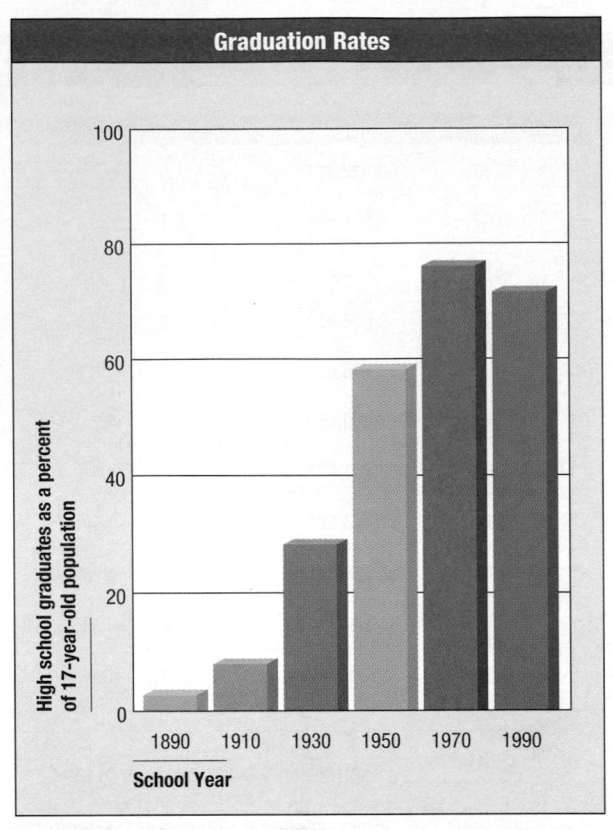

High school graduates as a percent of 17-year-old population

School Year

Life Expectancy

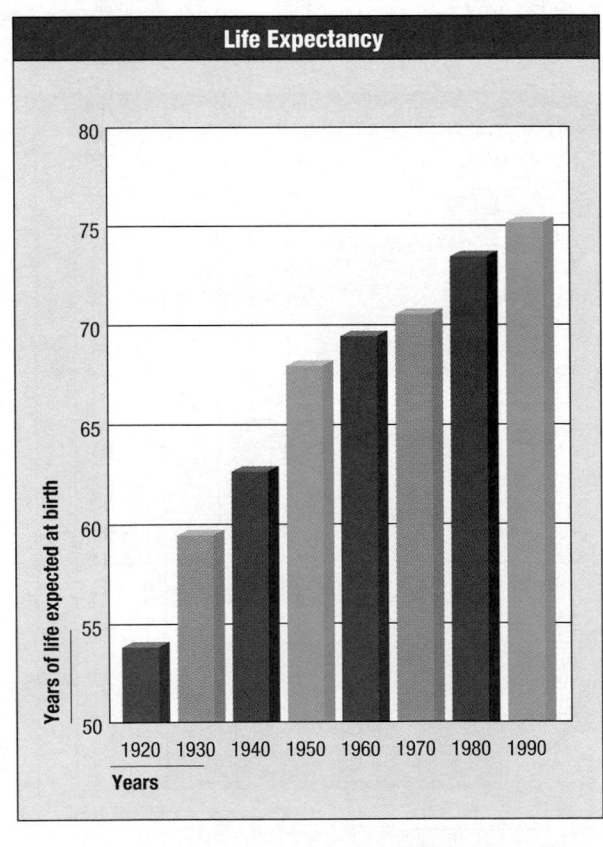

Years of life expected at birth

Years

The United States

STATE*	YEAR ADMITTED	POPULATION (1990)	LAND AREA (sq. mi.)	CAPITAL	LARGEST CITY	HOUSE REP. (1990)**
1. Delaware	1787	666,168	1,954	Dover	Wilmington	1
2. Pennsylvania	1787	11,881,643	44,819	Harrisburg	Philadelphia	21
3. New Jersey	1787	7,730,188	7,418	Trenton	Newark	13
4. Georgia	1788	6,478,216	57,918	Atlanta	Atlanta	11
5. Connecticut	1788	3,287,116	4,845	Hartford	Bridgeport	6
6. Massachusetts	1788	6,016,425	7,838	Boston	Boston	10
7. Maryland	1788	4,781,468	9,774	Annapolis	Baltimore	8
8. South Carolina	1788	3,486,703	30,111	Columbia	Columbia	6
9. New Hampshire	1788	1,109,252	8,969	Concord	Manchester	2
10. Virginia	1788	6,187,358	39,597	Richmond	Virginia Beach	11
11. New York	1788	17,990,455	47,223	Albany	New York	31
12. North Carolina	1789	6,628,637	48,718	Raleigh	Charlotte	12
13. Rhode Island	1790	1,003,464	1,045	Providence	Providence	2
14. Vermont	1791	562,758	9,249	Montpelier	Burlington	1
15. Kentucky	1792	3,685,296	39,732	Frankfort	Louisville	6
16. Tennessee	1796	4,877,185	41,219	Nashville	Memphis	9
17. Ohio	1803	10,847,115	40,952	Columbus	Columbus	19
18. Louisiana	1812	4,219,973	43,566	Baton Rouge	New Orleans	7
19. Indiana	1816	5,544,159	35,870	Indianapolis	Indianapolis	10
20. Mississippi	1817	2,573,216	46,913	Jackson	Jackson	5
21. Illinois	1818	11,430,602	55,593	Springfield	Chicago	20
22. Alabama	1819	4,040,587	50,750	Montgomery	Birmingham	7
23. Maine	1820	1,227,928	30,864	Augusta	Portland	2
24. Missouri	1821	5,117,073	68,898	Jefferson City	Kansas City	9
25. Arkansas	1836	2,350,725	52,075	Little Rock	Little Rock	4
26. Michigan	1837	9,295,297	56,809	Lansing	Detroit	16
27. Florida	1845	12,937,926	53,997	Tallahassee	Jacksonville	23
28. Texas	1845	16,986,510	261,194	Austin	Houston	30
29. Iowa	1846	2,776,755	55,874	Des Moines	Des Moines	5
30. Wisconsin	1848	4,891,769	54,313	Madison	Milwaukee	9
31. California	1850	29,760,021	155,973	Sacramento	Los Angeles	52
32. Minnesota	1858	4,375,099	79,616	St. Paul	Minneapolis	8
33. Oregon	1859	2,853,733	96,002	Salem	Portland	5
34. Kansas	1861	2,477,574	81,823	Topeka	Wichita	4
35. West Virginia	1863	1,793,477	24,086	Charleston	Charleston	3
36. Nevada	1864	1,201,833	109,805	Carson City	Las Vegas	2
37. Nebraska	1867	1,578,385	76,877	Lincoln	Omaha	3
38. Colorado	1876	3,294,394	103,729	Denver	Denver	6
39. North Dakota	1889	638,800	68,994	Bismarck	Fargo	1
40. South Dakota	1889	696,004	75,897	Pierre	Sioux Falls	1
41. Montana	1889	799,065	145,556	Helena	Billings	1
42. Washington	1889	4,887,941	66,581	Olympia	Seattle	9
43. Idaho	1890	1,006,749	82,750	Boise	Boise	2
44. Wyoming	1890	455,975	97,104	Cheyenne	Cheyenne	1
45. Utah	1896	1,727,784	82,168	Salt Lake City	Salt Lake City	3
46. Oklahoma	1907	3,145,585	68,678	Oklahoma City	Oklahoma City	6
47. New Mexico	1912	1,515,069	121,364	Sante Fe	Albuquerque	3
48. Arizona	1912	3,665,228	113,642	Phoenix	Phoenix	6
49. Alaska	1959	550,043	570,373	Juneau	Anchorage	1
50. Hawaii	1959	1,108,229	6,423	Honolulu	Honolulu	2
District of Columbia (Washington, D.C.)	–	606,900	61	–	–	–
United States of America	–	248,709,873	3,536,341	Washington, D.C.	New York	435

* Numbers denote the order in which states were admitted.
** Number of members in House of Representatives

Presidents
of the United States

★ ★

From George Washington to William J. Clinton, this presidential gallery introduces the forty-two Presidents and highlights biographical information on each.

** The Republican party during this period developed into today's Democratic party. Today's Republican party originated in 1854.

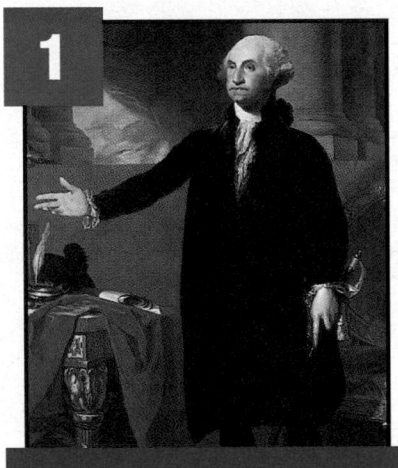

1

George Washington
1789–1797

Born: 1732
Died: 1799
Born in: Virginia
Elected from: Virginia
Age when elected: 56
Occupations: Planter, Soldier
Party: None
Vice President: John Adams

2

John Adams
1797–1801

Born: 1735
Died: 1826
Born in: Massachusetts
Elected from: Massachusetts
Age when elected: 61
Occupations: Teacher, Lawyer
Party: Federalist
Vice President: Thomas Jefferson

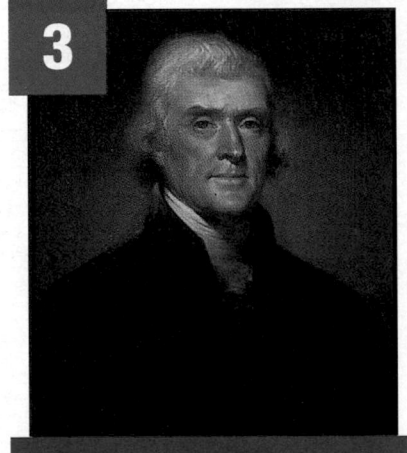

3

Thomas Jefferson
1801–1809

Born: 1743
Died: 1826
Born in: Virginia
Elected from: Virginia
Age when elected: 57
Occupations: Planter, Lawyer
Party: Republican**
Vice Presidents: Aaron Burr, George Clinton

James Madison
1809–1817

Born: 1751
Died: 1836
Born in: Virginia
Elected from: Virginia
Age when elected: 57
Occupation: Planter
Party: Republican**
Vice Presidents: George Clinton, Elbridge Gerry

James Monroe
1817–1825

Born: 1758
Died: 1831
Born in: Virginia
Elected from: Virginia
Age when elected: 58
Occupation: Lawyer
Party: Republican**
Vice President: Daniel D. Tompkins

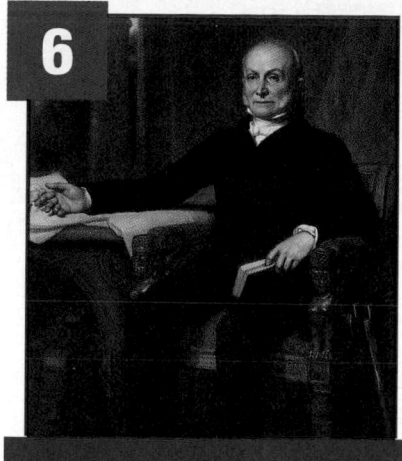

John Quincy Adams
1825–1829

Born: 1767
Died: 1848
Born in: Massachusetts
Elected from: Massachusetts
Age when elected: 57
Occupation: Lawyer
Party: Republican**
Vice President: John C. Calhoun

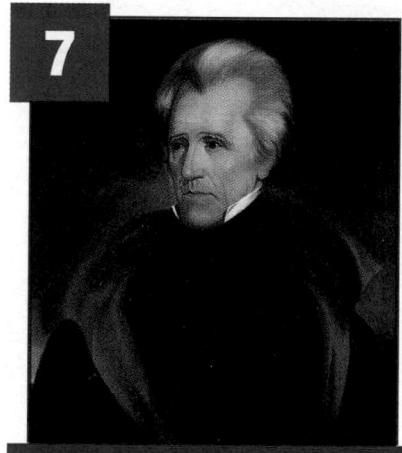

Andrew Jackson
1829–1837

Born: 1767
Died: 1845
Born in: South Carolina
Elected from: Tennessee
Age when elected: 61
Occupations: Lawyer, Soldier
Party: Democratic
Vice President: John C. Calhoun, Martin Van Buren

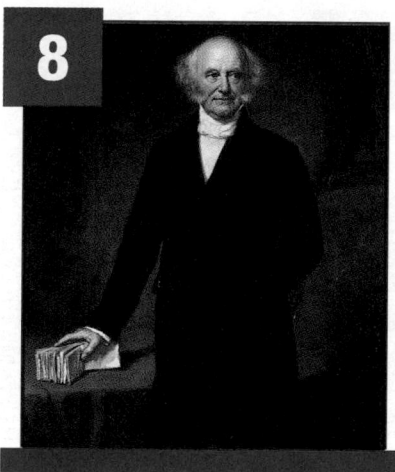

Martin Van Buren
1837–1841

Born: 1782
Died: 1862
Born in: New York
Elected from: New York
Age when elected: 54
Occupation: Lawyer
Party: Democratic
Vice President: Richard M. Johnson

William H. Harrison
1841

Born: 1773
Died: 1841
Born in: Virginia
Elected from: Ohio
Age when elected: 67
Occupations: Soldier, Planter
Party: Whig
Vice President: John Tyler

John Tyler
1841–1845

Born: 1790
Died: 1862
Born in: Virginia
Elected as V.P. from: Virginia
Succeeded: Harrison
Age when became President: 51
Occupation: Lawyer
Party: Whig
Vice President: None

James K. Polk
1845–1849

Born: 1795
Died: 1849
Born in: North Carolina
Elected from: Tennessee
Age when elected: 49
Occupation: Lawyer
Party: Democratic
Vice President: George M. Dallas

Zachary Taylor
1849–1850

Born: 1784
Died: 1850
Born in: Virginia
Elected from: Louisiana
Age when elected: 63
Occupation: Soldier
Party: Whig
Vice President: Millard Fillmore

Millard Fillmore
1850–1853

Born: 1800
Died: 1874
Born in: New York
Elected as V.P. from: New York
Succeeded: Taylor
Age when became President: 50
Occupation: Lawyer
Party: Whig
Vice President: None

Franklin Pierce
1853–1857

Born: 1804
Died: 1869
Born in: New Hampshire
Elected from: New Hampshire
Age when elected: 47
Occupation: Lawyer
Party: Democratic
Vice President: William R. King

James Buchanan
1857–1861

Born: 1791
Died: 1868
Born in: Pennsylvania
Elected from: Pennsylvania
Age when elected: 65
Occupation: Lawyer
Party: Democratic
Vice President: John G. Breckinridge

Abraham Lincoln
1861–1865

Born: 1809
Died: 1865
Born in: Kentucky
Elected from: Illinois
Age when elected: 51
Occupation: Lawyer
Party: Republican
Vice President: Hannibal Hamlin,
  Andrew Johnson

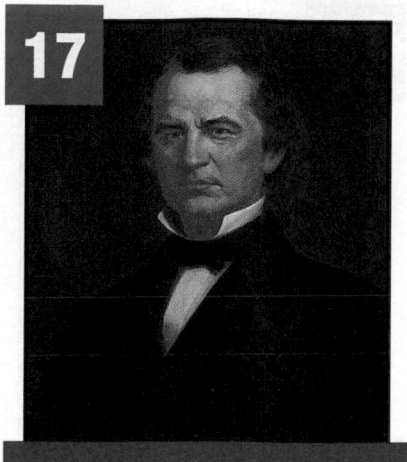

Andrew Johnson
1865–1869

Born: 1808
Died: 1875
Born in: North Carolina
Elected as V.P. from: Tennessee
Age when became President: 56
Succeeded: Lincoln
Occupation: Tailor
Party: Republican
Vice President: None

Ulysses S. Grant
1869–1877

Born: 1822
Died: 1885
Born in: Ohio
Elected from: Illinois
Age when elected: 46
Occupations: Farmer, Soldier
Party: Republican
Vice President: Schuyler Colfax,
  Henry Wilson

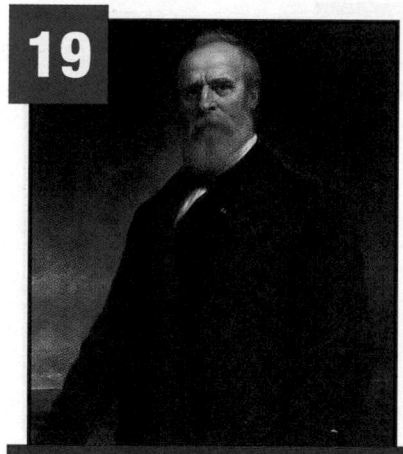

Rutherford B. Hayes
1877–1881

Born: 1822
Died: 1893
Born in: Ohio
Elected from: Ohio
Age when elected: 54
Occupation: Lawyer
Party: Republican
Vice President: William A. Wheeler

James A. Garfield
1881

Born: 1831
Died: 1881
Born in: Ohio
Elected from: Ohio
Age when elected: 49
Occupations: Lawyer, Politician
Party: Republican
Vice President: Chester A. Arthur

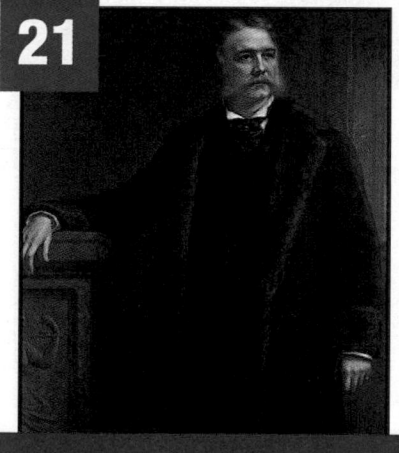

Chester A. Arthur
1881–1885

Born: 1830
Died: 1886
Born in: Vermont
Elected as V.P. from: New York
Succeeded: Garfield
Age when became President: 50
Occupations: Teacher, Lawyer
Party: Republican
Vice President: None

22 24

Grover Cleveland
1885–1889, 1893–1897

Born: 1837
Died: 1908
Born in: New Jersey
Elected from: New York
Age when elected: 47; 55
Occupation: Lawyer
Party: Democratic
Vice Presidents: Thomas A. Hendricks, Adlai E. Stevenson

23

Benjamin Harrison
1889–1893

Born: 1833
Died: 1901
Born in: Ohio
Elected from: Indiana
Age when elected: 55
Occupation: Lawyer
Party: Republican
Vice President: Levi P. Morton

25

William McKinley
1897–1901

Born: 1843
Died: 1901
Born in: Ohio
Elected from: Ohio
Age when elected: 53
Occupations: Teacher, Lawyer
Party: Republican
Vice Presidents: Garret Hobart, Theodore Roosevelt

26

Theodore Roosevelt
1901–1909

Born: 1858
Died: 1919
Born in: New York
Elected as V.P. from: New York
Succeeded: McKinley
Age when became President: 42
Occupations: Historian, Rancher
Party: Republican
Vice President: Charles W. Fairbanks

27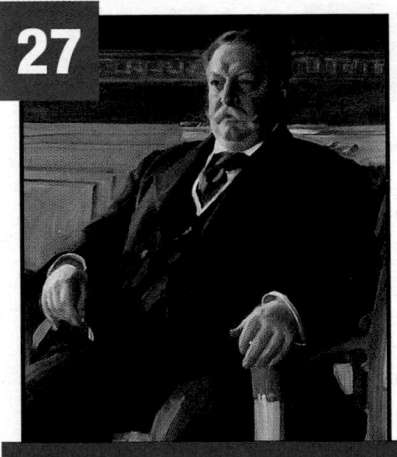

William H. Taft
1909–1913

Born: 1857
Died: 1930
Born in: Ohio
Elected from: Ohio
Age when elected: 51
Occupation: Lawyer
Party: Republican
Vice President: James S. Sherman

28

Woodrow Wilson
1913–1921

Born: 1856
Died: 1924
Born in: Virginia
Elected from: New Jersey
Age when elected: 55
Occupation: College Professor
Party: Democratic
Vice President: Thomas R. Marshall

Warren G. Harding
1921–1923

Born: 1865
Died: 1923
Born in: Ohio
Elected from: Ohio
Age when elected: 55
Occupations: Newspaper Editor, Publisher
Party: Republican
Vice President: Calvin Coolidge

Calvin Coolidge
1923–1929

Born: 1872
Died: 1933
Born in: Vermont
Elected as V.P. from: Massachusetts
Succeeded: Harding
Age when became President: 51
Occupation: Lawyer
Party: Republican
Vice President: Charles G. Dawes

Herbert C. Hoover
1929–1933

Born: 1874
Died: 1964
Born in: Iowa
Elected from: California
Age when elected: 54
Occupation: Engineer
Party: Republican
Vice President: Charles Curtis

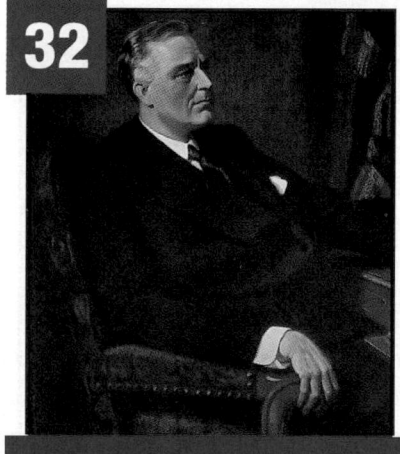

Franklin D. Roosevelt
1933–1945

Born: 1882
Died: 1945
Born in: New York
Elected from: New York
Age when elected: 50
Occupations: Lawyer
Party: Democratic
Vice Presidents: John N. Garner, Henry A. Wallace, Harry S Truman

Harry S. Truman
1945–1953

Born: 1884
Died: 1972
Born in: Missouri
Elected as V.P. from: Missouri
Succeeded: Roosevelt
Age when became President: 60
Occupation: Clerk, Farmer
Party: Democratic
Vice President: Alben W. Barkley

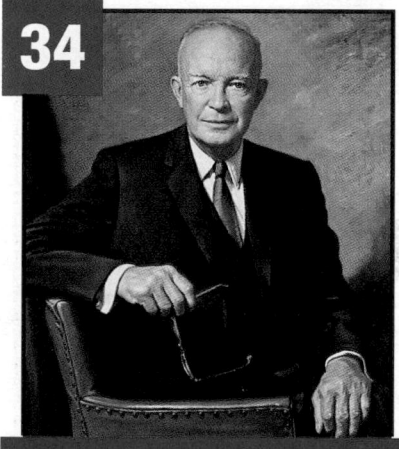

Dwight D. Eisenhower
1953–1961

Born: 1890
Died: 1969
Born in: Texas
Elected from: New York
Age when elected: 62
Occupation: Soldier
Party: Republican
Vice President: Richard M. Nixon

35

John F. Kennedy
1961–1963

Born: 1917
Died: 1963
Born in: Massachusetts
Elected from: Massachusetts
Age when elected: 43
Occupations: Author, Reporter
Party: Democratic
Vice President: Lyndon B. Johnson

36

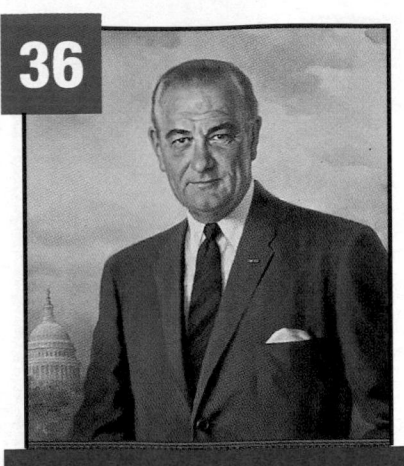

Lyndon B. Johnson
1963–1969

Born: 1908
Died: 1973
Born in: Texas
Elected as V.P. from: Texas
Succeeded: Kennedy
Age when became President: 55
Occupation: Teacher
Party: Democratic
Vice President: Hubert H. Humphrey

37

Richard M. Nixon
1969–1974

Born: 1913
Died: 1994
Born in: California
Elected from: New York
Age when elected: 55
Occupation: Lawyer
Party: Republican
Vice Presidents: Spiro T. Agnew,
 Gerald R. Ford

38

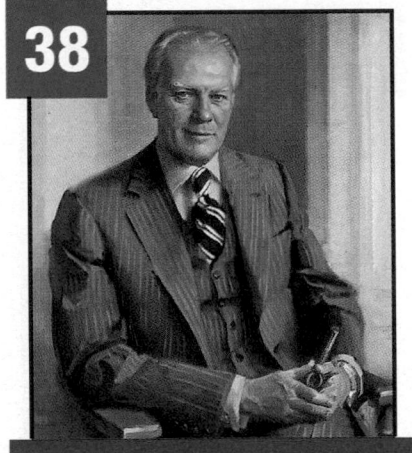

Gerald R. Ford
1974–1977

Born: 1913
Born in: Nebraska
Appointed by Nixon as V.P. upon
Agnew's resignation; assumed
presidency upon Nixon's resignation
Age when became President: 61
Occupation: Lawyer
Party: Republican
Vice President: Nelson R. Rockefeller

39

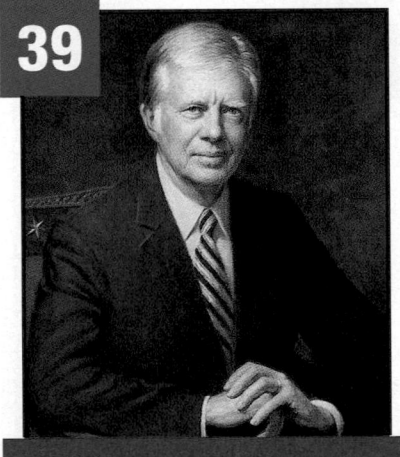

James E. Carter, Jr.
1977–1981

Born: 1924
Born in: Georgia
Elected from: Georgia
Age when elected: 52
Occupations: Business, Farmer
Party: Democratic
Vice President: Walter F. Mondale

40

Ronald W. Reagan
1981–1989

Born: 1911
Born in: Illinois
Elected from: California
Age when elected: 69
Occupations: Actor, Lecturer
Party: Republican
Vice President: George H.W. Bush

41

George H.W. Bush
1989–1993

Born: 1924
Born in: Massachusetts
Elected from: Texas
Age when elected: 64
Occupation: Business
Party: Republican
Vice President: J. Danforth Quayle

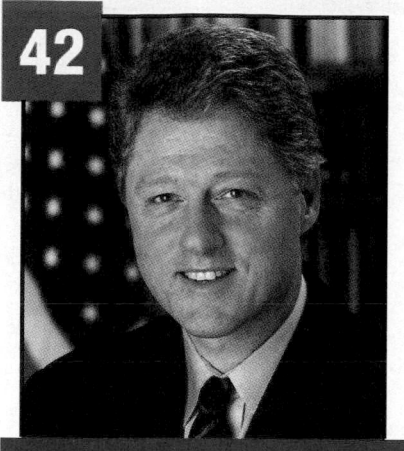

42

William J. Clinton
1993–

Born: 1946
Born in: Arkansas
Elected from: Arkansas
Age when elected: 46
Occupation: Lawyer
Party: Democratic
Vice President: Albert Gore, Jr.

Glossary

A

abolition The formal outlawing of slavery (p. 73)

abolitionism In the 1800s the movement to put an end to slavery in the United States (p. 155)

accommodation The policy under which certain African Americans accepted the results of white racism in order to achieve economic success (p. 283)

alliance A pact or association of nations joined in a common cause (p. 306)

amendment A written change or addition (p. 90)

amnesty An act by which the government grants pardon for crimes to a large group of individuals, usually in response to the group's acts of consolation (p. 185)

anarchism Opposition to any form of government; the theory that all governments should be abolished (p. 339)

annex To add or attach a new territory to an existing country (p. 294)

apartheid An official policy of racial segregation formerly mandated in South Africa (p. 880)

appeasement The policy of compromising or giving in to the demands of a hostile nation in the hope of maintaining peace (p. 496)

arbitration A method of settling a dispute by agreeing in advance to accept the decision of an impartial outsider (p. 271)

armistice An agreement to end hostilities (p. 222)

arms race Competition between the United States and the Soviet Union for greater military strength (p. 573)

assimilation The absorption of minority group members into the main culture of United States society (p. 737)

B

baby boom The unusually rapid population growth of the post-World War II period in the United States, lasting through the mid-1960s (p. 609)

backlash A strong, sudden reaction against an idea or policy (p. 809)

balance of power A condition in which the major powers are equal enough in strength to prevent the aggression of any and maintain the safety of all (p. 817)

bilingualism The use of two languages; the ability to use two languages with equal fluency (p. 737)

bipartisan coalition A group of Republicans and Democrats working together on issues (p. 906)

black codes Laws adopted in the South that severely restricted the rights of newly freed slaves (p. 185)

black power A movement to improve African American economic, political, and social conditions using African American leadership and organization, without the help of whites (p. 693)

black pride Pride in being African American; pride in one's African ancestry as well as one's American nationality (p. 691)

black separatism Concept, espoused by some African Americans in the United States, calling for the separation of the races (p.691)

blacklisting Efforts to brand people as Communists and prevent them from holding certain jobs (p. 647)

blitzkreig An intensive attack, often combining air and land forces, from the German blitzkrieg, or "lightning war"; in World War II, the German bombing raids on England (p. 496)

bolshevism A radical socialist ideology; from Bolshevik, the name of V.I. Lenin's left-wing majority party during the Russian Revolution (p. 322)

bond Certificate that earns interest and is redeemed for cash on a specific date (p. 529)

bootlegger A person who made, sold, or transported illegal liquor (p. 398)

boycott An organized agreement not to buy or use a certain product or deal with a certain company or nation, in order to exert pressure for change (pp. 675)

brinksmanship Practice of attempting to keep the peace among nations by letting it be known that one will never back down and is prepared to cross the brink of war (p. 579)

C

cabinet A body of people appointed by the President to lead the various departments of government and to serve as the President's official advisers (p. 113)

capital Accumulated money or other material wealth that is devoted to the production of more wealth; material wealth acquired in business by an individual or company (p. 356)

capitalism An economic system based on open competition in a free market, in which individuals and companies own the means of production and operate for profit (p. 276)

carpetbagger A Northern opportunist who moved to the South and took advantage of unsettled post-Civil War conditions; scornfully dubbed carpetbagger, after a kind of homemade luggage that many of them carried (p. 190)

checks and balances The system by which each of the three branches of government prevents the others from gaining excessive power (p. 84)

civil disobedience A strategy for causing social change by means of nonviolent resistance to unfair laws (p. 679)

civil liberties Freedom to enjoy the rights guaranteed by the constitution of the state or nation (p. 546)

civil rights The political, economic, and social rights of a citizen; particularly, those guaranteed under the United States Constitution, such as the right to vote and the right to equal treatment under the law (p. 669)

climate The specific set of meteorological conditions that characterize an area (p. 14)

closed shop A system in which all workers in an industry are required to be union members. (p. 633)

coalition A temporary alliance (of nations, parties, for example) formed for a specific action or purpose (p. 701)

cold war The United States-Soviet conflict that followed World War II in which the two powers avoided military confrontation but opposed each other's political and economic goals (p. 567)

commune A group of people who live communally, with collective ownership and use of property, often having shared goals, philosophies, and ways of life (p. 751)

community policing A method of police patrolling that involves sending foot patrols into neighborhoods and establishing better relations between the police and the public (p. 922)

compensation Money or something in return for a loss (p. 742)

conglomerate A firm that has holdings in a variety of unrelated industries (p. 601)

conquistadors Spanish explorers who conquered the new lands they discovered (p. 32)

conscientious objector A person who refuses military service because of moral or religious principles (p. 789)

conscription Compulsory enrollment in military service; the draft (p. 315)

consensus decision-making A management style, such as that of President Dwight Eisenhower, based on general agreement (p. 654)

conservative era A period in presidential politics in which the role of government is limited and individuals depend less on the government for assistance (p. 781)

constitution A written document of a plan of government (p. 73)

consumer price index A measure of the change in the cost of goods and services as compared with their cost in a fixed time period; also called the cost-of-living index (p. 528)

containment After World War II, the United States policy of securing the peace by trying to contain communism, or keep it from expanding beyond its current borders (pp. 566, 769)

corollary A proposition added to another as a natural consequence or effect, such as Teddy Roosevelt's corollary to the Monroe Doctrine (p. 297)

corporation A group of individuals authorized by law to act as a single entity; a business owned by many investors (p. 356)

counterculture A culture of young people with values that run counter to those of the established culture (p. 749)

coup The act of seizing power and overthrowing the government (p. 305)

covert operation. A secret or undercover government mission (p. 588)

coverture A British law under which a woman's inherited property belonged to her husband (p. 74)

credit A delayed payment plan in which a purchaser puts money down and pays the balance in installments; time allowed for payment of something sold on trust (p. 381)

crime bill A bill that has provisions for more police on the streets, building prisons, adding new applications to the death penalty, and banning assault weapons (p. 899)

cultural diffusion The spread of customs, ways of life, and other products of human thought and work from one cultural group to another (p. 752)

culture of poverty After World War II, the hungry, homeless and largely invisible members of a generally affluent American society (p. 619)

D

deferment The postponement of a person's induction into military service for reasons such as health or occupation (p. 789)

deficit spending A government policy of borrowing money in order to spend more than is received in taxes (p. 539)

demagogue A leader who gains power by appealing to people's emotions and prejudices (p. 467)

demobilization The postwar process of dismissing the troops from military service and shifting citizens and businesses back to peacetime pursuits (p. 599)

depression A period of extended and severe decline in a nation's economy, marked by low production and high unemployment (p. 421)

deregulate To remove restrictions and regulations (p. 859)

détente During the cold war, an attempt to lessen the tension between the United States and the Communist powers (p. 817)

diplomacy The art or practice of conducting international relations (p. 298)

direct primary An election open to all voters in a party; in a direct primary, candidates are chosen by the voters rather than by the party leaders (p. 252)

disarmament The act or policy of reducing or destroying military weapons (p. 351)

discretionary income Money to buy what is wanted in addition to what is needed (pp. 599–600)

discrimination The denial of rights because of someone's race, religion, age, sex, or other quality (p. 478)

dissident One who disagrees with established beliefs and policies; before Gorbachev's presidency, a citizen of the USSR who spoke out against Soviet policies (p. 840)

dogfight Name given to clashes between enemy aircraft (p. 308)

dole Money or goods given as charity; during the Great Depression, government relief payments; to be "on the dole" was to receive such payments regularly (p. 455)

domino theory A theory that if one country fell to communism, other countries in turn would fall, just like dominoes (p. 770)

doughboys Nickname for the United States infantrymen in World War I (p. 315)

dove A person who supports the withdrawal of United States troops from war and favors a negotiated end to war (p. 791)

draft The selection of persons for a particular compulsory assignment; a system of selecting persons to serve in the military (p. 789)

due process The legal procedures that safeguard an individual's rights (p. 716)

E

egalitarian A culture with no recognized authority figures; where all are considered equal (p. 23)

electronic media Forms of communication transmitted electronically and reaching the general public; primarily, radio and television (p. 656)

emancipation Freedom from bondage; particularly, freedom of African Americans from slavery (p. 176)

embargo A restriction or stoppage of trade (pp. 117, 837)

emerging nation A developing country in Asia, Latin America, or Africa (p. 588)

emigrate To leave one country to settle in another (p. 309)

enfranchisement Attainment of the rights of citizenship, especially the right to vote (p. 682)

entrepreneur A small business owner (p. 752)

eugenics In the early 1900s, a movement advocating improving the human race by controlling hereditary factors in mating (p. 284)

evangelist A fundamentalist preacher (p. 397)

expansionism The policy or process of increasing a nation's land area by acquiring new territory (p. 219)

extended family A family unit that includes not only parents and children but also other relatives such as grandparents, aunts, uncles, and cousins (p. 734)

external tax A tax levied on goods coming into an area, such as the tax the British Parliament imposed on sugar entering the American colonies (p. 58)

F

family leave Unpaid leave of absence for the birth or adoption of a child or for the illness of a family member (p. 899)

fascism A strongly nationalistic ideology, named for the Fascist party of Italy; a government characterized by racism and militarism; a repressive one-party dictatorship (p. 494)

fascist A follower of a political philosophy that preached nationalism and racism (p. 494)

federal regulation Control by the federal government rather than by private interests (p. 481)

feminist Activist who works to attain political, economic, and social rights for women equal to those of men (p. 726)

filibuster The tactic of making extended speeches to delay or prevent a vote on a piece of legislation (p. 687)

flapper The 1920s girl—at least the one promoted in advertising and movies; named for the open galoshes she flapped around in (pp. 382–383)

flatboat A flat-bottomed, square-ended craft that was typically used to transport goods along inland waterways in the early 1800s (p. 132)

foreclosure The legal procedure for reclaiming a piece of property when the buyer is unable to keep up the mortgage payments (p. 431)

frontier The area where colonist-settled lands bordered on lands of Native Americans (p. 130)

fugitive A person who has escaped from slavery and is running from the law (p. 169)

fundamentalism In the United States, a Protestant movement characterized by the belief that the words of the Bible were inspired by God and should be interpreted literally and followed closely (p. 397)

G

generation gap The differences in values, tastes, and attitudes between members of different age groups, especially adolescents and their parents (p. 749)

geography The study of people, places, and environments (p. 6)

gerrymandering Dividing voting districts in a way that increases or decreases representation by a certain group or party (p. 190)

glasnost A Russian word for a policy of openness, begun by Soviet President Gorbachev, encouraging free expression and an end to party censorship (p. 868)

global economy System of worldwide trade (p. 883)

gospel tradition A type of music that combines the words of traditional Protestant hymns with various African musical styles (p. 167)

government boarding school A school at which Native American children were taught white cultural traditions (p. 201)

gross national product (GNP) The total value of all goods and services produced in a nation in a given year (p. 527)

guerrilla warfare Fighting by small, independent bands, using tactics such as sabotage and sudden ambushes (p. 774)

H

hard money Currency consisting of gold or silver coins as opposed to paper (p. 82)

hawk A person who supports the war effort (p. 791)

hippie A member of the counterculture (p. 749)

history The study of events and people over time (p. 13)

holding company A company that owns controlling shares of stock in other companies (p. 270)

homestead Land awarded by the United States government to settlers who would live on it and farm it for five years, under the Homestead Act of 1862 (p. 196)

horizontal integration The merger of competing companies in an industry, such as oil refining, in order to dominate that industry (p. 209)

human/environment interaction The interdependence of people and their surroundings (p. 9)

human rights Basic rights and freedoms assumed to belong to all people everywhere (p. 839)

I

immigrant Person who enters a country to live there (p. 236)

impeachment Charges of misconduct brought against a public official (p. 830)

imperialism The policy of establishing economic, political, and military dominance over weaker nations on humanitarian and moral grounds (p. 295)

impressed Forced into public service, as American sailors forced to serve on British vessels in the late 1700s (p. 115)

indentured servant A person who agreed to work for a set number of years in return for passage to the Colonies (p. 40)

indigenous The people who originally inhabit an area; natives (p. 32)

industrial productivity The amount of goods produced by one hour of labor (p. 355)

industrialism The movement from agriculture to manufacturing as the main source of economic growth (p. 205)

industrialist A person who deals with the commercial production and sale of goods and services (p. 362)

inflation A sharp, continuing rise in prices caused by too much money and credit relative to the available goods (pp. 527, 837)

initiative A reform that allowed citizens to introduce a bill to a legislature or to bypass the legislature and propose a new law by petition (p. 253)

injunction A court order requiring an individual or company to do something, such as end a strike (p. 217)

internationalism A policy of cooperation and involvement among nations (p. 347)

internal tax A tax levied on goods produced and consumed within an area, such as the stamp tax imposed by the British Parliament on the American colonies (p. 58)

interventionism The policy of intervening, or interfering, in the affairs of another nation; in World War II the position of those who opposed isolationism and believed the United States should give all possible support, short of war, to the Allied forces (pp. 347, 500)

irreconcilables During World War I, a group of senators who opposed a League of Nations and could not be reconciled to voting for it (p. 325)

isolationism Avoidance of conflicts and alliances with other nations; indifference to affairs outside the United States; at the beginning of World War II, a policy of forming no alliances and taking no sides (p. 502)

K

kachina A sacred doll of the Pueblo peoples (p. 47)

L

land reform Redistribution of property to land-poor peasants (p. 572)

legislature A committee empowered to make laws (p. 48)

liberal era A period when government promoted social progress (p. 783)

liberate To free from outside control (p. 744)

liberation theology The philosophy of a movement of Christian activists working for social justice, especially in Latin America (p. 820)

limited war Beginning in the Truman era, a policy of avoiding global war by confining the fighting to one area and using conventional weapons, not nuclear power (p. 574)

location The position on the earth's surface (p. 7)

lynching A mob action in which a person is executed without a trial, often by hanging (p. 178)

M

majority More than 50 percent of a group (p. 89)

mandate A clear expression of the wishes of voters, expressed by election results (pp. 701, 857)

margin To "buy on margin" means that the brokerage house lends money to someone to buy securities. If the stock goes up, all the profits (minus the interest charged on the loan) are the purchaser's (p. 420)

martyr A person who voluntarily suffers death rather than renounce religious principles; a person who dies or endures great suffering for a cause (p. 691)

mass media The methods by which information and entertainment are transmitted to large numbers of people; includes newspapers, television, and radio (pp. 381, 441)

massive retaliation The cold war policy of the United States under which aggression against any ally would be met with an immediate all-out nuclear strike (p. 579)

materialism Placing more importance on money and material goods than on intellectual, spiritual, and artistic concerns (p. 390)

melting pot A society in which a number of racial, ethnic, and cultural groups are absorbed and blended together; from a vessel used for melting metals (p. 283)

merger Combining competing firms in an industry into a single larger company; combining several companies or corporations into one larger firm (p. 208)

migration The movement of people from one country or region to another (p. 535)

militant A person who is aggressive in promoting a cause (p. 682)

military-industrial complex The vast, interwoven military establishment and arms industry (p. 583)

militia group A citizen's military group that considers the government to be an enemy (p. 922)

mission A Spanish settlement built to convert Native Americans to Christianity (p. 37)

missionary One who travels to many lands to convert people to Christianity (p. 220)

mobilization Preparation for war, including both military and civilian efforts (p. 315)

moratorium An official authorization to suspend payments, as of a debt; an officially authorized period of waiting (p. 454)

movement A theme referring to the flow of people, goods, ideas, and information from one place to another (p. 8)

muckraker A writer whose investigative articles or books attacked abuses such as child labor or corruption (p. 244)

mutual deterrence A theory that as long as accurate missiles capable of complete destruction target each other's countries, neither country will risk starting a nuclear war (p. 866)

N

national debt In the late 1700s, the amount of money owed to Americans and to other countries after the American Revolution; the total amount of money owed by the federal government (p. 113)

national liberation Freeing a nation from control by another nation (p. 769)

national market The nationwide economic system made possible by the transportation network in the United States (p. 206)

nationalist movement The activities of a group focused on freeing a nation from foreign influence and control (p. 801)

nationalization The process of changing a property or industry from private to government ownership; after World War II Iran's declaration that its oil fields, with their British-owned factories, were the property of the Iranian government (p. 590)

nativism A preference for native-born Americans over immigrants (p. 294)

negotiate To reach an agreement (p. 800)

neoconservatism The conservative philosophy of the Reagan presidency that opposed excessive bureaucracy, federal spending, and government intervention in people's private lives (p. 857)

neutral Not choosing a side in a conflict (p. 115)

neutrality The policy of remaining impartial in a dispute, including not taking sides in a war; the policy of remaining unallied (p. 306)

nomadic Wandering from place to place (p. 23)

nonviolent resistance The act of peacefully demonstrating for a change in policy without fighting authorities (p. 676)

nullification Before the Civil War, the right claimed by some states to reject, or render null and void, any federal law they believed violated the Constitution (p. 153)

O

oligopoly The control of an entire industry, such as meat packing, by a few major producers (p. 356)

P

pacification program A policy in which entire villages are uprooted and the people forced to move to cities or refugee camps (p. 775)

pacifism Opposition to the use of force (p. 40)

pardon To forgive; to pass over without punishment (p. 831)

penny auction Staged sale of property for pennies to friends, who simply returned the property later (p. 431)

perestroika A Russian word for restructuring; Soviet President Gorbachev's name for his economic policy, which favors less government intervention and more private initiative (p. 868)

place A specific location (p. 8)

political machine A well-organized political organization that controls election results by awarding jobs and other favors in exchange for votes (p. 238)

pork barrel legislation Laws favoring projects of questionable necessity, bringing jobs and money into a legislator's district (p. 908)

pragmatist A person who is concerned with practical solutions to problems rather than with ideas and theories (p. 703)

presidio A Spanish settlement that served both as a trading center and as a garrison to defend Spanish territories (p. 37)

progressive A person who advocates reforms to confront the problems caused by industrialization and urbanization. (p. 243)

prohibition A ban on alcohol (p. 343)

propaganda A form of public information used to mold public opinion by employing techniques such as the use of emotionally charged language, name-calling, appeals to peer pressure, and the bandwagon approach (p. 317)

Q

quota A law limiting the number of immigrants (p. 401)

R

racism The idea that one race is superior to others, and that race determines a person's character or ability; prejudice and discrimination toward members of one racial group, usually a minority (p. 543)

radical Advocating political and social revolution (p. 338)

ratify To officially approve and accept (p. 81)

real income The amount of income earned, taking into account an increase in prices (p. 599)

realpolitik Practical politics; the view that a nation should pursue policies and make alliances based on its national interests (p. 817)

reapportionment A change in the number of legislative seats assigned to each state (p. 713)

recall A procedure that allows citizens to remove an elected official from office before the person's term officially ends (p. 253)

recession A period of declining productivity and reduced economic activity (p. 839)

referendum A process by which citizens vote directly for or against a political proposal or bill (p. 253)

region An area defined by one or more specific characteristics (p. 9)

regulatory commision A group whose responsibility it is to see that a company (or companies) is in compliance with existing laws (p. 275)

repatriation Return to a person's country of birth or citizenship (p. 433)

representation The right to be represented by delegates chosen in a free election; the election of officials who represent the views of a particular group (pp. 84, 735)

reservationists A group in the United States Congress who approved the idea of the League of Nations with reservations; they would support it if certain modifications were made to the proposal (p. 326)

resource management The scientific management of natural resources (p. 269)

revenue sharing A program through which the federal government returns some of its tax money to local governments (p. 810)

revivalism A religious movement that focused on individual religious experience rather than on church doctrine (p. 49)

revolution A violent effort to overthrow the government (p. 67)

right-to-work law Legislation outlawing union shops that require new workers to join (p. 633)

S

scientific management A management theory using efficiency experts to examine each work operation and find ways to minimize the time needed to complete it (p. 365)

scorched earth policy Policy of breaking the enemy's will by destroying food, shelter, and supplies (p. 178)

secede To withdraw formally from the Union (p. 153)

secession The act of officially withdrawing from a group (p. 172)

sectionalism A devotion to local interests over those of the larger group (p. 166)

sedentary Settled in one place (p. 23)

segregation The enforced separation of racial groups in schooling, housing, and other public areas (p. 668)

selectmen Elected officials in Puritan communities who decided such issues as taxes and land dispensation (p. 39)

self-determination The right of all people to decide what form of government they will live under (p. 305)

settlement house A neighborhood center providing educational and social services to needy people, established between 1889 and 1910 (p. 247)

sharecropping A system in which landowners provide farmers with land, seed, and supplies in exchange for a share in the crop (p. 189)

silent majority The great majority of Americans, whose opinions are not often heard (p. 809)

slave labor force A group of people enslaved by a master and made to work without pay (p. 85)

social gospel movement A movement emphasizing the application of Christian principles to social problems (p. 245)

socialism An economic theory advocating collective or government ownership of factories and other businesses instead of private ownership (p. 276)

sonar technology Technology that detects submerged objects by means of sound waves (p. 511)

Southern strategy A plan designed to appeal directly to Southern white conservatives (p. 812)

speakeasy A club where liquor was sold in violation of the law (p. 398)

speculation A risky business venture involving buying or selling property in the hope of making a large, quick profit; making investments in the stock market (p. 419)

speculator A person who buys property, such as land or bonds, in the hope that its value will go up (p. 113)

spoils system An arrangement by which victorious parties or candidates reward their supporters with jobs, contracts, etc. (p. 152)

stagflation An unusual economic condition that combines a stagnant economy with rising prices (p. 837)

standard of living The material well-being of the individuals or groups in a society (p. 377)

status quo The current situation or condition (p. 73)

status symbol A possession thought to reflect a person's wealth, prestige, or superior position in society (p. 441)

stock A share in business ownership (p. 418)

strike An organized work stoppage used to force an employer to meet certain demands, such as for better wages, hours, and conditions (p. 215)

subsidy A government grant of money to an individual or company for a purpose thought to benefit society (p. 457)

suburb A community at the edge of a large city (p. 235)

suburbia The suburbs of a city; the suburban culture (p. 607)

suffrage The right to vote (p. 70)

supply-side economics A theory based on the belief that the key to economic vitality is reducing taxes—especially those on wealthy individuals and large corporations—and that lowering taxes would encourage saving and investment, which would lead to business expansion and more jobs (p. 858)

syndicate A chain of newspapers under central ownership; an agency that provides articles or features to a number of newspapers or magazines (p. 390)

T

tabloid A newspaper with small pages and large type (p. 390)

tariff A tax or fee on imported goods (p. 146)

temperance Moderation in, or total abstinence from, the use of alcoholic beverages (p. 155)

tenement A city apartment building, often a crowded, run-down rental apartment building in the slums (p. 235)

termination policy A policy to end the reservation system and terminate all federal services to Native American groups (p. 624)

territorial integrity A nation's right to protect its land and control its trade (p. 299)

textile Fabric, especially woven or knitted; cloth (p. 141)

totalitarian A government controlled by a single person or party; suppressing freedom and controlling every aspect of life (p. 494)

trade deficit A gap in value between a country's imports and exports caused by a country's buying more than it sells, thus creating an unfavorable balance of trade (p. 881)

transcontinental railroad A railway completed in 1869, connecting the eastern and western ends of the United States (p. 197)

treason Betrayal of one's government (p. 59)

trust A legal combination of companies brought together to gain control of an industry and reduce competition (p. 239)

turnpike A road on which travelers must pay tolls (p. 143)

U

unconditional surrender A surrender without any concessions (p. 509)

undocumented immigrant A person who lacks the legal papers necessary for residence in the United States (p. 735)

unemployment The condition of being out of work; the number of unemployed persons relative to the potential labor force (p. 421)

unfunded mandate A law that businesses or states must comply with, but for which Congress supplies no money (p. 907)

union A group of workers who are organized for the purpose of gaining better wages, hours, and other benefits (Also labor union or trade union) (p. 215)

unionization The organization of the workers in a particular industry into unions (p. 467)

union shop A shop in which new workers are required to join the union (p. 633)

universal coverage Health insurance for all (p. 895)

urbanization The growth of cities; the assumption of an urban way of life (p. 235)

V

vegetation The collection of plants that grow in a specific area (p. 14)

vertical integration The effort of a firm to reduce costs by controlling all aspects of production in an industry and eliminating payment of independent suppliers (p. 209)

vigilante A person who, without authority, dispenses justice (p. 647)

W

wage Daily pay (p. 142)

welfare capitalism Programs adopted by employers in order to convince workers that they did not need unions; for example, providing employees with doctors and nurses and organizing employee athletic teams (p. 358)

western passage A direct western route from Europe to Asia (p. 31)

whistle-stop tour Brief appearances by a political candidate in many communities, usually made from the rear platform of a train (p. 636)

white-collar worker A professional or office worker (p. 366)

women's liberation A movement by women to gain economic, legal, political, and social rights equal to those of men (p. 725)

working poor Members of the United States workforce with earnings too low for them to rise above poverty (p. 885)

Glosario

A

abolition/abolición Prohibición formal de la esclavitud

abolitionism/abolicionismo Movimiento que en el siglo XIX puso fin a la esclavitud en los Estados Unidos

accomodation/acomodación Política bajo la cual determinados afro-americanos aceptaron los resultados del racismo blanco para tener éxito económico

alliance/alianza Pacto o asociación de naciones unidas en una causa común

amendment/enmienda Un cambio o adición por escrito

amnesty/amnistía Ley por la cual el gobierno indulta a un gran grupo de individuos por los crímenes cometidos, generalmente en respuesta a las acciones de consuelo del grupo

anarchism/anarquismo Oposición a cualquier forma de gobierno; teoría de que todos los gobiernos deberían ser abolidos

annex/anexionar Añadir o adjuntar un territorio nuevo a un país ya existente

apartheid/apartheid Política oficial de segregación racial antiguamente en Suráfrica

appeasement/apaciguamiento Política de compromiso o aceptación de las exigencias de una nación hostil con la esperanza de mantener la paz

arbitration/arbitraje Método de arreglar una disputa comprometiéndose de antemano a aceptar la decisión de una persona imparcial

armistice/armisticio Acuerdo de poner fin a las hostilidades

arms race/carrera armamentista Competición entre los Estados Unidos y la Unión Soviética para poseer mayor poder militar

assimilation/asimilación Absorción de miembros de grupos minoritarios en la cultura principal de la sociedad de los Estados Unidos

B

baby boom/baby boom El rápido crecimiento inusual de la población durante el período de posguerra de la Segunda Guerra Mundial en los Estados Unidos, que duró hasta la mitad de los años 60

backlash/reacción Reacción fuerte y súbita contra una idea o política

balance of power/equilibrio de poder Condición en la cual los poderes más importantes son suficientemente iguales en fuerza para evitar cualquier agresión y mantener la seguridad de todos

bilingualism/bilingüismo Uso de dos lenguas; la habilidad de hablar dos lenguas con la misma fluidez

bipartisan coalition/coalición bipartita Grupo de republicanos y demócratas que trabajaban juntos en algunos asuntos

black codes/códigos negros Leyes adoptadas en el sur que restringían severamente los derechos de los negros recién liberados

black power/poder negro Movimiento afro-americano de los 60 cuya meta era trabajar para lograr objetivos económicos, políticos y sociales para los afro-americanos utilizando sus líderes y su organización, sin la ayuda de los blancos

black pride/orgullo negro Orgullo de ser afro-americano; orgullo de ser de ascendencia africana y de tener la nacionalidad americana

black separatism/separatismo negro Concepto, defendido por algunos afro-americanos de los Estados Unidos, que exige la seperación de las razas

blacklisting/poner en la lista negra Esfuerzos para tachar a ciertas personas de comunistas e impedir que realizaran determinados trabajos

blitz(krieg) Ataque intensivo, a menudo combinando las fuerzas aéreas y terrestres; del alemán blitzkrieg, o "guerra relámpago", los bombardeos alemanes sobre Inglaterra durante la Segunda Guerra Mundial

bolshevism/bolchevismo Ideología socialista radical; de Bolchevique, nombre del partido mayoritario de izquierdas liderado por Lenin durante la revolución rusa

bond/obligación Título que gana interés y que puede cobrarse en metálico en una fecha concreta

bootlegger/contrabandista de licores Persona que hacía, vendía o transportaba licor ilegalmente

boycott/boicot Un acuerdo organizado de no comprar o utilizar un determinado producto o de no relacionarse con una determinada compañía o nación para ejercer presión y que así se realicen cambios

brinksmanship/política de la cuerda floja Práctica para intentar mantener la paz entre las naciones dando a conocer que una nación nunca cederá y que está lista para cruzar el umbral de la guerra

C

cabinet/gabinete Cuerpo de personas nombradas por el presidente para dirigir los diferentes departamentos del gobierno y servir de consejeros al presidente

capital/capital Dinero acumulado u otra riqueza material que está destinada a la creación de más riqueza; riqueza material adquirida en los negocios por un individuo o por una compañía

capitalism/capitalismo Sistema económoico basado en la competición abierta en un mercado libre, en el cual los individuos y las compañías poseen los medios de producción y trabajan para obtener beneficios

carpetbaggers/politicastros Oportunistas del norte que fueron al sur y se aprovecharon de las condiciones allí inestables; se les apodó con el nombre despreciativo de politicastros por una especie de equipaje casero que llevaban

checks and balances/cheques y balances Sistema por el cual cada una de las tres ramas del gobierno impide que las otras ganen excesivo poder

civil desobedience/desobediencia civil Estrategia para provocar un cambio social mediante resistencia no violenta contra las leyes injustas

civil liberties/libertades civiles Libertad para disfrutar de los derechos que garantiza la constitución del estado o la nación

civil rights/derechos civiles Derechos políticos, económicos y sociales de un ciudadano; particularmente los que garantiza la Constitución de los Estados Unidos, como el derecho al voto y el derecho a la igualdad de trato ante la ley

climate/clima Conjunto específico de condiciones meteorológicas que caracterizan una zona

closed shop/closed shop Sistema en el cual a todos los trabajadores de una empresa se les pide que sean miembros del sindicato

coalition/coalición Alianza temporal (de naciones, partidos, por ejemplo) formada para una acción o propósito específicos

cold war/guerra fría El conflicto estadounidense-soviético que siguió a la Segunda Guerra Mundial en el cual las dos potencias evitaron el enfrentamiento militar, pero se opusieron mutuamente a sus intereses políticos y económicos

commune/comuna Un grupo de personas que viven en comuna, con posesión y uso colectivo de la sociedad, a menudo con objetivos, filosofías y estilos de vida compartidos

community policing/policía de la comunidad Método de patrullar de la policía que consiste en enviar patrullas a pie a los vecindarios y establecer unas relaciones mejores entre la policía y el público

compensation/compensación Dinero u otro bien que se ofrece a cambio de una pérdida

conglomerate/conglomerado Una compañía que tiene holdings en una diversidad de industrias que no están relacionadas entre sí

conquistadors/conquistadores Exploradores españoles que conquistaron las nuevas tierras que descubrieron

conscientious objector/objetor de conciencia Persona que se niega a hacer el servicio militar debido a principios morales o religiosos

conscription/reclutamiento Alistamiento obligatorio al servicio militar

concensus decision-making/toma de decisiones por consenso Un estilo administrativo como el del presidente Dwight Eisenhower, basado en el acuerdo general

conservative era/era conservadora Período de la política presidencial en el cual el papel del gobierno está limitado y los individuos dependen menos de la ayuda del gobierno

consumer price index/índice de precios al consumo Medida de cambio en el costo de los bienes y servicios en comparación con su costo en un período de tiempo fijo; también llamado índice del costo de la vida

containment/contención Después de la Segunda Guerra Mundial, la política de los Estados Unidos de asegurar la paz tratando de contener el comunismo, o impidiendo que se extendiera más allá de sus fronteras reales

corollary/corolario Una proposición que se añade a otra como una consecuencia o efecto natural, como el corolario de Teddy Roosevelt a la Doctrina de Monroe

corporation/corporación Grupo de individuos al que la ley autoriza a actuar como a una sola entidad; negocio que pertenece a muchos inversores

counter culture/contracultura Cultura de la gente joven con valores que se oponen a los valores de la cultura convencional

coup/golpe de estado Acto de hacerse con el poder y derrocar al gobierno

covert operation/operación secreta Misión secreta o clandestina del gobierno

coverture/cobertura Ley británica por la cual la propiedad heredada de una mujer pertenecía a su marido

credit/crédito Plan de pago demorado en el cual el comprador pone parte del dinero y paga el balance a plazos; tiempo permitido para pagar algo que se ha vendido a crédito

crime bill/proyecto de ley criminal Proyecto de ley que tiene disposiciones para destinar más policías en las calles, construir cárceles, incluir nuevas solicitudes para la pena de muerte y prohibir armas de ataque

cultural diffusion/difusión cultural Expansión de las costumbres, estilos de vida y otros productos del trabajo y pensamiento humano de un grupo cultural a otro

culture of poverty/cultura de la pobreza Después de la Segunda Guerra Mundial, las personas que pasaban hambre, las personas sin hogar y el gran número de miembros invisibles de una sociedad americana en general acaudalada

D

deferment/prórroga Aplazamiento de la incorporación de una persona al servicio militar por razones de salud u ocupación

deficit spending/gasto de déficit Política del gobierno de tomar dinero prestado para poder gastar más dinero del obtenido por los impuestos

demagogue/demagogo Líder que gana poder apelando a las emociones y prejuicios de la gente

demobilization/desmobilización Proceso de la posguerra de licenciar a las tropas del servicio militar para que los ciudadanos y los negocios vuelvan a sus tareas y objetivos propios de un período de paz

depression/depresión Período de una larga y severa decadencia en la economía de una nación, marcado por una baja producción y un alto índice de desempleo

deregulation/desregulación Acción de suprimir restricciones y reglas

détente/détente Intento de disminuir la tensión entre los Estados Unidos y las potencias comunistas durante la guerra fría

diplomacy/diplomacia Arte en la práctica de dirigir relaciones internacionales

direct primary/elecciones primarias Elecciones abiertas a todos los votantes de un partido, en unas elecciones primarias, son los votantes los que eligen a los candidatos y no los líderes del partido

disarmament/desarmamento Ley o política de reducción o destrucción de las armas militares

discretionary income/renta discrecional Dinero para comprar lo que se quiere además de lo que se necesita

discrimination/discriminación Negación de los derechos de una persona debido a su raza, religión, edad, sexo u otra cualidad

dissident/disidente Persona que no está de acuerdo con la política o creencias establecidas; antes de la presidencia de Gorbachev, ciudadano de la Unión Soviética que se manifestaba en contra de la política soviética

dogfight/combate aéreo Nombre que recibían los enfrentamientos entre aviones enemigos

dole/subsidio de paro Dinero o bienes dados en calidad de caridad; durante la Gran Depresión, pagos de beneficencia del gobierno; estar "acogido a la beneficencia" consistía en recibir estos pagos regularmente

domino theory/teoría del dominó Teoría según la cual tras la caída de un país en el comunismo, otros países a su vez también caerían, igual que los dominós

doughboys/doughboys Apodo con el que se conocía a los soldados de infantería de los Estados Unidos durante la Primera Guerra Mundial

dove/paloma Persona que apoya la retirada de las tropas de los Estados Unidos de la guerra y está a favor de la negociación para poner fin a la guerra

draft/destacamento Selección de personas para una particular misión obligatoria; sistema de selección de personas para servir militarmente

due process/proceso de reconocimiento Procedimientos legales que salvaguardan los derechos de un individuo

E

egalitarian/igualitaria Cultura sin autoridades reconocidas, donde todas las personas se consideran iguales

electronic campaigning/campaña electrónica Estratégia de campaña política en la que un candidato intenta influenciar a los votantes mediante anuncios televisivos

electronic media/medios de comunicación electrónicos Formas de comunicación transmitida electrónicamente que llega a todo el público; radio y televisión principalmente

emancipation/emancipación Liberación de la esclavitud; en particular, liberación de la esclavitud de los afro-americanos

embargo/embargo Restricción o detención del comercio

emerging nation/nación emergente Países en vías de desarrollo de Asia, América Latina y África

emigrate/emigrar Dejar un país para establecerse en otro

enfranchisement/concesión de derechos políticos Obtención de los derechos de ciudadanía, especialmente el derecho al voto

entrepreneur/empresario Propietario de un pequeño negocio

eugenics/eugenesia Movimiento de principios del siglo XX para la mejora de la raza humana a través del control de los factores hereditarios mediante el emparejamiento

evangelist/evangelista Predicador fundamentalista

expansionism/expansionismo Política o proceso para incrementar el espacio físico de una nación adquiriendo nuevos territorios

extended family/familia ampliada Unidad familiar que incluye no sólo a los padres y a los hijos sino también a otros familiares, como abuelos, tíos y primos

external tax/impuesto exterior Impuesto exigido por los bienes que llegan a una zona, como el impuesto que impuso el Parlamento británico por el azúcar que llegaba a las colonias americanas

F

family leave/permiso familiar Permiso no pagado para ausentarse por el nacimiento o adopción de un hijo o por enfermedad de un miembro de la familia

fascism/fascismo Ideología altamente nacionalista cuyo nombre surgió para denominar al Partido fascista de Italia; gobierno caracterizado por el racismo y el militarismo; dictadura represiva de un solo partido

fascist/fascista Seguidor de una filosofía política que predicaba el nacionalismo y el racismo

federal regulation/regulación federal Control por parte del gobierno federal en vez de por parte de intereses privados

feminist/feminista Activista que trabaja para lograr derechos políticos, económicos y sociales para las mujeres iguales a los de los hombres

filibuster/obstruccionismo Táctica que consiste en dar largos discursos para demorar o impedir un voto para la creación de una ley

flapper/flapper Mujer característica de los años 20, por lo menos la que se promocionaba en la publicidad y en las películas; cuyo nombre hace referencia a los flecos de sus vestidos que giraban cuando se movían

flatboat/chalana Embarcación con el piso plano y los extremos cuadrados que se utilizaba para transportar bienes a lo largo de canales interiores a principios del siglo XIX

foreclosure/ejecución de una hipoteca Procedimiento legal para reclamar una parte de una propiedad cuando el comprador no puede mantener los pagos de la hipoteca

frontier/frontera Zona donde las tierras de los colonos establecidos hacían frontera con las tierras de los nativos americanos

fugitive/fugitivo Persona que escapó de la esclavitud y huía de la ley

fundamentalism/fundamentalismo Movimiento protestante en los Estados Unidos caracterizado por la creencia de que las palabras de la biblia fueron inspiradas por Dios y que por lo tanto deberían interpretarse literalmente y seguirse fielmente

G

generation gap/choque generacional Los diferentes valores, gustos y actitudes entre los miembros de grupos de diferentes edades, especialmente entre los adolescentes y sus padres

geography/geografía El estudio de la gente, lugares y entornos físicos

gerrymandering/división de los distritos electorales División de los distritos electorales de manera que aumente o disminuya la representación de un determinado grupo o partido

glasnost/glasnost Palabra rusa para denominar una política de apertura, empezó con el presidente Gorbachev, animando la libre expresión y poner fin a la censura de partido

global economy/economía global Sistema de comercio mundial

gospel tradition/tradición del gospel Tipo de música que combina las palabras de los himnos protestantes tradicionales con varios estilos de música africana

government boarding school/internado del gobierno Escuela en la que a los niños nativos americanos se les enseñaban las tradiciones culturales de los blancos

gross national product (GNP)/producto nacional bruto (PNB) El valor total de todos los bienes y servicios que se han producido en una nación en un año determinado

guerrilla warfare/guerra de guerrillas Lucha de bandas pequeñas e independientes, que utilizan tácticas como el sabotage y la emboscada

H

hard money/dinero fuerte Divisa consistente en monedas de oro o plata en oposición al papel moneda

hawk/halcón Persona que respalda el esfuerzo de la guerra

hippy/hippy Miembro de la contracultura

history/historia El estudio de los acontecimientos y de las personas a través del tiempo

holding company/holding Compañía que posee acciones predominantes del capital social en otras compañías

homestead/heredad Tierra concedida por el gobierno de los Estados Unidos a los colonos que allí vivieran y cultivaran durante cinco años, según la Ley de la heredad de 1862

horizontal integration/integración horizontal Fusión de compañías competitivas en una industria, como las de refinerías de petroleo, con la finalidad de dominar esa industria

human/environmental interaction/interacción ser humano/medio ambiente La interdependencia de las personas y el medio ambiente

human rights/derechos humanos Derechos y libertades básicas las cuales se asume que pertenecen a las personas de todos los lugares

I

immigrant/inmigrante Persona que entra en un país para vivir en él

impeachment/enjuiciamiento Cargos de mala conducta contra un funcionario público

imperialism/imperialismo Política que consiste en implantar un dominio económico, político y militar sobre naciones más debiles con motivos humanitarios y morales

impressment/requisición Práctica que consiste en forzar a la gente al servicio público, como los marineros americanos fueron forzados a sevir en los barcos británicos a finales del siglo XVIII

indentured servant/sirviente contratado Persona que aceptó trabajar por un número de años establecido a cambio de un pasaje para las colonias

indigenous/indígenas La gente que originariamente habita una zona; nativos

industrial productivity/productividad industrial Cantidad de bienes producidos en una hora de trabajo

industrialism/industrialismo El movimiento de la agricultura hacia la industria como la mayor fuente de crecimiento económico

industrialist/industrial Persona que se dedica a la producción comercial y a la venta de bienes y servicios

inflation/inflación Aumento agudo y continuo de los precios provocado por demasiado dinero y crédito relativo a los bienes disponibles

initiative/iniciativa Reforma que permitía a los ciudadanos introducir un decreto en una legislatura o evitar la legislatura y proponer una nueva ley por petición

injunction/requerimiento Una orden de la corte requiriendo que un individuo o una compañía haga algo, como terminar una huelga

internal tax/impuesto interior Impuesto exigido por los bienes que se producen y consumen dentro de una zona, como el impuesto del timbre fiscal impuesto por el Parlamento británico en las colonias americanas

interventionism/intervencionismo Política que consiste en intervenir, o interferir, en los asuntos de otra nación; en la Segunda Guerra Mundial la posición de aquellos que se oponían al aislacionismo y que creían que los Estados Unidos deberían ofrecer todo el apoyo posible a las fuerzas aliadas

irreconcilables/irreconciliables Durante la Primera Guerra Mundial un grupo de senadores que se opusieron a una Liga de Naciones y no pudieron reconciliarse para votar a su favor

isolationism/aislacionismo Evitar conflictos y alianzas con otras naciones; indiferencia a los asuntos que pasaban fuera de los Estados Unidos; a principios de la Segunda Guerra Mundial, política que consistía en no formar alianzas ni en ponerse de parte de nadie

K

kachina/kachina Muñeca sagrada de las gentes de Pueblo

L

land reform/reforma territorial Redistribución de propiedades a campesinos pobres sin tierras

legislature/legislatura Comité con poder para crear leyes

liberal era/era liberal Período en el que el gobierno promovió el progreso social

liberation theology/teología de liberación Filosofía de un movimiento de activistas cristianos que trabajaban a favor de la justicia social, especialmente en Latino América

limited war/guerra limitada Política que empezó con la era Truman y que consistía en evitar una guerra global confinando la lucha a una zona y utilizando armas covencionales, no poder nuclear

location/situación La posición sobre la superficie terrestre

lynching/linchamiento Una acción de la multitud en la que se ejecuta a una persona sin ser juzgada, generalmente en la horca

M

majority/mayoría Más del 50% de un grupo

mandate/mandato Una clara expresión de los deseos de los votantes, expresados en los resultados de las elecciones

margin/margen "Comprar al margen" significa que la casa de corretaje le presta dinero a alguien para comprar valores, si la bolsa sube, todos los beneficios (menos el interés que se cobra por el préstamo) son del comprador

martyr/mártir Persona que muere voluntariamente antes que renunciar a sus pricipios religiosos; persona que muere o que soporta un gran sufrimiento en defensa de una causa

mass media/medios de comunicación de masas Métodos mediante los cuales la información y el entretenimiento son transmitidos a un gran número de personas; incluyen periódicos, radio y televisión

massive retaliation/venganza masiva Política de la guerra fría de los Estados Unidos por la cual la agresión contra cualquier aliado se encontraría con una huelga nuclear incondicional

materialism/materialismo Dar más importancia al dinero y a los bienes materiales que a las cuestiones intelectuales, espirituales y artísticas

melting pot/crisol Sociedad en la cual un número de grupos raciales, étnicos y culturales se absorben y mezclan; de un recipiente que se utiliza para fundir metales

merger/fusión Conversión de compañías competitivas de una industria en una única compañía mayor; conversión de varias compañías o corporaciones en una compañía mayor

migration/migración Movimiento de gente de un país o región a otro

militant/militante Persona que es agresiva al promover una causa

military-industrial complex/complejo industrial militar El vasto y entrelazado establecimiento militar y la industria de las armas

militia group/grupo de milicia Grupo militar de ciudadanos que considera al gobierno como a un enemigo

mission/misión Colonia española construida para convertir al cristianismo a los nativos americanos

missionary/misionero Persona que viaja por muchos sitios para convertir a la gente al cristianismo

mobilization/mobilización Preparación para la guerra, incluyendo tanto esfuerzos militares como civiles

moratorium/moratoria Autorización oficial para suspender los pagos, como los de una deuda; un período de espera autorizado oficialmente

movement/movimiento Término que hace referencia al fluir de personas, bienes, ideas e información de un lugar a otro

muckracker/revelador de escándalos Escritor cuyos artículos de investigación o libros denunciaban abusos como el trabajo infantil o la corrupción

mutual deterrence/disuasión mútua Teoría que consiste en que siempre y cuando haya misiles precisos capaces de una destrucción total apuntando al otro país, ningún país se arriesgará a empezar una guerra nuclear

N

national debt/deuda nacional A finales del siglo XVII, la cantidad de dinero que se les debía a los americanos y a otros países después de la revolución americana; la cantidad total de dinero que se le debía al gobierno nacional

national liberation/liberación nacional Liberar a una nación del control de otra nación

national market/mercado nacional Sistema económico de dimensión nacional que es posible gracias a la red de transportes de los Estados Unidos

nationalist movement/movimiento nacionalista Las actividades de un grupo centradas en liberar a una nación de la influencia y control extranjero

nationalization/nacionalización El proceso de cambiar una propiedad o industria de un propietario privado al gobierno; después de la Segunda Guerra Mundial la declaración de Irán de que sus campos de petróleo, con sus fabricas pertenecientes a los británicos, eran propiedad del gobierno iraní

nativism/nativismo Preferencia de los americanos nativos por nacimiento sobre los inmigrantes

negotiate/negociar Llegar a un acuerdo

neoconservative/neoconservadora La filosofía conservadora de la presidencia Reagan que se oponía a la excesiva burocracia, al gasto federal y a la intervención del gobierno en la vida privada de las personas

neutral/neutral No estar de parte de nadie en un conflicto

neutrality/neutralidad Política que consistía en permanecer imparcial en una disputa, incluyendo el no ponerse de parte de nadie en una guerra; política de permanecer no aliado

nomadic/nómada Que va de un lugar a otro

nonviolent resistance/resistencia no violenta El acto de manifestarse pacíficamente para lograr un cambio en la política sin combatir a las autoridades

nullification/anulación Antes de la Guerra Civil, el derecho exigido por algunos estados para rechazar, o declarar nula cualquier ley federal que creían que violaba la Constitución

O

oligopoly/oligopolio El control de toda una industria, como la de envasado de carnes, por unos pocos productores importantes

P

pacification program/programa de pacificación Política bajo la cual pueblos enteros son desarraigados y se obliga a las personas a desplazarse hacia las ciudades o a campos de refugiados

pacifism/pacifismo Oposición al uso de la fuerza

pardon/perdón Perdonar; librarse del castigo

penny auction/subasta de penique Venta de propiedades que se realiza en un escenario para los amigos por tan solo unos peniques y que luego lo devuelven

perestroika/perestroika Palabra rusa que significa reestructura, nombre que denomina la política económica del presidente soviético Gorbachev, política que favorece una menor intervención del gobierno y una mayor iniciativa privada

place/lugar Una posición específica

political machine/máquina política Una organización política bien organizada que controla los resultados electorales ofreciendo trabajos y otros favores a cambio de votos

porkbarrel legislation/legislación de fondos públicos Leyes que favorecen proyectos de cuestionable necesidad, creando empleos y proporcionando dinero en un distrito de un legislador

pragmatist/pragmático Persona interesada en las soluciones prácticas a los problemas en vez de resolverlos con ideas y teorías

presidio/presidio Poblado español que servía tanto de centro de comercio como para defender territorios españoles

progressive/progresista Persona que defiende las reformas para hacer frente a los problemas causados por la industrialización y la urbanización

prohibition/prohibición Prohibir el alcohol

propaganda/propaganda Una forma de información pública que se utiliza para crear en el público una opinión mediante la utilización de técnicas como el uso de un lenguaje con carga emocional, llamar por el nombre de pila, apelación a la presión de los semejantes y un enfoque de triunfo

---
Q
---

quota/cupo Ley que limita el número de inmigrantes

R
---

racism/racismo La idea de que una raza es superior a las otras, y que la raza determina el carácter y la habilidad de una persona; prejuicio y discriminación hacia los miembros de un grupo racial, generalmente una minoría

radical/radical A favor de la revolución política y social

ratify/ratificar Aceptar y aprobar oficialmente

real income/renta neta La cantidad de los ingresos profesionales, teniendo en cuenta el aumento de los precios

realpolitik/realpolitik Política práctica; la visión de que una nación debería perseguir políticas y hacer alianzas basadas en sus intereses nacionales

reapportionment/nueva repartición Cambio en el número de escaños legislativos asignados a cada estado

recall/revocación Procedimiento que permite a los ciudadanos retirar de su cargo a un funcionario elegido antes de que termine su período de mandato

recession/recesión Período de productividad en declive y de una actividad económica reducida

referendum/referéndum Proceso por el cual los ciudadanos votan directamente a favor o en contra de una propuesta política o decreto de ley

region/región Una zona caracterizada por una o más cualidades específicas

regulatory commision/comisión reguladora Grupo cuya responsabilidad es la de ver que una compañía (o compañías) cumple las leyes existentes

repatriation/repatriación Retorno de una persona a su país natal o de ciudadanía

representation/representación El derecho a ser representado por delegados escogidos en elecciones libres; la elección de funcionarios que representen las ideas de un partido en concreto

reservationists/reservacionistas Un grupo del congreso que aprobó la idea de la Liga de Naciones con reservas; apoyarían la idea si se hacían ciertas modificaciones a dicha propuesta

resource management/administración de recursos La administración científica de los recursos naturales

revenue sharing/reparto de impuestos Programa a través del cual el gobierno federal devuelve parte del dinero de los impuestos a los gobiernos locales

revivalism/evangelismo Movimiento religioso que se centra más en la experiencia religiosa individual que en la doctrina de la iglesia

revolution/revolución Un esfuerzo violento para derrocar al gobierno

right-to-work law/ley de derecho al trabajo Legislación que prohibía las union shops que requerían la unión de más trabajadores

---
S
---

scientific management/gestión científica Una teoría de gestión que utiliza expertos eficientes para examinar cada operación de trabajo y encontrar formas de minimizar el tiempo que se necesita para completarlo

scorched earth policy/táctica de bloqueo del avance enemigo Táctica que consiste en romper la voluntad del enemigo destruyéndole la comida, el refugio y las municiones

secede/separarse Retirarse formalmente de la Unión

secession/secesión Acto de retirarse oficialmente de un grupo

sectionalism/seccionalismo Devoción de los intereses locales sobre los del grupo mayor

sedentary/sedentario Asentado en un lugar

segregation/segregación La separación forzosa de los grupos raciales en las escuelas, los alojamientos y otros lugares públicos

selectmen/concejales Funcionarios elegidos en las comunidades puritanas que decidían sobre las cuestiones de impuestos y de reparto de tierras

self-determination/autodeterminación El derecho que tienen todas las personas a decidir la forma de gobierno bajo el cual les gustaría vivir

settlement house/centro social Un centro en el vecindario que facilita servicios sociales y educativos a la gente necesitada, establecido entre 1889 y 1910

sharecroping/aparcería Sistema por el cual los propietarios de tierras proporcionan tierras, semillas y maquinaria a los granjeros a cambio de un porcentaje de la cosecha

silent majority/mayoría silenciosa La gran mayoría de los americanos, cuyas opiniones no son a menudo escuchadas

slave labor force/mano de obra esclava Grupo de personas que pertenecen a un amo quien les hace trabajar sin cobrar

social gospel movement/movimiento social de gospel Movimiento que enfatiza la aplicación de los principios cristianos a los problemas sociales

socialism/socialismo Teoría económica que defiende la propiedad colectiva o gubernamental de las fábricas y otros negocios en vez de la propiedad privada

sonar technology/tecnología sonar Tecnología que detecta objetos sumergidos mediante ondas sonoras

Southern strategy/estrategia sureña Plan diseñado para apelar directamente a los conservadores blancos del sur

speakeasy/despacho clandestino de bebidas Club donde se vende licor aun quebrantando la ley

speculation/especulación Aventura de negocios arriesgada que incluye la compra o venta de una propiedad con la esperanza de conseguir un gran beneficio rápidamente; invertir en la bolsa

speculator/especulador Persona que compra propiedades, como tierras o bonos, con la esperanza de que se incrementará su valor

spoils system/sistema de acaparamiento Acuerdo por el cual los partidos o candidatos victoriosos recompensan a sus seguidores con empleos, contratos, etc.

stagflation/inflación Condición económica inusual que combina una economía estancada con el aumento de los precios

standard of living/estilo de vida El bienestar material de los individuos o grupos de una sociedad

status quo/statu quo Estado de cosas en un determinado período

status symbol/símbolo de estatus La creencia de que las posesiones reflejaban la riqueza, prestigio o posición social superior de una persona en la sociedad

stocks/acciones Acciones de la propiedad del negocio

strike/huelga Paro organizado del trabajo que se utiliza para forzar al empleador a acceder a determinadas demandas, como mejores salarios, horarios y condiciones

subsidy/subsidio Dinero que concede el gobierno a un individuo o a una compañía con el propósito de beneficiar a la sociedad

suburb/suburbio Comunidad en las afueras de una gran ciudad

suburbia/suburbios Las afueras de una ciudad; la cultura suburbana

suffrage/sufragio Derecho al voto

supply-side economics/economía de supply-side Teoría basada en la creencia de que la clave de la vitalidad económica está en reducir los impuestos—especialmente los de los individuos ricos y las grandes compañías—y esta reducción de los impuestos animaría el ahorro y la inversión, lo cual llevaría a la expansión de los negocios y a la creación de más puestos de trabajo

syndicate/agencia de prensa Cadena de periódicos bajo dirección central; agencia que proporciona artículos o características a una serie de periódicos o revistas

T

tabloid/periódico sensacionalista Periódico de pequeñas páginas y grandes titulares—lectura ideal para los abarrotados y movedizos vagones del metro

tariff/tarifa Impuesto o cuota sobre los bienes importados

temperance/moderación Moderación, o abstinencia total, en el uso de bebidas alcohólicas

tenement/viviendas Edificio de apartamentos en la ciudad, a menudo un edificio de apartamentos poblados y de bajo alquiler en los barrios bajos

termination policy/política de terminación Política para poner fin al sistema de reserva y terminar con todos los servicios federales a los grupos de nativos americanos

territorial integrity/integridad territorial Protección de una nación de la violación de sus tierras y de sus derechos de comercio por otra nación

textile/industria textil Fábrica especialmente de prendas de lana y punto; telas

totalitarian/totalitario (Un gobierno) controlado por una sola persona o partido; que suprime la libertad y controla cada aspecto de la vida de las personas

trade deficit/déficit de comercio Un desequilibrio de los valores entre los bienes importados y exportados de un país debido a que dicho país ha comprado más de lo que ha vendido, creando así un balance desfavorable del comercio

transcontinental railroad/ferrocarril transcontinental Ferrocarril que se finalizó en 1869 y que unía los extremos este y oeste de los Estados Unidos

treason/traición Engaño del gobierno

trust/monopolio Combinación de compañías para ganar el control de una industria y reducir la competencia

turnpike/autovía Carretera en la que los conductores deben pagar peaje

U

unconditional surrender/rendición incondicional Rendición sin concesiones

undocumented immigrant/inmigrante indocumentado Persona que carece de los papeles legales necesarios para residir en los Estados Unidos

unemployment/desempleo La condición de estar sin trabajo; el número de personas desempleadas relativo al conjunto de trabajadores potenciales

unfunded mandate/mandato no remunerado Ley que los estados y los negocios deben acatar pero el congreso no proporciona dinero por ello

union/unión Grupo de trabajadores que están organizados con el propósito de ganar mejores salarios, horarios y otros beneficios (También sindicato)

unionization/sindicalización La organización de los trabajadores de una determinada industria dentro de los sindicatos

union shop/union shop Establecimiento que requería a sus nuevos trabajadores que se afiliaran al sindicato

universal coverage/cobertura universal Seguro sanitario que lo incluye todo

urbanization/urbanización El crecimiento de las ciudades; la pretensión de un estilo de vida urbano

V

vegetation/vegetación La colección de plantas que crecen en una zona específica

vertical integration/integración vertical El esfuerzo de una compañía para reducir costos mediante el control de todos los aspectos de producción de una industria y la eliminación del pago de proveedores independientes

vigilante/vigilante Persona que, sin autorización, administra justicia

W

wage/jornal Paga diaria

welfare capitalism/capitalismo benefactor Programas adoptados por los empleadores para convencer a los trabajadores de que no necesitan sindicatos; por ejemplo, proporcionando doctores y enfermeras a los empleados y organizando equipos de atletismo con los empleados

western passage/pasaje al oeste Una ruta directa hacia el oeste desde Europa hasta Asia

whistle-stop tour/gira por los apeaderos Breves apariciones de un cadidato político en muchas comunidades, generalmente en la plataforma trasera de un tren

white-collar worker/trabajador de cuello blanco Profesional o persona que trabaja en una oficina

women's liberation/liberación de la mujer Movimiento feminista para obtener los mismos derechos económicos, legales, políticos y sociales que los hombres

working poor/trabajo de pobres Miembros del cuerpo de trabajadores de los Estados Unidos cuyos salarios son demasiado bajos para permitirles salir de la pobreza

Index

Biddle, Tony, 490
big band era, 532–33
big business; in 1920s, 354–59, 362–68; Harding–Coolidge administrations and, 349–50; Hoover and, 350; during Progressive era, 243; Roosevelt, Theodore, and, 269–71, 277; Taft and, 273; in World War I, 317–18; after World War II, 601–02
Big Four, 324
Big Stick philosophy, 352
Big Three, 564
bilingualism, 737
Bill of Rights (1791), q101–103; debate over, c89, 90; need for, 90; ratification of, t90; Virginia State, 73. *See also* Constitution, United States.
Bingham, George Caleb, ptg37
Bird, Caroline, 434
Birmingham (Ala.), p410, p684, 684–85, 691
bison, p22
Black, Hugo, p714, 716
black Americans. *See* African Americans.
black cabinet, 478
Black Caucus, 899
black codes, 185
Blackfeet, 28
blacklisting, 357, 647, 651
"Black Man Talks of Reaping, A" (Bontemps), 392
Blackmun, Harry, 813
Black Muslims, 343, 692
Black Panther party, 694, p694, 811, p811
black power, 693
black pride, 691–92
black separatism, 691, 692
blacksmiths, p73
Black Star Line, 343
"Black Tuesday," ptg420, p428
Blake, James, 674
"Bleeding Kansas," 162, 171
blind, care for, 155
blitz, 501–02
blitzkrieg, 496, 510
blockade runners, 176
blood plasma, 550, 551
"Blowin' in the Wind" (Dylan), q748
blue-collar workers, 365–66
Blue Lake (N. Mex.), 742–43, 745
blues, the, 388–89
blue stars on flags, 528
Bly, Nellie, 288, p288
B&O. *See* Baltimore and Ohio Railroad (B&O).
Boardman, Barrington, q514
Bogart, Humphrey, 507, 651
Bolick, Clint, q915
Bolsheviks, and Red Scare in United States, 340, 406. *See also* Russian Revolution.
bombings; in Chicago, 216; in New York, 341; in Oklahoma City, 922
Bonaparte, Napoleon, 131–32
bonds, federal government, q94, 113–14
bonds, government. *See* government bonds.
Bonnin, Gertrude, 480
Bontemps, Arna, q392
bonus army, p426, 426–27, 456
"Boogie Woogie Bugle Boy of Company B" (Price and Raye), q526
Book of Daniel, The (Doctorow), q558–59
Book-of-the-Month Club, 390
books; in 1880s, 241; in 1920s, 389, 395; in 1930s, 440–41, 444–45
boom towns, during World War II, 536, 540–41
Boone, Daniel, p65, 130–31
Booth, John Wilkes, 180
bootleggers, 398–99
Borah, William, 325
Border Patrol, 406, p406
Bork, Robert, 829
Born on the Fourth of July (Kovic), q764–65
Bosnia, 896–97, m897

Boston (Mass.), 49, t68; Boston Massacre, p59, t59; Boston Tea Party, 59, 60; harbor, t59, 60; Hutchinson trial in, 42–45; Sugar Act protests, 57; Red Scare in, 340, 341; subway in, 235
Boston Harbor, t59, 59, 60
Boston Massacre, t59, p59, 59, 60
Boston Police Strike, 341
Boston Tea Party, 59
Boston University, 676
Boudinot, Elias, 139
Bourke-White, Margaret, p424
Boutros-Ghali, Boutros, q868
Bow, Clara, p395
Boxer Rebellion, 298
boxing, 387, 388
boycotts; of British goods, 59; civil rights and, 674–76, 678; embargo, 117, 141; grape, 733, 737, 738–41; Montgomery bus, 674–76; Supreme Court and, t358, 358; of tea ("Boston Tea Party"), 59, 60; by unions, 216
Boyle, Ralph ("Buzz"), 554
bracero program, 407, 623, 735
Brady, James, p899, 899
Brady Bill, 899
branches of government. *See* checks and balances; Constitution, United States.
Brandeis, Louis, p255, 255–56
Brant, Joseph, p46
Braun, Carol Mosely, 894
Brazil, 820
Brezhnev, Leonid, p818, 818, 840
Briand, Aristide, 351
Bridgeport (Conn.), 922–23
brinkmanship, 579
Britain, Battle of, 501–02
Brooke, R.N., ptg191
Brooklyn Bridge, 194, p195
Brooks, Jack, 833
Brooks, John, q619
Brooks, Preston, 171, crt171
"Brother, Can You Spare a Dime?" (Harburg), q424–25
Brotherhood of Sleeping Car Porters, 544
Brown, John, 162, ptg163, 171
Brown, Linda, 670
Brown, Pat, 826
Brown University, 244
Brown v. Board of Education (1954), 670–71
Bryan, William Jennings, 214, 309–10, p396, 396, 397
Buckland, William, p41
Buck, Pearl, 497
Budapest, 582
budget deficit, g839, g859, 860–61
Buena Vista, p169
buffalo; Native American uses of, 28, p29
Buffalo (N.Y.), 266, 433
Bulganin, Nikolai, 581
Bulgaria, 316, 564
Bulge, Battle of the, 511
Bullitt, Bill, 490
Bull Moose party, 276–78, crt277, m277
Bull Run, First Battle of, 174, m175
bulrush house, m28
Bunche, Ralph, q691
Bundy, McGeorge, 772
Bureau of Corporations, 349
Bureau of Indian Affairs, 743, 744, 746
Bureau of Investigation, 340. *See also* Federal Bureau of Investigation (FBI).
Bureau of Standards, 350
Burger, Warren, 813, c827, p827
Burgess-Norton Company, 317
burial sites; moundbuilder, 24–25, p25
Burlington Railroad, 270
Burma, 513
Burr, Aaron, 103, p116
Busch, Irma, q407

Bush, George, 877, q877; arms limitations and, 867–68; China and, 879–80; Clinton vs., 893–94, m893; Cuba and, 873; Dukakis vs., 877, p877; economy and, 882–85, crt883; education and, 923; environment and, 910; Iran-*contra* scandal and, 893–94; Persian Gulf War and, p878, 878–79; post-cold war problems and, 877–78; Reagan and, 876, 877; Soviet Union and, 867–68; taxes and, 883
business; in late 1800s, 208–09, 214; in 1920s, 349, 354–59, 362–68; in 1990s, 882–83; automobiles and, 379; cycles of, 1920–45, g549; during Great Depression, 424, 434–35; Hoover, Herbert, and, 350; managerial revolutions in, 208, 357; mass production in, 362–65; during Progressive era, 243; Reagan and, 857; Second New Deal and, 469–70; Taft, William Howard, and, 273; TVA and, 457–58; Whigs and, 153; white-collar workers in, 365–66; Wilson, Woodrow, and, 278–79; World War I and, 309, 310–11, 317–18; after World War II, 599, 601–02. *See also* big business; industry.
business administration, schools of, p357
business associations, p357
busing, school, 812–13
Butler, "Duckboards," p408
Butler Act, 396, 397
Butterfield, Alexander, c827, p827, 828–29
Byrnes, James F., 518

C

Cabeza de Vaca, Alvar Núñez, q2–3, 6
cabinet, the President's, 113
cable cars, 235
cable television, 859–60
Cabot, John (Giovanni Cabato), m31
Cahokia, settlement, 25
Calhoun, John C., 153, 169
California, m28; agriculture in, 198; anti-Chinese agitation in, 217, 405; Compromise of 1850 and, 169–70; federal budget cuts affect, 911; and grape boycott, 722, p723, 733, 736–37, 738–41, p740; Japanese immigration to, 301; Ku Klux Klan in, 400; Mexico and, 169, 219; migration to, m431, 431–32; primary in 1968, 780; southern, as part of Sunbelt, m814, 814–15; Spanish, 37; after World War II, 600, 603, 610; during World War II and, 535, 540–41. *See also* Japanese Americans.
Calley, William, 792–93
Cambodia, 769, m769, 770, 773, 774, 793, 798–99, 800, 825, 879
Camelot, 706
camera. *See* photography.
Campbell, Ben Nighthorse, 894
Camp David (Md), 98
Camp David Accord, p841, 841–42
Camp meeting, 150, 153
Canada, m31, 48, m161; NAFTA and, 881–82, 896; Newfoundland, 31, 37–38; Seven Years' War (French and Indian War) and, m48, 48–49; trade with, 881–82
canals, 128, p129, p144, 144–45, 149, 206
Cane Ridge (Ky.), 150, 153
Cantigny, 316
Capa, Robert, 489
Capone, Al, 399, p399
caravel, Portuguese, 31, p31
Caputo, Philip, q773, q774
Caribbean Sea, m297; in 1980s, m872; Seward and, 220–21; U.S. intervention in, t297. *See also* Bahamas; Cuba; Grenada; Haiti; Jamaica; Puerto Rico; Virgin Islands.
Carliss, George, 158

Dunkirk, 501, *p501*
Dunmore, Lord, *q75*
Dunne, Finley Peter, *q270*
Duplex Printing Press Co. v. *Deering* (1921), *t358*
DuPont; corporation, 365; family, 354
Dust Bowl, 430–31, *m431, m437*, 438–39, *m439*
Dutch, 39
Dutch East Indies, 513
Duvalier, François, 873
Duvalier, Jean-Claude, 873
Dylan, Bob, 748, *p748, q748*, 753, *q789*
Dynamic Sociology (Ward), 244
dysentery, 177, 309

E

Earhart, Amelia, 388
Earth Day, 784
earthworks, moundbuilder, 24–25, *p25*
Eastern Europe, 564, 565, 566, *t567*, 568. *See also* Europe.
Eastern North America, *m53, m57. See also* Atlantic Seaboard.
Eastern Woodland Native Americans, 25–27
East Germany, 571. *See also* Germany; Democratic Republic of (East).
East India Company, 59, *t59*
Eastland, James O., 683
Eastman, George, *t205*
East St. Louis (Ill.); Mississippian moundbuilder culture, 25
EC. *See* European Community (EC)
Eckford, Elizabeth Ann, 666
Economic Opportunity Act, 708
economy; in 1800s, 113–14, 140–49, *m181*; in 1920s, 354–55; automobiles and, 379; baby boom and, 610; under Bush, 882–85, 890, 892–93; under Carter, *g839*, 839; under Clinton, 903; in colonial era, 37, 39; credit and, 381; crises, *t423*; under Ford, 837–39, *g839*; global, 883; in Great Depression, 421–22; under Kennedy, 703; money and, 213; New Deal and, 456–58, 465; under Nixon, *g839*; under Reagan, 858–61; and recession beginning during Reconstruction, 190; Roosevelt, Theodore, and, 269–73; during World War II, 527–29; after World War II, 599–600, 632–33
Ederle, Gertrude, *p388*
Edison, Thomas Alva, *t205*, 205–06, 240, *p240*, 241
Edmund Pettus Bridge, *p688*
education; in 1920s, 383; in 1950s, 610, 613; in 1990s, 893, 923–24; African Americans and, 188–89, 190, 282; arms race and, 582; baby boom and, 610, 613; Bush and, 923; in business management, 357; civil rights in, 670–72; in colonial America, 39, *p39*, 46–47; evolution vs. Bible in, 396–97; free public, 39, 155; GI Bill and, 599, 600; higher levels of, 256–57, *c787*; length of school year, *g256*; literacy increases, 256–57; of Native Americans, 46–47; need to improve quality of, 923; property taxes as funding for, 924; public, 39; reform movement for public, 924; slaves and, 168; women and, *g726*, 727. *See also* schools.
Education, Department of, 923
Education Amendments Act (1972), 730
Edwards, Malenda, 140–41, *q140*
EEOC. *See* Equal Employment Opportunity Commission (EEOC).
egalitarianism, 43; Native American, 23, 138
Egypt, 590–91, 819, 841–42, 878
Ehrlichman, John, 825, *crt825*, 828, 829, *p829*
Eighteenth Amendment (1919), *q105*, 343–44,
402. *See also* Prohibition.
Eighth Amendment (1791), *q103*
"Eight-hour orphans," 538
Eightieth Congress, 631, 632–33, 635–36
Eisenhower, Dwight D., *p578, t581*, 578–83, *q579*; African Americans and, 509; arms race and, 579–81; on atomic bombing of Japan, *q517*; background of, 578, 579; Bulganin and Khrushchev and, 581, 584; business and, 654; "Chance for Peace" speech of, 580; CIA and, 588–590, 591–92; civil rights and, 671, 672; consensus decision making by, 653–54; on costs of armaments, *q580*; Cuba and, 654; election of, to presidency, 578, 653; emerging nations and, 588; as general in World War II, 510; during Great Depression, 426–27; interstate highway system and, *q603*, 654, *g654, m655*; Iran and, 587–88, 590; Korea and, 575, 578; Latin America and, 591–92; massive retaliation policy of, 579–80; McCarthy and, 646; on military-industrial complex, *q583*; Native Americans and, 624; New Look policy of, 579; Nixon and, 653, *p653*; "open skies" proposal, 581; reelected, 654; on religion, *q609*; social policies of, 654–55; Sputnik and, 582, 654; Suez crisis and, 590–91; Vietnam and, 770, 771
Eisenhower Doctrine, 591
El Alamein, 510
Elbe River, 562
elderly, poverty among, 620, *p620*
elections; in 1800s, 116, 146, 147, 151–52; Congressional, *q91–92, q105*; Presidential, *q96–97, q103, p146, p147*, 151–52, 153
Election of Senators, Direct, *q105*
electoral college, *q97, q103*
electors; District of Columbia, *q107*; presidential, *q97, q103*, 151
electricity; in 1920s, 377; appliance revolution, 442–43; during New Deal, 457–58, *p459*; Edison and, 205–06; lightbulb and, 205–06; to rural areas, 459, 539; use in motors, 206, 355; after World War II, 599
electronic bulletin boards (BBs), 87
Ellington, Edward ("Duke"), 533
Elliot, R. Brown, *p188*
Ellis, Clyde T., *q443*
Ellis Island, 236
Ellison, Ralph, *q668*
Ellsberg, Daniel, 799, 826
El Paso (Tex.), 735
El Salvador, 735, 820, 870–71, *p871*
emancipation, 176–77, *m179*
Emancipation Proclamation (1862), 176–77
Embargo Act (1807), 117, 141
embargo; of arms, to Yugoslav successor states, 896–97; of grain, to Soviet Union, 840; of military material for Japan, 504; of oil, by Saudi Arabia, 837–38
"Emergence of a Republican Majority, The" (Phillips), 811–12
Emergency Banking Act (1933), *c481*
Emergency Farm Mortgage Act (1933), *c481*
Emergency Price Control Act (EPCA) (1942), *t527*
Emergency Relief Act (1932), 426
emerging nations, 588–93
Emerson, Ralph Waldo, *q171*
Emlen, Anne, *q70*
Emperor Jones (O'Neill), *p391*
Empire State Building, 356, 447
employment; in manufacturing, 1899, *m263*; by profession, 1800–1960, *c211. See* working women; during World War II, 530–31. *See also* Equal Employment Opportunity Commission (EEOC); unemployment.
encomienda policy, 32
Endangered Species Act, 910, *p910*
Ends of Power, The (Haldeman), *q798*

Energy, Department of, *t841*
energy crisis, 836–38, 839
Enforcement Act (1870), 186, *t186*, 191
Engel v. *Vitale* (1962), *c715*, 716, *q716*
England; colonists and settlers from, 36–37, *t38*, 38–39, 41, 66–69, *p110–11. See also* African Americans; Slavery; Native Americans as, 32–34, 48; New Amsterdam and, 40. *See also* Great Britain *(for events after 1707).*
English Channel, swimming the, 388, *p388*
Enola Gay, 514
Enslaved Africans; African culture drawn on by, 166–67; family strength of, 166; life of, on plantations, 166–68; physical abuse of, 166; religion of, and, 166–67; resistance and revolt by, 167–68, *t168*; Underground Railroad and, 167
entitlement programs, 898, 908
environment; air pollution and, 910; agricultural effects, 9, 16–17; businesses and, 910; Carter and, 843; Civilian Conservation Corps (CCC) and, 455–56; cutbacks in protections for, 910–11; Gore, Albert, and, 893; government regulation of, 842–43; housing adaptations to, 28–29, *m28, p29*; landfills and, 900–01; logging industry and, 910; NAFTA and, 896; national parks and, 911; nuclear power and, 843; pollution of, 842–43, 910; Reagan and, 860; Roosevelt, Theodore, and, 910; during World War II, 536
Environmental Protection Agency (EPA), 810, 842–43, 860, 910
EPA. *See* Environmental Protection Agency (EPA).
EPCA. *See* Emergency Price Control Act (EPCA).
equality; concepts of, 23, 27, 43, 138
Equal Pay Act (1963), 726
Equal Rights Amendment (ERA), *t728*, 730–31, *m759*
Equiano, Olaudah, *q34–35*
ERA. *See* Equal Rights Amendment (ERA).
Erie Canal, 128, *p129, p144*, 144–45, 149
Eriksson, Leif, 31
Ervin, Sam J., 828, 829, *p829*
Escobedo v. *Illinois* (1964), *c715*, 716
Espionage Act (1917), 318, 319
Estevanico, 34
Estonia, 869
Ethiopia, Italian invasion of, 494
eugenics movement, 284, 405–06
Europe; alliances with countries in, 48, 68, 115, 116; in 1955, *m571*; in 1995, *m870*; Marshall Plan and, 568; Monroe Doctrine and, 219–20; neutrality during wars in, 115; and United States, in early twentieth century, 301; World War I and, *m307, m326*; World War II and, *m494, m511, m565*; Yalta agreements and, 564
European Community (EC), 817. *See also* European Union (formerly European Community).
European land claims (1763), *m48*
Europeans; colonial settlements of, 36–41, *t38*, 49; diseases brought by, 32–33; explorations by (1492–1550), *m31*; imported culture of, 33–34, 36–41, *p110–11*
European Union (formerly European Community), 896
evangelists, 397–98, 857
Evans, Hiram Wesley, 400–01
Evans, Oliver, 158
Everett, Edward, *p137*, 137–38
Evers, Charles, *p803*
Evers, Medgar, 686
Everything We Had, q775, q801
excise tax scandal, 190
executive branch, 84, *c85*; Constitutional description of, *q96*, 96–99

Credits

TEXT

17 From *The Mapping of America* by Seymour I. Schwartz and Ralph E. Ehrenberg. Harry N. Abrams, Inc., Publishers, New York. Copyright © 1980 **24** From *Castaways, The Narrative of Alvar Núñez Cabeza de Vaca*, edited by Enrique Pupo-Walker, translated by Frances M. López-Morillas. University of California Press. Copyright © 1993 by The Regents of the University of California. **126** Excerpt from *Roots* by Alex Haley. Copyright © 1976 by Alex Haley. Used by permission of Doubleday, a division of Bantam Doubleday Dell Publishing Group, Inc. **230** From *Sister Carrie* by Theodore Dreiser. Copyright © 1900 by Doubleday, Page, and Co. **334** Reprinted with permission of Charles Scribner's Sons, an imprint of Macmillan Publishing Company, from *The Great Gatsby* (Authorized Text) by F. Scott Fitzgerald. Copyright © 1991, 1992 by Eleanor Lanahan, Matthew J. Bruccoli and Samuel J. Lanahan as Trustees under Agreement dated July 3, 1975 Created by Frances Scott Fitzgerald Smith. Copyright 1925 by Charles Scribner's Sons, renewal copyright 1953 by Frances Scott Fitzgerald Lanahan. **346** From *American Tapestry* by Tom Tiede. Copyright © 1988 by Tom Tiede. Reprinted with permission of Pharos Books. **353** Reprinted with permission of Macmillan Publishing Company from *The Man Nobody Knows* by Bruce Barton. Copyright 1925 by the Bobbs-Merrill Company, Inc. Copyright renewed 1952 by Bruce Barton. **365** From *White Collar: The American Middle Class* by C. Wright Mills. Copyright © 1951 by Oxford University Press, Inc.; renewed by Yaraslava Mills. Reprinted by permission of Oxford University Press, Inc. **376** Excerpt from *Babbitt* by Sinclair Lewis, copyright 1922 by Harcourt Brace Jovanovich, Inc., and renewed 1950 by Sinclair Lewis, reprinted by permission of Oxford University Press, Inc. **392** Reprinted by permission of Harold Ober Associates Incorporated. Copyright 1963 by Arna Bontemps. **414** From *The Grapes of Wrath* by John Steinbeck. Copyright © 1939, 1967 by John Steinbeck. Reprinted by permission of Viking Penguin, a division of Penguin Books USA Inc. **425, 431, 435, 441, 443** From *Hard Times: An Oral History of the Great Depression* by Studs Terkel. Copyright © 1970 by Studs Terkel. Reprinted by permission of Pantheon Books, a division of Random House Inc. **424** Copyright © 1932 (renewed) Warner Bros. Inc. All rights reserved. Used by permission. **488** From *Ernie's War: The Best of Ernie Pyle's World War II Dispatches* by David Nichols. Copyright © 1986 by David Nichols. Reprinted by permission of Random House Inc. **508, 512, 524, 548** From *The Good War: An Oral History of World War II* by Studs Terkel. Copyright © 1984 by Studs Terkel. Reprinted by permission of Pantheon Books, a division of Random House Inc. **526** "Boogie Woogie Bugle Boy": Words and music by Don Raye and Hughie Prince. Copyright © 1940, 1941 by MCA Music Publishing, a division of MCA, Inc., New York, NY 10019. Copyright renewed. Used by permission. All Rights Reserved. **528, 534** From *The Home Front* by Archie Satterfield, published by Playboy Press. Copyright © 1981 by Archie Satterfield. Reprinted by permission of the author. **538** Reprinted with permission from The Crisis Magazine. **548** From *Wyoming's War Years, 1941–1945* by T.A. Larson, University of Wyoming Press. Copyright © 1954. Reprinted by permission of T.A. Larson. **549** From "American Business Activity from 1790 to Today," Fifty-Ninth Edition, January 1988. Reprinted with permission of Ameritrust Company N.A. **558** From *The Book of Daniel* by E.L. Doctorow. Copyright © 1971 by E.L. Doctorow. Reprinted by permission of Random House Inc. **608** From the song "Little Boxes." Words and music by Malvina Reynolds. Copyright © 1962 Schroder Music Company (ASCAP). Renewed 1990 by Nancy Schimmel. Used by permission. **612** From *The Stories of John Cheever*, copyright © 1978. Reprinted by permission of Alfred A. Knopf Inc. **622** From James Baldwin's *Notes of a Native Son.* Copyright 1955. Reprinted by permission of Beacon Press. **635** Excerpt from *Off the Record: The Private Papers of Harry S Truman* edited by Robert H. Ferrell. Copyright © 1980 by Robert H. Ferrell. Reprinted by permission of HarperCollins Publishers. **664** From *Meridian* by Alice Walker. copyright © 1976, Harcourt Brace Jovanovich, Publishers, Orlando, Florida **688** Excerpt from *Stand Up for America* by George C. Wallace. Copyright © 1976 by George C. Wallace. Used by permission of Doubleday, a division of Bantam Doubleday Dell Publishing Group, Inc. **688** From *Selma, Lord, Selma: Girlhood Memories of the Civil-Rights Days*, by Sheyann Webb and Rachel West Nelson, as told to Frank Sikora, © 1980 The University of Alabama Press. Used by permission. **693** From *The Panther and the Lash* by Langston Hughes. Copyright 1951 by Langston Hughes. Reprinted by permission of Alfred A. Knopf. **748** "Blowin' in the Wind" by Bob Dylan. Copyright © transferred 1990 to Special Rider Music. All rights reserved. International copyright secured. Reprinted by permission; "Like a Rolling Stone," by Bob Dylan. Copyright © 1965 Warner Bros. Inc. All rights reserved. Used by permission. **764** From *Born on the Fourth of July* by Ron Kovic. Copyright © 1976 by Ron Kovic. Reprinted by permission of McGraw Hill Publishing Company. **789** "The Times They Are A-Changin'," by Bob Dylan. Copyright © 1962, 1964 Warner Bros. Inc. All rights reserved. Used by permission. **852** Reprinted by permission of The Putnam Publishing Group from *The Joy Luck Club* by Amy Tan. Copyright © 1989 by Amy Tan.

MAPS

All interior maps by Mapping Specialists, Ltd., Madison, WI.

PHOTOGRAPHS

All border and background photos by John Soares with the exception of the *One Day in History* background photo by Doug Mindell. **Cover** N. Wright/National Motor Museum (c); Wesley Hitt/Liaison International (background) **Title page** Jeff Greenberg/Rainbow; **iv** Brown Brothers; **v** White House Historical Association; **vi** © Faith Ringgold Inc. (l); Photoplay Archives/LGI (r); **930,** © Larry Kunkel/FPG International Corp.; **944** ©FPG International Corp. (c, r); © Randy Wells/Allstock (l); **945** ©FPG International Corp(l); © Greg Ryan/Sally Beyer/Allstock (c); © Tom Bean/Allstock (r); **950** © Rick Iwaskai/Allstock; **950–957,** White House Historical Association.

The following credits are additions to or corrections of those found on page: **1** Laurie Platt Winfrey, Inc.; **17** World Perspectives; **115** New York State Historical Association, Cooperstown; **155** From the Collection of the Louisiana State Museum; **182** © 1984, Time-Life Books, Inc., from The Civil War Series, *Tenting Tonight,* photograph by Larry Sherer (bl); **199** Southern Pacific Lines; **201** S.J. Morrow Collection/W.H. Over State Museum; **202** Schmitt Collection/File photo by Ralph J. Brunke (l); **322** Courtesy Stephen White/© 1996 Artists Rights Society (ARS), New York/VG Bild-Kunst, Bonn (tr); **406** Photography Collection Harry Ransom Humanities Research Center, The University of Texas at Austin; **414** © The Dorothea Lange Collection, The Oakland Museum of California, The City of Oakland. Gift of Paul S. Taylor.; **425** © The Dorothea Lange Collection, The Oakland Museum of California, the city of Oakland. (br); **445** Cedar Rapids Museum of Art Archives, Gift of John B. Turner in Memory of Happy Young Turner (tr); **463** Brooklyn Museum (bl); **495** © Copyright ARS. Centro de Arte Reina Sofia, Madrid, Spain/Art Resource, NY; **523** Alfred Eisenstaedt/LIFE Magazine ©Time Inc.; **585** © TM 1995 Dr. Seuss Enterprises, L.P. All rights reserved. (tr); **586** From *War and Peace in the Nuclear Age* by J. Newhouse. Reprinted by permission of Random House/Photo by Ralph Brunke.; **600** (inset) Corry/Archive; **621** University of Kentucky Libraries; **649** UPI/Bettmann Newsphotos (t); **649** UPI/Bettmann (tr, tc, br); Motion Picture & Television Photo Archive (bc); **650** UPI/Bettmann, **651** UPI/Bettmann; **706** photo by Frank Wolfe, Courtesy Lyndon Baines Johnson Library (b); Courtesy Benny Andrews (t); **729** Courtesy of Ms. Magazine; **730** UPI/Bettmann (br); **733** © Paul Fusco/Magnum Photos; **753** © J. Marshall/Gamma Liaison (c); **754** Collection of John Jenkins III/© 1996 Andy Warhol Foundation for the Visual Arts/ARS, New York; **803** Primrose is a registered trademark of F.W. Woolworth Co. (l); **827** © Bill Swersey/Gamma Liaison (c); UPI/Bettmann (all others); **875** The Carson Collection (c); **880** © Savino/Sipa Press; **899** © Dirck Halstead/Gamma Liaison; **923** © Bill Pugliano/Gamma Liaison; **925** File photo by Ralph J. Brunke.

Diagraphics and Charts

Karl Gude **85, 142, 270, 645, 707, 895.** Arne Hurty **69, 165, 209;** Dennis Lowe **27, 529, 592, 790, 859;** David Puckett **296, 363, 379, 421, 503, 683;** All other charts and diagraphics by Ligature.